GOODE'S
WORLD ATLAS

20TH EDITION

John C. Hudson	Edward B. Espenshade, Jr.
EDITOR	EDITOR EMERITUS

CONTENTS

Goode's World Atlas

Copyright © 2000 by Rand McNally & Company; Sixth printing, Revised
Copyright © 1922, 1923, 1932, 1933, 1937, 1939, 1943, 1946, 1949, 1954, 1957,
1960, 1964, 1970, 1974, 1978, 1982, 1986, 1990, 1995 by Rand McNally & Company
Formerly *Goode's School Atlas*
Made in U.S.A.

Library of Congress Catalog Card Number 99-38535

Cover Photo: Dolomite Range
in northern Italy

CONTENTS, *continued*

Geographical Tables and Indexes [245–372]

INTRODUCTION

This is the twentieth edition of the Rand McNally **Goode's World Atlas**, which was first published more than seventy years ago. The name of Dr. J. Paul Goode, the original editor and distinguished cartographer who designed the early editions, has been retained to affirm the high standards that all those who have participated in the preparation of the atlas during these years have sought to attain.

Through the years, general-reference map coverage has been expanded; the number of thematic maps has been increased and their subject range broadened; and systematic improvements in symbolism, cartographic presentation, and map production and printing have been incorporated.

The twentieth edition continues this tradition. New maps include world forest regions and products, oceanic environments, three new ocean-floor maps, and eight new political maps. For the United States and Canada new or extensively revised maps of the grain trade, agricultural regions, and population density have been included.

Thematic maps, statistics, graphs, and various tables have been revised to incorporate the latest available data. The list of source materials and the index to thematic topics (subject index) have been revised. These additions and other revisions reflect the editors' and publisher's commitment to increasing the usefulness and quality of each edition of the Rand McNally **Goode's World Atlas**, thus maintaining it as a standard among world atlases.

Sources

Every effort was made to assemble the latest and most authentic source materials to use in this edition. In the general physical-political maps, data from national and state surveys, recent military maps, and hydrographic charts were utilized. Source materials for the specialized maps were even more varied (see the partial list of sources at the end of the atlas). They included published and unpublished documents in the form of maps, descriptions in articles and books, statistics, and correspondence with outside experts. Appreciation and thanks are expressed to the various agencies and organizations that cooperated. Noteworthy among them are: the United Nations (for demographic and economic statistics); the Food and Agriculture Organization of the United Nations (for production statistics on livestock, crops, and forest products and for statistics on world trade); the Office of the Geographer, Department of State (for the map, Surface Transport Facilities and other items); the Division of Foreign Agriculture, U.S. Department of Agriculture (for information on crop and live-stock distribution); various branches of the national military establishment; the National Oceanic and Atmospheric Administration (for information on temperature, wind pressure, and ocean currents); the Maritime Commission and the Department of Commerce (for statistics on ocean trade); the American Geographical Society (for permission to use the Miller cylindrical projection); the University of Chicago Press (for permission to use **Goode's** Homolosine equal-area projection); the McGraw-Hill Book Co. (for permission to use Glenn Trewartha's map of climatic regions); the Association of American Geographers (for permission to use Richard Murphy's map of landforms); and publications of the World Bank (for nutrition, health, and economic information).

Additional data sources consulted include: *World Oil* (for oil and gas data); International Labor Organization (for labor statistics); and the International Road Federation (for transportation data). The United Nations High Commissioner for refugees provided data for the refugees map.

Acknowledgments

The variety and complexity of problems involved in the preparation of a world atlas make the participation of specialists highly desirable. Of those who have contributed over the years the editors especially acknowledge: A. W. Küchler, Department of Geography, University of Kansas; Richard E. Murphy, late professor of geography, University of New Mexico; Erwin Raisz, late cartographer, Cambridge, Massachusetts; Glenn T. Trewartha, late professor of geography, University of Wisconsin; Derwent Whittlesey, late professor of geography, Harvard University; and Bogdan Zaborski, professor emeritus of geography, University of Ottawa.

The editors thank the entire Cartographic and Design staff of Rand McNally & Company for their continued outstanding contributions. We particularly appreciate the many years of valuable input we have received from Pat Healy and Jon Leverenz; the support of Dennis DeCock; and the help and dedication of Robert Argersinger, Greg Babiak, Brian Cantwell, Marzee Eckhoff, Winifred Farbman, Susan Hudson, Elizabeth Hunt, Jill Stift, and Barbara Strassheim. Ryan Baxter and Jeffrey Gray, Northwestern University, provided invaluable assistance in the preparation of several new maps in this edition.

With this edition, John C. Hudson, Professor of Geography at Northwestern University, assumes the editorship of **Goode's World Atlas** and Edward B. Espenshade, Jr., becomes editor emeritus. Professor Espenshade's tenure as editor, which spanned more than five decades, saw the innovation of most of the features that have made **Goode's World Atlas** the leading atlas in its field. He will continue to serve as an editorial advisor and as a source of inspiration for all who participate in the production of **Goode's**.

John C. Hudson
Edward B. Espenshade, Jr.

Geography and Maps

Geography is the science of location on the earth's surface. Its subject matter includes people, landforms, climate, and all other physical and human phenomena that make up the world's environments and give unique character to diverse places. Geographers construct maps that depict these patterns in order to better understand and explain them. Cartography is the branch of geography that focuses on the theory, methods, and techniques of mapping. Images derived from remote sensing, such as from an orbiting satellite, are now used routinely in mapping. The new technology has simultaneously produced more data for the mapmaker and a higher level and standard of accuracy for the map.

Geographic Education

For several decades geography instruction has been organized around five themes: location, place, human/environment interaction, movement, and regions. More recently, Geography for Life: National Geography Standards (National Geographic Research & Exploration, 1994) has provided a detailed list of objectives in geographic education.

The subject matter of geography is recognized as having six essential elements, beginning with the importance of understanding the **World in Spatial Terms**. Every geographically informed person should know how to use maps in studying the people, places, and environments of the Earth. **Places and Regions** are the localities, both small and large, with which individuals, groups, and whole cultures are identified. These human-defined regions stand apart from the ecosystems of the earth that are understood to be the result of complex **Physical Systems**. Human and physical regions come together in the study of **Human Settlements**, which focuses on the distribution of people, rates of demographic change, patterns of economic activity, and the network of connections and transactions that makes the systems function. Beyond these themes are broader issues of concern focusing on **Environment and Society**. Humans modify and affect their environments just as natural systems influence human activities. Resources are not fixed but rather are the subject of human appraisal as to their value, whether for use or for preservation. The **Uses of Geography** also include interpreting the past and planning for the future as well as interpreting the present.

Organization of the Atlas

Goode's World Atlas consists of three parts, beginning with *World Thematic Maps*, portraying the distribution of climatic regions, resources, landforms, and other major worldwide features. The second part is the *Regional Maps* section and main body of the atlas. It provides detailed reference maps for all inhabited land areas on a continent-by-continent basis. Thematic maps of the continents are also contained in this part. The third part contains a series of geographical tables, a glossary of geographical terms, the index of place names, a subject index, and a list of sources. The tables provide comparative data on a wide variety of topics. The index provides the locations of places named on the regional reference maps.

Cartographic Communication

To communicate information through a map, cartographers must assemble the geographic data, use their personal perception of the world to select the relevant information, and apply graphic techniques to produce the map. Readers must then be able to interpret the mapped data and relate it to their own experience and need for information. Thus, the success of any map depends on both the cartographer's and the map reader's knowledge and perception of the world and on their common understanding of a map's purpose and limitations.

The ability to understand maps and related imagery depends first on the reader's skill at recognizing how a curved, three-dimensional world is symbolized on a flat, two-dimensional map. Normally, we view the world horizontally (that is, our line of vision parallels the horizon), at the eye level about five and one-half to six feet above ground. Images appear directly in front and to either side of us, with our eyes encompassing all details as nonselectively as a camera. Less frequently, when we are atop a high platform or in an airplane, we view the world obliquely, as shown in *Figure 1*, in which both vertical and horizontal facets of objects can be seen. And only those persons at very high altitudes will view the world at a vertical angle (*Figure 2*). Yet maps are based on our ability to visualize the world from an overhead, or vertical, perspective.

A map differs from a purely vertical photograph in two important respects. First, in contrast to the single focal point of a photograph, a map is created as if the viewer were directly overhead at all points (See Figure 3). Second, just as our brains select from the myriad items in our field of vision those objects of interest or importance to us, so each map presents only those details necessary for a particular purpose-a map is not an inventory of all that is visible. Selectivity is one of a map's most important and useful characteristics.

Skill in reading maps is basically a matter of practice, but a fundamental grasp of cartographic principles and the symbols, scales, and projections commonly employed in creating maps is essential to comprehensive map use.

Map Data
When creating a map, the cartographer must select the objects to be shown, evaluate their relative importance, and find some way to simplify their form. The combined process is called *cartographic generalization*. In attempting to generalize data, the cartographer is limited by the purpose of the map, its scale, the methods to produce it, and the accuracy of the data.

Figure 1. Oblique aerial photograph of New York City.

Figure 2. High-altitude vertical photograph of New York City area.

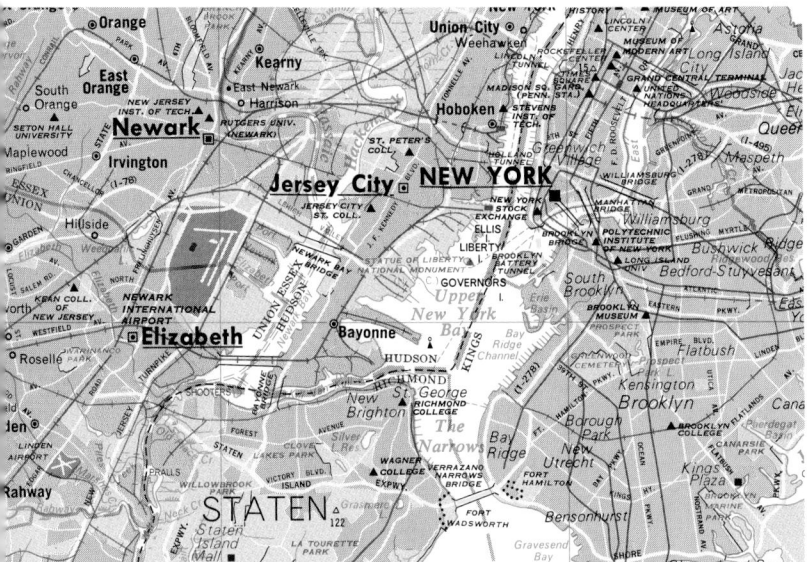

Figure 3. Map of New York City and environs.

Cartographic generalization consists of simplification, classification, symbolization, and induction.

Simplification involves omitting details that will clutter the map and confuse the reader. The degree of simplification depends on the purpose and scale of the map. If the cartographer is creating a detailed map of Canada and merely wants to show the location of the United States, he or she can draw a simplified outline of the country. However, if the map requires a precise identification of the states in New England and the Great Lakes region, the mapmaker will have to draw a more detailed outline, still being careful not to distract the reader from the main features of the Canadian map.

Classification of data is a way of reducing the information to a form that can be easily presented on a map. For example, portraying precise urban populations in the United States would require using as many different symbols as there are cities. Instead, the cartographer groups cities into population categories and assigns a distinct symbol to each one. With the help of a legend, the reader can easily decode the classifications.

Symbolization of information depends largely on the nature of the original data. Information can be *nominal* (showing differences in kind, such as land versus water, grassland versus forest); or *ordinal* (showing relative differences in quantities as well as kind, such as *major* versus *minor* ore deposits); or *interval* (degrees of temperature, inches of rainfall) or *ratio* (population densities), both expressing quantitative details about the data being mapped.

Cartographers use various shapes, colors, or patterns to symbolize these categories of data, and the particular nature of the information being communicated often determines how it is symbolized. Population density, for example, can be shown by the use of small dots or different intensities of color. However, if nominal data is being portrayed—for instance, the desert and fertile areas of Egypt—the mapmaker may want to use a different method of symbolizing the data, perhaps pattern symbols. The color, size, and style of type used for the different elements on a map are also important to symbolization.

Induction is the term cartographers use to describe the process whereby more information is represented on a map than is actually supplied by the original data. For instance, in creating a rainfall map, a cartographer may start with precise rainfall records for relatively few points on the map. After deciding the interval categories into which the data will be divided (e.g., thirty inches or more, fifteen to thirty inches, under fifteen inches), the mapmaker infers from the particular data points that nearby places receive the same or nearly the same amount of rainfall and draws the lines that distinguish the various rainfall regions accordingly. Obviously, generalizations arrived at through induction can never be as precise as the real-world patterns they represent. The map will only tell the reader that all the cities in a given area received about the same amount of rainfall; it will not tell exactly how much rain fell in any particular city in any particular time period.

Cartographers must also be aware of the map reader's perceptual limitations and preferences. During the past two decades, numerous experiments have helped determine how much information readers actually glean from a map and how symbols, colors, and shapes are recognized and interpreted. As a result, cartographers now have a better idea of what kind of rectangle to use; what type of layout or lettering suggests qualities such as power, stability, movement; and what colors are most appropriate.

Map Scale

Since part or all of the earth's surface may be portrayed on a single page of an atlas, the reader's first question should be: What is the relation of map size to the area represented? This proportional relationship is known as the *scale* of a map.

Scale is expressed as a ratio between the distance or area on the map and the same distance or area on the earth. The map scale is commonly represented in three ways: (1) as a simple fraction or ratio called the representative fraction, or RF; (2) as a written statement of map distance in relation to earth distance; and (3) as a graphic representation or a bar scale. All three forms of scale for distances are expressed on Maps A–D.

The RF is usually written as 1:62,500 (as in Map A), where 1 always refers to a unit of distance on the map. The ratio means that 1 centimeter or 1 millimeter or 1 foot on the map represents 62,500 centimeters or millimeters or feet on the earth's surface. The units of measure on both sides of the ratio must always be the same.

Maps may also include a *written statement* expressing distances in terms more familiar to the reader. In Map A the scale 1:62,500 is expressed as being (approximately) 1 inch to 1 mile; that is, 1 inch on the map represents roughly 1 mile on the earth's surface.

The *graphic scale* for distances is usually a bar scale, as shown in Maps A–D. A bar scale is normally subdivided, enabling the reader to measure distance directly on the map.

An *area scale* can also be used, in which one unit of area (square inches, square centimeters) is proportional to the same square units on the earth. The scale may be expressed as either $1:62,500^2$ or 1 to the square of 62,500. Area scales are used when the transformation of the globe to the flat map has been made so that areas are represented in true relation to their respective area on the earth.

When comparing map scales, it is helpful to remember that the *larger* the scale (see Map A) the smaller the area represented and the greater the amount of detail that a map can include. The *smaller* the scale (see Maps B, C, D) the larger the area covered and the less detail that can be presented.

Large-scale maps are useful when readers need such detailed information as the location of roadways, major buildings, city plans, and the like. On a smaller scale, the reader is able to place cities in relation to one another and recognize other prominent features of the region. At the smallest scale, the reader can get a broad view of several states and an idea of the total area. Finer details cannot be shown.

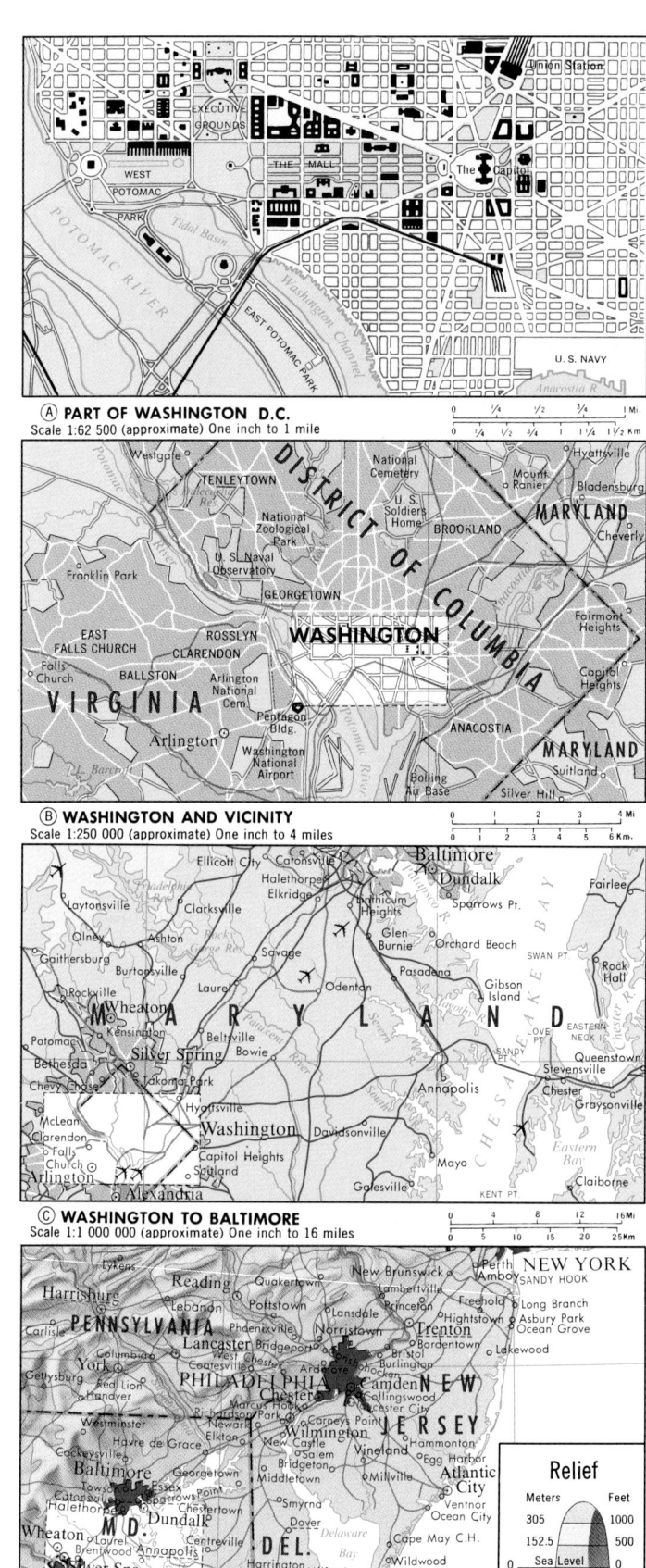

Ⓐ **PART OF WASHINGTON D.C.**
Scale 1:62 500 (approximate) One inch to 1 mile

Ⓑ **WASHINGTON AND VICINITY**
Scale 1:250 000 (approximate) One inch to 4 miles

Ⓒ **WASHINGTON TO BALTIMORE**
Scale 1:1 000 000 (approximate) One inch to 16 miles

Ⓓ **WASHINGTON TO NEW YORK**
Scale 1:4 000 000 one inch to 64 miles. Conic Projection

Map Projections

Every cartographer is faced with the problem of transforming the curved surface of the earth onto a flat plane with a minimum of distortion. The systematic transformation of locations on the earth (spherical surface) to locations on a map (flat surface) is called projection.

It is not possible to represent on a flat map the spatial relationships of angle, distance, direction, and area that only a globe can show faithfully. As a result, projection systems inevitably involve some distortion. On large-scale maps representing a few square miles, the distortion is generally negligible. But on maps depicting large countries, continents, or the entire world, the amount of distortion can be significant. Some maps of the Western Hemisphere, because of their projection, incorrectly portray Canada and Alaska as larger than the United States and Mexico, while South America looks considerably smaller than its northern neighbors.

One of the more practical ways map readers can become aware of projection distortions and learn how to make allowances for them is to compare the projection grid of a flat map with the grid of a globe. Some important characteristics of the globe grid are found listed on page xi.

There are an infinite number of possible map projections, all of which distort one or more of the characteristics of the globe in varying degrees. The projection system that a cartographer chooses depends on the size and location of the area being projected and the purpose of the map. In this atlas, most of the maps are drawn on projections that give a consistent area scale; good land and ocean shape; parallels that are parallel; and as consistent a linear scale as possible throughout the projection.

The transformation process is actually a mathematical one, but to aid in visualizing this process, it is helpful to consider the earth reduced to the scale of the intended map and then projected onto a simple geometric shape—a cylinder, cone, or plane. These geometric forms are then flattened to two dimensions to produce cylindrical, conic, and plane projections (see Figures 4, 5, and 6). Some of the projection systems used in this atlas are described on the following pages. By comparing these systems with the characteristics of a globe grid, readers can gain a clearer understanding of map distortion.

Mercator: This transformation—bearing the name of a famous sixteenth century cartographer—is conformal; that is, land masses are represented in their true shapes. Thus, for every point on the map, the angles shown are correct in every direction within a limited area. To achieve this, the projection increases latitudinal and longitudinal distances away from the equator. As a result, land *shapes* are correct, but their *areas* are distorted. The farther away from the equator, the greater the area distortion. For example, on a Mercator map, Alaska appears far larger than Mexico, whereas in fact Mexico's land area is greater. The Mercator projection is used in nautical navigation, because a line connecting any two points gives the compass direction between them. (See Figure 4.)

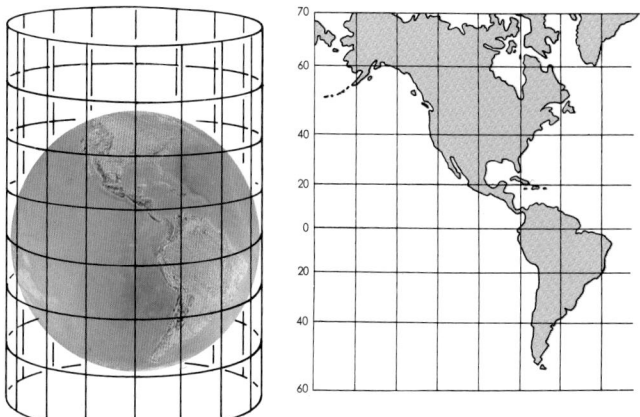

Figure 4.   Mercator Projection (right), based upon the projection of the globe onto a cylinder.

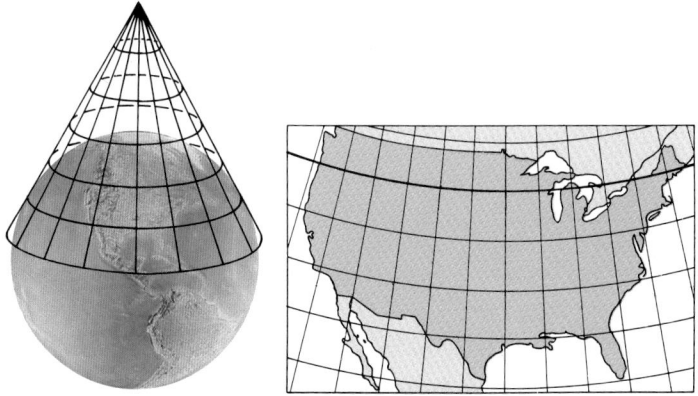

Figure 5.   Projection of the globe onto a cone and a resultant Conic Projection.

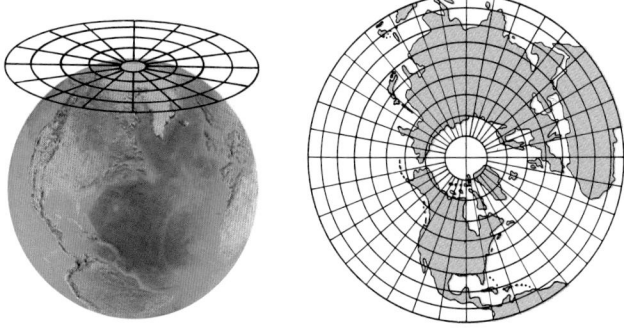

Figure 6.   Lambert Equal-Area Projection (right), which assumes the projection of the globe onto a plane surface.

Conic: In this transformation—a globe projected onto a tangent cone—meridians of longitude appear as straight lines, and lines of latitude appear as parallel arcs. The parallel of tangency (that is, where the cone is presumed to touch the globe) is called a standard parallel. In this projection, distortion increases in bands away from the standard parallel. Conic projections are helpful in depicting middle-latitude areas of east-west extension. (See Figure 5.)

Lambert Equal Area *(polar case):* This projection assumes a plane touching the globe at a single point. It shows true distances close to the center (the tangent point) but increasingly distorted ones away from it. The equal-area quality (showing land areas in their correct proportion) is maintained throughout; but in regions away from the center, distortion of shape increases. (See Figure 6.)

Miller Cylindrical: O. M. Miller suggested a modification to the Mercator projection to lessen the severe area distortion in the higher latitudes. The Miller projection is neither conformal nor equal-area. Thus, while shapes are less accurate than on the Mercator, the exaggeration of *size* of areas has been somewhat decreased. The Miller cylindrical is useful for showing the entire world in a rectangular format. (See Figure 7.)

Mollweide Homolographic: The Mollweide is an equal-area projection; the least distorted areas are ovals centered just above and below the center of the projection. Distance distortions increase toward the edges of the map. The Mollweide is used for world-distribution maps where a pleasing oval look is desired along with the equal-area quality. It is one of the bases used in the Goode's Interrupted Homolosine projection. (See Figure 8.)

Sinusoidal, or Sanson-Flamsteed: In this equal-area projection the scale is the same along all parallels and the central meridian. Distortion of shapes is less along the two main axes of the projection but increases markedly toward the edges. Maps depicting areas such as South America or Africa can make good use of the Sinusoidal's favorable characteristics by situating the land masses along the central meridian, where the shapes will be virtually undistorted. The Sinusoidal is also one of the bases used in the Goode's Interrupted Homolosine. (See Figure 9.)

Goode's Interrupted Homolosine: An equal-area projection, Goode's is composed of the Sinusoidal grid from the equator to about 40° N and 40° S latitudes; beyond these latitudes, the Mollweide is used. This grid is interrupted so that land masses can be projected with a minimum of shape distortion by positioning each section on a separate central meridian. Thus, the shapes as well as the sizes of land masses are represented with a high degree of fidelity. Oceans can also be positioned in this manner. (See Figure 10.)

Robinson: This projection was designed for Rand McNally to present an uninterrupted and visually correct map of the earth. It maintains overall shape and area relationships without extreme distortion and is widely used in classrooms and textbooks. (See Figure 11.)

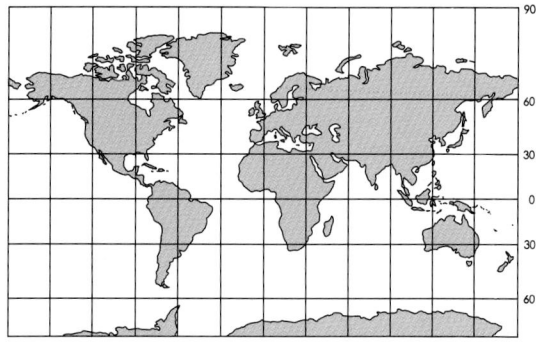

Figure 7. Miller Cylindrical Projection.

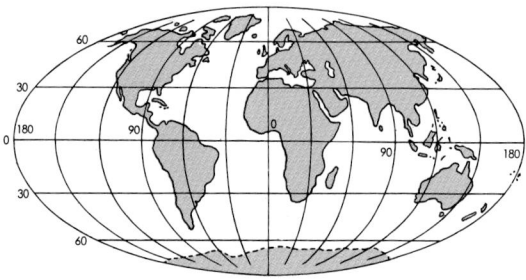

Figure 8. Mollweide Homolographic Projection.

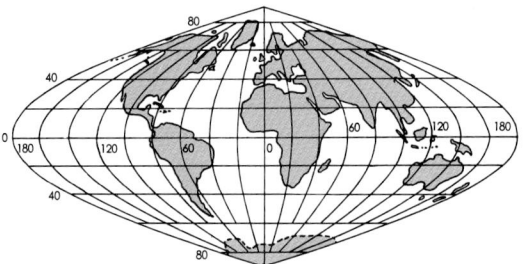

Figure 9. Sinusoidal Projection.

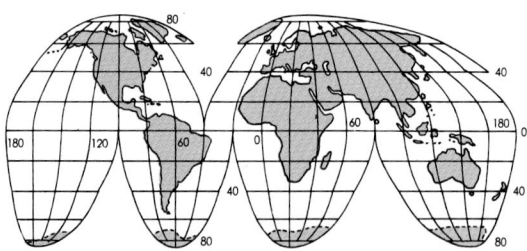

Figure 10. Goode's Interrupted Homolosine Projection.

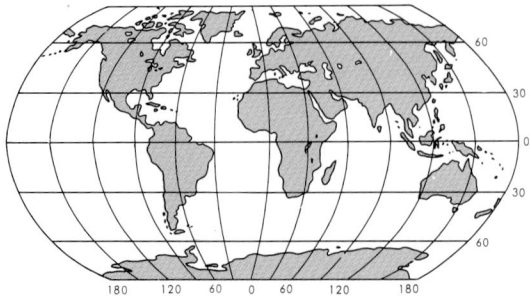

Figure 11. Robinson Projection.

Bonne: This equal-area transformation is mathematically related to the Sinusoidal. Distances are true along all parallels and the central meridian. Farther out from the central meridian, however, the increasing obliqueness of the grid's angles distorts shape and distance. This limits the area that can be usefully projected. Bonne projections, like conics, are best employed for relatively small areas in middle latitudes. (See Figure 12.)

Conic with Two Standard Parallels: The linear scale of this projection is consistent along two standard parallels instead of only one as in the simple conic. Since the spacing of the other parallels is reduced somewhat between the standard parallels and progressively enlarged beyond them, the projection does not exhibit the equal-area property. Careful selection of the standard parallels, however, provides good representation of limited areas. Like the Bonne projection, this system is widely used for areas in middle latitudes. (See Figure 13.)

Polyconic: In this system, the globe is projected onto a series of strips taken from tangent cones. Parallels are nonconcentric circles, and each is divided equally by the meridians, as on the globe. While distances along the straight central meridian are true, they are increasingly exaggerated along the curving meridians. Likewise, general representation of areas and shapes is good near the central meridian but progressively distorted away from it. Polyconic projections are used for middle-latitude areas to minimize all distortions and were employed for large-scale topographic maps. (See Figure 14.)

Lambert Conformal Conic: This conformal transformation system usually employs two standard parallels. Distortion increases away from the standard parallels, being greatest at the edges of the map. It is useful for projecting elongated east-west areas in the middle latitudes and is ideal for depicting the forty-eight contiguous states. It is also widely used for aeronautical and meteorological charts. (See Figure 15.)

Lambert Equal Area *(oblique and polar cases):* This equal-area projection can be centered at any point on the earth's surface, perpendicular to a line drawn through the globe. It maintains correct angles to all points on the map from its center (point of tangency), but distances become progressively distorted toward the edges. It is most useful for roughly circular areas or areas whose dimensions are nearly equal in two perpendicular directions.

The two most common forms of the Lambert projection are the oblique and the polar, shown in Figures 6 and 16. Although the meridians and parallels for the forms are different, the distortion characteristics are the same.

Important characteristics of the globe grid

1. All meridians of longitude are equal in length and meet at the Poles.
2. All lines of latitude are parallel and equally spaced on meridians.
3. The length, or circumference, of the parallels of latitude decreases as one moves from the equator to the Poles. For instance, the circumference of the parallel at 60° latitude is one-half the circumference of the equator.
4. Meridians of longitude are equally spaced on each parallel, but the distance between them decreases toward the Poles.
5. All parallels and meridians meet at right angles.

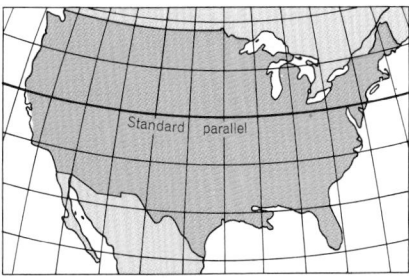

Figure 12.
Bonne Projection.

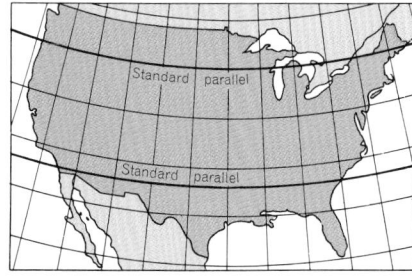

Figure 13.
Conic Projection with Two Standard Parallels.

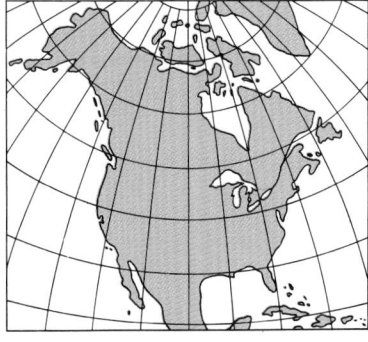

Figure 14.
Polyconic Projection.

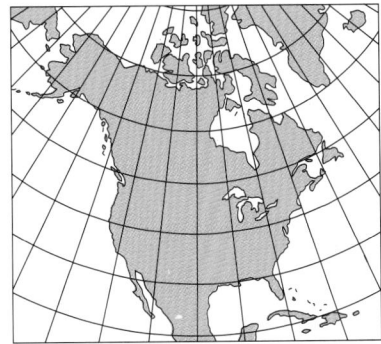

Figure 15.
Lambert Conformal Conic Projection.

Figure 16.
Lambert Equal-Area Projection (oblique case).

Edward B. Espenshade, Jr.
John C. Hudson

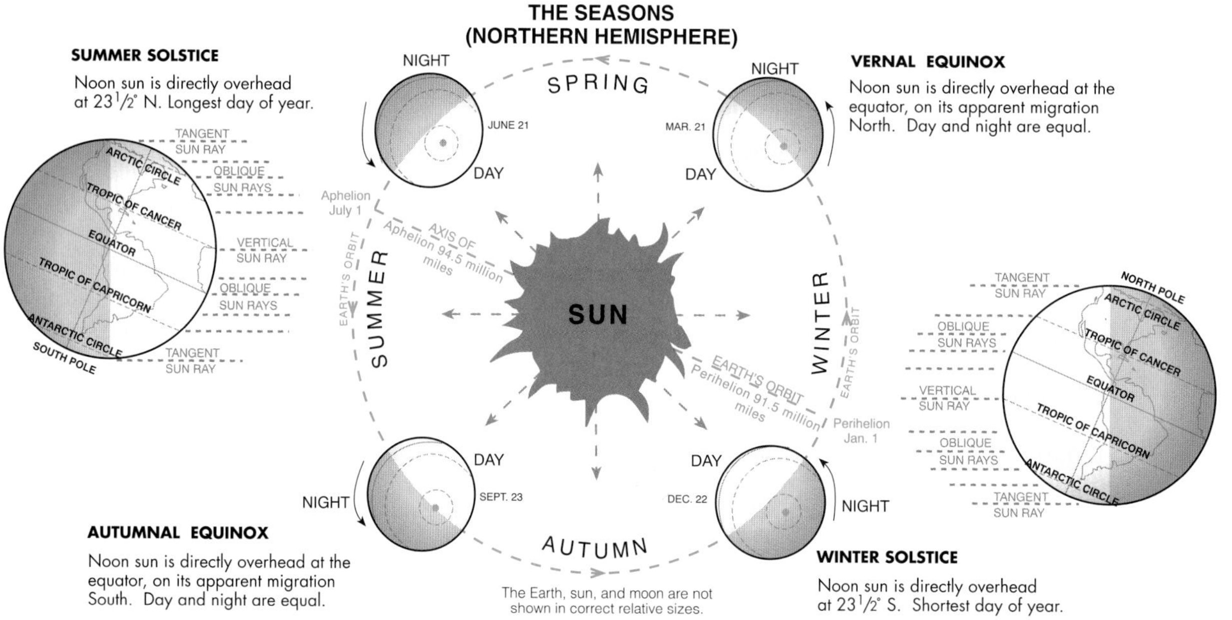

THE SEASONS
(NORTHERN HEMISPHERE)

SPRING

SUMMER

WINTER

AUTUMN

SUN

JUNE 21

MAR. 21

SEPT. 23

DEC. 22

NIGHT

DAY

NIGHT

DAY

DAY

NIGHT

DAY

NIGHT

Aphelion July 1

AXIS OF EARTH

Aphelion 94.5 million miles

EARTH'S ORBIT

EARTH'S ORBIT

EARTH'S ORBIT — Perihelion 91.5 million miles

Perihelion Jan. 1

SUMMER SOLSTICE
Noon sun is directly overhead at 23$\frac{1}{2}$° N. Longest day of year.

TANGENT SUN RAY
ARCTIC CIRCLE
OBLIQUE SUN RAYS
TROPIC OF CANCER
EQUATOR
VERTICAL SUN RAY
TROPIC OF CAPRICORN
OBLIQUE SUN RAYS
ANTARCTIC CIRCLE
SOUTH POLE
TANGENT SUN RAY

VERNAL EQUINOX
Noon sun is directly overhead at the equator, on its apparent migration North. Day and night are equal.

TANGENT SUN RAY
NORTH POLE
OBLIQUE SUN RAYS
ARCTIC CIRCLE
TROPIC OF CANCER
VERTICAL SUN RAY
EQUATOR
TROPIC OF CAPRICORN
OBLIQUE SUN RAYS
ANTARCTIC CIRCLE
TANGENT SUN RAY

AUTUMNAL EQUINOX
Noon sun is directly overhead at the equator, on its apparent migration South. Day and night are equal.

The Earth, sun, and moon are not shown in correct relative sizes.

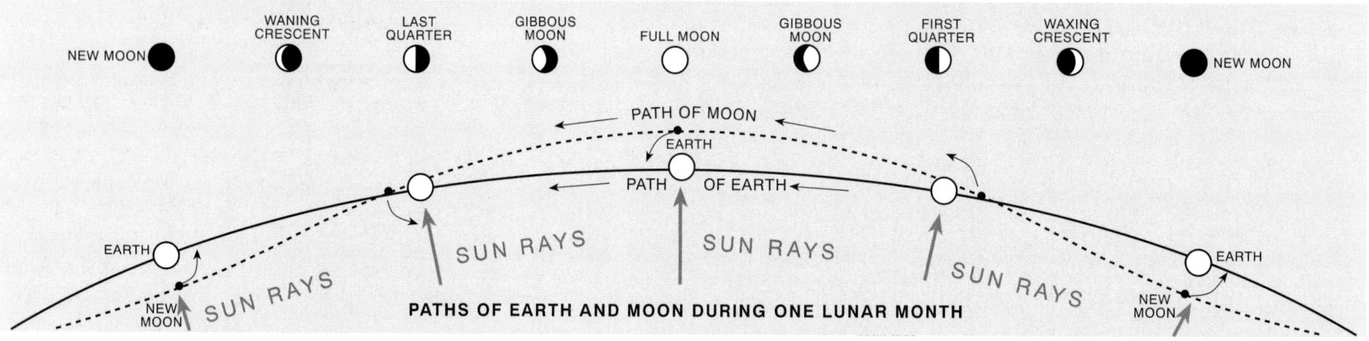

WINTER SOLSTICE
Noon sun is directly overhead at 23$\frac{1}{2}$° S. Shortest day of year.

NEW MOON | WANING CRESCENT | LAST QUARTER | GIBBOUS MOON | FULL MOON | GIBBOUS MOON | FIRST QUARTER | WAXING CRESCENT | NEW MOON

PATH OF MOON

EARTH

PATH OF EARTH

EARTH

SUN RAYS

SUN RAYS

SUN RAYS

EARTH

NEW MOON

SUN RAYS

NEW MOON

EARTH

PATHS OF EARTH AND MOON DURING ONE LUNAR MONTH

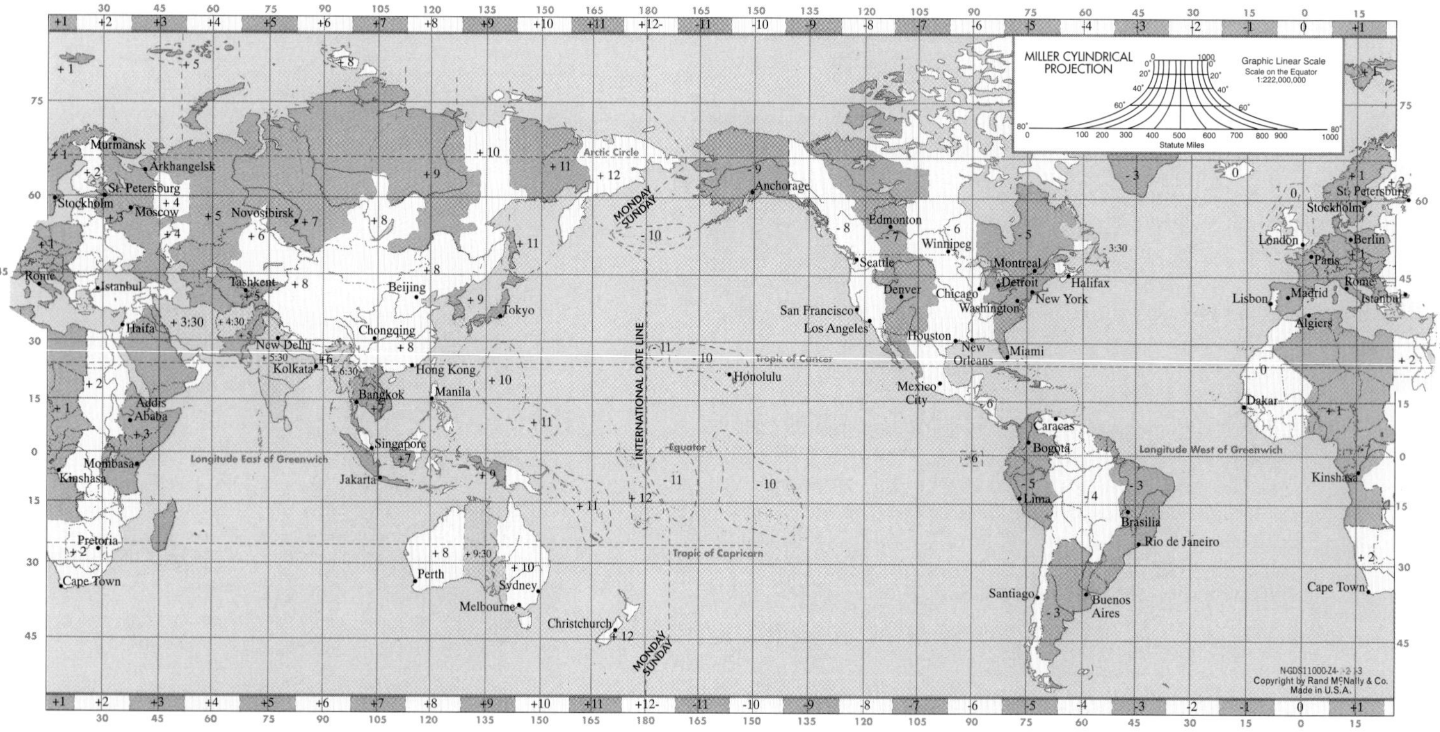

MILLER CYLINDRICAL PROJECTION

Graphic Linear Scale
Scale on the Equator
1:222,000,000

Statute Miles
0 100 200 300 400 500 600 700 800 900 1000

INTERNATIONAL DATE LINE

MONDAY SUNDAY

Arctic Circle

Tropic of Cancer

Equator

Tropic of Capricorn

Longitude East of Greenwich

Longitude West of Greenwich

NGDS11000-74- -2 -13
Copyright by Rand McNally & Co.
Made in U.S.A.

Time Zones

The surface of the earth is divided into 24 time zones. Each zone represents 15° of longitude or one hour of time. The time of the initial, or zero, zone is based on the central meridian of Greenwich and is adopted eastward and westward for a distance of 7$\frac{1}{2}$° of longitude. Each of the zones in turn is designated by a number representing the hours (+or-) by which its standard time differs from Greenwich mean time. These standard time zones are indicated by bands of orange and yellow. Areas which have a fractional deviation from standard time are shown in an intermediate color. The irregularities in the zones and the fractional deviations are due to political and economic factors.

(After U.S. Defense Mapping Agency)

WORLD THEMATIC MAPS

This section of the atlas consists of more than sixty thematic maps presenting world patterns and distributions. Together with accompanying graphs, these maps communicate basic information on mineral resources, agricultural products, trade, transportation, and other selected aspects of the natural and cultural geographical environment.

A thematic map uses symbols to show certain characteristics of, generally, one class of geographical information. This "theme" of a thematic map is presented upon a background of basic locational information–coastline, country boundaries, major drainage, etc. The map's primary concern is to communicate visually basic impressions of the distribution of the theme. For instance, on page 47 the distribution of cattle shown by point symbols impresses the reader with relative densities–the distribution of cattle is much more uniform throughout the United States than it is in China, and cattle are more numerous in the United States than in China.

Although it is possible to use a thematic map to obtain exact values of a quantity or commodity, it is not the purpose intended, any more than a thematic map is intended to be used to give precise distances from New York to Moscow. If one seeks precise statistics for each country, he may consult the bar graphs accompanying the maps or statistical tables such as those following page 244.

The map on this page is an example of a special class of thematic maps called cartograms. The cartogram assigns to a named earth region an area based on some value other than land surface area. In the cartogram below, and in all others appearing in this atlas, the areas assigned are proportional to their countries' populations. The result of mapping on this base is a meaningful way of portraying distributions such as natural increase which are causally related to existing size of population. On the other hand, natural increase is not causally related to earth area. In the thematic maps in this atlas, relative earth sizes have been considered when presenting the distributions.

Real and hypothetical geographical distributions are practically limitless but can be classed into point, line, area, or volume information relative to a specific location or area in the world. The thematic map, in communicating these fundamental classes of information, utilizes point, line, and area symbols. The symbols may be employed to show qualitative differences (difference in kind) of a certain category of information and may also show quantitative differences in the information (differences in amount). For example, the natural-vegetation map (page 24) was based upon information gathered by many observations over a period of time. It utilizes area symbols (color and pattern) to show the difference in the kind of vegetation as well as the extent. Quantitative factual information was shown on the annual-precipitation map, page 20, by means of isohyets (lines connecting points of equal rainfall). Also, area symbols were employed to show the intervals between the lines. In each of these thematic maps, there is one primary theme, or subject; the map communicates the information far better than volumes of words and tables could.

One of the most important aspects of the thematic-map section is use of the different maps to show comparisons and relationships among the distributions of various types of geographical information. For example, the relationship of dense population (page 30) to areas of intensive subsistence agriculture (page 38) and to manufacturing (page 55) is an important geographic concept.

The statistics communicated by the maps and graphs in this section are intended to give an idea of the relative importance of countries in the distributions mapped. The maps are not intended to take the place of statistical reference works. No single year affords a realistic base for production, trade, and certain economic and demographic statistics. Therefore, averages of data for three or four years have been used. Together with the maps, the averages and percentages provide the student with a realistic idea of the importance of specific areas.

POPULATION

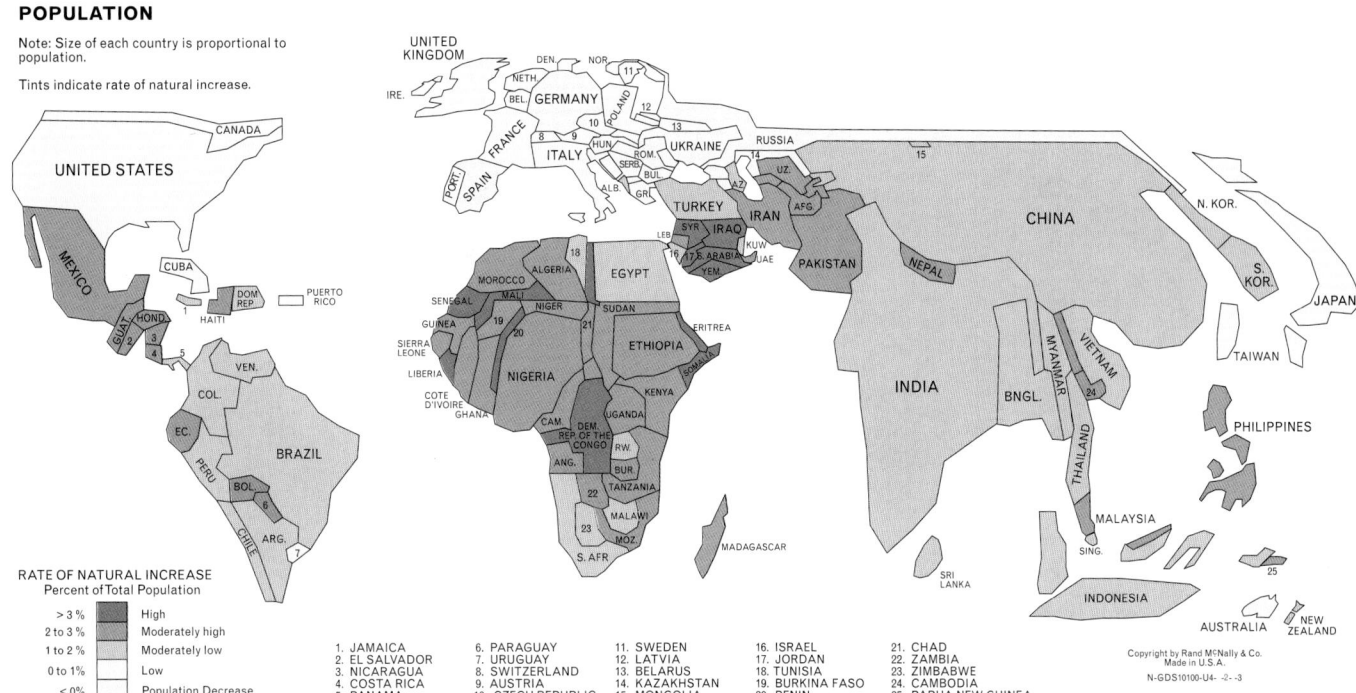

Note: Size of each country is proportional to population.

Tints indicate rate of natural increase.

RATE OF NATURAL INCREASE
Percent of Total Population

> 3 %	High
2 to 3 %	Moderately high
1 to 2 %	Moderately low
0 to 1%	Low
< 0%	Population Decrease

1. JAMAICA
2. EL SALVADOR
3. NICARAGUA
4. COSTA RICA
5. PANAMA
6. PARAGUAY
7. URUGUAY
8. SWITZERLAND
9. AUSTRIA
10. CZECH REPUBLIC
11. SWEDEN
12. LATVIA
13. BELARUS
14. KAZAKHSTAN
15. MONGOLIA
16. ISRAEL
17. JORDAN
18. TUNISIA
19. BURKINA FASO
20. BENIN
21. CHAD
22. ZAMBIA
23. ZIMBABWE
24. CAMBODIA
25. PAPUA NEW GUINEA

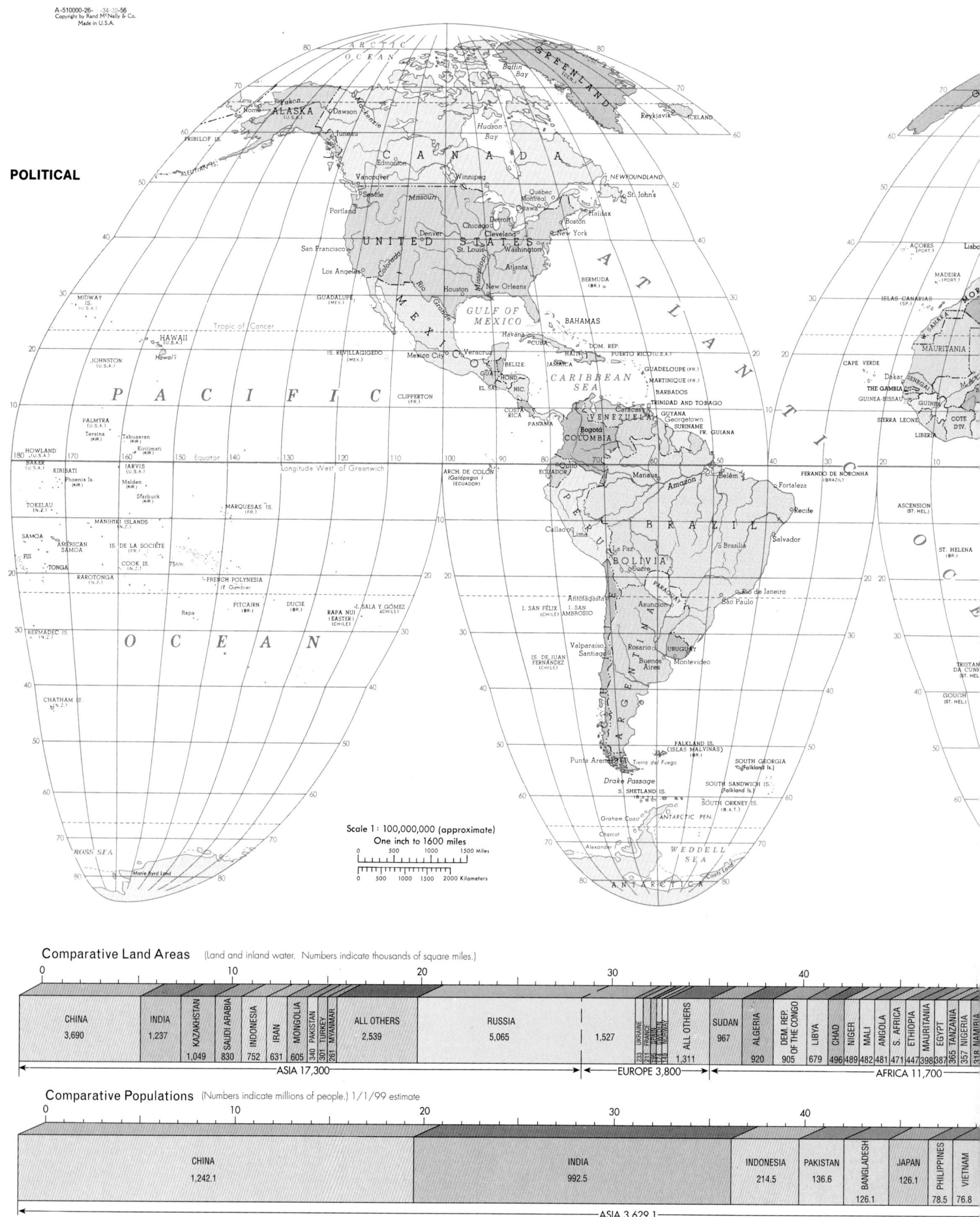

POLITICAL

Scale 1 : 100,000,000 (approximate)
One inch to 1600 miles

0   500   1000   1500 Miles

0   500 1000 1500 2000 Kilometers

Comparative Land Areas (Land and inland water. Numbers indicate thousands of square miles.)

0	10	20	30	40

| CHINA 3,690 | INDIA 1,237 | KAZAKHSTAN 1,049 | SAUDI ARABIA 830 | INDONESIA 752 | IRAN 631 | MONGOLIA 605 | PAKISTAN 340 | TURKEY 301 | MYANMAR 261 | ALL OTHERS 2,539 | RUSSIA 5,065 | 1,527 | UKRAINE 233 | FRANCE 211 | SPAIN 195 | SWEDEN 174 | NORWAY 149 | ALL OTHERS 1,311 | SUDAN 967 | ALGERIA 920 | DEM. REP. OF THE CONGO 905 | LIBYA 679 | CHAD 496 | NIGER 489 | MALI 482 | ANGOLA 481 | S. AFRICA 471 | ETHIOPIA 447 | MAURITANIA 398 | EGYPT 387 | TANZANIA 365 | NIGERIA 357 | NAMIBIA 318 |

←————————————————————————— ASIA 17,300 —————————————————————————→ ←——————— EUROPE 3,800 ———————→ ←——————————————————————————— AFRICA 11,700 ——————————————

Comparative Populations (Numbers indicate millions of people.) 1/1/99 estimate

0	10	20	30	40

| CHINA 1,242.1 | INDIA 992.5 | INDONESIA 214.5 | PAKISTAN 136.6 | BANGLADESH 126.1 | JAPAN 126.1 | PHILIPPINES 78.5 | VIETNAM 76.8 |

←——— ASIA 3,629.1 ——————————————————————————

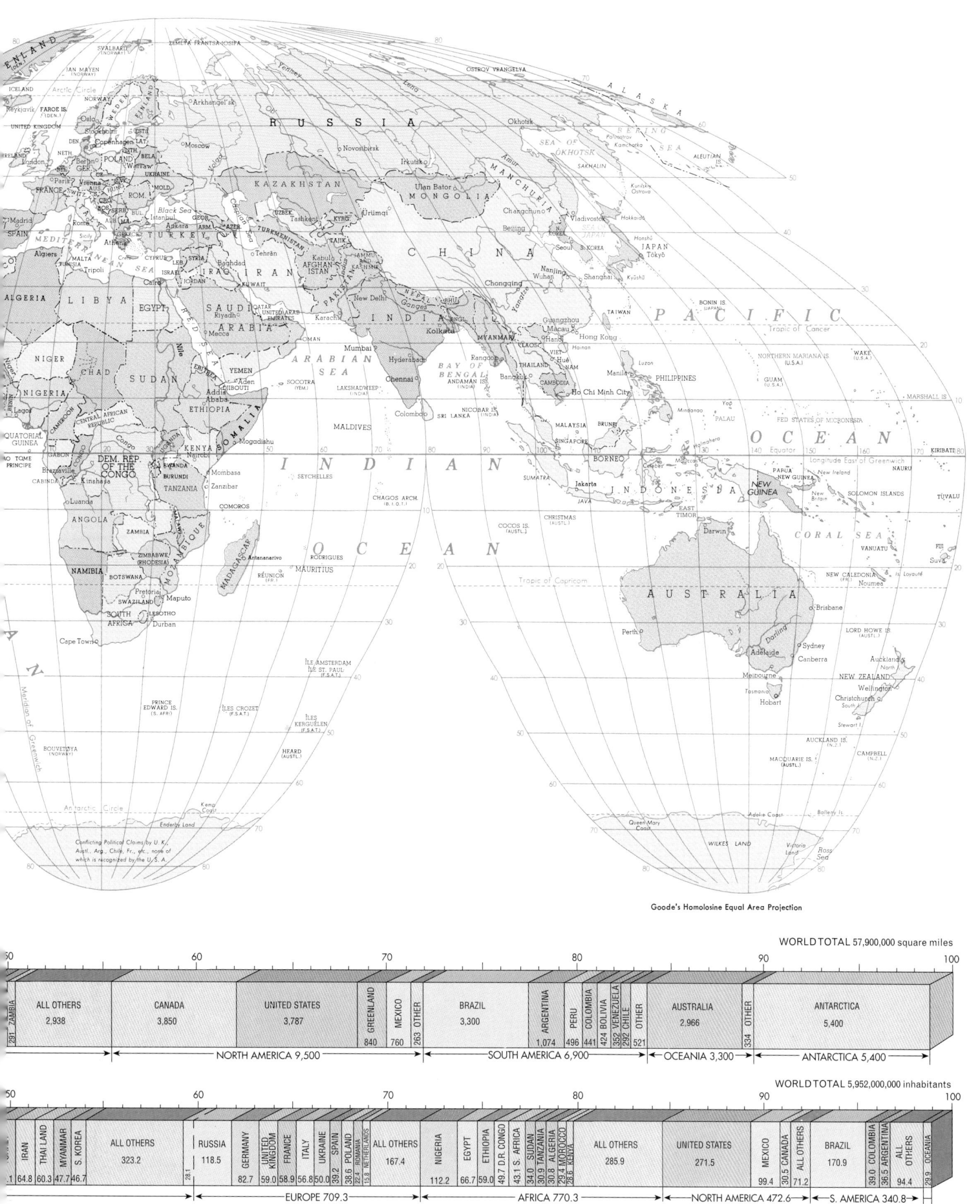

ENLAND
SVALBARD (NORWAY)
JAN MAYEN (NORWAY)
ZEMLYA FRANTSA-IOSIPA
OSTROV VRANGELYA
ALASKA
ICELAND
Arctic Circle
Reykjavik FAROE IS. (DEN.)
NORWAY
SWEDEN
FINLAND
Arkhangel'sk
Ob
Yenisey
Lena
BERING SEA
UNITED KINGDOM
Oslo
Stockholm
EST.
LAT.
Moscow
R U S S I A
Okhotsk
SEA OF OKHOTSK
Potorosy
Kamchatka
ALEUTIAN IS.
IRELAND
London
DEN.
Copenhagen
LITH.
BELA.
Novosibirsk
Irkutsk
Amur
SAKHALIN
Paris
NETH.
Berlin
GER.
POLAND
Warsaw
UKRAINE
KAZAKHSTAN
MANCHURIA
Kunlskiy Ostrova
FRANCE
SWITZ.
AUS.
Vienna
CZ.
SLVK.
MOLD.
Ulan Bator
M O N G O L I A
Changchun
Vladivostok
Hokkaido
Madrid
Rome
HUN.
SERB.
ROM.
BUL.
Black Sea
Istanbul
GEOR.
ARM.
AZER.
UZBEK.
Tashkent
KYRG.
Ürümqi
Beijing
Seoul
N. KOREA
S. KOREA
SEA OF JAPAN
JAPAN
Tokyo
Honshu
SPAIN
MEDITERRANEAN SEA
Sicily
Crete
GREECE
Athens
CYPRUS
TURKEY
Ankara
SYRIA
TURKMENISTAN
TAJIK.
C H I N A
Nanjing
Wuhan
Shanghai
Kyushu
Algiers
TUNISIA
MALTA
Tripoli
ISRAEL
Baghdad
IRAQ
IRAN
Tehran
Kabul
AFGHAN-
ISTAN
JAMMU
AND KASHMIR
Chongqing
Yangtze
PACIFIC
ALGERIA
LIBYA
EGYPT
Cairo
JORDAN
KUWAIT
SAUDI
ARABIA
Riyadh
QATAR
UNITED ARAB
EMIRATES
Karachi
PAKISTAN
New Delhi
NEPAL
BHU.
Ganges
I N D I A
BNGL.
Guangzhou
Macau
Hong Kong
Haikou
Hainan
TAIWAN
BONIN IS. (JAPAN)
Tropic of Cancer
WAKE (U.S.A.)
NIGER
CHAD
SUDAN
Nile
ERITREA
YEMEN
Aden
OMAN
Mecca
Mumbai
Hyderabad
Chennai
ARABIAN
SEA
Kolkata
MYANMAR
Rangoon
LAOS
THAILAND
VIET-
NAM
Hué
Hanoi
NORTHERN MARIANA IS. (U.S.A.)
GUAM (U.S.A.)
NIGERIA
Lagos
CAMEROON
CENTRAL AFRICAN
REPUBLIC
ETHIOPIA
Addis
Ababa
DJIBOUTI
SOMALIA
LAKSHADWEEP (INDIA)
Colombo
SRI LANKA
BAY OF
BENGAL
ANDAMAN IS. (INDIA)
NICOBAR IS. (INDIA)
Bangkok
CAMBODIA
Ho Chi Minh City
MALAYSIA
SINGAPORE
BRUNEI
Manila
PHILIPPINES
Mindanao
Yap
PALAU
FED. STATES OF MICRONESIA
MARSHALL IS.
EQUATORIAL
GUINEA
SAO TOME
PRINCIPE
GABON
Congo
DEM. REP.
OF THE
CONGO
UGANDA
RWANDA
BURUNDI
KENYA
Nairobi
Mogadishu
MALDIVES
SEYCHELLES
CHAGOS ARCH. (B.I.O.T.)
SUMATRA
Jakarta
JAVA
BORNEO
Celebes
I N D O N E S I A
EAST
TIMOR
Molucca
Halmahera
NEW
GUINEA
PAPUA
NEW GUINEA
New Ireland
New
Britain
SOLOMON ISLANDS
NAURU
KIRIBATI
Longitude East of Greenwich
Equator
Brazzaville
CABINDA
Kinshasa
Luanda
ANGOLA
ZAMBIA
TANZANIA
Mombasa
Zanzibar
MALAWI
COMOROS
CHRISTMAS
CHRISTMAS IS. (AUSTL.)
COCOS IS. (AUSTL.)
Darwin
CORAL SEA
TÜVALU
FIJI
Suva
VANUATU
NAMIBIA
BOTSWANA
ZIMBABWE
(RHODESIA)
MOZAMBIQUE
MADAGASCAR
Antananarivo
RÉUNION (FR.)
MAURITIUS
RODRIGUES
I N D I A N
O C E A N
Tropic of Capricorn
A U S T R A L I A
Perth
Darling
NEW CALEDONIA (FR.)
Nouméa
Île Loyauté
Brisbane
SOUTH
AFRICA
SWAZILAND
LESOTHO
Pretoria
Maputo
Durban
Cape Town
ÎLE AMSTERDAM
ÎLE ST. PAUL (F.S.A.T.)
Adelaide
Sydney
Canberra
LORD HOWE IS. (AUSTL.)
PRINCE
EDWARD IS.
(S. AFR.)
ÎLES CROZET (F.S.A.T.)
ÎLES
KERGUELEN (F.S.A.T.)
Melbourne
Tasmania
Hobart
NEW ZEALAND
Auckland
North I.
Wellington
Christchurch
South I.
Stewart I.
HEARD (AUSTL.)
AUCKLAND IS. (N.Z.)
MACQUARIE IS. (AUSTL.)
CAMPBELL (N.Z.)
BOUVETØYA (NORWAY)
Meridian of Greenwich
Antarctic Circle
Kemp Coast
Enderby Land
Conflicting Political Claims (by U. K.,
Austl., Arg., Chile, Fr., etc., none of
which is recognized by the U. S. A.
Adélie Coast
Queen Mary
Coast
WILKES LAND
Victoria
Land
Balleny Is.
Ross
Sea

Goode's Homolosine Equal Area Projection

WORLD TOTAL 57,900,000 square miles

	50	60	70	80	90	100

| ZAMBIA 291 | ALL OTHERS 2,938 | CANADA 3,850 | UNITED STATES 3,787 | GREENLAND 840 | MEXICO 760 | OTHER 263 | BRAZIL 3,300 | ARGENTINA 1,074 | PERU 496 | COLOMBIA 441 | BOLIVIA 424 | VENEZUELA 352 | CHILE 292 | OTHER 521 | AUSTRALIA 2,966 | OTHER 334 | ANTARCTICA 5,400 |

NORTH AMERICA 9,500 — SOUTH AMERICA 6,900 — OCEANIA 3,300 — ANTARCTICA 5,400

WORLD TOTAL 5,952,000,000 inhabitants

	50	60	70	80	90	100

| .1 | IRAN 64.8 | THAILAND 60.3 | MYANMAR 47.7 | S. KOREA 46.7 | ALL OTHERS 323.2 | 28.1 | RUSSIA 118.5 | GERMANY 82.7 | UNITED KINGDOM 59.0 | FRANCE 58.9 | ITALY 56.8 | UKRAINE 50.0 | SPAIN 39.2 | POLAND 38.6 | ROMANIA 22.4 | NETHERLANDS 15.8 | ALL OTHERS 167.4 | NIGERIA 112.2 | EGYPT 66.7 | ETHIOPIA 59.0 | D.R. CONGO 49.7 | S. AFRICA 43.1 | SUDAN 34.0 | TANZANIA 30.9 | ALGERIA 30.8 | MOROCCO 29.4 | KENYA 28.6 | ALL OTHERS 285.9 | UNITED STATES 271.5 | MEXICO 99.4 | CANADA 30.5 | ALL OTHERS 71.2 | BRAZIL 170.9 | COLOMBIA 39.0 | ARGENTINA 36.5 | ALL OTHERS 94.4 | OCEANIA 29.9 |

EUROPE 709.3 — AFRICA 770.3 — NORTH AMERICA 472.6 — S. AMERICA 340.8

4

PHYSICAL

Copyright by Rand McNally & Co.
Made in U.S.A.
N-GDS10000-A1- -1-|-3

Scale 1 : 100 000 000 (approximate)
One inch to 1,600 miles

0 500 1000 1500 2000 miles

0 500 1000 1500 2000 2500 Kilometers

Meters	Feet
3 050	10 000
1 525	5 000
610	2 000
305	1 000
0	SEA LEVEL 0
	BELOW SEA LEVEL
152.5	500
3 050	10 000
6 100	20 000

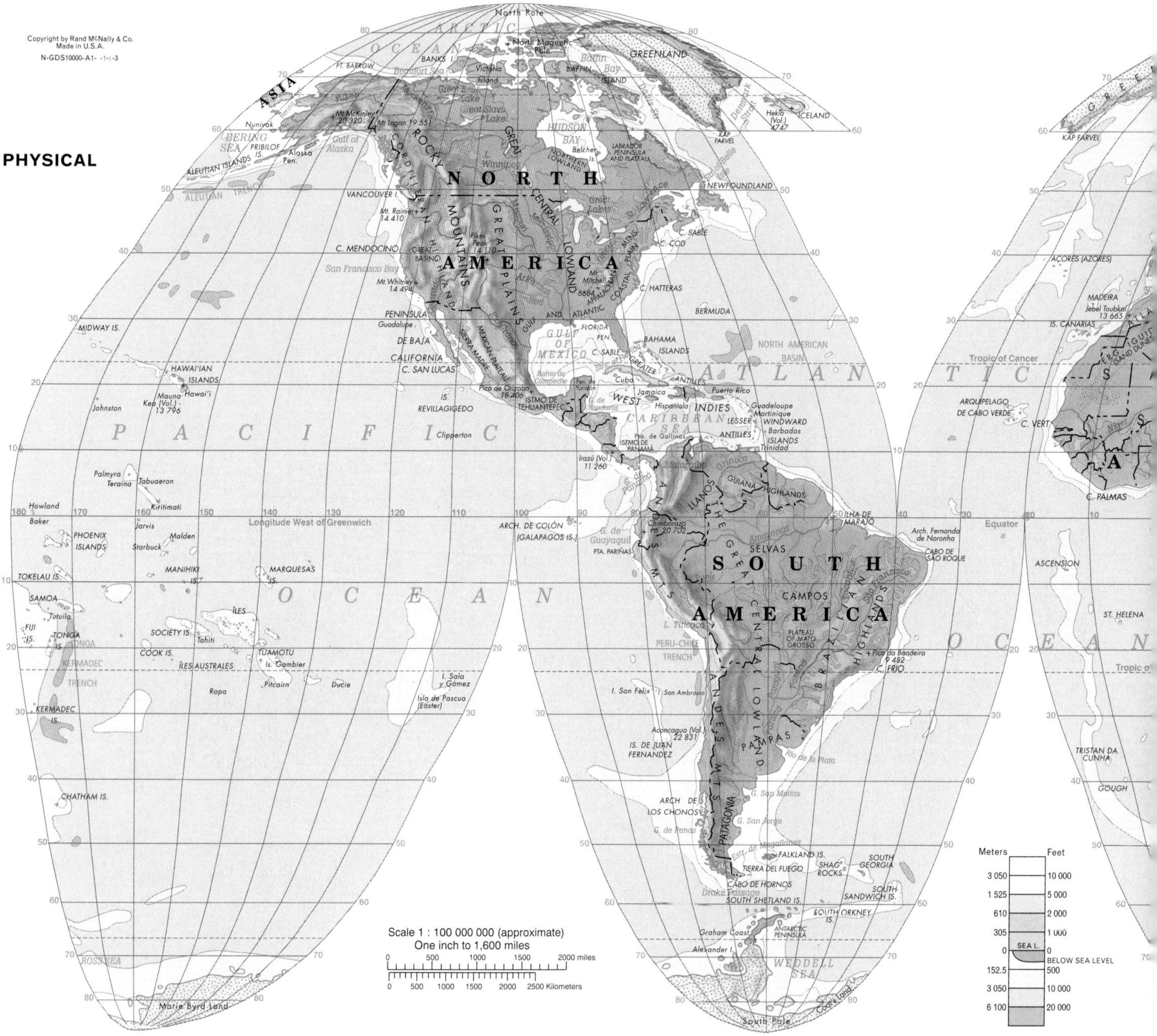

Land Elevations in Profile

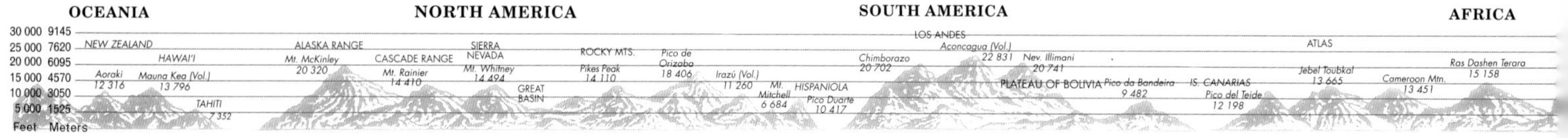

Ocean Depths in Profile

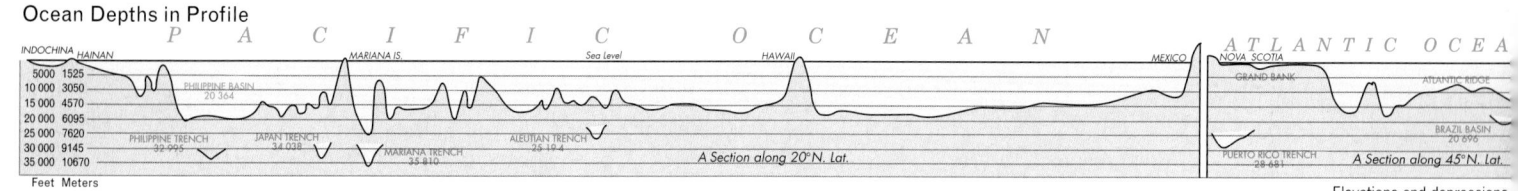

Elevations and depressions

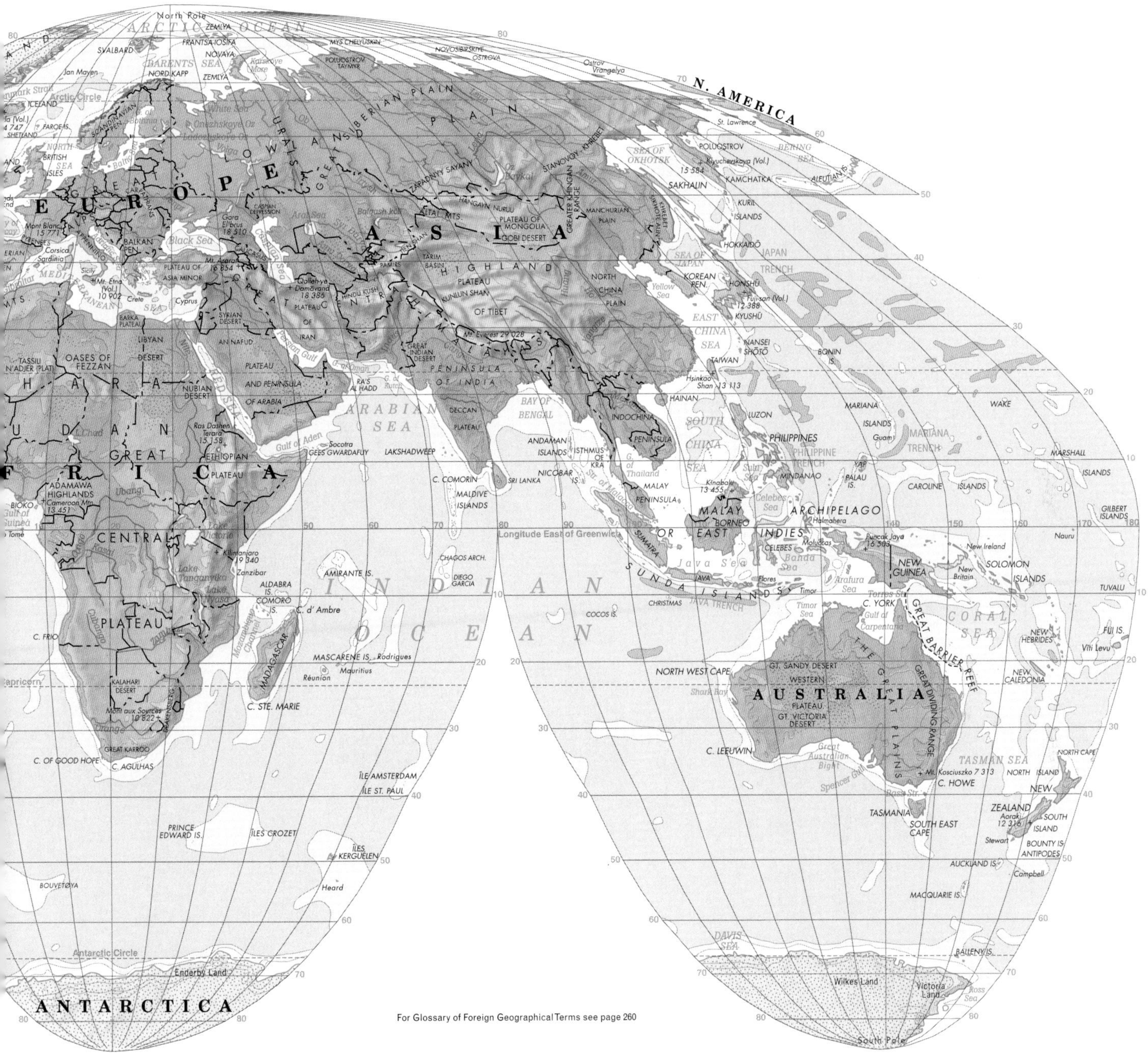

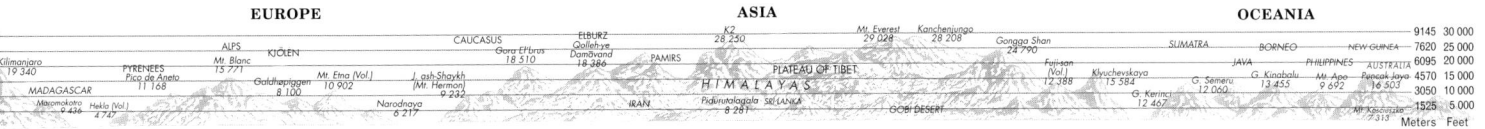

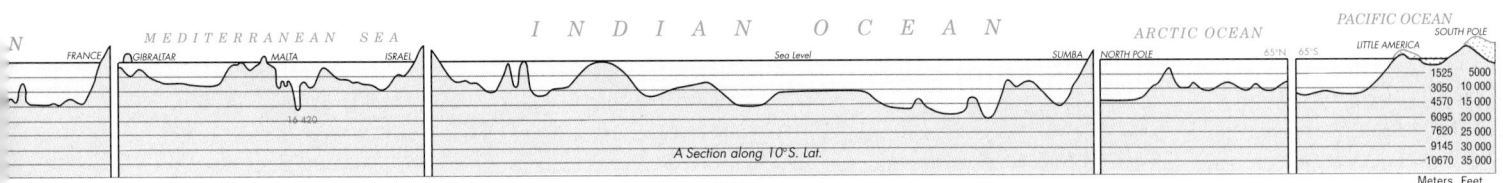

6

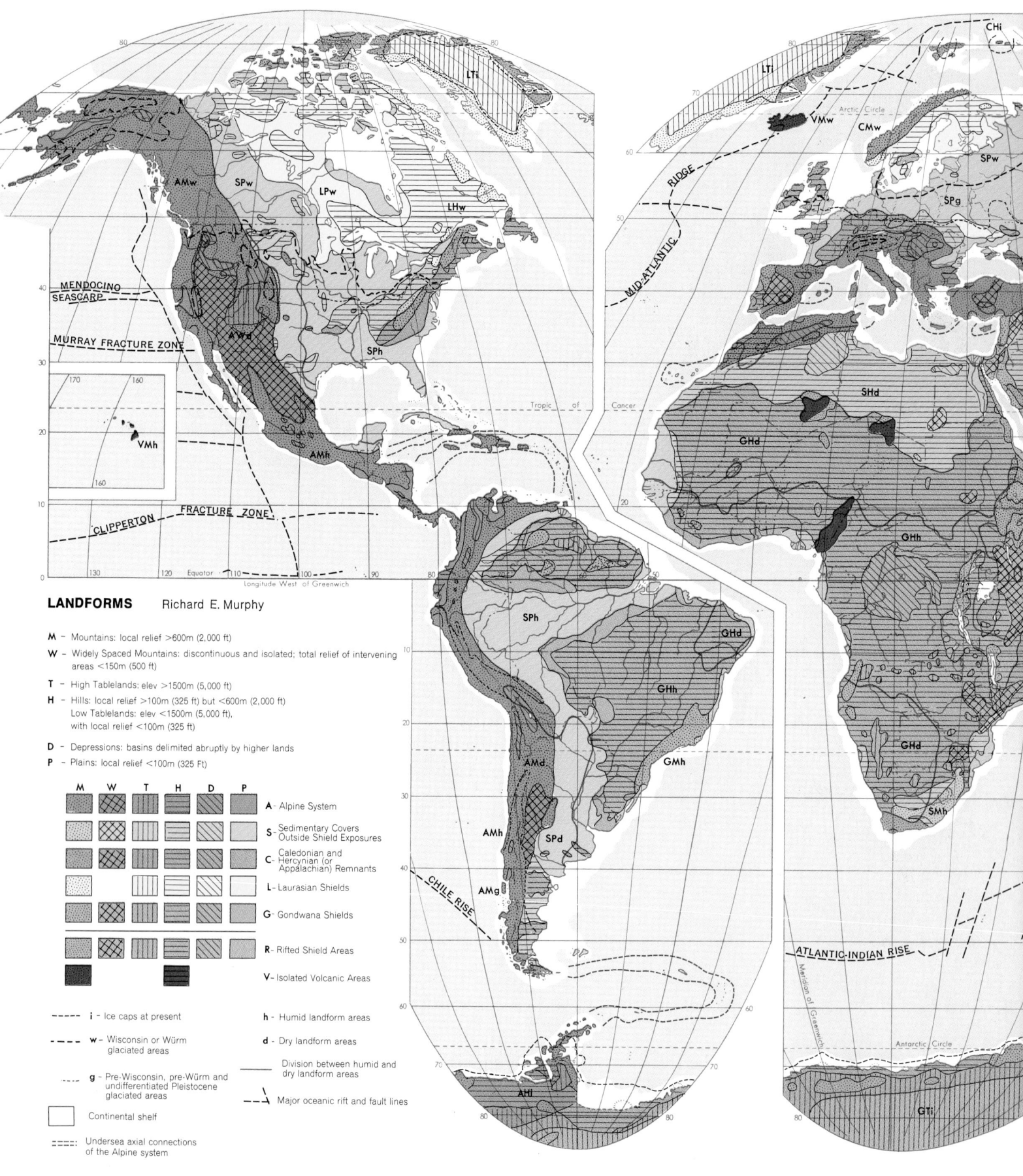

LANDFORMS   Richard E. Murphy

M – Mountains: local relief >600m (2,000 ft)

W – Widely Spaced Mountains: discontinuous and isolated; total relief of intervening areas <150m (500 ft)

T – High Tablelands: elev >1500m (5,000 ft)

H – Hills: local relief >100m (325 ft) but <600m (2,000 ft)
Low Tablelands: elev <1500m (5,000 ft), with local relief <100m (325 ft)

D – Depressions: basins delimited abruptly by higher lands

P – Plains: local relief <100m (325 Ft)

M   W   T   H   D   P

A - Alpine System

S - Sedimentary Covers Outside Shield Exposures

C - Caledonian and Hercynian (or Appalachian) Remnants

L - Laurasian Shields

G - Gondwana Shields

R - Rifted Shield Areas

V - Isolated Volcanic Areas

- - - - - **i** - Ice caps at present

- - - - - **w** - Wisconsin or Würm glaciated areas

- - - - - **g** - Pre-Wisconsin, pre-Würm and undifferentiated Pleistocene glaciated areas

h - Humid landform areas

d - Dry landform areas

——— Division between humid and dry landform areas

- - - - Major oceanic rift and fault lines

☐ Continental shelf

═══ Undersea axial connections of the Alpine system

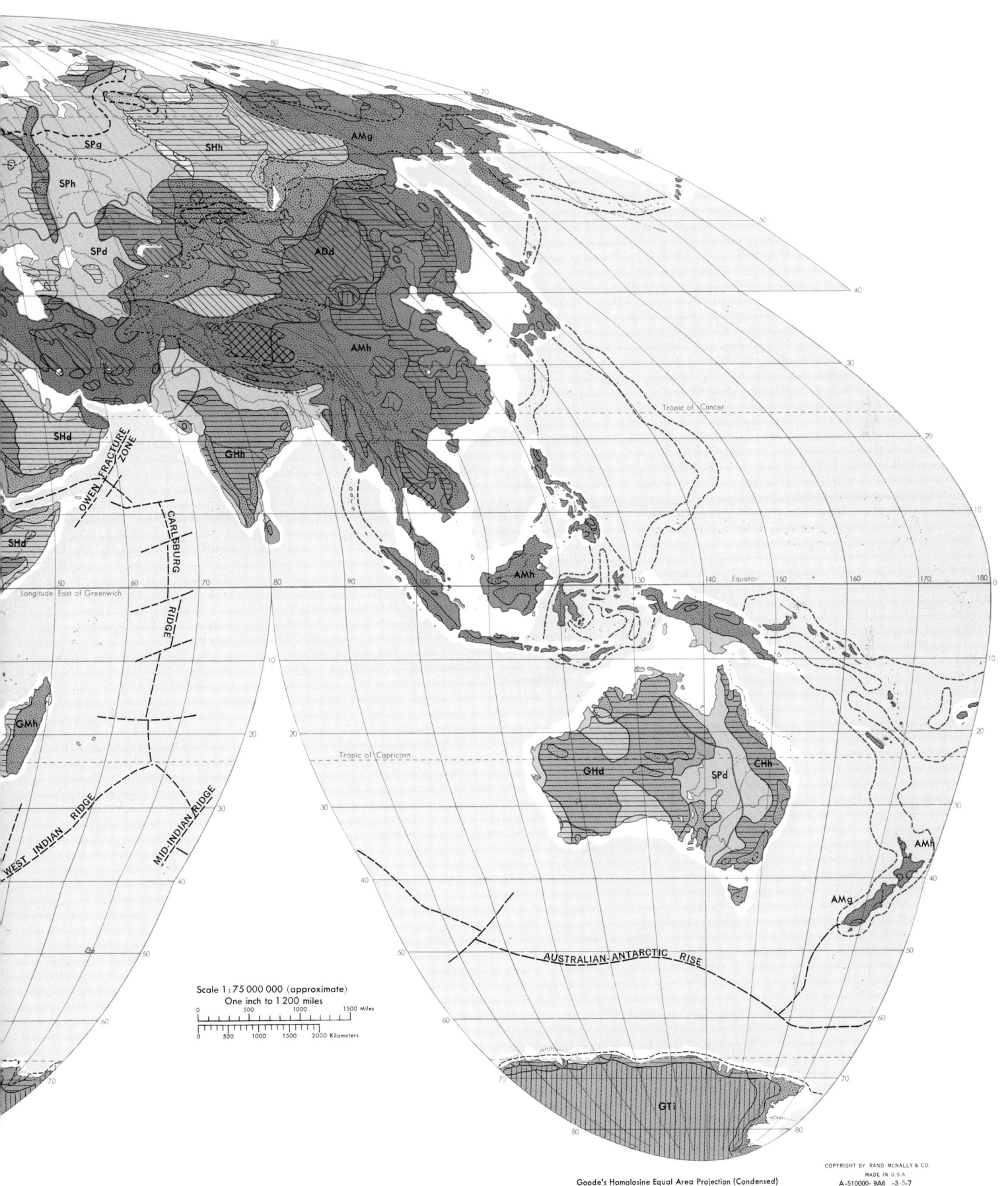

SPg

SHh

AMg

SPh

SPd

ADd

AMh

SHd

OWEN FRACTURE ZONE

CARLSBURG RIDGE

GHh

SHd

AMh

GMh

WEST INDIAN RIDGE

MID-INDIAN RIDGE

Tropic of Cancer

Equator

Longitude East of Greenwich

Tropic of Capricorn

GHd

SPd

CHh

AMh

AMg

AUSTRALIAN-ANTARCTIC RISE

Scale 1:75 000 000 (approximate)
One inch to 1 200 miles

0   500   1000   1500 Miles

0   500   1000   1500   2000 Kilometers

GTi

Goode's Homolosine Equal Area Projection (Condensed)

CONTINENTAL DRIFT

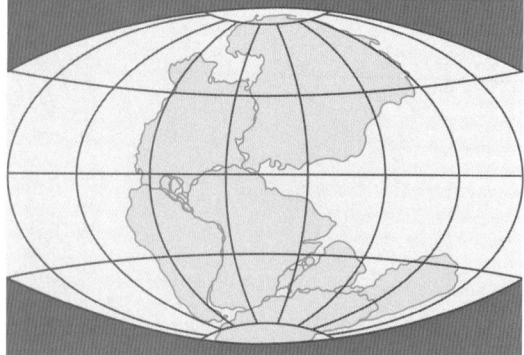

225 million years ago the supercontinent of Pangaea exists and Panthalassa forms the ancestral ocean. Tethys Sea separates Eurasia and Africa.

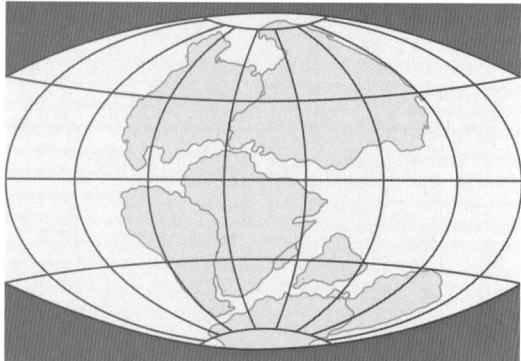

180 million years ago Pangaea splits, Laurasia drifts north. Gondwanaland breaks into South America/Africa, India, and Australia/Antarctica.

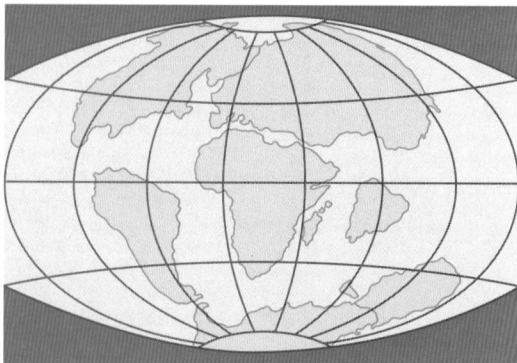

65 million years ago ocean basins take shape as South America and India move from Africa and the Tethys Sea closes to form the Mediterranean Sea.

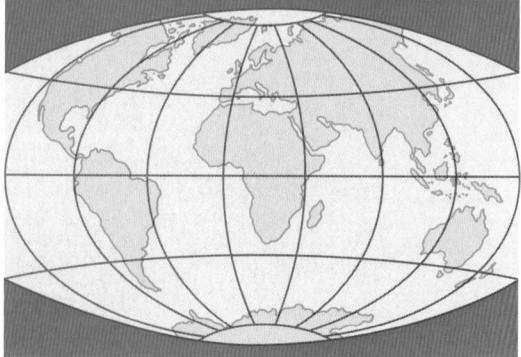

The present day: India has merged with Asia, Australia is free of Antarctica, and North America is free of Eurasia.

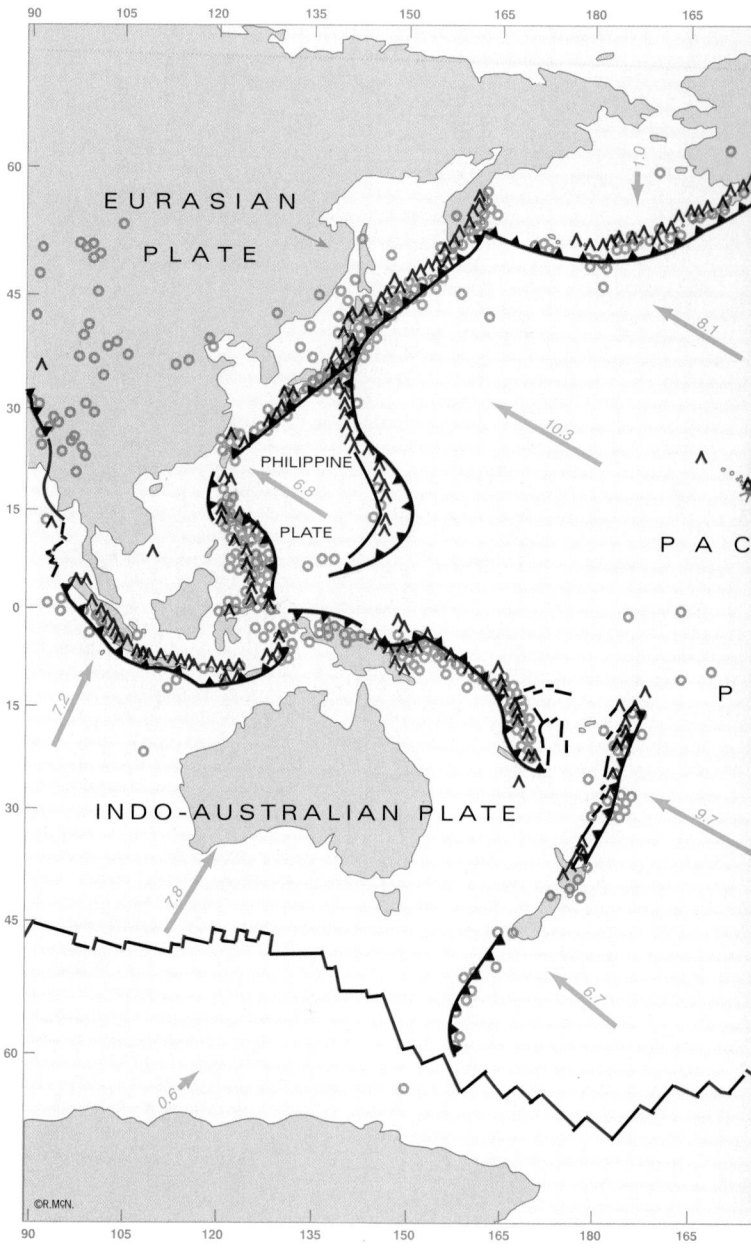

PLATE TECTONICS

Types of plate boundaries

Divergent: magma emerges from the earth's mantle at the mid-ocean ridges forming new crust and forcing the plates to spread apart at the ridges.

Convergent: plates collide at subduction zones where the denser plate is forced back into the earth's mantle forming deep ocean trenches.

Transform: plates slide past one another producing faults and fracture zones.

Other map symbols

Direction of plate movement

6.7 Length of arrow is proportional to the amount of plate movement (number indicates centimeters of movement per year)

○ Earthquake of magnitude 7.5 and above (from 10 A.D. to the present)

∧ Volcano (eruption since 1900)

✳ Selected hot spots

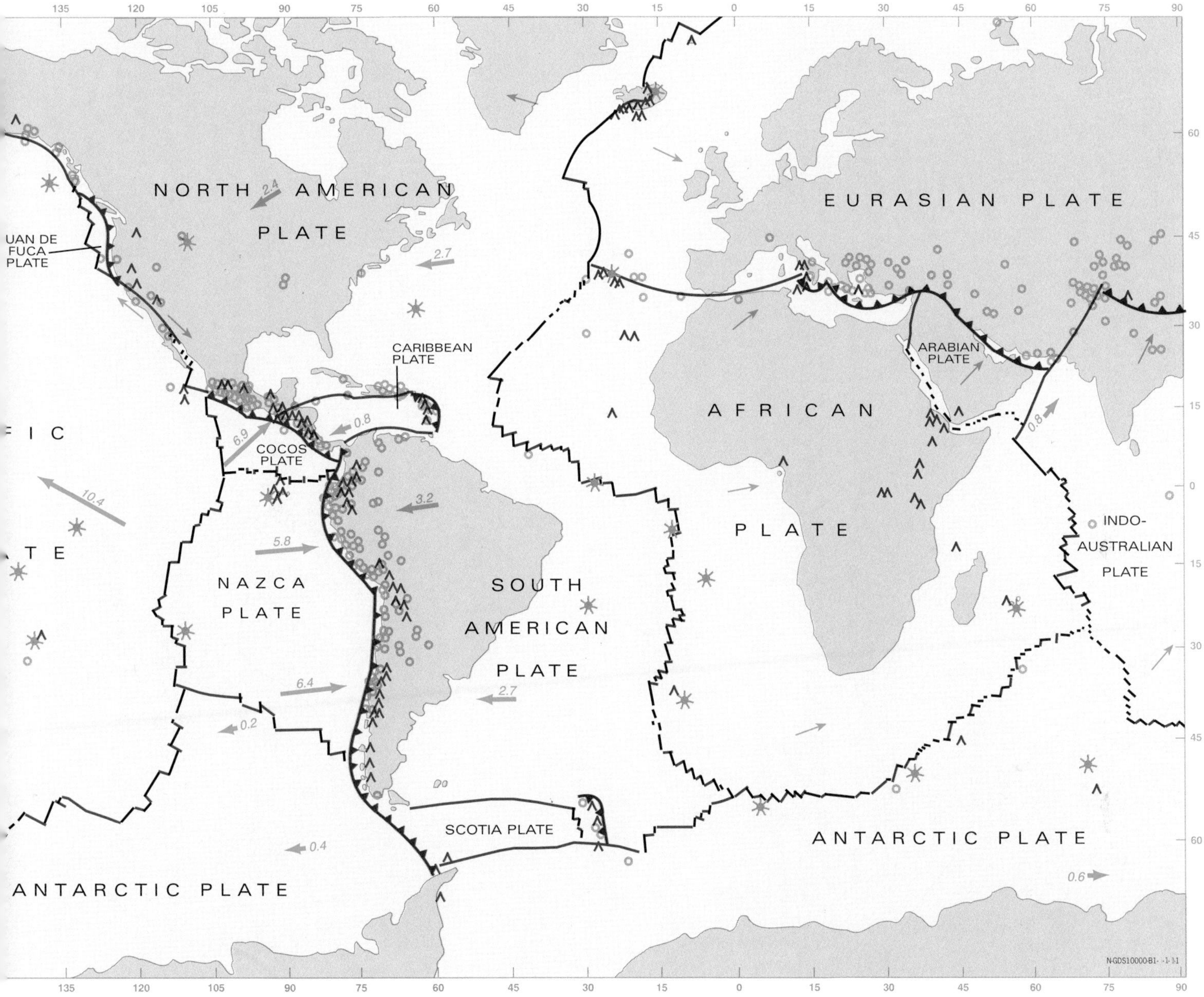

NORTH AMERICAN
PLATE

UAN DE
FUCA
PLATE

CARIBBEAN
PLATE

COCOS
PLATE

NAZCA
PLATE

SOUTH
AMERICAN
PLATE

SCOTIA PLATE

ANTARCTIC PLATE

EURASIAN PLATE

ARABIAN
PLATE

AFRICAN

PLATE

INDO-
AUSTRALIAN
PLATE

ANTARCTIC PLATE

The plate tectonic theory describes the movement of the earth's surface and subsurface and explains why surface features are where they are.

Stated concisely, the theory presumes the lithosphere - the outside crust and uppermost mantle of the earth - is divided into about a dozen major rigid plates and several smaller platelets that move relative to one another. The position and names of the plates are shown on the map above.

The motor that drives the plates is found deep in the mantle. The theory states that because of temperature differences in the mantle, slow convection currents circulate there. Where two molten currents converge and move upward, they separate, causing the crustal plates to bulge and move apart in mid-ocean regions. Transverse fractures disrupt these broad regions. Lava wells up at these points to cause volcanic activity and to form ridges. The plates grow larger by accretion along these mid-ocean ridges, cause vast regions of the crust to move apart, and force the plates to collide with one another. As the plates do so, they are destroyed at subduction zones, where the plates are consumed downward, back into the earth's mantle, forming deep ocean trenches. The diagrams to the right illustrate the processes.

Most of the earth's volcanic and seismic activities

occur where plates slide past each other at transform boundaries or collide along subduction zones. The friction and heat caused by the grinding motion of the subducted plates causes rock to liquify and rise to the surface as volcanoes and eventually form vast mountain ranges. Strong and deep earthquakes are common here.

Volcanoes and earthquakes also occur at random locations around the earth known as "hot spots". Hot rock from deep in the mantle rises to the surface creating some of the earth's tallest mountains. As the lithospheric plates move slowly over these stationary plumes of magma, island chains (such as the Hawaiian Islands) are formed.

The overall result of tectonic movement is that the crustal plates move slowly and inexorably as relatively rigid entitles, carrying the continents along with them. The history of this continental drifting is illustrated in the four maps to the left. It began with a single landmass called the supercontinent of Pangaea and the ancestral sea, the Panthalassa Ocean. Pangaea first split into a northern landmass called Laurasia and a southern block called Gondwanaland and subsequently into the continents we map today. The map of the future will be significantly different as the continents continue to drift.

Subduction
Zone

Ocean Ridge
Zone

Scale 1:72 000 000 at 40° latitude.

Scale 1:72 000 000 at 40° latitude. ROBINSON PROJECTION

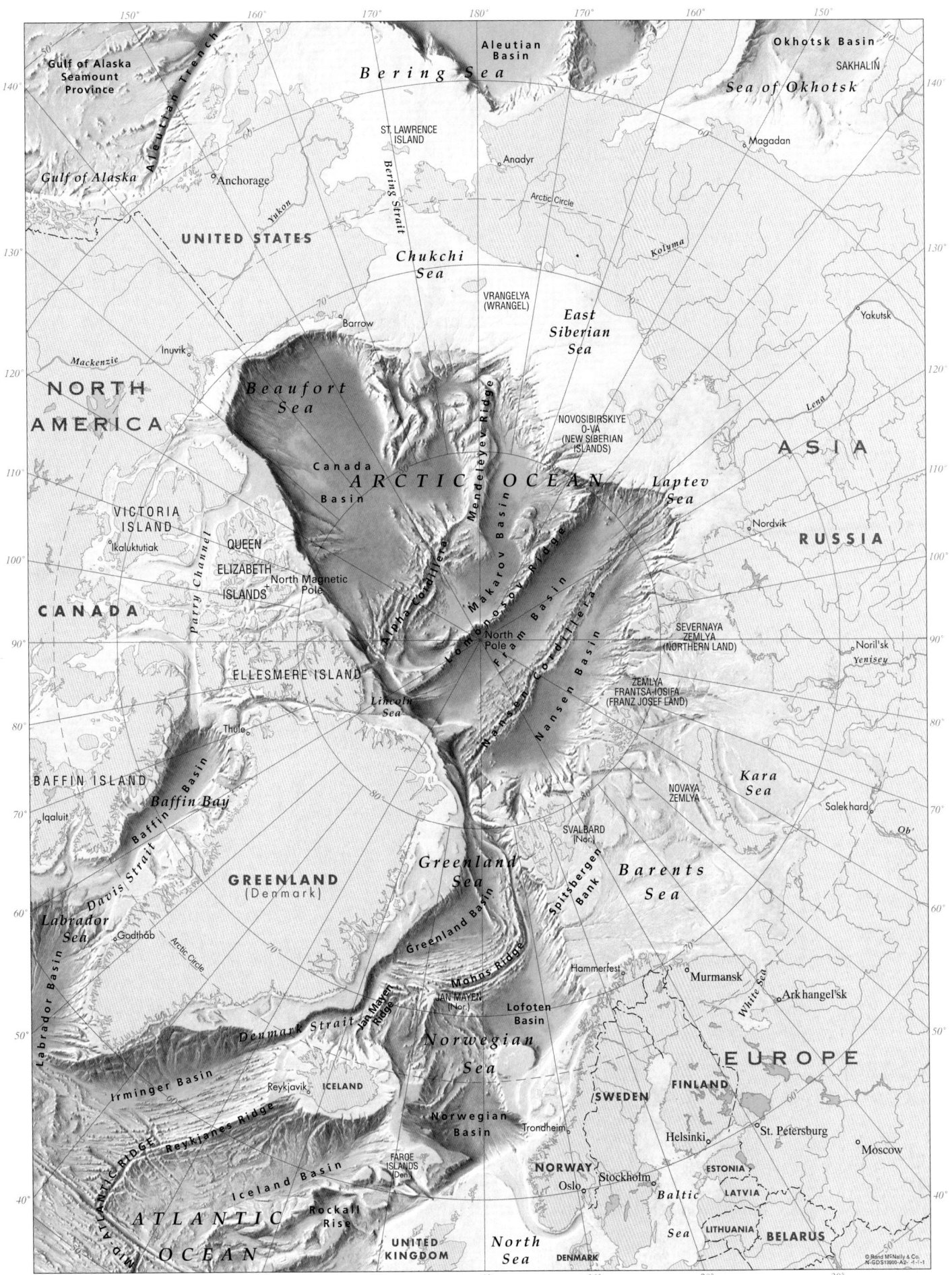

Scale 1:30 000 000. LAMBERT AZIMUTHAL EQUAL AREA PROJECTION

14

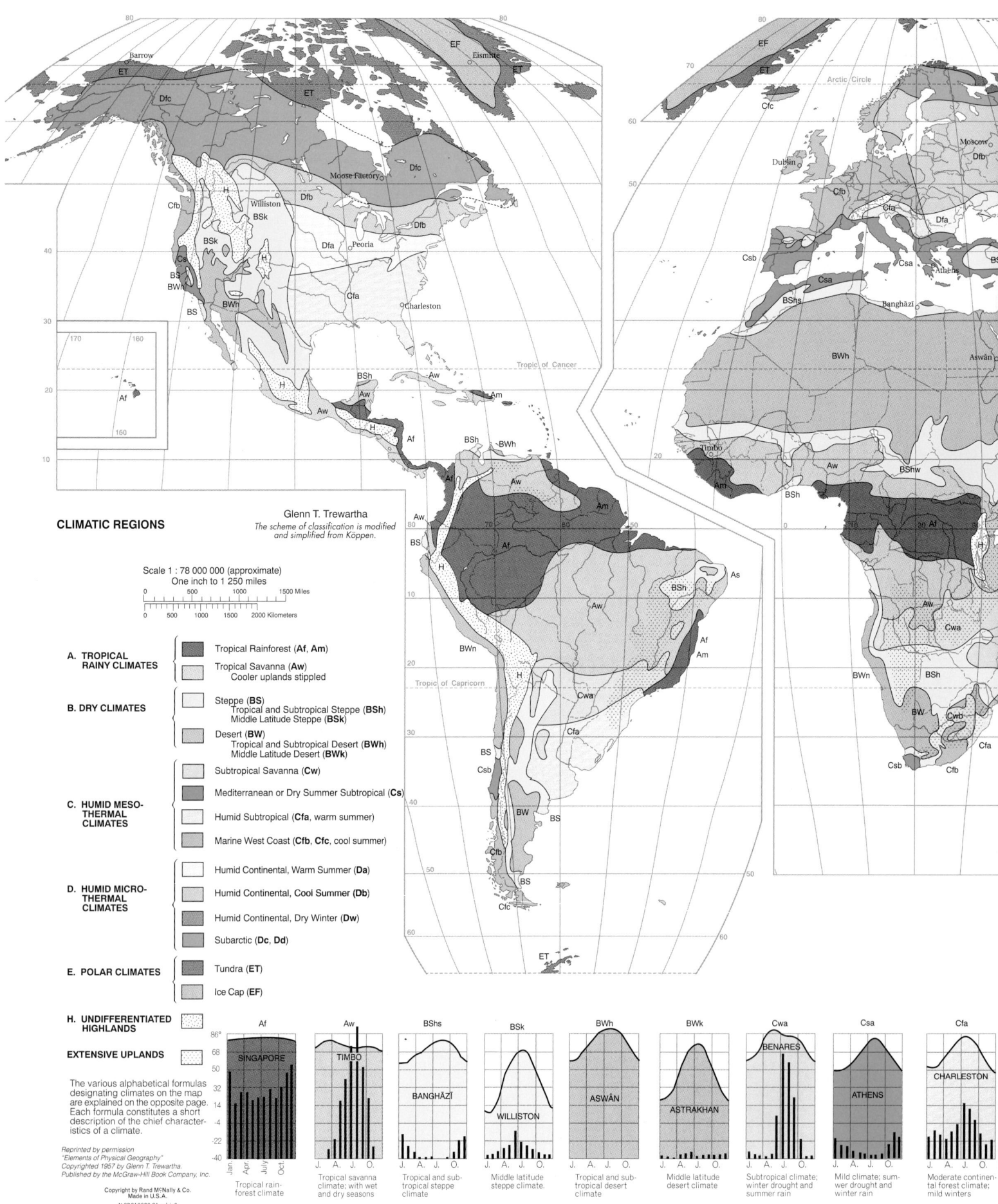

CLIMATIC REGIONS

Glenn T. Trewartha
*The scheme of classification is modified
and simplified from Köppen.*

Scale 1 : 78 000 000 (approximate)
One inch to 1 250 miles

0   500   1000   1500 Miles

0   500   1000   1500   2000 Kilometers

A. TROPICAL RAINY CLIMATES		Tropical Rainforest (**Af, Am**)
		Tropical Savanna (**Aw**) Cooler uplands stippled
B. DRY CLIMATES		Steppe (**BS**) Tropical and Subtropical Steppe (**BSh**) Middle Latitude Steppe (**BSk**)
		Desert (**BW**) Tropical and Subtropical Desert (**BWh**) Middle Latitude Desert (**BWk**)
C. HUMID MESO-THERMAL CLIMATES		Subtropical Savanna (**Cw**)
		Mediterranean or Dry Summer Subtropical (**Cs**)
		Humid Subtropical (**Cfa**, warm summer)
		Marine West Coast (**Cfb, Cfc**, cool summer)
D. HUMID MICRO-THERMAL CLIMATES		Humid Continental, Warm Summer (**Da**)
		Humid Continental, Cool Summer (**Db**)
		Humid Continental, Dry Winter (**Dw**)
		Subarctic (**Dc, Dd**)
E. POLAR CLIMATES		Tundra (**ET**)
		Ice Cap (**EF**)
H. UNDIFFERENTIATED HIGHLANDS		
EXTENSIVE UPLANDS		

The various alphabetical formulas
designating climates on the map
are explained on the opposite page.
Each formula constitutes a short
description of the chief characteristics of a climate.

*Reprinted by permission
"Elements of Physical Geography"
Copyrighted 1957 by Glenn T. Trewartha.
Published by the McGraw-Hill Book Company, Inc.*

Copyright by Rand McNally & Co.
Made in U.S.A.
N-GDS10000-C1- -1-1-2

Af	Aw	BShs	BSk	BWh	BWk	Cwa	Csa	Cfa
SINGAPORE	TIMBO	BANGHĀZĪ	WILLISTON	ASWÂN	ASTRAKHAN	BENARES	ATHENS	CHARLESTON
Tropical rain-forest climate	Tropical savanna climate; with wet and dry seasons	Tropical and sub-tropical steppe climate	Middle latitude steppe climate.	Tropical and sub-tropical desert climate	Middle latitude desert climate	Subtropical climate; winter drought and summer rain	Mild climate; sum-wer drought and winter rain	Moderate continen-tal forest climate; mild winters

86°
68
50
32
14
-4
-22
-40

J. A. J. O.

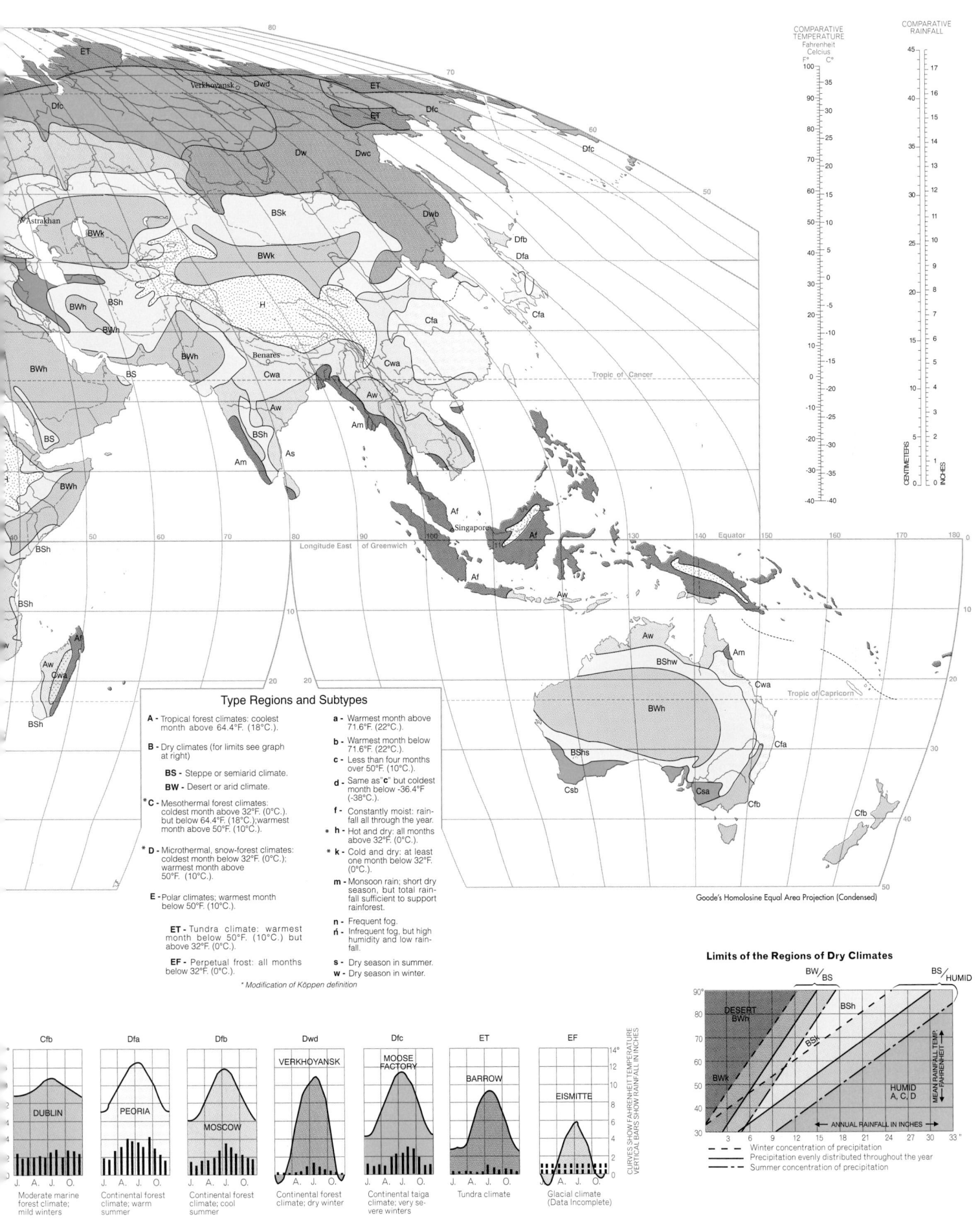

COMPARATIVE
TEMPERATURE
Fahrenheit
Celcius

COMPARATIVE
RAINFALL

Goode's Homolosine Equal Area Projection (Condensed)

Type Regions and Subtypes

A - Tropical forest climates: coolest month above 64.4°F. (18°C.).

B - Dry climates (for limits see graph at right)

    BS - Steppe or semiarid climate.

    BW - Desert or arid climate.

*C - Mesothermal forest climates: coldest month above 32°F. (0°C.). but below 64.4°F. (18°C.);warmest month above 50°F. (10°C.).

*D - Microthermal, snow-forest climates: coldest month below 32°F. (0°C.); warmest month above 50°F. (10°C.).

E - Polar climates; warmest month below 50°F. (10°C.).

    ET - Tundra climate: warmest month below 50°F. (10°C.) but above 32°F. (0°C.).

    EF - Perpetual frost: all months below 32°F. (0°C.).

    * Modification of Köppen definition

a - Warmest month above 71.6°F. (22°C.).

b - Warmest month below 71.6°F. (22°C.).

c - Less than four months over 50°F. (10°C.).

d - Same as "**c**" but coldest month below -36.4°F (-38°C.).

f - Constantly moist: rainfall all through the year.

* h - Hot and dry: all months above 32°F. (0°C.).

* k - Cold and dry: at least one month below 32°F. (0°C.).

m - Monsoon rain; short dry season, but total rainfall sufficient to support rainforest.

n - Frequent fog.

ń - Infrequent fog, but high humidity and low rainfall.

s - Dry season in summer.

w - Dry season in winter.

Limits of the Regions of Dry Climates

- - - Winter concentration of precipitation
——— Precipitation evenly distributed throughout the year
-·-·- Summer concentration of precipitation

CURVES SHOW FAHRENHEIT TEMPERATURE
VERTICAL BARS SHOW RAINFALL IN INCHES

Cfb	Dfa	Dfb	Dwd	Dfc	ET	EF
DUBLIN	PEORIA	MOSCOW	VERKHOYANSK	MOOSE FACTORY	BARROW	EISMITTE
Moderate marine forest climate; mild winters	Continental forest climate; warm summer	Continental forest climate; cool summer	Continental forest climate; dry winter	Continental taiga climate; very severe winters	Tundra climate	Glacial climate (Data Incomplete)

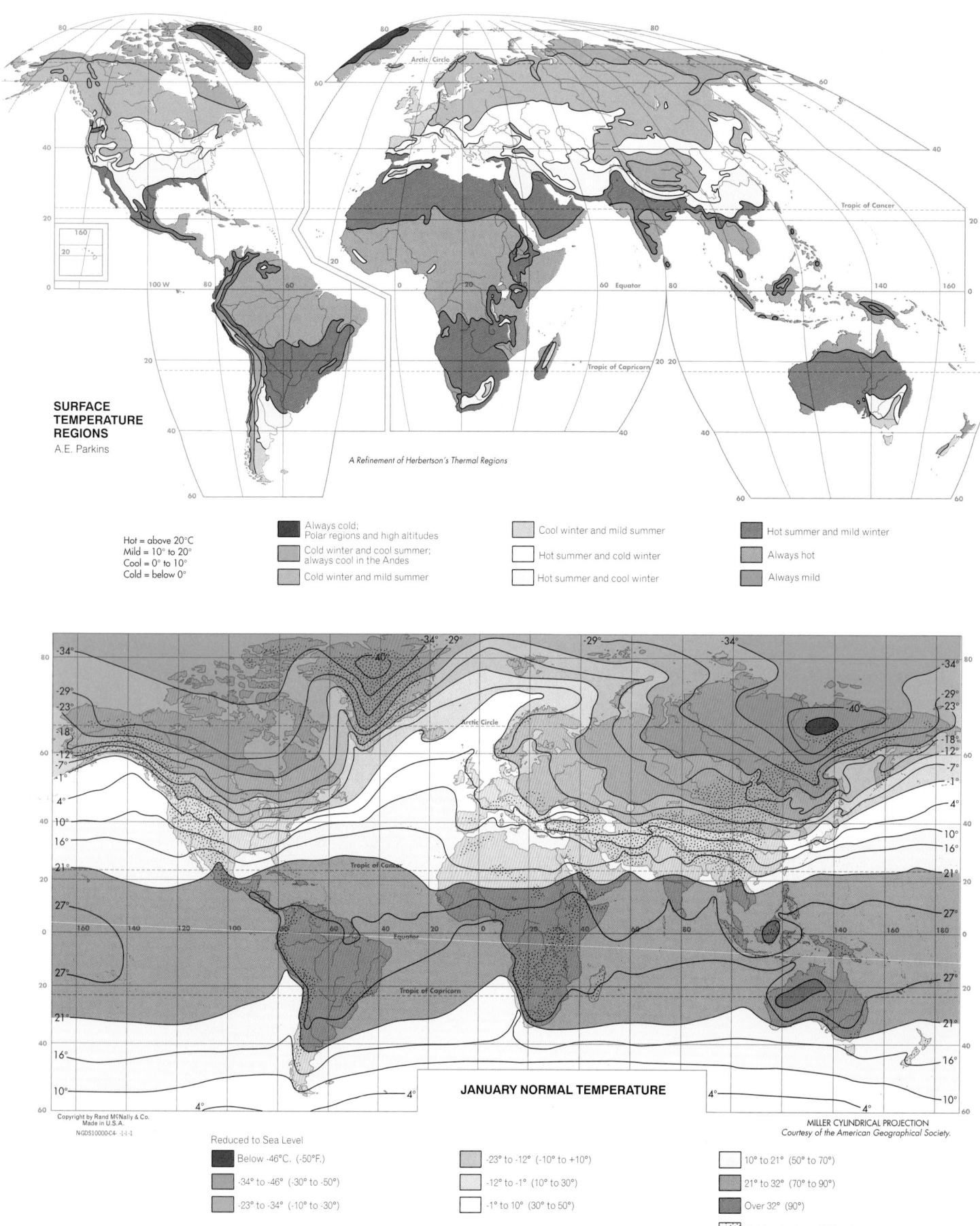

SURFACE TEMPERATURE REGIONS

A.E. Parkins

A Refinement of Herbertson's Thermal Regions

Hot = above 20°C
Mild = 10° to 20°
Cool = 0° to 10°
Cold = below 0°

- Always cold; Polar regions and high altitudes
- Cold winter and cool summer; always cool in the Andes
- Cold winter and mild summer
- Cool winter and mild summer
- Hot summer and cold winter
- Hot summer and cool winter
- Hot summer and mild winter
- Always hot
- Always mild

JANUARY NORMAL TEMPERATURE

Reduced to Sea Level

MILLER CYLINDRICAL PROJECTION
Courtesy of the American Geographical Society.

Copyright by Rand McNally & Co.
Made in U.S.A.
NGDS10000-C4- -14-1

- Below -46°C. (-50°F.)
- -34° to -46° (-30° to -50°)
- -23° to -34° (-10° to -30°)
- -23° to -12° (-10° to +10°)
- -12° to -1° (10° to 30°)
- -1° to 10° (30° to 50°)
- 10° to 21° (50° to 70°)
- 21° to 32° (70° to 90°)
- Over 32° (90°)
- Highlands above 1000 meters

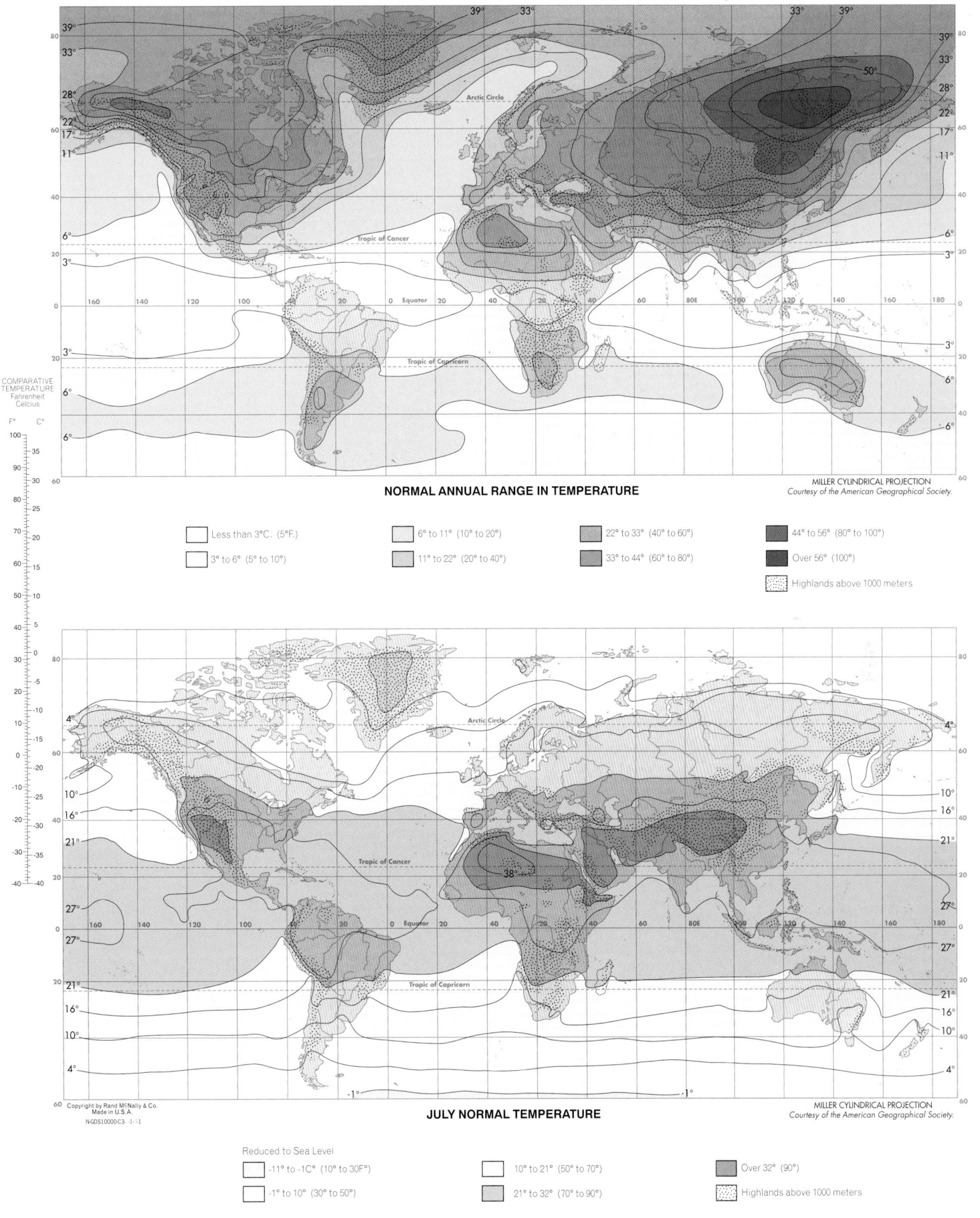

COMPARATIVE
TEMPERATURE
Fahrenheit
Celcius

NORMAL ANNUAL RANGE IN TEMPERATURE

MILLER CYLINDRICAL PROJECTION
Courtesy of the American Geographical Society.

	Less than 3°C. (5°F.)		6° to 11° (10° to 20°)		22° to 33° (40° to 60°)		44° to 56° (80° to 100°)
	3° to 6° (5° to 10°)		11° to 22° (20° to 40°)		33° to 44° (60° to 80°)		Over 56° (100°)
							Highlands above 1000 meters

JULY NORMAL TEMPERATURE

MILLER CYLINDRICAL PROJECTION
Courtesy of the American Geographical Society.

Reduced to Sea Level

	-11° to -1C° (10° to 30F°)		10° to 21° (50° to 70°)		Over 32° (90°)
	-1° to 10° (30° to 50°)		21° to 32° (70° to 90°)		Highlands above 1000 meters

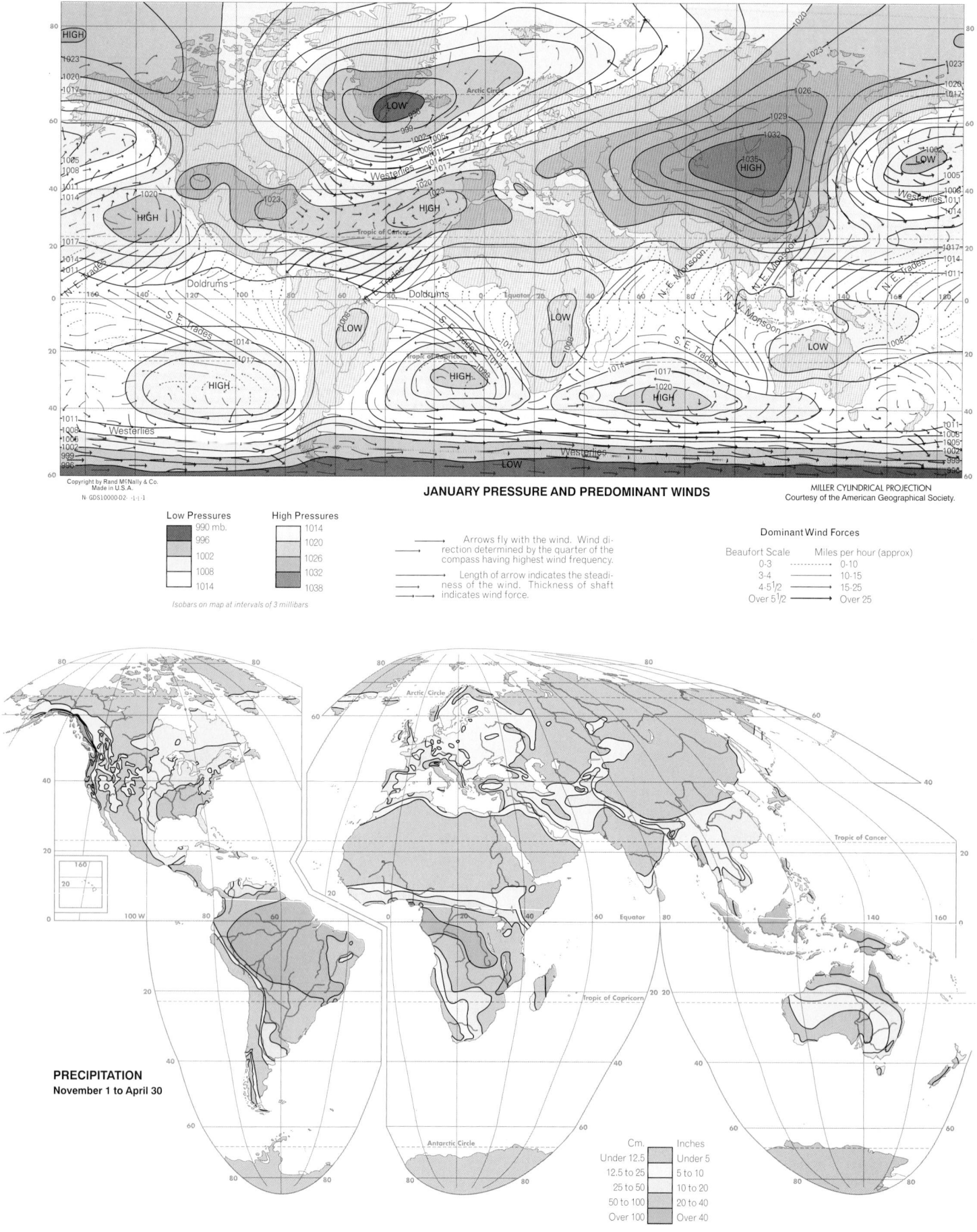

JANUARY PRESSURE AND PREDOMINANT WINDS

MILLER CYLINDRICAL PROJECTION
Courtesy of the American Geographical Society.

Copyright by Rand McNally & Co.
Made in U.S.A.
N- GDS10000-D2- -1-1-1

Low Pressures
990 mb.
996
1002
1008
1014

High Pressures
1014
1020
1026
1032
1038

Isobars on map at intervals of 3 millibars

Arrows fly with the wind. Wind direction determined by the quarter of the compass having highest wind frequency.

Length of arrow indicates the steadiness of the wind. Thickness of shaft indicates wind force.

Dominant Wind Forces

Beaufort Scale	Miles per hour (approx)
0-3	0-10
3-4	10-15
4-5½	15-25
Over 5½	Over 25

PRECIPITATION
November 1 to April 30

Cm.	Inches
Under 12.5	Under 5
12.5 to 25	5 to 10
25 to 50	10 to 20
50 to 100	20 to 40
Over 100	Over 40

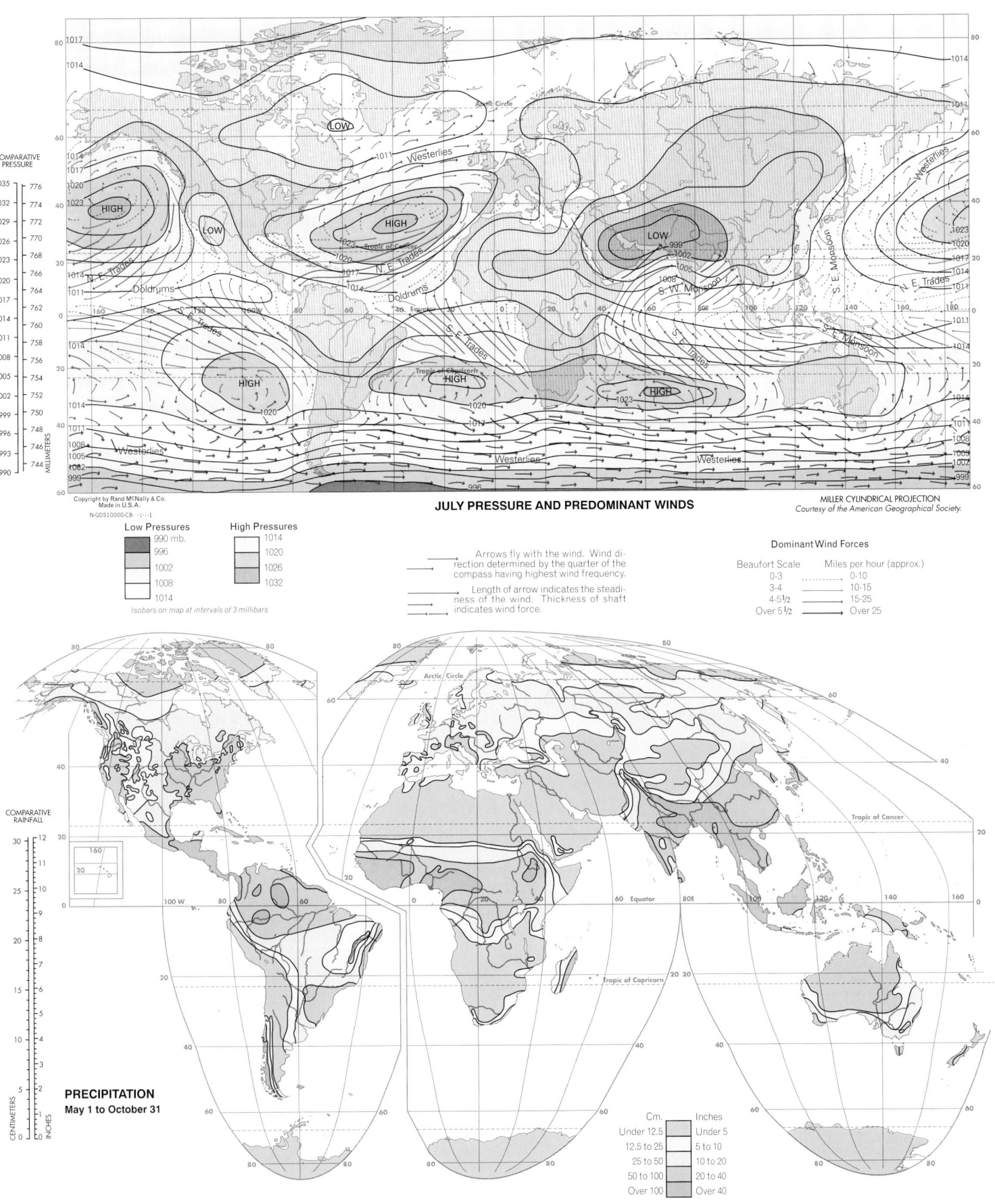

COMPARATIVE
PRESSURE

MILLIBARS	MILLIMETERS
1035	776
1032	774
1029	772
1026	770
1023	768
1020	766
1017	764
1014	762
1011	760
1008	758
1005	756
1002	754
999	752
996	750
993	748
990	746
	744

Copyright by Rand McNally & Co.
Made in U.S.A.

N-GDS10000-C8- -1-1-1

JULY PRESSURE AND PREDOMINANT WINDS

MILLER CYLINDRICAL PROJECTION
Courtesy of the American Geographical Society.

Low Pressures
- 990 mb.
- 996
- 1002
- 1008
- 1014

High Pressures
- 1014
- 1020
- 1026
- 1032

Isobars on map at intervals of 3 millibars

→ Arrows fly with the wind. Wind direction determined by the quarter of the compass having highest wind frequency.

→ Length of arrow indicates the steadiness of the wind. Thickness of shaft indicates wind force.

Dominant Wind Forces

Beaufort Scale	Miles per hour (approx.)
0-3	0-10
3-4	10-15
4-5½	15-25
Over 5½	Over 25

COMPARATIVE
RAINFALL

CENTIMETERS	INCHES
30	12
	11
25	10
	9
20	8
	7
15	6
	5
10	4
	3
5	2
	1
0	0

PRECIPITATION
May 1 to October 31

Cm.	Inches
Under 12.5	Under 5
12.5 to 25	5 to 10
25 to 50	10 to 20
50 to 100	20 to 40
Over 100	Over 40

ANNUAL PRECIPITATON AND OCEAN CURRENTS

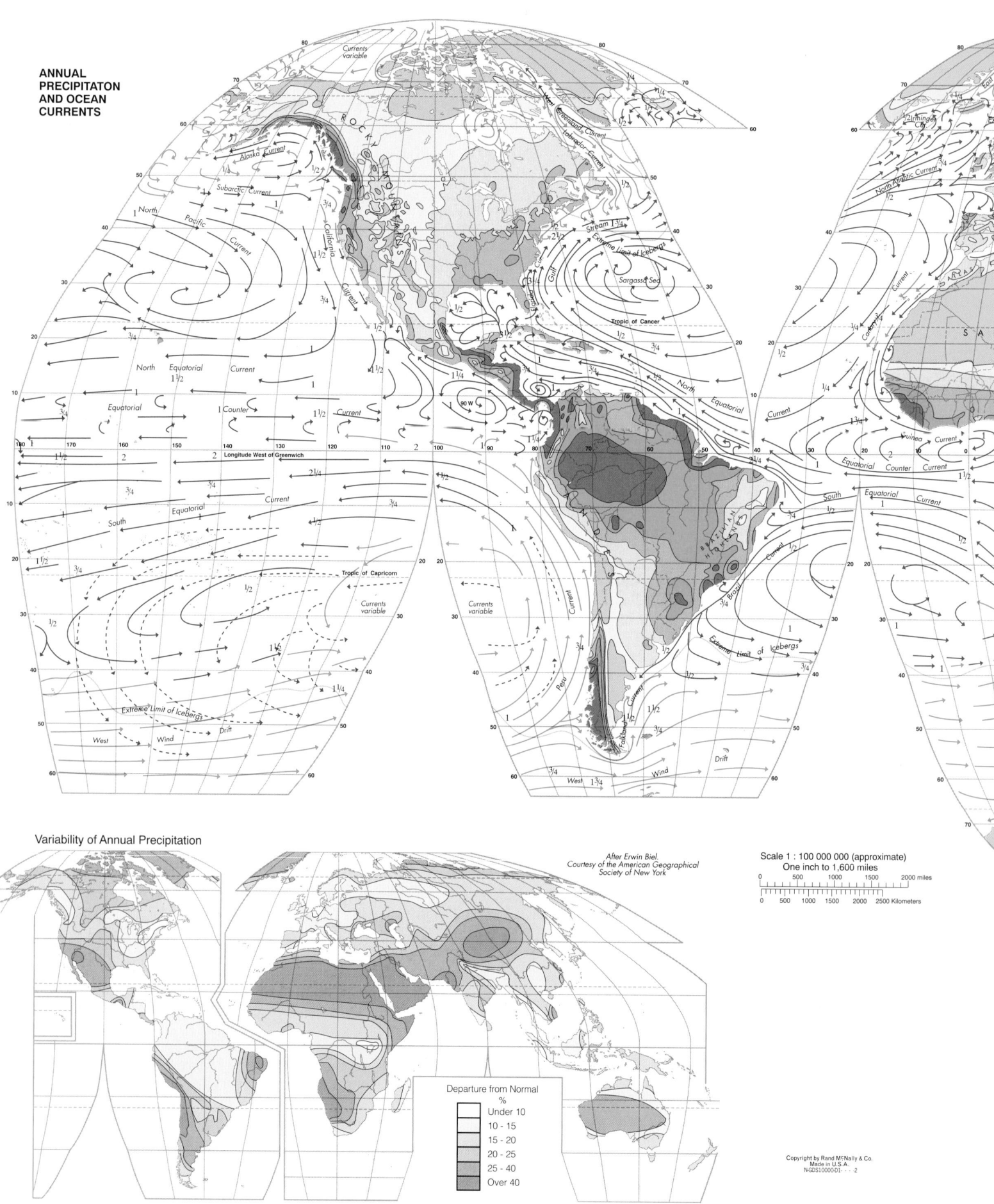

Variability of Annual Precipitation

After Erwin Biel.
Courtesy of the American Geographical
Society of New York

Scale 1 : 100 000 000 (approximate)
One inch to 1,600 miles

| 0 | 500 | 1000 | 1500 | 2000 miles |

| 0 | 500 | 1000 | 1500 | 2000 | 2500 Kilometers |

Departure from Normal
%
Under 10
10 - 15
15 - 20
20 - 25
25 - 40
Over 40

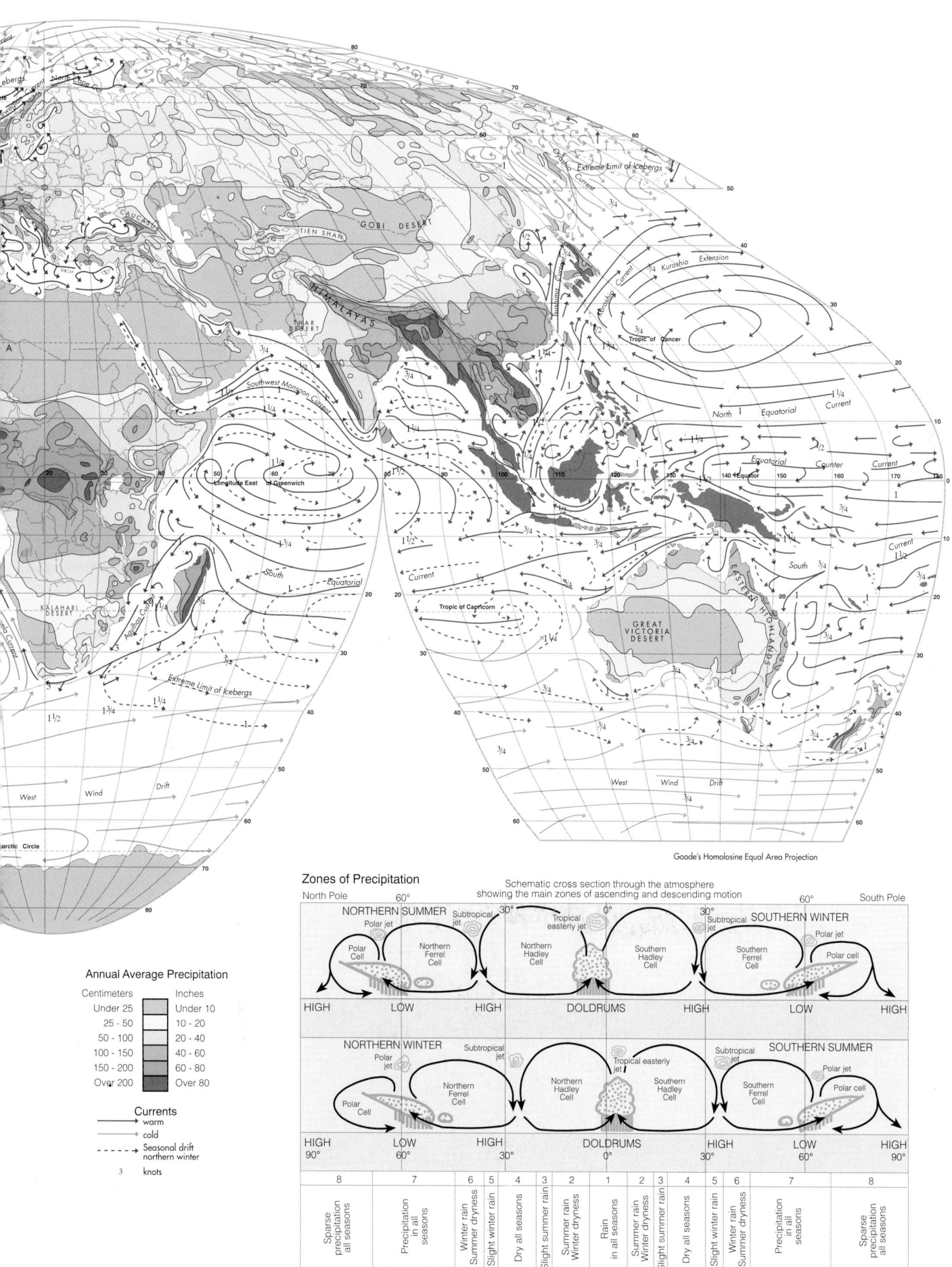

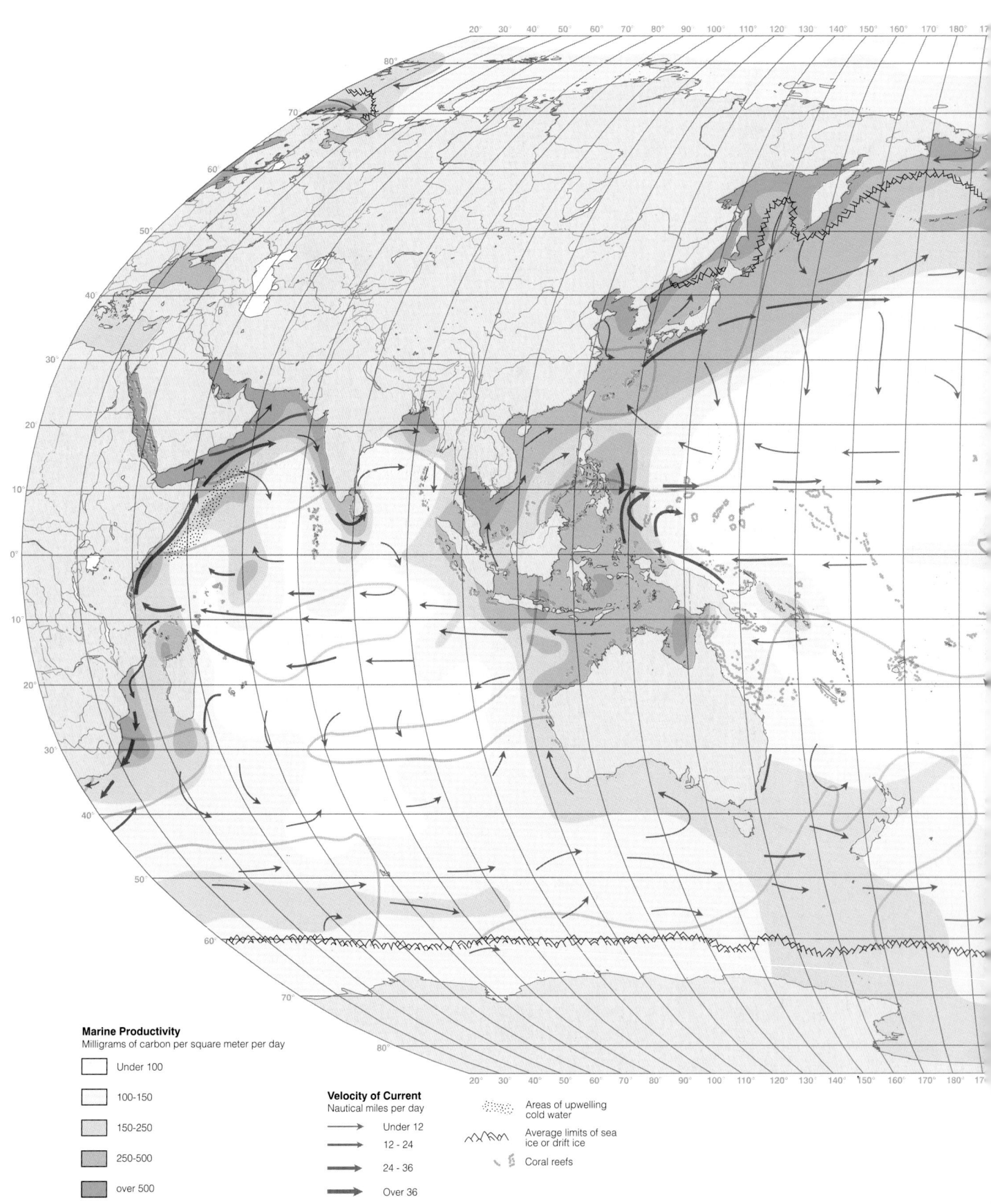

Marine Productivity
Milligrams of carbon per square meter per day

☐	Under 100
☐	100-150
☐	150-250
☐	250-500
☐	over 500

Velocity of Current
Nautical miles per day

→	Under 12
→	12 - 24
→	24 - 36
→	Over 36

Areas of upwelling cold water

Average limits of sea ice or drift ice

Coral reefs

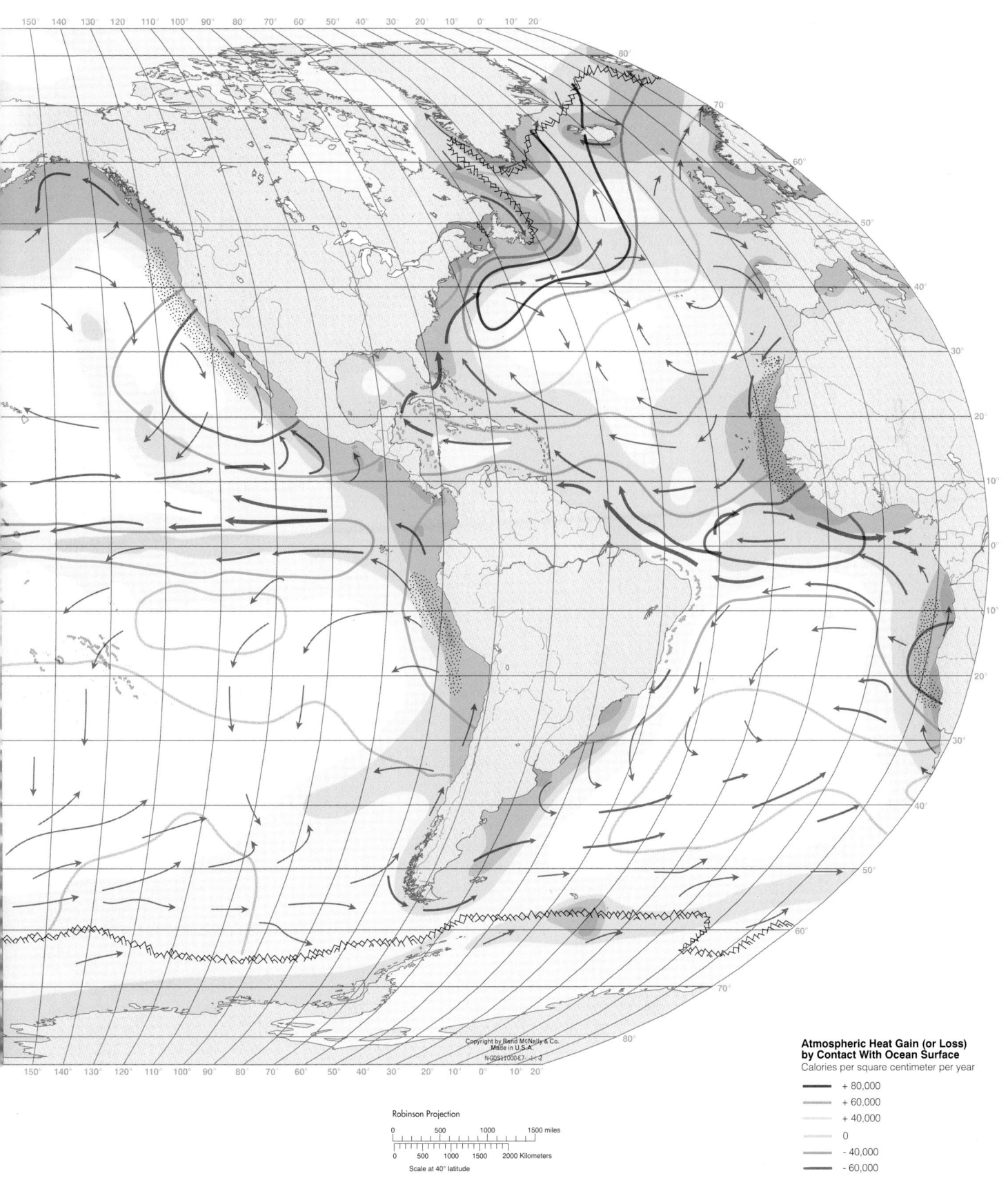

Atmospheric Heat Gain (or Loss) by Contact With Ocean Surface

Calories per square centimeter per year

———	+ 80,000
———	+ 60,000
———	+ 40,000
·······	0
———	- 40,000
———	- 60,000

Robinson Projection

0   500   1000   1500 miles

0   500   1000   1500   2000 Kilometers

Scale at 40° latitude

NATURAL VEGETATION

A.W. Küchler

Scale 1 : 78 000 000 (approximate)
One inch to 1 250 miles

0   500   1000   1500 Miles

0   500   1000   1500   2000 Kilometers

The various formulas are used to designate types of vegetation on this map. Each formula constitutes a short description of the chief characteristics of a vegetation. The classification is based on whether plants are woody or herbaceous, and if woody, whether they are broadleaf or needleleaf and evergreen or deciduous. The small letters are added to give more detail to the description.

All capital letters other than **G** and **L** imply trees, unless accompanied by **s** or **z**. The small letters refer to the capital letter immediately preceding them. Thus, **DsG** means that the vegetation consists of broadleaf deciduous shrubs (**Ds**) and of grass (**G**); **GBp** represents grass (**G**) with patches of broadleaf evergreen trees (**Bp**).

B - Broadleaf evergreen
D - Broadleaf deciduous
E - Needleleaf evergreen
G - Grass
L - Herbaceous plants other than grass
M - Mixed broadleaf deciduous and needleleaf evergreen
N - Needleleaf deciduous
S - Semideciduous: broadleaf evergreen and broadleaf deciduous

b - Vegetation largely or entirely absent
i - Plants sufficiently far apart that they frequently do not touch
p - Growth singly or in groups or patches
s - Shrubform, minimum height 3 feet
z - Dwarf shrubform, maximum height 3 feet

B		Broadleaf evergreen trees
Bs		Broadleaf evergreen, shrubform, minimum height 3 feet
Bsp		Broadleaf evergreen, shrubform, minimum height 3 feet, growth singly or in groups or patches
Bzi, Bz		Broadleaf evergreen, dwarf shrubform, maximum height 3 feet, plants sufficiently far apart that they frequently do not touch
D		Broadleaf deciduous trees
Di		Broadleaf deciduous trees, plants sufficiently far apart that they frequently do not touch

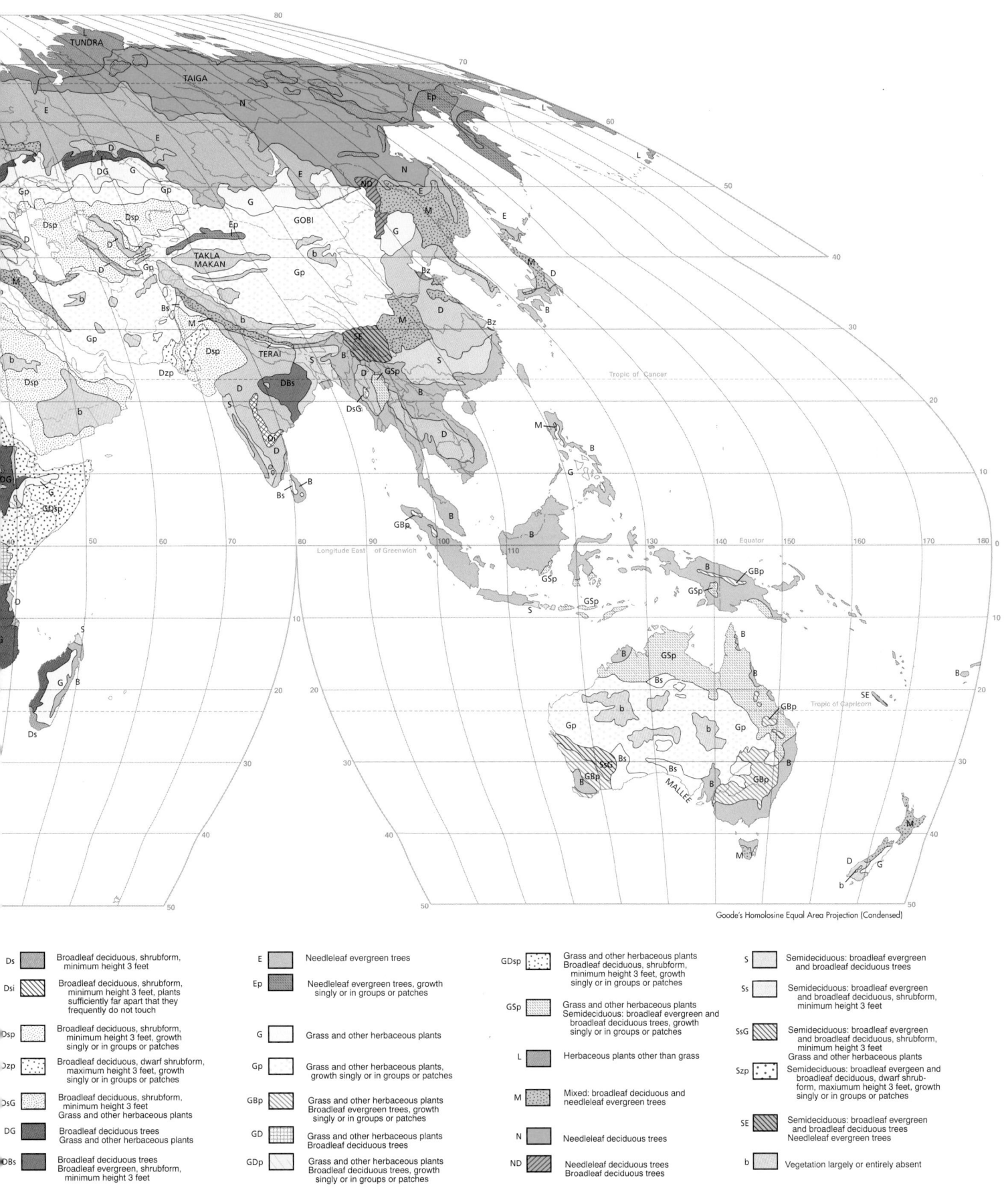

Goode's Homolosine Equal Area Projection (Condensed)

Ds		Broadleaf deciduous, shrubform, minimum height 3 feet
Dsi		Broadleaf deciduous, shrubform, minimum height 3 feet, plants sufficiently far apart that they frequently do not touch
Dsp		Broadleaf deciduous, shrubform, minimum height 3 feet, growth singly or in groups or patches
Dzp		Broadleaf deciduous, dwarf shrubform, maximum height 3 feet, growth singly or in groups or patches
DsG		Broadleaf deciduous, shrubform, minimum height 3 feet Grass and other herbaceous plants
DG		Broadleaf deciduous trees Grass and other herbaceous plants
DBs		Broadleaf deciduous trees Broadleaf evergreen, shrubform, minimum height 3 feet

E		Needleleaf evergreen trees
Ep		Needleleaf evergreen trees, growth singly or in groups or patches
G		Grass and other herbaceous plants
Gp		Grass and other herbaceous plants, growth singly or in groups or patches
GBp		Grass and other herbaceous plants Broadleaf evergreen trees, growth singly or in groups or patches
GD		Grass and other herbaceous plants Broadleaf deciduous trees
GDp		Grass and other herbaceous plants Broadleaf deciduous trees, growth singly or in groups or patches

GDsp		Grass and other herbaceous plants Broadleaf deciduous, shrubform, minimum height 3 feet, growth singly or in groups or patches
GSp		Grass and other herbaceous plants Semideciduous: broadleaf evergreen and broadleaf deciduous trees, growth singly or in groups or patches
L		Herbaceous plants other than grass
M		Mixed: broadleaf deciduous and needleleaf evergreen trees
N		Needleleaf deciduous trees
ND		Needleleaf deciduous trees Broadleaf deciduous trees

S		Semideciduous: broadleaf evergreen and broadleaf deciduous trees
Ss		Semideciduous: broadleaf evergreen and broadleaf deciduous, shrubform, minimum height 3 feet
SsG		Semideciduous: broadleaf evergreen and broadleaf deciduous, shrubform, minimum height 3 feet Grass and other herbaceous plants
Szp		Semideciduous: broadleaf evergreen and broadleaf deciduous, dwarf shrubform, maximum height 3 feet, growth singly or in groups or patches
SE		Semideciduous: broadleaf evergreen and broadleaf deciduous Needleleaf evergreen trees
b		Vegetation largely or entirely absent

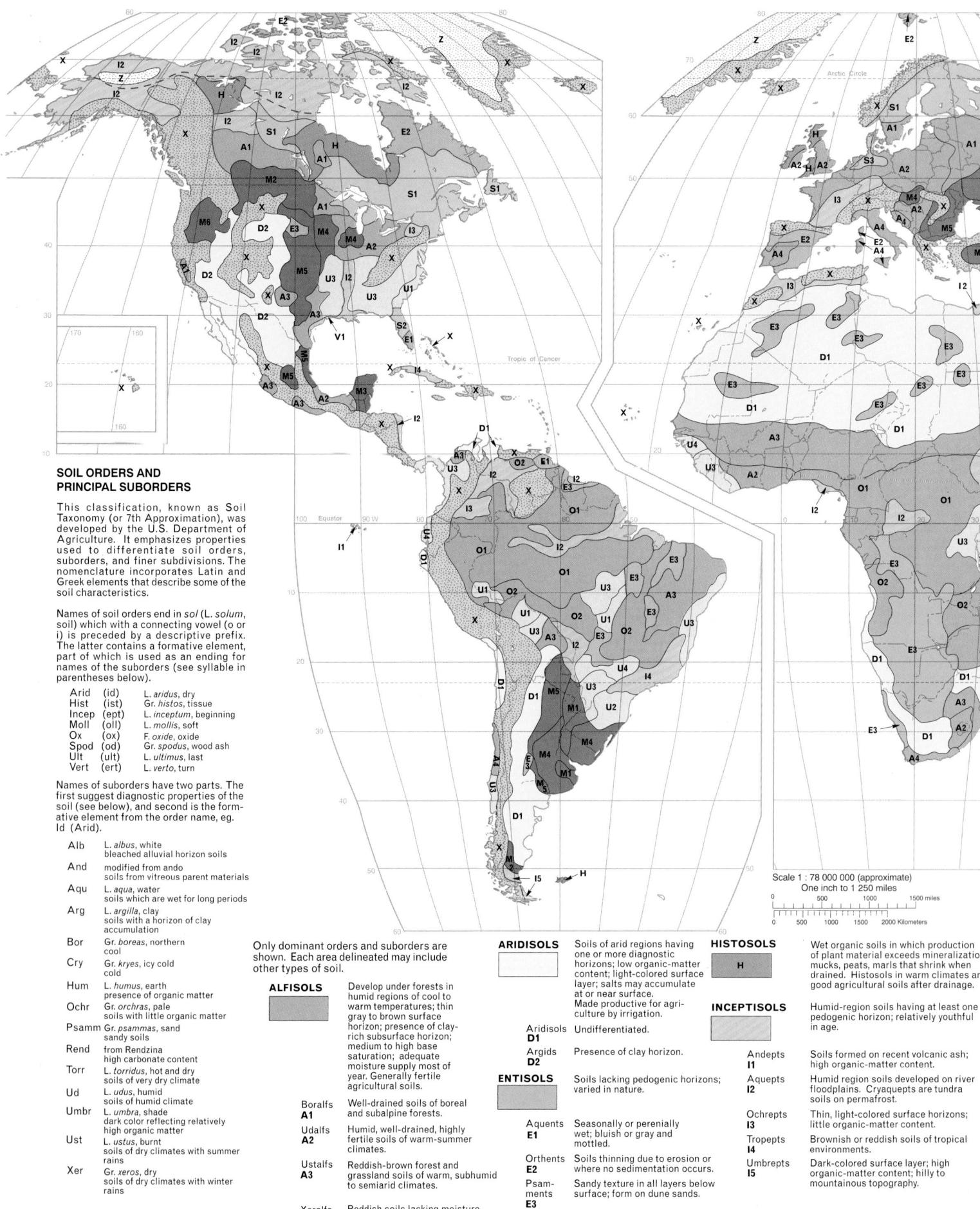

SOIL ORDERS AND PRINCIPAL SUBORDERS

This classification, known as Soil Taxonomy (or 7th Approximation), was developed by the U.S. Department of Agriculture. It emphasizes properties used to differentiate soil orders, suborders, and finer subdivisions. The nomenclature incorporates Latin and Greek elements that describe some of the soil characteristics.

Names of soil orders end in sol (L. solum, soil) which with a connecting vowel (o or i) is preceded by a descriptive prefix. The latter contains a formative element, part of which is used as an ending for names of the suborders (see syllable in parentheses below).

Arid	(id)	L. aridus, dry
Hist	(ist)	Gr. histos, tissue
Incep	(ept)	L. inceptum, beginning
Moll	(oll)	L. mollis, soft
Ox	(ox)	F. oxide, oxide
Spod	(od)	Gr. spodus, wood ash
Ult	(ult)	L. ultimus, last
Vert	(ert)	L. verto, turn

Names of suborders have two parts. The first suggest diagnostic properties of the soil (see below), and second is the formative element from the order name, eg. Id (Arid).

Alb	L. albus, white bleached alluvial horizon soils
And	modified from ando soils from vitreous parent materials
Aqu	L. aqua, water soils which are wet for long periods
Arg	L. argilla, clay soils with a horizon of clay accumulation
Bor	Gr. boreas, northern cool
Cry	Gr. kryes, icy cold cold
Hum	L. humus, earth presence of organic matter
Ochr	Gr. orchras, pale soils with little organic matter
Psamm	Gr. psammas, sand sandy soils
Rend	from Rendzina high carbonate content
Torr	L. torridus, hot and dry soils of very dry climate
Ud	L. udus, humid soils of humid climate
Umbr	L. umbra, shade dark color reflecting relatively high organic matter
Ust	L. ustus, burnt soils of dry climates with summer rains
Xer	Gr. xeros, dry soils of dry climates with winter rains

Only dominant orders and suborders are shown. Each area delineated may include other types of soil.

ALFISOLS

Develop under forests in humid regions of cool to warm temperatures; thin gray to brown surface horizon; presence of clay-rich subsurface horizon; medium to high base saturation; adequate moisture supply most of year. Generally fertile agricultural soils.

Boralfs A1	Well-drained soils of boreal and subalpine forests.
Udalfs A2	Humid, well-drained, highly fertile soils of warm-summer climates.
Ustalfs A3	Reddish-brown forest and grassland soils of warm, subhumid to semiarid climates.
Xeralfs A4	Reddish soils lacking moisture during summer in Mediterranean climate zones.

ARIDISOLS

Soils of arid regions having one or more diagnostic horizons; low organic-matter content; light-colored surface layer; salts may accumulate at or near surface. Made productive for agriculture by irrigation.

Aridisols D1	Undifferentiated.
Argids D2	Presence of clay horizon.

ENTISOLS

Soils lacking pedogenic horizons; varied in nature.

Aquents E1	Seasonally or perenially wet; bluish or gray and mottled.
Orthents E2	Soils thinning due to erosion or where no sedimentation occurs.
Psamments E3	Sandy texture in all layers below surface; form on dune sands.

HISTOSOLS

Wet organic soils in which production of plant material exceeds mineralization; mucks, peats, marls that shrink when drained. Histosols in warm climates are good agricultural soils after drainage.

INCEPTISOLS

Humid-region soils having at least one pedogenic horizon; relatively youthful in age.

Andepts I1	Soils formed on recent volcanic ash; high organic-matter content.
Aquepts I2	Humid region soils developed on river floodplains. Cryaquepts are tundra soils on permafrost.
Ochrepts I3	Thin, light-colored surface horizons; little organic-matter content.
Tropepts I4	Brownish or reddish soils of tropical environments.
Umbrepts I5	Dark-colored surface layer; high organic-matter content; hilly to mountainous topography.

Scale 1 : 78 000 000 (approximate)
One inch to 1 250 miles

0	500	1000	1500 miles
0	500 1000	1500	2000 Kilometers

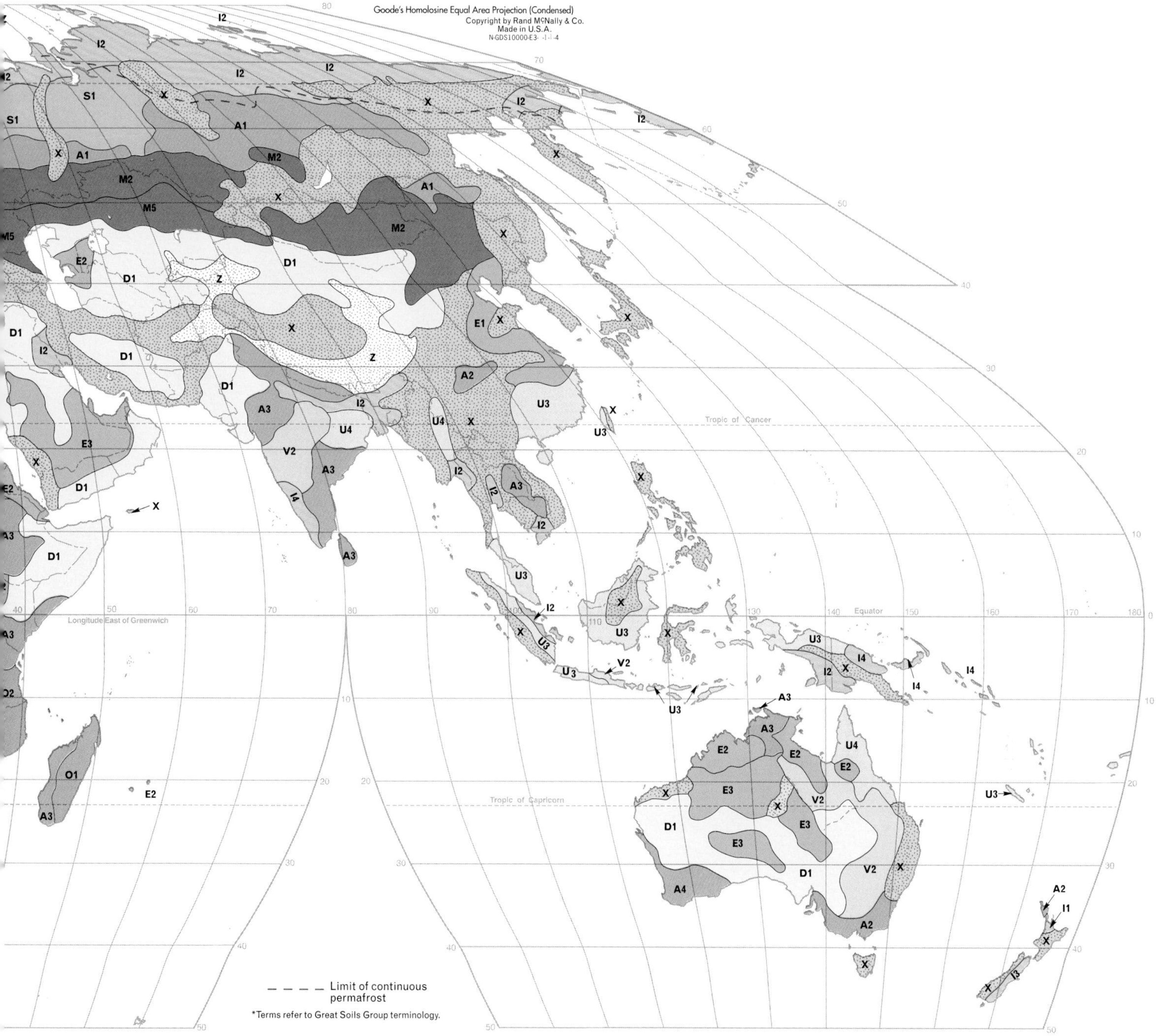

Goode's Homolosine Equal Area Projection (Condensed)
Copyright by Rand McNally & Co.
Made in U.S.A.
N-GDS10000-E3- -I-I -4

Tropic of Cancer

Equator

Longitude East of Greenwich

Tropic of Capricorn

— — — Limit of continuous permafrost

*Terms refer to Great Soils Group terminology.

MOLLISOLS Deep-profile soils with seasonal moisture deficit associated with grasslands; dark brown to black upper layer; may have subsurface horizon of calcium accumulation; high base saturation. Very productive for grain crops.

Albolls **M1** Soils with a grayish subsurface horizon over clay layer and a fluctuating water table.

Borolls **M2** Well-drained, fertile grassland soils of cool summers and cold winters.

Rendolls **M3** Formed on calcareous limestones.

Udolls **M4** Freely drained soils of humid regions with warm summers; excellent agricultural soils.

Ustolls **M5** Fertile agricultural soils of subhumid climates.

Xerolls **M6** Pronounced soil-moisture deficit during high-sun season; associated with Mediterranean climates.

OXISOLS Deeply weathered tropical and subtropical soils of low natural fertility; low base saturation; limited ability to hold soil nutrients against leaching; presence of plinthite (laterite) layers. Generally unsuited to large-scale agricultural production.

Orthox **O1** Hot and nearly always moist; associated with tropical rainforests.

Ustox **O2** Hot to warm forest and savanna soils with a drier season of low soil-moisture availability.

SPODOSOLS Soils of moist climates ranging from subtropical to cold conditions; include a spodic subsurface horizon incorporating active organic matter beneath a light-colored, leached, sandy horizon. Generally marginal for agriculture.

Spodo- sols **S1** Undifferentiated, mostly in high latitudes.

Aquods **S2** Seasonally wet developed on sandy parent material.

Humods **S3** Considerable organic matter present in subsurface horizon.

Orthods **S4** Subsurface accumulations of iron, aluminum, and organic matter.

ULTISOLS Tropical and subtropical soils with a variety of soil moisture regimes; subsurface clay horizon; low base saturation; very old soils characterized by long weathering of clay minerals; low ability to hold nutrients against leaching. Often marginal for agriculture.

Aquults **U1** Seasonally wet with mottled, gray subsurface horizon.

Humults **U2** Dark soils with high organic-matter content, warm temperatures.

Udults **U3** Low organic-matter content and temperate to hot conditions.

Ustults **U4** Seasonally dry, warm to hot conditions.

VERTISOLS Dark tropical and subtropical soils developed on heavy clays; deep shrinkage cracks appear during dry season which become filled with loose surface materials that absorb moisture and swell during wet season. Generally fertile and well suited to crop production.

Uderts **V1** Generally moist with limited period for shrinkage cracks to develop.

Usterts **V2** Over three months of shrinkage-crack formation.

MOUNTAIN SOILS Soils with various moisture and temperature regimes; mainly high altitude soils forming on steep slopes; soils vary greatly within a short distance.

X

Z Areas with little or no soils.

APPROXIMATE CORRELATION WITH OTHER SOIL CLASSIFICATION SYSTEMS

Soil Taxonomy	Great Soil Groups (former U.S. system)	Canadian system
Udalfs	Gray-brown Podzolic	Luvisolic Gray-Brown
Ustalfs	Reddish Chestnut; Red and Yellow Podzolic	
Aridisols	Desert and Reddish Desert Solonetz, Solonchak	
Entisols	Lithosols	Regosolic
Histosols	Bog	Organic
Inceptisol		Brunisolic
Orthents	Lithosols	
Aquepts	Humic Gley	Gleysolic
Cryaquept	Tundra	Cryosolic
Boralfs		Luvisolic Gray; Solonetzic
Borolls	Chernozem	Chernozemic, Solonetzic
	Chestnut Brown	
Rendolls	Rendzina	
Udolls	Prairie	
Ustolls	Brown	
Oxisols	Latosols	
Humod		Humic Podzolic
Orthods	Podzols	Podzolic
Udults	Red and Yellow Podzolic Reddish Brown Lateritic	
Vertisols	Rendzina	

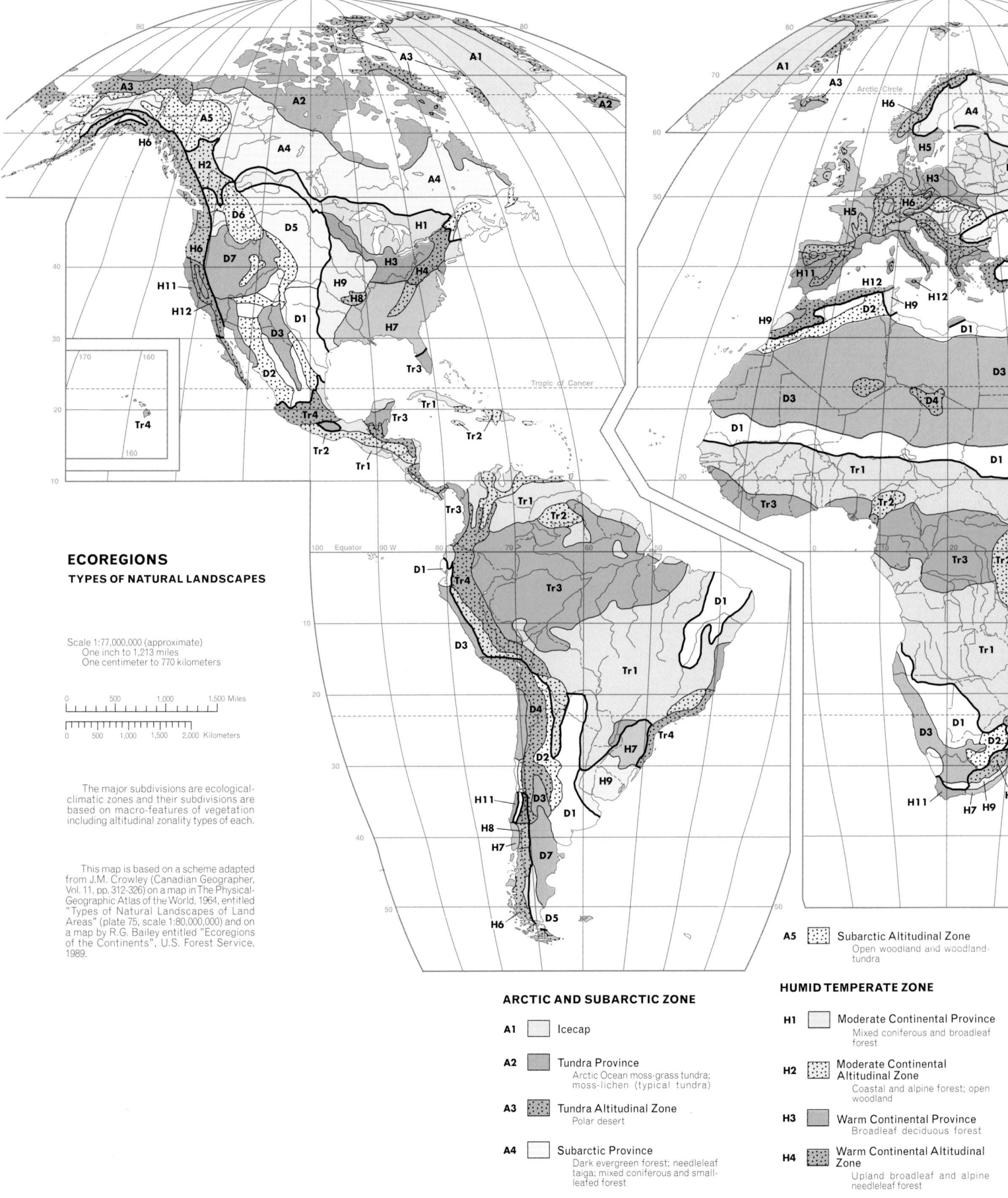

28

ECOREGIONS

TYPES OF NATURAL LANDSCAPES

Scale 1:77,000,000 (approximate)
One inch to 1,213 miles
One centimeter to 770 kilometers

500   1,000   1,500 Miles

0   500   1,000   1,500   2,000 Kilometers

The major subdivisions are ecological-climatic zones and their subdivisions are based on macro-features of vegetation including altitudinal zonality types of each.

This map is based on a scheme adapted from J.M. Crowley (Canadian Geographer, Vol. 11, pp. 312-326) on a map in The Physical-Geographic Atlas of the World, 1964, entitled "Types of Natural Landscapes of Land Areas" (plate 75, scale 1:80,000,000) and on a map by R.G. Bailey entitled "Ecoregions of the Continents", U.S. Forest Service, 1989.

A5 Subarctic Altitudinal Zone
Open woodland and woodland-tundra

ARCTIC AND SUBARCTIC ZONE

A1 Icecap

A2 Tundra Province
Arctic Ocean moss-grass tundra; moss-lichen (typical tundra)

A3 Tundra Altitudinal Zone
Polar desert

A4 Subarctic Province
Dark evergreen forest; needleleaf taiga; mixed coniferous and small-leafed forest

HUMID TEMPERATE ZONE

H1 Moderate Continental Province
Mixed coniferous and broadleaf forest

H2 Moderate Continental Altitudinal Zone
Coastal and alpine forest; open woodland

H3 Warm Continental Province
Broadleaf deciduous forest

H4 Warm Continental Altitudinal Zone
Upland broadleaf and alpine needleleaf forest

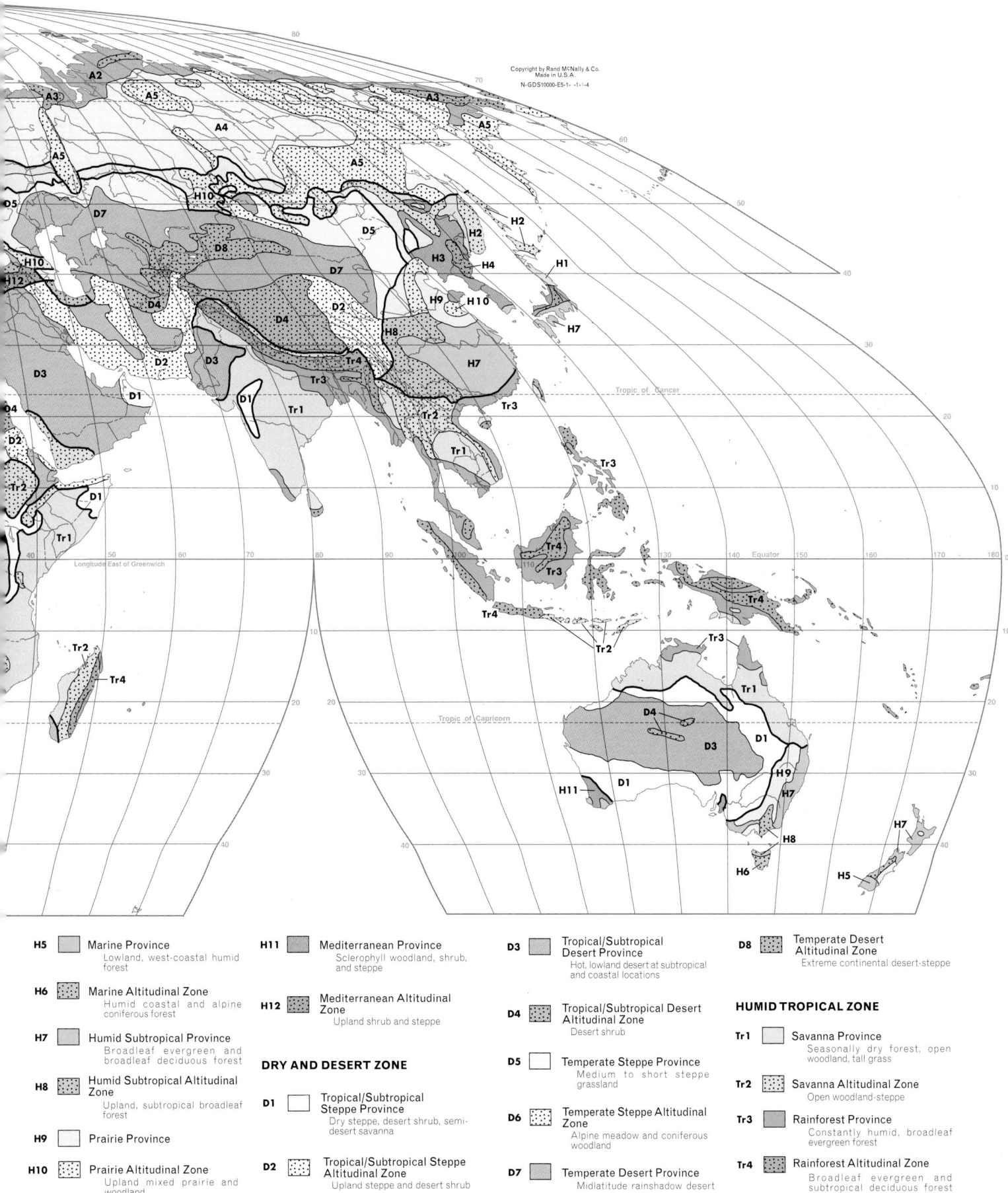

Copyright by Rand McNally & Co.
Made in U.S.A.
N-GDS10000-E5-1- -1-1-4

H5	Marine Province Lowland, west-coastal humid forest	**H11**	Mediterranean Province Sclerophyll woodland, shrub, and steppe	
H6	Marine Altitudinal Zone Humid coastal and alpine coniferous forest	**H12**	Mediterranean Altitudinal Zone Upland shrub and steppe	
H7	Humid Subtropical Province Broadleaf evergreen and broadleaf deciduous forest			
H8	Humid Subtropical Altitudinal Zone Upland, subtropical broadleaf forest		**DRY AND DESERT ZONE**	
H9	Prairie Province	**D1**	Tropical/Subtropical Steppe Province Dry steppe, desert shrub, semi-desert savanna	
H10	Prairie Altitudinal Zone Upland mixed prairie and woodland	**D2**	Tropical/Subtropical Steppe Altitudinal Zone Upland steppe and desert shrub	

D3	Tropical/Subtropical Desert Province Hot, lowland desert at subtropical and coastal locations	**D8**	Temperate Desert Altitudinal Zone Extreme continental desert-steppe	
D4	Tropical/Subtropical Desert Altitudinal Zone Desert shrub		**HUMID TROPICAL ZONE**	
D5	Temperate Steppe Province Medium to short steppe grassland	**Tr1**	Savanna Province Seasonally dry forest, open woodland, tall grass	
D6	Temperate Steppe Altitudinal Zone Alpine meadow and coniferous woodland	**Tr2**	Savanna Altitudinal Zone Open woodland-steppe	
D7	Temperate Desert Province Midlatitude rainshadow desert	**Tr3**	Rainforest Province Constantly humid, broadleaf evergreen forest	
		Tr4	Rainforest Altitudinal Zone Broadleaf evergreen and subtropical deciduous forest	

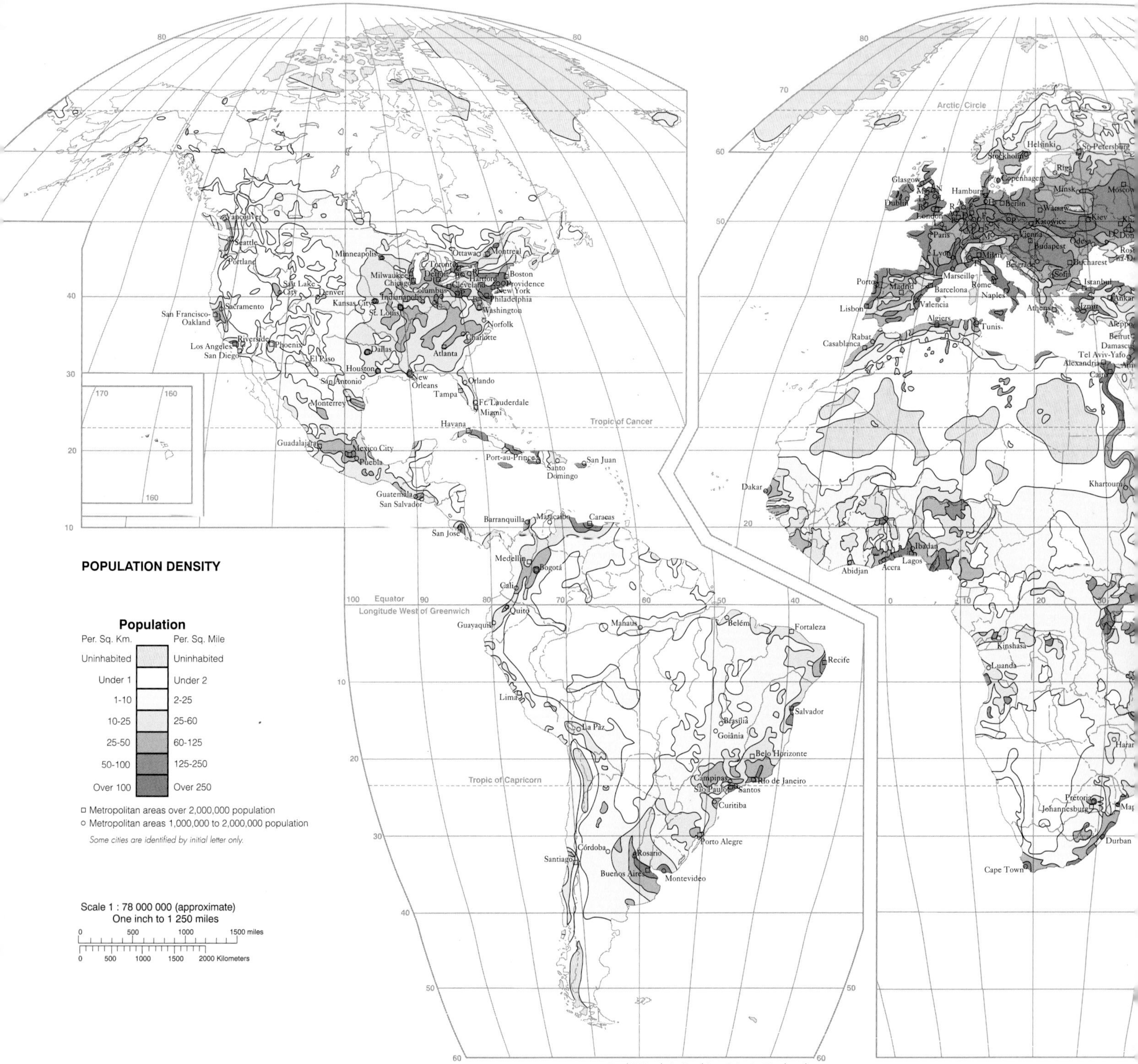

POPULATION DENSITY

Population

Per. Sq. Km.	Per. Sq. Mile
Uninhabited	Uninhabited
Under 1	Under 2
1-10	2-25
10-25	25-60
25-50	60-125
50-100	125-250
Over 100	Over 250

□ Metropolitan areas over 2,000,000 population
○ Metropolitan areas 1,000,000 to 2,000,000 population
Some cities are identified by initial letter only.

Scale 1 : 78 000 000 (approximate)
One inch to 1 250 miles

0   500   1000   1500 miles

0   500   1000   1500   2000 Kilometers

Goode's Homolosine Equal Area Projection (Condensed)

Population Density

per square kilometer (per square mile)

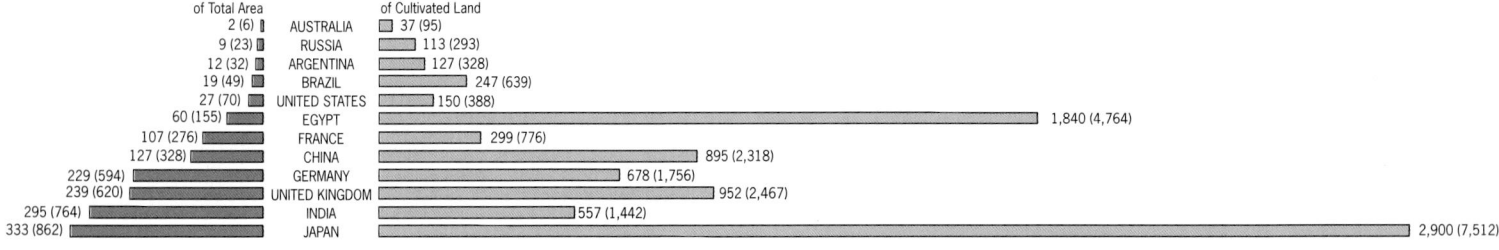

of Total Area		of Cultivated Land
2 (6)	AUSTRALIA	37 (95)
9 (23)	RUSSIA	113 (293)
12 (32)	ARGENTINA	127 (328)
19 (49)	BRAZIL	247 (639)
27 (70)	UNITED STATES	150 (388)
60 (155)	EGYPT	1,840 (4,764)
107 (276)	FRANCE	299 (776)
127 (328)	CHINA	895 (2,318)
229 (594)	GERMANY	678 (1,756)
239 (620)	UNITED KINGDOM	952 (2,467)
295 (764)	INDIA	557 (1,442)
333 (862)	JAPAN	2,900 (7,512)

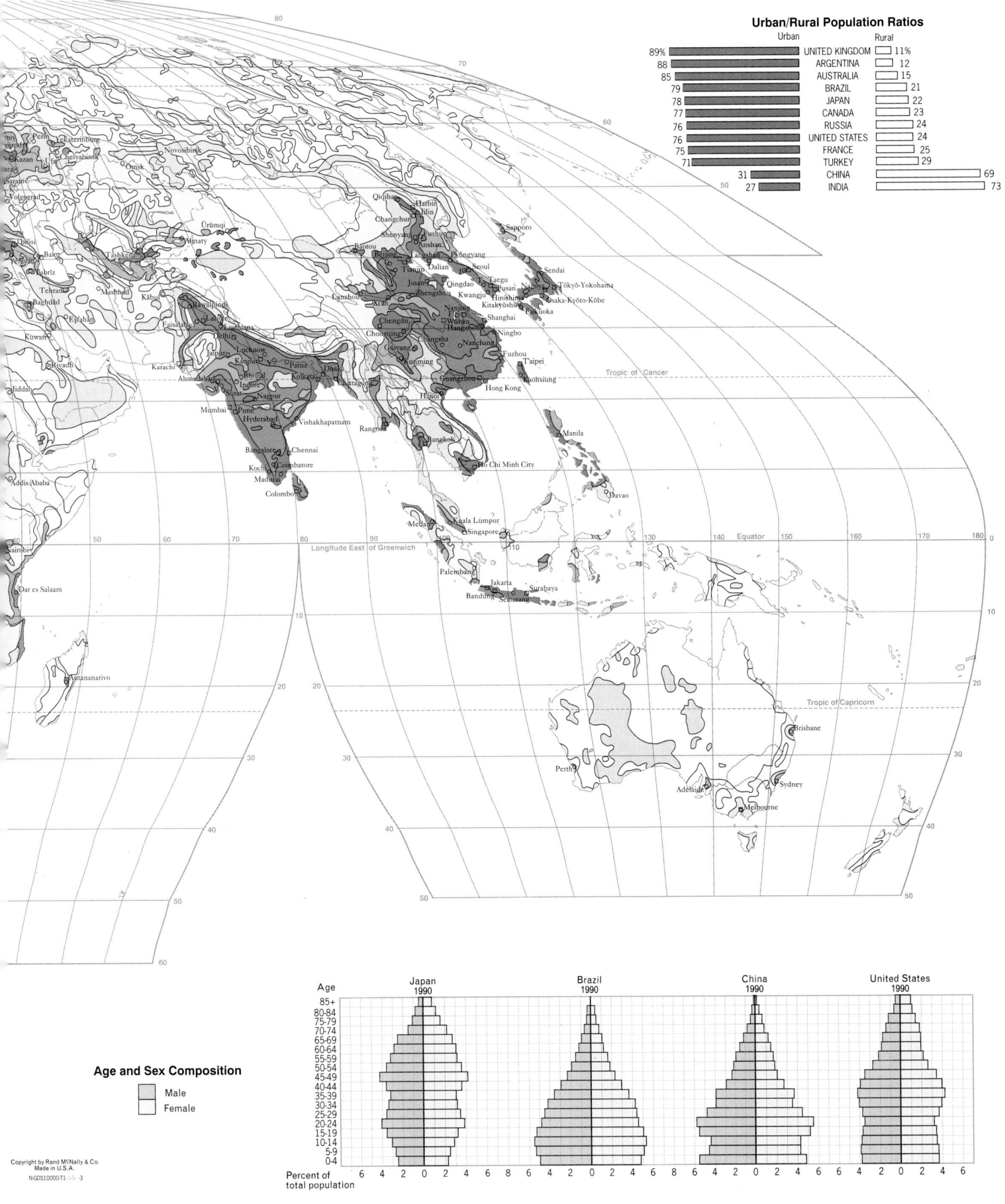

Urban/Rural Population Ratios

	Urban		Rural	
UNITED KINGDOM	89%		11%	
ARGENTINA	88		12	
AUSTRALIA	85		15	
BRAZIL	79		21	
JAPAN	78		22	
CANADA	77		23	
RUSSIA	76		24	
UNITED STATES	76		24	
FRANCE	75		25	
TURKEY	71		29	
CHINA	31		69	
INDIA	27		73	

Age and Sex Composition

Male

Female

Japan 1990

Brazil 1990

China 1990

United States 1990

Age
85+
80-84
75-79
70-74
65-69
60-64
55-59
50-54
45-49
40-44
35-39
30-34
25-29
20-24
15-19
10-14
5-9
0-4

Percent of total population

6 4 2 0 2 4 6   6 4 2 0 2 4 6 8   6 4 2 0 2 4 6   6 4 2 0 2 4 6

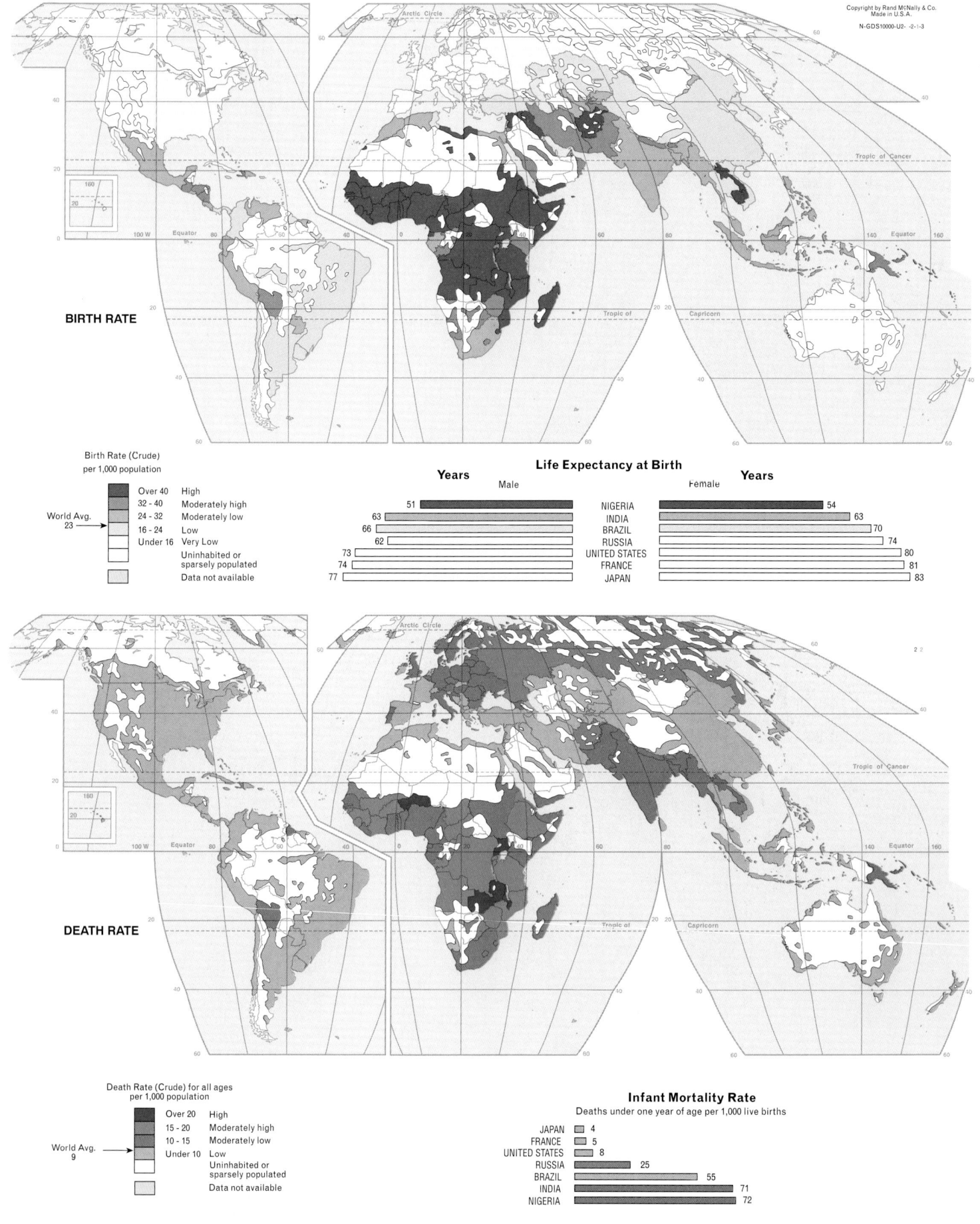

BIRTH RATE

Birth Rate (Crude)
per 1,000 population

	Over 40	High
	32 - 40	Moderately high
World Avg. 23 →	24 - 32	Moderately low
	16 - 24	Low
	Under 16	Very Low
		Uninhabited or sparsely populated
		Data not available

Life Expectancy at Birth

Years		Female	Years
Male			
51	NIGERIA	54	
63	INDIA	63	
66	BRAZIL	70	
62	RUSSIA	74	
73	UNITED STATES	80	
74	FRANCE	81	
77	JAPAN	83	

DEATH RATE

Death Rate (Crude) for all ages
per 1,000 population

	Over 20	High
	15 - 20	Moderately high
World Avg. 9 →	10 - 15	Moderately low
	Under 10	Low
		Uninhabited or sparsely populated
		Data not available

Infant Mortality Rate

Deaths under one year of age per 1,000 live births

JAPAN	4
FRANCE	5
UNITED STATES	8
RUSSIA	25
BRAZIL	55
INDIA	71
NIGERIA	72

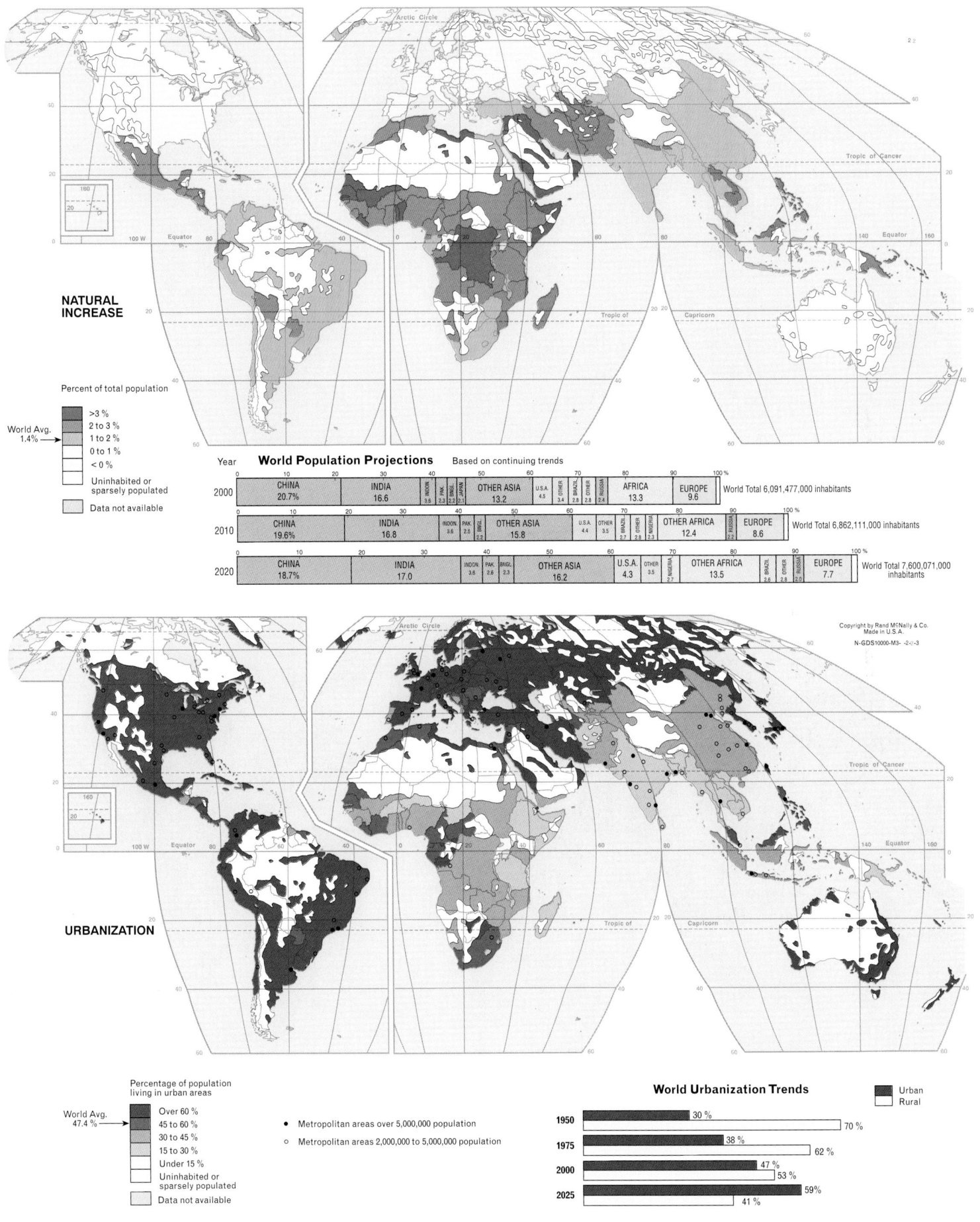

NATURAL INCREASE

Percent of total population

World Avg. 1.4% →

- >3 %
- 2 to 3 %
- 1 to 2 %
- 0 to 1 %
- < 0 %
- Uninhabited or sparsely populated
- Data not available

World Population Projections   Based on continuing trends

Year

| 2000 | CHINA 20.7% | INDIA 16.6 | INDON. 3.6 | PAK. 2.3 | BNGL. 2.2 | JAPAN 2.1 | OTHER ASIA 13.2 | U.S.A. 4.5 | OTHER 3.4 | BRAZIL 2.8 | OTHER 2.8 | RUSSIA 2.4 | AFRICA 13.3 | EUROPE 9.6 | World Total 6,091,477,000 inhabitants |

| 2010 | CHINA 19.6% | INDIA 16.8 | INDON. 3.6 | PAK. 2.5 | BNGL. 2.2 | OTHER ASIA 15.8 | U.S.A. 4.4 | OTHER 3.5 | BRAZIL 2.7 | OTHER 2.8 | NIGERIA 2.3 | OTHER AFRICA 12.4 | RUSSIA 2.2 | EUROPE 8.6 | World Total 6,862,111,000 inhabitants |

| 2020 | CHINA 18.7% | INDIA 17.0 | INDON. 3.6 | PAK. 2.8 | BNGL. 2.3 | OTHER ASIA 16.2 | U.S.A. 4.3 | OTHER 3.5 | NIGERIA 2.7 | OTHER AFRICA 13.5 | BRAZIL 2.6 | OTHER 2.8 | RUSSIA 2.0 | EUROPE 7.7 | World Total 7,600,071,000 inhabitants |

Copyright by Rand McNally & Co.
Made in U.S.A.
N-GDS10000-M3- -2-/-3

URBANIZATION

Percentage of population living in urban areas

World Avg. 47.4 % →

- Over 60 %
- 45 to 60 %
- 30 to 45 %
- 15 to 30 %
- Under 15 %
- Uninhabited or sparsely populated
- Data not available

● Metropolitan areas over 5,000,000 population
○ Metropolitan areas 2,000,000 to 5,000,000 population

World Urbanization Trends   ■ Urban □ Rural

1950	30 %	70 %
1975	38 %	62 %
2000	47 %	53 %
2025	59%	41 %

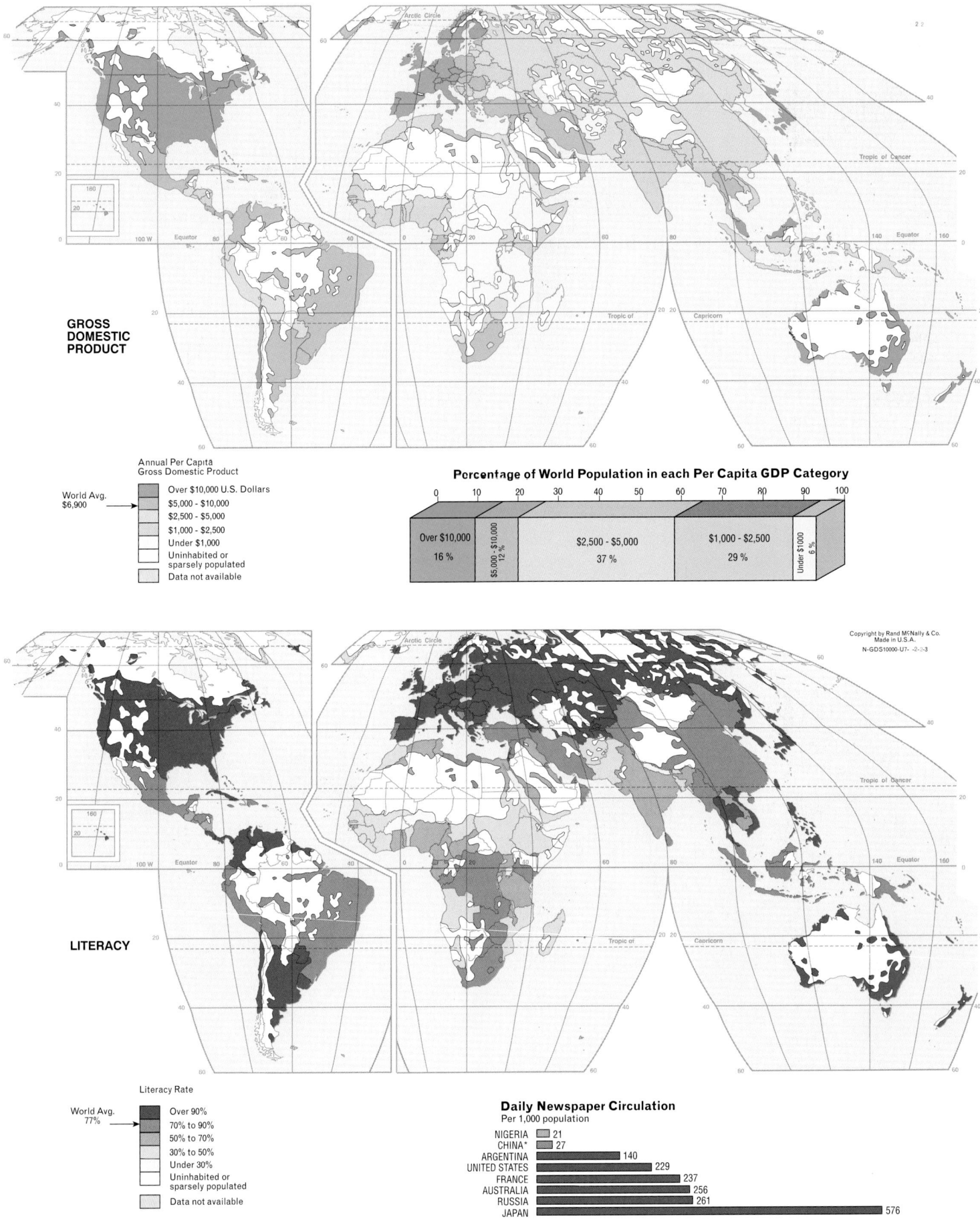

GROSS DOMESTIC PRODUCT

Annual Per Capita
Gross Domestic Product

World Avg.
$6,900 →

- Over $10,000 U.S. Dollars
- $5,000 - $10,000
- $2,500 - $5,000
- $1,000 - $2,500
- Under $1,000
- Uninhabited or sparsely populated
- Data not available

Percentage of World Population in each Per Capita GDP Category

Over $10,000	$5,000 - $10,000	$2,500 - $5,000	$1,000 - $2,500	Under $1000
16 %	12 %	37 %	29 %	6 %

Copyright by Rand McNally & Co.
Made in U.S.A.
N-GDS10000-U7- -2-2-3

LITERACY

Literacy Rate

World Avg.
77% →

- Over 90%
- 70% to 90%
- 50% to 70%
- 30% to 50%
- Under 30%
- Uninhabited or sparsely populated
- Data not available

Based on population 15 years
and over who can read and write.

Daily Newspaper Circulation
Per 1,000 population

NIGERIA	21
CHINA*	27
ARGENTINA	140
UNITED STATES	229
FRANCE	237
AUSTRALIA	256
RUSSIA	261
JAPAN	576

*Includes Data for Hong Kong

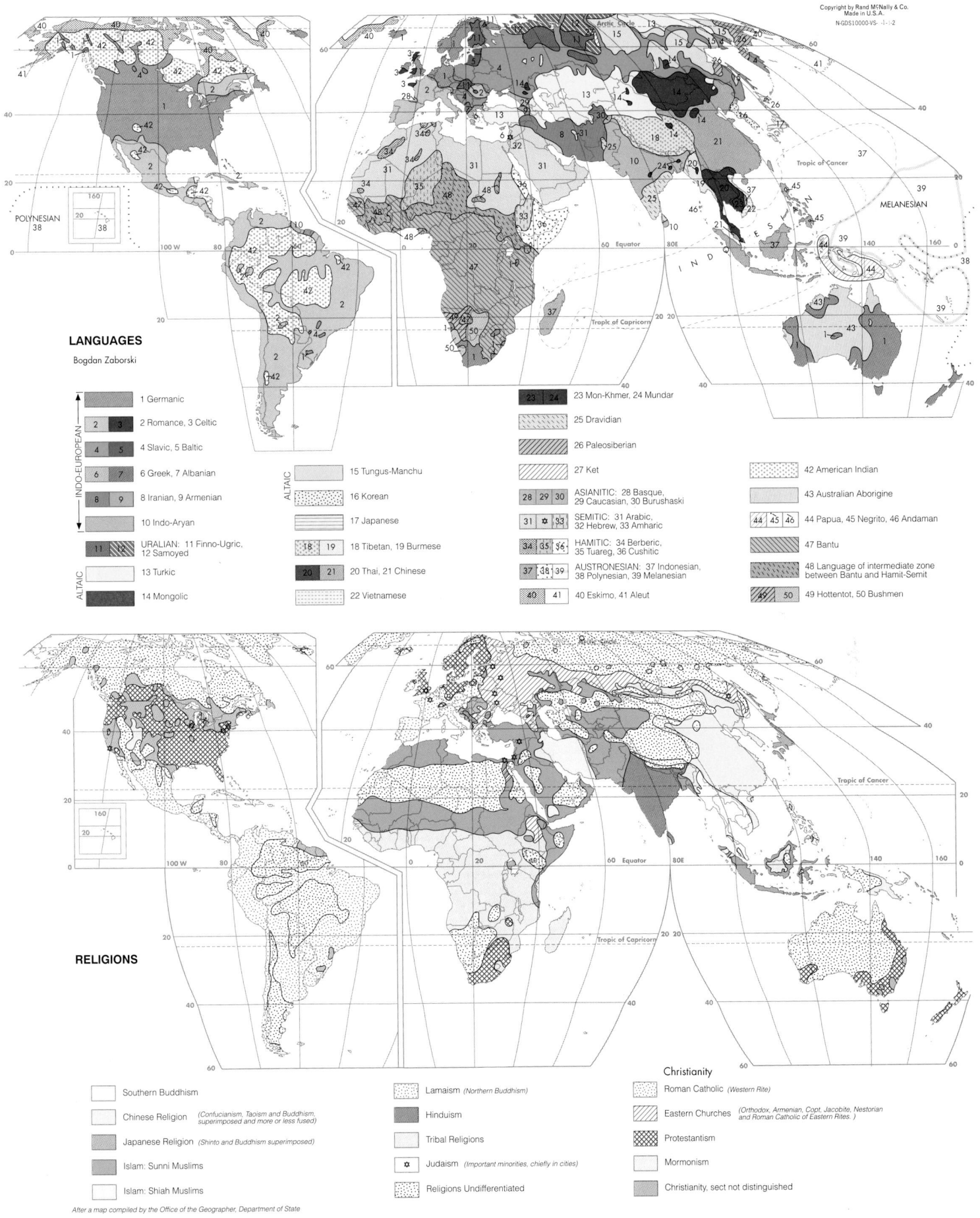

Copyright by Rand McNally & Co.
Made in U.S.A.
N-GDS10000-VS- -1-i-2

POLYNESIAN
38

LANGUAGES

Bogdan Zaborski

INDO-EUROPEAN

1	1 Germanic
2 3	2 Romance, 3 Celtic
4 5	4 Slavic, 5 Baltic
6 7	6 Greek, 7 Albanian
8 9	8 Iranian, 9 Armenian
10	10 Indo-Aryan

URALIC: 11 Finno-Ugric, 12 Samoyed

ALTAIC

13 Turkic

14 Mongolic

15 Tungus-Manchu

16 Korean

17 Japanese

18 19 · 18 Tibetan, 19 Burmese

20 21 · 20 Thai, 21 Chinese

22 Vietnamese

23 24 · 23 Mon-Khmer, 24 Mundar

25 Dravidian

26 Paleosiberian

27 Ket

28 29 30 · ASIANITIC: 28 Basque, 29 Caucasian, 30 Burushaski

31 ✿ 33 · SEMITIC: 31 Arabic, 32 Hebrew, 33 Amharic

34 35 36 · HAMITIC: 34 Berberic, 35 Tuareg, 36 Cushitic

37 38 39 · AUSTRONESIAN: 37 Indonesian, 38 Polynesian, 39 Melanesian

40 41 · 40 Eskimo, 41 Aleut

42 American Indian

43 Australian Aborigine

44 45 46 · 44 Papua, 45 Negrito, 46 Andaman

47 Bantu

48 Language of intermediate zone between Bantu and Hamit-Semit

49 50 · 49 Hottentot, 50 Bushmen

RELIGIONS

Southern Buddhism	Lamaism *(Northern Buddhism)*	**Christianity**
Chinese Religion *(Confucianism, Taoism and Buddhism, superimposed and more or less fused)*	Hinduism	Roman Catholic *(Western Rite)*
Japanese Religion *(Shinto and Buddhism superimposed)*	Tribal Religions	Eastern Churches *(Orthodox, Armenian, Copt, Jacobite, Nestorian and Roman Catholic of Eastern Rites.)*
Islam: Sunni Muslims	✿ Judaism *(Important minorities, chiefly in cities)*	Protestantism
Islam: Shiah Muslims	Religions Undifferentiated	Mormonism
		Christianity, sect not distinguished

After a map compiled by the Office of the Geographer, Department of State

CALORIE SUPPLY

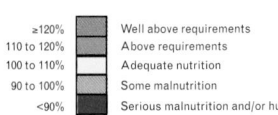

Note: Size of each country is proportional to population.

Calorie supply per capita
(percentage of requirements*)

≥120%	Well above requirements
110 to 120%	Above requirements
100 to 110%	Adequate nutrition
90 to 100%	Some malnutrition
<90%	Serious malnutrition and/or hunger
n.a.	Data not available

*Requirements estimated on the basis of
physiological needs for normal activity with
consideration of environmental temperature,
body weight, and age and sex distribution of
the population in various countries.
Estimates are for 1994-6.

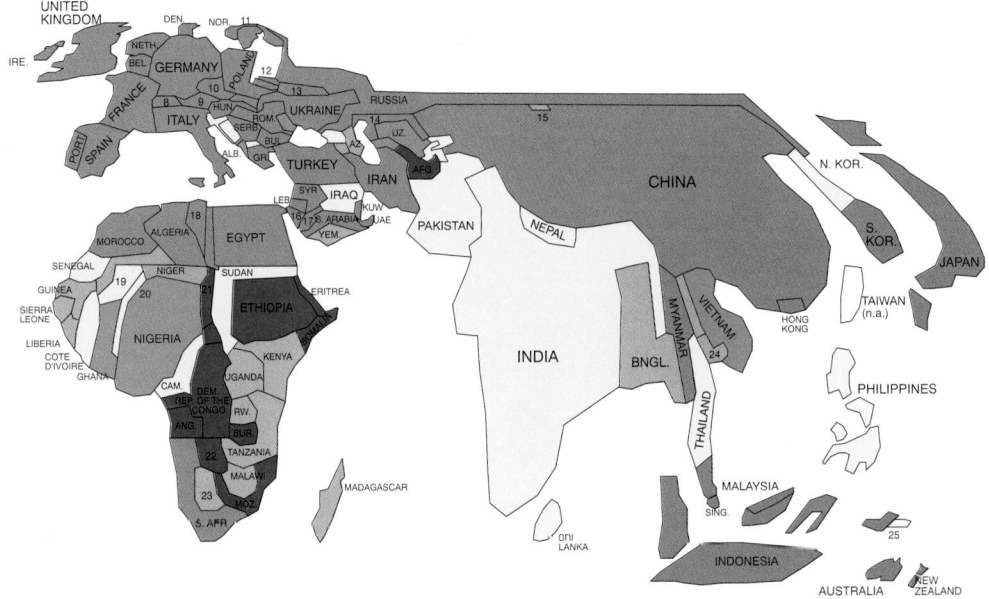

Copyright by Rand M&Nally & Co.
Made in U.S.A.
N-GDS10100-W5- -2-⅔-3

1. JAMAICA	6. PARAGUAY	11. SWEDEN	16. ISRAEL	21. CHAD
2. EL SALVADOR	7. URUGUAY	12. LATVIA	17. JORDAN	22. ZAMBIA
3. NICARAGUA	8. SWITZERLAND	13. BELARUS	18. TUNISIA	23. ZIMBABWE
4. COSTA RICA	9. AUSTRIA	14. KAZAKHSTAN	19. BURKINA FASO	24. CAMBODIA
5. PANAMA	10. CZECH REPUBLIC	15. MONGOLIA	20. BENIN	25. PAPUA NEW GUINEA

PROTEIN CONSUMPTION, 1996

Note: Size of each country is proportional to population.

Animal protein
as a % of diet

> 55 55 to 25 ≤ 25

Grams of protein
per capita per day

≥90			
75 to 90			
65 to 75			
50 to 65			
<50			

< 45   45 to 75   ≥ 75

Vegetable protein
as a % of diet

n.a. [ ] Data not available

Copyright by Rand M&Nally & Co.
Made in U.S.A.
N-GDS10100-W4- -2-⅔-3

PHYSICIANS

Note: Size of each country is proportional to population.

Population per Physician
- Less than 1,000
- 1,000 to 6,000
- 6,000 to 18,000
- Greater than 18,000

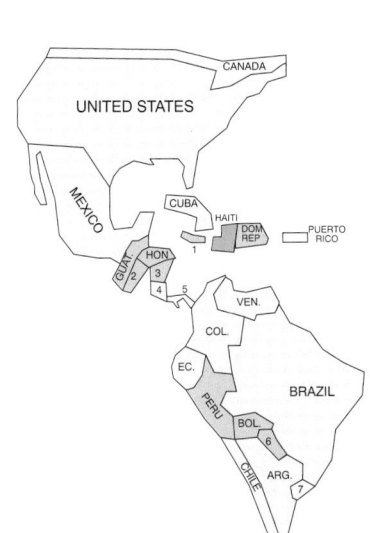
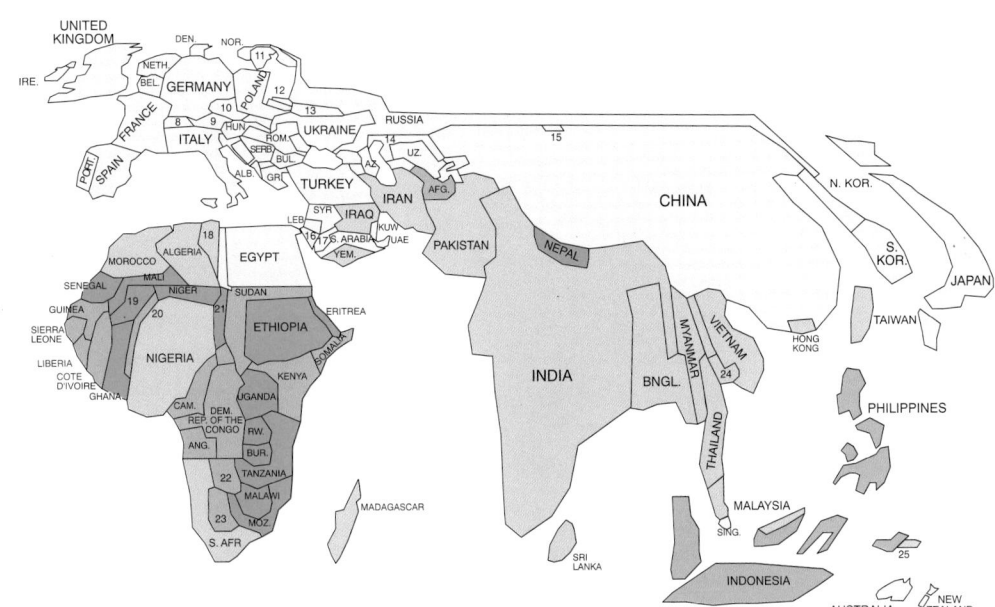

Copyright by Rand McNally & Co.
Made in U.S.A.
N-GDS10100-W3- -2-7-3

1. JAMAICA	6. PARAGUAY	11. SWEDEN	16. ISRAEL	21. CHAD
2. EL SALVADOR	7. URUGUAY	12. LATVIA	17. JORDAN	22. ZAMBIA
3. NICARAGUA	8. SWITZERLAND	13. BELARUS	18. TUNISIA	23. ZIMBABWE
4. COSTA RICA	9. AUSTRIA	14. KAZAKHSTAN	19. BURKINA FASO	24. CAMBODIA
5. PANAMA	10. CZECH REPUBLIC	15. MONGOLIA	20. BENIN	25. PAPUA NEW GUINEA

LIFE EXPECTANCY

Note: Size of each country is proportional to population.

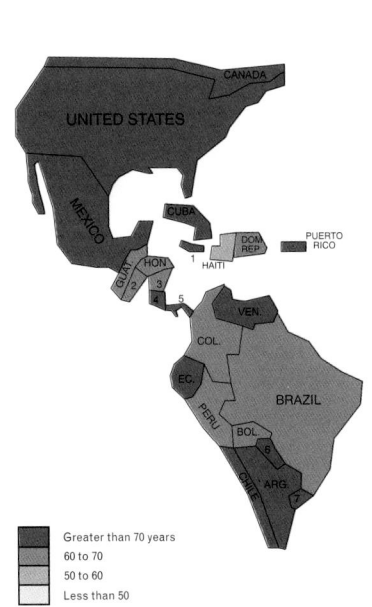
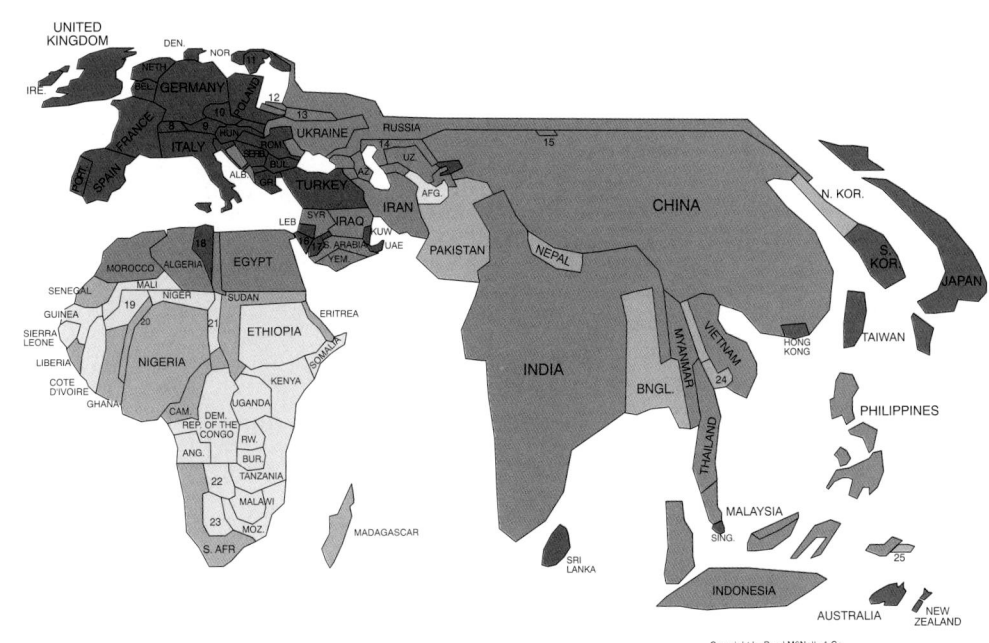

Copyright by Rand McNally & Co.
Made in U.S.A.

- Greater than 70 years
- 60 to 70
- 50 to 60
- Less than 50

Life Expectancy at Birth

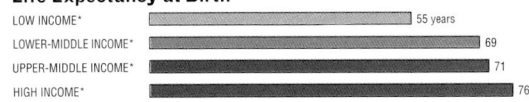

LOW INCOME* — 55 years
LOWER-MIDDLE INCOME* — 69
UPPER-MIDDLE INCOME* — 71
HIGH INCOME* — 76

*as defined by the World Bank

38

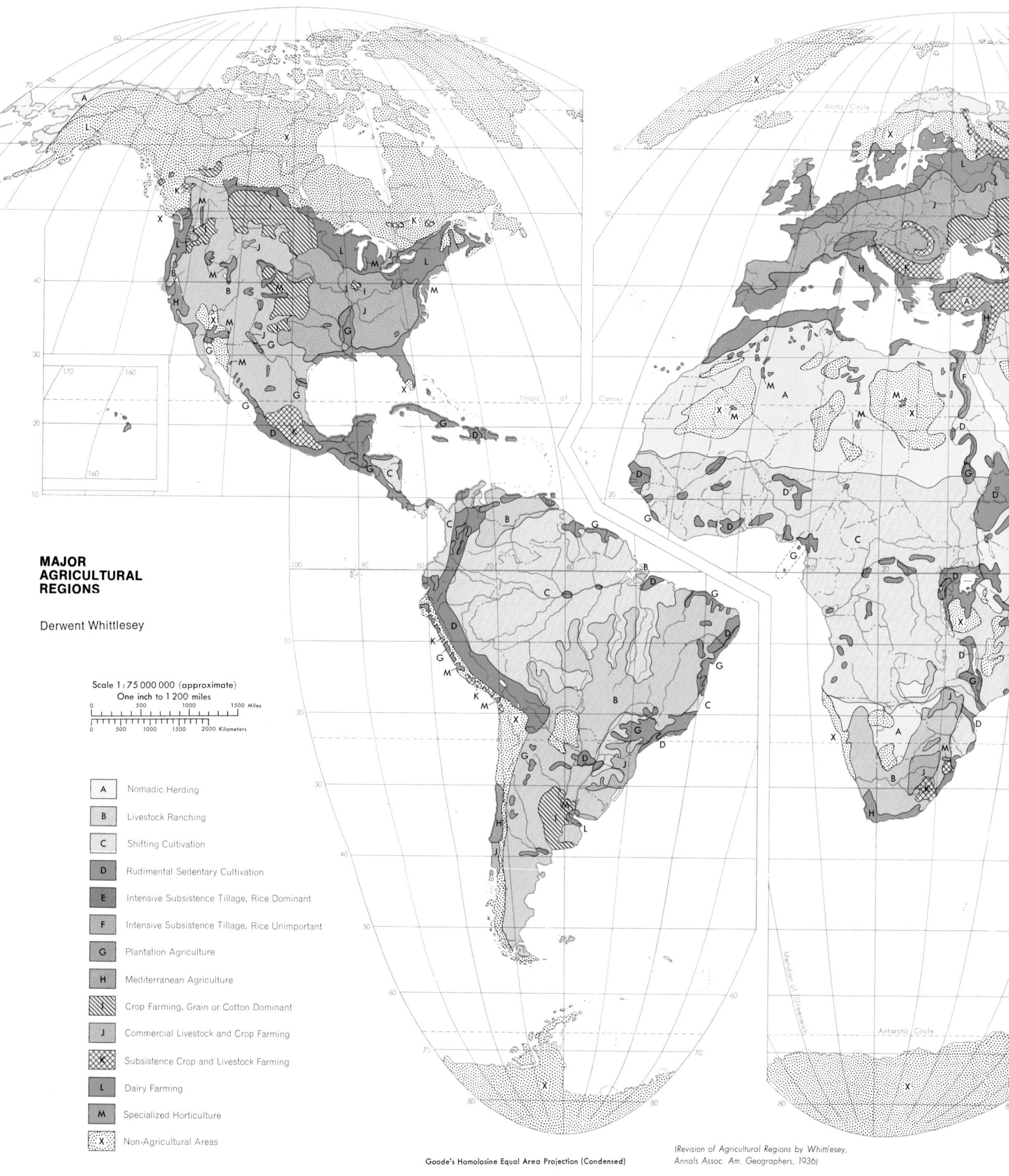

**MAJOR
AGRICULTURAL
REGIONS**

Derwent Whittlesey

Scale 1 : 75 000 000 (approximate)
One inch to 1 200 miles

A	Nomadic Herding
B	Livestock Ranching
C	Shifting Cultivation
D	Rudimental Sedentary Cultivation
E	Intensive Subsistence Tillage, Rice Dominant
F	Intensive Subsistence Tillage, Rice Unimportant
G	Plantation Agriculture
H	Mediterranean Agriculture
J	Crop Farming, Grain or Cotton Dominant
J	Commercial Livestock and Crop Farming
K	Subsistence Crop and Livestock Farming
L	Dairy Farming
M	Specialized Horticulture
X	Non-Agricultural Areas

Goode's Homolosine Equal Area Projection (Condensed)

(Revision of Agricultural Regions by Whittlesey,
Annals Assoc. Am. Geographers, 1936)

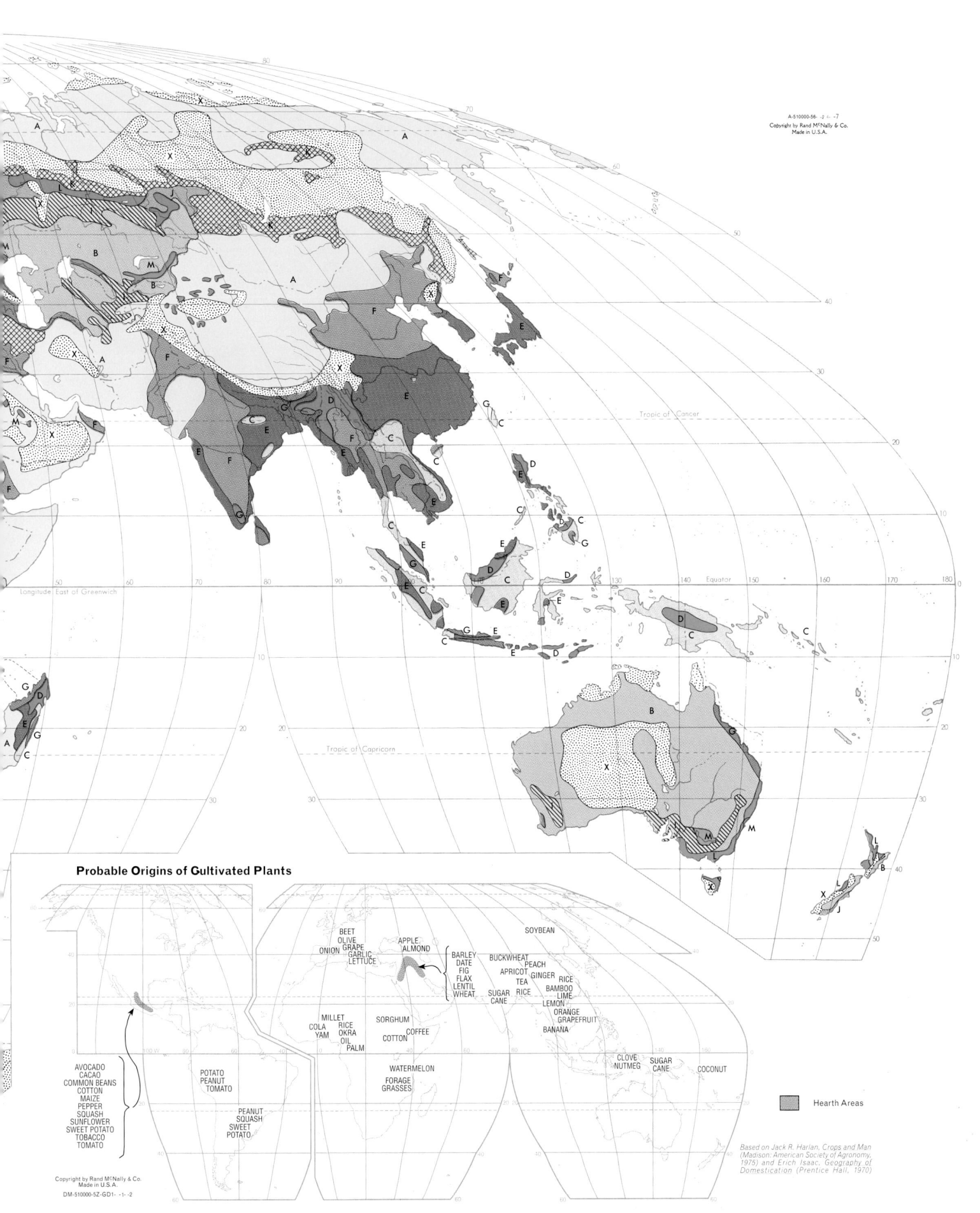

A-510000-56- -2 -7
Copyright by Rand McNally & Co.
Made in U.S.A.

Tropic of Cancer

Equator

Longitude East of Greenwich

Tropic of Capricorn

Probable Origins of Cultivated Plants

SOYBEAN

BEET
OLIVE
GRAPE   APPLE
ONION   GARLIC   ALMOND
LETTUCE
BARLEY   BUCKWHEAT
DATE   PEACH
FIG   APRICOT GINGER
FLAX   TEA   RICE
LENTIL   RICE   BAMBOO
WHEAT   LIME
SUGAR   LEMON
CANE   ORANGE
MILLET   GRAPEFRUIT
COLA   RICE   SORGHUM   BANANA
YAM   OKRA
OIL   COTTON   COFFEE
PALM

CLOVE
NUTMEG   SUGAR
WATERMELON   CANE   COCONUT

FORAGE
GRASSES

AVOCADO
CACAO
COMMON BEANS   POTATO
COTTON   PEANUT
MAIZE   TOMATO
PEPPER
SQUASH
SUNFLOWER   PEANUT
SWEET POTATO   SQUASH
TOBACCO   SWEET
TOMATO   POTATO

Hearth Areas

*Based on Jack R. Harlan, Crops and Man
(Madison: American Society of Agronomy,
1975) and Erich Isaac, Geography of
Domestication (Prentice Hall, 1970)*

Copyright by Rand McNally & Co.
Made in U.S.A.
DM-510000-5Z-GD1- -1- -2

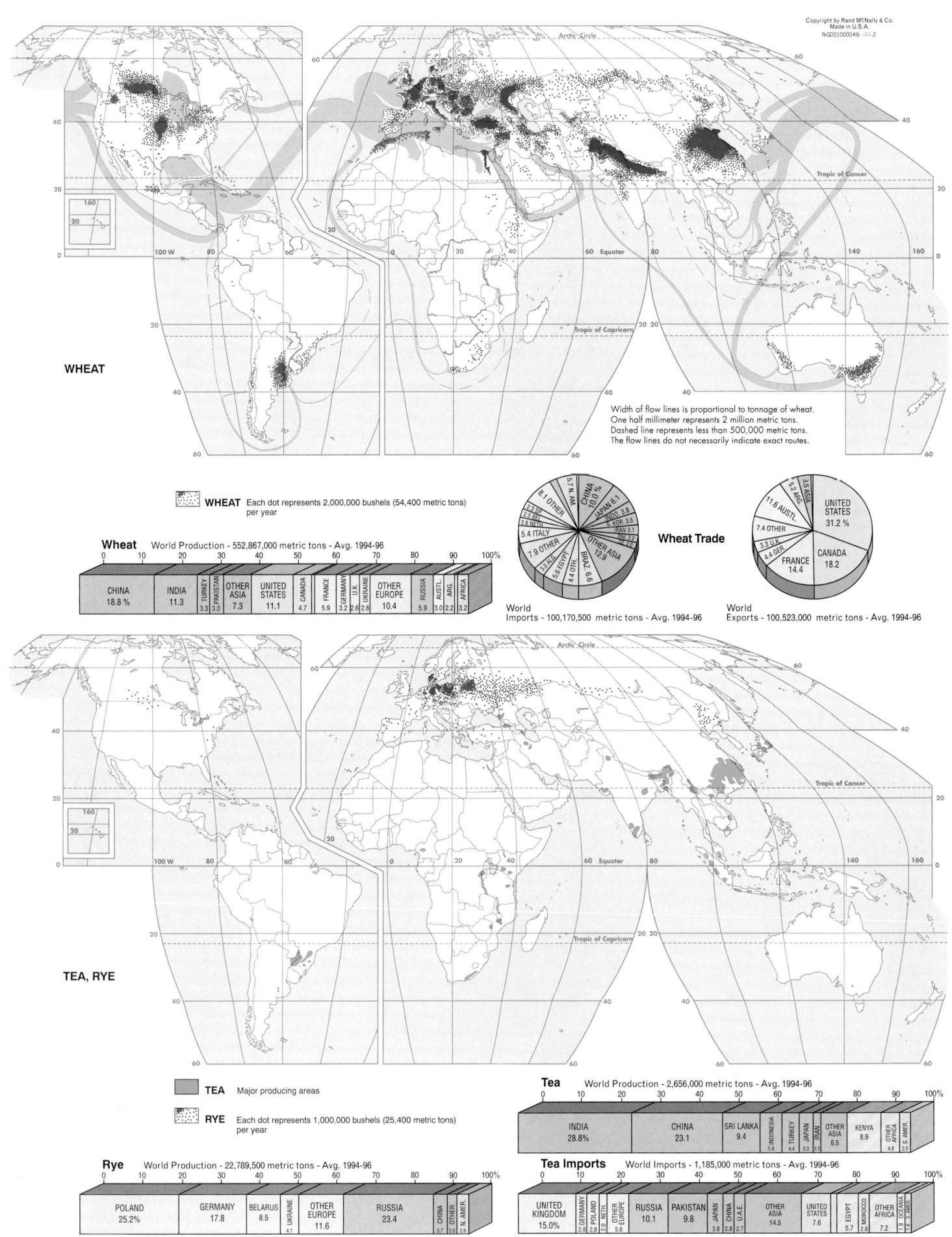

Copyright by Rand McNally & Co.
Made in U.S.A.
N-GDS10000-K6- -1-|-2

WHEAT

Width of flow lines is proportional to tonnage of wheat.
One half millimeter represents 2 million metric tons.
Dashed line represents less than 500,000 metric tons.
The flow lines do not necessarily indicate exact routes.

WHEAT Each dot represents 2,000,000 bushels (54,400 metric tons) per year

Wheat World Production - 552,867,000 metric tons - Avg. 1994-96

0	10	20	30	40	50	60	70	80	90	100%

| CHINA 18.8 % | INDIA 11.3 | TURKEY 3.3 | PAKISTAN 3.0 | OTHER ASIA 7.3 | UNITED STATES 11.1 | CANADA 4.7 | FRANCE 5.9 | GERMANY 3.2 | U.K. 2.6 | UKRAINE 2.6 | OTHER EUROPE 10.4 | RUSSIA 5.9 | AUSTL. 3.0 | ARG 2.2 | AFRICA 3.2 |

Wheat Trade

Wheat Imports pie:
CHINA 10.0 %, JAPAN 6.1, INDO. 3.8, S. KOR. 3.5, IRAN 3.1, IRAQ 2.2, OTHER ASIA 12.9, BRAZ. 6.6, EGYPT 5.6, 3.0 ALG., 7.9 OTHER, 5.4 ITALY, 2.6 NETH, 2.5 BEL, 2.3 SP, 8.1 OTHER, 5.7 N. AM.

World Imports - 100,170,500 metric tons - Avg. 1994-96

Wheat Exports pie:
UNITED STATES 31.2 %, CANADA 18.2, FRANCE 14.4, 4.4 GER., 3.3 U.K., 7.4 OTHER, 11.6 AUSTL., 5.2 ARG., 3.5 ASIA

World Exports - 100,523,000 metric tons - Avg. 1994-96

TEA, RYE

TEA Major producing areas

RYE Each dot represents 1,000,000 bushels (25,400 metric tons) per year

Tea World Production - 2,656,000 metric tons - Avg. 1994-96

0	10	20	30	40	50	60	70	80	90	100%

| INDIA 28.8% | CHINA 23.1 | SRI LANKA 9.4 | INDONESIA 5.8 | TURKEY 4.4 | JAPAN 3.3 | IRAN 2.9 | OTHER ASIA 6.5 | KENYA 8.9 | OTHER AFRICA 4.8 | S. AMER. 2.5 |

Rye World Production - 22,789,500 metric tons - Avg. 1994-96

0	10	20	30	40	50	60	70	80	90	100%

| POLAND 25.2% | GERMANY 17.8 | BELARUS 8.5 | UKRAINE 4.7 | OTHER EUROPE 11.6 | RUSSIA 23.4 | CHINA 3.7 | OTHER 2.0 | N. AMER. 2.0 |

Tea Imports World Imports - 1,185,000 metric tons - Avg. 1994-96

0	10	20	30	40	50	60	70	80	90	100%

| UNITED KINGDOM 15.0% | GERMANY 2.8 | POLAND 2.0 | NETH. 2.0 | OTHER EUROPE 5.8 | RUSSIA 10.1 | PAKISTAN 9.8 | JAPAN 3.8 | CHINA 2.8 | U.A.E. 2.7 | OTHER ASIA 14.5 | UNITED STATES 7.6 | EGYPT 5.7 | MOROCCO 2.8 | OTHER AFRICA 7.2 | OCEANIA 1.9 | S. AMER. 1.4 |

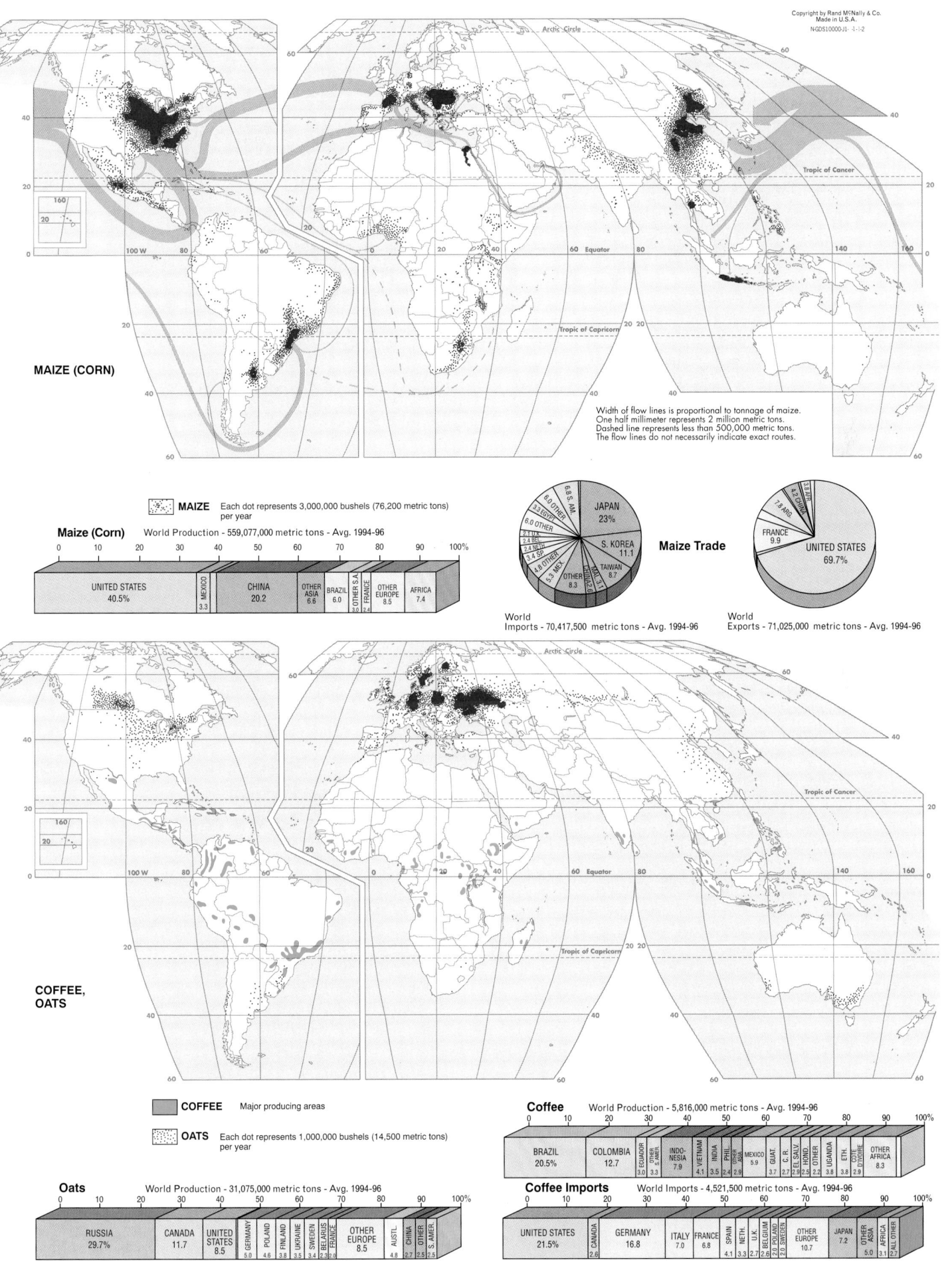

MAIZE (CORN)

Width of flow lines is proportional to tonnage of maize.
One half millimeter represents 2 million metric tons.
Dashed line represents less than 500,000 metric tons.
The flow lines do not necessarily indicate exact routes.

MAIZE Each dot represents 3,000,000 bushels (76,200 metric tons) per year

Maize (Corn) World Production - 559,077,000 metric tons - Avg. 1994-96

| UNITED STATES 40.5% | MEXICO 3.3 | CHINA 20.2 | OTHER ASIA 6.6 | BRAZIL 6.0 | OTHER S.A. 3.0 | FRANCE 2.4 | OTHER EUROPE 8.5 | AFRICA 7.4 |

Maize Trade

World Imports - 70,417,500 metric tons - Avg. 1994-96

Pie: JAPAN 23%, S. KOREA 11.1, TAIWAN 8.7, CHINA 3.1, OTHER 8.3, MEX 5.3, SP 4.8, NETH 3.4, BEL 2.4, U.X. 2.1, OTHER 6.0, 3.3 EGYPT, 6.0 OTHER, 6.8 S. AM.

World Exports - 71,025,000 metric tons - Avg. 1994-96

Pie: UNITED STATES 69.7%, FRANCE 9.9, ARG. 7.8, CHINA 4.2, AFR. 3.8

COFFEE, OATS

COFFEE Major producing areas

OATS Each dot represents 1,000,000 bushels (14,500 metric tons) per year

Coffee World Production - 5,816,000 metric tons - Avg. 1994-96

| BRAZIL 20.5% | COLOMBIA 12.7 | ECUADOR 3.0 | OTHER S. AMER. 3.3 | INDO-NESIA 7.9 | VIETNAM 4.1 | INDIA 3.5 | PHIL 2.9 | OTHER ASIA | MEXICO 5.9 | GUAT. 3.7 | C.R. 2.7 | EL SALV 2.7 | HOND 2.5 | OTHER 2.6 | UGANDA 3.8 | ETH. 3.8 | COTE D'IVOIRE 2.9 | OTHER AFRICA 8.3 |

Coffee Imports World Imports - 4,521,500 metric tons - Avg. 1994-96

| UNITED STATES 21.5% | CANADA 2.6 | GERMANY 16.8 | ITALY 7.0 | FRANCE 6.8 | SPAIN 4.1 | NETH. 3.3 | U.K. 2.7 | BELGIUM 2.6 | POLAND 2.0 | SWEDEN 2.0 | OTHER EUROPE 10.7 | JAPAN 7.2 | OTHER ASIA 5.0 | AFRICA 3.1 | ALL OTHER 2.7 |

Oats World Production - 31,075,000 metric tons - Avg. 1994-96

| RUSSIA 29.7% | CANADA 11.7 | UNITED STATES 8.5 | GERMANY 5.0 | POLAND 4.6 | FINLAND 3.8 | UKRAINE 3.5 | SWEDEN 3.4 | BELARUS 2.3 | FRANCE 2.0 | OTHER EUROPE 8.5 | AUSTL. 4.8 | CHINA 2.7 | OTHER 2.5 | S. AMER. 2.5 |

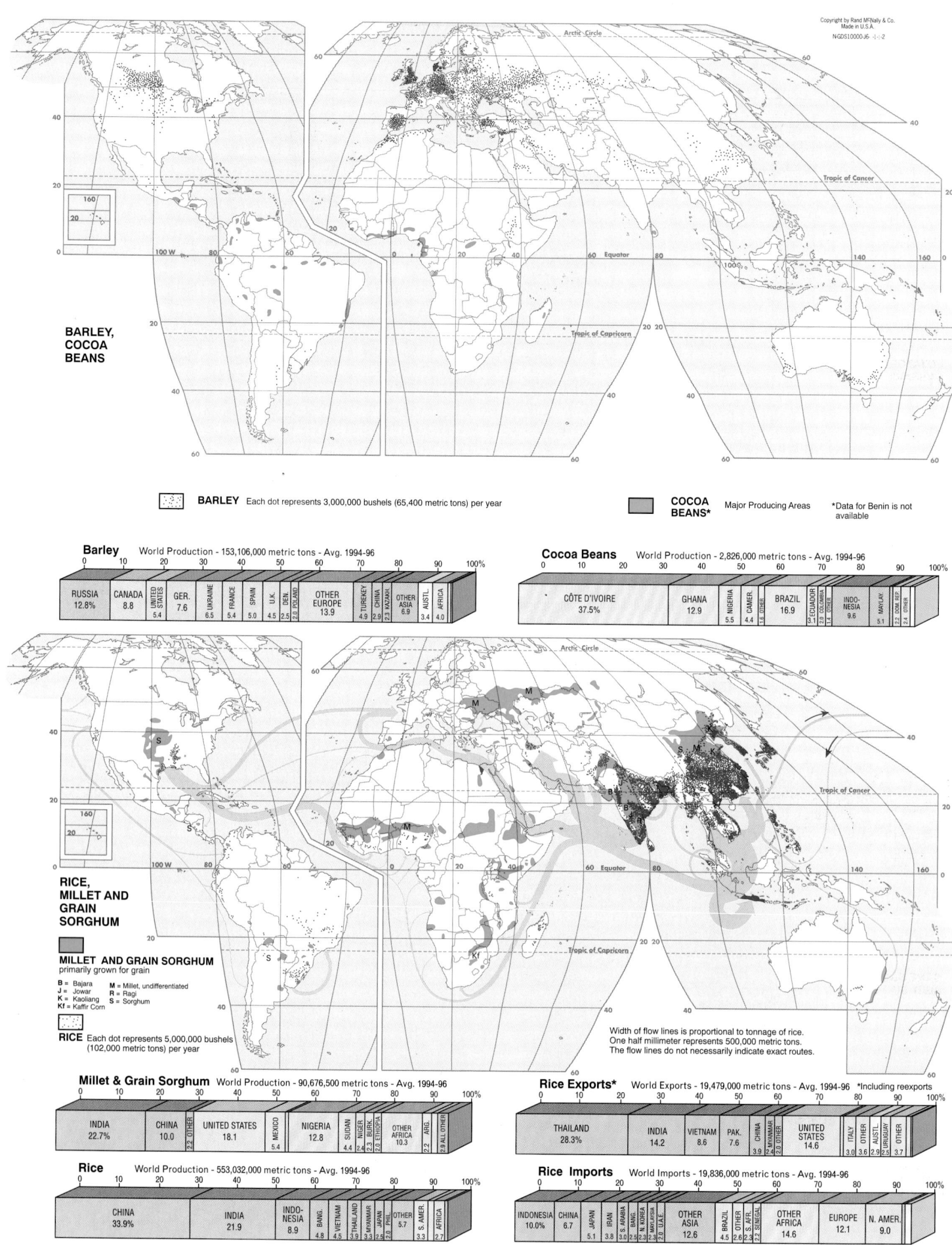

Copyright by Rand McNally & Co.
Made in U.S.A.
N-GDS10000-J6- -1-;-2

**BARLEY,
COCOA
BEANS**

BARLEY Each dot represents 3,000,000 bushels (65,400 metric tons) per year

**COCOA
BEANS*** Major Producing Areas

*Data for Benin is not available

Barley World Production - 153,106,000 metric tons - Avg. 1994-96

RUSSIA 12.8%	CANADA 8.8	UNITED STATES 5.4	GER. 7.6	UKRAINE 6.5	FRANCE 5.4	SPAIN 5.0	U.K. 4.5	DEN. 2.5	POLAND 2.0	OTHER EUROPE 13.9	TURKEY 4.9	CHINA 2.9	KAZAKH. 2.3	OTHER ASIA 6.9	AUSTL. 3.4	AFRICA 4.0

Cocoa Beans World Production - 2,826,000 metric tons - Avg. 1994-96

CÔTE D'IVOIRE 37.5%	GHANA 12.9	NIGERIA 5.5	CAMER. 4.4	BRAZIL 16.9	ECUADOR 3.1	COLOMBIA 2.0	OTHER 1.4	INDO-NESIA 9.6	MALAY. 5.1	DOM. REP. 2.2	OTHER 2.4

**RICE,
MILLET AND
GRAIN
SORGHUM**

MILLET AND GRAIN SORGHUM
primarily grown for grain

B = Bajara   M = Millet, undifferentiated
J = Jowar   R = Ragi
K = Kaoliang   S = Sorghum
Kf = Kaffir Corn

RICE Each dot represents 5,000,000 bushels (102,000 metric tons) per year

Width of flow lines is proportional to tonnage of rice.
One half millimeter represents 500,000 metric tons.
The flow lines do not necessarily indicate exact routes.

Millet & Grain Sorghum World Production - 90,676,500 metric tons - Avg. 1994-96

INDIA 22.7%	CHINA 10.0	OTHER 2.2	UNITED STATES 18.1	MEXICO 5.4	NIGERIA 12.8	SUDAN 4.4	NIGER 2.3	BURK. 2.0	ETHIOPIA 2.0	OTHER AFRICA 10.3	ARG. 2.2	ALL OTHER 2.9

Rice Exports* World Exports - 19,479,000 metric tons - Avg. 1994-96   *Including reexports

THAILAND 28.3%	INDIA 14.2	VIETNAM 8.6	PAK. 7.6	CHINA 3.9	MYANMAR 2.0	OTHER 2.0	UNITED STATES 14.6	ITALY 3.0	OTHER 3.6	AUSTL. 2.9	OTHER 3.7

Rice World Production - 553,032,000 metric tons - Avg. 1994-96

CHINA 33.9%	INDIA 21.9	INDO-NESIA 8.9	BANG. 4.8	VIETNAM 4.5	THAILAND 3.9	MYANMAR 3.3	JAPAN 2.0	OTHER 5.7	S. AMER. 3.3	AFRICA 2.7

Rice Imports World Imports - 19,836,000 metric tons - Avg. 1994-96

INDONESIA 10.0%	CHINA 6.7	JAPAN 5.1	IRAN 3.8	S. ARABIA 3.0	BANG. 2.5	N. KOREA 2.0	MALAYSIA 2.0	U.A.E. 2.0	OTHER ASIA 12.6	BRAZIL 4.5	OTHER 2.6	S. AFR. 2.2	SENEGAL 2.2	OTHER AFRICA 14.6	EUROPE 12.1	N. AMER. 9.0

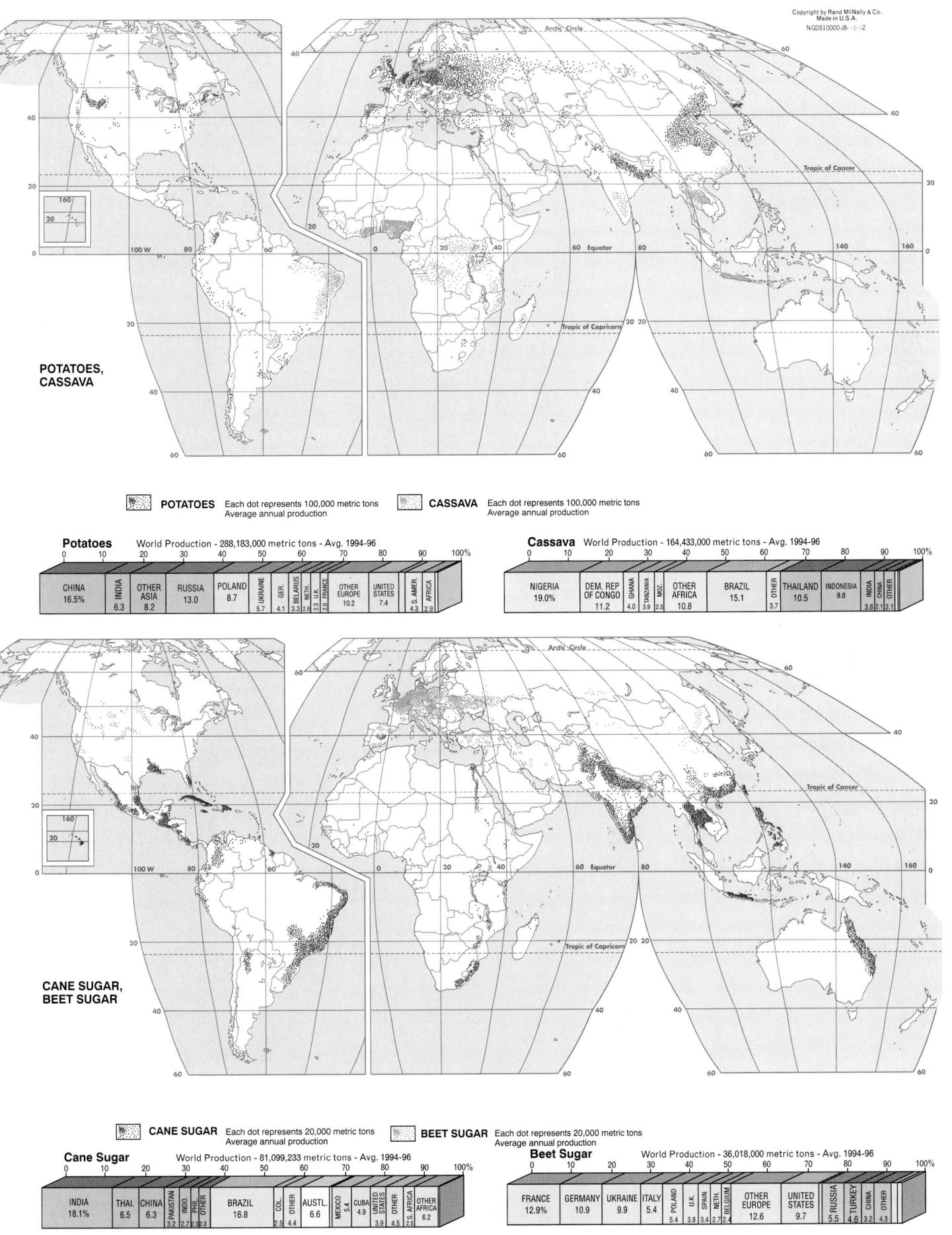

**POTATOES,
CASSAVA**

POTATOES Each dot represents 100,000 metric tons
Average annual production

CASSAVA Each dot represents 100,000 metric tons
Average annual production

Potatoes World Production - 288,183,000 metric tons - Avg. 1994-96

| 0 | 10 | 20 | 30 | 40 | 50 | 60 | 70 | 80 | 90 | 100% |

| CHINA 16.5% | INDIA 6.3 | OTHER ASIA 8.2 | RUSSIA 13.0 | POLAND 8.7 | UKRAINE 5.7 | GER. 4.1 | BELARUS 3.3 | NETH. 2.6 | U.K. 2.3 | FRANCE 2.0 | OTHER EUROPE 10.2 | UNITED STATES 7.4 | S. AMER. 4.3 | AFRICA 2.9 |

Cassava World Production - 164,433,000 metric tons - Avg. 1994-96

| 0 | 10 | 20 | 30 | 40 | 50 | 60 | 70 | 80 | 90 | 100% |

| NIGERIA 19.0% | DEM. REP OF CONGO 11.2 | GHANA 4.0 | TANZANIA 3.9 | MOZ. 2.5 | OTHER AFRICA 10.8 | BRAZIL 15.1 | OTHER 3.7 | THAILAND 10.5 | INDONESIA 9.8 | INDIA 3.6 | CHINA 2.1 | OTHER 3.1 |

**CANE SUGAR,
BEET SUGAR**

CANE SUGAR Each dot represents 20,000 metric tons
Average annual production

BEET SUGAR Each dot represents 20,000 metric tons
Average annual production

Cane Sugar World Production - 81,099,233 metric tons - Avg. 1994-96

| 0 | 10 | 20 | 30 | 40 | 50 | 60 | 70 | 80 | 90 | 100% |

| INDIA 18.1% | THAI. 6.5 | CHINA 6.3 | PAKISTAN 3.2 | INDO. 2.7 | PHIL. 2.3 | OTHER 2.3 | BRAZIL 16.8 | COL 2.5 | OTHER 4.4 | AUSTL. 6.6 | MEXICO 5.4 | CUBA 4.9 | UNITED STATES 3.9 | OTHER 4.5 | S. AFRICA 2.5 | OTHER AFRICA 6.2 |

Beet Sugar World Production - 36,018,000 metric tons - Avg. 1994-96

| 0 | 10 | 20 | 30 | 40 | 50 | 60 | 70 | 80 | 90 | 100% |

| FRANCE 12.9% | GERMANY 10.9 | UKRAINE 9.9 | ITALY 5.4 | POLAND 5.4 | U.K. 3.8 | SPAIN 3.4 | NETH. 2.7 | BELGIUM 2.4 | OTHER EUROPE 12.6 | UNITED STATES 9.7 | RUSSIA 5.5 | TURKEY 4.6 | CHINA 4.3 | OTHER |

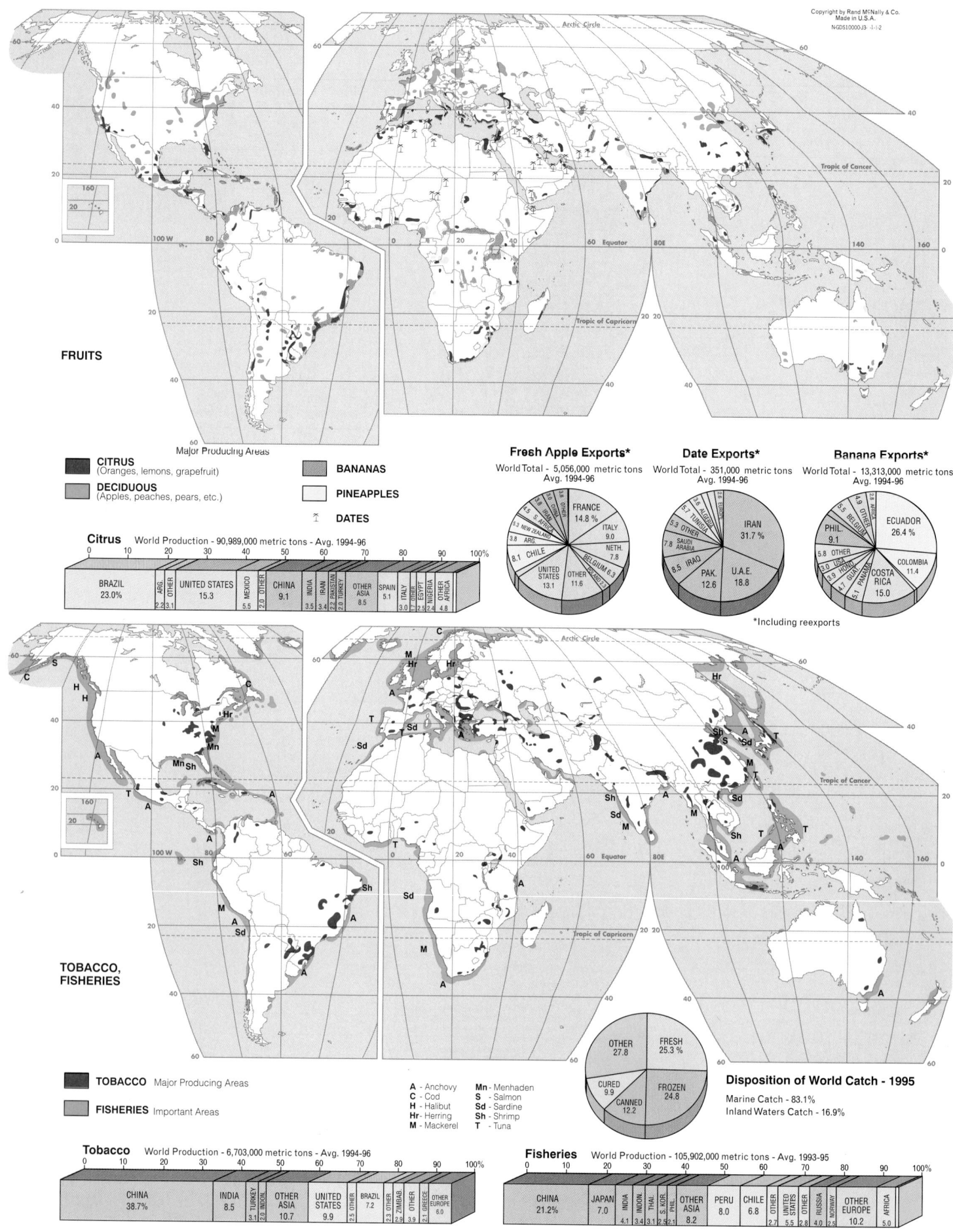

Copyright by Rand McNally & Co.
Made in U.S.A.
NGDS10000-J3- -I-I-2

FRUITS

Major Producing Areas

CITRUS
(Oranges, lemons, grapefruit)

DECIDUOUS
(Apples, peaches, pears, etc.)

BANANAS

PINEAPPLES

DATES

Fresh Apple Exports*
World Total - 5,056,000 metric tons
Avg. 1994-96

FRANCE 14.8 %
ITALY 9.0
NETH. 7.8
BELGIUM 6.3
OTHER 11.6
UNITED STATES 13.1
CHILE 8.1
ARG. 3.8
NEW ZEALAND 5.3
S. AFRICA 4.5
OTHER 3.8

Date Exports*
World Total - 351,000 metric tons
Avg. 1994-96

IRAN 31.7 %
U.A.E. 18.8
PAK. 12.6
IRAQ 8.5
SAUDI ARABIA 7.8
TUNISIA 5.3
OTHER 5.3
ALGERIA 2.6
OTHER 6.8

Banana Exports*
World Total - 13,313,000 metric tons
Avg. 1994-96

ECUADOR 26.4 %
COLOMBIA 11.4
COSTA RICA 15.0
PANAMA 5.1
HOND. 4.7
GUAT. 3.9
USA 3.0
OTHER 5.8
PHIL. 9.1
BELGIUM 5.5
OTHER 4.9

*Including reexports

Citrus World Production - 90,989,000 metric tons - Avg. 1994-96

	0	10	20	30	40	50	60	70	80	90	100%

BRAZIL 23.0% | ARG. 2.2 | OTHER 3.1 | UNITED STATES 15.3 | MEXICO 5.5 | CHINA 9.1 | INDIA 3.5 | IRAN 3.4 | PAKISTAN 2.2 | TURKEY 2.0 | OTHER ASIA 8.5 | SPAIN 5.1 | ITALY 3.0 | OTHER 2.7 | EGYPT 2.5 | NIGERIA 2.4 | OTHER AFRICA 4.8

TOBACCO, FISHERIES

A - Anchovy   Mn - Menhaden
C - Cod   S - Salmon
H - Halibut   Sd - Sardine
Hr - Herring   Sh - Shrimp
M - Mackerel   T - Tuna

TOBACCO Major Producing Areas

FISHERIES Important Areas

Disposition of World Catch - 1995

FRESH 25.3 %
FROZEN 24.8
CANNED 12.2
CURED 9.9
OTHER 27.8

Marine Catch - 83.1%
Inland Waters Catch - 16.9%

Tobacco World Production - 6,703,000 metric tons - Avg. 1994-96

	0	10	20	30	40	50	60	70	80	90	100%

CHINA 38.7% | INDIA 8.5 | TURKEY 3.1 | INDON. | OTHER ASIA 10.7 | UNITED STATES 9.9 | OTHER 2.5 | BRAZIL 7.2 | ZIMBAB. 2.3 | OTHER 2.9 | GREECE 2.1 | OTHER EUROPE 6.0

Fisheries World Production - 105,902,000 metric tons - Avg. 1993-95

	0	10	20	30	40	50	60	70	80	90	100%

CHINA 21.2% | JAPAN 7.0 | INDIA 4.1 | INDON. 3.4 | THAI. 3.1 | S. KOR. 2.5 | PHIL. 2.1 | OTHER ASIA 8.2 | PERU 8.0 | CHILE 6.8 | OTHER 2.7 | UNITED STATES 5.5 | OTHER 2.8 | RUSSIA 4.0 | NORWAY | OTHER EUROPE 10.2 | AFRICA 5.0

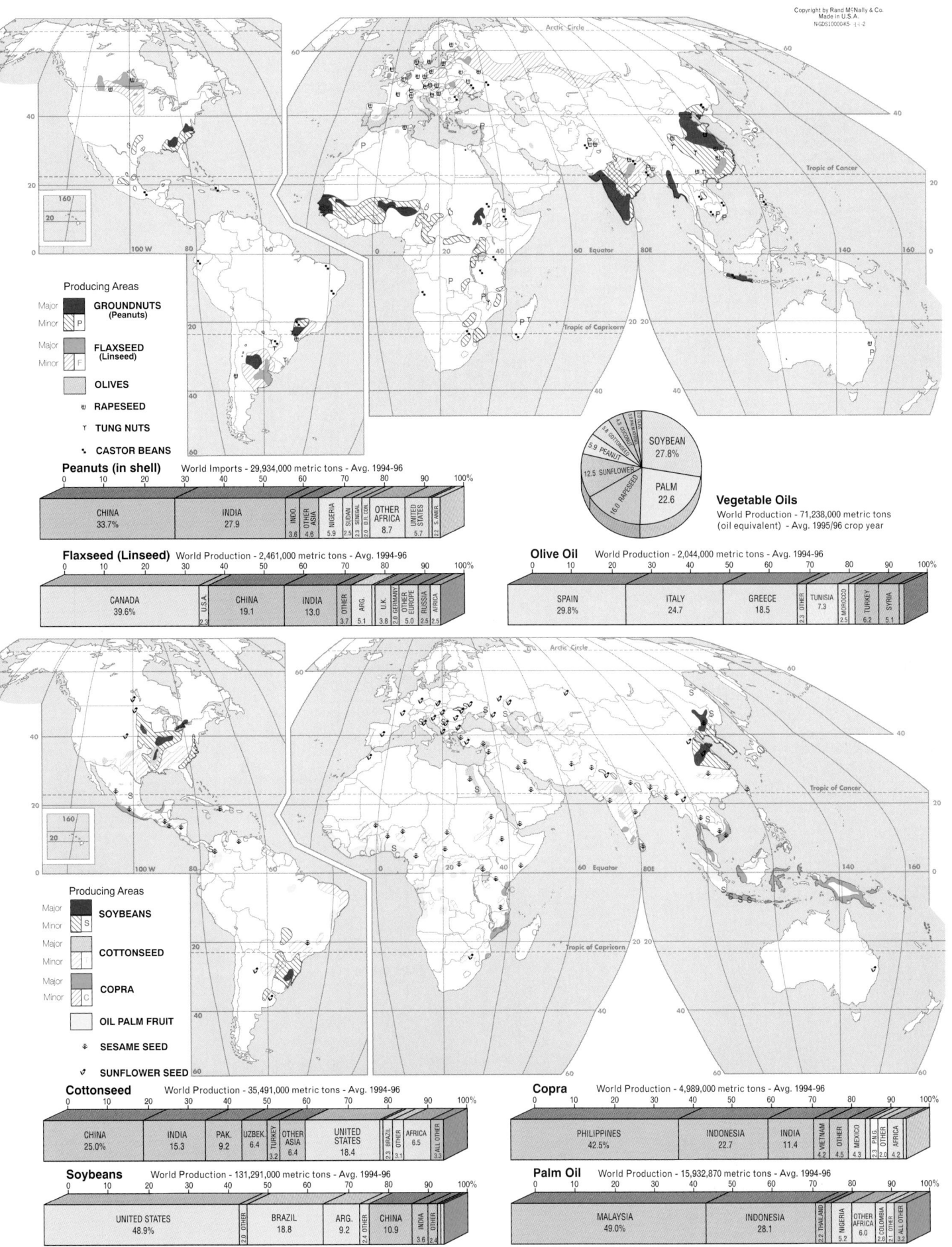

Copyright by Rand McNally & Co.
Made in U.S.A.
NGDS10000-K5-11-2

Producing Areas

Major / Minor — **GROUNDNUTS** (Peanuts) / P

Major / Minor — **FLAXSEED** (Linseed) / F

OLIVES

ᵂ **RAPESEED**

T **TUNG NUTS**

∴ **CASTOR BEANS**

Peanuts (in shell)   World Imports - 29,934,000 metric tons - Avg. 1994-96

CHINA 33.7%	INDIA 27.9	INDO. 3.6	OTHER ASIA 4.6	NIGERIA 5.9	SUDAN 2.5	SENEGAL 2.0	D.R. CON.	OTHER AFRICA 8.7	UNITED STATES 5.7	S. AMER. 2.2

Flaxseed (Linseed)   World Production - 2,461,000 metric tons - Avg. 1994-96

CANADA 39.6%	U.S.A. 2.3	CHINA 19.1	INDIA 13.0	OTHER 3.7	ARG. 5.1	U.K. 3.8	GERMANY 2.0	OTHER EUROPE 5.0	RUSSIA 2.5	AFRICA 2.5

Vegetable Oils

World Production - 71,238,000 metric tons
(oil equivalent) - Avg. 1995/96 crop year

Pie chart:
- SOYBEAN 27.8%
- PALM 22.6
- 16.0 RAPESEED
- 12.5 SUNFLOWER
- 5.9 PEANUT
- 5.4 COTTONSEED
- 4.8 COCONUT
- 2.8 OLIVE
- 2.2 OTHER

Olive Oil   World Production - 2,044,000 metric tons - Avg. 1994-96

SPAIN 29.8%	ITALY 24.7	GREECE 18.5	OTHER 2.3	TUNISIA 7.3	MOROCCO 2.5	TURKEY 6.2	SYRIA 5.1

Producing Areas

Major / Minor — **SOYBEANS** / S

Major / Minor — **COTTONSEED**

Major / Minor — **COPRA** / C

OIL PALM FRUIT

⚚ **SESAME SEED**

⚘ **SUNFLOWER SEED**

Cottonseed   World Production - 35,491,000 metric tons - Avg. 1994-96

CHINA 25.0%	INDIA 15.3	PAK. 9.2	UZBEK. 6.4	TURKEY 3.2	OTHER ASIA 6.4	UNITED STATES 18.4	BRAZIL 2.3	OTHER 3.1	AFRICA 6.5	ALL OTHER

Soybeans   World Production - 131,291,000 metric tons - Avg. 1994-96

UNITED STATES 48.9%	OTHER 2.0	BRAZIL 18.8	ARG. 9.2	OTHER 2.4	CHINA 10.9	INDIA 3.6	OTHER 2.4

Copra   World Production - 4,989,000 metric tons - Avg. 1994-96

PHILIPPINES 42.5%	INDONESIA 22.7	INDIA 11.4	VIETNAM 4.2	MEXICO 4.5	OTHER 4.3	AFRICA 2.0

Palm Oil   World Production - 15,932,870 metric tons - Avg. 1994-96

MALAYSIA 49.0%	INDONESIA 28.1	THAILAND 2.2	NIGERIA 5.2	OTHER AFRICA 6.0	COLOMBIA 2.1	ALL OTHER

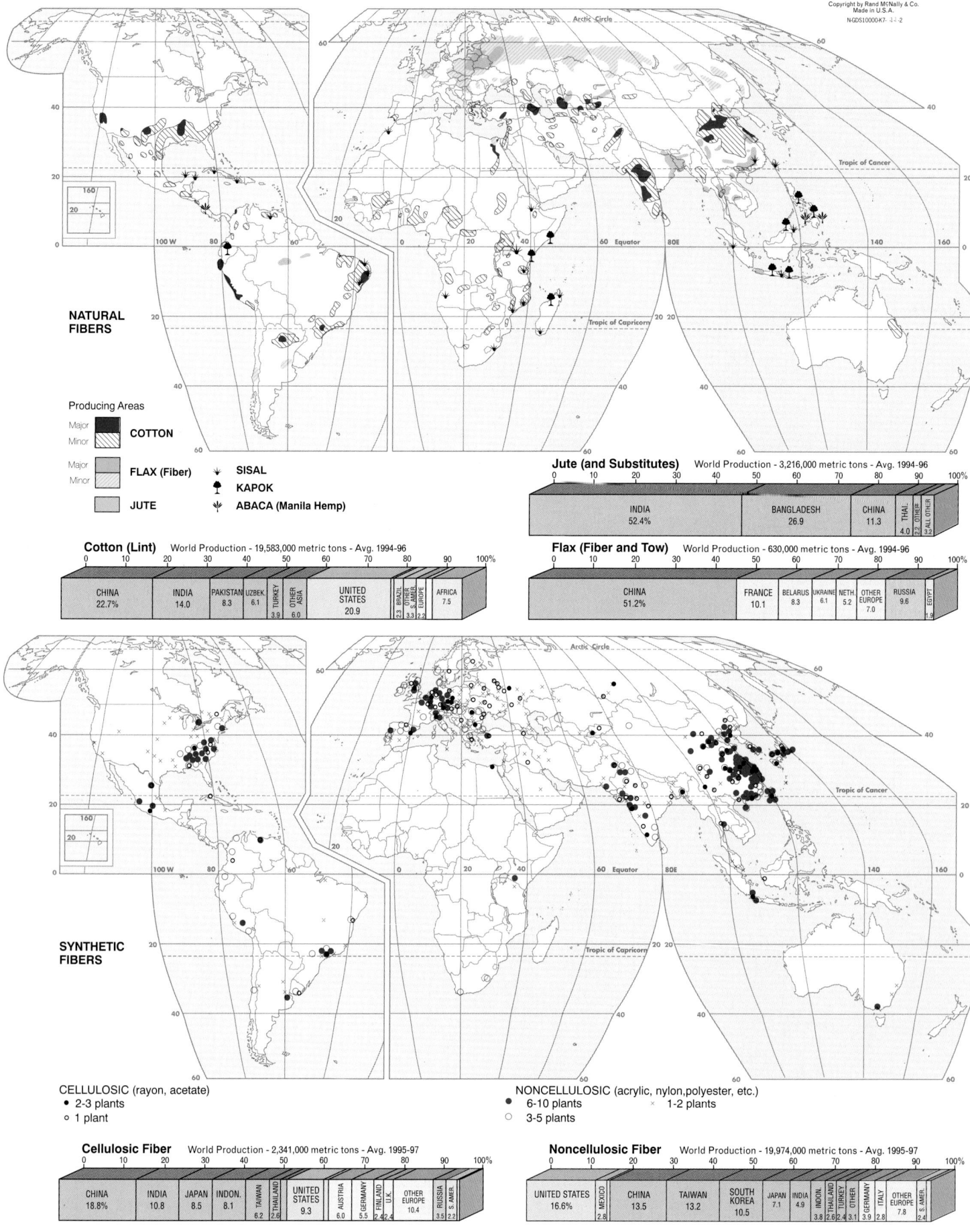

Copyright by Rand McNally & Co.
Made in U.S.A.
NGDS10000-K7-

NATURAL FIBERS

Producing Areas

Major / Minor **COTTON**

Major / Minor **FLAX (Fiber)**   ☤ **SISAL**

JUTE   ♠ **KAPOK**

    ⚚ **ABACA (Manila Hemp)**

Jute (and Substitutes) World Production - 3,216,000 metric tons - Avg. 1994-96

INDIA 52.4%	BANGLADESH 26.9	CHINA 11.3	THAI. 4.0	OTHER 2.2	ALL OTHER 3.2

Cotton (Lint) World Production - 19,583,000 metric tons - Avg. 1994-96

CHINA 22.7%	INDIA 14.0	PAKISTAN 8.3	UZBEK. 6.1	TURKEY 3.9	OTHER ASIA 6.0	UNITED STATES 20.9	BRAZIL 2.3	OTHER S. AMER. 3.3	EUROPE 2.2	AFRICA 7.5

Flax (Fiber and Tow) World Production - 630,000 metric tons - Avg. 1994-96

CHINA 51.2%	FRANCE 10.1	BELARUS 8.3	UKRAINE 6.1	NETH. 5.2	OTHER EUROPE 7.0	RUSSIA 9.6	EGYPT 1.9

SYNTHETIC FIBERS

CELLULOSIC (rayon, acetate)
● 2-3 plants
○ 1 plant

NONCELLULOSIC (acrylic, nylon, polyester, etc.)
● 6-10 plants   × 1-2 plants
○ 3-5 plants

Cellulosic Fiber World Production - 2,341,000 metric tons - Avg. 1995-97

CHINA 18.8%	INDIA 10.8	JAPAN 8.5	INDON. 8.1	TAIWAN 6.2	THAILAND 2.6	UNITED STATES 9.3	AUSTRIA 6.0	GERMANY 5.5	FINLAND 2.4	U.K. 2.4	OTHER EUROPE 10.4	RUSSIA 3.5	S. AMER. 2.2

Noncellulosic Fiber World Production - 19,974,000 metric tons - Avg. 1995-97

UNITED STATES 16.6%	MEXICO 2.8	CHINA 13.5	TAIWAN 13.2	SOUTH KOREA 10.5	JAPAN 7.1	INDIA 4.9	INDON. 3.8	THAILAND 2.6	TURKEY 2.4	OTHER 3.1	GERMANY 3.9	ITALY 2.8	OTHER EUROPE 7.8	S. AMER. 2.4

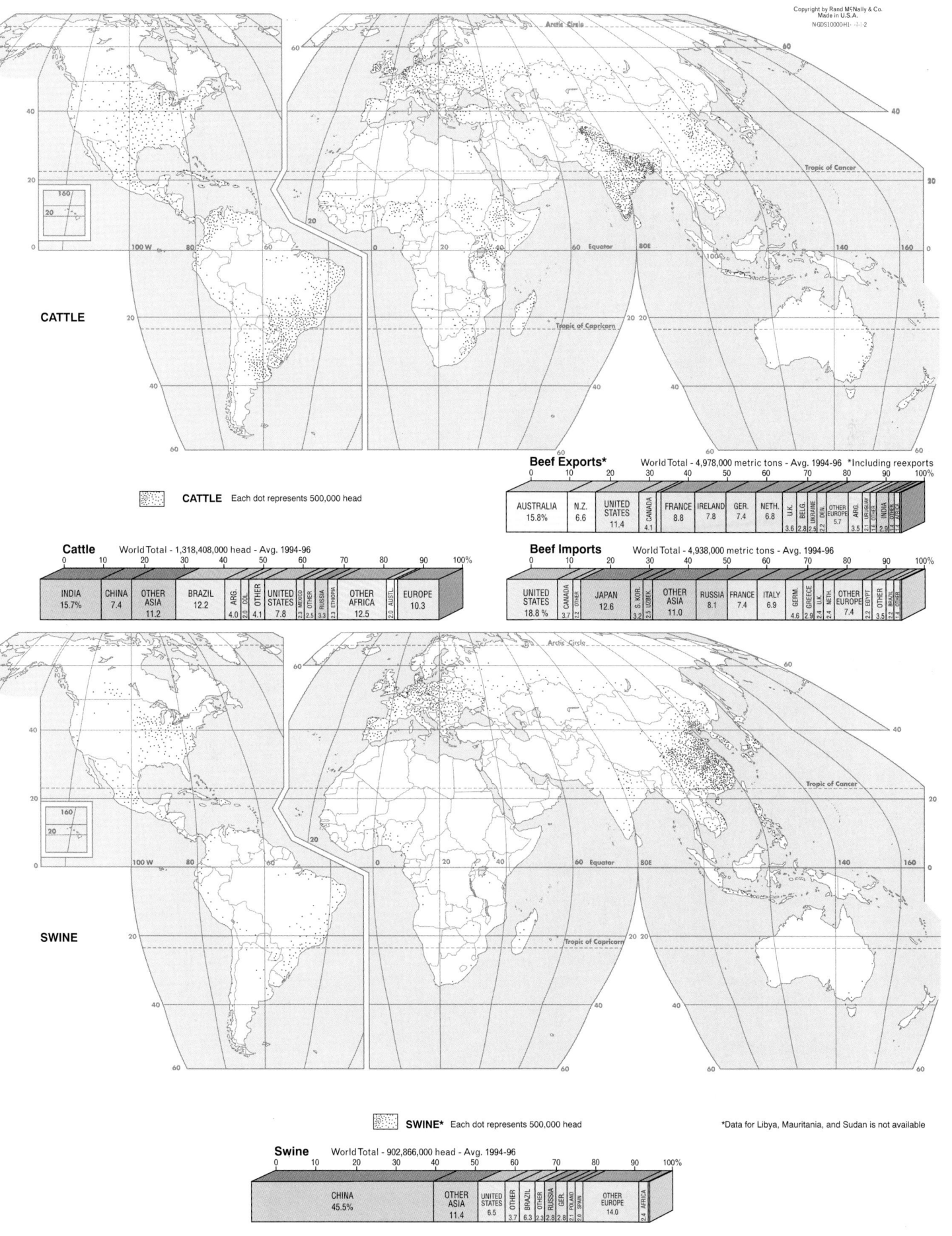

CATTLE

SWINE

CATTLE Each dot represents 500,000 head

SWINE* Each dot represents 500,000 head

*Data for Libya, Mauritania, and Sudan is not available

Cattle World Total - 1,318,408,000 head - Avg. 1994-96

0	10	20	30	40	50	60	70	80	90	100%

| INDIA 15.7% | CHINA 7.4 | OTHER ASIA 11.2 | BRAZIL 12.2 | ARG. 4.0 | COL. 2.0 | OTHER 4.1 | UNITED STATES 7.8 | MEXICO 2.3 | RUSSIA 2.5 | ETHIOPIA 3.3 | OTHER AFRICA 12.5 | AUSTL. 2.0 | EUROPE 10.3 |

Beef Exports* World Total - 4,978,000 metric tons - Avg. 1994-96 *Including reexports

0	10	20	30	40	50	60	70	80	90	100%

| AUSTRALIA 15.8% | N.Z. 6.6 | UNITED STATES 11.4 | CANADA 4.1 | FRANCE 8.8 | IRELAND 7.8 | GER. 7.4 | NETH. 6.8 | U.K. 3.6 | BELG. 2.8 | UKRAINE 2.5 | DEN. 2.2 | OTHER EUROPE 5.7 | ARG. 3.5 | URUGUAY 2.1 | INDIA 2.9 | OTHER 1.8 | BRAZIL 1.4 | AFRICA 1.4 |

Beef Imports World Total - 4,938,000 metric tons - Avg. 1994-96

0	10	20	30	40	50	60	70	80	90	100%

| UNITED STATES 18.8% | CANADA 3.7 | OTHER | JAPAN 12.6 | S. KOR. 3.2 | UZBEK. 2.5 | OTHER ASIA 11.0 | RUSSIA 8.1 | FRANCE 7.4 | ITALY 6.9 | GERM. 4.6 | GREECE 2.9 | U.K. 2.4 | NETH. | OTHER EUROPE 7.4 | EGYPT 2.2 | OTHER 3.5 | OTHER |

Swine World Total - 902,866,000 head - Avg. 1994-96

0	10	20	30	40	50	60	70	80	90	100%

| CHINA 45.5% | OTHER ASIA 11.4 | UNITED STATES 6.5 | OTHER 3.7 | BRAZIL 6.3 | OTHER 2.8 | RUSSIA 2.3 | GER. 2.1 | POLAND 2.0 | SPAIN 2.0 | OTHER EUROPE 14.0 | AFRICA 2.4 |

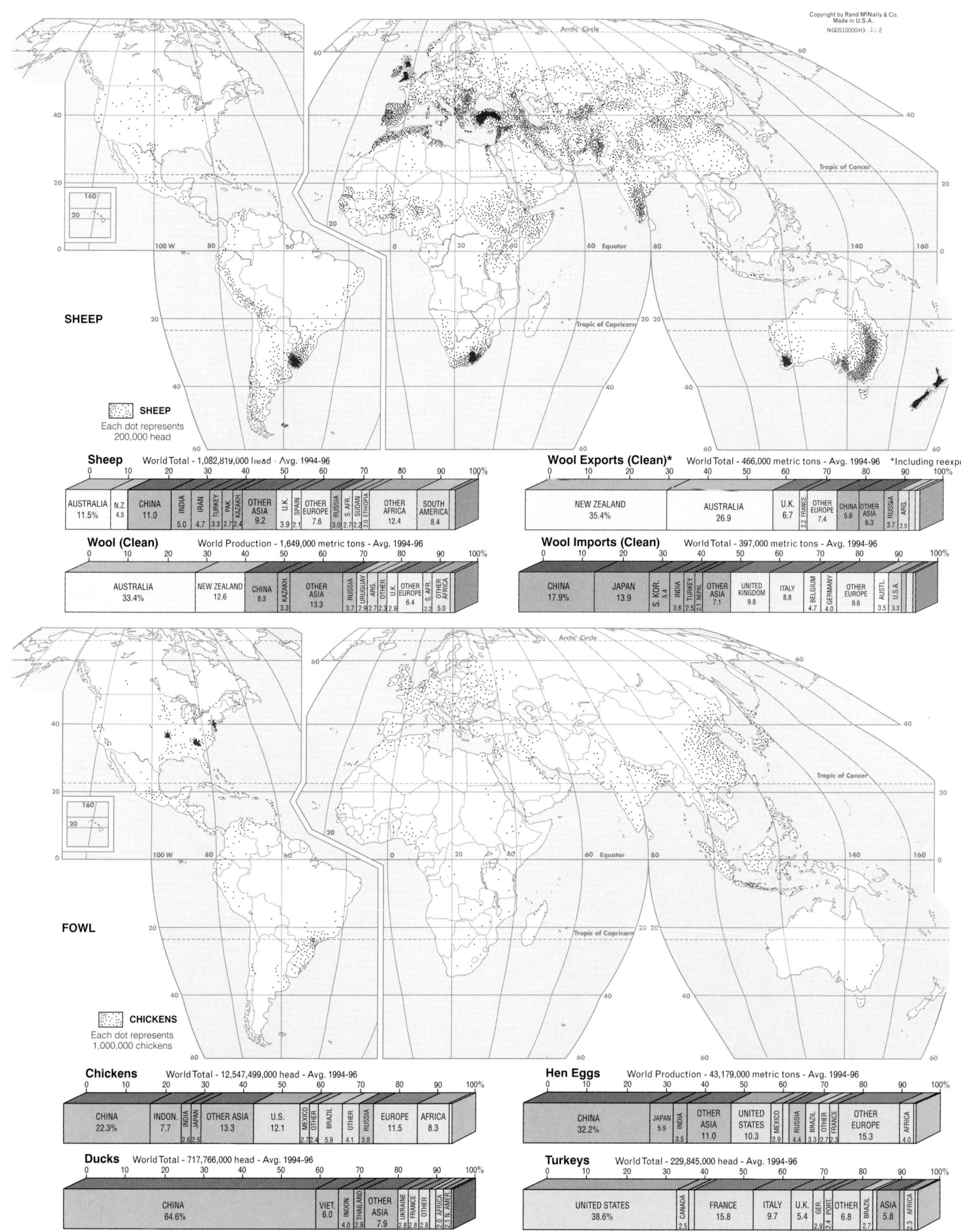

Copyright by Rand McNally & Co.
Made in U.S.A.
NGDS10000H3-⌐⌐2

SHEEP

SHEEP
Each dot represents
200,000 head

Sheep World Total - 1,082,819,000 head - Avg. 1994-96

AUSTRALIA 11.5%	N.Z. 4.5	CHINA 11.0	INDIA 5.0	IRAN 4.7	TURKEY 3.3	PAK 2.7	KAZAKH 2.4	OTHER ASIA 9.2	U.K. 3.9	SPAIN 2.1	OTHER EUROPE 7.6	RUSSIA 3.0 / S. AFR. 2.7 / SUDAN 2.2 / ETHIOPIA 2.0	OTHER AFRICA 12.4	SOUTH AMERICA 8.4	

Wool (Clean) World Production - 1,649,000 metric tons - Avg. 1994-96

AUSTRALIA 33.4%	NEW ZEALAND 12.6	CHINA 8.3	KAZAKH. 3.3	OTHER ASIA 13.3	RUSSIA 3.7 / URUGUAY 2.9 / ARG. 2.7 / OTHER 2.9	U.K. 6.4 / OTHER EUROPE	S. AFR. 2.2 / OTHER AFRICA 5.0

Wool Exports (Clean)* World Total - 466,000 metric tons - Avg. 1994-96   *Including reexports

NEW ZEALAND 35.4%	AUSTRALIA 26.9	U.K. 6.7	FRANCE 2.2	OTHER EUROPE 7.4	CHINA 5.6	OTHER ASIA 6.3	RUSSIA 3.7	ARG. 2.5

Wool Imports (Clean) World Total - 397,000 metric tons - Avg. 1994-96

CHINA 17.9%	JAPAN 13.9	S. KOR. 5.4	INDIA 3.6 / TURKEY 2.5 / NEPAL 2.1	OTHER ASIA 7.1	UNITED KINGDOM 9.8	ITALY 8.8	BELGIUM 4.7 / GERMANY 4.0	OTHER EUROPE 9.6	AUSTL. 3.5	U.S.A. 3.3	

FOWL

CHICKENS
Each dot represents
1,000,000 chickens

Chickens World Total - 12,547,499,000 head - Avg. 1994-96

CHINA 22.3%	INDON. 7.7	INDIA 2.6 / JAPAN 2.5	OTHER ASIA 13.3	U.S. 12.1	MEXICO 2.7 / BRAZIL 2.4	OTHER 5.9	RUSSIA 4.1 / 3.8	EUROPE 11.5	AFRICA 8.3	

Ducks World Total - 717,766,000 head - Avg. 1994-96

CHINA 64.6%	VIET. 6.0	INDON. 4.0	THAILAND 2.9	OTHER ASIA 7.9	UKRAINE 2.8 / FRANCE 2.8	OTHER EUROPE 2.8	AFRICA 2.0 / N. AMER. 2.1	

Hen Eggs World Production - 43,179,000 metric tons - Avg. 1994-96

CHINA 32.2%	JAPAN 5.9	INDIA 3.5	OTHER ASIA 11.0	UNITED STATES 10.3	MEXICO 2.9	RUSSIA 4.4	BRAZIL 3.3 / FRANCE 2.7	OTHER EUROPE 15.3	AFRICA 4.0	

Turkeys World Total - 229,845,000 head - Avg. 1994-96

UNITED STATES 38.6%	CANADA 2.5	FRANCE 15.8	ITALY 9.7	U.K. 5.4	GER. 2.9 / PORT. 2.4	OTHER 6.8	BRAZIL 3.3	ASIA 5.8	AFRICA 2.3

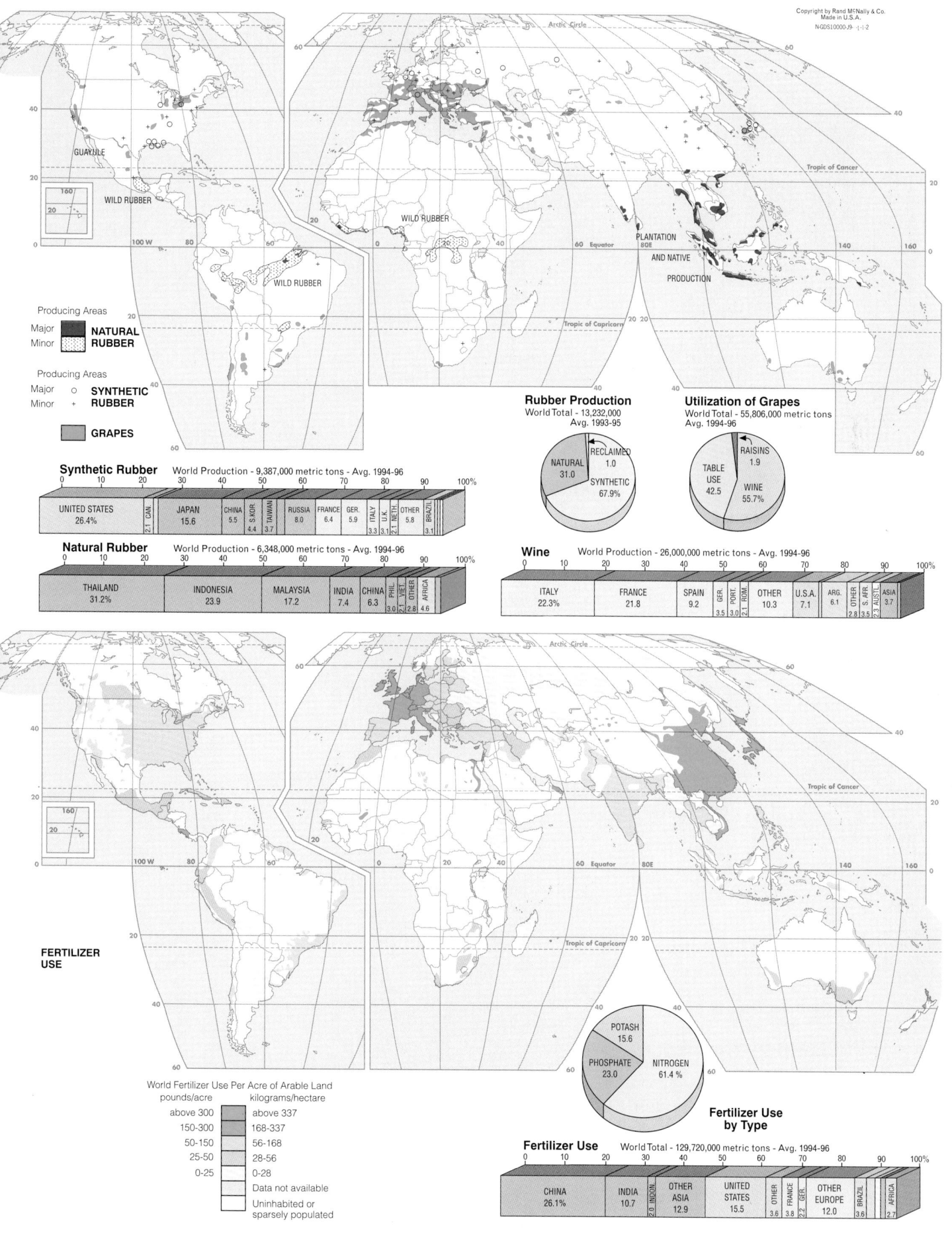

GUAYULE

WILD RUBBER

WILD RUBBER

WILD RUBBER

PLANTATION
80E
AND NATIVE
PRODUCTION

Producing Areas
Major — **NATURAL**
Minor — **RUBBER**

Producing Areas
Major ○ **SYNTHETIC**
Minor + **RUBBER**

GRAPES

Rubber Production
World Total - 13,232,000
Avg. 1993-95

NATURAL 31.0
RECLAIMED 1.0
SYNTHETIC 67.9%

Utilization of Grapes
World Total - 55,806,000 metric tons
Avg. 1994-96

TABLE USE 42.5
RAISINS 1.9
WINE 55.7%

Synthetic Rubber — World Production - 9,387,000 metric tons - Avg. 1994-96

| UNITED STATES 26.4% | CAN. 2.1 | JAPAN 15.6 | CHINA 5.5 | S.KOR. 4.4 | TAIWAN 3.7 | RUSSIA 8.0 | FRANCE 6.4 | GER. 5.9 | ITALY 3.3 | U.K. 3.1 | NETH. 2.1 | OTHER 5.8 | BRAZIL 3.1 |

Natural Rubber — World Production - 6,348,000 metric tons - Avg. 1994-96

| THAILAND 31.2% | INDONESIA 23.9 | MALAYSIA 17.2 | INDIA 7.4 | CHINA 6.3 | PHIL. 3.0 | VIET. 2.1 | OTHER 2.8 | AFRICA 4.6 |

Wine — World Production - 26,000,000 metric tons - Avg. 1994-96

| ITALY 22.3% | FRANCE 21.8 | SPAIN 9.2 | GER. 3.5 | PORT. 3.0 | ROM. 2.1 | OTHER 10.3 | U.S.A. 7.1 | ARG. 6.1 | OTHER 2.8 | S. AFR. 3.5 | AUSTL. 2.3 | ASIA 3.7 |

**FERTILIZER
USE**

Fertilizer Use by Type

POTASH 15.6
PHOSPHATE 23.0
NITROGEN 61.4 %

Fertilizer Use — World Total - 129,720,000 metric tons - Avg. 1994-96

| CHINA 26.1% | INDIA 10.7 | INDON. 2.0 | OTHER ASIA 12.9 | UNITED STATES 15.5 | OTHER 3.6 | FRANCE 2.2 | GER. 3.8 | OTHER EUROPE 12.0 | BRAZIL 3.6 | AFRICA 2.7 |

World Fertilizer Use Per Acre of Arable Land

pounds/acre	kilograms/hectare
above 300	above 337
150-300	168-337
50-150	56-168
25-50	28-56
0-25	0-28
Data not available	
Uninhabited or sparsely populated	

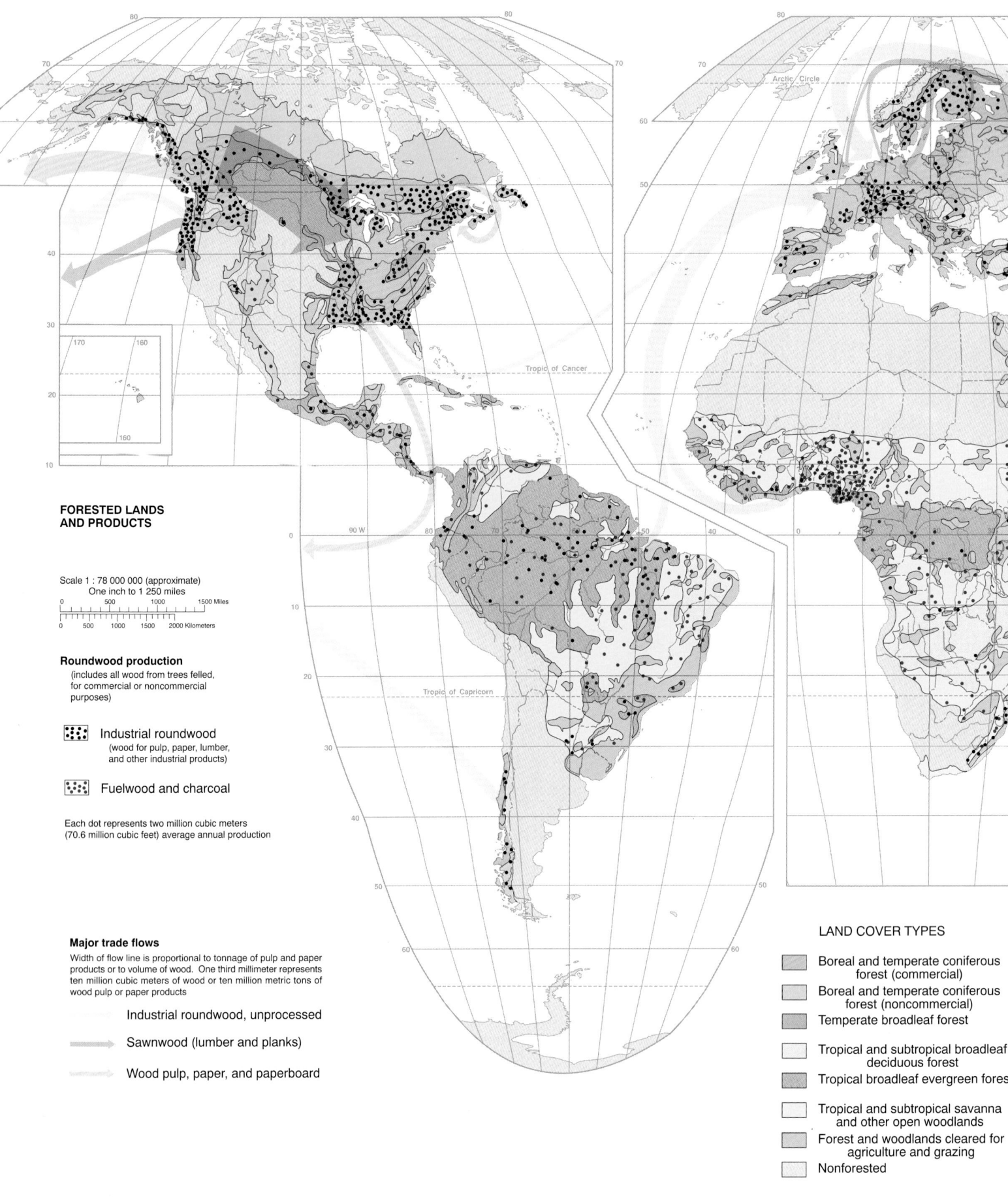

**FORESTED LANDS
AND PRODUCTS**

Scale 1 : 78 000 000 (approximate)
One inch to 1 250 miles

0   500   1000   1500 Miles

0   500   1000   1500   2000 Kilometers

Roundwood production
(includes all wood from trees felled,
for commercial or noncommercial
purposes)

Industrial roundwood
(wood for pulp, paper, lumber,
and other industrial products)

Fuelwood and charcoal

Each dot represents two million cubic meters
(70.6 million cubic feet) average annual production

Major trade flows
Width of flow line is proportional to tonnage of pulp and paper
products or to volume of wood. One third millimeter represents
ten million cubic meters of wood or ten million metric tons of
wood pulp or paper products

Industrial roundwood, unprocessed

Sawnwood (lumber and planks)

Wood pulp, paper, and paperboard

LAND COVER TYPES

Boreal and temperate coniferous
forest (commercial)

Boreal and temperate coniferous
forest (noncommercial)

Temperate broadleaf forest

Tropical and subtropical broadleaf
deciduous forest

Tropical broadleaf evergreen forest

Tropical and subtropical savanna
and other open woodlands

Forest and woodlands cleared for
agriculture and grazing

Nonforested

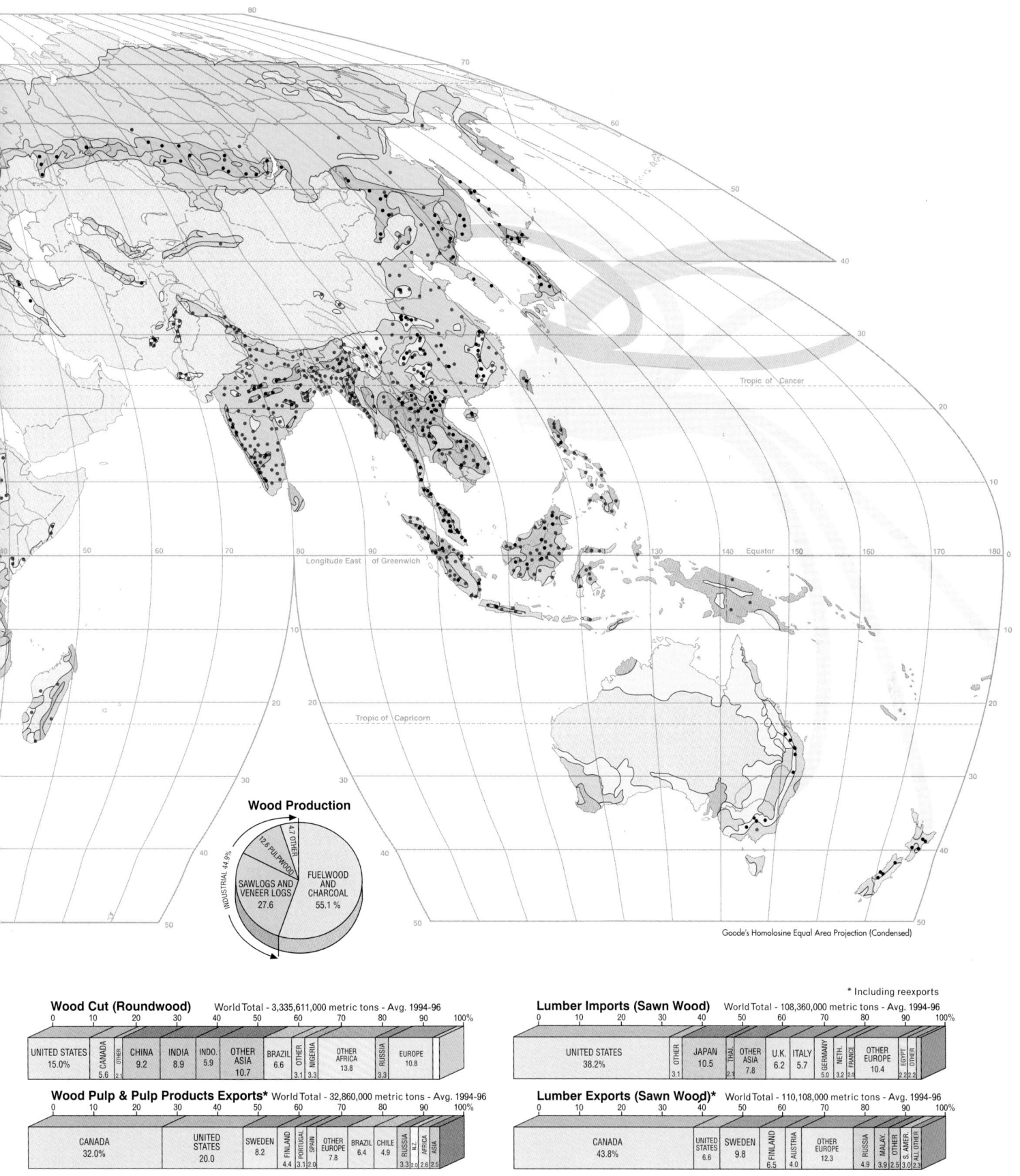

Wood Production

4.7 OTHER

12.6 PULPWOOD

INDUSTRIAL 44.9%

SAWLOGS AND VENEER LOGS 27.6

FUELWOOD AND CHARCOAL 55.1 %

Goode's Homolosine Equal Area Projection (Condensed)

Tropic of Cancer

Longitude East of Greenwich

Equator

Tropic of Capricorn

* Including reexports

Wood Cut (Roundwood) World Total - 3,335,611,000 metric tons - Avg. 1994-96

| 0 | 10 | 20 | 30 | 40 | 50 | 60 | 70 | 80 | 90 | 100% |

UNITED STATES 15.0% | CANADA 5.6 | OTHER 2.1 | CHINA 9.2 | INDIA 8.9 | INDO. 5.9 | OTHER ASIA 10.7 | BRAZIL 6.6 | OTHER 3.1 | NIGERIA 3.3 | OTHER AFRICA 13.8 | RUSSIA 3.3 | EUROPE 10.8

Lumber Imports (Sawn Wood) World Total - 108,360,000 metric tons - Avg. 1994-96

| 0 | 10 | 20 | 30 | 40 | 50 | 60 | 70 | 80 | 90 | 100% |

UNITED STATES 38.2% | OTHER 3.1 | JAPAN 10.5 | THAI. 2.1 | OTHER ASIA 7.8 | U.K. 6.2 | ITALY 5.7 | GERMANY 5.0 | NETH. 3.2 | FRANCE 2.9 | OTHER EUROPE 10.4 | EGYPT 2.2 | OTHER 2.2

Wood Pulp & Pulp Products Exports* World Total - 32,860,000 metric tons - Avg. 1994-96

| 0 | 10 | 20 | 30 | 40 | 50 | 60 | 70 | 80 | 90 | 100% |

CANADA 32.0% | UNITED STATES 20.0 | SWEDEN 8.2 | FINLAND 4.4 | PORTUGAL 3.1 | SPAIN 2.0 | OTHER EUROPE 7.8 | BRAZIL 6.4 | CHILE 4.9 | RUSSIA 3.3 | N.Z. 2.6 | AFRICA 2.6 | ASIA 2.5

Lumber Exports (Sawn Wood)* World Total - 110,108,000 metric tons - Avg. 1994-96

| 0 | 10 | 20 | 30 | 40 | 50 | 60 | 70 | 80 | 90 | 100% |

CANADA 43.8% | UNITED STATES 6.6 | SWEDEN 9.8 | FINLAND 6.5 | AUSTRIA 4.0 | OTHER EUROPE 12.3 | RUSSIA 4.9 | MALAY. 3.9 | OTHER 2.5 | S. AMER. 3.0 | ALL OTHER 2.3

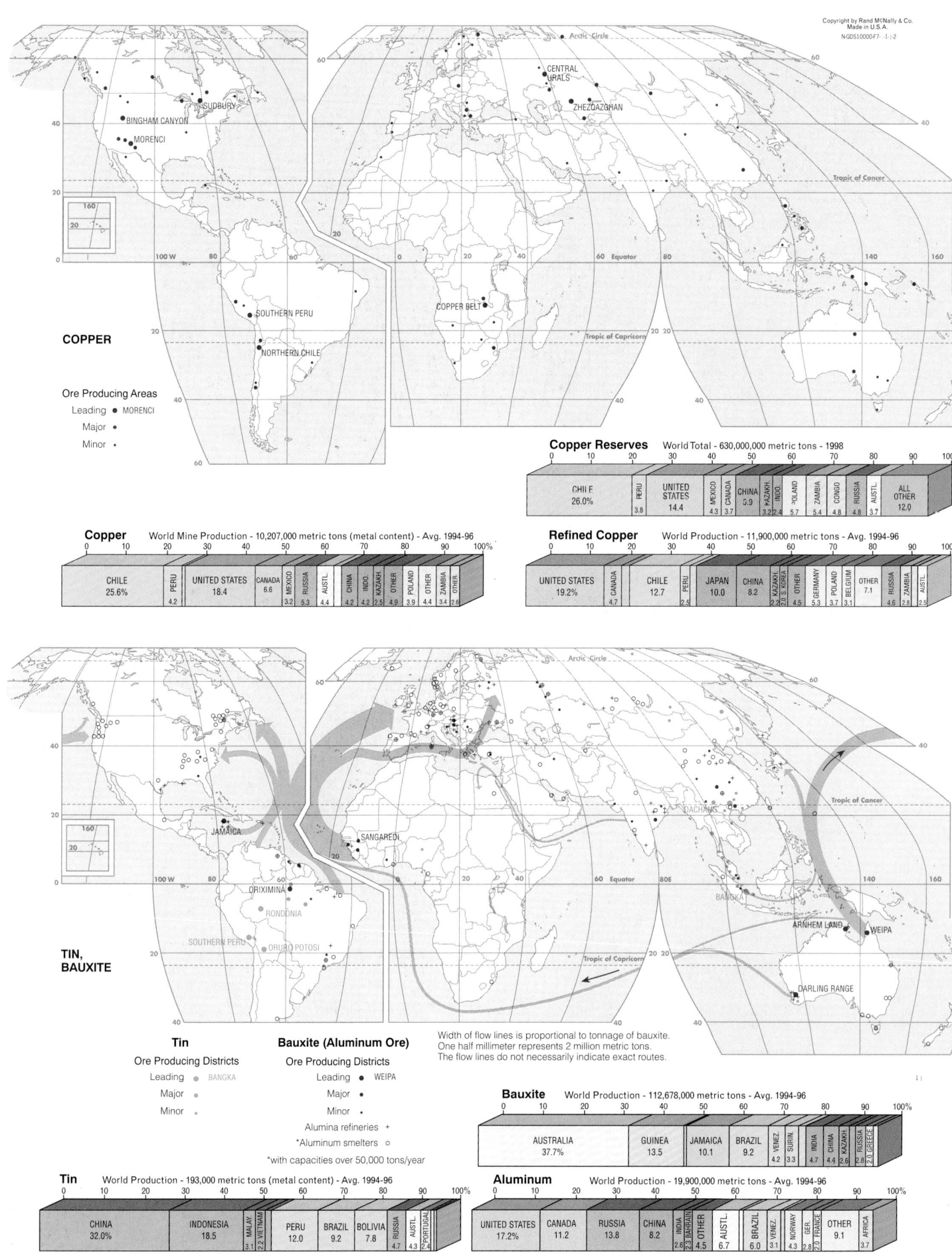

COPPER

Ore Producing Areas

Leading ● MORENCI

Major ●

Minor ·

Copper Reserves World Total - 630,000,000 metric tons - 1998

| 0 | 10 | 20 | 30 | 40 | 50 | 60 | 70 | 80 | 90 | 100% |

| CHILE 26.0% | PERU 3.8 | UNITED STATES 14.4 | MEXICO 4.3 | CANADA 3.7 | CHINA 5.9 | KAZAKH 3.2 | INDO 2.4 | POLAND 5.7 | ZAMBIA 5.4 | CONGO 4.8 | RUSSIA 3.7 | AUSTL | ALL OTHER 12.0 |

Copper World Mine Production - 10,207,000 metric tons (metal content) - Avg. 1994-96

| 0 | 10 | 20 | 30 | 40 | 50 | 60 | 70 | 80 | 90 | 100% |

| CHILE 25.6% | PERU 4.2 | UNITED STATES 18.4 | CANADA 6.6 | MEXICO 3.2 | RUSSIA 5.3 | AUSTL 4.4 | CHINA 4.2 | INDO 4.2 | KAZAKH 4.9 | OTHER 3.9 | POLAND | ZAMBIA 4.4 | OTHER 3.4 | 2.6 |

Refined Copper World Production - 11,900,000 metric tons - Avg. 1994-96

| 0 | 10 | 20 | 30 | 40 | 50 | 60 | 70 | 80 | 90 | 100% |

| UNITED STATES 19.2% | CANADA 4.7 | CHILE 12.7 | PERU 2.5 | JAPAN 10.0 | CHINA 8.2 | KAZAKH 2.2 | S. KOREA 2.1 | OTHER 4.5 | GERMANY 5.3 | POLAND 3.7 | BELGIUM 3.1 | OTHER 7.1 | RUSSIA 4.6 | ZAMBIA 2.8 | AUSTL 2.5 |

TIN, BAUXITE

Tin

Ore Producing Districts

Leading ● BANGKA

Major ●

Minor ·

Bauxite (Aluminum Ore)

Ore Producing Districts

Leading ● WEIPA

Major ●

Minor ·

Alumina refineries +

*Aluminum smelters ○

*with capacities over 50,000 tons/year

Width of flow lines is proportional to tonnage of bauxite.
One half millimeter represents 2 million metric tons.
The flow lines do not necessarily indicate exact routes.

Bauxite World Production - 112,678,000 metric tons - Avg. 1994-96

| 0 | 10 | 20 | 30 | 40 | 50 | 60 | 70 | 80 | 90 | 100% |

| AUSTRALIA 37.7% | GUINEA 13.5 | JAMAICA 10.1 | BRAZIL 9.2 | VENEZ. 4.2 | SURIN. 3.3 | INDIA 4.7 | CHINA 4.4 | KAZAKH 2.6 | RUSSIA 2.0 | GREECE |

Tin World Production - 193,000 metric tons (metal content) - Avg. 1994-96

| 0 | 10 | 20 | 30 | 40 | 50 | 60 | 70 | 80 | 90 | 100% |

| CHINA 32.0% | INDONESIA 18.5 | MALAY 3.1 | VIETNAM 2.2 | PERU 12.0 | BRAZIL 9.2 | BOLIVIA 7.8 | RUSSIA 4.7 | AUSTL 4.3 | PORTUGAL 2.4 |

Aluminum World Production - 19,900,000 metric tons - Avg. 1994-96

| 0 | 10 | 20 | 30 | 40 | 50 | 60 | 70 | 80 | 90 | 100% |

| UNITED STATES 17.2% | CANADA 11.2 | RUSSIA 13.8 | CHINA 8.2 | INDIA 2.6 | BAHRAIN 2.3 | OTHER 4.5 | AUSTL 6.7 | BRAZIL 6.0 | VENEZ. 3.1 | NORWAY 4.3 | GER. 2.8 | FRANCE 2.0 | OTHER 9.1 | AFRICA 3.7 |

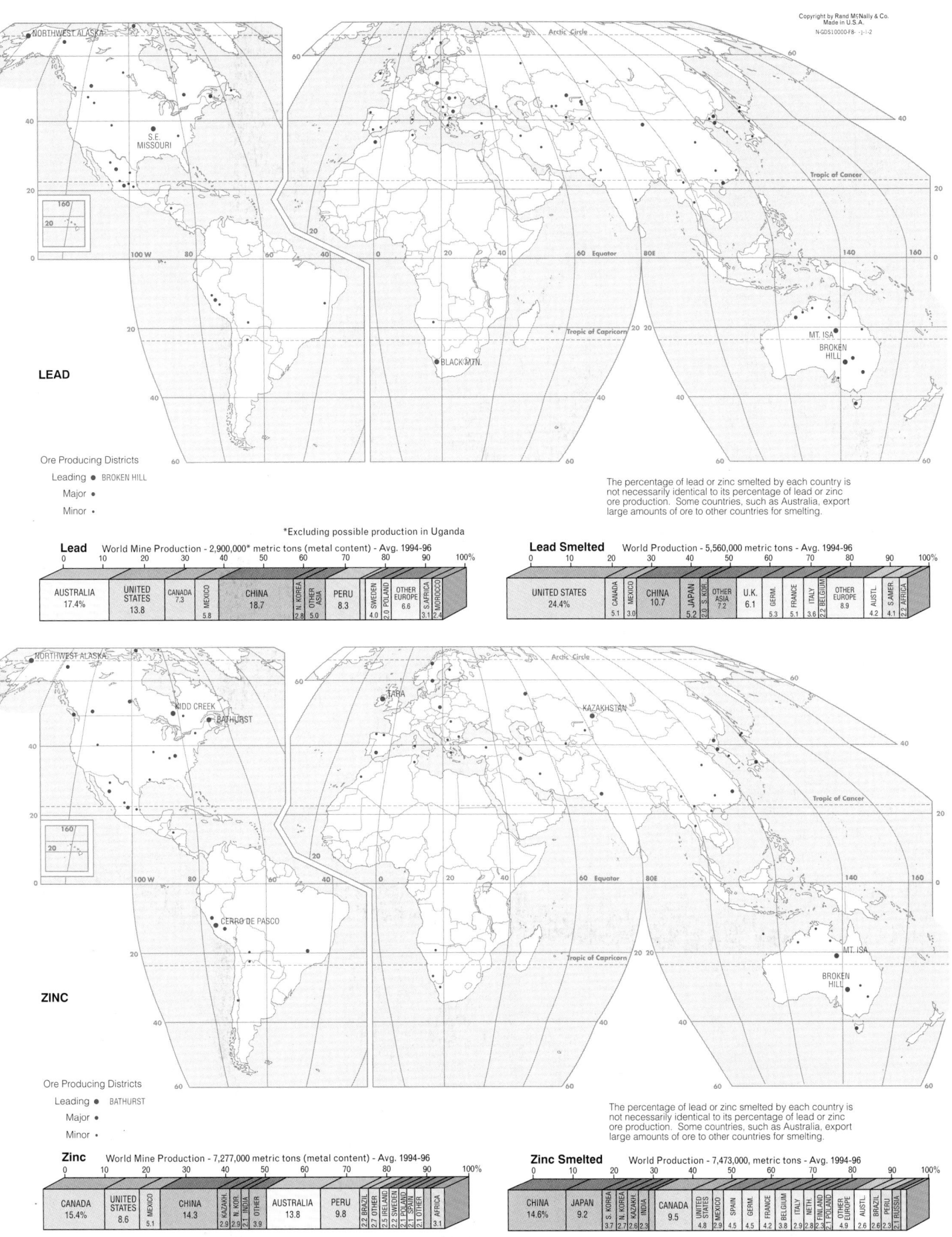

Copyright by Rand McNally & Co.
Made in U.S.A.
N-GDS10000-F8- -)-)-2

LEAD

Ore Producing Districts

Leading ● BROKEN HILL

Major ●

Minor ·

The percentage of lead or zinc smelted by each country is
not necessarily identical to its percentage of lead or zinc
ore production. Some countries, such as Australia, export
large amounts of ore to other countries for smelting.

*Excluding possible production in Uganda

Lead World Mine Production - 2,900,000* metric tons (metal content) - Avg. 1994-96

0	10	20	30	40	50	60	70	80	90	100%

| AUSTRALIA 17.4% | UNITED STATES 13.8 | CANADA 7.3 | MEXICO 5.8 | CHINA 18.7 | N. KOREA 2.8 | OTHER ASIA 5.0 | PERU 8.3 | SWEDEN 4.0 | POLAND 2.0 | OTHER EUROPE 6.6 | S.AFRICA 3.1 | MOROCCO 2.4 |

Lead Smelted World Production - 5,560,000 metric tons - Avg. 1994-96

0	10	20	30	40	50	60	70	80	90	100%

| UNITED STATES 24.4% | CANADA 5.1 | MEXICO 3.0 | CHINA 10.7 | JAPAN 5.2 | S. KOR. 2.0 | OTHER ASIA 7.2 | U.K. 6.1 | GERM. 5.3 | FRANCE 5.1 | ITALY 3.6 | BELGIUM 2.2 | OTHER EUROPE 8.9 | AUSTL. 4.2 | S.AMER. 4.1 | AFRICA 2.2 |

ZINC

Ore Producing Districts

Leading ● BATHURST

Major ●

Minor ·

The percentage of lead or zinc smelted by each country is
not necessarily identical to its percentage of lead or zinc
ore production. Some countries, such as Australia, export
large amounts of ore to other countries for smelting.

Zinc World Mine Production - 7,277,000 metric tons (metal content) - Avg. 1994-96

0	10	20	30	40	50	60	70	80	90	100%

| CANADA 15.4% | UNITED STATES 8.6 | MEXICO 5.1 | CHINA 14.3 | KAZAKH. 2.9 | N. KOR 2.9 | INDIA 2.1 | OTHER 3.9 | AUSTRALIA 13.8 | PERU 9.8 | BRAZIL 2.2 | OTHER 2.7 | IRELAND 2.5 | SWEDEN 2.2 | POLAND 2.1 | OTHER 2.1 | AFRICA 3.1 |

Zinc Smelted World Production - 7,473,000, metric tons - Avg. 1994-96

0	10	20	30	40	50	60	70	80	90	100%

| CHINA 14.6% | JAPAN 9.2 | S. KOREA 3.7 | N. KOREA 2.7 | KAZAKH 2.6 | INDIA 2.3 | CANADA 9.5 | UNITED STATES 4.8 | MEXICO 2.9 | SPAIN 4.5 | GERM. 4.2 | FRANCE 3.8 | ITALY 2.9 | NETH. 2.8 | FINLAND 2.1 | POLAND 2.1 | OTHER EUROPE 4.9 | AUSTL. 2.6 | PERU 2.3 | RUSSIA 3.1 |

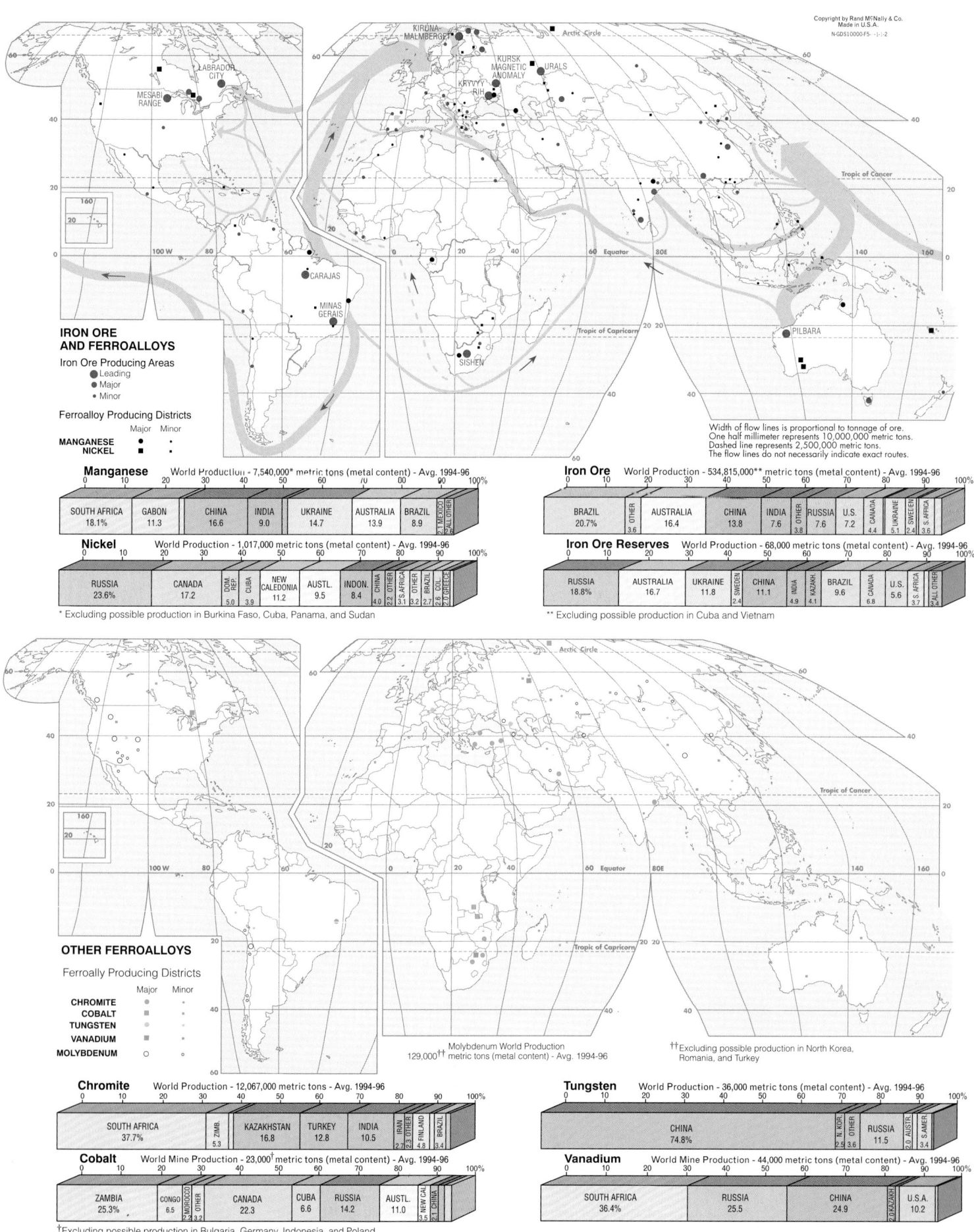

Copyright by Rand McNally & Co.
Made in U.S.A.
N-GDS10000-F5- -:-:-2

**IRON ORE
AND FERROALLOYS**

Iron Ore Producing Areas
● Leading
● Major
• Minor

Ferroalloy Producing Districts
	Major	Minor
MANGANESE	●	•
NICKEL	■	▪

Width of flow lines is proportional to tonnage of ore.
One half millimeter represents 10,000,000 metric tons.
Dashed line represents 2,500,000 metric tons.
The flow lines do not necessarily indicate exact routes.

Map labels: KIRUNA-MALMBERGET, LABRADOR CITY, MESABI RANGE, KURSK MAGNETIC ANOMALY, URALS, KRYVYY RIH, CARAJAS, MINAS GERAIS, SISHEN, PILBARA, Arctic Circle, Tropic of Cancer, Equator, Tropic of Capricorn

Manganese World Production - 7,540,000* metric tons (metal content) - Avg. 1994-96

SOUTH AFRICA 18.1%	GABON 11.3	CHINA 16.6	INDIA 9.0	UKRAINE 14.7	AUSTRALIA 13.9	BRAZIL 8.9	MEXICO 2.1	ALL OTHER 2.6

Nickel World Production - 1,017,000 metric tons (metal content) - Avg. 1994-96

RUSSIA 23.6%	CANADA 17.2	DOM. REP. 5.0	CUBA 3.9	NEW CALEDONIA 11.2	AUSTL. 9.5	INDON. 8.4	CHINA 4.0	OTHER 2.2	S.AFRICA 3.1	OTHER 3.2	BRAZIL 2.6	COL 2.6	GREECE 2.0

* Excluding possible production in Burkina Faso, Cuba, Panama, and Sudan

Iron Ore World Production - 534,815,000** metric tons (metal content) - Avg. 1994-96

BRAZIL 20.7%	OTHER 3.6	AUSTRALIA 16.4	CHINA 13.8	INDIA 7.6	OTHER 3.8	RUSSIA 7.6	U.S. 7.2	CANADA 4.4	UKRAINE 5.1	SWEDEN 2.4	S. AFRICA 3.6

Iron Ore Reserves World Production - 68,000 metric tons (metal content) - Avg. 1994-96

RUSSIA 18.8%	AUSTRALIA 16.7	UKRAINE 11.8	SWEDEN 2.4	CHINA 11.1	INDIA 4.9	KAZAKH. 4.1	BRAZIL 9.6	CANADA 6.8	U.S. 5.6	S. AFRICA 3.7	ALL OTHER 3.4

** Excluding possible production in Cuba and Vietnam

OTHER FERROALLOYS

Ferroally Producing Districts
	Major	Minor
CHROMITE	●	•
COBALT	■	▪
TUNGSTEN	●	•
VANADIUM	■	▪
MOLYBDENUM	○	○

Molybdenum World Production
129,000†† metric tons (metal content) - Avg. 1994-96

††Excluding possible production in North Korea, Romania, and Turkey

Chromite World Production - 12,067,000 metric tons - Avg. 1994-96

SOUTH AFRICA 37.7%	ZIMB. 5.3	KAZAKHSTAN 16.8	TURKEY 12.8	INDIA 10.5	IRAN 2.7	FINLAND 4.8	BRAZIL 3.4

Cobalt World Mine Production - 23,000† metric tons (metal content) - Avg. 1994-96

ZAMBIA 25.3%	CONGO 6.5	MOROCCO 2.2	OTHER 3.2	CANADA 22.3	CUBA 6.6	RUSSIA 14.2	AUSTL. 11.0	NEW CAL 3.5	CHINA 2.1

†Excluding possible production in Bulgaria, Germany, Indonesia, and Poland

Tungsten World Production - 36,000 metric tons (metal content) - Avg. 1994-96

CHINA 74.8%	N. KOR. 2.5	OTHER 3.6	RUSSIA 11.5	AUSTR. 2.0	S. AMER. 3.4

Vanadium World Mine Production - 44,000 metric tons (metal content) - Avg. 1994-96

SOUTH AFRICA 36.4%	RUSSIA 25.5	CHINA 24.9	KAZAKH. 2.0	U.S.A. 10.2

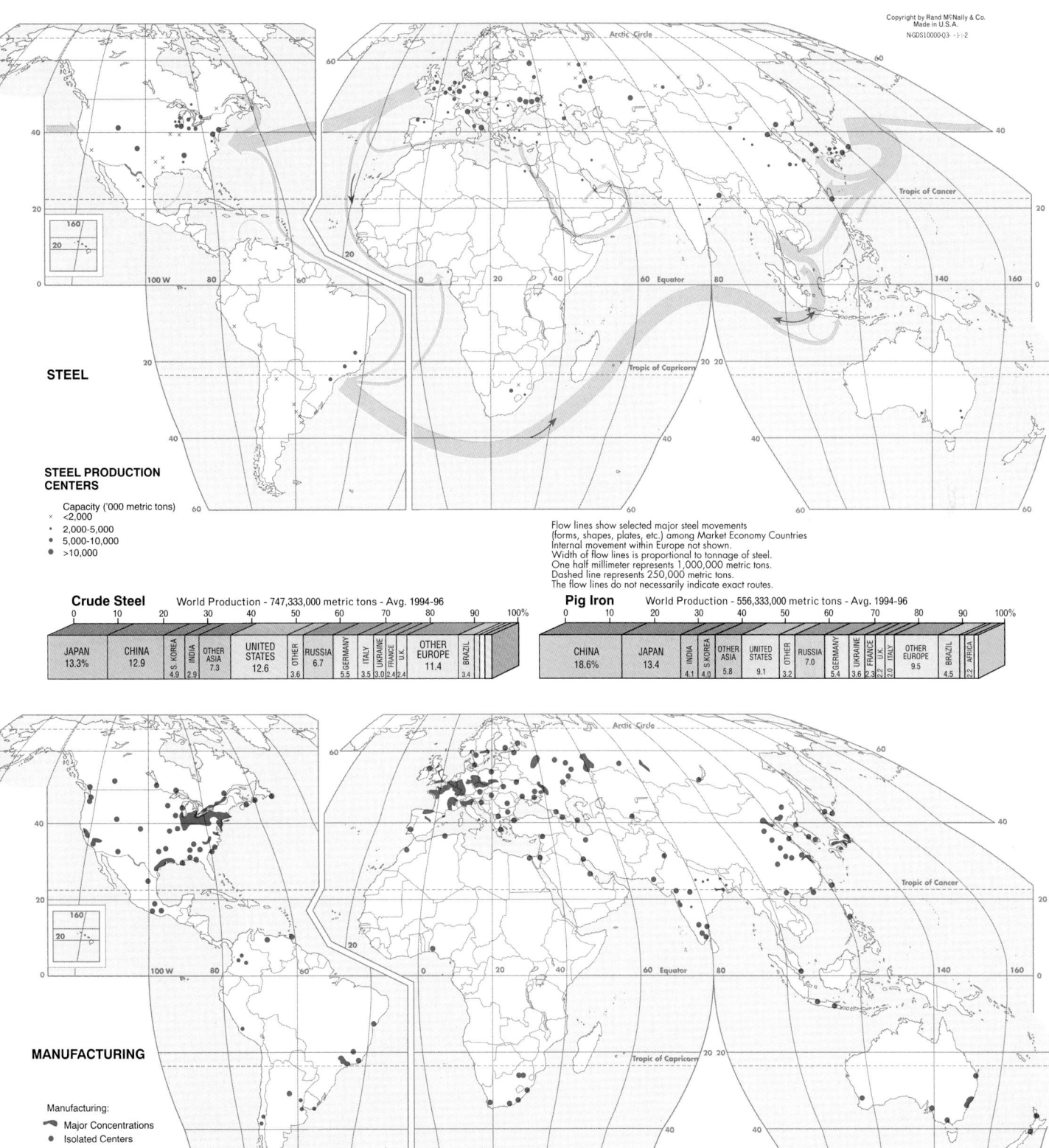

STEEL

STEEL PRODUCTION CENTERS

Capacity ('000 metric tons)
× <2,000
· 2,000-5,000
● 5,000-10,000
● >10,000

Flow lines show selected major steel movements
(forms, shapes, plates, etc.) among Market Economy Countries
Internal movement within Europe not shown.
Width of flow lines is proportional to tonnage of steel.
One half millimeter represents 1,000,000 metric tons.
Dashed line represents 250,000 metric tons.
The flow lines do not necessarily indicate exact routes.

Crude Steel — World Production - 747,333,000 metric tons - Avg. 1994-96

JAPAN 13.3%	CHINA 12.9	S. KOREA 4.9	INDIA 2.9	OTHER ASIA 7.3	UNITED STATES 12.6	OTHER 3.6	RUSSIA 6.7	GERMANY 5.5	ITALY 3.5	UKRAINE 3.0	FRANCE 2.4	U.K. 2.4	OTHER EUROPE 11.4	BRAZIL 3.4

Pig Iron — World Production - 556,333,000 metric tons - Avg. 1994-96

CHINA 18.6%	JAPAN 13.4	INDIA 4.1	S. KOREA 4.0	OTHER ASIA 5.8	UNITED STATES 9.1	OTHER 3.2	RUSSIA 7.0	GERMANY 5.4	UKRAINE 3.6	FRANCE 2.6	U.K. 2.2	ITALY 2.0	OTHER EUROPE 9.5	BRAZIL 4.5	AFRICA 2.2

MANUFACTURING

Manufacturing:
〜 Major Concentrations
● Isolated Centers

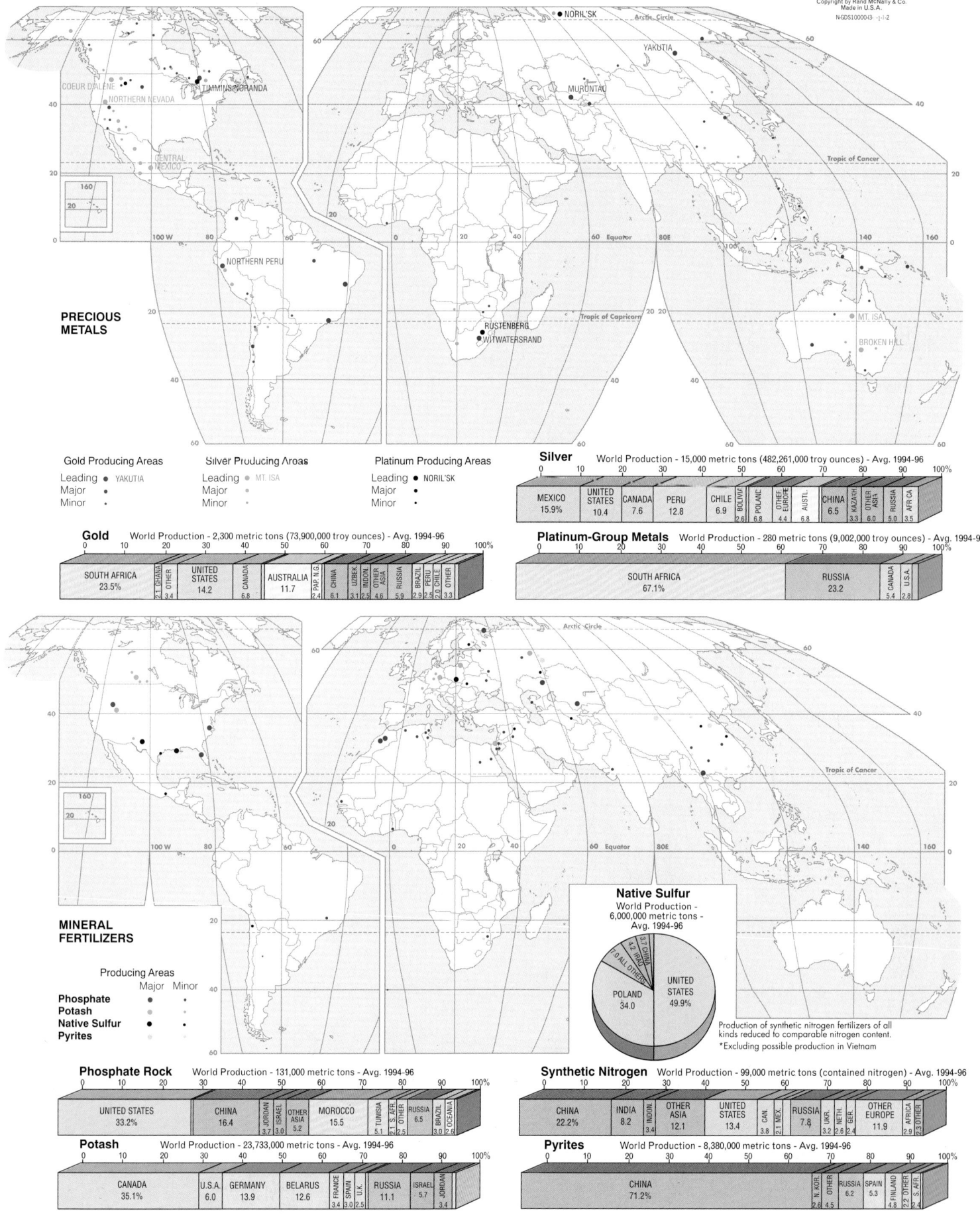

PRECIOUS METALS

Gold Producing Areas
Leading ● YAKUTIA
Major ●
Minor ·

Silver Producing Areas
Leading ● MT. ISA
Major ·
Minor ·

Platinum Producing Areas
Leading ● NORIL'SK
Major ·
Minor ·

Silver   World Production - 15,000 metric tons (482,261,000 troy ounces) - Avg. 1994-96

MEXICO 15.9%	UNITED STATES 10.4	CANADA 7.6	PERU 12.8	CHILE 6.9	BOLIVIA 2.6	POLAND 6.8	OTHER EUROPE 4.4	AUSTL. 6.8	CHINA 6.5	KAZAKH. 3.3	OTHER ASIA 6.0	RUSSIA 5.0	AFR CA 3.5

Gold   World Production - 2,300 metric tons (73,900,000 troy ounces) - Avg. 1994-96

SOUTH AFRICA 23.5%	GHANA 2.1	OTHER 3.4	UNITED STATES 14.2	CANADA 6.8	AUSTRALIA 11.7	PAP. N.G. 2.4	CHINA 6.1	UZBEK 3.1	INDON 2.5	OTHER ASIA 4.6	RUSSIA 5.9	BRAZIL 2.9	PERU 2.2	CHILE 3.3	OTHER

Platinum-Group Metals   World Production - 280 metric tons (9,002,000 troy ounces) - Avg. 1994-96

SOUTH AFRICA 67.1%	RUSSIA 23.2	CANADA 5.4	U.S.A. 2.8

MINERAL FERTILIZERS

Producing Areas
	Major	Minor
Phosphate	●	·
Potash	●	·
Native Sulfur	●	·
Pyrites	●	·

Native Sulfur
World Production -
6,000,000 metric tons -
Avg. 1994-96

UNITED STATES 49.9%
POLAND 34.0
ALL OTHER 9.0
IRAN 4.2
CHINA 3.3

Production of synthetic nitrogen fertilizers of all
kinds reduced to comparable nitrogen content.
*Excluding possible production in Vietnam

Phosphate Rock   World Production - 131,000 metric tons - Avg. 1994-96

UNITED STATES 33.2%	CHINA 16.4	JORDAN 3.0	OTHER ASIA 5.2	MOROCCO 15.5	TUNISIA 2.6	S. AFR. OTHER 2.5	RUSSIA 6.5	BRAZIL 3.0	OCEANIA

Synthetic Nitrogen   World Production - 99,000 metric tons (contained nitrogen) - Avg. 1994-96

CHINA 22.2%	INDIA 8.2	INDON 3.4	OTHER ASIA 12.1	UNITED STATES 13.4	CAN. 3.2	MEX. 2.1	RUSSIA 7.8	UKR. NETH. 2.6 GER. 2.4	OTHER EUROPE 11.9	AFRICA 2.9	OTHER 2.3

Potash   World Production - 23,733,000 metric tons - Avg. 1994-96

CANADA 35.1%	U.S.A. 6.0	GERMANY 13.9	BELARUS 12.6	FRANCE 3.4	SPAIN 3.0	U.K. 2.5	RUSSIA 11.1	ISRAEL 5.7	JORDAN 3.4

Pyrites   World Production - 8,380,000 metric tons - Avg. 1994-96

CHINA 71.2%	N. KOR. 2.6	OTHER 4.5	RUSSIA 6.2	SPAIN 5.3	FINLAND 4.8	OTHER 2.2	S. AFR.

Map labels: NORIL'SK, YAKUTIA, MURUNTAU, COEUR D'ALENE, NORTHERN NEVADA, TIMMINS/NORANDA, CENTRAL MEXICO, Arctic Circle, Tropic of Cancer, NORTHERN PERU, RUSTENBERG, WITWATERSRAND, Tropic of Capricorn, MT. ISA, BROKEN HILL, Equator

Copyright by Rand McNally & Co.
Made in U.S.A.
N-GDS10000-S4- 2-1-4

Arctic Circle

Tropic of Cancer

Equator

Tropic of Capricorn

NUCLEAR AND GEOTHERMAL POWER

Energy Producing Plants

- Nuclear
- Geothermal

GEOTHERMAL 0.4

NUCLEAR 17.3

HYDRO 19.3

THERMAL 63.0%

Electricity Production

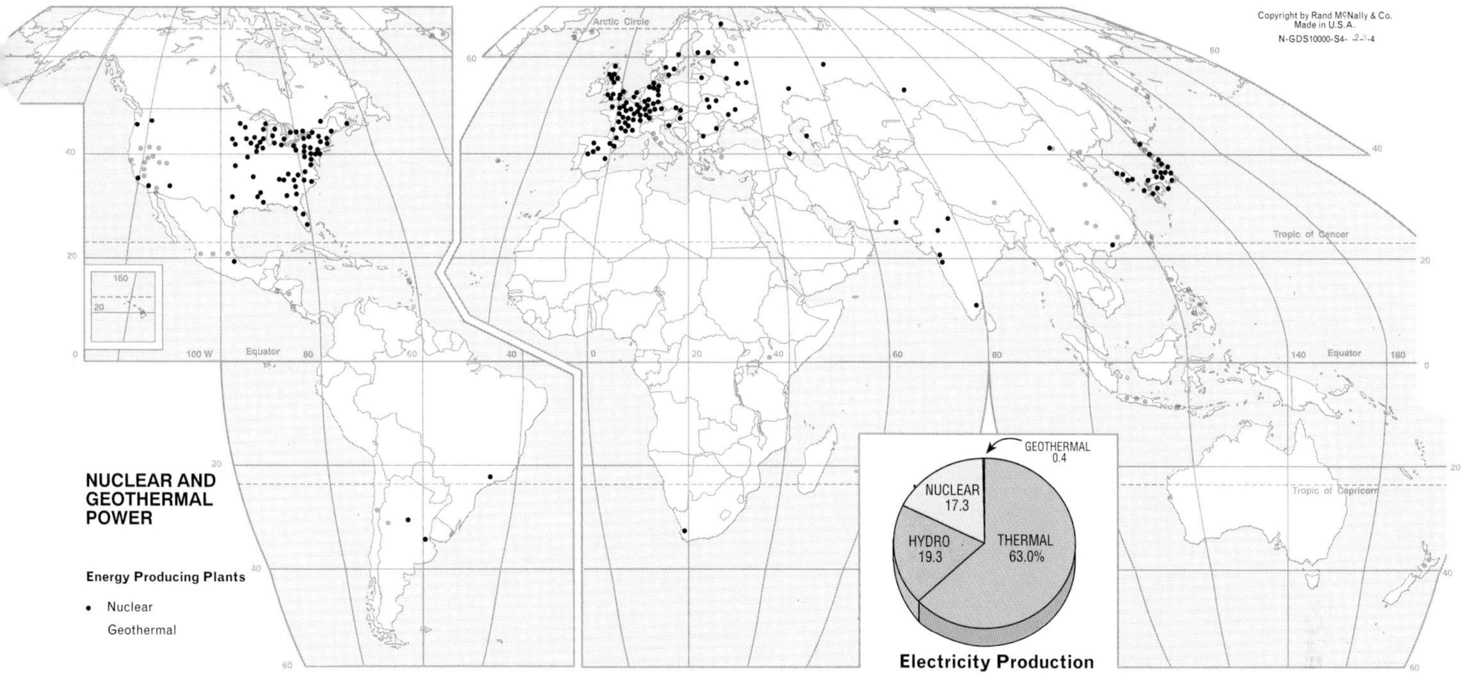

Nuclear Energy
World Production - 2,268,000 gigawatt hours - 1995

0	10	20	30	40	50	60	70	80	90	100%

| UNITED STATES 30.2% | CANADA 4.1 | FRANCE 16.9 | GER. 6.9 | U.K. 4.0 | SWEDEN 3.1 | SPAIN 2.5 | UKRAINE 2.4 | OTHER EUROPE 7.3 | JAPAN 13.0 | S. KOREA 3.0 | RUSSIA 4.5 |

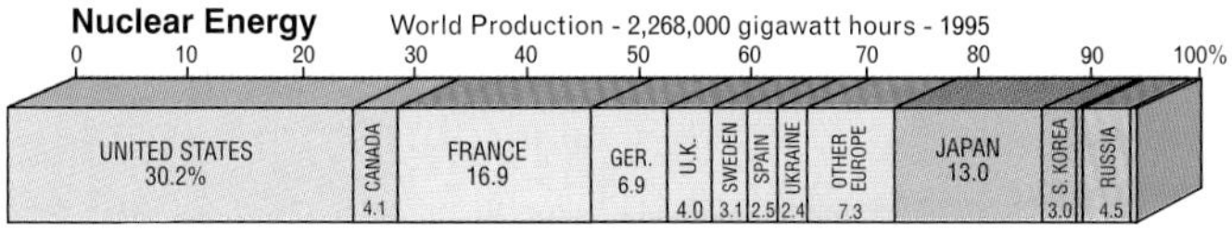

Geothermal Electricity
World Production - 48,000 gigawatt hours - 1995

0	10	20	30	40	50	60	70	80	90	100%

| UNITED STATES 37.6% | MEXICO 15.4 | OTHER 3.3 | PHILIPPINES 12.4 | JAPAN 6.7 | INDON. 3.8 | ITALY 7.2 | DENMARK 2.4 | OTHER EUROPE 4.5 | NEW ZEALAND 4.4 |

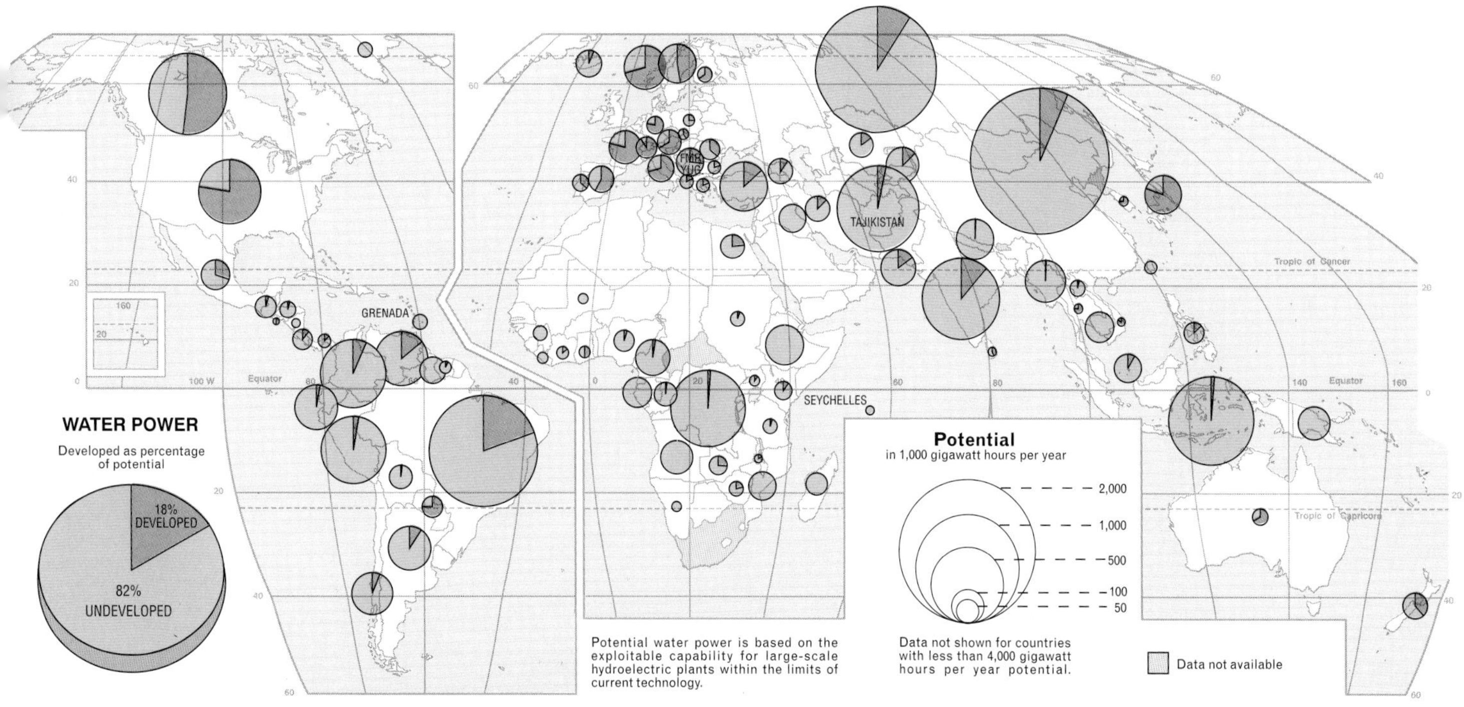

WATER POWER

Developed as percentage of potential

18% DEVELOPED

82% UNDEVELOPED

GRENADA

TAJIKISTAN

SEYCHELLES

Potential
in 1,000 gigawatt hours per year

- 2,000
- 1,000
- 500
- 100
- 50

Potential water power is based on the exploitable capability for large-scale hydroelectric plants within the limits of current technology.

Data not shown for countries with less than 4,000 gigawatt hours per year potential.

Data not available

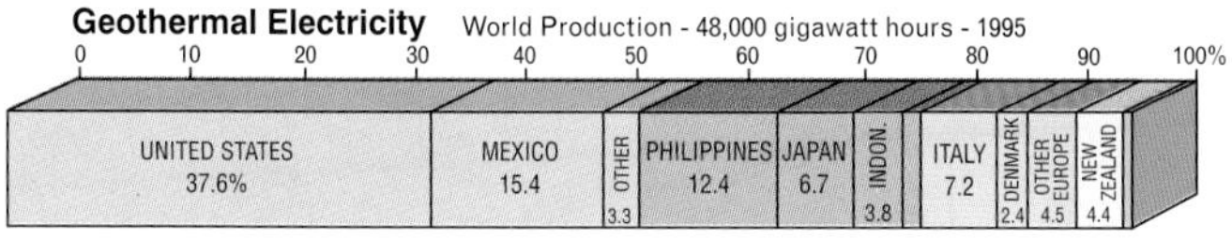

Developed Water Power (Total Capacity)
World Capacity - 708,931,000 kilowatts -1995

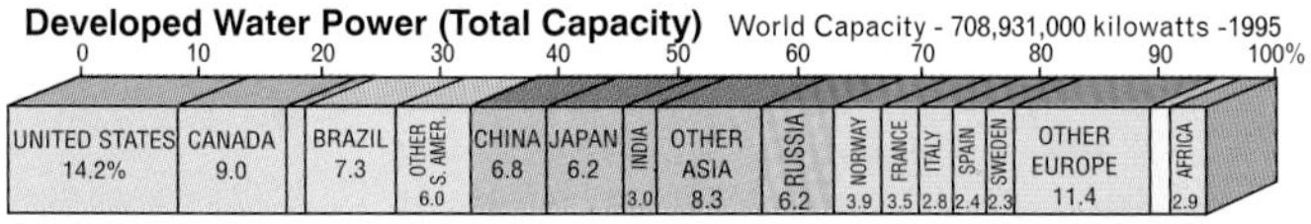

0	10	20	30	40	50	60	70	80	90	100%

| UNITED STATES 14.2% | CANADA 9.0 | BRAZIL 7.3 | OTHER S. AMER. | CHINA 6.8 | JAPAN 6.2 | INDIA | OTHER ASIA 8.3 | RUSSIA | NORWAY | FRANCE | ITALY | SWEDEN | OTHER EUROPE 11.4 | AFRICA 2.9 |

Potential Water Power
World Total - 14,503,000 gigawatt hours/year

0	10	20	30	40	50	60	70	80	90	100 %

| FORMER SOVIET UNION 23.0 % | CHINA 13.3 | INDON. 4.9 | INDIA 4.1 | OTHER ASIA 8.4 | BRAZIL 7.7 | COL. | PERU | OTHER S. AMER. 6.5 | CANADA 4.1 | U.S.A. 2.6 | D.R. CONGO 3.7 | OTHER AFRICA | EUROPE 6.6 |

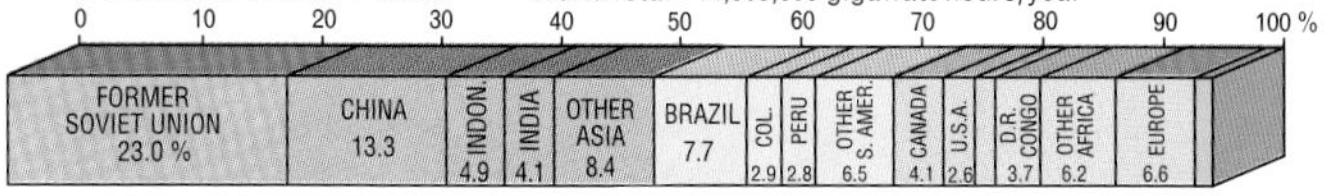

All Electricity
World Production - 13,098,000 gigawatt hours/year - 1995

0	10	20	30	40	50	60	70	80	90	100%

| UNITED STATES 25.8% | CANADA 4.1 | CHINA 8.0 | JAPAN 7.6 | INDIA 3.2 | OTHER ASIA 9.2 | RUSSIA 6.6 | GER. 4.1 | FRANCE 3.8 | U.K. 2.6 | OTHER EUROPE 14.2 | BRAZIL 2.1 | OTHER 2.3 | AFRICA 2.8 |

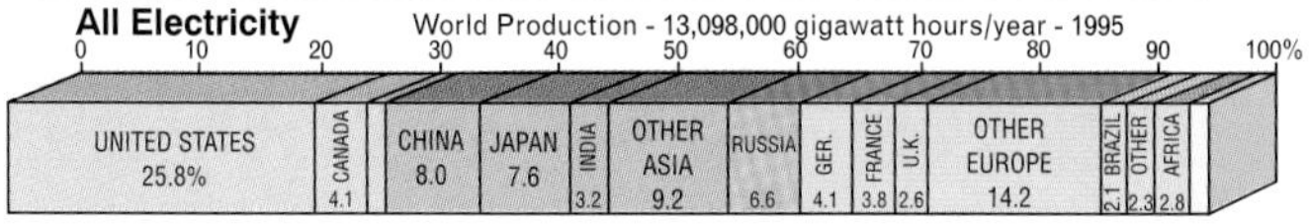

Hydroelectricity
World Production - 2,533,000 gigawatt hours/year - 1995

0	10	20	30	40	50	60	70	80	90	100%

| CANADA 13.1% | UNITED STATES 12.2 | BRAZIL 10.1 | VENEZ. 2.2 | OTHER S. AMER. 6.1 | CHINA 7.6 | JAPAN 3.6 | INDIA 2.8 | OTHER ASIA 8.0 | RUSSIA 7.0 | NORWAY 4.9 | FRANCE 3.0 | SWEDEN 2.7 | OTHER EUROPE 11.0 | AFRICA 2.3 |

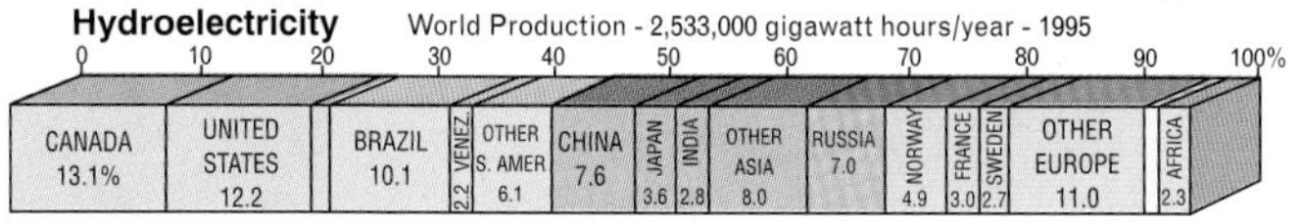

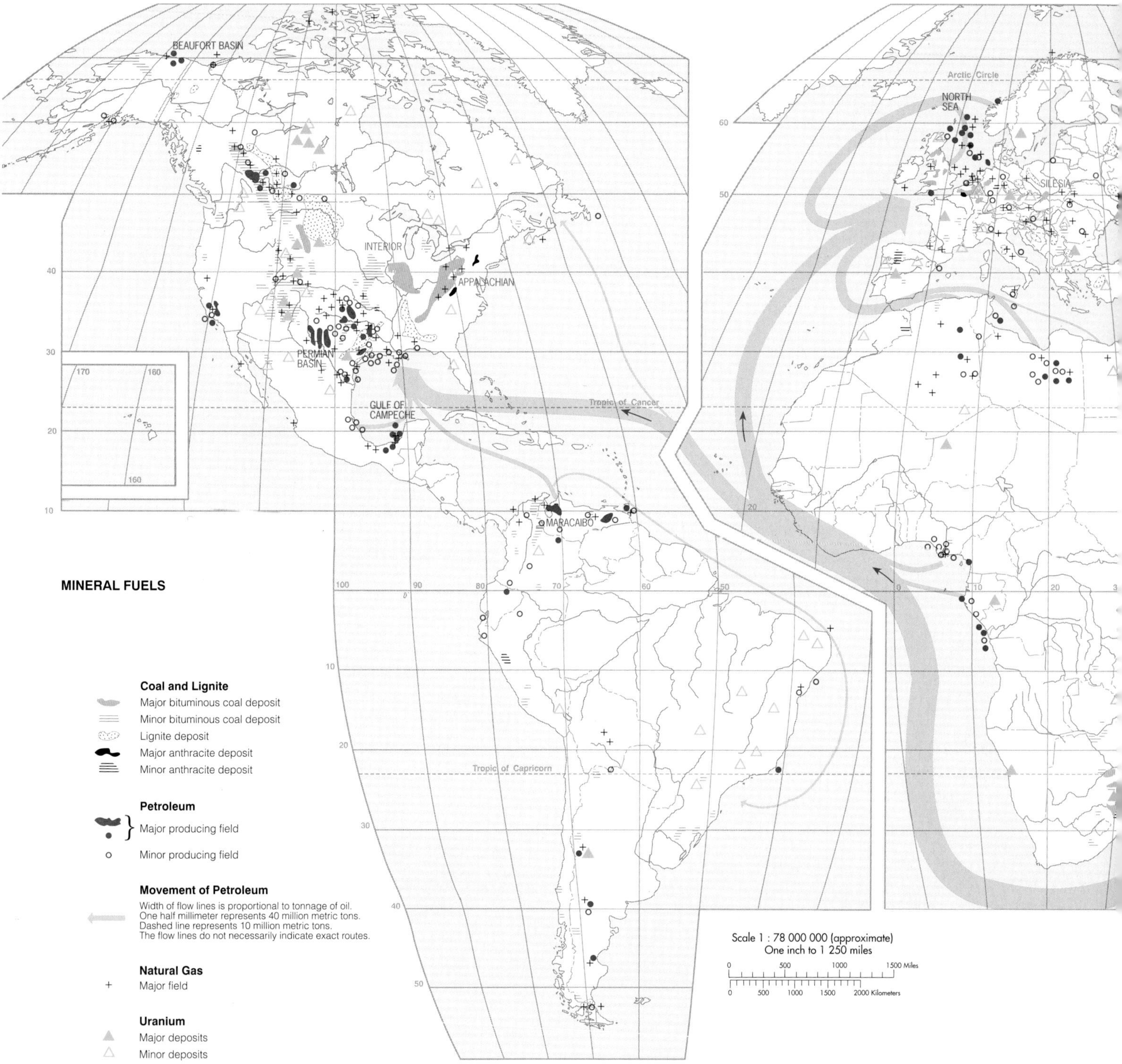

BEAUFORT BASIN

NORTH SEA

Arctic Circle

SILESIA

INTERIOR

APPALACHIAN

PERMIAN BASIN

GULF OF CAMPECHE

Tropic of Cancer

MARACAIBO

Tropic of Capricorn

MINERAL FUELS

Coal and Lignite

Major bituminous coal deposit

Minor bituminous coal deposit

Lignite deposit

Major anthracite deposit

Minor anthracite deposit

Petroleum

} Major producing field

o Minor producing field

Movement of Petroleum

Width of flow lines is proportional to tonnage of oil.
One half millimeter represents 40 million metric tons.
Dashed line represents 10 million metric tons.
The flow lines do not necessarily indicate exact routes.

Natural Gas

+ Major field

Uranium

▲ Major deposits

△ Minor deposits

Scale 1 : 78 000 000 (approximate)
One inch to 1 250 miles

0   500   1000   1500 Miles

0   500   1000   1500   2000 Kilometers

Coal   World Production - 4,645,332,000* metric tons - Avg. 1994-96

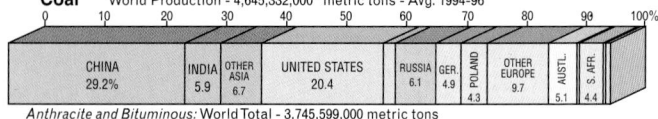

Anthracite and Bituminous: World Total - 3,745,599,000 metric tons

Coal Reserves   World Total - 1,035,786,456,000* metric tons - 1998

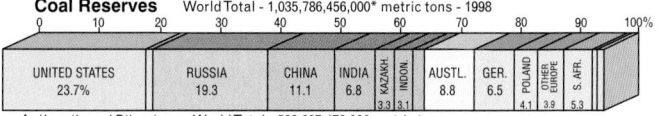

Anthracite and Bituminous: World Total - 523,607,472,000 metric tons
* Includes anthracite, subanthracite; bituminous, subbituminous, lignite, and brown coal

Petroleum   World Production - 3,100,472,000** metric tons (22,797,544,000 barrels) - Avg. 1994-96

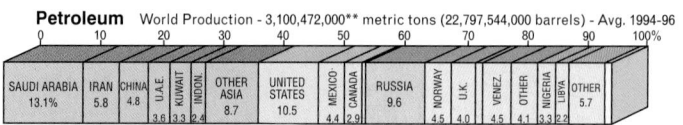

Petroleum Reserves   World Total - 157,769,452,000** metric tons (1,160,069,500,000 barrels) - 1997

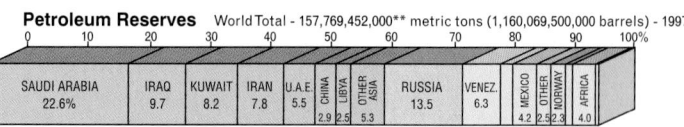

** Crude Petroleum

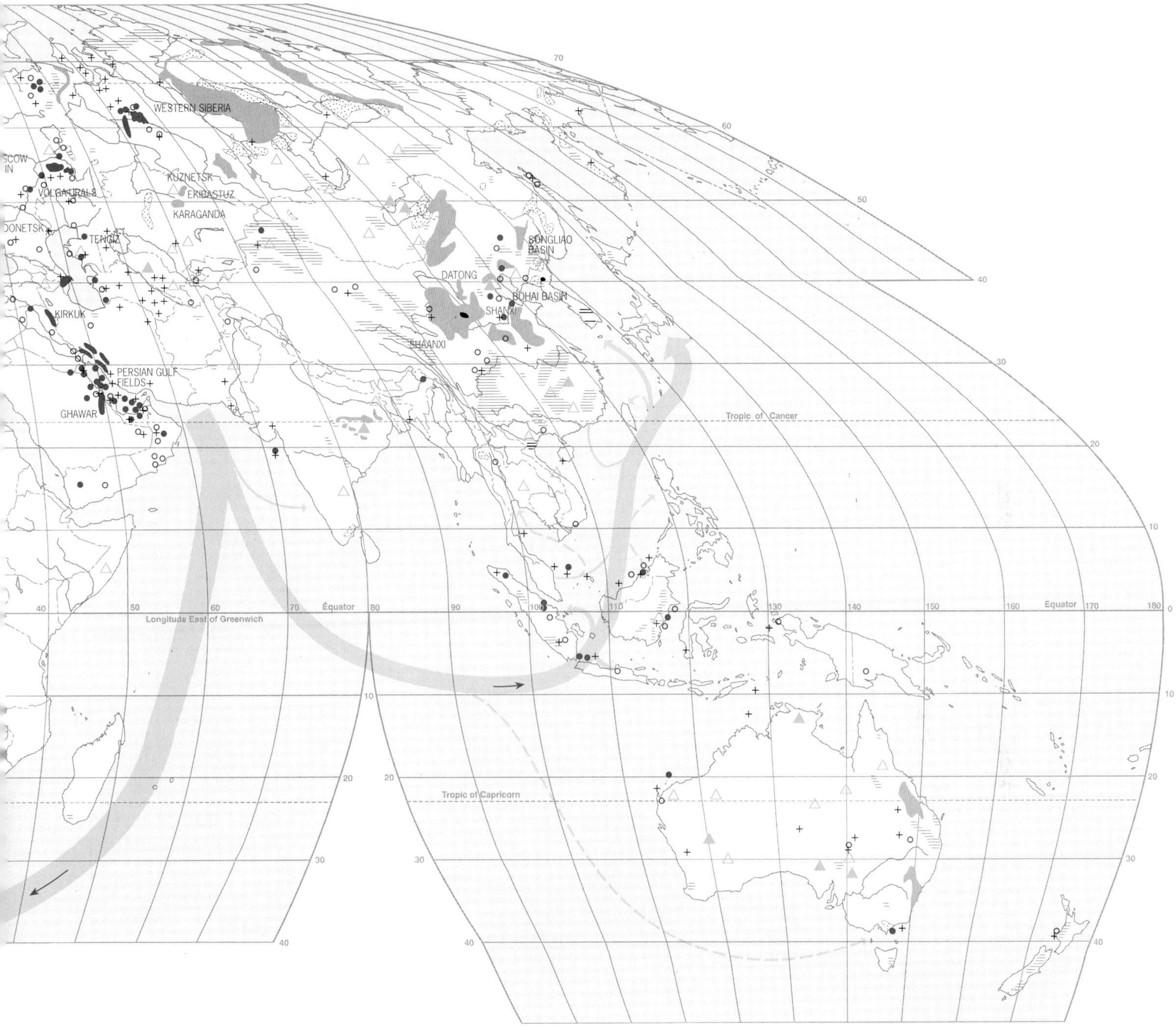

Map labels (from upper map):

WESTERN SIBERIA
KUZNETSK
EKIBASTUZ
KARAGANDA
SONGLIAO BASIN
DATONG
BOHAI BASIN
SHAN...
SHAANXI
SCOW IN
VOLGA–URALS
DONETSK
TENGIZ
KIRKUK
PERSIAN GULF FIELDS
GHAWAR

Tropic of Cancer
Équateur / Equator
Longitude East of Greenwich
Tropic of Capricorn

Goode's Homolosine Equal Area Projection (Condensed)

Natural Gas
World Production - 2,234,034,199,000 cubic meters - Avg. 1994-96

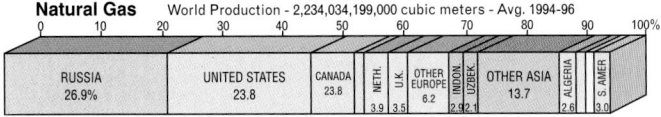

| RUSSIA 26.9% | UNITED STATES 23.8 | CANADA 23.8 | NETH. 3.9 | U.K. 3.5 | OTHER EUROPE 6.2 | INDON. 2.9 | UZBEK. 2.1 | OTHER ASIA 13.7 | ALGERIA 2.6 | S. AMER. 3.0 |

Natural Gas Reserves
World Total - 140,074,431,000 cubic meters - 1997

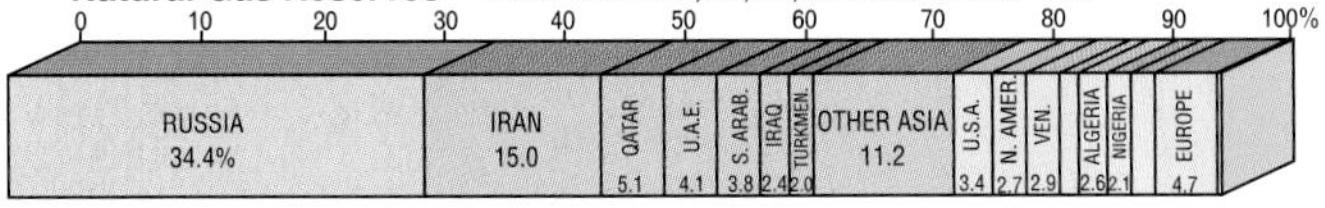

| RUSSIA 34.4% | IRAN 15.0 | QATAR 5.1 | U.A.E. 4.1 | S. ARAB. 3.8 | IRAQ 2.4 | TURKMEN. 2.0 | OTHER ASIA 11.2 | U.S.A. 3.4 | VEN. 2.7 | N. AMER. 2.9 | ALGERIA 2.6 | NIGERIA 2.1 | EUROPE 4.7 |

Uranium
World Production - 33,653 metric tons - Avg. 1994-96

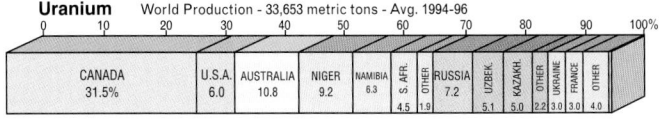

| CANADA 31.5% | U.S.A. 6.0 | AUSTRALIA 10.8 | NIGER 9.2 | NAMIBIA 6.3 | S. AFR. 4.5 | OTHER 1.9 | RUSSIA 7.2 | UZBEK. 5.1 | KAZAKH. 5.0 | OTHER 2.2 | UKRAINE 3.0 | FRANCE 3.0 | OTHER 4.0 |

Uranium Reserves
World Total - 3,414,000 metric tons - 1997

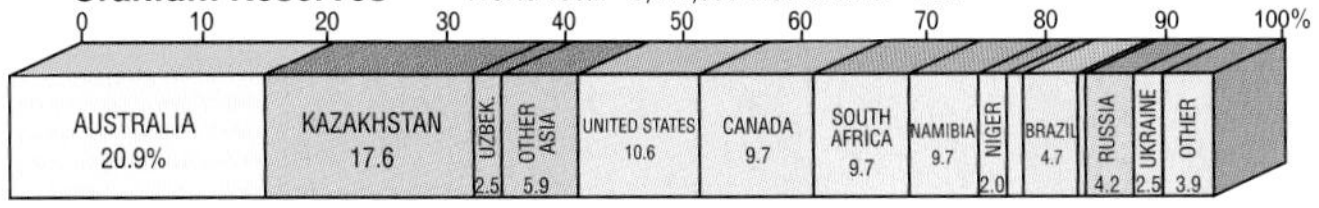

| AUSTRALIA 20.9% | KAZAKHSTAN 17.6 | UZBEK. 2.5 | OTHER ASIA 5.9 | UNITED STATES 10.6 | CANADA 9.7 | SOUTH AFRICA 9.7 | NAMIBIA 9.7 | NIGER 2.0 | BRAZIL 4.7 | RUSSIA 4.2 | UKRAINE 3.0 | OTHER 3.9 |

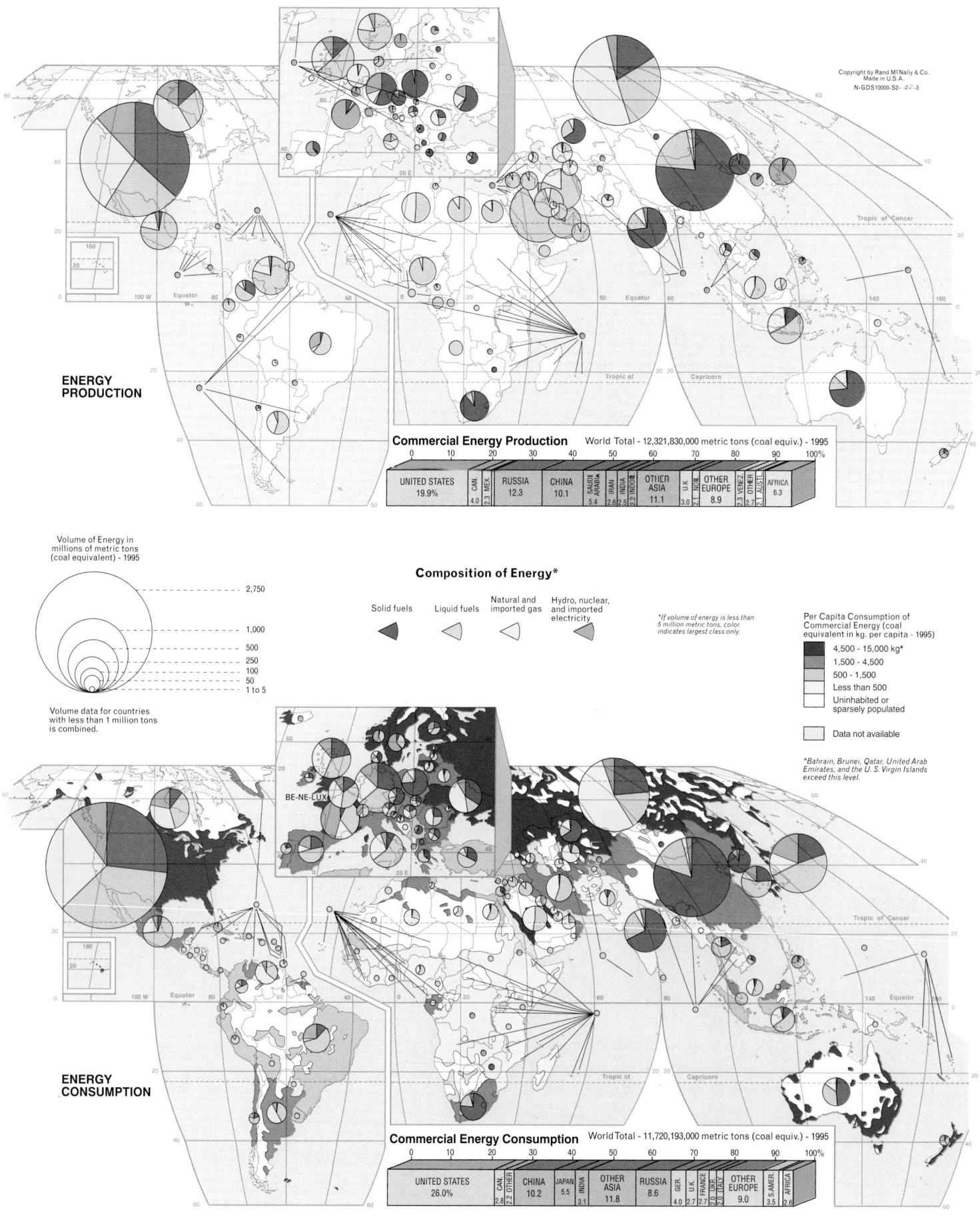

Copyright by Rand McNally & Co.
Made in U.S.A.
N-GDS10000-S2- -2-2-3

**ENERGY
PRODUCTION**

Commercial Energy Production World Total - 12,321,830,000 metric tons (coal equiv.) - 1995

UNITED STATES 19.9%	CAN 4.0	MEX 2.3	RUSSIA 12.3	CHINA 10.1	SAUDI ARABIA 5.4	IRAN 2.6	INDIA 2.5	OTHER ASIA 11.1	U.K. 3.0	NOR 2.1	OTHER EUROPE 8.9	VENEZ 2.2	OTHER 2.1	AUST 2.1	AFRICA 6.3

Volume of Energy in
millions of metric tons
(coal equivalent) - 1995

- 2,750
- 1,000
- 500
- 250
- 100
- 50
- 1 to 5

Volume data for countries
with less than 1 million tons
is combined.

Composition of Energy*

Solid fuels   Liquid fuels   Natural and imported gas   Hydro, nuclear, and imported electricity

*If volume of energy is less than
5 million metric tons, color
indicates largest class only.

Per Capita Consumption of
Commercial Energy (coal
equivalent in kg. per capita - 1995)

- 4,500 - 15,000 kg*
- 1,500 - 4,500
- 500 - 1,500
- Less than 500
- Uninhabited or sparsely populated

Data not available

*Bahrain, Brunei, Qatar, United Arab
Emirates, and the U. S. Virgin Islands
exceed this level.

BE-NE-LUX

**ENERGY
CONSUMPTION**

Commercial Energy Consumption World Total - 11,720,193,000 metric tons (coal equiv.) - 1995

UNITED STATES 26.0%	CAN 2.8	OTHER 2.2	CHINA 10.2	JAPAN 5.5	INDIA 3.1	OTHER ASIA 11.8	RUSSIA 8.6	GER 4.0	U.K. 2.7	FRANCE 2.7	ITA 2.0	OTHER EUROPE 9.0	S. AMER 3.5	AFRICA 2.6

Major Direction of Trade
EXPORTS TO

Europe → North America → Asia → South America →

Copyright by Rand McNally & Co.
Made in U.S.A.
N-GDS10000-O3- -2- -4

EXPORTS

Exports   World Total - $4,359,335,000,000 (U.S.) - Avg. 1993-95

| UNITED STATES 12.0% | CANADA 3.9 | GERMANY 10.2 | FRANCE 5.6 | U.K. 4.8 | ITALY 4.5 | NETH. 3.8 | BELG. 3.3 | OTHER EUROPE 12.2 | JAPAN 9.3 | CHINA 6.3 | S. KOR 2.1 | TAIWAN 2.2 | SING 2.2 | OTHER ASIA 8.5 | S. AMER 2.5 | AFRICA 2.2 |

Volume of Trade
(in millions of U.S. dollars - Avg. 1993-95)

— 500,000
— 200,000
— 100,000
— 50,000
— 20,000
— 10,000
— 500 - 2,000

If volume of trade is less than 10 billion dollars, color indicates major class only. If no symbol is shown, volume of trade is less than 500 million dollars.

Composition of Trade

Manufactured Articles   Food, Beverages, & Tobacco   Raw Materials   Fuel & Related Products   All other or undifferentiated

Major Direction of Trade
IMPORTS FROM

Europe → North America → Asia → South America →

IMPORTS

Imports   World Total - $4,414,745,000,000 (U.S.) - Avg. 1993-95

| UNITED STATES 15.7% | CANADA 3.5 | GERMANY 8.9 | FRANCE 5.4 | U.K. 5.3 | ITALY 4.0 | NETH. 3.4 | BELG. 3.0 | SPAIN 2.2 | OTHER EUROPE 10.4 | JAPAN 6.5 | CHINA 6.4 | S. KOR 2.4 | SING 2.4 | TAIWAN 2.1 | OTHER ASIA 9.1 | S. AMER 2.6 | AFRICA 2.4 |

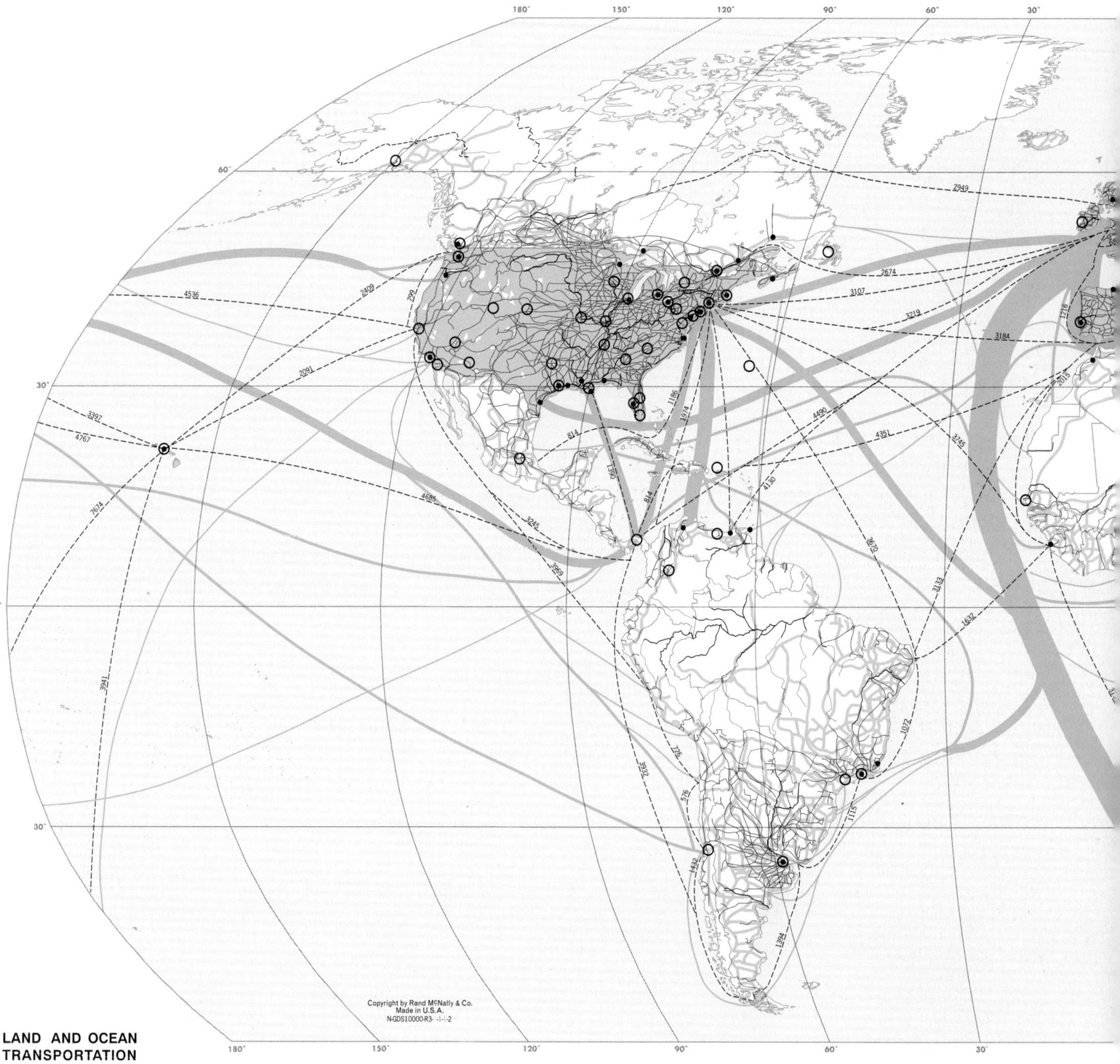

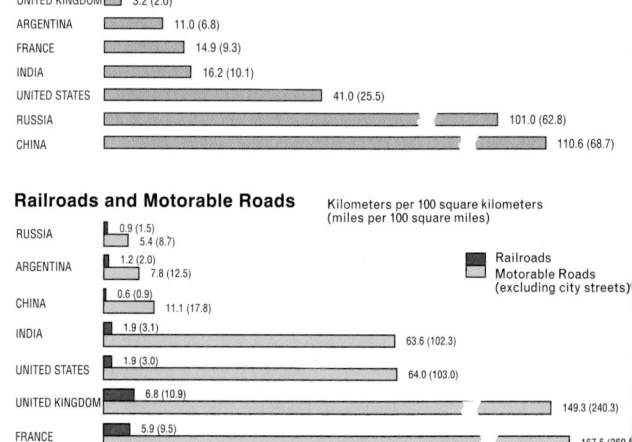

LAND AND OCEAN TRANSPORTATION

Vehicles   Per kilometer (mile) of motorable road

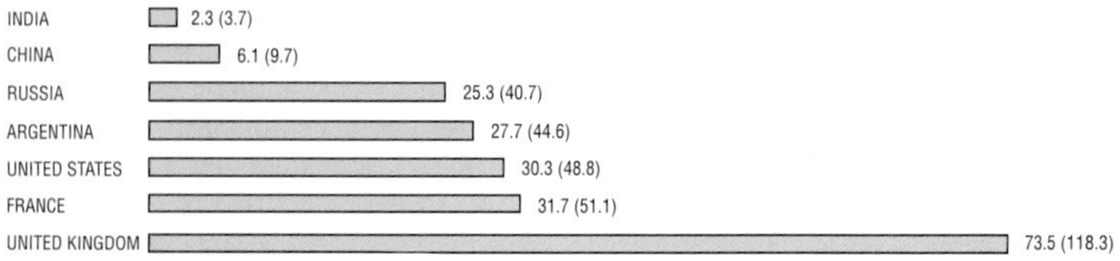

INDIA	2.3 (3.7)
CHINA	6.1 (9.7)
RUSSIA	25.3 (40.7)
ARGENTINA	27.7 (44.6)
UNITED STATES	30.3 (48.8)
FRANCE	31.7 (51.1)
UNITED KINGDOM	73.5 (118.3)

Persons per Vehicle

UNITED STATES	1.3
FRANCE	2.0
UNITED KINGDOM	2.2
ARGENTINA	5.5
RUSSIA	6.4
INDIA	179.1
CHINA	184.6

Inland Waterways   Thousands of kilometers (miles)

UNITED KINGDOM	3.2 (2.0)
ARGENTINA	11.0 (6.8)
FRANCE	14.9 (9.3)
INDIA	16.2 (10.1)
UNITED STATES	41.0 (25.5)
RUSSIA	101.0 (62.8)
CHINA	110.6 (68.7)

Railroads and Motorable Roads   Kilometers per 100 square kilometers (miles per 100 square miles)

■ Railroads
□ Motorable Roads (excluding city streets)

	Railroads	Motorable Roads
RUSSIA	0.9 (1.5)	5.4 (8.7)
ARGENTINA	1.2 (2.0)	7.8 (12.5)
CHINA	0.6 (0.9)	11.1 (17.8)
INDIA	1.9 (3.1)	63.6 (102.3)
UNITED STATES	1.9 (3.0)	64.0 (103.0)
UNITED KINGDOM	6.8 (10.9)	149.3 (240.3)
FRANCE	5.9 (9.5)	167.5 (269.5)

Copyright by Rand McNally & Co.
Made in U.S.A.
NGDS10000-R3- -i--i- -2

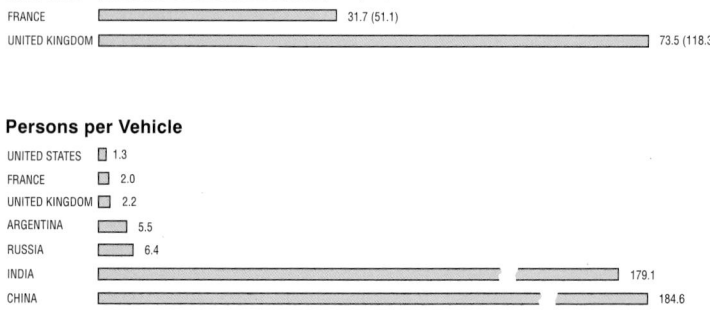

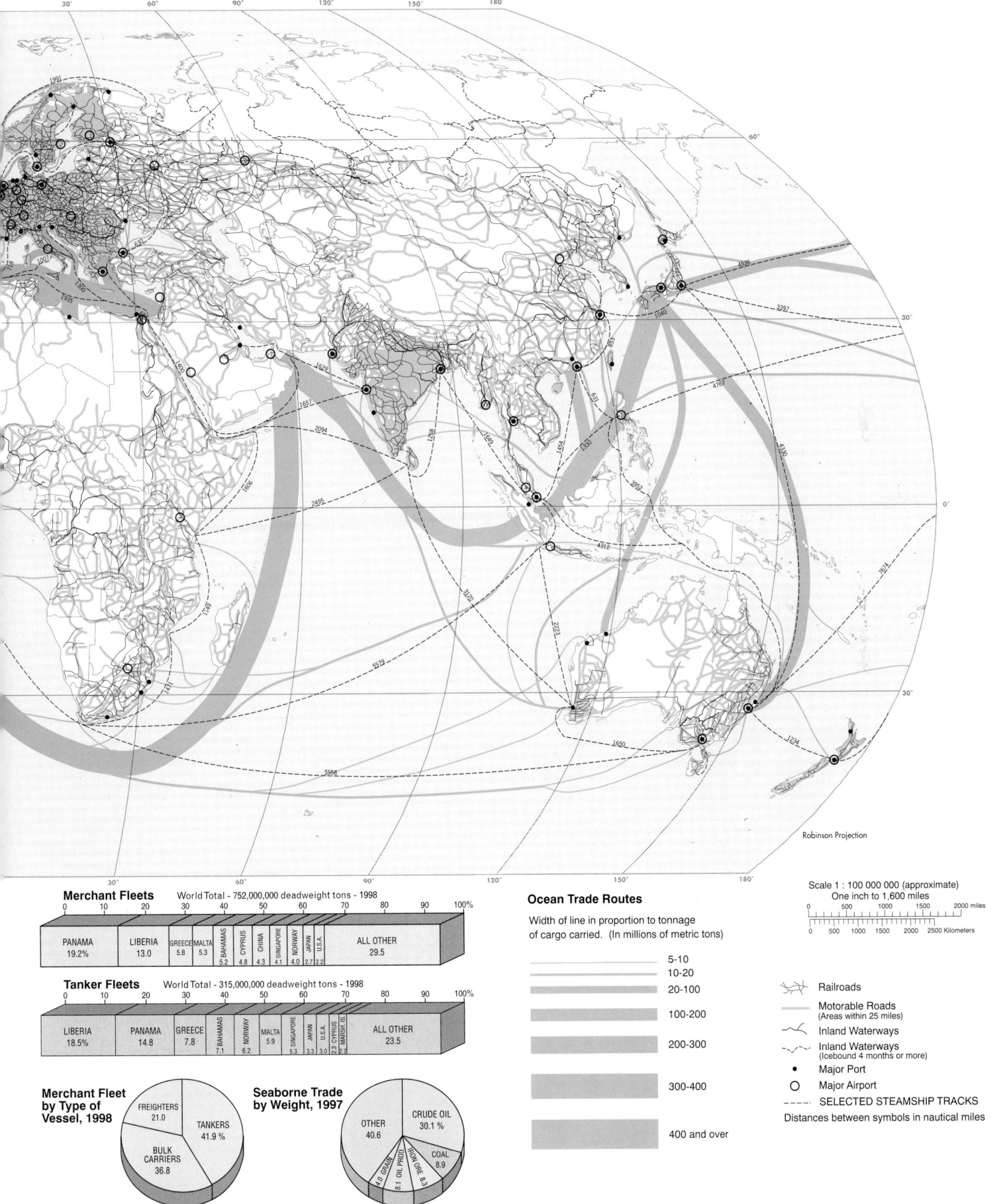

Robinson Projection

Merchant Fleets
World Total - 752,000,000 deadweight tons - 1998

0	10	20	30	40	50	60	70	80	90	100%

| PANAMA 19.2% | LIBERIA 13.0 | GREECE 5.8 | MALTA 5.3 | BAHAMAS 5.2 | CYPRUS 4.8 | CHINA 4.3 | SINGAPORE 4.1 | NORWAY 4.0 | JAPAN 2.7 | U.S.A. 2.2 | ALL OTHER 29.5 |

Tanker Fleets
World Total - 315,000,000 deadweight tons - 1998

0	10	20	30	40	50	60	70	80	90	100%

| LIBERIA 18.5% | PANAMA 14.8 | GREECE 7.8 | BAHAMAS 7.1 | NORWAY 6.2 | MALTA 5.9 | SINGAPORE 5.3 | JAPAN 3.3 | U.S.A. 3.0 | CYPRUS 2.3 | MARSH. IS. 2.2 | ALL OTHER 23.5 |

Merchant Fleet by Type of Vessel, 1998

FREIGHTERS 21.0
TANKERS 41.9 %
BULK CARRIERS 36.8

World Total - 752,000,000 deadweight tons - 1998

Seaborne Trade by Weight, 1997

OTHER 40.6
CRUDE OIL 30.1 %
COAL 8.9
IRON ORE 8.3
OIL PROD. 8.1
GRAIN 4.0

World Total - 5,074,000,000 metric tons - 1997

Ocean Trade Routes

Width of line in proportion to tonnage of cargo carried. (In millions of metric tons)

5-10
10-20
20-100
100-200
200-300
300-400
400 and over

Scale 1 : 100 000 000 (approximate)
One inch to 1,600 miles

0 500 1000 1500 2000 miles
0 500 1000 1500 2000 2500 Kilometers

Railroads
Motorable Roads (Areas within 25 miles)
Inland Waterways
Inland Waterways (Icebound 4 months or more)
• Major Port
○ Major Airport
---- SELECTED STEAMSHIP TRACKS
Distances between symbols in nautical miles

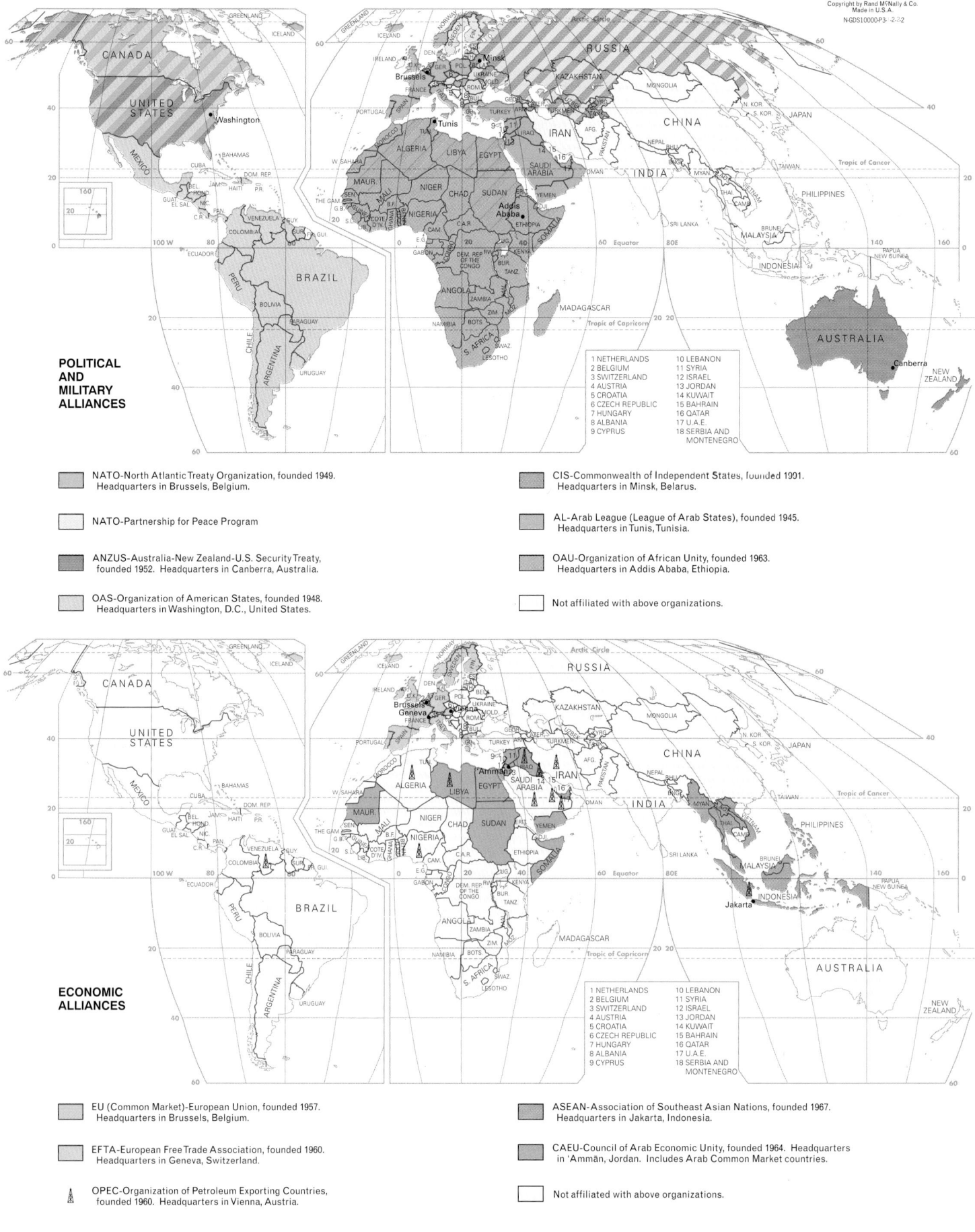

POLITICAL AND MILITARY ALLIANCES

1 NETHERLANDS	10 LEBANON
2 BELGIUM	11 SYRIA
3 SWITZERLAND	12 ISRAEL
4 AUSTRIA	13 JORDAN
5 CROATIA	14 KUWAIT
6 CZECH REPUBLIC	15 BAHRAIN
7 HUNGARY	16 QATAR
8 ALBANIA	17 U.A.E.
9 CYPRUS	18 SERBIA AND MONTENEGRO

NATO-North Atlantic Treaty Organization, founded 1949. Headquarters in Brussels, Belgium.

NATO-Partnership for Peace Program

ANZUS-Australia-New Zealand-U.S. Security Treaty, founded 1952. Headquarters in Canberra, Australia.

OAS-Organization of American States, founded 1948. Headquarters in Washington, D.C., United States.

CIS-Commonwealth of Independent States, founded 1991. Headquarters in Minsk, Belarus.

AL-Arab League (League of Arab States), founded 1945. Headquarters in Tunis, Tunisia.

OAU-Organization of African Unity, founded 1963. Headquarters in Addis Ababa, Ethiopia.

Not affiliated with above organizations.

ECONOMIC ALLIANCES

1 NETHERLANDS	10 LEBANON
2 BELGIUM	11 SYRIA
3 SWITZERLAND	12 ISRAEL
4 AUSTRIA	13 JORDAN
5 CROATIA	14 KUWAIT
6 CZECH REPUBLIC	15 BAHRAIN
7 HUNGARY	16 QATAR
8 ALBANIA	17 U.A.E.
9 CYPRUS	18 SERBIA AND MONTENEGRO

EU (Common Market)-European Union, founded 1957. Headquarters in Brussels, Belgium.

EFTA-European Free Trade Association, founded 1960. Headquarters in Geneva, Switzerland.

OPEC-Organization of Petroleum Exporting Countries, founded 1960. Headquarters in Vienna, Austria.

ASEAN-Association of Southeast Asian Nations, founded 1967. Headquarters in Jakarta, Indonesia.

CAEU-Council of Arab Economic Unity, founded 1964. Headquarters in 'Ammān, Jordan. Includes Arab Common Market countries.

Not affiliated with above organizations.

Copyright by Rand McNally & Co.
Made in U.S.A.
N-GDS10000-Y2- -3-i-4

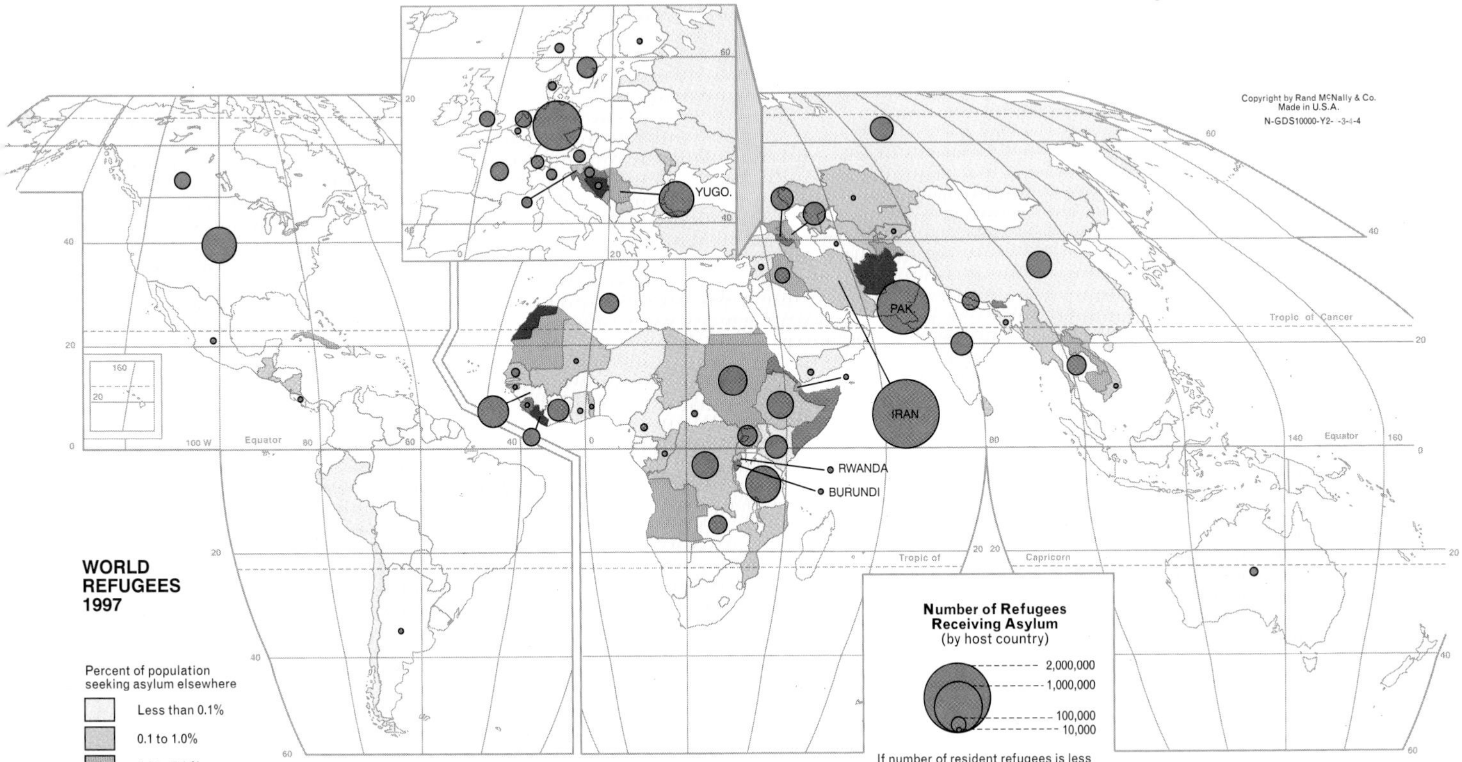

YUGO.

PAK.

IRAN

RWANDA

BURUNDI

WORLD REFUGEES 1997

Number of Refugees Receiving Asylum
(by host country)

- - - - 2,000,000
- - - - 1,000,000
- - - - 100,000
- - - - 10,000

If number of resident refugees is less than 10,000 people, no symbol is shown.

Percent of population seeking asylum elsewhere

- Less than 0.1%
- 0.1 to 1.0%
- 1.0 to 5.0 %
- 5.0 to 10.0%
- Greater than 10.0%

Excludes countries fled by 1,000 or fewer refugees. The origin of refugees is not always known and/or consistently reported by a number of countries.

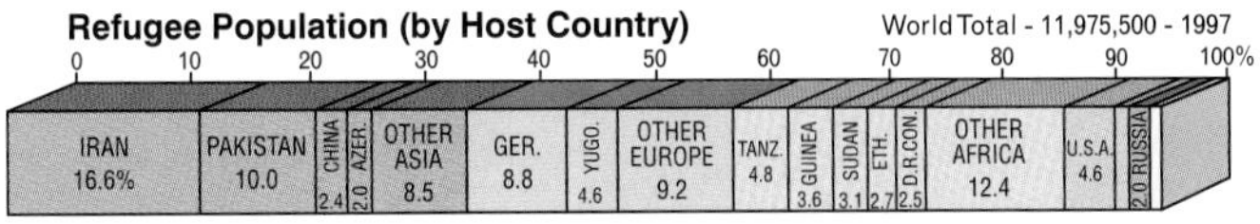

Refugee Population (by Host Country) World Total – 11,975,500 - 1997

0	10	20	30	40	50	60	70	80	90	100%

| IRAN 16.6% | PAKISTAN 10.0 | CHINA 2.4 | AZER. 2.0 | OTHER ASIA 8.5 | GER. 8.8 | YUGO. 4.6 | OTHER EUROPE 9.2 | TANZ. 4.8 | GUINEA 3.6 | SUDAN 3.1 | ETH. 2.7 | D.R.CON. 2.5 | OTHER AFRICA 12.4 | U.S.A. 4.6 | RUSSIA 2.0 |

Civil Conflicts

International Conflicts

Civil and International Conflicts

MAJOR CAUSES / FACTORS

- ○ Ethnic
- □ Religious
- + Political
- ⊕ Multiple or undifferentiated

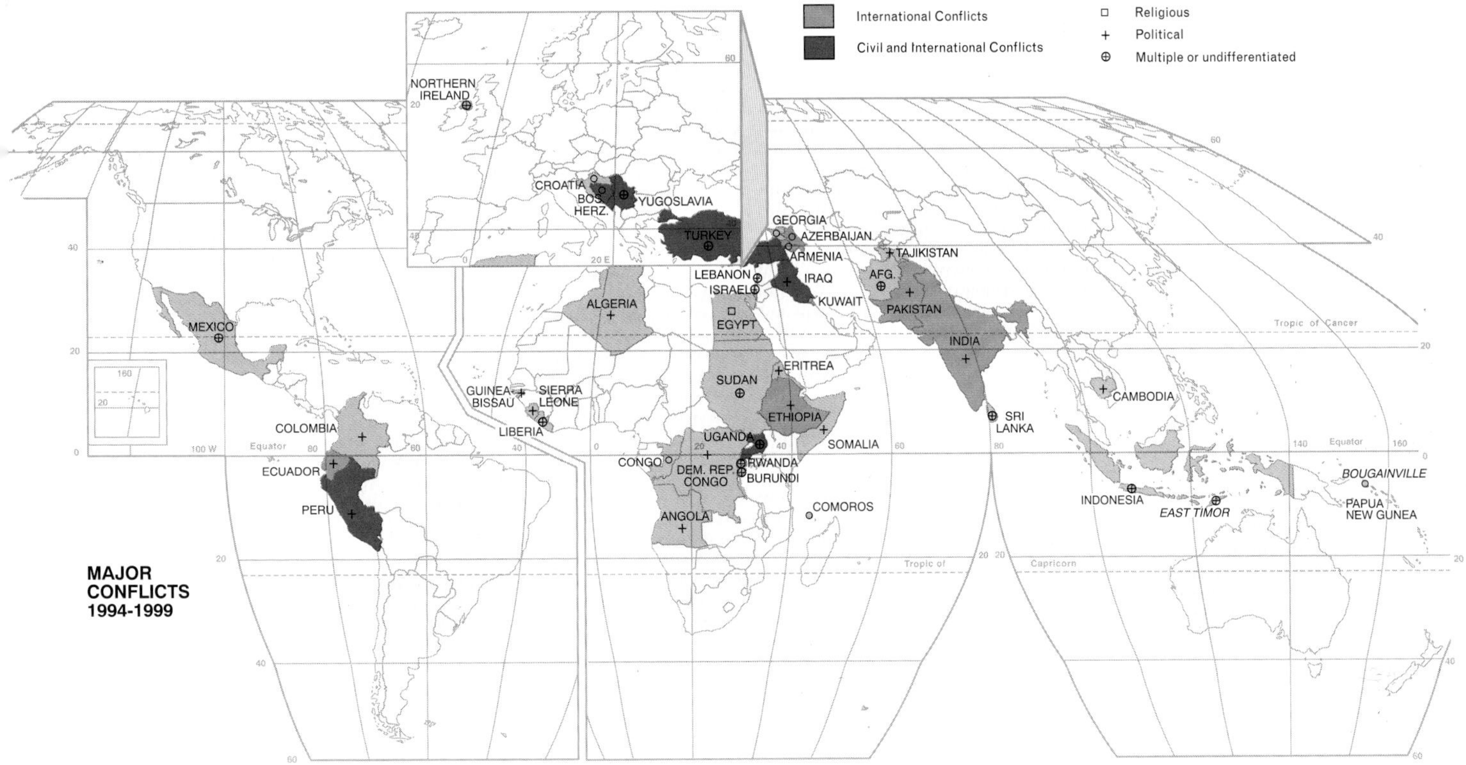

NORTHERN IRELAND

CROATIA
BOS. HERZ. YUGOSLAVIA

TURKEY

GEORGIA
AZERBAIJAN
ARMENIA   TAJIKISTAN

LEBANON   IRAQ   AFG.
ISRAEL   KUWAIT   PAKISTAN

ALGERIA   EGYPT

MEXICO

GUINEA   SIERRA
BISSAU   LEONE

LIBERIA

COLOMBIA

ECUADOR

PERU

ERITREA

SUDAN

ETHIOPIA

UGANDA
CONGO   SOMALIA
DEM. REP.   RWANDA
CONGO   BURUNDI

ANGOLA   COMOROS

INDIA

SRI LANKA

CAMBODIA

BOUGAINVILLE

INDONESIA   PAPUA
EAST TIMOR   NEW GUINEA

MAJOR CONFLICTS 1994-1999

REGIONAL MAPS

Basic continental and regional coverage of the world's land areas is provided by the following section of physical-political reference maps. The section falls into a continental arrangement: North America, South America, Europe, Asia, Australia, and Africa. Introducing each regional reference-map section are basic thematic maps.

To aid the student in acquiring concepts of the relative sizes of continents and of some of the countries and regions, uniform scales for comparable areas were used so far as possible. Continental maps are at a uniform scale of 1:40,000,000. In addition, most of the world is covered by a series of regional maps at scales of 1:16,000,000 and 1:12,000,000.

Maps at 1:10,000,000 provide even greater detail for parts of Europe, Africa, and Asia. The United States, parts of Canada, and much of Europe are mapped at 1:4,000,000. Ninety-two urbanized areas are shown at 1:1,000,000.

Many of the symbols used are self-explanatory. A complete legend below provides a key to the symbols on the reference maps in this atlas.

General elevation above sea level is shown by layer tints for altitudinal zones, each of which has a different hue and is defined by generalized contour lines. A legend is given on each map, reflecting this color gradation.

The surface configuration is represented by hill-shading, which gives the three-dimensional impression of landforms. This terrain representation is superimposed on the layer tints to convey a realistic and readily visualized impression of the surface. The combination of altitudinal tints and hill-shading best shows elevation, relief, steepness of slope, and ruggedness of terrain.

If the world used one alphabet and one language, no particular difficulty would arise in understanding place-names. However, some of the people of the world, the Chinese and the Japanese, for example, use nonalphabetic languages. Their symbols are transliterated into the Roman alphabet. In this atlas a "local-name" policy generally was used for naming cities and towns and local topographic and water features; however, for a few major cities and other well known features, Anglicized names were preferred. In these instances, local names may also be given in parentheses - for instance Moscow (Moskva), Vienna (Wien), Naples (Napoli). In countries where more than one official language is used, a name is in the dominant local language. The generic parts of local names for topographic and water features are self-explanatory in many cases because of the associated map symbols or type styles. A list of foreign generic names is given in the Glossary.

Place-names on the reference maps are listed in the Pronouncing Index, which is a distinctive feature of *Goode's World Atlas*.

Physical-Political Reference Map Legend

Cultural Features

Political Boundaries

International (over water) (Demarcated, Undemarcated, and Administrative)

Disputed de facto

Claim Boundary

Indefinite or Undefined

Secondary, State, Provincial, etc. (over water)

Parks, Indian Reservations

City Limits   Urbanized Areas

Neighborhoods, Sections of City

Populated Places

◉ 1,000,000 and over

◎ 250,000 to 1,000,000

⊙ 100,000 to 250,000

• 25,000 to 100,000

○ 0 to 25,000

TŌKYŌ National Capitals

Boise Secondary Capitals

Note: On maps at 1:20,000,000 and smaller the town symbols do not follow the specific population classification shown above. On all maps, type size indicates the relative importance of the city.

Transportation

Railroads

Railroads On 1:1,000,000 scale maps

Railroad Ferries

Roads

Major / Other On 1:1,000,000 scale maps

Major / Other On 1:4,000,000 scale maps

On other scale maps

Caravan Routes

✈ Airports

Other Cultural Features

Dams

Pipelines

▲ Points of Interest

Ruins

Land Features

△ Peaks, Spot Heights

= Passes

Sand

Contours

Water Features

Lakes and Reservoirs

Fresh Water

Fresh Water: Intermittent

Salt Water

Salt Water: Intermittent

Other Water Features

Salt Basins, Flats

Swamps

Ice Caps and Glaciers

Rivers

Intermittent Rivers

Aqueducts and Canals

Ship Channels

Falls

Rapids

Springs

△ Water Depths

Fishing Banks

Sand Bars

Reefs

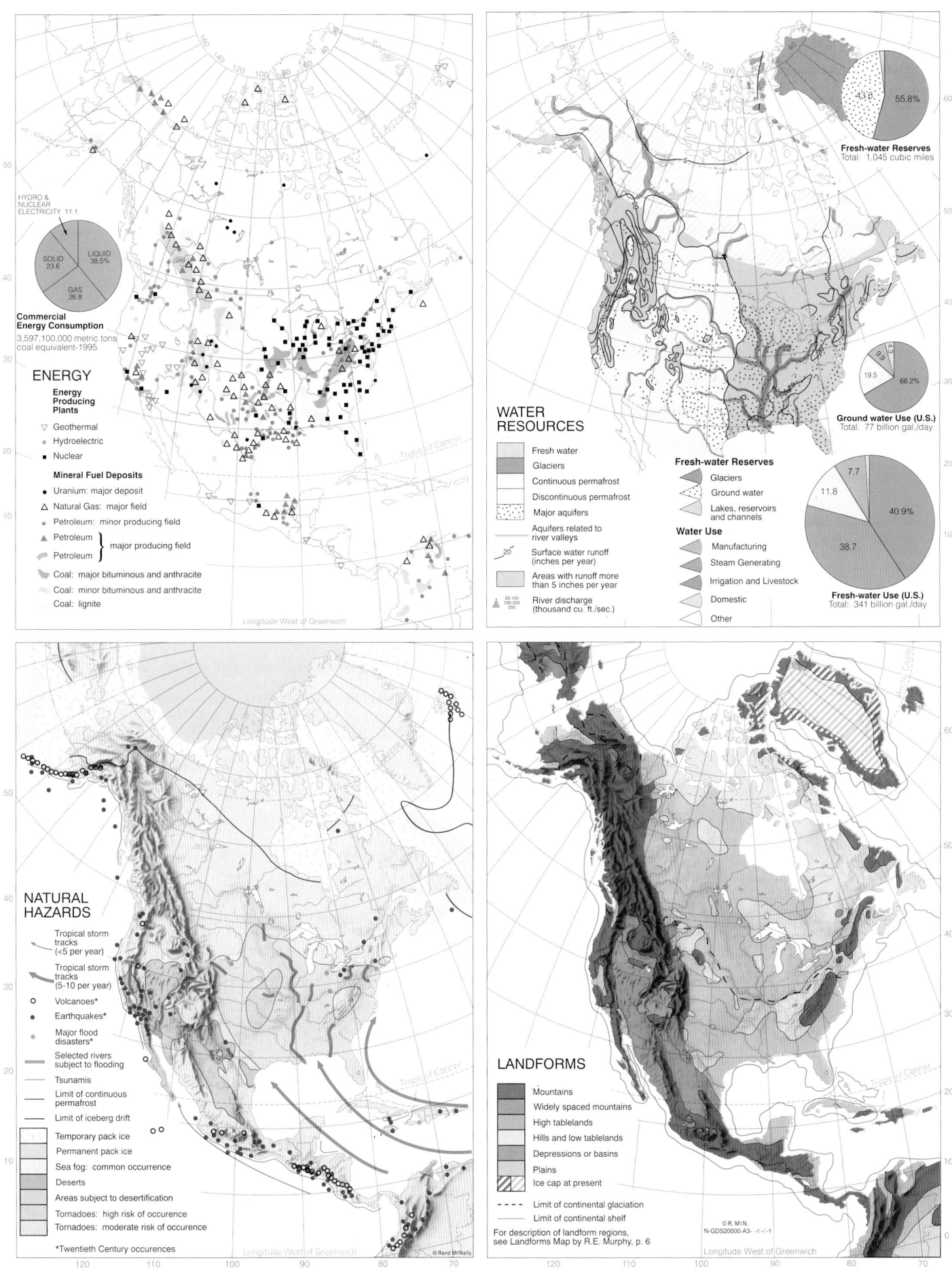

ENERGY

Commercial Energy Consumption
3,597,100,000 metric tons coal equivalent-1995

HYDRO & NUCLEAR ELECTRICITY 11.1
SOLID 23.6
LIQUID 38.5%
GAS 26.8

Energy Producing Plants
▽ Geothermal
● Hydroelectric
■ Nuclear

Mineral Fuel Deposits
● Uranium: major deposit
△ Natural Gas: major field
● Petroleum: minor producing field
▲ Petroleum } major producing field
◣ Petroleum
◣ Coal: major bituminous and anthracite
◤ Coal: minor bituminous and anthracite
Coal: lignite

Longitude West of Greenwich

WATER RESOURCES

Fresh water
Glaciers
Continuous permafrost
Discontinuous permafrost
Major aquifers
Aquifers related to river valleys
―20― Surface water runoff (inches per year)
Areas with runoff more than 5 inches per year
River discharge (thousand cu. ft./sec.) 25-100 / 100-250 / 250

Fresh-water Reserves
◣ Glaciers
◢ Ground water
◿ Lakes, reservoirs and channels

Water Use
◣ Manufacturing
◢ Steam Generating
◿ Irrigation and Livestock
◺ Domestic
▽ Other

Fresh-water Reserves
Total: 1,045 cubic miles
43.8 55.8%

Ground water Use (U.S.)
Total: 77 billion gal./day
4.3 9.9 19.5 66.2%

Fresh-water Use (U.S.)
Total: 341 billion gal./day
7.7 11.8 38.7 40.9%

NATURAL HAZARDS

↗ Tropical storm tracks (<5 per year)
↗ Tropical storm tracks (5-10 per year)
○ Volcanoes*
● Earthquakes*
● Major flood disasters*
▬ Selected rivers subject to flooding
― Tsunamis
― Limit of continuous permafrost
― Limit of iceberg drift
Temporary pack ice
Permanent pack ice
Sea fog: common occurrence
Deserts
Areas subject to desertification
Tornadoes: high risk of occurence
Tornadoes: moderate risk of occurence

*Twentieth Century occurences

Longitude West of Greenwich
© Rand McNally

LANDFORMS

Mountains
Widely spaced mountains
High tablelands
Hills and low tablelands
Depressions or basins
Plains
Ice cap at present

――― Limit of continental glaciation
――― Limit of continental shelf

For description of landform regions, see Landforms Map by R.E. Murphy, p. 6

© R. McN.
N-GDS20000-A3- -1-:1-1

Longitude West of Greenwich

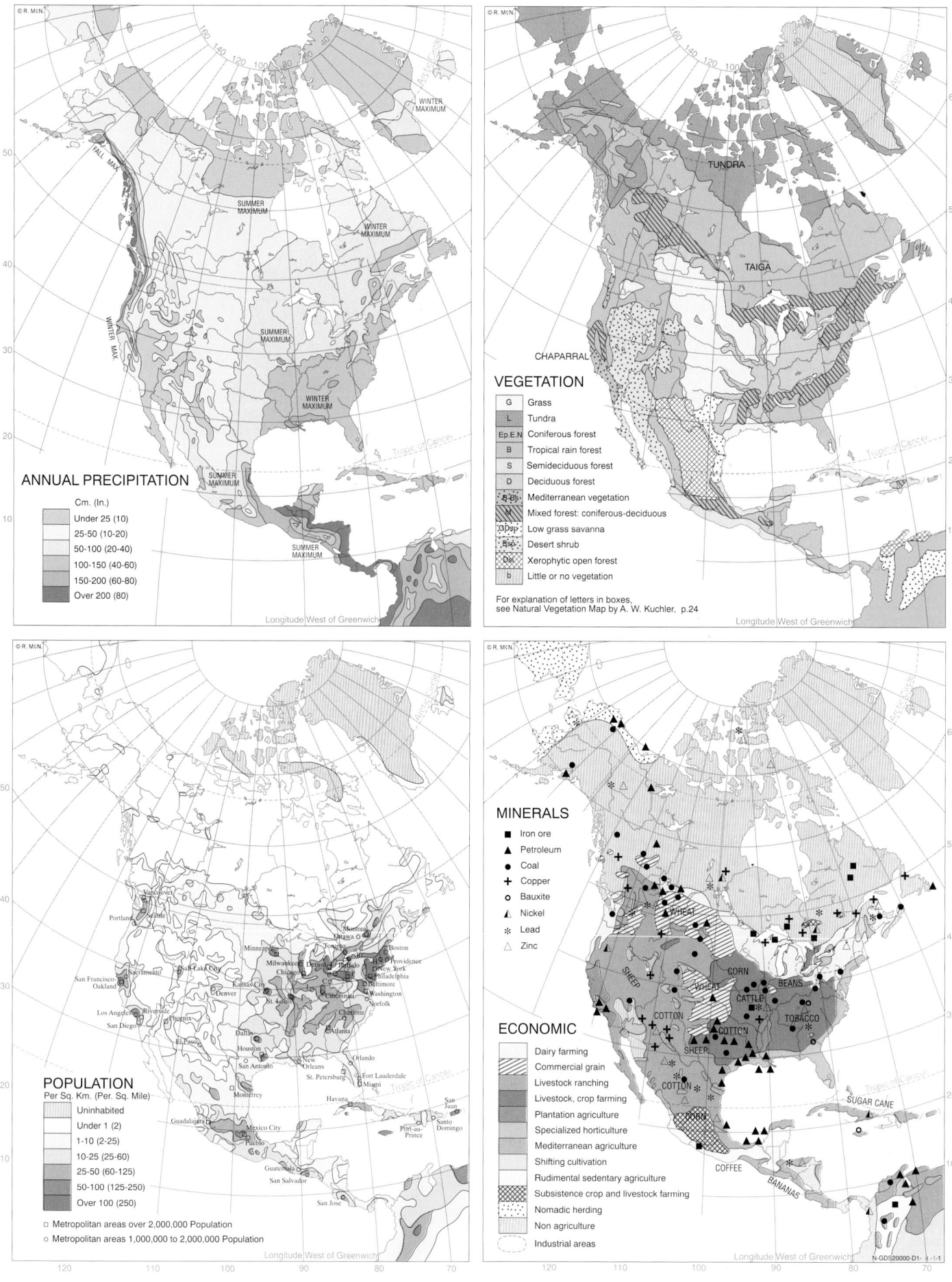

ANNUAL PRECIPITATION

Cm. (In.)

	Under 25 (10)
	25-50 (10-20)
	50-100 (20-40)
	100-150 (40-60)
	150-200 (60-80)
	Over 200 (80)

VEGETATION

G	Grass
L	Tundra
Ep.E.N	Coniferous forest
B	Tropical rain forest
S	Semideciduous forest
D	Deciduous forest
B.B.s	Mediterranean vegetation
M	Mixed forest: coniferous-deciduous
GDsp	Low grass savanna
Rsp	Desert shrub
Dei	Xerophytic open forest
b	Little or no vegetation

For explanation of letters in boxes,
see Natural Vegetation Map by A. W. Kuchler, p.24

POPULATION

Per Sq. Km. (Per. Sq. Mile)

	Uninhabited
	Under 1 (2)
	1-10 (2-25)
	10-25 (25-60)
	25-50 (60-125)
	50-100 (125-250)
	Over 100 (250)

□ Metropolitan areas over 2,000,000 Population

○ Metropolitan areas 1,000,000 to 2,000,000 Population

MINERALS

■	Iron ore
▲	Petroleum
●	Coal
+	Copper
○	Bauxite
◣	Nickel
✳	Lead
△	Zinc

ECONOMIC

	Dairy farming
	Commercial grain
	Livestock ranching
	Livestock, crop farming
	Plantation agriculture
	Specialized horticulture
	Mediterranean agriculture
	Shifting cultivation
	Rudimental sedentary agriculture
	Subsistence crop and livestock farming
	Nomadic herding
	Non agriculture
	Industrial areas

N-GDS20000-D1- a -1-1

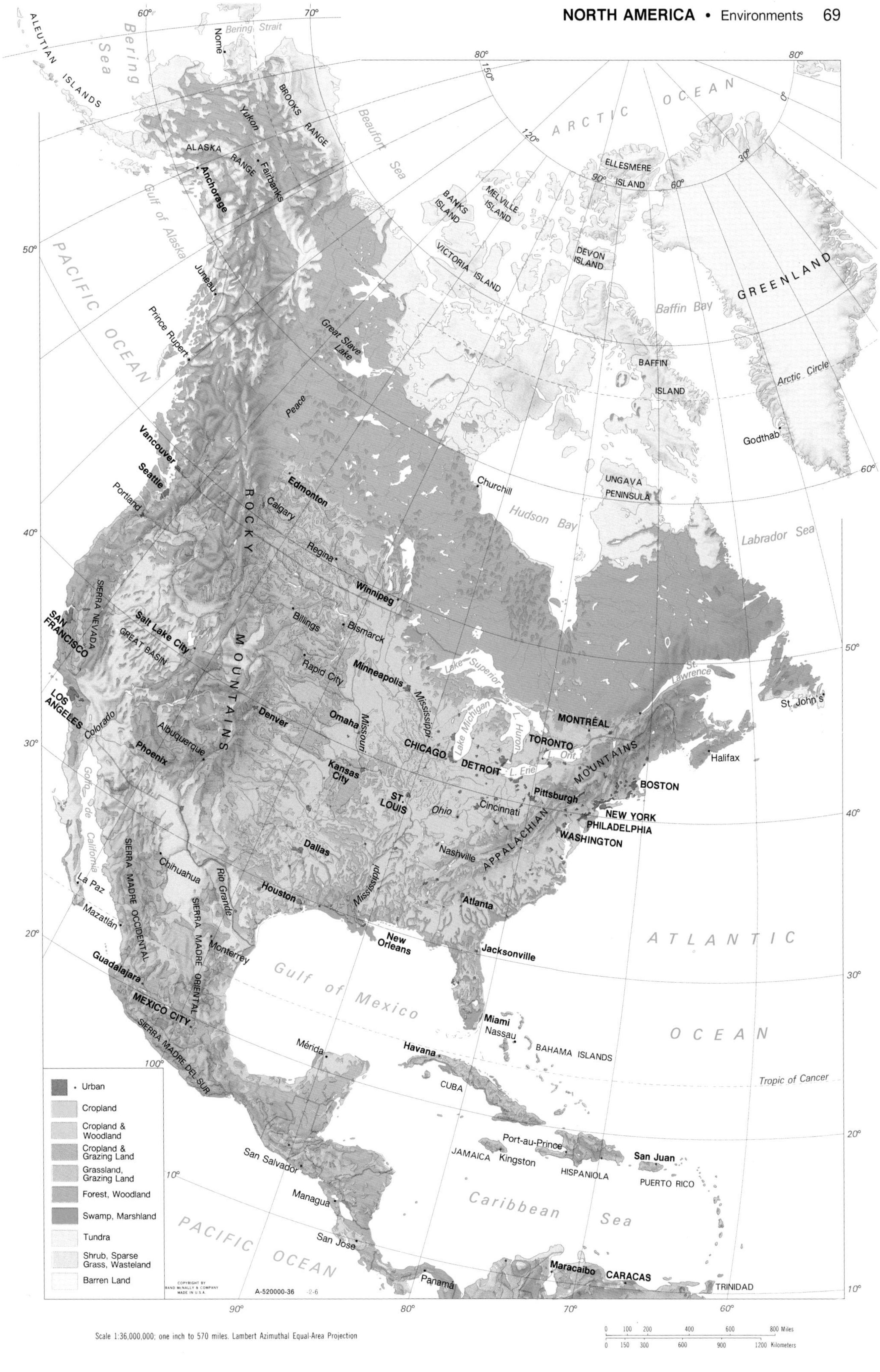

ARCTIC OCEAN

Bering Strait
Nome
BROOKS RANGE
Beaufort Sea
ALEUTIAN ISLANDS
Bering Sea
Yukon
ALASKA RANGE
Fairbanks
Anchorage
Gulf of Alaska
Juneau
Prince Rupert

ELLESMERE ISLAND
BANKS ISLAND
MELVILLE ISLAND
VICTORIA ISLAND
DEVON ISLAND
Baffin Bay
GREENLAND
BAFFIN ISLAND
Arctic Circle
Godthab

PACIFIC OCEAN

Great Slave Lake
Peace
Vancouver
Seattle
Portland
Edmonton
Calgary
ROCKY
Regina
Winnipeg
Billings
Bismarck
Churchill
Hudson Bay
UNGAVA PENINSULA
Labrador Sea
St. John's

SIERRA NEVADA
SAN FRANCISCO
Salt Lake City
GREAT BASIN
MOUNTAINS
Rapid City
Minneapolis
Lake Superior
L. Huron
St. Lawrence
Halifax

LOS ANGELES
Colorado
Denver
Omaha
Missouri
Mississippi
Lake Michigan
MONTRÉAL
TORONTO
L. Ont.
BOSTON
Albuquerque
Kansas City
CHICAGO
DETROIT
L. Erie
Pittsburgh
NEW YORK
PHILADELPHIA
WASHINGTON
Phoenix
ST. LOUIS
Ohio
Cincinnati
APPALACHIAN MOUNTAINS
Chihuahua
Dallas
Nashville
SIERRA MADRE OCCIDENTAL
Rio Grande
Houston
Mississippi
Atlanta
La Paz
SIERRA MADRE ORIENTAL
Monterrey
New Orleans
Jacksonville
Mazatlán
Golfo de California
Guadalajara
Gulf of Mexico
MEXICO CITY
SIERRA MADRE DEL SUR
Mérida
Miami
Nassau
BAHAMA ISLANDS
Havana
CUBA
Tropic of Cancer
San Salvador
Managua
San Jose
San José
Panamá
Port-au-Prince
JAMAICA
Kingston
HISPANIOLA
San Juan
PUERTO RICO
Caribbean Sea
Maracaibo
CARACAS
TRINIDAD

ATLANTIC OCEAN

PACIFIC OCEAN

Legend:
- Urban
- Cropland
- Cropland & Woodland
- Cropland & Grazing Land
- Grassland, Grazing Land
- Forest, Woodland
- Swamp, Marshland
- Tundra
- Shrub, Sparse Grass, Wasteland
- Barren Land

COPYRIGHT BY RAND McNALLY & COMPANY MADE IN U.S.A.
A-520000-36   -2-6

Scale 1:36,000,000; one inch to 570 miles. Lambert Azimuthal Equal-Area Projection

0 100 200 400 600 800 Miles
0 150 300 600 900 1200 Kilometers

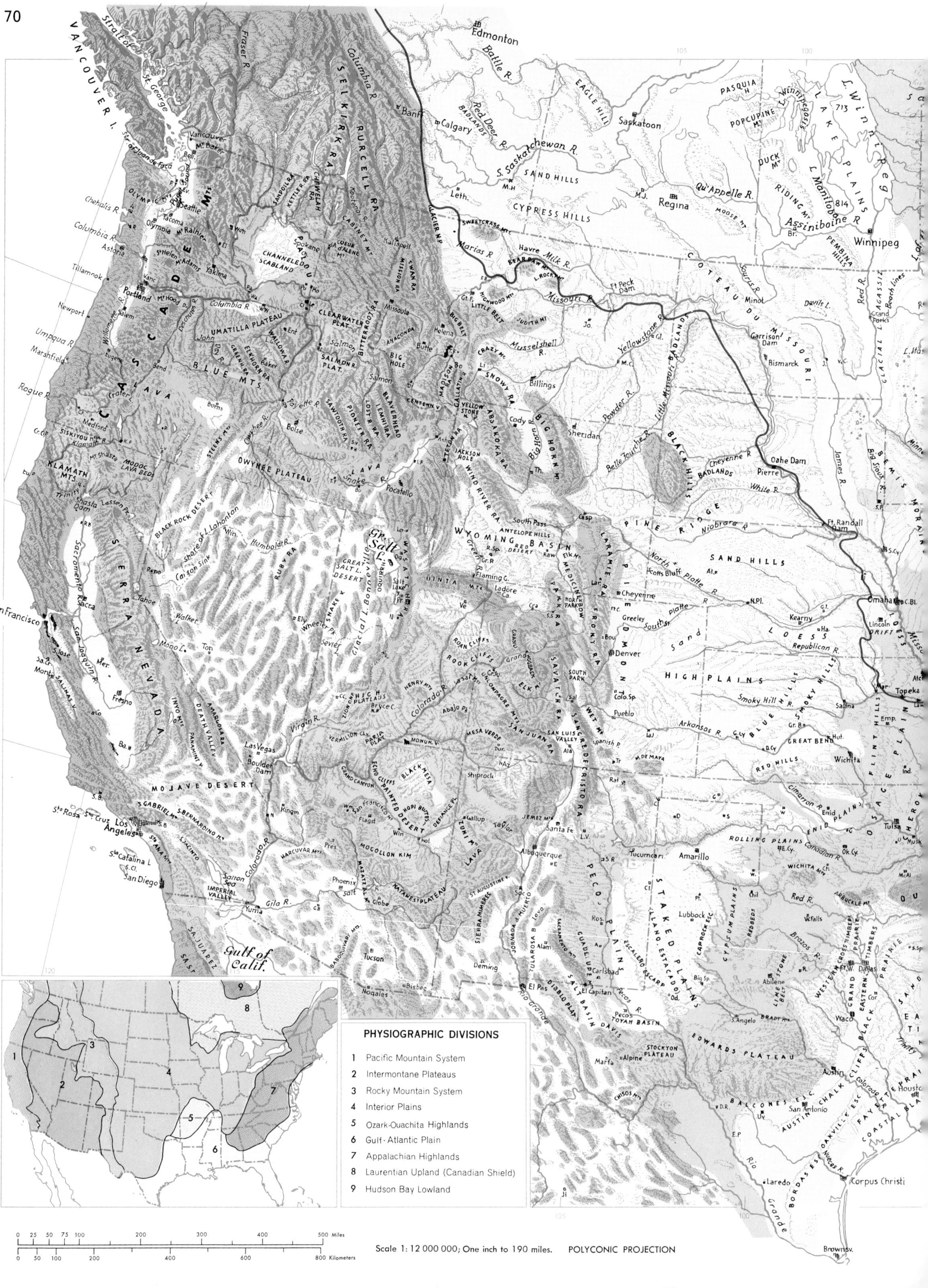

PHYSIOGRAPHIC DIVISIONS

1 Pacific Mountain System
2 Intermontane Plateaus
3 Rocky Mountain System
4 Interior Plains
5 Ozark-Ouachita Highlands
6 Gulf-Atlantic Plain
7 Appalachian Highlands
8 Laurentian Upland (Canadian Shield)
9 Hudson Bay Lowland

0 25 50 75 100   200   300   400   500 Miles

0   50   100   200   400   600   800 Kilometers

Scale 1 : 12 000 000; One inch to 190 miles.   POLYCONIC PROJECTION

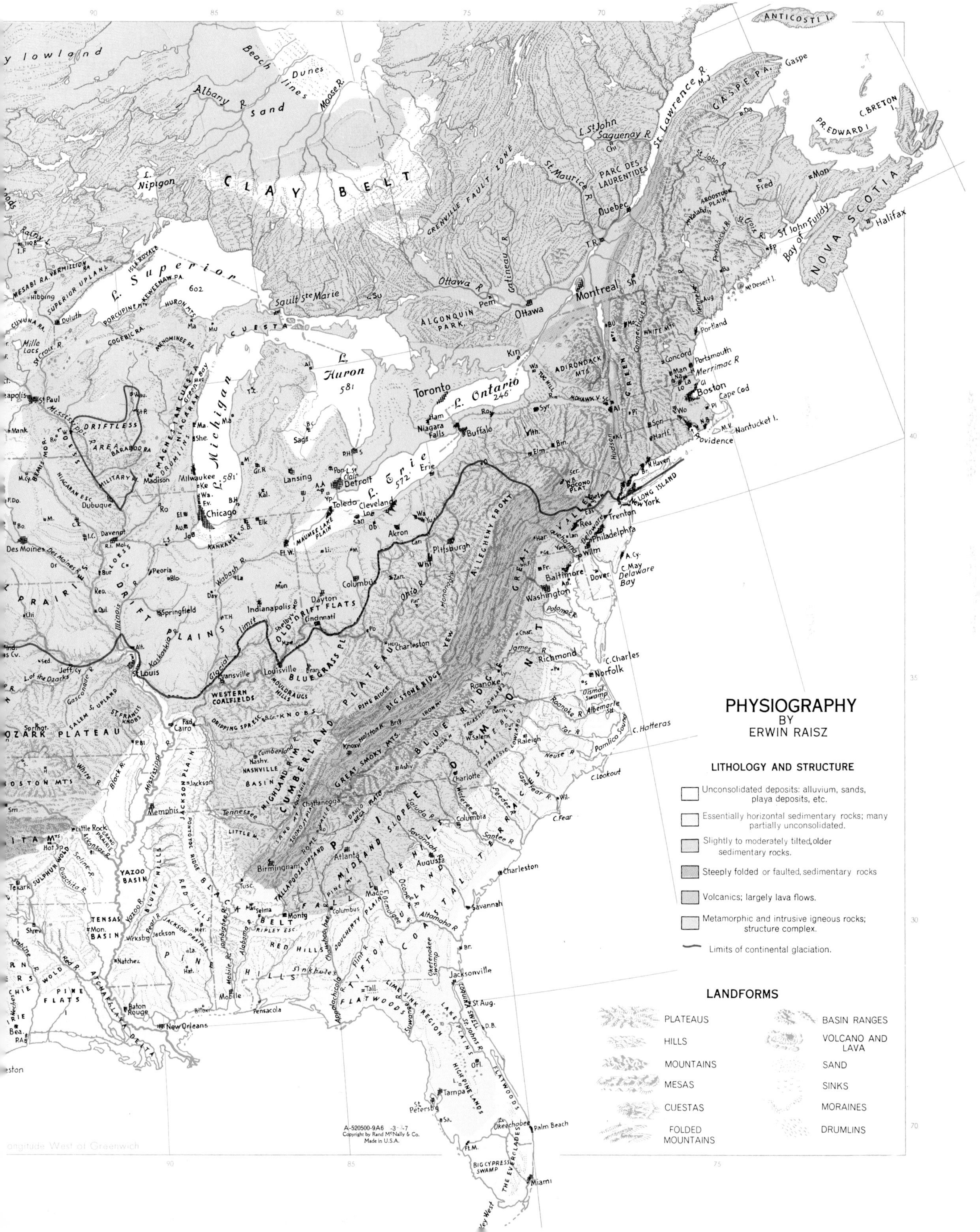

PHYSIOGRAPHY
BY ERWIN RAISZ

LITHOLOGY AND STRUCTURE

- Unconsolidated deposits: alluvium, sands, playa deposits, etc.
- Essentially horizontal sedimentary rocks; many partially unconsolidated.
- Slightly to moderately tilted, older sedimentary rocks.
- Steeply folded or faulted, sedimentary rocks.
- Volcanics; largely lava flows.
- Metamorphic and intrusive igneous rocks; structure complex.
- Limits of continental glaciation.

LANDFORMS

PLATEAUS	BASIN RANGES
HILLS	VOLCANO AND LAVA
MOUNTAINS	SAND
MESAS	SINKS
CUESTAS	MORAINES
FOLDED MOUNTAINS	DRUMLINS

A-520500-9A6 -3- -7
Copyright by Rand McNally & Co.
Made in U.S.A.

Map labels (selected):

Lowland · CLAY BELT · Albany R · Beach lines · Dunes · Sand · Moose R · ANTICOSTI I. · L. Nipigon · L. Superior · Duluth · Hibbing · MESABI RA · VERMILLION · SUPERIOR UPLAND · PORCUPINE MTS · KEWEENAW PA. · 602 · Sault Ste Marie · GRENVILLE FAULT ZONE · St Maurice R · PARC DES LAURENTIDES · Saguenay R · L St John · St Lawrence R · GASPE PA. · Gaspe · C. BRETON I. · PR. EDWARD I. · NOVA SCOTIA · Halifax · Bay of Fundy · St John · Quebec · Ottawa · Ottawa R · Gatineau R · ALGONQUIN PARK · Montreal · CUYUNA RA · GOGEBIC RA · MENOMINEE RA · HURON MTS · NIAGARA CUESTA · L. Huron 581 · L. Michigan 581 · Toronto · L. Ontario 246 · Niagara Falls · Buffalo · Hamilton · ADIRONDACK MTS · MOHAWK V. · GREEN MTS · WHITE MTS · Concord · Portsmouth · Portland · Boston · Cape Cod · Nantucket I. · Providence · DRIFTLESS AREA · BARABOO RA · DRUMLINS · MAGNESIAN CUESTA · St Paul · Milwaukee · Madison · Chicago · Lansing · Detroit · L. Erie 572 · Cleveland · Toledo · Akron · Erie · MAUMEE LAKE PLAIN · Dubuque · Davenport · Des Moines · LOESS · Peoria · Springfield · DRIFT PLAINS · Indianapolis · Dayton · Cincinnati · Columbus · Pittsburgh · ALLEGHENY FRONT · POCONO PLAT. · New York · LONG ISLAND · Trenton · Philadelphia · Wilmington · Dover · Delaware Bay · C. May · Baltimore · Washington · Potomac R · GREAT VALLEY · BLUE RIDGE · Richmond · Norfolk · C. Charles · C. Hatteras · Pamlico Sound · St Louis · Cairo · OZARK PLATEAU · ST FRANCIS KNOBS · SALEM UPLAND · BOSTON MTS · BLUEGRASS PLAIN · KNOBS · OLD DRIFT FLATS · WESTERN COALFIELDS · Louisville · Evansville · Charleston · Ohio R · CUMBERLAND PLATEAU · PINE RIDGE · BIG STONE RIDGE · Knoxville · GREAT SMOKY MTS · NASHVILLE BASIN · HIGHLAND RIM · Chattanooga · Memphis · JACKSON PLAIN · PONTOTOC RIDGE · Tennessee R · Roanoke · Roanoke R · Albemarle · C. Lookout · C. Fear · Raleigh · Neuse R · Charlotte · Columbia · PIEDMONT · FALL LINE · COASTAL PLAIN · Atlanta · Birmingham · TALLAPOOSA UPLAND · MIDLAND SLOPE · Montgomery · Columbus · Macon · Augusta · Charleston · Savannah · YAZOO BASIN · BLACK HILLS · BLUFF HILLS · RED HILLS · PINE HILLS · PINE FLATS · TENSAS BASIN · Jackson · Natchez · Baton Rouge · New Orleans · Mobile · Pensacola · Biloxi · Texarkana · Shreveport · Little Rock · Hot Springs · OUACHITA MTS · TIFTON UPLAND · FLATWOODS · LIME SINK REGION · Sinkholes · OKEFENOKEE SWAMP · Jacksonville · St Aug. · HIGH PINE LANDS · LAKE REGION · St Johns R · St Petersburg · Tampa · Okeechobee · Palm Beach · BIG CYPRESS SWAMP · THE EVERGLADES · Key West · Miami · DISMAL SWAMP · Longitude West of Greenwich

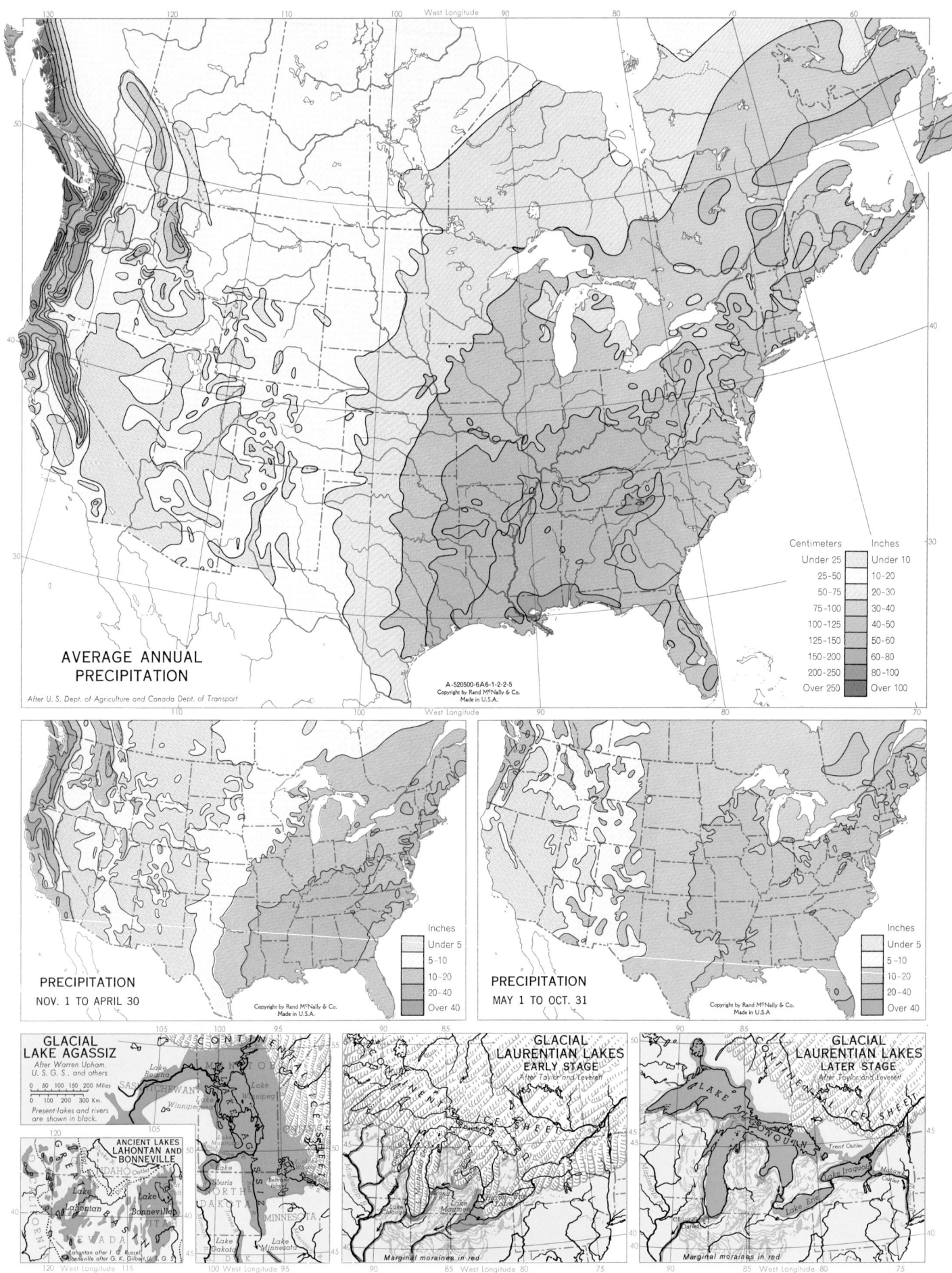

Centimeters	Inches
Under 25	Under 10
25–50	10–20
50–75	20–30
75–100	30–40
100–125	40–50
125–150	50–60
150–200	60–80
200–250	80–100
Over 250	Over 100

AVERAGE ANNUAL PRECIPITATION

After U. S. Dept. of Agriculture and Canada Dept. of Transport

A-520500-6A6-1-2-2-5
Copyright by Rand McNally & Co.
Made in U.S.A.

PRECIPITATION

NOV. 1 TO APRIL 30

Inches
Under 5
5–10
10–20
20–40
Over 40

Copyright by Rand McNally & Co.
Made in U.S.A

PRECIPITATION

MAY 1 TO OCT. 31

Inches
Under 5
5–10
10–20
20–40
Over 40

Copyright by Rand McNally & Co.
Made in U.S.A

GLACIAL LAKE AGASSIZ

After Warren Upham,
U. S. G. S. and others

0 50 100 150 200 Miles
0 100 200 300 Km.

Present lakes and rivers
are shown in black.

ANCIENT LAKES LAHONTAN AND BONNEVILLE

Lahontan after I. G. Russell
Bonneville after G. K. Gilbert, U. S. G. S.

GLACIAL LAURENTIAN LAKES EARLY STAGE

After Taylor and Leverett

Marginal moraines in red

GLACIAL LAURENTIAN LAKES LATER STAGE

After Taylor and Leverett

Marginal moraines in red

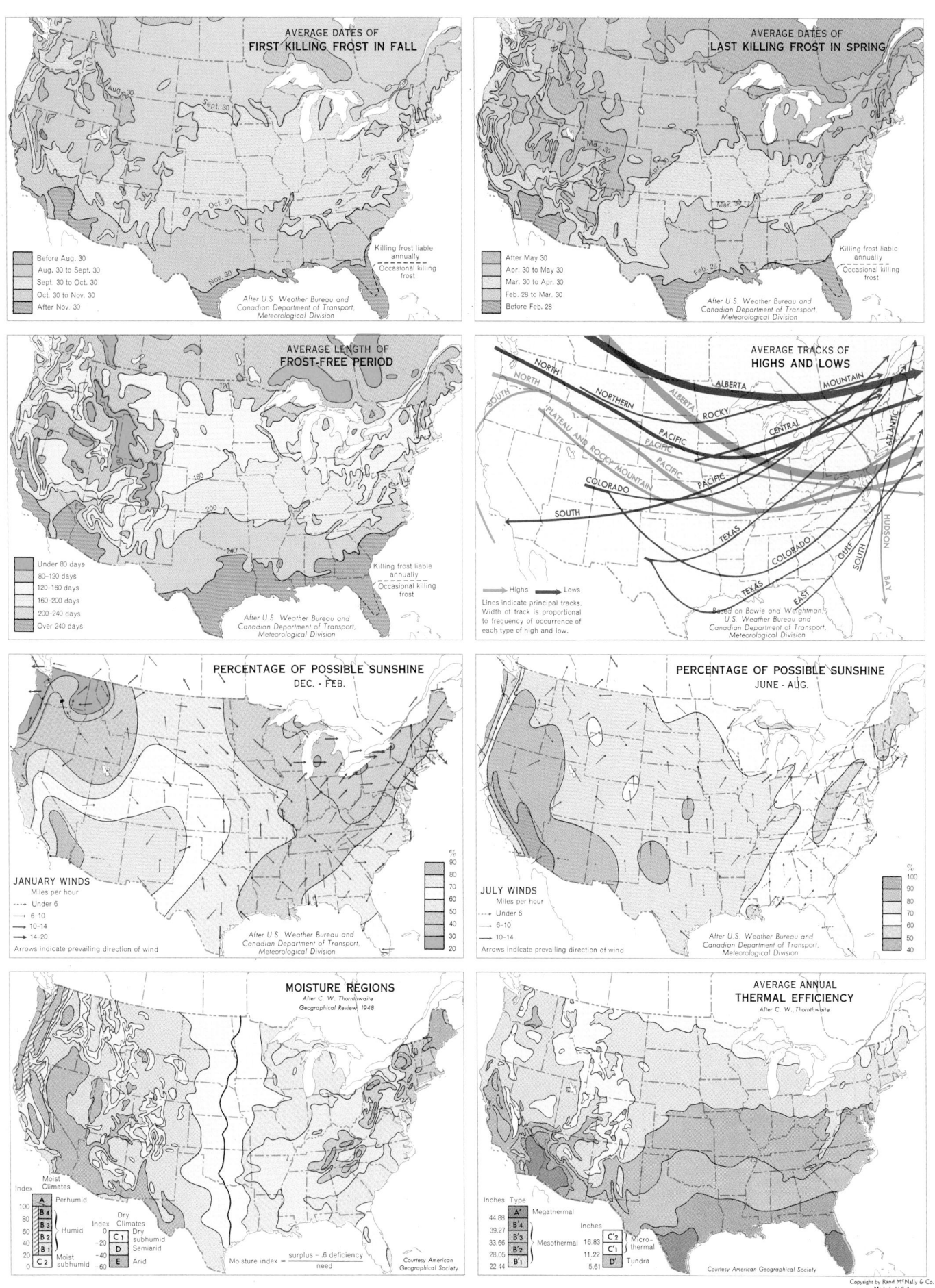

AVERAGE DATES OF
FIRST KILLING FROST IN FALL

Before Aug. 30
Aug. 30 to Sept. 30
Sept. 30 to Oct. 30
Oct. 30 to Nov. 30
After Nov. 30

Killing frost liable
annually
Occasional killing
frost

After U.S. Weather Bureau and
Canadian Department of Transport,
Meteorological Division

AVERAGE DATES OF
LAST KILLING FROST IN SPRING

After May 30
Apr. 30 to May 30
Mar. 30 to Apr. 30
Feb. 28 to Mar. 30
Before Feb. 28

Killing frost liable
annually
Occasional killing
frost

After U.S. Weather Bureau and
Canadian Department of Transport,
Meteorological Division

AVERAGE LENGTH OF
FROST-FREE PERIOD

Under 80 days
80–120 days
120–160 days
160–200 days
200–240 days
Over 240 days

Killing frost liable
annually
Occasional killing
frost

After U.S. Weather Bureau and
Canadian Department of Transport,
Meteorological Division

AVERAGE TRACKS OF
HIGHS AND LOWS

Highs   Lows
Lines indicate principal tracks.
Width of track is proportional
to frequency of occurrence of
each type of high and low.

Based on Bowie and Weightman,
U.S. Weather Bureau and
Canadian Department of Transport,
Meteorological Division

PERCENTAGE OF POSSIBLE SUNSHINE
DEC. - FEB.

JANUARY WINDS
Miles per hour
Under 6
6–10
10–14
14–20
Arrows indicate prevailing direction of wind

%
90
80
70
60
50
40
30
20

PERCENTAGE OF POSSIBLE SUNSHINE
JUNE - AUG.

JULY WINDS
Miles per hour
Under 6
6–10
10–14
Arrows indicate prevailing direction of wind

%
100
90
80
70
60
50
40

After U.S. Weather Bureau and
Canadian Department of Transport,
Meteorological Division

MOISTURE REGIONS
After C. W. Thornthwaite
Geographical Review, 1948

Moist
Climates
Index
100   A   Perhumid
80   B4
60   B3   Humid
40   B2
20   B1   Moist
0   C2   subhumid

Dry
Climates
Index
0   C1   Dry
        subhumid
-20   D   Semiarid
-40
-60   E   Arid

Moisture index = surplus − .6 deficiency / need

Courtesy American
Geographical Society

AVERAGE ANNUAL
THERMAL EFFICIENCY
After C. W. Thornthwaite

Inches   Type
44.88   A'   Megathermal
39.27   B'4
33.66   B'3   Mesothermal
28.05   B'2
22.44   B'1

Inches
16.83   C'2
11.22   C'1   Micro-
        thermal
5.61   D'   Tundra

Courtesy American Geographical Society

74

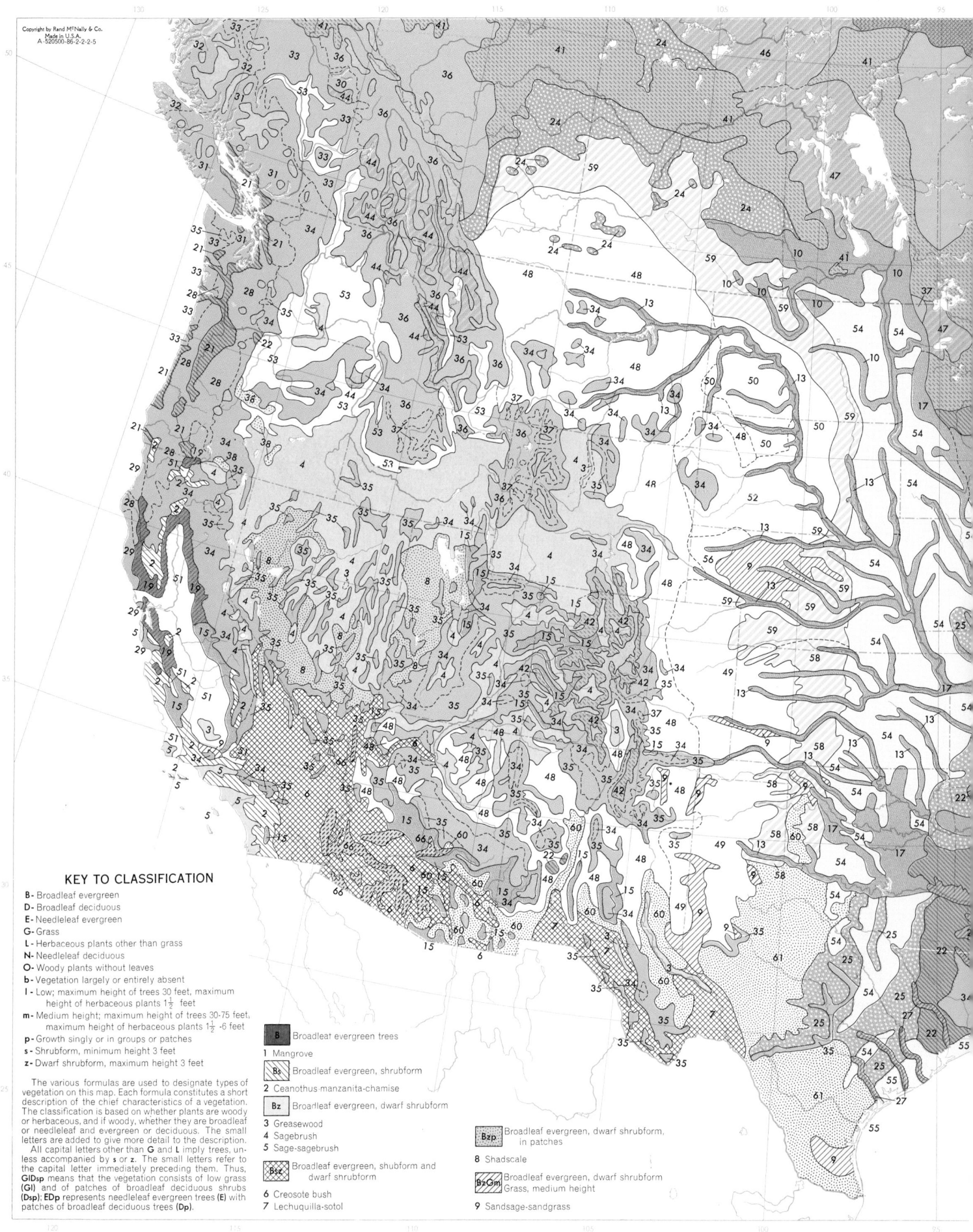

KEY TO CLASSIFICATION

- **B-** Broadleaf evergreen
- **D-** Broadleaf deciduous
- **E-** Needleleaf evergreen
- **G-** Grass
- **L-** Herbaceous plants other than grass
- **N-** Needleleaf deciduous
- **O-** Woody plants without leaves
- **b-** Vegetation largely or entirely absent
- **l-** Low; maximum height of trees 30 feet, maximum height of herbaceous plants 1½ feet
- **m-** Medium height; maximum height of trees 30-75 feet, maximum height of herbaceous plants 1½ -6 feet
- **p-** Growth singly or in groups or patches
- **s-** Shrubform, minimum height 3 feet
- **z-** Dwarf shrubform, maximum height 3 feet

The various formulas are used to designate types of vegetation on this map. Each formula constitutes a short description of the chief characteristics of a vegetation. The classification is based on whether plants are woody or herbaceous, and if woody, whether they are broadleaf or needleleaf and evergreen or deciduous. The small letters are added to give more detail to the description. All capital letters other than **G** and **L** imply trees, unless accompanied by **s** or **z**. The small letters refer to the capital letter immediately preceding them. Thus, **GlDsp** means that the vegetation consists of low grass (**Gl**) and of patches of broadleaf deciduous shrubs (**Dsp**); **EDp** represents needleleaf evergreen trees (**E**) with patches of broadleaf deciduous trees (**Dp**).

B Broadleaf evergreen trees

1 Mangrove

Bs Broadleaf evergreen, shrubform

2 Ceanothus-manzanita-chamise

Bz Broadleaf evergreen, dwarf shrubform

3 Greasewood

4 Sagebrush

5 Sage-sagebrush

Bsz Broadleaf evergreen, shubform and dwarf shrubform

6 Creosote bush

7 Lechuquilla-sotol

Bzp Broadleaf evergreen, dwarf shrubform, in patches

8 Shadscale

BzGm Broadleaf evergreen, dwarf shrubform Grass, medium height

9 Sandsage-sandgrass

0 25 50 75 100   200   300   400   500 Miles

0 50 100   200   400   600   800 Kilometers

Scale 1:14 000 000;   One inch to 220 miles

NATURAL VEGETATION

BY A. W. KÜCHLER

Based on "A Physiognomic Classification of Vegetation"
Annals of the Assoc. of American Geographers, Vol. 39, September, 1949

Longitude West of Greenwich

| **D** | Broadleaf deciduous trees |

10 Aspen-oak
11 Beech-maple
12 Beech-tulip tree-maple-basswood
13 Cottonwood-willow
14 Maple-basswood
15 Oak
16 Oak-ash-maple
17 Oak-hickory
18 Oak-tulip tree

| **DB** | Broadleaf deciduous trees
Broadleaf evergreen trees |

19 Oak-madrone

| **DE** | Broadleaf deciduous trees
Needleleaf evergreen trees |

20 Maple-yellow birch-hemlock-pine
21 Oak-Douglas fir
22 Oak-pine
23 Maple-beech-hemlock

| **D**/**Gmp** | Broadleaf deciduous trees
Grass, medium height, in patches |

24 Aspen-needle grass-wheat grass
25 Oak-hickory-bluestem

| **DN** | Broadleaf deciduous trees
Needleleaf deciduous trees |

26 Bay trees-bald cypress
27 Tupelo-gum-bald cypress

| **E** | Needleleaf evergreen trees |

28 Douglas fir
29 Douglas fir-redwood
30 Hemlock-arbor vitae
31 Hemlock-arbor vitae-Douglas fir
32 Hemlock-arbor vitae-fir
33 Hemlock-spruce
34 Pine
35 Pine-juniper
36 Pine-spruce
37 Spruce-fir

| **Esp** | Needleleaf evergreen, shrubform, in patches |

38 Juniper

| **EDp** | Needleleaf evergreen trees
Broadleaf deciduous trees, in patches |

39 Douglas fir-pine-aspen
40 Pine-spruce-birch
41 Spruce-aspen
42 Spruce-fir-aspen
43 Spruce-poplar-birch

| **EN** | Needleleaf evergreen trees
Needleleaf deciduous trees |

44 Hemlock-arbor vitae-Douglas fir-larch
45 Pine-bald cypress
46 Pine-spruce-larch
47 Spruce-larch

| **Gl** | Grass, low |

48 Grama grass
49 Grama grass-buffalo grass
50 Grama grass-needle grass
51 Needle grass-blue grass
52 Wheat grass
53 Wheat grass-blue grass

| **Gm** | Grass, medium height |

54 Bluestem
55 Broom grass-water grass
56 Marsh grass
57 Saw grass

| **Gml** | Grass, medium and low height |

58 Bluestem-bunch grass
59 Needle grass-wheat grass

| **Gl**/**Dsp** | Grass, low
Broadleaf deciduous, shrubform, in patches |

60 Bunch grass-oak

| **Gm**/**Dsp** | Grass, medium height
Broadleaf deciduous, shrubform, in patches |

61 Mesquite grass-mesquite

| **L** | Herbaceous plants other than grass |

62 Lichens, etc.

| **LEp** | Herbaceous plants other than grass
Needleleaf evergreen trees, in patches |

63 Lichens-spruce

| **LEp**/**Np** | Herbaceous plants other than grass
Needleleaf evergreen trees, in patches
Needleleaf deciduous trees, in patches |

64 Lichens-spruce-larch

| **N** | Needleleaf deciduous trees |

65 Bald cypress

| **Op** | Woody plants without leaves, in patches |

66 Palo verde-cacti-ocotillo

| **b** | Vegetation largely or entirely absent |

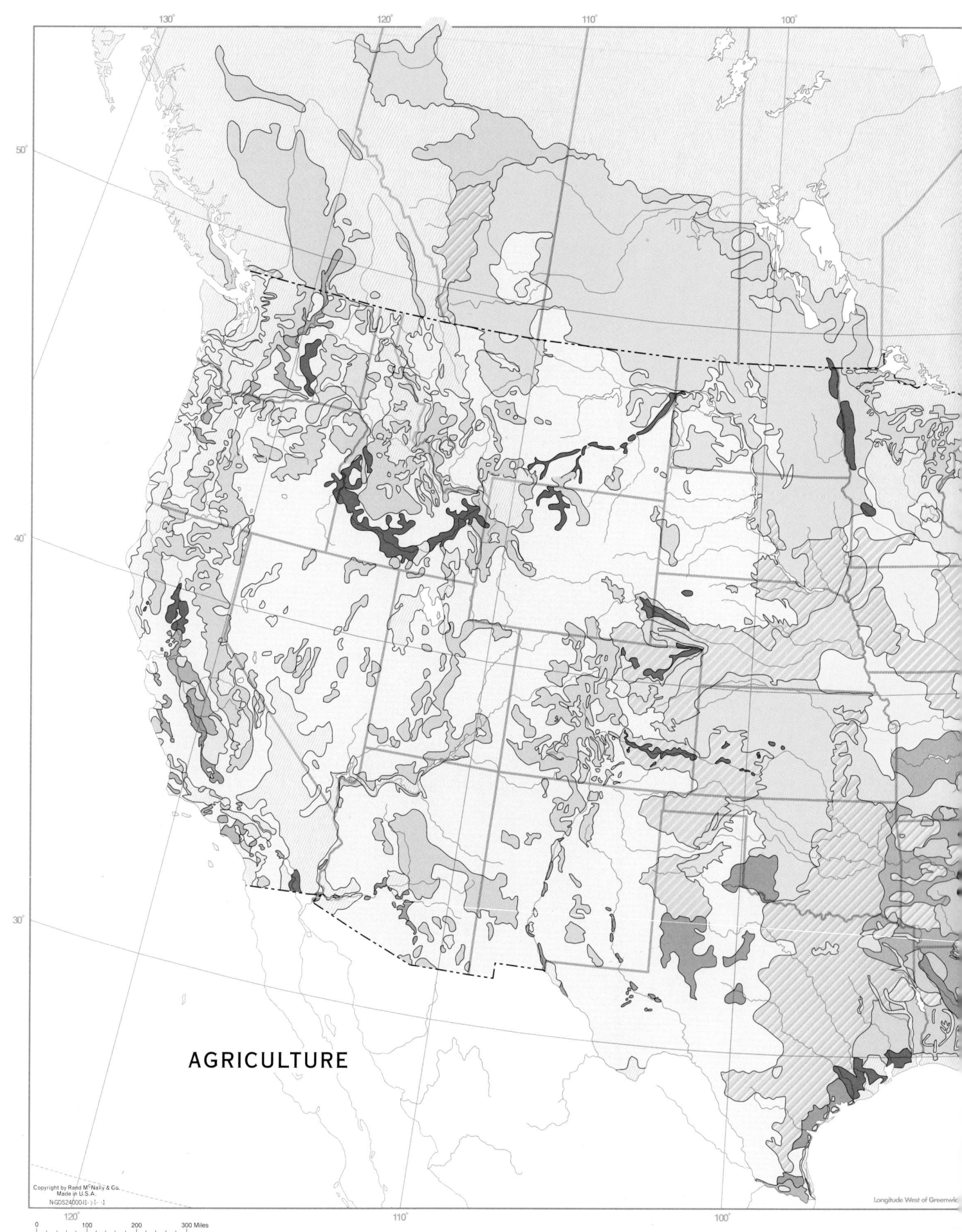

AGRICULTURE

Scale 1:15,000,000; One inch to 237 miles. One centimeter to 150 kilometers

0   100   200   300 Miles

0   100   200   300   400 Kilometers

Dairying

Fruits and Vegetables

Wheat, Barley, and Oilseeds

Cash Corn and Soybeans

Tobacco

Cotton

Livestock and Feed Grains: Beef

Livestock and Feed Grains: Hogs

Livestock and Feed Grains: Poultry

Livestock and Feed Grains: Mixed

Specialty Crops (Peanuts, Potatoes, Rice, Sugar)

Western Livestock Ranching

Western Feedlots

Agriculture and Forestry

Non-Agricultural Areas

ALBERS CONIC PROJECTION

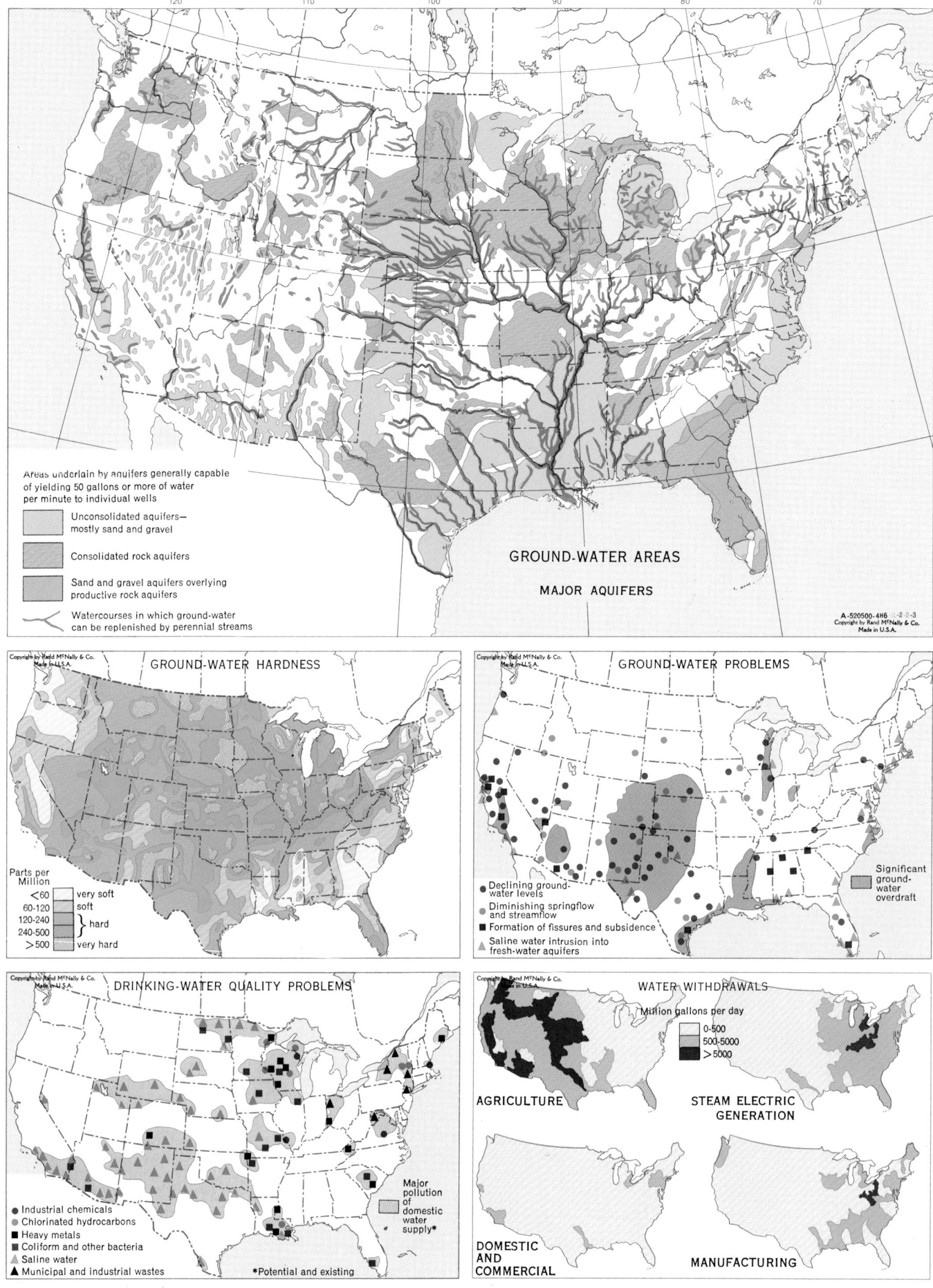

GROUND-WATER AREAS

MAJOR AQUIFERS

Areas underlain by aquifers generally capable
of yielding 50 gallons or more of water
per minute to individual wells

Unconsolidated aquifers—
mostly sand and gravel

Consolidated rock aquifers

Sand and gravel aquifers overlying
productive rock aquifers

Watercourses in which ground-water
can be replenished by perennial streams

A-520500-4H6
Copyright by Rand McNally & Co.
Made in U.S.A.

GROUND-WATER HARDNESS

Copyright by Rand McNally & Co.
Made in U.S.A.

Parts per
Million
<60   very soft
60-120   soft
120-240 } hard
240-500
>500   very hard

GROUND-WATER PROBLEMS

Copyright by Rand McNally & Co.
Made in U.S.A.

Declining ground-
water levels

Diminishing springflow
and streamflow

Formation of fissures and subsidence

Saline water intrusion into
fresh-water aquifers

Significant
ground-
water
overdraft

DRINKING-WATER QUALITY PROBLEMS

Copyright by Rand McNally & Co.
Made in U.S.A.

Industrial chemicals
Chlorinated hydrocarbons
Heavy metals
Coliform and other bacteria
Saline water
Municipal and industrial wastes

Major
pollution
of
domestic
water
supply*

*Potential and existing

WATER WITHDRAWALS

Copyright by Rand McNally & Co.
Made in U.S.A.

Million gallons per day
0-500
500-5000
>5000

AGRICULTURE

**STEAM ELECTRIC
GENERATION**

**DOMESTIC
AND
COMMERCIAL**

MANUFACTURING

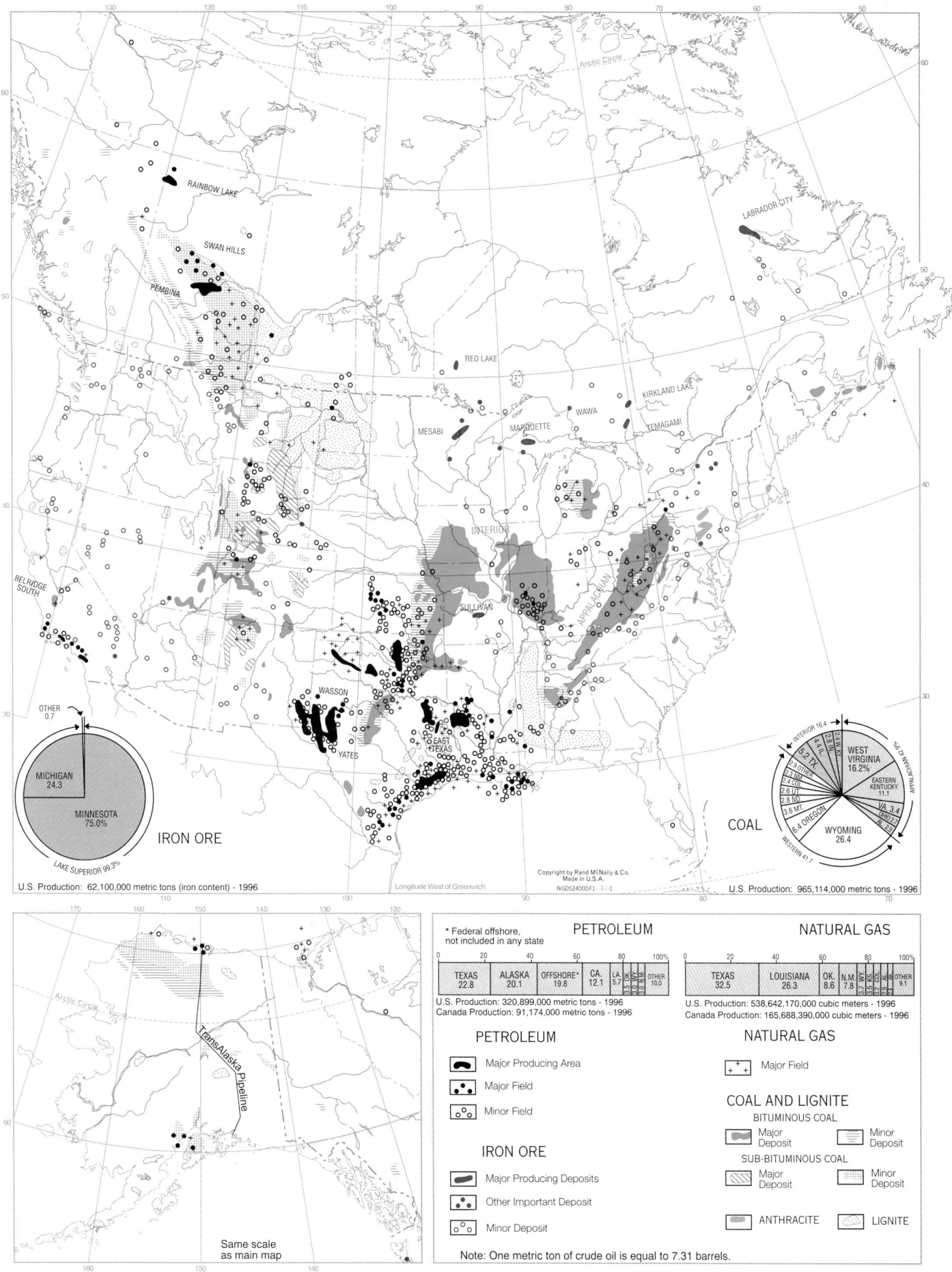

IRON ORE

OTHER
0.7

MICHIGAN
24.3

MINNESOTA
75.0%

LAKE SUPERIOR 99.3%

U.S. Production: 62,100,000 metric tons (iron content) - 1996

COAL

INTERIOR 16.4

5.2 TX

5.9 OTHER

2.3 NM

2.4 CO

2.6 UT

2.8 ND

3.6 MT

16.4 OREGON

WESTERN 41.7

WEST
VIRGINIA
16.2%

EASTERN
KENTUCKY
11.1

VA. 3.4

WYOMING
26.4

APPALACHIAN 28.3%

2.6 WV
4.4 IL

U.S. Production: 965,114,000 metric tons - 1996

RAINBOW LAKE

SWAN HILLS

PEMBINA

RED LAKE

KIRKLAND LAKE

WAWA

TEMAGAMI

MARQUETTE

MESABI

LABRADOR CITY

BELRIDGE
SOUTH

INTERIOR

SULLIVAN

APPALACHIAN

WASSON

YATES

EAST
TEXAS

Copyright by Rand McNally & Co.
Made in U.S.A.
N-GDS24000-FI· -1-1-1

Longitude West of Greenwich

Arctic Circle

TransAlaska Pipeline

Same scale
as main map

Scale 1:29,000,000; One inch to 457 miles.   ALBERS CONIC PROJECTION

*Federal offshore,
not included in any state

PETROLEUM

TEXAS 22.8	ALASKA 20.1	OFFSHORE* 19.8	CA. 12.1	LA 5.7	OK 3.9	WY 3.0	KS 2.6	NM 2.5	OTHER 10.0

U.S. Production: 320,899,000 metric tons - 1996
Canada Production: 91,174,000 metric tons - 1996

NATURAL GAS

TEXAS 32.5	LOUISIANA 26.3	OK. 8.6	N.M 7.8	WY 3.7	KS 3.5	CO 3.0	LA 2.4	OTHER 9.1

U.S. Production: 538,642,170,000 cubic meters - 1996
Canada Production: 165,688,390,000 cubic meters - 1996

PETROLEUM

Major Producing Area

Major Field

Minor Field

IRON ORE

Major Producing Deposits

Other Important Deposit

Minor Deposit

NATURAL GAS

Major Field

COAL AND LIGNITE

BITUMINOUS COAL

Major
Deposit

Minor
Deposit

SUB-BITUMINOUS COAL

Major
Deposit

Minor
Deposit

ANTHRACITE

LIGNITE

Note: One metric ton of crude oil is equal to 7.31 barrels.

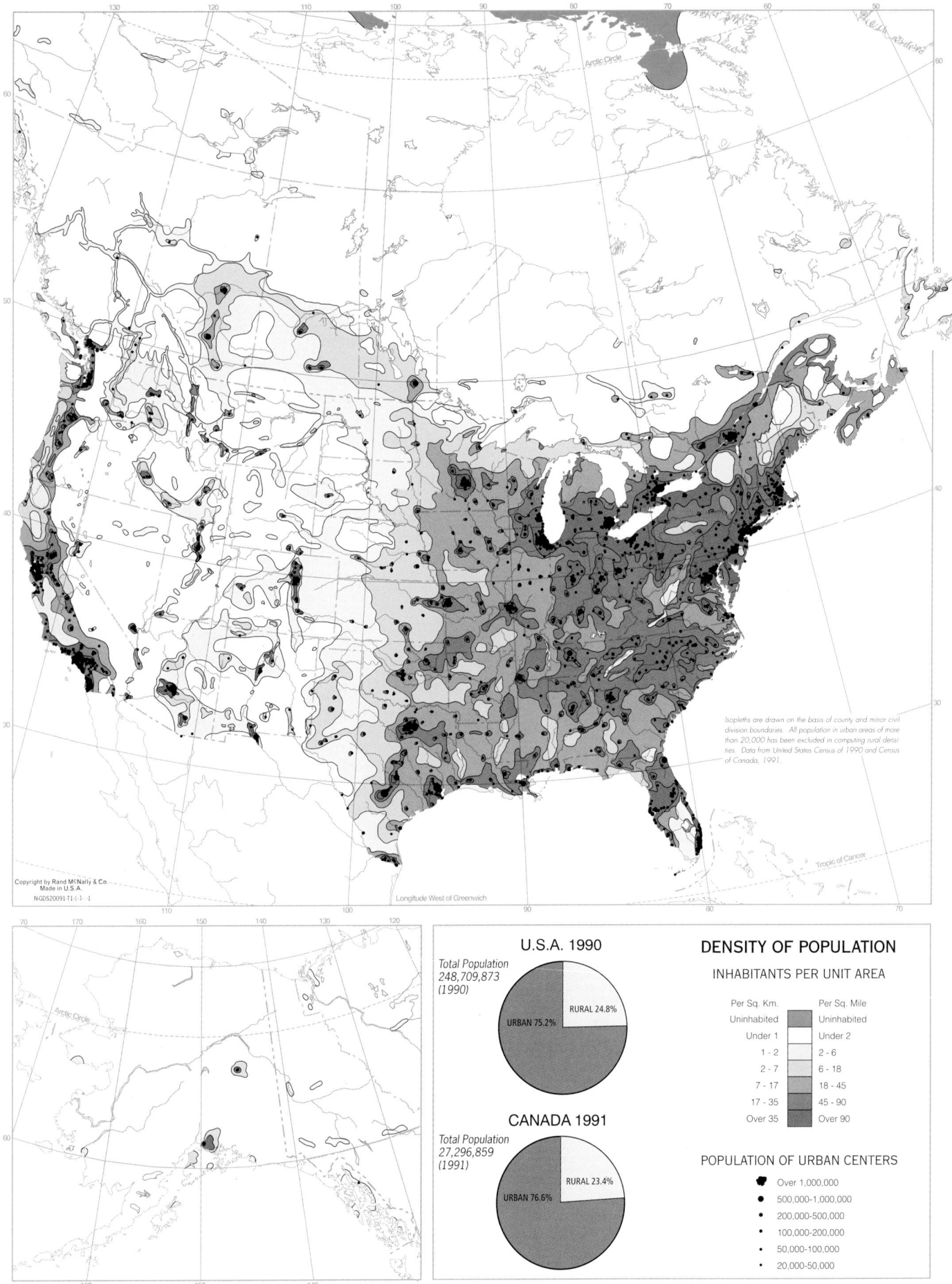

Isopleths are drawn on the basis of county and minor civil division boundaries. All population in urban areas of more than 20,000 has been excluded in computing rural densities. Data from United States Census of 1990 and Census of Canada, 1991.

Copyright by Rand M\`Nally & Co.
Made in U.S.A.
N-GDS20091-T1-1-1--1

Longitude West of Greenwich

U.S.A. 1990

Total Population
248,709,873
(1990)

URBAN 75.2% RURAL 24.8%

CANADA 1991

Total Population
27,296,859
(1991)

URBAN 76.6% RURAL 23.4%

DENSITY OF POPULATION

INHABITANTS PER UNIT AREA

Per Sq. Km.	Per Sq. Mile
Uninhabited	Uninhabited
Under 1	Under 2
1 - 2	2 - 6
2 - 7	6 - 18
7 - 17	18 - 45
17 - 35	45 - 90
Over 35	Over 90

POPULATION OF URBAN CENTERS

- Over 1,000,000
- 500,000-1,000,000
- 200,000-500,000
- 100,000-200,000
- 50,000-100,000
- 20,000-50,000

Scale 1:29,000,000; One inch to 457 miles.   ALBERS CONIC PROJECTION

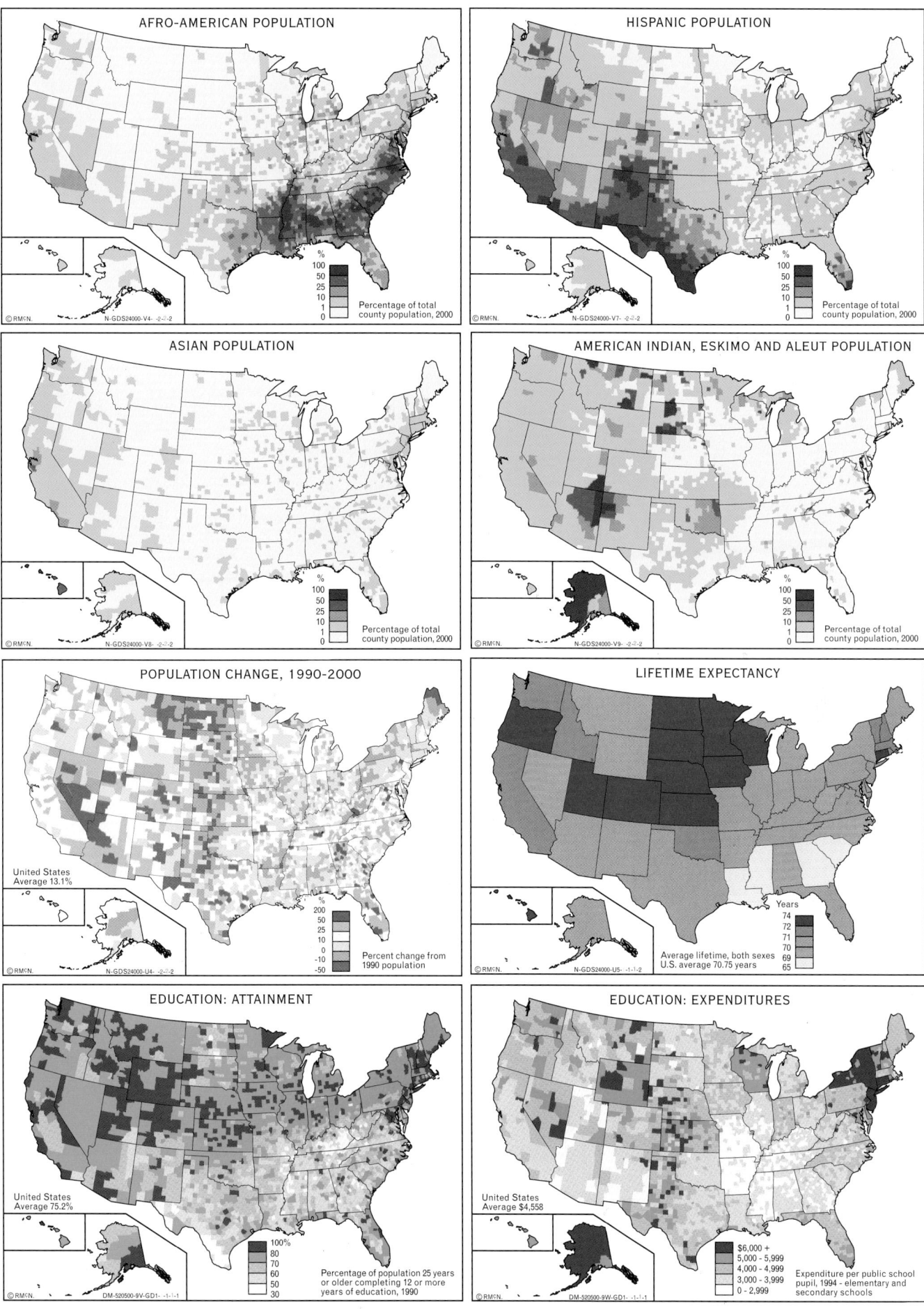

AFRO-AMERICAN POPULATION

%
100
50
25
10
1
0

Percentage of total
county population, 2000

HISPANIC POPULATION

%
100
50
25
10
1
0

Percentage of total
county population, 2000

ASIAN POPULATION

%
100
50
25
10
1
0

Percentage of total
county population, 2000

AMERICAN INDIAN, ESKIMO AND ALEUT POPULATION

%
100
50
25
10
1
0

Percentage of total
county population, 2000

POPULATION CHANGE, 1990-2000

United States
Average 13.1%

%
200
50
25
10
0
-10
-50

Percent change from
1990 population

LIFETIME EXPECTANCY

Years
74
72
71
70
69
65

Average lifetime, both sexes
U.S. average 70.75 years

EDUCATION: ATTAINMENT

United States
Average 75.2%

100%
80
70
60
50
30

Percentage of population 25 years
or older completing 12 or more
years of education, 1990

EDUCATION: EXPENDITURES

United States
Average $4,558

$6,000 +
5,000 - 5,999
4,000 - 4,999
3,000 - 3,999
0 - 2,999

Expenditure per public school
pupil, 1994 - elementary and
secondary schools

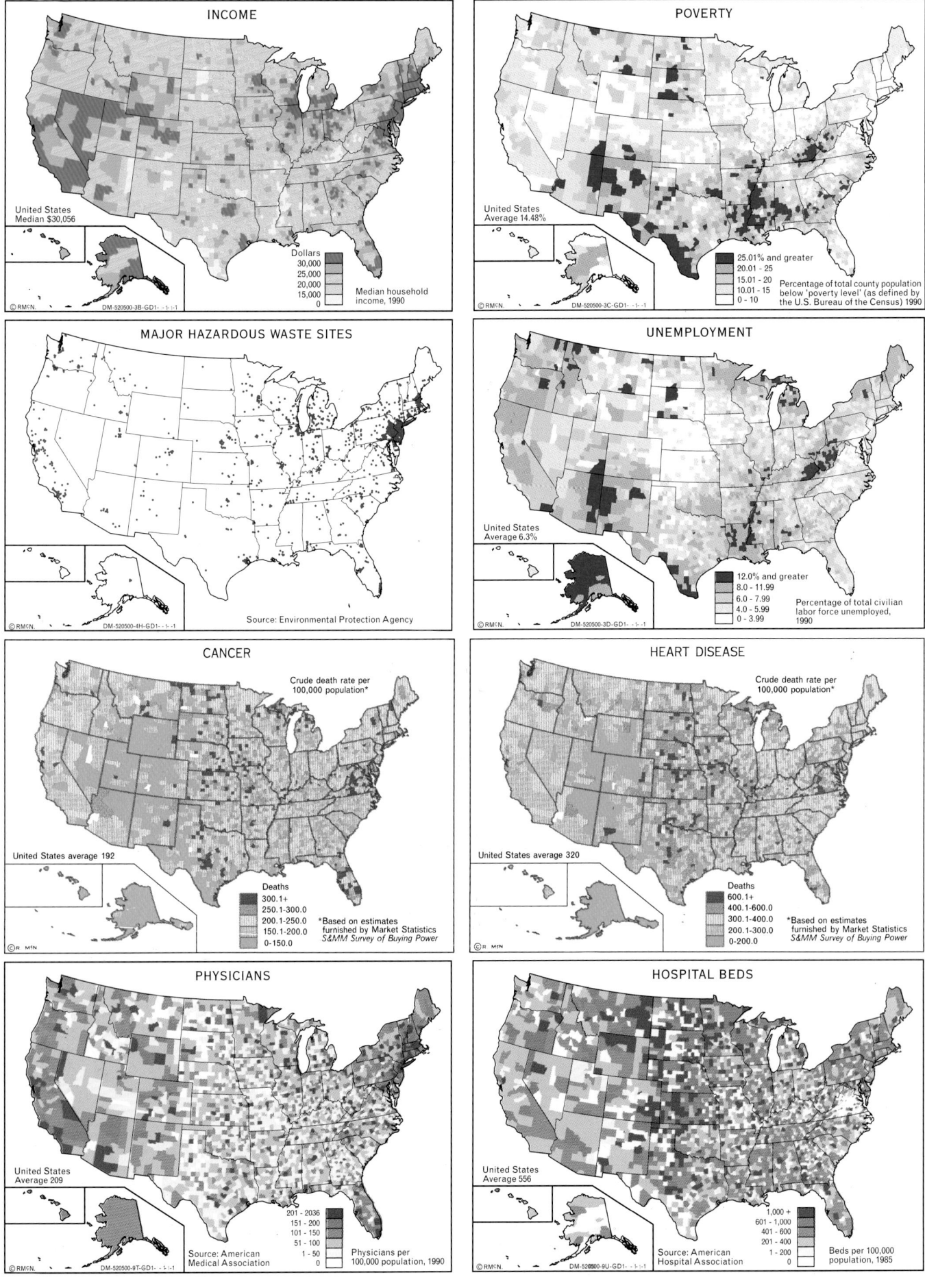

INCOME

United States
Median $30,056

Dollars
30,000
25,000
20,000
15,000
0

Median household
income, 1990

© RM©N. DM-520500-3B-GD1- -·-1-·-1

POVERTY

United States
Average 14.48%

25.01% and greater
20.01 - 25
15.01 - 20
10.01 - 15
0 - 10

Percentage of total county population
below 'poverty level' (as defined by
the U.S. Bureau of the Census) 1990

© RM©N. DM-520500-3C-GD1- -·-1-·-1

MAJOR HAZARDOUS WASTE SITES

Source: Environmental Protection Agency

© RM©N. DM-520500-4H-GD1- -·-1-·-1

UNEMPLOYMENT

United States
Average 6.3%

12.0% and greater
8.0 - 11.99
6.0 - 7.99
4.0 - 5.99
0 - 3.99

Percentage of total civilian
labor force unemployed,
1990

© RM©N. DM-520500-3D-GD1- -·-1-·-1

CANCER

Crude death rate per
100,000 population*

United States average 192

Deaths
300.1+
250.1-300.0
200.1-250.0
150.1-200.0
0-150.0

*Based on estimates
furnished by Market Statistics
S&MM Survey of Buying Power

© R M©N

HEART DISEASE

Crude death rate per
100,000 population*

United States average 320

Deaths
600.1+
400.1-600.0
300.1-400.0
200.1-300.0
0-200.0

*Based on estimates
furnished by Market Statistics
S&MM Survey of Buying Power

© R M©N

PHYSICIANS

United States
Average 209

201 - 2036
151 - 200
101 - 150
51 - 100
1 - 50
0

Physicians per
100,000 population, 1990

Source: American
Medical Association

© RM©N. DM-520500-9T-GD1- -·-1-·-1

HOSPITAL BEDS

United States
Average 556

1,000 +
601 - 1,000
401 - 600
201 - 400
1 - 200
0

Beds per 100,000
population, 1985

Source: American
Hospital Association

© RM©N. DM-520500-9U-GD1- -·-1-·-1

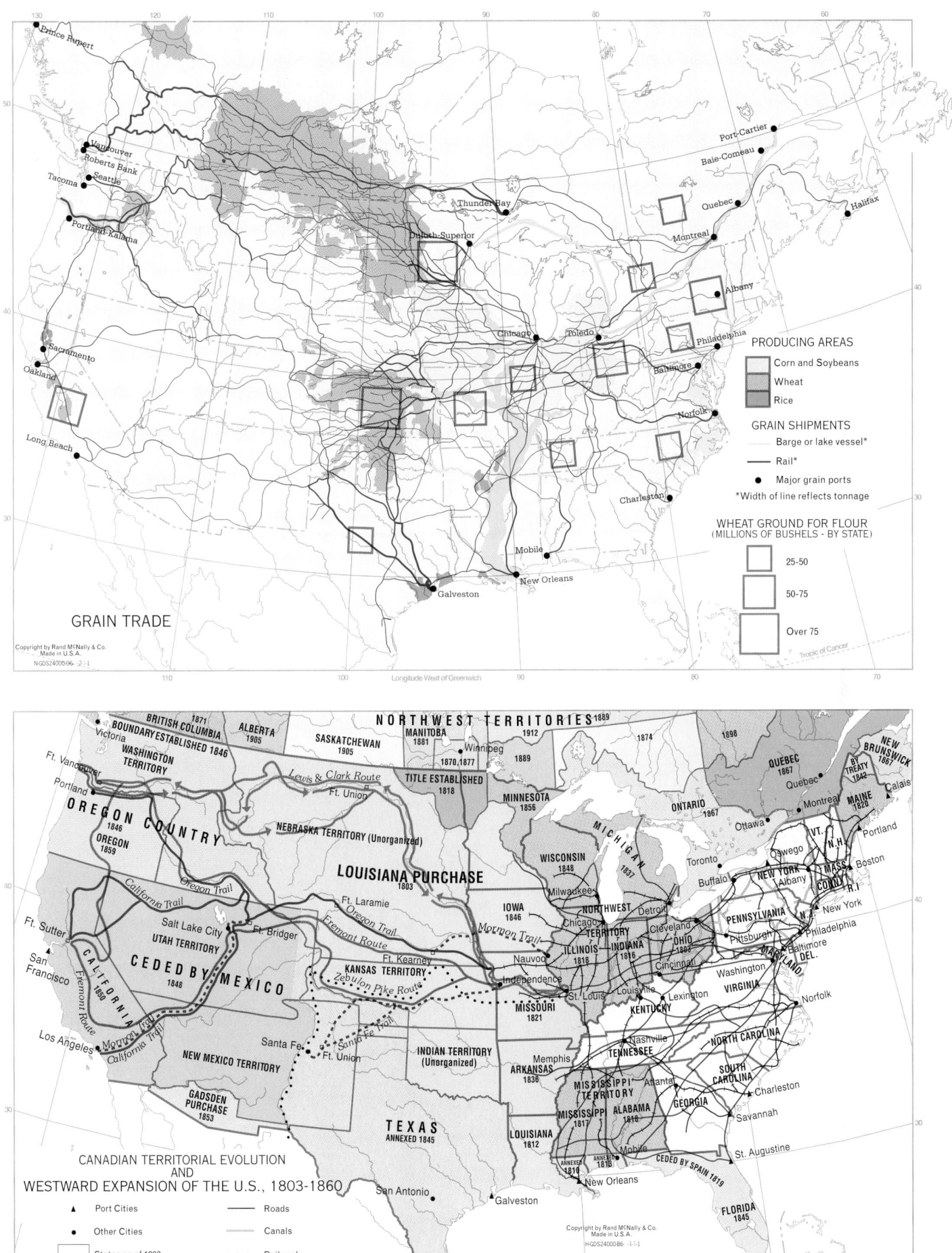

GRAIN TRADE

PRODUCING AREAS

Corn and Soybeans
Wheat
Rice

GRAIN SHIPMENTS

Barge or lake vessel*
Rail*
Major grain ports
*Width of line reflects tonnage

WHEAT GROUND FOR FLOUR
(MILLIONS OF BUSHELS - BY STATE)

25-50
50-75
Over 75

Copyright by Rand McNally & Co.
Made in U.S.A.
NGDS24000-06- -2-l-1

Longitude West of Greenwich

Tropic of Cancer

CANADIAN TERRITORIAL EVOLUTION
AND
WESTWARD EXPANSION OF THE U.S., 1803-1860

Port Cities   Roads
Other Cities   Canals
States as of 1803   Railroads

Copyright by Rand McNally & Co.
Made in U.S.A.
HGDS24000-86- -1-l-1

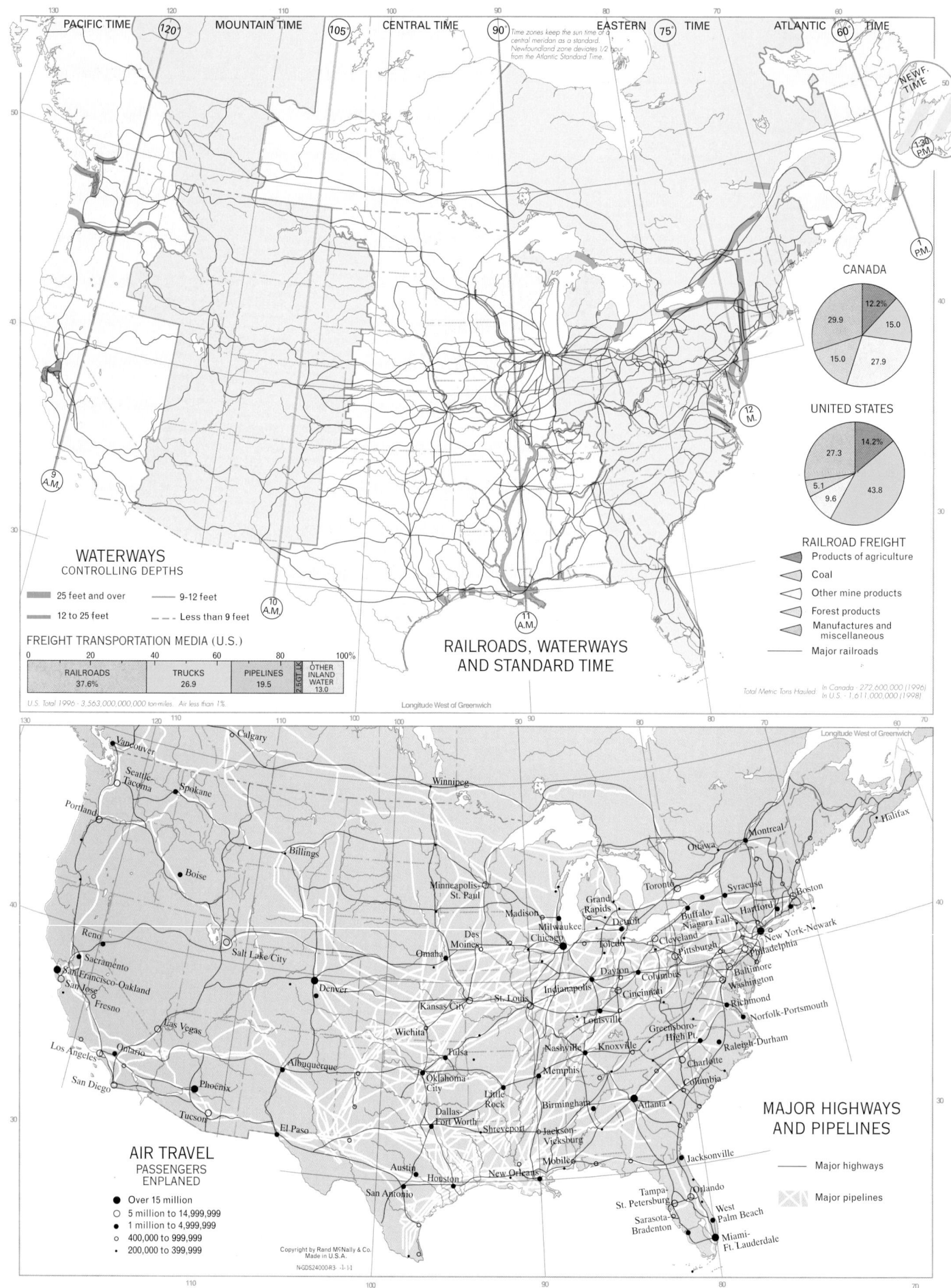

Time zones keep the sun time of a
central meridan as a standard.
Newfoundland zone deviates 1/2 hour
from the Atlantic Standard Time.

CANADA

12.2%
29.9   15.0
15.0   27.9

UNITED STATES

14.2%
27.3   43.8
5.1
9.6

RAILROAD FREIGHT
Products of agriculture
Coal
Other mine products
Forest products
Manufactures and
miscellaneous
— Major railroads

WATERWAYS
CONTROLLING DEPTHS

— 25 feet and over   — 9-12 feet
— 12 to 25 feet   --- Less than 9 feet

FREIGHT TRANSPORTATION MEDIA (U.S.)

0   20   40   60   80   100%
| RAILROADS | TRUCKS | PIPELINES | OTHER INLAND WATER |
| 37.6% | 26.9 | 19.5 | 13.0 |

2.5 GT. LK.

U.S. Total 1996 - 3,563,000,000,000 ton-miles. Air less than 1%

RAILROADS, WATERWAYS
AND STANDARD TIME

Longitude West of Greenwich

Total Metric Tons Hauled In Canada - 272,600,000 (1996)
In U.S. - 1,611,000,000 (1998)

Vancouver   Calgary
Seattle-
Tacoma   Spokane   Winnipeg
Portland
Billings   Halifax
Boise   Montreal
Minneapolis-   Ottawa
St. Paul   Grand   Toronto   Syracuse
Reno   Madison Rapids Detroit   Buffalo-   Boston
Salt Lake City   Milwaukee   Niagara Falls Hartford
Sacramento   Des Chicago Toledo Cleveland   New York-Newark
San Francisco-Oakland   Moines   Pittsburgh Philadelphia
San Jose   Denver   Omaha   Dayton Columbus   Baltimore
Fresno   St. Louis Indianapolis Cincinnati   Washington
Las Vegas   Kansas City   Richmond
Los Angeles Ontario   Wichita   Louisville   Norfolk-Portsmouth
San Diego   Tulsa   Nashville Knoxville Greensboro-   Raleigh-Durham
Phoenix   Albuquerque   Memphis   High Pt.
Tucson   Oklahoma Little   Charlotte
City   Rock Birmingham   Columbia
El Paso   Dallas-   Atlanta
Ft. Worth Shreveport Jackson-
Vicksburg
Austin   Houston   New Orleans   Jacksonville
San Antonio   Mobile
Tampa-   Orlando
St. Petersburg West
Sarasota-   Palm Beach
Bradenton   Miami-
Ft. Lauderdale

AIR TRAVEL
PASSENGERS
ENPLANED

● Over 15 million
○ 5 million to 14,999,999
• 1 million to 4,999,999
○ 400,000 to 999,999
· 200,000 to 399,999

MAJOR HIGHWAYS
AND PIPELINES

— Major highways
⊠ Major pipelines

Longitude West of Greenwich

Copyright by Rand McNally & Co.
Made in U.S.A.

N-GDS24000-R3 -1-1-1

Scale 1:29,000,000; One inch to 457 miles. ALBERS CONIC PROJECTION

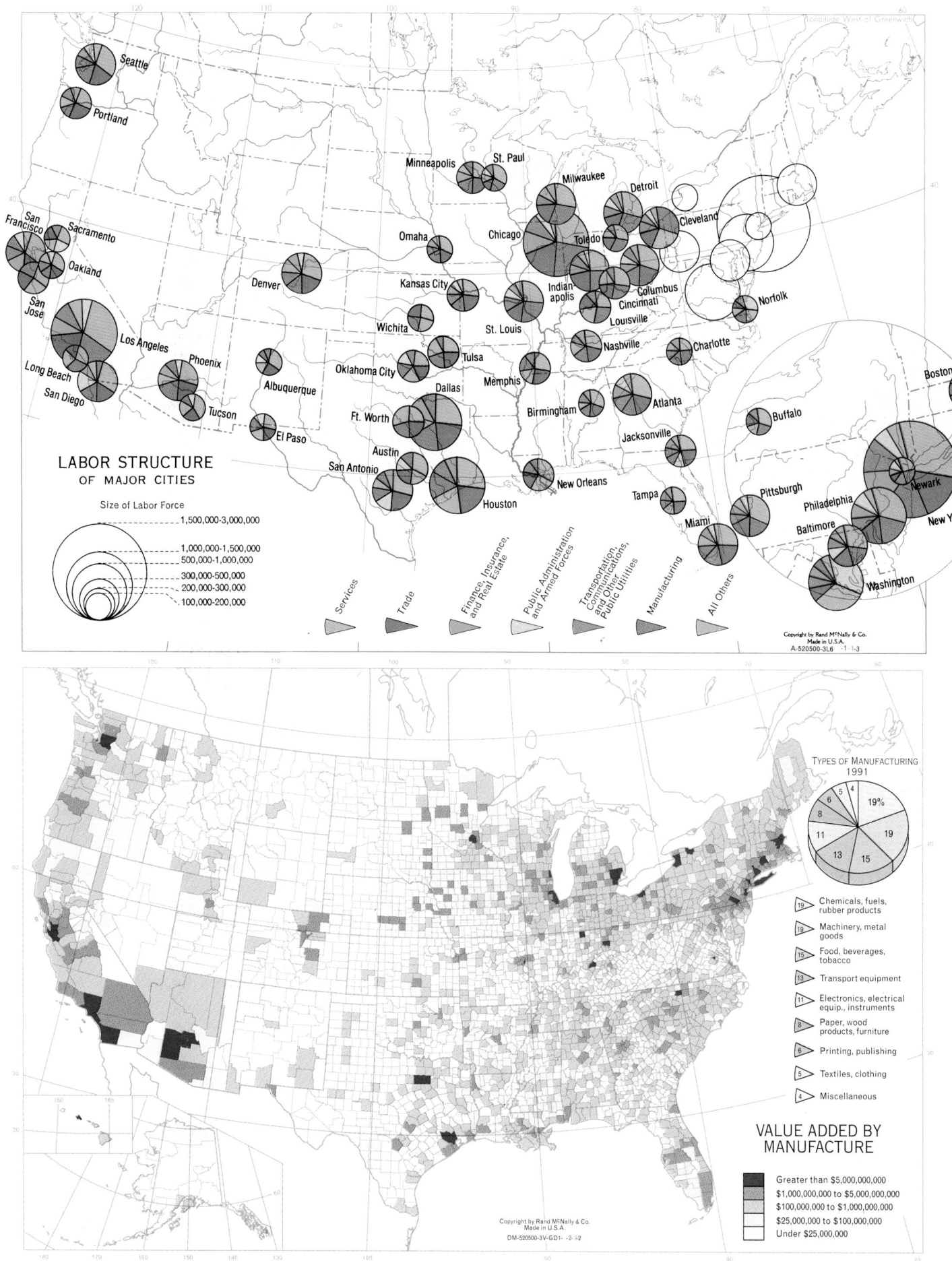

LABOR STRUCTURE
OF MAJOR CITIES

Size of Labor Force

1,500,000-3,000,000

1,000,000-1,500,000
500,000-1,000,000
300,000-500,000
200,000-300,000
100,000-200,000

Services

Trade

Finance, Insurance, and Real Estate

Public Administration and Armed Forces

Transportation, Communications, and Other Public Utilities

Manufacturing

All Others

Copyright by Rand McNally & Co.
Made in U.S.A.
A-520500-3L6 -1- 1-3

TYPES OF MANUFACTURING
1991

19%

19

15

13

11

8

6

5

4

19 Chemicals, fuels, rubber products

19 Machinery, metal goods

15 Food, beverages, tobacco

13 Transport equipment

11 Electronics, electrical equip., instruments

8 Paper, wood products, furniture

6 Printing, publishing

5 Textiles, clothing

4 Miscellaneous

VALUE ADDED BY
MANUFACTURE

Greater than $5,000,000,000

$1,000,000,000 to $5,000,000,000

$100,000,000 to $1,000,000,000

$25,000,000 to $100,000,000

Under $25,000,000

Copyright by Rand McNally & Co.
Made in U.S.A.
DM-520500-3V-GD1- -2- 42

Scale 1:12,000,000.

One inch to 190 miles.
One centimeter to 120 kilometers.

Albers Conic Projection.

0   50 100   200   300   400 Miles

0 50 100 150 200   300   400   500   600 Kilometers

FEDERAL LANDS AND INTERSTATE HIGHWAYS

Selected Highways and Federal Lands

National Parks, Monuments, Seashores, Preserves, Lakeshores, Recreation Areas

National Forests

National Grasslands

National Wildlife Refuges

Military Installations

Indian Reservations

Interstate Highways

Other Roads

U.S. Interstate Highways

Trans-Canada Highway

Other Canadian Roads

Copyright by Rand McNally & Co.
Made in U.S.A.

N-GDS24000-M5- -5-I-5

GREENLAND
North Pole
McKinley Sea
JAN MAYEN (Nor.)
GREENLAND SEA
SHETLAND IS. (Br.)
North Sea
UNITED KINGDOM
FAROE IS. (Den.)
IRELAND

ASIA
RUSSIA
POLUOSTROV KAMCHATKA
Anadyrskiy Zaliv
INTERNATIONAL DATE LINE
BERING SEA
WRANGELA
ARCTIC OCEAN
Lincoln Sea
GREENLAND (Denmark)
10,000
ICELAND
Reykjavík
Helja (Vol.) 4747

BEARING STRAIT
POINT BARROW
QUEEN ELIZABETH ISLANDS
Thule
KAP YORK
Baffin Bay
DISKO
Godhavn
Denmark Strait

PRIBILOF ISLANDS
ST. LAWRENCE
Nome
BROOKS RANGE
ALASKA
Fairbanks
Mt. McKinley 20,320
North Magnetic Pole
Mount Melville Sound
Gjoa Haven (Resolute)
KAP FARVEL
Angmagssalik
Godthåb
Julianehåb

ALEUTIAN ISLANDS
ALEUTIAN TROUGH
KODIAK ISLAND
Gulf of Alaska
ALASKA RANGE
Anchorage
Mt. Logan 19,550 Whitehorse
Inuvik
KLONDIKE REGION
Dawson
BANKS ISLAND
VICTORIA ISLAND
BOOTHIA PEN.
Great Bear Lake
Arctic Circle
Ft. Simpson
BAFFIN ISLAND
Foxe Basin
HUDSON STRAIT
CAPE CHIDLEY
UNGAVA BAY
Davis Strait
ATLANTIC OCEAN

Sitka
Juneau
QUEEN CHARLOTTE ISLANDS
Prince Rupert
COAST MOUNTAINS
Great Slave Lake
Athabasca Lake
Reindeer Lake
Churchill
HUDSON BAY
UNGAVA PEN.
LABRADOR
NEWFOUNDLAND
St. John's
C. RACE

VANCOUVER ISLAND
Vancouver
Seattle
Portland
CASCADE RANGE
Edmonton
Calgary
Nelson
CANADA
Saskatchewan
Regina
Lake Winnipeg
Winnipeg
Lake of the Woods
Lake Nipigon
LAURENTIAN HIGHLANDS
Québec
MONTRÉAL
Ottawa
Saint John
NOVA SCOTIA
CAPE BRETON ISLAND
Halifax
CAPE SABLE

Spokane
Butte
COAST RANGES
Mt. Shasta 14,162
SIERRA NEVADA
GREAT BASIN
Salt Lake City
ROCKY MOUNTAINS
GREAT PLAINS
Fargo
Duluth
Minneapolis
St. Paul
L. Superior
L. Michigan
L. Huron
Toronto
DETROIT
Cleveland
Buffalo
APPALACHIAN MTS.
Boston
CAPE COD
NEW YORK
PHILADELPHIA

San Francisco
Oakland
Pikes Peak 14,110
Mt. Whitney 14,494
Denver
Milwaukee
Omaha
CHICAGO
Kansas City
St. Louis
Cincinnati
Pittsburgh
Baltimore
Washington
Richmond
Chesapeake Bay
Norfolk
CAPE HATTERAS
BERMUDA (Br.)

LOS ANGELES
UNITED STATES
Wichita
Memphis
Birmingham
Atlanta
Savannah
Jacksonville
ATLANTIC OCEAN

El Paso
Fort Worth
Dallas
San Antonio
Houston
New Orleans
Mobile
Galveston
Florida
Miami

PACIFIC OCEAN

GUADALUPE (Mex.)
BAJA CALIFORNIA
Tropic of Cancer
CABO SAN LUCAS
Golfo de California
SIERRA MADRE OCCIDENTAL
MEXICO
SIERRA MADRE ORIENTAL
Tampico
Bahía de Campeche
GULF OF MEXICO
CAPE SABLE
Straits of Florida
HAVANA
CUBA
BAHAMAS
SAN SALVADOR
Tropic of Cancer
San Juan
PUERTO RICO (U.S.A.)
PUERTO RICO TRENCH
GUADELOUPE (Fr.)

ISLAS REVILLAGIGEDO (Mex.)
Guadalajara
MEXICO CITY
Popocatépetl 17,887
Pico de Orizaba 18,406 (Vol.)
Veracruz
YUCATÁN PEN.
Yucatán Channel
Golfo de Honduras
BELIZE
GUATEMALA
HONDURAS
EL SALVADOR
NICARAGUA
Windward Passage
HAITI
DOM. REP.
JAMAICA
Kingston
Port-au-Prince
Santo Domingo
WEST INDIES
MARTINIQUE (Fr.)
BARBADOS
TRINIDAD AND TOBAGO

CARIBBEAN SEA
PTA. DE GALLINAS
Caracas
Río Orinoco
CENTRAL AMERICA
COSTA RICA
PANAMA
Istmo de Panamá
G. de Panamá
SOUTH AMERICA
Bogotá

ISLA DEL COCO (Costa Rica)
ISLA DE MALPELO (Colombia)
Equator
Quito
Río Negro

40,000 SQ MI AREA

0   300   600
Miles

A-520000-26 -5-5-18
COPYRIGHT BY
RAND McNALLY & COMPANY
MADE IN U.S.A.

Longitude West 100° of Greenwich

0   200   400   600   800   1000 Miles
0   400   800   1200   1600 Kilometers

Scale 1:40 000 000; one inch to 630 miles. Lambert's Azimuthal Equal Area Projection
Elevations and depressions are given in feet

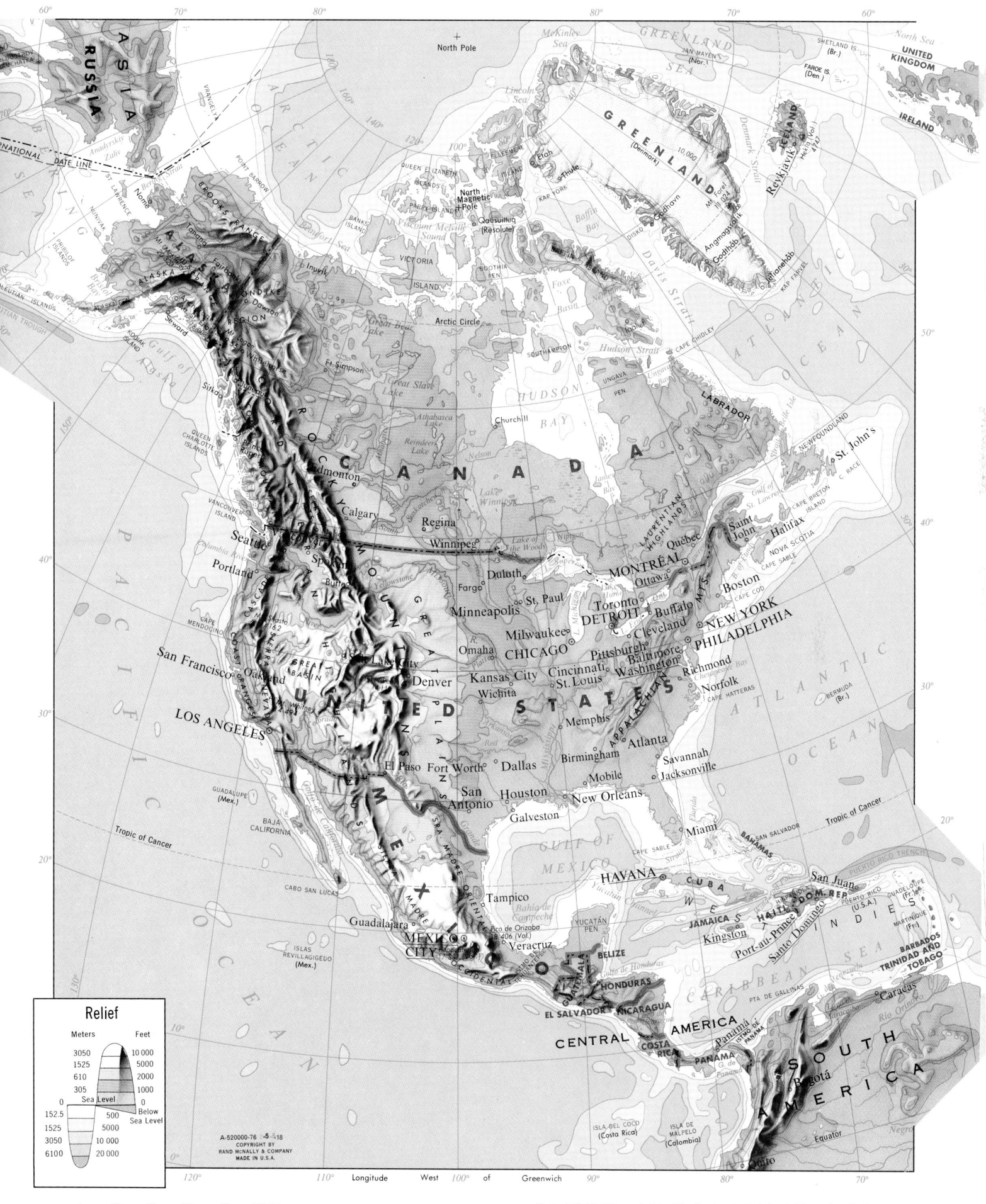

A-520000-76 -5- -18
COPYRIGHT BY
RAND McNALLY & COMPANY
MADE IN U.S.A.

Scale 1:40 000 000; one inch to 630 miles. Lambert's Azimuthal Equal Area Projection
Elevations and depressions are given in feet

ALASKA
U.S.A.
CANADA

KLONDIKE REGION

Mt. Logan
19 551
Mt. St. Elias 18 008
KLUANE NAT'L PARK

OGILVIE MTS.

RICHARDSON MTS.

IVVAVIK NAT'L PARK

VUNTUT NAT'L PARK

Old Crow

CAPE BATHURST

Tuktoyaktuk

Inuvik

Aklavik
Ft. McPherson

MELVILLE HILLS

TUKTUT NOGAIT NAT'L PARK

VICTORIA ISLAND

Kalaktutiak (Cambridge Bay)

KING WILLIAM I.

BOOTHIA PENINSULA

Ft. Good Hope

Kugluktuk (Coppermine)

WOLLASTON PEN.

Amundsen Gulf

Prince Albert Sound

C. BARING

Dolphin and Union Str.

Dease Strait

KENT PEN.

Coronation Gulf

Queen Maud Gulf

Y U K O N

Dawson

Mayo

MACKENZIE MTS.

PELLY MTS.

Whitehorse

Carcross

Frances

NAHANNI NAT'L PARK

Norman Wells

FRANKLIN MTS.

Arctic Circle

Great Bear Lake

N O R T H W E S T

T E R R I T O R I E S

N U N

PEACOCK HILLS

Contwoyto

Garry

Pelly

Back

Bathurst Inlet

Qamani'tuaq (Baker Lake)

Chesterfield Inlet

Iglulligaarjuk (Chesterfield Inlet)

Rankin Inlet

MacKay

Clinton-Colden

Dubawnt

Yathkyed

Kaskawulsh

Kluane

Yukon

Pelly

Teslin

HORN PLATEAU

Ft. Simpson

Yellowknife

Ft. Providence

Great Slave Lake

Lac la Martre

Nonacho

Aylmer

Nueltin

Thanne

Watson Lake

Liard

CAMERON HILLS

STIKINE RANGES

Telegraph Creek

Ft. Nelson

Churchill Peak 10 500

Fort Nelson

Ft. Liard

Hay River

Ft. Resolution

Ft. Smith

WOOD BUFFALO NAT'L PARK

CARIBOU MTS.

Ft. Fitzgerald

Uranium City

Selwyn

Churchill

Seal

R O C K Y

Williston Lake

Ft. St. John

Dawson Creek

Hazelton

Smithers

Terrace

Kitimat

Prince Rupert

CLEAR HILLS

Ft. Vermilion

Ft. Chipewyan

BUFFALO HEAD HILLS

BIRCH MTS.

Fort McMurray

Claire

Athabasca

Athabasca

Cree

Wollaston

Reindeer

Southern Indian

Lynn Lake

WAPUSK NAT'L PARK

C O A S T

B R I T I S H

Peace River

McLennan

High Prairie

Grande Prairie

Grouard Mission

CHEECHAM HILLS

Peter Pond Lake

Frobisher

Granville

Thompson

Sipiwesk

M A N I T O B

M O U N T A I N S

C O L U M B I A

SWAN HILLS

Smith

Athabasca

Lac La Biche

St. Paul

Meadow Lake

St. Walbur

Big River

PRINCE ALBERT NAT'L PARK

Lac la Ronge

Flin Flon

The Pas

Norway House

Cariboo

Vanderhoof

Prince George

Burns Lake

Ft. St. James

McBride

Mt. Robson 12 972

Whitecourt

Edson

Ft. Saskatchewan

Edmonton

JASPER NAT'L PARK

Mountain Park

Wetaskiwin

Vegreville

Vermilion

Lloydminster

North Battleford

Melfort

Tisdale

Prince Albert

Nipawin

Norway House

Lake Winnipeg

Berens River

Quesnel

Wells

Mt. Waddington 13 163

Blue River

GLACIER NAT'L PARK

MT. REVELSTOKE NAT'L PARK

Red Deer

Camrose

Ponoka

Lacombe

Innisfail

Wilkie

Biggar

Saskatoon

Humboldt

Big Quill

Wynyard

Canora

Winnipegosis

Dauphin

DUCK MTN.

RIDING MOUNTAIN NAT'L PARK

Minnedosa

Ocean Falls

Port Alice

Campbell River

Courtenay

Powell River

Clinton

Lillooet

Kamloops

BANFF NAT'L PARK

YOHO NAT'L PARK

KOOTENAY NAT'L PARK

REVELSTOKE NAT'L PARK

SELKIRK MTS.

Banff

Olds

Drumheller

Hanna

Rosetown

Kindersley

Outlook

Watrous

Yorkton

Kamsack

Melville

Russell

Gypsumville

VANCOUVER ISLAND

NOOTKA

Nanaimo

Port Alberni

Duncan

Vancouver

North Vancouver

Burnaby

Merritt

Vernon

Kelowna

Princeton

Penticton

Kimberley

Cranbrook

Nelson

Creston

Fernie

High River

Bassano

Claresholm

Red Deer

Medicine Hat

Swift Current

Diefenbaker

Moose Jaw

Indian Head

Qu'Appelle

Minnedosa

Neepawa

Portage la Prairie

Selkirk

Brandon

Victoria

Hope

Chilliwack

Oliver

Grand Forks

Rossland

Trail

Macleod

Cardston

Magrath

Taber

Lethbridge

Maple Creek

Gravelbourg

Assiniboia

Weyburn

Shaunavon

Estevan

Virden

Boissevain

Carman

Morden

Morris

Steinbach

Emerson

WATERTON GLACIER INT. PEACE PARK

CANADA

U.S.A.

Govenlock

Milk

Souris

Williston

Minot

Grand Forks

Fargo

SEATTLE

Tacoma

Olympia

Spokane

Moscow

Great Falls

Helena

Butte

M O N T A N A

LITTLE BELT MTS.

BIG BELT MTS.

NORTH DAKOTA

Bismarck

Valley City

WASHINGTON

Mt. Rainier 14 410

Mt. Adams 12 276

Yakima

Walla Walla

Moscow

BITTERROOT RANGE

Missouri

Vancouver

Portland

Salem

Eugene

Mt. Hood 11 239

Columbia

Pendleton

Baker

O R E G O N

I D A H O

Salmon

Yellowstone

Great Falls

Granite Peak 12 799

Billings

WYO.

SOUTH DAKOTA

Continued on pages 104-105

Longitude West of Greenwich

Scale 1: 12 000 000; one inch to 190 miles. Conic Projection

Elevations and depressions are given in feet

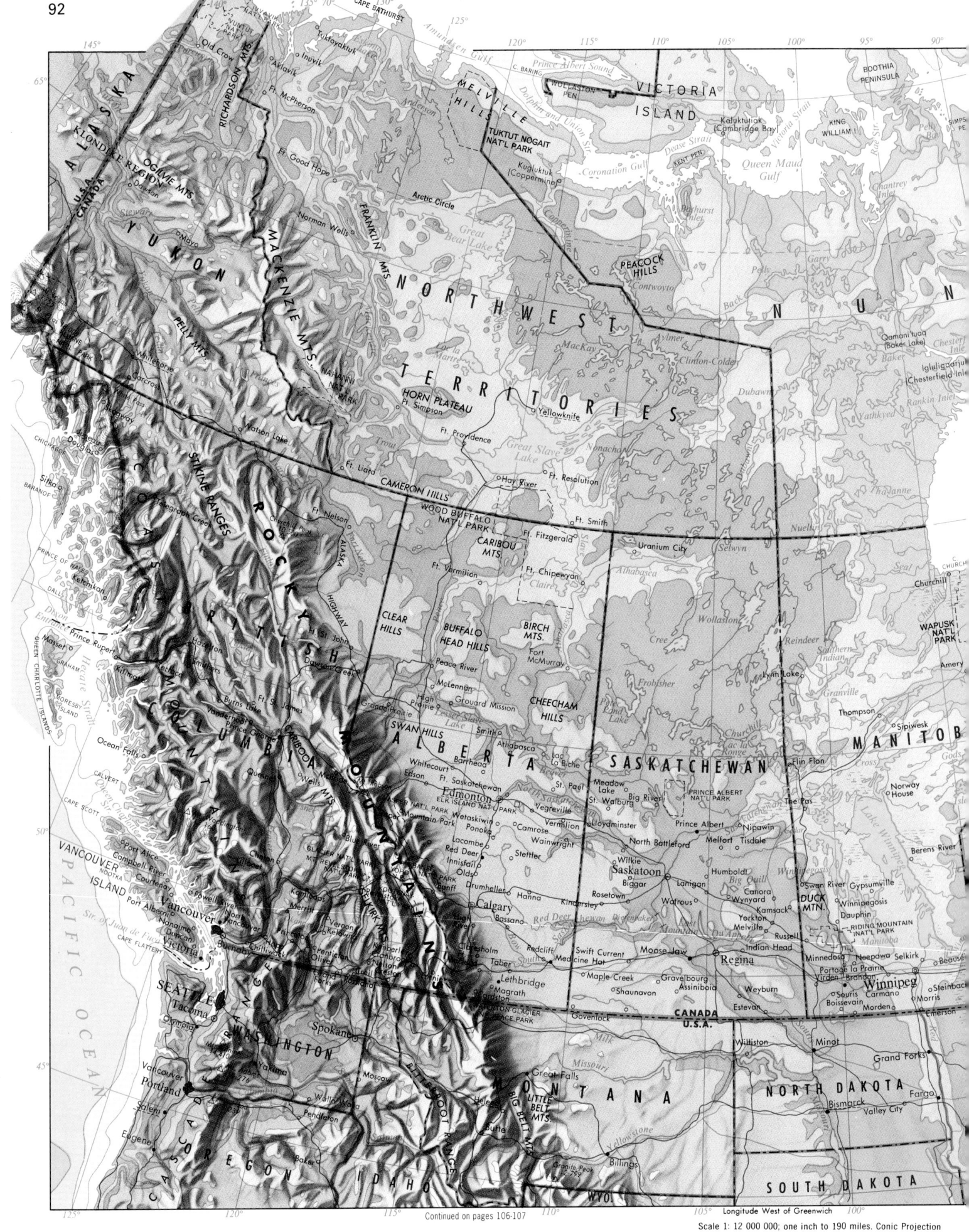

Continued on pages 106-107

Scale 1: 12 000 000; one inch to 190 miles. Conic Projection

Elevations and depressions are given in feet

Longitude West of Greenwich

Relief

Meters		Feet
3050		10 000
1525		5000
610		2000
305		1000
152.5		500
0	Sea Level	0
152.5		500
1525		5000

A-520220-76   6-49
COPYRIGHT BY
RAND McNALLY & COMPANY
MADE IN U.S.A.

Continued on pages 114-115   Longitude West of Greenwich

Scale 1:4 000 000; one inch to 64 miles. Conic Projection
Elevations and depressions are given in feet.

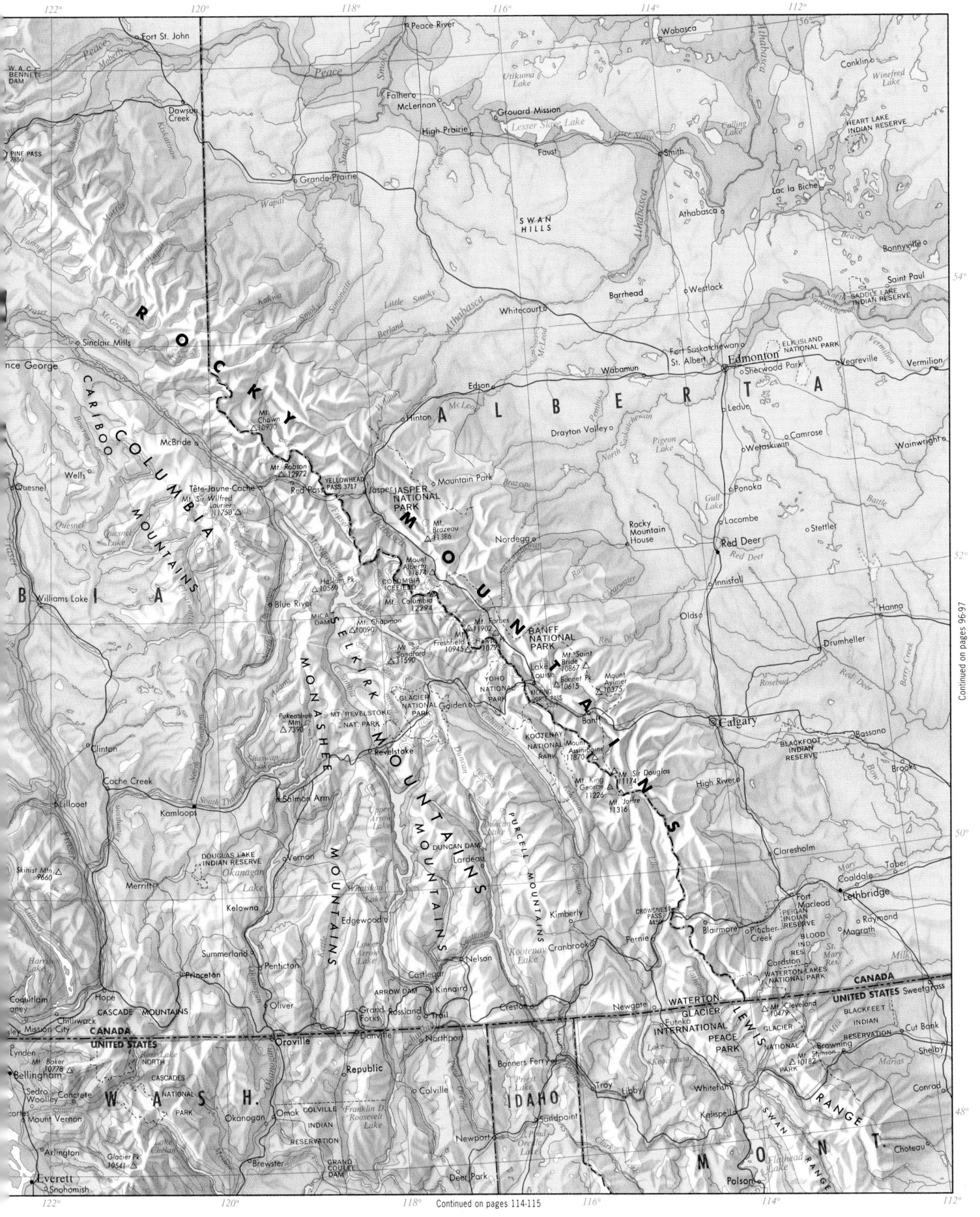

Continued on pages 96-97

Continued on pages 114-115

0 10 20 30 40 50 60 70 80 90 100 110 120 Miles

0 20 40 60 80 100 120 140 160 180 200 Kilometers

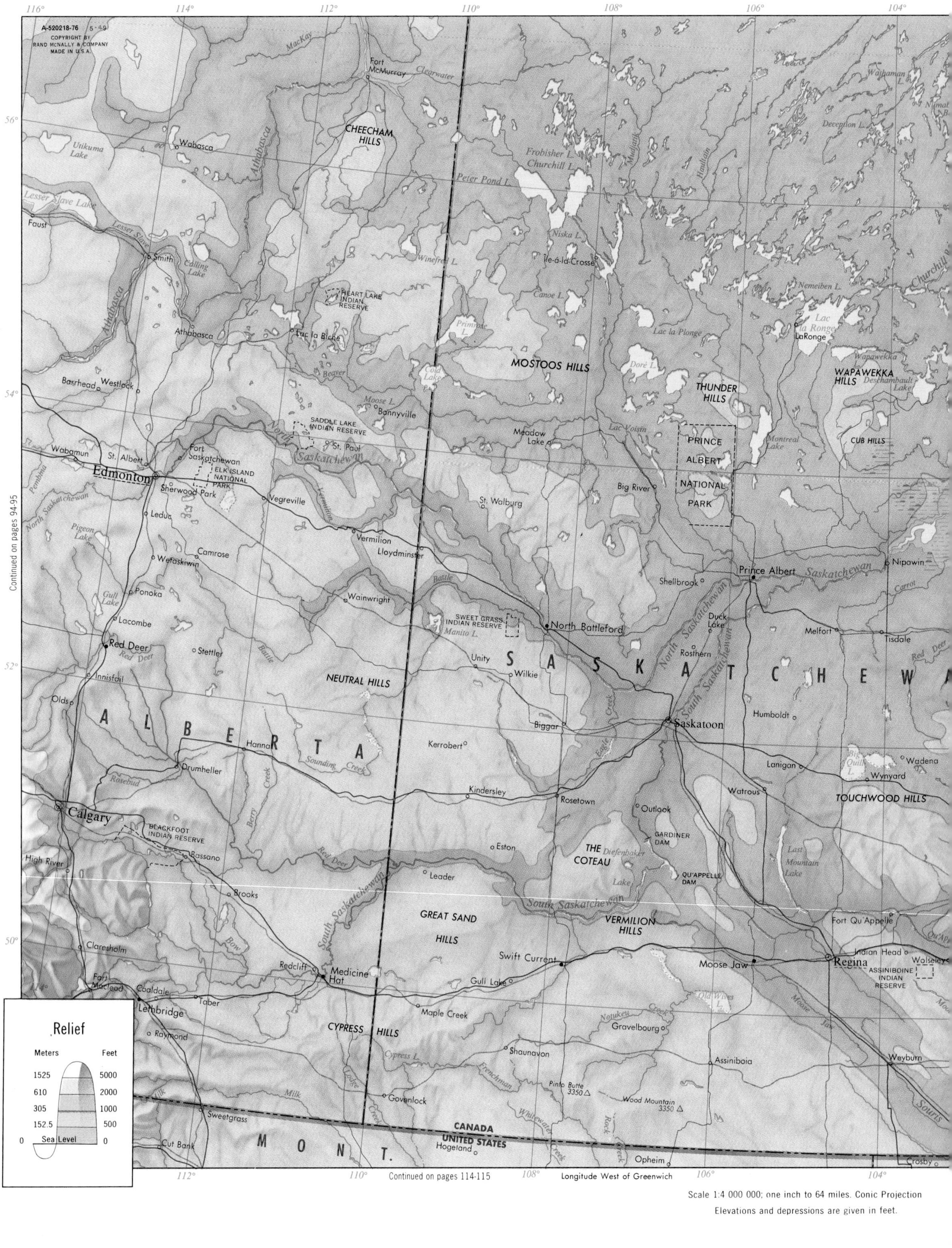

A-520218-76 5-49
COPYRIGHT BY
RAND McNALLY & COMPANY
MADE IN U.S.A.

116°   114°   112°   110°   108°   106°   104°

56°

MacKay

Fort
McMurray   Clearwater

CHEECHAM
HILLS

Utikuma
Lake

Wabasca

Peter Pond L.

Frobisher L.
Churchill L.

Decension L.

Lesser Slave Lake

Faust

Lesser Slave

Winefred L.

Niska L.

Île-à-la-Crosse

Nemeiben L.

Smith
Calling
Lake

Athabasca

HEART LAKE
INDIAN
RESERVE

Canoe L.

Lac la Plonge

Doré L.

Lac
la Ronge
LaRonge

Wapawekka

54°

Barrhead   Westlock

Lac la Biche

Primose
L.

MOSTOOS HILLS

WAPAWEKKA
HILLS

Deschambault
Lake

Beaver

Cold
Lake

Moose L.

Bonnyville

THUNDER
HILLS

CUB HILLS

Wabamun   St. Albert

North

SADDLE LAKE
INDIAN RESERVE

Meadow
Lake

Lac Voisin

PRINCE

Montreal
Lake

Pembina

Fort
Saskatchewan
ELK ISLAND
NATIONAL
PARK

St. Paul

Saskatchewan

ALBERT

Edmonton
Sherwood Park

Vegreville

Big River

NATIONAL

Ledue

St. Walburg

PARK

Pigeon
Lake

Camrose

Vermilion
Lloydminster

Wetaskiwin

Battle

Shellbrook

Prince Albert   Saskatchewan   Nipawin

Gull
Lake   Ponoka

Wainwright

North

Duck
Lake

52°

Lacombe

SWEET GRASS
INDIAN RESERVE

Rosthern

Melfort   Tisdale

Red Deer

Stettler

Manito L.

North Battleford

Saskatchewan

Red Deer

Innisfail

Battle

Unity

Wilkie

SASKATCHEW

Humboldt

Olds

NEUTRAL HILLS

Creek

Saskatoon

Big
Quill L.   Wadena

ALBERTA

Hanna

Biggar

South

Wynyard

Drumheller

Sounding   Creek

Kerrobert

Lanigan

Watrous

TOUCHWOOD HILLS

Rosebud

Berry   Creek

Kindersley

Rosetown

Eagle

Calgary

BLACKFOOT
INDIAN RESERVE

Bassano

Outlook

GARDINER
DAM

Last
Mountain
Lake

High River

Eston

THE
COTEAU

Diefenbaker

QU'APPELLE
DAM

Bow

Red Deer

Leader

Lake

Brooks

South   Saskatchewan

VERMILION
HILLS

Fort Qu'Appelle

50°

Claresholm

South Saskatchewan

GREAT SAND

HILLS

Swift Current

Moose Jaw

Regina

Indian Head   Walseley

Redcliff   Medicine
Hat

Gull Lake

ASSINIBOINE
INDIAN
RESERVE

Fort
Macleod

Coaldale

Taber

Maple Creek

Notukeu

Old Wives

Moose

Lethbridge

CYPRESS HILLS

Gravelbourg

Assiniboia

Weyburn

Raymond

Cypress L.

Shaunavon

Pinto Butte
3350

Wood Mountain
3350

Milk

Frenchman

Sweetgrass

Govenlock

Whitemud

Rock

Souris

CANADA
UNITED STATES

Cut Bank

MONT.

Hogeland

Opheim   Crosby

Continued on pages 114-115   Longitude West of Greenwich

Relief

Meters		Feet
1525		5000
610		2000
305		1000
152.5		500
0	Sea Level	0

Continued on pages 94-95

Scale 1:4 000 000; one inch to 64 miles. Conic Projection
Elevations and depressions are given in feet.

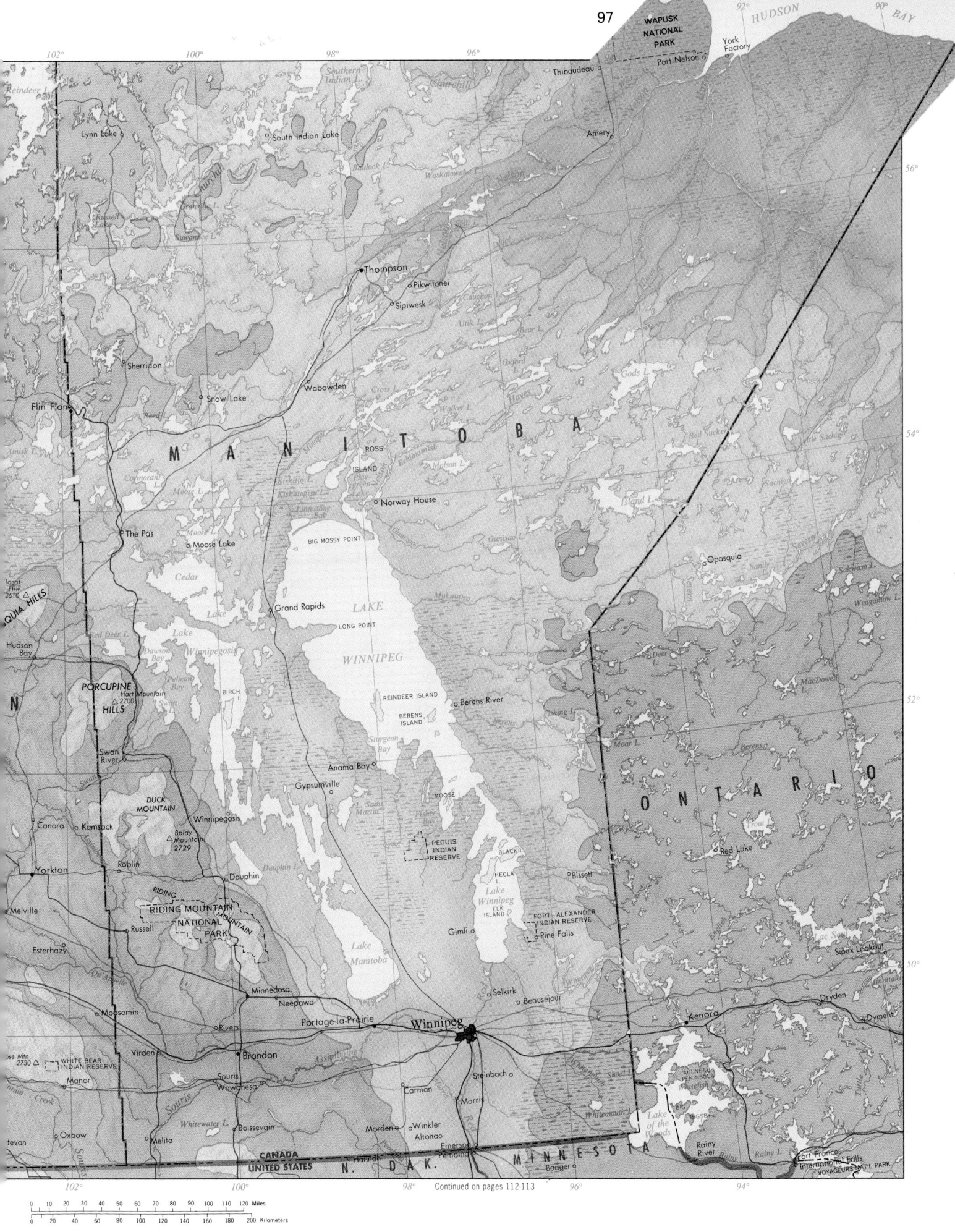

WAPUSK
NATIONAL
PARK

HUDSON BAY

York
Factory

Thibaudeau
Port Nelson

Amery

Southern
Indian L.

Churchill

Lynn Lake
South Indian Lake

Reindeer L.

Baldock L.

Waskaiowaka

Nelson

56°

Russell
Lake

Granville L.

Sisiwance L.

Sherridon

Thompson
Pikwitonei

Sipiwesk

Cauchon L.

Bear L.

Oxford
L.

Gods L.

Flin Flon

Snow Lake

Wabowden

Cross L.

Walker L.

Echimamish

Hayes

Uuk L.

Little Sachigo

Red Sucker
L.

Sachigo

M A N I T O B A

54°

Amisk L.

Cormorant L.

Moose L.

Minago

ROSS
ISLAND

Molson L.

Island L.

Idout
Hill
2610

The Pas

Moose Lake

Pine
Creek

Limestone
Bay

Norway House

Opasquia

Sandy

Sachigo L.

Salwaso L.

QUIA HILLS

Cedar

Lake

BIG MOSSY POINT

Guneau

Gunisao L.

Mukutawa

Weagamow L.

Hudson
Bay

Red Deer L.

Dawson
Bay

Lake

Grand Rapids

LAKE

LONG POINT

WINNIPEG

MacDowell
L.

52°

PORCUPINE

Hart Mountain
2700

HILLS

Swan

Pelican
Bay

BIRCH

Winnipegosis

REINDEER ISLAND

BERENS
ISLAND

Berens River

Berens

Deer
L.

Fishing L.

Trout

N

Swan
River

Sturgeon
Bay

Moar L.

Berens R.

Canora

Kamsack

DUCK
MOUNTAIN

Winnipegosis

Baldy
Mountain
2729

L. Saint
Martin

MOOSE I.

Fisher
Bay

Red Lake

O N T A R I O

Yorkton

Roblin

Dauphin

Gypsumville

Dauphin L.

PEGUIS
INDIAN
RESERVE

BLACK I.

HECLA
I.

Bissett

Mac Sec

Melville

RIDING
RIDING MOUNTAIN

MOUNTAIN

NATIONAL
PARK

Russell

Lake
Manitoba

Lake
Winnipeg
ELK
ISLAND

FORT ALEXANDER
INDIAN RESERVE

Pine Falls

Sioux Lookout

50°

Esterhazy

Minnedosa

Neepawa

Gimli

Selkirk

Beauséjour

Dryden

Qu'Appelle

Moosomin

Rivers

Portage-la-Prairie

Winnipeg

Kenora

Dymen

ose Mtn.
2730

WHITE BEAR
INDIAN RESERVE

Virden

Brandon

Assiniboine

Steinbach

Wood L.

Skool L.

Dryberry

Whitefish

Manor

Souris

Wawanesa

Carman

Morris

KGSB

Lake
of the
Woods

Rainy
River

Fort Frances

Oxbow

Melita

Boissevain

Morden

Winkler
Altona

Whitewater L.

tevan

Hannah

Pembina

Badger

Emerson

Whitemouth L.

Whitefish

Rainy L.

International Falls
VOYAGEURS NAT'L PARK

Continued on pages 112-113

CANADA
UNITED STATES

N. DAK.

MINNESOTA

102°   100°   98°   96°   94°

0 10 20 30 40 50 60 70 80 90 100 110 120 Miles

0   20   40   60   80   100   120   140   160   180   200 Kilometers

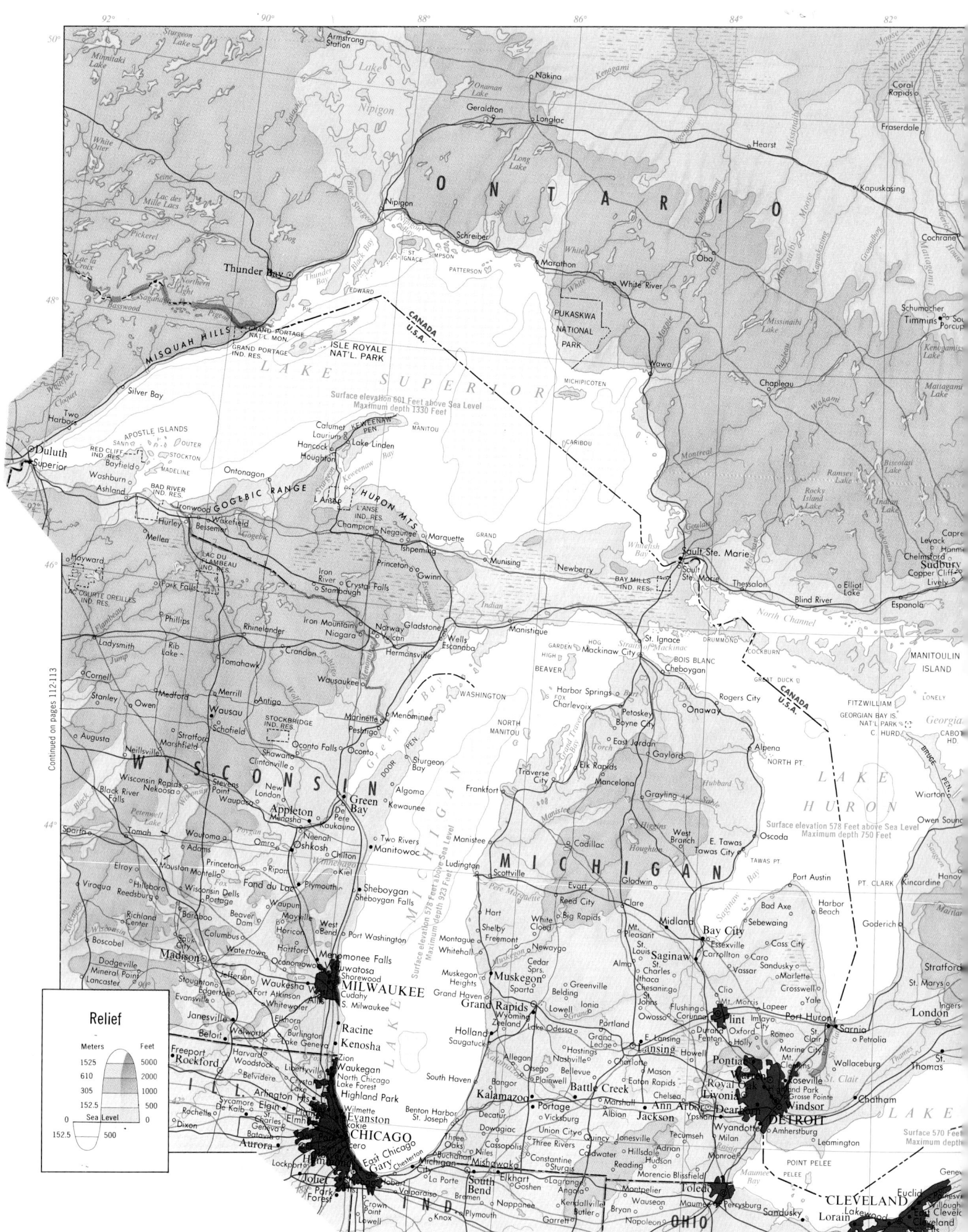

Continued on pages 112-113

Relief

Meters	Feet
1525	5000
610	2000
305	1000
152.5	500
0 Sea Level	0
152.5	500

ONTARIO

WISCONSIN

MICHIGAN

ILLINOIS

INDIANA

OHIO

LAKE SUPERIOR
Surface elevation 601 Feet above Sea Level
Maximum depth 1330 Feet

LAKE HURON
Surface elevation 578 Feet above Sea Level
Maximum depth 750 Feet

LAKE MICHIGAN
Surface elevation 578 Feet above Sea Level
Maximum depth 923 Feet

Thunder Bay

Duluth
Superior

MILWAUKEE

CHICAGO

Madison

Green Bay

Grand Rapids

Lansing

DETROIT

CLEVELAND

Toledo

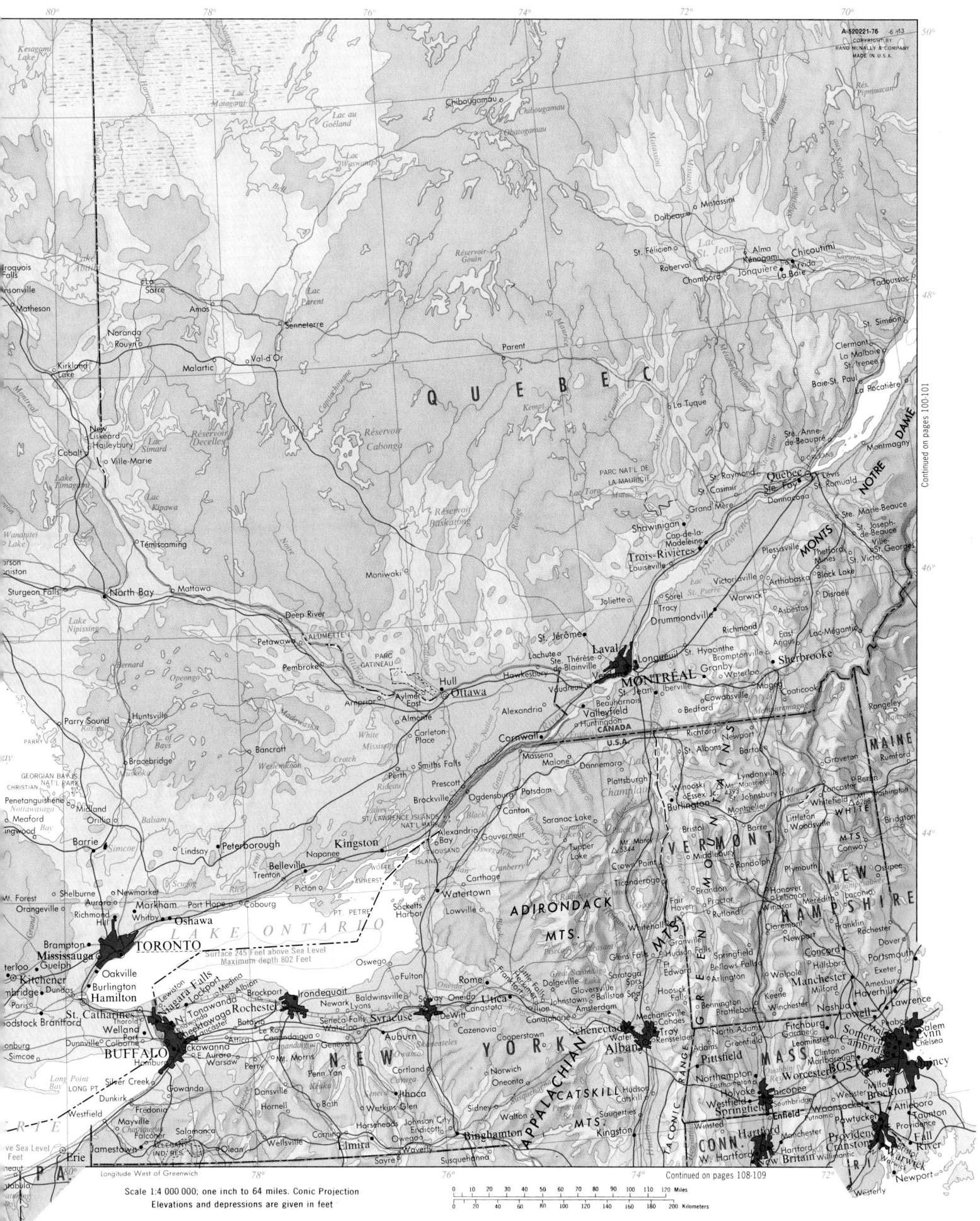

Continued on pages 100-101

Continued on pages 108-109

Scale 1:4 000 000; one inch to 64 miles. Conic Projection
Elevations and depressions are given in feet

0 10 20 30 40 50 60 70 80 90 100 110 120 Miles

0 20 40 60 80 100 120 140 160 180 200 Kilometers

Longitude West of Greenwich

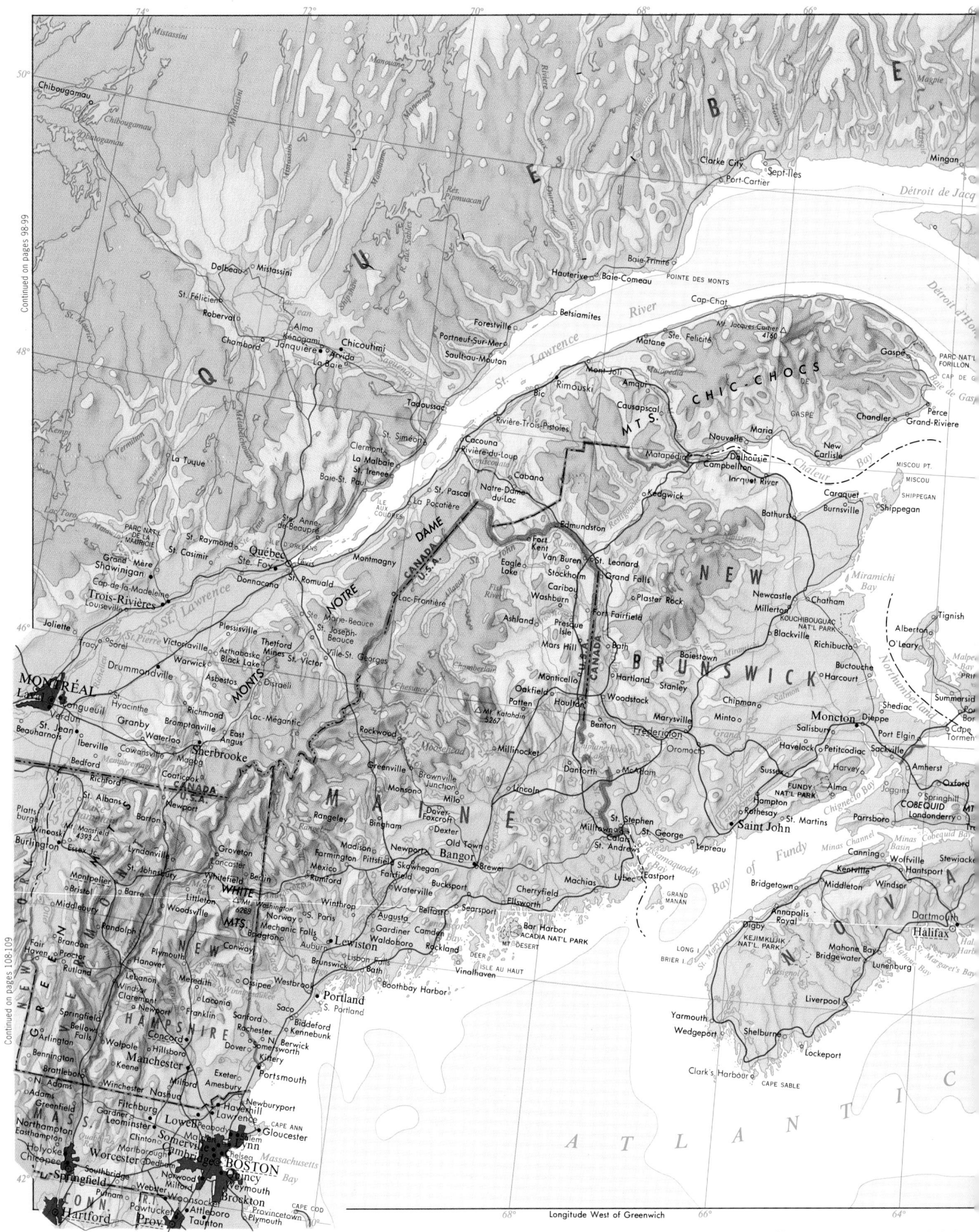

Continued on pages 98-99

Continued on pages 108-109

Longitude West of Greenwich

Scale 1:4 000 000; one inch to 64 miles. Conic Projection
Elevations and depressions are given in feet

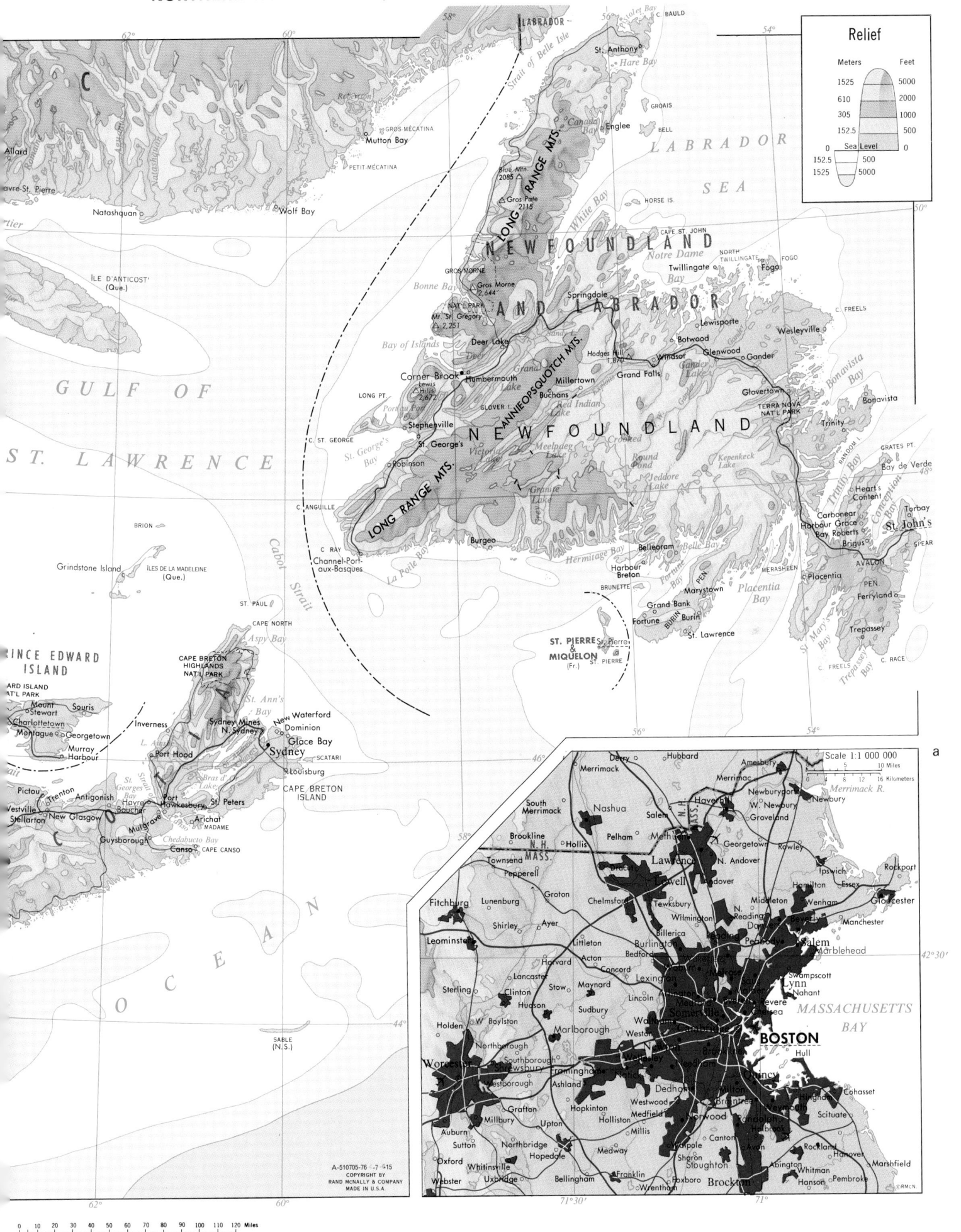

Relief

Meters		Feet
1525		5000
610		2000
305		1000
152.5		500
0	Sea Level	0
152.5		500
1525		5000

Scale 1:1 000 000

a

0 10 20 30 40 50 60 70 80 90 100 110 120 Miles
0 20 40 60 80 100 120 140 160 180 200 Kilometers

a

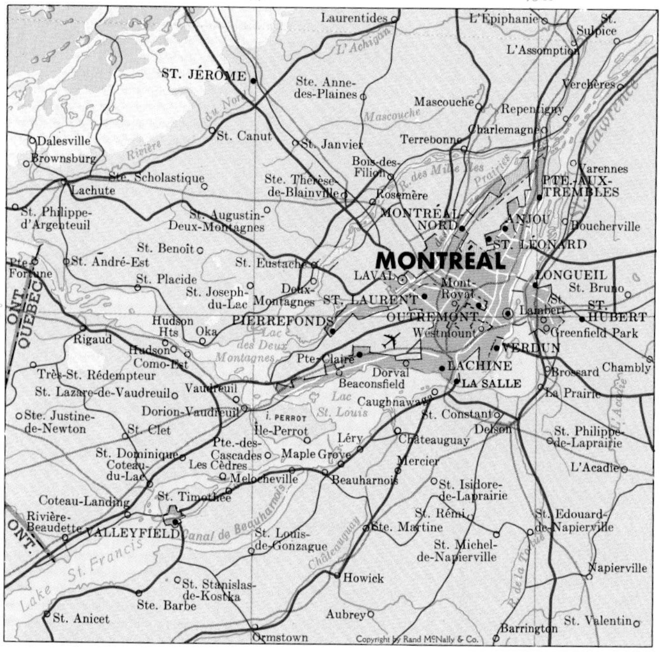

L'Épiphanie
Laurentides
L'Assomption
St. Sulpice
ST. JÉROME
Ste. Anne-des-Plaines
Mascouche
Repentigny
Charlemagne
Verchères
Dalesville
St. Canut
St. Janvier
Terrebonne
Brownsburg
Lachute
Bois-des-Filion
PTE.-AUX-TREMBLES
Ste. Scholastique
Ste. Thérèse-de-Blainville
Varennes
Boucherville
St. Augustin-Deux-Montagnes
Rosemère
St. Philippe-d'Argenteuil
St. Benoît
MONTRÉAL NORD
ANJOU
St. Eustache
Oka
LAVAL
ST. LÉONARD
Pte. Fortune
St. André-Est
St. Placide
Mont-Royal
LONGUEUIL
St. Bruno
Rigaud
Hudson Hts.
Como-Est
St. Joseph-du-Lac
Deux Montagnes
ST. LAURENT
OUTREMONT
St. Lambert
ST. HUBERT
Trés-St.-Rédempteur
St. Lazare-de-Vaudreuil
Westmount
VERDUN
Greenfield Park
Dorion-Vaudreuil
Vaudreuil
Pte. Claire
Dorval
Beaconsfield
LACHINE
Brossard
Chambly
St. Clet
Île-Perrot
Caughnawaga
LA SALLE
La Prairie
St. Justine-de-Newton
St. Dominique
Coteau-du-Lac
Les Cèdres
Pte.-des-Cascades
Maple Grove
Léry
St. Constant
Delson
St. Philippe-de-Laprairie
Coteau-Landing
St. Timothée
Mercier
Beauharnois
L'Acadie
Rivière-Beaudette
VALLEYFIELD
Melocheville
Châteauguay
St. Isidore-de-Laprairie
St. Rémi
St. Édouard-de-Napierville
St. Louis-de-Gonzague
Ste. Martine
St. Michel-de-Napierville
St. Stanislas-de-Kostka
Howick
Napierville
St. Anicet
Ste. Barbe
Aubrey
Barrington
St. Valentin
Ormstown

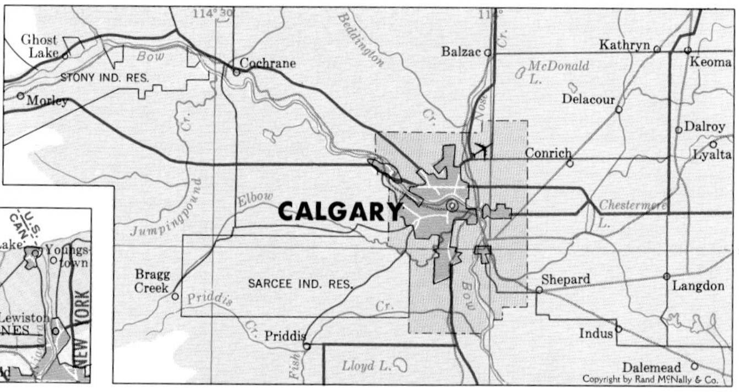

b

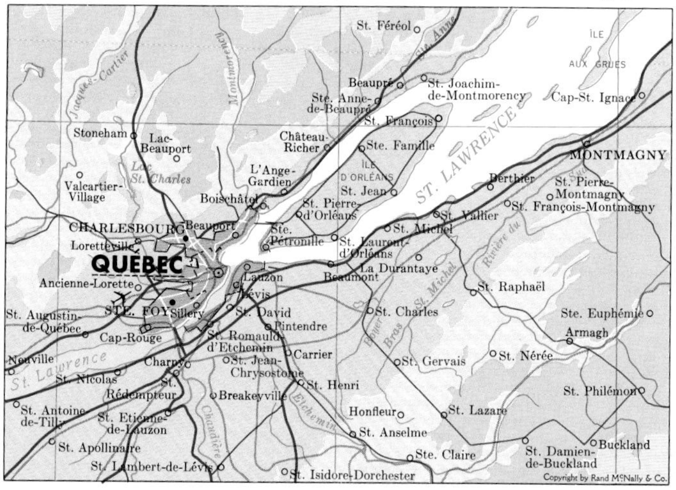

St. Féréol
Ste. Anne-de-Beaupré
St. Joachim-de-Montmorency
Cap-St. Ignac
Beaupré
ILE AUX GRUES
Stoneham
Lac-Beauport
St. François
Château-Richer
Ste. Famille
MONTMAGNY
Valcartier-Village
L'Ange-Gardien
St. Pierre
Perthier
St. Pierre-Montmagny
CHARLESBOURG
St. Jean
St. François-Montmagny
Loretteville
Ste. Pétronille
St. Michel
St. Vallier
QUÉBEC
Beauport
Ancienne-Lorette
St. Laurent d'Orléans
St. Charles
Ste. Euphémie
STE. FOY
Sillery
St. David
La Durantaye
Armagh
St. Augustin-de-Québec
Cap-Rouge
Charny
St. Romuald d'Etchemin
Beaumont
St. Raphaël
Norville
St. Jean-Chrysostome
Carrier
St. Gervais
St. Nérée
St. Antoine-de-Tilly
Rédempteur
Breakeyville
St. Henri
St. Nicolas
St. Étienne-de-Lauzon
Honfleur
St. Lazare
St. Philémon
St. Apollinaire
Ste. Anselme
Ste. Claire
St. Damien-de-Buckland
St. Lambert-de-Lévis
St. Isidore-Dorchester
Buckland

c

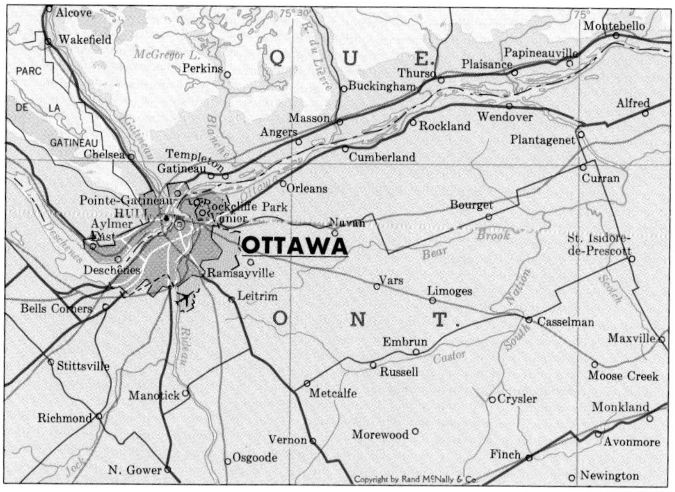

Alcove
Wakefield
McGregor L.
Perkins
Q   U   E.
Montebello
PARC
Papineauville
DE
LA
Thurso
Plaisance
GATINEAU
Buckingham
Chelsea
Masson
Rockland
Wendover
Alfred
Angers
Plantagenet
Templeton
Gatineau
Cumberland
Curran
Pointe-Gatineau
Orleans
HULL
Rockcliffe Park
Bourget
Aylmer
OTTAWA
Navan
St. Isidore-de-Prescott
Deschênes
Ramsayville
Vars
Limoges
Bells Corners
Leitrim
O   N   T.
Casselman
Stittsville
Embrun
Maxville
Manotick
Russell
Moose Creek
Richmond
Metcalfe
Crysler
Monkland
Vernon
Morewood
Avonmore
Osgoode
Finch
N. Gower
Newington

d

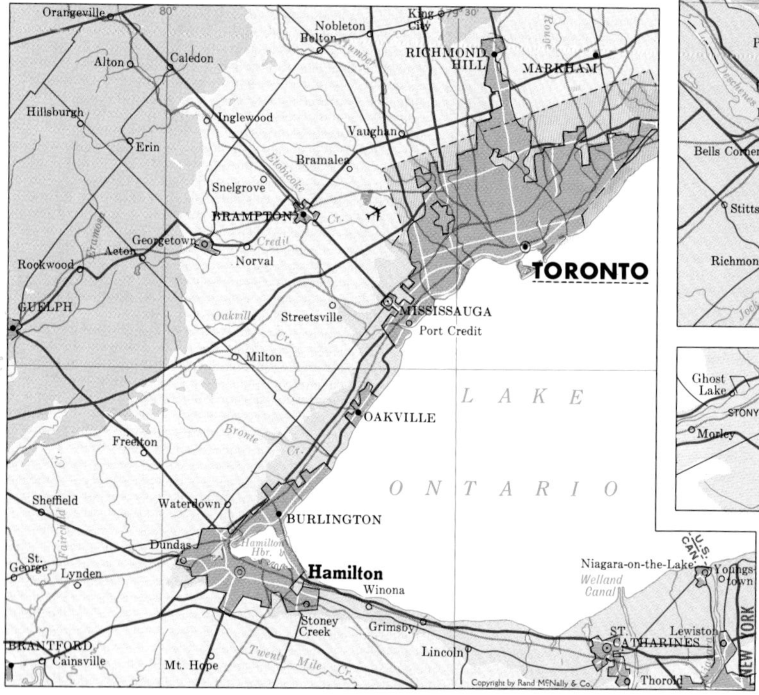

Orangeville
Nobleton
King
Alton
Caledon
Holton
RICHMOND HILL
MARKHAM
Hillsburgh
Inglewood
Vaughan
Erin
Bramalea
Snelgrove
BRAMPTON
Rockwood
Acton
Georgetown
Norval
GUELPH
TORONTO
Streetsville
MISSISSAUGA
Freelton
Milton
Port Credit
Sheffield
Waterdown
OAKVILLE
L A K E
St. George
Dundas
BURLINGTON
O N T A R I O
Lynden
Hamilton
Niagara-on-the-Lake
Youngstown
BRANTFORD
Stoney Creek
Winona
Welland Canal
Cainsville
Grimsby
Lewiston
Mt. Hope
Lincoln
ST. CATHARINES
NEW YORK
Thorold

e

Ghost Lake
Bow
Balzac
Kathryn
Keoma
STONY IND. RES.
Cochrane
McDonald L.
Morley
Delacour
Dalroy
Conrich
Lyalta
CALGARY
Bragg Creek
SARCEE IND. RES.
Shepard
Langdon
Priddis
Indus
Lloyd L.
Dalemead

f

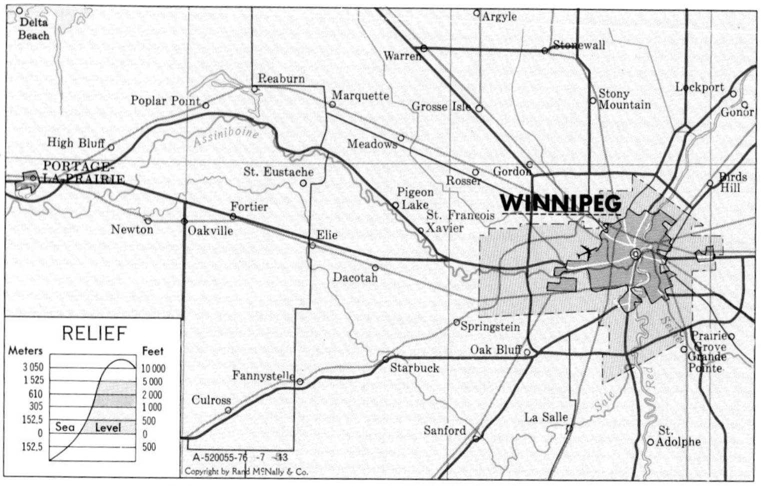

Delta Beach
Argyle
Stonewall
Warren
Reaburn
Marquette
Grosse Isle
Stony Mountain
Lockport
Poplar Point
Gonor
High Bluff
Meadows
PORTAGE-LA-PRAIRIE
St. Eustache
Pigeon Lake
Rosser
Gordon
Birds Hill
Fortier
St. François-Xavier
WINNIPEG
Newton
Oakville
Elie
Dacotah
Springstein
Prairie Grove
Grande Pointe
Fannystelle
Oak Bluff
Culross
Starbuck
La Salle
St. Adolphe
Sanford

RELIEF

Meters		Feet
3 050		10 000
1 525		5 000
610		2 000
305		1 000
152.5		500
0	Sea Level	0
152.5		500

A-520055-76-7-33

g

ALEXANDER IND. RES.
Morinville
Cardiff
Bruderheim
Rivière Qui Barre
Carbondale
Duagh
Fort Saskatchewan
Namao
Josephburg
Calahoo
Villeneuve
St. Albert
Oliver
Cannell
ELK ISLAND NAT'L PARK
EDMONTON
Bremner
Stony Plain
Clover Bar
Sherwood Park
Ardrossan
Spruce Grove
STONY PLAIN IND. RES.
Uncas
Devon
Hercules
N. Cooking Lake
Ellerslie
Cooking Lake
Buford
Calmar
Nisku
Looma
Beaumont
New Sarepta
Leduc

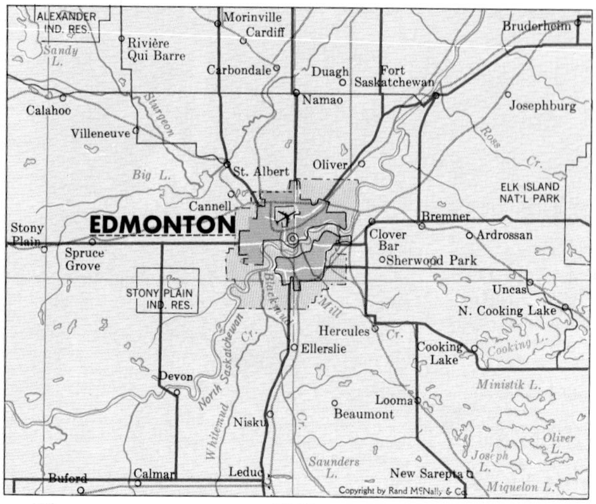

Scale 1:1 000 000; One inch to 16 miles.
Elevations and depressions are given in feet.

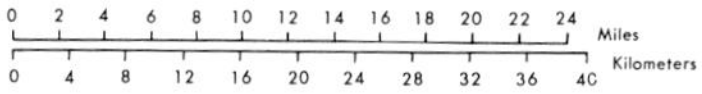

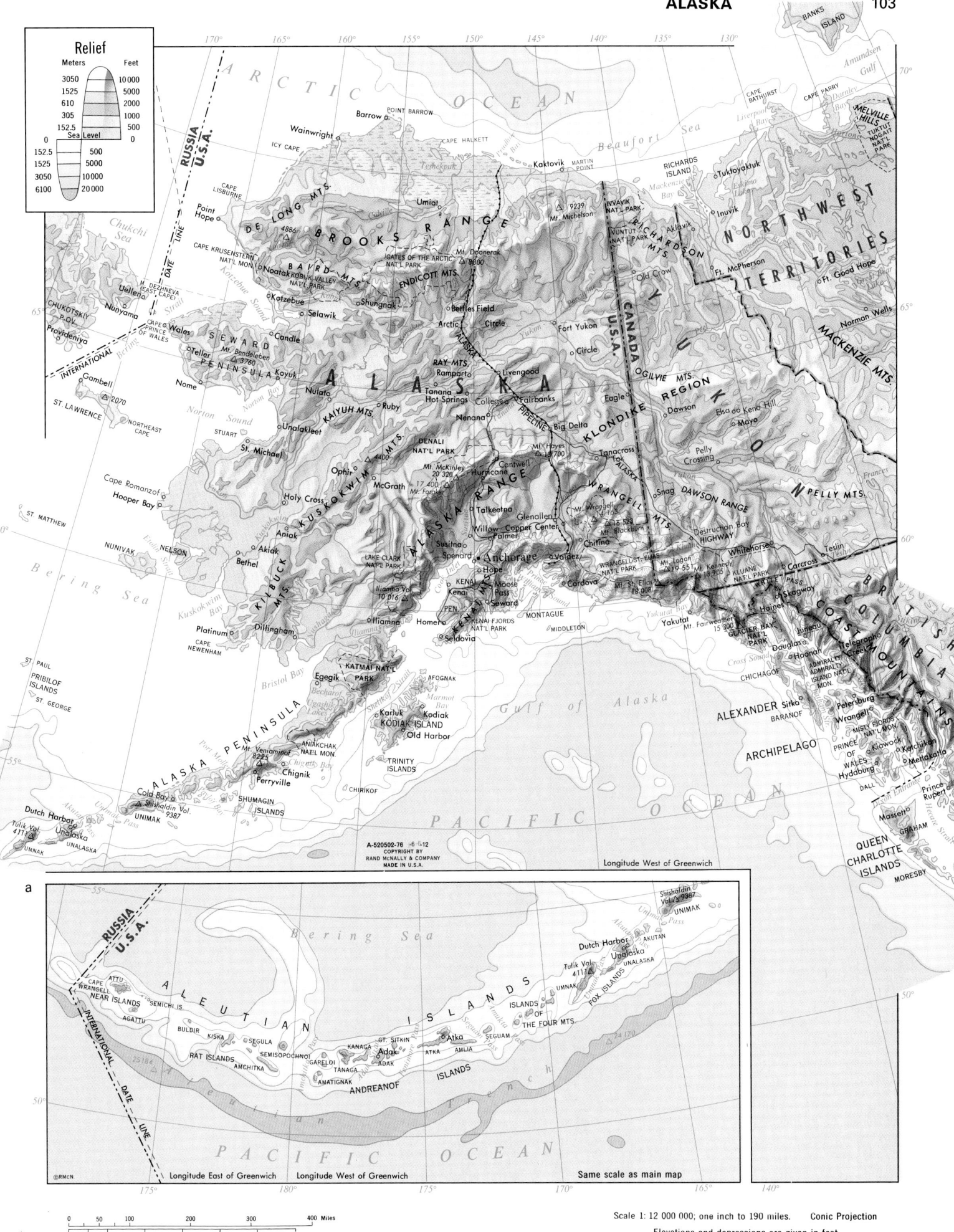

A-520502-76 -6-4-12
COPYRIGHT BY
RAND MCNALLY & COMPANY
MADE IN U.S.A.

Scale 1: 12 000 000; one inch to 190 miles.   Conic Projection

Elevations and depressions are given in feet

Continued on pages 90-91

A-520500-26 -921
COPYRIGHT BY
RAND McNALLY & COMPANY
MADE IN U.S.A.

a

Scale 1: 36 000 000

b

Scale 1: 36 000 000
One inch to 570 miles
©RMCN.

c   Longitude West of Greenwich

d   Scale 1: 3 400 000
©RMCN.

Same scale as main map

Longitude West of Greenwich

Scale 1:12 000 000; one inch to 190 miles. Polyconic Projection
Elevations and depressions are given in feet

Cities
and
Towns

0 to 50,000
50,000 to 500,000
500,000 to 1,000,000
1,000,000 and over

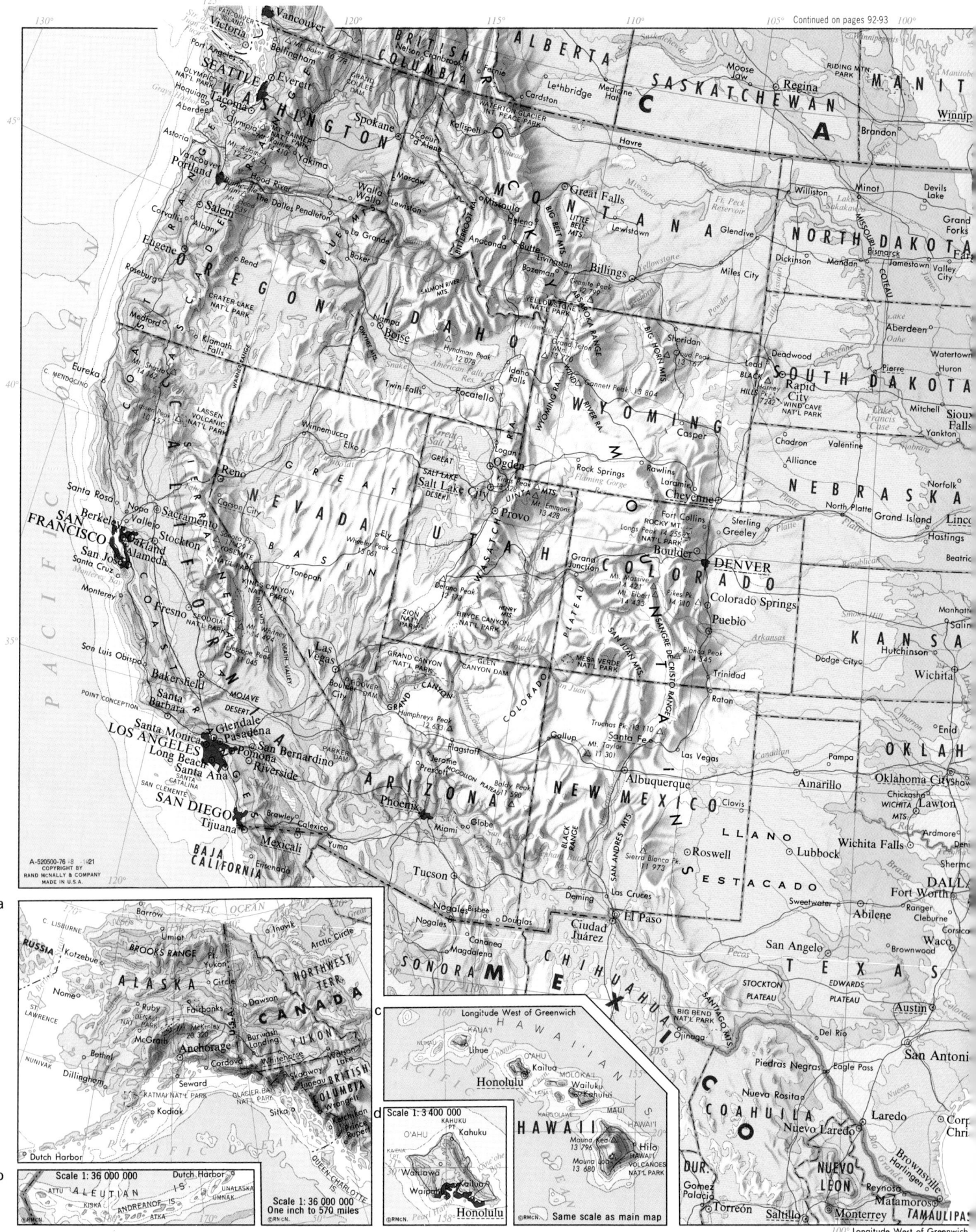

Continued on pages 92-93

Scale 1:12 000 000; one inch to 190 miles. Polyconic Projection
Elevations and depressions are given in feet

100° Longitude West of Greenwich

A-520500-76 -8 -21
COPYRIGHT BY
RAND McNALLY & COMPANY
MADE IN U.S.A.

a

b Scale 1: 36 000 000
Dutch Harbor
Scale 1: 36 000 000
One inch to 570 miles

c 160° Longitude West of Greenwich

d Scale 1: 3 400 000
Honolulu

Same scale as main map

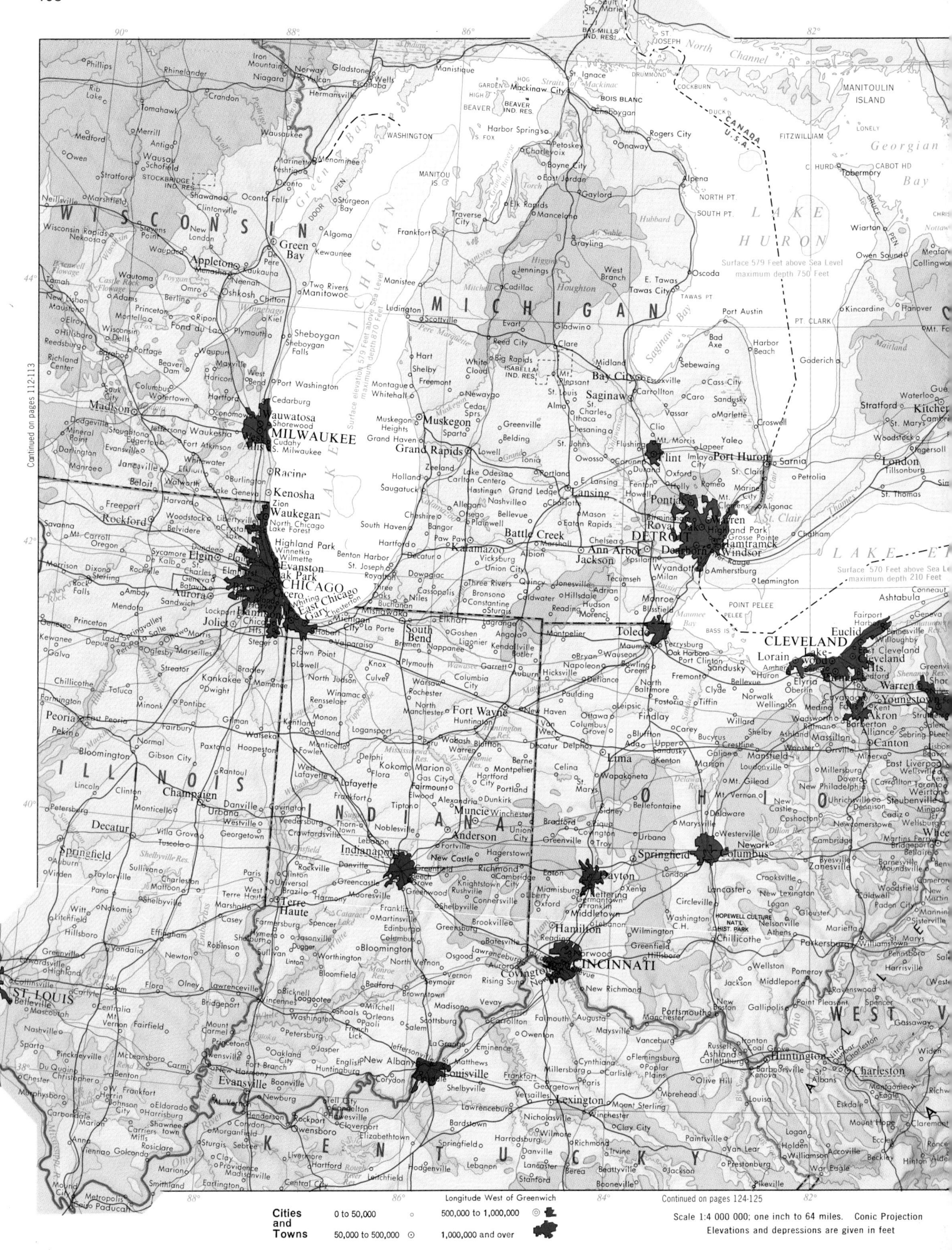

Continued on pages 112-113

Continued on pages 124-125

Longitude West of Greenwich

Cities and Towns

| | 0 to 50,000 | ○ | 500,000 to 1,000,000 | ◉ |
| | 50,000 to 500,000 | ⊙ | 1,000,000 and over | |

Scale 1:4 000 000; one inch to 64 miles. Conic Projection
Elevations and depressions are given in feet

Continued on pages 98-99

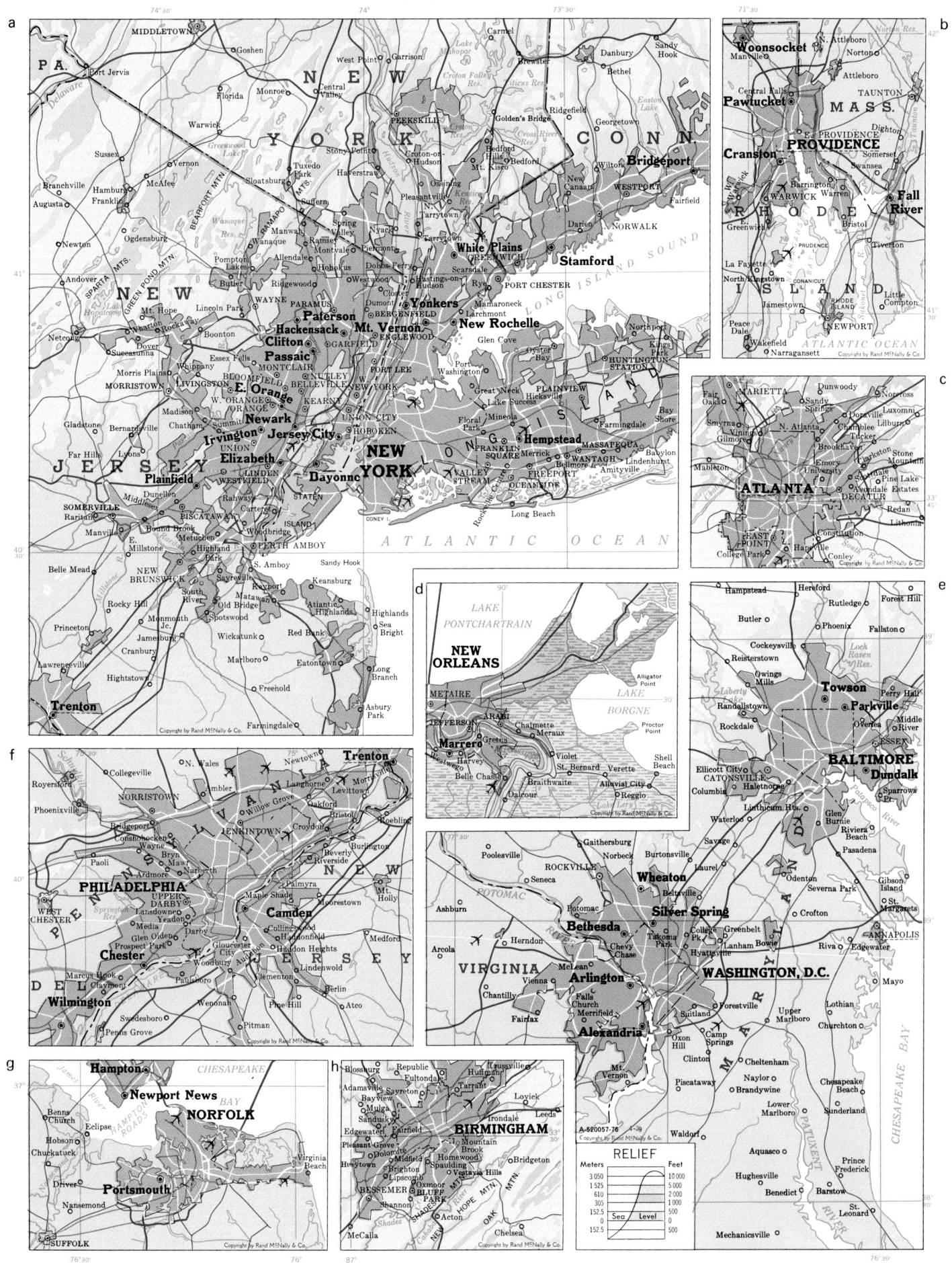

a

PA. MIDDLETOWN Goshen Lake
Mahopac Carmel
Port Jervis West Point Garrison Danbury Sandy
Hook
Florida Monroe Central
Valley Brewster Bethel
Warwick Ridgefield Georgetown
Sussex Stony Point Croton-on- New
Vernon Haverstraw Hudson Canaan WESTPORT **Bridgeport**
Branchville Franklin McAfee Tuxedo
Park Suffern Pleasantville N. Tarrytown Darien NORWALK Fairfield
Augusta Ramsey Spring **White Plains** Scarsdale
Andover Montvale Valley Nyack GREENWICH **Stamford**
SPARTA MTS. Pompton Allendale Piermont Rye PORT CHESTER
Lakes Hohokus Westwood Hastings-on- Glen Cove
NEW Mt. Hope Butler Ridgewood Dumont Hudson **New Rochelle**
Lincoln Park WAYNE PARAMUS **Yonkers** Larchmont
Rockaway BERGENFIELD **Mt. Vernon** Mamaroneck Oyster
Dover **Paterson** ENGLEWOOD Bay
Succasunna Boonton **Hackensack** GARFIELD FORT LEE Great Neck Northport
Morris Plains **Clifton** Port HUNTINGTON
Netcong Whippany Essex Fells NUTLEY **Passaic** Washington STATION
Morristown MONTCLAIR BLOOMFIELD NEW YORK Great Neck Bay
JERSEY Madison LIVINGSTON BELLEVILLE PLAINVIEW Shore
W. ORANGE KEARNY Hicksville
Chatham **E. Orange** UNION CITY Floral Mineola Farmingdale
ORANGE **Newark** HOBOKEN Park MASSAPEQUA
Gladstone Summit **Irvington Jersey City** FRANKLIN **Hempstead** WANTAGH
Bernardsville UNION SQUARE Merrick Lindenhurst
Far Hills **Elizabeth** **NEW YORK** Bellmore Amityville
Lyons LINDEN VALLEY FREEPORT Babylon
Plainfield WESTFIELD **Bayonne** STREAM OCEANSIDE
SOMERVILLE Rahway STATEN CONEY I. Long Beach
Raritan Carteret ISLAND
Manville Dunellen Woodbridge **ATLANTIC** **OCEAN**
Bound Brook PISCATAWAY PERTH AMBOY
E. Millstone Metuchen
Belle Mead Highland S. Amboy Sandy Hook
NEW Park
BRUNSWICK Sayreville Keansburg
Rocky Hill South Keyport Atlantic
River Matawan Highlands
Princeton Old Bridge Highlands
Monmouth Spotswood Sea
Jamesburg Jc. Bright
Cranbury Marlboro Red Bank
Lawrenceville Hightstown Eatontown
Long
Freehold Branch
Trenton
Asbury
Farmingdale Park
Copyright by Rand McNally & Co.

b

Woonsocket N. Attleboro Norton Res.
Manville Norton Attleboro
Central TAUNTON
Pawtucket Falls **MASS.**
E. PROVIDENCE Dighton
Cranston **PROVIDENCE** Somerset
**Fall
River**
RHODE Barrington Swansea
Warwick Warren Bristol
W. Greenwich Tiverton
La Fayette CONANICUT Little
North Kingstown Compton
ISLAND Jamestown PRUDENCE RHODE
I. Island NEWPORT
Peace Wakefield **ATLANTIC OCEAN**
Dale Narragansett
Copyright by Rand McNally & Co.

c

Dunwoody Norcross
Fair MARIETTA Sandy
Oaks Springs
Smyrna N. Atlanta Doraville Lilburn
Vining Chamblee Tucker
Mableton Emory Brookhaven Stone
University Clarkston Mountain
Avondale Pine Lake
ATLANTA Estates
DECATUR Redan
EAST Lithonia
POINT Constitution
College Park Hapeville Conley

d

LAKE
PONTCHARTRAIN
**NEW
ORLEANS**
Alligator
Point
LAKE
METAIRE BORGNE
JEFFERSON ARABI Proctor
Marrero Gretna Chalmette Point
Harvey Meraux
Belle Chasse Violet Shell
St. Bernard Verrette Beach
Braithwaite Allnvist City
Dalcour Reggio
Copyright by Rand McNally & Co.

e

Hampstead Hereford Forest Hill
Rutledge
Butler Phoenix Fallston
Cockeysville Loch
Reisterstown Owings Raven Perry Hall
Mills Res.
Randallstown **Towson**
Rockdale Liberty **Parkville**
Ellicott City Overlea Middle
CATONSVILLE River
Columbia Halethorpe ESSEX
BALTIMORE
Waterloo Linthicum Hts. **Dundalk**
Glen Sparrows
Burnie Riviera Pt.
Beach Pasadena
Gaithersburg Gibson
Poolesville Norbeck Burtonsville Island
ROCKVILLE Savage St.
Seneca Laurel Odenton Margarets
POTOMAC Severna Park
Ashburn Potomac **Wheaton** Beltsville Crofton
Arcola Takoma College Greenbelt ANNAPOLIS
Herndon Chevy Pk. Lanham Bowie Riva
Bethesda Chase Hyattsville Edgewater
VIRGINIA McLean **Silver Spring** Mayo
Vienna **WASHINGTON, D.C.**
Chantilly Falls **Arlington**
Church Suitland Upper
Fairfax Merrifield Forestville Marlboro
Churchton
Alexandria Oxon Camp
Hill Springs
Mt. Clinton Cheltenham Chesapeake
Vernon Naylor Beach
A-520057-76 4-39 Piscataway Brandywine Sunderland
Copyright by Rand McNally & Co. Lower
Marlboro
Waldorf Aquasco
Hughesville Prince
Frederick
Benedict Barstow
St.
Leonard
Mechanicsville

f

Royersford N. Wales Newtown
Collegeville Morris. **Trenton**
NORRISTOWN Ambler Langhorne Levittown
Phoenixville Willow Grove Oakford
Bridgeport JENKINTOWN Croydon Roebling
Conshohocken Bristol
Wayne Beverly
Paoli Bryn Narberth Riverside Mt.
Ardmore Mawr Palmyra Holly
PHILADELPHIA Maple Shade
UPPER Moorestown
WEST DARBY Cherry Hill
CHESTER Lansdowne Yeadon Collingswood Medford
Media Darby Haddonfield
Glen Olden Haddon Heights
Chester Prospect Park Woodbury Berlin
Marcus Hook Audubon
DEL. Claymont Paulsboro Clementon
Gloucester Lindenwold
Wilmington City Pine Hill
Penns Grove Wenonah Atco
Swedesboro Berlin
Pitman
Copyright by Rand McNally & Co.

g

Hampton CHESAPEAKE
BAY
Newport News
Benns **NORFOLK**
Church
Hobson Eclipse
Chuckatuck Virginia
Beach
Driver **Portsmouth**
Nansemond
SUFFOLK

h

Blossburg Republic Trussville
Fultondale Huffman
Adamsville Sayreton Tarrant
Bayview Leyick
Mulga Sandusky Irondale
BIRMINGHAM Leeds
Edgewater Fairfield
Pleasant Grove Mountain Bridgeton
Dolomite Brook
Hueytown Homewood
Midfield Spaulding
Brighton Vestavia Hills
Lipscomb Oxmoor
BESSEMER Bluff
Shannon Park
McCalla Acton
Chelsea
Copyright by Rand McNally & Co.

RELIEF

Meters		Feet
3 050		10 000
1 525		5 000
610		2 000
305		1 000
152.5		500
0	Sea Level	0
152.5		500

0 2 4 6 8 10 12 14 16 18 20 22 24 Miles
0 4 8 12 16 20 24 28 32 36 40 Kilometers

Scale 1:1 000 000; One inch to 16 miles.
Elevations and depressions are given in feet.

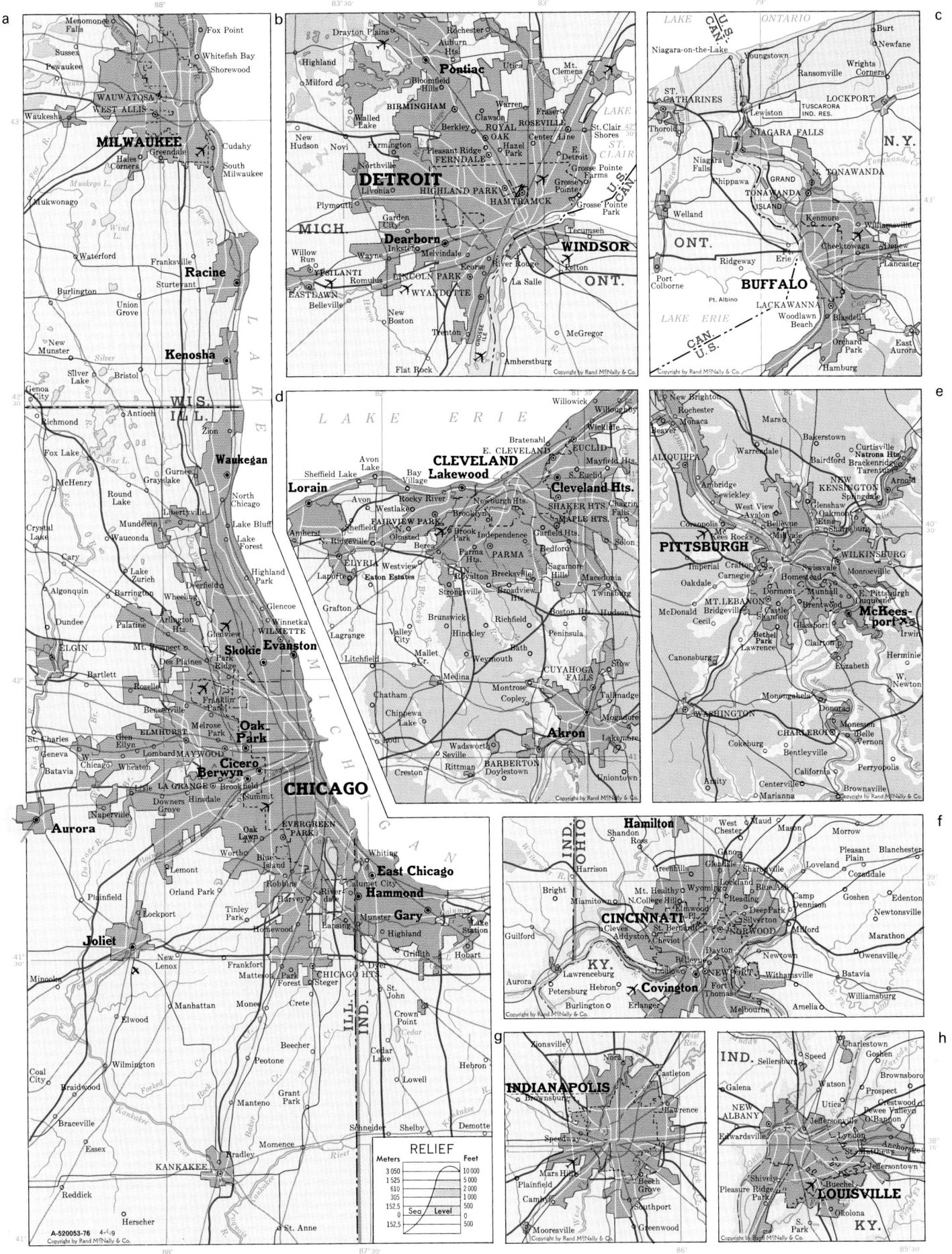

RELIEF

Meters		Feet
3 050		10 000
1 525		5 000
610		2 000
305		1 000
152.5		500
0	Sea Level	0
152.5		500

Scale 1:1 000 000; One inch to 16 miles.
Elevations and depressions are given in feet.

Miles: 0 2 4 6 8 10 12 14 16 18 20 22 24
Kilometers: 0 4 8 12 16 20 24 28 32 36 40

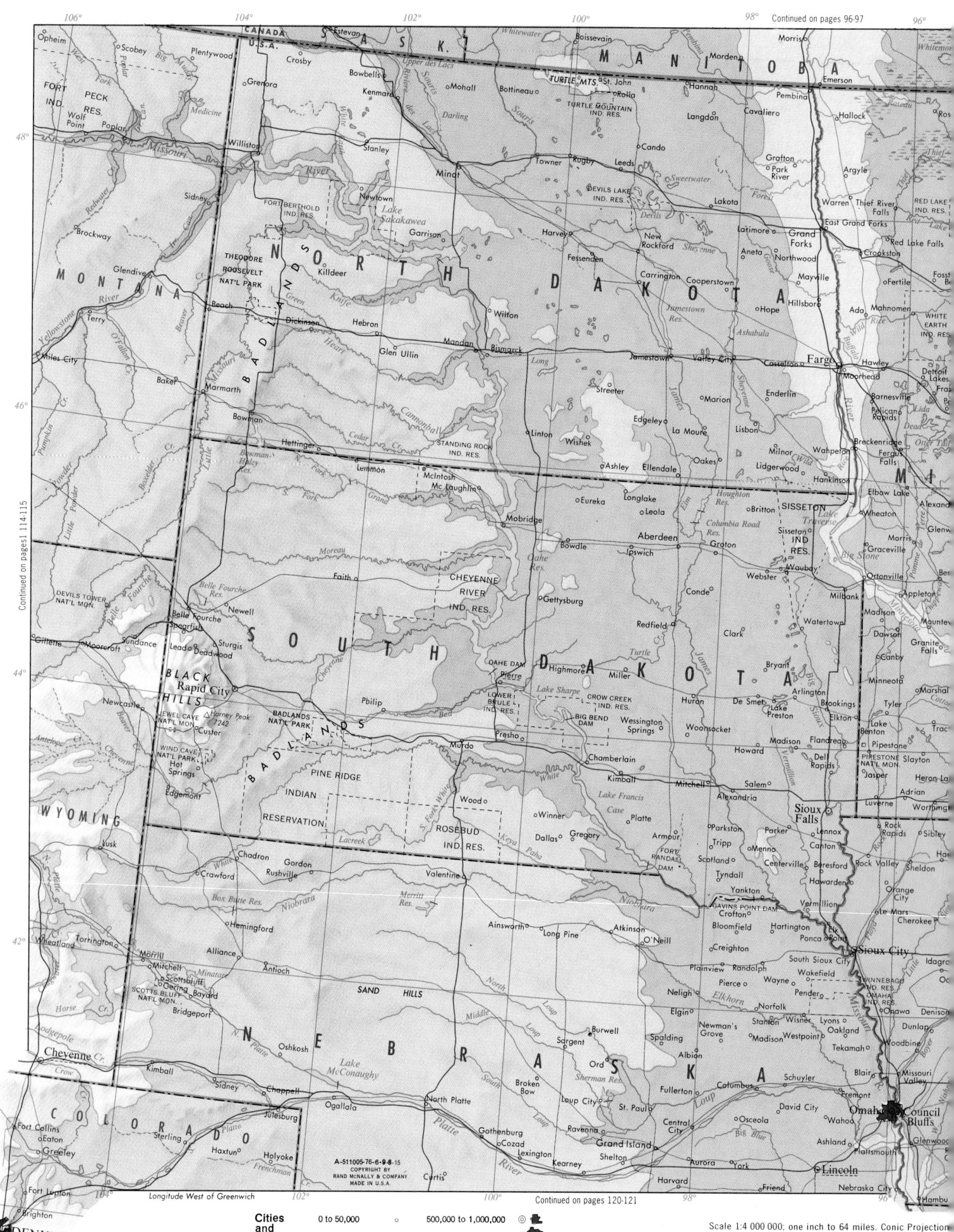

Continued on pages 96-97

106°   104°   102°   100°   98°   96°

CANADA
U.S.A.

S A S K.   M A N I T O B A

Opheim Scobey Plentywood
Crosby Estevan Whitewater Boissevain Morris
Peerless Big Muddy Bowbells Mohall Bottineau St. John Rolla Hannah Morden Emerson
FORT Grenora Kenmare Souris TURTLE MTS. Pembina Morris
PECK Wolf Williston Stanley Minot Towner Rugby Leeds Cando Langdon Cavalier Hallock
RES. Point Poplar TURTLE MOUNTAIN IND. RES. Grafton Argyle
48° Sidney Newtown Garrison Harvey New DEVILS LAKE Lakota Park Warren Thief River
FORT BERTHOLD Lake Rockford IND. RES. Northwood River East Grand Forks Falls RED LAKE
Brockway IND. RES. Sakakawea Fessenden Carrington Cooperstown Latimore Grand Crookston IND. RES. Red Lake Falls
Glendive THEODORE Killdeer Wilton Aneta Forks Fertile Fosst
MONTANA ROOSEVELT NORTH DAKOTA Mayville Hillsboro Ada Mahnomen WHITE
Terry NAT'L PARK Beach Dickinson Hebron Mandan Bismarck Carrington Hope EARTH
Miles City Baker Glen Ullin Jamestown Valley City Casselton Fargo IND. RES.
46° Marmarth Heart Long Streeter Marion Enderlin Moorhead Detroit
Bowman Edgeley La Moure Lisbon Barnesville Lakes
Hettinger STANDING ROCK Wishek Oakes Milnor Wahpeton Pelican Lida
Lemmon IND. RES. Ashley Ellendale Lidgerwood Breckenridge Rapids
McIntosh Longlake Hankinson Fergus MI
Mobridge Eureka Leola Britton Elbow Lake Falls
McLaughlin Bowdle Ipswich SISSETON Wheaton Alexand
Aberdeen Groton IND. Morris
CHEYENNE Gettysburg Webster Waubay RES. Graceville Glenw
44° Faith RIVER Conde Big Stone Ortonville
IND. RES. Redfield Clark Milbank Appleton
Highmore Miller Bryant Canby Mounte
SOUTH OAHE DAM Pierre CROW CREEK De Smet Arlington Granite
BLACK Rapid City DAKOTA Lake Sharpe IND. RES. Huron Brookings Falls
HILLS Philip LOWER BIG BEND Wessington Howard Elkton Minneota
Custer BADLANDS BRULE DAM Springs Woonsocket Madison Flandreau PIPESTONE Tyler
42° NAT'L PARK IND. RES. Murdo Presho Chamberlain Mitchell Salem Dell NAT'L MON. Pipestone
PINE RIDGE Kimball Alexandria Rapids Jasper Slayton
INDIAN Wood Winner Howard Parkston Parker Heron La
RESERVATION ROSEBUD Dallas Gregory Armour Tripp Centerville Adrian
Chadron IND. RES. FORT Menno Beresford Worthing
WYOMING Gordon Valentine RANDALL Scotland Hawarden Rock Rapids
Crawford Rushville DAM Tyndall Yankton Vermillion Sioux Falls

Cities
and
Towns

0 to 50,000 o   500,000 to 1,000,000 ⊚

50,000 to 500,000 ⊙   1,000,000 and over

Scale 1:4 000 000; one inch to 64 miles. Conic Projection
Elevations and depressions are given in feet

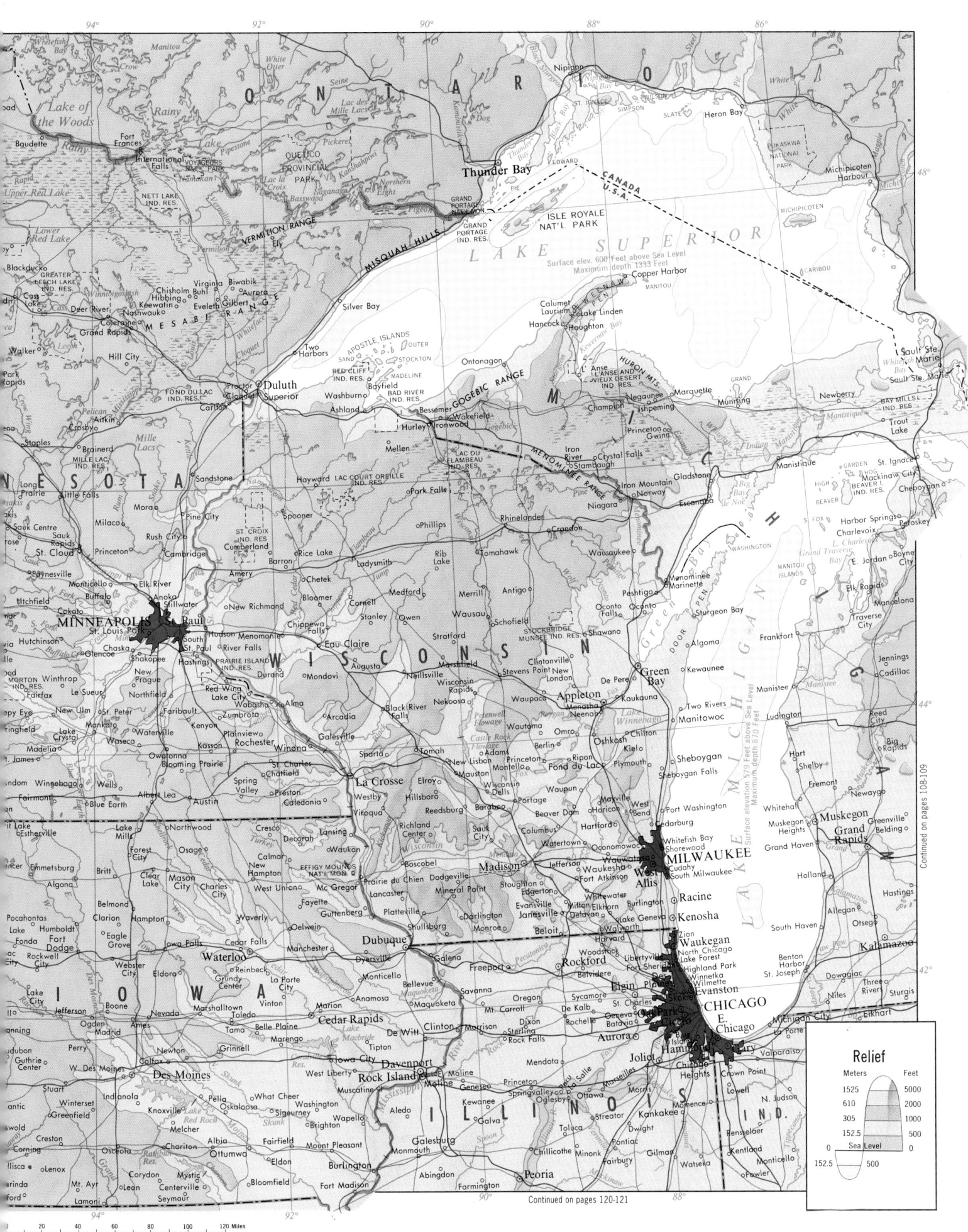

Continued on pages 108-109

Continued on pages 120-121

Relief

Meters		Feet
1525		5000
610		2000
305		1000
152.5		500
0	Sea Level	0
152.5		500

0 20 40 60 80 100 120 Miles
0 20 40 60 80 100 120 140 160 180 200 Kilometers

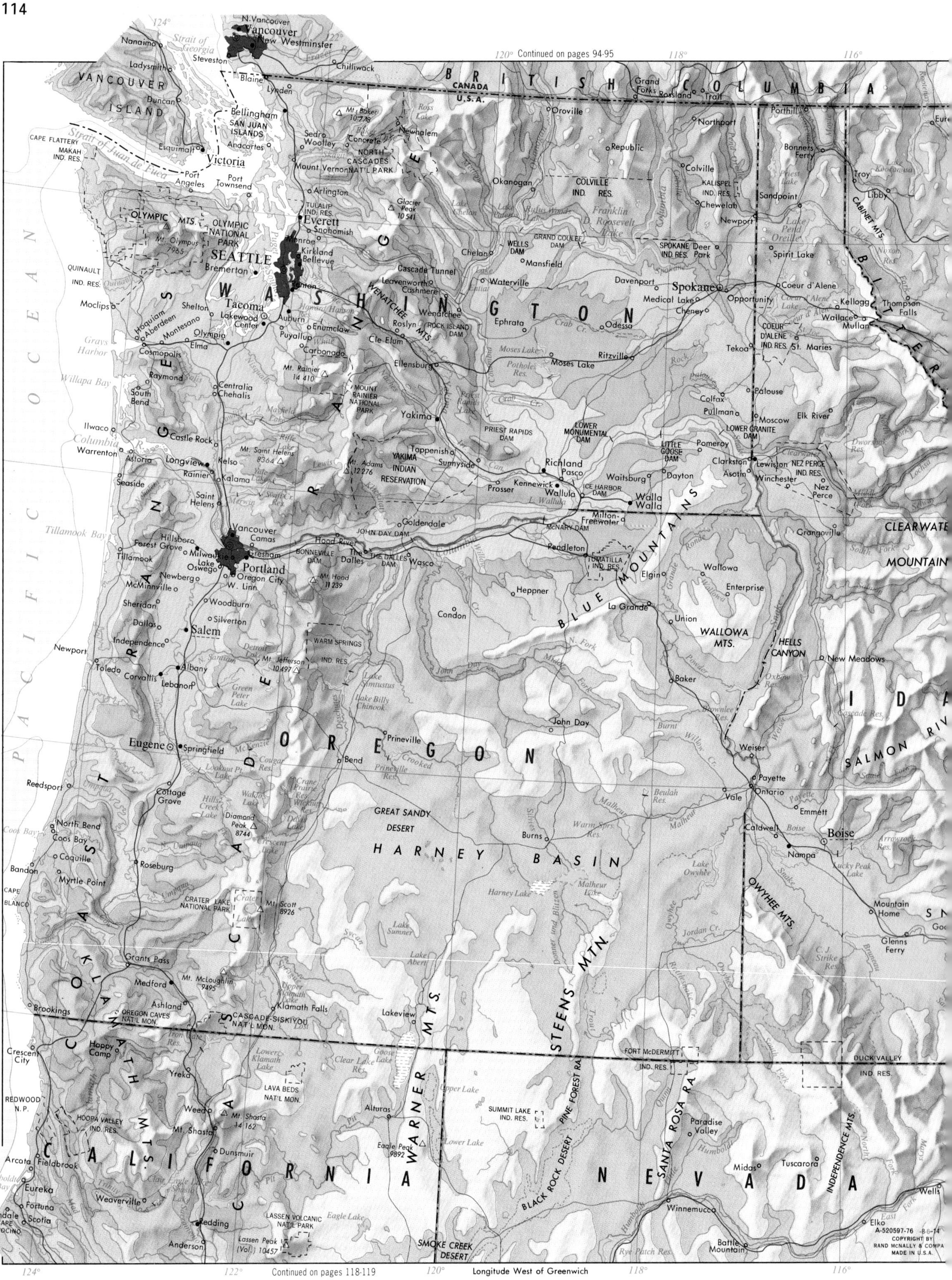

Continued on pages 94-95

BRITISH COLUMBIA

CANADA
U.S.A.

VANCOUVER ISLAND

Nanaimo
Ladysmith
Duncan
Esquimalt
Victoria
CAPE FLATTERY
MAKAH IND. RES.
Strait of Juan de Fuca
Port Angeles
Port Townsend

N. Vancouver
Vancouver
New Westminster
Steveston
Blaine
Lynden
Chilliwack
Bellingham
SAN JUAN ISLANDS
Anacortes
Sedro Woolley
Concrete
Mount Vernon
Arlington
Mt. Baker 10,778
Newhalem
Ross Lake
NORTH CASCADES NAT'L PARK
Strait of Georgia

Grand Forks
Rossland
Trail
Oroville
Northport
Republic
Colville
KALISPEL IND. RES.
Chewelah
Priest Ferry
Bonners Ferry
Troy
Libby
CABINET MTS.
Sandpoint
Newport
Lake Pend Oreille

OLYMPIC MTS.
OLYMPIC NATIONAL PARK
Mt. Olympus 7965
QUINAULT IND. RES.
Moclips
Hoquiam
Aberdeen
Montesano
Cosmopolis
Elma
Grays Harbor
Raymond
South Bend
Ilwaco

Everett
Snohomish
Monroe
SEATTLE
Bremerton
Kirkland
Bellevue
Renton
Tacoma
Lakewood Center
Auburn
Enumclaw
Puyallup
Carbonado
Olympia
Shelton
Centralia
Chehalis

Glacier Peak 10,541
Cascade Tunnel
Leavenworth
Cashmere
WENATCHEE MTS.
Wenatchee
Roslyn
Cle Elum
ROCK ISLAND DAM
Ellensburg

Chelan
Lake Chelan
Waterville
WELLS DAM
Mansfield
GRAND COULEE DAM
Davenport
Spokane
Medical Lake
Cheney
Opportunity
Coeur d'Alene
Kellogg
Wallace
Mullan
Thompson Falls
SPOKANE IND. RES.
Deer Park
Spirit Lake

Okanogan
COLVILLE IND. RES.
Lake Roosevelt
Franklin D. Roosevelt Lake

WASHINGTON

Mt. Rainier 14,410
MOUNT RAINIER NATIONAL PARK
Howard Hanson Res.
Yakima
Ephrata
Moses Lake
Ritzville
Odessa
Colfax
Pullman
Moscow
Elk River
Palouse
Tekoa
St. Maries
COEUR D'ALENE IND. RES.

Castle Rock
Warrenton
Astoria
Longview
Kelso
Rainier
Kalama
Saint Helens
Mt. Saint Helens 8364
Mt. Adams 12,276
YAKIMA INDIAN RESERVATION
Toppenish
Sunnyside
Goldendale
Prosser
Kennewick
Pasco
Richland
Wallula
Waitsburg
Dayton
Walla Walla
Milton-Freewater
Asotin
Clarkston
Lewiston
Winchester
NEZ PERCE IND. RES.
Nez Perce
PRIEST RAPIDS DAM
LOWER MONUMENTAL DAM
ICE HARBOR DAM
McNARY DAM
Pomeroy
LOWER GRANITE DAM
LITTLE GOOSE DAM
Dworshak Res.

COLUMBIA R.

Vancouver
Camas
Hillsboro
Forest Grove
Tillamook
Milwaukie
Lake Oswego
Gresham
Hood River
The Dalles
THE DALLES DAM
Wasco
BONNEVILLE DAM
JOHN DAY DAM
PORTLAND
Oregon City
W. Linn
Mt. Hood 11,239
McMinnville
Newberg
Woodburn
Sheridan
Dallas
Salem
Silverton
Independence
Albany
Corvallis
Lebanon
Toledo
Newport
WARM SPRINGS IND. RES.
Mt. Jefferson 10,497
Detroit Lake
Green Peter Lake

UMATILLA IND. RES.
Pendleton
Heppner
Elgin
La Grande
Union
Baker
BLUE MOUNTAINS
Wallowa
Enterprise
WALLOWA MTS.
HELLS CANYON
New Meadows
Grangeville
CLEARWATER MOUNTAINS

OREGON

Eugene
Springfield
Cottage Grove
Lookout Pt. Res.
Hills Creek Lake
Diamond Peak 8744
Crater Lake
CRATER LAKE NATIONAL PARK
Roseburg
Mt. Scott 8926
Prineville
Bend
Prineville Res.
Crooked R.
Lake Billy Chinook
Lake Simtustus
John Day
GREAT SANDY DESERT
HARNEY BASIN
Burns
Lake Sumner
Malheur Lake
Harney Lake
Beulah Res.
Warm Spgs. Res.
Vale
Ontario
Payette
Weiser
Emmett
Caldwell
Boise
Nampa
Lucky Peak Lake
Arrowrock Res.
OWYHEE MTS.
Mountain Home
Glenns Ferry
C.J. Strike Res.

North Bend
Coos Bay
Coquille
Bandon
CAPE BLANCO
Myrtle Point
Reedsport
COAST RANGE
UMPQUA R.

Grants Pass
Medford
Ashland
OREGON CAVES NAT'L MON.
KLAMATH MTS.
Mt. McLoughlin 9495
CASCADE-SISKIYOU NAT'L MON.
Klamath Falls
Upper Klamath Lake
Lake Abert
Lakeview
WARNER MTS.
STEENS MTN.
Lake Owyhee
Jordan Cr.
Owyhee R.

Brookings
Crescent City
Happy Camp
Yreka
Weed
Mt. Shasta 14,162
Dunsmuir
LAVA BEDS NAT'L MON.
Lower Klamath Lake
Clear Lake Res.
Goose Lake
Alturas
Upper Lake
Lower Lake
SUMMIT LAKE IND. RES.
FORT McDERMITT IND. RES.
PINE FOREST RA.
SANTA ROSA RA.
Paradise Valley
Midas
Tuscarora
INDEPENDENCE MTS.
DUCK VALLEY IND. RES.

REDWOOD N.P.
Arcata
Fieldbrook
Eureka
Fortuna
Scotia
Ferndale
CAPE MENDOCINO
Humboldt Bay
HOOPA VALLEY IND. RES.
Weaverville
Eagle Lake
LASSEN VOLCANIC NAT'L PARK
Lassen Peak (Vol.) 10,457
Redding
Anderson
Eagle Peak 9892
WARNER MTS.
BLACK ROCK DESERT
SMOKE CREEK DESERT
Winnemucca
Battle Mountain
Rye Patch Res.
Elko
Wells
East Fork

CALIFORNIA

NEVADA

IDAHO

SALMON RIVER

PACIFIC OCEAN

Tillamook Bay
Willapa Bay
Columbia R.
Coos Bay
Humboldt Bay

Longitude West of Greenwich

Scale 1: 4,000,000; one inch to 64 miles. Conic Projection
Elevations and depressions are given in feet

A-520597-76 8-6-14
COPYRIGHT BY
RAND McNALLY & COMPANY
MADE IN U.S.A.

Continued on pages 96-97

Continued on pages 112-113

Continued on pages 118-119

Relief

Meters		Feet
3050		10000
1525		5000
610		2000
305		1000
152.5		500
0	Sea Level	0
1525		500

0 20 40 60 80 100 120 Miles

0 20 40 60 80 100 120 140 160 180 200 Kilometers

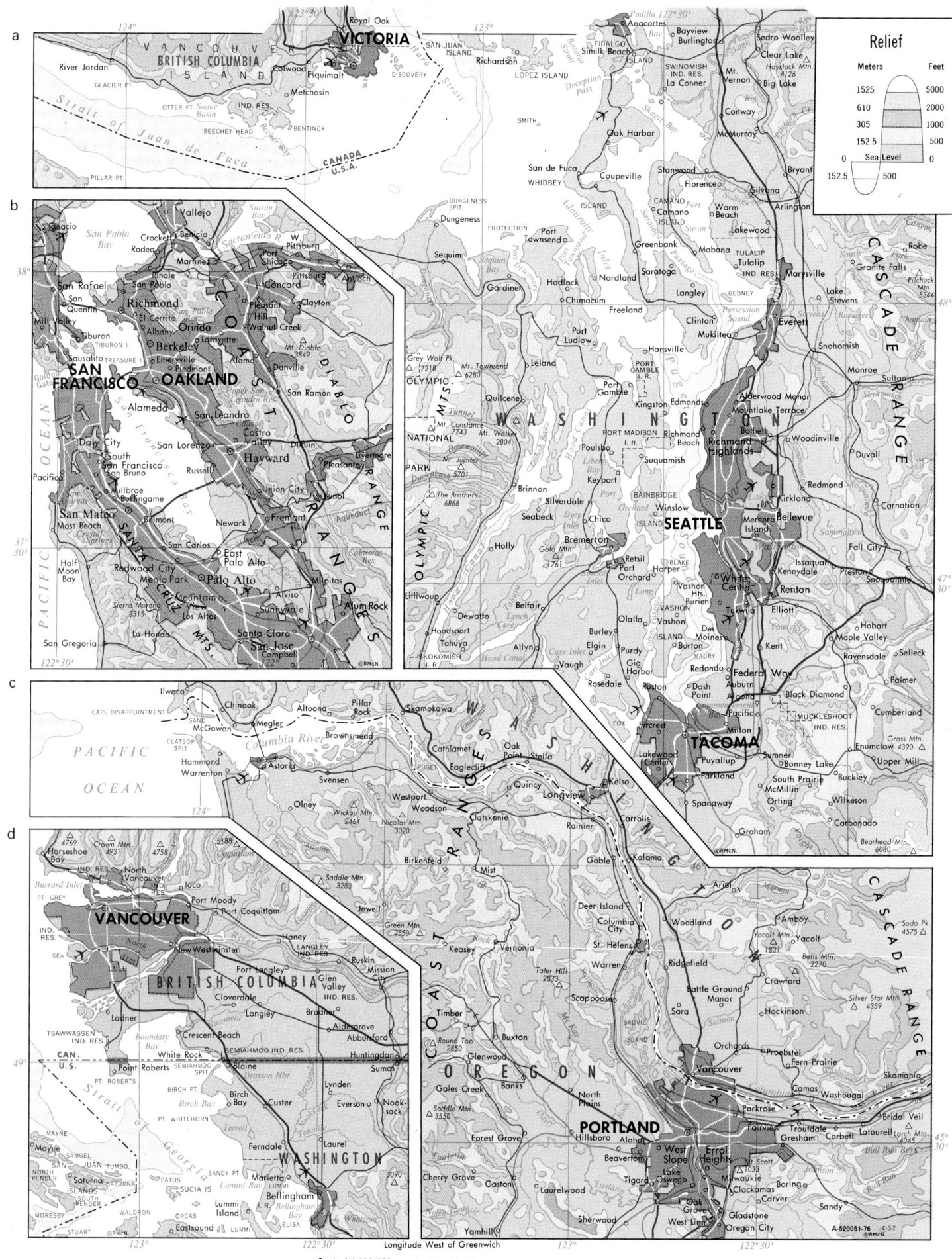

Scale 1:1 000 000; one inch to 16 miles.

Elevations and depressions are given in feet.

Longitude West of Greenwich

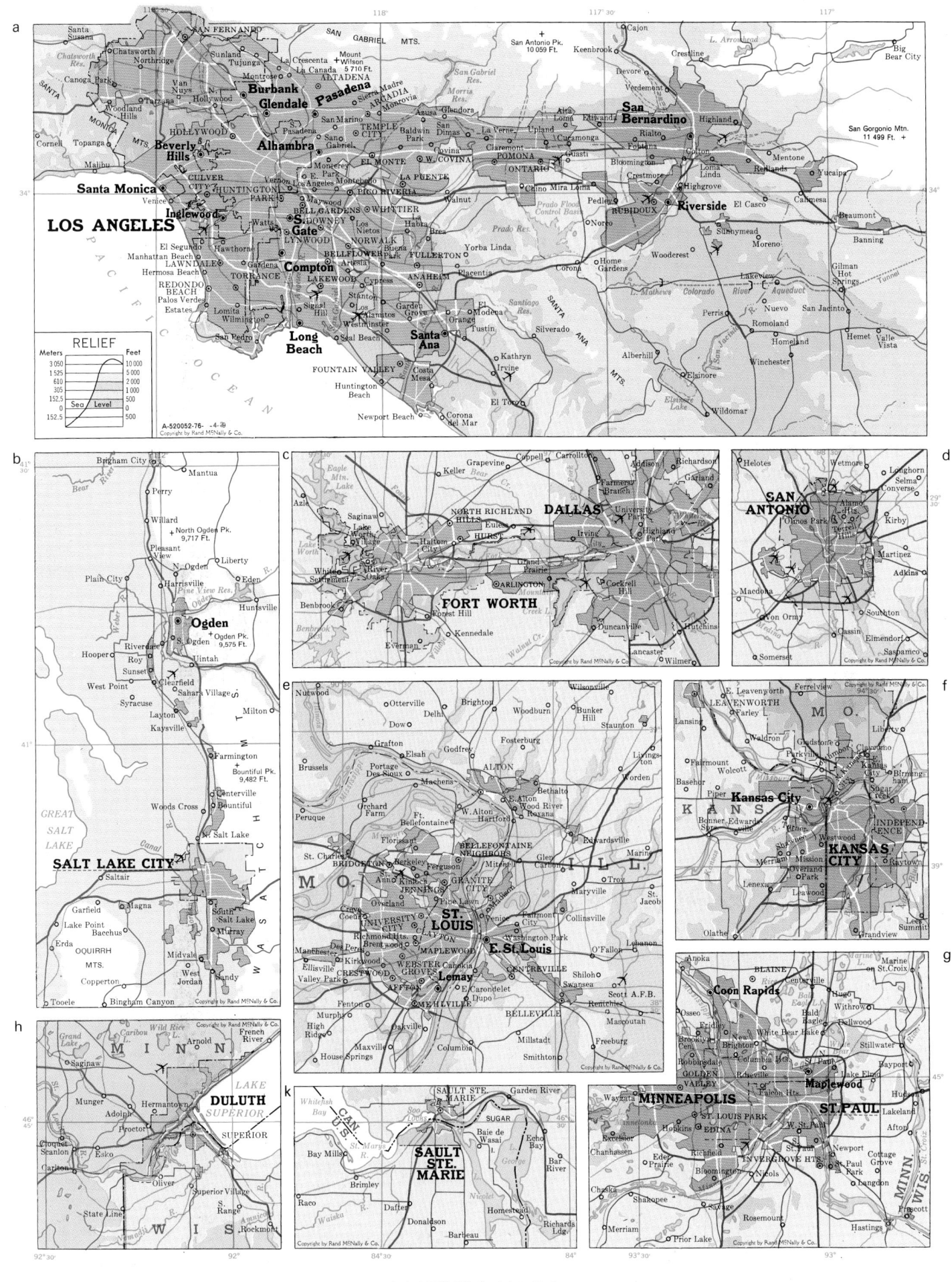

RELIEF

Meters	Feet
3 050	10 000
1 525	5 000
610	2 000
305	1 000
152.5	500
0	Sea Level 0
152.5	500

A-520052-76- -4-79
Copyright by Rand McNally & Co.

a — Los Angeles area

LOS ANGELES, Beverly Hills, Hollywood, Burbank, Glendale, Pasadena, Alhambra, Santa Monica, Inglewood, Compton, Long Beach, Santa Ana, Anaheim, Fullerton, Riverside, San Bernardino, Ontario, Pomona

b — Salt Lake City area

SALT LAKE CITY, Ogden, Great Salt Lake

c — Dallas–Fort Worth area

DALLAS, FORT WORTH, Arlington

d — San Antonio area

SAN ANTONIO

e — St. Louis area

ST. LOUIS, E. St. Louis, Maplewood, Lemay

f — Kansas City area

KANSAS CITY, Independence

g — Minneapolis–St. Paul area

MINNEAPOLIS, ST. PAUL, Coon Rapids, Maplewood

h — Duluth area

DULUTH, SUPERIOR, LAKE SUPERIOR

k — Sault Ste. Marie area

SAULT STE. MARIE

0 2 4 6 8 10 12 14 16 18 20 22 24 Miles
0 4 8 12 16 20 24 28 32 36 40 Kilometers

Scale 1:1 000 000; One inch to 16 miles.
Elevations and depressions are given in feet.

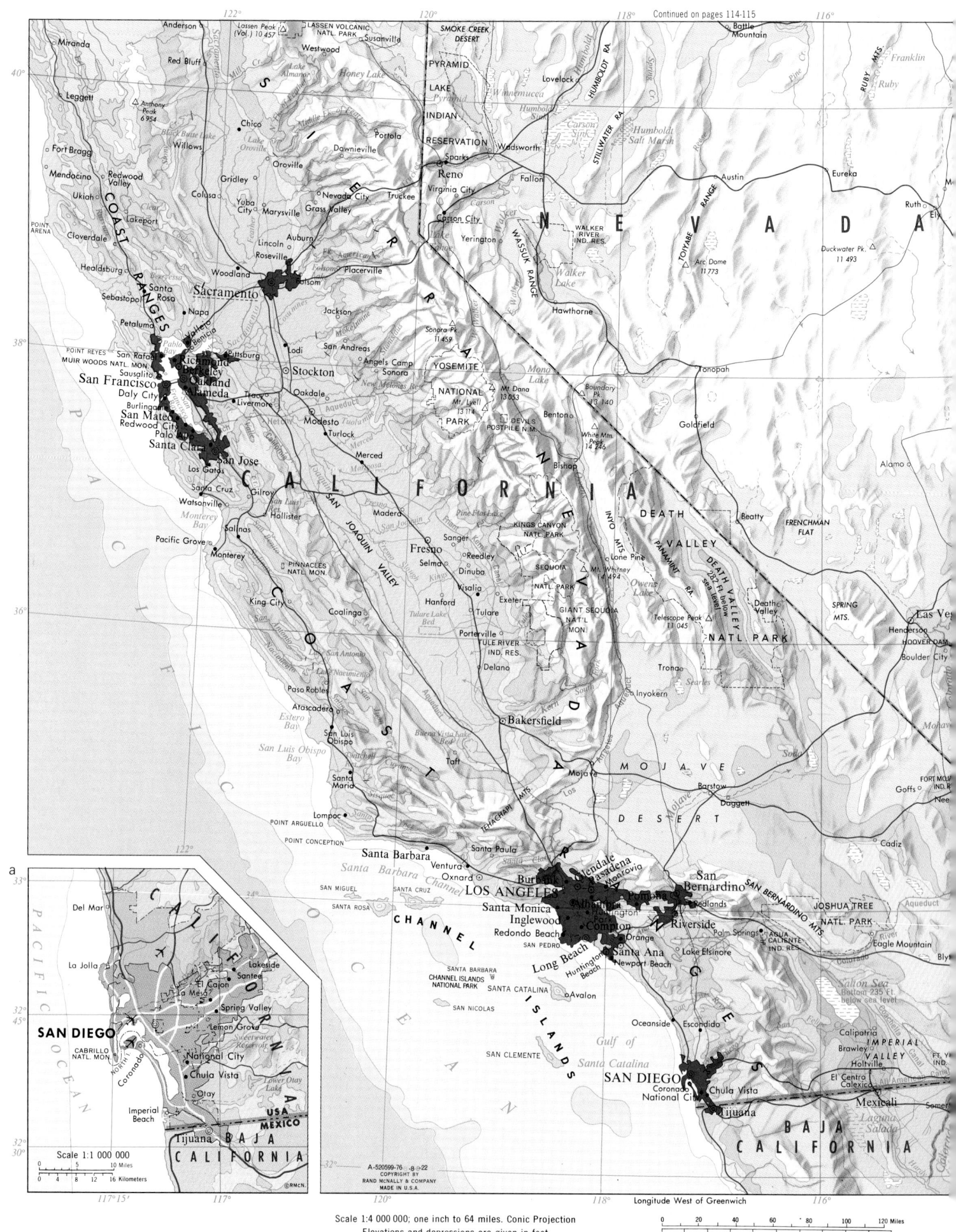

Continued on pages 114-115

a

SAN DIEGO

Scale 1:1 000 000

0   5   10 Miles

0 4   8 12 16 Kilometers

©RMcN.

A-520599-76 -8 0-22
COPYRIGHT BY
RAND McNALLY & COMPANY
MADE IN U.S.A.

Scale 1:4 000 000; one inch to 64 miles. Conic Projection
Elevations and depressions are given in feet

Longitude West of Greenwich

0   20   40   60   80   100   120 Miles

0 20 40 60 80 100 120 140 160 180 200 Kilometers

Continued on pages 120-121

Continued on pages 122-123

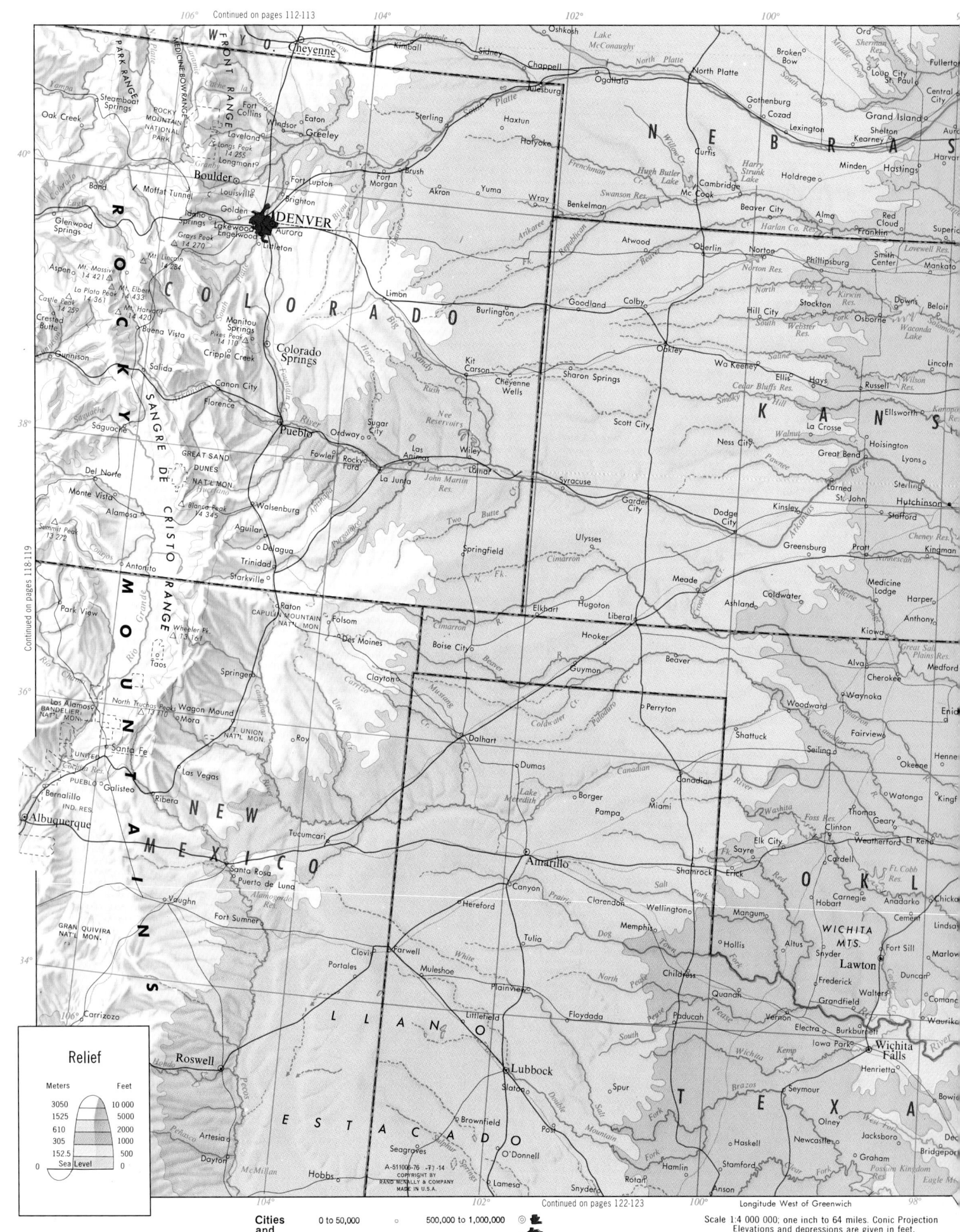

Continued on pages 112-113

Continued on pages 118-119

Continued on pages 122-123

Relief

Meters	Feet
3050	10 000
1525	5000
610	2000
305	1000
152.5	500
0 Sea Level	0

Cities and Towns

| 0 to 50,000 | ○ | 500,000 to 1,000,000 | ◎ |
| 50,000 to 500,000 | ⊙ | 1,000,000 and over | ▓ |

Scale 1:4 000 000; one inch to 64 miles. Conic Projection
Elevations and depressions are given in feet.

Longitude West of Greenwich

A-511006-76 -77 -14
COPYRIGHT BY
RAND McNALLY & COMPANY
MADE IN U.S.A.

Continued on pages 112-113

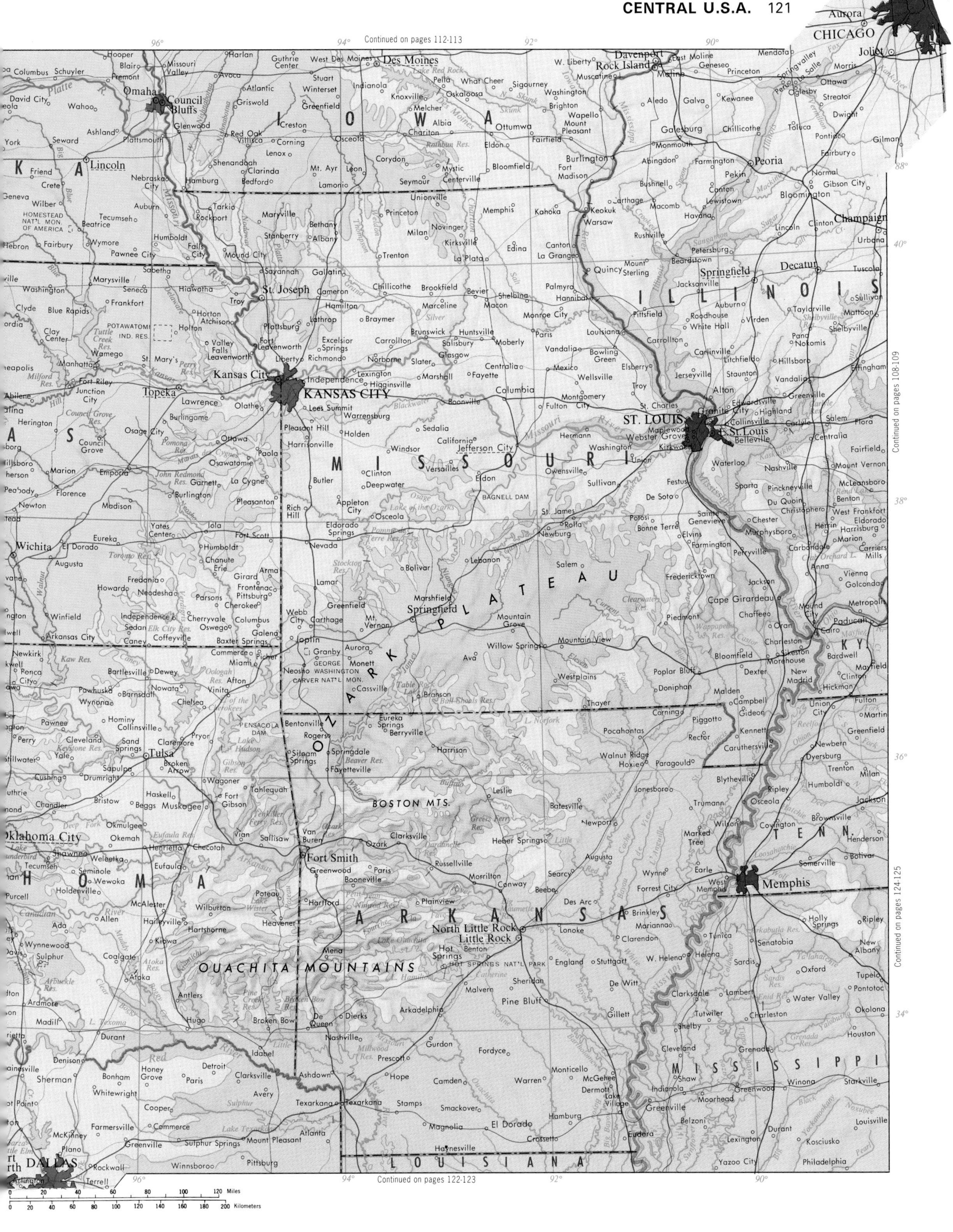

Continued on pages 108-109

Continued on pages 124-125

Continued on pages 122-123

CHICAGO
Aurora
Joliet

IOWA
Des Moines
Council Bluffs
Omaha

ILLINOIS
Springfield
Decatur
Champaign
Bloomington
Peoria

KANSAS
Lincoln
Topeka
Wichita

KANSAS CITY

MISSOURI
ST. LOUIS
St. Louis
Jefferson City
Columbia
Springfield

OZARK PLATEAU

BOSTON MTS.

OKLAHOMA
Oklahoma City
Tulsa
Fort Smith

ARKANSAS
Little Rock
North Little Rock
Hot Springs

OUACHITA MOUNTAINS

TENN.
Memphis

KY.
Cairo
Paducah

MISSISSIPPI

LOUISIANA

DALLAS

Scale
0 20 40 60 80 100 120 Miles
0 20 40 60 80 100 120 160 200 Kilometers

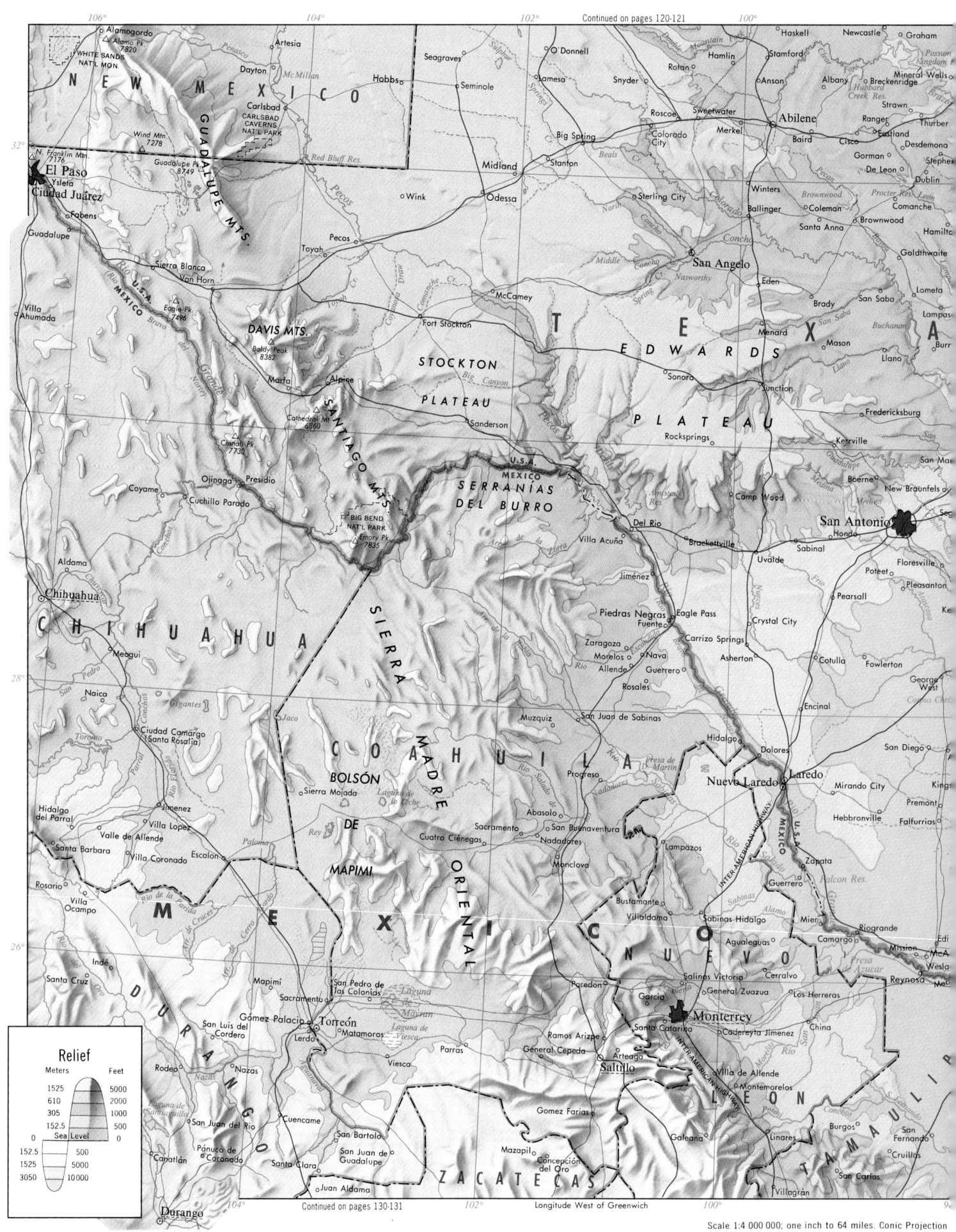

Continued on pages 120-121

NEW MEXICO

TEXAS

EDWARDS

PLATEAU

STOCKTON

PLATEAU

CHIHUAHUA

SERRANÍAS
DEL BURRO

SIERRA

MADRE

COAHUILA

ORIENTAL

BOLSÓN

DE

MAPIMI

MEXICO

DURANGO

NUEVO

LEON

ZACATECAS

TAMAULIPAS

DAVIS MTS.

SANTIAGO MTS.

Relief

Meters		Feet
1525		5000
610		2000
305		1000
152.5		500
0	Sea Level	0
152.5		500
1525		5000
3050		10000

Longitude West of Greenwich

Scale 1:4 000 000; one inch to 64 miles. Conic Projection
Elevations and depressions are given in feet

Continued on pages 120-121

Continued on pages 124-125

Scale 1:1 000 000

Cities	0 to 50,000	500,000 to 1,000,000
and		
Towns	50,000 to 500,000	1,000,000 and over

A-511007-76
COPYRIGHT BY
RAND McNALLY & COMPANY
MADE IN U.S.A.

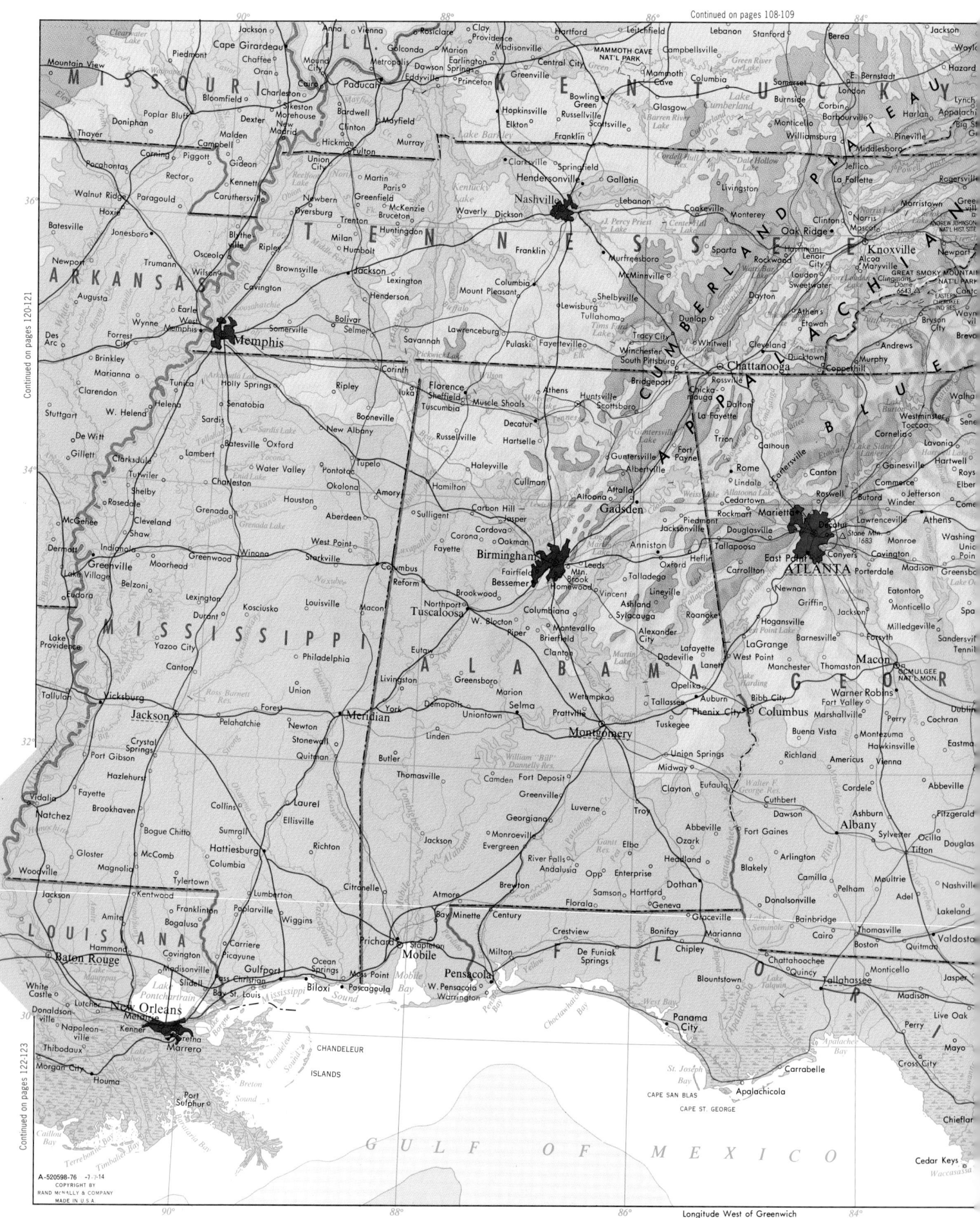

Continued on pages 108-109

Continued on pages 120-121

Continued on pages 122-123

Longitude West of Greenwich

Scale 1:4 000 000; one inch to 64 miles. Conic Projection
Elevations and depressions are given in feet

A-520598-76 -7-7-14
COPYRIGHT BY
RAND McNALLY & COMPANY
MADE IN U.S.A.

GULF OF MEXICO

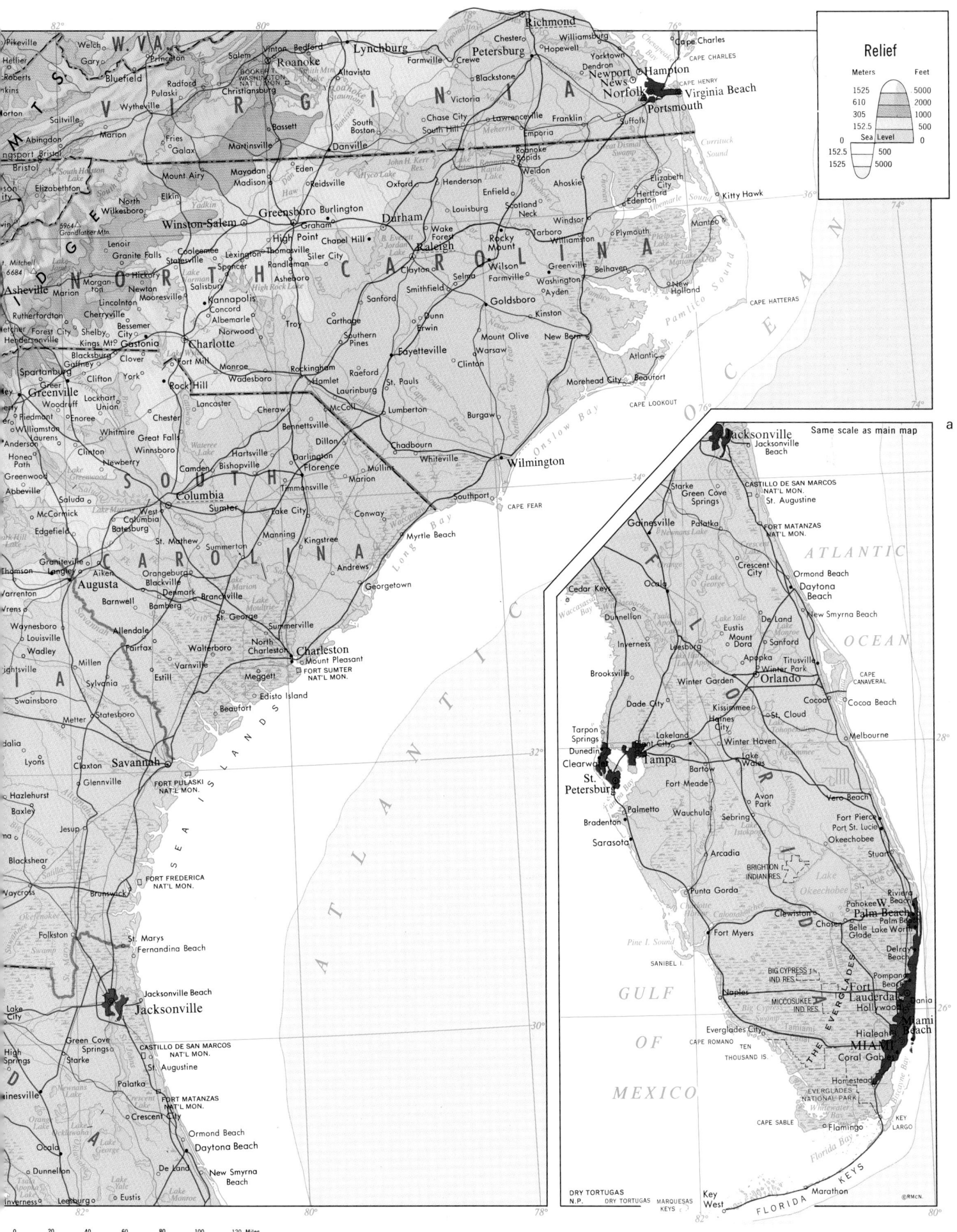

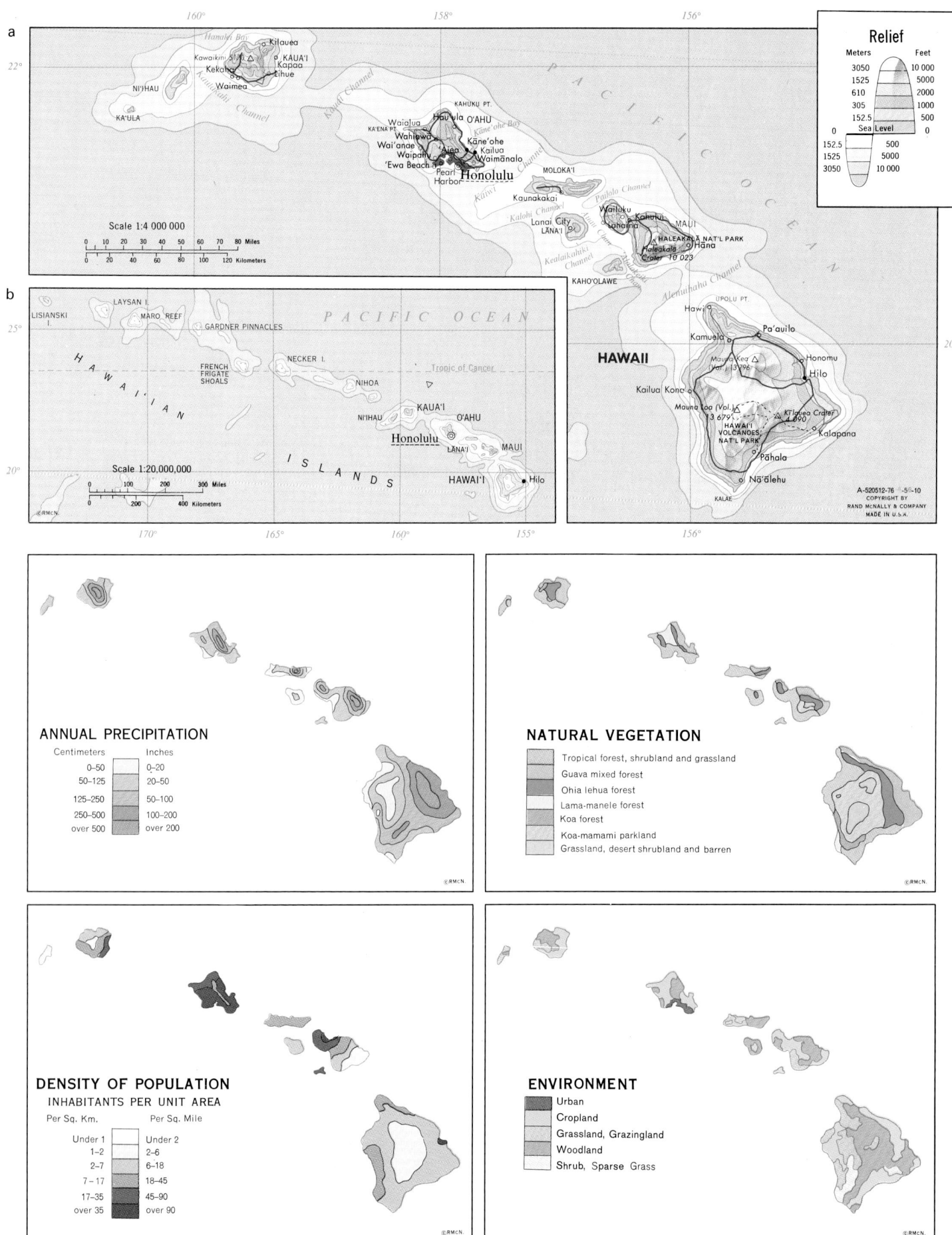

a

160°   158°   156°

22°

Relief

Meters	Feet
3050	10 000
1525	5000
610	2000
305	1000
152.5	500
0	Sea Level	0
152.5	500
1525	5000
3050	10 000

Hanalei Bay

Kilauea
Kawaikini △   KAUA'I
Kekaha   Kapaa
              Lihue
Waimea

NI'IHAU

KA'ULA

PACIFIC

Scale 1:4 000 000

0 10 20 30 40 50 60 70 80 Miles

0 20 40 60 80 100 120 Kilometers

KAHUKU PT.
Hau'ula O'AHU
Waialua
KA'ENA PT.   Kāne'ohe
Wahiawa   Kailua
Wai'anae   'Aiea   Waimānalo
Waipahu
'Ewa Beach   Pearl   Honolulu
              Harbor

MOLOKA'I

Kaunakakai

Wailuku Kahului
Lanai City Lahaina   MAUI
LĀNA'I   HALEAKALĀ NAT'L PARK
              Haleakalā Hāna
              Crater 10 023

KAHO'OLAWE

ALENUIHAHA Channel
UPOLU PT.

b

LAYSAN I.
LISIANSKI I.   MARO REEF
GARDNER PINNACLES

PACIFIC OCEAN

25°   20°

H
A
W
A
I
I
A
N

FRENCH
FRIGATE
SHOALS

NECKER I.

NIHOA

Tropic of Cancer

KAUA'I
NI'IHAU   O'AHU
Honolulu
LĀNA'I MAUI

I
S
L
A
N
D
S

Scale 1:20,000,000

0 100 200 300 Miles

0 200 400 Kilometers

HAWAI'I
Hilo

20°   20°

HAWAII

Hawi
Kamuela   Pa'auilo
Mauna Kea △   Honomu
(Vol.) 13,796   Hilo
Kailua Kona
Mauna Loa (Vol.) △   △ Kilauea Crater
13,679   4,090
HAWAI'I
VOLCANOES   Kalapana
NAT'L PARK
              Pāhala
Nā'ālehu
KALAE

A-520512-76 -5-10
COPYRIGHT BY
RAND McNALLY & COMPANY
MADE IN U.S.A.

170°   165°   160°   155°   156°

ANNUAL PRECIPITATION

Centimeters	Inches
0–50	0–20
50–125	20–50
125–250	50–100
250–500	100–200
over 500	over 200

NATURAL VEGETATION

Tropical forest, shrubland and grassland
Guava mixed forest
Ohia lehua forest
Lama-manele forest
Koa forest
Koa-mamami parkland
Grassland, desert shrubland and barren

DENSITY OF POPULATION
INHABITANTS PER UNIT AREA

Per Sq. Km.	Per Sq. Mile
Under 1	Under 2
1–2	2–6
2–7	6–18
7–17	18–45
17–35	45–90
over 35	over 90

ENVIRONMENT

Urban
Cropland
Grassland, Grazingland
Woodland
Shrub, Sparse Grass

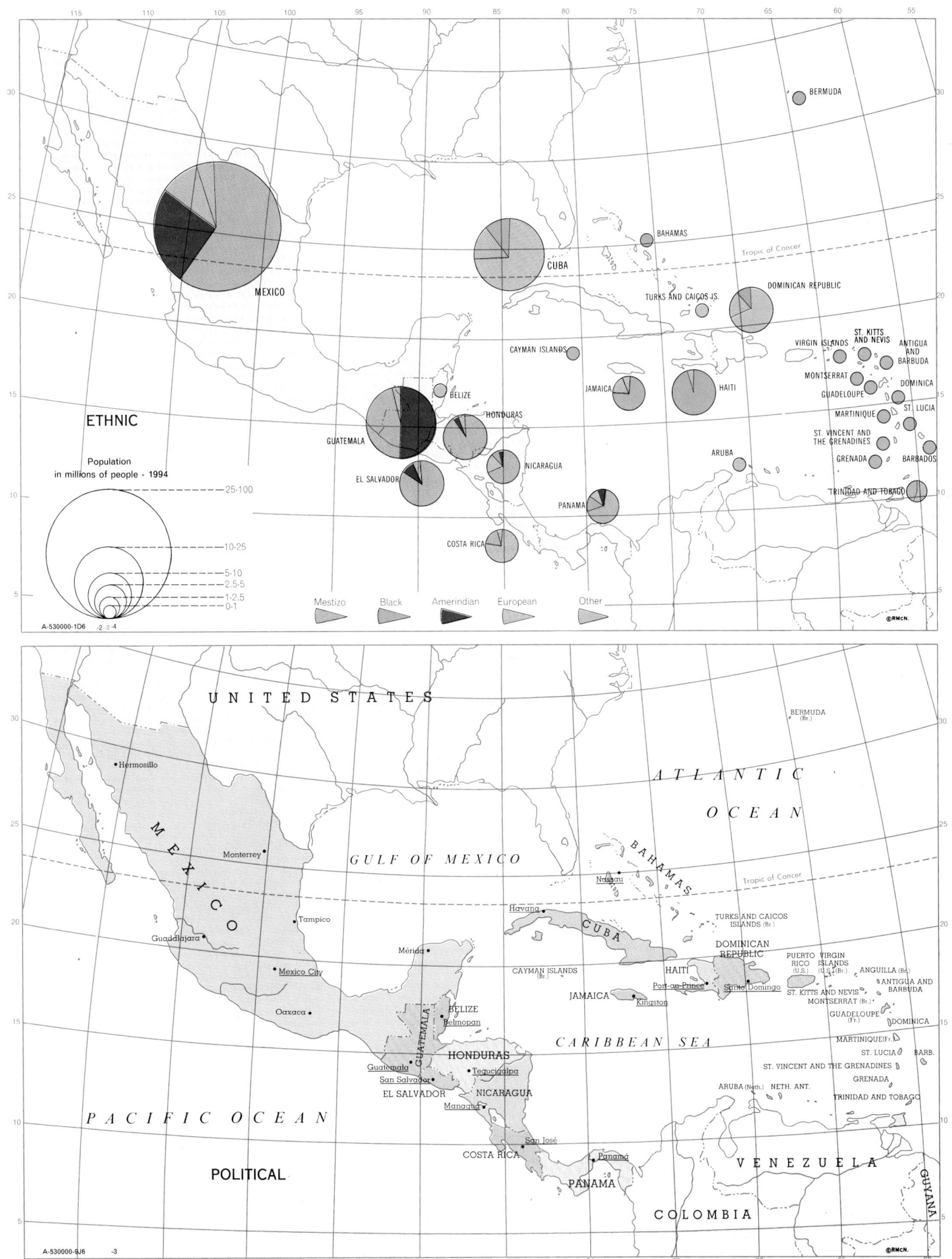

ETHNIC

Population
in millions of people - 1994

- 25-100
- 10-25
- 5-10
- 2.5-5
- 1-2.5
- 0-1

A-530000-1D6   -2 -2 -4

Mestizo   Black   Amerindian   European   Other

BERMUDA

MEXICO

CUBA

BAHAMAS

DOMINICAN REPUBLIC

TURKS AND CAICOS IS.

CAYMAN ISLANDS

BELIZE

HONDURAS

GUATEMALA

JAMAICA

HAITI

ST. KITTS AND NEVIS

VIRGIN ISLANDS

ANTIGUA AND BARBUDA

MONTSERRAT

DOMINICA

GUADELOUPE

MARTINIQUE

ST. LUCIA

ST. VINCENT AND THE GRENADINES

EL SALVADOR

NICARAGUA

ARUBA

GRENADA

BARBADOS

PANAMA

TRINIDAD AND TOBAGO

COSTA RICA

©RMCN.

POLITICAL

UNITED STATES

ATLANTIC OCEAN

Tropic of Cancer

• Hermosillo

M E X I C O

• Monterrey

GULF OF MEXICO

BAHAMAS

Nassau

• Tampico

Havana

CUBA

• Guadalajara

• Mérida

CAYMAN ISLANDS (Br.)

DOMINICAN REPUBLIC

TURKS AND CAICOS ISLANDS (Br.)

PUERTO RICO (U.S.)

VIRGIN ISLANDS (U.S.)(Br.)

ANGUILLA (Br.)

• Mexico City

HAITI

Port-au-Prince

Santo Domingo

ANTIGUA AND BARBUDA

ST. KITTS AND NEVIS

MONTSERRAT (Br.)

GUADELOUPE (Fr.)

DOMINICA

• Oaxaca

BELIZE

Belmopan

JAMAICA

Kingston

CARIBBEAN SEA

GUATEMALA

HONDURAS

Guatemala

Tegucigalpa

San Salvador

MARTINIQUE(Fr.)

ST. LUCIA

BARB.

ST. VINCENT AND THE GRENADINES

GRENADA

EL SALVADOR

NICARAGUA

Managua

ARUBA (Neth.)

NETH. ANT.

TRINIDAD AND TOBAGO

PACIFIC OCEAN

San José

COSTA RICA

Panamá

VENEZUELA

GUYANA

PANAMA

COLOMBIA

BERMUDA (Br.)

A-530000-9J6   -3

©RMCN.

Scale 1:16 000 000; one inch to 250 miles. Polyconic Projection
Elevations and depressions are given in feet

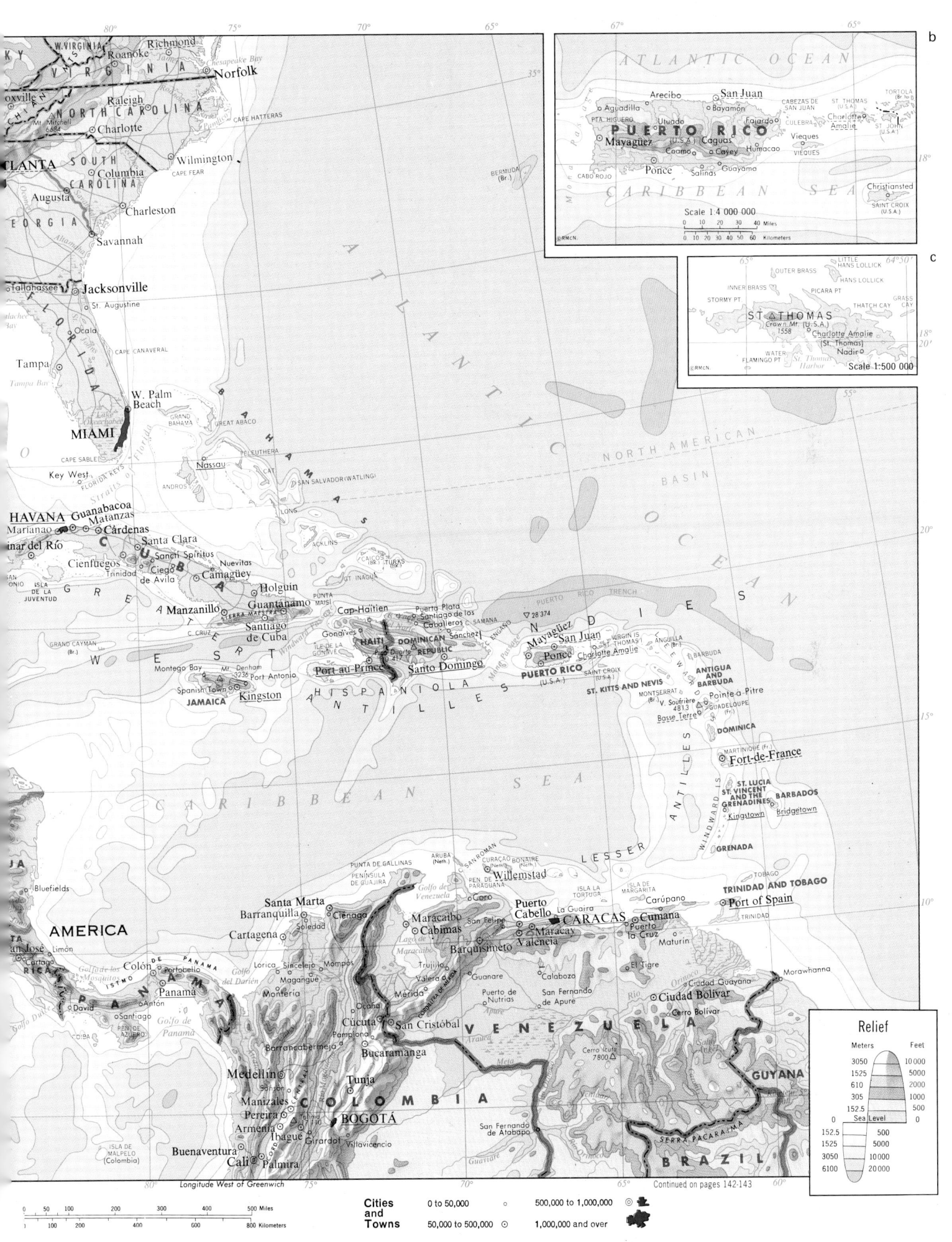

b

ATLANTIC OCEAN

Arecibo • San Juan
• Aguadilla ○ Bayamón   CABEZAS DE   ST. THOMAS   TORTOLA
PTA. HIGÜERO   SAN JUAN   (Br. Is.)
Utuado   ○   Fajardo   ○   Charlotte   ST. JOHN
PUERTO RICO   Amalie   (U.S.A.)
(U.S.A.)   ○ Caguas   CULEBRA
Mayagüez   ○ Cayey ○ Humacao   Vieques
○ Coamo   VIEQUES
CABO ROJO   ○ Salinas ○ Guayama

Ponce

CARIBBEAN   SEA   Christiansted
SAINT CROIX
(U.S.A.)

©RMcN.   18°

Scale 1:4 000 000
0 10 20 30 40 Miles
0 10 20 30 40 50 60 Kilometers

c

LITTLE   64°50'
HANS LOLLICK
OUTER BRASS   HANS LOLLICK
INNER BRASS   PICARA PT   THATCH CAY   GRASS
STORMY PT   CAY
ST. THOMAS
Crown Mt. (U.S.A.)   18°
1558   Charlotte Amalie   20'
(St. Thomas)
WATER   Nadir
FLAMINGO PT St. Thomas
©RMcN.   Harbor   Scale 1:500 000

Cities
and   0 to 50,000   ○   500,000 to 1,000,000   ◎
Towns   50,000 to 500,000   ⊙   1,000,000 and over

Continued on pages 142-143

Relief
Meters   Feet
3050   10 000
1525   5000
610   2000
305   1000
152.5   500
0   Sea Level   0
152.5   500
1525   5000
3050   10 000
6100   20 000

0   50 100   200   300   400   500 Miles
1 100 200   400   600   800 Kilometers

Longitude West of Greenwich

a

HIDALGO

TLAXCALA

MÉXICO

Morelos
Cuautitlán
Tecamac
Teotihuacán
Otumba
Apan

Nicolás Romero
Tutitlán
Acolman
Chiconautla
Pyramids of Teotihuacán
Calpulalpan

Cahuacán
Coacalco
Tepexpan

San Bartolo
Atizapán
Tlalnepantla
Tepetlaoxtoc

Ixtlahuaca
Cerro La Catedral 13 000
Mazatla
San Jerónimo
Nanacamilpa

Jiquipilco
Atzcapotzalco
Naucalpan de Juárez
Gustavo A. Madero
Lago de Texcoco (Dry Lake)
Texcoco

Temoaya
Mimiapan
Chimalpa
MEXICO CITY
Coatlinchán

Huixquilucan
Cuajimalpa
Nezahualcóyotl
Chicoloapan

Toluca
Lerma
Villa Obregón Contreras
Ixtacalco
Ixtapalapa
Los Reyes
Río Frío
HY.

Capultitlán
Metepec
Mexicalcingo
San Andrés
Tláhuac
Ayotla INTER-AMERICAN
Ixtapaluca
Texmelucan

Cerro Muneco 12 655
Tlálpan
Xochimilco
Chalco

Almoloya
Ajusco
Topilejo
Tecómitl

PUEBLA

Nevado de Toluca 14 409
Coatepec
Cerro Ajusco 12 850
Oxtotepec
Milpa Alta
Tlalmanalco
Tenango
Amecameca

DISTRITO FEDERAL

Iztaccihuatl 17 343

Tenango
Tres Cumbres
Ozumba
Volcán Popocatépetl 17 887

Huitzilac
Tepoztlán
Tlalnepantla

MORELOS
Tlayacapan

Scale 1:1 000 000

Cuernavaca

©RMCN

Laguna Almagre

Tropic of Cancer

PTA. JEREZ

Laguna de San Andres

tamira
Ciudad Madero
Tampico
Villa Cuauhtémoc
Tampico Alto

CABO ROJO
ARRECIFE BLANQUILLA
ISLA DE LOBOS

Laguna Tamiahua

luama
Tancoco
Tamiahua
Alamo
Túxpan

ARRECIFE TANQUIJO
ARRECIFE TÚXPAN

Tihuatlán

apalapa
Poza Rica
Tecolutla
Gutiérrez Zamora
Furbero
Nautla
Coyutla
Coxquihui

tlalpan
Cuetzalan del Progreso
Tlapacoyan
Misantla

atlán
Atempan
Jalacingo
Altotonga
Naolinco

apoaxtla
Teziutlán
Las Vigas
Perote
Xalapa

Libres
Nauchampatepetl 14 048
Coatepec

Teocelo

GULF OF MEXICO

Vega de Alatorre

PUNTA ZEMPOALA

Antigua Veracruz

B A H Í A   D E   C A M P E C H E

YUCATÁN

Sisal
Hunucmá

Maxcanú
Halachó

Calkini
Dzitbalché
Hecelchakán

Lerma
Campeche

Seybaplaya

Champotón

Pustunich

CAMPECHE

Sabancuy

Chicbul
Mamantel

manta
Tlatlauqui
Tlacolula

San Juan
xtenco

Antigua Veracruz

Veracruz

ARRECIFE CABEZA

Ciudad Serdán
Huatusco
Coscomatepec
Pico de Orizaba (Vol.) 18 406
Medellín

aca
Acatzingo de Hidalgo
Orizaba
Córdoba
Tlalixcoyan

oyatempan
Heroica Nogales
Omealca
Cotaxtla

Alvarado

ISLA DEL CARMEN
Laguna de Términos

Jlacotepec
Maltrata
Tehuacan
San Martín (Vol.) 6000
PTA. ZAPOTLÁN

San Pedro
Ciudad del Carmen

PUNTA FONTERA

Palizada

San Gabriel Chilac
Ajalpan
Zoquitlán
Tlacotalpan
Santiago Tuxtla
San Andrés Tuxtla

Paraíso
Frontera

Chazumba
Zinacatepec
Huatla de Jiménez
Ojitlán (S. Lucas)
Catemaco

Coatzacoalcos (Puerto México)

Allende
Comalcalco
Jalpa

Jánuta

atlalcingo
S. Miguel
Teotitlán del Camino
Jalapa de Díaz (San Felipe)
Tuxtepec

Pajápan

Cunduacán

Balancán

Tepelmeme
San Juan Evangelista
Jaltipan
Cosoleacaque

Cárdenas
Villahermosa
San Carlos
Emiliano Zapata

MEXICO
GUATEMALA

Huajuapan de León
Coixtlahuaca
Cuicatlán
Acayucan
Minatitlán
Texistepec

Jalmanguillo
Teapa
Tacotalpa
Palenque

azulapan
Progreso
Tejúpan (Santiago)
Playa Vicente
Sayula

Pichucalco
Tenosique

Pedro y San Pablo
Nochixtlán (Asunción)
Talea de Castro (San Miguel)
Villa Alta (San Ildefonso)
Jesús Carranza
Puebla Viejo

Chapultenango

Tlaxiaco
Sta. María Asunción
Ixtlán de Juárez
Hidalgo Yalalag
Zempoaltepetl 11 142

Tecpatán
Pantepec
Simojovel
Bachajón

errero
Chalcatongo
San Mateo (Etlatongo)
Oaxaca
Zacatepec (Santiago)
Mazatlán (San Juan)
Guichicovi (San Juan)

Compainalá
Jitotol
Ococingo

MESETA DE AGUA ESCONDIDA

Yosonotú (Sta. Catarina)
Zaachila
Zimatlán de Alvarez
Tlacolula de Matamoros
Ixtepec
Ixtaltepec (Asunción)
Zanatepec (Sto. Domingo)

Cancuc
Oxchuc
Amatenango

ndujía Sta. Cruz
Ocotlán de Morelos
Táviche
INTER-AMERICAN HY.
Union Hidalgo
Las Cruces

Berriozabal
Ozocoautla
Tuxtla Gutiérrez 9400
Bohom
San Cristóbal de las Casas
Chiapa de Corzo
Acala

Tlaxiaco
Sola de Vega (S. Miguel)
Ejutla de Crespo
Jalapa del Marqués
Juchitán de Zaragoza

Cintalapa
Suchiapa
Teopisca
Las Rosas

azolotitlán (Sta. María)
Miahuatlán
Las Vacas
Tehuantepec Sto. Domingo
Ixhuatán (San Francisco) 8202

Villa Flores
Venustiano Carranza
Comitán

amiltepec
Loxicha (Sta. Catarina)
Salina Cruz
Arriaga
Tonalá

Socoltenango
La Concordia
Trinitaria

ISTMO DE TEHUANTEPEC

O A X A C A

S I E R R A   D E   O A X A C A

SIERRA SUR

Pluma Hidalgo

Pochutla (San Pedro)

Puerto Ángel

Golfo de Tehuantepec

Laguna Superior
Laguna Inferior
Mar Muerto

SA. CUCHUMATANES

GUATEMALA

SIERRA MADRE
COR. DE CHIAPAS

Mapastepec
Cuauhtemoc
Jacatenango
Pijijiapan

Continued on pages 132-133

0   20   40   60   80   100   120 Miles
0   20   40   60   80   100   120   140   160   180   200 Kilometers

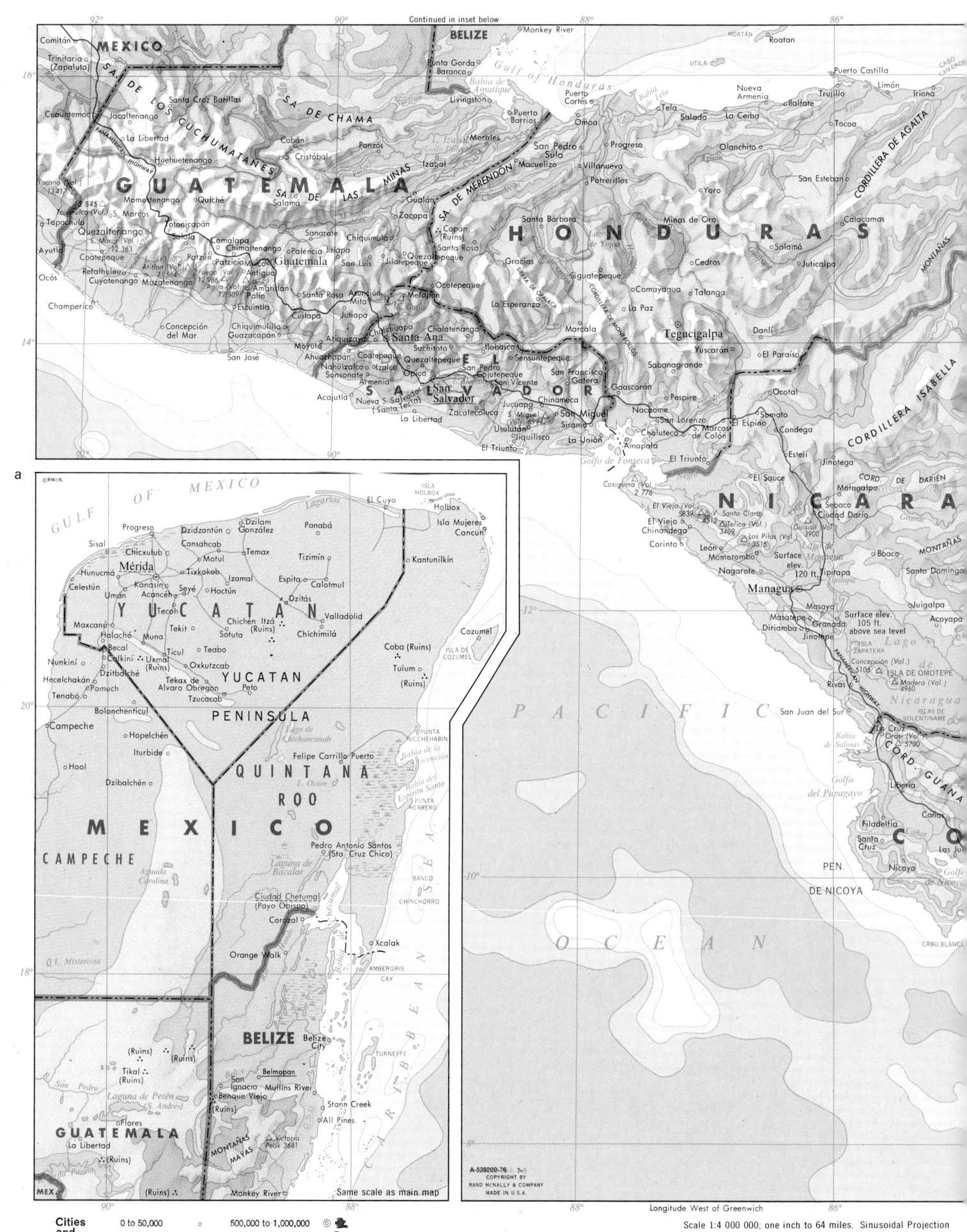

Cities
and
Towns

| 0 to 50,000 | o | 500,000 to 1,000,000 | ⊚ |
| 50,000 to 500,000 | ⊙ | 1,000,000 and over | |

Scale 1:4 000 000; one inch to 64 miles. Sinusoidal Projection

Elevations and depressions are given in feet

Longitude West of Greenwich

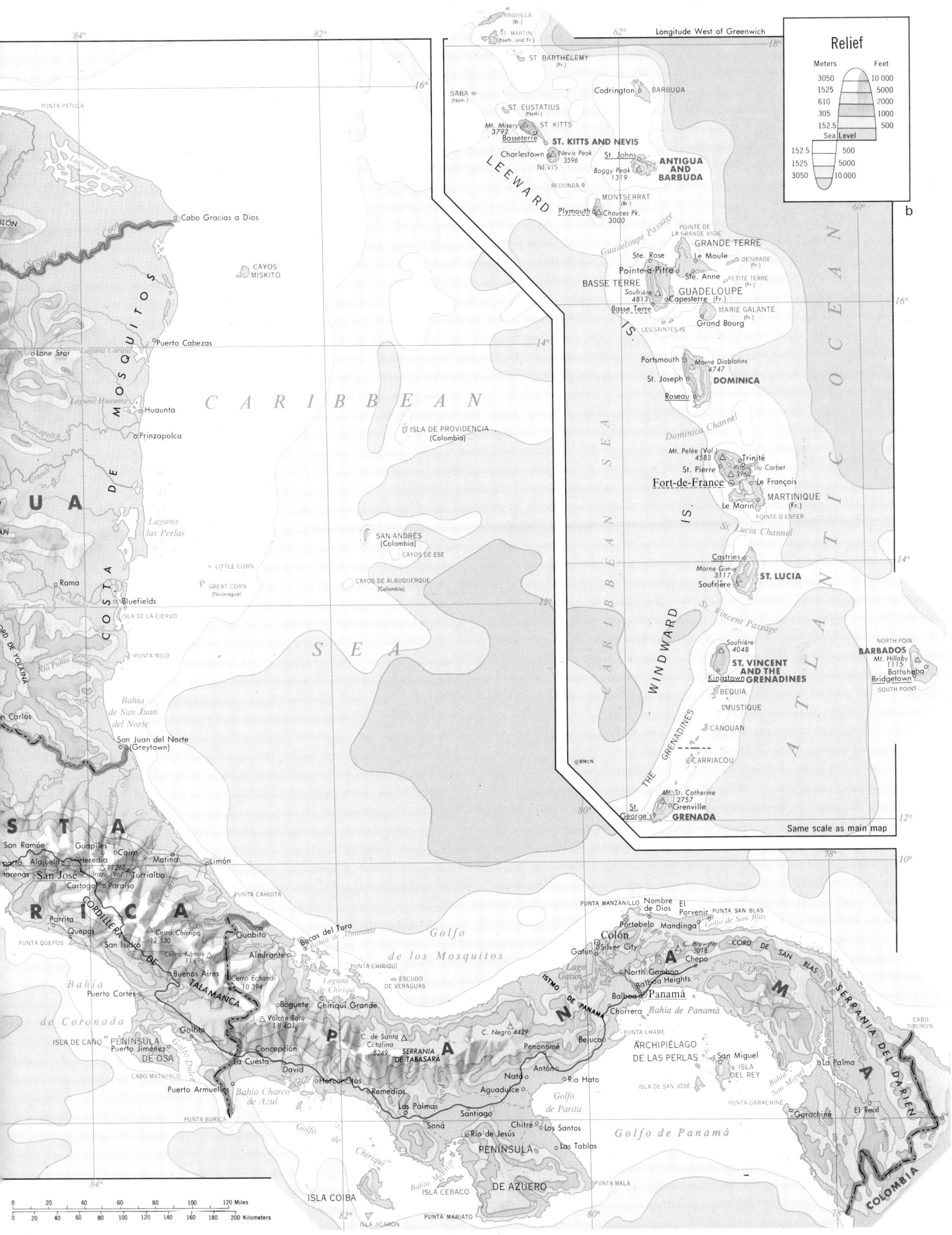

GULF

OF

MEXICO

FLORIDA

SANIBEL

Naples

Big Cypress Swamp

SEMINOLE IND. RES.

CAPE ROMANO

TEN THOUSAND ISLANDS

Everglades

EVERGLADES

THE EVERGLADES

EVERGLADES NATIONAL PARK

Homestead

Whitewater Bay

CAPE SABLE

Delray Beach

Dania

Fort Lauderdale

MIAMI

Miami Beach

Biscayne Bay

LITTLE BAHAMA BANK

SETTLEMENT PT.

West End

Freeport

PINDER POINT

GRAND BAHAMA

GREAT SALE CAY

LITTLE ABACO

GRAND BAHAMA

Carrion Crow Harbor

GREAT ISAAC

BROTHERS

LITTLE ISAAC

Northwest Providence Channel

GREAT ABACO

The Marls

Marsh Harbour

ELBOW

Cherokee Sound

MORES

GORDA CAY

Cross Harbor

CORNWALL

SOUTHWEST PT.

Cherokee Sound

Florida Bay

PINE IS.

KEY LARGO

Straits of Florida

FLORIDA KEYS

Key West

MARQUESAS KEYS

DRY TORTUGAS

Santaren Channel

DOG ROCKS

NORTH ELBOW CAYS

CAY SAL

CAY SAL BANK

DAMAS CAYS

ANGUILLA CAYS

Nicholas Channel

HURRICANE FLATS

Tropic of Cancer

NORTH BIMINI

SOUTH BIMINI

Barnett Harbor

N. CAT CAY

Dollar Harbor

RIDING ROCKS

ORANGE CAY

GREAT STIRRUP CAY

GREAT HARBOUR CAY

BERRY ISLANDS

BONDS CAY

WHALE CAY

FRAZIERS HOG CAY

JOULTER'S CAYS

Nicolls Town

Staniard Creek

WILLIAMS

SIMMS PT.

ANDROS ISLAND

North Bight

Middle Bight

South Bight

Turner Sound

NEW PROVIDENCE

Nassau

PARADISE

SHIP CHANNEL CAY

HIGHBORNE CAY

SALVADOR PT.

GREEN CAY

BOOBY ROCK

TONGUE OF THE OCEAN

SNAP PT.

CURLY CUT CAYS

ARCHIPIELAGO DE LOS COLORADOS

Santa Lucía

Pan de Guajaibon 2532

HAVANA

CIUDAD DE LA HABANA

Marianao

Guanabacoa

Regla

Guanajay

San Antonio de los Baños

Artemisa

Candelaria

HABANA

Bejucal

Güines

Güira de Melena

Batabanó

Union de Reyes

Alacranes

Matanzas

Cárdenas

Corralillo

Martí

Jovellanos

Pedro Betancourt

Colón

Quemado de Güines

MATANZAS

Sagua la Grande

Santo Domingo

Esperanza

ARCHIPIELAGO DE SABANA

CAYO BLANCOS

Bahia de Cárdenas

Bahia de Santa Clara

CAYO FRAGOSO

CAYO

CAYO SANTA MARÍA

VILLA CLARA

Santa Clara

Remedios

Caibarién

Camajuaní

Zulueta

Yaguajay

CAYO COCO

Bahia Buena Vista

Morón

CAYO GUILLERMO

Old Bahama Channel

CAYO LOBOS

CAYO CRUZ

CAYO PAREDON GRANDE

LOS PORGANOS

Consolación del Sur

Los Palacios

PINAR DEL RIO

SIERRA

VUELTA ABAJO

Pinar del Rio

San Juan y Martinez

Mantua

Guane

Bahía de Guadiana

PEN. DE GUANAHACABIBES

CABO FRANCES

CABO CORRIENTES

PTA. FRANCES

CABO PEPE

Ensenada de Cortés

CAYOS DE SAN FELIPE

CAYOS DE LOS INDIOS

Nueva Gerona

ISLA DE LA JUVENTUD

Santa Fé

CAYO DE DIOS

ISLAS DE MANGLES

ARCHIPIELAGO DE LOS CANARREOS

CAYOS DE JUAN LUIS

CAYO LARGO

CAYO ROSARIO

CAYO CANTILES

PUNTA GORDA

PENINSULA DE ZAPATA

Ensenada de la Broa

GOLFO DE BATABANO

CAYOS LAGUNA

Bordenón

Jagüey Grande

Rodas

Lajas

Cruces

Palmira

Cienfuegos

CIENFUEGOS

Bahia Cochinos

Bahia Cienfuegos

Pico San Juan

Casilda

SIERRA DE TRINIDAD

Trinidad

Placetas

Florida

SANCTI SPIRITUS

Sancti Spiritus

Jatibonico

CIEGO DE AVILA

Ciego de Avila

Júcaro

CAYO GUAJABA

CAYO SABINAL

CAMAGÜEY

Camagüey

Minas

Santa Lucía

Nuevitas

Bahia de Nuevitas

Fomento

Tunas de Zaza

CAYOS ANA MARÍA

BANCO JARDINES

BANCO XAGUA

CAYOS CINCO BALAS

CAYOS DE LAS DOCE LEGUAS

Canal de Caballones

LABERINTO DE LAS DOCE LEGUAS

Santa Cruz del Sur

GOLFO DE GUACANAYABO

Guayabal

Puerto Padre

LAS TUNAS

Victoria de las Tunas

Manzanillo

Campechuela

Niquero

Pico Ojo del Toro 1748

CABO CRUZ

GRANMA

SIERRA

Pico Turquino 2005

CARIBBEAN

CAYMAN ISLANDS

LITTLE CAYMAN

CAYMAN BRAC (Br.)

George Town

GRAND CAYMAN

SEA

Montego Bay

Falmouth

St. Ann's Bay

GALINA

Lucea

SOUTH NEGRIL PT.

Savanna la Mar

JAMAICA

Mt. Denham 2256

Bull Head 2720

Annotto Bay

Port Ma

Spanish To

Kingsto

Black River

May Pen

GT. PEDRO BLUFF

PORTLAND

Portland Bight

Relief

Meters	Feet
3050	10 000
1525	5000
610	2000
305	1000
152.5	500
0	Sea Level
152.5	500
1525	5000
3050	10 000
6100	20 000

Cities and Towns

0 to 50,000 ○

50,000 to 500,000 ⊙

500,000 to 1,000,000 ◎

1,000,000 and over

Longitude West of Greenwich

Scale 1:4 000 000; one inch to 64 miles. Conic Projection

Elevations and depressions are given in feet.

Scale 1:1 000 000

GULF OF MEXICO

HAVANA
(La Habana)

Cojimar
Playa de Guanaba

Playa de Santa Fé
Guanabacoa
Regla
Campo Florido
Baracoa
Marianao
San Francisco de Paula
Cotorro
Arroya Arena
Calabazar
Bauta
Rancho Boyeros
Cuatro Caminos
Cainito del Guayabal
Managua
San José de las Lajas
Santiago de las Vegas
La Sabina
Bejucal
Ensenada de Arigüanabo
Buenaventura
San Antonio
del los Baños
Ceiba del Agua
△ 950
San Antonio de las Vegas
©RMcN

ATLANTIC

OCEAN

JAMES PT.
Governor's Harbour
PALMETTO PT.
ELEUTHERA
Rock Sound
Arthur's Town
NORTHEAST PT.
LITTLE SAN SALVADOR
CAT
Old Bight
COLUMBUS PT.
HAWKS NEST PT.
SAN SALVADOR
(WATLING)
(Columbus, Oct. 12, 1492)
SOUTHWEST PT.
CONCEPTION
LEE STOCKING
CAPE STA. MARIA
Rolleville
RUM CAY
GREAT EXUMA
George Town
LITTLE EXUMA
HOG CAY
LONG
Clarence Town
JUMENTO CAYS
WATER CAY
SAMANA OR ATWOOD CAY
FLAMINGO CAY
CAP VERDE
BIRD ROCK
CROOKED
JAMAICA CAY
NORTHEAST PT.
SEAL CAYS
FORTUNE
PLANA OR FLAT CAYS
NURSE CAY
DIANA BANK
FISH CAY
RACCOON CAY
ACKLINS
Abraham's Bay
GREAT RAGGED
SALINA PT.
MAYAGUANA
COLUMBUS BANK
MIRA POR VOS ISLETS
CASTLE
CAY VERDE
CAY STA. DOMINGO
HOGSTY REEF
PROVIDENCIALES
NORTH CAICOS
GRAND CAICOS
CAPE COMETE
EAST CAICOS
WEST CAICOS
CAICOS IS. (Br.)
GRAND TURK
Grand Turk
LITTLE INAGUA
SOUTH CAICOS
TURKS IS. (Br.)
BROWN BANK
NORTHEAST PT.
WEST SAND SPIT
PALMETTO PT.
AMBERGRIS CAYS
SALT CAY
SEAL CAYS
MOUCHOIR PASSAGE
MOUCHOIR BANK
GREAT INAGUA
Matthew Town
The Lake
SILVER BANK
Gibara
CABO LUCRECIA
Banes
Holguin
Antilla
Bahía de Nipe
Mayari
Sagua de Tánamo
HOLGUIN
CUCHILLAS DE TOAR
3100
Baracoa
SANTIAGO DE CUBA
SA. DE PURIAL
Alto Songo
Soriano
San Luis
Caney
Pico Piedra
PUNTA MAISI
Bahía de Ovando
Santiago de Cuba
Guantánamo
Yateras
Caimanera
Naval Station (U.S.A.)
Bahía de Guantánamo
ILE DE LA TORTUE
Port de Paix
CABO ISABELA
Le Borgne
Cap-Haïtien
Monte Cristi
CORDILLERA SEPTENTRIONAL
Puerto Plata
CABO FRANCÉS VIEJO
CAP ST. NICOLAS
Le Môle
Limbé
Fort Liberté
Guayubin
Dajabón
Santiago Rodríguez
Gasper Hernández
Bahía Escocesa
PTE. PLATEFORME
Grande Rivière du Nord
Ouanaminthe
Vallière
Santiago de los Caballeros
Salcedo
Moca
Nagua
CABO SAMANA
Gonaïves
St. Michel de l'Atalaye
Hinche
La Vega
Jarabacoa
Cotui
Sánchez
Samaná
Bahía de Samaná
CABO SAN RAFAEL
GOLFE DES GONAIVES
Pic Bonhomme
5883
DOMINICAN
Riva
Sabana de la Mar
CORDILLERA ORIENTAL
St. Marc
Pico Duarte
10417
Hato Mayor
Miches
POINT OUEST
ILE DE LA GONAVE
Mirebalais
CORDILLERA CENTRAL
Mte. Tina
7285
Bayaguana
Los Llanos
Seibo
Jérémie
ILE GRANDE CAYEMITE
2544
San Juan
Xamasá
La Romana
HAITI
Canal du Sud
Léogane
Lascahobas
SIERRA DE NEIBA
REPUBLIC
Catalina
CAP DAME MARIE
Petion-ville
Neiba
Azua
San Cristóbal
Santo Domingo
S. Pedro de Macoris
FORMIGAS BANK
Anse d'Hainault
MASSIF DE LA HOTTE
Miragoane
Petit Goave
MASSIF DE LA SELLE
6778
Duvergé
Barahona
Bani
NAVASSA (U.S.A.)
Tiburon
7920
Aquin
SIERRA DE BAHORUCO
PTA. PALENQUE
Coteaux
Les Cayes
Jacmel Belle-Anse
Enriquillo
HISPANIOLA
SAONA
MORANT PT.
Roche à Bateau
ILE A VACHE
POINTE A GRAVOIS
Oviedo
CABO FALSO
BEATA
CABO BEATA
ALTO VELO

Windward Passage

Tropic of Cancer

10 20 30 40 50 60 70 80 90 100 110 120 Miles
20 40 60 80 100 120 140 160 180 200 Kilometers

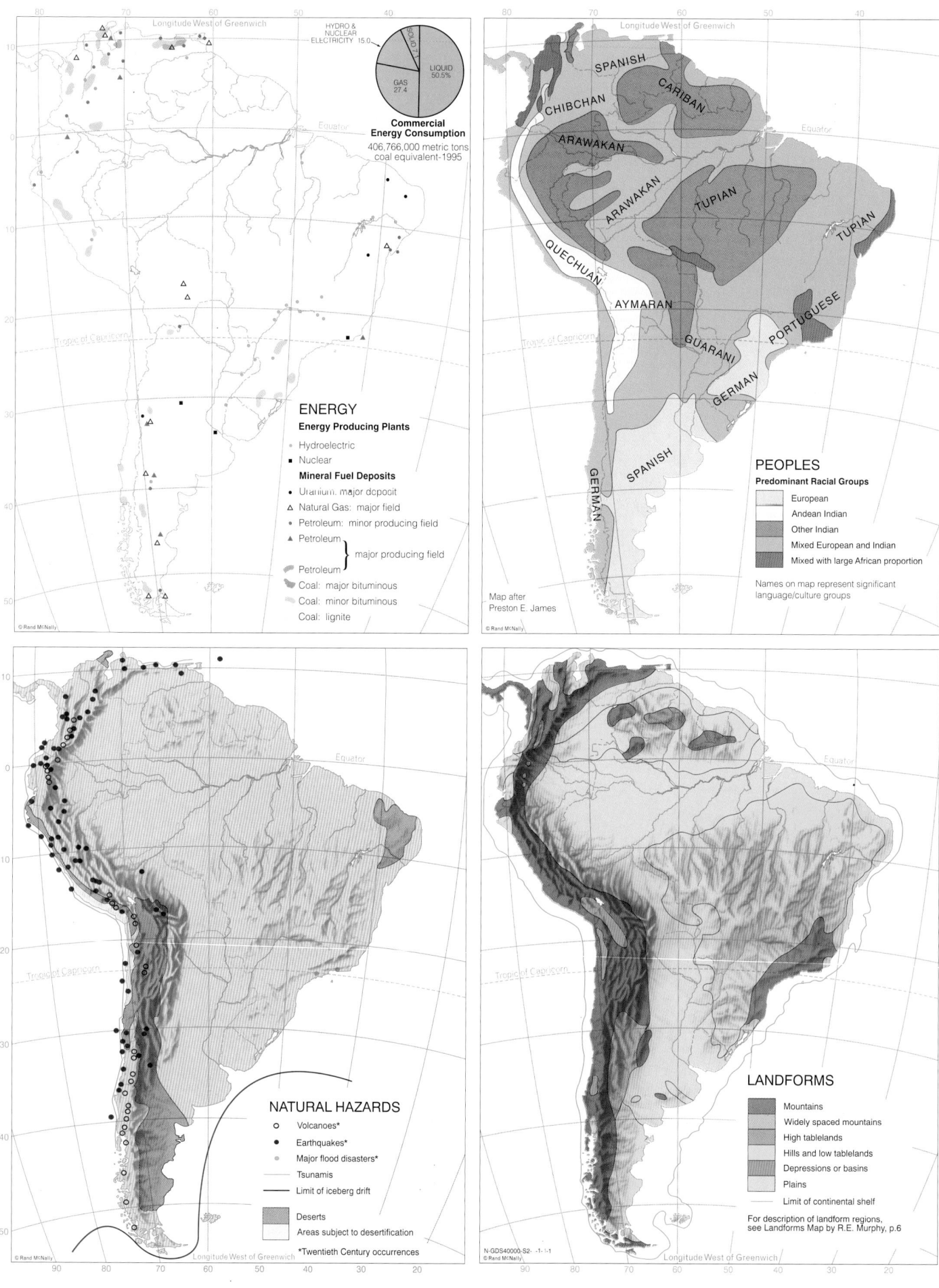

ENERGY

Energy Producing Plants

• Hydroelectric

■ Nuclear

Mineral Fuel Deposits

• Uranium: major deposit

△ Natural Gas: major field

• Petroleum: minor producing field

▲ Petroleum

⬤ Petroleum } major producing field

Coal: major bituminous

Coal: minor bituminous

Coal: lignite

© Rand McNally

HYDRO & NUCLEAR ELECTRICITY 15.0

SOLID 7.1

LIQUID 50.5%

GAS 27.4

Commercial Energy Consumption

406,766,000 metric tons coal equivalent-1995

PEOPLES

Predominant Racial Groups

European

Andean Indian

Other Indian

Mixed European and Indian

Mixed with large African proportion

Names on map represent significant language/culture groups

Map after Preston E. James

© Rand McNally

SPANISH

CHIBCHAN

ARAWAKAN

CARIBAN

ARAWAKAN

TUPIAN

QUECHUAN

AYMARAN

TUPIAN

GUARANI

PORTUGUESE

GERMAN

SPANISH

GERMAN

NATURAL HAZARDS

○ Volcanoes*

● Earthquakes*

● Major flood disasters*

— Tsunamis

— Limit of iceberg drift

Deserts

Areas subject to desertification

*Twentieth Century occurrences

© Rand McNally

LANDFORMS

Mountains

Widely spaced mountains

High tablelands

Hills and low tablelands

Depressions or basins

Plains

— Limit of continental shelf

For description of landform regions, see Landforms Map by R.E. Murphy, p.6

N-GDS40000-S2- -1- 1-1
© Rand McNally

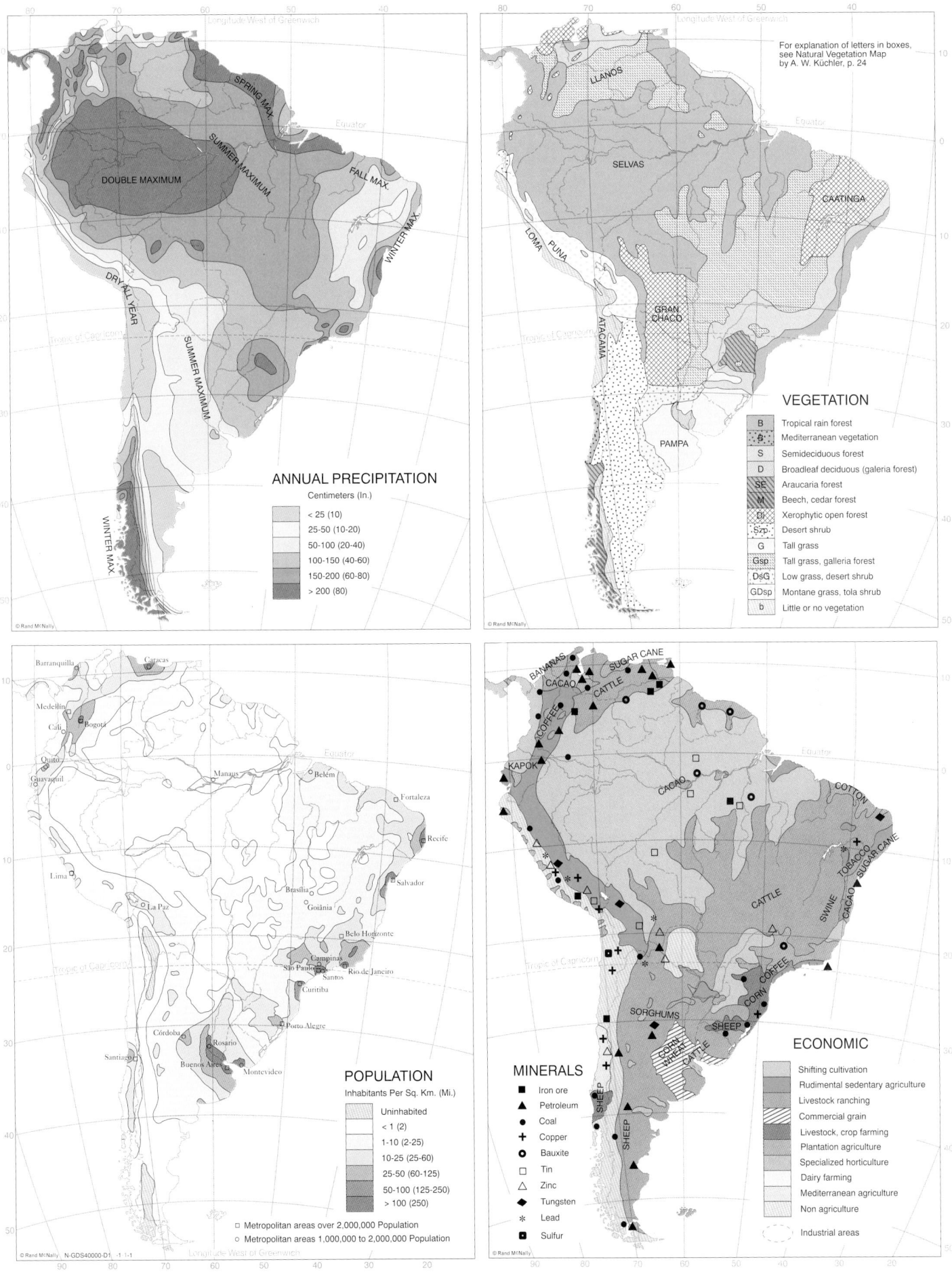

ANNUAL PRECIPITATION

Centimeters (In.)

- < 25 (10)
- 25-50 (10-20)
- 50-100 (20-40)
- 100-150 (40-60)
- 150-200 (60-80)
- > 200 (80)

SPRING MAX.
SUMMER MAXIMUM
FALL MAX.
WINTER MAX.
DOUBLE MAXIMUM
DRY ALL YEAR
SUMMER MAXIMUM
WINTER MAX.

VEGETATION

B	Tropical rain forest
Φ	Mediterranean vegetation
S	Semideciduous forest
D	Broadleaf deciduous (galeria forest)
SE	Araucaria forest
M	Beech, cedar forest
Dl	Xerophytic open forest
Szp	Desert shrub
G	Tall grass
Gsp	Tall grass, galleria forest
DsG	Low grass, desert shrub
GDsp	Montane grass, tola shrub
b	Little or no vegetation

LLANOS
SELVAS
CAATINGA
LOMA
PUNA
ATACAMA
GRAN CHACO
PAMPA

For explanation of letters in boxes, see Natural Vegetation Map by A. W. Küchler, p. 24

POPULATION

Inhabitants Per Sq. Km. (Mi.)

- Uninhabited
- < 1 (2)
- 1-10 (2-25)
- 10-25 (25-60)
- 25-50 (60-125)
- 50-100 (125-250)
- > 100 (250)

□ Metropolitan areas over 2,000,000 Population
○ Metropolitan areas 1,000,000 to 2,000,000 Population

Barranquilla, Caracas, Medellín, Cali, Bogotá, Quito, Guayaquil, Lima, La Paz, Santiago, Córdoba, Rosario, Buenos Aires, Montevideo, Manaus, Belém, Fortaleza, Recife, Salvador, Brasília, Goiânia, Belo Horizonte, Campinas, São Paulo, Santos, Rio de Janeiro, Curitiba, Porto Alegre

MINERALS

- ■ Iron ore
- ▲ Petroleum
- ● Coal
- + Copper
- ◎ Bauxite
- □ Tin
- △ Zinc
- ◆ Tungsten
- ＊ Lead
- ▣ Sulfur

ECONOMIC

- Shifting cultivation
- Rudimental sedentary agriculture
- Livestock ranching
- Commercial grain
- Livestock, crop farming
- Plantation agriculture
- Specialized horticulture
- Dairy farming
- Mediterranean agriculture
- Non agriculture
- Industrial areas

BANANAS, SUGAR CANE, CACAO, CATTLE, COFFEE, KAPOK, CACAO, COTTON, TOBACCO, SUGAR CANE, CATTLE, SWINE, CACAO, COFFEE, CORN, SORGHUMS, SHEEP, CORN, WHEAT, CATTLE, SHEEP

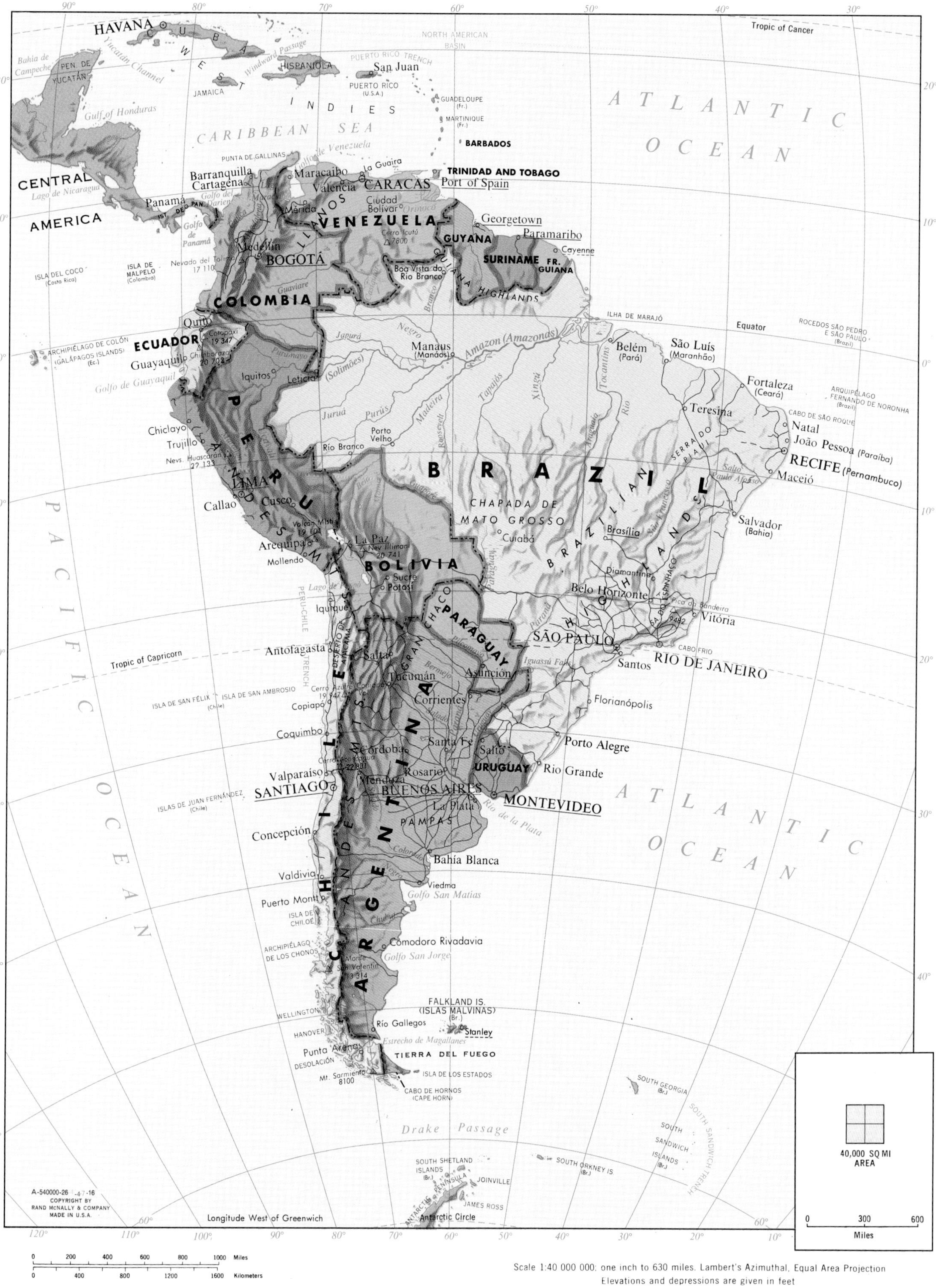

HAVANA

CUBA

Bahía de Campeche

PEN. DE YUCATÁN

Yucatán Channel

WEST

JAMAICA

HISPANIOLA

San Juan

PUERTO RICO (U.S.A.)

PUERTO RICO TRENCH

Gulf of Honduras

Lago de Nicaragua

CENTRAL

AMERICA

Panamá

IST. DE PAN.

Golfo de Darién

Golfo de Panamá

ISLA DE MALPELO (Colombia)

ISLA DEL COCO (Costa Rica)

CARIBBEAN SEA

NORTH AMERICAN BASIN

GUADELOUPE (Fr.)

MARTINIQUE (Fr.)

BARBADOS

Windward Passage

PUNTA DE GALLINAS

Golfo de Venezuela

La Guaira

TRINIDAD AND TOBAGO

Port of Spain

Barranquilla

Cartagena

Maracaibo

Valencia

CARACAS

Mérida

Ciudad Bolívar

Orinoco

VENEZUELA

Cerro Icutú △ 7800

Georgetown

Paramaribo

Medellín

BOGOTÁ

GUYANA

SURINAME

FR. GUIANA

Cayenne

Boa Vista do Rio Branco

GUIANA HIGHLANDS

COLOMBIA

Quito

ECUADOR

Cotopaxi 19 347

Chimborazo 20 704

Guayaquil

Golfo de Guayaquil

Iquitos

Leticia

Napo

ILHA DE MARAJÓ

Equator

ROCEDOS SÃO PEDRO E SÃO PAULO (Brazil)

ARQUIPÉLAGO DE COLÓN (GALÁPAGOS ISLANDS) (Ec.)

Negro

Manaus (Manáos)

Amazon (Amazonas)

Belém (Pará)

São Luís (Maranhão)

ARQUIPÉLAGO FERNANDO DE NORONHA (Brazil)

Chiclayo

Trujillo

Nevs. Huascarán 22 133

Japurá

Putumayo

Solimões

Juruá

Purús

Jutaí

Madeira

Porto Velho

Rio Branco

Tapajós

Xingu

Tocantins

Teresina

Fortaleza (Ceará)

Natal

João Pessoa (Paraíba)

CABO DE SÃO ROQUE

RECIFE (Pernambuco)

Maceió

P E R U

LIMA

Callao

Cusco

Volcán Misti 19 101

Arequipa

Mollendo

La Paz

Nev. Illimani 20 741

Lago de Titicaca

Sucre

Potosí

BOLIVIA

B R A Z I L

CHAPADA DE MATO GROSSO

Cuiabá

Diamantina

Serrado Mar

Salto Paulo Afonso

Salvador (Bahia)

Brasília

Belo Horizonte

Pico da Bandeira 9482

Vitória

A N D E S

CORDILLERA

PERU-CHILE TRENCH

Iquique

Antofagasta

Tropic of Capricorn

ISLA DE SAN FÉLIX

ISLA DE SAN AMBROSIO (Chile)

Copiapó

Cerro 19 947

Coquimbo

Valparaíso

SANTIAGO

ISLAS DE JUAN FERNÁNDEZ (Chile)

Concepción

Valdivia

Puerto Montt

ISLA DE CHILOÉ

ARCHIPIÉLAGO DE LOS CHONOS

GRAN CHACO

Salta

Tucumán

Corrientes

Córdoba

Santa Fe

Rosario

Mendoza

BUENOS AIRES

La Plata

PAMPAS

Bahía Blanca

PARAGUAY

SÃO PAULO

Asunción

Iguassú Falls

Santos

CABO FRIO

RIO DE JANEIRO

Florianópolis

Porto Alegre

URUGUAY

Salto

Rio Grande

MONTEVIDEO

Río de la Plata

Colorado

Viedma

Golfo San Matías

Monte San Valentín 13 314

Comodoro Rivadavia

Golfo San Jorge

A R G E N T I N A

C H I L E

ANDES

FALKLAND IS. (ISLAS MALVINAS) (Br.)

WELLINGTON I.

HANOVER I.

Río Gallegos

Stanley

Punta Arenas

DESOLACIÓN I.

Estrecho de Magallanes

Mt. Sarmiento 8100

TIERRA DEL FUEGO

ISLA DE LOS ESTADOS

CABO DE HORNOS (CAPE HORN)

SOUTH GEORGIA (Br.)

ATLANTIC OCEAN

PACIFIC OCEAN

Drake Passage

SOUTH SHETLAND ISLANDS (Br.)

SOUTH ORKNEY IS. (Br.)

SOUTH SANDWICH ISLANDS (Br.)

JOINVILLE I.

ANTARCTIC PENINSULA

JAMES ROSS I.

Antarctic Circle

Longitude West of Greenwich

Tropic of Cancer

40,000 SQ MI AREA

0 300 600
Miles

0 200 400 600 800 1000 Miles

0 400 800 1200 1600 Kilometers

Scale 1:40 000 000: one inch to 630 miles. Lambert's Azimuthal, Equal Area Projection
Elevations and depressions are given in feet

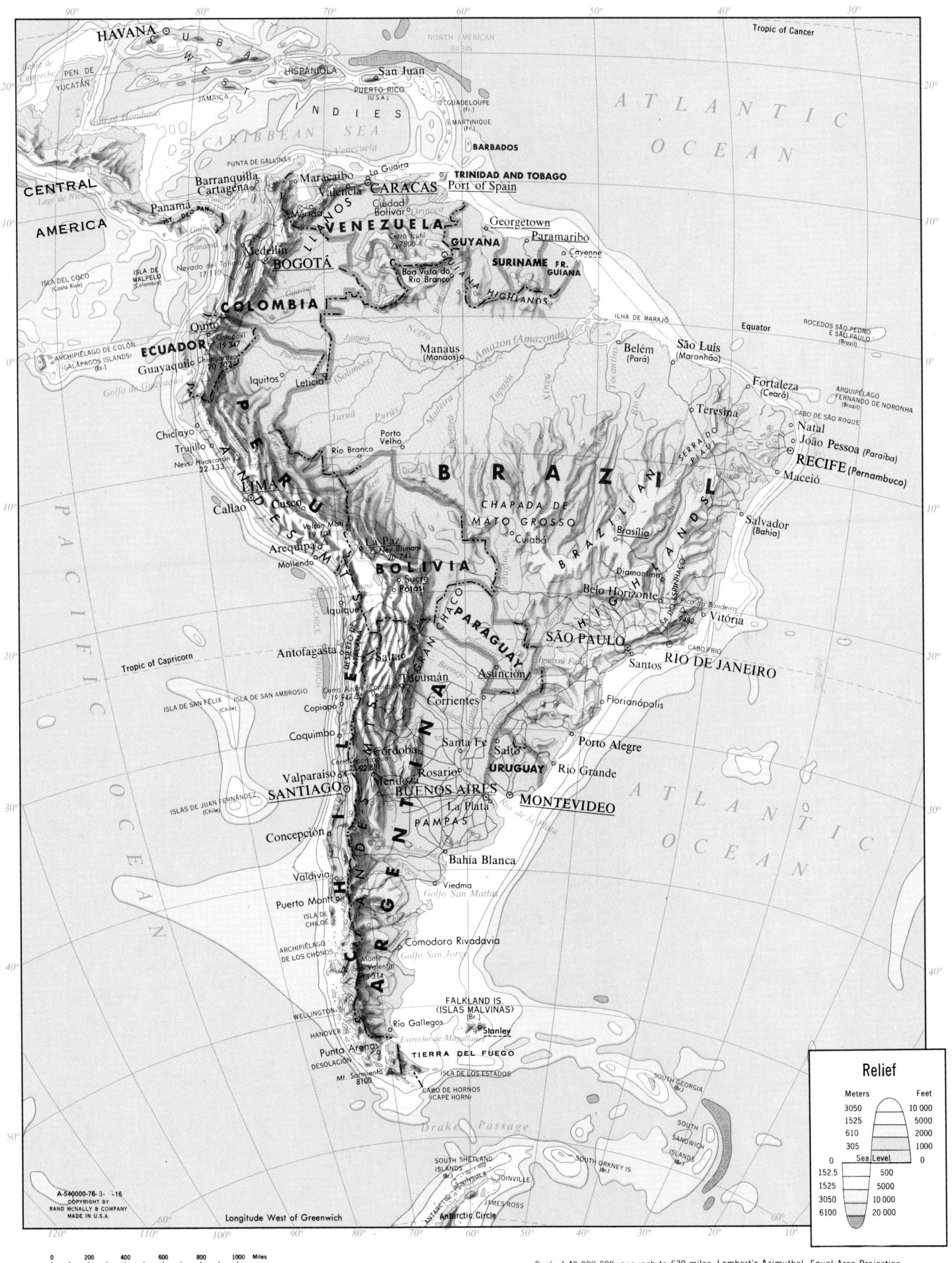

Longitude West of Greenwich

Scale 1:40 000 000; one inch to 630 miles. Lambert's Azimuthal, Equal Area Projection
Elevations and depressions are given in feet

Relief

Meters		Feet
3050		10 000
1525		5000
610		2000
305		1000
0	Sea Level	0
152.5		500
1525		5000
3050		10 000
6100		20 000

CUBA

JAMAICA
Kingston   HISPANIOLA

San Juan
PUERTO
RICO

C a r i b b e a n   S e a

A T L A N T I C

O C E A N

Barranquilla   Maracaibo   **CARACAS**   Port of Spain
TRINIDAD

Panamá

L L A N O S   *Orinoco*

Georgetown

BOGOTÁ

Quito   *Negro*   *Equator*

Belém

Iquitos   Manaus   *Amazon*   Fortaleza

S E L V A S

Rio Branco   *São Francisco*   Recife

LIMA

Salvador

Cuiabá
M A T O
G R O S S O   Brasília
La Paz

Iquique   *G R A N   C H A C O*   Belo Horizonte

Paraná   **SÃO
PAULO**   **RIO DE JANEIRO**

Tropic of Capricorn   Asunción

San Miguel
de Tucumán

Porto Alegre

Córdoba

P A C I F I C   **SANTIAGO**   **BUENOS AIRES**

Montevideo

O C E A N   *P A M P A*   *A T L A N T I C*

Bahía Blanca   *O C E A N*

Puerto Montt

P A T A G O N I A

FALKLAND
ISLANDS

Punta Arenas   TIERRA
DEL FUEGO

SOUTH
GEORGIA

Drake   Passage

A-540000-36   -2-8
COPYRIGHT BY
RAND MCNALLY & COMPANY
MADE IN U.S.A.

■	Urban
	Cropland
	Cropland & Woodland
	Cropland & Grazing Land
	Grassland, Grazing Land
	Forest, Woodland
	Swamp, Marshland
	Shrub, Sparse Grass, Wasteland
	Barren Land

Scale 1:36,000,000; one inch to 570 miles   Lambert Azimuthal Equal-Area Projection

0   100   200   400   600   800 Miles

0   150   300   600   900   1200 Kilometers

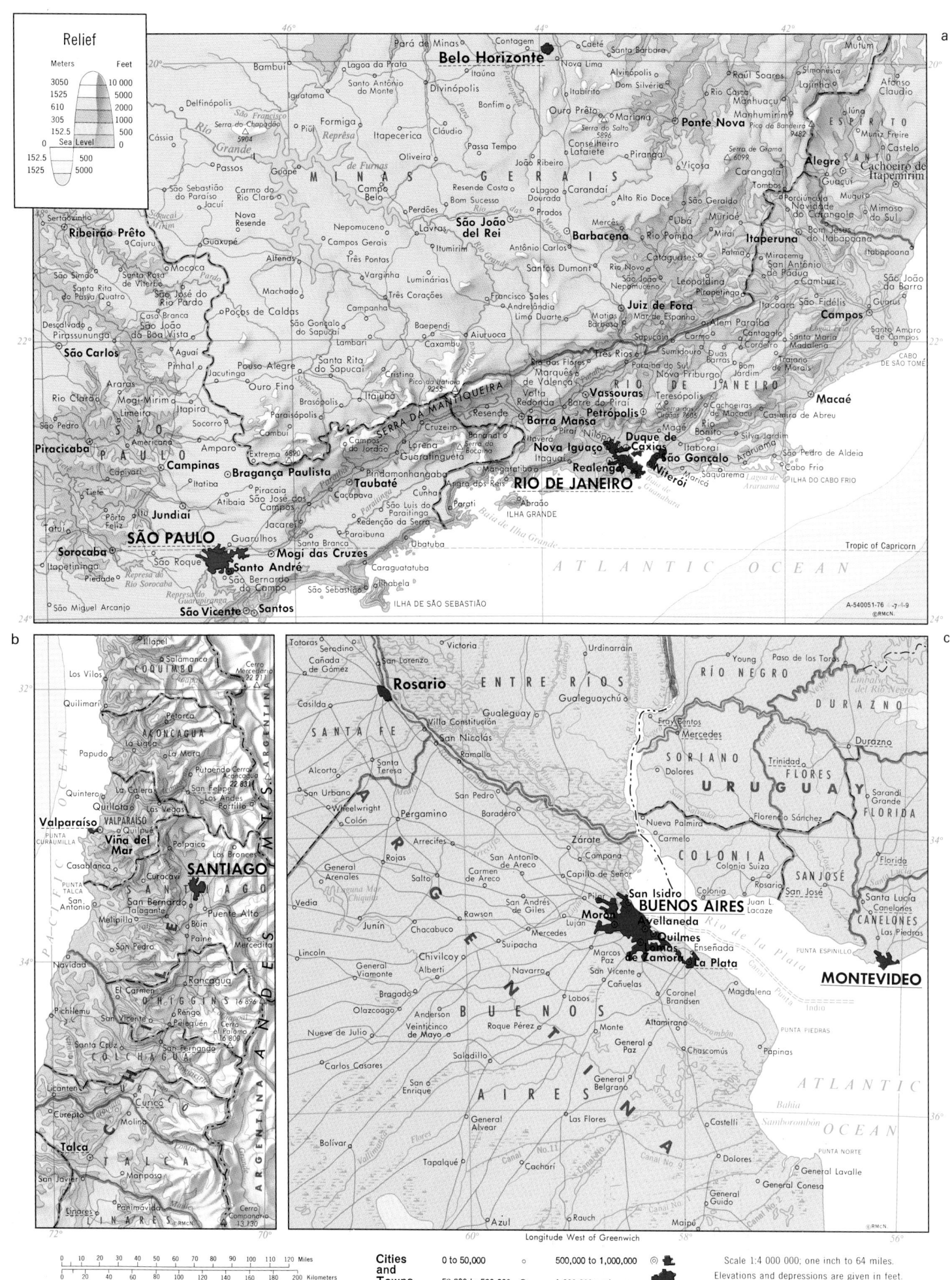

Relief

Meters	Feet
3050	10 000
1525	5000
610	2000
305	1000
152.5	500
0	Sea Level 0
152.5	500
1525	5000

BELO HORIZONTE

SÃO PAULO

RIO DE JANEIRO

ATLANTIC OCEAN

Tropic of Capricorn

b

SANTIAGO

c

Rosario

BUENOS AIRES

MONTEVIDEO

Longitude West of Greenwich

0 10 20 30 40 50 60 70 80 90 100 110 120 Miles
0 20 40 60 80 100 120 140 160 180 200 Kilometers

Cities and Towns

0 to 50,000	○
50,000 to 500,000	⊙
500,000 to 1,000,000	◎
1,000,000 and over	⬤

Scale 1:4 000 000; one inch to 64 miles.
Elevations and depressions are given in feet.

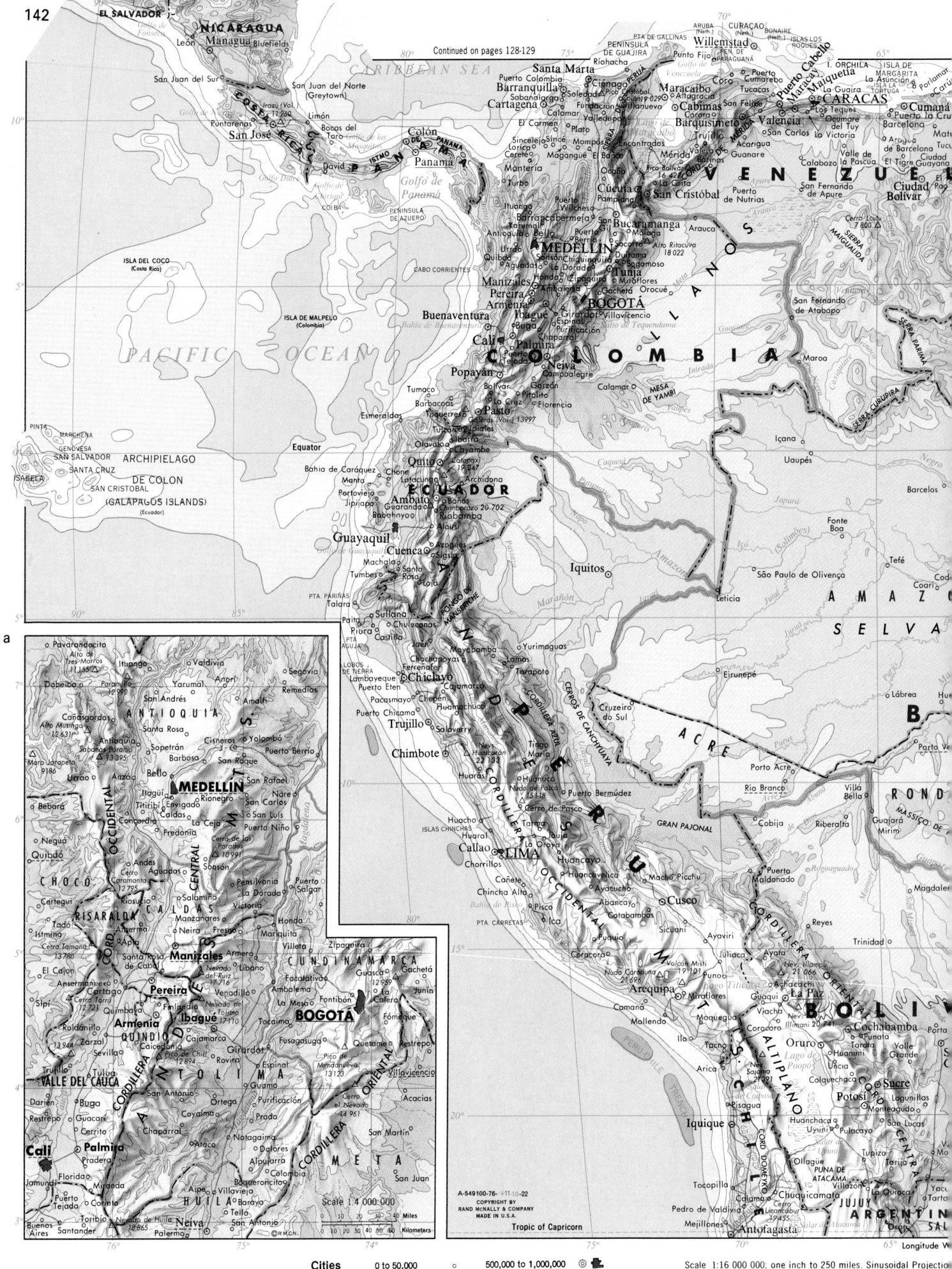

Continued on pages 128-129

Cities
and
Towns

0 to 50,000	o	500,000 to 1,000,000	
50,000 to 500,000	⊙	1,000,000 and over	

Scale 1:16 000 000; one inch to 250 miles. Sinusoidal Projection
Elevations and depressions are given in feet

Scale 1:4 000 000

A-549100-76- -11-10-22
COPYRIGHT BY
RAND McNALLY & COMPANY
MADE IN U.S.A.

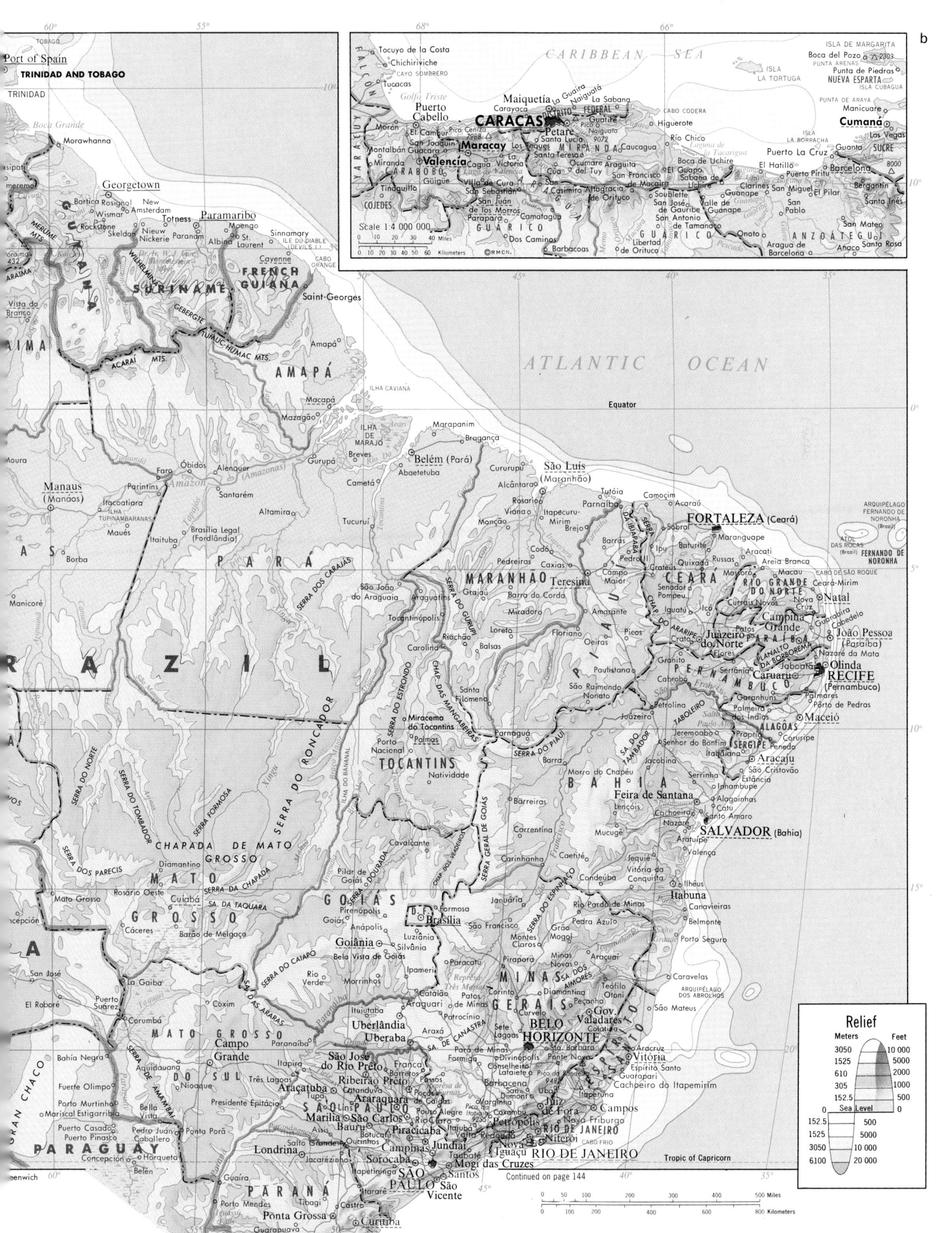

b

TOBAGO
Port of Spain
TRINIDAD AND TOBAGO
TRINIDAD

CARIBBEAN SEA

ISLA DE MARGARITA
Boca del Pozo
PUNTA ARENAS
Punta de Piedras
NUEVA ESPARTA
ISLA CUBAGUA

Tocuyo de la Costa
Chichiriviche
CAYO SOMBRERO
Tucacas
Golfo Triste
Puerto Cabello
El Cambur
Morón
Montalbán Guacara
Miranda
Valencia
CARABOBO
Güigüe
Villa de Cura
San Sebastián
COJEDES
Tinaquillo
San Juan de los Morros
Camatagua
Parapara
Dos Caminos
Barbacoas

Maiquetía
Carayaca
CARACAS
Maracay
La Victoria
Cagua
Cúa

PUNTA DE ARAYA
Manicuare
Cumaná
SUCRE
Las Vegas
Puerto La Cruz
El Hatillo
Barcelona
Puerto Píritu
Clarines
San Miguel
El Pilar
Bergantín

GUÁRICO
Libertad de Orituco
ANZOÁTEGUI
Aragua de Barcelona
Santa Rosa

Scale 1:4 000 000

ATLANTIC OCEAN

Morawhanna
Georgetown
New Amsterdam
Wismar
Rockstone
Skeldon
Nieuw Nickerie
Paranam
Albina
St. Laurent
Paramaribo
Moengo
Totness
Sinnamary
Cayenne
Saint-Georges

SURINAME
FRENCH GUIANA

Amapá
Macapá
Mazagão
ILHA DE MARAJÓ
Breves
Belém (Pará)
Abaetetuba
Cametá
Tucuruí

Equator

São Luís (Maranhão)
Alcântara
Rosário
Parnaíba
Tutóia
Camocim
Acaraú
FORTALEZA (Ceará)
Sobral
Maranguape
Baturité
Ipu
Aracati
Areia Branca
Mossoró
Macau
CABO DE SÃO ROQUE
ARQUIPÉLAGO FERNANDO DE NORONHA (Brazil)
ATOL DAS ROCAS (Brazil)
FERNANDO DE NORONHA

Manaus (Manáos)
Itacoatiara
Parintins
Óbidos
Alenquer
Santarém
Altamira

B R A Z I L

P A R Á

MARANHÃO
Teresina
Grajaú
Barra do Corda
Carolina
Balsas
Floriano
Oeiras
Picos
PIAUÍ
Amarante
CEARÁ
Quixadá
Russas
Iguatu
Crateús
RIO GRANDE DO NORTE
Currais Novos
Natal
Nova Cruz
Campina Grande
PARAÍBA
João Pessoa (Paraíba)
Juazeiro do Norte
Crato
Flores
Nazaré da Mata
Caruaru
Olinda
RECIFE (Pernambuco)
PERNAMBUCO
Garanhuns
Palmares
Pôrto de Pedras
Palmeira dos Índios
ALAGOAS
Maceió

TOCANTINS
Miracema do Tocantins
Porto Nacional
Palmas
Natividade
Barreiras
Correntina
BAHIA
Morro do Chapéu
Jacobina
Senhor do Bonfim
Serrinha
Feira de Santana
SERGIPE
Aracaju
Estância
Penedo
Propriá
Itabaiana
São Cristóvão

Corumbá
MATO GROSSO DO SUL
Campo Grande
Três Lagoas
Bela Vista

MATO GROSSO
Cuiabá
CHAPADA DE MATO GROSSO
Diamantino
Rosário Oeste

GOIÁS
Pirenópolis
Anápolis
Goiânia
D.F.
Brasília
Formosa
Luziânia
Silvânia
Ipameri
Catalão

MINAS GERAIS
Januária
Montes Claros
Pirapora
Paracatú
Araguari
Uberlândia
Uberaba
Araxá
BELO HORIZONTE
Gov. Valadares
Teófilo Otoni

SALVADOR (Bahia)
Valença
Jequié
Ilhéus
Itabuna
Vitória da Conquista
Canavieiras
Belmonte
Porto Seguro
Caravelas
ARQUIPÉLAGO DOS ABROLHOS

Vitória
Espírito Santo
Guarapari
Cachoeiro do Itapemirim
Campos
CABO FRIO

SÃO PAULO
São José do Rio Prêto
Ribeirão Prêto
Franca
Araçatuba
Marília
Bauru
São Carlos
Piracicaba
Campinas
Jundiaí
Sorocaba
SÃO PAULO
Santos
São Vicente

RIO DE JANEIRO
Petrópolis
Niterói
RIO DE JANEIRO
Nova Friburgo
Juiz de Fora
Barra Mansa
Volta Redonda

PARANÁ
Londrina
Ponta Grossa
Curitiba
Guaratuba

PARAGUAY

Tropic of Capricorn

Relief

Meters	Feet
3050	10 000
1525	5000
610	2000
305	1000
152.5	500
Sea Level	
152.5	500
1525	5000
3050	10 000
6100	20 000

Continued on page 144

Continued on pages 142-143

BOLIVIA
PARAGUAY
GRAN CHACO
CHACO
PUNA DE ATACAMA
Tropic of Capricorn

Tocopilla
Pedro de Valdivia
Mejillones
Antofagasta
Chuquicamata
Calama
Cerro Llincancabur 19,455
Tupiza
La Quiaca
Villazón
Tarija
Yacuiba
Tartagal
Orán
Puerto Olimpo
Bella Vista
Mariscal Estigarribia
Ponta Porã
Pedro Juan Caballero

Taltal
Chañaral
Caldera
Copiapó
Cerro Azufre (Copiapó) Vol. 19,947
Huasco
Vallenar
Freirina

TUCUMÁN
SANTIAGO DEL ESTERO
CATAMARCA
LA RIOJA
SAN JUAN
CÓRDOBA
SANTA FE
ENTRE RÍOS
CORRIENTES
MISIONES
RIO GRANDE DO SUL
URUGUAY

Salta
Jujuy
San Pedro
San Antonio de los Cobres
Metán
Nevados de Cachi 22,047
Llullaillaco 22,116
Salar de Atacama

Tucumán
Bella Vista
Monteros
Andalgalá
La Banda
Santiago del Estero
Villa Ángela
Catamarca
Añatuya
Frias
Tostado

Concepción
Horqueta
Formosa
Resistencia
Corrientes
Paso de los Libres
Uruguaiana

Asunción
Luque
Villarrica
Caazapá
Encarnación
Posadas

Coquimbo
La Serena
Tongoy
Ovalle
Illapel
Los Vilos
Quillota
Viña del Mar
Valparaíso
San Antonio
Melipilla

SANTIAGO
San Juan
Mendoza
San Luis
San Rafael
Cerro Aconcagua 22,831
Cerro Tupungato 21,555
Cerro Mercedario 22,211

Córdoba
Villa Dolores
Río Tercero
Río Cuarto
Villa María
Villa Mercedes
Rosario
San Nicolás
Pergamino
Junín

Santa Fe
Paraná
Rafaela
Concordia
Salto
Paysandú
Gualeguaychú
Mercedes
Durazno
Melo

BUENOS AIRES
La Plata
Avellaneda
MONTEVIDEO
Maldonado
Rocha

Rancagua
San Fernando
Constitución
Cauquenes
Talca
Linares
San Carlos
Parral
Chillán
Talcahuano
Concepción
Coronel
Lota
Los Ángeles
Angol
Lebú
Victoria
Lautaro
Temuco
Valdivia
Corral
La Unión
Osorno
Puerto Varas
Puerto Montt
Ancud
Castro
ISLA DE CHILOÉ

LA PAMPA
Santa Rosa
General Pico
General Acha
Neuquén
General Roca
Zapala
Chaele Choel

RÍO NEGRO
CHUBUT
SANTA CRUZ
PATAGONIA

Carmen de Patagones
Viedma
San Antonio Oeste
Golfo San Matías
PENÍNSULA VALDÉS
Puerto Madryn
Trelew
Rawson
PTA. DELGADA
Comodoro Rivadavia
Golfo San Jorge
Puerto Deseado
Puerto Santa Cruz
San Julián
Río Gallegos
Puerto Natales
Punta Arenas
TIERRA DEL FUEGO
Ushuaia
CABO DE HORNOS (CAPE HORN)

ARCHIPIÉLAGO DE LOS CHONOS
PENÍNSULA DE TAITAO
Golfo de Penas
Cerro Valentín
WELLINGTON
CAMPANA
Cerro Chaltel / Mte. Fitzroy 10,958
MESETA DE LAS VIZCACHAS
ARCHIPIÉLAGO MADRE DE DIOS
HANOVER
ISLA SANTA INÉS
PEN. DE BRUNSWICK
Estrecho de Magallanes
ISLAS DIEGO RAMÍREZ

FALKLAND IS. (ISLAS MALVINAS) (Br.) (Claimed by Argentina)
Stanley
BANCO BURDWOOD
ISLA DE LOS ESTADOS

Bahía Blanca
Bahía Grande
Bahía San Blas

PACIFIC OCEAN
ATLANTIC OCEAN

BRAZIL
SÃO PAULO
MINAS GERAIS
BELO HORIZONTE
RIO DE JANEIRO
PARANÁ
SANTA CATARINA

São José do Rio Prêto
Ribeirão Prêto
Araçatuba
Bauru
Marília
Londrina
Ponta Grossa
Curitiba
Paranaguá
São Francisco do Sul
Joinville
Blumenau
Itajaí
Florianópolis
Laguna
Tubarão
Caxias do Sul
PORTO ALEGRE
Pelotas
Rio Grande

Relief

Meters	Feet
3050	10 000
1525	5000
610	2000
305	1000
152.5	500
0	Sea Level
152.5	500
1525	5000
3050	10 000
6100	20 000

Below Sea Level

a — BUENOS AIRES
Scale 1:1 000 000

Tigre
San Fernando
San Isidro
Olivos
Vicente López
Villa Ballester
General San Martín
General Sarmiento
Bella Vista
Hurlingham
Morón
San Justo
Avellaneda
Lanús
Quilmes
Bernal
Banfield
Lomas de Zamora
Temperley
Almirante Brown
Esteban Echeverría
Burzaco
Longchamps
Ezeiza
RÍO DE LA PLATA

b — RIO DE JANEIRO
Scale 1:1 000 000

SERRA DAS ARARAS
Teresópolis
Petrópolis
Vassouras
Paracambi
Japeri
Queimados
Nova Iguaçu
Duque de Caxias
São João de Meriti
Nilópolis
Campo Grande
Santa Cruz
Jacarepaguá
RIO DE JANEIRO
Niterói
São Gonçalo
Magé
Baía de Guanabara
Copacabana
ATLANTIC OCEAN

A-549200-76
COPYRIGHT BY RAND McNALLY & COMPANY
MADE IN U.S.A.

Longitude West of Greenwich

Scale 1:16 000 000, one inch to 250 miles. Sinusoidal Projection
Elevations and depressions are given in feet

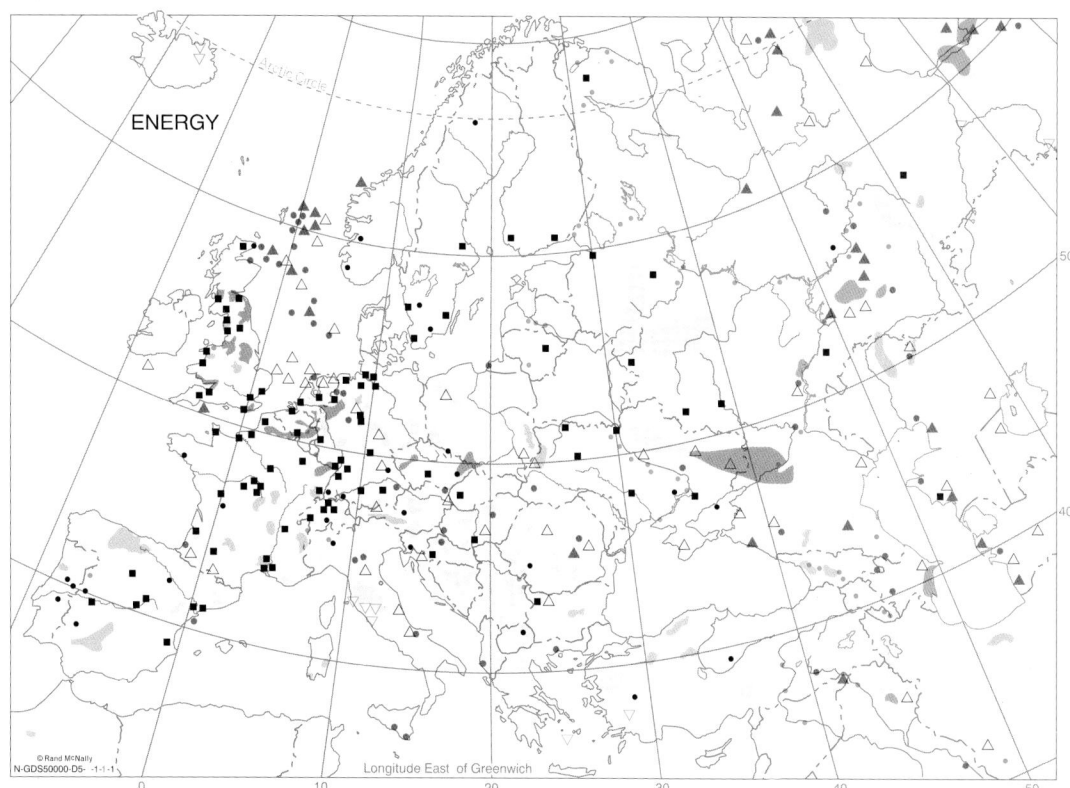

ENERGY

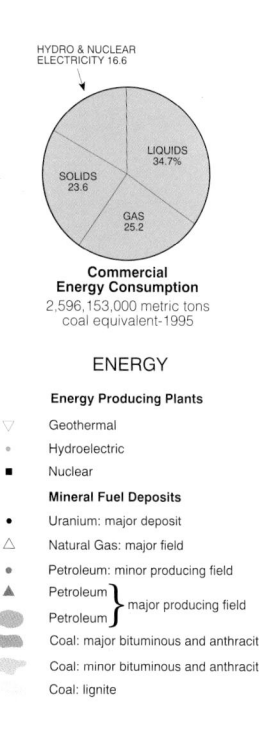

HYDRO & NUCLEAR
ELECTRICITY 16.6

LIQUIDS
34.7%

SOLIDS
23.6

GAS
25.2

**Commercial
Energy Consumption**
2,596,153,000 metric tons
coal equivalent-1995

ENERGY

Energy Producing Plants

▽ Geothermal

• Hydroelectric

■ Nuclear

Mineral Fuel Deposits

• Uranium: major deposit

△ Natural Gas: major field

• Petroleum: minor producing field

▲ Petroleum } major producing field
⬭ Petroleum }

⬭ Coal: major bituminous and anthracite

⬭ Coal: minor bituminous and anthracite

Coal: lignite

© Rand McNally
N-GDS50000-D5- -1-1-1

Longitude East of Greenwich

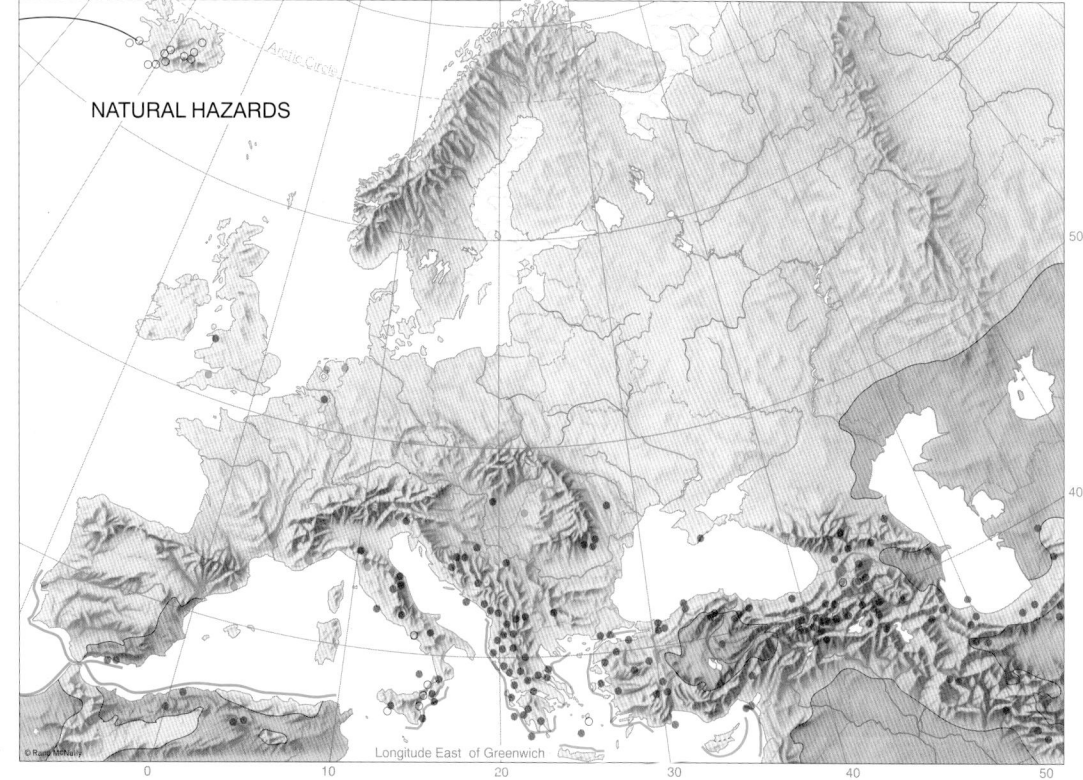

NATURAL HAZARDS

NATURAL HAZARDS

○ Volcanoes*

● Earthquakes*

● Major flood disasters*

—— Tsunamis

—— Limit of iceburg drift

Temporary pack ice

Areas subject to desertification

*Twentieth Century occurrences

© Rand McNally

Longitude East of Greenwich

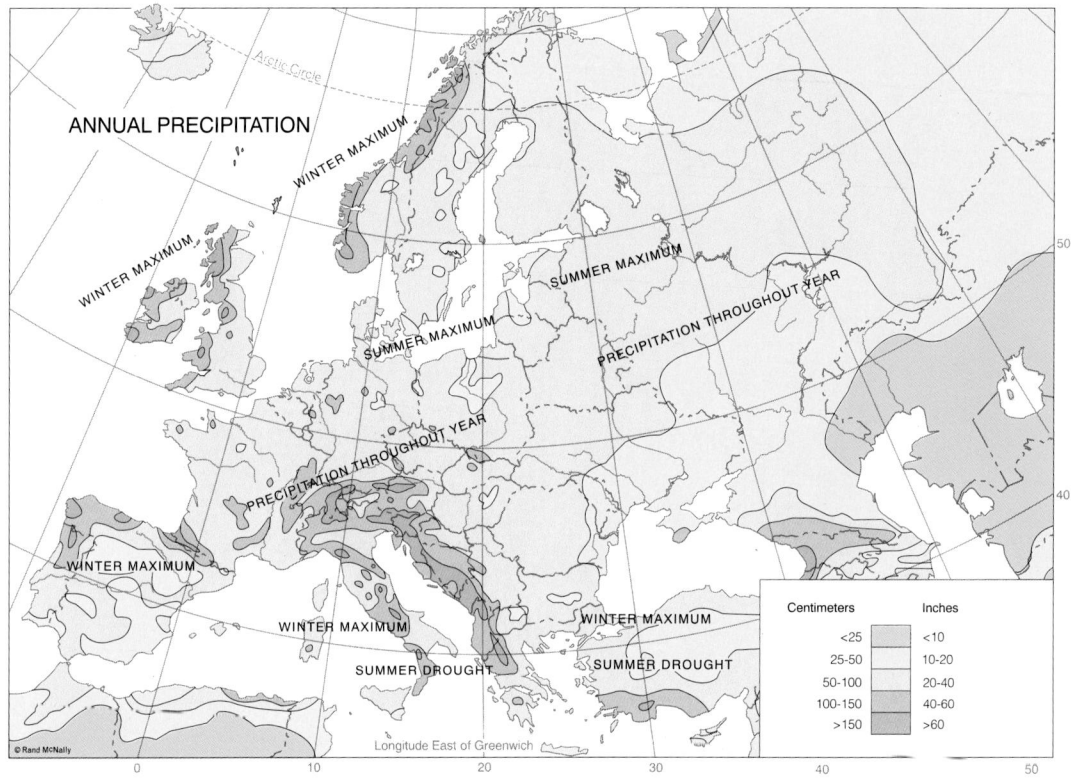

ANNUAL PRECIPITATION

WINTER MAXIMUM

WINTER MAXIMUM

SUMMER MAXIMUM

SUMMER MAXIMUM

PRECIPITATION THROUGHOUT YEAR

PRECIPITATION THROUGHOUT YEAR

WINTER MAXIMUM

WINTER MAXIMUM

WINTER MAXIMUM

SUMMER DROUGHT

SUMMER DROUGHT

Longitude East of Greenwich

© Rand McNally

Centimeters	Inches
<25	<10
25-50	10-20
50-100	20-40
100-150	40-60
>150	>60

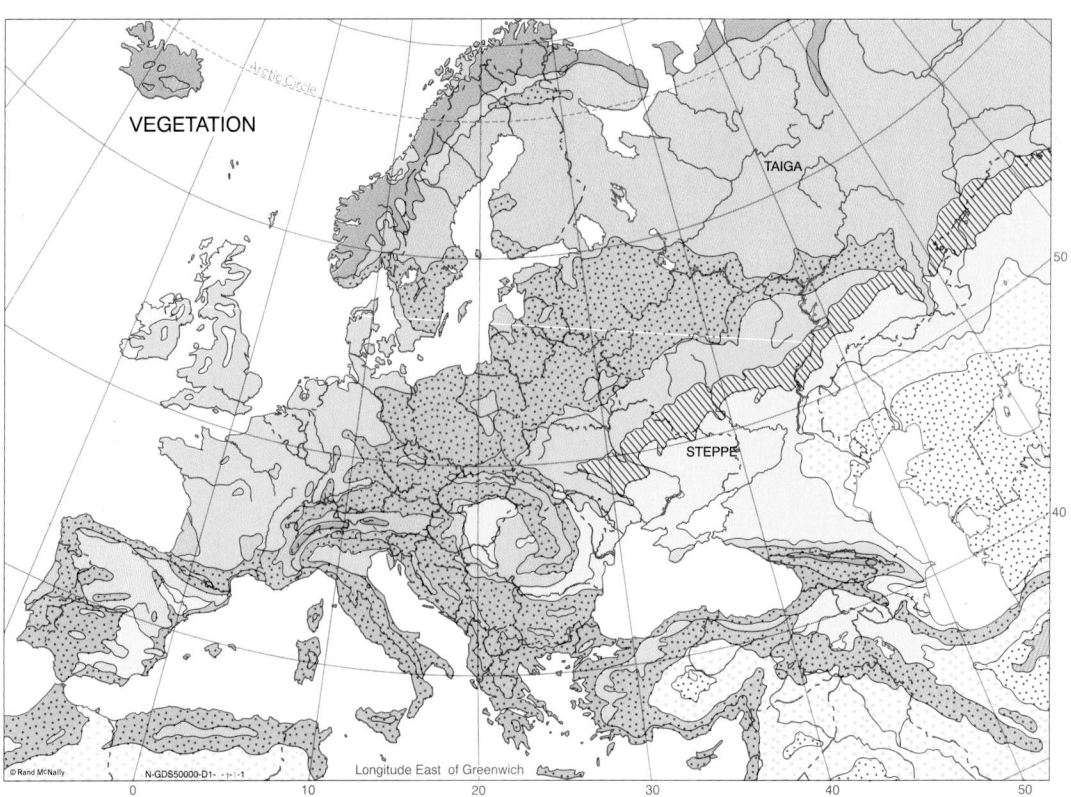

VEGETATION

TAIGA

STEPPE

Longitude East of Greenwich

© Rand McNally

N-GDS50000-D1-

VEGETATION

E	Coniferous forest
B,Bs	Mediterranean vegetation
M	Mixed forest: coniferous-deciduous
S	Semi-deciduous forest
D	Deciduous forest
DG	Wooded steppe
G	Grass (steppe)
Gp	Short grass
Dsp	Desert shrub
L	Heath and moor
L	Alpine vegetation, tundra
b	Little or no vegetation

For explanation of letters in boxes,
see Natural Vegetation Map
by A. W. Kuchler, p. 24

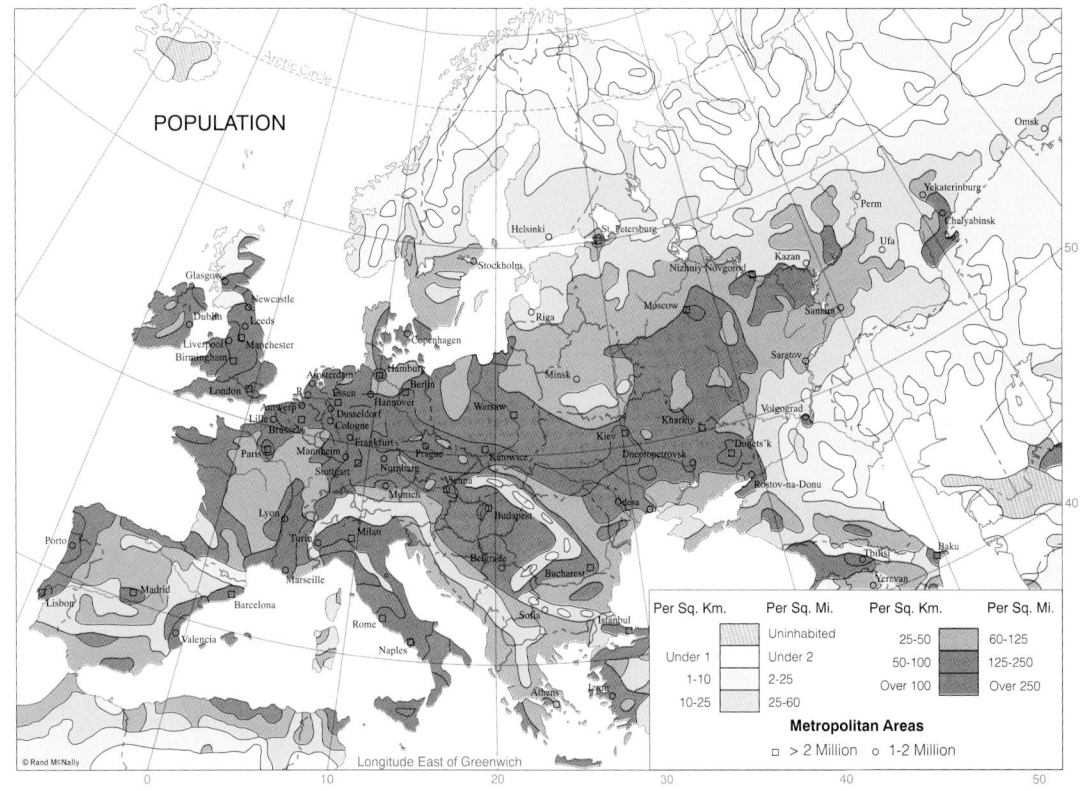

POPULATION

Per Sq. Km.	Per Sq. Mi.	Per Sq. Km.	Per Sq. Mi.
Uninhabited		25-50	60-125
Under 1	Under 2	50-100	125-250
1-10	2-25	Over 100	Over 250
10-25	25-60		

Metropolitan Areas

□ > 2 Million   ○ 1-2 Million

Longitude East of Greenwich

© Rand McNally

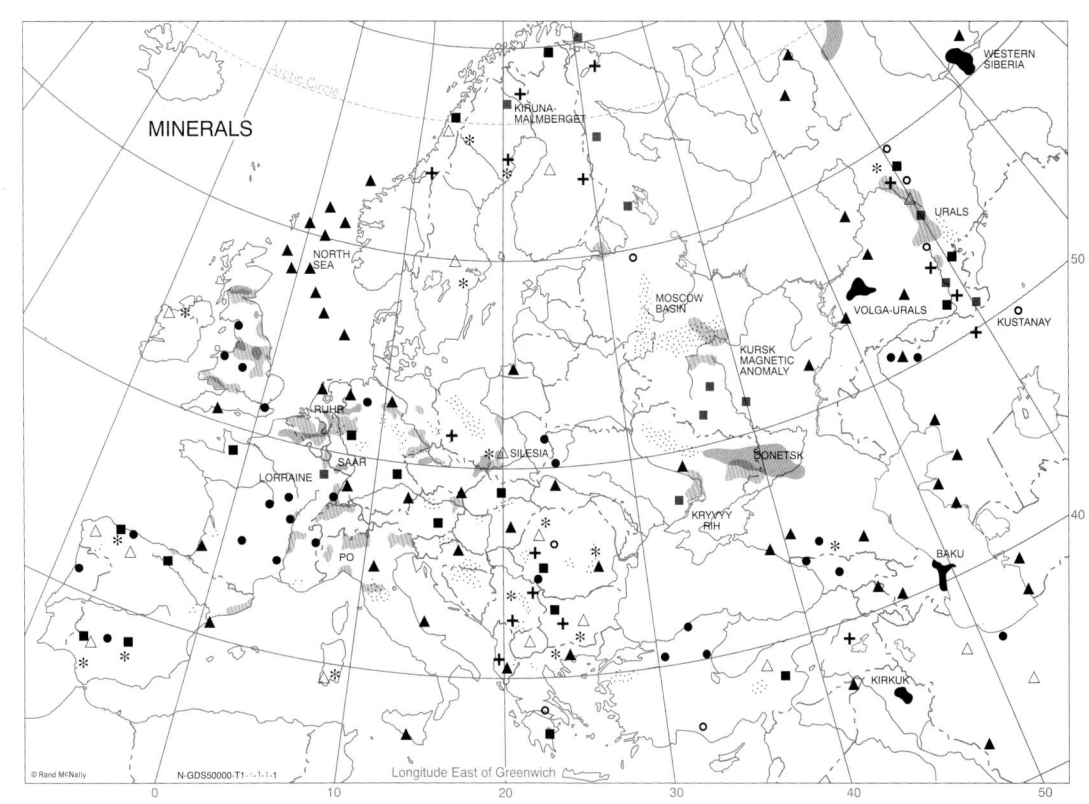

MINERALS

- Industrial areas
- Major coal deposits
- Major petroleum deposits
- Lignite deposits
- ▲ Minor petroleum deposits
- ● Minor coal deposits
- ■ Major iron ore
- ■ Minor iron ore
- ✳ Lead
- ○ Bauxite
- △ Zinc
- ✚ Copper

© Rand McNally   N-GDS50000-T1-·-1-·-1   Longitude East of Greenwich

Urban
Cropland
Cropland & Woodland
Cropland & Grazing Land
Grassland, Grazing Land
Forest, Woodland
Swamp, Marshland
Tundra
Shrub, Sparse Grass,
Wasteland (pattern)
Barren Land
Oasis

Longitude West of Greenwich 0° Longitude East of Greenwich

Scale 1: 16,000,000; one inch to 250 miles. Conic Projection

0 50 100   200   300   400   500 Miles
0   100   200   400   600   800 Kilometers

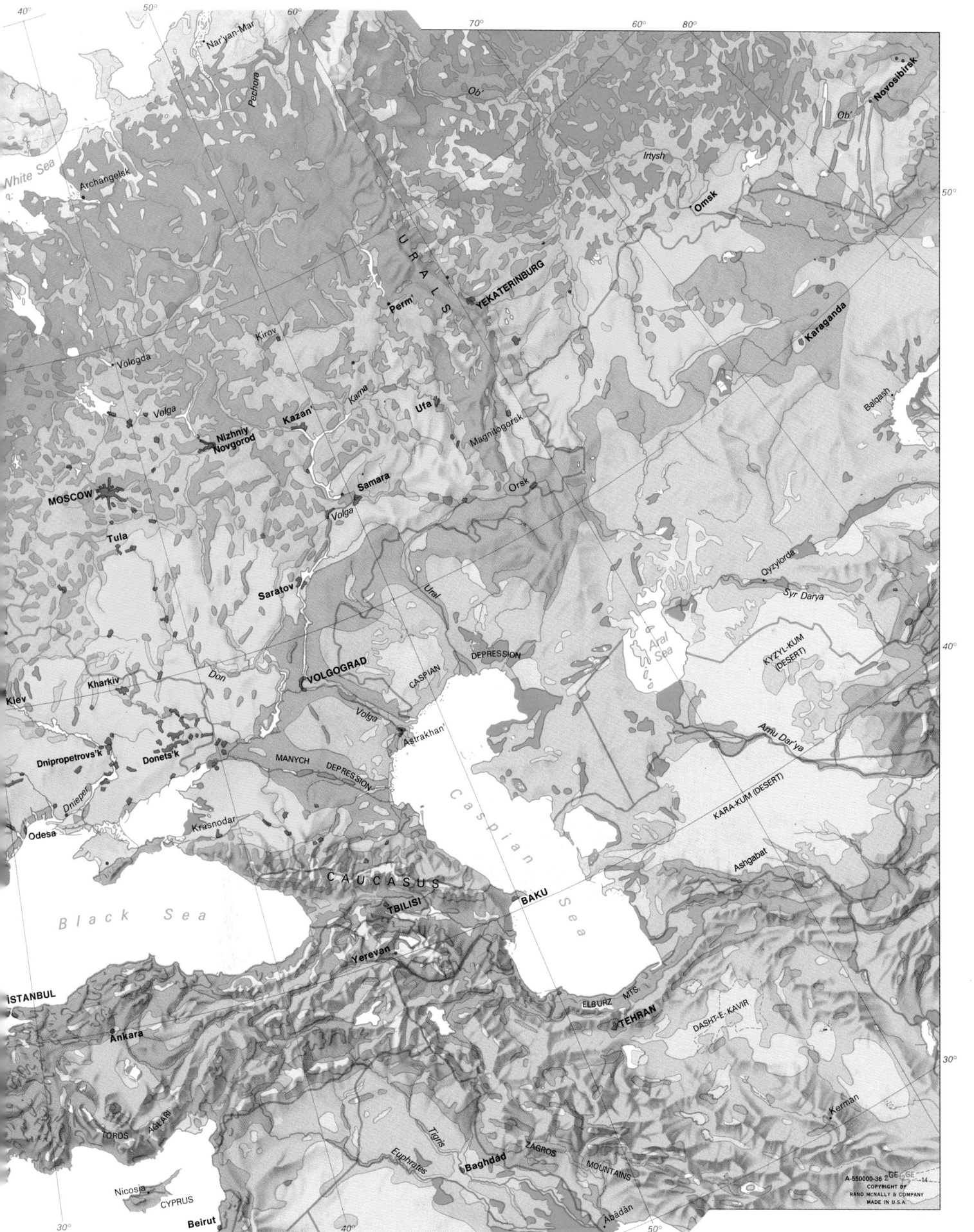

40° 50° 60° 70° 60° 80°

White Sea

Nar'yan-Mar

Pechora

Ob'

Irtysh

Novosibirsk

Ob'

Archangelsk

Omsk

50°

U R A L S

YEKATERINBURG

Perm

Karaganda

Kirov

Vologda

Kama

Ufa

Volga

Kazan

Magnitogorsk

Balqash

Nizhniy
Novgorod

Orsk

MOSCOW

Samara

Volga

Qyzylorda

Syr Darya

Tula

Saratov

Ural

DEPRESSION

Aral
Sea

KYZYL-KUM
(DESERT)

40°

Kiev

Kharkiv

Don

VOLGOGRAD

CASPIAN

Volga

Amu Dar'ya

Dnipropetrovs'k

Donets'k

Astrakhan'

KARA-KUM (DESERT)

Dnieper

MANYCH   DEPRESSION

Odesa

Krasnodar

Ashgabat

C A U C A S U S

Caspian

ISTANBUL

Black   Sea

TBILISI

BAKU

Sea

Yerevan

ELBURZ MTS.

TEHRAN

DASHT-E-KAVIR

30°

Ankara

TOROS

AĞLASI

Tigris

ZAGROS

Kerman

Nicosia

CYPRUS

Euphrates

Baghdad

MOUNTAINS

Beirut

Abādān

30° 40° 50°

Scale 1:16 000 000; one inch to 250 miles. Conic Projection
Elevations and depressions are given in feet.

PHYSIOGRAPHIC PROVINCES

0 ——— 400
Miles

FENNO-SCANDIAN SHIELD

AREA OF LATEST GLACIATION

NORTH EUROPEAN GLACIATED PLAIN

Western Uplands (Mostly old rocks) ☐ | Great European Plain ☐ | Central Uplands ☐ | Alpine System ☐

EUROPE DURING THE ICE AGE

THE GREAT ICE CAP (at its largest extent)

Tundra ☐ | Forest ☐ | Steppe ☐

PHYSIOGRAPHY
BY
ERWIN RAISZ

LITHOLOGY AND STRUCTURE

☐ Unconsolidated deposits: alluvium, sands, bottom lands.

☐ Essentially horizontal sediments, also uplands and terraces in the plains.

☐ Moderately folded sedimentary rocks.

☐ Strongly folded and faulted rocks. The "Younger Series" in Norway.

☐ Metamorphic and intrusive igneous rocks.

☐ volcanics, lava flows, basalts, etc.

LANDFORMS

PLATEAUS | CUESTAS | SAND

HILLS | FOLDED MOUNTAINS | SINKS

MOUNTAINS | BASIN RANGES | MORAINES

MESAS | VOLCANO AND LAVA | DRUMLINS

0 50 100 200 300 400 500 Miles
0 100 200 400 600 800 Kilometers

EUROPE LANGUAGES
BY
BOGDAN ZABORSKI

Scale 1:16,500,000; one inch to 260 miles Conic Projection

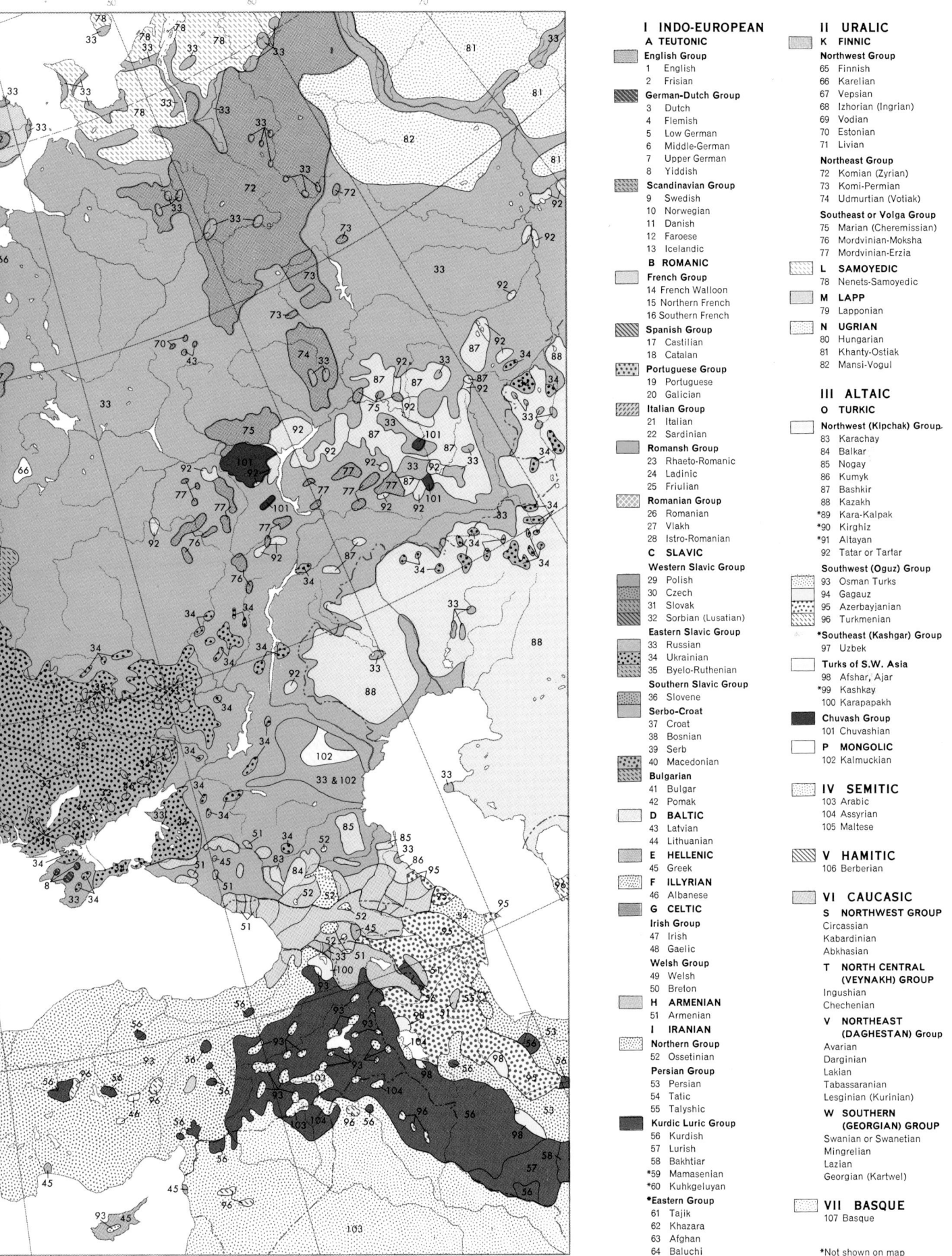

I INDO-EUROPEAN
A TEUTONIC
English Group
1   English
2   Frisian
German-Dutch Group
3   Dutch
4   Flemish
5   Low German
6   Middle-German
7   Upper German
8   Yiddish
Scandinavian Group
9   Swedish
10 Norwegian
11 Danish
12 Faroese
13 Icelandic
B ROMANIC
French Group
14 French Walloon
15 Northern French
16 Southern French
Spanish Group
17 Castilian
18 Catalan
Portuguese Group
19 Portuguese
20 Galician
Italian Group
21 Italian
22 Sardinian
Romansh Group
23 Rhaeto-Romanic
24 Ladinic
25 Friulian
Romanian Group
26 Romanian
27 Vlakh
28 Istro-Romanian
C SLAVIC
Western Slavic Group
29 Polish
30 Czech
31 Slovak
32 Sorbian (Lusatian)
Eastern Slavic Group
33 Russian
34 Ukrainian
35 Byelo-Ruthenian
Southern Slavic Group
36 Slovene
Serbo-Croat
37 Croat
38 Bosnian
39 Serb
40 Macedonian
Bulgarian
41 Bulgar
42 Pomak
D BALTIC
43 Latvian
44 Lithuanian
E HELLENIC
45 Greek
F ILLYRIAN
46 Albanese
G CELTIC
Irish Group
47 Irish
48 Gaelic
Welsh Group
49 Welsh
50 Breton
H ARMENIAN
51 Armenian
I IRANIAN
Northern Group
52 Ossetinian
Persian Group
53 Persian
54 Tatic
55 Talyshic
Kurdic Luric Group
56 Kurdish
57 Lurish
58 Bakhtiar
*59 Mamasenian
*60 Kuhkgeluyan
*Eastern Group
61 Tajik
62 Khazara
63 Afghan
64 Baluchi

II URALIC
K FINNIC
Northwest Group
65 Finnish
66 Karelian
67 Vepsian
68 Izhorian (Ingrian)
69 Vodian
70 Estonian
71 Livian
Northeast Group
72 Komian (Zyrian)
73 Komi-Permian
74 Udmurtian (Votiak)
Southeast or Volga Group
75 Marian (Cheremissian)
76 Mordvinian-Moksha
77 Mordvinian-Erzia
L SAMOYEDIC
78 Nenets-Samoyedic
M LAPP
79 Lapponian
N UGRIAN
80 Hungarian
81 Khanty-Ostiak
82 Mansi-Vogul

III ALTAIC
O TURKIC
Northwest (Kipchak) Group.
83 Karachay
84 Balkar
85 Nogay
86 Kumyk
87 Bashkir
88 Kazakh
*89 Kara-Kalpak
*90 Kirghiz
*91 Altayan
92 Tatar or Tartar
Southwest (Oguz) Group
93 Osman Turks
94 Gagauz
95 Azerbayjanian
96 Turkmenian
*Southeast (Kashgar) Group
97 Uzbek
Turks of S.W. Asia
98 Afshar, Ajar
*99 Kashkay
100 Karapapakh
Chuvash Group
101 Chuvashian
P MONGOLIC
102 Kalmuckian

IV SEMITIC
103 Arabic
104 Assyrian
105 Maltese

V HAMITIC
106 Berberian

VI CAUCASIC
S NORTHWEST GROUP
Circassian
Kabardinian
Abkhasian
**T NORTH CENTRAL
(VEYNAKH) GROUP**
Ingushian
Chechenian
**V NORTHEAST
(DAGHESTAN) Group**
Avarian
Darginian
Lakian
Tabassaranian
Lesginian (Kurinian)
**W SOUTHERN
(GEORGIAN) GROUP**
Swanian or Swanetian
Mingrelian
Lazian
Georgian (Kartwel)

VII BASQUE
107 Basque

*Not shown on map

Scale 1: 16 000 000; one inch to 250 miles. Conic Projection

Elevations and depressions are given in feet

Continued on pages 194-195

Relief

Meters		Feet
3050		10 000
1525		5000
610		2000
305		1000
152.5		500
Sea Level	0	0
152.5		Below Sea Level
1525		5000
3050		10 000

Scale 1: 16 000 000; one inch to 250 miles. Conic Projection

Elevations and depressions are given in feet

Continued on pages 230–231

0	50	100	200	300	400	500 Miles
0	100	200	400	600		800 Kilometers

Continued on pages 184-185

Continued on pages 198-199

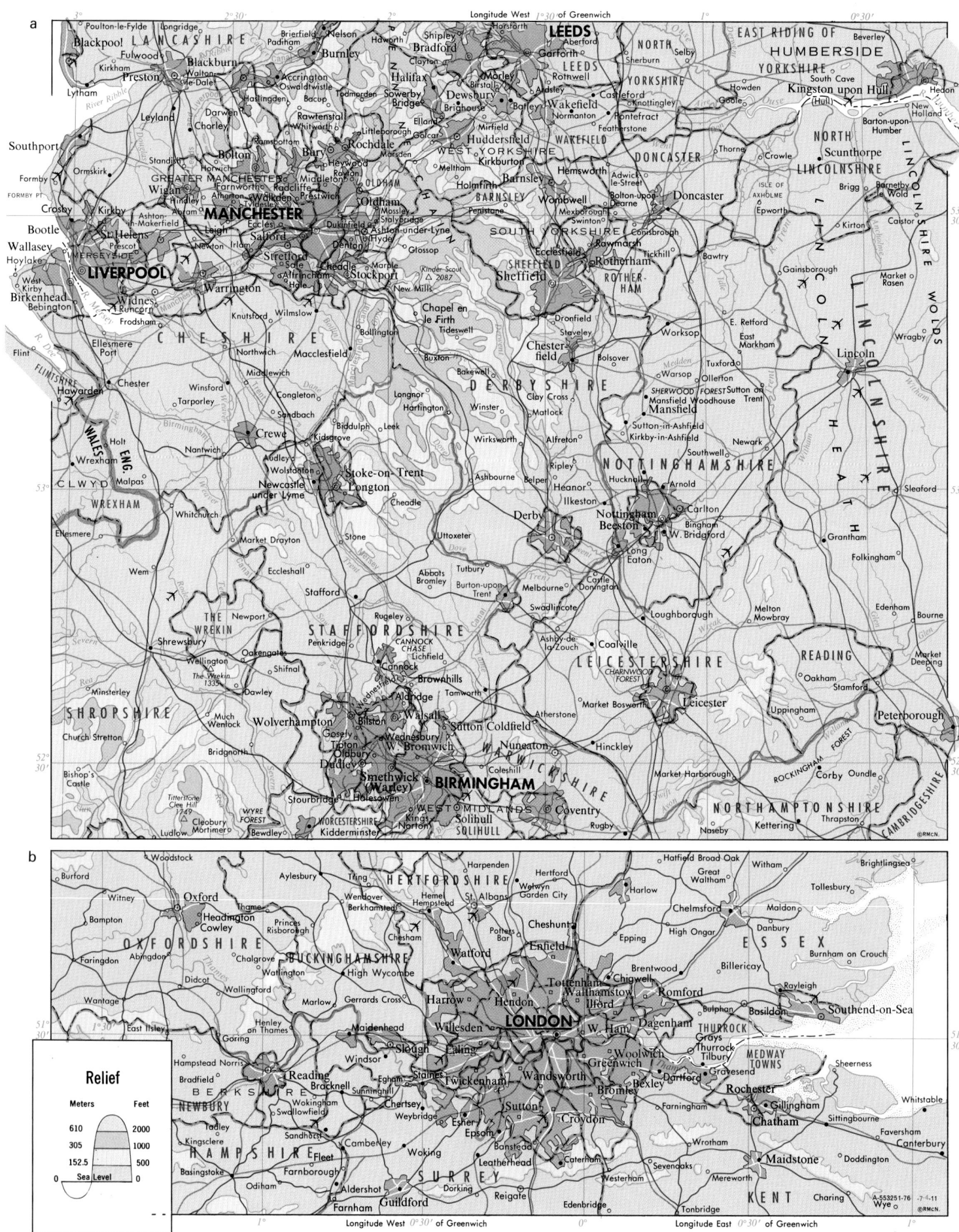

Relief

Meters	Feet
610	2000
305	1000
152.5	500
0 Sea Level	0

Scale 1:1 000 000; one inch to 16 miles.
Elevations and depressions are given in feet.

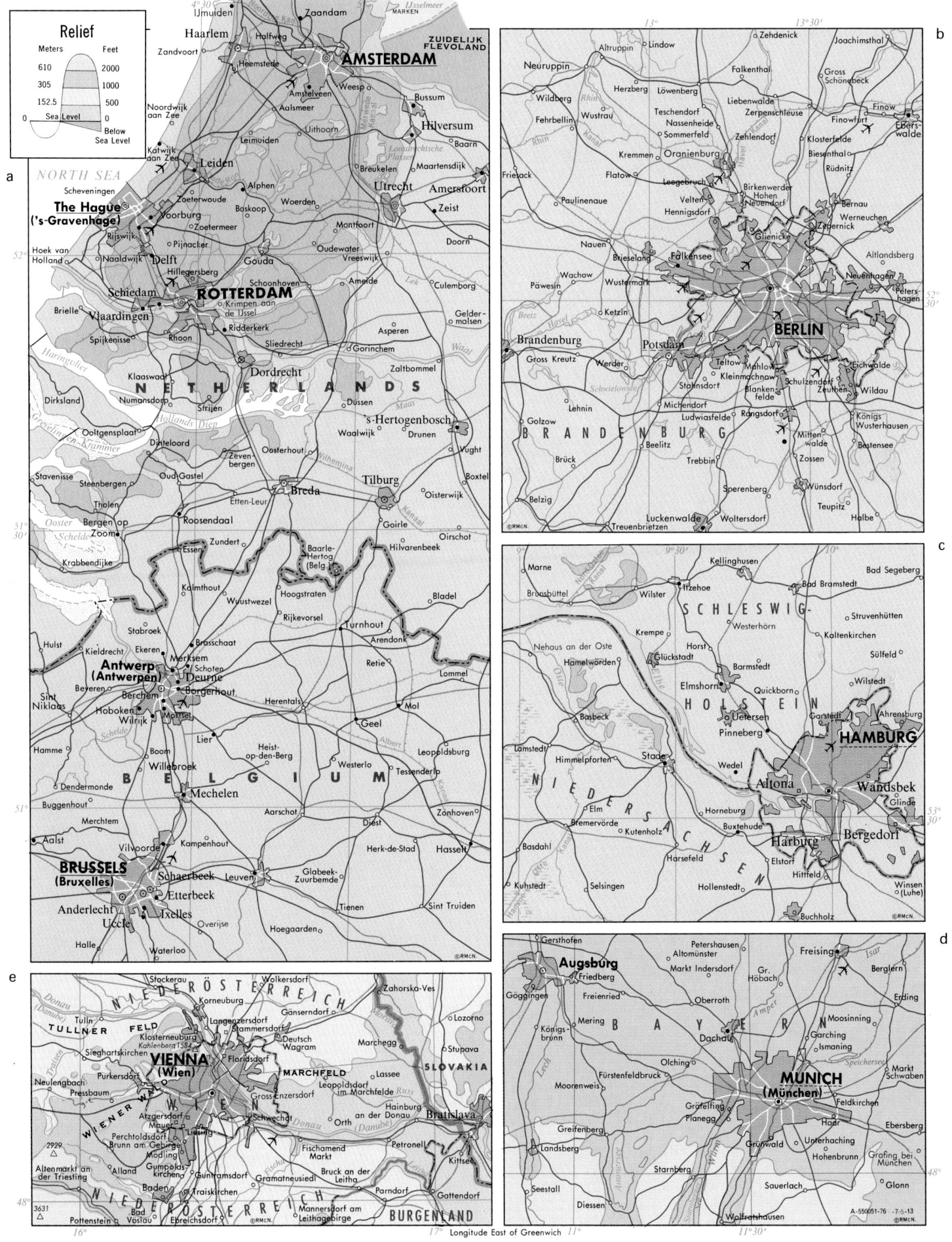

Relief

Meters		Feet
610		2000
305		1000
152.5		500
0	Sea Level	0
		Below Sea Level

a

NORTH SEA

IJmuiden
Zaandam
MARKEN
IJsselmeer

Haarlem
Halfweg
ZUIDELIJK
FLEVOLAND

Zandvoort
Heemstede

AMSTERDAM

Noordwijk aan Zee
Amstelveen
Weesp
Bussum

Aalsmeer
Uithoorn

Katwijk aan Zee
HILVERSUM

Leiden
Leimuiden
Baarn

Zoeterwoude
Alphen
Breukelen
Maartensdijk
Amersfoort

Scheveningen
Boskoop
Woerden
Utrecht
Zeist

The Hague
('s-Gravenhage)
Voorburg
Zoetermeer
Montfoort
Doorn

Rijswijk
Pijnacker
Oudewater
Vreeswijk

Hoek van
Holland
Naaldwijk
Delft
Gouda
Ameide
Culemborg

Hillegersberg
Schoonhoven
Gelder-
malsen

Schiedam
ROTTERDAM
Krimpen aan
de IJssel

Brielle
Ridderkerk
Asperen

Vlaardingen
Rhoon
Sliedrecht
Gorinchem

Spijkenisse
Zaltbommel

Klaaswaal
Dordrecht
Waal

NETHERLANDS

Dirksland
Numansdorp
Dussen

Oltgensplaat
Strijen
's-Hertogenbosch

Stavenisse
Waalwijk
Drunen
Vught

Steenbergen
Zevenbergen
Oosterhout

Tholen
Oud Gastel
Wilhelmina
Boxtel

Bergen op
Zoom
Breda
Tilburg
Oisterwijk

Krabbendijke
Roosendaal
Goirle
Oirschot

Essen
Zundert
Hilvarenbeek

Kalmhout
Baarle-
Hertog
(Belg.)

Wuustwezel
Hoogstraten
Bladel

Rijkevorsel
Turnhout
Lommel

Stabroek
Brasschaat
Arendonk

Kieldrecht
Schoten
Merksem
Retie

Antwerp
(Antwerpen)
Deurne
Herentals
Mol

Beveren
Borgerhout
Geel

Berchem
Leopoldsburg

Hoboken
Wilrijk
Lier
Westerlo
Tessenderlo

Sint
Niklaas
Heist-
op-den-Berg

Hamme
Boom

Dendermonde
Willebroek
Mechelen
Zonhoven

BELGIUM

Buggenhout
Aarschot
Hasselt

Merchtem
Diest
Herk-de-Stad

Aalst
Vilvoorde
Kampenhout

BRUSSELS
(Bruxelles)
Schaerbeek
Leuven
Glabbeek-
Zuurbemde

Anderlecht
Etterbeek
Tienen
Sint Truiden

Uccle
Ixelles
Overijse

Halle
Hoegaarden

Waterloo

b

Zehdenick
Joachimsthal

Altruppin
Lindow

Neuruppin
Falkenthal
Gross
Schönebeck

Herzberg
Löwenberg
Liebenwalde

Wildberg
Teschendorf
Zerpenschleuse
Finow

Fehrbellin
Wustrau
Nassenheide
Finowfurt
Ebers-
walde

Sommerfeld
Zehlendorf
Klosterfelde
Rüdnitz

Kremmen
Oranienburg
Biesenthal

Friesack
Flatow
Leegebruch
Birkenwerder
Bernau

Paulinenaue
Velten
Hohen
Neuendorf
Werneuchen

Nauen
Brieselang
Hennigsdorf
Glienicke

Wachow
Falkensee
Zepernick
Altlandsberg

Päwesin
Wustermark
Neuenhagen

Ketzin
BERLIN
Peters-
hagen

Brandenburg
Potsdam
Teltow
Mahlow
Eichwalde

Gross Kreutz
Werder
Kleinmachnow
Zeuthen
Wildau

Stahnsdorf
Blanken-
felde

Golzow
Lehnin
Michendorf
Rangsdorf
Königs
Wusterhausen

Ludwigsfelde
Mitten-
walde
Bastensee

BRANDENBURG

Brück
Beelitz
Zossen

Trebbin

Belzig
Sperenberg
Wünsdorf
Teupitz

Luckenwalde
Woltersdorf
Halbe

Treuenbrietzen

c

Marne
Kellinghusen
Bad Segeberg

Brunsbüttel
Wilster
Itzehoe
Bad Bramstedt

SCHLESWIG-
Struvenhütten

Westerhörn
Kaltenkirchen

Krempe
Horst
Barmstedt
Sülfeld

Nehaus an der Oste
Hamelwörden
Glückstadt
HOLSTEIN

Elmshorn
Quickborn
Wilstedt

Ottensen
Uetersen
Garstedt
Ahrensburg

Bosbeck
Pinneberg
HAMBURG

Lamstedt
Stade
Altona
Wandsbek

Himmelpforten
Wedel
Glinde

Elm
Horneburg
Bergedorf

Bremervörde
Buxtehude
Harburg

Basdahl
Kutenholz
Elstorf
Winsen
(Luhe)

Harsefeld
Hittfeld

Kuhstedt
Selsingen
Hollenstedt
Buchholz

d

Gersthofen
Petershausen
Freising
Isar

Augsburg
Friedberg
Altomünster
Berglern

Göggingen
Freienried
Markt Indersdorf
Gr.
Höbach
Erding

Königs-
brunn
Mering
Oberroth
Moosinning

BAYERN

Olching
Dachau
Garching
Ismaning

Fürstenfeldbruck

Moorenweis
MUNICH
(München)
Feldkirchen

Landsberg
Gräfelfing
Haar
Ebersberg

Greifenberg
Planegg
Unterhaching
Grafing bei
München

Grünwald
Hohenbrunn

Starnberg
Sauerlach
Glonn

Seestall
Wolfratshausen

e

Stockerau
Wolkersdorf

NIEDERÖSTERREICH
Zahorska-Ves

Tulln
Korneuburg
Gänserndorf

Donau
Langenzersdorf
Lozorno

TULLNER
FELD
Klosterneuburg
Deutsch
Wagram
Stupava

Kahlenberg 1584
Floridsdorf
Marchegg

Sieghartskirchen
VIENNA
(Wien)
Lassee

Neulengbach
Purkersdorf
Gross-Enzersdorf
SLOVAKIA

Pressbaum
WIENER
Leopoldsdorf
im Marchfelde

WIEN
Schwechat
Hainburg
an der Donau
Bratislava

Atzgersdorf
Orth
(Danube)

2929
Mauer
Liesing
Fischamend

Perchtoldsdorf
Petronell
Kittsee

Brunn am
Gebirge
Mödling
Gramatneusiedl

Gumpolds-
kirchen
Bruck an der
Leitha

Altenmarkt an
der Triesting
Baden
Parndorf
Gattendorf

3631
Bad
Vöslau
Traiskirchen
Mannersdorf am
Leithagebirge

Pottenstein
Ebreichsdorf
BURGENLAND

NIEDERÖSTERREICH

16°
17° Longitude East of Greenwich
11°
11°30'

0 5 10 15 20 Miles
0 4 8 12 16 20 24 28 32 Kilometers

Scale 1:1 000 000; one inch to 16 miles.
Elevations and depressions are given in feet.

A-550051-76 -7-5-13

Continued on pages 180-181

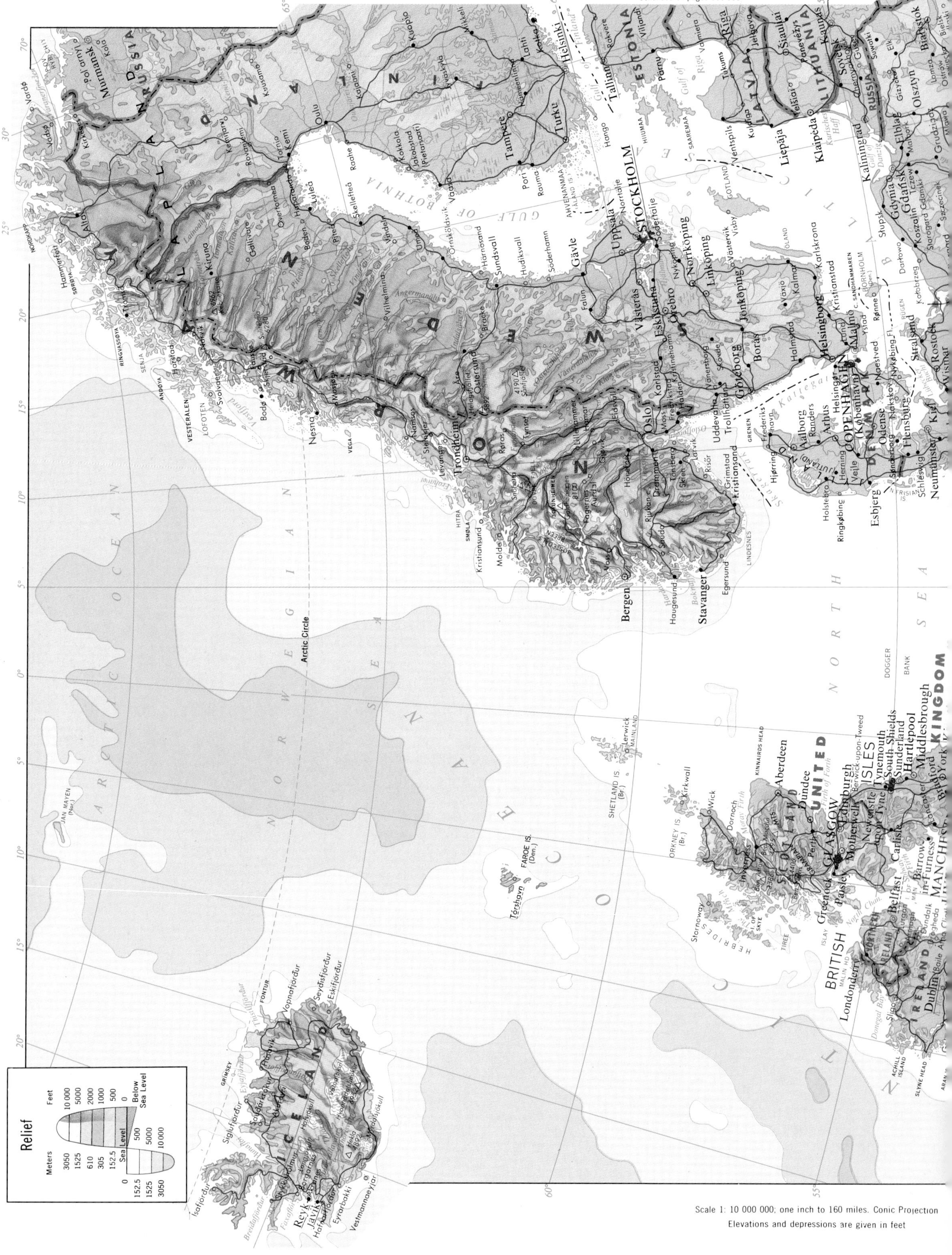

BELARUS

RUSSIA

Murmansk Kola

Vardø NORDKAPP Vadsø

LAPLAND

Hammerfest SØRØYA Kirkenes

FINLAND

Oulu

Kemi Tornio

Luleå Kiruna Gällivare Boden

Skellefteå

Umeå

GULF OF BOTHNIA

Kuopio Mikkeli

Tampere Lahti

Turku Helsinki

Kokkola (Karleby) Pori Rauma

Vaasa

ESTONIA Tallinn Narva

Gulf of Riga Riga

LATVIA Šiauliai

LITHUANIA Kaunas

RUSSIA

Klaipeda Kaliningrad

GOTLAND Visby

Gdynia Gdańsk Olsztyn

Białystok

STOCKHOLM Uppsala Norrtälje

SWEDEN

Gävle Falun Västerås Eskilstuna Örebro

Norrköping Linköping Jönköping

Göteborg Borås

Helsingborg Kristianstad Karlskrona Kalmar

Malmö COPENHAGEN København

DENMARK Århus Ålborg Randers Odense

Esbjerg Herning Vejle Kolding

Flensburg Kiel Rostock

NORWAY Oslo Moss Drammen Tønsberg

Trondheim Røros Lillehammer Hamar

Bergen Haugesund Stavanger Egersund

Kristiansand Arendal

LINDESNES

NORTH SEA

ARCTIC OCEAN

NORWEGIAN SEA

Arctic Circle

JAN MAYEN (Nor.)

FAROE IS. (Den.)

Tórshavn

SHETLAND IS. (Br.) Lerwick MAINLAND

ORKNEY IS. (Br.) Kirkwall

Wick

Stornoway HEBRIDES

SKYE ISLAY TIREE

UNITED KINGDOM

Aberdeen Dundee Edinburgh GLASGOW Greenock Paisley Motherwell

SCOTLAND

Inverness Dornoch

Newcastle upon Tyne South Shields Sunderland Hartlepool Middlesbrough Tynemouth

Carlisle Barrow-in-Furness MANCHESTER York Bradford

Belfast Londonderry NORTHERN IRELAND

Dublin IRELAND Sligo

BRITISH ISLES

ICELAND Reykjavík Ísafjörður Seyðisfjörður Vopnafjörður Eskifjörður

DOGGER BANK

NORTH SEA

Relief

Meters	Feet
3050	10 000
1525	5000
610	2000
305	1000
152.5	500
0	0 Sea Level
	Below Sea Level
Sea Level 0	
152.5	500
1525	5000
3050	10 000

Scale 1: 10 000 000; one inch to 160 miles. Conic Projection

Elevations and depressions are given in feet

MEDITERRANEAN SEA
TYRRHENIAN SEA
ADRIATIC SEA
IONIAN SEA
LIGURIAN SEA
BAY OF BISCAY
ENGLISH CHANNEL
FRANCE
SPAIN
PORTUGAL
ITALY
GERMANY
AUSTRIA
HUNGARY
POLAND
CZECH REP.
SLOVAKIA
CROATIA
BOSNIA AND HERZEGOVINA
SERBIA AND MONTENEGRO
ALBANIA
TUNISIA
ALGERIA
MOROCCO
ENGLAND
NETHERLANDS
BELGIUM
UKRAINE
ATLAS MOUNTAINS
PARIS
MADRID
ROME
LISBON
BARCELONA
LONDON
BERLIN
MUNICH
VIENNA
PRAGUE (PRAHA)
BUDAPEST
NAPLES
MILAN
BRUSSELS
AMSTERDAM
CORSICA (Fr.)
SARDINIA (It.)
BALEARS (Sp.)
MALTA
Longitude East of Greenwich
Longitude West of Greenwich
A-559400-76 -13-10-26
COPYRIGHT BY RAND McNALLY & COMPANY MADE IN U.S.A.
0 50 100 150 200 250 300 Miles
0 100 200 300 400 500 Kilometers

Continued on pages 160-161

Scale 1:10 000 000; one inch to 160 miles. Bonne's Projection
Elevations and depressions are given in feet

Continued on pages 180-181

The Turkish Republic of Northern Cyprus
unilaterally declared its independence
on Nov. 15, 1983.

Areas occupied by Israel since 1967.

| | 50 | 100 | 150 | 200 | 250 | 300 Miles |
| 100 | 200 | 300 | 400 | | 500 Kilometers |

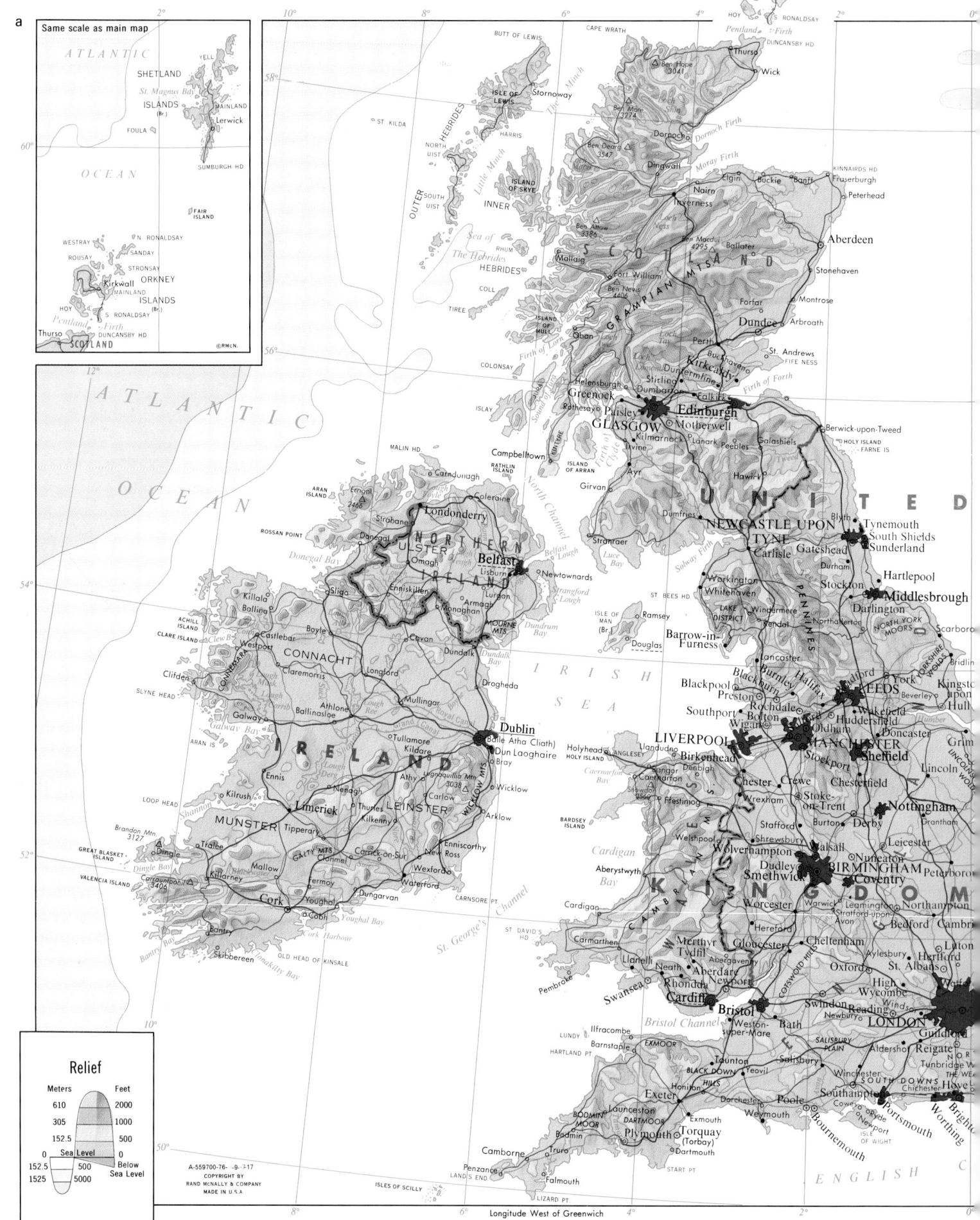

a

Same scale as main map

Relief

Meters		Feet
610		2000
305		1000
152.5		500
0	Sea Level	0
152.5		500 Below
1525		5000 Sea Level

A-559700-76- -9- 3-17
COPYRIGHT BY
RAND McNALLY & COMPANY
MADE IN U.S.A.

Longitude West of Greenwich

Scale 1: 4 000 000; one inch to 64 miles. Conic Projection

Elevations and depressions are given in feet

Continued on pages 166-167

Continued on pages 168-169

Continued on pages 170-171

Longitude East of Greenwich

0 10 20 30 40 50 60 70 80 90 100 110 120 Miles

0 20 40 60 80 100 120 140 160 180 200 Kilometers

NORWAY

SWEDEN

DENMARK

GERMANY

NETHERLANDS

BELGIUM

FRANCE

NORTH SEA

DOGGER BANK
60—120 Ft.

Skagerrak

Kattegat

BALTIC SEA

COPENHAGEN (København)

HAMBURG

Bremen

Hannover

AMSTERDAM

ROTTERDAM

The Hague ('s-Gravenhage)

ANTWERP

BRUSSELS

DÜSSELDORF

COLOGNE (Köln)

FRANKFURT AM MAIN

LUX.

Relief

Meters		Feet
1525		5000
610		2000
305		1000
152.5		500
0	Sea Level	0
152.5		Below Sea Level
		500

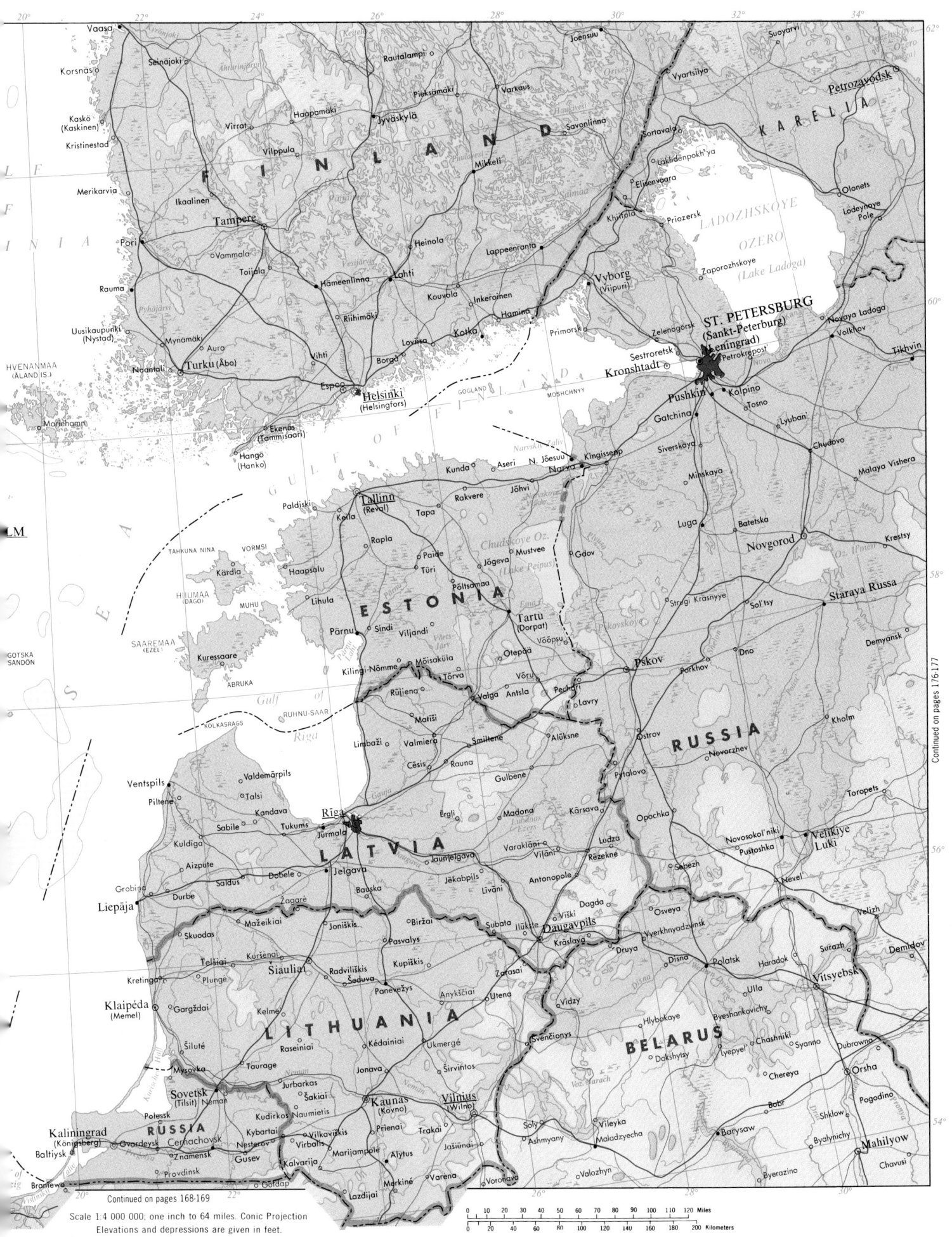

Continued on pages 176-177

Continued on pages 168-169

Scale 1:4 000 000; one inch to 64 miles. Conic Projection
Elevations and depressions are given in feet.

| 0 | 10 | 20 | 30 | 40 | 50 | 60 | 70 | 80 | 90 | 100 | 110 | 120 Miles |

| 0 | 20 | 40 | 60 | 80 | 100 | 120 | 140 | 160 | 180 | 200 Kilometers |

Continued on pages 166-167

Continued on pages 170-171

Continued on pages 174-175

Longitude East of Greenwich

Scale 1:4 000 000; one inch to 64 miles. Conic Projection
Elevations and depressions are given in feet

Continued on pages 166-167

Continued on pages 176-177

Relief

Meters	Feet
3050	10 000
1525	5000
610	2000
305	1000
152.5	500
0	Sea Level	0
	Below Sea Level

RUSSIA
LITHUANIA
BELARUS
UKRAINE
MOLDOVA
SLOVAKIA
HUNGARY
ROMANIA
TRANSYLVANIA
GALICIA
CARPATHIAN MOUNTAINS
MASURIA
POLAND

Minsk
Vilnius
Warsaw (Warszawa)
Budapest
Bratislava

0 10 20 30 40 50 60 70 80 90 100 110 120 Miles
0 20 40 60 80 100 120 140 160 180 200 Kilometers

Continued on pages 164-165

Relief

Meters		Feet
3050		10 000
1525		5000
610		2000
305		1000
152.5		500
0	Sea Level	0
152.5		500
1525		5000

UNITED KINGDOM

Honiton
Exeter
Launceston
Dorchester
Exmouth
Plymouth
Torquay
(Torbay)
Dartmouth
START POINT

Southampton
Poole
Weymouth
Bournemouth
Cowes
Ryde
Newport
ISLE OF WIGHT
Portsmouth
Chichester
Worthing
Hove
Brighton

Folkestone
Dover
Dunkerque
Lewes
Hastings
Bexhill
Eastbourne
Boulogne-sur-Mer
Étaples
Berck

Calais
St. Omer
Armentières
Béthune
Bruay-en-Artois
Arras
Abbeville
St. Valéry-sur-Somme
Le Tréport
Dieppe

Roeselare
Ieper
Kortrijk
Lille
Tourcoing
Roubaix
Douai
Denain
Valenciennes
Cambrai
Crécy-en-Ponthieu
Albert
Bohain-en-Vermandois
Péronne
Guise
St. Quentin

Gent
Aalst
Anderlecht
BRUSSELS
Leuven
BELGIUM
Nivelles
Mons
Maubeuge
Charleroi
Namur
Dinant
Givet

CHANNEL

ENGLISH

C. DE LA HAGUE
ALDERNEY
GUERNSEY
St. Peter Port
SARK
CHANNEL ISLANDS
(Br.)
JERSEY
St. Helier

Cherbourg
Valognes
PTE. DE BARFLEUR
Baie de la Seine
Carentan
Bayeux
Caen
Saint-Lô
Lisieux

Fécamp
Le Havre
Trouville
Honfleur
Pont-Audemer
Elbeuf
Louviers
Évreux

Bolbec
Yvetot
Rouen
Gisors
Vernon
Mantes-la-Jolie

Neufchâtel-en-Bray
Montdidier
Beauvais
Méru
Pontoise

Amiens
Corbie
Roye
Compiègne
Creil
Senlis

St. Quentin
Charleville-Mézières
Laon
Soissons
Reims
Rethel
Vouziers
Sedan

Golfe de St. Malo

St. Pol-de-Léon
Morlaix
Landerneau
MTS. D'ARRÉE
Carhaix-Plouguer
Brest
Douarnenez
PTE. DU RAZ
Audierne
Pont-l'Abbé
Quimper

Guingamp
St. Brieuc
Lamballe
Dinard
St. Malo
Dinan

Granville
Avranches
Montfort
Fougères
Vitré
Rennes
Laval

Conde
Flers
Argentan
Alençon
Sablé-sur-Sarthe

COLLINES DE NORMANDIE
COTESDUPERCHE

Dreux
Rambouillet
Chartres
L'Aigle
Nogent-le-Rotrou

Versailles
Boulogne-Billancourt
Argenteuil
St-Denis
Clichy
PARIS

Meaux
Étampes
Fontainebleau
Nemours
Pithiviers
Corbeil-Essonnes
Romilly-sur-Seine
Montereau-faut-Yonne

Château-Thierry
Épernay
Châlons-sur-Marne
Vitry-le-François
Arcis-sur-Aube
Bar-le-Duc
Joinville
Chaumont

CHAMPAGNE

NORMANDIE

BRETAGNE

Lannion
Pontivy
Concarneau
ÎLES DE GLÉNAN

Lorient
ÎLE DE GROIX
Hennebont
Vannes
Quiberon
BELLE-ÎLE

Ploërmel
Redon
Châteaubriant
St. Nazaire

Pornic
ÎLE DE NOIRMOUTIER
Nantes
Ancenis

Angers
Trélazé
Saumur
Chemillé
Cholet
Thouars

Tours
Amboise
Chinon
Loudun
Loches

Château-Renault
Blois
Vierzon
Mehun-sur-Yèvre

Vendôme
Orléans
Châteaudun

Montargis
Joigny
Auxerre
Sens

Gien
Briare
Cosne-sur-Loire
Clamecy
Avallon

Romorantin-Lanthenay
Bourges

Montbard
Dijon

SOLOGNE

FRANCE

MORVAN
CÔTE D'OR

L. de Grand Lieu
ÎLE D'YEU
La Roche-sur-Yon
Les Sables-d'Olonne
Fontenay-le-Comte
Luçon

Pertuis Breton
ÎLE DE RÉ
La Rochelle
Surgères
Rochefort
ÎLE D'OLÉRON

Bressuire
Parthenay
Châtellerault
Poitiers
Le Blanc
Descartes
Issoudun

St. Florent-sur-Cher
St. Amand-Mont Rond
Châteauroux
Argenton-sur-Creuse
Montmorillon

Moulins
Nevers
Autun
Le Creusot
Chalon-sur-Saône
Montceau
Paray-le-Monial
Digoin
Cluny
Mâcon

HAUTEURS DE GÂTINE

BAY OF BISCAY

Marennes
La Tremblade
Royan
Cognac
Saintes
St. Jean-d'Angely

Ruffec
Confolens
St. Junien
Guéret

Limoges
Aubusson
Ussel

Montluçon
Commentry
Vichy
Riom
Clermont-Ferrand

Roanne
Villefranche
Tarare
Thiers
Amplepuis

PLATEAUX DU LIMOUSIN

Barbezieux
Jonzac
Angoulême
St. Yrieix-la-Perche
Brive-la-Gaillarde
Tulle

Bort-les-Orgues
Puy de Sancy
6185
Issoire
Ambert
Montbrison
St. Chamond
Rive-de-Gier
Firminy
St. Étienne
Annonay
Yssingeaux

Lyon
Villeurbanne
Oullins
Givors

AUVERGNE

MASSIF CENTRAL

Blanquefort
Mérignac
Pessac
Bègles
Bordeaux
Libourne
Coutras

Bergerac
Périgueux

Argentat
Salat-la-Canéda
Aurillac
Murat
Plomb du Cantal
St. Flour
Le Puy
Mt-Mézenc
5751
Privas
Valence
Romans
Aubenas
Le Teil

Arcachon
Bassin d'Arcachon
La Teste-de-Buch

La Réole
Marmande
Tonneins

Langon
Cahors
Figeac
Decazeville
Aubin
Mende
Langogne
Bagnols-sur-Cèze
Orange

Labouheyre
Étang de Biscarosse

Villeneuve-sur-Lot
Agen
Moissac
Villefranche-de-Rouergue
Rodez
Millau

LANDES

LOT

Nérac
Condom
Castelsarrasin
Montauban
Gaillac
Albi
Carmaux

St. Affrique
Lodève
Montpellier
Lunel
Miramas
Arles

GASCOGNE

CÉVENNES

Mont-de-Marsan
Verdun
Auch

Dax
Aire-sur-l'Adour
Orthez
Pau
Tarbes

Toulouse
Muret
Bazièges
Castelnaudary
Baziège
Castres

Béziers
Agde
Sète

Golfe du Lion

Biarritz
Bayonne
St. Jean-de-Luz
Irún
Oloron-Ste-Marie

St. Gaudens
St. Girons
Foix
Pamiers
Carcassonne
Limoux
Sigean
Narbonne
Perpignan

Roncesvalles
Bagnères-de-Bigorre
Bagnères-de-Luchon
Lourdes
Tarascon
Quillan
Ax-les-Thermes
Prades
Rivesaltes
Port Vendres
C. DE CREUS

PYRÉNÉES

Pamplona
Jaca
Mt. Perdido
11007
Pico de Aneto
11168
SPAIN
ANDORRA
Andorra

Tafalla

MEDITERRANEAN SEA

Longitude West of Greenwich
Longitude East of Greenwich

Continued on pages 172-173

A-550900-76 1-76-14
COPYRIGHT BY
RAND MCNALLY & COMPANY
MADE IN U.S.A.

a

Miramas
St. Chamas
Istres
Berre-l'Étang
Rognac
Équille
Aix-en-Provence
Gardanne
Simiane

Étang de Berre
Marignane
Victoret
Vitrolles
Allauch

PORT-DE-BOUC
Lavéra
Martigues
Châteauneuf
L'Estaque
Les Pennes
Mirabeau

La Couronne
Carro
Sausset-les-Pins
Carry-le-Rouet
Madrague

Marseille

Golfe du Lion

La Madrague
CÔTE DE LA GINESTE 1073

©RMcN.

Scale 1:1 000 000
0 4 8 12 16 Kilometers
0   5   10 Miles

Scale 1:4 000 000; one inch to 64 miles. Conic Projection
Elevations and depressions are given in feet

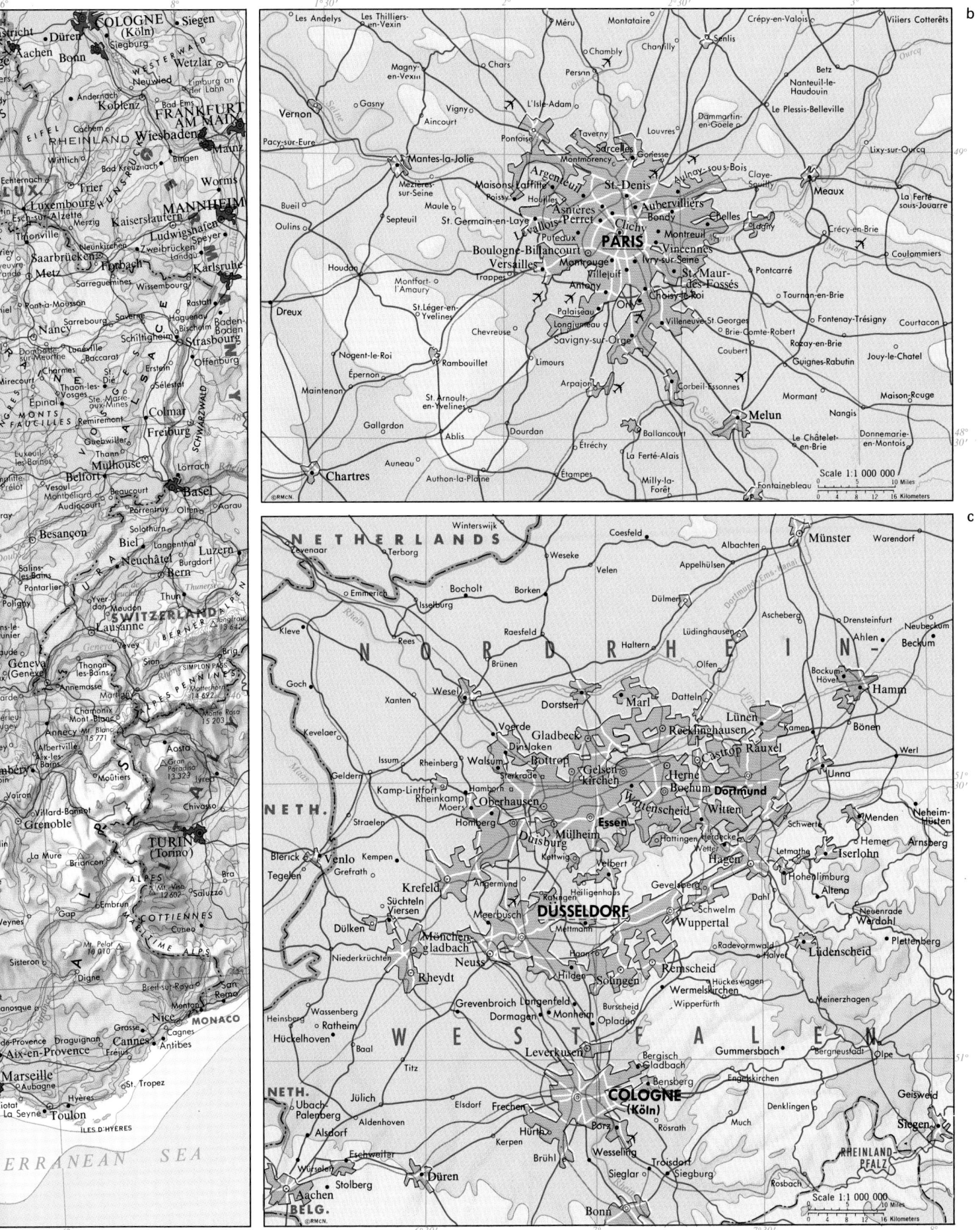

b

c

Scale 1:1 000 000

Scale 1:1 000 000

BAY OF BISCAY

CORDILLERA CANTABRICA

BASQUE PROVINCES

ATLANTIC OCEAN

MADRID

LISBON
(Lisboa)

Sevilla

Córdoba

Granada

Málaga

Gibraltar (Br.)

Strait of Gibraltar

MOROCCO

MEDITERRANEAN

Relief

Meters		Feet
3050		10000
1525		5000
610		2000
305		1000
152.5		500
0	Sea Level	0
152.5		500
1525		5000
3050		10000

A-552900-76   -6-12
COPYRIGHT BY
RAND McNALLY & COMPANY
MADE IN U.S.A.

Scale 1:4 000 000, one inch to 64 miles. Conic Projection
Elevations and depressions are given in feet

Longitude West of Greenwich

Continued on pages 170-171

a

S. Lorenzo de
El Escorial
SA. DEL HOYO
4606
Colmenar
Viejo
Fuente el Saz
El Escorial
Galapagar
S. Sebastián
de los Reyes
Algete
El Pardo
Valdemorillo
Las Rozas
de Madrid
Fuencarral
Barajas
de Madrid
Torrejón
de Ardoz
Alcalá de
Henares
Pozuelo de Alarcón
MADRID
Vicálvaro
S. Fernando de Henares
Brunete
Alcorcón
Vallecas
Loeches
Villaviciosa de Odón
Leganés
Getafe
Arganda
Campo Real
Móstoles
Navalcarnero
Valdilecha
Carabaña
Parla
Pinto
S. Martín
de la Vega
Morata
de Tajuña
Perales
de Tajuña
Scale 1:1 000 000
0   5   10 Miles
0 4 8 12 16 Kilometers   ©RMcN.

b

Mafra
Alhandra
Samora Correia
São João
das Lampas
Cheleiros
Alverca
Montelavar
Almargem
do Bispo
Loures
Sacavém
Montijo
Colares
Sintra
Odivelas
Amadora
LISBON
(Lisboa)
CABO
DA ROCA
Queluz
Barcarena
Carnaxide
Alcochete
Alcabideche
Estoril
Oeiras
Almada
Moita
Cascais
Barreiro
Seixal
Albos
Vedros
Pinhal Novo
Costa de Caparica
Coina
Palmela
ATLANTIC
OCEAN
Setúbal
Ba. de
Setúbal
Scale 1:1 000 000
0   5   10 Miles
0 4 8 12 16 Kilometers
CABO ESPICHEL
Sesimbra
Comporta

c

Frattamaggiore
Acerra
Nola
Avellino
Arzano
Pomigliano d'Arco
Marano di Napoli
Monteforte
Irpino
NAPLES
(Napoli)
Somma Vesuviana
3710
Pozzuoli
Vesuvio
4190
Sarno
Mercato
S. Severino
Bacoli
Portici
Torre
del Greco
S. Giuseppe
Vesuviano
I. DI PROCIDA
C. MISENO
Procida
Torre Annunziata
Pompeii Ruins
Angri
Nocera Inf.
Cava de'
Tirreni
Forio
2585
Ischia
Castellammare
di Stabia
4734
Gragnano
Salerno
I. D'ISCHIA
Golfo di Napoli
Sorrento
Amalfi
TYRRHENIAN
Golfo di Salerno
SEA
I. DI CAPRI
1932
Capri
PUNTA
CAMPANELLA
Scale 1:1 000 000
0   5   10 Miles
0 4 8 12 16 Kilometers

d

Pyrgi
Caere
Monterotondo
Veio
Mentana
Guidonia
Cerveteri
Ladispoli
Guidonia
ROME
(Roma)
Tivoli
Villa
Adriana
VATICAN CITY
Fregene
Frascati
Fiumicino
Marino
Ostia Antica
COLLI ALBANI
3114
Zagarolo
Lido di Roma
Laurentum
Albano Laziale
Genzano di Roma
Pomezia
Velletri
Lanuvio
Aprília
AGRO
PONTINO
Cisterna di
Latina
TYRRHENIAN
SEA
Anzio
Nettuno
Scale 1:1 000 000
0   5   10 Miles
0 4 8 12 16 Kilometers   ©RMcN.

Longitude East of Greenwich

0   20   40   60   80   100   120 Miles
0 20 40 60 80 100 140 160 180 200 Kilometers

Continued on pages 168-169

Continued on pages 170-171

BRENNER PASS

AUSTRIA

SWITZERLAND

Jungfrau 13,642

Matterhorn 14,672

SIMPLON PASS

ALPI LEPONTINE

RHAETIAN ALPS

St. Moritz

Merano   Bressanone   Lienz

Bolzano

TRENTINO-ALTO ADIGE

DOLOMITI

Trento

Pieve di Cadore

Tolmezzo

CARNIC ALPS

KARAWANKEN

Villach   Klagenfurt   Dravograd   Murska Sobota   Maribor

Ptuj   Čakovec

Varaždin   Koprivnica

FRIULI-VENEZIA GIULIA

Kranj   Celje

Triglav

SLOVENIA

Ljubljana

CROATIA

Zagreb

Bjelovar   Virovitica

Daruvar

Sisak   Petrinja

Kutina

BOSNA

Banja Luka

Sion   Aosta   Gran Paradiso   Ivrea   Biella

TURIN (Torino)

Pinerolo   Chivasso   Casale Monferrato   Asti   Alessandria

Locarno   Bellinzona   Lugano   Sondrio

Como   Lecco   Bergamo   Brescia

LOMBARDIA

Varese   Busto Arsizio   Gallarate   Monza

MILAN (Milano)

Novara   Pavia   Lodi   Crema   Cremona   Mantova (Mantua)

Vigevano   Piacenza   Codogno

Verona   Vicenza   Padova (Padua)   Treviso

VENETO

Mestre   Venice (Venezia)

Gulf of Venice

Rovigo   Adria   Chioggia   Cavarzere

Ferrara   Modena   Bologna

EMILIA-ROMAGNA

Parma   Reggio nell'Emilia   Carpi

Comacchio   Ravenna

Genoa (Genova)   Savona

LIGURIA

La Spezia   Carrara   Massa

Golfo di Genova

Rapallo   Sestri Levante

Nice   S. Remo   Ventimiglia

MONACO

FRANCE   Albenga   Imperia

MARITIME ALPS

Cuneo   Mondovì   Saluzzo   Fossano

LIGURIAN SEA

ISOLA DI GORGONA

CAPRAIA

Livorno (Leghorn)   Pisa   Lucca   Pistoia   Prato

Florence (Firenze)   Empoli   Pontedera

TOSCANA

Siena   Arezzo   Volterra   Grosseto

Piombino   Portoferraio

ISOLA D'ELBA   PIANOSA

DI MONTECRISTO   I. DEL GIGLIO   I. DI GIANNUTRI

Orbetello   Civitavecchia

C. CORSE

CORSICA

Bastia   Calvi   Corte   Mt. Cinto 8878   Mt. Incudine 6982

Ajaccio   Sartène   Porto-Vecchio   Bonifacio

Strait of Bonifacio

CAPRERA PT.   CAPRERA

ASINARA   Porto Torres   Sassari   Alghero   Ozieri

Tempio Pausania   Olbia

Golfo dell' Asinara

C. COMINO

Bosa   Nuoro   Dorgali   C. COMINO

Golfo di Orosei

Cuglieri   Oristano   Arborea   Lanusei

SARDINIA   Punta la Marmora 6017

Golfo di Oristano

Villacidro   Iglesias   Cagliari   Quartu Sant'Elena

Carloforte   I. DI S. PIETRO   I. DI S. ANTIOCO

Golfo di Cagliari   C. CARBONARA   C. SPARTIVENTO

TYRRHENIAN SEA

VATICAN CITY

ROME (Roma)

Frascati   Albano Laziale   Tivoli   Guidonia

Velletri   Aprilia   Anzio   Sabaudia   Terracina   Gaeta

LAZIO   Viterbo   Orvieto   Rieti   Terni

UMBRIA   Perugia   Assisi   Foligno   Spoleto   Todi

MARCHE   Ancona   Jesi   Macerata   Fermo   Recanati   Fabriano

Urbino   Pesaro   Fano   Senigallia

SAN MARINO   Rimini   Cesena   Forlì   Faenza   Imola

San Benedetto del Tronto   Ascoli Piceno   Teramo

Mt. Corno 9554   Pescara   Chieti   Ortona   Vasto   Termoli

ABRUZZI   L'Aquila   Avezzano   Sulmona   Mt. Amaro 9163

MOLISE   Campobasso   Isernia   Larino

Cassino   Frosinone   Sora   Ferentino

CAMPANIA   Caserta   Santa Maria   Aversa   Benevento   Avellino

NAPLES (Napoli)   Pozzuoli   Vesuvio 4190   Nola   Salerno

ISOLA D'ISCHIA   ISOLE PONZIANE   Golfo di Gaeta

Torre del Greco   Sorrento   I. DI CAPRI   Golfo di Salerno

Eboli   Battipaglia

PUGLIA   Foggia   Manfredonia   Monte Sant'Angelo

TESTA DEL GARGANO   Vieste

Cerignola   Andria   Barletta   Trani   Molfetta   Bitonto

Corato   Ruvo   Altamura   Gravina   Matera

BASILICATA   Potenza   Pisticci

Golfo di Manfredonia   ISOLE TREMITI

PIANOSA   PALAGRUŽA (Cro.)

Golfo di Policastro

CALABRIA   Cosenza   Castrovillari   Rossano   Coriglia

Golfo di Sant' Eufemia   Nicastro   Vibo Valentia   Polistena

STROMBOLI (VOL)   ISOLE EOLIE   FILICUDI   SALINA   PANAREA   LIPARI   ALICUDI   VULCANO

DI USTICA

Messina   Reggio di Calabria   C. SPARTIVENTO

Palermo   Monreale   Bagheria   Cefalù   Milazzo   Barcellona

Trapani   Marsala   Alcamo   Salemi   Castelvetrano   Mazara del Vallo

ISOLE EGADI   Partinico   Corleone   Termini

SICILY   Mt. Etna (Vol) 10,902   Taormina   Acireale   Catania   Enna

Caltanissetta   Agrigento   Sciacca   Gela   Caltagirone   Augusta

ADRIATIC SEA

ISTRA   Poreč   Rovinj   Pula   Pazin

Rijeka (Fiume)   KRK   CRES   RAB   Senj   Otočac

VELIKA KAPELA   Ogulin   Slunj   Bihać

VELEBIT   Gospić   Otočac

OTOK SUSAK   LOSINJ   Veli Lošinj   PAG   Karlobag

MOLAT   UNIJE   Zadar   Benkovac   Knin

DUGI OTOK   KORNAT   Skradin   Šibenik

DINARA   Livno   Sinj   Trogir   Split

DALMATIA   ŠOLTA   BRAČ   HVAR   Makarska

Vis   VIS   BIŠEVO   SUŠAC   KORČULA   Blato   LASTOVO

Sofia Laka   Kobarid   Idrija   Gorizia   Monfalcone

G. of Trieste   Trieste   Piran   Portorož   Koper

Postojna   Cerknica   Kočevje   Čabar

Novo Mesto   Brežice   Krško

Karlovac   Ozalj   Duga Resa

Bosanski Novi   Bosanska Dubica   Bosanska Gradiška   Prijedor

Sanski Most   Ključ   Jajce   Donji Vakuf   Bugojno

AEGEAN SEA

a   AKRA SPATHA   Kissamos   Kolpos Khanion   Khaniá   Khóra Sfakíon

Same scale as main map

Kólpos Almiroú   Réthimnon   DIA   Iráklion (Candia)   Neápoli

AKRA SIDHEROS   Kólpos Mirabéllou   Sitía

CRETE (Greece)   Áno Viánnos   Ierápetra

AKRA LITHINON   GÁVDHOS

MEDITERRANEAN SEA

©RMcN.

Scale 1:4 000 000; one inch to 64 miles. Conic Projection
Elevations and depressions are given in feet

Relief

Feet	
5000	
2000	
1000	
500	
Sea Level	
0	

Meters	
1525	
610	
305	
152.5	
0	
152.5	

Continued on pages 166-167

Cities and Towns

0 to 50,000	○
50,000 to 500,000	⊙
500,000 to 1,000,000	◉
1,000,000 and over	

Scale 1:4 000 000; one inch to 64 miles. Conic Projection
Elevations and depressions are given in feet

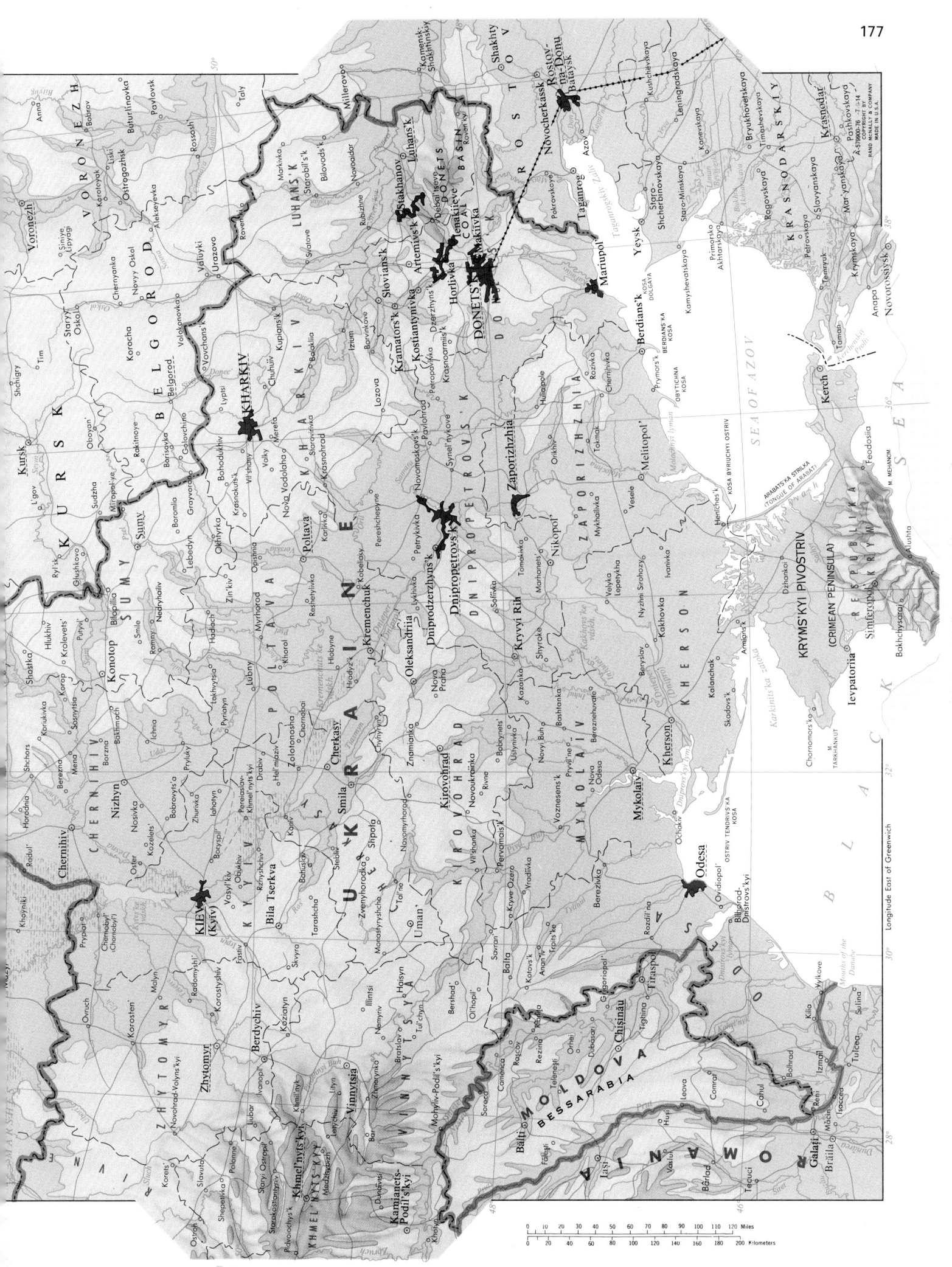

Longitude East of Greenwich

0 10 20 30 40 50 60 70 80 90 100 110 120 Miles
0 20 40 60 80 100 120 140 160 180 200 Kilometers

Cities and regions:

V O R O N E Z H
K U R S K
B E L G O R O D
L U H A N S'K
S U M Y
K H A R K I V
P O L T A V A
C H E R N I H I V
K Y I V
K I R O V O H R A D
D N I P R O P E T R O V S'K
Z A P O R I Z H Z H I A
K H E R S O N
M Y K O L A I V
D O N E T S'K
R O S T O V
K R A S N O D A R S K I Y
U K R A I N E
Z H Y T O M Y R
V I N N Y T S' Y A
K H M E L' N Y T S' K Y I
M O L D O V A
B E S S A R A B I A
R O M A N I A

DONETS BASIN
TENAKIIEVE COAL

KRYMS'KYI PIVOSTRIV
(CRIMEAN PENINSULA)
RESPUBLIKA KRYM

SEA OF AZOV
B L A C K   S E A

Voronezh, Anna, Bobrov, Pavlovsk, Buturlinovka, Taly, Millerovo, Kamensk-Shakhtinskiy, Shakhty, Novocherkassk, Rostov-na-Donu, Bataysk, Krasnodar, Novorossiysk

KYIV (Kyyiv), KHARKIV, DONETS'K, Makiivka, Horlivka, Artemivs'k, Stakhanov, Luhans'k, Kramators'k, Slovians'k, Kostiantynivka, Dzerzhyns'k, Yenakiieve, Debal'tseve, Rovenky, Mariupol', Berdians'k, Melitopol', Zaporizhzhia, Dnipropetrovs'k, Dniprodzerzhyns'k, Kryvyi Rih, Nikopol', Kherson, Mykolaiv, Odesa, Simferopol', Yevpatoriia, Kerch, Feodosiia, Sevastopol', Bakhchysarai

Poltava, Sumy, Konotop, Nizhyn, Chernihiv, Cherkasy, Kirovohrad, Bila Tserkva, Vinnytsia, Zhytomyr, Berdychiv, Khmel'nyts'kyi, Kamianets'-Podil's'kyi, Chişinău, Tiraspol', Galaţi, Brăila

Scale 1:20 000 000; one inch to 315 miles
Lambert's Azimuthal, Equal Area Projection
Elevations and depressions are given in f

Relief

Meters		Feet
3050		10 000
1525		5000
610		2000
305		1000
152.5		500
0	Sea Level	0
152.5	Below	500
1525	Sea Level	5000
3050		10 000

SEVERNAYA ZEMLYA
(NORTHERN LAND)

P-OV
GORY TAYMYR
BYRRANGA

CHUKOTSKOYE NAGOR'YE

VRANGELYA
(WRANGEL I.)

M. SHELAGSKIY

CHUKOTSKIY
P-OV

Arctic Circle

KORYAKSKIY KHREBET

Nordvik

Ust'-Olenek

Tiksi

Khatanga

Bulun

KHREBET

CHERSKOGO

KHREBET GYDAN (KOLYMSKIY)

P-OV
KAMCHATKA

Verkhoyansk

VERKHOYANSKIY KHREBET

Magadan

Petropavlovsk-
Kamchatskiy

Noril'sk
GORY
PUTORANA

Yakutsk

DZHUGDZHUR KHREBET

SAKHALIN

SEA
OF
OKHOTSK

Turukhansk

Tura

Aldan

PATOM
PLATEAU

STANOVOY KHREBET

Komsomol'sk-
na-Amure

Aleksandrovsk

Poronaysk

Yenisеysk

Kirensk

KHREBET BUREINSKIY

Yuzhno-Sakhalinsk

Krasnoyarsk

BAYKAL'SKIY KHREBET

YABLONOVYY KHREBET

Khabarovsk

SIKHOTE ALIN'

Abakan

SAYAN

KHREBET

Irkutsk

Ulan-Ude

Chita

NERCHINSKIY KHREBET

GREATER KHINGAN RANGE

Blagoveshchensk

Birobidzhan

HOKKAIDO

Sapporo

Kyzyl

TANNU-OLA

Petrovsk-Zabaykal'skiy

Kyakhta

HARBIN

Vladivostok

LESSER KHINGAN RANGE

MANCHURIA

Ulan Bator
(Ulaanbaatar)

MONGOLIA

Qiqihar

Jilin

CHANGCHUN

NORTH
KOREA

HONSHU

Uliastay

HANGAYN NURUU

FUSHUN

SHENYANG

SOUTH
KOREA

KYOTO

KOBE
OSAKA

GOBI OR SHAMO
(DESERT)

CHINA

Chengde

SEOUL

PUSAN

Hami

Zhangjiakou

BEIJING

TIANJIN

Baoding

Lüshun Dalian

YELLOW
SEA

Longitude East of Greenwich

0   100   200   300   400   500   600 Miles

0   200   400   600   800   1000 Kilometers

Continued on pages 160-161

Scale 1:10 000 000; one inch to 160 miles. Conic Projection
Elevations and depressions are given in feet.

Continued on pages 162-163

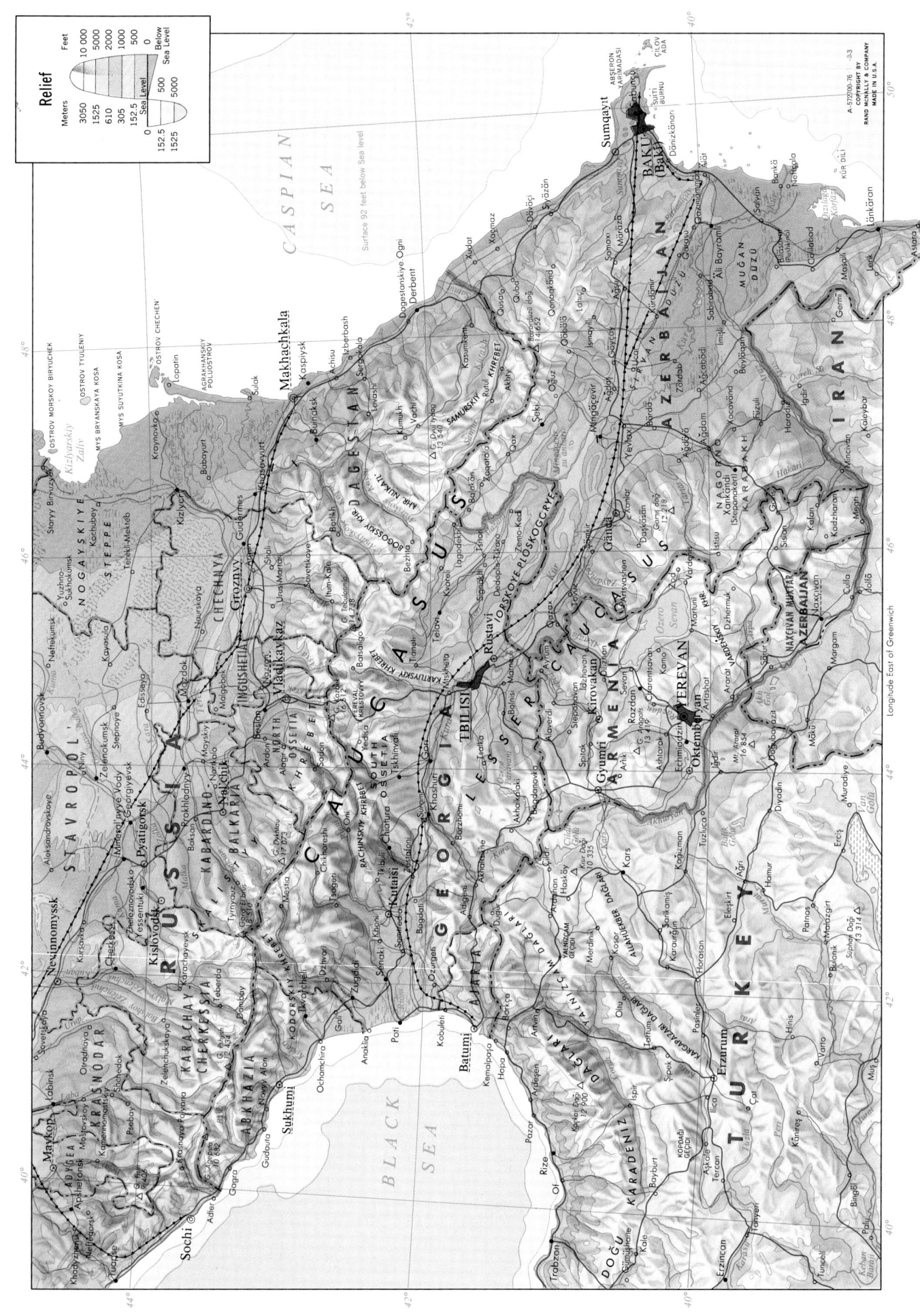

Relief

Meters	Feet
3050	10 000
1525	5000
610	2000
305	1000
152.5	500
0	Sea Level
	0 Below
	Sea Level
152.5	500
1525	5000

CASPIAN SEA

BLACK SEA

R U S S I A

G E O R G I A

A R M E N I A

A Z E R B A I J A N

T U R K E Y

I R A N

C A U C A S U S

L E S S E R   C A U C A S U S

Scale 1:4 000 000; one inch to 64 miles. Conic Projection
Elevations and depressions are given in feet

0 10 20 30 40 50 60 70 80 90 100 110 120 Miles
0 20 40 60 80 100 120 140 160 180 200 Kilometers

Longitude East of Greenwich

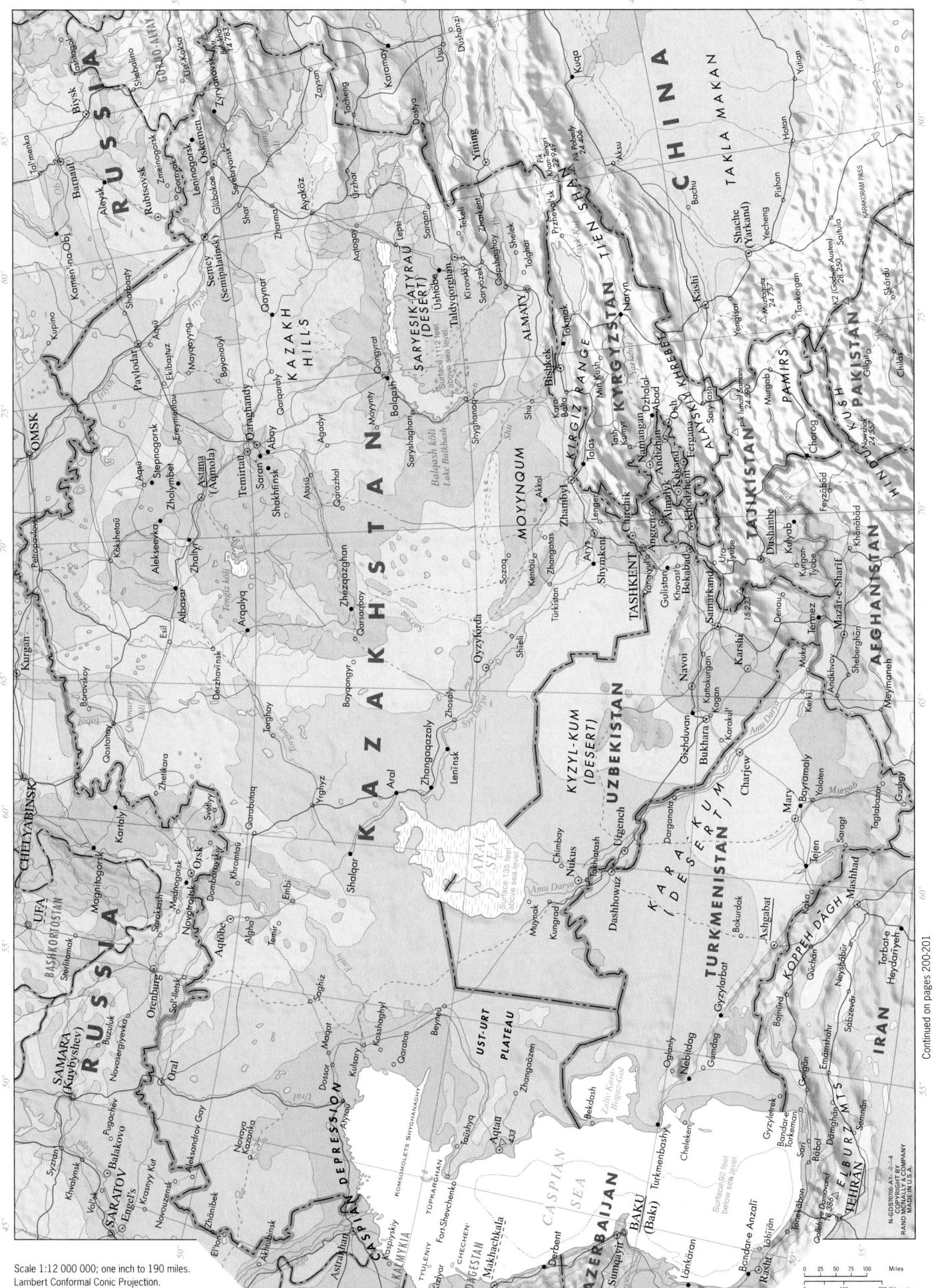

Continued on pages 200-201

Scale 1:12 000 000; one inch to 190 miles.
Lambert Conformal Conic Projection.
Elevations and depressions are given in feet.

0 25 50 75 100 Miles
0 100 200 Kilometers

N-GUS78700-A1—2-4
COPYRIGHT BY
RAND MCNALLY & COMPANY
MADE IN U.S.A.

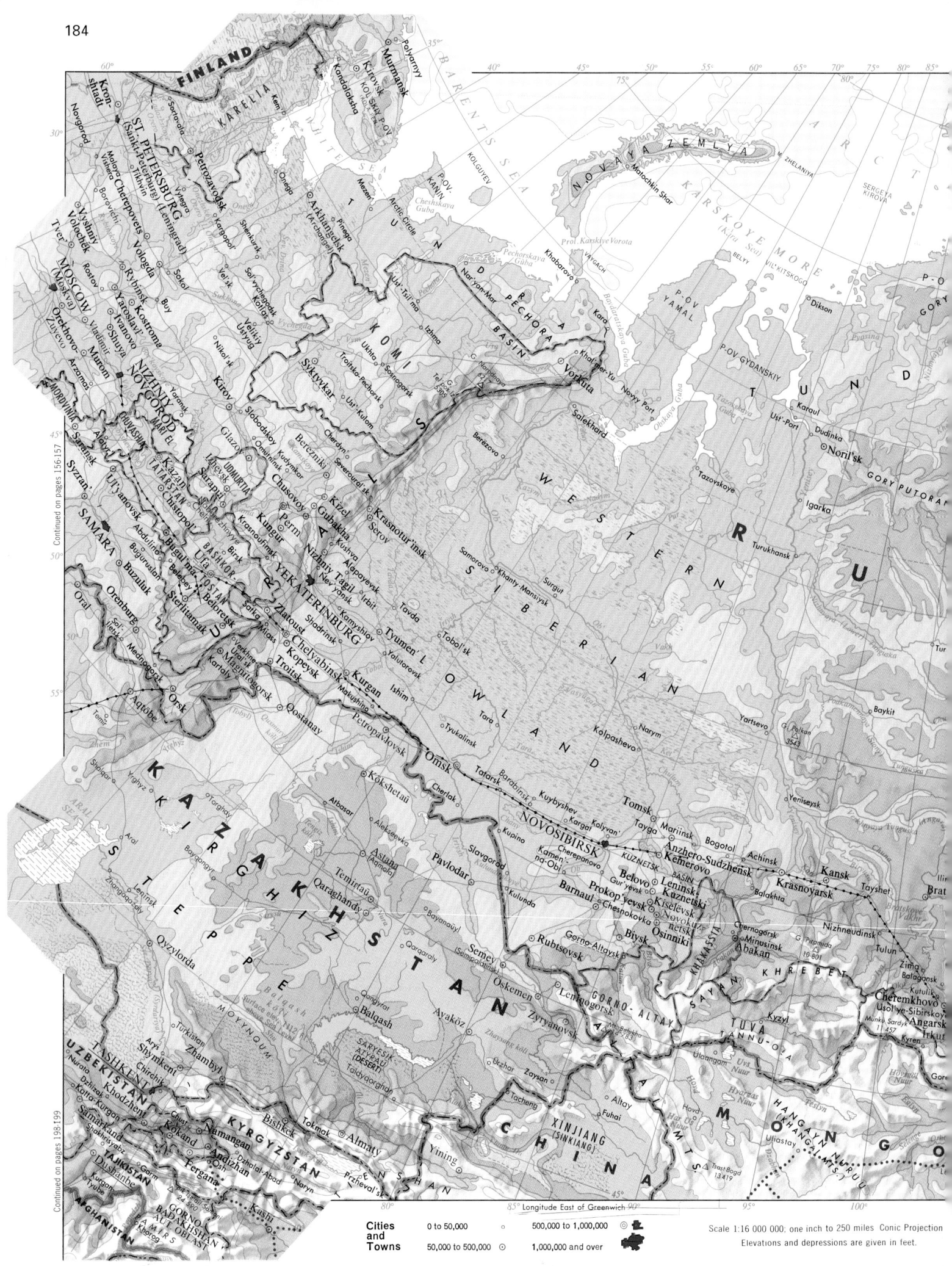

FINLAND

KARELIA

BARENTS SEA

NOVAYA ZEMLYA

KARSKOYE MORE

ST. PETERSBURG
(Sankt-Peterburg)
(Leningrad)

MOSCOW
(Moskva)

NIZHNIY
NOVGOROD

MORDVINIA

KOMI

PECHORA BASIN

TUNDRA

YAMAL

P-OV
GYDANSKIY

TUNDRA

Vorkuta

WESTERN

SIBERIAN

LOWLAND

RU

SAMARA

BASHKOR-
TOSTAN

YEKATERINBURG

Chelyabinsk
Magnitogorsk

K A Z A K H S T A N

ARAL
SEA

KIRGIZ
STEPPE

MOYNKUM

SARYESIK
ATYRAU
(DESERT)

NOVOSIBIRSK

KUZNETSK
BASIN

Krasnoyarsk

KHAKASSIA

GORNO-
ALTAY

SAYAN
KHREBET

TUVA
TANNU-OLA

Angarsk

HANGAYN
NURUU

M O N G O L I A

ALTAY

UZBEKISTAN

TASHKENT

KYRGYZSTAN

Bishkek

Almaty

C H I N A

XINJIANG
(SINKIANG)

TAJIKISTAN
Dushanbe

AFGHANISTAN

GORNO-
BADAKHSHAN

Continued on pages 156-157

Continued on pages 198-199

85° Longitude East of Greenwich

**Cities
and
Towns**

| 0 to 50,000 | ○ | 500,000 to 1,000,000 | ◉ |
| 50,000 to 500,000 | ⊙ | 1,000,000 and over | ● |

Scale 1:16 000 000; one inch to 250 miles Conic Projection
Elevations and depressions are given in feet.

Continued on pages 204-205

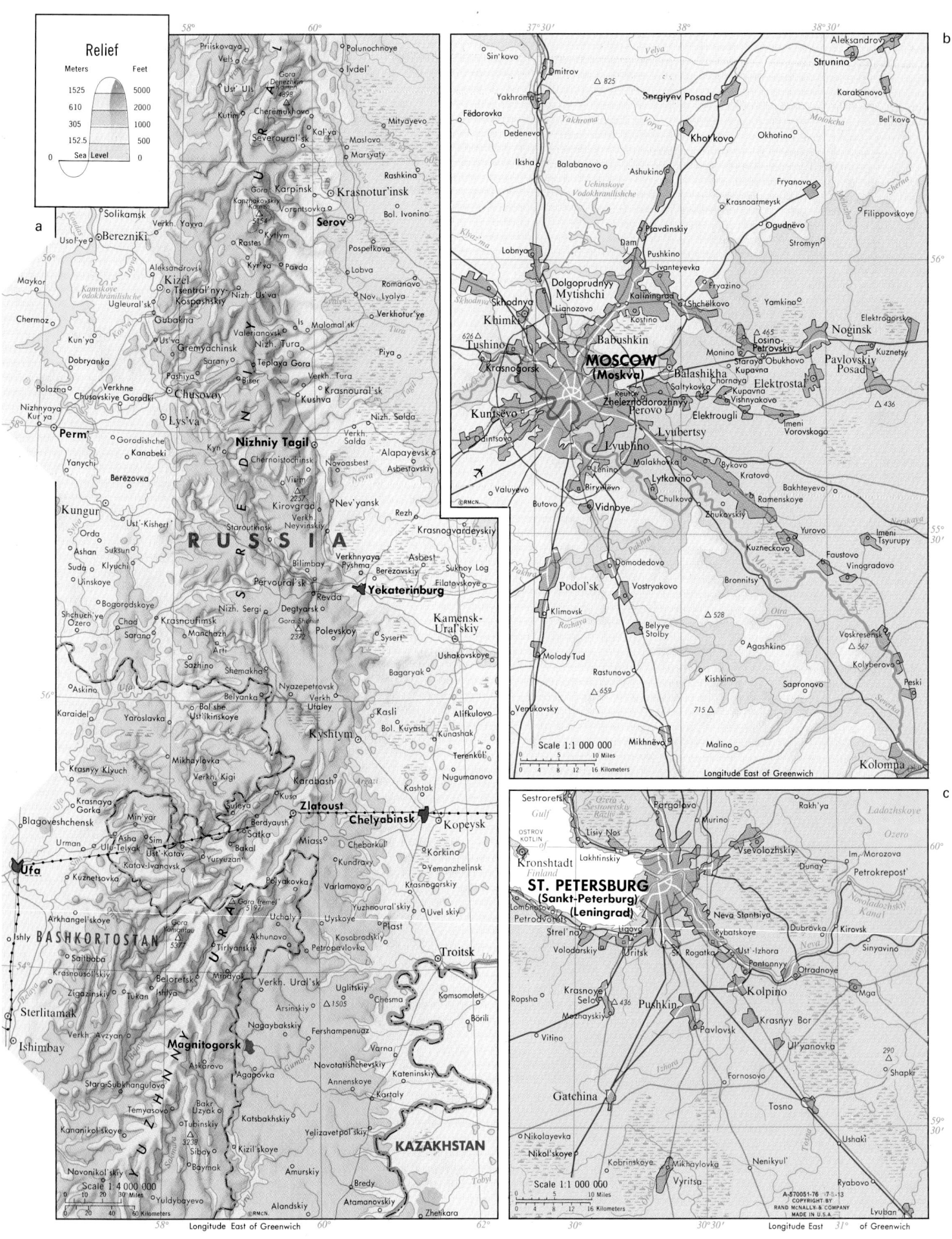

Relief

Meters		Feet
1525		5000
610		2000
305		1000
152.5		500
Sea Level		

a

b

Scale 1:1 000 000

0   5   10 Miles

0 4 8 12 16 Kilometers

Longitude East of Greenwich

MOSCOW
(Moskva)

c

ST. PETERSBURG
(Sankt-Peterburg)
(Leningrad)

Scale 1:1 000 000

0   5   10 Miles

0 4 8 12 16 Kilometers

Longitude East of Greenwich

KAZAKHSTAN

BASHKORTOSTAN

R U S S I A

Scale 1:4 000 000

0 10 20 30 Miles

0 20 40 60 Kilometers

Longitude East of Greenwich

©RMcN.

A-570051-76   7-3-13
COPYRIGHT BY
RAND McNALLY & COMPANY
MADE IN U.S.A.

Cities
and
Towns

| 0 to 50,000 | ○ | 500,000 to 1,000,000 | ◎ |
| 50,000 to 500,000 | ⊙ | 1,000,000 and over | |

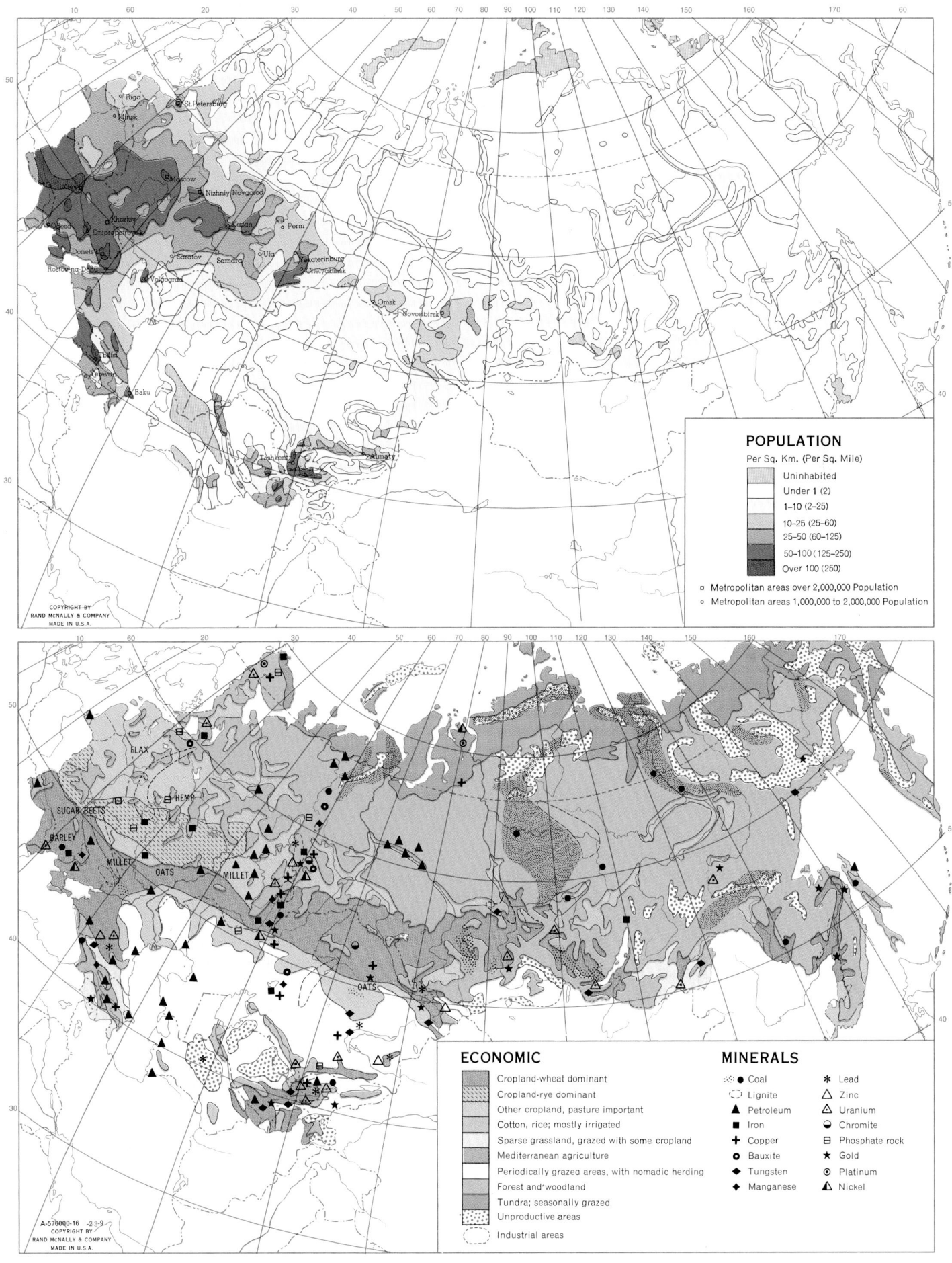

POPULATION

Per Sq. Km. (Per Sq. Mile)

- Uninhabited
- Under 1 (2)
- 1–10 (2–25)
- 10–25 (25–60)
- 25–50 (60–125)
- 50–100 (125–250)
- Over 100 (250)

▫ Metropolitan areas over 2,000,000 Population
○ Metropolitan areas 1,000,000 to 2,000,000 Population

COPYRIGHT BY
RAND McNALLY & COMPANY
MADE IN U.S.A.

ECONOMIC

- Cropland-wheat dominant
- Cropland-rye dominant
- Other cropland, pasture important
- Cotton, rice; mostly irrigated
- Sparse grassland, grazed with some cropland
- Mediterranean agriculture
- Periodically grazed areas, with nomadic herding
- Forest and woodland
- Tundra; seasonally grazed
- Unproductive areas
- Industrial areas

MINERALS

● Coal	✳ Lead
Lignite	△ Zinc
▲ Petroleum	△ Uranium
■ Iron	◒ Chromite
✛ Copper	⊟ Phosphate rock
◉ Bauxite	★ Gold
◆ Tungsten	◉ Platinum
◆ Manganese	◬ Nickel

A-570000-16 -2-3-9
COPYRIGHT BY
RAND McNALLY & COMPANY
MADE IN U.S.A.

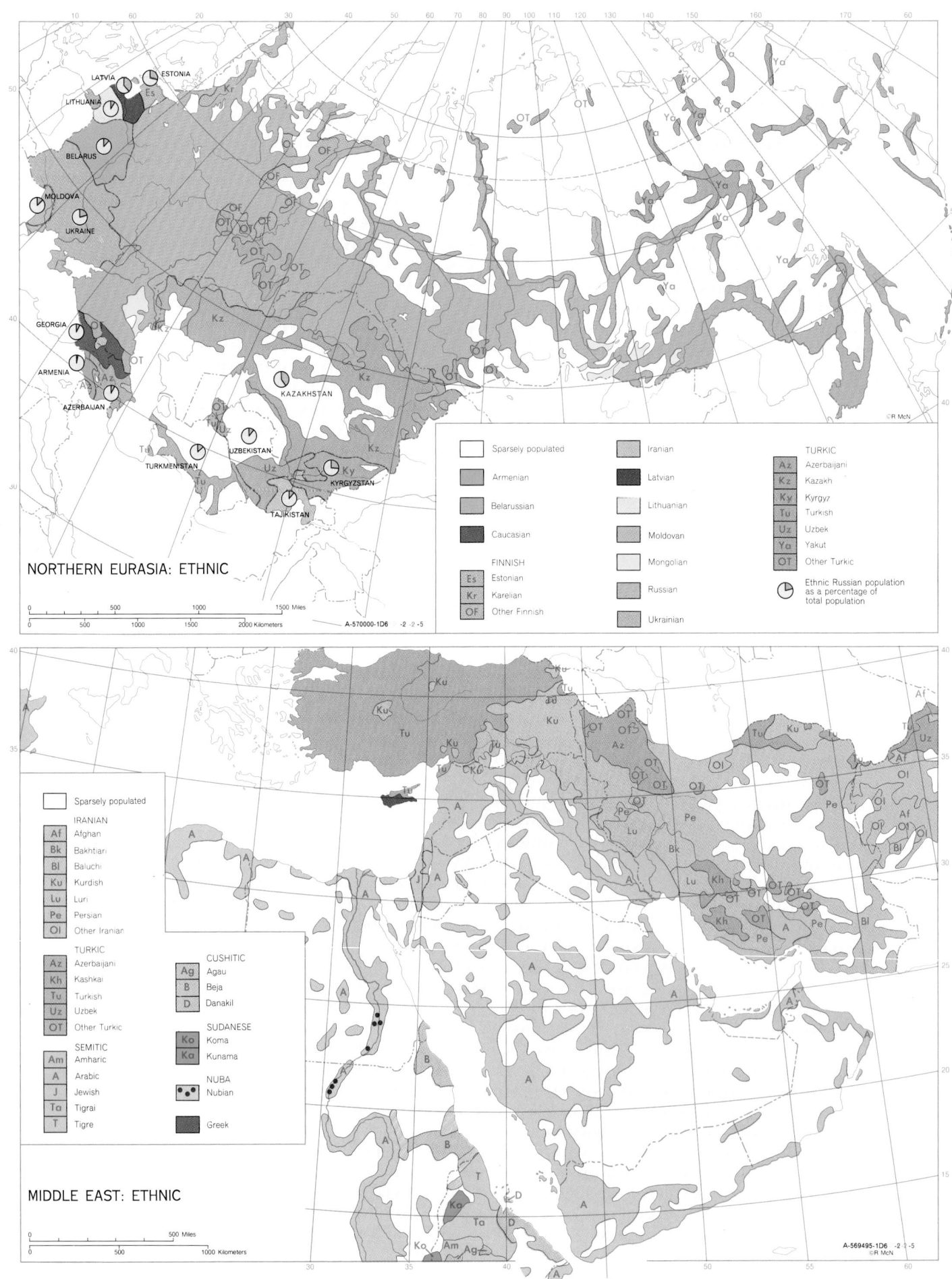

NORTHERN EURASIA: ETHNIC

LATVIA
ESTONIA
LITHUANIA
BELARUS
MOLDOVA
UKRAINE
GEORGIA
ARMENIA
AZERBAIJAN
TURKMENISTAN
UZBEKISTAN
KYRGYZSTAN
TAJIKISTAN
KAZAKHSTAN

0   500   1000   1500 Miles
0   500   1000   1500   2000 Kilometers
A-570000-1D6   -2 -2 -5

Sparsely populated	Iranian
Armenian	Latvian
Belarussian	Lithuanian
Caucasian	Moldovan
FINNISH	Mongolian
Es Estonian	Russian
Kr Karelian	Ukrainian
OF Other Finnish	

TURKIC
Az Azerbaijani
Kz Kazakh
Ky Kyrgyz
Tu Turkish
Uz Uzbek
Ya Yakut
OT Other Turkic

Ethnic Russian population as a percentage of total population

MIDDLE EAST: ETHNIC

Sparsely populated

IRANIAN
Af Afghan
Bk Bakhtiari
Bl Baluchi
Ku Kurdish
Lu Luri
Pe Persian
Ol Other Iranian

TURKIC
Az Azerbaijani
Kh Kashkai
Tu Turkish
Uz Uzbek
OT Other Turkic

SEMITIC
Am Amharic
A Arabic
J Jewish
Ta Tigrai
T Tigre

CUSHITIC
Ag Agau
B Beja
D Danakil

SUDANESE
Ko Koma
Ka Kunama

NUBA
Nubian

Greek

0   500 Miles
0   500   1000 Kilometers
A-569495-1D6   -2 -1 -5
©R McN

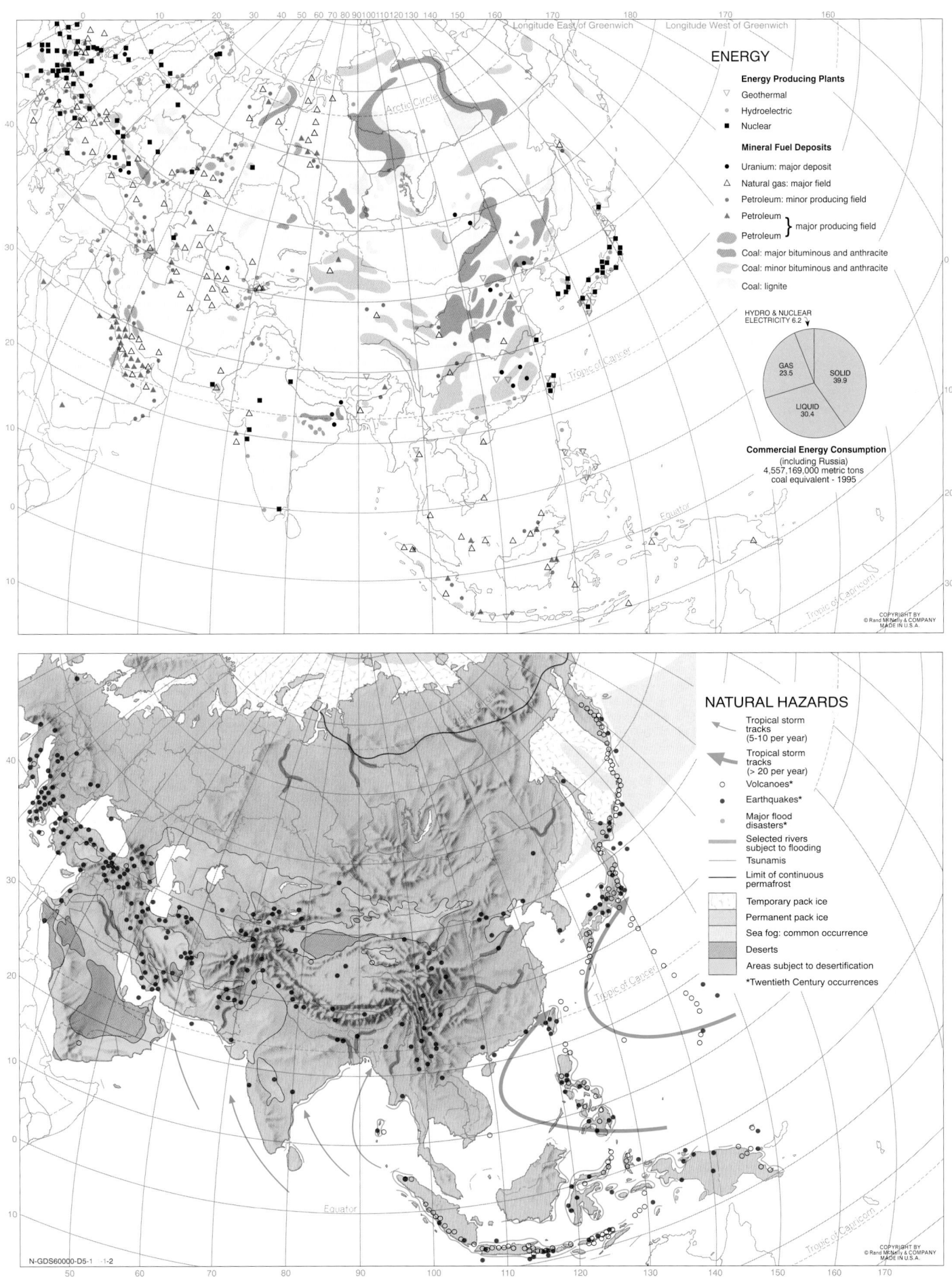

ENERGY

Energy Producing Plants
▽ Geothermal
● Hydroelectric
■ Nuclear

Mineral Fuel Deposits
● Uranium: major deposit
△ Natural gas: major field
● Petroleum: minor producing field
▲ Petroleum }
  Petroleum } major producing field
Coal: major bituminous and anthracite
Coal: minor bituminous and anthracite
Coal: lignite

HYDRO & NUCLEAR
ELECTRICITY 6.2

GAS 23.5
SOLID 39.9
LIQUID 30.4

Commercial Energy Consumption
(including Russia)
4,557,169,000 metric tons
coal equivalent - 1995

NATURAL HAZARDS

← Tropical storm tracks (5-10 per year)
← Tropical storm tracks (> 20 per year)
○ Volcanoes*
● Earthquakes*
● Major flood disasters*
Selected rivers subject to flooding
Tsunamis
Limit of continuous permafrost
Temporary pack ice
Permanent pack ice
Sea fog: common occurrence
Deserts
Areas subject to desertification
*Twentieth Century occurrences

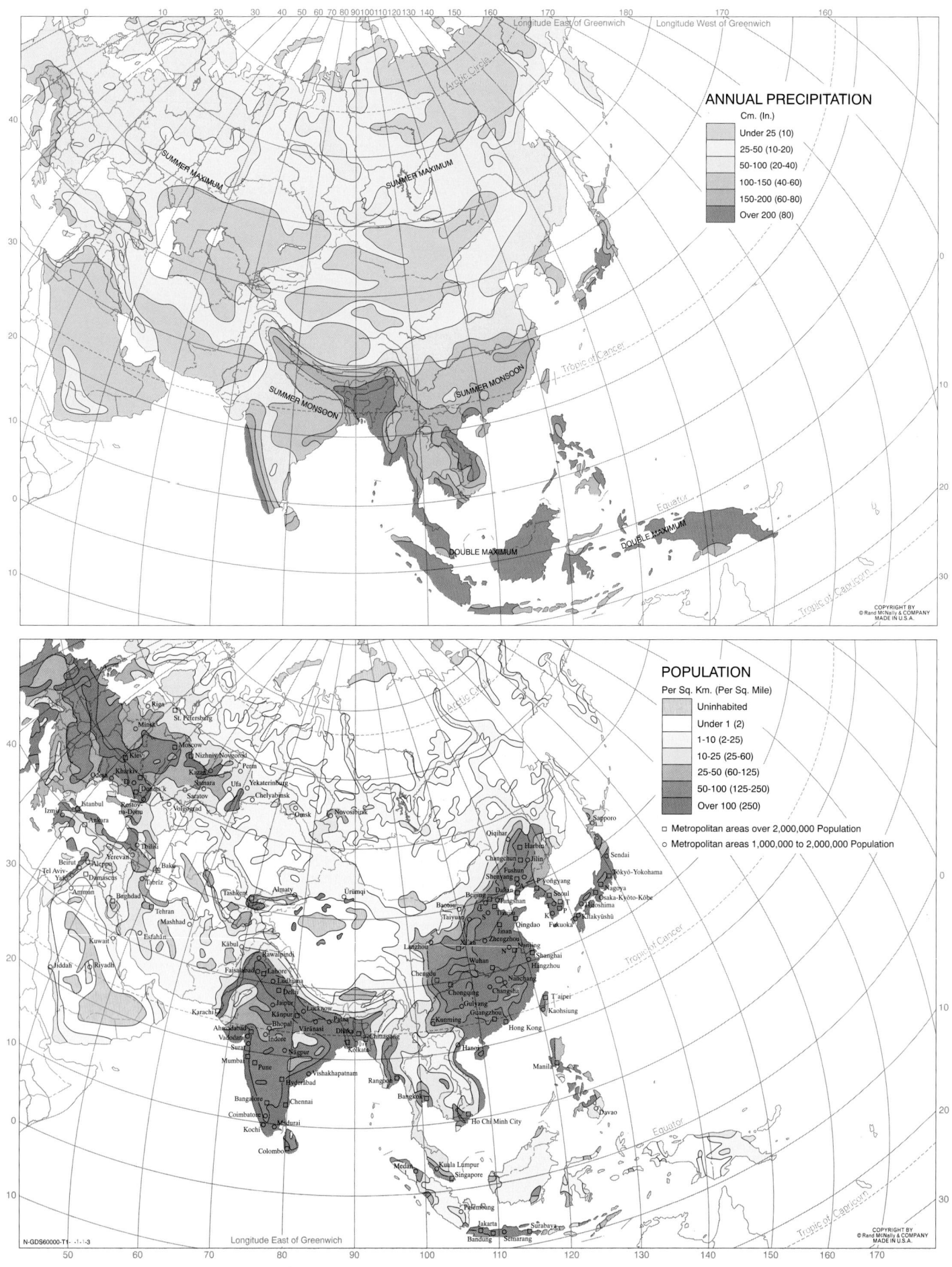

ANNUAL PRECIPITATION

Cm. (In.)

Under 25 (10)
25-50 (10-20)
50-100 (20-40)
100-150 (40-60)
150-200 (60-80)
Over 200 (80)

POPULATION

Per Sq. Km. (Per Sq. Mile)

Uninhabited
Under 1 (2)
1-10 (2-25)
10-25 (25-60)
25-50 (60-125)
50-100 (125-250)
Over 100 (250)

□ Metropolitan areas over 2,000,000 Population
○ Metropolitan areas 1,000,000 to 2,000,000 Population

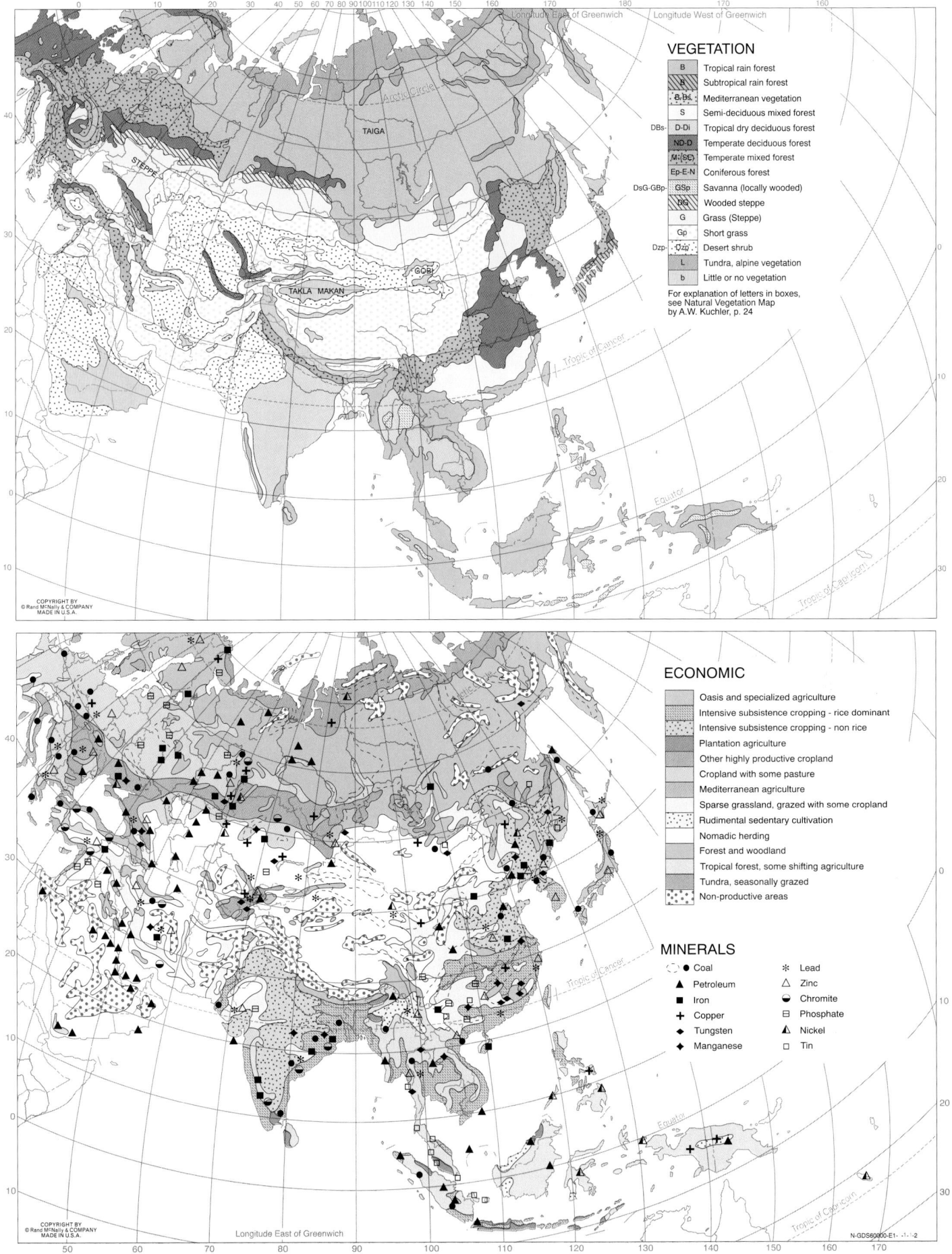

VEGETATION

- B — Tropical rain forest
- B — Subtropical rain forest
- B-Bs — Mediterranean vegetation
- S — Semi-deciduous mixed forest
- DBs- / D-Di — Tropical dry deciduous forest
- ND-D — Temperate deciduous forest
- M-(SE) — Temperate mixed forest
- Ep-E-N — Coniferous forest
- DsG-GBp- / GSp — Savanna (locally wooded)
- DG — Wooded steppe
- G — Grass (Steppe)
- Gp — Short grass
- Dzp- / Dzp — Desert shrub
- L — Tundra, alpine vegetation
- b — Little or no vegetation

For explanation of letters in boxes,
see Natural Vegetation Map
by A.W. Kuchler, p. 24

ECONOMIC

- Oasis and specialized agriculture
- Intensive subsistence cropping - rice dominant
- Intensive subsistence cropping - non rice
- Plantation agriculture
- Other highly productive cropland
- Cropland with some pasture
- Mediterranean agriculture
- Sparse grassland, grazed with some cropland
- Rudimental sedentary cultivation
- Nomadic herding
- Forest and woodland
- Tropical forest, some shifting agriculture
- Tundra, seasonally grazed
- Non-productive areas

MINERALS

- ● Coal
- ▲ Petroleum
- ■ Iron
- ✛ Copper
- ◆ Tungsten
- ◆ Manganese
- ✳ Lead
- △ Zinc
- ◖ Chromite
- ⊟ Phosphate
- ▲ Nickel
- ☐ Tin

Longitude East of Greenwich

N-GDS60000-E1- -1-·-2

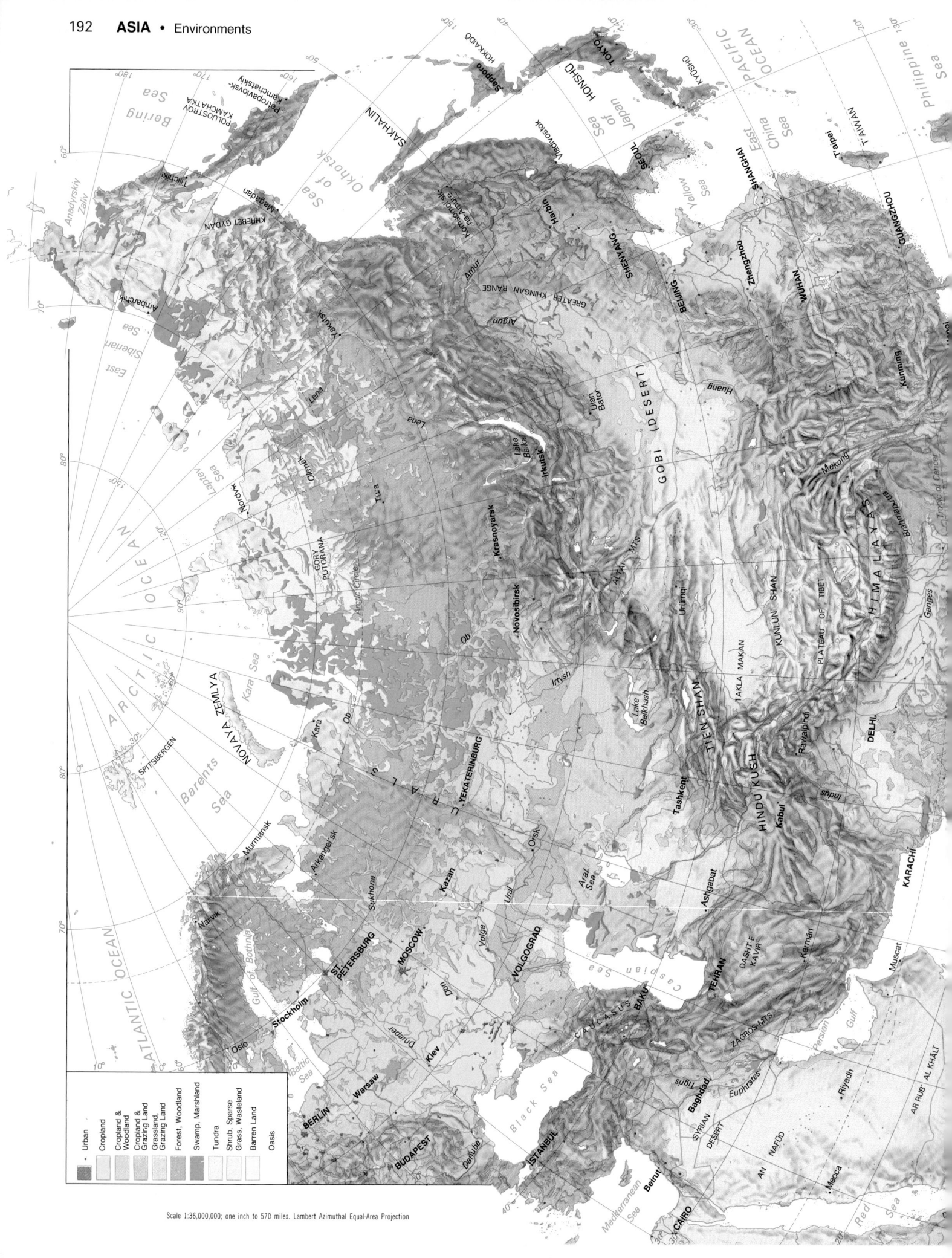

Scale 1:36,000,000; one inch to 570 miles. Lambert Azimuthal Equal-Area Projection

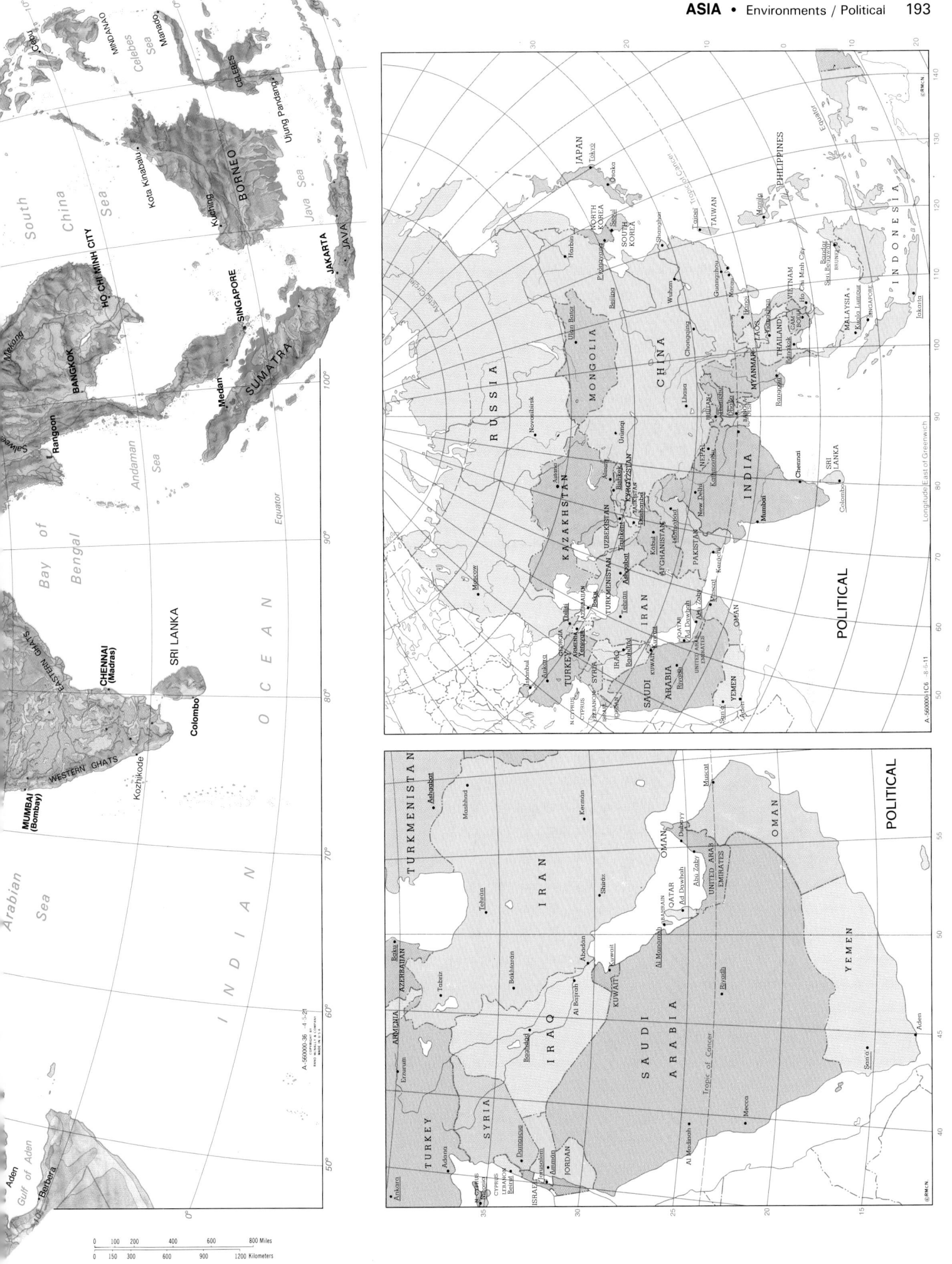

POLITICAL

POLITICAL

Scale 1:40 000 000; one inch to 630 miles. Lambert's Azimuthal, Equal Area Projection
Elevations and depressions are given in feet

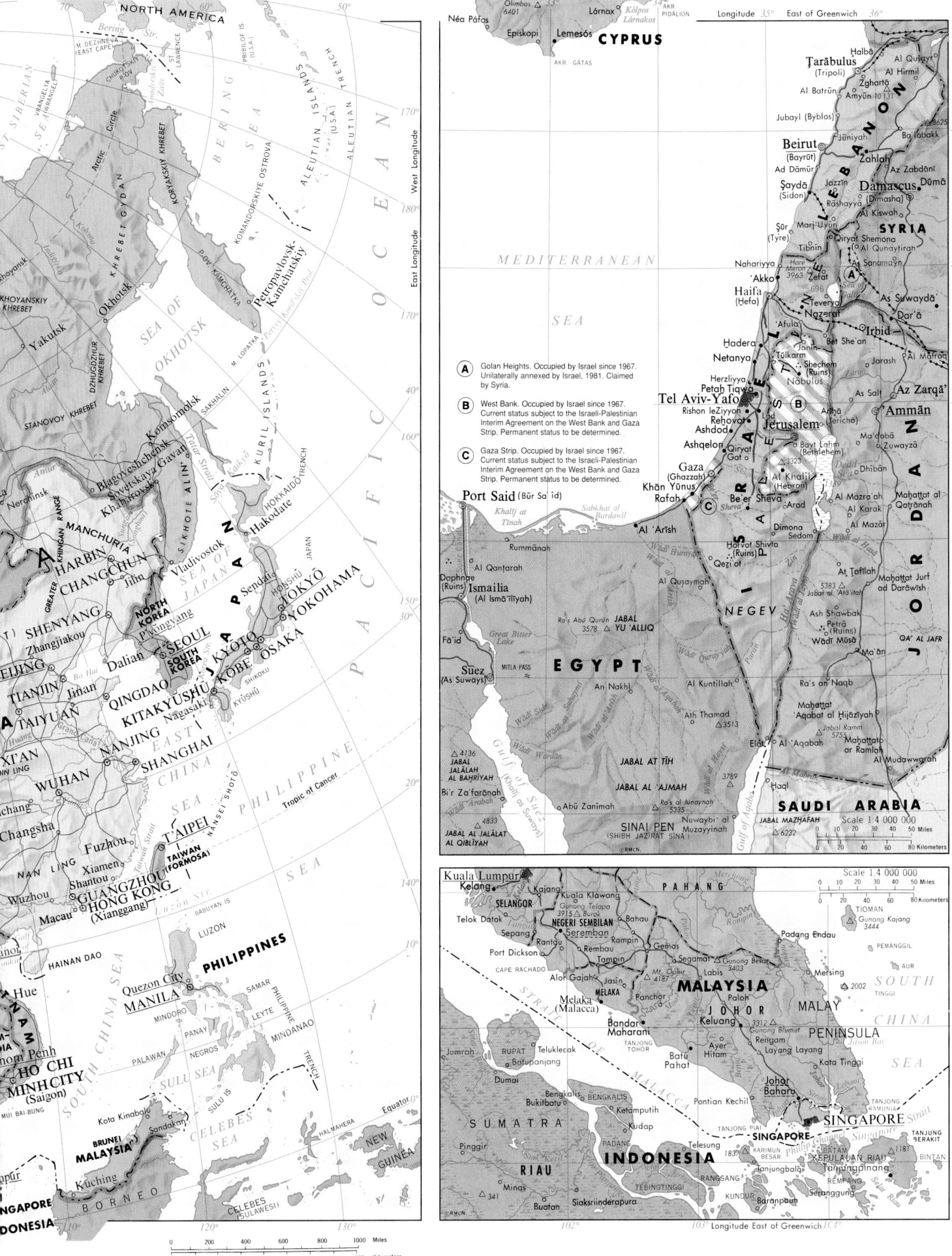

Longitude 35° East of Greenwich   36°

CYPRUS

Ólimbos 33°
6401
Néa Páfos
Episkopi
Lemesós
AKR. GÁTAS
Lárnax   Kólpos   AKR.
Lárnakos   PIDÁLION

MEDITERRANEAN

SEA

Tarābulus
(Tripoli)
Al Batrūn
Jubayl (Byblos)
Halba
Al Qusayr
Al Hirmil
Zgharta
Amyūn 10131
8625

Beirut
(Bayrūt)
Ad Dāmūr
Şaydā
(Sidon)
Jazzīn
Şūr
(Tyre)
Marj 'Uyūn
Tibnin
Naharriyya
'Akko
Haifa
(Hefa)
Hadera
Netanya
Herzliyya
Petah Tiqwa
Tel Aviv-Yafo
Rishon leZiyyon
Rehovot
Ashdod
Ashqelon
Gaza
(Ghazzah)
Khān Yūnus
Rafah
Zahlah
Az Zabdānī
Ba'labakk
Damascus
(Dimashq)
Dūmā
Rāshayyā
Al Kiswah
SYRIA
Al Qunaytirah
Qiryat Shemona
Sanamayn
Hare
Meron
3963
Zefat
696
Teverya
Nazerat
'Afula
Janin
Tülkarm
Shechem
(Ruins)
Nābulus
Arīhā
(Jericho)
Qiryat
Gat
Bayt Lahm
(Bethlehem)
3329
Al Khalil
(Hebron)
Be'er
Sheva
Be'er Sheva
Arad
Sedom
Bet She'an
Irbid
Jarash
Al Mafraq
As Suwaydā'
Dar'ā
Az Zarqā'
As Salt
Ma'dabā
Amman
Zuwayza
Dhiban
Al Mazra'ah
Al Karak
Al Mazar
Mahattat al
Qatrānah

(A) Golan Heights. Occupied by Israel since 1967. Unilaterally annexed by Israel, 1981. Claimed by Syria.

(B) West Bank. Occupied by Israel since 1967. Current status subject to the Israeli-Palestinian Interim Agreement on the West Bank and Gaza Strip. Permanent status to be determined.

(C) Gaza Strip. Occupied by Israel since 1967. Current status subject to the Israeli-Palestinian Interim Agreement on the West Bank and Gaza Strip. Permanent status to be determined.

Port Said (Būr Sa'īd)
Khalij at
Tīnah
Sabkhat al
Bardawil
Al 'Arīsh
Rummānah
Al Qantarah
Daphnae
(Ruins)
Ismailia
(Al Ismā'īlīyah)
Fā'id
Great Bitter
Lake
Al Qusaymah
Qezi'ot
Horvot Shivta
(Ruins)
Dimona
At Tafilah
Mahattat Jurf
ad Darāwīsh
5383
Jabal al 'Atā'itah
Ash Shawbak
Petrā
(Ruins)
Wādī Mūsā
Ma'ān
QA' AL JAFR
Ra's Abū Qurūn
3578
**JABAL
YU 'ALLIQ**
NEGEV

EGYPT
Suez
(As Suways)
MITLA PASS
An Nakhl
Al Kuntillah
Ra's an Naqb
'Aqabat al Hijāzīyah
Mahattat
ar Ramlah
Jabal Ramm
5755
Al Mudawwarah
Elāt
Al 'Aqabah
Haql
SAUDI ARABIA
4136
**JABAL
JALĀLAH
AL BAHRĪYAH**
Bi'r Za'farānah
JABAL AT TĪH
JABAL AL 'AJMAH
3789
4833
**JABAL AL JALĀLAT
AL QIBLĪYAH**
Abū Zanīmah
Ra's al Junaynah
5335
Nuwaybi' al
Muzayyinah
3513
JABAL MAZHAFAH
6232
SINAI PEN
(SHIBH JAZĪRAT SĪNĀ)

Scale 1:4 000 000
0 10 20 30 40 50 Miles
0   20   40   60   80 Kilometers

Scale 1:4 000 000
0 10 20 30 40 50 Miles
0   20   40   60   80 Kilometers

Kuala Lumpur
Kelang
Telok Datok
Port Dickson
CAPE RACHADO
SELANGOR
Kajang
Sepang
Rantau
NEGERI SEMBILAN
Seremban
Kuala Klawang
Gunong Telapa
3915
Burok
Bahau
Rembau
Tampin
Alor Gajah
Jasin
Melaka
(Malacca)
Panchor
Bandar
Maharani
Bukit
Hitam
Batu
Pahat
Jumrah
Teluklecak
RUPAT
Batupanjang
Dumai
Bengkalis
BENGKALIS
Bukitbatu
SUMATRA
Ketamputih
Kudap
Pinggir
Telesung
341
Minas
Buatan
Siaksriinderapura
RIAU
INDONESIA
PAHANG
Merchong
Rompin
Segamat
Gemas
Mt. Ophir
4187
Labis
Gunong Besar
3403
Gunong Blumut
3312
Rengam
Keluang
Layang Layang
JOHOR
MALAYSIA
Pontian Kechil
TANJONG
PIAI
Padang Endau
Mersing
Kota Tinggi
Ayer
**Johor
Baharu**
SINGAPORE
SINGAPORE
Pianggil
TIOMAN
Gunong Kajang
3444
PEMANGGIL
AUR
TINGGI
2002
**MALAY
PENINSULA**
Jason Bay
**SOUTH
CHINA
SEA**
TANJONG
BERAKIT
BATAM
KEPULAUAN RIAU
Tanjungbalai
Tanjungpinang
BINTAN
Sengga
RANGSANG
KUNDUR
Baranpauh
TEBINGTINGGI
Serangggung

200 400 600 800 1000 Miles
400   800   1200   1600 Kilometers

Continued on pages 229

Relief

Meters | Feet
3050 | 10 000
1525 | 5000
610 | 2000
305 | 1000
0 | Sea Level | Below Sea Level
| | 500
152.5 | 1525 | 5000
3050 | 10 000
6100 | 20 000

A-519695-76 -24-2-46
COPYRIGHT BY
RAND M9NALLY & COMPANY
MADE IN U.S.A.

Longitude East of Greenwich

Scale 1:40 000 000; one inch to 630 miles. Lambert's Azimuthal, Equal Area Projection
Elevations and depressions are given in feet

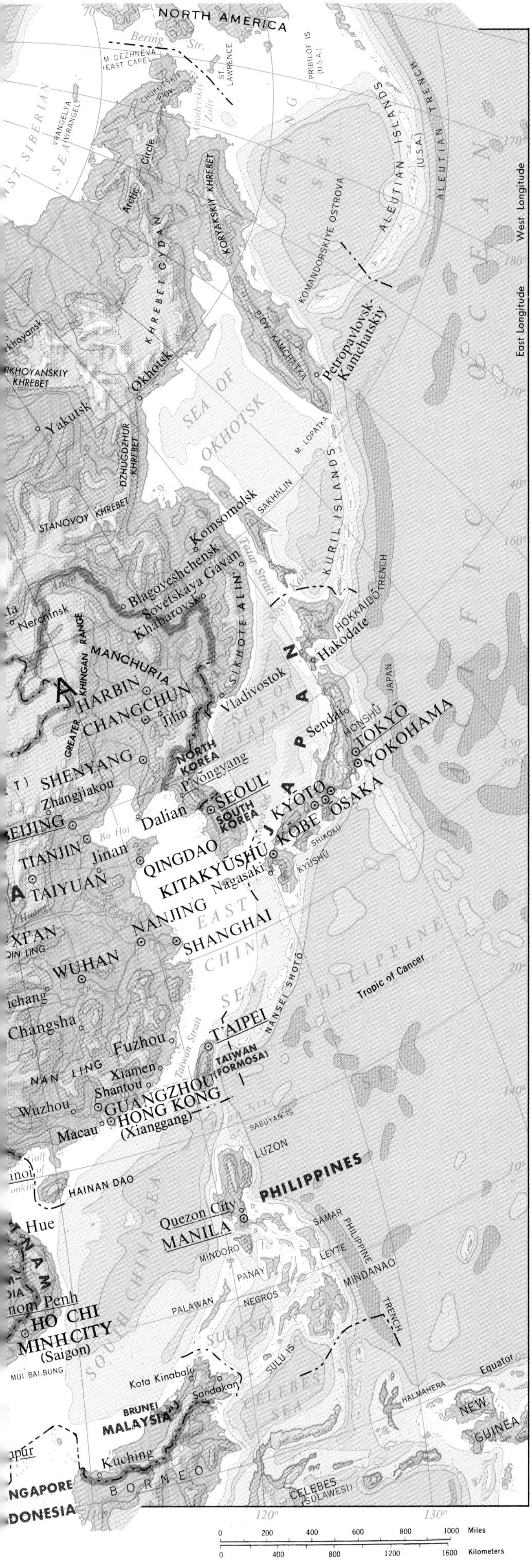
NORTH AMERICA
Bering Str.
M. DEZHNEVA (EAST CAPE)
ST. LAWRENCE
PRIBILOF IS. (U.S.A.)
BERING SEA
ALEUTIAN ISLANDS (U.S.A.)
ALEUTIAN TRENCH
KOMANDORSKIYE OSTROVA
East Longitude
West Longitude
KHREBET GYDAN
KORYAKSKIY KHREBET
Arctic Circle
Okhotsk
VERKHOYANSKIY KHREBET
Yakutsk
Petropavlovsk-Kamchatskiy
P-OV KAMCHATKA
SEA OF OKHOTSK
M. LOPATKA
DZHUGDZHUR KHREBET
STANOVOY KHREBET
SAKHALIN
KURIL ISLANDS
KURIL TRENCH
Komsomolsk
Tatar Strait
Nerchinsk
Blagoveshchensk
Sovetskaya Gavan
Khabarovsk
SIKHOTE ALIN
MANCHURIA
GREATER KHINGAN RANGE
HARBIN
CHANGCHUN
Jilin
Vladivostok
SEA OF JAPAN
HOKKAIDO
Hakodate
JAPAN
JAPAN TRENCH
Sendai
HONSHU
TOKYO
YOKOHAMA
NORTH KOREA
P'yongyang
SHENYANG
Zhangjiakou
BEIJING
TIANJIN
Bo Hai
Dalian
SEOUL
SOUTH KOREA
KYOTO
KOBE
OSAKA
SHIKOKU
KYUSHU
QINGDAO
KITAKYUSHU
Nagasaki
Jinan
TAIYUAN
NANJING
SHANGHAI
EAST CHINA SEA
XI'AN
WUHAN
Yichang
Changsha
NANSEI SHOTO
Tropic of Cancer
PHILIPPINE SEA
Fuzhou
Xiamen
Shantou
T'AIPEI
TAIWAN (FORMOSA)
Taiwan Strait
NAN LING
GUANGZHOU
HONG KONG (Xianggang)
Wuzhou
Macau
BABUYAN IS.
LUZON
PHILIPPINES
HAINAN DAO
Hue
Quezon City
MANILA
SAMAR
MINDORO
PANAY
LEYTE
NEGROS
PALAWAN
MINDANAO
PHILIPPINE TRENCH
SOUTH CHINA SEA
Phnom Penh
HO CHI MINH CITY (Saigon)
SULU SEA
SULU IS.
MUI BAI-BUNG
Kota Kinabalu
Sandakan
CELEBES SEA
HALMAHERA
Equator
BRUNEI
MALAYSIA
NEW GUINEA
Kuching
BORNEO
CELEBES (SULAWESI)
SINGAPORE
INDONESIA
PACIFIC OCEAN
120°
130°
0 200 400 600 800 1000 Miles
0 400 800 1200 1600 Kilometers

a

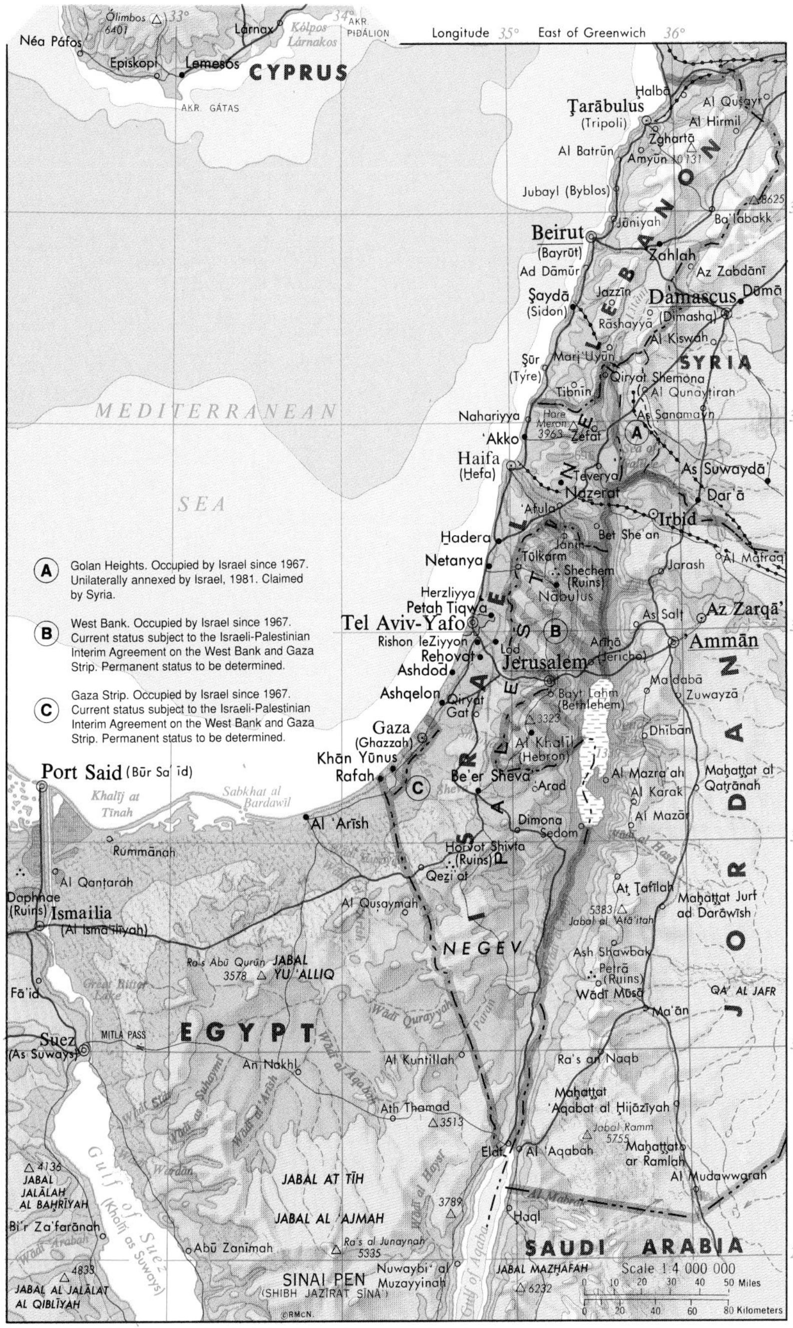
Néa Páfos
Ólimbos 6401
Lárnax
Kólpos Lárnakos
AKR. PIDÁLION
Episkopí
Lemesós
CYPRUS
AKR. GÁTAS
Longitude 35° East of Greenwich 36°
Ḩalbā
Ţarābulus (Tripoli)
Al Quşayr
Al Hirmil
Zgharta
Al Batrūn
Amyūn
Jubayl (Byblos)
Jūniyah
Ba'labakk
Beirut (Bayrūt)
Zahlah
Ad Dāmūr
Az Zabdānī
Şaydā (Sidon)
Jazzīn
Damascus (Dimashq)
Dūmā
Rāshayyā
Al Kiswah
Şūr (Tyre)
Marj 'Uyūn
Qiryat Shemona
SYRIA
LEBANON
Tibnīn
Al Qunayţirah
MEDITERRANEAN SEA
Nahariyya
Har Meron 3963
'Akko
Zefat
Haifa (Ḩefa)
Teverya
As Suwaydā'
Nazerat
Dar'ā
'Afula
Irbid
Bet She'an
Ḩadera
Jenin
Al Mafraq
Netanya
Ţūlkarm
Shechem (Ruins)
Nābulus
Jarash
Herzliyya
Petah Tiqwa
As Salt
Az Zarqā'
Tel Aviv-Yafo
Rishon leZiyyon
Lod
Rehovot
'Ammān
Ariḩā (Jericho)
Jerusalem
Ashdod
Ashqelon
Mādabā
Zuwayzā
Qiryat Gat
Bayt Laḩm (Bethlehem)
Gaza (Ghazzah)
Dhībān
Al Khalīl (Hebron)
Khān Yūnus
Rafah
Port Said (Būr Sa'īd)
Be'er Sheva'
Al Mazra'ah
Maḩaţţat al Qaţrānah
Arad
Al Karak
Khalīj at Tīnah
Sabkhat al Bardawīl
Dimona
Al Mazār
Al 'Arīsh
Sedom
Rummānah
Horvot Shivta (Ruins)
Qezi'ot
Aţ Ţafīlah
Al Qanţarah
Daphnae (Ruins)
Al Quşaymah
Maḩaţţat Jurf ad Darāwīsh
Ismailia (Al Ismā'īlīyah)
5383 Jabal al 'Aţā'iţah
ISRAEL
JORDAN
NEGEV
Ash Shawbak
Ra's Abū Qurūn 3578
JABAL YU'ALLIQ
Petra (Ruins)
Wādī Mūsā
Fā'id
Great Bitter Lake
QA' AL JAFR
Ma'ān
Suez (As Suways)
MITLA PASS
EGYPT
An Nakhl
Al Kuntillah
Ra's an Naqb
Ath Thamad 3513
Maḩaţţat 'Aqabat al Ḩijāzīyah
Jabal Ramm 5755
Elat
Al 'Aqabah
Maḩaţţat ar Ramlah
4136 JABAL JALĀLAH AL BAḨRĪYAH
JABAL AT TĪH
Al Mudawwarah
Gulf of Suez (Khalīj as Suways)
JABAL AL 'AJMAH
3789
Ḩaql
Bi'r Za'farānah
SAUDI ARABIA
Abū Zanīmah
Ra's al Junaynah 5335
4833 JABAL AL JALĀLAT AL QIBLĪYAH
SINAI PEN. (SHIBH JAZĪRAT SĪNĀ')
Nuwaybi' al Muzayyinah
JABAL MAZḨAFAH 6232
Gulf of Aqaba
Scale 1:4 000 000
0 10 20 30 40 50 Miles
0 20 40 60 80 Kilometers
©RMCN.
34° 33° 32° 31° 30° 29°
Ⓐ Golan Heights. Occupied by Israel since 1967. Unilaterally annexed by Israel, 1981. Claimed by Syria.
Ⓑ West Bank. Occupied by Israel since 1967. Current status subject to the Israeli-Palestinian Interim Agreement on the West Bank and Gaza Strip. Permanent status to be determined.
Ⓒ Gaza Strip. Occupied by Israel since 1967. Current status subject to the Israeli-Palestinian Interim Agreement on the West Bank and Gaza Strip. Permanent status to be determined.

b

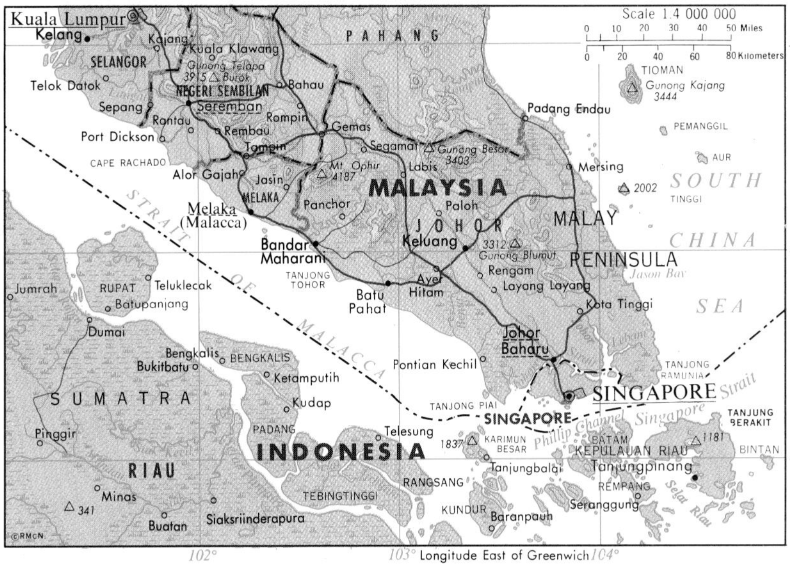
Kuala Lumpur
Kelang
Kajang
Kuala Klawang
PAHANG
SELANGOR
Gunong Telapa 3915
Buroh
NEGERI SEMBILAN
Seremban
Bahau
Telok Datok
Sepang
Rantau
Rembau
Rompin
Gemas
Port Dickson
Tampin
Segamat
Gunong Besar 3403
CAPE RACHADO
Alor Gajah
Jasin
Mt. Ophir 4187
Labis
Mersing
MELAKA
Melaka (Malacca)
Panchor
MALAYSIA
Paloh
JOHOR
Bandar Maharani
Keluang
Gunong Blumut 3312
MALAY PENINSULA
TANJONG TOHOR
Rengam
Jumrah
RUPAT
Teluklecak
Batu Pahat
Ayer Hitam
Layang Layang
Batupanjang
Kota Tinggi
Dumai
Johor Baharu
STRAIT OF MALACCA
Bengkalis
BENGKALIS
Bukitbatu
Ketamputih
Pontian Kechil
TANJONG RAMUNIA
SUMATRA
Kudap
TANJONG PIAI
SINGAPORE
Singapore Strait
TANJUNG BERAKIT
Pinggir
PADANG
Telesung
1837
KARIMUN BESAR
Phillip Channel
BATAM
KEPULAUAN RIAU
1181
BINTAN
INDONESIA
Tanjungbalai
Tanjungpinang
RIAU
RANGSANG
REMPANG
Minas
TEBINGTINGGI
KUNDUR
Serangoon
341
Buatan
Siaksriinderapura
Baranpauh
Scale 1:4 000 000
0 10 20 30 40 50 Miles
0 20 40 60 80 Kilometers
TIOMAN
Gunong Kajang 3444
PEMANGGIL
AUR
2002
TINGGI
SOUTH CHINA SEA
Jason Bay
3° 2° 1°
102°
103° Longitude East of Greenwich 104°
©RMCN.

BLACK SEA

RUSSIA

CAUCASUS

GEORGIA

AZERBAIJAN

ARMENIA

KAZA...

UZBEKISTAN

TURKESTAN

KARA-KUM (DESERT)

TURKMENISTAN

CASPIAN SEA

İSTANBUL
Bursa
İzmir
Ankara

T U R K E Y

K U R D I S T A N

Aleppo
SYRIA
Damascus
LEBANON
Beirut
ISRAEL
Tel Aviv-Yafo
Jerusalem
Gaza

MEDITERRANEAN SEA

NORTH CYPRUS
CYPRUS

Areas occupied by Israel since 1967

ALEXANDRIA (Al Iskandariyah)
CAIRO (Al Qāhirah)
Suez (As Suways)

EGYPT

JORDAN
Amman

IRAQ
BAGHDAD
Karbalā'
An Najaf
An Nāşirīyah
Al Başrah

SYRIAN DESERT

AN NAFŪD

JABAL SHAMMAR

S A U D I

N A J D

A R A B I A

A L H I J Ā Z

RED SEA

Mecca (Makkah)
Jiddah
At Ţā'if

Medina (Al Madīnah)
Yanbu'

Riyadh (Ar Riyāḍ)

KUWAIT
Kuwait (Al Kuwayt)

PERSIAN GULF

BAHRAIN
Al Manāmah
QATAR
Ad Dawhah
Abū Ẓaby
UNITED ARAB EMIRATES
Dubayy
Muscat
OMAN

I R A N

TEHRAN
Eşfahān
Shīrāz
Kermān
Ābādān
Ahvāz

DASHT-E KAVĪR DESERT

PLATEAU OF IRAN

ELBURZ MTS
Mashhad

AFGHA...

GULF OF OMAN

AR RUB' AL KHĀLĪ

JABAL AL AKHDAR

Tropic of Cancer

NAJRAN
Şa'dah
San'ā'
YEMEN
Aden ('Adan)
Al Hudaydah

HADRAMAWT
Al Mukallā

GULF OF ADEN

SUQUTRA (SOCOTRA) (Yemen)

DJIBOUTI
SOMALIA
ERITREA
ETHIOPIA
SUDAN

Continued on pages 230-231

Relief

Meters		Feet
3050		10 000
1525		5000
610		2000
305		1000
152.5		500
0	Sea Level	0
	Below Sea Level	
152.5		500
1525		5000
3050		10 000

A-569400-76 24-21-43
COPYRIGHT BY
RAND McNALLY & COMPANY
MADE IN U.S.A.

Scale 1:16 000 000; one inch to 250 miles. Polyconic Projection
Elevations and depressions are given in feet

Longitude East of Greenwich

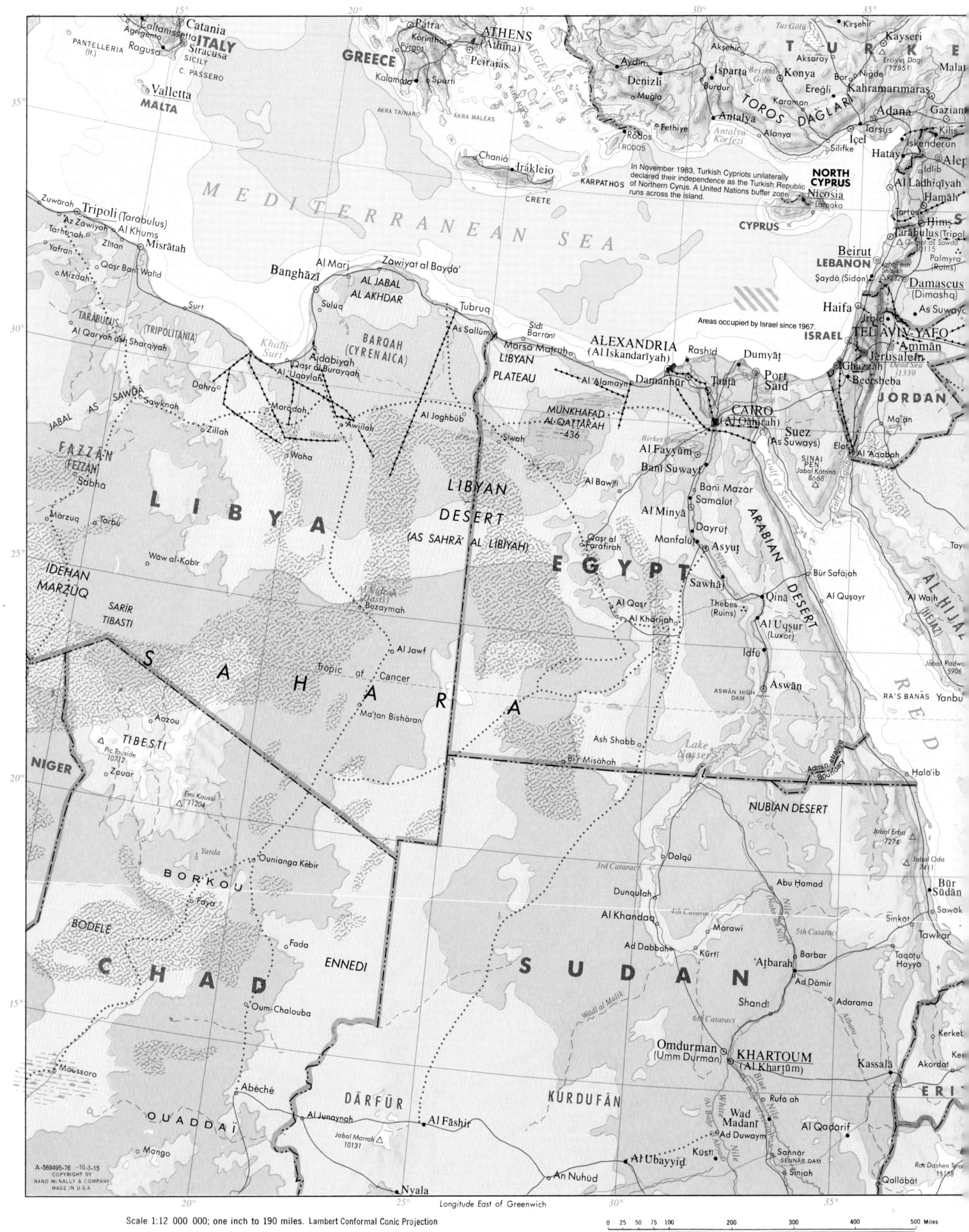

Scale 1:12 000 000; one inch to 190 miles. Lambert Conformal Conic Projection

Elevations and depressions are given in feet

0 25 50 75 100   200   300   400   500 Miles

0   100   200   400   600   800 Kilometers

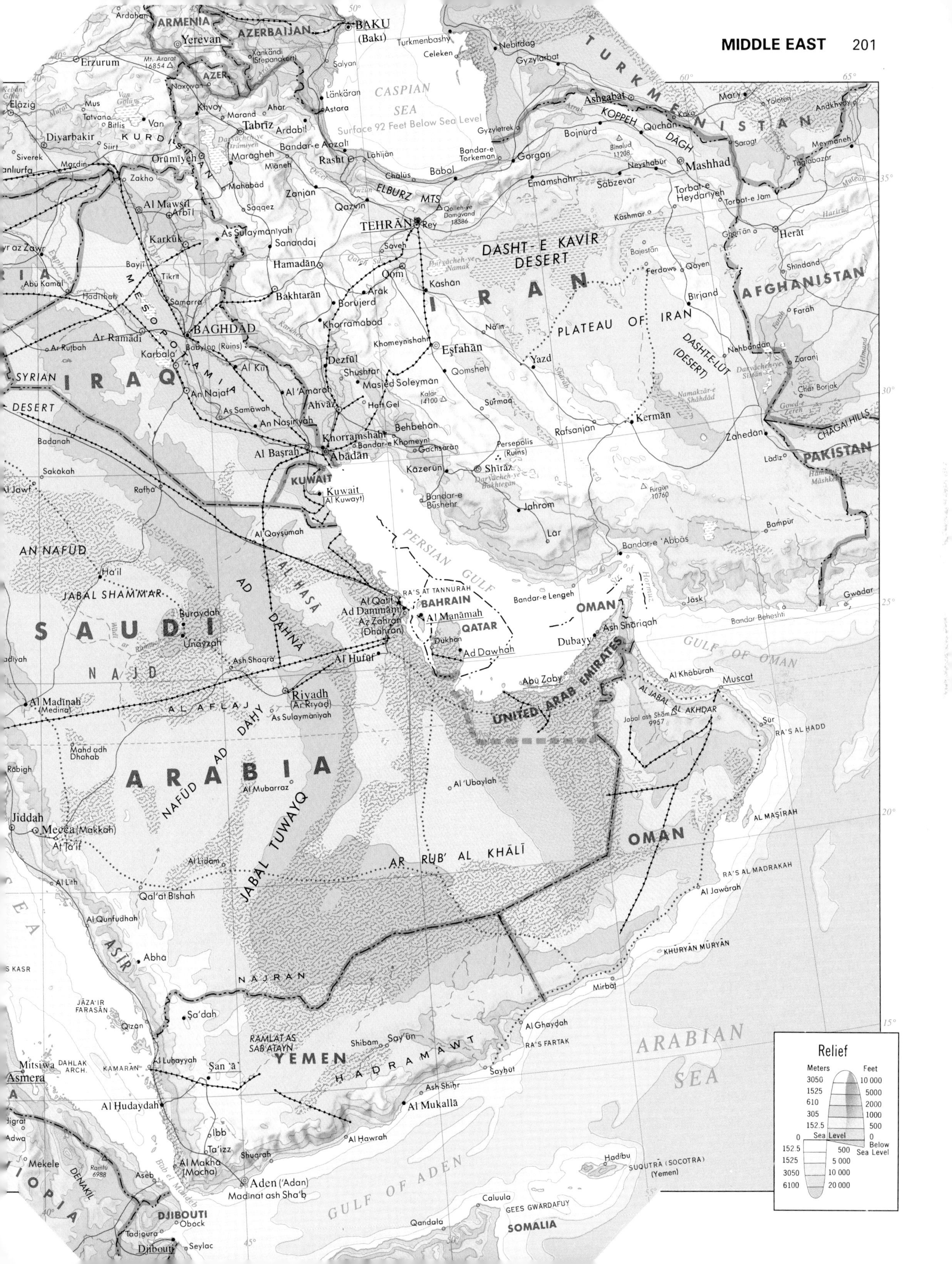

ARMENIA
Ardahan
AZERBAIJAN
Yerevan
•BAKU
(Bakı)
Erzurum
Turkmenbashy
Nebitdag
TURKMENISTAN
Celeken
Gyzylarbat
Ashgabat
Mary
Yöleten
Andkhvoy
Mt. Ararat
16854 △
AZER.
Naxçıvan
Xankändi
(Stepanakert)
Salyan
KOPPEH
DAGH
Quchan
Kaka
Meymaneh
Elazig
Mus
Tatvana
Van Gölü
Khvoy
Marand
Ahar
Astara
Länkäran
Gyzyletrek
Bojnurd
Saragt
Tagtabazar
Bitlis
Van
Siirt
Oromiyeh
Marägheh
Rasht
Lähijän
Bandar-e
Torkeman
Gorgan
Binalud
11208
Neyshäbür
Mashhad
Sabzevar
Diyarbakir
Mianeh
Bandar-e Anzali
Chälüs
Babol
Emämshahr
Torbat-e
Heydariyeh
Torbat-e Jam
Tabriz
Ardabil
CASPIAN SEA
Surface 92 Feet Below Sea Level
ELBURZ MTS
Kashmar
Ghariän
Herät
anlıurfa
Mardin
Zakho
KURDISTAN
Orūmīyeh
Maragheh
Zanjan
Qazvin
Qolleh-ye
Damgvand
18386
TEHRĀN
Rey
PLATEAU OF IRAN
Ferdows
Qäyen
Shindand
Al Mawsil
Arbil
Karkūk
Saqqez
As Sulaymaniyah
Sanandaj
Saveh
Qom
DASHT-E KAVIR DESERT
Bajestän
Birjand
AFGHANISTAN
Bayji
Tikrit
Samarra
Hamadān
Arāk
Kashan
Na'in
Yazd
DASHT-E-LŪT
(DESERT)
Farāh
r az Zawr
Abu Kamal
Hadithah
Babylon (Ruins)
Bakhtarän
Borujerd
Khorramabad
Eşfahān
Qomsheh
DASHT-E-LŪT
(DESERT)
Nehbandān
Zaranj
BAGHDAD
Al Küt
Dezful
Shushtar
Masjed Soleymän
Kalar
14100 △
Haft Gel
Surmaq
Rafsanjän
Kerman
Zähedän
Ladiz
Chäh Borjak
Gowd-e
Zereh
CHAGAI HILLS
Ar Ramadi
Karbala
An Najaf
Al 'Amärah
Ahväz
Behbehän
Persepolis
(Ruins)
Zähedän
PAKISTAN
Ar Rutbah
SYRIAN
DESERT
IRAQ
MESOPOTAMIA
As Samawah
An Näsirīyah
Khorramshahr
Bandar-e Khomeyni
Abädän
Gachsārān
Kazerün
Shiraz
Daryächeh-ye
Bakhtegän
Jahrom
Lär
Rafsanjän
Kermän
Bampür
Mäshkel
Badanah
Al Basrah
KUWAIT
Bandar-e
Büshehr
Bandar-e 'Abbās
Jäsk
Gwadar
Sakakah
Rafha
Kuwait
(Al Kuwayt)
PERSIAN GULF
Bandar-e Lengeh
OMAN
Hormuz
Bandar Beheshti
Al Jawf
Al Qaysūmah
AN NAFUD
Ha'il
JABAL SHAMMAR
Buraydah
Unayzah
AD DAHNA
AL HASA
RA'S AT TANNURAH
Ad Dammam
Az Zahrān
(Dhahran)
BAHRAIN
Al Manämah
QATAR
Dukhän
Ash Shāriqah
Dubayy
GULF OF OMAN
Al Khābūrah
Muscat
SAUDI
NAJD
Ash Shaqra
As Sulaymaniyah
Al Hufuf
Ad Dawhah
UNITED ARAB EMIRATES
Abū Zaby
Jabal ash Sham
9957
AL JABAL
AL AKHDAR
Sür
RA'S AL HADD
Al Madinah
(Medina)
Riyadh
(Ar Riyad)
AL AFLAJ
AD DAHY
Al 'Ubaylah
OMAN
Mahd adh
Dhahab
ARABIA
AD DAHY
NAFÜD
Al Mubarraz
JABAL TUWAYQ
Räbigh
Al Lidam
Qal'at Bishah
AR RUB' AL KHĀLĪ
RA'S AL MADRAKAH
Al Jawärah
Jiddah
Mecca (Makkah)
At Ta'if
Al Qunfudhah
Al Lith
ASIR
Abha
NAJRAN
AL MAŞIRAH
Mirbät
KHŪRYĀN MŪRYĀN
Al Ghaydah
RA'S FARTAK
ARABIAN SEA
S KASR
JĀZA'IR
FARASAN
Qizan
Sa'dah
RAMLAT AS
SAB'ATAYN
Shibam
Say'un
HADRAMAWT
Sayhüt
Ash Shihr
Mitsiwa
DAHLAK ARCH.
Asmera
A
KAMARAN
Al Luhayyah
San'a
YEMEN
Ibb
Al Mukallā
RELIEF
grat
Adwa
Al Hudaydah
Ta'izz
Shuqrah
Al Hawrah
SUQUTRĀ (SOCOTRA)
(Yemen)
Hadibu
Mekele
Ramlu
6988
Al Makha
(Mocha)
Bäb el Mandeb
Aden ('Adan)
Madinat ash Sha'b
Caluula
GEES GWARDAFUY
Adwa
ETHIOPIA
DENAKIL
DJIBOUTI
Obock
Tadjoura
Djibouti
Seylac
GULF OF ADEN
Qandala
SOMALIA

Relief

Meters	Feet
3050	10 000
1525	5000
610	2000
305	1000
152.5	500
0 Sea Level	0 Sea Level
152.5	Below Sea Level 500
1525	5 000
3050	10 000
6100	20 000

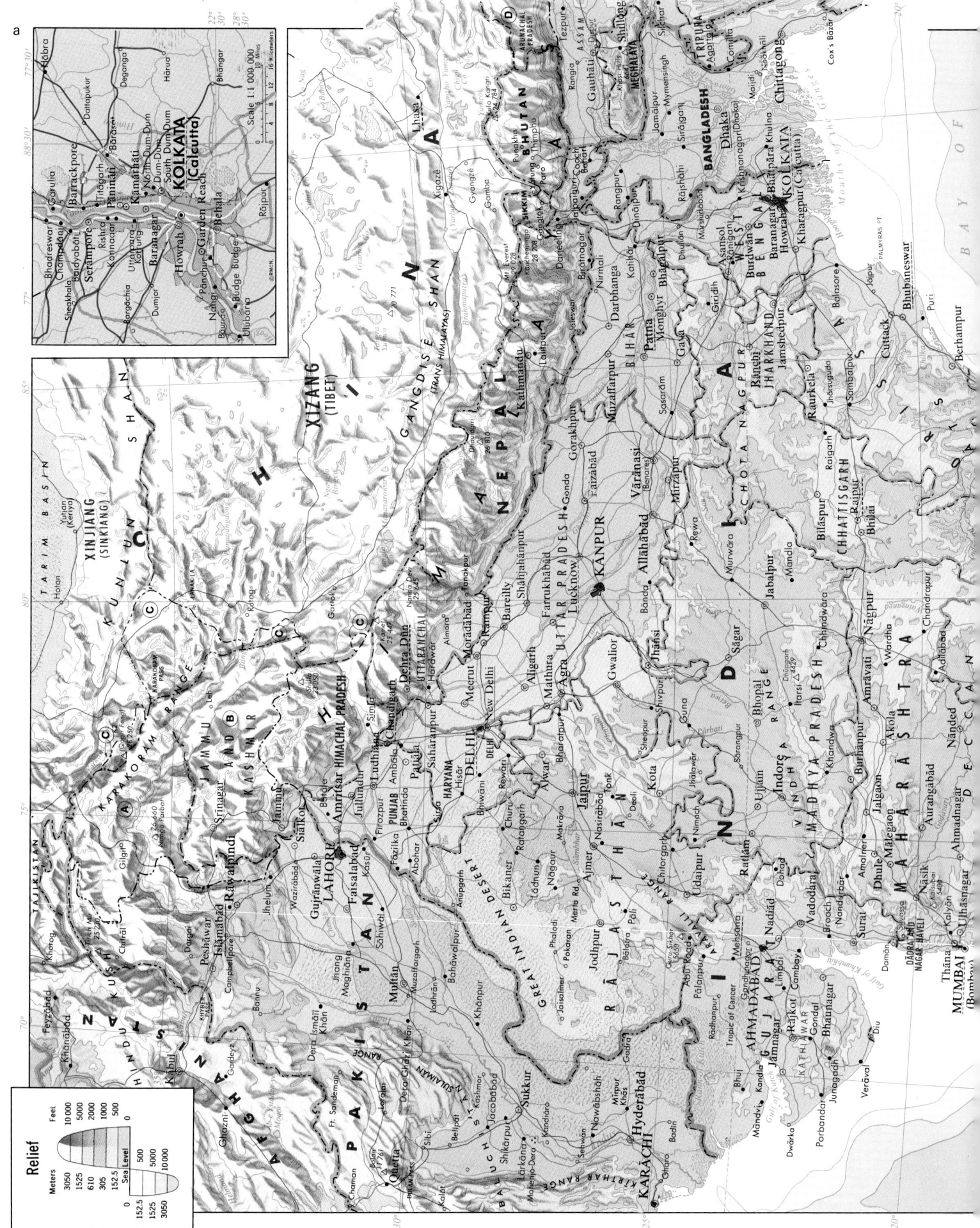

a

KOLKATA
(Calcutta)

Scale 1:1 000 000

Relief

Meters	Feet
3050	10 000
1525	5000
610	2000
305	1000
152.5	500
0	Sea Level 0

Scale 1:10 000 000; one inch to 160 miles. Lambert Conformal Conic Projection
Elevations and depressions are given in feet

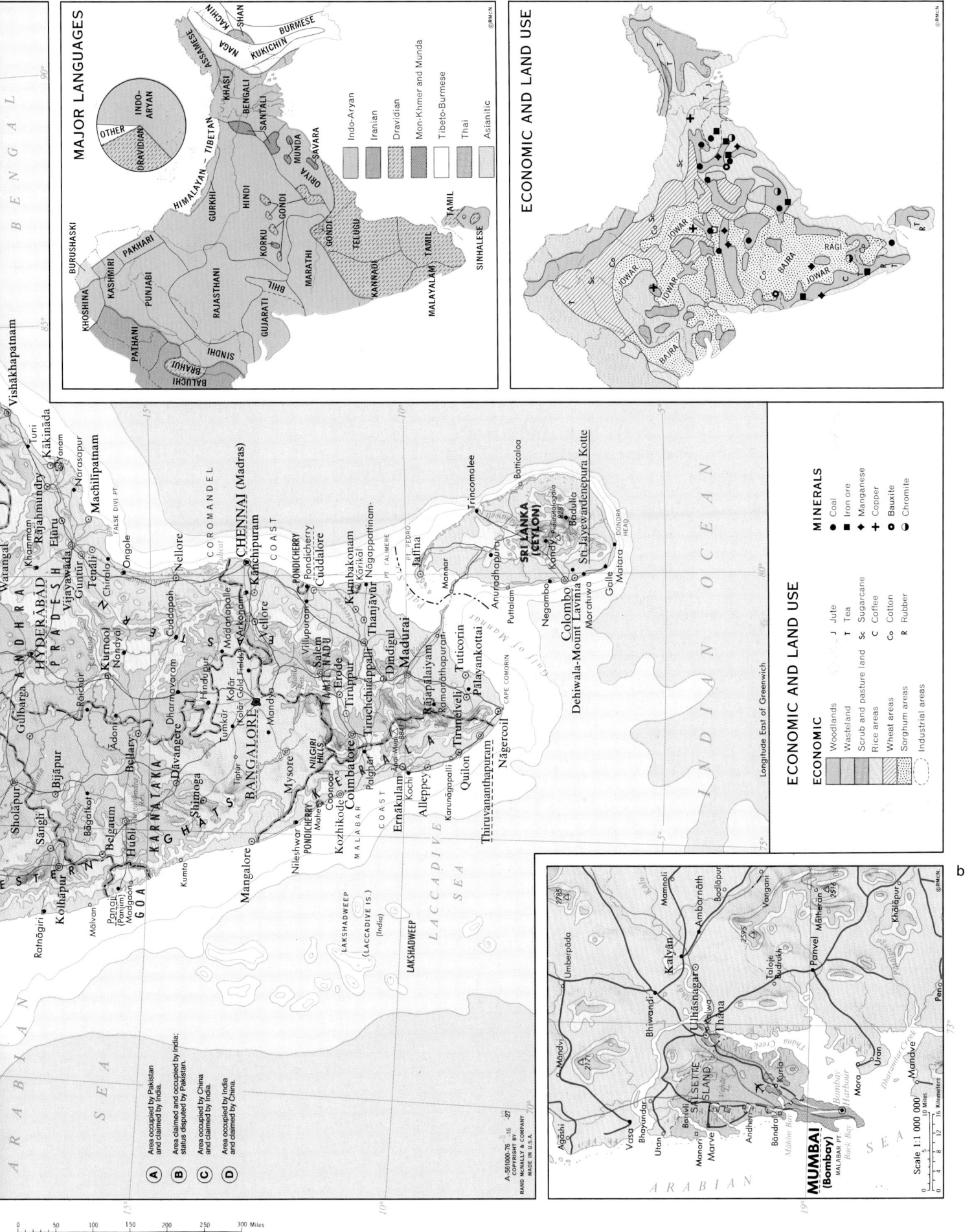

Continued on pages 184-185

Continued on pages 198-199

Scale 1:16 000 000; one inch to 250 miles. Polyconic Projection
Elevations and depressions are given in feet

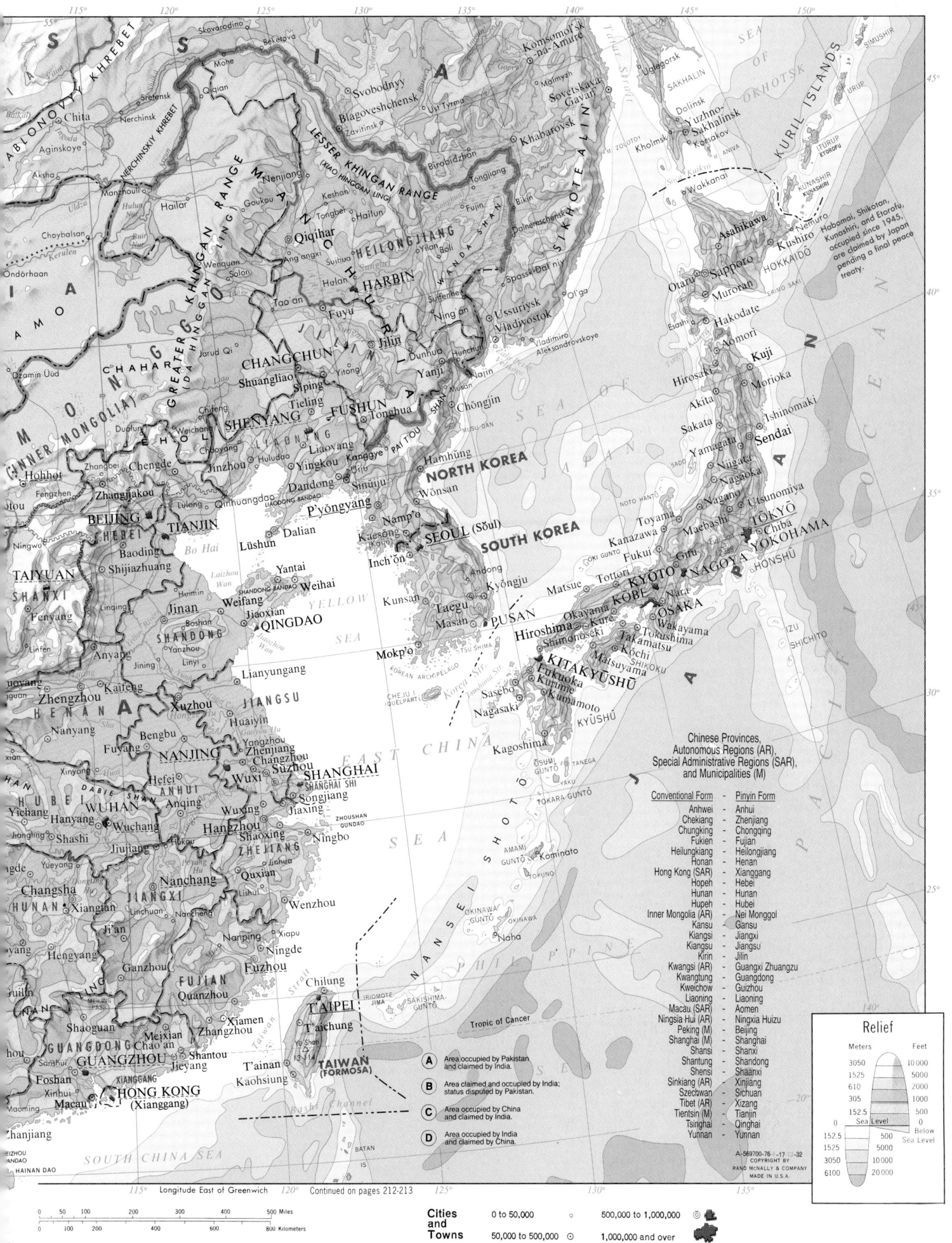

Chinese Provinces,
Autonomous Regions (AR),
Special Administrative Regions (SAR),
and Municipalities (M)

Conventional Form	-	Pinyin Form
Anhwei	-	Anhui
Chekiang	-	Zhejiang
Chungking	-	Chongqing
Fukien	-	Fujian
Heilungkiang	-	Heilongjiang
Honan	-	Henan
Hong Kong (SAR)	-	Xianggang
Hopeh	-	Hebei
Hunan	-	Hunan
Hupeh	-	Hubei
Inner Mongolia (AR)	-	Nei Monggol
Kansu	-	Gansu
Kiangsi	-	Jiangxi
Kiangsu	-	Jiangsu
Kirin	-	Jilin
Kwangsi (AR)	-	Guangxi Zhuangzu
Kwangtung	-	Guangdong
Kweichow	-	Guizhou
Liaoning	-	Liaoning
Macau (SAR)	-	Aomen
Ningsia Hui (AR)	-	Ningxia Huizu
Peking (M)	-	Beijing
Shanghai (M)	-	Shanghai
Shansi	-	Shanxi
Shantung	-	Shandong
Shensi	-	Shaanxi
Sinkiang (AR)	-	Xinjiang
Szechwan	-	Sichuan
Tibet (AR)	-	Xizang
Tientsin (M)	-	Tianjin
Tsinghai	-	Qinghai
Yunnan	-	Yunnan

A-569700-76 -17 ⌐-32
© COPYRIGHT BY
RAND MC NALLY & COMPANY
MADE IN U.S.A.

(A) Area occupied by Pakistan and claimed by India.

(B) Area claimed and occupied by India; status disputed by Pakistan.

(C) Area occupied by China and claimed by India.

(D) Area occupied by India and claimed by China.

Relief

Meters		Feet
3050		10 000
1525		5000
610		2000
305		1000
152.5		500
0	Sea Level	0
		Below
152.5		500 Sea Level
1525		5000
3050		10 000
6100		20 000

Longitude East of Greenwich   Continued on pages 212-213

0 50 100   200   300   400   500 Miles
0   100   200   400   600   800 Kilometers

Cities and Towns

0 to 50,000	○	500,000 to 1,000,000	◎
50,000 to 500,000	⊙	1,000,000 and over	■

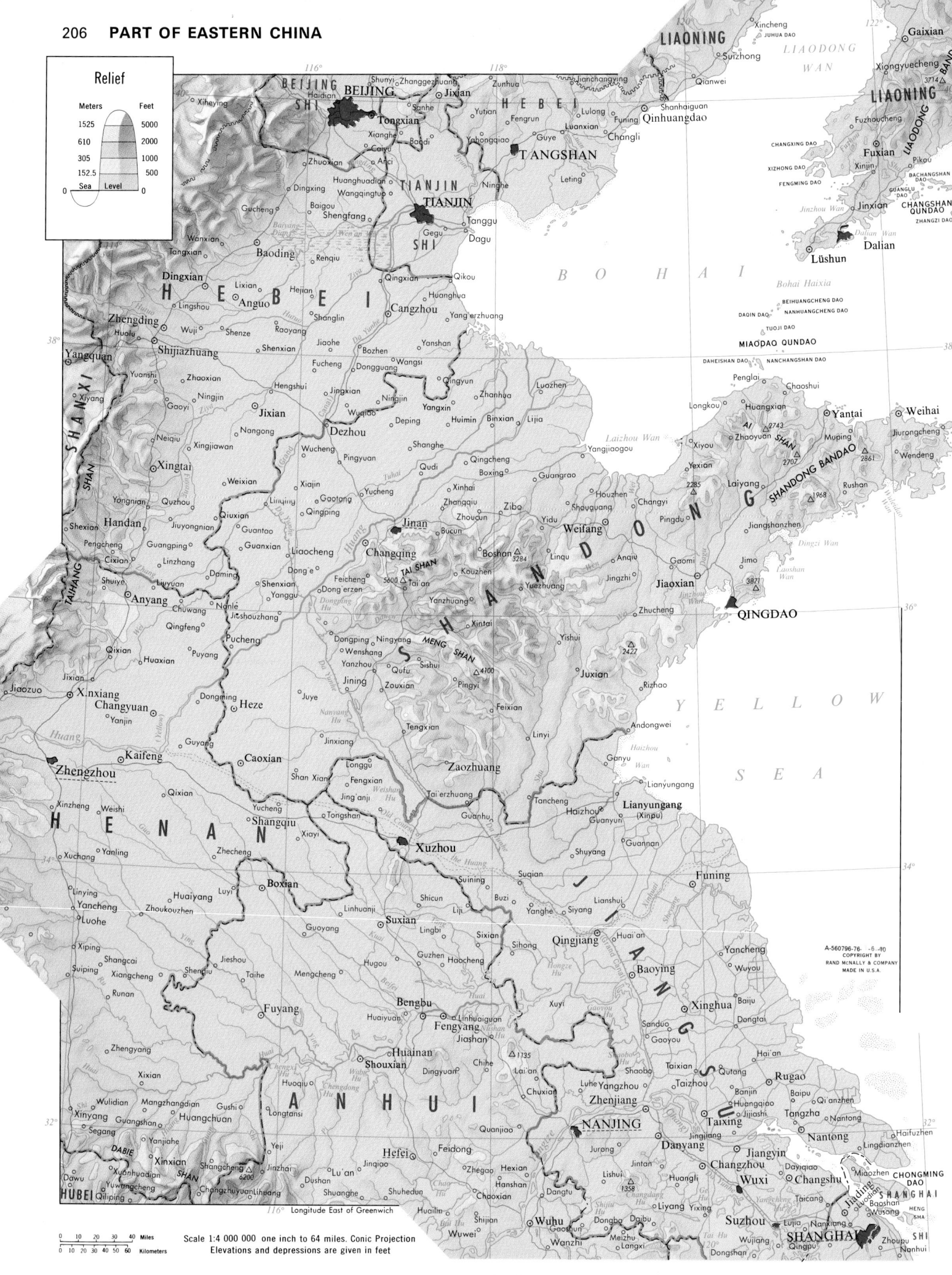

Relief

Meters	Feet
1525	5000
610	2000
305	1000
152.5	500
Sea Level	0

LIAONING

Gaixian

Xincheng
Juhua Dao
Suizhong
Xiongyuecheng
Pikou
LIAODONG WAN
Qianwei
Fuzhoucheng
LIAODONG BANDAO
Xiongyuecheng
Fuxian
Xinjin
3714

CHANGXING DAO
XIZHONG DAO
FENGMING DAO
BACHANGSHAN DAO
CHANGSHAN QUNDAO
GUANGLU DAO
ZHANGZI DAO

Lüshun
Dalian
Jinxian
Jinzhou Wan
Dalian Wan

BEIJING SHI
Xiheying
Haidian
BEIJING
Shunyi
Zhangjiazhuang
Zunhua
Jixian
Qianchangying

Tongxian
Sanhe
Yutian
Fengrun
Luanxian
Lulong
Fuling
Qinhuangdao
Shanhaiguan

Xiangge
Caiyu
Baodi
HEBEI
Guye
Changli

Zhuoxian
Anci
Ninghe
TANGSHAN
Leting
Changli

Dingxing
Wangqingtuo
TIANJIN SHI
Tanggu

Baigou
Shengfang
TIANJIN
Gegu
Dagu

Gucheng
Baiyang Dian

Wanxian
Renqiu
Qingxian
Qikou
Huanghua

Baoding

Tangxian
Lixian
Hejian
Yang'erzhuang

Dingxian
HEBEI
Shanglin
Cangzhou
Luozhen

Lingshou
Anguo
Raoyang
Yanshan

Zhengding
Wuji
Shenze
Bozhen
Zhanhua

Huolu
Shijiazhuang
Shenxian
Wangsi
Qingyun

Yangquan
Yuanshi
Hengshui
Jingxian
Ningjin
Yangxin
Huimin
Binxian
Lijia

SHANXI
Xiyang
Zhaoxian
Fucheng
Deping
Shanghe

Ningjin
Wucheng
Pingyuan
Shanghe
Qingcheng

Gaoyi
Jixian
Dezhou
Yucheng
Zhouan
Zibo
Weifang

SHAN
Neiqiu
Xingjiawan
Xiajin
Gaotang
Xinhai
Zhangqiu

Xingtai
Weixian
Linqing
Qingping
Changqing
JINAN
Bucun
Yidu
Changyi
Anqiu

Yongnian
Quzhou
Qiuxian
Guantao
Liaocheng
Dong'e
TAI SHAN
Boshan
3284

Handan
Guangping
Jiuyongnian
Daming
Shenxian
Yanggu
Feicheng
Tai'an
Kouzhen
Yuezhuang
Jingzhi
Jiaoxian

Shexian
Pengcheng
Linzhang
Nanle
Jishouzhang
Dongping Hu
Yanzhuang
Zhucheng

Cixian
Shuiye
Chuwang
Liuyuan

Anyang
Qingfeng
Pucheng
Xintai
2427

TAIHANG
Qixian
Huaxian
Puyang
Meng Shan
Yishui

Jiaozuo
Jixian
Guyang
Dongping
Ningyang
Sishui
4100
Pingyi

Xinxiang
Changyuan
Heze
Juye
Wenshang
Yanzhou
Qufu
Zouxian
Feixian
Linyi

Xinzheng
Yanjin
Caoxian
Jinxiang
Tengxian
Andongwei

Zhengzhou
Weishi
Yucheng
Longgu
Shan Xian
Tai'erzhuang
Rizhao

HENAN
Kaifeng
Guyang
Fengxian
Jing'anji
Weishan Hu
Zaozhuang
Tancheng
Haizhou
Lianyungang (Xinpu)

Xuchang
Qixian
Shangqiu
Tongshan
Guanhu
Guanyun

Linying
Yanling
Zhecheng
Xiayi
Old Canal
Xuzhou
Shuyang
Guannan

Yancheng
Huaiyang
Luyi
Suining
Shicun
Liji
Siyang

Luohe
Zhoukouzhen
Shangqiu
Buzi
Yanghe
Sihong
JIANGSU
Funing

Xiping
Shangcai
Jieshou
Taihe
Guoyang
Guzhen
Haocheng
Qingjiang
Huai'an
Yancheng

Suiping
Xiangcheng
Shengqiu
Mengcheng
Suixian
Lingbi
Sixian
Qingjiang
Huai an
Wuyou

Runan
ANHUI
Fuyang
Hugou
Bengbu
Xuyi
Baoying
Baiju

Zhengyang
Huaiyuan
Gaoyou Hu
Xinghua
Dongtai

Xixian
Shouxian
Linhuaiguan
Hongze Hu
Sanduo
Gaoyou

Dabie
Wulidian
Mangzhangdian
Gushi
Longtansi
Fengyang
Jiashan
1135
Shaobo
Taixian
Qutang
Rugao

Xinyang
Guangshan
Huangchuan
Dingyuan
Chihe
Lai'an
Luhe
Yangzhou
Taizhou
Banjin
Baipu

SHAN
Segang
Yanjiahe
Yeji
Huainan
Chuxian
Zhenjiang
Huangqiao
Qi'anzhen

Dawu
Xinxian
Shangcheng
Jinzhai
Lu'an
Hefei
Hexian
Hanshan
Dangtu
Danyang
Taixing
Nantong

HUBEI
Qiliping
Zhangzhuyuanliuhuang
Shuanghe
Chaoxian
NANJING
Jiangyin
Changzhou
Wuxi
Changshu
Jiading

Xinyang
6200
Huaiqiao
Jurong
Jintan
Shanghai
CHONGMING DAO

Longtansi
Dushan
Shuhedun
Dangshan
Lishui
Changzhou
Wuxi
Changshu
SHANGHAI SHI

Chaoxian
Jinjiao
Feidong
Yixing
Wujiang
Suzhou
Lujia
Nanxiang

ANHUI
Hefei
Zhegao
Wuhu
Gaochun
Liyang
Taicang
Baoshan

Dongba
Daiju
Tai Hu
SHANGHAI

Wanzhi
Meizhou
Langxi
Wusong

BOHAI

Bohai Haixia

BEIHUANGCHENG DAO

DAQIN DAO
NANHUANGCHENG DAO

TUOJI DAO

MIAODAO QUNDAO

DAHEISHAN DAO
NANCHANGSHAN DAO

Penglai
Chaoshui

Longkou
Huangxian
Yantai
Weihai

AI SHAN
2743
Zhaoyuan
Muping
Jiurongcheng

Yexian
Laiyang
Rushan
Wendeng

SHANDONG BANDAO
2861

2285
Jiangshanzhen
1968

SHANDONG
Changyi
Pingdu
Dingzi Wan

Shouguang
Gaomi
Jimo
Laoshan Wan

Linqu
3871
QINGDAO

YELLOW

SEA

Haizhou Wan

Ganyu

Lianyungang

A-560796-76-　-6-　10
COPYRIGHT BY
RAND McNALLY & COMPANY
MADE IN U.S.A.

Longdianzhen
Haifuzhen
HENG SHA

Zhapu
Zhoushan

Scale 1:4 000 000 one inch to 64 miles. Conic Projection
Elevations and depressions are given in feet

0　10　20　30　40 Miles
0 10 20 30 40 50 60 Kilometers

Longitude East of Greenwich

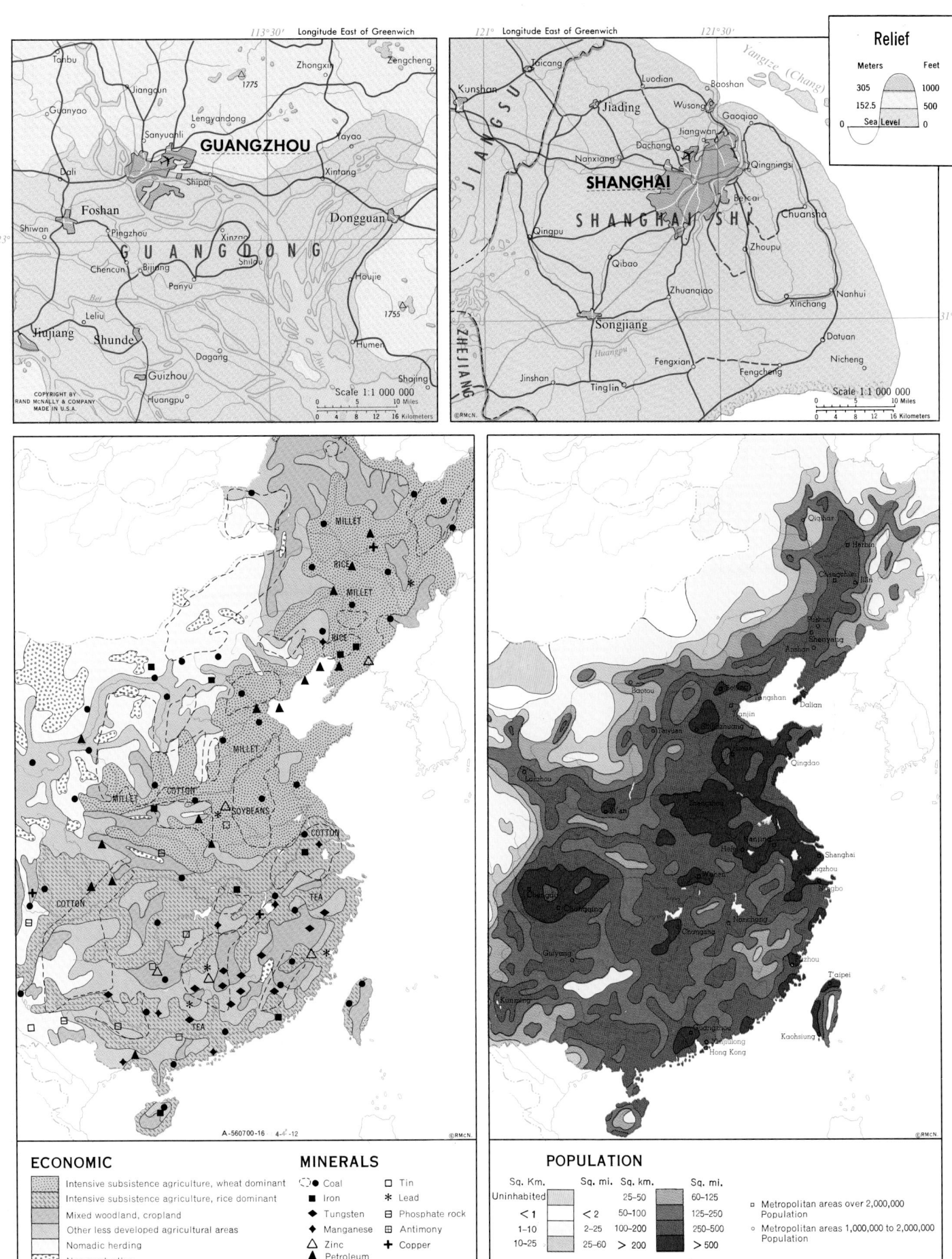

GUANGZHOU

Longitude East of Greenwich

Tanbu
Zhongxin
Zengcheng
Jiangcun
1775
Guanyao
Lengyandong
Yayao
Sanyuanli
GUANGZHOU
Xintang
Dali
Shipai
Dongguan
Foshan
Pingzhou
Xinzao
Houjie
GUANGDONG
Chencun
Bijiang
Shilou
Panyu
1755
Shiwan
Leliu
Dagang
Humen
Jiujiang
Shunde
Guizhou
Shajing
Huangpu

Scale 1:1 000 000

SHANGHAI

Longitude East of Greenwich

JIANGSU
Taicang
Luodian
Yangtze (Chang)
Kunshan
Baoshan
Jiading
Wusong
Gaoqiao
Nanxiang
Jiangwan
Dachang
Qingpu
SHANGHAI
Qingningsi
Qibao
SHANGHAI SHI
Beicai
Chuansha
Songjiang
Zhoupu
Zhuangqiao
Xinchang
Nanhui
Jinshan
Fengxian
Fengcheng
Datuan
Tingjian
Nicheng

ZHEJIANG

Scale 1:1 000 000

Relief

Meters	Feet
305	1000
152.5	500
0	Sea Level	0

ECONOMIC

- Intensive subsistence agriculture, wheat dominant
- Intensive subsistence agriculture, rice dominant
- Mixed woodland, cropland
- Other less developed agricultural areas
- Nomadic herding
- Non-productive

MINERALS

- ● Coal
- ■ Iron
- ◆ Tungsten
- ◆ Manganese
- △ Zinc
- ▲ Petroleum
- □ Tin
- ✳ Lead
- ⊟ Phosphate rock
- ⊞ Antimony
- ✛ Copper

POPULATION

Sq. Km.	Sq. mi.	Sq. km.	Sq. mi.
Uninhabited		25–50	60–125
<1	<2	50–100	125–250
1–10	2–25	100–200	250–500
10–25	25–60	>200	>500

- ▫ Metropolitan areas over 2,000,000 Population
- ∘ Metropolitan areas 1,000,000 to 2,000,000 Population

Continued on page 210

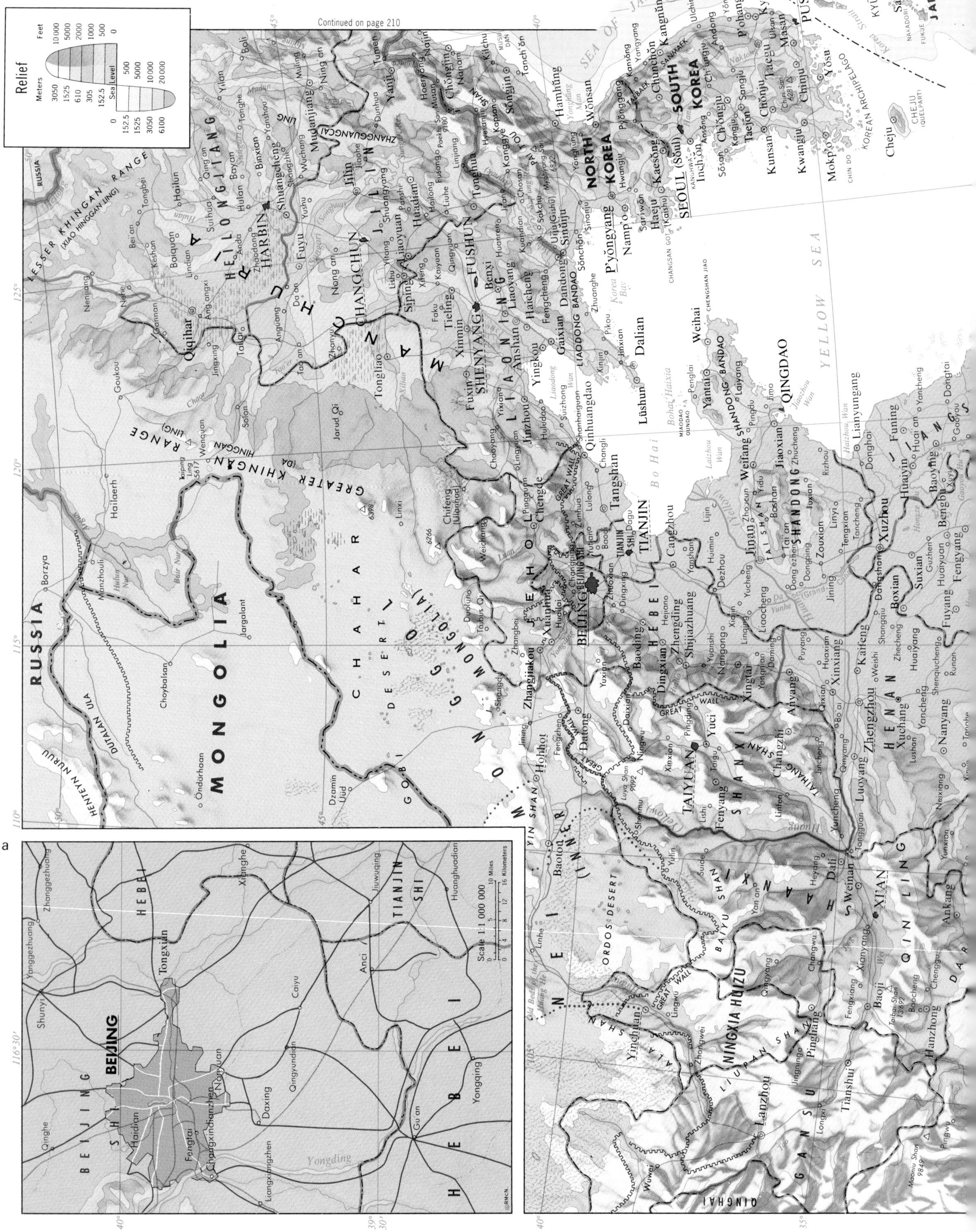

Relief

Feet
10000
5000
2000
1000
500
0

Meters
3050
1525
610
305
152.5
Sea Level
0
152.5
1525
3050
6100

| 500 |
| 5000 |
| 10000 |
| 20000 |

SEA OF JAPAN

JAPAN
KYUSHU
Sasebo
Fukue
FUKIE
SHIKOKU
Pusan
KOREA STRAIT

Korea Strait
Tsushima
NAADOR (IKI)

RUSSIA
MONGOLIA
CHINA

LESSER KHINGAN RANGE (XIAO HINGGAN LING)
GREATER KHINGAN RANGE (DA HINGGAN LING)
HENTEYN NURUU
DUTAAN ULA

HEILONGJIANG
JILIN
LIAONING
NEI MONGGOL (INNER MONGOLIA)
CHAHAR
GOBI DESERT
ORDOS DESERT
HEBEI
SHANXI
SHAANXI
SHANDONG
HENAN
NINGXIA HUIZU
GANSU
QINGHAI

NORTH KOREA
SOUTH KOREA
SEOUL (Sŏul)
Pyŏngyang
Hamhŭng
Wŏnsan
Nampʻo
Kaesŏng
Inchʻŏn
Taejŏn
Taegu
Pusan
Masan
Kwangju
Mokpo
Cheju (QUELPART)
CHEJU (QUELPART)
CHEJU
CHIN DO
KOREAN ARCHIPELAGO

Harbin
Qiqihar
Changchun
Shenyang
Fushun
Benxi
Anshan
Dalian
Lüshun
Yantai
Weihai
QINGDAO
Jinan
TIANJIN
BEIJING
Shijiazhuang
TAIYUAN
Baotou
Hohhot
Datong
Yinchuan
Lanzhou
Tianshui
XI'AN

YELLOW SEA
Bo Hai
Liaodong Wan
Bohai Haixia
Laizhou Wan
Korea Bay

LIAODONG BANDAO
SHANDONG BANDAO
MIAODAO QUNDAO
CHENGSHAN JIAO

TAIHANG SHAN
YIN SHAN
LIUPAN SHAN
QIN LING
DABA SHAN
BAYU SHAN
TAISHAN
Tai Shan

GREAT WALL

Yellow R. (Huang He)
Yongding

Scale 1:10 000 000; one inch to 160 miles. Lambert Conformal Conic Projection
Elevations and depressions are given in feet

a

BEIJING SHI
TIANJIN SHI
HEBEI

BEIJING
Haidian
Fengtai
Tongxian
Shunyi
Daxing
Gu'an
Yongqing
Anci

Scale 1:1 000 000
0 5 10 Miles
0 4 8 12 16 Kilometers

Cities and Towns

| 0 to 50,000 | ○ | 500,000 to 1,000,000 | ◎ |
| 50,000 to 500,000 | ⊙ | 1,000,000 and over | |

RMcN

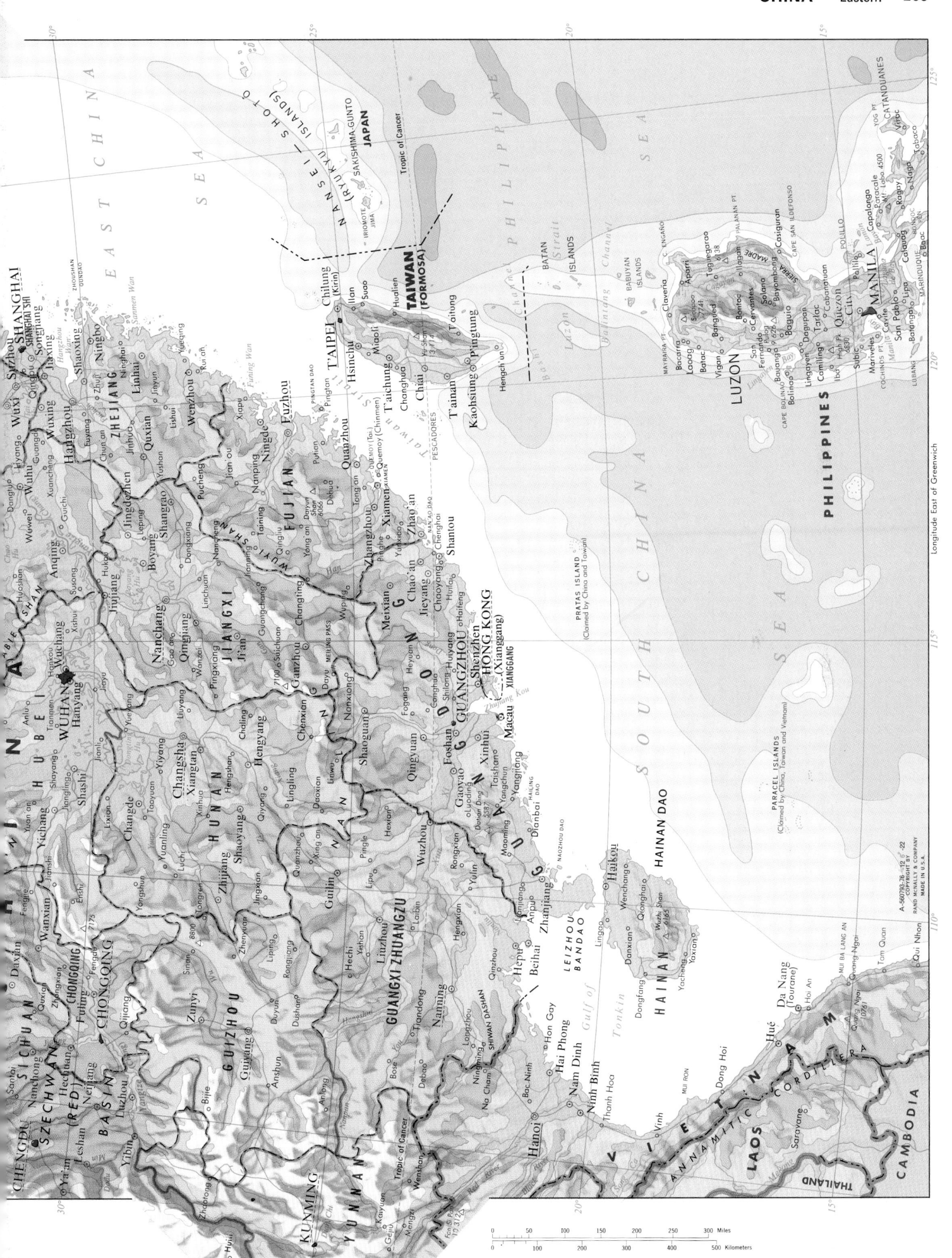

Continued on pages 208-209

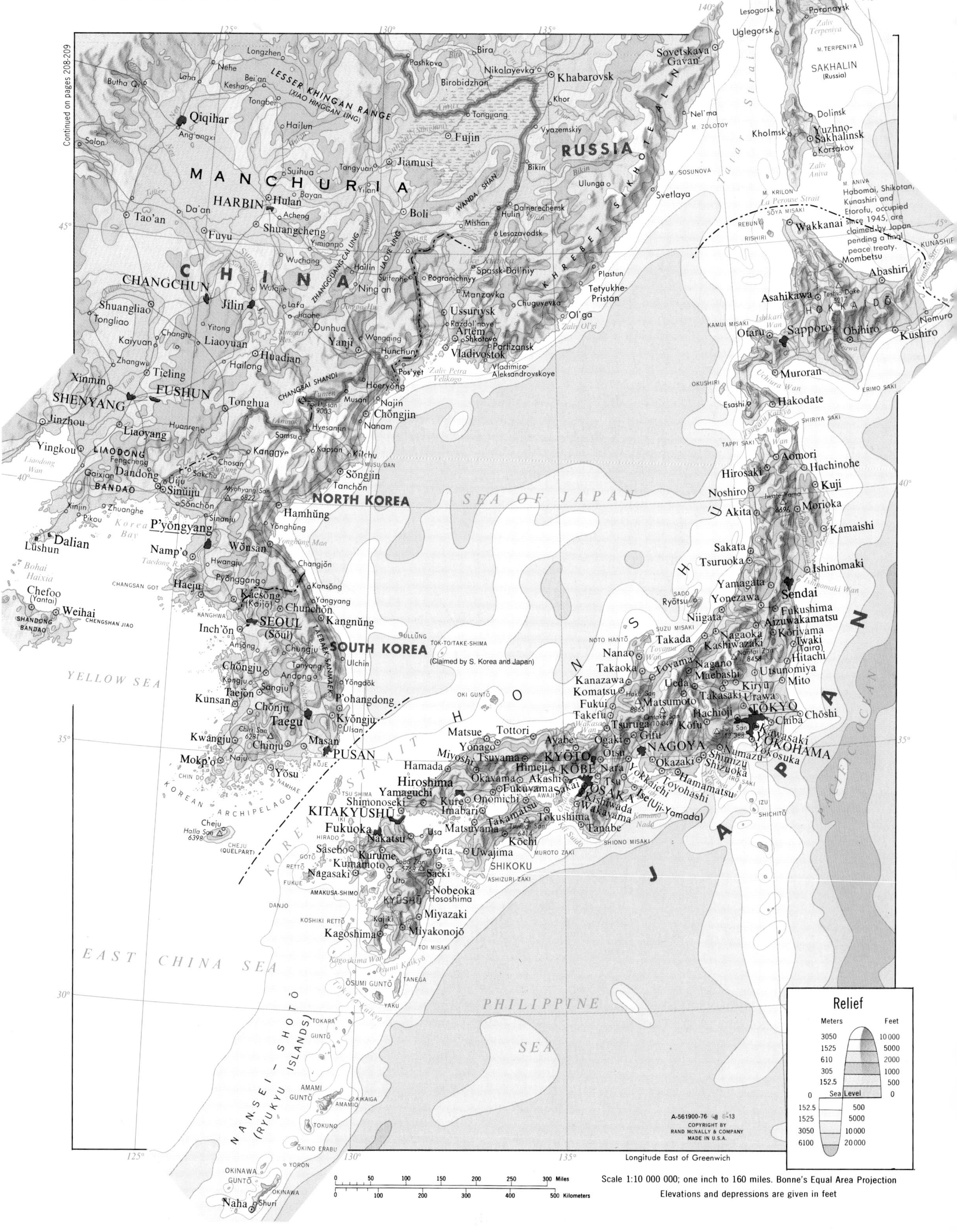

RUSSIA

SAKHALIN (Russia)

MANCHURIA
HARBIN
CHINA
CHANGCHUN
SHENYANG
FUSHUN
LIAODONG BANDAO

LESSER KHINGAN RANGE (XIAO HINGGAN LING)

WANDA SHAN

KHREBET SIKHOTE ALIN

Qiqihar
Ang'angxi
Nehe
Butha Qi
Laha
Bei'an
Keshan
Hailun
Tongken
Suihua
Bayan
Acheng
Hulan
Shuangcheng
Da'an
Tao'an
Fuyu
Jiamusi
Fujin
Tangyuan
Yilan
Boli
Mishan
Hulin
Lesozavodsk
Dalnerechensk
Spassk-Dal'niy
Manzovka
Chuguyevka
Plastun
Tetyukhe-Pristan
Svetlaya
Ulunga
Bikin
Khor
Vyazemskiy
Tongjiang
Khabarovsk
Nikolayevka
Pashkovo
Bira
Birobidzhan
Longzhen

Harbin
Shuangliao
Tongliao
Kaiyuan
Zhangwu
Xinmin
Jinzhou
Yingkou
Gaixian
Pikou
Zhuanghe
Xinjin
Lüshun
Dalian

Changchun
Jilin
Yitong
Liaoyuan
Huadian
Hailong
Huanren
Liaoyang
Fengcheng
Dandong
Siniju
Uiju
Tonghua

Yanji
Hunchun
Pos'yet
Vladivostok
Ussuriysk
Razdol'noye
Artëm
Shkotovo
Partizansk
Nakhodka
Suifenhe
Pogranichnyy
Hailin
Ning'an
Wuchang
Lafa
Jiaohe
Dunhua
Wangqing

CHANGBAI SHANDI

NORTH KOREA
P'yŏngyang
Namp'o
Wŏnsan
Hamhŭng
Hoeryŏng
Najin
Chŏngjin
Nanam
Musan
Kilchu
Kapsan
Samsu
Kanggye
Chosan
Hyesanjin
Songjin
Yŏnghŭng
Changjŏn
Hwangju
Pyŏnggang
Kaesŏng (Kaijō)
Haeju
Sariwŏn

SOUTH KOREA
SEOUL (Sŏul)
Inch'ŏn
Suwŏn
Chunchŏn
Kangnŭng
Wŏnju
Ch'ŏngju
Ch'ŏnan
Taejŏn
Chŏnju
Kunsan
Kwangju
Mokp'o
Sunch'ŏn
Chinju
Masan
PUSAN
Taegu
Kyŏngju
Ulsan
P'ohangdong
Yŏngdŏk
Andong
Yŏngju

Cheju (Quelpart)
Halla San 6398

KOREA BAY
Korea Bay
Taedong R.
YELLOW SEA
EAST CHINA SEA
SEA OF JAPAN
KOREA STRAIT
KOREAN ARCHIPELAGO

Bohai Haixia
Chefoo (Yantai)
Weihai
Shandong Bandao
Chengshan Jiao
Lüshun

HOKKAIDŌ
Wakkanai
Asahikawa
Sapporo
Otaru
Muroran
Hakodate
Obihiro
Kushiro
Nemuro
Abashiri
Mombetsu
Esashi

Habomai, Shikotan, Kunashiri and Etorofu, occupied since 1945, are claimed by Japan pending a final peace treaty.

KUNASHIRI
La Perouse Strait
Soya Misaki
Rebun
Rishiri
Tsugaru Kaikyō

HONSHU
JAPAN
TOKYO
Yokohama
Kawasaki
Yokosuka
Chiba
Chōshi
NAGOYA
KYOTO
OSAKA
KOBE
Nara
Sakai
Wakayama
Otsu
Gifu
Ōgaki
Yokkaichi
Tsu
Toyohashi
Hamamatsu
Shizuoka
Numazu
Shimizu
Fuji
Kōfu
Hachiōji
Urawa
Takasaki
Maebashi
Utsunomiya
Mito
Hitachi
Iwaki (Taira)
Kiryū
Ueda
Matsumoto
Nagano
Takada
Nagaoka
Kashiwazaki
Niigata
Sado
Ryōtsu
Nanao
Toyama
Takaoka
Kanazawa
Komatsu
Fukui
Takefu
Tsuruga

Aomori
Hachinohe
Kuji
Morioka
Kamaishi
Hirosaki
Noshiro
Akita
Sakata
Tsuruoka
Yamagata
Yonezawa
Sendai
Ishinomaki
Fukushima
Aizuwakamatsu
Kōriyama

Sendai
Kōfu

Matsue
Tottori
Yonago
Miyoshi
Tsuyama
Himeji
Akashi
Okayama
Fukuyama
Onomichi
Kure
Hiroshima
Yamaguchi
Shimonoseki
Iwakuni

SHIKOKU
Takamatsu
Tokushima
Matsuyama
Kōchi
Uwajima
Imabari

KYŪSHŪ
KITAKYŪSHŪ
Fukuoka
Nakatsu
Kurume
Kumamoto
Ōita
Saeki
Nobeoka
Hososhima
Miyazaki
Miyakonojō
Kagoshima
Kajiki
Sasebo
Nagasaki
Usa
Matsuyama

PACIFIC OCEAN
PHILIPPINE SEA

NANSEI-SHOTŌ (RYUKYU ISLANDS)
AMAMI
OKINAWA
Naha
Shuri
Okinawa Guntō
Yoron
Tokuno
Okino Erabu

TOK-TO/TAKE-SHIMA (Claimed by S. Korea and Japan)

OKI GUNTŌ

Relief

Meters		Feet
3050		10 000
1525		5000
610		2000
305		1000
152.5		500
0	Sea Level	0
152.5		500
1525		5000
3050		10000
6100		20000

A-561900-76
COPYRIGHT BY
RAND MCNALLY & COMPANY
MADE IN U.S.A.

Longitude East of Greenwich

Scale 1:10 000 000; one inch to 160 miles. Bonne's Equal Area Projection
Elevations and depressions are given in feet

0 50 100 150 200 250 300 Miles
0 100 200 300 400 500 Kilometers

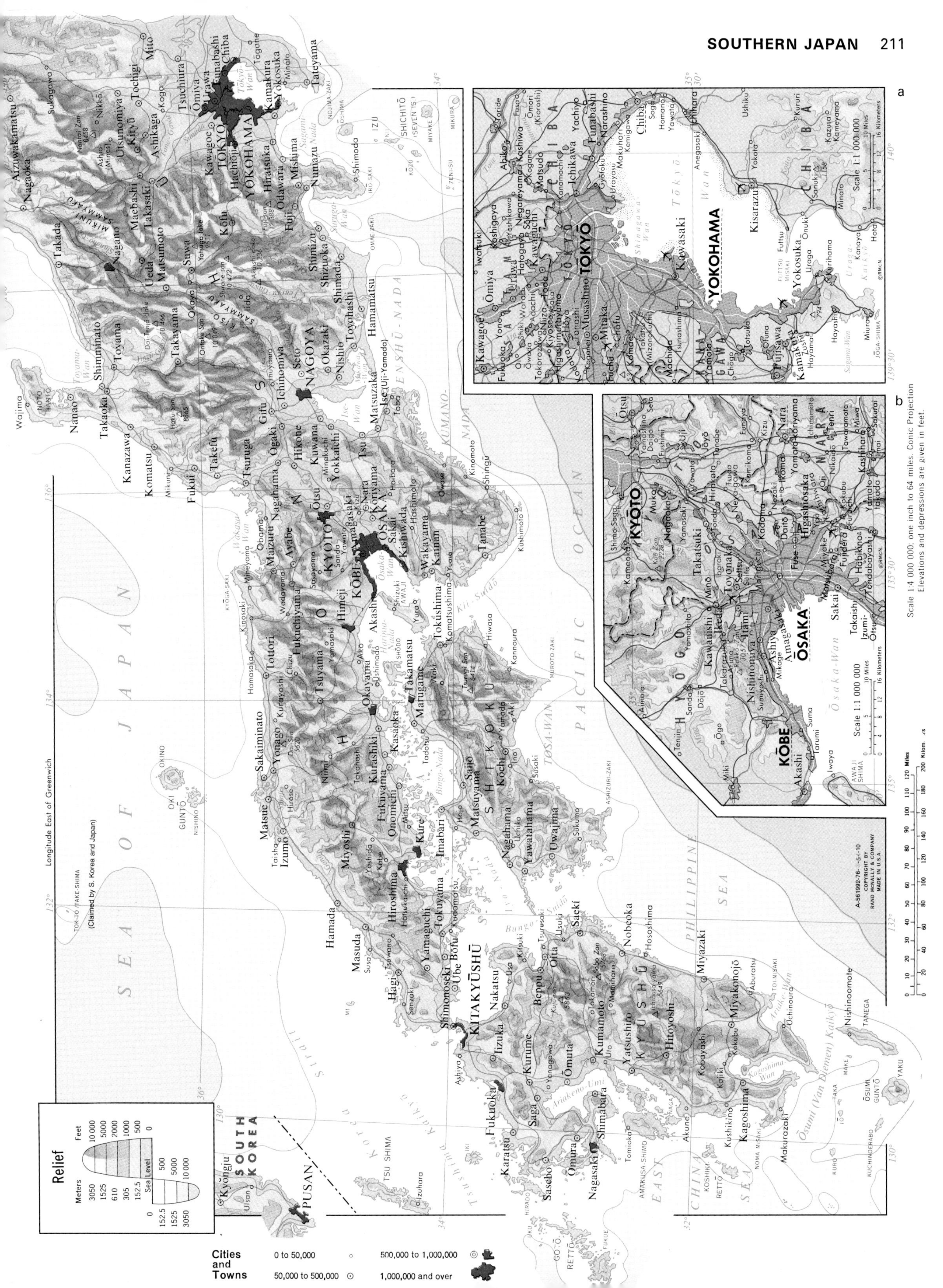

a

b

Scale 1:4 000 000; one inch to 64 miles. Conic Projection
Elevations and depressions are given in feet.

Relief

Meters	Feet
3050	10 000
1525	5000
610	2000
305	1000
152.5	500
0	Sea Level
152.5	500
1525	5000
3050	10 000

Cities and Towns

| 0 to 50,000 | 500,000 to 1,000,000 |
| 50,000 to 500,000 | 1,000,000 and over |

Scale 1:1 000 000

Scale 1:1 000 000

A-561092-76---5---10
COPYRIGHT BY
RAND McNALLY & COMPANY
MADE IN U.S.A.

Main map labels (selection):

SEA OF JAPAN
PACIFIC OCEAN
PHILIPPINE SEA
EAST CHINA SEA
SOUTH KOREA
PUSAN
TŌKYŌ
YOKOHAMA
NAGOYA
KYŌTO
ŌSAKA
KŌBE
KITAKYŪSHŪ
HONSHŪ
SHIKOKU
KYŪSHŪ

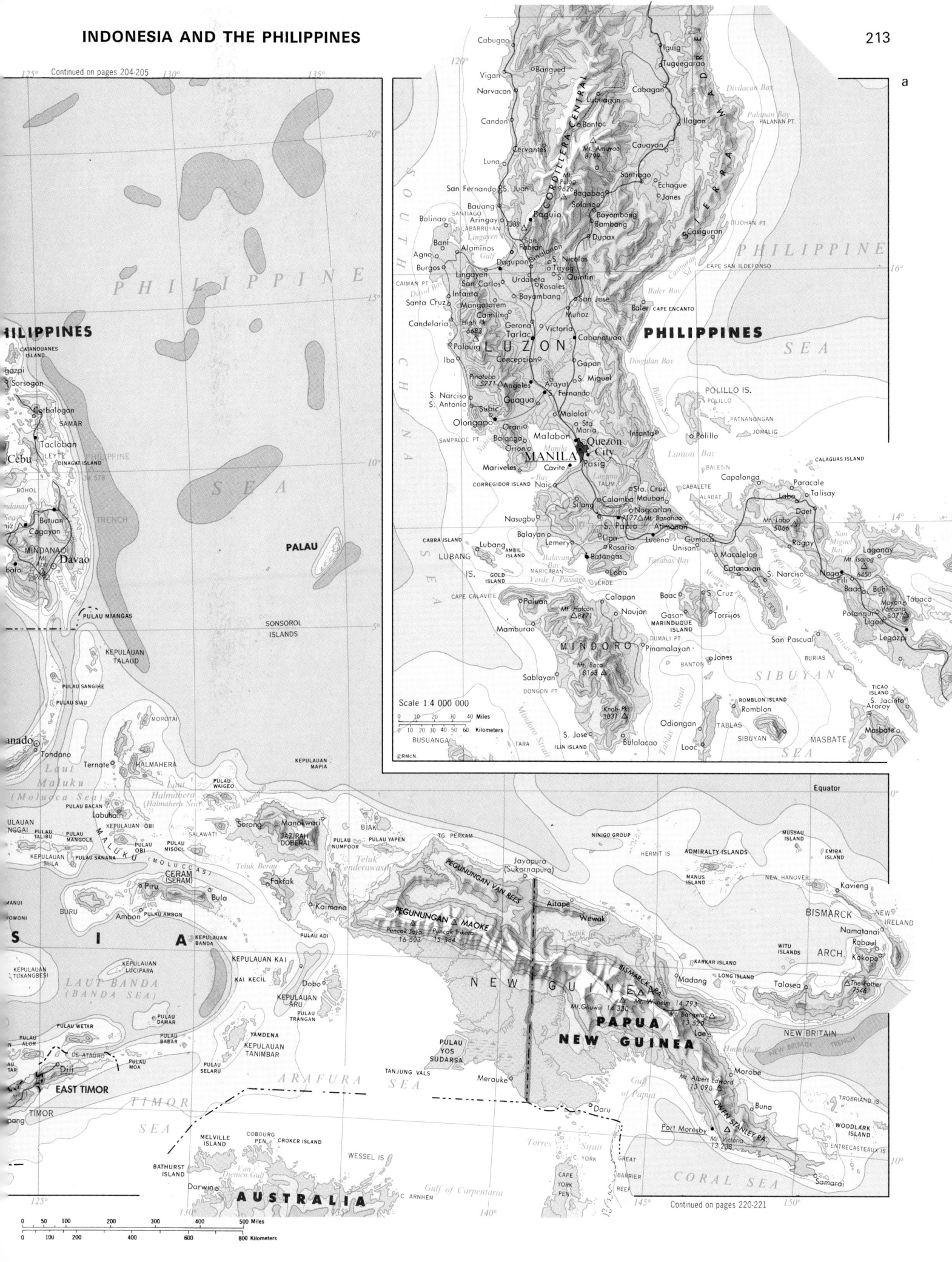

Continued on pages 204-205

PHILIPPINE

SEA

SOUTH CHINA SEA

PHILIPPINE SEA

PHILIPPINES

LUZON

PINATUBO

MANILA

Quezon City

Pasig

MINDORO

MARINDUQUE ISLAND

SIBUYAN SEA

MASBATE

TABLAS

Scale 1:4 000 000

0 10 20 30 40 Miles

0 10 20 30 40 50 60 Kilometers

©RMcN

PHILIPPINES

CELEBES

SULAWESI

Tacloban

SAMAR

Cebu

BOHOL

MINDANAO

Davao

PULAU MIANGAS

SONSOROL ISLANDS

PALAU

KEPULAUAN TALAUD

KEPULAUAN SANGIHE

PULAU SIAU

MOROTAI

HALMAHERA

KEPULAUAN MAPIA

Ternate

Laut Maluku (Molucca Sea)

Halmahera (Halmahera Sea)

PULAU WAIGEO

Sorong

Manokwari

BIAK

JAZIRAH DOBERAI

PULAU NUMFOOR

PULAU YAPEN

Teluk Cenderawasih

PEGUNUNGAN VAN REES

Jayapura (Sukarnapura)

Aitape

Wewak

NINIGO GROUP

HERMIT IS.

ADMIRALTY ISLANDS

MANUS ISLAND

MUSSAU ISLAND

EMIRA ISLAND

NEW HANOVER

Kavieng

BISMARCK ARCH.

NEW IRELAND

Namatanai

Rabaul

Kokopo

MALUKU (MOLUCCAS)

CERAM (SERAM)

Piru

Bula

Ambon

PULAU AMBON

BURU

KEPULAUAN OBI

PULAU MISOOL

Fakfak

Kaimana

PULAU ADI

NEW GUINEA

PEGUNUNGAN MAOKE

Puncak Jaya 16 503

Puncak Trikora 15 584

Sepik

KARKAR ISLAND

Madang

LONG ISLAND

Talasea

WITU ISLANDS

The Father 7546

BISMARCK RA.

Mt. Giluwe 14 330

Mt. Wilhelm 14 793

Mt. Bangeta 13 520

Lae

Morobe

NEW BRITAIN

NEW BRITAIN TRENCH

KEPULAUAN SULA

KEPULAUAN BANDA

KEPULAUAN KAI

KAI KECIL

Dobo

KEPULAUAN ARU

PULAU TRANGAN

Laut Banda (BANDA SEA)

KEPULAUAN LUCIPARA

PULAU DAMAR

YAMDENA

KEPULAUAN TANIMBAR

PULAU BABAR

PULAU SELARU

PULAU YOS SUDARSA

TANJUNG VALS

Merauke

Daru

PAPUA NEW GUINEA

Mt. Albert Edward 13 090

Port Moresby

OWEN STANLEY RA.

Mt. Victoria 13 238

Buna

Gulf of Papua

TROBRIAND IS.

WOODLARK ISLAND

D'ENTRECASTEAUX IS.

Samarai

CORAL SEA

GREAT BARRIER REEF

CAPE YORK

YORK PEN

PULAU WETAR

PULAU ALOR

DE ATAURO

Dili

EAST TIMOR

TIMOR

TIMOR SEA

ARAFURA SEA

PULAU MOA

MELVILLE ISLAND

BATHURST ISLAND

COBOURG PEN

CROKER ISLAND

WESSEL IS.

Van Diemen Gulf

Darwin

C. ARNHEM

Gulf of Carpentaria

AUSTRALIA

Torres Strait

Continued on pages 220-221

0 50 100   200   300   400   500 Miles

0   100   200   400   600   800 Kilometers

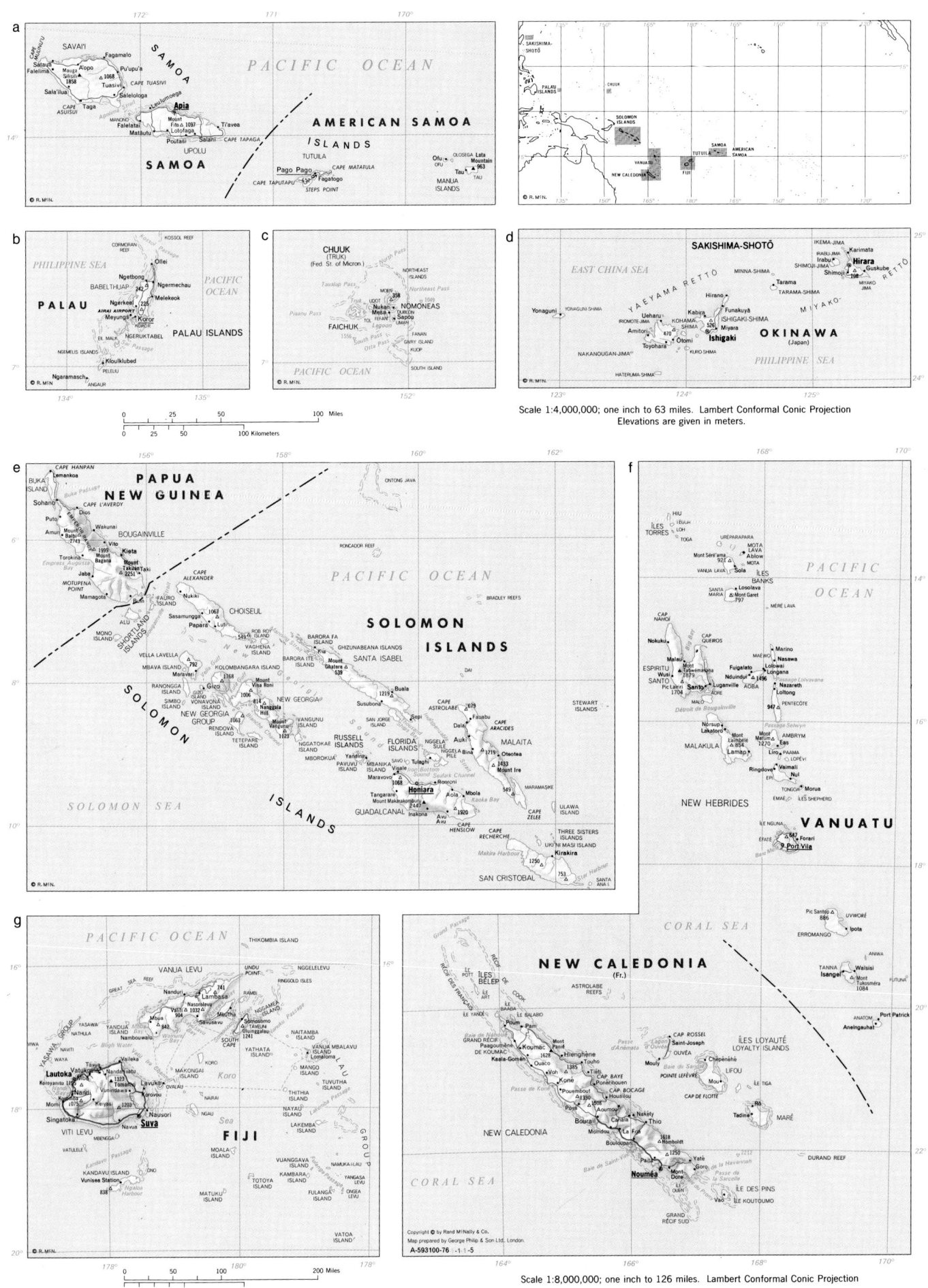

a

SAMOA

PACIFIC OCEAN

SAVAI'I
Fagamalo
A'opo
Pu'upu'a
Sataua
Mauga
Falelima
Sili'uli
Silisili
1858
CAPE TUASIVI
Tuasivi
Sala'ilua
Taga
Salelologa
Lauulumoega
CAPE ASUISUI
Poutasi
Ti'avea
Mount
Falelatai
Fito
1097
Lotofaga
Matautu
CAPE TAPAGA
UPOLU
APIA

AMERICAN SAMOA

ISLANDS

TUTUILA

Ofu
OLOSEGA
Lata
OFU
Mountain
Tau
963
TAU

Pago Pago
CAPE MATATULA
Fagatogo
CAPE TAPUTAPU
Fagatogo
STEPS POINT
MANUA
ISLANDS

© R. MSN.

b

PALAU

PHILIPPINE
SEA

KOSSOL REEF
CORMORAN
REEF
Ollei
Ngetbong
PACIFIC
Ngermechau
OCEAN
BABELTHUAP
242
Melekeok
Ngerkeai
225
Meyungs
Koror
AIRAI AIRPORT
NGERUKTABEL
PALAU ISLANDS
EIL MALK
NGEMELIS ISLANDS
Kloulklubed
PELELIU
Ngaramasch
ANGAUR

© R. MSN.

c

CHUUK
(TRUK)
(Fed. St. of Micron.)

Tannlop Pass
NORTHEAST
ISLANDS
Northeast Pass
MOEN
358
Pisann Pass
Nukan
NOMONEAS
Sapoq
UDOT
FEFAN
FAICHUK
FANAN
1556
South Pass
UMAN
GMRY ISLAND
KUOP
SOUTH ISLAND

PACIFIC OCEAN

© R. MSN.

d

SAKISHIMA-SHOTŌ

IKEMA-JIMA
Karimata
IRABUU-JIMA
SHIMOJI-JIMA
Hirara
EAST CHINA SEA
MINNA-SHIMA
Guskube
198
Tarama
Shimoji
MIYAKO-
JIMA
Yonaguni
YONAGUNI-SHIMA
TARAMA-SHIMA
Hirano
RETTO
Uehara
Funakuyā
Kabira
ISHIGAKI-SHIMA
Amitori
KOHAMA-
Miyara
520
OKINAWA
IROMOTE-JIMA
470
Ishigaki
(Japan)
Ōtomi
NAKANOUGAN-JIMA
Toyohara
KURO SHIMA
PHILIPPINE SEA
HATERUMA-SHIMA

© R. MSN.

YAEYAMA RETTO

MIYAKO

Scale 1:4,000,000; one inch to 63 miles. Lambert Conformal Conic Projection
Elevations are given in meters.

Scale bar:
0　25　50　100 Miles
0　25　50　100 Kilometers

e

CAPE HANPAN
Lemankoa
BUKA
ISLAND
Buka Passage
PAPUA
Sohano
CAPE L'AVERDY
NEW GUINEA
Puto
Dios
Amun
Wakunai
Mount
BOUGAINVILLE
Balbi
2743
Torokina
Vito
1999
Mount
Kieta
Bagana
ONTONG JAVA
Jaba
2251
Takun
MOTUPENA
Mamagota
Buin
POINT
FAURO
Nukiki
ISLAND
CHOISEUL
1067
ALU
Sasamungga
RONCADOR REEF
MONO
Papara
Luti
ISLAND
SHORTLAND
BRADLEY REEFS
ISLANDS
548
VELLA LAVELLA
ROB ROY
BARORA FA
ISLAND
ISLAND
SOLOMON
Maravari
792
GHIZUNABEANA ISLANDS
RANONGGA
Gizo
KOLOMBANGARA ISLAND
BARORA ITE
ISLAND
SANTA ISABEL
SIMBO
1768
Mount
ISLAND
1006
Vina Roni
Buala
SOLOMON
814
NEW GEORGIA
Mount
Susubona
Nggala
1063
Hill
VANGUNU
Sepi
1219
ISLAND
Mount
SAN JORGE
ISLANDS
RENDOVA
1123
ISLAND
ISLAND
Dala
CAPE
TETEPARE ISLAND
NGGATOKAE
PAVUVU
ASTROLABE
629
Fauabu
SOLOMON SEA
MBOROKUA
ISLAND
FLORIDA
NGGELA
1219
CAPE
RUSSELL
ISLANDS
SULE
Auki
ARACIDES
ISLANDS
NGGELA
Oloteotea
MBANIKA
PILE
MALAITA
Yandina
ISLAND
SAVO
Visale
1433
Maravovo
Tulaghi
Mount Ire
Tangarare
Honiara
Aola
Mount Makarakomburu
Ronoroni
Mbola
549
2447
Inakona
Kaoka Bay
Avu
1920
CAPE
GUADALCANAL
Avu
ZELEE
CAPE
ULAWA
HENSLOW
ISLAND
THREE SISTERS
CAPE
ISLANDS
RECHERCHE
UKI NI MASI ISLAND
1250
Kirakira
Makira Harbour
753
Star Harbour
SAN CRISTOBAL
SANTA
ANA I.

PACIFIC OCEAN

SOLOMON
ISLANDS

STEWART
ISLANDS

DAI

MARAMASIKE

© R. MSN.

f

HIU
ÎLES
LOH
TORRES
TOGA
UREPARAPARA
MOTA
Mont Sere'ama
LAVA
924
Ablow
VANUA LAVA
MOTA
ÎLES
Sola
BANKS
SANTA
Losolava
MARIA
Mont Garet
797
MÈRÈ LAVA
CAP
Nokaku
QUEIROS
ESPIRITU
Marino
Malao
MAEWO
Nasawa
SANTO
Fuigalato
Longana
Mount Tabwemasana
Ndundui
1496
Pic Lairn
Santo
Luganville
AOBA
1704
Nazareth
MALO
Loftong
Norsup
PENTECÔTE
947
Lakatoro
Mont
MALAKULA
Lambele
AMBRYM
Lamap
854
Eas
1270
LOPEVI
Liro
PAAMA
Ringdove
Vaimali
EPI
Nul
TONGOA
Morua
EMAE
ÎLES SHEPHERD
ÎLE NGUNA
Forari
EFATE
647
Port Vila

PACIFIC
OCEAN

Passage Lolovave

Détroit de Bougainville

Passage Selwyn

NEW HEBRIDES

VANUATU

g

PACIFIC OCEAN
THIKOMBIA ISLAND
VANUA LEVU
UNDU
POINT
Nanduri
741
NGGELELEVU
Lambasa
RINGGOLD ISLES
GREAT
SEA
Valili
1032
REEF
Nasorolevu
Mbua
Savusavu
642
NAITAMBA
YANDUA
TAVEUNI
ISLAND
ISLAND
1241
VANUA MBALAVU
Somosomo
SOUTH
VANUA
YASAWA
CAPE
YATHATA
Nambouwalu
LOMALOMA
GROUP
ISLAND
MANGO
NATHULA
KORO
ISLAND
NAVITI
Bligh Water
THITHIA
WAYA
NAIRAI
ISLAND
TUVUTHA
MAKONGAI
ISLAND
Taveu
ISLAND
NAYAU
Lautoka
Vatukoula
OVALAU
LAKEMBA
KORO
Vaileka
Koronyanitu
1323
ISLAND
Mba
Tomaniivi
NAMUKA-I-LAU
Nandi
1323
Nausori
KAMBARA
Nandarivatu
Korovou
YANGASA
Momi
1075
1203
Suva
NGAU
LEVU
Keiyasi
MBENGGA
Sea
FULANGA
ONGEA
Singatoka
FIJI
LEVU
MOALA
VATULELE
ISLAND
LAKEMBA
NAYAU
TOTOYA
ISLAND
KANDAVU
GROUP
VUANGGAVA
ISLAND
Vunisea Station
ONO
NAMUKA-I-LAU
838
Ngaloa Harbour
VANGGAVA
MATUKU
FULANGA
ISLAND
ONGEA
LEVU
VATOA
ISLAND

© R. MSN.

NEW CALEDONIA
(Fr.)

CORAL SEA
Pic Santo
886
UVWORE
ERROMANGO
Ipota
RECIF DE
Grand Passage
ÎLE POTT
ÎLES
BELEP
RÉCIFS
ÎLE ART
ASTROLABE
ANIWA
REEFS
COOK
TANNA
Waisisi
ÎLE BALABIO
Isangel
Mont Tukosmera
1084
ÎLE YANDE
Poum
Pam
ANATOM
Port Patrick
Baie de
Aneingauhat
DE FRANÇAIS
GRAND RÉCIF
Mont
Koumac
Panié
CAP ROSSEL
PAAGOUMENE
Saint-Joseph
1628
Touho
OUVÉA
DE KOUMAC
KAALA-GOMEN
Kaala-Gomen
Hienghène
1350
Poindimié
ÎLES LOYAUTÉ
Koné
1385
CAP BAYE
Mouly
LOYALTY ISLANDS
Pouembout
Ponérihouen
Baie de Chasseloup
Voh
CAP BOCAGE
LIFOU
Houailou
Chépénéhé
Poya
CAP DE FLOTTE
Mou
LE TIGA
Bourail
1618
Kouaoua
POINTE LEFÈVRE
Moindou
Canala
Nakéty
Tadine
Houndbo
Thio
MARE
La Foa
CAP
Boulouparis
1250
ASTROLABE
RÉCIFS
Paita
Goro
Île de la Havannah
DURAND REEF
Mont
Nouméa
Dore
Yate
Passe
NEW CALEDONIA
Mont
de la Sarcelle
ÎLE DES PINS
CORAL SEA
Vao
ÎLE KOUTOUMO
GRAND
RÉCIF SUD

Copyright © by Rand McNally & Co.
Map prepared by George Philip & Son Ltd, London.
A-593100-76 -1-1-5

Scale 1:8,000,000; one inch to 126 miles. Lambert Conformal Conic Projection
Elevations are given in meters.

Scale bar:
0　50　100　200 Miles
0　50　100　200 Kilometers

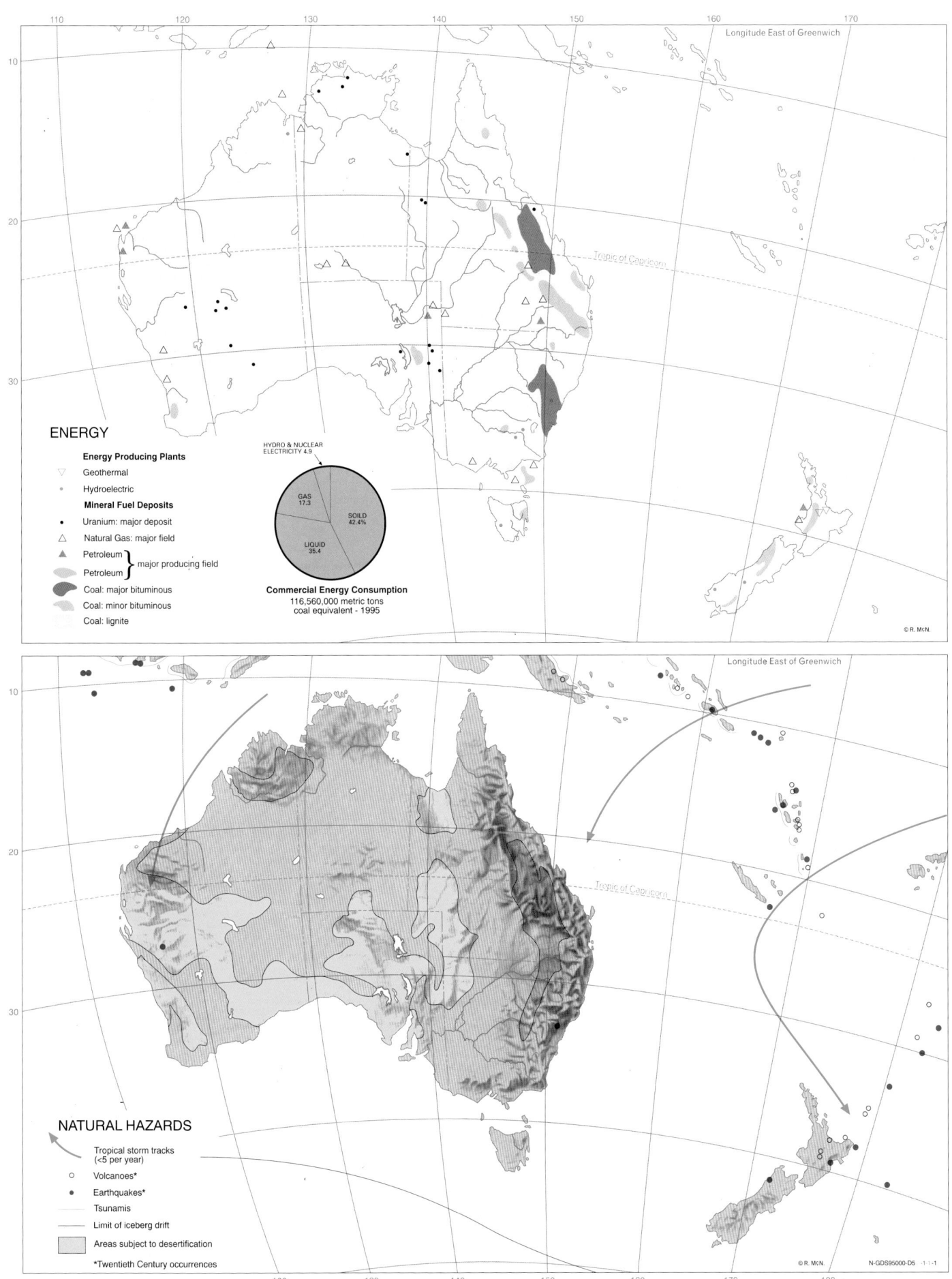

ENERGY

Energy Producing Plants

▽ Geothermal

· Hydroelectric

Mineral Fuel Deposits

· Uranium: major deposit

△ Natural Gas: major field

▲ Petroleum ⎫

        ⎬ major producing field

   Petroleum ⎭

  Coal: major bituminous

  Coal: minor bituminous

  Coal: lignite

HYDRO & NUCLEAR
ELECTRICITY 4.9

GAS
17.3

SOILD
42.4%

LIQUID
35.4

Commercial Energy Consumption
116,560,000 metric tons
coal equivalent - 1995

© R. McN.

Longitude East of Greenwich

Tropic of Capricorn

NATURAL HAZARDS

   Tropical storm tracks
   (<5 per year)

○ Volcanoes*

· Earthquakes*

   Tsunamis

   Limit of iceberg drift

   Areas subject to desertification

*Twentieth Century occurrences

© R. McN.   N-GDS95000-D5 -1-1-1

Longitude East of Greenwich

Tropic of Capricorn

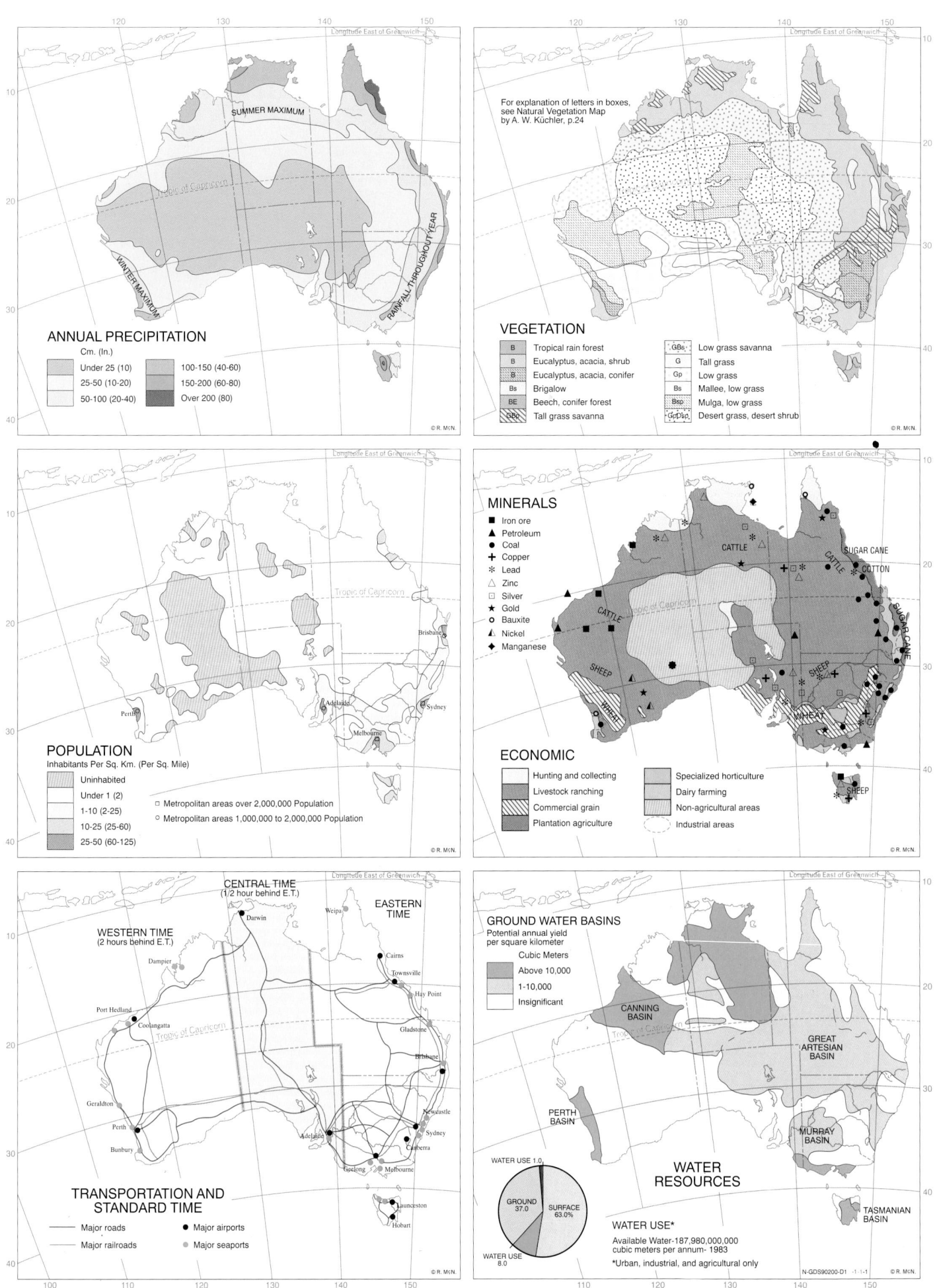

ANNUAL PRECIPITATION

Cm. (In.)

- Under 25 (10)
- 25-50 (10-20)
- 50-100 (20-40)
- 100-150 (40-60)
- 150-200 (60-80)
- Over 200 (80)

© R. McN.

VEGETATION

For explanation of letters in boxes, see Natural Vegetation Map by A. W. Küchler, p.24

- B Tropical rain forest
- B Eucalyptus, acacia, shrub
- B Eucalyptus, acacia, conifer
- Bs Brigalow
- BE Beech, conifer forest
- GBo Tall grass savanna
- GBs Low grass savanna
- G Tall grass
- Gp Low grass
- Bs Mallee, low grass
- Bsp Mulga, low grass
- GpDp Desert grass, desert shrub

© R. McN.

POPULATION

Inhabitants Per Sq. Km. (Per Sq. Mile)

- Uninhabited
- Under 1 (2)
- 1-10 (2-25)
- 10-25 (25-60)
- 25-50 (60-125)

□ Metropolitan areas over 2,000,000 Population
○ Metropolitan areas 1,000,000 to 2,000,000 Population

© R. McN.

MINERALS

- ■ Iron ore
- ▲ Petroleum
- ● Coal
- + Copper
- ✳ Lead
- △ Zinc
- □ Silver
- ★ Gold
- ○ Bauxite
- ▲ Nickel
- ◆ Manganese

ECONOMIC

- Hunting and collecting
- Livestock ranching
- Commercial grain
- Plantation agriculture
- Specialized horticulture
- Dairy farming
- Non-agricultural areas
- Industrial areas

© R. McN.

TRANSPORTATION AND STANDARD TIME

CENTRAL TIME (1/2 hour behind E.T.)
EASTERN TIME
WESTERN TIME (2 hours behind E.T.)

—— Major roads
—— Major railroads
● Major airports
● Major seaports

© R. McN.

GROUND WATER BASINS

Potential annual yield per square kilometer
Cubic Meters

- Above 10,000
- 1-10,000
- Insignificant

CANNING BASIN
GREAT ARTESIAN BASIN
PERTH BASIN
MURRAY BASIN
TASMANIAN BASIN

WATER RESOURCES

WATER USE 1.0
GROUND 37.0
SURFACE 63.0%
WATER USE 8.0

WATER USE*

Available Water-187,980,000,000 cubic meters per annum- 1983

*Urban, industrial, and agricultural only

N-GDS90200-D1 -1-1-1   © R. McN.

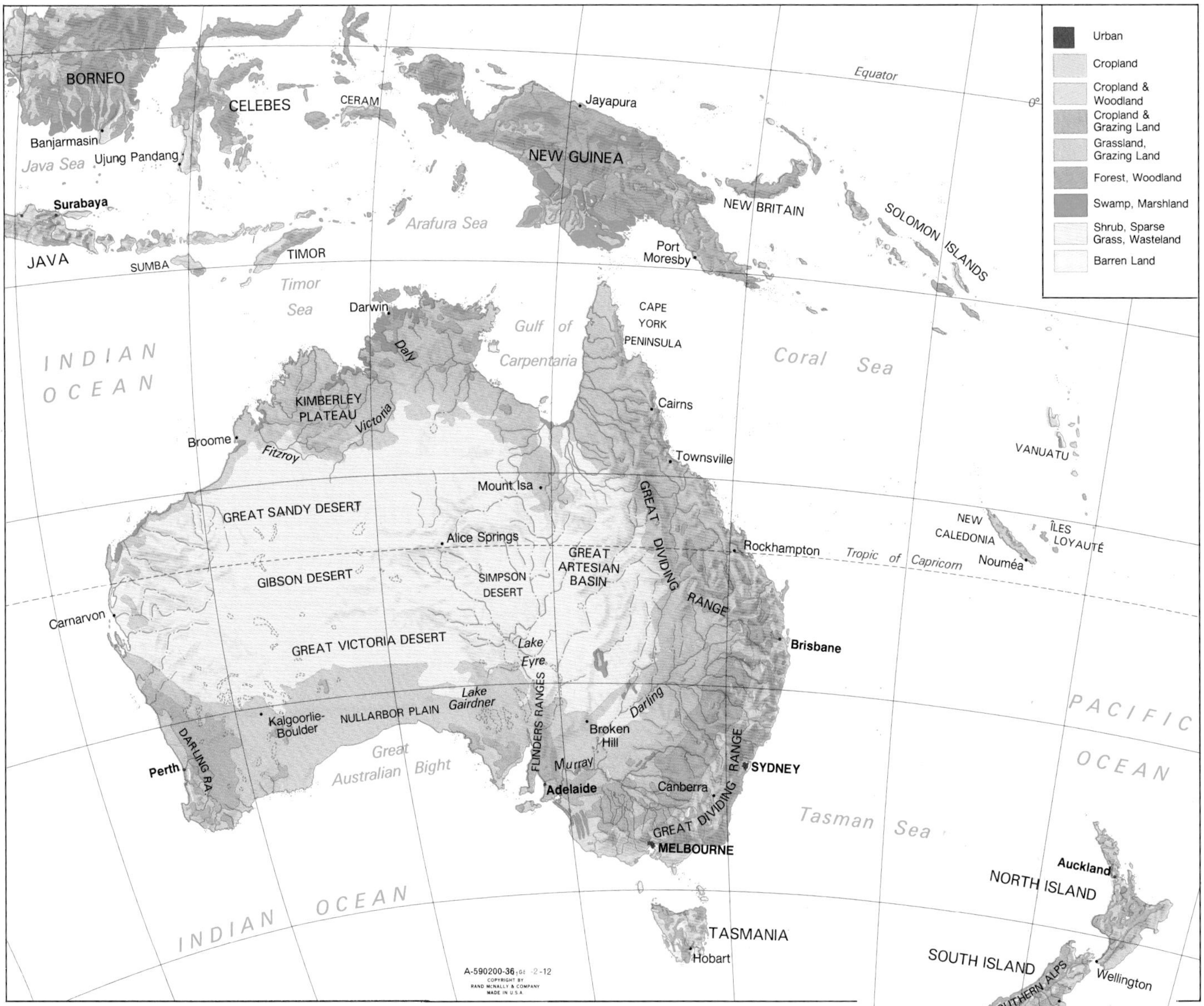

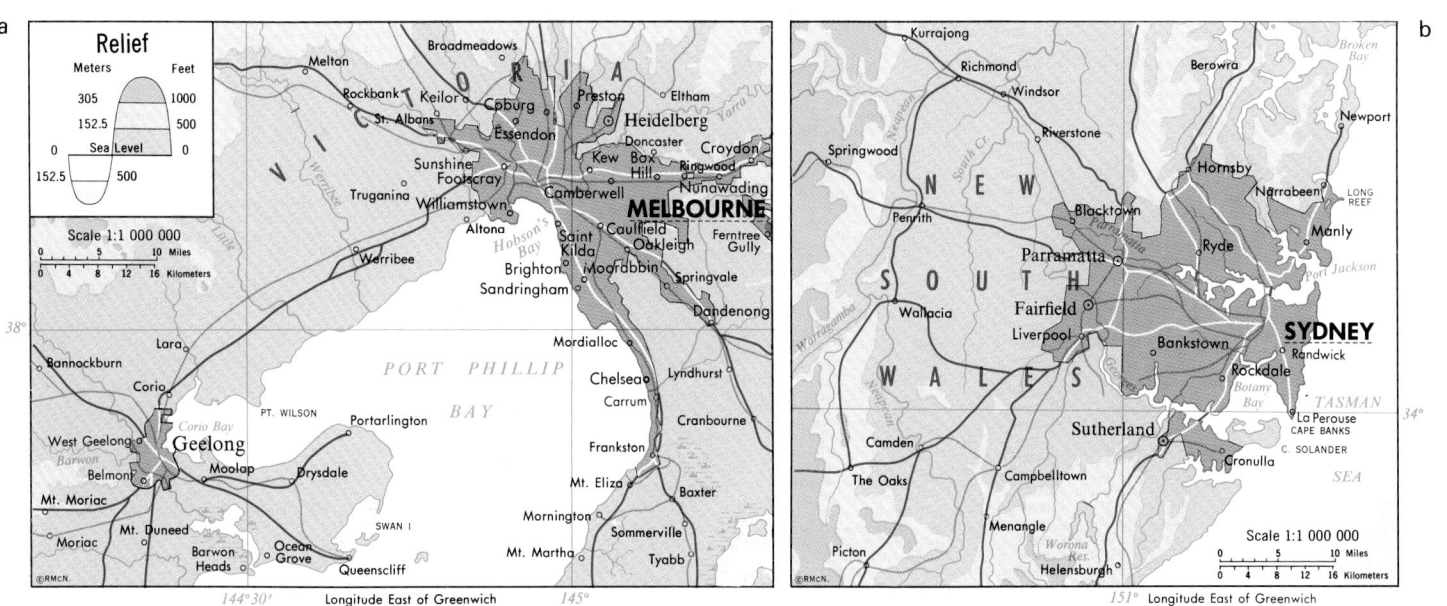

Urban
Cropland
Cropland & Woodland
Cropland & Grazing Land
Grassland, Grazing Land
Forest, Woodland
Swamp, Marshland
Shrub, Sparse Grass, Wasteland
Barren Land

BORNEO
CELEBES
CERAM
Banjarmasin
Ujung Pandang
Java Sea
Surabaya
JAVA
SUMBA
TIMOR
Jayapura
NEW GUINEA
NEW BRITAIN
Port Moresby
SOLOMON ISLANDS
Equator
Arafura Sea
Timor Sea
Darwin
Daly
Gulf of Carpentaria
CAPE YORK PENINSULA
Coral Sea
VANUATU
NEW CALEDONIA
ÎLES LOYAUTÉ
Nouméa
INDIAN OCEAN
KIMBERLEY PLATEAU
Victoria
Broome
Fitzroy
GREAT SANDY DESERT
Mount Isa
Cairns
Townsville
GREAT DIVIDING RANGE
Alice Springs
GIBSON DESERT
SIMPSON DESERT
GREAT ARTESIAN BASIN
Rockhampton
Tropic of Capricorn
Carnarvon
GREAT VICTORIA DESERT
Lake Eyre
Brisbane
Darling
Kalgoorlie-Boulder
NULLARBOR PLAIN
Lake Gairdner
FLINDERS RANGES
Broken Hill
Murray
SYDNEY
PACIFIC OCEAN
Perth
DARLING RA.
Great Australian Bight
Adelaide
Canberra
GREAT DIVIDING RANGE
Tasman Sea
INDIAN OCEAN
MELBOURNE
TASMANIA
Hobart
Auckland
NORTH ISLAND
SOUTH ISLAND
SOUTHERN ALPS
Wellington
Christchurch
STEWART ISLAND
Dunedin

Scale 1:36,000,000; one inch to 570 miles. Lambert Azimuthal Equal-Area Projection

A-590200-36
COPYRIGHT BY
RAND McNALLY & COMPANY
MADE IN U.S.A.

0 100 200 400 600 800 Miles
0 150 300 600 900 1200 Kilometers

a

Relief

Meters		Feet
305		1000
152.5		500
0	Sea Level	0
152.5		500

Scale 1:1 000 000

0 5 10 Miles
0 4 8 12 16 Kilometers

Broadmeadows
Melton
Rockbank
Keilor
Coburg
Preston
Eltham
St. Albans
Essendon
Heidelberg
Doncaster
VICTORIA
Sunshine
Kew
Bay
Hill
Croydon
Ringwood
Footscray
Camberwell
Nunawading
Truganina
Williamstown
MELBOURNE
Altona
Saint Kilda
Caulfield
Oakleigh
Ferntree Gully
Hobson's Bay
Brighton
Moorabbin
Springvale
Werribee
Sandringham
Dandenong
Lara
Mordialloc
Bannockburn
Corio
PORT PHILLIP BAY
Chelsea
Lyndhurst
Corio Bay
Portarlington
Carrum
Cranbourne
West Geelong
Geelong
Belmont
Moolap
Drysdale
Frankston
Mt. Moriac
Mt. Duneed
SWAN I.
Mt. Eliza
Baxter
Moriac
Barwon Heads
Ocean Grove
Mornington
Sommerville
Queenscliff
Mt. Martha
Tyabb

38°
PT. WILSON
144°30'   Longitude East of Greenwich   145°

b

Kurrajong
Broken Bay
Richmond
Berowra
Windsor
Newport
Springwood
Riverstone
Hornsby
Narrabeen
LONG REEF
Penrith
Blacktown
NEW
Ryde
Manly
Port Jackson
Parramatta
SOUTH
Wallacia
Fairfield
SYDNEY
Liverpool
Bankstown
Randwick
WALES
Rockdale
Botany Bay
La Perouse
CAPE BANKS
Camden
Sutherland
C. SOLANDER
TASMAN
The Oaks
Campbelltown
Cronulla
SEA
Menangle
Picton
Helensburgh

Scale 1:1 000 000

0 5 10 Miles
0 4 8 12 16 Kilometers

34°
151°   Longitude East of Greenwich

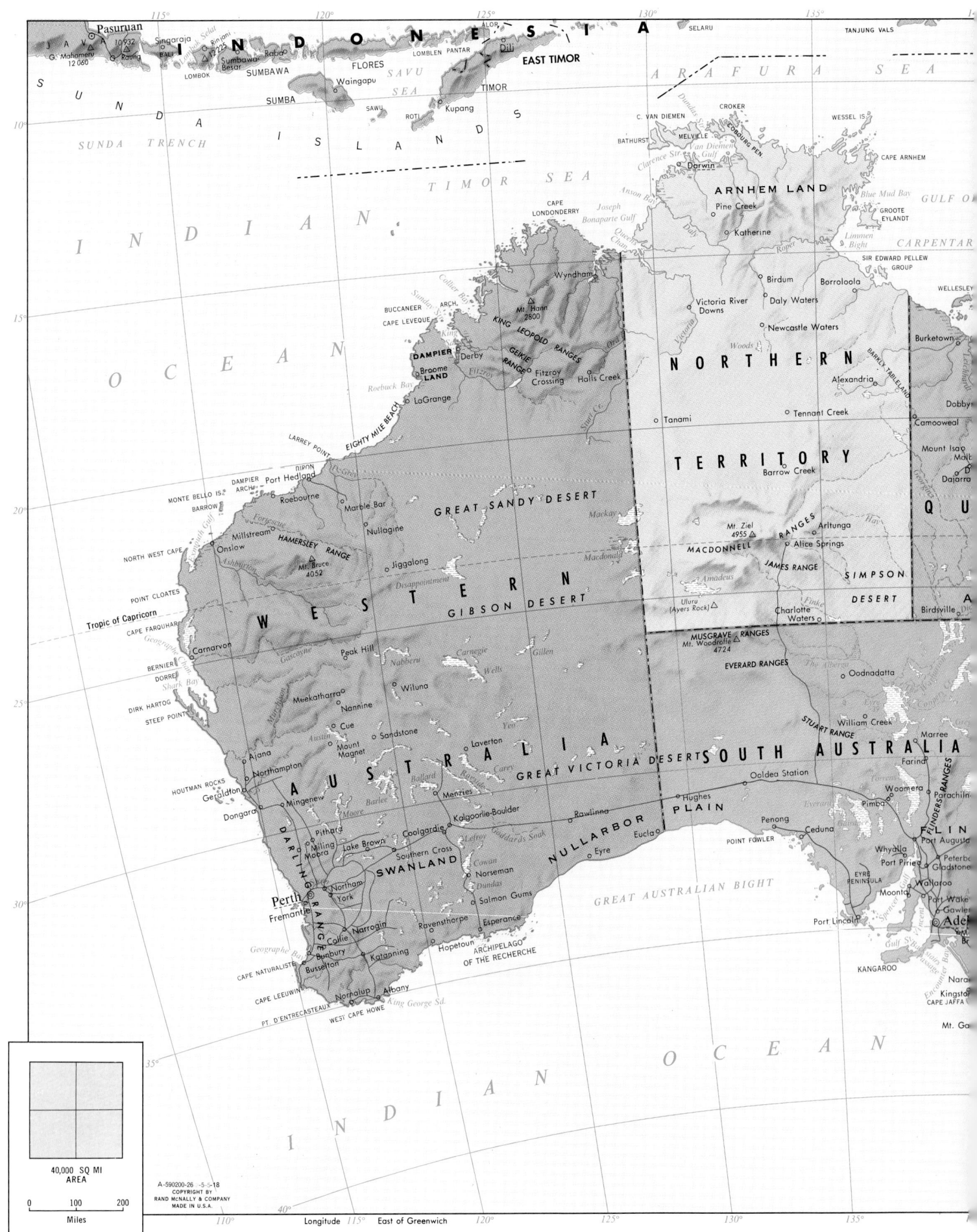

40,000 SQ MI
AREA

0   100   200
Miles

Scale 1:16 000 000; one inch to 250 miles. Lambert's Azimuthal, Equal Area Projection
Elevations and depressions are given in feet

Longitude 115°   East of Greenwich

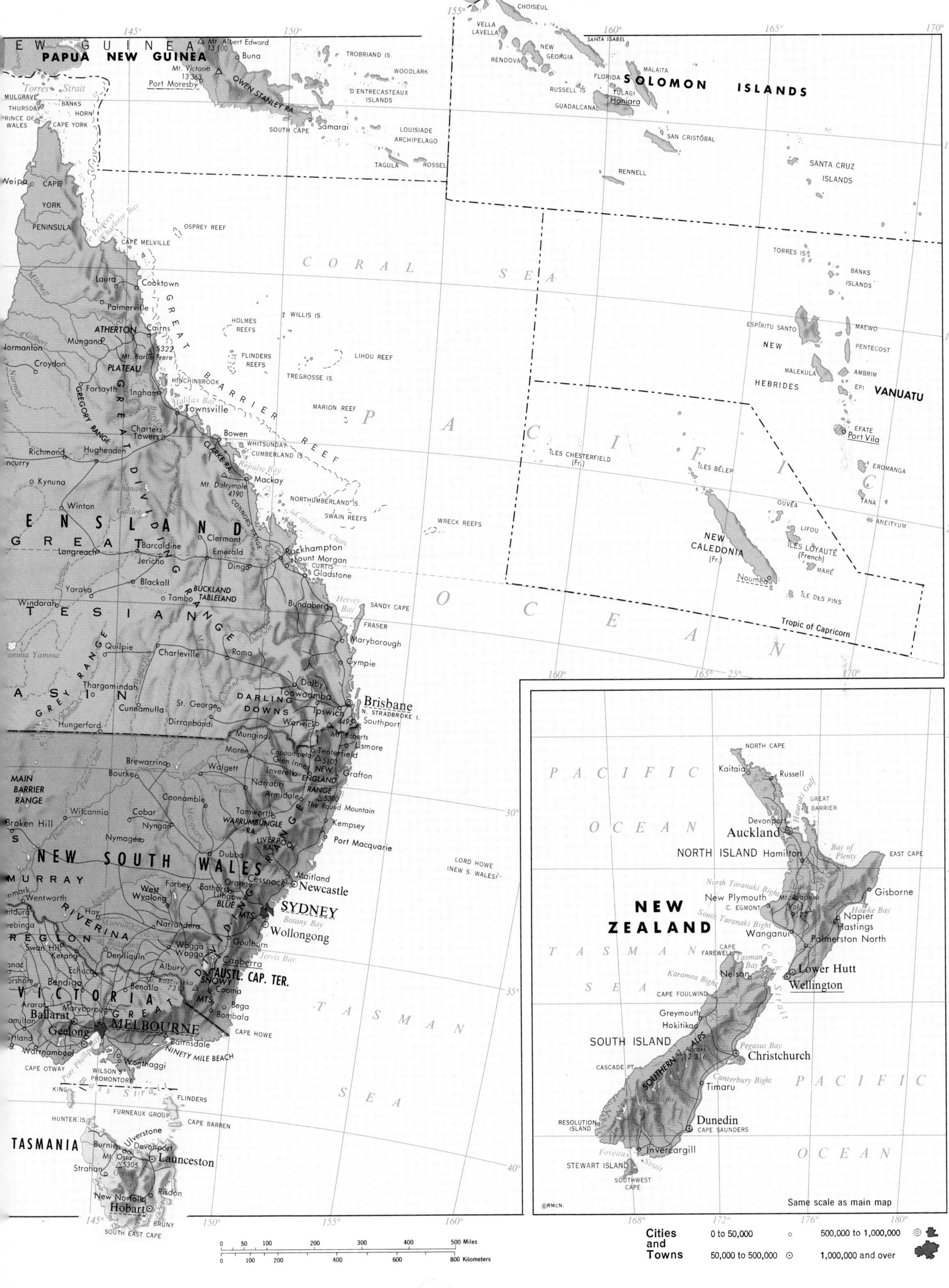

NEW GUINEA
PAPUA NEW GUINEA
Mt. Albert Edward
13,100
Buna
TROBRIAND IS.
Mt. Victoria
13,363
Port Moresby
WOODLARK
OWEN STANLEY RA.
D'ENTRECASTEAUX ISLANDS
Torres Strait
MULGRAVE
THURSDAY
BANKS
HORN
PRINCE OF WALES
CAPE YORK
Samarai
SOUTH CAPE
LOUISIADE ARCHIPELAGO
TAGULA ROSSEL

CHOISEUL
VELLA LAVELLA
RENDOVA
NEW GEORGIA
SANTA ISABEL
RUSSELL IS.
FLORIDA
MALAITA
TULAGI
Honiara
SOLOMON ISLANDS
GUADALCANAL
SAN CRISTÓBAL
RENNELL
SANTA CRUZ ISLANDS

Weipa
CAPE YORK PENINSULA
OSPREY REEF
CAPE MELVILLE

CORAL SEA

TORRES IS.
BANKS ISLANDS
ESPÍRITU SANTO
MAEWO
NEW
PENTECOST
HEBRIDES
MALEKULA
AMBRIM
EPI
VANUATU

Laura
Cooktown
Palmerville
HOLMES REEFS
WILLIS IS.
LIHOU REEF
ATHERTON
Mungana
Cairns
Mt. Bartle Frere
5,322
FLINDERS REEFS
TREGROSSE IS.
PLATEAU
Forsayth
Ingham
HINCHINBROOK
MARION REEF
Townsville

EFATE
Port Vila

Normanton
Croydon
Charters Towers
Richmond
Hughenden
Mt. Dalrymple
4,190
Bowen
WHITSUNDAY
CUMBERLAND IS.
Mackay
NORTHUMBERLAND IS.
SWAIN REEFS
WRECK REEFS

ÎLES CHESTERFIELD (Fr.)
ÎLES BÉLEP
 OUVÉA
MARÉ
LIFOU
ÎLES LOYAUTÉ (French)
NEW CALEDONIA (Fr.)
Nouméa
ÎLE DES PINS

EROMANGA
TANA
ANEITYUM

PACIFIC OCEAN

Kynuna
Winton
QUEENSLAND
GREAT
Longreach
Barcaldine
Jericho
Clermont
Emerald
Dingo
Rockhampton
Mount Morgan
CURTIS
Gladstone
Yaraka
Blackall
Tambo
BUCKLAND TABLELAND
Bundaberg
Hervey Bay
SANDY CAPE
Windorah
DIVIDING
Quilpie
Charleville
Roma
Maryborough
Gympie
Thargomindah
Cunnamulla
St. George
Dirranbandi
RANGE
Dalby
Toowoomba
Ipswich
Warwick
Brisbane
N. STRADBROKE I.
Southport

Tropic of Capricorn

NEW SOUTH WALES
Bourke
Brewarrina
Walgett
Moree
Narrabri
Tamworth
Lismore
Grafton
Kempsey
Port Macquarie
Tenterfield
Glen Innes
Inverell
Armidale
NEW ENGLAND RANGE
The Round Mountain
5,300
WARRUMBUNGLE RA.
LIVERPOOL RANGE
Newcastle
Maitland
Cessnock
BLUE MTS.
SYDNEY
Wollongong
Goulburn
Jervis Bay
Botany Bay

LORD HOWE (NEW S. WALES)

Broken Hill
Wilcannia
Cobar
Nymagee
Nyngan
Dubbo
Orange
Bathurst
Lithgow
Forbes
West Wyalong
Wagga Wagga
Albury
Narrandera
Hay
Deniliquin
Echuca
AUSTL. CAP. TER.
Canberra
Cooma
Mt. Kosciusko
7,316
SNOWY MTS.
Bega
Bombala

VICTORIA
MELBOURNE
Geelong
Ballarat
Bendigo
Maryborough
Bairnsdale
NINETY MILE BEACH
CAPE HOWE
Warrnambool
Wonthaggi
CAPE OTWAY
WILSON'S PROMONTORY
Port Phillip

Swan Hill
Kerang
Benalla
GREAT
DIVIDING RANGE

BASS STRAIT
KING
FLINDERS
FURNEAUX GROUP
HUNTER IS.
CAPE BARREN

TASMANIA
Burnie
Ulverstone
Devonport
Mt. Ossa
5,305
Launceston
Risdon
New Norfolk
Hobart
BRUNY
SOUTH EAST CAPE

TASMAN SEA

New Zealand inset (a)

PACIFIC OCEAN

NORTH CAPE
Kaitaia
Russell
GREAT BARRIER
Devonport
Auckland
Hauraki Gulf
Bay of Plenty
NORTH ISLAND
Hamilton
EAST CAPE

NEW ZEALAND

North Taranaki Bight
New Plymouth
C. EGMONT
South Taranaki Bight
Wanganui
Mt. Egmont
Gisborne
Hawke Bay
Napier
Hastings
Palmerston North

TASMAN SEA

CAPE FAREWELL
Tasman Bay
Nelson
Karamea Bight
CAPE FOULWIND
Lower Hutt
Wellington
Cook Strait

SOUTH ISLAND
Greymouth
Hokitika
SOUTHERN ALPS
Mt. Cook
12,316
Pegasus Bay
Christchurch
Canterbury Bight
CASCADE PT.
Timaru
RESOLUTION ISLAND
Dunedin
CAPE SAUNDERS
Foveaux Strait
Invercargill
STEWART ISLAND
SOUTHWEST CAPE

PACIFIC OCEAN

Same scale as main map

Cities and Towns

Cities and Towns		
0 to 50,000	○	500,000 to 1,000,000
50,000 to 500,000	⊙	1,000,000 and over

0 50 100 200 300 400 500 Miles
0 200 400 600 800 Kilometers

Continued on pages 212-213

INDONESIA

Pasuruan

JAVA
G. Mahameru 12 060
G. Raung 10 932
BALI
Singaraja
Rindjani 12 225
Rupa
Sumbawa Besar
LOMBOK
Besar
SUMBAWA

FLORES

LOMBLEN PANTAR
ALOR
Dili
EAST TIMOR

Waingapu

SUMBA

SAVU SEA

SAWU
ROTI
Kupang
TIMOR

SELARU
TANJUNG VALS

ARAFURA SEA

SUNDA ISLANDS

SUNDA Selat

TIMOR SEA

CAPE LONDONDERRY

Joseph Bonaparte Gulf

C. VAN DIEMEN
CROKER
Van Diemen Gulf
MELVILLE
BATHURST
Clarence Str.
Cobourg PEN.
Darwin

WESSEL IS.
CAPE ARNHEM
Blue Mud Bay
GROOTE EYLANDT
Limmen Bight
GULF OF
CARPENTARIA

ARNHEM LAND
Pine Creek
Katherine

SUNDA TRENCH

INDIAN OCEAN

Wyndham

Mt Hann 2800

KING LEOPOLD RANGES

BUCCANEER ARCH.
CAPE LEVEQUE

King Sd.

Derby

GEIKIE RANGE
Fitzroy Crossing
Halls Creek

Birdum

Victoria River Downs
Daly Waters
Newcastle Waters

SIR EDWARD PELLEW GROUP
WELLESLEY
Borroloola
Burketown

DAMPIER
Broome
LAND

Roebuck Bay

LaGrange

EIGHTY MILE BEACH

LARREY POINT

NORTHERN

TERRITORY

Tanami

Tennant Creek

Dobbyn
Camooweal
Mount Isa
Malbo
Dajarra

QU

MONTE BELLO IS.
BARROW
DAMPIER ARCH.
Port Hedland
RIPON
Roebourne

NORTH WEST CAPE

Millstream
Onslow

HAMERSLEY RANGE
Mt. Bruce 4052

Marble Bar

Nullagine

GREAT SANDY DESERT

Jiggalong

Disappointment

WESTERN

Barrow Creek

Mt. Ziel 4955
MACDONNELL RANGES
Arltunga
Alice Springs
JAMES RANGE

Amadeus

SIMPSON

DESERT

A

POINT CLOATES

Tropic of Capricorn

CAPE FARQUHAR

Carnarvon

BERNIER
DORRE
Shark Bay

GIBSON DESERT

Carnegie

Gilben

Uluru (Ayers Rock)

MUSGRAVE RANGES
Mt. Woodroffe 4724

EVERARD RANGES

Charlotte Waters

Birdsville

Peak Hill
Nabberu

Wells

The Alberga

Oodnadatta

DIRK HARTOG
STEEP POINT

Meekatharra
Nannine

Cue
Mount Magnet
Sandstone

Wiluna

AUSTRALIA

Yeo

Laverton

GREAT VICTORIA DESERT

SOUTH AUSTRALIA

STUART RANGE
William Creek
Marree
Farina

Cooper

Gregor

HOUTMAN ROCKS
Geraldton
Northampton

Dongara

Ajana

Ballard

Menzies

Oldea Station

Hughes

Penong

Ceduna

Woomera
Pimba
Parachilna

FLINDERS RANGES

Mingenew

Coolgardie
Kalgoorlie-Boulder
Norseman

Rawlinna
Eucla

NULLARBOR PLAIN

Eyre

POINT FOWLER

Port Augusta
Port Pirie
Whyalla
Gladstone

Pithara
Miling
Moora
Lake Brown
Southern Cross

SWANLAND

DARLING RANGE

Perth
Fremantle
Northam
York
Narrogin

Cowan
Dundas

Salmon Gums

Ravensthorpe

Esperance

Hopetoun

ARCHIPELAGO OF THE RECHERCHE

GREAT AUSTRALIAN BIGHT

Port Lincoln

EYRE PENINSULA

Moonta
Wallaroo
Port Wakefield
Gawler
Adela

Collie
Bunbury
Busselton

CAPE NATURALISTE

Katanning
Albany

CAPE LEEUWIN
Nornalup
PT. D'ENTRECASTEAUX
WEST CAPE HOWE
King George Sd.

KANGAROO

Naraco
Kingston
CAPE JAFFA

Mt. Gam

INDIAN OCEAN

Relief

Meters		Feet
3050		10 000
1525		5000
610		2000
305		1000
152.5		500
0	Sea Level	0
		Below
152.5		500 Sea Level
1525		5000
3050		10 000
6100		20 000

Longitude   East of Greenwich

Scale 1:16 000 000; one inch to 250 miles. Lambert's Azimuthal, Equal Area Projection
Elevations and depressions are given in feet

NEW GUINEA
PAPUA NEW GUINEA
Mt. Albert Edward 13,100
Buna
Mt. Victoria 13,363
Port Moresby
OWEN STANLEY RA.
TROBRIAND IS.
WOODLARK
D'ENTRECASTEAUX ISLANDS
SOUTH CAPE
Samarai
LOUISIADE ARCHIPELAGO
TAGULA   ROSSEL

Torres Strait
MULGRAVE
BANKS
THURSDAY
HORN
PRINCE OF WALES
CAPE YORK

VELLA LAVELLA
CHOISEUL
RENDOVA
NEW GEORGIA
SANTA ISABEL
FLORIDA
RUSSELL IS.
TULAGI
Honiara
GUADALCANAL
SAN CRISTOBAL
RENNELL
SOLOMON ISLANDS

SANTA CRUZ ISLANDS

TORRES IS.
BANKS ISLANDS

ESPÍRITU SANTO
NEW HEBRIDES
MAEWO
PENTECOST
MALEKULA
AMBRIM
EPI
VANUATU
EFATE
Port Vila
EROMANGA
TANA
ANEITYUM

Veipa
CAPE YORK
YORK PENINSULA
ormanton
Croydon
Mungana
ATHERTON PLATEAU
Mt. Bartle Frere 5322
Cairns
HINCHINBROOK I.
Halifax Bay
Townsville
CAPE MELVILLE
Laura
Cooktown
Palmerville
Forsayth
Ingham

GREAT BARRIER REEF
OSPREY REEF
HOLMES REEFS
WILLIS IS.
FLINDERS REEFS
LIHOU REEF
TREGROSSE IS.
MARION REEF

CORAL SEA

ÎLES CHESTERFIELD (Fr.)
ÎLES BÉLEP
OUVÉA
NEW CALEDONIA (Fr.)
Nouméa
LIFOU
ÎLES LOYAUTÉ (French)
MARÉ
ÎLE DES PINS

PACIFIC OCEAN

Tropic of Capricorn

Normanton
Richmond
Kynuna
Winton
QUEENSLAND
GREAT DIVIDING RANGE
GREGORY RANGE
Charters Towers
Hughenden
Bowen
WHITSUNDAY
CUMBERLAND IS.
Repulse Bay
Mackay
Mt. Dalrymple 4190
CONNORS RANGE
NORTHUMBERLAND IS.
SWAIN REEFS
Capricorn Chan.
WRECK REEFS

Longreach
Barcaldine
Jericho
Blackall
Clermont
Emerald
Dingo
Rockhampton
Mount Morgan
CURTIS
Gladstone
BUCKLAND TABLELAND

GREAT ARTESIAN BASIN
Yaraka
Tambo
Windorah
Quilpie
Charleville
Roma
Bundaberg
Hervey Bay
SANDY CAPE
FRASER
Maryborough
Gympie

Thargomindah
Cunnamulla
St. George
Dirranbandi
DARLING DOWNS
Dalby
Toowoomba
Ipswich
Warwick
Brisbane
N. STRADBROKE I.
Southport

GREAT DIVIDING RANGE
MAIN BARRIER RANGE

Hungerford
Brewarrina
Bourke
Walgett
Mungindi
Moree
Mt. Roberts 4495
Tenterfield
Glen Innes 5100
Inverell
Lismore
Grafton
NEW ENGLAND RANGE
Armidale 5290
The Round Mountain
Kempsey
Port Macquarie

Wilcannia
Cobar
Nyngan
Coonamble
Narrabri
Tamworth
WARRUMBUNGLE RA.
LIVERPOOL RANGE
Broken Hill
NEW SOUTH WALES
Nymagee
Dubbo
Cessnock
Maitland
Newcastle

LORD HOWE I.
(NEW S. WALES)

MURRAY
RIVERINA REGION
Wentworth
Hay
Swan Hill
Forbes
West Wyalong
Orange
Bathurst
Lithgow
BLUE MTS.
SYDNEY
Botany Bay
Wollongong

Narrandera
Wagga Wagga
Goulburn
Jervis Bay
Albury
Canberra
AUSTL. CAP. TER.
SNOWY MTS.
Mt. Kosciusko 7310
Cooma
Bega
Bombala
CAPE HOWE

VICTORIA
Kerang
Echuca
Bendigo
Benalla
GREAT DIVIDING RANGE
Bairnsdale
NINETY MILE BEACH

Ararat
Maryborough
Ballarat
Geelong
MELBOURNE
Warrnambool
CAPE OTWAY
Port Phillip Bay
WILSON'S PROMONTORY

KING
HUNTER IS.
FURNEAUX GROUP
FLINDERS
CAPE BARREN
TASMANIA
Burnie
Ulverstone
Devonport
Mt. Ossa 5305
Launceston
Strahan
New Norfolk
Hobart
BRUNY
SOUTH EAST CAPE

TASMAN SEA

a

NEW ZEALAND

PACIFIC OCEAN
NORTH CAPE
Kaitaia
Russell
Devonport
Auckland
NORTH ISLAND
Hamilton
GREAT BARRIER
Bay of Plenty
EAST CAPE
Hauraki Gulf

North Taranaki Bight
New Plymouth
Mt. Egmont
C. EGMONT
South Taranaki Bight
Gisborne
Napier
Hastings
Wanganui
Palmerston North
Lower Hutt
Wellington

TASMAN SEA
CAPE FAREWELL
Tasman Bay
Karamea Bight
Nelson
Cook Strait
CAPE FOULWIND
Greymouth
Hokitika
SOUTH ISLAND
SOUTHERN ALPS
Mt. Cook 12,316
Pegasus Bay
Christchurch
Canterbury Bight
Timaru

CASCADE PT.
RESOLUTION ISLAND
Dunedin
CAPE SAUNDERS
Invercargill
STEWART ISLAND
SOUTHWEST CAPE
Foveaux Strait
PACIFIC OCEAN

Same scale as main map

0   50 100   200   300   400   500 Miles
0   100   200   400   600   800 Kilometers

Cities and Towns
0 to 50,000
50,000 to 500,000
500,000 to 1,000,000
1,000,000 and over

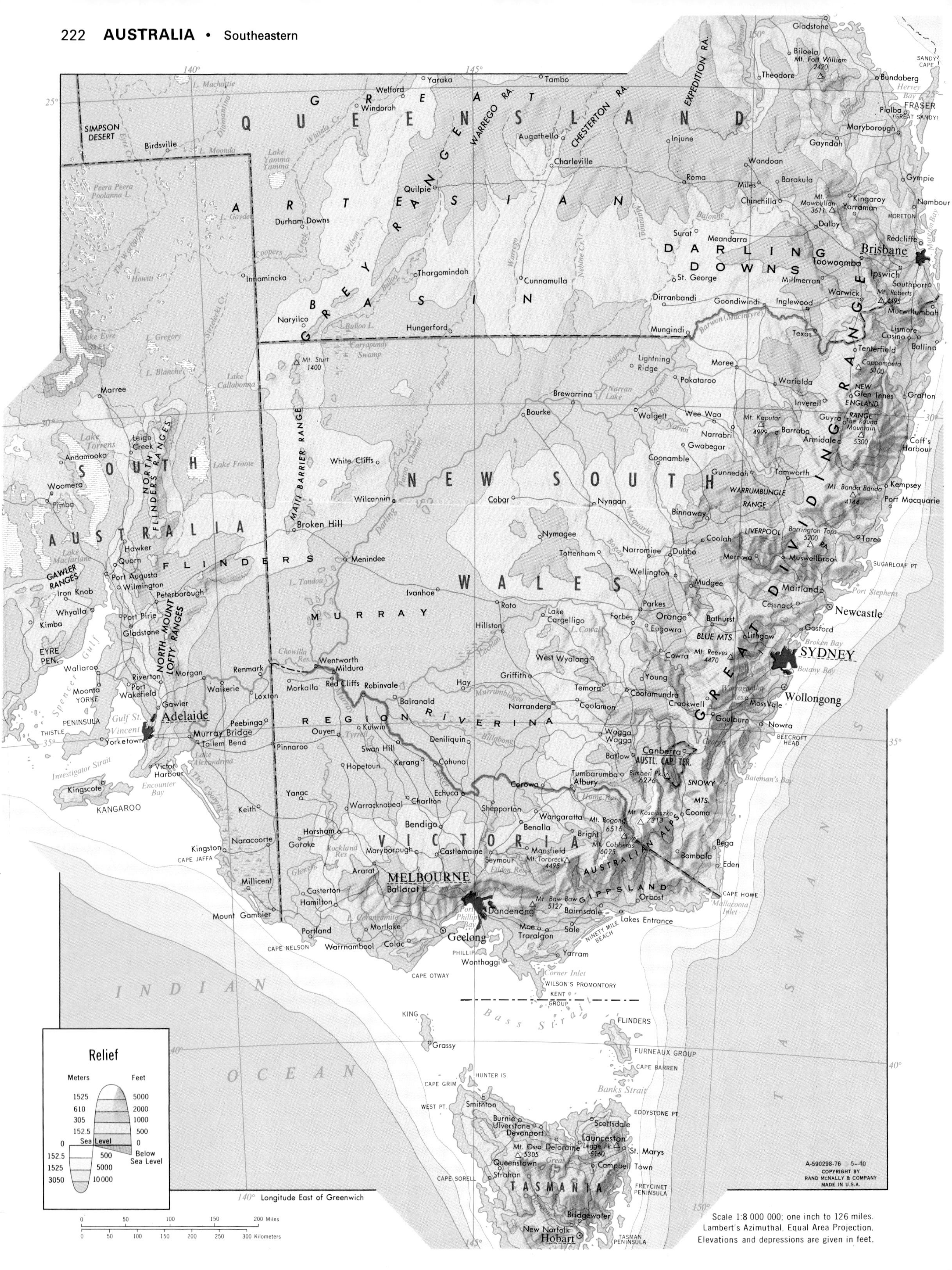
QUEENSLAND
GREAT ARTESIAN BASIN
GREY RANGE
WARREGO RA.
CHESTERTON RA.
EXPEDITION RA.
SIMPSON DESERT
DARLING DOWNS
SOUTH AUSTRALIA
NEW SOUTH WALES
VICTORIA
TASMANIA
FLINDERS RANGES
NORTH FLINDERS RANGES
NORTH MOUNT LOFTY RANGES
GAWLER RANGES
MAIN BARRIER RANGE
MURRAY
RIVERINA REGION
GREAT DIVIDING RANGE
NEW ENGLAND RANGE
LIVERPOOL RA.
WARRUMBUNGLE RANGE
BLUE MTS.
SNOWY MTS.
AUSTRALIAN ALPS
GIPPSLAND
AUSTL. CAP. TER.
INDIAN OCEAN
TASMAN SEA
Bass Strait
Banks Strait
Spencer Gulf
Gulf St. Vincent
Investigator Strait
Encounter Bay
Port Phillip Bay
Lake Eyre
Lake Torrens
Lake Frome
Lake Gairdner
Lake Callabonna
Lake Blanche
Lake Gregory
L. Machattie
Lake Yamma Yamma
L. Goyder
L. Howitt
L. Tandou
L. Cowal
Chowilla Res.
Caryapundy Swamp
Lake Alexandrina
Mt. Sturt 1400
Mt. Fort William 2420
Mt. Mowbullan 3611
Mt. Roberts 4495
Cappoompeta 5100
The Round Mountain 5300
Mt. Kaputar 4999
Mt. Banda Banda 4144
Barrington Tops 5200
Mt. Reeves 4470
Bimberi Pk. 6276
Mt. Kosciusko 7313
Mt. Bogong 6516
Mt. Cobberas 6025
Mt. Torbreck 4495
Mt. Baw Baw 5127
Mt. Ossa 5305
Legge Pk. 5160
Gladstone
Biloela
Theodore
Bundaberg
Maryborough
Gayndah
Gympie
Nambour
Kingaroy
Yarraman
Dalby
Redcliffe
Brisbane
Ipswich
Toowoomba
Southport
Warwick
Murwillumbah
Lismore
Casino
Ballina
Tenterfield
Grafton
Glen Innes
Inverell
Armidale
Coff's Harbour
Tamworth
Kempsey
Port Macquarie
Taree
Muswellbrook
Maitland
Newcastle
Gosford
SYDNEY
Wollongong
Nowra
Goulburn
Canberra
Cooma
Bega
Eden
Bombala
Birdsville
Windorah
Yaraka
Tambo
Augathella
Charleville
Injune
Roma
Wandoan
Miles
Chinchilla
Surat
Meandarra
St. George
Dirranbandi
Goondiwindi
Inglewood
Millmerran
Quilpie
Durham Downs
Innamincka
Thargomindah
Cunnamulla
Hungerford
Naryilco
Mungindi
Moree
Lightning Ridge
Brewarrina
Bourke
Walgett
Wee Waa
Narrabri
Gwabegar
Coonamble
Gunnedah
Coonabarabran
Binnaway
Coolah
Merriwa
Dubbo
Narromine
Wellington
Mudgee
Nyngan
Cobar
Nymagee
Tottenham
Parkes
Orange
Bathurst
Lithgow
Forbes
Eugowra
Cowra
Young
West Wyalong
Lake Cargelligo
Hillston
Griffith
Temora
Cootamundra
Crookwell
Wagga Wagga
Narrandera
Coolamon
Batlow
Tumbarumba
Albury
Corowa
Deniliquin
Hay
Roto
Ivanhoe
Menindee
Broken Hill
White Cliffs
Wilcannia
Wentworth
Mildura
Red Cliffs
Robinvale
Balranald
Morkalla
Ouyen
Kulwin
Swan Hill
Kerang
Cohuna
Echuca
Shepparton
Wangaratta
Benalla
Bright
Mansfield
Seymour
Bendigo
Castlemaine
Maryborough
Charlton
Warracknabeal
Hopetoun
Yanac
Horsham
Goroke
Ararat
Ballarat
MELBOURNE
Geelong
Dandenong
Colac
Mortlake
Warrnambool
Portland
Hamilton
Casterton
Mount Gambier
Millicent
Naracoorte
Kingston
Keith
Pinnaroo
Tailem Bend
Murray Bridge
Peebinga
Loxton
Waikerie
Renmark
Morgan
Adelaide
Gawler
Riverton
Port Wakefield
Moonta
Wallaroo
Yorketown
Victor Harbour
Kingscote
KANGAROO
Port Pirie
Gladstone
Peterborough
Port Augusta
Wilmington
Quorn
Hawker
Whyalla
Iron Knob
Kimba
Woomera
Pimba
Andamooka
Leigh Creek
Marree
Moe
Traralgon
Sale
Bairnsdale
Lakes Entrance
Orbost
Yarram
Wonthaggi
NINETY MILE BEACH
CAPE HOWE
CAPE OTWAY
CAPE NELSON
CAPE JAFFA
WILSON'S PROMONTORY
KENT GROUP
KING
Grassy
FLINDERS
FURNEAUX GROUP
CAPE BARREN
HUNTER IS.
CAPE GRIM
WEST PT.
EDDYSTONE PT.
Smithton
Burnie
Ulverstone
Devonport
Deloraine
Launceston
Scottsdale
St. Marys
Campbell Town
Queenstown
Strahan
CAPE SORELL
FREYCINET PENINSULA
Bridgewater
New Norfolk
Hobart
TASMAN PENINSULA
SANDY CAPE
FRASER (GREAT SANDY)
MORETON
SUGARLOAF PT
Port Stephens
Broken Bay
Botany Bay
BEECROFT HEAD
Bateman's Bay
EYRE PEN.
YORKE PENINSULA
THISTLE
Relief
Meters Feet
1525 5000
610 2000
305 1000
152.5 500
0 Sea Level 0
152.5 500 Below Sea Level
1525 5000
3050 10 000
140° Longitude East of Greenwich
0 50 100 150 200 Miles
0 50 100 150 200 250 300 Kilometers
A-590298-76 5-10
COPYRIGHT BY RAND McNALLY & COMPANY MADE IN U.S.A.
Scale 1:8 000 000; one inch to 126 miles.
Lambert's Azimuthal, Equal Area Projection.
Elevations and depressions are given in feet.

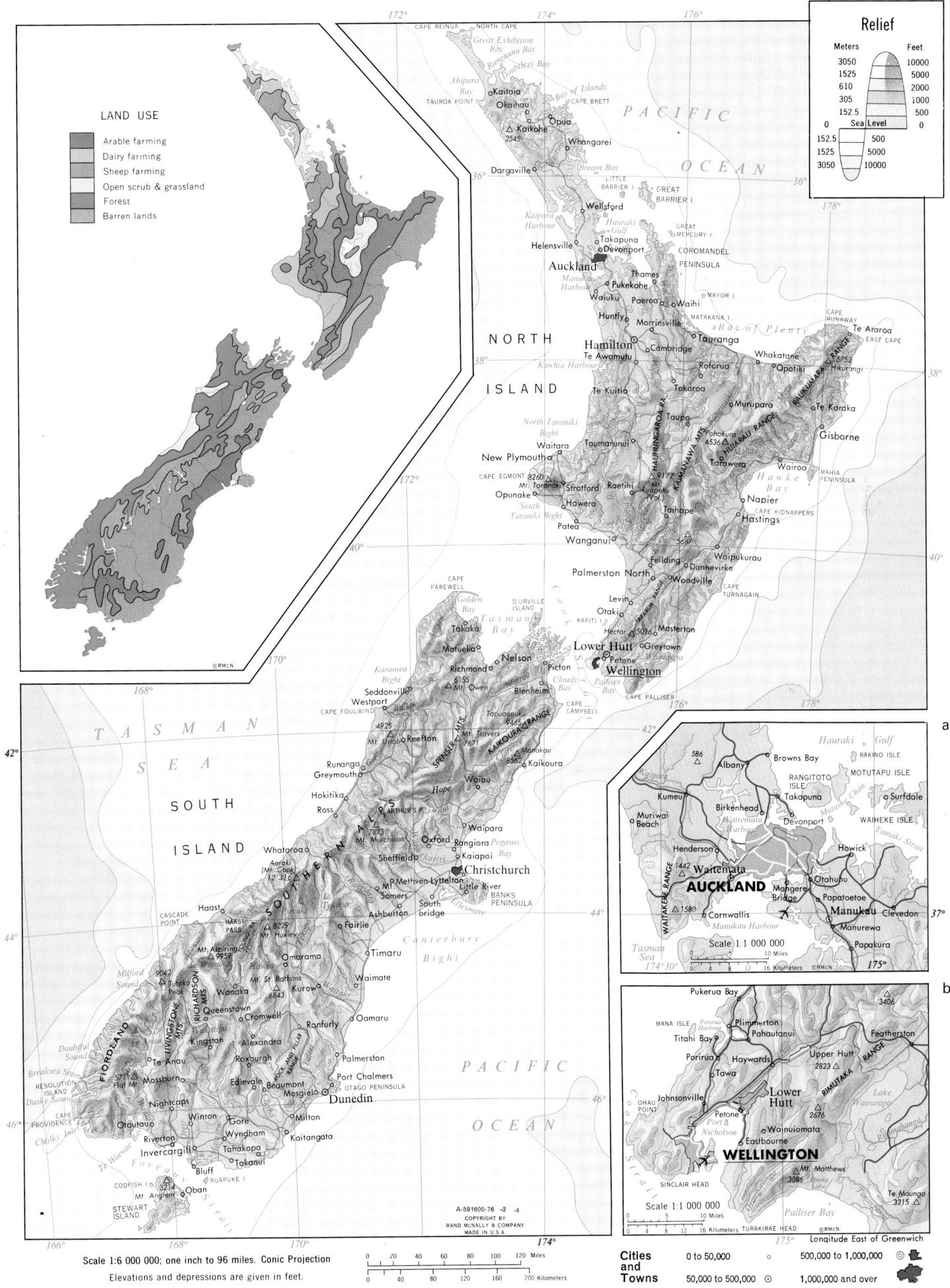

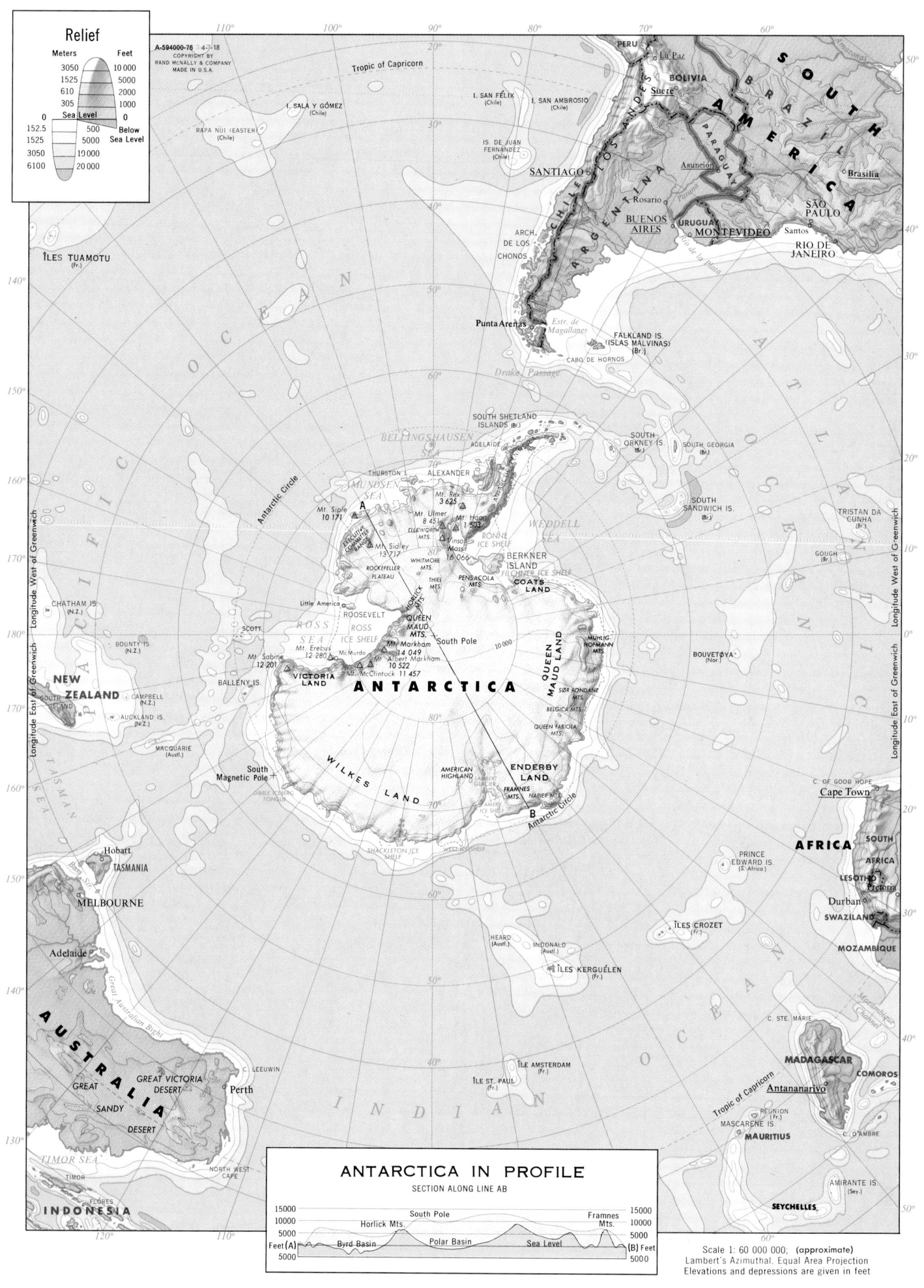

Relief

Meters		Feet
3050		10 000
1525		5000
610		2000
305		1000
0	Sea Level	0
152.5		500
1525		5000
3050		19 000
6100		20 000

A-594000-76 4-7-18
COPYRIGHT BY
RAND McNALLY & COMPANY
MADE IN U.S.A.

Tropic of Capricorn

SOUTH AMERICA

PERU
La Paz
BOLIVIA
Sucre
BRAZIL
PARAGUAY
Asunción
SANTIAGO
Rosario
São PAULO
Brasília
ARCH. DE LOS CHONOS
BUENOS AIRES
URUGUAY
MONTEVIDEO
RIO DE JANEIRO
Santos

I. SALA Y GÓMEZ (Chile)
RAPA NUI (EASTER) (Chile)
I. SAN FÉLIX (Chile)
I. SAN AMBROSIO (Chile)
IS. DE JUAN FERNÁNDEZ (Chile)

Punta Arenas
Estr. de Magallanes
FALKLAND IS. (ISLAS MALVINAS) (Br.)
CABO DE HORNOS

Drake Passage

ÎLES TUAMOTU (Fr.)

SOUTH SHETLAND ISLANDS (Br.)
Adelaide
BELLINGSHAUSEN SEA
AMUNDSEN SEA
Antarctic Circle

SOUTH ORKNEY IS. (Br.)
SOUTH GEORGIA (Br.)
SOUTH SANDWICH IS. (Br.)
WEDDELL SEA
TRISTAN DA CUNHA (Br.)
GOUGH (Br.)

THURSTON I.
ALEXANDER
Mt. Rex 3 625
Mt. Ulmer 8 451
Mt. Hagg 1 503
Mt. Siple 10 171
EXECUTIVE COMMITTEE RANGE
ELLSWORTH MTS.
Vinson Massif 16 066
Mt. Sidley 13 717
WHITMORE MTS.
ROCKEFELLER PLATEAU
THIEL MTS.
RONNE ICE SHELF
BERKNER ISLAND
FILCHNER ICE SHELF
PENSACOLA MTS.
COATS LAND

Little America
Scott
ROSS SEA
Roosevelt
ROSS ICE SHELF
HORLICK MTS.
QUEEN MAUD MTS.
CHATHAM IS. (N.Z.)
BOUNTY IS. (N.Z.)

BOUVETØYA (Nor.)

Mt. Sabine 12 201
Mt. Erebus 12 280
McMurdo
Mt. Markham 14 049
Mt. Albert Markham 10 522
Mt. McClintock 11 457
South Pole
VICTORIA LAND
BALLENY IS.
ANTARCTICA
QUEEN MAUD LAND
MÜHLIG-HOFMANN MTS.
SØR RONDANE MTS.
BELGICA MTS.
QUEEN FABIOLA MTS.

NEW ZEALAND
SOUTH ISLAND
CAMPBELL I. (N.Z.)
AUCKLAND IS. (N.Z.)
MACQUARIE (Austl.)
10 000

C. OF GOOD HOPE
Cape Town

South Magnetic Pole
AMERICAN HIGHLAND
LAMBERT GLACIER
ENDERBY LAND
FRAMNES MTS.
NAPIER MTS.
DIBBLE ICEBERG TONGUE
WILKES LAND

Antarctic Circle

PRINCE EDWARD IS. (S. Africa)

AFRICA
SOUTH AFRICA
LESOTHO
Pretoria
Durban
SWAZILAND
MOZAMBIQUE

Hobart
TASMANIA
MELBOURNE
SHACKLETON ICE SHELF
WEST ICE SHELF
TASMAN SEA

ÎLES CROZET (Fr.)

Adelaide
HEARD (Austl.)
McDONALD (Austl.)
ÎLES KERGUÉLEN (Fr.)

C. LEEUWIN
GREAT VICTORIA DESERT
Perth
AUSTRALIA
GREAT SANDY DESERT

ÎLE AMSTERDAM (Fr.)
ÎLE ST. PAUL (Fr.)

Tropic of Capricorn
RÉUNION (Fr.)
MASCARENE (Fr.)
MAURITIUS
C. D'AMBRE

MADAGASCAR
COMOROS
Antananarivo

TIMOR SEA
NORTH WEST CAPE
TIMOR
FLORES
INDONESIA

INDIAN OCEAN

AMIRANTE IS. (Sey.)
SEYCHELLES

ANTARCTICA IN PROFILE
SECTION ALONG LINE AB

15000	South Pole	15000
10000	Horlick Mts.	Framnes Mts. 10000
5000		5000
Feet (A)	Byrd Basin Polar Basin Sea Level	(B) Feet
5000		5000

Scale 1: 60 000 000; (approximate)
Lambert's Azimuthal, Equal Area Projection
Elevations and depressions are given in feet

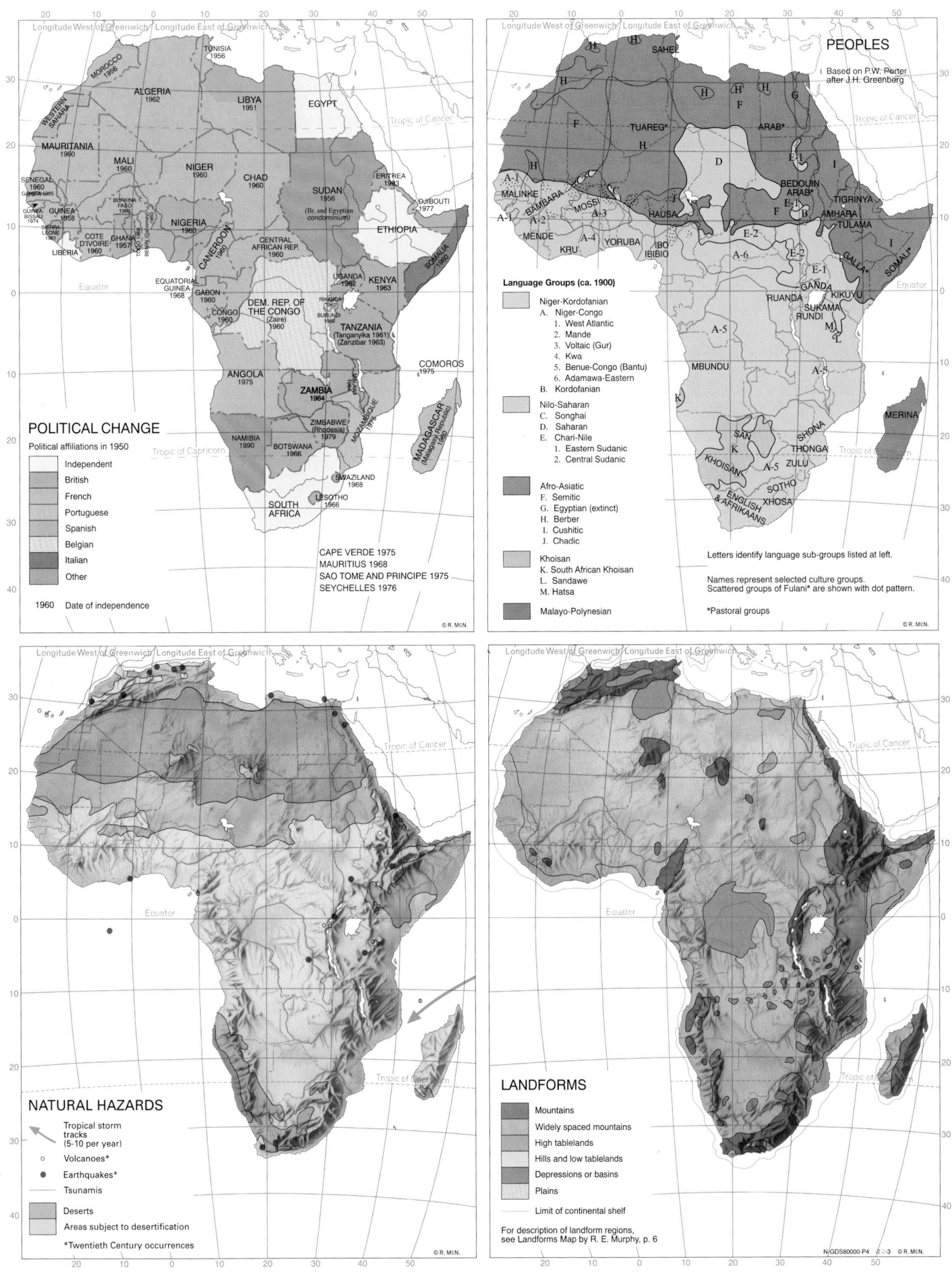

POLITICAL CHANGE

Political affiliations in 1950

- Independent
- British
- French
- Portuguese
- Spanish
- Belgian
- Italian
- Other

1960   Date of independence

CAPE VERDE 1975
MAURITIUS 1968
SAO TOME AND PRINCIPE 1975
SEYCHELLES 1976

TUNISIA 1956
MOROCCO 1956
ALGERIA 1962
LIBYA 1951
EGYPT
WESTERN SAHARA
MAURITANIA 1960
MALI 1960
NIGER 1960
CHAD 1960
SUDAN 1956 (Br. and Egyptian condominium)
ERITREA 1993
DJIBOUTI 1977
SENEGAL 1960
GAMBIA 1965
GUINEA BISSAU 1974
GUINEA 1958
BURKINA FASO 1960
SIERRA LEONE 1961
COTE D'IVOIRE 1960
GHANA 1957
TOGO 1960
BENIN (Dahomey) 1960
NIGERIA 1960
CAMEROON 1960
CENTRAL AFRICAN REP. 1960
ETHIOPIA
SOMALIA 1960
LIBERIA
EQUATORIAL GUINEA 1968
GABON 1960
CONGO 1960
DEM. REP. OF THE CONGO (Zaire) 1960
RWANDA 1962
BURUNDI 1962
UGANDA 1962
KENYA 1963
TANZANIA (Tanganyika 1961) (Zanzibar 1963)
COMOROS 1975
ANGOLA 1975
ZAMBIA 1964
MALAWI 1964
ZIMBABWE (Rhodesia) 1979
MOZAMBIQUE 1975
MADAGASCAR (Malagasy Republic) 1960
NAMIBIA 1990
BOTSWANA 1966
SWAZILAND 1968
LESOTHO 1966
SOUTH AFRICA

PEOPLES

Based on P.W. Porter after J.H. Greenberg

Language Groups (ca. 1900)

Niger-Kordofanian
A. Niger-Congo
    1. West Atlantic
    2. Mande
    3. Voltaic (Gur)
    4. Kwa
    5. Benue-Congo (Bantu)
    6. Adamawa-Eastern
B. Kordofanian

Nilo-Saharan
C. Songhai
D. Saharan
E. Chari-Nile
    1. Eastern Sudanic
    2. Central Sudanic

Afro-Asiatic
F. Semitic
G. Egyptian (extinct)
H. Berber
I. Cushitic
J. Chadic

Khoisan
K. South African Khoisan
L. Sandawe
M. Hatsa

Malayo-Polynesian

Letters identify language sub-groups listed at left.

Names represent selected culture groups.
Scattered groups of Fulani* are shown with dot pattern.

*Pastoral groups

SAHEL
TUAREG*
ARAB*
BEDOUIN ARAB*
TIGRINYA
AMHARA
TULAMA
GALLA*
SOMALI*
MALINKE
BAMBARA
MOSSI
HAUSA
MENDE
KRU
YORUBA
IBO
IBIBIO
RUANDA
GANDA
KIKUYU
SUKAMA
RUNDI
MBUNDU
SAN
SHONA
KHOISAN
THONGA
ZULU
SOTHO
XHOSA
ENGLISH & AFRIKAANS
MERINA

NATURAL HAZARDS

→ Tropical storm tracks (5–10 per year)
○ Volcanoes*
● Earthquakes*
— Tsunamis
   Deserts
   Areas subject to desertification

*Twentieth Century occurrences

LANDFORMS

- Mountains
- Widely spaced mountains
- High tablelands
- Hills and low tablelands
- Depressions or basins
- Plains

— Limit of continental shelf

For description of landform regions,
see Landforms Map by R. E. Murphy, p. 6

N/GDS80000-P4   22-3   © R. McN.

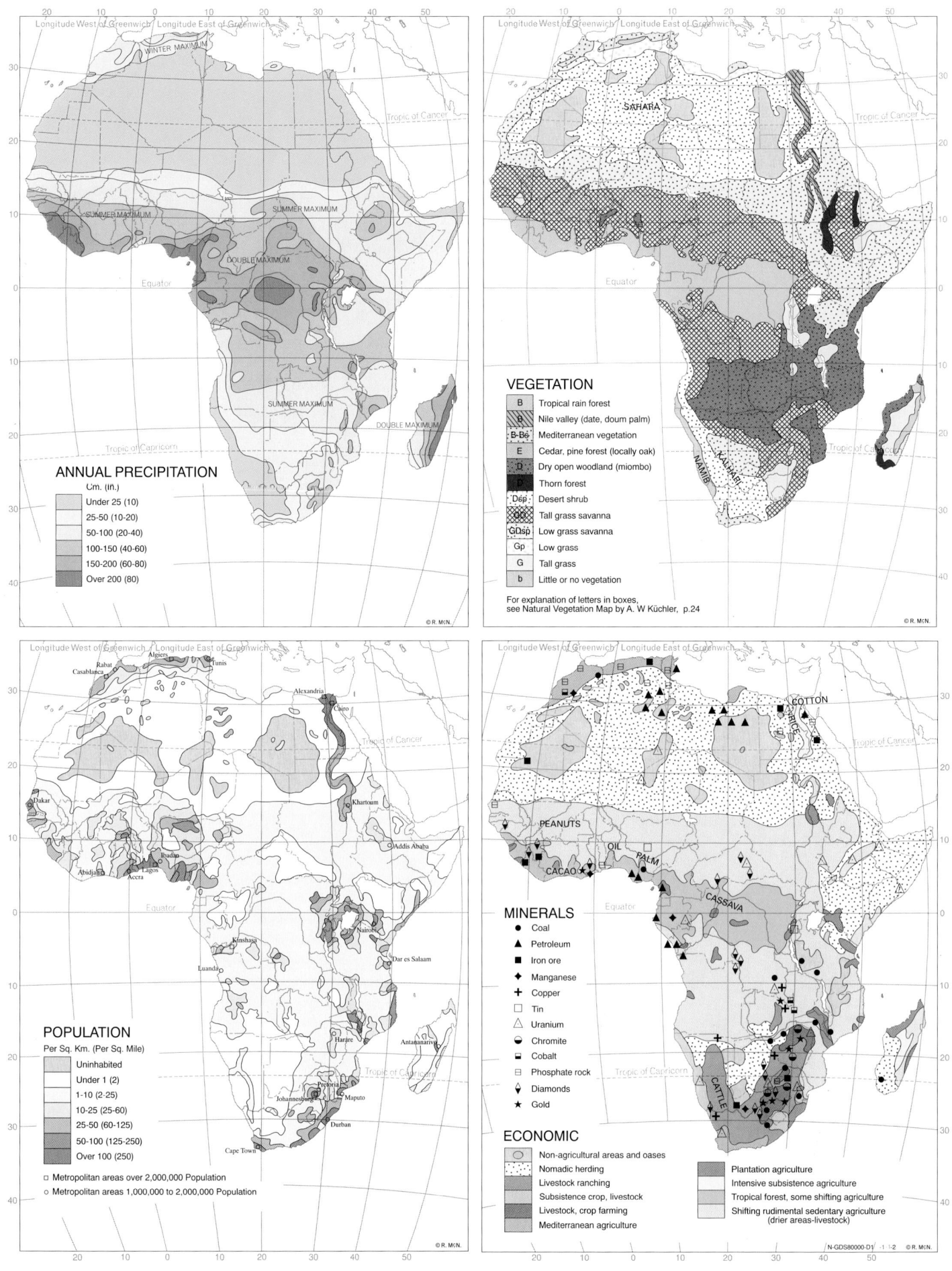

ANNUAL PRECIPITATION

Cm. (In.)

- Under 25 (10)
- 25-50 (10-20)
- 50-100 (20-40)
- 100-150 (40-60)
- 150-200 (60-80)
- Over 200 (80)

VEGETATION

B	Tropical rain forest
B	Nile valley (date, doum palm)
B-Be	Mediterranean vegetation
E	Cedar, pine forest (locally oak)
D	Dry open woodland (miombo)
P	Thorn forest
Dsp	Desert shrub
GD	Tall grass savanna
GDsp	Low grass savanna
Gp	Low grass
G	Tall grass
b	Little or no vegetation

For explanation of letters in boxes,
see Natural Vegetation Map by A. W Küchler, p.24

POPULATION

Per Sq. Km. (Per Sq. Mile)

- Uninhabited
- Under 1 (2)
- 1-10 (2-25)
- 10-25 (25-60)
- 25-50 (60-125)
- 50-100 (125-250)
- Over 100 (250)

□ Metropolitan areas over 2,000,000 Population
○ Metropolitan areas 1,000,000 to 2,000,000 Population

MINERALS

- ● Coal
- ▲ Petroleum
- ■ Iron ore
- ◆ Manganese
- + Copper
- □ Tin
- △ Uranium
- ◐ Chromite
- ⬓ Cobalt
- ⊟ Phosphate rock
- ⬦ Diamonds
- ★ Gold

ECONOMIC

- Non-agricultural areas and oases
- Nomadic herding
- Livestock ranching
- Subsistence crop, livestock
- Livestock, crop farming
- Mediterranean agriculture
- Plantation agriculture
- Intensive subsistence agriculture
- Tropical forest, some shifting agriculture
- Shifting rudimental sedentary agriculture (drier areas-livestock)

N-GDS80000-D1 -1 1-2   © R. McN.

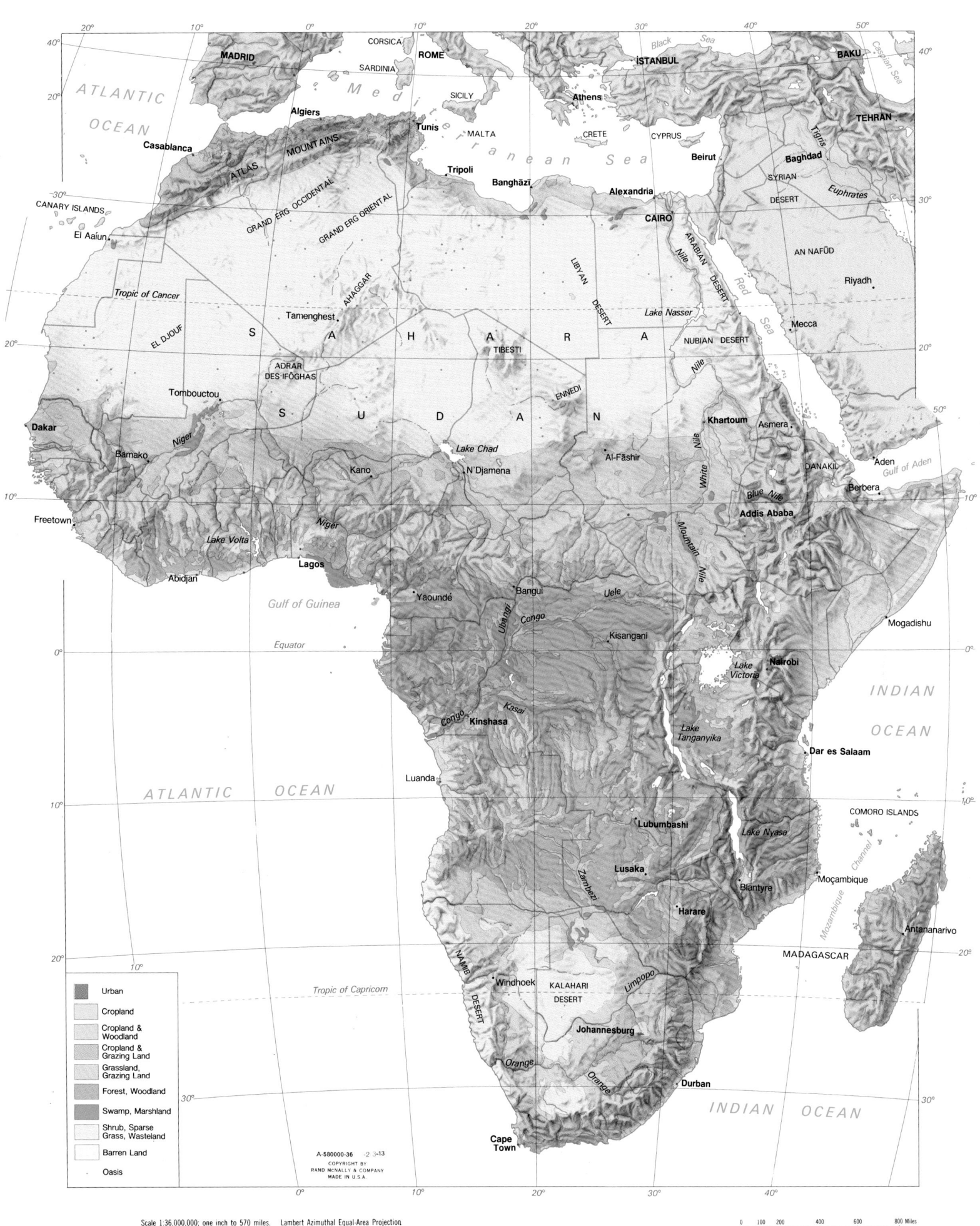

ATLANTIC OCEAN

Mediterranean Sea

MADRID

ROME

CORSICA

SARDINIA

Black Sea

İSTANBUL

BAKU

Caspian Sea

Athens

TEHRĀN

Algiers

Tunis

SICILY

MALTA

CRETE

CYPRUS

Beirut

Baghdad

Tigris

SYRIAN DESERT

Euphrates

Casablanca

ATLAS MOUNTAINS

Tripoli

Banghāzī

Alexandria

CAIRO

ARABIAN DESERT

AN NAFŪD

CANARY ISLANDS

GRAND ERG OCCIDENTAL

GRAND ERG ORIENTAL

LIBYAN DESERT

Nile

Red Sea

Riyadh

El Aaíun

Tropic of Cancer

Lake Nasser

Mecca

EL DJOUF

S   A   H   A   R   A

AHAGGAR

Tamenghest

TIBESTI

NUBIAN DESERT

Nile

Tombouctou

ADRAR DES IFÓGHAS

S   U   D   A   N

ENNEDI

Khartoum

Asmera

DANAKIL

Aden

Gulf of Aden

Dakar

Niger

Al-Fāshir

Nile

White

Blue Nile

Berbera

Bamako

Kano

Lake Chad

N'Djamena

Addis Ababa

Freetown

Niger

Lake Volta

Lagos

Abidjan

Gulf of Guinea

Yaoundé

Bangui

Uele

Mountain Nile

Mogadishu

Equator

Ubangi

Congo

Kisangani

Lake Victoria

Nairobi

INDIAN OCEAN

Congo

Kasai

Kinshasa

Lake Tanganyika

Dar es Salaam

Luanda

ATLANTIC OCEAN

Lubumbashi

Lake Nyasa

COMORO ISLANDS

Lusaka

Zambezi

Blantyre

Moçambique

Harare

Mozambique Channel

MADAGASCAR

Antananarivo

NAMIB DESERT

Windhoek

KALAHARI DESERT

Limpopo

Tropic of Capricorn

Johannesburg

Orange

Orange

Durban

INDIAN OCEAN

Cape Town

Legend:
- Urban
- Cropland
- Cropland & Woodland
- Cropland & Grazing Land
- Grassland, Grazing Land
- Forest, Woodland
- Swamp, Marshland
- Shrub, Sparse Grass, Wasteland
- Barren Land
- Oasis

A-580000-36   -2 3-13
COPYRIGHT BY
RAND McNALLY & COMPANY
MADE IN U.S.A.

Scale 1:36,000,000; one inch to 570 miles.   Lambert Azimuthal Equal-Area Projection

0   100   200   400   600   800 Miles

0   150   300   600   900   1200 Kilometers

Scale 1:40 000 000; one inch to 630 miles. Lambert's Azimuthal, Equal Area Projection
Elevations and depressions are given in feet.

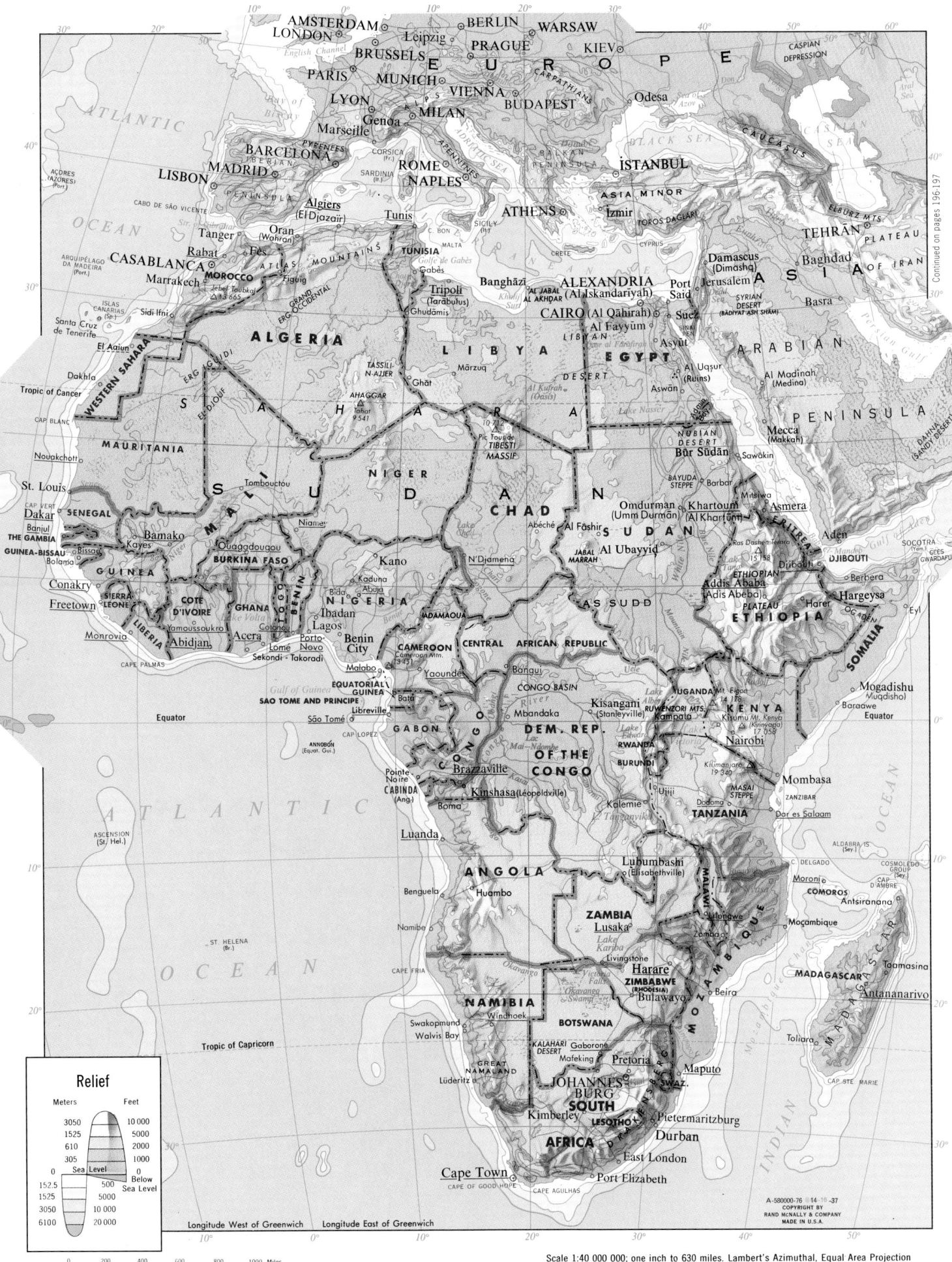

Continued on pages 196-197

Relief

Meters	Feet
3050	10 000
1525	5000
610	2000
305	1000
0 Sea Level	0 Below Sea Level
152.5	500
1525	5000
3050	10 000
6100	20 000

Longitude West of Greenwich   Longitude East of Greenwich

| 0 | 200 | 400 | 600 | 800 | 1000 Miles |
| 0 | 400 | | 800 | 1200 | 1600 Kilometers |

Scale 1:40 000 000; one inch to 630 miles. Lambert's Azimuthal, Equal Area Projection
Elevations and depressions are given in feet.

A-580000-76 14-16-37
COPYRIGHT BY
RAND McNALLY & COMPANY
MADE IN U.S.A.

a

Continued on pages 156-157

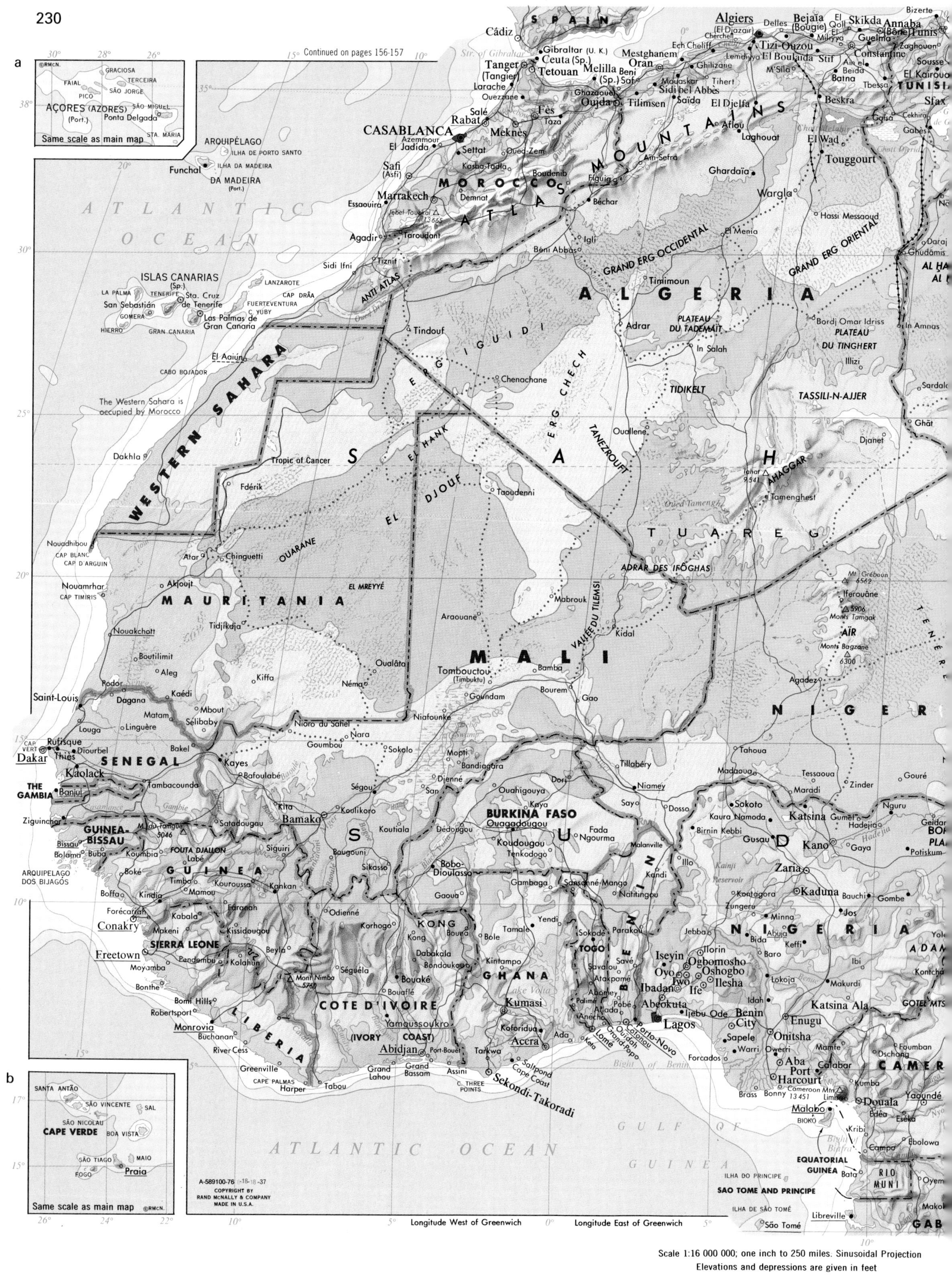

AÇORES (AZORES) (Port.)

GRACIOSA
FAIAL
PICO
TERCEIRA
SÃO JORGE
SÃO MIGUEL
Ponta Delgada
STA. MARIA

Same scale as main map

ARQUIPÉLAGO
ILHA DE PORTO SANTO
Funchal
ILHA DA MADEIRA
DA MADEIRA (Port.)

A T L A N T I C

O C E A N

ISLAS CANARIAS (Sp.)

LA PALMA
TENERIFE
San Sebastián
Sta. Cruz de Tenerife
LANZAROTE
CAP DRÂA
C. YÚBY
FUERTEVENTURA
GOMERA
Las Palmas de Gran Canaria
HIERRO
GRAN CANARIA

CABO BOJADOR

The Western Sahara is occupied by Morocco.

Tropic of Cancer

WESTERN SAHARA

El Aaiún

Dakhla

Fdérik

Nouadhibou
CAP BLANC
CAP D'ARGUIN

Atar
Chinguetti

Nouamhar
CAP TIMIRIS

Akjoujt

M A U R I T A N I A

Tidjikdja

Nouakchott

Boutilimit
Aleg

Kiffa

Kaédi

Saint-Louis

Rosso
Dagana

Matam
Louga
Sélibaby

CAP VERT
Rufisque
Dakar
Thiès
Diourbel
Linguère

Kaolack

SENEGAL

Bakel

THE GAMBIA
Banjul

Kayes
Bafoulabé

Ziguinchor

GUINEA-BISSAU

Bissau
Bolama
Buba

ARQUIPÉLAGO DOS BIJAGÓS

Boké
Boffa

GUINEA

Kindia

Forécariah
Conakry

Freetown

Moyamba

SIERRA LEONE

Bonthe

Bomi Hills
Robertsport

Monrovia
Buchanan

River Cess

LIBERIA

Greenville

Harper
CAPE PALMAS
Tabou

A T L A N T I C   O C E A N

b

CAPE VERDE

SANTA ANTÃO
SÃO VICENTE
SAL
SÃO NICOLAU
BOA VISTA
SÃO TIAGO
MAIO
FOGO
Praia

Same scale as main map

S P A I N

Cádiz
Str. of Gibraltar
Gibraltar (U.K.)
Tanger (Tangier)
Larache
Ceuta (Sp.)
Tetouan
Melilla (Sp.)
Beni Saf
Salé
Rabat
Fès
Taza
CASABLANCA
El Jadida
Azemmour
Settat
Meknès
Oued-Zem
Kasba-Tadla
Safi (Asfi)
Boudenib
MOROCCO
Marrakech
Demnat
Essaouira
Jebel Toubkal 13665
Agadir
Taroudant
Sidi Ifni
Tiznit
ANTI ATLAS
CAP DRÂA

Oujda
Tilimsen
Saïda
El Djelfa
Aflou
Laghouat
Béchar
Figuig
Aïn-Sefra
Ghardaïa
El Menia

ALGERIA

Algiers (El Djazair)
Delles
Bejaïa (Bougie)
El Kseur
Skikda
Annaba
Bône
Tunis
TUNISIA
Oran
Mostghanem
Constantine
Sétif
Batna
Tébessa
Sousse
Sfax
Gabès
El Wad
Touggourt
Wargla
Hassi Messaoud
Bordj Omar Idriss
In Amnas
PLATEAU DU TINGHERT
Illizi
TASSILI-N-AJJER
Ghât
Djanet

GRAND ERG OCCIDENTAL
GRAND ERG ORIENTAL
Timimoun
Adrar
PLATEAU DU TADEMAÏT
In Salah
Chenachane
TIDIKELT
Ouallene

S A H A R A

ERG IGUIDI
ERG CHECH
TANEZROUFT
EL HANK
EL DJOUF
Taoudenni
Oued Tamanrasset
Tahat 9541 AHAGGAR
Tamanghest

T U A R E G

ADRAR DES IFÔGHAS
Mt. Gréboun 6562
Iferouâne 5906
Monts Tamgak
AÏR
Monts Bagzane 6300
Agadez
TÉNÉRÉ

Tindouf

Taoudenni

Mabrouk

Araouane

VALLÉE DU TILEMSI

Kidal

M A L I

Bamba
Tombouctou (Timbuktu)
Goundam
Bourem
Gao
Niafunké

N I G E R

Tidjikdja

EL MREYYÉ

OUARANE

Oualâta

Néma

Nioro du Sahel

Nara
Goumbou
Sokolo

Tahoua
Tillabéry
Madaoua
Tessaoua
Goure
Zinder
Maradi
Sokoto
Katsina
Gumel
Nguru
Hadejia
Kano
Gusau
Gaya
Zaria
Kaduna
Bauchi
Gombe
Potiskum

Bandiagara
Mopti
Djenné
Ségou
San
Koutiala
Bobo-Dioulasso
Ouahigouya
Kaya
Niamey
Dosso
Dédougou
BURKINA FASO
Ouagadougou
Fada Ngourma
Tenkodogo
Tillabéry
Malanville
Birnin Kebbi
Kandi
Illo
Kainji Reservoir
Kontagora
Zungeru
Minna
Abuja
Jos
N I G E R I A
ADAMA

Kita
Bamako
Koulikoro
Bougouni
Sikasso

Satadougou
Siguiri
Kouroussa
Kankan
Odienné
Korhogo
KONG
Kong
Bouna
Dabakala
Bondoukou
Kintampo
Tamale
Yendi
Sokodé
Parakou
TOGO
Iseyin
Oyo
Ilorin
Ogbomosho
Oshogbo
Ilesha
Iwo
Ibadan
Ife
Lokoja
Makurdi
Katsina Ala
GOTEL MTS.
Keffi
Baro
Ibi

GUINEA

Timbo
FOUTA DJALLON
Labé
Mamou
Dalaba
M. du Tamgué 5046
Kindia
Kabala
Kissidougou
Beyla
Mt. Nimba 5748
Séguéla
Bouaké
Bouaflé
COTE D'IVOIRE (IVORY COAST)
Gagnoa
Yamoussoukro
Abidjan
Port-Bouet

Faranah
Koidu
Macenta

Pendembu
Kolahun

Zinguinchor

Gambaga
Natitingou
Bole
Salaga
GHANA
Kumasi
Koforidua
Accra
Tarkwa
Takoradi
Ada
Keta
Lomé
Anecho
Grand-Popo
Cotonou
Porto-Novo
Lagos
Benin City
Sapele
Warri
Forcados
Brass
Bonny
Calabar
Aba
Port Harcourt
Owerri
Enugu
Onitsha
CAMER
Mamfe
Kumba
Yaoundé
Malabo
BIOKO
Douala
Edéa
Eséka
Kribi

Bight of Benin

G U L F   O F   G U I N E A

Grand Bassam
Assini
C. THREE POINTS
Cape Coast
Sekondi-Takoradi
Salpond

Grand Lahou

EQUATORIAL GUINEA
Bata
RIO MUNI
SÃO TOME AND PRINCIPE
ILHA DO PRINCIPE
ILHA DE SÃO TOMÉ
São Tomé
Libreville
GAB

Cameroon Mtn. 13451
Ebolowa
Oyem
Campo

A T L A N T I C   O C E A N

Longitude West of Greenwich

Longitude East of Greenwich

Scale 1:16 000 000; one inch to 250 miles. Sinusoidal Projection
Elevations and depressions are given in feet

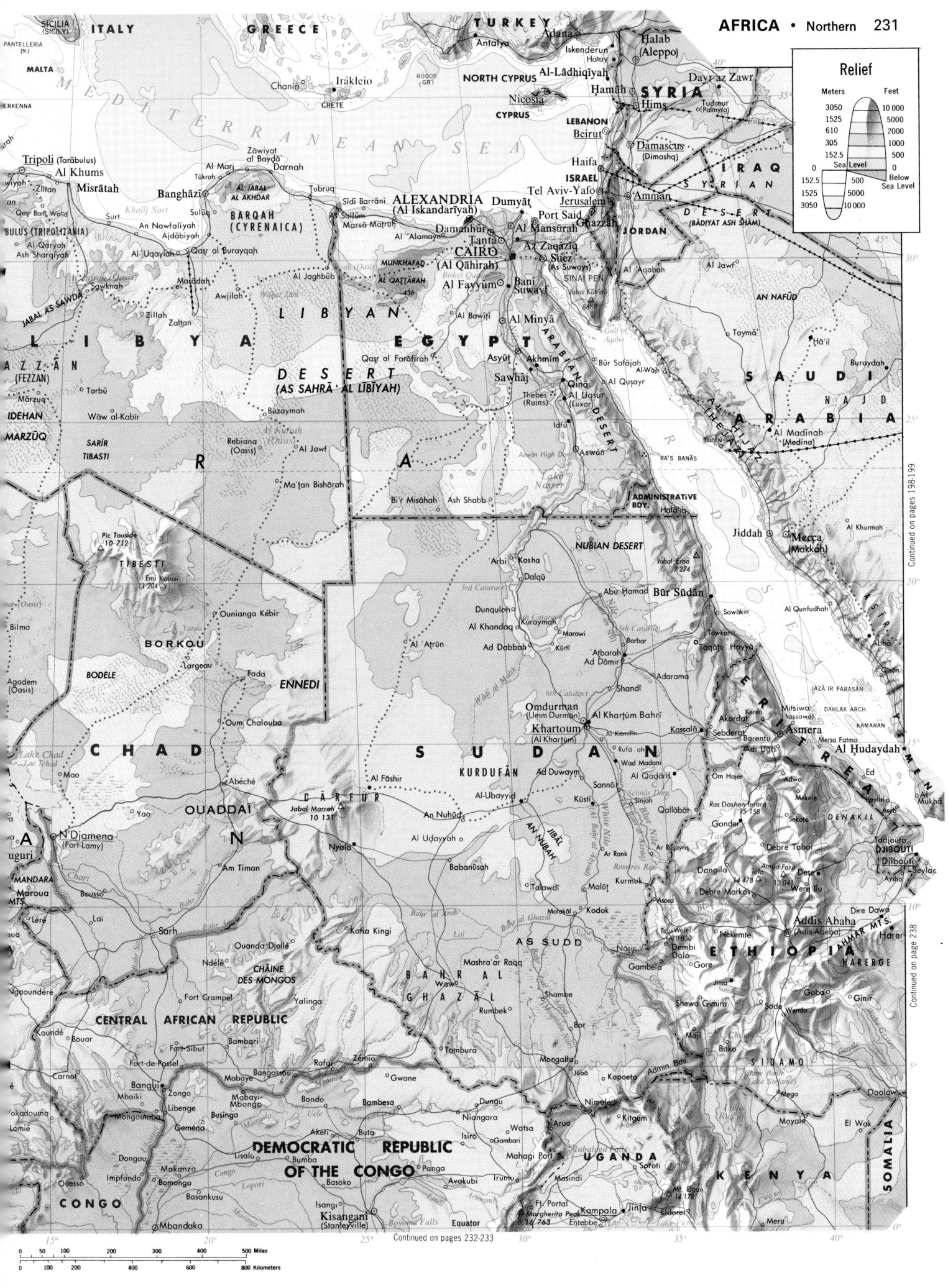

Relief

Meters	Feet
3050	10 000
1525	5000
610	2000
305	1000
152.5	500
0 Sea Level	0
152.5	500
1525	5000 Below
3050	10 000 Sea Level

SICILIA (SICILY) ITALY
PANTELLERIA (It.)
MALTA
ERKENNA
GREECE
TURKEY
Chania CRETE
RODOS (GR)
NORTH CYPRUS
Nicosia
CYPRUS
Antalya
Adana
Iskenderun
Hatay
Al-Lādhiqīyah
Halab (Aleppo)
Ḥamāh
SYRIA
Dayr az Zawr
Tudmur (Palmyra)
Ḥimṣ
LEBANON
Beirut
Damascus (Dimashq)
SYRIAN DESERT (BĀDIYAT ASH SHĀM)
IRAQ
Al Jawf
Haifa
Tel Aviv-Yafo
Jerusalem
ISRAEL
Amman
JORDAN
Al 'Aqabah
MEDITERRANEAN SEA
Tripoli (Tarābulus)
Al Khums
Misrātah
Zlitan
Qaṣr Bin Walīd
Banghāzī
AL JABAL AL AKHDAR
Zāwiyat al Bayḍā
Darnah
Ṭūbruq
Sīdī Barrānī
As Sallūm
Marsá Maṭrūḥ
ALEXANDRIA (Al Iskandarīyah)
Dumyāṭ
Port Said
Ghazzah
El 'Alamayn
Damanhūr
Tanṭā
Al Manṣūrah
Az Zaqāzīq
CAIRO (Al Qāhirah)
Suez (As Suways)
SINAI PEN.
Jabal Kātrīn 8668
AN NAFŪD
Ṭaymā'
Ḥā'il
Buraydah
SAUDI ARABIA
NAJD
Surt
Khalīj Surt
Ajdābiyah
An Nawfalīyah
Al 'Uqaylah
Qaṣr al Burayqah
Marādah
Awjilah
Al Jaghbūb
Siwa (Oasis)
MUNKHAFAD AL QAṬṬĀRAH -436
Birket Qārūn
Al Fayyūm
Banī Suwayf
Al Minyā
ARABIAN DESERT
Bür Safājah
Al-Wajh
Al Madīnah (Medina)
BARQAH (CYRENAICA)
LIBYA
Dawnah
Zillah
Zaltan
JABAL AS SAWDĀ
LIBYAN DESERT (AS SAHRĀ' AL LĪBĪYAH)
Qaṣr al Farāfirah
Asyūṭ
Akhmīm
Sawhāj
Thebes (Ruins)
Qinā
Al Uqṣur (Luxor)
Idfū
Aswān
Aswān High Dam
Al Quṣayr
RA'S BANĀS
Yanbu'
FEZZAN
Tarbū
Marzūq
Wāw al-Kabīr
SARĪR TIBASTI
Rebiana (Oasis)
Al Jawf
Ma'tan Bishārah
Bi'r Misāhah
Ash Shabb
Lake Nasser
ADMINISTRATIVE BDY.
Ḥalā'ib
Jiddah
Mecca (Makkah)
Al Khurmah
IDEHAN MARZŪQ
ÁZZĀN
SAHA RA
Buzaymah
Al Kufrah (Oasis)
Pic Touside 10 712
TIBESTI
Emi Koussi 11 204
BORKOU
Largeau
Fada
ENNEDI
Ounianga Kébir
Al 'Aṭrūn
Arbi
Kosha
Dalgū
3rd Cataract
Dunqulah
Al Khandaq
Ad Dabbah
Kuraymah
Marawi
4th Cataract
Kürtī
Abū Ḥamad
5th Cataract
Atbarah
Ad Dāmir
Barbar
Bür Sūdān
Sawākin
NUBIAN DESERT
Jabal Erba 7274
Al Qunfudhah
Abhā
Bilma
Agadem (Oasis)
BODELE
Oum Chalouba
CHAD
Mao
Abéché
DARFUR
Jabal Marrah 10 131
Al Fāshir
Nyala
KURDUFĀN
Al-Ubayyiḍ
An Nuhūd
Al Udayyah
Babanūsah
AN NUBAH
JIBĀL NUBAH
SUDAN
Wādī al Malik
Shandī
6th Cataract
Omdurman (Umm Durman)
Khartoum (Al Khartūm)
Al Khartūm Baḥrī
Al Kāmilīn
Rufa'ah
Wad Madanī
Ad Duwaym
Sannār
Al Qaḍārif
ERITREA
Kassalā
Sebderat
Barentu
Adi Ugrī
Akordat
Mitsiwa (Massawa)
DAHLAK ARCH.
KAMARAN
Asmera
Al Ḥudaydah
YEMEN
Al Mukhā
JAZĀ'IR FARASAN
N'Djamena (Fort-Lamy)
Maroua
MANDARA MTS.
Bousso
Lai
Ndélé
CHAÎNE DES MONGOS
Yalinga
Am Timan
Nyala
Talawdī
Kūstī
Sinjah
Sennār Dam
Qallābāt
Gonder
Om Hajer
Adwa
Mekele
Ras Dashen Terara 15 158
Sekota
Dese
Wera Ilu
Asosa
Kurmuk
Malūṭ
Rank
Malakāl
Kodok
AS SUDD
Mashra'ar Raqq
Waw
Rumbek
Shambe
Bor
BAHR AL GHAZĀL
Ouanda Djallé
Zémio
Yalinga
Rafai
Tambura
Nāṣir
Gambela
Jima
SIDAMO
Goba
Ginir
Dangila
Debre Tabor
Debre Markos
Addis Ababa (Ādīs Ābeba)
AHMAR MTS.
HARERGE
Harer
Dire Dawa
ETHIOPIA
Shewa Gimira
Sode
Wenda
Maji
Bako
CENTRAL AFRICAN REPUBLIC
Koundé
Bouar
Carnot
Fort-Sibut
Bambari
Bangassou
Mobaye
Bangui
Mongala
Jūba
Kapoeta
Admin. Bdy.
Shew Bahir Lake Stefanie
Mega
Moyale
El Wak
SOMALIA
DEMOCRATIC REPUBLIC OF THE CONGO
CONGO
Mbandaka
Dongou
Impfondo
Bomongo
Lisala
Bumba
Basankusu
Isangani
Kisangani (Stanleyville)
Boyoma Falls
Akeli
Buta
Panga
Avakubi
Niangara
Watsa
Gombari
Isiro
Mahagi Port
UGANDA
Arua
Nimule
Masindi
Soroti
Jinja
Kampala
Entebbe
Ft. Portal
Margherita Peak 16 763
Mt. Elgon 14 178
Eldoret
KENYA
Meru
Equator

Continued on pages 198-199
Continued on page 238
Continued on pages 232-233

0 50 100 200 300 400 500 Miles
0 100 200 400 600 800 Kilometers

Continued on pages 230-231

Scale 1:16 000 000; one inch to 250 miles. Sinusoidal Projection
Elevations and depressions are given in feet

b

c

Scale 1:1 000 000

Scale 1:4 000 000

Longitude East of Greenwich

Relief

Meters		Feet
3050		10 000
1525		5000
610		2000
305		1000
152.5		500
0	Sea Level	0
152.5		500
1525		5000
3050		10 000

234

Scale 1:10,000,000; one inch to 160 miles. Lambert Azimuthal Equal Area Projection
Elevations and depressions are given in feet.

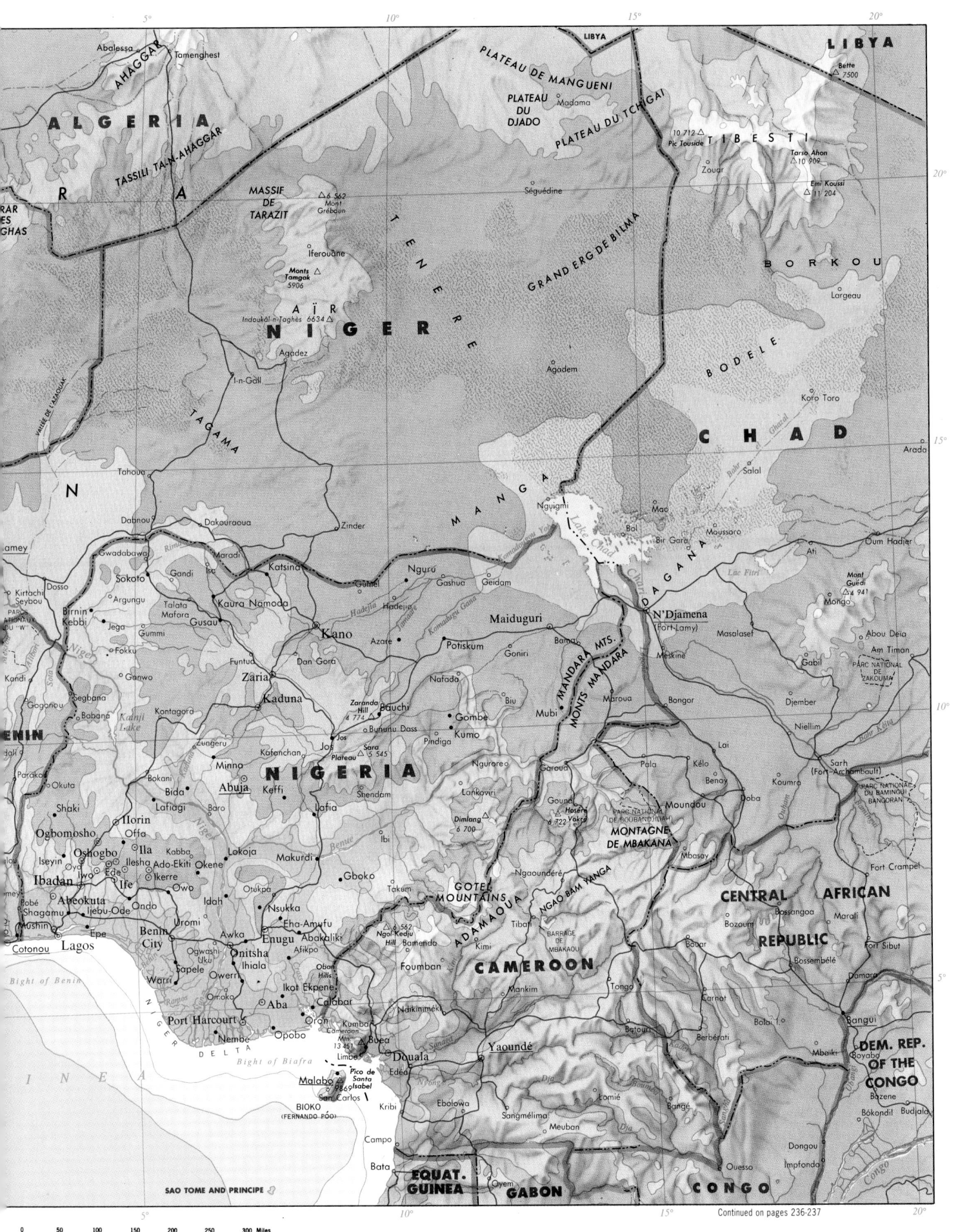

Abalessa
AHAGGAR
Tamenghest
ALGERIA
TASSILI TA-N-AHAGGAR
RÁR
ES
GHAS
MASSIF
DE
TARAZIT
△ 6 562
Mont
Grébaun
Iferouâne
Monts
Tamgak
5906
AÏR
Indoukâl-n-Taghès 6634 △
NIGER
Agadez
In-Gall
TAGAMA
TÉNÉRÉ
Séguédine

PLATEAU DE MANGUENI
LIBYA
PLATEAU
DU
DJADO
Madama
PLATEAU DU TCHIGAI
10 712 △
Pic Touside
TIBESTI
Zouar
Tarso Ahon
△ 10 909
Emi Koussi
△ 11 204

LIBYA
Bette △
7500

BORKOU
Largeau

GRAND ERG DE BILMA

Agadem

BODÉLÉ

Koro Toro

CHAD
Arada
15°

N
Tahoua
Dabnou
Dakouraoua
Zinder
amey
Dosso
Gwadabawa
Maradi
Sokoto
Gandi
Argungu
Katsina
Kirtachi
Seybou
Talata
Mafara
Kaura Namoda
Guidel
Nguru
Gashua
Geidam
Gumel
PARC
ATIONAL
DU "W"
Birnin
Kebbi
Jega
Gummi
Gusau
Hadejia
Hadejia
Maiduguri
Kandi
Fokku
Kano
Azare
Potiskum
Goniri
Gogonou
Funtua
Dan Gora
Nafada
Biu
Gombe
Kumo
Pindiga
Segbana
Babana
Zungeru
Kontagora
Zaria
Zaranda
Hill
4 774
Bauchi
Bununu Dass
EMIN
Parakou
Okuta
Bokani
Bida
Minna
Kafanchan
Jos
Plateau
Sara
△ 5 545
Nguroreo
dali
Shaki
Lafiagi
Baro
Abuja
Keffi
Shendam
Lankoviri
Ilorin
Offa
NIGERIA
Lafia
Ogbomosho
Ibi
Dimlang △
6 700
Ila
Kabba
Okene
Ado-Ekiti
Makurdi
Iseyin
Oyo
Ikerre
Owo
Otukpa
Ibadan
Ede
Ife
Idah
Takum
Pobé
Ondo
Gboko
Abeokuta
Ijebu-Ode
Nsukka
Eha-Amufu
GOTEL
MOUNTAINS
Mushin
Shagamu
Epe
Benin
City
Awka
Onitsha
Enugu
Abakaliki
Afikpo
Ngol-Kedju
Hill
△ 6 562
Bamenda
Cotonou
Lagos
Ogwashi-
Uku
Ihiala
Foumban
Sapele
Owerri
Oban
Hills
Warri
Ikot Ekpene
CAMEROON
Aba
Calabar
Mankim
Port Harcourt
Oron
Kumba
Ndikinimék
Nembe
Opobo
Cameroon
Mtn.
13 451
Buea
Bight of Benin
Malabo
Pico de
Santa Isabel
9869
Douala
San Carlos
Limbé
BIOKO
(FERNANDO PÓO)
Kribi
Edéa
Bight of Biafra
Campo
INEA
Bata
Ebolowa
EQUAT.
GUINEA
Sangmélima
GABON
SAO TOME AND PRINCIPE
Meuban

Nguigmi
Lake Chad
Mao
Bol
Bir Gara
MANGA
N'Djamena
(Fort-Lamy)
DAGANA
Meskine
Maroua
Bama
Mubi
MANDARA MTS.
MONTS MANDARA
Garoua
Pala
Goundi
Hosere
Vokra
6 722
PARC NATIONAL
DE BOUBANDJIDAH
Tiban
Kimi
BARRAGE
DE
MBAKAOU
Ngaoundéré
ADAMAOUA
NGAO BAM YANGA
Yaoundé
Lomié
Dja

Moussoro
Lac Fitri
Salal
Mongo
Mont Guédi
△ 4 941
Abou Deïa
Am Timan
Gabil
Djember
Niellim
Lai
Kélo
Benoy
Doba
Koumra
Bongor
Sarh
(Fort-Archambault)
PARC NATIONAL
DU BAMINGUI
BANGORAN
Moundou
MONTAGNE
DE MBAKANA
Mbasay
Bozoum
Bossangoa
CENTRAL AFRICAN
REPUBLIC
Marali
Fort Crampel
Bouar
Bossembélé
Carnot
Tongo
Batouri
Berbérati
Bangui
Bolai
Fort Sibut
Damar
DEM. REP.
OF THE
CONGO
Mbaïki
Boyabo
Bazene
Bókondil
Budjala
Dongou
Impfondo
Ouesso
CONGO

Continued on pages 236-237

0   50   100   150   200   250   300 Miles
0   100   200   300   400   500 Kilometers

Continued on pages 234-235

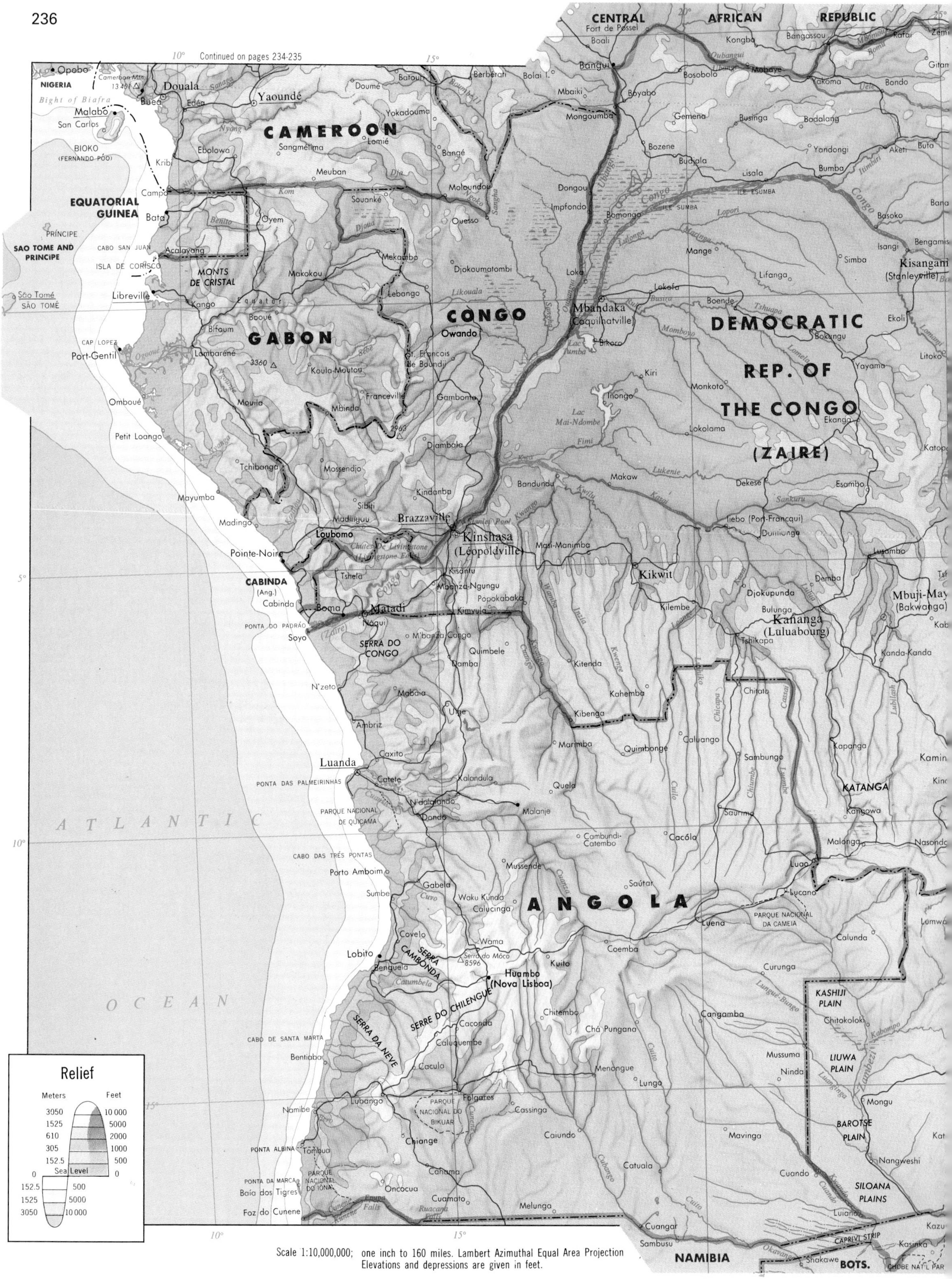

NIGERIA

Opobo

Bight of Biafra

Malabo

San Carlos

BIOKO
(FERNANDO PÓO)

EQUATORIAL
GUINEA

Bata

SAO TOME AND
PRINCIPE

PRÍNCIPE

CABO SAN JUAN

ISLA DE CORISCO

São Tomé
SÃO TOMÉ

Douala

Buea

Edéa

Cameroon Mtn.
13 451 △

Kribi

Campo

Acalayong

Libreville

CAP LOPEZ

Port-Gentil

Omboué

Petit Loango

Mayumba

Madingo

Pointe-Noire

CAMEROON

Yaoundé

Sangmélima

Ebolowa

Meuban

Oyem

MONTS
DE CRISTAL

Kango

Baoué

Bitam

GABON

Lambaréné

Mouila

Mbinda

3360 △

Koula-Moutou

Franceville

2963 △

Djambala

Doumé

Lomié

Yokadouma

Souanké

Mekambo

Makokou

Lebango

Sibiti

Madingou

Loubomo

Tshela

Boma

Soyo

N'zeto

Mabaia

Ambriz

Caxito

Luanda

Batouri

Bangé

Dja

Moloundou

Ouesso

Djokoumatombi

Owando

Gamboma

Mossendjo

Kindamba

Brazzaville

Kinshasa
(Léopoldville)

Kisantu

Mbanza-Ngungu

Nóqui

M'banza Congo

Quimbele

Damba

Uíge

N'dalatando

Dondo

Berbérati

Bolai

Mbaiki

Mongoumba

Impfondo

Likouala

Mbandaka
(Coquilhatville)

Bikoro

Inongo

Lac
Mai-Ndombe

Fimi

Makaw

Bandundu

Masi-Manimba

Popokabaka

Kitenda

Kibenga

Kahemba

Marimba

Quela

Malanje

Bolai

Bangui

Boyabo

Bomongo

Loka

Lac
Tumba

Lukenie

Tshuapa

Busira

Boende

Dekese

Kwilu

Kwango

Kikwit

Kilembe

Bulunga

Tshikapa

Kananga
(Luluabourg)

Djokupunda

Chitato

Caluango

Quimbonge

Sambungo

Calandula

CENTRAL

Fort de Possel

Kongbo

AFRICAN

REPUBLIC

Bangassou

Mobaye

Rafai

Zemi

Gitan

Bosobolo

Yakoma

Bondo

Gemena

Businga

Bodalang

Yandongi

Buta

Lisala

Bumba

Budjala

Itimbiri

Aketi

Bengamisa

Isangi

Basoko

Bana

Simba

Lifanga

Mange

Boende

Kisangani
(Stanleyville)

Ekoli

Lokofa

Bokungu

Yayama

Litoko

Monkoto

Lokolama

Ekanga

Esambo

Tshela

DEMOCRATIC

REP. OF

THE CONGO

(ZAIRE)

Ile Esumba

Demba

Lusambo

Mbuji-Mayi
(Bakwanga)

Kanda-Kanda

Kapanga

KATANGA

Kangowa

Malonga

Nasondo

Lubamba

Kamin

Luau

Lucano

Luena

PARQUE NACIONAL
DA CAMEIA

Calunda

Lomw

Curunga

Mussuma

Ninda

KASHIJI
PLAIN

Chitokolok

LIUWA
PLAIN

BAROTSE
PLAIN

SILOANA
PLAINS

ANGOLA

Mussende

Saútar

Cacóla

Camundi-
Catembo

Cambundi-
Catembo

Gabela

Waku Kúnda

Calucinga

Covelo

Wama

Serra do Môco
8596 △

Kuito

Coemba

Luena

Huambo
(Nova Lisboa)

SERRA DO CHILENGUE

Chitembo

Chá Pungana

Cangamba

Lobito

Benguela

SERRA
CAMBONDA

SERRA DA NEVE

Caconda

Caluquembe

Cacula

Caconda

Menongue

Lungo

Mavinga

Cangamba

Namibe

Lubango

PARQUE
NACIONAL DO
BIKUAR

Folgares

Cassinga

Caiundo

Mussuma

Mongu

Nangweshi

Chiange

Cahama

Caundo

Cuango

Catuala

Mavinga

Ponta Albina

Tômbua

PONTA DA MARCA

Baía dos Tigres

PARQUE
NACIONAL
DO IONA

Oncocua

Cuamato

Ruacaná

Cuamato

Melunga

Chobe

Luiana

CAPRIVI STRIP

Kazu

Foz do Cunene

Cuangar

Sambusu

Shakawe

Okavango

NAMIBIA

BOTS.

CHOBE NATL PAR

Kasinka

Kat

ATLANTIC

OCEAN

PONTA DO PADRÃO

CABINDA
(Ang.)

Cabinda

SERRA DO
CONGO

PONTA DAS PALMEIRINHAS

Catete

PONTA DAS TRÊS PONTAS

Porto Amboim

Sumbe

CABO DAS TRÊS PONTAS

PARQUE NACIONAL
DE QUICAMA

CABO DE SANTA MARTA

Bentiaba

Matadi

Kimvula

Lac
Tumba

Mombo

Lomami

Lopori

Lulonga

Kasai

Lubilash

Chicapa

Chiumbe

Cuilo

Cuango

Kwango

Cuanza

Cuvo

Cuito

Cubango

Cuando

Cassai

Luena

Kasai

Lungué-Bungo

Zambeze

Matadi

Relief		
Meters		Feet
3050		10 000
1525		5000
610		2000
305		1000
152.5		500
0	Sea Level	0
152.5		500
1525		5000
3050		10 000

Scale 1:10,000,000; one inch to 160 miles. Lambert Azimuthal Equal Area Projection
Elevations and depressions are given in feet.

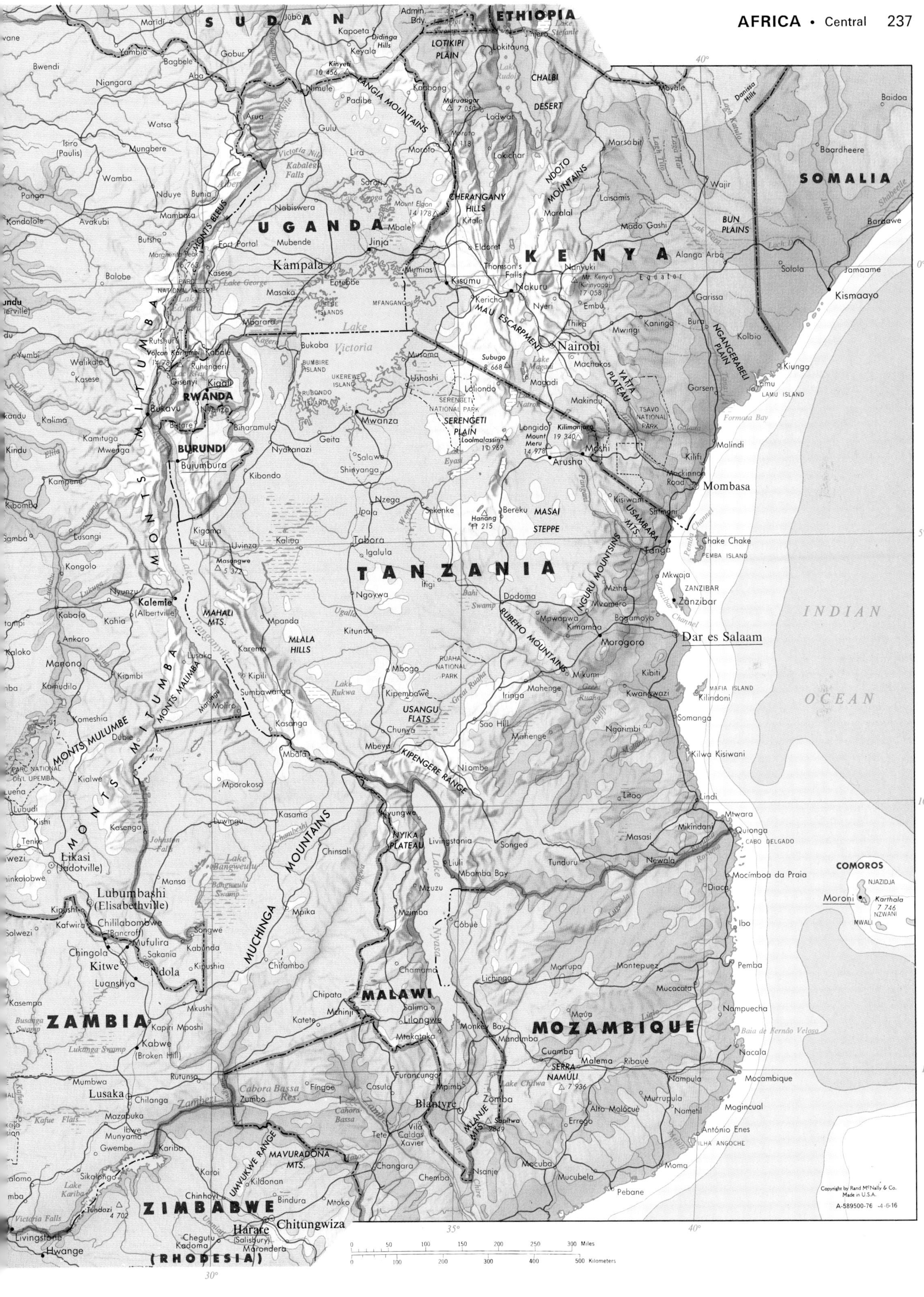
SUDAN
ETHIOPIA
SOMALIA
UGANDA
KENYA
RWANDA
BURUNDI
TANZANIA
ZAMBIA
MALAWI
MOZAMBIQUE
ZIMBABWE
(RHODESIA)
COMOROS
INDIAN OCEAN
Juba
Maridi
Yambio
Bagbele
Gobur
Kapoeta
Didinga Hills
Keyala
Kinyeti 10 456
Nimule
Aba
Bwendi
Niangara
Watsa
Isiro (Paulis)
Mungbere
Wamba
Panga
Nduye
Bunia
Kondolole
Avakubi
Mambasa
Butsha
Balobe
Admin Bay
Lotikipi Plain
Lokitaung
Chalbi Desert
Lake Stefanie
Moyale
Danissa Hills
Baidoa
Kaabong
Padibe
Rangia Mountains
Muruasigar 7 050
Lodwar
Marsabit
Baardheere
Arua
Gulu
Lira
Moroto
Lokichar
Ndoto Mountains
Wajir
Kabalega Falls
Lake Albert
Soroti
Lake Kyoga
Mount Elgon 14 178
Cherangany Hills
Kitale
Maralal
Laisamis
Bun Plains
Bardawe
Nabiswera
Mbale
Mado Gashi
Monts Bleus
Fort Portal
Mubende
Jinja
Eldoret
Kampala
Thomson's Falls
Nanyuki
Mt. Kenya (Kirinyaga) 17 058
Alanga Arba
Sołola
Jamaame
Kismaayo
Equator
Margherita Peak 16 763
Kasese
Lake George
Entebbe
Mumias
Kisumu
Nakuru
Parc National Albert
Masaka
Sese Islands
Mfangano
Kericho
Mau Escarpment
Nyeri
Embu
Garissa
Lake Edward
Mbarara
Lake Victoria
Thika
Mwingi
Kaninga
Bura
Ngangerabeli Plain
Kolbio
Rutshuru
Bukoba
Nairobi
Volcan Karisimbi 14 787
Kabale
Ruhengeri
Kigali
Gisenyi
Bumbire Island
Musoma
Subugo 8 668
Lake Magadi
Machakos
Yatta Plateau
Kiunga
Lamu
Lamu Island
Walikale
Kasese
Ukerewe Island
Ushashi
Loliondo
Magadi
Garsen
Rubondo Island
Serengeti National Park
Lake Natron
Makindu
Tsavo National Park
Formosa Bay
Bukavu
Nyanza
Kalima
Kindu
Kamituga
Mwenga
Bitare
Biharamulo
Mwanza
Geita
Serengeti Plain
Loolmalassin 10 969
Longido
Mount Meru 14 978
Kilimanjaro 19 340
Moshi
Arusha
Malindi
Kilifi
Bujumbura
Nyakanazi
Salawe
Shinyanga
Lake Eyasi
Mackinnon Road
Mombasa
Kampene
Kibondo
Kibombo
Monts Mitumba
Nzega
Ipala
Sekenke
Hanang 11 215
Bereku
Masai Steppe
Kisiwani
Usambara Mts.
Shimoni
Pemba Channel
Kigoma
Ujiji
Uvinza
Kaliua
Tabora
Igalula
Chake Chake
Pemba Island
Tanga
Samba
Lusangi
Kongolo
Masangwe 5 372
Nguru Mountains
Mkwaja
Zanzibar
Zanzibar Channel
Nyunzu
Kalemie (Albertville)
Itigi
Ngoywa
Bahi Swamp
Dodoma
Mziha
Mvomero
Kabalo
Kahia
Mahali Mts.
Lake Tanganyika
Mpanda
Ugalla
Rubeho Mountains
Mpwapwa
Kimamba
Bagamoyo
Ankoro
Kitunda
Mlala Hills
Morogoro
Dar es Salaam
Kaloko
Manono
Lusaka
Karema
Ruaha National Park
Mbogo
Mikumi
Kibiti
Kiambi
Kipili
Monts Malimba
Lake Rukwa
Great Ruaha
Mafia Island
Kilindoni
Kwangwazi
Kamudilo
Sumbawanga
Kipembawe
Iringa
Mahenge
Moliro
Usangu Flats
Komeshia
Monts Mulumbe
Dubie
Kasanga
Chunya
Sao Hill
Mahenge
Ngarimbi
Somanga
Lake Mweru
Mbala
Mbeya
Kipengere Range
Njombe
Kilwa Kisiwani
Parc National de l'Upemba
Kialwe
Mporokoso
Litoo
Lindi
Lubudi
Kishi
Kasama
Nyungwe
Mtwara
Tenke
Kasenga
Luwingu
Nyika Plateau
Livingstonia
Songea
Masasi
Mikindani
Quionga
Cabo Delgado
Likasi (Jadotville)
Johnston Falls
Chambeshi
Chinsali
Muchinga Mountains
Lake Nyasa
Lake Bangweulu
Liuli
Tunduru
Newala
Mocímboa da Praia
Mansa
Bangweulu Swamp
Mbamba Bay
Mzuzu
Njazidja
Moroni
Karthala 7 746
Nzwani
Mwali
Diaca
Lubumbashi (Elisabethville)
Kipushi
Chililabombwe (Bancroft)
Kafwira
Mzimba
Mpika
Cóbuè
Ibo
Songwe
Solwezi
Mufulira
Chingola
Sakania
Kitwe
Ndola
Kabunda
Kipushia
Chitambo
Chamama
Marrupa
Montepuez
Pemba
Luanshya
Lichinga
Mucacata
Kasempa
Chipata
Mchinji
Salima
Lilongwe
Maúa
Nampuecha
Busanga Swamp
Katete
Monkey Bay
Mandimba
Baia de Fernão Veloso
Mkushi
Kapiri Mposhi
Kabwe (Broken Hill)
Lukanga Swamp
Mtakataka
Cuamba
Malema
Ribauê
Nacala
Rutunsa
Serra Namúli 7 936
Mumbwa
Cabora Bassa Res.
Fingoe
Lake Chilwa
Nampula
Moçambique
Lusaka
Chilanga
Zumbo
Zambezi
Casula
Furancungo
Mpimbe
Zomba
Murrupula
Kafue Flats
Mazabuka
Cahora Bassa
Blantyre
Mlanje Mts.
Sapitwa 9 849
Alto Molócuè
Nametil
Mogincual
Munyama
Ibwe
Gwembe
Tete
Vila Caldas Xavier
Erregó
António Enes
Ilha Angoche
Kariba
Umvukwe Range
Mavuradona Mts.
Mocuba
Moma
Sikalongo
Lake Kariba
Karoi
Kildonan
Changara
Chemba
Nsanje
Mucubela
Chinhoyi
Bindura
Mtoko
Pebane
Tundazi 4 702
Victoria Falls
Livingstone
Hwange
Chegutu
Kadoma
Harare (Salisbury)
Chitungwiza
Marondera
30°
35°
40°
0°
5°
10°
15°
0 50 100 150 200 250 300 Miles
0 100 200 300 400 500 Kilometers
Copyright by Rand McNally & Co. Made in U.S.A.
A-589500-76 -4-6-16

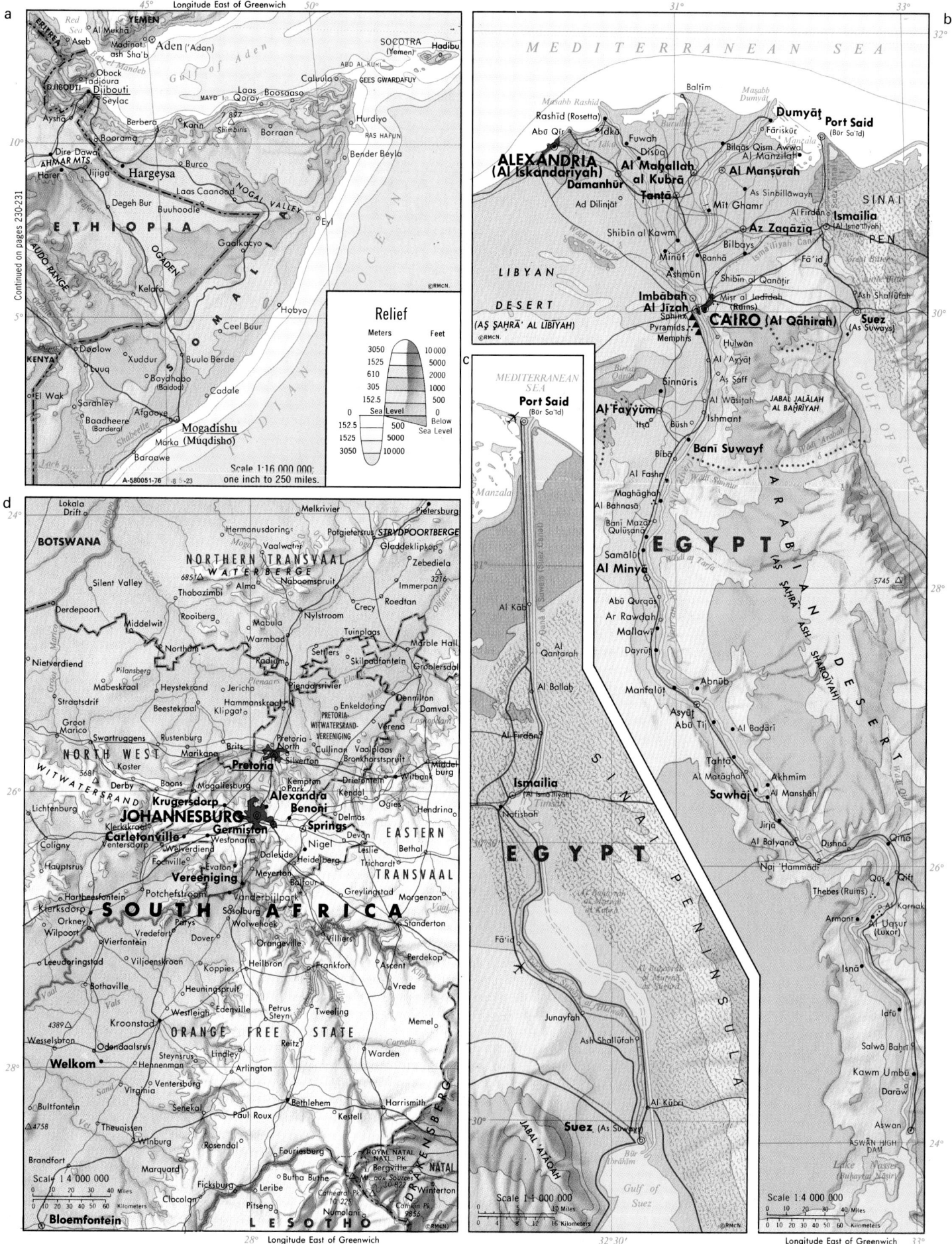

a

Longitude East of Greenwich

45°
50°

Red Sea

YEMEN

Al Mukhā

Madīnat ash Sha'b

Aden ('Adan)

Gulf of Aden

SOCOTRA (Yemen)

Hadībū

Aseb

ERITREA

Obock

Tadjoura

Djibouti

DJIBOUTI

Seylac

Aysha

MAYD I.

Laas Qoray

Boosaaso

Caluula

GEES GWARDAFUY

ABD AL KURI

RAS HAFUN

Dire Dawa

Hārer

Jijiga

Hargeysa

Berbera

Karin

Shimbīris 2407

Hurdiyo

Bender Beyla

AHMAR MTS.

Boorama

Burco

Laas Caanood

Degeh Bur

Buuhoodle

NOGAL VALLEY

Eyl

E T H I O P I A

OGADEN

S O M A L I A

Ke'afo

Gaalkacyo

KENYA

Dóolow

Xuddur

Buulo Berde

Ceel Buur

Hobyo

El Wak

Luuq

Baydhabo (Baidoa)

Afgooye

Cadale

Sarahley

Baadheere (Barderal)

Mogadishu (Muqdisho)

Marka

Baraawe

INDIAN OCEAN

©RMCN

Continued on pages 230-231

Relief

Meters		Feet
3050		10 000
1525		5000
610		2000
305		1000
152.5		500
0 Sea Level		0
152.5		Below Sea Level
1525		5000
3050		10 000

Scale 1:16 000 000
one inch to 250 miles.

A-580051-76 -8 5 -23

b

31°
33°
32°

M E D I T E R R A N E A N   S E A

Baltīm

Maşabb Dumyāţ

Maşabb Rashīd

Rashīd (Rosetta)

Abū Qīr

Idkū

Fuwah

Disūq

Burullus

Dumyāţ

Port Said (Bûr Sa'īd)

Fāriskūr

Bilqās Qism Awwal

Al Manzilah

ALEXANDRIA (Al Iskandarīyah)

Al Maḥallah al Kubrā

Al Manşūrah

Manzala

Damanhūr

Tantā

As Sinbillāwayn

SINAI PEN.

Ad Dilinjāt

Mīt Ghamr

Al Firdān

Ismailia (Al Ismā'īlīyah)

Shibīn al Kawm

Az Zaqāzīq

Banhā

Fā'id

Great Bitter Lake

Minūf

Bilbays

Ismailiyah Can.

LIBYAN

Ashmūn

Shibīn al Qanāţir

Ash Shallūfah

DESERT (AŞ ŞAḤRĀ' AL LĪBĪYAH)

Imbābah

Al Jīzah

Mişr al Jadīdah (Ruins)

CAIRO (Al Qāhirah)

Suez (As Suways)

©RMCN

Pyramids

Sphinx

Memphis

Ḥulwān

Al 'Ayyāţ

30°

GULF OF SUEZ

c

MEDITERRANEAN SEA

Port Said (Bûr Sa'īd)

Al Kāb

Manzala

Sinnūris

Aş Şaff

Birkat Qārūn

Al Fayyūm

Iţsā

Al Wāsiţah

JABAL JALĀLAH AL BAḤRĪYAH

Būsh

Ishmant

Bani Suwayf

Bibā

Al Fashn

Wādī Arabah

Maghāghah

Al Bahnasā

Banī Mazār

Qulūşanā

Samālūṭ

Al Minyā

E G Y P T

Abū Qurqāş

Ar Rawdah

Mallawī

Dayrūţ

AŞ ŞAḤRĀ' ASH SHARQĪYAH

Al Qanţarah

Al Ballah

Abnūb

Manfalūţ

Al Firdān

Asyūţ

Abū Tīj

Al Badārī

Ismailia (Al Ismā'īlīyah)

Nafīshah

Tahtā

Al Marāghah

Akhmīm

Al Manshāh

Sawhāj

S I N A I   P E N I N S U L A

Fā'id

Jirjā

Al Balyanā

Dishnā

Qinā

Naj' Ḥammādī

Thebes (Ruins)

Qūş

Qifṭ

Junayfah

Armant

Al Karnak

Al Uqsur (Luxor)

Isnā

Idfū

Salwā Baḥrī

Kawm Umbū

Darāw

Suez (As Suways)

JABAL ATAQAH

Gulf of Suez

ASWĀN HIGH DAM

Lake Nasser (Buḥayrat Nāşir)

Aswan

Al Kūbrī

Ash Shallūfah

Scale 1:4 000 000

d

Lokala Drift

Melkrivier

Pietersburg

BOTSWANA

Hermanusdoring

Potgietersrus

STRYDPOORTBERGE

Gladdeklipkop

NORTHERN TRANSVAAL

WATERBERGE

Vaalwater

Mogol

Silent Valley

6851 3216

Alma

Zebediela

Immerpan

Derdepoort

Thabazimbi

Naboomspruit

Middelwit

Rooiberg

Crecy

Roedtan

Nietverdiend

Mabula

Nylstroom

Tuinplaas

Marble Hall

Northam

Warmbad

Settlers

Skilpadfontein

Groblersdal

Straatsdrif

Pilansberg

Radium

Jericho

Hammanskraal

Enkeldoring

Dennilton

Groot Marico

Rustenburg

Klipgat

Plienaars

PRETORIA-WITWATERSRAND-VEREENIGING

Verena

NORTH WEST

568?

Koster

Marikana

Brits

Pretoria North

Cullinan

Vaalplaas

Bronkhorstspruit

Middelburg

Swartruggens

Derby

Magaliesburg

PRETORIA

Silverton

Witbank

Lichtenburg

Boons

Kempton Park

Driefontein

Kendal

Ogies

Hendrina

Krugersdorp

Alexandra

Benoni

JOHANNESBURG

Germiston

Springs

Delmas

Devon

Leslie

Bethal

EASTERN TRANSVAAL

Coligny

Klerksdorp

Carletonville

Venterspost

Welverdiend

Nigel

Westonaria

Fochville

Evaton

Heidelberg

Tlchardt

Hauptrus

Vereeniging

Meyerton

Balfour

Greylingstad

Morgenzon

WITWATERSRAND

Potchefstroom

Vanderbijlpark

Standerton

Hartbeesfontein

S O U T H   A F R I C A

Sasolburg

Wolwehoek

Klerksdorp

Parys

Villiers

Orkney

Vredefort

Dover

Orangeville

Perdekop

Wilpoort

Vierfontein

Frankfort

Ascent

Leeudoringstad

Viljoenskroon

Koppies

Heilbron

Vrede

Memel

Bothaville

Heuningspruit

Petrus Steyn

Tweeling

4389

Kroonstad

Lindley

Reitz

Warden

Welkom

O R A N G E   F R E E   S T A T E

Odendaalsrus

Steynsrus

Virginia

Senekal

Arlington

DRAKENSBERG

4758

Theunissen

Winburg

Paul Roux

Bethlehem

Harrismith

Brandfort

Rosendal

Fouriesburg

NATAL

Marquard

Ficksburg

Leribe

Clocolan

Pitseng

Butha Buthe

Winterton

Scale 1:4 000 000

ROYAL NATAL NATL. PK.

Bergville

Cathedral Pk.

Bloemfontein

Numonat

L E S O T H O

28° Longitude East of Greenwich

33° Longitude East of Greenwich

24°

28°

26°

28°

32°30'

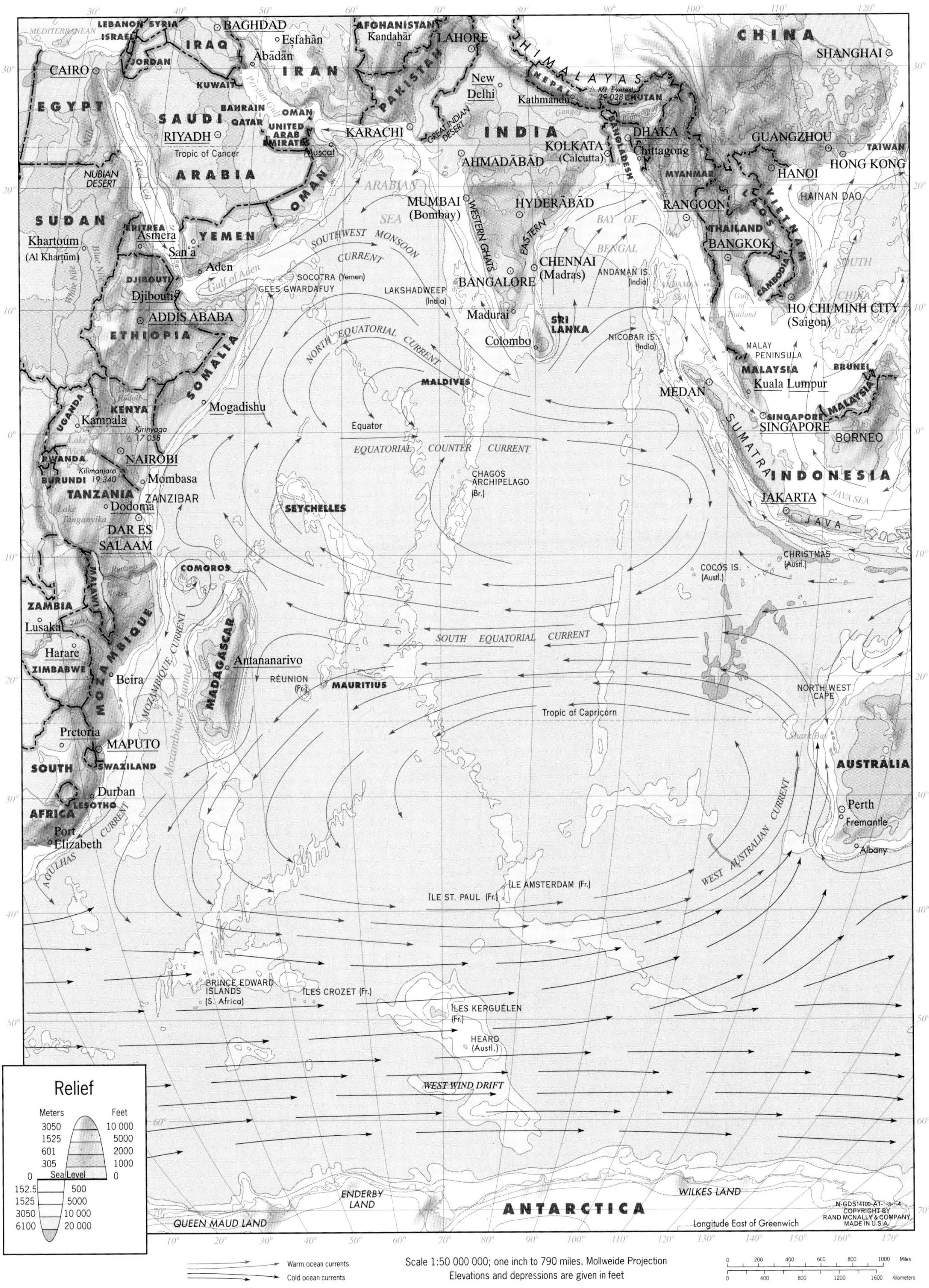

MEDITERRANEAN SEA
LEBANON SYRIA
ISRAEL
JORDAN
IRAQ BAGHDAD
Esfahān
Abādān
AFGHANISTAN
Kandahār
LAHORE
HIMALAYAS
NEPAL
Mt. Everest 29,028
BHUTAN
CHINA
SHANGHAI

CAIRO
KUWAIT
IRAN
New Delhi
Kathmandu
Ganges
GUANGZHOU
TAIWAN

EGYPT
SAUDI
BAHRAIN
QATAR
OMAN
UNITED ARAB EMIRATES
Muscat
Tropic of Cancer
RIYADH
PAKISTAN
GREAT INDIAN DESERT
KARACHI
INDIA
KOLKATA (Calcutta)
DHAKA
Chittagong
BANGLADESH
MYANMAR
HANOI
HONG KONG
HAINAN DAO

NUBIAN DESERT
ARABIA
AHMADĀBĀD
HYDERĀBĀD
RANGOON
THAILAND
BANGKOK

SUDAN
Red Sea
YEMEN
ERITREA
Asmera
San'a
MUMBAI (Bombay)
ARABIAN SEA
WESTERN GHATS
EASTERN GHATS
BAY OF BENGAL
LAOS
VIETNAM
CAMBODIA
SOUTH CHINA SEA

Khartoum (Al Khartūm)
Blue Nile
Aden
Gulf of Aden
SOUTHWEST MONSOON CURRENT
SOCOTRA (Yemen)
GEES GWARDAFUY
CHENNAI (Madras)
ANDAMAN IS. (India)
ANDAMAN SEA
Gulf of Thailand
HO CHI MINH CITY (Saigon)

DJIBOUTI
Djibouti
LAKSHADWEEP (India)
BANGALORE
MALAY PENINSULA
BRUNEI

ADDIS ABABA
ETHIOPIA
NORTH EQUATORIAL CURRENT
Madurai
Colombo
SRI LANKA
NICOBAR IS. (India)
MALAYSIA
Kuala Lumpur

SOMALIA
MALDIVES
MEDAN
SINGAPORE

UGANDA
KENYA
Kampala
Lake Rudolf
Kirinyaga 17,058
NAIROBI
Mombasa
Mogadishu
Equator
EQUATORIAL COUNTER CURRENT
CHAGOS ARCHIPELAGO (Br.)
BORNEO
SUMATRA
INDONESIA

RWANDA
BURUNDI
Lake Victoria
Kilimanjaro 19,340
TANZANIA
ZANZIBAR
Dodoma
JAKARTA
JAVA SEA
JAVA

DAR ES SALAAM
SEYCHELLES

MALAWI
Revuma
Lake Nyasa
COMOROS
SOUTH EQUATORIAL CURRENT
COCOS IS. (Austl.)
CHRISTMAS (Austl.)

ZAMBIA
Lusaka
Zambezi
MOZAMBIQUE CURRENT
MADAGASCAR
Antananarivo
NORTH WEST CAPE

Harare
ZIMBABWE
Beira
MOZAMBIQUE
Mozambique Channel
RÉUNION (Fr.)
MAURITIUS
Tropic of Capricorn
Shark Bay

Pretoria
MAPUTO
SWAZILAND
LESOTHO
AUSTRALIA
Perth
Fremantle

SOUTH AFRICA
Durban
Port Elizabeth
AGULHAS CURRENT
WEST AUSTRALIAN CURRENT
Albany

ÎLE ST. PAUL (Fr.)
ÎLE AMSTERDAM (Fr.)

PRINCE EDWARD ISLANDS (S. Africa)
ÎLES CROZET (Fr.)
ÎLES KERGUÉLEN (Fr.)
HEARD (Austl.)

WEST WIND DRIFT

ENDERBY LAND
QUEEN MAUD LAND
ANTARCTICA
WILKES LAND
Longitude East of Greenwich

N-GDS14100-AT- -9-'14
COPYRIGHT BY
RAND MCNALLY & COMPANY
MADE IN U.S.A.

Relief

Meters	Feet
3050	10 000
1525	5000
601	2000
305	1000
0 Sea Level	0
152.5	500
1525	5000
3050	10 000
6100	20 000

→ Warm ocean currents
→ Cold ocean currents

Scale 1:50 000 000; one inch to 790 miles. Mollweide Projection
Elevations and depressions are given in feet

0 200 400 600 800 1000 Miles
0 400 800 1200 1600 Kilometers

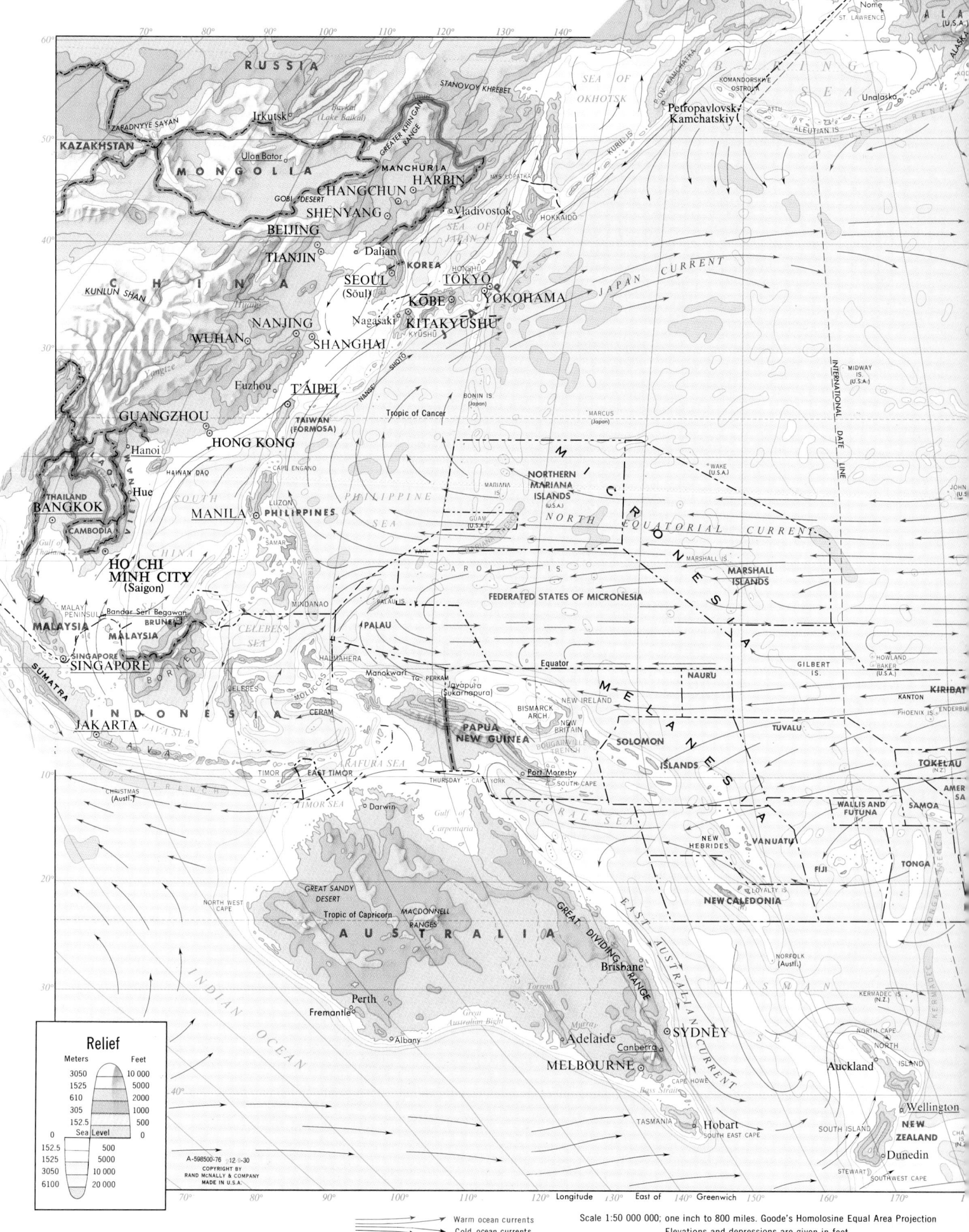

Relief

Meters		Feet
3050		10 000
1525		5000
610		2000
305		1000
152.5		500
0	Sea Level	0
152.5		500
1525		5000
3050		10 000
6100		20 000

A-598500-76 12 9-30
COPYRIGHT BY
RAND McNALLY & COMPANY
MADE IN U.S.A.

Warm ocean currents
Cold ocean currents

Scale 1:50 000 000; one inch to 800 miles. Goode's Homolosine Equal Area Projection
Elevations and depressions are given in feet

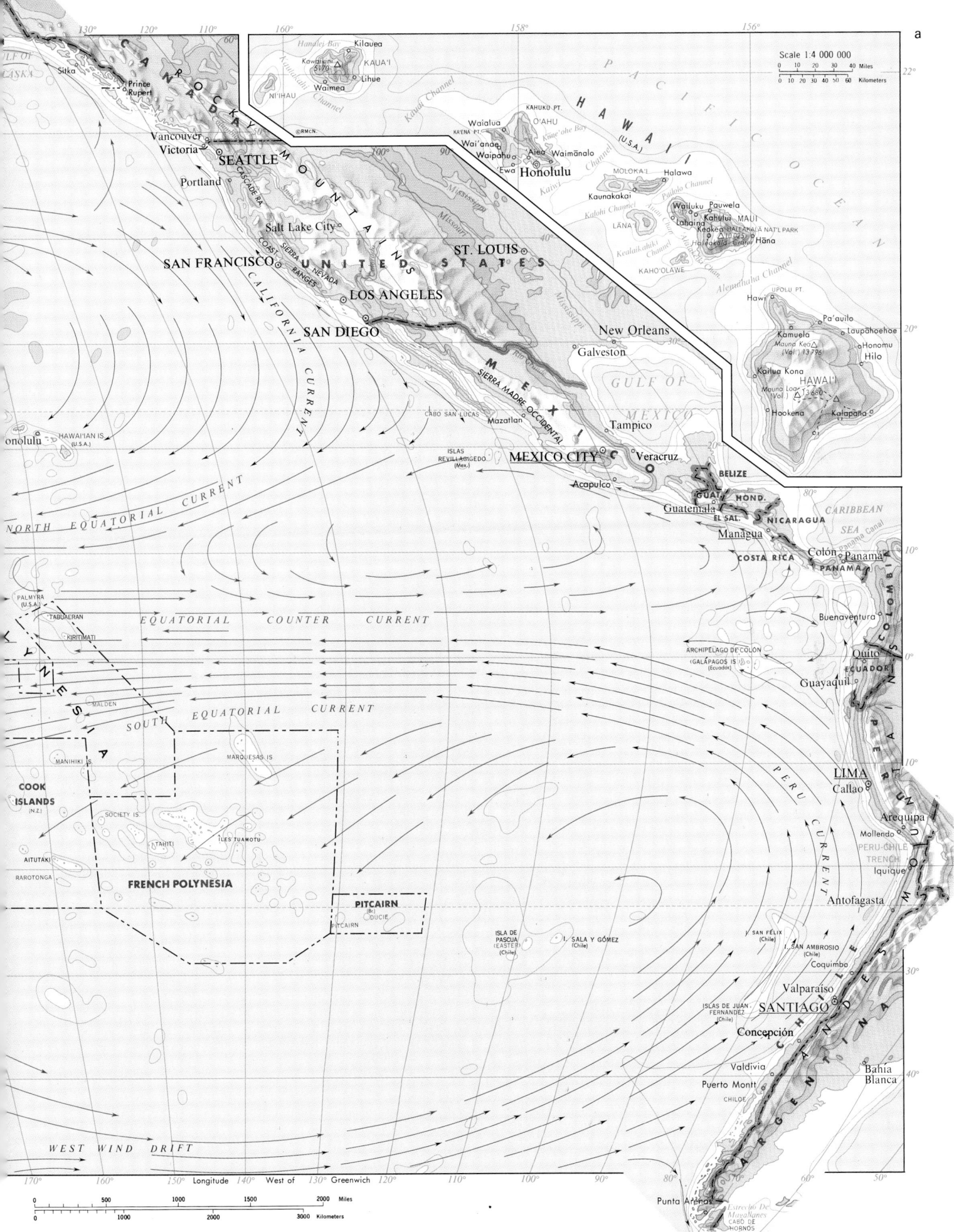

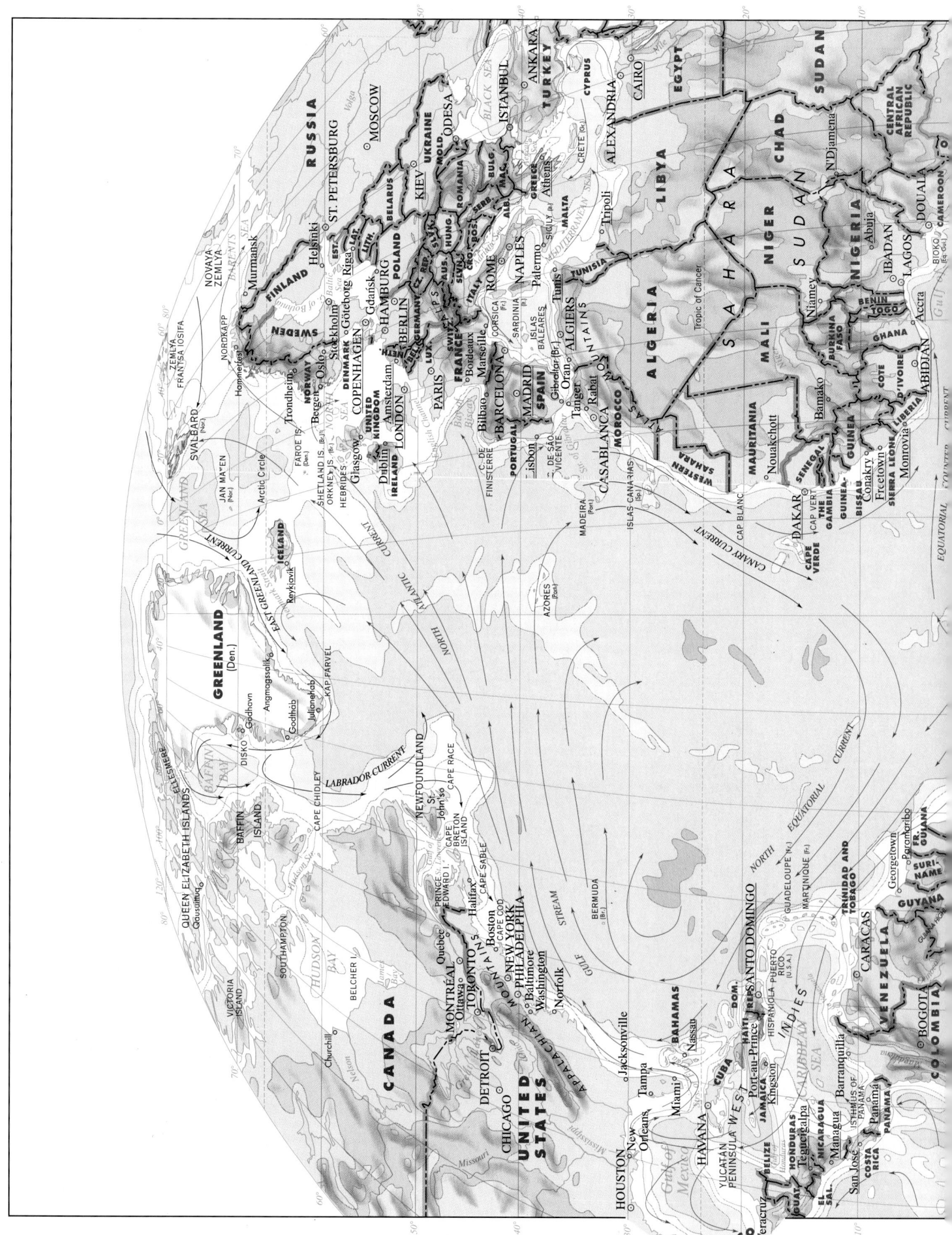

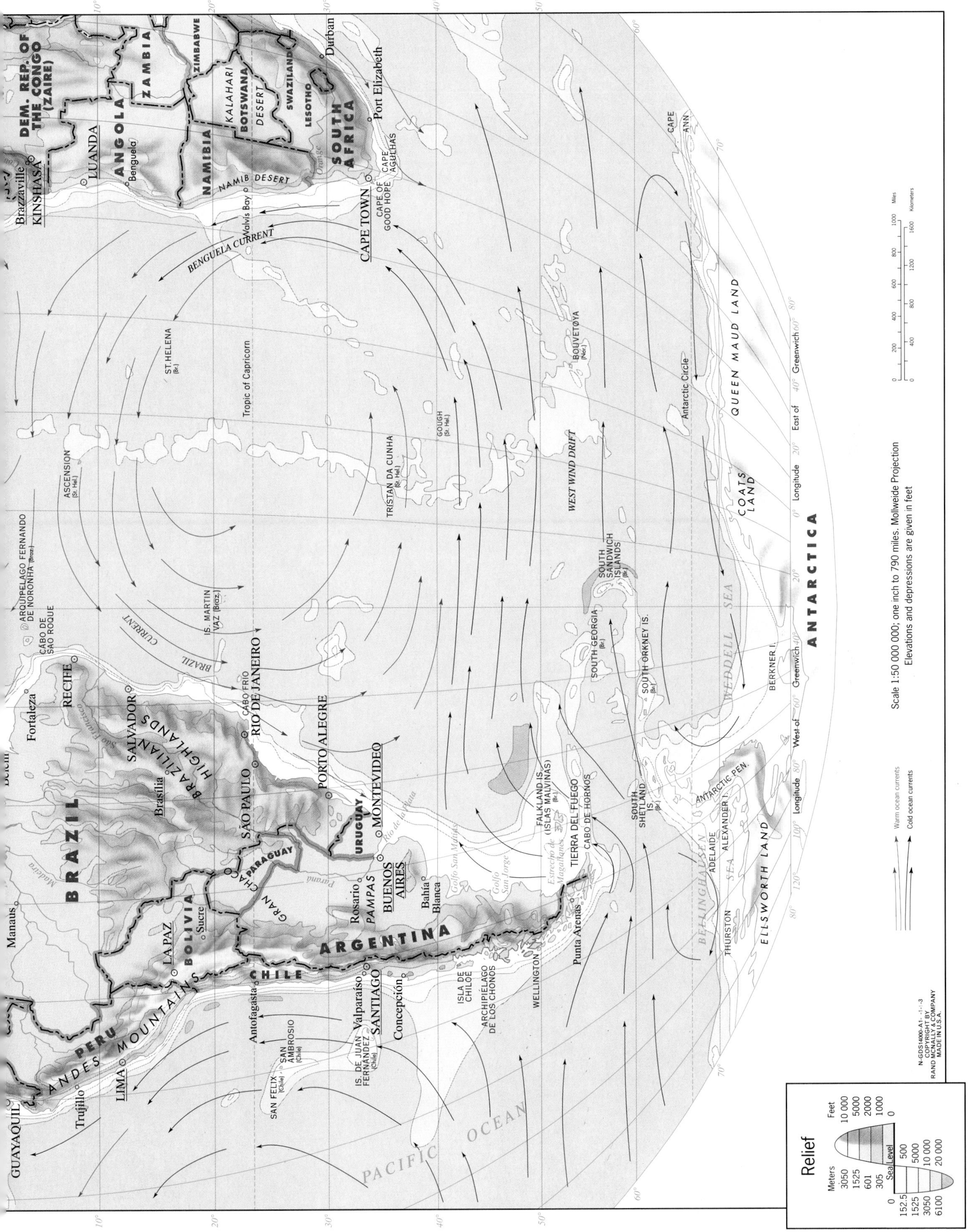

DEM. REP. OF THE CONGO (ZAIRE)

Brazzaville
KINSHASA

ZAMBIA
ZIMBABWE
ANGOLA
LUANDA
Benguela

NAMIBIA
KALAHARI DESERT
BOTSWANA
SWAZILAND
LESOTHO

Durban

SOUTH AFRICA
Port Elizabeth

NAMIB DESERT
Walvis Bay
Orange

CAPE TOWN
CAPE OF GOOD HOPE
CAPE AGULHAS

CAPE ANN

BENGUELA CURRENT

QUEEN MAUD LAND

St. HELENA (Br.)

Tropic of Capricorn

BOUVETØYA (Nor.)

Antarctic Circle

COATS LAND

ASCENSION (St. Hel.)

GOUGH (St. Hel.)

WEST WIND DRIFT

ARQUIPÉLAGO FERNANDO DE NORONHA (Braz.)

CABO DE SÃO ROQUE

TRISTAN DA CUNHA (St. Hel.)

WEDDELL SEA

IS. MARTIN VAZ (Braz.)

ANTARCTICA

BRAZIL CURRENT

SOUTH SANDWICH ISLANDS (Br.)

Manaus

BRAZIL

RECIFE
Fortaleza

SALVADOR
BRAZILIAN HIGHLANDS

Brasília

SÃO PAULO

PORTO ALEGRE

CABO FRIO
RIO DE JANEIRO

SOUTH GEORGIA (Br.)

SOUTH ORKNEY IS. (Br.)

BERKNER I.

ELLSWORTH LAND

PARAGUAY
GRAN CHACO

URUGUAY
MONTEVIDEO
Rio de la Plata

BUENOS AIRES
Rosario
PAMPAS
Bahía Blanca

FALKLAND IS. (ISLAS MALVINAS) (Br.)

TIERRA DEL FUEGO
CABO DE HORNOS

SOUTH SHETLAND IS. (Br.)

ANTARCTIC PEN.

ALEXANDER I.

BELLINGSHAUSEN SEA

THURSTON I.

LA PAZ
BOLIVIA
Sucre

ARGENTINA

Golfo San Matías
Golfo San Jorge
Estrecho de Magallanes

Punta Arenas

ADELAIDE

PERU
LIMA
Trujillo

ANDES MOUNTAINS

CHILE

Antofagasta
SAN FÉLIX (Chile)
SAN AMBROSIO (Chile)

Valparaíso
SANTIAGO
Concepción

IS. DE JUAN FERNÁNDEZ (Chile)

ISLA DE CHILOÉ

ARCHIPIÉLAGO DE LOS CHONOS

WELLINGTON

GUAYAQUIL

PACIFIC OCEAN

Longitude West of
Longitude East of Greenwich
Longitude Greenwich

Scale 1:50 000 000; one inch to 790 miles. Mollweide Projection
Elevations and depressions are given in feet

Warm ocean currents
Cold ocean currents

N-GD514000-A1-...-3
COPYRIGHT BY
RAND McNALLY & COMPANY
MADE IN U.S.A.

Miles
Kilometers
0 200 400 600 800 1000
0 400 800 1200 1600

Relief

Meters	Feet
3050	10 000
1525	5000
601	2000
305	1000
0 Sea Level	Sea Level 0
152.5	500
1525	5000
3050	10 000
6100	20 000

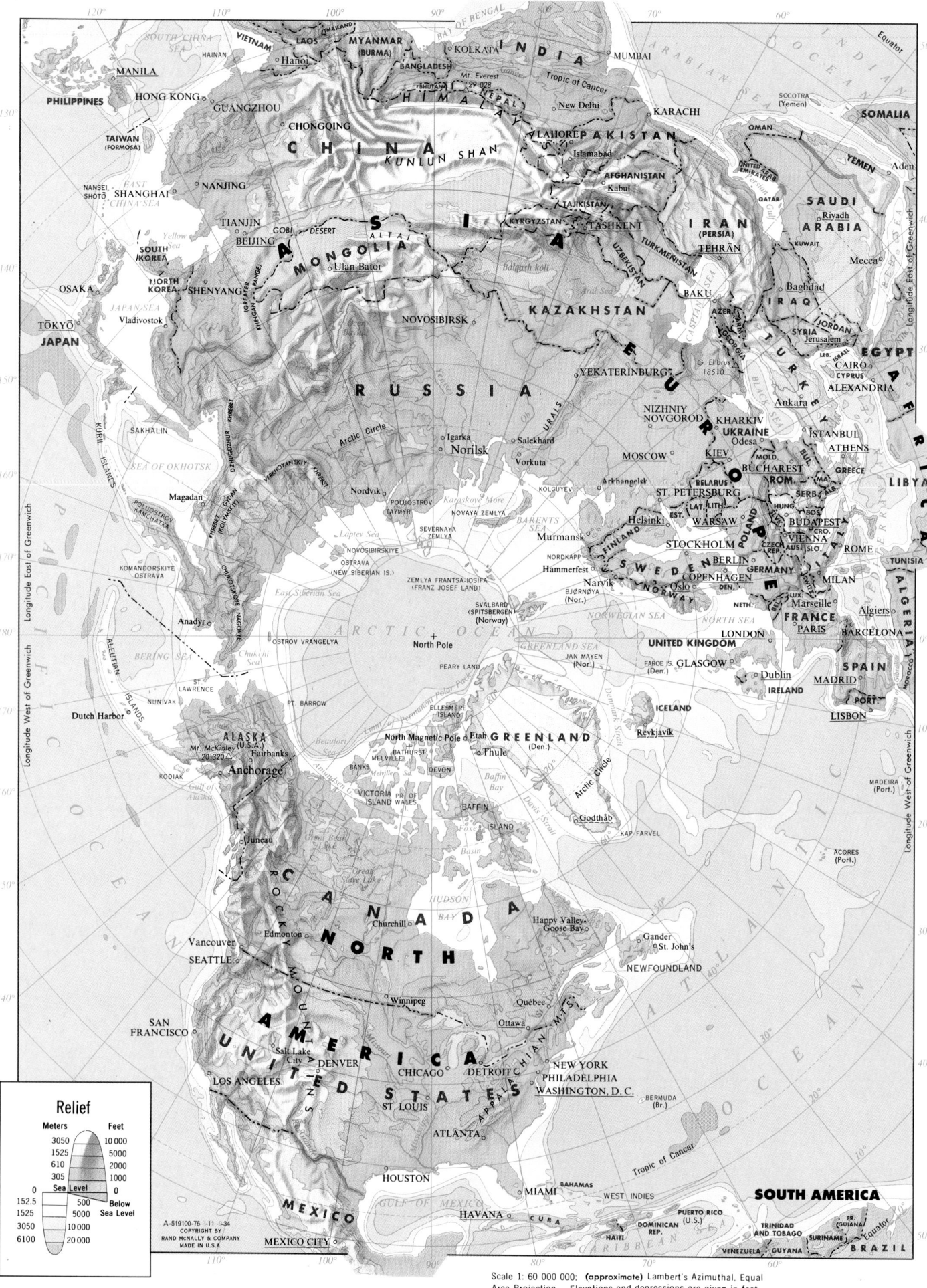

Relief

Meters	Feet
3050	10 000
1525	5000
610	2000
305	1000
0	Sea Level
Sea Level	
152.5	500
1525	5000 Below
3050	10 000 Sea Level
6100	20 000

A-519100-76 -11 -34
COPYRIGHT BY
RAND McNALLY & COMPANY
MADE IN U.S.A.

Scale 1: 60 000 000; (approximate) Lambert's Azimuthal, Equal
Area Projection   Elevations and depressions are given in feet

WORLD POLITICAL INFORMATION TABLE

This table gives the area, population, population density, political status, capital, and predominant languages for every country in the world. The political units listed are categorized by political status in the form of government column of the table, as follows: A—independent countries; B—internally independent political entities which are under the protection of another country in matters of defense and foreign affairs; C—colonies and other dependent political units; and D—the major administrative subdivisions of Australia, Canada, China, the United Kingdom, and the United States. For comparison, the table also includes the continents and the world. All footnotes appear at the end of the table.

The populations are estimates for January 1, 2002, made by Rand McNally on the basis of official data, United Nations estimates, and other available information. Area figures include inland water.

REGION OR POLITICAL DIVISION	Area Sq. Mi.	Est. Pop. 1/1/02	Pop. Per Sq. Mi.	Form of Government and Ruling Power		Capital	Predominant Languages
Afars and Issas see Djibouti							
† Afghanistan	251,826	27,280,000	108	Transitional	A	Kābol (Kabul)	Dari, Pashto, Uzbek, Turkmen
Africa	11,700,000	832,590,000	71				
Alabama	52,237	4,470,000	86	State (U.S.)	D	Montgomery	English
Alaska	615,230	640,000	1.0	State (U.S.)	D	Juneau	English, indigenous
† Albania	11,100	3,525,000	318	Republic	A	Tiranë	Albanian, Greek
Alberta	255,541	3,090,000	12	Province (Canada)	D	Edmonton	English
† Algeria	919,595	32,005,000	35	Republic	A	Algiers (El Djazaïr)	Arabic, Berber dialects, French
American Samoa	90	68,000	756	Unincorporated territory (U.S.)	C	Pago Pago	Samoan, English
† Andorra	175	68,000	389	Parliamentary co-principality (Spanish and French)	B	Andorra	Catalan, Spanish (Castilian), French
† Angola	481,354	10,480,000	22	Republic	A	Luanda	Portuguese, indigenous
Anguilla	35	12,000	342	Dependent territory (U.K. protection)	B	The Valley	English
Anhui	53,668	60,275,000	1,123	Province (China)	D	Hefei	Chinese (Mandarin)
Antarctica	5,400,000	(1)					
† Antigua and Barbuda	171	67,000	393	Parliamentary state	A	St. John's	English, local dialects
Aomen (Macau)	6.6	445,000	67,424	Special administrative region (China)	D	Aomen (Macau)	Chinese (Cantonese), Portuguese
† Argentina	1,073,519	37,600,000	35	Republic	A	Buenos Aires and Viedma(4)	Spanish, English, Italian, German, French
Arizona	114,006	5,380,000	47	State (U.S.)	D	Phoenix	English
Arkansas	53,182	2,700,000	51	State (U.S.)	D	Little Rock	English
† Armenia	11,506	3,335,000	290	Republic	A	Yerevan	Armenian, Russian
Aruba	75	70,000	940	Self-governing territory (Netherlands protection)	B	Oranjestad	Dutch, Papiamento, English, Spanish
Ascension	34	1,000	29	Dependency (St. Helena)	C	Georgetown	English
Asia	17,300,000	3,761,165,000	217				
† Australia	2,969,910	19,455,000	6.6	Federal parliamentary state	A	Canberra	English, indigenous
Australian Capital Territory	911	325,000	357	Territory (Australia)	D	Canberra	English
† Austria	32,378	8,160,000	252	Federal republic	A	Vienna (Wien)	German
† Azerbaijan	33,437	7,785,000	233	Republic	A	Baku (Bakı)	Azeri, Russian, Armenian
† Bahamas	5,382	300,000	56	Parliamentary State	A	Nassau	English, Creole
† Bahrain	267	650,000	2,436	Monarchy	A	Al Manāmah	Arabic, English, Farsi, Urdu
† Bangladesh	55,598	132,315,000	2,380	Republic	A	Dhaka	Bangla, English
† Barbados	166	275,000	1,657	Parliamentary state	A	Bridgetown	English
Beijing (Peking)	6,487	14,160,000	2,183	Autonomous city (China)	D	Beijing (Peking)	Chinese (Mandarin)
† Belarus	80,155	10,340,000	129	Republic	A	Minsk	Belarussian, Russian
Belau see Palau							
† Belgium	11,787	10,265,000	871	Constitutional monarchy	A	Brussels (Bruxelles)	Dutch (Flemish), French, German
† Belize	8,866	260,000	29	Parliamentary state	A	Belmopan	English, Spanish, Mayan, Garifuna
† Benin	43,475	6,690,000	154	Republic	A	Porto-Novo and Cotonou	French, Fon, Yoruba, indigenous
Bermuda	21	64,000	3,048	Dependent territory (U.K.)	C	Hamilton	English
† Bhutan	17,954	2,070,000	115	Monarchy (Indian protection)	B	Thimphu	Dzongkha, Tibetan and Nepalese dialects
† Bolivia	424,165	8,375,000	20	Republic	A	La Paz and Sucre	Aymara, Quechua, Spanish
† Bosnia and Herzegovina	19,741	3,950,000	200	Republic	A	Sarajevo	Serbo-Croatian
† Botswana	224,712	1,590,000	7.1	Republic	A	Gaborone	English, Tswana
† Brazil	3,300,172	175,260,000	53	Federal republic	A	Brasília	Portuguese, Spanish, English, French
British Columbia	364,764	4,115,000	11	Province (Canada)	D	Victoria	English
British Indian Ocean Territory	23	(1)		Dependent territory (U.K.)	C		English
† Brunei	2,226	345,000	155	Monarchy	A	Bandar Seri Begawan	Malay, English, Chinese
† Bugaria	42,855	7,665,000	179	Republic	A	Sofia (Sofiya)	Bulgarian, Turkish
† Burkina Faso	105,869	12,435,000	117	Republic	A	Ouagadougou	French, indigenous
Burma see Myanmar							
† Burundi	10,745	6,300,000	586	Republic	A	Bujumbura	French, Kirundi, Swahili
California	158,869	34,750,000	219	State (U.S.)	D	Sacramento	English
† Cambodia	69,898	12,630,000	181	Constitutional monarchy	A	Phnum Pénh (Phnom Penh)	Khmer, French
† Cameroon	183,568	15,995,000	87	Republic	A	Yaoundé	English, French, indigenous
† Canada	3,855,103	31,750,000	8.2	Federal parliamentary state	A	Ottawa	English, French
† Cape Verde	1,557	405,000	260	Republic	A	Praia	Portuguese, Crioulo
Cayman Islands	100	36,000	360	Dependent territory (U.K.)	C	George Town	English
† Central African Republic	240,536	3,610,000	15	Republic	A	Bangui	French, Sango, Arabic, indigenous
Ceylon see Sri Lanka							
† Chad	495,755	8,850,000	18	Republic	A	N'Djamena	Arabic, French, indigenous
Channel Islands	75	155,000	2,067	Two crown dependencies (U.K. protection)			English, French
† Chile	292,135	15,415,000	53	Republic	A	Santiago	Spanish
† China (excl. Taiwan)	3,690,045	1,278,720,000	347	Socialist republic	A	Beijing (Peking)	Chinese dialects
Chongqing	31,815	31,115,000	978	Autonomous city (China)	D	Chongqing	Chinese (Mandarin)
Christmas Island	52	3,000	58	External territory (Australia)	C	Settlement	English, Chinese, Malay
Cocos (Keeling) Islands	5.4	600	111	External territory (Australia)	C	West Island	English, Cocos-Malay, Malay
† Colombia	440,831	40,680,000	92	Republic	A	Bogotá	Spanish
Colorado	104,100	4,465,000	43	State (U.S.)	D	Denver	English
† Comoros (excl. Mayotte)	863	605,000	701	Federal Islamic republic	A	Moroni	Arabic, French, Comoran
† Congo	132,047	2,925,000	22	Republic	A	Brazzaville	French, Lingala, Kikongo, indigenous
† Congo, Democratic Republic of the (Zaire)	905,446	54,455,000	60	Republic	A	Kinshasa	French, Kikongo, Lingala, Swahili, Tshiluba, Kingwana
Connecticut	5,544	3,435,000	620	State (U.S.)	D	Hartford	English
Cook Islands	91	21,000	231	Self-governing territory (New Zealand protection)	B	Avarua	English, Maori
† Costa Rica	19,730	3,805,000	193	Republic	A	San José	Spanish
† Cote d'Ivoire (Ivory Coast)	124,518	16,600,000	133	Republic	A	Abidjan and Yamoussoukro	French, Dioula and other
† Croatia	21,829	4,365,000	200	Republic	A	Zagreb	Serbo-Croatian

REGION OR POLITICAL DIVISION	Area Sq. Mi.	Est. Pop. 1/1/02	Pop. Per Sq. Mi.	Form of Government and Ruling Power		Capital	Predominant Languages
† Cuba	42,804	11,205,000	262	Socialist republic	A	Havana (La Habana)	Spanish
† Cyprus	2,277	625,000	275	Republic	A	Nicosia (Levkosía)	Greek, English
Cyprus, North[2]	1,295	140,000	108	Republic	A	Nicosia (Lefkoşa)	Turkish
† Czech Republic	30,450	10,260,000	337	Republic	A	Prague (Praha)	Czech, Slovak
Delaware	2,396	800,000	334	State (U.S.)	D	Dover	English
† Denmark	16,639	5,360,000	322	Constitutional monarchy	A	Copenhagen (København)	Danish
District of Columbia	68	570,000	8,382	Federal district (U.S.)	D	Washington	English
† Djibouti	8,958	465,000	52	Republic	A	Djibouti	French, Arabic, Somali, Afar
† Dominica	305	70,000	230	Republic	A	Roseau	English, French
† Dominican Republic	18,704	8,650,000	462	Republic	A	Santo Domingo	Spanish
† East Timor	5,743	795,000	138	Republic	A	Dili	Portuguese, Tetum, Bahasa Indonesia (Malay), indigenous
† Ecuador	105,037	13,315,000	127	Republic	A	Quito	Spanish, Quechua, indigenous
† Egypt	386,662	70,125,000	181	Socialist republic	A	Cairo (Al Qāhirah)	Arabic
Ellice Islands see Tuvalu							
† El Salvador	8,124	6,295,000	775	Republic	A	San Salvador	Spanish, Nahua
England	50,352	50,365,000	1,000	Administrative division (U.K.)	D	London	English
† Equatorial Guinea	10,831	490,000	45	Republic	A	Malabo	Spanish, indigenous, English
† Eritrea	36,170	4,380,000	121	Republic	A	Asmera	Tigre, Kunama, Cushitic dialects, Nora Bana, Arabic
† Estonia	17,413	1,420,000	82	Republic	A	Tallinn	Estonian, Latvian, Lithuanian, Russian
† Ethiopia	446,953	66,780,000	149	Federal republic	A	Addis Ababa (Adis Abeba)	Amharic, Tigrinya, Orominga, Guaraginga, Somali, Arabic
Europe	3,800,000	728,975,000	192				
Falkland Islands[3]	4,700	3,000	0.6	Dependent territory (U.K.)	C	Stanley	English
Faroe Islands	540	46,000	85	Self-governing territory (Danish protection)	B	Tórshavn	Danish, Faroese
† Fiji	7,056	850,000	120	Republic	A	Suva	English, Fijian, Hindustani
† Finland	130,559	5,180,000	40	Republic	A	Helsinki (Helsingfors)	Finnish, Swedish, Lapp, Russian
Florida	59,928	16,570,000	276	State (U.S.)	D	Tallahassee	English
† France (excl. Overseas Departments)	208,482	59,660,000	286	Republic	A	Paris	French
French Guiana	32,253	180,000	5.6	Overseas department (France)	C	Cayenne	French
French Polynesia	1,360	255,000	188	Overseas territory (France)	C	Papeete	French, Tahitian
Fujian	46,332	35,235,000	760	Province (China)	D	Fuzhou	Chinese dialects
† Gabon	103,347	1,225,000	12	Republic	A	Libreville	French, Fang, indigenous
† Gambia, The	4,127	1,435,000	348	Republic	A	Banjul	English, Malinke, Wolof, Fula, indigenous
Gansu	173,746	25,985,000	150	Province (China)	D	Lanzhou	Chinese (Mandarin), Mongolian, Tibetan dialects
Gaza Strip	139	1,200,000	8,633	Israeli territory with limited self-government			Arabic
Georgia	58,977	8,460,000	143	State (U.S.)	D	Atlanta	English
† Georgia	26,911	4,975,000	185	Republic	A	Tbilisi	Georgian, Russian, Armenian, Azeri
† Germany	137,822	83,145,000	603	Federal republic	A	Berlin	German
† Ghana	92,098	20,070,000	218	Republic	A	Accra	English, Akan and other indigenous
Gibraltar	2.3	28,000	12,174	Dependent territory (U.K.)	C	Gibraltar	English, Spanish, Italian, Portuguese, Russian
Gilbert Islands see Kiribati							
Golan Heights	454	36,000	79	Occupied by Israel			Arabic, Hebrew
Great Britain see United Kingdom							
† Greece	50,949	10,635,000	209	Republic	A	Athens (Athínai)	Greek, English, French
Greenland	840,004	56,000	0.07	Self-governing territory (Danish protection)	B	Godthåb	Danish, Greenlandic, Inuit dialects
† Grenada	133	89,000	670	Parliamentary state	A	St. George's	English, French
Guadeloupe (incl. Dependencies)	657	435,000	662	Overseas department (France)	C	Basse-Terre	French, Creole
Guam	217	160,000	737	Unincorporated territory (U.S.)	C	Hagåtña	English, Chamorro, Japanese
Guangdong	68,649	89,085,000	1,298	Province (China)	D	Guangzhou (Canton)	Chinese dialects, Miao-Yao
Guangxi Zhuangzu	91,236	45,190,000	495	Autonomous region (China)	D	Nanning	Chinese dialects, Thai, Miao-Yao
† Guatemala	42,042	13,145,000	313	Republic	A	Guatemala	Spanish, Amerindian
Guernsey (incl. Dependencies)	30	64,000	2,126	Crown dependency (U.K. protection)	B	St. Peter Port	English, French
† Guinea	94,926	7,690,000	81	Republic	A	Conakry	French, indigenous
† Guinea-Bissau	13,948	1,330,000	95	Republic	A	Bissau	Portuguese, Crioulo, indigenous
Guizhou	65,637	35,575,000	542	Province (China)	D	Guiyang	Chinese (Mandarin), Thai, Miao-Yao
† Guyana	83,000	695,000	8.4	Republic	A	Georgetown	English, indigenous
Hainan	13,205	8,020,000	607	Province (China)	D	Haikou	Chinese, Min, Tai
† Haiti	10,714	7,015,000	655	Republic	A	Port-au-Prince	Creole, French
Hawaii	6,459	1,230,000	190	State (U.S.)	D	Honolulu	English, Hawaiian, Japanese
Hebei	73,359	68,160,000	929	Province (China)	D	Shijiazhuang	Chinese (Mandarin)
Heilongjiang	181,082	37,080,000	205	Province (China)	D	Harbin	Chinese dialects, Mongolian, Tungus
Henan	64,479	93,320,000	1,447	Province (China)	D	Zhengzhou	Chinese (Mandarin)
Holland see Netherlands							
† Honduras	43,277	6,485,000	150	Republic	A	Tegucigalpa	Spanish, indigenous
Hubei	72,356	60,990,000	843	Province (China)	D	Wuhan	Chinese dialects
Hunan	81,082	64,820,000	799	Province (China)	D	Changsha	Chinese dialects, Miao-Yao
† Hungary	35,919	10,090,000	281	Republic	A	Budapest	Hungarian
† Iceland	39,769	280,000	7.0	Republic	A	Reykjavík	Icelandic
Idaho	83,574	1,330,000	16	State (U.S.)	D	Boise	English
Illinois	57,918	12,505,000	216	State (U.S.)	D	Springfield	English
† India (incl. part of Jammu and Kashmir)	1,222,559	1,037,955,000	849	Federal republic	A	New Delhi	English, Hindi, Telugu, Bengali, indigenous
Indiana	36,420	6,125,000	168	State (U.S.)	D	Indianapolis	English
† Indonesia	735,310	230,260,000	313	Republic	A	Jakarta	Bahasa Indonesia (Malay), English, Dutch, indigenous
Iowa	56,276	2,920,000	52	State (U.S.)	D	Des Moines	English
† Iran	630,578	66,365,000	105	Islamic republic	A	Tehrān	Farsi, Turkish dialects, Kurdish
† Iraq	169,235	23,665,000	140	Republic	A	Baghdād	Arabic, Kurdish, Assyrian, Armenian
† Ireland	27,133	3,860,000	142	Republic	A	Dublin (Baile Átha Cliath)	English, Irish Gaelic
Isle of Man	221	74,000	335	Crown dependency (U.K. protection)	B	Douglas	English, Manx Gaelic
† Israel (excl. Occupied Areas)	8,019	5,985,000	746	Republic	A	Jerusalem (Yerushalayim)	Hebrew, Arabic
† Italy	116,342	57,700,000	496	Republic	A	Rome (Roma)	Italian, German, French, Slovene
Ivory Coast see Cote d'Ivoire							
Jamaica	4,244	2,670,000	629	Parliamentary state	A	Kingston	English, Creole
† Japan	145,850	126,880,000	870	Constitutional monarchy	A	Tōkyō	Japanese
Jersey	45	90,000	2,009	Crown dependency (U.K. protection)	B	St. Helier	English, French
Jiangsu	39,614	75,205,000	1,898	Province (China)	D	Nanjing (Nanking)	Chinese dialects
Jiangxi	64,325	41,815,000	650	Province (China)	D	Nanchang	Chinese dialects
Jilin	72,201	27,575,000	382	Province (China)	D	Changchun	Chinese (Mandarin), Mongolian, Korean

REGION OR POLITICAL DIVISION	Area Sq. Mi.	Est. Pop. 1/1/02	Pop. Per Sq. Mi.	Form of Government and Ruling Power		Capital	Predominant Languages
† Jordan	35,135	5,230,000	149	Constitutional monarchy	A	'Ammān	Arabic
Kansas	82,282	2,695,000	33	State (U.S.)	D	Topeka	English
† Kazakhstan	1,049,156	16,735,000	16	Republic	A	Astana (Akmola)	Kazakh, Russian
Kentucky	40,411	4,075,000	101	State (U.S.)	D	Frankfort	English
† Kenya	224,961	30,960,000	138	Republic	A	Nairobi	English, Swahili, indigenous
† Kiribati	313	95,000	303	Republic	A	Bairiki	English, Gilbertese
† Korea, North	46,540	22,100,000	475	Socialist republic	A	P'yŏngyang	Korean
† Korea, South	38,230	48,120,000	1,259	Republic	A	Seoul (Sŏul)	Korean
† Kuwait	6,880	2,075,000	302	Constitutional monarchy	A	Kuwait (Al Kuwayt)	Arabic, English
† Kyrgyzstan	76,641	4,785,000	62	Republic	A	Bishkek	Kirghiz, Russian
† Laos	91,429	5,705,000	62	Socialist republic	A	Viangchan (Vientiane)	Lao, French, English
† Latvia	24,595	2,375,000	97	Republic	A	Rīga	Latvian, Russian, Lithuanian
† Lebanon	4,016	3,655,000	910	Republic	A	Beirut (Bayrūt)	Arabic, French, Armenian, English
† Lesotho	11,720	2,195,000	187	Constitutional monarchy	A	Maseru	English, Sesotho, Zulu, Xhosa
Liaoning	56,255	42,710,000	759	Province (China)	D	Shenyang	Chinese (Mandarin), Mongolian
† Liberia	38,250	3,255,000	85	Republic	A	Monrovia	English, indigenous
† Libya	679,362	5,305,000	7.8	Socialist republic	A	Tripoli (Tarābulus)	Arabic
† Liechtenstein	62	33,000	534	Constitutional monarchy	A	Vaduz	German
† Lithuania	25,213	3,605,000	143	Republic	A	Vilnius	Lithuanian, Polish, Russian
Louisiana	49,651	4,465,000	90	State (U.S.)	D	Baton Rouge	English
† Luxembourg	999	445,000	446	Constitutional monarchy	A	Luxembourg	French, Luxembourgish, German
† Macedonia	9,928	2,050,000	206	Republic	A	Skopje	Macedonian, Albanian
† Madagascar	226,658	16,225,000	72	Republic	A	Antananarivo	Malagasy, French
Maine	33,741	1,290,000	38	State (U.S.)	D	Augusta	English
† Malawi	45,747	10,625,000	232	Republic	A	Lilongwe	Chichewa, English
† Malaysia	127,320	22,445,000	176	Federal constitutional monarchy	A	Kuala Lumpur and Putrajaya[4]	Malay, Chinese dialects, English, Tamil
† Maldives	115	315,000	2,737	Republic	A	Male'	Divehi
† Mali	482,077	11,170,000	23	Republic	A	Bamako	French, Bambara, indigenous
† Malta	122	395,000	3,238	Republic	A	Valletta	English, Maltese
Manitoba	250,116	1,150,000	4.6	Province (Canada)	D	Winnipeg	English
† Marshall Islands	70	72,000	1,029	Republic (U.S. protection)	A	Majuro (island)	English, indigenous, Japanese
Martinique	436	420,000	963	Overseas department (France)	C	Fort-de-France	French, Creole
Maryland	12,297	5,405,000	440	State (U.S.)	D	Annapolis	English
Massachusetts	9,241	6,390,000	691	State (U.S.)	D	Boston	English
† Mauritania	397,956	2,790,000	7.0	Republic	A	Nouakchott	Arabic, Pular, Soninke, Wolof
† Mauritius (incl. Dependencies)	788	1,195,000	1,517	Republic	A	Port Louis	English, Creole, Bhojpuri, French, Hindi, Tamil, others
Mayotte[5]	144	165,000	1,146	Territorial collectivity (France)	C	Mamoutzou	French, Swahili (Mahorian)
† Mexico	758,452	102,640,000	135	Federal republic	A	Mexico City (Ciudad de México)	Spanish, indigenous
Michigan	96,705	10,010,000	104	State (U.S.)	D	Lansing	English
† Micronesia, Federated States of	271	135,000	498	Republic (U.S. protection)	A	Palikir	English, indigenous
Midway Islands	2.0		(1)	Unincorporated territory (U.S.)	C		English
Minnesota	86,943	4,995,000	57	State (U.S.)	D	St. Paul	English
Mississippi	48,286	2,860,000	59	State (U.S.)	D	Jackson	English
Missouri	69,709	5,645,000	81	State (U.S.)	D	Jefferson City	English
† Moldova	13,012	4,435,000	341	Republic	A	Chişinău (Kishinev)	Romanian (Moldovan), Russian
† Monaco	0.8	32,000	40,000	Constitutional monarchy	A	Monaco	French, English, Italian, Monegasque
† Mongolia	604,829	2,675,000	4.4	Republic	A	Ulan Bator (Ulaanbaatar)	Khalkha Mongol, Turkish dialects, Russian, Chinese
Montana	147,046	905,000	6.2	State (U.S.)	D	Helena	English
Montserrat	39	8,000	205	Dependent territory (U.K.)	C	Plymouth	English
† Morocco (excl. Western Sahara)	172,414	30,905,000	179	Constitutional monarchy	A	Rabat	Arabic, Berber dialects, French
† Mozambique	308,642	19,495,000	63	Republic	A	Maputo	Portuguese, indigenous
† Myanmar (Burma)	261,228	42,120,000	161	Provisional military government	A	Rangoon (Yangon)	Burmese, indigenous
† Namibia	317,818	1,810,000	5.7	Republic	A	Windhoek	English, Afrikaans, German, indigenous
† Nauru	8.1	12,000	1,481	Republic	A	Yaren District	Nauruan, English
Nebraska	77,358	1,715,000	22	State (U.S.)	D	Lincoln	English
Nei Monggol (Inner Mongolia)	456,759	24,020,000	53	Autonomous region (China)	D	Hohhot	Mongolian
† Nepal	56,827	25,580,000	450	Constitutional monarchy	A	Kathmandu	Nepali, Maithali, Bhojpuri, other indigenous
† Netherlands	16,164	16,025,000	991	Constitutional monarchy	A	Amsterdam and The Hague ('s-Gravenhage)	Dutch
Netherlands Antilles	309	215,000	696	Self-governing territory (Netherlands protection)	B	Willemstad	Dutch, Papiamento, English
Nevada	110,567	2,150,000	19	State (U.S.)	D	Carson City	English
New Brunswick	28,150	760,000	27	Province (Canada)	D	Fredericton	English, French
New Caledonia	7,172	205,000	29	Overseas territory (France)	C	Nouméa	French, indigenous
New Hampshire	9,283	1,270,000	137	State (U.S.)	D	Concord	English
New Hebrides see Vanuatu							
New Jersey	8,215	8,510,000	1,036	State (U.S.)	D	Trenton	English
New Mexico	121,598	1,835,000	15	State (U.S.)	D	Santa Fe	English, Spanish
New South Wales	309,129	6,705,000	22	State (Australia)	D	Sydney	English
New York	53,989	19,020,000	352	State (U.S.)	D	Albany	English
† New Zealand	104,454	3,885,000	37	Parliamentary state	A	Wellington	English, Maori
Newfoundland and Labrador	156,453	530,000	3.4	Province (Canada)	D	St. John's	English
† Nicaragua	50,054	4,970,000	99	Republic	A	Managua	Spanish, English, indigenous
† Niger	489,192	10,495,000	21	Provisional military government	A	Niamey	French, Hausa, Djerma, indigenous
† Nigeria	356,669	128,285,000	360	Transitional military government	A	Abuja	English, Hausa, Fulani, Yorbua, Ibo, indigenous
Ningxia Huizu	25,637	5,730,000	224	Autonomous region (China)	D	Yinchuan	Chinese (Mandarin)
Niue	100	2,000	20	Self-governing territory (New Zealand protection)	B	Alofi	English, indigenous
Norfolk Island	14	2,000	143	External territory (Australia)	C	Kingston	English, Norfolk
North America	9,500,000	488,780,000	51				
North Carolina	52,672	8,240,000	156	State (U.S.)	D	Raleigh	English
North Dakota	70,704	630,000	8.9	State (U.S.)	D	Bismarck	English
Northern Ireland	5,467	1,705,000	312	Administrative division (U.K.)	D	Belfast	English
Northern Mariana Islands	184	76,000	413	Commonwealth (U.S. protection)	B	Saipan (island)	English, Chamorro, Carolinian
Northern Territory	520,902	200,000	0.4	Territory (Australia)	D	Darwin	English, indigenous
Northwest Territories	519,734	41,000	0.1	Territory (Canada)	D	Yellowknife	English, indigenous
† Norway (incl. Svalbard and Jan Mayen)	149,405	4,515,000	30	Constitutional monarchy	A	Oslo	Norwegian, Lapp, Finnish
Nova Scotia	21,345	945,000	44	Province (Canada)	D	Halifax	English
Nunavut	808,185	29,000	0.04	Territory (Canada)	D	Iqaluit	English, indigenous
Oceania (incl. Australia)	3,300,000	31,415,000	9.5				
Ohio	44,828	11,380,000	254	State (U.S.)	D	Columbus	English
Oklahoma	69,903	3,465,000	50	State (U.S.)	D	Oklahoma City	English

REGION OR POLITICAL DIVISION	Area Sq. Mi.	Est. Pop. 1/1/02	Pop. Per Sq. Mi.	Form of Government and Ruling Power	Capital	Predominant Languages
† Oman	82,030	2,665,000	32	Monarchy	A	Masqat	Arabic, English, Baluchi, Urdu, Indian dialects
Ontario	415,598	11,970,000	29	Province (Canada)	D	Toronto	English
Oregon	97,132	3,495,000	36	State (U.S.)	D	Salem	English
† Pakistan (incl. part of Jammu and Kashmir)	339,732	146,145,000	430	Federal Islamic republic	A	Islāmābād	English, Urdu, Punjabi, Sindhi, Pashto
† Palau (Belau)	196	19,000	97	Republic	A	Koror and Melekeok(4)	Angaur, English, Japanese, Palauan, Sonsorolese, Tobi
† Panama	29,157	2,865,000	98	Republic	A	Panamá	Spanish, English
† Papua New Guinea	178,704	5,110,000	29	Parliamentary state	A	Port Moresby	English, Motu, Pidgin, indigenous
† Paraguay	157,048	5,810,000	37	Republic	A	Asunción	Spanish, Guarani
Pennsylvania	46,058	12,290,000	267	State (U.S.)	D	Harrisburg	English
† Peru	496,225	27,720,000	56	Republic	A	Lima	Quechua, Spanish, Aymara
† Philippines	115,831	83,685,000	722	Republic	A	Manila	English, Pilipino, Tagalog
Pitcairn (incl. Dependencies)	19	100	5.3	Dependent territory (U.K.)	C	Adamstown	English, Tahitian
† Poland	120,728	38,630,000	320	Republic	A	Warsaw (Warszawa)	Polish
† Portugal	35,516	10,075,000	284	Republic	A	Lisbon (Lisboa)	Portuguese
Prince Edward Island	2,185	140,000	64	Province (Canada)	D	Charlottetown	English
Puerto Rico	3,515	3,950,000	1,124	Commonwealth (U.S. protection)	B	San Juan	Spanish, English
† Qatar	4,412	780,000	177	Monarchy	A	Ad Dawḥah	Arabic, English
Qinghai	277,994	5,260,000	19	Province (China)	D	Xining	Tibetan dialects, Mongolian, Turkish dialects, Chinese (Mandarin)
Quebec	595,391	7,425,000	12	Province (Canada)	D	Québec	French, English
Queensland	668,208	3,740,000	5.6	State (Australia)	D	Brisbane	English
Reunion	967	740,000	765	Overseas department (France)	C	Saint-Denis	French, Creole
Rhode Island	1,231	1,065,000	865	State (U.S.)	D	Providence	English
Rhodesia see Zimbabwe							
† Romania	91,699	22,340,000	244	Republic	A	Bucharest (București)	Romanian, Hungarian, German
† Russia	6,592,849	145,215,000	22	Federal republic	A	Moscow (Moskva)	Russian, Tatar, Ukrainian
† Rwanda	10,169	7,355,000	723	Republic	A	Kigali	French, Kinyarwanda, Kiswahili
St. Helena (incl. Dependencies)	121	7,000	58	Dependent territory (U.K.)	C	Jamestown	English
† St. Kitts and Nevis	104	39,000	375	Parliamentary state	B	Basseterre	English
† St. Lucia	238	160,000	672	Parliamentary state	A	Castries	English, French
St. Pierre and Miquelon	93	7,000	75	Territorial collectivity (France)	C	Saint-Pierre	French
† St. Vincent and the Grenadines	150	115,000	767	Parliamentary state	A	Kingstown	English, French
† Samoa	1,093	180,000	165	Constitutional monarchy	A	Apia	English, Samoan
† San Marino	24	28,000	1,186	Republic	A	San Marino	Italian
† Sao Tome and Principe	372	170,000	457	Republic	A	São Tomé	Portuguese, Fang
Saskatchewan	251,366	1,015,000	4.0	Province (Canada)	D	Regina	English
† Saudi Arabia	830,000	23,130,000	28	Monarchy	A	Riyadh (Ar Riyāḍ)	Arabic
Scotland	30,421	5,110,000	168	Administrative division (U.K.)	D	Edinburgh	English, Scots Gaelic
† Senegal	75,951	10,435,000	137	Republic	A	Dakar	French, Wolof, Fulani, Serer, indigenous
† Serbia and Montenegro (Yugoslavia)	39,449	10,665,000	270	Republic	A	Belgrade (Beograd)	Serbo-Croatian, Albanian
† Seychelles	176	80,000	455	Republic	A	Victoria	English, French, Creole
Shaanxi	79,151	36,410,000	460	Province (China)	D	Xi'an (Sian)	Chinese (Mandarin)
Shandong	59,074	91,510,000	1,549	Province (China)	D	Jinan	Chinese (Mandarin)
Shanghai	2,394	17,125,000	7,153	Autonomous city (China)	D	Shanghai	Chinese (Wu)
Shanxi	60,232	33,445,000	555	Province (China)	D	Taiyuan	Chinese (Mandarin)
Sichuan	188,263	83,865,000	445	Province (China)	D	Chengdu	Chinese (Mandarin), Tibetan dialects, Miao-Yao
† Sierra Leone	27,925	5,525,000	198	Transitional military government	A	Freetown	English, Krio, Mende, Temne, indigenous
† Singapore	246	4,375,000	17,814	Republic	A	Singapore	Chinese (Mandarin), English, Malay, Tamil
† Slovakia	18,933	5,420,000	286	Republic	A	Bratislava	Slovak, Hungarian
† Slovenia	7,821	1,930,000	247	Republic	A	Ljubljana	Slovenian, Serbo-Croatian
† Solomon Islands	10,954	490,000	45	Parliamentary state	A	Honiara	English, indigenous
† Somalia	246,201	7,620,000	31	None	A	Mogadishu (Muqdisho)	Arabic, Somali, English, Italian
† South Africa	470,693	43,645,000	93	Republic	A	Pretoria, Cape Town, and Bloemfontein	Afrikaans, English, Xhosa, Zulu, other indigenous
South America	6,900,000	352,960,000	51				
South Australia	379,724	1,525,000	4.0	State (Australia)	D	Adelaide	English
South Carolina	31,189	4,085,000	131	State (U.S.)	D	Columbia	English
South Dakota	77,121	755,000	9.8	State (U.S.)	D	Pierre	English
South Georgia (incl. Dependencies)(3)	1,450	(1)		Dependent territory (U.K.)	C	Grytviken Harbour	English
South West Africa see Namibia							
† Spain	194,885	40,060,000	206	Constitutional monarchy	A	Madrid	Spanish (Castilian), Catalan, Galician, Basque
Spanish North Africa(6)	12	150,000	12,500	Five possessions (Spain)	C		Spanish, Arabic, Berber dialects
Spanish Sahara see Western Sahara							
† Sri Lanka	24,962	19,495,000	781	Socialist republic	A	Colombo and Sri Jayewardenepura Kotte	English, Sinhala, Tamil
† Sudan	967,500	36,585,000	38	Provisional military government	A	Khartoum (Al Kharṭūm)	Arabic, Nubian and other indigenous, English
† Suriname	63,251	435,000	6.9	Republic	A	Paramaribo	Dutch, Sranan Tongo, English, Hindustani, Javanese
† Swaziland	6,704	1,115,000	166	Monarchy	A	Mbabane and Lobamba	English, siSwati
† Sweden	173,732	8,875,000	51	Constitutional monarchy	A	Stockholm	Swedish, Lapp, Finnish
† Switzerland	15,943	7,295,000	458	Federal republic	A	Bern (Berne)	German, French, Italian, Romansch
† Syria	71,498	16,940,000	237	Socialist republic	A	Damascus (Dimashq)	Arabic, Kurdish, Armenian, Aramaic, Circassian
Taiwan	13,901	22,460,000	1,616	Republic	A	T'aipei	Chinese (Mandarin), Taiwanese (Min), Hakka
† Tajikistan	55,251	6,650,000	120	Republic	A	Dushanbe	Tajik, Uzbek, Russian
† Tanzania	364,900	36,705,000	101	Republic	A	Dar es Salaam and Dodoma	English, Swahili, indigenous
Tasmania	26,409	475,000	18	State (Australia)	D	Hobart	English
Tennessee	42,146	5,760,000	137	State (U.S.)	D	Nashville	English
Texas	267,277	21,515,000	80	State (U.S.)	D	Austin	English, Spanish
† Thailand	198,115	62,080,000	313	Constitutional monarchy	A	Bangkok (Krung Thep)	Thai, indigenous
Tianjin (Tientsin)	4,363	10,150,000	2,326	Autonomous city (China)	D	Tianjin (Tientsin)	Chinese (Mandarin)
† Togo	21,925	5,220,000	238	Provisional military government	A	Lomé	French, Ewe, Mina, Kabye, Dagomba
Tokelau	4.6	1,500	326	Island territory (New Zealand)	C		English, Tokelauan
† Tonga	288	105,000	364	Constitutional monarchy	A	Nuku'alofa	Tongan, English
† Trinidad and Tobago	1,980	1,165,000	588	Republic	A	Port of Spain	English, Hindi, French, Spanish
Tristan da Cunha	40	300	7.5	Dependency (St. Helena)	C	Edinburgh	English

REGION OR POLITICAL DIVISION	Area Sq. Mi.	Est. Pop. 1/1/02	Pop. Per Sq. Mi.	Form of Government and Ruling Power		Capital	Predominant Languages
† Tunisia	63,170	9,760,000	155	Republic	A	Tunis	Arabic, French
† Turkey	302,541	66,905,000	221	Republic	A	Ankara	Turkish, Kurdish, Arabic
† Turkmenistan	188,457	4,645,000	25	Republic	A	Ashgabat	Turkmen, Russian, Uzbek
Turks and Caicos Islands	193	18,000	93	Dependent territory (U.K.)	C	Grand Turk	English
† Tuvalu	10	11,000	1,100	Parliamentary state	A	Funafuti	Tuvaluan, English
† Uganda	93,104	24,335,000	261	Republic	A	Kampala	English, Luganda, Swahili, indigenous
† Ukraine	233,090	48,570,000	208	Republic	A	Kiev (Kyïv)	Ukrainian, Russian, Romanian, Polish
† United Arab Emirates	32,278	2,425,000	75	Federation of monarchs	A	Abū Ẓaby (Abu Dhabi)	Arabic, Farsi, English, Hindi, Urdu
† United Kingdom	94,249	59,715,000	634	Parliamentary monarchy	A	London	English, Welsh, Scots Gaelic
† United States	3,717,796	279,310,000	75	Federal republic	A	Washington	English, Spanish
Upper Volta see Burkina Faso							
† Uruguay	68,500	3,375,000	49	Republic	A	Montevideo	Spanish
Utah	84,904	2,285,000	27	State (U.S.)	D	Salt Lake City	English
† Uzbekistan	172,742	25,355,000	147	Republic	A	Tashkent	Uzbek, Russian
† Vanuatu	4,707	195,000	41	Republic	A	Port Vila	Bislama, English, French
Vatican City	0.2	1,000	5,000	Monarchical-sacerdotal state	A	Vatican City	Italian, Latin, other
† Venezuela	352,145	24,105,000	68	Federal republic	A	Caracas	Spanish, Amerindian
Vermont	9,615	615,000	64	State (U.S.)	D	Montpelier	English
Victoria	87,807	4,920,000	56	State (Australia)	D	Melbourne	English
† Vietnam	127,428	80,520,000	632	Socialist republic	A	Hanoi	Vietnamese, French, Chinese, English, Khmer, indigenous
Virginia	42,326	7,230,000	171	State (U.S.)	D	Richmond	English
Virgin Islands (U.S.)	171	125,000	731	Unincorporated territory (U.S.)	C	Charlotte Amalie	English, Spanish, Creole
Wake Island	3.0	(1)		Unincorporated territory (U.S.)	C		English
Wales	8,015	2,960,000	369	Administrative division (U.K.)	D	Cardiff	English, Welsh Gaelic
Wallis and Futuna	99	15,000	152	Overseas territory (France)	C	Mata-Utu	French, Wallisian
Washington	70,637	6,030,000	85	State (U.S.)	D	Olympia	English
West Bank (incl. Jericho and East Jerusalem)	2,263	2,125,000	939	Israeli territory with limited self-government			Arabic, Hebrew
Western Australia	976,792	1,940,000	2.0	State (Australia)	D	Perth	English
Western Sahara	102,703	250,000	2.4	Occupied by Morocco	C		Arabic
West Virginia	24,231	1,800,000	74	State (U.S.)	D	Charleston	English
Wisconsin	65,499	5,415,000	83	State (U.S.)	D	Madison	English
Wyoming	97,818	495,000	5.1	State (U.S.)	D	Cheyenne	English
Xianggang (Hong Kong)	425	6,920,000	16,282	Special administrative region (China)	D	Hong Kong (Xianggang)	Chinese (Cantonese), English, Putonghua
Xinjiang Uygur (Sinkiang)	617,764	19,710,000	32	Autonomous region (China)	D	Ürümqi	Turkish dialects, Mongolian, Tungus, English
Xizang (Tibet)	471,045	2,670,000	5.7	Autonomous region (China)	D	Lhasa	Tibetan dialects
† Yemen	203,850	18,385,000	90	Republic	A	Sanaa (Ṣan'ā')	Arabic
Yugoslavia see Serbia and Montenegro							
Yukon Territory	186,272	30,000	0.2	Territory (Canada)	D	Whitehorse	English, Inuktitut, indigenous
Yunnan	152,124	43,545,000	286	Province (China)	D	Kunming	Chinese (Mandarin), Tibetan dialects, Khmer, Miao-Yao
Zaire see Congo, Democratic Republic of the							
† Zambia	290,586	9,865,000	34	Republic	A	Lusaka	English, Tonga, Lozi, other indigenous
Zhejiang	39,305	47,370,000	1,205	Province (China)	D	Hangzhou	Chinese dialects
† Zimbabwe	150,873	11,375,000	75	Republic	A	Harare (Salisbury)	English, Shona, Sindebele
WORLD	57,900,000	6,195,885,000	107				

† Member of the United Nations (2002).
... None, or not applicable.
(1) No Permanent Population
(2) North Cyprus unilaterally declared its independence from Cyprus in 1983.
(3) Claimed by Argentina.
(4) Future capital.
(5) Claimed by Comoros.
(6) Comprises Ceuta, Melilla, and several small islands.

WORLD DEMOGRAPHIC TABLE

CONTINENT / Country	Population Estimate 1/1/99	Pop. Per Sq. Mile	Urban[1] Population Projected 2000	%[1] Urban	Crude Birth[2] Rate per '000 - 1996	Crude Death[2,4] Rate per '000 - 1996	Natural[2] Increase % - 1996	Infant[2] Mortality 1996	Lifetime Expectance[3] 1998 Male	Lifetime Expectance[3] 1998 Female
NORTH AMERICA										
Bahamas	282,000	52	267,000	88.5	19	6	1.3	23	70	79
Belize	233,000	26	112,000	46.5	33	6	2.7	34	73	76
Canada	30,450,000	8	23,645,000	77.1	13	7	0.6	6	75	81
Costa Rica	3,639,000	184	1,970,000	51.9	24	4	2.0	14	74	79
Cuba	11,075,000	259	8,727,000	77.9	14	7	0.8	8	74	78
Dominica	66,000	216	50,000	71.0	18	5	1.3	10	74	80
Dominican Republic	8,064,000	431	5,537,000	65.2	24	6	1.8	48	69	73
El Salvador	5,797,000	714	2,947,000	46.6	28	6	2.2	32	66	71
Guatemala	12,170,000	289	4,932,000	40.4	34	7	2.7	51	65	70
Haiti	6,833,000	638	2,727,000	34.9	38	16	2.2	104	57	60
Honduras	5,931,000	137	3,042,000	46.9	33	6	2.8	42	68	72
Jamaica	2,644,000	623	1,451,000	56.1	22	6	1.6	16	72	77
Mexico	99,430,000	131	73,553,000	74.4	26	5	2.2	25	69	75
Nicaragua	4,650,000	93	3,038,000	64.7	34	6	2.8	46	67	70
Panama	2,757,000	95	1,649,000	57.8	23	5	1.8	30	72	76
St. Lucia	153,000	643	57,000	37.8	22	6	1.6	20	66	74
Trinidad and Tobago	1,110,000	561	993,000	74.1	16	7	0.9	18	71	75
United States	271,490,000	72	214,504,000	77.2	15	8	0.7	8	73	80
SOUTH AMERICA										
Argentina	36,500,000	34	33,089,000	89.4	19	9	1.1	28	70	77
Bolivia	7,904,000	19	5,400,000	64.8	32	11	2.2	68	60	63
Brazil	170,860,000	52	137,527,000	81.3	21	9	1.2	55	66	70
Chile	14,880,000	51	12,868,000	84.6	18	6	1.2	14	71	78
Colombia	38,950,000	88	29,154,000	74.9	21	5	1.7	26	67	73
Ecuador	12,450,000	119	7,892,000	62.4	25	6	2.0	35	67	73
Guyana	706,000	9	334,000	38.2	19	10	0.9	51	64	70
Paraguay	5,362,000	34	3,077,000	56.0	31	4	2.7	23	69	73
Peru	26,365,000	53	18,674,000	72.8	24	6	1.8	52	66	69
Suriname	430,000	7	236,000	52.3	24	6	1.8	29	69	74
Uruguay	3,297,000	48	2,990,000	91.3	17	9	0.8	15	70	76
Venezuela	23,005,000	65	21,113,000	87.4	24	5	1.9	30	70	76
EUROPE										
Albania	3,347,000	302	1,367,000	39.1	22	8	1.5	49	70	76
Austria	8,136,000	251	5,361,000	64.7	11	10	0.1	7	74	80
Belarus	10,405,000	130	7,654,000	74.4	12	14	-0.1	13	65	75
Belgium	10,180,000	864	9,985,000	97.4	11	10	0.1	7	74	81
Bosnia and Herzegovina	3,427,000	174	1,872,000	43.1	6	16	-1.0	43	71	76
Bulgaria	8,215,000	192	5,820,000	70.1	8	14	-0.5	16	68	75
Croatia	4,675,000	214	2,589,000	57.7	10	11	-0.2	10	68	77
Czech Republic	10,280,000	338	6,755,000	66.3	10	11	-0.1	8	68	75
Denmark	5,347,000	321	4,522,000	85.7	12	11	0.1	7	73	79
Estonia	1,414,000	81	1,053,000	74.3	11	14	-0.3	17	64	75
Finland	5,154,000	39	3,366,000	65.0	12	10	0.2	5	73	80
France	58,890,000	279	44,630,000	75.6	11	9	0.2	5	74	81
Germany	82,700,000	600	72,386,000	87.5	10	11	-0.2	6	74	80
Greece	10,685,000	210	6,368,000	60.1	11	9	0.1	8	76	81
Hungary	10,195,000	284	6,568,000	67.0	11	15	-0.4	12	65	74
Iceland	272,000	7	260,000	92.3	15	7	0.9	4	76	81
Ireland	3,626,000	134	2,092,000	58.5	14	8	0.5	7	73	79
Italy	56,760,000	488	38,317,000	67.0	10	10	z	7	75	79
Latvia	2,368,000	96	1,781,000	74.3	11	15	-0.4	21	63	75
Lithuania	3,592,000	142	2,755,000	74.7	13	13	z	17	65	76
Luxembourg	427,000	427	391,000	91.1	12	9	0.3	7	73	80
Macedonia	2,016,000	203	1,385,000	62.0	13	8	0.5	30	70	76
Moldova	4,459,000	343	2,460,000	55.2	16	12	0.5	48	64	72
Netherlands	15,770,000	976	14,181,000	89.4	12	8	0.4	6	75	81
Norway	4,430,000	30	3,269,000	74.2	12	10	0.2	6	74	81
Poland	38,600,000	318	25,389,000	65.6	12	10	0.2	12	67	76
Portugal	9,925,000	279	3,719,000	38.0	11	10	z	8	72	79
Romania	22,360,000	244	13,100,000	58.2	10	12	-0.3	23	67	73
Serbia and Montenegro	11,205,000	284	6,286,000	59.9	13	10	0.4	23	70	75
Slovakia	5,395,000	285	3,283,000	61.1	13	9	0.3	11	67	75
Slovenia	1,971,000	252	1,007,000	52.6	8	9	-0.1	7	69	78
Spain	39,150,000	201	30,895,000	77.6	8	9	-0.1	7	75	81
Sweden	8,899,000	51	7,414,000	83.3	13	11	0.2	6	76	82
Switzerland	7,268,000	456	4,638,000	62.6	12	9	0.3	6	75	82
Ukraine	49,965,000	214	36,838,000	72.5	11	15	-0.4	23	64	74
United Kingdom	59,040,000	626	52,198,000	89.5	13	11	0.2	6	75	79
Russia	146,630,000	22	113,567,000	77.7	10	16	-0.6	25	62	74
ASIA										
Afghanistan	25,315,000	101	5,600,000	21.9	43	18	2.5	150	45	46
Armenia	3,416,000	297	2,562,000	70.0	16	8	0.9	39	70	76
Azerbaijan	7,883,000	236	4,483,000	57.3	22	9	1.4	75	68	76
Bahrain	622,000	2,330	570,000	92.2	24	3	2.0	17	71	75
Bangladesh	126,110,000	2,268	27,172,000	21.2	31	11	1.9	102	58	58
Brunei	319,000	143	235,000	72.2	26	5	2.0	24	73	77
Cambodia	11,485,000	164	2,631,000	23.5	44	16	2.8	108	53	55
China	1,242,070,000	337	444,333,000[5]	34.3[5]	17	7	1.0	39	68	72
Cyprus	615,000	270	n.a.	n.a.	n.a.	n.a.	n.a.	n.a.	76	80
Georgia	5,085,000	189	3,289,000	60.7	13	12	0.1	23	70	78
India	992,470,000	802	286,323,000	28.4	26	10	1.6	71	63	63
Indonesia	214,530,000	285	85,458,000	40.2	24	8	1.5	63	63	67
Iran	64,830,000	103	47,085,000	61.6	34	7	2.7	53	69	70
Iraq	22,070,000	130	17,752,000	76.8	43	7	3.7	60	67	70
Israel	5,353,000	668	5,541,000	91.2	20	6	1.4	8	75	79
Japan	126,060,000	864	99,724,000	78.9	10	8	0.2	4	77	83
Jordan	4,491,000	128	4,697,000	74.2	37	4	3.3	32	68	72
Kazakhstan	16,835,000	16	10,442,000	61.7	19	10	0.9	63	67	75
Korea, North	21,230,000	456	15,021,000	62.8	23	5	1.7	26	69	75
Korea, South	46,650,000	1,220	40,395,000	86.2	16	6	1.1	8	69	76
Kuwait	1,952,000	284	1,919,000	97.6	20	2	1.8	11	74	78
Kyrgyzstan	4,531,000	59	1,821,000	40.1	26	9	1.7	78	67	74
Laos	5,334,000	58	1,336,000	23.5	42	14	2.8	97	52	55
Lebanon	3,534,000	880	2,951,000	89.7	28	6	2.2	37	68	72
Malaysia	21,155,000	166	12,767,000	57.3	26	5	2.1	24	70	74
Mongolia	2,599,000	4	1,738,000	63.5	26	9	1.7	70	64	67

CONTINENT / Country	Population Estimate 1/1/99	Pop. Per Sq. Mile	Urban[1] Population Projected 2000	%[1] Urban	Crude Birth[2] Rate per '000 - 1996	Crude Death[2,4] Rate per '000 - 1996	Natural[2] Increase % - 1996	Infant[2] Mortality 1996	Lifetime Expectancy[3] Male 1998	Lifetime Expectancy[3] Female 1998
Myanmar	47,700,000	183	13,661,000	27.7	30	12	1.8	81	59	62
Nepal	23,995,000	422	2,893,000	11.9	37	13	2.4	79	57	57
Oman	2,405,000	29	2,282,000	84.0	38	4	3.3	27	69	73
Pakistan	136,620,000	402	57,792,000	37.0	36	11	2.5	97	63	65
Philippines	78,530,000	678	43,985,000	58.6	30	7	2.3	36	67	70
Qatar	710,000	161	554,000	92.5	21	4	1.7	20	70	75
Saudi Arabia	21,140,000	25	18,572,000	85.7	38	5	3.3	46	70	73
Singapore	3,511,000	14,272	3,587,000	100.0	16	5	1.2	5	74	79
Sri Lanka	19,040,000	763	4,434,000	23.6	18	6	1.2	21	71	75
Syria	16,955,000	237	8,784,000	54.5	40	6	3.4	40	67	71
Taiwan	22,010,000	1,583	n.a./6	n.a./6	15	6	0.9	7	72	79
Tajikistan	6,059,000	110	2,102,000	32.9	34	8	2.5	113	69	74
Thailand	60,330,000	305	13,057,000	21.6	17	7	1.0	33	65	72
Turkey	65,090,000	216	49,517,000	75.3	22	6	1.7	43	67	71
Turkmenistan	4,332,000	23	2,038,000	45.5	29	9	2.0	82	64	70
United Arab Emirates	2,323,000	72	2,099,000	85.9	26	3	2.3	20	74	77
Uzbekistan	23,940,000	139	10,606,000	42.4	30	8	2.2	80	68	73
Vietnam	76,790,000	603	15,891,000	19.7	23	7	1.6	38	65	70
Yemen	16,660,000	82	6,886,000	38.0	45	10	3.6	72	51	52
AFRICA										
Algeria	30,805,000	33	18,727,000	59.3	29	6	2.3	49	68	70
Angola	11,020,000	23	4,371,000	34.2	45	18	2.7	139	47	51
Benin	6,202,000	143	2,630,000	42.3	47	14	3.3	105	47	51
Botswana	1,456,000	6	1,191,000	73.6	33	17	1.6	54	65	69
Burkina Faso	11,420,000	108	2,226,000	18.5	47	20	2.7	118	45	48
Burundi	5,634,000	524	625,000	9.0	43	15	2.8	102	49	53
Cameroon	15,240,000	83	7,401,000	48.9	42	14	2.9	79	57	60
Cape Verde	403,000	259	272,000	62.2	44	8	3.6	54	66	68
Central African Republic	3,410,000	14	1,499,000	41.2	40	18	2.2	112	48	53
Chad	7,458,000	15	1,729,000	23.8	44	17	2.7	120	48	51
Comoros	554,000	642	237,000	33.2	46	10	3.6	75	58	59
Congo	2,688,000	20	1,865,000	62.5	39	17	2.2	108	48	52
Congo, Democratic Republic of the	49,735,000	55	15,670,000	30.3	48	17	3.1	108	50	53
Cote d'Ivoire	15,630,000	126	7,046,000	46.5	42	16	2.7	82	49	51
Djibouti	444,000	50	572,000	83.3	43	15	2.7	107	49	52
Egypt	66,660,000	172	31,297,000	45.9	28	9	1.9	73	65	67
Equatorial Guinea	460,000	42	218,000	48.2	40	14	2.6	98	48	52
Eritrea	3,907,000	108	714,000	18.7	46	16	3.0	119	51	55
Ethiopia	59,040,000	132	11,679,000	17.7	46	18	2.9	123	48	52
Gabon	1,217,000	12	682,000	55.2	28	14	1.5	90	54	57
Gambia, The	1,314,000	318	404,000	32.5	46	15	3.1	118	45	49
Ghana	18,695,000	203	7,644,000	38.4	35	11	2.4	80	56	60
Guinea	7,508,000	79	2,577,000	32.8	43	19	2.4	134	46	47
Guinea-Bissau	1,220,000	87	280,000	23.7	40	16	2.3	116	44	47
Kenya	28,580,000	127	10,043,000	33.1	33	10	2.3	55	53	55
Lesotho	2,110,000	180	641,000	28.0	33	14	1.9	82	61	66
Liberia	2,852,000	75	1,560,000	47.9	43	12	3.1	108	56	59
Libya	4,934,000	7	5,597,000	87.6	44	8	3.7	60	64	68
Madagascar	14,665,000	65	5,133,000	29.5	43	14	2.8	94	58	61
Malawi	9,922,000	217	1,686,000	15.4	42	24	1.7	140	44	45
Mali	10,275,000	21	3,773,000	30.0	51	19	3.2	103	46	50
Mauritania	2,543,000	6	1,489,000	57.7	47	15	3.2	82	52	55
Mauritius	1,175,000	1,491	487,000	41.3	19	6	1.2	17	68	75
Morocco	29,390,000	170	16,035,000	55.3	27	6	2.2	43	64	68
Mozambique	19,895,000	64	7,869,000	40.2	46	19	2.7	126	45	48
Namibia	1,635,000	5	708,000	40.9	37	8	2.9	47	60	63
Niger	9,815,000	20	2,222,000	20.6	54	25	3.0	118	47	50
Nigeria	112,170,000	314	56,651,000	44.0	43	13	3.0	72	51	54
Rwanda	8,055,000	792	472,000	6.2	39	20	1.9	119	45	48
Sao Tome and Principe	152,000	409	68,000	46.7	34	9	2.6	61	62	66
Senegal	9,885,000	130	4,463,000	47.0	45	12	3.4	64	50	52
Sierra Leone	5,182,000	186	1,783,000	36.6	47	18	2.9	136	39	43
Somalia	6,993,000	28	3,170,000	27.5	44	13	3.1	121	47	51
South Africa	43,140,000	92	23,291,000	50.4	28	10	1.8	49	62	68
Sudan	34,010,000	35	10,772,000	36.1	41	11	2.9	76	54	56
Swaziland	975,000	145	351,000	35.7	43	11	3.2	88	58	62
Tanzania	30,935,000	85	9,376,000	27.8	41	19	2.2	106	50	53
Togo	4,992,000	228	1,556,000	33.3	46	11	3.6	84	55	59
Tunisia	9,448,000	150	6,445,000	65.5	24	5	1.9	35	68	71
Uganda	22,485,000	242	3,180,000	14.2	46	21	2.5	99	42	44
Zambia	9,561,000	33	4,067,000	44.5	45	24	2.1	96	45	47
Zimbabwe	11,105,000	74	4,387,000	35.3	32	18	1.4	73	50	52
OCEANIA										
Australia	18,735,000	6	15,954,000	84.7	14	7	0.7	6	75	81
Fiji	808,000	115	359,000	42.3	23	6	1.7	17	71	75
Kiribati	85,000	272	32,000	37.3	31	12	1.9	98	53	56
Micronesia, Federated States of	132,000	487	42,000	29.7	28	6	2.2	36	66	70
New Zealand	3,644,000	35	3,268,000	86.9	16	8	0.8	7	73	79
Papua New Guinea	4,652,000	26	838,000	17.4	33	10	2.3	60	57	59
Samoa	228,000	209	38,000	21.5	31	6	2.5	34	68	71
Solomon Islands	448,000	41	87,000	19.7	38	4	3.4	26	70	74
Tonga	108,000	375	46,000	46.4	24	7	1.7	20	66	71
Vanuatu	187,000	40	38,000	20.1	31	9	2.2	65	66	70

This table presents data, where available, for most independent nations having an area greater than 200 square miles

n.a. - not available

z - negligible

(1) Source: United Nations World Urbanization Prospects

(2) Source: United Nations Bureau of the Census World Population Profile

(3) Source: United States Central Intelligence Agency World Factbook

(4) Deaths under one year of age per 1,000 live births

(5) Includes data for Taiwan

(6) Data included with China

WORLD AGRICULTURE TABLE

CONTINENT / Country	Area square miles	1994 Area in Agriculture[1] %	Wheat[1]	1994-1996 Avg. Production Rice[1] '000 metric tons	Corn[1]	Cattle[1] '000	1994-1996 Avg. Swine[1] '000	Sheep[1] '000	1994-96 Avg. Agricultural Exports	Imports '000,000 of US $
NORTH AMERICA										
Bahamas	5,382	46	0.9%	0	0	z	1	5	6	$7	$2
Belize	8,866	506	5.7%	0	10	30	61	23	3	$2	$1
Canada	3,849,674	287,645	7.5%	25,917	0	7,289	12,712	11,137	633	$15,586	$2,619
Costa Rica	19,730	11,042	56.0%	0	179	29	1,726	317	3	$111	$37
Cuba	42,804	25,815	60.3%	0	277	87	4,633	1,667	310	$4	$94
Dominica	305	69	22.8%	0	0	z	13	5	8	z	$2
Dominican Republic	18,704	15,097	80.7%	0	443	37	2,368	933	133	$3	$62
El Salvador	8,124	6,039	74.3%	0	57	581	1,224	275	5	$8	$66
Guatemala	42,042	17,421	41.4%	25	30	1,099	1,911	774	525	$69	$42
Haiti	10,714	5,425	50.6%	0	100	201	1,243	412	131	$1	$5
Honduras	43,277	13,784	31.9%	1	37	638	2,175	600	13	$30	$12
Jamaica	4,244	1,942	45.8%	0	z	4	437	193	1	$5	$28
Mexico	759,533	411,197	54.1%	3,665	378	18,205	29,678	15,843	5,864	$484	$1,253
Nicaragua	50,054	28,510	57.0%	0	227	298	1,762	387	4	$11	$8
Panama	29,157	8,243	28.3%	0	198	110	1,450	254	0	$3	$19
St. Lucia	238	81	34.1%	0	0	z	12	14	13	$1	$7
Trinidad and Tobago	1,980	514	25.9%	0	13	5	36	32	12	$2	$4
United States	3,787,425	1,622,585	42.8%	61,587	8,210	226,663	102,410	58,719	9,020	$20,308	$14,445
SOUTH AMERICA										
Argentina	1,073,519	653,281	60.9%	12,222	836	10,761	52,222	3,167	20,709	$713	$390
Bolivia	424,165	137,915	32.5%	103	285	557	6,010	2,406	7,870	$93	$22
Brazil	3,300,172	946,717	28.7%	2,329	10,572	33,649	161,490	35,935	18,258	$2,230	$1,058
Chile	292,135	59,652	20.4%	1,294	144	937	3,788	1,461	4,597	$1,523	$220
Colombia	440,831	172,135	39.0%	81	1,729	1,084	25,758	2,510	2,540	$463	$308
Ecuador	105,037	31,386	29.9%	22	1,327	578	5,012	2,595	1,697	$114	$97
Guyana	83,000	6,664	8.0%	0	480	3	253	22	130	$8	$3
Paraguay	157,048	92,567	58.9%	376	101	644	9,551	2,517	386	$276	$4
Peru	496,225	120,695	24.3%	133	1,249	750	4,407	2,459	12,481	$123	$132
Suriname	63,251	344	0.5%	0	227	z	100	26	7	z	$1
Uruguay	68,500	57,235	83.6%	498	799	103	10,535	273	20,394	$281	$106
Venezuela	352,144	84,440	24.0%	z	717	1,098	14,204	3,339	782	$17	$503
EUROPE										
Albania	11,100	4,347	39.2%	365	z	208	837	100	2,460	n.a.	$20
Austria	32,377	13,622	42.1%	1,265	0	1,543	2,309	3,700	363	$1,626	$1,655
Belarus	80,155	36,085	45.0%	423	0	3	5,436	4,027	235	n.a.	n.a.
Belgium	11,783	5,722/2	48.6%/2	1,665/2	0	220/2	3,175/2	7,075/2	163/2	$1,706/2	$2,751/2
Bosnia and Herzegovina	19,741	7,722	39.1%	259	0	552	326	178	279	n.a.	n.a.
Bulgaria	42,855	23,780	55.5%	2,993	6	1,430	673	2,066	3,515	$196	$105
Croatia	21,829	8,927	40.9%	789	0	1,769	491	1,239	441	$606	$477
Czech Republic	30,450	16,510	54.2%	3,754	0	124	2,060	3,985	165	$606	$477
Denmark	16,639	10,390	62.4%	4,321	0	0	2,096	10,950	153	$1,276	$1,123
Estonia	17,413	5,614	32.2%	78	0	0	418	444	65	n.a.	n.a.
Finland	130,559	9,189	7.0%	392	0	0	1,198	1,330	91	$2,564	$832
France	211,208	115,942	54.9%	32,443	121	13,409	20,428	14,561	10,794	$3,403	$5,893
Germany	137,822	66,826	48.5%	17,741	0	2,584	15,916	24,837	2,368	$4,840	$10,579
Greece	50,949	35,629	69.9%	2,222	209	1,976	579	955	9,154	$377	$552
Hungary	35,919	23,637	65.8%	4,466	12	5,143	946	4,797	1,059	$256	$420
Iceland	39,769	8,803	22.1%	0	0	0	73	42	469	$8	$24
Ireland	27,137	16,954	62.5%	642	0	0	6,417	1,509	5,782	$396	$322
Italy	116,336	60,622	52.1%	8,062	1,368	8,495	7,296	8,144	10,604	$1,375	$9,909
Latvia	24,595	9,807	39.9%	267	0	0	589	512	91	n.a.	n.a.
Lithuania	25,213	13,564	53.8%	708	0	0	1,201	1,242	39	$104	$72
Luxembourg	999	n.a./3	n.a./3	n.a./3	0	n.a./3	n.a./3	n.a./3	n.a./3	n.a./3	n.a./3
Macedonia	9,928	5,004	50.4%	329	12	147	282	177	2,415	n.a.	n.a.
Moldova	13,012	9,873	75.9%	930	0	882	825	1,080	1,360	$9	$15
Netherlands	16,164	7,610	47.1%	1,139	0	78	4,642	14,307	1,705	$6,378	$3,540
Norway	149,405	3,977	2.7%	296	0	0	992	762	2,503	$542	$729
Poland	121,196	72,228	59.6%	8,301	0	259	7,379	19,283	711	$505	$739
Portugal	35,516	15,259	43.0%	410	143	782	1,319	2,387	5,897	$857	$1,003
Romania	91,699	57,135	62.3%	5,649	21	9,625	3,645	8,327	10,926	$229	$169
Serbia and Montenegro	39,449	23,946	60.7%	2,568	0	5,306	1,895	4,110	2,654	$116	$205
Slovakia	18,933	9,444	49.9%	1,932	0	622	946	2,098	412	$248	$157
Slovenia	7,820	3,042	38.9%	158	0	288	483	585	22	$127	$358
Spain	194,885	118,981	61.1%	4,494	499	2,895	5,510	18,377	22,466	$1,214	$2,894
Sweden	173,732	12,958	7.5%	1,643	0	0	1,798	2,330	472	$4,204	$1,059
Switzerland	15,943	6,104	38.3%	631	0	228	1,761	1,617	439	$474	$1,319
Ukraine	233,090	161,625	69.3%	14,559	80	2,256	19,596	14,129	4,706	n.a.	n.a.
United Kingdom	94,249	65,815	69.8%	14,575	0	0	11,827	7,609	42,532	$2,092	$5,583
RUSSIA										
Russia	6,592,849	847,910	12.9%	32,388	458	1,240	43,969	25,349	32,745	n.a.	n.a.
ASIA										
Afghanistan	251,826	146,926	58.3%	2,483	333	310	1,500	0	14,267	$49	$11
Armenia	11,506	4,942	43.0%	156	0	5	501	81	645	n.a.	n.a.
Azerbaijan	33,436	16,486	49.3%	689	4	13	1,645	37	4,580	n.a.	n.a.
Bahrain	267	35	13.0%	0	0	0	12	0	18	z	$30
Bangladesh	55,598	33,680	60.6%	1,248	26,631	2	23,773	0	1,075	$184	$272
Brunei	2,226	50	2.3%	0	1	0	2	5	0	z	$13
Cambodia	69,898	20,483	29.3%	0	2,971	55	2,733	2,071	0	n.a.	n.a.
China	3,690,045	2,059,735	55.8%	104,027	185,459	113,049	96,968	410,228	118,796	$4,011	$8,691
Cyprus	2,277	571	25.1%	11	0	0	65	367	260	$7	$40
Georgia	26,911	11,857	44.1%	120	0	375	966	362	783	n.a.	n.a.
India	1,237,061	699,188	56.5%	62,742	120,994	9,300	207,107	14,389	54,139	$309	$1,234
Indonesia	752,409	162,050	21.5%	0	49,162	8,141	11,578	8,193	7,212	$2,690	$2,092
Iran	630,578	243,085	38.5%	10,704	2,415	652	8,347	0	50,891	$139	$543
Iraq	169,235	36,795	21.7%	1,293	323	114	1,060	0	5,367	z	$12
Israel	8,019	2,243	28.0%	177	0	3	390	136	335	$304	$413
Japan	145,850	19,625	13.5%	496	13,780	z	4,911	10,257	23	$2,405	$15,921
Jordan	35,135	4,529	12.9%	60	0	6	62	0	2,067	$28	$74
Kazakhstan	1,049,155	856,374	81.6%	7,740	231	164	8,093	2,017	25,457	n.a.	n.a.
Korea, North	46,540	7,915	17.0%	117	2,313	1,986	1,200	3,150	363	n.a.	n.a.
Korea, South	38,230	8,197	21.4%	8	6,797	78	3,162	6,311	2	$1,314	$5,890
Kuwait	6,880	552	8.0%	z	0	1	18	0	306	z	$79
Kyrgyzstan	76,641	40,232	52.5%	783	7	154	950	134	5,368	n.a.	n.a.
Laos	91,429	6,371	7.0%	0	1,469	61	1,138	1,723	0	$82	$3
Lebanon	4,016	1,243	31.0%	57	0	5	69	55	244	$18	$95
Malaysia	127,320	30,444	23.9%	0	2,095	43	710	3,260	258	$3,712	$792
Mongolia	604,829	457,413	75.6%	265	0	0	3,018	25	13,761	n.a.	n.a.

CONTINENT / Country	Area square miles	1994 Area in Agriculture[1] square miles	%	Wheat[1]	Rice[1]	Corn[1]	Cattle[1] '000	Swine[1] '000	Sheep[1] '000	Exports	Imports
				1994-1996 Avg. Production '000 metric tons			1994-1996 Avg.			1994-96 Avg. Agricultural '000,000 of US $	
Myanmar	261,228	40,235	15.4%	92	17,997	292	9,889	2,967	324	$247	$7
Nepal	56,827	17,475	30.8%	951	3,399	1,317	6,798	639	897	z	$57
Oman	82,030	4,104	5.0%	1	0	0	144	0	149	z	$37
Pakistan	339,732	102,355	30.1%	16,374	5,859	1,287	17,848	0	29,071	$287	$547
Philippines	115,831	41,120	35.5%	0	11,063	4,212	2,028	8,731	30	$182	$511
Qatar	4,412	251	5.7%	z	0	z	13	0	191	z	$14
Saudi Arabia	830,000	477,992	57.6%	1,689	0	6	251	0	7,640	z	$342
Singapore	246	4	1.6%	0	0	0	z	187	0	$1,060	$937
Sri Lanka	24,962	8,969	35.9%	0	2,518	33	1,684	89	17	$115	$88
Syria	71,498	53,228	74.4%	3,989	z	217	769	1	12,150	$160	$90
Taiwan	13,900	4,170[4]	30.0%[4]	0	2,021	252	6	16,451	0	$1,542	$3,726
Tajikistan	55,251	17,297	31.3%	252	22	42	1,199	28	1,947	n.a.	n.a.
Thailand	198,115	82,027	41.4%	1	21,819	4,217	7,231	4,624	69	$2,491	$2,377
Turkey	300,948	155,015	51.5%	18,015	227	1,917	11,867	16	35,659	$275	$1,646
Turkmenistan	188,456	124,957	66.3%	790	86	92	1,161	123	6,083	n.a.	n.a.
United Arab Emirates	32,278	1,436	4.4%	1	0	4	69	0	357	$262	$188
Uzbekistan	172,742	106,741	61.8%	2,150	425	200	5,373	316	8,922	n.a.	n.a.
Vietnam	127,428	27,359	21.5%	0	24,963	1,286	3,635	16,272	0	$946	$121
Yemen	203,850	67,973	33.3%	164	0	59	1,169	0	3,784	$16	$18
AFRICA											
Algeria	919,595	153,050	16.6%	1,732	2	z	1,255	6	17,570	$9	$300
Angola	481,354	222,008	46.1%	4	23	270	3,103	800	242	z	$14
Benin	43,475	6,629	15.2%	0	18	531	1,282	571	842	$40	$8
Botswana	224,711	100,386	44.7%	1	0	13	2,389	4	243	n.a.	n.a.
Burkina Faso	105,869	36,413	34.4%	0	80	286	4,347	563	5,812	$268	$8
Burundi	10,745	8,494	79.1%	9	36	140	403	85	340	$6	$5
Cameroon	183,568	35,367	19.3%	z	65	618	4,890	1,407	3,793	$499	$29
Cape Verde	1,557	259	16.6%	0	0	9	19	472	9	z	$4
Central African Republic	240,535	19,382	8.1%	0	11	70	2,798	547	172	$61	$1
Chad	495,755	186,316	37.6%	2	89	99	4,642	18	2,293	$143	$4
Comoros	863	514	59.5%	0	17	4	50	0	18	z	z
Congo	132,047	39,324	29.8%	0	1	20	70	46	113	$134	$4
Congo, Democratic Republic of the	905,446	88,417	9.8%	9	432	1,170	1,142	1,160	1,052	$11	$6
Cote d'Ivoire	124,518	76,081	61.1%	0	956	546	1,258	369	1,282	$840	$10
Djibouti	8,958	5,019	56.0%	0	0	z	190	0	470	$1	$26
Egypt	386,662	12,606	3.3%	5,298	4,755	4,938	3,030	27	4,171	$187	$715
Equatorial Guinea	10,831	1,290	11.9%	0	0	0	5	5	36	$6	z
Eritrea	36,170	28,595	79.1%	11	0	11	1,307	0	1,527	n.a.	n.a.
Ethiopia	446,953	117,652	26.3%	1,653	0	2,533	29,725	21	21,750	$83	$21
Gabon	103,347	19,923	19.3%	0	1	29	38	207	172	$216	$5
Gambia, The	4,127	1,448	35.1%	0	20	12	315	14	158	z	$2
Ghana	92,098	49,807	54.1%	0	193	994	1,217	363	2,234	$45	$23
Guinea	94,926	46,795	49.3%	0	612	80	2,091	43	572	n.a.	n.a.
Guinea-Bissau	13,948	5,494	39.4%	0	128	13	475	310	255	$1	z
Kenya	224,961	99,691	44.3%	310	60	2,640	13,468	104	5,600	$90	$66
Lesotho	11,720	8,977	76.6%	17	0	133	583	61	1,202	n.a.	n.a.
Liberia	38,250	8,985	23.5%	0	67	0	36	120	210	$55	$1
Libya	679,362	59,517	8.8%	163	0	1	135	0	4,433	$17	$73
Madagascar	226,658	104,652	46.2%	7	2,436	171	10,309	1,593	794	$20	$9
Malawi	45,747	13,699	29.9%	2	55	1,498	690	237	100	$7	$4
Mali	482,077	127,413	26.4%	4	453	286	5,603	63	5,435	$202	$3
Mauritania	397,955	153,398	38.5%	z	57	7	1,179	0	5,589	$3	$3
Mauritius	788	436	55.4%	0	0	1	37	17	7	$10	$58
Morocco	172,414	118,579	68.8%	4,177	42	163	2,378	10	14,322	$137	$481
Mozambique	308,642	182,162	59.0%	2	118	723	1,280	174	121	$16	$12
Namibia	317,818	149,614	47.1%	4	0	25	2,019	19	2,409	n.a.	n.a.
Niger	489,191	57,683	11.8%	4	68	5	1,987	39	3,772	$1	$1
Nigeria	356,669	280,695	78.7%	40	2,823	6,539	16,322	7,159	14,000	$19	$28
Rwanda	10,169	7,124	70.1%	5	5	66	461	83	260	$3	$6
Sao Tome and Principe	372	162	43.6%	0	0	4	4	2	2	z	z
Senegal	75,951	31,139	41.0%	0	155	101	2,808	320	4,800	$20	$19
Sierra Leone	27,925	10,587	37.9%	0	384	8	380	50	328	$1	$2
Somalia	246,201	170,077	69.1%	1	2	146	5,133	9	13,333	$10	$8
South Africa	471,009	382,239	81.2%	2,177	3	9,437	12,996	1,581	28,951	$1,016	$522
Sudan	967,499	483,590	50.0%	479	2	41	22,017	0	23,367	$253	$12
Swaziland	6,704	5,127	76.5%	z	2	108	642	30	26	n.a.	n.a.
Tanzania	364,900	150,309	41.2%	66	690	2,463	13,888	335	3,955	$96	$12
Togo	21,925	10,039	45.8%	0	41	342	246	850	1,145	$36	$3
Tunisia	63,170	34,170	54.1%	1,017	0	0	672	6	6,253	$28	$290
Uganda	93,104	33,205	35.7%	9	79	857	5,213	920	1,890	$8	$4
Zambia	290,586	136,189	46.9%	51	10	1,056	2,633	288	65	$6	$9
Zimbabwe	150,873	77,521	51.4%	201	z	1,925	4,745	263	489	$126	$43
OCEANIA											
Australia	2,966,155	1,782,624	60.1%	16,389	1,008	253	25,955	2,652	124,849	$3,965	$902
Fiji	7,056	1,672	23.7%	0	18	2	349	120	7	$18	$2
Kiribati	313	143	45.6%	0	0	0	9	9	0	$1	$1
Micronesia, Federated States of	271	n.a.	n.a.	0	z	z	9	21	0	n.a.	n.a.
New Zealand	104,454	64,120	61.4%	255	0	171	9,059	426	48,215	$2,261	$142
Papua New Guinea	178,703	2,819	1.6%	0	1	2	107	1,383	4	$231	$6
Samoa	1,093	475	43.4%	0	0	0	26	179	0	z	$2
Solomon Islands	10,954	371	3.4%	0	0	0	10	55	0	$40	z
Tonga	288	201	69.7%	0	0	0	9	85	0	$1	$3
Vanuatu	4,707	560	11.9%	0	0	1	151	60	0	$2	$2

This table presents data, where available, for most independent nations having an area greater than 200 square miles

n.a. - not available

z - negligible

Footnotes:

(1) Source: United Nations Food and Agriculture Organization

(2) Includes data for Luxembourg

(3) Data included with Belgium

(4) Source: United States Central Intelligence Agency *World Factbook*

WORLD ECONOMIC TABLE

CONTINENT / Country	Commercial Energy Production 1995[1] Total '000 met. tons coal equiv.	Solid Fuels %	Liquid Fuels %	Gas Fuels %	Hydro. & Nuclear %	1994-96 Average Production '000 metric tons Coal[3]	Petroleum[3]	Iron ore[2]	Bauxite[2]	Trade: 1993-95 Average[4] '000,000 of US $ Fuel Exports	Fuel Imports	Manufactures Exports	Manufactures Imports
NORTH AMERICA													
Bahamas	n.a.	n.a.	n.a.	n.a.	n.a.	0	0	0	0	$161	$987	$6	$73
Belize	n.a.	n.a.	n.a.	n.a.	n.a.	0	0	0	0	z	$31	$16	$182
Canada	496,012	11.4%	31.3%	42.2%	15.1%	74,556	89,155	23,562	0	$15,251	$5,546	$105,581	$128,329
Costa Rica	1,019	0.0%	0.0%	0.0%	100.0%	0	0	0	0	$19	$275	$560	$2,361
Cuba	1,582	0.0%	95.7%	3.5%	0.8%	0	1,327	0	0	z	$199	$4	$1,445
Dominica	2	0.0%	0.0%	0.0%	100.0%	0	0	0	0	z	$7	$16	$76
Dominican Republic	245	0.0%	0.0%	0.0%	100.0%	0	50	0	0	z	$681	$490	$1,450
El Salvador	926	0.0%	0.0%	0.0%	100.0%	0	0	0	0	$4	$232	$384	$1,737
Guatemala	847	0.0%	66.8%	1.8%	31.4%	0	507	2	0	$35	$354	$472	$2,065
Haiti	20	0.0%	0.0%	0.0%	100.0%	0	0	0	0	z	$55	$58	$262
Honduras	295	0.0%	0.0%	0.0%	100.0%	0	0	0	0	z	$131	$82	$834
Jamaica	15	0.0%	0.0%	0.0%	100.0%	0	0	0	11,428	$18	$463	$838	$1,429
Mexico	282,781	2.2%	78.1%	14.6%	5.2%	8,981	134,984	5,058	0	$3,838	$1,096	$28,950	$41,755
Nicaragua	677	0.0%	0.0%	0.0%	100.0%	0	0	0	0	$2	$154	$79	$539
Panama	297	0.0%	0.0%	0.0%	100.0%	0	50	0	0	$19	$324	$119	$1,738
St. Lucia	n.a.	n.a.	n.a.	n.a.	n.a.	0	0	0	0	z	$23	$30	$200
Trinidad and Tobago	17,530	0.0%	53.2%	46.8%	0.0%	0	6,492	0	0	$955	$7	$511	$847
United States	2,444,217	36.3%	22.9%	28.3%	12.5%	946,597	325,733	38,527	100	$9,894	$56,402	$402,512	$544,765
SOUTH AMERICA													
Argentina	95,425	0.3%	54.9%	38.0%	6.8%	321	35,097	10	0	$1,724	$799	$5,621	$16,751
Bolivia	7,387	0.0%	31.7%	65.4%	2.9%	0	1,336	1	0	$139	$59	$177	$1,043
Brazil	93,543	3.5%	55.1%	7.0%	34.3%	4,300	35,771	110,780	10,398	$386	$4,740	$22,945	$27,891
Chile	6,840	18.1%	13.9%	34.9%	33.1%	1,126	532	5,225	0	$37	$1,166	$1,658	$10,247
Colombia	76,510	31.6%	55.6%	7.3%	5.5%	26,204	27,434	328	0	$2,126	$332	$3,318	$9,200
Ecuador	30,094	0.0%	96.1%	1.2%	2.8%	0	19,075	0	0	$1,320	$205	$287	$2,848
Guyana	1	0.0%	0.0%	0.0%	100.0%	0	0	0	2,082	z	$139	$30	$299
Paraguay	5,110	0.0%	0.0%	0.0%	100.0%	0	0	0	0	$1	$138	$115	$1,546
Peru	11,138	1.3%	81.3%	2.3%	15.2%	144	6,244	3,834	0	$246	$609	$673	$5,187
Suriname	550	0.0%	71.5%	0.0%	28.5%	0	339	0	3,767	$224	$47	$25	$180
Uruguay	921	0.0%	0.0%	0.0%	100.0%	0	0	0	0	$17	$271	$733	$1,973
Venezuela	284,511	1.6%	76.5%	19.5%	2.4%	4,289	138,845	9,615	4,749	$12,884	$101	$2,380	$8,570
EUROPE													
Albania	1,337	4.5%	55.6%	1.2%	38.6%	136	513	0	1	n.a.	$7	n.a.	$404
Austria	8,696	5.5%	17.8%	22.3%	54.3%	1,203	1,088	561	0	$622	$2,511	$42,138	$47,371
Belarus	4,100	24.9%	67.3%	7.7%	0.0%	0	1,898	0	0	n.a.	n.a.	n.a.	n.a.
Belgium	15,761	1.6%	0.0%	0.0%	98.4%	655	596	0	0	$3,696/5	$8,122/5	$108,879/5	$92,485/5
Bosnia and Herzegovina	516	66.1%	0.0%	0.0%	33.7%	2,716	0	57	75	n.a.	n.a.	n.a.	n.a.
Bulgaria	14,449	52.8%	0.4%	0.4%	46.3%	28,636	46	300	0	n.a.	n.a.	n.a.	n.a.
Croatia	3,845	2.7%	14.2%	66.3%	16.8%	171	1,679	0	1	$367	$676	$3,146	$3,881
Czech Republic	41,234	86.1%	0.5%	0.7%	12.8%	71,831	159	0	0	$688	$1,377	$13,392	$13,682
Denmark	20,402	0.0%	64.2%	35.1%	0.7%	0	9,580	0	0	$1,149	$1,268	$26,294	$27,310
Estonia	3,730	100.0%	0.0%	0.0%	0.0%	12,976	0	0	0	n.a.	n.a.	n.a.	n.a.
Finland	11,630	25.0%	0.0%	0.0%	75.0%	0	0	0	0	$587	$2,035	$25,764	$17,132
France	166,032	4.7%	2.5%	2.7%	90.1%	8,845	2,471	523	0	$5,834	$16,030	$186,918	$180,096
Germany	199,956	56.4%	2.1%	11.4%	30.1%	251,043	2,920	18	0	$4,400	$25,076	$386,350	$287,197
Greece	11,917	90.0%	5.5%	0.6%	3.9%	57,995	451	807	2,283	$996	$2,253	$4,611	$15,837
Hungary	18,307	24.6%	17.3%	29.6%	28.6%	14,314	1,752	0	965	$341	$1,622	$7,235	$10,515
Iceland	931	0.0%	0.0%	0.0%	100.0%	0	0	0	0	z	$111	$187	$1,182
Ireland	5,316	30.2%	0.0%	67.1%	2.7%	1	50	0	0	$144	$887	$25,713	$20,340
Italy	42,928	0.3%	17.4%	60.4%	21.8%	321	4,645	0	11	$2,553	$12,865	$175,169	$117,345
Latvia	473	23.7%	0.0%	0.0%	76.3%	0	0	0	0	n.a.	n.a.	n.a.	n.a.
Lithuania	4,687	0.4%	3.9%	0.0%	95.7%	0	151	0	0	$358	$873	$1,215	$1,464
Luxembourg	102	0.0%	0.0%	0.0%	100.0%	0	0	0	0	n.a./6	n.a./6	n.a./6	n.a./6
Macedonia	2,889	96.6%	0.0%	0.0%	3.4%	4,098	0	9	0	$4	$257	$111	$233
Moldova	34	0.0%	0.0%	0.0%	100.0%	60	0	0	0	n.a.	n.a.	$111	$233
Netherlands	102,559	0.0%	4.9%	93.6%	1.5%	0	3,317	0	0	$11,447	$11,062	$102,370	$106,491
Norway	258,250	0.1%	76.8%	17.3%	5.8%	279	138,870	1,301	0	$17,100	$814	$9,653	$22,641
Poland	135,480	95.7%	0.3%	3.7%	0.4%	200,175	242	0	0	$1,442	$2,124	$12,816	$17,178
Portugal	1,092	0.0%	0.0%	0.0%	100.0%	143	99	6	0	$559	$2,285	$15,487	$20,122
Romania	43,328	24.7%	23.0%	47.6%	4.7%	40,614	6,747	173	178	$620	$1,821	$4,654	$4,626
Serbia and Montenegro	12,027	69.6%	10.8%	8.1%	11.5%	38,397	1,120	28	128	$59	$726	$2,123	$2,676
Slovakia	6,629	14.8%	1.3%	5.2%	78.7%	2,720	70	232	0	$317	$1,381	$5,632	$4,579
Slovenia	3,214	31.6%	0.1%	0.7%	67.6%	4,851	2	0	0	$85	$513	$6,332	$5,769
Spain	38,977	34.9%	2.9%	1.5%	60.6%	29,336	748	884	0	$1,214	$8,102	$59,352	$68,483
Sweden	34,575	1.0%	0.0%	0.0%	99.0%		4	12,591	0	$1,592	$4,025	$54,523	$41,464
Switzerland	13,666	0.0%	0.0%	0.0%	100.0%	0	50	0	0	$135	$1,912	$63,266	$56,311
Ukraine	118,908	58.5%	4.9%	18.7%	17.9%	82,775	3,233	27,367	0	n.a.	n.a.	n.a.	n.a.
United Kingdom	364,154	12.4%	51.4%	26.9%	9.3%	49,059	122,967	0	0	$12,761	$8,141	$170,708	$185,386
Russia	1,512,045	16.1%	28.8%	51.2%	3.9%	281,935	297,509	40,500	3,133	n.a.	n.a.	n.a.	n.a.
ASIA													
Afghanistan	280	1.8%	0.0%	79.6%	18.2%	5	0	0	0	z	$4	$56	$284
Armenia	349	0.0%	0.0%	0.0%	100.0%	0	0	0	0	n.a.	n.a.	n.a.	n.a.
Azerbaijan	21,124	0.0%	63.3%	35.7%	0.9%	0	8,851	92	0	n.a.	n.a.	n.a.	n.a.
Bahrain	12,507	0.0%	28.0%	72.0%	0.0%	0	1,929	0	0	$2,223	$1,242	$609	$1,956
Bangladesh	9,287	0.0%	0.2%	99.4%	0.5%	0	65	0	0	$35	$830	$2,096	$2,813
Brunei	26,531	0.0%	46.5%	53.5%	0.0%	0	8,035	0	0	$2,281	$6	$30	$1,322
Cambodia	9	0.0%	0.0%	0.0%	100.0%	0	0	0	0	n.a.	n.a.	n.a.	n.a.
China/7	1,237,323	78.5%	17.3%	1.9%	2.3%	1,357,825	149,923	74,017	4,967	$8,341	$7,570	$234,342	$236,627
Cyprus	n.a.	n.a.	n.a.	n.a.	n.a.	0	0	0	0	$16	$240	$519	$2,027
Georgia	904	3.7%	31.6%	0.8%	64.0%	59	66	0	0	n.a.	n.a.	n.a.	n.a.
India	310,950	73.1%	15.3%	7.9%	3.7%	273,233	32,173	40,579	5,269	$489	$6,705	$19,618	$14,391
Indonesia	266,739	13.5%	53.9%	31.3%	1.3%	39,724	75,459	195	1,080	$10,354	$2,531	$20,627	$24,599
Iran	323,134	0.3%	81.7%	17.7%	0.3%	993	181,135	4,433	122	$14,418	$76	$743	$9,081
Iraq	58,207	0.0%	92.7%	7.2%	0.1%	0	27,986	0	0	$463	$2	$2	$594
Israel	40	0.0%	17.5%	72.5%	10.0%	0	7	0	0	z	$1,548	$15,065	$21,159
Japan	132,624	3.9%	0.8%	2.3%	93.0%	6,831	553	1	0	$2,405	$45,773	$381,625	$154,377
Jordan	5	0.0%	60.0%	0.0%	40.0%	0	1	0	0	z	$460	$721	$2,159
Kazakhstan	108,856	65.7%	27.1%	6.3%	0.9%	88,048	18,478	7,033	2,879	n.a.	n.a.	n.a.	n.a.
Korea, North	89,425	96.8%	0.0%	0.0%	3.2%	71,587	0	5,033	0	n.a.	n.a.	n.a.	n.a.
Korea, South	29,251	12.6%	0.0%	0.0%	87.4%	6,036	149	111	0	$2,022	$15,314	$94,328	$72,713
Kuwait	162,606	0.0%	92.6%	7.4%	0.0%	0	101,664	0	0	$10,864	$36	$539	$5,815
Kyrgyzstan	2,029	24.4%	6.3%	2.0%	67.3%	1,767	88	0	0	n.a.	n.a.	n.a.	n.a.
Laos	107	0.9%	0.0%	0.0%	99.1%	1	0	0	0	z	$120	$91	$275
Lebanon	90	0.0%	0.0%	0.0%	100.0%	0	0	0	0	$3	$898	$427	$3,710
Malaysia	89,147	0.1%	55.5%	43.3%	1.0%	77	33,466	160	188	$4,191	$1,402	$44,721	$52,235
Mongolia	2,472	100.0%	0.0%	0.0%	0.0%	7,741	0	0	0				

CONTINENT / Country	Commercial Energy Production 1995[1] Total '000 met. tons coal equiv.	Solid Fuels %	Liquid Fuels %	Gas Fuels %	Hydro. & Nuclear %	1994-96 Average Production '000 metric tons Coal[3]	Petroleum[3]	Iron ore[2]	Bauxite[2]	Trade: 1993-95 Average[4] '000,000 of US $ Fuel Exports	Fuel Imports	Manufactures Exports	Manufactures Imports
Myanmar	2,866	1.9%	24.0%	67.5%	6.6%	77	766	0	0	$67	$27	$53	$878
Nepal	120	0.0%	0.0%	0.0%	100.0%	12	0	0	0	z	$222	$363	$540
Oman	64,018	0.0%	95.1%	4.9%	0.0%	0	42,106	0	0	$4,343	$65	$767	$2,873
Pakistan	28,997	7.1%	13.6%	69.0%	10.3%	3,224	2,765	0	4	$73	$1,642	$6,099	$5,711
Philippines	9,191	9.7%	2.2%	0.0%	88.1%	1,744	190	0	0	$209	$2,136	$5,795	$13,417
Qatar	48,612	0.0%	62.8%	37.2%	0.0%	0	22,627	0	0	$2,387	$14	$760	$1,590
Saudi Arabia	660,695	0.0%	91.9%	8.1%	0.0%	0	406,540	0	0	$40,702	$53	$3,151	$20,907
Singapore	n.a.	n.a.	n.a.	n.a.	n.a.	0	199	0	0	$6,553	$8,435	$80,851	$86,639
Sri Lanka	554	0.0%	0.0%	0.0%	100.0%	0	0	0	0	$7	$293	$2,382	$3,474
Syria	44,178	0.0%	92.3%	7.0%	0.7%	0	28,771	0	0	$1,607	$142	$1,269	$2,920
Taiwan	n.a.	n.a.	n.a.	n.a.	n.a.	223	62	0	0	$675	$6,300	$89,342	$66,722
Tajikistan	1,903	1.3%	4.8%	2.3%	91.5%	57	55	0	0	n.a.	n.a.	n.a.	n.a.
Thailand	29,662	39.0%	17.7%	40.4%	2.8%	18,206	2,780	46	0	$323	$3,943	$33,721	$46,790
Turkey	26,882	63.9%	18.7%	0.8%	16.6%	55,358	3,426	3,134	407	$239	$3,820	$13,652	$20,070
Turkmenistan	44,210	0.0%	16.2%	83.8%	0.0%	0	3,686	0	0	n.a.	n.a.	n.a.	n.a.
United Arab Emirates	196,363	0.0%	80.7%	19.3%	0.0%	0	110,923	0	0	$1,026	$670	$9,277	$16,040
Uzbekistan	74,513	1.7%	19.2%	78.0%	1.2%	3,342	5,043	0	0	$1,322	$299	$551	$3,163
Vietnam	20,715	36.0%	53.1%	0.0%	10.9%	7,072	8,096	0	0	$780	$806	$35	$1,446
Yemen	24,308	0.0%	100.0%	0.0%	0.0%	0	16,884	0	0				
AFRICA													
Algeria	170,503	0.0%	51.3%	48.6%	0.0%	21	59,964	1,067	0	$8,911	$94	$349	$6,099
Angola	38,244	0.0%	99.0%	0.6%	0.4%	0	31,286	0	0	$3,034	$54	$3	$1,260
Benin	127	0.0%	100.0%	0.0%	0.0%	0	181	0	0	$7	$49	$5	$369
Botswana	n.a.	n.a.	n.a.	n.a.	n.a.	852	0	0	0	n.a.	n.a.	n.a.	n.a.
Burkina Faso	9	0.0%	0.0%	0.0%	100.0%	0	0	0	0	$1	$66	$61	$316
Burundi	20	30.0%	0.0%	0.0%	70.0%	0	0	0	0	z	$41	$3	$134
Cameroon	7,584	0.0%	95.7%	0.0%	4.3%	1	4,972	0	0	$530	$29	$143	$867
Cape Verde	n.a.	n.a.	n.a.	n.a.	n.a.	0	0	0	0	z	$17	z	$85
Central African Republic	10	0.0%	0.0%	0.0%	100.0%	0	0	0	0	z	$3	$38	$109
Chad	n.a.	n.a.	n.a.	n.a.	n.a.	0	0	0	0	z	$3	$26	$143
Comoros	z	z	z	z	z	0	0	0	0	z	$6	$4	$36
Congo	13,140	0.0%	99.6%	0.0%	0.4%	0	9,560	0	0	$892	$8	$22	$445
Congo, Democratic Republic of the	2,457	3.9%	66.6%	0.0%	29.5%	95	1,423	0	0	$33	$47	$25	$288
Cote d'Ivoire	647	0.0%	79.0%	0.0%	21.0%	0	510	0	0	$69	$327	$141	$1,370
Djibouti	n.a.	n.a.	n.a.	n.a.	n.a.	0	0	0	0	z	$16	$1	$107
Egypt	86,314	0.0%	77.5%	20.9%	1.5%	33	45,294	1,679	0	$1,138	$121	$1,236	$6,099
Equatorial Guinea	357	0.0%	100.0%	0.0%	0.0%	0	496	0	0	z	$3	$2	$28
Eritrea	n.a.	n.a.	n.a.	n.a.	n.a.	0	0	0	0	n.a.	n.a.	n.a.	n.a.
Ethiopia	228	0.0%	0.0%	0.0%	100.0%	0	0	0	0	$21	$110	$18	$647
Gabon	27,248	0.0%	95.6%	4.0%	0.3%	0	17,571	0	0	$2,125	$20	$27	$666
Gambia, The	n.a.	n.a.	n.a.	n.a.	n.a.	0	0	0	0	z	$18	z	$124
Ghana	751	0.0%	0.0%	0.0%	100.0%	0	189	0	593	$5	$463	$11	$1,016
Guinea	23	0.0%	0.0%	0.0%	100.0%	0	0	0	15,200	n.a.	n.a.	n.a.	n.a.
Guinea-Bissau	n.a.	n.a.	n.a.	n.a.	n.a.	0	0	0	0	z	$3	$2	$34
Kenya	739	0.0%	0.0%	0.0%	100.0%	0	50	0	0	$211	$456	$471	$1,500
Lesotho	n.a.	n.a.	n.a.	n.a.	n.a.	0	0	0	0	n.a.	n.a.	n.a.	n.a.
Liberia	22	0.0%	0.0%	0.0%	100.0%	0	0	0	0	$2	$62	$4	$109
Libya	106,811	0.0%	92.1%	7.9%	0.0%	0	68,974	0	0	$8,112	$14	$404	$3,377
Madagascar	43	0.0%	0.0%	0.0%	100.0%	0	0	0	0	$5	$67	$48	$313
Malawi	96	0.0%	0.0%	0.0%	100.0%	54	0	0	0	z	$54	$18	$393
Mali	28	0.0%	0.0%	0.0%	100.0%	0	0	0	0	z	$108	$5	$293
Mauritania	3	0.0%	0.0%	0.0%	100.0%	0	0	7,000	0	z	$53	$2	$195
Mauritius	17	0.0%	0.0%	0.0%	100.0%	0	0	0	0	z	$131	$979	$1,351
Morocco	764	84.9%	0.9%	4.3%	9.7%	643	13	26	0	$89	$1,053	$2,073	$4,296
Mozambique	44	86.4%	0.0%	0.0%	13.6%	38	0	0	11	$14	$127	$17	$581
Namibia	n.a.	n.a.	n.a.	n.a.	n.a.	0	0	0	0	n.a.	n.a.	n.a.	n.a.
Niger	173	100.0%	0.0%	0.0%	0.0%	172	0	0	0	$2	$86	$4	$180
Nigeria	138,317	0.0%	95.1%	4.3%	0.5%	50	101,128	117	0	$9,443	$476	$29	$5,317
Rwanda	20	0.0%	0.0%	0.0%	100.0%	0	0	0	0	z	$26	z	$147
Sao Tome and Principe	1	0.0%	0.0%	0.0%	100.0%	0	0	0	0	z	z	z	$15
Senegal	n.a.	n.a.	n.a.	n.a.	n.a.	0	0	0	0	$89	$164	$164	$528
Sierra Leone	n.a.	n.a.	n.a.	n.a.	n.a.	0	0	0	245	z	$3	$34	$102
Somalia	n.a.	n.a.	n.a.	n.a.	n.a.	0	0	0	0	$6	$1	$1	$125
South Africa	168,238	88.8%	7.6%	1.5%	2.2%	202,793	9,432	19,275	0	$2,007	$2,420	$11,151	$18,124
Sudan	116	0.0%	0.0%	0.0%	100.0%	0	205	0	0	$5	$138	$4	$654
Swaziland	n.a.	n.a.	n.a.	n.a.	n.a.	53	0	0	0	n.a.	n.a.	n.a.	n.a.
Tanzania	190	2.6%	0.0%	0.0%	97.4%	5	0	0	0	$26	$328	$78	$983
Togo	1	0.0%	0.0%	0.0%	100.0%	0	0	0	0	z	$22	$15	$175
Tunisia	6,301	0.0%	96.7%	3.3%	0.1%	0	4,432	127	0	$395	$504	$3,688	$5,030
Uganda	96	0.0%	0.0%	0.0%	100.0%	0	0	0	0	$2	$184	$2	$534
Zambia	1,255	24.1%	0.0%	0.0%	75.9%	383	0	0	0	$3	$209	$186	$670
Zimbabwe	2,412	87.9%	0.0%	0.0%	12.1%	3,278	0	108	0	$19	$202	$686	$1,736
OCEANIA													
Australia	261,022	73.7%	13.2%	12.3%	0.8%	238,596	27,597	87,518	42,484	$9,125	$2,707	$14,476	$45,855
Fiji	53	0.0%	0.0%	0.0%	100.0%	0	0	0	0	z	$91	$194	$567
Kiribati	n.a.	n.a.	n.a.	n.a.	n.a.	0	0	0	0	z	$3	z	$16
Micronesia, Federated States of	n.a.	n.a.	n.a.	n.a.	n.a.	0	0	0	0	n.a.	n.a.	n.a.	n.a.
New Zealand	17,264	16.4%	13.9%	35.4%	34.3%	3,211	1,786	767	0	$207	$639	$3,550	$9,859
Papua New Guinea	9,454	0.0%	98.2%	1.2%	0.6%	0	5,185	0	0	$5	$97	$252	$1,035
Samoa	3	0.0%	0.0%	0.0%	100.0%	0	0	0	0	z	$11	z	$55
Solomon Islands	n.a.	n.a.	n.a.	n.a.	n.a.	0	0	0	0	z	$17	z	$74
Tonga	n.a.	n.a.	n.a.	n.a.	n.a.	0	0	0	0	z	$8	$1	$36
Vanuatu	n.a.	n.a.	n.a.	n.a.	n.a.	0	0	0	0	z	$14	$3	$45

This table presents data, where available, for most independent nations having an area greater than 200 square miles

n.a. - not available

z - negligible

Footnotes:

(1) Source: United Nations *Energy Statistics Yearbook*

(2) Source: United States Geological Survey *Minerals Yearbook*

(3) Source: United States Energy Information Administration *International Energy Annual*

(4) Source: Derived from United Nations *Handbook of International Trade and Development Statistics*

(5) Includes data for Luxembourg

(6) Data included with Belgium

(7) Excluding Taiwan

WORLD ENVIRONMENT TABLE

CONTINENT / Country	Area Square Miles	1996 Protected Land[1] (sq mi)	%	Endangered Species 1996[1] (Critically Endangered, Endangered and Vulnerable) Mammal	Bird	Reptile	Amphib.	Fish	Invrt.	Forest Cover[2] Total 1995 Sq. Miles	Change: 1990-95 %
NORTH AMERICA											
Bahamas	5,382	563	10.5%	4	4	7	0	1	1	610	-12.2%
Belize	8,866	3,525	39.8%	5	1	5	0	4	1	7,575	-1.7%
Canada	3,849,674	367,995	9.6%	7	5	3	1	13	11	944,294	0.4%
Costa Rica	19,730	4,650	23.6%	14	13	7	1	0	9	4,819	-14.2%
Cuba	42,804	7,370	17.2%	9	13	7	0	4	3	7,112	-6.0%
Dominica	305	66	21.5%	1	2	4	0	0	0	178	0.0%
Dominican Republic	18,704	n.a.	n.a.	4	11	10	1	0	2	6,108	-7.7%
El Salvador	8,124	20	0.2%	2	0	6	0	0	1	405	-15.3%
Guatemala	42,042	8,365	19.9%	8	4	9	0	0	8	14,830	-9.7%
Haiti	10,714	37	0.3%	4	11	6	1	0	2	81	-16.0%
Honduras	43,277	4,366	10.1%	7	4	7	0	0	2	15,888	153.1%
Jamaica	4,244	379	8.9%	4	7	8	4	0	5	676	-31.1%
Mexico	759,533	61,683	8.1%	64	36	18	3	86	40	213,850	-4.4%
Nicaragua	50,054	6,322	12.6%	4	3	7	0	0	2	21,467	-11.9%
Panama	29,157	5,974	20.5%	17	10	7	0	1	2	10,811	-10.2%
St. Lucia	238	37	15.7%	0	3	6	0	0	0	19	-16.7%
Trinidad and Tobago	1,980	81	4.1%	1	3	5	0	0	0	622	-7.5%
United States	3,787,425	767,743	20.3%	35	50	28	24	123	594	820,525	1.4%
SOUTH AMERICA											
Argentina	1,073,519	35,236	3.3%	27	41	5	5	1	11	131,051	-1.3%
Bolivia	424,165	68,798	16.2%	24	27	3	0	0	1	186,526	-5.7%
Brazil	3,300,172	203,367	6.2%	71	103	15	5	12	34	2,127,960	-2.3%
Chile	292,135	54,584	18.7%	16	18	1	3	4	0	30,471	-1.8%
Colombia	440,831	36,159	8.2%	35	64	15	0	5	0	204,588	-2.4%
Ecuador	105,037	60,045	57.2%	28	53	12	0	1	23	43,000	-7.8%
Guyana	83,000	226	0.3%	10	3	8	0	0	1	71,726	-0.2%
Paraguay	157,048	5,410	3.4%	10	26	3	0	0	0	44,506	-12.4%
Peru	496,225	26,102	5.3%	46	64	9	1	0	2	260,858	-1.6%
Suriname	63,251	3,105	4.9%	10	2	6	0	0	0	56,838	-0.4%
Uruguay	68,500	183	0.3%	5	11	0	0	0	1	3,143	-0.2%
Venezuela	352,144	216,373	61.4%	24	22	14	0	5	1	169,866	-5.4%
EUROPE											
Albania	11,100	396	3.6%	2	7	1	0	7	3	4,039	0.0%
Austria	32,377	9,464	29.2%	7	5	1	0	7	41	14,969	0.0%
Belarus	80,155	3,380	4.2%	4	4	0	0	0	6	28,463	4.9%
Belgium	11,783	332	2.8%	6	3	0	0	1	13	2,737/3	0.0%/3
Bosnia and Herzegovina	19,741	103	0.5%	10	2	0	1	6	6	10,463	0.0%
Bulgaria	42,855	1,930	4.5%	13	12	1	0	8	7	12,510	0.1%
Croatia	21,829	1,531	7.0%	10	4	0	1	20	8	10,154	0.0%
Czech Republic	30,450	4,933	16.2%	7	6	0	0	6	17	7,765	5.1%
Denmark	16,639	5,327	32.0%	3	2	0	0	0	10	1,610	0.0%
Estonia	17,413	2,071	11.9%	4	2	0	0	1	3	6,637	2.6%
Finland	130,559	10,968	8.4%	4	4	0	0	1	8	77,332	-0.4%
France	211,208	21,515	10.2%	13	7	3	2	3	61	58,047	5.7%
Germany	137,822	37,140	26.9%	8	5	0	0	7	29	41,467	0.0%
Greece	50,949	1,316	2.6%	13	10	6	1	16	9	25,147	12.1%
Hungary	35,919	2,506	7.0%	8	10	1	0	11	26	11,127	4.5%
Iceland	39,769	3,786	9.5%	1	0	0	0	0	0	42	0.0%
Ireland	27,137	252	0.9%	2	1	0	0	1	2	2,201	14.0%
Italy	116,336	8,509	7.3%	10	7	4	4	9	41	25,081	0.4%
Latvia	24,595	3,173	12.9%	4	6	0	0	1	6	7,046	0.0%
Lithuania	25,213	2,492	9.9%	5	4	0	0	1	5	7,629	2.9%
Luxembourg	999	144	14.4%	3	1	0	0	0	4	n.a./4	n.a./4
Macedonia	9,928	700	7.1%	10	3	1	0	4	2	3,815	-0.1%
Moldova	13,012	195	1.5%	2	7	1	0	9	5	1,378	0.0%
Netherlands	16,164	1,861	11.5%	6	3	0	0	1	9	1,290	0.0%
Norway	149,405	8,056	5.4%	4	3	0	0	1	8	31,170	1.7%
Poland	121,196	11,309	9.3%	10	6	0	0	2	13	33,714	0.7%
Portugal	35,516	2,331	6.6%	13	7	0	1	9	67	11,100	4.4%
Romania	91,699	4,206	4.6%	16	11	2	0	11	21	24,116	-0.1%
Serbia and Montenegro	39,449	1,309	3.3%	12	8	1	0	13	19	6,830	0.0%
Slovakia	18,933	4,095	21.6%	8	4	0	0	7	20	7,680	0.6%
Slovenia	7,820	464	5.9%	10	3	0	1	5	38	4,158	0.0%
Spain	194,885	16,378	8.4%	19	10	6	3	10	57	32,386	0.0%
Sweden	173,732	14,111	8.1%	5	4	0	0	1	13	94,305	0.0%
Switzerland	15,943	2,875	18.0%	6	4	0	0	4	25	4,363	0.0%
Ukraine	233,090	3,469	1.5%	15	10	2	0	12	13	35,676	0.3%
United Kingdom	94,249	19,305	20.5%	4	2	0	0	1	10	9,228	2.8%
Russia	6,592,849	199,494	3.0%	31	38	5	0	13	26	2,947,890	0.0%
ASIA											
Afghanistan	251,826	844	0.3%	11	13	1	1	0	1	5,398	-29.7%
Armenia	11,506	824	7.2%	4	5	3	0	0	6	1,290	14.4%
Azerbaijan	33,436	1,844	5.5%	11	8	3	0	5	6	3,822	0.0%
Bahrain	267	3	1.2%	1	1	0	0	0	0	0	0.0%
Bangladesh	55,598	378	0.7%	18	30	13	0	0	0	3,900	-4.2%
Brunei	2,226	468	21.0%	9	14	4	0	2	0	1,676	-3.1%
Cambodia	69,898	12,614	18.0%	23	18	9	0	5	0	37,954	-7.7%
China	3,690,045	263,657	7.1%	75	90	15	1	28	4	514,763/5	-0.3%/5
Cyprus	2,277	302	13.2%	3	4	3	0	0	1	541	0.0%
Georgia	26,911	754	2.8%	10	5	7	0	3	9	11,537	0.0%
India	1,237,061	55,259	4.5%	75	73	16	3	4	22	250,986	0.1%
Indonesia	752,409	133,251	17.7%	128	104	19	0	60	29	423,905	-4.7%
Iran	630,578	32,058	5.1%	20	14	8	2	7	3	5,961	-8.4%
Iraq	169,235	2	0.0%	7	12	2	0	2	2	320	0.0%
Israel	8,019	1,257	15.7%	13	8	5	0	0	10	394	0.0%
Japan	145,850	9,880	6.8%	29	33	8	10	7	45	97,089	-0.3%
Jordan	35,135	1,151	3.3%	7	4	1	0	0	3	174	-11.8%
Kazakhstan	1,049,155	28,329	2.7%	15	15	1	1	5	4	40,556	10.1%
Korea, North	46,540	1,219	2.6%	7	19	0	0	0	1	23,823	0.0%
Korea, South	38,230	2,640	6.9%	6	19	0	0	0	1	29,444	-0.8%
Kuwait	6,880	105	1.5%	1	3	2	0	0	0	19	0.0%
Kyrgyzstan	76,641	2,679	3.5%	6	5	1	0	0	3	2,819	0.0%
Laos	91,429	10,642	11.6%	30	27	7	0	4	0	48,012	-5.6%
Lebanon	4,016	19	0.5%	5	5	2	0	0	1	201	-33.3%
Malaysia	127,320	5,897	4.6%	42	34	14	0	14	3	59,734	-11.5%
Mongolia	604,829	62,275	10.3%	12	14	0	0	0	3	36,317	0.0%
Myanmar	261,228	670	0.3%	31	44	20	0	1	2	104,831	-6.7%

CONTINENT / Country	Area Square Miles	1996 Protected Land[1]	%	Endangered Species 1996[1] (Critically Endangered, Endangered and Vulnerable) Mammal	Bird	Reptile	Amphib.	Fish	Invrt.	Forest Cover[2] Total 1995 Sq. Miles	Change: 1990-95 %
Nepal	56,827	4,905	8.6%	28	27	5	0	0	1	18,618	-5.4%
Oman	82,030	13,236	16.1%	9	5	4	0	3	1	0	0.0%
Pakistan	339,732	14,458	4.3%	13	25	6	0	1	0	6,749	-13.6%
Philippines	115,831	5,614	4.8%	49	86	7	2	26	18	26,124	-16.2%
Qatar	4,412	6	0.1%	0	1	2	0	0	0	0	0.0%
Saudi Arabia	830,000	318,774	38.4%	9	11	2	0	0	1	857	-3.9%
Singapore	246	11	4.6%	6	9	1	0	1	1	15	0.0%
Sri Lanka	24,962	3,357	13.4%	14	11	8	0	8	2	6,934	-5.3%
Syria	71,498	0	0.0%	4	7	3	0	0	3	846	-10.6%
Taiwan	13,900	1,520	10.9%	10	13	3	0	6	1	n.a./6	n.a./6
Tajikistan	55,251	2,266	4.1%	5	9	1	0	1	2	1,583	0.0%
Thailand	198,115	27,325	13.8%	34	45	16	0	14	1	44,904	-12.4%
Turkey	300,948	4,980	1.7%	15	14	12	2	18	9	34,193	0.0%
Turkmenistan	188,456	7,634	4.1%	11	12	2	0	5	3	14,494	0.0%
United Arab Emirates	32,278	0	0.0%	3	4	2	0	1	0	232	0.0%
Uzbekistan	172,742	3,160	1.8%	7	11	0	0	3	1	35,209	14.1%
Vietnam	127,428	3,842	3.0%	38	47	12	1	3	0	35,201	-6.9%
Yemen	203,850	0	0.0%	5	13	2	0	0	2	35	0.0%
AFRICA											
Algeria	919,595	22,745	2.5%	15	8	1	0	1	11	7,185	-5.9%
Angola	481,354	31,588	6.6%	17	13	5	0	0	6	85,715	-5.1%
Benin	43,475	4,875	11.2%	9	1	2	0	0	0	17,857	-6.1%
Botswana	224,711	40,536	18.0%	5	7	0	0	0	0	53,734	-2.5%
Burkina Faso	105,869	11,024	10.4%	6	1	1	0	0	0	16,490	-3.6%
Burundi	10,745	564	5.3%	5	6	0	0	0	3	1,224	-2.2%
Cameroon	183,568	8,099	4.4%	32	14	3	1	26	4	75,668	-3.2%
Cape Verde	1,557	0	0.0%	1	3	3	0	1	0	181	193.8%
Central African Republic	240,535	21,026	8.7%	11	2	1	0	0	0	115,560	-2.1%
Chad	495,755	44,379	9.0%	14	3	1	0	0	1	42,568	-4.1%
Comoros	863	0	0.0%	3	6	2	0	1	4	35	-25.0%
Congo	132,047	6,563	5.0%	10	3	2	0	0	1	75,433	-1.1%
Congo, Democratic Republic of the	905,446	56,515	6.2%	38	26	3	0	1	45	421,797	-3.3%
Cote d'Ivoire	124,518	7,666	6.2%	16	12	4	1	0	1	21,116	-2.7%
Djibouti	8,958	39	0.4%	3	3	2	0	0	0	85	0.0%
Egypt	386,662	3,065	0.8%	15	11	6	0	0	1	131	0.0%
Equatorial Guinea	10,831	0	0.0%	12	4	2	1	0	2	6,876	-2.6%
Eritrea	36,170	1,933	5.3%	6	3	3	0	0	0	1,089	0.0%
Ethiopia	446,953	72,200	16.2%	35	20	1	0	0	4	52,429	-2.2%
Gabon	103,347	2,792	2.7%	12	4	3	0	0	1	68,954	-2.5%
Gambia, The	4,127	87	2.1%	4	1	1	0	0	0	351	-4.2%
Ghana	92,098	4,897	5.3%	13	10	4	0	0	0	34,834	-6.1%
Guinea	94,926	631	0.7%	11	12	3	1	0	3	24,583	-5.5%
Guinea-Bissau	13,948	0	0.0%	4	1	3	0	0	1	8,915	-2.2%
Kenya	224,961	17,522	7.8%	43	24	5	0	20	15	4,988	-1.3%
Lesotho	11,720	26	0.2%	2	5	0	0	1	1	23	0.0%
Liberia	38,250	499	1.3%	11	13	3	1	0	2	17,402	-2.9%
Libya	679,362	668	0.1%	11	2	3	0	0	0	1,544	0.0%
Madagascar	226,658	4,756	2.1%	46	28	17	2	13	14	58,325	-4.1%
Malawi	45,747	4,087	8.9%	7	9	0	0	0	8	12,892	-7.6%
Mali	482,077	17,498	3.6%	13	6	1	0	0	0	44,730	-4.7%
Mauritania	397,955	6,741	1.7%	14	3	3	0	0	0	2,147	0.0%
Mauritius	788	61	7.7%	4	10	6	0	0	32	46	0.0%
Morocco	172,414	1,225	0.7%	18	11	2	0	1	7	14,807	-1.5%
Mozambique	308,642	26,946	8.7%	13	14	5	0	2	7	65,105	-3.3%
Namibia	317,818	43,304	13.6%	11	8	3	1	3	1	47,776	-1.7%
Niger	489,191	37,429	7.7%	11	2	1	0	0	1	9,892	0.0%
Nigeria	356,669	11,666	3.3%	26	9	4	0	0	1	53,205	-4.2%
Rwanda	10,169	1,531	15.1%	9	6	0	0	0	2	965	-0.8%
Sao Tome and Principe	372	0	0.0%	3	9	2	0	0	2	216	0.0%
Senegal	75,951	8,657	11.4%	13	6	7	0	0	0	28,498	-3.3%
Sierra Leone	27,925	592	2.1%	9	12	3	0	0	4	5,054	-14.0%
Somalia	246,201	2,025	0.8%	18	8	2	0	3	1	2,911	-0.8%
South Africa	471,009	25,657	5.4%	33	16	19	9	27	101	32,815	-0.9%
Sudan	967,499	47,294	4.9%	21	9	3	0	0	1	160,669	-4.1%
Swaziland	6,704	232	3.5%	5	6	0	0	0	0	564	0.0%
Tanzania	364,900	101,397	27.8%	33	30	4	0	19	46	125,522	-4.7%
Togo	21,925	1,657	7.6%	8	1	3	0	0	0	4,807	-7.0%
Tunisia	63,170	172	0.3%	11	6	2	0	0	5	2,143	-2.6%
Uganda	93,104	18,978	20.4%	18	10	1	0	28	10	23,568	-4.6%
Zambia	290,586	87,449	30.1%	11	10	0	0	0	6	121,228	-4.0%
Zimbabwe	150,873	19,293	12.8%	9	9	0	0	0	2	33,629	-2.8%
OCEANIA											
Australia	2,966,155	403,742	13.6%	58	45	37	25	37	281	157,947	0.2%
Fiji	7,056	77	1.1%	4	9	6	1	0	2	3,224	-2.1%
Kiribati	313	103	32.9%	0	4	2	0	0	1	0	0.0%
Micronesia, Federated States of	271	0	0.0%	6	6	2	0	0	4	n.a.	n.a.
New Zealand	104,454	24,455	23.4%	3	44	11	1	8	15	30,440	2.8%
Papua New Guinea	178,703	3,993	2.2%	57	31	10	0	13	11	142,622	-1.8%
Samoa	1,093	44	4.1%	2	6	2	0	0	1	525	-5.6%
Solomon Islands	10,954	32	0.3%	20	18	4	0	0	5	9,224	-1.0%
Tonga	288	14	4.8%	0	2	3	0	0	1	0	0.0%
Vanuatu	4,707	13	0.3%	3	6	3	0	0	1	3,475	-4.1%

This table presents data, where available, for most independent nations having an area greater than 200 square miles

Amphib. - Amphibian

Invrt. - Invertebrate

n.a. - not available

Footnotes:

(1) Source: World Conservation Monitoring Centre (WCMC) and World Conservation Union (IUCN); data reprinted by permission

(2) Source: United Nations Food and Agriculture Organization *State of the World's Forests*

(3) Includes data for Luxembourg

(4) Data included with Belgium

(5) Includes data for Taiwan

(6) Data included with China

WORLD COMPARISONS

General Information

Equatorial diameter of the earth, 7,926.38 miles.
Polar diameter of the earth, 7,899.80 miles.
Mean diameter of the earth, 7,917.52 miles.
Equatorial circumference of the earth, 24,901.46 miles.
Polar circumference of the earth, 24,855.34 miles.
Mean distance from the earth to the sun, 93,020,000 miles.
Mean distance from the earth to the moon, 238,857 miles.
Total area of the earth, 197,000,000 square miles.

Highest elevation on the earth's surface, Mt. Everest, Asia, 29,028 feet.
Lowest elevation on the earth's land surface, shores of the Dead Sea, Asia, 1,339 feet below sea level.
Greatest known depth of the ocean, southwest of Guam, Pacific Ocean, 35,810 feet.
Total land area of the earth (incl. inland water and Antarctica), 57,900,000 square miles.

Area of Africa, 11,700,000 square miles.
Area of Antarctica, 5,400,000 square miles.
Area of Asia, 17,300,000 square miles.
Area of Europe, 3,800,000 square miles.
Area of North America, 9,500,000 square miles.
Area of Oceania (incl. Australia) 3,300,000 square miles.
Area of South America, 6,900,000 square miles.
Population of the earth (est. 1/1/99), 5,952,000,000.

Principal Islands and Their Areas

ISLAND	Area (Sq. Mi.)
Baffin I., Canada	195,928
Banks I., Canada	27,038
Borneo (Kalimantan), Asia	287,298
Bougainville, Papua New Guinea	3,591
Cape Breton I., Canada	3,981
Celebes (Sulawesi), Indonesia	73,057
Ceram (Seram), Indonesia	7,191
Corsica, France	3,367
Crete, Greece	3,190
Cuba, N. America	42,780
Cyprus, Asia	3,572
Devon I., Canada	21,331
Ellesmere I., Canada	75,767
Flores, Indonesia	5,502
Great Britain, U.K.	88,795
Greenland, N. America	840,004
Guadalcanal, Solomon Is.	2,060
Hainan Dao, China	13,127
Hawaii, U.S.	4,021
Hispaniola, N. America	29,300
Hokkaidō, Japan	32,245
Honshū, Japan	89,176
Iceland, Europe	39,769
Ireland, Europe	32,587
Jamaica, N. America	4,247
Java (Jawa), Indonesia	51,038
Kodiak I., U.S.	3,670
Kyūshū, Japan	17,129
Leyte, Philippines	2,785
Long Island, U.S.	1,377
Luzon, Philippines	40,420
Madagascar, Africa	226,642
Melville I., Canada	16,274
Mindanao, Philippines	36,537
Mindoro, Philippines	3,759
Negros, Philippines	4,907
New Britain, Papua New Guinea	14,093
New Caledonia, Oceania	6,467
Newfoundland, Canada	42,031
New Guinea, Asia-Oceania	308,882
New Ireland, Papua New Guinea	3,475
North East Land, Norway	6,350
North I., New Zealand	44,333
Novaya Zemlya, Russia	31,892
Palawan, Philippines	4,550
Panay, Philippines	4,446
Prince of Wales I., Canada	12,872
Puerto Rico, N. America	3,514
Sakhalin, Russia	29,498
Samar, Philippines	5,050
Sardinia, Italy	9,301
Shikoku, Japan	7,258
Sicily, Italy	9,926
Somerset I., Canada	9,570
Southampton I., Canada	15,913
South I., New Zealand	57,708
Spitsbergen, Norway	15,260
Sri Lanka, Asia	24,942
Sumatra (Sumatera), Indonesia	182,860
Taiwan, Asia	13,900
Tasmania, Australia	26,178
Tierra del Fuego, S. America	18,600
Timor, Asia	5,743
Vancouver I., Canada	12,079
Victoria I., Canada	83,897
Vrangelya (Wrangel), Russia	2,819

Principal Lakes, Oceans, Seas, and Their Areas

LAKE Country	Area (Sq. Mi.)
Arabian Sea	1,492,000
Aral Sea, Kazakhstan-Uzbekistan	14,900
Arctic Ocean	5,400,000
Athabasca, L., Canada	3,064
Atlantic Ocean	31,800,000
Balqash kölï (L. Balkhash), Kazakhstan	7,066
Baltic Sea, Europe	163,000
Baykal, Ozero (L. Baikal), Russia	12,162
Bering Sea, Asia-N.A.	876,000
Black Sea, Europe-Asia	178,000
Caribbean Sea, N.A.-S.A.	1,063,000
Caspian Sea, Asia-Europe	143,244
Chad, L., Cameroon-Chad-Nigeria	6,300
Erie, L., Canada-U.S.	9,910
Eyre, L., Australia	3,700
Gairdner, L., Australia	1,660
Great Bear Lake, Canada	12,095
Great Salt Lake, U.S.	1,680
Great Slave Lake, Canada	11,030
Hudson Bay, Canada	475,000
Huron, L., Canada-U.S.	23,000
Indian Ocean	28,900,000
Japan, Sea of, Asia	389,000
Koko Nor (Qinghai Hu), China	1,650
Ladozhskoye Ozero (L. Ladoga), Russia	6,834
Manitoba, L., Canada	1,785
Mediterranean Sea, Europe-Africa-Asia	967,000
Mexico, Gulf of, N. America	596,000
Michigan, L., U.S.	22,300
Nicaragua, Lago de, Nicaragua	3,150
North Sea, Europe	222,000
Nyasa, L., Malawi-Mozambique-Tanzania	11,150
Onezhskoye Ozero (L. Onega), Russia	3,753
Ontario, L., Canada-U.S.	7,540
Pacific Ocean	63,800,000
Red Sea, Africa-Asia	169,000
Rudolf, L., Ethiopia-Kenya	2,473
Superior, L., Canada-U.S.	31,700
Tanganyika, L., Africa	12,350
Titicaca, Lago, Bolivia-Peru	3,200
Torrens, L., Australia	2,278
Vänern (L.), Sweden	2,156
Van Gölü (L.), Turkey	1,420
Victoria, L., Kenya-Tanzania-Uganda	26,820
Winnipeg, L., Canada	9,416
Winnipegosis, L., Canada	2,075
Yellow Sea, China-Korea	480,000

Principal Mountains and Their Heights

MOUNTAIN Country	Elev. (Ft.)
Aconcagua, Cerro, Argentina	22,831
Annapurna, Nepal	26,504
Aoraki, New Zealand	12,316
Api, Nepal	23,399
Apo, Philippines	9,692
Ararat, Mt., Turkey	16,854
Barú, Volcán, Panama	11,401
Bangueta, Mt., Papua New Guinea	13,520
Belukha, Mt., Kazakhstan-Russia	14,783
Bia, Phu, Laos	9,249
Blanc, Mont (Monte Bianco), France-Italy	15,771
Blanca Pk., Colorado, U.S.	14,345
Bolívar, Venezuela	16,427
Bonete, Cerro, Argentina	22,546
Borah Pk., Idaho, U.S.	12,662
Boundary Pk., Nevada, U.S.	13,140
Cameroon Mtn., Cameroon	13,451
Carrauntoohil, Ireland	3,406
Chaltel, Cerro (Monte Fitzroy), Argentina-Chile	10,958
Chimborazo, Ecuador	20,702
Chirripó, Cerro, Costa Rica	12,530
Colima, Nevado de, Mexico	13,911
Cotopaxi, Ecuador	19,347
Cristóbal Colón, Pico, Colombia	19,029
Damāvand, Qolleh-ye, Iran	18,386
Dhawalāgiri, Nepal	26,810
Duarte, Pico, Dominican Rep.	10,417
Dufourspitze (Monte Rosa), Italy-Switzerland	15,203
Elbert, Mt., Colorado, U.S.	14,433
El'brus, Gora, Russia	18,510
Elgon, Mt., Kenya-Uganda	14,178
Erciyeş Dağı, Turkey	12,848
Etna, Mt., Italy	10,902
Everest, Mt., China-Nepal	29,028
Fairweather, Mt., Alaska-Canada	15,300
Folādī, Koh-e, Afghanistan	16,847
Foraker, Mt., Alaska, U.S.	17,400
Fuji-san, Japan	12,388
Galdhøpiggen, Norway	8,100
Gannett Pk., Wyoming, U.S.	13,804
Gasherbrum, China-Pakistan	26,470
Gerlachovský štít, Slovakia	8,711
Giluwe, Mt., Papua New Guinea	14,331
Gongga Shan, China	24,790
Grand Teton, Wyoming, U.S.	13,770
Grossglockner, Austria	12,457
Hadūr Shu'ayb, Yemen	12,008
Haleakala Crater, Hawaii, U.S.	10,023
Hekla, Iceland	4,892
Hood, Mt., Oregon, U.S.	11,239
Huascarán, Nevado, Peru	22,133
Huila, Nevado de, Colombia	18,865
Hvannadalshnúkur, Iceland	6,952
Illampu, Nevado, Bolivia	21,066
Illimani, Nevado, Bolivia	20,741
Iztaccíhuatl, Mexico	17,159
Jaya, Puncak, Indonesia	16,503
Jungfrau, Switzerland	13,642
K2, China-Pakistan	28,250
Kāmet, China-India	25,447
Kānchenjunga, India-Nepal	28,208
Kātrīnā, Jabal, Egypt	8,668
Kebnekaise, Sweden	6,926
Kenya, Mt. (Kirinyaga), Kenya	17,058
Kerinci, Gunung, Indonesia	12,467
Kilimanjaro, Tanzania	19,340
Kinabalu, Gunong, Malaysia	13,455
Klyuchevskaya, Russia	15,584
Kommunizma, Pik, Tajikistan	24,590
Kosciuszko, Mt., Australia	7,313
Koussi, Emi, Chad	11,204
Kula Kangri, Bhutan	24,784
La Selle, Massif de, Haiti	8,793
Lassen Pk., California, U.S.	10,457
Llullaillaco, Volcán, Argentina-Chile	22,110
Logan, Mt., Canada	19,551
Longs Pk., Colorado, U.S.	14,255
Makālu, China-Nepal	27,825
Margherita Peak, Congo, D.R.C.-Uganda	16,763
Markham, Mt., Antarctica	14,049
Maromokotro, Madagascar	9,436
Massive, Mt., Colorado, U.S.	14,421
Matterhorn, Italy-Switzerland	14,692
Mauna Kea, Hawaii, U.S.	13,796
Mauna Loa, Hawaii, U.S.	13,679
Mayon Volcano, Philippines	8,077
McKinley, Mt., Alaska, U.S.	20,320
Meron, Hare, Israel	3,963
Meru, Mt., Tanzania	14,978
Misti, Volcán, Peru	19,101
Mitchell, Mt., North Carolina, U.S.	6,684
Môco, Serra do, Angola	8,596
Moldoveanu, Romania	8,346
Mulhacén, Spain (continental)	11,424
Musala, Bulgaria	9,596
Muztag, China	25,338
Muztagata, China	24,757
Namjagbarwa Feng, China	25,446
Nanda Devi, India	25,645
Nānga Parbat, Pakistan	26,660
Narodnaya, Gora, Russia	6,217
Nevis, Ben, United Kingdom	4,406
Ojos del Salado, Nevado, Argentina-Chile	22,615
Ólimbos, Cyprus	6,401
Ólympos, Greece	9,570
Olympus, Mt., Washington, U.S.	7,965
Orizaba, Pico de, Mexico	18,406
Paektu San, North Korea-China	9,003
Paricutín, Mexico	9,186
Parnassós, Greece	8,061
Pelée, Montagne, Martinique	4,583
Pidurutalagala, Sri Lanka	8,281
Pikes Pk., Colorado, U.S.	14,110
Pobedy, pik, China-Kyrgyzstan	24,406
Popocatépetl, Volcán, Mexico	17,930
Pulog, Mt., Philippines	9,626
Rainier, Mt., Washington, U.S.	14,410
Ramm, Jabal, Jordan	5,755
Ras Dashen Terara, Ethiopia	15,158
Rinjani, Gunung, Indonesia	12,224
Robson, Mt., Canada	12,972
Roraima, Mt., Brazil-Guyana-Venezuela	9,432
Ruapehu, Mt., New Zealand	9,177
St. Elias, Mt., Alaska, U.S.-Canada	18,008
Sajama, Nevado, Bolivia	21,391
Semeru, Gunung, Indonesia	12,060
Shām, Jabal ash, Oman	9,957
Shasta, Mt., California, U.S.	14,162
Snowdon, Wales, U.K.	3,560
Tahat, Algeria	9,541
Tajumulco (Vol.), Guatemala	13,845
Taranaki, Mt., New Zealand	8,260
Tirich Mīr, Pakistan	25,230
Tomanivi (Victoria), Fiji	4,341
Toubkal, Jebel, Morocco	13,665
Triglav, Slovenia	9,396
Trikora, Puncak, Indonesia	15,584
Tupungato, Cerro, Argentina-Chile	21,555
Turquino, Pico, Cuba	6,470
Uluru (Ayers Rock), Australia	2,844
Uncompahgre Pk., Colorado, U.S.	14,309
Vesuvio (Vesuvius), Italy	4,190
Victoria, Mt., Papua New Guinea	13,238
Vinson Massif, Antarctica	16,066
Waddington, Mt., Canada	13,163
Washington, Mt., New Hampshire, U.S.	6,288
Whitney, Mt., California, U.S.	14,494
Wilhelm, Mt., Papua New Guinea	14,793
Wrangell, Mt., Alaska, U.S.	14,163
Xixabangma Feng (Gosainthan), China	26,286
Yü Shan, Taiwan	13,114
Zugspitze, Austria-Germany	9,718

Principal Rivers and Their Lengths

RIVER Continent	Length (Mi.)
Albany, N. America	610
Aldan, Asia	1,412
Amazonas-Ucayali, S. America	4,000
Amu Darya, Asia	1,578
Amur, Asia	2,744
Amur-Argun, Asia	2,761
Araguaia, S. America	1,367
Arkansas, N. America	1,459
Athabasca, N. America	765
Brahmaputra, Asia	1,770
Branco, S. America	580
Brazos, N. America	870
Canadian, N. America	906
Churchill, N. America	1,000
Colorado, N. America (U.S.-Mexico)	1,450
Columbia, N. America	1,243
Congo (Zaïre), Africa	2,880
Cumberland, N. America	720
Danube, Europe	1,776
Darling, Australia	864
Dnepr (Dnieper), Europe	1,367
Dniester, Europe	840
Don, Europe	1,162
Elbe, Europe	720
Euphrates, Asia	1,510
Fraser, N. America	851
Ganges, Asia	1,560
Gila, N. America	630
Godāvari, Asia	930
Green, N. America	730
Huang (Yellow), Asia	3,395
Indus, Asia	1,800
Irrawaddy, Asia	1,300
Juruá, S. America	1,250
Kama, Europe	1,122
Kasai, Africa	1,338
Kolyma, Asia	1,323
Lena, Asia	2,734
Limpopo, Africa	1,100
Loire, Europe	625
Mackenzie, N. America	2,635
Madeira, S. America	2,013
Magdalena, S. America	950
Marañón, S. America	1,000
Mekong, Asia	2,600
Meuse, Europe	575
Mississippi, N. America	2,348
Mississippi-Missouri, N. America	3,740
Missouri, N. America	2,315
Murray, Australia	1,566
Negro, S. America	1,305
Neman, Europe	582
Niger, Africa	2,600
Nile, Africa	4,145
North Platte, N. America	618
Ob'-Irtysh, Asia	3,362
Oder, Europe	565
Ohio, N. America	981
Oka, Europe	932
Orange, Africa	1,300
Orinoco, S. America	1,600
Ottawa, N. America	790
Paraguay, S. America	1,610
Paraná, S. America	2,796
Parnaíba, S. America	850
Peace, N. America	1,195
Pechora, Europe	1,124
Pecos, N. America	735
Pilcomayo, S. America	1,550
Plata-Paraná, S. America	3,030
Purús, S. America	1,860
Red, N. America	1,270
Rhine, Europe	820
Rhône, Europe	505
Rio Grande, N. America	1,885
Roosevelt, S. America	950
St. Lawrence, N. America	800
Salado, S. America	870
Salween (Nu), Asia	1,750
São Francisco, S. America	1,988
Saskatchewan-Bow, N. America	1,205
Sava, Europe	585
Snake, N. America	1,038
Sungari (Songhua), Asia	1,140
Syr Darya, Asia	1,370
Tagus, Europe	625
Tarim, Asia	1,328
Tennessee, N. America	652
Tigris, Asia	1,180
Tisa, Europe	607
Tobol, Asia	989
Tocantins, S. America	1,640
Ucayali, S. America	1,220
Ural, Asia	1,509
Uruguay, S. America	1,025
Verkhnyaya Tunguska (Angara), Asia	1,105
Vilyuy, Asia	1,647
Volga, Europe	2,194
White, N. America (Ark.-Mo.)	720
Wisła (Vistula), Europe	630
Xiang, Asia	930
Xingu, S. America	1,230
Yangtze (Chang), Asia	3,915
Yellowstone, N. America	671
Yenisey, Asia	2,543
Yukon, N. America	1,979
Zambezi, Africa	1,700

PRINCIPAL CITIES OF THE WORLD

Abidjan, Cote d'Ivoire . . . 1,929,079
Accra, Ghana (1,390,000) . . . 949,113
Addis Ababa, Ethiopia (2,200,000) . . 2,084,588
Adelaide, Australia (1,045,854) . . . 16,115
Ahmadābād, India (4,519,278) . . . 3,515,361
Alexandria (Al Iskandarīyah), Egypt (3,350,000) . . . 2,926,859
Algiers (El Djazaïr), Algeria (2,547,983) . . . 1,507,241
Almaty, Kazakhstan (1,190,000) . . . 1,156,200
'Ammān, Jordan (1,500,000) . . . 963,490
Amsterdam, Netherlands (1,121,303) . . . 727,053
Ankara (Angora), Turkey (2,650,000) . . . 2,559,471
Antananarivo, Madagascar . . . 1,250,000
Antwerp (Antwerpen), Belgium (1,140,000) . . . 467,518
Asmera, Eritrea . . . 358,100
Asunción, Paraguay (700,000) . . . 502,426
Athens (Athínai), Greece (3,150,000) . 772,072
Atlanta, Georgia, U.S. (3,746,400) . . . 416,474
Auckland, New Zealand (855,571) . . . 315,668
Baghdād, Iraq . . . 3,841,268
Baku (Bakı), Azerbaijan (2,020,000) . 1,080,500
Baltimore, Maryland, U.S. (2,256,200) . . . 651,154
Bamako, Mali . . . 658,275
Bandung, Indonesia (2,220,000) . . . 2,058,122
Bangalore, India (5,686,844) . . . 4,292,223
Bangkok (Krung Thep), Thailand (7,060,000) . . . 5,620,591
Barcelona, Spain (4,000,000) . . . 1,496,266
Beijing (Peking), China (7,320,000) . 6,690,000
Beirut, Lebanon (1,675,000) . . . 509,000
Belém, Brazil (965,000) . . . 140,337
Belfast, N. Ireland, U.K. (730,000) . . . 296,700
Belgrade (Beograd), Serbia and Montenegro (1,554,826) . . . 1,136,786
Belo Horizonte, Brazil (4,055,000) . . 1,366,301
Berlin, Germany (4,220,000) . . . 3,425,759
Birmingham, England, U.K. (2,705,000) . . . 965,928
Bishkek, Kyrgyzstan . . . 631,300
Bogotá, Colombia (5,290,000) . . . 4,931,796
Bonn, Germany (600,000) . . . 304,841
Boston, Massachusetts, U.S. (4,714,000) . . . 589,141
Brasília, Brazil . . . 1,947,133
Bratislava, Slovakia . . . 451,395
Brazzaville, Congo . . . 693,712
Bremen, Germany (790,000) . . . 546,698
Brisbane, Australia (1,488,883) . . . 806,746
Brussels (Bruxelles), Belgium (2,385,000) . . . 136,424
Bucharest (București), Romania (2,300,000) . . . 2,067,545
Budapest, Hungary (2,450,000) . . . 1,906,798
Buenos Aires, Argentina (11,000,000) . . . 2,960,976
Cairo (Al Qāhirah), Egypt (9,300,000) . . . 6,068,695
Cali, Colombia (1,735,000) . . . 1,641,498
Canberra, Australia (324,536) . . . 298,847
Cape Town, South Africa (1,900,000) . . 854,616
Caracas, Venezuela (4,000,000) . . . 1,822,465
Casablanca, Morocco (3,400,000) . . 3,022,000
Changchun, China . . . 2,470,000
Chelyabinsk, Russia (1,320,000) . . . 1,086,300
Chengdu, China . . . 2,760,000
Chennai (Madras), India (6,424,624) . . . 4,216,268
Chicago, Illinois, U.S. (8,854,900) . . . 2,896,016
Chișinău (Kishinev), Moldova . . . 676,700
Chittagong, Bangladesh (2,342,662) . . . 1,566,070
Chongqing (Chungking), China . . . 3,870,000
Cincinnati, Ohio, U.S. (1,704,900) . . . 331,285
Cleveland, Ohio, U.S. (2,186,200) . . . 478,403
Cologne (Köln), Germany (1,830,000) . . . 964,311
Colombo, Sri Lanka (2,050,000) . . . 612,000
Columbus, Ohio, U.S. (1,243,700) . . . 711,470
Conakry, Guinea . . . 950,000
Copenhagen (København), Denmark (2,030,000) . . . 499,148
Cordoba, Argentina (1,260,000) . . . 1,179,067
Curitiba, Brazil (2,595,000) . . . 1,586,848
Dakar, Senegal . . . 1,490,450
Dalian (Lüda), China . . . 2,400,000
Dallas, Texas, U.S. (4,809,300) . . . 1,188,580
Damascus (Dimashq), Syria (2,230,000) . . . 1,549,932
Dar es Salaam, Tanzania . . . 1,096,000
Delhi, India (12,791,458) . . . 9,817,439
Denver, Colorado, U.S. (2,148,100) . . . 554,636
Detroit, Michigan, U.S. (4,668,000) . . . 951,270
Dhaka (Dacca), Bangladesh (6,537,308) . . . 3,637,892
Dnipropetrovs'k, Ukraine (1,590,000) . . . 1,147,000
Donets'k, Ukraine (2,090,000) . . . 1,088,000
Dresden, Germany (860,000) . . . 459,222
Dublin (Baile Átha Cliath), Ireland (1,175,000) . . . 481,854
Durban, South Africa (1,740,000) . . . 715,669
Düsseldorf, Germany (1,200,000) . . . 529,062
Edinburgh, Scotland, U.K. (640,000) . . 401,910
Essen, Germany (5,040,000) . . . 608,732
Faisalabad, Pakistan . . . 1,104,209
Florence (Firenze), Italy (640,000) . . . 381,762
Fortaleza, Brazil (2,780,000) . . . 788,956
Frankfurt am Main, Germany (1,960,000) . . . 643,469
Fukuoka, Japan (2,000,000) . . . 1,284,795
Gdańsk (Danzig), Poland (885,000) . . . 457,937
Geneva (Génève), Switzerland (470,000) . . . 171,042
Genoa (Genova), Italy (800,000) . . . 655,704
Glasgow, Scotland, U.K. (1,870,000) . . 662,954
Goiânia, Brazil . . . 1,075,761
Guadalajara, Mexico (3,669,021) . . . 1,646,183
Guangzhou (Canton), China . . . 3,750,000
Guatemala, Guatemala (1,500,000) . . . 823,301
Guayaquil, Ecuador . . . 1,508,444
Ḩalab, Syria (1,640,000) . . . 1,591,400
Hamburg, Germany (2,460,000) . . . 1,704,731
Hannover, Germany (1,015,000) . . . 520,670
Hanoi, Vietnam (1,275,000) . . . 905,939
Harare, Zimbabwe (1,470,000) . . . 1,189,103
Harbin, China . . . 3,120,000
Havana (La Habana), Cuba (2,285,000) . . . 2,189,716
Helsinki, Finland (1,075,000) . . . 512,686
Hiroshima, Japan (1,600,000) . . . 1,108,888
Ho Chi Minh City (Saigon), Vietnam (3,300,000) . . . 2,796,229
Hong Kong (Xianggang), China (4,770,000) . . . 1,250,993
Honolulu, Hawaii, U.S. (881,500) . . . 371,657
Houston, Texas, U.S. (4,178,400) . . . 1,953,631
Hyderābād, India (5,533,640) . . . 3,449,878
Ibadan, Nigeria . . . 1,144,000
Indianapolis, Indiana, U.S. (1,397,100) . . . 781,870
İstanbul, Turkey (7,550,000) . . . 6,620,241
İzmir, Turkey (1,900,000) . . . 1,757,414
Jakarta, Indonesia (10,200,000) . . . 8,227,746
Jerusalem, Israel (685,000) . . . 633,700
Jiddah, Saudi Arabia . . . 1,300,000
Jinan, China . . . 2,150,000
Johannesburg, South Africa (4,000,000) . . . 712,507
Kābol, Afghanistan . . . 1,424,400
Kampala, Uganda . . . 773,463
Kānpur, India (2,690,486) . . . 2,540,069
Kansas City, Missouri, U.S. (1,584,200) . . . 441,545
Kaohsiung, Taiwan (1,900,000) . . . 1,401,239
Karāchi, Pakistan (5,300,000) . . . 4,901,627
Katowice, Poland (2,755,000) . . . 343,158
Kazan', Russia (1,175,000) . . . 1,100,800
Kharkiv, Ukraine (1,950,000) . . . 1,555,000
Khartoum (Al Kharṭūm), Sudan (1,450,000) . . . 473,597
Kiev (Kyïv), Ukraine (3,250,000) . . . 2,630,000
Kingston, Jamaica (830,000) . . . 516,500
Kinshasa, Dem. Rep. of the Congo . . . 3,000,000
Kitakyūshū, Japan (1,550,000) . . . 1,019,598
Kōbe, Japan (*Ōsaka) . . . 1,423,792
Kolkata (Calcutta), India (13,216,546) . . . 4,580,544
Kuala Lumpur, Malaysia (2,500,000) . . . 1,297,526
Kunming, China . . . 1,500,000
Kuwait (Al Kuwayt), Kuwait (1,126,000) . . . 28,859
Kyōto, Japan (*Ōsaka) . . . 1,463,822
Lagos, Nigeria (3,800,000) . . . 1,213,000
Lahore, Pakistan (3,025,000) . . . 2,707,215
La Paz, Bolivia (1,487,854) . . . 792,611
Leeds, England, U.K. (1,530,000) . . . 424,194
Liège, Belgium (747,000) . . . 194,596
Lille, France (1,143,125) . . . 184,657
Lima, Peru (4,608,010) . . . 371,122
Lisbon (Lisboa), Portugal (2,350,000) . . . 663,394
Liverpool, England, U.K. (1,515,000) . . . 481,786
London, England, U.K. (12,000,000) . . . 7,650,944
Los Angeles, California, U.S. (13,144,700) . . . 3,694,820
Luanda, Angola . . . 1,459,900
Lucknow, India (2,266,933) . . . 2,207,340
Lusaka, Zambia . . . 982,362
Lyon, France (1,648,216) . . . 445,452
Madrid, Spain (4,690,000) . . . 2,882,860
Managua, Nicaragua . . . 864,201
Manaus, Brazil . . . 1,394,724
Manchester, England, U.K. (2,760,000) . . . 402,889
Manila, Philippines (11,200,000) . . . 1,654,761
Mannheim, Germany (1,525,000) . . . 310,475
Maputo, Mozambique . . . 966,837
Maracaibo, Venezuela . . . 1,249,670
Marseille, France (1,516,340) . . . 798,430
Mashhad, Iran . . . 1,887,405
Mecca (Makkah), Saudi Arabia . . . 550,000
Medan, Indonesia . . . 1,730,052
Medellín, Colombia (2,290,000) . . . 1,551,160
Melbourne, Australia (3,040,000) . . . 48,560
Memphis, Tennessee, U.S. (1,080,900) . . . 650,100
Mexico City, Mexico (17,786,983) . . . 8,605,539
Miami, Florida, U.S. (5,060,000) . . . 362,470
Milan (Milano), Italy (3,790,000) . . . 1,305,591
Milwaukee, Wisconsin, U.S. (1,619,000) . . . 596,974
Minneapolis, Minnesota, U.S. (2,726,600) . . . 382,618
Minsk, Belarus (1,722,000) . . . 1,661,000
Mogadishu, Somalia . . . 600,000
Monterrey, Mexico (3,236,604) . . . 1,110,909
Montevideo, Uruguay (1,650,000) . . . 1,303,182
Montréal, Canada (3,326,510) . . . 1,016,376
Moscow (Moskva), Russia (12,850,000) . . . 8,389,700
Mumbai (Bombay), India (16,368,084) . . . 11,914,398
Munich (München), Germany (1,930,000) . . . 1,205,923
Nagoya, Japan (5,250,000) . . . 2,152,184
Nāgpur, India (2,122,965) . . . 2,051,320
Nairobi, Kenya . . . 2,143,254
Nanjing, China . . . 2,490,000
Naples (Napoli), Italy (3,150,000) . . . 1,046,987
Nashville, Tennessee, U.S. (926,600) . . . 545,524
New Delhi, India (*Delhi) . . . 294,783
New Orleans, Louisiana, U.S. (1,247,700) . . . 484,674
New York, New York, U.S. (19,549,900) . . . 8,008,278
Nizhniy Novgorod, Russia (1,950,000) . . . 1,364,900
Novosibirsk, Russia (1,505,000) . . . 1,402,400
Nürnberg, Germany (1,065,000) . . . 489,758
Odesa, Ukraine (1,150,000) . . . 1,046,000
Oklahoma City, Oklahoma, U.S. (986,900) . . . 506,132
Omsk, Russia (1,190,000) . . . 1,157,600
Ōsaka, Japan (17,050,000) . . . 2,602,421
Oslo, Norway (773,498) . . . 504,040
Ottawa, Canada (1,010,498) . . . 323,340
Panamá, Panama (995,000) . . . 415,964
Paris, France (11,174,743) . . . 2,125,246
Perm', Russia (1,110,000) . . . 1,017,100
Perth, Australia (1,244,320) . . . 10,195
Philadelphia, Pennsylvania, U.S. (5,843,000) . . . 1,517,550
Phnum Pénh (Phnom Penh), Cambodia . . . 570,155
Phoenix, Arizona, U.S. (3,198,100) . . 1,321,045
Pittsburgh, Pennsylvania, U.S. (2,002,700) . . . 334,563
Poona (Pune), India (3,755,525) . . . 2,540,069
Port-au-Prince, Haiti (1,425,594) . . . 846,247
Portland, Oregon, U.S. (1,810,200) . . . 529,121
Porto Alegre, Brazil (3,375,000) . . . 1,304,998
Prague (Praha), Czech Republic (1,328,000) . . . 1,214,174
Pretoria, South Africa (1,100,000) . . . 525,583
Providence, Rhode Island, U.S. (1,030,400) . . . 173,618
Puebla, Mexico (2,343,073) . . . 1,271,673
Pusan, South Korea (3,800,000) . . . 3,797,566
P'yŏngyang, North Korea . . . 2,355,000
Qingdao, China . . . 2,300,000
Québec, Canada (671,889) . . . 167,264
Quezon City, Philippines (*Manila) . . 1,989,419
Quito, Ecuador (1,300,000) . . . 1,100,847
Rabat, Morocco (1,200,000) . . . 717,000
Recife, Brazil (3,160,000) . . . 1,421,993
Rīga, Latvia (1,000,000) . . . 874,200
Rio de Janerio, Brazil (10,465,000) . 5,851,914
Riyadh, Saudi Arabia . . . 1,250,000
Rome (Roma), Italy (3,235,000) . . . 2,649,765
Rosario, Argentina (1,190,000) . . . 894,645
Rostov-na-Donu, Russia (1,160,000) . . . 1,017,300
Rotterdam, Netherlands (1,089,979) . . 539,000
St. Louis, Missouri, U.S. (2,345,800) . . 348,189
St. Petersburg (Leningrad), Russia (6,000,000) . . . 4,728,200
Salt Lake City, Utah, U.S. (1,018,500) . . . 181,743
Salvador, Brazil (2,855,000) . . . 2,439,823
Samara, Russia (1,450,000) . . . 1,168,000
San Antonio, Texas, U.S. (1,432,100) . . . 1,144,646
San Diego, California, U.S. (2,775,400) . . . 1,223,400
San Francisco, California, U.S. (6,071,300) . . . 776,733
San José, Costa Rica (996,194) . . . 309,672
San Juan, Puerto Rico (1,967,627) . . . 421,958
San Salvador, El Salvador (1,250,000) . . . 415,346
Santiago, Chile (4,740,000) . . . 4,295,593
Santo Domingo, Dominican Rep. . . . 1,609,966
Santos, Brazil . . . 415,543
São Paulo, Brazil (17,380,000) . . . 9,713,692
Sapporo, Japan (2,000,000) . . . 1,757,025
Sarajevo, Bosnia and Herzegovina . . . 367,703
Saratov, Russia (1,135,000) . . . 881,000
Seattle, Washington, U.S. (3,095,700) . . . 563,662
Seoul (Sŏul), South Korea (15,850,000) . . . 10,627,790
Shanghai, China (11,010,000) . . . 8,930,000
Shenyang (Mukden), China . . . 4,050,000
Singapore, Singapore (4,400,000) . . 4,017,700
Skopje, Macedonia . . . 440,577
Sofia (Sofiya), Bulgaria (1,280,000) . . 1,190,126
Stockholm, Sweden (1,491,726) . . . 674,452
Stuttgart, Germany (2,020,000) . . . 585,274
Surabaya, Indonesia . . . 2,473,272
Sydney, Australia (3,741,290) . . . 11,115
Taegu, South Korea . . . 2,228,834
T'aipei, Taiwan (6,200,000) . . . 2,706,453
Taiyuan, China . . . 1,720,000
Tampa, Florida, U.S. (1,005,500) . . . 303,447
Tashkent, Uzbekistan (2,325,000) . . . 2,113,300
Tbilisi, Georgia (1,460,000) . . . 1,279,000
Tegucigalpa, Honduras . . . 576,661
Tehrān, Iran (8,800,000) . . . 6,758,845
Tel Aviv-Yafo, Israel (1,890,000) . . . 348,100
The Hague ('s-Gravenhage), Netherlands (701,211) . . . 440,743
Tianjin (Tientsin), China . . . 5,000,000
Tiranë, Albania . . . 243,000
Tōkyō, Japan (30,300,000) . . . 7,967,614
Toronto, Canada (4,263,757) . . . 2,385,421
Tripoli (Tarābulus), Libya (960,000) . . . 591,062
Tunis, Tunisia (1,300,000) . . . 674,142
Turin (Torino), Italy (1,550,000) . . . 921,485
Ufa, Russia (1,110,000) . . . 1,088,900
Ulan Bator, Mongolia . . . 649,797
Valencia, Spain (1,340,000) . . . 739,014
Vancouver, Canada (1,831,665) . . . 514,008
Venice (Venezia), Italy (420,000) . . . 297,743
Vienna (Wien), Austria (1,950,000) . . 1,609,631
Vilnius, Lithuania . . . 578,639
Vladivostok, Russia . . . 613,100
Volgograd (Stalingrad), Russia (1,358,000) . . . 1,000,000
Warsaw (Warszawa), Poland (2,300,000) . . . 1,615,369
Washington, D.C., U.S. (4,657,700) . . . 572,059
Wellington, New Zealand (375,000) . . . 150,301
Winnipeg, Canada (667,209) . . . 618,477
Wuhan, China . . . 3,870,000
Xi'an, China . . . 2,410,000
Xinjiulong (New Kowloon), China (*Hong Kong) . . . 1,526,910
Yangon (Rangoon), Myanmar (2,800,000) . . . 2,705,039
Yekaterinburg, Russia (1,530,000) . . 1,272,900
Yerevan, Armenia (1,315,000) . . . 1,199,000
Yokohama, Japan (*Tōkyō) . . . 3,307,136
Zagreb, Croatia . . . 867,865
Zurich, Switzerland (870,000) . . . 365,043

Metropolitan area populations are shown in parentheses.
* City is located within the metropolitan area of another city; for example, Kyōto, Japan is located in the Ōsaka metropolitan area.

GLOSSARY OF FOREIGN GEOGRAPHICAL TERMS

Annam . . . Annamese
Arab . . . Arabic
Bantu . . . Bantu
Bur . . . Burmese
Camb . . . Cambodian
Celt . . . Celtic
Chn . . . Chinese
Czech . . . Czech
Dan . . . Danish
Du . . . Dutch
Fin . . . Finnish
Fr . . . French
Ger . . . German
Gr . . . Greek
Hung . . . Hungarian
Ice . . . Icelandic
India . . . India
Indian . . . American Indian
Indon . . . Indonesian
It . . . Italian
Jap . . . Japanese
Kor . . . Korean
Mal . . . Malayan
Mong . . . Mongolian
Nor . . . Norwegian
Per . . . Persian
Pol . . . Polish
Port . . . Portuguese
Rom . . . Romanian
Rus . . . Russian
Siam . . . Siamese
So. Slav . . . Southern Slavonic
Sp . . . Spanish
Swe . . . Swedish
Tib . . . Tibetan
Tur . . . Turkish
Yugo . . . Yugoslav

å, Nor., Swe . . . brook, river
aa, Dan., Nor . . . brook
aas, Dan., Nor . . . ridge
āb, Per . . . water, river
abad, India, Per . . . town, city
ada, Tur . . . island
adrar, Berber . . . mountain
air, Indon . . . stream
akrotírion, Gr . . . cape
älf, Swe . . . river
alp, Ger . . . mountain
altipiano, It . . . plateau
alto, Sp . . . height
archipel, Fr . . . archipelago
archipiélago, Sp . . . archipelago
arquipélago, Port . . . archipelago
arroyo, Sp . . . brook, stream
ås, Nor., Swe . . . ridge
austral, Sp . . . southern
baai, Du . . . bay
bab, Arab . . . gate, port
bach, Ger . . . brook, stream
backe, Swe . . . hill
bad, Ger . . . bath, spa
bahía, Sp . . . bay, gulf
bahr, Arab . . . river, sea, lake
baia, It . . . bay, gulf
baía, Port . . . bay
baie, Fr . . . bay, gulf
bajo, Sp . . . depression
bak, Indon . . . stream
bakke, Dan., Nor . . . hill
balkan, Tur . . . mountain range
bana, Jap . . . point, cape
banco, Sp . . . bank
bandar, Mal., Per.
. . . town, port, harbor
bang, Siam . . . village
bassin, Fr . . . basin
batang, Indon., Mal . . . river
ben, Celt . . . mountain, summit
bender, Arab . . . harbor, port
bereg, Rus . . . coast, shore
berg, Du., Ger., Nor., Swe.
. . . mountain, hill
bir, Arab . . . well
birkat, Arab . . . lake, pond, pool
bit, Arab . . . house
bjaerg, Dan., Nor . . . mountain
bocche, It . . . mouth
boğazı, Tur . . . strait
bois, Fr . . . forest, wood
boloto, Rus . . . marsh
bolsón, Sp.
. . . flat-floored desert valley
boreal, Sp . . . northern
borg, Dan., Nor., Swe . . . castle, town
borgo, It . . . town, suburb
bosch, Du . . . forest, wood
bouche, Fr . . . river mouth
bourg, Fr . . . town, borough
bro, Dan., Nor., Swe . . . bridge
brücke, Ger . . . bridge
bucht, Ger . . . bay, bight
bugt, Dan., Nor., Swe . . . bay, gulf
bulu, Indon . . . mountain
burg, Du., Ger . . . castle, town
buri, Siam . . . town
burun, burnu, Tur . . . cape
by, Dan., Nor., Swe . . . village
caatinga, Port. (Brazil)
. . . open brushland
cabezo, Sp . . . summit
cabo, Port., Sp . . . cape
campo, It., Port., Sp . . . plain, field
campos, Port. (Brazil) . . . plains
cañón, Sp . . . canyon
cap, Fr . . . cape
capo, It . . . cape
casa, It., Port., Sp . . . house
castello, It., Port . . . castle, fort
castillo, Sp . . . castle
càte, Fr . . . hill
çay, Tur . . . stream, river
cayo, Sp . . . rock, shoal, islet
cerro, Sp . . . mountain, hill
champ, Fr . . . field
chang, Chn . . . village, middle
château, Fr . . . castle
chen, Chn . . . market town
chiang, Chn . . . river
chott, Arab . . . salt lake
chou, Chn. capital of district; island
chu, Tib . . . water, stream
cidade, Port . . . town, city
cima, Sp . . . summit, peak
città, It . . . town, city
ciudad, Sp . . . town, city
cochilha, Port . . . ridge
col, Fr . . . pass
colina, Sp . . . hill
cordillera, Sp . . . mountain chain
costa, It., Port., Sp . . . coast
côte, Fr . . . coast
cuchilla, Sp . . . mountain ridge
dağ, Tur . . . mountain(s)
dake, Jap . . . peak, summit
dal, Dan., Du., Nor., Swe . . . valley
dan, Kor . . . point, cape
danau, Indon . . . lake
dar, Arab . . . house, abode, country
darya, Per . . . river, sea
dasht, Per . . . plain, desert
deniz, Tur . . . sea
désert, Fr . . . desert
deserto, It . . . desert
desierto, Sp . . . desert
détroit, Fr . . . strait
dijk, Du . . . dam, dike
djebel, Arab . . . mountain
do, Kor . . . island
dorf, Ger . . . village
dorp, Du . . . village
duin, Du . . . dune
dzong, Tib.
. . . fort, administrative capital
eau, Fr . . . water
ecuador, Sp . . . equator
eiland, Du . . . island
elv, Dan., Nor . . . river, stream
embalse, Sp . . . reservoir
erg, Arab . . . dune, sandy desert
est, Fr., It . . . east
estado, Sp . . . state
este, Port., Sp . . . east
estrecho, Sp . . . strait
étang, Fr . . . pond, lake
état, Fr . . . state
eyjar, Ice . . . islands
feld, Ger . . . field, plain
festung, Ger . . . fortress
fiume, It . . . river
fjäll, Swe . . . mountain
fjärd, Swe . . . bay, inlet
fjeld, Nor . . . mountain, hill
fjord, Dan., Nor . . . fiord, inlet
fjördur, Ice . . . fiord, inlet
fleuve, Fr . . . river
flod, Dan., Swe . . . river
flói, Ice . . . bay, marshland
fluss, Ger . . . river
foce, It . . . river mouth
fontein, Du . . . a spring
forêt, Fr . . . forest
fors, Swe . . . waterfall
forst, Ger . . . forest
fos, Dan., Nor . . . waterfall
fu, Chn . . . town, residence
fuente, Sp . . . spring, fountain
fuerte, Sp . . . fort
furt, Ger . . . ford
gang, Kor . . . stream, river
gangri, Tib . . . mountain
gat, Dan., Nor . . . channel
gàve, Fr . . . stream
gawa, Jap . . . river
gebergte, Du . . . mountain range
gebiet, Ger . . . district, territory
gebirge, Ger . . . mountains
ghat, India . . . pass, mountain range
gobi, Mong . . . desert
gol, Mong . . . river
göl, gölü, Tur . . . lake
golf, Du., Ger . . . gulf, bay
golfe, Fr . . . gulf, bay
golfo, It., Port., Sp . . . gulf, bay
gomba, gompa, Tib . . . monastery
gora, Rus., So. Slav . . . mountain
góra, Pol . . . mountain
gorod, Rus . . . town
grad, Rus., So. Slav . . . town
guba, Rus . . . bay, gulf
gundung, Indon . . . mountain
guntō, Jap . . . archipelago
gunung, Mal . . . mountain
haf, Swe . . . sea, ocean
hafen, Ger . . . port, harbor
haff, Ger . . . gulf, inland sea
hai, Chn . . . sea, lake
hama, Jap . . . beach, shore
hamada, Arab . . . rocky plateau
hamn, Swe . . . harbor
hāmūn, Per . . . swampy lake, plain
hantō, Jap . . . peninsula
hassi, Arab . . . well, spring
haus, Ger . . . house
haut, Fr . . . summit, top
hav, Dan., Nor . . . sea, ocean
havn, Dan., Nor . . . harbor, port
havre, Fr . . . harbor, port
háza, Hung . . . house, dwelling of
heim, Ger . . . hamlet, home
hem, Swe . . . hamlet, home
higashi, Jap . . . east
hisar, Tur . . . fortress
hissar, Arab . . . fort
ho, Chn . . . river
hoek, Du . . . cape
hof, Ger . . . court, farmhouse
höfn, Ice . . . harbor
hoku, Jap . . . north
holm, Dan., Nor., Swe . . . island
hora, Czech . . . mountain
horn, Ger . . . peak
hoved, Dan., Nor . . . cape
hsien, Chn . . . district, district capital
hu, Chn . . . lake
hügel, Ger . . . hill
huk, Dan., Swe . . . point
hus, Dan., Nor., Swe . . . house
île, Fr . . . island
ilha, Port . . . island
indsö, Dan., Nor . . . lake
insel, Ger . . . island
insjö, Swe . . . lake
irmak, irmagi, Tur . . . river
isla, Sp . . . island
isola, It . . . island
istmo, It., Sp . . . isthmus
järvi, jaur, Fin . . . lake
jebel, Arab . . . mountain
jima, Jap . . . island
jökel, Nor . . . glacier
joki, Fin . . . river
jökull, Ice . . . glacier
kaap, Du . . . cape
kai, Jap . . . bay, gulf, sea
kaikyō, Jap . . . channel, strait
kalat, Per . . . castle, fortress
kale, Tur . . . fort
kali, Mal . . . creek, river
kand, Per . . . village
kang, Chn . . . mountain ridge; village
kap, Dan., Ger . . . cape
kapp, Nor., Swe . . . cape
kasr, Arab . . . fort, castle
kawa, Jap . . . river
kefr, Arab . . . village
kei, Jap . . . creek, river
ken, Jap . . . prefecture
khor, Arab . . . bay, inlet
khrebet, Rus . . . mountain range
kiang, Chn . . . large river
king, Chn . . . capital city, town
kita, Jap . . . north
ko, Jap . . . lake
köbstad, Dan . . . market-town
kol, Mong . . . lake
kólpos, Gr . . . gulf
kong, Chn . . . river
kopf, Ger . . . head, summit, peak
köpstad, Swe . . . market-town
körfezi, Tur . . . gulf
kosa, Rus . . . spit
kou, Chn . . . river mouth
köy, Tur . . . village
kraal, Du. (Africa) . . . native village
ksar, Arab . . . fortified village
kuala, Mal . . . bay, river mouth
kuh, Per . . . mountain
kum, Tur . . . sand
kuppe, Ger . . . summit
küste, Ger . . . coast
kyo, Jap . . . town, capital
la, Tib . . . mountain pass
labuan, Mal . . . anchorage, port
lac, Fr . . . lake
lago, It., Port., Sp . . . lake
lagoa, Port . . . lake, marsh
laguna, It., Port., Sp . . . lagoon, lake
lahti, Fin . . . bay, gulf
län, Swe . . . county
landsby, Dan., Nor . . . village
liehtao, Chn . . . archipelago
liman, Tur . . . bay, port
ling, Chn . . . pass, ridge, mountain
llanos, Sp . . . plains
loch, Celt. (Scotland) . . . lake, bay
loma, Sp . . . long, low hill
lough, Celt. (Ireland) . . . lake, bay
machi, Jap . . . town
man, Kor . . . bay
mar, Port., Sp . . . sea
mare, It., Rom . . . sea
marisma, Sp . . . marsh, swamp
mark, Ger . . . boundary, limit
massif, Fr . . . block of mountains
mato, Port . . . forest, thicket
me, Siam . . . river
meer, Du., Ger . . . lake, sea
mer, Fr . . . sea
mesa, Sp . . . flat-topped mountain
meseta, Sp . . . plateau
mina, Port., Sp . . . mine
minami, Jap . . . south
minato, Jap . . . harbor, haven
misaki, Jap . . . cape, headland
mont, Fr . . . mount, mountain
montagna, It . . . mountain
montagne, Fr . . . mountain
montaña, Sp . . . mountain
monte, It., Port., Sp.
. . . mount, mountain
more, Rus., So. Slav . . . sea
morro, Port., Sp . . . hill, bluff
mühle, Ger . . . mill
mund, Ger . . . mouth, opening
mündung, Ger . . . river mouth
mura, Jap . . . township
myit, Bur . . . river
mys, Rus . . . cape
nada, Jap . . . sea
nadi, India . . . river, creek
naes, Dan., Nor . . . cape
nafud, Arab . . . desert of sand dunes
nagar, India . . . town, city
nahr, Arab . . . river
nam, Siam . . . river, water
nan, Chn., Jap . . . south
näs, Nor., Swe . . . cape
nez, Fr . . . point, cape
nishi, nisi, Jap . . . west
njarga, Fin . . . peninsula
nong, Siam . . . marsh
noord, Du . . . north
nor, Mong . . . lake
nord, Dan., Fr., Ger., It.,
Nor., Swe . . . north
norte, Port., Sp . . . north
nos, Rus . . . cape
nyasa, Bantu . . . lake
ö, Dan., Nor., Swe . . . island
occidental, Sp . . . western
ocna, Rom . . . salt mine
odde, Dan., Nor . . . point, cape
oeste, Port., Sp . . . west
oka, Jap . . . hill
oost, Du . . . east
oriental, Sp . . . eastern
óros, Gr . . . mountain
ost, Ger., Swe . . . east
öster, Dan., Nor., Swe . . . eastern
ostrov, Rus . . . island
oued, Arab . . . river, stream
ouest, Fr . . . west
ozero, Rus . . . lake
pää, Fin . . . mountain
padang, Mal . . . plain, field
pampas, Sp. (Argentina)
. . . grassy plains
pará, Indian (Brazil) . . . river
pas, Fr . . . channel, passage
paso, Sp . . . mountain pass, passage
passo, It., Port.
mountain pass, passage, strait
patam, India . . . city, town
pei, Chn . . . north
pélagos, Gr . . . open sea
pegunungan, Indon . . . mountains
peña, Sp . . . rock
peresheyek, Rus . . . isthmus
pertuis, Fr . . . strait
peski, Rus . . . desert
pic, Fr . . . mountain peak
pico, Port., Sp . . . mountain peak
piedra, Sp . . . stone, rock
ping, Chn . . . plain, flat
planalto, Port . . . plateau
planina, Yugo . . . mountains
playa, Sp . . . shore, beach
pnom, Camb . . . mountain
pointe, Fr . . . point
polder, Du., Ger . . . reclaimed marsh
polje, So. Slav . . . plain, field
poluostrov, Rus . . . peninsula
pont, Fr . . . bridge
ponta, Port . . . point, headland
ponte, It., Port . . . bridge
pore, India . . . city, town
porthmós, Gr . . . strait
porto, It., Port . . . port, harbor
potamós, Gr . . . river
p'ov, Rus . . . peninsula
prado, Sp . . . field, meadow
presqu'île, Fr . . . peninsula
proliv, Rus . . . strait
pu, Chn . . . commercial village
pueblo, Sp . . . town, village
puerto, Sp . . . port, harbor
pulau, Indon . . . island
punkt, Ger . . . point
punt, Du . . . point
punta, It., Sp . . . point
pur, India . . . city, town
puy, Fr . . . peak
qal'a, qal'at, Arab . . . fort, village
qasr, Arab . . . fort, castle
rann, India . . . wasteland
ra's, Arab . . . cape, head
reka, Rus., So. Slav . . . river
reprêsa, Port . . . reservoir
rettō, Jap . . . island chain
ría, Sp . . . estuary
ribeira, Port . . . stream
riberão, Port . . . river
rio, It., Port . . . stream, river
río, Sp . . . river
rivière, Fr . . . river
roca, Sp . . . rock
rt, Yugo . . . cape
rūd, Per . . . river
saari, Fin . . . island
sable, Fr . . . sand
sahara, Arab . . . desert, plain
saki, Jap . . . cape
sal, Sp . . . salt
salar, Sp . . . salt flat, salt lake
salto, Sp . . . waterfall
san, Jap., Kor . . . mountain, hill
sat, satul, Rom . . . village
schloss, Ger . . . castle
sebkha, Arab . . . salt marsh
see, Ger . . . lake, sea
şehir, Tur . . . town, city
selat, Indon . . . stream
selvas, Port. (Brazil)
. . . tropical rain forests
seno, Sp . . . bay
serra, Port . . . mountain chain
serranía, Sp . . . mountain ridge
seto, Jap . . . strait
severnaya, Rus . . . northern
shahr, Per . . . town, city
shan, Chn . . . mountain, hill, island
shatt, Arab . . . river
shi, Jap . . . city
shima, Jap . . . island
shōtō, Jap . . . archipelago
si, Chn . . . west, western
sierra, Sp . . . mountain range
sjö, Nor., Swe . . . lake, sea
sö, Dan., Nor . . . lake, sea
söder, södra, Swe . . . south
song, Annam . . . river
sopka, Rus . . . peak, volcano
source, Fr . . . a spring
spitze, Ger . . . summit, point
staat, Ger . . . state
stad, Dan., Du., Nor., Swe.
. . . city, town
stadt, Ger . . . city, town
stato, It . . . state
step', Rus . . . treeless plain, steppe
straat, Du . . . strait
strand, Dan., Du., Ger., Nor.,
Swe . . . shore, beach
stretto, It . . . strait
strom, Ger
. . . river, stream
ström, Dan., Nor., Swe.
. . . stream, river
stroom, Du . . . stream, river
su, suyu, Tur . . . water, river
sud, Fr., Sp . . . south
süd, Ger . . . south
suidō, Jap . . . channel
sul, Port . . . south
sund, Dan., Nor., Swe . . . sound
sungai, sungei, Indon., Mal . . . river
sur, Sp . . . south
syd, Dan., Nor., Swe . . . south
tafelland, Ger . . . plateau
take, Jap . . . peak, summit
tal, Ger . . . valley
tanjung, tanjong, Mal . . . cape
tao, Chn . . . island
târg, târgul, Rom . . . market, town
tell, Arab . . . hill
teluk, Indon . . . bay, gulf
terra, It . . . land
terre, Fr . . . earth, land
thal, Ger . . . valley
tierra, Sp . . . earth, land
tō, Jap . . . east; island
tonle, Camb . . . river, lake
top, Du . . . peak
torp, Swe . . . hamlet, cottage
tsangpo, Tib . . . river
tsi, Chn . . . village, borough
tso, Tib . . . lake
tsu, Jap . . . harbor, port
tundra, Rus . . . treeless arctic plains
tung, Chn . . . east
tuz, Tur . . . salt
udde, Swe . . . cape
ufer, Ger . . . shore, riverbank
ujung, Indon . . . point, cape
umi, Jap . . . sea, gulf
ura, Jap . . . bay, coast, creek
ust'ye, Rus . . . river mouth
valle, It., Port., Sp . . . valley
vallée, Fr . . . valley
valli, It . . . lake
vár, Hung . . . fortress
város, Hung . . . town
varoš, So. Slav . . . town
veld, Du . . . open plain, field
verkh, Rus . . . top, summit
ves, Czech . . . village
vest, Dan., Nor., Swe . . . west
vik, Swe . . . cove, bay
vila, Port . . . town
villa, Sp . . . town
villar, Sp . . . village, hamlet
ville, Fr . . . town, city
vostok, Rus . . . east
wad, wādī, Arab.
. . . intermittent stream
wald, Ger . . . forest, woodland
wan, Chn., Jap . . . bay, gulf
weiler, Ger . . . hamlet, village
westersch, Du . . . western
wüste, Ger . . . desert
yama, Jap . . . mountain
yarimada, Tur . . . peninsula
yug, Rus . . . south
zaki, Jap . . . cape
zaliv, Rus . . . bay, gulf
zapad, Rus . . . west
zee, Du . . . sea
zemlya, Rus . . . land
zuid, Du . . . south

ABBREVIATIONS OF GEOGRAPHICAL NAMES AND TERMS

Ab., Can.	Alberta, Can.
Afg.	Afghanistan
Afr.	Africa
Ak., U.S.	Alaska, U.S.
Al., U.S.	Alabama, U.S.
Alb.	Albania
Alg.	Algeria
Am. Sam.	American Samoa
And.	Andorra
Ang.	Angola
Ant.	Antarctica
Antig.	Antigua and Barbuda
aq.	Aqueduct
Ar., U.S.	Arkansas, U.S.
Arg.	Argentina
Arm.	Armenia
arpt.	Airport
Aus.	Austria
Austl.	Australia
Az., U.S.	Arizona, U.S.
Azer.	Azerbaijan
b.	Bay, Gulf, Inlet, Lagoon
Bah.	Bahamas
Bahr.	Bahrain
Barb.	Barbados
B.C., Can.	British Columbia, Can.
Bdi.	Burundi
Bel.	Belgium
Bela.	Belarus
Ber.	Bermuda
Bhu.	Bhutan
bk.	Undersea Bank
bldg.	Building
Blg.	Bulgaria
Bngl.	Bangladesh
Bol.	Bolivia
Bos.	Bosnia and Herzegovina
Bots.	Botswana
Braz.	Brazil
Bru.	Brunei
Br. Vir. Is.	British Virgin Islands
bt.	Bight
Burkina	Burkina Faso
c.	Cape, Point
Ca., U.S.	California, U.S.
Cam.	Cameroon
Camb.	Cambodia
can.	Canal
Can.	Canada
C.A.R.	Central African Republic
Cay. Is.	Cayman Islands
C. Iv.	Cote d'Ivoire
clf.	Cliff, Escarpment
co.	County, Parish
Co., U.S.	Colorado, U.S.
Col.	Colombia
Com.	Comoros
cont.	Continent
Cook Is.	Cook Islands
C.R.	Costa Rica
Cro.	Croatia
cst.	Coast, Beach
Ct., U.S.	Connecticut, U.S.
C.V.	Cape Verde
Cyp.	Cyprus
Czech Rep.	Czech Republic
d.	Delta
D.C., U.S.	District of Columbia, U.S.
De., U.S.	Delaware, U.S.
Den.	Denmark
dep.	Dependency, Colony
depr.	Depression
dept.	Department, District
des.	Desert
Dji.	Djibouti
Dom.	Dominica
Dom. Rep.	Dominican Republic
D.R.C.	Democratic Republic of the Congo
Ec.	Ecuador
educ.	Educational Facility
El Sal.	El Salvador
Eng., U.K.	England, U.K.
Eq. Gui.	Equatorial Guinea
Erit.	Eritrea
Est.	Estonia
est.	Estuary
Eth.	Ethiopia
E. Timor	East Timor
Eur.	Europe
Falk. Is.	Falkland Islands
Far. Is.	Faroe Islands
Fin.	Finland
fj.	Fjord
Fl., U.S.	Florida, U.S.
for.	Forest, Moor
Fr.	France
Fr. Gu.	French Guiana
Fr. Poly.	French Polynesia
Ga., U.S.	Georgia, U.S.
Gam.	The Gambia
Gaza	Gaza Strip
Geor.	Georgia
Ger.	Germany
Grc.	Greece
Gren.	Grenada
Grnld.	Greenland
Guad.	Guadeloupe
Guat.	Guatemala
Guern.	Guernsey
Gui.	Guinea
Gui.-B.	Guinea-Bissau
Guy.	Guyana
Hi., U.S.	Hawaii, U.S.
hist.	Historic Site, Ruins
hist. reg.	Historic Region
Hond.	Honduras
Hung.	Hungary
i.	Island
Ia., U.S.	Iowa, U.S.
ice	Ice Feature, Glacier
Ice.	Iceland
Id., U.S.	Idaho, U.S.
Il., U.S.	Illinois, U.S.
In., U.S.	Indiana, U.S.
Indon.	Indonesia
I. of Man	Isle of Man
I.R.	Indian Reservation
Ire.	Ireland
is.	Islands
Isr.	Israel
isth.	Isthmus
Jam.	Jamaica
Jord.	Jordan
Kaz.	Kazakhstan
Kir.	Kiribati
Kor., N.	Korea, North
Kor., S.	Korea, South
Ks., U.S.	Kansas, U.S.
Kuw.	Kuwait
Ky., U.S.	Kentucky, U.S.
Kyrg.	Kyrgyzstan
l.	Lake, Pond
La., U.S.	Louisiana, U.S.
Lat.	Latvia
Leb.	Lebanon
Leso.	Lesotho
Lib.	Liberia
Liech.	Liechtenstein
Lith.	Lithuania
Lux.	Luxembourg
Ma., U.S.	Massachusetts, U.S.
Mac.	Macedonia
Madag.	Madagascar
Malay.	Malaysia
Mald.	Maldives
Marsh. Is.	Marshall Islands
Mart.	Martinique
Maur.	Mauritania
May.	Mayotte
Mb., Can.	Manitoba, Can.
Md., U.S.	Maryland, U.S.
Me., U.S.	Maine, U.S.
Mex.	Mexico
Mi., U.S.	Michigan, U.S.
Micron.	Micronesia, Federated States of
Mn., U.S.	Minnesota, U.S.
Mo., U.S.	Missouri, U.S.
Mol.	Moldova
Mong.	Mongolia
Monts.	Montserrat
Mor.	Morocco
Moz.	Mozambique
Ms., U.S.	Mississippi, U.S.
Mt., U.S.	Montana, U.S.
mth.	River Mouth or Channel
mtn.	Mountain
mts.	Mountains
Mwi.	Malawi
Mya.	Myanmar
N.A.	North America
N.B., Can.	New Brunswick, Can.
N.C., U.S.	North Carolina, U.S.
N. Cal.	New Caledonia
N. Cyp.	North Cyprus
N.D., U.S.	North Dakota, U.S.
Ne., U.S.	Nebraska, U.S.
neigh.	Neighborhood
Neth.	Netherlands
Neth. Ant.	Netherlands Antilles
Nf., Can.	Newfoundland and Labrador, Can.
N.H., U.S.	New Hampshire, U.S.
Nic.	Nicaragua
Nig.	Nigeria
N. Ire., U.K.	Northern Ireland, U.K.
N.J., U.S.	New Jersey, U.S.
N.M., U.S.	New Mexico, U.S.
N. Mar. Is.	Northern Mariana Islands
Nmb.	Namibia
Nor.	Norway
N.S., Can.	Nova Scotia, Can.
N.T., Can.	Northwest Territories, Can.
Nu., Can.	Nunavut, Can.
Nv., U.S.	Nevada, U.S.
N.Y., U.S.	New York, U.S.
N.Z.	New Zealand
o.	Ocean
Oc.	Oceania
Oh., U.S.	Ohio, U.S.
Ok., U.S.	Oklahoma, U.S.
On., Can.	Ontario, Can.
Or., U.S.	Oregon, U.S.
p.	Pass
Pa., U.S.	Pennsylvania, U.S.
Pak.	Pakistan
Pan.	Panama
Pap. N. Gui.	Papua New Guinea
Para.	Paraguay
P.E., Can.	Prince Edward Island, Can.
pen.	Peninsula
Phil.	Philippines
Pit.	Pitcairn
pl.	Plain, Flat
plat.	Plateau, Highland
Pol.	Poland
Port.	Portugal
P.R.	Puerto Rico
prov.	Province, Region
pt. of i.	Point of Interest
Qc., Can.	Quebec, Can.
r.	River, Creek
Reu.	Reunion
rec.	Recreational Site, Park
reg.	Physical Region
rel.	Religious Institution
res.	Reservoir
rf.	Reef, Shoal
R.I., U.S.	Rhode Island, U.S.
Rom.	Romania
Rw.	Rwanda
S.A.	South America
S. Afr.	South Africa
Sau. Ar.	Saudi Arabia
S.C., U.S.	South Carolina, U.S.
sci.	Scientific Station
Scot., U.K.	Scotland, U.K.
S.D., U.S.	South Dakota, U.S.
sea feat.	Undersea Feature
Sen.	Senegal
Serb.	Serbia and Montenegro
Sey.	Seychelles
S. Geor.	South Georgia
Sing.	Singapore
Sk., Can.	Saskatchewan, Can.
S.L.	Sierra Leone
Slvk.	Slovakia
Slvn.	Slovenia
S. Mar.	San Marino
Sol. Is.	Solomon Islands
Som.	Somalia
Sp. N. Afr.	Spanish North Africa
Sri L.	Sri Lanka
St. Hel.	St. Helena
St. K./N.	St. Kitts and Nevis
St. Luc.	St. Lucia
St. P./M.	St. Pierre and Miquelon
strt.	Strait, Channel, Sound
S. Tom./P.	Sao Tome and Principe
St. Vin.	St. Vincent and the Grenadines
Sur.	Suriname
Sval.	Svalbard
sw.	Swamp, Marsh
Swaz.	Swaziland
Swe.	Sweden
Switz.	Switzerland
Tai.	Taiwan
Taj.	Tajikistan
Tan.	Tanzania
T./C. Is.	Turks and Caicos Islands
ter.	Territory
Thai.	Thailand
Tn., U.S.	Tennessee, U.S.
trans.	Transportation Facility
Trin.	Trinidad and Tobago
Tun.	Tunisia
Tur.	Turkey
Turkmen.	Turkmenistan
Tx., U.S.	Texas, U.S.
U.A.E.	United Arab Emirates
Ug.	Uganda
U.K.	United Kingdom
Ukr.	Ukraine
Ur.	Uruguay
U.S.	United States
Ut., U.S.	Utah, U.S.
Uzb.	Uzbekistan
Va., U.S.	Virginia, U.S.
val.	Valley, Watercourse
Ven.	Venezuela
Viet.	Vietnam
V.I.U.S.	Virgin Islands (U.S.)
vol.	Volcano
Vt., U.S.	Vermont, U.S.
Wa., U.S.	Washington, U.S.
W.B.	West Bank
Wi., U.S.	Wisconsin, U.S.
W. Sah.	Western Sahara
wtfl.	Waterfall
W.V., U.S.	West Virginia, U.S.
Wy., U.S.	Wyoming, U.S.
Yk., Can.	Yukon Territory, Can.
Zam.	Zambia
Zimb.	Zimbabwe

PRONUNCIATION OF GEOGRAPHICAL NAMES

Key to the Sound Values of Letters and Symbols Used in the Index to Indicate Pronunciation

ă-ăt; băttle
ă-fin*ă*l; appe*ă*l
ā-rāte; elāte
å-senåte; inanimåte
ä-ärm; cälm
ȧ-ȧsk; bȧth
ȧ-sof*ȧ*; m*ȧ*rine (short neutral or indeterminate sound)
â-fâre; prepâre
ch-choose; church
dh-as th in other; either
ē-bē; ēve
ė-ėvent; crėate
ĕ-bĕt; ĕnd
ĕ-rec*ĕ*nt (short neutral or indeterminate sound)
ẽ-cratẽr; cindẽr
g-gō; gāme
gh-guttural g
ĭ-bĭt; wĭll
ĭ-(short neutral or indeterminate sound)
ī-rīde; bīte
ᴋ-gutteral k as *ch* in German *ich*
ng-sing
ŋ-baŋk; liŋger
ɴ-indicates nasalized
ŏ-nŏd; ŏdd
ŏ-c*ŏ*mmit; c*ŏ*nnect
ō-ōld; bōld
ȯ-ȯbey; hȯtel
ô-ôrder; nôrth
oi-boil
o͞o-fo͞od; ro͞ot
ò-as oo in foot; wood
ou-out; thou
s-soft; so; sane
sh-dish; finish
th-thin; thick
ū-pūre; cūre
ů-ůnite; ůsůrp
û-ûrn; fûr
ŭ-stŭd; ŭp
ŭ-circ*ŭ*s; s*ŭ*bmit
ü-as in French *tu*
zh-as *z* in a*z*ure
'-indeterminate vowel sound

In many cases the spelling of foreign geographical names does not even remotely indicate the pronunciation to an American, i.e., Słupsk in Poland is pronounced swȯpsk; Jujuy in Argentina is pronounced ho͞ohwē', La Spezia in Italy is lä-spĕ'zyä.

This condition is hardly surprising, however, when we consider that in our own language Worcester, Massachusetts, is pronounced wȯs'tẽr; Sioux City, Iowa, so͞o sĭ'tĭ; Schuylkill Haven, Pennsylvania, sko͞ol'kĭl hā-vĕn; Poughkeepsie, New York, p*ŏ*-kĭp'sė.

The indication of pronunciation of geographic names presents several peculiar problems:

1. Many foreign tongues use sounds that are not present in the English language and which an American cannot normally articulate. Thus, though the nearest English equivalent sound has been indicated, only approximate results are possible.

2. There are several dialects in each foreign tongue which cause variation in the local pronunciation of names. This also occurs in identical names in the various divisions of a great language group, as the Slavic or the Latin.

3. Within the United States there are marked differences in pronunciation, not only of local geographic names, but also of common words, indicating that the sound and tone values for letters as well as the placing of the emphasis vary considerably from one part of the country to another.

4. A number of different letters and diacritical combinations could be used to indicate essentially the same or approximate pronunciations.

Some variation in pronunciation other than that indicated in this index may be encountered, but such a difference does not necessarily indicate that either is in error, and in many cases it is a matter of individual choice as to which is preferred. In fact, an exact indication of pronunciation of many foreign names using English letters and diacritical marks is extremely difficult and sometimes impossible.

PRONOUNCING INDEX

This universal index includes in a single alphabetical list approximately 30,000 names of features that appear on the reference maps. Each name is followed by a page reference and geographical coordinates.

Abbreviation and Capitalization Abbreviations of names on the maps have been standardized as much as possible. Names that are abbreviated on the maps are generally spelled out in full in the index. Periods are used after all abbreviations regardless of local practice. The abbreviation "St." is used only for "Saint". "Sankt" and other forms of this term are spelled out.

Most initial letters of names are capitalized, except for a few Dutch names, such as "s-Gravenhage". Capitalization of noninitial words in a name generally follows local practice.

Alphabetization Names are alphabetized in the order of the letters of the English alphabet. Spanish *ll* and *ch*, for example, are not treated as direct letters. Furthermore, diacritical marks are disregarded in alphabetization — German or Scandinavian *ä* or *ö* are treated as *a* or *o*.

The names of physical features may appear inverted, since they are always alphabetized under the proper, not the generic, part of the name, thus: "Gibraltar, Strait of". Otherwise every entry, whether consisting of one word or more, is alphabetized as a single continuous entity. "Lakeland", for example, appears after "La Crosse" and before "La Salle". Names beginning with articles (Le Harve, Den Helder, Al Manāmah, Ad Dawhah) are not inverted.

In the case of identical names, towns are listed first, then political divisions, then physical features.

Generic Terms Except for cities, the names of all features are followed by terms that represent broad classes of features, for example, Mississippi, r. or Alabama, state. A list of all abbreviations used in the index is on page 261.

Country names and the names of features that extend beyond the boundaries of one county are followed by the name of the continent in which each is located. Country designations follow the names of all other places in the index. The locations of places in the United States and the United Kingdom are further defined by abbreviations that include the state or political division in which each is located.

Pronunciations Pronunciations are included for most names listed. An explanation of the pronunciation system used appears on page 261.

Page References and Geographical Coordinates The geographical coordinates and page references are found in the last columns of each entry.

If a page contains several maps or insets, a lowercase letter identifies the specific map or inset.

Latitude and longitude coordinates for point features, such as cities and mountain peaks, indicate the location of the symbols. For extensive areal features, such as countries or mountain ranges, or linear features, such as canals and rivers, locations are given for the position of the type as it appears on the map.

PLACE (Pronunciation)	PAGE	LAT.	LONG.
A			
Aachen, Ger. (ä′kĕn)	161	50°46′N	6°07′E
Aalborg, Den. (ôl′bôr)	154	57°02′N	9°55′E
Aalen, Ger. (ä′lĕn)	168	48°49′N	10°08′E
Aalsmeer, Neth.	159a	52°16′N	4°44′E
Aalst, Bel.	165	50°58′N	4°00′E
Aarau, Switz. (ä′rōu)	161	47°22′N	8°03′E
Aarschot, Bel.	159a	50°59′N	4°51′E
Aba, D.R.C.	237	3°52′N	30°14′E
Aba, Nig.	230	5°06′N	7°21′E
Ābādān, Iran (ä-bŭ-dän′)	198	30°15′N	48°30′E
Abaetetuba, Braz. (ä′bä-ĕ-tĕ-tōō′bä)	143	1°44′S	48°45′W
Abajo Peak, mtn., Ut., U.S. (ä-bá′hō)	119	37°51′N	109°28′W
Abakaliki, Nig.	235	6°21′N	8°06′E
Abakan, Russia (ŭ-bá-kän′)	179	53°43′N	91°28′E
Abakan, r., Russia (u-bá-kän′)	184	53°00′N	91°06′E
Abancay, Peru (ä-bän-kä′ē)	142	13°44′S	72°46′W
Abashiri, Japan (ä-bä-shē′rē)	210	44°00′N	144°13′E
Abasolo, Mex. (ä-bä-sō′lō)	130	24°05′N	98°24′W
Abasolo, Mex. (ä-bä-sō′lō)	122	27°13′N	101°25′W
Abaya, Lake, l., Eth. (ä-bä′yä)	231	6°24′N	38°22′E
'Abbāsah, Tur'at al, can., Egypt	238d	30°45′N	32°15′E
Abbeville, Fr. (ab-vēl′)	161	50°08′N	1°49′E
Abbeville, Al., U.S. (ăb′ĕ-vĭl)	124	31°35′N	85°15′W
Abbeville, Ga., U.S. (ăb′ĕ-vĭl)	124	31°53′N	83°23′W
Abbeville, La., U.S.	123	29°59′N	92°07′W
Abbeville, S.C., U.S.	125	34°09′N	82°25′W
Abbiategrasso, Italy (äb-byä′tä-gräs′sō)	174	45°23′N	8°52′E
Abbots Bromley, Eng., U.K. (ăb′ŭts brŭm′lē)	158a	52°49′N	1°52′W
Abbotsford, Can. (ăb′ŭts-fĕrd)	116d	49°03′N	122°17′W
'Abd al Kūrī, i., Yemen (äbd-ĕl-kò′rē)	238a	12°12′N	51°00′E
Abdulino, Russia (äb-dò-lē′nō)	180	53°42′N	53°40′E
Abengourou, C. Iv.	234	6°44′N	3°29′W
Abeokuta, Nig. (ä-bā-ō-kōō′tä)	230	7°10′N	3°26′E
Abercorn see Mbala, Zam.	232	8°50′S	31°22′E
Aberdare, Wales, U.K. (ăb-ĕr-dâr′)	164	51°45′N	3°35′W
Aberdeen, Scot., U.K.	154	57°10′N	2°05′W
Aberdeen, Ms., U.S. (ăb-ĕr-dēn′)	124	33°49′N	88°33′W
Aberdeen, S.D., U.S. (ăb-ĕr-dēn′)	104	45°28′N	98°29′W
Aberdeen, Wa., U.S. (ăb-ĕr-dēn′)	104	47°00′N	123°48′W
Aberford, Eng., U.K. (ăb′ĕr-fĕrd)	158a	53°49′N	1°21′W
Abergavenny, Wales, U.K. (ăb′ĕr-gá-vĕn′ĭ)	164	51°45′N	3°05′W
Abert, Lake, l., Or., U.S. (ā′bĕrt)	114	42°39′N	120°24′W
Aberystwyth, Wales, U.K. (ă-bĕr-ĭst′with)	164	52°25′N	4°04′W
Abidjan, C. Iv. (ä-bĕd-zhäɴ′)	230	5°19′N	4°02′W
Abiko, Japan (ä-bē-kō)	211a	35°53′N	140°01′E
Abilene, Ks., U.S. (ăb′ĭ-lēn)	121	38°54′N	97°12′W
Abilene, Tx., U.S.	104	32°25′N	99°45′W
Abingdon, Eng., U.K.	158b	51°38′N	1°17′W
Abingdon, Il., U.S. (ăb′ĭng-dŭn)	113	40°48′N	90°21′W
Abingdon, Va., U.S.	125	36°42′N	81°57′W
Abington, Ma., U.S. (ăb′ĭng-tŭn)	101a	42°07′N	70°57′W
Abiquiu Reservoir, res., N.M., U.S.	119	36°26′N	106°42′W
Abitibi, l., Can. (ăb-ĭ-tĭb′ĭ)	93	48°27′N	80°20′W
Abitibi, r., Can.	93	49°30′N	81°10′W
Abkhazia, state, Geor.	181	43°10′N	40°45′E
Ablis, Fr. (ä-blē′)	171b	48°31′N	1°50′E
Abnūb, Egypt (äb-nōōb′)	238b	27°18′N	31°11′E
Åbo see Turku, Fin.	154	60°28′N	22°12′E
Abohar, India	202	30°12′N	74°13′E
Aboisso, C. Iv.	234	5°28′N	3°12′W
Abomey, Benin (ăb-ô-mā′)	230	7°11′N	1°59′E
Abony, Hung. (ŏ′bô-ny′)	169	47°12′N	20°00′E
Abou Deïa, Chad	235	11°27′N	19°17′E
Abra, r., Phil. (ä′brä)	213a	17°16′N	120°38′E
Abraão, Braz. (äbrå-oun′)	141a	23°10′S	44°10′W
Abraham's Bay, b., Bah.	135	22°20′N	73°50′W
Abram, Eng., U.K. (ā′brăm)	158a	53°31′N	2°36′W
Abrantes, Port. (à-brän′tĕs)	172	39°28′N	8°13′W
Abrolhos, Arquipélago dos, is., Braz.	143	17°58′S	38°40′W
Abruka, i., Est. (ä-brò′kä)	167	58°09′N	22°30′E
Abruzzi e Molise, hist. reg., Italy	174	42°10′N	13°55′E
Absaroka Range, mts., U.S. (äb-sä-rō-kä)	106	44°50′N	109°47′W
Abşeron Yarımadası, pen., Azer.	181	40°20′N	50°30′E
Abū Arīsh, Sau. Ar.	198	16°48′N	43°00′E
Abu Dhabi see Abū Ẓaby, U.A.E.	198	24°15′N	54°28′E
Abuja, Nig.	230	9°12′N	7°11′E
Abū Ḩamad, Sudan (ä′bōō hä′-mĕd)	231	19°37′N	33°21′E
Abū Kamāl, Syria	198	34°45′N	40°46′E
Abunã, r., S.A. (ä-bōō-nä′)	142	10°25′S	67°00′W
Abū Qīr, Egypt (ä′bōō kēr′)	238b	31°18′N	30°06′E
Abū Qurūn, Ra's, mtn., Egypt	197a	30°22′N	33°32′E
Aburatsu, Japan (ä′bò-rät′sōō)	211	31°33′N	131°22′E
Abu Road, India (ä′bōō)	199	24°38′N	72°45′E
Abū Tīj, Egypt	238b	27°03′N	31°19′E
Abū Ẓaby, U.A.E.	198	24°15′N	54°28′E
Abū Zanīmah, Egypt	197a	29°03′N	33°08′E
Abyy, Russia	179	68°24′N	134°00′E
Acacias, Col. (ä-kä′sēäs)	142a	3°59′N	73°44′W
Acadia National Park, rec., Me., U.S. (ä-kā′dĭ-á)	107	44°19′N	68°01′W
Acajutla, El Sal. (ä-kä-hōōt′lä)	132	13°37′N	89°50′W
Acala, Mex. (ä-kä′lä)	131	16°38′N	92°49′W
Acalayong, Eq. Gui.	236	1°05′N	9°40′E
Acámbaro, Mex. (ä-käm′bä-rō)	130	20°03′N	100°42′W
Acancéh, Mex. (ä-kän-sĕ′)	132a	20°50′N	89°27′W
Acapetlahuaya, Mex. (ä-kä-pĕt′lä-hwä′yä)	130	18°24′N	100°04′W
Acaponeta, Mex. (ä-kä-pō-nā′tä)	130	22°31′N	105°25′W
Acaponeta, r., Mex. (ä-kä-pō-nä′tä)	130	22°47′N	105°23′W
Acapulco, Mex. (ä-kä-pōōl′kō)	128	16°49′N	99°57′W
Acaraí Mountains, mts., S.A.	143	1°30′N	57°40′W
Acarigua, Ven. (äkä-rē′gwä)	142	9°29′N	69°11′W
Acatlán de Osorio, Mex. (ä-kät-län′dä ō-sō′rē-ō)	130	18°11′N	98°04′W
Acatzingo de Hidalgo, Mex.	131	18°58′N	97°47′W
Acayucan, Mex. (ä-kä-yōō′kän)	131	17°56′N	94°55′W
Accoville, W.V., U.S. (ăk′kō-vĭl)	108	37°45′N	81°50′W
Accra, Ghana (ä′krá)	230	5°33′N	0°13′W
Accrington, Eng., U.K. (ăk′rĭng-tŭn)	158a	53°45′N	2°22′W
Acerra, Italy (ä-chĕ′r-rä)	173c	40°42′N	14°22′E
Achacachi, Bol. (ä-chä-kä′chē)	142	16°11′S	68°32′W
Acheloós, r., Grc.	175	38°45′N	21°26′E
Achill Island, i., Ire. (ä-chĭl′)	160	53°55′N	10°05′W
Achinsk, Russia (ä-chĕnsk′)	184	56°13′N	90°32′E
Acireale, Italy (ä-chē-rä-ä′lä)	174	37°37′N	15°12′E
Acklins, i., Bah. (ăk′lĭns)	129	22°30′N	73°55′W
Acklins, The Bight of, b., Bah. (ăk′lĭns)	135	22°35′N	74°20′W
Acolman, Mex. (ä-kōl-má′n)	131a	19°38′N	98°56′W
Acoma Indian Reservation, I.R., N.M., U.S.	119	34°52′N	107°40′W
Aconcagua, prov., Chile (ä-kôn-kä′gwä)	141b	32°20′S	71°00′W
Aconcagua, r., Chile (ä-kôn-kä′gwä)	141b	32°43′S	70°53′W
Aconcagua, Cerro, mtn., Arg. (ä-kôn-kä′gwä)	144	32°38′S	70°00′W
Açores (Azores), is., Port.	229	37°44′N	29°25′W
A Coruña, Spain	154	43°20′N	8°20′W
Acoyapa, Nic. (ä-kō-yä′pä)	132	11°54′N	85°11′W
Acqui, Italy (äk′kwē)	174	44°41′N	8°22′W
Acre, state, Braz. (ä′krä)	142	8°40′S	70°45′W
Acre, r., S.A.	142	10°33′S	68°34′W
Acton, Can. (ăk′tŭn)	102d	43°38′N	80°02′W
Acton, Al., U.S. (ăk′tŭn)	110h	33°21′N	86°49′W
Acton, Ma., U.S. (ăk′tŭn)	101a	42°29′N	71°26′W
Actopan, Mex. (äk-tō-pän′)	130	20°16′N	98°57′W
Actópan, r., Mex. (äk-tō-pän′)	131	19°25′N	96°31′W
Acuitzio del Canje, Mex. (ä-kwēt′zē-ō dĕl kän′hä)	130	19°28′N	101°21′W
Acul, Baie de l', b., Haiti (ä-kōōl′)	135	19°55′N	72°20′W
Ada, Mn., U.S. (ā′dŭ)	112	47°17′N	96°32′W
Ada, Oh., U.S. (ā′dŭ)	108	40°45′N	83°45′W
Ada, Ok., U.S. (ā′dŭ)	121	34°45′N	96°43′W

āt; finál; rāte; senáte; ärm; ásk; sofá; fâre; ch-choose; dh-as th in other; bē; ĕvent; bĕt; recĕnt; cratĕr; g-gō; gh-guttural g; bĭt; ĭ-short neutral; rīde; κ-guttural k as ch in German ich;

PLACE (Pronunciation)	PAGE	LAT.	LONG.
Ada, Serb. (ä′dä)	175	45°48′N	20°06′E
Adachi, Japan	211a	35°50′N	39°36′E
Adak, Ak., U.S. (ă-dăk′)	103a	56°50′N	176°48′W
Adak, i., Ak., U.S. (ă-dăk′)	103a	51°40′N	176°28′W
Adak Strait, strt., Ak., U.S. (ă-dăk′)	103a	51°42′N	177°16′W
Adamaoua, mts., Afr.	230	6°30′N	11°50′E
Adams, Ma., U.S. (ăd′ămz)	109	42°35′N	73°10′W
Adams, Wi., U.S. (ăd′ămz)	113	43°55′N	89°48′W
Adams, r., Can. (ăd′ămz)	95	51°30′N	119°20′W
Adams, Mount, mtn., Wa., U.S. (ăd′ămz)	106	46°15′N	121°19′W
Adamsville, Al., U.S. (ăd′ămz-vĭl)	110h	33°36′N	86°57′W
Adana, Tur. (ä′dä-nä)	198	37°05′N	35°20′E
Adapazarı, Tur. (ä-dä-pä-zä′rē)	163	40°45′N	30°20′E
Adarama, Sudan (ä-dä-rä′mä)	231	17°11′N	34°56′E
Adda, r., Italy (äd′dä)	174	45°43′N	9°31′E
Ad Dabbah, Sudan	231	18°04′N	30°58′E
Ad Dahnā, des., Sau. Ar.	198	26°05′N	47°15′E
Ad-Dāmir, Sudan (ad-dä′mĕr)	231	17°38′N	33°57′E
Ad Dammām, Sau. Ar.	198	26°27′N	49°59′E
Ad Dāmūr, Leb.	197a	33°44′N	35°27′E
Ad Dawhah, Qatar	198	25°02′N	51°28′E
Ad Dilam, Sau. Ar.	198	23°47′N	47°03′E
Ad Dilinjāt, Egypt	238b	30°48′N	30°32′E
Addis Ababa, Eth.	231	9°00′N	38°44′E
Addison, Tx., U.S. (ă′dĭ-sŭn)	117c	32°58′N	96°50′W
Addo, S. Afr. (ădō)	233c	33°33′S	25°43′E
Ad Duwaym, Sudan (ad-dò-ām′)	231	13°56′N	32°22′E
Addyston, Oh., U.S. (ăd′ē-stŭn)	111f	39°09′N	84°42′W
Adel, Ga., U.S. (ā-dĕl′)	124	31°08′N	83°55′W
Adelaide, Austl. (ăd′ē-lād)	218	34°46′S	139°08′E
Adelaide, S. Afr. (ăd-ĕl′ād)	233c	32°41′S	26°07′E
Adelaide Island, i., Ant. (ăd′ē-lād)	224	67°15′S	68°40′W
Aden ('Adan), Yemen (ä′dĕn)	198	12°48′N	45°00′E
Aden, Gulf of, b.	198	11°45′N	45°45′E
Adi, Pulau, i., Indon. (ä′dē)	213	4°25′S	133°52′E
Adige, r., Italy (ä′dē-jā)	162	46°38′N	10°43′E
Adigrat, Eth.	201	14°17′N	39°28′E
Adilābād, India (ŭ-dĭl-ă-băd′)	202	19°47′N	78°30′E
Adirondack Mountains, mts., N.Y., U.S. (ăd-ĭ-rŏn′dăk)	107	43°45′N	74°40′W
Adis Abeba *see* Addis Ababa, Eth.	231	9°00′N	38°44′E
Adi Ugri, Erit. (ä-dē ōō′grē)	231	14°54′N	38°52′E
Adjud, Rom. (äd′zhòd)	169	46°05′N	27°12′E
Adkins, Tx., U.S.	117d	29°22′N	98°18′W
Admiralty, i., Ak., U.S. (ăd′mĭ-răl-tē)	103	57°50′N	133°50′W
Admiralty Inlet, Wa., U.S. (ăd′mĭ-răl-tē)	116a	48°10′N	122°45′W
Admiralty Island National Monument, rec., Ak., U.S. (ăd′mĭ-răl-tē)	103	57°50′N	137°30′W
Admiralty Islands, is., Pap. N. Gui. (ăd′mĭ-răl-tē)	213	1°40′S	146°45′E
Ado-Ekiti, Nig.	235	7°38′N	5°12′E
Adolph, Mn., U.S. (ā′dolf)	117h	46°47′N	92°17′W
Ādoni, India	203	15°42′N	77°18′E
Adour, r., Fr. (à-dōōr′)	161	43°43′N	0°38′W
Adra, Spain (ä′drä)	172	36°45′N	3°02′W
Adrano, Italy (ä-drä′nō)	174	37°42′N	14°52′E
Adrar, Alg.	230	27°53′N	0°15′W
Adria, Italy (ä′drē-ä)	174	45°03′N	12°01′E
Adrian, Mi., U.S. (ā′drĭ-ăn)	108	41°55′N	84°00′W
Adrian, Mn., U.S. (ā′drĭ-ăn)	112	43°39′N	95°56′W
Adrianople *see* Edirne, Tur.	154	41°41′N	26°35′E
Adriatic Sea, sea, Eur.	156	43°30′N	14°27′E
Adwa, Eth.	231	14°02′N	38°58′E
Adwick-le-Street, Eng., U.K. (ăd′wĭk-lē-strēt′)	158a	53°35′N	1°11′W
Adycha, r., Russia (ä′dĭ-chà)	185	66°11′N	136°45′E
Adygea, prov., Russia	180	45°00′N	40°00′E
Adz′va, r., Russia (ädz′và)	180	67°00′N	59°20′E
Aegean Sea, sea (ē-jē′ăn)	156	39°04′N	24°56′E
A Estrada, Spain	172	42°42′N	8°29′W
Affton, Mo., U.S.	117e	38°33′N	90°20′W
Afghanistan, nation, Asia (ăf-găn-ĭ-stăn′)	198	33°00′N	63°00′E
Afgooye, Som. (äf-gô′ĭ)	238a	2°08′N	45°08′E
Afikpo, Nig.	235	5°53′N	7°56′E
Aflou, Alg. (ä-flōō′)	230	33°59′N	2°04′E
Afognak, i., Ak., U.S. (ä-fŏg-nák′)	103	58°28′N	151°35′W
A Fonsagrada, Spain	172	43°08′N	7°07′W
Afonso Claudio, Braz. (äl-fōn′sō-klou′dēō)	141a	20°05′S	41°05′W
Afragola, Italy (ä-frà′gō-lä)	173c	40°40′N	14°19′E
Africa, cont.	229	10°00′N	22°00′E
Afton, Mn., U.S. (ăf′tŭn)	117g	44°54′N	92°47′W
Afton, Ok., U.S. (ăf′tŭn)	121	36°42′N	94°56′W
Afton, Wy., U.S. (ăf′tŭn)	115	42°42′N	110°52′W
'Afula, Isr. (ä-fò′là)	197a	32°36′N	35°17′E
Afyon, Tur. (ä-fē-ōn)	198	38°45′N	30°20′E
Agadem, Niger (ä′gà-dĕm)	231	16°50′N	13°17′E
Agadez, Niger (ä′gà-dĕs)	230	16°58′N	7°59′E
Agadir, Mor. (ä-gà-dēr)	230	30°30′N	9°37′W
Agalta, Cordillera de, mts., Hond. (kôr-dēl-yĕ′rä-dĕ-ä-gä′l-tä)	132	15°15′N	85°42′W
Agapovka, Russia (ä-gä-pôv′kä)	186a	53°18′N	59°10′E
Agartala, India	202	23°53′N	91°22′E
Agāshi, India	203b	19°28′N	72°46′E
Agashkino, Russia (à-gàsh′kĭ-nô)	186b	55°18′N	38°13′E
Agattu, i., Ak., U.S. (à′gä-tōō)	103a	52°14′N	173°40′E
Agboville, C. Iv.	234	5°56′N	4°13′W
Ağdam, Azer. (äg′dăm)	181	40°00′N	47°00′E
Agde, Fr. (ägd)	170	43°19′N	3°30′E
Agen, Fr. (à-zhăN′)	161	44°13′N	0°31′E
Agiásos, Grc.	175	39°06′N	26°25′E
Aginskoye, Russia (ä-hĭn′skô-yĕ)	179	51°15′N	113°15′E
Ágios Efstrátios, i., Grc.	163	39°30′N	24°58′E
Agíou Órous, Kólpos, b., Grc.	175	40°15′N	24°00′E
Agno, Phil. (äg′nō)	213a	16°07′N	119°49′E
Agno, r., Phil.	213a	15°42′N	120°28′E
Agnone, Italy (än-yō′nā)	174	41°49′N	14°23′E
Agogo, Ghana	234	6°47′N	1°04′W
Agra, India (ä′grä)	199	27°18′N	78°00′E
Ağrı, Tur.	181	39°50′N	43°10′E
Agri, r., Italy (ä′grē)	174	40°15′N	16°21′E
Agrínio, Grc.	163	38°38′N	21°06′E
Agua, vol., Guat. (ä′gwä)	132	14°28′N	90°43′W
Agua Blanca, Río, r., Mex. (rē′ō-ä-gwä-blä′n-kä)	130	21°46′N	102°54′W
Agua Brava, Laguna de, l., Mex.	130	22°04′N	105°40′W
Agua Caliente Indian Reservation, I.R., Ca., U.S. (ä′gwä kal-yĕn′tä)	118	33°50′N	116°24′W
Aguada, Cuba (ä-gwä′dä)	134	22°25′N	80°50′W
Aguada, l., Mex. (ä-gwä′dä)	132a	18°46′N	89°40′W
Aguadas, Col. (ä-gwä′dás)	142	5°37′N	75°27′W
Aguadilla, P.R. (ä-gwä-dēl′yä)	129b	18°27′N	67°10′W
Aguadulce, Pan. (ä-gwä-dōōl′sā)	133	8°15′N	80°33′W
Agua Escondida, Meseta de, plat., Mex.	131	16°54′N	91°35′W
Agua Fria, r., Az., U.S. (ä′gwä frē-ä)	119	33°43′N	112°22′W
Agua Fria National Monument, rec., Az., U.S.	119	34°13′N	112°03′W
Aguai, Braz. (ägwä-ē′)	141a	22°04′S	46°57′W
Agualeguas, Mex. (ä-gwä-lä′gwäs)	122	26°19′N	99°33′W
Aguán, r., Hond. (ä-gwà′n)	132	15°22′N	87°00′W
Aguanaval, r., Mex. (à-guä-nä-väl′)	122	25°12′N	103°28′W
Aguanus, r., Can. (ä-gwä′nŭs)	101	50°45′N	62°03′W
Aguascalientes, Mex. (ä′gwäs-käl-yĕn′tās)	128	21°52′N	102°17′W
Aguascalientes, state, Mex. (ä′gwäs-käl-yĕn′tās)	130	22°00′N	102°18′W
Águeda, Port. (ä-gwä′dä)	172	40°36′N	8°26′W
Agueda, r., Eur. (ä-gĕ-dä)	172	40°50′N	6°44′W
Aguelhok, Mali	234	19°28′N	0°52′E
Aguilar, Spain	172	37°32′N	4°39′W
Aguilar, Co., U.S. (ä-gē-lär′)	120	37°24′N	104°38′W
Aguilas, Spain (ä-gē-läs)	162	37°26′N	1°35′W
Aguililla, Mex. (ä-gē-lēl-yä)	130	18°44′N	102°44′W
Aguilillа, r., Mex. (ä-gē-lēl-yä)	130	18°30′N	102°48′W
Aguja, Punta, c., Peru (pŭn′tä à-gōō′ hä)	142	6°00′S	81°15′W
Agulhas, Cape, c., S. Afr. (ä-gōōl′yäs)	232	34°47′S	20°00′E
Agusan, r., Phil. (ä-gōō′sän)	213	8°12′N	126°07′E
Ahaggar, mts., Alg. (à-hà-gär′)	230	23°14′N	6°00′E
Ahar, Iran	201	38°28′N	47°04′E
Ahlen, Ger. (ä′lĕn)	168	51°45′N	7°52′E
Ahmadābād, India (ŭ-mĕd-ā-băd′)	199	23°04′N	72°38′E
Ahmadnagar, India (ä′mûd-nŭ-gûr)	199	19°09′N	74°45′E
Ahmar Mountains, mts., Eth.	231	9°22′N	42°00′E
Ahoskie, N.C., U.S. (ā-hŏs′kē)	125	36°15′N	77°00′W
Ahrensburg, Ger. (ä′rĕns-bòrg)	159c	53°40′N	10°14′E
Ahrweiler, Ger. (är′vī-lĕr)	168	50°34′N	7°05′E
Ähtärinjärvi, l., Fin.	167	62°46′N	24°25′E
Ahuacatlán, Mex. (ä-wä-kät-län′)	130	21°05′N	104°28′W
Ahuachapán, El Sal. (ä-wä-chä-pän′)	132	13°57′N	89°53′W
Ahualulco, Mex. (ä-wä-lōōl′kō)	130	20°43′N	103°57′W
Ahuatempan, Mex. (ä-wä-tĕm-pän)	130	18°11′N	98°02′W
Åhus, Swe. (ô′hòs)	166	55°56′N	14°19′E
Ahvāz, Iran	198	31°15′N	48°54′E
Ahvenanmaa (Åland), is., Fin. (ä′vĕ-nàn-mô) (ô′lănd)	160	60°36′N	19°55′E
'Aiea, Hi., U.S.	126a	21°18′N	157°52′W
Aígina, Grc.	175	37°43′N	23°35′E
Aígina, i., Grc.	175	37°43′N	23°35′E
Aígio, Grc.	175	38°13′N	22°04′E
Aiken, S.C., U.S. (ā′kĕn)	125	33°32′N	81°43′W
Aimorès, Serra dos, mts., Braz. (sĕ′r-rä-dôs-ī-mō-rĕ′s)	143	17°40′S	42°38′W
Aimoto, Japan (ī-mò-tō)	211b	34°59′N	135°09′E
Aincourt, Fr. (ăN-kōō′r)	171b	49°04′N	1°47′E
Aïn el Beïda, Alg.	230	35°57′N	7°25′E
Ainsworth, Ne., U.S. (ānz′wûrth)	112	42°32′N	99°51′W
Aïn Témouchent, Alg. (ä′ĕntĕ-mōō-shaN′)	162	35°20′N	1°23′W
Aïn Wessara, Alg. (ĕn ōō-sā-rá)	173	35°25′N	2°50′E
Aipe, Col. (ī′pĕ)	142a	3°13′N	75°15′W
Aïr, mts., Niger	230	18°00′N	8°30′E
Aire, r., Eng., U.K.	158a	53°42′N	1°00′W
Aire-sur-l'Adour, Fr. (âr)	170	43°42′N	0°17′W
Airhitam, Selat, strt., Indon.	197b	0°58′N	102°38′E
Ai Shan, mts., China (äī′shän)	206	37°27′N	120°35′E
Aisne, r., Fr. (ĕn)	161	49°28′N	3°32′E
Aitape, Pap. N. Gui. (ä-ē-tä′pâ)	213	3°00′S	142°10′E
Aitkin, Mn., U.S. (āt′kĭn)	113	46°32′N	93°43′W
Aitolikó, Grc.	175	38°27′N	21°21′E
Aitos, Blg. (ä-ē′tōs)	175	42°42′N	27°17′E
Aitutaki, i., Cook Is. (ī-tōō-tä′kē)	241	19°00′S	162°00′W
Aiud, Rom. (ä′ē-òd)	163	46°19′N	23°40′E
Aiuruoca, Braz. (äē′ōō-rōōō′-kà)	141a	21°57′S	44°36′W
Aiuruoca, r., Braz.	141a	22°11′S	44°35′W
Aix-en-Provence, Fr. (ĕks-prô-vŏNs)	161	43°32′N	5°27′E
Aix-les-Bains, Fr. (ĕks′-lā-băN′)	171	45°42′N	5°56′E
Aizpute, Lat. (ä′ēz-pōō-tĕ)	167	56°44′N	21°37′E
Aizuwakamatsu, Japan	210	37°27′N	139°51′E
Ajaccio, Fr. (ä-yät′chō)	154	41°55′N	8°42′E
Ajalpan, Mex. (ä-häl′pän)	131	18°21′N	97°14′W
Ajana, Austl. (ăj-ăn′ĕr)	218	28°00′S	114°45′E
Ajaria, state, Geor.	182	41°40′N	42°00′E
Ajdābiyah, Libya	231	30°56′N	20°16′E
Ajjer, Tassili-n-, plat., Alg.	230	25°40′N	6°57′E
Ajmah, Jabal al, mts., Egypt	197a	29°12′N	34°03′E
Ajman, U.A.E.	198	25°15′N	54°30′E
Ajmer, India (ŭj-mēr′)	199	26°26′N	74°42′E
Ajo, Az., U.S. (ä′hô)	119	32°20′N	112°55′W
Ajuchitlán del Progreso, Mex. (ä-hōō-chet-lån)	130	18°11′N	100°32′W
Ajusco, Mex. (ä-hōō′s-kō)	131a	19°13′N	99°12′W
Ajusco, Cerro, mtn., Mex. (sĕ′r-rô-ä-hōō′s-kō)	131a	19°12′N	99°16′W
Akaishi-dake, mtn., Japan (ä-kī-shē dä′kä)	211	35°30′N	138°00′E
Akashi, Japan (ä′kä-shē)	210	34°38′N	134°59′E
Aketi, D.R.C. (ä-kå-tē)	231	2°44′N	23°46′E
Akhaltsikhe, Geor. (äkä′l-tsĭ-kĕ)	181	41°40′N	42°50′E
Akhdar, Al Jabal al, mts., Libya	231	32°00′N	22°00′E
Akhḑar, Al Jabal al, mts., Oman	198	23°30′N	56°43′W
Akhisar, Tur. (äk-hĭs-sär′)	163	38°58′N	27°58′E
Akhtarskaya, Bukhta, b., Russia (bōōk′tä àx-tär′skà-yà)	177	45°53′N	38°22′E
Akhtopol, Blg. (äк′tô-pōl)	175	42°08′N	27°54′E
Akhunovo, Russia (ä-kû′nô-vô)	186a	54°13′N	59°36′E
Aki, Japan (ä′kē)	211	33°31′N	133°51′E
Akiak, Ak., U.S. (äk′yák)	103	61°00′N	161°02′W
Akimiski, i., Can. (ä-kĭ-mĭ′skĭ)	93	52°54′N	80°22′W
Akita, Japan (ä′kē-tä)	205	39°40′N	140°12′E
Akjoujt, Maur.	230	19°45′N	14°23′W
'Akko, Isr.	197a	32°56′N	35°05′E
Aklavik, Can. (äk′lä-vĭk)	90	68°28′N	135°26′W
'Aklé′Âouâna, dunes, Afr.	234	18°07′N	6°00′W
Ako, Japan (ä′kō)	211	34°44′N	134°22′E
Akola, India (à-kō′lä)	199	20°47′N	77°00′E
Akordat, Erit.	231	15°34′N	37°54′E
Akpatok, i., Can. (äk′pà-tŏk)	93	60°30′N	67°10′W
Akranes, Ice.	160	64°18′N	21°40′W
Akron, Co., U.S. (ăk′rŭn)	120	40°09′N	103°14′W
Akron, Oh., U.S. (ăk′rŭn)	105	41°05′N	81°30′W
Aksaray, Tur. (äk-sà-rī′)	163	38°30′N	34°05′E
Akşehır, Tur. (äk′shå-hēr)	163	38°20′N	31°20′E
Akşehır Gölü, l., Tur. (äk′shå-hēr)	198	38°40′N	31°30′E
Aksha, Russia (äk′shà)	179	50°28′N	113°00′E
Aksu, China (ä-kŭ-sōō)	204	41°29′N	80°15′E
Akune, Japan (ä′kò-nå)	211	32°03′N	130°16′E
Akureyri, Ice. (ä-kò-rå′rē)	160	65°39′N	18°01′W
Akutan, i., Ak., U.S. (ä-kōō-tän′)	103a	53°58′N	169°54′W
Akwatia, Ghana	234	6°04′N	0°49′W
Alabama, state, U.S. (ăl-à-băm′à)	105	32°50′N	87°30′W
Alabama, r., Al., U.S. (ăl-à-băm′à)	107	31°20′N	87°39′W
Alabat, i., Phil. (ä-lä-bät′)	213a	14°14′N	122°05′E
Alacam, Tur. (ä-lä-chäm′)	181	41°30′N	35°40′E
Alacant, Spain	162	38°20′N	0°30′W
Alacranes, Cuba (ä-lä-krä′nås)	134	22°45′N	81°35′W
Al Aflaj, des., Sau. Ar.	198	24°00′N	44°47′E
Alagôas, state, Braz. (ä-lä-gō′äzh)	143	9°50′S	36°33′W
Alagoinhas, Braz. (ä-lä-gō-ēn′yäzh)	143	12°13′S	38°12′W
Alagón, Spain (ä-lä-gōn′)	172	41°46′N	1°07′W
Alagón, r., Spain (ä-lä-gōn′)	172	39°53′N	6°42′W
Alahuatán, r., Mex. (ä-lä-wä-tä′n)	130	18°30′N	100°00′W
Alajuela, C.R. (ä-lä-hwa′lä)	133	10°01′N	84°14′W
Alajuela, Lago, l., Pan. (ä-lä-hwa′lä)	128a	9°15′N	79°34′W
Alaköl, l., Kaz.	183	45°45′N	81°13′E
'Alalakeiki Channel, strt., Hi., U.S. (ä-lä-lä-kä′kē)	126a	20°40′N	156°30′W
Al 'Alamayn, Egypt	231	30°53′N	28°52′E
Al 'Amārah, Iraq	201	31°50′N	47°09′E
Alameda, Ca., U.S. (ăl-à-mā′dà)	104	37°46′N	122°15′W
Alameda, r., Ca., U.S. (ăl-à-mā′dà)	116b	37°36′N	122°02′W
Alaminos, Phil. (ä-lä-mē′nôs)	213a	16°09′N	119°58′E
Al 'Amirīyah, Egypt	163	31°01′N	29°52′E
Alamo, Mex. (ä′lä-mô)	131	20°55′N	97°41′W
Alamo, Ca., U.S. (ă′là-mō)	116b	37°51′N	122°02′W
Alamo, Nv., U.S. (ă′là-mō)	118	37°22′N	115°10′W
Alamo, r., Mex. (ä′lä-mô)	122	26°33′N	99°35′W
Alamogordo, N.M., U.S. (ăl-à-mō-gôr′dō)	119	32°55′N	106°00′W
Alamo Heights, Tx., U.S. (ă′là-mō)	117d	29°28′N	98°27′W
Alamo Indian Reservation, I.R., N.M., U.S.	119	34°30′N	107°30′W
Alamo Peak, mtn., N.M., U.S. (ă′là-mō pēk)	122	32°50′N	105°55′W
Alamosa, Co., U.S. (ăl-à-mō′sà)	119	37°25′N	105°50′W
Åland *see* Ahvenanmaa, is., Fin.	160	60°36′N	19°55′E
Alandskiy, Russia (ä-länt′skĭ)	186a	52°14′N	59°48′E
Alanga Arba, Kenya	237	0°07′N	40°25′E
Alanya, Tur.	163	36°40′N	32°10′E
Alaotra, l., Madag. (ä-lä-ō′trà)	233	17°15′S	48°17′E
Alapayevsk, Russia (ä-lä-pä′yĕfsk)	178	57°50′N	61°35′E
Al 'Aqabah, Jord.	198	29°32′N	35°00′E
Alaquines, Mex. (ā-lä-kē′nås)	130	22°07′N	99°35′W
Al 'Arīsh, Egypt (ä-rēsh′)	197a	31°08′N	33°48′E
Alaska, state, U.S. (à-lăs′kà)	106a	64°00′N	150°00′W
Alaska, Gulf of, b., Ak., U.S. (à-lăs′kà)	103	57°42′N	147°40′W
Alaska Highway, Ak., U.S. (à-lăs′kà)	103	63°00′N	142°00′W
Alaska Peninsula, pen., Ak., U.S. (à-lăs′kà)	103	55°50′N	162°10′W
Alaska Range, mts., Ak., U.S. (à-lăs′kà)	103	62°00′N	152°18′W
Al 'Atrūn, Sudan	231	18°13′N	26°44′E
Alatyr′, Russia (ä′lä-tür)	178	54°55′N	46°30′E
Alazani, r., Asia	182	41°05′N	46°40′E
Alba, Italy (äl′bä)	174	44°41′N	8°02′E
Albacete, Spain (äl-bä-thā′tā)	162	39°00′N	1°49′W
Albachten, Ger. (äl-bä′ĸ-tĕn)	171c	51°55′N	7°31′E
Alba de Tormes, Spain (äl-bà dā tôr′mās)	172	40°48′N	5°28′W
Alba Iulia, Rom. (äl-bä yōō′lyà)	163	46°05′N	23°32′E

ng-sing; ŋ-baŋk; N-nasalized n; nŏd; cŏmmit; ōld; ōbey; ôrder; oi-boil; fōōd; ò-as oo in foot; ou-out; s-soft; sh-dish; th-thin; pūre; ûnite; ûrn; stŭd; circŭs; ü-as in French tu; ′-indeterminate vowel.

PLACE (Pronunciation)	PAGE	LAT.	LONG.
Albani, Colli, hills, Italy	173d	41°46'N	12°45'E
Albania, nation, Eur. (ăl-bā'nĭ-ȧ)	154	41°45'N	20°00'E
Albano, Lago, l., Italy (lä'-gō äl-bä'nō)	173d	41°45'N	12°44'E
Albano Laziale, Italy (äl-bä'nō lät-zē-ä'lā)	174	41°44'N	12°43'E
Albany, Austl. (ôl'bȧ-nĭ)	218	35°00'S	118°00'E
Albany, Ca., U.S. (ôl'bȧ-nĭ)	116b	37°54'N	122°18'W
Albany, Ga., U.S. (ôl'bȧ-nĭ)	105	31°35'N	84°10'W
Albany, Mo., U.S. (ôl'bȧ-nĭ)	121	40°14'N	94°18'W
Albany, N.Y., U.S. (ôl'bȧ-nĭ)	105	42°40'N	73°50'W
Albany, Or., U.S. (ôl'bȧ-nĭ)	104	44°38'N	123°06'W
Albany, r., Can. (ôl'bȧ-nĭ)	93	51°45'N	83°30'W
Al Başrah, Iraq	198	30°35'N	47°59'E
Al Batrūn, Leb. (äl-bä-trōōn')	197a	34°16'N	35°39'E
Albemarle, N.C., U.S. (ăl'bē-märl)	125	35°24'N	80°36'W
Albemarle Sound, strt., N.C., U.S. (ăl'bē-märl)	107	36°00'N	76°17'W
Albenga, Italy (äl-bĕŋ'gä)	174	44°04'N	8°13'E
Alberche, r., Spain (äl-bĕr'chā)	172	40°08'N	4°19'W
Alberga, The, r., Austl. (ăl-bŭr'gȧ)	220	27°15'S	135°00'E
Albergaria-a-Velha, Port.	172	40°47'N	8°31'W
Alberhill, Ca., U.S. (ăl'bēr-hĭl)	117a	33°43'N	117°23'W
Albert, Fr. (àl-bâr')	170	50°00'N	2°49'E
Albert, l., Afr. (ăl'bērt) (àl-bâr')	231	1°50'N	30°40'E
Albert, Parc National, rec., D.R.C.	237	0°05'N	29°30'E
Alberta, prov., Can. (ăl-bûr'tȧ)	90	54°33'N	117°10'W
Alberta, Mount, mtn., Can. (ăl-bûr'tȧ)	95	52°18'N	117°28'W
Albert Edward, Mount, mtn., Pap. N. Gui. (ăl'bērt ĕd'wērd)	213	8°25'S	147°25'E
Alberti, Arg. (àl-bĕ'r-tē)	141c	35°01'S	60°16'W
Albert Kanaal, can., Bel.	159a	51°07'N	5°07'E
Albert Lea, Mn., U.S. (ăl'bērt lē')	113	43°38'N	93°24'W
Albert Nile, r., Ug.	237	3°25'N	31°35'E
Alberton, Can. (ăl'bēr-tŭn)	100	46°49'N	64°04'W
Alberton, S. Afr.	233b	26°16'S	28°08'E
Albertville *see* Kalemie, D.R.C.	232	5°56'S	29°12'E
Albertville, Fr. (àl-bêr-vēl')	171	45°42'N	6°25'E
Albertville, Al., U.S. (ăl'bērt-vĭl)	124	34°15'N	86°10'W
Albi, Fr. (äl-bē')	161	43°54'N	2°07'E
Albia, Ia., U.S. (ăl-bĭ-ȧ)	113	41°01'N	92°44'W
Albina, Sur. (äl-bē'nä)	143	5°30'N	54°33'W
Albina, Ponta, c., Ang.	236	15°51'S	11°44'E
Albino, Point, c., Can. (äl-bē'nō)	111c	42°50'N	79°05'W
Albion, Mi., U.S. (ăl'bĭ-ŭn)	108	42°15'N	84°50'W
Albion, Ne., U.S. (ăl'bĭ-ŭn)	112	41°42'N	98°00'W
Albion, N.Y., U.S. (ăl'bĭ-ŭn)	109	43°15'N	78°10'W
Alboran, Isla del, i., Spain (ē's-lä-dĕl-äl-bō-rä'n)	156	35°58'N	3°02'W
Albuquerque, N.M., U.S. (ăl-bŭ-kûr'kē)	104	35°05'N	106°40'W
Albuquerque, Cayos de, is., Col.	133	12°12'N	81°24'W
Alburquerque, Spain (äl-bōōr-kĕr'kā)	172	39°13'N	6°58'W
Albury, Austl. (ôl'bēr-ē)	219	36°00'S	147°00'E
Alcabideche, Port. (äl-kà-bē-dā'chā)	173b	38°43'N	9°24'W
Alcácer do Sal, Port. (äb'ĭ-lēn)	172	38°24'N	8°33'W
Alcalá de Henares, Spain (äl-kä-lä' dā ā-na'räs)	173a	40°29'N	3°22'W
Alcalá la Real, Spain (äl-kä-lä'lä rā-äl')	172	37°27'N	3°57'W
Alcamo, Italy (äl'kà-mō)	174	37°58'N	13°03'E
Alcanadre, r., Spain (äl-kä-nä'drā)	173	41°41'N	0°18'W
Alcanar, Spain (äl-kä-när')	173	40°35'N	0°27'E
Alcañiz, Spain (äl-kän-yēth')	162	41°03'N	0°08'W
Alcântara, Braz. (äl-kän'tá-rá)	143	2°17'S	44°29'W
Alcaraz, Spain (äl-kä-räth')	172	38°39'N	2°28'W
Alcaudete, Spain (äb'ĭng-dŭn)	172	37°38'N	4°05'W
Alcázar de San Juan, Spain (äl-kä'thär dā sän hwän')	162	39°22'N	3°12'W
Alcira, Spain (ä-thē'rä)	173	39°09'N	0°26'W
Alcoa, Tn., U.S. (ăl-kō'ȧ)	124	35°45'N	84°00'W
Alcobendas, Spain (äl-kō-bĕn'dàs)	173a	40°32'N	3°39'W
Alcochete, Port. (äl-kō-chā'ta)	173b	38°45'N	8°58'W
Alcoi, Spain	162	38°42'N	0°30'W
Alcorcón, Spain	173a	40°22'N	3°50'W
Alcorta, Arg. (àl-kôr'tä)	141c	33°32'S	61°08'W
Alcova Reservoir, res., Wy., U.S. (äl-kō'vȧ)	115	42°31'N	106°33'W
Alcove, Can. (äl-kōv')	102c	45°41'N	75°55'W
Alcúdia, Badia d', b., Spain	173	39°48'N	3°20'E
Aldabra Islands, is., Sey. (äl-dä'brä)	233	9°16'S	46°17'E
Aldama, Mex. (äl-dä'mä)	130	22°54'N	98°04'W
Aldama, Mex. (äl-dä'mä)	122	28°50'N	105°54'W
Aldan, Russia	179	58°46'N	125°19'E
Aldan, r., Russia	179	63°00'N	134°00'E
Aldan Plateau, plat., Russia	185	57°42'N	130°28'E
Aldanskaya, Russia	179	61°52'N	135°29'E
Aldenhoven, Ger. (äl'dĕn-hō'vĕn)	171c	50°54'N	6°18'E
Aldergrove, Can. (ôl'dēr-grōv)	116d	49°03'N	122°28'W
Alderney, i., Guern. (ôl'dēr-nĭ)	170	49°43'N	2°11'W
Aldershot, Eng., U.K. (ôl'dēr-shŏt)	164	51°14'N	0°46'W
Alderson, W.V., U.S. (ôl-dēr-sŭn)	108	37°40'N	80°40'W
Alderwood Manor, Wa., U.S. (ôl'dēr-wŏd măn'ŏr)	116a	47°49'N	122°18'W
Aldridge-Brownhills, Eng., U.K.	158a	52°38'N	1°55'W
Aledo, Il., U.S. (ȧ-lē'dō)	121	41°12'N	90°47'W
Aleg, Maur.	230	17°03'N	13°55'W
Alegre, Braz. (àlĕ'grĕ)	141a	20°41'S	41°32'W
Alegre, r., Braz. (àlĕ'grĕ)	144b	22°22'S	43°34'W
Alegrete, Braz. (ä-lā-grā'tā)	144	29°46'S	55°44'W
Aleksandrov, Russia (ä-lyĕk-sän' drôf)	180	56°24'N	38°45'E
Aleksandrovsk, Russia (ä-lyĕk-sän'drôfsk)	186a	59°11'N	57°36'E
Aleksandrovsk, Russia (ä-lyĕk-sän'drôfsk)	179	51°02'N	142°21'E
Aleksandrów Kujawski, Pol. (ä-lĕk-säh'drōōv kōō-yav'skē)	169	52°54'N	18°45'E
Alekseyevka, Russia (ä-lyĕk-sā-yĕf'kȧ)	177	50°39'N	38°40'E
Aleksin, Russia (äb'ĭng-tŭn)	176	54°31'N	37°07'E
Aleksinac, Serb. (á-lyĕk-sē-nák')	175	43°33'N	21°42'E
Alemán, Presa, res., Mex. (prä'sä-lē-mà'n)	131	18°20'N	96°35'W
Alem Paraíba, Braz. (ä-lĕ'm-pá-rāē'bá)	141a	21°54'S	42°40'W
Alençon, Fr. (à-läɴ-sôɴ')	161	48°26'N	0°08'E
Alenquer, Braz. (ä-lĕŋ-kĕr')	143	1°58'S	54°44'W
Alenquer, Port. (ä-lĕŋ-kĕr')	172	39°04'N	9°01'W
Alentejo, hist. reg., Port. (ä-lĕŋ-tā'zhō)	172	38°05'N	7°45'W
Alenuihaha Channel, strt., Hi., U.S. (ä'lå-nōō-ē-hä'hä)	126a	20°20'N	156°05'W
Aleppo, Syria (ȧ-lĕp-ō)	198	36°10'N	37°18'E
Alès, Fr. (ä-lĕs')	161	44°07'N	4°06'E
Alessandria, Italy (ä-lĕs-sän'drē-ä)	162	44°53'N	8°35'E
Ålesund, Nor. (ô'lĕ-sòn')	166	62°28'N	6°14'E
Aleutian Islands, is., Ak., U.S. (ȧ-lu'shăn)	106b	52°40'N	177°30'W
Aleutian Trench, deep	103a	50°40'N	177°10'E
Alevina, Mys, c., Russia	179	58°49'N	151°44'E
Alexander Archipelago, is., Ak., U.S. (ăl-ĕg-zăn'dēr)	103	57°05'N	138°10'W
Alexander City, Al., U.S.	124	32°55'N	85°55'W
Alexander Indian Reserve, I.R., Can.	102g	53°47'N	114°00'W
Alexander Island, i., Ant.	224	71°00'S	71°00'W
Alexandra, S. Afr. (ál-ex-än'drȧ)	238c	26°07'S	28°07'E
Alexandria, Austl. (ăl-ĕg-zăn'drĭ-ȧ)	218	19°00'S	136°56'E
Alexandria, Can. (ăl-ĕg-zăn'drĭ-ȧ)	99	45°50'N	74°35'W
Alexandria, Egypt (ăl-ĕg-zăn'drĭ-ȧ)	231	31°12'N	29°58'E
Alexandria, Rom. (ăl-ĕg-zăn'drĭ-ȧ)	175	43°55'N	25°21'E
Alexandria, S. Afr. (ăl-ĕx-än-drĭ-ȧ)	233c	33°40'S	26°26'E
Alexandria, In., U.S. (ăl-ĕg-zăn'drĭ-ȧ)	108	40°20'N	85°20'W
Alexandria, La., U.S. (ăl-ĕg-zăn'drĭ-ȧ)	105	31°18'N	92°28'W
Alexandria, Mn., U.S. (ăl-ĕg-zăn'drĭ-ȧ)	112	45°53'N	95°23'W
Alexandria, S.D., U.S. (ăl-ĕg-zăn'drĭ-ȧ)	112	43°39'N	97°45'W
Alexandria, Va., U.S. (ăl-ĕg-zăn'drĭ-ȧ)	105	38°50'N	77°05'W
Alexandria Bay, N.Y., U.S. (ăl-ĕg-zăn'drĭ-ȧ)	109	44°20'N	75°55'W
Alexandroúpoli, Grc.	163	40°41'N	25°51'E
Alfaro, Spain (äl-fārō)	172	42°08'N	1°43'W
Al-Fāshir, Sudan (äl-fä'shēr)	231	13°38'N	25°21'E
Al Fashn, Egypt	238b	28°47'N	30°53'E
Al Fayyūm, Egypt	231	29°14'N	30°48'E
Alfeiós, r., Grc.	175	37°33'N	21°50'E
Alfenas, Braz. (äl-fĕ'nàs)	141a	21°26'S	45°55'W
Al Firdān, Egypt (äl-fer-dän')	238b	30°43'N	32°20'E
Alfred, Can. (ăl'frĕd)	102c	45°34'N	74°52'W
Alfreton, Eng., U.K. (ăl'fēr-tŭn)	158a	53°06'N	1°23'W
Algarve, hist. reg., Port. (äl-gär'vĕ)	172	37°15'N	8°12'W
Algeciras, Spain (äl-hā-thē'räs)	172	36°08'N	5°25'W
Algeria, nation, Afr. (ăl-gē'rĭ-ȧ)	230	28°45'N	1°00'E
Algete, Spain (äl-hā'tä)	173a	40°36'N	3°30'W
Al Ghaydah, Yemen	201	16°12'N	52°15'E
Alghero, Italy (äl-gâ'rō)	162	40°32'N	8°22'E
Algiers, Alg. (ăl-jērs)	230	36°51'N	2°56'E
Algoa, Tx., U.S. (ăl-gō'ȧ)	123a	29°24'N	95°11'W
Algoma, Wa., U.S.	116a	47°17'N	122°15'W
Algoma, Wi., U.S.	113	44°38'N	87°29'W
Algona, Ia., U.S.	113	43°04'N	94°11'W
Algonac, Mi., U.S. (ăl'gô-năk)	108	42°35'N	82°30'W
Algonquin, Il., U.S. (ăl-gŏŋ'kwĭn)	111a	42°10'N	88°17'W
Algonquin Provincial Park, rec., Can.	107	45°50'N	78°20'W
Alhama de Granada, Spain (äl-hä'mä-dĕ-grä-nä'dä)	172	37°00'N	3°59'W
Alhama de Murcia, Spain	172	37°50'N	1°24'W
Alhambra, Ca., U.S. (ăl-hăm'brȧ)	117a	34°05'N	118°08'W
Al Ḩammān, Egypt	163	30°46'N	29°42'E
Alhandra, Port. (äl-yän'drȧ)	173b	38°55'N	9°01'W
Alhaurín, Spain (äl-lou-rēn')	172	36°40'N	4°40'W
Al Ḩawrah, Yemen	201	13°49'N	47°37'E
Al Ḩawţah, Yemen	198	15°58'N	48°26'E
Al Ḩijāz, reg., Sau. Ar.	198	23°45'N	39°08'E
Al Hirmil, Leb.	197a	34°23'N	36°22'E
Alhos Vedros, Port. (äl'yōs'vā'drōs)	173b	38°39'N	9°02'W
Alhucemas, Baie d', b., Afr.	172	35°18'N	3°50'W
Al Ḩudaydah, Yemen	198	14°43'N	43°03'E
Al Hufūf, Sau. Ar.	198	25°15'N	49°43'E
Al Ḩulwān, Egypt (äl-hĕl'wän)	238b	29°51'N	31°20'E
Aliákmonas, r., Grc.	163	40°26'N	22°17'E
Äli Bayramlı, Azer.	182	39°56'N	48°56'E
Alibori, r., Benin	235	11°40'N	2°55'E
Alice, S. Afr. (ăl-ĭs)	233c	32°47'S	26°51'E
Alice, Tx., U.S. (ăl'ĭs)	122	27°45'N	98°04'W
Alice, Punta, c., Italy (ä-lē'chĕ)	175	39°23'N	17°10'E
Alice Arm, Can.	94	55°29'N	129°29'W
Alicedale, S. Afr. (ăl'ĭs-dāl)	233c	33°18'S	26°04'E
Alice Springs, Austl. (ăl'ĭs)	218	23°38'S	133°56'E
Alicudi, i., Italy (ä-lē-kōō'dē)	174	38°34'N	14°21'E
Alifkulovo, Russia (ä-lĭf-kû'lô-vô)	186a	55°57'N	62°06'E
Alīgarh, India (ä-lē-gŭr')	199	27°58'N	78°08'E
Alingsås, Swe. (à'lĭŋ-sôs)	166	57°57'N	12°30'E
Aliquippa, Pa., U.S. (ăl-ĭ-kwĭp'ȧ)	111e	40°37'N	80°15'W
Al Iskandarīyah *see* Alexandria, Egypt	238b	31°12'N	29°58'E
Aliwal North, S. Afr. (ä-lē-wäl')	232	31°09'S	28°26'E
Al Jafr, Qa'al, pl., Jord.	197a	30°15'N	36°24'E
Al Jaghbūb, Libya	231	29°46'N	24°32'E
Al Jawārah, Oman	201	18°55'N	57°17'E
Al Jawf, Libya	231	24°14'N	23°15'E
Al Jawf, Sau. Ar.	198	29°45'N	39°30'E
Aljezur, Port. (äl-zhā-zōōr')	172	37°18'N	8°52'W
Al Jīzah, Egypt	238b	30°01'N	31°12'E
Al Jubayl, Sau. Ar.	198	27°01'N	49°40'E
Al Jufrah, oasis, Libya	231	29°30'N	15°16'E
Al Junaynah, Sudan	200	13°27'N	22°27'E
Aljustrel, Port. (äl-zhōō-strĕl')	172	37°44'N	8°23'W
Al Kāb, Egypt	238d	30°56'N	32°19'E
Al Kāmilīn, Sudan (käm-lēn')	231	15°09'N	33°06'E
Al Karak, Jord. (kĕ-räk')	197a	31°11'N	35°42'E
Al Karnak, Egypt (kär'nak)	238b	25°42'N	32°43'E
Al Khābūrah, Oman	198	23°45'N	57°30'E
Al Khalīl, W.B.	197a	31°31'N	35°07'E
Al Khandaq, Sudan (kän-däk')	231	18°38'N	30°29'E
Al Khārijah, Egypt	200	25°26'N	30°33'E
Al Khums, Libya	231	32°35'N	14°10'E
Al Khurmah, Sau. Ar.	198	21°37'N	41°44'E
Al Kiswah, Syria	197a	33°31'N	36°13'E
Alkmaar, Neth. (älk-mär')	165	52°39'N	4°42'E
Al Kufrah, oasis, Libya	231	24°45'N	22°45'E
Al Kuntillah, Egypt	197a	29°59'N	34°42'E
Al Kūt, Iraq	201	32°30'N	45°49'E
Al Kuwayt, Kuw. (äl-kōō-wit)	198	29°04'N	47°59'E
Al Lādhiqīyah, Syria	198	35°32'N	35°51'E
Allagash, r., Me., U.S. (ăl'ȧ-găsh)	100	46°50'N	69°24'W
Allāhābād, India (ŭl-ŭ-hä-bäd')	199	25°32'N	81°53'E
All American Canal, can., Ca., U.S. (âl á-mĕr'ĭ-kăn)	118	32°43'N	115°12'W
Alland, Aus.	159e	48°04'N	16°05'E
Allariz, Spain (äl-yä-rēth')	162	42°10'N	7°48'W
Allatoona Lake, res., Ga., U.S. (ăl'á-tōōn'ȧ)	124	34°05'N	84°57'W
Allauch, Fr. (ä-lĕ'ō)	170a	43°21'N	5°30'E
Allaykha, Russia (ä-lī'ĸȧ)	179	70°32'N	148°53'E
Allegan, Mi., U.S. (ăl'ē-găn)	108	42°30'N	85°55'W
Allegany Indian Reservation, I.R., N.Y., U.S. (ăl-ē-gā'nĭ)	109	42°05'N	78°55'W
Allegheny, r., Pa., U.S. (ăl-ē-gā'nĭ)	109	41°10'N	79°20'W
Allegheny Front, mtn., U.S. (ăl-ē-gā'nĭ)	108	38°12'N	80°03'W
Allegheny Mountains, mts., U.S. (ăl-ē-gā'nĭ)	107	37°35'N	81°55'W
Allegheny Plateau, plat., U.S. (ăl-ē-gā'nĭ)	108	39°00'N	81°15'W
Allegheny Reservoir, res., U.S. (ăl-ē-gā'nĭ)	109	41°50'N	78°55'W
Allen, Ok., U.S. (ăl'ĕn)	121	34°51'N	96°26'W
Allen, Lough, l., Ire. (lŏk ăl'ĕn)	164	54°07'N	8°09'W
Allendale, N.J., U.S. (ăl'ĕn-dāl)	110a	41°02'N	74°08'W
Allendale, S.C., U.S. (ăl'ĕn-dāl)	125	33°00'N	81°19'W
Allende, Mex. (äl-yĕn'då)	131	18°23'N	92°49'W
Allende, Mex.	122	28°20'N	100°50'W
Allentown, Pa., U.S. (ălĕn-toun)	105	40°35'N	75°30'W
Alleppey, India (á-lĕp'ē)	203	9°33'N	76°22'E
Aller, r., Ger. (äl'ĕr)	168	52°43'N	9°50'E
Alliance, Ne., U.S. (ȧ-lī'ăns)	104	42°06'N	102°53'W
Alliance, Oh., U.S. (ȧ-lī'ăns)	108	40°55'N	81°10'W
Al Lidām, Sau. Ar.	198	20°45'N	44°12'E
Allier, r., Fr. (à-lyā')	170	46°43'N	3°03'E
Alligator Point, c., La., U.S. (al'ĭ-gā-tēr)	110d	30°57'N	89°41'W
Allinge, Den. (äl'ĭŋ-ĕ)	166	55°16'N	14°48'E
Al Līth, Sau. Ar.	201	20°09'N	40°16'E
All Pines, Belize (ôl pīnz)	132a	16°55'N	88°15'W
Al Luḩayyah, Yemen	198	15°58'N	42°48'E
Alluvial City, La., U.S.	110d	29°51'N	89°42'W
Allyn, Wa., U.S. (ăl'ĭn)	116a	47°23'N	122°51'W
Alma, Can. (ăl'mȧ)	100	45°36'N	64°59'W
Alma, Can.	91	48°29'N	71°42'W
Alma, S. Afr.	238c	24°30'S	28°05'E
Alma, Ga., U.S.	125	31°33'N	82°31'W
Alma, Mi., U.S.	108	43°25'N	84°40'W
Alma, Ne., U.S.	120	40°08'N	99°21'W
Alma, Wi., U.S.	113	44°21'N	91°57'W
Alma-Ata *see* Almaty, Kaz.	183	43°19'N	77°08'E
Almada, Port. (äl-mä'dä)	173b	38°40'N	9°09'W
Almadén, Spain (äl-má-dhān')	172	38°47'N	4°50'W
Al Madīnah, Sau. Ar.	198	24°26'N	39°42'E
Al Mafraq, Jord.	197a	32°21'N	36°13'E
Almagre, Laguna, l., Mex. (lä-gô'nä-äl-mä'grĕ)	131	23°48'N	97°45'W
Almagro, Spain (äl-mä'grō)	172	38°52'N	3°41'W
Al Maḩallah al Kubrá, Egypt	238b	30°58'N	31°10'E
Al Manāmah, Bahr.	198	26°01'N	50°33'E
Almanor, Lake, l., Ca., U.S. (ăl-măn'ŏr)	118	40°11'N	121°20'W
Almansa, Spain (äl-män'sä)	172	38°52'N	1°09'W
Al Manshāh, Egypt	238b	26°31'N	31°46'E
Almansor, r., Port. (äl-män-sôr)	172	38°41'N	8°27'W
Al Manşūrah, Egypt	231	31°02'N	31°25'E
Al Manzilah, Egypt (män'za-la)	238b	31°09'N	32°05'E
Almanzora, r., Spain (äl-män-thō'rä)	172	37°20'N	2°25'W
Al Marāghah, Egypt	238b	26°41'N	31°35'E
Almargem do Bispo, Port. (äl-mär-zhĕɴ)	173b	38°51'N	9°16'W
Al-Marj, Libya	231	32°44'N	21°08'E
Al Maşīrah, i., Oman	198	20°43'N	58°58'E
Almaty (Alma-Ata), Kaz.	183	43°19'N	77°08'E
Almaty, val., Sau. Ar.	197a	29°16'N	35°12'E
Al Mawşil, Iraq	198	36°00'N	42°53'E
Almazán, Spain (äl-mä-thän')	172	41°30'N	2°33'W
Al Mazār, Jord.	197a	31°04'N	35°41'E
Al Mazra'ah, Jord.	197a	31°17'N	35°33'E
Almeirim, Port. (äl-māī-rēɴ')	172	39°13'N	8°31'W
Almelo, Neth. (äl'mē-lō)	165	52°20'N	6°42'E

ăt; finăl; rāte; senåte; ärm; åsk; sofȧ; fâre; ch-choose; dh-as th in other; bē; ēvent; bĕt; recĕnt; cratēr; g-gō; gh-guttural g; bĭt; ĭ-short neutral; rīde; ĸ-guttural k as ch in German ich;

266 Andrew Johnson National Historic Site – Archidona PRONOUNCING INDEX

PLACE (Pronunciation)	PAGE	LAT.	LONG.
Andrew Johnson National Historic Site, rec., Tn., U.S. (ăn′drōō jŏn′sŭn)	125	36°15′N	82°55′W
Andrews, N.C., U.S. (ăn′drōōz)	124	35°12′N	83°48′W
Andrews, S.C., U.S. (ăn′drōōz)	125	33°25′N	79°32′W
Andria, Italy (än′drê-ä)	163	41°17′N	15°55′E
Ándros, Grc. (àn′dhrôs)	175	37°50′N	24°54′E
Ándros, i., Grc. (àn′drôs)	163	37°59′N	24°55′E
Androscoggin, r., Me., U.S. (ăn-drŭs-kŏg′ĭn)	100	44°25′N	70°45′W
Andros Island, i., Bah. (ăn′drŏs)	129	24°30′N	78°00′W
Anefis i-n-Darane, Mali	234	18°03′N	0°36′E
Anegasaki, Japan (ä′nâ-gä-sä′kê)	211a	35°29′N	140°02′E
Aneityum, i., Vanuatu (ä-nâ-ē′tê-ŭm)	221	20°15′S	169°49′E
Aneta, N.D., U.S. (ă-nē′tȧ)	112	47°41′N	97°57′W
Aneto, Pico de, mtn., Spain (pê′kō-dĕ-ä-nĕ′tô)	156	42°35′N	0°38′E
Angamacutiro, Mex. (än′gä-mä-kōō-tē′rô)	130	20°08′N	101°44′W
Angangueo, Mex. (än-gäŋ′gwâ-ō)	130	19°36′N	100°18′W
Ang′angxi, China (äŋ-äŋ-shyē)	205	47°05′N	123°58′E
Angarsk, Russia	179	52°48′N	104°15′E
Ånge, Swe. (ông′ä)	166	62°31′N	15°39′E
Angel, Salto, wtfl., Ven. (säl′tō-á′n-hĕl)	142	5°44′N	62°27′W
Ángel de la Guarda, i., Mex. (á′n-hĕl-dĕ-lä-gwä′r-dä)	128	29°30′N	113°00′W
Angeles, Phil. (än′hâ-lās)	213a	15°09′N	120°35′E
Ängelholm, Swe. (ĕng′ĕl-hôlm)	166	56°14′N	12°50′E
Angelina, r., Tx., U.S. (ăn-jê lē′nȧ)	123	31°30′N	94°53′W
Angels Camp, Ca., U.S. (ān′jĕls kămp′)	118	38°03′N	120°33′W
Ångermanälven, r., Swe.	160	64°10′N	17°30′E
Angermund, Ger. (àn′ngĕr-mŭnd)	171c	51°20′N	6°47′E
Angermünde, Ger. (äng′ĕr-mûn-dĕ)	168	53°02′N	14°00′E
Angers, Can. (äɴ-zhā′)	102c	45°31′N	75°29′W
Angers, Fr.	170	47°29′N	0°36′W
Angkor, hist., Camb. (äng′kôr)	212	13°52′N	103°50′E
Anglesey, i., Wales, U.K. (ăŋ′g′l-sê)	164	53°35′N	4°28′W
Angleton, Tx., U.S. (aŋ′g′l-tŭn)	123a	29°10′N	95°25′W
Angmagssalik, Grnld. (äŋ-mä′sä-lĭk)	89	65°40′N	37°40′W
Angoche, Ilha, i., Moz. (ê′lä-än-gō′chå)	233	16°20′S	40°00′E
Angol, Chile (aŋ-gōl′)	144	37°47′S	72°43′W
Angola, In., U.S. (ăŋ-gō′lȧ)	108	41°35′N	85°00′W
Angola, nation, Afr. (ăŋ-gō′lȧ)	232	14°15′S	16°00′E
Angora see Ankara, Tur.	198	39°55′N	32°50′E
Angoulême, Fr. (äŋ′gōō-lâm′)	170	45°40′N	0°09′E
Angra dos Reis, Braz. (aŋ′grä dōs rā′ês)	141a	23°01′S	44°17′W
Angri, Italy (ä′n-grē)	173c	40°30′N	14°35′E
Anguang, China (än-gůäŋ)	208	45°28′N	123°42′E
Anguilla, dep., N.A.	129	18°15′N	62°54′W
Anguilla Cays, is., Bah. (ăŋ-gwĭl′ȧ)	134	23°30′N	79°35′W
Anguille, Cape, c., Can. (käp′-äŋ-gē′yē)	101	47°55′N	59°25′W
Anguo, China (än-gwô)	206	38°27′N	115°19′E
Anholt, i., Den. (än′hŏlt)	166	56°43′N	11°34′E
Anhui, prov., China (än-hwā)	205	31°30′N	117°15′E
Aniak, Ak., U.S. (ä-nyȧ′k)	103	61°32′N	159°35′W
Aniakchak National Monument, rec., Ak., U.S.	104	56°50′N	157°50′W
Animas, r., Co., U.S. (ä′nê-más)	119	37°03′N	107°50′W
Anina, Rom. (ä-nē′nä)	175	45°03′N	21°50′E
Anita, Pa., U.S. (ȧ-nē′ȧ)	109	41°05′N	79°00′W
Aniva, Mys, c., Russia (mĭs á-nē′vá)	210	46°08′N	143°13′E
Aniva, Zaliv, b., Russia (zä′lĭf ä-nē′vá)	210	46°30′N	143°00′E
Anjou, Can.	102a	45°37′N	73°33′W
Ankang, China (än-käŋ)	204	32°38′N	109°10′E
Ankara, Tur. (än′kȧ-rȧ)	198	39°55′N	32°50′E
Anklam, Ger. (än′kläm)	168	53°52′N	13°43′E
Ankoro, D.R.C. (ăŋ-kō′rō)	232	6°45′S	26°57′E
Anloga, Ghana	234	5°47′N	0°50′E
Anlong, China (än-loŋ)	209	25°01′N	105°32′E
Anlu, China (än′lōō)	209	31°18′N	113°40′E
Ann, Cape, c., Ma., U.S. (kăp ăn′)	109	42°40′N	70°40′W
Anna, Russia (än′ä)	177	51°31′N	40°27′E
Anna, Il., U.S. (ăn′ȧ)	121	37°28′N	89°15′W
Annaba, Alg.	230	36°57′N	7°39′E
Annaberg-Bucholz, Ger. (än′ä-bĕrgh)	168	50°35′N	13°02′E
An Nafūd, des., Sau. Ar.	198	28°30′N	40°30′E
An Najaf, Iraq (än nä-jäf′)	198	32°00′N	44°25′E
An Nakhl, Egypt	197a	29°55′N	33°45′E
Annamese Cordillera, mts., Asia	212	17°34′N	105°38′E
Annapolis, Md., U.S. (ă-năp′ô-lĭs)	105	39°00′N	76°25′W
Annapolis Royal, Can.	100	44°45′N	65°31′W
Ann Arbor, Mi., U.S. (ăn är′bẽr)	105	42°15′N	83°45′W
An Nāşirīyah, Iraq	198	31°08′N	46°15′E
An Nawfalīyah, Libya	231	30°57′N	17°38′E
Annecy, Fr. (àn sē′)	171	45°54′N	6°07′E
Annemasse, Fr. (än′mäs′)	171	46°09′N	6°13′E
Annette Island, i., Ak., U.S.	94	55°13′N	131°30′W
An Nhon, Viet.	212	13°55′N	109°00′E
Annieopsquotch Mountains, mts., Can.	101	48°37′N	57°17′W
Anniston, Al., U.S. (ăn′ĭs-tŭn)	105	33°39′N	85°47′W
Annobón, i., Eq. Gui.	229	2°00′S	3°30′E
Annonay, Fr. (án′ĭs-tsiŭn)	170	45°16′N	4°36′E
Annotto Bay, Jam. (än-nō′tō)	134	18°15′N	76°45′W
An Nuhūd, Sudan	231	12°39′N	28°18′E
Anoka, Mn., U.S. (ȧ-nō′kȧ)	117g	45°12′N	93°24′W
Anori, Col. (á-nō′rē)	142a	7°01′N	75°09′W
Áno Viánnos, Grc.	174a	35°02′N	25°26′E
Anpu, China (än-pōō)	204	21°28′N	110°00′E
Anqiu, China (än-chyô)	206	36°26′N	119°12′E
Ansbach, Ger. (äns′bäk)	168	49°18′N	10°35′E
Anse à Veau, Haiti (äɴs′ ä-vō′)	135	18°30′N	73°25′W
Anse d′Hainault, Haiti (äɴs′dĕnō)	135	18°30′N	74°25′W
Anserma, Col. (á′n-sĕ′r-má)	142a	5°13′N	75°47′W
Ansermanuevo, Col. (á′n-sĕ′r-má-nwĕ′vō)	142a	4°47′N	75°59′W
Anshan, China	208	41°00′N	123°00′E
Anshun, China (än-shōōn′)	204	26°12′N	105°50′E
Anson, Tx., U.S. (ăn′sŭn)	122	32°45′N	99°52′W
Anson Bay, b., Austl.	220	13°10′S	130°00′E
Ansŏng, Kor., S. (än′sŭng′)	210	37°00′N	127°12′E
Ansongo, Mali	234	15°40′N	0°30′E
Ansonia, Ct., U.S. (ăn-sōnĭ-ȧ)	109	41°20′N	73°05′W
Antalya, Tur. (än-tä′lê-ä)	163	37°00′N	30°50′E
Antalya Körfezi, b., Tur.	163	36°40′N	31°20′E
Antananarivo, Madag.	233	18°51′S	47°40′E
Antarctica, cont.	224	80°15′S	127°00′E
Antarctic Peninsula, pen., Ant.	224	70°00′S	65°00′W
Antelope Creek, r., Wy., U.S. (ăn′tê-lōp)	115	43°29′N	105°42′W
Antequera, Spain (än-tĕ-kĕ′rä)	162	37°01′N	4°34′W
Anthony, Ks., U.S. (ăn′thô-nê)	120	37°08′N	98°01′W
Anthony Peak, mtn., Ca., U.S.	118	39°51′N	122°58′W
Anti Atlas, mts., Mor.	230	28°45′N	9°30′W
Antibes, Fr. (äɴ-tēb′)	171	43°36′N	7°12′E
Anticosti, Île d′, i., Can. (ăn-tĭ-kŏs′tê)	93	49°30′N	62°00′W
Antigo, Wi., U.S. (ăn′tĭ-gō)	113	45°09′N	89°11′W
Antigonish, Can. (ăn-tĭ-gô-nêsh′)	101	45°35′N	61°55′W
Antigua, Guat. (än-tē′gwä)	128	14°32′N	90°43′W
Antigua, r., Mex.	131	19°16′N	96°36′W
Antigua and Barbuda, nation, N.A.	129	17°15′N	61°15′W
Antigua Veracruz, Mex. (än-tē′gwä vā-rä-krōōz′)	131	19°18′N	96°17′W
Antilla, Cuba (än-tē′lyä)	135	20°50′N	75°50′W
Antioch, Ca., U.S. (ăn′tĭ-ŏk)	116b	38°00′N	121°48′W
Antioch, Il., U.S.	111a	42°29′N	88°06′W
Antioch, Ne., U.S.	112	42°05′N	102°36′W
Antioquia, Col. (än tê ō′kê′ä)	142	6°34′N	75°49′W
Antioquia, dept., Col.	142a	6°48′N	75°42′W
Antlers, Ok., U.S. (ănt′lẽrz)	121	34°14′N	95°38′W
Antofagasta, Chile (än-tô-fä-gäs′tä)	144	23°32′S	70°21′W
Antofalla, Salar de, pl., Arg. (sá-lár′de án′tô-fä′lä)	144	26°00′S	67°52′W
Antón, Pan. (än-tōn′)	129	8°24′N	80°15′W
Antongila, Helodrano, b., Madag.	233	16°15′S	50°15′E
Antônio Carlos, Braz. (än-tō′nēō-ká′r-lôs)	141a	21°19′S	43°45′W
António Enes, Moz. (ăn-to′nyō ĕn′ĕs)	233	16°14′S	39°58′E
Antonito, Co., U.S. (ăn-tô-nē′tō)	120	37°04′N	106°01′W
Antonopole, Lat. (än′tô-nô-pō lyĕ)	167	56°19′N	27°11′E
Antony, Fr.	171b	48°45′N	2°18′E
Antsirabe, Madag. (änt-sê-rä′bä)	233	19°49′S	47°16′E
Antsiranana, Madag.	233	12°18′S	49°16′E
Antsla, Est. (ănt′slȧ)	167	57°49′N	26°29′E
Antuco, vol., S.A. (än-tōō′kō)	144	37°30′S	72°30′W
Antwerp, Bel.	154	51°13′N	4°24′E
Antwerpen see Antwerp, Bel.	154	51°13′N	4°24′E
Anūpgarh, India (ŭ-nôp′gŭr)	202	29°22′N	73°20′E
Anuradhapura, Sri L. (ŭ-nōō′rä-dŭ-pōō′rŭ)	203	8°24′N	80°25′E
Anxi, China (än-shyē)	204	40°36′N	95°49′E
Anyang, China (än′yäng)	205	36°05′N	114°22′E
Anykščiai, Lith. (anĭksh-chä′ê)	167	55°34′N	25°04′E
Anzhero-Sudzhensk, Russia (än′zhâ-rô-sôd′zhĕnsk)	178	56°08′N	86°08′E
Anzio, Italy (änt′zê-ō)	174	41°28′N	12°39′E
Anzoátegui, dept., Ven. (àn-zôȧ′tĕ-gê)	143b	9°38′N	64°45′W
Aoba, i., Vanuatu	214f	15°25′S	167°50′E
Aomori, Japan (äô-mō′rê)	205	40°45′N	140°52′E
Aoraki (Cook, Mount), mtn., N.Z.	221a	43°27′S	170°13′E
Aosta, Italy (ä-ôs′tä)	174	45°45′N	7°20′E
Aouk, Bahr, r., Afr. (ä-ōk′)	231	9°30′N	20°45′E
Aoukâr, reg., Maur.	234	18°00′N	9°40′W
Apalachicola, Fl., U.S. (ăp-ȧ-lăch-ĭ-kō′lȧ)	124	29°43′N	84°59′W
Apan, Mex. (ä-pá′n)	130	19°43′N	98°27′W
Apango, Mex. (ä-päŋ′gō)	130	17°41′N	99°22′W
Apaporis, r., S.A. (ä-pä-pô′rĭs)	142	0°48′N	72°32′W
Aparri, Phil. (ä-pär′rē)	212	18°15′N	121°40′E
Apasco, Mex. (ä-pá′s-kō)	130	20°33′N	100°43′W
Apatin, Serb. (ŏ′pŏ-tĭn)	175	45°40′N	19°00′E
Apatzingán de la Constitución, Mex.	130	19°07′N	102°21′W
Apeldoorn, Neth. (ä′pĕl-dōōrn)	161	52°14′N	5°55′E
Apennines see Appennino, mts., Italy	156	43°48′N	11°06′E
Apía, Col. (á-pē′ä)	142a	5°07′N	75°58′W
Apia, Samoa	214a	13°50′S	171°44′W
Apipilulco, Mex. (ä-pĭ-pĭ-lōōl′kō)	130	18°09′N	99°40′W
Apishapa, r., Co., U.S. (ăp-ĭ-shä′pȧ)	120	37°40′N	104°08′W
Apizaco, Mex. (ä-pê-zä′kō)	130	19°18′N	98°11′W
Apo, Mount, mtn., Phil. (ä′pō)	213	6°56′N	125°05′E
Apopka, Fl., U.S. (ă-pŏp′kȧ)	125a	28°37′N	81°30′W
Apopka, Lake, l., Fl., U.S.	125a	28°38′N	81°50′W
Apostle Islands, is., Wi., U.S. (ȧ-pŏs′l)	113	47°05′N	90°55′W
Appalachia, Va., U.S. (ăpȧ-lăch′ĭ-ȧ)	125	36°54′N	82°49′W
Appalachian Mountains, mts., N.A. (ăp-ȧ-lăch′ĭ-ȧn)	107	37°20′N	82°00′W
Appalachicola, r., Fl., U.S. (ăpȧ-lăch′ĭ-cōlā)	107	30°11′N	85°00′W
Äppelbo, Swe. (ĕp-ĕl-bōō)	166	60°30′N	14°02′E
Appelhülsen, Ger. (ä′pĕl-hül′sĕn)	171c	51°55′N	7°26′E
Appennino, mts., Italy (äp-pĕn-nĕ′nô)	156	43°48′N	11°06′E
Appleton, Mn., U.S. (ăp′l-tŭn)	112	45°10′N	96°01′W
Appleton, Wi., U.S.	105	44°14′N	88°27′W
Appleton City, Mo., U.S.	121	38°10′N	94°02′W
Appomattox, r., Va., U.S. (ăp-ô-măt′ŭks)	125	37°22′N	78°09′W
Aprília, Italy (ȧ-prē′lyȧ)	174	41°36′N	12°40′E
Apsheronsk, Russia	182	44°28′N	39°44′E
Apt, Fr. (äpt)	171	43°54′N	5°19′E
Apure, r., Ven. (ä-pōō′rā)	142	8°08′N	68°46′W
Apurimac, r., Peru (ä-pōō-rê-mäk′)	142	11°39′S	73°48′W
Aqaba, Gulf of, b. (ä′kȧ-bȧ)	198	28°30′N	34°40′E
Aqabah, Wādī al, r., Egypt	197a	29°48′N	34°05′E
Aqmola see Astana, Kaz.	183	51°10′N	71°43′E
Aqtaū, Kaz.	183	43°35′N	51°05′E
Aqtöbe, Kaz.	183	50°20′N	57°00′E
Aquasco, Md., U.S. (ȧ′gwă′scô)	110e	38°35′N	76°44′W
Aquidauana, Braz. (ä-kē-däwä′nä)	143	20°24′S	55°46′W
Aquin, Haiti (ä-kăn′)	135	18°20′N	73°25′W
Ara, r., Japan (ä-rä)	211a	35°40′N	139°52′E
Arab, Baḩr al, r., Sudan	231	9°46′N	26°52′E
′Arabah, Wādī, val., Egypt	238b	29°02′N	32°10′E
Arabats′ka Strilka (Tongue of Arabat), spit, Ukr.	177	45°50′N	35°05′E
Arabi, La., U.S.	110d	29°58′N	90°01′W
Arabian Desert, des., Egypt (ȧ-rā′bĭ-ăn)	231	27°06′N	32°49′E
Arabian Sea, sea (ȧ-rā′bĭ-ăn)	196	16°00′N	65°15′E
Aracaju, Braz. (ä-rä′kä-zhōō′)	143	11°00′S	37°01′W
Aracati, Braz. (ä-rä′kä-tē′)	143	4°31′S	37°41′W
Araçatuba, Braz. (ä-rä-sá-tōō′bä)	143	21°14′S	50°19′W
Aracena, Spain	172	37°53′N	6°34′W
Arachthos, r., Grc. (är′äk-thôs)	175	39°10′N	21°05′E
Aracruz, Braz. (ä-rä-krōō′s)	143	19°58′S	40°11′W
′Arad, Isr.	197a	31°20′N	35°15′E
Arad, Rom. (ŏ′rŏd)	163	46°10′N	21°18′E
Arafura Sea, sea (ä-rä-fōō′rä)	213	8°40′S	130°00′E
Aragats, Gora, mtn., Arm.	182	40°32′N	44°14′E
Aragon, hist. reg., Spain (ä-rä-gōn′)	173	40°55′N	0°45′W
Aragón, r., Spain	172	42°35′N	1°10′W
Aragua, dept., Ven. (ä-rä′gwä)	143b	10°00′N	67°05′W
Aragua de Barcelona, Ven.	142	9°29′N	64°48′W
Araguaía, r., Braz. (ä-rä-gwä′yä)	143	8°37′S	49°43′W
Araguari, Braz. (ä-rä-gwä′rê)	143	18°43′S	48°03′W
Araguatins, Braz. (ä-rä-gwä-tēns)	143	5°41′S	48°04′W
Aragüita, Ven. (ärä-gwē′tá)	143b	10°13′N	66°28′W
Araj, oasis, Egypt (ä-räj′)	163	29°05′N	26°51′E
Arāk, Iran	198	34°08′N	49°57′E
Arakan Yoma, mts., Mya. (ŭ-rŭ-kŭn′yō′mȧ)	199	19°51′N	94°13′E
Aral, Kaz.	183	46°47′N	62°00′E
Aral Sea, sea, Asia	178	45°17′N	60°02′E
Aralsor köli, l., Kaz. (ȧ-räl′sôr′)	181	49°00′N	48°20′E
Aramberri, Mex. (ä-räm-bĕr-rē′)	130	24°05′N	99°47′W
Arana, Sierra, mts., Spain	172	37°17′N	3°28′W
Aranda de Duero, Spain (ä-rän′dä dā dwā′rō)	172	41°43′N	3°45′W
Arandas, Mex. (ä-rän′däs)	130	20°43′N	102°18′W
Aran Island, i., Ire. (ăr′ăn)	164	54°58′N	8°33′W
Aran Islands, is., Ire.	160	53°04′N	9°59′W
Aranjuez, Spain (ä-rän-hwāth′)	162	40°02′N	3°24′W
Aransas Pass, Tx., U.S. (ȧ-răn′sȧs pȧs)	123	27°55′N	97°09′W
Araouane, Mali	230	18°54′N	3°33′W
Arapkir, Tur. (ä-räp-kēr′)	163	39°00′N	38°10′E
Araraquara, Braz. (ä-rä-rä-kwä′rä)	143	21°47′S	48°08′W
Araras, Braz. (ä-rá′räs)	141a	22°21′S	47°22′W
Araras, Serra das, mts., Braz. (sĕ′r-rä-däs-ä-rä′räs)	143	18°03′S	53°23′W
Araras, Serra das, mts., Braz.	144b	22°24′S	43°15′W
Araras, Serra das, mts., Braz. (sĕ′r-rä-däs-ä-rä′räs)	144	23°30′S	53°00′W
Ararat, Austl. (ăr′ărăt)	219	37°17′S	142°56′E
Ararat, Mount, mtn., Tur.	198	39°50′N	44°20′E
Arari, l., Braz. (ä-rá′rē)	143	0°30′S	48°50′W
Araripe, Chapada do, hills, Braz. (shä-pä′dä-dô-ä-rä-rē′pě)	143	5°55′S	40°42′W
Araruama, Braz. (ä-rä-rōō-ă′mä)	141a	22°53′S	42°19′W
Araruama, Lagoa de, l., Braz.	141a	23°00′S	42°15′W
Aras, r., Asia (ä-räs)	198	39°15′N	47°10′E
Aratuípe, Braz. (ä-rä-tōō-ē′pě)	143	13°12′S	38°58′W
Arauca, Col. (ä-rou′kä)	142	6°56′N	70°45′W
Arauca, r., S.A.	142	7°13′N	68°43′W
Aravalli Range, mts., India (ä-rä′vŭ-lê)	199	24°15′N	72°40′E
Araya, Punta de, c., Ven. (pŭn′tá-dĕ-ä-rä′yá)	143b	10°40′N	64°15′W
Arayat, Phil. (ä-rä′yät)	213a	15°10′N	120°44′E
′Arbi, Sudan	231	20°36′N	29°57′E
Arbīl, Iraq	198	36°10′N	44°00′E
Arboga, Swe. (är-bō′gä)	166	59°26′N	15°50′E
Arborea, Italy (är-bō-rĕ′ä)	174	39°50′N	8°36′E
Arbroath, Scot., U.K. (är-brōth′)	164	56°36′N	2°25′W
Arcachon, Fr. (är-kä-shôn′)	161	44°39′N	1°12′W
Arcachon, Bassin d′, Fr. (bä-sĕn′ där-kä-shôn′)	170	44°42′N	1°50′W
Arcadia, Ca., U.S. (är-kā′dĭ-ȧ)	117a	34°08′N	118°02′W
Arcadia, Fl., U.S.	125a	27°12′N	81°51′W
Arcadia, La., U.S.	123	32°33′N	92°56′W
Arcadia, Wi., U.S.	113	44°15′N	91°30′W
Arcata, Ca., U.S. (är-kȧ′tȧ)	114	40°54′N	124°05′W
Arc Dome Mountain, mtn., Nv., U.S. (ärk dōm)	118	38°51′N	117°21′W
Arcelia, Mex. (är-sä′lê-ä)	130	18°19′N	100°14′W
Archbald, Pa., U.S. (ärch′bôld)	109	41°30′N	75°35′W
Arches National Park, rec., Ut., U.S. (är′ches)	119	38°45′N	109°35′W
Archidona, Ec. (är-chê-do′nä)	142	1°01′S	77°49′W
Archidona, Spain (är-chē-dô′nä)	172	37°08′N	4°24′W

ăt; finȧl; rāte; senāte; ärm; ȧsk; sofȧ; fâre; ch-choose; dh-as th in other; bē; êvent; bĕt; recĕnt; cratẽr; g-gō; gh-guttural g; bĭt; ĭ-short neutral; rīde; ĸ-guttural k as ch in German ich;

PRONOUNCING INDEX

Arcis-sur-Aube – Atacama 267

PLACE (Pronunciation)	PAGE	LAT.	LONG.
Arcis-sur-Aube, Fr. (är-sēs′sûr-ōb′)	170	48°31′N	4°04′E
Arco, Id., U.S. (är′kō)	115	43°39′N	113°15′W
Arcola, Tx., U.S.	123a	29°30′N	95°28′W
Arcola, Va., U.S. (är′cōlă)	110e	38°57′N	77°32′W
Arcos de la Frontera, Spain (är′kōs-dĕ-lä-frôn-tĕ′rä)	172	36°44′N	5°48′W
Arctic Ocean, o.	244	85°00′N	170°00′E
Arda, r., Blg. (är′dä)	175	41°36′N	25°18′E
Ardabīl, Iran	198	38°15′N	48°00′E
Ardahan, Tur. (är-dȧ-hän′)	181	41°10′N	42°40′E
Ardatov, Russia (är-dȧ-tôf′)	180	54°58′N	46°10′E
Ardennes, mts., Eur. (ȧr-dĕn′)	161	50°01′N	5°12′E
Ardila, r., Eur. (är-dē′lȧ)	172	38°10′N	7°15′W
Ardmore, Ok., U.S. (ärd′mōr)	104	34°10′N	97°08′W
Ardmore, Pa., U.S.	110f	40°01′N	75°18′W
Ardrossan, Can. (är-dros′ȧn)	102g	53°33′N	113°08′W
Ardsley, Eng., U.K. (ärdz′lē)	158a	53°43′N	1°33′W
Åre, Swe.	160	63°12′N	13°12′E
Arecibo, P.R. (ä-rā-sē′bō)	129b	18°28′N	66°45′W
Areia Branca, Braz. (ä-rĕ′yä-brá′n-kä)	143	4°58′S	37°02′W
Arena, Point, c., Ca., U.S. (ä-rā′nȧ)	118	38°57′N	123°40′W
Arenas, Punta, c., Ven. (pŏn′tä-rĕ′näs)	143b	10°57′N	64°24′W
Arenas de San Pedro, Spain	172	40°12′N	5°04′W
Arendal, Nor. (ä′rĕn-däl)	166	58°29′N	8°44′E
Arendonk, Bel.	159a	51°19′N	5°07′E
Arequipa, Peru (ä-rā-kē′pä)	142	16°27′S	71°30′W
Arezzo, Italy (ä-rĕt′sō)	162	43°28′N	11°54′E
Arga, r., Spain (är′gä)	172	42°35′N	1°55′W
Arganda, Spain (är-gän′dä)	173a	40°18′N	3°27′W
Argazi, l., Russia (ăr′gä-zĭ)	186a	55°24′N	60°37′E
Argazi, r., Russia	186a	55°33′N	57°30′E
Argentan, Fr. (ȧr-zhäɴ-täɴ′)	170	48°45′N	0°01′W
Argentat, Fr. (ár-zhäɴ-tä′)	170	45°07′N	1°57′E
Argenteuil, Fr. (är-zhäɴ-tû′y′)	170	48°56′N	2°15′E
Argentina, nation, S.A. (är-jĕn-tē′nȧ)	144	35°30′S	67°00′W
Argentino, l., Arg. (är-κĕn-tē′nō)	144	50°15′S	72°45′W
Argenton-sur-Creuse, Fr. (är-zhäɴ′tôɴ-sür-krôs)	170	46°34′N	1°28′E
Argolikos Kólpos, b., Grc.	175	37°20′N	23°00′E
Argonne, mts., Fr. (ä′r-gôn)	171	49°21′N	5°54′E
Argos, Grc. (är′gŏs)	175	37°38′N	22°45′E
Argostóli, Grc.	175	38°10′N	20°30′E
Arguello, Point, c., Ca., U.S. (är-gwāl′yō)	118	34°35′N	120°40′W
Arguin, Cap d′, c., Maur.	230	20°28′N	17°46′W
Argun′, r., Asia (ár-gōōn′)	179	50°00′N	119°00′E
Argungu, Nig.	235	12°45′N	4°31′E
Argyle, Can. (är′gīl)	102f	50°11′N	97°27′W
Argyle, Mn., U.S.	112	48°21′N	96°48′W
Århus, Den. (ôr′hōōs)	160	56°09′N	10°10′E
Ariakeno-Umi, b., Japan (ä-rē′ä-kä′nō ōō′nē)	211	33°03′N	130°18′E
Ariake-Wan, b., Japan (ä′rē-ä′kå wän)	211	31°19′N	131°15′E
Ariano, Italy (ä-rē-ä′nō)	174	41°09′N	15°11′E
Ariari, r., Col. (ä-ryà′rē)	142a	3°34′N	73°42′W
Aribinda, Burkina	234	14°14′N	0°52′W
Arica, Chile (ä-rē′kä)	142	18°34′S	70°14′W
Arichat, Can. (ä-rĭ-shät′)	101	45°31′N	61°01′W
Ariège, r., Fr. (ȧ-rē-ĕzh′)	170	43°26′N	1°29′E
Ariel, Wa., U.S. (â′rĭ-ĕl)	116c	45°57′N	122°34′W
Arieș, r., Rom.	169	46°25′N	23°15′E
Ariguanabo, Lago de, l., Cuba (lä′gô-dĕ-ä-rē-gwä-nä′bô)	135a	22°52′N	82°33′W
Arikaree, r., Co., U.S. (ă-rĭ-kȧ-rē′)	120	39°51′N	102°18′W
Arima, Japan (ä′rē-mä′)	211b	34°48′N	135°16′E
Aringay, Phil. (ä-rĭŋ-gä′ē)	213a	16°25′N	120°20′E
Arinos, r., Braz. (ä-rē′nōzsh)	143	12°09′S	56°49′W
Aripuanã, r., Braz. (ȧ-rē-pwän′yȧ)	143	7°06′S	60°29′W
′Arīsh, Wādī al, r., Egypt (ȧ-rēsh′)	197a	30°36′N	34°07′E
Aristazabal Island, i., Can.	94	52°30′N	129°20′W
Arizona, state, U.S. (ăr-ĭ-zō′nȧ)	104	34°00′N	113°00′W
Arjona, Spain (är-hō′nä)	172	37°58′N	4°03′W
Arka, r., Russia	185	60°45′N	142°30′E
Arkabutla Lake, res., Ms., U.S. (är-kȧ-bŭt′lă)	124	34°48′N	90°00′W
Arkadelphia, Ar., U.S. (är-kȧ-dĕl′fĭ-ȧ)	121	34°06′N	93°05′W
Arkansas, state, U.S. (är′kăn-sô) (är-kăn′sȧs)	105	34°50′N	93°40′W
Arkansas, r., U.S.	106	37°30′N	97°00′W
Arkansas City, Ks., U.S.	121	37°04′N	97°02′W
Arkhangelsk (Archangel), Russia (ár-κän′gĕlsk)	178	64°30′N	40°25′E
Arkhangel′skoye, Russia (är-kän-gĕl′skô-yĕ)	186a	54°25′N	56°48′E
Arklow, Ire. (ärk′lō)	164	52°47′N	6°10′W
Arkonam, India (är-kō-näm′)	203	13°05′N	79°43′E
Arlanza, r., Spain (är-län-thä′)	172	42°08′N	3°45′W
Arlanzón, r., Spain (är-län-thōn′)	172	42°12′N	3°58′W
Arlberg Tunnel, trans., Aus. (ärl′bĕrgh)	168	47°05′N	10°15′E
Arles, Fr. (ärl)	170	43°42′N	4°38′E
Arlington, S. Afr.	238c	28°02′S	27°52′E
Arlington, Ga., U.S. (är′lĭng-tun′)	124	31°25′N	84°42′W
Arlington, Ma., U.S.	101a	42°26′N	71°13′W
Arlington, S.D., U.S. (är′lĕng-tŭn)	112	44°23′N	97°09′W
Arlington, Tx., U.S. (ár′lĭng-tŭn)	117c	32°44′N	97°07′W
Arlington, Va., U.S.	110e	38°55′N	77°10′W
Arlington, Vt., U.S.	109	43°05′N	73°05′W
Arlington, Wa., U.S.	116a	48°11′N	122°08′W
Arlington Heights, Il., U.S. (är′lĕng-tŭn-hī′ts)	111a	42°05′N	87°59′W
Arltunga, Austl. (ärl-tòŋ′gȧ)	218	23°19′S	134°45′E
Arma, Ks., U.S. (är′mȧ)	121	37°34′N	94°43′W
Armagh, Can. (är-mä′) (är-mäκ′)	102b	46°45′N	70°36′W
Armagh, N. Ire., U.K.	160	54°21′N	6°25′W
Armant, Egypt (är-mänt′)	238b	25°37′N	32°32′E
Armaro, Col. (är-má′rō)	142a	4°58′N	74°54′W
Armavir, Russia (ár-má-vĭr′)	178	45°00′N	41°00′E
Armenia, Col. (ár-mĕ′nē-ȧ)	142	4°33′N	75°40′W
Armenia, El Sal. (är-mä′nē-ä)	132	13°44′N	89°31′W
Armenia, nation, Asia	178	41°00′N	44°39′E
Armentières, Fr. (ár-mäɴ-tyâr′)	170	50°43′N	2°53′E
Armeria, Río de, r., Mex. (rē′ō-dĕ-är-mā-rē′ä)	130	19°36′N	104°10′W
Armherstburg, Can. (ärm′hĕrst-bōōrgh)	98	42°06′N	83°06′W
Armians′k, Ukr.	177	46°06′N	33°42′E
Armidale, Austl. (är′mĭ-dāl)	219	30°27′S	151°50′E
Armour, S.D., U.S. (är′mẽr)	112	43°18′N	98°21′W
Armstrong Station, Can. (ärm′strŏng)	91	50°21′N	89°00′W
Arnedo, Spain (är-nā′dō)	172	42°12′N	2°03′W
Arnhem, Neth. (ärn′hĕm)	161	51°58′N	5°56′E
Arnhem, Cape, c., Austl.	220	12°15′S	137°00′E
Arnhem Land, reg., Austl. (ärn′hĕm-lănd)	220	13°15′S	133°00′E
Arno, r., Italy (ä′r-nô)	162	43°30′N	11°00′E
Arnold, Eng., U.K. (är′nŭld)	158a	53°00′N	1°08′W
Arnold, Mn., U.S. (ár′nŭld)	117h	46°53′N	92°06′W
Arnold, Pa., U.S.	111e	40°35′N	79°45′W
Arnprior, Can. (ärn-prī′ẽr)	99	45°25′N	76°20′W
Arnsberg, Ger. (ärns′bĕrgh)	171c	51°25′N	8°02′E
Arnstadt, Ger. (ärn′shtät)	168	50°51′N	10°57′E
Aroab, Nmb. (är′ō-ȧb)	232	25°40′S	19°45′E
Aroostook, r., Me., U.S. (ȧ-rōs′tòk)	100	46°44′N	68°15′W
Aroroy, Phil. (ä-rō-rō′ē)	213a	12°30′N	123°24′E
Arpajon, Fr. (ăr-pä-jō′n)	171b	48°35′N	2°15′E
Arpoador, Ponta do, c., Braz. (pō′n-tä-dō-är′pōä-dō′r)	144b	22°59′S	43°11′W
Arraiolos, Port. (är-rī-ō′lōzh)	172	38°47′N	7°59′W
Ar Ramādī, Iraq	198	33°26′N	43°19′E
Arran, Island of, Scot., U.K. (ă′răn)	164	55°25′N	5°25′W
Ar Rank, Sudan	231	11°45′N	32°53′E
Arras, Fr. (ȧ-räs′)	161	50°21′N	2°40′E
Ar Rawḍah, Egypt	238b	27°47′N	30°52′E
Arrecifes, Arg. (är-rā-sē′fās)	141c	34°03′S	60°05′W
Arrecifes, r., Arg.	141c	34°07′S	59°50′W
Arrée, Monts d′, mts., Fr. (är-rā′)	170	48°27′N	4°00′W
Arriaga, Mex. (är-rēä′gä)	131	16°15′N	93°54′W
Arrone, r., Italy	173d	41°57′N	12°17′E
Arrow Creek, r., Mt., U.S. (ăr′ō)	115	47°29′N	109°53′W
Arrowhead, Lake, l., Ca., U.S. (lăk ăr′ōhĕd)	117a	34°17′N	117°13′W
Arrowrock Reservoir, res., Id., U.S. (ăr′ō-rŏk)	114	43°40′N	115°30′W
Arroya Arena, Cuba (är-rô′yä-rĕ′nä)	135a	23°01′N	82°30′W
Arroyo de la Luz, Spain (är-rō′yō-dĕ-lä-lōō′z)	172	39°39′N	6°46′W
Arroyo Seco, Mex. (är-rō′yō sä′kō)	130	21°31′N	99°44′W
Ar Rub′ al Khālī, des., Asia	198	20°00′N	51°00′E
Ar Ruṭbah, Iraq	201	33°02′N	40°17′E
Arsen′yev, Russia	179	44°13′N	133°32′E
Arsinskiy, Russia (är-sĭn′skĭ)	186a	53°46′N	59°54′E
Árta, Grc. (är′tä)	163	39°08′N	21°02′E
Arteaga, Mex. (är-tä-ä′gä)	122	25°28′N	100°50′W
Artëm, Russia (ár-tyôm′)	179	43°28′N	132°29′E
Artemisa, Cuba (är-tā-mē′sä)	134	22°50′N	82°45′W
Artemivs′k, Ukr.	181	48°37′N	38°00′E
Artesia, N.M., U.S. (är-tē′sĭ-ȧ)	120	32°44′N	104°23′W
Arthabaska, Can.	99	46°03′N	71°54′W
Arthur′s Town, Bah.	135	24°40′N	75°40′W
Arti, Russia (är′tĭ)	186a	56°20′N	58°38′E
Artibonite, r., N.A. (är-tē-bō-nē′tä)	135	19°00′N	72°25′W
Aru, Kepulauan, is., Indon.	213	6°20′S	133°00′E
Arua, Ug. (ä′rōō-ä)	231	3°01′N	30°55′E
Aruba, i., Aruba (ä-rōō′bȧ)	129	12°29′N	70°00′W
Arunachal Pradesh, state, India	199	27°35′N	92°56′E
Arusha, Tan. (ȧ-rōō′shä)	232	3°22′S	36°41′E
Arvida, Can.	91	48°26′N	71°11′W
Arvika, Swe. (är-vē′kȧ)	166	59°41′N	12°35′E
Arzamas, Russia (är-zä-mäs′)	180	55°20′N	43°52′E
Arziw, Alg.	162	35°50′N	0°20′W
Arzúa, Spain	172	42°54′N	8°19′W
Aš, Czech Rep. (äsh′)	168	50°12′N	12°13′E
Asahi-Gawa, r., Japan (ȧ-sä′hē-gä′wä)	211	35°01′N	133°40′E
Asahikawa, Japan	205	43°50′N	142°09′E
Asaka, Japan (ä-sä′kä)	211a	35°47′N	139°36′E
Asansol, India	199	23°45′N	86°58′E
Asbest, Russia (äs-bĕst′)	180	57°02′N	61°28′E
Asbestos, Can. (ăs-bĕs′tŏs)	99	45°49′N	71°52′W
Asbestovskiy, Russia	186a	57°46′N	61°23′E
Asbury Park, N.J., U.S. (ăz′bĕr-ĭ)	110a	40°13′N	74°01′W
Ascención, Bahía de la, b., Mex.	132a	19°39′N	87°30′W
Ascensión, Mex. (äs-sĕn-sē-ōn′)	130	24°21′N	99°54′W
Ascension, i., St. Hel. (ȧ-sĕn′shŭn)	229	8°00′S	13°00′W
Ascent, S. Afr. (ăs-ĕnt′)	238c	27°14′S	29°06′E
Aschaffenburg, Ger. (ä-shäf′ĕn-bòrgh)	168	49°58′N	9°12′E
Ascheberg, Ger. (ä′shĕ-bĕrg)	171c	51°47′N	7°38′E
Aschersleben, Ger. (äsh′ĕrs-lā-bĕn)	168	51°46′N	11°28′E
Ascoli Piceno, Italy (äs′kô-lēpē-chā′nō)	174	42°50′N	13°55′E
Aseb, Erit.	231	12°52′N	43°39′E
Asenovgrad, Blg.	175	42°00′N	24°49′E
Aseri, Est. (ȧ′sĕ-rĭ)	167	59°26′N	26°58′E
Asha, Russia (ä′shä)	186a	55°01′N	57°17′E
Ashabula, l., N.D., U.S. (ăsh′ȧ-bū-lă)	112	47°07′N	97°51′W
Ashan, Russia (ä′shän)	186a	57°08′N	56°25′E
Ashbourne, Eng., U.K. (ăsh′bŭrn)	158a	53°01′N	1°44′W
Ashburn, Ga., U.S. (ăsh′bŭrn)	124	31°42′N	83°42′W
Ashburn, Va., U.S.	110e	39°02′N	77°30′W
Ashburton, r., Austl. (ăsh′bûr-tŭn)	220	22°30′S	115°30′E
Ashby-de-la-Zouch, Eng., U.K. (ăsh′bĭ-dē-lȧ zōōsh′)	158a	52°44′N	1°23′W
Ashdod, Isr.	197a	31°46′N	34°39′E
Ashdown, Ar., U.S. (ăsh′doun)	121	33°41′N	94°07′W
Asheboro, N.C., U.S. (ăsh′bŭr-ô)	125	35°41′N	79°50′W
Asherton, Tx., U.S. (ăsh′ẽr-tŭn)	122	28°26′N	99°45′W
Asheville, N.C., U.S. (ăsh′vĭl)	105	35°35′N	82°35′W
Ash Fork, Az., U.S.	119	35°13′N	112°29′W
Ashgabat, Turkmen.	183	37°57′N	58°23′E
Ashikaga, Japan (ä′shē-kä′gȧ)	211	36°22′N	139°26′E
Ashiya, Japan (ä′shē-yä′)	211	33°54′N	130°40′E
Ashiya, Japan	211b	34°44′N	135°18′E
Ashizuri-Zaki, c., Japan (ä-shē-zò-rē zä-kē)	210	32°43′N	133°04′E
Ashland, Al., U.S. (ăsh′lȧnd)	124	33°15′N	85°50′W
Ashland, Ks., U.S.	120	37°11′N	99°46′W
Ashland, Ky., U.S.	108	38°25′N	82°40′W
Ashland, Ma., U.S.	101a	42°16′N	71°28′W
Ashland, Me., U.S.	100	46°37′N	68°26′W
Ashland, Ne., U.S.	112	41°02′N	96°23′W
Ashland, Oh., U.S.	108	40°50′N	82°15′W
Ashland, Or., U.S.	114	42°12′N	122°42′W
Ashland, Pa., U.S.	109	40°45′N	76°20′W
Ashland, Wi., U.S.	105	46°34′N	90°55′W
Ashley, N.D., U.S. (ăsh′lē)	112	46°03′N	99°23′W
Ashley, Pa., U.S.	109	41°15′N	75°55′W
Ashmūn, Egypt (ásh-mōōn′)	238b	30°19′N	30°57′E
Ashmyany, Bela.	167	54°27′N	25°55′E
Ashqelon, Isr. (äsh′kĕ-lōn)	197a	31°40′N	34°36′E
Ash Shabb, Egypt (shĕb)	231	22°34′N	29°52′E
Ash Shallūfah, Egypt (shäl′lò-fȧ)	238b	30°09′N	32°33′E
Ash Shaqrā′, Sau. Ar.	198	25°10′N	45°08′E
Ash Shāriqah, U.A.E.	201	25°22′N	55°23′E
Ash Shawbak, Jord.	197a	30°31′N	35°35′E
Ash Shiḥr, Yemen	198	14°45′N	49°32′E
Ashtabula, Oh., U.S. (ăsh-tȧ-bū′lȧ)	105	41°55′N	80°50′W
Ashton, Id., U.S. (ăsh′tŭn)	115	44°04′N	111°28′W
Ashton-in-Makerfield, Eng., U.K. (ăsh′tŭn-ĭn-măk′ẽr-fēld)	158a	53°29′N	2°39′W
Ashton-under-Lyne, Eng., U.K. (ăsh′tŭn-ŭn-dẽr-līn′)	158a	53°29′N	2°04′W
Ashuanipi, l., Can. (ăsh-wȧ-nĭp′ĭ)	93	52°40′N	67°42′W
Ashukino, Russia (ȧ-shōō′kinô)	186b	56°10′N	37°57′E
Asia, cont.	196	50°00′N	100°00′E
Asia Minor, reg., Tur. (ā′zhȧ)	157	38°18′N	31°18′E
Asientos, Mex. (ä-sē-ĕn′tōs)	130	22°13′N	102°05′W
Asilah, Mor.	172	35°30′N	6°05′W
Asinara, i., Italy	174	41°02′N	8°22′E
Asinara, Golfo dell′, b., Italy (gôl′fō-dĕl-ä-sē-nä′rä)	174	40°58′N	8°28′E
Asīr, reg., Sau. Ar. (ä-sēr′)	198	19°30′N	42°00′E
Askarovo, Russia (äs-kä-rô′vô)	186a	53°21′N	58°32′E
Askersund, Swe. (äs′kĕr-sònd)	166	58°43′N	14°53′E
Askino, Russia (äs′kĭ-nô)	186a	56°06′N	56°29′E
Asmara *see* Asmera, Erit.	230	15°17′N	38°56′E
Asmera, Erit. (äs-mä′rä)	231	15°17′N	38°56′E
Asnieres, Fr. (ä-nyâr′)	171b	48°55′N	2°18′E
Asosa, Eth.	231	10°13′N	34°28′E
Asotin, Wa., U.S. (ȧ-sō′tĭn)	114	46°19′N	117°01′W
Aspen, Co., U.S. (ăs′pĕn)	119	39°15′N	106°55′W
Asperen, Neth.	159a	51°52′N	5°07′E
Aspy Bay, b., Can. (ăs′pē)	101	46°55′N	60°25′W
Aş Şaff, Egypt	238b	29°33′N	31°23′E
As Sallūm, Egypt	231	31°35′N	25°05′E
As Salt, Jord.	197a	32°02′N	35°44′E
Assam, state, India (ăs-săm′)	199	26°00′N	91°00′E
As Samāwah, Iraq	201	31°18′N	45°17′E
Assens, Den. (äs′sĕns)	166	55°16′N	9°54′E
As Sinbillāwayn, Egypt	238b	30°53′N	31°37′E
Assini, C. Iv. (ȧ-sē-nē′)	230	4°52′N	3°16′W
Assiniboia, Can.	90	49°38′N	105°59′W
Assiniboine, r., Can. (ă-sĭn′ĭ-boin)	97	50°03′N	97°57′W
Assiniboine, Mount, mtn., Can.	95	50°52′N	115°39′W
Assis, Braz. (ä-sē′s)	143	22°39′S	50°21′W
Assisi, Italy	162	43°04′N	12°37′E
As-Sudd, reg., Sudan	231	8°45′N	30°45′E
As Sulaymānīyah, Iraq	198	35°47′N	45°23′E
As Sulaymānīyah, Sau. Ar.	201	24°09′N	46°19′E
As Suwaydā′, Syria	198	32°41′N	36°41′E
Astakós, Grc. (äs′tä-kôs)	175	38°42′N	21°00′E
Astana (Aqmola), Kaz.	183	51°10′N	71°43′E
Astara, Azer.	181	38°30′N	48°50′E
Asti, Italy (äs′tē)	162	44°54′N	8°12′E
Astorga, Spain (äs-tôr′gä)	172	42°28′N	6°03′W
Astoria, Or., U.S. (ăs-tō′rĭ-ȧ)	104	46°11′N	123°51′W
Astrakhan′, Russia (äs-trá-kän′)	178	46°15′N	48°00′E
Astrida, Rw. (äs-trē′dȧ)	232	2°37′S	29°48′E
Asturias, hist. reg., Spain (äs-tōō′ryäs)	172	43°21′N	6°00′W
Astypalaia, i., Grc.	163	36°31′N	26°19′E
Asunción *see* Ixtaltepec, Mex.	131	16°33′N	95°04′W
Asunción *see* Nochistlán, Mex.	130	21°23′N	102°52′W
Asunción, Para. (ä-sōōn-syōn′)	144	25°25′S	57°30′W
Asunción Mita, Guat. (ä-sōōn-syō′n-mē′tä)	132	14°19′N	89°43′W
Aswān, Egypt (ä-swän′)	231	24°05′N	32°57′E
Aswān High Dam, dam, Egypt	231	23°58′N	32°53′E
Atacama, Desierto de, des., Chile (dĕ-syĕ′r-tô-dĕ-ä-tä-kä′mä)	139	23°50′S	69°00′W

ng-sing; ŋ-baŋk; ɴ-nasalized n; nŏd; cŏmmit; ōld; ôbey; ôrder; oi-boil; fōōd; ò-as oo in foot; ou-out; s-soft; sh-dish; th-thin; pūre; ûnite; ûrn; stŭd; circŭs; ü-as in French tu; ′-indeterminate vowel.

268 Atacama – Babylon PRONOUNCING INDEX

PLACE (Pronunciation)	PAGE	LAT.	LONG.
Atacama, Puna de, plat., Bol. (po͞o′nä-dĕ-ä-tä-kȧ′mä)	142	21°35′S	66°58′W
Atacama, Puna de, reg., Chile (po͞o′nä-dĕ-ȧtä-kȧ′mä)	144	23°15′S	68°45′W
Atacama, Salar de, l., Chile (sȧ-lȧr′dĕ-ȧtä-kȧ′mä)	144	23°38′S	68°15′W
Ataco, Col. (ä-tȧ′kō)	142a	3°36′N	75°22′W
Atacora, Chaîne de l′, mts., Benin	234	10°15′N	1°15′E
Atā ′itah, Jabal al, mtn., Jord.	197a	30°48′N	35°19′E
Atamanovskiy, Russia (ä-tä-mä′nôv-skĭ)	186a	52°15′N	60°47′E
′Atāqah, Jabal, mts., Egypt	238d	29°59′N	32°20′E
Atar, Maur. (ä-tär′)	230	20°45′N	13°16′W
Atascadero, Ca., U.S. (ăt-ăs-kȧ-dâ′rō)	118	35°29′N	120°40′W
Atascosa, r., Tx., U.S. (ăt-ăs-kō′sȧ)	122	28°50′N	98°17′W
Atauro, Ilha de, i., E. Timor (dĕ-ä-tä′o͞o-rō)	213	8°20′S	126°15′E
Atbara, r., Afr.	231	17°14′N	34°27′E
′Aţbarah, Sudan (ät′bȧ-rä)	231	17°45′N	33°15′E
Atbasar, Kaz. (ät′bä-sär′)	183	51°42′N	68°28′E
Atchafalaya, r., La., U.S.	123	30°53′N	91°51′W
Atchafalaya Bay, b., La., U.S. (ăch-ȧ-fȧ-lī′ȧ)	123	29°25′N	91°30′W
Atchison, Ks., U.S. (ăch′ĭ-sŭn)	105	39°33′N	95°08′W
Atco, N.J., U.S. (ăt′kō)	110f	39°46′N	74°53′W
Atempan, Mex. (ä-tĕm-pȧ′n)	131	19°49′N	97°25′W
Atenguillo, r., Mex. (ä-tĕn-gē′l-yō)	130	20°18′N	104°35′W
Athabasca, Can. (ăth-ȧ-băs′kȧ)	90	54°43′N	113°17′W
Athabasca, l., Can.	92	59°04′N	109°10′W
Athabasca, r., Can.	92	57°30′N	112°00′W
Athens (Athína), Grc.	175	38°00′N	23°38′E
Athens, Al., U.S. (ăth′ĕnz)	124	34°47′N	86°58′W
Athens, Ga., U.S.	105	33°55′N	83°24′W
Athens, Oh., U.S.	108	39°20′N	82°10′W
Athens, Pa., U.S.	109	42°00′N	76°30′W
Athens, Tn., U.S.	124	35°26′N	84°36′W
Athens, Tx., U.S.	123	32°13′N	95°51′W
Atherstone, Eng., U.K. (ăth′ẽr-stŭn)	150a	52°34′N	1°33′W
Atherton, Eng., U.K. (ăth′ẽr-tŭn)	158a	53°32′N	2°29′W
Atherton Plateau, plat., Austl. (ădh-ĕr-tŏn)	221	17°00′S	144°30′E
Athi, r., Kenya (ä′tē)	233	2°43′S	38°30′E
Athína *see* Athens, Grc.	154	38°00′N	23°38′E
Athlone, Ire. (ăth-lōn′)	160	53°24′N	7°30′W
Áthos, mtn., Grc. (ăth′ŏs)	175	40°10′N	24°15′E
Ath Thamad, Egypt	197a	29°41′N	34°17′E
Athy, Ire. (ȧ-thī)	164	52°59′N	7°08′W
Ati, Chad	235	13°13′N	18°20′E
Atibaia, Braz. (ä-tē-bȧ′yă)	141a	23°08′S	46°32′W
Atikonak, l., Can.	93	52°34′N	63°49′W
Atimonan, Phil. (ä-tē-mō′nän)	213a	13°59′N	121°56′E
Atiquizaya, El Sal. (ä′tē-kē-zä′yä)	132	14°00′N	89°42′W
Atitlan, vol., Guat. (ä-tē-tlän′)	132	14°35′N	91°11′W
Atitlan, Lago, l., Guat. (ä-tē-tlän′)	132	14°38′N	91°23′W
Atizapán, Mex. (ä′tē-zȧ-pän′)	131a	19°33′N	99°16′W
Atka, Ak., U.S. (ăt′kȧ)	103a	52°18′N	174°18′W
Atka, i., Ak., U.S.	106b	51°58′N	174°30′W
Atkarsk, Russia (åt-kärsk′)	181	51°50′N	45°00′E
Atkinson, Ne., U.S. (ăt′kĭn-sŭn)	112	42°32′N	98°58′W
Atlanta, Ga., U.S. (ăt-lăn′tȧ)	105	33°45′N	84°23′W
Atlanta, Tx., U.S.	121	33°09′N	94°09′W
Atlantic, Ia., U.S. (ăt-lăn′tĭk)	113	41°23′N	94°58′W
Atlantic, N.C., U.S.	125	34°54′N	76°20′W
Atlantic City, N.J., U.S.	105	39°20′N	74°30′W
Atlantic Highlands, N.J., U.S.	110a	40°25′N	74°04′W
Atlantic Ocean, o.	4	5°00′S	25°00′W
Atlas Mountains, mts., Afr. (ăt′lăs)	230	31°22′N	4°57′W
Atliaca, Mex. (ät-lē-ä′kä)	130	17°38′N	99°24′W
Atlin, l., Can. (ăt′lĭn)	92	59°34′N	133°20′W
Atlixco, Mex. (ät-lēz′kō)	130	18°52′N	98°27′W
Atmore, Al., U.S. (ât′mōr)	124	31°01′N	87°31′W
Atoka, Ok., U.S. (ȧ-tō′kȧ)	121	34°23′N	96°07′W
Atoka Reservoir, res., Ok., U.S.	121	34°30′N	96°05′W
Atotonilco el Alto, Mex.	130	20°35′N	102°32′W
Atotonilco el Grande, Mex.	130	20°17′N	98°41′W
Atoui, r., Afr. (ȧ-to͞o-ē′)	230	21°00′N	15°32′W
Atoyac, Mex. (ä-tō-yäk′)	130	20°01′N	103°28′W
Atoyac, r., Mex.	130	18°35′N	98°16′W
Atoyac, r., Mex.	131	16°27′N	97°28′W
Atoyac de Alvarez, Mex. (ä-tō-yäk′dā äl′vä-rāz)	130	17°13′N	100°29′W
Atoyatempan, Mex. (ä-tō′yȧ-tĕm-pän′)	131	18°47′N	97°54′W
Atrak, r., Asia	198	37°45′N	56°30′E
Ätran, r., Swe.	166	57°02′N	12°43′E
Atrato, Río, r., Col. (rē′ō-ä-trä′tō)	142	7°15′N	77°18′W
Aţ Ţafīlah, Jord. (tä-fē′la)	197a	30°50′N	35°36′E
Aţ Ţā′if, Sau. Ar.	198	21°03′N	41°00′E
Attalla, Al., U.S. (ȧ-tăl′yȧ)	124	34°01′N	86°05′W
Attawapiskat, r., Can. (ăt′ȧ-wȧ-pĭs′kăt)	93	52°31′N	86°22′W
Attersee, l., Aus.	168	47°57′N	13°25′E
Attica, N.Y., U.S. (ăt′ĭ-kȧ)	109	42°55′N	78°15′W
Attleboro, Ma., U.S. (ăt′′l-bŭr-ō)	110b	41°56′N	71°15′W
Attow, Ben, mtn., Scot., U.K. (bĕn ăt′tō)	164	57°15′N	5°25′W
Attoyac Bay, Tx., U.S. (ă-toi′yăk)	123	31°45′N	94°23′W
Attu, i., Ak., U.S. (ät-to͞o′)	106b	53°08′N	173°18′E
Aţ Ţūr, Egypt	163	28°09′N	33°47′E
Aţ Ţurayf, Sau. Ar.	198	31°32′N	38°30′E
Åtvidaberg, Swe. (ōt-vē′dȧ-bĕrgh)	166	58°12′N	15°55′E
Atwood, Ks., U.S. (ăt′wo͝od)	120	39°48′N	101°06′W
Atyraū, Kaz.	183	47°10′N	51°50′E
Atzcapotzalco, Mex. (ät′zkä-pō-tzäl′kō)	130	19°29′N	99°11′W
Atzgersdorf, Aus.	159e	48°10′N	16°17′E
Auau Channel, strt., Hi., U.S. (ä′o͝o-ä′o͝o)	126a	20°55′N	156°50′W
Aubagne, Fr. (ō-bän′y′)	171	43°18′N	5°34′E
Aube, r., Fr. (ōb)	170	48°42′N	3°49′E
Aubenas, Fr. (ōb-nä′)	170	44°37′N	4°22′E
Aubervilliers, Fr. (ō-bĕr-vē-yā′)	171b	48°54′N	2°23′E
Aubin, Fr. (ō-băɴ′)	170	44°29′N	2°12′E
Aubrey, Can. (ô-brē′)	102a	45°08′N	73°47′W
Auburn, Al., U.S. (ô′bŭrn)	124	32°35′N	85°26′W
Auburn, Ca., U.S.	118	38°52′N	121°05′W
Auburn, Il., U.S.	121	39°36′N	89°46′W
Auburn, In., U.S.	108	41°20′N	85°05′W
Auburn, Ma., U.S.	101a	42°11′N	71°51′W
Auburn, Me., U.S.	105	44°04′N	70°24′W
Auburn, Ne., U.S.	121	40°23′N	95°50′W
Auburn, N.Y., U.S.	109	42°55′N	76°35′W
Auburn, Wa., U.S.	116a	47°18′N	122°14′W
Auburn Heights, Mi., U.S.	111b	42°37′N	83°13′W
Aubusson, Fr. (ō-bü-sôɴ′)	170	45°57′N	2°10′E
Auch, Fr. (ōsh)	161	43°38′N	0°35′E
Aucilla, r., Fl., U.S. (ô-sĭl′ȧ)	124	30°15′N	83°55′W
Auckland, N.Z. (ôk′lănd)	221a	36°53′S	174°45′E
Auckland Islands, is., N.Z.	3	50°30′S	166°30′E
Aude, r., Fr. (ōd)	170	42°55′N	2°08′E
Audierne, Fr. (ō-dyĕrn′)	170	48°02′N	4°31′W
Audincourt, Fr. (ō-dăn-ko͞or′)	171	47°30′N	6°49′E
Audley, Eng., U.K. (ôd′lĭ)	158a	53°03′N	2°18′W
Audo Range, mts., Eth.	238a	6°58′N	41°18′E
Audubon, Ia., U.S. (ô′do͝o-bŏn)	113	41°43′N	94°57′W
Audubon, N.J., U.S.	110f	39°54′N	75°04′W
Aue, Ger. (ou′ē)	168	50°35′N	12°44′E
Augathella, Austl. (ôr′gȧ′thĕ-lȧ)	222	25°49′S	146°40′E
Augrabiesvalle, wtfl., S. Afr.	232	28°30′S	20°00′E
Augsburg, Ger. (ouks′bo͝orgh)	161	48°23′N	10°55′E
Augusta, Ar., U.S. (ô-gŭs′tȧ)	121	35°16′N	91°21′W
Augusta, Ga., U.S.	105	33°26′N	82°00′W
Augusta, Ks., U.S.	121	37°41′N	96°58′W
Augusta, Ky., U.S.	108	38°45′N	84°00′W
Augusta, Me., U.S.	105	44°19′N	69°42′W
Augusta, N.J., U.S.	110a	41°07′N	74°44′W
Augusta, Wi., U.S.	113	44°40′N	91°09′W
Augustow, Pol. (ou-go͝os′to͝of)	169	53°52′N	23°00′E
Auki, Sol. Is.	214e	8°46′S	160°42′E
Aulnay-sous-Bois, Fr. (ō-nĕ′so͞o-bwä′)	171b	48°56′N	2°30′E
Aulne, r., Fr. (ōn)	170	48°08′N	3°53′W
Auneau, Fr. (ō-nĕü)	171b	48°28′N	1°45′E
Auob, r., Afr. (ä′wŏb)	232	25°00′S	19°00′E
Aur, i., Malay.	197b	2°27′N	104°51′E
Aura, Fin.	167	60°38′N	22°32′E
Aurangābād, India (ou-rŭŋ-gä-bäd′)	199	19°56′N	75°19′E
Aurdal, Nor. (äŭr-däl)	160	60°54′N	9°24′E
Aurès, Massif de l′, mts., Alg.	162	35°16′N	5°53′E
Aurillac, Fr. (ō-rē-yȧk′)	161	44°57′N	2°27′E
Aurora, Can.	99	43°59′N	79°25′W
Aurora, Co., U.S.	120	39°44′N	104°50′W
Aurora, Il., U.S. (ô-rō′rȧ)	105	41°45′N	88°18′W
Aurora, In., U.S.	111f	39°04′N	84°55′W
Aurora, Mn., U.S.	113	47°31′N	92°17′W
Aurora, Mo., U.S.	121	36°58′N	93°42′W
Aurora, Ne., U.S.	120	40°54′N	98°01′W
Aursunden, l., Nor. (äûr-sûndĕn)	166	62°42′N	11°10′E
Au Sable, r., Mi., U.S. (ô-sā′b′l)	108	44°40′N	84°25′W
Ausable, r., N.Y., U.S.	109	44°25′N	73°50′W
Austin, Mn., U.S. (ôs′tĭn)	113	43°40′N	92°58′W
Austin, Nv., U.S.	118	39°30′N	117°05′W
Austin, Tx., U.S.	104	30°15′N	97°42′W
Austin, l., Austl.	220	27°45′S	117°30′E
Austin Bayou, Tx., U.S. (ôs′tĭn bī-o͞o′)	123a	29°17′N	95°21′W
Australia, nation, Oc.	218	25°00′S	135°00′E
Australian Alps, mts., Austl.	222	37°10′S	147°55′E
Australian Capital Territory, ter., Austl. (ôs-trā′lĭ-ăn)	219	35°30′S	148°40′E
Austria, nation, Eur. (ôs′trĭ-ȧ)	154	47°15′N	11°53′E
Authon-la-Plaine, Fr. (ō-tō′ɴ-lă-plĕ′n)	171b	48°27′N	1°58′E
Autlán, Mex. (ä-o͞ot-län′)	128	19°47′N	104°24′W
Autun, Fr. (ō-tŭɴ′)	170	46°58′N	4°14′E
Auvergne, mts., Fr. (ō-vĕrn′y′)	170	45°12′N	2°31′E
Auxerre, Fr. (ō-sâr′)	161	47°48′N	3°32′E
Ava, Mo., U.S. (ā′vȧ)	121	36°56′N	92°40′W
Avakubi, D.R.C. (ä-vȧ-ko͞o′bē)	231	1°20′N	27°34′E
Avallon, Fr. (ȧ-vȧ-lôɴ′)	170	47°30′N	3°58′E
Avalon, Ca., U.S.	118	33°21′N	118°22′W
Avalon, Pa., U.S. (ăv′ȧ-lŏn)	111e	40°31′N	80°05′W
Aveiro, Port. (ä-vā′ro͝o)	162	40°38′N	8°38′W
Avelar, Braz. (ä′vĕ-lȧ′r)	144b	22°20′S	43°25′W
Avellaneda, Arg. (ä-vĕl-yä-nā′dhä)	144	34°40′S	58°23′W
Avellino, Italy (ä-vĕl-lē′nō)	174	40°40′N	14°46′E
Averøya, i., Nor. (ävĕr-ûē)	166	63°40′N	7°16′E
Aversa, Italy (ä-vĕr′sä)	174	40°58′N	14°13′E
Avery, Tx., U.S. (ā′vẽr-ĭ)	121	33°34′N	94°46′W
Avesta, Swe. (ä-vĕs′tä)	166	60°16′N	16°09′E
Aveyron, r., Fr. (ä-vâ-rôɴ)	170	44°07′N	1°45′E
Avezzano, Italy (ä-våt-sä′nō)	174	42°03′N	13°27′E
Avigliano, Italy (ä-vēl-yä′nō)	174	40°45′N	15°44′E
Avignon, Fr. (ȧ-vē-nyôɴ′)	161	43°55′N	4°50′E
Ávila, Spain (ä-vē-lä)	172	40°39′N	4°42′W
Avilés, Spain (ä-vē-lās′)	162	43°33′N	5°55′W
Aviño, Spain	172	43°36′N	8°05′W
Avoca, Ia., U.S. (ȧ-vō′kȧ)	121	41°29′N	95°16′W
Avon, Ct., U.S. (ā′vŏn)	109	41°40′N	72°50′W
Avon, Ma., U.S. (ā′vŏn)	101a	42°08′N	71°03′W
Avon, Oh., U.S.	111d	41°27′N	82°02′W
Avon, r., Eng., U.K. (ā′vŭn)	164	52°05′N	1°55′W
Avondale, Ga., U.S.	110c	33°47′N	84°16′W
Avon Lake, Oh., U.S.	111d	41°31′N	82°01′W
Avonmore, Can. (ä′vōɴ-mōr)	102c	45°11′N	74°58′W
Avon Park, Fl., U.S. (ā′vŏn pärk′)	125a	27°35′N	81°29′W
Avranches, Fr. (ȧ-vränsh′)	170	48°43′N	1°34′W
Awaji-Shima, i., Japan	210	34°32′N	135°02′E
Awe, Loch, l., Scot., U.K. (lŏĸ ôr)	164	56°22′N	5°04′W
Awjilah, Libya	231	29°07′N	21°21′E
Ax-les-Thermes, Fr. (äks′lā tĕrm′)	170	42°43′N	1°50′E
Axochiapan, Mex. (äks-ō-chyä′pän)	130	18°29′N	98°49′W
Ay, r., Russia	180	55°55′N	57°55′E
Ayabe, Japan (ä′yä-bĕ)	210	35°16′N	135°17′E
Ayachi, Arin′, mtn., Mor.	162	32°29′N	4°57′W
Ayacucho, Arg. (ä-yä-ko͞o′chō)	144	37°05′S	58°30′W
Ayacucho, Peru	142	13°12′S	74°03′W
Ayaköz, Kaz.	183	48°00′N	80°12′E
Ayamonte, Spain (ä-yä-mō′n-tĕ)	162	37°14′N	7°28′W
Ayan, Russia (ȧ-yän′)	179	56°26′N	138°18′E
Ayata, Bol. (ä-yä′tä)	142	15°17′S	68°43′W
Ayaviri, Peru (ä-yä-vē′rē)	142	14°46′S	70°38′W
Aydar, r., Eur. (ī-där′)	177	49°15′N	38°48′E
Ayden, N.C., U.S. (ā′dĕn)	125	35°27′N	77°25′W
Aydın, Tur. (āĭy-dĕn)	198	37°40′N	27°40′E
Ayer, Ma., U.S. (âr)	101a	42°33′N	71°36′W
Ayer Hitam, Malay.	197b	1°55′N	103°11′E
Ayers Rock *see* Uluru, mtn., Austl.	220	25°23′S	131°05′E
Aylesbury, Eng., U.K. (ālz′bẽr-ĭ)	164	51°47′N	0°49′W
Aylmer, l., Can. (āl′mẽr)	92	64°27′N	108°22′W
Aylmer, Mount, mtn., Can.	95	51°19′N	115°26′W
Aylmer East, Can. (āl′mẽr)	99	45°24′N	75°50′W
Ayo el Chico, Mex. (ä′yō el chē′kō)	130	20°31′N	102°21′W
Ayon, i., Russia (ī-ôn′)	179	69°50′N	168°40′E
Ayorou, Niger	234	14°44′N	0°55′E
Ayotla, Mex. (ä-yōt′lä)	131a	19°18′N	98°55′W
Ayoun el Atrous, Maur.	234	16°40′N	9°37′W
Ayr, Scot., U.K. (âr)	164	55°27′N	4°40′W
Aysha, Eth.	231	10°40′N	42°32′E
Ayutla, Guat. (ȧ-yo͞ot′lä)	132	14°44′N	92°11′W
Ayutla, Mex.	130	16°50′N	99°16′W
Ayutla, Mex.	130	20°09′N	104°20′W
Ayvalık, Tur. (āĭy-wă-lĭk)	163	39°19′N	26°40′E
Azaouad, reg., Mali	234	18°00′N	3°20′W
Azaouak, Vallée de l′, val., Afr.	235	15°50′N	3°10′E
Azare, Nig.	235	11°40′N	10°11′E
Azemmour, Mor. (ȧ-zē-mo͞or′)	230	33°20′N	8°21′W
Azerbaijan, nation, Asia	178	40°30′N	47°30′E
Azle, Tx., U.S. (ȧz′lē)	117c	35°54′N	97°33′W
Azogues, Ec. (ä-sō′gās)	142	2°47′S	78°45′W
Azores *see* Açores, is., Port.	229	37°44′N	29°25′W
Azov, Russia (ȧ-zôf′) (ä-zōf)	181	47°07′N	39°19′E
Azov, Sea of, sea, Eur.	178	46°00′N	36°20′E
Aztec, N.M., U.S. (ăz′tĕk)	119	36°40′N	108°00′W
Aztec Ruins National Monument, rec., N.M., U.S.	119	36°50′N	108°00′W
Azua, Dom. Rep. (ä′swä)	135	18°30′N	70°45′W
Azuaga, Spain (ä-thwä′gä)	172	38°15′N	5°42′W
Azucar, Presa de, res., Mex.	122	26°06′N	98°44′W
Azuero, Península de, pen., Pan.	129	7°30′N	80°34′W
Azufre, Cerro (Copiapó), mtn., Chile	144	27°10′S	69°00′W
Azul, Arg. (ä-so͞ol′)	144	36°46′S	59°51′W
Azul, Cordillera, mts., Peru	142	7°15′S	75°30′W
Azul, Sierra, mts., Mex.	130	23°20′N	98°28′W
Azusa, Ca., U.S. (ȧ-zo͞o′sȧ)	117a	34°08′N	117°55′W
Aẓ Ẓahrān (Dhahran), Sau. Ar.	198	26°13′N	50°00′E
Az Zaqāzīq, Egypt	231	30°36′N	31°36′E
Az Zarqā′, Jord.	197a	32°03′N	36°07′E
Az Zāwiyah, Libya	230	32°28′N	11°55′E

B

PLACE (Pronunciation)	PAGE	LAT.	LONG.
Baadheere (Bardera), Som.	238a	2°13′N	42°24′E
Baal, Ger. (bäl)	171c	51°02′N	6°17′E
Baao, Phil. (bä′ō)	213a	13°27′N	123°22′E
Baarle-Hertog, Bel.	159a	51°26′N	4°57′E
Baarn, Neth.	159a	52°12′N	5°18′E
Babaeski, Tur. (bä′bä-ĕs′kĭ)	175	41°25′N	27°05′E
Babahoyo, Ec. (bä-bä-ō′yō)	142	1°56′S	79°24′W
Babana, Nig.	235	10°36′N	3°50′E
Babanango, S. Afr.	233c	28°24′S	31°11′E
Babanūsah, Sudan	231	11°30′N	27°55′E
Babar, Pulau, i., Indon. (bä′bȧr)	213	7°50′S	129°15′E
Bab-el-Mandeb *see* Mandeb, Bab-el-, strt.	198	13°17′N	42°49′E
Babelthuap, i., Palau	214b	7°30′N	134°36′E
Babia, Arroyo de la, r., Mex.	122	28°26′N	101°50′W
Babine, r., Can.	94	55°10′N	127°00′W
Babine Lake, l., Can. (băb′ēn)	92	54°45′N	126°00′W
Bābol, Iran	198	36°30′N	52°48′E
Babruysk, Bela.	180	53°07′N	29°13′E
Babushkin, Russia (bä′bo͝osh-kĭn)	184	51°47′N	106°08′W
Babushkin, Russia	176	55°52′N	37°42′E
Babuyan Islands, is., Phil. (bä-bo͞o-yän′)	212	19°30′N	122°38′E
Babyak, Blg. (bäb′zhȧk)	175	41°59′N	23°42′E
Babylon, N.Y., U.S. (băb′ĭ-lŏn)	110a	40°42′N	73°19′W
Babylon, hist., Iraq	198	32°15′N	45°23′E

ăt; finăl; rāte; senåte; ärm; ȧsk; sofȧ; fâre; ch-choose; dh-as th in other; bē; ēvent; bĕt; recĕnt; cratẽr; g-gō; gh-guttural g; bĭt; ĭ-short neutral; rīde; ĸ-guttural k as ch in German ich;

PRONOUNCING INDEX Bacalar – Bangor 269

PLACE (Pronunciation)	PAGE	LAT.	LONG.
Bacalar, Laguna de, l., Mex. (lä-gōō-nä-dĕ-bä-kä-lär′)	132a	18°50′N	88°31′W
Bacan, Pulau, i., Indon.	213	0°30′S	127°00′E
Bacarra, Phil. (bä-kär′rä)	209	18°22′N	120°40′E
Bacău, Rom.	163	46°34′N	27°00′E
Baccarat, Fr. (bȧ-kȧ-rȧ′)	171	48°29′N	6°42′E
Bacchus, Ut., U.S. (băk′ŭs)	117b	40°40′N	112°06′W
Bachajón, Mex. (bä-chä-hōn′)	131	17°08′N	92°18′W
Bachu, China (bä-chōō)	204	39°50′N	78°23′E
Back, r., Can.	92	65°30′N	104°15′W
Bačka Palanka, Serb. (bäch′kä pälän-kä)	175	45°14′N	19°24′E
Bačka Topola, Serb. (bäch′kä tô′pô-lä′)	175	45°48′N	19°38′E
Back Bay, India (băk)	203b	18°55′N	72°45′E
Backstairs Passage, strt., Austl. (băk-stârs′)	220	35°50′S	138°15′E
Bac Lieu, Viet.	212	9°45′N	105°50′E
Bac Ninh, Viet. (bäk′nēn′′)	209	21°10′N	106°02′E
Baco, Mount, mtn., Phil. (bä′kō)	213a	12°50′N	121°11′E
Bacoli, Italy (bä-kō-lē′)	173c	40°33′N	14°05′E
Bacolod, Phil. (bä-kō′lôd)	213	10°42′N	123°03′E
Bácsalmás, Hung. (bäch′ôl-mäs)	169	46°07′N	19°18′E
Bacup, Eng., U.K. (băk′ŭp)	158a	53°42′N	2°12′W
Bad, r., S.D., U.S. (băd)	112	44°04′N	100°58′W
Badajoz, Spain (bȧ-dhä-hōth′)	162	38°52′N	6°56′W
Badalona, Spain (bä-dhä-lō′nä)	173	41°27′N	2°15′E
Badanah, Sau. Ar.	198	30°49′N	40°45′E
Bad Axe, Mi., U.S. (băd′ ăks)	108	43°50′N	82°55′W
Bad Bramstedt, Ger. (bät bräm′shtĕt)	159c	53°55′N	9°53′E
Baden, Aus. (bä′dĕn)	168	48°00′N	16°14′E
Baden, Switz.	168	47°28′N	8°17′E
Baden-Baden, Ger. (bä′dĕn-bä′dĕn)	161	48°46′N	8°11′E
Bad Freienwalde, Ger. (bät frī′ĕn-väl′dĕ)	168	52°47′N	14°00′E
Bad Hersfeld, Ger. (bät hĕrsh′fĕlt)	168	50°53′N	9°43′E
Badīn, Pak.	202	24°47′N	69°51′E
Bad Ischl, Aus. (bät ĭsh′′l)	168	47°46′N	13°37′E
Bad Kissingen, Ger. (bät kĭs′ĭng-ĕn)	168	50°12′N	10°05′E
Bad Kreuznach, Ger. (bät kroits′näk)	168	49°52′N	7°53′E
Badlands, reg., N.D., U.S. (băd′ lănds)	112	46°43′N	103°22′W
Badlands, reg., S.D., U.S.	112	43°43′N	102°36′W
Badlands National Park, rec., S.D., U.S.	112	43°56′N	102°37′W
Badlāpur, India	203b	19°12′N	73°12′E
Badogo, Mali	234	11°02′N	8°13′W
Bad Oldesloe, Ger. (bät ôl′dĕs-lōē)	168	53°48′N	10°21′E
Bad Reichenhall, Ger. (bät rī′kĕn-häl)	168	47°43′N	12°53′E
Bad River Indian Reservation, I.R., Wi., U.S. (băd)	113	46°41′N	90°36′W
Bad Segeberg, Ger. (bät sĕ′gĕ-bōōrgh)	159c	53°56′N	10°18′E
Bad Tölz, Ger. (bät tûltz)	168	47°46′N	11°35′E
Badulla, Sri L.	203	6°55′N	81°07′E
Bad Vöslau, Aus.	159e	47°58′N	16°13′E
Badwater Creek, r., Wy., U.S. (băd′wô-tēr)	115	43°13′N	107°55′W
Baena, Spain (bä-ā′nä)	162	37°38′N	4°20′W
Baependi, Braz. (bä-å-pĕn′dĭ)	141a	21°57′S	44°51′W
Baffin Bay, b., N.A. (băf′ĭn)	89	72°00′N	65°00′W
Baffin Bay, b., Tx., U.S.	123	27°11′N	97°35′W
Baffin Island, i., Can.	89	67°20′N	71°00′W
Bāfq, Iran (bäfk)	198	31°48′N	55°23′E
Bafra, Tur. (bäf′rä)	163	41°30′N	35°50′E
Bagabag, Phil. (bä-gä-bäg′)	213a	16°38′N	121°16′E
Bāgalkot, India	203	16°14′N	75°40′E
Bagamoyo, Tan. (bä-gä-mō′yō)	233	6°26′S	38°54′E
Bagaryak, Russia (bȧ-gȧr-yäk′)	186a	56°13′N	61°32′E
Bagbele, D.R.C.	237	4°21′N	29°17′E
Bagdad *see* Baghdād, Iraq	198	33°14′N	44°22′E
Baghdād, Iraq (bȧgh-dȧd′)(băg′dăd)	198	33°14′N	44°22′E
Bagheria, Italy (bä-gå-rē′ä)	174	38°03′N	13°32′E
Bagley, Mn., U.S. (băg′lē)	112	47°31′N	95°24′W
Bagnara, Italy (bän-yä′rä)	174	38°17′N	15°52′E
Bagnell Dam, Mo., U.S. (băg′nĕl)	121	38°13′N	92°40′W
Bagnères-de-Bigorre, Fr. (bän-yâr′dē-bē-gor′)	170	43°04′N	0°09′E
Bagnères-de-Luchon, Fr. (bän-yâr′ dē-lu chôN′)	170	42°46′N	0°36′E
Bagnols-sur-Ceze, Fr. (bä-nyôl′)	170	44°09′N	4°37′E
Bago, Mya.	212	17°17′N	96°29′E
Bagoé, r., Mali (bȧ-gō′å)	230	12°22′N	6°34′W
Baguio, Phil. (bä-gē-ō′)	212	16°24′N	120°36′E
Bagzane, Monts, mtn., Niger	230	18°40′N	8°40′E
Bahamas, nation, N.A. (bȧ-hā′mȧs)	129	26°15′N	76°00′W
Bahau, Malay.	197b	2°48′N	102°25′E
Bahāwalpur, Pak. (bŭ-hä′wŭl-pōōr)	199	29°29′N	71°41′E
Bahia, state, Braz.	143	11°05′S	43°00′W
Bahía, Islas de la, i., Hond. (ē′s-läs-dĕ-lä-bä-ē′ä)	128	16°15′N	86°30′W
Bahía Blanca, Arg. (bä-ē′ä blän′kä)	144	38°45′S	62°07′W
Bahía de Caráquez, Ec. (bä-ē′ä dā kä-rä′kĕz)	142	0°45′S	80°29′W
Bahía Negra, Para. (bä-ē′ä nā′grä)	143	20°11′S	58°05′W
Bahi Swamp, sw., Tan.	237	6°05′S	35°10′E
Bahoruco, Sierra de, mts., Dom. Rep. (sē-ĕ′r-rä-dĕ-bä-ō-rōō′kô)	135	18°10′N	71°25′W
Bahrain, nation, Asia (bä-rān′)	198	26°15′N	51°17′E
Baḥr al Ghazāl, hist. reg., Sudan (bär ĕl ghä-zäl′)	231	7°56′N	27°15′E
Baḥrīyah, oasis, Egypt (bȧ-hȧ-rē′yä)	163	28°34′N	29°01′E
Baía dos Tigres, Ang.	236	16°36′S	11°43′E
Baia Mare, Rom. (bä′yä mä′rä)	163	47°40′N	23°35′E
Baidyabāṭī, India	202a	22°47′N	88°21′E
Baie-Comeau, Can.	100	49°13′N	68°10′W
Baie de Wasai, Mi., U.S. (bā dē wä-sä′ē)	117k	46°27′N	84°15′W
Baie-Saint Paul, Can. (bā′sănt-pôl′)	91	47°27′N	70°30′W
Baigou, China (bī-gō)	206	39°08′N	116°02′E
Baihe, China (bī-hŭ)	208	32°30′N	110°15′E
Bai Hu, l., China (bī-hōō)	206	31°22′N	117°38′E
Baiju, China (bī-jyōō)	206	33°04′N	120°17′E
Baikal, Lake *see* Baykal, Ozero, l., Russia	179	53°00′N	109°28′E
Bailén, Spain (bä-ē-lān′)	172	38°05′N	3°48′W
Băileşti, Rom. (bȧ-ī-lĕsh′tē)	175	44°01′N	23°21′E
Bainbridge, Ga., U.S. (bān′brĭj)	124	30°52′N	84°35′W
Bainbridge Island, i., Wa., U.S.	116a	47°39′N	122°32′W
Baipu, China (bī-pōō)	206	32°15′N	120°47′E
Baiquan, China (bī-chyuän)	208	47°22′N	126°00′E
Baird, Tx., U.S. (bârd)	122	32°22′N	99°28′W
Bairdford, Pa., U.S. (bârd′fōrd)	111e	40°37′N	79°53′W
Baird Mountains, mts., Ak., U.S.	103	67°35′N	160°10′W
Bairnsdale, Austl. (bârnz′dāl)	219	37°50′S	147°39′E
Baïse, r., Fr. (bä-ēz′)	170	43°52′N	0°23′E
Baiyang Dian, l., China (bī-yäŋ-dĭĕn)	206	39°00′N	115°45′E
Baiyu Shan, mts., China (bī-yōō shän)	208	37°02′N	108°30′E
Baja, Hung. (bŏ′yō)	169	46°11′N	18°55′E
Baja California, state, Mex. (bä-hä)	128	30°15′N	117°25′W
Baja California, pen., Mex.	89	28°00′N	113°30′W
Baja California Sur, state, Mex.	128	26°00′N	113°30′W
Bajo, Canal, can., Spain	173a	40°36′N	3°41′W
Bakal, Russia (bä′kȧl)	186a	54°57′N	58°50′E
Baker, Mt., U.S. (bā′kēr)	115	46°21′N	104°12′W
Baker, Or., U.S.	104	44°46′N	117°52′W
Baker, i., Oc.	2	1°00′N	176°00′W
Baker, l., Can.	92	63°51′N	96°10′W
Baker, Mount, mtn., Wa., U.S.	106	48°46′N	121°52′W
Baker Creek, r., Il., U.S.	111a	41°13′N	87°47′W
Bakersfield, Ca., U.S. (bā′kērz-fēld)	104	35°23′N	119°00′W
Bakerstown, Pa., U.S. (bā′kerz-toun)	111e	40°39′N	79°56′W
Bakewell, Eng., U.K. (băk′wĕl)	158a	53°12′N	1°40′W
Bakhchysarai, Ukr.	177	44°46′N	33°54′E
Bakhmach, Ukr. (bȧk-mäch′)	177	51°09′N	32°47′E
Bakhtarān, Iran	198	34°01′N	47°00′E
Bakhtegan, Daryācheh-ye, l., Iran	198	29°29′N	54°31′E
Bakhteyevo, Russia	186b	55°35′N	38°32′E
Bako, Eth. (bä′kō)	231	5°47′N	36°39′E
Bakony, mts., Hung. (bȧ-kōn′y′)	169	46°57′N	17°30′E
Bakoye, r., Afr. (bȧ-kō′ē)	230	12°47′N	9°35′W
Bakr Uzyak, Russia (bȧkr ōōz′yȧk)	186a	52°59′N	58°43′E
Baku (Bakı), Azer. (bȧ-kōō′)	178	40°28′N	49°45′E
Bakwanga *see* Mbuji-Mayi, D.R.C.	236	6°09′S	23°28′E
Balabac Island, i., Phil. (bä′lä-bäk)	212	8°00′N	116°28′E
Balabac Strait, strt., Asia	212	7°23′N	116°30′E
Ba′labakk, Leb.	197a	34°00′N	36°13′E
Balabanovo, Russia (bȧ-lȧ-bä′nô-vô)	186b	56°10′N	37°44′E
Balagansk, Russia (bä-lä-gänsk′)	184	53°58′N	103°09′E
Balaguer, Spain (bä-lä-gĕr′)	173	41°48′N	0°50′E
Balakhta, Russia (bȧ′läk-tȧ′)	179	55°22′N	91°43′E
Balakliia, Ukr.	177	49°28′N	36°51′E
Balakovo, Russia (bȧ′lȧ-kô′vô)	181	52°00′N	47°40′E
Balancán, Mex. (bä-läŋ-kän′)	131	17°47′N	91°32′W
Balanga, Phil. (bä-läŋ′gä)	213a	14°41′N	120°31′E
Ba Lang An, Mui, c., Viet.	209	15°18′N	109°10′E
Balashikha, Russia (bȧ-lä′shĭ-kȧ)	186b	55°48′N	37°58′E
Balashov, Russia (bȧ′lȧ-shôf)	181	51°30′N	43°00′E
Balasore, India (bä-lȧ-sōr′)	199	21°38′N	86°59′E
Balassagyarmat, Hung. (bô′lôsh-shô-dyôr′môt)	169	48°04′N	19°19′E
Balaton Lake, l., Hung. (bô′lô-tôn)	163	46°47′N	17°55′E
Balayan, Phil. (bä-lä-yän′)	213a	13°56′N	120°44′E
Balayan Bay, b., Phil.	213a	13°46′N	120°46′E
Balboa Heights, Pan. (bäl-bô′ä)	133	8°59′N	79°33′W
Balboa Mountain, mtn., Pan.	128a	9°05′N	79°44′W
Balcarce, Arg. (bäl-kär′sä)	144	37°49′S	58°17′W
Balchik, Blg.	175	43°24′N	28°13′E
Bald Eagle, Mn., U.S. (bôld ē′g′l)	117g	45°06′N	93°01′W
Bald Eagle Lake, l., Mn., U.S.	117g	45°08′N	93°03′W
Baldock Lake, l., Can.	97	56°33′N	97°57′W
Baldwin Park, Ca., U.S. (bôld′wĭn)	117a	34°05′N	117°58′W
Baldwinsville, N.Y., U.S. (bôld′wĭns-vĭl)	109	43°10′N	76°20′W
Baldy Mountain, mtn., Can.	97	51°28′N	100°44′W
Baldy Peak, mtn., Az., U.S. (bôl′dē)	106	33°55′N	109°35′W
Baldy Peak, mtn., Tx., U.S. (bôl′dē pēk)	122	30°38′N	104°11′W
Balearic Islands *see* Balears, Illes, is., Spain	156	39°25′N	1°28′E
Balearic Sea, sea, Spain (băl-ē-ăr′ĭk)	173	39°40′N	1°05′E
Balears, Illes, is., Spain	156	39°25′N	1°28′E
Baleine, Grande Rivière de la, r., Can.	93	55°00′N	75°30′W
Baler, Phil. (bä-lar′)	213a	15°46′N	121°33′E
Baler Bay, b., Phil.	213a	15°51′N	121°40′E
Balesin, i., Phil.	213a	14°28′N	122°10′E
Baley, Russia (bȧl-yā′)	185	51°29′N	116°12′E
Balfate, Hond. (bäl-fä′tē)	132	15°48′N	86°24′W
Balfour, S. Afr. (băl′fŏor)	238c	26°41′S	28°37′E
Bali, i., Indon. (bä′lē)	212	8°00′S	115°22′E
Balıkeşir, Tur. (balĭk′ĭysĭr)	181	39°40′N	27°50′E
Balikpapan, Indon. (bä′lēk-pä′pän)	212	1°13′S	116°52′E
Balintang Channel, strt., Phil. (bä-lĭn-täng′)	212	19°50′N	121°08′E
Balkan Mountains *see* Stara Planina, mts., Blg.	156	42°50′N	24°45′E
Balkh, Afg. (bälk)	199	36°48′N	66°50′E
Balkhash, Lake *see* Balqash köli, l., Kaz.	183	45°58′N	72°15′E
Ballancourt, Fr. (bä-läN-kōr′)	171b	48°31′N	2°23′E
Ballarat, Austl. (băl′ȧ-răt)	219	37°37′S	144°00′E
Ballard, l., Austl. (băl′ȧrd)	220	29°15′S	120°45′E
Ballater, Scot., U.K. (băl′ȧ-tēr)	164	57°05′N	3°06′W
Balleny Islands, is., Ant. (băl′ĕ nē)	224	67°00′S	164°00′E
Ballina, Austl. (băl-ĭ-nä′)	222	28°50′S	153°35′E
Ballina, Ire.	164	54°06′N	9°05′W
Ballinasloe, Ire. (băl′ĭ-nȧ-slō′)	164	53°20′N	8°09′W
Ballinger, Tx., U.S. (băl′ĭn-jēr)	122	31°45′N	99°58′W
Ballston Spa, N.Y., U.S. (bôls′tŭn spä′)	109	43°05′N	73°50′W
Balmazújváros, Hung. (bŏl′mŏz-ōō′y′vä′rŏsh)	169	47°35′N	21°23′E
Balobe, D.R.C.	237	0°05′N	28°00′E
Balonne, r., Austl. (băl-ōn′)	221	27°00′S	149°10′E
Bālotra, India	202	25°56′N	72°12′E
Balqash, Kaz.	183	46°58′N	75°00′E
Balqash köli, l., Kaz.	183	45°58′N	72°15′E
Balranald, Austl. (băl′-rȧn-ăld)	222	34°42′S	143°30′E
Balsam, l., Can. (bôl′sȧm)	99	44°30′N	78°50′W
Balsas, Braz. (bäl′säs)	143	7°09′S	46°04′W
Balsas, r., Mex.	128	18°00′N	101°00′W
Balta, Ukr. (bäl′tȧ)	181	47°57′N	29°38′E
Bălţi, Mol.	181	47°47′N	27°57′E
Baltic Sea, sea, Eur. (bôl′tĭk)	156	55°20′N	16°50′E
Baltīm, Egypt (bȧl-tēm′)	238b	31°33′N	31°04′E
Baltimore, Md., U.S. (bôl′tĭ-mŏr)	105	39°20′N	76°38′W
Baltiysk, Russia (bäl-tēysk′)	167	54°40′N	19°55′E
Baluarte, Río del, Mex. (rē′ō-dĕl-bä-lōō′r-tĕ)	130	23°09′N	105°42′W
Baluchistān, hist. reg., Asia (bȧ-lŏŏ-chĭ-stän′)	199	27°30′N	65°30′E
Balzac, Can. (bôl′zăk)	102e	51°10′N	114°01′W
Bama, Nig.	235	11°30′N	13°41′E
Bamako, Mali (bä-mä-kō′)	230	12°39′N	8°00′W
Bambang, Phil. (bäm-bäng′)	213a	16°24′N	121°08′E
Bambari, C.A.R. (bäm-bȧ-rē)	231	5°44′N	20°40′E
Bamberg, Ger. (bäm′bĕrgh)	161	49°53′N	10°52′E
Bamberg, S.C., U.S. (băm′bûrg)	125	33°17′N	81°04′W
Bamenda, Cam.	235	5°56′N	10°10′E
Bamingui, r., C.A.R.	235	7°35′N	19°45′E
Bampton, Eng., U.K. (băm′tŭn)	158b	51°42′N	1°33′W
Bampūr, Iran (bŭm-pōōr′)	198	27°15′N	60°22′E
Bam Yanga, Ngao, mts., Cam.	235	8°20′N	14°40′E
Banahao, Mount, mtn., Phil. (bä-nä-hä′ō)	213a	14°04′N	121°45′E
Banalia, D.R.C.	237	1°33′N	25°20′E
Banamba, Mali	234	13°33′N	7°27′W
Bananal, Braz. (bä-nä-näl′)	141a	22°42′S	44°17′W
Bananal, Ilha do, i., Braz. (ē′lä-dô-bä-nä-näl′)	143	12°09′S	50°27′W
Banās, r., India (băn-äs′)	199	25°20′N	75°20′E
Banās, Ra′s, c., Egypt	231	23°48′N	36°39′E
Banat, reg., Rom. (bä-nät′)	175	45°35′N	21°05′E
Bancroft, Can. (băn′krŏft)	91	45°05′N	77°55′W
Bancroft *see* Chililabombwe, Zam.	237	12°18′S	27°43′E
Bānda, India (bän′dä)	199	25°36′N	80°21′E
Banda, Kepulauan, is., Indon.	213	4°40′S	129°56′E
Banda, Laut (Banda Sea), sea, Indon.	213	6°05′S	127°28′E
Banda Aceh, Indon.	212	5°10′N	95°10′E
Banda Banda, Mount, mtn., Austl. (băn′dȧ băn′dȧ)	222	31°09′S	152°15′E
Bandama Blanc, r., C. Iv. (băn-dä′mä)	234	6°15′N	5°00′W
Bandar Beheshtī, Iran	198	25°18′N	60°45′E
Bandar-e ‘Abbās, Iran (bän-där′ ȧb-bäs′)	198	27°04′N	56°22′E
Bandar-e Būshehr, Iran	198	28°48′N	50°53′E
Bandar-e Lengeh, Iran	198	26°44′N	54°47′E
Bandar-e Torkeman, Iran	198	37°05′N	54°08′E
Bandar Lampung, Indon.	212	5°16′S	105°06′E
Bandar Maharani, Malay. (bän-där′ mä-hä-rä′nē)	197b	2°02′N	102°34′E
Bandar Seri Begawan, Bru.	212	5°00′N	114°59′E
Bande, Spain	172	42°02′N	7°58′W
Bandeira, Pico da, mtn., Braz. (pē′kō dä bän dā′rä)	143	20°27′S	41°47′W
Bandelier National Monument, rec., N.M., U.S. (băn-dĕ-lēr′)	119	35°50′N	106°45′W
Banderas, Bahía de, b., Mex. (bä-ē′ä dĕ bän-dĕ′räs)	130	20°38′N	105°35′W
Bandirma, Tur. (bän-dĭr′mȧ)	163	40°25′N	27°50′E
Bandon, Or., U.S. (băn′dŭn)	114	43°06′N	124°25′W
Bāndra, India	203b	19°04′N	72°49′E
Bandundu, D.R.C.	232	3°18′S	17°20′E
Bandung, Indon.	212	7°00′S	107°22′E
Banes, Cuba (bä′näs)	135	21°00′N	75°45′W
Banff, Can. (bănf)	90	51°10′N	115°34′W
Banff, Scot., U.K.	164	57°39′N	2°37′W
Banff National Park, rec., Can.	92	51°38′N	116°22′W
Bánfield, Arg. (bä′n-fyĕ′ld)	144a	34°44′S	58°24′W
Banfora, Burkina	234	10°38′N	4°46′W
Bangalore, India (băŋ′gȧ′lôr)	199	13°03′N	77°39′E
Bangassou, C.A.R. (bäN-gȧ-sōō′)	231	4°47′N	22°49′E
Bangeta, Mount, mtn., Pap. N. Gui.	213	6°20′S	147°00′E
Banggai, Kepulauan, is., Indon. (bäng-gī′)	213	1°05′S	123°45′E
Banggi, Pulau, i., Malay.	212	7°12′N	117°10′E
Banghāzī, Libya	231	32°07′N	20°04′E
Bangka, i., Indon. (bäŋ′kȧ)	212	2°24′S	106°55′E
Bangkalan, Indon. (bäng-kȧ-län′)	212	6°07′S	112°50′E
Bangkok, Thai.	212	13°50′N	100°29′E
Bangladesh, nation, Asia	199	24°15′N	90°00′E
Bangong Co, l., Asia (bäŋ-gôŋ tswo)	202	33°40′N	79°30′E
Bangor, Wales, U.K. (băŋ′ŏr)	164	53°13′N	4°05′W
Bangor, Me., U.S. (băn′gēr)	105	44°47′N	68°47′W

ng-sing; ŋ-baŋk; N-nasalized n; nŏd; cŏmmit; ōld; ôbey; ôrder; oi-boil; fōōd; ŏ-as oo in foot; ou-out; s-soft; sh-dish; th-thin; pūre; ûnite; ûrn; stŭd; circŭs; ü-as in French tu; ′-indeterminate vowel.

270 Bangor – Bayard PRONOUNCING INDEX

PLACE (Pronunciation)	PAGE	LAT.	LONG.
Bangor, Mi., U.S.	108	42°20'N	86°05'W
Bangor, Pa., U.S.	109	40°55'N	75°10'W
Bangs, Mount, mtn., Az., U.S. (băngs)	119	36°45'N	113°50'W
Bangued, Phil. (bän-gād′)	213a	17°36'N	120°38'E
Bangui, C.A.R. (bäɴ-gē′)	231	4°22'N	18°35'E
Bangweulu, Lake, l., Zam. (băng-wĕ-ōō′lōō)	232	10°55'S	30°10'E
Bangweulu Swamp, sw., Zam.	237	11°25'S	30°10'E
Bani, Dom. Rep. (bä′-nĕ)	135	18°15'N	70°25'W
Bani, Phil. (bä′nē)	213a	16°11'N	119°51'E
Bani, r., Mali	230	13°00'N	5°30'W
Bánica, Dom. Rep. (bä′-nē-kä)	135	19°00'N	71°35'W
Banī Mazār, Egypt	200	28°29'N	30°48'E
Banister, r., Va., U.S. (băn′ĭs-tẽr)	125	36°45'N	79°17'W
Banī Suwayf, Egypt	231	29°05'N	31°06'E
Banja Luka, Bos. (bän-yä-lōō′kȧ)	163	44°45'N	17°11'E
Banjarmasin, Indon. (bän-jĕr-mä′sĕn)	212	3°18'S	114°32'E
Banjin, China (bän-jyĭn)	206	32°23'N	120°14'E
Banjul, Gam.	230	13°28'N	16°39'W
Bankberg, mts., S. Afr. (bäŋk′bûrg)	233c	32°18'S	25°15'E
Banks, Or., U.S. (bănks)	116c	45°37'N	123°07'W
Banks, i., Austl.	221	10°10'S	143°08'E
Banks, Cape, c., Austl.	217b	34°01'S	151°17'E
Banks Island, i., Can.	89	73°00'N	123°00'W
Banks Island, i., Can.	94	53°25'N	130°10'W
Banks Islands, is., Vanuatu	221	13°38'S	168°23'E
Banks Peninsula, pen., N.Z.	223	43°45'S	172°20'E
Banks Strait, strt., Austl.	222	40°45'S	148°00'E
Bankstown, Austl.	217b	33°55'S	151°02'E
Bann, r., N. Ire., U.K. (băn)	164	54°50'N	6°29'W
Banning, Ca., U.S. (băn′ĭng)	117a	33°56'N	116°53'W
Bannockburn, Austl.	217a	38°03'S	144°11'E
Bannu, Pak.	202	33°03'N	70°39'E
Baños, Ec. (bä′-nyŏs)	142	1°30'S	78°22'W
Banská Bystrica, Slvk. (bän′skä bē′strē-tzä)	161	48°46'N	19°10'E
Bansko, Blg. (bän′skō)	175	41°51'N	23°33'E
Banstead, Eng., U.K. (băn′stĕd)	158b	51°18'N	0°09'W
Banton, i., Phil. (bän-tōn′)	213a	12°54'N	121°55'E
Bantry, Ire. (băn′trĭ)	164	51°39'N	9°30'W
Bantry Bay, b., Ire.	164	51°25'N	10°09'W
Banyak, Kepulauan, is., Indon.	212	2°08'N	97°15'E
Banyuwangi, Indon. (bän-jô-wän′gē)	212	8°15'S	114°15'E
Baocheng, China (bou-chŭŋ)	208	33°15'N	106°58'E
Baodi, China (bou-dē)	208	39°44'N	117°19'E
Baoding, China (bou-dĭŋ)	205	38°52'N	115°31'E
Baoji, China (bou-jyē)	208	34°10'N	106°58'E
Baoshan, China (bou-shän)	204	25°14'N	99°03'E
Baoshan, China	206	31°25'N	121°29'E
Baotou, China (bou-tō)	205	40°28'N	110°10'E
Baoying, China (bou-yĭŋ)	208	33°14'N	119°20'E
Bapsfontein, S. Afr. (băps-fŏn-tān′)	233b	26°01'S	28°26'E
Baqueroncito, Col. (bä-kĕ-rŏ′n-sē-tô)	142a	3°18'N	74°40'W
Baraawe, Som.	238a	1°20'N	44°00'E
Barabinsk, Russia (bȧ′rȧ-bĭnsk)	184	55°18'N	78°00'E
Baraboo, Wi., U.S. (bâr′ȧ-bōō)	113	43°29'N	89°44'W
Baracoa, Cuba (bä-rä-kō′ä)	135	20°20'N	74°25'W
Baracoa, Cuba	135a	23°03'N	82°34'W
Baradères, Baie des, b., Haiti (bä-rä-dâr′)	135	18°35'N	73°35'W
Baradero, Arg. (bä-rä-dĕ′ŏ)	141c	33°50'S	59°30'W
Barahona, Dom. Rep. (bä-rä-ô′nä)	135	18°15'N	71°10'W
Barajas de Madrid, Spain (bä-rä′häs dā mä-drēdh′)	173a	40°28'N	3°35'W
Baranagar, India	202	22°38'N	88°25'E
Baranavichy, Bela. (bä′rä-nô-vē′chê)	180	53°08'N	25°59'E
Baranco, Belize (bä-räŋ′kô)	132	16°01'N	88°55'W
Baranof, i., Ak., U.S. (bä-rä′nôf)	103	56°48'N	136°08'W
Baranpauh, Indon.	197b	0°40'N	103°28'E
Barão de Melgaço, Braz. (bä-rouɴ-dĕ-mĕl-gä′sô)	143	16°12'S	55°48'W
Bārāsat, India	202a	22°42'N	88°29'E
Barataria Bay, b., La., U.S.	123	29°13'N	89°50'W
Baraya, Col. (bä-rȧ′yä)	142a	3°10'N	75°04'W
Barbacena, Braz. (bär-bä-sā′nȧ)	143	21°15'S	43°46'W
Barbacoas, Col. (bär-bä-kō′äs)	142	1°39'N	78°12'W
Barbacoas, Ven. (bä-bä-kô′äs)	143b	9°30'N	66°58'W
Barbados, nation, N.A. (bär-bā′dōz)	129	13°30'N	59°00'W
Barbar, Sudan	231	18°11'N	34°00'E
Barbastro, Spain (bär-bäs′trō)	173	42°05'N	0°05'E
Barbeau, Mi., U.S. (bȧr-bō′)	117k	46°17'N	84°16'W
Barberton, S. Afr.	232	25°48'S	31°04'E
Barberton, Oh., U.S. (bär′bẽr-tŭn)	111d	41°01'N	81°37'W
Barbezieux, Fr. (bärb′zyû′)	170	45°30'N	0°11'W
Barbosa, Col. (bär-bô′-sä)	142a	6°26'N	75°19'W
Barboursville, W.V., U.S. (bär′bẽrs-vĭl)	108	38°20'N	82°20'W
Barbourville, Ky., U.S.	124	36°52'N	83°58'W
Barbuda, i., Antig. (bär-bōō′dȧ)	129	17°45'N	61°15'W
Barcaldine, Austl. (bär′kôl-dīn)	219	23°33'S	145°17'E
Barcarrota, Spain (bär-kär-rō′tä)	172	38°31'N	6°50'W
Barcellona, Italy (bä-chĕl-lō′nä)	174	38°07'N	15°15'E
Barcelona, Spain (bär-thå-lō′nä)	154	41°25'N	2°08'E
Barcelona, Ven. (bär-så-lō′nä)	142	10°09'N	64°41'W
Barcelos, Braz. (bär-sĕ′lôs)	142	1°04'S	63°00'W
Barcelos, Port. (bär-thå-lōs)	172	41°34'N	8°39'W
Bardawīl, Sabkhat al, b., Egypt	197a	31°20'N	33°24'E
Bardejov, Czech Rep. (bär′dyĕ-yôf)	169	49°18'N	21°18'E
Bardsey Island, i., Wales, U.K. (bärd′sê)	164	52°45'N	4°50'W
Bardstown, Ky., U.S. (bärds′toun)	108	37°50'N	85°30'W
Bardwell, Ky., U.S. (bärd′wĕl)	124	36°51'N	88°57'W
Bareilly, India	199	28°21'N	79°25'E
Barents Sea, sea, Eur. (bä′rĕnts)	178	72°14'N	37°28'E
Barentu, Erit. (bä-rĕn′tōō)	231	15°06'N	37°39'E
Barfleur, Pointe de, c., Fr. (bȧr-flûr′)	170	49°43'N	1°17'W
Barguzin, Russia (bär′gōō-zĭn)	179	53°44'N	109°28'E
Bar Harbor, Me., U.S. (bär här′bẽr)	100	44°22'N	68°13'W
Bari, Italy (bä′rē)	154	41°08'N	16°53'E
Barinas, Ven. (bä-rē′näs)	142	8°36'N	70°14'W
Baring, Cape, c., Can. (bâr′ĭng)	92	70°07'N	119°48'W
Barisan, Pegunungan, mts., Indon. (bä-rē-sän′)	212	2°38'S	101°45'E
Barito, r., Indon. (bä-rē′tō)	212	2°10'S	114°38'E
Barka, r., Afr.	231	16°44'N	37°34'E
Barkley Sound, strt., Can.	94	48°53'N	125°20'W
Barkly East, S. Afr. (bärk′lē ēst)	233c	30°58'S	27°37'E
Barkly Tableland, plat., Austl. (bär′klê)	220	18°15'S	137°05'E
Barkol, China (bär-kůl)	204	43°43'N	92°50'E
Bârlad, Rom.	163	46°15'N	27°43'E
Bar-le-Duc, Fr. (băr-lē-dük′)	171	48°47'N	5°05'E
Barlee, l., Austl. (bär-lē′)	220	29°45'S	119°00'E
Barletta, Italy (bär-lĕt′tä)	163	41°19'N	16°20'E
Barmstedt, Ger. (bärm′shtĕt)	159c	53°47'N	9°46'E
Barnaul, Russia (bär-nä-ōl′)	178	53°18'N	83°23'E
Barnesboro, Pa., U.S. (bärnz′bẽr-ô)	109	40°45'N	78°50'W
Barnesville, Ga., U.S. (bärnz′vĭl)	124	33°03'N	84°10'W
Barnesville, Mn., U.S.	112	46°38'N	96°25'W
Barnesville, Oh., U.S.	108	39°55'N	81°10'W
Barnet, Vt., U.S. (bär′nĕt)	109	44°20'N	72°00'W
Barnetby le Wold, Eng., U.K. (bär′nĕt-bĭ)	158a	53°34'N	0°26'W
Barnett Harbor, b., Bah.	134	25°40'N	79°20'W
Barnsdall, Ok., U.S. (bärnz′dôl)	121	36°38'N	96°14'W
Barnsley, Eng., U.K. (bärnz′lĭ)	158a	53°33'N	1°29'W
Barnsley, co., Eng., U.K.	158a	53°33'N	1°30'W
Barnstaple, Eng., U.K. (bärn′stā-p'l)	164	51°06'N	4°05'W
Barnwell, S.C., U.S. (bärn′wĕl)	125	33°14'N	81°23'W
Baro, Nig. (bä′rô)	230	8°37'N	6°25'E
Baroda, India (bär-rō′dä)	199	22°21'N	73°12'E
Barotse Plain, pl., Zam.	236	15°50'S	22°55'E
Barqah (Cyrenaica), hist. reg., Libya	231	31°09'N	21°45'E
Barquisimeto, Ven. (bär-kē-sē-mā′tō)	142	10°04'N	69°16'W
Barra, Braz. (bär′rä)	143	11°04'S	43°11'W
Barraba, Austl.	222	30°22'S	150°36'E
Barrackpore, India	202a	22°46'N	88°21'E
Barra do Corda, Braz. (bär′rä dō cōr-dä)	143	5°33'S	45°13'W
Barra Mansa, Braz. (bär′rä män′sä)	141a	22°35'S	44°09'W
Barrancabermeja, Col. (bär-räŋ′kä-bēr-mā′hä)	142	7°06'N	73°49'W
Barranquilla, Col. (bär-rän-kēl′yä)	142	10°57'N	75°00'W
Barras, Braz. (bȧ′r-räs)	143	4°13'S	42°14'W
Barre, Vt., U.S. (băr′ē)	109	44°15'N	72°30'W
Barreiras, Braz. (bär-rā′räs)	143	12°13'S	44°59'W
Barreiro, Port. (bär-rĕ′ê-rô)	162	38°39'N	9°05'W
Barren, r., Ky., U.S.	124	37°00'N	86°20'W
Barren, Cape, c., Austl. (băr′ĕn)	221	40°20'S	149°00'E
Barren, Nosy, is., Madag.	233	18°18'S	43°57'E
Barren River Lake, res., Ky., U.S.	124	36°45'N	86°02'W
Barretos, Braz. (bär-rā′tôs)	143	20°40'S	48°36'W
Barrhead, Can. (băr′hĕd)	90	54°08'N	114°24'W
Barrie, Can. (băr′ĭ)	91	44°25'N	79°45'W
Barrington, Can. (bă-rĕng-tŏn)	102a	45°07'N	73°35'W
Barrington, Il., U.S.	111a	42°09'N	88°08'W
Barrington, R.I., U.S.	110b	41°44'N	71°16'W
Barrington Tops, mtn., Austl.	222	32°00'S	151°25'E
Bar River, Can. (bär)	117k	46°27'N	84°02'W
Barron, Wi., U.S. (băr′ŭn)	113	45°24'N	91°51'W
Barrow, Ak., U.S. (băr′ō)	106a	71°20'N	156°00'W
Barrow, i., Austl.	220	20°50'S	115°00'E
Barrow, r., Ire. (bă-rō)	164	52°35'N	7°05'W
Barrow, Point, c., Ak., U.S.	103	71°20'N	156°00'W
Barrow Creek, Austl.	218	21°23'S	133°55'E
Barrow-in-Furness, Eng., U.K.	160	54°10'N	3°15'W
Barstow, Ca., U.S. (bär′stō)	118	34°53'N	117°03'W
Barstow, Md., U.S.	110e	38°32'N	76°37'W
Barth, Ger. (bärt)	168	54°20'N	12°43'E
Bartholomew Bayou, r., U.S. (bär-thŏl′ō-mū bī-ōō′)	121	33°53'N	91°45'W
Barthurst, Can. (bär-thŭrst′)	91	47°38'N	65°40'W
Bartica, Guy. (bär′tĭ-kȧ)	143	6°23'N	58°32'W
Bartın, Tur. (bär′tĭn)	163	41°35'N	32°12'E
Bartle Frere, Mount, mtn., Austl. (bärt′'l frēr′)	221	17°30'S	145°46'E
Bartlesville, Ok., U.S. (bär′tlz-vĭl)	121	36°44'N	95°58'W
Bartlett, Il., U.S. (bärt′lĕt)	111a	41°59'N	88°11'W
Bartlett, Tx., U.S.	123	30°48'N	97°25'W
Barton, Vt., U.S. (bär′tŭn)	109	44°45'N	72°05'W
Barton-upon-Humber, Eng., U.K. (bär′tŭn-ŭp′ŏn-hŭm′bẽr)	158a	53°41'N	0°26'W
Bartoszyce, Pol. (bär-tô-shĭ′tsȧ)	169	54°15'N	20°50'E
Bartow, Fl., U.S. (bär′tō)	125a	27°51'N	81°50'W
Barvinkove, Ukr.	177	48°55'N	36°59'E
Barwon, r., Austl. (bär′wŭn)	221	30°00'S	147°30'E
Barwon Heads, Austl.	217a	38°17'S	144°29'E
Barycz, r., Pol. (bä′rĭch)	168	51°30'N	16°38'E
Barysaw, Bela.	180	54°16'N	28°33'E
Basankusu, D.R.C. (bä-sän-kōō′sōō)	231	1°14'N	19°45'E
Basbeck, Ger. (bäs′bĕk)	159c	53°40'N	9°11'E
Basdahl, Ger. (bäs′däl)	159c	53°27'N	9°00'E
Basehor, Ks., U.S. (bās′hôr)	117f	39°08'N	94°55'W
Basel, Switz. (bä′z'l)	161	47°32'N	7°35'E
Bashee, r., S. Afr. (bă-shē′)	233c	31°47'S	28°25'E
Bashi Channel, strt., Asia (băsh′ē)	205	21°20'N	120°22'E
Bashkortostan, prov., Russia	180	54°12'N	57°15'E
Bashtanka, Ukr. (bȧsh-tän′kȧ)	177	47°32'N	32°31'E
Basilan Island, i., Phil.	212	6°37'N	122°07'E
Basildon, Eng., U.K.	165	51°35'N	0°25'E
Basilicata, hist. reg., Italy (bä-zē-lê-kä′tä)	174	40°30'N	15°55'E
Basin, Wy., U.S. (bā′sĭn)	115	44°22'N	108°02'W
Basingstoke, Eng., U.K. (bā′zĭng-stōk)	158b	51°14'N	1°06'W
Baška, Cro. (bäsh′ka)	174	44°58'N	14°44'E
Baskale, Tur. (bäsh-kä′lĕ)	181	38°10'N	44°00'E
Baskatong, Réservoir, res., Can.	99	46°50'N	75°50'W
Baskunchak, l., Russia	181	48°20'N	46°40'E
Basoko, D.R.C. (bȧ-sō′kō)	231	0°52'N	23°50'E
Basque Provinces, hist. reg., Spain	172	43°00'N	2°46'W
Basra *see* Al Başrah, Iraq	198	30°35'N	47°59'E
Bassano, Can. (băs-săn′ō)	90	50°47'N	112°28'W
Bassano del Grappa, Italy	174	45°46'N	11°44'E
Bassari, Togo	234	9°15'N	0°47'E
Bassas da India, i., Reu. (bäs′säs dä ēn′dê-ä)	233	21°23'S	39°42'E
Basse Terre, Guad. (bȧs′ târ′)	129	16°00'N	61°43'W
Basseterre, St. K./N.	133b	17°20'N	62°42'W
Basse Terre, i., Guad.	133b	16°10'N	62°14'W
Bassett, Va., U.S. (băs′sĕt)	125	36°45'N	81°58'W
Bass Islands, is., Oh., U.S. (băs)	108	41°40'N	82°50'W
Bass Strait, strt., Austl.	221	39°40'S	145°40'E
Basswood, l., N.A. (băs′wŏd)	113	48°10'N	91°36'W
Båstad, Swe. (bô′stät)	166	56°26'N	12°46'E
Bastia, Fr. (bäs′tē-ä)	161	42°43'N	9°27'E
Bastogne, Bel. (bås-tôn′y′)	165	50°02'N	5°45'E
Bastrop, La., U.S. (băs′trŭp)	123	32°47'N	91°55'W
Bastrop, Tx., U.S.	123	30°08'N	97°18'W
Bastrop Bayou, Tx., U.S.	123a	29°07'N	95°22'W
Bata, Eq. Gui. (bä′tä)	230	1°51'N	9°45'E
Batabano, Golfo de, b., Cuba (gôl-fô-dĕ-bä-tä-bä′nô)	134	22°10'N	83°05'W
Batāla, India	202	31°54'N	75°18'E
Batam, i., Indon. (bä-täm′)	197b	1°03'N	104°00'E
Batang, China (bä-täŋ)	204	30°08'N	99°00'E
Batangas, Phil. (bä-tän′gäs)	212	13°45'N	121°04'E
Batan Islands, is., Phil. (bä-tän′)	212	20°58'N	122°20'E
Bátaszék, Hung. (bä′tá-sĕk)	169	46°07'N	18°40'E
Batavia, Il., U.S. (bȧ-tā′vĭ-ȧ)	111a	41°51'N	88°18'W
Batavia, N.Y., U.S.	109	43°00'N	78°15'W
Batavia, Oh., U.S.	111f	39°05'N	84°10'W
Bataysk, Russia (bȧ-tīsk′)	181	47°08'N	39°44'E
Bătdâmbâng, Camb. (bát-tam-băng′)	212	13°14'N	103°15'E
Batesburg, S.C., U.S. (bāts′bûrg)	125	33°53'N	81°34'W
Batesville, Ar., U.S. (bāts′vĭl)	121	35°46'N	91°39'W
Batesville, In., U.S.	108	39°15'N	85°15'W
Batesville, Ms., U.S.	124	34°17'N	89°55'W
Batetska, Russia (bȧ-tĕ′tskȧ)	176	58°36'N	30°21'E
Bath, Can. (bȧth)	100	46°31'N	67°36'W
Bath, Eng., U.K.	161	51°24'N	2°20'W
Bath, Me., U.S.	100	43°54'N	69°50'W
Bath, N.Y., U.S.	109	42°25'N	77°20'W
Bath, Oh., U.S.	111d	41°11'N	81°38'W
Bathsheba, Barb.	133b	13°13'N	60°30'W
Bathurst, Austl. (băth′ŭrst)	219	33°28'S	149°30'E
Bathurst *see* Banjul, Gam.	230	13°28'N	16°39'W
Bathurst, S. Afr. (bât-hûrst)	233c	33°26'S	26°53'E
Bathurst, i., Austl.	220	11°19'S	130°13'E
Bathurst, Cape, c., Can. (bath′-ûrst)	92	70°33'N	127°55'W
Bathurst Inlet, b., Can.	92	68°10'N	108°00'W
Batia, Benin	234	10°54'N	1°29'E
Batley, Eng., U.K. (băt′lĭ)	158a	53°43'N	1°37'W
Batna, Alg. (bät′nä)	230	35°41'N	6°12'E
Baton Rouge, La., U.S. (băt′ŭn rōōzh′)	105	30°28'N	91°10'W
Batticaloa, Sri L.	203	7°40'N	81°10'E
Battle, r., Can.	96	52°20'N	111°59'W
Battle Creek, Mi., U.S. (băt′'l krēk′)	105	42°20'N	85°15'W
Battle Ground, Wa., U.S. (băt′'l ground)	116c	45°47'N	122°32'W
Battle Harbour, Can. (băt′'l här′bẽr)	91	52°17'N	55°33'W
Battle Mountain, Nv., U.S.	114	40°40'N	116°56'W
Battonya, Hung. (bät-tô′nyä)	169	46°17'N	21°00'E
Batu, Kepulauan, is., Indon. (bä′tōō)	212	0°10'S	98°00'E
Batumi, Geor. (bŭ-tōō′mē)	178	41°40'N	41°30'E
Batu Pahat, Malay.	212	1°51'N	102°56'E
Batupanjang, Indon.	197b	1°42'N	101°35'E
Bauang, Phil. (bä′wäng)	213a	16°31'N	120°19'E
Bauchi, Nig. (bȧ-ōō′chê)	230	10°19'N	9°50'E
Bauld, Cape, c., Can.	93a	51°38'N	55°25'W
Bāuria, India	202a	22°29'N	88°08'E
Bauru, Braz. (bou-rōō′)	143	22°21'S	48°57'W
Bauska, Lat. (bou′skȧ)	167	56°24'N	24°12'E
Bauta, Cuba (bä′ōō-tä)	135a	22°59'N	82°33'W
Bautzen, Ger. (bout′sĕn)	161	51°11'N	14°27'E
Bavaria *see* Bayern, hist. reg., Ger.	168	49°00'N	11°16'E
Baw Baw, Mount, mtn., Austl.	222	37°50'S	146°17'E
Bawean, Pulau, i., Indon. (bȧ′vē-än)	212	5°50'S	112°40'E
Bawtry, Eng., U.K. (bôtrĭ)	158a	53°26'N	1°01'W
Baxley, Ga., U.S. (băks′lĭ)	125	31°47'N	82°22'W
Baxter, Austl.	217a	38°12'S	145°10'E
Baxter Springs, Ks., U.S. (băks′tẽr sprĭngs′)	121	37°01'N	94°44'W
Bay, Laguna de, l., Phil. (lä-gōō′nä dȧ bä′ē)	213a	14°24'N	121°13'E
Bayaguana, Dom. Rep. (bä-yä-gwä′nä)	135	18°45'N	69°40'W
Bay al Kabīr, Wadi, val., Libya	162	29°52'N	14°28'E
Bayambang, Phil. (bä-yäm-bäng′)	213a	15°50'N	120°26'E
Bayamo, Cuba (bä-yä′mō)	134	20°25'N	76°35'W
Bayamón, P.R.	129b	18°27'N	66°13'W
Bayan, China (bä-yän)	208	46°00'N	127°20'E
Bayanaūyl, Kaz.	183	50°43'N	75°37'E
Bayard, Ne., U.S. (bā′ẽrd)	112	41°45'N	103°20'W

PRONOUNCING INDEX   Bayard – Bengamisa   271

PLACE (Pronunciation)	PAGE	LAT.	LONG.
Bayard, N.M., U.S.	119	32°45'N	108°07'W
Bayard, W.V., U.S.	109	39°15'N	79°20'W
Bayburt, Tur. (bä'ĭ-bòrt)	181	40°15'N	40°10'E
Bay City, Mi., U.S. (bā)	105	43°35'N	83°55'W
Bay City, Tx., U.S.	123	28°59'N	95°58'W
Baydaratskaya Guba, b., Russia	180	69°20'N	66°10'E
Bay de Verde, Can.	101	48°05'N	52°54'W
Baydhabo (Baidoa), Som.	238a	3°19'N	44°20'E
Baydrag, r., Mong.	204	46°09'N	98°52'E
Bayern, state, Ger.	159d	48°05'N	11°30'E
Bayern (Bavaria), hist. reg., Ger. (bī'ĕrn) (bȧ-vâ-rĭ-ȧ)	168	49°00'N	11°16'E
Bayeux, Fr. (bȧ-yû')	161	49°19'N	0°41'W
Bayfield, Wi., U.S. (bā'fēld)	113	46°48'N	90°51'W
Baykal, Ozero (Lake Baikal), l., Russia	179	53°00'N	109°28'E
Baykal'skiy Khrebet, mts., Russia	179	53°30'N	107°30'E
Baykit, Russia (bī-kēt')	179	61°43'N	96°39'E
Baymak, Russia (bäy'mäk)	186a	52°35'N	58°21'E
Bay Mills, Mi., U.S. (bā mĭlls)	117k	46°27'N	84°36'W
Bay Mills Indian Reservation, I.R., Mi., U.S.	113	46°19'N	85°03'W
Bay Minette, Al., U.S. (bā'mĭn-ĕt')	124	30°52'N	87°44'W
Bayombong, Phil. (bä-yôm-bŏng')	213a	16°28'N	121°09'E
Bayonne, Fr. (bȧ-yôn')	154	43°28'N	1°30'W
Bayonne, N.J., U.S. (bā-yōn')	110a	40°40'N	74°07'W
Bayou Bodcau Reservoir, res., La., U.S. (bī'yōō bŏd'kō)	107	32°49'N	93°22'W
Bayport, Mn., U.S. (bā'pōrt)	117g	45°02'N	92°46'W
Bayqongyr, Kaz.	183	47°46'N	66°11'E
Bayramiç, Tur.	175	39°48'N	26°35'E
Bayreuth, Ger. (bī-roit')	168	49°56'N	11°35'E
Bay Roberts, Can. (bā rŏb'ĕrts)	101	47°36'N	53°16'W
Bays, Lake of, l., Can. (bās)	99	45°15'N	79°00'W
Bay Saint Louis, Ms., U.S. (bā' sânt lōō'ĭs)	124	30°19'N	89°20'W
Bay Shore, N.Y., U.S. (bā' shôr)	110a	40°44'N	73°15'W
Bayt Lahm, W.B. (bĕth'lē-hĕm)	197a	31°42'N	35°13'E
Baytown, Tx., U.S. (bā'town)	123a	29°44'N	95°01'W
Bayview, Al., U.S. (bā'vū)	110h	33°34'N	86°59'W
Bayview, Wa., U.S.	116a	48°29'N	122°28'W
Bay Village, Oh., U.S. (bā)	111d	41°29'N	81°56'W
Baza, Spain (bä'thä)	162	37°29'N	2°46'W
Baza, Sierra de, mts., Spain	172	37°19'N	2°48'W
Bazar-Dyuzi, mtn., Azer. (bä'zär-dyōōz'ĕ)	181	41°20'N	47°40'E
Bazaruto, Ilha do, i., Moz. (bä-zä-rōō'tō)	232	21°42'S	36°10'E
Bazièɡe, Fr.	170	43°25'N	1°41'E
Be, Nosy, i., Madag.	233	13°14'S	47°28'E
Beach, N.D., U.S. (bēch)	112	46°55'N	104°00'W
Beachy Head, c., Eng., U.K. (bēchē hĕd)	165	50°40'N	0°25'E
Beacon, N.Y., U.S. (bē'kŭn)	109	41°30'N	73°55'W
Beaconsfield, Can. (bē'kŭnz-fēld)	102a	45°26'N	73°51'W
Beals Creek, r., Tx., U.S. (bēls)	122	32°10'N	101°14'W
Bear, r., Ut., U.S.	117b	41°28'N	112°10'W
Bear, r., U.S.	115	42°17'N	111°42'W
Bear Brook, r., Can.	102c	45°24'N	75°15'W
Bear Creek, Mt., U.S. (bâr krēk)	115	45°11'N	109°07'W
Bear Creek, r., Al., U.S. (bâr)	124	34°27'N	88°00'W
Bear Creek, r., Tx., U.S.	117c	32°56'N	97°09'W
Beardstown, Il., U.S. (bērds'toun)	121	40°01'N	90°26'W
Bearfort Mountain, mtn., N.J., U.S. (bē'fŏrt)	110a	41°08'N	74°23'W
Bearhead Mountain, mtn., Wa., U.S. (bâr'hĕd)	116a	47°01'N	121°49'W
Bear Lake, l., Can.	97	55°08'N	96°00'W
Bear Lake, l., Id., U.S.	115	41°56'N	111°10'W
Bear River Range, mts., U.S.	115	41°50'N	111°30'W
Beas de Segura, Spain (bā'äs dā sā-gōō'rä)	172	38°16'N	2°53'W
Beata, i., Dom. Rep. (bĕ-ä'tä)	135	17°40'N	71°40'W
Beata, Cabo, c., Dom. Rep. (kä'bō-bĕ-ä'tä)	135	17°40'N	71°20'W
Beatrice, Ne., U.S. (bē'ȧ-trĭs)	104	40°16'N	96°45'W
Beatty, Nv., U.S. (bēt'ē)	118	36°58'N	116°48'W
Beattyville, Ky., U.S. (bēt'ē-vĭl)	108	37°35'N	83°40'W
Beaucaire, Fr. (bō-kâr')	170	43°49'N	4°37'E
Beaucourt, Fr. (bō-kōōr')	171	47°30'N	6°54'E
Beaufort, N.C., U.S. (bō'frt)	125	34°43'N	76°40'W
Beaufort, S.C., U.S.	125	32°25'N	80°40'W
Beaufort Sea, sea, N.A.	103	70°30'N	138°40'W
Beaufort West, S. Afr.	232	32°20'S	22°45'E
Beauharnois, Can. (bō-är-nwä')	99	45°23'N	73°52'W
Beaumont, Can.	102b	46°50'N	71°01'W
Beaumont, Can.	102g	53°22'N	113°18'W
Beaumont, Ca., U.S. (bō'mŏnt)	117a	33°57'N	116°57'W
Beaumont, Tx., U.S.	105	30°05'N	94°06'W
Beaune, Fr. (bōn)	170	47°02'N	4°49'E
Beauport, Can. (bō-pôr')	102b	46°52'N	71°11'W
Beauséjour, Can.	90	50°04'N	96°33'W
Beauvais, Fr. (bō-vĕ')	170	49°25'N	2°05'E
Beaver, Ok., U.S. (bē'vēr)	120	36°46'N	100°31'W
Beaver, Pa., U.S.	111e	40°42'N	80°18'W
Beaver, Ut., U.S.	119	38°15'N	112°40'W
Beaver, i., Mi., U.S.	108	45°40'N	85°30'W
Beaver, r., Can.	92	54°20'N	111°10'W
Beaver City, Ne., U.S.	120	40°08'N	99°52'W
Beaver Creek, r., Co., U.S.	120	39°42'N	103°37'W
Beaver Creek, r., Ks., U.S.	120	39°44'N	101°05'W
Beaver Creek, r., Mt., U.S.	112	46°45'N	104°18'W
Beaver Creek, r., Wy., U.S.	112	43°46'N	104°25'W
Beaver Dam, Wi., U.S.	113	43°29'N	88°50'W
Beaverhead, r., Mt., U.S.	115	45°25'N	112°35'W
Beaverhead Mountains, mts., Mt., U.S. (bē'vēr-hĕd)	115	44°33'N	112°59'W
Beaver Indian Reservation, I.R., Mi., U.S.	108	45°40'N	85°30'W
Beaverton, Or., U.S. (bē'vēr-tŭn)	116c	45°29'N	122°49'W
Bebington, Eng., U.K. (bē'bĭng-tŭn)	158a	53°20'N	2°59'W
Bečej, Serb. (bĕ'chā)	175	45°36'N	20°03'E
Béchar, Alg.	230	31°39'N	2°14'W
Becharof, l., Ak., U.S. (bĕk-ȧ-rôf)	103	57°58'N	156°58'W
Becher Bay, b., Can. (bēch'ēr)	116a	48°18'N	123°37'W
Beckley, W.V., U.S. (bĕk'lĭ)	108	37°40'N	81°15'W
Bédarieux, Fr. (bā-dȧ-ryû')	170	43°36'N	3°11'E
Beddington Creek, r., Can. (bĕd'ĕng tŭn)	102e	51°14'N	114°13'W
Bedford, Can. (bĕd'fērd)	99	45°10'N	73°00'W
Bedford, S. Afr.	233c	32°43'S	26°19'E
Bedford, Eng., U.K.	161	52°10'N	0°25'W
Bedford, Ia., U.S.	113	40°40'N	94°41'W
Bedford, In., U.S.	108	38°50'N	86°30'W
Bedford, Ma., U.S.	101a	42°30'N	71°17'W
Bedford, N.Y., U.S.	110a	41°12'N	73°38'W
Bedford, Oh., U.S.	111d	41°23'N	81°32'W
Bedford, Pa., U.S.	109	40°05'N	78°20'W
Bedford, Va., U.S.	125	37°19'N	79°27'W
Bedford Hills, N.Y., U.S.	110a	41°14'N	73°41'W
Beebe, Ar., U.S. (bē'bē)	121	35°04'N	91°54'W
Beecher, Il., U.S. (bē'chûr)	111a	41°20'N	87°38'W
Beechey Head, c., Can. (bē'chĭ hĕd)	116a	48°19'N	123°40'W
Beech Grove, In., U.S. (bēch grōv)	111g	39°43'N	86°05'W
Beecroft Head, c., Austl. (bē'krŏft)	222	35°03'S	151°15'E
Beelitz, Ger. (bĕ'lētz)	159b	52°14'N	12°59'E
Be'er Sheva', Isr. (bēr-shē'bȧ)	197a	31°15'N	34°48'E
Be'er Sheva', r., Isr.	197a	31°23'N	34°30'E
Beestekraal, S. Afr.	238c	25°22'S	27°34'E
Beeston, Eng., U.K. (bēs't'n)	158a	52°55'N	1°11'W
Beetz, r., Ger. (bĕtz)	159b	52°28'N	12°37'E
Beeville, Tx., U.S. (bē'vĭl)	123	28°24'N	97°44'W
Bega, Austl. (bā'gȧ)	219	36°50'S	149°49'E
Beggs, Ok., U.S. (bĕgz)	121	35°46'N	96°06'W
Bégles, Fr. (bĕ'gl')	170	44°47'N	0°34'W
Begoro, Ghana	234	6°23'N	0°23'W
Behala, India	202a	22°31'N	88°19'E
Behbehān, Iran	201	30°35'N	50°14'E
Behm Canal, can., Ak., U.S.	94	55°41'N	131°35'W
Bei, r., China (bā)	207a	22°54'N	113°08'E
Bei'an, China (bā-än)	208	48°05'N	126°26'E
Beicai, China (bā-tsī)	207b	31°12'N	121°33'E
Beifei, r., China (bā-fā)	206	33°14'N	117°03'E
Beihai, China (bā-hī)	204	21°30'N	109°10'E
Beihuangcheng Dao, i., China (bā-hûäŋ-chŭŋ dou)	206	38°23'N	120°55'E
Beijing, China	205	39°55'N	116°23'E
Beijing Shi, prov., China (bā-jyĭŋ shr)	208	40°07'N	116°00'E
Beira, Moz. (bā'rȧ)	232	19°45'N	34°58'E
Beira, hist. reg., Port. (bĕ'y-rä)	172	40°38'N	8°00'W
Beirut, Leb. (bā-rōōt')	198	33°53'N	35°30'E
Beja, Port. (bā'zhä)	162	38°03'N	7°53'W
Béja, Tun.	162	36°52'N	9°20'E
Bejaïa (Bougie), Alg.	230	36°46'N	5°00'E
Bejar, Spain	172	40°25'N	5°43'W
Bejestān, Iran	198	34°30'N	58°22'E
Bejucal, Cuba (bā-hōō-käl')	134	22°56'N	82°23'W
Bejuco, Pan. (bĕ-κōō'kō)	133	8°37'N	79°54'W
Békés, Hung. (bā'kāsh)	169	46°45'N	21°08'E
Békéscsaba, Hung. (bā'kāsh-chô'bô)	163	46°39'N	21°06'E
Beketova, Russia (bĕkĕ-to'vȧ)	185	53°23'N	125°21'E
Bela Crkva, Serb. (bĕ'lä tsĕrk'vä)	175	44°53'N	21°25'E
Belalcázar, Spain (bāl-ȧ-kä'thär)	172	38°35'N	5°12'W
Belarus, nation, Eur.	178	53°30'N	25°33'E
Belau *see* Palau, nation, Oc.	3	7°15'N	134°30'E
Bela Vista de Goiás, Braz.	143	16°57'S	48°47'W
Belawan, Indon. (bå-lä'wån)	212	3°43'N	98°43'E
Belaya, r., Russia (byĕ'lī-yȧ)	181	52°30'N	56°15'E
Belcher Islands, is., Can. (bĕl'chēr)	93	56°20'N	80°40'W
Belding, Mi., U.S. (bĕl'dĭng)	108	43°05'N	85°25'W
Belebey, Russia (byĕ'lĕ-bā'ĭ)	180	54°00'N	54°10'E
Belém, Braz. (bā-lĕN')	143	1°18'S	48°27'W
Belén, Para. (bā-lān')	144	23°30'S	57°09'W
Belen, N.M., U.S. (bĕ-lån')	119	34°40'N	106°45'W
Bélep, Îles, is., N. Cal.	221	19°30'S	164°00'E
Belëv, Russia (byĕl'yĕf)	180	53°49'N	36°06'E
Belfair, Wa., U.S. (bĕl'far)	116a	47°27'N	122°50'W
Belfast, N. Ire., U.K.	154	54°36'N	5°45'W
Belfast, Me., U.S. (bĕl'fast)	100	44°25'N	69°01'W
Belfast, Lough, b., N. Ire., U.K. (lŏκ bĕl'fȧst)	164	54°45'N	6°00'W
Belford Roxo, Braz.	144b	22°46'S	43°24'W
Belfort, Fr. (bā-fôr')	161	47°40'N	7°50'E
Belgaum, India	199	15°57'N	74°32'E
Belgium, nation, Eur. (bĕl'jĭ-ŭm)	154	51°00'N	2°52'E
Belgorod, Russia (byĕl'gŭ-rut)	181	50°36'N	36°32'E
Belgorod, prov., Russia	177	50°40'N	36°42'E
Belgrade (Beograd), Serb.	154	44°48'N	20°32'E
Belhaven, N.C., U.S. (bĕl'hā-vĕn)	125	35°33'N	76°37'W
Belington, W.V., U.S. (bĕl'ĭng-tŭn)	109	39°00'N	79°55'W
Belitung, i., Indon.	212	3°30'S	107°30'E
Belize, nation, N.A.	128	17°00'N	88°40'W
Belize, r., Belize	132a	17°16'N	88°56'W
Belize City, Belize (bĕ-lēz')	128	17°31'N	88°10'W
Bel'kovo, Russia (byĕl'kô-vô)	186b	56°15'N	38°49'E
Bel'kovskiy, i., Russia (byĕl-kôf'skĭ)	185	75°45'N	137°00'E
Bell, i., Can. (bĕl)	101	50°45'N	55°35'W
Bell, r., Can.	99	49°25'N	77°15'W
Bella Bella, Can.	94	52°10'N	128°07'W
Bella Coola, Can.	94	52°22'N	126°46'W
Bellaire, Oh., U.S. (bĕl-âr')	108	40°00'N	80°45'W
Bellaire, Tx., U.S.	123a	29°43'N	95°28'W
Bellary, India (bĕl-lä'rē)	199	15°15'N	76°56'E
Bella Union, Ur. (bĕ'l-yȧ-ōō-nyô'n)	144	30°18'S	57°26'W
Bella Vista, Arg. (bā'lyȧ vēs'tȧ)	144	27°07'S	65°14'W
Bella Vista, Arg.	144	28°35'S	58°53'W
Bella Vista, Arg.	144a	34°35'S	58°41'W
Bella Vista, Para.	143	22°16'S	56°14'W
Belle-Anse, Haiti	135	18°15'N	72°00'W
Belle Bay, b., Can. (bĕl)	101	47°35'N	55°15'W
Belle Chasse, La., U.S. (bĕl shäs')	110d	29°52'N	90°00'W
Bellefontaine, Oh., U.S. (bel-fōn'tān)	108	40°25'N	83°50'W
Bellefontaine Neighbors, Mo., U.S.	117e	38°46'N	90°13'W
Belle Fourche, S.D., U.S. (bĕl' fōōrsh')	112	44°28'N	103°50'W
Belle Fourche, r., Wy., U.S.	112	44°29'N	104°40'W
Belle Fourche Reservoir, res., S.D., U.S.	112	44°51'N	103°44'W
Bellegarde, Fr. (bĕl-gärd')	171	46°06'N	5°50'E
Belle Glade, Fl., U.S. (bĕl glād)	125a	26°39'N	80°37'W
Belle-Île, i., Fr. (bĕlēl')	161	47°15'N	3°30'W
Belle Isle, Strait of, strt., Can.	93	51°35'N	56°30'W
Belle Mead, N.J., U.S. (bĕl mēd)	110a	40°28'N	74°40'W
Belleoram, Can.	101	47°31'N	55°25'W
Belle Plaine, Ia., U.S. (bĕl plān')	113	41°52'N	92°19'W
Belle Vernon, Pa., U.S. (bĕl vûr'nŭn)	111e	40°08'N	79°52'W
Belleville, Can. (bĕl'vĭl)	99	44°15'N	77°25'W
Belleville, Il., U.S.	117e	38°31'N	89°59'W
Belleville, Ks., U.S.	121	39°49'N	97°37'W
Belleville, Mi., U.S.	111b	42°12'N	83°29'W
Belleville, N.J., U.S.	110a	40°47'N	74°09'W
Bellevue, Ia., U.S. (bĕl'vū)	113	42°14'N	90°26'W
Bellevue, Ky., U.S.	111f	39°06'N	84°29'W
Bellevue, Mi., U.S.	108	42°30'N	85°00'W
Bellevue, Oh., U.S.	108	41°15'N	82°45'W
Bellevue, Pa., U.S.	111e	40°30'N	80°04'W
Bellevue, Wa., U.S.	116a	47°37'N	122°12'W
Belley, Fr. (bĕ-lē')	171	45°46'N	5°41'E
Bellflower, Ca., U.S. (bĕl-flou'ēr)	117a	33°53'N	118°08'W
Bell Gardens, Ca., U.S.	117a	33°59'N	118°11'W
Bellingham, Ma., U.S. (bĕl'ĭng-hăm)	101a	42°05'N	71°28'W
Bellingham, Wa., U.S.	104	48°46'N	122°29'W
Bellingham Bay, b., Wa., U.S.	116d	48°44'N	122°34'W
Bellingshausen Sea, sea, Ant. (bĕl'ĭngz houz'n)	224	72°00'S	80°30'W
Bellinzona, Switz. (bĕl-ĭn-tsō'nä)	168	46°10'N	9°09'E
Bellmore, N.Y., U.S. (bĕl-mōr)	110a	40°40'N	73°31'W
Bello, Col. (bĕ'l-yô)	142	6°20'N	75°33'W
Bellow Falls, Vt., U.S. (bĕl'ōz fôls)	109	43°10'N	72°30'W
Bellpat, Pak.	202	29°08'N	68°00'E
Bell Peninsula, pen., Can.	93	63°50'N	81°16'W
Bells Corners, Can.	102c	45°20'N	75°49'W
Bells Mountain, mtn., Wa., U.S. (bĕls)	116c	45°50'N	122°21'W
Belluno, Italy (bĕl-lōō'nō)	174	46°08'N	12°14'E
Bell Ville, Arg. (bĕl vēl')	144	32°33'S	62°36'W
Bellville, S. Afr.	232a	33°54'S	18°38'E
Bellville, Tx., U.S. (bĕl'vĭl)	123	29°57'N	96°15'W
Bélmez, Spain (bĕl'mĕth)	172	38°17'N	5°17'W
Belmond, Ia., U.S. (bĕl'mŏnd)	113	42°49'N	93°37'W
Belmont, Ca., U.S.	116b	37°34'N	122°18'W
Belmonte, Braz. (bĕl-mōn'tȧ)	143	15°58'S	38°47'W
Belmopan, Belize	128	17°15'N	88°47'W
Belogorsk, Russia	179	51°09'N	128°32'E
Belo Horizonte, Braz. (bĕ'lôre-sô'n-tĕ)	143	19°54'S	43°56'W
Beloit, Ks., U.S. (bē-loit')	120	39°26'N	98°06'W
Beloit, Wi., U.S.	105	42°31'N	89°04'W
Belomorsk, Russia (byĕl-ô-môrsk')	180	64°30'N	34°42'E
Beloretsk, Russia (byĕ'lō-rĕtsk)	180	53°58'N	58°25'E
Belosarayskaya, Kosa, c., Ukr.	177	46°43'N	37°18'E
Belovo, Russia (byĕ'lŭ-vû)	184	54°25'N	86°18'E
Beloye, l., Russia	180	60°10'N	38°05'E
Belozersk, Russia (byĕ-lŭ-zyôrsk')	180	60°00'N	38°00'E
Belper, Eng., U.K. (bĕl'pēr)	158a	53°01'N	1°28'W
Belt, Mt., U.S. (bĕlt)	115	47°11'N	110°58'W
Belt Creek, r., Mt., U.S.	115	47°19'N	110°58'W
Belton, Tx., U.S. (bĕl'tŭn)	123	31°04'N	97°27'W
Belton Lake, l., Tx., U.S.	123	31°15'N	97°35'W
Beltsville, Md., U.S. (belts-vĭl)	110e	39°03'N	76°56'W
Belukha, Mount, mtn., Asia	178	49°47'N	86°23'E
Belvidere, Il., U.S. (bĕl-vē-dēr')	113	42°14'N	88°52'W
Belvidere, N.J., U.S.	109	40°50'N	75°05'W
Belyando, r., Austl. (bĕl-yän'dō)	221	22°09'S	146°48'E
Belyanka, Russia (byĕl'yán-kȧ)	186a	56°04'N	59°16'E
Belyy, Russia (byĕ'lē)	180	55°52'N	32°58'E
Belyy, i., Russia	178	73°19'N	72°00'E
Belyye Stolby, Russia (byĕ'lĭ-ye stôl'bĭ)	186b	55°20'N	37°52'E
Belzig, Ger. (bĕl'tsēg)	159b	52°08'N	12°35'E
Belzoni, Ms., U.S. (bĕl-zō'nē)	124	33°09'N	90°30'W
Bembe, Ang. (bĕn'bĕ)	232	7°00'S	14°20'E
Bembézar, r., Spain (bĕm-bā-thär')	172	38°00'N	5°18'W
Bemidji, Mn., U.S. (bē-mĭj'ĭ)	113	47°28'N	94°54'W
Bena Dibele, D.R.C. (bĕn'ȧ dē-bĕ'lĕ)	232	4°00'S	22°49'E
Benalla, Austl. (bĕn-ăl'ȧ)	219	36°30'S	146°00'E
Benares *see* Vārānasi, India	199	25°25'N	83°00'E
Benavente, Spain (bā-nä-vĕn'tä)	162	42°01'N	5°43'W
Benbrook, Tx., U.S. (bĕn'brōōk)	117c	32°41'N	97°27'W
Benbrook Reservoir, res., Tx., U.S.	117c	32°35'N	97°30'W
Bend, Or., U.S. (bĕnd)	104	44°04'N	121°17'W
Bendeleben, Mount, mtn., Ak., U.S. (bĕn-dĕl-bĕn)	103	65°18'N	163°45'W
Bender Beyla, Som.	238a	9°40'N	50°45'E
Bendigo, Austl. (bĕn'dĭ-gō)	219	36°39'S	144°20'E
Benedict, Md., U.S. (bĕnĕ'dĭct)	110e	38°31'N	76°41'W
Benešov, Czech Rep. (bĕn'ĕ-shôf)	168	49°48'N	14°40'E
Benevento, Italy (bā-nā-vĕn'tō)	162	41°08'N	14°46'E
Bengal, Bay of, b., Asia (bĕn-gôl')	196	17°30'N	87°00'E
Bengamisa, D.R.C.	237	0°57'N	25°10'E

ng-sing; ŋ-baŋk; N-nasalized n; nŏd; cŏmmit; ōld; ôbey; ôrder; oi-boil; fōōd; ò-as oo in foot; ou-out; s-soft; sh-dish; th-thin; pūre; ûnite; ûrn; stŭd; circŭs; ü-as in French tu; '-indeterminate vowel.

272 Bengbu – Bijou Creek PRONOUNCING INDEX

PLACE (Pronunciation)	PAGE	LAT.	LONG.
Bengbu, China (bŭŋ-bo͞o)	205	32°52'N	117°22'E
Benghazi *see* Banghāzī, Libya	230	32°07'N	20°04'E
Bengkalis, Indon. (bĕng-kä'lĭs)	212	1°29'N	102°06'E
Bengkulu, Indon.	212	3°46'S	102°18'E
Benguela, Ang. (bĕn-gĕl'á)	232	12°35'S	13°25'E
Beni, r., Bol. (bā'nē)	142	13°41'S	67°30'W
Béni-Abbas, Alg. (bā'nē ä-bĕs')	230	30°11'N	2°13'W
Benicia, Ca., U.S. (bē-nĭsh'ĭ-á)	116b	38°03'N	122°09'W
Benin, nation, Afr.	230	8°00'N	2°00'E
Benin, r., Nig. (bĕn-ēn')	235	5°55'N	5°15'E
Benin, Bight of, b., Afr.	230	5°30'N	3°00'E
Benin City, Nig.	230	6°19'N	5°41'E
Beni Saf, Alg. (bā'nē säf')	230	35°23'N	1°20'W
Benito, r., Eq. Gui.	236	1°35'N	10°45'E
Benkelman, Ne., U.S. (bĕn-kĕl-mán)	120	40°05'N	101°35'W
Benkovac, Cro. (bĕn'kō-váts)	174	44°02'N	15°41'E
Bennettsville, S.C., U.S. (bĕn'ĕts vĭl)	125	34°35'N	79°41'W
Bennington, Vt., U.S. (bĕn'ĭng-tŭn)	109	42°55'N	73°15'W
Benns Church, Va., U.S. (bĕnz' chûrch')	110g	36°47'N	76°35'W
Benoni, S. Afr. (bĕ-nō'nī)	232	26°11'S	28°19'E
Benoy, Chad	235	8°59'N	16°19'E
Benque Viejo, Belize (bĕn-kĕ bīĕ'hō)	132a	17°07'N	89°07'W
Bensberg, Ger.	171c	50°58'N	7°09'E
Bensenville, Il., U.S. (bĕn'sĕn-vĭl)	111a	41°57'N	87°56'W
Bensheim, Ger. (bĕns-hīm)	168	49°42'N	8°38'E
Benson, Az., U.S. (bĕn-sŭn)	119	32°00'N	110°20'W
Benson, Mn., U.S.	112	45°18'N	95°36'W
Bentiaba, Ang.	236	14°15'S	12°21'E
Bentleyville, Pa., U.S. (bent'lē vĭl)	111e	40°07'N	80°01'W
Benton, Can.	100	45°59'N	67°36'W
Benton, Ar., U.S. (bĕn'tŭn)	121	34°34'N	92°34'W
Benton, Ca., U.S.	118	37°44'N	118°22'W
Benton, Il., U.S.	108	38°00'N	88°55'W
Benton Harbor, Mi., U.S. (bĕn'tŭn här'bēr)	108	42°05'N	86°30'W
Bentonville, Ar., U.S. (bĕn'tŭn-vĭl)	121	36°22'N	94°11'W
Benue, r., Afr. (bā'no͞o-å)	230	0°00'N	8°00'E
Benut, r., Malay.	197b	1°43'N	103°20'E
Benwood, W.V., U.S. (bĕn-wo͝od)	108	39°55'N	80°45'W
Benxi, China (bŭn-shyē)	208	41°25'N	123°50'E
Beograd *see* Belgrade, Serb.	154	44°48'N	20°32'E
Beppu, Japan (bĕ'po͞o)	211	33°16'N	131°30'E
Bequia Island, i., St. Vin. (bĕk-ē'ä)	133b	13°00'N	61°08'W
Berakit, Tanjung, c., Indon.	197b	1°16'N	104°44'E
Berat, Alb. (bĕ-rät')	175	40°43'N	19°59'E
Berau, Teluk, b., Indon.	213	2°22'S	131°40'E
Berazategui, Arg. (bĕ-rä-zá'tĕ-gē)	144a	34°46'S	58°14'W
Berbera, Som. (bûr'bûr-á)	238a	10°25'N	45°05'E
Berbérati, C.A.R.	235	4°16'N	15°47'E
Berck, Fr. (bĕrk)	170	50°26'N	1°36'E
Berdians'k, Ukr.	181	46°45'N	36°47'E
Berdians'ka kosa, c., Ukr.	177	46°38'N	36°42'E
Berdyaush, Russia (bĕr'dyáûsh)	186a	55°10'N	59°12'E
Berdychiv, Ukr.	178	49°53'N	28°32'E
Berea, Ky., U.S. (bē-rē'á)	124	37°30'N	84°19'W
Berea, Oh., U.S.	111d	41°22'N	81°51'W
Berehove, Ukr.	169	48°13'N	22°40'E
Bereku, Tan.	237	4°27'S	35°44'E
Berens, r., Can. (bĕr'ĕnz)	97	52°15'N	96°30'W
Berens Island, i., Can.	97	52°18'N	97°40'W
Berens River, Can.	90	52°22'N	97°02'W
Beresford, S.D., U.S. (bĕr'ĕs-fērd)	112	43°05'N	96°46'W
Berettyóújfalu, Hung. (bĕ'rĕt-tyō-o͞o'y'fô-lo͞o)	169	47°14'N	21°33'E
Berezhany, Ukr. (bĕr-yĕ'zhá-nĕ)	169	49°25'N	24°58'E
Berezivka, Ukr.	177	47°12'N	30°56'E
Berezna, Ukr. (bĕr-yôz'ná)	177	51°32'N	31°47'E
Bereznehuvate, Ukr.	177	47°19'N	32°58'E
Berezniki, Russia (bĕr-yôz'nyē-kē)	180	59°25'N	56°46'E
Berëzovka, Russia	186a	57°35'N	57°19'E
Berëzovo, Russia (bĭr-yô'zē-vû)	178	64°10'N	65°10'E
Berëzovskiy, Russia (bĕr-yô'zôf-skĭ)	186a	56°54'N	60°47'E
Berga, Spain (bĕr'gä)	173	42°05'N	1°52'E
Bergama, Tur. (bĕr'gä-mä)	198	39°08'N	27°09'E
Bergamo, Italy (bĕr'gä-mō)	162	45°43'N	9°41'E
Bergantin, Ven. (bĕr-gän-tē'n)	143b	10°04'N	64°23'W
Bergara, Spain	172	43°08'N	2°23'W
Bergedorf, Ger. (bĕr'gē-dôrf)	159c	53°29'N	10°12'E
Bergen, Ger. (bĕr'gĕn)	168	54°26'N	13°26'E
Bergen, Nor.	154	60°24'N	5°20'E
Bergenfield, N.J., U.S.	110a	40°55'N	73°59'W
Bergen op Zoom, Neth.	165	51°29'N	4°16'E
Bergerac, Fr. (bĕr-zhē-rák')	161	44°49'N	0°28'E
Bergisch Gladbach, Ger. (bĕrg'ĭsh-glät'bäk)	171c	50°59'N	7°08'E
Berglern, Ger. (bĕrgh'lĕrn)	159d	48°24'N	11°55'E
Bergneustadt, Ger.	171c	51°01'N	7°39'E
Bergville, S. Afr. (bĕrg'vĭl)	233c	28°46'S	29°22'E
Berhampur, India	199	19°19'N	84°48'E
Bering Sea, sea (bē'rĭng)	240	58°00'N	175°00'W
Bering Strait, strt.	106a	64°50'N	169°50'W
Berja, Spain (bĕr'hä)	172	36°50'N	2°56'W
Berkeley, Ca., U.S. (bûrk'lĭ)	104	37°52'N	122°17'W
Berkeley, Mo., U.S.	117e	38°45'N	90°20'W
Berkeley Springs, W.V., U.S. (bûrk'lĭ springz)	109	39°40'N	78°10'W
Berkhamsted, Eng., U.K. (bĕrk'hăm'stĕd)	158b	51°44'N	0°34'W
Berkley, Mi., U.S. (bûrk'lĭ)	111b	42°30'N	83°10'W
Berkovitsa, Blg. (bĕ-kō'vē-tsá)	175	43°14'N	23°08'E
Berkshire, hist. reg., Eng., U.K.	158b	51°23'N	1°07'W
Berland, r., Can.	95	54°00'N	117°10'W
Berlenga, is., Port. (bĕr-lĕn'gäzh)	172	39°25'N	9°33'W
Berlin, Ger. (bĕr-lēn')	154	52°31'N	13°28'E

PLACE (Pronunciation)	PAGE	LAT.	LONG.
Berlin, S. Afr. (bĕr-lĭn)	233c	32°53'S	27°36'E
Berlin, N.H., U.S. (bûr-lĭn)	109	44°25'N	71°10'W
Berlin, N.J., U.S.	110f	39°47'N	74°56'W
Berlin, Wi., U.S. (bûr-lĭn')	113	43°58'N	88°58'W
Bermejo, r., S.A. (bĕr-mā'hō)	144	25°05'S	61°00'W
Bermeo, Spain (bĕr-mā'yō)	172	43°23'N	2°43'W
Bermuda, dep., N.A.	129	32°20'N	65°45'W
Bern, Switz. (bĕrn)	154	46°55'N	7°25'E
Bernal, Arg. (bĕr-näl')	144a	34°43'S	58°17'W
Bernalillo, N.M., U.S. (bĕr-nä-lē'yō)	119	35°20'N	106°30'W
Bernard, l., Can. (bēr-närd')	109	45°45'N	79°25'W
Bernardsville, N.J., U.S. (bûr nărds'vĭl)	110a	40°43'N	74°34'W
Bernau, Ger. (bĕr'nou)	168	52°40'N	13°35'E
Bernburg, Ger. (bĕrn'bo͝orgh)	168	51°48'N	11°43'E
Berndorf, Aus. (bĕrn'dôrf)	168	47°57'N	16°05'E
Berne, In., U.S. (bûrn)	108	40°40'N	84°55'W
Berner Alpen, mts., Switz.	168	46°29'N	7°30'E
Bernier, i., Austl. (bĕr-nēr')	220	24°58'S	113°15'E
Bernina, Pizzo, mtn., Eur.	168	46°23'N	9°58'E
Bero, r., Ang.	236	15°10'S	12°20'E
Beroun, Czech Rep. (bā'rōn)	168	49°57'N	14°03'E
Berounka, r., Czech Rep. (bĕ-rōn'ká)	168	49°53'N	13°40'E
Berowra, Austl.	217b	33°36'S	151°10'E
Berre, Étang de, l., Fr. (ā-tôn' dē bâr')	170a	43°27'N	5°07'E
Berre-l'Étang, Fr. (bâr'lā-tôn')	170a	43°28'N	5°11'E
Berriozabal, Mex. (bā'rēō-zä-bäl')	131	16°47'N	93°16'W
Berriyyane, Alg.	162	32°50'N	3°49'E
Berry Creek, r., Can.	96	51°15'N	111°40'W
Berryessa, r., Ca., U.S. (bĕ'rĭ ĕs'á)	118	38°35'N	122°33'W
Berry Islands, is., Bah.	134	25°40'N	77°50'W
Berryville, Ar., U.S. (bĕr'ē-vĭl)	121	36°21'N	93°34'W
Bershad', Ukr. (byĕr'shät)	177	48°22'N	29°31'E
Berthier, Can.	102b	46°56'N	70°44'W
Bertrand, r., Wa., U.S. (bûr'trănd)	116d	48°58'N	122°31'W
Berwick, Pa., U.S. (bûr'wĭk)	109	41°05'N	76°10'W
Berwick-upon-Tweed, Eng., U.K. (bĕr'ĭk)	160	55°45'N	2°01'W
Berwyn, Il., U.S. (bûr'wĭn)	111a	41°49'N	87°47'W
Beryslav, Ukr.	177	46°49'N	33°24'E
Besalampy, Madag. (bĕz-á-lám-pē')	233	16°48'S	44°40'E
Besançon, Fr. (bĕ-säN-sôn)	161	47°14'N	6°02'E
Besar, Gunong, mtn., Malay.	197b	2°31'N	103°09'E
Besed', r., Eur. (byĕ'syĕt)	176	52°58'N	31°36'E
Beskid Mountains, mts., Eur.	169	49°23'N	19°00'E
Beskra, Alg.	230	34°52'N	5°39'E
Beslan, Russia	182	43°12'N	44°33'E
Bessarabia, hist. reg., Mol.	177	47°00'N	28°30'E
Bességes, Fr. (bĕ-sĕzh')	170	44°20'N	4°07'E
Bessemer, Al., U.S. (bĕs'ē-mēr)	110h	33°24'N	86°58'W
Bessemer, Mi., U.S.	113	46°29'N	90°04'W
Bessemer City, N.C., U.S.	125	35°16'N	81°17'W
Bestensee, Ger. (bĕs'tĕn-zā)	159b	52°15'N	13°39'E
Betanzos, Spain (bĕ-tän'thōs)	172	43°18'N	8°14'W
Betatakin Ruin, Az., U.S. (bĕt-á-tăk'ĭn)	119	36°40'N	110°29'W
Bethal, S. Afr. (bĕth'ăl)	238c	26°27'S	29°28'E
Bethalto, Il., U.S. (bá-thăl'tō)	117e	38°54'N	90°03'W
Bethanien, Nmb.	232	26°20'S	16°10'E
Bethany, Mo., U.S.	121	40°15'N	94°04'W
Bethel, Ak., U.S. (bĕth'ĕl)	106a	60°50'N	161°50'W
Bethel, Ct., U.S.	110a	41°22'N	73°24'W
Bethel, Vt., U.S.	109	43°50'N	72°40'W
Bethel Park, Pa., U.S.	111e	40°19'N	80°02'W
Bethesda, Md., U.S. (bĕ-thĕs'dá)	110e	39°00'N	77°10'W
Bethlehem, S. Afr.	232	28°14'S	28°18'E
Bethlehem, Pa., U.S. (bĕth'lē-hĕm)	109	40°40'N	75°25'W
Bethlehem *see* Bayt Lahm, W.B.	197a	31°42'N	35°13'E
Béthune, Fr. (bā-tün')	170	50°32'N	2°37'E
Betroka, Madag. (bĕ-trōk'á)	233	23°13'S	46°17'E
Bet She'an, Isr.	197a	32°30'N	35°30'E
Betsiamites, Can.	91	48°57'N	68°36'W
Betsiamites, r., Can.	100	49°11'N	69°20'W
Betsiboka, r., Madag. (bĕt-sĭ-bō'ká)	233	16°47'S	46°45'E
Bettles Field, Ak., U.S. (bĕt'tŭls)	103	66°58'N	151°48'W
Betwa, r., India (bĕt'wá)	199	25°00'N	78°00'E
Betz, Fr. (bĕ)	171b	49°09'N	2°58'E
Beveren, Bel.	159a	51°13'N	4°14'E
B. Everett Jordan Lake, res., N.C., U.S.	125	35°45'N	79°00'W
Beverly, Ma., U.S.	101a	42°34'N	70°53'W
Beverly, N.J., U.S.	110f	40°03'N	74°56'W
Beverly Hills, Ca., U.S.	117a	34°05'N	118°24'W
Bevier, Mo., U.S. (bē-vēr')	121	39°44'N	92°36'W
Bewdley, Eng., U.K. (būd'lĭ)	158a	52°22'N	2°19'W
Bexhill, Eng., U.K. (bĕks'hĭl)	165	50°49'N	0°25'E
Bexley, Eng., U.K. (bĕks'ly)	158b	51°26'N	0°09'E
Beyla, Gui. (bā'lá)	230	8°41'N	8°37'W
Beylul, Erit.	231	13°15'N	42°21'E
Beypazari, Tur. (bā-pá-zä'rĭ)	163	40°10'N	31°40'E
Beyşehir, Tur.	181	38°00'N	31°45'E
Beysugskiy, Liman, b., Russia (lĭ-män' bĕy-so͞og'skĭ)	177	46°07'N	38°35'E
Bezhetsk, Russia (byĕ-zhĕtsk')	180	57°46'N	36°40'E
Bezhitsa, Russia (byĕ-zhĭ'tsá)	180	53°19'N	34°18'E
Béziers, Fr. (bā-zyā')	161	43°21'N	3°12'E
Bhadreswar, India	202a	22°49'N	88°22'E
Bhāgalpur, India (bä'gŭl-po͝or)	199	25°15'N	86°59'E
Bhamo, Mya. (bŭ-mō')	199	24°00'N	96°15'E
Bhāngar, India	202a	22°30'N	88°36'E
Bharatpur, India (bērt'po͝or)	199	27°21'N	77°33'E
Bhatinda, India (bŭ-tĭn-dá)	199	30°19'N	74°56'E
Bhātpāra, India	199	22°52'N	88°24'E

PLACE (Pronunciation)	PAGE	LAT.	LONG.
Bhaunagar, India (bäv-nŭg'ŭr)	199	21°45'N	72°58'E
Bhayandar, India	203b	19°20'N	72°50'E
Bhilai, India	202	21°14'N	81°23'E
Bhīma, r., India (bē'má)	199	18°00'N	74°45'E
Bhiwandi, India	203b	19°18'N	73°03'E
Bhiwāni, India	202	28°53'N	76°08'E
Bhopāl, India (bō-päl)	199	23°20'N	77°25'E
Bhubaneswar, India (bo͝o-bû-năsh'vûr)	199	20°21'N	85°53'E
Bhuj, India (bo͞oj)	199	23°22'N	69°39'E
Bhutan, nation, Asia (bo͞o-tän')	199	27°15'N	90°30'E
Biafra, Bight of, b., Afr.	230	4°05'N	7°10'E
Biak, i., Indon. (bē'ăk)	213	1°00'S	136°00'E
Biała Podlaska, Pol. (byä'wä pōd-läs'kä)	169	52°01'N	23°08'E
Białograd, Pol.	168	54°00'N	16°01'E
Bialystok, Pol. (byä-wĭs'tōk)	154	53°08'N	23°12'E
Biankouma, C. Iv.	234	7°44'N	7°37'W
Biarritz, Fr. (byä-rēts')	161	43°27'N	1°39'W
Bibb City, Ga., U.S. (bĭb' sĭ'tē)	124	32°31'N	84°56'W
Biberach, Ger. (bē'bĕräk)	168	48°06'N	9°49'E
Bibiani, Ghana	234	6°28'N	2°20'W
Bic, Can. (bĭk)	100	48°22'N	68°42'W
Bicknell, In., U.S. (bĭk'nĕl)	108	38°45'N	87°20'W
Bicske, Hung. (bĭsh'kē)	169	47°29'N	18°38'E
Bida, Nig. (bē'dä)	230	9°05'N	6°01'E
Biddeford, Me., U.S. (bĭd'ē-fērd)	100	43°29'N	70°29'W
Biddulph, Eng., U.K. (bĭd'ŭlf)	158a	53°07'N	2°10'W
Biebrza, r., Pol. (byĕb'zhá)	169	53°18'N	22°25'E
Biel, Switz. (bēl)	168	47°09'N	7°12'E
Bielefeld, Ger. (bē'lē-fĕlt)	161	52°01'N	8°35'E
Biella, Italy (byĕl'lä)	174	45°34'N	8°05'E
Bielsk Podlaski, Pol. (byĕlsk pŭd-lä'skĭ)	161	52°47'N	23°14'E
Bien Hoa, Viet.	212	10°59'N	106°49'E
Bienville, Lac, l., Can.	93	55°32'N	72°45'W
Biesenthal, Ger. (bē'sĕn-täl)	159b	52°46'N	13°38'E
Biferno, r., Italy (bē-fĕr'nō)	174	41°49'N	14°46'E
Bifoum, Gabon	236	0°22'S	10°23'E
Biga, Tur. (bē'ghá)	175	40°13'N	27°14'E
Big Bay de Noc, Mi., U.S. (bĭg bā dē nok')	113	45°48'N	86°41'W
Big Bayou, Ar., U.S. (bĭg'bī'yo͞o)	121	33°04'N	91°28'W
Big Bear City, Ca., U.S. (bĭg bâr)	117a	34°16'N	116°51'W
Big Belt Mountains, mts., Mt., U.S. (bĭg bĕlt)	106	46°53'N	111°43'W
Big Bend Dam, S.D., U.S. (bĭg bĕnd)	112	44°11'N	99°33'W
Big Bend National Park, rec., Tx., U.S.	106	29°15'N	103°15'W
Big Black, r., Ms., U.S. (bĭg blăk)	124	32°05'N	90°49'W
Big Blue, r., Ne., U.S. (bĭg blo͞o)	121	40°53'N	97°00'W
Big Canyon, Tx., U.S. (bĭg kăn'yŭn)	122	30°27'N	102°19'W
Big Cypress Indian Reservation, I.R., Fl., U.S.	125a	26°19'N	81°11'W
Big Cypress Swamp, sw., Fl., U.S. (bĭg sī'prĕs)	125a	26°02'N	81°20'W
Big Delta, Ak., U.S. (bĭg dĕl'tá)	103	64°08'N	145°48'W
Big Fork, r., Mn., U.S. (bĭg fôrk)	113	48°08'N	93°47'W
Biggar, Can.	90	52°04'N	108°00'W
Big Hole, r., Mt., U.S. (bĭg hōl)	115	45°53'N	113°15'W
Big Hole National Battlefield, Mt., U.S. (bĭg hōl băt''l-fēld)	115	45°44'N	113°35'W
Bighorn, r., U.S.	106	45°30'N	108°00'W
Bighorn Lake, res., Mt., U.S.	115	45°00'N	108°10'W
Bighorn Mountains, mts., U.S. (bĭg hôrn)	106	44°47'N	107°40'W
Big Island, i., Can.	97	49°10'N	94°40'W
Big Lake, Wa., U.S. (bĭg lāk)	116a	48°24'N	122°14'W
Big Lake, l., Can.	102g	53°35'N	113°47'W
Big Lake, l., Wa., U.S.	116a	48°24'N	122°14'W
Big Lost, r., Id., U.S. (lôst)	115	43°56'N	113°38'W
Big Mossy Point, c., Can.	97	53°45'N	97°50'W
Big Muddy, r., Il., U.S.	108	37°50'N	89°00'W
Big Muddy Creek, r., Mt., U.S. (bĭg mud'ĭ)	115	48°53'N	105°02'W
Bignona, Sen.	234	12°49'N	16°14'W
Big Porcupine Creek, r., Mt., U.S. (pôr'kū-pīn)	115	46°38'N	107°04'W
Big Quill Lake, l., Can.	92	51°55'N	104°22'W
Big Rapids, Mi., U.S. (bĭg răp'ĭdz)	108	43°40'N	85°30'W
Big River, Can.	90	53°50'N	107°01'W
Big Sandy, r., Az., U.S. (bĭg sănd'ē)	119	34°59'N	113°36'W
Big Sandy, r., Ky., U.S.	108	38°15'N	82°35'W
Big Sandy, r., Wy., U.S.	115	42°08'N	109°35'W
Big Sandy Creek, r., Co., U.S.	120	39°08'N	103°36'W
Big Sandy Creek, r., Mt., U.S.	115	48°20'N	110°08'W
Bigsby Island, i., Can.	97	49°04'N	94°35'W
Big Sioux, r., U.S. (bĭg so͞o)	112	44°34'N	97°00'W
Big Spring, Tx., U.S. (bĭg sprĭng)	122	32°15'N	101°28'W
Big Stone, l., Mn., U.S. (bĭg stōn)	112	45°29'N	96°40'W
Big Stone Gap, Va., U.S.	125	36°50'N	82°50'W
Big Sunflower, r., Ms., U.S. (sŭn-flou'ēr)	124	32°57'N	90°40'W
Big Timber, Mt., U.S. (bĭg'tĭm-bēr)	115	45°50'N	109°57'W
Big Wood, r., Id., U.S. (bĭg wo͝od)	115	43°02'N	114°30'W
Bihār, state, India (bē-här')	199	25°30'N	87°00'E
Biharamulo, Tan. (bē-hä-rä-mo͞o'lō)	232	2°38'S	31°20'E
Bihorului, Munţii, mts., Rom.	169	46°37'N	22°37'E
Bijagós, Arquipélago dos, is., Gui.-B.	230	11°20'N	17°10'W
Bijāpur, India	203	16°53'N	75°42'E
Bijeljina, Bos.	175	44°44'N	19°15'E
Bijelo Polje, Serb. (bē'yĕ-lō pō'lyĕ)	175	43°02'N	19°48'E
Bijiang, China (bē-jyän)	207a	22°57'N	113°15'E
Bijie, China (bē-jyĕ)	209	27°20'N	105°18'E
Bijou Creek, r., Co., U.S. (bē'zho͞o)	120	39°41'N	104°13'W

ăt; finăl; rāte; senāte; ärm; åsk; sofá; fâre; ch-choose; dh-as th in other; bē; ēvent; bĕt; recĕnt; cratēr; g-gō; gh-guttural g; bĭt; ĭ-short neutral; rīde; κ-guttural k as ch in German ich;

PLACE (Pronunciation)	PAGE	LAT.	LONG.
Bīkaner, India (bĭ-kă'nûr)	199	28°07'N	73°19'E
Bikin, Russia (bẻ-kēn')	210	46°41'N	134°29'E
Bikin, r., Russia	210	46°37'N	135°55'E
Bikoro, D.R.C. (bẻ-kō'rȯ)	232	0°45'S	18°07'E
Bikuar, Parque Nacional do, rec., Ang.	236	15°07'S	14°40'E
Bilāspur, India (bẻ-läs'po͞or)	199	22°08'N	82°12'E
Bila Tserkva, Ukr.	181	49°48'N	30°09'E
Bilauktaung, mts., Asia	212	14°40'N	98°50'E
Bilbao, Spain (bĭl-bä'ō)	154	43°12'N	2°48'W
Bilbays, Egypt	238b	30°26'N	31°37'E
Bileća, Bos. (bē'lĕ-chä)	175	42°52'N	18°26'E
Bilecik, Tur. (bē-lĕd-zhēk')	163	40°10'N	29°58'E
Bilé Karpaty, mts., Eur.	169	48°53'N	17°35'E
Biłgoraj, Pol. (bēw-gō'rī)	169	50°31'N	22°43'E
Bilhorod-Dnistrovs'kyi, Ukr.	181	46°09'N	30°19'E
Bilimbay, Russia (bē'lĭm-bȧy)	186a	56°59'N	59°53'E
Billabong, r., Austl. (bĭl'ă-bŏng)	221	35°15'S	145°20'E
Billerica, Ma., U.S. (bĭl'rĭk-ȧ)	101a	42°33'N	71°16'W
Billericay, Eng., U.K.	158b	51°38'N	0°25'E
Billings, Mt., U.S. (bĭl'ĭngz)	104	45°47'N	108°29'W
Bill Williams, r., Az., U.S. (bĭl-wĭl'yumz)	119	34°10'N	113°50'W
Bilma, Niger (bēl'mä)	231	18°41'N	13°20'E
Bilopillia, Ukr.	181	51°10'N	34°19'E
Bilovods'k, Ukr.	177	49°12'N	39°36'E
Biloxi, Ms., U.S. (bĭ-lŏk'sĭ)	105	30°24'N	88°50'W
Bilqās Qism Awwal, Egypt	238b	31°14'N	31°25'E
Bimberi Peak, mtn., Austl. (bĭm'bĕrĭ)	222	35°45'S	148°50'E
Binalonan, Phil. (bē-nä-lô'nän)	213a	16°03'N	120°35'E
Bingen, Ger. (bĭn'gĕn)	168	49°57'N	7°54'E
Bingham, Eng., U.K. (bĭng'ăm)	158a	52°57'N	0°57'W
Bingham, Me., U.S.	100	45°03'N	69°51'W
Bingham Canyon, Ut., U.S.	117b	40°33'N	112°09'W
Binghamton, N.Y., U.S. (bĭng'ȧm-tŭn)	105	42°05'N	75°55'W
Bingo-Nada, b., Japan (bĭn'gō nä-dä)	211	34°06'N	133°14'E
Binjai, Indon.	212	3°59'N	108°00'E
Binnaway, Austl. (bĭn'ă-wā)	222	31°42'S	149°22'E
Bintan, i., Indon. (bĭn'tän)	197b	1°09'N	104°43'E
Bintimani, mtn., S.L.	234	9°13'N	11°07'W
Bintulu, Malay. (bēn'to͞o-lo͞o)	212	3°07'N	113°06'E
Binxian, China	208	45°40'N	127°20'E
Binxian, China (bĭn-shyän)	206	37°27'N	117°58'E
Bio Gorge, val., Ghana	234	8°30'N	2°05'W
Bioko (Fernando Póo), i., Eq. Gui.	230	3°35'N	7°45'E
Bira, Russia (bē'rȧ)	210	49°00'N	133°18'E
Bira, r., Russia	210	48°55'N	132°25'E
Birātnagar, Nepal (bĭ-rät'nŭ-gŭr)	202	26°35'N	87°18'E
Birbka, Ukr.	169	49°36'N	24°18'E
Birch Bay, Wa., U.S. (bûrch)	116d	48°55'N	122°45'W
Birch Bay, b., Wa., U.S.	116d	48°55'N	122°52'W
Birch Island, i., Can.	97	52°25'N	99°55'W
Birch Mountains, mts., Can.	92	57°36'N	113°10'W
Birch Point, c., Wa., U.S.	116d	48°57'N	122°50'W
Bird Island, i., S. Afr. (bẽrd)	233c	33°51'S	26°21'E
Bird Rock, i., Bah. (bŭrd)	135	22°50'N	74°20'W
Birds Hill, Can. (bûrds)	102f	49°58'N	97°00'W
Birdsville, Austl. (bûrdz'vĭl)	218	25°50'S	139°31'E
Birdum, Austl. (bûrd'ŭm)	218	15°45'S	133°25'E
Birecik, Tur. (bē-rĕd-zhēk')	163	37°10'N	37°50'E
Bir Gara, Chad	235	13°11'N	15°58'E
Bīrjand, Iran (bēr'jănd)	198	33°07'N	59°16'E
Birkenfeld, Or., U.S.	116c	45°59'N	123°20'W
Birkenhead, Eng., U.K. (bûr'kĕn-hĕd)	164	53°23'N	3°02'W
Birkenwerder, Ger. (bēr'kĕn-vĕr-dĕr)	159b	52°41'N	13°22'E
Birmingham, Eng., U.K.	154	52°29'N	1°53'W
Birmingham, Al., U.S. (bûr'mĭng-häm)	105	33°31'N	86°49'W
Birmingham, Mi., U.S.	111b	42°32'N	83°13'W
Birmingham, Mo., U.S.	117f	39°10'N	94°22'W
Birmingham Canal, can., Eng., U.K.	158a	53°07'N	2°40'W
Bi'r Misāhah, Egypt	231	22°16'N	28°04'E
Birnin Kebbi, Nig.	230	12°32'N	4°12'E
Birobidzhan, Russia (bē'rȯ-bẻ-jän')	179	48°42'N	133°28'E
Birsk, Russia (bĭrsk)	178	55°25'N	55°30'E
Birstall, Eng., U.K. (bûr'stôl)	158a	53°44'N	1°39'W
Biryulëvo, Russia (bēr-yo͞ol'yô-vô)	186b	55°35'N	37°39'E
Biryusa, r., Russia (bēr-yo͞o'sä)	184	56°43'N	97°30'E
Bi'r Za'farānah, Egypt	197a	29°07'N	32°38'E
Biržai, Lith. (bẻr-zhä'ẻ)	167	56°11'N	24°45'E
Bisbee, Az., U.S. (bĭz'bē)	104	31°30'N	109°55'W
Biscay, Bay of, b., Eur. (bĭs'kā')	156	45°19'N	3°51'W
Biscayne Bay, b., Fl., U.S. (bĭs-kān')	125a	25°22'N	80°15'W
Bischeim, Fr. (bĭsh'hīm)	171	48°40'N	7°48'E
Biscotasi Lake, l., Can.	98	47°20'N	81°55'W
Biser, Russia (bē'sĕr)	186a	58°24'N	58°54'E
Biševo, is., Serb. (bē'shĕ-vō)	174	42°58'N	15°50'E
Bishkek, Kyrg.	183	42°49'N	74°42'E
Bisho, S. Afr.	232	32°50'S	27°20'E
Bishop, Ca., U.S. (bĭsh'ŭp)	118	37°22'N	118°25'W
Bishop, Tx., U.S.	123	27°35'N	97°46'W
Bishop's Castle, Eng., U.K. (bĭsh'ŏps käs''l)	158a	52°29'N	2°57'W
Bishopville, S.C., U.S. (bĭsh'ŭp-vĭl)	125	34°11'N	80°13'W
Bismarck, N.D., U.S. (bĭz'märk)	104	46°48'N	100°46'W
Bismarck Archipelago, is., Pap. N. Gui.	213	3°15'S	150°45'E
Bismarck Range, mts., Pap. N. Gui.	213	5°15'S	144°15'E
Bissau, Gui.-B. (bẻ-sa'o͞o)	234	11°51'N	15°35'W
Bissett, Can.	97	51°01'N	95°45'W
Bistineau, l., La., U.S. (bĭs-tĭ-nō')	123	32°19'N	93°45'W
Bistrita, Rom. (bĭs-trĭt-sȧ)	163	47°09'N	24°29'E
Bistrita, r., Rom.	169	47°08'N	25°47'E
Bitlis, Tur. (bĭt-lēs')	198	38°30'N	42°00'E
Bitola, Mac. (bẻ'tô-lä) (mȯ'nä-stẻr)	174	41°02'N	21°22'E
Bitonto, Italy (bẻ-tôn'tō)	174	41°08'N	16°42'E
Bitter Creek, r., Wy., U.S. (bĭt'ẽr)	115	41°36'N	108°29'W
Bitterfeld, Ger. (bĭt'ẽr-fĕlt)	168	51°39'N	12°19'E
Bitterroot, r., Mt., U.S.	115	46°28'N	114°10'W
Bitterroot Range, mts., U.S. (bĭt'ẽr-o͞ot)	106	47°15'N	115°13'W
Bityug, r., Russia (bĭt'yo͞og)	177	51°23'N	40°33'E
Biu, Nig.	235	10°35'N	12°13'E
Biwabik, Mn., U.S. (bẻ-wä'bĭk)	113	47°32'N	92°24'W
Biwa-ko, l., Japan (bẻ-wä'kō)	211	35°03'N	135°51'E
Biya, r., Russia (bĭ'yȧ)	184	52°22'N	87°28'E
Biysk, Russia (bēsk)	178	52°32'N	85°28'E
Bizana, S. Afr. (bĭz-änä)	233c	30°51'S	29°54'E
Bizerte, Tun. (bẻ-zĕrt')	230	37°23'N	9°52'E
Bjelovar, Cro. (byĕ-lō'vär)	174	45°54'N	16°53'E
Bjørnafjorden, b., Nor.	166	60°11'N	5°26'E
Bla, Mali	234	12°57'N	5°46'W
Black, l., Mi., U.S. (blăk)	108	45°25'N	84°15'W
Black, l., N.Y., U.S.	109	44°30'N	75°35'W
Black, r., Asia	212	21°00'N	103°30'E
Black, r., Can.	98	49°20'N	81°15'W
Black, r., Az., U.S.	119	33°35'N	109°35'W
Black, r., N.Y., U.S.	109	43°45'N	75°20'W
Black, r., S.C., U.S.	125	33°55'N	80°10'W
Black, r., Wi., U.S.	113	44°07'N	90°56'W
Black, r., U.S.	121	35°47'N	91°22'W
Blackall, Austl. (blăk'ŭl)	219	24°23'S	145°37'E
Black Bay, b., Can. (blăk)	98	48°36'N	88°32'W
Blackburn, Eng., U.K. (blăk'bûrn)	164	53°45'N	2°28'W
Blackburn Mount, mtn., Ak., U.S.	103	61°50'N	143°12'W
Black Butte Lake, res., Ca., U.S.	118	39°45'N	122°20'W
Black Canyon of the Gunnison National Park, rec., Co., U.S.	119	38°34'N	107°43'W
Black Diamond, Wa., U.S. (dī'mŭnd)	116a	47°19'N	122°00'W
Black Down Hills, hills, Eng., U.K. (blăk'doun)	164	50°58'N	3°19'W
Blackduck, Mn., U.S. (blăk'dŭk)	113	47°41'N	94°33'W
Blackfeet Indian Reservation, I.R., Mt., U.S.	115	48°40'N	113°00'W
Blackfoot, Id., U.S. (blăk'fo̤t)	115	43°11'N	112°23'W
Blackfoot, r., Mt., U.S.	115	46°53'N	113°33'W
Blackfoot Indian Reservation, I.R., Mt., U.S.	115	48°49'N	112°53'W
Blackfoot Indian Reserve, I.R., Can.	95	50°45'N	113°00'W
Blackfoot Reservoir, res., Id., U.S.	115	42°53'N	111°23'W
Black Forest *see* Schwarzwald, for., Ger.	168	47°54'N	7°57'E
Black Hills, mts., U.S.	106	44°08'N	103°47'W
Black Island, i., Can.	97	51°10'N	96°30'W
Black Lake, Can.	99	46°02'N	71°24'W
Black Mesa, Az., U.S. (blăk māsȧ)	119	36°33'N	110°40'W
Blackmud Creek, r., Can. (blăk'mŭd)	102g	53°28'N	113°34'W
Blackpool, Eng., U.K. (blăk'po͞ol)	164	53°49'N	3°02'W
Black Range, mts., N.M., U.S.	106	33°15'N	107°55'W
Black River, Jam. (blăk')	134	18°00'N	77°50'W
Black River Falls, Wi., U.S.	113	44°18'N	90°51'W
Black Rock Desert, des., Nv., U.S. (rŏk)	114	40°55'N	119°00'W
Blacksburg, S.C., U.S. (blăks'bûrg)	125	35°09'N	81°30'W
Black Sea, sea	157	43°01'N	32°16'E
Blackshear, Ga., U.S. (blăk'shĭr)	125	31°20'N	82°15'W
Blackstone, Va., U.S. (blăk'stȯn)	125	37°04'N	78°00'W
Black Sturgeon, r., Can. (stû'jŭn)	98	49°12'N	88°41'W
Blacktown, Austl. (blăk'toun)	217b	33°47'S	150°55'E
Blackville, Can. (blăk'vĭl)	100	46°44'N	65°50'W
Blackville, S.C., U.S.	125	33°21'N	81°19'W
Black Volta (Volta Noire), r., Afr.	230	11°30'N	4°00'W
Black Warrior, r., Al., U.S. (blăk wŏr'ĭ-ẽr)	124	32°37'N	87°42'W
Blackwater, r., Ire. (blăk-wô'tẽr)	164	52°05'N	9°02'W
Blackwater, r., Mo., U.S.	121	38°53'N	93°22'W
Blackwater, r., Va., U.S.	125	37°07'N	77°10'W
Blackwell, Ok., U.S. (blăk'wĕl)	121	36°47'N	97°19'W
Bladel, Neth.	159a	51°22'N	5°15'E
Blagodarnoye, Russia (blä'gȯ-där-nō'yĕ)	181	45°00'N	43°30'E
Blagoevgrad, Blg.	175	42°01'N	23°06'E
Blagoveshchensk, Russia (blä'gŏ-vyĕsh'chĕnsk)	179	50°16'N	127°47'E
Blagoveshchensk, Russia	186a	55°03'N	56°00'E
Blaine, Mn., U.S. (blān)	117g	45°11'N	93°14'W
Blaine, Wa., U.S.	116d	48°59'N	122°49'W
Blaine, W.V., U.S.	109	39°25'N	79°10'W
Blair, Ne., U.S. (blâr)	112	41°33'N	96°09'W
Blairmore, Can.	95	49°38'N	114°25'W
Blairsville, Pa., U.S. (blârs'vĭl)	109	40°30'N	79°40'W
Blake, i., Wa., U.S. (blāk)	116a	47°37'N	122°28'W
Blakely, Ga., U.S. (blāk'lẻ)	124	31°22'N	84°55'W
Blanc, Cap, c., Afr.	230	20°39'N	18°08'W
Blanc, Mont, mtn., Eur. (môɴ bläɴ)	156	45°50'N	6°53'E
Blanca, Bahía, b., Arg. (bä-ē'ä-blȧn'kä)	144	39°30'S	61°00'W
Blanca Peak, mtn., Co., U.S. (blăŋ'kȧ)	106	37°36'N	105°22'W
Blanche, r., Can.	102c	45°34'N	75°38'W
Blanche, Lake, l., Austl. (blănch)	222	29°20'S	139°12'E
Blanchester, Oh., U.S. (blăn'chĕs-tẽr)	111f	39°18'N	83°58'W
Blanco, r., Mex.	130	24°05'N	99°21'W
Blanco, r., Mex.	131	18°42'N	96°03'W
Blanco, Cabo, c., Arg. (bläŋ'kȯ)	144	47°08'S	65°47'W
Blanco, Cabo, c., C.R. (kȧ'bȯ-blăŋ'kō)	132	9°29'N	85°15'W
Blanco, Cape, c., Or., U.S. (blăn'kō)	114	42°53'N	124°38'W
Blancos, Cayo, i., Cuba (kä'yō-blăŋ'kōs)	134	23°15'N	80°55'W
Blanding, Ut., U.S.	119	37°40'N	109°31'W
Blankenfelde, Ger. (blän'kĕn-fĕl-dĕ)	159b	52°20'N	13°24'E
Blanquefort, Fr.	170	44°53'N	0°38'W
Blanquilla, Arrecife, i., Mex. (är-rĕ-sē'fĕ-blän-kẻ'l-yä)	131	21°32'N	97°14'W
Blantyre, Mwi. (blăn-tīyr)	232	15°47'S	35°00'E
Blasdell, N.Y., U.S. (blāz'dĕl)	111c	42°48'N	78°51'W
Blato, Cro. (blä'tō)	174	42°55'N	16°47'E
Blaye-et-Sainte Luce, Fr. (blā'ā-săɴt-lüs')	170	45°08'N	0°40'W
Blażowa, Pol. (bwä-zhō'vȧ)	169	49°51'N	22°05'E
Bleus, Monts, mts., D.R.C.	237	1°10'N	30°10'E
Blind River, Can. (blīnd)	91	46°10'N	83°09'W
Blissfield, Mi., U.S. (blĭs-fēld)	108	41°50'N	83°50'W
Blithe, r., Eng., U.K. (blĭth)	158a	52°22'N	1°49'W
Blitta, Togo	234	8°19'N	0°59'E
Block, i., R.I., U.S. (blŏk)	109	41°05'N	71°35'W
Bloedel, Can.	94	50°07'N	125°23'W
Bloemfontein, S. Afr. (blo͞om'fŏn-tān)	232	29°09'S	26°16'E
Blois, Fr. (blwä)	161	47°36'N	1°21'E
Blood Indian Reserve, I.R., Can.	95	49°30'N	113°10'W
Bloomer, Wi., U.S. (blo͞om'ẽr)	113	45°07'N	91°30'W
Bloomfield, Ia., U.S.	113	40°44'N	92°21'W
Bloomfield, In., U.S. (blo͞om'fēld)	108	39°00'N	86°55'W
Bloomfield, Mo., U.S.	121	36°54'N	89°55'W
Bloomfield, Ne., U.S.	112	42°36'N	97°40'W
Bloomfield, N.J., U.S.	110a	40°48'N	74°12'W
Bloomfield Hills, Mi., U.S.	111b	42°35'N	83°15'W
Blooming Prairie, Mn., U.S. (blo͞om'ĭng prā'rĭ)	113	43°52'N	93°04'W
Bloomington, Ca., U.S. (blo͞om'ĭng-tŭn)	117a	34°04'N	117°24'W
Bloomington, Il., U.S.	105	40°30'N	89°00'W
Bloomington, In., U.S.	108	39°10'N	86°35'W
Bloomington, Mn., U.S.	117g	44°50'N	93°18'W
Bloomsburg, Pa., U.S. (blo͞omz'bûrg)	109	41°00'N	76°25'W
Blossburg, Al., U.S. (blŏs'bûrg)	110h	33°38'N	86°57'W
Blossburg, Pa., U.S.	109	41°45'N	77°00'W
Bloubergstrand, S. Afr.	232a	33°48'S	18°28'E
Blountstown, Fl., U.S. (blŭnts'tun)	124	30°24'N	85°02'W
Bludenz, Aus. (blo͞o-dĕnts')	168	47°09'N	9°50'E
Blue Ash, Oh., U.S. (blo͞o ăsh)	111f	39°14'N	84°23'W
Blue Earth, Mn., U.S. (blo͞o ûrth)	113	43°38'N	94°05'W
Blue Earth, r., Mn., U.S.	113	43°55'N	94°16'W
Bluefield, W.V., U.S. (blo͞o'fēld)	125	37°15'N	81°11'W
Bluefields, Nic. (blo͞o'fēldz)	129	12°03'N	83°45'W
Blue Island, Il., U.S.	111a	41°39'N	87°41'W
Blue Mesa Reservoir, res., Co., U.S.	119	38°25'N	107°00'W
Blue Mountain, mtn., Can.	101	50°28'N	57°11'W
Blue Mountains, mts., Austl.	221	33°35'S	149°00'E
Blue Mountains, mts., Jam.	134	18°05'N	76°35'W
Blue Mountains, mts., U.S.	106	45°15'N	118°50'W
Blue Mud Bay, b., Austl. (bo͞o mŭd)	220	13°20'S	136°45'E
Blue Nile, r., Afr.	231	12°30'N	34°00'E
Blue Rapids, Ks., U.S. (blo͞o răp'ĭdz)	121	39°40'N	96°41'W
Blue Ridge, mtn., U.S. (blo͞o rĭj)	107	35°30'N	82°50'W
Blue River, Can.	90	52°05'N	119°17'W
Blue River, r., Mo., U.S.	117f	38°55'N	94°33'W
Bluff, Ut., U.S.	119	37°18'N	109°34'W
Bluff Park, Al., U.S.	110h	33°24'N	86°52'W
Bluffton, In., U.S. (blŭf-tŭn)	108	40°40'N	85°15'W
Bluffton, Oh., U.S.	108	40°50'N	83°55'W
Blumenau, Braz. (blo͞o'mĕn-ou)	144	26°53'S	48°58'W
Blumut, Gunong, mtn., Malay.	197b	2°03'N	103°34'E
Blyth, Eng., U.K. (blīth)	164	55°03'N	1°34'W
Blythe, Ca., U.S.	119	33°37'N	114°37'W
Blytheville, Ar., U.S. (blīth'vĭl)	121	35°55'N	89°51'W
Bo, S.L.	234	7°56'N	11°21'W
Boac, Phil.	213a	13°26'N	121°50'E
Boaco, Nic. (bȯ-ä'kō)	132	12°24'N	85°41'W
Bo'ai, China (bwo-ī)	208	35°10'N	113°08'E
Boa Vista, i., C.V. (bō-ä-vēsh'tȧ)	230b	16°01'N	23°52'W
Boa Vista do Rio Branco, Braz.	143	2°46'N	60°45'W
Bobo Dioulasso, Burkina (bō'bȯ-dyo͞o-lȧs-sō')	230	11°12'N	4°18'W
Bobr, Bela. (bȯ'b'r)	176	54°19'N	29°11'E
Bóbr, r., Pol. (bŭ'br)	168	51°44'N	15°13'E
Bobrov, Russia (bŭb-rôf')	181	51°07'N	40°01'E
Bobrovyts'a, Ukr.	177	50°43'N	31°27'E
Bobrynets', Ukr.	177	48°04'N	32°10'E
Boca del Pozo, Ven. (bô-kä-dĕl-pȯ'zŏ)	143b	11°00'N	64°21'W
Boca de Uchire, Ven. (bô-kä-dĕ-o͞o-chē'rĕ)	143b	10°09'N	65°27'W
Bocaina, Serra da, mtn., Braz. (sĕ'r-rä-dȧ-bȯ-kä'ē-nä)	141a	22°47'S	44°39'W
Bocas, Mex. (bō'käs)	130	22°29'N	101°03'W
Bocas del Toro, Pan. (bō'käs dĕl tō'rō)	133	9°24'N	82°15'W
Bochnia, Pol. (bōκ'nyä)	169	49°58'N	20°28'E
Bocholt, Ger. (bō'κōlt)	171c	51°50'N	6°37'E
Bochum, Ger.	168	51°29'N	7°13'E
Bockum-Hövel, Ger. (bō'κȯm-hû'fĕl)	171c	51°41'N	7°45'E
Bodalang, D.R.C.	236	3°14'N	22°14'E
Bodaybo, Russia (bō-dī'bō)	179	57°12'N	114°46'E
Bodele, depr., Chad (bō-dȧ-lā')	231	16°45'N	17°05'E
Boden, Swe.	160	65°51'N	21°29'E
Bodensee, l., Eur. (bō'dĕn zā)	156	47°48'N	9°22'E
Bodmin, Eng., U.K. (bŏd'mĭn)	164	50°29'N	4°45'W
Bodmin Moor, Eng., U.K. (bŏd'mĭn mȯr)	164	50°36'N	4°43'W
Bodrum, Tur.	181	37°10'N	27°07'E
Boende, D.R.C. (bô-ĕn'dȧ)	232	0°13'S	20°52'E
Boerne, Tx., U.S. (bō'ẽrn)	122	29°49'N	98°44'W
Boesmans, r., S. Afr.	233c	33°29'S	26°09'E
Boeuf, r., U.S. (bĕf)	123	32°23'N	91°57'W

274 Boffa – Bowie PRONOUNCING INDEX

PLACE (Pronunciation)	PAGE	LAT.	LONG.
Boffa, Gui. (bôf'á)	230	10°10'N	14°02'W
Bōfu, Japan (bō'fōō)	211	34°03'N	131°35'E
Bogalusa, La., U.S. (bō-gá-lōō'sá)	123	30°48'N	89°52'W
Bogan, r., Austl. (bŏ'gĕn)	222	32°10'S	147°40'E
Bogense, Den. (bŏ'gĕn-sĕ)	166	55°34'N	10°09'E
Boggy Peak, mtn., Antig. (bŏg'ĭ-pēk)	133b	17°03'N	61°50'W
Bogong, Mount, mtn., Austl.	222	36°50'S	147°15'E
Bogor, Indon.	212	6°45'S	106°45'E
Bogoroditsk, Russia (bō-gŏ'rô-dĭtsk)	176	53°48'N	38°06'E
Bogorodsk, Russia	180	56°02'N	43°40'E
Bogorodskoye, Russia (bô-gô-rôd'skô-yĕ)	186a	56°43'N	56°53'E
Bogotá, Col.	142	4°36'N	74°05'W
Bogotol, Russia (bŏ'gô-tŏl)	179	56°15'N	89°45'E
Boguchar, Russia (bŏ'gŏ-chär)	181	49°40'N	41°00'E
Bogue Chitto, Ms., U.S. (nôr'fēld)	124	31°26'N	90°25'W
Boguete, Pan. (bō-gĕ'tĕ)	133	8°54'N	82°29'W
Bo Hai, b., China	205	38°30'N	120°00'E
Bohai Haixia, strt., China (bwo-hī hī-shyä)	208	38°05'N	121°40'E
Bohain-en-Vermandois, Fr. (bô-ăN-ŏN-vâr-mäN-dwä')	170	49°58'N	3°22'E
Bohemia *see* Čechy, hist. reg., Czech Rep.	168	49°51'N	13°55'E
Bohemian Forest, mts., Eur. (bô-hē'mĭ-ăn)	156	49°35'N	12°27'E
Bohodukhiv, Ukr.	181	50°10'N	35°31'E
Bohol, i., Phil. (bô-hôl')	213	9°28'N	124°35'E
Bohom, Mex. (bŏ-ô'm)	131	16°47'N	92°42'W
Bohuslav, Ukr.	177	49°34'N	30°51'W
Boiestown, Can. (boiz'toun)	100	46°27'N	66°25'W
Bois Blanc, i., Mi., U.S. (boi' blănk)	108	45°45'N	84°30'W
Boischâtel, Can. (bwä-shä-tĕl')	102b	46°54'N	71°08'W
Bois-des-Filion, Can. (bōō-ä'dĕ-fē-yôN')	102a	45°40'N	73°46'W
Boise, Id., U.S. (boi'zē)	104	43°38'N	116°12'W
Boise, r., Id., U.S.	114	43°43'N	116°30'W
Boise City, Ok., U.S.	120	36°42'N	102°30'W
Boissevain, Can. (bois'vān)	90	49°14'N	100°03'W
Bojador, Cabo, c., W. Sah.	230	26°21'N	16°08'W
Bojnūrd, Iran	198	37°29'N	57°13'E
Bokani, Nig.	235	9°26'N	5°13'E
Boknafjorden, b., Nor.	160	59°12'N	5°37'E
Boksburg, S. Afr. (bŏks'bûrgh)	233b	26°13'N	28°15'E
Bokungu, D.R.C.	236	0°41'S	22°19'E
Bol, Chad	235	13°28'N	14°43'E
Bolai I, C.A.R.	235	4°20'N	17°21'E
Bolama, Gui.-B. (bô-lä'mä)	230	11°34'S	15°41'W
Bolan, mtn., Pak. (bô-län')	202	30°13'N	67°09'E
Bolaños, Mex. (bō-län'yôs)	130	21°40'N	103°48'W
Bolaños, r., Mex.	130	21°26'N	103°54'W
Bolan Pass, p., Pak.	199	29°50'N	67°10'E
Bolbec, Fr. (bôl-bĕk')	170	49°37'N	0°26'E
Bole, Ghana (bō'lå)	230	9°02'N	2°29'W
Bolesławiec, Pol. (bō-lĕ-slä'vyĕts)	168	51°15'N	15°35'E
Bolgatanga, Ghana	234	10°46'N	0°52'W
Bolhrad, Ukr.	181	45°41'N	28°38'E
Boli, China (bwo-lē)	205	45°40'N	130°38'E
Bolinao, Phil. (bō-lē-nä'ô)	213a	16°24'N	119°53'E
Bolívar, Arg. (bô-lē'vär)	144	36°15'S	61°05'W
Bolívar, Col.	142	1°46'N	76°58'W
Bolivar, Mo., U.S. (bŏl'ĭ-vȧr)	121	37°37'N	93°22'W
Bolivar, Tn., U.S.	124	35°14'N	88°56'W
Bolívar, Pico, mtn., Ven.	142	8°44'N	70°54'W
Bolivar Peninsula, pen., Tx., U.S. (bŏl'ĭ-vȧr)	123a	29°25'N	94°40'W
Bolivia, nation, S.A. (bô-lĭv'ĭ-ȧ)	142	17°00'S	64°00'W
Bolkhov, Russia (bôl-κôf')	180	53°27'N	35°59'E
Bollin, r., Eng., U.K. (bŏl'ĭn)	158a	53°18'N	2°11'W
Bollington, Eng., U.K. (bôl'ĭng-tŭn)	158a	53°18'N	2°06'W
Bollnäs, Swe. (bôl'nĕs)	166	61°22'N	16°20'E
Bolmen, l., Swe. (bôl'mĕn)	166	56°58'N	13°25'E
Bolobo, D.R.C. (bō'lô-bô)	232	2°14'S	16°18'E
Bologna, Italy (bô-lōn'yä)	154	44°30'N	11°18'E
Bologoye, Russia (bŏ-lŏ-gô'yĕ)	180	57°52'N	34°02'E
Bolonchenticul, Mex. (bô-lôn-chĕn-tē-kōō'l)	132a	20°03'N	89°47'W
Bolondrón, Cuba (bô-lôn-drōn')	134	22°45'N	81°25'W
Bolseno, Lago di, l., Italy (lä'gō-dē-bôl-sā'nô)	174	42°35'N	11°40'E
Bol'shaya Anyuy, r., Russia	185	67°58'N	161°15'E
Bol'shaya Chuya, r., Russia	185	58°15'N	111°40'E
Bol'shaya Kinel', r., Russia	180	53°20'N	52°40'E
Bol'she Ust'ikinskoye, Russia (bôl'she ŏs-tyĭ-kēn'skô-yĕ)	186a	55°58'N	58°18'E
Bol'shoy Begichëv, i., Russia	179	74°30'N	114°40'E
Bol'shoye Ivonino, Russia (ĭ-vô'nĭ-nô)	186a	59°41'N	61°12'E
Bol'shoy Kuyash, Russia (bôl'-shôy kōō'yásh)	186a	55°52'N	61°07'E
Bolsover, Eng., U.K. (bōl'zō-vĕr)	158a	53°14'N	1°17'W
Boltaña, Spain (bôl-tä'nä)	173	42°28'N	0°03'E
Bolton, Can. (bōl'tŭn)	102d	43°53'N	79°44'W
Bolton, Eng., U.K.	164	53°35'N	2°26'W
Bolton-upon-Dearne, Eng., U.K. (bōl'tŭn-ŭp'ŏn-dûrn)	158a	53°31'N	1°19'W
Bolu, Tur. (bō'lŏ)	163	40°45'N	31°45'E
Bolva, r., Russia (bôl'vä)	176	53°30'N	34°30'E
Bolvadin, Tur. (bŏl-vä-dēn')	163	38°50'N	30°50'E
Bolzano, Italy (bôl-tsä'nō)	162	46°31'N	11°22'E
Boma, D.R.C. (bō'mä)	232	5°51'S	13°03'E
Bombala, Austl. (bŭm-bä'lå)	219	36°55'S	149°07'E
Bombay *see* Mumbai, India	199	18°58'N	72°50'E
Bombay Harbour, b., India	203b	18°55'N	72°52'E
Bomi Hills, Lib.	230	7°00'N	11°00'W
Bom Jardim, Braz. (bôn zhär-dēN')	141a	22°10'S	42°25'W
Bom Jesus do Itabapoana, Braz.	141a	21°08'S	41°51'W
Bømlo, i., Nor. (bûmlô)	166	59°47'N	4°57'E
Bomongo, D.R.C.	231	1°22'N	18°21'E
Bom Sucesso, Braz. (bôn-sōō-sĕ'sō)	141a	21°02'S	44°44'W
Bomu *see* Mbomou, r., Afr.	231	4°50'N	24°00'E
Bon, Cap, c., Tun. (bôN)	162	37°04'N	11°13'E
Bonaire, i., Neth. Ant. (bô-nâr')	142	12°10'N	68°15'W
Bonavista, Can. (bō-nȧ-vĭs'tȧ)	93a	48°39'N	53°07'W
Bonavista Bay, b., Can.	93a	48°45'N	53°20'W
Bond, Co., U.S. (bŏnd)	120	39°53'N	106°40'W
Bondo, D.R.C. (bôn'dô)	184	3°49'N	23°40'E
Bondoc Peninsula, pen., Phil. (bôn-dŏk')	213a	13°24'N	122°30'E
Bondoukou, C. Iv. (bŏn-dōō'kōō)	230	8°02'N	2°48'W
Bonds Cay, i., Bah. (bŏnds kē)	134	25°30'N	77°45'W
Bondy, Fr.	171b	48°54'N	2°28'E
Bône *see* Annaba, Alg.	230	36°57'N	7°39'E
Bone, Teluk, b., Indon.	212	4°09'S	121°00'E
Bonete, Cerro, mtn., Arg. (bô'nĕtĕh çĕrrô)	144	27°50'S	68°35'W
Bonfim, Braz. (bôN-fē'N)	141a	20°20'S	44°15'W
Bongor, Chad	235	10°17'N	15°22'E
Bonham, Tx., U.S. (bŏn'ăm)	121	33°35'N	96°09'W
Bonhomme, Pic, mtn., Haiti	135	19°10'N	72°20'W
Bonifacio, Fr. (bō-nē-fä'chō)	174	41°23'N	9°10'E
Bonifacio, Strait of, strt., Eur.	162	41°14'N	9°02'E
Bonifay, Fl., U.S. (bŏn-ĭ-fā')	124	30°46'N	85°40'W
Bonin Islands, is., Japan (bō'nĭn)	241	26°30'N	141°00'E
Bonn, Ger. (bōn)	154	50°44'N	7°06'E
Bonne Bay, b., Can. (bŏn)	101	49°33'N	57°55'W
Bonners Ferry, Id., U.S. (bonĕrz fĕr'ĭ)	114	48°41'N	116°19'W
Bonner Springs, Ks., U.S. (bŏn'ĕr sprĭngz)	117f	39°04'N	94°52'W
Bonne Terre, Mo., U.S. (bŏn târ')	121	37°55'N	90°32'W
Bonnet Peak, mtn., Can. (bŏn'ĭt)	95	51°26'N	115°53'W
Bonneville Dam, dam, U.S. (bŏn'ē-vĭl)	114	45°37'N	121°57'W
Bonny, Nig. (bŏn'ē)	230	4°29'N	7°13'E
Bonny Lake, Wa., U.S. (bŏn'ē lăk)	116a	47°11'N	122°11'W
Bonnyville, Can. (bŏnē-vĭl)	95	54°16'N	110°44'W
Bonorva, Italy (bô-nôr'vä)	174	40°26'N	8°46'E
Bonthain, Indon. (bôn-tīn')	212	5°30'S	119°52'E
Bonthe, S.L.	230	7°32'N	12°30'W
Bontoc, Phil. (bôn-tŏk')	213a	17°10'N	121°01'E
Booby Rocks, is., Bah. (bōō'bĭ rŏks)	134	23°55'N	77°00'W
Booker T. Washington National Monument, rec., Va., U.S. (bŏŏk'ĕr tē wŏsh'ĭng-tŭn)	125	37°07'N	79°45'W
Boom, Bel.	159a	51°05'N	4°22'E
Boone, Ia., U.S. (bōōn)	113	42°04'N	93°51'W
Booneville, Ar., U.S. (bōōn'vĭl)	121	35°09'N	93°54'W
Booneville, Ky., U.S.	108	37°25'N	83°40'W
Booneville, Ms., U.S.	124	34°37'N	88°35'W
Boons, S. Afr.	238c	25°59'S	27°15'E
Boonton, N.J., U.S. (bōōn'tŭn)	110a	40°54'N	74°24'W
Boonville, In., U.S.	108	38°00'N	87°15'W
Boonville, Mo., U.S.	121	38°57'N	92°44'W
Boorama, Som.	238a	10°05'N	43°08'E
Boosaaso, Som.	238a	11°19'N	49°10'E
Boothbay Harbor, Me., U.S. (bōōth'bā här'bĕr)	100	43°51'N	69°39'W
Boothia, Gulf of, b., Can. (bōō'thĭ-ȧ)	93	69°04'N	86°04'W
Boothia Peninsula, pen., Can.	89	73°30'N	95°00'W
Bootle, Eng., U.K. (bōō't'l)	158a	53°29'N	3°02'W
Bor, Sudan (bôr)	231	6°13'N	31°35'E
Bor, Tur. (bōr)	181	37°50'N	34°40'E
Boraha, Nosy, i., Madag.	233	16°58'S	50°15'E
Borah Peak, mtn., Id., U.S. (bō'rä)	115	44°12'N	113°47'W
Borås, Swe. (bô'rōs)	160	57°43'N	12°55'E
Borāzjān, Iran (bō-räz-jän')	198	29°13'N	51°13'E
Borba, Braz. (bôr'bä)	143	4°23'S	59°31'W
Borborema, Planalto da, plat., Braz. (plä-nàl'tô-dä-bôr-bō-rĕ'mä)	143	7°35'S	36°40'W
Bordeaux, Fr. (bôr-dō')	154	44°50'N	0°37'W
Bordentown, N.J., U.S. (bôr'dĕn-toun)	109	40°05'N	74°40'W
Bordj-bou-Arréridj, Alg. (bôrj-bōō-á-rā-rēj')	162	36°03'N	4°48'E
Bordj Omar Idriss, Alg.	230	28°06'N	6°34'E
Borgarnes, Ice.	160	64°31'N	21°40'W
Borger, Tx., U.S. (bôr'gĕr)	120	35°40'N	101°23'W
Borgholm, Swe. (bôrg-hŏlm')	166	56°52'N	16°40'E
Borgne, l., La., U.S. (bôrn'y')	123	30°03'N	89°36'W
Borgomanero, Italy (bôr'gō-mä-nâ'rō)	174	45°40'N	8°28'E
Borgo Val di Taro, Italy (bô'r-zhō-väl-dē-tá'rō)	174	44°29'N	9°44'E
Borili, Kaz.	186a	53°36'N	61°55'E
Boring, Or., U.S. (bōring)	116c	45°26'N	122°22'W
Borisoglebsk, Russia (bŏ-rē-sô-glyĕpsk')	178	51°20'N	42°00'E
Borisovka, Russia (bŏ-rē-sôf'kȧ)	181	50°38'N	36°00'E
Borivli, India	203b	19°15'N	72°48'E
Borja, Spain (bôr'hä)	172	41°50'N	1°33'W
Borken, Ger. (bōr'kĕn)	171c	51°50'N	6°51'E
Borkou, reg., Chad (bôr-kōō')	231	18°11'N	18°28'E
Borkum, i., Ger. (bōr'kōōm)	168	53°31'N	6°50'E
Borlänge, Swe. (bôr-lĕŋ'gĕ)	166	60°30'N	15°24'E
Borneo, i., Asia	212	0°25'N	112°39'E
Bornholm, i., Den. (bôrn-hôlm)	156	55°16'N	15°15'E
Boromlia, Ukr.	177	50°36'N	34°58'E
Boromo, Burkina	234	11°45'N	2°56'W
Borovan, Blg. (bō-rô-vän')	175	43°24'N	23°47'E
Borovichi, Russia (bŏ-rô-vē'chê)	178	58°22'N	33°56'E
Borovsk, Russia (bô'rŏvsk)	176	55°13'N	36°26'E
Borraan, Som.	238a	10°38'N	48°30'E
Borracha, Isla la, i., Ven. (ē's-lä-là-bôr-rä'chä)	143b	10°18'N	64°44'W
Borriana, Spain	162	39°53'N	0°05'W
Borroloola, Austl. (bŏr-rô-lōō'lȧ)	218	16°15'S	136°19'E
Borshchiv, Ukr.	169	48°47'N	26°04'E
Bort-les-Orgues, Fr. (bôr-lā-zôrg)	170	45°26'N	2°26'E
Borūjerd, Iran	198	33°45'N	48°53'E
Boryslav, Ukr.	169	49°17'N	23°24'E
Boryspil', Ukr.	177	50°17'N	30°54'E
Borzna, Ukr. (bôrz'ná)	181	51°15'N	32°26'E
Borzya, Russia (bôrz'yá)	179	50°37'N	116°53'E
Bosa, Italy (bō'sä)	174	40°18'N	8°34'E
Bosanska Dubica, Bos. (bō'sän-skä dōō'bĭt-sä)	174	45°10'N	16°49'E
Bosanska Gradiška, Bos. (bō'sän-skä grä-dĭsh'kä)	175	45°08'N	17°15'E
Bosanski Novi, Bos. (bō's sän-skĭ nō'vē)	174	45°00'N	16°22'E
Bosanski Petrovac, Bos. (bō'sän-skĭ pĕt'rō-väts)	174	44°33'N	16°23'E
Bosanski Šamac, Bos. (bō'sän-skĭ shä'máts)	175	45°03'N	18°30'E
Boscobel, Wi., U.S. (bŏs'kô-bĕl)	113	43°08'N	90°44'W
Bose, China (bwo-sŭ)	209	24°00'N	106°38'E
Boshan, China (bwo-shan)	205	36°32'N	117°51'E
Boskoop, Neth.	159a	52°04'N	4°39'E
Boskovice, Czech Rep. (bŏs'kō-vē-tsĕ)	168	49°26'N	16°37'E
Bosna, r., Serb.	175	44°19'N	17°54'E
Bosnia and Herzegovina, nation, Eur.	175	44°15'N	17°30'E
Bosobolo, D.R.C.	236	4°11'N	19°54'E
Bosporus *see* İstanbul Boğazı, strt., Tur.	198	41°10'N	29°10'E
Bossangoa, C.A.R.	235	6°29'N	17°27'E
Bossier City, La., U.S. (bŏsh'ēr)	123	32°31'N	93°42'W
Bosten Hu, l., China (bwo-stŭn hōō)	204	42°06'N	88°01'E
Boston, Ga., U.S. (bôs'tŭn)	124	30°47'N	83°47'W
Boston, Ma., U.S.	105	42°15'N	71°07'W
Boston Heights, Oh., U.S.	111d	41°15'N	81°30'W
Boston Mountains, mts., Ar., U.S.	107	35°46'N	93°32'W
Botany Bay, b., Austl. (bŏt'á-nĭ)	221	33°58'S	151°11'E
Botevgrad, Blg.	175	42°54'N	23°41'E
Bothaville, S. Afr. (bō'tā-vĭl)	238c	27°24'S	26°38'E
Bothell, Wa., U.S. (bŏth'ĕl)	116a	47°46'N	122°12'W
Bothnia, Gulf of, b., Eur. (bŏth'nĭ-á)	156	63°40'N	21°30'E
Botoşani, Rom. (bō-tō-shán'ĭ)	169	47°46'N	26°40'E
Botswana, nation, Afr. (bŏtswănă)	232	22°10'S	23°13'E
Bottineau, N.D., U.S. (bŏt-ĭ-nō')	112	48°48'N	100°28'W
Bottrop, Ger. (bōt'trōp)	168	51°31'N	6°56'E
Botwood, Can. (bŏt'wŏd)	93a	49°08'N	55°21'W
Bouafle, C. Iv. (bō-á-flā')	230	6°59'N	5°45'W
Bouar, C.A.R. (bōō-är)	231	5°57'N	15°36'E
Bou Areg, Sebkha, Mor.	172	35°09'N	3°02'W
Boubandjidah, Parc National de, rec., Cam.	235	8°20'N	14°40'E
Boucherville, Can. (bōō-shā-vēl')	102a	45°37'N	73°27'W
Boudenib, Mor. (bōō-dĕ-nēb')	230	32°14'N	3°04'W
Boudette, Mn., U.S. (bōō-dĕt)	113	48°42'N	94°34'W
Boudouaou, Alg.	173	36°44'N	3°25'E
Boufarik, Alg. (bōō-fà-rēk')	173	36°35'N	2°55'E
Bougainville, i., Pap. N. Gui.	214e	6°00'S	155°00'E
Bougainville Trench, deep (bōō-găN-vēl')	241	7°00'S	152°00'E
Bougie *see* Bejaïa, Alg.	230	36°46'N	5°00'E
Bougouni, Mali (bōō-gōō-nē')	230	11°27'N	7°30'W
Bouïra, Alg. (boo-ē'rá)	162	36°25'N	3°55'E
Bouïra-Sahary, Alg. (bwē-rá sá'á-rē)	173	35°16'N	3°23'E
Bouka, r., Gui.	234	11°05'N	10°40'W
Boulder, Co., U.S.	104	40°02'N	105°19'W
Boulder, r., Mt., U.S.	115	46°10'N	112°07'W
Boulder City, Nv., U.S.	104	35°57'N	114°50'W
Boulder Peak, mtn., Id., U.S.	115	43°53'N	114°33'W
Boulogne-Billancourt, Fr. (bōō-lôn'y'-bē-yäN-kōōr')	170	48°50'N	2°14'E
Boulogne-sur-Mer, Fr. (bōō-lôn'y-sür-mâr')	161	50°44'N	1°37'E
Boumba, r., Cam.	235	3°20'N	14°40'E
Bouna, C. Iv. (bōō-nä')	230	9°16'N	3°00'W
Bouna, Parc National de, rec., C. Iv.	234	9°20'N	3°35'W
Boundary Bay, b., N.A. (boun'dá-rĭ)	116d	49°03'N	122°59'W
Boundary Peak, mtn., Nv., U.S.	118	37°52'N	118°20'W
Bound Brook, N.J., U.S. (bound brŏk)	110a	40°34'N	74°32'W
Bountiful, Ut., U.S. (boun'tĭ-fŏl)	117b	40°55'N	111°53'W
Bountiful Peak, mtn., Ut., U.S. (boun'tĭ-fŏl)	117b	40°58'N	111°49'W
Bounty Islands, is., N.Z.	5	47°42'S	179°05'E
Bourail, N. Cal.	214f	21°34'S	165°30'E
Bourem, Mali (bōō-rĕm')	230	16°43'N	0°15'W
Bourg-en-Bresse, Fr. (bōōr-gĕN-brĕs')	161	46°12'N	5°13'E
Bourges, Fr. (bōōrzh)	161	47°06'N	2°22'E
Bourget, Can. (bōōr-zhĕ')	102c	45°26'N	75°09'W
Bourgoin, Fr. (bōōr-gwăN')	171	45°46'N	5°17'E
Bourke, Austl. (bŭrk)	219	30°10'S	146°00'E
Bourne, Eng., U.K. (bōrn)	158a	52°46'N	0°22'W
Bournemouth, Eng., U.K. (bôrn'mŭth)	164	50°44'N	1°55'W
Bou Saâda, Alg. (bōō-sä'dä)	162	35°13'N	4°17'E
Bousso, Chad (bōō-sô')	231	10°33'N	16°45'E
Boutilimit, Maur.	230	17°30'N	14°54'W
Bouvetøya, i., Ant.	3	55°00'S	3°00'E
Bow, r., Can. (bō)	92	50°35'N	112°15'W
Bowbells, N.D., U.S. (bō'bĕls)	112	48°50'N	102°16'W
Bowdle, S.D., U.S. (bōd''l)	112	45°28'N	99°42'W
Bowen, Austl. (bō'ĕn)	219	20°02'S	148°14'E
Bowie, Md., U.S. (bōō'ĭ) (bō'ē)	110e	38°59'N	76°47'W
Bowie, Tx., U.S.	121	33°34'N	97°50'W

PRONOUNCING INDEX Bowling Green – Brownsville 275

PLACE (Pronunciation)	PAGE	LAT.	LONG.
Bowling Green, Ky., U.S. (bōlĭng grēn)	105	37°00'N	86°26'W
Bowling Green, Mo., U.S.	121	39°19'N	91°09'W
Bowling Green, Oh., U.S.	108	41°25'N	83°40'W
Bowman, N.D., U.S. (bō'mǎn)	112	46°11'N	103°23'W
Bowron, r., Can. (bō'rŭn)	95	53°20'N	121°10'W
Boxelder Creek, r., Mt., U.S. (bŏks'ĕl-dẽr)	112	45°35'N	104°28'W
Box Elder Creek, r., Mt., U.S.	115	47°17'N	108°37'W
Box Hill, Austl.	217a	37°49'S	145°08'E
Boxian, China (bwo shyĕn)	208	33°52'N	115°47'E
Boxing, China (bwo-shyĭŋ)	206	37°09'N	118°08'E
Boxtel, Neth.	159a	51°40'N	5°21'E
Boyabo, D.R.C.	236	3°43'N	18°46'E
Boyang, China (bwo-yäŋ)	209	29°00'N	116°42'E
Boyer, r., Can. (boi'ẽr)	102b	46°45'N	70°56'W
Boyer, r., Ia., U.S.	112	41°45'N	95°36'W
Boyle, Ire. (boil)	164	53°59'N	8°15'W
Boyne, r., Ire. (boin)	164	53°40'N	6°40'W
Boyne City, Mi., U.S.	108	45°15'N	85°05'W
Boyoma Falls, wtfl., D.R.C.	231	0°30'N	25°12'E
Boysen Reservoir, res., Wy., U.S.	115	43°19'N	108°11'W
Bozcaada, Tur. (bōz-cä'dä)	175	39°50'N	26°05'E
Bozca Ada, i., Tur.	175	39°50'N	26°00'E
Bozeman, Mt., U.S. (bōz'mǎn)	104	45°41'N	111°00'W
Bozene, D.R.C.	236	2°56'N	19°12'E
Bozhen, China (bwo-jŭn)	206	38°05'N	116°35'E
Bozoum, C.A.R.	235	6°19'N	16°23'E
Bra, Italy (brä)	174	44°41'N	7°52'E
Bracciano, Lago di, l., Italy (lä'gō-dē-brä-chä'nō)	174	42°05'N	12°00'E
Bracebridge, Can. (brās'brĭj)	99	45°05'N	79°20'W
Braceville, Il., U.S. (brās'vĭl)	111a	41°13'N	88°16'W
Bräcke, Swe. (brĕk'kĕ)	160	62°44'N	15°28'E
Brackenridge, Pa., U.S. (brăk'ĕn-rĭj)	111e	40°37'N	79°44'W
Brackettville, Tx., U.S. (brăk'ĕt-vĭl)	122	29°19'N	100°24'W
Braço Maior, mth., Braz.	143	11°00'S	51°00'W
Braço Menor, mth., Braz. (brä'zō-mē-nō'r)	143	11°38'S	50°00'W
Bradano, r., Italy (brä-dä'nō)	174	40°43'N	16°22'E
Bradenton, Fl., U.S. (brā'dĕn-tŭn)	125a	27°28'N	82°35'W
Bradfield, Eng., U.K. (brăd'fēld)	158b	51°25'N	1°08'W
Bradford, Eng., U.K. (brăd'fẽrd)	160	53°47'N	1°44'W
Bradford, Oh., U.S.	108	40°10'N	84°30'W
Bradford, Pa., U.S.	109	42°00'N	78°40'W
Bradley, Il., U.S. (brăd'lĭ)	111a	41°09'N	87°52'W
Bradner, Can. (brăd'nẽr)	116d	49°05'N	122°26'W
Brady, Tx., U.S. (brā'dĭ)	122	31°09'N	99°21'W
Braga, Port. (brä'gä)	162	41°20'N	8°25'W
Bragado, Arg. (brä-gä'dō)	144	35°07'S	60°28'W
Bragança, Braz. (brä-gän'sä)	143	1°02'S	46°50'W
Bragança, Port.	172	41°48'N	6°46'W
Bragança Paulista, Braz. (brä-gän'sä-pä'ōō-lē's-tà)	144	22°58'S	46°31'W
Bragg Creek, Can. (brăg)	102e	50°57'N	114°35'W
Brahmaputra, r., Asia (brä'mà-pōō'trà)	199	26°45'N	92°45'E
Brāhui, mts., Pak.	199	28°32'N	66°15'E
Braidwood, Il., U.S. (brād'wŏŏd)	111a	41°16'N	88°13'W
Brăila, Rom. (brē'ēlà)	154	45°15'N	27°58'E
Brainerd, Mn., U.S. (brān'ẽrd)	113	46°20'N	94°09'W
Braintree, Ma., U.S. (brān'trē)	101a	42°14'N	71°00'W
Braithwaite, La., U.S. (brīth'wīt)	110d	29°52'N	89°57'W
Brakpan, S. Afr. (brăk'păn)	233b	26°15'S	28°22'E
Bralorne, Can. (brā'lôrn)	95	50°47'N	122°49'W
Bramalea, Can.	102d	43°48'N	79°41'W
Brampton, Can. (brămp'tŭn)	99	43°41'N	79°46'W
Branca, Pedra, mtn., Braz. (pĕ'drä-brä'ɴ-kä)	144b	22°55'S	43°28'W
Branchville, N.J., U.S. (brănch'vĭl)	110a	41°09'S	74°44'W
Branchville, S.C., U.S.	125	33°17'N	80°48'W
Branco, r., Braz. (bräŋ'kō)	143	2°21'N	60°38'W
Brandberg, mtn., Nmb.	232	21°15'S	14°15'E
Brandenburg, Ger. (brän'dĕn-bŏŏrgh)	161	52°25'N	12°33'E
Brandenburg, state, Ger.	159b	52°15'N	13°00'E
Brandenburg, hist. reg., Ger.	168	52°12'N	13°31'E
Brandfort, S. Afr. (brăn'd-fŏrt)	238c	28°42'S	26°29'E
Brandon, Can. (brăn'dŭn)	90	49°50'N	99°57'W
Brandon, Vt., U.S.	109	43°45'N	73°05'W
Brandon Mountain, mtn., Ire. (brăn-dŏn)	164	52°15'N	10°12'W
Brandywine, Md., U.S. (brăndĭ'wīn)	110e	38°42'N	76°51'W
Branford, Ct., U.S. (brăn'fẽrd)	109	41°15'N	72°50'W
Braniewo, Pol. (brä-nyĕ'vō)	169	54°23'N	19°50'E
Brańsk, Pol. (brän' sk)	169	52°44'N	22°51'E
Branson, Mo., U.S.	121	36°39'N	93°13'W
Brantford, Can. (brănt'fẽrd)	99	43°09'N	80°17'W
Bras d'Or Lake, l., Can. (brä-dôr')	101	45°52'N	60°50'W
Brasília, Braz. (brä-sē'lyä)	143	15°49'S	47°39'W
Brasilia Legal, Braz.	143	3°45'S	55°46'W
Brasópolis, Braz. (brä-sō'pō-lēs)	141a	22°30'S	45°36'W
Braşov, Rom.	163	45°39'N	25°35'E
Brass, Nig. (brăs)	230	4°28'N	6°28'E
Brasschaat, Bel. (bräs'kät)	159a	51°19'N	4°30'E
Bratenahl, Oh., U.S. (bră'tĕn-ôl)	111d	41°34'N	81°36'W
Bratislava, Slvk. (brä'tĭs-lä-vä)	154	48°09'N	17°07'E
Bratsk, Russia (brätsk)	179	56°10'N	102°04'E
Bratskoye Vodokhranilishche, res., Russia	179	56°10'N	102°05'E
Bratslav, Ukr. (brät'sláf)	177	48°48'N	28°59'E
Brattleboro, Vt., U.S. (brăt''l-bŭr-ō)	109	42°50'N	72°35'W
Braunau, Aus. (brou'nou)	168	48°15'N	13°05'E
Braunschweig, Ger. (broun'shvīgh)	161	52°16'N	10°32'E
Bråviken, r., Swe.	166	58°40'N	16°40'E
Brawley, Ca., U.S. (brô'lĭ)	104	32°59'N	115°32'W
Bray, Ire. (brā)	164	53°10'N	6°05'W
Braymer, Mo., U.S. (brā'mẽr)	121	39°34'N	93°47'W
Brays Bay, Tx., U.S. (brās'bĭ'yōō)	123a	29°41'N	95°33'W
Brazeau, r., Can.	95	52°55'N	116°10'W
Brazeau, Mount, mtn., Can. (bră-zō')	95	52°33'N	117°21'W
Brazil, In., U.S. (brȧ-zĭl')	108	39°30'N	87°00'W
Brazil, nation, S.A.	143	9°00'S	53°00'W
Brazilian Highlands, mts., Braz. (brȧ zĭl yȧn hī-lǎndz)	139	14°00'S	48°00'W
Brazos, r., Tx., U.S. (brä'zōs)	106	33°10'N	98°50'W
Brazos, Clear Fork, r., Tx., U.S.	122	32°56'N	99°14'W
Brazos, Double Mountain Fork, r., Tx., U.S.	120	33°23'N	101°21'W
Brazos, Salt Fork, r., Tx., U.S. (sôlt fôrk)	120	33°20'N	101°57'W
Brazzaville, Congo (brȧ-zȧ-vēl')	232	4°16'S	15°17'E
Brčko, Bos. (bĕrch'kō)	175	44°54'N	18°46'E
Brda, r., Pol. (bẽr-dä)	169	53°18'N	17°55'E
Brea, Ca., U.S. (brē'ȧ)	117a	33°55'N	117°54'W
Breakeyville, Can.	102b	46°40'N	71°13'W
Breckenridge, Mn., U.S. (brĕk'ĕn-rĭj)	112	46°17'N	96°35'W
Breckenridge, Tx., U.S.	122	32°46'N	98°53'W
Brecksville, Oh., U.S. (brĕks'vĭl)	111d	41°19'N	81°38'W
Břeclav, Czech Rep. (brzhĕl'láf)	168	48°46'N	16°54'E
Breda, Neth. (brā-dä')	165	51°35'N	4°47'E
Bredasdorp, S. Afr. (brā'das-dôrp)	232	34°15'S	20°00'E
Bredy, Russia (brĕ'dĭ)	186a	52°25'N	60°23'E
Bregenz, Aus. (brā'gĕnts)	168	47°30'N	9°46'E
Bregovo, Blg. (brĕ'gō-vō)	175	44°07'N	22°45'E
Breidafjördur, b., Ice.	160	65°15'N	22°50'W
Breidbach, S. Afr. (brĕd'băk)	233c	32°54'S	27°26'E
Breil-sur-Roya, Fr. (brĕ'y')	171	43°57'N	7°36'E
Brejo, Braz. (brå'zhō)	143	3°33'S	42°46'W
Bremangerlandet, i., Nor.	166	61°51'N	4°25'E
Bremen, Ger. (brā-mĕn)	154	53°05'N	8°50'E
Bremen, In., U.S. (brē'mĕn)	108	41°25'N	86°05'W
Bremerhaven, Ger. (brām-ẽr-hä'fĕn)	160	53°33'N	8°38'E
Bremerton, Wa., U.S. (brĕm'ẽr-tŭn)	114	47°34'N	122°38'W
Bremervörde, Ger. (brĕ'mẽr-fûr-dĕ)	159c	53°29'N	9°09'E
Bremner, Can. (brĕm'nẽr)	102g	53°34'N	113°14'W
Bremond, Tx., U.S. (brĕm'ŭnd)	123	31°11'N	96°40'W
Brenham, Tx., U.S. (brĕn'ăm)	123	30°10'N	96°24'W
Brenner Pass, p., Eur. (brĕn'ẽr)	161	47°00'N	11°30'E
Brentwood, Eng., U.K. (brĕnt'wŏŏd)	165	51°37'N	0°18'E
Brentwood, Md., U.S.	109	39°00'N	76°55'W
Brentwood, Mo., U.S.	117e	38°37'N	90°21'W
Brentwood, Pa., U.S.	111e	40°22'N	79°59'W
Brescia, Italy (brā'shä)	162	45°33'N	10°15'E
Bressanone, Italy (brĕs-sä-nō'nä)	174	46°42'N	11°40'E
Bressuire, Fr. (grĕ-swēr')	170	46°49'N	0°14'W
Brest, Bela.	178	52°06'N	23°43'E
Brest, Fr. (brĕst)	154	48°24'N	4°30'W
Brest, prov., Bela.	176	52°30'N	26°50'E
Bretagne, hist. reg., Fr. (brĕ-täɴ'yĕ)	170	48°00'N	3°00'W
Breton, Pertuis, strt., Fr. (pâr-twē'brĕ-tôɴ')	170	46°18'N	1°43'W
Breton Sound, strt., La., U.S. (brĕt'ŭn)	124	29°38'N	89°15'W
Breukelen, Neth.	159a	52°09'N	5°00'E
Brevard, N.C., U.S. (brē-värd')	125	35°14'N	82°45'W
Breves, Braz. (brā'vĕzh)	143	1°32'S	50°13'W
Brevik, Nor. (brĕ'vĕk)	166	59°04'N	9°39'E
Brewarrina, Austl. (brōō-ẽr-rē'nȧ)	219	29°54'S	146°50'E
Brewer, Me., U.S. (brōō'ẽr)	100	44°46'N	68°46'W
Brewerville, Lib.	234	6°26'N	10°47'W
Brewster, N.Y., U.S. (brōō'stẽr)	110a	41°23'N	73°38'W
Brewster, Cerro, mtn., Pan. (sĕ'r-rō-brōō'stẽr)	133	9°19'N	79°15'W
Brewton, Al., U.S. (brōō'tŭn)	124	31°06'N	87°04'W
Brežice, Slvn. (brĕ'zhē-tsĕ)	174	45°55'N	15°37'E
Breznik, Blg. (brĕs'nĕk)	175	42°44'N	22°55'E
Briancon, Fr. (brē-äɴ-sôɴ')	171	44°54'N	6°39'E
Briare, Fr. (brē-är')	170	47°40'N	2°46'E
Bridal Veil, Or., U.S. (brīd'ăl vāl)	116c	45°33'N	122°10'W
Bridge Point, c., Bah. (brĭj)	134	25°35'N	76°40'W
Bridgeport, Al., U.S. (brĭj'pôrt)	124	34°55'N	85°42'W
Bridgeport, Ct., U.S.	105	41°12'N	73°12'W
Bridgeport, Il., U.S.	108	38°40'N	87°45'W
Bridgeport, Ne., U.S.	112	41°40'N	103°06'W
Bridgeport, Oh., U.S.	108	40°00'N	80°45'W
Bridgeport, Pa., U.S.	110f	40°06'N	75°21'W
Bridgeport, Tx., U.S.	121	33°13'N	97°46'W
Bridgeton, Al., U.S. (brĭj'tŭn)	110h	33°27'N	86°39'W
Bridgeton, Mo., U.S.	117e	38°45'N	90°23'W
Bridgeton, N.J., U.S.	109	39°30'N	75°15'W
Bridgetown, Barb. (brĭj' toun)	129	13°08'N	59°37'W
Bridgetown, Can.	100	44°51'N	65°18'W
Bridgeville, Pa., U.S. (brĭj'vĭl)	111e	40°22'N	80°07'W
Bridgewater, Austl. (brĭj'wô-tẽr)	222	42°50'S	147°28'E
Bridgewater, Can.	91	44°23'N	64°31'W
Bridgnorth, Eng., U.K. (brĭj'nôrth)	158a	52°32'N	2°25'W
Bridgton, Me., U.S. (brĭj'tŭn)	100	44°04'N	70°45'W
Bridlington, Eng., U.K. (brĭd'lĭng-tŭn)	164	54°06'N	0°10'W
Brie-Comte-Robert, Fr. (brē-kôɴt-ĕ-rō-bâr')	171b	48°42'N	2°37'E
Brielle, Neth.	159a	51°54'N	4°08'E
Brierfield, Eng., U.K. (brī'ẽr fēld)	158a	53°49'N	2°14'W
Brierfield, Al., U.S. (brī'ẽr-fēld)	124	33°01'N	86°55'W
Brier Island, i., Can. (brī'ẽr)	100	44°16'N	66°24'W
Brieselang, Ger. (brē'zĕ-läng)	159b	52°36'N	12°59'E
Briey, Fr. (brē-ĕ')	171	49°15'N	5°57'E
Brig, Switz. (brēg)	161	46°17'N	7°59'E
Brigg, Eng., U.K. (brĭg)	158a	53°33'N	0°29'W
Brigham City, Ut., U.S. (brĭg'ăm)	117b	41°31'N	112°01'W
Brighouse, Eng., U.K. (brĭg'hous)	158a	53°42'N	1°47'W
Bright, Austl. (brīt)	222	36°43'S	147°00'E
Bright, In., U.S. (brīt)	111f	39°13'N	84°51'W
Brightlingsea, Eng., U.K. (brī't-lĭng-sē)	158b	51°50'N	1°00'E
Brighton, Austl.	217a	37°55'S	145°00'E
Brighton, Eng., U.K.	161	50°47'N	0°07'W
Brighton, Al., U.S. (brīt'ŭn)	110h	33°27'N	86°56'W
Brighton, Co., U.S.	120	39°58'N	104°49'W
Brighton, Ia., U.S.	113	41°11'N	91°47'W
Brighton, Il., U.S.	117e	39°03'N	90°08'W
Brighton Indian Reservation, I.R., Fl., U.S.	125a	27°05'N	81°25'W
Brihuega, Spain (brē-wā'gä)	172	40°32'N	2°52'W
Brimley, Mi., U.S. (brĭm'lē)	117k	46°24'N	84°34'W
Brindisi, Italy (brēn'dē-zē)	154	40°38'N	17°57'E
Brinje, Cro. (brēn'yĕ)	174	45°00'N	15°08'E
Brinkley, Ar., U.S. (brĭŋk'lĭ)	121	34°52'N	91°12'W
Brinnon, Wa., U.S. (brĭn'ŭn)	116a	47°41'N	122°54'W
Brion, i., Can. (brē-ôɴ')	101	47°47'N	61°29'W
Brioude, Fr. (brē-ōōd')	170	45°18'N	3°22'E
Brisbane, Austl. (brĭz'bån)	222	27°30'S	153°10'E
Bristol, Eng., U.K.	161	51°29'N	2°39'W
Bristol, Ct., U.S. (brĭs'tŭl)	109	41°40'N	72°55'W
Bristol, Pa., U.S.	110f	40°06'N	74°51'W
Bristol, R.I., U.S.	110b	41°41'N	71°14'W
Bristol, Tn., U.S.	105	36°35'N	82°10'W
Bristol, Va., U.S.	105	36°36'N	82°00'W
Bristol, Vt., U.S.	109	44°10'N	73°00'W
Bristol, Wi., U.S.	111a	42°32'N	88°04'W
Bristol Bay, b., Ak., U.S.	103	58°05'N	158°54'W
Bristol Channel, strt., Eng., U.K.	161	51°20'N	3°47'W
Bristow, Ok., U.S. (brĭs'tō)	121	35°50'N	96°25'W
British Columbia, prov., Can. (brĭt'ĭsh kŏl'ŭm-bĭ-ȧ)	90	56°00'N	124°53'W
British Indian Ocean Territory, dep., Afr.	2	7°00'S	72°00'E
British Isles, is., Eur.	156	54°00'N	4°00'W
Brits, S. Afr.	238c	25°39'S	27°47'E
Britstown, S. Afr. (brĭts'toun)	232	30°30'S	23°40'E
Britt, Ia., U.S. (brĭt)	113	43°05'N	93°47'W
Brittany see Bretagne, hist. reg., Fr.	170	48°00'N	3°00'W
Britton, S.D., U.S. (brĭt'ŭn)	112	45°47'N	97°44'W
Brive-la-Gaillarde, Fr. (brēv-lä-gī-yärd'ĕ)	161	45°10'N	1°31'E
Briviesca, Spain (brē-vyās'kȧ)	172	42°34'N	3°21'W
Brno, Czech Rep. (b'r'nō)	154	49°18'N	16°37'E
Broa, Ensenada de la, b., Cuba	134	22°30'N	82°00'W
Broach, India	202	21°47'N	72°58'E
Broad, r., Ga., U.S. (brôd)	124	34°15'N	83°14'W
Broad, r., N.C., U.S.	125	35°38'N	82°40'W
Broadmeadows, Austl. (brôd'mĕd-ōz)	217a	37°40'S	144°53'E
Broadview Heights, Oh., U.S. (brôd'vū)	111d	41°18'N	81°41'W
Brockport, N.Y., U.S. (brŏk'pōrt)	109	43°15'N	77°55'W
Brockton, Ma., U.S. (brŏk'tŭn)	101a	42°04'N	71°01'W
Brockville, Can. (brŏk'vĭl)	91	44°35'N	75°40'W
Brockway, Mt., U.S. (brŏk'wā)	115	47°24'N	105°41'W
Brodnica, Pol. (brōd'nĭt-sȧ)	169	53°16'N	19°26'E
Brody, Ukr. (brō'dĭ)	181	50°05'N	25°10'E
Broken Arrow, Ok., U.S. (brō'kĕn ăr'ō)	121	36°03'N	95°48'W
Broken Bay, b., Austl.	222	33°34'S	151°20'E
Broken Bow, Ne., U.S. (brō'kĕn bō)	112	41°24'N	99°37'W
Broken Bow, Ok., U.S.	121	34°02'N	94°43'W
Broken Hill, Austl. (brōk'ĕn)	219	31°55'S	141°35'E
Broken Hill see Kabwe, Zam.	232	14°27'S	28°27'E
Bromley, Eng., U.K. (brŭm'lĭ)	158b	51°23'N	0°01'E
Bromptonville, Can. (brŭmp'tŭn-vĭl)	99	45°30'N	72°00'W
Brønderslev, Den. (brûn'dẽr-slĕv)	166	57°15'N	9°56'E
Bronkhorstspruit, S. Afr.	238c	25°50'S	28°48'E
Bronnitsy, Russia (brô-nyĭ'tsĭ)	176	55°26'N	38°16'E
Bronson, Mi., U.S. (brŏn'sŭn)	108	41°55'N	85°15'W
Bronte Creek, r., Can.	102d	43°25'N	79°53'W
Brood, r., S.C., U.S. (brōōd)	125	34°46'N	81°25'W
Brookfield, Il., U.S. (brŏŏk'fēld)	111a	41°49'N	87°51'W
Brookfield, Mo., U.S.	121	39°45'N	93°04'W
Brookhaven, Ga., U.S. (brŏŏk'hāv'n)	110c	33°52'N	84°21'W
Brookhaven, Ms., U.S.	124	31°35'N	90°26'W
Brookings, Or., U.S. (brŏŏk'ĭngs)	114	42°04'N	124°16'W
Brookings, S.D., U.S.	112	44°18'N	96°47'W
Brookline, Ma., U.S. (brŏŏk'līn)	101a	42°20'N	71°08'W
Brookline, N.H., U.S.	101a	42°44'N	71°37'W
Brooklyn, Oh., U.S. (brŏŏk'lĭn)	111d	41°26'N	81°44'W
Brooklyn Center, Mn., U.S.	117g	45°05'N	93°21'W
Brook Park, Oh., U.S. (brŏŏk)	111d	41°24'N	81°50'W
Brooks, Can.	95	50°35'N	111°53'W
Brooks Range, mts., Ak., U.S. (brŏŏks)	106a	68°20'N	159°00'W
Brooksville, Fl., U.S. (brŏŏks'vĭl)	125a	28°32'N	82°28'W
Brookville, In., U.S. (brŏŏk'vĭl)	108	39°20'N	85°00'W
Brookville, Pa., U.S.	109	41°10'N	79°00'W
Brookwood, Al., U.S. (brŏŏk'wŏŏd)	124	33°15'N	87°17'W
Broome, Austl. (brōōm)	218	18°00'S	122°15'E
Brossard, Can.	102a	45°26'N	73°28'W
Brothers, is., Bah. (brŭd'hẽrs)	134	26°05'N	79°00'W
Broumov, Czech Rep. (brōō'mōf)	168	50°33'N	15°55'E
Brown Bank, bk.	135	21°30'N	74°35'W
Brownfield, Tx., U.S. (broun'fēld)	120	33°11'N	102°16'W
Browning, Mt., U.S. (broun'ĭng)	115	48°37'N	113°05'W
Brownsboro, Ky., U.S. (brounz'bō-rō)	111h	38°22'N	85°30'W
Brownsburg, Can. (brouns'bûrg)	102a	45°40'N	74°24'W
Brownsburg, In., U.S.	111g	39°51'N	86°23'W
Brownsmead, Or., U.S. (brounz'-mēd)	116c	46°13'N	123°33'W
Brownstown, In., U.S. (brounz'toun)	108	38°50'N	86°00'W
Brownsville, Pa., U.S. (brounz'vĭl)	111e	40°01'N	79°53'W
Brownsville, Tn., U.S.	124	35°35'N	89°15'W

ng-sing; ŋ-baŋk; ɴ-nasalized n; nŏd; cŏmmit; ōld; ŏbey; ôrder; oi-boil; fōōd; ŏŏ-as oo in foot; ou-out; s-soft; sh-dish; th-thin; pūre; ûnite; ûrn; stŭd; circŭs; ü-as in French tu; '-indeterminate vowel.

276 Brownsville – Byeshankovichy PRONOUNCING INDEX

PLACE (Pronunciation)	PAGE	LAT.	LONG.
Brownsville, Tx., U.S.	104	25°55'N	97°30'W
Brownville Junction, Me., U.S. (broun'vĭl)	100	45°20'N	69°04'W
Brownwood, Tx., U.S. (broun'wŏŏd)	104	31°44'N	98°58'W
Brownwood, l., Tx., U.S.	122	31°55'N	99°15'W
Brozas, Spain (brō'thäs)	172	39°37'N	6°44'W
Bruce, Mount, mtn., Austl. (brōōs)	220	22°35'S	118°15'E
Bruce Peninsula, pen., Can.	98	44°50'N	81°20'W
Bruceton, Tn., U.S. (brōōs'tŭn)	124	36°02'N	88°14'W
Bruchsal, Ger. (brŏŏk'zäl)	168	49°08'N	8°34'E
Bruck, Aus. (brŏŏk)	168	47°25'N	15°14'E
Bruck, Aus.	168	48°01'N	16°47'E
Brück, Ger. (brük)	159b	52°12'N	12°45'E
Bruderheim, Can. (brōō'dĕr-hīm)	102g	53°47'N	112°56'W
Brugge, Bel.	161	51°13'N	3°05'E
Brühl, Ger. (brül)	171c	50°49'N	6°54'E
Bruneau, r., Id., U.S. (brōō-nō')	114	42°47'N	115°43'W
Brunei, nation, Asia (brŏŏ-nī')	212	4°52'N	113°38'E
Brünen, Ger. (brü'nĕn)	171c	51°43'N	6°41'E
Brunete, Spain (brōō-nā'tā)	173a	40°24'N	4°00'W
Brunette, i., Can. (brŏŏ-nĕt')	101	47°16'N	55°54'W
Brunn am Gebirge, Aus. (brōōn'äm gĕ-bĭr'gĕ)	159e	48°07'N	16°18'E
Brunsbüttel, Ger. (brŏŏns'büt-tĕl)	159c	53°58'N	9°10'E
Brunswick, Ga., U.S. (brŭnz'wĭk)	105	31°08'N	81°30'W
Brunswick, Md., U.S.	109	39°20'N	77°35'W
Brunswick, Me., U.S.	100	43°54'N	69°57'W
Brunswick, Mo., U.S.	121	39°25'N	93°07'W
Brunswick, Oh., U.S.	111d	41°14'N	81°50'W
Brunswick, Península de, pen., Chile	144	53°25'S	71°15'W
Bruny, i., Austl. (brōō'nē)	221	43°30'S	147°50'E
Brush, Co., U.S. (brŭsh)	120	40°14'N	103°40'W
Brusque, Braz. (brōō's-kōō'ĕ)	144	27°15'S	48°45'W
Brussels, Bel.	154	50°51'N	4°21'E
Brussels, Il., U.S. (brŭs'ĕls)	117e	38°57'N	90°36'W
Bruxelles *see* Brussels, Bel.	154	50°51'N	4°21'E
Bryan, Oh., U.S. (brī'ăn)	108	41°25'N	84°30'W
Bryan, Tx., U.S.	123	30°40'N	96°22'W
Bryansk, Russia	178	53°15'N	34°22'E
Bryansk, prov., Russia	176	52°43'N	32°25'E
Bryant, S.D., U.S. (brī'ănt)	112	44°35'N	97°29'W
Bryant, Wa., U.S.	116a	48°14'N	122°10'W
Bryce Canyon National Park, rec., Ut., U.S. (brīs)	106	37°35'N	112°15'W
Bryn Mawr, Pa., U.S. (brĭn mär')	110f	40°02'N	75°20'W
Bryson City, N.C., U.S. (brīs'ŭn)	124	35°25'N	83°25'W
Bryukhovetskaya, Russia (b'ryŭk'ô-vyĕt-skä'yä)	177	45°56'N	38°58'E
Buala, Sol. Is.	214e	8°08'S	159°35'E
Buatan, Indon.	197b	0°45'N	101°49'E
Buba, Gui.-B. (bōō'bȧ)	230	11°39'N	14°58'W
Bucaramanga, Col. (bōō-kä'rä-mäŋ'gä)	142	7°12'N	73°14'W
Buccaneer Archipelago, is., Austl. (bŭk-ȧ-nēr')	220	16°05'S	122°00'E
Buchach, Ukr. (bŏ'chȧch)	169	49°04'N	25°25'E
Buchanan, Lib. (bû-kăn'ăn)	230	5°57'N	10°02'W
Buchanan, Mi., U.S.	108	41°50'N	86°25'W
Buchanan, l., Austl. (bû-kăn'nŏn)	221	21°40'S	145°00'E
Buchanan, l., Tx., U.S. (bû-kăn'ăn)	122	30°55'N	98°40'W
Buchans, Can.	101	48°49'N	56°52'W
Bucharest, Rom.	154	44°23'N	26°10'E
Buchholz, Ger. (bōōk'hōltz)	159c	53°19'N	9°53'E
Buck Creek, r., In., U.S. (bŭk)	111g	39°43'N	85°58'W
Buckhannon, W.V., U.S. (bŭk-hăn'ŭn)	108	39°00'N	80°10'W
Buckhaven, Scot., U.K. (bŭk-hā'v'n)	164	56°10'N	3°10'W
Buckie, Scot., U.K. (bŭk'ī)	164	57°40'N	2°50'W
Buckingham, Can. (bŭk'ĭng-ăm)	102c	45°35'N	75°25'W
Buckingham, can., India (bŭk'ĭng-ăm)	203	15°18'N	79°50'E
Buckinghamshire, co., Eng., U.K.	158b	51°45'N	0°48'W
Buckland, Can. (bŭk'lănd)	102b	46°37'N	70°33'W
Buckland Tableland, reg., Austl.	221	24°31'S	148°00'E
Buckley, Wa., U.S. (bŭk'lē)	116a	47°10'N	122°02'W
Bucksport, Me., U.S. (bŭks'pôrt)	100	44°35'N	68°47'W
Buctouche, Can. (bük-tōōsh')	100	46°28'N	64°43'W
Bucun, China (bōō-tsŏn)	206	36°38'N	117°26'E
Bucureşti *see* Bucharest, Rom.	154	44°23'N	26°10'E
Bucyrus, Oh., U.S. (bû-sī'rŭs)	108	40°50'N	82°55'W
Budapest, Hung. (bōō'dȧ-pĕsht')	154	47°30'N	19°05'E
Budge Budge, India	202a	22°28'N	88°08'E
Budjala, D.R.C.	236	2°39'N	19°42'E
Budyonnovsk, Russia	182	44°46'N	44°09'E
Buea, Cam.	235	4°09'N	9°14'E
Buechel, Ky., U.S. (bĕ-chûl')	111h	38°12'N	85°38'W
Bueil, Fr. (bwā')	171b	48°55'N	1°27'E
Buena Park, Ca., U.S. (bwā'nȧ pärk)	117a	33°52'N	118°00'W
Buenaventura, Col. (bwā'nä-vĕn-tōō'rȧ)	142	3°46'N	77°09'W
Buenaventura, Cuba	135a	22°53'N	82°22'W
Buenaventura, Bahía de, b., Col.	142	3°45'N	79°23'W
Buena Vista, Co., U.S. (bū'nȧ vĭs'tȧ)	120	38°51'N	106°07'W
Buena Vista, Ga., U.S.	124	32°15'N	84°30'W
Buena Vista, Va., U.S.	109	37°45'N	79°20'W
Buena Vista, Bahía, b., Cuba (bä-ē'ä-bwĕ-nä-vē's-tä)	134	22°30'N	79°10'W
Buena Vista Lake Bed, l., Ca., U.S. (bū'nȧ vĭs'tȧ)	118	35°14'N	119°17'W
Buendia, Embalse de, res., Spain	172	40°30'N	2°45'W
Buenos Aires, Arg. (bwā'nōs ī'rās)	144	34°20'S	58°30'W
Buenos Aires, Col.	142a	3°01'N	76°34'W
Buenos Aires, C.R.	133	9°10'N	83°21'W
Buenos Aires, prov., Arg.	144	36°15'S	61°45'W
Buenos Aires, l., S.A.	144	46°30'S	72°15'W
Buffalo, Mn., U.S. (bŭf'ȧ lō)	113	45°10'N	93°50'W
Buffalo, N.Y., U.S.	105	42°54'N	78°51'W
Buffalo, Tx., U.S.	123	31°28'N	96°04'W
Buffalo, Wy., U.S.	115	44°19'N	106°42'W
Buffalo, r., S. Afr.	233c	28°35'S	30°27'E
Buffalo, r., Ar., U.S.	121	35°56'N	92°58'W
Buffalo, r., Tn., U.S.	124	35°24'N	87°10'W
Buffalo Bayou, Tx., U.S.	123a	29°46'N	95°32'W
Buffalo Creek, r., Mn., U.S.	113	44°46'N	94°28'W
Buffalo Head Hills, hills, Can.	92	57°16'N	116°18'W
Buford, Can. (bū'fûrd)	102g	53°15'N	113°55'W
Buford, Ga., U.S. (bū'fērd)	124	34°05'N	84°00'W
Bug (Zakhidnyy Buh), r., Eur.	169	52°29'N	21°20'E
Buga, Col. (bōō'gä)	142	3°54'N	76°17'W
Buggenhout, Bel.	159a	51°01'N	4°10'E
Buglandsfjorden, l., Nor.	166	58°53'N	7°55'E
Bugojno, Bos. (bŏ-gō ī nō)	175	44°03'N	17°28'E
Bugul'ma, Russia (bŏ-gōl'mȧ)	178	54°40'N	52°40'E
Buguruslan, Russia (bŏ-gŏ-rŏs-lȧn')	178	53°30'N	52°32'E
Buhi, Phil. (bōō'ē)	213a	13°26'N	123°31'E
Buhl, Id., U.S. (būl)	115	42°36'N	114°45'W
Buhl, Mn., U.S.	113	47°28'N	92°49'W
Buin, Chile (bŏ-ēn')	141b	33°44'S	70°44'W
Buinaksk, Russia (bŏ'ē-näksk)	181	42°40'N	47°20'E
Buir Nur, l., Asia (bōō-ēr nōōr)	205	47°50'N	117°00'E
Bujalance, Spain (bōō-hä-län'thā)	172	37°54'N	4°22'W
Bujumbura, Bdi.	237	3°23'S	29°22'E
Buka Island, i., Pap. N. Gui.	214e	5°15'S	154°35'E
Bukama, D.R.C. (bōō-kä'mä)	232	9°08'S	26°00'E
Bukavu, D.R.C.	232	2°30'S	28°52'E
Bukhara, Uzb. (bŏ-kä'rä)	183	39°31'N	64°22'E
Bukitbatu, Indon.	197b	1°25'N	101°58'E
Bukittinggi, Indon.	212	0°25'S	100°28'E
Bukoba, Tan.	232	1°20'S	31°49'E
Bukovina, hist. reg., Eur. (bŏ-kô'vĭ-nȧ)	169	48°06'N	25°20'E
Bula, Indon. (bōō'lä)	213	3°00'S	130°30'E
Bulalacao, Phil. (bōō-lä-lä'kä-ō)	213a	12°30'N	121°20'E
Bulawayo, Zimb. (bōō-lȧ-wā'yō)	232	20°12'S	28°43'E
Buldir, i., Ak., U.S. (bŭl dĭr)	103a	52°22'N	175°50'E
Bulgaria, nation, Eur. (bŏŏl-gā'rĭ-ă)	154	42°12'N	24°13'E
Bulkley Ranges, mts., Can. (bŭlk'lē)	94	54°30'N	127°30'W
Bullaque, r., Spain (bŏŏ-lä'kā)	172	39°15'N	4°13'W
Bullas, Spain (bōōl'yäs)	172	38°07'N	1°48'W
Bullfrog Creek, r., Ut., U.S.	119	37°45'N	110°55'W
Bull Harbour, Can. (hăr'bēr)	94	50°45'N	127°55'W
Bull Head, mtn., Jam.	134	18°10'N	77°15'W
Bull Run, r., Or., U.S. (bŏŏl)	116c	45°26'N	122°11'W
Bull Run Reservoir, res., Or., U.S.	116c	45°29'N	122°11'W
Bull Shoals Reservoir, res., U.S. (bŏŏl shōlz)	107	36°35'N	92°57'W
Bulpham, Eng., U.K. (bōōl'făn)	158b	51°33'N	0°21'E
Bultfontein, S. Afr. (bŏŏlt'fŏn-tān')	238c	28°18'S	26°10'E
Bulun, Russia (bōō-lōōn')	179	70°48'N	127°27'E
Bulungu, D.R.C. (bōō-lōŋ'gōō)	236	6°04'S	21°54'E
Bulwer, S. Afr. (bŏŏl-wēr)	233c	29°49'S	29°48'E
Bumba, D.R.C. (bōōm'bȧ)	231	2°11'N	22°28'E
Bumbire Island, i., Tan.	237	1°40'S	32°05'E
Buna, Pap. N. Gui. (bōō'nȧ)	213	8°58'S	148°38'E
Bunbury, Austl. (bŭn'bŭrĭ)	218	33°25'S	115°45'E
Bundaberg, Austl. (bŭn'dȧ-bûrg)	219	24°45'S	152°18'E
Bunguran Utara, Kepulauan, is., Indon.	212	3°22'N	108°00'E
Bunia, D.R.C.	237	1°34'N	30°15'E
Bunker Hill, Il., U.S. (bŭnk'ēr hĭl)	117e	39°03'N	89°57'W
Bunkie, La., U.S. (bŭŋ'kĭ)	123	30°55'N	92°10'W
Bun Plains, pl., Kenya	237	0°55'N	40°35'E
Bununu Dass, Nig.	235	10°00'N	9°31'E
Buor-Khaya, Guba, b., Russia	185	71°45'N	131°00'E
Buor Khaya, Mys, c., Russia	179	71°47'N	133°22'E
Bura, Kenya	237	1°06'S	39°57'E
Buraydah, Sau. Ar.	198	26°23'N	44°14'E
Burbank, Ca., U.S. (bûr'bănk)	117a	34°11'N	118°19'W
Burco, Som.	238a	9°20'N	45°45'E
Burdekin, r., Austl. (bûr'dĕ-kĭn)	221	19°22'S	145°07'E
Burdur, Tur. (bŏŏr-dŏŏr')	163	37°50'N	30°15'E
Burdwān, India (bŏŏd-wän')	199	23°29'N	87°53'E
Bureinskiy, Khrebet, mts., Russia	179	51°15'N	133°30'E
Bureya, Russia (bŏŏrā'ȧ)	179	49°55'N	130°00'E
Bureya, r., Russia (bŏ-rā'yä)	185	51°00'N	131°15'E
Burford, Eng., U.K. (bûr-fērd)	158b	51°46'N	1°38'W
Burgas, Blg. (bŏŏr-gäs')	163	42°29'N	27°30'E
Burgas, Gulf of, b., Blg.	163	42°30'N	27°40'E
Burgaw, N.C., U.S. (bûr'gô)	125	34°31'N	77°56'W
Burgdorf, Switz. (bŏrg'dôrf)	168	47°04'N	7°37'E
Burgenland, state, Aus.	159e	47°58'N	16°57'E
Burgeo, Can.	101	47°36'N	57°34'W
Burgess, Va., U.S.	109	37°53'N	76°21'W
Burgo de Osma, Spain	172	41°35'N	3°02'W
Burgos, Mex. (bŏŏr'gōs)	122	24°57'N	98°47'W
Burgos, Phil.	213a	16°03'N	119°52'E
Burgos, Spain (bōō'r-gōs)	162	42°20'N	3°44'W
Burgsvik, Swe. (bŏrgs'vĭk)	166	57°04'N	18°18'E
Burhānpur, India (bŏŏr'hän-pōōr)	199	21°26'N	76°08'E
Burias Island, i., Phil. (bōō'rē-äs)	213a	12°56'N	122°56'E
Burias Pass, strt., Phil. (bōō'rē-äs)	213a	13°04'N	123°11'E
Burica, Punta, c., N.A. (pōō'n-tä-bōō'rē-kä)	133	8°02'N	83°12'W
Burien, Wa., U.S. (bū'rĭ-ĕn)	116a	47°28'N	122°20'W
Burin, Can. (bûr'ĭn)	93a	47°02'N	55°10'W
Burin Peninsula, pen., Can.	101	47°00'N	55°40'W
Burkburnett, Tx., U.S. (bûrk-bûr'nĕt)	120	34°04'N	98°35'W
Burke, Vt., U.S. (bûrk)	109	44°40'N	72°00'W
Burke Channel, strt., Can.	94	52°07'N	127°38'W
Burketown, Austl. (bûrk'toun)	218	17°50'S	139°30'E
Burkina Faso, nation, Afr.	230	13°00'N	2°00'W
Burley, Id., U.S. (bûr'lĭ)	115	42°31'N	113°48'W
Burley, Wa., U.S.	116a	47°25'N	122°38'W
Burlingame, Ca., U.S. (bûr'lĭn-gām)	116b	37°35'N	122°22'W
Burlingame, Ks., U.S.	121	38°45'N	95°49'W
Burlington, Can. (bûr'lĭng-tŭn)	99	43°19'N	79°48'W
Burlington, Co., U.S.	120	39°17'N	102°26'W
Burlington, Ia., U.S.	105	40°48'N	91°05'W
Burlington, Ks., U.S.	121	38°10'N	95°46'W
Burlington, Ky., U.S.	111f	39°01'N	84°44'W
Burlington, Ma., U.S.	101a	42°31'N	71°13'W
Burlington, N.C., U.S.	125	36°05'N	79°26'W
Burlington, N.J., U.S.	110f	40°04'N	74°52'W
Burlington, Vt., U.S.	105	44°30'N	73°15'W
Burlington, Wa., U.S.	116a	48°28'N	122°20'W
Burlington, Wi., U.S.	111a	42°41'N	88°16'W
Burma *see* Myanmar, nation, Asia	194	21°00'N	95°15'E
Burnaby, Can.	90	49°14'N	122°58'W
Burnet, Tx., U.S. (bûrn'ĕt)	122	30°46'N	98°14'W
Burnham on Crouch, Eng., U.K. (bûrn'ăm-ŏn-krouch)	158b	51°38'N	0°48'E
Burnie, Austl. (bûr'nē)	219	41°15'S	146°05'E
Burnley, Eng., U.K. (bûrn'lē)	164	53°47'N	2°19'W
Burns, Or., U.S. (bûrnz)	114	43°35'N	119°05'W
Burnside, Ky., U.S. (bûrn'sīd)	124	36°57'N	84°33'W
Burns Lake, Can. (bûrnz lăk)	90	54°14'N	125°46'W
Burnsville, Can. (bûrnz'vĭl)	100	47°44'N	65°07'W
Burnt, r., Or., U.S. (bûrnt)	114	44°26'N	117°53'W
Burntwood, r., Can.	97	55°53'N	97°30'W
Burrard Inlet, b., Can. (bûr'ȧrd)	116d	49°19'N	123°15'W
Burr Gaabo, Som.	233	1°14'N	51°47'E
Burro, Serranías del, mts., Mex. (sĕr-rä-nē'äs dĕl bōō'r-rō)	122	29°39'N	102°07'W
Bursa, Tur. (bōōr'sȧ)	198	40°10'N	28°10'E
Būr Safājah, Egypt	231	26°57'N	33°56'E
Burscheid, Ger. (bŏŏr'shīd)	171c	51°05'N	7°07'E
Būr Sūdān, Sudan (sōō-dăn')	231	19°30'N	37°10'E
Burt, N.Y., U.S. (bûrt)	111c	43°19'N	78°45'W
Burt, l., Mi., U.S. (bûrt)	108	45°25'N	84°45'W
Burton, Wa., U.S. (bûr'tŭn)	116a	47°24'N	122°28'W
Burton, Lake, res., Ga., U.S.	124	34°46'N	83°40'W
Burtonsville, Md., U.S. (bûrtŏns-vĭl)	110e	39°07'N	76°57'W
Burton-upon-Trent, Eng., U.K. (bûr'tŭn-ŭp'-ŏn-trĕnt)	164	52°48'N	1°37'W
Buru, i., Indon.	213	3°30'S	126°30'E
Burullus, l., Egypt	238b	31°20'N	30°58'E
Burundi, nation, Afr.	232	3°00'S	29°30'E
Burwell, Ne., U.S. (bûr'wĕl)	112	41°46'N	99°08'W
Bury, Eng., U.K. (bĕr'ĭ)	158a	53°36'N	2°17'W
Buryatia, prov., Russia	185	55°15'N	112°00'E
Bury Saint Edmunds, Eng., U.K. (bĕr'ĭ-sānt ĕd'mŭndz)	165	52°14'N	0°44'E
Burzaco, Arg. (bōōr-zá'kō)	144a	34°50'S	58°23'W
Busanga Swamp, sw., Zam.	237	14°10'S	25°50'E
Būsh, Egypt (bōōsh)	238b	29°13'N	31°08'E
Bushmanland, hist. reg., S. Afr. (bŏŏsh-măn-lănd)	232	29°15'S	18°45'E
Bushnell, Il., U.S. (bŏŏsh'nĕl)	121	40°33'N	90°28'W
Businga, D.R.C. (bō-sĭŋ'gȧ)	231	3°20'N	20°53'E
Busira, r., D.R.C.	236	0°05'S	19°20'E
Bus'k, Ukr.	169	49°58'N	24°39'E
Busselton, Austl. (bŭs'l-tŭn)	218	33°40'S	115°30'E
Bussum, Neth.	159a	52°16'N	5°10'E
Bustamante, Mex. (bōōs-tȧ-män'tā)	122	26°34'N	100°30'W
Busto Arsizio, Italy (bōōs'tō är-sēd'zē-ō)	174	45°47'N	8°51'E
Busuanga, i., Phil. (bōō-swäŋ'gä)	213a	12°20'N	119°43'E
Buta, D.R.C. (bōō'tȧ)	231	2°48'N	24°44'E
Butha Buthe, Leso. (bōō-thȧ-bōō'thȧ)	233c	28°49'S	28°16'E
Butler, Al., U.S. (bŭt'lēr)	124	32°05'N	88°10'W
Butler, In., U.S.	108	41°25'N	84°50'W
Butler, Md., U.S.	110e	39°32'N	76°46'W
Butler, N.J., U.S.	110a	41°00'N	74°20'W
Butler, Pa., U.S.	109	40°50'N	79°55'W
Butovo, Russia (bŏ-tô'vô)	186b	55°33'N	37°36'E
Butsha, D.R.C.	237	0°57'N	29°13'E
Buttahatchee, r., Al., U.S. (bŭt-ȧ-hăch'ē)	124	34°02'N	88°05'W
Butte, Mt., U.S. (būt)	104	46°00'N	112°31'W
Butterworth, S. Afr. (bŭ tēr'wûrth)	233c	32°20'S	28°09'E
Butt of Lewis, c., Scot., U.K. (bŭt ŏv lū'ĭs)	164	58°34'N	6°15'W
Butuan, Phil. (bōō-tōō'än)	213	8°40'N	125°33'E
Buturlinovka, Russia (bōō-tōō'lē-nôf'ka)	181	50°47'N	40°35'E
Buuhoodle, Som.	238a	8°15'N	46°20'E
Buulo Berde, Som.	238a	3°53'N	45°30'E
Buxtehude, Ger.	159c	53°29'N	9°42'E
Buxton, Eng., U.K. (bŭks't'n)	158a	53°15'N	1°55'W
Buxton, Or., U.S.	116c	45°41'N	123°11'W
Buy, Russia (bwē)	178	58°30'N	41°48'E
Büyükmenderes, r., Tur.	198	37°50'N	28°20'E
Buzău, Rom. (bōō-zĕ'ō)	175	45°09'N	26°51'E
Buzău, r., Rom.	177	45°17'N	27°22'E
Buzaymah, Libya	231	25°14'N	22°13'E
Buzi, China (bōō-dz)	206	33°48'N	118°13'E
Buzuluk, Russia (bŏ-zŏ-lŏk')	178	52°50'N	52°10'E
Bwendi, D.R.C.	237	4°01'N	26°41'E
Byala, Blg.	175	43°26'N	25°44'E
Byala Slatina, Blg. (byä'la slä'tēnä)	175	43°26'N	23°56'E
Byalynichy, Bela. (byĕl-ĭ-nĭ'chĭ)	176	54°02'N	29°42'E
Byarezina, r., Bela. (bĕr-yĕ'zē-nȧ)	176	53°20'N	29°05'E
Byaroza, Bela.	169	52°29'N	24°59'E
Byblos *see* Jubayl, Leb.	197a	34°07'N	35°38'E
Bydgoszcz, Pol. (bĭd'gŏshch)	160	53°07'N	18°00'E
Byelorussia *see* Belarus, nation, Eur.	178	53°30'N	25°33'E
Byerazino, Bela. (bĕr-yä'zē-nô)	176	53°51'N	28°54'E
Byeshankovichy, Bela.	176	55°04'N	29°29'E

ăt; finăl; rāte; senāte; ärm; åsk; sofȧ; fâre; ch-choose; dh-as th in other; bē; ēvent; bĕt; recĕnt; cratẽr; g-gō; gh-guttural g; bĭt; ĭ-short neutral; rīde; κ-guttural k as ch in German ich;

PRONOUNCING INDEX Byesville – Camp Indian Reservation 277

PLACE (Pronunciation)	PAGE	LAT.	LONG.
Byesville, Oh., U.S. (bīz-vĭl)	108	39°55'N	81°35'W
Bygdin, l., Nor. (bügh-dĭn')	166	61°24'N	8°31'E
Byglandsfjord, Nor. (bügh'länds-fyôr)	166	58°40'N	7°49'E
Bykhaw, Bela.	176	53°32'N	30°15'E
Bykovo, Russia (bĭ-kô'vô)	186b	55°38'N	38°05'E
Byrranga, Gory, mts., Russia	184	74°15'N	94°28'E
Bytantay, r., Russia (byän'täy)	185	68°15'N	132°15'E
Bytom, Pol. (bĭ'tŭm)	161	50°21'N	18°55'E
Bytosh', Russia (bī-tôsh')	176	53°48'N	34°06'E
Bytow, Pol. (bĭ'tŭf)	169	54°10'N	17°30'E
C			
Cabagan, Phil. (kä-bä-gän')	213a	17°27'N	121°50'E
Cabalete, i., Phil. (kä-bä-lā'tå)	213a	14°19'N	122°00'E
Caballones, Canal de, strt., Cuba (kä-nä'l-dĕ-kä-bäl-yô'nĕs)	134	20°45'N	79°20'W
Caballo Reservoir, res., N.M., U.S. (kä-bä-lyō')	119	33°00'N	107°20'W
Cabanatuan, Phil. (kä-bä-nä-twän')	213a	15°30'N	120°56'E
Cabano, Can. (kä-bä-nō')	100	47°41'N	68°54'W
Cabarruyan, i., Phil. (kä-bä-rōō'yän)	213a	16°21'N	120°10'E
Cabedelo, Braz. (kä-bē-dā'lō)	143	6°58'S	34°49'W
Cabeza, Arrecife, i., Mex.	131	19°07'N	95°52'W
Cabeza del Buey, Spain (kȧ-bā'thä dĕl bwā')	172	38°43'N	5°18'W
Cabimas, Ven. (kä-bē'mäs)	142	10°21'N	71°27'W
Cabinda, Ang.	232	5°33'S	12°12'E
Cabinda, hist. reg., Ang. (kä-bĭn'dȧ)	232	5°10'S	10°00'E
Cabinet Mountains, mts., Mt., U.S. (kăb'ĭ-nĕt)	114	48°13'N	115°52'W
Cabo Frio, Braz. (kä'bō-frē'ō)	141a	22°53'S	42°02'W
Cabo Frio, Ilha do, Braz. (ē'lä-dô-kä'bô frē'ô)	141a	23°01'S	42°00'W
Cabo Gracias a Dios, Hond. (kȧ'bô-grä-syäs-ä-dyô's)	133	15°00'N	83°13'W
Cabonga, Réservoir, res., Can.	99	47°25'N	76°35'W
Cabora Bassa Reservoir, res., Moz.	232	15°45'S	32°00'E
Cabot Head, c., Can. (kăb'ŭt)	98	45°15'N	81°20'W
Cabot Strait, strt., Can. (kăb'ŭt)	93a	47°35'N	60°00'W
Cabra, Spain (käb'rä)	172	37°28'N	4°29'W
Cabra, i., Phil.	213a	13°55'N	119°55'E
Cabrera, Illa de, i., Spain	173	39°08'N	2°57'E
Cabrera, Sierra de la, mts., Spain	172	42°15'N	6°45'W
Cabriel, r., Spain (kä-brē-ĕl')	172	39°25'N	1°20'W
Cabrillo National Monument, rec., Ca., U.S. (kä-brēl'yō)	118a	32°41'N	117°03'W
Cabuçu, r., Braz. (kä-bōō'-sōō)	144b	22°57'S	43°36'W
Cabugao, Phil. (kä-bōō'gä-ô)	213a	17°48'N	120°28'E
Čačak, Serb. (chä'chák)	175	43°51'N	20°22'E
Caçapava, Braz. (kä'sä-pä'vä)	141a	23°05'S	45°52'W
Cáceres, Braz. (kä'sĕ-rĕs)	143	16°11'S	57°32'W
Cáceres, Spain (kä'thå-rās)	162	39°28'N	6°20'W
Cachapoal, r., Chile (kä-chä-pô-ä'l)	141b	34°23'S	70°19'W
Cache, r., Ar., U.S. (kăsh)	121	35°24'N	91°12'W
Cache Creek, Can.	95	50°48'N	121°19'W
Cache Creek, r., Ca., U.S. (kăsh)	118	38°53'N	122°24'W
Cache la Poudre, r., Co., U.S. (kàsh lá pōōd'r')	120	40°43'N	105°39'W
Cachi, Nevados de, mtn., Arg. (nĕ-vá'dôs-dĕ-kà'chē)	144	25°05'S	66°40'W
Cachinal, Chile (kä-chē-näl')	144	24°57'S	69°33'W
Cachoeira, Braz. (kä-shô-ā'rä)	143	12°32'S	38°47'W
Cachoeirá do Sul, Braz. (kä-shô-ā'rä-dô-sōō'l)	144	30°02'S	52°49'W
Cachoeiras de Macacu, Braz. (kä-shô-ā'räs-dĕ-mä-kà'kōō)	141a	22°28'S	42°39'W
Cachoeiro de Itapemirim, Braz.	143	20°51'S	41°06'W
Cacólo, Ang.	236	10°07'S	19°17'E
Caconda, Ang. (kä-kōn'dä)	232	13°43'S	15°06'E
Cacouna, Can.	100	47°54'N	69°31'W
Cacula, Ang.	236	14°29'S	14°10'E
Cadale, Som.	238a	2°45'N	46°15'E
Caddo, l., La., U.S. (kăd'ō)	123	32°37'N	94°15'W
Cadereyta, Mex. (kä-då-rā'tä)	130	20°42'N	99°47'W
Cadereyta Jimenez, Mex. (kä-dä-rā'tä hĕ-mā'nāz)	122	25°36'N	99°59'W
Cadi, Sierra de, mts., Spain (sē-ĕ'r-rä-dĕ-kä'dē)	173	42°17'N	1°34'E
Cadillac, Mi., U.S. (kăd'ĭ-lăk)	108	44°15'N	85°25'W
Cádiz, Spain (kà'dēz)	154	36°34'N	6°20'W
Cadiz, Ca., U.S. (kā'dĭz)	118	34°33'N	115°30'W
Cadiz, Oh., U.S.	108	40°15'N	81°00'W
Cádiz, Golfo de, b., Spain (gôl-fô-dĕ-kà'dēz)	162	36°50'N	7°00'W
Caen, Fr. (käN)	161	49°13'N	0°22'W
Caernarfon, Wales, U.K.	160	53°08'N	4°17'W
Caernarfon Bay, b., Wales, U.K.	164	53°09'N	4°56'W
Cagayan, Phil. (kä-gä-yän')	213	8°13'N	124°30'E
Cagayan, r., Phil.	212	16°45'N	121°55'E
Cagayan Islands, is., Phil.	212	9°40'N	120°30'E
Cagayan Sulu, i., Phil. (kä-gä-yän sōō'lōō)	212	7°00'N	118°30'E
Cagli, Italy (käl'yē)	174	43°35'N	12°40'E
Cagliari, Italy (käl'yä-rē)	154	39°16'N	9°08'E
Cagliari, Golfo di, b., Italy (gôl-fō-dē-käl'yä-rē)	162	39°08'N	9°12'E
Cagnes, Fr. (kän'y')	171	43°40'N	7°14'E
Cagua, Ven. (kä'gwä)	143b	10°12'N	67°27'W
Caguas, P.R. (kä'gwäs)	129b	18°12'N	66°01'W
Cahaba, r., Al., U.S. (kȧ hä-bä)	124	32°50'N	87°15'W
Cahama, Ang. (kä-à'mä)	232	16°17'S	14°19'E
Cahokia, Il., U.S. (kȧ-hō'kĭ-ȧ)	117e	38°34'N	90°11'W
Cahora-Bassa, wtfl., Moz.	237	15°40'S	32°50'E
Cahors, Fr. (kȧ-ôr')	161	44°27'N	1°27'E
Cahuacán, Mex. (kä-wä-kä'n)	131a	19°38'N	99°25'W
Cahuita, Punta, c., C.R. (pōō'n-tä-kä-wē'tȧ)	133	9°47'N	82°41'W
Cahul, Mol.	177	45°49'N	28°17'E
Caibarién, Cuba (kī-bä-rē-ĕn')	134	22°35'N	79°30'W
Caicedonia, Col. (kī-sĕ-dô-nēä)	142a	4°21'N	75°48'W
Caicos Bank, bk. (kī'kōs)	135	21°35'N	72°00'W
Caicos Islands, is., T./C. Is.	129	21°45'N	71°50'W
Caicos Passage, strt., N.A.	135	21°55'N	72°45'W
Caillou Bay, b., La., U.S. (kȧ-yōō')	123	29°07'N	91°00'W
Caimanera, Cuba (kī-mä-nā'rä)	135	20°00'N	75°10'W
Caiman Point, c., Phil. (kī'män)	213a	15°56'N	119°33'E
Caimito, r., Pan. (kä-ē-mē'tô)	128a	8°50'N	79°45'W
Caimito del Guayabal, Cuba (kä-ē-mē'tō-dĕl-gwä-yä-bä'l)	135a	22°57'N	82°36'W
Cairns, Austl. (kârnz)	219	17°02'S	145°49'E
Cairo, C.R. (kī'rō)	133	10°06'N	83°47'W
Cairo, Egypt	231	30°00'N	31°17'E
Cairo, Ga., U.S. (kā'rō)	124	30°48'N	84°12'W
Cairo, Il., U.S.	105	36°59'N	89°11'W
Caistor, Eng., U.K. (kâs'tēr)	158a	53°30'N	0°20'W
Caiundo, Ang.	236	15°46'S	17°28'E
Caiyu, China (tsī-yōō)	206	39°39'N	116°36'E
Cajamarca, Col. (kä-kä-mä'r-kä)	142a	4°25'N	75°25'W
Cajamarca, Peru (kä-hä-mär'kä)	142	7°16'S	78°30'W
Čajniče, Bos. (chī'nĭ-chĕ)	175	43°32'N	19°04'E
Cajon, Ca., U.S. (kȧ-hōn')	117a	34°18'N	117°28'W
Cajuru, Braz. (kȧ-zhōō'rōō)	141a	21°17'S	47°17'W
Čakovec, Cro. (chȧ'kō-vĕts)	174	46°23'N	16°27'E
Cala, S. Afr. (cä-lȧ)	233c	31°33'S	27°41'E
Calabar, Nig. (kăl-ȧ-bär')	230	4°57'N	8°19'E
Calabazar, Cuba (kä-lä-bä-zä'r)	135a	23°02'N	82°25'W
Calabozo, Ven. (kä-lä-bō'zō)	142	8°48'N	67°27'W
Calabria, hist. reg., Italy (kä-lä'brē-ä)	174	39°26'N	16°23'E
Calafat, Rom. (kȧ-lȧ-fȧt')	175	43°59'N	22°56'E
Calaguas Islands, is., Phil. (kä-läg'wäs)	213a	14°30'N	123°06'E
Calahoo, Can. (kă-lȧ-hōō')	102g	53°42'N	113°58'W
Calahorra, Spain (kä-lä-ôr'rä)	162	42°18'N	1°58'W
Calais, Fr. (kȧ-lĕ')	154	50°56'N	1°51'E
Calais, Me., U.S.	105	45°11'N	67°15'W
Calama, Chile (kä-lä'mä)	144	22°17'S	68°58'W
Calamar, Col. (kä-lä-mär')	142	10°24'N	75°00'W
Calamar, Col.	142	1°55'N	72°33'W
Calamba, Phil. (kä-läm'bä)	213a	14°12'N	121°10'E
Calamian Group, is., Phil. (kä-lä-myän')	212	12°14'N	118°38'E
Calañas, Spain (kä-län'yäs)	172	37°41'N	6°52'W
Calanda, Spain	173	40°53'N	0°20'W
Calapan, Phil. (kä-lä-pän')	213a	13°25'N	121°11'E
Călăraşi, Rom. (kŭ-lŭ-rash'ĭ)	163	44°09'N	27°20'E
Calatayud, Spain (kä-lä-tä-yōōdh')	162	41°23'N	1°37'W
Calauag Bay, b., Phil.	213a	14°07'N	122°10'E
Calaveras Reservoir, res., Ca., U.S. (kăl-ȧ-vĕr'ăs)	116b	37°29'N	121°47'W
Calavite, Cape, c., Phil. (kä-lä-vē'tä)	213a	13°29'N	120°00'E
Calcasieu, r., La., U.S. (kăl'kȧ-shū)	123	30°22'N	93°08'W
Calcasieu Lake, l., La., U.S.	123	29°58'N	93°08'W
Calcutta see Kolkata, India (kăl-kŭt'ȧ)	199	22°32'N	88°22'E
Caldas, Col. (kä'l-däs)	142a	6°06'N	75°38'W
Caldas, dept., Col.	142a	5°20'N	75°38'W
Caldas da Rainha, Port. (käl'däs dä rīn'yȧ)	172	39°25'N	9°08'W
Calder, r., Eng., U.K. (kôl'dẽr)	158a	53°39'N	1°30'W
Caldera, Chile (käl-dā'rä)	144	27°02'S	70°53'W
Calder Canal, can., Eng., U.K.	158a	53°48'N	2°25'W
Caldwell, Id., U.S. (kôld'wĕl)	114	43°40'N	116°43'W
Caldwell, Ks., U.S.	121	37°04'N	97°36'W
Caldwell, Oh., U.S.	108	39°40'N	81°30'W
Caldwell, Tx., U.S.	123	30°30'N	96°40'W
Caledon, Can. (kăl'ē-dŏn)	102d	43°52'N	79°59'W
Caledonia, Mn., U.S. (kăl-ē-dō'nĭ-ȧ)	113	43°38'N	91°31'W
Calella, Spain (kä-lĕl'yä)	173	41°37'N	2°39'E
Calera Victor Rosales, Mex. (kä-lā'rä-vē'k-tôr-rô-sä'lĕs)	130	22°57'N	102°42'W
Calexico, Ca., U.S. (kȧ-lĕk'sĭ-kō)	104	32°41'N	115°30'W
Calgary, Can. (kăl'gȧ-rĭ)	90	51°03'N	114°05'W
Calhoun, Ga., U.S. (käl-hōōn')	124	34°30'N	84°56'W
Cali, Col. (kä'lē)	142	3°26'N	76°30'W
Caliente, Nv., U.S. (käl-yĕn'tä)	119	37°38'N	114°30'W
California, Mo., U.S. (kăl-ĭ-fôr'nĭ-ȧ)	121	38°38'N	92°38'W
California, Pa., U.S.	111e	40°03'N	79°53'W
California, state, U.S.	104	38°10'N	121°20'W
California, Golfo de, b., Mex. (gôl-fô-dĕ-kä-lē-fôr-nyä)	128	30°30'N	113°45'W
California Aqueduct, aq., Ca., U.S.	118	37°10'N	121°10'W
Călimani, Munţii, mts., Rom.	169	47°05'N	24°47'E
Calimere, Point, c., India	203	10°20'N	80°20'E
Calimesa, Ca., U.S. (kă-lĭ-mä'sȧ)	117a	34°00'N	117°04'W
Calipatria, Ca., U.S. (kăl-ĭ-păt'rĭ-ȧ)	118	33°03'N	115°30'W
Calkini, Mex. (käl-kē-nē')	131	20°21'N	90°06'W
Callabonna, Lake, l., Austl. (călă'bŏnȧ)	222	29°35'S	140°28'E
Callao, Peru (käl-yä'ō)	142	12°02'S	77°07'W
Calling, l., Can. (kôl'ĭng)	95	55°15'N	113°12'W
Calmar, Can. (kăl'mär)	102g	53°16'N	113°49'W
Calmar, Ia., U.S.	113	43°12'N	91°54'W
Caloosahatchee, r., Fl., U.S. (kȧ-loo-sȧ-hăch'ē)	125a	26°45'N	81°41'W
Calotmul, Mex. (kä-lôt-mōōl)	132a	20°58'N	88°11'W
Calpulalpan, Mex. (käl-pōō-läl'pän)	130	19°35'N	98°33'W
Caltagirone, Italy (käl-tä-jē-rō'nå)	162	37°14'N	14°32'E
Caltanissetta, Italy (käl-tä-nē-sĕt'tä)	162	37°30'N	14°02'E
Caluango, Ang.	236	8°21'S	19°40'E
Calucinga, Ang.	236	11°18'S	16°12'E
Calumet, Mi., U.S. (kă-lū-mĕt')	113	47°15'N	88°29'W
Calumet, Lake, l., Il., U.S.	111a	41°43'N	87°36'W
Calumet City, Il., U.S.	111a	41°37'N	87°33'W
Calunda, Ang.	236	12°06'S	23°23'E
Caluquembe, Ang.	236	13°47'S	14°44'E
Caluula, Som.	238a	11°53'N	50°40'E
Calvert, Tx., U.S. (kăl'vẽrt)	123	30°59'N	96°41'W
Calvert Island, i., Can.	92	51°35'N	128°00'W
Calvi, Fr. (käl'vē)	174	42°33'N	8°35'E
Calvillo, Mex. (käl-vēl'yō)	131	21°51'N	102°44'E
Calvinia, S. Afr. (kăl-vĭn'ĭ-ȧ)	232	31°20'S	19°50'E
Cam, r., Eng., U.K. (kăm)	165	52°15'N	0°05'E
Camagüey, Cuba (kä-mä-gwā')	129	21°25'N	78°00'W
Camagüey, prov., Cuba	134	21°30'N	78°10'W
Camajuani, Cuba (kä-mä-hwä'nē)	134	22°25'N	79°50'W
Camano, Wa., U.S. (kä-mä'no)	116a	48°10'N	122°32'W
Camano Island, i., Wa., U.S.	116a	48°11'N	122°29'W
Camargo, Mex. (kä-mär gō)	122	26°19'N	98°49'W
Camarón, Cabo, c., Hond. (kȧ'bô-kä-mä-rōn')	132	16°06'N	85°05'W
Camas, Wa., U.S. (kăm'ȧs)	116c	45°36'N	122°24'W
Camas Creek, r., Id., U.S.	115	44°10'N	112°09'W
Camatagua, Ven. (kä-mä-tȧ'gwä)	143b	9°49'N	66°55'W
Ca Mau, Mui, c., Viet.	212	8°36'N	104°43'E
Cambay, India (kăm-bā')	202	22°22'N	72°39'E
Cambodia, nation, Asia	212	12°15'N	104°00'E
Cambonda, Serra, mts., Ang.	236	12°10'S	14°15'E
Camborne, Eng., U.K. (kăm'bôrn)	164	50°15'N	5°28'W
Cambrai, Fr. (käN-brĕ')	161	50°10'N	3°15'E
Cambrian Mountains, mts., Wales, U.K. (kăm'brĭ-ăn)	164	52°05'N	4°05'W
Cambridge, Can.	99	43°22'N	80°19'W
Cambridge, Eng., U.K. (kām'brĭj)	161	52°12'N	0°11'E
Cambridge, Ma., U.S.	101a	42°23'N	71°07'W
Cambridge, Md., U.S.	109	38°35'N	76°10'W
Cambridge, Mn., U.S.	113	45°35'N	93°14'W
Cambridge, Ne., U.S.	120	40°17'N	100°10'W
Cambridge, Oh., U.S.	108	40°00'N	81°35'W
Cambridge Bay see Kaluktutiak, Can.	92	69°15'N	105°00'W
Cambridge City, In., U.S.	108	39°45'N	85°15'W
Cambridgeshire, co., Eng., U.K.	158a	52°26'N	0°19'W
Cambuci, Braz. (käm-bōō'sē)	141a	21°35'S	41°54'W
Cambundi-Catembo, Ang.	236	10°09'S	17°31'E
Camby, In., U.S. (kăm'bē)	111g	39°40'N	86°19'W
Camden, Austl.	217b	34°03'S	150°42'E
Camden, Al., U.S. (kăm'dĕn)	124	31°58'N	87°15'W
Camden, Ar., U.S.	121	33°36'N	92°49'W
Camden, Me., U.S.	100	44°11'N	69°05'W
Camden, N.J., U.S.	105	39°56'N	75°06'W
Camden, S.C., U.S.	125	34°14'N	80°37'W
Cameia, Parque Nacional da, rec., Ang.	236	11°40'S	21°20'E
Camenca, Mol.	177	48°02'N	28°43'E
Cameron, Mo., U.S. (kăm'ẽr-ŭn)	121	39°44'N	94°14'W
Cameron, Tx., U.S.	123	30°52'N	96°57'W
Cameron, W.V., U.S.	108	39°40'N	80°35'W
Cameron Hills, hills, Can.	92	60°13'N	120°20'W
Cameroon, nation, Afr.	230	5°48'N	11°00'E
Cameroon Mountain, mtn., Cam.	230	4°12'N	9°11'E
Camiling, Phil. (kä-mē-lĭng')	213a	15°42'N	120°24'E
Camilla, Ga., U.S. (kȧ-mĭl'ȧ)	124	31°13'N	84°12'W
Caminha, Port. (kä-mĭn'yȧ)	172	41°52'N	8°44'W
Camoçim, Braz. (kä-mô-sēN')	143	2°56'S	40°55'W
Camooweal, Austl.	218	20°00'S	138°13'E
Campana, Arg. (käm-pä'nä)	141c	34°10'S	58°58'W
Campana, i., Chile (käm-pän'yä)	144	48°20'S	75°15'W
Campanario, Spain (kä-pä-nä'rē-ō)	172	38°51'N	5°36'W
Campanella, Punta, c., Italy (pô'n-tä-käm-pä-nĕ'lä)	173c	40°20'N	14°21'E
Campanha, Braz. (käm-pän-yäN')	141a	21°51'S	45°24'W
Campania, hist. reg., Italy (käm-pän'yä)	174	41°00'N	14°40'E
Campbell, Ca., U.S. (kăm'bĕl)	116b	37°17'N	121°57'W
Campbell, Mo., U.S.	121	36°29'N	90°04'W
Campbell, is., N.Z.	3	52°30'S	169°00'E
Campbellpore, Pak.	202	33°49'N	72°24'E
Campbell River, Can.	90	50°01'N	125°15'W
Campbellsville, Ky., U.S. (kăm'bĕlz-vĭl)	124	37°19'N	85°20'W
Campbellton, Can. (kăm'bĕl-tŭn)	91	48°00'N	66°40'W
Campbelltown, Austl. (kăm'bĕl-toun)	217b	34°04'S	150°49'E
Campbelltown, Scot., U.K. (kăm'b'l-toun)	164	55°25'N	5°50'W
Camp Dennison, Oh., U.S. (dĕ'nĭ-sŏn)	111f	39°12'N	84°17'W
Campeche, Mex. (käm-pā'chå)	128	19°51'N	90°32'W
Campeche, state, Mex.	128	18°55'N	90°20'W
Campeche, Bahía de, b., Mex. (bä-ē'ä-dĕ-käm-pā'chā)	128	19°30'N	93°40'W
Campechuela, Cuba (käm-på-chwā'lä)	134	20°15'N	77°15'W
Camperdown, S. Afr. (kăm'pẽr-doun)	233c	29°44'S	30°33'E
Câmpina, Rom.	175	45°08'N	25°47'E
Campina Grande, Braz. (käm-pē'nä grän'dĕ)	143	7°15'S	35°49'W
Campinas, Braz. (käm-pē'näzh)	143	22°53'S	47°03'W
Camp Indian Reservation, I.R., Ca., U.S. (kămp)	118	32°39'N	116°26'W

PLACE (Pronunciation)	PAGE	LAT.	LONG.
Campo, Cam. (käm'pō)	230	2°22'N	9°49'E
Campoalegre, Col. (kä'm-pô-älĕ'grĕ)	142	2°34'N	75°20'W
Campobasso, Italy (käm'pô-bäs'sō)	174	41°35'N	14°39'E
Campo Belo, Braz.	141a	20°52'S	45°15'W
Campo de Criptana, Spain (käm'pō dā krēp-tä'nä)	172	39°24'N	3°09'W
Campo Florido, Cuba (kä'm-pō flô-rē'dō)	135a	23°07'N	82°07'W
Campo Grande, Braz. (käm-pô grän'dĕ)	143	20°28'S	54°32'W
Campo Grande, Braz.	144b	22°54'S	43°33'W
Campo Maior, Braz. (käm-pô mä-yôr')	143	4°48'S	42°12'W
Campo Maior, Port.	172	39°03'N	7°06'W
Campo Real, Spain (käm'pô rå-äl')	173a	40°21'N	3°23'W
Campos, Braz. (kä'm-pôs)	143	21°46'S	41°19'W
Campos do Jordão, Braz. (kä'm-pôs-dô-zhôr-dou'n)	141a	22°45'S	45°35'W
Campos Gerais, Braz. (kä'm-pôs-zhĕ-rä'ēs)	141a	21°17'S	45°43'W
Camps Bay, S. Afr. (kămps)	232a	33°57'S	18°22'E
Camp Springs, Md., U.S. (cămp sprĭngz)	110e	38°48'N	76°55'W
Câmpulung, Rom.	163	45°15'N	25°03'E
Câmpulung Moldovenesc, Rom.	169	47°31'N	25°36'E
Camp Wood, Tx., U.S. (kămp wo͝od)	122	29°39'N	100°02'W
Camrose, Can. (kăm-rōz)	90	53°01'N	112°50'W
Camu, r., Dom. Rep. (kä'mo͞o)	135	19°05'N	70°15'W
Canada, nation, N.A. (kăn'á-dá)	90	50°00'N	100°00'W
Canada Bay, b., Can.	101	50°43'N	56°10'W
Cañada de Gómez, Arg. (kä-nyä'dä-dĕ-gô'mĕz)	144	32°49'S	61°24'W
Canadian, Tx., U.S. (kȧ-nā'dĭ-ăn)	120	35°54'N	100°24'W
Canadian, r., U.S.	106	35°30'N	102°30'W
Canajoharie, N.Y., U.S. (kăn-á-jō-hăr'ê)	109	42°55'N	74°35'W
Çanakkale, Tur. (chä-näk-kä'lĕ)	163	40°10'N	26°26'E
Çanakkale Boğazi (Dardanelles), strt., Tur.	163	40°05'N	25°50'E
Canandaigua, N.Y., U.S. (kăn-ăn-dā'gwá)	109	42°55'N	77°20'W
Canandaigua, l., N.Y., U.S.	109	42°45'N	77°20'W
Cananea, Mex. (kä-nä-nĕ'ä)	128	31°00'N	110°20'W
Canarias, Islas (Canary Is.), is., Spain (ê's-läs-kä-nä'ryäs)	229	29°15'N	16°30'W
Canarreos, Archipiélago de los, is., Cuba	134	21°35'N	82°20'W
Canary Islands *see* Canarias, Islas, is., Spain	229	29°15'N	16°30'W
Cañas, C.R. (kä'-nyäs)	132	10°26'N	85°06'W
Cañas, r., C.R.	132	10°20'N	85°21'W
Cañasgordas, Col. (kä'nyäs-gô'r-däs)	142a	6°44'N	76°01'W
Canastota, N.Y., U.S. (kăn-ȧs-tō'tȧ)	109	43°05'N	75°45'W
Canastra, Serra de, mts., Braz. (sĕ'r-rä-dĕ-kä-nä's-trä)	143	19°53'S	46°57'W
Canatlán, Mex. (kä-nät-län')	122	24°30'N	104°45'W
Canaveral, Cape, c., Fl., U.S.	107	28°30'N	80°23'W
Canavieiras, Braz. (kä-nä-vē-â'räs)	143	15°40'S	38°49'W
Canberra, Austl. (kăn'bĕr-á)	219	35°21'S	149°10'E
Canby, Mn., U.S. (kăn'bĭ)	112	44°43'N	96°15'W
Canchyuaya, Cerros de, mts., Peru (sĕ'r-rôs-dĕ-kän-cho͞o-á'ïä)	142	7°30'S	74°30'W
Cancuc, Mex. (kän-ko͞ok)	131	16°58'N	92°17'W
Cancún, Mex.	132a	21°25'N	86°50'W
Candelaria, Cuba (kän-dĕ-lä'ryä)	134	22°45'N	82°55'W
Candelaria, Phil. (kän-då-lä'rē-ä)	213a	15°39'N	119°55'E
Candelaria, r., Mex. (kän-dĕ-lä-ryä)	131	18°25'N	91°21'W
Candeleda, Spain (kän-dhå-lā'dhä)	172	40°09'N	5°18'W
Candia *see* Iráklion, Grc.	154	35°20'N	25°10'E
Candle, Ak., U.S. (kăn'd'l)	103	65°00'N	162°04'W
Cando, N.D., U.S. (kăn'dō)	112	48°27'N	99°13'W
Candon, Phil. (kän-dōn')	213a	17°13'N	120°26'E
Canelones, Ur. (kä-nĕ-lô-nĕs)	141c	34°32'S	56°19'W
Canelones, dept., Ur.	141c	34°34'S	56°15'W
Cañete, Peru (kän-yā'tâ)	142	13°06'S	76°17'W
Caney, Cuba (kä-nā') (kā'nĭ)	135	20°05'N	75°45'W
Caney, Ks., U.S. (kā'nĭ)	121	37°00'N	95°57'W
Caney Fork, r., Tn., U.S.	124	36°10'N	85°50'W
Cangamba, Ang.	232	13°40'S	19°54'E
Cangas, Spain (kän'gäs)	172	42°15'N	8°43'W
Cangas de Narcea, Spain (kä'n-gäs-dĕ-när-sĕ-ä)	172	43°08'N	6°36'W
Cangzhou, China (tsäŋ-jō)	208	38°21'N	116°53'E
Caniapiscau, l., Can.	93	54°10'N	71°13'E
Caniapiscau, r., Can.	93	57°00'N	68°45'W
Canicatti, Italy (kä-nê-kät'tē)	174	37°18'N	13°58'E
Cañitas, Mex. (kän-yē'täs)	130	23°38'N	102°44'W
Cannell, Can.	102g	53°35'N	113°38'W
Cannelton, In., U.S. (kăn'ĕl-tŭn)	108	37°55'N	86°45'W
Cannes, Fr. (kȧn)	161	43°34'N	7°05'E
Canning, Can. (kăn'ĭng)	100	45°09'N	64°25'W
Cannock, Eng., U.K. (kăn'ŭk)	158a	52°41'N	2°02'W
Cannock Chase, reg., Eng., U.K. (kăn'ŭk chās)	158a	52°43'N	1°54'W
Cannon, r., Mn., U.S. (kăn'ŭn)	113	44°18'N	93°24'W
Cannonball, r., N.D., U.S. (kăn'ŭn-bâl)	112	46°17'N	101°35'W
Caño, Isla de, i., C.R. (ê's-lä-dĕ-kä'nō)	133	8°38'N	84°00'W
Canoga Park, Ca., U.S. (kä-nō'gȧ)	117a	34°07'N	118°36'W
Canoncito Indian Reservation, I.R., N.M., U.S.	119	35°00'N	107°05'W
Canon City, Co., U.S. (kăn'yŭn)	120	38°27'N	105°16'W
Canonsburg, Pa., U.S. (kăn'ŭnz-bûrg)	111e	40°16'N	80°11'W
Canoochee, r., Ga., U.S. (kȧ-no͞o'chē)	125	32°25'N	82°11'W
Canora, Can. (kȧ-nōrȧ)	90	51°37'N	102°26'W
Canosa, Italy (kä-nō'sä)	174	41°14'N	16°03'E
Canouan, i., St. Vin.	133b	12°44'N	61°10'W
Cansahcab, Mex.	132a	21°11'N	89°05'W
Canso, Can. (kăn'sō)	101	45°20'N	61°00'W
Canso, Cape, c., Can.	101	45°21'N	60°46'W
Canso, Strait of, strt., Can.	101	45°37'N	61°25'W
Cantabrica, Cordillera, mts., Spain	156	43°05'N	6°05'W
Cantagalo, Braz. (kän-tä-gà'lo)	141a	21°59'S	42°22'W
Cantanhede, Port. (kän-tän-yā'dâ)	172	40°22'N	8°35'W
Canterbury, Eng., U.K. (kăn'tĕr-bĕr-ê)	165	51°17'N	1°06'E
Canterbury Bight, b., N.Z.	221a	44°15'S	172°08'E
Cantiles, Cayo, i., Cuba (ky-ō-kän-tē'lås)	134	21°40'N	82°00'W
Canton *see* Guangzhou, China	205	23°07'N	113°15'E
Canton, Ga., U.S.	124	34°13'N	84°29'W
Canton, Il., U.S.	121	40°34'N	90°02'W
Canton, Ma., U.S.	101a	42°09'N	71°09'W
Canton, Mo., U.S.	121	40°08'N	91°33'W
Canton, Ms., U.S.	124	32°36'N	90°01'W
Canton, N.C., U.S.	125	35°32'N	82°50'W
Canton, Oh., U.S.	105	40°50'N	81°25'W
Canton, Pa., U.S.	109	41°50'N	76°45'W
Canton, S.D., U.S.	112	43°17'N	96°37'W
Cantu, Italy (kän-to͞o')	174	45°43'N	9°09'E
Cañuelas, Arg. (kä-nyòĕ'-läs)	141c	35°03'S	58°45'W
Canyon, Tx., U.S. (kăn'yŭn)	120	34°59'N	101°57'W
Canyon, r., Wa., U.S.	116a	48°09'N	121°48'W
Canyon de Chelly National Monument, rec., Az., U.S.	119	36°14'N	110°00'W
Canyon Ferry Lake, res., Mt., U.S.	115	46°33'N	111°37'W
Canyonlands National Park, rec., Ut., U.S.	119	38°10'N	110°00'W
Canyons of the Ancients National Monument, rec., Co., U.S.	119	37°30'N	108°50'W
Caoxian, China (tsou shyĕn)	206	34°48'N	115°33'E
Capalonga, Phil. (kä-pä-lôŋ'gä)	213a	14°20'N	122°30'E
Capannori, Italy (kä-pän'nô-rē)	174	43°50'N	10°30'E
Capaya, r., Ven. (kä-pä-ïä)	143b	10°28'N	66°15'W
Cap-Chat, Can. (kȧp-shä')	91	48°02'N	65°20'W
Cap-de-la-Madeleine, Can. (kȧp dē lȧ mȧ-d'lĕn')	99	46°23'N	72°30'W
Cape Breton, i., Can. (kāp brĕt'ŭn)	101	45°48'N	59°50'W
Cape Breton Highlands National Park, rec., Can.	91	46°45'N	60°45'W
Cape Charles, Va., U.S. (kāp chärlz)	125	37°13'N	76°02'W
Cape Coast, Ghana	230	5°05'N	1°15'W
Cape Fear, r., N.C., U.S. (kāp fēr)	107	35°00'N	79°00'W
Cape Flats, pl., S. Afr. (kāp flăts)	232a	34°01'S	18°37'E
Cape Girardeau, Mo., U.S. (jē-rär-dō')	105	37°17'N	89°32'W
Cape Krusenstern National Monument, rec., Ak., U.S.	103	67°30'N	163°40'W
Cape May, N.J., U.S. (kāp mā)	109	38°55'N	74°50'W
Cape May Court House, N.J., U.S.	109	39°05'N	75°00'W
Cape Romanzof, Ak., U.S. (rō' män zôf)	103	61°50'N	165°45'W
Capesterre, Guad.	133b	16°02'N	61°37'W
Cape Tormentine, Can.	100	46°08'N	63°47'W
Cape Town, S. Afr. (kāp toun)	232	33°48'S	18°28'E
Cape Verde, nation, Afr.	230b	15°48'N	26°02'W
Cape York Peninsula, pen., Austl. (kāp yôrk)	221	12°30'S	142°35'E
Cap-Haïtien, Haiti (kȧp ȧ-ē-syăn')	129	19°45'N	72°15'W
Capilla de Señor, Arg. (kä-pēl'yä dā sān-yôr')	141c	34°18'S	59°07'W
Capitachouane, r., Can.	99	47°50'N	76°45'W
Capitol Reef National Park, rec., Ut., U.S. (kăp'ĭ-tŏl)	119	38°15'N	111°10'W
Capivari, Braz. (kä-pē-vá'rê)	141a	22°59'S	47°29'W
Capivari, r., Braz.	144b	22°39'S	43°19'W
Capoompeta, mtn., Austl. (kȧ-po͞om-pē'tȧ)	221	29°15'S	152°12'E
Capraia, i., Italy (kä-prä'yä)	162	43°02'N	9°51'E
Caprara Point, c., Italy (kä-prä'rä)	174	41°08'N	8°20'E
Capreol, Can.	99	46°43'N	80°56'W
Caprera, i., Italy (kä-prā'rä)	174	41°12'N	9°28'E
Capri, Italy	173c	40°18'N	14°16'E
Capri, Isola di, i., Italy (ê'-sō-lä-dē-kä'prē)	173c	40°19'N	14°10'E
Capricorn Channel, strt., Austl. (kăp'rĭ-kôrn)	221	22°27'S	151°24'E
Caprivi Strip, hist. reg., Nmb.	232	18°00'S	22°00'E
Cap-Rouge, Can. (kȧp ro͞ozh')	102b	46°45'N	71°21'W
Cap-Saint Ignace, Can. (kĭp săn-tē-nyȧs')	102b	47°02'N	70°27'W
Capua, Italy (kä'pwä)	162	41°07'N	14°14'E
Capulhuac, Mex. (kä-pòl-hwák')	130	19°33'N	99°43'W
Capulin Mountain National Monument, rec., N.M., U.S. (kȧ-pū'lĭn)	120	36°15'N	103°58'W
Capultitlán, Mex. (kä-pòl-tē-tlà'n)	131a	19°15'N	99°40'W
Caquetá (Japurá), r., S.A.	142	0°20'S	73°00'W
Carabaña, Spain (kä-rä-bän'yä)	173a	40°16'N	3°15'W
Carabelle, Fl., U.S. (kăr'á-bĕl)	124	29°50'N	84°40'W
Carabobo, dept., Ven. (kä-rä-bô'-bô)	143b	10°07'N	68°06'W
Caracal, Rom. (kȧ-rȧ-kȧl')	175	44°06'N	24°22'E
Caracas, Ven. (kä-rä'käs)	142	10°30'N	66°58'W
Carácuaro de Morelos, Mex. (kä-rä'kwä-rō-dĕ-mō-rĕ-lôs)	130	18°44'N	101°04'W
Caraguatatuba, Braz. (kä-rä-gwä-tȧ-to͞o'bä)	141a	23°37'S	45°26'W
Carajás, Serra dos, mts., Braz. (sĕ'r-rä-dôs-kä-rä-zhá's)	143	5°58'S	51°45'W
Caramanta, Cerro, mtn., Col. (sĕ'r-rô-kä-rä-mà'n-tä)	142a	5°29'N	76°01'W
Carangola, Braz. (kä-rän'gō'lä)	141a	20°46'S	42°02'W
Caraquet, Can. (kä-rȧ-kĕt')	91	47°48'N	64°57'W
Carata, Laguna, l., Nic. (lä-gò'nä-kä-rä'tä)	133	13°59'N	83°41'W
Caratasca, Laguna, l., Hond. (lä-gò'nä-kä-rä-täs'kä)	133	15°20'N	83°45'W
Caravaca, Spain (kä-rä-vä'kä)	172	38°05'N	1°51'W
Caravelas, Braz. (kȧ-rä-vĕl'äzh)	143	17°46'S	39°06'W
Carayaca, Ven. (kȧ-rä-ïä'kä)	143b	10°32'N	67°07'W
Caràzinho, Braz. (kä-rȧ'zē-nyŏ)	144	28°22'S	52°33'W
Carballiño, Spain	162	42°26'N	8°04'W
Carballo, Spain (kär-bäl'yō)	172	43°13'N	8°40'W
Carbet, Pitons du, mtn., Mart.	133b	14°40'N	61°05'W
Carbon, r., Wa., U.S. (kär'bŏn)	116a	47°06'N	122°08'W
Carbonado, Wa., U.S. (kȧr-bō-nä'dō)	116a	47°05'N	122°03'W
Carbonara, Cape, c., Italy (kär-bō-nä'rä)	162	39°08'N	9°33'E
Carbondale, Can. (kär'bŏn-dāl)	102g	53°45'N	113°32'W
Carbondale, Il., U.S.	108	37°42'N	89°12'W
Carbondale, Pa., U.S.	109	41°35'N	75°30'W
Carbonear, Can. (kär-bō-nēr')	101	47°45'N	53°14'W
Carbon Hill, Al., U.S. (kär'bŏn hĭl)	124	33°53'N	87°34'W
Carcaixent, Spain	173	39°09'N	0°29'W
Carcans, Étang de, l., Fr. (ā-tan-dĕ-kär-kän)	170	45°12'N	1°00'W
Carcassonne, Fr. (kȧr-kȧ-sôn')	161	43°12'N	2°23'E
Carcross, Can. (kär'krôs)	90	60°18'N	134°54'W
Cárdenas, Cuba (kär'då-näs)	129	23°00'N	81°10'W
Cárdenas, Mex. (ká'r-dĕ-näs)	131	17°59'N	93°23'W
Cárdenas, Mex.	130	22°01'N	99°38'W
Cárdenas, Bahía de, b., Cuba (bä-ē'ä-dĕ-kär'då-näs)	134	23°10'N	81°10'W
Cardiff, Can. (kär'dĭf)	102g	53°46'N	113°36'W
Cardiff, Wales, U.K.	161	51°30'N	3°18'W
Cardigan, Wales, U.K. (kär'dĭ-găn)	161	52°05'N	4°40'W
Cardigan Bay, b., Wales, U.K.	161	52°35'N	4°40'W
Cardston, Can. (kärds'tŭn)	90	49°12'N	113°18'W
Carei, Rom. (kä-rā')	169	47°42'N	22°28'E
Carentan, Fr. (ka-rŏn-tän')	170	49°19'N	1°14'W
Carey, Oh., U.S. (kā'rê)	108	40°55'N	83°25'W
Carey, l., Austl. (kâr'ē)	220	29°20'S	123°35'E
Carhaix-Plouguer, Fr. (kär-ĕ')	170	48°17'N	3°37'W
Caribbean Sea, sea (kăr-ĭ-bē'ăn)	129	14°30'N	75°30'W
Caribe, Arroyo, r., Mex. (är-rō'ï-kä-rē'bĕ)	131	18°18'N	90°38'W
Cariboo Mountains, mts., Can. (kă'rĭ-bo͞o)	92	53°00'N	121°00'W
Caribou, Me., U.S.	100	46°51'N	68°01'W
Caribou, i., Can.	98	47°22'N	85°42'W
Caribou Lake, l., Mn., U.S.	117h	46°54'N	92°16'W
Caribou Mountains, mts., Can.	92	59°20'N	115°30'W
Carinhanha, Braz. (kä-rĭ-nyän'yä)	143	14°14'S	43°44'W
Carini, Italy (kä-rē'nē)	174	38°09'N	13°10'E
Carleton Place, Can. (kärl'tŭn)	99	45°15'N	76°10'W
Carletonville, S. Afr.	238c	26°20'S	27°23'E
Carlinville, Il., U.S. (kär'lĭn-vĭl)	121	39°16'N	89°52'W
Carlisle, Eng., U.K. (kär-līl')	154	54°54'N	3°03'W
Carlisle, Ky., U.S.	108	38°20'N	84°00'W
Carlisle, Pa., U.S.	109	40°10'N	77°15'W
Carloforte, Italy (kär'lô-fôr-tȧ)	174	39°11'N	8°28'E
Carlos Casares, Arg. (kär-lôs-kä-sä'rĕs)	144	35°38'S	61°17'W
Carlow, Ire. (kär'lō)	164	52°50'N	7°00'W
Carlsbad, N.M., U.S. (kärlz'băd)	122	32°24'N	104°12'W
Carlsbad Caverns National Park, rec., N.M., U.S.	122	32°08'N	104°30'W
Carlton, Eng., U.K. (kärl'tŭn)	158a	52°58'N	1°05'W
Carlton, Mn., U.S.	117h	46°40'N	92°26'W
Carlton Center, Mi., U.S. (kärl'tŭn sĕn'tĕr)	108	42°45'N	85°20'W
Carlyle, Il., U.S. (kärlīl')	121	38°37'N	89°23'W
Carmagnola, Italy (kär-mä-nyô'lä)	174	44°52'N	7°48'E
Carman, Can. (kär'măn)	90	49°32'N	98°00'W
Carmarthen, Wales, U.K. (kär-mär'thĕn)	164	51°50'N	4°20'W
Carmaux, Fr. (kȧr-mō')	170	44°05'N	2°09'E
Carmel, N.Y., U.S. (kär'mĕl)	110a	41°25'N	73°42'W
Carmelo, Ur. (kär-mĕ'lo)	141c	33°59'S	58°15'W
Carmen, Isla del, i., Mex. (ê's-lä-dĕl-kä'r-mĕn)	131	18°43'N	91°40'W
Carmen, Laguna del, l., Mex. (lä-gò'nä-dĕl-kä'r-mĕn)	131	18°15'N	93°26'W
Carmen de Areco, Arg. (kär'mĕn' dā ä-rä'kō)	141c	34°21'S	59°50'W
Carmen de Patagones, Arg. (ká'r-mĕn-dĕ-pä-tä-gô'nĕs)	144	41°00'S	63°00'W
Carmi, Il., U.S. (kär'mī)	108	38°05'N	88°10'W
Carmo, Braz. (ká'r-mô)	141a	21°57'S	42°45'W
Carmo do Rio Clara, Braz. (ká'r-mô-dô-rē'ô-klä'rä)	141a	20°57'S	46°04'W
Carmona, Spain	172	37°28'N	5°38'W
Carnarvon, Austl. (kär-när'vŭn)	218	24°45'S	113°45'E
Carnarvon, S. Afr.	232	31°00'S	22°15'E
Carnation, Wa., U.S. (kär-nā'shŭn)	116a	47°39'N	121°55'W
Carnaxide, Port. (kär-nä-shē'dĕ)	173b	38°44'N	9°15'W
Carndonagh, Ire. (kärn-dō-nä')	164	55°15'N	7°15'W
Carnegie, Ok., U.S. (kär-nĕg'ĭ)	120	35°06'N	98°38'W
Carnegie, Pa., U.S.	111e	40°24'N	80°06'W
Carneys Point, N.J., U.S. (kär'nĕs)	109	39°45'N	75°25'W
Carnic Alps, mts., Eur.	161	46°43'N	12°38'E
Carnot, Alg. (kär nō')	173	36°15'N	1°40'E
Carnot, C.A.R.	231	5°00'N	15°52'E
Carnsore Point, c., Ire. (kärn'sôr)	164	52°10'N	6°16'W
Caro, Mi., U.S. (kâ'rō)	108	43°30'N	83°25'W
Carolina, Braz. (kä-rô-lē'nä)	143	7°26'S	47°16'W

PRONOUNCING INDEX Carolina – Celestún 279

PLACE (Pronunciation)	PAGE	LAT.	LONG.
Carolina, S. Afr. (kăr-ŏ-lī'nȧ)	232	26°07'S	30°09'E
Carolina, I., Mex. (kä-rō-lē'nä)	132a	18°41'N	89°40'W
Caroline Islands, is., Oc.	5	8°00'N	140°00'E
Caroni, r., Ven. (kä-rō'nē)	142	5°49'N	62°57'W
Carora, Ven. (kä-rô'rä)	142	10°09'N	70°12'W
Carpathians, mts., Eur. (kär-pā'thĭ-ăn)	156	49°23'N	20°14'E
Carpații Meridionali (Transylvanian Alps), mts., Rom.	156	45°30'N	23°30'E
Carpentaria, Gulf of, b., Austl. (kär-pĕn-târ'ĭȧ)	220	14°45'S	138°50'E
Carpentras, Fr. (kär-päN-träs')	171	44°04'N	5°01'E
Carpi, Italy	174	44°48'N	10°54'E
Carrara, Italy (kä-rä'rä)	162	44°05'N	10°05'E
Carrauntoohil, Ire. (kă-răn-tōō'ĭl)	164	52°01'N	9°48'W
Carretas, Punta, c., Peru (pōō'n-tä-kär-rē'tĕ'rás)	142	14°15'S	76°25'W
Carriacou, i., Gren.	133b	12°28'N	61°20'W
Carrick-on-Sur, Ire. (kăr'-ĭk)	164	52°20'N	7°35'W
Carrier, Can. (kăr'ĭ-ĕr)	102b	46°43'N	71°05'W
Carriere, Ms., U.S. (kȧ-rēr')	124	30°37'N	89°37'W
Carriers Mills, Il., U.S. (kăr'ĭ-ĕrs)	108	37°40'N	88°40'W
Carrington, N.D., U.S. (kăr'ĭng-tŭn)	112	47°26'N	99°06'W
Carr Inlet, Wa., U.S. (kăr ĭn'lĕt)	116a	47°20'N	122°42'W
Carrion Crow Harbor, b., Bah. (kăr'ĭŭn krō)	134	26°35'N	77°55'W
Carrión de los Condes, Spain (kär-rē-ōn' dā los kōn'dâs)	172	42°20'N	4°35'W
Carrizo Creek, r., N.M., U.S. (kär-rē'zō)	120	36°22'N	103°39'W
Carrizo Springs, Tx., U.S.	122	28°32'N	99°51'W
Carrizozo, N.M., U.S. (kär-rē-zō'zō)	119	33°40'N	105°55'W
Carroll, Ia., U.S. (kăr'ŭl)	113	42°03'N	94°51'W
Carrollton, Ga., U.S. (kăr-ŭl-tŭn)	124	33°35'N	85°05'W
Carrollton, Il., U.S.	121	39°18'N	90°22'W
Carrollton, Ky., U.S.	108	38°45'N	85°15'W
Carrollton, Mi., U.S.	108	43°30'N	83°55'W
Carrollton, Mo., U.S.	121	39°21'N	93°29'W
Carrollton, Oh., U.S.	108	40°35'N	81°10'W
Carrollton, Tx., U.S.	117c	32°58'N	96°53'W
Carrols, Wa., U.S. (kăr'ŭlz)	116c	46°05'N	122°51'W
Carrot, r., Can.	96	53°12'N	103°50'W
Carry-le-Rouet, Fr. (kä-rē'lĕ-rö-ā')	170a	43°20'N	5°10'E
Carsamba, Tur. (chär-shäm'bä)	163	41°05'N	36°40'E
Carson, r., Nv., U.S. (kär'sŭn)	118	39°15'N	119°25'W
Carson City, Nv., U.S.	104	39°10'N	119°45'W
Carson Sink, Nv., U.S.	118	39°51'N	118°25'W
Cartagena, Col. (kär-tä-hā'nä)	142	10°30'N	75°40'W
Cartagena, Spain (kär-tä-kĕ'nä)	154	37°46'N	1°00'W
Cartago, Col. (kär-tä'gō)	142a	4°44'N	75°54'W
Cartago, C.R.	129	9°52'N	83°56'W
Cartaxo, Port. (kär-tä'shō)	172	39°10'N	8°48'W
Carteret, N.J., U.S. (kär'tē-ret)	110a	40°35'N	74°13'W
Cartersville, Ga., U.S. (kär'tērs-vĭl)	124	34°09'N	84°47'W
Carthage, Tun.	230	37°04'N	10°18'E
Carthage, Il., U.S. (kär'thāj)	121	40°27'N	91°09'W
Carthage, Mo., U.S.	121	37°10'N	94°18'W
Carthage, N.C., U.S.	125	35°22'N	79°25'W
Carthage, N.Y., U.S.	109	44°00'N	75°45'W
Carthage, Tx., U.S.	123	32°09'N	94°20'W
Carthcart, S. Afr. (cärth-cȧ't)	233c	32°18'S	27°11'E
Cartwright, Can. (kärt'rīt)	91	53°36'N	57°00'W
Caruaru, Braz. (kä-rò-ȧ-rōō')	143	8°19'S	35°52'W
Carúpano, Ven. (kä-rōō'pä-nō)	142	10°45'N	63°21'W
Caruthersville, Mo., U.S. (kȧ-rŭdh'ērz-vĭl)	121	36°09'N	89°41'W
Carver, Or., U.S. (kärv'ēr)	116c	45°24'N	122°30'W
Carvoeiro, Cabo, c., Port. (ká'bō-kär-vô-ĕ'y-rō)	172	39°22'N	9°24'W
Cary, Il., U.S. (kā'rē)	111a	42°13'N	88°14'W
Casablanca, Chile (kä-sä-bläŋ'kä)	141b	33°19'S	71°24'W
Casablanca, Mor.	230	33°32'N	7°41'W
Casa Branca, Braz. (kä'sä-brȧ'N-kä)	141a	21°47'S	47°04'W
Casa Grande, Az., U.S. (kä'sä grän'dā)	119	32°50'N	111°45'W
Casa Grande Ruins National Monument, rec., Az., U.S.	119	33°00'N	111°33'W
Casale Monferrato, Italy (kä-sä'lā)	174	45°08'N	8°26'E
Casalmaggiore, Italy (kä-säl-mäd-jō'rä)	174	45°00'N	10°24'E
Casamance, r., Sen. (kä-sä-mäns')	230	12°30'N	15°00'W
Cascade Mountains, mts., N.A.	95	49°10'N	121°00'W
Cascade Point, c., N.Z. (kăs-kād')	221a	43°59'S	168°23'E
Cascade Range, mts., N.A.	106	42°50'N	122°20'W
Cascade-Siskiyou National Monument, rec., Or., U.S.	114	42°05'N	122°30'W
Cascade Tunnel, trans., Wa., U.S.	114	47°41'N	120°53'W
Cascais, Port. (käs-kȧ-ēzh)	172	38°42'N	9°25'W
Case Inlet, Wa., U.S. (kās)	116a	47°22'N	122°47'W
Caseros, Arg. (kä-sā'rôs)	144a	34°35'S	58°34'W
Caserta, Italy (kä-zĕr'tä)	174	41°04'N	14°21'E
Casey, Il., U.S. (kā'sĭ)	108	39°20'N	88°00'W
Cashmere, Wa., U.S. (kăsh'mĭr)	114	47°30'N	120°28'W
Casiguran, Phil. (käs-sē-gōō'rän)	213a	16°15'N	122°10'E
Casiguran Sound, strt., Phil.	213a	16°02'N	121°51'E
Casilda, Arg. (kä-sē'l-dä)	144	33°02'S	61°11'W
Casilda, Cuba	134	21°50'N	80°00'W
Casimiro de Abreu, Braz. (kä'sē-mē'ro-dĕ-á-brĕ'ōō)	141a	22°30'S	42°11'W
Casino, Austl. (kȧ-sē'nō)	222	28°35'S	153°10'E
Casiquiare, r., Ven. (kä-sē-kyä'rä)	142	2°11'N	66°15'W
Caspe, Spain (käs'pā)	173	41°18'N	0°02'W
Casper, Wy., U.S. (kăs'pēr)	104	42°51'N	106°18'W
Caspian Depression, depr. (kăs'pĭ-ăn)	178	47°40'N	52°35'E
Caspian Sea, sea	178	40°00'N	52°00'E
Cass, W.V., U.S. (kăs)	109	38°25'N	79°55'W
Cass, l., Mn., U.S.	113	47°23'N	94°28'W
Cassai (Kasai), r., Afr. (kä-sä'ē)	232	11°30'S	21°00'E
Cass City, Mi., U.S. (kăs)	108	43°35'N	83°10'W
Casselman, Can. (kăs''l-mȧn)	102c	45°18'N	75°05'W
Casselton, N.D., U.S. (kăs''l-tŭn)	112	46°53'N	97°14'W
Cássia, Braz. (ká'syä)	141a	20°36'S	46°53'W
Cassin, Tx., U.S. (kăs'ĭn)	117d	29°16'N	98°29'W
Cassinga, Ang.	232	15°05'S	16°15'E
Cassino, Italy (käs-sē'nō)	162	41°30'N	13°50'E
Cass Lake, Mn., U.S. (kăs)	113	47°23'N	94°37'W
Cassopolis, Mi., U.S. (kăs-ŏ'pô-lĭs)	108	41°55'N	86°00'W
Cassville, Mo., U.S. (kăs'vĭl)	121	36°41'N	93°52'W
Castanheira de Pêra, Port. (käs-tän-yā'rä-dĕ-pĕ'rä)	172	40°00'N	8°07'W
Castellammare di Stabia, Italy	173c	40°26'N	14°29'E
Castelli, Arg. (kás-tĕ'zhē)	141c	36°07'S	57°48'W
Castelló de la Plana, Spain	162	39°59'N	0°05'W
Castelnaudary, Fr. (kás'tĕl-nō-dȧ-rē')	170	43°20'N	1°57'E
Castelo, Braz. (käs-tĕ'lô)	141a	20°37'S	41°13'W
Castelo Branco, Port. (käs-tā'lò bräŋ'kò)	162	39°48'N	7°37'W
Castelo de Vide, Port. (käs-tā'lò dĭ vē'dĭ)	172	39°25'N	7°25'W
Castelsarrasin, Fr. (kás'tĕl-sȧ-rȧ-zăN')	170	44°03'N	1°05'E
Castelvetrano, Italy (käs'tĕl-vē-trä'nō)	174	37°43'N	12°50'E
Castilla, Peru (kȧs-tē'l-yä)	142	5°18'S	80°40'W
Castilla La Nueva, hist. reg., Spain (käs-tē'lyä lä nwā'vä)	172	39°15'N	3°55'W
Castilla La Vieja, hist. reg., Spain (käs-tēl'yä lä vyā'hä)	172	40°48'N	4°24'W
Castillo de San Marcos National Monument, rec., Fl., U.S. (käs-tē'lyä de-sän mär-kōs)	125	29°55'N	81°25'W
Castle, i., Bah. (kȧs''l)	135	22°05'N	74°20'W
Castlebar, Ire. (kȧs''l-bär)	164	53°55'N	9°15'W
Castle Dale, Ut., U.S. (kȧs'l dāl)	119	39°15'N	111°00'W
Castle Donington, Eng., U.K. (dŏn'ĭng-tŭn)	158a	52°50'N	1°21'W
Castleford, Eng., U.K. (kȧs'l-fērd)	158a	53°43'N	1°21'W
Castlegar, Can. (kȧs''l-gär)	95	49°19'N	117°40'W
Castlemaine, Austl. (kăs''l-mān)	222	37°05'S	144°10'E
Castle Peak, mtn., Co., U.S.	119	39°00'N	106°50'W
Castle Rock, Wa., U.S. (kȧs''l-rŏk)	114	46°17'N	122°53'W
Castle Rock Flowage, res., Wi., U.S.	113	44°03'N	89°48'W
Castle Shannon, Pa., U.S. (shăn'ŭn)	111e	40°22'N	80°02'W
Castleton, In., U.S. (kȧs''l-tŏn)	111g	39°54'N	86°03'W
Castor, r., Can. (kăs'tôr)	102c	45°16'N	75°14'W
Castor, r., Mo., U.S.	121	36°59'N	89°53'W
Castres, Fr. (kȧs'tr')	170	43°36'N	2°13'E
Castries, St. Luc. (kȧs-trē')	133b	14°01'N	61°00'W
Castro, Braz. (käs'trò)	143	24°56'S	50°00'W
Castro, Chile (käs'tro)	144	42°27'S	73°48'W
Castro Daire, Port. (käs'trò dīr'ĭ)	172	40°56'N	7°57'W
Castro del Río, Spain (käs-trō-dĕl rē'ō)	172	37°42'N	4°28'W
Castrop Rauxel, Ger. (käs'trōp rou'ksĕl)	171c	51°33'N	7°19'E
Castro-Urdiales, Spain	162	43°23'N	3°11'W
Castro Valley, Ca., U.S.	116b	37°42'N	122°05'W
Castro Verde, Port. (käs-trō vĕr'dĕ)	172	37°43'N	8°05'W
Castrovillari, Italy (käs'trō-vēl-lyä'rē)	174	39°48'N	16°11'E
Castuera, Spain (käs-tò-ā'rä)	172	38°43'N	5°33'W
Casula, Moz.	237	15°25'S	33°40'E
Cat, i., Bah.	135	24°30'N	75°30'W
Catacamas, Hond. (kä-tä-kä'mäs)	132	14°52'N	85°55'W
Cataguases, Braz. (kä-tä-gwá'sĕs)	141a	21°23'S	42°42'W
Catahoula, l., La., U.S. (kăt-ȧ-hò'lȧ)	123	31°35'N	92°20'W
Catalão, Braz. (kä-tä-louN')	143	18°09'S	47°42'W
Catalina, i., Dom. Rep. (kä-tä-lē'nä)	135	18°20'N	69°00'W
Catalunya, hist. reg., Spain	173	41°23'N	0°50'E
Catamarca, Arg. (kä-tä-mä'r-kä)	144	28°29'S	65°45'W
Catamarca, prov., Arg. (kä-tä-mär'kä)	144	27°15'S	67°15'W
Catanaun, Phil. (kä-tä-nä'wän)	213a	13°36'N	122°20'E
Catanduanes Island, i., Phil. (kä-tän-dwä'nĕs)	213	13°55'N	125°00'E
Catanduva, Braz. (kä-tän-dōō'vä)	143	21°12'S	48°47'W
Catania, Italy (kä-tä'nyä)	154	37°30'N	15°09'E
Catania, Golfo di, b., Italy (gôl-fô-dē-kȧ-tä'nyä)	174	37°24'N	15°28'E
Catanzaro, Italy (kä-tän-dzä'rō)	163	38°53'N	16°34'E
Catarroja, Spain (kä-tär-rō'hä)	173	39°24'N	0°25'W
Catawba, r., N.C., U.S. (kȧ-tô'bȧ)	125	35°25'N	80°55'W
Catbalogan, Phil. (kät-bä-lō'gän)	213	11°45'N	124°52'E
Catemaco, Mex. (kä-tā-mä'kō)	131	18°26'N	95°06'W
Catemaco, Lago, l., Mex. (lä'gô-kä-tä-mä'kō)	131	18°23'N	95°04'W
Caterham, Eng., U.K. (kā'tēr-ŭm)	158b	51°16'N	0°04'W
Catete, Ang. (kä-tĕ'tĕ)	232	9°06'S	13°43'E
Cathedral Mountain, mtn., Tx., U.S. (kȧ-thē'drăl)	122	30°09'N	103°46'W
Cathedral Peak, mtn., Afr. (kă-thē'drăl)	233c	28°53'S	29°04'E
Catherine, Lake, l., Ar., U.S. (kă-thēr-ĭn)	121	34°26'N	92°47'W
Cathkin Peak, mtn., Afr. (kăth'kĭn)	232	29°08'S	29°22'E
Cathlamet, Wa., U.S. (kăth-lăm'ĕt)	116c	46°12'N	123°22'W
Catlettsburg, Ky., U.S. (kăt'lĕts-bûrg)	108	38°20'N	82°35'W
Catoche, Cabo, c., Mex. (kä-tō'chĕ)	128	21°30'N	87°15'W
Catonsville, Md., U.S. (kā'tŭnz-vĭl)	110e	39°16'N	76°45'W
Catorce, Mex. (kä-tôr'sä)	130	23°41'N	100°51'W
Catskill, N.Y., U.S. (kăts'kĭl)	109	42°15'N	73°50'W
Catskill Mountains, mts., N.Y., U.S.	107	42°20'N	74°35'W
Cattaraugus Indian Reservation, I.R., N.Y., U.S. (kăt'tȧ-rȧ-gŭs)	109	42°30'N	79°05'W
Catu, Braz. (kȧ-tōō)	143	12°26'S	38°12'W
Catuala, Ang.	236	16°29'S	19°03'E
Catumbela, r., Ang. (kä'tŏm-bĕl'ȧ)	236	12°40'S	14°10'E
Cauayan, Phil. (kou-ä'yän)	213a	16°56'N	121°46'E
Cauca, r., Col. (kou'kä)	142	7°30'N	75°26'W
Caucagua, Ven. (käō-kȧ'gwä)	143b	10°17'N	66°22'W
Caucasus, mts.	178	43°20'N	42°00'E
Cauchon Lake, l., Can. (kô-shōn')	97	55°25'N	96°30'W
Caughnawaga, Can.	102a	45°24'N	73°41'W
Caulfield, Austl.	217a	37°53'S	145°03'E
Caulonia, Italy (kou-lō'nyä)	174	38°24'N	16°22'E
Cauquenes, Chile (kou-kā'nās)	144	35°54'S	72°14'W
Caura, r., Ven. (kou'rä)	142	6°48'N	64°40'W
Causapscal, Can.	100	48°22'N	67°14'W
Caution, Cape, c., Can. (kô'shŭn)	94	51°10'N	127°47'W
Cauto, r., Cuba (kou'tō)	134	20°33'N	76°20'W
Cauvery, r., India	199	12°00'N	77°00'E
Cava, Braz. (kȧ'vä)	144b	22°41'S	43°26'W
Cava de' Tirreni, Italy (kä'vä-dĕ-tēr-rĕ'nē)	173c	40°27'N	14°43'E
Cávado, r., Port. (kä-vä'dō)	172	41°43'N	8°08'W
Cavalcante, Braz. (kä-väl-kän'tā)	143	13°45'S	47°33'W
Cavalier, N.D., U.S. (kăv-ȧ-lēr')	112	48°45'N	97°39'W
Cavally, r., Afr.	234	4°40'N	7°30'W
Cavan, Ire. (kăv'ăn)	164	54°01'N	7°00'W
Cavarzere, Italy (kä-vär'dzȧ-rā)	174	45°08'N	12°06'E
Cavendish, Vt., U.S. (kăv'ĕn-dĭsh)	109	43°25'N	72°35'W
Caviana, Ilha, i., Braz. (kä-vyä'nä)	143	0°45'N	49°33'W
Cavite, Phil. (kä-vē'tä)	213a	14°30'N	120°54'E
Caxambu, Braz. (kä-shä'm-bōō)	143	22°00'S	44°45'W
Caxias, Braz. (kä'shē-äzh)	143	4°48'S	43°16'W
Caxias do Sul, Braz. (kä'shē-äzh-dô-sōō'l)	144	29°13'S	51°03'W
Caxito, Ang. (kä-shē'tō)	232	8°33'S	13°36'E
Cayambe, Ec. (kȧ-īä'm-bĕ)	142	0°03'N	79°09'W
Cayenne, Fr. Gu. (kā-ĕn')	143	4°56'N	52°18'W
Cayetano Rubio, Mex. (kä-yĕ-tȧ-nô-rōō'byô)	130	20°37'N	100°21'W
Cayey, P.R.	129b	18°05'N	66°12'W
Cayman Brac, i., Cay. Is. (kī-män' bräk)	134	19°45'N	79°50'W
Cayman Islands, dep., N.A.	134	19°30'N	80°30'W
Cay Sal Bank, bk. (kē-săl)	134	23°55'N	80°20'W
Cayuga, l., N.Y., U.S. (kā-yōō'gȧ)	109	42°35'N	76°35'W
Cazalla de la Sierra, Spain	172	37°55'N	5°48'W
Cazaux, Étang de, l., Fr. (ā-tăN' dĕ kä-zō')	170	44°32'N	0°59'W
Cazenovia, N.Y., U.S. (kăz-ē-nō'vĭ-ä)	109	42°55'N	75°50'W
Cazenovia Creek, r., N.Y., U.S.	111c	42°49'N	78°45'W
Čazma, Cro. (chäz'mä)	174	45°44'N	16°39'E
Cazombo, Ang. (kä-zô'm-bō)	232	11°54'S	22°52'E
Cazones, r., Mex. (kä-zō'nĕs)	131	20°37'N	97°28'W
Cazones, Ensenada de, b., Cuba (ĕn-sĕ-nä-dä-dĕ-kä-zō'nås)	134	22°05'N	81°30'W
Cazones, Golfo de, b., Cuba (gôl-fô-dĕ-kä-zō'nås)	134	21°55'N	81°15'W
Cazorla, Spain (kä-thôr'lå)	172	37°55'N	2°58'W
Cea, r., Spain (thā'ä)	172	42°18'N	5°10'W
Ceará-Mirim, Braz. (sā-ä-rä'mē-rē'N)	143	6°00'S	35°13'W
Cebaco, Isla, i., Pan. (ē's-lä-sȧ-bä'kō)	133	7°27'N	81°08'W
Cebolla Creek, r., Co., U.S. (sē-bōl'yȧ)	119	38°15'N	107°10'W
Cebreros, Spain (sĕ-brĕ'rôs)	172	40°28'N	4°28'W
Cebu, Phil. (sā-bōō')	213	10°22'N	123°49'E
Čechy (Bohemia), hist. reg., Czech Rep.	168	49°51'N	13°55'E
Cecil, Pa., U.S. (sē'sĭl)	111e	40°20'N	80°10'W
Cedar, r., Ia., U.S.	113	42°23'N	92°07'W
Cedar, r., Wa., U.S.	116c	45°56'N	122°32'W
Cedar, West Fork, r., Ia., U.S.	113	42°49'N	93°10'W
Cedar Bayou, Tx., U.S.	123a	29°54'N	94°58'W
Cedar Breaks National Monument, rec., Ut., U.S.	119	37°35'N	112°55'W
Cedarburg, Wi., U.S. (sē'dĕr bûrg)	113	43°23'N	88°00'W
Cedar City, Ut., U.S.	119	37°40'N	113°10'W
Cedar Creek, r., N.D., U.S.	112	46°05'N	102°10'W
Cedar Falls, Ia., U.S.	113	42°31'N	92°29'W
Cedar Keys, Fl., U.S.	124	29°06'N	83°03'W
Cedar Lake, In., U.S.	111a	41°22'N	87°27'W
Cedar Lake, l., In., U.S.	111a	41°23'N	87°25'W
Cedar Lake, res., Can.	92	53°10'N	100°00'W
Cedar Rapids, Ia., U.S.	105	42°00'N	91°43'W
Cedar Springs, Mi., U.S.	108	43°15'N	85°40'W
Cedartown, Ga., U.S. (sē'dēr-toun)	124	34°00'N	85°15'W
Cedarville, S. Afr. (cĕdȧr'vĭl)	233c	30°23'S	29°04'E
Cedral, Mex. (sā-dräl')	130	23°47'N	100°42'W
Cedros, Hond. (sā'drōs)	132	14°36'N	87°07'W
Cedros, i., Mex.	128	28°10'N	115°10'W
Ceduna, Austl. (sē-dò'nȧ)	218	32°15'S	133°55'E
Ceel Buur, Som.	238a	4°35'N	46°40'E
Cega, r., Spain (thā'gä)	172	41°25'N	4°27'W
Cegléd, Hung. (tsā'glād)	169	47°10'N	19°49'E
Ceglie, Italy (chĕ'lyĕ)	175	40°39'N	17°32'E
Cehegín, Spain (thā-ȧ-hēn')	172	38°05'N	1°48'W
Ceiba del Agua, Cuba (sā'bä-dĕl-ȧ'gwä)	135a	22°53'N	82°38'W
Cekhira, Tun.	230	34°17'N	10°00'E
Celaya, Mex. (sā-lä'yä)	128	20°33'N	100°49'W
Celebes (Sulawesi), i., Indon.	212	2°15'S	120°30'E
Celebes Sea, sea, Asia	212	3°45'N	121°52'E
Celestún, Mex. (sĕ-lĕs-tōō'n)	132a	20°57'N	90°18'W

ng-sing; ŋ-baŋk; N-nasalized n; nŏd; cŏmmit; ōld; ŏbey; ôrder; oi-boil; fōōd; ò-as oo in foot; ou-out; s-soft; sh-dish; th-thin; pūre; ûnite; ûrn; stŭd; circŭs; ü-as in French tu; '-indeterminate vowel.

PLACE (Pronunciation)	PAGE	LAT.	LONG.
Celina, Oh., U.S. (sẽlī′na)	108	40°30′N	84°35′W
Celje, Slvn. (tsĕl′yĕ)	174	46°13′N	15°17′E
Celle, Ger. (tsĕl′ĕ)	161	52°37′N	10°05′E
Cement, Ok., U.S. (sė-mĕnt′)	120	34°56′N	98°07′W
Cenderawasih, Teluk, b., Indon.	213	2°20′S	135°30′E
Ceniza, Pico, mtn., Ven. (pē′kô-sĕ-nē′zä)	143b	10°24′N	67°26′W
Center, Tx., U.S. (sĕn′tẽr)	123	31°50′N	94°10′W
Center Hill Lake, res., Tn., U.S. (sĕn′tẽr-hĭl)	124	36°02′N	86°00′W
Center Line, Mi., U.S. (sĕn′tẽr līn)	111b	42°29′N	83°01′W
Centerville, Ia., U.S. (sĕn′tẽr-vĭl)	113	40°44′N	92°48′W
Centerville, Mn., U.S.	117g	45°10′N	93°03′W
Centerville, Pa., U.S.	111e	40°02′N	79°58′W
Centerville, S.D., U.S.	112	43°07′N	96°56′W
Centerville, Ut., U.S.	117b	40°55′N	111°53′W
Central, Cordillera, mts., Bol. (kôr-dēl-yĕ′rä-sĕn-trä′l)	142	19°18′S	65°29′W
Central, Cordillera, mts., Col.	142a	3°58′N	75°55′W
Central, Cordillera, mts., Dom. Rep.	135	19°05′N	71°30′W
Central, Cordillera, mts., Phil. (kôr-dēl-yĕ′rä-sĕn′träl)	213a	17°05′N	120°55′E
Central African Republic, nation, Afr.	231	7°50′N	21°00′E
Central America, reg., N.A. (ä-mĕr′ĭ-kȧ)	128	10°45′N	87°15′W
Central City, Ky., U.S. (sĕn′trăl)	124	37°15′N	87°09′W
Central City, Ne., U.S. (sĕn′trăl sĭ′tĭ)	112	41°07′N	98°00′W
Central Falls, R.I., U.S. (sĕn′trăl fôlz)	110b	41°54′N	71°23′W
Centralia, Il., U.S. (sĕn-trā′lĭ-ȧ)	108	38°35′N	89°05′W
Centralia, Mo., U.S.	121	39°11′N	92°07′W
Centralia, Wa., U.S.	114	46°42′N	122°58′W
Central Plateau, plat., Russia	180	55°00′N	33°30′E
Central Valley, N.Y., U.S.	110a	41°19′N	74°07′W
Centreville, Il., U.S. (sĕn′tẽr-vĭl)	117e	38°33′N	90°06′W
Centreville, Md., U.S.	109	39°05′N	76°05′W
Century, Fl., U.S. (sĕn′tū-rĭ)	124	30°57′N	87°15′W
Ceram (Seram), i., Indon.	213	2°45′S	129°30′E
Céret, Fr.	170	42°29′N	2°47′E
Cerignola, Italy (chā-rē-nyô′lä)	174	41°16′N	15°55′E
Cerknica, Slvn. (tsĕr′knē-tsȧ)	174	45°48′N	14°21′E
Cern′achovsk, Russia (chĕr-nyä′κôfsk)	180	54°38′N	21°49′E
Cerralvo, Mex. (sĕr-räl′vō)	122	26°05′N	99°37′W
Cerralvo, i., Mex.	128	24°00′N	109°59′W
Cerrito, Col. (sĕr-rē′-tô)	142a	3°41′N	76°17′W
Cerritos, Mex. (sĕr-rē′tôs)	130	22°26′N	100°16′W
Cerro de Pasco, Peru (sĕr′rō dā päs′kō)	142	10°45′S	76°14′W
Cerro Gordo, Arroyo de, r., Mex. (är-rô-yō-dĕ-sĕ′r-rô-gôr-dō)	122	26°12′N	104°06′W
Certegui, Col. (sĕr-tĕ′gē)	142a	5°21′N	76°35′W
Cervantes, Phil. (sĕr-vän′täs)	213a	16°59′N	120°42′E
Cervera del Río Alhama, Spain	172	42°02′N	1°55′W
Cerveteri, Italy (chĕr-vĕ′tĕ-rē)	173d	42°00′N	12°06′E
Cesena, Italy (chĕ′sĕ-nä)	174	44°08′N	12°16′E
Cēsis, Lat. (sā′sĭs)	167	57°19′N	25°17′E
Česká Lípa, Czech Rep. (chĕs′kä lē′pa)	168	50°41′N	14°31′E
České Budějovice, Czech Rep. (chĕs′kā bōō′dyĕ-yô-vēt-sĕ)	161	49°00′N	14°30′E
Českomoravská Vysočina, hills, Czech Rep.	168	49°21′N	15°40′E
Český Těšín, Czech Rep.	169	49°43′N	18°22′E
Çeşme, Tur. (chĕsh′mĕ)	175	38°20′N	26°20′E
Cessnock, Austl.	219	32°58′S	151°15′E
Cestos, r., Lib.	234	5°40′N	9°25′W
Cetinje, Serb. (tsĕt′in-yĕ)	154	42°23′N	18°55′E
Ceuta, Sp. N. Afr. (thā-ōō′tä)	230	36°04′N	5°36′W
Cévennes, reg., Fr. (sā-vĕn′)	161	44°20′N	3°48′E
Ceylon *see* Sri Lanka, nation, Asia	203	8°45′N	82°30′E
Chabot, Lake, l., Ca., U.S. (sha′bŏt)	116b	37°44′N	122°06′W
Chacabuco, Arg. (chä-kä-bōō′kō)	141c	34°37′S	60°27′W
Chacaltianguis, Mex. (chä-käl-tē-äŋ′gwēs)	131	18°18′N	95°50′W
Chachapoyas, Peru (chä-chä-poi′yäs)	142	6°16′S	77°48′W
Chaco, prov., Arg. (chä′kō)	144	26°00′S	60°45′W
Chaco Culture National Historic Park, rec., N.M., U.S. (chä′kô)	119	36°05′N	108°00′W
Chad, Russia (chäd)	186a	56°33′N	57°11′E
Chad, nation, Afr.	231	17°48′N	19°00′E
Chad, Lake, l., Afr.	231	13°55′N	13°40′E
Chadbourn, N.C., U.S. (chăd′bŭrn)	125	34°19′N	78°55′W
Chadron, Ne., U.S. (chăd′rŭn)	104	42°50′N	103°10′W
Chafarinas, Islas, is., Sp. N. Afr.	172	35°08′N	2°20′W
Chaffee, Mo., U.S. (chăf′ē)	121	37°10′N	89°39′W
Chāgal Hills, hills, Afg.	198	29°15′N	63°28′E
Chagodoshcha, r., Russia (chä-gō-dôsh-chä)	176	59°08′N	35°13′E
Chagres, r., Pan. (chä′grĕs)	133	9°18′N	79°22′W
Chagrin, r., Oh., U.S. (shȧ′grĭn)	111d	41°34′N	81°24′W
Chagrin Falls, Oh., U.S. (shȧ′grĭn fôls)	111d	41°26′N	81°23′W
Chahar, hist. reg., China (chä-här)	205	44°25′N	115°00′E
Chake Chake, Tan.	237	5°15′S	39°46′E
Chalatenango, El Sal. (chäl-ä-tĕ-näŋ′gō)	132	14°04′N	88°54′W
Chalbi Desert, des., Kenya	237	3°40′N	36°50′E
Chalcatongo, Mex. (chäl-kä-tôŋ′gō)	131	17°04′N	97°41′W
Chalchihuites, Mex. (chäl-chē-wē′tās)	130	23°28′N	103°57′W
Chalchuapa, El Sal. (chäl-chwä′pä)	132	14°01′N	89°39′W
Chalco, Mex. (chäl-kō)	131a	19°15′N	98°54′W
Chaleur Bay, b., Can. (shȧ-lûr′)	93	47°58′N	65°33′W
Chalgrove, Eng., U.K. (chăl′grôv)	158b	51°38′N	1°05′W
Chaling, China (chä′lĭng)	209	27°00′N	113°31′E

PLACE (Pronunciation)	PAGE	LAT.	LONG.
Chalkída, Grc.	163	38°28′N	23°38′E
Chalmette, La., U.S. (shăl-mĕt′)	110d	29°57′N	89°57′W
Châlons-sur-Marne, Fr. (shȧ-lôn′sür-märn)	161	48°57′N	4°23′E
Chalon-sur-Saône, Fr.	161	46°47′N	4°54′E
Chaltel, Cerro (Monte Fitzroy), mtn., S.A. (sĕ′r-rô-chäl′tĕl)	144	48°10′S	73°18′W
Chālūs, Iran	201	36°38′N	51°26′E
Chama, Rio, r., N.M., U.S. (chä′mä)	119	36°19′N	106°31′W
Chama, Sierra de, mts., Guat. (sē-ĕ′r-rä-dĕ-chä-mä)	132	15°48′N	90°20′W
Chamama, Mwi.	237	12°55′S	33°43′E
Chaman, Pak. (chŭm-än′)	199	30°58′N	66°21′E
Chambal, r., India (chŭm-bäl′)	199	24°30′N	75°30′E
Chamberlain, S.D., U.S. (chām′bẽr-lĭn)	112	43°48′N	99°21′W
Chamberlain, l., Me., U.S.	100	46°15′N	69°10′W
Chambersburg, Pa., U.S. (chām′bẽrz-bûrg)	109	40°00′N	77°40′W
Chambéry, Fr. (shäm-bā-rē′)	161	45°35′N	5°54′E
Chambeshi, r., Zam.	237	10°35′S	31°20′E
Chamblee, Ga., U.S. (chăm-blē′)	110c	33°55′N	84°18′W
Chambly, Can. (shän-blē′)	102a	45°27′N	73°17′W
Chambly, Fr.	171b	49°11′N	2°14′E
Chambord, Can.	91	48°22′N	72°01′W
Chame, Punta, c., Pan. (pô′n-tä-chä′mȧ)	133	8°41′N	79°27′W
Chamelecón, r., Hond. (chä-mĕ-lĕ-kô′n)	132	15°09′N	88°42′W
Chamo, l., Eth.	231	5°58′N	37°00′E
Chamonix-Mont-Blanc, Fr. (shȧ-mō-nē′)	171	45°55′N	6°50′E
Champagne, reg., Fr. (shäm-pän′yĕ)	170	48°53′N	4°48′E
Champaign, Il., U.S. (shăm-pān′)	105	40°10′N	88°15′W
Champdāni, India	202a	22°48′N	88°21′E
Champerico, Guat. (chăm-pȧ-rē′kō)	132	14°18′N	91°55′W
Champion, Mi., U.S. (chăm′pĭ-ŭn)	113	46°30′N	87°59′W
Champlain, Lake, l., N.A. (shăm-plān′)	107	44°45′N	73°20′W
Champlitte-et-le Prálot, Fr. (shäN-plēt′)	171	47°38′N	5°28′E
Champotón, Mex. (chäm-pō-tōn′)	131	19°21′N	90°43′W
Champotón, r., Mex.	131	19°19′N	90°15′W
Chañaral, Chile (chän-yä-räl′)	144	26°20′S	70°46′W
Chances Peak, vol., Monts.	133b	16°43′N	62°10′W
Chandeleur Islands, is., La., U.S. (shăn-dē-lōōr′)	124	29°53′N	88°35′W
Chandeleur Sound, strt., La., U.S.	124	29°47′N	89°08′W
Chandīgarh, India	199	30°51′N	77°13′E
Chandler, Can. (chăn′dlẽr)	91	48°21′N	64°41′W
Chandler, Ok., U.S.	121	35°42′N	96°52′W
Chandrapur, India	199	19°58′N	79°21′E
Chang *see* Yangtze, r., China	205	30°30′N	117°25′E
Changane, r., Moz.	232	22°42′S	32°46′E
Changara, Moz.	237	16°54′S	33°14′E
Changchun, China (chäŋ-chòn)	205	43°55′N	125°25′E
Changdang Hu, l., China (chäŋ-däŋ hōō)	206	31°37′N	119°29′E
Changde, China (chäŋ-dŭ)	205	29°00′N	111°38′E
Changhua, Tai. (chäng′hwä′)	209	24°02′N	120°32′E
Changjŏn, Kor., N. (chäng′jŭn′)	210	38°40′N	128°05′E
Changli, China (chäŋ-lē)	208	39°46′N	119°10′E
Changning, China (chäŋ-nĭŋ)	204	24°34′N	99°49′E
Changping, China (chäŋ-pĭŋ)	208	40°12′N	116°10′E
Changqing, China (chäŋ-chyĭŋ)	206	36°33′N	116°42′E
Changsan Got, c., Kor., N.	210	38°06′N	124°50′E
Changsha, China (chäŋ-shä)	205	28°20′N	113°00′E
Changshan Qundao, is., China (chäŋ-shän chyòn-dou)	206	39°08′N	122°26′E
Changshu, China (chäŋ-shōō)	206	31°40′N	120°45′E
Changting, China	209	25°50′N	116°18′E
Changwu, China (chäng′wōō′)	208	35°12′N	107°45′E
Changxindianzhen, China (chäŋ-shyĭn-dĭĕn-jŭn)	208a	39°49′N	116°12′E
Changxing Dao, i., China (chäŋ-shyĭŋ dou)	206	39°38′N	121°10′E
Changyi, China (chäŋ-yē)	206	36°51′N	119°23′E
Changyuan, China (chyäŋ-yuän)	206	35°10′N	114°41′E
Changzhi, China (chäŋ-jr)	208	35°58′N	112°58′E
Changzhou, China (chäŋ-jō)	205	31°47′N	119°56′E
Changzhuyuan, China (chäŋ-jōō-yuän)	206	31°33′N	115°17′E
Chanhassen, Mn., U.S. (shăn′hăs-sĕn)	117g	44°52′N	93°32′W
Chaniá, Grc.	162	35°31′N	24°01′E
Channel Islands, is., Eur. (chăn′ĕl)	156	49°15′N	3°30′W
Channel Islands, is., Ca., U.S.	118	33°30′N	119°15′W
Channel-Port-aux-Basques, Can.	91	47°35′N	59°11′W
Channelview, Tx., U.S. (chănĕlvū)	123a	29°46′N	95°07′W
Chantada, Spain (chän-tä′dä)	172	42°38′N	7°36′W
Chanthaburi, Thai.	212	12°37′N	102°04′E
Chantilly, Fr. (shäN-tē-yē′)	171b	49°12′N	2°30′E
Chantilly, Va., U.S. (shăn′tĭlē)	110e	38°53′N	77°26′W
Chantrey Inlet, b., Can. (chăn-trē)	92	67°49′N	95°00′W
Chanute, Ks., U.S. (shȧ-nōōt′)	105	37°41′N	95°27′W
Chany, l., Russia (chä′nē)	178	54°15′N	77°31′E
Chao′an, China (chou-än)	205	23°48′N	116°35′E
Chao Hu, l., China	209	31°45′N	116°59′E
Chao Phraya, r., Thai.	212	16°13′N	99°33′E
Chaor, r., China (chou-r)	208	47°20′N	121°40′E
Chaoshui, China (chou-shwā)	206	37°43′N	120°56′E
Chaoxian, China (chou shyĕn)	206	31°37′N	117°50′E
Chaoyang, China	205	41°32′N	120°20′E
Chaoyang, China (chou-yäŋ)	209	23°18′N	116°32′E
Chapada, Serra da, mts., Braz. (sĕ′r-rä-dä-shä-pä′dä)	143	14°57′S	54°34′W

PLACE (Pronunciation)	PAGE	LAT.	LONG.
Chapadão, Serra do, mtn., Braz. (sĕ′r-rä-dô-shä-pȧ-dou′N)	141a	20°31′S	46°20′W
Chapala, Mex. (chä-pä′lä)	130	20°18′N	103°10′W
Chapala, Lago de, l., Mex. (lä′gô-dĕ-chä-pä′lä)	128	20°14′N	103°02′W
Chapalagana, r., Mex. (chä-pä-lä-gȧ′nä)	130	22°11′N	104°09′W
Chaparral, Col. (chä-pär-rä′l)	142	3°44′N	75°28′W
Chapayevsk, Russia (châ-pī′ĕfsk)	180	53°00′N	49°30′E
Chapel Hill, N.C., U.S. (chăp′′l hĭl)	125	35°55′N	79°05′W
Chaplain, l., Wa., U.S. (chăp′lĭn)	116a	47°58′N	121°50′W
Chapleau, Can. (chăp-lō′)	91	47°43′N	83°28′W
Chapman, Mount, mtn., Can. (chăp′mȧn)	95	51°50′N	118°20′W
Chapman′s Bay, b., S. Afr. (chăp′mȧns bā)	232a	34°06′S	18°17′E
Chappell, Ne., U.S. (chă-pĕl′)	112	41°06′N	102°29′W
Chapultenango, Mex. (chä-pòl-tē-näŋ′gō)	131	17°19′N	93°08′W
Chá Pungana, Ang.	236	13°44′S	18°39′E
Chār Borjak, Afg.	201	30°17′N	62°03′E
Charcas, Mex. (chär′käs)	130	23°09′N	101°09′W
Charco de Azul, Bahía, b., Pan.	133	8°14′N	82°45′W
Charente, r., Fr. (shȧ-räNt′)	170	45°48′N	0°28′W
Chari, r., Afr. (shä-rē′)	235	12°45′N	14°55′E
Charing, Eng., U.K. (chȧ′rĭng)	158b	51°13′N	0°49′E
Chariton, Ia., U.S. (châr′ĭ-tŭn)	113	41°02′N	93°16′W
Chariton, r., Mo., U.S.	121	40°24′N	92°38′W
Charjew, Turkmen.	183	38°52′N	63°37′E
Charlemagne, Can. (shärl-mäny′)	102a	45°43′N	73°29′W
Charleroi, Bel. (shȧr-lē-rwä′)	161	50°25′N	4°35′E
Charleroi, Pa., U.S. (shär′lē-roi)	111e	40°08′N	79°54′W
Charles, Cape, c., Va., U.S. (chärlz)	109	37°05′N	75°48′W
Charlesbourg, Can. (shȧrl-bōōr′)	102b	46°51′N	71°16′W
Charles City, Ia., U.S. (chärlz)	113	43°03′N	92°40′W
Charleston, Il., U.S. (chärlz′tŭn)	108	39°30′N	88°10′W
Charleston, Mo., U.S.	121	36°53′N	89°20′W
Charleston, Ms., U.S.	124	34°00′N	90°02′W
Charleston, S.C., U.S.	105	32°47′N	79°56′W
Charleston, W.V., U.S.	105	38°20′N	81°35′W
Charlestown, St. K./N.	133b	17°10′N	62°32′W
Charlestown, In., U.S. (chärlz′toun)	111h	38°46′N	85°39′W
Charleville, Austl. (chär′lē-vĭl)	219	20°16′S	146°28′E
Charleville Mézières, Fr. (shärl-vēl′)	170	49°48′N	4°41′E
Charlevoix, Mi., U.S. (shär′lē-voi)	108	45°20′N	85°15′W
Charlevoix, Lake, l., Mi., U.S.	113	45°17′N	85°43′W
Charlotte, Mi., U.S. (shär′lŏt)	108	42°35′N	84°50′W
Charlotte, N.C., U.S.	105	35°15′N	80°50′W
Charlotte Amalie, V.I.U.S. (shär-lŏt′ĕ ä-mä′lĭ-ȧ)	129	18°21′N	64°54′W
Charlotte Harbor, b., Fl., U.S.	125a	26°49′N	82°00′W
Charlotte Lake, l., Can.	94	52°07′N	125°30′W
Charlottenberg, Swe. (shär-lŭt′ĕn-bĕrg)	166	59°53′N	12°17′E
Charlottesville, Va., U.S. (shär′lŏtz-vĭl)	105	38°00′N	78°25′W
Charlottetown, Can. (shär′lŏt-toun)	91	46°14′N	63°08′W
Charlotte Waters, Austl. (shär′lŏt)	218	26°00′S	134°50′E
Charmes, Fr. (shärm)	171	48°23′N	6°19′E
Charnwood Forest, for., Eng., U.K. (chärn′wŏŏd)	158a	52°42′N	1°15′W
Charny, Can. (shär-nē′)	102b	46°43′N	71°16′W
Chars, Fr. (shär)	171b	49°09′N	1°57′E
Chārsadda, Pak. (chŭr-sä′dä)	199a	34°17′N	71°43′E
Charters Towers, Austl. (chär′tẽrz)	219	20°03′S	146°20′E
Chartres, Fr. (shärt′r′)	161	48°26′N	1°29′E
Chascomús, Arg. (chäs-kō-mōōs′)	144	35°32′S	58°01′W
Chase City, Va., U.S. (chās)	125	36°45′N	78°27′W
Chashniki, Bela. (chäsh′nyē-kē)	176	54°51′N	29°08′E
Chaska, Mn., U.S. (chăs′kȧ)	117g	44°48′N	93°36′W
Châteaudun, Fr. (shä-tō-dăN′)	170	48°04′N	1°23′E
Château-Gontier, Fr. (chȧ-tō-gôN′tyā′)	170	47°48′N	0°43′W
Châteauguay, Can. (chȧ-tō-gā)	102a	45°22′N	73°45′W
Châteauguay, r., N.A.	102a	45°13′N	73°51′W
Châteauneuf, Fr.	170a	43°23′N	5°11′E
Château-Renault, Fr. (shȧ-tō-rē-nō′)	170	47°36′N	0°57′E
Château-Richer, Can. (shȧ-tō′rē-shā′)	102b	47°00′N	71°01′W
Châteauroux, Fr. (shȧ-tō-rōō′)	161	46°47′N	1°39′E
Château-Thierry, Fr. (shȧ-tō′ty-ĕr-rē′)	170	49°03′N	3°22′E
Châtellerault, Fr. (shä-tĕl-rō′)	161	46°48′N	0°31′E
Chatfield, Mn., U.S. (chăt′fēld)	113	43°50′N	92°10′W
Chatham, Can. (chăt′ȧm)	91	42°25′N	82°10′W
Chatham, Can.	91	47°02′N	65°28′W
Chatham, Eng., U.K. (chăt′ŭm)	165	51°23′N	0°32′E
Chatham, N.J., U.S. (chăt′ȧm)	110a	40°44′N	74°23′W
Chatham, Oh., U.S.	111d	41°06′N	82°01′W
Chatham Islands, is., N.Z.	2	44°00′S	178°00′W
Chatham Sound, strt., Can.	94	54°32′N	130°35′W
Chatham Strait, strt., Ak., U.S.	103	57°00′N	134°40′W
Chatsworth, Ca., U.S. (chătz′wûrth)	117a	34°16′N	118°36′W
Chatsworth Reservoir, res., Ca., U.S.	117a	34°15′N	118°41′W
Chattahoochee, Fl., U.S. (chăt-tȧ-hōō′ chee)	124	30°42′N	84°47′W
Chattahoochee, r., U.S.	107	32°00′N	85°10′W
Chattanooga, Tn., U.S. (chăt-ȧ-nōō′gȧ)	105	35°01′N	85°15′W
Chattooga, r., Ga., U.S. (chă-tōō′gȧ)	124	34°47′N	83°13′W
Chaudière, r., Can. (shō-dyĕr′)	99	46°26′N	71°10′W
Chaumont, Fr. (shō-môN′)	161	48°08′N	5°07′E
Chaunskaya Guba, b., Russia	185	69°15′N	170°00′E
Chauny, Fr. (shō-nē′)	170	49°40′N	3°09′E
Chau-phu, Viet.	212	10°49′N	104°57′E

ăt; finăl; rāte; senāte; ärm; ȧsk; sofȧ; fâre; ch-choose; dh-as th in other; bē; ēvent; bĕt; recĕnt; cratẽr; g-gō; gh-guttural g; bĭt; ĭ-short neutral; rīde; κ-guttural k as ch in German ich;

PRONOUNCING INDEX

Chautauqua – Chippewa Lake 281

PLACE (Pronunciation)	PAGE	LAT.	LONG.
Chautauqua, l., N.Y., U.S. (shȧ-tô´kwȧ)	109	42°10′N	79°25′W
Chavaniga, Russia	180	66°02′N	37°50′E
Chaves, Port. (chä´vězh)	172	41°44′N	7°30′W
Chavinda, Mex. (chä-vē´n-dä)	130	20°01′N	102°27′W
Chavusi, Bela.	176	53°57′N	30°58′E
Chazumba, Mex. (chä-zȯm´bä)	131	18°11′N	97°41′W
Cheadle, Eng., U.K. (chē´d'l)	158a	52°59′N	1°59′W
Cheat, W.V., U.S. (chēt)	109	39°35′N	79°40′W
Cheb, Czech Rep. (κěb)	168	50°05′N	12°23′E
Chebarkul', Russia (chě-bår-kûl´)	186a	54°59′N	60°22′E
Cheboksary, Russia (chyě-bôk-sä´rě)	180	56°00′N	47°20′E
Cheboygan, Mi., U.S. (shě-boi´găn)	108	45°40′N	84°30′W
Chech, Erg, des., Alg.	230	24°45′N	2°07′W
Chechen', i., Russia (chyěch´ěn)	181	44°00′N	48°10′E
Chechnya, prov., Russia	182	43°30′N	45°50′E
Checotah, Ok., U.S. (chě-kō´tȧ)	121	35°27′N	95°32′W
Chedabucto Bay, b., Can. (chěd-ȧ-bŭk-tō)	101	45°23′N	61°10′W
Cheduba Island, i., Mya.	212	18°45′N	93°01′E
Cheecham Hills, hills, Can. (chēē´hăm)	96	56°20′N	111°10′W
Cheektowaga, N.Y., U.S. (chēk-tŏ-wä´gȧ)	111c	42°54′N	78°46′W
Chefoo *see* Yantai, China	205	37°32′N	121°22′E
Chegutu, Zimb.	232	18°18′S	30°10′E
Chehalis, Wa., U.S. (chě-hā´lĭs)	114	46°39′N	122°58′W
Chehalis, r., Wa., U.S.	114	46°47′N	123°17′W
Cheju, Kor., S. (chě´jōō´)	210	33°29′N	126°40′E
Cheju (Quelpart), i., Kor., S.	210	33°20′N	126°25′E
Chekalin, Russia (chě-kä´lĭn)	176	54°05′N	36°13′E
Chela, Serra da, mts., Ang. (sěr´rȧ dā shā´lȧ)	232	15°30′S	13°30′E
Chelan, Wa., U.S. (chě-lăn´)	114	47°51′N	119°59′W
Chelan, Lake, l., Wa., U.S.	114	48°09′N	120°20′W
Cheleiros, Port. (shě-la´rōzh)	173b	38°54′N	9°19′W
Chéliff, r., Alg. (shā-lēf)	230	36°00′N	2°00′E
Chelles, Fr.	171b	48°53′N	2°36′E
Chełm, Pol. (κělm)	161	51°08′N	23°30′E
Chełmno, Pol. (κělm´nō)	169	53°20′N	18°25′E
Chelmsford, Can.	98	46°35′N	81°12′W
Chelmsford, Eng., U.K. (chělm´s-fērd)	165	51°44′N	0°28′E
Chelmsford, Ma., U.S.	101a	42°36′N	71°21′W
Chelsea, Austl.	217a	38°05′S	145°08′E
Chelsea, Can.	102c	45°30′N	75°46′W
Chelsea, Al., U.S. (chěl´sē)	110h	33°20′N	86°38′W
Chelsea, Ma., U.S.	101a	42°23′N	71°02′W
Chelsea, Mi., U.S.	108	42°20′N	84°00′W
Chelsea, Ok., U.S.	121	36°32′N	95°23′W
Cheltenham, Eng., U.K. (chělt´nŭm)	164	51°57′N	2°06′W
Cheltenham, Md., U.S. (chěltēn-hăm)	110e	38°45′N	76°50′W
Chelyabinsk, Russia (chěl-yä-bėnsk´)	178	55°10′N	61°25′E
Chelyuskin, Mys, c., Russia (chěl-yȯs´-kĭn)	179	77°45′N	104°45′E
Chemba, Moz.	237	17°08′S	34°52′E
Chemnitz, Ger.	161	50°48′N	12°53′E
Chemung, r., N.Y., U.S. (shě-mŭng)	109	42°20′N	77°25′W
Chën, Gora, mtn., Russia	179	65°13′N	142°12′E
Chenāb, r., Asia (chě-näb)	199	30°30′N	71°30′E
Chenachane, Alg. (shē-nȧ-shän´)	230	26°14′N	4°14′W
Chencun, China (chŭn-tsȯn)	207a	22°58′N	113°14′E
Cheney, Wa., U.S. (chē´nȧ)	114	47°29′N	117°34′W
Chengde, China (chŭŋ-dŭ)	205	40°50′N	117°50′E
Chengdong Hu, l., China (chŭŋ-dȯŋ hōō)	206	32°22′N	116°32′E
Chengdu, China (chŭŋ-dōō)	204	30°30′N	104°10′E
Chenggu, China (chŭŋ-gōō)	208	33°05′N	107°25′E
Chenghai, China (chŭŋ-hī)	209	23°22′N	116°40′E
Chengshan Jiao, c., China (jyou chŭŋ-shän)	208	37°28′N	122°40′E
Chengxi Hu, l., China (chŭŋ-shyē hōō)	206	32°31′N	116°04′E
Chennai (Madras), India	199	13°08′N	80°15′E
Chenxian, China (chŭn-shyěn)	209	25°40′N	113°00′E
Chepén, Peru (chě-pě´n)	142	7°17′S	79°24′W
Chepo, Pan. (chā´pō)	133	9°12′N	79°06′W
Chepo, r., Pan.	133	9°10′N	78°36′W
Cher, r., Fr. (shâr)	161	47°14′N	1°34′E
Cherán, Mex. (chā-rän´)	130	19°41′N	101°54′W
Cherangany Hills, hills, Kenya	237	1°25′N	35°20′E
Cheraw, S.C., U.S. (chē´rô)	125	34°40′N	79°52′W
Cherbourg, Fr. (shär-bȯr´)	154	49°39′N	1°43′W
Cherdyn', Russia (chěr-dyēn´)	178	60°25′N	56°32′E
Cheremkhovo, Russia (chěr´yěm-kô-vō)	179	52°58′N	103°18′E
Cherëmukhovo, Russia (chěr-yě-mû-kô-vȯ)	186a	60°20′N	60°00′E
Cherepanovo, Russia (chěr´yě pä-nô´vō)	178	54°13′N	83°22′E
Cherepovets, Russia (chěr-yě-pô´vyětz)	178	59°08′N	37°59′E
Chereya, Bela. (chěr-ā´yä)	176	54°38′N	29°16′E
Chergui, i., Tun.	162	34°50′N	11°40′E
Chergui, Chott ech, l., Alg. (chěr gē)	162	34°12′N	0°10′W
Cherkasy, Ukr.	177	49°26′N	32°03′E
Cherkasy, prov., Ukr.	177	48°58′N	30°55′E
Cherkessk, Russia	182	44°14′N	42°04′E
Cherlak, Russia (chĭr-läk´)	178	54°04′N	74°28′E
Chermoz, Russia (chěr-môz´)	180	58°47′N	56°08′E
Chern', Russia (chěrn)	176	53°28′N	36°49′E
Chërnaya Kalitva, r., Russia (chôr´nȧ yȧ kȧ-lēt´vȧ)	177	50°15′N	39°16′E
Chernihiv, Ukr.	181	51°23′N	31°15′E
Chernihiv, prov., Ukr.	177	51°28′N	31°18′E
Chernihivka, Ukr.	177	47°08′N	36°20′E
Chernivtsi, Ukr.	178	48°18′N	25°56′E

PLACE (Pronunciation)	PAGE	LAT.	LONG.
Chernobyl' *see* Chornobai, Ukr.	176	51°17′N	30°14′E
Chernogorsk, Russia (chěr-nŏ-gôrsk´)	184	54°01′N	91°07′E
Chernoistochinsk, Russia (chěr-nôy-stô´chĭnsk)	186a	57°44′N	59°55′E
Chernyanka, Russia (chěrn-yäŋ´kä)	177	50°56′N	37°48′E
Cherokee, Ia., U.S. (chěr-ȯ-kē´)	112	42°43′N	95°33′W
Cherokee, Ks., U.S.	121	37°21′N	94°50′W
Cherokee, Ok., U.S.	120	36°44′N	98°22′W
Cherokee Lake, res., Tn., U.S.	124	36°22′N	83°22′W
Cherokees, Lake of the, res., Ok., U.S. (chěr-ȯ-kēz´)	107	36°32′N	95°14′W
Cherokee Sound, Bah.	134	26°15′N	76°55′W
Cherryfield, Me., U.S. (chěr´ĭ-fēld)	100	44°37′N	67°56′W
Cherry Grove, Or., U.S.	116c	45°27′N	123°15′W
Cherryvale, Ks., U.S.	121	37°16′N	95°33′W
Cherryville, N.C., U.S. (chěr´ĭ-vĭl)	125	35°32′N	81°22′W
Cherskogo, Khrebet, mts., Russia	179	67°15′N	140°00′E
Chertsey, Eng., U.K.	158b	51°24′N	0°30′W
Chervonoye, Vozyera, l., Bela. (chěr-vô´nȯ-yě)	176	52°24′N	28°00′E
Chervyen', Bela. (chěr´vyěn)	176	53°43′N	28°26′E
Cherykaw, Bela.	176	53°34′N	31°22′E
Chesaning, Mi., U.S. (chěs´ȧ-nĭng)	108	43°10′N	84°10′W
Chesapeake, Va., U.S. (chěs´ȧ-pēk)	110g	36°48′N	76°16′W
Chesapeake Bay, b., U.S.	107	38°20′N	76°15′W
Chesapeake Beach, Md., U.S.	110e	38°42′N	76°33′W
Chesham, Eng., U.K. (chěsh´ŭm)	158b	51°41′N	0°37′W
Cheshire, Mi., U.S. (chěsh´ĭr)	108	42°25′N	86°00′W
Cheshire, co., Eng., U.K.	158a	53°16′N	2°30′W
Chëshskaya Guba, b., Russia	178	67°25′N	46°00′E
Cheshunt, Eng., U.K.	158b	51°43′N	0°02′W
Chesma, Russia (chěs´mȧ)	186a	53°50′N	60°42′E
Chesnokovka, Russia (chěs-nŏ-kôf´kȧ)	178	53°28′N	83°41′E
Chester, Eng., U.K. (chěs´tēr)	164	53°12′N	2°53′W
Chester, Il., U.S.	121	37°54′N	89°48′W
Chester, Pa., U.S.	110f	39°51′N	75°22′W
Chester, S.C., U.S.	125	34°42′N	81°11′W
Chester, Va., U.S.	125	37°20′N	77°24′W
Chester, W.V., U.S.	108	40°35′N	80°30′W
Chesterfield, Eng., U.K. (chěs´tēr-fēld)	164	53°14′N	1°26′W
Chesterfield, Îles, is., N. Cal.	221	19°38′S	160°08′E
Chesterfield Inlet *see* Igluligaarjuk, Can.	92	63°19′N	91°11′W
Chesterfield Inlet, b., Can.	93	63°59′N	92°09′W
Chestermere Lake, l., Can. (chěs´tē-mēr)	102e	51°03′N	113°45′W
Chesterton, In., U.S. (chěs´těr-tŭn)	108	41°35′N	87°05′W
Chestertown, Md., U.S. (chěs´tēr-toun)	109	39°15′N	76°05′W
Chesuncook, l., Me., U.S. (chěs´ŭn-kȯk)	100	46°03′N	69°40′W
Chetek, Wi., U.S. (chě´těk)	113	45°18′N	91°41′W
Chetumal, Bahía de, b., N.A. (bă-ē-ă dě chět-ōō-mäl´)	128	18°07′N	88°05′W
Chevelon Creek, r., Az., U.S. (shěv´ȧ-lŏn)	119	34°35′N	111°00′W
Cheviot, Oh., U.S. (shěv´ĭ-ŭt)	111f	39°10′N	84°37′W
Chevreuse, Fr. (shě-vrûz´)	171b	48°42′N	2°02′E
Chevy Chase, Md., U.S. (shěvĭ chās)	110e	38°58′N	77°06′W
Chew Bahir, Afr. (stěf-a-nē)	231	4°46′N	37°31′E
Chewelah, Wa., U.S. (chē-wē´lä)	114	48°17′N	117°42′W
Cheyenne, Wy., U.S. (shī-ěn´)	104	41°10′N	104°49′W
Cheyenne, r., U.S.	106	44°20′N	102°15′W
Cheyenne River Indian Reservation, I.R., S.D., U.S.	112	45°07′N	100°46′W
Cheyenne Wells, Co., U.S.	120	38°46′N	102°21′W
Chhattisgarh, state, India	199	23°00′N	83°00′E
Chhindwāra, India	202	22°08′N	78°57′E
Chiai, Tai. (chĭ´ī´)	209	23°28′N	120°28′E
Chiange, Ang.	236	15°45′S	13°48′E
Chiang Mai, Thai.	212	18°38′N	98°44′E
Chiang Rai, Thai.	212	19°53′N	99°48′E
Chiapa, Río de, r., Mex.	132	16°00′N	92°20′W
Chiapa de Corzo, Mex. (chě-ä´pä dā kŏr´zō)	131	16°44′N	93°01′W
Chiapas, state, Mex. (chě-ä´päs)	128	17°10′N	93°00′W
Chiapas, Cordilla de, mts., Mex. (kŏr-dēl-yě´rä-dě-chyȧ´räs)	131	15°55′N	93°15′W
Chiari, Italy (kyä´rē)	174	45°31′N	9°57′E
Chiasso, Switz.	168	45°50′N	8°57′E
Chiatura, Geor.	182	42°17′N	43°17′E
Chiautla, Mex. (chyä-ōōt´lȧ)	130	18°16′N	98°37′W
Chiavari, Italy (kyä-vä´rē)	174	44°18′N	9°21′E
Chiba, Japan (chē´bȧ)	205	35°37′N	140°08′E
Chiba, dept., Japan	211a	35°47′N	140°02′E
Chibougamau, Can. (chē-bōō´gä-mou)	91	49°57′N	74°23′W
Chibougamau, l., Can.	99	49°53′N	74°21′W
Chicago, Il., U.S. (shĭ-kô-gō) (chĭ-kä´gō)	105	41°49′N	87°37′W
Chicago Heights, Il., U.S.	111a	41°30′N	87°38′W
Chicapa, r., Afr. (chē-kä´pä)	232	7°45′S	20°25′E
Chicbul, Mex. (chēk-bōō´l)	131	18°45′N	90°56′W
Chic-Chocs, Monts, mts., Can.	93	48°38′N	66°37′W
Chichagof, i., Ak., U.S. (chě-chä´gôf)	103	57°50′N	137°00′W
Chichancanab, Lago de, l., Mex. (lä´gô-dě-chē-chän-kä-nä´b)	132a	19°50′N	88°28′W
Chichén Itzá, hist., Mex.	132a	20°40′N	88°35′W
Chichester, Eng., U.K. (chĭch´ěs-tēr)	164	50°50′N	0°55′W
Chichimilá, Mex. (chē-chē-mě´lä)	132a	20°36′N	88°14′W
Chichiriviche, Ven. (chē-chē-rē-vē-chě)	143b	10°56′N	68°17′W
Chickamauga, Ga., U.S. (chĭk-ȧ-mô´gȧ)	124	34°50′N	85°15′W
Chickamauga Lake, res., Tn., U.S.	124	35°18′N	85°22′W

PLACE (Pronunciation)	PAGE	LAT.	LONG.
Chickasawhay, r., Ms., U.S. (chĭk-ȧ-sô´wā)	124	31°45′N	88°45′W
Chickasha, Ok., U.S. (chĭk´ȧ-shā)	104	35°04′N	97°56′W
Chiclana de la Frontera, Spain (chě-klä´nä)	172	36°25′N	6°09′W
Chiclayo, Peru (chě-klä´yō)	142	6°46′S	79°50′W
Chico, Ca., U.S. (chē´kō)	118	39°43′N	121°51′W
Chico, Wa., U.S.	116a	47°37′N	122°43′W
Chico, r., Arg.	144	44°30′S	66°00′W
Chico, r., Arg.	144	49°15′S	69°30′W
Chico, r., Phil.	213a	17°33′N	121°24′E
Chicoloapan, Mex. (chě-kō-lwä´pän)	131a	19°24′N	98°54′W
Chiconautla, Mex.	131a	19°39′N	99°01′W
Chicontepec, Mex. (chě-kōn´tě-pěk´)	130	20°58′N	98°08′W
Chicopee, Ma., U.S. (chĭk´ȯ-pē)	109	42°10′N	72°35′W
Chicoutimi, Can. (shē-kōō´tē-mē´)	91	48°26′N	71°04′W
Chicxulub, Mex. (chēk-sōō-lōō´b)	132a	21°10′N	89°30′W
Chiefland, Fl., U.S. (chēf´lȧnd)	125	29°30′N	82°50′W
Chiemsee, l., Ger. (κēm zā)	168	47°58′N	12°20′E
Chieri, Italy (kyâ´rē)	174	45°03′N	7°48′E
Chieti, Italy (kyě´tē)	162	42°22′N	14°22′E
Chifeng, China (chr-fŭŋ)	205	42°18′N	118°52′E
Chignanuapan, Mex. (chē´g-ŋä-nwä-pȧ´n)	130	19°49′N	98°02′W
Chignecto Bay, b., Can. (shĭg-něk´tō)	100	45°33′N	64°50′W
Chignik, Ak., U.S. (chĭg´nĭk)	103	56°14′N	158°12′W
Chignik Bay, b., Ak., U.S.	103	56°18′N	157°22′W
Chigu Co, l., China (chr-gōō tswo)	202	28°55′N	91°47′E
Chigwell, Eng., U.K.	158b	51°38′N	0°05′E
Chihe, China (chr-hŭ)	206	32°32′N	117°57′E
Chihuahua, Mex. (chě-wä´wä)	128	28°37′N	106°06′W
Chihuahua, state, Mex.	128	29°00′N	107°30′W
Chikishlyar, Turkmen. (chě-kěsh-lyär´)	183	37°40′N	53°50′E
Chilanga, Zam.	237	15°34′S	28°17′E
Chilapa, Mex. (chě-lä´pä)	130	17°34′N	99°14′W
Chilchota, Mex. (chěl-chō´tä)	130	19°40′N	102°04′W
Chilcotin, r., Can. (chĭl-kō´tĭn)	94	52°20′N	124°15′W
Childress, Tx., U.S. (chīld´rěs)	120	34°26′N	100°11′W
Chile, nation, S.A. (chē´lā)	144	35°00′S	72°00′W
Chilecito, Arg. (chě-lå-sē´tō)	144	29°06′S	67°25′W
Chilengue, Serra do, mts., Ang.	236	13°20′S	15°00′E
Chilibre, Pan. (chē-lě´brě)	128a	9°09′N	79°37′W
Chililabombwe, Zam.	237	12°18′S	27°43′E
Chilka, l., India	202	19°26′N	85°42′E
Chilko, r., Can. (chĭl´kō)	94	51°53′N	123°53′W
Chilko Lake, l., Can.	94	51°20′N	124°05′W
Chillán, Chile (chēl-yän´)	144	36°44′S	72°06′W
Chillicothe, Il., U.S. (chĭl-ĭ-kŏth´ě)	108	41°55′N	89°30′W
Chillicothe, Mo., U.S.	121	39°46′N	93°32′W
Chillicothe, Oh., U.S.	108	39°20′N	83°00′W
Chilliwack, Can. (chĭl´ĭ-wăk)	90	49°10′N	121°57′W
Chiloé, Isla de, i., Chile	144	42°30′S	73°55′W
Chilpancingo de los Bravo, Mex.	128	17°32′N	99°30′W
Chilton, Wi., U.S. (chĭl´tŭn)	113	44°00′N	88°12′W
Chilung, Tai. (chĭ´lung)	205	25°02′N	121°48′E
Chilwa, Lake, l., Afr.	232	15°12′S	36°30′E
Chimacum, Wa., U.S. (chĭm´ä-kŭm)	116a	48°01′N	122°47′W
Chimalpa, Mex. (chē-mäl´pä)	131a	19°26′N	99°22′W
Chimaltenango, Guat. (chě-mäl-tå-näŋ´gō)	132	14°39′N	90°48′W
Chimaltitan, Mex. (chěmäl-tē-tän´)	130	21°36′N	103°50′W
Chimbay, Uzb. (chĭm-bī´)	183	43°00′N	59°44′E
Chimborazo, mtn., Ec. (chěm-bȯ-rä´zō)	142	1°35′S	78°45′W
Chimbote, Peru (chěm-bō´tå)	142	9°02′S	78°33′W
China, Mex. (chē´nä)	122	25°43′N	99°13′W
China, nation, Asia (chī´nȧ)	204	36°45′N	93°00′E
Chinameca, El Sal. (Chě-nä-mā´kä)	132	13°31′N	88°18′W
Chinandega, Nic. (chē-nän-dā´gä)	132	12°38′N	87°08′W
Chinati Peak, mtn., Tx., U.S. (chĭ-nä´tē)	122	29°56′N	104°29′W
Chincha Alta, Peru (chĭn´chä äl´tä)	142	13°24′S	76°04′W
Chinchas, Islas, is., Peru (ě´s-läs-chē´n-chäs)	142	11°27′S	79°05′W
Chinchilla, Austl. (chĭn-chĭl´ȧ)	222	26°44′S	150°36′E
Chinchorro, Banco, bk., Mex. (bä´n-kô-chēn-chô´r-rŏ)	132a	18°43′N	87°25′W
Chincilla de Monte Aragon, Spain	172	38°54′N	1°43′W
Chinde, Moz. (shěn´dě)	232	17°39′S	36°34′E
Chin Do, i., Kor., S.	210	34°30′N	125°43′E
Chindwin, r., Mya. (chĭn-dwĭn)	199	23°30′N	94°34′E
Chingola, Zam. (chĭng-gōlä)	232	12°32′S	27°52′E
Chinguar, Ang. (chĭng-gär)	232	12°35′S	16°15′E
Chinguetti, Maur. (chěŋ-gět´ě)	230	20°34′N	12°34′W
Chinhoyi, Zimb.	232	17°22′S	30°12′E
Chinju, Kor., S. (chĭn´jōō)	210	35°13′N	128°10′E
Chinko, r., C.A.R. (shĭn´kȯ)	231	6°37′N	24°31′E
Chinmen *see* Quemoy, Tai.	209	24°30′N	118°20′E
Chino, Ca., U.S. (chē´nō)	117a	34°01′N	117°42′W
Chinon, Fr. (shē-nôɴ´)	170	47°09′N	0°13′E
Chinook, Mt., U.S. (shĭn-ȯk´)	115	48°35′N	109°15′W
Chinsali, Zam.	237	10°34′S	32°03′E
Chinteche, Mwi. (chĭn-tě´chě)	232	11°48′S	34°14′E
Chioggia, Italy (kyôd´jä)	174	45°12′N	12°17′E
Chíos, Grc. (kē´ȯs)	163	38°23′N	26°09′E
Chíos, i., Grc.	163	38°20′N	25°45′E
Chipata, Zam.	232	13°39′S	32°40′E
Chipera, Moz. (zhě-pě´rä)	232	15°16′S	32°30′E
Chipley, Fl., U.S. (chĭp´lĭ)	124	30°45′N	85°33′W
Chipman, Can. (chĭp´mȧn)	100	46°11′N	65°53′W
Chipola, r., Fl., U.S. (chĭ-pō´lȧ)	124	30°40′N	85°14′W
Chippawa, Can. (chĭp´ě-wä)	111c	43°03′N	79°03′W
Chippewa, r., Mn., U.S. (chĭp´ě-wä)	112	45°07′N	95°41′W
Chippewa, r., Wi., U.S.	113	45°07′N	91°19′W
Chippewa Falls, Wi., U.S.	113	44°55′N	91°26′W
Chippewa Lake, Oh., U.S.	111d	41°04′N	81°54′W

282 Chiputneticook Lakes – Clearwater PRONOUNCING INDEX

PLACE (Pronunciation)	PAGE	LAT.	LONG.
Chiputneticook Lakes, l., N.A. (chĭ-pȯt-nĕt′ĭ-kȯk)	100	45°47′N	67°45′W
Chiquimula, Guat. (chē-kė-mo͞o′lä)	132	14°47′N	89°31′W
Chiquimulilla, Guat. (chē-kē-mo͞o-lė′l-yä)	132	14°08′N	90°23′W
Chiquinquira, Col. (chė-kēŋ′kė-rä′)	142	5°33′N	73°49′W
Chirala, India	203	15°52′N	80°22′E
Chirchik, Uzb. (chĭr-chēk′)	183	41°28′N	69°18′E
Chire (Shire), r., Afr.	237	17°15′S	35°25′E
Chiricahua National Monument, rec., Az., U.S. (chĭ-rā-cä′hwä)	119	32°02′N	109°18′W
Chirikof, i., Ak., U.S. (chĭ′rĭ-kôf)	103	55°50′N	155°35′W
Chiriquí, Punta, c., Pan. (pȯ′n-tä-chē-rė-kē′)	133	9°13′N	81°39′W
Chiriquí Grande, Pan. (chē-rė-kē′ grän′dā)	133	8°57′N	82°08′W
Chiri San, mtn., Kor., S. (chĭ′rĭ-sän′)	210	35°20′N	127°39′E
Chiromo, Mwi.	232	16°34′S	35°13′E
Chirpan, Blg.	163	42°12′N	25°19′E
Chirripó, Río, r., C.R.	133	9°50′N	83°20′W
Chisasibi, Can.	91	53°40′N	78°58′W
Chisholm, Mn., U.S. (chĭz′ŭm)	113	47°28′N	92°53′W
Chişinău, Mol.	178	47°02′N	28°52′E
Chistopol′, Russia (chĭs-tô′pȯl-y′)	178	55°21′N	50°37′E
Chita, Russia (chė-tȧ′)	179	52°09′N	113°39′E
Chitambo, Zam.	237	12°55′S	30°39′E
Chitato, Ang.	236	7°20′S	20°47′E
Chitembo, Ang.	236	13°34′S	16°40′E
Chitina, Ak., U.S. (chĭ-tē′nȧ)	103	61°28′N	144°35′W
Chitokoloki, Zam.	236	13°50′S	23°13′E
Chitorgarh, India	202	24°59′N	74°42′E
Chitrāl, Pak. (chē-träl′)	199	35°58′N	71°48′E
Chittagong, Bngl. (chĭt-ȧ-gông′)	199	22°26′N	90°51′E
Chitungwiza, Zimb.	232	17°51′S	31°05′E
Chiumbe, r., Afr. (chė-ȯm′bȧ)	232	9°45′S	21°00′E
Chivasso, Italy (kė-väs′sō)	174	45°13′N	7°52′E
Chivhu, Zimb.	232	18°59′S	30°58′E
Chivilcoy, Arg. (chē-vėl-koi′)	144	34°51′S	60°03′W
Chixoy, r., Guat. (chē-ĸoi′)	132	15°40′N	90°35′W
Chizu, Japan (chė-zo͞o′)	211	35°16′N	134°15′E
Chloride, Az., U.S. (klō′rīd)	119	35°25′N	114°15′W
Chmielnik, Pol. (ĸmyĕl′nėĸ)	169	50°36′N	20°46′E
Choapa, r., Chile (chȯ-ȧ′pä)	141b	31°56′S	70°48′W
Choctawhatchee, r., Fl., U.S.	124	30°37′N	85°56′W
Choctawhatchee Bay, b., Fl., U.S. (chôk-tô-hăch′ė)	124	30°15′N	86°32′W
Chodziez, Pol. (ĸōj′yĕsh)	168	52°59′N	16°55′E
Choele Choel, Arg. (chȯ-ĕ′lĕ-chȯĕ′l)	144	39°14′S	65°46′W
Chōfu, Japan (chō′fo͞o′)	211a	35°39′N	139°33′E
Chōgo, Japan (chō-gō)	211a	35°25′N	139°28′E
Choiseul, i., Sol. Is. (shwä-zûl′)	221	7°30′S	157°30′E
Choisy-le-Roi, Fr.	171b	48°46′N	2°25′E
Chojnice, Pol. (ĸoĭ-nē-tsĕ)	169	53°41′N	17°34′E
Cholet, Fr. (shȯ-lĕ′)	161	47°06′N	0°54′W
Cholula, Mex. (chō-lo͞o′lä)	130	19°04′N	98°19′W
Choluteca, Hond. (chō-lo͞o-tā′kä)	132	13°18′N	87°12′W
Choluteco, r., Hond.	132	13°34′N	86°59′W
Chomutov, Czech Rep. (kō′mȯ-tȯf)	168	50°27′N	13°23′E
Chona, r., Russia (chō′nä)	185	60°45′N	109°15′E
Chone, Ec. (chô′nĕ)	142	0°48′S	80°06′W
Chŏngjin, Kor., N. (chŭng-jĭn′)	205	41°48′N	129°46′E
Chŏngju, Kor., S. (chŭng-jo͞o′)	210	36°35′N	127°30′E
Chongming Dao, i., China (chȯŋ-mĭŋ dou)	209	31°40′N	122°30′E
Chongqing, China (chȯŋ-chyĭŋ)	204	29°38′N	107°30′E
Chongqing, prov., China	204	30°00′N	108°00′E
Chŏnju, Kor., S. (chŭn-jo͞o′)	210	35°48′N	127°08′E
Chonos, Archipiélago de los, is., Chile	144	44°35′N	76°15′W
Chorley, Eng., U.K. (chôr′lĭ)	158a	53°40′N	2°38′W
Chornaya, neigh., Russia	186b	55°45′N	38°04′E
Chornobai, Ukr.	177	51°17′N	30°14′E
Chornobay, Ukr. (chĕr-nō-bī′)	177	49°41′N	32°24′E
Chornomors′ke, Ukr.	181	45°29′N	32°43′E
Chorrillos, Peru (chôr-rē′l-yōs)	142	12°17′S	76°55′W
Chortkiv, Ukr.	169	49°01′N	25°48′E
Chosan, Kor., N. (chō-sän′)	210	40°44′N	125°48′E
Chosen, Fl., U.S. (chō′z′n)	125a	26°41′N	80°41′W
Chōshi, Japan (chō′shē)	210	35°40′N	140°55′E
Choszczno, Pol. (chȯsh′chnô)	168	53°10′N	15°25′E
Chota Nagpur, plat., India	202	23°40′N	82°50′E
Choteau, Mt., U.S. (shō′tō)	115	47°51′N	112°10′W
Chowan, r., N.C., U.S. (chȯ-wän′)	125	36°13′N	76°46′W
Chowilla Reservoir, res., Austl.	222	34°05′S	141°20′E
Chown, Mount, mtn., Can. (choun)	95	53°24′N	119°22′W
Choybalsan, Mong.	205	47°50′N	114°15′E
Christchurch, N.Z. (krīst′chûrch)	221a	43°30′S	172°38′E
Christian, i., Can. (krĭs′chăn)	99	44°50′N	80°00′W
Christiansburg, Va., U.S. (krĭs′chănz-bûrg)	125	37°08′N	80°25′W
Christiansted, V.I.U.S.	129b	17°45′N	64°44′W
Christmas Island, dep., Oc.	212	10°35′S	105°40′E
Christopher, Il., U.S. (krĭs′tȯ-fẽr)	121	37°58′N	89°04′W
Chrudim, Czech Rep. (ĸro͞o′dyėm)	168	49°57′N	15°46′E
Chrzanów, Pol. (ĸzhä′nȯf)	169	50°08′N	19°24′E
Chuansha, China (chůän-shä)	207b	31°12′N	121°41′E
Chubut, prov., Arg. (chȯ-bo͞ot′)	144	44°00′S	69°15′W
Chubut, r., Arg. (chȯ-bo͞ot′)	144	43°05′S	69°00′W
Chuckatuck, Va., U.S. (chŭck ȧ-tŭck)	110g	36°51′N	76°35′W
Chucunaque, r., Pan. (cho͞o-ko͞o-nä′kȧ)	133	8°36′N	77°48′W
Chudovo, Russia (chȯ′dȯ-vȯ)	176	59°03′N	31°56′E
Chudskoye Ozero, l., Eur. (chȯt′skȯ-yĕ)	180	58°43′N	26°45′E

PLACE (Pronunciation)	PAGE	LAT.	LONG.
Chuguchak, hist. reg., China (cho͞o′go͞o-chäk′)	204	46°09′N	83°58′E
Chuguyevka, Russia (chȯ-go͞o′yĕf-kȧ)	210	43°58′N	133°49′E
Chugwater Creek, r., Wy., U.S. (chŭg′wô-tẽr)	112	41°43′N	104°54′W
Chuhuïv, Ukr.	181	49°52′N	36°40′E
Chukotskiy Poluostrov, pen., Russia	179	66°12′N	175°00′W
Chukotskoye Nagor′ye, mts., Russia	179	66°00′N	166°00′E
Chula Vista, Ca., U.S. (cho͞o′lȧ vĭs′tȧ)	118a	32°38′N	117°05′W
Chulkovo, Russia (cho͞ol-kô vô)	186b	55°33′N	38°04′E
Chulucanas, Peru	142	5°13′S	80°13′W
Chulum, r., Russia	184	57°52′N	84°45′E
Chumikan, Russia (cho͞o-mē-kän′)	179	54°47′N	135°09′E
Chun′an, China (chȯn-än)	209	29°38′N	119°00′E
Chunchŏn, Kor., S. (chȯn-chŭn′)	210	37°51′N	127°46′E
Chungju, Kor., S. (chŭng′jo͞o′)	210	37°00′N	128°19′E
Chungking *see* Chongqing, China	204	29°38′N	107°30′E
Chunya, Tan.	237	8°32′S	33°25′E
Chunya, r., Russia (chȯn′yä′)	184	61°45′N	101°28′E
Chuquicamata, Chile (cho͞o-kė-kä-mä′tä)	144	22°08′S	68°57′W
Chur, Switz. (ko͞or)	161	46°51′N	9°32′E
Churchill, Can. (chûrch′ĭl)	91	58°50′N	94°10′W
Churchill, r., Can.	92	58°00′N	95°00′W
Churchill, Cape, c., Can.	93	59°07′N	93°50′W
Churchill Falls, wtfl., Can.	93	53°35′N	64°27′W
Churchill Lake, l., Can.	96	56°12′N	108°40′W
Churchill Peak, mtn., Can.	92	58°10′N	125°14′W
Church Stretton, Eng., U.K. (chûrch strĕt′ŭn)	158a	52°32′N	2°49′W
Churchton, Md., U.S.	110e	38°49′N	76°33′W
Churu, India	202	28°22′N	75°00′E
Churumuco, Mex. (cho͞o-ro͞o-mo͞o′kō)	130	18°39′N	101°40′W
Chuska Mountains, mts., Az., U.S. (chŭs-kȧ)	119	36°21′N	109°11′W
Chusovaya, r., Russia (cho͞o-sô-vä′yȧ)	180	58°08′N	58°35′E
Chusovoy, Russia (cho͞o-sô-vȯy′)	178	58°18′N	57°50′E
Chust, Uzb. (chȯst)	183	41°05′N	71°28′E
Chuuk (Truk), is., Micron.	214c	7°25′N	151°47′E
Chuvashia, prov., Russia	180	55°45′N	46°00′E
Chuviscar, r., Mex. (cho͞o-vės-kär′)	122	28°34′N	105°36′W
Chuwang, China (cho͞o-wäŋ)	206	36°08′N	114°53′E
Chuxian, China (cho͞o shyĕn)	208	32°19′N	118°19′E
Chuxiong, China (cho͞o-shyȯŋ)	204	25°19′N	101°34′E
Chyhyryn, Ukr.	177	49°02′N	32°39′E
Cicero, Il., U.S. (sĭs′ẽr-ō)	111a	41°50′N	87°46′W
Cide, Tur. (jē′dĕ)	163	41°50′N	33°00′E
Ciechanów, Pol. (tsyĕ-kä′nȯf)	169	52°52′N	20°39′E
Ciego de Avila, Cuba (syā′gō dā ä′vė-lä)	129	21°50′N	78°45′W
Ciego de Avila, prov., Cuba	134	22°00′N	78°40′W
Ciempozuelos, Spain (thyĕm-pȯ-thwā′lōs)	172	40°09′N	3°36′W
Ciénaga, Col. (syā′nä-gä)	142	11°01′N	74°15′W
Cienfuegos, Cuba (syĕn-fwā′gōs)	129	22°10′N	80°30′W
Cienfuegos, prov., Cuba	134	22°15′N	80°40′W
Cienfuegos, Bahía, b., Cuba (bä-ē′ä-syĕn-fwā′gōs)	134	22°00′N	80°35′W
Ciervo, Isla de la, i., Nic. (ė′s-lä-dĕ-lä-syĕ′r-vô)	133	11°56′N	83°20′W
Cieszyn, Pol. (tsyĕ′shėn)	169	49°47′N	18°45′E
Cieza, Spain (thyā′thä)	172	38°13′N	1°25′W
Cigüela, r., Spain	172	39°53′N	2°54′W
Cihuatlán, Mex. (sē-wä-tlȧ′n)	130	19°13′N	104°36′W
Cihuatlán, r., Mex.	130	19°11′N	104°30′W
Cijara, Embalse de, res., Spain	172	39°25′N	5°00′W
Cilician Gates, p., Tur.	181	37°30′N	35°30′E
Cimarron, r., Co., U.S.	120	37°13′N	102°30′W
Cimarron, r., U.S. (sĭm-ȧ-rōn′)	106	36°26′N	98°27′W
Cinca, r., Spain (thēŋ′kä)	173	42°09′N	0°08′E
Cincinnati, Oh., U.S. (sĭn-sĭ-nȧt′ĭ)	105	39°08′N	84°30′W
Cinco Balas, Cayos, is., Cuba (kä′yōs-thēŋ′kō bä′läs)	134	21°05′N	79°25′W
Cintalapa, Mex. (sėn-tä-lä′pä)	131	16°41′N	93°44′W
Cinto, Monte, mtn., Fr. (chēn′tō)	161	42°24′N	8°54′E
Circle, Ak., U.S. (sûr′k′l)	106a	65°49′N	144°22′W
Circleville, Oh., U.S. (sûr′k′lvĭl)	108	39°35′N	83°00′W
Cirebon, Indon.	212	6°50′S	108°33′E
Ciri Grande, r., Pan. (sē′rē-grȧ′n′dĕ)	128a	8°55′N	80°04′W
Cisco, Tx., U.S. (sĭs′kō)	122	32°23′N	98°57′W
Cisneros, Col. (sės-nĕ′rȯs)	142a	6°33′N	75°05′W
Cisterna di Latina, Italy (chēs-tĕ′r-nä-dē-lä-tė′nä)	173d	41°36′N	12°53′E
Cistierna, Spain (thės-tyĕr′nä)	172	42°48′N	5°08′W
Citronelle, Al., U.S. (cĭt-rȯ′nēl)	124	31°05′N	88°15′W
Cittadella, Italy (chēt-tä-dĕl′lä)	174	45°39′N	11°51′E
Città di Castello, Italy (chēt-tä′dē käs-tĕl′lō)	174	43°27′N	12°17′E
Ciudad Altamirano, Mex. (syo͞o-dä′d-äl-tä-mē-rä′nȯ)	130	18°24′N	100°38′W
Ciudad Bolívar, Ven. (syo͞o-dhädh′ bȯ-lē′vär)	142	8°07′N	63°41′W
Ciudad Camargo, Mex.	128	27°42′N	105°10′W
Ciudad Chetumal, Mex.	128	18°30′N	88°17′W
Ciudad Darío, Nic. (syo͞o-dhädh′dä′rė-ō)	132	12°44′N	86°08′W
Ciudad de la Habana, prov., Cuba	134	23°20′N	82°10′W
Ciudad del Carmen, Mex. (syo͞o-dä′d-dĕl-kȧ′r-mĕn)	128	18°39′N	91°49′W
Ciudad del Maíz, Mex. (syo͞o-dhädh′del mä-ēz′)	130	22°24′N	99°37′W
Ciudad Fernández, Mex. (syo͞o-dhädh′fĕr-nän′dĕz)	130	21°56′N	100°03′W

PLACE (Pronunciation)	PAGE	LAT.	LONG.
Ciudad García, Mex. (syo͞o-dhädh′gär-sē′ä)	128	22°39′N	103°02′W
Ciudad Guayana, Ven.	142	8°30′N	62°45′W
Ciudad Guzmán, Mex. (syo͞o-dhädh′gȯz-män)	128	19°40′N	103°29′W
Ciudad Hidalgo, Mex. (syo͞o-dä′d-ė-dä′l-gȯ)	130	19°41′N	100°35′W
Ciudad Juárez, Mex. (syo͞o-dhädh hwä′rāz)	128	31°44′N	106°28′W
Ciudad Madero, Mex. (syo͞o-dä′d-mä-dĕ′rȯ)	131	22°16′N	97°52′W
Ciudad Mante, Mex. (syo͞o-dä′d-mȧn′tĕ)	128	22°34′N	98°58′W
Ciudad Manual Doblado, Mex. (syo͞o-dä′d-män-wāl′dō-blä′dō)	130	20°43′N	101°57′W
Ciudad Obregón, Mex. (syo͞o-dhädh-ô-brĕ-gô′n)	128	27°40′N	109°58′W
Ciudad Real, Spain (thyo͞o-dhädh′rā-äl′)	172	38°59′N	3°55′W
Ciudad Rodrigo, Spain (thyo͞o-dhädh′rȯ-drē′gō)	162	40°38′N	6°34′W
Ciudad Serdán, Mex. (syo͞o-dä′d-sĕr-dȧ′n)	131	18°58′N	97°26′W
Ciudad Victoria, Mex. (syo͞o-dhädh′vėk-tō′rė-ä)	128	23°43′N	99°09′W
Ciutadella, Spain	173	40°00′N	3°52′E
Civitavecchia, Italy (chē′vė-tä-vĕk′kyä)	174	42°06′N	11°49′E
Cixian, China (tsē shyĕn)	206	36°22′N	114°23′E
Clackamas, Or., U.S. (klăc-kȧ′măs)	116c	45°25′N	122°34′W
Claire, l., Can. (klâr)	92	58°33′N	113°16′W
Clair Engle Lake, l., Ca., U.S.	114	40°51′N	122°41′W
Clairton, Pa., U.S. (klărtŭn)	111e	40°17′N	79°53′W
Clanton, Al., U.S. (klăn′tŭn)	124	32°50′N	86°38′W
Clare, Mi., U.S. (klâr)	108	43°50′N	84°45′W
Clare Island, i., Ire.	164	53°46′N	10°00′W
Claremont, Ca., U.S. (klâr′mŏnt)	117a	34°06′N	117°43′W
Claremont, N.H., U.S. (klâr′mŏnt)	109	43°20′N	72°20′W
Claremont, W.V., U.S.	108	37°55′N	81°00′W
Claremore, Ok., U.S. (klâr′mōr)	121	36°16′N	95°37′W
Claremorris, Ire. (klâr-mŏr′ĭs)	164	53°46′N	9°05′W
Clarence Strait, strt., Austl. (klăr′ĕns)	220	12°15′S	130°05′E
Clarence Strait, strt., Ak., U.S.	94	55°25′N	132°00′W
Clarence Town, Bah.	135	23°05′N	75°00′W
Clarendon, Ar., U.S. (klâr′ĕn-dŭn)	121	34°42′N	91°17′W
Clarendon, Tx., U.S.	120	34°55′N	100°52′W
Clarens, S. Afr. (clâ-rĕns)	233c	28°34′S	28°26′E
Claresholm, Can. (klâr′ĕs-hōlm)	90	50°02′N	113°35′W
Clarinda, Ia., U.S. (klȧ-rĭn′dȧ)	112	40°42′N	95°00′W
Clarines, Ven. (klä-rē′nĕs)	143b	9°57′N	65°10′W
Clarion, Ia., U.S. (klăr′i-ŭn)	113	42°43′N	93°45′W
Clarion, Pa., U.S.	109	41°10′N	79°25′W
Clark, S.D., U.S. (klärk)	112	44°52′N	97°45′W
Clark, Point, c., Can.	98	44°05′N	81°50′W
Clarkdale, Az., U.S. (klärk-dāl)	119	34°45′N	112°05′W
Clarke City, Can.	91	50°12′N	66°38′W
Clarke Range, mts., Austl.	221	20°30′S	148°00′E
Clark Fork, r., Mt., U.S.	114	47°50′N	115°35′W
Clarksburg, W.V., U.S. (klärkz′bûrg)	105	39°15′N	80°20′W
Clarksdale, Ms., U.S. (klärks-dāl)	124	34°10′N	90°31′W
Clark′s Harbour, Can. (klärks)	100	43°26′N	65°38′W
Clarks Hill Lake, res., U.S. (klärk-hĭl)	107	33°50′N	82°35′W
Clarkston, Ga., U.S. (klärks′tŭn)	110c	33°49′N	84°15′W
Clarkston, Wa., U.S.	114	46°24′N	117°01′W
Clarksville, Ar., U.S. (klärks-vĭl)	121	35°28′N	93°26′W
Clarksville, Tn., U.S.	124	36°30′N	87°23′W
Clarksville, Tx., U.S.	121	33°37′N	95°02′W
Clatskanie, Or., U.S.	116c	46°04′N	123°11′W
Clatskanie, r., Or., U.S. (klăt-skā′nė)	116c	46°06′N	123°11′W
Clatsop Spit, Or., U.S. (klăt-sŏp)	116c	46°13′N	124°04′W
Cláudio, Braz. (klou′-dēō)	141a	20°26′S	44°44′W
Claveria, Phil. (klä-vȧ-rē′ä)	209	18°38′N	121°08′E
Clawson, Mi., U.S. (klô′s′n)	111b	42°32′N	83°09′W
Claxton, Ga., U.S. (klăks′tŭn)	125	32°07′N	81°54′W
Clay, Ky., U.S. (klā)	124	37°28′N	87°50′W
Clay Center, Ks., U.S. (klā sĕn′tēr)	121	39°23′N	97°08′W
Clay City, Ky., U.S. (klā sĭ′tĭ)	108	37°50′N	83°55′W
Claycomo, Mo., U.S. (kla-kō′mo)	117f	39°12′N	94°30′W
Clay Cross, Eng., U.K. (klā krŏs)	158a	53°10′N	1°25′W
Claye-Souilly, Fr. (klĕ-so͞o-yē′)	171b	48°56′N	2°43′E
Claymont, De., U.S. (klā-mŏnt)	110f	39°48′N	75°28′W
Clayton, Eng., U.K.	158a	53°47′N	1°49′W
Clayton, Al., U.S. (klā′tŭn)	124	31°52′N	85°25′W
Clayton, Ca., U.S.	116b	37°56′N	121°56′W
Clayton, Mo., U.S.	117e	38°39′N	90°20′W
Clayton, N.C., U.S.	125	35°40′N	78°27′W
Clayton, N.M., U.S.	120	36°26′N	103°12′W
Clear, l., Ca., U.S.	118	39°05′N	122°50′W
Clear Boggy Creek, r., Ok., U.S. (klēr bŏg′ĭ krēk)	121	34°21′N	96°22′W
Clear Creek, r., Az., U.S.	119	34°40′N	111°05′W
Clear Creek, r., Tx., U.S.	123a	29°34′N	95°13′W
Clear Creek, r., Wy., U.S.	115	44°35′N	106°20′W
Clearfield, Pa., U.S. (klēr-fēld)	109	41°00′N	78°25′W
Clearfield, Ut., U.S.	117b	41°07′N	112°01′W
Clear Hills, Can.	90	57°11′N	119°20′W
Clear Lake, Ia., U.S.	113	43°09′N	93°23′W
Clear Lake, Wa., U.S.	116a	48°27′N	122°14′W
Clear Lake Reservoir, res., Ca., U.S.	114	41°53′N	121°00′W
Clearwater, Fl., U.S. (klēr-wô′tēr)	125a	27°43′N	82°45′W
Clearwater, r., Can.	95	52°00′N	114°50′W
Clearwater, r., Can.	96	56°10′N	110°40′W
Clearwater, r., Can.	95	52°00′N	120°10′W
Clearwater, r., Id., U.S.	114	46°27′N	116°33′W

PRONOUNCING INDEX

Clearwater – Comacchio 283

PLACE (Pronunciation)	PAGE	LAT.	LONG.
Clearwater, Middle Fork, r., Id., U.S.	114	46°10'N	115°48'W
Clearwater, North Fork, r., Id., U.S.	114	46°34'N	116°08'W
Clearwater, South Fork, r., Id., U.S.	114	45°46'N	115°53'W
Clearwater Mountains, mts., Id., U.S.	114	45°56'N	115°15'W
Cleburne, Tx., U.S. (klē'bŭrn)	104	32°21'N	97°23'W
Cle Elum, Wa., U.S. (klē ĕl'ŭm)	114	47°12'N	120°55'W
Clementon, N.J., U.S. (klē'mĕn-tŭn)	110f	39°49'N	75°00'W
Cleobury Mortimer, Eng., U.K. (klēō-bĕr'ĭ môr'tĭ-mĕr)	158a	52°22'N	2°29'W
Clermont, Austl. (klĕr'mŏnt)	219	23°02'S	147°46'E
Clermont, Can.	99	47°45'N	70°20'W
Clermont-Ferrand, Fr. (klĕr-môn'fĕr-räN')	154	45°47'N	3°03'E
Cleveland, Ms., U.S. (klēv'lănd)	124	33°45'N	90°42'W
Cleveland, Oh., U.S.	105	41°30'N	81°42'W
Cleveland, Ok., U.S.	121	36°18'N	96°28'W
Cleveland, Tn., U.S.	124	35°09'N	84°52'W
Cleveland, Tx., U.S.	123	30°18'N	95°05'W
Cleveland Heights, Oh., U.S.	111d	41°30'N	81°35'W
Cleveland Peninsula, pen., Ak., U.S.	94	55°45'N	132°00'W
Cleves, Oh., U.S. (klē'vĕs)	111f	39°10'N	84°45'W
Clew Bay, b., Ire. (klōō)	164	53°47'N	9°45'W
Clewiston, Fl., U.S. (klē'wĭs-tŭn)	125a	26°44'N	80°55'W
Clichy, Fr. (klē-shē')	170	48°54'N	2°18'E
Clifden, Ire. (klĭf'dĕn)	164	53°31'N	10°04'W
Clifton, Az., U.S. (klĭf'tŭn)	119	33°05'N	109°20'W
Clifton, N.J., U.S.	110a	40°52'N	74°09'W
Clifton, S.C., U.S.	125	35°00'N	81°47'W
Clifton, Tx., U.S.	123	31°45'N	97°31'W
Clifton Forge, Va., U.S.	109	37°50'N	79°50'W
Clinch, r., Tn., U.S. (klĭnch)	124	36°30'N	83°19'W
Clingmans Dome, mtn., U.S. (klĭng'măns dōm)	124	35°37'N	83°26'W
Clinton, Can. (klĭn-'tŭn)	90	51°05'N	121°35'W
Clinton, Ia., U.S.	113	41°50'N	90°13'W
Clinton, Il., U.S.	108	40°10'N	88°55'W
Clinton, In., U.S.	108	39°40'N	87°25'W
Clinton, Ky., U.S.	124	36°39'N	88°56'W
Clinton, Ma., U.S.	101a	42°25'N	71°41'W
Clinton, Md., U.S.	110e	38°46'N	76°54'W
Clinton, Mo., U.S.	121	38°23'N	93°46'W
Clinton, N.C., U.S.	125	34°58'N	78°20'W
Clinton, Ok., U.S.	120	35°31'N	98°56'W
Clinton, S.C., U.S.	125	34°27'N	81°53'W
Clinton, Tn., U.S.	124	36°05'N	84°08'W
Clinton, Wa., U.S.	116a	47°59'N	122°22'W
Clinton, r., Mi., U.S.	111b	42°36'N	83°00'W
Clinton-Colden, l., Can.	92	63°58'N	106°34'W
Clintonville, Wi., U.S. (klĭn'tŭn-vĭl)	113	44°37'N	88°46'W
Clio, Mi., U.S. (klē'ō)	108	43°10'N	83°45'W
Cloates, Point, c., Austl. (klōts)	220	22°47'S	113°45'E
Clocolan, S. Afr.	238c	28°56'S	27°35'E
Clonakilty Bay, b., Ire. (klŏn-ȧ-kĭltē)	164	51°30'N	8°50'W
Cloncurry, Austl. (klŏn-kŭr'ē)	218	20°58'S	140°42'E
Clonmel, Ire. (klŏn-mĕl)	164	52°21'N	7°45'W
Cloquet, Mn., U.S. (klō-kā')	117h	46°42'N	92°28'W
Closter, N.J., U.S. (klōs'tẽr)	110a	40°58'N	73°57'W
Cloud Peak, mtn., Wy., U.S. (kloud)	106	44°23'N	107°11'W
Clover, S.C., U.S. (klō'vẽr)	125	35°08'N	81°08'W
Clover Bar, Can. (klō'vẽr bär)	102g	53°34'N	113°20'W
Cloverdale, Can.	116d	49°06'N	122°44'W
Cloverdale, Ca., U.S. (klō'vẽr-dāl)	118	38°47'N	123°03'W
Cloverport, Ky., U.S. (klō'vẽr pōrt)	108	37°50'N	86°35'W
Clovis, N.M., U.S. (klō'vĭs)	104	34°24'N	103°11'W
Cluj-Napoca, Rom.	154	46°46'N	23°34'E
Clun, r., Eng., U.K. (klŭn)	158a	52°25'N	2°56'W
Cluny, Fr. (klü-nē')	170	46°27'N	4°40'E
Clutha, r., N.Z. (klōō'thȧ)	221a	45°52'S	169°30'E
Clwyd, hist. reg., Wales, U.K.	158a	53°01'N	2°59'W
Clyde, Ks., U.S.	121	39°34'N	97°23'W
Clyde, Oh., U.S.	108	41°15'N	83°00'W
Clyde, r., Scot., U.K.	164	55°35'N	3°50'W
Clyde, Firth of, b., Scot., U.K. (fûrth ŏv klīd)	164	55°28'N	5°01'W
Côa, r., Port. (kō'ä)	172	40°28'N	6°55'W
Coacalco, Mex. (kō-ä-käl'kō)	131a	19°37'N	99°06'W
Coachella, Canal, can., Ca., U.S. (kō'chĕl-lȧ)	118	33°15'N	115°25'W
Coahuayana, Río de, r., Mex. (rē'ō-dĕ-kô-ä-wä-yä'nä)	130	19°00'N	103°33'W
Coahuayutla, Mex. (kō'ä-wī-yōōt'lä)	130	18°19'N	101°44'W
Coahuila, state, Mex. (kō-ä-wē'lä)	128	27°30'N	103°00'W
Coal City, Il., U.S. (kōl sĭ'tĭ)	111a	41°17'N	88°17'W
Coalcomán, Río de, r., Mex. (rē'ō-dĕ-kō-äl-kō-män')	130	18°45'N	103°15'W
Coalcomán, Sierra de, mts., Mex.	130	18°30'N	102°45'W
Coalcomán de Matamoros, Mex.	130	18°46'N	103°10'W
Coaldale, Can. (kōl'dāl)	95	49°43'N	112°37'W
Coalgate, Ok., U.S. (kōl'gāt)	121	34°44'N	96°13'W
Coal Grove, Oh., U.S. (kōl grōv)	108	38°20'N	82°40'W
Coalinga, Ca., U.S. (kō-ȧ-lĭŋ'gȧ)	118	36°09'N	120°23'W
Coalville, Eng., U.K. (kōl'vĭl)	158a	52°43'N	1°21'W
Coamo, P.R. (kō-ä'mō)	129b	18°05'N	66°21'W
Coari, Braz. (kō-är'ē)	142	4°06'S	63°10'W
Coast Mountains, mts., N.A. (kōst)	92	54°10'N	128°00'W
Coast Ranges, mts., U.S.	106	41°28'N	123°30'W
Coatepec, Mex. (kō-ä-tā-pĕk)	130	19°23'N	98°44'W
Coatepec, Mex.	131a	19°08'N	99°25'W
Coatepec, Mex.	131	19°26'N	96°56'W
Coatepeque, El Sal.	132	13°56'N	89°30'W
Coatepeque, Guat. (kō-ä-tā-pä'kȧ)	132	14°40'N	91°52'W
Coatesville, Pa., U.S. (kōts'vĭl)	109	40°00'N	75°50'W
Coatetelco, Mex. (kō-ä-tȧ-tĕl'kō)	130	18°43'N	99°17'W
Coaticook, Can. (kō'tĭ-ko̍ok)	99	45°10'N	71°55'W
Coatlinchán, Mex. (kô-ä-tlē'n-chä'n)	131a	19°26'N	98°52'W
Coats, i., Can. (kōts)	93	62°23'N	82°11'W
Coats Land, reg., Ant.	224	74°00'S	30°00'W
Coatzacoalcos, Mex.	128	18°09'N	94°26'W
Coatzacoalcos, r., Mex.	131	17°40'N	94°41'W
Coba, hist., Mex. (kô'bä)	132a	20°23'N	87°23'W
Cobalt, Can. (kō'bôlt)	91	47°21'N	79°40'W
Cobán, Guat. (kō-bän')	128	15°28'N	90°19'W
Cobar, Austl.	219	31°28'S	145°50'E
Cobberas, Mount, mtn., Austl. (cŏ-bĕr-ăs)	222	36°45'S	148°15'E
Cobequid Mountains, mts., Can.	100	45°35'N	64°10'W
Cobh, Ire. (kôv)	154	51°52'N	8°09'W
Cobija, Bol. (kō-bē'hä)	142	11°12'S	68°49'W
Cobourg, Can. (kō'bo̍orgh)	91	43°55'N	78°05'W
Cobre, r., Jam. (kō'brā)	134	18°05'N	77°00'W
Coburg, Austl.	217a	37°45'S	144°58'E
Coburg, Ger. (kō'bōōrg)	168	50°16'N	10°57'E
Cocentaina, Spain (kō-thān-tä-ē'nȧ)	173	38°44'N	0°27'W
Cochabamba, Bol.	142	17°24'S	66°09'W
Cochinos, Bahía, b., Cuba (bä-ē'ä-kō-chē'nōs)	134	22°05'N	81°10'W
Cochinos Banks, bk.	134	22°20'N	76°15'W
Cochiti Indian Reservation, I.R., N.M., U.S.	119	35°37'N	106°20'W
Cochran, Ga., U.S. (kŏk'răn)	124	32°23'N	83°23'W
Cochrane, Can. (kŏk'răn)	91	49°01'N	81°06'W
Cochrane, Can.	102e	51°11'N	114°28'W
Cockburn, i., Can. (kŏk-bûrn)	98	45°55'N	83°25'W
Cockeysville, Md., U.S. (kŏk'ĭz-vĭl)	110e	39°30'N	76°40'W
Cockrell Hill, Tx., U.S. (kŏk'rĕl)	117c	32°44'N	96°53'W
Coco, r., N.A.	129	14°55'N	83°45'W
Coco, Cayo, i., Cuba (kä'-yō-kô'kô)	134	22°30'S	78°30'W
Coco, Isla del, i., C.R. (ē's-lä-dĕl-kô-kô)	128	5°33'N	87°02'W
Cocoa, Fl., U.S. (kō'kō)	125a	28°21'N	80°44'W
Cocoa Beach, Fl., U.S.	125a	28°20'N	80°35'W
Cocoli, Pan. (kô-kô'lē)	128a	8°58'N	79°36'W
Coconino, Plateau, plat., Az., U.S. (kō kō nē'nō)	119	35°45'N	112°28'W
Cocos (Keeling) Islands, is., Oc. (kō'kôs) (kē'lĭng)	3	11°50'S	90°50'E
Coco Solito, Pan. (kô-kô-sô-lē'tô)	128a	9°21'N	79°53'W
Cocula, Mex. (kō-kōō'lä)	130	20°23'N	103°47'W
Cocula, r., Mex.	130	18°17'N	99°45'W
Cod, Cape, pen., Ma., U.S.	107	41°42'N	70°15'W
Codajás, Braz. (kō-dä-häzh')	142	3°44'S	62°09'W
Codera, Cabo, c., Ven. (kȧ'bô-kô-dĕ'rä)	143b	10°35'N	66°06'W
Codogno, Italy (kô-dō'nyō)	174	45°08'N	9°43'E
Codrington, Antig. (kŏd'rĭng-tŭn)	133b	17°39'N	61°49'W
Cody, Wy., U.S. (kō'dĭ)	115	44°31'N	109°02'W
Coelho da Rocha, Braz.	144b	22°47'S	43°23'W
Coemba, Ang.	236	12°08'S	18°05'E
Coesfeld, Ger. (kûs'fĕld)	171c	51°56'N	7°10'E
Coeur d'Alene, Id., U.S. (kûr dȧ-lān')	104	47°43'N	116°35'W
Coeur d'Alene, r., Id., U.S.	114	47°26'N	116°35'W
Coeur d'Alene Indian Reservation, I.R., Id., U.S.	114	47°18'N	116°45'W
Coeur d'Alene Lake, l., Id., U.S.	114	47°32'N	116°39'W
Coffeyville, Ks., U.S. (kŏf'ĭ-vĭl)	105	37°01'N	95°38'W
Coff's Harbour, Austl.	222	30°20'S	153°10'E
Cofimvaba, S. Afr. (căfĭm'vä-bȧ)	233c	32°01'S	27°37'E
Coghinas, r., Italy (kō'gē-nás)	174	40°31'N	9°00'E
Cognac, Fr. (kôn-yak')	161	45°41'N	0°22'W
Cohasset, Ma., U.S. (kô-hăs'ĕt)	101a	42°14'N	70°48'W
Cohoes, N.Y., U.S. (kô-hōz')	109	42°50'N	73°40'W
Coig, r., Arg. (kô'ĕk)	144	51°15'N	71°00'W
Coimbatore, India (kô-ēm-bȧ-tōr')	199	11°03'N	76°56'E
Coimbra, Port. (kô-ēm'brä)	154	40°14'N	8°23'W
Coín, Spain (kô-ēn')	172	36°40'N	4°45'W
Coina, Port. (kô-ē'nȧ)	173b	38°35'N	9°03'W
Coina, r., Port. (kô'y-nä)	173b	38°35'N	9°02'W
Coipasa, Salar de, pl., Bol. (sä-lä'r-dĕ-koi-pä'-sä)	142	19°12'S	69°13'W
Coixtlahuaca, Mex. (kō-ĕks'tlä-wä'kä)	131	17°42'N	97°17'W
Cojedes, dept., Ven. (kô-kĕ'dĕs)	143b	9°50'N	68°21'W
Cojimar, Cuba (kô-hē-mär')	135a	23°10'N	82°19'W
Cojutepeque, El Sal. (kô-hô-tĕ-pā'kȧ)	132	13°45'N	88°50'W
Cokato, Mn., U.S. (kô-kā'tō)	113	45°03'N	94°11'W
Cokeburg, Pa., U.S. (kōk bûgh)	111e	40°06'N	80°03'W
Colac, Austl. (kŏ'lȧc)	222	38°25'S	143°40'E
Colares, Port. (kō-lä'rĕs)	173b	38°47'N	9°27'W
Colatina, Braz. (kô-lä-tē'nä)	143	19°33'S	40°42'W
Colby, Ks., U.S. (kōl'bĭ)	120	39°23'N	101°04'W
Colchagua, prov., Chile (kôl-chȧ'gwä)	141b	34°42'S	71°24'W
Colchester, Eng., U.K. (kōl'chĕs-tẽr)	165	51°52'N	0°50'E
Cold Lake, l., Can. (kōld)	96	54°33'N	110°05'W
Coldwater, Ks., U.S. (kōld'wô-tẽr)	120	37°14'N	99°21'W
Coldwater, Mi., U.S.	108	41°55'N	85°00'W
Coldwater, r., Ms., U.S.	124	34°25'N	90°12'W
Coldwater Creek, r., Tx., U.S.	120	36°10'N	101°45'W
Coleman, Tx., U.S. (kōl'mȧn)	122	31°50'N	99°25'W
Colenso, S. Afr. (kŏ-lĕnz'ô)	233c	28°48'S	29°49'E
Coleraine, N. Ire., U.K.	164	55°08'N	6°40'W
Coleraine, Mn., U.S. (kōl-rān')	113	47°16'N	93°29'W
Coleshill, Eng., U.K. (kōlz'hĭl)	158a	52°30'N	1°42'W
Colfax, Ia., U.S. (kōl'făks)	113	41°40'N	93°13'W
Colfax, La., U.S.	123	31°31'N	92°42'W
Colfax, Wa., U.S.	114	46°53'N	117°21'W
Colhué Huapi, l., Arg. (kôl-wā'ōä'pē)	144	45°30'S	68°45'W
Coligny, S. Afr.	238c	26°20'S	26°18'E
Colima, Mex. (kōlē'mä)	128	19°13'N	103°45'W
Colima, state, Mex.	130	19°10'N	104°00'W
Colima, Nevado de, mtn., Mex. (nĕ-vä'dô-dĕ-kō-lē'mä)	128	19°30'N	103°38'W
Coll, i., Scot., U.K. (kōl)	164	56°42'N	6°23'W
College, Ak., U.S.	103	64°43'N	147°50'W
College Park, Ga., U.S. (kŏl'ĕj)	110c	33°39'N	84°27'W
College Park, Md., U.S.	110e	38°59'N	76°58'W
Collegeville, Pa., U.S. (kŏl'ĕj-vĭl)	110f	40°11'N	75°27'W
Collie, Austl. (kŏl'ē)	218	33°20'S	116°20'E
Collier Bay, b., Austl. (kŏl-yẽr)	220	15°30'S	123°30'E
Collingswood, N.J., U.S. (kŏl'ĭngz-wo̍od)	110f	39°54'N	75°04'W
Collingwood, Can.	99	44°30'N	80°20'W
Collins, Ms., U.S. (kŏl'ĭns)	124	31°40'N	89°34'W
Collinsville, Il., U.S. (kŏl'ĭnz-vĭl)	117e	38°41'N	89°59'W
Collinsville, Ok., U.S.	121	36°21'N	95°50'W
Colmar, Fr. (kôl'mär)	161	48°03'N	7°25'E
Colmenar de Oreja, Spain (kôl-mā-när'dāōrā'hä)	172	40°06'N	3°25'W
Colmenar Viejo, Spain (kôl-mā-när'vyā'hō)	172	40°40'N	3°46'W
Cologne, Ger.	154	50°56'N	6°57'E
Colombia, Col. (kô-lôm'bē-ä)	142a	3°23'N	74°48'W
Colombia, nation, S.A.	142	3°30'N	72°30'W
Colombo, Sri L. (kô-lôm'bō)	203	6°58'N	79°52'E
Colón, Arg. (kō-lōn')	141c	33°55'S	61°08'W
Colón, Cuba (kô-lô'n)	134	22°45'N	80°55'W
Colón, Mex. (kō-lōn')	130	20°46'N	100°02'W
Colón, Pan. (kō-lōn')	129	9°22'N	79°54'W
Colón, Archipiélago de, is., Ec.	142	0°10'S	87°45'W
Colón, Montañas de, mts., Hond. (môn-tä'n-yäs-dĕ-kô-lô'n)	133	14°58'N	84°39'W
Colonia, Ur. (kō-lō'nē-ä)	144	34°27'S	57°50'W
Colonia, dept., Ur.	141c	34°08'S	57°50'W
Colonia Suiza, Ur. (kô-lô'nêä-sōē'zä)	141c	34°17'S	57°15'W
Colonna, Capo, c., Italy	175	39°02'N	17°15'E
Colonsay, i., Scot., U.K. (kŏl-ôn-sā')	165	56°08'N	6°08'E
Coloradas, Lomas, Arg. (lô'mäs-kō-lō-rä'däs)	144	43°30'S	68°00'W
Colorado, state, U.S.	104	39°30'N	106°55'W
Colorado, r., Arg.	144	38°30'S	66°00'W
Colorado, r., N.A.	106	36°00'N	113°30'W
Colorado, r., Tx., U.S.	106	30°08'N	97°33'W
Colorado City, Tx., U.S. (kŏl-ô-rä'dō sĭ'tĭ)	122	32°24'N	100°50'W
Colorado National Monument, rec., Co., U.S.	119	39°00'N	108°40'W
Colorado Plateau, plat., U.S.	106	36°20'N	109°25'W
Colorado River Aqueduct, aq., Ca., U.S.	118	33°38'N	115°43'W
Colorado River Indian Reservation, I.R., Az., U.S.	119	34°03'N	114°02'W
Colorados, Archipiélago de los, is., Cuba	134	22°25'N	84°25'W
Colorado Springs, Co., U.S. (kŏl-ô-rä'dō)	104	38°49'N	104°48'W
Colotepec, r., Mex. (kô-lô'tĕ-pĕk)	131	15°56'N	96°57'W
Colotlán, Mex. (kô-lô-tlän')	130	22°06'N	103°14'W
Colotlán, r., Mex.	130	22°09'N	103°17'W
Colquechaca, Bol. (kôl-kā-chä'kä)	142	18°47'S	66°02'W
Colstrip, Mt., U.S. (kōl'strip)	115	45°54'N	106°38'W
Colton, Ca., U.S. (kōl'tŭn)	117a	34°04'N	117°20'W
Columbia, Il., U.S. (kô-lŭm'bĭ-ȧ)	117e	38°26'N	90°12'W
Columbia, Ky., U.S.	124	37°06'N	85°15'W
Columbia, Md., U.S.	110e	39°15'N	76°51'W
Columbia, Mo., U.S.	105	38°55'N	92°19'W
Columbia, Ms., U.S.	124	31°15'N	89°49'W
Columbia, Pa., U.S.	109	40°00'N	76°25'W
Columbia, S.C., U.S.	105	34°00'N	81°00'W
Columbia, Tn., U.S.	124	35°36'N	87°02'W
Columbia, r., N.A.	92	46°00'N	120°00'W
Columbia, Mount, mtn., Can.	95	52°09'N	117°25'W
Columbia City, In., U.S.	108	41°10'N	85°30'W
Columbia City, Or., U.S.	116c	45°53'N	112°49'W
Columbia Heights, Mn., U.S.	117g	45°03'N	93°15'W
Columbia Icefield, ice, Can.	95	52°08'N	117°26'W
Columbia Mountains, mts., N.A.	95	51°30'N	118°30'W
Columbiana, Al., U.S. (kô-ŭm-bĭ-ă'nȧ)	124	33°10'N	86°35'W
Columbretes, is., Spain (kô-lōōm-brĕ'tĕs)	173	39°54'N	0°54'E
Columbus, Ga., U.S. (kô-lŭm'bŭs)	105	32°29'N	84°56'W
Columbus, In., U.S.	108	39°15'N	85°55'W
Columbus, Ks., U.S.	121	37°10'N	94°50'W
Columbus, Ms., U.S.	124	33°30'N	88°25'W
Columbus, Mt., U.S.	115	45°39'N	109°15'W
Columbus, Ne., U.S.	112	41°25'N	97°25'W
Columbus, N.M., U.S.	119	31°50'N	107°40'W
Columbus, Oh., U.S.	105	40°00'N	83°00'W
Columbus, Tx., U.S.	123	29°44'N	96°34'W
Columbus, Wi., U.S.	113	43°20'N	89°01'W
Columbus Bank, bk. (kô-lŭm'bŭs)	135	22°05'N	75°30'W
Columbus Grove, Oh., U.S.	108	40°55'N	84°05'W
Columbus Point, c., Bah.	135	24°10'N	75°15'W
Colusa, Ca., U.S. (kô-lū'sȧ)	118	39°12'N	122°01'W
Colville, Wa., U.S. (kŏl'vĭl)	114	48°33'N	117°53'W
Colville, r., Ak., U.S.	103	69°00'N	156°25'W
Colville Indian Reservation, I.R., Wa., U.S.	114	48°15'N	119°00'W
Colville R, Wa., U.S.	114	48°25'N	117°58'W
Colvos Passage, strt., Wa., U.S. (kŏl'vōs)	116a	47°24'N	122°32'W
Colwood, Can. (kŏl'wo̍od)	116a	48°26'N	123°30'W
Comacchio, Italy (kô-mäk'kyō)	174	44°42'N	12°12'E

ng-sing; ŋ-baŋk; N-nasalized n; nŏd; cŏmmit; ōld; ôbey; ôrder; oi-boil; fōōd; o̍-as oo in foot; ou-out; s-soft; sh-dish; th-thin; pūre; ûnite; ûrn; stŭd; circŭs; ü-as in French tu; '-indeterminate vowel.

284 Comala – Cosamaloápan PRONOUNCING INDEX

PLACE (Pronunciation)	PAGE	LAT.	LONG.
Comala, Mex. (kō-mä-lä′)	130	19°22′N	103°47′W
Comalapa, Guat. (kō-mä-lä′-pä)	132	14°43′N	90°56′W
Comalcalco, Mex. (kō-mäl-käl′kō)	131	18°16′N	93°13′W
Comanche, Ok., U.S. (kô-man′chē)	121	34°20′N	97°58′W
Comanche, Tx., U.S.	122	31°54′N	98°37′W
Comanche Creek, r., Tx., U.S.	122	31°02′N	102°47′W
Comayagua, Hond. (kō-mä-yä′gwä)	128	14°24′N	87°36′W
Combahee, r., S.C., U.S. (kŏm-bȧ-hē′)	125	32°42′N	80°40′W
Comer, Ga., U.S. (kŭm′ẽr)	124	34°02′N	83°07′W
Comete, Cape, c., T./C. Is. (kô-mā′tȧ)	135	21°45′N	71°25′W
Comilla, Bngl. (kō-mĭl′ä)	199	23°33′N	91°17′E
Comino, Cape, c., Italy (kô-mē′nō)	174	40°30′N	9°48′E
Comitán, Mex. (kô-mē-tän′)	128	16°16′N	92°09′W
Commencement Bay, b., Wa., U.S. (kŏ-mĕns′mĕnt bā)	116a	47°17′N	122°21′W
Commentry, Fr. (kô-mäN-trē′)	170	46°16′N	2°44′E
Commerce, Ga., U.S. (kŏm′ẽrs)	124	34°10′N	83°27′W
Commerce, Ok., U.S.	121	36°57′N	94°54′W
Commerce, Tx., U.S.	121	33°15′N	95°52′W
Como, Italy (kō′mō)	162	45°48′N	9°03′E
Como, Lago di, l., Italy (lä′gō-dē-kō′mō)	162	46°00′N	9°30′E
Comodoro Rivadavia, Arg.	144	45°47′S	67°31′W
Como-Est, Can.	102a	45°27′N	74°08′W
Comonfort, Mex. (kô-mōn-fô′rt)	130	20°43′N	100°47′W
Comorin, Cape, c., India (kŏ′mô-rĭn)	203	8°05′N	78°05′E
Comoros, nation, Afr.	233	12°30′S	42°45′E
Comox, Can. (kō′mŏks)	94	49°40′N	124°55′W
Companario, Cerro, mtn., S.A. (sĕ′r-rô-kôm-pä-nä′ryô)	141b	35°54′S	70°23′W
Compiègne, Fr. (kôN-pyĕn′y′)	161	49°25′N	2°49′E
Comporta, Port. (kôm-pôr′tȧ)	173b	38°24′N	8°48′W
Compostela, Mex. (kōm-pô-stā′lä)	130	21°14′N	104°54′W
Compton, Ca., U.S. (kŏmpt′tŭn)	117a	33°54′N	118°14′W
Comrat, Mol. (kôm-răt′)	181	46°17′N	28°38′E
Conakry, Gui. (kô-nȧ-krē′)	230	9°31′N	13°43′W
Conanicut, i., R.I., U.S. (kŏn′ȧ-nĭ-kŭt)	110b	41°34′N	71°20′W
Conasauga, r., Ga., U.S. (kŏ-nȧ)	124	34°40′N	84°51′W
Concarneau, Fr. (kôN-kär-nō′)	170	47°54′N	3°52′W
Concepción, Bol. (kôn-sĕp′syōn′)	143	15°47′S	61°08′W
Concepción, Chile	144	36°51′S	72°59′W
Concepción, Pan.	133	8°31′N	82°38′W
Concepción, Para.	144	23°29′S	57°18′W
Concepcion, Phil.	213a	15°19′N	120°40′E
Concepción, vol., Nic.	132	11°36′N	85°43′W
Concepción, r., Mex.	128	30°25′N	112°20′W
Concepción del Mar, Guat. (kôn-sĕp-syōn′dĕl mär′)	132	14°07′N	91°23′W
Concepción del Oro, Mex. (kôn-sĕp-syōn′ dĕl ō′rō)	128	24°39′N	101°24′W
Concepción del Uruguay, Arg. (kôn-sĕp-syō′n-dĕl-ōō-rōō-gwī′)	144	32°31′S	58°10′W
Conception, i., Bah.	135	23°50′N	75°05′W
Conception, Point, c., Ca., U.S.	106	34°27′N	120°28′W
Conception Bay, b., Can. (kŏn-sĕp′shŭn)	101	47°50′N	52°50′W
Concho, r., Tx., U.S. (kŏn′chō)	122	31°34′N	100°00′W
Conchos, r., Mex.	128	29°30′N	105°00′W
Conchos, r., Mex. (kōn′chōs)	122	25°03′N	99°00′W
Concord, Ca., U.S. (kŏŋ′kẽrd)	116b	37°58′N	122°02′W
Concord, Ma., U.S.	101a	42°28′N	71°21′W
Concord, N.C., U.S.	125	35°23′N	80°11′W
Concord, N.H., U.S.	105	43°10′N	71°30′W
Concordia, Arg. (kŏn-kôr′dĭ-ȧ)	144	31°18′S	57°59′W
Concordia, Col.	142a	6°04′N	75°54′W
Concordia, Mex. (kôn-kô′r-dyä)	130	23°17′N	106°06′W
Concordia, Ks., U.S.	121	39°32′N	97°39′W
Concrete, Wa., U.S. (kŏn-′krēt)	114	48°33′N	121°44′W
Conde, Fr.	170	48°50′N	0°36′W
Conde, S.D., U.S. (kŏn-dē′)	112	45°10′N	98°06′W
Condega, Nic. (kŏn-dĕ′gä)	132	13°20′N	86°27′W
Condeúba, Braz. (kōn-dā-ōō′bä)	143	14°47′S	41°44′W
Condom, Fr.	170	43°58′N	0°22′E
Condon, Or., U.S. (kŏn′dŭn)	114	45°14′N	120°10′W
Conecun, r., Al., U.S. (kô-nē′kŭ)	124	31°05′N	86°52′W
Conegliano, Italy (kō-nâl-yä′nō)	174	45°59′N	12°17′E
Conejos, r., Co., U.S. (kô-nā′hōs)	119	37°07′N	106°19′W
Conemaugh, Pa., U.S. (kŏn′ē-mô)	109	40°25′N	78°50′W
Coney Island, i., N.Y., U.S. (kō′nĭ)	110a	40°34′N	73°27′W
Confolens, Fr. (kôN-fä-läN′)	170	46°01′N	0°41′E
Congaree, r., S.C., U.S. (kŏŋ-gȧ-rē′)	125	33°53′N	80°55′W
Conghua, China (tsôŋ-hwä)	209	23°30′N	113°40′E
Congleton, Eng., U.K. (kŏŋ′g′l-tŭn)	158a	53°10′N	2°13′W
Congo, nation, Afr. (kŏn′gō)	232	3°00′S	13°48′E
Congo (Zaire), r., Afr. (kŏn′gō)	229	2°00′S	17°00′E
Congo, Democratic Republic of the (Zaire), nation, Afr.	232	1°00′S	22°15′E
Congo, Serra do, mts., Ang.	236	6°25′S	13°30′E
Congo Basin, basin, D.R.C.	229	2°47′N	20°58′E
Conisbrough, Eng., U.K. (kŏn′ĭs-bŭr-ŏ)	158a	53°29′N	1°13′W
Coniston, Can.	99	46°29′N	80°51′W
Conklin, Can. (kŏŋk′lĭn)	95	55°38′N	111°05′W
Conley, Ga., U.S. (kŏn′lĭ)	110c	33°38′N	84°19′W
Conn, Lough, l., Ire. (lŏk kŏn)	164	53°56′N	9°25′W
Connacht, hist. reg., Ire. (cŏn′ât)	164	53°50′N	8°45′W
Conneaut, Oh., U.S. (kŏn-ē-ôt′)	108	41°55′N	80°35′W
Connecticut, state, U.S. (kŏ-nĕt′ĭ-kŭt)	105	41°40′N	73°10′W
Connecticut, r., U.S.	107	43°55′N	72°15′W
Connellsville, Pa., U.S. (kŏn′nĕlz-vĭl)	109	40°00′N	79°40′W
Connemara, mts., Ire. (kŏn-nē-mȧ′rȧ)	164	53°30′N	9°54′W
Connersville, In., U.S. (kŏn′ẽrz-vĭl)	108	39°35′N	85°10′W
Connors Range, mts., Austl. (kŏn′nŏrs)	221	22°15′S	149°00′E
Conrad, Mt., U.S. (kŏn′răd)	115	48°11′N	111°56′W
Conrich, Can. (kŏn′rĭch)	102e	51°06′N	113°51′W
Conroe, Tx., U.S. (kŏn′rō)	123	30°18′N	95°23′W
Conselheiro Lafaiete, Braz.	143	20°40′S	43°46′W
Conshohocken, Pa., U.S. (kŏn-shô-hŏk′ĕn)	110f	40°04′N	75°18′W
Consolación del Sur, Cuba (kōn-sô-lä-syōn′)	134	22°30′N	83°55′W
Con Son, is., Viet.	212	8°30′N	106°28′E
Constance, Mount, mtn., Wa., U.S. (kŏn′stăns)	116a	47°46′N	123°08′W
Constanța, Rom. (kōn-stan′tsȧ)	154	44°12′N	28°36′E
Constantina, Spain (kōn-stän-tē′nä)	172	37°52′N	5°39′W
Constantine, Alg. (kôN-stäN′tēn′)	230	36°28′N	6°38′E
Constantine, Mi., U.S. (kŏn′stăn-tēn)	108	41°50′N	85°40′W
Constitución, Chile (kōn′stĭ-tōō-syōn′)	144	35°24′S	72°25′W
Constitution, Ga., U.S. (kŏn-stĭ-tū′shŭn)	110c	33°41′N	84°20′W
Contagem, Braz. (kōn-tá′zhĕm)	141a	19°54′S	44°05′W
Contepec, Mex. (kōn-tĕ-pĕk′)	130	20°04′N	100°07′W
Contreras, Mex. (kôn-trĕ′räs)	131a	19°18′N	99°14′W
Contwoyto, l., Can.	92	65°42′N	110°50′W
Converse, Tx., U.S. (kŏn′vẽrs)	117d	29°31′N	98°17′W
Conway, Ar., U.S. (kŏn′wā)	121	35°06′N	92°27′W
Conway, N.H., U.S.	109	44°00′N	71°10′W
Conway, S.C., U.S.	125	33°49′N	79°01′W
Conway, Wa., U.S.	116a	48°20′N	122°20′W
Conyers, Ga., U.S. (kŏn′yẽrz)	124	33°41′N	84°01′W
Cooch Behār, India (kōoch bē-här′)	199	26°25′N	89°34′E
Cook, Cape, c., Can. (kŏok)	94	50°08′N	127°55′W
Cook, Mount see Aoraki, mtn., N.Z.	221a	43°27′S	170°13′E
Cookeville, Tn., U.S. (kŏok′vĭl)	124	36°07′N	85°30′W
Cooking Lake, Can. (kŏok′ĭng)	102g	53°25′N	113°08′W
Cooking Lake, l., Can.	102g	53°25′N	113°02′W
Cook Inlet, b., Ak., U.S.	103	60°50′N	151°38′W
Cook Islands, dep., Oc.	2	20°00′S	158°00′W
Cook Strait, strt., N.Z.	221a	40°37′S	174°15′E
Cooktown, Austl. (kŏok′toun)	219	15°40′S	145°20′E
Cooleemee, N.C., U.S. (kōō-lē′mē)	125	35°50′N	80°32′W
Coolgardie, Austl. (kōōl-gär′dē)	218	31°00′S	121°25′E
Cooma, Austl. (kōō′mȧ)	219	36°22′S	149°10′E
Coonamble, Austl. (kōō-năm′b′l)	219	31°00′S	148°30′E
Coonoor, India	203	10°22′N	76°15′E
Coon Rapids, Mn., U.S. (kōn)	117g	45°09′N	93°17′W
Cooper, Tx., U.S. (kōōp′ẽr)	121	33°23′N	95°40′W
Cooper Center, Ak., U.S.	103	61°54′N	15°30′W
Coopers Creek, r., Austl. (kōō′pẽrz)	221	27°32′S	141°19′E
Cooperstown, N.D., U.S.	112	47°26′N	98°07′W
Cooperstown, N.Y., U.S. (kōōp′ẽrs-toun)	109	42°45′N	74°55′W
Coosa, Al., U.S. (kōō′sȧ)	124	32°43′N	86°25′W
Coosa, r., U.S.	107	34°00′N	86°00′W
Coosawattee, r., Ga., U.S.	124	34°37′N	84°45′W
Coos Bay, Or., U.S. (kōōs)	114	43°21′N	124°12′W
Coos Bay, b., Or., U.S.	114	43°19′N	124°40′W
Cootamundra, Austl. (kōtȧ-mŭnd′rȧ)	222	34°25′S	148°00′E
Copacabana, Braz. (kô′pä-kȧ-bá′nä)	144b	22°57′S	43°11′W
Copalita, r., Mex. (kō-pä-lē′tä)	131	15°55′N	96°06′W
Copán, hist., Hond. (kō-pän′)	132	14°50′N	89°10′W
Copano Bay, b., Tx., U.S. (kō-pän′ō)	123	28°08′N	97°25′W
Copenhagen (København), Den.	154	55°43′N	12°27′E
Copiapó, Chile (kō-pyä-pō′)	144	27°16′S	70°28′W
Copley, Oh., U.S. (kŏp′lē)	111d	41°06′N	81°38′W
Copparo, Italy (kôp-pä′rō)	174	44°53′N	11°50′E
Coppell, Tx., U.S. (kŏp′pĕl)	117c	32°57′N	97°00′W
Copper, r., Ak., U.S. (kŏp′ẽr)	103	62°38′N	145°00′W
Copper Cliff, Can.	98	46°28′N	81°04′W
Copper Harbor, Mi., U.S.	113	47°27′N	87°53′W
Copperhill, Tn., U.S. (kŏp′ẽr hĭl)	124	35°00′N	84°22′W
Coppermine see Kugluktuk, Can.	92	67°46′N	115°19′W
Coppermine, r., Can.	92	66°48′N	114°59′W
Copper Mountain, mtn., Ak., U.S.	94	55°14′N	132°36′W
Copperton, Ut., U.S. (kŏp′ẽr-tŭn)	117b	40°34′N	112°06′W
Coquilee, Or., U.S. (kō-kēl′)	114	43°11′N	124°11′W
Coquilhatville see Mbandaka, D.R.C.	232	0°04′N	18°16′E
Coquimbo, Chile (kô-kēm′bō)	144	29°58′S	71°31′W
Coquimbo, prov., Chile	141b	31°50′S	71°05′W
Coquitlam Lake, l., Can. (kō-kwĭt-lȧm)	116d	49°23′N	122°44′W
Corabia, Rom. (kô-rä′bĭ-ȧ)	163	43°45′N	24°29′E
Coracora, Peru (kō′rä-kō′rä)	142	15°12′S	73°42′W
Coral Gables, Fl., U.S.	125a	25°43′N	80°14′W
Coral Rapids, Can. (kŏr′ăl)	91	50°18′N	81°49′W
Coral Sea, sea, Oc. (kŏr′ăl)	221	13°30′S	150°00′E
Coralville Reservoir, res., Ia., U.S.	113	41°45′N	91°50′W
Corangamite, Lake, l., Austl. (cŏr-ăng′á-mĭt)	222	38°05′S	142°55′E
Coraopolis, Pa., U.S. (kō-rä-ŏp′ō-lĭs)	111e	40°30′N	80°09′W
Corato, Italy (kô′rä-tô)	174	41°08′N	16°28′E
Corbeil-Essonnes, Fr. (kôr-bā′yĕ-sŏn′)	170	48°31′N	2°29′E
Corbett, Or., U.S. (kôr′bĕt)	116c	45°31′N	122°17′W
Corbie, Fr. (kôr-bē′)	170	49°55′N	2°27′E
Corbin, Ky., U.S. (kôr′bĭn)	124	36°55′N	84°06′W
Corby, Eng., U.K. (kôr′bĭ)	158a	52°29′N	0°38′W
Corcovado, mtn., Braz. (kôr-kô-vä′dô)	144b	22°57′S	43°13′W
Corcovado, Golfo, b., Chile (kôr-kô-vä′dhō)	144	43°40′S	75°00′W
Cordeiro, Braz. (kôr-dā′rō)	141a	22°03′S	42°22′W
Cordele, Ga., U.S. (kôr-dēl′)	124	31°55′N	83°50′W
Cordell, Ok., U.S. (kôr-dĕl′)	120	35°19′N	98°58′W
Córdoba, Arg. (kôr′dô-vä)	144	30°20′S	64°03′W
Córdoba, Mex. (kô′r-dô-bä)	128	18°53′N	96°54′W
Córdoba, Spain (kô′r-dô-bä)	172	37°55′N	4°45′W
Córdoba, prov., Arg. (kôr′dô-vä)	144	32°00′S	64°00′W
Córdoba, Sierra de, mts., Arg.	144	31°15′S	64°30′W
Cordova, Ak., U.S. (kôr′dô-vä)	106a	60°34′N	145°38′W
Cordova, Al., U.S. (kôr′dô-ȧ)	124	33°45′N	86°22′W
Cordova Bay, b., Ak., U.S.	94	54°55′N	132°35′W
Corfu see Kérkira, i., Grc.	156	39°33′N	19°36′E
Corigliano, Italy (kō-rē-lyä′nō)	174	39°35′N	16°30′E
Corinth see Kórinthos, Grc.	154	37°56′N	22°54′E
Corinth, Ms., U.S. (kŏr′ĭnth)	124	34°55′N	88°30′W
Corinto, Braz. (kô-rē′n-tō)	143	18°20′S	44°16′W
Corinto, Col.	142a	3°09′N	76°12′W
Corinto, Nic. (kōr-ĭn′to)	132	12°30′N	87°12′W
Corio, Austl.	217a	38°05′S	144°22′E
Corio Bay, b., Austl.	217a	38°07′S	144°25′E
Corisco, Isla de, i., Eq. Gui.	236	0°50′N	8°40′E
Cork, Ire. (kôrk)	154	51°54′N	8°25′W
Cork Harbour, b., Ire.	164	51°44′N	8°15′W
Corleone, Italy (kôr-lå-ō′nä)	174	37°48′N	13°18′E
Cormorant Lake, l., Can.	97	54°13′N	100°47′W
Cornelia, Ga., U.S. (kôr-nē′lyȧ)	124	34°31′N	83°30′W
Cornelis, r., S. Afr. (kôr-nē′lĭs)	238c	27°48′S	29°15′E
Cornell, Ca., U.S. (kôr-nĕl′)	117a	34°06′N	118°46′W
Cornell, Wi., U.S.	113	45°10′N	91°10′W
Corner Brook, Can. (kôr′nẽr)	91	48°57′N	57°57′W
Corner Inlet, b., Austl.	222	38°55′S	146°45′E
Corning, Ar., U.S. (kôr′nĭng)	121	36°26′N	90°35′W
Corning, Ia., U.S.	113	40°58′N	94°40′W
Corning, N.Y., U.S.	109	42°10′N	77°05′W
Corno, Monte, mtn., Italy (kôr′nō)	162	42°28′N	13°37′E
Cornwall, Bah.	134	25°55′N	77°15′W
Cornwall, Can. (kôrn′wôl)	99	45°05′N	74°35′W
Coro, Ven. (kō′rô)	142	11°22′N	69°43′W
Corocoro, Bol. (kō-rô-kō′rô)	142	17°15′S	68°21′W
Coromandel Coast, cst., India (kŏr-ô-man′dĕl)	199	13°30′N	80°30′E
Coromandel Peninsula, pen., N.Z.	223	36°50′S	176°00′E
Corona, Al., U.S. (kō-rō′nȧ)	124	33°42′N	87°28′W
Corona, Ca., U.S.	117a	33°52′N	117°34′W
Coronada, Bahía de, b., C.R. (bä-ē′ä-dĕ-kô-rô-nä′dō)	133	8°47′N	84°04′W
Corona del Mar, Ca., U.S. (kô-rō′nȧ dĕl mär)	117a	33°36′N	117°53′W
Coronado, Ca., U.S. (kŏr-ô-nä′dō)	118a	32°42′N	117°12′W
Coronation Gulf, b., Can. (kŏr-ō-nā′shŭn)	92	68°07′N	112°50′W
Coronel, Chile (kō-rō-nĕl′)	144	37°00′S	73°10′W
Coronel Brandsen, Arg. (kŏ-rō-nĕl-brá′nd-sĕn)	141c	35°09′S	58°15′W
Coronel Dorrego, Arg. (kŏ-rō-nĕl-dôr-rĕ′gô)	144	38°43′S	61°16′W
Coronel Oviedo, Para. (kŏ-rō-nĕl-ō-vē′dô)	144	25°28′S	56°22′W
Coronel Pringles, Arg. (kŏ-rō-nĕl-prēn′glĕs)	144	37°54′S	61°22′W
Coronel Suárez, Arg. (kŏ-rō-nĕl-swä′rās)	144	37°27′S	61°49′W
Corowa, Austl. (cŏr-ô-wȧ)	222	36°02′S	146°23′E
Corozal, Belize (cŏr-ŏth-äl′)	132a	18°25′N	88°23′W
Corpus Christi, Tx., U.S. (kôr′pŭs krĭs′tē)	104	27°48′N	97°24′W
Corpus Christi Bay, b., Tx., U.S.	123	27°47′N	97°14′W
Corpus Christi Lake, l., Tx., U.S.	122	28°08′N	98°20′W
Corral, Chile (kô-räl′)	144	39°57′S	73°15′W
Corral de Almaguer, Spain (kô-räl′dā äl-mä-gâr′)	172	39°45′N	3°10′W
Corralillo, Cuba (kō-rä-lē-yō)	134	23°00′N	80°40′W
Corregidor Island, i., Phil. (kō-rā-hē-dōr′)	213a	14°21′N	120°25′E
Correntina, Braz. (kō-rĕn-tē-nȧ)	143	13°18′S	44°33′W
Corrib, Lough, l., Ire. (lŏk kŏr′ĭb)	164	53°25′N	9°19′W
Corrientes, Arg. (kō-ryĕn′tās)	144	27°25′S	58°39′W
Corrientes, prov., Arg.	144	28°45′S	58°00′W
Corrientes, Cabo, c., Col. (kȧ′bô-kō-ryĕn′tās)	142	5°34′N	77°35′W
Corrientes, Cabo, c., Cuba (kȧ′bô-kôr-rē-ĕn′tĕs)	134	21°50′N	84°25′W
Corrientes, Cabo, c., Mex.	128	20°25′N	105°41′W
Corry, Pa., U.S. (kŏr′ĭ)	109	41°55′N	79°40′W
Corse, Cap, c., Fr. (kôrs)	161	42°59′N	9°19′E
Corsica, i., Fr. (kôr′sē-kä)	156	42°10′N	8°55′E
Corsicana, Tx., U.S. (kôr-sĭ-kăn′ȧ)	104	32°06′N	96°28′W
Cortazar, Mex. (kôr-tä-zär)	130	20°30′N	100°57′W
Corte, Fr. (kôr′tȧ)	174	42°18′N	9°10′E
Cortegana, Spain (kôr-tå-gä′nä)	172	37°54′N	6°48′W
Cortés, Ensenada de, b., Cuba (ĕn-sĕ-nä-dä-dĕ-kôr-tās′)	134	22°05′N	83°45′W
Cortez, Co., U.S.	119	37°21′N	108°35′W
Cortland, N.Y., U.S. (kôrt′lănd)	109	42°35′N	76°10′W
Cortona, Italy (kôr-tō′nä)	174	43°16′N	12°00′E
Corubal, r., Gui.-B.	234	11°43′N	14°40′W
Coruche, Port. (kō-rōō′she)	172	38°58′N	8°34′W
Çoruh, r., Asia (chō-rōōk′)	181	40°30′N	41°10′E
Çorum, Tur. (chô-rōōm′)	198	40°34′N	34°45′E
Corunna, Mi., U.S. (kō-rŭn′ȧ)	108	43°00′N	84°05′W
Coruripe, Braz. (kō-rō-rē′pĭ)	143	10°09′S	36°13′W
Corvallis, Or., U.S. (kŏr-văl′ĭs)	104	44°34′N	123°17′W
Corve, r., Eng., U.K. (kôr′vē)	158a	52°28′N	2°43′W
Corydon, Ia., U.S.	113	40°45′N	93°20′W
Corydon, In., U.S. (kŏr′ĭ-dŭn)	108	38°10′N	86°05′W
Corydon, Ky., U.S.	108	37°45′N	87°40′W
Cosamaloápan, Mex. (kō-sá-mä-lwä′pän)	131	18°21′N	95°48′W

PLACE (Pronunciation)	PAGE	LAT.	LONG.
Coscomatepec, Mex. (kôs'kōmä-tĕ-pĕk')	131	19°04'N	97°03'W
Cosenza, Italy (kō-zĕnt'sä)	163	39°18'N	16°15'E
Coshocton, Oh., U.S. (kō-shŏk'tŭn)	108	40°15'N	81°55'W
Cosigüina, vol., Nic.	132	12°59'N	87°35'W
Cosmoledo Group, is., Sey. (kŏs-mō-lā'dō)	233	9°42'S	47°45'E
Cosmopolis, Wa., U.S. (kŏz-mŏp'ō-lĭs)	114	46°58'N	123°47'W
Cosne-sur-Loire, Fr. (kōn-sür-lwär')	170	47°25'N	2°57'E
Cosoleacaque, Mex. (kō sō lā-ä-kä'kē)	131	18°01'N	94°38'W
Costa de Caparica, Port.	173b	38°40'N	9°12'W
Costa Mesa, Ca., U.S. (kŏs'tȧ mā'sȧ)	117a	33°39'N	118°54'W
Costa Rica, nation, N.A. (kŏs'tȧ rē'kȧ)	129	10°30'N	84°30'W
Cosumnes, r., Ca., U.S. (kŏ-sŭm'nĕz)	118	38°21'N	121°17'W
Cotabambas, Peru (kō-tä-bäm'bäs)	142	13°49'S	72°17'W
Cotabato, Phil. (kō-tä-bä'tō)	213	7°06'N	124°13'E
Cotaxtla, Mex. (kō-täs'tlä)	131	18°49'N	96°22'W
Cotaxtla, r., Mex.	131	18°54'N	96°21'W
Coteau-du-Lac, Can. (cō-tō'dü-läk)	102a	45°17'N	74°11'W
Coteau-Landing, Can.	102a	45°15'N	74°13'W
Coteaux, Haiti	135	18°15'N	74°05'W
Cote d'Ivoire (Ivory Coast), nation, Afr.	230	7°43'N	6°30'W
Côte d'Or, reg., Fr.	170	47°02'N	4°35'E
Cotija de la Paz, Mex. (kō-tē'-kä-dĕ-lä-pá'z)	130	19°46'N	102°43'W
Cotonou, Benin (kō-tō-nōō')	230	6°21'N	2°26'E
Cotopaxi, mtn., Ec. (kō-tō-păk'sē)	142	0°40'S	78°26'W
Cotorro, Cuba (kō-tôr-rō)	135a	23°03'N	82°17'W
Cotswold Hills, hills, Eng., U.K. (kŭtz'wōld)	164	51°35'N	2°16'W
Cottage Grove, Mn., U.S. (kŏt'āj grōv)	117g	44°50'N	92°52'W
Cottage Grove, Or., U.S.	114	43°48'N	123°04'W
Cottbus, Ger. (kōtt'bōōs)	161	51°47'N	14°20'E
Cottonwood, r., Mn., U.S. (kŏt'ŭn-wŏd)	112	44°25'N	95°35'W
Cotulla, Tx., U.S. (kŏ-tŭl'lȧ)	122	28°26'N	99°14'W
Coubert, Fr. (kōō-bâr')	171b	48°40'N	2°43'E
Coudersport, Pa., U.S. (kou'dẽrz-port)	109	41°45'N	78°00'W
Coudres, Île aux, i., Can.	100	47°17'N	70°12'W
Coulommiers, Fr. (kōō-lô-myā')	171b	48°49'N	3°05'E
Coulto, Serra do, mts., Braz. (sĕ'r-rä-dō-kō-ô'tô)	144b	22°33'S	43°27'W
Council Bluffs, Ia., U.S. (koun'sĭl blŭf)	105	41°16'N	95°53'W
Council Grove, Ks., U.S. (koun'sĭl grōv)	121	38°39'N	96°30'W
Coupeville, Wa., U.S. (kōōp'vĭl)	116a	48°13'N	122°41'W
Courantyne, r., S.A. (kôr'ăntĭn)	143	4°28'N	57°42'W
Courtenay, Can. (cōōrt-nā')	90	49°41'N	125°00'W
Coushatta, La., U.S. (kou-shăt'ȧ)	123	32°02'N	93°21'W
Coutras, Fr. (kōō-trá')	170	45°02'N	0°07'W
Covelo, Ang.	236	12°06'S	13°55'E
Coventry, Eng., U.K. (kŭv'ĕn-trĭ)	164	52°25'N	1°29'W
Covina, Ca., U.S. (kô-vē'nȧ)	117a	34°06'N	117°54'W
Covington, Ga., U.S. (kŭv'ĭng-tŭn)	124	33°36'N	83°50'W
Covington, In., U.S.	108	40°10'N	87°15'W
Covington, Ky., U.S.	105	39°05'N	84°31'W
Covington, La., U.S.	123	30°30'N	90°06'W
Covington, Oh., U.S.	108	40°10'N	84°20'W
Covington, Ok., U.S.	121	36°18'N	97°32'W
Covington, Tn., U.S.	124	35°33'N	89°40'W
Covington, Va., U.S.	108	37°50'N	80°00'W
Cowal, Lake, l., Austl. (kou'ăl)	222	33°30'S	147°10'E
Cowan, l., Austl. (kou'ăn)	220	32°00'S	122°30'E
Cowansville, Can.	99	45°13'N	72°47'W
Cow Creek, r., Or., U.S. (kou)	114	42°45'N	123°35'W
Cowes, Eng., U.K. (kouz)	164	50°43'N	1°25'W
Cowichan Lake, l., Can.	94	48°54'N	124°20'W
Cowlitz, r., Wa., U.S. (kou'lĭts)	114	46°30'N	122°45'W
Cowra, Austl. (kou'rȧ)	222	33°50'S	148°33'E
Coxim, Braz. (kō-shēn')	143	18°32'S	54°43'W
Coxquihui, Mex. (kōz-kē-wē')	131	20°10'N	97°34'W
Cox's Bāzār, Bngl.	202	21°32'N	92°00'E
Coyaima, Col. (kō-yä'ē-mä)	142a	3°48'N	75°11'W
Coyame, Mex. (kō-yä'mā)	122	29°26'N	105°05'W
Coyanosa Draw, Tx., U.S. (kō yá-nō'sä)	122	30°55'N	103°07'W
Coyoacán, Mex. (kô-yō-á-kän')	130	19°21'N	99°10'W
Coyote, r., Ca., U.S. (kī'ōt)	116b	37°37'N	121°57'W
Coyuca de Benítez, Mex. (kō-yōō'kä dā bā-nē'tāz)	130	17°04'N	100°06'W
Coyuca de Catalán, Mex. (kō-yōō'kä dā kä-tä-län')	130	18°19'N	100°41'W
Coyutla, Mex. (kō-yōō'tlä)	131	20°13'N	97°40'W
Cozad, Ne., U.S. (kō'zăd)	120	40°53'N	99°59'W
Cozaddale, Oh., U.S. (kō-zăd-dāl)	111f	39°16'N	84°09'W
Cozoyoapan, Mex. (kô-zō-yô-ä-pá'n)	130	16°45'N	98°17'W
Cozumel, Mex. (kŏ-zōō-mĕ'l)	132a	20°31'N	86°55'W
Cozumel, Isla de, i., Mex. (ē's-lä-dĕ-kŏ-zōō-mĕ'l)	128	20°26'N	87°10'W
Crab Creek, r., Wa., U.S. (krăb)	114	46°47'N	119°43'W
Crab Creek, r., Wa., U.S.	114	47°21'N	119°09'W
Cradock, S. Afr. (kră'dŭk)	232	32°12'S	25°38'E
Crafton, Pa., U.S. (krăf'tŭn)	111e	40°26'N	80°04'W
Craig, Co., U.S. (krāg)	115	40°32'N	107°31'W
Craiova, Rom. (krá-yō'vá)	163	44°18'N	23°50'E
Cranberry, l., N.Y., U.S. (krăn'bĕr-ĭ)	109	44°10'N	74°50'W
Cranbourne, Austl.	217a	38°07'S	145°16'E
Cranbrook, Can. (krăn'brŏk)	90	49°31'N	115°46'W
Cranbury, N.J., U.S. (krăn'bē-rĭ)	110a	40°19'N	74°31'W
Crandon, Wi., U.S. (krăn'dŭn)	113	45°35'N	88°55'W
Crane Prairie Reservoir, res., Or., U.S.	114	43°50'N	121°55'W
Cranston, R.I., U.S. (krăns'tŭn)	110b	41°46'N	71°25'W
Crater Lake, l., Or., U.S. (krā'tēr)	114	43°00'N	122°08'W
Crater Lake National Park, rec., Or., U.S.	114	42°58'N	122°40'W
Craters of the Moon National Monument, rec., Id., U.S. (krā'tēr)	115	43°28'N	113°15'W
Crateús, Braz. (krä-tā-ōōzh')	143	5°09'S	40°35'W
Crato, Braz. (krä'tō)	143	7°19'S	39°13'W
Crawford, Ne., U.S. (krô'fērd)	112	42°41'N	103°25'W
Crawford, Wa., U.S.	116c	45°49'N	122°24'W
Crawfordsville, In., U.S. (krô'fērdz-vĭl)	108	40°00'N	86°55'W
Crazy Mountains, mts., Mt., U.S. (krā'zĭ)	115	46°11'N	110°25'W
Crazy Woman Creek, r., Wy., U.S.	115	44°08'N	106°40'W
Crecy, S. Afr. (krĕ-sē)	238c	24°38'S	28°52'E
Crécy-en-Brie, Fr. (krā-sē'-ĕN-brē')	171b	48°52'N	2°55'E
Crécy-en-Ponthieu, Fr.	170	50°13'N	1°48'E
Credit, r., Can.	102d	43°41'N	79°55'W
Cree, l., Can. (krē)	92	57°35'N	107°52'W
Creighton, S. Afr. (cre-tŏn)	233c	30°02'S	29°52'E
Creighton, Ne., U.S. (krā'tŭn)	112	42°27'N	97°54'W
Creil, Fr. (krĕ'y')	170	49°18'N	2°28'E
Crema, Italy (krā'mä)	174	45°21'N	9°53'E
Cremona, Italy (krā-mō'nä)	162	45°09'N	10°02'E
Crépy-en-Valois, Fr. (krā-pē'ĕN-vä-lwä')	171b	49°14'N	2°53'E
Cres, Cro. (tsrĕs)	174	44°58'N	14°21'E
Crescent Beach, Can.	116d	49°03'N	122°58'W
Crescent City, Ca., U.S. (krĕs'ĕnt)	114	41°46'N	124°13'W
Crescent City, Fl., U.S.	125	29°26'N	81°35'W
Crescent Lake, l., Fl., U.S. (krĕs'ĕnt)	125	29°33'N	81°30'W
Crescent Lake, l., Or., U.S.	114	43°25'N	121°58'W
Cresco, Ia., U.S. (krĕs'kō)	113	43°23'N	92°07'W
Crested Butte, Co., U.S. (krĕst'ĕd būt)	119	38°50'N	107°00'W
Crestline, Ca., U.S. (krĕst-līn)	117a	34°15'N	117°17'W
Crestline, Oh., U.S.	108	40°50'N	82°40'W
Crestmore, Ca., U.S. (krĕst'môr)	117a	34°02'N	117°23'W
Creston, Can. (krĕs'tŭn)	90	49°06'N	116°31'W
Creston, Ia., U.S.	113	41°04'N	94°22'W
Creston, Oh., U.S.	111d	40°59'N	81°54'W
Crestview, Fl., U.S. (krĕst'vū)	124	30°44'N	86°35'W
Crestwood, Ky., U.S. (krĕst'wŏd)	111h	38°20'N	85°28'W
Crestwood, Mo., U.S.	117e	38°33'N	90°23'W
Crete, Il., U.S. (krēt)	111a	41°26'N	87°38'W
Crete, Ne., U.S.	121	40°38'N	96°56'W
Crete, i., Grc.	156	35°15'N	24°30'E
Creus, Cap de, c., Spain	173	42°16'N	3°18'E
Creuse, r., Fr. (krûz)	170	46°51'N	0°49'E
Creve Coeur, Mo., U.S. (krēv kŏr)	117e	38°40'N	90°27'W
Crevillent, Spain	173	38°12'N	0°48'W
Crewe, Eng., U.K. (krōō)	164	53°06'N	2°27'W
Crewe, Va., U.S.	125	37°09'N	78°08'W
Crimean Peninsula *see* Kryms'kyi Pivostriv, pen., Ukr.	181	45°18'N	33°30'E
Crimmitschau, Ger. (krĭm'ĭt-shou)	168	50°49'N	12°22'E
Cripple Creek, Co., U.S. (krĭp''l)	120	38°44'N	105°12'W
Crisfield, Md., U.S. (krĭs-fēld)	109	38°00'N	75°50'W
Cristal, Monts de, mts., Gabon	236	0°50'N	10°30'E
Cristina, Braz. (krēs-tē'-nä)	141a	22°13'S	45°15'W
Cristóbal Colón, Pico, mtn., Col. (pē'kō-krēs-tô'bäl-kō-lôn')	142	11°00'N	74°00'W
Crişul Alb, r., Rom. (krē'shōōl älb)	169	46°20'N	22°15'E
Crna, r., Serb. (ts'r'nà)	175	41°03'N	21°46'E
Crna Gora (Montenegro), state, Serb.	175	42°55'N	18°52'E
Črnomelj, Slvn. (ch'r'nō-māl')	174	45°35'N	15°11'E
Croatia, nation, Eur.	174	45°24'N	15°18'E
Crockett, Ca., U.S. (krŏk'ĕt)	116b	38°03'N	122°14'W
Crockett, Tx., U.S.	123	31°19'N	95°28'W
Crofton, Md., U.S.	110e	39°01'N	76°43'W
Crofton, Ne., U.S.	112	42°44'N	97°32'W
Croix, Lac la, l., N.A. (läk lä krōō-ä')	113	48°19'N	91°53'W
Croker, i., Austl. (krō'kȧ)	220	10°45'S	132°25'E
Cronulla, Austl. (krō-nŭl'ȧ)	217b	34°03'S	151°09'E
Crooked, i., Bah.	135	22°45'N	74°10'W
Crooked, l., Can.	101	48°25'N	56°05'W
Crooked, r., Can.	95	54°30'N	122°55'W
Crooked, r., Or., U.S.	114	44°07'N	120°30'W
Crooked Creek, r., Il., U.S. (krōōk'ĕd)	121	40°21'N	90°49'W
Crooked Island Passage, strt., Bah.	135	22°40'N	74°50'W
Crookston, Mn., U.S. (krŏks'tŭn)	112	47°44'N	96°35'W
Crooksville, Oh., U.S. (krŏks'vĭl)	108	39°45'N	82°05'W
Crosby, Eng., U.K.	158a	53°30'N	3°02'W
Crosby, Mn., U.S. (krôz'bĭ)	113	46°29'N	93°58'W
Crosby, N.D., U.S.	112	48°55'N	103°18'W
Crosby, Tx., U.S.	123a	29°55'N	95°04'W
Cross, l., La., U.S.	123	32°33'N	93°58'W
Cross, r., Nig.	235	5°35'N	8°05'E
Cross City, Fl., U.S.	124	29°55'N	83°25'W
Crossett, Ar., U.S. (krôs'ĕt)	121	33°08'N	92°00'W
Cross Lake, l., Can.	92	54°45'N	97°30'W
Cross River Reservoir, res., N.Y., U.S. (krôs)	110a	41°14'N	73°34'W
Cross Sound, strt., Ak., U.S. (krŏs)	103	58°12'N	137°20'W
Crosswell, Mi., U.S. (krŏz'wĕl)	108	43°15'N	82°35'W
Croswell, i., Serb.	174	44°50'N	14°31'E
Crotch, l., Can.	99	44°55'N	76°55'W
Crotone, Italy (krō-tō'nĕ)	175	39°05'N	17°08'E
Croton Falls Reservoir, res., N.Y., U.S. (krōtŭn)	110a	41°22'N	73°44'W
Croton-on-Hudson, N.Y., U.S. (krō'tŭn-ŏn hŭd'sŭn)	110a	41°12'N	73°53'W
Crow, l., Can.	113	49°13'N	93°29'W
Crow Agency, Mt., U.S.	115	45°36'N	107°27'W
Crow Creek, r., Co., U.S.	120	41°08'N	104°25'W
Crow Creek Indian Reservation, I.R., S.D., U.S.	112	44°17'N	99°17'W
Crow Indian Reservation, I.R., Mt., U.S. (krō)	115	45°26'N	108°12'W
Crowle, Eng., U.K. (kroul)	158a	53°36'N	0°49'W
Crowley, La., U.S. (krou'lē)	123	30°13'N	92°22'W
Crown Mountain, mtn., Can. (kroun)	116d	49°24'N	123°05'W
Crown Mountain, mtn., V.I.U.S.	129c	18°22'N	64°58'W
Crown Point, In., U.S. (kroun point')	111a	41°25'N	87°22'W
Crown Point, N.Y., U.S.	109	44°00'N	73°25'W
Crowsnest Pass, p., Can.	95	49°39'N	114°45'W
Crow Wing, r., Mn., U.S. (krō)	113	44°50'N	94°01'W
Crow Wing, r., Mn., U.S.	113	46°42'N	94°48'W
Crow Wing, North Fork, r., Mn., U.S.	113	45°16'N	94°28'W
Crow Wing, South Fork, r., Mn., U.S.	113	44°59'N	94°42'W
Croydon, Austl. (kroi'dŭn)	219	18°15'S	142°15'E
Croydon, Austl.	217a	37°48'S	145°17'E
Croydon, Eng., U.K.	161	51°22'N	0°06'W
Croydon, Pa., U.S.	110f	40°05'N	74°55'W
Crozet, Îles, is., Afr. (krō-zĕ')	3	46°20'S	51°30'E
Cruces, Cuba (krōō'sås)	134	22°20'N	80°20'W
Cruces, Arroyo de, r., Mex. (är-rō'yô-dĕ-krōō'sĕs)	122	26°17'N	104°32'W
Cruillas, Mex. (krōō-ēl'yäs)	122	24°45'N	98°31'W
Cruz, Cabo, c., Cuba (ká'-bô-krōōz)	129	19°50'N	77°45'W
Cruz, Cayo, i., Cuba (kä'yō-krōōz)	134	22°15'N	77°50'W
Cruz Alta, Braz. (krōōz äl'tä)	144	28°41'S	54°02'W
Cruz del Eje, Arg. (krōō's-dĕl-ĕ-kĕ)	144	30°46'S	64°45'W
Cruzeiro, Braz. (krōō-zā'rō)	141a	22°36'S	44°57'W
Cruzeiro do Sul, Braz. (krōō-zā'rō dò sōōl)	142	7°34'S	72°40'W
Crysler, Can.	102c	45°13'N	75°09'W
Crystal City, Tx., U.S. (krĭs'tăl sĭ'tĭ)	122	28°40'N	99°50'W
Crystal Falls, Mi., U.S. (krĭs'tăl fôls)	113	46°06'N	88°21'W
Crystal Lake, Il., U.S. (krĭs'tăl lăk)	111a	42°15'N	88°18'W
Crystal Springs, Ms., U.S. (krĭs'tăl sprĭngz)	124	31°58'N	90°20'W
Crystal Springs, oasis, Ca., U.S.	116b	37°31'N	122°26'W
Csongrád, Hung. (chôn'gräd)	169	46°42'N	20°09'E
Csorna, Hung. (chôr'nä)	169	47°39'N	17°11'E
Cúa, Ven. (kōō'ä)	143b	10°10'N	66°54'W
Cuajimalpa, Mex. (kwä-hē-mäl'pä)	131a	19°21'N	99°18'W
Cuale, Sierra del, mts., Mex. (sē-ĕ'r-rä-dĕl-kwä'lĕ)	130	20°20'N	104°58'W
Cuamato, Ang. (kwä-mä'tō)	236	17°05'S	15°09'E
Cuamba, Moz.	237	14°49'S	36°33'E
Cuando, Ang. (kwän'dō)	236	16°32'S	22°07'E
Cuando, r., Afr.	232	14°30'S	20°00'E
Cuangar, Ang.	236	17°36'S	18°39'E
Cuango, r., Afr.	232	9°00'S	18°00'E
Cuanza, r., Ang. (kwän'zä)	232	9°45'S	15°00'E
Cuarto, r., Arg.	144	33°00'S	63°25'W
Cuatro Caminos, Cuba (kwä'trô-kä-mē'nōs)	135a	23°01'N	82°13'W
Cuatro Ciénegas, Mex. (kwä'trō syā'nâ-gäs)	122	26°59'N	102°03'W
Cuauhtemoc, Mex. (kwä-ōō-tĕ-mŏk')	131	15°43'N	91°57'W
Cuautepec, Mex. (kwä-ōō-tĕ-pĕk)	130	16°41'N	99°04'W
Cuautepec, Mex.	130	20°01'N	98°19'W
Cuautitlán, Mex. (kwä-ōō-tēt-län')	131a	19°40'N	99°12'W
Cuautla, Mex. (kwä-ōō'tlä)	130	18°47'N	98°57'W
Cuba, Port. (kōō'bà)	172	38°10'N	7°55'W
Cuba, nation, N.A. (kū'bȧ)	129	22°00'N	79°00'W
Cubagua, Isla, i., Ven. (ē's-lä-kōō-bä'gwä)	143b	10°48'N	64°10'W
Cubango (Okavango), r., Afr. (kōō-băŋ'gō)	232	17°10'S	18°20'E
Cub Hills, hills, Can. (kŭb)	96	54°20'N	104°30'W
Cucamonga, Ca., U.S. (kōō-kȧ-mŏŋ'gȧ)	117a	34°05'N	117°35'W
Cuchi, Ang.	232	14°40'S	16°50'E
Cuchillo Parado, Mex. (kōō-chē'lyô pä-rä'dō)	122	29°26'N	104°52'W
Cuchumatanes, Sierra de los, mts., Guat.	132	15°35'N	91°10'W
Cúcuta, Col. (kōō'kōō-tä)	142	7°56'N	72°30'W
Cudahy, Wi., U.S. (kŭd'ȧ-hĭ)	111a	42°57'N	87°52'W
Cuddalore, India (kŭd ȧ-lōr')	199	11°49'N	79°46'E
Cuddapah, India (kŭd'ȧ-pä)	199	14°31'N	78°52'E
Cue, Austl. (kū)	218	27°30'S	118°10'E
Cuéllar, Spain (kwā'lyär')	172	41°24'N	4°15'W
Cuenca, Ec. (kwĕn'kä)	142	2°52'S	78°54'W
Cuenca, Spain	162	40°05'N	2°07'W
Cuenca, Sierra de, mts., Spain (sē-ĕ'r-rä-dĕ-kwĕ'n-kä)	172	40°02'N	1°50'W
Cuencame, Mex. (kwĕn-kä-mä')	122	24°52'N	103°42'W
Cuerámaro, Mex. (kwä-rä'mä-rō)	130	20°39'N	101°44'W
Cuernavaca, Mex. (kwĕr-nä-vä'kä)	128	18°55'N	99°15'W
Cuero, Tx., U.S. (kwā'rō)	123	29°05'N	97°16'W
Cuetzalá del Progreso, Mex. (kwĕt-zä-lä dĕl prō-grĕ'sō)	130	18°07'N	99°51'W
Cuetzalan del Progreso, Mex.	131	20°02'N	97°33'W
Cuevas del Almanzora, Spain (kwĕ'väs-dĕl-äl-män-zō-rä)	162	37°19'N	1°54'W
Cuglieri, Italy (kōō-lyâ'rĕ)	174	40°11'N	8°37'E
Cuicatlán, Mex. (kwē-kä-tlän')	131	17°46'N	96°57'W
Cuilapa, Guat. (kò-ē-lä'pä)	132	14°16'N	90°20'W
Cuilo (Kwilu), r., Afr.	236	9°15'S	19°30'E

D

ăt; finäl; rāte; senåte; ärm; ásk; sofá; fâre; ch-choose; dh-as th in other; bē; ĕvent; bĕt; recĕnt; cratẽr; g-gō; gh-guttural g; bĭt; ī-short neutral; rīde; κ-guttural k as ch in German ich;

PRONOUNCING INDEX Davenport – Diablotins 287

PLACE (Pronunciation)	PAGE	LAT.	LONG.
Davenport, Wa., U.S.	114	47°39'N	118°07'W
David, Pan. (dá-vēdh')	129	8°27'N	82°27'W
David City, Ne., U.S. (dā'vĭd)	112	41°15'N	97°10'W
David-Gorodok, Bela. (dá-vēt' gô-rō'dôk)	181	52°02'N	27°14'E
Davis, Ok., U.S. (dā'vĭs)	121	34°34'N	97°08'W
Davis, W.V., U.S.	109	39°15'N	79°25'W
Davis Lake, l., Or., U.S.	114	43°38'N	121°43'W
Davis Mountains, mts., Tx., U.S.	122	30°45'N	104°17'W
Davis Strait, strt., N.A.	89	66°00'N	60°00'W
Davlekanovo, Russia	180	54°15'N	55°05'E
Davos, Switz. (dä'vōs)	168	46°47'N	9°50'E
Dawa, r., Afr.	231	4°30'N	40°30'E
Dawāsir, Wādī ad, val., Sau. Ar.	198	20°48'N	44°07'E
Dawei, Mya.	212	14°04'N	98°19'E
Dawen, r., China (dä-wŭn)	206	35°58'N	116°53'E
Dawley, Eng., U.K. (dô'lĭ)	158a	52°38'N	2°28'W
Dawna Range, mts., Mya. (dô'ná)	212	17°02'N	98°01'E
Dawson, Can. (dô'sŭn)	90	64°04'N	139°22'W
Dawson, Ga., U.S.	124	31°45'N	84°29'W
Dawson, Mn., U.S.	112	44°54'N	96°03'W
Dawson, r., Austl.	221	24°20'S	149°45'E
Dawson Bay, b., Can.	97	52°55'N	100°50'W
Dawson Creek, Can.	90	55°46'N	120°14'W
Dawson Range, mts., Can.	103	62°15'N	138°10'W
Dawson Springs, Ky., U.S.	124	37°10'N	87°40'W
Dawu, China (dä-wōō)	206	31°33'N	114°07'E
Dax, Fr. (dáks)	161	43°42'N	1°06'W
Daxian, China (dä-shyĕn)	204	31°12'N	107°30'E
Daxing, China (dä-shyĭŋ)	208a	39°44'N	116°19'E
Dayiqiao, China (dä-yē-chyou)	206	31°43'N	120°40'E
Dayr az Zawr, Syria (dá-ēr-ēz-zôr')	198	35°15'N	40°01'E
Dayton, Ky., U.S. (dā'tŭn)	111f	39°07'N	84°28'W
Dayton, N.M., U.S.	120	32°44'N	104°23'W
Dayton, Oh., U.S.	105	39°54'N	84°15'W
Dayton, Tn., U.S.	124	35°30'N	85°00'W
Dayton, Tx., U.S.	123	30°03'N	94°53'W
Dayton, Wa., U.S.	114	46°18'N	117°59'W
Daytona Beach, Fl., U.S. (dā-tō'ná)	105	29°11'N	81°02'W
Dayu, China (dä-yōō)	209	25°20'N	114°20'E
Da Yunhe (Grand Canal), can., China (dä yòn-hŭ)	205	35°00'N	117°00'E
Dayville, Ct., U.S. (dā'vĭl)	109	41°50'N	71°55'W
De Aar, S. Afr. (dē-är')	232	30°45'S	24°05'E
Dead, l., Mn., U.S. (dĕd)	112	46°28'N	96°00'W
Dead Sea, l., Asia	198	31°30'N	35°30'E
Deadwood, S.D., U.S. (dĕd'wòd)	104	44°23'N	103°43'W
Deal Island, Md., U.S. (dēl-ī'lănd)	109	38°10'N	75°55'W
Dean, r., Can. (dēn)	94	52°45'N	125°30'W
Dean Channel, strt., Can.	94	52°33'N	127°13'W
Deán Funes, Arg. (dĕ-á'n-fōō-nĕs)	144	30°26'S	64°12'W
Dearborn, Mi., U.S. (dēr'bŭrn)	111b	42°18'N	83°15'W
Dearg, Ben, mtn., Scot., U.K. (bĕn dŭrg)	164	57°48'N	4°59'W
Dease Strait, strt., Can. (dēz)	92	68°50'N	108°20'W
Death Valley, Ca., U.S.	118	36°18'N	116°26'W
Death Valley, val., Ca., U.S.	106	36°30'N	117°00'W
Death Valley National Park, rec., U.S.	118	36°34'N	117°00'W
Debal'tseve, Ukr.	177	48°23'N	38°29'E
Debao, China (dŭ-bou)	204	23°18'N	106°40'E
Debar, Mac. (dĕ'bär)(dā'brä)	175	41°31'N	20°32'E
Dęblin, Pol. (dăN'blĭn)	169	51°34'N	21°49'E
Dębno, Pol. (dĕb-nô')	168	52°47'N	13°43'E
Debo, Lac, l., Mali	234	15°15'N	4°40'W
Debrecen, Hung. (dĕ'brĕ-tsĕn)	154	47°32'N	21°40'E
Debre Markos, Eth.	231	10°15'N	37°45'E
Debre Tabor, Eth.	231	11°57'N	38°09'E
Decatur, Al., U.S. (dē-kā'tŭr)	124	34°35'N	87°00'W
Decatur, Ga., U.S.	110c	33°47'N	84°18'W
Decatur, Il., U.S.	105	39°50'N	88°59'W
Decatur, In., U.S.	108	40°50'N	84°55'W
Decatur, Mi., U.S.	108	42°10'N	86°00'W
Decatur, Tx., U.S.	121	33°14'N	97°33'W
Decazeville, Fr. (dē-käz'vēl')	161	44°33'N	2°16'E
Deccan, plat., India (dĕk'ăn)	199	19°05'N	76°40'E
Deception Lake, l., Can.	96	56°33'N	104°15'W
Deception Pass, p., Wa., U.S. (dē-sĕp'shŭn)	116a	48°24'N	122°44'W
Děčín, Czech Rep. (dyĕ'chēn)	168	50°47'N	14°14'E
Decorah, Ia., U.S. (dē-kō'rá)	113	43°18'N	91°48'W
Dedenevo, Russia (dyĕ-dyĕ'nyĕ-vô)	186b	56°14'N	37°31'E
Dedham, Ma., U.S. (dĕd'ăm)	101a	42°15'N	71°11'W
Dedo do Deus, mtn., Braz. (dĕ-dô-dô-dĕ'ōōs)	144b	22°30'S	43°02'W
Dédougou, Burkina (dā-dò-gōō')	230	12°38'N	3°28'W
Dee, r., Scot., U.K.	164	57°05'N	2°25'W
Dee, r., U.K.	158a	53°15'N	3°05'E
Deep, r., N.C., U.S. (dēp)	125	35°36'N	79°32'W
Deep Fork, r., Ok., U.S.	121	35°35'N	96°42'W
Deep River, Can.	99	46°06'N	77°20'W
Deepwater, Mo., U.S. (dep-wô-tēr)	121	38°15'N	93°46'W
Deer, i., Me., U.S.	100	44°07'N	68°38'W
Deerfield, Il., U.S. (dēr'fēld)	111a	42°10'N	87°51'W
Deer Island, Or., U.S.	116c	45°56'N	122°51'W
Deer Lake, Can.	93a	49°10'N	57°25'W
Deer Lake, l., Can.	97	52°40'N	94°30'W
Deer Lodge, Mt., U.S. (dēr lŏj)	115	46°23'N	112°42'W
Deer Park, Oh., U.S.	111f	39°12'N	84°24'W
Deer Park, Wa., U.S.	114	47°58'N	117°28'W
Deer River, Mn., U.S.	113	47°20'N	93°49'W
Defiance, Oh., U.S. (dē-fī'ăns)	108	41°15'N	84°20'W
DeFuniak Springs, Fl., U.S. (dē fū'nĭ-ăk)	124	30°42'N	86°06'W
Deganga, India	202a	22°41'N	88°41'E
Degeh Bur, Eth.	238a	8°10'N	43°25'E
Deggendorf, Ger. (dĕ'ghĕn-dôrf)	168	48°50'N	12°59'E
Degollado, Mex. (dā-gō-lyä'dō)	130	20°27'N	102°11'W
DeGrey, r., Austl. (dē grā')	220	20°20'S	119°25'E
Degtyarsk, Russia (dĕg-ty'arsk)	186a	56°42'N	60°05'E
Dehiwala-Mount Lavinia, Sri L.	203	6°47'N	79°55'E
Dehra Dūn, India (dā'rŭ)	199	30°09'N	78°07'E
Dehua, China (dŭ-hwä)	209	25°30'N	118°15'E
Dej, Rom. (dāzh)	163	47°09'N	23°53'E
De Kalb, Il., U.S. (dē kălb')	108	41°54'N	88°46'W
Dekese, D.R.C.	236	3°27'S	21°24'E
Delacour, Can. (dĕ-lä-kōōr')	102e	51°09'N	113°45'W
Delagua, Co., U.S. (dĕl-ä'gwä)	120	37°19'N	104°42'W
De Land, Fl., U.S. (dē lănd')	125	29°00'N	81°19'W
Delano, Ca., U.S. (dĕl'á-nō)	118	35°47'N	119°15'W
Delano Peak, mtn., Ut., U.S.	106	38°25'N	112°25'W
Delavan, Wi., U.S. (dĕl'á-văn)	113	42°39'N	88°38'W
Delaware, Oh., U.S. (dĕl'á-wâr)	108	40°15'N	83°05'W
Delaware, state, U.S.	105	38°40'N	75°30'W
Delaware, r., Ks., U.S.	121	39°45'N	95°47'W
Delaware, r., U.S.	109	41°50'N	75°20'W
Delaware Bay, b., U.S.	107	39°05'N	75°10'W
Delaware Reservoir, res., Oh., U.S.	109	40°30'N	83°05'E
Delémont, Switz. (dē-lā-môN')	168	47°21'N	7°18'E
De Leon, Tx., U.S. (dē lē-ŏn')	122	32°06'N	98°33'W
Delft, Neth. (dĕlft)	165	52°01'N	4°20'E
Delfzijl, Neth.	165	53°20'N	6°50'E
Delgada, Punta, c., Arg. (pōō'n-tä-dĕl-gä'dä)	144	43°46'S	63°46'W
Delgado, Cabo, c., Moz. (ká'bô-dĕl-gä'dō)	233	10°40'S	40°35'E
Delhi, India	199	28°54'N	77°13'E
Delhi, Il., U.S. (dĕl'hī)	117e	39°03'N	90°16'W
Delhi, La., U.S.	123	32°26'N	91°29'W
Delhi, state, India	199	28°30'N	76°50'E
Delitzsch, Ger. (dā'lĭch)	168	51°32'N	12°18'E
Dellansjöarna, l., Swe.	166	61°57'N	16°25'E
Delles, Alg. (dĕ'lĕs')	230	36°59'N	3°40'E
Dell Rapids, S.D., U.S. (dĕl)	112	43°50'N	96°43'W
Dellwood, Mn., U.S. (dĕl'wòd)	117g	45°05'N	92°58'W
Del Mar, Ca., U.S. (dĕl mär')	118a	32°57'N	117°16'W
Delmas, S. Afr. (dĕl'más)	238c	26°08'S	28°43'E
Delmenhorst, Ger. (dĕl'mĕn-hôrst)	168	53°03'N	8°38'E
Del Norte, Co., U.S. (dĕl nôrt')	119	37°40'N	106°25'W
De-Longa, i., Russia	179	76°21'N	148°56'E
De Long Mountains, mts., Ak., U.S. (dē'lŏng)	103	68°38'N	162°30'W
Deloraine, Austl. (dĕ-lŭ-rān)	222	41°30'S	146°40'E
Delphi, In., U.S. (dĕl'fī)	108	40°35'N	86°40'W
Delphos, Oh., U.S. (dĕl'fŏs)	108	40°50'N	84°20'W
Delray Beach, Fl., U.S. (dĕl-rā')	125a	26°27'N	80°05'W
Del Rio, Tx., U.S. (dĕl rē'ō)	104	29°21'N	100°52'W
Delson, Can. (dĕl'sŭn)	102a	45°24'N	73°32'W
Delta, Co., U.S.	119	38°45'N	108°05'W
Delta, Ut., U.S.	119	39°20'N	112°35'W
Delta Beach, Can.	102f	50°10'N	98°20'W
Delvine, Alb. (dĕl'vē-ná)	175	39°58'N	20°10'E
Dëma, r., Russia (dyĕm'ä)	180	53°40'N	54°30'E
Demba, D.R.C.	236	5°30'S	22°16'E
Dembi Dolo, Eth.	231	8°46'N	34°46'E
Demidov, Russia (dzyĕ'mē-dô'f)	176	55°16'N	31°32'E
Deming, N.M., U.S. (dĕm'ĭng)	104	32°15'N	107°45'W
Demmin, Ger. (dĕm'mēn)	168	53°54'N	13°04'E
Demnat, Mor. (dĕm-nät)	230	31°58'N	7°03'W
Demopolis, Al., U.S. (dē-mŏp'ô-lĭs)	124	32°30'N	87°50'W
Demotte, In., U.S. (dē'mŏt)	111a	41°12'N	87°13'W
Dempo, Gunung, mtn., Indon. (dĕm'pō)	212	4°04'S	103°11'E
Dem'yanka, r., Russia (dyĕm-yän'kä)	184	59°07'N	72°58'E
Demyansk, Russia (dyĕm-yänsk')	176	57°39'N	32°26'E
Denain, Fr. (dē-năN')	170	50°23'N	3°21'E
Denakil Plain, pl., Eth.	231	12°45'N	41°01'E
Denali National Park, rec., Ak., U.S.	106a	63°48'N	153°02'W
Denbigh, Wales, U.K. (dĕn'bĭ)	164	53°15'N	3°25'W
Dendermonde, Bel.	159a	51°02'N	4°04'E
Dendron, Va., U.S. (dĕn'drŭn)	125	37°02'N	76°53'W
Denezhkin Kamen, Gora, mtn., Russia (dzyĕ-ŋĕ'zhkĕn kămĭēŋ)	186a	60°26'N	59°35'E
Denham, Mount, mtn., Jam.	129	18°20'N	77°30'W
Den Helder, Neth. (dĕn hĕl'dĕr)	165	52°55'N	5°45'E
Dénia, Spain	173	38°48'N	0°06'E
Deniliquin, Austl. (dĕ-nĭl'ĭ-kwĭn)	219	35°20'S	144°52'E
Denison, Ia., U.S. (dĕn'ĭ-sŭn)	112	42°01'N	95°22'W
Denison, Tx., U.S.	104	33°45'N	97°02'W
Denizli, Tur. (dĕn-ĭz-lē')	163	37°40'N	29°10'E
Denklingen, Ger. (dĕn'klēn-gĕn)	171c	50°54'N	7°40'E
Denmark, S.C., U.S. (dĕn'märk)	125	33°18'N	81°09'W
Denmark, nation, Eur.	154	56°14'N	8°30'E
Denmark Strait, strt., Eur.	89	66°30'N	27°00'W
Dennilton, S. Afr. (dĕn-ĭl-tŭn)	238c	25°18'S	29°13'E
Dennison, Oh., U.S. (dĕn'ĭ-sŭn)	108	40°25'N	81°20'W
Denpasar, Indon.	212	8°35'S	115°10'E
Denton, Eng., U.K. (dĕn'tŭn)	158a	53°27'N	2°07'W
Denton, Md., U.S.	109	38°55'N	75°50'W
Denton, Tx., U.S.	121	33°12'N	97°06'W
D'Entrecasteaux, Point, c., Austl. (dăN-tr'-kás-tō')	220	34°50'S	114°45'E
D'Entrecasteaux Islands, is., Pap. N. Gui. (dăN-tr'-kás-tō')	213	9°45'S	152°00'E
Denver, Co., U.S. (dĕn'vēr)	104	39°44'N	104°59'W
Deoli, India	202	25°52'N	75°23'E
De Pere, Wi., U.S. (dē pēr')	113	44°25'N	88°04'W
Depew, N.Y., U.S. (dē-pū')	111c	42°55'N	78°43'W
Deping, China (dŭ-pĭŋ)	206	37°28'N	116°57'E
Depue, Il., U.S. (dē pū)	108	41°15'N	89°55'W
De Queen, Ar., U.S. (dē kwēn')	121	34°02'N	94°21'W
De Quincy, La., U.S. (dē kwĭn'sĭ)	123	30°27'N	93°27'W
Dera, Lach, r., Afr. (läk dā'rä)	238a	0°45'N	41°26'E
Dera, Lak, r., Afr.	231	0°45'N	41°30'E
Dera Ghāzi Khān, Pak. (dā'rŭ gä-zē' kan')	199	30°09'N	70°39'E
Dera Ismāīl Khān, Pak. (dā'rŭ ĭs-mä-ēl' kăn')	202	31°55'N	70°51'E
Derbent, Russia (dĕr-bĕnt')	181	42°00'N	48°10'E
Derby, Austl. (där'bē)(dûr'bē)	218	17°20'S	123°40'E
Derby, S. Afr. (där'bĭ)	238c	25°55'S	27°02'E
Derby, Eng., U.K. (där'bē)	161	52°55'N	1°29'W
Derby, Ct., U.S. (dûr'bē)	109	41°20'N	73°05'W
Derbyshire, co., Eng., U.K.	158a	53°11'N	1°30'W
Derdepoort, S. Afr.	238c	24°39'S	26°21'E
Derg, Lough, l., Ire. (lŏk dĕrg)	164	53°00'N	8°09'W
De Ridder, La., U.S. (dē rĭd'ēr)	123	30°50'N	93°18'W
Dermott, Ar., U.S. (dûr'mŏt)	121	33°32'N	91°24'W
Derry, N.H., U.S. (dâr'ĭ)	101a	42°53'N	71°22'W
Derventa, Bos. (dĕr'ven-tá)	175	44°58'N	17°58'E
Derwent, r., Austl. (dĕr'wĕnt)	222	42°21'S	146°30'E
Derwent, r., Eng., U.K.	158a	52°54'N	1°24'W
Des Arc, Ar., U.S. (dāz ärk')	121	34°59'N	91°31'W
Descalvado, Braz. (dĕs-käl-vá-dô)	141a	21°55'S	47°37'W
Descartes, Fr.	170	46°58'N	0°42'E
Deschambault Lake, l., Can.	96	54°40'N	103°35'W
Deschênes, Can.	102c	45°23'N	75°47'W
Deschenes, Lake, l., Can.	102c	45°25'N	75°53'W
Deschutes, r., Or., U.S. (dā-shōōt')	114	44°25'N	121°21'W
Desdemona, Tx., U.S. (dĕz-dē-mō'ná)	122	32°16'N	98°33'W
Dese, Eth.	231	11°00'N	39°51'E
Deseado, r., Arg. (dā-sā-ä'dhō)	144	46°50'S	67°45'W
Desirade Island, i., Guad. (dā-zē-rás')	133b	16°21'N	60°51'W
De Smet, S.D., U.S. (dē smĕt')	112	44°23'N	97°33'W
Des Moines, Ia., U.S. (dē moin')	105	41°35'N	93°37'W
Des Moines, N.M., U.S.	120	36°42'N	103°48'W
Des Moines, Wa., U.S.	116a	46°24'N	122°20'W
Des Moines, r., U.S.	107	42°30'N	94°20'W
Desna, r., Eur. (dyĕs-ná')	181	51°55'N	31°45'E
Desolación, i., Chile (dĕ-sò-lä-syō'n)	144	53°05'S	74°00'W
De Soto, Mo., U.S. (dē sō'tō)	121	38°07'N	90°32'W
Des Peres, Mo., U.S. (dĕs pĕr'ĕs)	117e	38°36'N	90°26'W
Des Plaines, Il., U.S. (dĕs plānz')	111a	42°02'N	87°54'W
Des Plaines, r., U.S.	111a	41°39'N	87°56'W
Dessau, Ger. (dĕsòu)	161	51°50'N	12°15'E
Detmold, Ger. (dĕt'mōld)	168	51°57'N	8°55'E
Detroit, Mi., U.S. (dē-troit')	105	42°22'N	83°10'W
Detroit, Tx., U.S.	121	33°41'N	95°16'W
Detroit Lake, res., Or., U.S.	114	44°42'N	122°10'W
Detroit Lakes, Mn., U.S. (dē-troit'lākz)	112	46°48'N	95°51'W
Detva, Slvk. (dyĕt'vá)	169	48°32'N	19°21'E
Deurne, Bel.	159a	51°13'N	4°27'E
Deutsch Wagram, Aus.	159e	48°19'N	16°34'E
Deux-Montagnes, Can.	102a	45°33'N	73°53'W
Deux Montagnes, Lac des, l., Can.	102a	45°28'N	74°00'W
Deva, Rom. (dā'vä)	163	45°52'N	22°52'E
Dévaványa, Hung. (dā'vô-vän-yô)	169	47°01'N	20°58'E
Develi, Tur. (dĕ'vå-lē)	181	38°20'N	35°10'E
Deventer, Neth. (dĕv'ĕn-tēr)	165	52°14'N	6°07'E
Devils, r., Tx., U.S.	122	29°55'N	101°10'W
Devils Island *see* Diable, Île du, i., Fr. Gu.	143	5°15'N	52°40'W
Devils Lake, N.D., U.S.	104	48°10'N	98°55'W
Devils Lake, l., N.D., U.S. (dĕv''lz)	112	47°57'N	99°04'W
Devils Lake Indian Reservation, I.R., N.D., U.S.	112	48°08'N	99°40'W
Devils Postpile National Monument, rec., Ca., U.S.	118	37°42'N	119°12'W
Devils Tower National Monument, rec., Wy., U.S.	115	44°38'N	105°07'W
Devoll, r., Alb.	175	40°55'N	20°10'E
Devon, Can.	102g	53°23'N	113°43'W
Devon, S. Afr. (dĕv'ŭn)	238c	26°23'S	28°47'E
Devonport, Austl. (dĕv'ŭn-pôrt)	219	41°20'S	146°30'E
Devonport, N.Z.	221a	36°50'S	174°45'E
Devore, Ca., U.S. (dē-vôr')	117a	34°13'N	117°24'W
Dewatto, Wa., U.S. (dē-wát'ō)	116a	47°27'N	123°04'W
Dewey, Ok., U.S. (dū'ĭ)	121	36°48'N	95°55'W
De Witt, Ar., U.S. (dē wĭt')	121	34°17'N	91°22'W
De Witt, Ia., U.S.	113	41°46'N	90°34'W
Dewsbury, Eng., U.K. (dūz'bēr-ĭ)	158a	53°42'N	1°39'W
Dexter, Me., U.S. (dĕks'tēr)	100	45°01'N	69°19'W
Dexter, Mo., U.S.	121	36°46'N	89°56'W
Dezfūl, Iran	198	32°14'N	48°37'E
Dezhnëva, Mys, c., Russia (dyĕzh'nyĭf)	196	68°00'N	172°00'W
Dezhou, China (dŭ-jō)	208	37°28'N	116°17'E
Dhahran *see* Az̧ Z̧ahrān, Sau. Ar.	198	26°13'N	50°00'E
Dhaka, Bngl. (dă'kä) (dăk'á)	199	23°45'N	90°29'E
Dharamtar Creek, r., India	203b	18°49'N	72°54'E
Dharmavaram, India	203	14°32'N	77°43'E
Dhawalāgiri, mtn., Nepal	199	28°42'N	83°31'E
Dhībān, Jord.	197a	31°30'N	35°46'E
Dhidhimótikhon, Grc.	175	41°20'N	26°27'E
Dhule, India	199	20°58'N	74°43'E
Día, i., Grc. (dē'ä)	174a	35°27'N	25°17'E
Diable, Île du, i., Fr. Gu.	143	5°15'N	52°40'W
Diablo, Mount, mtn., Ca., U.S. (dyä'blō)	116b	37°52'N	121°55'W
Diablo Heights, Pan. (dyá'blō)	128a	8°58'N	79°34'W
Diablo Range, mts., Ca., U.S.	116b	37°47'N	121°50'W
Diablotins, Morne, mtn., Dom.	133b	15°31'N	61°24'W

ng-sing; ŋ-baŋk; N-nasalized n; nŏd; cŏmmit; ōld; ôbey; ôrder; oi-boil; fōōd; ò-as oo in foot; ou-out; s-soft; sh-dish; th-thin; pūre; ůnite; ûrn; stŭd; circŭs; ü-as in French tu; '-indeterminate vowel.

ăt; fīnăl; rāte; senāte; ärm; ásk; sofá; fâre;   ch-choose;   dh-as th in other;   bē; ĕvent; bĕt; recĕnt; crātēr;   g-gō; gh-guttural g;   bĭt; ī-short neutral; rīde;   ᴋ-guttural k as ch in German ich;

PRONOUNCING INDEX

Douglas Channel – East Cleveland 289

PLACE (Pronunciation)	PAGE	LAT.	LONG.
Douglas Channel, strt., Can.	94	53°30'N	129°12'W
Douglas Lake, res., Tn., U.S. (dŭg′lăs)	124	36°00'N	83°35'W
Douglas Lake Indian Reserve, I.R., Can.	95	50°10'N	120°49'W
Douglasville, Ga., U.S. (dŭg′lăs-vĭl)	124	33°45'N	84°47'W
Dourada, Serra, mts., Braz. (sĕ′r-rä-dôōō-rà′dă)	143	15°11'S	49°57'W
Dourdan, Fr. (dōōr-däN′)	171b	48°32'N	2°01'E
Douro, r., Port. (dō′ò-rô)	172	41°03'N	8°12'W
Dove, r., Eng., U.K. (dŭv)	158a	52°53'N	1°47'W
Dover, S. Afr.	238c	27°05'S	27°44'E
Dover, Eng., U.K.	154	51°08'N	1°19'E
Dover, De., U.S. (dō vẽr)	105	39°10'N	75°30'W
Dover, N.H., U.S.	109	43°15'N	71°00'W
Dover, N.J., U.S.	110a	40°53'N	74°33'W
Dover, Oh., U.S.	108	40°35'N	81°30'W
Dover, Strait of, strt., Eur.	156	50°50'N	1°15'W
Dover-Foxcroft, Me., U.S. (dō′vẽr fŏks′krŏft)	100	45°10'N	69°15'W
Dovre Fjell, mts., Nor. (dŏv′rĕ fyĕl′)	156	62°03'N	8°36'E
Dow, Il., U.S. (dou)	117e	39°01'N	90°20'W
Dowagiac, Mi., U.S. (dô-wô′jăk)	108	42°00'N	86°05'W
Downers Grove, Il., U.S. (dou′nẽrz grōv)	111a	41°48'N	88°00'W
Downey, Ca., U.S. (dou′nĭ)	117a	33°56'N	118°08'W
Downieville, Ca., U.S. (dou′nĭ-nĭl)	118	39°35'N	120°48'W
Downs, Ks., U.S. (dounz)	120	39°29'N	98°32'W
Doylestown, Oh., U.S. (doilz′toun)	111d	40°58'N	81°43'W
Drâa, Cap, c., Mor. (drà)	230	28°39'N	12°15'W
Drâa, Oued, r., Afr.	230	28°00'N	9°31'W
Drabiv, Ukr.	177	49°57'N	32°14'E
Drac, r., Fr. (dräk)	171	44°50'N	5°47'E
Dracut, Ma., U.S. (dră′kŭt)	101a	42°40'N	71°19'W
Draganovo, Blg. (drä-gä-nō′vô)	175	43°13'N	25°45'E
Drăgăşani, Rom. (drä-gà-shän′ĭ)	175	44°39'N	24°18'E
Draguignan, Fr. (drä-gēn-yäN′)	171	43°35'N	6°28'E
Drahichyn, Bela.	169	52°10'N	25°11'E
Drakensberg, mts., Afr. (drä′kĕnz-bĕrgh)	232	29°15'S	29°07'E
Drake Passage, strt. (drāk păs′ĭj)	139	57°00'S	65°00'W
Dráma, Grc. (drä′mä)	163	41°09'N	24°10'E
Drammen, Nor. (dräm′ĕn)	160	59°45'N	10°15'E
Drau (Drava), r., Eur. (drou)	168	46°44'N	13°45'E
Drava, r., Eur. (drä′vä)	156	45°45'N	17°30'E
Dravograd, Slvn. (drä′vô-gräd′)	174	46°37'N	15°01'E
Drawsko Pomorskie, Pol. (dräv′skō pō-mōr′skyĕ)	168	53°31'N	15°50'E
Drayton Harbor, b., Wa., U.S. (drā′tŭn)	116d	48°58'N	122°40'W
Drayton Plains, Mi., U.S.	111b	42°41'N	83°23'W
Drayton Valley, Can.	95	53°13'N	114°59'W
Drensteinfurt, Ger. (drĕn′shtīn-fōōrt)	171c	51°47'N	7°44'E
Dresden, Ger. (drās′dĕn)	154	51°05'N	13°45'E
Dreux, Fr. (drû)	170	48°44'N	1°24'E
Driefontein, S. Afr.	238c	25°53'S	29°10'E
Drin, r., Alb. (drēn)	175	42°13'N	20°13'E
Drina, r., Serb. (drē′nä)	163	44°09'N	19°30'E
Drinit, Pellg i, b., Alb.	175	41°42'N	19°17'E
Dr. Ir. W. J. van Blommestein Meer, res., Sur.	143	4°45'N	55°05'W
Drissa, r., Eur.	176	55°44'N	28°58'E
Driver, Va., U.S.	110g	36°50'N	76°30'W
Dröbak, Nor. (drû′bäk)	166	59°40'N	10°35'E
Drobeta-Turnu Severin, Rom.	163	43°54'N	24°49'E
Drogheda, Ire. (drō′hē-dȧ)	160	53°43'N	6°15'W
Drohobych, Ukr.	169	49°21'N	23°31'E
Drôme, r., Fr. (drōm)	170	44°42'N	4°53'E
Dronfield, Eng., U.K. (drŏn′fēld)	158a	53°18'N	1°28'W
Drumheller, Can. (drŭm-hĕl-ẽr)	90	51°28'N	112°42'W
Drummond, i., Mi., U.S. (drŭm′ŭnd)	108	46°00'N	83°50'W
Drummondville, Can. (drŭm′ŭnd-vĭl)	91	45°53'N	72°33'W
Drumright, Ok., U.S. (drŭm′rīt)	121	35°59'N	96°37'W
Drunen, Neth.	159a	51°41'N	5°10'E
Drut′, r., Bela. (drōōt)	176	53°40'N	29°45'E
Druya, Bela. (drò′yà)	176	55°45'N	27°26'E
Drwęca, r., Pol. (d′r-vān′tsȧ)	169	53°06'N	19°13'E
Dryden, Can. (drī-dĕn)	91	49°47'N	92°50'W
Drysdale, Austl.	217a	38°11'S	144°34'E
Dry Tortugas, is., Fl., U.S. (tôr-tōō′gäz)	125a	24°37'N	82°45'W
Dry Tortugas National Park, rec., Fl., U.S.	125a	24°42'N	83°02'W
Dschang, Cam. (dshäng)	230	5°34'N	10°09'E
Duabo, Lib.	234	5°40'N	8°05'W
Duagh, Can.	102g	53°43'N	113°24'W
Duarte, Pico, mtn., Dom. Rep. (dŭĭ′ärtĕh pēcô)	129	19°00'N	71°00'W
Duas Barras, Braz. (dōō′äs-bà′r-räs)	141a	22°03'S	42°30'W
Dubai see Dubayy, U.A.E.	198	25°18'N	55°26'E
Dubăsari, Mol.	177	47°16'N	29°11'E
Dubawnt, l., Can. (dōō-bônt′)	92	63°27'N	103°30'W
Dubawnt, r., Can.	92	61°30'N	103°49'W
Dubayy, U.A.E.	198	25°18'N	55°26'E
Dubbo, Austl. (dŭb′ō)	219	32°20'S	148°42'E
Dubie, D.R.C.	237	8°33'S	28°32'E
Dublin, Ire.	154	53°20'N	6°15'W
Dublin, Ca., U.S. (dŭb′lĭn)	116b	37°42'N	121°56'W
Dublin, Ga., U.S.	125	32°33'N	82°55'W
Dublin, Tx., U.S.	122	32°05'N	98°20'W
Dubna, Russia	176	56°44'N	37°10'E
Dubno, Ukr. (dōō′b-nô)	169	50°24'N	25°44'E
Du Bois, Pa., U.S. (dò-bois′)	109	41°10'N	78°45'W
Dubovka, Russia (dò-bôf′kȧ)	181	49°00'N	44°50'E
Dubrovka, Russia (dōō-brôf′kȧ)	186c	59°51'N	30°56'E
Dubrovnik, Cro. (dò′brôv-nĕk) (rä-gōō′sä)	154	42°40'N	18°10'E
Dubrowna, Bela.	176	54°39'N	30°54'E
Dubuque, Ia., U.S. (dò-būk′)	105	42°30'N	90°43'W
Duchesne, Ut., U.S. (dò-shān′)	119	40°12'N	110°23'W
Duchesne, r., Ut., U.S.	119	40°20'N	110°50'W
Duchess, Austl. (dŭch′ĕs)	218	21°30'S	139°55'E
Ducie Island, i., Pit. (dü-sē′)	2	25°30'S	126°20'W
Duck, r., Tn., U.S.	124	35°55'N	87°40'W
Duckabush, r., Wa., U.S. (dŭk′ȧ-bòsh)	116a	47°41'N	123°09'W
Duck Lake, Can.	96	52°47'N	106°13'W
Duck Mountain, mtn., Can.	97	51°35'N	101°00'W
Ducktown, Tn., U.S. (dŭk′toun)	124	35°03'N	84°20'W
Duck Valley Indian Reservation, I.R., Id., U.S.	114	42°02'N	115°49'W
Duckwater Peak, mtn., Nv., U.S. (dŭk-wô-tẽr)	118	39°00'N	115°31'W
Duda, r., Col. (dōō′dä)	142a	3°25'N	74°23'W
Dudinka, Russia (dōō-dĭn′kȧ)	178	69°15'N	85°42'E
Dudley, Eng., U.K. (dŭd′lĭ)	161	52°28'N	2°07'E
Duero, r., Eur.	156	41°30'N	4°30'W
Dufourspitze, mtn., Eur.	168	45°55'N	7°52'E
Dugger, In., U.S. (dŭg′ẽr)	108	39°00'N	87°10'W
Dugi Otok, i., Serb. (dōō′gē ō′tôk)	174	44°03'N	14°40'E
Duisburg, Ger. (dōō′ĭs-bòrgh)	161	51°26'N	6°46'E
Dukhān, Qatar	201	25°25'N	50°48'E
Dukhovshchina, Russia (dōō-ĸôfsh-′chēnȧ)	176	55°13'N	32°26'E
Dukinfield, Eng., U.K. (dŭk′ĭn-fēld)	158a	53°28'N	2°05'W
Dukla Pass, p., Eur. (dò′klä)	161	49°25'N	21°44'E
Dulce, Golfo, b., C.R. (gōl′fô dōōl′sä)	129	8°25'N	83°13'W
Dülken, Ger. (dül′kĕn)	171c	51°15'N	6°21'E
Dülmen, Ger. (dül′mĕn)	171c	51°50'N	7°17'E
Duluth, Mn., U.S. (dò-lōōth′)	105	46°50'N	92°07'W
Dumai, Indon.	197b	1°39'N	101°30'E
Dumali Point, c., Phil. (dōō-mä′lē)	213a	13°07'N	121°42'E
Dumas, Tx., U.S.	120	35°52'N	101°58'W
Dumbarton, Scot., U.K. (dŭm′bär-tŭn)	164	56°00'N	4°35'W
Dum-Dum, India	202a	22°37'N	88°25'E
Dumfries, Scot., U.K. (dŭm-frēs′)	164	55°05'N	3°40'W
Dumjor, India	202a	22°37'N	88°14'E
Dumont, N.J., U.S. (dōō′mŏnt)	110a	40°56'N	74°00'W
Dumyāt, Egypt	231	31°22'N	31°50'E
Dunaföldvär, Hung. (dò′nô-fûld′vär)	169	46°48'N	18°55'E
Dunaïvtsi, Ukr.	177	48°52'N	26°51'E
Dunajec, r., Pol. (dò-nä′yĕts)	169	49°52'N	20°53'E
Dunaújváros, Hung.	169	46°57'N	18°55'E
Dunay, Russia (dōō′nĭ)	186c	59°59'N	30°57'E
Dunbar, W.V., U.S.	108	38°20'N	81°45'W
Duncan, Can. (dŭn′kăn)	90	48°47'N	123°42'W
Duncan, Ok., U.S.	121	34°29'N	97°56'W
Duncan, r., Can.	95	50°30'N	116°45'W
Duncan Dam, dam, Can.	95	50°15'N	116°55'W
Duncan Lake, l., Can.	95	50°20'N	117°00'W
Duncansby Head, c., Scot., U.K. (dŭn′kănz-bĭ)	164	58°40'N	3°01'W
Duncanville, Tx., U.S. (dŭn′kăn-vĭl)	117c	32°39'N	96°55'W
Dundalk, Ire. (dŭn′kôk)	160	54°00'N	6°18'W
Dundalk, Md., U.S.	110e	39°16'N	76°31'W
Dundalk Bay, b., Ire. (dŭn′dôk)	164	53°55'N	6°15'W
Dundas, Can. (dŭn-dăs′)	99	43°16'N	79°58'W
Dundas, l., Austl. (dŭn-dȧs)	220	32°15'S	122°00'E
Dundas Island, i., Can.	94	54°33'N	130°55'W
Dundas Strait, strt., Austl.	220	10°35'S	131°15'E
Dundedin, Fl., U.S. (dŭn-ē′dĭn)	125a	28°00'N	82°43'W
Dundee, S. Afr.	233c	28°14'S	30°16'E
Dundee, Scot., U.K.	154	56°30'N	2°55'W
Dundee, Il., U.S. (dŭn-dē)	111a	42°06'N	88°17'W
Dundrum Bay, b., N. Ire., U.K. (dŭn-drŭm′)	164	54°13'N	5°47'W
Dunedin, N.Z.	221a	45°48'S	170°32'E
Dunellen, N.J., U.S. (dŭn-ĕl′l′n)	110a	40°36'N	74°28'W
Dunfermline, Scot., U.K. (dŭn-fẽrm′lĭn)	164	56°05'N	3°30'W
Dungarvan, Ire. (dŭn-gàr′vȧn)	164	52°06'N	7°50'W
Dungeness, Wa., U.S. (dŭnj-nĕs′)	116a	48°09'N	123°07'W
Dungeness, r., Wa., U.S.	116a	48°03'N	123°10'W
Dungeness Spit, Wa., U.S.	116a	48°11'N	123°03'W
Dunhua, China (dòn-hwä)	205	43°18'N	128°10'E
Dunkerque, Fr. (dŭN-kĕrk′)	161	51°02'N	2°37'E
Dunkirk, In., U.S. (dŭn′kûrk)	108	40°20'N	85°25'W
Dunkwa, Ghana	234	5°22'N	1°12'W
Dun Laoghaire, Ire. (dŭn-lā′rĕ)	160	53°16'N	6°09'W
Dunlap, Ia., U.S. (dŭn′lăp)	112	41°53'N	95°33'W
Dunlap, Tn., U.S.	124	35°23'N	85°23'W
Dunmore, Pa., U.S. (dŭn′mōr)	109	41°25'N	75°30'W
Dunn, N.C., U.S. (dŭn)	125	35°18'N	78°37'W
Dunnellon, Fl., U.S. (dŭn-ĕl′ŏn)	125	29°02'N	82°28'W
Dunnville, Can. (dŭn′vĭl)	99	42°55'N	79°40'W
Dunqulah, Sudan	231	19°21'N	30°19'E
Dunsmuir, Ca., U.S. (dŭnz′mūr)	114	41°08'N	122°17'W
Dunwoody, Ga., U.S. (dŭn-wòd′ĭ)	110c	33°57'N	84°20'W
Duolun, China (dwô-lōōn)	205	42°12'N	116°15'E
Du Page, r., Il., U.S. (dōō pāj)	111a	41°41'N	88°11'W
Du Page, East Branch, r., Il., U.S.	111a	41°42'N	88°09'W
Du Page, West Branch, r., Il., U.S.	111a	41°42'N	88°09'W
Dupax, Phil. (dōō′päks)	213a	16°16'N	121°06'E
Dupo, Il., U.S. (dū′pō)	117e	38°31'N	90°12'W
Duque de Caxias, Braz. (dōō′kĕ-dĕ-kȧ′shyàs)	141a	22°46'S	43°18'W
Duquesne, Pa., U.S. (dò-kān′)	111e	40°22'N	79°51'W
Du Quoin, Il., U.S. (dò-kwoin′)	121	38°01'N	89°14'W
Durance, r., Fr. (dü-räNs′)	161	43°46'N	5°52'E
Durand, Mi., U.S. (dů-rănd′)	108	42°50'N	84°00'W
Durand, Wi., U.S.	113	44°37'N	91°58'W
Durango, Mex. (dōō-rä′n-gô)	128	24°02'N	104°42'W
Durango, Co., U.S. (dò-răn′gō)	119	37°15'N	107°55'W
Durango, state, Mex.	128	25°00'N	106°00'W
Durant, Ms., U.S. (dů-rănt′)	124	33°05'N	89°50'W
Durant, Ok., U.S.	121	33°59'N	96°23'W
Duratón, r., Spain (dōō-rä-tōn′)	172	41°30'N	3°55'W
Durazno, Ur. (dōō-räz′nō)	144	33°21'S	56°31'W
Durazno, dept., Ur.	141c	33°00'S	56°35'W
Durban, S. Afr. (dûr′băn)	232	29°48'S	31°00'E
Durbanville, S. Afr. (dûr-bȧn′vĭl)	232a	33°50'S	18°39'E
Durbe, Lat. (dōōr′bĕ)	167	56°36'N	21°24'E
Đurđevac, Cro.	163	46°03'N	17°03'E
Düren, Ger. (dü′rĕn)	171c	50°48'N	6°30'E
Durham, Eng., U.K. (dûr′ăm)	164	54°47'N	1°46'W
Durham, N.C., U.S.	105	36°00'N	78°55'W
Durham Downs, Austl.	222	27°30'S	141°55'E
Durrës, Alb. (dòr′ĕs)	154	41°19'N	19°27'E
Duryea, Pa., U.S. (dōōr-yā′)	109	41°20'N	75°50'W
Dushan, China	206	31°38'N	116°16'E
Dushan, China (dōō-shän)	209	25°50'N	107°42'E
Dushanbe, Taj.	183	38°30'N	68°45'E
Düsseldorf, Ger. (düs′ĕl-dôrf)	161	51°14'N	6°47'E
Dussen, Neth.	159a	51°43'N	4°58'E
Dutalan Ula, mts., Mong.	208	49°25'N	112°40'E
Dutch Harbor, Ak., U.S. (dŭch här′bẽr)	106a	53°58'N	166°30'W
Duvall, Wa., U.S. (dōō′vâl)	116a	47°44'N	121°59'W
Duwamish, r., Wa., U.S. (dōō-wăm′ĭsh)	116a	47°24'N	122°18'W
Duyun, China (dōō-yòn)	204	26°18'N	107°40'E
Dvinskaya Guba, b., Russia	180	65°10'N	38°40'E
Dwārka, India	202	22°18'N	68°59'E
Dwight, Il., U.S. (dwīt)	108	41°00'N	88°20'W
Dworshak Res, Id., U.S.	114	46°45'N	115°50'W
Dyat′kovo, Russia (dyät′kō-vō)	176	53°36'N	34°19'E
Dyer, In., U.S. (dī′ẽr)	111a	41°30'N	87°31'W
Dyersburg, Tn., U.S. (dī′ẽrz-bûrg)	124	36°02'N	89°23'W
Dyersville, Ia., U.S. (dī′ẽrz-vĭl)	113	42°28'N	91°09'W
Dyes Inlet, Wa., U.S. (dīz)	116a	47°37'N	122°45'W
Dykhtau, Gora, mtn., Russia	182	43°03'N	43°08'E
Dyment, Can. (dī′mĕnt)	97	49°37'N	92°19'W
Dzamïn Üüd, Mong.	205	44°38'N	111°32'E
Dzaoudzi, May. (dzou′dzĭ)	233	12°44'S	45°15'E
Dzavhan, r., Mong.	204	48°19'N	94°08'E
Dzerzhinsk, Russia	180	56°20'N	43°50'E
Dzerzhyns′k, Ukr.	177	48°26'N	37°50'E
Dzhalal-Abad, Kyrg. (jȧ-läl′ȧ-bät′)	183	40°56'N	73°00'E
Dzhambul see Zhambyl, Kaz.	183	42°51'N	71°29'E
Dzhankoi, Ukr.	181	45°43'N	34°22'E
Dzhizak, Uzb. (dzhĕ′zäk)	183	40°13'N	67°58'E
Dzhugdzhur Khrebet, mts., Russia (jòg-jōōr′)	179	56°15'N	137°00'E
Działoszyce, Pol. (jyä-wō-shĕ′tsĕ)	169	50°21'N	20°22'E
Dzibalchén, Mex. (zē-bäl-chĕ′n)	132a	19°25'N	89°39'W
Dzidzantún, Mex. (zēd-zän-tōō′n)	132a	21°18'N	89°00'W
Dzierżoniów, Pol. (dzyĕr-zhôn′yŭf)	168	50°44'N	16°38'E
Dzilam González, Mex. (zē-lä′m-gôn-zä′lĕz)	132a	21°21'N	88°53'W
Dzitás, Mex. (zē-tà′s)	132a	20°47'N	88°32'W
Dzungaria, reg., China (dzòŋ-gä′rĭ-ȧ)	204	44°39'N	86°13'E
Dzungarian Gate, p., Asia	204	45°00'N	88°00'E
Dzyarzhynsk, Bela.	176	53°41'N	27°14'E

E

PLACE (Pronunciation)	PAGE	LAT.	LONG.
Eagle, W.V., U.S.	108	38°10'N	81°20'W
Eagle, r., Co., U.S.	119	39°32'N	106°28'W
Eaglecliff, Wa., U.S. (ē′gl-klĭf)	116c	46°10'N	123°13'W
Eagle Creek, r., In., U.S.	111g	39°54'N	86°17'W
Eagle Grove, Ia., U.S.	113	42°39'N	93°55'W
Eagle Lake, Me., U.S.	100	47°03'N	68°38'W
Eagle Lake, Tx., U.S.	123	29°37'N	96°20'W
Eagle Lake, l., Ca., U.S.	114	40°45'N	120°52'W
Eagle Mountain, Ca., U.S.	118	33°49'N	115°27'W
Eagle Mountain L, Tx., U.S.	117c	32°56'N	97°27'W
Eagle Pass, Tx., U.S.	104	28°49'N	100°30'W
Eagle Pk, Ca., U.S.	114	41°18'N	120°11'W
Ealing, Eng., U.K. (ē′lĭng)	158b	51°29'N	0°19'W
Earle, Ar., U.S. (ûrl)	121	35°14'N	90°28'W
Earlington, Ky., U.S. (ûr′lĭng-tŭn)	124	37°15'N	87°31'W
Easley, S.C., U.S. (ēz′lĭ)	125	34°48'N	82°37'W
East, Mount, mtn., Pan.	128a	9°09'N	79°46'W
East Alton, Il., U.S. (ôl′tŭn)	117e	38°53'N	90°08'W
East Angus, Can. (ăŋ′gŭs)	99	45°35'N	71°40'W
East Aurora, N.Y., U.S. (ô-rō′rȧ)	111c	42°46'N	78°38'W
East Bay, b., Tx., U.S.	123a	29°30'N	94°41'W
East Bernstadt, Ky., U.S. (bûrn′stát)	124	37°09'N	84°08'W
Eastbourne, Eng., U.K. (ēst′bôrn)	165	50°48'N	0°16'E
East Caicos, i., T./C. Is. (kī′kōs)	135	21°40'N	71°35'W
East Cape, c., N.Z.	221a	37°37'S	178°33'E
East Cape see Dezhnëva, Mys, c., Russia	196	68°00'N	172°00'W
East Carondelet, Il., U.S. (kȧ-rŏn′dĕ-lĕt)	117e	38°33'N	90°14'W
East Cherokee Indian Reservation, I.R., N.C., U.S.	124	35°33'N	83°12'W
East Chicago, In., U.S. (shĭ-kô′gō)	111a	41°39'N	87°29'W
East China Sea, sea, Asia	205	30°28'N	125°52'E
East Cleveland, Oh., U.S. (klēv′lănd)	111d	41°33'N	81°35'W

ng-sing; ŋ-baŋk; N-nasalized n; nŏd; cŏmmit; ōld; ôbey; ôrder; oi-boil; fōōd; ò-as oo in foot; ou-out; s-soft; sh-dish; th-thin; pūre; ûnite; ûrn; stŭd; circŭs; ü-as in French tu; ′-indeterminate vowel.

290 East Cote Blanche Bay – Ellice Islands PRONOUNCING INDEX

PLACE (Pronunciation)	PAGE	LAT.	LONG.
East Cote Blanche Bay, b., La., U.S. (kōt blänsh′)	123	29°30′N	92°07′W
East Des Moines, r., Ia., U.S. (dē moin′)	113	42°57′N	94°17′W
East Detroit, Mi., U.S. (dē-troit′)	111b	42°28′N	82°57′W
Easter Island see Pascua, Isla de, i., Chile	241	26°50′S	109°00′W
Eastern Ghāts, mts., India	199	13°50′N	78°45′E
Eastern Turkestan, hist. reg., China (tòr-kĕ-stän′)(tûr-kĕ-stăn′)	204	39°40′N	78°20′E
East Grand Forks, Mn., U.S. (grănd fôrks)	112	47°56′N	97°02′W
East Greenwich, R.I., U.S. (grĭn′ĭj)	110b	41°40′N	71°27′W
Easthampton, Ma., U.S. (ēst-hămp′tŭn)	109	42°15′N	72°45′W
East Hartford, Ct., U.S. (härt′fērd)	109	41°45′N	72°35′W
East Helena, Mt., U.S. (hĕ-hē′nȧ)	115	46°31′N	111°50′W
East Ilsley, Eng., U.K. (ĭl′slē)	158b	51°30′N	1°18′W
East Jordan, Mi., U.S. (jôr′dăn)	108	45°05′N	85°05′W
East Kansas City, Mo., U.S. (kăn′zȧs)	117f	39°09′N	94°30′W
Eastland, Tx., U.S. (ēst′lănd)	122	32°24′N	98°47′W
East Lansing, Mi., U.S. (lăn′sĭng)	108	42°45′N	84°30′W
Eastlawn, Mi., U.S.	111b	42°15′N	83°35′W
East Leavenworth, Mo., U.S. (lĕv′ĕn-wûrth)	117f	39°18′N	94°50′W
East Liverpool, Oh., U.S. (lĭv′ēr-pōōl)	108	40°40′N	80°35′W
East London, S. Afr. (lŭn′dŭn)	232	33°02′S	27°54′E
East Los Angeles, Ca., U.S. (lōs ăŋ′hȧ-lās)	117a	34°01′N	118°09′W
Eastmain, r., Can. (ēst′mān)	93	52°12′N	73°19′W
Eastman, Ga., U.S. (ēst′măn)	124	32°10′N	83°11′W
East Millstone, N.J., U.S. (mĭl′stōn)	110a	40°30′N	74°35′W
East Moline, Il., U.S. (mô-lēn′)	113	41°31′N	90°28′W
East Nishnabotna, r., Ia., U.S. (nĭsh-nȧ-bŏt′nȧ)	112	40°53′N	95°23′W
Easton, Md., U.S. (ēs′tŭn)	109	38°45′N	76°05′W
Easton, Pa., U.S.	109	40°45′N	75°15′W
Easton L, Ct., U.S.	110a	41°10′N	73°17′W
East Orange, N.J., U.S. (ŏr′ĕnj)	110a	40°46′N	74°12′W
East Pakistan see Bangladesh, nation, Asia	199	24°15′N	90°00′E
East Palo Alto, Ca., U.S.	116b	37°27′N	122°07′W
East Peoria, Il., U.S. (pē-ō′rĭ-ȧ)	108	40°40′N	89°30′W
East Pittsburgh, Pa., U.S. (pĭts′bûrg)	111e	40°24′N	79°50′W
East Point, Ga., U.S.	110c	33°41′N	84°27′W
Eastport, Me., U.S. (ēst′pōrt)	100	44°53′N	67°01′W
East Providence, R.I., U.S. (prŏv′ĭ-dĕns)	110b	41°49′N	71°22′W
East Retford, Eng., U.K. (rĕt′fērd)	158a	53°19′N	0°56′W
East Riding of Yorkshire, co., Eng., U.K.	158a	53°45′N	0°40′W
East Rochester, N.Y., U.S. (rŏch′ĕs-tēr)	109	43°10′N	77°30′W
East Saint Louis, Il., U.S.	105	38°38′N	90°10′W
East Siberian Sea, sea, Russia (sī-bĭr′y′n)	179	73°00′N	153°28′E
Eastsound, Wa., U.S. (ēst-sound)	116d	48°42′N	122°42′W
East Stroudsburg, Pa., U.S. (stroudz′bûrg)	109	41°00′N	75°10′W
East Syracuse, N.Y., U.S. (sĭr′ȧ-kūs)	109	43°05′N	76°00′W
East Tavaputs Plateau, plat., Ut., U.S. (tă-vă′-pŭts)	119	39°25′N	109°45′W
East Tawas, Mi., U.S. (tô′wăs)	108	44°15′N	83°30′W
East Timor, nation, Asia	213	9°00′S	125°30′E
East Walker, r., U.S. (wôk′ēr)	118	38°36′N	119°02′W
Eaton, Co., U.S. (ē′tŭn)	120	40°31′N	104°42′W
Eaton, Oh., U.S.	108	39°45′N	84°40′W
Eaton Estates, Oh., U.S.	111d	41°19′N	82°01′W
Eaton Rapids, Mi., U.S. (răp′ĭdz)	108	42°30′N	84°40′W
Eatonton, Ga., U.S. (ē′tŭn-tŭn)	124	33°20′N	83°24′W
Eatontown, N.J., U.S. (ē′tŭn-toun)	110a	40°18′N	74°04′W
Eau Claire, Wi., U.S. (ō klâr′)	105	44°47′N	91°32′W
Ebeltoft, Den. (ĕ′bĕl-tŭft)	166	56°11′N	10°39′E
Ebensburg, Pa., U.S.	109	40°29′N	78°44′W
Ebersberg, Ger. (ĕ′bĕrs-bĕrgh)	159d	48°05′N	11°58′E
Ebingen, Ger. (ā′bĭng-ĕn)	168	48°13′N	9°04′E
Eboli, Italy (ĕb′ō-lē)	174	40°38′N	15°04′E
Ebolowa, Cam.	230	2°54′N	11°09′E
Ebreichsdorf, Aus.	159e	47°58′N	16°24′E
Ebrié, Lagune, b., C. Iv.	234	5°20′N	4°50′W
Ebro, r., Spain (ā′brō)	156	42°00′N	2°00′W
Eccles, Eng., U.K. (ĕk″lz)	158a	53°29′N	2°20′W
Eccles, W.V., U.S.	108	37°45′N	81°10′W
Eccleshall, Eng., U.K.	158a	52°51′N	2°15′W
Eceabat, Tur.	175	40°10′N	26°21′E
Echague, Phil. (ā-chä′gwä)	213a	16°43′N	121°40′E
Echandi, Cerro, mtn., N.A. (sĕ′r-rô-ĕ-chä′nd)	133	9°05′N	82°51′W
Ech Cheliff, Alg.	230	36°14′N	1°32′E
Echimamish, r., Can.	97	54°15′N	97°30′W
Echmiadzin, Arm.	182	40°10′N	44°18′E
Echo Bay, Can. (ĕk′ō)	117k	46°29′N	84°04′W
Echoing, r., Can. (ĕk′ō-ĭng)	97	55°15′N	91°30′W
Echternach, Lux. (ĕk′tēr-näk)	171	49°48′N	6°25′E
Echuca, Austl. (ē-chō′kȧ)	219	36°10′S	144°47′E
Écija, Spain (ā′thē-hä)	162	37°20′N	5°07′W
Eckernförde, Ger.	168	54°27′N	9°51′E
Eclipse, Va., U.S. (ē-klĭps′)	110g	36°55′N	76°29′W
Ecorse, Mi., U.S. (ē-kôrs′)	111b	42°15′N	83°09′W
Ecuador, nation, S.A. (ĕk′wȧ-dôr)	142	0°00′N	78°30′W
Ed, Erit.	231	13°57′N	41°37′E
Eddyville, Ky., U.S. (ĕd′ĭ-vĭl)	124	37°03′N	88°03′W
Ede, Nig.	235	7°44′N	4°27′E
Edéa, Cam. (ĕ-dā′ä)	230	3°48′N	10°08′E
Eden, Tx., U.S.	122	31°13′N	99°51′W
Eden, Ut., U.S.	117b	41°18′N	111°49′W
Eden, r., Eng., U.K. (ē′dĕn)	164	54°40′N	2°35′W
Edenbridge, Eng., U.K. (ē′dĕn-brĭj)	158b	51°11′N	0°05′E
Edenham, Eng., U.K. (ē′d′n-ăm)	158a	52°46′N	0°25′W
Eden Prairie, Mn., U.S. (prâr′ĭ)	117g	44°51′N	93°29′W
Edenton, N.C., U.S. (ē′dĕn-tŭn)	125	36°02′N	76°37′W
Edenton, Oh., U.S.	111f	39°14′N	84°02′W
Edenvale, S. Afr. (ĕd′ĕn-väl)	233b	26°09′S	28°10′E
Edenville, S. Afr. (ĕd′n-vĭl)	238c	27°33′S	27°42′E
Eder, r., Ger. (ā′dēr)	168	51°05′N	8°52′E
Édessa, Grc.	163	40°48′N	22°04′E
Edgefield, S.C., U.S. (ĕj′fēld)	125	33°52′N	81°55′W
Edgeley, N.D., U.S. (ĕj′lĭ)	112	46°24′N	98°43′W
Edgemont, S.D., U.S. (ĕj′mŏnt)	112	43°19′N	103°50′W
Edgerton, Wi., U.S. (ĕj′ēr-tŭn)	113	42°49′N	89°06′W
Edgewater, Al., U.S. (ĕj-wô-tēr)	110h	33°31′N	86°52′W
Edgewater, Md., U.S.	110e	38°58′N	76°35′W
Edgewood, Can. (ĕj′wŏd)	95	49°47′N	118°08′W
Edina, Mn., U.S. (ē-dī′nȧ)	117g	44°55′N	93°20′W
Edina, Mo., U.S.	121	40°10′N	92°11′W
Edinburg, In., U.S. (ĕd′′n-bûrg)	108	39°20′N	85°55′W
Edinburg, Tx., U.S.	122	26°18′N	98°08′W
Edinburgh, Scot., U.K. (ĕd′′n-bŭr-ō)	154	55°57′N	3°10′W
Edirne, Tur.	175	41°41′N	26°35′E
Edisto, r., S.C., U.S. (ĕd′ĭs-tō)	125	33°10′N	80°50′W
Edisto, North Fork, r., S.C., U.S.	125	33°42′N	81°24′W
Edisto, South Fork, r., S.C., U.S.	125	33°43′N	81°35′W
Edisto Island, S.C., U.S.	125	32°32′N	80°20′W
Edmond, Ok., U.S. (ĕd′mŭnd)	121	35°39′N	97°29′W
Edmonds, Wa., U.S. (ĕd′mŭndz)	116a	47°49′N	122°23′W
Edmonton, Can.	90	53°33′N	113°28′W
Edmundston, Can. (ĕd′mŭn-stŭn)	91	47°22′N	68°20′W
Edna, Tx., U.S. (ĕd′nȧ)	123	28°59′N	96°39′W
Edremit, Tur. (ĕd-rĕ-mēt′)	163	39°35′N	27°00′E
Edremit Körfezi, b., Tur.	175	39°28′N	26°35′E
Edson, Can. (ĕd′sŭn)	90	53°35′N	116°26′W
Edward, i., Can. (ĕd′wērd)	98	48°21′N	88°29′W
Edward, l., Afr.	232	0°25′S	29°40′E
Edwardsville, Il., U.S. (ĕd′wērdz-vĭl)	117e	38°49′N	89°58′W
Edwardsville, In., U.S.	111h	38°17′N	85°53′W
Edwardsville, Ks., U.S.	117f	39°04′N	94°49′W
Eel, r., Ca., U.S. (ēl)	114	40°39′N	124°15′W
Eel, r., In., U.S.	108	40°50′N	85°55′W
Efate, i., Vanuatu (ā-fä′tä)	221	18°02′S	168°29′E
Effigy Mounds National Monument, rec., Ia., U.S. (ĕf′ĭ-jü mounds)	113	43°04′N	91°15′W
Effingham, Il., U.S. (ĕf′ĭng-hăm)	108	39°05′N	88°30′W
Ega, r., Spain (ā′gä)	172	42°40′N	2°20′W
Egadi, Isole, is., Italy (ĕ′sō-lĕ-ĕ′gä-dē)	162	38°01′N	12°00′E
Egegik, Ak., U.S. (ĕg′ĕ-jĭt)	103	58°10′N	157°22′W
Eger, Hung. (ĕ gĕr)	169	47°53′N	20°24′E
Egersund, Nor. (ĕ′ghĕr-sōn′)	160	58°29′N	6°01′E
Egg Harbor, N.J., U.S. (ĕg här′bēr)	109	39°30′N	74°35′W
Egham, Eng., U.K. (ĕg′ŭm)	158b	51°24′N	0°33′W
Egiyn, r., Mong.	204	49°41′N	100°40′E
Egmont, Cape, c., N.Z. (ĕg′mŏnt)	221a	39°18′S	173°49′E
Egypt, nation, Afr. (ē′jĭpt)	231	26°58′N	27°01′E
Eha-Amufu, Nig.	235	6°40′N	7°46′E
Eibar, Spain (ā′ē-bär)	172	43°12′N	2°20′W
Eichstätt, Ger. (īk′shtät)	168	48°54′N	11°14′E
Eichwalde, Ger. (īk′väl-dĕ)	159b	52°22′N	13°37′E
Eidfjord, Nor. (ĕĭd′fyôr)	166	60°28′N	7°04′E
Eidsvoll, Nor. (ĭdhs′vôl)	160	60°19′N	11°15′E
Eifel, mts., Ger. (ī′fĕl)	168	50°08′N	6°30′E
Eighty Mile Beach, cst., Austl.	220	19°00′S	121°00′E
Eilenburg, Ger. (ī′lĕn-bòrgh)	168	51°27′N	12°38′E
Einbeck, Ger. (īn′bĕk)	168	51°49′N	9°52′E
Eindhoven, Neth. (īnd′hō-vĕn)	165	51°29′N	5°20′E
Eisenach, Ger. (ī′zĕn-äk)	161	50°58′N	10°18′E
Eisenhüttenstadt, Ger.	168	52°08′N	14°40′E
Eivissa, Spain	173	38°55′N	1°24′E
Eivissa, i., Spain	156	38°55′N	1°24′E
Ejea de los Caballeros, Spain	172	42°07′N	1°05′W
Ejura, Ghana	234	7°23′N	1°22′W
Ejutla de Crespo, Mex. (ā-hōt′lä dā krās′pō)	131	16°34′N	96°44′W
Ekanga, D.R.C.	236	2°23′S	23°14′E
Ekenäs, Fin. (ĕ′kĕ-nâs)	167	59°59′N	23°25′E
Ekeren, Bel.	159a	51°17′N	4°27′E
Ekoli, D.R.C.	236	0°23′S	24°16′E
El Aaiún, W. Sah.	230	26°45′N	13°15′W
El Affroun, Alg. (ĕl ȧf-froun′)	173	36°28′N	2°38′E
Elands, r., S. Afr. (ēlånds)	233c	31°48′S	26°09′E
Elands, r., S. Afr.	238c	25°11′S	28°52′E
El Arahal, Spain (ĕl ä-rä-äl′)	172	37°17′N	5°32′W
El Arba, Alg.	173	36°35′N	3°10′E
Elat, Isr.	198	29°34′N	34°57′E
Elazığ, Tur. (ĕl-ä′zĕz)	198	38°40′N	39°00′E
Elba, Al., U.S. (ĕl′bȧ)	124	31°25′N	86°01′W
Elba, Isola d′, i., Italy (ē-sō lä-d-ĕl′bȧ)	162	42°42′N	10°25′E
El Banco, Col. (ĕl băn′cô)	142	8°58′N	74°01′W
Elbansan, Alb. (ĕl-bä-sän′)	163	41°08′N	20°05′E
Elbe (Labe), r., Eur. (ĕl′bĕ)(lä′bĕ)	156	52°30′N	11°30′E
Elbert, Mount, mtn., Co., U.S. (ĕl′bērt)	106	39°05′N	106°25′W
Elberton, Ga., U.S. (ĕl′bēr-tŭn)	125	34°05′N	82°53′W
Elbeuf, Fr. (ĕl-bûf′)	161	49°16′N	0°59′E
El Beyadh, Alg.	162	33°42′N	1°06′E
Elbistan, Tur. (ĕl-bē-stän′)	163	38°20′N	37°10′E
Elbląg, Pol. (ĕl′blăng)	160	54°11′N	19°25′E
El Bonillo, Spain (ĕl bō-nēl′yō)	172	38°56′N	2°31′W
El Boulaïda, Alg.	230	36°33′N	2°45′E
Elbow, r., Can. (ĕl′bō)	102e	51°03′N	114°24′W
Elbow Cay, i., Bah.	134	26°25′N	76°55′W
Elbow Lake, Mn., U.S.	112	46°00′N	95°59′W
El′brus, Gora, mtn., Russia (ĕl′brŏs′)	178	43°20′N	42°25′E
Elbrus, Mount see El′brus, Gora, mtn., Russia	178	43°20′N	42°25′E
Elburz Mountains, mts., Iran (ĕl′bòrz′)	198	36°30′N	51°00′E
El Cajon, Col. (ĕl-kä-kô′n)	142a	4°50′N	76°35′W
El Cajon, Ca., U.S.	118a	32°48′N	116°58′W
El Cambur, Ven. (käm-bōōr′)	143b	10°24′N	68°06′W
El Campo, Tx., U.S. (kăm′pō)	123	29°13′N	96°17′W
El Carmen, Chile (kȧ′r-mĕn)	141b	34°14′S	71°23′W
El Carmen, Col. (kȧ′r-mĕn)	142	9°54′N	75°12′W
El Casco, Ca., U.S. (kăs′kô)	117a	33°59′N	117°08′W
El Centro, Ca., U.S. (sĕn′trō)	118	32°47′N	115°33′W
El Cerrito, Ca., U.S. (sĕr-rē′tō)	116b	37°55′N	122°19′W
El Cuyo, Mex.	132a	21°30′N	87°42′W
Elda, Spain (ĕl′dä)	173	38°28′N	0°44′W
El Djelfa, Alg.	230	34°40′N	3°17′E
El Djouf, des., Afr. (ĕl djōōf)	230	21°45′N	7°05′W
Eldon, Ia., U.S. (ĕl-dŭn)	113	40°55′N	92°15′W
Eldon, Mo., U.S.	121	38°21′N	92°36′W
Eldora, Ia., U.S. (ĕl-dō′rȧ)	113	42°21′N	93°08′W
El Dorado, Ar., U.S. (ĕl dô-rä′dō)	105	33°13′N	92°39′W
Eldorado, Il., U.S.	108	37°50′N	88°30′W
El Dorado, Ks., U.S.	121	37°49′N	96°51′W
Eldorado Springs, Mo., U.S. (sprĭngz)	121	37°51′N	94°02′W
Eldoret, Kenya (ĕl-dō-rĕt′)	237	0°31′N	35°17′E
El Ebano, Mex. (ā-bä′nō)	130	22°13′N	98°26′W
Electra, Tx., U.S. (ē-lĕk′trȧ)	120	34°02′N	98°54′W
Electric Peak, mtn., Mt., U.S. (ē-lĕk′trĭk)	115	45°03′N	110°52′W
Elek, r.	181	51°20′N	53°10′E
Elektrogorsk, Russia (ĕl-yĕk′trō-gôrsk)	186b	55°53′N	38°48′E
Elektrostal′, Russia (ĕl-yĕk′trō-stál)	186b	55°47′N	38°27′E
Elektrougli, Russia	186b	55°43′N	38°13′E
Elephant Butte Reservoir, res., N.M., U.S. (ĕl′ē-fănt būt)	106	33°25′N	107°10′W
El Escorial, Spain (ĕl-ĕs-kō-ryä′l)	173a	40°38′N	4°08′W
El Espino, Nic. (ĕl-ĕs-pē′nō)	132	13°26′N	86°48′W
Eleuthera, i., Bah. (ē-lū′thēr-ȧ)	129	25°05′N	76°10′W
Eleuthera Point, c., Bah.	134	24°35′N	76°05′W
Eleven Point, r., Mo., U.S. (ē-lĕv′ĕn)	121	36°53′N	91°39′W
Elgin, Scot., U.K.	164	57°40′N	3°30′W
Elgin, Il., U.S. (ĕl′jĭn)	111a	42°03′N	88°16′W
Elgin, Ne., U.S.	112	41°58′N	98°04′W
Elgin, Or., U.S.	114	45°34′N	117°58′W
Elgin, Tx., U.S.	123	30°21′N	97°22′W
Elgin, Wa., U.S.	116a	47°23′N	122°42′W
Elgon, Mount, mtn., Afr. (ĕl′gŏn)	231	1°00′N	34°25′E
El Grara, Alg.	162	32°50′N	4°26′E
El Grullo, Mex. (grōōl-yô)	130	19°46′N	104°10′W
El Guapo, Ven. (gwȧ′pô)	143b	10°07′N	66°00′W
El Hank, reg., Afr.	230	23°44′N	6°45′W
El Hatillo, Ven. (ä-tē′l-yô)	143b	10°08′N	65°13′W
Elie, Can. (ē′lē)	102f	49°55′N	97°45′W
Elila, r., D.R.C. (ĕ-lē′lȧ)	232	3°30′S	28°00′E
Elisa, i., Wa., U.S. (ē-lī′sȧ)	116d	48°43′N	122°37′W
Élisabethville see Lubumbashi, D.R.C.	232	11°40′S	27°28′E
Elisenvaara, Russia (ā-lē′sĕn-vä′rȧ)	167	61°25′N	29°46′E
Elizabeth, La., U.S. (ē-lĭz′ȧ-bĕth)	123	30°50′N	92°47′W
Elizabeth, N.J., U.S.	110a	40°40′N	74°13′W
Elizabeth, Pa., U.S.	111e	40°16′N	79°53′W
Elizabeth City, N.C., U.S.	125	36°15′N	76°15′W
Elizabethton, Tn., U.S. (ē-lĭz-ȧ-bĕth′tŭn)	125	36°19′N	82°12′W
Elizabethtown, Ky., U.S. (ē-lĭz′ȧ-bĕth-toun)	108	37°40′N	85°55′W
El Jadida, Mor.	230	33°14′N	8°34′W
Ełk, Pol.	160	53°53′N	22°23′E
Elk, r., Can.	95	50°00′N	115°00′W
Elk, r., Tn., U.S.	124	35°05′N	86°36′W
Elk, r., W.V., U.S.	108	38°30′N	81°05′W
El Kairouan, Tun. (kĕr-ò-än)	230	35°46′N	10°04′E
Elk City, Ok., U.S. (ĕlk)	120	35°23′N	99°23′W
El Kef, Tun. (xĕf′)	162	36°14′N	8°42′E
Elkhart, In., U.S. (ĕlk′härt)	108	41°40′N	86°00′W
Elkhart, Ks., U.S.	120	37°00′N	101°54′W
Elkhart, Tx., U.S.	123	31°38′N	95°35′W
Elkhorn, Wi., U.S. (ĕlk′hôrn)	113	42°39′N	88°32′W
Elkhorn, r., Ne., U.S.	112	42°06′N	97°46′W
Elkin, N.C., U.S. (ĕl′kĭn)	125	36°15′N	80°50′W
Elk Island, i., Can.	97	50°45′N	96°32′W
Elk Island National Park, rec., Can. (ĕlk ī′lănd)	92	53°37′N	112°45′W
Elko, Nv., U.S. (ĕl′kō)	104	40°51′N	115°46′W
Elk Point, S.D., U.S.	112	42°41′N	96°41′W
Elk Rapids, Mi., U.S. (răp′ĭdz)	108	44°55′N	85°25′W
Elk River, Id., U.S. (rĭv′ēr)	114	46°47′N	116°11′W
Elk River, Mn., U.S.	113	45°17′N	93°33′W
Elkton, Ky., U.S. (ĕlk′tŭn)	124	36°47′N	87°08′W
Elkton, Md., U.S.	109	39°35′N	75°50′W
Elkton, S.D., U.S.	112	44°15′N	96°28′W
Elland, Eng., U.K. (el′ănd)	158a	53°41′N	1°50′W
Ellen, Mount, mtn., Ut., U.S. (ĕl′ĕn)	119	38°05′N	110°50′W
Ellendale, N.D., U.S. (ĕl′ĕn-dāl)	112	46°01′N	98°33′W
Ellensburg, Wa., U.S. (ĕl′ĕnz-bûrg)	114	47°00′N	120°31′W
Ellenville, N.Y., U.S. (ĕl′ĕn-vĭl)	109	41°40′N	74°25′W
Ellerslie, Can. (ĕl′ērz-lē)	102g	53°25′N	113°30′W
Ellesmere, Eng., U.K. (ĕlz′mēr)	158a	52°55′N	2°54′W
Ellesmere Island, i., Can.	89	81°00′N	80°00′W
Ellesmere Port, Eng., U.K.	158a	53°17′N	2°54′W
Ellice Islands see Tuvalu, nation, Oc.	3	5°20′S	174°00′E

ăt; fināl; rāte; senāte; ärm; åsk; sofȧ; fâre; ch-choose; dh-as th in other; bē; ēvent; bĕt; recĕnt; cratēr; g-gō; gh-guttural g; bĭt; ĭ-short neutral; rīde; κ-guttural k as ch in German ich;

PRONOUNCING INDEX

Ellicott City – Estarreja 291

PLACE (Pronunciation)	PAGE	LAT.	LONG.
Ellicott City, is., Md., U.S. (ĕl′ĭ-kŏt sĭ′tē)	110e	39°16′N	76°48′W
Ellicott Creek, r., N.Y., U.S.	111c	43°00′N	78°46′W
Elliot, S. Afr.	233c	31°19′S	27°52′E
Elliot, Wa., U.S. (el′ĭ-ŭt)	116a	47°28′N	122°08′W
Elliotdale, S. Afr. (ĕl-ĭ-ŏt′dāl)	233c	31°58′S	28°42′E
Elliot Lake, Can.	98	46°23′N	82°39′W
Ellis, Ks., U.S. (ĕl′ĭs)	120	38°56′N	99°34′W
Ellisville, Mo., U.S.	117e	38°35′N	90°35′W
Ellisville, Ms., U.S. (ĕl′ĭs-vĭl)	124	31°37′N	89°10′W
Ellsworth, Ks., U.S. (ĕlz′wûrth)	120	38°43′N	98°14′W
Ellsworth, Me., U.S.	100	44°33′N	68°26′W
Ellsworth Mountains, mts., Ant.	224	77°00′S	90°00′W
Ellwangen, Ger. (ĕl′väŋ-gĕn)	168	48°47′N	10°08′E
Elm, Ger. (ĕlm)	159c	53°31′N	9°13′E
Elm, r., S.D., U.S.	112	45°47′N	98°28′W
Elm, r., W.V., U.S.	108	38°30′N	81°05′W
Elma, Wa., U.S. (ĕl′mȧ)	114	47°02′N	123°20′W
El Mahdia, Tun. (mä-dēȧ)(mä′dē-ȧ)	162	35°30′N	11°09′E
Elmendorf, Tx., U.S. (ĕl′mĕn-dôrf)	117d	29°16′N	98°20′W
El Menia, Alg.	230	30°39′N	2°52′E
Elm Fork, Tx., U.S. (ĕlm fôrk)	117c	32°55′N	96°56′W
Elmhurst, Il., U.S. (ĕlm′hûrst)	111a	41°54′N	87°56′W
El Miliyya, Alg. (mē′ä)	230	36°30′N	6°16′E
Elmira, N.Y., U.S. (ĕl-mī′rȧ)	109	42°05′N	76°50′W
Elmira Heights, N.Y., U.S.	109	42°10′N	76°50′W
El Modena, Ca., U.S. (mô-dē′nô)	117a	33°47′N	117°48′W
El Mohammadia, Alg.	173	35°35′N	0°05′E
El Monte, Ca., U.S. (mŏn′tȧ)	117a	34°04′N	118°02′W
El Morro National Monument, rec., N.M., U.S.	119	35°05′N	108°20′W
Elmshorn, Ger. (ĕlms′hôrn)	168	53°45′N	9°39′E
Elmwood Place, Oh., U.S. (ĕlm′wo͝od plās)	111f	39°11′N	84°30′W
Elokomin, r., Wa., U.S. (ê-lō′kô-mĭn)	116c	46°16′N	123°16′W
El Oro, Mex. (ô-rô)	130	19°49′N	100°04′W
El Pao, Ven. (ĕl pä′ō)	142	8°08′N	62°37′W
El Paraíso, Hond. (pä-rä-ē′sō)	132	13°55′N	86°35′W
El Pardo, Spain (pä′r-dô)	173a	40°31′N	3°47′W
El Paso, Tx., U.S. (pas′ō)	104	31°47′N	106°27′W
El Pilar, Ven. (pē-lä′r)	143b	9°56′N	64°48′W
El Porvenir, Pan. (pôr-vä-nēr′)	133	9°34′N	78°55′W
El Puerto de Santa María, Spain	172	36°36′N	6°18′W
El Qala, Alg.	162	36°52′N	8°23′E
El Qoll, Alg.	230	37°02′N	6°29′E
El Real, Pan. (rā-äl)	133	8°07′N	77°43′W
El Reno, Ok., U.S. (rē′nō)	121	35°31′N	97°57′W
Elroy, Wi., U.S. (ĕl′roi)	113	43°44′N	90°17′W
Elsa, Can.	103	63°55′N	135°25′W
Elsah, Il., U.S. (ĕl′zȧ)	117e	38°57′N	90°22′W
El Salto, Mex. (säl′tō)	130	23°48′N	105°22′W
El Salvador, nation, N.A.	128	14°00′N	89°30′W
El Sauce, Nic. (ĕl-sȧ′ô-sĕ)	132	13°00′N	86°40′W
Elsberry, Mo., U.S. (ĕlz′bĕr-ĭ)	121	39°09′N	90°44′W
Elsdorf, Ger. (ĕls′dōrf)	171c	50°56′N	6°35′E
El Segundo, Ca., U.S. (sêgŭn′dō)	117a	33°55′N	118°24′W
Elsinore, Ca., U.S. (ĕl′sĭ-nôr)	117a	33°40′N	117°19′W
Elsinore Lake, l., Ca., U.S.	117a	33°38′N	117°21′W
Elstorf, Ger. (ĕls′tōrf)	159c	53°25′N	9°48′E
Eltham, Austl. (ĕl′thăm)	217a	37°43′S	145°08′E
El Tigre, Ven. (tē′grĕ)	142	8°49′N	64°15′W
El′ton, l., Russia	181	49°10′N	47°00′E
El Toro, Ca., U.S. (tō′rō)	117a	33°37′N	117°42′W
El Triunfo, El Sal.	132	13°17′N	88°32′W
El Triunfo, Hond. (ĕl-trē-o͞o′n-fô)	132	13°06′N	87°00′W
Elūru, India	199	16°44′N	80°09′E
El Vado Res, N.M., U.S.	119	36°37′N	106°30′W
Elvas, Port. (ĕl′väzh)	162	38°53′N	7°11′W
Elverum, Nor. (ĕl′vĕ-ro͝om)	166	60°53′N	11°33′E
El Viejo, Nic. (ĕl-vyĕ′κō)	132	12°10′N	87°10′W
El Viejo, vol., Nic.	132	12°44′N	87°03′W
Elvins, Mo., U.S. (ĕl′vĭnz)	121	37°49′N	90°31′W
El Wad, Alg.	230	33°23′N	6°49′E
El Wak, Kenya (wäk′)	231	3°00′N	41°00′E
Elwell, Lake, res., Mt., U.S.	115	48°22′N	111°17′W
Elwood, Il., U.S. (ĕ′wo͝od)	111a	41°24′N	88°07′W
Elwood, In., U.S.	108	40°15′N	85°50′W
Elx, Spain	173	38°15′N	0°42′W
Ely, Eng., U.K. (ē′lĭ)	165	52°25′N	0°17′E
Ely, Mn., U.S.	113	47°54′N	91°53′W
Ely, Nv., U.S.	104	39°16′N	114°53′W
Elyria, Oh., U.S. (ê-lĭr′ĭ-ȧ)	111d	41°22′N	82°07′W
Ema, r., Est. (å′mȧ)	167	58°25′N	27°00′E
Emāmshahr, Iran	198	36°25′N	55°01′E
Emån, r., Swe.	166	57°15′N	15°46′E
Embarrass, r., Il., U.S. (ĕm-băr′ăs)	108	39°15′N	88°05′W
Embrun, Can. (ĕm′brŭn)	102c	45°16′N	75°17′W
Embrun, Fr. (äɴ-brûɴ′)	171	44°35′N	6°32′E
Embu, Kenya	237	0°32′S	37°27′E
Emden, Ger. (ĕm′dĕn)	168	53°21′N	7°15′E
Emerson, Can. (ĕm′ẽr-sŭn)	90	49°00′N	97°12′W
Emeryville, Ca., U.S. (ĕm′ẽr-ĭ-vĭl)	116b	37°50′N	122°17′W
Emi Koussi, mtn., Chad (ā′mê ko͞o-sē′)	231	19°50′N	18°30′E
Emiliano Zapata, Mex. (ĕ-mē-lyä′nô-zä-pä′tä)	131	17°45′N	91°46′W
Emilia-Romagna, hist. reg., Italy (ĕ-mēl′yä rô-mä′n-yä)	174	44°35′N	10°48′E
Eminence, Ky., U.S. (ĕm′ĭ-nĕns)	108	38°25′N	85°15′W
Emira Island, i., Pap. N. Gui. (ā-mê-rä′)	213	1°40′S	150°28′E
Emmen, Neth. (ĕm′ĕn)	165	52°48′N	6°55′E
Emmerich, Ger. (ĕm′ẽr-ĭk)	171c	51°51′N	6°16′E
Emmetsburg, Ia., U.S. (ĕm′ĕts-bûrg)	113	43°07′N	94°41′W
Emmett, Id., U.S. (ĕm′ĕt)	114	43°53′N	116°30′W
Emmons, Mount, mtn., Ut., U.S. (ĕm′ŭnz)	106	40°43′N	110°20′W
Emory Peak, mtn., Tx., U.S. (ĕ′mō-rē pēk)	122	29°13′N	103°20′W
Empoli, Italy (ām′pô-lē)	174	43°43′N	10°55′E
Emporia, Ks., U.S. (ĕm-pō′rĭ-ȧ)	104	38°24′N	96°11′W
Emporia, Va., U.S.	125	37°40′N	77°34′W
Emporium, Pa., U.S. (ĕm-pō′rĭ-ŭm)	109	41°30′N	78°15′W
Empty Quarter see Ar Rub′al Khālī, des., Asia	198	20°00′N	51°00′E
Ems, r., Ger. (ĕms)	168	52°52′N	7°16′E
Ems-Weser Kanal, can., Ger.	168	52°23′N	8°11′E
Enånger, Swe. (ĕn-ôŋ′gĕr)	166	61°36′N	16°55′E
Encantada, Cerro de la, mtn., Mex. (sĕ′r-rô-dĕ-lä-ĕn-kän-tä′dä)	128	31°58′N	115°15′W
Encanto, Cape, c., Phil. (ĕn-kän′tō)	213a	15°44′N	121°46′E
Encarnación, Para. (ĕn-kär-nä-syōn′)	144	27°26′S	55°52′W
Encarnación de Díaz, Mex. (ĕn-kär-nä-syōn dā dē′äz)	130	21°34′N	102°15′W
Encinal, Tx., U.S. (ĕn′sĭ-nôl)	122	28°02′N	99°22′W
Encontrados, Ven. (ĕn-kōn-trä′dōs)	142	9°01′N	72°10′W
Encounter Bay, b., Austl. (ĕn-koun′tẽr)	220	35°50′S	138°45′E
Endako, r., Can.	94	54°05′N	125°30′W
Endau, r., Malay.	197b	2°29′N	103°40′E
Enderbury, i., Kir. (ĕn′dẽr-bŭrĭ)	240	2°00′S	171°00′W
Enderby Land, reg., Ant. (ĕn′dẽr bĭ)	224	72°00′S	52°00′E
Enderlin, N.D., U.S. (ĕn′dẽr-lĭn)	112	46°38′N	97°37′W
Endicott, N.Y., U.S. (ĕn′dĭ-kŏt)	109	42°05′N	76°00′W
Endicott Mountains, mts., Ak., U.S.	103	67°30′N	153°45′W
Enez, Tur.	175	40°42′N	26°05′E
Enfer, Pointe d′, c., Mart.	133b	14°21′N	60°48′W
Enfield, Eng., U.K.	158b	51°38′N	0°06′W
Enfield, Ct., U.S. (ĕn′fēld)	109	41°55′N	72°35′W
Enfield, N.C., U.S.	125	36°10′N	77°41′W
Engaño, Cabo, c., Dom. Rep. (kä′-bô- ĕn-gä-nô)	129	18°40′N	68°30′W
Engcobo, S. Afr. (ĕŋg-cô-bô)	233c	31°41′S	27°59′E
Engel′s, Russia (ĕn′gĕls)	181	51°20′N	45°40′E
Engelskirchen, Ger. (ĕn′gĕls-kĕr′κĕn)	171c	50°59′N	7°25′E
Enggano, Pulau, i., Indon. (ĕng-gä′nō)	212	5°22′S	102°18′E
England, Ar., U.S. (ĭŋ′glănd)	121	34°33′N	91°58′W
England, state, U.K. (ĭŋ′glănd)	154	51°35′N	1°40′W
Englewood, Co., U.S. (ĕn′g′l-wo͝od)	120	39°39′N	105°00′W
Englewood, N.J., U.S.	110a	40°54′N	73°59′W
English, In., U.S. (ĭn′glĭsh)	108	38°15′N	86°25′W
English, r., Can.	93	50°31′N	94°12′W
English Channel, strt., Eur.	156	49°45′N	3°06′W
Enguera, Spain (ān′gārä)	173	38°58′N	0°42′W
Enid, Ok., U.S. (ē′nĭd)	104	36°25′N	97°52′W
Enid Lake, res., Ms., U.S.	124	34°13′N	89°47′W
Enkeldoring, S. Afr. (ĕŋ′k′l-dôr-ĭng)	238c	25°24′S	28°43′E
Enköping, Swe. (ĕn′kû-pĭng)	166	59°39′N	17°05′E
Ennedi, mts., Chad (ĕn-nĕd′ē)	231	16°45′N	22°45′E
Ennis, Ire. (ĕn′ĭs)	164	52°54′N	9°05′W
Ennis, Tx., U.S.	123	32°20′N	96°38′W
Enniscorthy, Ire. (ĕn-ĭs-kôr′thĭ)	164	52°33′N	6°27′W
Enniskillen, N. Ire., U.K. (ĕn-ĭs-kĭl′ĕn)	164	54°20′N	7°25′W
Ennis Lake, res., Mt., U.S.	115	45°15′N	111°30′W
Enns, r., Aus. (ĕns)	161	47°37′N	14°35′E
Enoree, S.C., U.S. (ê-nō′rē)	125	34°43′N	81°58′W
Enoree, r., S.C., U.S.	125	34°35′N	81°55′W
Enriquillo, Dom. Rep. (ĕn-rê-kē′l-yô)	135	17°55′N	71°15′W
Enriquillo, Lago, l., Dom. Rep. (lä′gô-ĕn-rê-kē′l-yô)	135	18°35′N	71°35′W
Enschede, Neth. (ĕns′κä-dĕ)	161	52°10′N	6°50′E
Enseñada, Arg.	141c	34°50′S	57°55′W
Ensenada, Mex. (ĕn-sĕ-nä′dä)	128	32°00′N	116°30′W
Enshi, China (ŭn-shr)	204	30°18′N	109°25′E
Enshū-Nada, b., Japan (ĕn′sho͞o nä-dä)	211	34°25′N	137°14′E
Entebbe, Ug.	231	0°04′N	32°28′E
Enterprise, Al., U.S. (ĕn′tẽr-prīz)	124	31°20′N	85°50′W
Enterprise, Or., U.S.	114	45°25′N	117°16′W
Entiat, L, Wa., U.S.	114	45°43′N	120°11′W
Entraygues, Fr. (ĕɴ-trĕg′)	170	44°39′N	2°33′E
Entre Rios, prov., Arg.	144	31°30′S	59°00′W
Enugu, Nig. (ĕ-no͞o′go͞o)	230	6°27′N	7°27′E
Enumclaw, Wa., U.S. (ĕn′ŭm-klô)	116a	47°12′N	121°59′W
Envigado, Col. (ĕn-vē-gá′dō)	142a	6°10′N	75°34′W
Eolie, Isole, is., Italy (ē′sō-lĕ-ĕ-ō′lyĕ)	162	38°43′N	14°43′E
Epe, Nig.	235	6°37′N	3°59′E
Épernay, Fr. (ā-pĕr-nĕ′)	161	49°02′N	3°54′E
Épernon, Fr. (ā-pĕr-nôɴ′)	171b	48°36′N	1°41′E
Ephraim, Ut., U.S. (ē′frā-ĭm)	119	39°20′N	111°40′W
Ephrata, Wa., U.S. (ēfrā′tȧ)	114	47°18′N	119°35′W
Epi, Vanuatu (ā′pê)	219	16°59′S	168°29′E
Épila, Spain (ā′pê-lä)	172	41°38′N	1°15′W
Épinal, Fr. (ā-pē-nál′)	161	48°11′N	6°27′E
Episkopi, Cyp.	197a	34°38′N	32°55′E
Epping, Eng., U.K. (ĕp′ĭng)	158b	51°41′N	0°06′E
Epsom, Eng., U.K.	158b	51°20′N	0°16′W
Epupa Falls, wtfl., Afr.	236	17°00′S	13°05′E
Epworth, Eng., U.K. (ĕp′wûrth)	158a	53°31′N	0°50′W
Equatorial Guinea, nation, Afr.	230	2°00′N	7°15′E
Équilles, Fr.	170a	43°34′N	5°21′E
Eramosa, r., Can. (ĕr-ȧ-mō′sȧ)	102d	43°39′N	80°08′W
Erba, Jabal, mtn., Sudan (ĕr-bȧ)	231	20°53′N	36°45′E
Erciyeş Dağı, mtn., Tur.	163	38°30′N	35°36′E
Erding, Ger. (ĕr′dĕng)	159d	48°19′N	11°54′E
Erechim, Braz. (ĕ-rĕ-shê′ɴ)	144	27°43′S	52°11′W
Ereğli, Tur. (ĕ-rā′ĭ-le)	163	37°40′N	34°00′E
Ereğli, Tur.	163	41°15′N	31°25′E
Erfurt, Ger. (ĕr′fo͝ort)	161	50°59′N	11°04′E
Ergene, r., Tur. (ĕr′gĕ-nĕ)	175	41°17′N	26°50′E
Erges, r., Eur. (ĕr′-zhĕs)	172	39°45′N	7°01′W
Ērgļi, Lat.	167	56°54′N	25°38′E
Eria, r., Spain (ā-rē′ä)	172	42°10′N	6°08′W
Erick, Ok., U.S. (âr′ĭk)	120	35°14′N	99°51′W
Erie, Ks., U.S. (ē′rĭ)	121	37°35′N	95°17′W
Erie, Pa., U.S.	105	42°05′N	80°05′W
Erie, Lake, l., N.A.	107	42°15′N	81°25′W
Erimo Saki, c., Japan (ā′rē-mō sä-kē)	205	41°53′N	143°20′E
Erin, Can. (ĕ′rĭn)	102d	43°46′N	80°04′W
Eritrea, nation, Afr. (ā-rê-trā′ȧ)	231	16°15′N	38°30′E
Erlangen, Ger. (ĕr′läng-ĕn)	168	49°36′N	11°03′E
Erlanger, Ky., U.S. (ẽr′lăng-ẽr)	111f	39°01′N	84°36′W
Ermoúpoli, Grc.	175	37°30′N	24°56′E
Ernākulam, India	199	9°58′N	76°23′E
Erne, Lower Lough, l., N. Ire., U.K.	164	54°30′N	7°40′W
Erne, Upper Lough, l., N. Ire., U.K. (lŏk ûrn)	164	54°20′N	7°24′W
Erode, India	203	11°20′N	77°45′E
Eromanga, i., Vanuatu	221	18°58′S	169°18′E
Eros, La., U.S. (ē′rŏs)	123	32°23′N	92°22′W
Errego, Moz.	237	16°02′S	37°14′E
Errigal, mtn., Ire. (ĕr-ĭ-gôl′)	164	55°02′N	8°07′W
Errol Heights, Or., U.S.	116c	45°29′N	122°38′W
Erstein, Fr. (ĕr′shtīn)	171	48°27′N	7°40′E
Erwin, N.C., U.S. (ûr′wĭn)	125	35°16′N	78°40′W
Erwin, Tn., U.S.	125	36°07′N	82°25′W
Erzgebirge, mts., Eur. (ĕrts′gĕ-bē′gĕ)	156	50°29′N	12°40′E
Erzincan, Tur. (ĕr-zĭn-jän′)	198	39°50′N	39°30′E
Erzurum, Tur. (ĕrz′ro͞om′)	198	39°55′N	41°10′E
Esambo, D.R.C.	236	3°40′S	23°24′E
Esashi, Japan (ĕs′ä-shê)	205	41°50′N	140°10′E
Esbjerg, Den. (ĕs′byĕrgh)	160	55°29′N	8°25′E
Escalante, Ut., U.S. (ĕs-kȧ-lăn′tē)	119	37°50′N	111°40′W
Escalante, r., Ut., U.S.	119	37°40′N	111°20′W
Escalón, Mex.	122	26°45′N	104°20′W
Escambia, r., Fl., U.S. (ĕs-kăm′bĭ-ȧ)	124	30°38′N	87°20′W
Escanaba, Mi., U.S. (ĕs-kȧ-nô′bȧ)	105	45°44′N	87°05′W
Escanaba, r., Mi., U.S.	113	46°10′N	87°22′W
Escarpada Point, Phil.	212	18°40′N	122°45′E
Esch-sur-Alzette, Lux.	171	49°32′N	6°21′E
Eschwege, Ger. (ĕsh′vā-gē)	168	51°11′N	10°02′E
Eschweiler, Ger. (ĕsh′vī-lẽr)	171c	50°49′N	6°15′E
Escondido, Ca., U.S. (ĕs-kŏn-dē′dō)	118	33°07′N	117°00′W
Escondido, r., Nic.	133	12°04′N	84°09′W
Escondido, Río, r., Mex. (rē′ō-ĕs-kōn-dē′dô)	122	28°30′N	100°45′W
Escudo de Veraguas, i., Pan. (ĕs-ko͞o′dä dā vā-rä′gwäs)	133	9°07′N	81°25′W
Escuinapa, Mex. (ĕs-kwē-nä′pä)	128	22°49′N	105°44′W
Escuintla, Guat. (ĕs-kwēn′tlä)	132	14°16′N	90°47′W
Ese, Cayos de, i., Col.	133	12°24′N	81°07′W
Eşfahān, Iran	198	32°38′N	51°30′E
Esgueva, r., Spain (ĕs-gĕ′vä)	172	41°48′N	4°10′W
Esher, Eng., U.K.	158b	51°23′N	0°22′W
Eshowe, S. Afr. (ĕsh′ô-wê)	233c	28°54′S	31°28′E
Esiama, Ghana	234	4°56′N	2°21′W
Eskdale, W.V., U.S. (ĕsk′dāl)	108	38°05′N	81°25′W
Eskifjördur, Ice. (ĕs′kê-fyŭr′do͞or)	154	65°04′N	14°01′W
Eskilstuna, Swe. (å′shĕl-stü-na)	160	59°23′N	16°28′E
Eskimo Lakes, l., Can. (es′kĭ-mō)	92	69°40′N	130°10′W
Eskişehir, Tur. (ĕs-kê-shĕ′h′r)	198	39°40′N	30°20′E
Esko, Mn., U.S. (ĕs′kô)	117h	46°27′N	92°22′W
Esla, r., Spain (ĕs-lä)	172	41°50′N	5°48′W
Eslöv, Swe. (ĕs′lûv)	166	55°50′N	13°17′E
Esmeraldas, Ec. (ĕs-mȧ-räl′däs)	142	0°58′N	79°45′W
Espanola, Can. (ĕs-pȧ-nō′lȧ)	91	46°11′N	81°59′W
Esparta, C.R. (ĕs-pär′tä)	133	9°59′N	84°40′W
Esperance, Austl. (ĕs′pê-răns)	218	33°45′S	122°07′E
Esperanza, Cuba (ĕs-pĕ-rä′n-zä)	134	22°30′N	80°10′W
Espichel, Cabo, c., Port. (kȧ′bō-ĕs-pē-shĕl′)	172	38°25′N	9°13′W
Espinal, Col. (ĕs-pê-näl′)	142	4°10′N	74°53′W
Espinhaço, Serra do, mts., Braz. (sĕ′r-rä-dô-ĕs-pê-nȧ-sô)	143	16°00′S	44°00′W
Espinillo, Punta, c., Ur. (po͞o′n-tä-ĕs-pê-nē′l-yô)	141c	34°49′S	56°27′W
Espírito Santo, Braz. (ĕs-pē′rē-tō-sän′tô)	143	20°27′S	40°18′W
Espírito Santo, state, Braz.	143	19°57′S	40°58′W
Espiritu Santo, i., Vanuatu (ĕs-pē′rê-to͞o sän′tō)	221	15°45′S	166°50′E
Espíritu Santo, Bahía del, b., Mex.	132a	19°25′N	87°28′W
Espita, Mex. (ĕs-pē′tä)	132a	20°57′N	88°22′W
Espoo, Fin.	167	60°13′N	24°41′E
Es Port de Pollença, Spain	173	39°50′N	3°00′E
Esposende, Port. (ĕs-pō-zĕn′dā)	172	41°33′N	8°45′W
Esquel, Arg. (ĕs-kĕ′l)	144	42°47′S	71°22′W
Esquimalt, Can. (ĕs-kwī′mŏlt)	94	48°26′N	123°24′W
Essaouira, Mor.	230	31°34′N	9°44′W
Essen, Bel.	159a	51°28′N	4°27′E
Essen, Ger. (ĕs′sĕn)	154	51°26′N	6°59′E
Essendon, Austl.	217a	37°46′S	144°55′E
Essequibo, r., Guy. (ĕs-ā-kē′bō)	143	4°26′N	58°17′W
Essex, Il., U.S.	111a	41°11′N	88°11′W
Essex, Ma., U.S.	101a	42°38′N	70°47′W
Essex, Md., U.S.	110e	39°19′N	76°29′W
Essex, Vt., U.S.	109	44°30′N	73°05′W
Essex Fells, N.J., U.S. (ĕs′ĕks fĕlz)	110a	40°50′N	74°16′W
Essexville, Mi., U.S. (ĕs′ĕks-vĭl)	108	43°35′N	83°50′W
Esslingen, Ger. (ĕs′slēn-gĕn)	168	48°45′N	9°19′E
Estacado, Llano, pl., U.S. (yä-nō ĕs-tȧcȧ-dō′)	106	33°50′N	103°20′W
Estância, Braz. (ĕs-tän′sĭ-ä)	143	11°17′S	37°18′W
Estarreja, Port. (ĕ-tär-rā′zhä)	172	40°44′N	8°39′W

292 Estats – Felipe Carrillo Puerto PRONOUNCING INDEX

PLACE (Pronunciation)	PAGE	LAT.	LONG.
Estats, Pique d', mtn., Eur.	173	42°43′N	1°30′E
Estcourt, S. Afr. (ĕst-coort)	233c	29°04′S	29°53′E
Este, Italy (ĕs′tā)	174	45°13′N	11°40′E
Estella, Spain (ĕs-tāl′yä)	172	42°40′N	2°01′W
Estepa, Spain (ĕs-tā′pä)	172	37°18′N	4°54′W
Estepona, Spain (ĕs-tå-pō′nä)	172	36°26′N	5°08′W
Esterhazy, Can. (ĕs′tẽr-hā-zē)	97	50°40′N	102°08′W
Estero Bay, b., Ca., U.S. (ĕs-tā′rōs)	118	35°22′N	121°04′W
Estevan, Can. (ĕ-stē′văn)	90	49°07′N	103°05′W
Estevan Group, is., Can.	94	53°05′N	129°40′W
Estherville, Ia., U.S. (ĕs′tẽr-vĭl)	113	43°24′N	94°49′W
Estill, S.C., U.S. (ĕs′tĭl)	125	32°46′N	81°15′W
Eston, Can.	96	51°10′N	108°45′W
Estonia, nation, Eur.	178	59°10′N	25°00′E
Estoril, Port. (ĕs-tô-rēl′)	173b	38°45′N	9°24′W
Estrêla, mtn., Port. (mäl-you′ɴ-dä-ĕs-trĕ′lä)	172	40°20′N	7°38′W
Estrêla, r., Braz. (ĕs-trĕ′lȧ)	144b	22°39′S	43°16′W
Estrêla, Serra da, mts., Port. (sĕr′rȧ dä ĕs-trā′lȧ)	172	40°25′N	7°45′W
Estremadura, hist. reg., Port. (ĕs-trā-mä-dōō′rȧ)	172	39°00′N	8°36′W
Estremoz, Port. (ĕs-trā-mōzh′)	172	38°50′N	7°35′W
Estrondo, Serra do, mts., Braz. (sĕr′-rȧ dȯ ĕs-trȯn′-dȯ)	143	9°52′S	48°56′W
Esumba, Île, i., D.R.C.	236	2°00′N	21°12′E
Esztergom, Hung. (ĕs′tẽr-gōm)	169	47°46′N	18°45′E
Etah, Grnld. (ē′tă)	89	78°20′N	72°42′W
Étampes, Fr. (ā-täɴp′)	170	48°26′N	2°09′E
Étaples, Fr. (ā-täp′l′)	170	50°32′N	1°38′E
Etchemin, r., Can. (ĕch′ĕ-mĭn)	102b	46°39′N	71°03′W
Ethiopa, nation, Afr. (ē-thē-ō′pē-ȧ)	231	7°53′N	37°55′E
Eticoga, Gui.-B.	234	11°09′N	16°08′W
Etiwanda, Ca., U.S. (ĕ-tĭ-wän′dȧ)	117a	34°07′N	117°31′W
Etna, Pa., U.S. (ĕt′nȧ)	111e	40°30′N	79°55′W
Etna, Mount, vol., Italy	156	37°48′N	15°00′E
Etobicoke Creek, r., Can.	102d	43°44′N	79°48′W
Etolin Strait, strt., Ak., U.S. (ĕt ō lĭn)	103	60°35′S	165°40′W
Etoshapan, pl., Nmb. (ėtō′shä)	232	19°07′S	15°30′E
Etowah, Tn., U.S. (ĕt′ȯ-wä)	124	35°18′N	84°31′W
Etowah, r., Ga., U.S.	124	34°23′N	84°19′W
Étréchy, Fr. (ā-trā-shē′)	171b	48°29′N	2°12′E
Etten-Leur, Neth.	159a	51°34′N	4°38′E
Etterbeek, Bel. (ĕt′ẽr-bāk)	159a	50°51′N	4°24′E
Etzatlán, Mex. (ĕt-zä-tlän′)	130	20°44′N	104°04′W
Eucla, Austl. (ū′klȧ)	218	31°45′S	128°50′E
Euclid, Oh., U.S. (ū′klĭd)	111d	41°34′N	81°32′W
Eudora, Ar., U.S. (u-dō′rȧ)	121	33°07′N	91°16′W
Eufaula, Al., U.S. (ů-fô′lȧ)	124	31°53′N	85°09′W
Eufaula, Ok., U.S.	121	35°16′N	95°35′W
Eufaula Reservoir, res., Ok., U.S.	121	35°00′N	94°45′W
Eugene, Or., U.S. (ů-jēn′)	104	44°02′N	123°06′W
Euless, Tx., U.S. (ū′lĕs)	117c	32°50′N	97°05′W
Eunice, La., U.S. (ū′nĭs)	123	30°30′N	92°25′W
Eupen, Bel. (oi′pĕn)	165	50°39′N	6°05′E
Euphrates, r., Asia (ů-frā′tēz)	198	36°00′N	40°00′E
Eure, r., Fr. (ûr)	170	49°03′N	1°22′E
Eureka, Ca., U.S. (û-rē′kȧ)	104	40°45′N	124°10′W
Eureka, Ks., U.S.	121	37°48′N	96°17′W
Eureka, Mt., U.S.	114	48°53′N	115°07′W
Eureka, Nv., U.S.	118	39°33′N	115°58′W
Eureka, S.D., U.S.	112	45°46′N	99°38′W
Eureka, Ut., U.S.	119	39°55′N	112°10′W
Eureka Springs, Ar., U.S.	121	36°24′N	93°43′W
Europe, cont. (ū′rŭp)	156	50°00′N	15°00′E
Eustis, Fl., U.S. (ūs′tĭs)	125	28°50′N	81°41′W
Eutaw, Al., U.S. (ū-tå)	124	32°48′N	87°50′W
Eutsuk Lake, l., Can. (ōōt′sŭk)	94	53°20′N	126°44′W
Evanston, Il., U.S. (ĕv′ăn-stŭn)	105	42°03′N	87°41′W
Evanston, Wy., U.S.	115	41°17′N	111°02′W
Evansville, In., U.S. (ĕv′ănz-vĭl)	105	38°00′N	87°30′W
Evansville, Wi., U.S.	113	42°46′N	89°19′W
Evart, Mi., U.S. (ĕv′ẽrt)	108	43°55′N	85°10′W
Evaton, S. Afr. (ĕv′ȧ-tŏn)	238c	26°32′S	27°53′E
Eveleth, Mn., U.S. (ĕv′ē-lĕth)	113	47°27′N	92°35′W
Everard, l., Austl. (ĕv′ẽr-ȧrd)	220	31°20′S	134°10′E
Everard Ranges, mts., Austl.	220	27°15′S	132°00′E
Everest, Mount, mtn., Asia (ĕv′ẽr-ĕst)	199	28°00′N	86°57′E
Everett, Ma., U.S. (ĕv′ẽr-ĕt)	101a	42°24′N	71°03′W
Everett, Wa., U.S. (ĕv′ẽr-ĕt)	104	47°59′N	122°11′W
Everett Mountains, mts., Can.	93	62°34′N	68°00′W
Everglades, The, sw., Fl., U.S.	125a	25°35′N	80°55′W
Everglades City, Fl., U.S. (ĕv′ẽr-glādz)	125a	25°50′N	81°25′W
Everglades National Park, rec., Fl., U.S.	107	25°39′N	80°57′W
Evergreen, Al., U.S. (ĕv′ẽr-grēn)	124	31°25′N	87°56′W
Evergreen Park, Il., U.S.	111a	41°44′N	87°42′W
Everman, Tx., U.S. (ĕv′ẽr-măn)	117c	32°38′N	97°17′W
Everson, Wa., U.S. (ĕv′ẽr-sŭn)	116d	48°55′N	122°21′W
Évora, Port. (ĕv′ȯ-rä)	162	38°35′N	7°54′W
Évreux, Fr. (ā-vrû′)	161	49°02′N	1°11′E
Evrótas, r., Grc. (ĕv-rō′täs)	175	37°15′N	22°17′E
Évvoia, i., Grc.	163	38°38′N	23°45′E
'Ewa Beach, Hi., U.S. (ē′wä)	126a	21°17′N	158°03′W
Ewaso Ng'iro, r., Kenya	231	0°59′N	37°47′E
Excelsior, Mn., U.S. (ĕk-sel′sĭ-ŏr)	117g	44°54′N	93°35′W
Excelsior Springs, Mo., U.S.	121	39°20′N	94°13′W
Exe, r., Eng., U.K. (ĕks)	164	50°57′N	3°37′W
Exeter, Eng., U.K.	161	50°45′N	3°33′W
Exeter, Ca., U.S. (ĕk′sė-tẽr)	118	36°18′N	119°09′W
Exeter, N.H., U.S.	109	43°00′N	71°00′W
Exmoor, for., Eng., U.K. (ĕks′mȯr)	164	51°10′N	3°55′W
Exmouth, Eng., U.K. (ĕks′mŭth)	164	50°40′N	3°20′W
Exmouth Gulf, b., Austl.	220	21°45′S	114°30′E
Exploits, r., Can. (ĕks-ploits′)	101	48°50′N	56°15′W
Extórrax, r., Mex. (ĕx-tó′rȧx)	130	21°04′N	99°39′W
Extrema, Braz. (ĕsh-trĕ′mä)	141a	22°52′S	46°19′W
Extremadura, hist. reg., Spain (ĕks-trā-mä-doo′rä)	172	38°43′N	6°30′W
Exuma Sound, strt., Bah. (ĕk-sōō′mä)	134	24°20′N	76°20′W
Eyasi, Lake, l., Tan. (å-yä′sė)	232	3°25′S	34°55′E
Eyjafjördur, b., Ice.	160	66°21′N	18°20′W
Eyl, Som.	238a	7°53′N	49°45′E
Eyrarbakki, Ice.	160	63°51′N	20°52′W
Eyre, Austl. (âr)	218	32°15′S	126°20′E
Eyre, l., Austl.	220	28°43′S	137°50′E
Eyre Peninsula, pen., Austl.	220	33°30′S	136°00′E
Ezeiza, Arg. (ĕ-zā′zä)	144a	34°52′S	58°31′W
Ezine, Tur. (å′zĭ-nå)	175	39°47′N	26°18′E

F

PLACE (Pronunciation)	PAGE	LAT.	LONG.
Faaborg, Den. (fô′bȯrg)	166	55°06′N	10°19′E
Fabens, Tx., U.S. (fā′bĕnz)	122	31°30′N	106°07′W
Fabriano, Italy (fä-brē-ä′nȯ)	174	43°20′N	12°55′E
Fada, Chad (fä′dä)	231	17°06′N	21°18′E
Fada Ngourma, Burkina (fä′dä′′n gōōr′mä)	230	12°04′N	0°21′E
Faddeya, i., Russia (fȧd-yā′)	179	76°12′N	145°00′E
Faenza, Italy (fä-ĕnd′zä)	174	44°16′N	11°53′E
Fafe, Port. (fä′fā)	172	41°30′N	8°10′W
Fafen, r., Eth.	238a	8°15′N	42°40′E
Făgăras, Rom. (fȧ-gä′räsh)	175	45°50′N	24°55′E
Fagerness, Nor. (fä′ghẽr-nĕs)	160	61°00′N	9°10′E
Fagnano, l., S.A. (fäk-nä′nȯ)	144	54°35′S	68°20′W
Faguibine, Lac, l., Mali	234	16°50′N	4°20′W
Faial, i., Port. (fä-yä′l)	230a	38°40′N	29°19′W
Fā'id, Egypt (fä-yēd′)	238d	30°19′N	32°18′E
Fairbanks, Ak., U.S. (fâr′bănks)	106a	64°50′N	147°48′W
Fairbury, Il., U.S. (fâr′bĕr ĭ)	108	40°45′N	88°25′W
Fairbury, Ne., U.S.	121	40°09′N	97°11′W
Fairchild Creek, r., Can. (fâr′chīld)	102d	43°18′N	80°10′W
Fairfax, Mn., U.S. (fâr′făks)	113	44°29′N	94°44′W
Fairfax, S.C., U.S.	125	32°29′N	81°13′W
Fairfax, Va., U.S.	110e	38°51′N	77°20′W
Fairfield, Austl.	217b	33°52′S	150°57′E
Fairfield, Al., U.S. (fâr′fēld)	110h	33°30′N	86°50′W
Fairfield, Ct., U.S.	110a	41°08′N	73°22′W
Fairfield, Ia., U.S.	113	41°00′N	91°59′W
Fairfield, Il., U.S.	108	38°25′N	88°20′W
Fairfield, Me., U.S.	100	44°35′N	69°38′W
Fairhaven, Ma., U.S. (fâr-hā′vĕn)	109	41°35′N	70°55′W
Fair Haven, Vt., U.S.	109	43°35′N	73°15′W
Fair Island, i., Scot., U.K. (fâr)	164a	59°34′N	1°41′W
Fairmont, Mn., U.S. (fâr′mŏnt)	113	43°39′N	94°26′W
Fairmont, W.V., U.S.	108	39°30′N	80°10′W
Fairmont City, Il., U.S.	117e	38°39′N	90°05′W
Fairmount, In., U.S.	108	40°25′N	85°45′W
Fairmount, Ks., U.S.	117f	39°12′N	95°55′W
Fair Oaks, Ga., U.S. (fâr ōks)	110c	33°56′N	84°33′W
Fairport, N.Y., U.S. (fâr′pōrt)	109	43°05′N	77°30′W
Fairport Harbor, Oh., U.S.	108	41°45′N	81°15′W
Fairview, Ok., U.S. (fâr′vū)	120	36°16′N	98°28′W
Fairview, Or., U.S.	116c	45°32′N	112°26′W
Fairview, Ut., U.S.	119	39°35′N	111°30′W
Fairview Park, Oh., U.S.	111d	41°27′N	81°52′W
Fairweather, Mount, mtn., N.A. (fâr-wĕdh′ẽr)	103	59°12′N	137°22′W
Faisalabad, Pak.	199	31°29′N	73°06′E
Faith, S.D., U.S. (fāth)	112	45°02′N	120°02′W
Faizābād, India	199	26°50′N	82°17′E
Fajardo, P.R.	129b	18°20′N	65°40′W
Fakfak, Indon.	213	2°56′S	132°25′E
Faku, China (fä-kōō)	208	42°28′N	123°20′E
Falcón, dept., Ven. (fäl-kô′n)	143b	11°00′N	68°28′W
Falconer, N.Y., U.S. (fô′k′n-ẽr)	109	42°10′N	79°10′W
Falcon Heights, Mn., U.S. (fô′k′n)	117g	44°59′N	93°10′W
Falcon Reservoir, res., N.A. (fôk′n)	122	26°47′N	99°03′W
Făleşti, Mol.	177	47°33′N	27°46′E
Falfurrias, Tx., U.S. (făl′fōō-rē′ȧs)	122	27°15′N	98°08′W
Falher, Can. (făl′ẽr)	95	55°44′N	117°12′W
Falkenberg, Swe. (fäl′kĕn-bĕrgh)	166	56°54′N	12°25′E
Falkensee, Ger. (fäl′kĕn-zā)	159b	52°34′N	13°05′E
Falkenthal, Ger. (fäl′kĕn-täl)	159b	52°54′N	13°18′E
Falkirk, Scot., U.K. (fôl′kûrk)	164	55°59′N	3°55′W
Falkland Islands, dep., S.A. (fôk′lănd)	144	50°45′S	61°00′W
Falköping, Swe. (fäl′chûp-ĭng)	166	58°09′N	13°30′E
Fall City, Wa., U.S.	116a	47°34′N	121°53′W
Fall Creek, r., In., U.S. (fôl)	111g	39°52′N	86°04′W
Fallon, Nv., U.S. (făl′ŭn)	118	39°30′N	118°48′W
Fall River, Ma., U.S.	105	41°42′N	71°07′W
Falls Church, Va., U.S. (fôlz chûrch)	110e	38°53′N	77°10′W
Falls City, Ne., U.S.	121	40°04′N	95°37′W
Fallston, Md., U.S. (făls′ton)	110e	39°32′N	76°26′W
Falmouth, Jam.	134	18°30′N	77°40′W
Falmouth, Eng., U.K. (făl′mŭth)	164	50°08′N	5°04′W
Falmouth, Ky., U.S.	108	38°40′N	84°20′W
False Divi Point, c., India	203	15°45′N	80°50′E
Falster, i., Den. (fäls′tĕr)	166	54°48′N	11°58′E
Fălticeni, Rom. (fŭl-tė-chån′y′)	169	47°27′N	26°17′E
Falun, Swe. (fä-lōōn′)	160	60°38′N	15°35′E
Famagusta, N. Cyp. (fä-mä-gōōs′tä)	163	35°08′N	33°59′E
Famatina, Sierra de, mts., Arg.	144	29°00′S	67°50′W
Fangxian, China (fäŋ-shyĕn)	208	32°05′N	110°45′E
Fanning, i., Can.	102f	49°45′N	97°46′W
Fano, Italy (fä′nō)	174	43°49′N	13°01′E
Fanø, i., Den. (fän′û)	166	55°24′N	8°10′E
Fan Si Pan, mtn., Viet.	209	22°25′N	103°50′E
Farafangana, Madag. (fä-rä-fäŋ-gä′nä)	233	23°18′S	47°59′E
Farāh, Afg. (fä-rä′)	198	32°15′N	62°13′E
Farallón, Punta, c., Mex. (pō′n-tä-fä-rä-lōn)	130	19°21′N	105°03′W
Faranah, Gui. (fä-rä′nä)	230	10°02′N	10°44′W
Farasān, Jaza'ir, is., Sau. Ar.	198	16°45′N	41°08′E
Faregh, Wadi al, r., Libya (wädė ĕl fä-rĕg′)	163	30°10′N	19°34′E
Farewell, Cape, c., N.Z. (fâr-wĕl′)	221a	40°37′S	172°40′E
Fargo, N.D., U.S. (fär′gō)	104	46°53′N	96°48′W
Far Hills, N.J., U.S. (fär hĭlz)	110a	40°41′N	74°38′W
Faribault, Mn., U.S. (fâ′rĭ-bō)	113	44°19′N	93°16′W
Farilhōes, is., Port. (fä-rė-lyôɴzh′)	172	39°28′N	9°32′W
Faringdon, Eng., U.K. (fă′rĭng-dŏn)	158b	51°38′N	1°35′W
Fāriskūr, Egypt (fä-rės-kōōr′)	238b	31°19′N	31°46′E
Farit, Amba, mtn., Eth.	231	10°51′N	37°52′E
Farley, Mo., U.S. (fär′lē)	117f	39°16′N	94°49′W
Farmers Branch, Tx., U.S.	117c	32°56′N	96°53′W
Farmersburg, In., U.S. (fär′mẽrz-bûrg)	108	39°15′N	87°25′W
Farmersville, Tx., U.S. (fär′mẽrz-vĭl)	121	33°11′N	96°22′W
Farmingdale, N.J., U.S. (färm′ĕng-dāl)	110a	40°11′N	74°10′W
Farmingdale, N.Y., U.S.	110a	40°44′N	73°26′W
Farmingham, Ma., U.S. (färm-ĭng-hăm)	101a	42°17′N	71°25′W
Farmington, Il., U.S. (färm-ĭng-tŭn)	121	40°42′N	90°01′W
Farmington, Me., U.S.	100	44°40′N	70°10′W
Farmington, Mi., U.S.	111b	42°28′N	83°23′W
Farmington, Mo., U.S.	121	37°46′N	90°26′W
Farmington, N.M., U.S.	119	36°40′N	108°10′W
Farmington, Ut., U.S.	117b	40°59′N	111°53′W
Farmville, N.C., U.S. (färm-vĭl)	125	35°35′N	77°35′W
Farmville, Va., U.S.	125	37°15′N	78°23′W
Farnborough, Eng., U.K. (färn′bŭr-ȯ)	158b	51°15′N	0°45′W
Farne Islands, is., Eng., U.K. (färn)	164	55°40′N	1°32′W
Farnham, Can. (fär′năm)	109	45°15′N	72°55′W
Farningham, Eng., U.K. (fär′nĭng ŭm)	158b	51°22′N	0°14′E
Farnworth, Eng., U.K. (färn′wŭrth)	158a	53°34′N	2°24′W
Faro, Braz. (fä′rȯ)	143	2°05′S	56°32′W
Faro, Port.	162	37°01′N	7°57′W
Farodofay, Madag.	233	24°59′S	46°58′E
Faroe Islands, is., Eur.	156	62°00′N	5°45′W
Fårön, i., Swe.	167	57°57′N	19°10′E
Farquhar, Cape, c., Austl. (fär′kwȧr)	220	23°50′S	112°55′E
Farrell, Pa., U.S. (făr′ĕl)	108	41°10′N	80°30′W
Farrukhābād, India (fŭ-rȯk-hä-bäd′)	199	27°29′N	79°35′E
Fársala, Grc.	175	39°18′N	22°25′E
Farsund, Nor. (fär′sȯn)	166	58°05′N	6°47′E
Fartak, Ra's, c., Yemen	198	15°43′N	52°17′E
Fartura, Serra da, mts., Braz. (sĕ′r-rä-dȧ-fär-tōō′rä)	144	26°40′S	53°15′W
Farvel, Kap, c., Grnld.	89	60°00′N	44°00′W
Farwell, Tx., U.S. (fär′wĕl)	120	34°24′N	103°03′W
Fasano, Italy (fä-zä′nō)	175	40°50′N	17°22′E
Fastiv, Ukr.	177	50°04′N	29°57′E
Fatëzh, Russia	176	52°06′N	35°51′E
Fatima, Port.	173	39°36′N	9°36′E
Fatsa, Tur. (fät′sä)	163	40°50′N	37°30′E
Faucilles, Monts, mts., Fr. (môɴ′ fō-sēl′)	171	48°07′N	6°13′E
Fauske, Nor.	160	67°15′N	15°24′E
Faust, Can. (foust)	95	55°19′N	115°38′W
Faustovo, Russia	186b	55°27′N	38°29′E
Faversham, Eng., U.K. (fă′vẽr-sh′m)	158b	51°19′N	0°54′E
Faxaflói, b., Ice.	160	64°33′N	22°40′W
Fayette, Al., U.S. (få-yĕt′)	124	33°40′N	87°54′W
Fayette, Ia., U.S.	113	42°49′N	91°49′W
Fayette, Mo., U.S.	121	39°09′N	92°41′W
Fayette, Ms., U.S.	124	31°43′N	91°00′W
Fayetteville, Ar., U.S. (få-yĕt′vĭl)	121	36°03′N	94°08′W
Fayetteville, N.C., U.S.	125	35°02′N	78°54′W
Fayetteville, Tn., U.S.	124	35°10′N	86°33′W
Fazao, Forêt Classée du, for., Togo	234	8°50′N	0°40′E
Fazilka, India	202	30°30′N	74°02′E
Fazzān (Fezzan), hist. reg., Libya	231	26°45′N	13°01′E
Fdérik, Maur.	230	22°45′N	12°38′W
Fear, Cape, c., N.C., U.S. (fēr)	125	33°52′N	77°48′W
Feather, r., Ca., U.S. (fĕth′ẽr)	118	38°56′N	121°41′W
Feather, Middle Fork of, r., Ca., U.S.	118	39°49′N	121°10′W
Feather, North Fork of, r., Ca., U.S.	118	40°00′N	121°20′W
Featherstone, Eng., U.K. (fĕdh′ẽr stŭn)	158a	53°39′N	1°21′W
Fécamp, Fr. (fā-käɴ′)	161	49°45′N	0°20′E
Federal, Distrito, dept., Ven. (dės-trė′tȯ-fĕ-dĕ-rä′l)	143b	10°34′N	66°55′W
Federal Way, Wa., U.S.	116a	47°20′N	122°20′W
Fëdorovka, Russia (fyô′dō-rôf-kȧ)	186b	56°15′N	37°14′E
Fehmarn, i., Ger. (fā′märn)	168	54°28′N	11°15′E
Fehrbellin, Ger. (fĕr′bĕl-lēn)	159b	52°49′N	12°46′E
Feia, Logoa, l., Braz. (lȯ-gôä-fĕ′yä)	141a	21°54′S	41°15′W
Feicheng, China (fā-chŭŋ)	206	36°18′N	116°45′E
Feidong, China (fā-dȯŋ)	206	31°53′N	117°28′E
Feira de Santana, Braz. (fĕ′ê-rä dā sänt-än′ä)	143	12°16′S	38°46′W
Feixian, China (fā-shyĕn)	206	35°17′N	117°59′E
Felanitx, Spain (fā-lä-nēch′)	162	39°29′N	3°09′E
Feldkirch, Aus. (fĕlt′kĭrk)	168	47°15′N	9°36′E
Feldkirchen, Ger. (fĕld′kĕr-ĸĕn)	159d	48°09′N	11°44′E
Felipe Carrillo Puerto, Mex.	132a	19°36′N	88°04′W

ăt; finăl; rāte; senåte; ärm; ȧsk; sofȧ; fâre; ch-choose; dh-as th in other; bē; ėvent; bĕt; recĕnt; cratẽr; g-gō; gh-guttural g; bĭt; ĭ-short neutral; rīde; ĸ-guttural k as ch in German ich;

PRONOUNCING INDEX

Feltre – Fort Bellefontaine 293

PLACE (Pronunciation)	PAGE	LAT.	LONG.
Feltre, Italy (fĕl'trä)	174	46°02'N	11°56'E
Femunden, I., Nor.	160	62°17'N	11°40'E
Fengcheng, China (fŭŋ-chŭŋ)	208	40°28'N	124°03'E
Fengcheng, China	207b	30°55'N	121°38'E
Fengdu, China (fŭŋ-dōō)	204	29°58'N	107°50'E
Fengjie, China (fŭŋ-jyĕ)	204	31°02'N	109°30'E
Fengming Dao, i., China (fŭŋ-mĭŋ dou)	206	39°19'N	121°15'E
Fengrun, China (fŭŋ-rŏn)	206	39°51'N	118°06'E
Fengtai, China (fŭŋ-tī)	208a	39°51'N	116°19'E
Fengxian, China (fŭŋ-shyĕn)	207b	30°55'N	121°26'E
Fengxian, China	206	34°41'N	116°36'E
Fengxiang, China (fŭŋ-shyäŋ)	204	34°25'N	107°20'E
Fengyang, China (fŭng'yăng')	208	32°55'N	117°32'E
Fengzhen, China (fŭŋ-jŭn)	205	40°28'N	113°20'E
Fennimore Pass, strt., Ak., U.S. (fĕn-ĭ-mōr)	103a	51°40'N	175°38'W
Fenoarivo Atsinanana, Madag.	233	17°30'S	49°31'E
Fenton, Mi., U.S. (fĕn-tŭn)	108	42°50'N	83°40'W
Fenton, Mo., U.S.	117e	38°31'N	90°27'W
Fenyang, China	205	37°20'N	111°48'E
Feodosiia, Ukr.	181	45°02'N	35°21'E
Ferdows, Iran	198	34°00'N	58°13'E
Ferentino, Italy (fā-rĕn-tē'nō)	174	41°42'N	13°18'E
Fergana, Uzb.	183	40°23'N	71°46'E
Fergus Falls, Mn., U.S. (fûr'gŭs)	104	46°17'N	96°03'W
Ferguson, Mo., U.S. (fûr-gŭ-sŭn)	117e	38°45'N	90°18'W
Ferkéssédougou, C. Iv.	234	9°36'N	5°12'W
Fermo, Italy (fĕr'mō)	174	43°10'N	13°43'E
Fermoselle, Spain (fĕr-mō-sāl'yā)	172	41°20'N	6°23'W
Fermoy, Ire. (fûr-moi')	164	52°05'N	8°06'W
Fernandina Beach, Fl., U.S. (fûr-năn-dē'nȧ)	125	30°38'N	81°29'W
Fernando de Noronha, Arquipélago, is., Braz.	143	3°51'S	32°25'W
Fernando Póo see Bioko, i., Eq. Gui.	230	3°35'N	7°45'E
Fernán-Núñez, Spain (fĕr-nän'nōōn'yāth)	172	37°42'N	4°43'W
Fernão Veloso, Baia de, b., Moz.	237	14°20'S	40°55'E
Ferndale, Ca., U.S. (fûrn'dāl)	114	40°34'N	124°18'W
Ferndale, Mi., U.S.	111b	42°27'N	83°08'W
Ferndale, Wa., U.S.	116d	48°51'N	122°36'W
Fernie, Can. (fûr'nĭ)	90	49°30'N	115°03'W
Fern Prairie, Wa., U.S. (fûrn prâr'ĭ)	116c	45°38'N	122°25'W
Ferrara, Italy (fĕr-rä'rä)	162	44°50'N	11°37'E
Ferrat, Cap, c., Alg. (kăp fĕr-rät)	173	35°49'N	0°29'W
Ferreira do Alentejo, Port.	172	38°03'N	8°06'W
Ferreira do Zezere, Port. (fĕr-rĕ'ē-rä dŏ zā-zā'rĕ)	172	39°49'N	8°17'W
Ferrelview, Mo., U.S. (fĕr'rĕl-vū)	117f	39°18'N	94°40'W
Ferreñafe, Peru (fĕr-rĕn-yä'fē)	142	6°38'S	79°48'W
Ferriday, La., U.S. (fĕr'ĭ-dā)	123	31°38'N	91°33'W
Ferrol, Spain	154	43°30'N	8°12'W
Fershampenuaz, Russia (fĕr-shäm'pĕn-wäz)	186a	53°32'N	59°50'E
Fertile, Mn., U.S. (fur'tĭl)	112	47°33'N	96°18'W
Fès, Mor. (fĕs)	230	34°08'N	5°00'W
Fessenden, N.D., U.S. (fĕs'ĕn-dĕn)	112	47°39'N	99°40'W
Festus, Mo., U.S. (fĕst'ŭs)	121	38°12'N	90°22'W
Fethiye, Tur. (fĕt-hē'yĕ)	163	36°40'N	29°05'E
Feuilles, Rivière aux, r., Can.	93	58°30'N	70°50'W
Ffestiniog, Wales, U.K.	164	52°59'N	3°58'W
Fianarantsoa, Madag. (fyȧ-nä'rȧn-tsō'ȧ)	233	21°21'S	47°15'E
Ficksburg, S. Afr. (fĭks'bûrg)	238c	28°53'S	27°53'E
Fidalgo Island, i., Wa., U.S. (fĭ-dăl'gō)	116a	48°28'N	122°39'W
Fieldbrook, Ca., U.S. (fēld'brŏk)	114	40°59'N	124°02'W
Fier, Alb. (fyĕr)	175	40°43'N	19°34'E
Fife Ness, c., Scot., U.K. (fīf'nes')	164	56°15'N	2°19'W
Fifth Cataract, wtfl., Sudan	231	18°27'N	33°38'E
Figeac, Fr. (fē-zhäk')	170	44°37'N	2°02'E
Figeholm, Swe. (fē-ghĕ-hōlm)	166	57°24'N	16°33'E
Figueira da Foz, Port. (fē-gwĕy-rä-dȧ-fôz)	172	40°10'N	8°50'W
Figuig, Mor.	230	32°20'N	1°30'W
Fiji, nation, Oc. (fē'jē)	3	18°40'S	175°00'E
Filadelfia, C.R. (fĭl-ȧ-dĕl'fĭ-ȧ)	132	10°26'N	85°37'W
Filatovskoye, Russia (fĭ-lä'tŏf-skô-yĕ)	186a	56°49'N	62°20'E
Filchner Ice Shelf, ice, Ant. (fĭlk'nĕr)	224	80°00'S	35°00'W
Filicudi, i., Italy (fē'le-kōō'dē)	174	38°34'N	14°39'E
Filippovskoye, Russia (fĭ-lĭ-pôf'skô-yĕ)	186b	56°06'N	38°38'E
Filipstad, Swe. (fĭl'ĭps-städh)	166	59°44'N	14°09'E
Fillmore, Ut., U.S. (fĭl'môr)	119	39°00'N	112°20'W
Filsa, Nor.	166	60°35'N	12°03'E
Fimi, r., D.R.C.	232	2°43'S	17°50'E
Finch, Can. (fĭnch)	102c	45°09'N	75°06'W
Findlay, Oh., U.S. (fĭnd'lā)	108	41°05'N	83°40'W
Fingoe, Moz.	237	15°12'S	31°50'E
Finke, r., Austl. (fĭŋ'kē)	220	25°25'S	134°30'E
Finland, nation, Eur. (fĭn'lȧnd)	154	62°45'N	26°13'E
Finland, Gulf of, b., Eur. (fĭn'lȧnd)	156	59°35'N	23°35'E
Finlandia, Col. (fēn-lä'n-dêä)	142a	4°38'N	75°39'W
Finlay, r., Can. (fĭn'lā)	92	57°45'N	125°30'W
Finow, Ger. (fē'nōv)	159b	52°50'N	13°44'E
Finowfurt, Ger. (fē'nō-fōōrt)	159b	52°50'N	13°41'E
Fircrest, Wa., U.S. (fûr'krĕst)	116a	47°14'N	122°31'W
Firenze see Florence, Italy	154	43°47'N	11°15'E
Firenzuola, Italy (fē-rĕnt-swô'lä)	174	44°08'N	11°21'E
Firozpur, India	199	30°58'N	74°39'E
Fischa, r., Aus.	159e	48°04'N	16°33'E
Fischamend Markt, Aus.	159e	48°07'N	16°37'E
Fish, r., Nmb. (fĭsh)	232	28°00'S	17°30'E
Fish Cay, i., Bah.	135	22°30'N	74°20'W
Fish Creek, r., Can. (fĭsh)	102e	50°52'N	114°21'W
Fisher, La., U.S. (fĭsh'ẽr)	123	31°28'N	93°30'W
Fisher Bay, b., Can.	97	51°30'N	97°16'W
Fisher Channel, strt., Can.	94	52°10'N	127°42'W
Fisher Strait, strt., Can.	93	62°43'N	84°28'W
Fisterra, Cabo de, c., Spain	156	42°52'N	9°48'W
Fitchburg, Ma., U.S. (fĭch'bûrg)	109	42°35'N	71°48'W
Fitri, Lac, l., Chad	235	12°50'N	17°28'E
Fitzgerald, Ga., U.S. (fĭts-jĕr'ăld)	124	31°42'N	83°17'W
Fitz Hugh Sound, strt., Can. (fĭts hū)	94	51°40'N	127°57'W
Fitzroy, r., Austl. (fĭts-roi')	220	18°00'S	124°05'E
Fitzroy, r., Austl.	221	23°45'S	150°02'E
Fitzroy, Monte (Cerro Chaltel), mtn., S.A.	144	48°10'S	73°18'W
Fitzroy Crossing, Austl.	218	18°08'S	126°00'E
Fitzwilliam, i., Can. (fĭts-wĭl'yŭm)	98	45°30'N	81°45'W
Fiume see Rijeka, Cro.	162	45°22'N	14°24'E
Fiumicino, Italy (fyōō-mē-chē'nō)	173d	41°47'N	12°19'E
Fjällbacka, Swe. (fyĕl'bäk-ȧ)	166	58°37'N	11°17'E
Flagstaff, S. Afr. (flăg'stäf)	233c	31°06'S	29°31'E
Flagstaff, Az., U.S. (flăg-stȧf)	104	35°15'N	111°40'W
Flagstaff, l., Me., U.S. (flăg-stȧf)	109	45°05'N	70°30'W
Flåm, Nor. (flôm)	166	60°50'N	7°00'E
Flambeau, r., Wi., U.S. (flăm-bō')	113	45°32'N	91°05'W
Flaming Gorge Reservoir, res., U.S.	106	41°13'N	109°30'W
Flamingo, Fl., U.S. (flȧ-mĭŋ'gô)	125	25°10'N	80°55'W
Flamingo Cay, i., Bah. (flȧ-mĭŋ'gô)	135	22°50'N	75°50'W
Flamingo Point, c., V.I.U.S.	129c	18°19'N	65°00'W
Flanders, hist. reg., Fr. (flăn'dẽrz)	165	50°53'N	2°29'E
Flandreau, S.D., U.S. (flăn'drō)	112	44°02'N	96°35'W
Flathead, r., N.A.	95	49°30'N	114°30'W
Flathead, Middle Fork, r., Mt., U.S.	115	48°30'N	113°47'W
Flathead, North Fork, r., N.A.	115	48°45'N	114°20'W
Flathead, South Fork, r., Mt., U.S.	115	48°05'N	113°45'W
Flathead Indian Reservation, I.R., Mt., U.S.	115	47°30'N	114°25'W
Flathead Lake, l., Mt., U.S. (flăt'hĕd)	106	47°57'N	114°20'W
Flatow, Ger.	159b	52°44'N	12°58'E
Flat Rock, Mi., U.S. (flăt rŏk)	111b	42°06'N	83°17'W
Flattery, Cape, c., Wa., U.S. (flăt'ẽr-ĭ)	114	48°22'N	124°45'W
Flatwillow Creek, r., Mt., U.S. (flat wĭl'ô)	115	46°45'N	108°47'W
Flekkefjord, Nor. (flăk'kē-fyōr)	166	58°19'N	6°38'E
Flemingsburg, Ky., U.S. (flĕm'ĭngz-bûrg)	108	38°25'N	83°45'W
Flensburg, Ger. (flĕns'bŏrgh)	160	54°48'N	9°27'E
Flers, Fr. (flĕr)	161	48°43'N	0°37'W
Fletcher, N.C., U.S.	125	35°26'N	82°30'W
Flinders, i., Austl.	221	39°35'S	148°10'E
Flinders, r., Austl.	221	18°48'S	141°07'E
Flinders, reg., Austl. (flĭn'dẽrz)	220	32°15'S	138°45'E
Flinders Reefs, rf., Austl.	221	17°30'S	149°02'E
Flin Flon, Can. (flĭn flŏn)	90	54°46'N	101°53'W
Flint, Wales, U.K.	158a	53°15'N	3°07'W
Flint, Mi., U.S.	105	43°00'N	83°45'W
Flint, r., Ga., U.S. (flĭnt)	107	31°25'N	84°15'W
Flintshire, co., Wales, U.K.	158a	53°13'N	3°00'W
Flora, Il., U.S. (flō'rȧ)	108	38°40'N	88°25'W
Flora, In., U.S.	108	40°25'N	86°30'W
Florala, Al., U.S. (flŏr-ăl'ȧ)	124	31°01'N	86°19'W
Floral Park, N.Y., U.S. (flôr'ăl pärk)	110a	40°42'N	73°42'W
Florence, Italy	154	43°47'N	11°15'E
Florence, Al., U.S. (flŏr'ĕns)	105	34°46'N	87°40'W
Florence, Az., U.S.	119	33°00'N	111°25'W
Florence, Co., U.S.	120	38°23'N	105°08'W
Florence, Ks., U.S.	121	38°14'N	96°56'W
Florence, S.C., U.S.	125	34°10'N	79°45'W
Florence, Wa., U.S.	116a	48°13'N	122°21'W
Florencia, Col. (flō-rĕn'sē-ȧ)	142	1°31'N	75°13'W
Florencio Sánchez, Ur. (flō-rĕn-sēō-sá'n-chĕz)	141c	33°52'S	57°24'W
Florencio Varela, Arg. (flō-rĕn'sē-o vä-rā'lä)	144a	34°50'S	58°16'W
Flores, Braz. (flō'rĕzh)	143	7°57'S	37°48'W
Flores, Guat.	132a	16°53'N	89°54'W
Flores, dept., Ur.	141c	33°33'S	57°00'W
Flores, i., Indon.	212	8°14'S	121°08'E
Flores, r., Arg.	141c	36°13'S	60°28'W
Flores, Laut (Flores Sea), sea, Indon.	212	7°09'S	120°30'E
Floresville, Tx., U.S. (flō'rĕs-vĭl)	122	29°10'N	98°08'W
Floriano, Braz. (flō-rȧ-ä'nŏ)	143	6°17'S	42°58'W
Florianópolis, Braz. (flō-rē-ä-nō'pō-lēs)	144	27°30'S	48°30'W
Florida, Col. (flō-rē'dä)	142a	3°20'N	76°12'W
Florida, Cuba	134	22°10'N	79°50'W
Florida, S. Afr.	233b	26°11'S	27°56'E
Florida, Ur. (flŏ-rē-dhä)	144	34°06'S	56°14'W
Florida, N.Y., U.S. (flŏr'ĭ-dȧ)	110a	41°20'N	74°21'W
Florida, state, U.S. (flŏr'ĭ-dȧ)	105	30°30'N	84°40'W
Florida, dept., Ur. (flŏ-rē'dhä)	141c	33°48'S	56°15'W
Florida, i., Sol. Is.	221	8°56'S	159°45'E
Florida, Straits of, strt., N.A.	129	24°10'N	81°00'W
Florida Bay, b., Fl., U.S. (flŏr'ĭ-dȧ)	125a	24°55'N	80°55'W
Florida Keys, is., Fl., U.S.	107	24°33'N	81°20'W
Florida Mountains, mts., N.M., U.S.	119	32°10'N	107°35'W
Florido, Río, r., Mex. (flō-rē'dō)	122	27°21'N	104°48'W
Floridsdorf, Aus. (flō'rĭds-dôrf)	159e	48°16'N	16°25'E
Florina, Grc. (flō-rē'nä)	163	40°48'N	21°24'E
Florissant, Mo., U.S. (flŏr'ĭ-sȧnt)	117e	38°47'N	90°20'W
Floyd, r., la., U.S. (floid)	112	42°38'N	96°15'W
Floydada, Tx., U.S. (floi-dā'dȧ)	120	33°59'N	101°19'W
Floyds Fork, r., Ky., U.S. (floi-dz)	111h	38°08'N	85°30'W
Flumendosa, r., Italy	174	39°45'N	9°18'E
Flushing, Mi., U.S. (flûsh'ĭng)	108	43°05'N	83°50'W
Fly, r. (flī)	213	8°00'S	141°45'E
Foča, Bos. (fō'chä)	175	43°29'N	18°48'E
Fochville, S. Afr. (fŏk'vĭl)	238c	26°29'S	27°29'E
Focşani, Rom. (fŏk-shä'nê)	169	45°41'N	27°17'E
Fogang, China (fwo-gäŋ)	209	23°50'N	113°35'E
Foggia, Italy (fôd'jä)	163	41°30'N	15°34'E
Fogo, Can. (fō'gō)	101	49°43'N	54°17'W
Fogo, i., Can.	99	49°40'N	54°13'W
Fogo, i., C.V.	230b	14°46'N	24°51'W
Fohnsdorf, Aus. (fōns'dôrf)	168	47°13'N	14°40'E
Föhr, i., Ger. (fûr)	168	54°47'N	8°30'E
Foix, Fr. (fwä)	170	42°58'N	1°34'E
Fokku, Nig.	235	11°40'N	4°31'E
Folādī, Koh-e, mtn., Afg.	199	34°38'N	67°32'E
Folgares, Ang.	236	14°54'S	15°08'E
Foligno, Italy (fō-lēn'yō)	174	42°58'N	12°41'E
Folkeston, Eng., U.K.	165	51°05'N	1°18'E
Folkingham, Eng., U.K. (fō'kĭng-ăm)	158a	52°53'N	0°24'W
Folkston, Ga., U.S.	125	30°50'N	82°01'W
Folsom, Ca., U.S.	118	38°40'N	121°10'W
Folsom, N.M., U.S. (fŏl'sŭm)	120	36°47'N	103°56'W
Fomento, Cuba (fō-mĕ'n-tō)	134	21°35'N	78°20'W
Fómeque, Col. (fŏ'mĕ-kĕ)	142a	4°29'N	73°52'W
Fonda, la., U.S. (fŏn'dȧ)	113	42°33'N	94°51'W
Fond du Lac, Wi., U.S. (fŏn dū lăk')	105	43°47'N	88°29'W
Fond du Lac Indian Reservation, I.R., Mn., U.S.	113	46°44'N	93°04'W
Fondi, Italy (fŏn'dē)	174	41°23'N	13°25'E
Fonseca, Golfo de, b., N.A. (gôl-fō-dĕ-fŏn-sā'kä)	128	13°09'N	87°55'W
Fontainebleau, Fr. (fôɴ-tĕn-blō')	161	48°24'N	2°42'E
Fontana, Ca., U.S. (fŏn-tă'nȧ)	117a	34°06'N	117°27'W
Fonte Boa, Braz. (fōn'tȧ bō'ȧ)	142	2°32'S	66°05'W
Fontenay-le-Comte, Fr. (fônt-nĕ'lē-kônt')	170	46°28'N	0°53'W
Fontenay-Trésigny, Fr. (fôɴ-te-nā' tra-sēn-yē')	171b	48°43'N	2°53'E
Fontenelle Reservoir, res., Wy., U.S.	115	42°05'N	110°05'W
Fontera, Punta, c., Mex. (pōō'n-tä-fōn-tē'rä)	131	18°36'N	92°43'W
Fontibón, Col. (fōn-tē-bôn')	142a	4°42'N	74°09'W
Fontur, c., Ice.	156	66°21'N	14°02'W
Foothills, S. Afr. (fŏt-hĭls)	233b	25°55'S	27°36'E
Footscray, Austl.	217a	37°48'S	144°54'E
Foraker, Mount, mtn., Ak., U.S. (fŏr'ȧ-kẽr)	103	62°40'N	152°40'W
Forbach, Fr. (fŏr'bäk)	171	49°12'N	6°54'E
Forbes, Austl. (fôrbz)	219	33°24'S	148°05'E
Forbes, Mount, mtn., Can.	95	51°52'N	116°56'W
Forchheim, Ger. (fŏrk'hīm)	168	49°43'N	11°05'E
Fordyce, Ar., U.S. (fôr'dīs)	121	33°48'N	92°24'W
Forécariah, Gui. (fōr-kȧ-rē'ä')	230	9°26'N	13°06'W
Forel, Mont, mtn., Grnld.	89	65°50'N	37°41'W
Forest, Ms., U.S. (fŏr'ĕst)	124	32°22'N	89°29'W
Forest, r., N.D., U.S.	112	48°08'N	97°45'W
Forest City, la., U.S.	113	43°14'N	93°40'W
Forest City, N.C., U.S.	125	35°20'N	81°52'W
Forest City, Pa., U.S.	109	41°35'N	75°30'W
Forest Grove, Or., U.S. (grōv)	116c	45°31'N	123°07'W
Forest Hill, Md., U.S.	110e	39°35'N	76°26'W
Forest Hill, Tx., U.S.	117c	32°40'N	97°16'W
Forestville, Can. (fŏr'ĕst-vĭl)	100	48°45'N	69°06'W
Forestville, Md., U.S.	110e	38°51'N	76°55'W
Forez, Monts du, mts., Fr. (môn dü fō-rā')	170	44°55'N	3°43'E
Forfar, Scot., U.K. (fôr'fȧr)	164	57°10'N	2°55'W
Forillon, Parc National, rec., Can.	100	48°50'N	64°05'W
Forio, mtn., Italy (fō'ryō)	173c	40°29'N	13°55'E
Forked Creek, r., Il., U.S. (fôrk'd)	111a	41°16'N	88°01'W
Forked Deer, r., Tn., U.S.	124	35°53'N	89°29'W
Forli, Italy (fōr-lē')	162	44°13'N	12°03'E
Formby, Eng., U.K. (fôrm'bê)	158a	53°34'N	3°04'W
Formby Point, c., Eng., U.K.	158a	53°33'N	3°06'W
Formentera, Isla de, i., Spain (ē's-lä-dĕ-fôr-mĕn-tā'rä)	162	38°43'N	1°25'E
Formiga, Braz. (fôr-mē'gȧ)	143	20°27'S	45°25'W
Formigas Bank, bk. (fŏr-mē'gäs)	135	18°30'N	75°40'W
Formosa, Arg. (fōr-mō'sä)	144	27°25'S	58°12'W
Formosa, Braz.	143	15°32'S	47°10'W
Formosa, prov., Arg.	144	24°30'S	60°45'W
Formosa, Serra, mts., Braz. (sĕ'r-rä)	143	12°59'S	55°11'W
Formosa Bay, b., Kenya	237	2°45'S	40°30'E
Formosa Strait see Taiwan Strait, strt., Asia	205	24°30'N	120°00'E
Fornosovo, Russia (fôr-nô'sô vô)	186c	59°35'N	30°34'E
Forrest City, Ar., U.S. (for'ĕst sĭ'tĭ)	121	35°00'N	90°46'W
Forsayth, Austl. (fôr-sīth')	219	18°33'S	143°42'E
Forshaga, Swe. (fôrs'hä'gä)	166	59°34'N	13°25'E
Forst, Ger. (fôrst)	161	51°45'N	14°38'E
Forsyth, Ga., U.S. (fôr-sīth')	124	33°02'N	83°56'W
Forsyth, Mt., U.S.	115	46°15'N	106°41'W
Fort Albany, Can. (fôrt ôl'bȧ nĭ)	91	52°20'N	81°30'W
Fort Alexander Indian Reserve, I.R., Can.	97	50°27'N	96°15'W
Fortaleza, Braz. (fôr'tä-lā'zȧ)	143	3°35'S	38°31'W
Fort Apache Indian Reservation, I.R., Az., U.S. (ȧ-păch'ē)	119	34°02'N	110°27'W
Fort Atkinson, Wi., U.S. (ăt'kĭn-sŭn)	113	42°55'N	88°46'W
Fort Beaufort, S. Afr. (bō'fôrt)	233c	32°47'S	26°39'E
Fort Belknap Indian Reservation, I.R., Mt., U.S.	115	48°16'N	108°38'W
Fort Bellefontaine, Mo., U.S. (bĕl-fŏn-tān')	117f	38°50'N	90°15'W

ng-sing; ŋ-baŋk; ɴ-nasalized n; nŏd; cŏmmit; ōld; ôbey; ôrder; oi-boil; fōōd; ŏ-as oo in foot; ou-out; s-soft; sh-dish; th-thin; pūre; ûnite; ûrn; stŭd; circŭs; ü-as in French tu; '-indeterminate vowel.

ăt; finăl; rāte; senåte; ärm; àsk; sofà; fåre; ch-choose; dh-as th in other; bē; ĕvent; bĕt; recĕnt; cratẽr; g-gō; gh-guttural g; bĭt; ĭ-short neutral; rīde; κ-guttural k as ch in German ich;

PRONOUNCING INDEX

Frydlant – Gattendorf 295

PLACE (Pronunciation)	PAGE	LAT.	LONG.
Frydlant, Czech Rep. (frēd′länt)	168	50°56′N	15°05′E
Fucheng, China (fōō-chŭŋ)	206	37°53′N	116°08′E
Fuchu, Japan (fōō′chōō)	211a	35°41′N	139°29′E
Fuchun, r., China (fōō-chòn)	209	29°50′N	120°00′E
Fuego, vol., Guat. (fwā′gō)	132	14°29′N	90°52′W
Fuencarral, Spain (fuān-kär-räl′)	173a	40°29′N	3°42′W
Fuensalida, Spain (fwān-sä-lē′dä)	172	40°04′N	4°15′W
Fuente, Mex. (fwĕ′n-tĕ′)	122	28°39′N	100°34′W
Fuente de Cantos, Spain (fwĕn′tā dā kän′tōs)	172	38°15′N	6°18′W
Fuente el Saz, Spain (fwĕn′tå ĕl säth′)	173a	40°39′N	3°30′W
Fuenteobejuna, Spain	172	38°15′N	5°30′W
Fuentesaúco, Spain (fwĕn-tå-sä-ōō′kō)	172	41°18′N	5°25′W
Fuerte, Río del, r., Mex. (rē′ō-dĕl-fōō-ĕ′r-tĕ)	128	26°15′N	108°50′W
Fuerte Olimpo, Para. (fwĕr′tå ō-lēm-pō)	144	21°10′S	57°49′W
Fuerteventura Island, i., Spain (fwĕr′tå-vĕn-tōō′rä)	230	28°24′N	13°21′W
Fuhai, China	204	47°01′N	87°07′E
Fuji, Japan (jōō′jê)	211	35°11′N	138°44′E
Fuji, r., Japan	211	35°20′N	138°23′E
Fujian, prov., China (fōō-jyĕn)	205	25°40′N	117°30′E
Fujidera, Japan	211b	34°34′N	135°37′E
Fujin, China (fōō-jyĭn)	205	47°13′N	132°11′E
Fuji San, mtn., Japan (fōō′jê sän)	205	35°23′N	138°44′E
Fujisawa, Japan (fōō′jê-sä′wa)	211a	35°20′N	139°29′E
Fujiyama see Fuji San, mtn., Japan	205	35°23′N	138°44′E
Fukuchiyama, Japan (fō′kò-chê-yä′ma)	211	35°18′N	135°07′E
Fukue, i., Japan (fò-kōō′ā)	210	32°40′N	129°02′E
Fukui, Japan (fōō′kōō-ê)	205	36°05′N	136°14′E
Fukuoka, Japan (fōō′kò-ō′kà)	205	33°35′N	130°23′E
Fukuoka, Japan	211a	35°52′N	139°31′E
Fukushima, Japan (fōō′kò-shē′mà)	210	37°45′N	140°29′E
Fukuyama, Japan (fōō′kò-yä′mà)	210	34°31′N	133°21′E
Fulda, Ger.	161	50°33′N	9°41′E
Fulda, r., Ger. (fòl′dä)	168	51°05′N	9°40′E
Fuling, China (fōō-lĭŋ)	204	29°40′N	107°30′E
Fullerton, Ca., U.S. (fòl′ẽr-tŭn)	117a	33°53′N	117°56′W
Fullerton, La., U.S.	123	31°00′N	93°00′W
Fullerton, Ne., U.S.	112	41°21′N	97°59′W
Fulton, Ky., U.S. (fŭl′tŭn)	124	36°30′N	88°53′W
Fulton, Mo., U.S.	121	38°51′N	91°56′W
Fulton, N.Y., U.S.	109	43°20′N	76°25′W
Fultondale, Al., U.S. (fŭl′tŭn-dāl)	110h	33°37′N	86°48′W
Funabashi, Japan (fōō′nà-bä′shē)	211	35°43′N	139°59′E
Funaya, Japan (fōō-nä′yä)	211b	34°45′N	135°52′E
Funchal, Port. (fòn-shäl′)	230	32°41′N	16°15′W
Fundación, Col. (fōōn-dä-syō′n)	142	10°43′N	74°13′W
Fundão, Port. (fòn-douN′)	172	40°08′N	7°32′W
Fundy, Bay of, b., Can. (fŭn′dĭ)	93	45°00′N	66°00′W
Fundy National Park, rec., Can.	93	45°38′N	65°00′W
Funing, China (fōō-nĭŋ)	208	33°55′N	119°54′E
Funing, China	206	39°55′N	119°16′E
Funing Wan, b., China	209	26°48′N	120°35′E
Funtua, Nig.	235	11°31′N	7°17′E
Furancungo, Moz.	237	14°55′S	33°35′E
Furbero, Mex. (fōōr-bĕ′rô)	131	20°21′N	97°32′W
Furgun, mtn., Iran	198	28°47′N	57°00′E
Furmanov, Russia (fûr-mä′nôf)	180	57°14′N	41°11′E
Furnas, Represa de, res., Braz.	143	21°00′S	46°00′W
Furneaux Group, is., Austl. (fûr′nō)	221	40°15′S	146°27′E
Fürstenfeld, Aus. (für′stĕn-fĕlt)	168	47°02′N	16°03′E
Fürstenfeldbruck, Ger. (fur′stĕn-fĕld′brōōk)	159d	48°11′N	11°16′E
Fürstenwalde, Ger. (für′stĕn-väl-dĕ)	168	52°21′N	14°04′E
Fürth, Ger. (fürt)	161	49°28′N	11°03′E
Furuichi, Japan (fōō′rò-ē′chê)	211b	34°33′N	135°37′E
Fusa, Japan (fōō′sä)	211a	35°52′N	140°08′E
Fuse, Japan	211b	34°40′N	135°33′E
Fushimi, Japan (fōō′shē-mê)	211b	34°57′N	135°47′E
Fushun, China (fōō′shōōn′)	205	41°50′N	124°00′E
Fusong, China (fōō-sōŋ)	208	42°12′N	127°12′E
Futtsu, Japan (fōō′tsōō′)	211a	35°19′N	139°49′E
Futtsu Misaki, c., Japan (fōōt′tsōō′ mê-sä′kē)	211a	35°19′N	139°46′E
Fuwah, Egypt (fōō′wà)	238b	31°13′N	30°35′E
Fuxian, China (fōō shyĕn)	206	39°36′N	121°59′E
Fuxin, China (fōō-shyĭn)	208	42°05′N	121°40′E
Fuyang, China (fōō-yäŋ)	205	32°53′N	115°48′E
Fuyang, China	209	30°10′N	119°58′E
Fuyang, r., China (fōō-yäŋ)	206	36°59′N	114°48′E
Fuyu, China (fōō-yōō)	205	45°20′N	125°00′E
Fuzhou, China (fōō-jō)	205	26°02′N	119°18′E
Fuzhou, r., China	206	39°38′N	121°43′E
Fuzhoucheng, China (fōō-jō-chŭŋ)	206	39°46′N	121°44′E
Fyn, i., Den. (fü′n)	166	55°24′N	10°33′E
Fyne, Loch, l., Scot., U.K. (fīn)	164	56°14′N	5°10′W
Fyresvatn, l., Nor.	166	59°04′N	7°55′E

G

PLACE (Pronunciation)	PAGE	LAT.	LONG.
Gaalkacyo, Som.	238a	7°00′N	47°30′E
Gabela, Ang.	236	10°48′S	14°20′E
Gabès, Tun. (gä′bĕs)	230	33°51′N	10°04′E
Gabès, Golfe de, b., Tun.	230	32°22′N	10°59′E
Gabil, Chad	235	11°09′N	18°12′E
Gąbin, Pol. (gôN′bēn)	169	52°23′N	19°47′E
Gabon, nation, Afr. (gå-bôN′)	232	0°30′S	10°45′E
Gaborone, Bots.	232	24°28′S	25°59′E
Gabriel, r., Tx., U.S. (gā′brī-ĕl)	123	30°38′N	97°15′W
Gabrovo, Blg. (gäb′rô-vō)	175	42°52′N	25°19′E
Gachsārān, Iran	201	30°12′N	50°47′E
Gacko, Bos. (gäts′kô)	175	43°10′N	18°34′E
Gadsden, Al., U.S. (gădz′dĕn)	105	34°00′N	86°00′W
Găeşti, Rom. (gä-yĕsh′tê)	175	44°43′N	25°21′E
Gaeta, Italy (gä-å′tä)	174	41°18′N	13°34′E
Gaffney, S.C., U.S. (găf′nĭ)	125	35°04′N	81°47′W
Gafsa, Tun. (gäf′sä)	230	34°16′N	8°37′E
Gagarin, Russia	176	55°32′N	34°58′E
Gagnoa, C. Iv.	234	6°08′N	5°56′W
Gagra, Geor.	182	43°20′N	40°15′E
Gaillac-sur-Tarn, Fr. (gà-yäk′sür-tärn′)	170	43°54′N	1°52′E
Gaillard Cut, reg., Pan. (gä-ĕl-yä′rd)	128a	9°03′N	79°42′W
Gainesville, Fl., U.S. (gānz′vĭl)	105	29°40′N	82°20′W
Gainesville, Ga., U.S.	124	34°16′N	83°48′W
Gainesville, Tx., U.S.	121	33°38′N	97°08′W
Gainsborough, Eng., U.K. (gānz′bŭr-ō)	158a	53°23′N	0°46′W
Gairdner, Lake, l., Austl. (gârd′nẽr)	220	32°20′S	136°30′E
Gaithersburg, Md., U.S. (gā′thẽrs′bûrg)	110e	39°08′N	77°13′W
Gaixian, China (gī-shyĕn)	208	40°25′N	122°20′E
Galana, r., Kenya	237	3°00′S	39°30′E
Galapagar, Spain (gä-lä-pä-gär′)	173a	40°36′N	4°00′W
Galapagos Islands see Colón, Archipiélago de, is., Ec.	142	0°10′S	87°45′W
Galaria, r., Italy	173d	41°58′N	12°21′E
Galashiels, Scot., U.K. (găl-ȧ-shēlz)	164	55°40′N	2°57′W
Galaţi, Rom.	154	45°25′N	28°05′E
Galatina, Italy (gä-lä-tē′nä)	175	40°10′N	18°12′E
Galaxídi, Grc.	175	38°26′N	22°22′E
Galdhøpiggen, mtn., Nor.	166	61°37′N	8°17′E
Galeana, Mex. (gä-lå-ä′nä)	122	24°50′N	100°04′W
Galena, Il., U.S. (gȧ-lē′nȧ)	113	42°26′N	90°27′W
Galena, In., U.S.	111h	38°21′N	85°55′W
Galena Peak, mtn., Tx., U.S.	123a	29°44′N	95°14′W
Galera, Cerro, mtn., Pan. (sĕ′r-rô-gä-lĕ′rä)	128a	8°55′N	79°38′W
Galeras, vol., Col. (gä-lĕ′räs)	142	0°57′N	77°27′W
Gales, r., Or., U.S. (gālz)	116c	45°33′N	123°11′W
Galesburg, Il., U.S. (gālz′bûrg)	105	40°56′N	90°21′W
Galesville, Wi., U.S. (gālz′vĭl)	113	44°04′N	91°22′W
Galeton, Pa., U.S. (gāl′tŭn)	109	41°45′N	77°40′W
Galich, Russia (gäl′ĭch)	180	58°20′N	42°38′E
Galicia, hist. reg., Pol. (gȧ-lĭsh′ĭ-ȧ)	169	49°48′N	21°05′E
Galicia, hist. reg., Spain (gä-lē′thyä)	172	43°35′N	8°03′W
Galilee, l., Austl. (găl′ĭ-lē)	221	22°23′S	145°09′E
Galilee, Sea of, l., Isr.	197a	32°53′N	35°45′E
Galina Point, c., Jam. (gä-lē′nä)	134	18°25′N	76°50′W
Galion, Oh., U.S. (găl′ĭ-ŭn)	108	40°45′N	82°50′W
Galisteo, N.M., U.S. (gä-lĭs-tå′ō)	120	35°20′N	106°00′W
Gallarate, Italy (gäl-lä-rä′tä)	174	45°37′N	8°48′E
Gallardon, Fr. (gä-lär-dôN′)	171b	48°31′N	1°40′E
Gallatin, Mo., U.S. (găl′ȧ-tĭn)	121	39°55′N	93°58′W
Gallatin, Tn., U.S.	124	36°23′N	86°28′W
Gallatin, r., Mt., U.S.	115	45°12′N	111°10′W
Galle, Sri L. (gäl)	203	6°13′N	80°10′E
Gállego, r., Spain (gäl-yä′gō)	173	42°27′N	0°37′W
Gallinas, Punta de, c., Col. (gä-lyē′näs)	142	12°10′N	72°10′W
Gallipoli, Italy (gäl-lē′pô-lē)	175	40°03′N	17°58′E
Gallipoli see Gelibolu, Tur. (gäl-lē′pô-lē)	163	40°25′N	26°40′E
Gallipoli Peninsula, pen., Tur.	175	40°23′N	25°10′E
Gallipolis, Oh., U.S. (găl-ĭ-pô-lēs)	108	38°50′N	82°10′W
Gällivare, Swe. (yĕl-ĭ-vär′ĕ)	160	68°06′N	20°29′E
Gallo, r., Spain (gäl′yō)	172	40°43′N	1°42′W
Gallup, N.M., U.S. (găl′ŭp)	104	35°30′N	108°45′W
Galty Mountains, mts., Ire.	164	52°19′N	8°20′W
Galva, Il., U.S. (găl′vȧ)	121	41°11′N	90°02′W
Galveston, Tx., U.S. (găl′vĕs-tŭn)	105	29°18′N	94°48′W
Galveston Bay, b., Tx., U.S.	107	29°39′N	94°45′W
Galveston I, Tx., U.S.	123a	29°12′N	94°53′W
Galway, Ire.	154	53°16′N	9°05′W
Galway Bay, b., Ire. (gôl′wā)	164	53°10′N	9°47′W
Gamba, China (gäm-bä)	202	28°23′N	89°42′E
Gambaga, Ghana (gäm-bä′gä)	230	10°32′N	0°26′W
Gambela, Eth. (găm-bā′lȧ)	231	8°15′N	34°33′E
Gambia (Gambie), r., Afr.	234	13°20′N	15°55′W
Gambia, The, nation, Afr.	230	13°38′N	19°38′W
Gambie, r., Afr.	230	12°30′N	13°00′W
Gamboma, Congo (gäm-bō′mä)	232	1°53′S	15°51′E
Gamleby, Swe. (gäm′lĕ-bü)	166	57°54′N	16°20′E
Gan, r., China (gän)	209	26°50′N	115°00′E
Gäncä, Azer.	180	40°40′N	46°22′E
Gandak, r., India	202	26°37′N	84°22′E
Gander, Can. (găn′dẽr)	91	48°57′N	54°34′W
Gander, r., Can.	101	49°10′N	54°35′W
Gander Lake, l., Can.	101	48°55′N	55°40′W
Gandhinagar, India	202	23°30′N	72°47′E
Gandi, Nig.	235	12°55′N	5°49′E
Gandía, Spain (gän-dē′ä)	173	38°56′N	0°10′W
Gangdisê Shan (Trans Himalayas), mts., China	204	30°25′N	83°43′E
Ganges, r., Asia (găn′jēz)	199	24°00′N	89°30′E
Ganges, Mouths of the, mth., Asia (găn′jēz)	199	21°18′N	88°40′E
Gangi, Italy (gän′jē)	174	37°48′N	14°15′E
Gangtok, India	199	27°15′N	88°30′E
Gannan, China (gän-nän)	208	47°50′N	123°30′E
Gannett Peak, mtn., Wy., U.S. (găn′ĕt)	106	43°10′N	109°38′W
Gano, Oh., U.S. (ă′nô)	111f	39°18′N	84°24′W
Gänserndorf, Aus.	159e	48°21′N	16°43′E
Gansu, prov., China (gän-sōō)	204	38°50′N	101°10′E
Ganwo, Nig.	235	11°13′N	4°42′E
Ganyu, China (gän-yōō)	206	34°52′N	119°07′E
Ganzhou, China (gän-jō)	205	25°50′N	114°30′E
Gao, Mali (gä′ō)	230	16°16′N	0°03′W
Gao'an, China (gou-än)	209	28°30′N	115°02′E
Gaomi, China (gou-mē)	206	36°23′N	119°46′E
Gaoqiao, China (gou-chyou)	207b	31°21′N	121°35′E
Gaoshun, China (gou-shòn)	206	31°22′N	118°50′E
Gaotang, China (gou-täŋ)	206	36°52′N	116°12′E
Gaoyao, China (gou-you)	209	23°08′N	112°25′E
Gaoyi, China (gou-yē)	206	37°37′N	114°39′E
Gaoyou, China (gou-yō)	208	32°46′N	119°26′E
Gaoyou Hu, l., China (kä′ō-yōō′hōō)	205	32°42′N	118°40′E
Gap, Fr. (gȧp)	161	44°34′N	6°08′E
Gapan, Phil. (gä-pän)	213a	15°18′N	120°56′E
Gar, China	204	31°11′N	80°35′E
Garanhuns, Braz. (gä-rän-yònsh′)	143	8°49′S	36°28′W
Garber, Ok., U.S. (gár′bẽr)	121	36°28′N	97°35′W
Garching, Ger. (gär′kĕng)	159d	48°15′N	11°39′E
Garcia, Mex. (gär-sē′ä)	122	25°50′N	100°37′W
García de la Cadena, Mex.	130	21°14′N	103°26′W
Garda, Lago di, l., Italy (lä-gō-dē-gär′dä)	162	45°43′N	10°26′E
Gardanne, Fr. (gȧr-dán′)	170a	43°28′N	5°29′E
Gardelegen, Ger. (gär-dē-lā′ghĕn)	168	52°32′N	11°22′E
Garden, i., Mi., U.S. (gär′d′n)	108	45°50′N	85°50′W
Gardena, Ca., U.S. (gär-dē′nȧ)	117a	33°53′N	118°19′W
Garden City, Ks., U.S.	120	37°58′N	100°52′W
Garden City, Mi., U.S.	111b	42°20′N	83°21′W
Garden Grove, Ca., U.S. (gär′d′n grōv)	117a	33°47′N	117°56′W
Garden Reach, India	202a	22°33′N	88°17′E
Garden River, Can.	117k	46°33′N	84°10′W
Gardeyz, Afg.	202	33°43′N	69°09′E
Gardiner, Me., U.S. (gärd′nẽr)	100	44°12′N	69°46′W
Gardiner, Mt., U.S.	115	45°03′N	110°43′W
Gardiner, Wa., U.S.	116a	48°03′N	122°55′W
Gardiner Dam, dam, Can.	96	51°17′N	106°51′W
Gardner, Ma., U.S.	109	42°35′N	72°00′W
Gardner Canal, strt., Can.	94	53°28′N	128°15′W
Gardner Pinnacles, Hi., U.S.	126b	25°10′N	167°00′W
Gareloi, i., Ak., U.S. (gär-lōō-ä′)	103a	51°40′N	178°48′W
Garfield, N.J., U.S. (gär′fēld)	110a	40°53′N	74°06′W
Garfield, Ut., U.S.	117b	40°45′N	112°10′W
Garfield Heights, Oh., U.S.	111d	41°25′N	81°36′W
Gargaliánoi, Grc. (gär-gä-lyä′nē)	175	37°07′N	21°50′E
Gargždai, Lith. (gärgzh′dī)	167	55°43′N	20°09′E
Garibaldi, Mount, mtn., Can. (gär-ĭ-băl′dê)	94	49°51′N	123°01′W
Garin, Arg. (gä-rē′n)	144a	34°25′S	58°44′W
Garissa, Kenya	237	0°28′S	39°38′E
Garland, Tx., U.S. (gär′lănd)	117c	32°55′N	96°39′W
Garland, Ut., U.S.	115	41°45′N	112°10′W
Garm, Taj.	183	39°12′N	70°28′E
Garmisch-Partenkirchen, Ger. (gär′mēsh pär′tĕn-kĕr′kĕn)	168	47°38′N	11°10′E
Garnett, Ks., U.S. (gär′nĕt)	121	38°16′N	95°15′W
Garonne, r., Fr. (gȧ-rôn)	156	44°00′N	1°00′E
Garoua, Cam. (gär′wä)	231	9°18′N	13°24′E
Garrett, In., U.S. (găr′ĕt)	108	41°20′N	85°10′W
Garrison, N.D., U.S.	112	47°38′N	101°24′W
Garrison, N.Y., U.S. (găr′ĭ-sŭn)	110a	41°23′N	73°57′W
Garrovillas, Spain (gä-rô-vēl′yäs)	172	39°42′N	6°30′W
Garry, l., Can. (găr′ĭ)	92	66°16′N	99°23′W
Garsen, Kenya	237	2°16′S	40°07′E
Garson, Can.	99	46°34′N	80°52′W
Garstedt, Ger. (gär′shtĕt)	159c	53°40′N	9°58′E
Garulia, India	202a	22°48′N	88°23′E
Garwolin, Pol. (gär-vō′lēn)	169	51°54′N	21°40′E
Gary, In., U.S. (gā′rĭ)	105	41°35′N	87°21′W
Gary, W.V., U.S. (fĭl′bẽrt)	125	37°21′N	81°33′W
Garzón, Col. (gär-thōn′)	142	2°13′N	75°44′W
Gasan, Phil. (gä-sän′)	213a	13°19′N	121°52′E
Gasan-Kuli, Turkmen.	183	37°25′N	53°55′E
Gas City, In., U.S. (găs)	108	40°30′N	85°40′W
Gascogne, reg., Fr. (gäs-kôn′yĕ)	170	43°45′N	1°49′W
Gasconade, r., Mo., U.S. (găs-kô-nād′)	121	37°46′N	92°15′W
Gascoyne, r., Austl. (găs-koin′)	220	25°15′S	117°00′E
Gashland, Mo., U.S. (găsh′-lănd)	117f	39°15′N	94°35′W
Gashua, Nig.	235	12°54′N	11°00′E
Gasny, Fr. (gäs-nē′)	171b	49°05′N	1°36′E
Gaspé, Can.	91	48°50′N	64°29′W
Gaspé, Péninsule de, pen., Can.	93	48°30′N	65°00′W
Gasper Hernández, Dom. Rep. (gäs-pär′ ĕr-nän′dāth)	135	19°40′N	70°15′W
Gassaway, W.V., U.S. (găs′ȧ-wā)	108	38°40′N	80°45′W
Gaston, Or., U.S. (găs′tŭn)	116c	45°26′N	123°08′W
Gastonia, N.C., U.S. (găs-tō′nĭ-ȧ)	125	35°15′N	81°14′W
Gastre, Arg. (gäs-trĕ)	144	42°12′S	68°50′W
Gata, Cabo de, c., Spain (kå′bô-dĕ-gä′tä)	162	36°42′N	2°00′W
Gata, Sierra de, mts., Spain (syĕr′rȧ dā gä′tä)	162	40°12′N	6°39′W
Gatchina, Russia (gä-chē′nȧ)	180	59°33′N	30°08′E
Gátes, Akrotírion, c., Cyp.	197a	34°30′N	33°15′E
Gateshead, Eng., U.K. (gāts′hĕd)	164	54°56′N	1°38′W
Gates of the Arctic National Park, rec., Ak., U.S.	103	67°45′N	153°30′W
Gatesville, Tx., U.S. (gāts′vĭl)	123	31°26′N	97°34′W
Gâtine, Hauteurs de, hills, Fr.	170	46°40′N	0°50′W
Gatineau, Can. (gà′tē-nō)	102c	45°29′N	75°38′W
Gatineau, r., Can.	99	45°45′N	75°50′W
Gatineau, Parc de la, rec., Can.	99	45°32′N	75°53′W
Gattendorf, Aus.	159e	48°01′N	17°00′E

PLACE (Pronunciation)	PAGE	LAT.	LONG.
Gatun, Pan. (gä-tōōn')	133	9°16'N	79°25'W
Gatun, r., Pan.	128a	9°21'N	79°40'W
Gatún, Lago, l., Pan.	133	9°13'N	79°24'W
Gatun Locks, trans., Pan.	128a	9°16'N	79°57'W
Gauhāti, India	199	26°09'N	91°51'E
Gauja, r., Lat. (gå'ŏ-yå)	167	57°10'N	24°30'E
Gaula, r., Nor.	166	62°55'N	10°45'E
Gávdos, i., Grc. (gäv'dôs)	163	34°48'N	24°08'E
Gavins Point Dam, Ne., U.S. (gă'-vĭns)	112	42°47'N	97°47'W
Gāvkhūnī, Bātlāq-e, l., Iran	198	31°40'N	52°48'E
Gävle, Swe. (yĕv'lĕ)	154	60°40'N	17°07'E
Gävlebukten, b., Swe.	166	60°45'N	17°30'E
Gavrilov Posad, Russia (gá-vrê-lôf'ka po-sát)	176	56°34'N	40°09'E
Gavrilov-Yam, Russia (gá'vrê-lôf yäm')	176	57°17'N	39°49'E
Gawler, Austl. (gô'lẽr)	218	34°35'S	138°47'E
Gawler Ranges, mts., Austl.	222	32°35'S	136°30'E
Gaya, India (gŭ'yä)(gī'á)	199	24°53'N	85°00'E
Gaya, Nig. (gä'yä)	230	11°58'N	9°05'E
Gaylord, Mi., U.S. (gā'lôrd)	108	45°00'N	84°35'W
Gayndah, Austl. (gān'dăh)	222	25°43'S	151°33'E
Gaza, Gaza	198	31°30'N	34°29'E
Gaziantep, Tur. (gä-zē-än'tĕp)	198	37°10'N	37°30'E
Gbarnga, Lib.	234	7°00'N	9°29'W
Gdańsk, Pol. (g'dänsk)	154	54°20'N	18°40'E
Gdov, Russia (g'dôf')	180	58°44'N	27°51'E
Gdynia, Pol. (g'dĕn'yà)	160	54°29'N	18°30'E
Geary, Ok., U.S. (gē'rĭ)	120	35°36'N	98°19'W
Géba, r., Gui.-B.	234	12°25'N	14°35'W
Gebo, Wy., U.S. (gĕb'ō)	115	43°49'N	108°13'W
Ged, La., U.S. (gĕd)	123	30°07'N	93°36'W
Gediz, r., Tur.	163	38°44'N	28°45'E
Gedney, i., Wa., U.S. (gĕd-nē)	116a	48°01'N	122°18'W
Gedser, Den.	166	54°35'N	12°08'E
Geel, Bel.	159a	51°09'N	5°01'E
Geelong, Austl. (jē-lông')	219	38°06'S	144°13'E
Gegu, China (gŭ-gōō)	206	39°00'N	117°30'E
Ge Hu, l., China (gŭ hōō)	206	31°37'N	119°57'E
Geidam, Nig.	230	12°57'N	11°57'E
Geikie Range, mts., Austl. (gē'kē)	220	17°35'S	125°32'E
Geislingen, Ger. (gīs'lĭng-ĕn)	168	48°37'N	9°52'E
Geist Reservoir, res., In., U.S. (gēst)	111g	39°57'N	85°59'W
Geita, Tan.	237	2°52'S	32°10'E
Gejiu, China (gŭ-jĭo)	209	23°32'N	102°50'E
Geldermalsen, Neth.	159a	51°53'N	5°18'E
Geldern, Ger. (gĕl'dĕrn)	171c	51°31'N	6°20'E
Gelibolu, Tur. (gĕ-lĭb'ô-lò)	163	40°25'N	26°40'E
Gelsenkirchen, Ger. (gĕl-zĕn-kĭrk-ĕn)	168	51°31'N	7°05'E
Gemas, Malay. (jĕm'ás)	197b	2°35'N	102°37'E
Gemena, D.R.C.	231	3°15'N	19°46'E
Gemlik, Tur. (gĕm'lĭk)	163	40°30'N	29°10'E
Genale (Jubba), r., Afr.	238a	5°15'N	41°00'E
General Alvear, Arg. (gĕ-nĕ-räl'äl-vĕ-ä'r)	141c	36°04'S	60°02'W
General Arenales, Arg. (ä-rĕ-nä'lĕs)	141c	34°19'S	61°16'W
General Belgrano, Arg. (bĕl-grá'nô)	141c	35°45'S	58°32'W
General Cepeda, Mex. (sĕ-pĕ'dä)	122	25°24'N	101°29'W
General Conesa, Arg. (kô-nĕ'sä)	141c	36°30'S	57°19'W
General Guido, Arg. (gē'dô)	141c	36°41'S	57°48'W
General Lavalle, Arg. (lå-vá'l-yĕ)	141c	36°25'S	56°55'W
General Madariaga, Arg. (män-dá-rēä'gä)	144	36°59'S	57°14'W
General Paz, Arg. (pá'z)	141c	35°30'S	58°20'W
General Pedro Antonio Santos, Mex.	130	21°37'N	98°58'W
General Pico, Arg. (pē'kô)	144	36°46'S	63°44'W
General Roca, Arg. (rô-kä)	144	39°01'S	67°31'W
General San Martín, Arg. (sän-mår-tē'n)	144a	34°35'S	58°32'W
General Sarmiento (San Miguel), Arg.	144a	34°33'S	58°43'W
General Viamonte, Arg. (vēä'môn-tĕ)	141c	35°01'S	60°59'W
General Zuazua, Mex. (zwä'zwä)	122	25°54'N	100°07'W
Genesee, r., N.Y., U.S. (jĕn-ē-sē')	109	42°25'N	78°10'W
Geneseo, Il., U.S. (jē-nĕsē'ō)	108	41°28'N	90°11'W
Geneva (Genève), Switz.	154	46°14'N	6°04'E
Geneva, Al., U.S. (jĕ-nē'vá)	124	31°03'N	85°50'W
Geneva, Il., U.S.	111a	41°53'N	88°18'W
Geneva, Ne., U.S.	121	40°32'N	97°37'W
Geneva, N.Y., U.S.	109	42°50'N	77°00'W
Geneva, Oh., U.S.	108	41°45'N	80°55'W
Geneva, Lake, l., Switz.	161	46°28'N	6°30'E
Genève see Geneva, Switz.	154	46°14'N	6°04'E
Genil, r., Spain (hå-nēl')	172	37°15'N	4°05'W
Genoa, Italy	154	44°23'N	9°52'E
Genoa, Ne., U.S. (jen'ô-á)	121	41°26'N	97°43'W
Genoa City, Wi., U.S.	111a	42°31'N	88°19'W
Genova, Golfo di, b., Italy (gôl-fô-dē-jĕn'ō-vä)	156	44°10'N	8°45'E
Genovesa, i., Ec. (ĕ's-lä-gĕ-nō-vĕ-sä)	142	0°08'N	90°15'W
Gent, Bel.	161	51°05'N	3°40'E
Genthin, Ger. (gĕn-tēn')	168	52°24'N	12°10'E
Genzano di Roma, Italy (gzhĕnt-zá'-nô-dē-rô'mä)	173d	41°43'N	12°49'E
Geographe Bay, b., Austl. (jē-ô-graf')	220	33°00'S	114°00'E
Geographe Channel, strt., Austl. (jēô'grā-fĭk)	220	24°15'S	112°50'E
George, l., N.Y., U.S. (jôrj)	109	43°40'N	73°30'W
George, Lake, l., N.A. (jôrg)	117k	46°26'N	84°09'W
George, Lake, l., Ug.	237	0°02'N	30°25'E
George, Lake, l., Fl., U.S. (jôr-ĭj)	125	29°10'N	81°50'W
George, Lake, l., In., U.S.	111a	41°31'N	87°17'W
Georges, r., Austl.	217b	33°57'S	151°00'E
George Town, Bah.	135	23°30'N	75°50'W
Georgetown, Can. (jôrg-toun)	102d	43°39'N	79°56'W
Georgetown, Can. (jôr-ĭj-toun)	101	46°11'N	62°32'W
George Town, Cay. Is.	134	19°20'N	81°20'W
Georgetown, Guy. (jôrj'toun)	143	7°45'N	58°04'W
George Town, Malay.	212	5°21'N	100°09'E
Georgetown, Ct., U.S.	110a	41°15'N	73°25'W
Georgetown, De., U.S.	109	38°40'N	75°20'W
Georgetown, Il., U.S.	108	40°00'N	87°40'W
Georgetown, Ky., U.S.	108	38°10'N	84°35'W
Georgetown, Ma., U.S. (jôrg-toun)	101a	42°43'N	71°00'W
Georgetown, Md., U.S.	109	39°25'N	75°55'W
Georgetown, S.C., U.S. (jôr-ĭj-toun)	125	33°22'N	79°17'W
Georgetown, Tx., U.S. (jôrg-toun)	123	30°37'N	97°40'W
George Washington Birthplace National Monument, rec., Va., U.S. (jôrj wŏsh'ĭng-tŭn)	109	38°10'N	77°00'W
George Washington Carver National Monument, rec., Mo., U.S. (jôrg wăsh-ĭng-tŭn kär'vẽr)	121	36°58'N	94°21'W
George West, Tx., U.S.	122	28°20'N	98°07'W
Georgia, nation, Asia	178	42°17'N	43°00'E
Georgia, state, U.S. (jôr'ji-ă)	105	32°40'N	83°50'W
Georgia, Strait of, strt., N.A.	94	49°20'N	124°00'W
Georgiana, Al., U.S. (jôr-jē-ăn'á)	124	31°39'N	86°44'W
Georgian Bay, b., Can.	93	45°15'N	80°50'W
Georgian Bay Islands National Park, rec., Can.	98	45°20'N	81°40'W
Georgina, r., Austl. (jôr-jē'ná)	220	22°00'S	138°15'E
Georgiyevsk, Russia (gyôr-gyĕfsk')	181	44°05'N	43°30'E
Gera, Ger. (gā'rä)	161	50°52'N	12°06'E
Geral, Serra, mts., Braz. (sĕr'rá zhă-räl')	144	28°30'S	51°00'W
Geral de Goiás, Serra, mts., Braz. (zhă-räl'-dĕ-gô-yá's)	143	14°22'S	45°40'W
Geraldton, Austl. (jĕr'ăld-tŭn)	218	28°40'S	114°35'E
Geraldton, Can.	91	49°43'N	87°00'W
Gérgal, Spain (gĕr'gäl)	172	37°08'N	2°29'W
Gering, Ne., U.S. (gē'rĭng)	112	41°49'N	103°41'W
Gerlachovský štít, mtn., Slvk.	169	49°12'N	20°08'E
Germantown, Oh., U.S. (jûr'mán-toun)	108	39°35'N	84°25'W
Germany, nation, Eur. (jûr'má-nĭ)	154	51°00'N	10°00'E
Germiston, S. Afr. (jûr'mĭs-tŭn)	232	26°19'S	28°11'E
Gerona, Phil. (hā-rō'nä)	213a	15°36'N	120°36'E
Gerrards Cross, Eng., U.K. (jĕrărds krŏs)	158b	51°34'N	0°33'W
Gers, r., Fr. (zhĕr)	173	43°25'N	0°30'E
Gersthofen, Ger. (gĕrst-hō'fĕn)	159d	48°26'N	10°54'E
Getafe, Spain (hā-tä'fā)	172	40°19'N	3°44'W
Gettysburg, Pa., U.S. (gĕt'ĭs-bûrg)	109	39°50'N	77°15'W
Gettysburg, S.D., U.S.	112	45°01'N	99°59'W
Gevelsberg, Ger. (gĕ-fĕls'bĕrgh)	171c	51°18'N	7°20'E
Ghāghra, r., India	199	26°00'N	83°00'E
Ghana, nation, Afr. (gän'ä)	230	8°00'N	2°00'W
Ghanzi, Bots. (gän'zē)	232	21°30'S	22°00'E
Ghardaïa, Alg. (gär-dä'ē-ä)	230	32°29'N	3°38'E
Gharo, Pak.	202	24°50'N	68°35'E
Ghāt, Libya	230	24°52'N	10°16'E
Ghazāl, Bahr al-, r., Sudan	231	9°30'N	30°00'E
Ghazal, Bahr el, r., Chad (bär ĕl ghä-zäl')	235	14°30'N	17°00'E
Ghazzah see Gaza, Gaza	198	31°30'N	34°29'E
Gheorgheni, Rom.	163	46°48'N	25°30'E
Gherla, Rom. (gĕr'lä)	169	47°01'N	23°55'E
Ghilizane, Alg.	230	35°43'N	0°43'E
Ghorīān, Afg.	201	34°21'N	61°30'E
Ghost Lake, Can.	102e	51°15'N	114°46'W
Ghudāmis, Libya	230	30°07'N	9°26'E
Giannitsá, Grc.	175	40°47'N	22°26'E
Giannutri, Isola di, i., Italy (jän-nōō'trē)	174	42°15'N	11°06'E
Giant Sequoia National Monument, rec., Ca., U.S.	118	36°10'N	118°35'W
Gibara, Cuba (hē-bä'rä)	134	21°05'N	76°10'W
Gibeon, Nmb. (gĭb'ē-ŭn)	232	25°15'S	17°30'E
Gibraleón, Spain (hē-brä-lå-ōn')	172	37°24'N	7°00'W
Gibraltar, dep., Eur. (gĭ-bräl-tă'r)	154	36°08'N	5°22'W
Gibraltar, Strait of, strt.	156	35°55'N	5°45'W
Gibson City, Il., U.S. (gĭb'sŭn)	108	40°25'N	88°20'W
Gibson Desert, des., Austl.	220	24°45'S	123°15'E
Gibson Island, Md., U.S.	110e	39°05'N	76°26'W
Gibson Reservoir, res., Ok., U.S.	121	36°07'N	95°08'W
Giddings, Tx., U.S. (gĭd'ĭngz)	123	30°11'N	96°55'W
Gideon, Mo., U.S. (gĭd'ē-ŭn)	121	36°27'N	89°56'W
Gien, Fr. (zhē-ăN')	161	47°43'N	2°37'E
Giessen, Ger. (gēs'sĕn)	168	50°35'N	8°40'E
Gifu, Japan (gē'fōō)	205	35°25'N	136°45'E
Gig Harbor, Wa., U.S. (gĭg)	116a	47°20'N	122°36'W
Giglio, Isola del, i., Italy (jēl'yō)	174	42°23'N	10°55'E
Gijón, Spain (hē-hōn')	154	43°33'N	5°37'W
Gila, r., U.S. (hē'lá)	106	33°00'N	110°00'W
Gila Bend, Az., U.S.	119	32°59'N	112°41'W
Gila Cliff Dwellings National Monument, rec., N.M., U.S.	119	33°15'N	108°20'W
Gila River Indian Reservation, I.R., Az., U.S.	119	33°11'N	112°38'W
Gilbert, Mn., U.S. (gĭl'bẽrt)	113	47°27'N	92°29'W
Gilbert, r., Austl. (gĭl-bẽrt)	221	17°15'S	142°09'E
Gilbert, Mount, mtn., Can.	94	50°51'N	124°20'W
Gilbert Islands, is., Kir.	241	0°30'S	174°00'E
Gilboa, Mount, mtn., S. Afr. (gĭl-bŏá)	233c	29°13'S	30°17'E
Gilford Island, i., Can. (gĭl'fẽrd)	94	50°45'N	126°25'W
Gilgit, Pak. (gĭl'gĭt)	199	35°58'N	73°48'E
Gil Island, i., Can. (gĭl)	94	53°13'N	129°15'W
Gillen, l., Austl. (jĭl'ĕn)	220	26°15'S	125°15'E
Gillett, Ar., U.S. (jĭ-lĕt')	121	34°07'N	91°22'W
Gillette, Wy., U.S.	115	44°17'N	105°30'W
Gillingham, Eng., U.K. (gĭl'ĭng ăm)	165	51°23'N	0°33'E
Gilman, Il., U.S. (gĭl'măn)	108	40°45'N	87°55'W
Gilman Hot Springs, Ca., U.S.	117a	33°49'N	116°57'W
Gilmer, Tx., U.S. (gĭl'mẽr)	123	32°43'N	94°57'W
Gilmore, Ga., U.S. (gĭl'môr)	110c	33°51'N	84°29'W
Gilo, r., Eth.	231	7°40'N	34°17'E
Gilroy, Ca., U.S. (gĭl-roi')	118	37°00'N	121°34'W
Giluwe, Mount, mtn., Pap. N. Gui.	213	6°04'S	144°00'E
Gimli, Can. (gĭm'lē)	97	50°39'N	97°00'W
Gimone, r., Fr. (zhē-mōn')	170	43°26'N	0°36'E
Ginir, Eth.	231	7°13'N	40°44'E
Ginosa, Italy (jē-nō'zä)	174	40°35'N	16°48'E
Gioia del Colle, Italy (jô'yä dĕl kôl'lā)	174	40°48'N	16°55'E
Girard, Ks., U.S. (jĭ-rărd')	121	37°30'N	94°50'W
Girardot, Col. (hē-rär-dōt')	142	4°19'N	74°47'W
Giresun, Tur. (ghĕr'ĕ-sòn')	198	40°55'N	38°20'E
Giridih, India (jē-rē-dē)	199	24°12'N	86°18'E
Girona, Spain	162	41°55'N	2°48'E
Gironde, r., Fr. (zhē-rônd')	156	45°31'N	1°00'W
Girvan, Scot., U.K. (gûr'vān)	164	55°15'N	5°01'W
Gisborne, N.Z. (gĭz'bŭrn)	221a	38°40'S	178°08'E
Gisenyi, Rw.	232	1°43'S	29°15'E
Gisors, Fr. (zhē-zôr')	170	49°19'N	1°47'E
Gitambo, D.R.C.	236	4°21'N	24°45'E
Gitega, Bdi.	232	3°39'S	30°05'E
Giurgiu, Rom. (jòr'jò)	175	43°53'N	25°58'E
Givet, Fr. (zhē-vĕ')	170	50°08'N	4°47'E
Givors, Fr. (zhē-vôr')	170	45°35'N	4°46'E
Giza see Al Jīzah, Egypt	238b	30°01'N	31°12'E
Gizhiga, Russia (gē'zhi-gà)	179	61°59'N	160°46'E
Gizo, Sol. Is.	214e	8°06'S	156°51'E
Gizycko, Pol. (gĭ'zhĭ-ko)	160	54°03'N	21°48'E
Gjirokastër, Alb.	163	40°04'N	20°10'E
Gjøvik, Nor. (gyû'vĕk)	160	60°47'N	10°36'E
Glabeek-Zuurbemde, Bel.	159a	50°52'N	4°59'E
Glace Bay, Can. (gläs bā)	101	46°12'N	59°57'W
Glacier Bay National Park, rec., Ak., U.S. (glā'shẽr)	106a	58°40'N	136°50'W
Glacier National Park, rec., Can.	92	51°45'N	117°35'W
Glacier Peak, mtn., Wa., U.S.	114	48°07'N	121°10'W
Glacier Point, c., Can.	116a	48°24'N	123°59'W
Gladbeck, Ger. (gläd'bĕk)	168	51°35'N	6°59'E
Gladdeklipkop, S. Afr.	238c	24°17'S	29°36'E
Gladstone, Austl. (glăd'stōn)	219	23°45'S	152°00'E
Gladstone, Austl.	218	33°15'S	138°20'E
Gladstone, Mi., U.S.	113	45°50'N	87°04'W
Gladstone, N.J., U.S.	110a	40°43'N	74°39'W
Gladstone, Or., U.S.	116c	45°23'N	122°36'W
Gladwin, Mi., U.S. (glăd'wĭn)	108	44°00'N	84°25'W
Glåma, r., Nor.	156	61°30'N	10°30'E
Glarus, Switz. (glä'ròs)	168	47°02'N	9°03'E
Glasgow, Scot., U.K. (glås'gō)	154	55°54'N	4°25'W
Glasgow, Ky., U.S.	124	37°00'N	85°55'W
Glasgow, Mo., U.S.	121	39°14'N	92°48'W
Glasgow, Mt., U.S.	115	48°14'N	106°39'W
Glassport, Pa., U.S. (glås'pōrt)	111e	40°19'N	79°53'W
Glauchau, Ger. (glou'kou)	168	50°51'N	12°28'E
Glazov, Russia (glä'zôf)	178	58°05'N	52°52'E
Glen, r., Eng., U.K. (glĕn)	158a	52°44'N	0°18'W
Glénan, Îles de, is., Fr. (ĕl-dĕ-glā-năn')	170	47°43'N	4°42'W
Glen Burnie, Md., U.S. (bûr'nē)	110e	39°10'N	76°38'W
Glen Canyon, p., Ut., U.S.	119	37°10'N	110°50'W
Glen Canyon Dam, dam, Az., U.S. (glĕn kăn'yŭn)	106	36°57'N	111°25'W
Glen Canyon National Recreation Area, rec., U.S.	119	37°00'N	111°20'W
Glen Carbon, Il., U.S. (kär'bŏn)	117e	38°45'N	89°59'W
Glencoe, S. Afr. (glĕn-cō)	233c	28°14'S	30°09'E
Glencoe, Il., U.S.	111a	42°08'N	87°45'W
Glencoe, Mn., U.S. (glĕn'kō)	113	44°44'N	94°07'W
Glen Cove, N.Y., U.S. (kōv)	110a	40°51'N	73°38'W
Glendale, Az., U.S. (glĕn'dāl)	119	33°30'N	112°15'W
Glendale, Ca., U.S.	104	34°09'N	118°15'W
Glendale, Oh., U.S.	111f	31°16'N	84°22'W
Glendive, Mt., U.S. (glĕn'dīv)	104	47°08'N	104°41'W
Glendo, Wy., U.S.	115	42°32'N	104°54'W
Glendora, Ca., U.S. (glĕn-dō'rá)	117a	34°08'N	117°52'W
Glenelg, r., Austl.	222	37°20'S	141°30'E
Glen Ellyn, Il., U.S. (glĕn ĕl'-lĕn)	111a	41°53'N	88°04'W
Glen Innes, Austl. (ĭn'ĕs)	219	29°45'S	152°02'E
Glenns Ferry, Id., U.S. (fĕr'ĭ)	114	42°58'N	115°21'W
Glen Olden, Pa., U.S. (ōl'd'n)	110f	39°54'N	75°17'W
Glenomra, La., U.S. (glĕn-mō'rá)	123	30°58'N	92°36'W
Glenrock, Wy., U.S. (glĕn'rŏk)	115	42°50'N	105°53'W
Glens Falls, N.Y., U.S. (glĕnz fôlz)	109	43°20'N	73°40'W
Glenshaw, Pa., U.S. (glĕn'shô)	111e	40°33'N	79°57'W
Glen Valley, Can.	116d	49°09'N	122°30'W
Glenview, Il., U.S. (glĕn'vū)	111a	42°04'N	87°48'W
Glenville, Ga., U.S. (glĕn'vĭl)	125	31°55'N	81°56'W
Glenwood, Ia., U.S.	112	41°03'N	95°44'W
Glenwood, Mn., U.S.	112	45°39'N	95°23'W
Glenwood, N.M., U.S.	119	33°19'N	108°52'W
Glenwood Springs, Co., U.S.	119	39°35'N	107°20'W
Glienicke, Ger. (glē'nē-kĕ)	159b	52°38'N	13°19'E
Glinde, Ger. (glĕn'dĕ)	159c	53°32'N	10°13'E
Glittertinden, mtn., Nor.	166	61°39'N	8°33'E
Gliwice, Pol. (gwĭ-wĭt'sĕ)	161	50°18'N	18°40'E
Globe, Az., U.S. (glōb)	104	33°20'N	110°50'W
Głogów, Pol. (gwō'gōōv)	161	51°40'N	16°04'E
Glommen, r., Nor. (glôm'ĕn)	166	60°03'N	11°15'E
Glonn, Ger. (glônn)	159d	47°59'N	11°52'E

ăt; finăl; rāte; senăte; ärm; åsk; sofá; fâre; ch-choose; dh-as th in other; bē; ēvent; bĕt; recĕnt; cratẽr; g-gō; gh-guttural g; bĭt; ĭ-short neutral; rīde; K-guttural k as ch in German ich;

PRONOUNCING INDEX

Glorieuses – Grand Rapids 297

PLACE (Pronunciation)	PAGE	LAT.	LONG.
Glorieuses, Îles, is., Reu.	233	11°28'S	47°50'E
Glossop, Eng., U.K. (glŏs'ŭp)	158a	53°26'N	1°57'W
Gloster, Ms., U.S. (glŏs'tẽr)	124	31°10'N	91°00'W
Gloucester, Eng., U.K. (glŏs'tẽr)	161	51°54'N	2°11'W
Gloucester, Ma., U.S.	101a	42°37'N	70°40'W
Gloucester City, N.J., U.S.	110f	39°53'N	75°08'W
Glouster, Oh., U.S. (glŏs'tẽr)	108	39°35'N	82°05'W
Glover Island, i., Can. (glŭv'ẽr)	101	48°44'N	57°45'W
Gloversville, N.Y., U.S. (glŭv'ẽrz-vĭl)	109	43°05'N	74°20'W
Glovertown, Can. (glŭv'ẽr-toun)	101	48°41'N	54°02'W
Glückstadt, Ger. (glük-shtät)	159c	53°47'N	9°25'E
Glushkovo, Russia (glòsh'kô-vō)	177	51°21'N	34°43'E
Gmünden, Aus. (g'mòn'dĕn)	168	47°57'N	13°47'E
Gniezno, Pol. (g'nyăz'nô)	161	52°32'N	17°34'E
Gnjilane, Serb. (gnyē'lä-nĕ)	175	42°28'N	21°27'E
Goa, state, India (gō'ä)	199	15°45'N	74°00'E
Goascorán, Hond. (gō-äs'kō-rän')	132	13°37'N	87°43'W
Goba, Eth. (gō'bä)	231	7°17'N	39°58'E
Gobabis, Nmb. (gō-bä'bĭs)	232	22°25'S	18°50'E
Gobi , des., Asia (gō'be)	204	43°29'N	103°15'E
Goble, Or., U.S. (gō'b'l)	116c	46°01'N	122°53'W
Goch, Ger. (gôk)	171c	51°35'N	6°10'E
Godāvari, r., India (gô-dä'vŭ-rē)	199	19°00'N	78°30'E
Goddards Soak, sw., Austl. (gŏd'ȧrdz)	220	31°20'S	123°30'E
Goderich, Can. (gōd'rĭch)	98	43°45'N	81°45'W
Godfrey, Il., U.S. (gŏd'frē)	117e	38°57'N	90°12'W
Godhavn, Grnld. (gōdh'håvn)	89	69°15'N	53°30'W
Gods, r., Can. (ŏodz)	97	55°17'N	93°35'W
Gods Lake, Can.	91	54°40'N	94°09'W
Godthåb, Grnld. (gŏt'hòb)	89	64°10'N	51°32'W
Goéland, Lac au, l., Can.	99	49°47'N	76°41'W
Goffs, Ca., U.S. (gôfs)	118	34°57'N	115°06'W
Gogebic, l., Mi., U.S. (gô-gē'bĭk)	113	46°24'N	89°25'W
Gogebic Range, mts., Mi., U.S.	113	46°37'N	89°48'W
Göggingen, Ger. (gûg'gĕn-gĕn)	159d	48°21'N	10°53'E
Gogland, i., Russia	167	60°04'N	26°55'E
Gogonou, Benin	235	10°50'N	2°50'E
Gogorrón, Mex. (gō-gô-rōn')	130	21°51'N	100°54'W
Goiânia, Braz. (gô-yá'nyä)	143	16°41'S	48°57'W
Goiás, Braz. (gô-yá's)	143	15°57'S	50°10'W
Goiás, state, Braz.	143	16°00'S	48°00'W
Goirle, Neth.	159a	51°31'N	5°06'E
Gökçeada, i., Tur.	175	40°10'N	25°27'E
Göksu, r., Tur. (gûk'soo')	181	36°40'N	33°30'E
Gol, Nor. (gûl)	166	60°58'N	8°54'E
Golax, Va., U.S. (gō'lăks)	125	36°41'N	80°56'W
Golcar, Eng., U.K. (gŏl'kȧr)	158a	53°38'N	1°52'W
Golconda, Il., U.S. (gŏl-kŏn'dȧ)	121	37°21'N	88°32'W
Gołdap, Pol. (gôl'dăp)	169	54°17'N	22°17'E
Golden, Can.	95	51°18'N	116°58'W
Golden, Co., U.S.	120	39°44'N	105°15'W
Goldendale, Wa., U.S. (gōl'dĕn-dāl)	114	45°49'N	120°48'W
Golden Gate, strt., Ca., U.S. (gōl'dĕn gāt)	116b	37°48'N	122°32'W
Golden Hinde, mtn., Can. (hīnd)	94	49°40'N	125°45'W
Golden's Bridge, N.Y., U.S.	110a	41°17'N	73°41'W
Golden Valley, Mn., U.S.	117g	44°58'N	93°23'W
Goldfield, Nv., U.S. (gōld'fēld)	118	37°42'N	117°15'W
Gold Hill, mtn., Pan.	128a	9°03'N	79°08'W
Gold Mountain, mtn., Wa., U.S. (gōld)	116a	47°33'N	122°48'W
Goldsboro, N.C., U.S. (gōldz-bûr'ô)	125	35°23'N	77°59'W
Goldthwaite, Tx., U.S. (gōld'thwāt)	122	31°27'N	98°34'W
Goleniów, Pol. (gô-lĕ-nyŭf')	168	53°33'N	14°51'E
Golets-Purpula, Gora, mtn., Russia	179	59°08'N	115°22'E
Golfito, C.R. (gōl-fē'tō)	133	8°40'N	83°12'W
Goliad, Tx., U.S. (gō-lĭ-ăd')	123	28°40'N	97°12'W
Golo, r., Fr.	174	42°28'N	9°18'E
Golo Island, i., Phil. (gō'lō)	213a	13°38'N	120°17'E
Golovchino, Russia (gō-lôf'chĕ-nō)	177	50°34'N	35°52'E
Golyamo Konare, Blg. (gō'lå-mō-kō'nä-rĕ)	175	42°16'N	24°33'E
Golzow, Ger. (gōl'tsōv)	159b	52°17'N	12°36'E
Gombe, Nig.	230	10°19'N	11°02'E
Gomera Island, i., Spain (gô-mā'rä)	230	28°00'N	18°01'W
Gomez Farias, Mex. (gō'māz fä-rē'ás)	122	24°59'N	101°02'W
Gómez Palacio, Mex. (pä-lä'syō)	128	25°35'N	103°30'W
Gonaïves, Haiti (gō-nà-ēv')	129	19°25'N	72°45'W
Gonaïves, Golfe des, b., Haiti (gō-nà-ēv')	135	19°20'N	73°20'W
Gonâve, Île de la, i., Haiti (gô-nàv')	129	18°50'N	73°30'W
Gonda, India	202	27°13'N	82°00'E
Gondal, India	202	22°02'N	70°47'E
Gonder, Eth.	231	12°39'N	37°30'E
Gonesse, Fr. (gô-nĕs')	171b	48°59'N	2°28'E
Gongga Shan, mtn., China (gôn-gä shän)	204	29°16'N	101°46'E
Goniri, Nig.	235	11°30'N	12°20'E
Gonō, r., Japan (gō'nō)	211	35°00'N	132°25'E
Gonor, Can. (gō'nŏr)	102f	50°04'N	96°57'W
Gonubie, S. Afr. (gŏn'ōō-bē)	233c	32°56'S	28°02'E
Gonzales, Mex. (gôn-zá'lĕs)	130	22°47'N	98°26'W
Gonzales, Tx., U.S. (gŏn-zä'lĕz)	123	29°31'N	97°25'W
González Catán, Arg. (gōn-zá'lĕz-kä-tá'n)	144a	34°47'S	58°39'W
Good Hope, Cape of, c., S. Afr. (kāp ov gōōd hōp)	232	34°21'S	18°29'E
Good Hope Mountain, mtn., Can.	94	51°09'N	124°10'W
Gooding, Id., U.S. (gòd'ĭng)	115	42°55'N	114°43'W
Goodland, In., U.S. (gòd'lănd)	108	40°50'N	87°15'W
Goodland, Ks., U.S.	120	39°19'N	101°43'W
Goodwood, S. Afr. (gòd'wòd)	232a	33°54'S	18°33'E
Goole, Eng., U.K. (gōōl)	158a	53°42'N	0°52'W
Goose, r., N.D., U.S.	112	47°40'N	97°41'W
Gooseberry Creek, r., Wy., U.S. (gōōs-bĕr'ĭ)	115	44°04'N	108°35'W
Goose Creek, r., Id., U.S. (gōōs)	115	42°07'N	113°53'W
Goose Lake, l., Ca., U.S.	114	41°56'N	120°35'W
Gorakhpur, India (gō'rŭk-pōōr)	199	26°45'N	82°39'E
Gorda, Punta, c., Cuba (pōō'n-tä-gôr-dä)	134	22°25'N	82°10'W
Gorda Cay, i., Bah. (gôr'dä)	134	26°05'N	77°30'W
Gordon, Can. (gôr'dŭn)	102f	50°00'N	97°20'W
Gordon, Ne., U.S.	112	42°47'N	102°14'W
Gore, Eth. (gō'rĕ)	231	8°12'N	35°34'E
Gorgān, Iran	198	36°44'N	54°30'E
Gorgona, Isola di, Italy (gôr-gō'nä)	162	43°27'N	9°55'E
Gori, Geor. (gō'rē)	181	42°00'N	44°08'E
Gorinchem, Neth. (gō'rĭn-kĕm)	159a	51°50'N	4°59'E
Goring, Eng., U.K. (gôr'ĭng)	158b	51°30'N	1°08'W
Gorizia, Italy (gô-rē'tsē-yä)	174	45°56'N	13°40'E
Gor'kiy *see* Nizhniy Novgorod, Russia	178	56°15'N	44°05'E
Gor'kovskoye, res., Russia	178	56°38'N	43°40'E
Gorlice, Pol. (gôr-lē'tsĕ)	169	49°38'N	21°11'E
Görlitz, Ger. (gûr'lĭts)	161	51°10'N	15°01'E
Gorman, Tx., U.S. (gôr'măn)	122	32°13'N	98°40'W
Gorna Oryakhovitsa, Blg. (gôr'nä-ôr-yĕk'ô-vē-tsá)	175	43°08'N	25°40'E
Gornji Milanovac, Serb. (gôrn'yē-mē'la-nô-väts)	175	44°02'N	20°29'E
Gorno-Altay, prov., Russia	184	51°00'N	86°00'E
Gorno-Altaysk, Russia (gôr'nŭ'ŭl-tīsk')	178	51°58'N	85°58'E
Gorodishche, Russia (gô-rô'dĭsh-chĕ)	186a	57°57'N	57°03'E
Gorodok, Russia	179	50°30'N	103°58'E
Gorontalo, Indon. (gō-rōn-tä'lo)	213	0°40'N	123°04'E
Gorzów Wielkopolski, Pol. (gō-zhōōv'vyĕl-ko-pōl'skē)	160	53°44'N	15°15'E
Gosely, Eng., U.K.	158a	52°33'N	2°10'W
Goshen, In., U.S. (gō'shĕn)	108	41°35'N	85°50'W
Goshen, Ky., U.S.	111h	38°24'N	85°34'W
Goshen, N.Y., U.S.	110a	41°24'N	74°19'W
Goshen, Oh., U.S.	111f	39°14'N	84°09'W
Goshute Indian Reservation, I.R., Ut., U.S. (gō-shōōt')	119	39°50'N	114°00'W
Goslar, Ger. (gôs'lär)	168	51°55'N	10°25'E
Gospa, r., Ven. (gôs-pä)	143b	9°43'N	64°23'W
Gostivar, Mac. (gos'tē-vär)	175	41°46'N	20°58'E
Gostynin, Pol. (gôs-tē'nĭn)	169	52°24'N	19°30'E
Göta, r., Swe. (gōĕtä)	166	58°11'N	12°03'E
Göta Kanal, can., Swe. (yû'tȧ)	166	58°35'N	15°24'E
Göteborg, Swe. (yû'tĕ-bôrgh)	154	57°39'N	11°56'E
Gotel Mountains, mts., Afr.	235	7°05'N	11°20'E
Gotera, El Sal. (gō-tā'rä)	132	13°41'N	88°06'W
Gotha, Ger. (gō'tȧ)	161	50°47'N	10°43'E
Gothenburg *see* Göteborg, Swe.	154	57°39'N	11°56'E
Gothenburg, Ne., U.S. (gŏth'ĕn-bûrg)	120	40°57'N	100°08'W
Gotland, i., Swe.	156	57°35'N	17°35'E
Gotska Sandön, i., Swe.	167	58°24'N	19°15'E
Göttingen, Ger. (gŭt'ĭng-ĕn)	168	51°32'N	9°57'E
Gouda, Neth. (gou'dä)	159a	52°00'N	4°42'E
Gough, i., St. Hel. (gŏf)	2	40°00'S	10°00'W
Gouin, Réservoir, res., Can.	93	48°15'N	74°15'W
Goukou, China (gō-kō)	205	48°45'N	121°42'E
Goulais, r., Can.	98	46°45'N	84°10'W
Goulburn, Austl. (gōl'bŭrn)	219	34°47'S	149°40'E
Goumbati, mtn., Sen.	234	13°08'N	12°06'W
Goumbou, Mali (gōōm-bōō')	230	14°59'N	7°27'W
Gouna, Cam.	235	8°32'N	13°34'E
Goundam, Mali (gōōn-dän')	230	16°29'N	3°37'W
Gouverneur, N.Y., U.S. (gŭv-ẽr-nōōr')	109	44°20'N	75°25'W
Govenlock, Can. (gŭvĕn-lŏk)	90	49°15'N	109°48'W
Governador, Ilha do, i., Braz. (gô-vĕr-nä-dō-'r-ē-lá'dō)	144b	22°48'S	43°13'W
Governador Portela, Braz. (pōr-tĕ'lá)	144b	22°28'S	43°30'W
Governador Valadares, Braz. (vä-lä-dä'rĕs)	143	18°47'S	41°45'W
Governor's Harbour, Bah.	134	25°15'N	76°15'W
Gowanda, N.Y., U.S. (gô-wŏn'dȧ)	109	42°30'N	78°55'W
Goya, Arg. (gō'yä)	144	29°06'S	59°12'W
Göyçay, Azer. (gĕ-ôk'chī)	181	40°40'N	47°40'E
Goyt, r., Eng., U.K. (goit)	158a	53°19'N	2°03'W
Graaff-Reinet, S. Afr. (gräf'rī'nĕt)	232	32°10'S	24°40'E
Gračac, Cro. (grä'chäts)	174	44°16'N	15°50'E
Gračanica, Bos.	175	44°42'N	18°18'E
Graceville, Fl., U.S. (grās'vĭl)	124	30°57'N	85°30'W
Graceville, Mn., U.S.	112	45°33'N	96°25'W
Gracias, Hond. (grä'sē-äs)	132	14°35'N	88°37'W
Graciosa Island, i., Port. (grä-syō'sä)	230a	39°07'N	27°30'W
Gradačac, Bos. (gra-dä'chats)	163	44°50'N	18°28'E
Grado, Spain (grä'dō)	172	43°24'N	6°04'W
Gräfelfing, Ger. (grä'fĕl-fēng)	159d	48°07'N	11°27'E
Grafing bei München, Ger. (grä'fēng)	159d	48°03'N	11°58'E
Grafton, Austl. (graf'tŭn)	219	29°38'S	153°05'E
Grafton, Il., U.S.	117e	38°58'N	90°26'W
Grafton, Ma., U.S.	101a	42°13'N	71°41'W
Grafton, N.D., U.S.	112	48°24'N	97°25'W
Grafton, Oh., U.S.	111d	41°16'N	82°04'W
Grafton, W.V., U.S.	108	39°20'N	80°00'W
Gragnano, Italy (grän-yä'nô)	173c	40°27'N	14°32'E
Graham, N.C., U.S. (grā'ăm)	125	36°03'N	79°23'W
Graham, Tx., U.S.	120	33°07'N	98°34'W
Graham, Wa., U.S.	116a	47°03'N	122°18'W
Graham, i., Can.	92	53°50'N	132°40'W
Grahamstown, S. Afr. (grā'ăms'toun)	233c	33°19'S	26°33'E
Grajewo, Pol. (grä-yā'vo)	169	53°38'N	22°28'E
Grama, Serra de, mtn., Braz. (sĕ'r-rä-dĕ-grá'mà)	141a	20°42'S	42°28'W
Gramada, Blg. (grä'mä-dä)	175	43°46'N	22°41'E
Gramatneusiedl, Aus.	159e	48°02'N	16°29'E
Grampian Mountains, mts., Scot., U.K. (grăm'pĭ-ăn)	156	56°30'N	4°55'W
Granada, Nic. (grä-nä'dhä)	128	11°55'N	85°58'W
Granada, Spain (grä-nä'dä)	162	37°13'N	3°37'W
Gran Bajo, reg., Arg. (grán'bá'kō)	144	47°35'S	68°45'W
Granbury, Tx., U.S. (grăn'bĕr-ĭ)	123	32°26'N	97°45'W
Granby, Can. (grăn'bĭ)	91	45°30'N	72°40'W
Granby, Mo., U.S.	121	36°54'N	94°15'W
Granby, l., Co., U.S.	120	40°07'N	105°40'W
Gran Canaria Island, i., Spain (grän'kä-nä'rē-ä)	230	27°39'N	15°39'W
Gran Chaco, reg., S.A. (grán'chá'kō)	144	25°30'S	62°15'W
Grand, i., Mi., U.S.	113	46°37'N	86°38'W
Grand, l., Can.	100	45°59'N	66°15'W
Grand, l., Me., U.S.	100	45°17'N	67°42'W
Grand, r., Can.	99	43°45'N	80°20'W
Grand, r., Mi., U.S.	108	42°58'N	85°13'W
Grand, r., Mo., U.S.	121	39°50'N	93°52'W
Grand, r., S.D., U.S.	112	45°40'N	101°55'W
Grand, North Fork, r., U.S.	112	45°52'N	102°49'W
Grand, South Fork, r., S.D., U.S.	112	45°38'N	102°56'W
Grand Bahama, i., Bah.	129	26°35'N	78°30'W
Grand Bank, Can. (grănd băngk)	93a	47°06'N	55°47'W
Grand Bassam, C. Iv. (grän bá-sän')	230	5°12'N	3°44'W
Grand Bourg, Guad. (grän bōōr')	133b	15°54'N	61°20'W
Grand Caicos, i., T./C. Is. (grănd kä-ē'kōs)	135	21°45'N	71°50'W
Grand Canal *see* Da Yunhe, can., China	205	35°00'N	117°00'E
Grand Canal, can., Ire.	164	53°21'N	7°15'W
Grand Canyon, Az., U.S.	119	36°05'N	112°10'W
Grand Canyon, p., Az., U.S.	106	35°50'N	113°16'W
Grand Canyon National Park, rec., Az., U.S.	106	36°15'N	112°20'W
Grand Canyon-Parashant National Monument, rec., Az., U.S.	119	36°25'N	113°45'W
Grand Cayman, i., Cay. Is. (kī'măn)	129	19°15'N	81°15'W
Grand Coulee Dam, dam, Wa., U.S. (kōō'lē)	106	47°58'N	119°28'W
Grande, r., Arg.	141b	35°25'S	70°14'W
Grande, r., Bol.	142	16°49'S	63°19'W
Grande, r., Braz.	143	19°48'S	49°54'W
Grande, r., Mex.	131	17°37'N	96°41'W
Grande, r., Nic. (grän'dĕ)	133	13°01'N	84°21'W
Grande, r., Ur.	141c	33°19'S	57°15'W
Grande, Arroyo, r., Mex. (är-rō'yō-grä'n-dĕ)	130	23°30'N	98°45'W
Grande, Bahía, b., Arg. (bä-ē'ä-grán'dĕ)	144	50°45'S	68°00'W
Grande, Boca, mth., Ven. (bŏ'kä-grä'n-dĕ)	143	8°46'N	60°17'W
Grande, Cuchilla, mts., Ur. (kōō-chē'l-yä)	144	33°00'S	55°15'W
Grande, Ilha, i., Braz. (grän'dĕ)	141a	23°11'S	44°14'W
Grande, Rio, r., N.A. (grän'dä)	106	26°50'N	99°10'W
Grande, Salinas, l., Arg. (sä-lē'nás)	144	29°45'S	65°00'W
Grande, Salto, wtfl., Braz. (säl-tô)	143	16°18'S	39°38'W
Grande Cayemite, Île, i., Haiti	135	18°45'N	73°45'W
Grande de Otoro, r., Hond. (grä'dą dä ō-tō'rō)	132	14°42'N	88°21'W
Grande de Santiago, Río, r., Mex. (rēō-grä'n-dĕ-dĕ-sän-tyá'gō)	128	20°30'N	104°00'W
Grande Pointe, Can. (grănd point')	102f	49°47'N	97°03'W
Grande Prairie, Can. (prâr'ĭ)	90	55°10'N	118°48'W
Grand Erg Occidental, des., Alg.	230	30°00'N	1°00'E
Grand Erg Oriental, des., Alg.	230	30°00'N	7°00'E
Grande Rivière du Nord, Haiti (rē-vyâr' dü nôr')	135	19°35'N	72°10'W
Grande Ronde, r., Or., U.S. (rŏnd')	114	45°32'N	117°52'W
Gran Desierto, des., Mex. (grän-dĕ-syĕ'r-tô)	119	32°14'N	114°28'W
Grande Terre, i., Guad.	133b	16°28'N	61°13'W
Grande Vigie, Pointe de la, c., Guad. (grănd vē-gē')	133b	16°32'N	61°25'W
Grand Falls, Can. (fôlz)	93a	48°56'N	55°40'W
Grandfather Mountain, mtn., N.C., U.S. (grănd-fä-thẽr)	125	36°07'N	81°48'W
Grandfield, Ok., U.S. (grănd'fēld)	120	34°13'N	98°39'W
Grand Forks, Can. (fôrks)	90	49°02'N	118°27'W
Grand Forks, N.D., U.S.	104	47°55'N	97°05'W
Grand Haven, Mi., U.S. (hā'v'n)	108	43°05'N	86°15'W
Grand Island, Ne., U.S. (ī'lȧnd)	104	40°56'N	98°20'W
Grand Island, i., N.Y., U.S.	111c	43°03'N	78°58'W
Grand Junction, Co., U.S. (jŭngk'shŭn)	104	39°05'N	108°35'W
Grand Lake, l., Can. (lāk)	93a	49°00'N	57°10'W
Grand Lake, l., La., U.S.	123	29°57'N	91°25'W
Grand Lake, l., Mn., U.S.	117h	46°54'N	92°26'W
Grand Ledge, Mi., U.S. (lĕj)	108	42°45'N	84°50'W
Grand Lieu, Lac de, l., Fr. (grän'-lyû)	170	47°00'N	1°45'W
Grand Manan, i., Can. (mȧ-năn)	100	44°40'N	66°50'W
Grand Mère, Can. (grän mâr')	91	46°36'N	72°43'W
Grândola, Port. (grăn'dô-lȧ)	172	38°10'N	8°36'W
Grand Portage Indian Reservation, I.R., Mn., U.S. (pōr'tĭj)	113	47°54'N	89°34'W
Grand Portage National Monument, rec., Mi., U.S.	113	47°59'N	89°47'W
Grand Prairie, Tx., U.S. (prĕ'rē)	117c	32°45'N	97°00'W
Grand Rapids, Can.	97	53°08'N	99°20'W
Grand Rapids, Mi., U.S. (răp'ĭdz)	105	43°00'N	85°45'W
Grand Rapids, Mn., U.S.	113	47°16'N	93°33'W

ng-sing; ŋ-baŋk; ɴ-nasalized n; nŏd; cŏmmit; ōld; ôbey; ôrder; oi-boil; fōōd; ò-as oo in foot; ou-out; s-soft; sh-dish; th-thin; pūre; ûnite; ûrn; stŭd; circŭs; ü-as in French tu; '-indeterminate vowel.

298 Grand-Riviere – Guadalajara

PRONOUNCING INDEX

PLACE (Pronunciation)	PAGE	LAT.	LONG.
Grand-Riviere, Can.	100	48°26'N	64°30'W
Grand Staircase-Escalante National Monument, rec., Ut., U.S.	119	37°25'N	111°30'W
Grand Teton, mtn., Wy., U.S.	106	43°46'N	110°50'W
Grand Teton National Park, rec., Wy., U.S. (tē'tŏn)	115	43°54'N	110°15'W
Grand Traverse Bay, b., Mi., U.S. (trăv'ērs)	108	45°00'N	85°30'W
Grand Turk, T./C. Is. (tûrk)	135	21°30'N	71°10'W
Grand Turk, i., T./C. Is.	135	21°30'N	71°10'W
Grandview, Mo., U.S. (grănd'vyōō)	117f	38°53'N	94°32'W
Granger, Wy., U.S. (grān'jēr)	115	41°37'N	109°58'W
Grangeville, Id., U.S. (grānj'vĭl)	114	45°56'N	116°08'W
Granite City, Il., U.S. (grăn'ĭt sĭt'ĭ)	117e	38°42'N	90°09'W
Granite Falls, Mn., U.S. (fôlz)	112	44°46'N	95°34'W
Granite Falls, N.C., U.S.	125	35°49'N	81°25'W
Granite Falls, Wa., U.S.	116a	48°05'N	121°59'W
Granite Lake, l., Can.	101	48°01'N	57°00'W
Granite Peak, mtn., Mt., U.S.	106	45°13'N	109°48'W
Graniteville, S.C., U.S. (grăn'ĭt-vĭl)	125	33°35'N	81°50'W
Granito, Braz. (grä-nē'tō)	143	7°39'S	39°34'W
Granma, prov., Cuba	134	20°10'N	76°50'W
Gränna, Swe. (grĕn'à)	166	58°02'N	14°38'E
Granollers, Spain (grä-nôl-yĕrs')	173	41°36'N	2°19'E
Gran Pajonal, reg., Peru (grä'n-pä-kô-näl')	142	11°14'S	71°45'W
Gran Paradiso, mtn., Italy	174	45°32'N	7°16'E
Gran Piedra, mtn., Cuba (grän-pyĕ'drä)	135	20°00'N	75°40'W
Grantham, Eng., U.K. (grăn'tăm)	164	52°54'N	0°38'W
Grant Park, Il., U.S. (grănt pärk)	111a	41°14'N	87°39'W
Grants Pass, Or., U.S. (grănts pås)	114	42°26'N	123°20'W
Granville, Fr. (gräN-vēl')	161	48°52'N	1°35'W
Granville, N.Y., U.S. (grăn'vĭl)	109	43°25'N	73°15'W
Granville, l., Can.	92	56°18'N	100°30'W
Grão Mogol, Braz. (grouN' mō-gōl')	143	16°34'S	42°35'W
Grapevine, Tx., U.S. (grāp'vīn)	117c	32°56'N	97°05'W
Gräsö, i., Swe.	166	60°30'N	18°35'E
Grass, r., N.Y., U.S.	109	44°45'N	75°10'W
Grass Cay, i., V.I.U.S.	129c	18°22'N	64°50'W
Grasse, Fr. (gräs)	171	43°39'N	6°57'E
Grass Mountain, mtn., Wa., U.S. (gràs)	116a	47°13'N	121°48'W
Grates Point, c., Can. (grāts)	101	48°09'N	52°57'W
Gravelbourg, Can. (grăv'ĕl-bôrg)	90	49°53'N	106°34'W
Gravesend, Eng., U.K. (grāvz'ĕnd')	158b	51°26'N	0°22'E
Gravina, Italy (grä-vē'nä)	174	40°48'N	16°27'E
Gravois, Pointe à, c., Haiti (grà-vwä')	135	18°00'N	74°20'W
Gray, Fr. (grå)	171	47°26'N	5°35'E
Grayling, Mi., U.S. (grā'lĭng)	108	44°40'N	84°40'W
Grays Harbor, b., Wa., U.S. (grās)	106	46°55'N	124°23'W
Grayslake, Il., U.S. (grāz'lāk)	111a	42°20'N	88°20'W
Grays Peak, mtn., Co., U.S. (grāz)	120	39°29'N	105°52'W
Grays Thurrock, Eng., U.K. (thŭ'rŏk)	158b	51°28'N	0°19'E
Grayvoron, Russia (grä-ē'vô-rôn)	177	50°28'N	35°41'E
Graz, Aus. (gräts)	154	47°05'N	15°26'E
Great Abaco, i., Bah. (ä'bä-kō)	129	26°30'N	77°05'W
Great Artesian Basin, basin, Austl. (är-tēzh-ăn bā-sĭn)	221	23°16'S	143°37'E
Great Australian Bight, b., Austl. (ôs-trā'lĭ-ăn bĭt)	220	33°30'S	127°00'E
Great Bahama Bank, bk. (bȧ-hā'mȧ)	134	25°00'N	78°50'W
Great Barrier, i., N.Z. (băr'ĭ-ēr)	221a	36°10'S	175°30'E
Great Barrier Reef, rf., Austl. (bȧ-rĭ-ēr rēf)	221	16°43'S	146°34'E
Great Basin, basin, U.S. (grāt bā's'n)	106	40°08'N	117°10'W
Great Bear Lake, l., Can. (bâr)	92	66°10'N	119°53'W
Great Bend, Ks., U.S. (bĕnd)	120	38°41'N	98°46'W
Great Bitter Lake, l., Egypt	238b	30°24'N	32°27'E
Great Blasket Island, i., Ire. (blăs'kĕt)	164	52°05'N	10°55'W
Great Corn Island, i., Nic.	133	12°10'N	82°54'W
Great Dismal Swamp, sw., U.S. (dĭz'măl)	125	36°35'N	76°34'W
Great Divide Basin, basin, Wy., U.S. (dĭ-vīd' bā's'n)	115	42°10'N	108°10'W
Great Dividing Range, mts., Austl. (dĭ-vī-dĭng rānj)	221	35°16'S	146°38'E
Great Duck, i., Can. (dŭk)	98	45°40'N	83°22'W
Greater Antilles, is., N.A.	129	20°30'N	79°15'W
Greater Khingan Range, mts., China (dä hĭŋ-gän lĭŋ)	205	46°30'N	120°00'E
Greater Leech Indian Reservation, I.R., Mn., U.S. (grāt'ēr lēch)	113	47°39'N	94°27'W
Greater Manchester, hist. reg., Eng., U.K.	158a	53°34'N	2°41'W
Greater Sunda Islands, is., Asia	212	4°00'S	108°00'E
Great Exuma, i., Bah. (ĕk-sōō'mä)	134	23°35'N	76°00'W
Great Falls, Mt., U.S. (fôlz)	104	47°30'N	111°15'W
Great Falls, S.C., U.S.	125	34°32'N	80°53'W
Great Guana Cay, i., Bah. (gwä'nä)	134	24°00'N	76°20'W
Great Harbor Cay, i., Bah. (kē)	134	25°45'N	77°50'W
Great Inagua, i., Bah. (ē-nä'gwä)	129	21°00'N	73°15'W
Great Indian Desert, des., Asia	199	27°35'N	71°37'E
Great Isaac, i., Bah. (ī'zăk)	134	26°05'N	79°05'W
Great Karroo, plat., S. Afr. (grāt kȧ'rōō)	232	32°45'S	22°00'E
Great Limpopo Transfrontier Park, rec., Afr.	232	22°00'S	31°30'E
Great Namaland, hist. reg., Nmb.	232	25°45'S	16°15'E
Great Neck, N.Y., U.S. (nĕk)	110a	40°48'N	73°44'W
Great Nicobar Island, i., India (nĭk-ō-bär')	212	7°00'N	94°18'E
Great Pedro Bluff, c., Jam.	134	17°50'N	78°05'W
Great Pee Dee, r., S.C., U.S. (pē-dē')	107	34°01'N	79°26'W
Great Plains, pl., N.A. (plāns)	89	45°00'N	104°00'W
Great Ragged, i., Bah.	135	22°10'N	75°45'W
Great Ruaha, r., Tan.	232	7°30'S	37°00'E
Great Salt Lake, l., Ut., U.S. (sôlt lāk)	106	41°19'N	112°48'W
Great Salt Lake Desert, des., Ut., U.S.	106	41°00'N	113°30'W
Great Salt Plains Reservoir, res., Ok., U.S.	120	36°56'N	98°14'W
Great Sand Dunes National Monument, rec., Co., U.S.	120	37°56'N	105°25'W
Great Sand Hills, hills, Can. (sănd)	96	50°35'N	109°05'W
Great Sandy Desert, des., Austl. (săn'dē)	220	21°50'S	123°10'E
Great Sandy Desert, des., Or., U.S. (săn'dĭ)	114	43°43'N	120°44'W
Great Sitkin, i., Ak., U.S. (sĭt-kĭn)	103a	52°18'N	176°22'W
Great Slave Lake, l., Can. (slāv)	92	61°37'N	114°58'W
Great Smoky Mountains National Park, rec., U.S. (smōk-ē)	107	35°43'N	83°20'W
Great Stirrup Cay, i., Bah. (stĭr-ŭp)	134	25°50'N	77°55'W
Great Victoria Desert, des., Austl. (vĭk-tō'rĭ-ȧ)	220	29°45'S	124°30'E
Great Wall, hist., China	204	38°00'N	109°00'E
Great Waltham, Eng., U.K. (wôl'thŭm)	158b	51°47'N	0°27'E
Great Yarmouth, Eng., U.K. (yär-mŭth)	161	52°35'N	1°45'E
Grebbestad, Swe. (grĕb-bĕ-städh)	166	58°42'N	11°15'E
Gréboun, Mont, mtn., Niger	230	20°00'N	8°35'E
Gredos, Sierra de, mts., Spain (syĕr'rä dā grā'dōs)	172	40°13'N	5°30'W
Greece, nation, Eur. (grēs)	154	39°00'N	21°30'E
Greeley, Co., U.S. (grē'lĭ)	104	40°25'N	104°41'W
Green, r., Ky., U.S. (grēn)	124	37°13'N	86°30'W
Green, r., N.D., U.S.	112	47°05'N	103°05'W
Green, r., Ut., U.S.	119	38°30'N	110°05'W
Green, r., Wa., U.S.	116a	47°17'N	121°57'W
Green, r., Wy., U.S.	115	41°08'N	110°27'W
Green, r., U.S.	106	38°30'N	110°10'W
Greenbank, Wa., U.S. (grēn'bănk)	116a	48°06'N	122°35'W
Green Bay, Wi., U.S.	105	44°30'N	88°04'W
Green Bay, b., U.S.	107	44°55'N	87°40'W
Green Bayou, Tx., U.S.	123a	29°53'N	95°13'W
Greenbelt, Md., U.S. (grēn'bĕlt)	110e	38°59'N	76°53'W
Greencastle, In., U.S. (grēn-kás''l)	108	39°40'N	86°50'W
Green Cay, i., Bah.	134	24°05'N	77°10'W
Green Cove Springs, Fl., U.S. (kōv)	125	29°56'N	81°42'W
Greendale, Wi., U.S. (grēn'dāl)	111a	42°56'N	87°59'W
Greenfield, Ia., U.S.	113	41°16'N	94°30'W
Greenfield, In., U.S. (grēn'fēld)	108	39°45'N	85°40'W
Greenfield, Ma., U.S.	109	42°35'N	72°35'W
Greenfield, Mo., U.S.	121	37°23'N	93°48'W
Greenfield, Oh., U.S.	108	39°15'N	83°25'W
Greenfield, Tn., U.S.	124	36°08'N	88°45'W
Greenfield Park, Can.	102a	45°29'N	73°29'W
Greenhills, Oh., U.S. (grēn-hĭls)	111f	39°16'N	84°31'W
Greenland, dep., N.A. (grēn'lănd)	89	74°00'N	40°00'W
Greenland Sea, sea	244	77°00'N	1°00'W
Green Mountain, mtn., Or., U.S.	116c	45°52'N	123°24'W
Green Mountain Reservoir, res., Co., U.S.	119	39°50'N	106°20'W
Green Mountains, mts., N.A.	107	43°10'N	73°05'W
Greenock, Scot., U.K. (grēn'ŭk)	160	55°55'N	4°45'W
Green Peter Lake, res., Or., U.S.	114	44°28'N	122°30'W
Green Pond Mountain, mtn., N.J., U.S. (pŏnd)	110a	41°00'N	74°32'W
Greenport, N.Y., U.S.	109	41°06'N	72°22'W
Green River, Ut., U.S. (grēn rĭv'ēr)	119	39°00'N	110°05'W
Green River, Wy., U.S.	115	41°32'N	109°26'W
Green River Lake, res., Ky., U.S.	124	37°15'N	85°15'W
Greensboro, Al., U.S. (grēnz'bŭro)	124	32°42'N	87°36'W
Greensboro, Ga., U.S. (grēns-bûr'ō)	124	33°34'N	83°11'W
Greensboro, N.C., U.S.	105	36°04'N	79°45'W
Greensburg, In., U.S. (grēnz'bûrg)	108	39°20'N	85°30'W
Greensburg, Ks., U.S. (grēns-bûrg)	120	37°36'N	99°17'W
Greensburg, Pa., U.S.	109	40°20'N	79°30'W
Greenville, Lib.	230	5°01'N	9°03'W
Greenville, Al., U.S. (grēn'vĭl)	124	31°49'N	86°39'W
Greenville, Il., U.S.	121	38°52'N	89°22'W
Greenville, Ky., U.S.	124	37°11'N	87°11'W
Greenville, Me., U.S.	100	45°26'N	69°35'W
Greenville, Mi., U.S.	108	43°10'N	85°25'W
Greenville, Ms., U.S.	105	33°25'N	91°00'W
Greenville, N.C., U.S.	125	35°35'N	77°22'W
Greenville, Oh., U.S.	108	40°05'N	84°35'W
Greenville, Pa., U.S.	108	41°20'N	80°25'W
Greenville, S.C., U.S.	105	34°50'N	82°25'W
Greenville, Tn., U.S.	125	36°08'N	82°50'W
Greenville, Tx., U.S.	123	33°09'N	96°07'W
Greenwich, Eng., U.K.	158b	51°28'N	0°00'
Greenwich, Ct., U.S.	110a	41°01'N	73°37'W
Greenwood, Ar., U.S. (grēn-wŏŏd)	121	35°13'N	94°15'W
Greenwood, In., U.S.	111g	39°37'N	86°07'W
Greenwood, Ms., U.S.	124	33°30'N	90°09'W
Greenwood, S.C., U.S.	125	34°10'N	82°10'W
Greenwood, Lake, res., S.C., U.S.	125	34°17'N	81°55'W
Greenwood Lake, l., N.Y., U.S.	110a	41°13'N	74°20'W
Greer, S.C., U.S. (grēr)	125	34°55'N	81°56'W
Grefrath, Ger. (grĕf'rät)	171c	51°20'N	6°21'E
Gregory, S.D., U.S. (grĕg'ō-rĭ)	112	43°12'N	99°27'W
Gregory, Lake, l., Austl. (grĕg'ō-rē)	220	28°47'S	139°15'E
Gregory Range, mts., Austl.	221	19°23'S	143°45'E
Greifenberg, Ger. (grī'fĕn-bĕrgh)	159d	48°04'N	11°06'E
Greifswald, Ger. (grīfs'vält)	168	54°05'N	13°24'E
Greiz, Ger. (grīts)	168	50°39'N	12°14'E
Gremyachinsk, Russia (grâ'myá-chĭnsk)	186a	58°35'N	57°53'E
Grenada, Ms., U.S. (grē-nä'da)	124	33°45'N	89°47'W
Grenada, nation, N.A.	129	12°02'N	61°15'W
Grenada Lake, res., Ms., U.S.	124	33°52'N	89°30'W
Grenadines, The, is., N.A. (grĕn'ȧ-dēnz)	133b	12°37'N	61°35'W
Grenen, c., Den.	160	57°43'N	10°31'E
Grenoble, Fr. (grē-nō'bl')	161	45°14'N	5°45'E
Grenora, N.D., U.S. (grē-nō'rȧ)	112	48°38'N	103°55'W
Grenville, Can. (grĕn'vĭl)	109	45°40'N	74°35'W
Grenville, Gren.	133b	12°07'N	61°38'W
Gresham, Or., U.S. (grĕsh'ăm)	116c	45°30'N	122°25'W
Gretna, La., U.S. (grĕt'nȧ)	110d	29°56'N	90°03'W
Grevelingen Krammer, r., Neth.	159a	51°42'N	4°03'E
Grevenbroich, Ger. (grĕ'fĕn-broik)	171c	51°05'N	6°36'E
Grey, r., Can. (grā)	101	47°53'N	57°00'W
Grey, Point, c., Can.	116d	49°22'N	123°16'W
Greybull, Wy., U.S. (grā'bŏŏl)	115	44°28'N	108°05'W
Greybull, r., Wy., U.S.	115	44°13'N	108°43'W
Greylingstad, S. Afr. (grā-lĭng'shtȧt)	238c	26°40'S	29°13'E
Greymouth, N.Z. (grā'mouth)	221a	42°27'S	171°17'E
Grey Range, mts., Austl.	221	28°40'S	142°05'E
Greytown, S. Afr. (grā'toun)	233c	29°07'S	30°38'E
Grey Wolf Peak, mtn., Wa., U.S. (grā wŏlf)	116a	48°53'N	123°12'W
Gridley, Ca., U.S. (grĭd'lĭ)	118	39°22'N	121°43'W
Griffin, Ga., U.S. (grĭf'ĭn)	124	33°15'N	84°16'W
Griffith, Austl. (grĭf-ĭth)	222	34°16'S	146°10'E
Griffith, In., U.S.	111a	41°31'N	87°26'W
Grigoriopol', Mol. (grĭ'gor-i-ō'pōl)	177	47°09'N	29°18'E
Grijalva, r., Mex. (grē-häl'vä)	131	17°25'N	93°23'W
Grim, Cape, c., Austl. (grĭm)	222	40°43'S	144°30'E
Grimma, Ger. (grĭm'ȧ)	168	51°14'N	12°43'E
Grimsby, Can. (grĭmz'bĭ)	102d	43°11'N	79°33'W
Grimsby, Eng., U.K.	160	53°35'N	0°05'W
Grímsey, i., Ice. (grĭms'å)	160	66°30'N	17°50'W
Grimstad, Nor. (grĭm-städh)	160	58°21'N	8°30'E
Grindstone Island, Can.	101	47°25'N	61°51'W
Grinnell, Ia., U.S. (grĭ-nĕl')	113	41°44'N	92°44'W
Griswold, Ia., U.S. (grĭz'wŭld)	112	41°11'N	95°05'W
Groais Island, i., Can.	101	50°57'N	55°35'W
Grobina, Lat. (grō'bĭnĭa)	167	56°35'N	21°10'E
Groblersdal, S. Afr.	238c	25°11'S	29°25'E
Grodzisk, Pol. (grō'jēsk)	168	52°14'N	16°22'E
Grodzisk Masowiecki, Pol. (grō'jēsk mä-zō-vyĕts'ke)	169	52°06'N	20°40'E
Groesbeck, Tx., U.S. (grōs'bĕk)	123	31°32'N	96°31'W
Groix, Île de, i., Fr. (ēl dē grwä')	170	47°39'N	3°28'W
Grójec, Pol. (grò'yĕts)	169	51°53'N	20°52'E
Gronau, Ger. (grō'nou)	168	52°12'N	7°05'E
Groningen, Neth. (grō'nĭng-ĕn)	160	53°13'N	6°30'E
Groote Eylandt, i., Austl. (grō'tē ī'länt)	220	13°50'S	137°30'E
Grootfontein, Nmb. (grōt'fŏn-tān')	232	19°30'S	18°15'E
Groot-Kei, r., Afr. (kē)	233c	32°17'S	27°30'E
Grootkop, mtn., S. Afr.	232a	34°11'S	18°23'E
Groot Marico, S. Afr.	238c	25°36'S	26°23'E
Groot Marico, r., Afr.	238c	25°13'S	26°20'E
Groot-Vis, r., S. Afr.	233c	33°04'S	26°08'E
Groot Vloer, pl., S. Afr. (grōt' vlòr')	232	30°00'S	21°00'E
Gros-Mécatina, i., Can.	101	50°50'N	58°33'W
Gros Morne, mtn., Can. (grō môrn')	101	49°36'N	57°48'W
Gros Morne National Park, rec., Can.	93a	49°45'N	59°15'W
Gros Pate, mtn., Can.	101	50°16'N	57°25'W
Grosse Island, i., Mi., U.S. (grōs)	111b	42°08'N	83°09'W
Grosse Isle, Can. (ĭl')	102f	50°04'N	97°27'W
Grossenhain, Ger. (grōs'ĕn-hīn)	168	51°17'N	13°33'E
Gross-Enzersdorf, Aus.	159e	48°13'N	16°33'E
Grosse Pointe, Mi., U.S. (point')	111b	42°23'N	82°54'W
Grosse Pointe Farms, Mi., U.S. (färm)	111b	42°25'N	82°53'W
Grosse Pointe Park, Mi., U.S. (pärk)	111b	42°23'N	82°55'W
Grosseto, Italy (grôs-sā'tō)	174	42°46'N	11°09'E
Grossglockner, mtn., Aus.	161	47°06'N	12°45'E
Gross Höbach, Ger. (hû'bäk)	159d	48°21'N	11°36'E
Gross Kreutz, Ger. (kroitz)	159b	52°24'N	12°47'E
Gross Schönebeck, Ger. (shō'nē-bĕk)	159b	52°54'N	13°32'E
Gros Ventre, r., Wy., U.S. (grōvĕn't'r)	115	43°38'N	110°34'W
Groton, Ct., U.S. (grŏt'ŭn)	109	41°20'N	72°00'W
Groton, Ma., U.S.	101a	42°37'N	71°34'W
Groton, S.D., U.S.	112	45°25'N	98°04'W
Grottaglie, Italy (grôt-täl'yā)	175	40°32'N	17°26'E
Grouard Mission, Can.	90	55°31'N	116°09'W
Groveland, Ma., U.S. (grōv'land)	101a	42°25'N	71°02'W
Groveton, N.H., U.S. (grōv'tŭn)	109	44°35'N	71°30'W
Groveton, Tx., U.S.	123	31°04'N	95°07'W
Groznyy, Russia (grŏz'nĭ)	178	43°20'N	45°40'E
Grudziądz, Pol. (grōō'jŏnts)	160	53°30'N	18°48'E
Grues, Île aux, i., Can. (ō grü)	102b	47°05'N	70°32'W
Grundy Center, Ia., U.S. (grŭn'dĭ sĕn'tēr)	113	42°22'N	92°45'W
Gruñidora, Mex. (grōō-nyē-dō'rō)	130	24°10'N	101°49'W
Grünwald, Ger. (grōōn'väld)	159d	48°04'N	11°34'E
Gryazi, Russia (gryä'zĭ)	176	52°31'N	39°59'E
Gryazovets, Russia (gryä'zō-vĕts)	180	58°52'N	40°14'E
Gryfice, Pol. (grĭ'fĭ-tsĕ)	168	53°55'N	15°11'E
Gryfino, Pol. (grĭ'fē-nō)	168	53°16'N	14°30'E
Guabito, Pan. (gwä-bē'tō)	133	9°30'N	82°33'W
Guacanayabo, Golfo de, b., Cuba (gôl-fô-dĕ-gwä-kä-nä-yä'bō)	134	20°30'N	77°40'W
Guacara, Ven. (gwá'kä-rä)	143b	10°16'N	67°48'W
Guadalajara, Mex. (gwä-dhä-lä-hä'rä)	128	20°41'N	103°21'W

ăt; finȧl; rāte; senāte; ärm; ȧsk; sofȧ; fâre; ch-choose; dh-as th in other; bē; ēvent; bĕt; recĕnt; cratēr; g-gō; gh-guttural g; bĭt; ĭ-short neutral; rīde; κ-guttural k as ch in German ich;

PRONOUNCING INDEX

Guadalajara – Haines City 299

PLACE (Pronunciation)	PAGE	LAT.	LONG.
Guadalajara, Spain (gwä-dä-lä-kä′rä)	162	40°37′N	3°10′W
Guadalcanal, Spain (gwä-dhäl-kä-näl′)	172	38°05′N	5°48′W
Guadalcanal, i., Sol. Is.	221	9°48′S	158°43′E
Guadalcázar, Mex. (gwä-dhäl-kä′zär)	130	22°38′N	100°24′W
Guadalete, r., Spain (gwä-dhä-lā′tå)	172	36°53′N	5°38′W
Guadalhorce, r., Spain (gwä-dhäl-ôr′thä)	172	37°05′N	4°50′W
Guadalimar, r., Spain (gwä-dhä-lē-mär′)	172	38°29′N	2°53′W
Guadalope, r., Spain (gwä-dä-lô-pě)	173	40°48′N	0°10′W
Guadalquivir, Río, r., Spain (rē′ō-gwä-dhäl-kē-vēr′)	156	37°30′N	5°00′W
Guadalupe, Mex.	122	31°23′N	106°06′W
Guadalupe, i., Mex.	128	29°00′N	118°45′W
Guadalupe, r., Tx., U.S. (gwä-dhä-lo͞o′på)	122	29°54′N	99°03′W
Guadalupe, Sierra de, mts., Spain (syĕr′rä dā gwä-dhä-lo͞o′pä)	162	39°30′N	5°25′W
Guadalupe Mountains, mts., N.M., U.S.	122	32°00′N	104°55′W
Guadalupe Peak, mtn., Tx., U.S.	122	31°55′N	104°55′W
Guadarrama, r., Spain (gwä-dhär-rä′mä)	173a	40°34′N	3°58′W
Guadarrama, Sierra de, mts., Spain (gwä-dhär-rä′mä)	156	41°00′N	3°40′W
Guadatentin, r., Spain	172	37°43′N	1°58′W
Guadeloupe, dep., N.A. (gwä-dē-lo͞op)	129	16°40′N	61°10′W
Guadeloupe Passage, strt., N.A.	133b	16°26′N	62°00′W
Guadiana, r., Eur. (gwä-dvä′nä)	156	39°00′N	6°00′W
Guadiana, Bahía de, b., Cuba (bä-ē′ä-dĕ-gwä-dhē-ä′nä)	134	22°10′N	84°35′W
Guadiana Alto, r., Spain (äl′tō)	172	39°02′N	2°52′W
Guadiana Menor, r., Spain (mā′nôr)	172	37°43′N	2°45′W
Guadiaro, r., Spain (gwä-dhē-ä′rō)	172	36°38′N	5°25′W
Guadiela, r., Spain (gwä-dhē-ā′lä)	172	40°27′N	2°05′W
Guadix, Spain (gwä-dēsh′)	172	37°18′N	3°09′W
Guaira, Braz. (gwä-ē-rä)	143	24°03′S	54°02′W
Guaire, r., Ven. (gwī′rĕ)	143b	10°25′N	66°43′W
Guajaba, Cayo, i., Cuba (kä′yō-gwä-hä′bä)	134	21°50′N	77°35′W
Guajará Mirim, Braz. (gwä-zhä-rä′mē-rēɴ′)	142	10°58′S	65°12′W
Guajira, Península de, pen., S.A.	142	12°35′N	73°00′W
Gualán, Guat. (gwä-län′)	132	15°08′N	89°21′W
Gualeguay, Arg. (gwä-lĕ-gwä′y)	144	33°10′S	59°20′W
Gualeguay, r., Arg.	144	32°49′S	59°05′W
Gualicho, Salina, l., Arg. (sä-lē′nä-gwä-lē′chō)	144	40°20′S	65°15′W
Guam, i., Oc. (gwäm)	3	14°00′N	143°20′E
Guamo, Col. (gwä′mō)	142a	4°02′N	74°58′W
Gu'an, China (go͞o-än)	208a	39°25′N	116°18′E
Guan, r., China (gůän)	206	31°56′N	115°19′E
Guanabacoa, Cuba (gwä-nä-bä-kō′ä)	129	23°08′N	82°19′W
Guanabara, Baía de, b., Braz.	141a	22°44′S	43°09′W
Guanacaste, Cordillera, mts., C.R.	132	10°54′N	85°27′W
Guanacevi, Mex. (gwä-nä-sĕ-vē′)	128	25°30′N	105°45′W
Guanahacabibes, Península de, pen., Cuba	134	21°55′N	84°35′W
Guanajay, Cuba (gwä-nä-hī′)	134	22°55′N	82°40′W
Guanajuato, Mex. (gwä-nä-hwä′tō)	128	21°01′N	101°16′W
Guanajuato, state, Mex.	128	21°00′N	101°00′W
Guanape, Ven. (gwä-nä′pĕ)	143b	9°55′N	65°32′W
Guanape, r., Ven.	143b	9°52′N	65°20′W
Guanare, Ven. (gwä-nä′rå)	142	8°57′N	69°47′W
Guanduçu, r., Braz. (gwä′n-do͞o′so͞o)	144b	22°50′S	43°40′W
Guane, Cuba (gwä′nå)	134	22°10′N	84°05′W
Guangchang, China (gůäŋ-chäŋ)	209	26°50′N	116°18′E
Guangde, China (gůäŋ-dŭ)	209	30°40′N	119°20′E
Guangdong, prov., China (gůäŋ-dôŋ)	205	23°45′N	113°15′E
Guanglu Dao, i., China (gůäŋ-lo͞o dou)	206	39°13′N	122°21′E
Guangping, China (gůäŋ-pĭŋ)	206	36°30′N	114°57′E
Guangrao, China (gůäŋ-rou)	206	37°04′N	118°24′E
Guangshan, China (gůäŋ-shän)	206	32°02′N	114°53′E
Guangxi Zhuangzu, prov., China (gůäŋ-shyē)	204	24°00′N	108°30′E
Guangzhou, China	204	23°07′N	113°15′W
Guanhu, China (gůän-ho͞o)	206	34°26′N	117°59′E
Guannan, China (gůän-nän)	206	34°17′N	119°17′E
Guanta, Ven. (gwän′tä)	143b	10°15′N	64°35′W
Guantánamo, Cuba (gwän-tä′nä-mô)	135	20°10′N	75°10′W
Guantánamo, prov., Cuba	135	20°10′N	75°05′W
Guantánamo, Bahía de, b., Cuba	135	19°35′N	75°35′W
Guantao, China (gůän-tou)	206	36°39′N	115°25′E
Guanxian, China (gůän-shyĕn)	206	36°30′N	115°28′E
Guanyao, China (gůän-you)	207a	23°13′N	113°04′E
Guanyun, China (gůän-yòn)	206	34°28′N	119°16′E
Guapiles, C.R. (gwä-pē-lĕs)	133	10°05′N	83°54′W
Guapimirim, Braz. (gwä-pē-mē-rē′ɴ)	144b	22°31′S	42°59′W
Guaporé, r., S.A. (gwä-pô-rā′)	142	12°11′S	63°47′W
Guaqui, Bol. (guä′kē)	142	16°42′S	68°47′W
Guara, Sierra de, mts., Spain (sē-ĕ′r-rä-dĕ-gwä′rä)	173	42°24′N	0°15′W
Guarabira, Braz. (gwä-rä-bē′rá)	143	6°49′S	35°27′W
Guaranda, Ec. (gwä-rán′dä)	142	1°39′S	78°57′W
Guarapari, Braz. (gwä-rä-pä′rē)	143	20°34′S	40°31′W
Guarapiranga, Represa do, res., Braz.	141a	23°45′S	46°44′W
Guarapuava, Braz. (gwä-rä-pwä′vá)	144	25°29′S	51°26′W
Guarda, Port. (gwär′dä)	172	40°32′N	7°17′W
Guardiato, r., Spain	172	38°10′N	5°05′W
Guarena, Spain (gwä-rā′nyä)	172	38°52′N	6°08′W
Guaribe, r., Ven. (gwä-rē′bĕ)	143b	9°48′N	65°17′W
Guárico, dept., Ven.	143b	9°42′N	67°25′W
Guarulhos, Braz. (gwá-rō′l-yôs)	141a	23°28′S	46°30′W
Guarus, Braz. (gwá′ro͞os)	141a	21°44′S	41°19′W
Guasca, Col. (gwäs′kä)	142a	4°52′N	73°52′W
Guasipati, Ven. (gwä-sē-pä′tē)	143	7°26′N	61°57′W
Guastalla, Italy (gwäs-täl′lä)	174	44°53′N	10°39′E
Guasti, Ca., U.S. (gwäs′tĭ)	117a	34°04′N	117°35′W
Guatemala, Guat. (guä-tå-mä′lä)	128	14°37′N	90°32′W
Guatemala, nation, N.A.	128	15°45′N	91°45′W
Guatire, Ven. (gwä-tē′rĕ)	143b	10°28′N	66°34′W
Guaviare, r., Col.	142	3°35′N	69°28′W
Guayabal, Cuba (gwä-yä-bä′l)	134	20°40′N	77°40′W
Guayalejo, r., Mex. (gwä-yä-lĕ′hô)	130	23°24′N	99°09′W
Guayama, P.R. (gwä-yä′mä)	129b	18°00′N	66°08′W
Guayamouc, r., Haiti	135	19°05′N	72°00′W
Guayaquil, Ec. (gwī-ä-kēl′)	142	2°16′S	79°53′W
Guayaquil, Golfo de, b., Ec. (gôl-fô-dĕ)	142	3°03′S	82°12′W
Guaymas, Mex. (gwä′y-mäs)	128	27°49′N	110°58′W
Guayubin, Dom. Rep. (gwá-yo͞o-bē′n)	135	19°40′N	71°25′W
Guazacapán, Guat. (gwä-zä-kä-pän′)	132	14°04′N	90°26′W
Gubakha, Russia (go͞o-bä′kå)	178	58°53′N	57°35′E
Gubbio, Italy (go͞ob′byô)	174	43°23′N	12°36′E
Guben, Ger.	168	51°57′N	14°43′E
Gucheng, China (go͞o-chŭŋ)	206	39°09′N	115°43′E
Gúdar, Sierra de, mts., Spain	173	40°28′N	0°47′W
Gudena, r., Den.	166	56°20′N	9°47′E
Gudermes, Russia	182	43°20′N	46°08′E
Gudvangen, Nor. (go͞odh′väŋ-gĕn)	166	60°52′N	6°45′E
Guebwiller, Fr. (gĕb-vē-lâr′)	171	47°53′N	7°10′E
Guédi, Mont, mtn., Chad	235	12°14′N	18°58′E
Guelma, Alg. (gwĕl′mä)	230	36°32′N	7°17′E
Guelph, Can. (gwĕlf)	99	43°33′N	80°15′W
Güere, r., Ven. (gwĕ′rĕ)	143b	9°39′N	65°00′W
Guéret, Fr. (gā-rĕ′)	170	46°09′N	1°52′E
Guernsey, dep., Eur.	170	49°28′N	2°35′W
Guernsey, i., Guern. (gûrn′zĭ)	161	49°27′N	2°36′W
Guerrero, Mex. (gĕr-rā′rō)	122	26°47′N	99°20′W
Guerrero, Mex.	122	28°20′N	100°24′W
Guerrero, state, Mex.	128	17°45′N	100°15′W
Gueydan, La., U.S. (gā′dăn)	123	30°01′N	92°31′W
Guia de Pacobaíba, Braz. (gwē′ä-dĕ-pä′kō-bī′bä)	144b	22°42′S	43°10′W
Guiana Highlands, mts., S.A.	139	3°20′N	60°00′W
Guichi, China (gwā-chr)	209	30°35′N	117°28′E
Guichicovi, Mex. (gwē-chē-kō′vē)	131	16°58′N	95°10′W
Guidonia, Italy (gwē-dō′nyá)	174	42°00′N	12°45′E
Guiglo, C. Iv.	234	6°33′N	7°29′W
Guignes-Rabutin, Fr. (gēɴ′yĕ)	171b	48°38′N	2°48′E
Güigüe, Ven. (gwē′gwĕ)	143b	10°05′N	67°48′W
Guija, Lago, l., N.A. (gē′hä)	132	14°16′N	89°21′W
Guildford, Eng., U.K. (gĭl′fērd)	164	51°13′N	0°34′W
Guilford, In., U.S. (gĭl′fērd)	111f	39°10′N	84°55′W
Guilin, China (gwā-lĭn)	205	25°18′N	110°22′E
Guimarães, Port. (gē-mä-rǎnsh′)	172	41°27′N	8°22′W
Guinea, nation, Afr. (gĭn′ē)	230	10°48′N	12°28′W
Guinea, Gulf of, b., Afr.	230	2°00′N	1°00′E
Guinea-Bissau, nation, Afr. (gĭn′ē)	230	12°00′N	20°00′W
Guingamp, Fr. (găɴ-gäɴ′)	170	48°35′N	3°10′W
Guir, r., Mor.	162	31°55′N	2°48′W
Güira de Melena, Cuba (gwē′rä dā må-lā′nä)	134	22°45′N	82°30′W
Güiria, Ven. (gwē-rē′ä)	142	10°43′N	62°16′W
Guise, Fr. (guēz)	170	49°54′N	3°37′E
Guisisil, vol., Nic. (gē-sē-sēl′)	132	12°40′N	86°11′W
Guiyang, China (gwā-yäŋ)	204	26°45′N	107°00′E
Guizhou, China (gwā-jō)	207a	22°46′N	113°15′E
Guizhou, prov., China	204	27°00′N	106°10′E
Gujānwāla, Pak. (gòj-rän′va-lá)	199	32°08′N	74°14′E
Gujarat, India	199	22°54′N	72°00′E
Gulbarga, India (gòl-bûr′gá)	199	17°25′N	76°52′E
Gulbene, Lat. (gòl-bā′nĕ)	167	57°09′N	26°49′E
Gulfport, Ms., U.S. (gŭlf′pōrt)	124	30°24′N	89°05′W
Gulja *see* Yining, China	204	43°58′N	80°40′E
Gull Lake, Can.	96	50°10′N	108°25′W
Gull Lake, l., Can.	95	52°35′N	114°00′W
Gulu, Ug.	237	2°47′N	32°18′E
Gumaca, Phil. (go͞o-mä-kä′)	213a	13°55′N	122°06′E
Gumbeyka, r., Russia (gòm-bĕy′ká)	186a	53°20′N	59°42′E
Gumel, Nig.	230	12°39′N	9°22′E
Gummersbach, Ger. (gòm′ĕrs-bäk)	168	51°02′N	7°34′E
Gummi, Nig.	235	12°09′N	5°09′E
Gumpoldskirchen, Aus.	159e	48°04′N	16°15′E
Guna, India	202	24°44′N	77°17′E
Gunisao, r., Can. (gŭn-*i*-sā′ō)	97	53°40′N	97°35′W
Gunisao Lake, l., Can.	97	53°35′N	96°10′W
Gunnedah, Austl. (gŭ′nē-dä)	222	31°00′S	150°10′E
Gunnison, Co., U.S. (gŭn′ĭ-sŭn)	119	38°33′N	106°56′W
Gunnison, Ut., U.S.	119	39°10′N	111°50′W
Gunnison, r., Co., U.S.	119	38°45′N	108°20′W
Guntersville, Al., U.S. (gŭn′tērz-vĭl)	124	34°20′N	86°19′W
Guntersville Lake, res., Al., U.S.	124	34°30′N	86°20′W
Guntramsdorf, Aus.	159e	48°04′N	16°19′E
Guntūr, India (gòn′to͞or)	199	16°22′N	80°29′E
Guoyang, China (gwô-yäŋ)	206	33°32′N	116°10′E
Gurdon, Ar., U.S. (gûr′dŭn)	121	33°56′N	93°10′W
Gurgueia, r., Braz.	143	8°12′S	43°49′W
Guri, Embalse, res., Ven.	142	7°30′N	63°00′W
Gurnee, Il., U.S. (gûr′nē)	111a	42°22′N	87°55′W
Gurskøy, i., Nor. (go͞orskûē)	166	62°18′N	5°20′E
Gurupi, Serra do, mts., Braz. (sĕ′r-rä-dô-go͞o-ro͞o-pē′)	143	5°32′S	47°02′W
Guru Sikhar, mtn., India	202	29°42′N	72°50′E
Gur'yevsk, Russia (go͞or-yĭfsk′)	178	54°17′N	85°56′E
Gusau, Nig. (go͞o-zä′o͞o)	230	12°12′N	6°40′E
Gusev, Russia (go͞o′sĕf)	167	54°35′N	22°15′E
Gushi, China (go͞o-shr)	206	32°11′N	115°39′E
Gushiago, Ghana	234	9°55′N	0°12′W
Gusinje, Serb. (go͞o-sēn′yĕ)	175	42°34′N	19°54′E
Gus'-Khrustal'nyy, Russia (go͞os-kro͞o-stäl′ny′)	180	55°39′N	40°41′E
Gustavo A. Madero, Mex. (go͞os-tä′vô-á-mä-dĕ′rô)	130	19°29′N	99°07′W
Güstrow, Ger. (güs′trō)	168	53°48′N	12°12′E
Gütersloh, Ger. (gü′tĕrs-lo)	168	51°54′N	8°22′E
Guthrie, Ok., U.S. (gŭth′rĭ)	121	35°52′N	97°26′W
Guthrie Center, Ia., U.S.	113	41°41′N	94°33′W
Gutiérrez Zamora, Mex. (go͞o-tĭ-âr′räz zä-mō′rä)	131	20°27′N	97°17′W
Guttenberg, Ia., U.S. (gŭt′ĕn-bûrg)	113	42°48′N	91°09′W
Guyana, nation, S.A. (gŭy′ănă)	143	7°45′N	59°00′W
Guyang, China (go͞o-yäŋ)	206	34°56′N	114°57′E
Guye, China (go͞o-yŭ)	206	39°46′N	118°23′E
Guymon, Ok., U.S. (gī′mŏn)	120	36°41′N	101°29′W
Guysborough, Can. (gīz′bŭr-ô)	101	45°23′N	61°30′W
Guzhen, China (go͞o-jŭn)	208	33°20′N	117°18′E
Gvardeysk, Russia (gvár-dĕysk′)	167	54°39′N	21°11′E
Gwadabawa, Nig.	235	13°20′N	5°15′E
Gwādar, Pak. (gwä′dŭr)	198	25°15′N	62°29′E
Gwalior, India	199	26°13′N	78°10′E
Gwane, D.R.C. (gwän)	231	4°43′N	25°50′E
Gwardafuy, Gees, c., Som.	238a	11°55′N	51°30′E
Gwda, r., Pol.	168	53°27′N	16°52′E
Gwembe, Zam.	237	16°30′S	27°35′E
Gweru, Zimb.	232	19°15′S	29°48′E
Gwinn, Mi., U.S. (gwĭn)	113	46°15′N	87°30′W
Gyaring Co, l., China	202	30°37′N	88°33′E
Gydan, Khrebet (Kolymskiy), mts., Russia	179	61°45′N	155°00′E
Gydanskiy Poluostrov, pen., Russia	178	70°42′N	76°03′E
Gympie, Austl. (gĭm′pē)	219	26°20′S	152°50′E
Gyöngyös, Hung. (dyûn′dyûsh)	163	47°47′N	19°55′E
Györ, Hung. (dyûr)	163	47°40′N	17°37′E
Gyōtoku, Japan (gyō′tô-ko͞o′)	211a	35°42′N	139°56′E
Gypsumville, Can. (jĭp′sŭm′vĭl)	90	51°45′N	98°35′W
Gýtheio, Grc.	175	36°50′N	22°37′E
Gyula, Hung. (dyò′lä)	169	46°38′N	21°18′E
Gyumri, Arm.	181	40°40′N	43°50′E
Gyzylarbat, Turkmen.	183	38°55′N	56°33′E

H

PLACE (Pronunciation)	PAGE	LAT.	LONG.
Haan, Ger. (hän)	171c	51°12′N	7°00′E
Haapamäki, Fin. (häp′ä-mĕ-kē)	167	62°16′N	24°20′E
Haapsalu, Est. (häp′sä-lò)	167	58°56′N	23°33′E
Haar, Ger. (här)	159d	48°06′N	11°44′E
Ha'Arava (Wādī al Jayb), val., Asia	197a	30°33′N	35°10′E
Haarlem, Neth. (här′lĕm)	165	52°22′N	4°37′E
Habana, prov., Cuba (hä-vä′nä)	134	22°45′N	82°25′W
Hābra, India	202a	22°49′N	88°38′E
Hachinohe, Japan (hä′chē-nō′hå)	210	40°29′N	141°40′E
Hachiōji, Japan (hä′chē-ō′jē)	210	35°39′N	139°18′E
Hackensack, N.J., U.S. (hăk′ĕn-săk)	110a	40°54′N	74°03′W
Ḩadd, Ra's al, c., Oman	198	22°29′N	59°46′E
Haddonfield, N.J., U.S. (hăd′ŭn-fēld)	110f	39°53′N	75°02′W
Haddon Heights, N.J., U.S. (hăd′ŭn hīts)	110f	39°53′N	75°03′W
Hadejia, Nig. (hä-dā′jä)	230	12°30′N	9°59′E
Hadejia, r., Nig.	230	12°15′N	10°00′E
Hadera, Isr. (ká-dĕ′rá)	197a	32°26′N	34°55′E
Haderslev, Den. (hä′dhĕrs-lĕv)	166	55°17′N	9°28′E
Hadiach, Ukr.	181	50°22′N	33°59′E
Ḩadīdū, Yemen	198	12°40′N	53°50′E
Hadlock, Wa., U.S. (hăd′lŏk)	116a	48°02′N	122°46′W
Ḩaḑramawt, reg., Yemen	198	15°22′N	48°40′E
Hadūr Shu'ayb, mtn., Yemen	198	15°45′N	43°45′E
Haeju, Kor., N. (hä′ĕ-jŭ)	210	38°03′N	125°42′E
Hafnarfjördur, Ice.	160	64°02′N	21°32′W
Haft Gel, Iran	201	31°27′N	49°27′E
Hafun, Ras, c., Som. (hä-fo͞on′)	238a	10°15′N	51°35′E
Hageland, Mt., U.S. (hăge′lând)	115	48°53′N	108°43′W
Hagen, Ger. (hä′gĕn)	168	51°21′N	7°29′E
Hagerstown, In., U.S. (hä′gĕrz-toun)	108	39°55′N	85°10′W
Hagerstown, Md., U.S.	105	39°40′N	77°45′W
Hagi, Japan (hä′gĭ)	211	34°25′N	131°25′E
Hague, Cap de la, c., Fr. (dē lä äg′)	170	49°44′N	1°55′W
Haguenau, Fr. (ág′nō′)	171	48°47′N	7°48′E
Hai'an, China (hī-än)	206	32°35′N	120°25′E
Haibara, Japan (hä′ē-bä′rä)	211	34°29′N	135°57′E
Haicheng, China (hī-chŭŋ)	208	40°58′N	122°45′E
Haidian, China (hī-dĭĕn)	206	39°59′N	116°17′E
Haifa, Isr. (hä′ē-fá)	198	32°48′N	35°00′E
Haifeng, China (hä′ē-fĕng′)	209	23°00′N	115°20′E
Haifuzhen, China (hī-fo͞o-jŭn)	206	31°57′N	121°48′E
Haikou, China (hī-kō)	209	20°00′N	110°20′E
Ḩā'il, Sau. Ar.	198	27°30′N	41°47′E
Hailar, China	205	49°10′N	118°40′E
Hailey, Id., U.S. (hā′lĭ)	115	43°31′N	114°19′W
Haileybury, Can.	99	47°27′N	79°38′W
Haileyville, Ok., U.S. (hā′lĭ-vĭl)	121	34°51′N	95°34′W
Hailing Dao, i., China (hī-lĭŋ dou)	209	21°30′N	112°15′E
Hailong, China (hī-loŋ)	208	42°32′N	125°52′E
Hailun, China (hä′ē-lo͞on′)	205	47°18′N	126°50′E
Hainan, prov., China	204	19°00′N	109°30′E
Hainan Dao, i., China (hī-nän dou)	205	19°00′N	111°10′E
Hainburg, Aus.	168	48°09′N	16°57′E
Haines, Ak., U.S. (hānz)	103	59°10′N	135°38′W
Haines City, Fl., U.S.	125a	28°05′N	81°38′W

ăt; finăl; rāte; senāte; ärm; åsk; sofá; fâre; ch-choose; dh-as th in other; bē; ĕvent; bĕt; recĕnt; cratêr; g-gō; gh-guttural g; bĭt; ĭ-short neutral; rīde; ᴋ-guttural k as ch in German ich;

PRONOUNCING INDEX

Hawaii – Hindupur 301

PLACE (Pronunciation)	PAGE	LAT.	LONG.
Hawaii, state, U.S.	106c	20°00'N	157°40'W
Hawai'i, i., Hi., U.S. (häw wī'ē)	106c	19°30'N	155°30'W
Hawai'ian Islands, is., Hi., U.S. (hä-wī'ǎn)	106c	22°00'N	158°00'W
Hawai'i Volcanoes National Park, rec., Hi., U.S.	106c	19°30'N	155°25'W
Hawarden, Ia., U.S. (hā'wàr-dĕn)	112	43°00'N	96°28'W
Hawi, Hi., U.S. (hä'wē)	126a	20°16'N	155°48'W
Hawick, Scot., U.K. (hô'ĭk)	164	55°25'N	2°55'W
Hawke Bay, b., N.Z. (hôk)	221a	39°17'S	177°20'E
Hawker, Austl. (hô'kẽr)	222	31°58'S	138°12'E
Hawkesbury, Can. (hôks'bẽr-ĭ)	99	45°35'N	74°35'W
Hawkinsville, Ga., U.S. (hô'kĭnz-vĭl)	124	32°15'N	83°30'W
Hawks Nest Point, c., Bah.	135	24°05'N	75°30'W
Hawley, Mn., U.S. (hô'lĭ)	112	46°52'N	96°18'W
Haworth, Eng., U.K. (hā'wûrth)	158a	53°50'N	1°57'W
Hawthorne, Ca., U.S. (hô'thôrn)	117a	33°55'N	118°22'W
Hawthorne, Nv., U.S.	118	38°33'N	118°39'W
Haxtun, Co., U.S. (hăks'tŭn)	120	40°39'N	102°38'W
Hay, r., Austl. (hā)	220	23°00'S	136°45'E
Hay, r., Can.	92	60°21'N	117°14'W
Hayama, Japan (hä-yä'mä)	211a	35°16'N	139°35'E
Hayashi, Japan (hä-yä'shē)	211a	35°13'N	139°38'E
Hayden, Az., U.S. (hā'dĕn)	119	33°00'N	110°50'W
Hayes, r., Can.	93	55°25'N	93°55'W
Hayes, Mount, mtn., Ak., U.S. (hāz)	103	63°32'N	146°40'W
Haynesville, La., U.S. (hānz'vĭl)	123	32°55'N	93°08'W
Hayrabolu, Tur.	175	41°14'N	27°05'E
Hay River, Can.	90	60°50'N	115°53'W
Hays, Ks., U.S. (hāz)	120	38°51'N	99°20'W
Haystack Mountain, mtn., Wa., U.S. (hā-stăk')	116a	48°26'N	122°07'W
Hayward, Ca., U.S. (hā'wẽrd)	116b	37°40'N	122°06'W
Hayward, Wi., U.S.	113	46°01'N	91°31'W
Hazard, Ky., U.S. (hăz'ǎrd)	124	37°13'N	83°10'W
Hazelhurst, Ga., U.S. (hā'z'l-hûrst)	125	31°50'N	82°36'W
Hazelhurst, Ms., U.S.	124	31°52'N	90°23'W
Hazel Park, Mi., U.S.	111b	42°28'N	83°06'W
Hazelton, Can. (hā'z'l-tŭn)	90	55°15'N	127°40'W
Hazelton Mountains, mts., Can.	94	55°00'N	128°00'W
Hazleton, Pa., U.S.	109	41°00'N	76°00'W
Headland, Al., U.S. (hĕd'lănd)	124	31°22'N	85°20'W
Healdsburg, Ca., U.S. (hēldz'bûrg)	118	38°37'N	122°52'W
Healdton, Ok., U.S. (hēld'tŭn)	121	34°13'N	97°28'W
Heanor, Eng., U.K. (hēn'ŏr)	158a	53°01'N	1°22'W
Heard Island, i., Austl. (hûrd)	3	53°10'S	74°35'E
Hearne, Tx., U.S. (hûrn)	123	30°53'N	96°35'W
Hearst, Can. (hûrst)	91	49°36'N	83°40'W
Heart, r., N.D., U.S. (härt)	112	46°46'N	102°34'W
Heart Lake Indian Reserve, I.R., Can.	95	55°02'N	111°30'W
Heart's Content, Can. (härts kŏn'tĕnt)	101	47°52'N	53°22'W
Heavener, Ok., U.S. (hēv'nẽr)	121	34°52'N	94°36'W
Hebbronville, Tx., U.S. (hē'brŭn-vĭl)	122	27°18'N	98°40'W
Hebei, prov., China (hŭ-bā)	205	39°15'N	115°40'E
Heber City, Ut., U.S. (hē'bẽr)	119	40°30'N	111°25'W
Heber Springs, Ar., U.S.	121	35°28'N	91°59'W
Hebgen Lake, res., Mt., U.S. (hĕb'gĕn)	115	44°47'N	111°38'W
Hebrides, is., Scot., U.K.	156	57°00'N	6°30'W
Hebrides, Sea of the, sea, Scot., U.K.	164	57°00'N	7°00'W
Hebron, Can. (hēb'rŭn)	91	58°11'N	62°56'W
Hebron, In., U.S.	111a	41°19'N	87°13'W
Hebron, Ky., U.S.	111f	39°04'N	84°43'W
Hebron, N.D., U.S.	112	46°54'N	102°04'W
Hebron, Ne., U.S.	121	40°11'N	97°36'W
Hebron *see* Al Khalīl, W.B.	197a	31°31'N	35°07'E
Heby, Swe. (hĭ'bü)	166	59°56'N	16°48'E
Hecate Strait, strt., Can. (hĕk'ǎ-tē)	92	53°00'N	131°00'W
Hecelchakán, Mex. (ā-sĕl-chä-kän')	131	20°10'N	90°09'W
Hechi, China (hŭ-chr)	209	24°50'N	108°18'E
Hechuan, China (hŭ-chyuän)	204	30°00'N	106°20'E
Hecla Island, i., Can.	97	51°08'N	96°45'W
Hedemora, Swe. (hĭ-dĕ-mō'rä)	166	60°16'N	15°55'E
Hedon, Eng., U.K. (hĕ-dŭn)	158a	53°44'N	0°12'W
Heemstede, Neth.	159a	52°20'N	4°36'E
Heerlen, Neth.	165	50°55'N	5°58'E
Hefei, China (hŭ-fā)	205	31°51'N	117°15'E
Heflin, Al., U.S. (hĕf'lĭn)	124	33°40'N	85°33'W
Heide, Ger. (hī'dē)	168	54°13'N	9°06'E
Heidelberg, Austl. (hī'dĕl-bûrg)	217a	37°45'S	145°04'E
Heidelberg, Ger. (hīdĕl-bĕrgh)	161	49°24'N	8°43'E
Heidelberg, S. Afr.	238c	26°32'S	28°22'E
Heidenheim, Ger. (hī'dĕn-hīm)	168	48°41'N	10°09'E
Heilbron, S. Afr. (hīl'brōn)	238c	27°17'S	27°58'E
Heilbronn, Ger. (hīl'brōn)	161	49°09'N	9°16'E
Heiligenhaus, Ger. (hī'lē-gĕn-houz)	171c	51°19'N	6°58'E
Heiligenstadt, Ger. (hī'lē-gĕn-shtät)	168	51°21'N	10°10'E
Heilongjiang, prov., China (hā-lôŋ-jyäŋ)	205	46°36'N	128°07'E
Heinola, Fin. (hå-nō'lå)	167	61°13'N	26°03'E
Heinsberg, Ger. (hīnz'bĕrgh)	171c	51°04'N	6°07'E
Heist-op-den-Berg, Bel.	159a	51°05'N	4°14'E
Hejaz *see* Al Ḩijāz, reg., Sau. Ar.	198	23°45'N	39°08'E
Hejian, China (hŭ-jyĕn)	208	38°28'N	116°05'E
Hekla, vol., Ice.	156	63°53'N	19°37'W
Hel, Pol. (hāl)	169	54°37'N	18°53'E
Helagsfjället, mtn., Swe.	160	62°54'N	12°24'E
Helan Shan, mts., China (hŭ-län shän)	204	38°02'N	105°20'E
Helena, Ar., U.S. (hē-lē'nà)	105	34°33'N	90°35'W
Helena, Mt., U.S. (hĕ-lē'nǎ)	104	46°35'N	112°01'W
Helensburgh, Austl. (hĕl'ĕnz-bŭr-ō)	217b	34°11'S	150°59'E
Helensburgh, Scot., U.K.	164	56°01'N	4°53'W
Helgoland, i., Ger. (hĕl'gô-länd)	168	54°13'N	7°30'E
Hellier, Ky., U.S. (hĕl'yẽr)	125	37°16'N	82°27'W
Hellín, Spain (ĕl-yén')	162	38°30'N	1°40'W
Hells Canyon, p., U.S.	114	45°20'N	116°45'W
Helmand, r., Afg. (hĕl'mŭnd)	198	31°00'N	63°48'E
Hel'miaziv, Ukr.	177	49°49'N	31°54'E
Helmond, Neth. (hĕl'mŏnt) (ĕl'môN')	165	51°35'N	5°04'E
Helmstedt, Ger. (hĕlm'shtĕt)	168	52°14'N	11°03'E
Helotes, Tx., U.S. (hē'lōts)	117d	29°35'N	98°41'W
Helper, Ut., U.S. (hĕlp'ẽr)	119	39°40'N	110°55'W
Helsingborg, Swe. (hĕl'sĭng-bôrgh)	160	56°04'N	12°40'E
Helsingfors *see* Helsinki, Fin.	154	60°10'N	24°53'E
Helsingør, Den. (hĕl-sĭng-ûr')	160	56°03'N	12°33'E
Helsinki, Fin. (hĕl'sĕn-kē)	154	60°10'N	24°53'E
Hemel Hempstead, Eng., U.K. (hĕm'ĕl hĕmp'stĕd)	158b	51°43'N	0°29'W
Hemer, Ger.	171c	51°22'N	7°46'E
Hemet, Ca., U.S. (hĕm'ĕt)	117a	33°45'N	116°57'W
Hemingford, Ne., U.S. (hĕm'ĭng-fẽrd)	112	42°21'N	103°30'W
Hemphill, Tx., U.S. (hĕmp'hĭl)	123	31°20'N	93°48'W
Hempstead, N.Y., U.S. (hĕmp'stĕd)	110a	40°42'N	73°37'W
Hempstead, Tx., U.S.	123	30°07'N	96°05'W
Hemse, Swe. (hĕm'sē)	166	57°15'N	18°25'E
Hemsön, i., Swe.	166	62°43'N	18°22'E
Henan, prov., China (hŭ-nän)	205	33°58'N	112°33'E
Henares, r., Spain (å-nä'rås)	172	40°50'N	2°55'W
Henderson, Ky., U.S. (hĕn'dẽr-sŭn)	108	37°50'N	87°30'W
Henderson, N.C., U.S.	125	36°18'N	78°24'W
Henderson, Nv., U.S.	118	36°09'N	115°04'W
Henderson, Tn., U.S.	124	35°25'N	88°40'W
Henderson, Tx., U.S.	123	32°09'N	94°48'W
Hendersonville, N.C., U.S. (hĕn'dẽr-sŭn-vĭl)	125	35°17'N	82°28'W
Hendersonville, Tn., U.S.	124	36°18'N	86°37'W
Hendon, Eng., U.K. (hĕn'dŭn)	158b	51°34'N	0°13'W
Hendrina, S. Afr. (hĕn-drē'nǎ)	238c	26°10'S	29°44'E
Hengch'un, Tai. (hĕng'chŭn')	209	22°00'N	120°42'E
Hengelo, Neth. (hĕŋgĕ-lō)	165	52°20'N	6°45'E
Hengshan, China (hĕng'shän')	209	27°20'N	112°40'E
Hengshui, China (hĕng'shōō-ē')	206	37°43'N	115°42'E
Hengxian, China (hŭŋ shyĕn)	209	22°40'N	109°20'E
Hengyang, China	205	26°58'N	112°30'E
Heniches'k, Ukr.	181	46°11'N	34°47'E
Henley on Thames, Eng., U.K. (hĕn'lē ŏn tĕmz)	158b	51°31'N	0°54'W
Henlopen, Cape, c., De., U.S. (hĕn-lō'pĕn)	109	38°45'N	75°05'W
Hennebont, Fr. (ĕn-bôn')	170	47°47'N	3°16'W
Hennenman, S. Afr.	238c	27°59'S	27°03'E
Hennessey, Ok., U.S. (hĕn'ĕ-sĭ)	121	36°04'N	97°53'W
Hennigsdorf, Ger. (hĕ'nĕngz-dōrf)	159b	52°39'N	13°12'E
Hennops, r., S. Afr. (hĕn'ŏps)	233b	25°51'S	27°57'E
Hennopsrivier, S. Afr.	233b	25°50'S	27°59'E
Henrietta, Ok., U.S. (hĕn-rĭ-ĕt'ǎ)	121	35°25'N	95°58'W
Henrietta, Tx., U.S. (hen-rĭ-ĕ'tǎ)	120	33°47'N	98°11'W
Henrietta Maria, Cape, c., Can. (hĕn-rĭ-ĕt'ǎ)	93	55°10'N	82°20'W
Henry Mountains, mts., Ut., U.S. (hĕn'rĭ)	106	37°55'N	110°45'W
Henrys Fork, r., Id., U.S.	115	43°52'N	111°55'W
Henteyn Nuruu, mtn., Russia	208	49°40'N	111°00'E
Hentiyn Nuruu, mts., Mong.	204	49°25'N	107°51'E
Henzada, Mya.	199	17°38'N	95°28'E
Heppner, Or., U.S. (hĕp'nẽr)	114	45°21'N	119°33'W
Hepu, China (hŭ-pōō)	209	21°28'N	109°10'E
Herāt, Afg. (hĕ-rät')	198	34°28'N	62°13'E
Hercules, Can.	102g	53°27'N	113°20'W
Herdecke, Ger. (hĕr'dĕ-kĕ)	171c	51°24'N	7°26'E
Heredia, C.R. (ā-rā'dhē-ä)	133	10°04'N	84°06'W
Hereford, Eng., U.K. (hĕrĕ'fẽrd)	164	52°05'N	2°44'W
Hereford, Md., U.S.	110e	39°35'N	76°42'W
Hereford, Tx., U.S. (hĕr'ĕ-fẽrd)	120	34°47'N	102°25'W
Hereford and Worcester, co., Eng., U.K.	158a	52°24'N	2°15'W
Herencia, Spain (å-rān'thē-ä)	172	39°23'N	3°22'W
Herentals, Bel.	159a	51°10'N	4°51'E
Herford, Ger. (hĕr'fōrt)	168	52°06'N	8°42'E
Herington, Ks., U.S. (hĕr'ĭng-tŭn)	121	38°41'N	96°57'W
Herisau, Switz. (hā'rē-zou)	168	47°23'N	9°18'E
Herk-de-Stad, Bel.	159a	50°56'N	5°13'E
Herkimer, N.Y., U.S. (hûr'kĭ-mẽr)	109	43°05'N	75°00'W
Hermansville, Mi., U.S. (hûr'mǎns-vĭl)	108	45°40'N	87°35'W
Hermantown, Mn., U.S. (hẽr'mǎn-toun)	117h	46°46'N	92°12'W
Hermanusdorings, S. Afr.	238c	24°08'S	27°46'E
Herminie, Pa., U.S. (hûr-mĭ'nē)	111e	40°16'N	79°45'W
Hermitage Bay, b., Can. (hûr'mĭ-tĕj)	101	47°35'N	56°05'W
Hermit Islands, is., Pap. N. Gui. (hûr'mĭt)	213	1°48'S	144°55'E
Hermosa Beach, Ca., U.S. (hẽr-mō'sá)	117a	33°51'N	118°24'W
Hermosillo, Mex. (ĕr-mō-sē'l-yō)	128	29°00'N	110°57'W
Herndon, Va., U.S. (hĕrn'don)	110e	38°58'N	77°22'W
Herne, Ger. (hĕr'nĕ)	171c	51°32'N	7°13'E
Herning, Den. (hĕr'nĭng)	160	56°08'N	8°55'E
Heron, l., Mn., U.S. (hĕr'ŭn)	112	43°42'N	95°23'W
Heron Lake, Mn., U.S.	112	43°48'N	95°20'W
Herrero, Punta, Mex. (pō'n-tä-ĕr-rĕ'rō)	132a	19°18'N	87°24'W
Herrin, Il., U.S. (hĕr'ĭn)	108	37°50'N	89°00'W
Herschel, S. Afr. (hĕr'-shĕl)	233c	30°37'S	27°12'E
Herscher, Il., U.S. (hĕr'shẽr)	111a	41°03'N	88°06'W
Herstal, Bel. (hĕr'stäl)	165	50°42'N	5°32'E
Hertford, Eng., U.K.	164	51°48'N	0°05'W
Hertford, N.C., U.S. (hûrt'fẽrd)	125	36°10'N	76°30'W
Hertfordshire, co., Eng., U.K.	158b	51°46'N	0°05'W
Hertzberg, Ger. (hĕrtz'bĕrgh)	159b	52°54'N	12°58'E
Hervás, Spain	172	40°16'N	5°51'W
Herzliyya, Isr.	197a	32°10'N	34°49'E
Hessen, hist. reg., Ger. (hĕs'ĕn)	168	50°42'N	9°00'E
Hetch Hetchy Aqueduct, Ca., U.S. (hĕtch hĕt'chĭ ǎk'wē-dŭkt)	118	37°27'N	120°54'W
Hettinger, N.D., U.S. (hĕt'ĭn-jẽr)	112	45°58'N	102°36'W
Heuningspruit, S. Afr.	238c	27°28'S	27°26'E
Hexian, China (hŭ shyĕn)	209	24°20'N	111°28'E
Hexian, China	206	31°44'N	118°20'E
Heyang, China (hŭ-yäŋ)	208	35°18'N	110°18'E
Heystekrand, S. Afr.	238c	25°16'S	27°14'E
Heyuan, China (hŭ-yůän)	209	23°48'N	114°45'E
Heywood, Eng., U.K. (hā'wŏŏd)	158a	53°36'N	2°12'W
Heze, China (hŭ-dzŭ)	206	35°13'N	115°28'E
Hialeah, Fl., U.S. (hī-à-lē'ăh)	125a	25°49'N	80°18'W
Hiawatha, Ks., U.S. (hī-ǎ-wô'thǎ)	121	39°50'N	95°33'W
Hiawatha, Ut., U.S.	119	39°25'N	111°05'W
Hibbing, Mn., U.S. (hĭb'ĭng)	105	47°26'N	92°58'W
Hickman, Ky., U.S. (hĭk'mǎn)	124	34°33'N	89°10'W
Hickory, N.C., U.S. (hĭk'ô-rĭ)	125	35°43'N	81°21'W
Hicksville, N.Y., U.S.	108	41°15'N	84°45'W
Hicksville, N.Y., U.S. (hĭks'vĭl)	110a	40°47'N	73°25'W
Hico, Tx., U.S. (hī'kō)	122	32°00'N	98°02'W
Hidalgo, Mex. (ē-dhäl'gō)	130	24°14'N	99°25'W
Hidalgo, Mex.	122	27°49'N	99°53'W
Hidalgo, state, Mex.	128	20°45'N	99°30'W
Hidalgo del Parral, Mex. (ē-dä'l-gō-dĕl-pär-rà'l)	128	26°55'N	105°40'W
Hidalgo Yalalag, Mex. (ē-dhäl'gō-yä-lä-läg)	131	17°12'N	96°11'W
Hierro Island, i., Spain (yĕ'r-rô)	230	27°37'N	18°29'W
Higashimurayama, Japan	211a	35°46'N	139°28'E
Higashiōsaka, Japan	211b	34°40'N	135°44'E
Higgins, l., Mi., U.S. (hĭg'ĭnz)	108	44°20'N	84°45'W
Higginsville, Mo., U.S. (hĭg'ĭnz-vĭl)	121	39°05'N	93°44'W
High, i., Mi., U.S.	108	45°45'N	85°45'W
High Bluff, Can.	102f	50°01'N	98°08'W
Highborne Cay, i., Bah. (hī'bôrn kē)	134	24°45'N	76°50'W
Highgrove, Ca., U.S. (hī'grōv)	117a	34°01'N	117°20'W
High Island, Tx., U.S.	123a	29°34'N	94°24'W
Highland, Ca., U.S. (hī'lǎnd)	117a	34°08'N	117°13'W
Highland, Il., U.S.	121	38°44'N	89°41'W
Highland, In., U.S.	111a	41°33'N	87°28'W
Highland, Mi., U.S.	111b	42°38'N	83°37'W
Highland Park, Il., U.S.	111a	42°11'N	87°47'W
Highland Park, Mi., U.S.	111b	42°24'N	83°06'W
Highland Park, N.J., U.S.	110a	40°30'N	74°25'W
Highland Park, Tx., U.S.	117c	32°49'N	96°48'W
Highlands, N.J., U.S. (hī-lǎndz)	110a	40°24'N	73°59'W
Highlands, Tx., U.S.	123a	29°49'N	95°01'W
Highmore, S.D., U.S. (hī'mōr)	112	44°30'N	99°26'W
High Ongar, Eng., U.K. (on'gẽr)	158b	51°43'N	0°15'E
High Peak, mtn., Phil.	213a	15°38'N	120°05'E
High Point, N.C., U.S.	125	35°55'N	80°00'W
High Prairie, Can.	90	55°26'N	116°29'W
High Ridge, Mo., U.S.	117e	38°27'N	90°32'W
High River, Can.	90	50°35'N	113°52'W
High Rock Lake, res., N.C., U.S. (hī'-rŏk)	125	35°40'N	80°15'W
High Springs, Fl., U.S.	125	29°48'N	82°38'W
High Tatra Mountains, mts., Eur.	169	49°15'N	19°40'E
Hightstown, N.J., U.S. (hīts-toun)	110a	40°16'N	74°32'W
High Wycombe, Eng., U.K. (wĭ-kŭm)	164	51°36'N	0°45'W
Higuero, Punta, c., P.R.	129b	18°21'N	67°11'W
Higuerote, Ven. (ē-gĕ-rô'tĕ)	143b	10°29'N	66°06'W
Higüey, Dom. Rep. (ē-gwĕ'y)	135	18°40'N	68°45'W
Hiiumaa, i., Est. (hē'ŏm-ô)	180	58°47'N	22°05'E
Hikone, Japan (hē'kō-nĕ)	211	35°15'N	136°15'E
Hildburghausen, Ger. (hĭld'bōrg hou-zĕn)	168	50°26'N	10°45'E
Hilden, Ger. (hēl'dĕn)	171c	51°10'N	6°56'E
Hildesheim, Ger. (hĭl'dĕs-hīm)	161	52°08'N	9°56'E
Hillaby, Mount, mtn., Barb. (hĭl'ǎ-bĭ)	133b	13°15'N	59°35'W
Hill City, Ks., U.S. (hĭl)	120	39°22'N	99°54'W
Hill City, Mn., U.S.	113	46°58'N	93°38'W
Hillegersberg, Neth.	159a	51°57'N	4°29'E
Hillerød, Den. (hē'lĕ-rûdh)	166	55°56'N	12°17'E
Hillsboro, Il., U.S. (hĭlz'bŭr-ō)	121	39°09'N	89°28'W
Hillsboro, Ks., U.S.	121	38°22'N	97°11'W
Hillsboro, N.D., U.S.	112	47°23'N	97°05'W
Hillsboro, N.H., U.S.	109	43°05'N	71°55'W
Hillsboro, Oh., U.S.	108	39°10'N	83°40'W
Hillsboro, Or., U.S.	116c	45°31'N	122°59'W
Hillsboro, Tx., U.S.	123	32°01'N	97°06'W
Hillsboro, Wi., U.S.	113	43°39'N	90°20'W
Hillsburgh, Can. (hĭlz'bûrg)	102d	43°48'N	80°09'W
Hills Creek Lake, res., Or., U.S.	114	43°41'N	122°26'W
Hillsdale, Mi., U.S. (hĭls-dāl)	119	41°55'N	84°35'W
Hilo, Hi., U.S. (hē'lō)	106c	19°44'N	155°01'W
Hilvarenbeek, Neth.	159a	51°29'N	5°10'E
Hilversum, Neth. (hĭl'vẽr-sŭm)	159a	52°13'N	5°10'E
Himachal Pradesh, India	199	32°00'N	77°30'E
Himalayas, mts., Asia	199	29°30'N	85°02'E
Himeji, Japan (hē'mā-jē)	210	34°50'N	134°42'E
Himmelpforten, Ger. (hē'mĕl-pfōr-tĕn)	159c	53°37'N	9°19'E
Ḩimş, Syria	198	34°44'N	36°43'E
Hinche, Haiti (hēn'chå) (ăNsh)	135	19°10'N	72°05'W
Hinchinbrook, i., Austl. (hĭn-chĭn-brŏŏk)	220	18°23'S	146°57'W
Hinckley, Eng., U.K. (hĭnk'lĭ)	158a	52°32'N	1°21'W
Hindley, Eng., U.K. (hĭnd'lĭ)	158a	53°32'N	2°35'W
Hindu Kush, mts., Asia (hĭn'dōō kōōsh')	199	35°15'N	68°44'E
Hindupur, India (hĭn'dōō-pōōr)	203	13°52'N	77°34'E

ng-sing; ŋ-baŋk; N-nasalized n; nŏd; cŏmmit; ōld; ôbey; ôrder; oi-boil; fōōd; ŏŏ-as oo in foot; ou-out; s-soft; sh-dish; th-thin; pūre; ůnite; ûrn; stŭd; circŭs; ü-as in French tu; '-indeterminate vowel.

302 Hingham – Hualapai Mountains PRONOUNCING INDEX

PLACE (Pronunciation)	PAGE	LAT.	LONG.
Hingham, Ma., U.S. (hĭng′ăm)	101a	42°14′N	70°53′W
Hinkley, Oh., U.S. (hĭnk′-lĭ)	111d	41°14′N	81°45′W
Hinojosa del Duque, Spain (ē-nō-kō′sä)	172	38°30′N	5°09′W
Hinsdale, Il., U.S. (hĭnz′dāl)	111a	41°48′N	87°56′W
Hinton, Can. (hĭn′tŭn)	95	53°25′N	117°34′W
Hinton, W.V., U.S. (hĭn′tŭn)	108	37°40′N	80°55′W
Hirado, i., Japan (hē′rä-dō)	210	33°19′N	129°18′E
Hirakata, Japan (hē′rä-kä′tä)	211b	34°49′N	135°40′E
Hirara, Japan	214d	24°48′N	125°17′E
Hiratsuka, Japan (hē-rät-sōō′kȧ)	211	35°20′N	139°19′E
Hirosaki, Japan (hē′rō-sä′kē)	205	40°31′N	140°38′E
Hirose, Japan (hē′rō-sä)	211	35°20′N	133°11′E
Hiroshima, Japan (hē-rō-shē′mȧ)	205	34°22′N	132°25′E
Hirson, Fr. (ēr-sôN′)	170	49°54′N	4°00′E
Hisar, India	202	29°15′N	75°47′E
Hispaniola, i., N.A. (hĭ′spăn-ĭ-ō-lȧ)	129	17°30′N	73°15′W
Hitachi, Japan (hē-tä′chē)	210	36°42′N	140°47′E
Hitchcock, Tx., U.S. (hĭch′kŏk)	123a	29°21′N	95°01′W
Hitoyoshi, Japan (hē′tō-yō′shē)	211	32°13′N	130°45′E
Hitra, i., Nor. (hĭträ)	160	63°34′N	7°37′E
Hittefeld, Ger. (hē′tĕ-fĕld)	159c	53°23′N	9°59′E
Hiwasa, Japan (hē′wȧ-sä)	211	33°44′N	134°31′E
Hiwassee, r., Tn., U.S. (hī-wôs′sē)	124	35°10′N	84°35′W
Hjälmaren, l., Swe.	160	59°07′N	16°05′E
Hjo, Swe. (yō)	166	58°19′N	14°11′E
Hjørring, Den. (jûr′ĭng)	160	57°27′N	9°59′E
Hlobyne, Ukr.	177	49°22′N	33°17′E
Hlohovec, Slvk. (hlō′ho-vĕts)	169	48°24′N	17°49′E
Hlukhiv, Ukr.	181	51°42′N	33°52′E
Hlybokaye, Bela.	180	55°08′N	27°44′E
Hobart, Austl. (hō′bȧrt)	219	43°00′S	147°30′E
Hobart, In., U.S.	111a	41°31′N	87°15′W
Hobart, Ok., U.S.	120	35°02′N	99°06′W
Hobart, Wa., U.S.	116a	47°25′N	121°58′W
Hobbs, N.M., U.S. (hŏbs)	120	32°41′N	103°15′W
Hoboken, Bel. (hō′bō kĕn)	159a	51°11′N	4°20′E
Hoboken, N.J., U.S.	110a	40°43′N	74°03′W
Hobro, Den. (hô-brô′)	166	56°38′N	9°47′E
Hobson, Va., U.S. (hŏb′sŭn)	110g	36°54′N	76°31′W
Hobson's Bay, b., Austl. (hŏb′sŭnz)	217a	37°54′S	144°45′E
Hobyo, Som.	238a	5°24′N	48°28′E
Ho Chi Minh City, Viet.	212	10°46′N	106°34′E
Hockinson, Wa., U.S. (hŏk′ĭn-sŭn)	116c	45°44′N	122°29′W
Hoctún, Mex. (ôk-tōō′n)	132a	20°52′N	89°10′W
Hodgenville, Ky., U.S. (hŏj′ĕn-vĭl)	108	37°35′N	85°45′W
Hodges Hill, mtn., Can. (hŏj′ĕz)	101	49°04′N	55°53′W
Hódmezövásárhely, Hung. (hōd′mĕ-zû-vō′shôr-hĕl-y′)	169	46°24′N	20°21′E
Hodna, Chott el, l., Alg.	162	35°20′N	3°27′E
Hodonin, Czech Rep. (hē′dō-nén)	169	48°50′N	17°06′E
Hoegaarden, Bel.	159a	50°46′N	4°55′E
Hoek van Holland, Neth.	159a	51°59′N	4°05′E
Hoeryŏng, Kor., N. (hwĕr′yŭng)	210	42°28′N	129°39′E
Hof, Ger. (hōf)	168	50°19′N	11°55′E
Hofsjökull, ice, Ice. (hôfs′yü′kōōl)	160	64°55′N	18°40′W
Hog, i., Mi., U.S.	108	45°50′N	85°20′W
Hogansville, Ga., U.S. (hō′gănz-vĭl)	124	33°10′N	84°54′W
Hog Cay, i., Bah.	135	23°35′N	75°30′W
Hogsty Reef, rf., Bah.	135	21°45′N	73°50′W
Hohenbrunn, Ger. (hō′hĕn-brōōn)	159d	48°03′N	11°42′E
Hohenlimburg, Ger. (hō′hĕn lĕm′bōōrg)	171c	51°20′N	7°35′E
Hohen Neuendorf, Ger. (hō′hĕn noi′ĕn-dōrf)	159b	52°40′N	13°22′E
Hohe Tauern, mts., Aus. (hō′ĕ tou′ĕrn)	168	47°11′N	12°12′E
Hohhot, China (hŭ-hōō-tŭ)	205	41°05′N	111°50′E
Hohoe, Ghana	234	7°09′N	0°28′E
Hohokus, N.J., U.S. (hō-hō-kŭs)	110a	41°01′N	74°08′W
Hoi An, Viet.	209	15°48′N	108°30′E
Hoisington, Ks., U.S. (hoi′zĭng-tŭn)	120	38°30′N	98°46′W
Hojo, Japan (hō′jō)	211	33°58′N	132°50′E
Hokitika, N.Z. (hō-kĭ-tē′kä)	221a	42°43′S	170°59′E
Hokkaidō, i., Japan (hŏk′kĭ-dō)	210	43°30′N	142°45′E
Holbaek, Den. (hôl′bĕk)	166	55°42′N	11°40′E
Holbox, Mex. (ôl-bō′x)	132a	21°33′N	87°19′W
Holbox, Isla, i., Mex. (ē′s-lä-ôl-bō′x)	132a	21°40′N	87°21′W
Holbrook, Az., U.S. (hōl′brŏŏk)	119	34°55′N	110°15′W
Holbrook, Ma., U.S.	101a	42°10′N	71°01′W
Holden, Ma., U.S. (hōl′dĕn)	101a	42°21′N	71°51′W
Holden, Mo., U.S.	121	38°42′N	94°00′W
Holden, W.V., U.S.	108	37°45′N	82°05′W
Holdenville, Ok., U.S. (hōl′dĕn-vĭl)	121	35°05′N	96°25′W
Holdrege, Ne., U.S. (hōl′drĕj)	120	40°25′N	99°28′W
Holguín, Cuba (ôl-gēn′)	129	20°55′N	76°15′W
Holguín, prov., Cuba	134	20°40′N	76°15′W
Holidaysburg, Pa., U.S. (hŏl′ĭ-dāz-bûrg)	109	40°30′N	78°30′W
Hollabrunn, Aus.	168	48°33′N	16°04′E
Holland, Mi., U.S. (hŏl′ănd)	108	42°45′N	86°10′W
Hollands Diep, strt., Neth.	159a	51°43′N	4°25′E
Hollenstedt, Ger. (hō′lĕn-shtĕt)	159c	53°22′N	9°43′E
Hollis, N.H., U.S. (hŏl′ĭs)	101a	42°30′N	71°29′W
Hollis, Ok., U.S.	120	34°39′N	99°56′W
Hollister, Ca., U.S. (hŏl′ĭs-tēr)	118	36°50′N	121°25′W
Holliston, Ma., U.S. (hŏl′ĭs-tŭn)	101a	42°12′N	71°25′W
Holly, Mi., U.S. (hŏl′ĭ)	108	42°45′N	83°30′W
Holly, Wa., U.S.	116a	47°34′N	122°58′W
Holly Springs, Ms., U.S. (hŏl′ĭ sprĭngz)	124	34°45′N	89°28′W
Hollywood, Ca., U.S. (hŏl′ē-wŏŏd)	117a	34°06′N	118°20′W
Hollywood, Fl., U.S.	125a	26°00′N	80°11′W
Holmes Reefs, rf., Austl. (hōmz)	221	16°33′S	148°43′E
Holmestrand, Nor. (hôl′mĕ-strän)	166	59°29′N	10°17′E
Holmsbu, Nor. (hôlms′bōō)	166	59°36′N	10°26′E
Holmsjön, l., Swe.	166	62°23′N	15°43′E
Holstebro, Den. (hôl′stĕ-brô)	160	56°22′N	8°39′E
Holstein, hist. reg., Ger.	168	54°10′N	9°40′E
Holston, r., Tn., U.S. (hōl′stŭn)	124	36°02′N	83°42′W
Holt, Eng., U.K. (hōlt)	158a	53°05′N	2°53′W
Holton, Ks., U.S. (hōl′tŭn)	121	39°27′N	95°43′W
Holy Cross, Ak., U.S. (hō′lĭ krôs)	103	62°10′N	159°40′W
Holyhead, Wales, U.K. (hŏl′ē-hĕd)	164	53°18′N	4°45′W
Holy Island, i., Eng., U.K.	164	55°43′N	1°48′W
Holy Island, i., Wales, U.K. (hō′lĭ)	164	53°15′N	4°45′W
Holyoke, Co., U.S. (hōl′yōk)	120	40°36′N	102°18′W
Holyoke, Ma., U.S.	109	42°10′N	72°40′W
Homano, Japan (hō-mä′nō)	211a	35°33′N	140°08′E
Homberg, Ger. (hōm′bĕrgh)	171c	51°27′N	6°42′E
Hombori, Mali	234	15°17′N	1°42′W
Home Gardens, Ca., U.S. (hōm gär′d′nz)	117a	33°53′N	117°32′W
Homeland, Ca., U.S. (hōm′lănd)	117a	33°44′N	117°07′W
Homer, Ak., U.S. (hō′mēr)	103	59°42′N	151°30′W
Homer, La., U.S.	123	32°46′N	93°05′W
Homer Youngs Peak, mtn., Mt., U.S.	115	45°19′N	113°41′W
Homestead, Fl., U.S. (hōm′stĕd)	125a	25°27′N	80°28′W
Homestead, Mi., U.S.	117k	46°20′N	84°07′W
Homestead, Pa., U.S.	111e	40°29′N	79°55′W
Homestead National Monument of America, rec., Ne., U.S.	121	40°16′N	96°51′W
Homewood, Al., U.S. (hōm′wŏŏd)	110h	33°28′N	86°48′W
Homewood, Il., U.S.	111a	41°34′N	87°40′W
Hominy, Ok., U.S. (hŏm′ĭ-nĭ)	121	36°25′N	96°24′W
Homochitto, r., Ms., U.S. (hō-mō-chĭt′ō)	124	31°23′N	91°15′W
Homyel′, Bela.	180	52°20′N	31°03′E
Homyel′, prov., Bela.	176	52°18′N	29°00′E
Honda, Col. (hōn′dȧ)	142	5°13′N	74°45′W
Honda, Bahía, b., Cuba (bä-ē′ä-ō′n-dä)	134	23°10′N	83°20′W
Hondo, Tx., U.S.	122	29°20′N	99°08′W
Hondo, r., N.M., U.S.	120	33°22′N	105°06′W
Hondo, Río, r., N.A. (hon-dō′)	132a	18°16′N	88°32′W
Honduras, nation, N.A. (hŏn-dōō′rȧs)	128	14°30′N	88°00′W
Honduras, Gulf of, b., N.A.	128	16°30′N	87°30′W
Honea Path, S.C., U.S. (hŭn′ĭ păth)	125	34°25′N	82°16′W
Hønefoss, Nor. (hē′nĕ-fôs)	160	60°10′N	10°15′E
Honesdale, Pa., U.S. (hōnz′dāl)	109	41°30′N	75°15′W
Honey Grove, Tx., U.S. (hŭn′ĭ grōv)	121	33°35′N	95°54′W
Honey Lake, l., Ca., U.S. (hŭn′ĭ)	118	40°11′N	120°34′W
Honfleur, Can. (ôN-flûr′)	102b	46°39′N	70°53′W
Honfleur, Fr. (ôN-flûr′)	170	49°26′N	0°13′E
Hon Gay, Viet.	209	20°58′N	107°10′E
Hong Kong (Xianggang), China	205	21°45′N	115°00′E
Hongshui, r., China (hōŋ-shwä)	204	24°30′N	105°00′E
Honguedo, Détroit d′, strt., Can.	100	49°08′N	63°45′W
Hongze Hu, l., China	205	33°17′N	118°37′E
Honiara, Sol. Is.	219	9°26′S	159°57′E
Honiton, Eng., U.K. (hŏn′ĭ-tŏn)	164	50°49′N	3°10′W
Honolulu, Hi., U.S. (hŏn-ō-lōō′lōō)	106c	21°18′N	157°50′W
Honomu, Hi., U.S. (hŏn′ō-mōō)	126a	19°50′N	155°04′W
Honshū, i., Japan	205	36°00′N	138°00′E
Hood, Mount, mtn., Or., U.S.	106	45°20′N	121°43′W
Hood Canal, b., Wa., U.S. (hŏŏd)	116a	47°45′N	122°45′W
Hood River, Or., U.S.	104	45°42′N	121°30′W
Hoodsport, Wa., U.S. (hŏŏdz′pōrt)	116a	47°25′N	123°09′W
Hoogly, r., India (hōōg′lĭ)	199	21°35′N	87°50′E
Hoogstraten, Bel.	159a	51°24′N	4°46′E
Hooker, Ok., U.S. (hŏŏk′ēr)	120	36°49′N	101°13′W
Hool, Mex. (ōō′l)	132a	19°32′N	90°22′W
Hoonah, Ak., U.S. (hōō′nä)	103	58°05′N	135°25′W
Hoopa Valley Indian Reservation, I.R., Ca., U.S.	114	41°18′N	123°35′W
Hooper, Ne., U.S. (hŏŏp′ēr)	121	41°37′N	96°31′W
Hooper, Ut., U.S.	117b	41°10′N	112°08′W
Hooper Bay, Ak., U.S.	103	61°32′N	166°02′W
Hoopeston, Il., U.S. (hōōps′tŭn)	108	40°35′N	87°40′W
Hoosick Falls, N.Y., U.S. (hōō′sĭk)	109	42°55′N	73°15′W
Hoover Dam, Nv., U.S. (hōō′vēr)	118	36°00′N	115°06′W
Hoover Dam, dam, U.S.	106	36°00′N	114°27′W
Hopatcong, Lake, l., N.J., U.S. (hō-păt′kong)	110a	40°57′N	74°38′W
Hope, Ak., U.S. (hōp)	103	60°54′N	149°48′W
Hope, Ar., U.S.	121	33°41′N	93°35′W
Hope, N.D., U.S.	112	47°17′N	97°45′W
Hope, Ben, mtn., Scot., U.K. (bĕn hōp)	164	58°25′N	4°25′W
Hopedale, Can. (hōp′dāl)	91	55°26′N	60°11′W
Hopedale, Ma., U.S. (hōp′dāl)	101a	42°08′N	71°33′W
Hopelchén, Mex. (o-pĕl-chĕ′n)	132a	19°47′N	89°51′W
Hopes Advance, Cap, c., Can. (hōps ăd-vans′)	93	61°05′N	69°35′W
Hopetoun, Austl. (hōp′toun)	218	33°50′S	120°15′E
Hopetown, S. Afr. (hōp′toun)	232	29°35′S	24°10′E
Hopewell, Va., U.S. (hōp′wĕl)	125	37°14′N	77°15′W
Hopewell Culture National Historical Park, rec., Oh., U.S.	108	39°25′N	83°00′W
Hopi Indian Reservation, I.R., Az., U.S. (hō′pē)	119	36°20′N	110°30′W
Hopkins, Mn., U.S. (hŏp′kĭns)	117g	44°55′N	93°24′W
Hopkinsville, Ky., U.S. (hŏp′kĭns-vĭl)	105	36°50′N	87°28′W
Hopkinton, Ma., U.S. (hŏp′kĭn-tŭn)	101a	42°14′N	71°31′W
Hoquiam, Wa., U.S. (hō′kwĭ-ăm)	104	47°00′N	123°53′W
Horconcitos, Pan. (ŏr-kôn-sē′-tôs)	133	8°18′N	82°11′W
Horgen, Switz. (hôr′gĕn)	168	47°16′N	8°35′E
Horicon, Wi., U.S. (hŏr′ĭ-kŏn)	113	43°26′N	88°40′W
Horlivka, Ukr.	181	48°17′N	38°03′E
Hormuz, Strait of, strt., Asia (hôr′mŭz′)	198	26°30′N	56°30′E
Horn, i., Austl. (hôrn)	221	10°30′S	143°30′E
Horn, Cape *see* Hornos, Cabo de, c., Chile	144	56°00′S	67°00′W
Hornavan, l., Swe.	160	65°54′N	16°17′E
Horneburg, Ger. (hôr′nĕ-bōrgh)	159c	53°30′N	9°35′E
Hornell, N.Y., U.S. (hôr-nĕl′)	109	42°20′N	77°40′W
Hornos, Cabo de, c., Chile	144	56°00′S	67°00′W
Horn Plateau, plat., Can.	92	62°12′N	120°29′W
Hornsby, Austl. (hôrnz′bĭ)	217b	33°43′S	151°06′E
Horodenka, Ukr.	169	48°40′N	25°30′E
Horodnia, Ukr.	177	51°54′N	31°31′E
Horodok, Ukr.	169	49°47′N	23°39′E
Horqueta, Para. (ŏr-kĕ′tä)	144	23°20′S	57°00′W
Horse Creek, r., Co., U.S. (hôrs)	120	38°49′N	103°48′W
Horse Creek, r., Wy., U.S.	112	41°33′N	104°39′W
Horse Islands, is., Can.	101	50°11′N	55°45′W
Horsens, Den. (hôrs′ĕns)	166	55°50′N	9°49′E
Horseshoe Bay, Can. (hôrs-shōō)	116d	49°23′N	123°16′W
Horsforth, Eng., U.K. (hôrs′fŭrth)	158a	53°50′N	1°38′W
Horsham, Austl. (hôr′shăm) (hôrs′ăm)	219	36°42′S	142°17′E
Horst, Ger. (hôrst)	159c	53°49′N	9°37′E
Horten, Nor. (hôr′tĕn)	166	59°26′N	10°27′E
Horton, Ks., U.S. (hôr′tŭn)	121	39°38′N	95°32′W
Horton, r., Ak., U.S. (hôr′tŭn)	103	68°38′N	122°00′W
Horwich, Eng., U.K. (hŏr′ĭch)	158a	53°36′N	2°33′W
Horyn′, r., Eur. (gō′rĕn′)	169	50°55′N	26°07′E
Hososhima, Japan (hō′sō-shē′mä)	210	32°25′N	131°40′E
Hoste, i., Chile (ŏs′tā)	144	55°20′S	70°45′W
Hostotipaquillo, Mex. (ôs-tō′tĭ-pä-kēl′yō)	130	21°09′N	104°05′W
Hota, Japan (hō′tä)	211a	35°08′N	139°50′E
Hotan, China (hwô-tän)	204	37°11′N	79°50′E
Hotan, r., China	204	39°09′N	81°08′E
Hoto Mayor, Dom. Rep. (ô-tô-mä-yô′r)	135	18°45′N	69°10′W
Hot Springs, Ak., U.S. (hŏt sprĭngs)	103	65°00′N	150°20′W
Hot Springs, Ar., U.S.	105	34°29′N	93°02′W
Hot Springs, S.D., U.S.	112	43°28′N	103°32′W
Hot Springs, Va., U.S.	109	38°00′N	79°55′W
Hot Springs National Park, rec., Ar., U.S.	107	34°30′N	93°00′W
Hotte, Massif de la, mts., Haiti	135	18°25′N	74°00′W
Hotville, Ca., U.S. (hŏt′vĭl)	118	32°50′N	115°24′W
Houdan, Fr. (ōō-däN′)	171b	48°47′N	1°36′E
Houghton, Mi., U.S. (hō′tŭn)	113	47°06′N	88°36′W
Houghton, l., Mi., U.S.	108	44°20′N	84°45′W
Houilles, Fr. (ōō-yĕs′)	171b	48°55′N	2°11′E
Houjie, China (hwô-jyĕ)	207a	22°58′N	113°39′E
Houlton, Me., U.S. (hōl′tŭn)	100	46°07′N	67°50′W
Houma, La., U.S. (hōō′mȧ)	123	29°36′N	90°43′W
Housatonic, r., U.S. (hōō-sȧ-tŏn′ĭk)	109	41°50′N	73°25′W
House Springs, Mo., U.S. (hous sprĭngs)	117e	38°24′N	90°34′W
Houston, Ms., U.S. (hūs′tŭn)	124	33°53′N	89°00′W
Houston, Tx., U.S.	105	29°46′N	95°21′W
Houston Ship Channel, strt., Tx., U.S.	123a	29°38′N	94°57′W
Houtbaai, S. Afr.	232a	34°03′S	18°22′E
Houtman Rocks, is., Austl. (hout′män)	220	28°15′S	112°45′E
Houzhen, China (hwô-jŭn)	206	36°59′N	118°59′E
Hovd, Mong.	204	48°08′N	91°40′E
Hovd Gol, r., Mong.	204	49°06′N	91°16′E
Hove, Eng., U.K. (hōv)	164	50°50′N	0°09′W
Hövsgöl Nuur, l., Mong.	204	51°11′N	99°11′E
Howard, Ks., U.S. (hou′ărd)	121	37°27′N	96°10′W
Howard, S.D., U.S.	112	44°01′N	97°31′W
Howden, Eng., U.K. (hou′dĕn)	158a	53°44′N	0°52′W
Howe, Cape, c., Austl. (hou)	221	37°30′S	150°40′E
Howell, Mi., U.S. (hou′ĕl)	108	42°40′N	84°00′W
Howe Sound, strt., Can.	94	49°22′N	123°18′W
Howick, Can. (hou′ĭk)	102a	45°11′N	73°51′W
Howick, S. Afr.	233c	29°29′S	30°16′E
Howland, i., Oc. (hou′lănd)	2	1°00′N	176°00′W
Howrah, India (hou′rä)	199	22°33′N	88°20′E
Howse Peak, mtn., Can.	95	51°30′N	116°40′W
Howson Peak, mtn., Can.	94	54°25′N	127°45′W
Hoxie, Ar., U.S. (kŏh′sĭ)	121	36°03′N	91°00′W
Hoy, i., Scot., U.K. (hoi)	164a	58°53′N	3°10′W
Hōya, Japan	211a	35°45′N	139°35′E
Hoylake, Eng., U.K. (hoi-lāk′)	158a	53°23′N	3°11′W
Hoyo, Sierra del, mts., Spain (sē-ĕ′r-rä-dĕl-ô′yô)	173a	40°39′N	3°56′W
Hradec Králové, Czech Rep.	161	50°12′N	15°50′E
Hradyz′k, Ukr.	177	49°12′N	33°06′E
Hranice, Czech Rep. (hrän′yē-tsĕ)	169	49°33′N	17°45′E
Hröby, Swe. (hûr′bü)	166	55°50′N	13°41′E
Hrodna, Bela.	180	53°40′N	23°49′E
Hron, r., Slvk.	169	48°22′N	18°42′E
Hrubieszów, Pol. (hrōō-byä′shōōf)	169	50°48′N	23°54′E
Hsawnhsup, Mya.	204	24°29′N	94°45′E
Hsinchu, Tai. (hsĭn′chōō′)	209	24°48′N	121°00′E
Huadian, China (hwä-dĭĕn)	208	42°38′N	126°45′E
Huai, r., China (hwī)	205	32°07′N	114°38′E
Huai′an, China (hwī-än)	208	33°31′N	119°11′E
Huailai, China	208	40°20′N	115°45′E
Huailin, China (hwī-lĭn)	206	31°27′N	117°36′E
Huainan, China	206	32°38′N	117°02′E
Huaiyang, China (hōōäī′yang)	208	33°45′N	114°54′E
Huaiyuan, China (hwī-yüän)	208	32°53′N	117°13′E
Huajicori, Mex. (wä-jē-kō′rē)	130	22°41′N	105°24′W
Huajuapan de León, Mex. (wäj-wä′päm dā lā-ōn′)	131	17°46′N	97°45′W
Hualapai Indian Reservation, I.R., Az., U.S. (wälȧpī)	119	35°41′N	113°38′W
Hualapai Mountains, mts., Az., U.S.	119	34°53′N	113°54′W

ăt; finăl; rāte; senȧte; ärm; ȧsk; sofȧ; fâre; ch-choose; dh-as th in other; bē; ēvent; bĕt; recĕnt; cratēr; g-gō; gh-guttural g; bĭt; ĭ-short neutral; rīde; K-guttural k as ch in German ich;

ng-sing;　ŋ-baŋk;　N-nasalized n;　nŏd;　cŏmmit;　ōld;　ȯbey;　ôrder;　oi-boil;　fōōd;　ȯ-as oo in foot;　ou-out;　s-soft;　sh-dish;　th-thin;　pūre;　ūnite;　ûrn;　stŭd;　circŭs;　ü-as in French tu;　′-indeterminate vowel.

304 Iijoki – Isla-Cristina PRONOUNCING INDEX

PLACE (Pronunciation)	PAGE	LAT.	LONG.
Iijoki, r., Fin. (ē'yô'kĭ)	180	65°28'N	27°00'E
Iizuka, Japan (ē'ē-zò-kà)	211	33°39'N	130°39'E
Ijebu-Ode, Nig. (ē-jĕ'bōō ōdå)	230	6°50'N	3°56'E
IJmuiden, Neth.	159a	52°27'N	4°36'E
IJsselmeer, l., Neth. (ī'sĕl-mār)	165	52°46'N	5°14'E
Ikaalinen, Fin. (ē'kä-lĭ-nĕn)	167	61°47'N	22°55'E
Ikaría, i., Grc. (ē-kä'ryà)	175	37°43'N	26°07'E
Ikeda, Japan (ē'kå-dä)	211b	34°49'N	135°26'E
Ikerre, Nig.	235	7°31'N	5°14'E
Ikhtiman, Blg. (ėk'tē-män)	175	42°26'N	23°49'E
Iki, i., Japan (ē'kė)	210	33°46'N	129°44'E
Ikoma, Japan	211b	34°41'N	135°43'E
Ikoma, Tan. (ė-kō'mä)	232	2°08'S	34°47'E
Iksha, Russia (ĭk'shà)	186b	56°10'N	37°30'E
Ila, Nig.	235	8°01'N	4°55'E
Ilagan, Phil.	213a	17°09'N	121°52'E
Ilan, Tai. (ē'län')	209	24°50'N	121°42'E
Iława, Pol. (ė-lä'vå)	169	53°35'N	19°36'E
Île-à-la-Crosse, Can.	96	55°34'N	108°00'W
Ilebo, D.R.C.	232	4°19'S	20°35'E
Ilek, Russia (ē'lyĕk)	181	51°30'N	53°10'E
Île-Perrot, Can. (yl-pĕ-rōt')	102a	45°21'N	73°54'W
Ilesha, Nig.	230	7°38'N	4°45'E
Ilford, Eng., U.K. (ĭl'fērd)	158b	51°33'N	0°06'E
Ilfracombe, Eng., U.K. (ĭl-frȧ-kōōm')	164	51°13'N	4°08'W
Ilhabela, Braz. (ē'lä-bĕ'lä)	141a	23°47'S	45°21'W
Ilha Grande, Baía de, b., Braz. (ēl'yà grän'dĕ)	141a	23°17'S	44°25'W
Ílhavo, Port. (ēl'yà-vō)	162	40°36'N	8°41'W
Ilhéus, Braz. (ē-lĕ'ōōs)	143	14°52'S	39°00'W
Ili, r., Asia	184	44°30'N	76°45'E
Iliamna, Ak., U.S. (ē-lē-äm'nà)	103	59°45'N	155°05'W
Iliamna, Ak., U.S.	103	60°18'N	153°25'W
Iliamna, l., Ak., U.S.	103	59°25'N	155°30'W
Ilim, r., Russia (ė-lyėm')	184	57°28'N	103°00'E
Ilimsk, Russia (ė-lyėmsk')	179	56°47'N	103°43'E
Ilin Island, i., Phil. (ē-lyēn')	213a	12°16'N	120°57'E
Ilion, N.Y., U.S. (ĭl'ĭ-ŭn)	109	43°00'N	75°05'W
Ilkeston, Eng., U.K. (ĭl'kĕs-tŭn)	158a	52°58'N	1°19'W
Illampu, Nevado, mtn., Bol. (nĕ-vá'dô-ēl-yäm-pōō')	142	15°50'S	68°15'W
Illapel, Chile (ē-zhä-pĕ'l)	144	31°37'S	71°10'W
Iller, r., Ger. (ĭlĕr)	168	47°52'N	10°06'E
Illimani, Nevado, mtn., Bol. (nĕ-vá'dô-ēl-yē-mä'nē)	142	16°50'S	67°38'W
Illinois, state, U.S. (ĭl-ĭ-noi') (ĭl-ĭ-noiz')	105	40°25'N	90°40'W
Illinois, r., Il., U.S.	107	39°00'N	90°30'W
Illintsi, Ukr.	177	49°07'N	29°13'E
Illizi, Alg.	230	26°35'N	8°24'E
Il'men, l., Russia (ô'zē-rô el''men'') (ĭl'mĕn)	180	58°18'N	32°00'E
Ilo, Peru	142	17°46'S	71°13'W
Ilobasco, El Sal. (ē-lò-bäs'kô)	132	13°57'N	88°46'W
Iloilo, Phil. (ē-lô-ē'lō)	212	10°49'N	122°33'E
Ilopango, Lago, l., El Sal. (ē-lô-päŋ'gō)	132	13°48'N	88°50'W
Ilorin, Nig. (ē-lô-rēn')	230	8°30'N	4°32'E
Ilūkste, Lat.	167	55°59'N	26°20'E
Ilwaco, Wa., U.S. (ĭl-wā'kô)	116c	46°19'N	124°02'W
Ilych, r., Russia (ė'l'ĭch)	180	62°30'N	57°30'E
Imabari, Japan (ē'mä-bä'rė)	210	34°05'N	132°58'E
Imai, Japan (ė-mī')	211b	34°30'N	135°47'E
Iman, r., Russia (ė-män')	210	45°40'N	134°31'E
Imandra, l., Russia (ē-män'drà)	180	67°40'N	32°30'E
Imbābah, Egypt (ēm-bä'bà)	238b	30°06'N	31°09'E
Imeni Morozova, Russia (ĭm-yĕ'nyĭ mô rô'zô và)	186c	59°58'N	31°02'E
Imeni Moskvy, Kanal (Moscow Canal), can., Russia (kà-näl'ĭm-yă'nĭ mŏs-kvĭ)	176	56°33'N	37°15'E
Imeni Tsyurupy, Russia	186b	55°30'N	38°39'E
Imeni Vorovskogo, Russia	186b	55°43'N	38°21'E
Imlay City, Mi., U.S. (ĭm'lā)	108	43°00'N	83°15'W
Immenstadt, Ger. (ĭm'ĕn-shtät)	168	47°34'N	10°12'E
Immerpan, S. Afr. (ĭmĕr-pän)	238c	24°29'S	29°14'E
Imola, Italy (ē'mô-lä)	174	44°19'N	11°43'E
Imotski, Cro. (ė-môts'kė)	175	43°25'N	17°15'E
Impameri, Braz.	143	17°44'S	48°03'W
Impendle, S. Afr. (ĭm-pĕnd'lå)	233c	29°38'S	29°54'E
Imperia, Italy (ėm-pä'rē-ä)	162	43°52'N	8°00'E
Imperial, Pa., U.S. (ĭm-pē'rĭ-ăl)	111e	40°27'N	80°15'W
Imperial Beach, Ca., U.S.	118a	32°34'N	117°08'W
Imperial Valley, Ca., U.S.	118	33°00'N	115°22'W
Impfondo, Congo (ĭmp-fōn'dō)	231	1°37'N	18°04'E
Imphāl, India (ĭmp'hŭl)	199	24°42'N	94°00'E
Ina, r., Japan (ė-nä')	211b	34°56'N	135°21'E
Inaja Indian Reservation, I.R., Ca., U.S. (ė-nä'hä)	118	32°56'N	116°37'W
Inari, l., Fin.	160	69°02'N	26°22'E
Inca, Spain (ēŋ'kä)	173	39°43'N	2°53'E
Ince Burun, c., Tur. (ĭn'jå)	163	42°00'N	35°00'E
Inch'ŏn, Kor., S. (ĭn'chŭn)	205	37°26'N	126°46'E
Incudine, Monte, mtn., Fr. (ēn-kōō-dē'nå) (äɴ-kü-dēn')	174	41°53'N	9°17'E
Indalsälven, r., Swe.	160	62°50'N	16°50'E
Independence, Ks., U.S. (ĭn-dė-pĕn'dĕns)	121	37°14'N	95°42'W
Independence, Mo., U.S.	117f	39°06'N	94°26'W
Independence, Oh., U.S.	111d	41°23'N	81°39'W
Independence, Or., U.S.	114	44°49'N	123°13'W
Independence Mountains, mts., Nv., U.S.	114	41°15'N	116°02'W
Inder köli, l., Kaz.	181	48°20'N	52°10'E
India, nation, Asia (ĭn'dĭ-ȧ)	199	23°00'N	77°30'E
Indian, l., Mi., U.S. (ĭn'dĭ-ăn)	113	46°04'N	86°34'W
Indian, r., N.Y., U.S.	109	44°05'N	75°45'W
Indiana, Pa., U.S. (ĭn-dĭ-än'ȧ)	109	40°40'N	79°10'W
Indiana, state, U.S.	105	39°50'N	86°45'W
Indianapolis, In., U.S. (ĭn-dĭ-ăn-ăp'ô-lĭs)	105	39°45'N	86°08'W
Indian Arm, b., Can. (ĭn'dĭ-ăn ärm)	116d	49°21'N	122°55'W
Indian Head, Can.	90	50°29'N	103°44'W
Indian Lake, l., Can.	98	47°00'N	82°00'W
Indian Ocean, o.	5	10°00'S	70°00'E
Indianola, Ia., U.S. (ĭn-dĭ-ăn-ō'lȧ)	113	41°22'N	93°33'W
Indianola, Ms., U.S.	124	33°29'N	90°35'W
Indigirka, r., Russia (ēn-dė-gēr'kà)	185	67°45'N	145°45'E
Indio, r., Pan. (ē'n-dyô)	128a	9°13'N	79°28'W
Indochina, reg., Asia (ĭn-dō-chī'nà)	212	17°22'N	105°18'E
Indonesia, nation, Asia (ĭn'dô-nē-zhȧ)	212	4°38'S	118°45'E
Indore, India (ĭn-dōr')	199	22°48'N	76°51'E
Indragiri, r., Indon. (ĭn-drà-jē'rė)	212	0°27'S	102°05'E
Indrāvati, r., India (ĭn-drŭ-vä'tė)	199	19°00'N	82°00'E
Indre, r., Fr. (äɴ'dr')	170	47°13'N	0°29'E
Indus, Can. (ĭn'dŭs)	102e	50°55'N	113°45'W
Indus, r., Asia	199	26°43'N	67°41'E
Indwe, S. Afr. (ĭnd'wå)	233c	31°30'S	27°21'E
Inebolu, Tur. (ė-nå-bō'lōō)	163	41°50'N	33°40'E
Inego, Tur. (ė'nå-gŭ)	181	40°05'N	29°20'E
Infanta, Phil. (ēn-fän'tä)	213a	14°44'N	121°39'E
Infanta, Phil.	213a	15°50'N	119°53'E
Inferror, Laguna, l., Mex. (lä-gō'nä-ēn-fĕr-rôr)	131	16°18'N	94°40'W
Infiernillo, Presa de, res., Mex.	130	18°50'N	101°50'W
Infiesto, Spain (ēn-fyĕ's-tô)	172	43°21'N	5°24'W
I-n-Gall, Niger	235	16°47'N	6°56'E
Ingersoll, Can. (ĭn'gēr-sŏl)	98	43°05'N	81°00'W
Ingham, Austl. (ĭng'ăm)	219	18°45'S	146°14'E
Ingles, Cayos, is., Cuba (kä-yōs-ē'n-glĕ's)	134	21°55'N	82°35'W
Inglewood, Can.	102d	43°48'N	79°56'W
Inglewood, Ca., U.S. (ĭn'g'l-wòd)	117a	33°57'N	118°22'W
Ingoda, r., Russia (ēn-gō'dȧ)	186	51°29'N	112°32'E
Ingolstadt, Ger. (ĭŋ'gŏl-shtät)	168	48°46'N	11°27'E
Ingur, r., Geor. (ēn-gōōr')	181	42°30'N	42°00'E
Ingushetia, prov., Russia	182	43°15'N	45°00'E
Inhambane, Moz. (ēn-äm-bä'-nĕ)	232	23°47'S	35°28'E
Inhambupe, Braz. (ēn-yäm-bōō'pä)	143	11°47'S	38°13'W
Inharrime, Moz. (ēn-yär-rē'mä)	232	24°17'S	35°07'E
Inhomirim, Braz. (ē-nô-mė-rē'ɴ)	144b	22°34'S	43°11'W
Inhul, r., Ukr.	177	47°22'N	32°52'E
Inhulets', r., Ukr.	177	47°12'N	33°12'E
Inírida, r., Col. (ē-nē-rē'dä)	142	2°25'N	70°38'W
Injune, Austl. (ĭn'jōn)	222	25°52'S	148°30'E
Inkeroinem, Fin. (ĭn'kĕr-oi-nĕn)	167	60°42'N	26°50'E
Inkster, Mi., U.S. (ĭngk'stēr)	111b	42°18'N	83°19'W
Inn, r., Eur. (ĭn)	161	48°00'N	12°00'E
Innamincka, Austl. (ĭnn-ȧ'mĭn-kȧ)	222	27°50'S	140°48'E
Inner Brass, i., V.I.U.S. (bräs)	129c	18°23'N	64°58'W
Inner Hebrides, is., Scot., U.K.	164	57°20'N	6°20'W
Inner Mongolia *see* Nei Monggol, prov., China	204	40°15'N	105°00'E
Innisfail, Can.	90	52°02'N	113°57'W
Innsbruck, Aus. (ĭns'bròk)	161	47°15'N	11°25'E
Ino, Japan (ē'nô)	211	33°34'N	133°23'E
Inongo, D.R.C. (ē-nôŋ'gō)	232	1°57'S	18°16'E
Inowrocław, Pol. (ē-nô-vrôts'läf)	169	52°48'N	18°16'E
In Salah, Alg.	230	27°13'N	2°22'E
Inscription House Ruin, Az., U.S. (ĭn'skrĭp-shŭn hous rōō'ĭn)	119	36°45'N	110°47'W
International Falls, Mn., U.S. (ĭn'tēr-năsh'ŭn-ăl fôlz)	105	48°34'N	93°26'W
Inuvik, Can.	90	68°40'N	134°10'W
Inuyama, Japan (ē'nōō-yä'mä)	211	35°24'N	137°01'E
Invercargil, N.Z. (ĭn-vĕr-kär'gĭl)	223	46°25'S	168°27'E
Inverel, Austl. (ĭn-vēr-el')	219	29°50'S	151°32'E
Invergrove Heights, Mn., U.S. (ĭn'vēr-grōv)	117g	44°51'N	93°01'W
Inverness, Can. (ĭn-vēr-nĕs')	101	46°14'N	61°18'W
Inverness, Scot., U.K.	160	57°30'N	4°07'W
Inverness, Fl., U.S.	125	28°48'N	82°22'W
Investigator Strait, strt., Austl. (ĭn-vĕst'ĭ'gā-tôr)	222	35°33'S	137°00'E
Inyangani, mtn., Zimb. (ēn-yän-gä'nė)	232	18°06'S	32°37'E
Inyokern, Ca., U.S.	118	35°39'N	117°51'W
Inyo Mountains, mts., Ca., U.S. (ĭn'yō)	106	36°55'N	118°04'W
Inzer, r., Russia (ĭn'zĕr)	186a	54°24'N	57°17'E
Inzia, r., D.R.C.	236	5°55'S	17°50'E
Ioánnina, Grc. (yô-ä'nė-nà)	163	39°39'N	20°52'E
Ioco, Can.	116d	49°18'N	122°53'W
Iola, Ks., U.S. (ī-ō'lȧ)	121	37°55'N	95°23'W
Iôna, Parque Nacional do, rec., Ang.	236	16°35'S	12°00'E
Ionia, Mi., U.S. (ī-ō'nĭ-à)	108	43°00'N	85°10'W
Ionian Islands, is., Grc. (ī-ō'nĭ-ăn)	163	39°10'N	20°05'E
Ionian Sea, sea, Eur.	156	38°59'N	18°48'E
Iori, r., Asia	182	41°03'N	46°17'E
Íos, i., Grc. (ī'ŏs)	175	36°48'N	25°25'E
Iowa, state, U.S. (ī'ô-wȧ)	105	42°05'N	94°20'W
Iowa, r., Ia., U.S.	113	41°55'N	92°20'W
Iowa City, Ia., U.S.	105	41°39'N	91°31'W
Iowa Falls, Ia., U.S.	113	42°32'N	93°16'W
Iowa Park, Tx., U.S.	120	33°57'N	98°39'W
Ipala, Tan.	237	4°30'S	32°53'E
Ipeirus, hist. reg., Grc.	175	39°35'N	20°45'E
Ipel', r., Eur. (ē'pĕl)	169	48°08'N	19°00'E
Ipiales, Col. (ē-pė-ä'lås)	142	0°48'N	77°45'W
Ipoh, Malay.	212	4°45'N	101°05'E
Ipswich, Austl. (ĭps'wĭch)	219	27°40'S	152°50'E
Ipswich, Eng., U.K.	161	52°05'N	1°05'E
Ipswich, Ma., U.S.	101a	42°41'N	70°50'W
Ipswich, S.D., U.S.	112	45°26'N	99°01'W
Ipu, Braz. (ē-pōō)	143	4°11'S	40°45'W
Iput', r., Eur. (ė-pòt')	181	52°53'N	31°57'E
Iqaluit, Can.	91	63°48'N	68°31'W
Iquique, Chile (ē-kē'kĕ)	142	20°16'S	70°07'W
Iquitos, Peru (ė-kē'tōs)	142	3°39'S	73°18'W
Irákleio, Grc.	154	35°20'N	25°10'E
Iran, nation, Asia (ē-rän')	198	31°15'N	53°30'E
Iran, Plateau of, plat., Iran	198	32°28'N	58°00'E
Iran Mountains, mts., Asia	212	2°30'N	114°30'E
Irapuato, Mex. (ē-rä-pwä'tō)	130	20°41'N	101°24'W
Iraq, nation, Asia (ē-räk')	198	32°00'N	42°30'E
Irazú, vol., C.R. (ē-rä-zōō')	133	9°58'N	83°54'W
Irbid, Jord. (ĕr-bēd')	200	32°33'N	35°51'E
Irbit, Russia (ĕr-bĕt')	178	57°40'N	63°10'E
Irébou, D.R.C. (ē-rā'bōō)	232	0°40'S	17°48'E
Ireland, nation, Eur. (īr-lănd)	154	53°33'N	8°00'W
Iremel', Gora, mtn., Russia (gå-rä'ĭ-rĕ'mĕl)	186a	54°32'N	58°52'E
Irene, S. Afr. (ī-rē-nē)	233b	25°53'S	28°13'E
Irîgui, reg., Mali	234	16°45'N	5°35'W
Iriklinskoye Vodokhranilishche, res., Russia	181	52°20'N	58°50'E
Iringa, Tan. (ė-rĭŋ'gä)	232	7°46'S	35°42'E
Iriomote Jima, i., Japan (ērē'-ō-mō-tā)	205	24°20'N	123°30'E
Iriona, Hond. (ē-rė-ō'nä)	132	15°53'N	85°12'W
Irish Sea, sea, Eur. (ī'rĭsh)	156	53°55'N	5°25'W
Irkutsk, Russia (ĭr-kòtsk')	179	52°16'N	104°00'E
Irlam, Eng., U.K. (ûr'lăm)	158a	53°26'N	2°26'W
Irois, Cap des, c., Haiti	135	18°25'N	74°50'W
Iron Bottom Sound, strt., Sol. Is.	214e	9°15'S	160°00'E
Irondale, Al., U.S. (ī'ērn-dăl)	110h	33°32'N	86°43'W
Iron Gate, val., Eur.	175	44°43'N	22°32'E
Iron Knob, Austl. (ī-ăn nŏb)	222	32°47'S	137°10'E
Iron Mountain, Mi., U.S. (ī'ērn)	113	45°49'N	88°04'W
Iron River, Mi., U.S.	113	46°09'N	88°39'W
Ironton, Oh., U.S. (ī'ērn-tŭn)	108	38°30'N	82°45'W
Ironwood, Mi., U.S. (ī'ērn-wòd)	113	46°28'N	90°10'W
Ironwood Forest National Monument, rec., Az., U.S.	119	32°30'N	111°25'W
Iroquois, r., Il., U.S. (ĭr'ô-kwoi)	108	40°55'N	87°20'W
Iroquois Falls, Can.	91	48°41'N	80°39'W
Irō-Saki, c., Japan (ē'rō sä'kē)	210	34°35'N	138°54'E
Irpin, r., Ukr.	177	50°13'N	29°55'E
Irrawaddy, r., Mya. (ĭr-ȧ-wäd'ė)	199	23°27'N	96°25'E
Irtysh, r., Asia (ĭr-tĭsh')	178	59°00'N	69°00'E
Irumu, D.R.C. (ė-rò'mōō)	231	1°30'N	29°52'E
Irun, Spain (ė-rōōn')	172	43°20'N	1°47'W
Irvine, Scot., U.K.	164	55°39'N	4°40'W
Irvine, Ca., U.S. (ûr'vĭn)	117a	33°40'N	117°45'W
Irvine, Ky., U.S.	108	37°40'N	84°00'W
Irving, Tx., U.S. (ûr'vēng)	117c	32°49'N	96°57'W
Irvington, N.J., U.S. (ûr'vēng-tŭn)	110a	40°43'N	74°15'W
Irwin, Pa., U.S. (ûr'wĭn)	111e	40°19'N	79°42'W
Is, Russia (ēs)	186a	58°48'N	59°44'E
Isa, Nig.	235	13°14'N	6°24'E
Isaacs, Mount, mtn., Pan. (ē-sä-ä'ks)	128a	9°22'N	79°31'W
Isabela, i., Ec. (ē-sä-bā'lä)	142	0°47'S	91°35'W
Isabela, Cabo, c., Dom. Rep. (kå'bô-ē-sä-bĕ'lä)	135	20°00'N	71°00'W
Isabella, Cordillera, mts., Nic. (kôr-dēl-yĕ'rä-ē-sä-bĕlä)	132	13°20'N	85°37'W
Isabella Indian Reservation, I.R., Mi., U.S. (ĭs-à-bĕl'-lȧ)	108	43°35'N	84°55'W
Isaccea, Rom. (ē-säk'chä)	177	45°16'N	28°26'E
Ísafjördur, Ice. (ēs'ȧ-fȳr-dòr)	160	66°09'N	22°39'W
Isangi, D.R.C. (ē-säŋ'gē)	204	0°46'N	24°15'E
Isar, r., Ger. (ē'zär)	161	48°30'N	12°30'E
Isarco, r., Italy (ė-sär'kō)	174	46°37'N	11°25'E
Isarog, Mount, mtn., Phil. (ē-sä-rò-g)	213a	13°40'N	123°23'E
Ischia, Italy (ēs'kyä)	173c	40°29'N	13°58'E
Ischia, Isola d', i., Italy (dĕ'sh-kyä)	162	40°26'N	13°55'E
Ise, Japan (ĭs'hĕ) (ū'gē-yä'mä'dà)	210	34°30'N	136°43'E
Iseo, Lago d', l., Italy (lä-'gō-dē-ē-zĕ'ō)	174	45°50'N	9°55'E
Isére, r., Fr. (ė-zâr')	161	45°15'N	5°15'E
Iserlohn, Ger. (ē'zĕr-lōn)	171c	51°22'N	7°42'E
Isernia, Italy (ė-zĕr'nyä)	174	41°35'N	14°14'E
Ise-Wan, b., Japan (ē'sĕ wän)	210	34°49'N	136°44'E
Iseyin, Nig.	230	7°58'N	3°36'E
Ishigaki, Japan	214d	24°20'N	124°09'E
Ishikari Wan, b., Japan (ē'shē-kä-rē wän)	210	43°30'N	141°05'E
Ishim, Russia (ĭsh-ĕm')	178	56°07'N	69°13'E
Ishim, r., Asia	178	53°17'N	67°45'E
Ishimbay, Russia (ē-shēm-bī')	186a	53°28'N	56°02'E
Ishinomaki, Japan (ĭsh-nō-mä'kē)	205	38°22'N	141°22'E
Ishinomaki Wan, b., Japan (ē-shē-nō-mä'kē wän)	210	38°10'N	141°40'E
Ishly, Russia (ĭsh'lĭ)	186a	54°13'N	55°55'E
Ishlya, Russia (ĭsh'lyà)	186a	53°54'N	57°48'E
Ishmant, Egypt	238b	29°17'N	31°15'E
Ishpeming, Mi., U.S. (ĭsh'pė-mĭng)	113	46°28'N	87°42'W
Isipingo, S. Afr. (ĭs-ĭ-pĭng-gō)	233c	29°59'S	30°58'E
Isiro, D.R.C.	231	2°47'N	27°37'E
İskenderun, Tur. (ĭs-kĕn'dĕr-ōōn)	198	36°45'N	36°15'E
İskenderun Körfezi, b., Tur.	163	36°22'N	35°25'E
İskilip, Tur. (ĕs'kĭ-lĕp')	163	40°40'N	34°30'E
Iskŭr, r., Blg. (ĭs'k'r)	175	43°05'N	23°37'E
Isla-Cristina, Spain (ī'lä-krē-stē'nä)	172	37°13'N	7°20'W

ăt; finăl; rāte; senåte; ärm; åsk; sofȧ; fâre; ch-choose; dh-as th in other; bē; ėvent; bĕt; recĕnt; cratēr; g-gō; gh-guttural g; bĭt; ĭ-short neutral; rīde; ĸ-guttural k as ch in German ich;

PLACE (Pronunciation)	PAGE	LAT.	LONG.
Islāmābād, Pak.	199	33°55'N	73°05'E
Isla Mujeres, Mex. (ē's-lä-mōō-kĕ'rĕs)	132a	21°25'N	86°53'W
Island Lake, l., Can.	93	53°47'N	94°25'W
Islands, Bay of, b., Can. (ī'lăndz)	101	49°10'N	58°15'W
Islay, i., Scot., U.K. (ī'lā)	160	55°55'N	6°35'W
Isle, r., Fr. (ēl)	170	45°02'N	0°29'E
Isle of Axholme, reg., Eng., U.K. (ăks'-hōm)	158a	53°33'N	0°48'W
Isle of Man, dep., Eur. (măn)	164	54°26'N	4°21'W
Isle Royale National Park, rec., Mi., U.S. (īl'roi-ăl')	107	47°57'N	88°37'W
Isleta, N.M., U.S. (ēs-lā'tá) (ī-lē'tá)	119	34°55'N	106°45'W
Isleta Indian Reservation, I.R., N.M., U.S.	119	34°55'N	106°45'W
Ismailia, Egypt (ēs-mā-ēl'ēá)	238b	30°35'N	32°17'E
Ismā'īlīyah Canal, can., Egypt	238b	30°25'N	31°45'E
Ismail Samani, pik, mtn., Taj.	183	38°57'N	72°01'E
Ismaning, Ger. (ēz'mä-nēng)	159d	48°14'N	11°41'E
Isparta, Tur. (ē-spär'tá)	198	37°50'N	30°40'E
Israel, nation, Asia	198	32°40'N	34°00'E
Issaquah, Wa., U.S. (ĭz'sā-kwăh)	116a	47°32'N	122°02'W
Isselburg, Ger. (ē'sĕl-bōōrg)	171c	51°50'N	6°28'E
Issoire, Fr. (ē-swár')	170	45°32'N	3°13'E
Issoudun, Fr. (ē-sōō-dăN')	170	46°56'N	2°00'E
Issum, Ger. (ē'sōōm)	171c	51°32'N	6°24'E
Issyk-Kul, Ozero, l., Kyrg.	183	42°13'N	76°12'E
İstanbul, Tur. (ē-stän-bōōl')	198	41°02'N	29°00'E
İstanbul Boğazı (Bosporus), strt., Tur.	198	41°10'N	29°10'E
Istiaía, Grc. (ĭs-tyī'yä)	175	38°58'N	23°11'E
Istmina, Col. (ēst-mē'nä)	142a	5°10'N	76°40'W
Istokpoga, Lake, l., Fl., U.S. (ĭs-tŏk-pō'gá)	125a	27°20'N	81°33'W
Istra, pen., Serb. (ē-strä)	174	45°18'N	13°48'E
Istranca Dağlari, mts., Eur. (ĭ-strän'já)	175	41°50'N	27°25'E
Istres, Fr. (ēs'tr')	170a	43°30'N	5°00'E
Itabaiana, Braz. (ē-tä-bä-yá-nä)	143	10°42'S	37°17'W
Itabapoana, Braz. (ē-tä'-bä-pôá'nä)	141a	21°19'S	40°58'W
Itabapoana, r., Braz.	141a	21°11'S	41°18'W
Itabirito, Braz. (ē-tä-bē-rē'tô)	141a	20°15'S	43°46'W
Itabuna, Braz. (ē-tä-bōō'ná)	143	14°47'S	39°17'W
Itacoara, Braz. (ē-tä-kō'ä-rä)	141a	21°41'S	42°04'W
Itacoatiara, Braz. (ē-tá-kwá-tyä'rá)	143	3°03'S	58°18'W
Itagüí, Col. (ē-tä'gwē)	142a	6°11'N	75°36'W
Itagui, r., Braz.	144b	22°53'S	43°43'W
Itaipava, Braz. (ē-tī-pá'-vä)	144b	22°23'S	43°09'W
Itaipu, Braz. (ē-tī'pōō)	144b	22°58'S	43°02'W
Itaituba, Braz. (ē-tä'ī-tōō'bá)	143	4°12'S	56°00'W
Itajái, Braz. (ē-tä-zhī')	144	26°52'S	48°39'W
Italy, Tx., U.S.	123	32°11'N	96°51'W
Italy, nation, Eur. (ĭt'á-lē)	154	43°58'N	11°14'E
Itambi, Braz. (ē-tä'm-bē)	144b	22°44'S	42°57'W
Itami, Japan (ē'tä'mē')	211b	34°47'N	135°25'E
Itapecerica, Braz. (ē-tä-pĕ-sĕ-rē'kà)	141a	20°29'S	45°08'W
Itapecuru-Mirim, Braz. (ē-tä-pĕ'kōō-rōō-mē-rēN')	143	3°17'S	44°15'W
Itaperuna, Braz. (ē-tá'pâ-rōō'nä)	143	21°12'S	41°53'W
Itapetininga, Braz. (ē-tä-pĕ-tē-nēN-gä)	143	23°37'S	48°03'W
Itapira, Braz. (ē-tá-pē'rá)	143	20°42'S	51°19'W
Itapira, Braz.	141a	22°27'S	46°47'W
Itarsi, India	202	22°43'N	77°45'E
Itasca, Tx., U.S. (ī-tăs'ká)	123	32°09'N	97°08'W
Itasca, l., Mn., U.S.	112	47°13'N	95°14'W
Itatiaia, Pico da, mtn., Braz. (pē'-kô-dá-ē-tä-tyá'ēä)	143	22°18'S	44°41'W
Itatiba, Braz. (ē-tä-tē'bä)	141a	23°01'S	46°48'W
Itaúna, Braz. (ē-tä-ōō'nä)	141a	20°05'S	44°35'W
Ithaca, Mi., U.S. (ĭth'á-ká)	108	43°20'N	84°35'W
Ithaca, N.Y., U.S.	105	42°25'N	76°30'W
Itháka, i., Grc. (ē'thä-kĕ)	175	38°27'N	20°48'E
Itigi, Tan.	237	5°42'S	34°29'E
Itimbiri, r., D.R.C.	236	2°40'N	23°30'E
Itoko, D.R.C. (ē-tō'kō)	232	1°13'S	22°07'E
Itu, Braz. (ē-tōō')	141a	23°16'S	47°16'W
Ituango, Col. (ē-twäŋ'gō)	142	7°07'N	75°44'W
Ituiutaba, Braz. (ē-tōō-ēōō-tä'bä)	143	18°56'S	49°17'W
Itumirim, Braz. (ē-tōō-mē-rē'N)	141a	21°20'S	44°51'W
Itundujia Santa Cruz, Mex. (ē-tōōn-dōō-hē'ä sä'n-tä krōō'z)	131	16°50'N	97°43'W
Iturbide, Mex. (ē'tōōr-bē'dhā)	132a	19°38'N	89°31'W
Iturup, i., Russia (ē-tōō-rōōp')	185	45°35'N	147°15'E
Ituzaingo, Arg. (ē-tōō-zä-ē'n-gô)	144a	34°40'S	58°40'W
Itzehoe, Ger. (ē'tzĕ-hō)	168	53°55'N	9°31'E
Iuka, Ms., U.S. (ī-ū'ká)	124	34°47'N	88°10'W
Iúna, Braz. (ē-ōō'-nä)	141a	20°22'S	41°32'W
Ivanhoe, Austl. (ĭv'ăn-hō)	222	32°53'S	144°10'E
Ivanivka, Ukr.	176	46°43'N	34°33'E
Ivano-Frankivs'k, Ukr.	181	48°53'N	24°46'E
Ivanopil', Ukr.	177	49°51'N	28°11'E
Ivanovo, Russia (ē-vä'nô-vō)	178	57°02'N	41°54'E
Ivanovo, prov., Russia	176	56°55'N	40°30'E
Ivanteyevka, Russia (ē-vän-tyĕ'yĕf-ká)	186b	55°58'N	37°56'E
Ivdel', Russia (ĭv'dyĕl)	186a	60°42'N	60°27'E
Iviza see Eivissa, i., Spain	156	38°55'N	1°24'E
Ivohibé, Madag. (ē-vō-hē-bā')	233	22°28'S	46°59'E
Ivory Coast see Cote d'Ivoire, nation, Afr.	230	7°43'N	6°30'W
Ivrea, Italy (ē-vrĕ'ä)	162	45°25'N	7°54'E
Ivry-sur-Seine, Fr.	171b	48°49'N	2°23'E
Ivujivik, Can.	91	62°17'N	77°52'W
Ivvavik National Park, rec., Can.	103	69°10'N	139°30'W
Iwaki, Japan	210	37°03'N	140°57'E
Iwate Yama, mtn., Japan (ē-wä-tĕ-yä'mä)	210	39°50'N	140°56'E
Iwatsuki, Japan	211a	35°48'N	139°43'E
Iwaya, Japan (ē'wá-yá)	211b	34°35'N	135°01'E
Iwo, Nig.	230	7°38'N	4°11'E
Ixcateopán, Mex. (ēs-kä-tä-ō-pän')	130	18°29'N	99°49'W
Ixelles, Bel.	159a	50°49'N	4°23'E
Ixhautlán, Mex. (ēs-wát-län')	130	20°41'N	98°01'W
Ixhuatán, Mex. (ēs-hwä-tän')	131	16°19'N	94°30'W
Ixmiquilpan, Mex. (ēs-mē-kēl'pän)	130	20°30'N	99°12'W
Ixopo, S. Afr.	233c	30°10'S	30°04'E
Ixtacalco, Mex. (ēs-tá-käl'kō)	131a	19°23'N	99°07'W
Ixtaltepec, Mex. (ēs-täl-tĕ-pĕk')	131	16°33'N	95°04'W
Ixtapalapa, Mex. (ēs'tä-pä-lä'pä)	131a	19°21'N	99°06'W
Ixtapaluca, Mex. (ēs'tä-pä-lōō'kä)	131a	19°18'N	98°53'W
Ixtepec, Mex. (ēks-tĕ'pĕk)	131	16°37'N	95°09'W
Ixtlahuaca, Mex. (ēs-tlä-wä'kä)	130	19°34'N	99°46'W
Ixtlán de Juárez, Mex. (ēs-tlän' dā hwä'rāz)	131	17°20'N	96°29'W
Ixtlán del Río, Mex. (ēs-tlän'dĕl rē'ō)	130	21°05'N	104°22'W
Iya, r., Russia	184	53°45'N	99°30'E
Iyo-Nada, b., Japan (ē'yō nä-dä)	211	33°33'N	132°07'E
Izabal, Guat. (ē'zä-bäl')	132	15°23'N	89°10'W
Izabal, Lago, l., Guat.	132	15°30'N	89°04'W
Izalco, El Sal. (ē-zäl'kō)	132	13°50'N	89°40'W
Izamal, Mex. (ē-zä-mä'l)	132a	20°55'N	89°00'W
Izberbash, Russia	182	42°33'N	47°52'E
Izhevsk, Russia (ē-zhyĕfsk')	178	56°50'N	53°15'E
Izhma, Russia (ĭzh'má)	180	65°00'N	54°05'E
Izhma, r., Russia	180	64°00'N	53°00'E
Izhora, r., Russia (ēz'hô-rá)	186c	59°36'N	30°20'E
Izmaïl, Ukr.	181	45°00'N	28°49'E
İzmir, Tur. (ĭz-mēr')	198	38°25'N	27°05'E
Izmit, Tur. (ĭz-mĭt')	163	40°45'N	29°45'E
Iznajar, Embalse de, res., Spain	172	37°15'N	4°30'W
Iztaccíhuatl, mtn., Mex.	130	19°10'N	98°38'W
Izuhara, Japan (ē'zōō-hä'rä)	211	34°11'N	129°18'E
Izumi-Ōtsu, Japan (ē'zōō-mōō ō'tsōō)	211b	34°30'N	135°24'E
Izumo, Japan (ē'zōō-mō)	211	35°22'N	132°45'E
Izu Shichitō, is., Japan	205	34°32'N	139°25'E

J

PLACE (Pronunciation)	PAGE	LAT.	LONG.
Jabal, Bahr al, r., Sudan	231	7°30'N	31°00'E
Jabalpur, India	199	23°18'N	79°59'E
Jablonec nad Nisou, Czech Rep. (yäb'lô-nyĕts)	168	50°43'N	15°12'E
Jablunkov Pass, p., Eur. (yäb'lōn-kôf)	169	49°31'N	18°35'E
Jaboatão, Braz. (zhä-bô-á-touN)	143	8°14'S	35°08'W
Jaca, Spain (hä'kä)	173	42°35'N	0°30'W
Jacala, Mex. (hä-kà'lä)	130	21°01'N	99°11'W
Jacaltenango, Guat. (hä-kál-tĕ-näŋ'gō)	132	15°39'N	91°41'W
Jacarézinho, Braz. (zhä-kä-rĕ'zē-nyō)	143	23°13'S	49°58'W
Jachymov, Czech Rep. (yä'chĭ-môf)	168	50°22'N	12°51'E
Jacinto City, Tx., U.S. (hä-sēn'tō) (já-sĭn'tō)	123a	29°45'N	95°14'W
Jacksboro, Tx., U.S. (jăks'bŭr-ô)	120	33°13'N	98°11'W
Jackson, Al., U.S. (jăk'sŭn)	124	31°31'N	87°52'W
Jackson, Ca., U.S.	118	38°22'N	120°47'W
Jackson, Ga., U.S.	124	33°19'N	83°55'W
Jackson, Ky., U.S.	124	37°32'N	83°17'W
Jackson, La., U.S.	123	30°50'N	91°13'W
Jackson, Mi., U.S.	105	42°15'N	84°25'W
Jackson, Mn., U.S.	112	43°37'N	95°00'W
Jackson, Mo., U.S.	121	37°23'N	89°40'W
Jackson, Ms., U.S.	105	32°17'N	90°10'W
Jackson, Oh., U.S.	108	39°00'N	82°40'W
Jackson, Tn., U.S.	105	35°37'N	88°49'W
Jackson, Port, b., Austl.	217b	33°50'S	151°18'E
Jackson Lake, l., Wy., U.S.	115	43°57'N	110°28'W
Jacksonville, Al., U.S. (jăk'sŭn-vĭl)	124	33°52'N	85°45'W
Jacksonville, Fl., U.S.	105	30°20'N	81°40'W
Jacksonville, Il., U.S.	105	39°43'N	90°12'W
Jacksonville, Tx., U.S.	123	31°58'N	95°18'W
Jacksonville Beach, Fl., U.S.	125	31°18'N	81°25'W
Jacmel, Haiti (zhák-mĕl')	135	18°15'N	72°30'W
Jaco, l., Mex. (hä'kō)	122	27°51'N	103°50'W
Jacobābad, Pak.	202	28°22'N	68°30'E
Jacobina, Braz. (zhä-kô-bē'ná)	143	11°13'S	40°30'W
Jacques-Cartier, r., Can.	102b	47°04'N	71°28'W
Jacques Cartier, Détroit de, strt., Can.	100	50°07'S	63°58'W
Jacques-Cartier, Mont, mtn., Can.	100	48°59'N	66°00'W
Jacquet River, Can. (zhá-kĕ') (jăk'ĕt)	100	47°55'N	66°00'W
Jacutinga, Braz. (zhá-kōō-tēn'gä)	141a	22°17'S	46°36'W
Jadebusen, b., Ger.	168	53°28'N	8°17'E
Jadotville see Likasi, D.R.C.	232	10°59'S	26°44'E
Jaén, Peru (Kä-ĕ'n)	142	5°38'S	78°49'W
Jaen, Spain	162	37°45'N	3°48'W
Jaffa, Cape, c., Austl. (jăf'ă)	220	36°58'S	139°29'E
Jaffna, Sri L. (jăf'ná)	203	9°44'N	80°09'E
Jagüey Grande, Cuba (hä'gwā grän'dā)	134	22°35'N	81°05'W
Jahore Strait, strt., Asia	197b	1°22'N	103°37'E
Jahrom, Iran	198	28°30'N	53°28'E
Jaibo, r., Cuba (hä-ē'bō)	135	20°10'N	75°20'W
Jaipur, India	199	27°00'N	75°50'E
Jaisalmer, India	202	27°00'N	70°54'E
Jajce, Bos. (yī'tsĕ)	175	44°20'N	17°19'E
Jajpur, India	199	20°49'N	86°37'E
Jakarta, Indon. (yä-kär'tä)	212	6°17'S	106°45'E
Jakobstad, Fin. (yá'kōb-stádh)	160	63°33'N	22°31'E
Jalacingo, Mex. (hä-lä-sĭŋ'gō)	131	19°47'N	97°16'W
Jalālābād, Afg. (jŭ-lä-lá-bäd)	199a	34°25'N	70°27'E
Jalālah al Baḥrīyah, Jabal, mts., Egypt	238b	29°20'N	32°00'E
Jalapa, Guat. (hä-lä'pá)	132	14°38'N	89°58'W
Jalapa de Díaz, Mex.	131	18°06'N	96°33'W
Jalapa del Marqués, Mex. (dĕl mär-kās')	131	16°30'N	95°29'W
Jaleswar, Nepal	202	26°50'N	85°55'E
Jalgaon, India	202	21°08'N	75°33'E
Jalisco, Mex. (hä-lēs'kō)	130	21°27'N	104°54'W
Jalisco, state, Mex.	128	20°07'N	104°45'W
Jalón, r., Spain (hä-lōn')	172	41°22'N	1°46'W
Jalostotitlán, Mex. (hä-lōs-tē-tlán')	130	21°09'N	102°30'W
Jalpa, Mex. (häl'pä)	131	18°12'N	93°06'W
Jalpa, Mex. (häl'pä)	130	21°40'N	103°04'W
Jalpan, Mex. (häl'pän)	130	21°13'N	99°31'W
Jaltepec, Mex. (häl-tâ-pĕk')	131	17°20'N	95°15'W
Jaltipan, Mex. (häl-tâ-pän')	131	17°59'N	94°42'W
Jaltocan, Mex. (häl-tô-kän')	130	21°08'N	98°32'W
Jamaare, r., Nig.	235	11°50'N	10°10'E
Jamaica, nation, N.A.	129	17°45'N	78°00'W
Jamaica Cay, i., Bah.	135	22°45'N	75°55'W
Jamālpur, Bngl.	202	24°56'N	89°58'E
Jamay, Mex. (hä-mī')	130	20°16'N	102°43'W
Jambi, Indon. (mäm'bē)	212	1°45'S	103°28'E
James, r., Mo., U.S.	121	36°51'N	93°22'W
James, r., Va., U.S.	107	37°35'N	77°50'W
James, r., U.S.	106	46°25'N	98°55'W
James, Lake, res., N.C., U.S.	125	36°07'N	81°48'W
James Bay, b., Can. (jāmz)	93	53°53'N	80°40'W
Jamesburg, N.J., U.S. (jāmz'bûrg)	110a	40°21'N	74°26'W
James Point, c., Bah.	134	25°20'N	76°30'W
James Range, mts., Austl.	220	24°15'S	133°30'E
James Ross, i., Ant.	139	64°20'S	58°20'W
Jamestown, S. Afr.	233c	31°07'S	26°49'E
Jamestown, N.D., U.S.	104	46°54'N	98°42'W
Jamestown, N.Y., U.S. (jāmz'toun)	105	42°05'N	79°15'W
Jamestown, R.I., U.S.	110b	41°30'N	71°21'W
Jamestown Reservoir, res., N.D., U.S.	112	47°16'N	98°40'W
Jamiltepec, Mex. (hä-mēl-tâ-pĕk)	131	16°16'N	97°54'W
Jammerbugten, b., Den.	166	57°20'N	9°28'E
Jammu, India	199	32°50'N	74°52'E
Jammu and Kashmir, state, India (kásh-mēr')	199	34°30'N	76°00'E
Jammu and Kashmīr, hist. reg., Asia (kásh-mēr')	199	39°10'N	75°05'E
Jāmnagar, India (jäm-nû'gŭr)	199	22°33'N	70°03'E
Jamshedpur, India (jäm'shĕd-pōōr)	199	22°52'N	86°11'E
Jándula, r., Spain (hän'dōō-lá)	172	38°28'N	3°52'W
Janesville, Wi., U.S. (jānz'vĭl)	113	42°41'N	89°03'W
Janin, W.B.	197a	32°27'N	35°19'E
Jan Mayen, i., Nor. (yän mī'ĕn)	160	70°59'N	8°05'W
Jánoshalma, Hung. (yä'nôsh-hôl-mô)	169	46°17'N	19°18'E
Janów Lubelski, Pol. (yä'nōōf lŭ-bĕl'skĭ)	169	50°40'N	22°25'E
Januária, Braz. (zhä-nwä'rē-ä)	143	15°31'S	44°17'W
Japan, nation, Asia (já-păn')	205	36°30'N	133°30'E
Japan, Sea of, sea, Asia (já-păn')	205	40°08'N	132°55'E
Japeri, Braz. (zhá-pĕ'rē)	144b	22°38'S	43°40'W
Japurá (Caquetá), r., S.A.	142	2°00'S	68°00'W
Jarabacoa, Dom. Rep. (Kä-rä-bä-kō'ä)	135	19°05'N	70°40'W
Jaral del Progreso, Mex. (hä-räl dĕl prô-grā'sō)	130	20°21'N	101°05'W
Jarama, r., Spain (hä-rä'mä)	172	40°33'N	3°30'W
Jarash, Jord.	197a	32°17'N	35°53'E
Jardines, Banco, bk., Cuba (bä'n-kō-här-dē'nás)	134	21°45'N	81°40'W
Jargalant, Mong.	208	46°28'N	115°10'E
Jari, r., Braz. (zhä-rē)	143	0°28'N	53°00'W
Jarocin, Pol. (yä-rō'tsyēn)	169	51°58'N	17°31'E
Jarosław, Pol. (yá-rōs-wáf)	161	50°01'N	22°41'E
Jarud Qi, China (jya-lōō-tŭ shyē)	205	44°35'N	120°40'E
Jasin, Malay.	197b	2°19'N	102°26'E
Jašiūnai, Lith. (dzá-shōō-ná'yē)	167	54°27'N	25°25'E
Jāsk, Iran (jäsk)	198	25°46'N	57°48'E
Jasło, Pol. (yás'wō)	169	49°44'N	21°28'E
Jason Bay, b., Malay.	197b	1°53'N	104°14'E
Jasonville, In., U.S. (jā'sŭn-vĭl)	108	39°10'N	87°15'W
Jasper, Can.	90	52°53'N	118°05'W
Jasper, Al., U.S. (jăs'pēr)	124	33°50'N	87°17'W
Jasper, Fl., U.S.	125	30°30'N	82°56'W
Jasper, In., U.S.	108	38°20'N	86°55'W
Jasper, Mn., U.S.	112	43°51'N	96°22'W
Jasper, Tx., U.S.	123	30°55'N	93°59'W
Jasper National Park, rec., Can.	92	53°09'N	117°45'W
Jászapáti, Hung. (yäs'ô-pä-tē)	169	47°29'N	20°10'E
Jászberény, Hung.	169	47°30'N	19°56'E
Jatibonico, Cuba (hä-tē-bō-nē'kô)	134	22°00'N	79°15'W
Jauja, Peru (Kä-ô'K)	142	11°43'S	75°32'W
Jaumave, Mex. (hou-mä'vâ)	130	23°23'N	99°24'W
Jaunjelgava, Lat. (youn'yĕl'gá-vá)	180	56°37'N	25°06'E
Java (Jawa), i., Indon.	212	8°35'S	111°11'E
Javari, r., S.A. (Kä-vä-rē)	142	4°25'S	72°07'W
Java Trench, deep	212	9°45'S	107°30'E
Jawa, Laut (Java Sea), sea, Indon.	212	5°10'S	110°30'E
Jawor, Pol. (yä'vôr)	168	51°04'N	16°12'E
Jaworzno, Pol. (yä-vôzh'nô)	169	50°11'N	19°18'E
Jaya, Puncak, mtn., Indon.	213	4°00'S	137°00'E
Jayapura, Indon.	212	2°30'S	140°45'W
Jayb, Wādī al (Ha'Arava), val., Asia	197a	30°33'N	35°10'E

ng-sing; ŋ-baŋk; N-nasalized n; nŏd; cŏmmit; ōld; ōbey; ôrder; oi-boil; fōōd; ŏ-as oo in foot; ou-out; s-soft; sh-dish; th-thin; pūre; ûnite; ûrn; stŭd; circŭs; ü-as in French tu; '-indeterminate vowel.

PLACE (Pronunciation)	PAGE	LAT.	LONG.
Jazzīn, Leb.	197a	33°34'N	35°37'E
Jeanerette, La., U.S. (jĕn-ĕr-et') (zhän-rĕt')	123	29°54'N	91°41'W
Jebba, Nig. (jĕb'ȧ)	230	9°07'N	4°46'E
Jeddore Lake, l., Can.	101	48°07'N	55°35'W
Jędrzejów, Pol. (yăɴ-dzhă'yôf)	169	50°38'N	20°18'E
Jefferson, Ga., U.S. (jĕf'ẽr-sŭn)	124	34°05'N	83°35'W
Jefferson, Ia., U.S.	113	42°10'N	94°22'W
Jefferson, La., U.S.	110d	29°57'N	90°04'W
Jefferson, Tx., U.S.	123	32°47'N	94°21'W
Jefferson, Wi., U.S.	113	42°59'N	88°45'W
Jefferson, r., Mt., U.S.	115	45°37'N	112°22'W
Jefferson, Mount, mtn., Or., U.S.	114	44°41'N	121°50'W
Jefferson City, Mo., U.S.	105	38°34'N	92°10'W
Jeffersontown, Ky., U.S. (jĕf'ẽr-sŭn-toun)	111h	38°11'N	85°34'W
Jeffersonville, In., U.S. (jĕf'ẽr-sŭn-vĭl)	111h	38°17'N	85°44'W
Jega, Nig.	235	12°15'N	4°23'E
Jehol, hist. reg., China (jĕ-hŏl)	205	42°31'N	118°12'E
Jēkabpils, Lat. (yĕk'áb-pĭls)	180	56°29'N	25°50'E
Jelenia Góra, Pol. (yĕ-lĕn'yȧ gó'rá)	168	50°53'N	15°43'E
Jelgava, Lat.	167	56°39'N	23°42'E
Jellico, Tn., U.S. (jĕl'ĭ-kō)	124	36°34'N	84°06'W
Jemez Indian Reservation, I.R., N.M., U.S.	119	35°35'N	106°45'W
Jena, Ger. (yā'nä)	161	50°55'N	11°37'E
Jenkins, Ky., U.S. (jĕŋ'kĭnz)	125	37°09'N	82°38'W
Jenkintown, Pa., U.S. (jĕŋ'kĭn-toun)	110f	40°06'N	75°08'W
Jennings, La., U.S. (jĕn'ĭngz)	123	30°14'N	92°40'W
Jennings, Mi., U.S.	108	44°20'N	85°20'W
Jennings, Mo., U.S.	117e	38°43'N	90°16'W
Jequitinhonha, r., Braz. (zhĕ-kē-tēŋ-ō'n-yä)	143	16°47'S	41°19'W
Jérémie, Haiti (zhā-rå-mē')	135	18°40'N	74°10'W
Jeremoabo, Braz. (zhĕ-rä-mō-ȧ'bō)	143	10°03'S	38°13'W
Jerez, Punta, c., Mex. (pōō'n-tä-kĕ-rāz')	131	23°04'N	97°44'W
Jerez de la Frontera, Spain	162	36°42'N	6°09'W
Jerez de los Caballeros, Spain	172	38°20'N	6°45'W
Jericho, Austl. (jĕr'ĭ-kō)	219	23°38'S	146°24'E
Jericho, S. Afr. (jĕr-ĭkô)	238c	25°16'N	27°47'E
Jericho see Arīḥā, W.B.	197a	31°51'N	35°28'E
Jerome, Az., U.S. (jė-rōm')	104	34°45'N	112°10'W
Jerome, Id., U.S.	115	42°44'N	114°31'W
Jersey, dep., Eur.	170	49°15'N	2°10'W
Jersey, i., Jersey (jûr'zĭ)	161	49°13'N	2°07'W
Jersey City, N.J., U.S.	105	40°43'N	74°05'W
Jersey Shore, Pa., U.S.	109	41°10'N	77°15'W
Jerseyville, Il., U.S. (jẽr'zė-vĭl)	121	39°07'N	90°18'W
Jerusalem, Isr. (jė-rōō'sá-lĕm)	198	31°46'N	35°14'E
Jesup, Ga., U.S. (jĕs'ŭp)	125	31°36'N	81°53'W
Jesús Carranza, Mex. (hē-sōō's-kär-rä'n-zä)	131	17°26'N	95°01'W
Jewel, Or., U.S. (jū'ĕl)	116c	45°56'N	123°30'W
Jewel Cave National Monument, rec., S.D., U.S.	112	43°44'N	103°52'W
Jhālawār, India	199	24°30'N	76°00'E
Jhang Maghiāna, Pak.	202	31°21'N	72°19'E
Jhānsi, India (jän'sė)	199	25°29'N	78°32'E
Jharkhand, state, India	199	23°30'N	85°00'E
Jhārsuguda, India	202	22°51'N	84°13'E
Jhelum, Pak.	199	32°59'N	73°43'E
Jhelum, r., Asia (jā'lŭm)	199	31°40'N	71°51'E
Jiading, China (jyä-dĭŋ)	206	31°23'N	121°15'E
Jialing, r., China (jyä-lĭŋ)	204	32°30'N	105°30'E
Jiamusi, China	210	46°50'N	130°21'E
Ji'an, China (jyē-än)	205	27°15'N	115°10'E
Ji'an, China	208	41°00'N	126°04'E
Jianchangying, China (jyĕn-chäŋ-yĭŋ)	206	40°09'N	118°47'E
Jiangcun, China (jyän-tsōn)	207a	23°16'N	113°14'E
Jiangling, China (jyäŋ-lĭŋ)	205	30°30'N	112°10'E
Jiangshanzhen, China (jyäŋ-shän-jŭn)	206	36°39'N	120°31'E
Jiangsu, prov., China (jyäŋ-sōō)	205	33°45'N	120°30'E
Jiangwan, China (jyäŋ-wän)	207b	31°18'N	121°29'E
Jiangxi, prov., China (jyäŋ-shyē)	205	28°15'N	116°00'E
Jiangyin, China (jyäŋ-yĭn)	209	31°54'N	120°15'E
Jianli, China (jyĕn-lē)	209	29°50'N	112°52'E
Jianning, China (jyĕn-nĭŋ)	209	26°50'N	116°55'E
Jian'ou, China (jyĕn-ō)	209	27°10'N	118°18'E
Jianshi, China (jyĕn-shr)	209	30°40'N	109°45'E
Jiaohe, China	206	38°03'N	116°18'E
Jiaohe, China (jyou-hŭ)	208	43°40'N	127°20'E
Jiaoxian, China (jyou shyĕn)	205	36°18'N	120°01'E
Jiaozuo, China (jyou-dzwô)	206	35°15'N	113°18'E
Jiashan, China (jyä-shän)	206	32°41'N	118°00'E
Jiaxing, China (jyä-shyĭŋ)	205	30°45'N	120°50'E
Jiayu, China (jyä-yōō)	209	30°00'N	114°00'E
Jiazhou Wan, b., China (jyä-jō wän)	205	36°10'N	119°55'E
Jicarilla Apache Indian Reservation, I.R., N.M., U.S. (kĕ-kȧ-rĕl'yȧ)	119	36°45'N	107°00'W
Jicarón, Isla, i., Pan. (kē-kä-rōn')	133	7°14'N	81°41'W
Jiddah, Sau. Ar.	198	21°30'N	39°15'E
Jieshou, China	206	33°17'N	115°20'E
Jieyang, China (jyĕ-yäŋ)	205	23°38'N	116°20'E
Jiggalong, Austl. (jĭg'ȧ-lông)	218	23°20'S	120°45'E
Jiguani, Cuba (kē-gwä-nē')	134	20°20'N	76°30'W
Jigüey, Bahía, b., Cuba (bä-ē'ä-kĕ'gwā)	134	22°15'N	78°10'W
Jihlava, Czech Rep. (yē'hlá-vȧ)	161	49°23'N	15°33'E
Jijel, Alg.	161	36°49'N	5°47'E
Jijia, r., Rom.	169	47°35'N	27°02'E
Jijiashi, China (jyē-jyä-shr)	206	32°10'N	120°17'E
Jijiga, Eth.	238a	9°15'N	42°48'E
Jilin, China (jyē-lĭn)	205	43°58'N	126°40'E
Jilin, prov., China	205	44°20'N	124°50'E
Jiloca, r., Spain (kē-lō'kä)	172	41°13'N	1°30'W
Jilotepeque, Guat. (kē-lô-tĕ-pĕ'kĕ)	132	14°39'N	89°36'W
Jima, Eth.	231	7°41'N	36°52'E
Jimbolia, Rom. (zhĭm-bô'lyä)	175	45°45'N	20°44'E
Jiménez, Mex. (kĕ-mā'nāz)	130	24°12'N	98°29'W
Jiménez, Mex.	122	27°09'N	104°55'W
Jiménez, Mex.	122	29°03'N	100°42'W
Jiménez del Téul, Mex. (tĕ-ōō'l)	130	21°28'N	103°51'W
Jimo, China (jyē-mwo)	208	36°22'N	120°28'E
Jim Thorpe, Pa., U.S. (jĭm' thôrp')	109	40°50'N	75°45'W
Jinan, China (jyē-nän)	205	36°40'N	117°01'E
Jincheng, China (jyĭn-chŭŋ)	208	35°30'N	112°50'E
Jindřichův Hradec, Czech Rep. (yĕn'd'r-zhĭ-kōōf hrä'dĕts)	168	49°09'N	15°02'E
Jing, r., China (jyĭŋ)	208	34°40'N	108°20'E
Jing'anji, China (jyĭŋ-än-jē)	206	34°30'N	116°55'E
Jingdezhen, China (jyĭŋ-dŭ-jŭn)	209	29°18'N	117°18'E
Jingjiang, China (jyĭŋ-jyäŋ)	206	32°02'N	120°15'E
Jingning, China (jyĭŋ-nĭŋ)	208	35°28'N	105°50'E
Jingpo Hu, l., China (jyĭŋ-pwo hōō)	208	44°10'N	129°00'E
Jingxian, China (jyĭŋ shyĕn)	209	26°32'N	109°45'E
Jingxian, China	206	37°43'N	116°17'E
Jingxing, China (jyĭŋ-shyĭŋ)	208	47°00'N	123°00'E
Jingzhi, China (jyĭŋ-jr)	206	36°19'N	119°23'E
Jinhua, China (jyĭn-hwä)	205	29°10'N	119°42'E
Jining, China (jyē-nĭŋ)	205	35°26'N	116°34'E
Jining, China	208	41°00'N	113°10'E
Jinja, Ug. (jĭn'jä)	231	0°26'N	33°12'E
Jinotega, Nic. (kē-nô-tā'gä)	132	13°07'N	86°00'W
Jinotepe, Nic. (kē-nô-tā'på)	132	11°52'N	86°12'W
Jinqiao, China (jyĭn-chyou)	206	31°46'N	116°46'E
Jinshan, China (jyĭn-shän)	207b	30°53'N	121°09'E
Jinta, China (jyĭn-tä)	204	40°11'N	98°45'E
Jintan, China (jyĭn-tän)	206	31°47'N	119°34'E
Jin Xian, China (jyĭn shyĕn)	208	39°04'N	121°40'E
Jinxiang, China (jyĭn-shyäŋ)	206	35°03'N	116°20'E
Jinyun, China (jyĭn-yôn)	209	28°40'N	120°08'E
Jinzhai, China (jyĭn-jī)	206	31°41'N	115°51'E
Jinzhou, China (jyĭn-jō)	205	41°00'N	121°00'E
Jinzhou Wan, b., China (jyĭn-jō wän)	206	39°07'N	121°17'E
Jinzū-Gawa, r., Japan (jĕn'zōō gä'wä)	211	36°26'N	137°18'E
Jipijapa, Ec. (kē-pē-hä'pä)	142	1°36'S	80°52'W
Jiquilisco, El Sal. (kē-kē-lē's-kô)	132	13°18'N	88°32'W
Jiquilpan de Juárez, Mex. (kē-kēl'pän dā hwä'rāz)	130	20°00'N	102°43'W
Jiquipilco, Mex. (hē-kē-pē'l-kô)	131a	19°32'N	99°37'W
Jitotol, Mex. (kē-tô-tōl')	131	17°03'N	92°54'W
Jiu, r., Rom.	175	44°45'N	23°17'E
Jiujiang, China (jyô-jyän)	207a	22°50'N	113°02'E
Jiujiang, China	205	29°43'N	116°00'E
Jiuquan, China (jyô-chyän)	204	39°46'N	98°26'E
Jiurongcheng, China (jyô-rôŋ-chŭŋ)	206	37°23'N	122°31'E
Jiushouzhang, China (jyô-shō-jäŋ)	206	35°59'N	115°52'E
Jiuwuqing, China (jyô-wōō-chyĭŋ)	208a	32°31'N	116°51'E
Jiuyongnian, China (jyô-yôŋ-nĭĕn)	206	36°41'N	114°46'E
Jixian, China (jyē shyĕn)	206	35°25'N	114°03'E
Jixian, China	206	37°37'N	115°33'E
Jixian, China	206	40°03'N	117°25'E
Jiyun, r., China (jyē-yōōm)	206	39°35'N	117°34'E
Joachimsthal, Ger.	159b	52°58'N	13°45'E
João Pessoa, Braz.	143	7°09'S	34°45'W
João Ribeiro, Braz. (zhô-uɴ-rē-bā'rō)	141a	20°42'S	44°03'W
Jobabo, r., Cuba (hō-bä'bä)	134	20°50'N	77°15'W
Jock, r., Can. (jŏk)	102c	45°08'N	75°51'W
Jocotepec, Mex. (jô-kō-tå-pĕk')	130	20°17'N	103°26'W
Jodar, Spain (hō'där)	172	37°54'N	3°20'W
Jodhpur, India (hōd'pōōr)	199	26°23'N	73°00'E
Joensuu, Fin. (yô-ĕn'sōō)	167	62°35'N	29°46'E
Joffre, Mount, mtn., Can. (jŏ'f'r)	95	50°32'N	115°13'W
Jõgeva, Est. (yû'gĕ-vȧ)	167	58°45'N	26°23'E
Joggins, Can. (jŏ'gĭnz)	100	45°42'N	64°27'W
Johannesburg, S. Afr. (yô-hän'ĕs-bôrgh)	232	26°08'S	27°54'E
John Day, r., Or., U.S. (jŏn'dā)	114	44°46'N	120°15'W
John Day, Middle Fork, r., Or., U.S.	114	44°53'N	119°04'W
John Day, North Fork, r., Or., U.S.	114	45°03'N	118°50'W
John Day Dam, Or., U.S.	114	45°40'N	120°15'W
John H. Kerr Reservoir, res., U.S.	107	36°30'N	78°38'W
John Martin Reservoir, res., Co., U.S. (jŏn mär'tĭn)	120	37°57'N	103°04'W
Johnson, r., Or., U.S. (jŏn'sŭn)	116c	45°27'N	122°20'W
Johnsonburg, Pa., U.S. (jŏn'sŭn-bûrg)	109	41°30'N	78°40'W
Johnson City, Il., U.S. (jŏn'sŭn)	108	37°50'N	88°55'W
Johnson City, N.Y., U.S.	109	42°10'N	76°00'W
Johnson City, Tn., U.S.	105	36°17'N	82°23'W
Johnston, i., Oc. (jŏn'stŭn)	2	17°00'N	168°00'W
Johnstone Strait, strt., Can.	94	50°25'N	126°00'W
Johnston Falls, wtfl., Afr.	237	10°35'S	28°50'E
Johnstown, N.Y., U.S. (jonz'toun)	109	43°00'N	74°20'W
Johnstown, Pa., U.S.	105	40°20'N	78°50'W
Johor, r., Malay. (jŭ-hōr')	197b	1°39'N	103°52'E
Johor Baharu, Malay.	212	1°28'N	103°46'E
Jõhvi, Est. (yû'vĭ)	167	59°21'N	27°21'E
Joigny, Fr. (zhwán-yē')	170	47°58'N	3°26'E
Joinville, Braz. (zhwăɴ-vēl')	144	26°18'S	48°47'W
Joinville, Fr.	171	48°28'N	5°05'E
Joinville, i., Ant.	139	63°00'S	53°30'W
Jojutla, Mex. (hō-hōō'tlä)	130	18°39'N	99°11'W
Jola, Mex. (kô'lä)	130	21°08'N	104°26'W
Joliet, Il., U.S. (jō-lĭ-ĕt')	111a	41°32'N	88°05'W
Joliette, Can. (zhô-lyĕt')	91	46°01'N	73°30'W
Jolo, Phil. (hō-lō)	212	5°59'N	121°05'E
Jolo Island, i., Phil.	212	5°55'N	121°15'E
Jomalig, i., Phil. (hô-mä'lēg)	213a	14°44'N	122°34'E
Jomulco, Mex. (hô-mōōl'kō)	130	21°08'N	104°24'W
Jonacatepec, Mex.	130	18°39'N	98°46'W
Jonava, Lith. (yō-nä'vá)	167	55°05'N	24°15'E
Jones, Phil. (jōnz)	213a	12°56'N	122°05'E
Jones, Phil.	213a	16°35'N	121°39'E
Jonesboro, Ar., U.S. (jōnz'bûro)	105	35°49'N	90°42'W
Jonesboro, La., U.S.	123	32°14'N	92°43'W
Jonesville, La., U.S. (jōnz'vĭl)	123	31°35'N	91°50'W
Jonesville, Mi., U.S.	108	42°00'N	84°45'W
Jong, r., S.L.	234	8°10'N	12°10'W
Joniškis, Lith. (yô'nĭsh-kĭs)	167	56°14'N	23°36'E
Jönköping, Swe. (yûn'chû-pĭng)	160	57°47'N	14°10'E
Jonquiere, Can. (zhôɴ-kyâr')	91	48°25'N	71°15'W
Jonuta, Mex. (hô-nōō'tä)	131	18°07'N	92°09'W
Jonzac, Fr. (zhôɴ-zák')	170	45°27'N	0°27'W
Joplin, Mo., U.S. (jŏp'lĭn)	105	37°05'N	94°31'W
Jordan, nation, Asia (jôr'dăn)	198	30°15'N	38°00'E
Jordan, r., Asia	197a	32°05'N	35°35'E
Jordan, r., Ut., U.S.	117b	40°42'N	111°56'W
Jorhāt, India (jôr-hät')	199	26°43'N	94°16'E
Jorullo, Volcán de, vol., Mex. (vôl-kä'n-dĕ-hô-rōōl'yō)	130	18°54'N	101°38'W
José C. Paz, Arg.	144a	34°32'S	58°44'W
Joseph Bonaparte Gulf, b., Austl. (jô'sĕf bô'nȧ-pärt)	220	13°30'S	128°40'E
Josephburg, Can.	102g	53°45'N	113°06'W
Joseph Lake, l., Can. (jô'sĕf lăk)	102g	53°18'N	113°06'W
Joshua Tree National Park, rec., Ca., U.S. (jô'shū-ȧ trē)	118	34°02'N	115°53'W
Jos Plateau, plat., Nig. (jôs)	235	9°53'N	9°05'E
Jostedalsbreen, ice, Nor. (yôstĕ-däls-brĕĕn)	160	61°40'N	6°55'E
Jotunheimen, mts., Nor.	160	61°44'N	8°11'E
Joulter's Cays, is., Bah. (jōl'tẽrz)	134	25°20'N	78°10'W
Jouy-le-Chatel, Fr. (zhwē-lĕ-shä-tĕl')	171b	48°40'N	3°07'E
Jovellanos, Cuba (hō-vĕl-yä'nōs)	134	22°50'N	81°10'W
J. Percy Priest Lake, res., Tn., U.S.	124	36°00'N	86°45'W
Juan Aldama, Mex. (kōȧ'n-äl-dá'mä)	130	24°16'N	103°21'W
Juan de Fuca, Strait of, strt., N.A. (hwän' dā fōō'kä)	92	48°25'N	124°37'W
Juan de Nova, Île, i., Reu.	233	17°18'S	43°07'E
Juan Diaz, r., Pan. (kōōȧ'n-dē'äz)	128a	9°05'N	79°30'W
Juan Fernández, Islas de, is., Chile	139	33°30'S	79°00'W
Juan L. Lacaze, Ur. (hōōȧ'n-ĕ'lĕ-lä-kä'zĕ)	141c	34°25'S	57°28'W
Juan Luis, Cayos de, is., Cuba (ka-yōs-dĕ-hwän lōō-ēs')	134	22°15'N	82°00'W
Juárez, Arg. (hōōȧ'rĕz)	144	37°42'S	59°46'W
Juázeiro, Braz. (zhōōȧ'zā'rô)	143	9°27'S	40°28'W
Juazeiro do Norte, Braz. (zhōōȧ'zā'rô-dô-nôr-tĕ)	143	7°16'S	38°57'W
Jubayl, Leb. (jōō-bīl')	197a	34°07'N	35°38'E
Jubba (Genale), r., Afr.	238a	1°30'N	42°25'E
Juby, Cap, c., Mor. (yōō'bė)	230	28°01'N	13°21'W
Júcar, r., Spain (hōō'kär)	162	39°10'N	1°22'W
Júcaro, Cuba (hōō'ká-rô)	134	21°40'N	78°50'W
Juchipila, Mex. (hōō-chė-pē'lȧ)	130	21°26'N	103°09'W
Juchitán, Mex. (hōō-chė-tän')	128	16°15'N	95°00'W
Juchitlán, Mex. (hōō-chē-tlän)	130	20°05'N	104°07'W
Jucuapa, El Sal. (kōō-kwä'pä)	132	13°30'N	88°24'W
Judenburg, Aus. (jōō'dĕn-bûrg)	168	47°10'N	14°40'E
Judith, r., Mt., U.S. (jōō'dĭth)	115	47°20'N	109°36'W
Juhua Dao, i., China (jyōō-hwä dou)	206	40°30'N	120°47'E
Juigalpa, Nic. (hwė-gäl'pä)	132	12°02'N	85°24'W
Juiz de Fora, Braz. (zhò-ēzh' dā fō'rä)	143	21°47'S	43°20'W
Jujuy, Arg. (hōō-hwē')	144	24°14'S	65°15'W
Jujuy, prov., Arg. (hōō-hwē')	144	23°00'S	65°45'W
Jukskei, r., S. Afr.	233b	25°58'S	27°58'E
Julesburg, Co., U.S. (jōōlz'bûrg)	120	40°59'N	102°16'W
Juliaca, Peru (hōō-lė-ä'kä)	142	15°26'S	70°12'W
Julian Alps, mts., Serb.	162	46°05'N	14°05'E
Julianehåb, Grnld.	89	60°07'N	46°20'W
Jülich, Ger. (yü'lĕk)	171c	50°55'N	6°22'E
Jullundur, India	199	31°29'N	75°39'E
Julpaiguri, India	202	26°35'N	88°48'E
Jumento Cays, is., Bah. (hōō-mĕn'tō)	135	23°05'N	75°40'W
Jumilla, Spain (hōō-mēl'yä)	172	38°28'N	1°20'W
Jump, r., Wi., U.S. (jŭmp)	113	45°18'N	90°53'W
Jumpingpound Creek, r., Can. (jŭmp-ĭng-pound)	102e	51°01'N	114°34'W
Jumrah, Indon.	197b	1°48'N	101°04'E
Junagādh, India (jò-nä'gŭd)	199	21°33'N	70°25'E
Junayfah, Egypt	238d	30°11'N	32°26'E
Junaynah, Ra's al, mtn., Egypt	197a	29°02'N	33°58'E
Junction, Tx., U.S. (jŭnk'shŭn)	122	30°29'N	99°48'W
Junction City, Ks., U.S.	121	39°01'N	96°49'W
Jundiaí, Braz.	143	23°11'S	46°52'W
Juneau, Ak., U.S. (jōō'nō)	106a	58°25'N	134°30'W
Jungfrau, mtn., Switz. (yòng'frou)	168	46°30'N	7°59'E
Junín, Arg. (hōō-nē'n)	144	34°35'S	60°56'W
Junín, Col.	142a	4°47'N	73°39'W
Juniyah, Leb. (jōō-nē'ĕ)	197a	33°59'N	35°38'E
Jupiter, r., Can.	100	49°40'N	63°20'W
Jupiter, Mount, mtn., Wa., U.S.	116a	47°42'N	123°04'W
Jur, r., Sudan (jòr)	231	6°38'N	27°52'E
Jura, mts., Eur. (zhü-rá')	161	46°55'N	6°49'E
Jura, i., Scot., U.K. (jōō'rȧ)	164	56°09'N	6°45'W
Jura, Sound of, strt., Scot., U.K. (jōō'rȧ)	164	55°45'N	5°55'W
Jurbarkas, Lith. (yōōr-bär'käs)	167	55°06'N	22°50'E
Jūrmala, Lat.	167	56°57'N	23°37'E
Jurong, China (jyōō-roŋ)	206	31°58'N	119°12'E
Juruá, r., S.A.	142	5°30'S	67°30'W
Juruena, r., Braz. (zhōō-rōōĕ'nä)	143	12°22'S	58°34'W

PRONOUNCING INDEX

Jutiapa – Kara-Kum 307

PLACE (Pronunciation)	PAGE	LAT.	LONG.
Jutiapa, Guat. (hōō-tē-ä'pä)	132	14°16'N	89°55'W
Juticalpa, Hond. (hōō-tē-käl'pä)	128	14°35'N	86°17'W
Jutland *see* Jylland, reg., Den.	160	56°04'N	9°00'E
Juventino Rosas, Mex.	130	20°38'N	101°02'W
Juventud, Isla de la, i., Cuba	129	21°40'N	82°45'W
Juxian, China (jyōō shyĕn)	208	35°35'N	118°50'E
Juxtlahuaca, Mex. (hōōs-tlä-hwä'kä)	130	17°20'N	98°02'W
Juye, China (jyōō-yŭ)	206	35°25'N	116°05'E
Južna Morava, r., Serb. (ů'zhnä mô'rä-vä)	175	42°30'N	22°00'E
Jylland, reg., Den.	160	56°04'N	9°00'E
K			
K2(Qogir Feng), mtn., Asia	199	36°06'N	76°38'E
Kaabong, Ug.	237	3°31'N	34°08'E
Kaalfontein, S. Afr. (kärl-fŏn-tān)	233b	26°02'S	28°16'E
Kaappunt, c., S. Afr.	232a	34°21'S	18°30'E
Kabaena, Pulau, i., Indon. (kä-bȧ-ā'nȧ)	212	5°35'S	121°07'E
Kabala, S.L. (kȧ-bä'lȧ)	230	9°43'N	11°39'W
Kabale, Ug.	237	1°15'S	29°59'E
Kabalega Falls, wtfl., Ug.	231	2°15'N	31°41'E
Kabalo, D.R.C. (kä-bä'lō)	232	6°03'S	26°55'E
Kabambare, D.R.C. (kä-bäm-bä'rȧ)	232	4°47'S	27°45'E
Kabardino-Balkaria, prov., Russia	180	43°30'N	43°30'E
Kabba, Nig.	235	7°50'N	6°03'E
Kabe, Japan (kä'bā)	211	34°32'N	132°30'E
Kabinakagami, r., Can.	98	49°00'N	84°15'W
Kabinda, D.R.C. (kä-bĕN'dä)	232	6°08'S	24°29'E
Kabompo, r., Zam. (kȧ-bôm'pō)	232	14°00'S	23°40'E
Kabongo, D.R.C. (kȧ-bông'ō)	232	7°58'S	25°10'E
Kabot, Gui.	234	10°48'N	14°57'W
Kaboudia, Ra's, c., Tun.	162	35°17'N	11°28'E
Kābul, Afg. (kä'bo͝ol)	199	34°39'N	69°14'E
Kabul, r., Asia (kä'bo͝ol)	199	34°44'N	69°43'E
Kabunda, D.R.C.	237	12°25'S	29°22'E
Kabwe, Zam.	232	14°27'S	28°27'E
Kachuga, Russia (kȧ-cho͞o-gȧ)	179	54°09'N	105°43'E
Kadei, r., Afr.	235	4°00'N	15°10'E
Kadnikov, Russia (käd'nē-kôf)	180	59°30'N	40°10'E
Kadoma, Japan	211b	34°43'N	135°36'E
Kadoma, Zimb.	232	18°21'S	29°55'E
Kaduna, Nig. (kä-do͞o'nä)	230	10°33'N	7°27'E
Kaduna, r., Nig.	235	9°30'N	6°00'E
Kaédi, Maur. (kä-ā-dē')	230	16°09'N	13°30'W
Ka'ena Point, c., Hi., U.S. (kä'ā-nä)	106d	21°33'N	158°19'W
Kaesŏng, Kor., N. (kä'ĕ-sŭng) (kĭ'jō)	205	38°00'N	126°35'E
Kafanchan, Nig.	235	9°36'N	8°17'E
Kafia Kingi, Sudan (kä'fē-ȧ kĭŋ'gē)	231	9°17'N	24°28'E
Kafue, Zam. (kä'fo͞o)	232	15°45'S	28°17'E
Kafue, r., Zam.	232	15°45'S	26°30'E
Kafue Flats, sw., Zam.	237	16°15'S	26°30'E
Kafue National Park, rec., Zam.	237	15°00'S	25°35'E
Kafwira, D.R.C.	237	12°10'S	27°33'E
Kagal'nik, r., Russia (kä-gäl''nēk)	177	46°58'N	39°25'E
Kagera, r., Afr. (kä-gā'rȧ)	232	1°10'S	31°10'E
Kagoshima, Japan (kä'gô-shē'mȧ)	205	31°35'N	130°31'E
Kagoshima-Wan, b., Japan (kä'gô-shē'mä wän)	210	31°24'N	130°39'E
Kahayan, r., Indon.	212	1°45'S	113°40'E
Kahemba, D.R.C.	236	7°17'S	19°00'E
Kahia, D.R.C.	237	6°21'S	28°24'E
Kahoka, Mo., U.S. (kȧ-hō'kȧ)	121	40°26'N	91°42'W
Kaho'olawe, i., Hi., U.S. (kä-hō͞o-lä'wē)	106c	20°28'N	156°48'W
Kahramanmaraş, Tur.	198	37°40'N	36°50'W
Kahshahpiwi, r., Can.	113	48°24'N	90°56'W
Kahuku Point, c., Hi., U.S. (kä-ho͞o'ko͞o)	106d	21°50'N	157°50'W
Kahului, Hi., U.S.	106c	20°53'N	156°28'W
Kai, Kepulauan, is., Indon.	213	5°35'S	132°45'E
Kaiang, Malay.	197b	3°00'N	101°47'E
Kaiashk, r., Can.	98	49°40'N	89°30'W
Kaibab Indian Reservation, I.R., Az., U.S. (kī'ē-bȧb)	119	36°55'N	112°45'W
Kaibab Plat, Az., U.S.	119	36°30'N	112°10'W
Kaidu, r., China (kī-do͞o)	204	42°35'N	84°04'E
Kaieteur Fall, wtfl., Guy. (kī-ĕ-to͞or')	143	4°48'N	59°24'W
Kaifeng, China (kī-fŭŋ)	205	34°48'N	114°22'E
Kai Kecil, i., Indon.	213	5°45'S	132°40'E
Kailua, Hi., U.S. (kä'ē-lo͞o'ä)	106c	21°18'N	157°43'W
Kailua Kona, Hi., U.S.	126a	19°49'N	155°59'W
Kaimana, Indon.	213	3°32'S	133°47'E
Kaimanawa Mountains, mts., N.Z.	223	39°10'S	176°00'E
Kainan, Japan (kä'ē-nän')	211	34°09'N	135°14'E
Kainji Lake, res., Nig.	230	10°25'N	4°50'E
Kaiserslautern, Ger. (kī-zĕrs-lou'tĕrn)	161	49°26'N	7°46'E
Kaitaia, N.Z. (kä-ē-tä'ē-ȧ)	221a	35°30'S	173°28'E
Kaiwi Channel, strt., Hi., U.S. (käē-wē)	106c	21°10'N	157°38'W
Kaiyuan, China (kī-yuän)	209	23°42'N	103°20'E
Kaiyuan, China	208	42°30'N	124°00'E
Kaiyuh Mountains, mts., Ak., U.S. (kī-yo͞o')	103	64°25'N	157°38'W
Kajaani, Fin. (kä'yȧ-nē)	160	64°15'N	27°16'E
Kajang, Gunong, mtn., Malay.	197b	2°47'N	104°05'E
Kajiki, Japan (kä'jē-kē)	210	31°44'N	130°41'E
Kakhovka, Ukr. (kä-Kôf'kȧ)	177	46°46'N	33°32'E
Kakhovs'ke vodoskhovyshche, res., Ukr.	178	47°21'N	33°33'E
Kākināda, India	199	16°58'N	82°18'E
Kaktovik, Ak., U.S. (kăk-tō'vĭk)	103	70°08'N	143°51'W
Kakwa, r., Can. (kăk'wȧ)	95	54°00'N	118°55'W
Kalach, Russia (kȧ-läch')	181	50°15'N	40°55'E
Kaladan, r., Asia	204	21°07'N	93°04'E
Kalae, c., Hi., U.S.	126a	18°55'N	155°41'W
Kalahari Desert, des., Afr. (kä-lä-hä'rē)	232	23°00'S	22°03'E
Kalama, Wa., U.S. (kȧ-lăm'ȧ)	116c	46°01'N	122°50'W
Kalama, r., Wa., U.S.	116c	46°03'N	122°47'W
Kalamáta, Grc.	154	37°04'N	22°08'E
Kalamazoo, Mi., U.S. (kăl-ȧ-mȧ-zo͞o')	105	42°20'N	85°40'W
Kalamazoo, r., Mi., U.S.	108	42°35'N	86°00'W
Kalanchak, Ukr. (kä-län-chäk')	177	46°17'N	33°14'E
Kalandula, Ang. (do͞o'kȧ dȧ brä-gäN'sä)	232	9°06'S	15°57'E
Kalaotoa, Pulau, i., Indon.	212	7°22'S	122°30'E
Kalapana, Hi., U.S. (kä-lä-pä'nä)	126a	19°25'N	155°00'W
Kalar, mtn., Iran	198	31°43'N	51°41'E
Kalāt, Pak. (kŭ-lät')	199	29°05'N	66°36'E
Kalemie, D.R.C.	232	5°56'S	29°12'E
Kalgan *see* Zhangjiakou, China	205	40°45'N	114°58'E
Kalgoorlie-Boulder, Austl. (kăl-go͞or'lē)	218	30°45'S	121°35'E
Kaliakra, Nos, c., Blg.	163	43°25'N	28°42'E
Kalima, D.R.C.	237	2°34'S	26°37'E
Kaliningrad, Russia	178	54°42'N	20°32'E
Kaliningrad, Russia (kä-lē-nēn'grät)	186b	55°55'N	37°49'E
Kalinkavichy, Bela.	176	52°07'N	29°19'E
Kalispel Indian Reservation, I.R., Wa., U.S. (kăl-ĭ-spĕl')	114	48°25'N	117°30'W
Kalispell, Mt., U.S. (kăl'ĭ-spĕl)	104	48°12'N	114°18'W
Kalisz, Pol. (kä'lēsh)	161	51°45'N	18°05'E
Kaliua, Tan.	237	5°04'S	31°48'E
Kalixälven, r., Swe.	160	67°12'N	22°00'E
Kalmar, Swe. (käl'mär)	160	56°40'N	16°19'E
Kalmarsund, strt., Swe. (käl'mär)	166	56°30'N	16°17'E
Kal'mius, r., Ukr. (käl''myo͞os)	177	47°15'N	37°38'E
Kalmykiya, prov., Russia	181	46°56'N	46°00'E
Kalocsa, Hung. (kä'lô-chä)	169	46°32'N	19°00'E
Kalohi Channel, strt., Hi., U.S. (kä-lō'hĭ)	126a	20°55'N	157°15'W
Kaloko, D.R.C.	237	6°47'S	25°48'E
Kalomo, Zam. (kä-lō'mō)	232	17°02'S	26°30'E
Kalsubai Mount, mtn., India	202	19°43'N	73°47'E
Kaltenkirchen, Ger. (käl'tĕn-kēr-kĕn)	159c	53°50'N	9°57'E
Kālu, r., India	203b	19°18'N	73°14'E
Kaluga, Russia (kȧ-lo͞o'gä)	178	54°29'N	36°12'E
Kaluga, prov., Russia	176	54°10'N	35°00'E
Kaluktutiak (Cambridge Bay), Can.	90	69°15'N	105°00'W
Kalundborg, Den. (kȧ-lo͞on''bôr')	166	55°42'N	11°07'E
Kalush, Ukr. (kä'lo͞osh)	169	49°02'N	24°24'E
Kalvarija, Lith. (käl-vä-rē'yȧ)	167	54°24'N	23°17'E
Kalwa, India	203b	19°12'N	72°59'E
Kal'ya, Russia (käl'yȧ)	186a	60°17'N	59°58'E
Kalyān, India	202	19°16'N	73°07'E
Kalyazin, Russia (käl-yȧ'zēn)	176	57°13'N	37°55'E
Kama, r., Russia (kä'mä)	178	56°10'N	53°50'E
Kamaishi, Japan (kä'mä-ē'shē)	210	39°16'N	142°03'E
Kamakura, Japan (kä'mä-ko͞o'rä)	211	35°19'N	139°33'E
Kamarān, i., Yemen	198	15°19'N	41°47'E
Kāmārhāti, India	202a	22°41'N	88°23'E
Kambove, D.R.C. (käm-bō'vē)	232	10°58'S	26°43'E
Kamchatka, r., Russia	185	54°15'N	158°38'E
Kamchatka, Poluostrov, pen., Russia	185	55°19'N	157°45'E
Kamen, Ger. (kä'mĕn)	171c	51°35'N	7°40'E
Kamenjak, Rt, c., Cro. (kȧ'mĕ-nyäk)	174	44°45'N	13°57'E
Kamen'-na-Obi, Russia (kä-mĭny'nŭ ô'bē)	178	53°43'N	81°28'E
Kamensk-Shakhtinskiy, Russia (kä'mĕnsk shäk'tĭn-skĭ)	177	48°17'N	40°16'E
Kamensk-Ural'skiy, Russia (kä'mĕnsk o͞o-räl'skĭ)	180	56°27'N	61°55'E
Kamenz, Ger. (kä'mĕnts)	168	51°16'N	14°05'E
Kameoka, Japan (kä'mā-ōkä)	211b	35°01'N	135°35'E
Kämet, mtn., Asia	202	30°50'N	79°42'E
Kamianets'-Podil's'kyi, Ukr.	181	48°41'N	26°34'E
Kamianka-Buz'ka, Ukr.	169	50°06'N	24°20'E
Kamień Pomorski, Pol.	168	53°57'N	14°48'E
Kamikoma, Japan (kä'mē-kō'mä)	211b	34°45'N	135°50'E
Kamina, D.R.C.	232	8°44'S	25°00'E
Kaministikwia, r., Can. (kȧ-mĭ-nĭ-stĭk'wĭ-ȧ)	113	48°40'N	89°41'W
Kamituga, D.R.C.	237	3°04'S	28°11'E
Kamloops, Can. (kăm'lo͞ops)	90	50°40'N	120°20'W
Kamp, r., Aus. (kämp)	168	48°30'N	15°45'E
Kampala, Ug. (käm-pä'lä)	231	0°19'N	32°25'E
Kampar, r., Indon. (käm'pär)	212	0°30'N	101°30'E
Kampene, D.R.C.	237	3°36'S	26°40'E
Kampenhout, Bel.	159a	50°56'N	4°33'E
Kamp-Lintfort, Ger. (kämp-lĕnt'fōrt)	171c	51°30'N	6°34'E
Kâmpóng Saôm, Camb.	212	10°40'N	103°50'E
Kâmpóng Thum, Camb. (kŏm'pŏng-tŏm)	212	12°41'N	104°29'E
Kâmpôt, Camb. (käm'pōt)	212	10°41'N	104°07'E
Kampuchea *see* Cambodia, nation, Asia	212	12°15'N	104°00'E
Kamsack, Can. (kăm'săk)	90	51°34'N	101°54'W
Kamskoye, res., Russia	178	59°08'N	56°30'E
Kamudilo, D.R.C.	237	7°42'S	27°18'E
Kamuela, Hi., U.S.	126a	20°01'N	155°40'W
Kamui Misaki, c., Japan	210	43°25'N	139°35'E
Kámuk, Cerro, mtn., C.R. (sĕ'r-rô-kä-mo͞o'k)	133	9°18'N	83°02'W
Kamyshevatskaya, Russia	177	46°24'N	37°58'E
Kamyshin, Russia (kä-mwēsh'ĭn)	178	50°08'N	45°20'E
Kamyshlov, Russia (kä-mēsh'lôf)	178	56°50'N	62°32'E
Kan, r., Russia (kän)	184	56°30'N	94°17'E
Kanab, Ut., U.S. (kăn'ăb)	119	37°00'N	112°30'W
Kanabeki, Russia (kȧ-nä'byĕ-kĭ)	186a	57°48'N	57°16'E
Kanab Plateau, plat., Az., U.S.	119	36°31'N	112°55'W
Kanaga, i., Ak., U.S. (kă-nă'gă)	103a	52°02'N	177°38'W
Kanagawa, dept., Japan (kä'nä-gä'wä)	211a	35°29'N	139°32'E
Kanā'is, Ra's al, c., Egypt	163	31°14'N	28°08'E
Kanamachi, Japan (kä-nä-mä'chē)	211a	35°46'N	139°52'E
Kananga, D.R.C.	232	6°14'S	22°17'E
Kananikol'skoye, Russia	186a	52°48'N	57°29'E
Kanasín, Mex. (kä-nä-sē'n)	132a	20°54'N	89°31'W
Kanatak, Ak., U.S. (kă-nă'tŏk)	103	57°35'N	155°48'W
Kanawha, r., W.V., U.S. (kȧ-nô'wȧ)	107	37°55'N	81°50'W
Kanaya, Japan (kä-nä'yä)	211a	35°10'N	139°49'E
Kanazawa, Japan (kä'nȧ-zä'wȧ)	205	36°34'N	136°38'E
Kānchenjunga, mtn., Asia (kĭn-chĭn-jòn'gȧ)	199	27°30'N	88°18'E
Kānchipuram, India	199	12°55'N	79°43'E
Kandahār, Afg.	199	31°43'N	65°58'E
Kanda Kanda, D.R.C. (kän'dȧ kän'dȧ)	232	6°56'S	23°36'E
Kandalaksha, Russia (kȧn-dȧ-lȧk'shȧ)	178	67°10'N	33°05'E
Kandalakshskiy Zaliv, b., Russia	180	66°20'N	35°00'E
Kandava, Lat. (kän'dȧ-vȧ)	167	57°03'N	22°45'E
Kandi, Benin (käN-dē')	230	11°08'N	2°56'E
Kandiāro, Pak.	202	27°09'N	68°12'E
Kandla, India (kŭnd'lŭ)	202	23°00'N	70°20'E
Kandy, Sri L. (kän'dē)	203	7°18'N	80°42'E
Kane, Pa., U.S. (kān)	109	41°40'N	78°50'W
Kāne'ohe, Hi., U.S. (kä-nā-ō'hā)	126a	21°25'N	157°47'W
Kāne'ohe Bay, b., Hi., U.S.	106d	21°32'N	157°40'W
Kanevskaya, Russia (kȧ-nyĕf'skȧ)	177	46°07'N	38°58'E
Kangaroo, i., Austl. (kăŋ-gȧ-ro͞o')	220	36°05'S	137°05'E
Kangāvar, Iran (kŭŋ'gȧ-vär)	198	34°37'N	46°45'E
Kangean, Kepulauan, is., Indon. (käŋ'gē-än)	212	6°50'S	116°22'E
Kanggye, Kor., N. (käng'gyĕ)	205	40°55'N	126°40'E
Kanghwa, i., Kor., S. (käng'hwä)	210	37°38'N	126°00'E
Kangnŭng, Kor., S. (käng'nó ng)	210	37°42'N	128°50'E
Kango, Gabon (käN-gō)	232	0°09'N	10°08'E
Kangowa, D.R.C.	236	9°55'S	22°48'E
Kanin, Poluostrov, pen., Russia	178	68°00'N	45°00'E
Kaningo, Kenya	237	0°49'S	38°32'E
Kanin Nos, Mys, c., Russia	180	68°40'N	44°00'E
Kaniv, Ukr.	177	49°46'N	31°27'E
Kanivs'ke vodoskhovyshche, res., Ukr.	178	50°10'N	30°40'E
Kanjiža, Serb. (kä'nyē-zhä)	175	46°05'N	20°02'E
Kankakee, Il., U.S. (kăŋ-kȧ-kē')	108	41°07'N	87°53'W
Kankakee, r., Il., U.S.	108	41°15'N	88°15'W
Kankan, Gui. (käN-käN) (kän-kän')	230	10°23'N	9°18'W
Kannapolis, N.C., U.S. (kăn-ăp'ō-lĭs)	125	35°30'N	80°38'W
Kannoura, Japan (kä'nō-ō͞o'rä)	211	33°34'N	134°18'E
Kano, Nig. (kä'nō)	230	12°00'N	8°30'E
Kanonkop, mtn., S. Afr.	232a	33°49'S	18°37'E
Kanopolis Reservoir, res., Ks., U.S. (kăn-ŏp'ō-lĭs)	120	38°44'N	98°01'W
Kānpur, India (kän'pûr)	202	26°30'N	80°10'E
Kansas, state, U.S. (kăn'zȧs)	104	38°30'N	99°40'W
Kansas, r., Ks., U.S.	121	39°08'N	95°52'W
Kansas City, Ks., U.S.	105	39°06'N	94°39'W
Kansas City, Mo., U.S.	105	39°05'N	94°35'W
Kansk, Russia	179	56°14'N	95°43'E
Kansŏng, Kor., S.	210	38°09'N	128°29'E
Kantang, Thai. (kän'täng')	212	7°26'N	99°28'E
Kantchari, Burkina	234	12°29'N	1°31'E
Kanton, i., Kir.	240	3°50'S	174°00'W
Kantunilkin, Mex. (kän-to͞o-nēl-kē'n)	132a	21°07'N	87°30'W
Kanzhakovskiy Kamen, Gora, mtn., Russia (kȧn-zhä'kôvs-kēē kä'mĭen)	186a	59°38'N	59°12'E
Kaohsiung, Tai. (kä-ō-syông')	205	22°35'N	120°25'E
Kaolack, Sen.	230	14°09'N	16°04'W
Kaouar, oasis, Niger	231	19°16'N	13°09'E
Kapaa, Hi., U.S.	126a	22°06'N	159°20'W
Kapanga, D.R.C.	236	8°21'S	22°35'E
Kapfenberg, Aus. (kȧp'fĕn-bĕrgh)	168	47°27'N	15°16'E
Kapiri Mposhi, Zam.	237	13°58'S	28°41'E
Kapoeta, Sudan	231	4°45'N	33°35'E
Kaposvár, Hung. (kô'pôsh-vär)	169	46°21'N	17°45'E
Kapsan, Kor., N. (käp'sän')	210	40°59'N	128°22'E
Kapuskasing, Can.	91	49°28'N	82°22'W
Kapuskasing, r., Can.	98	48°55'N	82°55'W
Kapustin Yar, Russia (kä'pôs-tĕn yär')	181	48°30'N	45°40'E
Kaputar, Mount, mtn., Austl. (kă-pû-tăr)	222	30°11'S	150°11'E
Kapuvár, Hung. (kô'po͞o-vär)	169	47°35'N	17°02'E
Kara, Russia (kärȧ)	178	68°42'N	65°30'E
Kara, r., Russia	180	68°30'N	65°20'E
Karabalā', Iraq (kŭr'bȧ-lä)	198	32°31'N	43°58'E
Karabanovo, Russia (kä'rȧ-bȧ-nō-vō)	176	56°19'N	38°43'E
Karabash, Russia (kó-rȧ-bäsh')	186a	55°27'N	60°14'E
Kara-Bogaz-Gol, Zaliv, b., Turkmen. (kȧ-rä' bŭ-gäs')	183	41°30'N	53°40'E
Karachay-Cherkessia, prov., Russia	182	44°00'N	42°00'E
Karachev, Russia (kȧ-rȧ-chôf')	180	53°08'N	34°54'E
Karāchi, Pak.	199	24°59'N	68°56'E
Karaganda *see* Qaraghandy, Kaz.	183	49°42'N	73°18'E
Karaidel', Russia (kä'rī-dĕl)	186a	55°52'N	56°54'E
Karakoram Pass, p., Asia	199	35°35'N	77°45'E
Karakoram Range, mts., India (kä'rä kō'rŏm)	199	35°24'N	76°38'E
Karakorum, hist., Mong.	204	47°25'N	102°22'E
Kara-Kum, des., Turkmen.	183	40°00'N	57°00'E

308 Kara Kum Canal – Keshan PRONOUNCING INDEX

PLACE (Pronunciation)	PAGE	LAT.	LONG.
Kara Kum Canal, can., Turkmen.	183	37°35'N	61°50'E
Karaman, Tur. (kä-rä-män')	163	37°10'N	33°00'E
Karamay, China (kär-äm-ā)	204	45°37'N	84°53'E
Karamea Bight, b., N.Z. (kȧ-rȧ-mē'ȧ bĭt)	221a	41°20'S	171°30'E
Kara Sea *see* Karskoye More, sea, Russia	178	74°00'N	68°00'E
Karashahr (Yanqui), China (kä-rä-shä-är) (yän-chyē)	204	42°14'N	86°28'E
Karatsu, Japan (kä'rä-tso͞o)	211	33°28'N	129°59'E
Karaul, Russia (kä-rä-ōl')	184	70°13'N	83°46'E
Karawanken, mts., Eur.	168	46°32'N	14°07'E
Karcag, Hung. (kär'tsäg)	169	47°18'N	20°58'E
Kárditsa, Grc.	175	39°23'N	21°57'E
Kärdla, Est. (kĕrd'lȧ)	167	58°59'N	22°44'E
Karelia, prov., Russia	184	62°30'N	32°35'E
Karema, Tan.	232	6°49'S	30°26'E
Kargat, Russia (kär-gät')	178	55°17'N	80°07'E
Karghalik *see* Yecheng, China	204	37°54'N	77°25'E
Kargopol', Russia (kär-gō-pōl'')	178	61°30'N	38°50'E
Kariba, Lake, res., Afr.	232	17°15'S	27°55'E
Karibib, Nmb. (kȧr'ȧ-bĭb)	232	21°55'S	15°50'E
Kārikāl, India (kä-rē-käl')	203	10°58'N	79°49'E
Karimata, Kepulauan, is., Indon. (kä-rē-mä'tä)	212	1°08'S	108°10'E
Karimata, Selat, strt., Indon.	212	1°00'S	107°10'E
Karimun Besar, i., Indon.	197b	1°10'N	103°28'E
Karimunjawa, Kepulauan, is., Indon. (kä'rē-mo͞on-yä'vä)	212	5°36'S	110°15'E
Karin, Som. (kȧr'ĭn)	238a	10°43'N	45°50'E
Karkar Island, i., Pap. N. Gui. (kär'kär)	213	4°50'S	146°45'E
Karkheh, r., Iran	198	32°45'N	47°50'E
Karkinits'ka zatoka, b., Ukr.	177	45°50'N	32°45'E
Karkūk, Iraq	198	35°28'N	44°22'E
Karlivka, Ukr.	177	49°26'N	35°08'E
Karlobag, Cro. (kär-lō-bäg')	174	44°30'N	15°03'E
Karlovac, Cro. (kär'lō-väts)	163	45°29'N	15°16'E
Karlovo, Blg. (kär'lō-vō)	175	42°39'N	24°48'E
Karlovy Vary, Czech Rep. (kär'lō-vē vä'rē)	161	50°13'N	12°53'E
Karlshamn, Swe. (kärls'häm)	166	56°11'N	14°50'E
Karlskrona, Swe. (kärls'krō-nä)	160	56°10'N	15°33'E
Karlsruhe, Ger. (kärls'ro͞o-ē)	161	49°00'N	8°23'E
Karlstad, Swe. (kärl'städ)	154	59°25'N	13°28'E
Karluk, Ak., U.S. (kär'lŭk)	103	57°30'N	154°22'W
Karmøy, i., Nor. (kärm-ûe)	166	59°14'N	5°00'E
Karnataka, state, India	199	14°55'N	75°00'E
Karnobat, Blg. (kär-nō'bät)	175	42°39'N	26°59'E
Karonga, Mwi. (kȧ-rōŋ'gȧ)	232	9°52'S	33°57'E
Kárpathos, i., Grc.	163	35°34'N	27°26'E
Karpinsk, Russia (kär'pĭnsk)	186a	59°46'N	60°00'E
Kars, Tur. (kärs)	198	40°35'N	43°00'E
Kārsava, Lat. (kär'sä-vä)	167	56°46'N	27°39'E
Karshi, Uzb. (kär'shē)	183	38°30'N	66°08'E
Karskiye Vorota, Proliv, strt., Russia	178	70°30'N	58°07'E
Karskoye More (Kara Sea), sea, Russia	178	74°00'N	68°00'E
Kartaly, Russia (kȧr'tȧ lē)	178	53°05'N	60°40'E
Karunagapalli, India	203	9°09'N	76°34'E
Karvina, Czech Rep.	169	49°50'N	18°30'E
Kasai (Cassai), r., Afr.	232	3°45'S	19°10'E
Kasama, Zam. (kȧ-sä'mȧ)	232	10°13'S	31°12'E
Kasanga, Tan. (kȧ-säŋ'gȧ)	232	8°28'S	31°09'E
Kasaoka, Japan (kä'sä-ō'kȧ)	211	34°33'N	133°29'E
Kasba-Tadla, Mor. (käs'bȧ-täd'lȧ)	230	32°37'N	5°57'W
Kasempa, Zam. (kȧ-sĕm'pȧ)	232	13°27'S	25°50'E
Kasenga, D.R.C. (kȧ-seŋ'gȧ)	232	10°22'S	28°38'E
Kasese, D.R.C.	237	1°38'S	27°07'E
Kasese, Ug.	237	0°10'N	30°05'E
Kāshān, Iran (kä-shän')	198	33°52'N	51°15'E
Kashgar *see* Kashi, China	204	39°29'N	76°00'E
Kashi (Kashgar), China (kä-shr) (käsh-gär)	204	39°29'N	76°00'E
Kashihara, Japan (kä'shē-hä'rä)	211b	34°31'N	135°48'E
Kashiji Plain, pl., Zam.	236	13°25'S	22°30'E
Kashin, Russia (kä-shēn')	176	57°20'N	37°38'E
Kashira, Russia (kä-shē'rȧ)	176	54°49'N	38°11'E
Kashiwa, Japan (kä'shē-wä)	211a	35°51'N	139°58'E
Kashiwara, Japan	211b	34°35'N	135°38'E
Kashiwazaki, Japan (kä'shē-wä-zä'kē)	210	37°06'N	138°17'E
Kāshmar, Iran	201	35°12'N	58°27'E
Kashmir *see* Jammu and Kashmir, state, India	199	34°30'N	76°00'E
Kashmor, Pak.	202	28°33'N	69°34'E
Kashtak, Russia (käsh'tȧk)	186a	55°18'N	61°25'E
Kasimov, Russia (kȧ-sē'môf)	180	54°56'N	41°23'E
Kaskanak, Ak., U.S. (kăs-kă'năk)	103	60°00'N	158°00'W
Kaskaskia, r., Il., U.S. (kăs-kăs'kĭ-ȧ)	108	39°10'N	88°50'W
Kaskattama, r., Can. (kăs-kă-tä'mȧ)	97	56°28'N	90°55'W
Kaskö (Kaskinen), Fin. (käs'kû) (käs'kē-nĕn)	167	62°24'N	21°18'E
Kasli, Russia (käs'lĭ)	180	55°53'N	60°46'E
Kasongo, D.R.C. (kä-sôŋ'gō)	232	4°31'S	26°42'E
Kásos, i., Grc.	163	35°20'N	26°55'E
Kaspiysk, Russia	182	42°52'N	47°38'E
Kassándras, Kólpos, b., Grc.	175	40°10'N	23°35'E
Kassel, Ger. (käs'ĕl)	161	51°19'N	9°30'E
Kasson, Mn., U.S. (kăs'ŭn)	113	44°01'N	92°45'W
Kastamonu, Tur. (kä-stȧ-mō'no͞o)	198	41°20'N	33°50'E
Kastoría, Grc. (kȧs-tō'rĭ-ȧ)	163	40°28'N	21°17'E
Kasūr, Pak.	202	31°10'N	74°29'E
Kataba, Zam.	237	16°05'S	25°10'E
Katahdin, Mount, mtn., Me., U.S. (kȧ-tä'dĭn)	100	45°56'N	68°57'W
Katanga, hist. reg., D.R.C. (kȧ-täŋ'gȧ)	232	8°30'S	25°00'E
Katanning, Austl. (kȧ-tăn'ĭng)	218	33°45'S	117°45'E
Katav-Ivanovsk, Russia (kä'täf ĭ-vä'nôfsk)	186a	54°46'N	58°13'E
Kateninskiy, Russia (kȧtyĕ'nĭs-kĭ)	186a	53°12'N	61°05'E
Kateríni, Grc.	175	40°18'N	22°36'E
Katete, Zam.	237	14°05'S	32°07'E
Katherine, Austl. (kăth'ẽr-ĭn)	218	14°15'S	132°20'E
Kāthiāwār, pen., India (kä'tyȧ-wär')	199	22°10'N	70°20'E
Kathmandu, Nepal (kät-män-do͞o')	199	27°49'N	85°21'E
Kathryn, Can. (kăth'rĭn)	102e	51°13'N	113°42'W
Kathryn, Ca., U.S.	117a	33°42'N	117°45'W
Katihār, India	202	25°39'N	87°39'E
Katiola, C. Iv.	234	8°08'N	5°06'W
Katmai National Park, rec., Ak., U.S. (kăt'mī)	106a	58°38'N	155°00'W
Katompi, D.R.C.	237	6°11'S	26°20'E
Katopa, D.R.C.	237	2°45'S	25°06'E
Katowice, Pol.	154	50°15'N	19°00'E
Katrineholm, Swe. (kȧ-trē'nĕ-hōlm)	166	59°01'N	16°10'E
Katsbakhskiy, Russia (kȧts-băk'skĭ)	186a	52°57'N	59°37'E
Katsina, Nig. (kät'sē-nȧ)	230	13°00'N	7°32'E
Katsina Ala, Nig.	230	7°10'N	9°17'E
Katsura, r., Japan (kä'tso-rä)	211b	34°55'N	135°43'E
Katta-Kurgan, Uzb. (kȧ-tȧ-kōr-gän')	183	39°45'N	66°42'E
Kattegat, strt., Eur. (kăt'ĕ-găt)	156	56°57'N	11°25'E
Katumba, D.R.C.	237	7°45'S	25°18'E
Katun', r., Russia (kȧ-tōn')	184	51°30'N	86°18'E
Katwijk aan Zee, Neth.	159a	52°12'N	4°23'E
Kaua'i, i., Hi., U.S.	106c	22°09'N	159°15'W
Kauai Channel, strt., Hi., U.S. (kä-o͞o-ä'ē)	106c	21°35'N	158°52'W
Kaufbeuren, Ger. (kouf'boi-rĕn)	168	47°52'N	10°38'E
Kaufman, Tx., U.S. (kôf'mȧn)	123	32°36'N	96°18'W
Kaukauna, Wi., U.S. (kô-kô'nȧ)	113	44°17'N	88°15'W
Kaulakahi Channel, strt., Hi., U.S. (kä'o͞o-lȧ-kä'hē)	126a	22°00'N	159°55'W
Kaunakakai, Hi., U.S. (kä'o͞o-nȧ-kä'kī)	126a	21°06'N	156°59'W
Kaunas, Lith. (kou'nȧs) (kôv'nō)	178	54°42'N	23°54'E
Kaura Namoda, Nig.	230	12°35'N	6°35'E
Kavála, Grc. (kä-vä'lä)	163	40°55'N	24°24'E
Kavieng, Pap. N. Gui. (kä-vē-ĕng')	213	2°44'S	151°02'E
Kavīr, Dasht-e, des., Iran (dŭsht-ē-ka-vēr')	198	34°41'N	53°30'E
Kawagoe, Japan (kä-wä-gō'ȧ)	211	35°55'N	139°29'E
Kawaguchi, Japan (kä-wä-go͞o-chē)	211a	35°48'N	139°44'E
Kawaikini, mtn., Hi., U.S. (kä-wä'ē-kĭ-nĭ)	126a	22°05'N	159°33'W
Kawanishi, Japan (kä-wä'nē-shē)	211b	34°49'N	135°26'E
Kawasaki, Japan (kä-wä-sä'kē)	210	35°32'N	139°43'E
Kaxgar, r., China	204	39°30'N	75°00'E
Kaya, Burkina (kä'yä)	230	13°05'N	1°05'W
Kayan, r., Indon.	212	1°45'N	115°38'E
Kaycee, Wy., U.S. (kā-sē')	115	43°43'N	106°38'W
Kayes, Mali (kāz)	230	14°27'N	11°26'W
Kayseri, Tur. (kī'sĕ-rē)	198	38°45'N	35°20'E
Kazach'ye, Russia	179	70°46'N	135°47'E
Kazakhstan, nation, Asia	178	48°45'N	59°00'E
Kazan', Russia (kȧ-zän')	178	55°50'N	49°18'E
Kazanka, Ukr. (kȧ-zän'kȧ)	177	47°49'N	32°50'E
Kazanlŭk, Blg. (kȧ'zȧn-lĕk)	175	42°47'N	25°23'E
Kazbek, Gora, mtn. (kȧz-bĕk')	181	42°42'N	44°31'E
Kāzerūn, Iran	198	29°37'N	51°44'E
Kazincbarcika, Hung. (kô'zĭnts-bôr-tsĭ-ko)	169	48°15'N	20°39'E
Kazungula, Zam.	237	17°45'S	25°20'E
Kazusa Kameyama, Japan (kä-zo͞o-sä kä-mȧ'yä-mä)	211a	35°14'N	140°06'E
Kazym, r., Russia (kä-zēm')	184	63°30'N	67°41'E
Kéa, i., Grc.	175	37°36'N	24°13'E
Kealaikahiki Channel, strt., Hi., U.S. (kā-ä'lä-ē-kä-hē'kē)	126a	20°38'N	157°00'W
Keansburg, N.J., U.S. (kēnz'bûrg)	110a	40°26'N	74°08'W
Kearney, Ne., U.S. (kär'nĭ)	112	40°42'N	99°05'W
Kearny, N.J., U.S.	110a	40°46'N	74°09'W
Keasey, Or., U.S. (kēz'ĭ)	116c	45°51'N	123°20'W
Kebnekaise, mtn., Swe. (kĕp'nĕ-kä-ēs'ĕ)	156	67°53'N	18°10'E
Kecskemét, Hung. (kĕch'kĕ-māt)	163	46°52'N	19°42'E
Kedah, hist. reg., Malay. (kä'dä)	212	6°00'N	100°31'E
Kėdainiai, Lith. (kē-dī-nĭ-ĭ)	167	55°16'N	23°58'E
Kedgwick, Can. (kĕdj'wĭk)	100	47°39'N	67°21'W
Keenbrook, Ca., U.S. (kēn'bro͝ok)	117a	34°16'N	117°29'W
Keene, N.H., U.S. (kēn)	109	42°55'N	72°15'W
Keetmanshoop, Nmb. (kāt'mȧns-hōp)	232	26°30'S	18°05'E
Keet Seel Ruin, Az., U.S. (kēt sēl)	119	36°46'N	110°32'W
Keewatin, Mn., U.S. (kē-wä'tĭn)	113	47°24'N	93°03'W
Kefallonía, i., Grc.	163	38°08'N	20°58'E
Keffi, Nig. (kĕf'ē)	230	8°51'N	7°52'E
Ke Ga, Mui, c., Viet.	212	12°58'N	109°50'E
Kei, r., Afr. (kā)	233c	32°57'S	26°50'E
Keila, Est. (kā'lȧ)	167	59°19'N	24°25'E
Keilor, Austl.	217a	37°43'S	144°50'E
Kei Mouth, S. Afr.	233c	32°40'S	28°23'E
Keiskammahoek, S. Afr. (kās'kämä-ho͝ok')	233c	32°42'S	27°11'E
Kéita, Bahr, r., Chad	235	9°30'N	19°17'E
Keitele, l., Fin. (kā'tĕ-lĕ)	167	62°50'N	25°40'E
Kekaha, Hi., U.S.	126a	21°57'N	159°42'W
Kelafo, Eth.	238a	5°40'N	44°00'E
Kelang, Malay.	212	3°20'N	101°27'E
Kelang, r., Malay.	197b	3°00'N	101°40'E
Kelkit, r., Tur.	163	40°38'N	37°03'E
Keller, Tx., U.S. (kĕl'ẽr)	117c	32°56'N	97°15'W
Kellinghusen, Ger. (kĕ'lĕng-ho͞o-zĕn)	159c	53°57'N	9°43'E
Kellogg, Id., U.S. (kĕl'ŏg)	114	47°32'N	116°07'W
Kelme', Lith. (kĕl-mȧ)	167	55°36'N	22°53'E
Kélo, Chad	235	9°19'N	15°48'E
Kelowna, Can.	90	49°53'N	119°29'W
Kelsey Bay, Can. (kĕl'sē)	94	50°24'N	125°57'W
Kelso, Wa., U.S.	116c	46°09'N	122°54'W
Keluang, Malay.	197b	2°01'N	103°19'E
Kem', Russia (kĕm)	178	65°00'N	34°48'E
Kemah, Tx., U.S. (kē'mȧ)	123a	29°32'N	95°01'W
Kemerovo, Russia	178	55°31'N	86°05'E
Kemi, Fin. (kā'mē)	160	65°48'N	24°38'E
Kemi, r., Fin.	160	67°02'N	27°50'E
Kemigawa, Japan (kĕ'mē-gä'wä)	211a	35°38'N	140°07'E
Kemijarvi, Fin. (kā'mē-yĕr-vē)	160	66°48'N	27°21'E
Kemi-joki, l., Fin.	160	66°37'N	28°13'E
Kemmerer, Wy., U.S. (kĕm'ẽr-ẽr)	115	41°48'N	110°36'W
Kemp, l., Tx., U.S. (kĕmp)	120	33°55'N	99°22'W
Kempen, Ger. (kĕm'pĕn)	171c	51°22'N	6°25'E
Kempsey, Austl. (kĕmp'sē)	219	30°59'S	152°50'E
Kempt, l., Can. (kĕmpt)	99	47°28'N	74°00'W
Kempten, Ger. (kĕmp'tĕn)	161	47°44'N	10°17'E
Kempton Park, S. Afr. (kĕmp'tŏn pärk)	238c	26°07'S	28°29'E
Ken, r., India	202	25°00'N	79°55'E
Kenai, Ak., U.S. (kĕ-nī')	103	60°38'N	151°18'W
Kenai Fjords National Park, rec., Ak., U.S.	103	59°45'N	150°00'W
Kenai Mountains, mts., Ak., U.S.	103	60°00'N	150°00'W
Kenai Pen, Ak., U.S.	103	64°40'N	150°18'W
Kendal, S. Afr.	238c	26°03'S	28°58'E
Kendal, Eng., U.K. (kĕn'dȧl)	164	54°20'N	1°48'W
Kendallville, In., U.S. (kĕn'dăl-vĭl)	108	41°25'N	85°20'W
Kenedy, Tx., U.S. (kĕn'ĕ-dĭ)	123	28°49'N	97°50'W
Kenema, S.L.	234	7°52'N	11°12'W
Kenitra, Mor. (kĕ-nē'trȧ)	162	34°21'N	6°34'W
Kenmare, N.D., U.S. (kĕn-mâr')	112	48°41'N	102°05'W
Kenmore, N.Y., U.S. (kĕn'mōr)	111c	42°58'N	78°53'W
Kennebec, r., Me., U.S. (kĕn-ē-bĕk')	100	44°23'N	69°48'W
Kennebunk, Me., U.S. (kĕn-ē-buŋk')	100	43°24'N	70°33'W
Kennedale, Tx., U.S. (kĕn'-ē-dāl)	117c	32°38'N	97°13'W
Kennedy, Cape *see* Canaveral, Cape, c., Fl., U.S.	107	28°30'N	80°23'W
Kennedy, Mount, mtn., Can.	103	60°25'N	138°50'W
Kenner, La., U.S. (kĕn'ẽr)	123	29°58'N	90°15'W
Kennett, Mo., U.S. (kĕn'ĕt)	121	36°14'N	90°01'W
Kennewick, Wa., U.S. (kĕn'ē-wĭk)	114	46°12'N	119°06'W
Kenney Dam, dam, Can.	94	53°37'N	124°58'W
Kennydale, Wa., U.S. (kĕn-nē'dāl)	116a	47°31'N	122°12'W
Kénogami, Can. (kĕn-ō'gä-mē)	91	48°26'N	71°14'W
Kenogamissi Lake, l., Can.	98	48°15'N	81°31'W
Keno Hill, Can.	103	63°58'N	135°18'W
Kenora, Can. (kē-nō'rȧ)	91	49°47'N	94°29'W
Kenosha, Wi., U.S. (kē-nō'shȧ)	105	42°34'N	87°50'W
Kenova, W.V., U.S. (kē-nō'vȧ)	108	38°20'N	82°35'W
Kensico Reservoir, res., N.Y., U.S. (kĕn'sĭ-kō)	110a	41°08'N	73°45'W
Kent, Oh., U.S. (kĕnt)	108	41°05'N	81°20'W
Kent, Wa., U.S.	116a	47°23'N	122°14'W
Kentani, S. Afr. (kĕnt-änĭ')	233c	32°31'S	28°19'E
Kentland, In., U.S. (kĕnt'lănd)	108	40°50'N	87°25'W
Kenton, Oh., U.S. (kĕn'tŭn)	108	40°40'N	83°35'W
Kent Peninsula, pen., Can.	92	68°28'N	108°10'W
Kentucky, state, U.S. (kĕn-tŭk'ĭ)	105	37°30'N	87°35'W
Kentucky, res., U.S.	107	36°20'N	88°50'W
Kentucky, r., Ky., U.S.	107	38°15'N	85°01'W
Kentwood, La., U.S. (kĕnt'wo͝od)	123	30°56'N	90°31'W
Kenya, nation, Afr. (kĕn'yȧ)	232	1°00'N	36°53'E
Kenya, Mount (Kirinyaga), mtn., Kenya	233	0°10'S	37°20'E
Kenyon, Mn., U.S. (kĕn'yŭn)	113	44°15'N	92°58'W
Keokuk, Ia., U.S. (kē'ō-kŭk)	105	40°24'N	91°34'W
Keoma, Can. (kē-ō'mȧ)	102e	51°13'N	113°39'W
Kepenkeck Lake, l., Can.	101	48°13'N	54°45'W
Kępno, Pol. (kaŋ'pnō)	169	51°17'N	17°59'E
Kerala, state, India	199	16°38'N	76°00'E
Kerang, Austl. (kē-răng')	219	35°32'S	143°58'E
Kerch, Ukr.	178	45°20'N	36°26'E
Kerchenskiy Proliv, strt., Eur. (kĕr-chĕn'skĭ prô'lĭf)	177	45°08'N	36°35'E
Kerempe Burun, c., Tur.	163	42°00'N	33°20'E
Keren, Erit.	231	15°46'N	38°28'E
Kerguélen, Îles, is., Afr. (kĕr'gȧ-lĕn)	3	49°50'S	69°30'E
Kericho, Kenya	237	0°22'S	35°17'E
Kerinci, Gunung, mtn., Indon.	212	1°45'S	101°18'E
Keriya *see* Yutian, China	204	36°55'N	81°39'E
Keriya, r., China (kē'rē-yä)	204	37°13'N	81°59'E
Kerkebet, Erit.	200	16°18'N	37°24'E
Kerkenna, Îles, i., Tun. (kĕr'kĕn-nä)	230	34°49'N	11°37'E
Kerki, Turkmen. (kĕr'kē)	183	37°52'N	65°15'E
Kérkyra, Grc.	163	39°36'N	19°56'E
Kérkyra, i., Grc.	162	39°33'N	19°36'E
Kermadec Islands, is., N.Z. (kẽr-măd'ĕk)	3	30°30'S	177°00'E
Kermān, Iran (kĕr-män')	198	30°23'N	57°08'E
Kermānshāh *see* Bakhtarān, Iran	198	34°01'N	47°00'E
Kern, r., Ca., U.S.	118	35°31'N	118°37'W
Kern, South Fork, r., Ca., U.S.	118	35°40'N	118°15'W
Kerpen, Ger. (kĕr'pĕn)	171c	50°52'N	6°42'E
Kerrobert, Can.	96	51°53'N	109°13'W
Kerrville, Tx., U.S. (kûr'vĭl)	122	30°02'N	99°07'W
Kerulen, r., Asia (kĕr'o͞o-lĕn)	205	47°52'N	113°22'E
Kesagami Lake, l., Can.	99	50°23'N	80°15'W
Keşan, Tur. (kĕ'shȧn)	175	40°50'N	26°37'E
Keshan, China (kŭ-shän)	205	48°00'N	126°30'E

PRONOUNCING INDEX Kesour – Kitgum 309

PLACE (Pronunciation)	PAGE	LAT.	LONG.
Kesour, Monts des, mts., Alg.	162	32°51'N	0°30'W
Kestell, S. Afr. (kĕs'tĕl)	238c	28°19'S	28°43'E
Keszthely, Hung. (kĕst'hĕl-lĭ)	169	46°46'N	17°12'E
Ket', r., Russia (kyĕt)	184	58°30'N	84°15'E
Keta, Ghana	230	6°00'N	1°00'E
Ketamputih, Indon.	197b	1°25'N	102°19'E
Ketapang, Indon. (kĕ-tá-päng')	212	2°00'S	109°57'E
Ketchikan, Ak., U.S. (kĕch-ĭ-kăn')	106a	55°21'N	131°35'W
Kętrzyn, Pol. (kăn't'r-zĭn)	169	54°04'N	21°24'E
Kettering, Eng., U.K. (kĕt'ĕr-ĭng)	158a	52°23'N	0°43'W
Kettering, Oh., U.S.	108	39°40'N	84°15'W
Kettle, r., Can.	95	49°40'N	119°00'W
Kettle, r., Mn., U.S. (kĕt''l)	113	46°20'N	92°57'W
Kettwig, Ger. (kĕt'vēg)	171c	51°22'N	6°56'E
Kęty, Pol. (kăn tĭ)	169	49°54'N	19°16'E
Ketzin, Ger. (kĕ'tzēn)	159b	52°29'N	12°51'E
Keuka, l., N.Y., U.S. (kē-ū'ká)	109	42°30'N	77°10'W
Kevelaer, Ger. (kĕ'fĕ-lär)	171c	51°35'N	6°15'E
Kew, Austl.	217a	37°49'S	145°02'E
Kewanee, Il., U.S. (kē-wä'nē)	113	41°15'N	89°55'W
Kewaunee, Wi., U.S. (kē-wô'nē)	113	44°27'N	87°33'W
Keweenaw Bay, b., Mi., U.S. (kē'wē-nô)	113	46°59'N	88°15'W
Keweenaw Peninsula, pen., Mi., U.S.	113	47°28'N	88°12'W
Keya Paha, r., S.D., U.S. (kē-yá pä'hä)	112	43°11'N	100°10'W
Key Largo, i., Fl., U.S.	125a	25°11'N	80°15'W
Keyport, N.J., U.S. (kē'pōrt)	110a	40°26'N	74°12'W
Keyport, Wa., U.S.	116a	47°42'N	122°38'W
Keyser, W.V., U.S. (kī'sĕr)	109	39°25'N	79°00'W
Key West, Fl., U.S. (kē wĕst')	105	24°31'N	81°47'W
Kežmarok, Slvk. (kĕzh'má-rôk)	169	49°10'N	20°27'E
Khabarovo, Russia (kŭ-bár-ôvô)	178	69°31'N	60°41'E
Khabarovsk, Russia (кä-bä'rôfsk)	179	48°35'N	135°12'E
Khakassia, prov., Russia	184	52°32'N	89°33'E
Khālāpur, India	203b	18°48'N	73°17'E
Khalkidhiki, pen., Grc.	175	40°30'N	23°18'E
Khal'mer-Yu, Russia (kŭl-myĕr'-yōō')	178	67°52'N	64°25'E
Khalturin, Russia (кäl'tōō-rēn)	180	58°28'N	49°00'E
Khambhāt, Gulf of, b., India	199	21°20'N	72°27'E
Khammam, India	203	17°09'N	80°13'E
Khānābād, Afg.	202	36°43'N	69°11'E
Khandwa, India	202	21°53'N	76°22'E
Khaníon, Kólpos, b., Grc.	174a	35°35'N	23°55'E
Khanka, l., Asia (kän'ká)	179	45°09'N	133°28'E
Khānpur, Pak.	202	28°42'N	70°42'E
Khanty-Mansiysk, Russia (kŭn-te'mŭn-sēsk')	178	61°02'N	69°01'E
Khān Yūnus, Gaza	197a	31°21'N	34°19'E
Kharagpur, India (kŭ-rŭg'pŏr)	199	22°26'N	87°21'E
Kharkiv, Ukr.	178	50°00'N	36°10'E
Kharkiv, prov., Ukr.	177	49°33'N	35°55'E
Kharkov *see* Kharkiv, Ukr.	178	50°00'N	36°10'E
Kharlovka, Russia	180	68°47'N	37°20'E
Kharmanli, Blg. (кár-män'lē)	175	41°54'N	25°55'E
Khartoum, Sudan	231	15°34'N	32°36'E
Khasavyurt, Russia	182	43°15'N	46°37'E
Khāsh, Iran	198	28°08'N	61°08'E
Khāsh, r., Afg.	198	32°30'N	64°27'E
Khasi Hills, hills, India	199	25°38'N	91°55'E
Khaskovo, Blg. (кás'kô-vô)	163	41°56'N	25°32'E
Khatanga, Russia (кá-tän'gá)	179	71°48'N	101°47'E
Khatangskiy Zaliv, b., Russia (kä-tän'g-skē)	179	73°45'N	108°30'E
Khaybār, Sau. Ar.	198	25°45'N	39°28'E
Kherson, Ukr. (кĕr-sôn')	181	46°38'N	32°34'E
Kherson, prov., Ukr.	177	46°32'N	32°55'E
Khiitola, Russia (кhē'tō-lá)	167	61°14'N	29°40'E
Khimki, Russia (кēm'kī)	186b	55°54'N	37°27'E
Khmel'nyts'kyi, Ukr.	181	49°29'N	26°54'E
Khmel'nyts'kyy, prov., Ukr.	177	49°27'N	26°30'E
Khmil'nyk, Ukr.	177	49°34'N	27°58'E
Kholm, Russia (кôlm)	176	57°09'N	31°07'E
Kholmsk, Russia (кŭlmsk)	179	47°09'N	142°33'E
Khomeynīshahr, Iran	201	32°41'N	51°31'E
Khon Kaen, Thai.	212	16°37'N	102°41'E
Khopër, r., Russia (кô'pĕr)	181	52°00'N	43°00'E
Khor, Russia (кôr')	210	47°50'N	134°52'E
Khor, r., Russia	210	47°23'N	135°20'E
Khóra Sfakión, Grc.	174a	35°12'N	24°10'E
Khorog, Taj.	183	37°30'N	71°36'E
Khorol, Ukr. (кô'rôl)	177	49°48'N	33°17'E
Khorol, r., Ukr.	177	49°50'N	33°21'E
Khorramābād, Iran	201	33°30'N	48°20'E
Khorramshahr, Iran (kô-ram'shär)	198	30°36'N	48°15'E
Khot'kovo, Russia	186b	56°15'N	38°00'E
Khotyn, Ukr.	181	48°29'N	26°32'E
Khoyniki, Bela.	177	51°54'N	30°00'E
Khudzhand, Taj.	183	40°17'N	69°37'E
Khulna, Bngl.	199	22°50'N	89°38'E
Khūryān Mūryān, is., Oman	198	17°27'N	56°02'E
Khust, Ukr. (кôst)	169	48°10'N	23°18'E
Khvalynsk, Russia (кvá-lĭnsk')	181	52°30'N	48°00'E
Khvoy, Iran	198	38°32'N	45°01'E
Khyber Pass, p., Asia (kī'bĕr)	199	34°28'N	71°18'E
Kialwe, D.R.C.	237	9°22'S	27°08'E
Kiambi, D.R.C. (kyäm'bē)	232	7°20'S	28°01'E
Kiamichi, r., Ok., U.S. (kyá-mē'chē)	121	34°31'N	95°34'W
Kianta, l., Fin. (kyán'tá)	180	65°00'N	28°15'E
Kibenga, D.R.C.	236	7°55'S	17°35'E
Kibiti, Tan.	237	7°44'S	38°57'E
Kibombo, D.R.C.	237	3°54'S	25°55'E
Kibondo, Tan.	237	3°35'S	30°42'E
Kičevo, Mac. (kē'chĕ-vô)	175	41°30'N	20°59'E
Kickapoo, r., Wi., U.S. (kĭk'á-pōō)	113	43°20'N	90°55'W
Kicking Horse Pass, p., Can.	95	51°25'N	116°10'W
Kidal, Mali (kē-dál')	230	18°33'N	1°00'E
Kidderminster, Eng., U.K. (kĭd'ĕr-mĭn-stĕr)	158a	52°23'N	2°14'W
Kidd's Beach, S. Afr. (kĭdz)	233c	33°09'S	27°43'E
Kidsgrove, Eng., U.K. (kĭdz'grōv)	158a	53°05'N	2°15'W
Kiel, Ger. (kēl)	154	54°19'N	10°08'E
Kiel, Wi., U.S.	113	43°52'N	88°04'W
Kiel Bay, b., Ger.	168	54°33'N	10°19'E
Kiel Canal *see* Nord-Ostsee Kanal, can., Ger.	168	54°03'N	9°23'E
Kielce, Pol. (kyĕl'tsĕ)	169	50°50'N	20°41'E
Kieldrecht, Bel. (kēl'drĕĸt)	159a	51°17'N	4°09'E
Kiev (Kyïv), Ukr.	178	50°27'N	30°30'E
Kiffa, Maur. (kēf'á)	230	16°37'N	11°24'W
Kigali, Rw. (kē-gä'lē)	232	1°59'S	30°05'E
Kigoma, Tan. (kē-gō'mä)	232	4°57'S	29°38'E
Kii-Suido, strt., Japan (kē sōō-ē'dō)	210	33°53'N	134°55'E
Kikaiga, i., Japan	210	28°25'N	130°10'E
Kikinda, Serb. (ĸē'kēn-dä)	175	45°49'N	20°30'E
Kikládes, is., Grc.	162	37°30'N	24°45'E
Kikwit, D.R.C. (kē'kwēt)	232	5°02'S	18°49'E
Kil, Swe. (kēl)	166	59°30'N	13°15'E
Kilauea, Hi., U.S. (kē-lä-ōō-ā'ä)	126a	22°12'N	159°25'W
Kilauea Crater, depr., Hi., U.S.	126a	19°28'N	155°18'W
Kilbuck Mountains, mts., Ak., U.S. (kĭl-bŭk)	103	60°05'N	160°00'W
Kilchu, Kor., N. (kĭl'chò)	210	40°59'N	129°23'E
Kildare, Ire. (kĭl-dār')	164	53°09'N	7°05'W
Kilembe, D.R.C.	236	5°42'S	19°55'E
Kilgore, Tx., U.S.	123	32°23'N	94°53'W
Kilia, Ukr.	177	45°28'N	29°17'E
Kilifi, Kenya	237	3°38'S	39°51'E
Kilimanjaro, mtn., Tan. (kyl-ē-män-jä'rô)	233	3°09'S	37°19'E
Kilimatinde, Tan. (kĭl-ē-mä-tĭn'dá)	232	5°48'S	34°58'E
Kilindoni, Tan.	237	7°55'S	39°39'E
Kilingi-Nõmme, Est. (kē'lĭn-gē-nôm'mĕ)	167	58°08'N	25°03'E
Kilis, Tur. (kē'lēs)	163	36°50'N	37°20'E
Kilkenny, Ire. (kĭl-kĕn-ĭ)	161	52°40'N	7°30'W
Kilkis, Grc. (kĭl'kĭs)	175	40°59'N	22°51'E
Killala, Ire. (kĭ-lä'lá)	164	54°11'N	9°10'W
Killarney, Ire.	164	52°03'N	9°05'W
Killdeer, N.D., U.S. (kĭl'dēr)	112	47°22'N	102°45'W
Killiniq Island, i., Can.	93	60°32'N	63°56'W
Kilmarnock, Scot., U.K. (kĭl-mär'nŭk)	164	55°38'N	4°25'W
Kilrush, Ire. (kĭl'rŭsh)	164	52°40'N	9°16'W
Kilwa Kisiwani, Tan.	237	8°58'S	39°30'E
Kilwa Kivinje, Tan.	233	8°43'S	39°18'E
Kim, r., Cam.	235	5°40'N	11°17'E
Kimamba, Tan.	237	6°47'S	37°08'E
Kimba, Austl. (kĭm'bá)	222	33°08'S	136°25'E
Kimball, Ne., U.S. (kĭm-bál)	112	41°14'N	103°41'W
Kimball, S.D., U.S.	112	43°44'N	98°58'W
Kimberley, Can. (kĭm'bĕr-lĭ)	90	49°41'N	115°59'W
Kimberley, S. Afr.	232	28°40'S	24°50'E
Kimi, Cam.	235	6°05'N	11°30'E
Kimmirut (Lake Harbour), Can.	91	62°43'N	69°40'W
Kímolos, i., Grc. (kē'mô-lôs)	175	36°52'N	24°20'E
Kimry, Russia (kĭm'rē)	180	56°53'N	37°24'E
Kimvula, D.R.C.	236	5°44'S	15°58'E
Kinabalu, Gunong, mtn., Malay.	212	5°45'N	115°26'E
Kincardine, Can. (kĭn-kär'dĭn)	91	44°10'N	81°15'W
Kinda, D.R.C.	237	9°18'S	25°04'E
Kindanba, Congo	236	3°44'S	14°31'E
Kinder, La., U.S. (kĭn'dĕr)	123	30°30'N	92°50'W
Kindersley, Can. (kĭn'dĕrz-lē)	90	51°27'N	109°10'W
Kindia, Gui. (kĭn'dē-á)	230	10°04'N	12°51'W
Kindu, D.R.C.	232	2°57'S	25°56'E
Kinel'-Cherkassy, Russia	180	53°32'N	51°32'E
Kineshma, Russia (kē-nĕsh'má)	180	57°27'N	41°02'E
King, i., Austl. (kĭng)	221	39°35'S	143°40'E
Kingaroy, Austl. (kĭŋ'gă-roi)	222	26°37'S	151°50'E
King City, Can.	102d	43°56'N	79°32'W
King City, Ca., U.S. (kĭng sĭ'tĭ)	118	36°12'N	121°08'W
Kingcome Inlet, b., Can. (kĭng'kŭm)	94	50°50'N	126°10'W
Kingfisher, Ok., U.S. (kĭng'fĭsh-ĕr)	121	35°51'N	97°55'W
King George Sound, strt., Austl. (jôrj)	220	35°17'S	118°30'E
Kingisepp, Russia (kĭŋ-gē-sep')	180	59°22'N	28°38'E
King Leopold Ranges, mts., Austl. (lē'ô-pōld)	220	16°25'S	125°00'E
Kingman, Az., U.S. (kĭng'măn)	119	35°10'N	114°05'W
Kingman, Ks., U.S. (kĭng'măn)	120	37°38'N	98°07'W
Kings, r., Ca., U.S.	118	36°28'N	119°43'W
Kings Canyon National Park, rec., Ca., U.S. (kăn'yŭn)	106	36°52'N	118°53'W
Kingsclere, Eng., U.K. (kĭngs-clēr)	158b	51°18'N	1°15'W
Kingscote, Austl. (kĭngz'kŭt)	222	35°45'S	137°32'E
King's Lynn, Eng., U.K. (kĭngz lĭn')	165	52°45'N	0°20'E
Kings Mountain, N.C., U.S.	125	35°13'N	81°30'W
Kings Norton, Eng., U.K. (nôr'tŭn)	158a	52°25'N	1°54'W
King Sound, strt., Austl.	220	16°50'S	123°35'E
Kings Park, N.Y., U.S. (kĭngz pärk)	110a	40°53'N	73°16'W
Kings Peak, mtn., Ut., U.S.	106	40°46'N	110°20'W
Kingsport, Tn., U.S. (kĭngz'pōrt)	125	36°33'N	82°36'W
Kingston, Austl. (kĭngz'tŭn)	218	37°52'S	139°52'E
Kingston, Can.	91	44°15'N	76°30'W
Kingston, Jam.	129	18°00'N	76°45'W
Kingston, N.Y., U.S.	105	42°00'N	74°00'W
Kingston, Pa., U.S.	109	41°15'N	75°50'W
Kingston, Wa., U.S.	116a	47°04'N	122°29'W
Kingston upon Hull, Eng., U.K.	154	53°45'N	0°25'W
Kingstown, St. Vin. (kĭngz'toun)	129	13°10'N	61°14'W
Kingstree, S.C., U.S. (kĭngz'trē)	125	33°30'N	79°50'W
Kingsville, Tx., U.S. (kĭngz'vĭl)	123	27°32'N	97°52'W
King William Island, i., Can. (kĭng wĭl'yăm)	92	69°25'N	97°00'W
King William's Town, S. Afr. (kĭng-wĭl'-yŭmz-toun)	233c	32°53'S	27°24'E
Kinira, r., S. Afr.	233c	30°37'S	28°52'E
Kinloch, Mo., U.S. (kĭn-lŏk)	117e	38°44'N	90°19'W
Kinnaird, Can. (kĭn-ärd')	95	49°17'N	117°39'W
Kinnairds Head, c., Scot., U.K. (kĭn-ârds'hĕd)	160	57°42'N	3°55'W
Kinomoto, Japan (kē'nō-mō'tō)	211	33°53'N	136°07'E
Kinosaki, Japan (kē'nō-sä'kē)	211	35°38'N	134°47'E
Kinshasa, D.R.C.	232	4°18'S	15°18'E
Kinsley, Ks., U.S. (kĭnz'lĭ)	120	37°55'N	99°24'W
Kinston, N.C., U.S. (kĭnz'tŭn)	125	35°15'N	77°35'W
Kintampo, Ghana (kēn-täm'pō)	230	8°03'N	1°43'W
Kintyre, pen., Scot., U.K.	164	55°50'N	5°40'W
Kiowa, Ks., U.S. (kī'ô-wá)	120	37°01'N	98°30'W
Kiowa, Ok., U.S.	121	34°42'N	95°53'W
Kipawa, Lac, l., Can.	99	46°55'N	79°00'W
Kipembawe, Tan. (kē-pĕm-bä'wá)	232	7°39'S	33°24'E
Kipengere Range, mts., Tan.	237	9°10'S	34°00'E
Kipili, Tan.	237	7°26'S	30°36'E
Kipushi, D.R.C.	237	11°46'S	27°14'E
Kirakira, Sol. Is.	214e	10°27'S	161°55'E
Kirby, Tx., U.S. (kŭr'bĭ)	117d	29°29'N	98°23'W
Kirbyville, Tx., U.S. (kŭr'bĭ-vĭl)	123	30°39'N	93°54'W
Kirenga, r., Russia (kē-rĕn'gá)	185	56°30'N	108°18'E
Kirensk, Russia (kē-rĕnsk')	179	57°47'N	108°22'E
Kirgiz Range, mts., Asia	183	42°30'N	74°00'E
Kiri, D.R.C.	236	1°27'S	19°00'E
Kiribati, nation, Oc.	3	1°30'S	173°00'E
Kirin *see* Chilung, Tai.	205	25°02'N	121°48'E
Kiritimati, i., Kir.	2	2°20'N	157°40'W
Kirkby, Eng., U.K.	158a	53°29'N	2°54'W
Kirkby-in-Ashfield, Eng., U.K. (kûrk'bē-ĭn-ăsh'fēld)	158a	53°06'N	1°16'W
Kirkcaldy, Scot., U.K. (kĕr-kô'dĭ)	164	56°06'N	3°15'W
Kirkenes, Nor.	160	69°40'N	30°03'E
Kirkham, Eng., U.K. (kûrk'ăm)	158a	53°47'N	2°53'W
Kirkland, Wa., U.S. (kûrk'lănd)	116a	47°41'N	122°12'W
Kirklareli, Tur. (kêrk'lâr-ĕ'lē)	163	41°44'N	27°15'E
Kirksville, Mo., U.S. (kûrks'vĭl)	105	40°12'N	92°35'W
Kirkwall, Scot., U.K. (kûrk'wôl)	160	58°58'N	2°59'W
Kirkwood, S. Afr.	233c	33°26'S	25°24'E
Kirkwood, Mo., U.S. (kûrk'wòd)	117e	38°35'N	90°24'W
Kirn, Ger. (kērn)	168	49°47'N	7°23'E
Kirov, Russia	176	54°04'N	34°19'E
Kirov, Russia	178	58°35'N	49°35'E
Kirovakan, Arm.	182	40°48'N	44°30'E
Kirovgrad, Russia (kē'rŭ-vŭ-grad)	186a	57°26'N	60°03'E
Kirovohrad, Ukr.	181	48°33'N	32°17'E
Kirovohrad, prov., Ukr.	177	48°23'N	31°10'E
Kirovsk, Russia (kē-rôfsk')	186c	59°52'N	30°59'E
Kirovsk, Russia	178	67°40'N	33°58'E
Kirsanov, Russia (kēr-sá'nôf)	181	52°40'N	42°40'E
Kırşehir, Tur. (kêr-shĕ'hēr)	198	39°10'N	34°00'E
Kirtachi Seybou, Niger	235	12°48'N	2°29'E
Kirthar Range, mts., Pak. (kĭr-tŭr)	199	27°00'N	67°10'E
Kirton, Eng., U.K. (kûr'tŭn)	158a	53°29'N	0°35'W
Kiruna, Swe. (kē-rōō'nä)	160	67°49'N	20°08'E
Kirundu, D.R.C.	237	0°44'S	25°32'E
Kirwin Reservoir, res., Ks., U.S. (kûr'wĭn)	120	39°34'N	99°04'W
Kiryū, Japan	210	36°24'N	139°20'E
Kirzhach, Russia (kēr-zhák')	176	56°08'N	38°53'E
Kisaki, Tan. (kē-sá'kē)	233	7°37'S	37°43'E
Kisangani, D.R.C.	231	0°30'N	25°12'E
Kisarazu, Japan (kē'sá-rá'zōō)	211a	35°23'N	139°55'E
Kiselëvsk, Russia (kē-sĭ-lyôfsk')	178	54°00'N	86°39'E
Kishinev *see* Chişinău, Mol.	178	47°02'N	28°52'E
Kishiwada, Japan (kē'shē-wä'dä)	210	34°25'N	135°18'E
Kishkino, Russia (kĕsh'kĭ-nô)	186b	55°15'N	38°04'E
Kisiwani, Tan.	237	4°08'S	37°57'E
Kiska, i., Ak., U.S. (kĭs'kä)	106b	52°08'N	177°10'E
Kiskatinaw, r., Can.	95	55°10'N	120°20'W
Kiskittogisu Lake, l., Can.	97	54°05'N	99°00'W
Kiskitto Lake, l., Can. (kĭs-kĭ'tō)	97	54°16'N	98°34'W
Kiskunfélegyháza, Hung. (kĭsh'kòn-fā'lĕd-y'hä'zô)	169	46°42'N	19°52'E
Kiskunhalas, Hung. (kĭsh'kòn-hô'lôsh)	169	46°24'N	19°26'E
Kiskunmajsa, Hung. (kĭsh'kòn-mī'shô)	169	46°29'N	19°42'E
Kislovodsk, Russia	182	43°55'N	42°44'E
Kismaayo, Som.	233	0°18'S	42°30'E
Kiso-Gawa, r., Japan (kē'sō-gä'wä)	211	35°29'N	137°12'E
Kiso-Sammyaku, mts., Japan (kē'sō säm'myä-kōō)	211	35°47'N	137°39'E
Kissamos, Grc.	174a	35°13'N	23°35'E
Kissidougou, Gui. (kē'sē-dōō'gōō)	230	9°11'N	10°06'W
Kissimmee, Fl., U.S. (kĭ-sĭm'ē)	125a	28°17'N	81°25'W
Kissimmee, r., Fl., U.S.	125a	27°45'N	81°07'W
Kissimmee, Lake, l., Fl., U.S.	125a	27°58'N	81°17'W
Kisujszallás, Hung.	169	47°12'N	20°47'E
Kisumu, Kenya (kē'sōō-mōō)	232	0°06'S	34°45'E
Kita, Mali (kē'tá)	230	13°03'N	9°29'W
Kitakami Gawa, r., Japan	210	39°20'N	141°10'E
Kitakyūshū, Japan	205	33°53'N	130°50'E
Kitale, Kenya	237	1°01'N	35°00'E
Kit Carson, Co., U.S.	120	38°46'N	102°48'W
Kitchener, Can. (kĭch'ĕ-nĕr)	91	43°25'N	80°35'W
Kitenda, D.R.C.	236	6°53'S	17°21'E
Kitgum, Ug. (kĭt'gòm)	231	3°29'N	33°04'E

ng-sing; ŋ-baŋk; ɴ-nasalized n; nŏd; cŏmmit; ōld; ôbey; ôrder; oi-boil; fōōd; ò-as oo in foot; ou-out; s-soft; sh-dish; th-thin; pūre; ûnite; ûrn; stŭd; circŭs; ü-as in French tu; '-indeterminate vowel.

310 Kitimat – Kozhikode PRONOUNCING INDEX

PLACE (Pronunciation)	PAGE	LAT.	LONG.
Kitimat, Can. (kĭ´tĭ-măt)	90	54°03'N	128°33'W
Kitimat, r., Can.	94	53°50'N	129°00'W
Kitimat Ranges, mts., Can.	94	53°30'N	128°50'W
Kitlope, r., Can. (kĭt´lōp)	94	53°00'N	128°00'W
Kitsuki, Japan (kėt´sȯ-kė)	211	33°24'N	131°35'E
Kittanning, Pa., U.S. (kĭ-tăn´ĭng)	109	40°50'N	79°30'W
Kittatinny Mountains, mts., N.J., U.S. (kĭ-tŭ-tĭ´nė)	110a	41°16'N	74°44'W
Kittery, Me., U.S. (kĭt´ĕr-ĭ)	100	43°07'N	70°45'W
Kittsee, Aus.	159e	48°05'N	17°05'E
Kitty Hawk, N.C., U.S. (kĭt´ė hôk)	125	36°04'N	75°42'W
Kitunda, Tan.	237	6°48'S	33°13'E
Kitwe, Zam.	237	12°49'S	28°13'E
Kitzingen, Ger. (kĭt´zĭng-ĕn)	168	49°44'N	10°08'E
Kiunga, Kenya	237	1°45'S	41°29'E
Kivu, Lac, l., Afr.	232	1°45'S	28°55'E
Kīyose, Japan	211a	35°47'N	139°32'E
Kizel, Russia (kē´zĕl)	180	59°05'N	57°42'E
Kızıl, r., Tur.	198	40°00'N	34°00'E
Kizil'skoye, Russia (kĭz´ĭl-skô-yĕ)	186a	52°43'N	58°53'E
Kizlyar, Russia (kĭz-lyär´)	181	44°00'N	46°50'E
Kizlyarskiy Zaliv, b., Russia	182	44°33'N	46°55'E
Kizu, Japan (kē´zōō)	211	34°43'N	135°49'E
Klaas Smits, r., S. Afr.	233c	31°45'S	26°33'E
Klaaswaal, Neth.	159a	51°46'N	4°25'E
Kladno, Czech Rep. (kläd´nō)	168	50°10'N	14°05'E
Klagenfurt, Aus. (klä´gĕn-fȯrt)	161	46°38'N	14°19'E
Klaipéda, Lith. (klī´pȧ-dȧ)	180	55°43'N	21°10'E
Klamath, r., U.S.	114	41°40'N	123°25'W
Klamath Falls, Or., U.S.	104	42°13'N	121°49'W
Klamath Mountains, mts., Ca., U.S.	114	42°00'N	123°25'W
Klarälven, r., Swe.	160	60°40'N	13°00'E
Klaskanine, r., Or., U.S. (klăs´kȧ-nīn)	116c	46°02'N	123°43'W
Klatovy, Czech Rep. (klȧ´tȯ-vė)	161	49°23'N	13°18'E
Klawock, Ak., U.S. (klā´wăk)	103	55°32'N	133°10'W
Kleinmachnow, Ger. (klīn-mäĸ´nō)	159b	52°22'N	13°12'E
Klerksdorp, S. Afr. (klĕrks´dôrp)	238c	26°52'S	26°40'E
Klerksraal, S. Afr. (klĕrks´kräl)	238c	26°15'N	27°10'E
Kletnya, Russia (klyĕt´nyȧ)	176	53°19'N	33°14'E
Kleve, Ger. (klĕ´fĕ)	168	51°47'N	6°09'E
Klickitat, r., Wa., U.S.	114	46°01'N	121°07'W
Klimovichi, Bela. (klē-mȯ-vē´chė)	176	53°37'N	31°21'E
Klimovsk, Russia (klĭ´môfsk)	186b	55°21'N	37°32'E
Klin, Russia (klėn)	176	56°18'N	36°43'E
Klintehamn, Swe. (klēn´tē-häm)	166	57°24'N	18°14'E
Klintsy, Russia (klĭn´tsĭ)	181	52°46'N	32°14'E
Klip, r., S. Afr. (klĭp)	238c	27°18'N	29°25'E
Klipgat, S. Afr.	238c	25°26'S	27°57'E
Klippan, Swe. (klyp´pȧn)	166	56°08'N	13°09'E
Kłodzko, Pol. (klôd´skȯ)	168	50°26'N	16°38'E
Klondike Region, hist. reg., N.A. (klŏn´dīk)	90	64°12'N	142°38'W
Klosterfelde, Ger. (klōs´tĕr-fĕl-dĕ)	159b	52°47'N	13°29'E
Klosterneuburg, Aus. (klōs-tĕr-noi´bōōrgh)	159e	48°19'N	16°20'E
Kluane, l., Can.	92	61°15'N	138°40'W
Kluane National Park, rec., Can.	92	60°25'N	137°53'W
Kluczbork, Pol. (klōōch´bōrk)	169	50°59'N	18°15'E
Klyaz'ma, r., Russia (klyäz´mȧ)	176	55°49'N	39°19'E
Klyetsk, Bela. (klĕtsk)	176	53°04'N	26°43'E
Klyuchevskaya, vol., Russia (klyōō-chĕfskä´yä)	179	56°13'N	160°00'E
Klyuchi, Russia (klyōō´chĭ)	186a	57°03'N	57°20'E
Knezha, Blg. (knyā´zhȧ)	163	43°27'N	24°03'E
Knife, r., N.D., U.S. (nīf)	112	47°06'N	102°33'W
Knight Inlet, b., Can. (nīt)	94	50°41'N	125°40'W
Knightstown, In., U.S. (nīts´toun)	108	39°45'N	85°30'W
Knin, Cro. (knēn)	174	44°02'N	16°14'E
Knittelfeld, Aus.	161	47°13'N	14°50'E
Knob Peak, mtn., Phil. (nŏb)	213a	12°30'N	121°20'E
Knottingley, Eng., U.K. (nŏt´ĭng-lĭ)	158a	53°42'N	1°14'W
Knox, In., U.S. (nŏks)	108	41°15'N	86°40'W
Knox, Cape, c., Can.	94	54°12'N	133°20'W
Knoxville, Ia., U.S. (nŏks´vĭl)	113	41°19'N	93°05'W
Knoxville, Tn., U.S.	105	35°58'N	83°55'W
Knutsford, Eng., U.K. (nŭts´fĕrd)	158a	53°18'N	2°22'W
Knyszyn, Pol. (knĭ´shĭn)	169	53°16'N	22°59'E
Kobayashi, Japan (kō´bȧ-yä´shė)	211	31°58'N	130°59'E
Kōbe, Japan (kō´bĕ)	205	34°30'N	135°10'E
Kobeliaky, Ukr.	181	49°11'N	34°12'E
København *see* Copenhagen, Den.	154	55°43'N	12°27'E
Koblenz, Ger. (kō´blĕntz)	161	50°18'N	7°36'E
Kobozha, r., Russia (kȯ-bō´zhȧ)	176	58°55'N	35°18'E
Kobrinskoye, Russia (kô-brĭn´skô-yĕ)	186c	59°25'N	30°07'E
Kobryn, Bela. (kō´brėn´)	181	52°13'N	24°23'E
Kobuk, r., Ak., U.S. (kō´bŭk)	103	66°58'N	158°48'W
Kobuk Valley National Park, rec., Ak., U.S.	103	67°20'N	159°00'W
Kobuleti, Geor. (kȯ-bȯ-lyā´tė)	181	41°50'N	41°40'E
Kočani, Mac. (kô´chä-nĕ)	175	41°54'N	22°25'E
Kočevje, Slvn. (kô´chāv-ye)	174	45°38'N	14°51'E
Kocher, r., Ger. (kȯĸ´ĕr)	168	49°00'N	9°52'E
Kochi, India	203	9°58'N	76°19'E
Kōchi, Japan (kō´chė)	205	33°35'N	133°32'E
Kodaira, Japan	211a	35°43'N	139°29'E
Kodiak, Ak., U.S. (kō´dyăk)	106a	57°50'N	152°30'W
Kodiak Island, i., Ak., U.S.	103	57°24'N	153°32'W
Kodok, Sudan (ko´dŏk)	231	9°57'N	32°08'E
Koforidua, Ghana (kō fȯ-rĭ-dōō´ȧ)	230	6°03'N	0°17'W
Kōfu, Japan (kō´fōō´)	210	35°41'N	138°34'E
Koga, Japan (kō´gȧ)	211	36°13'N	139°40'E
Kogan, r., Gui.	234	11°30'N	14°05'W
Kogane, Japan (kō´gä-nȧ)	211a	35°50'N	139°56'E
Koganei, Japan (kō´gä-nā)	211a	35°42'N	139°31'E
Køge, Den. (kû´gĕ)	166	55°27'N	12°09'E
Køge Bugt, b., Den.	166	55°30'N	12°25'E
Kogoni, Mali	234	14°44'N	6°02'W
Kohīma, India (kȯ-ē´mȧ)	199	25°45'N	94°41'E
Kohyl'nyk, r., Eur.	177	46°08'N	29°10'E
Koito, r., Japan (kȯ´ê-tō)	211a	35°19'N	139°58'E
Kŏje, i., Kor., S. (kû´jĕ)	210	34°53'N	129°00'E
Kokand, Uzb. (kȯ-känt´)	183	40°27'N	71°07'E
Kokemäenjoki, r., Fin.	167	61°23'N	22°03'E
Kokhma, Russia (kôĸ´mȧ)	176	56°57'N	41°08'E
Kokkola, Fin. (kô´kȯ-lȧ)	160	63°47'N	22°58'E
Kokomo, In., U.S. (kō´kȯ-mȯ)	108	40°30'N	86°20'W
Koko Nor (Qinghai Hu), l., China (kō´kȯ nor) (chyĭŋ-hī hōō)	204	37°26'N	98°30'E
Kokopo, Pap. N. Gui. (kȯ-kȯ´pō)	213	4°25'S	152°27'E
Kökshetaū, Kaz.	183	53°15'N	69°13'E
Koksoak, r., Can. (kȯk´sȯ-ăk)	93	57°42'N	69°50'W
Kokstad, S. Afr. (kȯk´shtät)	233c	30°33'S	29°27'E
Kokubu, Japan (kō´kōō-bōō)	211	31°42'N	130°46'E
Kokuou, Japan (kȯ´kōō-ȯ´ōōo)	211b	34°34'N	135°39'E
Kola Peninsula *see* Kol'skiy Poluostrov, pen., Russia	178	67°15'N	37°40'E
Kolār (Kolār Gold Fields), India (kȯl-är´)	199	13°39'N	78°33'E
Kolárvo, Slvk. (kōl-árōvō)	169	47°54'N	17°59'E
Kolbio, Kenya	237	1°10'S	41°15'E
Kol'chugino, Russia (kȯl-chȯ´gė-nô)	176	56°19'N	39°29'E
Kolda, Sen.	234	12°53'N	14°57'W
Kolding, Den. (kŭl´dĭng)	166	55°29'N	9°24'E
Kole, D.R.C. (kō´lȧ)	232	3°19'S	22°46'E
Kolguyev, i., Russia (kȯl-gȯ´yĕf)	178	69°00'N	49°00'E
Kolhāpur, India	203	16°48'N	74°15'E
Kolin, Czech Rep. (kō´lēn)	168	50°01'N	15°11'E
Kolkasrags, c., Lat. (kôl-käs´rȧgz)	167	57°46'N	22°39'E
Kolkata (Calcutta), India	199	22°32'N	88°22'E
Köln *see* Cologne, Ger.	171c	50°56'N	6°57'E
Kolno, Pol. (kôw´nȯ)	169	53°23'N	21°56'E
Koło, Pol. (kô´wȯ)	169	52°11'N	18°37'E
Kołobrzeg, Pol. (kȯ-lôb´zhĕk)	160	54°10'N	15°35'E
Kolomna, Russia (kȧl-ȯm´nȧ)	180	55°06'N	38°47'E
Kolomyia, Ukr.	169	48°32'N	25°04'E
Kolp', r., Russia (kôlp)	176	59°18'N	35°32'E
Kolpashevo, Russia (kŭl pȧ shô´vȧ)	178	58°16'N	82°43'E
Kolpino, Russia (kôl´pė-nȯ)	180	59°45'N	30°37'E
Kolpny, Russia (kôlp´nyė)	176	52°14'N	36°54'E
Kol'skiy Poluostrov, pen., Russia	178	67°15'N	37°40'E
Kolva, r., Russia	180	61°00'N	57°00'E
Kolwezi, D.R.C. (kōl-wĕ´zē)	232	10°43'S	25°28'E
Kolyberovo, Russia (kȯ-lĭ-byâ´rô-vô)	186b	55°16'N	38°45'E
Kolyma, r., Russia	179	66°30'N	151°45'E
Kolymskiy Mountains *see* Gydan, Khrebet, mts., Russia	179	61°45'N	155°00'E
Kom, r., Afr.	236	2°15'N	12°05'E
Komadugu Gana, r., Nig.	235	12°15'N	11°10'E
Komae, Japan	211a	35°37'N	139°35'E
Komandorskiye Ostrova, is., Russia	197	55°40'N	167°13'E
Komárno, Slvk. (kȯ´mär-nȯ)	169	47°46'N	18°08'E
Komarno, Ukr.	169	49°38'N	23°42'E
Komárom, Hung. (kȯ´mä-rȯm)	169	47°45'N	18°06'E
Komatipoort, S. Afr. (kō-mä´tė-pōrt)	232	25°21'S	32°00'E
Komatsu, Japan (kō-mät´sōō)	210	36°23'N	136°26'E
Komatsushima, Japan (kō-mät´sōō-shė´mä)	211	34°04'N	134°32'E
Komeshia, D.R.C.	237	8°01'S	27°07'E
Komga, S. Afr. (kōm´gȧ)	233c	32°36'S	27°54'E
Komi, prov., Russia (kȯmė)	184	63°00'N	55°00'E
Kommetijie, S. Afr.	232a	34°09'S	18°19'E
Komoé, r., C. Iv.	234	5°40'N	3°40'W
Komsomolets, Kaz.	186a	53°45'N	62°04'E
Komsomol'sk-na-Amure, Russia	179	50°46'N	137°14'E
Kona, Mali	234	14°57'N	3°53'W
Konda, r., Russia (kȯn´dȧ)	180	60°50'N	64°00'E
Kondas, r., Russia (kȯn´dȧs)	186a	59°30'N	56°28'E
Kondoa, Tan. (kȯn-dō´ȧ)	232	4°52'S	36°00'E
Kondolole, D.R.C.	237	1°20'N	25°58'E
Koné, N. Cal.	214f	21°04'S	164°52'E
Kong, C. Iv. (kông)	230	9°05'N	4°41'W
Kongbo, C.A.R.	236	4°44'N	21°23'E
Kongolo, D.R.C. (kôŋ´gō´lō)	232	5°23'S	27°00'E
Kongsberg, Nor. (kŭngs´bĕrg)	166	59°40'N	9°36'E
Kongsvinger, Nor. (kŭngs´vĭŋ-gĕr)	166	60°12'N	12°00'E
Koni, D.R.C. (kō´nē)	232	10°32'S	27°27'E
Königsberg *see* Kaliningrad, Russia	178	54°42'N	20°32'E
Königsbrunn, Ger. (kû´nēgs-brōōn)	159d	48°16'N	10°53'E
Königs Wusterhausen, Ger. (kû´nēgs vōōs´tĕr-hou-zĕn)	159b	52°18'N	13°38'E
Konin, Pol. (kô´nyėn)	161	52°11'N	18°17'E
Kónitsa, Grc. (kȯ´nyē´tsȧ)	175	40°03'N	20°46'E
Konjic, Bos. (kôn´yēts)	175	43°38'N	17°59'E
Konju, Kor., S.	210	36°21'N	127°05'E
Konnagar, India	202a	22°41'N	88°22'E
Konotop, Ukr. (kȯ-nȯ-tôp´)	181	51°13'N	33°14'E
Konpienga, r., Burkina	234	11°15'N	0°35'E
Konqi, r., China (kȯn-chyē)	204	41°09'N	87°46'E
Końskie, Pol. (koin´´skyĕ)	169	51°12'N	20°26'E
Konstanz, Ger. (kȯn´shtänts)	168	47°39'N	9°10'E
Kontagora, Nig. (kōn-tȧ-gō´rä)	230	10°24'N	5°28'E
Konya, Tur. (kōn´yȧ)	198	36°55'N	32°25'E
Koocanusa, Lake, res., N.A.	114	49°00'N	115°10'W
Kootenay (Kootenai), r., N.A.	95	49°45'N	117°05'W
Kootenay Lake, l., Can.	95	49°35'N	116°50'W
Kootenay National Park, rec., Can. (kōō´tė-nȧ)	90	51°06'N	117°02'W
Kōō-zan, mtn., Japan (kōō´zän)	211b	34°53'N	135°32'E
Kopervik, Nor. (kô´pĕr-vėk)	166	59°18'N	5°20'E
Kopeysk, Russia (kȯ-pāsk´)	184	55°07'N	61°37'E
Köping, Swe. (chû´pĭng)	166	59°32'N	15°58'E
Kopparberg, Swe. (kŏp´pȧr-bĕrgh)	166	59°53'N	15°00'E
Koppeh Dāgh, mts., Asia	198	37°28'N	58°29'E
Koppies, S. Afr.	238c	27°15'S	27°35'E
Koprivnica, Cro. (kô´prēv-nė´tsȧ)	174	46°10'N	16°48'E
Kopychyntsi, Ukr.	169	49°06'N	25°55'E
Korčula, i., Serb. (kȯr´chōō-lȧ)	175	42°50'N	17°05'E
Korea, North, nation, Asia	205	40°00'N	127°00'E
Korea, South, nation, Asia	205	36°30'N	128°00'E
Korea Bay, b., Asia	208	39°18'N	123°50'E
Korean Archipelago, is., Kor., S.	205	34°05'N	125°35'E
Korea Strait, strt., Asia	205	33°30'N	128°30'E
Korets', Ukr.	169	50°35'N	27°13'E
Korhogo, C. Iv. (kȯr-hō´gō)	230	9°27'N	5°38'W
Korinthiakós Kólpos, b., Grc.	163	38°15'N	22°33'E
Kórinthos, Grc. (kȯ-rėn´thȯs) (kŏr´ĭnth)	154	37°56'N	22°54'E
Koriukivka, Ukr.	177	51°44'N	32°24'E
Kōriyama, Japan (kō´rė-yä´mä)	210	37°18'N	140°25'E
Korkino, Russia (kôr´kē-nŭ)	186a	54°53'N	61°25'E
Korla, China (kōr-lä)	204	41°37'N	86°03'E
Körmend, Hung. (kûr´mĕnt)	168	47°02'N	16°36'E
Kornat, i., Serb. (kȯr-nät´)	174	43°46'N	15°10'E
Korneuburg, Aus. (kȯr´noi-bȯrgh)	159e	48°22'N	16°21'E
Koro, Mali	234	14°04'N	3°05'W
Korocha, Russia (kȯ-rō´chȧ)	177	50°50'N	37°13'E
Korop, Ukr. (kō´rôp)	177	51°33'N	32°54'E
Koro Sea, sea, Fiji	214g	18°00'S	179°50'E
Korosten', Ukr. (kô´rȯs-tĕn)	181	50°51'N	28°39'E
Korostyshiv, Ukr.	177	50°19'N	29°05'E
Koro Toro, Chad	235	16°05'N	18°30'E
Korotoyak, Russia (kȯ´rȯ-tȯ-yȧk´)	177	51°00'N	39°06'E
Korsakov, Russia (kôr´sȧ-kôf´)	179	46°42'N	143°16'E
Korsnäs, Fin. (kôrs´nĕs)	167	62°51'N	21°17'E
Korsør, Den. (kôrs´ûr´)	166	55°19'N	11°08'E
Kortrijk, Bel.	165	50°49'N	3°10'E
Koryakskiy Khrebet, mts., Russia	179	62°00'N	168°45'E
Kosa Byriuchyi ostriv, i., Ukr.	177	46°07'N	35°12'E
Kościan, Pol. (kŭsh´tsyȧn)	168	52°05'N	16°38'E
Kościerzyna, Pol. (kŭsh tsyĕ-zhē´nȧ)	169	54°08'N	17°59'E
Kosciusko, Ms., U.S. (kŏs-ĭ-ŭs´kō)	124	33°04'N	89°35'W
Kosciuszko, Mount, mtn., Austl.	221	36°26'S	148°20'E
Kosha, Sudan	231	20°49'N	30°27'E
Koshigaya, Japan (kȯ´shė-gä´yä)	211a	35°53'N	139°48'E
Köshim, r., Kaz.	181	50°30'N	50°40'E
Kosi, r., India (kȯ´sē)	202	26°00'N	86°20'E
Košice, Slvk. (kō´shė-tsĕ´)	161	48°43'N	21°17'E
Kosmos, S. Afr. (kŏz´mŏs)	233b	25°45'S	27°51'E
Kosobrodskiy, Russia (kä-sô´brȯd-skĭ)	186a	54°14'N	60°53'E
Kosovo, hist. reg., Serb.	175	42°35'N	21°00'E
Kosovska Mitrovica, Serb. (kȯ´sôv-skä´ mė´trȯ-vė-tsä´)	175	42°51'N	20°50'E
Kostajnica, Cro. (kôs´tä-ė-nē´tsȧ)	174	45°14'N	16°32'E
Koster, S. Afr.	238c	25°52'S	26°52'E
Kostiantynivka, Ukr.	177	48°33'N	37°42'E
Kostino, Russia (kôs´tĭ-nô)	186b	55°54'N	37°51'E
Kostroma, Russia (kȯs-trȯ-mȧ´)	178	57°46'N	40°55'E
Kostroma, prov., Russia	176	57°50'N	41°10'E
Kostrzyn, Pol. (kôst´chėn)	161	52°35'N	14°38'E
Kos'va, r., Russia (kôs´vȧ)	186a	58°44'N	57°08'E
Koszalin, Pol. (kô-shä´lĭn)	160	54°12'N	16°10'E
Köszeg, Hung. (kû´sĕg)	168	47°21'N	16°32'E
Kota, India	199	25°17'N	75°49'E
Kota Baharu, Malay. (kō´tä bä´rōō)	212	6°15'N	102°23'E
Kotabaru, Indon.	212	3°22'S	116°15'E
Kota Kinabalu, Malay.	212	5°55'N	116°05'E
Kota Tinggi, Malay.	197b	1°43'N	103°54'E
Kotel, Blg. (kō-tĕl´)	175	42°54'N	26°28'E
Kotel'nich, Russia (kȯ-tyĕl´nėch)	180	58°15'N	48°20'E
Kotel'nyy, i., Russia (kȯ-tyĕl´nė)	179	74°51'N	134°09'E
Kotka, Fin. (kŏt´kȧ)	160	60°28'N	26°56'E
Kotlas, Russia (kôt´lȧs)	180	61°10'N	46°50'E
Kotlin, Ostrov, i., Russia (ȯs-trôf´ kôt´lĭn)	186c	60°02'N	29°49'E
Kotor, Serb.	175	42°25'N	18°46'E
Kotorosl', r., Russia (kȯ-tô´rȯsl)	176	57°18'N	39°08'E
Kotovs'k, Ukr.	177	47°49'N	29°31'E
Kotto, r., C.A.R.	231	5°17'N	22°04'E
Kotuy, r., Russia (kô-tōō´)	184	71°00'N	103°15'E
Kotzebue, Ak., U.S. (kȯt´sē-bōō)	106a	66°48'N	162°42'W
Kotzebue Sound, strt., Ak., U.S.	103	67°00'N	164°28'W
Kouchibouguac National Park, rec., Can.	100	46°53'N	65°35'W
Koudougou, Burkina (kōō-dōō´gōō)	230	12°15'N	2°22'W
Kouilou, r., Congo	232	4°30'S	12°00'E
Koula-Moutou, Gabon	236	1°08'S	12°29'E
Koulikoro, Mali (kōō-lė-kō´rȯ)	230	12°53'N	7°33'W
Koulouguidi, Mali	235	13°27'N	17°33'E
Koumac, N. Cal.	214f	20°33'S	164°17'E
Koumra, Chad	235	8°55'N	17°33'E
Koundara, Gui.	234	12°29'N	13°18'W
Kouroussa, Gui. (kōō-rōō´sä)	230	10°39'N	9°53'W
Koutiala, Mali (kōō-tė-ä´lä)	230	12°29'N	5°29'W
Kouvola, Fin. (kō´ȯ-vȯ-lä)	167	60°51'N	26°40'E
Kouzhen, China (kō-jŭn)	206	36°19'N	117°37'E
Kovda, l., Russia (kôv´dȧ)	180	66°45'N	32°00'E
Kovel', Ukr. (kō´vĕl)	181	51°13'N	24°45'E
Kovno *see* Kaunas, Lith.	178	54°42'N	23°54'E
Kovrov, Russia (kȯv-rôf´)	180	56°23'N	41°21'E
Koyuk, Ak., U.S. (kȯ-yōōk´)	103	65°00'N	161°18'W
Koyukuk, r., Ak., U.S. (kȯ-yōō´kȯk)	103	66°25'N	153°50'W
Kozáni, Grc.	163	40°16'N	21°51'E
Kozelets', Ukr. (kȯzĕ-lyĕts)	177	50°53'N	31°07'E
Kozel'sk, Russia (kȯ-zĕlsk´)	176	54°01'N	35°49'E
Kozhikode, India	199	11°19'N	75°49'E

ăt; finăl; rāte; senåte; ärm; åsk; sofȧ; fâre; ch-choose; dh-as th in other; bē; ėvent; bĕt; recĕnt; cratẽr; g-gō; gh-guttural g; bĭt; ĭ-short neutral; rīde; ĸ-guttural k as ch in German ich;

PRONOUNCING INDEX Koziatyn – Lábrea 311

PLACE (Pronunciation)	PAGE	LAT.	LONG.
Koziatyn, Ukr.	181	49°43'N	28°50'E
Kozienice, Pol. (kō-zyĕ-nē'tsĕ)	169	51°34'N	21°35'E
Koźle, Pol. (kôzh'lĕ)	169	50°19'N	18°10'E
Kozloduy, Blg. (kŭz'lô-dwē)	175	43°45'N	23°42'E
Kōzu, i., Japan (kō'zōō)	211	34°16'N	139°03'E
Kra, Isthmus of, isth., Asia	212	9°30'S	99°45'E
Kraai, r., S. Afr. (krä'ē)	233c	30°50'S	27°03'E
Krabbendijke, Neth.	159a	51°26'N	4°05'E
Krâchéh, Camb.	212	12°28'N	106°06'E
Kragujevac, Serb. (krä'gōō'yĕ-váts)	163	44°01'N	20°55'E
Kraków, Pol. (krä'kôf)	154	50°05'N	20°00'E
Kraljevo, Serb. (kräl'ye-vô)	163	43°39'N	20°48'E
Kramators'k, Ukr.	177	48°43'N	37°32'E
Kramfors, Swe. (kräm'fôrs)	166	62°54'N	17°49'E
Kranj, Slvn. (krän')	162	46°16'N	14°23'E
Kranskop, S. Afr. (kränz'kŏp)	233c	28°57'S	30°54'E
Krāslava, Lat. (kräs'lä-vä)	167	55°53'N	27°12'E
Kraslice, Czech Rep. (kräs'lē-tsĕ)	168	50°19'N	12°30'E
Krasnaya Gorka, Russia	186a	55°12'N	56°40'E
Krasnaya Sloboda, Russia	181	48°25'N	44°35'E
Kraśnik, Pol. (kräsh'nĭk)	169	50°53'N	22°15'E
Krasnoarmeysk, Russia (kräs'nô-ár-maśk')	186b	56°06'N	38°09'E
Krasnoarmiis'k, Ukr.	177	48°19'N	37°04'E
Krasnodar, Russia (kräs'nô-dár)	178	45°03'N	38°55'E
Krasnodarskiy, prov., Russia (krás-nô-där'skĭ ôb'lást)	177	45°25'N	38°10'E
Krasnogorsk, Russia	186b	55°49'N	37°20'E
Krasnogorskiy, Russia (kräs-nô-gôr'skĭ)	186a	54°36'N	61°15'E
Krasnogvardeyskiy, Russia (krå'sno-gvăr-dzyē ĕs-kēē)	186a	57°17'N	62°05'E
Krasnohrad, Ukr.	177	49°23'N	35°26'E
Krasnokamsk, Russia (kräs-nô-kämsk')	180	58°00'N	55°45'E
Krasnokuts'k, Ukr.	177	50°03'N	35°05'E
Krasnoslobodsk, Russia (kräs'nô-slôbôtsk')	180	54°20'N	43°50'E
Krasnotur'insk, Russia (krŭs-nŭ-tōō-rensk')	178	59°47'N	60°15'E
Krasnoufimsk, Russia (krŭs-nŭ-ōō-fēmsk')	178	56°38'N	57°46'E
Krasnoural'sk, Russia (kräs'nô-ōō-rälsk')	180	58°21'N	60°05'E
Krasnousol'skiy, Russia (kräs-nô-ô-sôl'skĭ)	186a	53°54'N	56°27'E
Krasnovishersk, Russia (kräs-nô-vēshersk')	180	60°22'N	57°20'E
Krasnoyarsk, Russia (kräs-nô-yársk')	179	56°13'N	93°12'E
Krasnoye Selo, Russia (kräs'nŭ-yŭ sâ'lô)	186c	59°44'N	30°06'E
Krasny Kholm, Russia (kräs'nē ĸōlm)	176	58°03'N	37°11'E
Krasnystaw, Pol. (kräs-nê-stáf')	169	50°59'N	23°11'E
Krasnyy Bor, Russia (kräs'nê bôr)	186c	59°41'N	30°40'E
Krasnyy Klyuch, Russia (kräs'nê'klyûch')	186a	55°24'N	56°43'E
Krasnyy Kut, Russia (krás-nê kōōt')	181	50°50'N	47°00'E
Kratovo, Mac. (krä'tô-vô)	175	42°04'N	22°12'E
Kratovo, Russia (krä'tô-vô)	186b	55°35'N	38°10'E
Krefeld, Ger. (krā'fĕlt)	171c	51°20'N	6°34'E
Kremenchuk, Ukr.	181	49°04'N	33°26'E
Kremenchuts'ke vodoskhovyshche, res., Ukr.	181	49°20'N	32°45'E
Kremenets', Ukr.	169	50°06'N	25°43'E
Kremmen, Ger. (krĕ'mĕn)	159b	52°45'N	13°02'E
Krempe, Ger. (krĕm'pĕ)	159c	53°50'N	9°29'E
Krems, Aus. (krĕms)	168	48°25'N	15°36'E
Krestovyy, Pereval, p., Geor.	182	42°32'N	44°28'E
Kresttsy, Russia (kråst'sê)	176	58°16'N	32°25'E
Kretinga, Lith. (krĕ-tĭn'gá)	167	55°55'N	21°17'E
Kribi, Cam. (krē'bê)	230	2°57'N	9°55'E
Krilon, Mys, c., Russia (mĭs krĭl'ôn)	210	45°58'N	142°00'E
Krimpen aan de IJssel, Neth.	159a	51°55'N	4°34'E
Krishna, r., India	199	16°00'N	79°00'E
Krishnanagar, India	202	23°29'N	88°33'E
Kristiansand, Nor. (krĭs-tyán-sän'')	154	58°09'N	7°59'E
Kristianstad, Swe. (krĭs-tyán-städ')	160	56°02'N	14°09'E
Kristiansund, Nor. (krĭs-tyán-sòn'')	160	63°07'N	7°49'E
Kristinehamn, Swe. (krês-tē'nĕ-häm')	160	59°20'N	14°05'E
Kristinestad, Fin. (krĭs-tē'nĕ-städh)	167	62°16'N	21°28'E
Kriva-Palanka, Mac. (krē-vá-pá-läŋ'ká)	175	42°12'N	22°21'E
Krivoy Rog *see* Kryvyi Rih, Ukr.	178	47°54'N	33°22'E
Križevci, Cro. (krē'zhĕv-tsĭ)	174	46°02'N	16°30'E
Krk, i., Serb. (k'rk)	174	45°06'N	14°33'E
Krnov, Czech Rep. (k'r'nôf)	169	50°05'N	17°41'E
Krokodil, r., S. Afr. (krŏ'kŏ-dĭl)	238c	24°25'S	27°08'E
Krolevets', Ukr.	181	51°33'N	33°21'E
Kromy, Russia (krō'mê)	176	52°44'N	35°41'E
Kronshtadt, Russia (krōn'shtät)	180	59°59'N	29°47'E
Kroonstad, S. Afr. (krōn'shtät)	232	27°40'S	27°15'E
Kropotkin, Russia (krá-pôt'kĭn)	181	45°25'N	40°30'E
Krosno, Pol. (krôs'nô)	169	49°41'N	21°46'E
Krotoszyn, Pol. (krō-tō'shĭn)	169	51°41'N	17°25'E
Krško, Slvn. (k'rsh'kô)	174	45°58'N	15°30'E
Krugersdorp, S. Afr. (krōō'gĕrz-dôrp)	232	26°06'S	27°46'E
Krung Thep *see* Bangkok, Thai.	212	13°50'N	100°29'E
Kruševac, Serb. (krò'shĕ-váts)	175	43°34'N	21°21'E
Kruševo, Mac.	175	41°20'N	21°15'E
Krychaw, Bela.	176	53°44'N	31°39'E
Krylbo, Swe. (krül'bô)	166	60°07'N	16°14'E
Krym, Respublika, prov., Ukr.	177	45°08'N	34°05'E
Krymskaya, Russia (krĭm'ská-yá)	177	44°58'N	38°01'E
Kryms'kyi Pivostriv (Crimean Peninsula), pen., Ukr.	181	45°18'N	33°30'E
Krynki, Pol. (krĭn'kê)	169	53°15'N	23°47'E
Kryve Ozero, Ukr.	177	47°57'N	30°21'E
Kryvyi Rih, Ukr.	178	47°54'N	33°22'E
Ksar Chellala, Alg.	173	35°12'N	2°20'E
Ksar-el-Kebir, Mor.	162	35°01'N	5°48'W
Ksar-es-Souk, Mor.	162	31°58'N	4°25'W
Kuai, r., China (kōō-ī)	206	33°30'N	116°56'E
Kuala Klawang, Malay.	197b	2°57'N	102°04'E
Kuala Lumpur, Malay. (kwä'lä lòm-pōōr')	212	3°08'N	101°42'E
Kuandian, China (kŭän-dĭĕn)	208	40°40'N	124°50'E
Kuban, r., Russia	181	45°20'N	40°05'E
Kubenskoye, l., Russia	180	59°40'N	39°40'E
Kuching, Malay. (kōō'chĭng)	212	1°30'N	110°26'E
Kuchinoerabo, i., Japan (kōō'chē nō ĕr'á-bō)	211	30°31'N	129°53'E
Kudamatsu, Japan (kōō'dá-mä'tsōō)	211	34°00'N	131°51'E
Kudap, Indon.	197b	1°14'N	102°30'E
Kudat, Malay. (kōō-dät')	212	6°56'N	116°48'E
Kudirkos Naumietis, Lith. (kōōdĭr-kôs ná'ô-mĕ'tĭs)	167	54°51'N	23°00'E
Kudymkar, Russia (kōō-dĭm-kär')	178	58°43'N	54°52'E
Kufstein, Aus. (kōōf'shtīn)	168	47°34'N	12°11'E
Kugluktuk (Coppermine), Can.	90	67°46'N	115°19'W
Kuhstedt, Ger. (kōō'shtĕ)	159c	53°23'N	8°58'E
Kuibyshev *see* Kuybyshev, Russia	178	53°10'N	50°05'E
Kuilsrivier, S. Afr.	232a	33°56'S	18°41'E
Kuito, Ang.	232	12°22'S	16°56'E
Kuji, Japan	205	40°11'N	141°46'E
Kujū-san, mtn., Japan (kōō'jò-săn')	211	33°07'N	131°14'E
Kukës, Alb. (kōō'kĕs)	175	42°03'N	20°25'E
Kula, Blg. (kōō'lá)	175	43°52'N	23°13'E
Kula, Tur.	163	38°32'N	28°30'E
Kula Kangri, mtn., Bhu.	199	33°11'N	90°36'E
Kular, Khrebet, mts., Russia (kò-lär')	185	69°00'N	131°45'E
Kuldīga, Lat. (kòl'dê-gá)	167	56°59'N	21°59'E
Kulebaki, Russia (kōō-lĕ-bäk'ĭ)	180	55°22'N	42°30'E
Kulmbach, Ger. (klòlm'bäĸ)	168	50°07'N	11°28'E
Kulunda, Russia (kò-lòn'dá)	178	52°38'N	79°00'E
Kulundinskoye, l., Russia	184	52°45'N	77°18'E
Kum, r., Kor., S. (kòm)	210	36°50'N	127°30'E
Kuma, r., Russia (kōō'mä)	181	44°50'N	45°10'E
Kumamoto, Japan (kōō'mä-mō'tô)	205	32°49'N	130°40'E
Kumano-Nada, b., Japan (kōō-mä'nō nä-dä)	211	34°03'N	136°36'E
Kumanovo, Mac. (kò-mä'nô-vô)	175	42°10'N	21°41'E
Kumasi, Ghana (kōō-mä'sê)	230	6°41'N	1°35'W
Kumba, Cam. (kòm'bá)	230	4°38'N	9°25'E
Kumbakonam, India (kòm'bŭ-kō'nŭm)	199	10°59'N	79°25'E
Kumkale, Tur.	175	39°59'N	26°10'E
Kumo, Nig.	235	10°03'N	11°13'E
Kumta, India	203	14°19'N	75°28'E
Kumul *see* Hami, China	204	42°58'N	93°14'E
Kunashak, Russia (kû-nä'shák)	186a	55°43'N	61°35'E
Kunashir (Kunashiri), i., Russia (kōō-nŭ-shēr')	205	44°00'N	145°45'E
Kunda, Est.	167	59°30'N	26°28'E
Kundravy, Russia (kōōn'drá-vĭ)	186a	54°50'N	60°14'E
Kundur, i., Indon.	197b	0°49'N	103°20'E
Kunene (Cunene), r., Afr.	232	17°05'S	12°35'E
Kungälv, Swe. (kŭng'ĕlf)	166	57°53'N	12°01'E
Kungsbacka, Swe. (kŭngs'bä-ká)	166	57°31'N	12°04'E
Kungur, Russia (kòn-gōōr')	178	57°27'N	56°53'E
Kunlun Shan, mts., China (kōōn-lōōn shän)	204	35°26'N	83°09'E
Kunming, China (kōōn-mĭŋ)	204	25°10'N	102°50'E
Kunsan, Kor., S. (kòn'sän')	205	35°54'N	126°46'E
Kunshan, China (kōōnshän)	207b	31°23'N	120°57'E
Kuntsëvo, Russia (kòn-tsyô'vô)	176	55°43'N	37°27'E
Kun'ya, Russia	186a	58°42'N	56°47'E
Kun'ya, r., Russia (kòn'yá)	176	56°45'N	30°53'E
Kuopio, Fin. (kò-ô'pê-ō)	160	62°48'N	28°30'E
Kupa, r., Serb.	174	45°32'N	14°50'E
Kupang, Indon.	213	10°14'S	123°37'E
Kupavna, Russia	186b	55°49'N	38°11'E
Kupians'k, Ukr.	181	49°44'N	37°38'E
Kupino, Russia (kōō-pĭ'nô)	178	54°00'N	77°47'E
Kupiškis, Lith. (kò-pĭsh'kĭs)	167	55°50'N	24°55'E
Kuqa, China (kōō-chyä)	204	41°34'N	82°44'E
Kür, r., Asia	181	41°10'N	45°40'E
Kurashiki, Japan (kōō'rä-shē'kê)	211	34°37'N	133°44'E
Kuraymah, Sudan	231	18°34'N	31°49'E
Kurayoshi, Japan (kōō'rá-yō'shê)	211	35°25'N	133°49'E
Kurdistan, hist. reg., Asia (kûrd'ĭ-stăn)	198	37°40'N	43°30'E
Kurdufān, hist. reg., Sudan (kòr-dô-fän')	231	14°08'N	28°39'E
Kŭrdzhali, Blg.	175	41°39'N	25°21'E
Kure, Japan (kōō'rĕ)	205	34°17'N	132°35'E
Kuressaare, Est. (kò'rĕ-sä'rĕ)	167	58°15'N	22°26'E
Kurgan, Russia (kòr-găn')	178	55°28'N	65°14'E
Kurgan-Tyube, Taj. (kòr-gän' tyò'bĕ)	183	38°00'N	68°49'E
Kurihama, Japan (kōō-rē-hä'mä)	211a	35°14'N	139°42'E
Kuril Islands, is., Russia (kōō'rĭl)	185	46°20'N	149°30'E
Kurisches Haff, b., Eur.	167	55°10'N	21°08'E
Kurla, neigh., India	203b	19°03'N	72°53'E
Kurmuk, Sudan (kòr'mōōk)	231	10°40'N	34°13'E
Kurnool, India (kòr-nōōl')	199	16°00'N	78°04'E
Kurrajong, Austl.	217b	33°33'S	150°40'E
Kuršenai, Lith. (kòr'shá-nī)	167	56°01'N	22°56'E
Kursk, Russia (kòrsk)	178	51°44'N	36°08'E
Kuršumlija, Serb. (kòr'shòm'lĭ-yá)	175	43°08'N	21°18'E
Kuruman, S. Afr. (kōō-rōō-män')	232	27°25'S	23°30'E
Kurume, Japan (kōō'rò-mĕ)	205	33°10'N	130°30'E
Kururi, Japan (kōō'rò-rê)	211a	35°17'N	140°05'E
Kusa, Russia (kōō'sá)	186a	55°19'N	59°27'E
Kushchëvskaya, Russia	177	46°34'N	39°40'E
Kushikino, Japan (kōō'shĭ-kē'nō)	211	31°44'N	130°19'E
Kushimoto, Japan (kōō'shĭ-mō'tō)	211	33°29'N	135°47'E
Kushiro, Japan (kōō'shē-rō)	205	43°00'N	144°22'E
Kushva, Russia (kōōsh'vá)	178	58°18'N	59°51'E
Kuskokwim, r., Ak., U.S.	103	61°32'N	160°36'W
Kuskokwim Bay, b., Ak., U.S. (kŭs'kô-kwĭm)	103	59°25'N	163°14'W
Kuskokwim Mountains, mts., Ak., U.S.	103	62°08'N	158°00'W
Kuskovak, Ak., U.S. (kŭs-kō'văk)	103	60°10'N	162°50'W
Kütahya, Tur. (kû-tä'hyá)	198	39°20'N	29°50'E
Kutaisi, Geor. (kōō-tŭ-ē'sê)	181	42°15'N	42°40'E
Kutch, Gulf of, b., India	199	22°45'N	68°33'E
Kutch, Rann of, sw., Asia	199	23°59'N	69°13'E
Kutenholz, Ger. (kōō'tĕn-hōlts)	159c	53°29'N	9°20'E
Kutim, Russia (kōō'tĭm)	186a	60°22'N	58°51'E
Kutina, Cro. (kōō'tē-ná)	174	45°29'N	16°48'E
Kutno, Pol. (kòt'nô)	161	52°14'N	19°22'E
Kutno, l., Russia	180	65°15'N	31°30'E
Kutulik, Russia (kò tōō'lyĭk)	179	53°12'N	102°51'E
Kuujjuaq, Can.	91	58°06'N	68°25'W
Kuusamo, Fin. (kōō'sá-mô)	160	65°59'N	29°10'E
Kuvshinovo, Russia (kòv-shē'nô-vô)	176	57°01'N	34°09'E
Kuwait *see* Al Kuwait, Kuw.	198	29°04'N	47°59'E
Kuwait, nation, Asia	198	29°00'N	48°45'E
Kuwana, Japan (kōō'wá-ná)	211	35°02'N	136°40'E
Kuybyshev *see* Samara, Russia	180	53°10'N	50°05'E
Kuybyshevskoye, res., Russia	178	53°40'N	49°00'E
Kuzneckovo, Russia	186b	55°29'N	38°22'E
Kuznetsk, Russia (kōōz-nyĕtsk')	180	53°00'N	46°30'E
Kuznetsk Basin, basin, Russia	178	56°30'N	86°15'E
Kuznetsovka, Russia (kòz-nyĕt'sôf-kȧ)	186a	54°41'N	56°40'E
Kuznetsovo, Russia (kòz-nyĕt-sô'vô)	176	56°39'N	36°55'E
Kuznetsy, Russia	186b	55°50'N	38°39'E
Kvarner Zaliv, b., Serb. (kvär'nĕr)	174	44°41'N	14°05'E
Kwa, r., D.R.C.	236	3°00'S	16°45'E
Kwahu Plateau, plat., Ghana	234	7°00'N	1°35'W
Kwando (Cuando), r., Afr.	236	16°50'S	22°40'E
Kwangju, Kor., S.	210	35°09'N	126°54'E
Kwango (Cuango), r., Afr. (kwäng'ō')	236	6°35'S	16°50'E
Kwangwazi, Tan.	237	7°47'S	38°15'E
Kwekwe, Zimb.	232	18°49'S	29°45'E
Kwenge, r., Afr. (kwĕŋ'gĕ)	232	6°45'S	18°23'E
Kwilu, r., Afr. (kwē'lōō)	232	4°00'S	18°00'E
Kyakhta, Russia (kyäĸ'ta)	179	51°00'N	107°30'E
Kyaukpyu, Mya. (chouk'pyoo')	199	19°19'N	93°33'E
Kybartai, Lith. (kē'bär-tī')	167	54°40'N	22°46'E
Kyïv *see* Kiev, Ukr.	178	50°27'N	30°30'E
Kyïvs'ke vodoskhovyshche, res., Ukr.	178	51°00'N	30°20'E
Kými, Grc.	175	38°38'N	24°05'E
Kyn, Russia (kĭn')	186a	57°52'N	58°42'E
Kynuna, Austl. (kī-nōō'ná)	219	21°30'S	142°12'E
Kyoga, Lake, l., Ug.	231	1°30'N	32°45'E
Kyōga-Saki, c., Japan (kyō'gä sa'kê)	211	35°46'N	135°14'E
Kyŏngju, Kor., S. (kyŭng'yōō)	205	35°48'N	129°12'E
Kyōto, Japan (kyō'tō')	205	35°00'N	135°46'E
Kyōto, dept., Japan	211b	34°56'N	135°42'E
Kyparissía, Grc.	163	37°17'N	21°43'E
Kyparissiakós Kólpos, b., Grc.	175	37°28'N	21°15'E
Kyren, Russia (kĭ-rĕn')	179	51°46'N	102°13'E
Kyrgyzstan, nation, Asia	178	41°45'N	74°38'E
Kyrönjoki, r., Fin.	167	63°03'N	22°20'E
Kyrya, Russia (kĕr'yá)	186a	59°18'N	59°03'E
Kyshtym, Russia (kĭsh-tĭm')	180	55°42'N	60°34'E
Kýthira, i., Grc.	163	36°15'N	22°56'E
Kýthnos, i., Grc.	175	37°24'N	24°10'E
Kytlym, Russia (kĭt'lĭm)	186a	59°30'N	59°15'E
Kyūshū, i., Japan	205	33°00'N	131°00'E
Kyustendil, Blg. (kyòs-tĕn-dĭl')	163	42°16'N	22°39'E
Kyyiv, prov., Ukr.	177	50°05'N	30°40'E
Kyzyl, Russia (kĭ zĭl)	179	51°37'N	93°38'E
Kyzyl-Kum, des., Asia	178	42°47'N	64°45'E

L

PLACE (Pronunciation)	PAGE	LAT.	LONG.
Laa, Aus.	168	48°42'N	16°23'E
La Almunia de Doña Godina, Spain	172	41°29'N	1°22'W
Laas Caanood, Som.	238a	8°24'N	47°20'E
La Asunción, Ven. (lä ä-sōōn-syōn')	142	11°02'N	63°57'W
La Baie, Can.	99	48°21'N	70°53'W
La Banda, Arg. (lä bän'dä)	144	27°48'S	64°12'W
La Barca, Mex. (lä bär'ká)	130	20°17'N	102°33'W
Laberge, Lake, l., Can. (lá-bĕrzh')	92	61°08'N	136°42'W
Laberinto de las Doce Leguas, is., Cuba	134	20°40'N	78°35'W
Labinsk, Russia	181	44°30'N	40°40'E
Labis, Malay. (läb'ĭs)	197b	2°23'N	103°01'E
La Bisbal, Spain (lä bēs-bäl')	173	41°55'N	3°00'E
Labo, Phil. (lä'bô)	213a	14°11'N	122°49'E
Labo, Mount, mtn., Phil.	213a	14°00'N	122°47'E
Labouheyre, Fr. (lá-bōō-âr')	170	44°14'N	0°58'W
Laboulaye, Arg. (lä-bô'ōō-lä-yĕ)	144	34°01'S	63°10'W
Labrador, reg., Can. (lăb'rá-dôr)	93	53°05'N	63°30'W
Labrador Sea, sea, Can.	101	50°38'N	55°00'W
Lábrea, Braz. (lä-brā'ä)	142	7°28'S	64°39'W

312 Labuan – L'Anse PRONOUNCING INDEX

PLACE (Pronunciation)	PAGE	LAT.	LONG.
Labuan, Pulau, i., Malay. (lä-bö-än')	212	5°28'N	115°11'E
Labuha, Indon.	213	0°43'S	127°35'E
L'Acadie, Can. (lȧ-kȧ-dē')	102a	45°18'N	73°22'W
L'Acadie, r., Can.	102a	45°24'N	73°21'W
La Calera, Chile (lä-kä-lĕ-rä)	141b	32°47'S	71°11'W
La Calera, Col.	142a	4°43'N	73°58'W
Lac Allard, Can.	100	50°38'N	63°28'W
La Canada, Ca., U.S. (lä kän-yä'dä)	117a	34°13'N	118°12'W
Lacantum, r., Mex. (lä-kän-to͞o'm)	131	16°13'N	90°52'W
La Carolina, Spain (lä kä-rô-lē'nä)	172	38°16'N	3°48'W
La Catedral, Cerro, mtn., Mex. (sĕ'r-rô-lä-kä-tĕ-drȧ'l)	131a	19°32'N	99°31'W
Lac-Beauport, Can. (läk-bō-pōr')	102b	46°58'N	71°17'W
Laccadive Islands *see* Lakshadweep, is., India	199	11°00'N	73°02'E
Laccadive Sea, sea, Asia	203	9°10'N	75°17'E
Lac Court Oreille Indian Reservation, I.R., Wi., U.S.	113	46°04'N	91°18'W
Lac du Flambeau Indian Reservation, I.R., Wi., U.S.	113	46°12'N	89°50'W
La Ceiba, Hond. (lȧ sēbä)	128	15°45'N	86°52'W
La Ceja, Col. (lä-sĕ-kä)	142a	6°02'N	75°25'W
Lac-Frontière, Can.	91	46°42'N	70°00'W
Lacha, l., Russia (lȧ'chä)	180	61°15'N	39°05'E
La Chaux de Fonds, Switz. (lȧ shō dē-fôN')	168	47°07'N	6°47'E
L'Achigan, r., Can. (lä-shē-gäN)	102a	45°49'N	73°48'W
Lachine, Can. (lȧ-shēn')	102a	45°26'N	73°40'W
Lachlan, r., Austl. (läk'lăn)	221	34°00'S	145°00'E
La Chorrera, Pan. (lȧchôr-rā'rä)	133	8°54'N	79°47'W
Lachute, Can. (lȧ-sho͞ot')	99	45°39'N	74°20'W
La Ciotat, Fr. (lȧ syô-tȧ')	171	43°13'N	5°35'E
Lackawanna, N.Y., U.S. (lak-ȧ-wŏn'ȧ)	111c	42°49'N	78°50'W
Lac La Biche, Can.	90	54°46'N	112°58'W
Lacombe, Can.	90	52°28'N	113°44'W
Laconia, N.H., U.S. (lȧ-kō'nĭ-ȧ)	109	43°30'N	71°30'W
La Conner, Wa., U.S. (lȧ kŏn'ẽr)	116a	48°23'N	122°30'W
Lacreek, l., S.D., U.S. (lȧ'krēk)	112	43°04'N	101°46'W
La Cresenta, Ca., U.S. (lȧ krĕs'ĕnt-ȧ)	117a	34°14'N	118°13'W
La Cross, Ks., U.S. (lȧ-krôs')	120	38°30'N	99°20'W
La Crosse, Wi., U.S.	105	43°48'N	91°14'W
La Cruz, Col. (lȧ kro͞oz')	142	1°37'N	77°00'W
La Cruz, C.R. (lä-kro͞o'z)	132	11°05'N	85°37'W
Lacs, Riviere des, r., N.D., U.S. (rē-vyĕr' de läk)	112	48°30'N	101°45'W
La Cuesta, C.R. (lä-kwĕ's-tä)	133	8°32'N	82°51'W
La Cygne, Ks., U.S. (lȧ-sēn'y') (lȧ-sēn')	121	38°20'N	94°45'W
Ladd, Il., U.S. (lăd)	108	41°25'N	89°25'W
Ladíspoli, Italy (lä-dē's-pô-lē)	173d	41°57'N	12°05'E
Lādīz, Iran	201	28°56'N	61°19'E
Ladner, Can. (lăd'nẽr)	94	49°05'N	123°05'W
Lādnun, India (läd'nōn)	202	27°45'N	74°20'E
Ladoga, Lake *see* Ladozhskoye Ozero, l., Russia	178	60°59'N	31°30'E
La Dorado, Col. (lä dô-rä'dä)	142	5°28'N	74°42'W
Ladozhskoye Ozero, Russia (lȧ-dôsh'skô-yĕ ô'zĕ-rô)	178	60°59'N	31°30'E
La Durantaye, Can. (lä dü-räN-tā')	102b	46°51'N	70°51'W
Lady Frere, S. Afr. (lā-dē frâ'r')	233c	31°48'S	27°16'E
Lady Grey, S. Afr.	233c	30°44'S	27°17'E
Ladysmith, Can. (lā'dĭ-smĭth)	94	48°58'N	123°49'W
Ladysmith, S. Afr.	232	28°38'S	29°48'E
Ladysmith, Wi., U.S.	113	45°27'N	91°07'W
Lae, Pap. N. Gui. (lä'â)	213	6°15'S	146°57'E
Laerdalsøyri, Nor.	166	61°08'N	7°26'E
La Esperanza, Hond. (lä ĕs-pâ-rän'zä)	132	14°20'N	88°21'W
Lafayette, Al., U.S.	124	32°52'N	85°25'W
Lafayette, Ca., U.S.	116b	37°53'N	122°07'W
Lafayette, Ga., U.S. (lä-fā-yĕt')	124	34°41'N	85°19'W
Lafayette, In., U.S.	105	40°25'N	86°55'W
Lafayette, La., U.S.	105	30°15'N	92°02'W
La Fayette, R.I., U.S.	110b	41°34'N	71°29'W
La Ferté-Alais, Fr. (lä-fĕr-tā'ä-lā')	171b	48°29'N	2°19'E
La Ferté-sous-Jouarre, Fr. (lȧ fĕr-tā'so͞o-zho͞o-är')	171b	48°56'N	3°07'E
Lafia, Nig.	235	8°30'N	8°30'E
Lafiagi, Nig.	235	8°52'N	5°25'E
La Flèche, Fr. (lȧ flāsh')	170	47°43'N	0°03'W
La Follete, Tn., U.S. (lä-fŏl'ĕt)	124	36°23'N	84°07'W
Lafourche, Bayou, r., La., U.S. (bä-yo͞o'lȧ-fo͞orsh')	123	29°25'N	90°15'W
La Gaiba, Braz. (lä-gī'bä)	143	17°54'S	57°32'W
La Galite, i., Tun. (gä-lēt)	162	37°36'N	8°03'E
Lågan, r., Nor. (lô'ghĕn)	156	61°00'N	10°00'E
Lagan, r., Swe.	166	56°34'N	13°25'E
Lagan, r., N. Ire., U.K. (lā'găn)	164	54°30'N	6°00'W
Lagarto, r., Pan. (lä-gä'r-tô)	128a	9°08'N	80°05'W
Lagartos, l., Mex. (lä-gä'r-tôs)	132a	21°32'N	88°15'W
Laghouat, Alg. (lä-gwät')	230	33°45'N	2°49'E
Lagkadás, Grc.	175	40°44'N	23°10'E
Lagny, Fr. (län-yē')	171b	48°53'N	2°41'E
Lagoa da Prata, Braz. (lä-gô'ä-dȧ-prä'tȧ)	141a	20°04'S	45°33'W
Lagoa Dourada, Braz. (lä-gô'ä-dō-rä'dä)	141a	20°55'S	44°03'W
Lagogne, Fr. (laN-gōn'y')	170	44°43'N	3°50'E
Lagonay, Phil.	213a	13°44'N	123°31'E
Lagos, Nig. (lä'gōs)	230	6°27'N	3°24'E
Lagos, Port. (lä'gôzh)	172	37°08'N	8°43'W
Lagos de Moreno, Mex. (lä'gōs dā mō-rā'nō)	128	21°21'N	101°55'W
La Grand' Combe, Fr. (lȧ grän kaNb')	170	44°12'N	4°03'E
La Grande, Or., U.S. (lȧ grănd')	104	45°20'N	118°06'W
La Grande, r., Can.	93	53°55'N	77°30'W
La Grange, Austl. (lä grānj)	218	18°40'S	122°00'E
La Grange, Ga., U.S. (lȧ-grānj')	105	33°01'N	85°00'W
La Grange, Il., U.S.	111a	41°49'N	87°53'W
Lagrange, In., U.S.	108	41°40'N	85°25'W
La Grange, Ky., U.S.	108	38°20'N	85°25'W
La Grange, Mo., U.S.	121	40°04'N	91°30'W
Lagrange, Oh., U.S.	111d	41°14'N	82°07'W
Lagrange, Tx., U.S.	123	29°55'N	96°50'W
La Grita, Ven. (lä grē'tȧ)	142	8°02'N	71°59'W
La Guaira, Ven. (lä gwä'ē-rä)	142	10°36'N	66°54'W
La Guardia, Spain (lä gwär'dē-ȧ)	172	41°55'N	8°48'W
Laguna, Braz. (lä-go͞o'nä)	144	28°19'S	48°42'W
Laguna, Cayos, is., Cuba (kä'yōs-lä-gō'nä)	134	22°15'N	82°45'W
Laguna Indian Reservation, I.R., N.M., U.S.	119	35°00'N	107°30'W
Lagunillas, Bol. (lä-go͞o-nēl'yäs)	142	19°42'S	63°38'W
Lagunillas, Mex. (lä-go͞o-nē'l-yäs)	130	21°34'N	99°41'W
La Habana *see* Havana, Cuba	129	23°08'N	82°23'W
La Habra, Ca., U.S. (lȧ hȧb'rȧ)	117a	34°56'N	117°57'W
Lahaina, Hi., U.S. (lä-hä'ē-nä)	126a	20°52'N	156°39'W
Lāhījān, Iran	201	37°12'N	50°01'E
Laholm, Swe. (lä'hôlm)	166	56°30'N	13°00'E
La Honda, Ca., U.S. (lä hŏn'dȧ)	116b	37°20'N	122°16'W
Lahore, Pak. (lä-hōr')	199	32°00'N	74°18'E
Lahr, Ger. (lär)	168	48°19'N	7°52'E
Lahti, Fin. (lä'tê)	160	60°59'N	27°39'E
Lai, Chad	231	9°29'N	16°18'E
Lai'an, China (lī-än)	206	32°27'N	118°25'E
Laibin, China (lī-bĭn)	209	23°42'N	109°20'E
L'Aigle, Fr. (lĕ'gl')	170	48°45'N	0°37'E
Laisamis, Kenya	237	1°36'N	37°48'E
Laiyang, China (läī'yäng)	208	36°59'N	120°42'E
Laizhou Wan, b., China (lī-jō wän)	205	37°22'N	119°19'E
Laja, Río de la, r., Mex. (rē'ō-dĕ-lä-lȧ'kä)	130	21°17'N	100°57'W
Lajas, Cuba (lä'häs)	134	22°25'N	80°20'W
Lajeado, Braz. (lä-zhĕä'dō)	144	29°24'S	51°46'W
Lajes, Braz. (lȧ'zhĕs)	144	27°47'S	50°17'W
Lajinha, Braz. (lä-zhē'nyä)	141a	20°08'S	41°36'W
La Jolla, Ca., U.S. (lȧ hoi'yȧ)	118a	32°51'N	117°16'W
La Jolla Indian Reservation, I.R., Ca., U.S.	118	33°19'N	116°21'W
La Junta, Co., U.S. (lȧ ho͞on'tȧ)	120	37°59'N	103°35'W
Lake Arthur, La., U.S. (är'thŭr)	123	30°06'N	92°40'W
Lake Barkley, res., U.S.	124	36°45'N	88°00'W
Lake Benton, Mn., U.S. (bĕn'tŭn)	112	44°15'N	96°17'W
Lake Bluff, Il., U.S. (blŭf)	111a	42°17'N	87°50'W
Lake Brown, Austl. (broun)	218	31°03'S	118°30'E
Lake Charles, La., U.S. (chärlz')	105	30°15'N	93°14'W
Lake City, Fl., U.S.	125	30°09'N	82°40'W
Lake City, Ia., U.S.	113	42°14'N	94°43'W
Lake City, Mn., U.S.	113	44°28'N	92°19'W
Lake City, S.C., U.S.	125	33°57'N	79°45'W
Lake Clark National Park, rec., Ak., U.S.	103	60°30'N	153°15'W
Lake Cowichan, Can. (kou'ĭ-chăn)	94	48°50'N	124°03'W
Lake Crystal, Mn., U.S. (krĭs'tăl)	113	44°05'N	94°12'W
Lake District, reg., Eng., U.K. (lāk)	164	54°25'N	3°20'W
Lake Elmo, Mn., U.S. (ĕlmō)	117g	45°00'N	92°53'W
Lake Forest, Il., U.S. (fŏr'ĕst)	111a	42°16'N	87°50'W
Lake Fork, r., Ut., U.S.	119	40°30'N	110°25'W
Lake Geneva, Wi., U.S. (jĕ-nē'vȧ)	113	42°36'N	88°28'W
Lake Havasu City, Az., U.S.	119	34°27'N	114°22'W
Lake June, Tx., U.S. (jo͞on)	117c	32°43'N	96°45'W
Lakeland, Fl., U.S. (lāk'lănd)	105	28°02'N	81°58'W
Lakeland, Ga., U.S.	124	31°02'N	83°02'W
Lakeland, Mn., U.S.	117g	44°57'N	92°47'W
Lake Linden, Mi., U.S. (lĭn'dĕn)	113	47°11'N	88°26'W
Lake Louise, Can. (lo͞o-ēz')	95	51°26'N	116°11'W
Lake Mead National Recreation Area, rec., U.S.	119	36°00'N	114°30'W
Lake Mills, Ia., U.S. (mĭlz')	113	43°25'N	93°32'W
Lakemore, Oh., U.S. (lāk-mōr)	111d	41°01'N	81°24'W
Lake Odessa, Mi., U.S.	108	42°50'N	85°15'W
Lake Oswego, Or., U.S. (ŏs-wē'go)	116c	45°25'N	122°40'W
Lake Placid, N.Y., U.S.	109	44°17'N	73°59'W
Lake Point, Ut., U.S.	117b	40°41'N	112°16'W
Lakeport, Ca., U.S. (lāk'pōrt)	118	39°03'N	122°54'W
Lake Preston, S.D., U.S. (prēs'tŭn)	112	44°21'N	97°23'W
Lake Providence, La., U.S. (prŏv'ĭ-dĕns)	123	32°48'N	91°12'W
Lake Red Rock, res., Ia., U.S.	113	41°30'N	93°15'W
Lake Sharpe, res., S.D., U.S.	112	44°30'N	100°00'W
Lakeside, Ca., U.S. (lāk'sīd)	118a	32°52'N	116°55'W
Lake Station, In., U.S.	111a	41°34'N	87°15'W
Lake Stevens, Wa., U.S.	116a	48°01'N	122°04'W
Lake Success, N.Y., U.S. (sŭk-sĕs')	110a	40°46'N	73°43'W
Lakeview, Or., U.S.	114	42°11'N	120°21'W
Lake Village, Ar., U.S.	121	33°20'N	91°17'W
Lake Wales, Fl., U.S. (wālz')	125a	27°54'N	81°35'W
Lakewood, Ca., U.S. (lāk'wŏd)	117a	33°50'N	118°09'W
Lakewood, Co., U.S.	120	39°44'N	105°06'W
Lakewood, Oh., U.S.	105	41°29'N	81°48'W
Lakewood, Pa., U.S.	109	40°05'N	74°10'W
Lakewood, Wa., U.S.	116a	48°09'N	122°13'W
Lakewood Center, Wa., U.S.	116a	47°10'N	122°31'W
Lake Worth, Fl., U.S. (wûrth')	125a	26°37'N	80°04'W
Lake Worth Village, Tx., U.S.	117c	32°49'N	97°26'W
Lake Zurich, Il., U.S. (tsü'rĭk)	111a	42°11'N	88°05'W
Lakhdenpokh'ya, Russia (l'äk-dĭe'npōkyȧ)	167	61°33'N	30°10'E
Lakhtinskiy, Russia (lȧk-tĭn'skĭ)	186c	59°59'N	30°10'E
Lakota, N.D., U.S. (lȧ-kō'tȧ)	112	48°04'N	98°21'W
Lakshadweep, state, India	199	10°10'N	72°50'E
Lakshadweep, is., India	199	11°00'N	73°02'E
La Libertad, El Sal.	132	13°29'N	89°20'W
La Libertad, Guat. (lä lē-bĕr-tädh')	132	15°31'N	91°44'W
La Libertad, Guat.	132a	16°46'N	90°12'W
La Ligua, Chile (lä lē'gwä)	141b	32°21'S	71°13'W
Lalín, Spain (lä-lē'n)	172	42°40'N	8°05'W
La Línea, Spain (lä lē'nā-ä)	162	36°11'N	5°22'W
Lalitpur, Nepal	199	27°23'N	85°24'E
La Louviere, Bel. (lȧ lo͞o-vyâr')	165	50°30'N	4°10'E
La Luz, Mex. (lä lo͞oz')	130	21°04'N	101°19'W
Lama-Kara, Togo	234	9°33'N	1°12'E
La Malbaie, Can. (lȧ mäl-bā')	91	47°39'N	70°10'W
La Mancha, reg., Spain (lä män'chä)	172	38°55'N	4°20'W
Lamar, Co., U.S. (lȧ-mär')	120	38°04'N	102°44'W
Lamar, Mo., U.S.	121	37°28'N	94°15'W
La Marmora, Punta, mtn., Italy (lä-mä'r-mô-rä)	162	40°00'N	9°28'E
La Marque, Tx., U.S. (lȧ-märk)	123a	29°23'N	94°58'W
Lamas, Peru (lä'mȧs)	142	6°24'S	76°41'W
Lamballe, Fr. (läN-bäl')	170	48°29'N	2°36'W
Lambari, Braz. (läm-bȧ'rē)	141a	21°58'S	45°22'W
Lambasa, Fiji	214g	16°26'S	179°24'E
Lambayeque, Peru (läm-bä-yā'kå)	142	6°41'S	79°58'W
Lambert, Ms., U.S. (lăm'bẽrt)	124	34°10'N	90°16'W
Lambertville, N.J., U.S. (lăm'bẽrt-vĭl)	109	40°20'N	75°00'W
Lame Deer, Mt., U.S. (lām dēr')	115	45°36'N	106°40'W
Lamego, Port. (lä-mā'gō)	172	41°07'N	7°47'W
La Mesa, Col.	142a	4°38'N	74°27'W
La Mesa, Ca., U.S. (lä mā'sä)	118a	32°46'N	117°01'W
Lamesa, Tx., U.S.	120	32°44'N	101°54'W
Lamía, Grc. (lȧ-mē'ȧ)	163	38°54'N	22°25'E
Lamon Bay, b., Phil. (lä-mōn')	212	14°35'N	121°52'E
La Mora, Chile (lä-mō'rä)	141b	32°28'S	70°56'W
La Moure, N.D., U.S. (lȧ mo͞or')	112	46°23'N	98°17'W
Lampa, r., Chile (lä'm-pä)	141b	33°15'S	70°55'W
Lampasas, Tx., U.S. (lăm-păs'ȧs)	122	31°06'N	98°10'W
Lampasas, r., Tx., U.S.	122	31°18'N	98°08'W
Lampazos, Mex. (läm-pä'zōs)	128	27°03'N	100°30'W
Lampedusa, i., Italy (läm-pȧ-do͞o'sä)	162	35°29'N	12°58'E
Lamstedt, Ger. (läm'shtĕt)	159c	53°38'N	9°06'E
Lamu, Kenya (lä'mo͞o)	233	2°16'S	40°54'E
Lamu Island, i., Kenya	237	2°25'S	40°50'E
La Mure, Fr. (lȧ mür')	171	44°55'N	5°50'E
Lan', r., Bela. (lȧn')	176	52°38'N	27°05'E
Lāna'i, i., Hi., U.S. (lä-nä'ē)	106c	20°48'N	157°06'W
Lanai City, Hi., U.S.	126a	20°50'N	156°56'W
Lanak La, p., China	199	34°40'N	79°50'E
Lanark, Scot., U.K. (lăn'ȧrk)	164	55°40'N	3°50'W
Lancashire, co., Eng., U.K. (lăŋ'kȧ-shĭr)	158a	53°49'N	2°42'W
Lancaster, Eng., U.K.	160	54°04'N	2°55'W
Lancaster, Ky., U.S.	108	37°35'N	84°30'W
Lancaster, Ma., U.S.	101a	42°28'N	71°40'W
Lancaster, N.H., U.S.	109	44°25'N	71°30'W
Lancaster, N.Y., U.S.	111c	42°54'N	78°42'W
Lancaster, Oh., U.S.	108	39°40'N	82°35'W
Lancaster, Pa., U.S.	105	40°05'N	76°20'W
Lancaster, Tx., U.S.	117c	32°36'N	96°45'W
Lancaster, Wi., U.S.	113	42°51'N	90°44'W
Lândana, Ang. (län-dä'nä)	232	5°15'S	12°07'E
Landau, Ger. (län'dou)	168	49°13'N	8°07'E
Lander, Wy., U.S. (lăn'dẽr)	115	42°49'N	108°24'W
Landerneau, Fr. (läN-dĕr-nō')	170	48°28'N	4°14'W
Landes, reg., Fr. (läNd)	170	44°22'N	0°52'W
Landsberg, Ger. (länds'bo͞orgh)	168	48°03'N	10°53'E
Lands End, c., Eng., U.K.	156	50°03'N	5°45'W
Landshut, Ger. (länts'ho͞ot)	161	48°32'N	12°09'E
Landskrona, Swe. (lȧns-krô'nȧ)	166	55°51'N	12°47'E
Lanett, Al., U.S. (lȧ-nĕt')	124	32°52'N	85°13'W
Langat, r., Malay.	197b	2°46'N	101°33'E
Langdon, Can. (lăng'dŭn)	102e	50°58'N	113°40'W
Langdon, Mn., U.S.	117g	44°49'N	92°56'W
L'Ange-Gardien, Can. (länzh gȧr-dyăN')	102b	46°55'N	71°06'W
Langeland, i., Den.	166	54°52'N	10°46'E
Langenzersdorf, Aus.	159e	48°30'N	16°22'E
Langesund, Nor. (läng'ĕ-sōn)	166	58°59'N	9°38'E
Langfjorden, b., Nor.	166	62°40'N	7°45'E
Langhorne, Pa., U.S. (lăng'hôrn)	110f	40°10'N	74°55'W
Langia Mountains, mts., Ug.	237	3°35'N	33°35'E
Langjökoll, ice, Ice. (läng-yû'ko͞ol)	160	64°40'N	20°31'W
Langla Co, l., China (läŋ-lä tswo)	202	30°42'N	80°40'E
Langley, Can. (lăng'lĭ)	95	49°06'N	122°39'W
Langley, S.C., U.S.	125	33°32'N	81°52'W
Langley, Wa., U.S.	116a	48°02'N	122°25'W
Langley Indian Reserve, I.R., Can.	116d	49°12'N	122°31'W
Langnau, Switz. (läng'nou)	168	46°56'N	7°46'E
Langon, Fr. (läN-gôN')	170	44°34'N	0°16'W
Langres, Fr. (läN'gr')	171	47°53'N	5°20'E
Langres, Plateau de, plat., Fr. (plä-tō'dē-läN'grĕ)	170	47°39'N	5°00'E
Langsa, Indon. (läng'sȧ)	212	4°33'N	97°52'E
Lang Son, Viet. (lăng'sŏn')	212	21°52'N	106°42'E
L'Anguille, r., Ar., U.S. (läN-gē'y')	121	35°23'N	90°52'W
Langxi, China (läŋ-shyē)	206	31°10'N	119°09'E
Langzhong, China (läŋ-jôŋ)	204	31°40'N	106°05'E
Lanham, Md., U.S. (lăn'ăm)	110e	38°58'N	76°54'W
Lanigan, Can. (lăn'ĭ-găn)	90	51°52'N	105°02'W
Länkäran, Azer. (lĕn-kô-rän')	178	38°52'N	48°58'E
Lankoviri, Nig.	235	9°00'N	11°25'E
Lansdale, Pa., U.S. (lănz'dāl)	109	40°20'N	75°15'W
Lansdowne, Pa., U.S.	110f	39°57'N	75°17'W
L'Anse, Mi., U.S. (läns)	113	46°43'N	88°28'W

ăt; finăl; rāte; senâte; ärm; ȧsk; sofȧ; fâre; ch-choose; dh-as th in other; bē; ēvent; bĕt; recĕnt; cratẽr; g-gō; gh-guttural g; bĭt; ĭ-short neutral; rīde; ĸ-guttural k as ch in German ich;

PRONOUNCING INDEX

L'Anse and Vieux Desert – Leivádia 313

PLACE (Pronunciation)	PAGE	LAT.	LONG.
L'Anse and Vieux Desert Indian Reservation, I.R., Mi., U.S.	113	46°41'N	88°12'W
Lansford, Pa., U.S. (lănz'fērd)	109	40°50'N	75°50'W
Lansing, Ia., U.S.	113	43°22'N	91°16'W
Lansing, Il., U.S.	111a	41°34'N	87°33'W
Lansing, Ks., U.S.	117f	39°15'N	94°53'W
Lansing, Mi., U.S.	105	42°45'N	84°35'W
Lanús, Arg. (lä-noos')	144a	34°42'S	58°24'W
Lanusei, Italy (lä-noo-sĕ'y)	174	39°51'N	9°34'E
Lanúvio, Italy (lä-noo'vyô)	173d	41°41'N	12°42'E
Lanzarote Island, i., Spain (län-zà-rō'tā)	230	29°04'N	13°03'W
Lanzhou, China (län-jō)	204	35°55'N	103°55'E
Laoag, Phil. (lä-wäg')	212	18°13'N	120°38'E
Laon, Fr. (läN)	170	49°36'N	3°35'E
La Oroya, Peru (lä-ô-rō'yä)	142	11°30'S	76°00'W
Laos, nation, Asia (lā-ōs) (là-ōs')	212	20°15'N	102°00'E
Laoshan Wan, b., China (lou-shän wän)	206	36°21'N	120°48'E
La Palma, Pan. (lä-päl'mä)	133	8°25'N	78°07'W
La Palma, Spain	172	37°24'N	6°36'W
La Palma Island, i., Spain	230	28°42'N	19°03'W
La Pampa, prov., Arg.	144	37°25'S	67°00'W
Lapa Rio Negro, Braz. (lä-pä-rē'ō-nĕ'grô)	144	26°12'S	49°56'W
La Paz, Arg. (lä päz')	144	30°48'S	59°47'W
La Paz, Bol.	142	16°31'S	68°03'W
La Paz, Hond.	132	14°15'N	87°40'W
La Paz, Mex. (lä-pá'z)	130	23°39'N	100°44'W
La Paz, Mex.	128	24°00'N	110°15'W
Lapeer, Mi., U.S. (lȧ-pēr')	108	43°05'N	83°15'W
La-Penne-sur-Huveaune, Fr. (la-pĕn'sür-ü-vōn')	170a	43°18'N	5°33'E
La Perouse, Austl.	217b	33°59'S	151°14'E
La Piedad Cabadas, Mex. (lä pyå-dhädh' kä-bä'dhäs)	130	20°20'N	102°04'W
Lapland, hist. reg., Eur. (lăp'lȧnd)	154	68°20'N	22°00'E
La Plata, Arg. (lä plä'tä)	144	34°54'S	57°57'W
La Plata, Mo., U.S. (lȧ plā'tȧ)	121	40°03'N	92°28'W
La Plata Peak, mtn., Co., U.S.	119	39°00'N	106°25'W
La Pocatière, Can. (lá pô-ká-tyâr')	99	47°24'N	70°01'W
La Poile Bay, b., Can. (lȧ pwäl')	101	47°38'N	58°20'W
La Porte, In., U.S. (lȧ pōrt')	108	41°35'N	86°45'W
Laporte, Oh., U.S.	111d	41°19'N	82°05'W
La Porte, Tx., U.S.	123a	29°40'N	95°01'W
La Porte City, Ia., U.S.	113	42°20'N	92°10'W
Lappeenranta, Fin. (lä'pēn-rän'tä)	167	61°04'N	28°08'E
La Prairie, Can. (lȧ-prå-rē')	102a	45°24'N	73°30'W
Lâpseki, Tur. (läp'sȧ-kē)	175	40°20'N	26°41'E
Laptev Sea, sea, Russia (läp'tyĭf)	179	75°39'N	120°00'E
La Puebla de Montalbán, Spain	172	39°54'N	4°21'W
La Puente, Ca., U.S. (pwĕn'tē)	117a	34°01'N	117°57'W
Lapuşul, r., Rom. (lä'poo-shool)	169	47°29'N	23°46'E
La Quiaca, Arg. (lä kē-ä'kä)	144	22°15'S	65°44'W
L'Aquila, Italy (lá'kē-lä)	162	42°22'N	13°24'E
Lār, Iran (lär)	198	27°31'N	54°12'E
Lara, Austl.	217a	38°02'S	144°24'E
Larache, Mor. (lä-räsh')	230	35°15'N	6°09'W
Laramie, Wy., U.S. (lăr'ȧ-mĭ)	104	41°20'N	105°40'W
Laramie, r., Co., U.S.	120	40°56'N	105°55'W
Larchmont, N.Y., U.S. (lärch'mŏnt)	110a	40°56'N	73°46'W
Larch Mountain, mtn., Or., U.S. (lärch)	116c	45°32'N	122°06'W
Laredo, Spain (lä-rā'dhō)	172	43°24'N	3°24'W
Laredo, Tx., U.S.	104	27°31'N	99°29'W
La Réole, Fr. (lá rā-ōl')	170	44°37'N	0°03'W
Largeau, Chad (lär-zhō')	231	17°55'N	19°07'E
Largo, Cayo, Cuba (kä'yō-lär'gō)	134	21°40'N	81°30'W
Larimore, N.D., U.S. (lăr'ĭ-môr)	112	47°53'N	97°38'W
Larino, Italy (lä-rē'nô)	174	41°48'N	14°54'E
La Rioja, Arg. (lä rē-ōhä)	144	29°18'S	67°42'W
La Rioja, prov., Arg. (lä-rē-ô'kä)	144	28°45'S	68°00'W
Lárisa, Grc. (lä'rē-sà)	163	39°38'N	22°25'E
Lārkāna, Pak.	202	27°40'N	68°12'E
Larnaka, Cyp.	163	34°55'N	33°37'E
Lárnakos, Kólpos, b., Cyp.	197a	36°50'N	33°45'E
Larned, Ks., U.S. (lär'nĕd)	120	38°09'N	99°07'W
La Robla, Spain (lä rōb'lä)	172	42°48'N	5°36'W
La Rochelle, Fr. (lá rô-shĕl')	154	46°10'N	1°09'W
La Roche-sur-Yon, Fr. (là rôsh'sûr-yôn')	161	46°39'N	1°27'W
La Roda, Spain (lä rō'dä)	172	39°13'N	2°08'W
La Romona, Dom. Rep. (lä-rä-mô'nä)	135	18°25'N	69°00'W
Larrey Point, c., Austl. (lăr'ē)	220	19°15'S	118°15'E
Laruns, Fr. (là-răNs')	170	42°58'N	0°28'W
Larvik, Nor. (lär'vĕk)	160	59°06'N	10°03'E
La Sabana, Ven. (lä-sä-bá'nä)	143b	10°38'N	66°24'W
La Sabina, Cuba (lä-sä-bē'nä)	135a	22°51'N	82°05'W
La Sagra, mtn., Spain (lä sä'grä)	162	37°56'N	2°35'W
La Sal, Ut., U.S. (lȧ sàl')	119	38°10'N	109°20'W
La Salle, Can. (lȧ sàl')	111b	42°14'N	83°06'W
La Salle, Can.	102a	45°26'N	73°39'W
La Salle, Can.	102f	49°41'N	97°16'W
La Salle, Il., U.S.	108	41°20'N	89°05'W
Las Animas, Co., U.S. (lȧs ă'nĭ-mȧs)	120	38°03'N	103°16'W
La Sarre, Can.	91	48°43'N	79°12'W
Lascahobas, Haiti (läs-kä-ō'bás)	135	19°00'N	71°55'W
Las Cruces, Mex. (läs-kroo'sĕs)	131	16°37'N	93°54'W
Las Cruces, N.M., U.S.	104	32°20'N	106°50'W
La Selle, Massif de, mtn., Haiti (lä'sĕl')	135	18°25'N	72°05'W
La Serena, Chile (lä-sĕ-rē'nä)	144	29°55'S	71°24'W
La Seyne, Fr. (lä-sân')	161	43°07'N	5°52'E
Las Flores, Arg. (läs flo'rĕs)	144	36°01'S	59°07'W
Lashio, Mya. (lăsh'ē-ō)	204	22°58'N	98°03'E
Las Juntas, C.R. (läs-kōō'n-täs)	132	10°15'N	85°00'W
Las Maismas, sw., Spain (läs-mī's-mäs)	172	37°05'N	6°25'W
La Solana, Spain (lä-sô-lä-nä)	172	38°56'N	3°13'W
Las Palmas, Pan.	133	8°08'N	81°30'W
Las Palmas de Gran Canaria, Spain (läs päl'mäs)	230	28°07'N	15°28'W
La Spezia, Italy (lä-spĕ'zyä)	154	44°07'N	9°48'E
Las Piedras, Ur. (läs-pyĕ'drás)	141c	34°42'S	56°08'W
Las Pilas, vol., Nic. (läs-pē'läs)	132	12°32'N	86°43'W
Las Rosas, Mex. (läs rō thäs)	131	16°24'N	92°23'W
Las Rozas de Madrid, Spain (läs rō'thas dā mä-dhrēd')	173a	40°29'N	3°53'W
Lassee, Aus.	159e	48°14'N	16°50'E
Lassen Peak, mtn., Ca., U.S. (lăs'ĕn)	106	40°30'N	121°32'W
Lassen Volcanic National Park, rec., Ca., U.S.	106	40°43'N	121°35'W
L'Assomption, Can. (lás-sôm-syôN)	102a	45°50'N	73°25'W
Lass Qoray, Som.	238a	11°13'N	48°19'E
Las Tablas, Pan. (läs tä'bläs)	133	7°48'N	80°16'W
Last Mountain, l., Can. (lȧst moun'tĭn)	92	51°05'N	105°10'W
Lastoursville, Gabon (lȧs-tōōr-vēl')	232	1°00'S	12°49'E
Las Tres Vírgenes, Volcán, vol., Mex. (vē'r-hĕ-nĕs)	128	26°00'N	111°45'W
Las Tunas, prov., Cuba	134	21°05'N	77°00'W
Las Vacas, Mex. (läs-vá'käs)	131	16°24'N	95°48'W
Las Vegas, Chile (läs-vĕ'gäs)	141b	32°50'S	70°59'W
Las Vegas, N.M., U.S.	104	35°36'N	105°13'W
Las Vegas, Nv., U.S. (läs vā'gäs)	104	36°12'N	115°10'W
Las Vegas, Ven. (läs-vĕ'gäs)	143b	10°26'N	64°08'W
Las Vigas, Mex.	131	19°38'N	97°03'W
Las Vizcachas, Meseta de, plat., Arg.	144	49°35'S	71°00'W
Latacunga, Ec. (lä-tä-kòŋ'gä)	142	1°02'S	78°33'W
Latakia *see* Al Lādhiqīyah, Syria	198	35°32'N	35°51'E
La Teste-de-Buch, Fr. (lä-tĕst-dĕ-büsh)	170	44°38'N	1°11'W
Lathrop, Mo., U.S. (lā'thrŭp)	121	39°32'N	94°21'W
La Tortuga, Isla, i., Ven. (ē's-lä-lä-tôr-tōō'gä)	142	10°55'N	65°18'W
Latorytsia, r., Eur.	169	48°27'N	22°30'E
Latourell, Or., U.S. (lȧ-tou'rĕl)	116c	45°32'N	122°13'W
La Tremblade, Fr. (lä-trĕN-bläd')	170	45°45'N	1°12'W
Latrobe, Pa., U.S. (lȧ-trōb')	109	40°25'N	79°15'W
La Tuque, Can. (lá'tük')	91	47°27'N	72°49'W
Lātūr, India (lä-tōōr')	202	18°20'N	76°35'E
Latvia, nation, Eur.	178	57°28'N	24°29'E
Lau Group, is., Fiji	214g	18°20'S	178°30'W
Launceston, Austl. (lôn'sĕs-tŭn)	219	41°35'S	147°22'E
Launceston, Eng., U.K. (lôrn'stŏn)	164	50°38'N	4°26'W
La Unión, Chile (lä-ōō-nyô'n)	144	40°15'S	73°04'W
La Unión, El Sal.	132	13°18'N	87°51'W
La Unión, Mex. (lä ōōn-nyōn')	130	17°59'N	101°48'W
La Unión, Spain	162	37°38'N	0°50'W
Laura, Austl. (lôrȧ)	219	15°40'S	144°45'E
Laurel, De., U.S. (lô'rĕl)	109	38°30'N	75°40'W
Laurel, Md., U.S.	110e	39°06'N	76°51'W
Laurel, Ms., U.S.	105	31°42'N	89°07'W
Laurel, Mt., U.S.	115	45°41'N	108°45'W
Laurel, Wa., U.S.	116d	48°52'N	122°29'W
Laurelwood, Or., U.S. (lô'rĕl-wòd)	116c	45°25'N	123°05'W
Laurens, S.C., U.S. (lô'rĕnz)	125	34°29'N	82°03'W
Laurentian Highlands, hills, Can. (lô'rĕn-tĭ-ȧn)	89	49°00'N	74°50'W
Laurentides, Can. (lô'rĕn-tīdz)	102a	45°51'N	73°46'W
Lauria, Italy (lou'rē-ä)	163	40°03'N	15°02'E
Laurinburg, N.C., U.S. (lô'rĭn-bûrg)	125	34°45'N	79°27'W
Laurium, Mi., U.S. (lô'rĭ-ŭm)	113	47°13'N	88°28'W
Lausanne, Switz. (lō-zȧn')	154	46°32'N	6°35'E
Laut, Pulau, i., Indon.	212	3°39'S	116°07'E
Lautaro, Chile (lou-tä'rô)	144	38°40'S	72°24'W
Laut Kecil, Kepulauan, is., Indon.	212	4°44'S	115°43'E
Lautoka, Fiji	214g	17°37'S	177°27'E
Lauzon, Can. (lō-zōN')	102b	46°50'N	71°10'W
Lava Beds National Monument, rec., Ca., U.S. (lä'vȧ bĕds)	114	41°38'N	121°44'W
Lavaca, r., Tx., U.S. (lȧ-vák'ȧ)	123	29°05'N	96°50'W
Lava Hot Springs, Id., U.S.	115	42°37'N	111°58'W
Laval, Can.	91	45°31'N	73°44'W
Laval, Fr. (lä-väl')	161	48°05'N	0°47'W
La Vecilla de Curueño, Spain	172	42°53'N	5°18'W
La Vega, Dom. Rep. (lä-vĕ'gä)	135	19°15'N	70°35'W
Lavello, Italy (lä-vĕl'lô)	174	41°05'N	15°50'E
La Verne, Ca., U.S. (lȧ vûrn')	117a	34°06'N	117°46'W
Laverton, Austl. (lā'vēr-tŭn)	218	28°45'S	122°30'E
La Victoria, Ven. (lä vēk-tō'rē-ä)	142	10°14'N	67°20'W
La Vila Joiosa, Spain	173	38°30'N	0°14'W
Lavonia, Ga., U.S. (lȧ-vō'nĭ-ȧ)	124	34°26'N	83°05'W
Lavon Reservoir, res., Tx., U.S.	123	33°06'N	96°20'W
Lavras, Braz. (lä'vräzh)	141a	21°15'S	44°59'W
Lávrio, Grc.	175	37°44'N	24°05'E
Lavry, Russia (lou'rȧ)	176	57°35'N	27°28'E
Lawndale, Ca., U.S. (lôn'dāl)	117a	33°54'N	118°22'W
Lawra, Ghana	234	10°39'N	2°52'W
Lawrence, In., U.S. (lô'rĕns)	111g	39°59'N	86°01'W
Lawrence, Ks., U.S.	105	38°57'N	95°13'W
Lawrence, Ma., U.S.	101a	42°42'N	71°09'W
Lawrence, Pa., U.S.	111e	40°18'N	80°07'W
Lawrenceburg, In., U.S. (lô'rĕns-bûrg)	111f	39°06'N	84°47'W
Lawrenceburg, Ky., U.S.	108	38°00'N	85°00'W
Lawrenceburg, Tn., U.S.	124	35°13'N	87°20'W
Lawrenceville, Ga., U.S. (lô-rĕns-vĭl)	124	33°56'N	83°57'W
Lawrenceville, Il., U.S.	108	38°45'N	87°45'W
Lawrenceville, N.J., U.S.	110a	40°17'N	74°44'W
Lawrenceville, Va., U.S.	125	36°43'N	77°52'W
Lawsonia, Md., U.S. (lô-sō'nĭ-ȧ)	109	38°00'N	75°50'W
Lawton, Ok., U.S. (lô'tŭn)	104	34°36'N	98°25'W
Lawz, Jabal al, mtn., Sau. Ar.	198	28°46'N	35°37'E
Layang Layang, Malay. (lä-yäng' lä-yäng')	197b	1°49'N	103°28'E
Laysan, i., Hi., U.S.	126b	26°00'N	171°00'W
Layton, Ut., U.S. (lā'tŭn)	117b	41°04'N	111°58'W
Lazdijai, Lith. (läzh'dē-yī')	167	54°12'N	23°35'E
Lazio (Latium), hist. reg., Italy	174	42°05'N	12°25'E
Lead, S.D., U.S. (lēd)	104	44°22'N	103°47'W
Leader, Can.	96	50°55'N	109°32'W
Leadville, Co., U.S. (lĕd'vĭl)	120	39°14'N	106°18'W
Leaf, r., Ms., U.S. (lēf)	124	31°43'N	89°20'W
League City, Tx., U.S. (lēg)	123a	29°31'N	95°05'W
Leamington, Can. (lĕm'ĭng-tŭn)	98	42°05'N	82°35'W
Leamington, Eng., U.K. (lĕ'mĭng-tŭn)	164	52°17'N	1°25'W
Leatherhead, Eng., U.K. (lĕdh'ēr-hĕd')	158b	51°17'N	0°20'W
Leavenworth, Ks., U.S. (lĕv'ĕn-wûrth)	105	39°19'N	94°54'W
Leavenworth, Wa., U.S.	114	47°35'N	120°39'W
Leawood, Ks., U.S. (lē'wòd)	117f	38°58'N	94°37'W
Łeba, Pol. (lā'bä)	169	54°45'N	17°34'E
Lebam, r., Malay.	197b	1°35'N	104°09'E
Lebango, Congo	236	0°22'N	14°49'E
Lebanon, Il., U.S. (lĕb'ȧ-nŭn)	117e	38°36'N	89°49'W
Lebanon, In., U.S.	108	40°00'N	86°30'W
Lebanon, Ky., U.S.	124	37°32'N	85°15'W
Lebanon, Mo., U.S.	121	37°40'N	92°43'W
Lebanon, N.H., U.S.	109	43°40'N	72°15'W
Lebanon, Oh., U.S.	108	39°25'N	84°10'W
Lebanon, Or., U.S.	114	44°31'N	122°53'W
Lebanon, Pa., U.S.	109	40°20'N	76°20'W
Lebanon, Tn., U.S.	124	36°10'N	86°16'W
Lebanon, nation, Asia	198	34°00'N	34°00'E
Lebedyan', Russia (lyĕ'bĕ-dyän')	180	53°03'N	39°08'E
Lebedyn, Ukr.	181	50°34'N	34°27'E
Le Blanc, Fr. (lĕ-blän')	170	46°38'N	0°59'E
Le Borgne, Haiti (lē bōrn'y')	135	19°50'N	72°30'W
Lębork, Pol. (lăN-bòrk')	169	54°33'N	17°46'E
Lebrija, Spain (lå-brē'hä)	172	36°55'N	6°06'W
Lecce, Italy (lĕt'chā)	163	40°22'N	18°11'E
Lecco, Italy (lĕk'kō)	174	45°52'N	9°28'E
Lech, r., Ger. (lĕk)	168	47°41'N	10°52'E
Le Châtelet-en-Brie, Fr. (lĕ-shä-tĕ-lā'ĕN-brē')	171b	48°29'N	2°50'E
Leche, Laguna de, l., Cuba (lä-gò'nä-dĕ-lĕ'chĕ)	134	22°10'N	78°30'W
Leche, Laguna de la, l., Mex.	122	27°16'N	102°45'W
Lecompte, La., U.S.	123	31°06'N	92°25'W
Le Creusot, Fr. (lĕkrü-zō)	161	46°48'N	4°23'E
Ledesma, Spain (lå-dĕs'mä)	172	41°05'N	5°59'W
Leduc, Can. (lĕ-dōōk')	95	53°16'N	113°33'W
Leech, l., Mn., U.S. (lēch)	113	47°06'N	94°16'W
Leeds, Eng., U.K.	154	53°48'N	1°33'W
Leeds, Al., U.S. (lēdz)	110h	33°33'N	86°33'W
Leeds, N.D., U.S.	112	48°18'N	99°24'W
Leeds, co., Eng., U.K.	158a	53°50'N	1°30'W
Leeds and Liverpool Canal, can., Eng., U.K. (lĭv'ēr-pōōl)	158a	53°36'N	2°38'W
Leegebruch, Ger. (lĕh'gĕn-brōōk)	159b	52°43'N	13°12'E
Leek, Eng., U.K. (lēk)	158a	53°06'N	2°01'W
Leer, Ger. (lār)	168	53°14'N	7°27'E
Leesburg, Fl., U.S. (lēz'bûrg)	125	28°49'N	81°53'W
Leesburg, Va., U.S.	109	39°10'N	77°30'W
Lees Summit, Mo., U.S.	117f	38°55'N	94°23'W
Lee Stocking, i., Bah.	134	23°45'N	76°05'W
Leesville, La., U.S. (lēz'vĭl)	123	31°09'N	93°17'W
Leetonia, Oh., U.S. (lē-tō'nĭ-ȧ)	108	40°50'N	80°45'W
Leeuwarden, Neth. (lā'wär-dĕn)	161	52°12'N	5°50'E
Leeuwin, Cape, c., Austl. (lōō'wĭn)	220	34°15'S	114°30'E
Leeward Islands, is., N.A. (lē'wērd)	123	17°00'N	62°15'W
Lefkáda, Grc.	175	38°49'N	20°43'E
Lefkáda, i., Grc.	163	38°42'N	20°22'E
Le François, Mart.	133b	14°37'N	60°55'W
Lefroy, l., Austl. (lē-froi')	220	31°30'S	122°00'E
Leganés, Spain (lå-gä'nás)	173a	40°20'N	3°46'W
Legazpi, Phil. (lå-gäs'pē)	213	13°09'N	123°44'E
Legge Peak, mtn., Austl. (lĕg)	222	41°33'S	148°10'E
Leggett, Ca., U.S.	118	39°51'N	123°42'W
Leghorn *see* Livorno, Italy	154	43°32'N	11°18'E
Legnano, Italy (lå-nyä'nō)	174	45°35'N	8°53'E
Legnica, Pol. (lĕk-nĭt'sȧ)	161	51°13'N	16°10'E
Leh, India (lā)	202	34°10'N	77°40'E
Le Havre, Fr. (lē áv'r')	154	49°31'N	0°07'E
Lehi, Ut., U.S. (lē'hī)	119	40°25'N	111°55'W
Lehman Caves National Monument, rec., Nv., U.S. (lē'mȧn)	119	38°54'N	114°08'W
Lehnin, Ger. (lĕh'nēn)	159b	52°19'N	12°45'E
Leicester, Eng., U.K. (lĕs'tēr)	154	52°37'N	1°08'W
Leicestershire, co., Eng., U.K.	158a	52°40'N	1°12'W
Leichhardt, r., Austl. (līk'härt)	220	18°30'S	139°45'E
Leiden, Neth. (lī'dĕn)	165	52°09'N	4°29'E
Leigh Creek, Austl. (lē krēk)	222	30°33'S	138°30'E
Leikanger, Nor. (lī'käŋ'gēr)	166	61°11'N	6°51'E
Leimuiden, Neth.	159a	52°13'N	4°40'E
Leine, r., Ger. (lī'nĕ)	168	51°58'N	9°56'E
Leinster, hist. reg., Ire. (lĕn-stēr)	164	52°45'N	7°19'W
Leipsic, Oh., U.S. (līp'sĭk)	108	41°05'N	84°00'W
Leipzig, Ger. (līp'tsĭk)	154	51°20'N	12°24'E
Leiria, Port. (lå-rē'ä)	172	39°45'N	8°50'W
Leitchfield, Ky., U.S. (lēch'fēld)	124	37°28'N	86°20'W
Leitha, r., Aus.	159e	48°04'N	16°57'E
Leitrim, Can.	102c	45°20'N	75°36'W
Leivádia, Grc.	175	38°25'N	22°51'E

ng-sing; ŋ-baŋk; N-nasalized n; nŏd; cŏmmit; ōld; ōbey; ôrder; oi-boil; fōōd; ò-as oo in foot; ou-out; s-soft; sh-dish; th-thin; pūre; ūnite; ûrn; stŭd; circŭs; ü-as in French tu; '-indeterminate vowel.

ăt; finăl; rāte; senâte; ärm; ásk; sofá; fâre; ch-choose; dh-as th in other; bē; ĕvent; bĕt; recĕnt; crātēr; g-gō; gh-guttural g; bĭt; ī-short neutral; rīde; κ-guttural k as ch in German ich;

316 Loma Linda – Łuków PRONOUNCING INDEX

PLACE (Pronunciation)	PAGE	LAT.	LONG.
Loma Linda, Ca., U.S. (lō'mȧ lĭn'dȧ)	117a	34°04'N	117°16'W
Lomami, r., D.R.C.	232	0°50'S	24°40'E
Lomas de Zamora, Arg. (lō'mäs dā zä-mō'rä)	141c	34°46'S	58°24'W
Lombard, Il., U.S. (lŏm-bärd)	111a	41°53'N	88°01'W
Lombardia, hist. reg., Italy (lôm-bär-dē'ä)	174	45°20'N	9°30'E
Lomblen, Pulau, i., Indon. (lŏm-blĕn')	213	8°08'S	123°45'E
Lombok, i., Indon. (lŏm-bŏk')	212	9°15'S	116°15'E
Lomé, Togo	230	6°08'N	1°13'E
Lomela, D.R.C. (lō-mā'lȧ)	232	2°19'S	23°33'E
Lomela, r., D.R.C.	232	0°35'S	21°20'E
Lometa, Tx., U.S. (lō-mē'tȧ)	122	31°10'N	98°25'W
Lomié, Cam. (lō-mē-ā')	235	3°10'N	13°37'E
Lomita, Ca., U.S. (lō-mē'tȧ)	117a	33°48'N	118°20'W
Lommel, Bel.	159a	51°14'N	5°21'E
Lommond, Loch, l., Scot., U.K. (lŏk lō'mŭnd)	164	56°15'N	4°40'W
Lomonosov, Russia (lô-mô'nô-sof)	186c	59°54'N	29°47'E
Lompoc, Ca., U.S. (lŏm-pŏk')	118	34°39'N	120°30'W
Łomża, Pol. (lôm'zhȧ)	169	53°11'N	22°04'E
Lonaconing, Md., U.S. (lō-nă-kō'nĭng)	109	39°35'N	78°55'W
London, Can. (lŭn'dŭn)	91	43°00'N	81°20'W
London, Eng., U.K.	154	51°30'N	0°07'W
London, Ky., U.S.	124	37°07'N	84°06'W
London, Oh., U.S.	108	39°50'N	83°30'W
Londonderry, Can. (lŭn'dŭn-dĕr-ĭ)	100	45°29'N	63°36'W
Londonderry, N. Ire., U.K.	160	55°00'N	7°19'W
Londonderry, Cape, c., Austl.	220	13°30'S	127°00'E
Londrina, Braz. (lôn-drē'nä)	143	21°53'S	51°17'W
Lonely, i., Can. (lōn'lĭ)	93	45°35'N	81°30'W
Lone Pine, Ca., U.S.	118	36°36'N	118°03'W
Lone Star, Nic.	133	13°58'N	84°25'W
Long, i., Bah.	129	23°25'N	75°10'W
Long, i., Can.	100	44°21'S	66°25'W
Long, l., N.D., U.S.	112	46°47'N	100°14'W
Long, l., Wa., U.S.	116a	47°29'N	122°36'W
Longa, r., Ang. (lôŋ'gȧ)	232	10°20'S	15°15'E
Long Bay, b., S.C., U.S.	125	33°30'N	78°54'W
Long Beach, Ca., U.S. (lông bēch)	104	33°46'N	118°12'W
Long Beach, N.Y., U.S.	110a	40°35'N	73°38'W
Long Branch, N.J., U.S. (lông brȧnch)	110a	40°18'N	73°59'W
Longdon, N.D., U.S. (lông'dŭn)	112	48°45'N	98°23'W
Long Eaton, Eng., U.K. (ē'tŭn)	158a	52°54'N	1°16'W
Longford, Ire. (lŏng'fērd)	164	53°43'N	7°40'W
Longgu, China (lôŋ-gōō)	206	34°52'N	116°48'E
Longhorn, Tx., U.S. (lông-hôrn)	117d	29°33'N	98°23'W
Longido, Tan.	237	2°44'S	36°41'E
Long Island, i., Pap. N. Gui.	213	5°10'S	147°30'E
Long Island, i., Ak., U.S.	94	54°54'N	132°45'W
Long Island, i., N.Y., U.S. (lông)	107	40°50'N	72°50'W
Long Island Sound, strt., U.S. (lông ī'lănd)	107	41°05'N	72°45'W
Longjumeau, Fr. (lôɴ-zhü-mō')	171b	48°42'N	2°17'E
Longkou, China (lôŋ-kō)	206	37°39'N	120°21'E
Longlac, Can. (lông'lăk)	91	49°41'N	86°28'W
Longlake, S.D., U.S. (lông-lāk)	112	45°52'N	99°06'W
Long Lake, l., Can.	98	49°10'N	86°45'W
Longmont, Co., U.S. (lông'mŏnt)	120	40°11'N	105°07'W
Longnor, Eng., U.K. (lông'nôr)	158a	53°11'N	1°52'W
Long Pine, Ne., U.S. (lông pīn)	112	42°31'N	99°42'W
Long Point, c., Can.	97	53°02'N	98°40'W
Long Point, c., Can.	101	48°48'N	58°46'W
Long Point, c., Can.	99	42°35'N	80°05'W
Long Point Bay, b., Can.	99	42°40'N	80°10'W
Long Range Mountains, mts., Can.	93a	48°00'N	58°30'W
Longreach, Austl. (lông'rēch)	219	23°32'S	144°17'E
Long Reach, r., Can.	100	45°26'N	66°05'W
Long Reef, c., Austl.	217b	33°45'S	151°22'E
Longridge, Eng., U.K. (lông'rĭj)	158a	53°51'N	2°37'W
Longs Peak, mtn., Co., U.S. (lôngz)	106	40°17'N	105°37'W
Longtansi, China (lôŋ-tä-sz)	206	32°12'N	115°53'E
Longton, Eng., U.K. (lông'tŭn)	158a	52°59'N	2°08'W
Longueuil, Can. (lôɴ-gû'y')	99	45°32'N	73°30'W
Longview, Tx., U.S.	123	32°29'N	94°44'W
Longview, Wa., U.S. (lông-vū)	114	46°06'N	123°02'W
Longville, La., U.S. (lông'vĭl)	123	30°36'N	93°14'W
Longwy, Fr. (lôɴ-wē')	171	49°32'N	6°14'E
Longxi, China (lôŋ-shyē)	204	35°00'N	104°40'E
Long Xuyen, Viet. (loung' sōō'yĕn)	212	10°31'N	105°28'E
Longzhou, China (lôŋ-jō)	204	22°20'N	107°02'E
Lonoke, Ar., U.S. (lō'nōk)	121	34°48'N	91°52'W
Lons-le-Saunier, Fr. (lôɴ-lē-sō-nyā')	171	46°40'N	5°33'E
Lontue, r., Chile (lōn-tōĕ')	141b	35°20'S	70°45'W
Looc, Phil. (lō-ōk')	213a	12°16'N	121°59'E
Loogootee, In., U.S.	108	38°40'N	86°55'W
Lookout, Cape, c., N.C., U.S. (lŏŏk'out)	125	34°34'N	76°38'W
Lookout Point Lake, res., Or., U.S.	114	43°51'N	122°38'W
Loolmalasin, mtn., Tan.	237	3°03'S	35°46'E
Looma, Can. (ŏ'mȧ)	102g	53°22'N	113°15'W
Loop Head, c., Ire. (lōōp)	164	52°32'N	9°59'W
Loosahatchie, r., Tn., U.S. (lōz-ȧ-hă'chē)	124	35°20'N	89°45'W
Loosdrechtsche Plassen, l., Neth.	159a	52°11'N	5°09'E
Lopatka, Mys, c., Russia (lô-pät'kȧ)	197	51°00'N	156°52'E
Lopez, Cap, c., Gabon	236	0°37'N	8°43'E
Lopez Bay, b., Phil. (lō'pāz)	213a	14°04'N	122°00'E
Lopez l, Wa., U.S.	116a	48°25'N	122°53'W
Lopori, r., D.R.C. (lō-pō'rē)	231	1°35'N	20°43'E
Lora, Spain (lō'rä)	172	37°40'N	5°31'W
Lorain, Oh., U.S. (lō-rān')	111d	41°28'N	82°10'W
Loralai, Pak. (lō-rŭ-lī')	199	30°31'N	68°35'E
Lorca, Spain (lôr'kä)	162	37°39'N	1°40'W
Lord Howe, i., Austl. (lôrd hou)	220	31°44'S	157°56'W
Lordsburg, N.M., U.S. (lôrdz'bûrg)	119	32°20'N	108°45'W
Lorena, Braz. (lō-rā'nȧ)	141a	22°45'S	45°07'W
Loreto, Braz. (lō-rā'tō)	143	7°09'S	45°10'W
Loretteville, Can. (lô-rĕt-vēl')	102b	46°51'N	71°21'W
Lorica, Col. (lō-rē'kä)	142	9°14'N	75°54'W
Lorient, Fr. (lō-rē'äɴ')	161	47°45'N	3°22'W
Lorn, Firth of, b., Scot., U.K. (fûrth ŏv lôrn')	164	56°10'N	6°09'W
Lörrach, Ger. (lûr'äĸ)	168	47°36'N	7°38'E
Lorraine, hist. reg., Fr.	171	49°00'N	6°00'E
Los Alamitos, Ca., U.S. (lōs ăl-ȧ-mē'tōs)	117a	33°48'N	118°04'W
Los Alamos, N.M., U.S. (ăl-ȧ-mōs')	119	35°53'N	106°20'W
Los Altos, Ca., U.S. (ăl-tōs')	116b	37°23'N	122°06'W
Los Andes, Chile (àn'dĕs)	141b	32°44'S	70°36'W
Los Angeles, Chile (äŋ'hā-lās)	144	37°27'S	72°15'W
Los Angeles, Ca., U.S.	104	34°03'N	118°14'W
Los Angeles, Ca., U.S.	118	34°03'N	118°14'W
Los Angeles, r., Ca., U.S.	117a	33°50'N	118°13'W
Los Angeles Aqueduct, Ca., U.S.	118	35°12'N	118°02'W
Los Bronces, Chile (lōs brō'n-sĕs)	141b	33°09'S	70°18'W
Loscha, r., Id., U.S. (lŏs'chȧ)	114	46°20'N	115°11'W
Los Estados, Isla de, i., Arg. (ē's-lä dĕ lōs ĕs-dōs)	144	54°45'S	64°25'W
Los Gatos, Ca., U.S. (gä'tōs)	118	37°13'N	121°59'W
Los Herreras, Mex. (ĕr-rā-räs)	122	25°55'N	99°23'W
Los llanos, Dom. Rep. (lōs ĕ-lä'nōs)	135	18°35'N	69°30'W
Los Indios, Cayos de, is., Cuba (kä'vōs dĕ lōs ē'n-dvō's)	134	21°50'N	83°10'W
Lošinj, i., Serb.	174	44°35'N	14°34'E
Losino Petrovskiy, Russia	186b	55°52'N	38°12'E
Los Nietos, Ca., U.S. (nyā'tōs)	117a	33°57'N	118°05'W
Los Palacios, Cuba	134	22°35'N	83°15'W
Los Pinos, r., Co., U.S. (pē'nōs)	119	36°58'N	107°35'W
Los Reyes, Mex.	128	19°35'N	102°29'W
Los Reyes, Mex.	131a	19°21'N	98°58'W
Los Santos, Pan. (săn'tōs)	133	7°57'N	80°24'W
Los Santos de Maimona, Spain (san'tōs)	172	38°38'N	6°30'W
Lost, r., Or., U.S.	114	42°07'N	121°30'W
Los Teques, Ven. (tĕ'kĕs)	142	10°22'N	67°04'W
Lost River Range, mts., Id., U.S. (rĭ'vēr)	115	44°23'N	113°48'W
Los Vilos, Chile (vē'lōs)	144	31°56'S	71°29'W
Lot, r., Fr. (lôt)	161	44°30'N	1°30'E
Lota, Chile (lō'tä)	144	37°11'S	73°14'W
Lothian, Md., U.S. (lōth'ĭăn)	110e	38°50'N	76°38'W
Lotikipi Plain, pl., Afr.	237	4°25'N	34°55'E
Lötschberg Tunnel, trans., Switz.	168	46°26'N	7°54'E
Louangphrabang, Laos (lōō-ang'prä-bäng')	212	19°47'N	102°15'E
Loudon, Tn., U.S. (lou'dŭn)	124	35°43'N	84°20'W
Loudonville, Oh., U.S. (lou'dŭn-vĭl)	108	40°40'N	82°15'W
Loudun, Fr.	170	47°03'N	0°00'
Loughborough, Eng., U.K. (lŭf'bŭr-ō)	158a	52°46'N	1°12'W
Louisa, Ky., U.S. (lōō'ēz-ȧ)	108	38°05'N	82°40'W
Louisade Archipelago, is., Pap. N. Gui.	221	10°44'S	153°58'E
Louisberg, N.C., U.S. (lōō'ĭs-bûrg)	125	36°05'N	79°19'W
Louisburg, Can. (lōō'ĭs-bourg)	101	45°55'N	59°58'W
Louiseville, Can.	99	46°17'N	72°58'W
Louisiana, Mo., U.S. (lōō-ē-zē-ăn'ȧ)	121	39°24'N	91°03'W
Louisiana, state, U.S.	105	30°50'N	92°50'W
Louis Trichardt, S. Afr. (lōō'ĭs trĭchärt)	232	22°52'S	29°53'E
Louisville, Co., U.S. (lōō'ĭs-vĭl) (lōō'ē-vĭl)	120	39°58'N	105°08'W
Louisville, Ga., U.S.	125	33°00'N	82°25'W
Louisville, Ky., U.S.	105	38°15'N	85°45'W
Louisville, Ms., U.S.	124	33°07'N	89°02'W
Louis XIV, Pointe, c., Can.	93	54°35'N	79°51'W
Louny, Czech Rep. (lō'nē)	168	50°20'N	13°47'E
Loup, r., Ne., U.S. (lōōp)	112	41°17'N	97°58'W
Loup City, Ne., U.S.	112	41°15'N	98°59'W
Lourdes, Fr. (lōōrd)	161	43°06'N	0°03'W
Lourenço Marques *see* Maputo, Moz.	232	26°50'S	32°30'E
Loures, Port. (lō'rĕzh)	173b	38°49'N	9°10'W
Lousa, Port. (lō'zȧ)	172	40°05'N	8°12'W
Louth, Eng., U.K. (louth)	164	53°27'N	0°02'W
Louvain *see* Leuven, Bel.	165	50°53'N	4°42'E
Louviers, Fr. (lōō-vyā')	170	49°13'N	1°11'E
Lovech, Blg. (lō'vĕts)	175	43°10'N	24°40'E
Loveland, Co., U.S. (lŭv'lănd)	120	40°24'N	105°04'W
Loveland, Oh., U.S.	111f	39°16'N	84°15'W
Lovell, Wy., U.S. (lŭv'ĕl)	115	44°50'N	108°23'W
Lovelock, Nv., U.S. (lŭv'lŏk)	118	40°10'N	118°37'W
Lovick, Al., U.S. (lŭ'vĭk)	110h	33°34'N	86°38'W
Loviisa, Fin. (lô'vē-sä)	167	60°28'N	26°10'E
Low, Cape, c., Can. (lō)	93	62°58'N	86°50'W
Lowa, r., D.R.C. (lō'wȧ)	232	1°30'S	27°18'E
Lowell, In., U.S.	111a	41°17'N	87°26'W
Lowell, Ma., U.S.	105	42°38'N	71°18'W
Lowell, Mi., U.S.	108	42°55'N	85°20'W
Löwenberg, Ger. (lû'vĕn-bĕrgh)	159b	52°53'N	13°09'E
Lower Brule Indian Reservation, I.R., S.D., U.S. (brü'lā)	112	44°15'N	100°21'W
Lower California *see* Baja California, pen., Mex.	89	28°00'N	113°30'W
Lower Granite Dam, dam, Wa., U.S.	114	46°40'N	117°26'W
Lower Hutt, N.Z. (hŭt)	221a	41°10'S	174°55'E
Lower Klamath Lake, l., Ca., U.S. (klăm'ȧth)	114	41°55'N	121°50'W
Lower Lake, l., Ca., U.S.	114	41°21'N	119°53'W
Lower Marlboro, Md., U.S. (lō'ēr märl'bōrō)	110e	38°40'N	76°42'W
Lower Monumental Dam, dam, Wa., U.S.	114	46°34'N	118°32'W
Lower Otay Lake, res., Ca., U.S. (ō'tā)	118a	32°37'N	116°46'W
Lower Red Lake, l., Mn., U.S.	113	47°58'N	94°31'W
Lower Saxony *see* Niedersachsen, state, Ger.	159c	53°30'N	9°30'E
Lowestoft, Eng., U.K. (lō'stŏf)	165	52°31'N	1°45'E
Łowicz, Pol. (lô'vĭch)	169	52°06'N	19°57'E
Lowville, N.Y., U.S. (lou'vĭl)	109	43°45'N	75°30'W
Loxicha, Mex.	131	16°03'N	96°46'W
Loxton, Austl. (lôks'tŭn)	222	34°25'S	140°38'E
Loyauté, Îles, is., N. Cal.	221	21°00'S	167°00'E
Loznica, Serb. (lōz'nē-tsȧ)	163	44°31'N	19°16'E
Lozova, Ukr.	181	48°53'N	36°23'E
Luama, r., D.R.C. (lōō'ä-mȧ)	232	4°17'S	27°45'E
Lu'an, China (lōō-än)	209	31°45'N	116°29'E
Luan, r., China	205	41°25'N	117°15'E
Luanda, Ang. (lōō-än'dä)	232	8°48'S	13°14'E
Luanguinga, r., Afr. (lōō-ä-gĭŋ'gȧ)	232	14°00'S	20°45'E
Luanshya, Zam.	237	13°08'S	28°24'E
Luanxian, China (luän shyĕn)	206	39°47'N	118°40'E
Luao, Ang.	236	10°42'S	22°12'E
Luarca, Spain (lwä'kä)	162	43°33'N	6°30'W
Lubaczów, Pol. (lōō-bä'chōf)	169	50°08'N	23°10'E
Lubán, Pol. (lōō'bän')	168	51°08'N	15°17'E
Lubānas Ezers, l., Lat. (lōō-bä'nȧs ā'zĕrs)	167	56°48'N	26°30'E
Lubang, Phil. (lōō-bäng')	213a	13°49'N	120°07'E
Lubang Islands, is., Phil.	212	13°47'N	119°56'E
Lubango, Ang.	232	14°55'S	13°30'E
Lubartów, Pol. (lōō-bär'tŏf)	169	51°27'N	22°37'E
Lubawa, Pol. (lōō-bä'vä)	169	53°31'N	19°47'E
Lübben, Ger. (lüb'ĕn)	168	51°56'N	13°53'E
Lubbock, Tx., U.S.	105	33°35'N	101°50'E
Lubec, Me., U.S. (lū'bĕk)	100	44°49'N	67°01'W
Lübeck, Ger. (lü'bĕk)	154	53°53'N	10°42'E
Lübecker Bucht, b., Ger. (lü'bĕ-kĕr bōōĸt)	160	54°10'N	11°20'E
Lubilash, r., D.R.C. (lōō-bē-lash')	232	7°35'S	23°55'E
Lubin, Pol. (lyŏ'bĭn)	168	51°24'N	16°14'E
Lublin, Pol. (lyŏ'blĕn')	154	51°14'N	22°33'E
Lubny, Ukr. (lŏb'nē)	181	50°01'N	33°02'E
Lubuagan, Phil. (lō-bwä-gä'n)	213a	17°24'N	121°11'E
Lubudi, D.R.C.	237	9°57'S	25°58'E
Lubudi, r., D.R.C. (lō-bō'dē)	232	10°00'S	24°30'E
Lubumbashi, D.R.C.	232	11°40'S	27°28'E
Lucano, Ang.	236	11°16'S	21°38'E
Lucca, Italy (lōōk'kä)	162	43°51'N	10°29'E
Lucea, Jam.	134	18°25'N	78°10'W
Luce Bay, b., Scot., U.K. (lūs)	164	54°45'N	4°45'W
Lucena, Phil. (lōō-sā'nä)	213a	13°55'N	121°36'E
Lucena, Spain (lōō-thā'nä)	162	37°25'N	4°28'W
Lučenec, Slvk. (lōō'châ-nyĕts)	161	48°19'N	19°41'E
Lucera, Italy (lōō-châ'rä)	174	41°31'N	15°22'E
Luchi, China	209	28°18'N	110°10'E
Lucin, Ut., U.S. (lū-sĕn')	115	41°23'N	113°59'W
Lucipara, Kepulauan, is., Indon.	213	5°45'S	128°15'E
Luckenwalde, Ger.	168	52°05'N	13°10'E
Lucknow, India (lŭk'nou)	199	26°54'N	80°58'E
Lucky Peak Lake, res., Id., U.S.	114	43°33'N	116°00'W
Luçon, Fr. (lü-sôɴ')	170	46°27'N	1°12'W
Lucrecia, Cabo, c., Cuba	135	21°05'N	75°30'W
Luda Kamchiya, r., Blg.	175	42°46'N	27°13'E
Lüdenscheid, Ger. (lü'dĕn-shīt)	171c	51°13'N	7°38'E
Lüderitz, Nmb. (lü'dēr-ĭts) (lü'dĕ-rĭts)	232	26°35'S	15°15'E
Lüderitz Bucht, b., Nmb.	232	26°35'S	14°30'E
Ludhiāna, India	199	31°00'N	75°52'E
Lüdinghausen, Ger.	171c	51°46'N	7°27'E
Ludington, Mi., U.S. (lŭd'ĭng-tŭn)	108	44°00'N	86°25'W
Ludlow, Eng., U.K. (lŭd'lō)	158a	52°22'N	2°43'W
Ludlow, Ky., U.S.	111f	39°05'N	84°33'W
Ludvika, Swe. (loodh-vē'kȧ)	166	60°10'N	15°09'E
Ludwigsburg, Ger.	168	48°53'N	9°14'E
Ludwigsfelde, Ger.	159b	52°18'N	13°16'E
Ludwigshafen, Ger.	168	49°29'N	8°26'E
Ludwigslust, Ger.	168	53°18'N	11°31'E
Ludza, Lat. (lōōd'zȧ)	167	56°33'N	27°45'E
Luebo, D.R.C. (lōō-ā'bō)	232	5°15'S	21°22'E
Luena, Ang.	232	11°45'S	19°55'E
Luena, D.R.C.	237	9°27'S	25°47'E
Lufira, r., D.R.C. (lōō-fē'rȧ)	232	9°32'S	27°15'E
Lufkin, Tx., U.S. (lŭf'kĭn)	123	31°21'N	94°43'W
Luga, Russia (lōō'gȧ)	180	58°43'N	29°52'E
Luga, r., Russia	176	59°00'N	29°25'E
Lugano, Switz. (lōō-gä'nō)	168	46°01'N	8°52'E
Lugenda, r., Moz.	233	12°05'S	38°15'E
Lugo, Italy (lōō'gō)	174	44°28'N	11°57'E
Lugo, Spain (lōō'gō)	162	43°01'N	7°32'W
Lugoj, Rom.	163	45°51'N	21°56'E
Luhans'k, Ukr.	178	48°34'N	39°18'E
Luhans'k, prov., Ukr.	177	49°30'N	38°35'E
Luhe, China (lōō-hŭ)	206	32°22'N	118°50'E
Luiana, Ang.	236	17°23'S	23°03'E
Luilaka, r., D.R.C. (lōō-ē-lä'kȧ)	232	2°18'S	21°15'E
Luis Moya, Mex. (lōōē's-mô-yä)	130	22°26'N	102°14'W
Luján, Arg. (lōō'hän')	141c	34°36'S	59°07'W
Luján, r., Arg.	141c	34°33'S	58°59'W
Lujia, China (lōō-jyä)	206	31°17'N	120°54'W
Lukanga Swamp, sw., Zam. (lōō-käŋ'gȧ)	232	14°30'S	27°25'E
Lukenie, r., D.R.C. (lōō-kā'nyā)	232	3°10'S	19°05'E
Lukolela, D.R.C.	232	1°03'S	17°01'E
Lukovit, Blg. (lōō'kō-vĕt')	175	43°13'N	24°07'E
Łuków, Pol. (wŏ'kōf)	169	51°57'N	22°25'E

ăt; fĭnăl; rāte; senăte; ärm; ȧsk; sofȧ; fâre; ch-choose; dh-as th in other; bē; ēvent; bĕt; recĕnt; cratēr; g-gō; gh-guttural g; bĭt; ĭ-short neutral; rīde; ĸ-guttural k as ch in German ich;

PRONOUNCING INDEX
Lukuga – Maḩaţţat Jurf ad Darāwīsh 317

PLACE (Pronunciation)	PAGE	LAT.	LONG.
Lukuga, r., D.R.C. (lōō-kōō′gȧ)	232	5°50′S	27°35′E
Lüleburgaz, Tur. (lü′lĕ-bòr-gäs′)	175	41°25′N	27°23′E
Luling, Tx., U.S. (lū′lĭng)	123	29°41′N	97°38′W
Lulong, China (lōō-lôŋ)	205	39°54′N	118°53′E
Lulonga, r., D.R.C.	236	1°00′N	18°37′E
Luluabourg *see* Kananga, D.R.C.	232	6°14′S	22°17′E
Lulu Island, i., Can.	116d	49°09′N	123°05′W
Lulu Island, i., Ak., U.S.	94	55°28′N	133°30′W
Lumajangdong Co, l., China	202	34°00′N	81°47′E
Lumber, r., N.C., U.S. (lŭm′bẽr)	125	34°45′N	79°10′W
Lumberton, Ms., U.S. (lŭm′bẽr-tŭn)	124	31°00′N	89°25′W
Lumberton, N.C., U.S.	125	34°47′N	79°00′W
Luminárias, Braz. (lōō-mē-ná′ryäs)	141a	21°32′S	44°53′W
Lummi, i., Wa., U.S.	116d	48°42′N	122°43′W
Lummi Bay, b., Wa., U.S. (lŭm′ĭ)	116d	48°47′N	122°44′W
Lummi Island, Wa., U.S.	116d	48°44′N	122°42′W
Lumwana, Zam.	237	11°50′S	25°10′E
Lün, Mong.	204	47°58′N	104°52′E
Luna, Phil. (lōō′nȧ)	213a	16°51′N	120°22′E
Lund, Swe. (lŭnd)	160	55°42′N	13°10′E
Lundy, i., Eng., U.K. (lŭn′dē)	164	51°12′N	4°50′W
Lüneburg, Ger. (lü′nē-bòrgh)	168	53°16′N	10°25′E
Lunel, Fr. (lü-nĕl′)	170	43°41′N	4°07′E
Lünen, Ger. (lü′nĕn)	171c	51°36′N	7°30′E
Lunenburg, Can. (lōō′nĕn-bûrg)	91	44°23′N	64°19′W
Lunenburg, Ma., U.S.	101a	42°36′N	71°44′W
Lunéville, Fr. (lü-nȧ-vel′)	171	48°37′N	6°29′E
Lunga, Ang.	236	14°42′S	18°32′E
Lungué-Bungo, r., Afr.	232	13°00′S	20°30′E
Lunsar, S.L.	234	8°41′N	12°32′W
Luodian, China (lwô-dĭĕn)	206	31°25′N	121°20′E
Luoding, China (lwô-dĭŋ)	209	23°42′N	111°35′E
Luohe, China (lwô-hŭ)	206	33°35′N	114°02′E
Luoyang, China (lwô-yäŋ)	205	34°45′N	112°32′E
Luozhen, China (lwô-jŭn)	206	37°45′N	118°29′E
Luque, Para. (loo′kä)	144	25°18′S	57°17′W
Luray, Va., U.S. (lū-rā′)	109	38°40′N	78°25′W
Lurgan, N. Ire., U.K. (lûr′găn)	160	54°27′N	6°28′W
Lúrio, Moz. (lōō′rê-ō)	233	13°17′S	40°29′E
Lúrio, Moz.	233	14°00′S	38°45′E
Lusaka, D.R.C.	237	7°10′S	29°27′E
Lusaka, Zam. (lō-sä′kȧ)	232	15°25′S	28°17′E
Lusambo, D.R.C. (lōō-säm′bō)	232	4°58′S	23°27′E
Lusanga, D.R.C.	232	5°13′S	18°43′E
Lusangi, D.R.C.	237	4°37′S	27°08′E
Lushan, China	208	33°45′N	113°00′E
Lushiko, r., Afr.	236	6°35′S	19°45′E
Lushoto, Tan. (lōō-shō′tō)	233	4°47′S	38°17′E
Lüshun, China (lü-shŭn)	205	38°49′N	121°15′E
Lusikisiki, S. Afr. (lōō-sê-kê-sē′kê)	233c	31°22′S	29°37′E
Lusk, Wy., U.S. (lŭsk)	112	42°46′N	104°27′W
Lūt, Dasht-e, des., Iran (dȧ′sht-ē-lōōt)	198	31°47′N	58°38′E
Lutcher, La., U.S. (lŭch′ẽr)	123	30°03′N	90°43′W
Luton, Eng., U.K. (lū′tŭn)	164	51°55′N	0°28′W
Luts'k, Ukr.	181	50°45′N	25°20′E
Luuq, Som.	238a	3°38′N	42°35′E
Luverne, Al., U.S. (lū-vûn′)	124	31°42′N	86°15′W
Luverne, Mn., U.S.	112	43°40′N	96°13′W
Luwingu, Zam.	237	10°15′S	29°55′E
Luxapallila Creek, r., U.S. (lŭk-sȧ-pôl′ĭ-lȧ)	124	33°36′N	88°08′W
Luxembourg, Lux.	154	49°38′N	6°30′E
Luxembourg, nation, Eur.	154	49°30′N	6°22′E
Luxeuil-les-Baines, Fr.	171	47°49′N	6°19′E
Luxomni, Ga., U.S. (lŭx′ôm-nī)	110c	33°54′N	84°07′W
Luxor *see* Al Uqşur, Egypt	231	25°38′N	32°59′E
Luya Shan, mtn., China	208	38°50′N	111°40′E
Luyi, China (lōō-yē)	206	33°52′N	115°32′E
Luzern, Switz. (lō-tsĕrn)	161	47°03′N	8°18′E
Luzhou, China (lōō-jō)	204	28°58′N	105°25′E
Luziânia, Braz. (lōō-zyà′nēȧ)	143	16°17′S	47°44′W
Luzon, i., Phil. (lōō-zŏn′)	212	17°10′N	119°45′E
Luzon Strait, strt., Asia	209	20°40′N	121°00′E
L'viv, Ukr.	178	49°50′N	24°00′E
L'vov *see* L'viv, Ukr.	178	49°50′N	24°00′E
Lyalta, Can.	102e	51°07′N	113°36′W
Lyalya, r., Russia (lyá′lyá)	186a	58°58′N	60°17′E
Lyaskovets, Blg.	175	43°07′N	25°41′E
Lydenburg, S. Afr. (lī′dĕn-bûrg)	232	25°06′S	30°21′E
Lyell, Mount, mtn., Ca., U.S. (lī′ĕl)	118	37°44′N	119°22′W
Lyepye', Bela. (lyĕ-pĕl′)	176	54°52′N	28°41′E
Lykens, Pa., U.S. (lī′kĕnz)	109	40°35′N	76°45′W
Lykhivka, Ukr.	177	48°52′N	33°57′E
Lyna, r., Eur. (lĭn′à)	169	53°56′N	20°30′E
Lynch, Ky., U.S. (lĭnch)	125	36°56′N	82°55′W
Lynchburg, Va., U.S. (lĭnch′bûrg)	105	37°23′N	79°08′W
Lynch Cove, Wa., U.S. (lĭnch)	116a	47°26′N	122°54′W
Lynden, Can. (lĭn′dĕn)	102d	43°14′N	80°08′W
Lynden, Wa., U.S.	116d	48°56′N	122°27′W
Lyndhurst, Austl.	217a	38°03′S	145°14′E
Lyndon, Ky., U.S. (lĭn′dŭn)	111h	38°15′N	85°36′W
Lyndonville, Vt., U.S. (lĭn′dŭn-vĭl)	109	44°35′N	72°00′W
Lynn, Ma., U.S. (lĭn)	105	42°28′N	70°57′W
Lynn Lake, Can. (lāk)	90	56°51′N	101°05′W
Lynwood, Ca., U.S. (lĭn′wŏod)	117a	33°56′N	118°13′W
Lyon, Fr. (lē-ôN′)	154	45°44′N	4°52′E
Lyons, Ga., U.S. (lī′ŭnz)	125	32°08′N	82°19′W
Lyons, Ks., U.S.	120	38°20′N	98°11′W
Lyons, Ne., U.S.	112	41°57′N	96°28′W
Lyons, N.J., U.S.	110a	40°41′N	74°33′W
Lyons, N.Y., U.S.	109	43°05′N	77°00′W
Lyptsi, Ukr.	177	50°11′N	36°25′E
Lysefjorden, b., Nor.	166	58°59′N	6°35′E
Lysekil, Swe. (lü′sĕ-kĕl)	166	58°17′N	11°22′E
Lys'va, Russia (lĭs′vá)	180	58°07′N	57°47′E
Lytham, Eng., U.K. (lĭth′ăm)	158a	53°44′N	2°58′W
Lytkarino, Russia	186b	55°35′N	37°55′E
Lyttelton, S. Afr. (lĭt′l′tŏn)	233b	25°51′S	28°13′E
Lyuban', Russia (lyōō′bán)	176	59°21′N	31°15′E
Lyubertsy, Russia (lyōō′bĕr-tsê)	176	55°40′N	37°55′E
Lyubim, Russia (lyōō-bĕm′)	176	58°24′N	40°39′E
Lyublino, Russia (lyōōb′lĭ-nô)	186b	55°41′N	37°45′E
Lyudinovo, Russia (lū-dē′novō)	176	53°52′N	34°28′E

M

PLACE (Pronunciation)	PAGE	LAT.	LONG.
Ma'ān, Jord. (mä-än′)	198	30°12′N	35°45′E
Maartensdijk, Neth.	159a	52°09′N	5°10′E
Maas (Meuse), r., Eur.	165	51°50′N	5°40′E
Maastricht, Neth. (mäs′trĭkt)	165	50°51′N	5°35′E
Mabaia, Ang.	236	7°13′S	14°03′E
Mabana, Wa., U.S. (mä-bä-nä)	116a	48°06′N	122°25′W
Mabank, Tx., U.S. (mā′bănk)	123	32°21′N	96°05′W
Mabeskraal, S. Afr.	238c	25°12′S	26°47′E
Mableton, Ga., U.S. (mā′b'l-tŭn)	110c	33°49′N	84°34′W
Mabrouk, Mali	230	19°27′N	1°16′W
Mabula, S. Afr. (mà′bōō-la)	238c	24°49′S	27°59′E
Macalelon, Phil. (mä-kä-lā-lōn′)	213a	13°46′N	122°09′E
Macau, Braz. (mä-ká′ò)	143	5°12′S	36°34′W
Macau, China	205	22°00′N	113°00′E
Macaya, Pico de, mtn., Haiti	135	18°25′N	74°00′W
Macclesfield, Eng., U.K. (măk′'lz-fēld)	158a	53°15′N	2°07′W
Macclesfield Canal, can., Eng., U.K. (măk′'lz-fēld)	158a	53°14′N	2°07′W
Macdona, Tx., U.S. (măk-dō′nä)	117d	29°20′N	98°42′W
Macdonald, l., Austl. (măk-dŏn′ăld)	220	23°40′S	127°40′E
Macdonnell Ranges, mts., Austl. (măk-dŏn′ĕl)	220	23°40′S	131°30′E
MacDowell Lake, l., Can. (măk-dou ĕl)	97	52°15′N	92°45′W
Macdui, Ben, mtn., Scot., U.K. (bĕn măk-dōō′ê)	160	57°06′N	3°45′W
Macedonia, Oh., U.S. (măs-ê-dō′nĭ-ȧ)	111d	41°19′N	81°30′E
Macedonia, nation, Eur.	175	41°50′N	22°00′E
Macedonia, hist. reg., Eur. (măs-ê-dō′nĭ-ȧ)	163	41°05′N	22°15′E
Maceió, Braz.	143	9°40′S	35°43′W
Macerata, Italy (mä-chå-rä′tä)	174	43°18′N	13°28′E
Macfarlane, Lake, l., Austl. (måc′fär-lān)	222	32°10′S	137°00′E
Machache, mtn., Leso.	233c	29°22′S	27°53′E
Machado, Braz. (mä-shá-dô)	141a	21°42′S	45°55′W
Machakos, Kenya	237	1°31′S	37°16′E
Machala, Ec. (mä-chá′lä)	142	3°18′S	78°54′W
Machens, Mo., U.S. (măk′ĕns)	117e	38°54′N	90°20′W
Machias, Me., U.S. (mȧ-chī′ăs)	100	44°22′N	67°29′W
Machida, Japan (mä-chê′dä)	211a	35°32′N	139°28′E
Machilīpatnam, India	199	16°22′N	81°10′E
Machu Picchu, Peru (mä′chò-pê′k-chò)	142	13°07′S	72°34′W
Măcin, Rom. (mȧ-chēn′)	177	45°15′N	28°09′E
Macina, reg., Mali	234	14°50′N	4°40′W
Mackay, Austl. (mȧ-kī′)	219	21°15′S	149°08′E
Mackay, Id., U.S. (măk-kā′)	115	43°55′N	113°38′W
Mackay, l., Austl. (mă-kī′)	220	22°30′S	127°45′E
MacKay, l., Can. (măk-kā′)	92	64°10′N	112°35′W
Mackenzie, r., Can.	92	63°38′N	124°23′W
Mackenzie Bay, b., Can.	103	69°20′N	137°10′W
Mackenzie Mountains, mts., Can. (mȧ-kĕn′zĭ)	92	63°41′N	129°27′W
Mackinaw, r., Il., U.S.	108	40°35′N	89°25′W
Mackinaw City, Mi., U.S. (măk′ĭ-nô)	108	45°45′N	84°45′W
Mackinnon Road, Kenya	237	3°44′S	39°03′E
Macleantown, S. Afr. (măk-lăn′toun)	233c	32°48′S	27°48′E
Maclear, S. Afr. (mȧ-klēr′)	232	31°06′S	28°23′E
Macomb, Il., U.S. (mȧ-kōōm′)	121	40°27′N	90°40′W
Mâcon, Fr. (mä-kôN)	161	46°19′N	4°51′E
Macon, Ga., U.S. (mā′kŏn)	105	32°49′N	83°39′W
Macon, Mo., U.S.	121	39°42′N	92°29′W
Macon, Ms., U.S.	124	32°07′N	88°31′W
Macquarie, r., Austl.	221	31°43′S	148°04′E
Macquarie Islands, is., Austl. (mȧ-kwŏr′ê)	3	54°36′S	158°45′E
Macuelizo, Hond. (mä-kwĕ-lē′zô)	132	15°22′N	88°32′W
Mad, r., Ca., U.S. (măd)	114	40°38′N	123°37′W
Madagascar, nation, Afr. (măd-ȧ-găs′kȧr)	233	18°05′S	43°12′E
Madame, i., Can. (mà-dàm′)	101	45°33′N	61°02′W
Madanapalle, India	203	13°06′N	78°09′E
Madang, Pap. N. Gui. (mä-däng′)	213	5°15′S	145°45′E
Madaoua, Niger (mà-dou′à)	230	14°04′N	6°03′E
Madawaska, r., Can. (măd-ȧ-wôs′kȧ)	99	45°20′N	77°25′W
Madeira, r., S.A.	142	6°48′S	62°43′W
Madeira, Arquipélago da, is., Port.	229	33°26′N	16°44′W
Madeira, Ilha da, i., Port. (mä-dā′rä)	230	32°41′N	16°15′W
Madeleine, Îles de la, is., Can.	93	47°30′N	61°45′W
Madelia, Mn., U.S. (mȧ-dē′lĭ-ȧ)	113	44°03′N	94°23′W
Madeline, i., Wi., U.S. (măd′ĕ-lĭn)	113	46°47′N	91°30′W
Madera, Ca., U.S. (mȧ-dā′rȧ)	118	36°57′N	120°04′W
Madera, vol., Nic.	132	11°27′N	85°30′W
Madgaon, India	203	15°09′N	73°58′E
Madhya Pradesh, state, India (mŭd′vŭ prŭ-dāsh′)	199	22°04′N	77°48′E
Madill, Ok., U.S. (mȧ-dĭl′)	121	34°04′N	96°45′W
Madīnat ash Sha'b, Yemen	198	12°45′N	44°00′E
Madingo, Congo	236	4°07′S	11°22′E
Madingou, Congo	236	4°09′S	13°34′E
Madison, Fl., U.S. (măd′ĭ-sŭn)	124	30°28′N	83°25′W
Madison, Ga., U.S.	124	33°34′N	83°29′W
Madison, Il., U.S.	117e	38°40′N	90°09′W
Madison, In., U.S.	108	38°45′N	85°25′W
Madison, Ks., U.S.	121	38°08′N	96°07′W
Madison, Me., U.S.	100	44°47′N	69°52′W
Madison, Mn., U.S.	112	44°59′N	96°13′W
Madison, N.C., U.S.	125	36°22′N	79°59′W
Madison, Ne., U.S.	112	41°49′N	97°27′W
Madison, N.J., U.S.	110a	40°46′N	74°25′W
Madison, S.D., U.S.	112	44°01′N	97°08′W
Madison, Wi., U.S.	105	43°05′N	89°23′W
Madison Res, Mt., U.S.	115	45°25′N	111°28′W
Madisonville, Ky., U.S. (măd′ĭ-sŭn-vĭl)	108	37°20′N	87°30′W
Madisonville, La., U.S.	123	30°22′N	90°10′W
Madisonville, Tx., U.S.	123	30°57′N	95°55′W
Madjori, Burkina	234	11°26′N	1°15′E
Mado Gashi, Kenya	237	0°44′N	39°10′E
Madona, Lat. (mà′dō′nà)	167	56°50′N	26°14′E
Madrakah, Ra's al, c., Oman	198	18°53′N	57°48′E
Madras *see* Chennai, India	199	13°08′N	80°15′E
Madre, Laguna, l., Mex. (lä-gōō′nä mä′drå)	123	25°08′N	97°41′W
Madre, Sierra, mts., N.A. (sē-ĕ′r-rä-mà′drĕ)	131	15°55′N	92°40′W
Madre, Sierra, mts., Phil.	213a	16°40′N	122°10′E
Madre de Dios, r., S.A. (mä′drå dä dê-ōs′)	142	12°07′S	68°02′W
Madre de Dios, Archipiélago, is., Chile (mä′drå dä dê-ōs′)	144	50°40′S	76°30′W
Madre del Sur, Sierra, mts., Mex. (sē-ĕ′r-rä-mä′drå dĕlsōōr′)	128	17°35′N	100°35′W
Madre Occidental, Sierra, mts., Mex.	128	29°30′N	107°30′W
Madre Oriental, Sierra, mts., Mex.	128	25°30′N	100°45′W
Madrid, Spain (mä-drê′d)	154	40°26′N	3°42′W
Madrid, Ia., U.S. (măd′rĭd)	113	41°51′N	93°48′W
Madridejos, Spain (mä-dhrê-dhä′hōs)	172	39°29′N	3°32′W
Madura, i., Indon. (mä-dōō′rä)	212	6°45′S	113°30′E
Madurai, India (mä-dōō′rä)	199	9°57′N	78°04′E
Madureira, Serra do, mtn., Braz. (sĕ′r-rä-dô-mä-dōō-rā′rȧ)	144b	22°49′S	43°30′W
Maebashi, Japan (mä-ĕ-bä′shê)	205	36°26′N	139°04′E
Maestra, Sierra, mts., Cuba (sē-ĕ′r-rà-mä-ās′trä)	129	20°05′N	77°05′W
Maewo, i., Vanuatu	221	15°17′S	168°16′E
Mafeking, S. Afr. (máf′ê′kĭng)	232	25°46′S	24°45′E
Mafra, Braz. (mä′frä)	144	26°21′N	49°59′W
Mafra, Port. (mäf′rȧ)	173b	38°56′N	9°20′W
Magadan, Russia (mȧ-gá-dän′)	179	59°39′N	150°43′E
Magadan Oblast, Russia	185	65°00′N	160°00′E
Magadi, Kenya	237	1°54′S	36°17′E
Magalies, r., S. Afr. (mä-gä′lyĕs)	233b	25°51′S	27°42′E
Magaliesberg, mts., S. Afr.	233b	25°45′S	27°43′E
Magaliesburg, S. Afr.	238c	26°01′S	27°32′E
Magallanes, Estrecho de, strt., S.A.	144	52°30′S	68°45′W
Magat, r., Phil. (mä-gät′)	213a	16°45′N	121°16′E
Magdalena, Arg. (mäg-dä-lā′nä)	141c	35°05′S	57°32′W
Magdalena, Bol.	142	13°17′S	63°57′W
Magdalena, Mex.	104	30°34′N	110°50′W
Magdalena, N.M., U.S.	119	34°10′N	107°45′W
Magdalena, i., Chile	144	44°45′S	73°15′W
Magdalena, r., Col.	142	7°45′N	74°04′W
Magdalena, Bahía, b., Mex. (bä-ē′ä-mäg-dä-lā′nä)	128	24°30′N	114°00′W
Magdeburg, Ger. (mäg′dĕ-bòrgh)	154	52°07′N	11°39′E
Magellan, Strait of *see* Magallanes, Estrecho de, strt., S.A.	144	52°30′S	68°45′W
Magenta, Italy (mȧ-jĕn′tȧ)	174	45°26′N	8°53′E
Magerøya, i., Nor.	160	71°10′N	24°11′E
Maggiore, Lago, l., Italy	162	46°03′N	8°25′E
Maghāghah, Egypt	238b	28°38′N	30°50′W
Maghniyya, Alg.	162	34°52′N	1°40′W
Magiscatzin, Mex. (mä-kês-kät-zēn′)	130	22°48′N	98°42′W
Maglaj, Bos. (mà′glä-ê)	175	44°34′N	18°12′E
Maglie, Italy (mäl′yā)	175	40°06′N	18°20′E
Magna, Ut., U.S. (măg′nȧ)	117b	40°43′N	112°06′W
Magnitogorsk, Russia (mäg-nyē′tô-gôrsk)	178	53°26′N	59°05′E
Magnolia, Ar., U.S. (măg-nō′lĭ-ȧ)	121	33°16′N	93°13′W
Magnolia, Ms., U.S.	124	31°08′N	90°27′W
Magny-en-Vexin, Fr. (mä-nyē′ĕN-vĕ-sàN′)	171b	49°09′N	1°45′E
Magog, Can. (mȧ-gŏg′)	99	45°15′N	72°10′W
Magpie, r., Can.	100	50°40′N	64°30′W
Magpie, r., Can.	98	48°13′N	84°50′W
Magpie, Lac, l., Can.	100	50°55′N	64°39′W
Magrath, Can.	90	49°25′N	112°52′W
Magude, Moz. (mä-gōō′då)	232	24°58′S	32°39′E
Magwe, Mya. (mŭg-wā′)	199	20°19′N	94°57′E
Mahābād, Iran	201	36°55′N	45°50′E
Mahahi Port, D.R.C. (mä-hä′gê)	231	2°14′N	31°12′E
Mahajanga, Madag.	233	15°12′S	46°26′E
Mahakam, r., Indon.	212	0°30′S	116°15′E
Mahali Mountains, mts., Tan.	237	6°20′S	30°00′E
Mahaly, Madag. (mà-hàl-ē′)	233	24°09′S	46°20′E
Mahanoro, Madag. (mà-hà-nô′rō)	233	19°57′S	48°47′E
Mahanoy City, Pa., U.S. (mä-hȧ-noi′)	109	40°50′N	76°10′W
Maḩaţţat al Qaţrānah, Jord.	197a	31°15′N	36°04′E
Maḩaţţat 'Aqabat al Ḩijāzīyah, Jord.	197a	29°45′N	35°55′E
Maḩaţţat ar Ramlah, Jord.	197a	29°31′N	35°57′E
Maḩaţţat Jurf ad Darāwīsh, Jord.	197a	30°41′N	35°51′E

ng-sing; ŋ-baŋk; N-nasalized n; nŏd; cŏmmit; ōld; ōbey; ôrder; oi-boil; fōōd; ò-as oo in foot; ou-out; s-soft; sh-dish; th-thin; pūre; ůnite; ûrn; stŭd; circŭs; ü-as in French tu; ′-indeterminate vowel.

318 Mahd adh-Dhahab – Mansfield PRONOUNCING INDEX

PLACE (Pronunciation)	PAGE	LAT.	LONG.
Mahd adh-Dhahab, Sau. Ar.	201	23°30'N	40°52'E
Mahe, India (mä-ā')	199	11°42'N	75°39'E
Mahenge, Tan. (mä-hĕŋ'gå)	232	7°38'S	36°16'E
Mahi, r., India	202	23°16'N	73°20'E
Mahilyow, Bela.	180	53°53'N	30°22'E
Mahilyow, prov., Bela.	176	53°28'N	30°15'E
Māhīm Bay, b., India	203b	19°03'N	72°45'E
Mahlabatini, S. Afr. (mä'lá-bà-tē'nê)	233c	28°15'S	31°29'E
Mahlow, Ger. (mä'lōv)	159b	52°23'N	13°24'E
Mahnomen, Mn., U.S. (mô-nō'mĕn)	112	47°18'N	95°58'W
Mahone Bay, Can. (mȧ-hōn')	100	44°27'N	64°23'W
Mahone Bay, b., Can.	100	44°30'N	64°15'W
Mahopac, Lake, l., N.Y., U.S. (mā-hō'păk)	110a	41°24'N	73°45'W
Mahwah, N.J., U.S. (mȧ-wä')	110a	41°05'N	74°09'W
Maidenhead, Eng., U.K. (măd'ĕn-hĕd)	158b	51°30'N	0°44'W
Maidstone, Eng., U.K.	165	51°17'N	0°32'E
Maiduguri, Nig. (mä'ē-dá-gōō'rê)	231	11°51'N	13°10'E
Maigualida, Sierra, mts., Ven. (sē-ĕ'r-rá-mī-gwä'lē-dē)	142	6°30'N	65°50'W
Maijdi, Bngl.	202	22°59'N	91°08'E
Maikop see Maykop, Russia	178	44°35'N	40°07'E
Main, r., Ger. (mīn)	168	49°49'N	9°20'E
Main Barrier Range, mts., Austl. (băr'ĭ-ĕr)	221	31°25'S	141°40'E
Mai-Ndombe, Lac, l., D.R.C.	232	2°16'S	19°00'E
Maine, state, U.S. (mān)	105	45°25'N	69°50'W
Mainland, i., Scot., U.K. (mān-lănd)	160	60°19'N	2°40'W
Maintenon, Fr. (măn-tē-nôn')	171b	48°35'N	1°35'E
Maintirano, Madag. (mä'ēn-tē-rä'nō)	233	18°05'S	44°08'E
Mainz, Ger. (mīnts)	154	49°59'N	8°16'E
Maio, i., C.V. (mä'yo)	230b	15°15'N	22°50'W
Maipo, S.A.	144	34°08'S	69°51'W
Maipo, r., Chile (mī'pô)	141b	33°45'S	71°08'W
Maiquetía, Ven. (mī-kĕ-tē'ä)	142	10°37'N	66°56'W
Maison-Rouge, Fr. (mā-zôn-rōōzh')	171b	48°34'N	3°09'E
Maisons-Laffitte, Fr.	171b	48°57'N	2°09'E
Maitland, Austl. (māt'lănd)	219	32°45'S	151°40'E
Maizuru, Japan (mä-ĭ'zōō-rōō)	211	35°26'N	135°15'E
Majene, Indon.	212	3°34'S	119°00'E
Maji, Eth.	231	6°14'N	35°34'E
Majorca see Mallorca, i., Spain	156	39°18'N	2°22'E
Makah Indian Reservation, I.R., Wa., U.S.	114	48°17'N	124°52'W
Makanya, Tan. (mä-kän'yä)	233	4°15'S	37°49'E
Makanza, D.R.C.	231	1°42'N	19°08'E
Makarakomburu, Mount, mtn., Sol. Is.	214e	9°43'S	160°02'E
Makarska, Cro. (mä'kär-skä)	175	43°17'N	17°05'E
Makar'yev, Russia	180	57°50'N	43°48'E
Makasar see Ujung Pandang, Indon.	212	5°08'S	119°28'E
Makasar, Selat (Makassar Strait), strt., Indon.	212	2°00'S	118°07'E
Makaw, D.R.C.	236	3°29'S	18°19'E
Make, i., Japan (mä'kå)	211	30°43'N	130°49'E
Makeni, S.L.	230	8°53'N	12°03'W
Makgadikgadi Pans, pl., Bots.	232	20°38'S	21°31'E
Makhachkala, Russia (mäĸ'äch-kä'lä)	181	43°00'N	47°40'E
Makhaleng, r., Leso.	233c	29°53'S	27°33'E
Makiïvka, Ukr.	181	48°03'N	38°00'E
Makindu, Kenya	237	2°17'S	37°49'E
Makkah see Mecca, Sau. Ar.	198	21°27'N	39°45'E
Makkovik, Can.	91	55°01'N	59°10'W
Makokou, Gabon (mȧ-kō-kōō')	230	0°34'N	12°52'E
Maków Mazowiecki, Pol. (mä'kōov mä-zō-vyĕts'kē)	169	52°51'N	21°07'E
Makuhari, Japan (mä-kōō-hä'rē)	211a	35°39'N	140°04'E
Makurazaki, Japan (mä'kō-rä-zä'kê)	211	31°16'N	130°18'E
Makurdi, Nig.	230	7°45'N	8°32'E
Makushin, Ak., U.S. (mȧ-kō'shĭn)	103	53°57'N	166°28'W
Makushino, Russia (mȧ-kō-shēn'ō)	178	55°03'N	67°43'E
Mala, Punta, c., Pan. (pô'n-tä-mä'lä)	133	7°32'N	79°44'W
Malabar Coast, cst., India (măl'ȧ-bär)	203	11°19'N	75°33'E
Malabar Point, c., India	203b	18°57'N	72°47'E
Malabo, Eq. Gui.	230	3°45'N	8°47'E
Malabon, Phil.	213a	14°39'N	120°57'E
Malacca, Strait of, strt., Asia (mȧ-lăk'ȧ)	212	4°15'N	99°44'E
Malad City, Id., U.S. (mȧ-lăd')	115	42°11'N	112°15'W
Maladzyecha, Bela.	180	54°18'N	26°57'E
Málaga, Col. (mȧ'lä-gä)	142	6°41'N	72°46'W
Málaga, Spain	154	36°45'N	4°25'W
Malagón, Spain (mä-lä-gōn')	172	39°12'N	3°52'W
Malaita, i., Sol. Is. (mȧ-lä'ē-tȧ)	221	8°38'S	161°15'E
Malakāl, Sudan (mȧ-lȧ-käl')	231	9°46'N	31°54'E
Malakhovka, Russia (mȧ-läk'ôf-kȧ)	186b	55°38'N	38°01'E
Malang, Indon.	212	8°06'S	112°50'E
Malanje, Ang. (mä-läŋ-gå)	232	9°32'S	16°20'E
Malanville, Benin	230	12°04'N	3°09'E
Mälaren, l., Swe.	160	59°38'N	16°55'E
Malartic, Can.	91	48°07'N	78°11'W
Malatya, Tur. (mȧ-lä'tyȧ)	198	38°30'N	38°15'E
Malawi, nation, Afr.	232	11°15'S	33°45'E
Malawi, Lake see Nyasa, Lake, l., Afr.	232	10°45'S	34°30'E
Malaya Vishera, Russia (vê-shä'rä)	178	58°51'N	32°13'E
Malay Peninsula, pen., Asia (mȧ-lā') (mā'lā)	212	6°00'N	101°00'E
Malaysia, nation, Asia (mȧ-lā'zhȧ)	212	4°10'N	101°22'E
Malbon, Austl. (măl'bŭn)	218	21°15'S	140°30'E
Malbork, Pol. (mäl'bōrk)	160	54°02'N	19°04'E
Malcabran, r., Port. (mäl-kä-brän')	173b	38°47'N	8°46'W
Malden, Ma., U.S. (môl'dĕn)	101a	42°26'N	71°04'W
Malden, Mo., U.S.	121	36°32'N	89°56'W
Malden, i., Kir.	2	4°20'S	154°30'W
Maldives, nation, Asia	194	4°30'N	71°30'E
Maldon, Eng., U.K. (môrl'dŏn)	158b	51°44'N	0°39'E
Maldonado, Ur. (mäl-dō-nä'dô)	144	34°54'S	54°57'W
Maldonado, Punta, c., Mex. (pōō'n-tä)	130	16°18'N	98°34'W
Maléas, Ákra, c., Grc.	163	36°31'N	23°13'E
Mālegaon, India	202	20°35'N	74°30'E
Malé Karpaty, mts., Slvk.	169	48°31'N	17°15'E
Malekula, i., Vanuatu (mä-lā-kōō'lä)	221	16°44'S	167°45'E
Malema, Moz.	237	14°57'S	37°20'E
Malheur, r., Or., U.S. (mȧ-lōōr')	114	43°45'N	117°41'W
Malheur Lake, l., Or., U.S. (mȧ-lōōr')	114	43°16'N	118°37'W
Mali, nation, Afr.	230	15°45'N	0°15'W
Malibu, Ca., U.S. (mă'lĭ-bōō)	117a	34°03'N	118°38'W
Malik, Wādī al, r., Sudan	231	16°48'N	29°30'E
Malimba, Monts, mts., D.R.C.	237	7°45'S	29°15'E
Malinalco, Mex. (mä-lē-näl'kō)	130	18°54'N	99°31'W
Malinaltepec, Mex. (mä-lē-näl-tȧ-pĕk')	130	17°01'N	98°41'W
Malindi, Kenya (mä-lēn'dê)	233	3°14'S	40°04'E
Malin Head, c., Ire.	160	55°23'N	7°24'W
Malino, Russia (mä'lĭ-nô)	186b	55°07'N	38°12'E
Malkara, Tur. (mäl'kȧ-rȧ)	175	40°51'N	26°52'E
Malko Tŭrnovo, Blg. (mäl'kō-t'r'nō-vȧ)	175	41°59'N	27°28'E
Mallaig, Scot., U.K.	164	56°59'N	5°55'W
Mallet Creek, Oh., U.S. (măl'ĕt)	111d	41°10'N	81°55'W
Mallorca, i., Spain	156	39°30'N	3°00'E
Mallow, Ire. (măl'ō)	164	52°07'N	9°04'W
Malmédy, Bel. (mȧl-mā-dē')	165	50°25'N	6°01'E
Malmesbury, S. Afr. (mämz'bēr-ĭ)	232	33°30'S	18°35'E
Malmköping, Swe. (mälm'chû'pĭng)	166	59°09'N	16°39'E
Malmö, Swe.	154	55°36'N	13°00'E
Malmyzh, Russia (mȧl-mēzh')	179	49°58'N	137°07'E
Malmyzh, Russia	180	56°30'N	50°48'E
Maloarkhangelsk, Russia (mä'lô-ȧr-кäŋ'gĕlsk)	176	52°26'N	36°29'E
Malolos, Phil. (mä-lō'lōs)	213a	14°51'N	120°49'E
Malomal'sk, Russia (mȧ-lō-mälsk'')	186a	58°47'N	59°55'E
Malone, N.Y., U.S. (mȧ-lōn')	109	44°50'N	74°20'W
Malonga, D.R.C.	236	10°24'S	23°10'E
Maloti Mountains, mts., Leso.	233c	29°00'S	28°29'E
Maloyaroslavets, Russia (mä'lō-yä-rō-slä-vyĕts)	176	55°01'N	36°25'E
Malozemel'skaya Tundra, reg., Russia	180	67°30'N	50°00'E
Malpas, Eng., U.K. (măl'pȧz)	158a	53°01'N	2°46'W
Malpelo, Isla de, i., Col. (mäl-pä'lō)	142	3°55'N	81°30'W
Malpeque Bay, b., Can. (môl-pĕk')	100	46°30'N	63°47'W
Malta, Mt., U.S. (môl'tȧ)	115	48°20'N	107°50'W
Malta, nation, Eur.	154	35°52'N	13°30'E
Maltahöhe, Nmb. (mäl'tä-hō'ē)	232	24°45'S	16°45'E
Maltrata, Mex. (mäl-trä'tä)	131	18°48'N	97°16'W
Maluku (Moluccas), is., Indon.	213	2°22'S	128°25'E
Maluku, Laut (Molucca Sea), sea, Indon.	213	0°15'N	125°41'E
Malūţ, Sudan	231	10°30'N	32°17'E
Mālvan, India	203	16°08'N	73°32'E
Malvern, Ar., U.S. (măl'vērn)	121	34°21'N	92°47'W
Malyn, Ukr.	177	50°44'N	29°15'E
Malynivka, Ukr.	177	49°50'N	36°43'E
Malyy Anyuy, r., Russia	185	67°52'N	164°30'E
Malyy Tamir, i., Russia	185	78°10'N	107°30'E
Mamantel, Mex. (mä-mȧn-tĕl')	131	18°36'N	91°06'W
Mamaroneck, N.Y., U.S. (măm'ȧ-rō-nĕk)	110a	40°57'N	73°44'W
Mambasa, D.R.C.	237	1°21'N	29°03'E
Mamburao, Phil. (mäm-bōō'rä-ō)	213a	13°14'N	120°35'E
Mamfe, Cam. (mäm'fĕ)	230	5°46'N	9°17'E
Mamihara, Japan (mä'mê-hä-rä)	211	32°41'N	131°12'E
Mammoth Cave, Ky., U.S. (măm'ŏth)	124	37°10'N	86°04'W
Mammoth Cave National Park, rec., Ky., U.S.	107	37°20'N	86°21'W
Mammoth Hot Springs, Wy., U.S. (măm'ŭth hôt sprĭngz)	115	44°55'N	110°50'W
Mamnoli, India	203b	19°17'N	73°15'E
Mamoré, r., S.A.	142	13°00'S	65°20'W
Mamou, Gui.	230	10°26'N	12°07'W
Mampong, Ghana	234	7°04'N	1°24'W
Mamry, Jezioro, l., Pol. (mäm'rĭ)	169	54°10'N	21°28'E
Man, C. Iv.	234	7°24'N	7°33'W
Manacor, Spain (mä-nä-kôr')	173	39°35'N	3°15'E
Manado, Indon.	213	1°29'N	124°50'E
Managua, Cuba (mä-nä'gwä)	135a	22°58'N	82°17'W
Managua, Nic.	128	12°10'N	86°16'W
Managua, Lago de, l., Nic. (lä'gō-dĕ)	132	12°28'N	86°10'W
Manakara, Madag. (mä-nä-kä'rŭ)	233	22°17'S	48°06'E
Manama see Al Manāmah, Bahr.	198	26°01'N	50°33'E
Mananara, r., Madag. (mä-nä-nä'rŭ)	233	23°15'S	48°15'E
Mananjary, Madag. (mä-nän-zhä'rê)	233	20°16'S	48°13'E
Manas, China	204	44°30'N	86°00'E
Manassas, Va., U.S. (mȧ-năs'ȧs)	109	38°45'N	77°30'W
Manaus, Braz. (mä-nä'ōōzh)	143	3°01'S	60°00'W
Mancelona, Mi., U.S. (măn-sē-lō'nȧ)	108	44°50'N	85°05'W
Mancha Real, Spain (män'chä rā-äl')	172	37°48'N	3°37'W
Manchazh, Russia (män'chȧsh)	186a	56°30'N	58°10'E
Manchester, Eng., U.K.	154	53°28'N	2°14'W
Manchester, Ct., U.S. (măn'chĕs-tēr)	109	41°45'N	72°30'W
Manchester, Ga., U.S.	124	32°50'N	84°37'W
Manchester, Ia., U.S.	113	42°30'N	91°30'W
Manchester, Ma., U.S.	101a	42°35'N	70°47'W
Manchester, Mo., U.S.	117e	38°36'N	90°31'W
Manchester, N.H., U.S.	105	43°00'N	71°30'W
Manchester, Oh., U.S.	108	38°40'N	83°35'W
Manchester Ship Canal, Eng., U.K.	158a	53°20'N	2°40'W
Manchuria, hist. reg., China (măn-chōō'rē-ȧ)	205	48°00'N	124°58'E
Mandal, Nor. (män'däl)	166	58°03'N	7°28'E
Mandalay, Mya. (măn'dȧ-lā)	199	22°00'N	96°08'E
Mandalselva, r., Nor.	166	58°25'N	7°30'E
Mandan, N.D., U.S. (măn'dăn)	104	46°49'N	100°54'W
Mandara Mountains, mts., Afr. (män-dä'rä)	231	10°15'N	13°23'E
Mandau Siak, r., Indon.	197b	1°03'N	101°25'E
Mandeb, Bab-el-, strt. (băb'ĕl măn-dĕb')	198	13°17'N	42°49'E
Mandimba, Moz.	237	14°21'S	35°39'E
Mandinga, Pan. (män-dĭŋ'gä)	133	9°32'N	79°04'W
Mandla, India	202	22°43'N	80°23'E
Mándra, Grc. (män'drä)	175	38°06'N	23°32'E
Mandritsara, Madag. (mȧn-drēt-sä'rȧ)	233	15°49'S	48°47'E
Manduria, Italy (män-dōō'rē-ä)	175	40°23'N	17°41'E
Mandve, India	203b	18°47'N	72°52'E
Māndvi, India (mŭnd'vē)	203b	19°29'N	72°53'E
Māndvi, India (mŭnd'vē)	199	22°54'N	69°23'E
Mandya, India	203	12°40'N	77°00'E
Manfredonia, Italy (män-frȧ-dô'nyä)	174	41°39'N	15°55'E
Manfredónia, Golfo di, b., Italy (gôl-fō-dē)	174	41°34'N	16°05'E
Mangabeiras, Chapada das, pl., Braz.	143	8°05'S	47°32'W
Mangalore, India (mŭŋ-gŭ-lōr')	199	12°53'N	74°52'E
Mangaratiba, Braz. (män-gä-rä-tē'bȧ)	141a	22°56'S	44°03'W
Mangatarem, Phil. (män'gȧ-tä'rĕm)	213a	15°48'N	120°18'E
Mange, D.R.C.	236	0°54'N	20°30'E
Mangkalihat, Tanjung, c., Indon.	212	1°25'N	119°55'E
Mangles, Islas de, Cuba (ē's-läs-dĕ-mäŋ'gläs) (măŋ'g'lz)	134	22°05'N	82°50'W
Mangoche, Mwi.	232	14°16'S	35°14'E
Mangoky, r., Madag. (män-gō'kē)	233	22°02'S	44°11'E
Mangole, Pulau, i., Indon.	213	1°35'S	126°22'E
Mangualde, Port. (män-gwäl'dĕ)	172	40°38'N	7°44'W
Mangueira, Lagoa da, l., Braz.	144	33°15'S	52°45'W
Mangum, Ok., U.S. (măŋ'gŭm)	120	34°52'N	99°31'W
Mangzhangdian, China (mäŋ-jäŋ-dĭĕn)	206	32°07'N	114°44'E
Manhattan, Il., U.S.	111a	41°25'N	87°29'W
Manhattan, Ks., U.S. (măn-hăt'ăn)	104	39°11'N	96°34'W
Manhattan Beach, Ca., U.S.	117a	33°53'N	118°24'W
Manhuaçu, Braz. (män-ōȧ'sōō)	141a	20°17'S	42°01'W
Manhumirim, Braz. (män-ōō-mē-rē'ɴ)	141a	22°30'S	41°57'W
Manicouagane, r., Can.	93	50°00'N	68°35'W
Manicouagane, Lac, res., Can.	93	51°30'N	68°19'W
Manicuare, Ven. (mä-nē-kwä'rē)	143b	10°35'N	64°10'W
Manihiki Islands, is., Cook Is. (mä'nē-hē'kê)	241	9°40'S	158°00'W
Manila, Phil.	212	14°37'N	121°00'E
Manila Bay, b., Phil. (mȧ-nĭl'ȧ)	213a	14°38'N	120°46'E
Manisa, Tur. (mä'nê-sȧ)	163	38°40'N	27°30'E
Manistee, Mi., U.S. (măn-ĭs-tē')	108	44°15'N	86°20'W
Manistee, r., Mi., U.S.	108	44°25'N	85°45'W
Manistique, Mi., U.S. (măn-ĭs-tēk')	113	45°58'N	86°16'W
Manistique, l., Mi., U.S.	113	46°14'N	85°30'W
Manistique, r., Mi., U.S.	113	46°05'N	86°09'W
Manitoba, prov., Can. (măn-ĭ-tō'bȧ)	90	55°12'N	97°29'W
Manitoba, Lake, l., Can.	92	51°00'N	98°45'W
Manito Lake, l., Can. (măn'ĭ-tō)	96	52°45'N	109°45'W
Manitou, i., Mi., U.S. (măn'ĭ-tōō)	113	47°21'N	87°33'W
Manitou, l., Can.	113	49°21'N	93°01'W
Manitou Islands, is., Mi., U.S.	108	45°05'N	86°00'W
Manitoulin Island, i., Can. (măn-ĭ-tōō'lĭn)	93	45°45'N	81°30'W
Manitou Springs, Co., U.S.	120	38°51'N	104°58'W
Manitowoc, Wi., U.S. (măn-ĭ-tō-wŏk')	113	44°05'N	87°42'W
Manitqueira, Serra da, mts., Braz.	141a	22°40'S	45°12'W
Maniwaki, Can.	99	46°23'N	76°00'W
Manizales, Col. (mä-nê-zä'läs)	142	5°05'N	75°31'W
Manjacaze, Moz. (man'yä-kä'zĕ)	232	24°37'S	33°49'E
Mankato, Ks., U.S. (măn-kā'tō)	120	39°45'N	98°12'W
Mankato, Mn., U.S.	105	44°10'N	93°59'W
Mankim, Cam.	235	5°01'N	12°00'E
Manlléu, Spain (män-lyā'ōō)	173	42°00'N	2°16'E
Mannar, Sri L. (mȧ-när')	203	9°48'N	80°03'E
Mannar, Gulf of, b., Asia	199	8°47'N	78°33'E
Mannheim, Ger. (män'hīm)	161	49°30'N	8°31'E
Manning, Ia., U.S. (măn'ĭng)	112	41°53'N	95°04'W
Manning, S.C., U.S.	125	33°41'N	80°12'W
Mannington, W.V., U.S. (măn'ĭng-tŭn)	108	39°30'N	80°55'W
Mano, r., Afr.	234	7°00'N	11°25'W
Man of War Bay, b., Bah.	135	21°05'N	74°05'W
Man of War Channel, strt., Bah.	134	22°45'N	76°10'W
Manokwari, Indon. (mȧ-nŏk-wä'rê)	213	0°56'S	134°10'E
Manono, D.R.C.	237	7°18'S	27°25'E
Manor, Can. (măn'ēr)	97	49°36'N	102°05'W
Manor, Wa., U.S.	116c	45°45'N	122°36'W
Manori, neigh., India	203b	19°13'N	72°43'E
Manosque, Fr. (mȧ-nôsh')	171	43°51'N	5°48'E
Manotick, Can.	102c	45°13'N	75°41'W
Manouane, r., Can.	99	50°15'N	70°30'W
Manouane, Lac, l., Can. (mȧ-nōō'ȧn)	100	50°36'N	70°50'W
Manresa, Spain (män-rā'sä)	162	41°44'N	1°52'E
Mansa, Zam.	232	11°12'S	28°53'E
Mansel, i., Can. (măn'sĕl)	91	61°56'N	81°10'W
Manseriche, Pongo de, reg., Peru (pŏ'n-gō-dĕ-män-sĕ-rē'chĕ)	142	4°15'S	77°45'W
Mansfield, Eng., U.K. (mănz'fēld)	158a	53°08'N	1°12'W
Mansfield, La., U.S.	123	32°02'N	93°43'W
Mansfield, Oh., U.S.	108	40°45'N	82°30'W
Mansfield, Wa., U.S.	114	47°48'N	119°39'W
Mansfield, Mount, mtn., Vt., U.S.	109	44°30'N	72°45'W

PRONOUNCING INDEX
Mansfield Woodhouse – Marystown 319

PLACE (Pronunciation)	PAGE	LAT.	LONG.
Mansfield Woodhouse, Eng., U.K. (wo͝od-hous)	158a	53°08'N	1°12'W
Manta, Ec. (män'tä)	142	1°03'S	80°16'W
Manteno, Il., U.S. (măn-tē-nō)	111a	41°15'N	87°50'W
Manteo, N.C., U.S.	125	35°55'N	75°40'W
Mantes-la-Jolie, Fr. (mänt-ĕ-lä-zhō-lē')	170	48°59'N	1°42'E
Manti, Ut., U.S. (măn'tī)	119	39°15'N	111°40'W
Mantova, Italy (män'tô-vä) (măn'tu̇-ȧ)	162	45°09'N	10°47'E
Mantua, Cuba (män-to͞o'ä)	134	22°20'N	84°15'W
Mantua *see* Mantova, Italy	162	45°09'N	10°47'E
Mantua, Ut., U.S. (măn'tu̇-ȧ)	117b	41°30'N	111°57'W
Manua Islands, is., Am. Sam.	214a	14°13'S	169°35'W
Manui, Pulau, i., Indon. (mä-no͞o'ē)	213	3°35'S	123°38'E
Manus Island, i., Pap. N. Gui. (mä'no͞os)	213	2°22'S	146°22'E
Manvel, Tx., U.S. (măn'vel)	123a	29°28'N	95°22'W
Manville, N.J., U.S. (măn'vĭl)	110a	40°33'N	74°36'W
Manville, R.I., U.S.	110b	41°57'N	71°27'W
Manzala Lake, l., Egypt	238b	31°14'N	32°04'E
Manzanares, Col. (män-sä-nä'rĕs)	142a	5°15'N	75°09'W
Manzanares, r., Spain (mänz-nä'rĕs)	173a	40°36'N	3°48'W
Manzanares, Canal del, Spain (kä-nä'l-dĕl-män-thä-nä'rĕs)	173a	40°20'N	3°38'W
Manzanillo, Cuba (män'zä-nēl'yō)	129	20°20'N	77°05'W
Manzanillo, Mex.	128	19°02'N	104°21'W
Manzanillo, Bahía de, b., Mex. (bä-ē'ä-dĕ-män-zä-nē'l-yō)	130	19°00'N	104°38'W
Manzanillo, Bahía de, b., N.A.	135	19°55'N	71°50'W
Manzanillo, Punta, c., Pan.	133	9°40'N	79°33'W
Manzhouli, China (män-jō-lē)	205	49°25'N	117°15'E
Manzovka, Russia (màn-zhô'f-kà)	210	44°16'N	132°13'E
Mao, Chad (mä'ô)	231	14°07'N	15°19'E
Mao, Dom. Rep.	135	19°35'N	71°10'W
Maó, Spain	162	39°52'N	4°15'E
Maoke, Pegunungan, mts., Indon.	213	4°00'S	138°00'E
Maoming, China	205	21°55'N	110°40'E
Maoniu Shan, mtn., China (mou-nĭō shän)	208	32°45'N	104°09'E
Mapastepec, Mex. (ma-päs-tå-pĕk')	131	15°24'N	92°52'W
Mapia, Kepulauan, i., Indon.	213	0°57'N	134°22'E
Mapimí, Mex. (mä-pê-mē')	122	25°50'N	103°50'W
Mapimí, Bolsón de, des., Mex. (bôl-sŏ'n-dĕ-mä-pē'mē)	122	27°27'N	103°20'W
Maple Creek, Can. (mā'p'l) (krēk)	90	49°55'N	109°27'W
Maple Grove, Can. (grōv)	102a	45°19'N	73°51'W
Maple Heights, Oh., U.S.	111d	41°25'N	81°34'W
Maple Shade, N.J., U.S. (shād)	110f	39°57'N	75°01'W
Maple Valley, Wa., U.S. (văl'ē)	116a	47°24'N	122°02'W
Maplewood, Mn., U.S. (wo͝od)	117g	45°00'N	93°03'W
Maplewood, Mo., U.S.	117e	38°37'N	90°20'W
Mapumulo, S. Afr. (mä-pä-mo͞o'lō)	233c	29°12'S	31°05'E
Maputo, Moz.	232	26°50'S	32°30'E
Maquela do Zombo, Ang. (mà-kā'lȧ dò zôm'bò)	232	6°08'S	15°15'E
Maquoketa, Ia., U.S. (mȧ-kō-kê-tȧ)	113	42°04'N	90°42'W
Maquoketa, r., Ia., U.S.	113	42°08'N	90°40'W
Mar, Serra do, mts., Braz. (sĕr'rȧ dò mär')	144	26°30'S	49°15'W
Maracaibo, Ven. (mä-rä-kī'bō)	142	10°38'N	71°45'W
Maracaibo, Lago de, l., Ven. (lä'gô-dĕ-mä-rä-kī'bō)	142	9°55'N	72°13'W
Maracay, Ven. (mä-rä-kăy')	142	10°15'N	67°35'W
Marādah, Libya	231	29°10'N	19°07'E
Maradi, Niger (mȧ-rȧ-dē')	230	13°29'N	7°06'E
Marāgheh, Iran	201	37°20'N	46°10'E
Maraisburg, S. Afr.	233b	26°12'S	27°57'E
Marais des Cygnes, r., Ks., U.S.	121	38°30'N	95°30'W
Marajó, Ilha de, i., Braz.	143	1°00'S	49°30'W
Maralal, Kenya	237	1°06'N	36°42'E
Marali, C.A.R.	235	6°01'N	18°24'E
Marand, Iran	201	38°26'N	45°46'E
Maranguape, Braz. (mä-räŋ-gwä'pĕ)	143	3°48'S	38°38'W
Maranhão, state, Braz. (mä-rän-youN)	143	5°15'S	45°52'W
Maranoa, r., Austl. (mä-rä-nō'ä)	221	27°01'S	148°03'E
Marano di Napoli, Italy (mä-rä'nô-dē-nä'pô-lē)	173c	40°39'N	14°12'E
Marañón, r., Peru (mä-rä-nyōn')	142	4°26'S	75°08'W
Marapanim, Braz. (mä-rä-pä-nē'N)	143	0°45'S	47°42'W
Marathon, Can.	91	48°50'N	86°10'W
Marathon, Fl., U.S. (măr'ȧ-thŏn)	125a	24°41'N	81°06'W
Marathon, Oh., U.S.	111f	39°09'N	83°59'W
Maravatio, Mex. (mä-rä-vä'tê-ō)	130	19°54'N	100°25'W
Marawi, Sudan	231	18°07'N	31°57'E
Marble Bar, Austl. (mär'b'l bär)	218	21°15'S	119°15'E
Marble Canal, can., Az., U.S. (mär'b'l)	119	36°21'N	111°48'W
Marblehead, Ma., U.S. (mär'b'l-hĕd)	101a	42°30'N	70°51'W
Marburg an der Lahn, Ger.	168	50°49'N	8°46'E
Marca, Ponta da, c., Ang.	236	16°31'S	11°42'E
Marcala, Hond. (mär-kä-lä)	132	14°08'N	88°01'W
Marceline, Mo., U.S. (mär-sê-lēn')	121	39°42'N	92°56'W
Marche, hist. reg., Italy (mär'kā)	174	43°35'N	12°33'E
Marchegg, Aus.	159e	48°18'N	16°55'E
Marchena, Spain (mär-chā'nä)	162	37°20'N	5°25'W
Marchena, i., Ec. (ĕ's-lä-mär-chĕ'nä)	142	0°29'N	90°31'W
Marchfeld, reg., Aus.	159e	48°14'N	16°37'E
Mar Chiquita, Laguna, l., Arg. (lä-go͞o'nä-mär-chê-kē'tä)	141c	34°25'S	61°10'W
Marcos Paz, Arg. (mär-kōs' päz)	141c	34°49'S	58°51'W
Marcus, i., Japan (mär'kŭs)	241	24°00'N	155°00'E
Marcus Hook, Pa., U.S. (mär'kŭs ho͝ok)	110f	39°49'N	75°25'W
Marcy, Mount, mtn., N.Y., U.S. (mär'sē)	109	44°10'N	73°55'W

PLACE (Pronunciation)	PAGE	LAT.	LONG.
Mar de Espanha, Braz. (mär-dĕ-ĕs-pä'nyȧ)	141a	21°53'S	43°00'W
Mar del Plata, Arg. (mär dĕl- plä'ta)	144	37°59'S	57°35'W
Mardin, Tur. (mär-dēn')	198	37°25'N	40°40'E
Maré, i., N. Cal. (mȧ-rā')	221	21°53'S	168°30'E
Maree, Loch, b., Scot., U.K. (mä-rē')	164	57°40'N	5°44'W
Marengo, Ia., U.S. (mȧ-rĕŋ'gō)	113	41°47'N	92°04'W
Marennes, Fr. (mȧ-rĕn')	170	45°49'N	1°08'W
Marfa, Tx., U.S. (mär'fȧ)	122	30°19'N	104°01'W
Margarita, Pan. (mär-go͞o-rē'tä)	128a	9°20'N	79°55'W
Margarita, Isla de, i., Ven. (mä-gȧ-rē'tȧ)	142	11°00'N	64°15'W
Margate, S. Afr. (mä-gāt')	233c	30°52'S	30°21'E
Margate, Eng., U.K. (mär'gāt)	165	51°21'N	1°17'E
Margherita Peak, mtn., Afr.	231	0°22'N	29°51'E
Marguerite, r., Can.	100	50°39'N	66°42'W
Marhanets', Ukr.	177	47°41'N	34°33'E
Maria, Can. (mȧ-rē'ȧ)	100	48°10'N	66°04'W
Mariager, Den. (mä-rê-ägh'ĕr)	166	56°38'N	10°00'E
Mariana, Braz. (mä-ryȧ'nä)	141a	20°23'S	43°24'W
Mariana Islands, is., Oc.	5	16°00'N	145°30'E
Marianao, Cuba (mä-rê-ä-nä'ō)	129	23°05'N	82°26'W
Mariana Trench, deep	241	12°00'N	144°00'E
Marianna, Ar., U.S. (mā-rĭ-ăn'ȧ)	121	34°45'N	90°45'W
Marianna, Fl., U.S.	124	30°46'N	85°14'W
Marianna, Pa., U.S.	111e	40°01'N	80°05'W
Mariano Acosta, Arg. (mä-rêä'nô-á-kōs'tä)	144a	34°28'S	58°48'W
Mariánské Lázně, Czech Rep. (mär'yȧn-skĕ'läz'nyĕ)	168	49°58'N	12°42'E
Marias, r., Mt., U.S. (mȧ-rī'ȧz)	115	48°15'N	110°50'W
Marías, Islas, is., Mex. (mä-rē'äs)	128	21°30'N	106°40'W
Mariato, Punta, c., Pan.	133	7°17'N	81°09'W
Maribo, Den. (mä'rê-bô)	166	54°46'N	11°29'E
Maribor, Slvn. (mä're-bôr)	154	46°33'N	15°37'E
Maricaban, i., Phil. (mä-rê-kä-bän')	213a	13°40'N	120°44'E
Mariefred, Swe. (mä-rē'ĕ-frĭd)	166	59°17'N	17°09'E
Marie Galante, i., Guad. (mȧ-rē' gȧ-länt')	133b	15°58'N	61°05'W
Mariehamn, Fin. (mȧ-rē'ê-häm''n)	167	60°07'N	19°57'E
Mari El, prov., Russia	180	56°30'N	48°00'E
Mariestad, Swe. (mä-rē'ĕ-städ')	166	58°43'N	13°45'E
Marietta, Ga., U.S. (mā-rĭ-ĕt'ȧ)	110c	33°57'N	84°33'W
Marietta, Oh., U.S.	108	39°25'N	81°30'W
Marietta, Ok., U.S.	121	33°53'N	97°07'W
Marietta, Wa., U.S.	116d	48°48'N	122°35'W
Mariinsk, Russia (mȧ-rē'ĭnsk)	184	56°15'N	87°28'E
Marijampole, Lith. (mä-rē-yäm-pô'lē)	167	54°33'N	23°26'E
Marikana, S. Afr. (mä'-rĭ-kä-nȧ)	238c	25°40'S	27°28'E
Marília, Braz. (mä-rē'lyȧ)	143	22°02'S	49°48'W
Marimba, Ang.	236	8°28'S	17°08'E
Marín, Spain	172	42°24'N	8°40'W
Marinduque Island, i., Phil. (mä-rēn-do͞o'kä)	213a	13°14'N	121°45'E
Marine, Il., U.S. (mȧ-rēn')	117e	38°48'N	89°47'W
Marine City, Mi., U.S.	108	42°45'N	82°30'W
Marine Lake, l., Mn., U.S.	117g	45°13'N	92°55'W
Marine on Saint Croix, Mn., U.S.	117g	45°11'N	92°47'W
Marinette, Wi., U.S. (măr-ĭ-nĕt')	105	45°04'N	87°40'W
Maringa, r., D.R.C. (mä-riŋ'gä)	231	0°30'N	21°00'E
Marinha Grande, Port. (mä-rēn'yȧ grän'dĕ)	172	39°49'N	8°53'W
Marion, Al., U.S. (măr'ĭ-ŭn)	124	32°36'N	87°19'W
Marion, Ia., U.S.	113	42°01'N	91°39'W
Marion, Il., U.S.	108	37°40'N	88°55'W
Marion, In., U.S.	105	40°35'N	85°45'W
Marion, Ks., U.S.	121	38°21'N	97°02'W
Marion, Ky., U.S.	124	37°19'N	88°05'W
Marion, N.C., U.S.	125	35°40'N	82°00'W
Marion, N.D., U.S.	112	46°37'N	98°20'W
Marion, Oh., U.S.	108	40°35'N	83°10'W
Marion, S.C., U.S.	125	34°08'N	79°23'W
Marion, Va., U.S.	125	36°48'N	81°33'W
Marion, Lake, res., S.C., U.S.	125	33°25'N	80°35'W
Marion Reef, rf., Austl.	221	18°57'S	151°31'E
Mariposa, Chile (mä-rê-pô'sä)	141b	35°33'S	71°21'W
Mariposa Creek, r., Ca., U.S.	118	37°14'N	120°30'W
Mariquita, Col. (mä-rē-kē'tä)	142a	5°13'N	74°52'W
Mariscal Estigarribia, Para.	144	22°03'S	60°28'W
Marisco, Ponta do, c., Braz. (pô'n-tä-dô-mä-rē's-kō)	144b	23°01'S	43°17'W
Maritime Alps, mts., Eur. (mȧ'rĭ-tīm ălps)	161	44°20'N	7°02'E
Mariupol', Ukr.	178	47°07'N	37°32'E
Mariveles, Phil.	213a	14°27'N	120°29'E
Marj Uyan, Leb.	197a	33°21'N	35°36'E
Marka, Som.	238a	1°45'N	44°47'E
Markaryd, Swe. (mär'kä-rüd)	166	56°30'N	13°34'E
Marked Tree, Ar., U.S. (märkt trē)	121	35°31'N	90°26'W
Marken, i., Neth.	159a	52°26'N	5°08'E
Market Bosworth, Eng., U.K. (bŏz'wûrth)	158a	52°37'N	1°23'W
Market Deeping, Eng., U.K. (dēp'ĭng)	158a	52°40'N	0°19'W
Market Drayton, Eng., U.K. (drā'tŭn)	158a	52°54'N	2°29'W
Market Harborough, Eng., U.K. (här'bŭr-ô)	158a	52°28'N	0°55'W
Market Rasen, Eng., U.K. (rā'zĕn)	158a	53°23'N	0°21'W
Markham, Can. (märk'ȧm)	99	43°53'N	79°15'W
Markham, Mount, mtn., Ant.	224	82°59'S	159°30'E
Markivka, Ukr.	177	49°32'N	39°34'E
Markovo, Russia (mär'kô-vô)	179	64°46'N	170°48'E
Markrāna, India	202	27°08'N	74°43'E
Marks, Russia	181	51°42'N	46°46'E
Marksville, La., U.S. (märks'vĭl)	123	31°09'N	92°05'W

PLACE (Pronunciation)	PAGE	LAT.	LONG.
Markt Indersdorf, Ger. (märkt ēn'dĕrs-dōrf)	159d	48°22'N	11°23'E
Marktredwitz, Ger. (märk-rĕd'vēts)	168	50°02'N	12°05'E
Markt Schwaben, Ger. (märkt shvä'bĕn)	159d	48°12'N	11°52'E
Marl, Ger. (märl)	171c	51°40'N	7°05'E
Marlboro, N.J., U.S.	110a	40°18'N	74°15'W
Marlborough, Ma., U.S.	101a	42°21'N	71°33'W
Marlette, Mi., U.S. (mär-lĕt')	108	43°25'N	83°05'W
Marlin, Tx., U.S. (mär'lĭn)	123	31°18'N	96°52'W
Marlinton, W.V., U.S. (mär'lĭn-tŭn)	108	38°15'N	80°10'W
Marlow, Eng., U.K. (mär'lō)	158b	51°33'N	0°46'W
Marlow, Ok., U.S.	121	34°38'N	97°56'W
Marls, The, b., Bah. (märls)	134	26°30'N	77°15'W
Marmande, Fr. (mȧr-mänd')	170	44°30'N	0°10'E
Marmara Denizi, sea, Tur.	198	40°40'N	28°00'E
Marmarth, N.D., U.S. (mär'mȧrth)	112	46°19'N	103°57'W
Mar Muerto, l., Mex. (mär-mòĕ'r-tô)	131	16°13'N	94°22'W
Marne, Ger. (mär'nĕ)	159c	53°57'N	9°01'E
Marne, r., Fr. (märn)	161	49°00'N	4°30'E
Maroa, Ven. (mä-rō'ä)	142	2°43'N	67°37'W
Maroantsetra, Madag. (mȧ-rō-äŋ-tsä'trȧ)	233	15°18'S	49°48'E
Maro Jarapeto, mtn., Col. (mä-rô-hä-rä-pĕ'tô)	142a	6°29'N	76°39'W
Maromokotro, mtn., Madag.	233	14°00'S	49°11'E
Marondera, Zimb.	232	18°10'S	31°36'E
Maroni, r., S.A. (mä-rō'nê)	143	3°02'N	53°54'W
Maro Reef, rf., Hi., U.S.	126b	25°15'N	170°00'W
Maroua, Cam. (mär'wä)	231	10°36'N	14°20'E
Marple, Eng., U.K. (mär'p'l)	158a	53°24'N	2°04'W
Marquard, S. Afr.	238c	28°41'S	27°26'E
Marquesas Islands, is., Fr. Poly. (mär-kĕ'säs)	2	8°50'S	141°00'W
Marquesas Keys, is., Fl., U.S. (mär-kē'zȧs)	125a	24°37'N	82°15'W
Marquês de Valença, Braz. (mȧr-kĕ's-dĕ-vä-lĕ'n-sȧ)	141a	22°16'S	43°42'W
Marquette, Can. (mȧr-kĕt')	102f	50°04'N	97°43'W
Marquette, Mi., U.S.	105	46°32'N	87°25'W
Marquez, Tx., U.S. (mär-kāz')	123	31°14'N	96°15'W
Marra, Jabal, mtn., Sudan (jĕb'ĕl mär'ä)	231	13°00'N	23°47'E
Marrakech, Mor. (mär-rä'kĕsh)	230	31°38'N	8°00'W
Marree, Austl. (măr'rē)	218	29°38'S	137°55'E
Marrero, La., U.S.	110d	29°55'N	90°06'W
Marrupa, Moz.	237	13°08'S	37°30'E
Mars, Pa., U.S. (märz)	111e	40°42'N	80°01'W
Marsabit, Kenya	237	2°20'N	37°59'E
Marsala, Italy (mär-sä'lä)	162	37°48'N	12°28'E
Marsden, Eng., U.K. (märz'dĕn)	158a	53°36'N	1°55'W
Marseille, Fr. (mȧr-sâ'y')	154	43°18'N	5°25'E
Marseilles, Il., U.S. (mär-sĕlz')	108	41°20'N	88°40'W
Marshall, Il., U.S. (mär'shȧl)	108	39°20'N	87°40'W
Marshall, Mi., U.S.	108	42°20'N	84°55'W
Marshall, Mn., U.S.	112	44°28'N	95°49'W
Marshall, Mo., U.S.	121	39°07'N	93°12'W
Marshall, Tx., U.S.	105	32°33'N	94°22'W
Marshall Islands, nation, Oc.	3	10°00'N	165°00'E
Marshalltown, Ia., U.S. (mär'shȧl-toun)	113	42°02'N	92°55'W
Marshallville, Ga., U.S. (mär'shȧl-vĭl)	124	32°29'N	83°55'W
Marshfield, Ma., U.S. (märsh'fēld)	101a	42°06'N	70°43'W
Marshfield, Mo., U.S.	121	37°20'N	92°53'W
Marshfield, Wi., U.S.	113	44°40'N	90°10'W
Marsh Harbour, Bah.	134	26°30'N	77°00'W
Mars Hill, In., U.S. (märz'hĭl')	111g	39°43'N	86°15'W
Mars Hill, Me., U.S.	100	46°34'N	67°54'W
Marstrand, Swe. (mär'stränd)	166	57°54'N	11°33'E
Marsyaty, Russia (märs'yȧ-tĭ)	186a	60°03'N	60°28'E
Mart, Tx., U.S. (märt)	123	31°32'N	96°49'W
Martaban, Gulf of, b., Mya. (mär-tŭ-bän')	212	16°34'N	96°58'E
Martapura, Indon.	212	3°19'S	114°45'E
Martha's Vineyard, i., Ma., U.S. (mär'thȧz vĭn'yȧrd)	109	41°25'N	70°35'W
Martigny, Switz. (mȧr-tê-nyē')	168	46°06'N	7°00'E
Martigues, Fr.	171	43°24'N	5°05'E
Martin, Tn., U.S. (mär'tĭn)	124	36°20'N	88°45'W
Martina Franca, Italy (mär-tē'nä fräŋ'kä)	175	40°43'N	17°21'E
Martinez, Ca., U.S. (mär-tē'nĕz)	116b	38°01'N	122°08'W
Martinez, Tx., U.S.	117d	29°25'N	98°20'W
Martinique, dep., N.A. (mȧr-tê-nēk')	129	14°50'N	60°40'W
Martin Lake, res., Al., U.S.	124	32°40'N	86°05'W
Martin Point, c., Ak., U.S.	103	70°10'N	142°00'W
Martinsburg, W.V., U.S. (mär'tĭnz-bûrg)	109	39°30'N	78°00'W
Martins Ferry, Oh., U.S. (mär'tĭnz)	108	40°05'N	80°45'W
Martinsville, In., U.S. (mär'tĭnz-vĭl)	108	39°25'N	86°25'W
Martinsville, Va., U.S.	125	36°40'N	79°53'W
Martos, Spain (mär'tōs)	172	37°43'N	3°58'W
Martre, Lac la, l., Can. (läk la märtr)	92	63°24'N	119°58'W
Marugame, Japan (mä'ro͞o-gä'mä)	211	34°19'N	133°48'E
Marungu, mts., D.R.C.	237	7°50'S	29°50'E
Marve, neigh., India	203b	19°12'N	72°43'E
Mary, Turkmen. (mä'rē)	183	37°45'N	61°47'E
Mar'yanskaya, Russia (mȧr-yän'skȧ-yȧ)	177	45°04'N	38°39'E
Maryborough, Austl. (mā'rĭ-bŭr-ô)	219	25°35'S	152°40'E
Maryborough, Austl.	219	37°00'S	143°50'E
Maryland, state, U.S. (mĕr'ĭ-lănd)	105	39°10'N	76°25'W
Marys, r., Nv., U.S. (mā'rĭz)	114	41°25'N	115°10'W
Marystown, Can. (mâr'ĭz-toun)	101	47°11'N	55°10'W

ng-sing; ŋ-baŋk; N-nasalized n; nŏd; cŏmmit; ōld; ôbey; ôrder; oi-boil; fo͞od; ȯ-as oo in foot; ou-out; s-soft; sh-dish; th-thin; pūre; ůnite; ûrn; stŭd; circŭs; ü-as in French tu; '-indeterminate vowel.

ăt; fīnăl; rāte; senăte; ärm; åsk; sofá; fâre; ch-choose; dh-as th in other; bē; ĕvent; bĕt; recĕnt; cratĕr; g-gō; gh-guttural g; bĭt; ĭ-short neutral; rīde; κ-guttural k as ch in German ich;

PRONOUNCING INDEX
Medanosa – Mezquitic 321

PLACE (Pronunciation)	PAGE	LAT.	LONG.
Medanosa, Punta, c., Arg. (po͞o´n-tä-mĕ-dä-nô´sä)	144	47°50'S	65°53'W
Medden, r., Eng., U.K. (mĕd´ĕn)	158a	53°14'N	1°05'W
Medellín, Col. (må-dhĕl-yēn´)	142	6°15'N	75°34'W
Medellín, Mex. (mĕ-dĕl-yĕ´n)	131	19°03'N	96°08'W
Medenine, Tun. (mā-dē-nēn´)	162	33°22'N	10°33'E
Medfeld, Ma., U.S. (mĕd´fēld)	101a	42°11'N	71°19'W
Medford, Ma., U.S. (mĕd´fērd)	101a	42°25'N	71°07'W
Medford, N.J., U.S.	110f	39°54'N	74°50'W
Medford, Ok., U.S.	121	36°47'N	97°44'W
Medford, Or., U.S.	104	42°19'N	122°52'W
Medford, Wi., U.S.	113	45°09'N	90°22'W
Media, Pa., U.S. (mē´dĭ-à)	110f	39°55'N	75°24'W
Mediaş, Rom. (mĕd-yäsh´)	169	46°09'N	24°21'E
Medical Lake, Wa., U.S. (mĕd´ĭ-kăl)	114	47°34'N	117°40'W
Medicine Bow, r., Wy., U.S.	115	41°58'N	106°30'W
Medicine Hat, Can. (mĕd´ĭ-sĭn hăt)	90	50°03'N	110°40'W
Medicine Lake, l., Mt., U.S. (mĕd´ĭ-sĭn)	115	48°24'N	104°15'W
Medicine Lodge, Ks., U.S.	120	37°17'N	98°37'W
Medicine Lodge, r., Ks., U.S.	120	37°20'N	98°57'W
Medina *see* Al Madīnah, Sau. Ar.	198	24°26'N	39°42'E
Medina, N.Y., U.S. (mē-dī´nà)	109	43°15'N	78°20'W
Medina, Oh., U.S.	111d	41°08'N	81°52'W
Medina, r., Tx., U.S.	122	29°45'N	99°13'W
Medina del Campo, Spain (må-dē´nä dĕl käm´pō)	162	41°18'N	4°54'W
Medina de Ríoseco, Spain (må-dē´nä dā rē-ō-sā´kō)	172	41°53'N	5°05'W
Medina Lake, l., Tx., U.S.	122	29°36'N	98°47'W
Medina Sidonia, Spain	172	36°28'N	5°58'W
Mediterranean Sea, sea (mĕd-ĭ-tēr-ā´nē-ăn)	162	36°22'N	13°25'E
Medjerda, Oued, r., Afr.	162	36°43'N	9°54'E
Mednogorsk, Russia	178	51°27'N	57°22'E
Medveditsa, r., Russia (mĕd-vyĕ´dē tsà)	181	50°10'N	43°40'E
Medvezhegorsk, Russia (mĕd-vyĕzh´yĕ-gôrsk´)	180	63°00'N	34°20'E
Medway, Ma., U.S. (mĕd´wā)	101a	42°08'N	71°23'W
Medway Towns, co., Eng., U.K.	158b	51°27'N	0°30'E
Medyn', Russia (mĕ-dēn´)	176	54°58'N	35°53'E
Medzhybizh, Ukr.	177	49°23'N	27°29'E
Meekatharra, Austl. (mē-kă-thăr´ă)	218	26°30'S	118°38'E
Meeker, Co., U.S. (mēk´ēr)	119	40°00'N	107°55'W
Meelpaeg Lake, l., Can. (mēl´pă-ĕg)	101	48°22'N	56°52'W
Meerane, Ger. (mā-rä´nĕ)	168	50°51'N	12°27'E
Meerbusch, Ger.	171c	51°15'N	6°41'E
Meerut, India (mē´rŭt)	199	28°59'N	77°43'E
Megalópoli, Grc.	175	37°22'N	22°08'E
Mégara, Grc. (mĕg´ā-rà)	175	37°59'N	23°21'E
Megget, S.C., U.S. (mĕg´ĕt)	125	32°44'N	80°15'W
Megler, Wa., U.S. (mĕg´lēr)	116c	46°15'N	123°52'W
Mehanom, Mys, c., Ukr.	177	44°48'N	35°17'E
Meherrin, r., Va., U.S. (mē-hĕr´ĭn)	125	36°40'N	77°49'W
Mehlville, Mo., U.S.	117e	38°30'N	90°19'W
Mehsāna, India	202	23°42'N	72°23'E
Mehun-sur-Yèvre, Fr. (mē-ŭɴ-sür-yĕvr´)	170	47°11'N	2°14'E
Meiling Pass, p., China (mā´lĭng´)	205	25°22'N	115°00'E
Meinerzhagen, Ger. (mī´nĕrts-hä-gĕn)	171c	51°06'N	7°39'E
Meiningen, Ger. (mī´nĭng-ĕn)	168	50°35'N	10°25'E
Meiringen, Switz.	168	46°45'N	8°11'E
Meissen, Ger.	168	51°11'N	13°28'E
Meizhu, China (mā-jo͞o)	206	31°17'N	119°12'E
Mejillones, Chile (må-κē-lyō´nås)	144	23°07'S	70°31'W
Mekambo, Gabon	236	1°01'N	13°56'E
Mekele, Eth.	231	13°31'N	39°19'E
Meknés, Mor. (mĕk´nĕs)(mĕk-nĕs´)	230	33°56'N	5°44'W
Mekong, r., Asia	212	18°00'N	104°30'E
Melaka, Malay.	212	2°11'N	102°15'E
Melaka, state, Malay.	197b	2°19'N	102°09'E
Melanesia, is., Oc.	240	13°00'S	164°00'E
Melbourne, Austl. (mĕl´bŭrn)	219	37°52'S	145°08'E
Melbourne, Eng., U.K.	158a	52°49'N	1°26'W
Melbourne, Fl., U.S.	125a	28°05'N	80°37'W
Melbourne, Ky., U.S.	111f	39°02'N	84°22'W
Melcher, Ia., U.S. (mĕl´chēr)	113	41°13'N	93°11'W
Melekess, Russia (mĕl-yĕk-ĕs)	180	54°14'N	49°39'E
Melenki, Russia (mĕ-lyĕn´kē)	180	55°25'N	41°34'E
Melfort, Can. (mĕl´fôrt)	90	52°52'N	104°36'W
Melghir, Chott, l., Alg.	230	33°52'N	5°22'E
Melilla, Sp. N. Afr. (mā-lēl´yä)	230	35°24'N	3°30'W
Melipilla, Chile (må-lē-pē´lyä)	144	33°40'S	71°12'W
Melita, Can.	97	49°11'N	101°09'W
Melitopol', Ukr. (mā-lē-tō´pōl-y´)	181	46°49'N	35°19'E
Melivoia, Grc.	175	39°42'N	22°47'E
Melkrivier, S. Afr.	238c	24°01'S	28°23'E
Mellen, Wi., U.S. (mĕl´ĕn)	113	46°20'N	90°40'W
Mellerud, Swe. (mål´ĕ-ro͞odh)	166	58°43'N	12°25'E
Melmoth, S. Afr.	233c	28°38'S	31°26'E
Melo, Ur. (mā´lō)	144	32°18'S	54°07'W
Melocheville, Can. (mĕ-lōsh-vēl´)	102a	45°24'N	73°56'W
Melozha, r., Russia (myĕ´lô-zhà)	186b	56°06'N	38°34'E
Melrose, Ma., U.S. (mĕl´rōz)	101a	42°29'N	71°06'W
Melrose, Mn., U.S.	113	45°39'N	94°49'W
Melrose Park, Il., U.S.	111a	41°54'N	87°52'W
Meltham, Eng., U.K. (mĕl´thăm)	158a	53°35'N	1°51'W
Melton, Austl. (mĕl´tŭn)	217a	37°41'S	144°35'E
Melton Mowbray, Eng., U.K. (mō´brâ)	158a	52°45'N	0°52'W
Melúli, r., Moz.	237	16°10'S	39°30'E
Melun, Fr. (mē-lŭɴ´)	161	48°32'N	2°40'E
Melunga, Ang.	236	17°16'S	16°24'E
Melville, Can. (mĕl´vĭl)	90	50°55'N	102°48'W
Melville, La., U.S.	123	30°39'N	91°45'W
Melville, i., Austl.	220	11°30'S	131°12'E
Melville, l., Can.	93	53°46'N	59°31'W
Melville, Cape, c., Austl.	221	14°15'S	145°50'E
Melville Hills, hills, Can.	92	69°18'N	124°57'W
Melville Peninsula, pen., Can.	93	67°44'N	84°09'W
Melvindale, Mi., U.S. (mĕl´vĭn-dāl)	111b	42°17'N	83°11'W
Melyana, Alg.	161	36°19'N	1°56'E
Mélykút, Hung. (mā´l´ko͞ot)	169	46°14'N	19°21'E
Memba, Moz. (mĕm´bà)	233	14°12'N	40°35'E
Memel *see* Klaipėda, Lith.	180	55°43'N	21°10'E
Memel, S. Afr. (mĕ´mĕl)	238c	27°42'S	29°35'E
Memmingen, Ger. (mĕm´ĭng-ĕn)	168	47°59'N	10°10'E
Memo, r., Ven. (mĕ´mō)	143b	9°32'N	66°30'W
Memphis, Mo., U.S. (mĕm´fĭs)	121	40°27'N	92°11'W
Memphis, Tn., U.S. (mĕm´fĭs)	105	35°07'N	90°03'W
Memphis, Tx., U.S.	120	34°42'N	100°33'W
Memphis, hist., Egypt	238b	29°50'N	31°12'E
Mena, Ukr. (mē-nà´)	177	51°31'N	32°14'E
Mena, Ar., U.S. (mē´nà)	121	34°35'N	94°09'W
Menangle, Austl.	217b	34°08'S	150°48'E
Menard, Tx., U.S. (mė-närd´)	122	30°56'N	99°48'W
Menasha, Wi., U.S. (mė-năsh´ȧ)	113	44°12'N	88°29'W
Mende, Fr. (mäɴd)	170	44°31'N	3°30'E
Menden, Ger. (mĕn´dĕn)	171c	51°26'N	7°47'E
Mendes, Braz. (mĕ´n-dĕs)	144b	22°32'S	43°44'W
Mendocino, Ca., U.S.	118	39°18'N	123°47'W
Mendocino, Cape, c., Ca., U.S. (mĕn´dō-sē´nō)	107	40°25'N	12°42'W
Mendota, Il., U.S. (mĕn-dō´tȧ)	113	41°34'N	89°06'W
Mendota, l., Wi., U.S.	113	43°09'N	89°41'W
Mendoza, Arg. (mĕn-dō´sä)	144	32°48'S	68°45'W
Mendoza, prov., Arg.	144	35°10'S	69°00'W
Mengcheng, China (mŭŋ-chŭŋ)	206	33°15'N	116°34'E
Meng Shan, mts., China (mŭŋ shän)	206	35°47'N	117°23'E
Mengzi, China	204	23°22'N	103°20'E
Menindee, Austl. (mĕ-nĭn-dē)	222	32°23'S	142°30'E
Menlo Park, Ca., U.S. (mĕn´lō pärk)	116b	37°27'N	122°11'W
Menno, S.D., U.S. (mĕn´ō)	112	43°14'N	97°34'W
Menominee, Mi., U.S. (mė-nŏm´ĭ-nē)	113	45°08'N	87°40'W
Menominee, r., Mi., U.S.	113	45°37'N	87°54'W
Menominee Falls, Wi., U.S. (fôls)	111a	43°11'N	88°06'W
Menominee Ra, Mi., U.S.	113	46°07'N	88°53'W
Menomonee, r., Wi., U.S.	111a	43°09'N	88°06'W
Menomonie, Wi., U.S.	113	44°53'N	91°55'W
Menongue, Ang.	236	14°36'S	17°48'E
Menorca (Minorca), i., Spain (mĕ-nō´r-kä)	156	40°05'N	3°58'E
Mentana, Italy (mĕn-tá´nä)	173d	42°02'N	12°40'E
Mentawai, Kepulauan, is., Indon. (mĕn-tä-vī´)	212	1°08'S	98°10'E
Menton, Fr. (mäɴ-tôɴ´)	171	43°46'N	7°37'E
Mentone, Ca., U.S. (mĕn´tōne)	117a	34°05'N	117°08'W
Mentz, l., S. Afr. (mĕnts)	233c	33°13'S	25°15'E
Menzel Bourguiba, Tun.	162	37°12'N	9°51'E
Menzelinsk, Russia (mĕn´zyĕ-lĕnsk´)	180	55°40'N	53°15'E
Menzies, Austl. (mĕn´zēz)	218	29°45'S	122°15'E
Meogui, Mex. (må-ō´gē)	122	28°17'N	105°28'W
Meppel, Neth. (mĕp´ĕl)	165	52°41'N	6°08'E
Meppen, Ger. (mĕp´ĕn)	168	52°40'N	7°18'E
Merabéllou, Kólpos, b., Grc.	174a	35°16'N	25°55'E
Meramec, r., Mo., U.S. (mĕr´à-mĕk)	121	38°06'N	91°06'W
Merano, Italy (må-rä´nō)	162	46°39'N	11°10'E
Merasheen, i., Can. (mĕ´rá-shēn)	101	47°30'N	54°15'W
Merauke, Indon. (må-rou´kä)	213	8°32'S	140°17'E
Meraux, La., U.S. (mē-ro´)	110d	29°56'N	89°56'W
Mercato San Severino, Italy	173c	40°34'N	14°38'E
Merced, Ca., U.S. (mĕr-sĕd´)	118	37°17'N	120°30'W
Merced, r., Ca., U.S.	118	37°25'N	120°31'W
Mercedario, Cerro, mtn., Arg. (mĕr-så-dhä´rē-ō)	144	31°58'S	70°07'W
Mercedes, Arg.	141c	34°41'S	59°26'W
Mercedes, Arg. (mĕr-sā´dhās)	144	29°04'S	58°01'W
Mercedes, Ur.	144	33°17'S	58°04'W
Mercedes, Tx., U.S.	123	26°09'N	97°55'W
Mercedita, Chile (mĕr-sĕ-dē´tä)	141b	33°51'S	71°10'W
Mercer Island, Wa., U.S. (mûr´sēr)	116a	47°35'N	122°15'W
Mercês, Braz. (mĕ-sĕ´s)	141a	21°13'S	43°20'W
Merchtem, Bel.	159a	50°57'N	4°13'E
Mercier, Can.	102a	45°19'N	73°45'W
Mercy, Cape, c., Can.	93	64°48'N	63°22'W
Meredith, N.H., U.S. (mĕr´ē-dĭth)	109	43°35'N	71°35'W
Merefa, Ukr. (mā-rĕf´à)	177	49°49'N	36°04'E
Merendón, Serranía de, mts., Hond.	132	15°01'N	89°05'W
Mereworth, Eng., U.K. (mĕ-rē wûrth)	158b	51°15'N	0°23'E
Mergui, Mya. (mĕr-gē´)	212	12°29'N	98°39'E
Mergui Archipelago, is., Mya.	212	12°04'N	97°02'E
Meric (Maritsa), r., Eur.	167	40°43'N	26°19'E
Mérida, Mex.	128	20°58'N	89°37'W
Mérida, Ven.	142	8°30'N	71°15'W
Mérida, Cordillera de, mts., Ven. (mĕ´rē-dhä)	142	8°30'N	70°45'W
Meriden, Ct., U.S. (mĕr´ĭ-dĕn)	109	41°30'N	72°50'W
Meridian, Ms., U.S. (mē-rĭd-ĭ-ăn)	105	32°21'N	88°41'W
Meridian, Tx., U.S.	123	31°56'N	97°37'W
Mérignac, Fr.	170	44°50'N	0°40'W
Merikarvia, Fin. (mā´rē-kár´vē-à)	167	61°51'N	21°30'E
Mering, Ger. (mĕ´rĕng)	159d	48°16'N	11°00'E
Merkel, Tx., U.S. (mûr´kĕl)	122	32°26'N	100°02'W
Merkinė, Lith.	167	54°10'N	24°10'E
Merksem, Bel.	159a	51°15'N	4°27'E
Merkys, r., Lith. (măr´kĭs)	169	54°23'N	25°00'E
Merlo, Arg. (mĕr-lō)	144a	34°40'S	58°44'W
Meron, Hare, mtn., Isr.	197a	32°58'N	35°25'E
Merriam, Ks., U.S. (mĕr-rĭ-yàm)	117f	39°01'N	94°42'W
Merriam, Mn., U.S.	117g	44°44'N	93°36'W
Merrick, N.Y., U.S. (mĕr´ĭk)	110a	40°40'N	73°33'W
Merrifield, Va., U.S. (mĕr´ĭ-fēld)	110e	38°50'N	77°12'W
Merrill, Wi., U.S. (mĕr´ĭl)	113	45°11'N	89°42'W
Merrimac, Ma., U.S. (mĕr´ĭ-măk)	101a	45°20'N	71°00'W
Merrimack, N.H., U.S.	101a	42°51'N	71°25'W
Merrimack, r., Ma., U.S. (mĕr´ĭ-măk)	109	43°10'N	71°30'W
Merritt, Can. (mĕr´ĭt)	90	50°07'N	120°47'W
Merryville, La., U.S. (mĕr´ĭ-vĭl)	123	30°46'N	93°34'W
Mersa Fatma, Erit.	231	14°54'N	40°14'E
Merseburg, Ger. (mĕr´zĕ-bo͞orgh)	168	51°21'N	11°59'E
Mersey, r., Eng., U.K. (mûr´zē)	158a	53°20'N	2°55'W
Merseyside, hist. reg., Eng., U.K.	158a	53°29'N	2°59'W
Mersing, Malay.	197b	2°25'N	103°51'E
Merta Road, India (mār´tŭ rōd)	202	26°50'N	73°54'E
Merthyr Tydfil, Wales, U.K. (mûr´thēr tĭd´vĭl)	164	51°46'N	3°30'W
Mértola Almodóvar, Port. (mĕr-tô-lá-äl-mô-dô´vär)	172	37°39'N	8°04'W
Méru, Fr. (mā-rü´)	170	49°14'N	2°08'E
Meru, Kenya (mā´ro͞o)	231	0°01'N	37°45'E
Meru, Mount, mtn., Tan.	237	3°15'S	36°43'E
Merume Mountains, mts., Guy. (mĕr-ü´mĕ)	143	5°45'N	60°15'W
Merwede Kanaal, can., Neth.	159a	52°15'N	5°01'E
Merwin, l., Wa., U.S. (mĕr´wĭn)	116c	45°58'N	122°27'W
Merzifon, Tur. (mĕr´ze-fōn)	198	40°50'N	35°30'E
Mesa, Az., U.S. (mā´sà)	119	33°25'N	111°50'W
Mesabi Range, mts., Mn., U.S. (mā-sŏb´bē)	113	47°17'N	93°04'W
Mesagne, Italy (mā-sän´yå)	175	40°34'N	17°51'E
Mesa Verde National Park, rec., Co., U.S. (vĕr´dē)	106	37°22'N	108°27'W
Mescalero Apache Indian Reservation, I.R., N.M., U.S. (mĕs-kä-lā´rō)	119	33°10'N	105°45'W
Meshchovsk, Russia (myĕsh´chĕfsk)	176	54°17'N	35°19'E
Mesilla, N.M., U.S. (må-sē´yä)	119	32°15'N	106°45'W
Meskine, Chad	235	11°25'N	15°21'E
Mesolóngi, Grc.	175	38°23'N	21°28'E
Mesopotamia, hist. reg., Asia	201	34°00'N	44°00'E
Mesquita, Braz.	144b	22°48'S	43°26'W
Messina, Italy (mĕ-sē´nà)	154	38°11'N	15°34'E
Messina, S. Afr.	232	22°17'S	30°13'E
Messina, Stretto di, strt., Italy (stĕ´t-tô dē)	163	38°10'N	15°34'E
Messíni, Grc.	175	37°05'N	22°00'E
Mestaganem, Alg.	230	36°04'N	0°11'E
Mestre, Italy (mĕs´trā)	174	45°29'N	12°15'E
Meta, dept., Col. (mĕ´tä)	142a	3°28'N	74°07'W
Meta, r., S.A.	142	4°33'N	72°09'W
Métabetchouane, r., Can. (mĕ-tá-bĕt-cho͞o-än´)	99	47°45'N	72°00'W
Metairie, La., U.S.	123	30°00'N	90°11'W
Metán, Arg. (mĕ-tá´n)	144	25°32'S	64°51'W
Metangula, Moz.	232	12°42'S	34°48'E
Metapán, El Sal. (må-täpän´)	132	14°21'N	89°26'W
Metcalfe, Can. (mĕt-käf)	102c	45°14'N	75°27'W
Metchosin, Can.	116a	48°22'N	123°33'W
Metepec, Mex. (må-tĕ-pĕk´)	130	18°56'N	98°31'W
Metepec, Mex.	130	19°15'N	99°36'W
Methow, r., Wa., U.S. (mĕt´hou) (mĕt hou´)	114	48°26'N	120°15'W
Methuen, Ma., U.S. (mē-thū´ĕn)	101a	42°44'N	71°11'W
Metković, Cro. (mĕt´kō-vĭch)	175	43°02'N	17°40'E
Metlakatla, Ak., U.S. (mĕt-lá-kăt´lá)	103	55°08'N	131°35'W
Metropolis, Il., U.S. (mē-trŏp´ō-lĭs)	121	37°09'N	88°46'W
Metter, Ga., U.S. (mĕt´ēr)	125	32°21'N	82°05'W
Mettmann, Ger. (mĕt´män)	171c	51°15'N	6°58'E
Metuchen, N.J., U.S. (mĕ-tŭ´chĕn)	110a	40°32'N	74°21'W
Metz, Fr. (mĕtz)	161	49°08'N	6°10'E
Metztitlán, Mex. (mĕtz-tĕt-län)	130	20°36'N	98°45'W
Meuban, Cam.	235	2°27'N	12°41'E
Meuse (Maas), r., Eur. (mûz) (müz)	165	50°32'N	5°22'E
Mexborough, Eng., U.K. (mĕks´bŭr-ô)	158a	53°30'N	1°17'W
Mexia, Tx., U.S. (må-hē´à)	123	31°32'N	96°29'W
Mexian, China	205	24°20'N	116°10'E
Mexicalcingo, Mex. (mĕ-kē-käl-sēn´go)	131a	19°13'N	99°34'W
Mexicali, Mex. (māk-sē-kä´lē)	128	32°28'N	115°29'W
Mexicana, Altiplanicie, plat., Mex.	130	22°38'N	102°33'W
Mexican Hat, Ut., U.S. (mĕk´sĭ-kăn hăt)	119	37°10'N	109°55'W
Mexico, Me., U.S. (mĕk´sĭ-kō)	100	44°34'N	70°33'W
Mexico, Mo., U.S.	121	39°09'N	91°51'W
Mexico, nation, N.A.	128	23°45'N	104°00'W
Mexico, Gulf of, b., N.A.	128	25°15'N	93°45'W
Mexico City, Mex. (mĕk´sĭ-kō)	128	19°28'N	99°09'W
Mexticacán, Mex. (mĕs´tē-kä-kän´)	130	21°12'N	102°43'W
Meyers Chuck, Ak., U.S.	94	55°44'N	132°15'W
Meyersdale, Pa., U.S. (mī´ērz-dāl)	109	39°55'N	79°00'W
Meyerton, S. Afr. (mī´ēr-tŭn)	238c	26°35'S	28°01'E
Meymaneh, Afg.	198	35°53'N	64°38'E
Mezen', Russia	178	65°50'N	44°05'E
Mezen', r., Russia	180	65°20'N	44°45'E
Mézenc, Mont, mtn., Fr. (mōɴ-mā-zĕɴ´)	170	44°55'N	4°12'E
Mezha, r., Eur. (myā´zhà)	176	55°53'N	31°44'E
Mézieres-sur-Seine, Fr. (mā-zyâr´sür-sân´)	171b	48°58'N	1°49'E
Mezőkövesd, Hung. (mĕ´zû-kû´vĕsht)	169	47°49'N	20°36'E
Mezötur, Hung. (mĕ´zû-to͞or)	169	47°00'N	20°36'E
Mezquital, Mex. (mâz-kē-täl´)	130	23°30'N	104°20'W
Mezquitic, Mex. (mâz-kē-tēk´)	130	22°25'N	103°43'W
Mezquitic, r., Mex.	130	22°25'N	103°45'W

ng-sing; ŋ-baŋk; ɴ-nasalized n; nŏd; cŏmmit; ōld; ôbey; ôrder; oi-boil; fo͞od; ŏo-as oo in foot; ou-out; s-soft; sh-dish; th-thin; pūre; ûnite; ûrn; stŭd; circŭs; ü-as in French tu; ´-indeterminate vowel.

322 Mfangano Island – Mississippi PRONOUNCING INDEX

PLACE (Pronunciation)	PAGE	LAT.	LONG.
Mfangano Island, i., Kenya	237	0°28'S	33°35'E
Mga, Russia (m'gà)	186c	59°45'N	31°04'E
Mglin, Russia (m'glēn')	176	53°03'N	32°52'W
Mia, Oued, r., Alg.	162	29°26'N	3°15'E
Miacatlán, Mex. (mē'ä-kä-tlän')	130	18°42'N	99°17'W
Miahuatlán, Mex. (mē'ä-wä-tlän')	131	16°20'N	96°38'W
Miajadas, Spain (mē-ä-hä'däs)	172	39°10'N	5°53'W
Miami, Az., U.S.	104	33°20'N	110°55'W
Miami, Fl., U.S.	105	25°45'N	80°11'W
Miami, Ok., U.S.	121	36°51'N	94°51'W
Miami, Tx., U.S.	120	35°41'N	100°39'W
Miami Beach, Fl., U.S.	125a	25°47'N	80°07'W
Miamisburg, Oh., U.S. (mī-ăm'iz-bûrg)	108	39°40'N	84°20'W
Miamitown, Oh., U.S. (mī-ăm'ĭ-toun)	111f	39°13'N	84°43'W
Mīāneh, Iran	198	37°15'N	47°13'E
Miangas, Pulau, i., Indon.	213	5°30'N	127°00'E
Miaoli, Tai. (mē-ou'lĭ)	209	24°30'N	120°48'E
Miaozhen, China (miou-jŭn)	206	31°44'N	121°28'E
Miass, Russia (mī-äs')	184	54°59'N	60°06'E
Miastko, Pol. (myäst'kô)	168	54°01'N	17°00'E
Miccosukee Indian Reservation, I.R., Fl., U.S.	125a	26°10'N	80°50'W
Michalovce, Slvk. (mē'ĸä-lôf'tsě)	169	48°44'N	21°56'E
Michel Peak, mtn., Can.	94	53°35'N	126°25'W
Michelson, Mount, mtn., Ak., U.S. (mĭch'ĕl-sŭn)	103	69°11'N	144°12'W
Michendorf, Ger. (mē'ĸĕn-dōrf)	159b	52°19'N	13°02'E
Miches, Dom. Rep. (mē'chĕs)	135	19°00'N	69°05'W
Michigan, state, U.S. (mĭsh-ĭ-găn)	105	45°55'N	87°00'W
Michigan, Lake, l., U.S.	107	43°20'N	87°10'W
Michigan City, In., U.S.	108	41°40'N	86°55'W
Michipicoten, r., Can.	113	47°56'N	84°42'W
Michipicoten Harbour, Can.	113	47°58'N	84°58'W
Michurinsk, Russia (mĭ-chōō-rĭnsk')	181	52°53'N	40°32'E
Mico, Punta, c., Nic. (pōō'n-tä-mē'kô)	133	11°38'N	83°24'W
Micronesia, is., Oc.	240	11°00'N	159°00'E
Micronesia, Federated States of, nation, Oc.	3	5°00'N	152°00'E
Midas, Nv., U.S. (mī'dås)	114	41°15'N	116°50'W
Middelfart, Den. (mēd'’l-färt)	166	55°30'N	9°45'E
Middle, r., Can.	94	55°00'N	125°50'W
Middle Andaman, i., India (ăn-dȧ-măn')	212	12°44'N	93°21'E
Middle Bayou, Tx., U.S.	123a	29°38'N	95°06'W
Middleburg, S. Afr. (mĭd'ĕl-bûrg)	232	31°30'S	25°00'E
Middleburg, S. Afr.	238c	25°47'S	29°30'E
Middlebury, Vt., U.S. (mĭd'’l-bĕr-ĭ)	109	44°00'N	73°10'W
Middle Concho, Tx., U.S. (kōn'chō)	122	31°21'N	100°50'W
Middle River, Md., U.S.	110e	39°20'N	76°27'W
Middlesboro, Ky., U.S. (mĭd'’lz-bŭr-ô)	124	36°36'N	83°42'W
Middlesbrough, Eng., U.K. (mĭd'’lz-brŭ)	160	54°35'N	1°18'W
Middlesex, N.J., U.S. (mĭd'’l-sĕks)	110a	40°34'N	74°30'W
Middleton, Can. (mĭd'’l-tŭn)	100	44°57'N	65°04'W
Middleton, Eng., U.K.	158a	53°34'N	2°12'W
Middletown, Ct., U.S.	109	41°35'N	72°40'W
Middletown, De., U.S.	109	39°30'N	75°40'W
Middletown, Ma., U.S.	101a	42°35'N	71°01'W
Middletown, N.Y., U.S.	109	41°26'N	74°25'W
Middletown, Oh., U.S.	108	39°30'N	84°25'W
Middlewich, Eng., U.K. (mĭd'’l-wĭch)	158a	53°11'N	2°27'W
Middlewit, S. Afr. (mĭd'l'wĭt)	238c	24°50'S	27°00'E
Midfield, Al., U.S.	110h	33°28'N	86°54'W
Midi, Canal du, Fr. (kä-näl-dü-mē-dē')	161	43°22'N	1°35'E
Mid Illovo, S. Afr. (mĭd ĭl'ô-vō)	233c	29°59'S	30°32'E
Midland, Can. (mĭd'lănd)	91	44°45'N	79°50'W
Midland, Mi., U.S.	108	43°40'N	84°20'W
Midland, Tx., U.S.	122	32°05'N	102°05'W
Midvale, Ut., U.S. (mĭd'vāl)	117b	40°37'N	111°54'W
Midway, Al., U.S. (mĭd'wā)	124	32°03'N	85°30'W
Midway Islands, is., Oc.	2	28°00'N	179°00'W
Midwest, Wy., U.S. (mĭd-wĕst')	115	43°25'N	106°15'W
Midye, Tur. (mēd'yĕ)	181	41°35'N	28°10'E
Międzyrzecz, Pol. (myăn-dzû'zhĕch)	168	52°26'N	15°35'E
Mielec, Pol. (myĕ'lĕts)	169	50°17'N	21°27'E
Mier, Mex. (myâr)	122	26°26'N	99°08'W
Mieres, Spain (myā'rās)	172	43°14'N	5°45'W
Mier y Noriega, Mex. (myâr'ē nô-rē-ā'gä)	130	23°28'N	100°08'W
Miguel Auza, Mex.	130	24°17'N	103°27'W
Miguel Pereira, Braz.	144b	22°27'S	43°28'W
Mijares, r., Spain	173	39°55'N	0°01'W
Mikage, Japan (mē'kä-gå)	211b	34°42'N	135°15'E
Mikawa-Wan, b., Japan (mē'kä-wä wän)	211	34°43'N	137°09'E
Mikhaylov, Russia (mē-ĸäy'lôf)	180	54°14'N	39°03'E
Mikhaylovka, Russia	186a	55°35'N	57°57'E
Mikhaylovka, Russia	186c	59°20'N	30°21'E
Mikhaylovka, Russia	181	50°05'N	43°10'E
Mikhnëvo, Russia (mĭk-nyô'vô)	186b	55°08'N	37°57'E
Miki, Japan (mē'kē)	211b	34°47'N	134°59'E
Mikindani, Tan. (mē-kēn-dä'nē)	233	10°17'S	40°07'E
Mikkeli, Fin. (mĭk'ĕ-lĭ)	160	61°42'N	27°14'E
Mikulov, Czech Rep. (mĭ'kōō-lôf)	168	48°47'N	16°39'E
Mikumi, Tan.	237	7°24'S	36°59'E
Mikuni, Japan (mē'kōō-nē)	211	36°09'N	136°14'E
Mikuni-Sammyaku, mts., Japan (säm'myä-kōō)	211	36°51'N	138°38'E
Mikura, i., Japan (mē'kōō-rä)	211	33°53'N	139°26'E
Milaca, Milaca, Mn., U.S. (mē-lăk'ȧ)	113	45°45'N	93°41'W
Milan (Milano), Italy (mē-lä'nō)	174	45°29'N	9°12'E
Milan, Mi., U.S. (mĭ'lăn)	108	42°05'N	83°40'W
Milan, Mo., U.S.	121	40°13'N	93°07'W
Milan, Tn., U.S.	124	35°54'N	88°47'W
Milâs, Tur. (mē'läs)	163	37°10'N	27°25'E
Milazzo, Italy	174	38°13'N	15°17'E
Milbank, S.D., U.S. (mĭl'băŋĸ)	112	45°13'N	96°38'W
Mildura, Austl. (mĭl-dū'rȧ)	219	34°10'S	142°18'E
Miles City, Mt., U.S. (mīlz)	104	46°24'N	105°50'W
Milford, Ct., U.S. (mĭl'fērd)	109	41°15'N	73°05'W
Milford, De., U.S.	109	38°55'N	75°25'W
Milford, Ma., U.S.	101a	42°09'N	71°31'W
Milford, Mi., U.S.	111b	42°35'N	83°36'W
Milford, N.H., U.S.	109	42°50'N	71°40'W
Milford, Oh., U.S.	111f	39°11'N	84°18'W
Milford, Ut., U.S.	119	38°20'N	113°05'W
Milford Sound, strt., N.Z.	223	44°35'S	167°47'E
Miling, Austl. (mĭl'' ng)	218	30°30'S	116°25'E
Milipitas, Ca., U.S. (mĭl-ĭ-pĭ'tås)	116b	37°26'N	121°54'W
Milk, r., N.A.	106	48°30'N	107°00'W
Millau, Fr. (mē-yō')	161	44°06'N	3°04'E
Millbrae, Ca., U.S. (mĭl'brā)	116b	37°36'N	122°23'W
Millbury, Ma., U.S. (mĭl'bĕr-ĭ)	101a	42°12'N	71°46'W
Mill Creek, r., Can. (mĭl)	102g	53°28'N	113°25'W
Mill Creek, r., Ca., U.S.	118	40°07'N	121°55'W
Milledgeville, Ga., U.S. (mĭl'ĕj-vĭl)	124	33°05'N	83°15'W
Mille Îles, Rivière des, r., Can. (rē-vyâr' dā mĭl'ĭl')	102a	45°41'N	73°40'W
Mille Lac Indian Reservation, I.R., Mn., U.S. (mĭl lăk')	113	46°14'N	94°13'W
Mille Lacs, l., Mn., U.S.	113	46°25'N	93°22'W
Mille Lacs, Lac des, l., Can. (läk dē mēl läks)	98	48°52'N	90°53'W
Millen, Ga., U.S. (mĭl'ĕn)	125	32°47'N	81°55'W
Miller, S.D., U.S. (mĭl'ēr)	112	44°31'N	99°00'W
Millerovo, Russia (mĭl'ĕ-rô-vô)	181	48°58'N	40°27'E
Millersburg, Ky., U.S. (mĭl'ērz-bûrg)	108	38°15'N	84°10'W
Millersburg, Oh., U.S.	108	40°35'N	81°55'W
Millersburg, Pa., U.S.	109	40°35'N	76°55'W
Millerton, Can. (mĭl'ēr-tŭn)	100	46°56'N	65°40'W
Millertown, Can. (mĭl'ēr-toun)	101	48°49'N	56°32'W
Millicent, Austl. (mĭl-ĭ-sĕnt)	222	37°30'S	140°20'E
Millinocket, Me., U.S. (mĭl-ĭ-nŏk'ĕt)	100	45°40'N	68°44'W
Millis, Ma., U.S. (mĭl-ĭs)	101a	42°10'N	71°22'W
Millstadt, Il., U.S. (mĭl'stăt)	117e	38°27'N	90°06'W
Millstone, r., N.J., U.S. (mĭl'stōn)	110a	40°27'N	74°38'W
Millstream, Austl. (mĭl'strēm)	218	21°45'S	117°10'E
Milltown, Can. (mĭl'toun)	100	45°13'N	67°19'W
Mill Valley, Ca., U.S. (mĭl)	116b	37°54'N	122°32'W
Millwood Reservoir, res., Ar., U.S.	121	33°00'N	94°00'W
Milly-la-Forêt, Fr. (mē-yē'-la-fō-rĕ')	171b	48°24'N	2°28'E
Milnerton, S. Afr. (mĭl'nēr-tŭn)	232a	33°52'S	18°30'E
Milnor, N.D., U.S. (mĭl'nēr)	112	46°17'N	97°29'W
Milo, Me., U.S.	100	44°16'N	69°01'W
Milos, i., Grc. (mē'lōs)	163	36°45'N	24°35'E
Milpa Alta, Mex. (mē'l-pä-ä'l-tä)	131a	19°11'N	99°01'W
Milton, Can.	102d	43°31'N	79°53'W
Milton, Fl., U.S. (mĭl'tŭn)	124	30°37'N	87°02'W
Milton, Pa., U.S.	109	41°00'N	76°50'W
Milton, Ut., U.S.	117b	41°04'N	111°44'W
Milton, Wa., U.S.	116a	47°15'N	122°20'W
Milton, Wi., U.S.	113	42°45'N	89°00'W
Milton-Freewater, Or., U.S.	114	45°57'N	118°25'W
Milvale, Pa., U.S. (mĭl'văl)	111e	40°29'N	79°58'W
Milville, N.J., U.S. (mĭl'vĭl)	109	39°25'N	75°00'W
Milwaukee, Wi., U.S.	105	43°03'N	87°55'W
Milwaukee, r., Wi., U.S.	111a	43°10'N	87°56'W
Milwaukie, Or., U.S. (mĭl-wô'kē)	114	45°27'N	122°38'W
Mimiapan, Mex. (mē-myä-pan')	131a	19°26'N	99°28'W
Mimoso do Sul, Braz. (mē-mô'sō-dô-sōō'l)	141a	21°03'S	41°21'W
Min, r., China (mēn)	205	26°03'N	118°30'E
Min, r., China	209	29°30'N	104°00'E
Mina, r., Alg. (mē'nȧ)	173	35°24'N	0°51'E
Minago, r., Can. (mĭ-nä'gō)	97	54°25'N	98°45'W
Minakuchi, Japan (mē'nȧ-kōō'chē)	211	34°59'N	136°06'E
Minas, Cuba (mē'näs)	134	21°30'N	77°35'W
Minas, Indon.	197b	0°52'N	101°29'E
Minas, Ur. (mē'näs)	144	34°18'S	55°12'W
Minas, Sierra de las, mts., Guat. (syĕr'rȧ dā läs mē'näs)	132	15°08'N	90°25'W
Minas Basin, b., Can. (mī'nȧs)	100	45°20'N	64°00'W
Minas Channel, strt., Can.	100	45°15'N	64°45'W
Minas de Oro, Hond. (mē'näs-dĕ-dĕ-ō-rô)	132	14°52'N	87°19'W
Minas de Riotinto, Spain (mē'näs dā rē-ô-tēn'tō)	172	37°43'N	6°35'W
Minas Novas, Braz. (mē'näzh nō'väzh)	143	17°20'S	42°19'W
Minatare, l., Ne., U.S. (mĭn'ȧ-târ)	112	41°56'N	103°07'W
Minatitlán, Mex. (mē-nä-tē-tlän')	128	17°59'N	94°33'W
Minatitlán, Mex.	130	19°21'N	104°02'W
Minato, Japan (mē'nȧ-tô)	211	35°13'N	139°52'E
Minch, The, strt., Scot., U.K.	156	58°04'N	6°04'W
Mindanao, i., Phil.	213	8°00'N	125°00'E
Mindanao Sea, sea, Phil.	213	8°55'N	124°00'E
Minden, Ger. (mĭn'dĕn)	168	52°17'N	8°58'E
Minden, La., U.S.	123	32°36'N	93°19'W
Minden, Ne., U.S.	120	40°30'N	98°54'W
Mindoro, i., Phil.	212	12°50'N	121°05'E
Mindoro Strait, strt., Phil.	213a	12°28'N	120°33'E
Mindyak, Russia (mēn'dyák)	186a	54°01'N	58°48'E
Mineola, N.Y., U.S. (mĭn-ē-ō'lȧ)	110a	40°43'N	73°38'W
Mineola, Tx., U.S.	123	32°39'N	95°31'W
Mineral del Chico, Mex. (mē-nȧ-räl'dĕl chē'kō)	130	20°13'N	98°46'W
Mineral del Monte, Mex. (mē-nȧ-räl dĕl mōn'tå)	130	20°18'N	98°39'W
Mineral'nyye Vody, Russia	181	44°10'N	43°15'E
Mineral Point, Wi., U.S. (mĭn'ēr-ăl)	113	42°50'N	90°10'W
Minerál Wells, Tx., U.S. (mĭn'ēr-ăl wĕlz)	122	32°48'N	98°06'W
Minerva, Oh., U.S. (mĭ-nur'vȧ)	108	40°45'N	81°10'W
Minervino, Italy (mē-nĕr-vē'nô)	174	41°07'N	16°05'E
Mineyama, Japan (mē-nĕ-yä'mä)	211	35°38'N	135°05'E
Mingäçevir, Azer.	182	40°45'N	47°03'E
Mingäçevir su anbarı, res., Azer.	182	40°50'N	46°50'E
Mingan, Can.	91	50°18'N	64°02'W
Mingenew, Austl. (mĭn'gĕ-nû)	218	29°15'S	115°45'E
Mingo Junction, Oh., U.S. (mĭŋ'gō)	108	40°15'N	80°40'W
Minho, hist. reg., Port. (mēn yō)	172	41°32'N	8°13'W
Minho (Miño), r., Eur. (mē'n-yō)	172	41°28'N	9°05'W
Ministik Lake, l., Can. (mĭ-nĭs'tĭk)	102g	53°23'N	113°05'W
Minna, Nig. (mĭn'ȧ)	230	9°37'N	6°33'E
Minneapolis, Ks., U.S. (mĭn-ē-ăp'ô-lĭs)	121	39°07'N	97°41'W
Minneapolis, Mn., U.S.	105	44°58'N	93°15'W
Minnedosa, Can. (mĭn-ē-dō'sȧ)	90	50°14'N	99°51'W
Minneota, Mn., U.S. (mĭn-ē-ō'tȧ)	112	44°34'N	95°59'W
Minnesota, state, U.S. (mĭn-ē-sō'tȧ)	105	46°10'N	90°20'W
Minnesota, r., Mn., U.S.	107	44°30'N	95°00'W
Minnetonka, l., Mn., U.S. (mĭn-ē-tôn'kȧ)	113	44°52'N	93°34'W
Minnitaki Lake, l., Can. (mĭ'nĭ-tä'kē)	97	49°58'N	92°00'W
Mino, r., Japan	211b	34°56'N	135°06'E
Minonk, Il., U.S. (mī'nŏnk)	108	40°55'N	89°00'W
Minooka, Il., U.S. (mĭ-nōō'kȧ)	111a	41°27'N	88°15'W
Minot, N.D., U.S.	104	48°13'N	101°17'W
Minsk, Bela. (mēnsk)	178	53°54'N	27°35'E
Minsk, prov., Bela.	176	53°50'N	27°43'E
Mińsk Mazowiecki, Pol. (mēn'sk mä-zō-vyĕt'skĭ)	169	52°10'N	21°35'E
Minsterley, Eng., U.K. (mĭnstēr-lē)	158a	52°38'N	2°55'W
Minto, Can.	100	46°05'N	66°05'W
Minto, l., Can.	93	57°18'N	75°50'W
Minturno, Italy (mēn-tōōr'nō)	174	41°17'N	13°44'E
Minūf, Egypt (mē-nōōf')	238b	30°26'N	30°55'E
Minusinsk, Russia (mē-nö-sēnsk')	179	53°47'N	91°45'E
Min'yar, Russia	186a	55°06'N	57°33'E
Miquelon Lake, l., Can. (mĭ'kē-lôn)	102g	53°16'N	112°55'W
Miquihuana, Mex. (mē-kē-wä'nä)	130	23°36'N	99°45'W
Mir, Bela. (mēr)	169	53°27'N	26°25'E
Miracema, Braz. (mē-rä-sĕ'mä)	141a	21°24'S	42°10'W
Miracema do Tocantins, Braz.	143	9°34'S	48°24'W
Mirador, Braz. (mē-rȧ-dōr')	143	6°19'S	44°12'W
Miraflores, Col. (mē-rä-flō'räs)	142	5°10'N	73°13'W
Miraflores, Peru	142	16°19'S	71°20'W
Miraflores Locks, trans., Pan.	128a	9°00'N	79°35'W
Miragoâne, Haiti (mē-rȧ-gwän')	135	18°25'N	73°05'W
Mira Loma, Ca., U.S. (mĭ'rȧ lō'mȧ)	117a	34°01'N	117°32'W
Miramar, Ca., U.S. (mĭr'ă-mär)	118a	32°53'N	117°08'W
Miramas, Fr.	170	43°35'N	5°00'E
Miramichi Bay, b., Can. (mĭr'ȧ-mē'shē)	100	47°08'N	65°08'W
Miranda, Col. (mē-rä'n-dä)	142a	3°14'N	76°11'W
Miranda, Ca., U.S.	118	40°14'N	123°49'W
Miranda, Ven.	143b	10°09'N	68°24'W
Miranda, dept., Ven.	143b	10°17'N	66°41'W
Miranda de Ebro, Spain (mē-rä'n-dä-dĕ-ĕ'brō)	172	42°42'N	2°59'W
Miranda do Douro, Port. (mē-rän'dä dô-dwĕ'rô)	172	41°30'N	6°17'W
Mirandela, Port. (mē-rän-dā'lȧ)	172	41°28'N	7°10'W
Mirando City, Tx., U.S. (mĭr-ăn'dō)	122	27°25'N	99°03'W
Mira Por Vos Islets, is., Bah. (mē'rä pôr vōs)	135	22°05'N	74°30'W
Mira Por Vos Pass, strt., Bah.	135	22°10'N	74°35'W
Mirbāţ, Oman	198	16°58'N	54°42'E
Mirebalais, Haiti (mēr-bȧ-lĕ')	135	18°50'N	72°05'W
Mirecourt, Fr. (mēr-kōōr')	171	48°20'N	6°08'E
Mirfield, Eng., U.K. (mûr'fēld)	158a	53°41'N	1°42'W
Miri, Malay. (mē'rē)	212	4°13'N	113°56'E
Mirim, Lagoa, l., S.A. (mē-rēɴ')	144	33°00'S	53°15'W
Miropol'ye, Ukr. (mē-rô-pôl'yĕ)	177	51°02'N	35°13'E
Mīrpur Khās, Pak. (mēr'pōōr käs)	202	25°36'N	69°10'E
Mirzāpur, India (mēr'zä-pōōr)	199	25°12'N	82°38'E
Misantla, Mex. (mē-sän'tlä)	131	19°55'N	96°49'W
Miscou, i., Can. (mĭs'kō)	100	47°58'N	64°35'W
Miscou Point, c., Can.	100	48°04'N	64°32'W
Miseno, Cape, c., Italy (mē-zĕ'nō)	173c	40°33'N	14°12'E
Misery, Mount, mtn., St. K./N. (mĭz'rē-ĭ)	133b	17°28'N	62°47'W
Mishan, China (mĭ'shäɴ)	210	45°32'N	132°19'E
Mishawaka, In., U.S. (mĭsh-ȧ-wôk'ȧ)	108	41°45'N	86°15'W
Mishina, Japan (mē'shē-mä)	211	35°09'N	138°56'E
Misiones, prov., Arg. (mē-syō'näs)	144	27°00'S	54°30'W
Miskito, Cayos, is., Nic.	133	14°34'N	82°30'W
Miskolc, Hung. (mĭsh'kôlts)	154	48°07'N	20°50'E
Misool, Pulau, i., Indon. (mē-sôl')	213	2°00'S	130°05'E
Misquah Hills, Mn., U.S. (mĭs-kwä' hĭlz)	113	47°50'N	90°30'W
Mişr al Jadīdah, Egypt	238b	30°06'N	31°35'E
Misrātah, Libya	231	32°23'N	14°58'E
Missinaibi, r., Can. (mĭs'ĭn-ă'ĕ-bē)	93	50°27'N	83°01'W
Missinaibi Lake, l., Can.	98	48°23'N	83°40'W
Mission, Ks., U.S. (mĭsh'ŭn)	117f	39°02'N	94°39'W
Mission, Tx., U.S.	122	26°14'N	98°19'W
Mission City, Can. (sĭ'tĭ)	95	49°08'N	112°18'W
Mississagi, r., Can.	98	46°35'N	83°30'W
Mississauga, Can.	99	43°34'N	79°37'W
Mississippi, state, U.S. (mĭs-ĭ-sĭp'ē)	105	32°30'N	89°45'W
Mississippi, l., Can.	99	45°05'N	76°15'W
Mississippi, r., U.S.	107	32°00'N	91°30'W

PRONOUNCING INDEX

Mississippi Sound – Monterotondo 323

PLACE (Pronunciation)	PAGE	LAT.	LONG.
Mississippi Sound, strt., Ms., U.S.	124	34°16'N	89°10'W
Missoula, Mt., U.S. (mĭ-zōō′lȧ)	104	46°55'N	114°00'W
Missouri, state, U.S. (mĭ-sōō′rē)	105	38°00'N	93°40'W
Missouri, r., U.S.	106	40°40'N	96°00'W
Missouri City, Tx., U.S.	123a	29°37'N	95°32'W
Missouri Coteau, hills, U.S.	106	47°30'N	101°00'W
Missouri Valley, Ia., U.S.	112	41°35'N	95°53'W
Mist, Or., U.S. (mĭst)	116c	46°00'N	123°15'W
Mistassini, Can. (mĭs-tȧ-sĭ′nē)	99	48°56'N	71°55'W
Mistassini, l., Can. (mĭs-tȧ-sĭ′nē)	93	50°48'N	73°30'W
Mistelbach, Aus. (mĭs′tĕl-bäk)	168	48°34'N	16°33'E
Misteriosa, Lago, l., Mex. (mēs-tē-ryō′sä)	132a	18°05'N	90°15'W
Misti, Volcán, vol., Peru	142	16°04'S	71°20'W
Mistretta, Italy (mē-strĕt′tä)	174	37°54'N	14°22'E
Misty Fjords National Monument, rec., Ak., U.S.	103	51°00'N	131°00'W
Mita, Punta de, c., Mex. (pōō′n-tä-dĕ-mē′tä)	130	20°44'N	105°34'W
Mitaka, Japan (mē′tä-kä)	211a	35°42'N	139°34'E
Mitchell, Il., U.S. (mĭch′ĕl)	117e	38°46'N	90°05'W
Mitchell, In., U.S.	108	38°45'N	86°25'W
Mitchell, Ne., U.S.	112	41°56'N	103°49'W
Mitchell, S.D., U.S.	104	43°42'N	98°01'W
Mitchell, Mount, mtn., N.C., U.S.	107	35°47'N	82°15'W
Mit Ghamr, Egypt	238b	30°43'N	31°20'E
Mitla Pass, p., Egypt	197a	30°03'N	32°40'E
Mito, Japan (mē′tō)	210	36°20'N	140°23'E
Mitsiwa, Erit.	231	15°40'N	39°19'E
Mitsu, Japan (mēt′sò)	211	34°21'N	132°49'E
Mittelland Kanal, can., Ger. (mĭt′ĕl-länd)	168	52°18'N	10°42'E
Mittenwalde, Ger. (mē′tĕn-väl-dĕ)	159b	52°16'N	13°33'E
Mittweida, Ger. (mĭt-vī′dä)	168	50°59'N	12°58'E
Mitumba, Monts, mts., D.R.C.	237	10°50'S	27°00'E
Mityayevo, Russia (mĭt-yä′yĕ-vô)	186a	60°17'N	61°02'E
Miura, Japan	211a	35°08'N	139°37'E
Miwa, Japan (mē′wä)	211b	34°32'N	135°51'E
Mixico, Guat. (mēs′kô)	132	14°37'N	90°37'W
Mixquiahuala, Mex. (mēs-kē-wä′lä)	130	20°12'N	99°13'W
Mixteco, r., Mex. (mēs-tā′kō)	130	17°45'N	98°10'W
Miyake, Japan (mē′yä-kå)	211b	34°35'N	135°34'E
Miyake, i., Japan (mē′yä-kå)	211	34°06'N	139°21'E
Miyakonojō, Japan	210	31°44'N	131°04'E
Miyazaki, Japan (mē′yä-zä′kē)	210	31°55'N	131°27'E
Miyoshi, Japan (mē-yō′shē′)	210	34°48'N	132°49'E
Mizdah, Libya (mēz′dä)	200	31°29'N	13°09'E
Mizil, Rom. (mē′zēl)	175	45°01'N	26°30'E
Mizoram, state, India	199	23°25'N	92°45'E
Mjölby, Swe. (myûl′bü)	166	58°20'N	15°09'E
Mjörn, l., Swe.	166	57°55'N	12°22'E
Mjösa, l., Nor. (myûsä)	160	60°41'N	11°25'E
Mkalama, Tan.	232	4°07'S	34°38'E
Mkushi, Zam.	237	13°40'S	29°20'E
Mkwaja, Tan.	237	5°47'S	38°51'E
Mladá Boleslav, Czech Rep. (mlä′dä bô′lĕ-slåf)	168	50°26'N	14°52'E
Mlala Hills, hills, Tan.	237	6°47'S	31°45'E
Mlanje Mountains, mts., Mwi.	237	15°55'S	35°30'E
Mława, Pol. (mwä′vå)	160	53°07'N	20°25'E
Mmabatho, S. Afr.	232	25°42'S	25°43'E
Moa, r., Afr.	234	7°40'N	11°15'W
Moa, Pulau, i., Indon.	213	8°30'S	128°30'E
Moab, Ut., U.S. (mō′ăb)	119	38°35'N	109°35'W
Moanda, Gabon	232	1°37'S	13°09'E
Moar Lake, l., Can. (môr)	97	52°00'N	95°09'W
Moba, D.R.C.	232	7°12'S	29°39'E
Mobaye, C.A.R. (mô-bä′y′)	231	4°19'N	21°11'E
Mobayi-Mbongo, D.R.C.	231	4°14'N	21°11'E
Moberly, Mo., U.S. (mō′bĕr-lĭ)	105	39°24'N	92°25'W
Mobile, Al., U.S. (mô-bēl′)	105	30°42'N	88°03'W
Mobile, r., Al., U.S.	124	31°15'N	88°00'W
Mobile Bay, b., Al., U.S.	107	30°26'N	87°56'W
Mobridge, S.D., U.S. (mō′brĭj)	112	45°32'N	100°26'W
Moca, Dom. Rep. (mō′kä)	135	19°25'N	70°35'W
Moçambique, Moz. (mō-säN-bē′kĕ)	237	15°03'S	40°42'E
Moçâmedes, Ang. (mô-zȧ-mĕ-dĕs)	232	15°10'S	12°09'E
Moçâmedes, hist. reg., Ang.	232	16°00'S	12°15'E
Mochitlán, Mex. (mō-chē-tlän′)	130	17°10'N	99°19'W
Mochudi, Bots. (mō-chō′dē)	232	24°13'S	26°07'E
Mocímboa da Praia, Moz. (mō-sē′ēm-bô-ȧ prä′ēȧ)	233	11°20'S	40°21'E
Moclips, Wa., U.S.	114	47°14'N	124°13'W
Môco, Serra do, mtn., Ang.	236	12°25'S	15°10'E
Mococa, Braz. (mô-kô′kȧ)	141a	21°29'S	46°58'W
Moctezuma, Mex. (mōk′tā-zōō′mä)	130	22°44'N	101°06'W
Mocuba, Moz.	237	16°50'S	36°59'E
Modderfontein, S. Afr.	233b	26°06'S	28°10'E
Modena, Italy (mô′dĕ-nä)	162	44°38'N	10°54'E
Modesto, Ca., U.S. (mô-dĕs′tō)	118	37°39'N	121°00'W
Mödling, Aus. (mûd′lĭng)	159e	48°06'N	16°17'E
Moelv, Nor.	166	60°55'N	10°40'E
Moengo, Sur.	143	5°43'N	54°19'W
Moenkopi, Az., U.S.	119	36°07'N	111°13'W
Moers, Ger. (mûrs)	171c	51°27'N	6°38'E
Moffat Tunnel, trans., Co., U.S. (môf′ăt)	120	39°52'N	106°20'W
Mogadishu (Muqdisho), Som.	238a	2°08'N	45°22'E
Mogadore, Oh., U.S. (mŏg-ȧ-dōr′)	111d	41°04'N	81°23'E
Mogaung, Mya. (mō-gä′ông)	199	25°30'N	96°52'E
Mogi das Cruzes, Braz. (mō-gē-däs-krōō′sĕs)	143	23°33'S	46°10'W
Mogi-Guaçu, r., Braz. (mô-gē-gwä′sōō)	141a	22°06'S	47°12'W
Mogilno, Pol. (mô-gēl′nô)	168	52°38'N	17°58'E
Mogi-Mirim, Braz. (mô-gē-mē-rē′N)	141a	22°26'S	46°57'W
Mogok, Mya. (mô-gōk′)	199	23°14'N	96°38'E
Mogol, r., S. Afr. (mô-gŏl)	238c	24°12'S	27°55'E
Mogollon Plateau, plat., Az., U.S.	106	34°15'N	110°45'W
Mogollon Rim, cliff, Az., U.S. (mō-gô-yōn′)	119	34°26'N	111°17'W
Moguer, Spain (mô-gĕr′)	172	37°15'N	6°50'W
Mohács, Hung. (mô′häch)	169	45°59'N	18°38'E
Mohale's Hoek, Leso.	233c	30°09'S	27°28'E
Mohall, N.D., U.S. (mō′hôl)	112	48°46'N	101°29'W
Mohave, l., Nv., U.S. (mô-hä′vā)	119	35°23'N	114°40'W
Mohe, China (mwo-hŭ)	205	53°33'N	122°30'E
Mohenjo-Dero, hist., Pak.	199	27°20'N	68°10'E
Mohyliv-Podil's'kyi, Ukr.	181	48°27'N	27°51'E
Mõisaküla, Est. (mēē′sȧ-kü′lä)	167	58°07'N	25°12'E
Moissac, Fr. (mwä-sák′)	170	44°07'N	1°05'E
Moita, Port. (mô-ē′tȧ)	173b	38°39'N	9°00'W
Mojave, Ca., U.S.	118	35°06'N	118°09'W
Mojave, r., Ca., U.S. (mô-hä′vā)	118	34°46'N	117°24'W
Mojave Desert, Ca., U.S.	118	35°05'N	117°30'W
Mojave Desert, des., Ca., U.S.	106	35°00'N	117°00'W
Mokhotlong, Leso.	233c	29°18'S	29°06'E
Mokp'o, Kor., S. (môk′pō′)	205	34°50'N	126°30'E
Mol, Bel.	159a	51°21'N	5°09'E
Moldavia *see* Moldova, nation, Eur.	178	48°00'N	28°00'E
Moldavia, hist. reg., Rom.	169	47°20'N	27°12'E
Molde, Nor. (môl′dĕ)	160	62°44'N	7°15'E
Moldova, nation, Eur.	178	48°00'N	28°00'E
Moldova, r., Rom.	169	47°17'N	26°27'E
Moldoveanu, Vârful, mtn., Rom.	175	45°33'N	24°38'E
Molepolole, Bots. (mō-lȧ-pô-lō′lȧ)	232	24°15'S	25°33'W
Molfetta, Italy (môl-fĕt′tä)	163	41°11'N	16°38'E
Molina, Chile (mô-lē′nä)	141b	35°07'S	71°17'W
Molina de Aragón, Spain (mô-lē′nä dĕ ä-rä-gô′n)	172	40°40'N	1°54'W
Molína de Segura, Spain (mô-lē′nä dĕ sĕ-gōō′rä)	172	38°03'N	1°07'W
Moline, Il., U.S. (mô-lēn′)	121	41°31'N	90°34'W
Moliro, D.R.C.	232	8°13'S	30°34'E
Moliterno, Italy (mōl-ē-tĕr′nō)	174	40°13'N	15°54'W
Mollendo, Peru (mō-lyĕn′dō)	142	17°02'S	71°59'W
Moller, Port, Ak., U.S. (pōrt mōl′ēr)	103	56°18'N	161°30'W
Mölndal, Swe. (mûln′däl)	166	57°39'N	12°01'E
Molochna, r., Ukr.	177	47°05'N	35°22'E
Molochnyĭ lyman, l., Ukr.	177	46°35'N	35°32'E
Molody Tud, Russia (mō-lō-dô′ē tōō′d)	186b	55°17'N	37°31'E
Moloka'i, i., Hi., U.S. (mō-lô kä′ē)	106c	21°15'N	157°05'W
Molokcha, r., Russia (mô′lôk-chä)	186b	56°15'N	38°29'E
Molopo, r., Afr. (mō-lō-pô)	232	27°45'S	20°45'E
Molson Lake, l., Can. (mōl′sŭn)	97	54°12'N	96°45'W
Molteno, S. Afr. (môl-tā′nô)	233c	31°24'S	26°23'E
Moluccas *see* Maluku, is., Indon.	213	2°22'S	128°25'E
Moma, Moz.	237	16°44'S	39°14'E
Mombasa, Kenya (mōm-bä′sä)	233	4°03'S	39°40'E
Mombetsu, Japan (môm′bĕt-sōō′)	210	44°21'N	142°48'E
Momence, Il., U.S. (mô-mĕns′)	111a	41°09'N	87°40'W
Momostenango, Guat. (mô-môs-tā-nän′gô)	132	15°02'N	91°25'W
Momotombo, Nic.	132	12°25'N	86°43'W
Mompog Pass, strt., Phil. (mōm-pōg′)	213a	13°35'N	122°09'E
Mompos, Col. (mōm-pōs′)	142	9°05'N	74°30'W
Momtblanc, Spain	173	41°20'N	1°08'E
Møn, i., Den. (mûn)	166	54°54'N	12°30'E
Monaca, Pa., U.S. (mŏ-nȧ′kō)	111e	40°41'N	80°17'W
Monaco, nation, Eur. (mŏn′ȧ-kō)	154	43°43'N	7°47'E
Monaghan, Ire. (mō′ȧ-găn)	164	54°16'N	7°20'W
Mona Passage, strt., N.A. (mō′nä)	129	18°00'N	68°10'W
Monarch Mountain, mtn., Can. (mŏn′ērk)	94	51°41'N	125°53'W
Monashee Mountains, mts., Can. (mŏ-nä′shē)	95	50°30'N	118°30'W
Monastir *see* Bitola, Mac.	174	41°02'N	21°22'E
Monastir, Tun. (môn-ȧs-tēr′)	162	35°49'N	10°56'E
Monastyrshchina, Russia (mô-nȧs-tērsh′chĭ-nȧ)	176	54°19'N	31°49'E
Monastyryshche, Ukr.	177	48°57'N	29°53'E
Monção, Braz. (mon-souN′)	143	3°39'S	45°23'W
Moncayo, mtn., Spain (môn-kä′yō)	172	41°44'N	1°48'W
Monchegorsk, Russia (mōn′chĕ-gôrsk)	180	69°00'N	33°35'E
Mönchengladbach, Ger. (mûn′kĕn glät′bäk)	168	51°12'N	6°28'E
Moncique, Serra de, mts., Port. (sĕr′rä dä môn-chē′kĕ)	172	37°22'N	8°37'W
Monclova, Mex. (môn-klō′vä)	128	26°53'N	101°25'W
Moncton, Can. (mŭngk′tŭn)	91	46°06'N	64°47'W
Mondêgo, r., Port. (mōn-dĕ′gō)	172	40°10'N	8°36'W
Mondego, Cabo, c., Port. (kä′bō môn-dā′gô)	172	40°12'N	8°55'W
Mondombe, D.R.C. (môn-dôm′bȧ)	232	0°45'S	23°06'E
Mondoñedo, Spain (môn-dô-nyā′dō)	172	43°35'N	7°18'W
Mondovi, Wi., U.S. (mŏn-dō′vĭ)	113	44°35'N	91°42'W
Monee, Il., U.S. (mō-nĭ)	111a	41°25'N	87°45'W
Monessen, Pa., U.S. (mō-nĕs′sen)	111e	40°09'N	79°53'W
Monett, Mo., U.S. (mô-nĕt′)	121	36°55'N	93°55'W
Monfalcone, Italy	174	45°49'N	13°30'E
Monforte de Lemos, Spain (môn-fôr′tä dĕ lĕ′môs)	172	42°30'N	7°30'W
Mongala, r., D.R.C. (mŏn-gäl′ȧ)	231	3°20'N	21°30'E
Mongalla, Sudan	231	5°11'N	31°46'E
Monghyr, India (mŏn-gēr′)	199	25°23'N	86°34'E
Mongo, r., Afr.	234	9°50'N	11°50'W
Mongolia, nation, Asia (mŏŋ-gō′lĭ-ȧ)	204	46°00'N	100°00'E
Mongos, Chaîne des, mts., C.A.R.	231	8°04'N	21°59'E
Mongoumba, C.A.R. (mŏŋ-gōōm′bȧ)	231	3°38'N	18°36'E
Mongu, Zam. (mŏŋ-gōō′)	232	15°15'S	23°09'E
Monkey Bay, Mwi.	237	14°05'S	34°55'E
Monkey River, Belize (mŭŋ′kĭ)	132a	16°22'N	88°33'W
Monkland, Can. (mŭngk-lănd)	102c	45°12'N	74°52'W
Monkoto, D.R.C. (môn-kō′tō)	232	1°38'S	20°39'E
Monmouth, Il., U.S. (mŏn′mŭth) (mŏn′mouth)	121	40°54'N	90°38'W
Monmouth Junction, N.J., U.S. (mŏn′mouth jŭngk′shŭn)	110a	40°23'N	74°33'W
Monmouth Mountain, mtn., Can. (mŏn′mŭth)	94	51°00'N	123°47'W
Mono, r., Afr.	234	7°20'N	1°25'E
Mono Lake, l., Ca., U.S. (mō′nō)	118	38°04'N	119°00'W
Monon, In., U.S. (mō′nŏn)	108	40°55'N	86°55'W
Monongah, W.V., U.S. (mô-nŏn′gȧ)	108	39°25'N	80°10'W
Monongahela, Pa., U.S. (mô-nŏn-gȧ-hē′lȧ)	111a	40°11'N	79°55'W
Monongahela, r., W.V., U.S.	108	39°30'N	80°10'W
Monopoli, Italy (mô-nô′pô-lê)	175	40°55'N	17°17'E
Monóvar, Spain (mô-nō′vär)	173	38°26'N	0°50'W
Monreale, Italy (mōn-rȧ-ä′lā)	174	38°04'N	13°15'E
Monroe, Ga., U.S. (mŭn-rō′)	124	33°47'N	83°43'W
Monroe, La., U.S.	105	32°30'N	92°06'W
Monroe, Mi., U.S.	108	41°55'N	83°25'W
Monroe, N.C., U.S.	125	34°58'N	80°34'W
Monroe, N.Y., U.S.	110a	41°19'N	74°11'W
Monroe, Ut., U.S.	119	38°35'N	112°10'W
Monroe, Wa., U.S.	116a	47°52'N	121°58'W
Monroe, Wi., U.S.	113	42°35'N	89°40'W
Monroe, Lake, l., Fl., U.S.	125	28°50'N	81°15'W
Monroe City, Mo., U.S.	121	39°38'N	91°41'W
Monroeville, Al., U.S. (mŭn-rō′vĭl)	124	31°33'N	87°19'W
Monroeville, Pa., U.S.	111e	40°26'N	79°46'W
Monrovia, Lib.	230	6°18'N	10°47'W
Monrovia, Ca., U.S. (mŏn-rō′vĭ-ȧ)	117a	34°09'N	118°00'W
Mons, Bel. (môN′)	161	50°29'N	3°55'E
Monson, Me., U.S. (mŏn′sŭn)	100	45°17'N	69°28'W
Mönsterås, Swe. (mŭn′stĕr-ôs)	166	57°04'N	16°24'E
Montagne Tremblant Provincial Park, rec., Can.	107	46°30'N	75°51'W
Montague, Can. (mŏn′tȧ-gū)	101	46°10'N	62°39'W
Montague, Mi., U.S.	108	43°30'N	86°25'W
Montague, i., Ak., U.S.	103	60°10'N	147°00'W
Montalbán, Ven. (mōnt-äl-bän)	143b	10°14'N	68°19'W
Montalegre, Port. (mōn-tä-lā′grĕ)	172	41°49'N	7°48'W
Montana, state, U.S. (mŏn-tăn′ȧ)	104	47°10'N	111°50'W
Montánchez, Spain (môn-tän′chāth)	172	39°18'N	6°09'W
Montargis, Fr. (môN-tȧr-zhē′)	161	47°59'N	2°42'E
Montataire, Fr. (môN-tȧ-târ)	171b	49°15'N	2°26'E
Montauban, Fr. (môN-tô-bäN′)	161	44°01'N	1°22'E
Montauk, N.Y., U.S.	109	41°03'N	71°57'W
Montauk Point, c., N.Y., U.S. (mŏn-tôk′)	109	41°05'N	71°55'W
Montbard, Fr. (môN-bȧr′)	170	47°40'N	4°19'E
Montbéliard, Fr. (môN-bā-lyȧr′)	171	47°32'N	6°45'E
Mont Belvieu, Tx., U.S. (mŏnt bĕl′vū)	123a	29°51'N	94°53'W
Montbrison, Fr. (môN-brē-zôN′)	170	45°38'N	4°06'E
Montceau, Fr. (môN-sō′)	170	46°39'N	4°22'E
Montclair, N.J., U.S. (mŏnt-klâr′)	110a	40°49'N	74°13'W
Mont-de-Marsan, Fr. (môN-dē-mȧr-säN′)	161	43°54'N	0°32'W
Montdidier, Fr. (môN-dē-dyā′)	170	49°42'N	2°33'E
Monte, Arg. (mŏ′n-tĕ)	141c	35°25'S	58°49'W
Monteagudo, Bol. (mōn′tȧ-ä-gōō′dhō)	142	19°49'S	63°48'W
Montebello, Can.	102c	45°40'N	74°56'W
Montebello, Ca., U.S. (mŏn-tē-bĕl′ō)	117a	34°01'N	118°06'W
Monte Bello Islands, is., Austl.	220	20°30'S	114°10'E
Monte Caseros, Arg. (mō′n-tĕ-kä-sĕ′rôs)	144	30°16'S	57°39'W
Montecillos, Cordillera de, mts., Hond.	132	14°19'N	87°52'W
Monte Cristi, Dom. Rep. (mô′n-tĕ-krē′s-tē)	135	19°50'N	71°40'W
Montecristo, Isola di, i., Italy (mōn′tȧ-krēs′tō)	174	42°20'N	10°19'E
Monte Escobedo, Mex. (mōn′tȧ ĕs-kô-bā′dhō)	130	22°18'N	103°34'W
Monteforte Irpino, Italy (mōn-tĕ-fō′r-tĕ ē′r-pē′nō)	173c	40°39'N	14°42'E
Montefrío, Spain (mōn-tȧ-frē′ō)	172	37°20'N	4°02'W
Montego Bay, Jam. (mŏn-tē′gō)	129	18°30'N	77°55'W
Montelavar, Port. (mōn-tĕ-lȧ-vär′)	173b	38°51'N	9°20'W
Montélimar, Fr. (môN-tā-lē-mär′)	161	44°33'N	4°47'E
Montellano, Spain (mōn-tȧ-lyä′nō)	172	37°00'N	5°34'W
Montello, Wi., U.S. (mŏn-tĕl′ō)	113	43°47'N	89°20'W
Montemorelos, Mex. (mōn′tȧ-mō-rā′lōs)	128	25°14'N	99°50'W
Montemor-o-Novo, Port. (mōN-tĕ-môr′ō-nô′vô)	172	38°39'N	8°11'W
Montenegro *see* Crna Gora, state, Serb.	175	42°55'N	18°52'E
Montenegro, reg., Moz.	237	13°07'S	39°00'E
Montepulciano, Italy (mōn′tȧ-pōōl-chä′nō)	174	43°05'N	11°48'E
Montereau-faut-Yonne, Fr. (môN-t′rō′fō-yôn′)	170	48°24'N	2°57'E
Monterey, Ca., U.S. (mŏn-tĕ-rā′)	104	36°36'N	121°53'W
Monterey, Tn., U.S.	124	36°06'N	85°15'W
Monterey Bay, b., Ca., U.S.	106	36°48'N	122°01'W
Monterey Park, Ca., U.S.	117a	34°04'N	118°08'W
Montería, Col. (mōn-tā-rā′ä)	142	8°47'N	75°57'W
Monteros, Arg. (mōn-tĕ′rôs)	144	27°14'S	65°29'W
Monterotondo, Italy (mōn-tĕ-rô-tô′n-dō)	173d	42°03'N	12°39'E

ng-sing; ŋ-baŋk; N-nasalized n; nŏd; cŏmmit; ōld; ôbey; ôrder; oi-boil; fōōd; ò-as oo in foot; ou-out; s-soft; sh-dish; th-thin; pūre; ûnite; ûrn; stŭd; circŭs; ü-as in French tu; ′-indeterminate vowel.

324 Monterrey – Mount Morgan PRONOUNCING INDEX

PLACE (Pronunciation)	PAGE	LAT.	LONG.
Monterrey, Mex. (mōn-tĕr-rā′)	128	25°43′N	100°19′W
Montesano, Wa., U.S. (mŏn-tē-sä′nō)	114	46°59′N	123°35′W
Monte Sant'Angelo, Italy (mô′n-tĕ sän ä′n-gzhĕ-lô)	163	41°43′N	15°59′E
Montes Claros, Braz. (môn-tĕs-klä′rôs)	143	16°44′S	43°41′W
Montevallo, Al., U.S. (môn-tē-văl′ō)	124	33°05′N	86°49′W
Montevarchi, Italy (mōn-tå-vär′kē)	174	43°30′N	11°45′E
Montevideo, Ur. (mōn′tå-vē-dhā′ō)	144	34°50′S	56°10′W
Montevideo, Mn., U.S. (mŏn′tå-vĕ-dhā′ō)	112	44°56′N	95°42′W
Monte Vista, Co., U.S. (mŏn′tē vĭs′tȧ)	119	37°35′N	106°10′W
Montezuma, Ga., U.S. (mŏn-tē-zōō′mȧ)	124	32°17′N	84°00′W
Montezuma Castle National Monument, rec., Az., U.S.	119	34°38′N	111°50′W
Montfoort, Neth.	159a	52°02′N	4°56′E
Montfor-l'Amaury, Fr. (mōN-fŏr′lä-mō-rē′)	171b	48°47′N	1°49′E
Montfort, Fr. (mōn-fŏr)	170	48°09′N	1°58′W
Montgomery, Al., U.S. (mŏnt-gŭm′ēr-ĭ)	105	32°23′N	86°17′W
Montgomery, W.V., U.S.	108	38°10′N	81°25′W
Montgomery City, Mo., U.S.	121	38°58′N	91°29′W
Monticello, Ar., U.S. (mŏn-tĭ-sĕl′ō)	121	33°38′N	91°47′W
Monticello, Fl., U.S.	124	30°32′N	83°53′W
Monticello, Ga., U.S.	124	33°00′N	83°11′W
Monticello, Ia., U.S.	113	42°14′N	91°13′W
Monticello, Il., U.S.	108	40°05′N	88°35′W
Monticello, In., U.S.	108	40°40′N	86°50′W
Monticello, Ky., U.S.	124	36°47′N	84°50′W
Monticello, Me., U.S.	100	46°19′N	67°53′W
Monticello, Mn., U.S.	113	45°18′N	93°48′W
Monticello, N.Y., U.S.	109	41°35′N	74°40′W
Monticello, Ut., U.S.	119	37°55′N	109°25′W
Montijo, Port. (môn-tē′zhō)	173b	38°42′N	8°58′W
Montijo, Spain (môn-tē′hō)	172	38°55′N	6°35′W
Montijo, Bahía, b., Pan. (bä-ē′ä môn-tē′hō)	129	7°36′N	81°11′W
Mont-Joli, Can. (môN zhô-lē′)	91	48°35′N	68°11′W
Montluçon, Fr. (môN-lü-sôN′)	161	46°20′N	2°35′E
Montmagny, Can. (môN-mán-yē′)	99	46°59′N	70°33′W
Montmorency, Fr. (môN′mô-rāN-sē′)	171b	48°59′N	2°19′E
Montmorency, r., Can. (mŏnt-mô-rĕn′sĭ)	102b	47°03′N	71°10′W
Montmorillon, Fr. (môN′mô-rē-yôN′)	170	46°26′N	0°50′E
Montone, r., Italy (môn-tô′nĕ)	174	44°03′N	11°45′E
Montoro, Spain (môn-tō′rō)	172	38°01′N	4°22′W
Montpelier, Id., U.S.	115	42°19′N	111°19′W
Montpelier, In., U.S. (mŏnt-pēl′yēr)	108	40°35′N	85°20′W
Montpelier, Oh., U.S.	108	41°35′N	84°35′W
Montpelier, Vt., U.S.	105	44°20′N	72°35′W
Montpellier, Fr. (môN-pĕ-lyā′)	161	43°38′N	3°53′E
Montréal, Can. (mŏn-trē-ôl′)	91	45°30′N	73°35′W
Montreal, r., Can.	99	47°50′N	80°30′W
Montreal, r., Can.	98	47°15′N	84°20′W
Montreal Lake, l., Can.	96	54°20′N	105°40′W
Montréal-Nord, Can.	102a	45°36′N	73°38′W
Montreuil, Fr.	171b	48°52′N	2°27′E
Montreux, Switz. (môn-trû′)	168	46°26′N	6°52′E
Montrose, Scot., U.K.	164	56°45′N	2°25′W
Montrose, Ca., U.S. (mŏnt-rōz)	117a	34°13′N	118°13′W
Montrose, Co., U.S. (mŏn-trōz′)	119	38°30′N	107°55′W
Montrose, Oh., U.S.	111d	41°08′N	81°38′W
Montrose, Pa., U.S. (mŏnt-rōz′)	109	41°50′N	75°50′W
Montrouge, Fr.	171b	48°49′N	2°19′E
Mont-Royal, Can.	102a	47°31′N	73°39′W
Monts, Pointe des, c., Can. (pwăNt′ dā môN′)	100	49°19′N	67°22′W
Mont Saint Martin, Fr. (mŏN săN mär-tăN′)	171	49°34′N	6°13′E
Montserrat, dep., N.A. (mŏnt-sĕ-răt′)	129	16°48′N	63°15′W
Montvale, N.J., U.S. (mŏnt-văl′)	110a	41°02′N	74°01′W
Monywa, Mya. (mŏn′yōō-wȧ)	199	22°02′N	95°16′E
Monza, Italy (mōn′tsä)	174	45°34′N	9°17′E
Monzón, Spain (mōn-thōn′)	173	41°54′N	0°09′E
Moody, Tx., U.S. (mōō′dĭ)	123	31°18′N	97°20′W
Mooi, r., S. Afr. (mōō′ĭ)	238c	26°34′S	27°03′E
Mooi, r., S. Afr.	233c	29°00′S	30°15′E
Mooirivier, S. Afr.	233c	29°14′S	29°59′E
Moolap, Austl.	217a	38°11′S	144°26′E
Moonta, Austl. (mōōn′tȧ)	218	34°05′S	137°42′E
Moora, Austl. (môr′ȧ)	218	30°35′S	116°12′E
Moorabbin, Austl.	217a	37°56′S	145°02′E
Moore, l., Austl. (mōr)	220	29°50′S	118°12′E
Moorenweis, Ger. (mō′rĕn-vīz)	159d	48°10′N	11°05′E
Moore Reservoir, res., Vt., U.S.	109	44°20′N	72°10′W
Moorestown, N.J., U.S. (mōrz′toun)	110f	39°58′N	74°56′W
Mooresville, In., U.S. (mōrz′vĭl)	111g	39°37′N	86°22′W
Mooresville, N.C., U.S.	125	35°34′N	80°48′W
Moorhead, Mn., U.S. (mōr′hĕd)	112	46°52′N	96°44′W
Moorhead, Ms., U.S.	124	33°25′N	90°30′W
Moose, r., Can.	93	51°01′N	80°42′W
Moose Creek, Can.	102c	45°16′N	74°58′W
Moosehead, Me., U.S. (mōōs′hĕd)	100	45°37′N	69°15′W
Moose Island, i., Can.	97	51°50′N	97°09′W
Moose Jaw, Can. (mōōs jô)	90	50°23′N	105°32′W
Moose Jaw, r., Can.	96	50°34′N	105°17′W
Moose Lake, Can.	97	53°40′N	100°28′W
Moose Mountain, mtn., Can.	97	49°45′N	102°37′W
Moose Mountain Creek, r., Can.	97	49°12′N	102°10′W
Moosilauke, mtn., N.H., U.S. (mōō-sĭ-lȧ′kē)	109	44°00′N	71°50′W
Moosinning, Ger. (mō′zē-nēng)	159d	48°17′N	11°51′E
Moosomin, Can. (mōō′sô-mĭn)	97	50°07′N	101°40′W
Moosonee, Can. (mōō′sô-nē)	91	51°20′N	80°44′W
Mopti, Mali (mŏp′tē)	230	14°30′N	4°12′W
Moquegua, Peru (mô-kā′gwä)	142	17°15′S	70°54′W
Mór, Hung. (mōr)	169	47°25′N	18°14′E
Mora, India	203b	18°54′N	72°56′E
Mora, Spain (mō-rä)	172	39°42′N	3°45′W
Mora, Swe. (mō′rä)	166	61°00′N	14°29′E
Mora, Mn., U.S. (mō′rȧ)	113	45°52′N	93°18′W
Mora, N.M., U.S.	120	35°58′N	105°17′W
Morādābād, India (mō-rä-dä-bäd′)	199	28°57′N	78°48′E
Morales, Guat. (mô-rä′lĕs)	132	15°29′N	88°46′W
Moramanga, Madag. (mō-rä-mäŋ′gä)	233	18°48′S	48°09′E
Morant Point, c., Jam. (mô-rănt′)	134	17°55′N	76°10′W
Morata de Tajuña, Spain (mô-rä′tä dā tä-hōō′nyä)	173a	40°14′N	3°27′W
Moratuwa, Sri L.	203	6°35′N	79°59′E
Morava (Moravia), hist. reg., Czech Rep.	168	49°21′N	16°57′E
Morava, r., Eur.	161	49°00′N	17°30′E
Moravia *see* Morava, hist. reg., Czech Rep.	168	49°21′N	16°57′E
Morawhanna, Guy. (mô-rȧ-hwä′nȧ)	143	8°12′N	59°33′W
Moray Firth, b., Scot., U.K. (mŭr′ā)	156	57°41′N	3°55′W
Mörbylånga, Swe. (mûr′bü-lôn′gȧ)	166	56°32′N	16°23′E
Morden, Can. (môr′dĕn)	90	49°11′N	98°05′W
Mordialloc, Austl. (môr-dĭ-ăl′ŏk)	217a	38°00′S	145°05′E
Mordvinia, prov., Russia	180	54°18′N	43°50′E
More, Ben, mtn., Scot., U.K. (bĕn môr)	164	58°09′N	5°01′W
Moreau, r., S.D., U.S. (mô-rō′)	112	45°13′N	102°22′W
Moree, Austl. (mō′rē)	219	29°20′S	149°50′E
Morehead, Ky., U.S.	108	38°10′N	83°25′W
Morehead City, N.C., U.S. (mōr′hĕd)	125	34°43′N	76°43′W
Morehouse, Mo., U.S. (mōr′hous)	121	36°49′N	89°41′W
Morelia, Mex. (mô-rā′lyä)	128	19°43′N	101°12′W
Morella, Spain (mô-rāl′yä)	173	40°38′N	0°07′W
Morelos, Mex. (mô-rā′lōs)	130	22°46′N	102°36′W
Morelos, Mex.	131a	19°41′N	99°29′W
Morelos, Mex.	122	28°24′N	100°51′W
Morelos, r., Mex.	122	26°27′N	99°35′W
Morena, Sierra, mtn., Ca., U.S. (syĕr′rä mô-rā′nä)	116b	37°24′N	122°19′W
Morena, Sierra, mts., Spain (syĕr′rä mô-rā′nä)	156	38°15′N	5°45′W
Morenci, Az., U.S. (mô-rĕn′sĭ)	119	33°05′N	109°25′W
Morenci, Mi., U.S.	108	41°50′N	84°50′W
Moreno, Arg. (mô-rĕ′nō)	144a	34°39′S	58°47′W
Moreno, Ca., U.S.	117a	33°55′N	117°09′W
Mores, i., Bah. (mōrz)	134	26°20′N	77°35′W
Moresby, i., Can. (mōrz′bĭ)	116d	48°43′N	123°15′W
Moresby Island, i., Can.	92	52°50′N	131°55′W
Moreton, i., Austl. (môr′tŭn)	222	26°53′S	152°42′E
Moreton Bay, b., Austl. (môr′tŭn)	222	27°12′S	153°10′E
Morewood, Can. (mōr′wŏod)	102c	45°11′N	75°17′W
Morgan, Mt., U.S. (môr′găn)	115	46°25′N	107°56′W
Morgan, Ut., U.S.	115	41°04′N	111°42′W
Morgan City, La., U.S.	123	29°41′N	91°11′W
Morganfield, Ky., U.S. (môr′găn-fēld)	108	37°40′N	87°55′W
Morgan's Bay, S. Afr.	233c	32°42′S	28°19′E
Morganton, N.C., U.S. (môr′găn-tŭn)	125	35°44′N	81°42′W
Morgantown, W.V., U.S. (môr′găn-toun)	109	39°40′N	79°55′W
Morga Range, mts., Afg.	199a	34°02′N	70°38′E
Morgenzon, S. Afr. (môr′gănt-sŏn)	238c	26°44′S	29°39′E
Moriac, Austl.	217a	38°15′S	144°20′E
Morice Lake, l., Can.	94	54°00′N	127°37′W
Moriguchi, Japan (mō′rē-gōō′chē)	211b	34°44′N	135°34′E
Morinville, Can. (mō′rĭn-vĭl)	102g	53°48′N	113°39′W
Morioka, Japan (mō′rē-ō′kȧ)	205	39°40′N	141°21′E
Morkoka, r., Russia (mŏr-kô′kȧ)	185	65°35′N	111°00′E
Morlaix, Fr. (mŏr-lĕ′)	161	48°36′N	3°48′W
Morley, Can. (mŏr′lē)	102e	51°10′N	114°51′W
Mormant, Fr.	171b	48°35′N	2°54′E
Morne Gimie, St. Luc. (mōrn′ zhē-mē′)	133b	13°53′N	61°03′W
Mornington, Austl.	217a	38°13′S	145°02′E
Morobe, Pap. N. Gui.	213	8°03′S	147°45′E
Morocco, nation, Afr. (mō-rŏk′ō)	230	32°00′N	7°00′W
Morogoro, Tan. (mō-rō-gō′rō)	233	6°49′S	37°40′E
Moroleón, Mex. (mō-rō-lā-ōn′)	130	20°07′N	101°15′W
Morombe, Madag. (mōō-rōōm′bā)	233	21°39′S	43°34′E
Morón, Arg. (mo-rŏ′n)	141c	34°39′S	58°37′W
Morón, Cuba (mô-rōn′)	134	22°05′N	78°35′W
Morón, Ven. (mô-rō′n)	143b	10°29′N	68°11′W
Morondava, Madag. (mō-rōn-dȧ′vȧ)	233	20°17′S	44°18′E
Morón de la Frontera, Spain (mô-rōn′dā läf rôn-tā′rä)	172	37°08′N	5°20′W
Morongo Indian Reservation, I.R., Ca., U.S. (mō-rôŋ′gō)	118	33°54′N	116°47′W
Moroni, Com.	233	11°41′S	43°16′E
Moroni, Ut., U.S. (mô-rō′nĭ)	119	39°30′N	111°40′W
Morotai, i., Indon. (mō-rō-tä′ē)	213	2°12′N	128°30′E
Moroto, Ug.	237	2°32′N	34°39′E
Morozovsk, Russia	181	48°20′N	41°50′E
Morrill, Ne., U.S. (mŏr′ĭl)	112	41°59′N	103°54′W
Morrilton, Ar., U.S. (mŏr′ĭl-tŭn)	121	35°09′N	92°42′W
Morrinhos, Braz. (mô-rēn′yōzh)	143	17°45′S	48°56′W
Morris, Can. (mŏr′ĭs)	90	49°21′N	97°22′W
Morris, Il., U.S.	108	41°20′N	88°25′W
Morris, Mn., U.S.	112	45°35′N	95°53′W
Morris, r., Can.	97	49°30′N	97°30′W
Morrison, Il., U.S. (mŏr′ĭ-sŭn)	113	41°48′N	89°58′W
Morris Reservoir, res., Ca., U.S.	117a	34°11′N	117°49′W
Morristown, N.J., U.S. (mŏr′rĭs-toun)	110a	40°48′N	74°29′W
Morristown, Tn., U.S.	124	36°10′N	83°18′W
Morrisville, Pa., U.S. (mŏr′ĭs-vĭl)	110f	40°12′N	74°46′W
Morro do Chapéu, Braz. (môr-ō dō-shä-pĕ′ōō)	143	11°34′S	41°03′W
Morrow, Oh., U.S. (mŏr′ō)	111f	39°21′N	84°07′W
Mors, i., Den.	166	56°46′N	8°38′E
Morshansk, Russia (môr-shánsk′)	180	53°25′N	41°35′E
Mortara, Italy (mŏr-tä′rä)	174	45°13′N	8°47′E
Morteros, Arg. (mŏr-tĕ′tôs)	144	30°47′S	62°00′W
Mortes, Rio das, r., Braz. (rēō-däs-mô′r-tĕs)	141a	21°04′S	44°29′W
Morton Indian Reservation, I.R., Mn., U.S. (mŏr′tŭn)	113	44°35′N	94°48′W
Mortsel, Bel. (môr-sĕl′)	159a	51°10′N	4°28′E
Morvan, mts., Fr. (mōr-väN′)	170	47°11′N	4°10′E
Morzhovets, i., Russia (môr′zhô-vyĕts′)	180	66°40′N	42°30′E
Mosal'sk, Russia (mō-zálsk′)	176	54°27′N	34°57′E
Moscavide, Port.	173b	38°47′N	9°06′W
Moscow (Moskva), Russia	178	55°45′N	37°37′E
Moscow, Id., U.S. (mŏs′kō)	104	46°44′N	116°57′W
Mosel (Moselle), r., Eur. (mō′sĕl) (mō-zĕl)	168	49°49′N	7°00′E
Moses, r., S. Afr.	238c	25°17′S	29°04′E
Moses Lake, Wa., U.S.	114	47°08′N	119°15′W
Moses Lake, l., Wa., U.S. (mō′zĕz)	114	47°09′N	119°30′W
Moshchnyy, is., Russia (môsh′chnĭ)	167	59°56′N	28°07′E
Moshi, Tan. (mō′shē)	233	3°21′S	37°20′E
Mosjøen, Nor.	160	65°50′N	13°10′E
Moskva *see* Moscow, Russia	178	55°45′N	37°37′E
Moskva, prov., Russia	176	55°38′N	36°48′E
Moskva, r., Russia	180	55°30′N	37°05′E
Mosonmagyaróvár, Hung.	169	47°51′N	17°16′E
Mosquitos, Costa de, cst., Nic. (kôs-tä-dĕ-mōs-kē′tō)	133	12°05′N	83°49′W
Mosquitos, Gulfo de los, b., Pan. (gōō′l-fô-dĕ-lôs-mōs-kē′tôs)	129	9°17′N	80°59′W
Moss, Nor. (môs)	160	59°29′N	10°39′E
Moss Beach, Ca., U.S. (môs bēch)	116b	37°32′N	122°31′W
Mosselbaai, S. Afr. (mō′sŭl bā)	232	34°06′S	22°23′E
Mossendjo, Congo	236	2°57′S	12°44′E
Mossley, Eng., U.K. (môs′lĭ)	158a	53°31′N	2°02′W
Moss Point, Ms., U.S. (môs)	124	30°25′N	88°32′W
Most, Czech Rep. (mōst)	168	50°32′N	13°37′E
Mostar, Bos. (môs′tär)	163	43°20′N	17°51′E
Móstoles, Spain (mōs-tō-lās)	173a	40°19′N	3°52′W
Mostoos Hills, hills, Can. (mŏs′tōōs)	96	54°50′N	108°45′W
Mosvatnet, l., Nor.	166	59°55′N	7°50′E
Motagua, r., N.A. (mō-tä′gwä)	132	15°29′N	88°39′W
Motala, Swe. (mō-tô′lä)	166	58°34′N	15°00′E
Motherwell, Scot., U.K. (mŭdh′ēr-wĕl)	160	55°45′N	4°05′W
Motril, Spain (mō-trēl′)	162	36°44′N	3°32′W
Motul, Mex. (mō-tōō′l)	132a	21°07′N	89°14′W
Mouaskar, Alg.	230	35°25′N	0°08′E
Mouchoir Bank, bk. (mōō-shwär′)	135	21°35′N	70°40′W
Mouchoir Passage, strt., T./C. Is.	135	21°05′N	71°05′W
Moudjéria, Maur.	234	17°53′N	12°20′W
Mouila, Gabon	236	1°52′S	11°01′E
Mouille Point, c., S. Afr.	232a	33°54′S	18°19′E
Moulins, Fr. (mōō-lăN′)	161	46°34′N	3°19′E
Moulouya, Oued, r., Mor. (mōō-lōō′yȧ)	230	34°00′N	4°00′W
Moultrie, Ga., U.S. (mōl′trĭ)	124	31°10′N	83°48′W
Moultrie, Lake, l., S.C., U.S.	125	33°12′N	80°00′W
Mound City, Il., U.S.	121	37°06′N	89°13′W
Mound City, Mo., U.S.	121	40°08′N	95°13′W
Moundou, Chad	235	8°34′N	16°05′E
Moundsville, W.V., U.S. (moundz′vĭl)	108	39°50′N	80°50′W
Mount, Cape, c., Lib.	234	6°47′N	11°20′W
Mountain Brook, Al., U.S. (moun′tĭn brŏok)	110h	33°30′N	86°45′W
Mountain Creek Lake, l., Tx., U.S.	117c	32°43′N	97°03′W
Mountain Grove, Mo., U.S. (grōv)	121	37°07′N	92°16′W
Mountain Home, Id., U.S. (hōm)	114	43°08′N	115°43′W
Mountain Park, Can. (pärk)	90	52°55′N	117°14′W
Mountain View, Ca., U.S. (moun′tĭn vū)	116b	37°25′N	122°07′W
Mountain View, Mo., U.S.	121	36°59′N	91°46′W
Mount Airy, N.C., U.S. (âr′ĭ)	125	36°28′N	80°37′W
Mount Ayliff, S. Afr. (ā′lĭf)	233c	30°48′S	29°24′E
Mount Ayr, Ia., U.S. (âr)	113	40°43′N	94°06′W
Mount Carmel, Il., U.S. (kär′mĕl)	108	38°25′N	87°45′W
Mount Carmel, Pa., U.S.	109	40°50′N	76°25′W
Mount Carooll, Il., U.S.	113	42°05′N	89°55′W
Mount Clemens, Mi., U.S. (klĕm′ĕnz)	111b	42°36′N	82°52′W
Mount Desert, i., Me., U.S. (dē-zûrt′)	100	44°15′N	68°08′W
Mount Dora, Fl., U.S. (dō′rȧ)	125a	28°45′N	81°38′W
Mount Duneed, Austl.	217a	38°15′S	144°20′E
Mount Eliza, Austl.	217a	38°11′S	145°05′E
Mount Fletcher, S. Afr. (flĕ′chēr)	233c	30°42′S	28°32′E
Mount Forest, Can. (fŏr′ĕst)	99	44°00′N	80°45′W
Mount Frere, S. Afr. (frâr′)	233c	30°54′S	29°02′E
Mount Gambier, Austl. (găm′bēr)	218	37°30′S	140°53′E
Mount Gilead, Oh., U.S. (gĭl′ĕăd)	108	40°30′N	82°50′W
Mount Healthy, Oh., U.S. (hĕlth′ē)	111f	39°14′N	84°32′W
Mount Holly, N.J., U.S. (hŏl′ĭ)	110f	39°59′N	74°47′W
Mount Hope, Can.	102d	43°09′N	79°55′W
Mount Hope, N.J., U.S. (hōp)	110a	40°55′N	74°32′W
Mount Hope, W.V., U.S.	108	37°55′N	81°10′W
Mount Isa, Austl. (ī′zȧ)	218	21°00′S	139°45′E
Mount Kisco, N.Y., U.S. (kĭs′kō)	110a	41°12′N	73°44′W
Mountlake Terrace, Wa., U.S. (mount lāk tĕr′ĭs)	116a	47°48′N	122°19′W
Mount Lebanon, Pa., U.S. (lĕb′ȧ-nŭn)	111e	40°22′N	80°03′W
Mount Magnet, Austl. (măg-nĕt)	218	28°00′S	118°00′E
Mount Martha, Austl.	217a	38°17′S	145°01′E
Mount Morgan, Austl. (môr-găn)	219	23°42′S	150°45′E

ăt; finȧl; rāte; senāte; ärm; ȧsk; sofȧ; fâre; ch-choose; dh-as th in other; bē; ēvent; bĕt; recĕnt; cratēr; g-gō; gh-guttural g; bĭt; ĭ-short neutral; rīde; K-guttural k as ch in German ich;

PRONOUNCING INDEX

Mount Moriac – Nabberu 325

PLACE (Pronunciation)	PAGE	LAT.	LONG.
Mount Moriac, Austl.	217a	38°13'S	144°12'E
Mount Morris, Mi., U.S. (mŏr'ĭs)	108	43°10'N	83°45'W
Mount Morris, N.Y., U.S.	109	42°45'N	77°50'W
Mount Nimba National Park, rec., C. Iv.	234	7°35'N	8°10'W
Mount Olive, N.C., U.S. (ŏl'ĭv)	125	35°11'N	78°05'W
Mount Peale, Ut., U.S.	119	38°26'N	109°16'W
Mount Pleasant, Ia., U.S. (plĕz'ănt)	113	40°59'N	91°34'W
Mount Pleasant, Mi., U.S.	108	43°35'N	84°45'W
Mount Pleasant, S.C., U.S.	125	32°46'N	79°51'W
Mount Pleasant, Tn., U.S.	124	35°31'N	87°12'W
Mount Pleasant, Tx., U.S.	123	33°10'N	94°56'W
Mount Pleasant, Ut., U.S.	119	39°35'N	111°20'W
Mount Prospect, Il., U.S. (prŏs'pĕkt)	111a	42°03'N	87°56'W
Mount Rainier National Park, rec., Wa., U.S. (rå-nēr')	106	46°47'N	121°17'W
Mount Revelstoke National Park, rec., Can. (rĕv'ĕl-stōk)	90	51°22'N	120°15'W
Mount Savage, Md., U.S. (săv'āj)	109	39°45'N	78°55'W
Mount Shasta, Ca., U.S. (shăs'tȧ)	114	41°18'N	122°17'W
Mount Sterling, Il., U.S. (stûr'lĭng)	121	39°59'N	90°44'W
Mount Sterling, Ky., U.S.	108	38°05'N	84°00'W
Mount Stewart, Can. (stū'ărt)	101	46°22'N	62°52'W
Mount Union, Pa., U.S. (ūn'yŭn)	109	40°25'N	77°50'W
Mount Vernon, Il., U.S. (vûr'nŭn)	108	38°20'N	88°50'W
Mount Vernon, In., U.S.	108	37°55'N	87°50'W
Mount Vernon, Mo., U.S.	121	37°09'N	93°48'W
Mount Vernon, N.Y., U.S.	110a	40°55'N	73°51'W
Mount Vernon, Oh., U.S.	108	40°25'N	82°30'W
Mount Vernon, Va., U.S.	110e	38°43'N	77°06'W
Mount Vernon, Wa., U.S.	114	48°25'N	122°20'W
Moura, Braz. (mō'rȧ)	143	1°33'S	61°38'W
Moura, Port.	172	38°08'N	7°28'W
Mourne Mountains, mts., N. Ire., U.K. (môrn)	164	54°10'N	6°09'W
Moussoro, Chad	235	13°39'N	16°29'E
Moûtiers, Fr. (mōō-tyår')	171	45°31'N	6°34'E
Mowbullan, Mount, mtn., Austl.	222	26°50'S	151°34'E
Moyahua, Mex. (mô-yä'wä)	130	21°16'N	103°10'W
Moyale, Kenya (mô-yä'lä)	231	3°28'N	39°04'E
Moyamba, S.L. (mô-yäm'bä)	230	8°10'N	12°26'W
Moyen Atlas, mts., Mor.	162	32°49'N	5°28'W
Moyeuvre-Grande, Fr.	171	49°15'N	6°26'E
Moyie, r., Id., U.S. (moi'yē)	114	38°50'N	116°10'W
Moyobamba, Peru (mō-yō-bäm'bä)	142	6°12'S	76°56'W
Moyuta, Guat. (mô-ē-ōō'tä)	132	14°01'N	90°05'W
Moyyero, r., Russia	184	67°15'N	104°10'E
Moyynqum, des., Kaz.	183	44°30'N	70°00'E
Mozambique, nation, Afr. (mō-zăm-bēk')	232	20°15'S	33°53'E
Mozambique Channel, strt., Afr. (mō-zăm-bek')	233	24°00'S	38°00'E
Mozdok, Russia (môz-dôk')	181	43°45'N	44°35'E
Mozhaysk, Russia (mô-zhäysk')	176	55°31'N	36°02'E
Mozhayskiy, Russia (mô-zhāy'skĭ)	186c	59°42'N	30°08'E
Mpanda, Tan.	237	6°22'S	31°02'E
Mpika, Zam.	237	11°54'S	31°26'E
Mpimbe, Mwi.	237	15°18'S	35°04'E
Mporokoso, Zam. ('m-pō-rō-kō'sō)	232	9°23'S	30°05'E
Mpwapwa, Tan. ('m-pwä'pwä)	232	6°21'S	36°29'E
Mqanduli, S. Afr. ('m-kän'dōō-lē)	233c	31°50'S	28°42'E
Mrągowo, Pol. (mrän'gō-vō)	169	53°52'N	21°18'E
M'Sila, Alg. (m'sē'lȧ)	230	35°47'N	4°34'E
Msta, r., Russia (m'stá')	180	58°30'N	33°00'E
Mstsislaw, Bela.	176	54°01'N	31°42'E
Mtakataka, Mwi.	237	14°12'S	34°32'E
Mtamvuna, r., Afr.	233c	30°43'S	29°53'E
Mtata, r., S. Afr.	233c	31°48'S	29°03'E
Mtsensk, Russia (m'tsĕnsk)	180	53°17'N	36°33'E
Mtwara, Tan.	237	10°16'S	40°11'E
Muar, r., Malay.	197b	2°18'N	102°43'E
Mubende, Ug.	237	0°35'N	31°23'E
Mubi, Nig.	235	10°18'N	13°20'E
Mucacata, Moz.	237	13°20'S	39°59'E
Much, Ger. (mōōk)	171c	50°54'N	7°24'E
Muchinga Mountains, mts., Zam.	237	12°40'S	30°50'E
Much Wenlock, Eng., U.K. (mŭch wĕn'lŏk)	158a	52°35'N	2°33'W
Muckalee Creek, r., Ga., U.S. (mŭk'ȧ lē)	124	31°55'N	84°10'W
Muckleshoot Indian Reservation, I.R., Wa., U.S. (mŭck''l-shōōt)	116a	47°21'N	122°04'W
Mucubela, Moz.	237	16°55'S	37°52'E
Mud, l., Mi., U.S. (mŭd)	113	46°12'N	84°32'W
Mudan, r., China (mōō-dän)	208	45°30'N	129°40'E
Mudanjiang, China (mōō-dän-jyäŋ)	208	44°28'N	129°38'E
Muddy, r., Nv., U.S. (mŭd'ĭ)	119	36°56'N	114°42'W
Muddy Boggy Creek, r., Ok., U.S. (mud'ĭ bôg'ĭ)	121	34°42'N	96°11'W
Muddy Creek, r., Ut., U.S. (mŭd'ĭ)	119	38°45'N	111°10'W
Mudgee, Austl. (mŭ-jē)	222	32°47'S	149°10'E
Mudjatik, r., Can.	96	56°23'N	107°40'W
Mufulira, Zam.	237	12°33'S	28°14'E
Muğla, Tur. (mōōg'lä)	198	37°10'N	28°20'E
Mühldorf, Ger. (mül-dôrf)	168	48°15'N	12°33'E
Mühlhausen, Ger. (mül'hou-zĕn)	168	51°13'N	10°25'E
Muhu, i., Est. (mōō'hōō)	167	58°41'N	22°55'E
Muir Woods National Monument, rec., Ca., U.S. (mūr)	118	37°54'N	123°22'W
Muizenberg, S. Afr. (mwĭz-ĕn-bûrg')	232a	34°07'S	18°28'E
Mukacheve, Ukr.	169	48°25'N	22°43'E
Mukden see Shenyang, China	204	41°45'N	123°22'E
Mukhtuya, Russia (mók-tōō'yȧ)	179	61°00'N	113°00'E
Mukilteo, Wa., U.S. (mū-kĭl-tā'ō)	116a	47°57'N	122°18'W
Muko, Japan (mōō'kō)	211b	34°57'N	135°43'E

PLACE (Pronunciation)	PAGE	LAT.	LONG.
Muko, r., Japan (mōō'kō)	211b	34°52'N	135°17'E
Mukutawa, r., Can.	97	53°10'N	97°28'W
Mukwonago, Wi., U.S. (mū-kwō-nă'gō)	111a	42°52'N	88°19'W
Mula, Spain (mōō'lä)	172	38°05'N	1°12'W
Mula, Al., U.S. (mŭl'gȧ)	110h	33°33'N	86°59'W
Mulde, r., Ger. (mól'dĕ)	168	50°30'N	12°30'E
Muleros, Mex. (mōō-lā'rōs)	130	23°44'N	104°00'W
Muleshoe, Tx., U.S.	120	34°13'N	102°43'W
Mulgrave, Can. (mŭl'grāv)	101	45°37'N	61°23'W
Mulhacén, mtn., Spain	162	37°04'N	3°18'W
Mülheim, Ger. (mül'hīm)	171c	51°25'N	6°53'E
Mulhouse, Fr. (mü-lōōz')	161	47°46'N	7°20'E
Muling, China (mōō-lĭŋ)	208	44°32'N	130°18'E
Muling, r., China	208	44°40'N	130°30'E
Mull, Island of, i., Scot., U.K. (mŭl)	164	56°40'N	6°19'W
Mullan, Id., U.S. (mŭl'ăn)	114	47°26'N	115°50'W
Müller, Pegunungan, mts., Indon. (mül'ĕr)	212	0°22'N	113°05'E
Mullingar, Ire. (mŭl-ĭn-gär)	164	53°31'N	7°26'W
Mullins, S.C., U.S. (mŭl'ĭnz)	125	34°11'N	79°13'W
Mullins River, Belize	132a	17°08'N	88°18'W
Multān, Pak. (mŏ-tän')	199	30°17'N	71°13'E
Multnomah Channel, strt., Or., U.S. (mŭl nō mȧ)	116c	45°41'N	122°53'W
Mulumbe, Monts, mts., D.R.C.	237	8°47'S	27°20'E
Mulvane, Ks., U.S. (mŭl-vān')	121	37°30'N	97°13'W
Mumbai (Bombay), India	199	18°58'N	72°50'E
Mumbwa, Zam. (mōm'bwä)	232	14°59'S	27°04'E
Mumias, Kenya	237	0°20'N	34°29'E
Muna, Mex. (mōō'nȧ)	132a	20°28'N	89°42'W
München see Munich, Ger.	154	48°08'N	11°35'E
Muncie, In., U.S. (mŭn'sĭ)	105	40°10'N	85°30'W
Mundelein, Il., U.S. (mŭn-dē-lĭn')	111a	42°16'N	88°00'W
Mundonueva, Pico de, mtn., Col. (pē'kō-dĕ-mōō'n-dō-nwĕ'vä)	142a	4°18'N	74°12'W
Muneco, Cerro, mtn., Mex. (sĕ'r-rō-mōō-nĕ'kō)	131a	19°13'N	99°20'W
Mungana, Austl. (mŭn-găn'ȧ)	219	17°15'S	144°18'E
Mungbere, D.R.C.	237	2°38'N	28°30'E
Munger, Mn., U.S. (mŭn'gēr)	117h	46°48'N	92°20'W
Mungindi, Austl. (mŭn-gĭn'dē)	219	29°00'S	148°45'E
Munhall, Pa., U.S. (mŭn'hôl)	111e	40°24'N	79°53'W
Munhango, Ang. (mōn-hän'gȧ)	232	12°15'S	18°55'E
Munich, Ger.	154	48°08'N	11°35'E
Munising, Mi., U.S. (mū'nĭ-sĭng)	113	46°24'N	86°41'W
Muniz Freire, Braz.	141a	20°29'S	41°25'W
Munku Sardyk, mtn., Asia (mōn'kō sär-dĭk')	179	51°45'N	100°30'E
Muñoz, Phil. (mōōn-nyōth')	213a	15°44'N	120°53'E
Münster, Ger. (mün'stĕr)	161	51°57'N	7°38'E
Munster, In., U.S. (mŭn'stēr)	111a	41°34'N	87°31'W
Munster, hist. reg., Ire. (mŭn-stēr)	164	52°30'N	9°24'W
Muntok, Indon. (mōn-tŏk')	212	2°05'S	105°11'E
Muong Sing, Laos (mōō'ông-sĭng')	212	21°06'N	101°17'E
Muping, China (mōō-pĭŋ)	206	37°23'N	121°36'E
Muqui, Braz. (mōō-kōē)	141a	20°56'S	41°20'W
Mur, r., Eur. (mōōr)	161	47°00'N	15°00'E
Muradiye, Tur. (mōō-rä'dē-yĕ)	181	39°00'N	43°40'E
Murat, Fr. (mü-rä)	170	45°05'N	2°56'E
Murat, r., Tur. (mōō-rät')	198	39°00'N	42°00'E
Murchison, r., Austl. (mûr'chĭ-sŭn)	220	26°45'S	116°15'E
Murcia, Spain (mōōr'thyä)	154	38°00'N	1°10'W
Murcia, hist. reg., Spain	172	38°35'N	1°51'W
Murdo, S.D., U.S. (mûr'dō)	112	43°53'N	100°42'W
Mureş, r., Rom. (mōō'rĕsh)	163	46°02'N	21°50'E
Muret, Fr. (mü-rĕ')	170	43°28'N	1°17'E
Murfreesboro, Tn., U.S. (mûr'frēz-bŭr-ō)	124	35°50'N	86°19'W
Murgab, Taj.	183	38°10'N	73°59'E
Murgab, r., Asia (mōōr-gäb')	198	37°07'N	62°32'E
Muriaé, r., Braz.	141a	21°20'S	41°40'W
Murino, Russia (mōō'rĭ-nō)	186c	60°03'N	30°28'E
Müritz, l., Ger. (mür'its)	168	53°20'N	12°33'E
Murmansk, Russia (mōōr-mänsk')	178	69°00'N	33°20'E
Murom, Russia (mōō'rōm)	178	55°30'N	42°00'W
Muroran, Japan (mōō'rō-rän)	205	42°21'N	141°05'E
Muros, Spain (mōō'rōs)	172	42°48'N	9°00'W
Muroto-Zaki, c., Japan (mōō'rō-tō zä'kē)	210	33°14'N	134°12'E
Murphy, Mo., U.S. (mŭr'fĭ)	117e	38°29'N	90°29'W
Murphy, N.C., U.S.	124	35°05'N	84°00'W
Murphysboro, Il., U.S. (mŭr'fĭz-bŭr-ō)	121	37°46'N	89°21'W
Murray, Ky., U.S. (mŭr'ĭ)	124	36°39'N	88°17'W
Murray, Ut., U.S.	117b	40°40'N	111°53'W
Murray, r., Austl.	220	34°20'S	140°00'E
Murray, r., Can.	95	55°00'N	121°00'W
Murray, Lake, res., S.C., U.S. (mŭr'ĭ)	125	34°07'N	81°18'W
Murray Bridge, Austl.	218	35°10'S	139°35'E
Murray Harbour, Can.	101	46°00'N	62°31'W
Murray Region, reg., Austl. (mŭ'rē)	221	33°20'S	142°30'E
Murrumbidgee, r., Austl. (mŭr-ŭm-bĭd'jē)	221	34°30'S	145°20'E
Murrupula, Moz.	237	15°27'S	38°47'E
Murshidābād, India (mòr'shē-dä-bäd')	202	24°08'N	88°11'E
Murska Sobota, Slvn. (mōōr'skä sō'bō-tä)	174	46°40'N	16°14'E
Muruasigar, mtn., Kenya	237	3°08'N	35°02'E
Murwāra, India	199	23°54'N	80°23'E
Murwillumbah, Austl. (mŭr-wĭl'lŭm-bŭ)	222	28°15'S	153°30'E
Mürz, r., Aus. (mürts)	168	47°30'N	15°21'E
Mürzzuschlag, Aus. (mürts'tsōō-shlägh)	168	47°37'N	15°41'E

PLACE (Pronunciation)	PAGE	LAT.	LONG.
Muş, Tur. (mōōsh)	181	38°55'N	41°30'E
Musala, mtn., Blg.	175	42°05'N	23°24'E
Musan, Kor., N. (mò'sän)	205	41°11'N	129°10'E
Musashino, Japan (mōō-sä'shē-nō)	211a	35°43'N	139°35'E
Muscat, Oman (mŭs-kăt')	198	23°23'N	58°30'E
Muscat and Oman see Oman, nation, Asia	198	20°00'N	57°45'E
Muscatine, Ia., U.S. (mŭs-kȧ-tēn)	113	41°26'N	91°00'W
Muscle Shoals, Al., U.S. (mŭs''l shōlz)	124	34°44'N	87°38'W
Musgrave Ranges, mts., Austl. (mŭs'grāv)	220	26°15'S	131°15'E
Mushie, D.R.C. (mŭsh'ē)	232	3°04'S	16°50'E
Mushin, Nig.	235	6°32'N	3°22'E
Musi, r., Indon. (mōō'sē)	212	2°40'S	103°42'E
Musinga, Alto, mtn., Col. (ä'l-tō-mōō-sē'n-gä)	142a	6°40'N	76°13'W
Muskego Lake, l., Wi., U.S. (mŭs-kē'gō)	111a	42°53'N	88°10'W
Muskegon, Mi., U.S. (mŭs-kē'gŭn)	105	43°15'N	86°20'W
Muskegon, r., Mi., U.S.	108	43°20'N	85°55'W
Muskegon Heights, Mi., U.S.	108	43°10'N	86°20'W
Muskingum, r., Oh., U.S. (mŭs-kĭŋ'gŭm)	108	39°45'N	81°55'W
Muskogee, Ok., U.S. (mŭs-kō'gē)	105	35°44'N	95°21'W
Muskoka, l., Can. (mŭs-kō'kȧ)	99	45°00'N	79°30'W
Musoma, Tan.	237	1°30'S	33°48'E
Mussau Island, i., Pap. N. Gui. (mōō-sä'ōō)	213	1°30'S	149°32'E
Musselshell, r., Mt., U.S. (mŭs''l-shĕl)	115	46°25'N	108°20'W
Mussende, Ang.	236	10°32'S	16°05'E
Mussuma, Ang.	236	14°14'S	21°59'E
Mustafakemalpaşa, Tur.	163	40°05'N	28°30'E
Mustang Bayou, Tx., U.S.	123a	29°22'N	95°12'W
Mustang Creek, r., Tx., U.S. (mŭs'tăng)	120	36°22'N	102°46'W
Mustang Island, i., Tx., U.S.	123	27°43'N	97°00'W
Mustique, i., St. Vin. (müs-tēk')	133b	12°53'N	61°03'W
Mustvee, Est. (mōōst'vĕ-ĕ)	167	58°50'N	26°54'E
Musu Dan, c., Kor., N. (mò'sò dän)	205	40°51'N	130°00'E
Muswellbrook, Austl. (mŭs'wŭnl-brók)	222	32°15'S	150°50'E
Mutare, Zimb.	232	18°49'S	32°39'E
Mutombo Mukulu, D.R.C. (mōō-tôm'bō mōō-kōō'lōō)	232	8°12'S	23°56'E
Mutsu Wan, b., Japan (mōōt'sōō wän)	210	41°20'N	140°55'E
Mutton Bay, Can. (mŭt''n)	101	50°48'N	59°02'W
Mutum, Braz. (mōō-tōō'm)	141a	19°48'S	41°24'W
Muzaffargarh, Pak.	202	30°09'N	71°15'E
Muzaffarpur, India	202	26°13'N	85°20'E
Muzon, Cape, c., Ak., U.S.	94	54°41'N	132°44'W
Muzquiz, Mex. (mōōz'kēz)	122	27°53'N	101°31'W
Muztagata, mtn., China	204	38°20'N	75°28'E
Mvomero, Tan.	237	6°20'S	37°25'E
Mvoti, r., S. Afr.	233c	29°18'S	30°52'E
Mwali, i., Com.	233	12°15'S	43°45'E
Mwanza, Tan. (mwän'zä)	232	2°31'S	32°54'E
Mwaya, Tan. (mwä'yä)	232	9°19'S	33°51'E
Mwenga, D.R.C.	237	3°02'S	28°26'E
Mweru, l., Afr.	232	8°50'S	28°50'E
Mwingi, Kenya	237	0°56'S	38°04'E
Myanmar (Burma), nation, Asia	194	21°00'N	95°15'E
Myingyan, Mya. (myĭng-yŭn')	199	21°37'N	95°26'E
Myitkyina, Mya. (myĭ'chē-nȧ)	199	25°33'N	97°25'E
Myjava, Slvk. (mûē'yȧ-vä)	169	48°45'N	17°33'E
Mykhailivka, Ukr.	177	47°16'N	35°12'E
Mykolaïv, Ukr.	178	46°58'N	32°02'E
Mykolaïv, prov., Ukr.	177	47°27'N	31°25'E
Mýkonos, i., Grc.	175	37°26'N	25°30'E
Mymensingh, Bngl.	199	24°48'N	90°28'E
Mynämäki, Fin.	167	60°41'N	21°58'E
Myohyang San, mtn., Kor., N. (myō'hyang)	210	40°00'N	126°12'E
Mýrdalsjökull, ice, Ice. (mür'däls-yû'kòl)	160	63°34'N	18°04'W
Myrhorod, Ukr.	181	49°56'N	33°36'E
Mýrina, Grc.	175	39°52'N	25°01'E
Myrtle Beach, S.C., U.S. (mûr't'l)	125	33°42'N	78°53'W
Myrtle Point, Or., U.S.	114	43°04'N	124°08'W
Mysen, Nor.	166	59°32'N	11°16'E
Myshikino, Russia (mēsh'kē-nō)	176	57°48'N	38°21'E
Mysore, India (mī-sōr')	199	12°31'N	76°42'E
Mysovka, Russia (mē'sôf-kȧ)	167	55°11'N	21°17'E
Mystic, Ia., U.S. (mĭs'tĭk)	113	40°47'N	92°54'W
Mytilíni, Grc.	163	39°09'N	26°35'E
Mytishchi, Russia (mē-tēsh'chi)	186b	55°55'N	37°46'E
Mziha, Tan.	237	5°54'S	37°47'E
Mzimba, Mwi. ('m-zĭm'bä)	232	11°52'S	33°34'E
Mzimkulu, r., Afr.	233c	30°12'S	29°57'E
Mzimvubu, r., S. Afr.	233c	31°22'S	29°20'E
Mzuzu, Mwi.	237	11°30'S	34°10'E

N

PLACE (Pronunciation)	PAGE	LAT.	LONG.
Naab, r., Ger. (näp)	168	49°38'N	12°15'E
Naaldwijk, Neth.	159a	52°00'N	4°11'E
Nā'ālehu, Hi., U.S.	126a	19°00'N	155°35'W
Naantali, Fin. (nän'tá-lē)	167	60°29'N	22°03'E
Nabberu, l., Austl. (năb'ēr-ōō)	220	26°05'S	120°35'E

ng-sing; ŋ-baŋk; ɴ-nasalized n; nŏd; cŏmmit; ōld; ôbey; ôrder; oi-boil; fōōd; ó-as oo in foot; ou-out; s-soft; sh-dish; th-thin; pūre; ûnite; ûrn; stŭd; circŭs; ü-as in French tu; '-indeterminate vowel.

326 Naberezhnyye Chelny – Nduye PRONOUNCING INDEX

PLACE (Pronunciation)	PAGE	LAT.	LONG.
Naberezhnyye Chelny, Russia	178	55°42'N	52°19'E
Nabeul, Tun. (nā-bûl')	230	36°34'N	10°45'E
Nabiswera, Ug.	237	1°28'N	32°16'E
Naboomspruit, S. Afr.	238c	24°32'S	28°43'E
Nābulus, W.B.	197a	32°13'N	35°16'E
Nacala, Moz. (nā-kă'là)	233	14°34'S	40°41'E
Nacaome, Hond. (nä-kä-ō'mä)	132	13°32'N	87°28'W
Na Cham, Viet. (nä chäm')	209	22°02'N	106°30'E
Naches, r., Wa., U.S. (năch'ĕz)	114	46°51'N	121°03'W
Náchod, Czech Rep. (näk'ôt)	168	50°25'N	16°08'E
Nacimiento, Lake, res., Ca., U.S. (nȧ-sĭ-myĕn'tô)	118	35°50'N	121°00'W
Nacogdoches, Tx., U.S. (năk'ō-dō'chĕz)	123	31°36'N	94°40'W
Nadadores, Mex. (nä-dä-dō'rās)	122	27°04'N	101°36'W
Nadiād, India	202	22°45'N	72°51'E
Nadir, V.I.U.S.	129c	18°19'N	64°53'W
Nădlac, Rom.	175	46°09'N	20°52'E
Nadvirna, Ukr.	169	48°37'N	24°35'E
Nadym, r., Russia (nȧ'dĭm)	184	64°30'N	72°48'E
Naestved, Den. (nĕst'vĭdh)	160	55°14'N	11°46'E
Nafada, Nig.	235	11°08'N	11°20'E
Nafishah, Egypt	238d	30°34'N	32°15'E
Náfplio, Grc.	175	37°33'N	22°46'E
Nafūd ad Dahy, des., Sau. Ar.	198	22°15'N	44°15'E
Nag, Co, l., China	202	31°38'N	91°18'E
Naga, Phil. (nä'gä)	213	13°37'N	123°12'E
Naga, i., Japan	211	32°09'N	130°16'E
Nagahama, Japan (nä'gä-hä'mä)	211	33°32'N	132°29'E
Nagahama, Japan	211	35°23'N	136°16'E
Nagaland, India	199	25°47'N	94°15'E
Nagano, Japan (nä'gä-nô)	205	36°42'N	138°12'E
Nagaoka, Japan (nä'gȧ-ō'kȧ)	205	37°22'N	138°49'E
Nagaoka, Japan	211b	34°54'N	135°42'E
Nāgappattinam, India	199	10°48'N	79°51'E
Nagarote, Nic. (nä-gä-rô'tĕ)	132	12°17'N	86°35'W
Nagasaki, Japan (nä'gȧ-sä'kê)	205	32°48'N	129°53'E
Nāgaur, India	202	27°19'N	73°41'E
Nagaybakskiy, Russia (nȧ-gáy-bäk'skĭ)	186a	53°33'N	59°33'E
Nagcarlan, Phil. (näg-kär-län')	213a	14°07'N	121°24'E
Nāgercoil, India	203	8°15'N	77°29'E
Nagorno Karabakh, hist. reg., Azer. (nu-gôr'nŭ-kŭ-rŭ-bäk')	181	40°10'N	46°50'E
Nagoya, Japan	205	35°09'N	136°53'E
Nāgpur, India (näg'po͝or)	199	21°12'N	79°09'E
Nagua, Dom. Rep. (nȧ'gwä)	135	19°20'N	69°40'W
Nagykanizsa, Hung. (nôd'y'kô'nê-shô)	163	46°27'N	17°00'E
Nagykőrös, Hung. (nôd'y'kū-rūsh)	169	47°02'N	19°46'E
Naha, Japan (nä'hä)	205	26°02'N	127°43'E
Nahanni National Park, rec., Can.	92	62°10'N	125°15'W
Nahant, Ma., U.S. (nȧ-hănt)	101a	42°26'N	70°55'W
Nahariyya, Isr.	197a	33°01'N	35°06'E
Nahuel Huapi, l., Arg. (nä'wĕl wä'pê)	144	41°00'S	71°30'W
Nahuizalco, El Sal. (nä-wê-zäl'kō)	132	13°50'N	89°43'W
Naic, Phil. (nä-ēk)	213a	14°20'N	120°46'E
Naica, Mex. (nä-ē'kä)	122	27°53'N	105°30'W
Naiguata, Pico, mtn., Ven. (pē'kô)	143b	10°32'N	66°44'W
Nain, Can. (nīn)	91	56°29'N	61°52'W
Nā'īn, Iran	201	32°52'N	53°05'E
Nairn, Scot., U.K. (nârn)	164	57°35'N	3°54'W
Nairobi, Kenya (nī-rō'bê)	232	1°17'S	36°49'E
Naivasha, Kenya (nī-vä'shȧ)	232	0°47'S	36°29'E
Najd, hist. reg., Sau. Ar.	198	25°18'N	42°38'E
Najin, Kor., N. (nä'jĭn)	205	42°04'N	130°35'E
Najran, des., Sau. Ar. (nŭj-rän')	198	17°29'N	45°30'E
Naju, Kor., S. (nä'jo͞o')	210	35°02'N	126°42'E
Najusa, r., Cuba (nä-ho͞o'sä)	134	20°55'N	77°55'W
Nakatsu, Japan (nä'käts-o͞o)	210	33°34'N	131°10'E
Nakhodka, Russia (nŭ-kôt'kŭ)	179	43°03'N	133°08'E
Nakhon Ratchasima, Thai.	212	14°56'N	102°14'E
Nakhon Sawan, Thai.	212	15°42'N	100°06'E
Nakhon Si Thammarat, Thai.	212	8°27'N	99°58'E
Nakło nad Notecia, Pol.	169	53°10'N	17°35'E
Nakskov, Den. (näk'skou)	160	54°51'N	11°06'E
Naktong, r., Kor., S. (näk'tŭng)	210	36°10'N	128°30'E
Nal'chik, Russia (nȧl-chĕk')	181	43°30'N	43°35'E
Nalón, r., Spain (nä-lōn')	172	43°15'N	5°38'W
Nālūt, Libya (nä-lo͞ot')	230	31°51'N	10°49'E
Namak, Daryacheh-ye, l., Iran	198	34°58'N	51°33'E
Namakan, l., Mn., U.S. (nă'mȧ-kȧn)	113	48°20'N	92°43'W
Namangan, Uzb. (nȧ-mȧn-gän')	183	41°08'N	71°59'E
Namao, Can.	102g	53°43'N	113°30'W
Namatanai, Pap. N. Gui. (nä'mä-tä-nä'ē)	213	3°43'S	152°26'E
Nambour, Austl. (năm'bòr)	222	26°48'S	153°00'E
Nam Co, l., China (näm tswo)	204	30°30'N	91°10'E
Nam Dinh, Viet. (näm dēnĸ')	212	20°30'N	106°10'E
Nametil, Moz.	237	15°43'S	39°21'E
Namhae, i., Kor., S. (näm'hī')	210	34°23'N	128°05'E
Namib Desert, des., Nmb. (nä-mēb')	232	18°45'S	12°45'E
Namibia, nation, Afr.	232	19°30'S	16°13'E
Namoi, r., Austl. (nämoi)	221	30°10'S	148°43'E
Namous, Oued en, r., Alg. (nȧ-mo͞os')	162	31°48'N	0°19'W
Nampa, Id., U.S. (năm'pȧ)	104	43°35'N	116°35'W
Namp'o, Kor., N.	205	38°47'N	125°28'E
Nampuecha, Moz.	237	13°59'S	40°18'E
Nampula, Moz.	237	15°07'S	39°15'E
Namsos, Nor. (näm'sôs)	160	64°28'N	11°14'E
Namu, Can.	94	51°53'N	127°50'W
Namuli, Serra, mts., Moz.	237	15°05'S	37°05'E
Namur, Bel. (nȧ-mür')	161	50°29'N	4°55'E
Namutoni, Nmb. (nȧ-mo͞o-tō'nê)	232	18°45'S	17°00'E
Nan, r., Thai.	212	18°11'N	100°29'E
Nanacamilpa, Mex. (nä-nä-kä-mē'l-pä)	131a	19°30'N	98°33'W
Nanaimo, Can. (nȧ-nī'mō)	90	49°10'N	123°56'W
Nanam, Kor., N. (nä'nän')	210	41°38'N	129°37'E
Nanao, Japan (nä'nä-ō)	210	37°03'N	136°59'E
Nan'ao Dao, i., China (nän-ou dou)	209	23°30'N	117°30'E
Nanchang, China (nän'chäng')	205	28°38'N	115°48'E
Nanchangshan Dao, i., China (nän-chäŋ-shän dou)	206	37°56'N	120°42'E
Nancheng, China (nän-chäŋ)	205	26°50'N	116°40'E
Nanchong, China (nän-chôŋ)	204	30°45'N	106°05'E
Nancy, Fr. (näN-sē')	161	48°42'N	6°11'E
Nancy Creek, r., Ga., U.S. (năn'cē)	110c	33°51'N	84°25'W
Nanda Devi, mtn., India (nän'dä dā'vē)	199	30°30'N	80°25'E
Nānded, India	202	19°13'N	77°21'E
Nandurbār, India	202	21°29'N	74°13'E
Nandyāl, India	203	15°54'N	78°09'E
Nanga Parbat, mtn., Pak.	202	35°20'N	74°35'E
Nangi, India	202a	22°30'N	88°14'E
Nangis, Fr. (näN-zhē')	171b	48°33'N	3°01'E
Nangong, China (nän-gôŋ)	208	37°22'N	115°22'E
Nangweshi, Zam.	236	16°26'S	23°17'E
Nanhuangcheng Dao, i., China (nän-hûäŋ-chŭŋ dou)	206	38°22'N	120°54'E
Nanhui, China	206	31°03'N	121°45'E
Nanjing, China (nän-jyĭŋ)	205	32°04'N	118°46'E
Nanjuma, r., China (nän-jyo͞o-mä)	206	39°37'N	115°45'E
Nanking see Nanjing, China	204	32°04'N	118°46'E
Nanle, China (nän-lŭ)	206	36°03'N	115°13'E
Nan Ling, mts., China	205	25°15'N	111°40'E
Nanliu, r., China (nän-lĭō)	209	22°00'N	109°18'E
Nannine, Austl. (nă-nēn')	218	25°50'S	118°30'E
Nanning, China (nän'nĭng')	204	22°56'N	108°10'E
Nanpan, r., China (nän-pän)	209	24°50'N	105°30'E
Nanping, China (nän-pĭŋ)	205	26°40'N	118°05'E
Nansei-shotō, is., Japan	205	27°30'N	127°00'E
Nansemond, Va., U.S. (năn'sê-mŭnd)	110g	36°46'N	76°32'W
Nantai Zan, mtn., Japan (nän-täê zän)	210	36°47'N	139°28'E
Nantes, Fr. (näNt')	154	47°13'N	1°37'W
Nanteuil-le-Haudouin, Fr. (näN-tû-lĕ-ō-dwăN')	171b	49°08'N	2°49'E
Nanticoke, Pa., U.S. (năn'tĭ-kōk)	109	41°10'N	76°00'W
Nantong, China (nän-tôŋ)	206	32°02'N	120°51'E
Nantong, China	206	32°08'N	121°06'E
Nantucket, i., Ma., U.S. (năn-tŭk'ĕt)	107	41°15'N	70°05'W
Nantwich, Eng., U.K. (nănt'wĭch)	158a	53°04'N	2°31'W
Nanxiang, China (nän-shyäŋ)	206	31°17'N	121°17'E
Nanxiong, China (nän-shôŋ)	209	25°10'N	114°20'E
Nanyang, China	205	33°00'N	112°42'E
Nanyang Hu, l., China (nän-yäŋ ho͞o)	206	35°14'N	116°24'E
Nanyuan, China (nän-yůän)	208a	39°48'N	116°24'E
Naolinco, Mex. (nä-o-lēŋ'kō)	131	19°39'N	96°50'W
Náousa, Grc. (nä'o͞o-sȧ)	175	40°38'N	22°05'E
Naozhou Dao, i., China (nou-jō dou)	209	20°58'N	110°58'E
Napa, Ca., U.S. (năp'ȧ)	104	38°20'N	122°17'W
Napanee, Can. (năp'ȧ-nē)	99	44°15'N	77°00'W
Naperville, Il., U.S. (nā'pēr-vĭl)	111a	41°46'N	88°09'W
Napier, N.Z. (nā'pĭ-ēr)	221a	39°30'S	177°00'E
Napierville, Can. (nā'pĭ-ē-vĭl)	102a	45°11'N	73°24'W
Naples (Napoli), Italy	154	40°37'N	14°12'E
Naples, Fl., U.S. (nā'p'lz)	125a	26°07'N	81°46'W
Napo, r., S.A. (nä'pō)	142	1°49'S	74°20'W
Napoleon, Oh., U.S. (nȧ-pō'lē-ŭn)	108	41°20'N	84°10'W
Napoleonville, La., U.S. (nȧ-pō'lê-ŭn-vĭl)	123	29°56'N	91°03'W
Napoli see Naples, Italy	154	40°37'N	14°12'E
Napoli, Golfo di, b., Italy	162	40°29'N	14°08'E
Nappanee, In., U.S. (năp'ȧ-nē)	108	41°30'N	86°00'W
Nara, Japan (nä'rä)	205	34°41'N	135°50'E
Nara, Mali	230	15°09'N	7°27'W
Nara, dept., Japan	211b	34°36'N	135°49'E
Nara, r., Russia	176	55°05'N	37°16'E
Narach, Vozyera, l., Bela.	176	54°51'N	27°00'E
Naracoorte, Austl. (nȧ-rȧ-ko͞on'tê)	218	36°50'S	140°50'E
Narashino, Japan	211a	35°41'N	140°01'E
Naraspur, India	203	16°32'N	81°43'E
Narbērth, Pa., U.S. (när'bûrth)	110f	40°01'N	75°17'W
Narbonne, Fr. (nȧr-bôn')	161	43°12'N	3°00'E
Nare, Col. (nä'rĕ)	142a	6°12'N	74°37'W
Narew, r., Pol. (när'ĕf)	169	52°43'N	21°19'E
Narmada, r., India	199	22°30'N	75°30'E
Narodnaya, Gora, mtn., Russia (nȧ-rôd'nȧ-yȧ)	178	65°10'N	60°10'E
Naro-Fominsk, Russia (nä'rô-mênsk')	180	55°23'N	36°43'E
Narrabeen, Austl. (năr-ȧ-bĭn)	217b	33°44'S	151°18'E
Narragansett, R.I., U.S. (năr-ȧ-găn'sĕt)	110b	41°26'N	71°27'W
Narragansett Bay, b., R.I., U.S.	109	41°20'N	71°15'W
Narrandera, Austl. (nȧ-rȧn-dē'rȧ)	219	34°40'S	146°40'E
Narrogin, Austl. (năr'ō-gĭn)	218	33°00'S	117°15'E
Narva, Est. (när'vȧ)	180	59°24'N	28°12'E
Narvacan, Phil. (när-vä-kän')	213a	17°27'N	120°29'E
Narva Jõesuu, Est. (nȧr'vȧ ô-ô-ă'so͞o-ô)	167	59°26'N	28°02'E
Narvik, Nor. (när'vêk)	154	68°21'N	17°18'E
Narvskiy Zaliv, b., Eur. (nȧr'vskĭ zä'lĭf)	167	59°35'N	27°25'E
Narvskoye, res., Eur.	167	59°18'N	28°14'E
Nar'yan-Mar, Russia (när'yȧn mär')	178	67°42'N	53°30'E
Naryilco, Austl. (när-ĭl'kō)	222	28°40'S	141°50'E
Narym, Russia (nä-rēm')	178	58°47'N	82°05'E
Naryn, r., Asia (nŭ-rĭn')	184	41°20'N	76°00'E
Naseby, Eng., U.K. (nāz'bĭ)	158a	52°23'N	0°59'W
Nashua, Mo., U.S. (năsh'ū-ȧ)	117f	39°18'N	94°34'W
Nashua, N.H., U.S.	105	42°47'N	71°23'W
Nashville, Ar., U.S. (năsh'vĭl)	121	33°56'N	93°50'W
Nashville, Ga., U.S.	124	31°12'N	83°15'W
Nashville, Il., U.S.	121	38°21'N	89°42'W
Nashville, Mi., U.S.	108	42°35'N	85°50'W
Nashville, Tn., U.S.	105	36°10'N	86°48'W
Nashwauk, Mn., U.S. (năsh'wôk)	113	47°21'N	93°12'W
Näsi, l., Fin.	160	61°42'N	24°05'E
Našice, Cro. (nä'shê-tsĕ)	163	45°29'N	18°06'E
Nasielsk, Pol. (nä'syĕlsk)	169	52°35'N	20°50'E
Nāsik, India (nä'sĭk)	199	20°02'N	73°49'E
Nāşir, Sudan (nä-zēr')	231	8°30'N	33°06'E
Nasirabād, India	202	26°13'N	74°48'E
Naskaupi, r., Can. (năs'kô-pĭ)	93	53°59'N	61°10'W
Nasondoye, D.R.C.	237	10°22'S	25°06'E
Nass, r., Can. (năs)	94	55°00'N	129°30'W
Nassau, Bah. (năs'ô)	129	25°05'N	77°20'W
Nassenheide, Ger. (nä'sĕn-hī-dĕ)	159b	52°49'N	13°13'E
Nasser, Lake, res., Egypt	231	23°50'N	32°50'E
Nasugbu, Phil. (nȧ-so͝og-bo͞o')	213a	14°05'N	120°37'E
Nasworthy Lake, l., Tx., U.S. (năz'wûr-thê)	122	31°17'N	100°30'W
Natagaima, Col. (nä-tä-gī'mä)	142a	3°38'N	75°07'W
Natal, Braz. (nä-täl')	143	6°00'S	35°13'W
Natashquan, Can. (nä-tăsh'kwăn)	91	50°11'N	61°49'W
Natashquan, r., Can.	101	50°35'N	61°35'W
Natchez, Ms., U.S. (năch'ĕz)	105	31°35'N	91°20'W
Natchitoches, La., U.S. (năk'ĭ-tŏsh) (nȧch-ĭ-tŏsh')	123	31°46'N	93°06'W
Natick, Ma., U.S. (nā'tĭk)	101a	42°17'N	71°21'W
National Bison Range, I.R., Mt., U.S. (năsh'ŭn-ăl bī's'n)	115	47°18'N	113°58'W
National City, Ca., U.S.	118a	32°38'N	117°01'W
Natitingou, Benin	230	10°19'N	1°22'E
Natividade, Braz. (nä-tê-vê-dä'dĕ)	143	11°43'S	47°34'W
Natron, Lake, l., Tan. (nā'trŏn)	232	2°17'S	36°10'E
Natrona Heights, Pa., U.S. (nā'trō nȧ)	111e	40°38'N	79°43'W
Naţrūn, Wādī an, val., Egypt	238b	30°33'N	30°12'E
Natuna Besar, i., Indon.	212	4°00'N	106°50'E
Natural Bridges National Monument, rec., Ut., U.S. (năt'ū-răl brĭj'ĕs)	119	37°20'N	110°20'W
Naturaliste, Cape, c., Austl. (năt-ū-rȧ-lĭst')	220	33°30'S	115°10'E
Nau, Cap de la, c., Spain	156	38°43'N	0°14'E
Naucalpan de Juárez, Mex.	131a	19°28'N	99°14'W
Nauchampatepetl, mtn., Mex. (nä͞oo-chäm-pä-tĕ'pĕtl)	131	19°32'N	97°09'W
Nauen, Ger. (nou'ĕn)	159b	52°36'N	12°53'E
Naugatuck, Ct., U.S. (nô'gȧ-tŭk)	109	41°25'N	73°05'W
Naujan, Phil. (nä-ô-hän')	213a	13°19'N	121°17'E
Naumburg, Ger. (noum'bôrgh)	168	51°10'N	11°50'E
Nauru, nation, Oc.	3	0°30'S	167°00'E
Nautla, Mex. (nä-o͞ot'lä)	128	20°14'N	96°44'W
Nava, Mex. (nä'vä)	122	28°25'N	100°44'W
Nava del Rey, Spain (nä-vä dĕl rā'ê)	172	41°22'N	5°04'W
Navahermosa, Spain (nä-vä-ĕr-mō'sä)	172	39°39'N	4°28'W
Navajas, Cuba (nä-vä-häs')	134	22°40'N	81°20'W
Navajo Hopi Joint Use Area, I.R., Az., U.S.	119	36°15'N	110°30'W
Navajo Indian Reservation, I.R., U.S. (năv'ȧ-hō)	119	36°31'N	109°24'W
Navajo National Monument, rec., Az., U.S.	119	36°43'N	110°39'W
Navajo Reservoir, res., N.M., U.S.	119	36°57'N	107°26'W
Navalcarnero, Spain (nä-väl'kär-nā'rō)	173a	40°17'N	4°05'W
Navalmoral de la Mata, Spain	172	39°53'N	5°32'W
Navan, Can. (nă'vȧn)	102c	45°25'N	75°26'W
Navarino, i., Chile (nȧ-vä-rē'nô)	144	55°30'S	68°15'W
Navarra, hist. reg., Spain (nä-vär'rä)	172	42°40'N	1°35'W
Navarro, Arg. (nä-vă'r-rō)	141c	35°00'S	59°16'W
Navasota, Tx., U.S. (năv-ȧ-sō'tȧ)	123	30°24'N	96°05'W
Navasota, r., Tx., U.S.	123	31°03'N	96°11'W
Navassa, i., N.A. (nȧ-văs'ȧ)	135	18°25'N	75°15'W
Navia, r., Spain (nä-vē'ä)	172	43°10'N	6°45'W
Navidad, Chile (nä-vê-dä'd)	141b	33°57'S	71°51'W
Navidad Bank, bk. (nä-vê-dädh')	135	20°05'N	69°00'W
Navidade do Carangola, Braz. (nȧ-vē-dä'dô-kȧ-răn-gô'la)	141a	21°04'S	41°58'W
Navojoa, Mex. (nä-vô-kô'ä)	128	27°00'N	109°40'W
Nawābshāh, Pak. (nȧ-wäb'shä)	202	26°20'N	68°30'E
Naxçıvan, Azer.	181	39°10'N	45°30'E
Naxçıvan Muxtar, state, Azer.	182	39°20'N	45°30'E
Náxos, i., Grc. (nák'sôs)	163	37°15'N	25°20'E
Nayarit, state, Mex. (nä-yä-rēt')	128	22°00'N	105°15'W
Nayarit, Sierra de, mts., Mex. (sē-ĕ'r-rä-dĕ)	130	23°20'N	105°07'W
Naye, Sen.	234	14°25'N	12°12'W
Naylor, Md., U.S. (nā'lŏr)	110e	38°43'N	76°46'W
Nazaré da Mata, Braz. (dä-mä-tä)	143	7°46'S	35°13'W
Nazas, Mex. (nä'zäs)	122	25°14'N	104°08'W
Nazas, r., Mex.	128	25°30'N	104°40'W
Nazerat, Isr.	197a	32°43'N	35°19'E
Nazilli, Tur. (nȧ-zĭ-lē')	181	37°40'N	28°10'E
Naziya, r., Russia (nȧ-zē'yȧ)	186c	59°48'N	31°18'E
Nazko, r., Can.	94	52°35'N	123°10'W
N'dalatando, Ang.	236	9°18'S	14°54'E
Ndali, Benin	235	9°51'N	2°43'E
Ndikiniméki, Cam.	235	4°46'N	10°50'E
N'Djamena, Chad	231	12°07'N	15°03'E
Ndola, Zam. (n'dō'lä)	232	12°58'S	28°38'E
Ndoto Mountains, mts., Kenya	237	1°55'N	37°05'E
Ndrhamcha, Sebkha de, l., Maur.	234	18°50'N	15°15'W
Nduye, D.R.C.	237	1°50'N	29°01'E

ăt; finăl; rāte; senāte; ärm; ȧsk; sofȧ; fâre; ch-choose; dh-as th in other; bē; ēvent; bĕt; recĕnt; cratẽr; g-gō; gh-guttural g; bĭt; ĭ-short neutral; rīde; ĸ-guttural k as ch in German ich;

PRONOUNCING INDEX

Neagh – New Providence 327

PLACE (Pronunciation)	PAGE	LAT.	LONG.
Neagh, Lough, l., N. Ire., U.K. (lŏk nā)	160	54°40′N	6°47′W
Néa Páfos, Cyp.	197a	34°46′N	32°27′E
Neapean, r., Austl.	217b	33°40′S	150°39′E
Neápoli, Grc.	175	36°35′N	23°08′E
Neápolis, Grc.	174a	35°17′N	25°37′E
Near Islands, is., Ak., U.S. (nēr)	103a	52°20′N	172°40′E
Neath, Wales, U.K. (nēth)	164	51°41′N	3°50′W
Nebine Creek, r., Austl. (nĕ-bēne′)	222	27°50′S	147°00′E
Nebitdag, Turkmen.	183	39°30′N	54°20′E
Nebraska, state, U.S. (nė-brăs′kȧ)	104	41°45′N	101°30′W
Nebraska City, Ne., U.S.	121	40°40′N	95°50′W
Nechako, r., Can.	94	53°45′N	124°55′W
Nechako Plateau, plat., Can. (nĭ-chă′kō)	94	54°00′N	124°30′W
Nechako Range, mts., Can.	94	53°20′N	124°30′W
Nechako Reservoir, res., Can.	94	53°25′N	125°10′W
Neches, r., Tx., U.S. (nĕch′ĕz)	123	31°03′N	94°40′W
Neckar, r., Ger. (nĕk′är)	168	49°16′N	9°06′E
Necker Island, i., Hi., U.S.	126b	24°00′N	164°00′W
Necochea, Arg. (nā-kỏ-chā′ä)	144	38°30′S	58°45′W
Nedryhailiv, Ukr.	177	50°49′N	33°52′E
Needham, Ma., U.S. (nēd′ăm)	101a	42°17′N	71°14′W
Needles, Ca., U.S. (nē′d'lz)	119	34°51′N	114°39′W
Neenah, Wi., U.S. (nē′nȧ)	113	44°10′N	88°30′W
Neepawa, Can.	90	50°13′N	99°29′W
Nee Reservoir, res., Co., U.S. (nee)	120	38°26′N	102°56′W
Negareyama, Japan (nå′gä-rå-yä′mä)	211a	35°52′N	139°54′E
Negaunee, Mi., U.S. (nė-gô′nė)	113	46°30′N	87°37′W
Negeri Sembilan, state, Malay. (nā′grė-sĕm-bė-län′)	197b	2°46′N	101°54′E
Negev, des., Isr. (nĕ′gĕv)	197a	30°34′N	34°43′E
Negombo, Sri L.	203	7°39′N	79°49′E
Negotin, Serb. (nĕ′gỏ-tėn)	175	44°13′N	22°33′E
Negro, r., Arg.	144	39°50′S	65°00′W
Negro, r., N.A.	132	13°01′N	87°10′W
Negro, r., S.A.	141c	33°17′S	58°18′W
Negro, r., S.A. (nā′grỏ)	142	0°18′S	63°21′W
Negro, Cerro, mtn., Pan. (sĕ′-rrỏ-nā′grỏ)	133	8°44′N	80°37′W
Negros, i., Phil. (nā′grōs)	212	9°50′N	121°45′E
Nehalem, r., Or., U.S. (nė-hăl′ĕm)	114	45°52′N	123°37′W
Nehaus an der Oste, Ger. (noi′houz) (ōz′tĕ)	159c	53°48′N	9°02′E
Nehbandān, Iran	201	31°32′N	60°02′E
Nehe, China (nŭ-hŭ)	208	48°23′N	124°58′E
Neheim-Hüsten, Ger. (nĕ′hīm)	171c	51°28′N	7°58′E
Neiba, Dom. Rep. (nå-ē′bä)	135	18°30′N	71°20′W
Neiba, Bahía de, b., Dom. Rep.	135	18°10′N	71°00′W
Neiba, Sierra de, mts., Dom. Rep. (sē-ĕr′rä-dĕ)	135	18°40′N	71°40′W
Neihart, Mt., U.S. (nī′hårt)	115	46°54′N	110°39′W
Neijiang, China (nā-jyäŋ)	209	29°38′N	105°01′E
Neillsville, Wi., U.S. (nēlz′vĭl)	113	44°35′N	90°37′W
Nei Monggol (Inner Mongolia), state, China	204	40°15′N	105°00′E
Neiqiu, China (nā-chyō)	206	37°17′N	114°32′E
Neira, Col. (nā′rä)	142a	5°10′N	75°32′W
Neisse, r., Eur. (nēs)	168	51°30′N	15°00′E
Neiva, Col. (nå-ē′vä) (nā′vä)	142	2°55′N	75°16′W
Neixiang, China (nā-shyäŋ)	208	33°00′N	111°38′E
Nekemte, Eth.	231	9°09′N	36°29′E
Nekoosa, Wi., U.S. (nė-ko͞o′sȧ)	113	44°19′N	89°54′W
Neligh, Ne., U.S. (nē′-lē)	112	42°06′N	98°02′W
Nel'kan, Russia (nĕl-kän′)	179	57°45′N	136°36′E
Nellore, India (nĕl-lōr′)	199	14°28′N	79°59′E
Nel'ma, Russia (nĕl-mä′)	210	47°34′N	139°05′E
Nelson, Can. (nĕl′sŭn)	90	49°29′N	117°17′W
Nelson, N.Z.	221a	41°15′S	173°22′E
Nelson, Eng., U.K.	158a	53°50′N	2°13′W
Nelson, i., Ak., U.S.	103	60°38′N	164°42′W
Nelson, r., Can.	97	56°50′N	93°40′W
Nelson, Cape, c., Austl.	222	38°29′S	141°20′E
Nelsonville, Oh., U.S. (nĕl′sŭn-vĭl)	108	39°30′N	82°15′W
Néma, Maur. (nā′mä)	230	16°37′N	7°15′W
Nemadji, r., Wi., U.S. (nĕ-măd′jė)	117h	46°33′N	92°16′W
Neman, Russia (ŋĕ′-mån)	167	55°02′N	22°01′E
Neman, r., Eur.	180	53°28′N	24°45′E
Nembe, Nig.	235	4°35′N	6°26′E
Nemeiben Lake, l., Can. (nĕ-mē′bȧn)	96	55°20′N	105°20′W
Nemours, Fr.	170	48°16′N	2°41′E
Nemuro, Japan (nā′mỏ-rō)	205	43°13′N	145°10′E
Nemuro Strait, strt., Asia	210	43°07′N	145°10′E
Nemyriv, Ukr.	177	48°56′N	28°51′E
Nen, r., China (nŭn)	205	47°07′N	123°28′E
Nen, r., Eng., U.K. (nĕn)	158a	52°32′N	0°19′W
Nenagh, Ire. (nē′nȧ)	164	52°50′N	8°05′W
Nenana, Ak., U.S. (nå-nä′nȧ)	103	64°28′N	149°18′W
Nenikyul', Russia (nĕ-nyē′kyûl)	186c	59°26′N	30°40′E
Nenjiang, China (nŭn-jyäŋ)	205	49°02′N	125°15′E
Neodesha, Ks., U.S. (nē-ỏ-dĕ-shô′)	121	37°24′N	95°41′W
Neosho, Mo., U.S.	121	36°51′N	94°22′W
Neosho, r., Ks., U.S. (nė-ō′shō)	121	38°07′N	95°40′W
Nepal, nation, Asia (nĕ-pôl′)	199	28°45′N	83°00′E
Nephi, Ut., U.S. (nē′fī)	119	39°40′N	111°50′W
Nepomuceno, Braz. (nĕ-pô-mo͞o-sĕ′no)	141a	21°15′S	45°13′W
Nera, r., Italy (nā′rä)	174	42°45′N	12°54′E
Nérac, Fr. (nā-råk′)	170	44°08′N	0°19′E
Nerchinsk, Russia (nyĕr′ chėnsk)	179	51°47′N	116°17′E
Nerchinskiy Khrebet, mts., Russia	179	50°30′N	118°30′E
Nerchinskiy Zavod, Russia (nyĕr′chėn-skĭzȧ-vôt′)	179	51°35′N	119°46′E
Nerekhta, Russia (nyĕ-rĕκ′tȧ)	176	57°29′N	40°34′E
Neretva, r., Serb. (nĕ′rĕt-vȧ)	175	43°08′N	17°50′E
Nerja, Spain (nĕr′hä)	172	36°45′N	3°53′W
Nerl', r., Russia (nyĕrl)	176	56°59′N	37°57′E
Nerskaya, r., Russia (nyĕr′skȧ-yȧ)	186b	55°31′N	38°46′E
Nerussa, r., Russia (nyå-ro͞o′sȧ)	176	52°24′N	34°20′E
Ness, Loch, l., Scot., U.K. (lŏκ nĕs)	164	57°23′N	4°20′W
Ness City, Ks., U.S. (nĕs)	120	38°27′N	99°55′W
Nesterov, Russia (nyĕs-tă′rôf)	167	54°39′N	22°38′E
Néstos (Mesta), r., Eur. (nās′tōs)	175	41°25′N	24°12′E
Netanya, Isr.	197a	32°19′N	34°52′E
Netcong, N.J., U.S. (nĕt′cŏnj)	110a	40°54′N	74°42′W
Netherlands, nation, Eur. (nĕdh′ĕr-lăndz)	154	53°01′N	3°57′E
Netherlands Guiana *see* Suriname, nation, S.A.	143	4°00′N	56°00′W
Nettilling, l., Can.	93	66°30′N	70°40′W
Nett Lake Indian Reservation, I.R., Mn., U.S. (nĕt lāk)	113	48°23′N	93°19′W
Nettuno, Italy (nĕt-to͞o′nô)	173d	41°28′N	12°40′E
Neubeckum, Ger. (noi′bĕ-ko͞om)	171c	51°48′N	8°01′E
Neubrandenburg, Ger. (noi-brän′dĕn-bȯrgh)	168	53°33′N	13°16′E
Neuburg, Ger. (noi′bȯrgh)	168	48°43′N	11°12′E
Neuchâtel, Switz. (nû-shȧ-tĕl′)	161	47°00′N	6°52′E
Neuchâtel, Lac de, l., Switz.	168	46°48′N	6°53′E
Neuenhagen, Ger. (noi′ĕn-hä-gĕn)	159b	52°31′N	13°41′E
Neuenrade, Ger. (noi′ĕn-rä-dĕ)	171c	51°17′N	7°47′E
Neufchâtel-en-Bray, Fr. (nû-shä-tĕl′ĕɴ-brā′)	170	49°43′N	1°25′E
Neulengbach, Aus.	159e	48°13′N	15°55′E
Neumarkt, Ger. (noi′märkt)	168	49°17′N	11°30′E
Neumünster, Ger. (noi′münstēr)	160	54°04′N	10°00′E
Neunkirchen, Aus. (noin′kĭrκ-ĕn)	168	47°43′N	16°05′E
Neuquén, Arg. (nĕ-ȯ-kān′)	144	38°52′S	68°12′W
Neuquén, prov., Arg.	144	39°40′S	70°45′W
Neuquén, r., Arg.	144	38°45′S	69°00′W
Neuruppin, Ger. (noi′ro͞o-pēn)	168	52°55′N	12°48′E
Neuse, r., N.C., U.S. (nūz)	125	36°12′N	78°50′W
Neusiedler See, l., Eur. (noi-zēd′lĕr)	168	47°54′N	16°31′E
Neuss, Ger. (nois)	171c	51°12′N	6°41′E
Neustadt, Ger. (noi′shtät)	168	49°21′N	8°08′E
Neustadt bei Coburg, Ger. (bī kō′bo͞orgh)	168	50°20′N	11°09′E
Neustadt in Holstein, Ger.	168	54°06′N	10°50′E
Neustrelitz, Ger. (noi-strā′lĭts)	168	53°21′N	13°05′E
Neutral Hills, hills, Can. (nū′trăl)	96	52°10′N	110°50′W
Neu Ulm, Ger. (noi ȯ lm′)	168	48°23′N	10°01′E
Neuville, Can. (nū′vĭl)	102b	46°39′N	71°35′W
Neuwied, Ger. (noi′vēdt)	168	50°26′N	7°28′E
Neva, r., Russia (nyĕ-vä′)	176	59°49′N	30°54′E
Nevada, Ia., U.S. (nė-vä′dȧ)	113	42°01′N	93°27′W
Nevada, Mo., U.S.	121	37°49′N	94°21′W
Nevada, state, U.S. (nĕ vȧ′dȧ)	104	39°30′N	117°00′W
Nevada, Sierra, mts., Spain (syĕr′rä nā-vä′dhä)	156	37°01′N	3°28′W
Nevada, Sierra, mts., U.S. (sē-ĕ′r-rä nė-vä′dȧ)	106	39°20′N	120°05′W
Nevado, Cerro el, mtn., Col. (sĕ′r-rỏ-ĕl-nĕ-vä′dỏ)	142a	4°02′N	74°08′W
Neva Stantsiya, Russia (nyĕ-vä′ stän′tsĭ-yȧ)	186c	59°53′N	30°30′E
Neve, Serra da, mts., Ang.	236	13°40′S	13°20′E
Nevel', Russia (nyĕ′vĕl)	180	56°03′N	29°57′E
Neveri, r., Ven. (nĕ-vĕ-rē)	143b	10°13′N	64°18′W
Nevers, Fr. (nẽ-vår′)	161	46°59′N	3°10′E
Neves, Braz.	144b	22°51′S	43°06′W
Nevesinje, Bos. (nĕ-vĕ′sėn-yĕ)	175	43°15′N	18°08′E
Nevinnomiyssk, Russia	182	44°38′N	41°56′E
Nevis, i., St. K./N. (nē′vĭs)	129	17°05′N	62°38′W
Nevis, Ben, mtn., Scot., U.K. (bĕn)	160	56°47′N	5°00′W
Nevis Peak, mtn., St. K./N.	133b	17°11′N	62°33′W
Nevşehir, Tur. (nĕv-shĕ′hėr)	163	38°40′N	34°35′E
Nev'yansk, Russia (nĕv-yänsk′)	178	57°29′N	60°14′E
New, r., Va., U.S. (nū)	125	37°20′N	80°35′W
Newala, Tan.	237	10°56′S	39°18′E
New Albany, In., U.S. (nû ôl′bȧ-nĭ)	111h	38°17′N	85°49′W
New Albany, Ms., U.S.	125	34°28′N	39°00′W
New Amsterdam, Guy. (ăm′stēr-dăm)	143	6°14′N	57°30′W
Newark, Eng., U.K. (nū′ẽrk)	158a	53°04′N	0°49′W
Newark, Ca., U.S. (nū′ẽrk)	116b	37°32′N	122°02′W
Newark, De., U.S. (no͞o′ärk)	109	39°40′N	75°45′W
Newark, N.J., U.S. (no͞o′ûrk)	105	40°44′N	74°10′W
Newark, N.Y., U.S. (nū′ẽrk)	109	43°05′N	77°10′W
Newark, Oh., U.S.	108	40°05′N	82°25′W
Newaygo, Mi., U.S. (nū′wā-go)	108	43°25′N	85°50′W
New Bedford, Ma., U.S. (bĕd′fẽrd)	105	41°35′N	70°55′W
Newberg, Or., U.S. (nū′bûrg)	108	45°17′N	122°58′W
New Bern, N.C., U.S. (bûrn)	105	35°05′N	77°05′W
Newbern, Tn., U.S.	124	36°05′N	89°12′W
Newberry, Mi., U.S. (nū′bĕr-ĭ)	113	46°22′N	85°31′W
Newberry, S.C., U.S.	125	34°15′N	81°40′W
New Boston, Mi., U.S. (bôs′tŭn)	111b	42°10′N	83°24′W
New Boston, Oh., U.S.	108	38°45′N	82°55′W
New Braunfels, Tx., U.S. (nū broun′fĕls)	122	29°43′N	98°07′W
New Brighton, Mn., U.S. (brī′tŭn)	117g	45°04′N	93°12′W
New Brighton, Pa., U.S.	111e	40°34′N	80°18′W
New Britain, Ct., U.S. (brĭt′'n)	109	41°40′N	72°45′W
New Britain, i., Pap. N. Gui.	213	6°45′S	149°38′E
New Brunswick, N.J., U.S. (brŭnz′wĭk)	110a	40°29′N	74°27′W
New Brunswick, prov., Can.	91	47°14′N	66°30′W
Newburg, In., U.S.	108	38°00′N	87°25′W
Newburg, Mo., U.S.	121	37°54′N	91°53′W
Newburgh, N.Y., U.S.	109	41°30′N	74°00′W
Newburgh Heights, Oh., U.S.	111d	41°27′N	81°40′W
Newbury, Eng., U.K. (nū′bẽr-ĭ)	164	51°24′N	1°26′W
Newbury, Ma., U.S.	101a	42°48′N	70°52′W
Newbury, co., Eng., U.K.	158b	51°25′N	1°15′W
Newburyport, Ma., U.S. (nū′bẽr-ĭ-pōrt)	101a	42°48′N	70°53′W
New Caledonia, dep., Oc.	219	21°28′S	164°40′E
New Canaan, Ct., U.S. (kā-nȧn)	110a	41°06′N	73°30′W
New Carlisle, Can. (kär-līl′)	91	48°01′N	65°20′W
Newcastle, Austl. (nū-kȧs′'l)	222	33°00′S	151°55′E
Newcastle, Can.	91	47°00′N	65°34′W
New Castle, De., U.S.	109	39°40′N	75°35′W
New Castle, In., U.S.	108	39°55′N	85°25′W
New Castle, Oh., U.S.	108	40°20′N	82°10′W
New Castle, Pa., U.S.	108	41°00′N	80°25′W
Newcastle, Tx., U.S.	120	33°13′N	98°44′W
Newcastle, Wy., U.S.	112	43°51′N	104°11′W
Newcastle under Lyme, Eng., U.K. (nů-kȧs′'l) (nů-käs′'l)	158a	53°01′N	2°14′W
Newcastle upon Tyne, Eng., U.K.	154	55°00′N	1°45′W
Newcastle Waters, Austl. (wô′tẽrz)	218	17°10′S	133°25′E
Newcomerstown, Oh., U.S. (nū′kŭm-ẽrz-toun)	108	40°15′N	81°40′W
New Croton Reservoir, res., N.Y., U.S. (krŏ′tôn)	110a	41°15′N	73°47′W
New Delhi, India (dĕl′hī)	199	28°43′N	77°18′E
Newell, S.D., U.S. (nū′ĕl)	112	44°43′N	103°26′W
New England Range, mts., Austl. (nů ĭŋ′glănd)	221	29°32′S	152°30′E
Newenham, Cape, c., Ak., U.S. (nū-ĕn-hăm)	103	58°40′N	162°32′W
Newfane, N.Y., U.S. (nū-fān)	111c	43°17′N	78°44′W
Newfoundland, i., Can.	93a	48°30′N	56°00′W
Newfoundland and Labrador, prov., Can.	91	48°15′N	56°53′W
Newgate, Can. (nů′gāt)	95	49°01′N	115°10′W
New Georgia, i., Sol. Is. (jôr′jĭ-ȧ)	221	8°08′S	158°00′E
New Georgia Group, is., Sol. Is.	214e	8°30′S	157°20′E
New Georgia Sound, strt., Sol. Is.	214e	8°00′S	158°10′E
New Glasgow, Can. (glȧs′gō)	91	45°35′N	62°36′W
New Guinea, i. (gĭne)	213	5°45′S	140°00′E
Newhalem, Wa., U.S. (nū hā′lŭm)	114	48°44′N	121°11′W
New Hampshire, state, U.S. (hămp′shĭr)	105	43°55′N	71°40′W
New Hampton, Ia., U.S. (hămp′tŭn)	113	43°03′N	92°20′W
New Hanover, S. Afr. (hăn′ỏvẽr)	233c	29°23′S	30°32′E
New Hanover, i., Pap. N. Gui.	213	2°37′S	150°15′E
New Harmony, In., U.S. (nū här′mỏ-nĭ)	108	38°10′N	87°55′W
New Haven, Ct., U.S. (hā′vĕn)	105	41°20′N	72°55′W
New Haven, In., U.S. (nū hāv′'n)	108	41°05′N	85°00′W
New Hebrides, is., Vanuatu	221	16°00′S	167°00′E
New Holland, Eng., U.K. (hŏl′ănd)	158a	53°42′N	0°21′W
New Holland, N.C., U.S.	125	35°27′N	76°14′W
New Hope Mountain, mtn., Al., U.S. (hōp)	110h	33°23′N	86°45′W
New Hudson, Mi., U.S. (hŭd′sŭn)	111b	42°30′N	83°36′W
New Iberia, La., U.S. (ī-bē′rĭ-ȧ)	123	30°00′N	91°50′W
Newington, Can. (nū′ėng-tŏn)	102c	45°07′N	75°00′W
New Ireland, i., Pap. N. Gui. (īr′lănd)	213	3°15′S	152°30′E
New Jersey, state, U.S. (jûr′zĭ)	105	40°30′N	74°50′W
New Kensington, Pa., U.S. (kĕn′zĭng-tŭn)	111e	40°34′N	79°35′W
Newkirk, Ok., U.S. (nū′kûrk)	121	36°52′N	97°03′W
New Lenox, Il., U.S. (lĕn′ŭk)	111a	41°31′N	87°58′W
New Lexington, Oh., U.S. (lĕk′sĭng-tŭn)	108	39°40′N	82°10′W
New Lisbon, Wi., U.S. (lĭz′bŭn)	113	43°52′N	90°11′W
New Liskeard, Can.	99	47°30′N	79°40′W
New London, Ct., U.S. (lŭn′dŭn)	109	41°20′N	72°05′W
New London, Wi., U.S.	113	44°24′N	88°45′W
New Madrid, Mo., U.S. (măd′rĭd)	121	36°34′N	89°31′W
Newman's Grove, Ne., U.S. (nū′măn grōv)	112	41°46′N	97°44′W
Newmarket, Can. (nū′mär-kĕt)	99	44°00′N	79°30′W
New Martinsville, W.V., U.S. (mär′tĭnz-vĭl)	108	39°35′N	80°50′W
New Meadows, Id., U.S.	114	44°58′N	116°20′W
New Mexico, state, U.S. (mĕk′sĭ-kō)	104	34°30′N	107°10′W
New Mills, Eng., U.K. (mĭlz)	158a	53°22′N	2°00′W
New Munster, Wi., U.S. (mŭn′stẽr)	111a	42°35′N	88°13′W
Newnan, Ga., U.S. (nū′năn)	124	33°22′N	84°47′W
New Norfolk, Austl. (nôr′fŏk)	219	42°50′S	147°17′E
New Orleans, La., U.S. (ôr′lê-ănz)	105	30°00′N	90°05′W
New Philadelphia, Oh., U.S. (fĭl-ȧ-dĕl′fĭ-ȧ)	108	40°30′N	81°30′W
New Plymouth, N.Z. (plĭm′ūth)	221a	39°04′S	174°13′E
Newport, Austl.	217b	33°39′S	151°19′E
Newport, Eng., U.K. (nū-pôrt)	164	50°41′N	1°25′W
Newport, Eng., U.K.	158a	52°46′N	2°22′W
Newport, Wales, U.K.	161	51°36′N	3°05′W
Newport, Ar., U.S. (nū′pōrt)	121	35°35′N	91°16′W
Newport, Ky., U.S.	105	39°05′N	84°30′W
Newport, Me., U.S.	100	44°49′N	69°20′W
Newport, Mn., U.S.	117g	44°52′N	92°59′W
Newport, N.H., U.S.	109	43°20′N	72°10′W
Newport, Or., U.S.	114	44°39′N	124°02′W
Newport, R.I., U.S.	109	41°29′N	71°16′W
Newport, Tn., U.S.	124	35°55′N	83°12′W
Newport, Vt., U.S.	109	44°55′N	72°15′W
Newport, Wa., U.S.	114	48°12′N	117°01′W
Newport Beach, Ca., U.S. (bēch)	117a	33°36′N	117°55′W
Newport News, Va., U.S.	105	36°59′N	76°24′W
New Prague, Mn., U.S. (nū prāg)	113	44°33′N	93°35′W
New Providence, i., Bah. (prŏv′ĭ-dĕns)	134	25°00′N	77°25′W

ng-sing; ŋ-baŋk; ɴ-nasalized n; nŏd; cŏmmit; ōld; ỏbey; ôrder; oi-boil; fo͞od; ȯ-as oo in foot; ou-out; s-soft; sh-dish; th-thin; pūre; ůnite; ûrn; stŭd; circŭs; ü-as in French tu; ′-indeterminate vowel.

328 New Richmond – Norman

PRONOUNCING INDEX

PLACE (Pronunciation)	PAGE	LAT.	LONG.
New Richmond, Oh., U.S. (rĭch′mŭnd)	108	38°55′N	84°15′W
New Richmond, Wi., U.S.	113	45°07′N	92°34′W
New Roads, La., U.S. (rōds)	123	30°42′N	91°26′W
New Rochelle, N.Y., U.S. (rū-shĕl′)	110a	40°55′N	73°47′W
New Rockford, N.D., U.S. (rŏk′fērd)	112	47°40′N	99°08′W
New Ross, Ire. (rôs)	164	52°25′N	6°55′W
New Sarepta, Can.	102g	53°17′N	113°09′W
New Siberian Islands *see* Novosibirskiye Ostrova, is., Russia	179	74°00′N	140°30′E
New Smyrna Beach, Fl., U.S. (smûr′nȧ)	125	29°00′N	80°57′W
New South Wales, state, Austl. (wālz)	219	32°45′S	146°14′E
Newton, Can. (nū′tŭn)	102f	49°56′N	98°04′W
Newton, Eng., U.K.	158a	53°27′N	2°37′W
Newton, Ia., U.S.	113	41°42′N	93°04′W
Newton, Il., U.S.	108	39°00′N	88°10′W
Newton, Ks., U.S.	121	38°03′N	97°22′W
Newton, Ma., U.S.	101a	42°21′N	71°13′W
Newton, Ms., U.S.	124	32°18′N	89°10′W
Newton, N.C., U.S.	125	35°40′N	81°19′W
Newton, N.J., U.S.	110a	41°03′N	74°45′W
Newton, Tx., U.S.	123	30°47′N	93°45′W
Newtonsville, Oh., U.S. (nū′tŭnz-vĭl)	111f	39°11′N	84°04′W
Newtown, N.D., U.S. (nū′toun)	112	47°57′N	102°25′W
Newtown, Oh., U.S.	111f	39°08′N	84°22′W
Newtown, Pa., U.S.	110f	40°13′N	74°56′W
Newtownards, N. Ire., U.K. (nu-t′n-ardz′)	164	54°35′N	5°39′W
New Ulm, Mn., U.S. (ŭlm)	113	44°18′N	94°27′W
New Waterford, Can. (wô′tēr-fērd)	91	46°15′N	60°05′W
New Westminster, Can. (wĕst′mĭn-stēr)	95	49°12′N	122°55′W
New York, N.Y., U.S. (yôrk)	105	40°40′N	73°58′W
New York, state, U.S.	105	42°45′N	78°05′W
New Zealand, nation, Oc. (zē′lȧnd)	221a	42°00′S	175°00′E
Nexapa, r., Mex. (nĕks-ä′pä)	130	18°32′N	98°29′W
Neya-gawa, Japan (nā′yä gä′wä)	211b	34°47′N	135°38′E
Neyshābūr, Iran	198	36°06′N	58°45′E
Neyva, r., Russia (nēy′vȧ)	186a	57°39′N	60°37′E
Nezahualcóyotl, Mex.	131a	19°27′N	99°03′W
Nez Perce, Id., U.S. (nĕz′ pûrs′)	114	46°16′N	116°15′W
Nez Perce Indian Reservation, I.R., Id., U.S.	114	46°20′N	116°30′W
Ngami, l., Bots. (n′gä′mē)	232	20°56′S	22°31′E
Ngangerabeli Plain, pl., Kenya	237	1°20′S	40°10′E
Ngangla Ringco, l., China (ŋäŋ-lä rĭŋ-tswo)	202	31°42′N	82°53′E
Ngarimbi, Tan.	237	8°28′S	38°36′E
Ngoko, r., Afr.	236	1°55′N	15°53′E
Ngol-Kedju Hill, mtn., Cam.	235	6°20′N	9°45′E
Ngong, Kenya (′n-gông)	232	1°27′S	36°39′E
Ngounié, r., Gabon	236	1°15′S	10°43′E
Ngoywa, Tan.	237	5°56′S	32°48′E
Ngqeleni, S. Afr. (′ng-kĕ-lā′nē)	233c	31°41′S	29°04′E
Nguigmi, Niger (′n-gĕg′mē)	231	14°15′N	13°07′E
Ngurore, Nig.	235	9°18′N	12°14′E
Nguru, Nig. (′n-gōō′rōō)	230	12°53′N	10°26′E
Nguru Mountains, mts., Tan.	237	6°10′S	37°35′E
Nha Trang, Viet. (nyä-träng′)	212	12°08′N	108°56′E
Niafounke, Mali	230	16°03′N	4°17′W
Niagara, Wi., U.S. (nī-ăg′ȧ-rȧ)	113	45°45′N	88°05′W
Niagara, r., N.A.	111c	43°12′N	79°03′W
Niagara Falls, Can.	111c	43°05′N	79°05′W
Niagara Falls, N.Y., U.S.	105	43°06′N	79°02′W
Niagara-on-the-Lake, Can.	102d	43°16′N	79°05′W
Niakaramandougou, C. Iv.	234	8°40′N	5°17′W
Niamey, Niger (nē-ä-mā′)	230	13°31′N	2°07′E
Niamtougou, Togo	234	9°46′N	1°06′E
Niangara, D.R.C. (nē-äŋ-gä′rȧ)	231	3°42′N	27°52′E
Niangua, r., Mo., U.S. (nī-ăŋ′gwȧ)	121	37°30′N	93°05′W
Nias, Pulau, i., Indon. (nē′äs′)	212	0°58′N	97°43′E
Nibe, Den. (nē′bĕ)	166	56°57′N	9°36′E
Nicaragua, nation, N.A. (nĭk-ȧ-rä′gwȧ)	128	12°45′N	86°15′W
Nicaragua, Lago de, l., Nic. (lä′gô dĕ)	128	11°45′N	85°28′W
Nicastro, Italy (nê-käs′trō)	163	38°39′N	16°15′E
Nicchehabin, Punta, c., Mex. (pōō′n-tä-nĕk-chĕ-ä-bē′n)	132a	19°50′N	87°20′W
Nice, Fr. (nēs)	154	43°42′N	7°21′E
Nicheng, China (nē-chŭŋ)	207b	30°54′N	121°48′E
Nichicun, l., Can. (nĭch′ĭ-kŭn)	93	53°07′N	72°10′W
Nicholas Channel, strt., N.A. (nĭk′ō-lȧs)	134	23°30′N	80°20′W
Nicholasville, Ky., U.S. (nĭk′ō-lȧs-vĭl)	108	37°55′N	84°35′W
Nicobar Islands, is., India (nĭk-ô-bär′)	212	8°28′N	94°04′E
Nicolai Mountain, mtn., Or., U.S. (nē-cō lī′)	116c	46°05′N	123°27′W
Nicolás Romero, Mex. (nē-kô-lá′s rô-mĕ′rô)	131a	19°38′N	99°20′W
Nicolet, Lake, l., Mi., U.S. (nĭ′kō-lĕt)	117k	46°22′N	84°14′W
Nicolls Town, Bah.	134	25°10′N	78°00′W
Nicols, Mn., U.S. (nĭk′ĕls)	117g	44°50′N	93°12′W
Nicomeki, r., Can.	116d	49°04′N	122°47′W
Nicosia, Cyp. (nē-kô-sē′ȧ)	198	35°10′N	33°22′E
Nicoya, C.R. (nē-kō′yä)	132	10°08′N	85°27′W
Nicoya, Golfo de, b., C.R. (gôl-fô-dĕ)	132	10°03′N	85°04′W
Nicoya, Península de, pen., C.R.	132	10°05′N	86°00′W
Nidzica, Pol. (nê-jēt′sȧ)	169	53°21′N	20°30′E
Niedere Tauern, mts., Aus.	168	47°15′N	13°41′E
Niederkrüchten, Ger. (nē′dĕr-krük-tĕn)	171c	51°12′N	6°14′E
Niederösterreich, state, Aus.	159e	48°24′N	16°20′E
Niedersachsen (Lower Saxony), state, Ger. (nē′dĕr-zäk-sĕn)	159c	53°30′N	9°30′E
Niellim, Chad	235	9°42′N	17°49′E
Nienburg, Ger. (nē′ĕn-bòrgh)	168	52°40′N	9°15′E
Nietverdiend, S. Afr.	238c	25°02′S	26°10′E
Nieuw Nickerie, Sur. (nê-nē′kĕ-rē′)	143	5°51′N	57°00′W
Nieves, Mex. (nyā′vås)	130	24°00′N	102°57′W
Niğde, Tur. (nĭg′dĕ)	163	37°55′N	34°40′E
Nigel, S. Afr. (nī′jĕl)	238c	26°26′S	28°27′E
Niger, nation, Afr. (nī′jēr)	230	18°02′N	8°30′E
Niger, r., Afr.	230	8°00′N	6°00′E
Niger Delta, d., Nig.	235	4°45′N	5°20′E
Nigeria, nation, Afr. (nī-jē′rĭ-ȧ)	230	8°57′N	6°30′E
Nihoa, i., Hi., U.S.	126b	23°15′N	161°30′W
Nii, i., Japan (nē)	211	34°26′N	139°23′E
Niigata, Japan (nē′ê-gä′tȧ)	205	37°47′N	139°04′E
Ni′ihau, i., Hi., U.S. (nē′ê-ha′ōō)	106c	21°50′N	160°05′W
Niimi, Japan (nē′mê)	211	34°59′N	133°28′E
Niiza, Japan	211a	35°48′N	139°34′E
Nijmegen, Neth. (nī′mȧ-gĕn)	165	51°50′N	5°52′E
Nikitinka, Russia (nê-kĭ′tĭn-kȧ)	176	55°33′N	33°19′E
Nikolayevka, Russia (nē-kô-lä′yĕf-kȧ)	186c	59°29′N	29°48′E
Nikolayevka, Russia	210	48°37′N	134°09′E
Nikolayevskiy, Russia	181	50°00′N	45°30′E
Nikolayevsk-na-Amure, Russia	179	53°18′N	140°49′E
Nikol′sk, Russia (nê-kôlsk′)	178	59°30′N	45°40′E
Nikol′skoye, Russia (nê-kôl′skô-yĕ)	186c	59°27′N	30°00′E
Nikopol, Blg. (nē′kô-pōl′)	163	43°41′N	24°52′E
Nikopol′, Ukr.	181	47°36′N	34°24′E
Nilahue, r., Chile (nē-lá′wĕ)	141b	34°36′S	71°50′W
Nile, r., Afr. (nīl)	231	27°30′N	31°00′E
Niles, Mi., U.S. (nīlz)	108	41°50′N	86°15′W
Niles, Oh., U.S.	108	41°15′N	80°45′W
Nileshwar, India	203	12°08′N	74°14′E
Nilgiri Hills, hills, India	203	12°05′N	76°22′E
Nilópolis, Braz. (nē-lô′pō-lēs)	141a	22°48′S	43°25′W
Nimach, India	202	24°32′N	74°51′E
Nimba, Mont, mtn., Afr. (nĭm′bȧ)	230	7°40′N	8°33′W
Nimba Mountains, mts., Afr.	234	7°30′N	8°35′W
Nîmes, Fr. (nēm)	154	43°49′N	4°22′E
Nimrod Reservoir, res., Ar., U.S. (nĭm′rŏd)	121	34°58′N	93°46′W
Nimule, Sudan (nê-mōō′lå)	231	3°38′N	32°12′E
Ninda, Ang.	236	14°47′S	21°24′E
Nine Mile Creek, r., Ut., U.S. (mīn′īmôd′)	119	39°50′N	110°30′W
Ninety Mile Beach, cst., Austl.	221	38°20′S	147°30′E
Nineveh, Iraq (nĭn′ĕ-vȧ)	198	36°30′N	43°10′E
Ning′an, China (nĭŋ-än)	205	44°20′N	129°20′E
Ningbo, China (nĭŋ-bwo)	205	29°56′N	121°30′E
Ningde, China (nĭŋ-dū)	205	26°38′N	119°33′E
Ninghai, China (nĭng′hī′)	209	29°20′N	121°20′E
Ninghe, China (nĭŋ-hŭ)	206	39°20′N	117°50′E
Ningjin, China (nĭŋ-jyĭn)	206	37°39′N	116°47′E
Ningjin, China	206	37°37′N	114°55′E
Ningming, China	209	22°22′N	107°06′E
Ningwu, China (nĭng′wōō′)	205	39°00′N	112°12′E
Ningxia Huizu, prov., China (nĭŋ-shyä)	204	37°10′N	106°00′E
Ningyang, China (nĭng′yäng′)	206	35°46′N	116°48′E
Ninh Binh, Viet. (nĕn bĕnk′)	212	20°22′N	106°00′E
Ninigo Group, is., Pap. N. Gui.	213	1°15′S	143°30′E
Ninnescah, r., Ks., U.S. (nĭn′ĕs-kä)	120	37°37′N	98°31′W
Nioaque, Braz. (nēō-á′-kĕ)	143	21°14′S	55°41′W
Niobrara, r., U.S. (nī-ô-brâr′ȧ)	106	42°46′N	98°46′W
Niokolo Koba, Parc National du, rec., Sen.	234	13°05′N	13°00′W
Nioro du Sahel, Mali (nê-ō′rō)	230	15°15′N	9°35′W
Nipawin, Can.	90	53°22′N	104°00′W
Nipe, Bahía de, b., Cuba (bä-ē′ä-dĕ-nē′pā)	135	20°50′N	75°30′W
Nipe, Sierra de, mts., Cuba (sē-ĕ′r-rȧ-dĕ)	135	20°20′N	75°50′W
Nipigon, Can. (nĭp′ĭ-gŏn)	91	48°58′N	88°17′W
Nipigon, l., Can.	93	49°37′N	89°55′W
Nipigon Bay, b., Can.	98	48°56′N	88°00′W
Nipisiguit, r., Can. (nĭ-pĭ′sĭ-kwĭt)	100	47°26′N	66°15′W
Nipissing, l., Can. (nĭp′ĭ-sĭng)	93	45°59′N	80°19′W
Niquero, Cuba (nē-kā′rō)	134	20°00′N	77°35′W
Nirmali, India	202	26°30′N	86°43′E
Niš, Serb.	154	43°19′N	21°54′E
Nisa, Port. (nē′sȧ)	172	39°32′N	7°41′W
Nišava, r., Eur. (nē′shȧ-vȧ)	175	43°17′N	22°17′E
Nishino, i., Japan (nēsh′ê-nô)	211	36°06′N	132°49′E
Nishinomiya, Japan (nēsh′ê-nô-mē′yȧ)	211b	34°44′N	135°21′E
Nishio, Japan (nēsh′ê-ô)	211	34°50′N	137°01′E
Niska Lake, l., Can. (nĭs′kȧ)	96	55°35′N	108°38′W
Nisko, Pol. (nēs′kô)	169	50°30′N	22°07′E
Nisku, Can. (nĭs-kū′)	102g	53°21′N	113°33′W
Nisqually, r., Wa., U.S. (nĭs-kwôl′ĭ)	114	46°51′N	122°33′W
Nissan, r., Swe.	166	57°06′N	13°22′E
Nisser, l., Nor. (nĭs′ĕr)	166	59°14′N	8°35′E
Nissum Fjord, b., Den.	166	56°24′N	7°35′E
Niterói, Braz. (nē-tĕ-rô′ĭ)	143	22°53′S	43°07′W
Nith, r., Scot., U.K. (nĭth)	164	55°13′N	3°55′W
Nitra, Slvk. (nē′trȧ)	169	48°18′N	18°04′E
Nitra, r., Slvk.	169	48°13′N	18°14′E
Nitro, W.V., U.S. (nī′trô)	108	38°25′N	81°50′W
Niue, dep., Oc. (nĭ′ŏ)	241	19°50′S	167°00′W
Nivelles, Bel. (nē′vĕl′)	165	50°33′N	4°17′E
Nixon, Tx., U.S. (nĭk′sŭn)	123	29°16′N	97°48′W
Nizāmābād, India	199	18°48′N	78°07′E
Nizhne-Angarsk, Russia (nyēzh′nyĭ-ŭngärsk′)	179	55°49′N	108°46′E
Nizhne-Chirskaya, Russia	181	48°20′N	42°50′E
Nizhne-Kolymsk, Russia (kô-lĕmsk′)	179	68°32′N	160°56′E
Nizhneudinsk, Russia (nĕzh′nyĭ-ōōdĕnsk′)	179	54°58′N	99°15′E
Nizhniye Sergi, Russia (nyĕzh′ nyē sĕr′gē)	180	56°41′N	59°19′E
Nizhniy Novgorod (Gor′kiy), Russia	178	56°15′N	44°05′E
Nizhniy Tagil, Russia (tŭgēl′)	178	57°54′N	59°59′E
Nizhnyaya Kur′ya, Russia (nyē′zhnyȧ-yȧ kōōr′yȧ)	186a	58°01′N	56°00′E
Nizhnyaya Salda, Russia (nyē′zhnya′ya säl′da′)	186a	58°05′N	60°43′E
Nizhnyaya Taymyra, r., Russia	184	72°30′N	95°18′E
Nizhnyaya Tunguska, r., Russia	179	64°13′N	91°30′E
Nizhnyaya Tura, Russia (tōō′rȧ)	186a	58°38′N	59°50′E
Nizhnyaya Us′va, Russia (ô′vȧ)	186a	59°05′N	58°53′E
Nizhyn, Ukr.	181	51°03′N	31°52′E
Nízke Tatry, mts., Slvk.	169	48°57′N	19°18′E
Njazidja, i., Com.	233	11°44′S	42°38′E
Njombe, Tan.	237	9°20′S	34°46′E
Njurunda, Swe. (nyōō-ròn′dȧ)	166	62°15′N	17°24′E
Nkala Mission, Zam.	237	15°55′S	26°00′E
Nkandla, S. Afr. (′n-känd′lä)	233c	28°40′S	31°06′E
Nkawkaw, Ghana	234	6°33′N	0°47′W
Nkhota, Mwi. (kō-tȧ kō-tȧ)	232	12°52′S	34°16′E
Noākhāli, Bngl.	199	22°52′N	91°08′E
Noatak, Ak., U.S. (nō-á′tȧk)	103	67°22′N	163°28′W
Noatak, r., Ak., U.S.	103	67°58′N	162°15′W
Nobeoka, Japan (nō-bȧ-ō′kȧ)	210	32°36′N	131°41′E
Noblesville, In., U.S. (nō′bl′z-vĭl)	108	40°00′N	86°00′W
Nobleton, Can. (nō′bl′tŭn)	102d	43°54′N	79°39′W
Nocera Inferiore, Italy (ĕn-fĕ-ryō′rĕ)	173c	40°30′N	14°38′E
Nochistlán, Mex. (nô-chēs-tlän′)	130	21°23′N	102°52′W
Nochixtlón, Mex. (ä-sòn-syōn′)	131	17°28′N	97°12′W
Nogales, Mex. (nō-gä′lĕs)	130	18°49′N	97°09′W
Nogales, Mex.	128	31°15′N	111°00′W
Nogales, Az., U.S. (nô-gä′lĕs)	104	31°20′N	110°55′W
Nogal Valley, val., Som. (nô′gäl)	238a	8°30′N	47°50′E
Nogent-le-Roi, Fr. (nŏ-zhon-lĕ-rwä′)	171b	48°39′N	1°32′E
Nogent-le-Rotrou, Fr. (rō-trōō′)	170	48°22′N	0°47′E
Noginsk, Russia (nô-gēnsk′)	180	55°52′N	38°28′E
Noguera Pallaresa, r., Spain	173	42°18′N	1°03′E
Noia, Spain	172	42°46′N	8°50′W
Noirmoutier, Île de, i., Fr. (nwár-mōō-tyā′)	161	47°03′N	3°08′W
Nojima-Zaki, c., Japan (nō′jē-mä zä-kê)	211	34°54′N	139°48′E
Nokomis, Il., U.S. (nô-kō′mĭs)	108	39°15′N	89°10′W
Nola, Italy (nô′lä)	174	40°41′N	14°32′E
Nolinsk, Russia (nô-lênsk′)	180	57°32′N	49°50′E
Noma Misaki, c., Japan (nô′mä mē′sä-kē)	211	31°25′N	130°09′E
Nombre de Dios, Mex. (nôm-brĕ-dĕ-dyô′s)	130	23°50′N	104°14′W
Nombre de Dios, Pan. (nô′m-brĕ)	133	9°34′N	79°28′W
Nome, Ak., U.S. (nōm)	106a	64°30′N	165°20′W
Nonacho, l., Can.	92	61°48′N	111°20′W
Nong′an, China (nôŋ-än)	208	44°25′N	125°10′E
Nongoma, S. Afr. (nōn-gō′mȧ)	232	27°48′S	31°45′E
Nooksack, Wa., U.S. (nòk′sāk)	116d	48°55′N	122°19′W
Nooksack, r., Wa., U.S.	116d	48°54′N	122°31′W
Noordwijk aan Zee, Neth.	159a	52°14′N	4°25′E
Noordzee Kanaal, can., Neth.	159a	52°27′N	4°42′E
Nootka, i., Can. (nōōt′kȧ)	92	49°32′N	126°42′W
Nootka Sound, strt., Can.	94	49°33′N	126°38′W
Nóqui, Ang. (nô-kē′)	232	5°51′S	13°25′E
Nor, r., China (nou′)	210	46°55′N	132°45′E
Nora, Swe.	166	59°32′N	14°56′E
Nora, In., U.S. (nō′rä)	111g	39°54′N	86°08′W
Noranda, Can.	99	48°15′N	79°01′W
Norbeck, Md., U.S. (nôr′bĕk)	110e	39°06′N	77°05′W
Norborne, Mo., U.S. (nôr′bôrn)	121	39°17′N	93°39′W
Norco, Ca., U.S. (nôr′kô)	117a	33°57′N	117°33′W
Norcross, Ga., U.S. (nôr′krôs)	110c	33°56′N	84°13′W
Nord, Riviere du, Can. (rēv-yĕr′ dü nōr)	102a	45°45′N	74°02′W
Nordegg, Can. (nûr′dĕg)	95	52°28′N	116°04′W
Norden, Ger. (nôr′dĕn)	168	53°35′N	7°14′E
Norderney, i., Ger. (nōr′dĕr-nĕy)	168	53°45′N	6°58′E
Nordfjord, b., Nor. (nô′fyôr)	166	61°50′N	5°35′E
Nordhausen, Ger. (nôrt′hau-zĕn)	161	51°30′N	10°48′E
Nordhorn, Ger. (nôrt′hôrn)	168	52°26′N	7°05′E
Nord Kapp, c., Nor.	180	71°11′N	25°48′E
Nordland, Wa., U.S. (nôrd′lȧnd)	116a	48°03′N	122°41′W
Nördlingen, Ger. (nûrt′lĭng-ĕn)	168	48°51′N	10°30′E
Nord-Ostsee Kanal (Kiel Canal), can., Ger. (nōrd-ōzt-zā) (kēl)	168	54°03′N	9°23′E
Nordrhein-Westfalen (North Rhine-Westphalia), state, Ger. (nôrd′hīn-vĕst-fä-lĕn)	171c	51°40′N	7°00′E
Nordvik, Russia (nôrd′vēk)	179	73°57′N	111°15′E
Nore, r., Ire. (nōr)	164	52°34′N	7°15′W
Norfolk, Ma., U.S. (nôr′fŏk)	101a	42°07′N	71°19′W
Norfolk, Ne., U.S.	104	42°10′N	97°25′W
Norfolk, Va., U.S.	105	36°55′N	76°15′W
Norfolk, i., Oc.	241	27°10′S	166°50′E
Norfork, Lake, l., Ar., U.S.	121	36°25′N	92°09′W
Noril′sk, Russia (nô rēlsk′)	178	69°00′N	87°11′E
Normal, Il., U.S. (nôr′mȧl)	108	40°35′N	89°00′W
Norman, r., Austl.	221	18°27′S	141°29′E
Norman, Lake, res., N.C., U.S.	107	35°30′N	80°53′W

ăt; finăl; rāte; senâte; ärm; åsk; sofȧ; fâre; ch-choose; dh-as th in other; bē; ēvent; bĕt; recĕnt; cratẽr; g-gō; gh-guttural g; bĭt; ĭ-short neutral; rīde; ᴋ-guttural k as ch in German ich;

PRONOUNCING INDEX

Normandie – Nowa Sól 329

PLACE (Pronunciation)	PAGE	LAT.	LONG.
Normandie, hist. reg., Fr. (nŏr-mäɴ-dē')	170	49°02'N	0°17'E
Normandie, Collines de, hills, Fr. (kō-lēn'dĕ-nŏr-män-dē')	170	48°46'N	0°50'W
Normandy see Normandie, hist. reg., Fr.	170	49°02'N	0°17'E
Normanton, Austl. (nôr'măn-tŭn)	219	17°45'S	141°10'E
Normanton, Eng., U.K.	158a	53°40'N	1°21'W
Norman Wells, Can.	90	65°26'N	127°00'W
Nornalup, Austl. (nôr-năl'ŭp)	218	35°00'S	117°00'E
Nørresundby, Den. (nû-rĕ-sôn'bü)	166	57°04'N	9°55'E
Norris, Tn., U.S. (nŏr'ĭs)	124	36°09'N	84°05'W
Norris Lake, res., Tn., U.S.	107	36°17'N	84°10'W
Norristown, Pa., U.S. (nŏr'ĭs-town)	110f	40°07'N	75°21'W
Norrköping, Swe. (nôr'chûp'ĭng)	154	58°37'N	16°10'E
Norrtälje, Swe. (nôr-tĕl'yĕ)	160	59°47'N	18°39'E
Norseman, Austl. (nôrs'măn)	218	32°15'S	122°00'E
Norte, Punta, c., Arg. (pōō'n-tä-nŏr'tĕ)	141c	36°17'S	56°46'W
Norte, Serra do, mts., Braz. (sĕ'r-rä-dô-nôr'te)	143	12°04'S	59°08'W
North, Cape, c., Can.	101	47°02'N	60°25'W
North Adams, Ma., U.S. (ăd'ămz)	109	42°40'N	73°05'W
Northam, Austl. (nôr-dhăm)	218	31°50'S	116°45'E
Northam, S. Afr. (nôr'thăm)	238c	24°52'S	27°16'E
North America, cont.	89	45°00'N	100°00'W
North American Basin, deep (á-mĕr'ĭ-kăn)	4	23°45'N	62°45'W
Northampton, Austl. (nôr-thămp'tŭn)	218	28°22'S	114°45'E
Northampton, Eng., U.K. (nôrth-ămp'tŭn)	161	52°14'N	0°56'W
Northampton, Ma., U.S.	109	42°20'N	72°45'W
Northampton, Pa., U.S.	109	40°45'N	75°30'W
Northamptonshire, co., Eng., U.K.	158a	52°25'N	0°47'W
North Andaman Island, i., India (ăn-dá-măn')	212	13°15'N	93°30'E
North Andover, Ma., U.S. (ăn'dô-vẽr)	101a	42°42'N	71°07'W
North Arm, mth., Can. (ärm)	116d	49°13'N	123°01'W
North Atlanta, Ga., U.S. (ăt-lăn'tá)	110c	33°52'N	84°20'W
North Attleboro, Ma., U.S. (ăt''l-bŭr-ô)	110b	41°59'N	71°18'W
North Baltimore, Oh., U.S. (bôl'tĭ-môr)	108	41°10'N	83°40'W
North Basque, Tx., U.S. (băsk)	122	31°56'N	98°01'W
North Battleford, Can. (băt''l-fẽrd)	90	52°47'N	108°17'W
North Bay, Can.	91	46°13'N	79°26'W
North Bend, Or., U.S. (bĕnd)	114	43°23'N	124°13'W
North Berwick, Me., U.S. (bûr'wĭk)	100	43°18'N	70°46'W
North Bight, b., Bah. (bīt)	134	24°30'N	77°40'W
North Bimini, i., Bah. (bĭ'mĭ-nê)	134	25°45'N	79°20'W
North Borneo see Sabah, hist. reg., Malay.	212	5°10'N	116°25'E
Northborough, Ma., U.S.	101a	42°19'N	71°39'W
Northbridge, Ma., U.S. (nôrth'brĭj)	101a	42°09'N	71°39'W
North Caicos, i., T./C. Is. (kī'kôs)	135	21°55'N	72°00'W
North Cape, c., N.Z.	221a	34°31'S	173°02'E
North Carolina, state, U.S. (kăr-ô-lī'ná)	105	35°40'N	81°30'W
North Cascades National Park, rec., Wa., U.S.	114	48°50'N	120°50'W
North Cat Cay, i., Bah.	134	25°35'N	79°20'W
North Channel, strt., Can.	98	46°10'N	83°20'W
North Channel, strt., U.K.	156	55°15'N	7°56'W
North Charleston, S.C., U.S. (chärlz'tŭn)	125	32°49'N	79°57'W
North Chicago, Il., U.S. (shĭ-kô'gō)	111a	42°19'N	87°51'W
North College Hill, Oh., U.S. (kŏl'ĕj hĭl)	111f	39°13'N	84°33'W
North Concho, Tx., U.S. (kŏn'chō)	122	31°40'N	100°48'W
North Cooking Lake, Can. (kôk'ĭng lăk)	102g	53°28'N	112°57'W
North Cyprus, nation, Asia	198	35°15'N	33°40'E
North Dakota, state, U.S. (dá-kō'tá)	104	47°20'N	101°55'W
North Downs, Eng., U.K. (dounz)	164	51°11'N	0°01'W
North Dum-Dum, India	202a	22°38'N	88°23'E
Northeast Cape, c., Ak., U.S. (nôrth-ēst)	103	63°15'N	169°04'W
Northeast Point, c., Bah.	135	21°25'N	73°00'W
Northeast Point, c., Bah.	135	22°45'N	73°50'W
Northeast Providence Channel, strt., Bah. (prŏv'ĭ-dĕns)	134	25°45'N	77°00'W
Northeim, Ger. (nôrt'hīm)	168	51°42'N	9°59'E
North Elbow Cays, is., Bah.	134	23°55'N	80°30'W
Northern Cheyenne Indian Reservation, I.R., Mt., U.S.	115	45°32'N	106°43'W
Northern Dvina see Severnaya Dvina, r., Russia	178	63°00'N	42°40'E
Northern Ireland, state, U.K. (ĭr'lănd)	154	54°48'N	7°00'W
Northern Land see Severnaya Zemlya, is., Russia	179	79°33'N	101°15'E
Northern Mariana Islands, dep., Oc. (mä-rē-ä'ná)	3	17°20'N	145°00'E
Northern Territory, ter., Austl.	218	18°15'S	133°00'E
Northern Yukon National Park, rec., Can.	103	69°00'N	140°00'W
Northfield, Mn., U.S. (nôrth'fēld)	113	44°28'N	93°11'W
North Flinders Ranges, mts., Austl. (flĭn'dẽrz)	222	31°55'S	138°45'E
North Foreland, Eng., U.K. (nôrth-fōr'lănd)	165	51°20'N	1°30'E
North Franklin Mountain, mtn., Tx., U.S. (frăŋ'klĭn)	122	31°55'N	106°30'W
North Frisian Islands, is., Eur.	160	55°16'N	8°15'E
North Gamboa, Pan. (găm-bô'ä)	133	9°07'N	79°40'W
North Gower, Can. (gŏw'ẽr)	102c	45°08'N	75°43'W
North Hollywood, Ca., U.S. (hŏl'ê-wŏd)	117a	34°10'N	118°23'W
North Island, i., N.Z.	221a	37°20'S	173°30'E
North Island, i., Ca., U.S.	118a	32°39'N	117°14'W
North Judson, In., U.S. (jŭd'sŭn)	108	41°15'N	86°50'W
North Kansas City, Mo., U.S. (kăn'zás)	117f	39°08'N	94°34'W
North Kingstown, R.I., U.S.	110b	41°34'N	71°26'W
North Lincolnshire, co., Eng., U.K.	158a	53°40'N	0°35'W
North Little Rock, Ar., U.S. (lĭt''l rŏk)	121	34°46'N	92°13'W
North Loup, r., Ne., U.S. (lōōp)	112	42°05'N	100°10'W
North Magnetic Pole, pt. of i.	244	77°19'N	101°49'W
North Manchester, In., U.S. (măn'chĕs-tẽr)	108	41°00'N	85°45'W
Northmoor, Mo., U.S. (nôth'mōōr)	117f	39°10'N	94°37'W
North Moose Lake, l., Can.	97	54°09'N	100°20'W
North Mount Lofty Ranges, mts., Austl.	222	33°50'S	138°30'E
North Ogden, Ut., U.S. (ŏg'dĕn)	117b	41°18'N	111°58'W
North Ogden Peak, mtn., Ut., U.S.	117b	41°23'N	111°59'W
North Olmsted, Oh., U.S. (ōlm-stĕd)	111d	41°25'N	81°55'W
North Ossetia, prov., Russia	180	43°00'N	44°15'E
North Pease, r., Tx., U.S. (pēz)	120	34°19'N	100°58'W
North Pender, i., Can. (pĕn'dẽr)	116d	48°48'N	123°16'W
North Plains, Or., U.S. (plānz)	116c	45°36'N	123°00'W
North Platte, Ne., U.S. (plăt)	104	41°08'N	100°45'W
North Platte, r., U.S.	106	41°20'N	102°40'W
North Point, c., Barb.	133b	13°22'N	59°36'W
North Point, c., Mi., U.S.	108	45°00'N	83°20'W
North Pole, pt. of i.	244	90°00'N	0°00'
Northport, Al., U.S. (nôrth'pōrt)	124	33°12'N	87°35'W
Northport, N.Y., U.S.	110a	40°53'N	73°20'W
Northport, Wa., U.S.	114	48°53'N	117°47'W
North Reading, Ma., U.S. (rĕd'ĭng)	101a	42°34'N	71°04'W
North Richland Hills, Tx., U.S.	117c	32°50'N	97°13'W
Northridge, Ca., U.S. (nôrth'ridj)	117a	34°14'N	118°32'W
North Ridgeville, Oh., U.S. (rĭj-vĭl)	111d	41°23'N	82°01'W
North Ronaldsay, i., Scot., U.K.	164a	59°21'N	2°23'W
North Royalton, Oh., U.S. (roi'ăl-tŭn)	111d	41°19'N	81°44'W
North Saint Paul, Mn., U.S. (sánt pôl')	113	45°01'N	92°59'W
North Santiam, r., Or., U.S. (săn'tyăm)	114	44°42'N	122°50'W
North Saskatchewan, r., Can. (săn-kăch'ê-wän)	92	54°00'N	111°30'W
North Sea, Eur.	154	56°09'N	3°16'E
North Skunk, r., Ia., U.S. (skŭnk)	113	41°39'N	92°46'W
North Stradbroke Island, i., Austl. (străd'brōk)	221	27°45'S	154°18'E
North Sydney, Can. (sĭd'nê)	101	46°13'N	60°15'W
North Taranaki Bight, N.Z. (tá-rá-nä'kĭ bīt)	221a	38°40'S	174°00'E
North Tarrytown, N.Y., U.S. (tăr'ĭ-toun)	110a	41°05'N	73°52'W
North Thompson, r., Can.	95	50°50'N	120°10'W
North Tonawanda, N.Y., U.S. (tŏn-á-wŏn'dá)	111c	43°02'N	78°53'W
North Truchas Peaks, mtn., N.M., U.S. (trōō'chäs)	106	35°58'N	105°40'W
North Twillingate, i., Can. (twĭl'ĭn-gāt)	100	35°58'N	105°37'W
North Uist, i., Scot., U.K. (û'ĭst)	164	57°37'N	7°22'W
Northumberland, N.H., U.S.	109	44°30'N	71°30'W
Northumberland Islands, is., Austl.	221	21°42'S	151°30'E
Northumberland Strait, strt., Can. (nôr thŭm'bẽr-lănd)	100	46°25'N	64°20'W
North Umpqua, r., Or., U.S. (ŭmp'kwă)	114	43°20'N	122°50'W
North Vancouver, Can. (văn-kōō'vẽr)	90	49°19'N	123°04'W
North Vernon, In., U.S. (vûr'nŭn)	108	39°05'N	85°45'W
Northville, Mi., U.S. (nôrth-vĭl)	111b	42°26'N	83°28'W
North Wales, Pa., U.S. (wālz)	110f	40°12'N	75°16'W
North West Cape, c., Austl. (nôrth'wĕst)	220	21°50'S	112°25'E
Northwest Cape Fear, r., N.C., U.S. (căp fēr)	125	34°34'N	79°46'W
North West Gander, r., Can. (găn'dẽr)	101	48°40'N	55°15'W
Northwest Providence Channel, strt., Bah. (prŏv'ĭ-dĕns)	134	26°15'N	78°45'W
Northwest Territories, ter., Can. (tĕr'ĭ-tō'rĭs)	90	65°00'N	120°00'W
Northwich, Eng., U.K. (nôrth'wĭch)	158a	53°15'N	2°31'W
North Wilkesboro, N.C., U.S. (wĭlks'bûrô)	125	36°08'N	81°10'W
Northwood, Ia., U.S. (nôrth'wŏd)	113	43°26'N	93°13'W
Northwood, N.D., U.S.	112	47°44'N	97°36'W
North Yamhill, r., Or., U.S. (yăm' hĭl)	116c	45°22'N	123°21'W
North York, Can.	99	43°47'N	79°25'W
North York Moors, for., Eng., U.K. (yôrk mōrz')	164	54°20'N	0°40'W
North Yorkshire, co., Eng., U.K.	158a	53°50'N	1°10'W
Norton, Ks., U.S. (nôr'tŭn)	120	39°40'N	99°54'W
Norton, Ma., U.S.	110b	41°58'N	71°08'W
Norton, Va., U.S.	125	36°54'N	82°36'W
Norton Bay, b., Ak., U.S.	103	64°22'N	162°18'W
Norton Reservoir, res., Ma., U.S.	110b	42°01'N	71°07'W
Norton Sound, strt., Ak., U.S.	103	63°48'N	164°50'W
Norval, Can. (nôr'văl)	102d	43°39'N	79°52'W
Norwalk, Ca., U.S. (nôr'wôk)	117a	33°54'N	118°05'W
Norwalk, Ct., U.S.	110a	41°06'N	73°25'W
Norwalk, Oh., U.S.	108	41°15'N	82°35'W
Norway, Me., U.S.	100	44°11'N	70°35'W
Norway, Mi., U.S.	113	45°47'N	87°55'W
Norway, nation, Eur. (nôr'wā)	154	63°48'N	11°17'E
Norway House, Can.	90	53°59'N	97°50'W
Norwegian Sea, sea, Eur. (nôr-wē'jăn)	160	66°54'N	1°43'E
Norwell, Ma., U.S. (nôr'wĕl)	101a	42°10'N	70°47'W
Norwich, Eng., U.K.	161	52°40'N	1°15'E
Norwich, Ct., U.S. (nôr'wĭch)	109	41°20'N	72°00'W
Norwich, N.Y., U.S.	109	42°35'N	75°30'W
Norwood, Ma., U.S. (nôr'wŏŏd)	101a	42°11'N	71°13'W
Norwood, N.C., U.S.	125	35°15'N	80°08'W
Norwood, Oh., U.S.	111f	39°10'N	84°27'W
Nose Creek, r., Can. (nōz)	102e	51°09'N	114°02'W
Noshiro, Japan (nō'shê-rō)	210	40°09'N	140°02'E
Nosivka, Ukr. (nô'sôf-ká)	177	50°54'N	31°35'E
Nossob, r., Afr. (nô'sŏb)	232	24°15'S	19°10'E
Noteć, r., Pol. (nô'tĕcn)	168	52°50'N	16°19'E
Notodden, Nor. (nōt'ôd'n)	166	59°35'N	9°15'E
Notre Dame, Monts, mts., Can.	100	46°35'N	70°35'W
Notre Dame Bay, b., Can. (nō't'r dám')	93a	49°45'N	55°15'W
Notre-Dame-du-Lac, Can.	100	47°37'N	68°51'W
Nottawasaga Bay, b., Can. (nŏt'á-wá-sä'gá)	99	44°45'N	80°35'W
Nottaway, r., Can. (nôt'á-wā)	93	50°58'N	78°02'W
Nottingham, Eng., U.K. (nŏt'ĭng-ăm)	161	52°58'N	1°09'W
Nottingham Island, i., Can.	93	62°58'N	78°53'W
Nottinghamshire, co., Eng., U.K.	158a	53°03'N	1°05'W
Nottoway, r., Va., U.S. (nôt'á-wā)	125	36°53'N	77°47'W
Notukeu Creek, r., Can.	96	49°55'N	106°30'W
Nouadhibou, Maur.	230	21°02'N	17°09'W
Nouakchott, Maur.	230	18°06'N	15°57'W
Nouamrhar, Maur.	230	19°22'N	16°31'W
Nouméa, N. Cal. (nōō-mā'ä)	219	22°16'S	166°27'E
Nouvelle, Can. (nōō-vĕl')	100	48°09'N	66°22'W
Nouvelle-France, Cap de, c., Can.	93	62°03'N	74°00'W
Nouzonville, Fr. (nōō-zôɴ-vēl')	170	49°51'N	4°43'E
Nova Cruz, Braz. (nō'vá-krōō'z)	143	6°22'S	35°20'W
Nova Friburgo, Braz. (frê-bōōr'gō)	143	22°18'S	42°31'W
Nova Iguaçu, Braz. (nō'vä-ē-gwä-sōō')	143	22°45'S	43°27'W
Nova Lima, Braz. (lē'mä)	141a	19°59'S	43°51'W
Nova Lisboa see Huambo, Ang.	232	12°44'S	15°47'E
Nova Mambone, Moz. (nō'vá-mám-bō'nĕ)	232	21°04'S	35°13'E
Nova Odesa, Ukr.	177	47°18'N	31°48'E
Nova Praha, Ukr.	177	48°34'N	32°54'E
Novara, Italy (nô-vä'rä)	162	45°24'N	8°38'E
Nova Resende, Braz.	141a	21°12'S	46°25'W
Nova Scotia, prov., Can. (skō'shá)	91	44°28'N	65°00'W
Nova Vodolaha, Ukr.	177	49°43'N	35°51'E
Novaya Ladoga, Russia (nô'vá-ya lä-dô-gá)	167	60°06'N	32°16'E
Novaya Lyalya, Russia (lyä'lyá)	186a	59°03'N	60°36'E
Novaya Sibir, i., Russia (sê-bēr')	179	75°00'N	149°00'E
Novaya Zemlya, i., Russia (zĕm-lyá')	178	72°00'N	54°46'E
Nova Zagora, Blg. (zä'gô-rá)	175	42°30'N	26°01'E
Novelda, Spain (nō-vĕl'dá)	173	38°22'N	0°46'W
Nové Mesto nad Váhom, Slvk. (nô'vĕ myĕs'tô)	169	48°44'N	17°47'E
Nové Zámky, Slvk. (zám'kĕ)	161	47°58'N	18°10'E
Novgorod, Russia (nôv'gô-rŏt)	180	58°32'N	31°16'E
Novgorod, prov., Russia	176	58°27'N	31°55'E
Novhorod-Sivers'kyi, Ukr.	181	52°01'N	33°14'E
Novi, Mi., U.S. (nō'vī)	111b	42°29'N	83°28'W
Novigrad, Cro. (nō'vĭ grád)	174	44°09'N	15°34'E
Novi Ligure, Italy (nô'vê)	174	44°43'N	8°48'E
Novinger, Mo., U.S. (nŏv'ĭn-jẽr)	121	40°14'N	92°43'W
Novi Pazar, Blg. (pä-zär')	175	43°22'N	27°26'E
Novi Pazar, Serb. (pä-zär')	163	43°08'N	20°30'E
Novi Sad, Serb. (säd')	154	45°15'N	19°53'E
Novoaidar, Ukr.	177	48°57'N	39°01'E
Novoasbest, Russia (nô-vô-äs-bĕst')	186a	57°43'N	60°14'E
Novocherkassk, Russia (nô'vô-chĕr-kásk')	181	47°25'N	40°04'E
Novokuznetsk, Russia (nô'vô-kô'z-nyĕ'tsk) (stá'lênsk)	178	53°43'N	86°59'E
Novo-Ladozhskiy Kanal, can., Russia (nô-vô-lä'dôzh-skĭ ká-näl')	167	59°54'N	31°19'E
Novo Mesto, Slvn. (nôvô măs'tô)	174	45°48'N	15°13'E
Novomoskovsk, Russia (nô'vô-môs-kôfsk')	178	54°06'N	38°08'E
Novomoskovs'k, Ukr.	181	48°37'N	35°12'E
Novomyrhorod, Ukr.	177	48°46'N	31°44'E
Novonikol'skiy, Russia (nô'vô-nyĭ-kôl'skĭ)	186a	52°28'N	57°12'E
Novorossiysk, Russia (nô'vô-rô-sĕsk')	178	44°43'N	37°48'E
Novorzhev, Russia (nô'vô-rzhêv')	176	57°01'N	29°17'E
Novo-Selo, Blg. (nô'vô-sĕ'lô)	175	44°09'N	22°46'E
Novosibirsk, Russia (nô'vô-sê-bērsk')	178	55°09'N	82°58'E
Novosibirskiye Ostrova (New Siberian Islands), is., Russia	179	74°00'N	140°30'E
Novosil', Russia (nô'vô-sĭl)	176	52°58'N	37°03'E
Novosokol'niki, Russia (nô'vô-sô-kôl'nē-kē)	176	56°18'N	30°07'E
Novotatishchevskiy, Russia (nô'vô-tá-tyĭsh'chĕv-skĭ)	186a	53°22'N	60°24'E
Novoukraïnka, Ukr.	181	48°18'N	31°33'E
Novouzensk, Russia (nô-vô-ô-zĕnsk')	181	50°40'N	48°08'E
Novozybkov, Russia (nô'vô-zĕp'kôf)	181	52°31'N	31°54'E
Novyi Buh, Ukr.	177	47°43'N	32°33'E
Nový Jičín, Czech Rep. (nô'vē yē'chên)	169	49°36'N	18°02'E
Novyy Oskol, Russia (ôs-kôl')	177	50°46'N	37°53'E
Novyy Port, Russia (nô'vē)	178	67°19'N	72°28'E
Nowa Sól, Pol. (nô'vá sŭl')	168	51°49'N	15°41'E

PLACE (Pronunciation)	PAGE	LAT.	LONG.
Nowata, Ok., U.S. (nô-wä'tȧ)	121	36°42'N	95°38'W
Nowood Creek, r., Wy., U.S.	115	44°02'N	107°37'W
Nowra, Austl. (nou'rȧ)	222	34°55'S	150°45'E
Nowy Dwór Mazowiecki, Pol. (nô'vĭ dvōōr mä-zo-vyĕts'ke)	169	52°26'N	20°46'E
Nowy Sącz, Pol. (nô'vē sônch')	169	49°36'N	20°42'E
Nowy Targ, Pol. (tärk')	169	49°29'N	20°02'E
Noxon Reservoir, res., Mt., U.S.	114	47°50'N	115°40'W
Noxubee, r., Ms., U.S. (nŏks'ū-bē)	124	33°20'N	88°55'W
Noyes Island, i., Ak., U.S. (noiz)	94	55°30'N	133°40'W
Nozaki, Japan (nō'zä-kē)	211b	34°43'N	135°39'E
Nqamakwe, S. Afr. ('n-gä-mä'kwå)	233c	32°13'S	27°57'E
Nqutu, S. Afr. ('n-kōō'tōō)	233c	28°17'S	30°41'E
Nsawam, Ghana	234	5°50'N	0°20'W
Ntshoni, mtn., S. Afr.	233c	29°34'S	30°03'E
Ntwetwe Pan, pl., Bots.	232	20°00'S	24°18'E
Nubah, Jibāl an, mts., Sudan	231	12°22'N	30°39'E
Nubian Desert, des., Sudan (nōō'bĭ-ăn)	231	21°13'N	33°09'E
Nudo Coropuna, mtn., Peru (nōō'dô kō-rō-pōō'nä)	142	15°53'S	72°04'W
Nudo de Pasco, mtn., Peru (dĕ pås'kô)	142	10°34'S	76°12'W
Nueces, r., Tx., U.S. (nů-ā'sås)	106	28°20'N	98°08'W
Nueltin, l., Can. (nwĕl'tin)	92	60°14'N	101°00'W
Nueva Armenia, Hond. (nwä'vä är-mā'nē-å)	132	15°47'N	86°32'W
Nueva Esparta, dept., Ven. (nwĕ'vä ĕs-pä'r-tä)	143b	10°50'N	64°35'W
Nueva Gerona, Cuba (kĕ-rô'nä)	134	21°55'N	82°45'W
Nueva Palmira, Ur. (päl-mē'rä)	141c	33°53'S	58°23'W
Nueva Rosita, Mex. (nòĕ'vä rô-sē'tä)	104	27°55'N	101°10'W
Nueva San Salvador, El Sal.	132	13°41'N	89°16'W
Nueve, Canal Numero, can., Arg.	141c	36°22'S	58°19'W
Nueve de Julio, Arg. (nwā'vå dā hōō'lyô)	144	35°26'S	60°51'W
Nuevitas, Cuba (nwä-vē'täs)	129	21°35'N	77°15'W
Nuevitas, Bahía de, b., Cuba (bä-ē'ä dĕ nwä-vē'täs)	134	21°30'N	77°05'W
Nuevo, Ca., U.S. (nwā'vō)	117a	33°48'N	117°09'W
Nuevo Laredo, Mex. (lä-rā'dhō)	128	27°29'N	99°30'W
Nuevo Leon, state, Mex. (lå-ōn')	128	26°00'N	100°00'W
Nuevo San Juan, Pan. (nwĕ'vô sän kōō-ä'n)	128a	9°14'N	79°43'W
Nugumanovo, Russia (nû-gû-mä'nô-vô)	186a	55°28'N	61°50'E
Nulato, Ak., U.S. (nōō-lä'tō)	103	64°40'N	158°18'W
Nullagine, Austl. (nŭ-lă'jēn)	218	22°00'S	120°07'E
Nullarbor Plain, pl., Austl. (nŭ-lär'bôr)	220	31°45'S	126°30'E
Numabin Bay, b., Can. (nōō-mä'bĭn)	96	56°30'N	103°08'W
Numansdorp, Neth.	159a	51°43'N	4°25'E
Numazu, Japan (nōō'mä-zōō)	210	35°06'N	138°55'E
Numfoor, Pulau, i., Indon.	213	1°20'S	134°48'E
Nun, r., Nig.	235	5°05'N	6°10'E
Nunavut, ter., Can.	90	70°00'N	95°00'W
Nunawading, Austl.	217a	37°49'S	145°10'E
Nuneaton, Eng., U.K. (nŭn'ē-tŭn)	164	52°31'N	1°28'W
Nunivak, i., Ak., U.S. (nōō'nĭ-văk)	106a	60°25'N	167°42'W
Nunyama, Russia (nûn-yä'må)	103	65°49'N	170°32'W
Nuoro, Italy (nwô'rō)	174	40°29'N	9°20'E
Nura, r., Kaz.	184	49°48'N	73°54'E
Nurata, Uzb. (nōōr'ät'å)	183	40°33'N	65°28'E
Nuremberg *see* Nürnberg, Ger.	154	49°28'N	11°07'E
Nürnberg, Ger. (nürn'bĕrgh)	154	49°28'N	11°07'E
Nurse Cay, i., Bah.	135	22°30'N	75°50'W
Nusabyin, Tur. (nōō'sī-bēn)	181	37°05'N	41°10'E
Nushagak, r., Ak., U.S. (nū-shă-găk')	103	59°28'N	157°40'W
Nushan Hu, l., China	206	32°50'N	117°59'E
Nushki, Pak. (nŭsh'kē)	199	29°30'N	66°02'E
Nuthe, r., Ger. (nōō'tē)	159b	52°15'N	13°11'E
Nutley, N.J., U.S. (nŭt'lē)	110a	40°49'N	74°09'W
Nutter Fort, W.V., U.S. (nŭt'ēr fôrt)	108	39°15'N	80°15'W
Nutwood, Il., U.S. (nŭt'wŏŏd)	117e	39°05'N	90°34'W
Nuwaybi 'al Muzayyinah, Egypt	197a	28°59'N	34°40'E
Nuweland, S. Afr.	232a	33°58'S	18°28'E
Nyack, N.Y., U.S. (nī'ăk)	110a	41°05'N	73°55'W
Nyainqêntanglha Shan, mts., China (nyä-ĭn-chyŭn-täŋ-lä shän)	204	29°55'N	88°08'E
Nyakanazi, Tan.	237	3°00'S	31°15'E
Nyala, Sudan	231	12°00'N	24°52'E
Nyanga, r., Gabon	236	2°45'S	10°30'E
Nyanza, Rw.	237	2°21'S	29°45'E
Nyasa, Lake, l., Afr. (nyä'sä)	232	10°45'S	34°30'E
Nyasvizh, Bela. (nyĕs'vēsh)	176	53°13'N	26°44'E
Nyazepetrovsk, Russia (nyä'zĕ-pĕ-trôvsk')	186a	56°04'N	59°38'E
Nyborg, Den. (nü'bôr'')	166	55°20'N	10°45'E
Nybro, Swe. (nü'brō)	166	56°44'N	15°56'E
Nyeri, Kenya	237	0°25'S	36°57'E
Nyika Plateau, plat., Mwi.	237	10°30'S	35°50'E
Nyíregyháza, Hung. (nyē'rĕd-y'hä'zä)	163	47°58'N	21°45'E
Nykøbing, Den. (nü'kû-bĭng)	160	56°46'N	8°47'E
Nykøbing, Den.	166	54°45'N	11°54'E
Nykøbing Sjaelland, Den.	166	55°55'N	11°37'E
Nyköping, Swe. (nü'chû-pĭng)	160	58°46'N	16°58'E
Nylstroom, S. Afr. (nĭl'strōm)	232	24°42'S	28°25'E
Nymagee, Austl. (nī-mȧ-gē')	219	32°17'S	146°18'E
Nymburk, Czech Rep. (nĕm'bòrk)	161	50°12'N	15°03'E
Nynäshamn, Swe. (nü-nĕs-häm'n)	166	58°53'N	17°55'E
Nyngan, Austl. (nĭŋ'gȧn)	219	31°31'S	147°25'E
Nyong, r., Cam. (nyông)	230	4°00'N	12°00'E
Nyou, Burkina	234	12°46'N	1°56'W
Nýřany, Czech Rep. (nêr-zhä'nê)	168	49°43'N	13°13'E
Nysa, Pol. (nē'sȧ)	169	50°29'N	17°20'E
Nytva, Russia	180	58°00'N	55°10'E
Nyungwe, Mwi.	237	10°16'S	34°07'E
Nyunzu, D.R.C.	237	5°57'S	28°01'E
Nyuya, r., Russia (nyōō'yȧ)	185	60°30'N	111°45'E
Nyzhni Sirohozy, Ukr.	177	46°51'N	34°25'E
Nzega, Tan.	237	4°13'S	33°11'E
N'zeto, Ang.	232	7°14'S	12°52'E
Nzi, r., C. Iv.	234	7°00'N	4°27'W
Nzwani, i., Com. (än-zhwän)	233	12°14'S	44°47'E

O

PLACE (Pronunciation)	PAGE	LAT.	LONG.
Oahe, Lake, res., U.S.	106	45°20'N	100°00'W
O'ahu, i., Hi., U.S. (ō-ä'hōō) (ō-ä'hü)	106c	21°38'N	157°48'W
Oak Bay, Can.	94	48°27'N	123°18'W
Oak Bluff, Can. (ōk blŭf)	102f	49°47'N	97°21'W
Oak Creek, Co., U.S. (ōk krēk')	115	40°20'N	106°50'W
Oakdale, Ca., U.S. (ōk'dāl)	118	37°45'N	120°52'W
Oakdale, Ky., U.S.	108	38°15'N	85°50'W
Oakdale, La., U.S.	123	30°49'N	92°40'W
Oakdale, Pa., U.S.	111e	40°24'N	80°11'W
Oakengates, Eng., U.K. (ōk'ĕn-gāts)	158a	52°41'N	2°27'W
Oakes, N.D., U.S. (ōks)	112	46°10'N	98°50'W
Oakfield, Me., U.S. (ōk'fēld)	100	46°08'N	68°10'W
Oakford, Pa., U.S. (ōk'fōrd)	110f	40°08'N	74°58'W
Oak Grove, Or., U.S. (grōv)	116c	45°25'N	122°38'W
Oakham, Eng., U.K. (ōk'ăm)	158a	52°40'N	0°38'W
Oak Harbor, Oh., U.S. (ōk'här'bēr)	108	41°30'N	83°05'W
Oak Harbor, Wa., U.S.	116a	48°18'N	122°39'W
Oakland, Ca., U.S. (ōk'lănd)	104	37°48'N	122°16'W
Oakland, Ne., U.S.	112	41°50'N	96°28'W
Oakland City, In., U.S.	108	38°20'N	87°20'W
Oak Lawn, Il., U.S.	111a	41°43'N	87°45'W
Oakleigh, Austl. (ōk'lå)	217a	37°54'S	145°05'E
Oakley, Id., U.S. (ōk'lĭ)	114	42°15'N	135°53'W
Oakley, Ks., U.S.	120	39°08'N	100°49'W
Oakman, Al., U.S. (ōk'măn)	124	33°42'N	87°20'W
Oakmont, Pa., U.S. (ōk'mōnt)	111e	40°31'N	79°50'W
Oak Mountain, mtn., Al., U.S.	110h	33°22'N	86°42'W
Oak Park, Il., U.S. (pärk)	111a	41°53'N	87°48'W
Oak Point, Wa., U.S.	116c	46°11'N	123°11'W
Oak Ridge, Tn., U.S. (rĭj)	124	36°01'N	84°15'W
Oakville, Can. (ōk'vĭl)	99	43°27'N	79°40'W
Oakville, Can.	102f	49°56'N	97°58'W
Oakville, Mo., U.S.	117e	38°27'N	90°18'W
Oakville Creek, r., Can.	102d	43°34'N	79°54'W
Oakwood, Tx., U.S. (ōk'wŏŏd)	123	31°36'N	95°48'W
Oatman, Az., U.S. (ōt'măn)	119	34°00'N	114°25'W
Oaxaca, Mex.	128	17°03'N	96°42'W
Oaxaca, state, Mex. (wä-hä'kä)	128	16°45'N	97°00'W
Oaxaca, Sierra de, mts., Mex. (sē-ĕ'r-rä dĕ)	131	16°15'N	97°25'W
Ob', r., Russia	178	62°15'N	67°00'E
Oba, Can. (ō'bå)	91	48°58'N	84°09'W
Obama, Japan (ō'bå-mä)	211	35°29'N	135°44'E
Oban, Scot., U.K. (ō'băn)	164	56°25'N	5°35'W
Oban Hills, hills, Nig.	235	5°35'N	8°30'E
O'Bannon, Ky., U.S. (ō-băn'nōn)	111h	38°17'N	85°30'W
O Barco de Valdeorras, Spain	172	42°26'N	6°58'W
Obatogamau, l., Can. (ō-bå-tō'găm-ô)	99	49°38'N	74°10'W
Oberhausen, Ger. (ō'bĕr-hou'zĕn)	171c	51°27'N	6°51'E
Oberlin, Ks., U.S. (ō'bĕr-lĭn)	120	39°49'N	100°30'W
Oberlin, Oh., U.S.	108	41°15'N	82°15'W
Oberroth, Ger. (ō'bĕr-rōt)	159d	48°19'N	11°20'E
Obi, Kepulauan, is., Indon. (ō'bē)	213	1°25'S	128°15'E
Obi, Pulau, i., Indon.	213	1°30'S	127°45'E
Óbidos, Braz. (ō'bē-dòzh)	143	1°57'S	55°32'W
Obihiro, Japan (ō'bē-hē'rō)	210	42°55'N	142°50'E
Obion, r., Tn., U.S.	124	36°10'N	89°25'W
Obion, North Fork, r., Tn., U.S. (ô-bī'ŏn)	124	35°49'N	89°06'W
Obitsu, r., Japan (ō'bēt'sōō)	211a	35°19'N	140°03'E
Obock, Dji. (ō-bŏk')	238a	11°55'N	43°15'E
Obol', r., Bela. (ô-bŏl')	176	55°24'N	29°24'E
Oboyan', Russia (ô-bô-yän')	181	51°14'N	36°16'E
Obskaya Guba, b., Russia	178	67°13'N	73°45'E
Obuasi, Ghana	234	6°14'N	1°39'W
Obukhiv, Ukr.	177	50°07'N	30°36'E
Obukhovo, Russia	186b	55°50'N	38°17'E
Obytichna kosa, spit, Ukr.	177	46°32'N	36°07'E
Ocala, Fl., U.S. (ô-kä'lȧ)	125	29°11'N	82°09'W
Ocampo, Mex. (ô-käm'pō)	130	22°49'N	99°23'W
Ocaña, Col. (ô-kän'yä)	142	8°15'N	73°37'W
Ocaña, Spain (ô-kä'n-yä)	172	39°58'N	3°31'W
Occidental, Cordillera, mts., Col.	142a	5°05'N	76°04'W
Occidental, Cordillera, mts., Peru	142	10°12'S	76°58'W
Ocean Beach, Ca., U.S. (ō'shăn bēch)	118a	32°44'N	117°14'W
Ocean Bight, b., Bah.	135	21°15'N	73°15'W
Ocean City, Md., U.S.	109	38°20'N	75°10'W
Ocean City, N.J., U.S.	109	39°15'N	74°35'W
Ocean Falls, Can. (Fôls)	90	52°21'N	127°40'W
Ocean Grove, Austl.	217a	38°16'S	144°32'E
Ocean Grove, N.J., U.S. (grōv)	109	40°10'N	74°00'W
Oceanside, Ca., U.S. (ō'shăn-sīd)	118	33°11'N	117°22'W
Oceanside, N.Y., U.S.	110a	40°38'N	73°39'W
Ocean Springs, Ms., U.S. (sprĭngs)	124	30°25'N	88°49'W
Ochakiv, Ukr.	177	46°38'N	31°33'E
Ochamchira, Geor.	182	42°44'N	41°28'E
Ochlockonee, r., Fl., U.S. (ŏk-lô-kō'nē)	124	30°10'N	84°38'W
Ocilla, Ga., U.S. (ô-sĭl'ȧ)	124	31°36'N	83°15'W
Ockelbo, Swe. (ôk'ĕl-bô)	166	60°54'N	16°35'E
Ocklawaha, Lake, res., Fl., U.S.	125	29°30'N	81°50'W
Ocmulgee, r., Ga., U.S.	124	32°25'N	83°30'W
Ocmulgee National Monument, rec., Ga., U.S. (ôk-mŭl'gē)	124	32°45'N	83°28'W
Ocoa, Bahía de, b., Dom. Rep.	135	18°20'N	70°40'W
Ococingo, Mex. (ô-kô-sē'n-gô)	131	17°03'N	92°18'W
Ocom, Lago, l., Mex. (ô-kô'm)	132a	19°26'N	88°18'W
Oconee, r., Ga., U.S. (ô-kō'nē)	107	32°45'N	83°00'W
Oconee, Lake, res., Ga., U.S.	124	33°30'N	83°15'W
Oconomowoc, Wi., U.S. (ô-kŏn'ô-mô-wŏk')	113	43°06'N	88°24'W
Oconto, Wi., U.S. (ô-kŏn'tō)	113	44°54'N	87°55'W
Oconto, r., Wi., U.S.	113	45°08'N	88°24'W
Oconto Falls, Wi., U.S.	113	44°53'N	88°11'W
Ocós, Guat. (ô-kōs')	132	14°31'N	92°12'W
Ocotal, Nic. (ō-kô-täl')	132	13°36'N	86°31'W
Ocotepeque, Hond. (ô-kō-tå-pā'kå)	132	14°25'N	89°13'W
Ocotlán, Mex. (ō-kô-tlän')	130	20°19'N	102°44'W
Ocotlán de Morelos, Mex. (dā mô-rā'lōs)	131	16°46'N	96°41'W
Ocozocoautla, Mex. (ô-kō'zô-kwä-ōō'tlä)	131	16°44'N	93°22'W
Ocumare del Tuy, Ven. (ô-kōō-mä'ra del twē')	142	10°07'N	66°47'W
Oda, Ghana	234	5°55'N	0°59'W
Odawara, Japan (ō'då-wä'rä)	211	35°15'N	139°10'E
Odda, Nor. (ôdh-å)	166	60°04'N	6°30'E
Odebolt, Ia., U.S. (ō'dē-bōlt)	112	42°20'N	95°14'W
Odemira, Port. (ō-då-mē'rå)	172	37°35'N	8°40'W
Ödemiş, Tur. (û'dĕ-mēsh)	163	38°12'N	28°00'E
Odendaalsrus, S. Afr. (ō'dĕn-däls-rûs')	238c	27°52'S	26°41'E
Odense, Den. (ō'dhĕn-sĕ)	160	55°24'N	10°20'E
Odenton, Md., U.S. (ō'dĕn-tŭn)	110e	39°05'N	76°43'W
Odenwald, for., Ger. (ō'dĕn-väld)	168	49°39'N	8°55'E
Oder, r., Eur. (ō'dĕr)	156	52°40'N	14°19'E
Oderhaff, l., Eur.	168	53°47'N	14°02'E
Odesa, Ukr.	178	46°28'N	30°44'E
Odesa, prov., Ukr.	177	46°05'N	29°48'E
Odessa, Tx., U.S. (ô-dĕs'ȧ)	122	31°52'N	102°21'W
Odessa, Wa., U.S.	114	47°20'N	118°42'W
Odiel, r., Spain (ō-dē-ĕl')	172	37°47'N	6°42'W
Odiham, Eng., U.K. (ŏd'ē-ăm)	158b	51°14'N	0°56'W
Odintsovo, Russia (ô-dēn'tsô-vô)	186b	55°40'N	37°16'E
Odiongan, Phil. (ō-dē-ôŋ'gän)	213a	12°24'N	121°59'E
Odivelas, Port. (ō-dē-vā'lyäs)	173b	38°47'N	9°11'W
Odobeşti, Rom. (ô-dô-bĕsh't')	169	45°46'N	27°08'E
O'Donnell, Tx., U.S. (ō-dŏn'ĕl)	120	32°59'N	101°51'W
Odorhei, Rom. (ô-dôr-hā')	169	46°18'N	25°17'E
Odra *see* Oder, r., Eur. (ô'drå)	156	52°40'N	14°19'E
Oeiras, Braz. (wå-ê-räzh')	143	7°05'S	42°01'W
Oeirás, Port. (ō-ĕ'y-rå's)	173b	38°42'N	9°18'W
Oelwein, Ia., U.S. (ōl'wīn)	113	42°40'N	91°56'W
O'Fallon, Il., U.S. (ō-făl'ŭn)	117e	38°36'N	89°55'W
O'Fallon Creek, r., Mt., U.S.	115	46°25'N	104°47'W
Ofanto, r., Italy (ô-făn'tō)	174	41°08'N	15°33'E
Offa, Nig.	235	8°09'N	4°44'E
Offenbach, Ger. (ôf'ĕn-băk)	168	50°06'N	8°50'E
Offenburg, Ger. (ôf'ĕn-bòrgh)	168	48°28'N	7°57'E
Ofuna, Japan (ō'fōō-nä)	211a	35°21'N	139°32'E
Ogaden Plateau, plat., Eth.	238a	6°45'N	44°53'E
Ogaki, Japan	210	35°21'N	136°36'E
Ogallala, Ne., U.S. (ō-gä-lä'lä)	112	41°08'N	101°44'W
Ogbomosho, Nig. (ŏg-bô-mō'shō)	230	8°08'N	4°15'E
Ogden, Ia., U.S. (ŏg'dĕn)	113	42°10'N	94°20'W
Ogden, Ut., U.S.	104	41°14'N	111°58'W
Ogden, r., Ut., U.S.	117b	41°16'N	111°54'W
Ogden Peak, mtn., Ut., U.S.	117b	41°11'N	111°51'W
Ogdensburg, N.J., U.S. (ŏg'dĕnz-bûrg)	110a	41°05'N	74°36'W
Ogdensburg, N.Y., U.S.	105	44°40'N	75°30'W
Ogeechee, r., Ga., U.S. (ô-gē'chē)	125	32°35'N	81°50'W
Ogies, S. Afr.	238c	26°03'S	29°04'E
Ogilvie Mountains, mts., Can. (ō'g'l-vĭ)	92	64°45'N	138°10'W
Oglesby, Il., U.S. (ō'g'lz-bĭ)	108	41°20'N	89°00'W
Oglio, r., Italy (ôl'yō)	174	45°15'N	10°19'E
Ogo, Japan (ō'gō)	211b	34°49'N	135°06'E
Ogou, r., Togo	234	8°05'N	1°30'E
Ogudnëvo, Russia (ôg-òd-nyô'vô)	186b	56°04'N	38°17'E
Ogulin, Cro. (ō-gōō-lēn')	174	45°17'N	15°11'E
Ogwashi-Uku, Nig.	235	6°10'N	6°31'E
O'Higgins, prov., Chile (ô-kē'gēns)	141b	34°17'S	70°52'W
Ohio, state, U.S. (ô'hī'ō)	105	40°30'N	83°15'W
Ohio, r., U.S.	107	37°25'N	88°05'W
Ohoopee, r., Ga., U.S. (ô-hōō'pe-mc)	125	32°32'N	82°38'W
Ohře, r., Eur. (ōr'zhĕ)	168	50°08'N	12°45'E
Ohrid, Mac. (ō'krēd)	175	41°08'N	20°46'E
Ohrid, Lake, l., Eur.	175	40°58'N	20°35'E
Ōi, Japan (oi')	211a	35°51'N	139°31'E
Oi-Gawa, r., Japan (ō'ē-gä'wȧ)	211	35°09'N	138°05'E
Oil City, Pa., U.S. (oil sĭ'tĭ)	109	41°25'N	79°40'W
Oirschot, Neth.	159a	51°30'N	5°20'E
Oise, r., Fr. (wäz)	161	49°30'N	2°56'E
Oisterwijk, Neth.	159a	51°34'N	5°13'E
Oita, Japan (ō'ē-tä)	210	33°14'N	131°38'E
Oji, Japan (ō'jē)	211b	34°36'N	135°43'E
Ojinaga, Mex. (ō-kē-nä'gä)	128	29°34'N	104°26'W
Ojitlán, Mex. (ōkē-tlän') (sän-lōō'käs)	131	18°04'N	96°23'W

ăt; finăl; rāte; senåte; ärm; åsk; sofȧ; fâre; ch-choose; dh-as th in other; bē; ēvent; bĕt; recĕnt; cratēr; g-gō; gh-guttural g; bĭt; ĭ-short neutral; rīde; ĸ-guttural k as ch in German ich;

PRONOUNCING INDEX

Ojo Caliente – Orikhiv 331

PLACE (Pronunciation)	PAGE	LAT.	LONG.
Ojo Caliente, Mex. (ōkō käl-yĕn′tä)	130	21°50′N	100°43′W
Ojocaliente, Mex. (ô-kô-kä-lyĕ′n-tĕ)	130	22°39′N	102°15′W
Ojo del Toro, Pico, mtn., Cuba (pē′kô-ô-kō-dĕl-tô′rô)	134	19°55′N	77°25′W
Oka, Can. (ō-kä)	102a	45°28′N	74°05′W
Oka, r., Russia (ô-kà′)	180	55°10′N	42°10′E
Oka, r., Russia (ō-kä′)	184	53°28′N	101°09′E
Oka, r., Russia (ô-kä′)	181	52°10′N	35°20′E
Okahandja, Nmb.	232	21°50′S	16°45′E
Okanagan (Okanogan), r., N.A. (ō′kȧ-näg′ǎn)	95	49°06′N	119°43′W
Okanagan Lake, l., Can.	92	50°00′N	119°28′W
Okano, r., Gabon (ō′kä′nō)	230	0°15′N	11°08′E
Okanogan, Wa., U.S.	114	48°20′N	119°34′W
Okanogan, r., Wa., U.S.	114	48°36′N	119°33′W
Okatibbee, r., Ms., U.S. (ō′kä-tĭb′ē)	124	32°37′N	88°54′W
Okatoma Creek, r., Ms., U.S. (ô-kä-tō′mä)	124	31°43′N	89°34′W
Okavango (Cubango), r., Afr.	232	18°00′S	20°00′E
Okavango Swamp, sw., Bots.	232	19°30′S	23°02′E
Okaya, Japan (ō′kȧ-yȧ)	211	36°04′N	138°01′E
Okayama, Japan (ō′kȧ-yä′mȧ)	205	34°39′N	133°54′E
Okazaki, Japan (ō′kȧ-zä′kê)	210	34°58′N	137°09′E
Okeechobee, Fl., U.S. (ō-kê-chō′bē)	125	27°15′N	80°50′W
Okeechobee, Lake, l., Fl., U.S.	107	27°00′N	80°49′W
Okeene, Ok., U.S. (ô-kēn′)	120	36°06′N	98°19′W
Okefenokee Swamp, sw., U.S. (ō′kê-fê-nō′kê)	125	30°54′N	82°20′W
Okemah, Ok., U.S. (ô-kē′mä)	121	35°26′N	96°18′W
Okene, Nig.	235	7°33′N	6°15′E
Okha, Russia (ŭ-kä′)	179	53°44′N	143°12′E
Okhotino, Russia (ô-kô′tĭ-nô)	186b	56°14′N	38°24′E
Okhotsk, Russia (ô-kôtsk′)	179	59°28′N	143°32′E
Okhotsk, Sea of, sea, Asia (ô-kôtsk′)	179	56°45′N	146°00′E
Okhtyrka, Ukr.	181	50°18′N	34°53′E
Okinawa, i., Japan	205	26°30′N	128°00′E
Okino, i., Japan (ō′kê-nô)	211	36°22′N	133°27′E
Ōkino Erabu, i., Japan (ō-kē′nô-å-rä′bōō)	210	27°18′N	129°00′E
Oklahoma, state, U.S. (ô-klȧ-hō′mȧ)	104	36°00′N	98°20′W
Oklahoma City, Ok., U.S.	104	35°27′N	97°32′W
Oklawaha, r., Fl., U.S. (ŏk-lȧ-wô′hô)	125	29°13′N	82°00′W
Okmulgee, Ok., U.S. (ôk-mŭl′gē)	121	35°37′N	95°58′W
Okolona, Ky., U.S. (ō-kô-lō′nȧ)	111h	38°08′N	85°41′W
Okolona, Ms., U.S.	124	33°59′N	88°43′W
Oktemberyan, Arm.	182	40°09′N	44°02′E
Okushiri, i., Japan (ō′koo-shē′rê)	210	42°12′N	139°30′E
Okuta, Nig.	235	9°14′N	3°15′E
Olalla, Wa., U.S. (ō-lä′lȧ)	116a	47°26′N	122°33′W
Olanchito, Hond. (ō′län-chē′tô)	132	15°28′N	86°35′W
Öland, i., Swe. (û-länd′)	156	57°03′N	17°15′E
Olathe, Ks., U.S. (ô-lā′thê)	117f	38°53′N	94°49′W
Olavarría, Arg. (ō-lä-vär-rē′ä)	144	36°49′N	60°15′W
Oława, Pol. (ô-lä′vȧ)	169	50°57′N	17°18′E
Olazoago, Arg. (ô-läz-kôä′gô)	141c	35°14′S	60°37′W
Olbia, Italy (ô′l-byä)	174	40°55′N	9°28′E
Olching, Ger. (ōl′kēng)	159d	48°13′N	11°21′E
Old Bahama Channel, strt., N.A. (bȧ-hā′mȧ)	134	22°45′N	78°30′W
Old Bight, Bah.	135	24°15′N	75°20′W
Old Bridge, N.J., U.S. (brĭj)	110a	40°24′N	74°22′W
Old Crow, Can. (crō)	90	67°51′N	139°58′W
Oldenburg, Ger. (ôl′dĕn-bòrgh)	160	53°09′N	8°13′E
Old Forge, Pa., U.S. (fôrj)	109	41°20′N	75°50′W
Oldham, Eng., U.K. (ōld′ȧm)	164	53°32′N	2°07′W
Oldham, co., Eng., U.K.	158a	53°35′N	2°05′W
Old Harbor, Ak., U.S. (här′bẽr)	103	57°18′N	153°20′W
Old Head of Kinsale, c., Ire. (ōld hĕd ŏv kĭn-sāl)	164	51°35′N	8°35′W
Old R, Tx., U.S.	123a	29°54′N	94°52′W
Olds, Can. (ōldz)	90	51°47′N	114°06′W
Old Tate, Bots.	232	21°18′S	27°43′E
Old Town, Me., U.S. (toun)	100	44°55′N	68°42′W
Old Wives Lake, l., Can. (wīvz)	96	50°05′N	106°00′W
Olean, N.Y., U.S. (ō-lê-ăn′)	105	42°05′N	78°25′W
Olecko, Pol. (ô-lĕt′skô)	169	54°02′N	22°29′E
Olekma, r., Russia (ô-lyĕk-mä′)	185	55°41′N	120°33′E
Olëkminsk, Russia (ô-lyĕk-mênsk′)	179	60°39′N	120°40′E
Oleksandriia, Ukr.	176	48°40′N	33°07′E
Olenëk, r., Russia (ô-lyĕ-nyôk′)	179	68°00′N	113°00′E
Oléron Île, d′, i., Fr. (ēl′ dō lā-rôn′)	161	45°52′N	1°58′W
Oleśnica, Pol. (ô-lĕsh-nĭ′tsȧ)	161	51°13′N	17°24′E
Olfen, Ger. (ōl′fĕn)	171c	51°43′N	7°22′E
Ol′ga, Russia (ôl′gȧ)	179	43°48′N	135°44′E
Ol′gi, Zaliv, b., Russia (zä′lĭf ôl′gĭ)	210	43°43′N	135°25′E
Olhão, Port. (ôl-youn′)	162	37°02′N	7°54′W
Ol′hopil′, Ukr.	177	48°11′N	29°28′E
Olievenhoutpoort, S. Afr.	233b	25°58′S	27°55′E
Ólimbos, mtn., Cyp.	197a	34°56′N	32°52′E
Olinda, Braz. (ô-lē′n-dä)	143	8°00′S	34°58′W
Olinda, Braz.	144b	22°49′S	43°25′W
Oliva, Spain (ô-lē′vä)	173	38°54′N	0°07′W
Oliva de la Frontera, Spain (ô-lē′vä dā)	172	38°33′N	6°55′W
Olive Hill, Ky., U.S. (ŏl′ĭv)	108	38°15′N	83°10′W
Oliveira, Braz. (ô-lē-vā′rä)	141a	20°42′S	44°49′W
Olivenza, Spain (ō-lê-vĕn′thä)	172	38°42′N	7°06′W
Oliver, Can. (ŏ′lĭ-vẽr)	90	49°11′N	119°33′W
Oliver, Can.	102g	53°38′N	113°21′W
Oliver, Wi., U.S. (ŏ′lĭvẽr)	117h	46°39′N	92°12′W
Oliver Lake, l., Can.	102g	53°19′N	113°00′W
Olivia, Mn., U.S. (ō-lĭv′ê-ȧ)	112	44°46′N	95°00′W
Olivos, Arg. (ôlē′vôs)	144a	34°30′S	58°29′W
Ollagüe, Chile (ô-lyä′gå)	142	21°17′S	68°17′W
Ollerton, Eng., U.K. (ôl′ẽr-tŭn)	158a	53°12′N	1°02′W
Olmos Park, Tx., U.S. (ōl′mŭs pärk′)	117d	29°27′N	98°32′W
Olney, Il., U.S. (ŏl′nĭ)	108	38°45′N	88°05′W
Olney, Or., U.S. (ŏl′nē)	116c	46°06′N	123°45′W
Olney, Tx., U.S.	120	33°24′N	98°43′W
Olomane, r., Can. (ō′lô mȧ′nĕ)	101	51°05′N	60°50′W
Olomouc, Czech Rep. (ô′lô-mōts)	161	49°37′N	17°15′E
Olonets, Russia (ô-lô′nĕts)	167	60°58′N	32°54′E
Olongapo, Phil.	212	14°49′S	120°17′E
Oloron, Gave d′, r., Fr. (gäv-dŏ-lō-rôn′)	170	43°21′N	0°44′W
Oloron-Sainte Marie, Fr. (ō-lô-rônt′sănt mȧ-rē′)	170	43°11′N	1°37′W
Olot, Spain (ô-lōt′)	162	42°09′N	2°30′E
Olpe, Ger. (ōl′pĕ)	171c	51°02′N	7°51′E
Olsnitz, Ger. (ôl′z′nētz)	168	50°25′N	12°11′E
Olsztyn, Pol. (ôl′shtĭn)	160	53°47′N	20°28′E
Olt, r., Rom.	163	44°09′N	24°40′E
Olten, Switz. (ôl′tĕn)	168	47°20′N	7°53′E
Olteniţa, Rom. (ôl-tā′nĭ-tsȧ)	175	44°05′N	26°39′E
Olvera, Spain (ôl-vĕ′rä)	172	36°55′N	5°16′W
Olympia, Wa., U.S. (ô-lĭm′pĭ-ȧ)	104	47°02′N	122°52′W
Olympic Mountains, mts., Wa., U.S.	114	47°54′N	123°58′W
Olympic National Park, rec., Wa., U.S. (ô-lĭm′pĭk)	106	47°54′N	123°00′W
Ólympos, mtn., Grc.	162	40°05′N	22°21′E
Olympus, Mount, mtn., Wa., U.S. (ô-lĭm′pŭs)	114	47°43′N	123°30′W
Olyphant, Pa., U.S. (ŏl′ĭ-fănt)	109	41°30′N	75°40′W
Olyutorskiy, Mys, c., Russia (ŭl-yōō′tŏr-skê)	179	59°49′N	167°16′E
Omae-Zaki, c., Japan (ō′mä-å zä′kê)	211	34°37′N	138°15′E
Omagh, N. Ire., U.K. (ō′mä)	164	54°35′N	7°25′W
Omaha, Ne., U.S. (ō′mȧ-hä)	105	41°18′N	95°57′W
Omaha Indian Reservation, I.R., Ne., U.S.	112	42°09′N	96°08′W
Oman, nation, Asia	198	20°00′N	57°45′E
Oman, Gulf of, b., Asia	198	24°24′N	58°58′E
Omaruru, Nmb. (ō-mä-rōō′rōō)	232	21°25′S	16°50′E
Ombrone, r., Italy (ôm-brō′nä)	174	42°48′N	11°18′E
Omdurman, Sudan	231	15°45′N	32°30′E
Omealca, Mex. (ōmå-äl′kō)	131	18°44′N	96°45′W
Ometepec, Mex. (ô-mā-tȧ-pĕk′)	130	16°41′N	98°27′W
Om Hajer, Eth.	231	14°06′N	36°46′E
Omineca, r., Can. (ō-mĭ-nĕk′ȧ)	94	55°50′N	125°45′W
Omineca Mountains, mts., Can.	94	56°00′N	125°00′W
Ōmiya, Japan (ō′mê-yȧ)	211	35°54′N	139°38′E
Omo, r., Eth. (ō′mō)	231	5°54′N	36°09′E
Omoa, Hond. (ô-mō′rä)	132	15°43′N	88°03′W
Omoko, Nig.	235	5°20′N	6°39′E
Omolon, r., Russia (ō′mō)	185	67°43′N	159°15′E
Ōmori, Japan (ō′mô-rê)	211a	35°50′N	140°09′E
Omotepe, Isla de, i., Nic. (ē′s-lä-dĕ-ō-mô-tā′pȧ)	132	11°32′N	85°30′W
Omro, Wi., U.S. (ŏm′rō)	113	44°01′N	89°46′W
Omsk, Russia (ômsk)	178	55°12′N	73°19′E
Ōmura, Japan (ō′mōō-rȧ)	211	32°56′N	129°57′E
Ōmuta, Japan (ō′mô-tȧ)	211	33°02′N	130°28′E
Omutninsk, Russia (ō′mōō-tnēnsk)	180	58°38′N	52°10′E
Onawa, Ia., U.S. (ŏn-ȧ-wȧ)	112	42°02′N	96°05′W
Onaway, Mi., U.S.	108	45°25′N	84°10′W
Oncócua, Ang.	236	16°34′S	13°28′E
Onda, Spain (ōn′dä)	173	39°58′N	0°13′W
Ondava, r., Slvk. (ōn′dȧ-vȧ)	169	48°51′N	21°40′E
Ondo, Nig.	235	7°04′N	4°47′E
Öndörhaan, Mong.	205	47°20′N	110°40′E
Onega, Russia (ô-nyĕ′gȧ)	178	63°50′N	38°08′E
Onega, r., Russia	180	63°20′N	39°20′E
Onega, Lake see Onezhskoye Ozero, l., Russia	180	62°02′N	34°35′E
Oneida, N.Y., U.S. (ô-nī′dȧ)	109	43°05′N	75°40′W
Oneida, l., N.Y., U.S.	109	43°10′N	76°00′W
O′Neill, Ne., U.S. (ō-nēl′)	112	42°28′N	98°38′W
Oneonta, N.Y., U.S. (ō-nê-ŏn′tȧ)	109	42°25′N	75°05′W
Onezhskaja Guba, b., Russia	180	64°30′N	36°00′E
Onezhskiy, Poluostrov, pen., Russia	180	64°30′N	37°40′E
Onezhskoye Ozero, Russia (ô-nâsh′skô-yĕ ô′zĕ-rô)	180	62°02′N	34°35′E
Ongiin Hiid, Mong.	204	46°00′N	102°46′E
Ongole, India	203	15°36′N	80°03′E
Onilahy, r., Madag.	233	23°41′S	45°00′E
Onitsha, Nig. (ô-nĭt′shȧ)	230	6°09′N	6°47′W
Onomichi, Japan (ō′nô-mē′chê)	210	34°27′N	133°12′E
Onon, r., Asia (ō′nôn)	179	49°00′N	112°00′E
Onoto, Ven. (ô-nŏ′tô)	143b	9°38′N	65°03′W
Onslow, Austl. (ŏnz′lō)	218	21°53′S	115°00′E
Onslow B, N.C., U.S. (ŏnz′lō)	125	34°22′N	77°35′W
Ontake San, mtn., Japan (ôn′tä-kä sän)	210	35°55′N	137°29′E
Ontario, Ca., U.S. (ŏn-tā′rĭ-ō)	117a	34°04′N	117°39′E
Ontario, Or., U.S.	114	44°02′N	116°57′W
Ontario, prov., Can.	91	50°47′N	88°50′W
Ontario, Lake, l., N.A.	107	43°35′N	79°05′W
Ontinyent, Spain	173	38°48′N	0°35′W
Ontonagon, Mi., U.S. (ŏn-tô-năg′ŏn)	113	46°50′N	89°20′W
Ōnuki, Japan (ō′nōō-kê)	211a	35°17′N	139°51′E
Oodnadatta, Austl. (ōōd′nȧ-dȧ′tȧ)	218	27°38′S	135°40′E
Ooldea Station, Austl. (ōōl-dā′ä)	218	30°35′S	132°08′E
Oologah Reservoir, res., Ok., U.S.	107	36°43′N	95°32′W
Ooltgensplaat, Neth.	159a	51°41′N	4°19′E
Oostanaula, r., Ga., U.S. (ōō-stȧ-nô′lȧ)	124	34°25′N	85°10′W
Oostende, Bel. (ōst-ĕn′dĕ)	161	51°14′N	2°55′E
Oosterhout, Neth.	159a	51°38′N	4°52′E
Ooster Schelde, r., Neth.	159a	51°40′N	3°40′E
Ootsa Lake, l., Can.	94	53°49′N	126°18′W
Opalaca, Sierra de, mts., Hond. (sē-sĕ′r-rä-dĕ-ô-pä-lä′kä)	132	14°30′N	88°29′W
Opasquia, Can. (ō-pās′kwê-ȧ)	97	53°16′N	93°53′W
Opatów, Pol. (ô-pä′tôf)	169	50°47′N	21°25′E
Opava, Czech Rep. (ō′pä-vä)	169	49°56′N	17°52′E
Opelika, Al., U.S. (ŏp-ê-lī′kȧ)	124	32°39′N	85°23′W
Opelousas, La., U.S. (ŏp-ê-lōō′sȧs)	123	30°33′N	92°04′W
Opeongo, l., Can. (ŏp-ê-ŏŋ′gō)	99	45°40′N	78°20′W
Opheim, Mt., U.S. (ô-fīm′)	115	48°51′N	106°19′W
Ophir, Ak., U.S. (ō′fẽr)	103	63°10′N	156°28′W
Ophir, Mount, mtn., Malay.	197b	2°22′N	102°37′E
Opico, El Sal. (ô-pē′kō)	132	13°50′N	89°23′W
Opinaca, r., Can. (ŏp-ĭ-nä′kȧ)	93	52°28′N	77°40′W
Opishnia, Ukr.	177	49°57′N	34°34′E
Opladen, Ger. (ōp′lä-dĕn)	171c	51°04′N	7°00′E
Opobo, Nig.	235	4°34′N	7°27′E
Opochka, Russia (ō-pôch′kȧ)	180	56°43′N	28°39′E
Opoczno, Pol. (ô-pôch′nô)	169	51°22′N	20°18′E
Opole, Pol. (ô-pôl′ä)	161	50°42′N	17°55′E
Opole Lubelskie, Pol. (ō-pō′lä lōō-bĕl′skyĕ)	169	51°09′N	21°58′E
Opp, Al., U.S. (ŏp)	124	31°18′N	86°15′W
Oppdal, Nor. (ôp′däl)	166	62°37′N	9°41′E
Opportunity, Wa., U.S. (ŏp-ŏr tū′nĭ tĭ)	116a	47°37′N	117°20′W
Oquirrh Mountains, mts., Ut., U.S. (ō′kwẽr)	117b	40°38′N	112°11′W
Oradea, Rom. (ô-räd′yä)	154	47°02′N	21°55′E
Oral, Kaz.	183	51°14′N	51°22′E
Oran, Alg. (ō-rän) (ō-rän′)	230	35°46′N	0°45′W
Orán, Arg. (ō-rà′n)	144	23°13′S	64°17′W
Oran, Mo., U.S. (ôr′ȧn)	121	37°05′N	89°39′W
Oran, Sebkha d′, l., Alg.	173	35°28′N	0°28′W
Orange, Austl. (ŏr′ĕnj)	219	33°15′S	149°08′E
Orange, Fr. (ô-ränzh′)	161	44°08′N	4°48′E
Orange, Ca., U.S.	117a	33°48′N	117°51′W
Orange, Ct., U.S.	109	41°15′N	73°00′W
Orange, N.J., U.S.	110a	40°46′N	74°14′W
Orange, Tx., U.S.	121	30°07′N	93°44′W
Orange, r., Afr.	232	29°15′S	17°30′E
Orange, Cabo, c., Braz. (kȧ-bô-rä′n-zhĕ)	143	4°25′N	51°30′W
Orangeburg, S.C., U.S. (ŏr′ĕnj-bûrg)	125	33°30′N	80°50′W
Orange Cay, i., Bah. (ŏr-ĕnj kē)	134	24°55′N	79°05′W
Orange City, Ia., U.S.	112	43°01′N	96°06′W
Orange Lake, l., Fl., U.S.	125	29°30′N	82°12′W
Orangeville, Can. (ŏr′ĕnj-vĭl)	99	43°55′N	80°06′W
Orangeville, S. Afr.	238c	27°05′S	28°13′E
Orange Walk, Belize (wôl′′k)	132a	18°09′N	88°32′W
Orani, Phil. (ō-rä′nê)	213a	14°47′N	120°32′E
Oranienburg, Ger. (ō-rä′nê-ĕn-bòrgh)	168	52°45′N	13°14′E
Oranjemund, Nmb.	232	28°33′S	16°20′E
Orăştie, Rom. (ô-rŭsh′tyå)	175	45°50′N	23°14′E
Orbetello, Italy (ôr-bȧ-tĕl′lō)	174	42°27′N	11°15′E
Orbigo, r., Spain (ôr-bē′gō)	172	42°30′N	5°55′W
Orbost, Austl. (ôr′bŭst)	222	37°43′S	148°20′E
Orcas, i., Wa., U.S. (ôr′kȧs)	116d	48°43′N	122°52′W
Orchard Farm, Mo., U.S. (ôr′chẽrd färm)	117e	38°53′N	90°27′W
Orchard Park, N.Y., U.S.	111c	42°46′N	78°46′W
Orchards, Wa., U.S. (ôr′chẽdz)	116c	45°40′N	122°33′W
Orchila, Isla, i., Ven.	142	11°47′N	66°34′W
Ord, Ne., U.S. (ôrd)	112	41°35′N	98°57′W
Ord, r., Austl.	220	17°30′S	128°40′E
Ord, Mount, mtn., Az., U.S.	119	33°55′N	109°40′W
Orda, Kaz. (ôr′dȧ)	181	48°50′N	47°30′E
Orda, Russia (ôr′dȧ)	186a	57°10′N	57°12′E
Ordes, Spain	172	43°00′N	8°24′W
Ordos Desert, des., China	204	39°12′N	108°10′E
Ordu, Tur. (ôr′dô)	163	41°00′N	37°50′E
Ordway, Co., U.S. (ôrd′wā)	120	38°11′N	103°46′W
Örebro, Swe. (û′rē-brō)	160	59°16′N	15°11′E
Oredezh, r., Russia (ô′rĕ-dĕzh)	186c	59°23′N	30°21′E
Oregon, Il., U.S.	113	42°01′N	89°21′W
Oregon, state, U.S.	104	43°40′N	121°50′W
Oregon Caves National Monument, rec., Or., U.S. (căvz)	114	42°05′N	123°13′W
Oregon City, Or., U.S.	116c	45°21′N	122°36′W
Öregrund, Swe. (û-rĕ-grònd)	166	60°20′N	18°26′E
Orekhovo, Blg.	175	43°43′N	23°59′E
Orekhovo-Zuyevo, Russia (ôr-yĕ′kô-vô zò′yĕ-vô)	178	55°46′N	39°00′E
Orël, Russia (ôr-yôl′)	176	52°59′N	36°05′E
Orël, prov., Russia	176	52°35′N	36°08′E
Orem, Ut., U.S. (ō′rĕm)	119	40°15′N	111°50′W
Ore Mountains see Erzgebirge, mts., Eur.	156	50°29′N	12°40′E
Orenburg, Russia (ô′rĕn-bōōrg)	178	51°50′N	55°05′E
Øresund, strt., Eur.	166	55°50′N	12°40′E
Órganos, Sierra de los, mts., Cuba (sē-ĕ′r-rä-dĕ-lôs-ô′r-gä-nôs)	134	22°20′N	84°10′W
Organ Pipe Cactus National Monument, rec., Az., U.S. (ôr′gȧn pīp kăk′tŭs)	119	32°14′N	113°05′W
Orgãos, Serra das, mtn., Braz. (sĕ′r-rä-däs-ôr-goun′s)	141a	22°30′S	43°01′W
Orhei, Mol.	181	47°27′N	28°49′E
Orhon, r., Mong.	204	48°33′N	103°07′E
Oriental, Cordillera, mts., Col. (kôr-dēl-yĕ′rä)	142a	3°30′N	74°27′W
Oriental, Cordillera, mts., Dom. Rep. (kôr-dĕl-yĕ′rä ô-ryĕ′n-tāl)	135	18°55′N	69°40′W
Oriental, Cordillera, mts., S.A. (kôr-dēl-yĕ′rä ô-rê-ĕn-täl′)	142	14°00′S	68°33′W
Orikhiv, Ukr.	177	47°34′N	35°51′E

ng-sing; ŋ-baŋk; ɴ-nasalized n; nŏd; cŏmmit; ōld; ôbey; ôrder; oi-boil; fōōd; ò-as oo in foot; ou-out; s-soft; sh-dish; th-thin; pūre; ûnite; ûrn; stŭd; circŭs; ü-as in French tu; ′-indeterminate vowel.

PLACE (Pronunciation)	PAGE	LAT.	LONG.
Oril', r., Ukr.	177	49°08'N	34°55'E
Orillia, Can. (ô-rĭl'ĭ-á)	91	44°35'N	79°25'W
Orin, Wy., U.S.	115	42°40'N	105°10'W
Orinda, Ca., U.S.	116b	37°53'N	122°11'W
Orinoco, r., Ven. (ō-rĭ-nō'kō)	142	8°32'N	63°13'W
Oriola, Spain	173	38°04'N	0°55'W
Orion, Phil. (ō-rē-ōn')	213a	14°37'N	120°34'E
Orissa, state, India (ŏ-rĭs'á)	199	25°09'N	83°50'E
Oristano, Italy (ô-rês-tä'nō)	162	39°53'N	8°38'E
Oristano, Golfo di, b., Italy (gôl-fô-dē-ô-rês-tä'nō)	174	39°53'N	8°12'E
Orituco, r., Ven. (ô-rē-tōō'kō)	143b	9°37'N	66°25'W
Oriuco, r., Ven. (ô-rēōō'kō)	143b	9°36'N	66°25'W
Orivesi, l., Fin.	167	62°15'N	29°55'E
Orizaba, Mex. (ô-rē-zä'bä)	129	18°52'N	97°05'W
Orizaba, Pico de, vol., Mex.	128	19°04'N	97°14'W
Orkanger, Nor.	166	63°19'N	9°54'W
Orkla, r., Nor. (ôr'klå)	166	62°55'N	9°50'E
Orkney, S. Afr. (ôrk'nĭ)	238c	26°58'S	26°39'E
Orkney Islands, is., Scot., U.K.	156	59°01'N	2°08'W
Orlando, S. Afr. (ôr-lăn-dô)	233b	26°15'S	27°56'E
Orlando, Fl., U.S. (ôr-lăn'dō)	105	28°32'N	81°22'W
Orland Park, Il., U.S. (ôr-lăn')	111a	41°38'N	87°52'W
Orleans, Can. (ôr-lå-äN')	102c	45°28'N	75°31'W
Orléans, Fr. (ôr-lā-äN')	154	47°55'N	1°56'E
Orleans, In., U.S. (ôr-lēnz')	108	38°40'N	86°25'W
Orléans, Île d', i., Can.	99	46°56'N	70°57'W
Orly, Fr.	171b	48°45'N	2°24'E
Ormond Beach, Fl., U.S. (ôr'mŏnd)	125	29°15'N	81°05'W
Ormskirk, Eng., U.K. (ôrms'kĕrk)	158a	53°34'N	2°53'W
Ormstown, Can. (ôrms'toun)	102a	45°07'N	74°00'W
Orneta, Pol. (ôr-nyĕ'tä)	169	54°07'N	20°10'E
Örnsköldsvik, Swe. (ûrn'skôlts-vēk)	160	63°10'N	18°32'E
Oro, Río del, r., Mex. (rē'ō dĕl ō'rō)	130	18°04'N	100°59'W
Oro, Río del, r., Mex.	119	26°04'N	105°40'W
Orobie, Alpi, mts., Italy (äl'pē-ô-rō'byĕ)	174	46°05'N	9°47'E
Oron, Nig.	235	4°48'N	8°14'E
Orosei, Golfo di, b., Italy (gôl-fô-dē-ō-rô-sā'ē)	174	40°12'N	9°45'E
Orosháza, Hung. (ô-rôsh-hä'sô)	169	46°33'N	20°31'E
Orosi, vol., C.R. (ō-rō'sē)	132	11°00'N	85°30'W
Oroville, Ca., U.S. (ōr'ō-vĭl)	118	39°29'N	121°34'W
Oroville, Wa., U.S.	114	48°55'N	119°25'W
Oroville, Lake, res., Ca., U.S.	118	39°32'N	121°25'W
Orreagal, Spain	172	43°00'N	1°17'W
Orrville, Oh., U.S. (ôr'vĭl)	108	40°45'N	81°50'W
Orsa, Swe. (ōr'sä)	166	61°08'N	14°35'E
Orsha, Bela. (ôr'shå)	180	54°29'N	30°28'E
Orsk, Russia (ôrsk)	178	51°15'N	58°50'E
Orşova, Rom. (ôr'shō-vä)	175	44°43'N	22°26'E
Ortega, Col. (ôr-tĕ'gä)	142a	3°56'N	75°12'W
Ortegal, Cabo, c., Spain (ká'bô-ôr-tå-gäl')	162	43°46'N	8°15'W
Orth, Aus.	159e	48°09'N	16°42'E
Orthez, Fr. (ôr-tĕz')	171	43°29'N	0°43'W
Órthrys, Óros, mtn., Grc.	175	39°00'N	22°15'E
Ortigueira, Spain (ôr-tê-gä'ê-rä)	162	43°40'N	7°50'W
Orting, Wa., U.S. (ôrt'ĭng)	116a	47°06'N	122°12'W
Ortona, Italy (ôr-tō'nä)	174	42°22'N	14°22'E
Ortonville, Mn., U.S. (ôr-tŭn-vĭl)	112	45°18'N	96°26'W
Orūmīyeh, Iran	198	37°30'N	45°15'E
Orūmīyeh, Daryacheh-ye, l., Iran	198	38°01'N	45°17'E
Oruro, Bol. (ō-rōō'rō)	142	17°57'S	66°59'W
Orvieto, Italy (ôr-vyå'tō)	174	42°43'N	12°08'E
Osa, Russia (ô'sá)	180	57°18'N	55°25'E
Osa, Península de, pen., C.R. (ō'sä)	133	8°30'N	83°25'W
Osage, Ia., U.S. (ō'sāj)	113	43°16'N	92°49'W
Osage, r., Mo., U.S.	121	38°10'N	93°12'W
Osage City, Ks., U.S. (ō'sāj sĭ'tĭ)	121	38°28'N	95°53'W
Ōsaka, Japan (ō'sä-kä)	205	34°40'N	135°27'E
Ōsaka, dept., Japan	211b	34°45'N	135°36'E
Ōsaka-Wan, b., Japan (wän)	210	34°34'N	135°16'E
Osakis, Mn., U.S. (ô-sā'kĭs)	112	45°51'N	95°09'W
Osakis, l., Mn., U.S.	113	45°55'N	94°55'W
Osawatomie, Ks., U.S. (ŏs-á-wăt'ô-mê)	121	38°29'N	94°57'W
Osborne, Ks., U.S. (ŏz'bŭrn)	120	39°25'N	98°42'W
Osceola, Ar., U.S. (ŏs-ê-ō'là)	121	35°42'N	89°58'W
Osceola, Ia., U.S.	113	41°04'N	93°45'W
Osceola, Mo., U.S.	121	38°02'N	93°41'W
Osceola, Ne., U.S.	112	41°11'N	97°34'W
Oscoda, Mi., U.S. (ŏs-kō'dá)	108	44°25'N	83°20'W
Osëtr, r., Russia (ô'sĕt'r)	176	54°27'N	38°15'E
Osgood, In., U.S. (ŏz'gŏŏd)	108	39°10'N	85°20'W
Osgoode, Can.	102c	45°09'N	75°37'W
Osh, Kyrg. (ôsh)	183	40°33'N	72°48'E
Oshawa, Can. (ŏsh'á-wá)	91	43°50'N	78°50'W
Ōshima, i., Japan (ō'shē'mä)	211	34°47'N	139°35'E
Oshkosh, Ne., U.S. (ŏsh'kŏsh)	112	41°24'N	102°22'W
Oshkosh, Wi., U.S.	105	44°01'N	88°35'W
Oshogbo, Nig.	230	7°47'N	4°34'E
Osijek, Cro. (ôs'ĭ-yĕk)	163	45°33'N	18°48'E
Osinniki, Russia (ŭ-sē'nyĭ-kē)	184	53°37'N	87°21'E
Oskaloosa, Ia., U.S. (ŏs-ká-lōō'sá)	113	41°16'N	92°40'W
Oskarshamn, Swe. (ôs'kärs-häm'n)	166	57°16'N	16°24'E
Oskarström, Swe. (ôs'kärs-strûm)	166	56°48'N	12°55'E
Öskemen, Kaz.	183	49°58'N	82°38'E
Oskil, r., Eur.	181	51°00'N	37°41'E
Oslo, Nor. (ôs'lō)	154	59°56'N	10°41'E
Oslofjorden, b., Nor.	166	59°03'N	10°35'E
Osmaniye, Tur.	163	37°10'N	36°30'E
Osnabrück, Ger. (ôs-nä-brük')	168	52°16'N	8°05'E
Osorno, Chile (ô-sō'r-nō)	144	40°42'S	73°13'W
Osøyra, Nor.	166	60°24'N	5°22'E
Osprey Reef, rf., Austl. (ŏs'prå)	221	14°00'S	146°45'E
Ossa, Mount, mtn., Austl. (ŏsá)	221	41°45'S	146°05'E
Osseo, Mn., U.S. (ŏs'sĕ-ō)	117g	45°07'N	93°24'W
Ossining, N.Y., U.S. (ŏs'ĭ-nĭng)	110a	41°09'N	73°51'W
Ossipee, N.H., U.S. (ŏs'ĭ-pê)	100	43°42'N	71°08'W
Ossjøen, l., Nor. (ôs-syûĕn)	166	61°20'N	12°00'E
Ostashkov, Russia (ôs-täsh'kôf)	180	57°07'N	33°04'E
Oster, Ukr. (ōs'tĕr)	177	50°55'N	30°52'E
Osterdalälven, r., Swe.	160	61°40'N	13°00'E
Østerfjord, b., Nor. (ûs'tĕr fyôr')	166	60°40'N	5°25'E
Östersund, Swe. (ûs'tĕr-sōōnd)	160	63°09'N	14°49'E
Östhammar, Swe. (ûst'häm'är)	166	60°16'N	18°21'E
Ostrava, Czech Rep.	154	49°51'N	18°18'E
Ostróda, Pol. (ôs'trŏt-å)	169	53°41'N	19°58'E
Ostrogozhsk, Russia (ôs-tr-gôzhk')	181	50°53'N	39°03'E
Ostroh, Ukr.	181	50°21'N	26°40'E
Ostrołęka, Pol. (ôs-trô-woN'kå)	169	53°04'N	21°35'E
Ostrov, Russia (ôs-trôf')	180	57°21'N	28°22'E
Ostrowiec Świętokrzyski, Pol. (ôs-trō'vyĕts shvyĕN-tō-kzhĭ'ske)	161	50°55'N	21°24'E
Ostrów Lubelski, Pol. (ôs'trŏf lōō'bĕl-skĭ)	169	51°32'N	22°49'E
Ostrów Mazowiecka, Pol. (mä-zô-vyĕt'skä)	161	52°47'N	21°54'E
Ostrów Wielkopolski, Pol. (ōs'trōōf vyĕl-kō-pōl'skē)	161	51°38'N	17°49'E
Ostrzeszów, Pol. (ôs-tzhä'shôf)	169	51°26'N	17°56'E
Ostuni, Italy (ôs-tōō'nē)	175	40°44'N	17°35'E
Osum, r., Alb. (ō'sōm)	175	40°37'N	20°00'E
Osuna, Spain (ô-sōō'nä)	172	37°18'N	5°05'W
Osveya, Bela. (ôs'vĕ-yå)	176	56°00'N	28°08'E
Oswaldtwistle, Eng., U.K. (ŏz-wáld-twĭs''l)	158a	53°44'N	2°23'W
Oswegatchie, r., N.Y., U.S. (ŏs-wê-găch'ĭ)	109	44°15'N	75°20'W
Oswego, Ks., U.S. (ŏs-wē'gō)	121	37°10'N	95°08'W
Oswego, N.Y., U.S.	105	43°25'N	76°30'W
Oświęcim, Pol. (ôsh-vyăN'tsyĭm)	169	50°02'N	19°17'E
Otaru, Japan (ô'tá-rŏ)	205	43°07'N	141°00'E
Otavalo, Ec. (ōta-vä'lō)	142	0°14'N	78°16'W
Otavi, Nmb. (ô-tä'vê)	232	19°35'S	17°20'E
Otay, Ca., U.S. (ō'tā)	118a	32°36'N	117°04'W
Otepää, Est.	167	58°03'N	26°30'E
Oti, r., Afr.	234	9°00'N	0°10'E
Otish, Monts, mts., Can. (ô-tĭsh')	93	52°15'N	70°20'W
Otjiwarongo, Nmb. (ŏt-jê-wà-rôn'gō)	232	20°20'S	16°25'E
Otočac, Cro. (ō'tô-chàts)	174	44°53'N	15°15'E
Otra, r., Nor.	166	59°13'N	7°20'E
Otra, r., Russia (ôt'rá)	186b	55°22'N	38°20'E
Otradnoye, Russia (ô-trä'd-nôyĕ)	186c	59°46'N	30°50'E
Otranto, Italy (ô'trän-tô) (ô-trän'tō)	175	40°07'N	18°30'E
Otranto, Strait of, strt., Eur.	156	40°30'N	18°45'E
Otsego, Mi., U.S. (ŏt-sē'gō)	108	42°25'N	85°45'W
Otsu, Japan (ō'tsŏ)	210	35°00'N	135°54'E
Otta, l., Nor. (ôt'tå)	166	61°53'N	8°40'E
Ottawa, Can. (ŏt'á-wá)	91	45°25'N	75°43'W
Ottawa, Il., U.S.	108	41°20'N	88°50'W
Ottawa, Ks., U.S.	121	38°37'N	95°16'W
Ottawa, Oh., U.S.	108	41°00'N	84°00'W
Ottawa, r., Can.	93	46°05'N	77°20'W
Otter Creek, r., Ut., U.S. (ŏt'ĕr)	119	38°20'N	111°55'W
Otter Creek, r., Vt., U.S.	109	44°05'N	73°15'W
Otter Point, c., Can.	116a	48°21'N	123°50'W
Otter Tail, l., Mn., U.S.	112	46°21'N	95°52'W
Otterville, Il., U.S. (ŏt'ĕr-vĭl)	117e	39°03'N	90°24'W
Ottery, S. Afr. (ŏt'ĕr-ĭ)	232a	34°02'S	18°31'E
Ottumwa, Ia., U.S. (ô-tŭm'wá)	105	41°00'N	92°26'W
Otukpa, Nig.	235	7°09'N	7°41'E
Otumba, Mex. (ô-tŭm'bä)	130	19°41'N	98°46'W
Otway, Cape, c., Austl. (ŏt'wā)	221	38°55'S	153°40'E
Otway, Seno, b., Chile (sĕ'nō-ō't-wā'y)	144	53°00'S	73°00'W
Otwock, Pol. (ôt'vôtsk)	169	52°05'N	21°18'E
Ouachita, r., U.S.	107	33°25'N	92°30'W
Ouachita Mountains, mts., U.S. (wŏsh'ĭ-tô)	107	34°29'N	95°01'W
Ouagadougou, Burkina (wä'gá-dōō'gōō)	230	12°22'N	1°31'W
Ouahigouya, Burkina (wä-ê-gōō'yä)	230	13°35'N	2°25'W
Oualâta, Maur. (wä-lä'tä)	230	17°11'N	6°50'W
Ouallene, Alg. (wäl-lân')	230	24°43'N	1°15'E
Ouanaminthe, Haiti	135	19°35'N	71°45'W
Ouarane, reg., Maur.	230	20°44'N	10°27'W
Ouarkoye, Burkina	234	12°05'N	3°40'W
Ouassel, r., Alg.	173	35°30'N	1°55'E
Oubangui (Ubangi), r., Afr. (ōō-bäN'gê)	236	4°30'N	20°35'E
Oude Rijn, r., Neth.	159a	52°09'N	4°33'E
Oudewater, Neth.	159a	52°01'N	4°52'E
Oud-Gastel, Neth.	159a	51°35'N	4°27'E
Oudtshoorn, S. Afr. (outs'hōrn)	232	33°33'S	23°36'E
Oued Rhiou, Alg.	173	35°55'N	0°57'E
Oued Tlelat, Alg.	173	35°33'N	0°28'W
Oued-Zem, Mor. (wĕd-zĕm')	230	33°05'N	5°49'W
Ouessant, Island d', i., Fr. (ēl-dwĕ-säN')	161	48°28'N	5°00'W
Ouesso, Congo	231	1°37'N	16°04'E
Ouest, Point, c., Haiti	135	19°00'N	73°25'W
Ouezzane, Mor. (wĕ-zan')	230	34°48'N	5°40'W
Ouham, r., Afr.	235	8°30'N	17°50'E
Ouidah, Benin (wē-dä')	230	6°25'N	2°05'E
Oujda, Mor.	230	34°41'N	1°45'W
Oulins, Fr. (ōō-läN')	171b	48°52'N	1°27'E
Oullins, Fr. (ōō-lăN')	170	45°44'N	4°46'E
Oulu, Fin. (ō'lō)	154	64°58'N	25°43'E
Oulujärvi, l., Fin.	160	64°20'N	25°48'E
Oum Chalouba, Chad (ōōm shä-lōō'bä)	231	15°48'N	20°30'E
Oum Hadjer, Chad	235	13°18'N	19°41'E
Ounas, r., Fin. (ō'nås)	160	67°46'N	24°40'E
Oundle, Eng., U.K. (ōn'd'l)	158a	52°28'N	0°28'W
Ounianga Kébir, Chad (ōō-nê-äŋ'gá kē-bēr')	231	19°04'N	20°22'E
Ouray, Co., U.S. (ōō-rā')	120	38°00'N	107°40'W
Ourense, Spain	172	42°20'N	7°52'W
Ourinhos, Braz. (ôò-rē'nyôs)	143	23°04'S	49°45'W
Ourique, Port. (ō-rē'kĕ)	172	37°39'N	8°10'W
Ouro Fino, Braz. (ōŭ-rô-fē'nō)	141a	22°18'S	46°21'W
Ouro Prêto, Braz. (ō'rò prä'tò)	144	20°24'S	43°30'W
Outardes, Rivière aux, r., Can.	93	50°53'N	68°50'W
Outer, i., Wi., U.S. (out'ĕr)	113	47°03'N	90°20'W
Outer Brass, i., V.I.U.S. (bräs)	129c	18°24'N	64°58'W
Outer Hebrides, is., Scot., U.K.	164	57°20'N	7°50'W
Outjo, Nmb. (ōt'yō)	232	20°05'S	17°10'E
Outlook, Can.	96	51°31'N	107°05'W
Outremont, Can. (ōō-trĕ-môN')	102a	45°31'N	73°36'W
Ouvéa, i., N. Cal.	221	20°43'S	166°48'E
Ouyen, Austl. (ōō-ĕn)	222	35°05'S	142°10'E
Ovalle, Chile (ō-väl'yā)	144	30°43'S	71°16'W
Ovando, Bahía de, b., Cuba (bä-ē'ä-dĕ-ō-vä'n-dō)	135	20°10'N	74°05'W
Ovar, Port. (ô-vär')	172	40°52'N	8°38'W
Overijse, Bel.	159a	50°46'N	4°32'E
Overland, Mo., U.S. (ō-vĕr-lănd)	117e	38°42'N	90°22'W
Overland Park, Ks., U.S.	117f	38°59'N	94°40'W
Overlea, Md., U.S. (ō'vĕr-lā)(ō'vĕr-lē)	110e	39°21'N	76°31'W
Övertornea, Swe.	160	66°19'N	23°31'E
Ovidiopol', Ukr.	177	46°15'N	30°28'E
Oviedo, Dom. Rep. (ō-vyĕ'dō)	135	17°50'N	71°25'W
Oviedo, Spain (ō-vê-ā'dhō)	154	43°22'N	5°50'W
Ovruch, Ukr.	177	51°19'N	28°51'E
Owada, Japan (ō'wä-dá)	211a	35°49'N	139°33'E
Owambo, hist. reg., Nmb.	232	18°10'S	15°00'E
Owando, Congo	232	0°29'S	15°55'E
Owasco, l., N.Y., U.S. (ō-wăsk'kō)	109	42°50'N	76°30'W
Owase, Japan (ō'wä-shê)	211	34°03'N	136°12'E
Owego, N.Y., U.S. (ō-wē'gō)	109	42°05'N	76°15'W
Owen, Wi., U.S. (ō'ĕn)	113	44°56'N	90°35'W
Owensboro, Ky., U.S. (ō'ĕnz-bŭr-ô)	105	37°45'N	87°05'W
Owens Lake, l., Ca., U.S.	118	37°13'N	118°20'W
Owen Sound, Can. (ō'ĕn)	91	44°30'N	80°55'W
Owen Stanley Range, mts., Pap. N. Gui. (stăn'lē)	213	9°00'S	147°30'E
Owensville, In., U.S. (ō'ĕnz-vĭl)	108	38°15'N	87°40'W
Owensville, Mo., U.S.	121	38°20'N	91°29'W
Owensville, Oh., U.S.	111f	39°08'N	84°07'W
Owenton, Ky., U.S. (ō'ĕn-tŭn)	108	38°35'N	84°55'W
Owerri, Nig. (ô-wĕr'ê)	230	5°26'N	7°04'E
Owings Mill, Md., U.S. (ōwĭngz mĭl)	110e	39°25'N	76°50'W
Owl Creek, r., Wy., U.S. (oul)	115	43°45'N	108°46'W
Owo, Nig.	235	7°15'N	5°37'E
Owosso, Mi., U.S. (ô-wŏs'ō)	108	43°00'N	84°15'W
Owyhee, r., U.S.	106	43°04'N	117°45'W
Owyhee, Lake, res., Or., U.S.	106	43°27'N	117°30'W
Owyhee, South Fork, r., Id., U.S.	114	42°07'N	116°43'W
Owyhee Mountains, mts., Id., U.S. (ô-wī'hê)	106	43°15'N	116°48'W
Oxbow, Can.	97	49°12'N	102°11'W
Oxchuc, Mex. (ôs-chōōk')	131	16°47'N	92°24'W
Oxford, Can. (ŏks'fērd)	100	45°44'N	63°52'W
Oxford, Eng., U.K.	161	51°43'N	1°16'W
Oxford, Al., U.S. (ŏks'fērd)	125	33°38'N	80°46'W
Oxford, Ma., U.S.	101a	42°07'N	71°52'W
Oxford, Mi., U.S.	108	42°50'N	83°15'W
Oxford, Ms., U.S.	124	34°22'N	89°30'W
Oxford, N.C., U.S.	125	36°17'N	78°35'W
Oxford, Oh., U.S.	108	39°30'N	84°45'W
Oxford Lake, l., Can.	97	54°51'N	95°37'W
Oxfordshire, co., Eng., U.K.	158b	51°36'N	1°30'W
Oxkutzcab, Mex. (ôx-kōō'tz-käb)	132a	20°18'N	89°22'W
Oxmoor, Al., U.S. (ŏks'mŏr)	110h	33°25'N	86°52'W
Oxnard, Ca., U.S. (ŏks'närd)	118	34°08'N	119°12'W
Oxon Hill, Md., U.S. (ŏks'ŏn hĭl)	110e	38°48'N	77°00'W
Oyapock, r., S.A. (ō-yá-pŏk')	143	2°45'N	52°15'W
Oyem, Gabon	230	1°37'N	11°35'E
Øyeren, l., Nor. (ûĭĕrĕn)	166	59°50'N	11°25'E
Oymyakon, Russia (oi-myŭ-kôn')	179	63°14'N	142°58'E
Oyo, Nig. (ō'yō)	230	7°51'N	3°56'E
Oyonnax, Fr. (ô-yô-näks')	171	46°16'N	5°40'E
Oyster Bay, N.Y., U.S.	110a	40°52'N	73°32'W
Oyster Bayou, Tx., U.S.	123a	29°41'N	94°33'W
Oyster Creek, r., Tx., U.S. (ois'tēr)	123a	29°13'N	95°29'W
Oyyl, r., Kaz.	181	49°30'N	55°10'E
Ozama, r., Dom. Rep. (ô-zä'mä)	135	18°45'N	69°55'W
Ozamiz, Phil. (ô-zä'mēz)	213	8°06'N	123°43'E
Ozark, Al., U.S. (ō'zärk)	124	31°28'N	85°28'W
Ozark, Ar., U.S.	121	35°29'N	93°49'W
Ozark Plateau, plat., U.S.	107	36°37'N	93°56'W
Ozarks, Lake of the, l., Mo., U.S. (ō'zärksz)	107	38°06'N	93°26'W
Ozëry, Russia (ô-zyô'rĕ)	176	54°53'N	38°31'E
Ozieri, Italy	162	40°38'N	8°53'E
Ozorków, Pol. (ô-zôr'kôf)	169	51°58'N	19°20'E
Ozuluama, Mex.	131	21°34'N	97°52'W
Ozumba, Mex.	131a	19°02'N	98°48'W
Ozurgeti, Geor.	182	41°56'N	42°00'E

ăt; finăl; rāte; senâte; ärm; åsk; sofá; fâre; ch-choose; dh-as th in other; bē; êvent; bĕt; recĕnt; cratĕr; g-gō; gh-guttural g; bĭt; ĭ-short neutral; rīde; K-guttural k as ch in German ich;

PRONOUNCING INDEX

Paarl – Paris 333

P

PLACE (Pronunciation)	PAGE	LAT.	LONG.
Paarl, S. Afr. (pärl)	232	33°45'S	18°55'E
Pa'auilo, Hi., U.S. (pä-ä-o͞o'ē-lō)	126a	20°03'N	155°25'W
Pabianice, Pol. (pä-byå-nē'tsĕ)	169	51°40'N	19°29'E
Pacaás Novos, Massiço de, mts., Braz.	142	11°03'S	64°02'W
Pacaraima, Serra, mts., S.A. (sĕr'rá pä-kä-rä-ē'mä)	142	3°45'N	62°30'W
Pacasmayo, Peru (pä-käs-mä'yō)	142	7°24'S	79°30'W
Pachuca, Mex. (pä-cho͞o'kä)	128	20°07'N	98°43'W
Pacific, Wa., U.S. (pȧ-sĭf'ĭk)	116a	47°16'N	122°15'W
Pacifica, Ca., U.S. (pȧ-sĭf'ĭ-kä)	116b	37°38'N	122°29'W
Pacific Beach, Ca., U.S.	118a	32°47'N	117°22'W
Pacific Grove, Ca., U.S.	118	36°37'N	121°54'W
Pacific Islands, Trust Territory of the *see* Palau, nation, Oc.	3	7°15'N	134°30'E
Pacific Ocean, o.	2	0°00'	170°00'W
Pacific Ranges, mts., Can.	94	51°00'N	125°30'W
Pacific Rim National Park, rec., Can.	94	49°00'N	126°00'W
Pacolet, r., S.C., U.S. (pă'cō-lĕt)	125	34°55'N	81°49'W
Pacy-sur-Eure, Fr. (pä-sē-sür-ûr')	171b	49°01'N	1°24'E
Padang, Indon. (pä-däng')	212	1°01'S	100°28'E
Padang, i., Indon.	197b	1°12'N	102°21'E
Padang Endau, Malay.	197b	2°39'N	103°38'E
Paden City, W.V., U.S. (pā'dĕn)	108	39°30'N	80°55'W
Paderborn, Ger. (pä-dĕr-bôrn')	168	51°43'N	8°46'E
Padibe, Ug.	237	3°28'N	32°50'E
Padiham, Eng., U.K. (păd'ĭ-hăm)	158a	53°48'N	2°19'W
Padilla, Mex. (pä-dēl'yä)	130	24°00'N	98°45'W
Padilla Bay, b., Wa., U.S. (pä-dĭl'lȧ)	116a	48°31'N	122°34'W
Padova, Italy (pä'dō-vä)(păd'û-ȧ)	162	45°24'N	11°53'E
Padre Island, i., Tx., U.S. (pä'drā)	123	27°09'N	97°15'W
Padua *see* Padova, Italy	162	45°24'N	11°53'E
Paducah, Ky., U.S.	105	37°05'N	88°36'W
Paducah, Tx., U.S.	120	34°01'N	100°18'W
Paektu-san, mtn., Asia (pâk'to͞o-sän')	210	42°00'N	128°03'E
Pag, i., Serb. (päg)	174	44°30'N	14°48'E
Pagai Selatan, Pulau, i., Indon.	212	2°48'S	100°22'E
Pagai Utara, Pulau, i., Indon.	212	2°45'S	100°02'E
Pagasitikós Kólpos, b., Grc.	175	39°15'N	23°00'E
Page, Az., U.S.	119	36°57'N	111°27'W
Pago Pago, Am. Sam.	214a	14°16'S	170°42'W
Pagosa Springs, Co., U.S. (pȧ-gō'sȧ)	120	37°15'N	107°05'W
Pāhala, Hi., U.S. (pä-hä'lä)	126a	19°11'N	155°28'W
Pahang, state, Malay.	197b	3°02'N	102°57'E
Pahang, r., Malay.	212	3°39'N	102°41'E
Pahokee, Fl., U.S. (pȧ-hō'kē)	125a	26°45'N	80°40'W
Paide, Est. (pī'dĕ)	167	58°54'N	25°30'E
Päijänne, l., Fin. (pĕ'ē-yĕn-nĕ)	160	61°38'N	25°05'E
Pailolo Channel, strt., Hi., U.S. (pä-ē-lō'lō)	126a	21°05'N	156°41'W
Paine, Chile (pī'nĕ)	141b	33°49'S	70°44'W
Painesville, Oh., U.S. (pānz'vĭl)	108	41°40'N	81°15'W
Painted Desert, des., Az., U.S. (pānt'ĕd)	120	36°15'N	111°35'W
Painted Rock Reservoir, res., Az., U.S.	119	33°00'N	113°05'W
Paintsville, Ky., U.S. (pānts'vĭl)	108	37°50'N	82°50'W
Paisley, Scot., U.K. (pāz'lĭ)	160	55°50'N	4°30'W
Paita, Peru (pä-ē'tä)	142	5°11'S	81°12'W
Pai T'ou Shan, mts., Kor., N.	205	40°30'N	127°20'E
Paiute Indian Reservation, I.R., Ut., U.S.	119	38°17'N	113°50'W
Pajápan, Mex. (pä-hä'pän)	131	18°16'N	94°41'W
Pakanbaru, Indon.	212	0°43'N	101°15'E
Pakhra, r., Russia (päk'rá)	186b	55°29'N	37°51'E
Pakistan, nation, Asia	199	28°00'N	67°30'E
Pakokku, Mya. (pä-kŏk'kō)	204	21°29'N	95°00'E
Paks, Hung. (pôksh)	169	46°38'N	18°53'E
Pala, Chad	235	9°22'N	14°54'E
Palacios, Tx., U.S. (pä-lä'syōs)	123	28°42'N	96°12'W
Palagruža, Otoci, is., Cro.	174	42°20'N	16°23'E
Palaiseau, Fr. (pȧ-lĕ-zō')	171b	48°44'N	2°16'E
Palana, Russia	179	59°07'N	159°58'E
Palanan Bay, b., Phil. (pä-lä'nän)	213a	17°14'N	122°35'E
Palanan Point, c., Phil.	213a	17°12'N	122°40'E
Pālanpur, India (pä'lŭn-po͞or)	199	24°08'N	73°29'E
Palapye, Bots. (pȧ-läp'yĕ)	232	22°34'S	27°28'E
Palatine, Il., U.S. (păl'ȧ-tīn)	111a	42°07'N	88°03'W
Palatka, Fl., U.S. (pȧ-lăt'kȧ)	125	29°39'N	81°40'W
Palau (Belau), nation, Oc. (pä-lä'ō)	3	7°15'N	134°30'E
Palauig, Phil. (pȧ-lou'ēg)	213a	15°27'N	119°54'E
Palawan, i., Phil. (pä-lä'wȧn)	212	9°50'N	117°38'E
Pālayankottai, India	203	8°50'N	77°50'E
Paldiski, Est. (päl'dĭ-skĭ)	167	59°22'N	24°04'E
Palembang, Indon. (pä-lĕm-bäng')	212	2°57'S	104°40'E
Palencia, Guat. (pä-lĕn'sē-ȧ)	132	14°40'N	90°22'W
Palencia, Spain (pä-lĕ'n-syä)	162	42°02'N	4°32'W
Palenque, Mex. (pä-lĕŋ'kā)	131	17°34'N	91°58'W
Palenque, Punta, c., Dom. Rep. (po͞o'n-tä)	135	18°10'N	70°10'W
Palermo, Col. (pä-lĕr'mō)	142a	2°53'N	75°26'W
Palermo, Italy	154	38°08'N	13°24'E
Palestine, Tx., U.S.	105	31°46'N	95°38'W
Palestine, hist. reg., Asia (păl'ĕs-tīn)	197a	31°33'N	35°00'E
Paletwa, Mya. (pŭ-lĕt'wä)	199	21°19'N	92°52'E
Palghāt, India	203	10°49'N	76°40'E
Pāli, India	202	25°53'N	73°18'E
Palín, Guat. (pä-lēn')	132	14°42'N	90°42'W
Palizada, Mex. (pä-lē-zä'dä)	131	18°17'N	92°04'W
Palk Strait, strt., Asia (pôk)	199	10°00'N	79°23'E
Palma, Braz. (päl'mä)	141a	21°23'S	42°18'W
Palma, Spain	154	39°35'N	2°38'E
Palma, Bahía de, b., Spain	173	39°24'N	2°37'E
Palma del Río, Spain	172	37°43'N	5°19'W
Palmares, Braz. (päl-má'rĕs)	143	8°46'S	35°28'W
Palmas, Braz. (päl'mäs)	144	26°20'S	51°56'W
Palmas, Braz.	143	10°08'S	48°18'W
Palmas, Cape, c., Lib.	230	4°22'N	7°44'W
Palma Soriano, Cuba (sō-rē-ä'nō)	134	20°15'N	76°00'W
Palm Beach, Fl., U.S. (päm bēch')	125a	26°43'N	80°03'W
Palmeira dos Índios, Braz. (pä-mā'rä-dōs-ē'n-dyōs)	143	9°26'S	36°33'W
Palmeirinhas, Ponta das, c., Ang.	236	9°05'S	13°00'E
Palmela, Port. (päl-mā'lä)	172	38°34'N	8°54'W
Palmer, Ak., U.S. (päm'ẽr)	103	61°38'N	149°15'W
Palmer, Wa., U.S.	116a	47°19'N	121°53'W
Palmerston North, N.Z. (päm'ẽr-stŭn)	221a	40°20'S	175°35'E
Palmerville, Austl. (päm'ẽr-vĭl)	219	16°08'S	144°15'E
Palmetto, Fl., U.S. (pȧl-mĕt'ō)	125a	27°32'N	82°34'W
Palmetto Point, c., Bah.	135	21°15'N	73°25'W
Palmi, Italy (päl'mē)	174	38°21'N	15°54'E
Palmira, Col. (päl-mē'rä)	142	3°33'N	76°17'W
Palmira, Cuba	134	22°15'N	80°25'W
Palmyra, Mo., U.S. (păl-mī'rȧ)	121	39°45'N	91°32'W
Palmyra, N.J., U.S.	110f	40°01'N	75°00'W
Palmyra, i., Oc.	2	6°00'N	162°20'W
Palmyra, hist., Syria	198	34°25'N	38°28'E
Palmyras Point, c., India	202	20°42'N	87°45'E
Palo Alto, Ca., U.S. (pä'lō äl'tō)	116b	37°27'N	122°09'W
Paloduro Creek, r., Tx., U.S. (pā-lō-do͞o'rō)	120	36°16'N	101°12'W
Paloh, Malay.	197b	2°11'N	103°12'E
Paloma, I., Mex. (pä-lō'mä)	122	26°53'N	104°02'W
Palomo, Cerro el, mtn., Chile (sĕ'r-rō-ĕl-pä-lō'mō)	141b	34°36'S	70°20'W
Palos, Cabo de, c., Spain (kȧ'bō-dĕ-pä'lōs)	162	39°38'N	0°43'W
Palos Verdes Estates, Ca., U.S. (pă'lŭs vûr'dĭs)	117a	33°48'N	118°24'W
Palouse, Wa., U.S. (pȧ-lo͞oz')	114	46°54'N	117°04'W
Palouse, r., Wa., U.S.	114	47°02'N	117°35'W
Palu, Tur. (pä-loo')	181	38°55'N	40°10'E
Paluan, Phil. (pä-lo͞o'än)	213a	13°25'N	120°29'E
Pamiers, Fr. (pȧ-myā')	161	43°07'N	1°34'E
Pamirs, mts., Asia	199	38°14'N	72°27'E
Pamlico, r., N.C., U.S. (păm'lĭ-kō)	125	35°25'N	76°59'W
Pamlico Sound, strt., N.C., U.S.	107	35°10'N	76°10'W
Pampa, Tx., U.S. (păm'pȧ)	104	35°32'N	100°56'W
Pampa de Castillo, pl., Arg. (pä'm-pä-dĕ-käs-tē'l-yō)	144	45°30'S	67°30'W
Pampana, r., S.L.	234	8°35'N	11°55'W
Pampanga, r., Phil. (päm-päŋ'gä)	213a	15°20'N	120°48'E
Pampas, reg., Arg. (päm'päs)	144	37°00'S	64°30'W
Pampilhosa do Botão, Port. (päm-pē-lyō'sȧ-dō-bō-touN')	172	40°21'N	8°32'W
Pamplona, Col. (päm-plō'nä)	142	7°19'N	72°41'W
Pamplona, Spain (päm-plō'nä)	162	42°49'N	1°39'W
Pamunkey, r., Va., U.S. (pȧ-mŭŋ'kĭ)	109	37°40'N	77°20'W
Pana, Il., U.S. (pā'nȧ)	108	39°25'N	89°05'W
Panagyurishte, Blg. (pȧ-nȧ-gyo͞o'rĕsh-tĕ)	175	42°30'N	24°11'E
Panaji (Panjim), India	199	15°33'N	73°52'E
Panamá, Pan.	129	8°58'N	79°32'W
Panama, nation, N.A.	129	9°00'N	80°00'W
Panamá, Istmo de, isth., Pan.	129	9°00'N	80°00'W
Panama Canal, can., Pan.	128a	9°20'N	79°55'W
Panama City, Fl., U.S. (păn-ȧ mä' sĭ'tĭ)	124	30°08'N	85°39'W
Panamint Range, mts., Ca., U.S. (păn-ȧ-mĭnt')	118	36°40'N	117°30'W
Panarea, i., Italy (pä-nä'rē-a)	174	38°37'N	15°05'E
Panaro, r., Italy (pä-nä'rō)	174	44°47'N	11°06'E
Panay, i., Phil. (pä-nī')	212	11°15'N	121°38'E
Pančevo, Serb. (pȧn'chĕ-vō)	163	44°52'N	20°42'E
Panchor, Malay.	197b	2°11'N	102°43'E
Pānchur, India	202a	22°31'N	88°17'E
Panda, D.R.C. (pän'dä')	232	10°59'S	27°24'E
Pan de Guajaibon, mtn., Cuba (pän dā gwä-jȧ-bōn')	134	22°50'N	83°20'W
Panevėžys, Lith. (pä'nyĕ-vāzh'ēs)	180	55°44'N	24°21'E
Panga, D.R.C. (päŋ'gä)	231	1°51'N	26°25'E
Pangani, Tan. (pän-gä'nē)	233	5°28'S	38°58'E
Pangani, r., Tan.	237	4°40'S	37°45'E
Pangkalpinang, Indon. (päng-käl'pē-näng')	212	2°11'S	106°04'E
Pangnirtung, Can.	91	66°08'N	65°26'W
Panguitch, Ut., U.S. (pän'gwĭch)	119	37°50'N	112°30'W
Panié, Mont, mtn., N. Cal.	214f	20°36'S	164°46'E
Pānihāti, India	202a	22°42'N	88°23'E
Panimávida, Chile (pä-nē-má'vē-dä)	141b	35°44'S	71°26'W
Panshi, China (pän-shē)	208	42°50'N	126°48'E
Pantar, Pulau, i., Indon. (pän'tär)	213	8°40'N	123°45'E
Pantelleria, i., Italy (pän-tĕl-lȧ-rē'ä)	162	36°43'N	11°59'E
Pantepec, Mex. (pän-tå-pĕk')	131	17°11'N	93°04'W
Panuco, Mex. (pä'no͞o-kō)	130	22°04'N	98°11'W
Pánuco, Mex. (pä'no͞o-kō)	130	23°25'N	105°55'W
Panuco, r., Mex.	128	21°59'N	98°20'W
Pánuco de Coronado, Mex. (pä'no͞o-kō dā kō-rō-nä'dhō)	122	24°33'N	104°20'W
Panvel, India	203b	18°59'N	73°06'E
Panyu, China (pä-yo͞o)	207a	22°56'N	113°22'E
Panzós, Guat. (pä-zós')	132	15°26'N	89°40'W
Pao, r., Ven. (pá'ō)	143b	9°52'N	67°57'W
Paola, Ks., U.S. (pȧ-ō'lȧ)	121	38°34'N	94°51'W
Paoli, In., U.S. (pȧ-ō'lī)	108	38°35'N	86°30'W
Paoli, Pa., U.S.	110f	40°03'N	75°29'W
Paonia, Co., U.S. (pā-ō'nyȧ)	119	38°50'N	107°40'W
Pápa, Hung. (pä'pō)	163	47°18'N	17°27'E
Papagayo, r., Mex. (pä-pä-gä'yō)	130	16°52'N	99°41'W
Papagayo, Golfo del, b., C.R. (gôl-fô-dĕl-pä-pä-gá'yō)	132	10°44'N	85°56'W
Papagayo, Laguna, l., Mex. (lä-ò-nä)	130	16°44'N	99°44'W
Papantla de Olarte, Mex. (pä-pän'tlä dā-ō-lä'r-tĕ)	128	20°30'N	97°15'W
Papatoapan, r., Mex. (pä-pä-tô-ä-pá'n)	131	18°00'N	96°22'W
Papenburg, Ger. (päp'ĕn-bŏrgh)	168	53°05'N	7°23'E
Papinas, Arg. (pä-pē'näs)	141c	35°30'S	57°19'W
Papineauville, Can. (pä-pē-nō'vēl)	102c	45°38'N	75°01'W
Papua, Gulf of, b., Pap. N. Gui. (păp-o͞o-ȧ)	213	8°20'S	144°45'E
Papua New Guinea, nation, Oc. (păp-o͞o-ȧ)(gĭne)	213	7°00'S	142°15'E
Papudo, Chile (pä-po͞o'dō)	141b	32°30'S	71°25'W
Paquequer Pequeno, Braz. (pä-kĕ-kĕ'r-pĕ-kĕ'nō)	144b	22°19'S	43°02'W
Para, r., Russia	176	53°45'N	40°58'E
Paracale, Phil. (pä-rä-kä'lå)	213a	14°17'N	122°47'E
Paracambi, Braz.	144b	22°36'S	43°43'W
Paracatu, Braz. (pä-rä-kä-to͞o')	143	17°17'S	46°43'W
Paracel Islands, is., Asia	212	16°40'N	113°00'E
Paraćin, Serb. (pá'rä-chēn)	163	43°51'N	21°26'E
Para de Minas, Braz. (pä-rä-dĕ-mē'näs)	143	19°52'S	44°37'W
Paradise, i., Bah.	134	25°05'N	77°20'W
Paradise Valley, Nv., U.S. (păr'ȧ-dīs)	114	41°28'N	117°32'W
Parados, Cerro de los, mtn., Col. (sĕ'r-rō-dĕ-lōs-pä-rä'dōs)	142a	5°44'N	75°13'W
Paragould, Ar., U.S. (păr'ȧ-go͞old)	121	36°03'N	90°29'W
Paraguaçu, r., Braz. (pä-rä-gwä-zo͞o')	143	12°25'S	39°46'W
Paraguay, nation, S.A. (păr'ȧ-gwā)	144	24°00'S	57°00'W
Paraguay, r., S.A. (pä-rä-gwä'y)	144	21°12'S	57°31'W
Paraíba, state, Braz. (pä-rä-ē'bä)	143	7°11'S	37°05'W
Paraíba, r., Braz.	141a	23°02'S	45°43'W
Paraíba do Sul, Braz. (dō-so͞o'l)	141a	22°10'S	43°18'W
Paraibuna, Braz. (pä-räē-bo͞o'nä)	141a	23°23'S	45°38'W
Paraíso, C.R.	133	9°50'N	83°53'W
Paraíso, Mex.	131	18°24'N	93°11'W
Paraiso, Pan. (pä-rä-ē'sō)	128a	9°02'N	79°38'W
Paraisópolis, Braz. (pä-räē-sō'pō-lēs)	141a	22°35'S	45°45'W
Paraitinga, r., Braz. (pä-rä-ē-tē'n-gä)	141a	23°15'S	45°24'W
Parakou, Benin (pȧ-rȧ-ko͞o')	230	9°21'N	2°37'E
Paramaribo, Sur. (pȧ-rȧ-má'rē-bō)	143	5°50'N	55°15'W
Paramatta, Austl. (păr-ȧ-măt'ȧ)	217b	33°49'S	150°59'E
Paramillo, mtn., Col. (pä-rä-mē'l-yō)	142a	7°06'N	75°55'W
Paramus, N.J., U.S.	110a	40°56'N	74°04'W
Paran, r., Asia	197a	30°05'N	34°50'E
Paraná, Arg.	144	31°44'S	60°32'W
Paraná, r., S.A.	144	24°00'S	54°00'W
Paranaíba, Braz. (pä-rä-nȧ-ē'bȧ)	143	19°43'S	51°13'W
Paranaíba, r., Braz.	143	18°58'S	50°44'W
Paraná Ibicuy, r., Arg.	141c	33°27'S	59°26'W
Paranam, Sur.	143	5°39'N	55°13'W
Paranápanema, r., Braz. (pä-rä'ná'pä-nĕ-mä)	143	22°28'S	52°15'W
Paraopeda, r., Braz. (pä-rä-o-pĕ'dä)	141a	20°09'S	44°14'W
Parapara, Ven. (pä-rä-pä-rä)	143b	9°44'N	67°17'W
Parati, Braz. (pä-rätē)	141a	23°14'S	44°43'W
Paray-le-Monial, Fr. (pȧ-rĕ'lē-mô-nyäl')	170	46°27'N	4°14'E
Pārbati, r., India	202	24°50'N	76°44'E
Parchim, Ger. (par'kĭm)	168	53°25'N	11°52'E
Parczew, Pol. (pär'chĕf)	169	51°38'N	22°53'E
Pardo, r., Braz. (pär'dō)	143	15°25'S	39°40'W
Pardo, r., Braz.	141a	21°32'S	46°40'W
Pardubice, Czech Rep. (pär'dō-bĭt-sĕ)	168	50°02'N	15°47'E
Parecis, Serra dos, mts., Braz. (sĕr'rȧ dōs pä-rå-sēzh')	143	13°45'S	59°28'W
Paredes de Nava, Spain (pä-rā'dås dā nä'vä)	172	42°10'N	4°41'W
Paredón, Mex.	122	25°56'N	100°58'W
Parent, Can.	91	47°59'N	74°30'W
Parent, Lac, l., Can.	99	48°40'N	77°00'W
Parepare, Indon.	212	4°01'S	119°38'E
Pargolovo, Russia (pȧr-gô'lô vô)	186c	60°04'N	30°18'E
Paria, r., Az., U.S.	119	37°07'N	111°51'W
Paria, Golfo de, b. (gôl-fô-dĕ-br-pä-rē-ä)	142	10°33'N	62°14'W
Paricutín, Volcán, vol., Mex.	130	19°27'N	102°14'W
Parida, Río de la, r., Mex. (rē'ō-dĕ-lä-pä-rē'dä)	122	26°23'N	104°40'W
Parima, Serra, mts., S.A. (sĕr'rȧ pä-rē'mä)	142	3°45'N	64°00'W
Pariñas, Punta, c., Peru (po͞o'n-tä-pä-rē'n-yäs)	142	4°30'S	81°23'W
Parintins, Braz. (pä-rĭn-tĭnzh')	143	2°34'S	56°30'W
Paris, Can.	99	43°15'N	80°23'W
Paris, Fr. (pȧ-rē')	154	48°51'N	2°20'E
Paris, Ar., U.S. (păr'ĭs)	121	35°17'N	93°43'W
Paris, Il., U.S.	108	39°35'N	87°40'W
Paris, Ky., U.S.	108	38°15'N	84°15'W
Paris, Mo., U.S.	121	39°27'N	91°59'W
Paris, Tn., U.S.	124	36°16'N	88°20'W
Paris, Tx., U.S.	105	33°39'N	95°33'W

334 Parita – Penistone PRONOUNCING INDEX

PLACE (Pronunciation)	PAGE	LAT.	LONG.
Parita, Golfo de, b., Pan. (gôl-fô-dĕ-pä-rē'tä)	133	8°06'N	80°10'W
Park City, Ut., U.S.	115	40°39'N	111°33'W
Parker, S.D., U.S. (pär'kẽr)	112	43°24'N	97°10'W
Parker Dam, dam, U.S.	106	34°20'N	114°00'W
Parkersburg, W.V., U.S. (pär'kẽrz-bûrg)	105	39°15'N	81°35'W
Parkes, Austl. (pärks)	222	33°10'S	148°10'E
Park Falls, Wi., U.S. (pärk)	113	45°55'N	90°29'W
Park Forest, Il., U.S.	111a	41°29'N	87°41'W
Parkland, Wa., U.S. (pärk'lănd)	116a	47°09'N	122°26'W
Park Range, mts., Co., U.S.	115	40°54'N	106°40'W
Park Rapids, Mn., U.S.	112	46°53'N	95°05'W
Park Ridge, Il., U.S.	111a	42°00'N	87°50'W
Park River, N.D., U.S.	112	48°22'N	97°43'W
Parkrose, Or., U.S. (pärk'rōz)	116c	45°33'N	122°33'W
Park Rynie, S. Afr.	233c	30°22'S	30°43'E
Parkston, S.D., U.S. (pärks'tŭn)	112	43°22'N	97°59'W
Parkville, Md., U.S.	110e	39°22'N	76°32'W
Parkville, Mo., U.S.	117f	39°12'N	94°41'W
Parla, Spain (pär'lä)	173a	40°14'N	3°46'W
Parma, Italy (pär'mä)	162	44°48'N	10°20'E
Parma, Oh., U.S.	111d	41°23'N	81°44'W
Parma Heights, Oh., U.S.	111d	41°23'N	81°36'W
Parnaíba, Braz. (pär-nä-ē'bä)	143	3°00'S	41°42'W
Parnaiba, r., Braz.	143	3°57'S	42°30'W
Parnassós, mtn., Grc.	175	38°36'N	22°35'E
Parndorf, Aus.	159e	48°00'N	16°52'E
Pärnu, Est. (pĕr'nōō)	180	58°24'N	24°29'E
Pärnu, r., Est.	167	58°40'N	25°05'E
Pärnu Laht, b., Est. (läkt)	167	58°15'N	24°17'E
Paro, Bhu. (pä'rô)	202	27°30'N	89°30'E
Paroo, r., Austl. (pä'rōō)	221	30°00'S	144°00'E
Páros, Grc. (pä'rôs) (pā'rŏs)	175	37°05'N	25°14'E
Páros, i., Grc.	163	37°11'N	25°00'E
Parow, S. Afr. (pă'rô)	232a	33°54'S	18°36'E
Parowan, Ut., U.S. (păr'ô-wăn)	119	37°50'N	112°50'W
Parral, Chile (pär-rä'l)	144	36°07'S	71°47'W
Parral, r., Mex.	122	27°25'N	105°08'W
Parramatta, r., Austl. (păr-ȧ-măt'ȧ)	217b	33°42'S	150°58'E
Parras, Mex. (pär-räs')	122	25°28'N	102°08'W
Parrita, C.R. (pär-rē'tä)	133	9°32'N	84°17'W
Parrsboro, Can. (pärz'bŭr-ô)	100	45°24'N	64°20'W
Parry, i., Can. (păr'ĭ)	99	45°15'N	80°00'W
Parry, Mount, mtn., Can.	94	52°53'N	128°45'W
Parry Islands, is., Can.	89	75°30'N	110°00'W
Parry Sound, Can.	91	45°20'N	80°00'W
Parsnip, r., Can. (pärs'nĭp)	95	54°45'N	122°20'W
Parsons, Ks., U.S. (pär's'nz)	105	37°20'N	95°16'W
Parsons, W.V., U.S.	109	39°05'N	79°40'W
Parthenay, Fr. (pȧr-t'nĕ')	170	46°39'N	0°16'W
Partinico, Italy (pär-tē'nê-kô)	174	38°02'N	13°11'E
Partizansk, Russia	179	43°15'N	133°19'E
Parys, S. Afr. (pȧ-rĭs')	238c	26°53'S	27°28'E
Pasadena, Ca., U.S. (păs-ȧ-dē'nȧ)	104	34°09'N	118°09'W
Pasadena, Md., U.S.	110e	39°06'N	76°35'W
Pasadena, Tx., U.S.	123a	29°43'N	95°13'W
Pascagoula, Ms., U.S. (păs-kȧ-gōō'lȧ)	124	30°22'N	88°33'W
Pascagoula, r., Ms., U.S.	124	30°52'N	88°48'W
Paşcani, Rom. (päsh-kän')	169	47°46'N	26°42'E
Pasco, Wa., U.S. (păs'kō)	114	46°13'N	119°04'W
Pascua, Isla de (Easter Island), i., Chile	241	26°50'S	109°00'W
Pasewalk, Ger. (pä'zĕ-välk)	168	53°31'N	14°01'E
Pashiya, Russia (pä'shĭ-yȧ)	186a	58°27'N	58°17'E
Pashkovo, Russia (pȧsh-kô'vô)	210	48°52'N	131°09'E
Pashkovskaya, Russia (pȧsh-kôf'skȧ-yȧ)	177	45°00'N	39°04'E
Pasig, Phil.	213a	14°34'N	121°05'E
Pasión, Río de la, r., Guat. (rē'ō-dĕ-lä-pä-syōn')	132a	16°31'N	90°11'W
Paso de los Libres, Arg. (pä-sô-dĕ-lôs-lē'brĕs)	144	29°33'S	57°05'W
Paso de los Toros, Ur. (tŏ'rôs)	141c	32°43'S	56°33'W
Paso Robles, Ca., U.S. (pă'sō rō'blĕs)	118	35°38'N	120°44'W
Pasquia Hills, hills, Can. (păs'kwē-ȧ)	97	53°13'N	102°37'W
Passaic, N.J., U.S. (pă-sā'ĭk)	110a	40°52'N	74°08'W
Passaic, r., N.J., U.S.	110a	40°42'N	74°26'W
Passamaquoddy Bay, b., N.A. (păs'ȧ-mȧ-kwŏd'ĭ)	100	45°06'N	66°59'W
Passa Tempo, Braz. (pä's-sä-tĕ'm-pô)	141a	20°40'S	44°29'W
Passau, Ger. (päs'ou)	161	48°34'N	13°27'E
Pass Christian, Ms., U.S. (pȧs krĭs'tyĕn)	124	30°20'N	89°15'W
Passero, Cape, c., Italy (päs-sĕ'rô)	156	36°34'N	15°13'E
Passo Fundo, Braz. (pä'sō fōn'dō)	144	28°16'S	52°13'W
Passos, Braz. (pä's-sōs)	143	20°45'S	46°37'W
Pastaza, r., S.A. (päs-tä'zä)	142	3°05'S	76°18'W
Pasto, Col. (päs'tô)	142	1°15'N	77°19'W
Pastora, Mex. (päs-tô-rä)	130	22°08'N	100°04'W
Pasuruan, Indon.	212	7°45'S	112°50'E
Pasvalys, Lith. (päs-vä-lēs')	167	56°04'N	24°23'E
Patagonia, reg., Arg. (păt-ȧ-gō'nĭ-ȧ)	144	46°45'S	69°30'W
Pātālganga, r., India	203b	18°52'N	73°08'E
Patapsco, r., Md., U.S. (pȧ-tăps'kō)	110e	39°12'N	76°30'W
Pateros, Lake, res., Wa., U.S.	114	48°05'N	119°45'W
Paterson, N.J., U.S. (păt'ẽr-sŭn)	110a	40°55'N	74°10'W
Pathein, Mya.	199	16°46'N	94°47'E
Pathfinder Reservoir, res., Wy., U.S. (păth'fīn-dẽr)	115	42°22'N	107°10'W
Patiāla, India (pŭt-ē-ä'lŭ)	199	30°25'N	76°28'E
Pati do Alferes, Braz. (pä-tē-dô-ál-fĕ'rĕs)	144b	22°25'S	43°25'W
Patna, India (pŭt'nŭ)	199	25°33'N	85°18'E

PLACE (Pronunciation)	PAGE	LAT.	LONG.
Patnanongan, i., Phil. (pät-nä-nôŋ'gän)	213a	14°50'N	122°25'E
Patoka, r., In., U.S. (pȧ-tō'kȧ)	108	38°25'N	87°25'W
Patom Plateau, plat., Russia	179	59°30'N	115°00'E
Patos, Braz. (pä'tōzh)	143	7°03'S	37°14'W
Patos, Wa., U.S. (pă'tōs)	116d	48°47'N	122°57'W
Patos, Lagoa dos, l., Braz. (lä'gō-ȧ dozh pä'tōzh)	144	31°15'S	51°30'W
Patos de Minas, Braz. (dĕ-mē'năzh)	143	18°39'S	46°31'W
Pátra, Grc.	163	38°15'N	21°48'E
Patraïkós Kólpos, b., Grc.	175	38°16'N	21°19'E
Patras *see* Pátrai, Grc.	163	38°15'N	21°48'E
Patrocínio, Braz. (pä-trō-sē'nê-ô)	143	18°48'S	46°47'W
Pattani, Thai. (pät'ȧ-nê)	212	6°56'N	101°13'E
Patten, Me., U.S. (păt''n)	100	45°59'N	68°27'W
Patterson, La., U.S. (păt'ẽr-sŭn)	123	29°41'N	91°20'W
Patterson, i., Can.	98	48°38'N	87°14'W
Patton, Pa., U.S.	109	40°40'N	78°45'W
Patuca, r., Hond.	133	15°22'N	84°31'W
Patuca, Punta, c., Hond. (pōō'n-tä-pä-tōō'kä)	133	15°55'N	84°05'W
Patuxent, r., Md., U.S. (pȧ-tŭk'sĕnt)	109	39°10'N	77°10'W
Pátzcuaro, Mex. (päts'kwä-rô)	130	19°30'N	101°36'W
Pátzcuaro, Lago de, l., Mex. (lä'gô-dĕ)	130	19°36'N	101°38'W
Patzicia, Guat. (pät-zē'syä)	132	14°36'N	90°57'W
Patzún, Guat. (pät-zōōn')	132	14°40'N	91°00'W
Pau, Fr. (pō)	161	43°18'N	0°23'W
Pau, Gave de, r., Fr. (gäv-dē)	170	43°33'N	0°51'W
Paulding, Oh., U.S. (pôl'dĭng)	108	41°05'N	84°35'W
Paulinenaue, Ger. (pou'lē-nĕ-nou-ĕ)	159b	52°40'N	12°43'E
Paulistano, Braz. (pá'ŏ-lēs-tá-nä)	143	8°13'S	41°06'W
Paulo Afonso, Salto, wtfl., Braz. (säl-tô-pou'lô äf-fōn'sô)	143	9°33'S	38°32'W
Paul Roux, S. Afr. (pôrl rōō)	238c	28°18'S	27°57'E
Paulsboro, N.J., U.S. (pôlz'bē-rô)	110f	39°50'N	75°16'W
Pauls Valley, Ok., U.S. (pôlz văl'ê)	121	34°43'N	97°13'W
Pavarandocito, Col. (pä-vä-rän-dô-sē'tô)	142a	7°18'N	76°32'W
Pavda, Russia (päv'da)	186a	59°16'N	59°32'E
Pavia, Italy (pä-vē'ä)	162	45°12'N	9°11'E
Pavlodar, Kaz. (páv-lô-dár')	183	52°17'N	77°23'E
Pavlof Bay, b., Ak., U.S. (păv-lōf)	103	55°20'N	161°20'W
Pavlohrad, Ukr.	181	48°32'N	35°52'E
Pavlovsk, Russia (páv-lôfsk')	177	50°28'N	40°05'E
Pavlovsk, Russia	186c	59°41'N	30°27'E
Pavlovskiy Posad, Russia (páv-lôf'skĭ pô-sát')	180	55°47'N	38°39'E
Pavuna, Braz. (pä-vōō'nȧ)	144b	22°48'S	43°21'W
Päwesin, Ger. (pă'vĕ-zēn)	159b	52°31'N	12°44'E
Pawhuska, Ok., U.S. (pô-hŭs'kȧ)	121	36°41'N	96°20'W
Pawnee, Ok., U.S. (pô-nē')	121	36°20'N	96°47'W
Pawnee, r., Ks., U.S.	120	38°18'N	99°42'W
Pawnee City, Ne., U.S.	121	40°08'N	96°09'W
Paw Paw, Mi., U.S. (pô'pô)	108	42°15'N	85°55'W
Paw Paw, r., Mi., U.S.	113	42°14'N	86°21'W
Pawtucket, R.I., U.S. (pô-tŭk'ĕt)	109	41°53'N	71°23'W
Paxoi, i., Grc.	175	39°14'N	20°15'E
Paxton, Il., U.S. (păks'tŭn)	108	40°35'N	88°00'W
Payette, Id., U.S. (pȧ-ĕt')	114	44°05'N	116°55'W
Payette, r., Id., U.S.	114	43°57'N	116°26'W
Payette, North Fork, r., Id., U.S.	114	44°10'N	116°10'W
Payette, South Fork, r., Id., U.S.	114	44°07'N	115°43'W
Pay-Khoy, Khrebet, mts., Russia	180	68°08'N	63°04'E
Payne, l., Can. (pān)	93	59°22'N	73°16'W
Paynesville, Mn., U.S. (pānz'vĭl)	113	45°23'N	94°43'W
Paysandú, Ur. (pī-sän-dōō')	144	32°16'S	57°55'W
Payson, Ut., U.S. (pā's'n)	119	40°05'N	111°45'W
Pazardzhik, Blg. (pä-zȧr-dzhek')	163	42°10'N	24°22'E
Pazin, Cro. (pä'zēn)	174	45°14'N	13°57'E
Peabody, Ks., U.S. (pē'bŏd-ĭ)	121	38°09'N	97°09'W
Peabody, Ma., U.S.	101a	42°32'N	70°56'W
Peace, r., Can.	92	57°30'N	117°30'W
Peace Creek, r., Fl., U.S. (pēs)	125a	27°16'N	81°53'W
Peace Dale, R.I., U.S. (dāl)	110b	41°27'N	71°30'W
Peace River, Can. (rĭv'ẽr)	90	56°14'N	117°17'W
Peacock Hills, hills, Can. (pē-kŏk' hĭlz)	92	66°08'N	109°55'W
Peak Hill, Austl.	218	25°38'S	118°50'E
Pearl, r., U.S. (pûrl)	107	30°30'N	89°45'W
Pearland, Tx., U.S. (pûrl'ănd)	123a	29°34'N	95°17'W
Pearl Harbor, Hi., U.S.	126a	21°20'N	157°53'W
Pearl Harbor, b., Hi., U.S.	106d	21°22'N	157°58'W
Pearsall, Tx., U.S. (pĕr'sôl)	122	28°53'N	99°06'W
Pearse Island, i., Can. (pērs)	94	54°51'N	130°21'W
Pearston, S. Afr. (pē'ērstŏn)	233c	32°36'S	25°09'E
Peary Land, reg., Grnld. (pēr'ĭ)	244	82°00'N	40°00'W
Pease, r., Tx., U.S. (pēz)	120	34°07'N	99°53'W
Peason, La., U.S. (pēz''n)	123	31°25'N	93°19'W
Pebane, Moz. (pĕ-bá'nĕ)	233	17°10'S	38°08'E
Pecan Bay, Tx., U.S. (pê-kăn')	122	32°04'N	99°15'W
Peçanha, Braz. (pâ-kän'yȧ)	143	18°37'S	42°26'W
Pecatonica, r., Il., U.S. (pĕk-ȧ-tŏn-ĭ-kȧ)	113	42°21'N	89°28'W
Pechenga, Russia (pyĕ'chĕŋ-gȧ)	180	69°30'N	31°10'E
Pechora, r., Russia	178	66°00'N	54°00'E
Pechora Basin, Russia (pyĕ-chô'rȧ)	178	67°55'N	58°37'E
Pechori, Russia (pĕt'sĕ-rĕ)	176	57°48'N	27°33'E
Pecos, N.M., U.S. (pā'kôs)	119	35°29'N	105°41'W
Pecos, Tx., U.S.	122	31°26'N	103°30'W
Pecos, r., U.S.	106	31°10'N	103°10'W
Pécs, Hung. (pāch)	163	46°04'N	18°15'E
Peddie, S. Afr.	233c	33°13'S	27°09'E
Pedley, Ca., U.S. (pĕd'lē)	117a	33°59'N	117°29'W

PLACE (Pronunciation)	PAGE	LAT.	LONG.
Pedra Azul, Braz. (pā'drä-zōō'l)	143	16°03'S	41°13'W
Pedreiras, Braz. (pĕ-drā'räs)	143	4°30'S	44°31'W
Pedro, Point, c., Sri L. (pē'drô)	203	9°50'N	80°14'E
Pedro Antonio Santos, Mex.	132a	18°55'N	88°13'W
Pedro Betancourt, Cuba (bā-täŋ-kōrt')	134	22°40'N	81°15'W
Pedro de Valdivia, Chile (pĕ'drô-dĕ-väl-dē'vê-ä)	144	22°32'S	69°55'W
Pedro do Rio, Braz. (dô-rē'ô)	144b	22°20'S	43°09'W
Pedro II, Braz. (pā'drò sā-gòn'dò)	143	4°20'S	41°27'W
Pedro Juan Caballero, Para. (hòá'n-kä-bäl-yĕ'rō)	144	22°40'S	55°42'W
Pedro Miguel, Pan. (mê-gāl')	128a	9°01'N	79°36'W
Pedro Miguel Locks, trans., Pan. (mê-gāl')	128a	9°01'N	79°36'W
Peebinga, Austl. (pê-bĭng'ȧ)	218	34°43'S	140°55'E
Peebles, Scot., U.K. (pē'b'lz)	164	55°40'N	3°15'W
Peekskill, N.Y., U.S. (pēks'kĭl)	110a	41°17'N	73°55'W
Pegasus Bay, b., N.Z. (pĕg'ȧ-sŭs)	221a	43°18'S	173°25'E
Pegnitz, r., Ger. (pĕgh-nēts)	168	49°38'N	11°40'E
Pego, Spain (pā'gō)	173	38°50'N	0°09'W
Peguis Indian Reserve, I.R., Can.	97	51°20'N	97°35'W
Pegu Yoma, mts., Mya. (pĕ-gōō'yō'mä)	199	19°16'N	95°59'E
Pehčevo, Mac. (pĕк'chĕ-vô)	175	41°42'N	22°57'E
Peigan Indian Reserve, I.R., Can.	95	49°35'N	113°40'W
Peipus, Lake *see* Chudskoye Ozero, l., Eur.	180	58°43'N	26°45'E
Peiraiás, Grc.	163	37°57'N	23°38'E
Pekin, Il., U.S. (pē'kĭn)	108	40°35'N	89°30'W
Peking *see* Beijing, China	205	39°55'N	116°23'E
Pelagie, Isole, is., Italy	162	35°46'N	12°32'E
Pélagos, i., Grc.	175	39°17'N	24°05'E
Pelahatchie, Ms., U.S. (pĕl-ȧ-hăch'ê)	124	32°17'N	89°48'W
Pelat, Mont, mtn., Fr. (pē-lá')	161	44°16'N	6°43'E
Peleduy, Russia (pyĕl-yĭ-dōō'ē)	179	59°50'N	112°47'E
Pelée, Mont, mtn., Mart. (pē-lā')	133b	14°49'N	61°10'W
Pelee, Point, c., Can.	98	41°55'N	82°30'W
Pelee Island, i., Can. (pē'lê)	98	41°45'N	82°30'W
Pelequén, Chile (pĕ-lĕ-kĕ'n)	141b	34°26'S	71°52'W
Pelham, Ga., U.S. (pĕl'hăm)	124	31°07'N	84°10'W
Pelham, N.H., U.S.	101a	42°43'N	71°22'W
Pelican, l., Mn., U.S.	113	46°36'N	94°00'W
Pelican Bay, b., Can.	97	52°45'N	100°20'W
Pelican Harbor, b., Bah. (pĕl'ĭ-kăn)	134	26°20'N	76°45'W
Pelican Rapids, Mn., U.S. (pĕl'ĭ-kăn)	112	46°34'N	96°05'W
Pella, Ia., U.S. (pĕl'ȧ)	113	41°25'N	92°50'W
Pellworm, i., Ger. (pĕl'vôrm)	168	54°33'N	8°25'E
Pelly, l., Can.	92	66°08'N	102°57'W
Pelly, r., Can.	92	62°20'N	133°00'W
Pelly Bay, b., Can. (pĕl'ĭ)	93	68°57'N	91°05'W
Pelly Crossing, Can.	103	62°50'N	136°50'W
Pelly Mountains, mts., Can.	92	61°50'N	133°05'W
Peloncillo Mountains, mts., Az., U.S. (pĕl-ôn-sĭl'lō)	119	32°40'N	109°20'W
Peloponnisos, pen., Grc.	175	37°28'N	22°14'E
Pelotas, Braz. (pā-lō'tăzh)	144	31°45'S	52°18'W
Pelton, Can. (pĕl'tŭn)	111b	42°15'N	82°57'W
Pelym, r., Russia	180	60°20'N	63°05'E
Pelzer, S.C., U.S. (pĕl'zẽr)	125	34°38'N	82°30'W
Pemanggil, i., Malay.	197b	2°37'N	104°41'E
Pematangsiantar, Indon.	212	2°58'N	99°03'E
Pemba, Moz. (pĕm'bȧ)	233	12°58'S	40°30'E
Pemba, Zam.	232	15°29'S	27°22'E
Pemba Channel, strt., Afr.	237	5°10'S	39°30'E
Pemba Island, i., Tan.	237	5°20'S	39°57'E
Pembina, N.D., U.S. (pĕm'bĭ-nȧ)	112	48°58'N	97°15'W
Pembina, r., Can.	95	53°05'N	114°30'W
Pembina, r., N.A.	97	49°08'N	98°20'W
Pembroke, Can. (pĕm' brōk)	91	45°50'N	77°00'W
Pembroke, Wales, U.K.	164	51°40'N	5°00'W
Pembroke, Ma., U.S. (pĕm'brōk)	101a	42°05'N	70°49'W
Pen, India	203b	18°44'N	73°06'E
Penafiel, Port. (pā-nȧ-fyĕl')	172	41°12'N	8°19'W
Peñafiel, Spain (pā-nyȧ-fyĕl')	172	41°38'N	4°08'W
Peñalara, mtn., Spain (pā-nyä-lä'rä)	162	40°52'N	3°57'W
Pena Nevada, Cerro, Mex.	130	23°47'N	99°52'W
Peñaranda de Bracamonte, Spain	172	40°54'N	5°11'W
Peñarroya-Pueblonuevo, Spain (pĕn-yär-rô'yä-pwĕ'blô-nwĕ'vô)	172	38°18'N	5°18'W
Peñas, Cabo de, c., Spain (kȧ'bô-dĕ-pā'nyäs)	172	43°42'N	6°12'W
Penas, Golfo de, b., Chile (gôl-fô-dĕ-pĕ'n-äs)	144	47°15'S	77°30'W
Penasco, r., Tx., U.S. (pā-nás'kō)	122	32°50'N	104°45'W
Pendembu, S.L. (pĕn-dĕm'bōō)	230	8°06'N	10°42'W
Pender, Ne., U.S. (pĕn'dẽr)	112	42°08'N	96°43'W
Penderisco, r., Col. (pĕn-dĕ-rē's-kô)	142a	6°30'N	76°21'W
Pendjari, Parc National de la, rec., Benin	234	11°25'N	1°30'E
Pendleton, Or., U.S. (pĕn'd'l-tŭn)	104	45°41'N	118°47'W
Pend Oreille, r., Wa., U.S.	114	48°44'N	117°20'W
Pend Oreille, Lake, l., Id., U.S. (pŏn-dô-rā')(pĕn-dô-rĕl')	106	48°09'N	116°38'W
Penedo, Braz. (pā-nā'dô)	143	10°17'S	36°28'W
Penetanguishene, Can. (pĕn'ē-tăŋ-gĭ-shēn')	99	44°45'N	79°55'W
Pengcheng, China (pŭŋ-chŭŋ)	206	36°24'N	114°11'E
Penglai, China (pŭŋ-lī)	208	37°49'N	120°45'E
Peniche, Port. (pĕ-nē'chå)	172	39°22'N	9°24'W
Peninsula, Oh., U.S. (pĕn-ĭn'sū-lȧ)	111d	41°14'N	81°32'W
Penistone, Eng., U.K. (pĕn'ĭ-stŭn)	158a	53°31'N	1°38'W

ăt; finăl; rāte; senâte; ärm; ȧsk; sofȧ; fâre; ch-choose; dh-as th in other; bē; ėvent; bĕt; recĕnt; cratẽr; g-gō; gh-guttural g; bĭt; ĭ-short neutral; rīde; к-guttural k as ch in German ich;

PRONOUNCING INDEX Penjamillo – Pillar Rocks 335

PLACE (Pronunciation)	PAGE	LAT.	LONG.
Penjamillo, Mex. (pěn-hä-mēl'yō)	130	20°06'N	101°56'W
Pénjamo, Mex. (pān'hä-mō)	130	20°27'N	101°43'W
Penk, r., Eng., U.K. (pěnk)	158a	52°41'N	2°10'W
Penkridge, Eng., U.K. (pěnk'rĭj)	158a	52°43'N	2°07'W
Penne, Italy (pěn'nä)	174	42°28'N	13°57'E
Penner, r., India (pěn'ẽr)	199	14°43'N	79°09'E
Pennines, hills, Eng., U.K. (pěn-īn')	164	54°30'N	2°10'W
Pennines, Alpes, mts., Eur.	168	46°02'N	7°07'E
Pennsboro, W.V., U.S. (pěnz'bŭr-ô)	108	39°10'N	81°00'W
Penns Grove, N.J., U.S. (pěnz grōv)	110f	39°44'N	75°28'W
Pennsylvania, state, U.S. (pěn-sĭl-vā'nĭ-*á*)	105	41°00'N	78°10'W
Penn Yan, N.Y., U.S. (pěn yăn')	109	42°40'N	77°00'W
Pennycutaway, r., Can.	97	56°10'N	93°25'W
Peno, l., Russia (pā'nô)	176	56°55'N	32°28'E
Penobscot, r., Me., U.S.	107	45°00'N	68°36'W
Penobscot Bay, b., Me., U.S. (pē-nŏb'skŏt)	100	44°20'N	69°00'W
Penong, Austl. (pē-nông')	218	32°00'S	133°00'E
Penrith, Austl.	217b	33°45'S	150°42'E
Pensacola, Fl., U.S. (pěn-s*á*-kō'l*á*)	105	30°25'N	87°13'W
Pensacola Dam, Ok., U.S.	121	36°27'N	95°02'W
Pensilvania, Col. (pěn-sēl-vä'nyä)	142a	5°31'N	75°05'W
Pentecost, i., Vanuatu (pěn'tē-kŏst)	221	16°05'S	168°28'E
Penticton, Can.	90	49°30'N	119°35'W
Pentland Firth, strt., Scot., U.K. (pěnt'l*ă*nd)	164	58°44'N	3°25'W
Penza, Russia (pěn'zȧ)	178	53°10'N	45°00'E
Penzance, Eng., U.K. (pěn-zăns')	164	50°07'N	5°40'W
Penzberg, Ger. (pěnts'běrgh)	168	47°43'N	11°21'E
Penzhina, r., Russia (pyĭn-zē-nŭ)	185	62°15'N	166°30'E
Penzhino, Russia	179	63°42'N	168°00'E
Penzhinskaya Guba, b., Russia	185	60°30'N	161°30'E
Peoria, Il., U.S. (pē-ō'rĭ-*á*)	105	40°45'N	89°35'W
Peotillos, Mex. (pā-ō-tel'yōs)	130	22°30'N	100°39'W
Peotone, Il., U.S. (pē'ō-tŏn)	111a	41°20'N	87°47'W
Pepacton Reservoir, res., N.Y., U.S. (pěp-ăc't*ŭ*n)	109	42°05'N	74°40'W
Pepe, Cabo, c., Cuba (kä'bô-pě'pě)	134	21°30'N	83°10'W
Pepperell, Ma., U.S. (pěp'ẽr-ěl)	101a	42°40'N	71°36'W
Peqin, Alb. (pě-kēn')	175	41°03'N	19°48'E
Perales, r., Spain (pā-rä'lās)	173a	40°24'N	4°07'W
Perales de Tajuña, Spain (dā tä-hōō'nyä)	173a	40°14'N	3°22'W
Perche, Collines du, hills, Fr.	170	48°25'N	0°40'E
Perchtoldsdorf, Aus. (pěrk'tôlts-dôrf)	159e	48°07'N	16°17'E
Perdekop, S. Afr.	238c	27°11'S	29°38'E
Perdido, r., Al., U.S. (pěr-dī'dō)	124	30°45'N	87°38'W
Perdido, Monte, mtn., Spain (pěr-dē'dō)	173	42°40'N	0°00'
Perdões, Braz. (pěr-dô'ěs)	141a	21°05'S	45°05'W
Pereiaslav-Khmel'nyts'kyi, Ukr.	181	50°05'N	31°25'E
Pereira, Col. (på-rā'rä)	142	4°49'N	75°42'W
Pere Marquette, Mi., U.S.	108	43°55'N	86°10'W
Pereshchepyne, Ukr.	177	49°02'N	35°19'E
Pereslavl'-Zalesskiy, Russia (pâ-rå-slåv''l zå-lyěs'kĭ)	180	56°43'N	38°52'E
Pergamino, Arg. (pěr-gä-mē'nō)	144	33°53'S	60°36'W
Perham, Mn., U.S. (pěr'h*ă*m)	112	46°37'N	95°35'W
Peribonca, r., Can. (pěr-ĭ-bŏŋ'kȧ)	93	50°30'N	71°00'W
Périgueux, Fr. (pā-rē-gû')	161	45°12'N	0°43'E
Perija, Sierra de, mts., Col. (sē-ě'r-rȧ-dě-pě-rē'кä)	142	9°25'N	73°30'W
Perkam, Tanjung, c., Indon.	213	1°20'S	138°45'E
Perkins, Can. (pẽr'k*ě*ns)	102c	45°37'N	75°37'W
Perlas, Archipiélago de las, is., Pan.	133	8°29'N	79°15'W
Perlas, Laguna las, l., Nic. (lä-gô'nä-dě-läs)	133	12°34'N	83°19'W
Perleberg, Ger. (pěr'lē-běrg)	168	53°06'N	11°51'E
Perm', Russia (pěrm)	178	58°00'N	56°15'E
Pernambuco *see* Recife, Braz.	143	8°09'S	34°59'W
Pernambuco, state, Braz. (pěr-näm-bōō'kō)	143	8°08'S	38°54'W
Pernik, Blg. (pěr-nēk')	163	42°36'N	23°04'E
Péronne, Fr. (pā-rôn')	170	49°57'N	2°49'E
Perote, Mex. (pě-rô'tě)	131	19°33'N	97°13'W
Perovo, Russia (på'rô-vô)	186b	55°43'N	37°47'E
Perpignan, Fr. (pěr-pē-nyäɴ')	161	42°42'N	2°48'E
Perris, Ca., U.S. (pěr'ĭs)	117a	33°46'N	117°14'W
Perros, Bahía, b., Cuba (bä-ē'ä-pā'rōs)	134	22°25'N	78°35'W
Perrot, Île, i., Can.	102a	45°23'N	73°57'W
Perry, Fl., U.S. (pěr'ĭ)	124	30°06'N	83°35'W
Perry, Ga., U.S.	124	32°27'N	83°44'W
Perry, Ia., U.S.	113	41°49'N	94°40'W
Perry, N.Y., U.S.	109	42°45'N	78°00'W
Perry, Ok., U.S.	121	36°17'N	97°18'W
Perry, Ut., U.S.	117b	41°27'N	112°02'W
Perry Hall, Md., U.S.	110e	39°24'N	76°29'W
Perryopolis, Pa., U.S. (pě-rē-ŏ'pô-lĭs)	111e	40°05'N	79°45'W
Perrysburg, Oh., U.S. (pěr'ĭz-bûrg)	108	41°35'N	83°35'W
Perryton, Tx., U.S. (pěr'ĭ-t*ŭ*n)	120	36°23'N	100°48'W
Perryville, Ak., U.S. (pěr-ĭ-vĭl)	103	55°58'N	159°28'W
Perryville, Mo., U.S.	121	37°41'N	89°52'W
Persan, Fr. (pěr-säɴ')	171b	49°09'N	2°15'E
Persepolis, hist., Iran (pěr-sěp'ô-lĭs)	198	30°15'N	53°08'E
Persian Gulf, b., Asia (pûr'zh*ă*n)	198	27°38'N	50°30'E
Perth, Austl. (pûrth)	218	31°50'S	116°10'E
Perth, Can.	99	44°40'N	76°15'W
Perth, Scot., U.K.	160	56°24'N	3°25'W
Perth Amboy, N.J., U.S. (ăm'boi)	110a	40°31'N	74°16'W
Pertuis, Fr. (pěr-tüē')	171	43°43'N	5°29'E
Peru, Il., U.S. (pē-rōō')	108	41°20'N	89°10'W
Peru, In., U.S.	108	40°45'N	86°00'W
Peru, nation, S.A.	142	10°00'S	75°00'W
Peru-Chile Trench, deep	139	25°00'S	71°30'W
Perugia, Italy (pā-rōō'jä)	162	43°08'N	12°24'E
Peruque, Mo., U.S. (pě rō'kě)	117e	38°52'N	90°36'W
Pervomais'k, Ukr.	181	48°04'N	30°52'E
Pervoural'sk, Russia (pěr-vô-ô-rálsk')	186a	56°54'N	59°58'E
Pesaro, Italy (pā'zä-rō)	162	43°54'N	12°55'E
Pescado, r., Ven. (pěs-kä'dō)	143b	9°33'N	65°32'W
Pescara, Italy (päs-kä'rä)	174	42°26'N	14°15'E
Pescara, r., Italy	174	42°18'N	13°22'E
Peschanyy müyisi, c., Kaz.	181	43°10'N	51°20'E
Pescia, Italy (pā'shä)	174	43°53'N	11°42'E
Peshāwar, Pak. (pě-shä'w*ŭ*r)	199	34°01'N	71°34'E
Peshtera, Blg.	175	42°03'N	24°19'E
Peshtigo, Wi., U.S. (pěsh'tē-gō)	113	45°03'N	87°46'W
Peshtigo, r., Wi., U.S.	113	45°15'N	88°14'W
Peski, Russia (pyâs'kĭ)	186b	55°13'N	38°48'E
Pêso da Régua, Port. (pā-sò-dä-rā'gwä)	172	41°09'N	7°47'W
Pespire, Hond. (pås-pē'rå)	132	13°35'N	87°20'W
Pesqueria, r., Mex. (pås-kå-rē'*á*)	122	25°55'N	100°25'W
Pessac, Fr.	170	44°48'N	0°38'W
Petacalco, Bahía de, b., Mex. (bä-ē'ä-dě-pě-tä-käl'kô)	130	17°55'N	102°00'W
Petah Tiqwa, Isr.	197a	32°05'N	34°53'E
Petaluma, Ca., U.S. (pét-*á*-lō'm*á*)	118	38°15'N	122°38'W
Petare, Ven. (pě-tä'rě)	143b	10°28'N	66°48'W
Petatlán, Mex. (pā-tä-tlän')	130	17°31'N	101°17'W
Petawawa, Can.	99	45°54'N	77°17'W
Petén, Laguna de, l., Guat. (lä-gò'nä-dě-på-tān')	132a	17°05'N	89°54'W
Petenwell Reservoir, res., Wi., U.S.	113	44°10'N	89°55'W
Peterborough, Austl.	218	32°53'S	138°58'E
Peterborough, Can. (pē'tẽr-bŭr-ô)	91	44°20'N	78°20'W
Peterborough, Eng., U.K.	164	52°35'N	0°14'W
Peterhead, Scot., U.K. (pē-tẽr-hěd')	164	57°36'N	3°47'W
Peter Pond Lake, l., Can. (pŏnd)	92	55°55'N	108°44'W
Petersburg, Ak., U.S. (pē'tẽrz-bûrg)	103	56°52'N	133°10'W
Petersburg, Il., U.S.	121	40°01'N	89°51'W
Petersburg, In., U.S.	108	38°30'N	87°15'W
Petersburg, Ky., U.S.	111f	39°04'N	84°52'W
Petersburg, Va., U.S.	105	37°12'N	77°30'W
Petershagen, Ger. (pě'těrs-hä-gěn)	159b	52°32'N	13°46'E
Petershausen, Ger. (pě'těrs-hou-zěn)	159d	48°25'N	11°29'E
Pétionville, Haiti	135	18°30'N	72°20'W
Petitcodiac, Can. (pē-tē-kô-dyåk')	100	45°56'N	65°10'W
Petite Terre, i., Guad. (pē-tēt'târ')	133b	16°12'N	61°00'W
Petit Goâve, Haiti (pē-tē' gô-áv')	135	18°25'N	72°50'W
Petit Jean Creek, r., Ar., U.S. (pē-tē'zhäɴ')	121	35°05'N	93°55'W
Petit Loango, Gabon	236	2°16'S	9°35'E
Petlalcingo, Mex. (pě-tläl-sěŋ'gô)	131	18°05'N	97°53'W
Peto, Mex. (pě'tô)	132a	20°07'N	88°49'W
Petorca, Chile (pā-tŏr'kȧ)	141b	32°14'S	70°55'W
Petoskey, Mi., U.S. (pě-tŏs-kĭ)	108	45°25'N	84°55'W
Petra, hist., Jord.	197a	30°21'N	35°25'E
Petra Velikogo, Zaliv, b., Russia	210	42°40'N	131°50'E
Petre, Point, c., Can.	99	43°50'N	77°00'W
Petrich, Blg. (pā'trĭch)	163	41°24'N	23°13'E
Petrified Forest National Park, rec., Az., U.S. (pět'rĭ-fīd fôr'ěst)	119	34°58'N	109°35'W
Petrinja, Cro. (pā'trēn-yȧ)	174	45°25'N	16°17'E
Petrodvorets, Russia (pyě-trô-dvô-ryěts')	186c	59°53'N	29°55'E
Petrokrepost', Russia (pyě'trô-krě-pôst)	180	59°56'N	31°03'E
Petrolia, Can. (pē-trō'lĭ-*á*)	98	42°50'N	82°10'W
Petrolina, Braz. (pě-trō-lē'n*á*)	143	9°18'S	40°28'W
Petronell, Aus.	159e	48°07'N	16°52'E
Petropavlivka, Ukr.	177	48°24'N	36°23'E
Petropavlovka, Russia	186a	54°10'N	59°50'E
Petropavlovsk, Kaz.	183	54°44'N	69°07'E
Petropavlovsk-Kamchatskiy, Russia (käm-chät'skĭ)	179	53°13'N	158°56'E
Petrópolis, Braz. (på-trô-pô-lēzh')	143	22°31'S	43°10'W
Petroşani, Rom.	175	45°24'N	23°24'E
Petrovsk, Russia (pyě-trôfsk')	181	52°20'N	45°15'E
Petrovskaya, Russia (pyě-trôf'skȧ-yȧ)	177	45°25'N	37°50'E
Petrovskoye, Russia	181	45°20'N	43°00'E
Petrovsk-Zabaykal'skiy, Russia (pyě-trôfskzä-bī-käl'skĭ)	179	51°13'N	109°08'E
Petrozavodsk, Russia (pyā'trô-zȧ-vôtsk')	178	61°46'N	34°25'E
Petrus Steyn, S. Afr.	238c	27°40'S	28°09'E
Petrykivka, Ukr.	177	48°43'N	34°29'E
Pewaukee, Wi., U.S. (pĭ-wô'kê)	111a	43°05'N	88°15'W
Pewaukee Lake, l., Wi., U.S.	111a	43°03'N	88°18'W
Pewee Valley, Ky., U.S. (pe wē)	111h	38°19'N	85°29'W
Peza, r., Russia (pyå'zȧ)	180	65°35'N	46°50'E
Pézenas, Fr. (pā-zē-nä')	170	43°26'N	3°24'E
Pforzheim, Ger. (pfôrts'hīm)	161	48°52'N	8°43'E
Phalodi, India	202	27°13'N	72°22'E
Phan Thiet, Viet. (p'hän')	212	11°30'N	108°43'E
Phelps Lake, l., N.C., U.S.	125	35°46'N	76°27'W
Phenix City, Al., U.S. (fē'nĭks)	124	32°29'N	85°00'W
Philadelphia, Ms., U.S. (fĭl-*á*-děl'phĭ-*á*)	124	32°45'N	89°07'W
Philadelphia, Pa., U.S.	105	40°00'N	75°13'W
Philip, S.D., U.S. (fĭl'ĭp)	112	44°03'N	101°35'W
Philippeville *see* Skikda, Alg.	230	36°58'N	6°51'E
Philippines, nation, Asia (fĭl'ĭ-pēnz)	213	14°25'N	125°00'E
Philippine Sea, sea (fĭl'ĭ-pēn)	241	16°00'N	133°00'E
Philippine Trench, deep	213	10°30'N	127°15'E
Philipsburg, Pa., U.S. (fĭl'lĭps-bẽrg)	109	40°55'N	78°10'W
Philipsburg, Wy., U.S.	115	46°19'N	113°19'W
Phillip, i., Austl. (fĭl'ĭp)	222	38°32'S	145°10'E
Phillip Channel, strt., Indon.	197b	1°04'N	103°40'E
Phillipi, W.V., U.S. (fĭ-lĭp'ĭ)	108	39°10'N	80°00'W
Phillips, Wi., U.S. (fĭl'ĭps)	113	45°41'N	90°24'W
Phillipsburg, Ks., U.S. (fĭl'lĭps-bẽrg)	120	39°44'N	99°19'W
Phillipsburg, N.J., U.S.	109	40°45'N	75°10'W
Phitsanulok, Thai.	212	16°51'N	100°15'E
Phnom Penh (Phnum Pénh), Camb. (nŏm'pěn')	212	11°39'N	104°53'E
Phnum Pénh *see* Phnom Penh, Camb.	212	11°39'N	104°53'E
Phoenix, Az., U.S. (fē'nĭks)	104	33°30'N	112°00'W
Phoenix, Md., U.S.	110e	39°31'N	76°40'W
Phoenix Islands, is., Kir.	2	4°00'S	174°00'W
Phoenixville, Pa., U.S. (fē'nĭks-vĭl)	110f	40°08'N	75°31'W
Phou Bia, mtn., Laos	212	19°36'N	103°00'E
Phra Nakhon Si Ayutthaya, Thai.	212	14°16'N	100°37'E
Phuket, Thai.	212	7°57'N	98°19'E
Phu Quoc, Dao, i., Viet.	212	10°13'N	104°00'E
Pi, r., China (bē)	206	32°06'N	116°31'E
Piacenza, Italy (pyä-chěnt'sä)	162	45°02'N	9°42'E
Pianosa, i., Italy (pyä-nō'sä)	174	42°13'N	15°45'E
Piave, r., Italy (pyä'vā)	174	45°45'N	12°15'E
Piazza Armerina, Italy (pyät'sȧ är-må-rē'nä)	174	37°23'N	14°26'E
Pibor, r., Sudan (pē'bôr)	231	7°21'N	32°54'E
Pic, r., Can. (pěk)	98	48°48'N	86°28'W
Picara Point, c., V.I.U.S. (pē-kä'rȧ)	129c	18°23'N	64°57'W
Picayune, Ms., U.S. (pĭk'ȧ yōōn)	124	30°32'N	89°41'W
Picher, Ok., U.S. (pĭch'ẽr)	121	36°58'N	94°49'W
Pichilemu, Chile (pē-chē-lě'mōō)	141b	34°22'S	72°01'W
Pichucalco, Mex. (pē-chōō-käl'kô)	131	17°34'N	93°06'W
Pickerel, l., Can. (pĭk'ẽr-ěl)	98	48°35'N	91°10'W
Pickwick Lake, res., U.S. (pĭk'wĭck)	124	35°04'N	88°05'W
Pico, Ca., U.S. (pē'kô)	117a	34°01'N	118°05'W
Pico Island, i., Port. (pē'kô)	230a	38°16'N	28°49'W
Pico Rivera, Ca., U.S.	117a	34°01'N	118°05'W
Picos, Braz. (pē'kōzh)	143	7°13'S	41°23'W
Picton, Austl. (pĭk'tŭn)	217b	34°11'S	150°37'E
Picton, Can.	99	44°00'N	77°15'W
Pictou, Can. (pĭk-tōō')	101	45°41'N	62°43'W
Pidálion, Akrotírion, c., Cyp.	197a	34°50'N	34°05'E
Pidurutalagala, mtn., Sri L. (pē'dô-rô-tä'lȧ-gä'lȧ)	203	7°00'N	80°46'E
Pidvolochys'k, Ukr.	177	49°32'N	26°16'E
Pie, i., Can. (pī)	98	48°10'N	89°07'W
Piedade, Braz. (pyä-dä'dě)	141a	23°42'S	47°25'W
Piedmont, Al., U.S. (pēd'mŏnt)	124	33°54'N	85°36'W
Piedmont, Ca., U.S.	116b	37°50'N	122°14'W
Piedmont, Mo., U.S.	121	37°09'N	90°42'W
Piedmont, S.C., U.S.	125	34°40'N	82°27'W
Piedmont, W.V., U.S.	109	39°30'N	79°05'W
Piedrabuena, Spain (pyā-drä-bwā'nä)	172	39°01'N	4°10'W
Piedras, Punta, c., Arg. (pōō'n-tä-pyě'dräs)	141c	35°25'S	57°10'W
Piedras Negras, Mex. (pyā'dräs nā'gräs)	128	28°41'N	100°33'W
Pieksämäki, Fin. (pyěk'sě-mě-kē)	167	62°18'N	27°14'E
Piemonte, hist. reg., Italy (pyě-mô'n-tě)	174	44°30'N	7°42'E
Pienaars, r., S. Afr.	238c	25°13'S	28°05'E
Pienaarsrivier, S. Afr.	238c	25°12'S	28°18'E
Pierce, Ne., U.S. (pērs)	112	42°11'N	97°33'W
Pierce, W.V., U.S.	109	39°15'N	79°30'W
Piermont, N.Y., U.S. (pēr'mŏnt)	110a	41°03'N	73°55'W
Pierre, S.D., U.S. (pēr)	104	44°22'N	100°20'W
Pierrefonds, Can.	102a	45°29'N	73°52'W
Piešt'any, Slvk.	169	48°36'N	17°48'E
Pietermaritzburg, S. Afr. (pē-tẽr-mȧ-rĭts-bûrg)	232	29°36'S	30°23'E
Pietersburg, S. Afr. (pē'tẽrz-bûrg)	232	23°56'S	29°30'E
Piet Retief, S. Afr. (pēt rě-tēf')	232	27°00'S	30°58'E
Pietrosu, Vârful, mtn., Rom.	169	47°35'N	24°49'E
Pieve di Cadore, Italy (pyā'vå dē kä-dō'rå)	162	46°26'N	12°22'E
Pigeon, r., N.A. (pĭj'*ŭ*n)	113	48°05'N	90°13'W
Pigeon Lake, Can.	102f	49°57'N	97°36'W
Pigeon Lake, l., Can.	95	53°00'N	114°00'W
Piggott, Ar., U.S. (pĭg-ŭt)	121	36°22'N	90°10'W
Pijijiapan, Mex. (pēkē-kē-ä'pän)	131	15°40'N	93°12'W
Pijnacker, Neth.	159a	52°01'N	4°25'E
Pikes Peak, mtn., Co., U.S. (pīks)	106	38°49'N	105°03'W
Pikeville, Ky., U.S. (pīk'vĭl)	108	37°28'N	82°31'W
Pikou, China (pē-kō)	208	39°25'N	122°19'E
Pikwitonei, Can. (pĭk'wĭ-tōn)	97	55°35'N	97°09'W
Piła, Pol. (pē'lȧ)	168	53°09'N	16°44'E
Pilansberg, mtn., S. Afr. (pē'*ă*ns'bûrg)	238c	25°08'S	26°55'E
Pilar, Arg. (pē'lär)	141c	34°27'S	58°55'W
Pilar, Para.	144	27°00'S	58°15'W
Pilar de Goiás, Braz. (dě-gô'yá's)	143	14°47'S	49°33'W
Pilchuck, r., Wa., U.S.	116a	48°03'N	121°58'W
Pilchuck Creek, r., Wa., U.S. (pĭl'chŭck)	116a	48°19'N	122°11'W
Pilchuck Mountain, mtn., Wa., U.S.	116a	48°03'N	121°48'W
Pilcomayo, r., S.A. (pēl-cō-mī'ô)	144	24°45'S	59°15'W
Pili, Phil. (pē'lē)	213a	13°34'N	123°17'E
Pilica, r., Pol. (pē-lēt'sä)	169	51°00'N	19°48'E
Pillar Point, c., Wa., U.S. (pĭl'*ă*r)	116a	48°14'N	124°06'W
Pillar Rocks, Wa., U.S.	116c	46°16'N	123°35'W

ng-sing; ŋ-baŋk; ɴ-nasalized n; nŏd; c*ŏ*mmit; ōld; ôbey; ôrder; oi-boil; fōōd; ŏ-as oo in foot; ou-out; s-soft; sh-dish; th-thin; pūre; ûnite; ûrn; stŭd; circ*ŭ*s; ü-as in French tu; '-indeterminate vowel.

PLACE (Pronunciation)	PAGE	LAT.	LONG.
Pilón, r., Mex. (pē-lōn′)	130	24°13′N	99°03′W
Pilot Point, Tx., U.S. (pī′lŭt)	121	33°24′N	97°00′W
Pilsen see Plzeň, Czech Rep.	154	49°46′N	13°25′E
Piltene, Lat. (pĭl′tĕ-nĕ)	167	57°17′N	21°40′E
Pimal, Cerra, mtn., Mex. (sĕ′r-rä-pē-mäl′)	130	22°58′N	104°19′W
Pimba, Austl. (pĭm′bȧ)	218	31°15′S	137°50′E
Pimville, neigh., S. Afr. (pĭm′vĭl)	233b	26°17′S	27°54′E
Pinacate, Cerro, mtn., Mex. (sĕ′r-rô-pē-nä-kä′tĕ)	128	31°45′N	113°30′W
Pinamalayan, Phil. (pē-nä-mä-lä′yän)	213a	13°04′N	121°31′E
Pinang see George Town, Malay.	212	5°21′N	100°09′E
Pınarbaşı, Tur. (pē′när-bä′shĭ)	163	38°50′N	36°10′E
Pinar del Río, Cuba (pē-när′ dĕl rē′ô)	129	22°25′N	83°35′W
Pinar del Río, prov., Cuba	134	22°45′N	83°25′W
Pinatubo, mtn., Phil. (pē-nä-tōō′bô)	213a	15°09′N	120°19′E
Pincher Creek, Can. (pĭn′chẽr krēk)	95	49°29′N	113°57′W
Pinckneyville, Il., U.S. (pĭnk′nĭ-vĭl)	121	38°06′N	89°22′W
Pińczów, Pol. (pēn′′chôf)	169	50°32′N	20°33′E
Pindamonhangaba, Braz. (pē′n-dä-mōnyä′n-gä-bä)	141a	22°56′S	45°26′W
Pinder Point, c., Bah.	134	26°35′N	78°35′W
Pindiga, Nig.	235	9°59′N	10°54′E
Píndos Óros, mts., Grc.	156	39°48′N	21°19′E
Pine, r., Can. (pīn)	95	55°30′N	122°20′W
Pine, r., Wi., U.S.	113	45°50′N	88°37′W
Pine Bluff, Ar., U.S. (pīn blŭf)	105	34°13′N	92°01′W
Pine City, Mn., U.S. (pīn)	113	45°50′N	93°01′W
Pine Creek, Austl.	218	13°45′S	132°00′E
Pine Creek, r., Nv., U.S.	118	40°15′N	116°17′W
Pine Falls, Can.	97	50°35′N	96°15′W
Pine Flat Lake, res., Ca., U.S.	118	36°52′N	119°18′W
Pine Forest Range, mts., Nv., U.S.	114	41°35′N	118°45′W
Pinega, Russia (pē-nyĕ′gȧ)	178	64°40′N	43°30′E
Pinega, r., Russia	180	64°10′N	42°30′E
Pine Hill, N.J., U.S. (pīn hĭl)	110f	39°47′N	74°59′W
Pineiós, r., Grc.	175	39°30′N	21°40′E
Pine Island Sound, strt., Fl., U.S.	125a	26°32′N	82°30′W
Pine Lake Estates, Ga., U.S. (lāk ĕs-tāts′)	110c	33°47′N	84°13′W
Pinelands, S. Afr. (pīn′lănds)	232a	33°57′S	18°30′E
Pine Lawn, Mo., U.S. (lôn)	117e	38°42′N	90°17′W
Pine Pass, p., Can.	95	55°22′N	122°40′W
Pinerolo, Italy (pē-nå-rô′lō)	174	44°47′N	7°18′E
Pines, Lake o' the, Tx., U.S.	123	32°50′N	94°40′W
Pinetown, S. Afr. (pīn′toun)	233c	29°47′S	30°52′E
Pine View Reservoir, res., Ut., U.S. (vū)	117b	41°17′N	111°54′W
Pineville, Ky., U.S. (pīn′vĭl)	124	36°48′N	83°43′W
Pineville, La., U.S.	123	31°20′N	92°25′W
Ping, r., Thai.	212	17°54′N	98°29′E
Pingding, China (pĭŋ-dĭŋ)	208	37°50′N	113°30′E
Pingdu, China (pĭŋ-dōō)	208	36°46′N	119°57′E
Pinggir, Indon.	197b	1°05′N	101°12′E
Pinghe, China (pĭŋ-hŭ)	209	24°30′N	117°02′E
Pingle, China (pĭŋ-lŭ)	209	24°30′N	110°22′E
Pingliang, China (pĭng′lyäng′)	204	35°12′N	106°50′E
Pingquan, China (pĭŋ-chyůän)	208	40°58′N	118°40′E
Pingtan, China (pĭŋ-tän)	209	25°30′N	119°45′E
Pingtan Dao, i., China (pĭŋ-tän dou)	209	25°40′N	119°45′E
P'ingtung, Tai.	209	22°40′N	120°35′E
Pingwu, China (pĭŋ-wōō)	208	32°20′N	104°40′E
Pingxiang, China (pĭŋ-shyäŋ)	209	27°40′N	113°50′E
Pingyi, China (pĭŋ-yē)	206	35°30′N	117°38′E
Pingyuan, China (pĭŋ-yůän)	206	37°11′N	116°26′E
Pingzhou, China (pĭŋ-jō)	207a	23°01′N	113°11′E
Pinhal, Braz. (pē-nyȧ′l)	141a	22°11′S	46°43′W
Pinhal Novo, Port. (nô vô)	173b	38°38′N	8°54′W
Pinhel, Port. (pēn-yĕl′)	172	40°45′N	7°03′W
Pini, Pulau, i., Indon.	212	0°07′S	98°38′E
Pinnacles National Monument, rec., Ca., U.S. (pĭn′ȧ-k'lz)	118	36°30′N	121°00′W
Pinneberg, Ger. (pĭn′ĕ-bĕrg)	159c	53°40′N	9°48′E
Pinole, Ca., U.S. (pĭ-nō′lē)	116b	38°01′N	122°17′W
Pinos-Puente, Spain (pwān′tå)	172	37°15′N	3°43′W
Pinotepa Nacional, Mex. (pē-nô-tā′pä nä-syô-näl′)	130	16°21′N	98°04′W
Pins, Île des, i., N. Cal.	221	22°44′S	167°44′E
Pinsk, Bela. (pēn′sk)	178	52°07′N	26°05′E
Pinta, i., Ec.	142	0°41′N	90°47′W
Pintendre, Can. (pĕn-tändr′)	102b	46°45′N	71°07′W
Pinto, Spain (pēn′tō)	173a	40°14′N	3°42′W
Pinto Butte, Can. (pĭn′tō)	96	49°22′N	107°25′W
Pioche, Nv., U.S. (pī-ō′chē)	119	37°56′N	114°28′W
Piombino, Italy (pyôm-bē′nō)	162	42°56′N	10°33′E
Pioneer Mountains, mts., Mt., U.S. (pī′ô-nēr′)	115	45°23′N	112°51′W
Piotrków Trybunalski, Pol. (pyōtr′kōōv trĭ-bōō-nal′skē)	161	51°23′N	19°44′E
Piper, Al., U.S. (pī′pẽr)	124	33°04′N	87°00′W
Piper, Ks., U.S.	117f	39°09′N	94°51′W
Pipe Spring National Monument, rec., Az., U.S. (pīp spring)	119	36°50′N	112°45′W
Pipestone, Mn., U.S. (pīp′stōn)	112	44°00′N	96°19′W
Pipestone National Monument, rec., Mn., U.S.	112	44°03′N	96°24′W
Pipmuacan, Réservoir, res., Can. (pĭp-mä-kän′)	99	49°45′N	70°00′W
Piqua, Oh., U.S. (pĭk′wȧ)	108	40°10′N	84°15′W
Piracaia, Braz. (pē-rä-kȧ′yä)	141a	23°04′S	46°20′W
Piracicaba, Braz. (pē-rä-sē-kä′bä)	143	22°43′S	47°39′W
Piraíba, r., Braz. (pä-rä-ē′bȧ)	141a	21°38′S	41°29′W
Piramida, mtn., Russia	179	54°00′N	96°00′E
Piran, Slvn. (pē-rå′n)	174	45°31′N	13°34′E
Piranga, Braz. (pē-rä′n-gä)	141a	20°41′S	43°17′W
Pirapetinga, Braz. (pē-rä-pĕ-tē′n-gä)	141a	21°40′S	42°20′W
Pirapora, Braz. (pē-rä-pō′rȧ)	143	17°39′S	44°54′W
Pirassununga, Braz. (pē-rä-sōō-nōō′n-gä)	141a	22°00′S	47°24′W
Pirenópolis, Braz. (pē-rĕ-nô′pō-lēs)	143	15°56′S	48°49′W
Piritu, Laguna de, l., Ven. (lä-gô′nä-dĕ-pē-rē′tōō)	143b	10°00′N	64°57′W
Pirmasens, Ger. (pĭr-mä-zĕns′)	168	49°12′N	7°34′E
Pirna, Ger. (pĭr′nä)	168	50°57′N	13°56′E
Pirot, Serb. (pē′rōt)	163	43°09′N	22°35′E
Pirtleville, Az., U.S. (pûr′t'l-vĭl)	119	31°25′N	109°35′W
Piru, Indon. (pē-rōō′)	213	3°15′S	128°25′E
Pisa, Italy (pē′sä)	162	43°52′N	10°24′E
Pisagua, Chile (pē-sä′gwä)	142	19°43′S	70°12′W
Piscataway, Md., U.S. (pĭs-kă-tă-wā)	110e	38°42′N	76°59′W
Piscataway, N.J., U.S.	110a	40°35′N	74°27′W
Pisco, Peru (pēs′kō)	142	13°43′S	76°07′W
Pisco, Bahía de, b., Peru	142	13°43′S	77°48′W
Piseco, l., N.Y., U.S. (pĭ-sā′kô)	109	43°25′N	74°35′W
Pisek, Czech Rep. (pē′sĕk)	161	49°18′N	14°08′E
Pisticci, Italy (pēs-tē′chē)	174	40°24′N	16°34′E
Pistoia, Italy (pēs-tô′yä)	162	43°57′N	11°54′E
Pisuerga, r., Spain (pē-swĕr′gä)	172	41°48′N	4°28′W
Pit, r., Ca., U.S. (pĭt)	114	40°58′N	121°42′W
Pitalito, Col. (pē-tä-lē′tō)	142	1°45′N	75°09′W
Pitcairn, dep., Oc.	2	25°04′S	130°05′W
Pitealven, r., Swe.	160	66°08′N	18°51′E
Piteşti, Rom. (pē-tĕsht′′)	175	44°51′N	24°51′E
Pithara, Austl. (pĭt′ărȧ)	218	30°27′S	116°45′E
Pithiviers, Fr. (pē-tē-vyā′)	170	48°12′N	2°14′E
Pitman, N.J., U.S. (pĭt′mȧn)	110f	39°44′N	75°08′W
Pitseng, Leso.	233c	29°03′S	28°13′E
Pitt, r., Can.	116d	49°19′N	122°39′W
Pitt Island, i., Can.	94	53°35′N	129°45′W
Pittsburg, Ca., U.S. (pĭts′bûrg)	116b	38°01′N	121°52′W
Pittsburg, Ks., U.S.	105	37°25′N	94°43′W
Pittsburg, Tx., U.S.	121	32°00′N	94°57′W
Pittsburgh, Pa., U.S.	105	40°26′N	80°01′W
Pittsfield, Il., U.S. (pĭts′fēld)	121	39°37′N	90°47′W
Pittsfield, Ma., U.S.	109	42°25′N	73°15′W
Pittsfield, Me., U.S.	100	44°45′N	69°44′W
Pittston, Pa., U.S. (pĭts′tŭn)	109	41°20′N	75°50′W
Piũi, Braz. (pē-ōō′ē)	141a	20°27′S	45°57′W
Piura, Peru (pē-ōō′rä)	142	5°13′S	80°46′W
Pivdennyi Buh, r., Ukr.	181	48°12′N	30°13′E
Piya, Russia (pē′yȧ)	186a	58°34′N	61°12′E
Placentia, Can.	101	47°15′N	53°58′W
Placentia, Ca., U.S. (plă-sĕn′shĭ-ȧ)	117a	33°52′N	117°50′W
Placentia Bay, b., Can.	93a	47°14′N	54°30′W
Placerville, Ca., U.S. (plăs′ẽr-vĭl)	118	38°43′N	120°47′W
Placetas, Cuba (plä-thā′täs)	134	22°10′N	79°40′W
Placid, l., N.Y., U.S. (plăs′ĭd)	109	44°20′N	74°00′W
Plain City, Ut., U.S. (plān)	117b	41°18′N	112°06′W
Plainfield, Il., U.S. (plān′fēld)	111a	41°37′N	88°12′W
Plainfield, In., U.S.	111g	39°42′N	86°23′W
Plainfield, N.J., U.S.	110a	40°38′N	74°25′W
Plainview, Ar., U.S. (plān′vū)	121	34°59′N	93°15′W
Plainview, Mn., U.S.	113	44°09′N	93°12′W
Plainview, Ne., U.S.	112	42°20′N	97°47′W
Plainview, Tx., U.S.	120	34°11′N	101°42′W
Plainwell, Mi., U.S. (plan′wĕl)	108	42°25′N	85°40′W
Plaisance, Can. (plĕ-zäns′)	102c	45°37′N	75°07′W
Plana or Flat Cays, is., Bah. (plä′nä)	135	22°35′N	73°35′W
Planegg, Ger. (plä′nĕg)	159d	48°06′N	11°27′E
Plano, Tx., U.S. (plā′nō)	121	33°01′N	96°42′W
Plantagenet, Can. (plän-tăzh-nĕ′)	102c	45°33′N	75°00′W
Plant City, Fl., U.S. (plȧnt sĭ′tĭ)	125a	28°00′N	82°07′W
Plaquemine, La., U.S. (plăk′mēn′)	123	30°17′N	91°14′W
Plasencia, Spain (plä-sĕn′thē-ä)	172	40°02′N	6°07′W
Plast, Russia (plást)	180	54°22′N	60°48′E
Plaster Rock, Can. (plȧs′tẽr rŏk)	100	46°54′N	67°24′W
Plastun, Russia (plȧs-tōōn′)	210	44°41′N	136°08′E
Plata, Río de la, est., S.A. (dālä plä′tä)	144	34°35′S	58°15′W
Platani, r., Italy (plä-tä′nē)	174	37°26′N	13°28′E
Plateforme, Pointe, c., Haiti	135	19°35′N	73°50′W
Platinum, Ak., U.S. (plăt′ĭ-nŭm)	103	59°00′N	161°27′W
Plato, Col. (plä′tō)	142	9°49′N	74°48′W
Platón Sánchez, Mex. (plä-tōn′ sän′chĕz)	130	21°14′N	98°20′W
Platte, S.D., U.S. (plăt)	112	43°22′N	98°51′W
Platte, r., Mo., U.S.	121	40°09′N	94°40′W
Platte, r., Ne., U.S.	106	40°50′N	100°40′W
Platteville, Wi., U.S. (plăt′vĭl)	113	42°44′N	90°31′W
Plattsburg, Mo., U.S. (plăts′bûrg)	121	39°33′N	94°26′W
Plattsburg, N.Y., U.S.	109	44°40′N	73°30′W
Plattsmouth, Ne., U.S. (plăts′mŭth)	112	41°00′N	95°53′W
Plauen, Ger. (plou′ĕn)	161	50°30′N	12°08′E
Playa de Guanabo, Cuba (plä-yä-dĕ-gwä-nä′bô)	135a	23°10′N	82°07′W
Playa de Santa Fé, Cuba	135a	23°05′N	82°31′W
Playas Lake, l., N.M., U.S. (plä′yȧs)	119	31°50′N	108°30′W
Playa Vicente, Mex. (vē-sĕn′tå)	131	17°49′N	95°49′W
Playa Vicente, r., Mex.	131	17°36′N	96°13′W
Playgreen Lake, l., Can. (plā′grēn)	97	54°00′N	98°10′W
Pleasant, l., N.Y., U.S. (plĕz′ănt)	109	43°25′N	74°25′W
Pleasant Grove, Al., U.S.	110h	33°29′N	86°57′W
Pleasant Hill, Ca., U.S.	116b	37°57′N	122°04′W
Pleasant Hill, Mo., U.S.	121	38°46′N	94°18′W
Pleasanton, Ca., U.S. (plĕz′ăn-tŭn)	116b	37°40′N	121°53′W
Pleasanton, Ks., U.S.	121	38°10′N	94°41′W
Pleasanton, Tx., U.S.	122	28°58′N	98°30′W
Pleasant Plain, Oh., U.S. (plĕz′ănt)	111f	39°17′N	84°06′W
Pleasant Ridge, Mi., U.S.	111b	42°28′N	83°09′W
Pleasant View, Ut., U.S. (plĕz′ănt vū)	117b	41°20′N	112°02′W
Pleasantville, N.Y., U.S. (plĕz′ănt-vĭl)	110a	41°08′N	73°47′W
Pleasure Ridge Park, Ky., U.S. (plĕzh′ẽr rĭj)	111h	38°09′N	85°49′W
Plenty, Bay of, b., N.Z. (plĕn′tē)	221a	37°30′S	177°10′E
Plentywood, Mt., U.S. (plĕn′tē-wŏd)	115	48°47′N	104°38′W
Ples, Russia (plyĕs)	176	57°26′N	41°29′E
Pleshcheyevo, l., Russia (plĕsh-chā′yĕ-vô)	176	56°50′N	38°22′E
Plessisville, Can. (plĕ-sē′vēl′)	99	46°12′N	71°47′W
Pleszew, Pol. (plĕ′zhĕf)	169	51°54′N	17°48′E
Plettenberg, Ger. (plĕ′tĕn-bĕrgh)	171c	51°13′N	7°53′E
Pleven, Blg. (plĕ′vĕn)	163	43°24′N	24°26′E
Pljevlja, Serb. (plĕv′lyä)	163	43°20′N	19°21′E
Płock, Pol. (pwôtsk)	161	52°32′N	19°44′E
Ploërmel, Fr. (plô-ĕr-mĕl′)	170	47°56′N	2°25′W
Ploieşti, Rom. (plô-yĕsht′′)	154	44°56′N	26°01′E
Plomári, Grc.	175	38°51′N	26°24′E
Plomb du Cantal, mtn., Fr. (plôɴ′dükäɴ-täl′)	161	45°30′N	2°49′E
Plonge, Lac la, l., Can. (plōɴzh)	96	55°08′N	107°25′W
Plovdiv, Blg. (plôv′dĭf) (fĭl-ĭp-ŏp′ô-lĭs)	154	42°09′N	24°43′E
Pluma Hidalgo, Mex. (plōō′mä ē-däl′gō)	131	15°54′N	96°23′W
Plunge, Lith. (plŏŋ′gä)	167	55°56′N	21°45′E
Plymouth, Monts.	133b	16°43′N	62°12′W
Plymouth, Eng., U.K. (plĭm′ŭth)	161	50°25′N	4°14′W
Plymouth, In., U.S.	108	41°20′N	86°20′W
Plymouth, Ma., U.S.	109	42°00′N	70°45′W
Plymouth, Mi., U.S.	111b	42°23′N	83°27′W
Plymouth, N.C., U.S.	125	35°50′N	76°44′W
Plymouth, N.H., U.S.	109	43°50′N	71°40′W
Plymouth, Pa., U.S.	109	41°15′N	75°55′W
Plymouth, Wi., U.S.	113	43°45′N	87°59′W
Plyussa, r., Russia (plyōō′sȧ)	176	58°33′N	28°30′E
Plzeň, Czech Rep.	154	49°45′N	13°23′E
Po, r., Italy	156	45°10′N	11°00′E
Pocahontas, Ar., U.S. (pō-kȧ-hŏn′tȧs)	121	36°15′N	91°01′W
Pocahontas, Ia., U.S.	113	42°43′N	94°41′W
Pocatello, Id., U.S. (pō-kȧ-tĕl′ō)	104	42°54′N	112°30′W
Pochëp, Russia (pô-chĕp′)	181	52°56′N	33°27′E
Pochinok, Russia (pô-chē′nôk)	176	54°14′N	32°27′E
Pochinski, Russia	180	54°40′N	44°50′E
Pochotitán, Mex. (pô-chô-tē-tä′n)	130	21°37′N	104°33′W
Pochutla, Mex.	131	15°46′N	96°28′W
Pocomoke City, Md., U.S. (pō-kō-mōk′)	109	38°05′N	75°35′W
Pocono Mountains, mts., Pa., U.S. (pō-cō′nō)	109	41°10′N	75°30′W
Poços de Caldas, Braz. (pō-sôs-dĕ-käl′dȧs)	143	21°48′S	46°34′W
Poder, Sen. (pô-dôr′)	230	16°35′N	15°04′W
Podgorica, Serb.	175	42°25′N	19°15′E
Podkamennaya Tunguska, r., Russia	179	61°43′N	93°45′E
Podol'sk, Russia (pō-dôl′′sk)	180	55°26′N	37°33′E
Poggibonsi, Italy (pôd-jē-bôn′sē)	174	43°27′N	11°12′E
Pogodino, Bela. (pô-gô′dē-nô)	180	54°17′N	31°00′E
P'ohangdong, Kor., S.	210	35°57′N	129°23′E
Pointe-à-Pitre, Guad. (pwăɴt′ ȧ pē-tr′)	129	16°15′N	61°32′W
Pointe-aux-Trembles, Can. (pōō-änt′ ō-tränbl)	102a	45°39′N	73°30′W
Pointe Claire, Can. (pōō-änt′ klĕr)	102a	45°27′N	73°48′W
Pointe-des-Cascades, Can. (käs-kädz′)	102a	45°19′N	73°58′W
Pointe Fortune, Can. (fôr′tūn)	102a	45°34′N	74°23′W
Pointe-Gatineau, Can. (pōō-änt′gä-tē-nō′)	102c	45°28′N	75°42′W
Pointe Noire, Congo	232	4°48′S	11°51′E
Point Hope, Ak., U.S. (hōp)	103	68°18′N	166°38′W
Point Pleasant, W.V., U.S. (plĕz′ănt)	108	38°50′N	82°10′W
Point Roberts, Wa., U.S. (rŏb′ẽrts)	116d	48°59′N	123°04′W
Poissy, Fr. (pwȧ-sē′)	171b	48°55′N	2°02′E
Poitiers, Fr. (pwȧ-tyā′)	161	46°35′N	0°18′E
Pokaran, India (pō′kŭr-ŭn)	202	27°00′N	72°05′E
Pokrov, Russia (pô-krôf)	176	55°56′N	39°09′E
Pokrovskoye, Russia (pô-krôf′skô-yĕ)	177	47°27′N	38°54′E
Pola, r., Russia (pō′lä)	176	57°44′N	31°53′E
Pola de Laviana, Spain (dĕ-lä-vyä′nä)	172	43°15′N	5°29′W
Pola de Siero, Spain	172	43°24′N	5°39′W
Poland, nation, Eur. (pō′lănd)	154	52°37′N	17°01′E
Polangui, Phil. (pô-läŋ′gē)	213a	13°18′N	123°29′E
Polatsk, Bela.	180	55°30′N	28°48′E
Polazna, Russia (pô′láz-nȧ)	186a	58°18′N	56°25′E
Polessk, Russia (pô′lĕsk)	167	54°50′N	21°14′E
Polevskoy, Russia (pô-lĕ′vs-kô′ĭ)	186a	56°28′N	60°14′E
Polgár, Hung. (pôl′gär)	169	47°54′N	21°10′E
Policastro, Golfo di, b., Italy	174	40°00′N	15°23′E
Polichnítos, Grc.	175	39°05′N	26°11′E
Poligny, Fr. (pō-lē-nyē′)	171	46°48′N	5°42′E
Polillo, Phil. (pō-lēl′yō)	213a	14°42′N	121°56′E
Polillo Islands, is., Phil.	199	15°05′N	122°15′E
Polillo Strait, strt., Phil.	213a	15°02′N	121°40′E
Polist', r., Russia (pō′lĭst)	176	57°42′N	31°02′E
Polistena, Italy (pō-lēs-tā′nä)	174	38°25′N	16°05′E
Polkan, Gora, mtn., Russia	179	60°18′N	92°08′E
Polochic, r., Guat. (pō-lō-chēk′)	132	15°19′N	89°45′W
Polonne, Ukr.	177	50°07′N	27°31′E
Polpaico, Chile (pôl-pȧ′y-kô)	141b	33°10′S	70°53′W
Polson, Mt., U.S. (pōl′sŭn)	115	47°40′N	114°10′W

ăt; finăl; rāte; senåte; ärm; ȧsk; sofȧ; fâre; ch-choose; dh-as th in other; bē; ēvent; bĕt; recĕnt; cratẽr; g-gō; gh-guttural g; bĭt; ĭ-short neutral; rīde; ĸ-guttural k as ch in German ich;

PRONOUNCING INDEX

Poltava – Pratas Island 337

PLACE (Pronunciation)	PAGE	LAT.	LONG.
Poltava, Ukr. (pôl-tä′vä)	178	49°35′N	34°33′E
Poltava, prov., Ukr.	177	49°53′N	32°58′E
Pōltsamaa, Est. (pŏlt′sȧ-mä)	167	58°39′N	26°00′E
Polunochnoye, Russia (pô-lōō-nô′ch-nô′yĕ)	186a	60°52′N	60°27′E
Poluy, r., Russia (pôl′wė)	184	65°45′N	68°15′E
Polyakovka, Russia (pŭl-yä′kôv-kȧ)	186a	54°38′N	59°42′E
Polyarnyy, Russia (pŭl-yär′nē)	178	69°10′N	33°30′E
Polygyros, Grc.	175	40°23′N	23°27′E
Polynesia, is., Oc.	240	4°00′S	156°00′W
Pomba, r., Braz. (pô′m-bȧ)	141a	21°28′S	42°28′W
Pomerania, hist. reg., Pol. (pŏm-ė-rā′nĭ-ȧ)	168	53°50′N	15°20′E
Pomeroy, S. Afr. (pŏm′ẽr-roi)	233c	28°36′S	30°26′E
Pomeroy, Wa., U.S. (pŏm′ẽr-oi)	114	46°28′N	117°35′W
Pomezia, Italy (pô-mĕ′t-zyä)	173d	41°41′N	12°31′E
Pomigliano d'Arco, Italy (pô-mē-lyȧ′nô-d-ä′r-kô)	173c	40°39′N	14°23′E
Pomme de Terre, Mn., U.S. (pôm dē tĕr′)	112	45°22′N	95°52′W
Pomona, Ca., U.S. (pô-mō′nȧ)	104	34°04′N	117°45′W
Pomorie, Blg.	163	42°24′N	27°41′E
Pompano Beach, Fl., U.S. (pŏm′pă-nô)	125a	26°12′N	80°07′W
Pompeii Ruins, hist., Italy	173c	40°31′N	14°29′E
Pompton Lakes, N.J., U.S. (pŏmp′tŏn)	110a	41°01′N	74°16′W
Pomuch, Mex. (pô-mōō′ch)	132a	20°12′N	90°10′W
Ponca, Ne., U.S. (pŏn′kȧ)	112	42°34′N	96°43′W
Ponca City, Ok., U.S.	121	36°42′N	97°07′W
Ponce, P.R. (pōn′sā)	129	18°01′N	66°43′W
Pondicherry, India	199	11°58′N	79°48′E
Pondicherry, state, India	199	11°50′N	74°50′E
Ponferrada, Spain (pôn-fĕr-rä′dhä)	162	42°33′N	6°38′W
Ponoka, Can. (pŏ-nō′kȧ)	90	52°42′N	113°35′W
Ponoy, Russia	180	66°58′N	41°00′E
Ponoy, r., Russia	180	67°00′N	39°00′E
Ponta Delgada, Port. (pôn′tȧ dĕl-gä′dȧ)	230a	37°40′N	25°45′W
Ponta Grossa, Braz. (grō′sȧ)	143	25°09′S	50°05′W
Pont-à-Mousson, Fr. (pôɴ′tȧ-mōōsôɴ′)	171	48°55′N	6°02′E
Pontarlier, Fr. (pôɴ′tȧr-lyā′)	171	46°53′N	6°22′E
Pont-Audemer, Fr. (pôɴ′tōd′mâr′)	170	49°23′N	0°28′E
Pontchartrain Lake, l., La., U.S. (pôɴ-shȧr-trăn′)	123	30°10′N	90°10′W
Ponteareas, Spain	172	42°09′N	8°23′W
Pontedera, Italy (pōn-tȧ-dā′rä)	174	43°37′N	10°37′E
Ponte de Sor, Port.	172	39°14′N	8°03′W
Pontefract, Eng., U.K. (pŏn′tė-frăkt)	158a	53°41′N	1°18′W
Ponte Nova, Braz. (pô′n-tĕ-nô′vȧ)	143	20°26′S	42°52′W
Pontevedra, Spain (pôn-tĕ-vĕ-drä)	162	42°28′N	8°38′W
Ponthierville *see* Ubundi, D.R.C.	232	0°21′S	25°29′E
Pontiac, Il., U.S. (pŏn′tĭ-ăk)	108	40°55′N	88°35′W
Pontiac, Mi., U.S.	105	42°37′N	83°17′W
Pontianak, Indon. (pôn-tė-ä′nȧk)	212	0°04′S	109°20′E
Pontian Kechil, Malay.	197b	1°29′N	103°24′E
Pontic Mountains, mts., Tur.	181	41°20′N	34°30′E
Pontivy, Fr. (pôɴ-tė-vē′)	170	48°05′N	2°57′W
Pontoise, Fr. (pôɴ-twȧz′)	170	49°03′N	2°05′E
Pontonnyy, Russia (pôn′tôn-nyĭ)	186c	59°47′N	30°39′E
Pontotoc, Ms., U.S. (pŏn-tô-tŏk′)	124	34°11′N	88°59′W
Pontremoli, Italy (pôn-trĕm′ô-lē)	174	44°21′N	9°50′E
Ponziane, Isole, i., Italy (ė′sō-lĕ)	162	40°55′N	12°58′E
Poole, Eng., U.K. (pōōl)	164	50°43′N	2°00′W
Poolesville, Md., U.S. (poolĕs-vĭl)	110e	39°08′N	77°26′W
Pooley Island, i., Can. (pōō′lē)	94	52°44′N	128°16′W
Poopó, Lago de, l., Bol.	142	18°45′S	67°07′W
Popayán, Col. (pō-pä-yän′)	142	2°21′N	76°43′W
Poplar, Mt., U.S. (pŏp′lẽr)	115	48°08′N	105°10′W
Poplar, r., Mt., U.S.	115	48°34′N	105°20′W
Poplar, West Fork, r., Mt., U.S.	115	48°59′N	106°06′W
Poplar Bluff, Mo., U.S. (blŭf)	121	36°43′N	90°22′W
Poplar Plains, Ky., U.S. (plāns)	108	38°20′N	83°40′W
Poplar Point, Can.	102f	50°04′N	97°57′W
Poplarville, Ms., U.S. (pŏp′lẽr-vĭl)	124	30°50′N	89°33′W
Popocatépetl Volcán, Mex. (pô-pô-kä-tā′pĕ′t'l)	128	19°01′N	98°38′W
Popokabaka, D.R.C. (pō′pô-kȧ-bä′kȧ)	232	5°42′S	16°35′E
Popovo, Blg. (pô′pô-vō)	175	43°23′N	26°17′E
Porbandar, India (pōr-bŭn′dŭr)	199	21°44′N	69°40′E
Porce, r., Col. (pôr-sĕ)	142a	7°11′N	74°55′W
Porcher Island, i., Can. (pôr′kẽr)	94	53°57′N	130°30′W
Porcuna, Spain (pôr-kōō′nä)	172	37°54′N	4°10′W
Porcupine, r., N.A.	103	67°38′N	140°07′W
Porcupine Creek, r., Mt., U.S.	115	48°27′N	106°24′W
Porcupine Hills, hills, Can.	97	52°30′N	101°45′W
Pordenone, Italy (pōr-dȧ-nō′nȧ)	174	45°58′N	12°38′E
Pori, Fin. (pô′rė)	160	61°29′N	21°45′E
Poriúncula, Braz.	141a	20°58′S	42°02′W
Porkhov, Russia (pôr′κôf)	180	57°46′N	29°33′E
Porlamar, Ven. (pôr-lä-mär′)	142	11°00′N	63°55′W
Pornic, Fr. (pôr-nēk′)	170	47°08′N	2°07′W
Poronaysk, Russia (pô′rô-nīsk)	179	49°21′N	143°23′E
Porrentruy, Switz. (pô-räɴ-trũē′)	168	47°25′N	7°02′E
Porsgrunn, Nor. (pôrs′gròn′)	166	59°09′N	9°36′E
Portachuelo, Bol. (pôrt-ä-chwā′lô)	142	17°20′S	63°12′W
Portage, Pa., U.S. (pôr′tāj)	109	40°25′N	78°35′W
Portage, Wi., U.S.	113	43°33′N	89°29′W
Portage Des Sioux, Mo., U.S. (dē sōō)	117e	38°56′N	90°21′W
Portage la Prairie, Can. (lä-prā′rĭ)	90	49°57′N	98°25′W
Port Alberni, Can. (pōr äl-bĕr-nē′)	90	49°14′N	124°48′W
Portalegre, Port. (pôr-tä-lā′grĕ)	162	39°18′N	7°26′W
Portales, N.M., U.S. (pôr-tä′lĕs)	120	34°10′N	103°11′W
Port Alfred, S. Afr.	232	33°36′S	26°55′E
Port Alice, Can. (ăl′ĭs)	90	50°23′N	127°27′W
Port Allegany, Pa., U.S. (ăl-ė-gā′nĭ)	109	41°50′N	78°10′W
Port Angeles, Wa., U.S. (ăn′jĕ-lĕs)	104	48°07′N	123°26′W
Port Antonio, Jam.	129	18°10′N	76°25′W
Portarlington, Austl.	217a	38°07′S	144°39′E
Port Arthur, Tx., U.S.	105	29°52′N	93°59′W
Port Augusta, Austl. (ô-gŭs′tă)	222	32°28′S	137°50′E
Port au Port Bay, b., Can. (pôr′tō pōr′)	101	48°41′N	58°45′W
Port-au-Prince, Haiti (prăɴs′)	129	18°35′N	72°20′W
Port Austin, Mi., U.S. (ôs′tĭn)	108	44°00′N	83°00′W
Port Blair, India (blâr)	212	12°07′N	92°45′E
Port Bolivar, Tx., U.S. (bŏl′ĭ-vȧr)	123a	29°22′N	94°46′W
Port Borden, Can. (bôr′dĕn)	100	46°15′N	63°42′W
Port-Bouët, C. Iv.	230	5°24′N	3°56′W
Port-Cartier, Can.	100	50°01′N	66°53′W
Port Chester, N.Y., U.S. (chĕs′tẽr)	110a	40°59′N	73°40′W
Port Chicago, Ca., U.S. (shĭ-kô′gō)	116b	38°03′N	122°01′W
Port Clinton, Oh., U.S. (klĭn′tŭn)	108	41°30′N	83°00′W
Port Colborne, Can.	99	42°53′N	79°13′W
Port Coquitlam, Can. (kô-kwĭt′lȧm)	95	49°16′N	122°46′W
Port Credit, Can. (krĕd′ĭt)	102d	43°33′N	79°35′W
Port-de-Bouc, Fr. (pôr-dē-bōōk′)	170a	43°24′N	5°00′E
Port de Paix, Haiti (pĕ)	135	19°55′N	72°50′W
Port Dickson, Malay. (dĭk′sŭn)	197b	2°33′N	101°49′E
Port Discovery, b., Wa., U.S. (dĭs-kŭv′ẽr-ĭ)	116a	48°05′N	122°55′W
Port Edward, S. Afr. (ĕd′wẽrd)	233c	31°04′S	30°14′E
Port Elgin, Can. (ĕl′jĭn)	100	46°03′N	64°05′W
Port Elizabeth, S. Afr. (ė-lĭz′ȧ-bĕth)	232	33°57′S	25°37′E
Porterdale, Ga., U.S. (pōr′tẽr-dāl)	124	33°34′N	83°53′W
Porterville, Ca., U.S. (pōr′tẽr-vĭl)	118	36°03′N	119°05′W
Port Francqui *see* Ilebo, D.R.C.	232	4°19′S	20°35′E
Port Gamble, Wa., U.S. (găm′bŭl)	116a	47°52′N	122°36′W
Port Gamble Indian Reservation, I.R., Wa., U.S.	116a	47°54′N	122°33′W
Port-Gentil, Gabon (zhäɴ-tē′)	232	0°43′S	8°47′E
Port Gibson, Ms., U.S.	124	31°56′N	90°57′W
Port Harcourt, Nig. (här′kŭrt)	230	4°43′N	7°05′E
Port Hardy, Can. (här′dĭ)	94	50°43′N	127°29′W
Port Hawkesbury, Can.	101	45°37′N	61°21′W
Port Hedland, Austl. (hĕd′lănd)	218	20°30′S	118°30′E
Porthill, Id., U.S.	114	49°00′N	116°30′W
Port Hood, Can. (hòd)	101	46°01′N	61°32′W
Port Hope, Can. (hōp)	99	43°55′N	78°10′W
Port Huron, Mi., U.S. (hū′rŏn)	105	43°00′N	82°30′W
Portici, Italy (pôr′tė-chė)	173c	40°34′N	14°20′E
Portillo, Chile (pôr-tē′l-yô)	141b	32°51′S	70°09′W
Portimão, Port. (pôr-tē-moůɴ)	172	37°09′N	8°34′W
Port Jervis, N.Y., U.S. (jûr′vĭs)	110a	41°22′N	74°41′W
Portland, Austl. (pōrt′lănd)	219	38°20′S	142°40′E
Portland, In., U.S.	108	40°25′N	85°00′W
Portland, Me., U.S.	105	43°40′N	70°16′W
Portland, Mi., U.S.	108	42°50′N	85°00′W
Portland, Or., U.S.	104	45°31′N	122°41′W
Portland, Tx., U.S.	123	27°53′N	97°20′W
Portland Bight, b., Jam.	134	17°45′N	77°05′W
Portland Canal, can., Ak., U.S.	94	55°10′N	130°08′W
Portland Inlet, b., Can.	94	54°50′N	130°15′W
Portland Point, c., Jam.	134	17°40′N	77°20′W
Port Lavaca, Tx., U.S. (lȧ-vä′kȧ)	123	28°36′N	96°38′W
Port Lincoln, Austl. (lĭŋ-kŭn)	218	34°39′S	135°50′E
Port Ludlow, Wa., U.S. (lŭd′lō)	116a	47°26′N	122°41′W
Port Macquarie, Austl. (mȧ-kwŏ′rĭ)	219	31°25′S	152°45′E
Port Madison Indian Reservation, I.R., Wa., U.S. (măd′ĭ-sŭn)	116a	47°46′N	122°38′W
Port Maria, Jam. (mȧ-rī′ȧ)	134	18°20′N	76°55′W
Port Moody, Can. (mōōd′ĭ)	95	49°17′N	122°51′W
Port Moresby, Pap. N. Gui. (mōrz′bė)	213	9°34′S	147°20′E
Port Neches, Tx., U.S. (nĕch′ĕz)	123	29°59′N	93°57′W
Port Nelson, Can. (nĕl′sŭn)	97	57°03′N	92°36′W
Portneuf-Sur-Mer, Can. (pôr-nûf′sür mẽr)	100	48°36′N	69°06′W
Port Nolloth, S. Afr. (nŏl′ŏth)	232	29°10′S	17°00′E
Porto (Oporto), Port. (pōr′tò)	154	41°10′N	8°38′W
Porto Acre, Braz. (ä′krĕ)	142	9°38′S	67°34′W
Porto Alegre, Braz. (ä-lā′grĕ)	144	29°58′S	51°11′W
Porto Amboim, Ang.	232	11°01′S	13°45′E
Portobelo, Pan. (pôr′tô-bā′lô)	129	9°32′N	79°40′W
Pôrto de Pedras, Braz. (pā′dräzh)	143	9°09′S	35°20′W
Pôrto Feliz, Braz. (fĕ-lē′s)	141a	23°12′S	47°30′W
Portoferraio, Italy (pōr′tô-fĕr-rä′yō)	174	42°47′N	10°20′E
Port of Spain, Trin. (spān)	143	10°44′N	61°24′W
Portogruaro, Italy (pōr′tô-grò-ä′rō)	174	45°48′N	12°49′E
Portola, Ca., U.S. (pôr′tō-lȧ)	118	39°47′N	120°29′W
Porto Mendes, Braz. (mĕ′n-dĕs)	143	24°41′S	54°13′W
Porto Murtinho, Braz. (mòr-tēn′yò)	143	21°43′S	57°43′W
Porto Nacional, Braz. (nȧ-syô-näl′)	143	10°43′S	48°14′W
Porto Novo, Benin (pōr′tô-nō′vō)	230	6°29′N	2°37′E
Port Orchard, Wa., U.S. (ôr′chẽrd)	116a	47°32′N	122°38′W
Port Orchard, b., Wa., U.S.	116a	47°40′N	122°39′W
Porto Santo, Ilha de, i., Port. (säɴ′tò)	230	32°41′N	16°15′W
Porto Seguro, Braz. (sā-gōō′rò)	143	16°26′S	38°59′W
Porto Torres, Italy (tôr′rĕs)	174	40°49′N	8°25′E
Porto-Vecchio, Fr. (vĕk′ė-ô)	174	41°36′N	9°17′E
Porto Velho, Braz. (vāl′yò)	142	8°45′S	63°43′W
Portoviejo, Ec. (pôr-tō-vyā′hō)	142	1°11′S	80°28′W
Port Phillip Bay, b., Austl. (fĭl′ĭp)	221	37°57′S	144°50′E
Port Pirie, Austl. (pĭ′rė)	218	33°10′S	138°00′E
Port Royal, b., Jam. (roi′ăl)	134	17°50′N	76°45′W
Port Said, Egypt	238d	31°15′N	32°19′E
Port Saint Johns, S. Afr. (sånt jŏnz)	232	31°37′S	29°32′E
Port Saint Lucie, Fl., U.S.	125a	27°20′N	80°20′W
Port Shepstone, S. Afr. (shĕps′tŭn)	232	30°45′S	30°23′E
Portsmouth, Dom.	133b	15°33′N	61°28′W
Portsmouth, Eng., U.K. (pôrts′mŭth)	154	50°45′N	1°03′W
Portsmouth, N.H., U.S.	105	43°05′N	70°50′W
Portsmouth, Oh., U.S.	105	38°45′N	83°00′W
Portsmouth, Va., U.S.	105	36°50′N	76°19′W
Port Sulphur, La., U.S. (sŭl′fẽr)	124	29°28′N	89°41′W
Port Susan, b., Wa., U.S. (sū-zȧn′)	116a	48°11′N	122°25′W
Port Townsend, Wa., U.S. (tounz′ĕnd)	116a	48°07′N	122°46′W
Port Townsend, b., Wa., U.S.	116a	48°05′N	122°47′W
Portugal, nation, Eur. (pōr′tu-găl)	154	38°15′N	8°08′W
Portugalete, Spain (pōr-tōō-gä-lā′tā)	172	43°18′N	3°05′W
Portuguese West Africa *see* Angola, nation, Ang.	232	14°15′S	16°00′E
Port Vendres, Fr.	170	42°32′N	3°07′E
Port Vila, Vanuatu	219	17°44′S	168°19′E
Port Wakefield, Austl. (wāk′fēld)	218	34°12′S	138°10′E
Port Washington, N.Y., U.S. (wôsh′ĭng-tŭn)	110a	40°49′N	73°42′W
Port Washington, Wi., U.S.	113	43°24′N	87°52′W
Posadas, Arg. (pō-sä′dhäs)	144	27°32′S	55°56′W
Posadas, Spain (pô-sä-däs)	172	37°48′N	5°09′W
Poshekhon'ye Volodarsk, Russia (pô-shyĕ′κŏn-yĕ vôl′ô-dȧrsk)	176	58°31′N	39°07′E
Poso, Danau, l., Indon. (pō′sō)	212	2°00′S	119°40′E
Pospelokova, Russia (pôs-pyĕl′kô-vȧ)	186a	59°25′N	60°50′E
Possession Sound, strt., Wa., U.S. (pŏ-zĕsh-ŭn)	116a	47°59′N	122°17′W
Possum Kingdom Reservoir, res., Tx., U.S. (pŏs′ŭm kĭng′dŭm)	122	32°58′N	98°12′W
Post, Tx., U.S. (pōst)	120	33°12′N	101°21′W
Postojna, Slvn. (pōs-tōynȧ)	174	45°45′N	14°13′E
Pos'yet, Russia (pos-yĕt′)	210	42°27′N	130°47′E
Potawatomi Indian Reservation, I.R., Ks., U.S. (pŏt-å-wā′tō mē)	121	39°30′N	96°11′W
Potchefstroom, S. Afr. (pŏch′ĕf-strōm)	232	26°42′S	27°06′E
Poteau, Ok., U.S. (pô-tō′)	121	35°03′N	94°37′W
Poteet, Tx., U.S. (pô-tēt)	122	29°05′N	98°35′W
Potenza, Italy (pô-tĕnt′sä)	163	40°39′N	15°49′E
Potenza, r., Italy	174	43°09′N	13°00′E
Potgietersrus, S. Afr. (pôt-κē′tẽrs-rûs)	232	24°09′S	29°04′E
Potholes Reservoir, res., Wa., U.S.	114	47°00′N	119°20′W
Poti, Geor. (pô′tė)	181	42°10′N	41°40′E
Potiskum, Nig.	230	11°43′N	11°05′E
Potomac, Md., U.S. (pô-tō′măk)	110e	39°01′N	77°13′W
Potomac, r., U.S. (pô-tō′măk)	107	38°15′N	76°55′W
Potosí, Bol.	142	19°35′S	65°45′W
Potosi, Mo., U.S. (pŏ-tō′sĭ)	121	37°56′N	90°46′W
Potosi, r., Mex. (pō-tô-sē′)	122	25°04′N	99°36′W
Potrerillos, Hond. (pō-trå-rēl′yôs)	132	15°13′N	87°58′W
Potsdam, Ger. (pôts′däm)	161	52°24′N	13°04′E
Potsdam, N.Y., U.S. (pŏts′dăm)	109	44°40′N	75°00′W
Pottenstein, Aus.	159e	47°58′N	16°06′E
Potters Bar, Eng., U.K. (pŏt′ĕz bär)	158b	51°41′N	0°12′W
Pottstown, Pa., U.S. (pŏts′toun)	109	40°15′N	75°40′W
Pottsville, Pa., U.S. (pôts′vĭl)	109	40°40′N	76°15′W
Poughkeepsie, N.Y., U.S. (pŏ-kĭp′sė)	105	41°45′N	73°55′W
Poulsbo, Wa., U.S. (pōlz′bò)	116a	47°44′N	122°38′W
Poulton-le-Fylde, Eng., U.K. (pōl′tŭn-lē-fīld′)	158a	53°52′N	2°59′W
Pouso Alegre, Braz. (pō′zò ä-lā′grĕ)	143	22°13′S	45°56′W
Póvoa de Varzim, Port. (pō-vō′ȧ dā vär′zēɴ)	162	41°23′N	8°44′W
Powder, r., Or., U.S.	114	44°55′N	117°35′W
Powder, r., U.S. (pou′dẽr)	106	45°18′N	105°37′W
Powder, South Fork, r., Wy., U.S.	115	43°13′N	106°54′W
Powder River, Wy., U.S.	115	43°06′N	106°55′W
Powell, Wy., U.S. (pou′ĕl)	115	44°44′N	108°44′W
Powell, Lake, res., U.S.	106	37°26′N	110°25′W
Powell Lake, l., Can.	94	50°10′N	124°13′W
Powell Point, c., Bah.	134	24°50′N	76°20′W
Powell Reservoir, res., Ky., U.S.	124	36°30′N	83°35′W
Powell River, Can.	90	49°52′N	124°33′W
Poyang Hu, l., China	205	29°20′N	116°28′E
Poygan, r., Wi., U.S. (poi′gȧn)	113	44°10′N	89°05′W
Požarevac, Serb. (pô′zhȧ′rĕ-vȧts)	175	44°38′N	21°12′E
Poza Rica, Mex. (pô-zô-rė′kä)	131	20°32′N	97°25′W
Poznań, Pol.	154	52°25′N	16°55′E
Pozoblanco, Spain (pô-thō-bläŋ′kō)	172	38°23′N	4°50′W
Pozos, Mex. (pô′zōs)	130	22°05′N	100°50′W
Pozuelo de Alarcón, Spain (pô-thwā′lō dā ä-lär-kōn′)	173a	40°27′N	3°49′W
Pozzuoli, Italy (pôt-swô′lē)	174	40°34′N	14°08′E
Pra, r., Ghana (prȧ)	234	5°45′N	1°35′W
Pra, r., Russia	176	55°00′N	40°13′E
Prachin Buri, Thai. (prä′chĕn)	212	13°59′N	101°15′E
Pradera, Col. (prä-dĕ′rä)	142a	3°24′N	76°13′W
Prades, Fr. (prȧd)	170	42°37′N	2°23′E
Prado, Col. (prädô)	142a	3°44′N	74°55′W
Prado Reservoir, res., Ca., U.S. (prä′dō)	117a	33°45′N	117°40′W
Prados, Braz. (prȧ′dôs)	141a	21°05′S	44°04′W
Prague, Czech Rep.	168	50°05′N	14°26′E
Praha *see* Prague, Czech Rep.	154	50°05′N	14°26′E
Praia, C.V. (prä′yȧ)	230b	15°00′N	23°30′W
Praia Funda, Ponta da, c., Braz. (pôn′tä-dȧ-prä′yȧ-fōō′n-dä)	144b	23°04′S	43°34′W
Prairie du Chien, Wi., U.S. (prā′rĭ dò shēn′)	113	43°02′N	91°10′W
Prairie Grove, Can. (prā′rĭ grōv)	102f	49°48′N	96°57′W
Prairie Island Indian Reservation, I.R., Mn., U.S.	113	44°42′N	92°32′W
Prairies, Rivière des, r., Can. (rē-vyâr′ dā prå-rē′)	102a	45°40′N	73°34′W
Pratas Island, i., Asia	209	20°40′N	116°30′E

ng-sing; ŋ-baŋk; ɴ-nasalized n; nŏd; cŏmmit; ōld; ôbey; ôrder; oi-boil; fōōd; ò-as oo in foot; ou-out; s-soft; sh-dish; th-thin; pūre; ůnite; ûrn; stŭd; circŭs; ü-as in French tu; ′-indeterminate vowel.

338 Prato – Purkersdorf PRONOUNCING INDEX

PLACE (Pronunciation)	PAGE	LAT.	LONG.
Prato, Italy (prä'tō)	174	43°53'N	11°03'E
Pratt, Ks., U.S. (prăt)	120	37°37'N	98°43'W
Prattville, Al., U.S. (prăt'vĭl)	124	32°28'N	86°27'W
Pravdinsk, Russia	167	54°26'N	21°00'E
Pravdinskiy, Russia (práv-dĕn'skĭ)	186b	56°03'N	37°52'E
Pravia, Spain (prä'vē-ä)	172	43°30'N	6°08'W
Pregolya, r., Russia (prĕ-gô'lă)	167	54°37'N	20°50'E
Premont, Tx., U.S. (prē-mŏnt')	122	27°20'N	98°07'W
Prenzlau, Ger. (prĕnts'lou)	168	53°19'N	13°52'E
Přerov, Czech Rep. (przhě'rôf)	161	49°28'N	17°28'E
Prescot, Eng., U.K. (prĕs'kŭt)	158a	53°25'N	2°48'W
Prescott, Can. (prĕs'kŭt)	109	44°45'N	75°35'W
Prescott, Ar., U.S.	121	33°47'N	93°23'W
Prescott, Az., U.S. (prĕs'kŏt)	104	34°30'N	112°30'W
Prescott, Wi., U.S. (prĕs'kŏt)	117g	44°45'N	92°48'W
Presho, S.D., U.S. (prĕsh'ō)	112	43°56'N	100°04'W
Presidencia Rogue Sáenz Peña, Arg.	144	26°52'S	60°15'W
Presidente Epitácio, Braz. (prā-sē-dĕn'tĕ å-pē-tä'syō)	143	21°56'S	52°01'W
Presidio, Tx., U.S. (prĕ-sĭ'dĭ-ō)	122	29°33'N	104°23'W
Presidio, Río del, r., Mex. (rē'ō-dĕl-prĕ-sē'dyô)	130	23°54'N	105°44'W
Prešov, Slvk. (prĕ'shôf)	161	49°00'N	21°18'E
Prespa, Lake, l., Eur. (prĕs'pä)	175	40°49'N	20°50'E
Prespuntal, r., Ven.	143b	9°55'N	64°32'W
Presque Isle, Me., U.S. (prĕsk'ēl')	100	46°41'N	68°03'W
Pressbaum, Aus.	159e	48°12'N	16°06'E
Prestea, Ghana	234	5°27'N	2°08'W
Preston, Austl.	217a	37°45'S	145°01'E
Preston, Eng., U.K. (prĕs'tŭn)	164	53°46'N	2°42'W
Preston, Id., U.S. (pres'tŭn)	115	42°05'N	111°54'W
Preston, Mn., U.S. (prĕs'tŭn)	113	43°42'N	92°06'W
Preston, Wa., U.S.	116a	47°31'N	121°56'W
Prestonburg, Ky., U.S. (prĕs'tŭn-bûrg)	108	37°35'N	82°50'W
Prestwich, Eng., U.K. (prĕst'wĭch)	158a	53°32'N	2°17'W
Pretoria, S. Afr. (prē-tō'rĭ-ă)	232	25°43'S	28°16'E
Pretoria North, S. Afr. (prĕ-tō'rĭ-ă nōōrd)	238c	25°41'S	28°11'E
Préveza, Grc. (prĕ'vå-zä)	175	38°58'N	20°44'E
Pribilof Islands, is., Ak., U.S. (prĭ'bĭ-lof)	103	57°00'N	169°20'W
Priboj, Serb. (prē'boi)	175	43°33'N	19°33'E
Price, Ut., U.S. (prīs)	119	39°35'N	110°50'W
Price, r., Ut., U.S.	119	39°21'N	110°35'W
Prichard, Al., U.S. (prĭt'chârd)	124	30°44'N	88°04'W
Priddis, Can. (prĭd'dĭs)	102e	50°53'N	114°20'W
Priddis Creek, r., Can.	102e	50°56'N	114°32'W
Priego, Spain (prē-ā'gō)	172	37°27'N	4°13'W
Prienai, Lith. (prē-ĕn'ī)	167	54°38'N	23°56'E
Prieska, S. Afr. (prē-ĕs'kȧ)	232	29°40'S	22°50'E
Priest Lake, l., Id., U.S. (prēst)	114	48°30'N	116°43'W
Priest Rapids Dam, Wa., U.S.	114	46°39'N	119°55'W
Priest Rapids Lake, res., Wa., U.S.	114	46°42'N	119°58'W
Priiskovaya, Russia (prĭ-ĭs'kô-va-yȧ)	186a	60°50'N	58°55'E
Prijedor, Bos. (prē'yĕ-dôr)	174	44°58'N	16°43'E
Prijepolje, Serb. (prē'yĕ-pô'lyĕ)	175	43°22'N	19°41'E
Prilep, Mac. (prē'lĕp)	163	41°20'N	21°35'E
Primorsk, Russia (prē-môrsk')	167	60°24'N	28°35'E
Primorsko-Akhtarskaya, Russia (prē-môr'skô äк-tär'skĭ-ē)	181	46°03'N	38°09'E
Primrose, S. Afr.	233b	26°11'S	28°11'E
Primrose Lake, l., Can.	96	54°55'N	109°45'W
Prince Albert, Can. (prĭns ăl'bērt)	90	53°12'N	105°46'W
Prince Albert National Park, rec., Can.	92	54°10'N	105°25'W
Prince Albert Sound, strt., Can.	92	70°23'N	116°57'W
Prince Charles Island, i., Can. (chärlz)	93	67°41'N	74°10'W
Prince Edward Island, prov., Can.	91	46°45'N	63°10'W
Prince Edward Islands, is., S. Afr.	224	46°36'S	37°57'E
Prince Edward National Park, rec., Can. (ĕd'wērd)	93	46°33'N	63°35'W
Prince Edward Peninsula, pen., Can.	109	44°00'N	77°15'W
Prince Frederick, Md., U.S. (prĭnce frĕdērĭk)	110e	38°33'N	76°35'W
Prince George, Can. (jôrj)	90	53°51'N	122°57'W
Prince of Wales, i., Austl.	221	10°47'S	142°15'E
Prince of Wales, i., Ak., U.S.	103	55°47'N	132°50'W
Prince of Wales, Cape, c., Ak., U.S. (wālz)	103	65°48'N	169°08'W
Prince Rupert, Can. (roo'pērt)	90	54°19'N	130°19'W
Princes Risborough, Eng., U.K. (prĭns'ĕz rĭz'brŭ)	158b	51°41'N	0°51'W
Princess Charlotte Bay, b., Austl. (shär'lŏt)	221	13°45'S	144°15'E
Princess Royal Channel, strt., Can. (roi'ăl)	94	53°10'N	128°37'W
Princess Royal Island, i., Can.	94	52°57'N	128°49'W
Princeton, Can. (prĭns'tŭn)	90	49°27'N	120°31'W
Princeton, Il., U.S.	108	41°20'N	89°25'W
Princeton, In., U.S.	108	38°20'N	87°35'W
Princeton, Ky., U.S.	124	37°07'N	87°52'W
Princeton, Mi., U.S.	113	46°16'N	87°33'W
Princeton, Mn., U.S.	113	45°34'N	93°36'W
Princeton, Mo., U.S.	121	40°23'N	93°34'W
Princeton, N.J., U.S.	109	40°21'N	74°40'W
Princeton, Wi., U.S.	113	43°50'N	89°09'W
Princeton, W.V., U.S.	125	37°21'N	81°05'W
Prince William Sound, strt., Ak., U.S. (wĭl'yăm)	103	60°40'N	147°10'W
Príncipe, i., S. Tom./P. (prēn'sē-pĕ)	230	1°37'N	7°25'E
Principe Channel, strt., Can. (prĭn'sĭ-pē)	94	53°28'N	129°45'W
Prineville, Or., U.S. (prīn'vĭl)	114	44°17'N	120°48'W

PLACE (Pronunciation)	PAGE	LAT.	LONG.
Prineville Reservoir, res., Or., U.S.	114	44°07'N	120°45'W
Prinzapolca, Nic. (prēn-zä-pōl'kä)	133	13°18'N	83°35'W
Prinzapolca, r., Nic.	133	13°23'N	84°23'W
Prior Lake, Mn., U.S. (prī'ēr)	117g	44°43'N	93°26'W
Priozërsk, Russia (prĭ-ô'zĕrsk)	167	61°03'N	30°08'E
Pripet, r., Eur.	181	51°50'N	29°45'E
Pripet Marshes, sw., Eur.	181	52°10'N	27°30'E
Priština, Serb. (prēsh'tĭ-nä)	163	42°39'N	21°12'E
Pritzwalk, Ger. (prēts'välk)	168	53°09'N	12°12'E
Privas, Fr. (prē-väs')	170	44°44'N	4°37'E
Prizren, Serb. (prē'zrĕn)	163	42°11'N	20°45'E
Procida, Italy (prô'chē-dä)	173c	40°31'N	14°02'E
Procida, Isola di, i., Italy	173c	40°32'N	13°57'E
Proctor, Mn., U.S. (prŏk'tēr)	117h	46°45'N	92°14'W
Proctor, Vt., U.S.	109	43°40'N	73°00'W
Proebstel, Wa., U.S. (prōb'stĕl)	116c	45°40'N	122°29'W
Proenca-a-Nova, Port. (prô-ān'sȧ-ä-nō'vȧ)	172	39°44'N	7°55'W
Progreso, Hond. (prô-grĕ'sô)	132	15°28'N	87°49'W
Progreso, Mex. (prô-grā'sō)	128	21°14'N	89°39'W
Progreso, Mex.	122	27°29'N	101°05'W
Prokhladnyy, Russia	182	43°46'N	44°00'E
Prokop'yevsk, Russia	184	53°53'N	86°45'E
Prokuplje, Serb. (prô'kòp'l-yĕ)	175	43°16'N	21°40'E
Prome, Mya.	212	18°46'N	95°15'E
Pronya, r., Bela. (prô'nyä)	176	54°08'N	30°58'E
Pronya, r., Russia	176	54°08'N	39°30'E
Prospect, Ky., U.S. (prŏs'pĕkt)	111h	38°21'N	85°36'W
Prospect Park, Pa., U.S. (prŏs'pĕkt pärk)	110f	39°53'N	75°18'W
Prosser, Wa., U.S. (prŏs'ēr)	114	46°10'N	119°46'W
Prostějov, Czech Rep. (prôs'tyĕ-yôf)	169	49°28'N	17°08'E
Protection, i., Wa., U.S. (prô-tĕk'shŭn)	116a	48°07'N	122°56'W
Protoka, r., Russia (prôt'ô-kȧ)	176	55°00'N	36°42'E
Provadiya, Blg. (prō-väd'ē-yȧ)	175	43°13'N	27°28'E
Providence, Ky., U.S. (prŏv'ĭ-dĕns)	108	37°25'N	87°45'W
Providence, R.I., U.S.	105	41°50'N	71°23'W
Providence, Ut., U.S.	115	41°42'N	111°50'W
Providencia, Isla de, i., Col.	133	13°21'N	80°55'W
Providenciales, i., T./C. Is.	135	21°50'N	72°15'W
Provideniya, Russia (prô-vĭ-dä'nĭ-yȧ)	103	64°30'N	172°54'W
Provincetown, Ma., U.S.	109	42°03'N	70°11'W
Provo, Ut., U.S. (prō'vō)	104	40°15'N	111°40'W
Prozor, Bos. (prô'zôr)	175	43°48'N	17°59'E
Prudence Island, i., R.I., U.S. (prōō'dĕns)	110b	41°38'N	71°20'W
Prudhoe Bay, b., Ak., U.S.	103	70°40'N	147°25'W
Prudnik, Pol. (prŏd'nĭk)	169	50°19'N	17°34'E
Prussia, hist. reg., Eur. (prŭsh'ȧ)	168	50°43'N	8°35'E
Pruszków, Pol. (prōsh'kôf)	169	52°09'N	20°50'E
Prut, r., Eur. (prōōt)	156	48°05'N	27°07'E
Pryluky, Ukr.	181	50°36'N	32°21'E
Prymors'k, Ukr.	177	46°43'N	36°21'E
Pryor, Ok., U.S. (prī'ēr)	121	36°16'N	95°19'W
Pryvil'ne, Ukr.	177	47°30'N	32°21'E
Przedbórz, Pol.	169	51°05'N	19°53'E
Przemyśl, Pol. (pzhĕ'mĭsh'l)	154	49°47'N	22°45'E
Przheval'sk, Kyrg. (p'r-zhĭ-välsk')	183	42°29'N	78°24'E
Psel, r., Eur.	181	49°45'N	33°42'E
Pskov, Russia (pskôf)	178	57°48'N	28°19'E
Pskov, prov., Russia	176	57°33'N	29°05'E
Pskovskoye Ozero, l., Eur. (p'skôv'skô'yĕ ôzē-rô)	180	58°05'N	28°15'E
Ptich', r., Bela. (p'tēch)	180	53°17'N	28°16'E
Ptuj, Slvn. (ptōō'ē)	174	46°24'N	15°54'E
Pucheng, China (pōō'chĕng')	209	28°02'N	118°25'E
Pucheng, China (pōō-chŭŋ)	206	35°43'N	115°22'E
Puck, Pol. (pòtsk)	169	54°43'N	18°23'E
Pudozh, Russia (pōō'dôzh)	180	61°50'N	36°50'E
Puebla, Mex. (pwā'blä)	128	19°02'N	98°11'W
Puebla, state, Mex.	131	19°00'N	97°45'W
Puebla de Don Fadrique, Spain	172	37°55'N	2°55'W
Pueblo, Co., U.S. (pwā'blō)	104	38°15'N	104°36'W
Pueblo Nuevo, Mex. (nwā'vô)	130	23°23'N	105°21'W
Pueblo Viejo, Mex. (vyā'hô)	131	17°23'N	93°46'W
Puente Alto, Chile (pwĕ'n-tĕ äl'tô)	141b	33°36'S	70°34'W
Puentedeume, Spain (pwĕn-tā-dhå-ōō'må)	172	43°28'N	8°09'W
Puente-Genil, Spain (pwĕn'tå-hå-nēl')	172	37°25'N	4°18'W
Puerco, Rio, r., N.M., U.S. (pwĕr'kō)	119	35°15'N	107°05'W
Puerto Aisén, Chile (pwĕ'r-tō ī'y-sĕ'n)	144	45°28'S	72°44'W
Puerto Angel, Mex. (pwĕ'r-tō äŋ'hål)	131	15°42'N	96°32'W
Puerto Armuelles, Pan. (pwe'r-tô är-mōō-ā'lyās)	133	8°18'N	82°52'W
Puerto Barrios, Guat. (pwĕ'r-tô bär'rē-ôs)	128	15°43'N	88°36'W
Puerto Bermúdez, Peru (pwĕ'r-tō bĕr-mōō'dāz)	142	10°17'S	74°57'W
Puerto Berrío, Col. (pwĕ'r-tō bĕr-rē'ō)	142	6°29'N	74°27'W
Puerto Cabello, Ven. (pwĕ'r-tō kä-bĕl'yō)	142	10°28'N	68°01'W
Puerto Cabezas, Nic. (pwĕ'r-tō kä-bā'zäs)	133	14°01'N	83°26'W
Puerto Casado, Para. (pwĕ'r-tō kä-sä'dō)	144	22°16'S	57°57'W
Puerto Castilla, Hond. (pwĕ'r-tō käs-tēl'yō)	132	16°01'N	86°01'W
Puerto Chicama, Peru (pwĕ'r-tō chē-kä'mä)	142	7°46'S	79°18'W
Puerto Colombia, Col. (pwĕ'r-tô kô-lôm'bē-ä)	142	11°08'N	75°09'W
Puerto Cortés, C.R. (pwĕ'r-tô kôr-tās')	133	9°00'N	83°37'W

PLACE (Pronunciation)	PAGE	LAT.	LONG.
Puerto Cortés, Hond. (pwĕ'r-tô kôr-tās')	128	15°48'N	87°57'W
Puerto Cumarebo, Ven. (pwĕ'r-tō kōō-mä-rĕ'bô)	142	11°25'N	69°17'W
Puerto de Luna, N.M., U.S. (pwĕr'tô då lōō'nä)	120	34°49'N	104°36'W
Puerto de Nutrias, Ven. (pwĕ'r-tō dĕ nōō-trē-ās')	142	8°02'N	69°19'W
Puerto Deseado, Arg. (pwĕ'r-tō dā-sā-ä'dhō)	144	47°38'S	66°00'W
Puerto de Somport, p., Eur.	173	42°51'N	0°25'W
Puerto Eten, Peru (pwĕ'r-tō ĕ-tĕ'n)	142	6°59'S	79°51'W
Puerto Jiménez, C.R. (pwĕ'r-tō кē-mĕ'nĕz)	133	8°35'N	83°23'W
Puerto La Cruz, Ven. (pwĕ'r-tō lä krōō'z)	142	10°14'N	64°38'W
Puertollano, Spain (pwĕ-tôl-yä'nō)	162	38°41'N	4°05'W
Puerto Madryn, Arg. (pwĕ'r-tō mä-drĕn')	144	42°45'S	65°01'W
Puerto Maldonado, Peru (pwĕ'r-tō mäl-dō-nä'dô)	142	12°43'S	69°01'W
Puerto Miniso, Mex. (pwĕ'r-tō mē-nē'sô)	130	16°06'N	98°02'W
Puerto Montt, Chile (pwĕ'r-tō mô'nt)	144	41°29'S	73°00'W
Puerto Natales, Chile (pwĕ'r-tō nä-tä'lĕs)	144	51°48'S	72°01'W
Puerto Niño, Col. (pwĕ'r-tō nē'n-yô)	142a	5°57'N	74°36'W
Puerto Padre, Cuba (pwĕ'r-tō pä'drā)	134	21°10'N	76°40'W
Puerto Peñasco, Mex. (pwĕ'r-tô pĕn-yä's-kô)	128	31°39'N	113°15'W
Puerto Pinasco, Para. (pwĕ'r-tō pē-ná's-kô)	144	22°31'S	57°50'W
Puerto Píritu, Ven. (pwĕ'r-tō pē'rē-tōō)	143b	10°05'N	65°04'W
Puerto Plata, Dom. Rep. (pwĕ'r-tô plä'tä)	129	19°50'N	70°40'W
Puerto Princesa, Phil. (pwĕr-tô prēn-sā'sä)	212	9°45'N	118°41'E
Puerto Rico, dep., N.A. (pwĕr'tô rē'kō)	129	18°16'N	66°50'W
Puerto Rico Trench, deep	129	19°45'N	66°30'W
Puerto Salgar, Col. (pwĕ'r-tō säl-gär')	142a	5°30'N	74°39'W
Puerto Santa Cruz, Arg. (pwĕ'r-tō sän'tä krōōz')	144	50°04'S	68°32'W
Puerto Suárez, Bol. (pwĕ'r-tō swä'råz)	143	18°55'S	57°39'W
Puerto Tejada, Col. (pwĕ'r-tō tĕ-кä'dä)	142	3°13'N	76°23'W
Puerto Vallarta, Mex. (pwĕ'r-tô väl-yär'tä)	130	20°36'N	105°13'W
Puerto Varas, Chile (pwĕ'r-tō vä'räs)	144	41°16'S	73°03'W
Puerto Wilches, Col. (pwĕ'r-tō vēl'c-hĕs)	142	7°19'N	73°54'W
Pugachëv, Russia (pōō'gá-chyôf)	181	52°00'N	48°40'E
Puget, Wa., U.S. (pū'jĕt)	116c	46°10'N	123°23'W
Puget Sound, strt., Wa., U.S.	114	47°49'N	122°26'W
Puglia (Apulia), hist. reg., Italy (pōō'lyä) (ä-pōō'lyä)	174	41°13'N	16°10'E
Pukaskwa National Park, rec., Can.	93	48°22'N	85°55'W
Pukeashun Mountain, mtn., Can.	95	51°12'N	119°14'W
Pukin, r., Malay.	197b	2°53'N	102°54'E
Pula, Cro. (pōō'lä)	162	44°52'N	13°55'E
Pulacayo, Bol. (pōō-lä-kä'yō)	142	20°12'S	66°33'W
Pulaski, Tn., U.S. (pů-lăs'kĭ)	124	35°11'N	87°03'W
Pulaski, Va., U.S.	125	37°00'N	81°45'W
Puławy, Pol. (pó-wä'vē)	169	51°24'N	21°59'E
Pulicat, r., India	203	13°58'N	79°52'E
Pullman, Wa., U.S. (pòl'măn)	114	46°44'N	117°10'W
Pulog, Mount, mtn., Phil. (pōō'lôg)	213a	16°38'N	120°53'E
Puma Yumco, l., China (pōō-mä yōōm-tswo)	202	28°30'N	90°10'E
Pumpkin Creek, r., Mt., U.S. (pŭmp'kĭn)	115	45°47'N	105°35'W
Punakha, Bhu. (pōō-nŭk'ŭ)	199	27°45'N	89°59'E
Punata, Bol. (pōō-nä'tä)	142	17°43'S	65°43'W
Pune, India	199	18°38'N	73°53'E
Punjab, state, India (pŭn'jäb')	199	31°00'N	75°30'E
Puno, Peru (pōō'nô)	142	15°58'S	70°02'W
Punta Arenas, Chile (pōō'n-tä-rĕ'näs)	144	53°09'S	70°48'W
Punta de Piedras, Ven. (pōō'n-tä dĕ pyĕ'dräs)	143b	10°54'N	64°06'W
Punta Gorda, Belize (pòn'tä gôr'dä)	132	16°07'N	88°50'W
Punta Gorda, Fl., U.S. (pŭn'tȧ gôr'dȧ)	125a	26°55'N	82°02'W
Punta Gorda, Río, r., Nic. (pōō'n-tä gô'r-dä)	133	11°34'N	84°13'W
Punta Indio, Canal, strt., Arg. (pōō'n-tä-ē'n-dyô)	141c	34°56'S	57°20'W
Puntarenas, C.R. (pònt-ä-rā'näs)	129	9°59'N	84°49'W
Punto Fijo, Ven. (pōō'n-tô fē'кô)	142	11°48'N	70°14'W
Punxsutawney, Pa., U.S. (pŭnk-sŭ-tô'nē)	109	40°55'N	79°00'W
Puquio, Peru (pōō'kyô)	142	14°43'S	74°02'W
Pur, r., Russia	184	65°30'N	77°30'E
Purcell, Ok., U.S. (pûr-sĕl')	121	35°01'N	97°22'W
Purcell Mountains, mts., N.A. (pûr-sĕl')	95	50°00'N	116°30'W
Purdy, Wa., U.S. (pûr'dē)	116a	47°23'N	122°37'W
Purépero, Mex. (pōō-rā'på-rō)	130	19°56'N	102°02'W
Purgatoire, r., Co., U.S. (pûr-gȧ-twär')	120	37°25'N	103°53'W
Puri, India (pó'rē)	199	19°52'N	85°51'E
Purial, Sierra de, mts., Cuba (sē-ĕ'r-rá-dĕ-pōō-rē-äl')	135	20°15'N	74°40'W
Purificación, Col. (pōō-rē-fē-kä-syōn')	142	3°52'N	74°54'W
Purificación, Mex. (pōō-rē-fē-kä-syô'n)	130	19°44'N	104°38'W
Purificación, r., Mex.	130	19°30'N	104°54'W
Purkersdorf, Aus.	159e	48°13'N	16°11'E

ăt; finăl; rāte; senåte; ärm; åsk; sofȧ; fâre; ch-choose; dh-as th in other; bē; ėvent; bĕt; recĕnt; cratēr; g-gō; gh-guttural g; bĭt; ĭ-short neutral; rīde; к-guttural k as ch in German ich;

PRONOUNCING INDEX

Puruandiro – Ramanāthapuram 339

PLACE (Pronunciation)	PAGE	LAT.	LONG.
Puruandiro, Mex. (pò-rōō-än'dė-rō)	130	20°04'N	101°33'W
Purús, r., S.A. (pōō-rōō's)	142	6°45'S	64°34'W
Pusan, Kor., S.	205	35°08'N	129°05'E
Pushkin, Russia (pòsh'kĭn)	180	59°43'N	30°25'E
Pushkino, Russia (pōōsh'kė-nỏ)	176	56°01'N	37°51'E
Pustoshka, Russia (pûs-tôsh'kȧ)	176	56°20'N	29°33'E
Pustunich, Mex. (pōōs-tōō'nẻch)	131	19°10'N	90°29'W
Putaendo, Chile (pōō-tä-ĕn-dỏ)	141b	32°37'S	70°42'W
Puteaux, Fr. (pü-tō')	171b	48°52'N	2°12'E
Putfontein, S. Afr. (pòt'fŏn-tān)	233b	26°08'S	28°24'E
Putian, China (pōō-tĭĕn)	209	25°40'N	119°02'E
Putla de Guerrero, Mex. (pōō'tlä-dĕ-gĕr-rĕ'rō)	131	17°03'N	97°55'W
Putnam, Ct., U.S. (pŭt'năm)	109	41°55'N	71°55'W
Putorana, Gory, mts., Russia	179	68°45'N	93°15'E
Puttalam, Sri L.	203	8°02'N	79°44'E
Putumayo, r., S.A. (pò-tōō-mä'yō)	142	1°02'S	73°50'W
Putung, Tanjung, c., Indon.	212	3°35'S	111°50'E
Putyvl', Ukr.	177	51°21'N	33°52'E
Puulavesi, l., Fin.	167	61°49'N	27°10'E
Puyallup, Wa., U.S. (pū-ăl'ŭp)	116a	47°12'N	122°18'W
Puyang, China (pōō-yäŋ)	208	35°42'N	114°58'E
Pweto, D.R.C. (pwā'tō)	232	8°29'S	28°58'E
Pyasina, r., Russia (pyä-sē'nȧ)	184	72°45'N	87°37'E
Pyatigorsk, Russia (pyȧ-tė-gôrsk')	181	44°00'N	43°00'E
Pyetrykaw, Bela.	176	52°09'N	28°30'E
Pyhäjärvi, l., Fin.	167	60°57'N	21°50'E
Pyinmana, Mya. (pyėn-mä'nŭ)	199	19°47'N	96°15'E
Pymatuning Reservoir, res., Pa., U.S. (pī-mȧ-tûn'ĭng)	108	41°40'N	80°30'W
Pyŏnggang, Kor., N. (pyŭng'gäng')	210	38°21'N	127°18'E
P'yŏngyang, Kor., N.	205	39°03'N	125°48'E
Pyramid, l., Nv., U.S. (pī'rȧ-mĭd)	118	40°02'N	119°50'W
Pyramid Lake Indian Reservation, I.R., Nv., U.S.	118	40°17'N	119°52'W
Pyramids, hist., Egypt	238b	29°53'N	31°10'E
Pyrenees, mts., Eur. (pĭr-e-nēz')	156	43°00'N	0°05'E
Pýrgos, Grc.	163	37°51'N	21°28'E
Pyriatyn, Ukr.	181	50°13'N	32°31'E
Pyrzyce, Pol. (pĕzhĭ'tsĕ)	168	53°09'N	14°53'E

Q

PLACE (Pronunciation)	PAGE	LAT.	LONG.
Qal'at Bishah, Sau. Ar.	198	20°01'N	42°30'E
Qamdo, China (chyäm-dwō)	204	31°06'N	96°30'E
Qandala, Som.	201	11°28'N	49°52'E
Qaraghandy (Karaganda), Kaz.	183	49°42'N	73°18'E
Qaraözen, r.	181	49°50'N	49°35'E
Qarqan *see* Qiemo, China	204	38°02'N	85°16'E
Qarqan, r., China	204	38°55'N	87°15'E
Qarqaraly, Kaz.	183	49°18'N	75°28'E
Qārūn, Birket, l., Egypt	231	29°34'N	30°34'E
Qaşr al Burayqah, Libya	231	30°25'N	19°20'E
Qasr al-Farāfirah, Egypt	231	27°04'N	28°13'E
Qaşr Banī Walīd, Libya	231	31°45'N	14°04'E
Qasr el Boukhari, Alg.	162	35°50'N	2°48'E
Qatar, nation, Asia (kä'tȧr)	198	25°00'N	52°45'E
Qaţārah, Munkhafaḑ al, depr., Egypt	231	30°07'N	27°30'E
Qausuittuq (Resolute), Can.	89	74°41'N	95°00'W
Qāyen, Iran	198	33°45'N	59°08'E
Qazvīn, Iran	198	36°10'N	49°59'E
Qeshm, Iran	198	26°51'N	56°10'E
Qeshm, i., Iran	198	26°52'N	56°15'E
Qezel Owzan, r., Iran	198	36°30'N	49°00'E
Qezi'ot, Isr.	197a	30°53'N	34°28'E
Qianwei, China (chyĕn-wā)	206	40°11'N	120°05'E
Qi'anzhen, China (chyē-än-jŭn)	206	32°16'N	120°59'E
Qibao, China (chyē-bou)	207b	31°06'N	121°16'E
Qiblīyah, Jabal al Jalālat al, mts., Egypt	197a	28°49'N	32°21'E
Qijiang, China (chyē-jyäŋ)	209	29°05'N	106°40'E
Qikou, China (chyē-kō)	206	38°37'N	117°33'E
Qilian Shan, mts., China (chyē-lĭĕn shän)	204	38°43'N	98°00'E
Qiliping, China (chyē-lē-pĭŋ)	206	31°28'N	114°41'E
Qindao, China (chyĭn-dou)	205	36°05'N	120°10'E
Qing'an, China (chyĭŋ-än)	208	46°50'N	127°30'E
Qingcheng, China (chyĭŋ-chŭŋ)	206	37°12'N	117°43'E
Qingfeng, China (chyĭŋ-fŭŋ)	206	35°52'N	115°05'E
Qinghai, prov., China (chyĭŋ-hī)	204	36°14'N	95°30'E
Qinghai Hu *see* Koko Nor, l., China	204	37°26'N	98°30'E
Qinghe, China (chyĭŋ-hŭ)	208a	40°08'N	116°16'E
Qingjiang, China (chyĭŋ-jyäŋ)	209	28°00'N	115°30'E
Qingjiang, China	206	33°34'N	118°58'E
Qingliu, China (chyĭŋ-lĭỏ)	209	26°15'N	116°50'E
Qingningsi, China (chyĭŋ-nĭŋ-sz)	207b	31°16'N	121°33'E
Qingping, China (chyĭŋ-pĭŋ)	206	36°46'N	116°03'E
Qingpu, China (chyĭŋ-pōō)	209	31°08'N	121°06'E
Qingxian, China (chyĭŋ shyĕn)	206	38°37'N	116°48'E
Qingyang, China (chyĭŋ-yäŋ)	204	36°02'N	107°42'E
Qingyuan, China (chyĭŋ-yỏän)	209	23°43'N	113°10'E
Qingyuan, China	208	42°05'N	125°00'E
Qingyun, China (chyĭŋ-yòn)	206	37°52'N	117°26'E
Qingyundian, China (chĭŋ-yòn-dĭĕn)	208a	39°41'N	116°31'E
Qinhuangdao, China (chyĭn-huaŋ-dou)	205	39°57'N	119°34'E
Qin Ling, mts., China (chyĭn lĭŋ)	204	33°25'N	108°58'E
Qinyang, China (chyĭn-yäŋ)	208	35°00'N	112°55'E
Qinzhou, China (chyĭn-jō)	209	22°00'N	108°35'E
Qionghai, China (chyỏŋ-hī)	209	19°10'N	110°28'E
Qiqian, China (chyē-chyĕn)	205	52°23'N	121°04'E
Qiqihar, China	205	47°18'N	124°00'E
Qiryat Gat, Isr.	197a	31°38'N	34°36'E
Qiryat Shemona, Isr.	197a	33°12'N	35°34'E
Qitai, China (chyē-tī)	204	44°07'N	89°04'E
Qiuxian, China (chyỏ shyĕn)	206	36°43'N	115°13'E
Qixian, China (chyē-shyĕn)	206	34°33'N	114°47'E
Qixian, China	208	35°36'N	114°13'E
Qiyang, China (chyē-yäŋ)	209	26°40'N	112°00'E
Qobda, r., Kaz. (kä-rȧ kôb'dȧ)	181	50°40'N	55°00'E
Qogir Feng *see* K2, mtn., Asia	199	36°06'N	76°38'E
Qom, Iran	198	34°28'N	50°53'E
Qongyrat, Kaz.	183	47°25'N	75°10'E
Qostanay, Kaz.	183	53°10'N	63°39'E
Quabbin Reservoir, res., Ma., U.S. (kwā'bĭn)	109	42°20'N	72°10'W
Quachita, Lake, l., Ar., U.S. (kwä shĭ'tô)	121	34°47'N	93°37'W
Quadra Island, i., Can.	94	50°08'N	125°16'W
Quakertown, Pa., U.S. (kwā'kẽr-toun)	109	40°30'N	75°20'W
Quanah, Tx., U.S. (kwä'nȧ)	120	34°19'N	99°43'W
Quang Ngai, Viet. (kwäng n'gä'ė)	212	15°05'N	108°58'E
Quang Ngai, mtn., Viet.	209	15°10'N	108°20'E
Quanjiao, China (chyuän-jyou)	206	32°06'N	118°17'E
Quanzhou, China (chyuän-jō)	205	24°58'N	118°40'E
Quanzhou, China	209	25°58'N	111°02'E
Qu'Appelle, r., Can.	92	50°30'N	104°00'W
Qu'Appelle Dam, dam, Can.	96	51°00'N	106°25'W
Quartu Sant'Elena, Italy (kwär-tōō' sänt a'lå-nä)	174	39°16'N	9°12'E
Quartzsite, Az., U.S.	119	33°40'N	114°13'W
Quatsino Sound, strt., Can. (kwŏt-sē'nō)	94	50°25'N	128°10'W
Quba, Azer. (kōō'bā)	181	41°05'N	48°30'E
Qūchān, Iran	201	37°06'N	58°30'E
Qudi, China	206	37°06'N	117°15'E
Québec, Can. (kwė-bĕk') (kå-bĕk')	102b	46°49'N	71°13'W
Quebec, prov., Can.	91	51°07'N	70°25'W
Quedlinburg, Ger. (kvĕd'lėn-bŏŏrgh)	168	51°45'N	11°10'E
Queen Bess, Can.	94	51°16'N	124°34'W
Queen Charlotte Islands, is., Can. (kwēn shär'lŏt)	92	53°30'N	132°25'W
Queen Charlotte Ranges, mts., Can.	94	53°00'N	132°00'W
Queen Charlotte Sound, strt., Can.	94	51°30'N	129°30'W
Queen Charlotte Strait, strt., Can. (strāt)	92	50°40'N	127°25'W
Queen Elizabeth Islands, is., Can. (ė-lĭz'ȧ-bĕth)	89	78°20'N	110°00'W
Queen Maud Gulf, b., Can. (mäd)	92	68°27'N	102°55'W
Queen Maud Land, reg., Ant.	224	75°00'S	10°00'E
Queen Maud Mountains, mts., Ant.	224	85°00'S	179°00'W
Queens Channel, strt., Austl. (kwēnz)	220	14°25'S	129°10'E
Queenscliff, Austl.	217a	38°16'S	144°39'E
Queensland, state, Austl. (kwēnz'lănd)	219	22°45'S	141°01'E
Queenstown, Austl. (kwēnz'toun)	222	42°00'S	145°40'E
Queenstown, S. Afr.	233c	31°54'S	26°53'E
Queimados, Braz. (kā-mȧ'dỏs)	144b	22°42'S	43°34'W
Quela, Ang.	236	9°16'S	17°02'E
Quelimane, Moz. (kā-lė-mä'nĕ)	233	17°48'S	37°05'E
Queluz, Port.	173b	38°45'N	9°15'W
Quemado de Güines, Cuba (kā-mä'dhä-dĕ-gwē'nĕs)	134	22°45'N	80°20'W
Quemoy, Tai.	209	24°30'N	118°20'E
Quemoy, i., Tai.	209	24°27'N	118°23'E
Quepos, C.R. (kā'pỏs)	133	9°26'N	84°10'W
Quepos, Punta, c., C.R. (pōō'n-tä)	133	9°23'N	84°20'W
Querétaro, Mex. (kå-rā'tä-rō)	128	20°37'N	100°25'W
Querétaro, state, Mex.	130	21°00'N	100°00'W
Quesada, Spain (kå-sä'dhä)	172	37°51'N	3°04'W
Quesnel, Can. (kā-nĕl')	90	52°59'N	122°30'W
Quesnel, r., Can.	95	52°15'N	122°00'W
Quesnel Lake, l., Can.	92	52°32'N	121°05'W
Quetame, Col. (kĕ-tä'mĕ)	142a	4°20'N	73°50'W
Quetta, Pak. (kwĕt'ä)	199	30°19'N	67°01'E
Quezaltenango, Guat. (kå-zäl'tå-näŋ'gō)	128	14°50'N	91°30'W
Quezaltepeque, El Sal. (kĕ-zäl'tĕ'pĕ-kĕ)	132	13°50'N	89°17'W
Quezaltepeque, Guat. (kå-zäl'tå-pā'kå)	132	14°39'N	89°26'W
Quezon City, Phil. (kā-zōn)	212	14°40'N	121°02'E
Qufu, China (chyōō-fōō)	206	35°37'N	116°54'E
Quibdo, Col. (kēb'dō)	142	5°42'N	76°41'W
Quiberon, Fr. (kė-bẽ-rôɴ')	170	47°29'N	3°08'W
Quiçama, Parque Nacional de, rec., Ang.	236	10°00'S	13°25'E
Quicksborn, Ger. (kvēks'bōrn)	159c	53°44'N	9°54'E
Quilcene, Wa., U.S. (kwĭl-sēn')	116a	47°50'N	122°53'W
Quilimari, Chile (kē-lē-mä'rē)	141b	32°06'S	71°28'W
Quillan, Fr. (kė-yäɴ')	170	42°53'N	2°13'E
Quillota, Chile (kėl-yō'tä)	144	32°52'S	71°14'W
Quilmes, Arg. (kēl'mās)	141c	34°43'S	58°16'W
Quilon, India (kwė-lōn')	203	8°58'N	76°16'E
Quilpie, Austl. (kwĭl'pė)	219	26°34'S	149°20'E
Quimbaya, Col. (kēm-bä'yä)	142a	4°38'N	75°46'W
Quimbele, Ang.	236	6°28'S	16°13'E
Quimbonge, Ang.	236	8°36'S	18°30'E
Quimper, Fr. (kăɴ-pĕr')	161	47°59'N	4°04'W
Quinalt, r., Wa., U.S.	114	47°23'N	124°10'W
Quinault Indian Reservation, I.R., Wa., U.S.	114	47°27'N	124°34'W
Quincy, Fl., U.S. (kwĭn'sė)	124	30°35'N	84°35'W
Quincy, Il., U.S.	105	39°55'N	91°23'W
Quincy, Ma., U.S.	101a	42°15'N	71°00'W
Quincy, Mi., U.S.	108	42°00'N	84°50'W
Quincy, Or., U.S.	116c	46°08'N	123°10'W
Qui Nhon, Viet. (kwĭnyỏn)	212	13°51'N	109°03'E
Quinn, r., Nv., U.S. (kwĭn)	114	41°42'N	117°45'W
Quintanar de la Orden, Spain (kēn-tä-när')	172	39°36'N	3°02'W
Quintana Roo, state, Mex. (rô'ỏ)	128	19°30'N	88°30'W
Quintero, Chile (kēn-tĕ'rỏ)	141b	32°48'S	71°30'W
Quionga, Moz.	237	10°37'S	40°30'E
Quiroga, Mex. (kē-rỏ'gä)	130	19°39'N	101°30'W
Quiroga, Spain (kē-rỏ'gä)	172	42°28'N	7°18'W
Quitman, Ga., U.S. (kwĭt'măn)	124	30°46'N	83°35'W
Quitman, Ms., U.S.	124	33°02'N	88°43'W
Quito, Ec. (kē'tō)	142	0°17'S	78°32'W
Qumbu, S. Afr. (kòm'bōō)	233c	31°10'S	28°48'E
Quorn, Austl. (kwôrn)	222	32°20'S	138°00'E
Qurayyah, Wādī, r., Egypt	197a	30°08'N	34°27'E
Qusmuryn köli, l., Kaz.	183	52°30'N	64°15'E
Qutang, China (chyōō-täŋ)	206	32°33'N	120°07'E
Quthing, Leso.	233c	30°35'S	27°42'E
Quxian, China (chyōō-shyĕn)	205	28°58'N	118°58'E
Quxian, China	209	30°40'N	106°48'E
Quzhou, China (chyoỏ-jō)	206	36°47'N	114°58'E
Qyzylorda, Kaz.	183	44°58'N	65°45'E

R

PLACE (Pronunciation)	PAGE	LAT.	LONG.
Raab (Raba), r., Eur. (räp)	168	46°55'N	15°55'E
Raahe, Fin. (rä'ĕ)	160	64°39'N	24°22'E
Rab, i., Serb. (räb)	174	44°45'N	14°40'E
Raba, Indon.	212	8°32'S	118°49'E
Raba (Raab), r., Eur.	169	47°28'N	17°12'E
Rabat, Mor. (rȧ-bät')	230	33°59'N	6°47'W
Rabaul, Pap. N. Gui. (rä'boul)	213	4°15'S	152°19'E
Rābigh, Sau. Ar.	201	22°48'N	39°01'E
Raccoon, r., Ia., U.S. (ră-kōōn')	113	42°07'N	94°45'W
Raccoon Cay, i., Bah.	135	22°25'N	75°50'W
Race, Cape, c., Can. (rās)	101	46°40'N	53°10'W
Rachado, Cape, c., Malay.	197b	2°26'N	101°29'E
Racibórz, Pol. (rä-chē'bōōzh)	169	50°06'N	18°14'E
Racine, Wi., U.S. (rȧ-sēn')	105	42°43'N	87°49'W
Raco, Mi., U.S. (rȧ cō)	117k	46°22'N	84°43'W
Rădăuţi, Rom.	163	47°53'N	25°55'E
Radcliffe, Eng., U.K. (răd'klĭf)	158a	53°34'N	2°20'W
Radevormwald, Ger. (rä'dĕ-fōrm-väld)	171c	51°12'N	7°22'E
Radford, Va., U.S. (răd'fẽrd)	125	37°06'N	81°33'W
Rādhanpur, India	202	23°57'N	71°38'E
Radium, S. Afr. (rā'dĭ-ŭm)	238c	25°06'S	28°18'E
Radom, Pol. (rä'dỏm)	161	51°24'N	21°11'E
Radomir, Blg. (rä'dỏ-mėr)	175	42°33'N	22°58'E
Radomsko, Pol. (rä-dôm'skỏ)	161	51°04'N	19°27'E
Radomyshl, Ukr. (rä-dỏ-mēsh''l)	181	50°30'N	29°13'E
Radul', Ukr. (rȧ'dōōl)	177	51°52'N	30°46'E
Radviliškis, Lith. (rȧd'vė-lēsh'kės)	167	55°49'N	23°31'E
Radwah, Jabal, mtn., Sau. Ar.	198	24°44'N	38°14'E
Radzyń Podlaski, Pol. (räd'zėn-y' pŭd-lä'skĭ)	169	51°49'N	22°40'E
Raeford, N.C., U.S. (rā'fẽrd)	125	34°57'N	79°15'W
Raesfeld, Ger. (răz'fĕld)	171c	51°46'N	6°50'E
Raeside, l., Austl. (rā'sīd)	220	29°20'S	122°30'E
Rae Strait, strt., Can. (rā)	92	68°40'N	95°03'W
Rafaela, Arg. (rä-fä-å'lä)	144	31°15'S	61°21'W
Rafah, Pak. (rä'fä)	197a	31°14'N	34°12'E
Rafsanjān, Iran	198	30°45'N	56°30'E
Raft, r., Id., U.S. (răft)	115	42°20'N	113°17'W
Ragay, Phil. (rä-gī')	213a	13°49'N	122°45'E
Ragay Gulf, b., Phil.	213a	13°44'N	122°38'E
Ragunda, Swe. (rä-gòn'dä)	166	63°07'N	16°24'E
Ragusa, Italy (rä-gōō'sä)	162	36°58'N	14°41'E
Rahachow, Bela.	180	53°07'N	30°04'E
Rahway, N.J., U.S. (rỏ'wā)	110a	40°37'N	74°16'W
Rāichūr, India (rä'ė-chōōr')	199	16°23'N	77°18'E
Raigarh, India (ri'gŭr)	199	21°57'N	83°32'E
Rainbow Bridge National Monument, rec., Ut., U.S. (rān'bō)	119	37°05'N	111°00'W
Rainbow City, Pan.	128a	9°20'N	79°53'W
Rainier, Or., U.S.	116c	46°05'N	122°56'W
Rainier, Mount, mtn., Wa., U.S. (rā-nēr')	106	46°52'N	121°46'W
Rainy, r., N.A.	107	48°50'N	94°41'W
Rainy Lake, l., N.A. (rān'ė)	93	48°43'N	94°29'W
Rainy River, Can.	91	48°43'N	94°29'W
Raipur, India (rä'jŭ-bōō-rė')	202	21°25'N	81°37'E
Raisin, r., Mi., U.S. (rā'zĭn)	108	42°00'N	83°35'W
Raitan, N.J., U.S. (rā-tăn)	110a	40°34'N	74°40'W
Rājahmundry, India (räj-ŭ-mŭn'drė)	199	17°03'N	81°51'E
Rajang, r., Malay.	212	2°10'N	113°30'E
Rājapālaiyam, India	203	9°30'N	77°33'E
Rājasthān, state, India (rä'jŭs-tän)	199	26°00'N	72°00'E
Rājkot, India (räj'kỏt)	199	22°20'N	70°48'E
Rājpur, India	202a	22°24'N	88°25'E
Rājshāhi, Bngl.	199	24°26'S	88°39'E
Rakhiv, Ukr.	169	48°02'N	24°13'E
Rakh'oya, Russia (räk'yȧ)	186c	60°06'N	30°50'E
Rakitnoye, Russia (rȧ-kēt'nỏ-yĕ)	181	50°51'N	35°53'E
Rakovník, Czech Rep.	168	50°07'N	13°45'E
Rakvere, Est. (rȧk'vĕ-rĕ)	180	59°22'N	26°14'E
Raleigh, N.C., U.S.	105	35°45'N	78°39'W
Ram, r., Can.	95	52°10'N	115°05'W
Rama, Nic. (rä'mä)	133	12°11'N	84°14'W
Ramallo, Arg. (rä-mä'l-yỏ)	141c	33°28'S	60°02'W
Ramanāthapuram, India	203	9°13'N	78°52'E

ng-sing; ŋ-baŋk; ɴ-nasalized n; nŏd; cŏmmit; ōld; ỏbey; ôrder; oi-boil; fōōd; ò-as oo in foot; ou-out; s-soft; sh-dish; th-thin; pūre; ůnite; ûrn; stŭd; circŭs; ü-as in French tu; '-indeterminate vowel.

340 Rambouillet – Revda PRONOUNCING INDEX

PLACE (Pronunciation)	PAGE	LAT.	LONG.
Rambouillet, Fr. (räɴ-bōō-yĕ′)	170	48°39'N	1°49'E
Rame Head, c., S. Afr.	233c	31°48'S	29°22'E
Ramenskoye, Russia (rá′mĕn-skô-yĕ)	176	55°34'N	38°15'E
Ramlat as Sab'atayn, reg., Asia	198	16°08'N	45°15'E
Ramm, Jabal, mtn., Jord.	197a	29°37'N	35°32'E
Râmnicu Sărat, Rom.	163	45°24'N	27°06'E
Râmnicu Vâlcea, Rom.	175	45°07'N	24°22'E
Ramos, Mex. (rä′mōs)	130	22°46'N	101°52'W
Ramos, r., Nig.	235	5°10'N	5°40'E
Ramos Arizpe, Mex. (ä-rēz′pà)	122	25°33'N	100°57'W
Rampart, Ak., U.S. (răm′pàrt)	103	65°28'N	150°18'W
Rampo Mountains, mts., N.J., U.S. (răm′pō)	110a	41°06'N	72°12'W
Rāmpur, India (räm′pōōr)	199	28°53'N	79°03'E
Ramree Island, i., Mya. (räm′rē′)	212	19°01'N	93°23'E
Ramsayville, Can. (răm′zê vĭl)	102c	45°23'N	75°34'W
Ramsbottom, Eng., U.K. (rămz′bŏt-ŭm)	158a	53°39'N	2°20'W
Ramsey, I. of Man (răm′zê)	164	54°20'N	4°25'W
Ramsey, N.J., U.S.	110a	41°03'N	74°09'W
Ramsey Lake, l., Can.	98	47°15'N	82°16'W
Ramsgate, Eng., U.K. (rămz′′gāt)	165	51°19'N	1°20'E
Ramu, r., Pap. N. Gui. (rä′mōō)	213	5°35'S	145°16'E
Rancagua, Chile (rän-kä′gwä)	144	34°10'S	70°43'W
Rance, r., Fr. (räɴs)	170	48°17'N	2°30'W
Rānchī, India	199	23°21'N	85°20'E
Rancho Boyeros, Cuba (rä′n-chô-bô-yĕ′rôs)	135a	23°00'N	82°23'W
Randallstown, Md., U.S. (răn′dălz-toun)	110e	39°22'N	76°48'W
Randers, Den. (rän′ĕrs)	160	56°28'N	10°03'E
Randfontein, S. Afr. (ránt′fŏn-tān)	233b	26°10'S	27°42'E
Randleman, N.C., U.S. (răn′d'l-măn)	125	35°49'N	79°50'W
Randolph, Ma., U.S. (răn′dôlf)	101a	42°10'N	71°03'W
Randolph, Ne., U.S.	112	42°22'N	97°22'W
Randolph, Vt., U.S.	109	43°55'N	72°40'W
Random Island, i., Can. (răn′dŭm)	101	48°12'N	53°25'W
Randsfjorden, Nor.	160	60°35'N	10°10'E
Randwick, Austl.	217b	33°55'S	151°15'E
Ranérou, Sen.	234	15°18'N	13°58'W
Rangeley, Me., U.S. (rānj′lê)	100	44°56'N	70°38'W
Rangeley, l., Me., U.S.	100	45°00'N	70°25'W
Ranger, Tx., U.S. (rān′jēr)	104	32°26'N	98°41'W
Rangia, India	202	26°32'N	91°39'E
Rangoon (Yangon), Mya. (ráŋ-gōōn′)	199	16°46'N	96°09'E
Rangpur, Bngl. (rŭng′pōōr)	199	25°48'N	89°19'E
Rangsang, i., Indon. (räng′säng′)	197b	0°53'N	103°05'E
Rangsdorf, Ger. (rängs′dōrf)	159b	52°17'N	13°25'E
Rānīganj, India (rä-nē-gŭnj′)	202	23°40'N	87°08'E
Rankin Inlet, b., Can. (răŋ′kĕn)	93	62°45'N	94°27'W
Ranova, r., Russia (rä′nô-vá)	176	53°55'N	40°03'E
Rantau, Malay.	197b	2°35'N	101°58'E
Rantekombola, Bulu, mtn., Indon.	212	3°22'S	119°50'E
Rantoul, Il., U.S. (răn-tōōl′)	108	40°25'N	88°05'W
Raoyang, China (rou-yäŋ)	206	38°16'N	115°45'E
Rapallo, Italy (rä-päl′lô)	174	44°21'N	9°14'E
Rapel, r., Chile (rä-pāl′)	141b	34°05'S	71°30'W
Rapid, r., Mn., U.S. (răp′ĭd)	113	48°21'N	94°50'W
Rapid City, S.D., U.S.	104	44°06'N	103°14'W
Rapla, Est. (räp′lá)	167	59°02'N	24°46'E
Rappahannock, r., Va., U.S. (răp′á-hăn′ŭk)	109	38°20'N	75°25'W
Raquette, l., N.Y., U.S. (răk′ĕt)	109	43°50'N	74°35'W
Raritan, r., N.J., U.S. (răr′ĭ-tăn)	110a	40°32'N	74°27'W
Rarotonga, Cook Is. (rä′rô-tŏŋ′gá)	2	20°40'S	163°00'W
Ra's an Naqb, Jord.	197a	30°00'N	35°29'E
Raşcov, Mol.	177	47°55'N	28°51'E
Ras Dashen Terara, mtn., Eth. (räs dä-shän′)	231	12°49'N	38°14'E
Raseiniai, Lith. (rä-syā′nyī)	167	55°23'N	23°04'E
Rashayya, Leb.	197a	33°30'N	35°50'E
Rashīd, Egypt (rá-shēd′) (rô-zĕt′á)	200	31°22'N	30°25'E
Rashîd, Masabb, mth., Egypt	238b	31°30'N	29°58'E
Rashkina, Russia (räsh′kĭ-ná)	186a	59°57'N	61°30'E
Rasht, Iran	198	37°13'N	49°45'E
Raška, Serb. (räsh′ká)	175	43°16'N	20°40'E
Rasskazovo, Russia (räs-kä′sô-vô)	181	52°40'N	41°40'E
Rastatt, Ger. (rä-shtät)	168	48°51'N	8°12'E
Rastes, Russia (rás′tĕs)	186a	59°24'N	58°49'E
Rastunovo, Russia (rás-tōō′nô-vô)	186b	55°15'N	37°50'E
Ratangarh, India (rŭ-tŭn′gŭr)	202	28°10'N	74°30'E
Ratcliff, Tx., U.S. (răt′klĭf)	123	31°22'N	95°09'W
Rathenow, Ger. (rä′tĕ-nō)	168	52°36'N	12°20'E
Rathlin Island, i., N. Ire., U.K. (răth-lĭn)	164	55°18'N	6°13'W
Ratingen, Ger. (rä′tēn-gĕn)	171c	51°18'N	6°51'E
Rat Islands, is., Ak., U.S. (răt)	103a	51°35'N	176°48'E
Ratlām, India	202	23°19'N	75°05'E
Ratnāgiri, India	203	17°04'N	73°24'E
Raton, N.M., U.S. (rá-tōn′)	104	36°52'N	104°26'W
Rattlesnake Creek, r., Or., U.S. (răt′′l snāk)	114	42°38'N	117°39'W
Rättvik, Swe. (rĕt′vēk)	166	60°54'N	15°07'E
Rauch, Arg. (rá′ōōch)	144	36°47'S	59°05'W
Raufoss, Nor. (rou′fôs)	166	60°44'N	10°30'E
Raúl Soares, Braz. (rä-ōō′l-sôä′rĕs)	141a	20°05'S	42°28'W
Rauma, Fin. (rä′ô·mà)	160	61°07'N	21°31'E
Rauna, Lat. (rāū′ná)	167	57°21'N	25°31'E
Raurkela, India	199	22°15'N	84°53'E
Rautalampi, Fin. (rä′ōō-tê-läm′pô)	167	62°39'N	26°25'E
Rava-Rus'ka, Ukr.	169	50°14'N	23°40'E
Ravenna, Italy (rä-vĕn′nä)	162	44°27'N	12°13'E
Ravenna, Ne., U.S. (rá-vĕn′á)	112	41°20'N	98°50'W
Ravenna, Oh., U.S.	108	41°10'N	81°20'W
Ravensburg, Ger. (rä′vĕns-bōōrgh)	168	47°48'N	9°35'E
Ravensdale, Wa., U.S. (rā′vĕnz-dāl)	116a	47°22'N	121°58'W
Ravensthorpe, Austl. (rā′vĕns-thôrp)	218	33°30'S	120°20'E
Ravenswood, W.V., U.S. (rā′vĕnz-wŏd)	108	38°55'N	81°50'W
Rāwalpindi, Pak. (rä-wŭl-pēn′dê)	199	33°40'N	73°10'E
Rawa Mazowiecka, Pol.	169	51°46'N	20°17'E
Rawandoz, Iraq	181	36°37'N	44°30'E
Rawicz, Pol. (rä′vĕch)	168	51°36'N	16°51'E
Rawlina, Austl. (rôr-lēnă)	218	31°13'S	125°45'E
Rawlins, Wy., U.S. (rô′lĭnz)	104	41°46'N	107°15'W
Rawson, Arg. (rô′sŭn)	144	43°16'S	65°09'W
Rawson, Arg.	141c	34°36'S	60°03'W
Rawtenstall, Eng., U.K. (rô′tĕn-stôl)	158a	53°42'N	2°17'W
Ray, Cape, c., Can. (rā)	93a	47°40'N	59°18'W
Raya, Bukit, mtn., Indon.	212	0°45'S	112°11'E
Raychikinsk, Russia (rī′chĭ-kĕnsk)	185	49°52'N	129°17'E
Rayleigh, Eng., U.K. (rā′lê)	158b	51°35'N	0°36'E
Raymond, Can. (rā′mŭnd)	95	49°27'N	112°39'W
Raymond, Wa., U.S.	114	46°41'N	123°42'W
Raymondville, Tx., U.S. (rā′mŭnd-vĭl)	121	26°30'N	97°46'W
Ray Mountains, mts., Ak., U.S.	103	65°40'N	151°45'W
Rayne, La., U.S. (rān)	123	30°12'N	92°15'W
Rayón, Mex. (rä-yōn′)	130	21°49'N	99°39'W
Rayton, S. Afr. (rā′tŭn)	233b	25°45'S	28°33'E
Raytown, Mo., U.S. (rā′toun)	117f	39°01'N	94°48'W
Rayville, La., U.S. (rā-vĭl)	123	32°28'N	91°46'W
Raz, Pointe du, c., Fr. (pwăɴt dü rä)	161	48°02'N	4°43'W
Razdan, Arm.	182	40°30'N	44°46'E
Razdol'noye, Russia (räz-dôl′nô-yĕ)	210	43°38'N	131°58'E
Razgrad, Blg.	163	43°32'N	26°32'E
Razlog, Blg. (räz′lôk)	175	41°54'N	23°32'E
Razorback Mountain, mtn., Can. (rā′zēr-băk)	94	51°35'N	124°42'W
Rea, r., Eng., U.K. (rē)	158a	52°25'N	2°31'W
Reaburn, Can. (rā′bûrn)	102f	50°06'N	97°53'W
Reading, Eng., U.K. (rĕd′ĭng)	161	51°25'N	0°58'W
Reading, Ma., U.S.	101a	42°32'N	71°07'W
Reading, Mi., U.S.	108	41°45'N	84°45'W
Reading, Oh., U.S.	111f	39°14'N	84°26'W
Reading, Pa., U.S.	105	40°20'N	75°55'W
Reading, co., Eng., U.K.	158a	52°37'N	0°40'W
Realengo, Braz. (rĕ-ä-län-gô)	141a	23°50'S	43°25'W
Rebiana, Libya	231	24°10'N	22°03'E
Rebun, i., Japan (rē′bōōn)	210	45°25'N	140°54'E
Recanati, Italy (rā-kä-nä′tê)	174	43°25'N	13°35'E
Recherche, Archipelago of the, is., Austl. (rē-shârsh′)	220	34°17'S	122°30'E
Rechytsa, Bela. (ryĕ′chĕt-sá)	181	52°22'N	30°24'E
Recife, Braz. (rā-sē′fĕ)	143	8°09'S	34°59'W
Recife, Kapp, c., S. Afr. (rå-sē′fĕ)	233c	34°03'S	25°43'E
Recklinghausen, Ger. (rĕk′lĭng-hou-zĕn)	171c	51°36'N	7°13'E
Reconquista, Arg. (rā-kôn-kēs′tä)	144	29°01'S	59°41'W
Rector, Ar., U.S. (rĕk′tēr)	121	36°16'N	90°21'W
Red, r., Asia	212	21°00'N	103°00'E
Red, r., N.A. (rĕd)	106	48°00'N	97°00'W
Red, r., Tn., U.S.	124	36°35'N	86°55'W
Red, r., U.S.	107	31°40'N	92°55'W
Red, North Fork, r., U.S.	120	35°20'N	100°08'W
Red, Prairie Dog Town Fork, r., U.S. (prā′rī)	120	34°54'N	101°31'W
Red, Salt Fork, r., U.S.	120	35°04'N	100°31'W
Redan, Ga., U.S. (rê-dăn′) (rĕd′ăn)	110c	33°44'N	84°09'W
Red Bank, N.J., U.S. (băngk)	110a	40°21'N	74°06'W
Red Bluff Reservoir, res., Tx., U.S.	122	32°03'N	103°52'W
Redby, Mn., U.S. (rĕd′bê)	113	47°52'N	94°55'W
Red Cedar, r., Wi., U.S. (sē′dēr)	113	45°03'N	91°48'W
Redcliff, Can. (rĕd′clĭf)	90	50°05'N	110°47'W
Redcliffe, Austl. (rĕd′clĭf)	222	27°20'S	153°12'E
Red Cliff Indian Reservation, I.R., Wi., U.S.	113	46°48'N	91°22'W
Red Cloud, Ne., U.S. (kloud)	120	40°06'N	98°32'W
Red Deer, Can. (dēr)	90	52°16'N	113°48'W
Red Deer, r., Can.	92	51°00'N	111°00'W
Red Deer, r., Can.	97	52°55'N	102°10'W
Red Deer Lake, l., Can.	97	52°58'N	101°28'W
Reddick, Il., U.S. (rĕd′dĭk)	111a	41°06'N	88°16'W
Redding, Ca., U.S. (rĕd′ĭng)	114	40°36'N	122°25'W
Redenção da Serra, Braz. (rĕ-dĕn-souɴ-dä-sĕ′r-rä)	141a	23°17'S	45°31'W
Redfield, S.D., U.S. (rĕd′fēld)	112	44°53'N	98°30'W
Red Fish Bar, Tx., U.S.	123a	29°29'N	94°53'W
Red Indian Lake, l., Can. (ĭn′dĭ-ăn)	93a	48°40'N	56°50'W
Red Lake, Can. (lāk)	91	51°02'N	93°49'W
Red Lake, r., Mn., U.S.	112	48°02'N	96°04'W
Red Lake Falls, Mn., U.S. (lăk fôls)	112	47°52'N	96°17'W
Red Lake Indian Reservation, I.R., Mn., U.S.	112	48°09'N	95°55'W
Redlands, Ca., U.S. (rĕd′lăndz)	117a	34°04'N	117°11'W
Red Lion, Pa., U.S. (lī′ŭn)	109	39°55'N	76°30'W
Red Lodge, Mt., U.S.	115	45°13'N	107°16'W
Redmond, Wa., U.S. (rĕd′mŭnd)	116a	47°40'N	122°07'W
Rednitz, r., Ger. (rĕd′nĕtz)	168	49°10'N	11°00'E
Red Oak, Ia., U.S. (ōk)	112	41°00'N	95°12'W
Redon, Fr. (rĕ-dôɴ′)	170	47°42'N	2°03'W
Redonda, Isla, i., Braz. (ē′s-lä-rĕ-dô′n-dä)	144b	23°05'S	43°11'W
Redonda Island, i., Antig. (rĕ-dŏn′dá)	133b	16°55'N	62°28'W
Redondela, Spain (rā-dhôn-dā′lä)	172	42°16'N	8°34'W
Redondo, Port. (rå-dôn′dò)	172	38°40'N	7°32'W
Redondo, Wa., U.S. (rē-dŏn′dō)	116a	47°21'N	122°19'W
Redondo Beach, Ca., U.S.	117a	33°50'N	118°23'W
Red Pass, Can. (pás)	95	52°59'N	118°59'W
Red Rock, r., Mt., U.S.	115	44°54'N	112°44'W
Red Sea, sea	198	23°15'N	37°00'E
Redstone, Can. (rĕd′stōn)	94	52°08'N	123°42'W
Red Sucker Lake, l., Can. (sŭk′ēr)	97	54°09'N	93°40'W
Redwater, r., Mt., U.S.	115	47°37'N	105°25'W
Red Willow Creek, r., Ne., U.S.	120	40°34'N	100°48'W
Red Wing, Mn., U.S.	113	44°34'N	92°35'W
Redwood City, Ca., U.S. (rĕd′ wŏod)	116b	37°29'N	122°13'W
Redwood Falls, Mn., U.S.	112	44°32'N	95°06'W
Redwood National Park, rec., Ca., U.S.	114	41°20'N	124°00'W
Redwood Valley, Ca., U.S.	118	39°15'N	123°12'W
Ree, Lough, l., Ire. (lŏκ′rē′)	160	53°30'N	7°45'W
Reed City, Mi., U.S. (rēd)	108	43°50'N	85°35'W
Reed Lake, l., Can.	97	54°37'N	100°30'W
Reedley, Ca., U.S. (rēd′lê)	118	36°37'N	119°27'W
Reedsburg, Wi., U.S. (rēdz′bûrg)	113	43°32'N	90°01'W
Reedsport, Or., U.S. (rēdz′pôrt)	114	43°42'N	124°08'W
Reelfoot Lake, res., Tn., U.S. (rēl′fŏt)	124	36°18'N	89°20'W
Rees, Ger. (rĕz)	171c	51°46'N	6°25'E
Reeves, Mount, mtn., Austl. (rēv's)	222	33°50'S	149°56'E
Reform, Al., U.S. (rê-fôrm′)	124	33°23'N	88°00'W
Refugio, Tx., U.S. (rå-fōō′hyô) (rĕ-fū′jō)	123	28°18'N	97°15'W
Rega, r., Pol. (rĕ-gä)	168	53°48'N	15°30'E
Regen, r., Ger. (rā′ghĕn)	168	49°09'N	12°21'E
Regensburg, Ger. (rā′ghĕns-bôrgh)	161	49°02'N	12°06'E
Reggio, La., U.S. (rĕg′jĭ-ō)	110d	29°50'N	89°46'W
Reggio di Calabria, Italy (rĕ′jô dē kä-lä′brē-ä)	163	38°07'N	15°42'E
Reggio nell' Emilia, Italy	162	44°43'N	10°34'E
Reghin, Rom. (rå-gēn′)	169	46°47'N	24°44'E
Regina, Can. (rê-jī′nà)	96	50°25'N	104°39'W
Regla, Cuba (rāg′lä)	134	23°08'N	82°20'W
Regnitz, r., Ger. (rĕg′nētz)	168	49°50'N	10°55'E
Reguengos de Monsaraz, Port.	172	38°26'N	7°30'W
Rehoboth, Nmb.	232	23°10'S	17°15'E
Rehovot, Isr.	197a	31°53'N	34°49'E
Reichenbach, Ger. (rī′κĕn-bäκ)	168	50°36'N	12°18'E
Reidsville, N.C., U.S. (rēdz′vĭl)	125	36°20'N	79°37'W
Reigate, Eng., U.K. (rī′gāt)	164	51°12'N	0°12'W
Reims, Fr. (răɴs)	154	49°16'N	4°00'E
Reina Adelaida, Archipiélago, is., Chile	144	52°00'S	74°15'W
Reinbeck, Ia., U.S. (rīn′bĕk)	113	42°22'N	92°34'W
Reindeer, l., Can. (rān′dēr)	92	57°36'N	101°23'W
Reindeer, r., Can.	96	55°45'N	103°30'W
Reindeer Island, i., Can.	97	52°25'N	98°00'W
Reinosa, Spain (rå-ê-nō′sä)	172	43°01'N	4°08'W
Reistertown, Md., U.S. (rēs′tēr-toun)	110e	39°28'N	76°50'W
Reitz, S. Afr.	238c	27°48'S	28°25'E
Rema, Jabal, mtn., Yemen	198	14°13'N	44°38'E
Rembau, Malay.	197b	2°36'N	102°06'E
Remedios, Col. (rĕ-mĕ′dyôs)	142a	7°03'N	74°42'W
Remedios, Cuba (rā-mā′dhē-ōs)	134	22°30'N	79°35'W
Remedios, Pan. (rĕ-mĕ′dyôs)	133	8°14'N	81°46'W
Remiremont, Fr. (rē-mēr-môɴ′)	171	48°01'N	6°35'E
Rempang, i., Indon.	197b	0°51'N	104°04'E
Remscheid, Ger. (rĕm′shīt)	171c	51°10'N	7°11'E
Rena, Nor.	166	61°08'N	11°17'E
Rendova, i., Sol. Is. (rĕn′dô-vá)	221	8°38'S	156°26'E
Rendsburg, Ger. (rĕnts′bôrgh)	168	54°19'N	9°39'E
Renfrew, Can. (rĕn′frōō)	91	45°30'N	76°30'W
Rengam, Malay. (rĕn′găm′)	197b	1°53'N	103°24'E
Rengo, Chile (rĕn′gō)	141b	34°22'S	70°50'W
Reni, Ukr. (ran′)	177	45°26'N	28°18'E
Renmark, Austl. (rĕn′märk)	218	34°10'S	140°50'E
Rennel, i., Sol. Is. (rĕn-nĕl′)	221	11°50'S	160°38'E
Rennes, Fr. (rĕn)	154	48°07'N	1°02'W
Reno, Nv., U.S. (rē′nō)	104	39°32'N	119°49'W
Reno, r., Italy (rā′nô)	174	44°10'N	10°55'E
Renovo, Pa., U.S. (rê-nō′vō)	109	41°20'N	77°50'W
Renqiu, China (rŭn-chyō)	206	38°44'N	116°05'E
Rensselaer, In., U.S. (rĕn′sĕ-lâr)	108	41°00'N	87°10'W
Rensselaer, N.Y., U.S. (rĕn′sē-lâr)	109	42°40'N	73°45'W
Rentchler, Il., U.S. (rĕnt′chlēr)	117e	38°30'N	89°52'W
Renton, Wa., U.S. (rĕn′tŭn)	116a	47°29'N	122°13'W
Repentigny, Can.	102a	45°47'N	73°26'W
Republic, Al., U.S. (rê-pŭb′lĭk)	110h	33°37'N	86°54'W
Republic, Wa., U.S.	114	48°38'N	118°44'W
Republican, r., U.S.	106	40°15'N	100°00'W
Republican, South Fork, r., Co., U.S. (rê-pŭb′lĭ-kăn)	120	39°35'N	102°28'W
Repulse Bay, b., Austl. (rê-pŭls′)	221	20°56'S	149°22'E
Requena, Spain (rå-kā′nä)	162	39°29'N	1°03'W
Resende, Braz. (rĕ-sĕ′n-dĕ)	141a	22°30'S	44°26'W
Resende Costa, Braz. (kôs-tä)	141a	20°55'S	44°12'W
Reshetylivka, Ukr.	177	49°34'N	34°04'E
Resistencia, Arg. (rā-sēs-tĕn′syä)	144	27°24'S	58°54'W
Reşiţa, Rom. (rā′shē-tá)	175	45°18'N	21°56'E
Resolute *see* Qausuittuq, Can.	89	74°41'N	95°00'W
Resolution, i., Can. (rĕz-ô-lū′shŭn)	93	61°30'N	63°58'W
Resolution Island, i., N.Z. (rĕz-ŏl-ûshûn)	221a	45°43'S	166°20'E
Restigouche, r., Can.	100	47°35'N	67°35'W
Restrepo, Col. (rĕs-trĕ′pô)	142a	3°49'N	76°31'W
Restrepo, Col.	142a	4°16'N	73°32'W
Retalhuleu, Guat. (rā-täl-ōō-lān′)	132	14°31'N	91°41'W
Rethel, Fr. (r-tĕl′)	170	49°34'N	4°20'E
Réthimnon, Grc.	174a	35°21'N	24°30'E
Retie, Bel.	159a	51°16'N	5°08'E
Retsil, Wa., U.S. (rĕt′sĭl)	116a	47°33'N	122°37'W
Reunion, dep., Afr. (rā-ü-nyôn′)	3	21°06'S	55°36'E
Reus, Spain (rā′ōōs)	162	41°08'N	1°05'E
Reutlingen, Ger. (roit′lĭng-ĕn)	168	48°29'N	9°14'E
Reutov, Russia (rĕ-ōō′ôf)	186b	55°45'N	37°52'E
Revda, Russia (ryâv′dá)	186a	56°48'N	59°57'E

ăt; finăl; rāte; senåte; ärm; ásk; sofá; fâre; ch-choose; dh-as th in other; bē; êvent; bĕt; recĕnt; cratēr; g-gō; gh-guttural g; bĭt; ĭ-short neutral; rīde; κ-guttural k as ch in German ich;

PRONOUNCING INDEX

Revelstoke – Rockingham Forest 341

PLACE (Pronunciation)	PAGE	LAT.	LONG.
Revelstoke, Can. (rĕv′ĕl-stōk)	90	51°00′N	118°12′W
Reventazón, Río, r., C.R. (rå-vĕn-tä-zōn′)	133	10°10′N	83°30′W
Revere, Ma., U.S. (rē-vēr′)	101a	42°24′N	71°01′W
Revillagigedo, Islas, is., Mex. (ē′s-läs-rĕ-vêl-yä-hĕ′gĕ-dô)	128	18°45′N	111°00′W
Revillagigedo Chan, Ak., U.S. (rĕ-vĭl′á-gĭ-gē′dō)	94	55°10′N	131°13′W
Revillagigedo Island, i., Ak., U.S.	94	55°35′N	131°23′W
Revin, Fr. (rē-văN)	170	49°56′N	4°34′E
Rewa, India (rā′wä)	199	24°41′N	81°11′E
Rewāri, India	202	28°19′N	76°39′E
Rexburg, Id., U.S. (rĕks′bûrg)	115	43°50′N	111°48′W
Rey, Iran	201	35°35′N	51°25′E
Rey, I., Mex. (rā)	122	27°00′N	103°33′W
Rey, Isla del, i., Pan. (ē′s-lä-dĕl-rā′ē)	133	8°20′N	78°40′W
Reyes, Bol. (rā′yĕs)	142	14°19′S	67°16′W
Reyes, Point, c., Ca., U.S.	118	38°00′N	123°00′W
Reykjanes, c., Ice. (rā′kyá-nĕs)	156	63°37′N	24°33′W
Reykjavík, Ice. (rā′kyá-vēk)	154	64°09′N	21°39′W
Reynosa, Mex. (rā-ē-nō′sä)	122	26°05′N	98°21′W
Rēzekne, Lat. (rā′zĕk-nĕ)	180	56°31′N	27°19′E
Rezh, Russia (rĕzh′)	186a	57°22′N	61°23′E
Rezina, Mol. (ryĕzh′ĕ-nĭ)	177	47°44′N	28°56′E
Rhaetian Alps, mts., Eur.	168	46°30′N	10°00′E
Rhaetien Alps, mts., Eur.	174	46°22′N	10°33′E
Rheinberg, Ger. (rīn′bĕrgh)	171c	51°33′N	6°37′E
Rheine, Ger. (rī′nĕ)	168	52°16′N	7°26′E
Rheinkamp, Ger.	171c	51°30′N	6°37′E
Rheinland, hist. reg., Ger.	168	50°05′N	6°40′E
Rheydt, Ger. (rĕ′yt)	171c	51°10′N	6°28′E
Rhin, r., Ger. (rĕn)	159b	52°52′N	12°49′E
Rhine, r., Eur.	156	50°34′N	7°21′E
Rhinelander, Wi., U.S. (rīn′lăn-dēr)	113	45°39′N	89°25′W
Rhin Kanal, can., Ger. (rēn kä-näl′)	159b	52°47′N	12°40′E
Rhiou, r., Alg.	173	35°45′N	1°18′E
Rhode Island, state, U.S. (rōd ī′lănd)	105	41°35′N	71°40′W
Rhode Island, i., R.I., U.S.	110b	41°31′N	71°14′W
Rhodes, S. Afr. (rōdz)	233c	30°48′S	27°56′E
Rhodes *see* Ródhos, i., Grc.	156	36°00′N	28°29′E
Rhodesia *see* Zimbabwe, nation, Afr.	232	17°50′S	29°30′E
Rhodope Mountains, mts., Eur. (rô′dô-pĕ)	156	42°00′N	24°08′E
Rhondda, Wales, U.K. (rŏn′dhá)	164	51°40′N	3°40′W
Rhône, r., Fr. (rōn)	156	44°30′N	4°45′E
Rhoon, Neth.	159a	51°52′N	4°24′E
Rhum, i., Scot., U.K. (rŭm)	164	57°00′N	6°20′W
Riachão, Braz. (rē-ä-shouN′)	143	7°15′S	46°30′W
Rialto, Ca., U.S. (rē-äl′tō)	117a	34°06′N	117°23′W
Riau, prov., Indon.	197b	0°56′N	101°25′E
Riau, Kepulauan, i., Indon.	212	0°30′N	104°55′E
Riau, Selat, strt., Indon.	197b	0°40′N	104°27′E
Riaza, r., Spain (rē-ä′thä)	172	41°25′N	3°25′W
Ribadavia, Spain (rē-bä-dhä′vē-ä)	172	42°18′N	8°06′W
Ribadeo, Spain (rē-bä-dhā′ō)	172	43°32′N	7°05′W
Ribadesella, Spain (rē′bä-dā-säl′yä)	172	43°30′N	5°02′W
Ribe, Den. (rē′bĕ)	166	55°20′N	8°45′E
Ribeirão Prêto, Braz. (rē-bā-rouN-prĕ′tô)	143	21°11′S	47°47′W
Ribera, N.M., U.S. (rē-bĕ′rä)	120	35°23′N	105°27′W
Riberalta, Bol. (rē-bå-räl′tä)	142	11°06′S	66°02′W
Rib Lake, Wi., U.S. (rĭb lāk)	113	45°20′N	90°11′W
Rîbniţa, Mol.	177	47°45′N	29°02′E
Rice, l., Can.	99	44°05′N	78°10′W
Rice Lake, Wi., U.S.	113	45°30′N	91°44′W
Rice Lake, l., Mn., U.S.	117g	45°10′N	93°09′W
Richards Island, i., Can. (rĭch′ĕrds)	103	69°45′N	135°30′W
Richards Landing, Can. (lănd′ĭng)	117k	46°18′N	84°02′W
Richardson, Tx., U.S. (rĭch′ĕrd-sŭn)	117c	32°56′N	96°44′W
Richardson, Wa., U.S.	116a	48°27′N	122°54′W
Richardson Mountains, mts., Can.	92	66°58′N	136°19′W
Richardson Mountains, mts., N.Z.	223	44°50′S	168°30′E
Richardson Park, De., U.S. (pärk)	109	39°45′N	75°35′W
Richelieu, r., Can. (rēsh′lyû′)	99	45°05′N	73°25′W
Richfield, Mn., U.S.	117g	44°53′N	93°17′W
Richfield, Oh., U.S.	111d	41°14′N	81°38′W
Richfield, Ut., U.S.	119	38°45′N	112°05′W
Richford, Vt., U.S. (rĭch′fērd)	109	45°00′N	72°35′W
Rich Hill, Mo., U.S. (rĭch hĭl)	121	38°05′N	94°21′W
Richibucto, Can. (rĭ-chĭ-bŭk′tō)	91	46°41′N	64°52′W
Richland, Ga., U.S. (rĭch′lănd)	124	32°05′N	84°40′W
Richland, Wa., U.S.	114	46°17′N	119°19′W
Richland Center, Wi., U.S. (sĕn′tēr)	113	43°20′N	90°25′W
Richmond, Austl. (rĭch′mŭnd)	219	20°47′S	143°14′E
Richmond, Austl.	217b	33°36′S	150°45′E
Richmond, Can.	102c	45°12′N	75°49′W
Richmond, Can.	99	45°40′N	72°07′W
Richmond, S. Afr.	233c	29°52′S	30°17′E
Richmond, Il., U.S.	111a	42°29′N	88°18′W
Richmond, In., U.S.	108	39°50′N	85°00′W
Richmond, Ky., U.S.	108	37°45′N	84°20′W
Richmond, Mo., U.S.	121	39°16′N	93°58′W
Richmond, Tx., U.S.	123	29°35′N	95°45′W
Richmond, Ut., U.S.	115	41°55′N	111°50′W
Richmond, Va., U.S.	105	37°35′N	77°30′W
Richmond Beach, Wa., U.S.	116a	47°47′N	122°23′W
Richmond Heights, Mo., U.S.	117e	38°38′N	90°20′W
Richmond Highlands, Wa., U.S.	116a	47°46′N	122°22′W
Richmond Hill, Can. (hĭl)	99	43°53′N	79°26′W
Richton, Ms., U.S. (rĭch′tŭn)	124	31°20′N	89°54′W
Richwood, W.V., U.S. (rĭch′wŏŏd)	108	38°10′N	80°30′W
Ridderkerk, Neth.	159a	51°52′N	4°35′E
Rideau, r., Can.	102c	45°17′N	75°41′W
Rideau Lake, l., Can. (rē-dō′)	99	44°40′N	76°20′W

PLACE (Pronunciation)	PAGE	LAT.	LONG.
Ridgefield, Ct., U.S. (rĭj′fēld)	110a	41°16′N	73°30′W
Ridgefield, Wa., U.S.	116c	45°49′N	122°40′W
Ridgeway, Can. (rĭj′wā)	111c	42°53′N	79°02′W
Ridgewood, N.J., U.S. (rĭdj′wŏŏd)	110a	40°59′N	74°08′W
Ridgway, Pa., U.S.	109	41°25′N	78°40′W
Riding Mountain, mtn., Can. (rīd′ĭng)	97	50°37′N	99°37′W
Riding Mountain National Park, rec., Can. (rīd′ĭng)	92	50°59′N	99°19′W
Riding Rocks, is., Bah.	134	25°20′N	79°10′W
Riebeek-Oos, S. Afr.	233c	33°14′S	26°09′E
Ried, Aus. (rēd)	168	48°13′N	13°30′E
Riesa, Ger. (rē′zá)	168	51°17′N	13°17′E
Rieti, Italy (rē-ā′tē)	162	42°25′N	12°51′E
Rievleidam, res., S. Afr.	233b	25°52′S	28°18′E
Riffe Lake, res., Wa., U.S.	114	46°20′N	122°10′W
Rifle, Co., U.S. (rī′f′l)	119	39°35′N	107°50′W
Rīga, Lat. (rē′gá)	178	56°55′N	24°05′E
Riga, Gulf of, b., Eur.	180	57°56′N	23°05′E
Rīgān, Iran	198	28°45′N	58°55′E
Rigaud, Can. (rē-gō′)	102a	45°29′N	74°18′W
Rigby, Id., U.S. (rĭg′bē)	115	43°40′N	111°55′W
Rigeley, W.V., U.S. (rĭj′lē)	109	39°40′N	78°45′W
Rīgestān, des., Afg.	198	30°53′N	64°42′E
Rigolet, Can. (rĭg-ō-lā′)	91	54°10′N	58°40′W
Riihimäki, Fin.	167	60°44′N	24°44′E
Rijeka, Cro. (rĭ-yĕ′kä)	162	45°22′N	14°24′E
Rijkevorsel, Bel.	159a	51°21′N	4°46′E
Rijswijk, Neth.	159a	52°03′N	4°19′E
Rika, r., Ukr. (rē′kà)	169	48°21′N	23°37′E
Rima, r., Nig.	235	13°30′N	5°50′E
Rimavska Sobota, Slvk. (rē′maf-skä sô′bô-tá)	169	48°25′N	20°01′E
Rimbo, Swe. (rēm′bŏŏ)	166	59°45′N	18°22′E
Rimini, Italy (rē′mē-nē)	162	44°03′N	12°33′E
Rimouski, Can. (rē-mōōs′kē)	91	48°27′N	68°32′W
Rincón de Romos, Mex. (rēn-kōn dā rō-mōs′)	130	22°13′N	102°21′W
Ringkøbing, Den. (rĭng′kûb-ĭng)	160	56°06′N	8°14′E
Ringkøbing Fjord, b., Den.	166	55°55′N	8°04′E
Ringsted, Den. (rĭng′stĕdh)	166	55°27′N	11°49′E
Ringvassøya, i., Nor. (rĭng′väs-ûē)	160	69°58′N	16°43′E
Ringwood, Austl.	217a	37°49′S	145°14′E
Rinjani, Gunung, mtn., Indon.	212	8°39′S	116°22′E
Río Abajo, Pan. (rē′ō-ä-bä′kō)	128a	9°01′N	78°30′W
Río Balsas, Mex. (rē′ō-bäl-säs)	130	17°59′N	99°45′W
Riobamba, Ec. (rē′ō-bäm-bä)	142	1°45′S	78°37′W
Rio Bonito, Braz. (rē′ŏŏ bō-nē′tŏŏ)	141a	22°44′S	42°38′W
Rio Branco, Braz. (rē′ŏŏ brän′kŏŏ)	142	9°57′S	67°50′W
Río Branco, Ur. (rĭō brăncō)	144	32°33′S	53°29′W
Rio Casca, Braz. (rē′ō-kà′s-kä)	141a	20°15′S	42°39′W
Río Chico, Ven. (rē′ō chē′kŏ)	143b	10°20′N	65°58′W
Rio Claro, Braz. (rē′ŏŏ klä′rŏŏ)	143	22°25′S	47°33′W
Río Cuarto, Arg. (rē′ō kwär′tō)	144	33°05′S	64°15′W
Rio das Flores, Braz. (rē′ō-däs-flō-rĕs)	141a	22°10′S	43°35′W
Rio de Janeiro, Braz. (rē′ŏŏ dā zhä-nā′ē-rŏŏ)	144b	22°50′S	43°20′W
Rio de Janeiro, state, Braz.	143	22°27′S	42°43′W
Río de Jesús, Pan.	133	7°54′N	80°59′W
Río Frío, Mex. (rē′ō-frē′ō)	131a	19°21′N	98°40′W
Río Gallegos, Arg. (rē′ō gä-lā′gōs)	144	51°43′S	69°15′W
Rio Grande, Braz. (rē′ŏŏ grän′dĕ)	144	31°04′S	52°14′W
Río Grande, Mex. (rē′ō grän′dā)	130	23°51′N	102°59′W
Riogrande, Tx., U.S. (rē′ō grän-dā)	122	26°23′N	98°48′W
Rio Grande do Norte, state, Braz.	143	5°26′S	37°20′W
Rio Grande do Sul, state, Braz. (rē′ŏŏ grän′dĕ-dŏŏ-sōō′l)	144	29°00′S	54°00′W
Ríohacha, Col. (rē′ō-ä′chä)	142	11°30′N	72°54′W
Río Hato, Pan. (rē′ō-ä′tō)	133	8°19′N	80°11′W
Riom, Fr. (rē-ôN′)	170	45°54′N	3°08′E
Rio Muni, hist. reg., Eq. Gui. (rē′ō mōō′nē)	230	1°47′N	8°33′E
Rionegro, Col. (rē′ō-nĕ′grō)	142a	6°09′N	75°22′W
Río Negro, prov., Arg. (rē′ō nā′grō)	144	40°15′S	68°15′W
Río Negro, dept., Ur. (rē′ō-nĕ′grō)	141c	32°48′S	57°45′W
Río Negro, Embalse del, res., Ur.	144	32°45′S	55°50′W
Rionero, Italy (rē-ō-nā′rō)	174	40°55′N	15°42′E
Rioni, r., Geor.	182	42°08′N	41°39′E
Rio Novo, Braz. (rē′ō-nô′vō)	141a	21°30′S	43°08′W
Rio Pardo de Minas, Braz. (rē′ō pär′dō-dĕ-mē′näs)	143	15°43′S	42°24′W
Rio Pombo, Braz. (rē′ō pôm′bä)	141a	21°17′S	43°09′W
Rio Sorocaba, Represa do, res., Braz.	141a	23°37′S	47°19′W
Ríosucio, Col. (rē′ō-sōō′syō)	142a	5°25′N	75°41′W
Río Tercero, Arg. (rē′ō dĕr-sĕ′rō)	144	32°12′S	63°59′W
Rio Verde, Braz. (vĕr′dĕ)	143	17°47′S	50°49′W
Ríoverde, Mex. (rē′ō-vĕr′dā)	128	21°54′N	99°59′W
Ripley, Eng., U.K. (rĭp′lē)	158a	53°03′N	1°24′W
Ripley, Ms., U.S.	124	34°44′N	88°55′W
Ripley, Tn., U.S.	124	35°44′N	89°34′W
Ripoll, Spain (rē-pōl′′)	173	42°10′N	2°10′E
Ripon, Wi., U.S. (rĭp′ŏn)	113	43°49′N	88°50′W
Ripon, i., Austl.	220	20°05′S	118°10′E
Ripon Falls, wtfl., Ug.	232	0°38′N	33°02′E
Risaralda, dept., Col.	142a	5°15′N	76°00′W
Risdon, Austl. (rĭz′dŭn)	219	42°37′S	147°32′E
Rishiri, i., Japan (rē-shē′rē)	210	45°10′N	141°08′E
Rishon le Ziyyon, Isr.	197a	31°57′N	34°48′E
Rishra, India	202a	22°42′N	88°22′E
Rising Sun, In., U.S. (rīz′ĭng sŭn)	108	38°55′N	84°55′W
Risor, Nor. (rēs′ûr)	160	58°44′N	9°10′E
Ritacuva, Alto, mtn., Col. (ä′l-tô-rē-tä-kōō′vä)	142	6°22′N	72°13′W
Rittman, Oh., U.S. (rĭt′năn)	111d	40°58′N	81°47′W
Ritzville, Wa., U.S. (rĭts′vĭl)	114	47°08′N	118°23′W

PLACE (Pronunciation)	PAGE	LAT.	LONG.
Riva, Dom. Rep. (rē′vä)	135	19°10′N	69°55′W
Riva, Italy (rē′vä)	174	45°54′N	10°49′E
Riva, Md., U.S. (rī′vä)	110e	38°57′N	76°36′W
Rivas, Nic. (rē′väs)	132	11°25′N	85°51′W
Rive-de-Gier, Fr. (rēv-dē-zhē-ā′)	170	45°32′N	4°37′E
Rivera, Ur. (rē-vā′rä)	144	30°52′S	55°32′W
River Cess, Lib. (rĭv′ĕr sĕs)	230	5°46′N	9°52′W
Riverdale, Il., U.S. (rĭv′ēr dāl)	111a	41°38′N	87°36′W
Riverdale, Ut., U.S.	117b	41°11′N	112°00′W
River Falls, Al., U.S.	124	31°20′N	86°25′W
River Falls, Wi., U.S.	113	44°48′N	92°38′W
Riverhead, N.Y., U.S. (rĭv′ēr hĕd)	109	40°55′N	72°40′W
Riverina, reg., Austl. (rĭv-ēr-ē′nä)	221	34°55′S	144°30′E
River Jordan, Can. (jôr′dăn)	116a	48°25′N	124°03′W
River Oaks, Tx., U.S. (ōkz)	117c	32°47′N	97°24′W
River Rouge, Mi., U.S. (rōōzh)	111b	42°16′N	83°09′W
Rivers, Can.	97	50°01′N	100°15′W
Riverside, Ca., U.S. (rĭv′ēr-sīd)	104	33°59′N	117°21′W
Riverside, N.J., U.S.	110f	40°02′N	74°58′W
Rivers Inlet, Can.	94	51°45′N	127°15′W
Riverstone, Austl.	217b	33°41′S	150°52′E
Riverton, Va., U.S.	109	39°00′N	78°15′W
Riverton, Wy., U.S.	115	43°02′N	108°24′W
Rivesaltes, Fr. (rēv′zält′)	170	42°48′N	2°48′E
Riviera Beach, Fl., U.S. (rĭv-ĭ-ēr′á bēch)	125a	26°46′N	80°04′W
Riviera Beach, Md., U.S.	110e	39°10′N	76°32′W
Rivière-Beaudette, Can.	102a	45°14′N	74°20′W
Rivière-du-Loup, Can. (rē-vyâr′ dü lōō′)	91	47°50′N	69°32′W
Rivière Qui Barre, Can. (rēv-yĕr′ kē-bär)	102g	53°47′N	113°51′W
Rivière-Trois-Pistoles, Can. (trwä′pēs-tôl′)	100	48°07′N	69°10′W
Rivne, Ukr.	177	48°11′N	31°46′E
Rivne, Ukr.	181	50°37′N	26°17′E
Rivne, prov., Ukr.	177	50°55′N	27°00′E
Riyadh, Sau. Ar.	198	24°31′N	46°47′E
Rize, Tur. (rē′zĕ)	163	41°00′N	40°30′E
Rizhao, China (rē-jou)	208	35°27′N	119°28′E
Rizzuto, Cape, c., Italy (rēt-sōō′tô)	175	38°53′N	17°05′E
Rjukan, Nor. (ryōō′kän)	160	59°53′N	8°30′E
Roanne, Fr. (rō-än′)	161	46°02′N	4°04′E
Roanoke, Al., U.S. (rō′á-nōk)	124	33°08′N	85°21′W
Roanoke, Va., U.S.	105	37°16′N	79°55′W
Roanoke, r., U.S.	107	36°17′N	77°22′W
Roanoke Rapids, N.C., U.S.	125	36°25′N	77°40′W
Roanoke Rapids Lake, res., N.C., U.S.	125	36°28′N	77°37′W
Roan Plateau, plat., Co., U.S. (rōn)	119	39°25′N	110°00′W
Roatan, Hond. (rō-ä-tän′)	132	16°18′N	86°33′W
Roatán, i., Hond.	132	16°19′N	86°46′W
Robbeneiland, i., S. Afr.	232a	33°48′S	18°22′E
Robbins, Il., U.S. (rŏb′ĭnz)	111a	41°39′N	87°42′W
Robbinsdale, Mn., U.S. (rŏb′ĭnz-dāl)	117g	45°03′N	93°22′W
Robe, Wa., U.S. (rōb)	116a	48°06′N	121°50′W
Roberts, Mount, mtn., Austl. (rŏb′ĕrts)	221	28°05′S	152°30′E
Roberts, Point, c., Wa., U.S. (rŏb′ĕrts)	116d	48°58′N	123°05′W
Robertson, Lac, l., Can.	101	51°00′N	59°10′W
Robertsport, Lib. (rŏb′ĕrts-pōrt)	230	6°45′N	11°22′W
Roberval, Can. (rŏb′ēr-văl) (rô-bĕr-vàl′)	91	48°32′N	72°15′W
Robinson, Can.	101	48°16′N	58°50′W
Robinson, Il., U.S. (rŏb′ĭn-sŭn)	108	39°00′N	87°45′W
Robinvale, Austl. (rŏb-ĭn′vāl)	222	34°45′S	142°45′E
Roblin, Can.	97	51°15′N	101°25′W
Robson, Mount, mtn., Can. (rŏb′sŭn)	95	53°07′N	119°09′W
Robstown, Tx., U.S. (rŏbz′toun)	123	27°46′N	97°41′W
Roca, Cabo da, c., Port. (ká′bō-dä-rô′kă)	172	38°47′N	9°30′W
Rocas, Atol das, atoll, Braz. (ä-tôl-däs-rō′kás)	143	3°50′S	33°46′W
Rocha, Ur. (rō′chás)	144	34°26′S	54°14′W
Rochdale, Eng., U.K. (rŏch′dāl)	164	53°37′N	2°09′W
Roche à Bateau, Haiti (rôsh à bá-tō′)	135	18°10′N	74°00′W
Rochefort, Fr. (rôsh-fōr′)	161	45°55′N	0°57′W
Rochelle, Il., U.S. (rō-shĕl′)	113	41°53′N	89°06′W
Rochester, Eng., U.K.	158a	51°24′N	0°30′E
Rochester, In., U.S. (rŏch′ĕs-tēr)	108	41°05′N	86°20′W
Rochester, Mi., U.S.	111b	42°41′N	83°09′W
Rochester, Mn., U.S.	105	44°01′N	92°30′W
Rochester, N.H., U.S.	109	43°20′N	71°00′W
Rochester, N.Y., U.S.	105	43°15′N	77°35′W
Rochester, Pa., U.S.	111e	40°42′N	80°16′W
Rock, r., Ia., U.S.	112	43°17′N	96°13′W
Rock, r., Or., U.S.	116c	45°34′N	122°52′W
Rock, r., Or., U.S.	116c	45°52′N	123°14′W
Rock, r., U.S.	107	41°40′N	90°00′W
Rockaway, N.J., U.S. (rŏck′á-wā)	110a	40°54′N	74°30′W
Rockbank, Austl.	217a	37°44′S	144°40′E
Rockcliffe Park, Can. (rŏk′klĭf pärk)	102c	45°27′N	75°40′W
Rock Creek, r., Can. (rŏk)	115	49°01′N	107°00′W
Rock Creek, r., Il., U.S.	111a	41°16′N	87°54′W
Rock Creek, r., Mt., U.S.	115	46°25′N	113°40′W
Rock Creek, r., Or., U.S.	114	45°30′N	120°06′W
Rock Creek, r., Wa., U.S.	114	47°09′N	117°50′W
Rockdale, Austl.	217b	33°57′S	151°08′E
Rockdale, Md., U.S.	110e	39°22′N	76°49′W
Rockdale, Tx., U.S. (rŏk′dāl)	123	30°39′N	97°00′W
Rock Falls, Il., U.S. (rŏk fôlz)	113	41°45′N	89°42′W
Rockford, Il., U.S. (rŏk′fērd)	105	42°16′N	89°07′W
Rockhampton, Austl. (rŏk-hămp′tŭn)	219	23°26′S	150°29′E
Rock Hill, S.C., U.S. (rŏk′hĭl)	105	34°55′N	81°01′W
Rockingham, N.C., U.S. (rŏk′ĭng-hăm)	125	34°54′N	79°45′W
Rockingham Forest, for., Eng., U.K. (rok′ĭng-hăm)	158a	52°29′N	0°43′W

ng-sing; ŋ-baŋk; N-nasalized n; nŏd; cŏmmit; ōld; ôbey; ôrder; oi-boil; fōōd; ŏŏ-as oo in foot; ou-out; s-soft; sh-dish; th-thin; pūre; ûnite; ûrn; stŭd; circŭs; ü-as in French tu; ′-indeterminate vowel.

342 Rock Island – Rumbek PRONOUNCING INDEX

PLACE (Pronunciation)	PAGE	LAT.	LONG.
Rock Island, Il., U.S.	105	41°31'N	90°37'W
Rock Island Dam, Wa., U.S. (ī lănd)	114	47°17'N	120°33'W
Rockland, Can. (rŏk'lănd)	102c	45°33'N	75°17'W
Rockland, Ma., U.S.	101a	42°07'N	70°55'W
Rockland, Me., U.S.	100	44°06'N	69°09'W
Rockland Reservoir, res., Austl.	222	36°55'S	142°20'E
Rockmart, Ga., U.S. (rŏk'märt)	124	33°58'N	85°00'W
Rockmont, Wi., U.S. (rŏk'mŏnt)	117h	46°34'N	91°54'W
Rockport, In., U.S. (rŏk'pōrt)	108	38°20'N	87°00'W
Rockport, Ma., U.S.	101a	42°39'N	70°37'W
Rockport, Mo., U.S.	121	40°25'N	95°30'W
Rockport, Tx., U.S.	123	28°03'N	97°03'W
Rock Rapids, Ia., U.S. (răp'ĭdz)	112	43°26'N	96°10'W
Rock Sound, strt., Bah.	134	24°50'N	76°05'W
Rocksprings, Tx., U.S. (rŏk sprĭngs)	122	30°02'N	100°12'W
Rock Springs, Wy., U.S.	104	41°35'N	109°13'W
Rockstone, Guy. (rŏk'stôn)	143	5°55'N	57°27'W
Rock Valley, Ia., U.S. (văl'ĭ)	112	43°13'N	96°17'W
Rockville, In., U.S. (rŏk'vĭl)	108	39°45'N	87°15'W
Rockville, Md., U.S.	110e	39°05'N	77°11'W
Rockville Centre, N.Y., U.S. (sĕn'tĕr)	110a	40°39'N	73°39'W
Rockwall, Tx., U.S. (rŏk'wôl)	121	32°55'N	96°23'W
Rockwell City, Ia., U.S. (rŏk'wĕl)	113	42°22'N	94°37'W
Rockwood, Can. (rŏk-wŏŏd)	102d	43°37'N	80°08'W
Rockwood, Me., U.S.	100	45°39'N	69°45'W
Rockwood, Tn., U.S.	124	35°51'N	84°41'W
Rocky, East Branch, r., Oh., U.S.	111d	41°13'N	81°43'W
Rocky, West Branch, r., Oh., U.S.	111d	41°17'N	81°54'W
Rocky Boys Indian Reservation, I.R., Mt., U.S.	115	48°08'N	109°34'W
Rocky Ford, Co., U.S.	120	38°02'N	103°43'W
Rocky Hill, N.J., U.S. (hĭl)	110a	40°24'N	74°38'W
Rocky Island Lake, I., Can.	98	46°56'N	83°04'W
Rocky Mount, N.C., U.S.	125	35°55'N	77°47'W
Rocky Mountain House, Can.	95	52°22'N	114°55'W
Rocky Mountain National Park, rec., Co., U.S.	106	40°29'N	106°06'W
Rocky Mountains, mts., N.A.	89	50°00'N	114°00'W
Rocky River, Oh., U.S.	111d	41°29'N	81°51'W
Rodas, Cuba (rō'dhäs)	134	22°20'N	80°35'W
Roden, r., Eng., U.K. (rō'dĕn)	158a	52°49'N	2°38'W
Rodeo, Mex. (rō-dā'ō)	122	25°12'N	104°34'W
Rodeo, Ca., U.S. (rō'dēō)	116b	38°02'N	122°16'W
Roderick Island, i., Can. (rŏd'ē-rĭk)	94	52°40'N	128°22'W
Rodez, Fr. (rō-dĕz')	161	44°22'N	2°34'E
Rodnei, Munţii, mts., Rom.	169	47°41'N	24°05'E
Rodniki, Russia (rôd'nē-kē)	180	57°08'N	41°48'E
Rodonit, Kep I, c., Alb.	175	41°38'N	19°01'E
Ródos, Grc.	163	36°24'N	28°15'E
Ródos, i., Grc.	162	36°00'N	28°29'E
Roebling, N.J., U.S. (rōb'lĭng)	110f	40°07'N	74°48'W
Roebourne, Austl. (rō'bŭrn)	218	20°50'S	117°15'E
Roebuck Bay, b., Austl. (rō'bŭck)	220	18°15'S	121°10'E
Roedtan, S. Afr.	238c	24°37'S	29°08'E
Roeselare, Bel.	165	50°55'N	3°05'E
Roesiger, I., Wa., U.S. (rōz'ĭ-gĕr)	116a	47°59'N	121°56'W
Roes Welcome Sound, strt., Can. (rōz)	93	64°10'N	87°23'W
Rogatica, Bos. (rō-gä'tē-tsä)	175	43°46'N	19°00'E
Rogers, Ar., U.S. (rŏj-ĕrz)	121	36°19'N	94°07'W
Rogers City, Mi., U.S.	108	45°30'N	83°50'W
Rogersville, Tn., U.S.	124	36°21'N	83°00'W
Rognac, Fr. (rŏn-yäk')	170a	43°29'N	5°15'E
Rogoaguado, I., Bol. (rō'gō-ä-gwä-dō)	142	12°42'S	66°46'W
Rogovskaya, Russia (rô-gôf'skà-yà)	177	45°43'N	38°42'E
Rogózno, Pol. (rô'gôzh-nō)	168	52°44'N	16°53'E
Rogue, r., Or., U.S. (rōg)	114	42°32'N	124°13'W
Rohatyn, Ukr.	169	49°22'N	24°37'E
Rojas, Arg. (rō'häs)	141c	34°11'S	60°42'W
Rojo, Cabo, c., Mex. (rō'hō)	131	21°35'N	97°16'W
Rojo, Cabo, c., P.R. (rō'hō)	129b	17°55'N	67°14'W
Rokel, r., S.L.	234	9°00'N	11°55'W
Rokkō-Zan, mtn., Japan (rôk'kō zän)	211b	34°46'N	135°16'E
Rokycany, Czech Rep. (rô'kĭ'tsà-nĭ)	168	49°44'N	13°37'E
Roldanillo, Col. (rôl-dä-nē'l-yō)	142a	4°24'N	76°09'W
Rolla, Mo., U.S.	121	37°56'N	91°45'W
Rolla, N.D., U.S.	112	48°52'N	99°32'W
Rolleville, Bah.	134	23°40'N	76°00'W
Roma, Austl. (rō'mà)	219	26°30'S	148°48'E
Roma see Rome, Italy	154	41°52'N	12°37'E
Roma, Leso.	233c	29°28'S	27°43'E
Romaine, r., Can. (rō-mĕn')	93	51°22'N	63°23'W
Roman, Rom. (rō'män)	169	46°56'N	26°57'E
Romania, nation, Eur. (rō-mā'nē-à)	154	46°18'N	22°53'E
Romano, Cape, c., Fl., U.S. (rō-mä'nō)	125a	25°48'N	82°00'W
Romano, Cayo, i., Cuba (kä'yō-rō-mä'nō)	134	22°15'N	78°00'W
Romanovo, Russia (rō-mä'nô-vô)	186a	59°09'N	61°24'E
Romans, Fr. (rō-mäɴ')	170	45°04'N	4°49'E
Romblon, Phil. (rōm-blōn')	213a	12°34'N	122°16'E
Romblon Island, i., Phil.	213a	12°33'N	122°17'E
Rome (Roma), Italy	154	41°52'N	12°37'E
Rome, Ga., U.S. (rōm)	105	34°14'N	85°10'W
Rome, N.Y., U.S.	109	43°15'N	75°25'W
Romeo, Mi., U.S. (rō'mē-ō)	108	42°50'N	83°00'W
Romford, Eng., U.K. (rŭm'fērd)	158b	51°35'N	0°11'E
Romilly-sur-Seine, Fr. (rō-mē-yē'sür-sān')	170	48°32'N	3°41'E
Romita, Mex. (rō-mē'tä)	130	20°53'N	101°32'W
Romny, Ukr. (rôm'nĭ)	181	50°46'N	33°31'E
Rømø, i., Den. (rûm'û)	166	55°08'N	8°17'E
Romoland, Ca., U.S. (rō'mō'lănd)	117a	33°44'N	117°11'W
Romorantin-Lanthenay, Fr. (rō-mō-räɴ-tăɴ')	170	47°24'N	1°46'E
Rompin, Malay.	197b	2°42'N	102°30'E
Rompin, r., Malay.	197b	2°54'N	103°10'E
Romsdalsfjorden, Nor.	166	62°40'N	7°05'W
Romulus, Mi., U.S. (rom'ū lŭs)	111b	42°14'N	83°24'W
Ron, Mui, c., Viet.	209	18°05'N	106°45'E
Ronan, Mt., U.S. (rō'năn)	115	47°28'N	114°03'W
Roncador, Serra do, mts., Braz. (sĕr'rà dō rôn-kä-dōr')	143	12°44'S	52°19'W
Ronceverte, W.V., U.S. (rŏn'sē-vûrt)	108	37°45'N	80°30'W
Ronda, Spain (rōn'dä)	181	36°45'N	5°10'W
Ronda, Sierra de, mts., Spain	172	36°35'N	5°03'W
Rondônia, state, Braz.	142	10°15'S	63°07'W
Ronge, Lac la, I., Can. (rōnzh)	92	55°10'N	105°00'W
Rongjiang, China (rôŋ-jyäŋ)	209	25°52'N	108°45'E
Rongxian, China	209	22°50'N	110°32'E
Rønne, Den. (rûn'ĕ)	160	55°08'N	14°46'E
Ronneby, Swe. (rōn'ĕ-bü)	166	56°13'N	15°17'E
Ronne Ice Shelf, ice, Ant.	224	77°30'S	38°00'W
Roodepoort, S. Afr. (rō'dĕ-pōrt)	233b	26°10'S	27°52'E
Roodhouse, Il., U.S. (rōōd'hous)	121	39°29'N	90°21'W
Rooiberg, S. Afr.	238c	24°46'S	27°42'E
Roosendaal, Neth. (rō'zĕn-däl)	159a	51°32'N	4°27'E
Roosevelt, Ut., U.S. (rōz'vĕlt)	119	40°20'N	110°00'W
Roosevelt, r., Braz. (rô'sĕ-vĕlt)	143	9°22'S	60°28'W
Roosevelt Island, i., Ant.	224	79°30'S	168°00'W
Root, r., Wi., U.S.	111a	42°49'N	87°54'W
Roper, r., Austl. (rōp'ēr)	220	14°50'S	134°00'E
Ropsha, Russia (rôp'shà)	186c	59°44'N	29°53'E
Roque Pérez, Arg. (rô'kĕ-pĕ'rĕz)	141c	35°23'S	59°22'W
Roques, Islas los, is., Ven.	142	12°25'N	67°40'W
Roraima, state, Braz. (rō'rĭy-mă)	142	2°00'N	62°15'W
Roraima, Mount, mtn., S.A. (rô-rä-ē'mä)	143	5°12'N	60°52'W
Røros, Nor. (rûr'ôs)	160	62°36'N	11°25'E
Ros', r., Ukr. (rôs)	177	49°40'N	30°22'E
Rosa, Monte, mtn., Italy (mōn'tā rō'zä)	162	45°56'N	7°51'E
Rosales, Mex. (rō-zä'läs)	122	28°15'N	100°43'W
Rosales, Phil. (rô-sä'lĕs)	213a	15°54'N	120°38'E
Rosamorada, Mex. (rō'zä-mō-rä'dhä)	130	22°06'N	105°16'W
Rosaria, Laguna, I., Mex. (lä-gö'nä-rō-sà'ryä)	131	17°50'N	93°51'W
Rosario, Arg. (rō-zä'rē-ō)	144	32°58'S	60°42'W
Rosario, Braz. (rō-zä'rē-ò)	143	2°49'S	44°15'W
Rosario, Mex.	122	26°31'N	105°40'W
Rosario, Mex.	130	22°58'N	105°54'W
Rosario, Phil.	213a	13°49'N	121°13'W
Rosario, Ur.	141c	34°19'S	57°24'E
Rosario, Cayo, i., Cuba (kä'yō-rō-sä'ryō)	134	21°40'N	81°55'W
Rosário do Sul, Braz. (rō-zä'rē-ò-dō-sōō'l)	144	30°17'S	54°52'W
Rosário Oeste, Braz. (ō'ĕst'ē)	143	14°47'S	56°20'W
Rosario Strait, strt., Wa., U.S.	116a	48°27'N	122°45'W
Rosbach, Ger. (rōz'bäĸ)	171c	50°47'N	7°38'E
Roscoe, Tx., U.S. (rôs'kō)	122	32°26'N	100°38'W
Roseau, Dom.	133b	15°17'N	61°23'W
Roseau, Mn., U.S. (rō-zō')	112	48°52'N	95°47'W
Roseau, r., Mn., U.S.	112	48°52'N	96°11'W
Roseberg, Or., U.S. (rōz'bûrg)	104	43°13'N	123°30'W
Rosebud, r., Can. (rōz'bŭd)	95	51°20'N	112°20'W
Rosebud Creek, r., Mt., U.S.	115	45°48'N	106°34'W
Rosebud Indian Reservation, I.R., S.D., U.S.	112	43°13'N	100°42'W
Rosedale, Ms., U.S.	124	33°49'N	90°56'W
Rosedale, Wa., U.S.	116a	47°20'N	122°39'W
Roseires Reservoir, res., Sudan	231	11°15'N	34°45'E
Roselle, Il., U.S. (rō-zĕl')	111a	41°59'N	88°05'W
Rosemère, Can. (rōz'mēr)	102a	45°38'N	73°48'W
Rosemount, Mn., U.S. (rōz'mount)	117g	44°44'N	93°08'W
Rosendal, S. Afr. (rō-sĕn'tăl)	238c	28°32'S	27°56'E
Rosenheim, Ger. (rō'zĕn-hĭm)	161	47°52'N	12°06'E
Roses, Golf de, b., Spain	173	42°10'N	3°20'E
Rosetown, Can. (rōz'toun)	90	51°33'N	108°00'W
Rosetta see Rashīd, Egypt	200	31°22'N	30°25'E
Rosettenville, neigh., S. Afr.	233b	26°15'S	28°04'E
Roseville, Ca., U.S. (rōz'vĭl)	118	38°44'N	121°19'W
Roseville, Mi., U.S.	111b	42°30'N	82°55'W
Roseville, Mn., U.S.	117g	45°01'N	93°10'W
Rosiclare, Il., U.S. (rōz'y-klâr)	108	37°30'N	88°15'W
Rosignol, Guy. (rōs-ĭg-nŏl)	143	6°16'N	57°37'W
Roşiori de Vede, Rom. (rô-shôr'ē dĕ vĕ-dĕ)	175	44°06'N	25°00'E
Roskilde, Den. (rôs'kēl-dĕ)	166	55°39'N	12°04'E
Roslavl', Russia (rôs'läv'l)	180	53°56'N	32°52'E
Roslyn, Wa., U.S. (rŏz'lĭn)	114	47°14'N	121°00'W
Rösrath, Ger. (rûz'rät)	171c	50°53'N	7°11'E
Ross, Oh., U.S. (rôs)	111f	39°19'N	84°39'W
Rossano, Italy (rō-sä'nō)	163	39°34'N	16°38'E
Rossan Point, c., Ire.	164	54°45'N	8°30'W
Ross Creek, r., Can.	102g	53°40'N	113°08'W
Rosseau, I., Can. (rôs-sō')	99	45°15'N	79°30'W
Rossel, i., Pap. N. Gui. (rô-sĕl')	221	11°31'S	154°00'E
Rosser, Can. (rôs'sĕr)	102f	49°59'N	97°27'W
Ross Ice Shelf, ice, Ant.	224	81°30'S	175°00'W
Rossignol, Lake, I., Can.	100	44°10'N	65°10'W
Ross Island, i., Can.	97	54°14'N	97°45'W
Ross Lake, res., Wa., U.S.	114	48°40'N	121°07'W
Rossland, Can. (rôs'lănd)	90	49°05'N	118°48'W
Rossosh', Russia (rôs'sŭsh)	181	50°12'N	39°32'E
Rossouw, S. Afr.	233c	31°12'S	27°18'E
Ross Sea, sea, Ant.	224	76°00'S	178°00'W
Rossvatnet, I., Nor.	160	65°36'N	13°08'E
Rossville, Ga., U.S. (rôs'vĭl)	124	34°57'N	85°22'W
Rosthern, Can.	96	52°41'N	106°25'W
Rostock, Ger. (rôs'tŭk)	160	54°04'N	12°06'E
Rostov, Russia	180	57°13'N	39°23'E
Rostov, prov., Russia	177	47°38'N	39°15'E
Rostov-na-Donu, Russia (rôstôv-nå-dô-nōō)	178	47°16'N	39°47'E
Roswell, Ga., U.S. (rŏz'wĕl)	124	34°02'N	84°21'W
Roswell, N.M., U.S.	104	33°23'N	104°32'W
Rotan, Tx., U.S. (rô-tăn')	120	32°51'N	100°27'W
Rothenburg, Ger.	168	49°20'N	10°10'E
Rotherham, Eng., U.K. (rŏdh'ēr-ăm)	158a	53°26'N	1°21'W
Rotherham, co., Eng., U.K.	158a	53°52'N	1°45'W
Rothesay, Can. (rôth'så)	100	45°23'N	66°00'W
Rothesay, Scot., U.K.	164	55°50'N	3°14'W
Rothwell, Eng., U.K.	158a	53°44'N	1°30'W
Roti, Pulau, i., Indon. (rō'tē)	212	10°30'S	122°52'E
Roto, Austl. (rō'tō)	222	33°07'S	145°30'E
Rotorua, N.Z.	223	38°07'S	176°17'E
Rotterdam, Neth. (rôt'ĕr-däm')	154	51°55'N	4°27'E
Rottweil, Ger. (rōt'vīl)	168	48°10'N	8°36'E
Roubaix, Fr. (rōō-bĕ')	170	50°42'N	3°10'E
Rouen, Fr. (rōō-äɴ')	154	49°25'N	1°05'E
Rouge, r., Can. (rōōzh)	102d	43°53'N	79°21'W
Rouge, r., Can.	99	46°40'N	74°50'W
Rouge, r., Mi., U.S.	111b	42°30'N	83°15'W
Rough River Reservoir, res., Ky., U.S.	108	37°45'N	86°10'W
Round Lake, Il., U.S.	111a	42°21'N	88°05'W
Round Pond, I., Can.	101	48°15'N	55°57'W
Round Rock, Tx., U.S.	123	30°31'N	97°41'W
Round Top, mtn., Or., U.S. (tŏp)	116c	45°41'N	123°22'W
Roundup, Mt., U.S. (round'ŭp)	115	46°25'N	108°35'W
Rousay, i., Scot., U.K. (rōō'zå)	164a	59°10'N	3°04'W
Rouyn, Can. (rōōn)	91	48°22'N	79°03'W
Rovaniemi, Fin. (rô'vå-nyĕ'mĭ)	160	66°29'N	25°45'E
Rovato, Italy (rô-vä'tō)	174	45°33'N	10°00'E
Roven'ki, Russia	177	49°54'N	38°54'E
Roven'ky, Ukr.	177	48°06'N	39°44'E
Rovereto, Italy (rō-vå-rā'tō)	174	45°53'N	11°05'E
Rovigo, Italy (rô-vē'gô)	174	45°05'N	11°48'E
Rovinj, Cro. (rō'ēn')	174	45°05'N	13°40'E
Rovira, Col. (rô-vē'rä)	142a	4°14'N	75°13'W
Rovuma (Ruvuma), r., Afr.	237	10°50'S	39°50'E
Rowley, Ma., U.S. (rou'lē)	101a	42°43'N	70°53'W
Roxana, Il., U.S. (rŏks'ăn-nà)	117e	38°51'N	90°05'W
Roxas, Phil. (rô-xäs)	212	11°30'N	122°47'E
Roxo, Cap, c., Sen.	234	12°20'N	16°43'W
Roy, N.M., U.S. (roi)	120	35°54'N	104°09'W
Roy, Ut., U.S.	117b	41°10'N	112°02'W
Royal, i., Bah.	134	25°30'N	76°50'W
Royal Canal, can., Ire. (roi-ăl)	164	53°28'N	6°45'W
Royal Natal National Park, rec., S. Afr.	233c	28°35'S	28°54'E
Royal Oak, Can. (roi'ăl ōk)	116a	48°30'N	123°24'W
Royal Oak, Mi., U.S.	111b	42°29'N	83°09'W
Royalton, Mi., U.S. (roi'ăl-tŭn)	108	42°00'N	86°25'W
Royan, Fr. (rwä-yäɴ')	170	45°40'N	1°02'W
Roye, Fr. (rwä)	170	49°43'N	2°40'E
Royersford, Pa., U.S. (rô'yĕrz-fērd)	110f	40°11'N	75°32'W
Royston, Ga., U.S. (roiz'tŭn)	124	34°15'N	83°06'W
Royton, Eng., U.K. (roi'tŭn)	158a	53°34'N	2°07'W
Rozay-en-Brie, Fr. (rō-zā-ĕɴ-brē')	171b	48°41'N	2°57'E
Rozdil'na, Ukr.	177	46°47'N	30°08'E
Rozhaya, r., Russia (rô'zhà-yà)	186b	55°20'N	37°37'E
Rozivka, Ukr.	177	47°14'N	36°35'E
Rožňava, Slvk. (rôzh'nyà-và)	169	48°39'N	20°32'E
Rtishchevo, Russia ('r-tĭsh'chĕ-vô)	181	52°15'N	43°40'E
Ru, r., China (rōō)	206	33°07'N	114°18'E
Ruacana Falls, wtfl., Afr.	232	17°15'S	14°45'E
Ruaha National Park, rec., Tan.	237	7°15'S	34°50'E
Ruapehu, vol., N.Z. (rò-à-pā'hōō)	221a	39°15'S	175°37'E
Rub' al Khali see Ar Rub' al Khālī, des., Asia	198	20°00'N	51°00'E
Rubeho Mountains, mts., Tan.	237	6°45'S	36°15'E
Rubidoux, Ca., U.S.	117a	33°59'N	117°24'W
Rubizhne, Ukr.	177	48°53'N	38°29'E
Rubondo Island, i., Tan.	237	2°10'S	31°55'E
Rubtsovsk, Russia	178	51°31'N	81°17'E
Ruby, Ak., U.S. (rōō'bē)	106a	64°38'N	155°22'W
Ruby, I., Nv., U.S.	118	40°11'N	115°20'W
Ruby, r., Mt., U.S.	115	45°06'N	112°10'W
Ruby Mountains, mts., Nv., U.S.	118	40°11'N	115°36'W
Rudkøbing, Den. (rōōdh'kûb-ĭng)	166	54°56'N	10°44'E
Rüdnitz, Ger. (rüd'nētz)	159b	52°44'N	13°38'E
Rudolf, Lake, I., Afr. (rōō'dŏlf)	231	3°30'N	36°05'E
Rufā'ah, Sudan (rōō-fä'ä)	231	14°52'N	33°30'E
Ruffec, Fr. (rü-fĕk')	170	46°03'N	0°11'E
Rufiji, r., Tan. (rò-fē'jē)	233	8°00'S	38°00'E
Rufisque, Sen. (rü-fēsk')	230	14°43'N	17°17'W
Rufunsa, Zam.	237	15°05'S	29°40'E
Rufus Woods, Wa., U.S.	114	48°02'N	119°33'W
Rugao, China (rōō-gou)	208	32°24'N	120°33'E
Rugby, Eng., U.K. (rŭg'bē)	158a	52°22'N	1°15'W
Rugby, N.D., U.S.	112	48°22'N	100°00'W
Rugeley, Eng., U.K. (rōōj'lē)	158a	52°46'N	1°56'W
Rügen, i., Ger. (rü'ghĕn)	156	54°28'N	13°47'E
Ruhnu-Saar, i., Est. (rōōnò-sä'âr)	167	57°46'N	23°15'E
Ruhr, r., Ger. (ròr)	168	51°18'N	8°17'E
Rui'an, China (rwā-än)	209	27°48'N	120°40'E
Ruiz, Mex. (rōē'z)	130	21°55'N	105°09'W
Ruiz, Nevado del, vol., Col. (nĕ-vá'dō-dĕl-rōōē'z)	142a	4°52'N	75°20'W
Rūjiena, Lat. (rò'yĭ-ă-nà)	167	57°54'N	25°19'E
Ruki, r., D.R.C.	236	0°05'S	18°55'E
Rukwa, Lake, I., Tan. (rōōk-wä')	232	8°00'S	32°25'E
Rum, r., Mn., U.S. (rŭm)	113	45°52'N	93°45'W
Ruma, Serb. (rōō'mà)	175	45°00'N	19°53'E
Rumbek, Sudan (rŭm'bĕk)	231	6°52'N	29°43'E

PRONOUNCING INDEX Rum Cay – Saint George 343

PLACE (Pronunciation)	PAGE	LAT.	LONG.
Rum Cay, i., Bah.	135	23°40'N	74°50'W
Rumford, Me., U.S. (rŭm'fẽrd)	100	44°32'N	70°35'W
Rummah, Wādī ar, val., Sau. Ar.	198	26°17'N	41°45'E
Rummānah, Egypt	197a	31°01'N	32°39'E
Runan, China (ro͞o-nän)	208	32°59'N	114°22'E
Runcorn, Eng., U.K. (rŭŋ'kôrn)	158a	53°20'N	2°44'W
Ruo, r., China (rwô)	204	41°15'N	100°46'E
Rupat, i., Indon. (ro͞o'pät)	197b	1°55'N	101°35'E
Rupat, Selat, strt., Indon.	197b	1°55'N	101°17'E
Rupert, Id., U.S. (ro͞o'pẽrt)	115	42°36'N	113°41'W
Rupert, Rivière de, r., Can.	93	51°35'N	76°30'W
Ruse, Blg. (ro͞o'sĕ) (rò'sĕ)	154	43°50'N	25°59'E
Rushan, China (ro͞o-shän)	206	36°54'N	121°31'E
Rush City, Mn., U.S.	113	45°40'N	92°59'W
Rushville, Il., U.S. (rŭsh'vĭl)	121	40°08'N	90°34'W
Rushville, In., U.S.	108	39°35'N	85°30'W
Rushville, Ne., U.S.	112	42°43'N	102°27'W
Rusizi, r., Afr.	237	3°00'S	29°05'E
Rusk, Tx., U.S. (rŭsk)	123	31°49'N	95°09'W
Ruskin, Can. (rŭs'kĭn)	116d	49°10'N	122°25'W
Russ, r., Aus.	159e	48°12'N	16°55'E
Russas, Braz. (ro͞o's-säs)	143	4°48'S	37°50'W
Russell, Can. (rŭs'ĕl)	90	50°47'N	101°15'W
Russell, Can.	102c	45°15'N	75°22'W
Russell, Ca., U.S.	116b	37°39'N	122°08'W
Russell, Ks., U.S.	120	38°51'N	98°51'W
Russell, Ky., U.S.	108	38°30'N	82°45'W
Russel Lake, l., Can.	97	56°15'N	101°30'W
Russell Islands, is., Sol. Is.	221	9°16'S	158°30'E
Russellville, Al., U.S. (rŭs'ĕl-vĭl)	124	34°29'N	87°44'W
Russellville, Ar., U.S.	121	35°16'N	93°08'W
Russelville, Ky., U.S.	124	36°48'N	86°51'W
Russia, nation, Russia	178	61°00'N	60°00'E
Russian, r., Ca., U.S. (rŭsh'ăn)	118	38°59'N	123°10'W
Rustavi, Geor.	182	41°33'N	45°02'E
Rustenburg, S. Afr. (rŭs'tĕn-bûrg)	238c	25°40'S	27°15'E
Ruston, La., U.S. (rŭs'tŭn)	123	32°32'N	92°39'W
Ruston, Wa., U.S.	116a	47°18'N	122°30'W
Rute, Spain (ro͞o'tā)	172	38°20'N	4°34'W
Ruth, Nv., U.S. (ro͞oth)	118	39°17'N	115°00'W
Ruthenia, hist. reg., Ukr.	169	48°25'N	23°00'E
Rutherfordton, N.C., U.S. (rŭdh'ẽr-fẽrd-tŭn)	125	35°23'N	81°58'W
Rutland, Vt., U.S.	109	43°35'N	72°55'W
Rutledge, Md., U.S. (rŭt'lĕdj)	110e	39°34'N	76°33'W
Rutog, China	204	33°29'N	79°26'E
Rutshuru, D.R.C. (ro͞ot-sho͞o'ro͞o)	232	1°11'S	29°27'E
Ruvo, Italy (ro͞o'vô)	174	41°07'N	16°32'E
Ruvuma, r., Afr.	237	11°30'S	37°00'E
Ruza, Russia (ro͞o'zà)	176	55°42'N	36°12'E
Ruzhany, Bela. (rò-zhän'ĭ)	169	52°49'N	24°54'E
Rwanda, nation, Afr.	232	2°10'S	29°37'E
Ryabovo, Russia (ryä'bô-vô)	186c	59°24'N	31°08'E
Ryazan', Russia (ryä-zän'')	178	54°37'N	39°43'E
Ryazan', prov., Russia	176	54°10'N	39°37'E
Ryazhsk, Russia (ryäzh'sk')	180	53°43'N	40°04'E
Rybachiy, Poluostrov, pen., Russia	180	69°50'N	33°20'E
Rybatskoye, Russia	186c	59°50'N	30°31'E
Rybinsk, Russia	178	58°02'N	38°52'E
Rybinskoye, res., Russia	178	58°23'N	38°15'E
Rybnik, Pol. (rĭb'nĕk)	169	50°06'N	18°37'E
Ryde, Eng., U.K. (rīd)	164	50°43'N	1°16'W
Rye, N.Y., U.S. (rī)	110a	40°58'N	73°42'W
Ryl'sk, Russia (rêl''sk)	181	51°33'N	34°42'E
Ryōtsu, Japan (ryōt'so͞o)	210	38°02'N	138°23'E
Rypin, Pol. (rĭ'pĕn)	169	53°04'N	19°25'E
Rysy, mtn., Eur.	169	49°12'N	20°04'E
Ryukyu Islands *see* Nansei-shotō, is., Japan	205	27°30'N	127°00'E
Rzeszów, Pol. (zhå-shöf)	161	50°02'N	22°00'E
Rzhev, Russia ('r-zhĕf)	178	56°16'N	34°17'E
Rzhyshchiv, Ukr.	177	49°58'N	31°05'E

S

PLACE (Pronunciation)	PAGE	LAT.	LONG.
Saale, r., Ger. (sä-lĕ)	168	51°14'N	11°52'E
Saalfeld, Ger. (säl'fĕlt)	168	50°38'N	11°20'E
Saarbrücken, Ger. (zähr'brü-kĕn)	161	49°15'N	7°01'E
Saaremaa, i., Est.	180	58°25'N	22°30'E
Saavedra, Arg. (sä-ä-vā'drä)	144	37°45'S	62°23'W
Saba, i., Neth. Ant. (sä'bä)	133b	17°39'N	63°20'W
Šabac, Serb. (shä'báts)	163	44°45'N	19°49'E
Sabadell, Spain (sä-bä-dhål')	162	41°32'N	2°07'E
Sabah, hist. reg., Malay.	212	5°10'N	116°25'E
Sabana, Archipiélago de, is., Cuba	134	23°05'N	80°00'W
Sabana, Río, r., Pan. (sä-bä'nä)	133	8°40'N	78°02'W
Sabana de la Mar, Dom. Rep. (sä-bä'nä dā lä mär')	135	19°05'N	69°30'W
Sabana de Uchire, Ven. (sä-bá'nä dě o͞o-chē'rě)	143b	10°02'N	65°32'W
Sabanagrande, Hond. (sä-bä'nä-grä'n-dě)	132	13°47'N	87°16'W
Sabanalarga, Col. (sä-bä'nä-lär'gä)	142	10°38'N	75°02'W
Sabanas Páramo, mtn., Col. (sä-bá'näs pá'rä-mô)	142a	6°28'N	76°08'W
Sabancuy, Mex. (sä-bäŋ-kwē')	131	18°58'N	91°09'W
Sabang, Indon. (sä'bäng)	212	5°52'N	95°26'E
Sabaudia, Italy (sä-bou'dê-ä)	174	41°19'N	13°00'E
Sabetha, Ks., U.S. (sá-bĕth'á)	121	39°54'N	95°49'W
Sabi (Rio Save), r., Afr. (sä'bê)	232	20°18'S	32°07'E
Sabile, Lat. (sá'bê-lĕ)	167	57°03'N	22°34'E
Sabinal, Tx., U.S. (sá-bī'nál)	122	29°19'N	99°27'W
Sabinal, Cayo, i., Cuba (kä'yō sä-bē-näl')	134	21°40'N	77°20'W
Sabinas, Mex.	128	28°05'N	101°30'W
Sabinas, r., Mex. (sä-bē'näs)	122	26°37'N	99°52'W
Sabinas, Río, r., Mex. (rē'ō sä-bē'näs)	122	27°25'N	100°33'W
Sabinas Hidalgo, Mex. (ê-däl'gô)	122	26°30'N	100°10'W
Sabine, Tx., U.S. (sá-bēn')	123	29°44'N	93°54'W
Sabine, r., U.S.	107	32°00'N	94°30'W
Sabine, Mount, mtn., Ant.	224	72°05'S	169°10'E
Sabine Lake, l., La., U.S.	123	29°53'N	93°41'W
Sablayan, Phil. (säb-lä-yän')	213a	12°49'N	120°47'E
Sable, Cape, c., Can. (sā'b'l)	93	43°25'N	65°24'W
Sable, Cape, c., Fl., U.S.	107	25°12'N	81°10'W
Sables, Rivière aux, r., Can.	99	49°00'N	70°20'W
Sablé-sur-Sarthe, Fr. (säb-lā-sür-särt')	170	47°50'N	0°17'W
Sablya, Gora, mtn., Russia	180	64°50'N	59°00'E
Sàbor, r., Port. (sä-bōr')	172	41°18'N	6°54'W
Sabunchu, Azer.	182	40°26'N	49°56'E
Sabzevār, Iran	201	36°13'N	57°42'E
Sac, r., Mo., U.S. (sôk)	121	38°11'N	93°45'W
Sacandaga Reservoir, res., N.Y., U.S. (sä-kăn-dâ'gá)	109	43°10'N	74°15'W
Sacavém, Port. (sä-kä-vĕN')	173b	38°47'N	9°06'W
Sacavém, r., Port.	173b	38°52'N	9°06'W
Sac City, Ia., U.S. (sôk)	112	42°25'N	95°00'W
Sachigo Lake, l., Can. (săch'ĭ-gō)	97	53°49'N	92°08'W
Sachsen, hist. reg., Ger. (zäk'sĕn)	168	50°45'N	12°17'E
Sacketts Harbor, N.Y., U.S. (săk'ĕts)	109	43°55'N	76°05'W
Sackville, Can. (săk'vĭl)	100	45°54'N	64°22'W
Saco, Me., U.S. (sô'kô)	100	43°30'N	70°28'W
Saco, r., Braz. (sä'kô)	144b	22°20'S	43°26'W
Saco, r., Me., U.S.	100	43°53'N	70°46'W
Sacramento, Mex.	122	25°45'N	103°22'W
Sacramento, Mex.	122	27°05'N	101°45'W
Sacramento, Ca., U.S. (săk-rá-mĕn'tō)	104	38°35'N	121°30'W
Sacramento, r., Ca., U.S.	118	40°20'N	122°07'W
Şa'dah, Yemen	198	16°50'N	43°45'E
Saddle Lake Indian Reserve, I.R., Can.	95	54°00'N	111°40'W
Saddle Mountain, mtn., Or., U.S. (săd''l)	116c	45°58'N	123°40'W
Sadiya, India (sŭ-dē'yä)	199	27°53'N	95°35'E
Sado, i., Japan (sä'dō)	205	38°05'N	138°26'E
Sado, r., Port. (sä'dò)	172	38°15'N	8°20'W
Saeby, Den. (sĕ'bü)	166	57°21'N	10°29'E
Saeki, Japan (sä'å-kĕ)	210	32°56'N	131°51'E
Säffle, Swe.	166	59°10'N	12°55'E
Safford, Az., U.S. (săf'fẽrd)	119	32°50'N	109°45'W
Safi, Mor. (sä'fê) (äs'fê)	230	32°24'N	9°09'W
Safīd Koh, Selseleh-ye, mts., Afg.	198	34°45'N	63°58'E
Saga, Japan (sä'gä)	211	33°15'N	130°18'E
Sagami-Nada, b., Japan (sä'gä'mê nä-dä)	211	35°06'N	139°24'E
Sagamore Hills, Oh., U.S. (săg'á-môr hĭlz)	111d	41°19'N	81°34'W
Saganaga, l., N.A. (să-gá-nă'gá)	113	48°13'N	91°17'W
Sāgar, India	199	23°55'N	78°45'E
Saghyz, r., Kaz.	181	48°30'N	56°10'E
Saginaw, Mi., U.S. (săg'ĭ-nô)	105	43°25'N	84°00'W
Saginaw, Mn., U.S.	117h	46°51'N	92°26'W
Saginaw, Tx., U.S.	117c	32°52'N	97°22'W
Saginaw Bay, b., Mi., U.S.	107	43°50'N	83°40'W
Saguache, Co., U.S. (sá-wăch') (sä-gwä'chê)	119	38°05'N	106°10'W
Saguache Creek, r., Co., U.S.	108	38°05'N	106°40'W
Sagua de Tánamo, Cuba (sä-gwä dĕ tá'nä-mō)	135	20°40'N	75°15'W
Sagua la Grande, Cuba (sä-gwä lä grä'n-dĕ)	134	22°45'N	80°05'W
Saguaro National Park, rec., Az., U.S. (säg-wä'rō)	119	32°12'N	110°40'W
Saguenay, r., Can. (săg-ē-nā')	93	48°20'N	70°15'W
Sagunt, Spain	173	38°58'N	1°29'E
Sagunto, Spain (sä-gón'tō)	162	39°40'N	0°17'W
Sahara, des., Afr. (sá-hä'rá)	230	23°44'N	1°40'W
Saharan Atlas, mts., Afr.	162	32°51'N	1°02'W
Sahāranpur, India (sŭ-hä'rŭn-po͞or')	199	29°58'N	77°41'E
Sahara Village, Ut., U.S. (sá-hä'rá)	117b	41°06'N	111°58'W
Sahel *see* Sudan, reg., Afr.	230	15°00'N	7°00'E
Sāhīwāl, Pak.	202	30°43'N	73°04'E
Sahuayo de Dias, Mex.	130	20°03'N	102°43'W
Saigon *see* Ho Chi Minh City, Viet.	212	10°46'N	106°34'E
Saijō, Japan (sä'ē-jô)	211	33°55'N	133°13'E
Saimaa, l., Fin. (sä'ĭ-mä)	160	61°24'N	28°45'E
Sain Alto, Mex. (sä-ēn' äl'tō)	130	23°35'N	103°13'W
Saint Adolphe, Can. (sånt a'dôlf) (săN' tà-dôlf')	102f	49°40'N	97°07'W
Saint Afrique, Fr. (săN' tá-frēk')	170	43°58'N	2°52'E
Saint Albans, Austl. (sånt ôl'bănz)	217a	37°44'S	144°47'E
Saint Albans, Eng., U.K.	164	51°44'N	0°20'W
Saint Albans, Vt., U.S.	109	44°50'N	73°05'W
Saint Albans, W.V., U.S.	108	38°20'N	81°50'W
Saint Albert, Can. (sånt ăl'bẽrt)	95	53°38'N	113°38'W
Saint Amand-Mont Rond, Fr. (săN't à-mäN' môN-rôN')	170	46°44'N	2°28'E
Saint André-Est, Can.	102a	45°33'N	74°19'W
Saint Andrews, Can.	91	45°05'N	67°03'W
Saint Andrews, Scot., U.K.	164	56°20'N	2°40'W
Saint Andrew's Channel, strt., Can.	101	46°06'N	60°28'W
Saint Anicet, Can. (sĕNt ä-nē-sĕ')	102a	45°07'N	74°23'W
Saint Ann, Mo., U.S. (sånt ăn')	117e	38°44'N	90°23'W
Sainte Anne, Guad.	133b	16°15'N	61°23'W
Saint Anne, Il., U.S.	111a	41°01'N	87°44'W
Sainte Anne, r., Can. (săNt ån') (sånt ăn')	99	46°55'N	71°46'W
Sainte-Anne, r., Can.	102b	47°07'N	70°50'W
Sainte Anne-des-Plaines, Can. (dā plĕN)	102a	45°46'N	73°49'W
Saint Ann's Bay, Jam.	134	18°25'N	77°15'W
Saint Anns Bay, b., Can. (ănz)	101	46°20'N	60°30'W
Saint Anselme, Can. (săN' tän-sĕlm')	102b	46°37'N	70°58'W
Saint Anthony, Can. (săN ăn'thô-nê)	91	51°24'N	55°35'W
Saint Anthony, Id., U.S. (sånt ăn'thô-nê)	115	43°59'N	111°42'W
Saint Antoine-de-Tilly, Can.	102b	46°40'N	71°31'W
Saint Apollinaire, Can. (săN' tá-pôl-ê-nâr')	102b	46°36'N	71°30'W
Saint Arnoult-en-Yvelines, Fr. (săN-tär-no͞o'ĕN-nēv-lēn')	171b	48°33'N	1°55'E
Saint Augustin-de-Québec, Can. (sĕN tō-güs-tēn')	102b	46°45'N	71°27'W
Saint Augustin-Deux-Montagnes, Can.	102a	45°38'N	73°59'W
Saint Augustine, Fl., U.S. (sånt ô'güs-tēn)	105	29°53'N	81°21'W
Sainte Barbe, Can. (sånt bärb')	102a	45°14'N	74°12'W
Saint Barthélemy, i., Guad.	133b	17°55'N	62°32'W
Saint Bees Head, c., Eng., U.K. (sånt bēz' hĕd)	164	54°30'N	3°40'W
Saint Benoit, Can. (sĕN bĕ-no͞o-ä')	102a	45°34'N	74°05'W
Saint Bernard, La., U.S. (bẽr-närd')	110d	29°52'N	89°52'W
Saint Bernard, Oh., U.S.	111f	39°10'N	84°30'W
Saint Bride, Mount, mtn., Can. (sånt brīd)	95	51°30'N	115°57'W
Saint Brieuc, Fr. (săN' brēs')	161	48°32'N	2°47'W
Saint Bruno, Can. (brū'nō)	102a	45°31'N	73°20'W
Saint Canut, Can. (săN' ká-nū')	102a	45°43'N	74°04'W
Saint Casimir, Can. (kà-zē-mēr')	99	46°45'N	72°34'W
Saint Catharines, Can. (kăth'á-rĭnz)	91	43°10'N	79°14'W
Saint Catherine, Mount, mtn., Gren.	133b	12°10'N	61°42'W
Saint Chamas, Fr. (sàN-shä-mä')	170a	43°32'N	5°03'E
Saint Chamond, Fr. (săN' shà-môN')	161	45°30'N	4°17'E
Saint Charles, Can. (săN' shärlz')	102b	46°47'N	70°57'W
Saint Charles, Il., U.S. (sånt chärlz')	111a	41°55'N	88°19'W
Saint Charles, Mi., U.S.	108	43°20'N	84°10'W
Saint Charles, Mn., U.S.	113	43°56'N	92°05'W
Saint Charles, Mo., U.S.	117e	38°47'N	90°29'W
Saint Charles, Lac, l., Can.	102b	46°56'N	71°21'W
Saint Christopher-Nevis *see* Saint Kitts and Nevis, nation, N.A.	128	17°24'N	63°30'W
Saint Clair, Mi., U.S. (sånt klâr)	108	42°55'N	82°30'W
Saint Clair, l., Can.	107	42°25'N	82°30'W
Saint Clair, r., Can.	98	42°45'N	82°25'W
Sainte Claire, Can.	102b	46°36'N	70°52'W
Saint Clair Shores, Mi., U.S.	111b	42°30'N	82°54'W
Saint Claude, Fr. (săN' klōd')	171	46°24'N	5°53'E
Saint Clet, Can. (săNt' klā')	102a	45°22'N	74°21'W
Saint Cloud, Fl., U.S. (sånt kloud')	125a	28°13'N	81°17'W
Saint Cloud, Mn., U.S.	105	45°33'N	94°08'W
Saint Constant, Can. (kŏN'stănt)	102a	45°23'N	73°34'W
Saint Croix, i., V.I.U.S. (sånt kroi')	129	17°40'N	64°43'W
Saint Croix, r., N.A. (kroi')	100	45°28'N	67°32'W
Saint Croix, r., U.S. (sånt kroi')	107	45°45'N	93°00'W
Saint Croix Indian Reservation, I.R., Wi., U.S.	113	45°40'N	92°21'W
Saint Croix Island, i., S. Afr. (săN krwä)	233c	33°48'S	25°45'E
Saint Damien-de-Buckland, Can. (sånt dā'mê-ĕn)	102b	46°37'N	70°39'W
Saint David, Can. (dā'vĭd)	102b	46°47'N	71°11'W
Saint David's Head, c., Wales, U.K.	164	51°54'N	5°25'W
Saint-Denis, Fr. (săN'dē-nē')	161	48°26'N	2°22'E
Saint Dizier, Fr. (dê-zyā')	161	48°49'N	4°55'E
Saint Dominique, Can. (sĕN dō-mē-nēk')	102a	45°19'N	74°09'W
Saint Edouard-de-Napierville, Can. (sĕN-tĕ-do͞o-är')	102a	45°14'N	73°31'W
Saint Elias, Mount, mtn., N.A. (sånt ê-lī'ăs)	92	60°25'N	141°00'W
Saint Étienne, Fr.	161	45°26'N	4°22'E
Saint Etienne-de-Lauzon, Can. (săN' tā-tyĕn')	102b	46°39'N	71°19'W
Sainte Euphémie, Can. (sĕNt û-fē-mē')	102b	46°47'N	70°27'W
Saint Eustache, Can. (săN' tû-stash')	102a	45°34'N	73°54'W
Saint Eustache, Can.	102f	49°58'N	97°47'W
Sainte Famille, Can. (săN't fà-mē'y')	102b	46°58'N	70°58'W
Saint Félicien, Can. (săN fā-lê-syăN')	91	48°39'N	72°28'W
Sainte Felicite, Can.	100	48°54'N	67°20'W
Saint Féréol, Can. (fa-rā-ôl')	102b	47°07'N	70°52'W
Saint Florent-sur-Cher, Fr. (săN' flô-räN'sür-shâr')	170	46°58'N	2°15'E
Saint Flour, Fr. (săN flo͞or')	170	45°02'N	3°09'E
Sainte Foy, Can. (sănt fwä)	99	46°47'N	71°18'W
Saint Francis, r., Ar., U.S.	121	35°56'N	90°27'W
Saint Francis Lake, l., Can. (săN frăn'sĭs)	99	45°00'N	74°20'W
Saint François, Can. (săN'frăn-swä')	102b	47°01'N	70°49'W
Saint François de Boundji, Congo	236	1°03'S	15°22'E
Saint Francois Xavier, Can.	102f	49°55'N	97°32'W
Saint Gaudens, Fr. (gō-dăNs')	170	43°07'N	0°43'E
Sainte Genevieve, Mo., U.S. (sånt jĕn'ĕ-vēv)	121	37°58'N	90°02'W
Saint George, Austl. (sånt jôrj')	219	28°02'S	148°40'E

ng-sing; ŋ-baŋk; N-nasalized n; nŏd; cŏmmit; ōld; ôbey; ôrder; oi-boil; fo͞od; ò-as oo in foot; ou-out; s-soft; sh-dish; th-thin; pūre; ûnite; ûrn; stŭd; circŭs; ü-as in French tu; '-indeterminate vowel.

344 Saint George – Salem PRONOUNCING INDEX

PLACE (Pronunciation)	PAGE	LAT.	LONG.
Saint George, Can. (săn jôrj′)	91	45°08′N	66°49′W
Saint George, Can. (săn′zhôrzh′)	102d	43°14′N	80°15′W
Saint George, S.C., U.S. (sånt jôrj′)	125	33°11′N	80°35′W
Saint George, Ut., U.S.	119	37°05′N	113°40′W
Saint George, i., Ak., U.S.	103	56°30′N	169°40′W
Saint George, Cape, c., Can.	93a	48°28′N	59°15′W
Saint George, Cape, c., Fl., U.S.	124	29°30′N	85°20′W
Saint George's, Can. (jôrj′ĕs)	91	48°26′N	58°29′W
Saint Georges, Fr. Gu.	143	3°48′N	51°47′W
Saint George's, Gren.	133b	12°02′N	61°57′W
Saint George's Bay, b., Can.	93a	48°20′N	59°00′W
Saint Georges Bay, b., Can.	101	45°49′N	61°45′W
Saint George's Channel, strt., Eur. (jôr-jĕz)	156	51°45′N	6°30′W
Saint Germain-en-Laye, Fr. (săn′ zhĕr-măn-än-lā′)	170	48°53′N	2°05′E
Saint Gervais, Can. (zhĕr-vĕ′)	102b	46°43′N	70°53′W
Saint Girons, Fr. (zhē-rôn′)	170	42°58′N	1°08′E
Saint Gotthard Pass, p., Switz.	168	46°33′N	8°34′E
Saint Gregory, Mount, mtn., Can. (sånt grĕg′ẽr-ė)	101	49°19′N	58°13′W
Saint Helena, i., St. Hel.	229	16°01′S	5°16′W
Saint Helenabaai, b., S. Afr.	232	32°25′S	17°15′E
Saint Helens, Eng., U.K. (sånt hĕl′ĕnz)	158a	53°27′N	2°44′W
Saint Helens, Or., U.S. (hĕl′ĕnz)	116c	45°52′N	122°49′W
Saint Helens, Mount, vol., Wa., U.S.	114	46°13′N	122°10′W
Saint Helier, Jersey (hyĕl′yẽr)	170	49°12′N	2°06′W
Saint Henri, Can. (săn′ hĕn′rē)	102b	46°41′N	71°04′W
Saint Hubert, Can.	102a	45°29′N	73°24′W
Saint Hyacinthe, Can.	91	45°35′N	72°55′W
Saint Ignace, Mi., U.S. (sånt ĭg′nås)	113	45°51′N	84°39′W
Saint Ignace, i., Can. (săn′ ĭg′nås)	98	48°47′N	88°14′W
Saint Irenee, Can. (săn′ tē-rå-nā′)	99	47°34′N	70°15′W
Saint Isidore-de-Laprairie, Can.	102a	45°18′N	73°41′W
Saint Isidore-de-Prescott, Can. (săn′ ĭz′ĭ-dôr-prĕs-kŏt)	102c	45°23′N	74°54′W
Saint Isidore-Dorchester, Can. (dŏr-chĕs′tẽr)	102b	46°35′N	71°05′W
Saint Jacob, Il., U.S. (jā-kŏb)	117e	38°43′N	89°46′W
Saint James, Mn., U.S. (sånt jāmz′)	113	43°58′N	94°37′W
Saint James, Mo., U.S.	121	37°59′N	91°37′W
Saint James, Cape, c., Can.	94	51°58′N	131°00′W
Saint Janvier, Can. (săn′ zhän-vyā′)	102a	45°43′N	73°56′W
Saint Jean, Can. (săn′ zhän′)	91	45°20′N	73°15′W
Saint Jean, Can.	102b	46°55′N	70°54′W
Saint Jean, Lac, l., Can.	93	48°35′N	72°00′W
Saint Jean-Chrysostome, Can. (krĭ-zōs-tōm′)	102b	46°43′N	71°12′W
Saint Jean-d'Angely, Fr. (dän-zhå-lē′)	170	45°56′N	0°33′W
Saint Jean-de-Luz, Fr. (dē lüz′)	170	43°23′N	1°40′W
Saint Jérôme, Can. (sånt jĕ-rōm′) (săn zhā-rōm′)	102a	45°47′N	74°00′W
Saint Joachim-de-Montmorency, Can. (sånt jō′*à*-kĭm)	102b	47°04′N	70°51′W
Saint John, Can. (sånt jŏn)	91	45°16′N	66°03′W
Saint John, In., U.S.	111a	41°27′N	87°29′W
Saint John, Ks., U.S.	120	37°59′N	98°44′W
Saint John, N.D., U.S.	112	48°57′N	99°42′W
Saint John, i., V.I.U.S.	129b	18°16′N	64°48′W
Saint John, r., N.A.	93	47°00′N	68°00′W
Saint John, Cape, c., Can.	101	50°00′N	55°32′W
Saint Johns, Antig.	133b	17°07′N	61°50′W
Saint John's, Can. (jŏns)	93a	47°34′N	52°43′W
Saint Johns, Az., U.S. (jŏnz)	119	34°30′N	109°25′W
Saint Johns, Mi., U.S.	108	43°05′N	84°35′W
Saint Johns, r., Fl., U.S.	107	29°54′N	81°32′W
Saint Johnsbury, Vt., U.S. (jŏnz′bĕr-ė)	109	44°25′N	72°00′W
Saint Joseph, Dom.	133b	15°25′N	61°26′W
Saint Joseph, Mi., U.S.	108	42°05′N	86°30′W
Saint Joseph, Mo., U.S. (sånt jō-sĕf)	105	39°44′N	94°49′W
Saint Joseph, i., Can.	108	46°15′N	83°55′W
Saint Joseph, l., Can. (jō′zhûf)	93	51°31′N	90°40′W
Saint Joseph, r., Mi., U.S. (sånt jō′sĕf)	108	41°45′N	85°50′W
Saint Joseph Bay, b., Fl., U.S. (jō′zhûf)	124	29°48′N	85°26′W
Saint Joseph-de-Beauce, Can. (sĕn zhō-zĕf′ *dē* bōs)	99	46°18′N	70°52′W
Saint Joseph-du-Lac, Can. (sĕn zhō-zĕf′ dü läk)	102a	45°32′N	74°00′W
Saint Joseph Island, i., Tx., U.S. (sånt jō-sĕf)	123	27°58′N	96°50′W
Saint Junien, Fr. (săn′zhü-nyăn′)	170	45°53′N	0°54′E
Sainte Justine-de-Newton, Can. (sånt jŭs-tēn′)	102a	45°22′N	74°22′W
Saint Kilda, Austl.	217a	37°52′S	144°59′E
Saint Kilda, i., Scot., U.K. (kĭl′*dà*)	164	57°50′N	8°32′W
Saint Kitts, i., St. K./N. (sånt kĭtts)	129	17°24′N	63°30′W
Saint Kitts and Nevis, nation, N.A.	129	17°24′N	63°30′W
Saint Lambert, Can.	109	45°29′N	73°29′W
Saint Lambert-de-Lévis, Can.	102b	46°35′N	71°12′W
Saint Laurent, Can. (săn′lō-rän)	102a	45°31′N	73°41′W
Saint Laurent, Fr. Gu.	143	5°27′N	53°56′W
Saint Laurent-d'Orleans, Can.	102b	46°52′N	71°00′W
Saint Lawrence, Can. (sånt lô′rĕns)	101	46°55′N	55°23′W
Saint Lawrence, i., Ak., U.S. (sånt lô′rĕns)	106a	63°10′N	172°12′W
Saint Lawrence, r., N.A.	93	48°24′N	69°30′W
Saint Lawrence, Gulf of, b., Can.	93	48°00′N	62°00′W
Saint Lazare, Can. (săn′lå-zår′)	102b	46°39′N	70°48′W
Saint Lazare-de-Vaudreuil, Can.	102a	45°24′N	74°08′W
Saint Léger-en-Yvelines, Fr. (sån-lā-zhĕ′ĕn-nēv-lēn′)	171b	48°43′N	1°45′E
Saint Leonard, Can. (sånt lĕn′ård)	100	47°10′N	67°56′W
Saint Léonard, Can.	102a	45°36′N	73°35′W
Saint Leonard, Md., U.S.	110e	38°29′N	76°31′W
Saint Lô, Fr.	161	49°07′N	1°05′W
Saint-Louis, Sen.	230	16°02′N	16°30′W
Saint Louis, Mi., U.S. (sånt lo͞o′ĭs)	108	43°25′N	84°35′W
Saint Louis, Mo., U.S. (sånt lo͞o′ĭs) (lo͞o′ė)	105	38°39′N	90°15′W
Saint Louis, r., Mn., U.S. (sånt lo͞o′ĭs)	113	46°57′N	92°58′W
Saint Louis, Lac, l., Can. (săn′ lo͞o-ē′)	102a	45°24′N	73°51′W
Saint Louis-de-Gonzague, Can. (săn′ lo͞o ē′)	102a	45°13′N	74°00′W
Saint Louis Park, Mn., U.S.	117g	44°56′N	93°21′W
Saint Lucia, nation, N.A.	129	13°54′N	60°40′W
Saint Lucia Channel, strt., N.A. (lū′shĭ-*à*)	133b	14°15′N	61°00′W
Saint Lucie Canal, can., Fl., U.S. (lū′sė)	125a	26°57′N	80°25′W
Saint Magnus Bay, b., Scot., U.K. (măg′nŭs)	164a	60°25′N	2°09′W
Saint Malo, Fr. (săn′ må-lō′)	161	48°40′N	2°02′W
Saint Malo, Golfe de, b., Fr. (gôlf-*dē*-sån-mä-lō′)	161	48°50′N	2°49′W
Saint Marc, Haiti (săn′ mårk′)	135	19°10′N	72°40′W
Saint-Marc, Canal de, strt., Haiti	135	19°05′N	73°15′W
Saint Marcellin, Fr. (mär-sĕ-lăn′)	171	45°08′N	5°15′E
Saint Margarets, Md., U.S.	110e	39°02′N	76°30′W
Sainte Marie, Cap, c., Madag.	233	25°31′S	45°00′E
Sainte-Marie-aux-Mines, Fr. (sån′tĕ-mä-rē′ō-mēn′)	171	48°14′N	7°08′E
Sainte Marie-Beauce, Can. (sånt′må-rē′)	99	46°27′N	71°03′W
Saint Maries, Id., U.S. (sånt mā′rēs)	114	47°18′N	116°34′W
Saint Martin, i., N.A. (mär′tĭn)	133b	18°06′N	62°54′W
Sainte Martine, Can.	102a	45°14′N	73°37′W
Saint Martins, Can. (mär′tĭnz)	100	45°21′N	65°32′W
Saint Martinville, La., U.S. (mär′tĭn-vĭl)	123	30°08′N	91°50′W
Saint Mary, r., Can. (mā′rė)	95	49°25′N	113°00′W
Saint Mary, Cape, c., Gam.	234	13°28′N	16°40′W
Saint Mary Reservoir, res., Can.	95	49°30′N	113°00′W
Saint Marys, Austl. (mā′rēz)	222	41°40′S	148°10′E
Saint Marys, Can.	98	43°15′N	81°10′W
Saint Marys, Ga., U.S.	125	30°43′N	81°35′W
Saint Mary's, Ks., U.S.	121	39°12′N	96°03′W
Saint Mary's, Oh., U.S.	108	40°30′N	84°25′W
Saint Marys, Pa., U.S.	109	41°25′N	78°30′W
Saint Marys, W.V., U.S.	108	39°20′N	81°15′W
Saint Marys, r., N.A.	117k	46°27′N	84°33′W
Saint Marys, r., U.S.	125	30°37′N	82°05′W
Saint Mary's Bay, b., Can.	101	46°50′N	53°47′W
Saint Mary's Bay, b., Can.	100	44°20′N	66°10′W
Saint Mathew, S.C., U.S. (măth′ū)	125	33°40′N	80°46′W
Saint Matthew, i., Ak., U.S.	103	60°25′N	172°10′W
Saint Matthews, Ky., U.S. (măth′ūz)	111h	38°15′N	85°39′W
Saint Maur-des-Fossés, Fr.	171b	48°48′N	2°29′E
Saint Maurice, r., Can. (săn′ mō-rēs′) (sånt mô′rĭs)	93	47°20′N	72°55′W
Saint Michael, Ak., U.S. (sånt mī′k*ĕ*l)	103	63°22′N	162°20′W
Saint Michel, Can. (săn′mē-shĕl′)	102b	46°52′N	70°54′W
Saint Michel, Bras, r., Can.	102b	46°47′N	70°51′W
Saint Michel-de-l'Atalaye, Haiti	135	19°25′N	72°20′W
Saint Michel-de-Napierville, Can.	102a	45°14′N	73°34′W
Saint Mihiel, Fr. (săn′ mē-yĕl′)	171	48°53′N	5°30′E
Saint Nazaire, Fr. (săn′nå-zâr′)	154	47°18′N	2°13′W
Saint Nérée, Can. (nā-rā′)	102b	46°43′N	70°43′W
Saint Nicolas, Can. (ne-kô-lä′)	102b	46°42′N	71°22′W
Saint Nicolas, Cap, c., Haiti	135	19°45′N	73°35′W
Saint Omer, Fr. (săn′tô-mâr′)	170	50°44′N	2°16′E
Saint Pascal, Can. (sĕn pā-skäl′)	100	47°32′N	69°48′W
Saint Paul, Can. (sånt pôl′)	90	53°59′N	111°17′W
Saint Paul, Mn., U.S.	105	44°57′N	93°05′W
Saint Paul, Ne., U.S.	112	41°13′N	98°28′W
Saint Paul, i., Can.	101	47°15′N	60°10′W
Saint Paul, i., Ak., U.S.	103	57°10′N	170°20′W
Saint Paul, r., Lib.	234	7°10′N	10°00′W
Saint Paul, Île, i., Afr.	3	38°43′S	77°31′E
Saint Paul Park, Mn., U.S. (pärk)	117g	44°51′N	93°00′W
Saint Pauls, N.C., U.S. (pôls)	125	34°47′N	78°57′W
Saint Peter, Mn., U.S. (pē tẽr)	113	44°20′N	93°56′W
Saint Peter Port, Guern.	170	49°27′N	2°35′W
Saint Petersburg (Sankt-Peterburg) (Leningrad), Russia	178	59°57′N	30°20′E
Saint Petersburg, Fl., U.S. (pē′tẽrz-bûrg)	105	27°47′N	82°38′W
Sainte Pétronille, Can. (sĕnt pĕt-rō-nēl′)	102b	46°51′N	71°08′W
Saint Philémon, Can. (săn fēl-mōn′)	102b	46°41′N	70°28′W
Saint Philippe-d'Argenteuil, Can. (săn′fe-lēp′)	102a	45°38′N	74°25′W
Saint Philippe-de-Lapairie, Can.	102a	45°20′N	73°28′W
Saint Pierre, Mart. (săn′pyâr′)	133b	14°45′N	61°12′W
Saint Pierre, St. P./M.	101	46°47′N	56°11′W
Saint Pierre, i., St. P./M.	101	46°47′N	56°11′W
Saint Pierre, Lac, l., Can.	99	46°07′N	72°45′W
Saint Pierre and Miquelon, dep., N.A.	93a	46°53′N	56°40′W
Saint Pierre-d'Orléans, Can.	102b	46°53′N	71°04′W
Saint Pierre-Montmagny, Can.	102b	46°55′N	70°37′W
Saint Placide, Can. (plăs′ĭd)	102a	45°32′N	74°11′W
Saint Pol-de-Léon, Fr. (săn-pô′*dē*-lā-ôn′)	170	48°41′N	4°00′W
Saint Quentin, Fr. (săn′kän-tăn′)	161	49°52′N	3°16′E
Saint Raphaël, Can. (rä-fā-ĕl′)	102b	46°48′N	70°46′W
Saint Raymond, Can.	99	46°50′N	71°51′W
Saint Rédempteur, Can. (săn rā-dănp-tûr′)	102b	46°42′N	71°18′W
Saint Rémi, Can. (sĕn rĕ-mē′)	102a	45°15′N	73°36′W
Saint Romuald-d'Etchemin, Can. (sĕn rō′mo͞o-äl)	99	46°45′N	71°14′W
Sainte Rose, Guad.	133b	16°19′N	61°45′W
Saintes, Fr.	170	45°44′N	0°41′W
Sainte Scholastique, Can. (skô-lås-tēk′)	102a	45°39′N	74°05′W
Saint Siméon, Can.	99	47°51′N	69°55′W
Saint Stanislas-de-Kostka, Can.	102a	45°11′N	74°08′W
Saint Stephen, Can. (stē′vĕn)	91	45°12′N	66°17′W
Saint Sulpice, Can.	102a	45°50′N	73°21′W
Saint Thérèse-de-Blainville, Can. (tē-rĕz′ dē blĕn-vēl′)	99	45°38′N	73°51′W
Saint Thomas, Can. (tŏm′*ås*)	91	42°45′N	81°15′W
Saint Thomas, i., V.I.U.S.	129	18°22′N	64°57′W
Saint Thomas Harbor, b., V.I.U.S. (tŏm′*ås*)	129c	18°19′N	64°56′W
Saint Timothée, Can. (tē-mô-tā′)	102a	45°17′N	74°03′W
Saint Tropez, Fr. (trô-pĕ′)	171	43°15′N	6°42′E
Saint Valentin, Can. (văl-*ĕn*-tĭn)	102a	45°07′N	73°19′W
Saint Valéry-sur-Somme, Fr. (vå-lā-rē′)	170	50°10′N	1°39′E
Saint Vallier, Can. (väl-yā′)	102b	46°54′N	70°49′W
Saint Victor, Can. (vĭk′tẽr)	99	46°09′N	70°56′W
Saint Vincent, Gulf, b., Austl. (vĭn′sĕnt)	222	34°55′S	138°00′E
Saint Vincent and the Grenadines, nation, N.A.	129	13°20′N	60°50′W
Saint Vincent Passage, strt., N.A.	133b	13°35′N	61°10′W
Saint Walburg, Can.	90	53°39′N	109°12′W
Saint Yrieix-la-Perche, Fr. (ē-rē-ĕ)	170	45°30′N	1°08′E
Saitama, dept., Japan (sī′tä-mä)	211a	35°52′N	139°40′E
Saitbaba, Russia (så-ĕt′bå-bå)	186a	54°06′N	56°42′E
Sajama, Nevada, mtn., Bol. (nĕ-vå′dä-sä-hä′mä)	142	18°13′S	68°53′W
Sakai, Japan (sä′kä-ė)	210	34°34′N	135°28′E
Sakaiminato, Japan	211	35°33′N	133°15′E
Sakākah, Sau. Ar.	198	29°58′N	40°03′E
Sakakawea, Lake, res., N.D., U.S.	106	47°49′N	101°58′W
Sakania, D.R.C. (så-ka′nĭ-å)	232	12°45′S	28°34′E
Sakarya, r., Tur. (så-kär′yå)	198	40°10′N	31°00′E
Sakata, Japan (sä′kä-tä)	205	38°56′N	139°57′E
Sakchu, Kor., N. (säk′chò)	210	40°29′N	125°09′E
Sakha (Yakutia), prov., Russia	185	65°21′N	117°13′E
Sakhalin, i., Russia (så-kå-lēn′)	179	52°00′N	143°00′E
Šakiai, Lith. (shä′kĭ-ī)	167	54°59′N	23°05′E
Sakishima-guntō, is., Japan (sä′kė-shē′ma gòn′tō′)	205	24°25′N	125°00′E
Sakmara, r., Russia	181	52°00′N	56°10′E
Sakomet, r., R.I., U.S. (sä-kō′mĕt)	110b	41°32′N	71°11′W
Sakurai, Japan	211b	34°31′N	135°51′E
Sakwaso Lake, l., Can. (s*à*-kwā′sō)	97	53°01′N	91°55′W
Sal, i., C.V. (säal)	230b	16°45′N	22°39′W
Sal, r., Russia (sàl)	181	47°30′N	43°00′E
Sal, Cay, i., Bah. (kē säl)	134	23°45′N	80°25′W
Sala, Swe. (sô′lä)	166	59°56′N	16°34′E
Sala Consilina, Italy (sä′lä kōn-sė-lē′nä)	174	40°24′N	15°38′E
Salada, Laguna, l., Mex. (lä-gò′nä-sä-lä′dä)	118	32°34′N	115°45′W
Saladillo, Arg. (sä-lä-dēl′yō)	144	35°38′S	59°48′W
Salado, Hond. (sä-lä′dhō)	132	15°44′N	87°03′W
Salado, r., Arg.	141c	35°53′S	58°12′W
Salado, r., Arg.	144	37°00′S	67°00′W
Salado, r., Arg. (sä-lä′dō)	144	26°05′S	63°35′W
Salado, r., Mex.	128	28°00′N	102°00′W
Salado, r., Mex. (sä-lä′dō)	131	18°30′N	97°29′W
Salado Creek, r., Tx., U.S.	117d	29°23′N	98°25′W
Salado de los Nadadores, Río, r., Mex. (dĕ-lōs-nä-dä-dō′rĕs)	122	27°26′N	101°35′W
Salal, Chad	235	14°51′N	17°13′E
Salamanca, Chile (sä-lä-mä′n-kä)	141b	31°48′S	70°57′W
Salamanca, Mex.	128	20°36′N	101°10′W
Salamanca, Spain (sä-lä-mä′n-kå)	154	40°54′N	5°42′W
Salamanca, N.Y., U.S. (săl-*à*-măŋ′k*à*)	109	42°10′N	78°45′W
Salamat, Bahr, r., Chad (bär sä-lä-mät′)	231	10°06′N	19°16′E
Salamina, Col. (sä-lä-mē′-nä)	142a	5°25′N	75°29′W
Salamína, Grc.	175	37°58′N	23°30′E
Salat-la-Canada, Fr.	170	44°52′N	1°13′E
Salaverry, Peru (sä-lä-vă′rē)	142	8°16′S	78°54′W
Salawati, i., Indon. (sä-lä-wä′tė)	213	1°07′S	130°52′E
Salawe, Tan.	237	3°19′S	32°52′E
Sala y Gómez, Isla, i., Chile	241	26°50′S	105°50′W
Salcedo, Dom. Rep. (säl-sä′dō)	135	19°25′N	70°30′W
Saldaña, r., Col. (säl-dà′n-yä)	142a	3°42′N	75°16′W
Saldanha, S. Afr.	232	32°55′S	18°05′E
Saldus, Lat. (sàl′dòs)	167	56°39′N	22°30′E
Sale, Austl. (sāl)	222	38°10′S	147°07′E
Sale, Eng., U.K.	158a	53°24′N	2°20′W
Sale, r., Can. (sål′rē-vyâr′)	102f	49°44′N	97°11′W
Salekhard, Russia (sŭ-lyĭ-kärt)	180	66°35′N	66°50′E
Salem, India	199	11°39′N	78°11′E
Salem, S. Afr.	233c	33°29′S	26°30′E
Salem, Il., U.S. (sā′lĕm)	108	38°40′N	89°00′W
Salem, In., U.S.	108	38°35′N	86°00′W
Salem, Ma., U.S.	101a	42°31′N	70°54′W
Salem, Mo., U.S.	121	37°36′N	91°33′W
Salem, N.H., U.S.	101a	42°46′N	71°16′W
Salem, N.J., U.S.	109	39°35′N	75°30′W
Salem, Oh., U.S.	108	40°55′N	80°50′W
Salem, Or., U.S.	104	44°55′N	123°03′W

ăt; fin*ă*l; rāte; senåte; ärm; åsk; sof*à*; fâre; ch-choose; dh-as th in other; bē; ėvent; bĕt; recĕnt; cratẽr; g-gō; gh-guttural g; bĭt; *ĭ*-short neutral; rīde; ĸ-guttural k as ch in German ich;

PRONOUNCING INDEX Salem – San Felipe 345

PLACE (Pronunciation)	PAGE	LAT.	LONG.
Salem, S.D., U.S.	112	43°43'N	97°23'W
Salem, Va., U.S.	125	37°16'N	80°05'W
Salem, W.V., U.S.	108	39°15'N	80°35'W
Salemi, Italy (sä-lå'mē)	174	37°49'N	12°48'E
Salerno, Italy (sä-lĕr'nô)	162	40°27'N	14°46'E
Salerno, Golfo di, b., Italy (gôl-fô-dē)	162	40°30'N	14°40'E
Salford, Eng., U.K. (săl'fērd)	164	53°26'N	2°19'W
Salgótarján, Hung. (shôl'gō-tôr-yän)	169	48°06'N	19°50'E
Salhyr, r., Ukr.	177	45°25'N	34°22'E
Salida, Co., U.S. (sá-lī'dá)	120	38°31'N	106°01'W
Salies-de-Béan, Fr.	170	43°27'N	0°58'W
Salima, Mwi.	237	13°47'S	34°26'E
Salina, Ks., U.S. (sá-lī'ná)	104	38°50'N	97°37'W
Salina, Ut., U.S.	119	39°00'N	111°55'W
Salina, i., Italy (sä-lē'nä)	174	38°35'N	14°48'E
Salina Cruz, Mex. (sä-lē'nä kro͞oz')	128	16°10'N	95°12'W
Salina Point, c., Bah.	135	22°10'N	74°20'W
Salinas, Mex.	128	22°38'N	101°42'W
Salinas, P.R.	129b	17°58'N	66°16'W
Salinas, Ca., U.S. (sá-lē'nás)	118	36°41'N	121°40'W
Salinas, r., Mex. (sä-lē'näs)	131	16°15'N	90°31'W
Salinas, r., Ca., U.S.	118	36°33'N	121°29'W
Salinas, Bahía de, b., N.A. (bä-ē'ä-dē-sá-lē'nás)	132	11°05'N	85°55'W
Salinas National Monument, rec., N.M., U.S.	119	34°10'N	106°05'W
Salinas Victoria, Mex. (sä-lē'näs vēk-tō'rē-ä)	122	25°59'N	100°19'W
Saline, r., Ar., U.S. (sá-lēn')	121	34°06'N	92°30'W
Saline, r., Ks., U.S.	120	39°05'N	99°43'W
Salins-les-Bains, Fr. (sá-làn'-lā-bàn')	171	46°55'N	5°54'E
Salisbury, Can.	100	46°03'N	65°05'W
Salisbury, Eng., U.K. (sôlz'bē-rē)	161	50°35'N	1°51'W
Salisbury, Md., U.S.	109	38°20'N	75°40'W
Salisbury, Mo., U.S.	121	39°24'N	92°47'W
Salisbury, N.C., U.S.	125	35°40'N	80°29'W
Salisbury *see* Harare, Zimb.	232	17°50'S	31°03'E
Salisbury Island, i., Can.	93	63°36'N	76°20'W
Salisbury Plain, pl., Eng., U.K.	164	51°15'N	1°52'W
Salkehatchie, r., S.C., U.S. (sô-kē-hăch'ē)	125	33°09'N	81°10'W
Sallisaw, Ok., U.S. (săl'ĭ-sô)	121	35°27'N	94°48'W
Salmon, Id., U.S. (săm'ŭn)	115	45°11'N	113°54'W
Salmon, r., Can.	94	54°00'N	123°50'W
Salmon, r., Can.	100	46°19'N	65°36'W
Salmon, r., Id., U.S.	106	45°30'N	115°45'W
Salmon, r., N.Y., U.S.	109	44°35'N	74°15'W
Salmon, r., Wa., U.S.	116c	45°44'N	122°36'W
Salmon, Middle Fork, r., Id., U.S.	114	44°50'N	114°52'W
Salmon Arm, Can.	95	50°42'N	119°16'W
Salmon Falls Creek, r., Id., U.S.	115	42°22'N	114°53'W
Salmon Gums, Austl. (gŭmz)	218	33°00'S	122°00'E
Salmon River Mountains, mts., Id., U.S.	106	44°15'N	115°44'W
Salon-de-Provence, Fr. (sá-lôn-dē-prô-văns')	171	43°48'N	5°09'E
Salonika *see* Thessaloníki, Grc.	154	40°38'N	22°59'E
Salonta, Rom. (sä-lôn'tä)	169	46°46'N	21°38'E
Saloum, r., Sen.	234	14°10'N	15°45'W
Salsette Island, i., India	203b	19°12'N	72°52'E
Sal'sk, Russia (sälsk)	181	46°30'N	41°20'E
Salt, r., Az., U.S. (sôlt)	106	33°28'N	111°35'W
Salt, r., Mo., U.S.	121	39°54'N	92°11'W
Salta, Arg. (säl'tä)	144	24°50'S	65°16'W
Salta, prov., Arg.	144	25°15'S	65°00'W
Saltair, Ut., U.S. (sôlt'âr)	117b	40°46'N	112°09'W
Salt Cay, i., T./C. Is.	135	21°20'N	71°15'W
Salt Creek, r., Il., U.S. (sôlt)	111a	42°01'N	88°01'W
Saltillo, Mex. (säl-tēl'yō)	128	25°24'N	100°59'W
Salt Lake City, Ut., U.S. (sôlt lāk sĭ'tĭ)	104	40°45'N	111°52'W
Salto, Arg. (säl'tō)	141c	34°17'S	60°15'W
Salto, Ur.	144	31°18'S	57°45'W
Salto, r., Mex.	130	22°16'N	99°18'W
Salto, Serra do, mtn., Braz. (sĕ'r-rä-dô)	141a	20°26'S	43°28'W
Salto Grande, Braz. (grän'dä)	143	22°57'S	49°58'W
Salton Sea, Ca., U.S. (sôlt'ŭn)	118	33°28'N	115°43'W
Salton Sea, l., Ca., U.S.	106	33°19'N	115°50'W
Saltpond, Ghana	230	5°16'N	1°07'W
Salt River Indian Reservation, I.R., Az., U.S. (sôlt rĭv'ēr)	119	33°40'N	112°01'W
Saltsjöbaden, Swe. (sält'shû-bäd'ĕn)	166	59°15'N	18°20'E
Saltspring Island, i., Can. (sält'sprĭng)	94	48°47'N	123°30'W
Saltville, Va., U.S. (sôlt'vĭl)	125	36°50'N	81°45'W
Saltykovka, Russia (sál-tē'kôf-ká)	186b	55°45'N	37°56'E
Salud, Mount, mtn., Pan. (sä-lo͞o'th)	128a	9°14'N	79°42'W
Saluda, S.C., U.S. (sá-lo͞o'dá)	125	34°02'N	81°46'W
Saluda, r., S.C., U.S.	125	34°07'N	81°48'W
Saluzzo, Italy (sä-lo͞ot'sō)	174	44°39'N	7°31'E
Salvador, Braz. (säl-vä-dōr') (bä-ē'á)	143	12°59'S	38°27'W
Salvador Lake, l., La., U.S.	123	29°45'N	90°20'W
Salvador Point, c., Bah.	134	24°30'N	77°45'W
Salvatierra, Mex. (säl-vä-tyĕr'rä)	130	20°13'N	100°52'W
Salween, r., Asia	196	21°00'N	98°00'E
Salyan, Azer.	181	39°40'N	49°10'E
Salzburg, Aus. (sälts'bŏŏrgh)	161	47°48'N	13°04'E
Salzwedel, Ger. (sälts-vä'dĕl)	168	52°51'N	11°10'E
Samālūt, Egypt (sä-mä-lo͞ot')	200	28°17'N	30°43'E
Samana, Cabo, c., Dom. Rep.	129	19°20'N	69°00'W
Samana or Atwood Cay, i., Bah.	135	23°05'N	73°45'W
Samar, i., Phil. (sä'mär)	213	11°30'N	126°07'E
Samara (Kuybyshev), Russia	180	53°10'N	50°05'E
Samara, r., Russia	181	52°50'N	50°35'E
Samara, r., Ukr. (sá-mä'rá)	177	48°47'N	35°30'E
Samarai, Pap. N. Gui. (sä-mä-rä'ē)	213	10°45'S	150°49'E
Samarinda, Indon.	212	0°30'S	117°10'E
Samarkand, Uzb. (sá-már-känt')	183	39°42'N	67°00'E
Şamaxı, Azer.	181	40°35'N	48°40'E
Samba, D.R.C.	237	4°38'S	26°22'E
Sambalpur, India (sŭm'bŭl-pòr)	199	21°30'N	84°05'E
Sāmbhar, r., India	202	27°00'N	74°58'E
Sambir, Ukr.	169	49°31'N	23°12'E
Samborombón, r., Arg.	141c	35°20'S	57°52'W
Samborombón, Bahía, b., Arg. (bä-ē'ä-säm-bô-rôm-bô'n)	141c	35°57'S	57°05'W
Sambre, r., Eur. (säN'br')	165	50°20'N	4°15'E
Sambungo, Ang.	236	8°39'S	20°43'E
Sammamish, r., Wa., U.S.	116a	47°43'N	122°08'W
Sammamish, Lake, l., Wa., U.S. (så-măm'ĭsh)	116a	47°35'N	122°02'W
Samoa, nation, Oc.	2	14°30'S	172°00'W
Samoa Islands, is., Oc.	214a	14°00'S	171°00'W
Samokov, Blg. (sä'mô-kôf)	175	42°20'N	23°33'E
Samora Correia, Port. (sä-mô'rä-kôr-rĕ'yä)	173b	38°55'N	8°52'W
Samorovo, Russia (sá-má-rô'vô)	184	60°47'N	69°13'E
Sámos, i., Grc. (sä'mŏs)	163	37°53'N	26°35'E
Samothráki, i., Grc.	163	40°23'N	25°10'E
Sampaloc Point, c., Phil. (säm-pä'lŏk)	213a	14°43'N	119°56'E
Sam Rayburn Reservoir, res., Tx., U.S.	123	31°10'N	94°15'W
Samson, Al., U.S. (săm'sŭn)	124	31°06'N	86°02'W
Samsu, Kor., N. (säm'so͞o')	210	41°12'N	128°00'E
Samsun, Tur. (sám'so͞on')	198	41°20'N	36°05'E
Samtredia, Geor. (sám'trĕ-dē)	181	42°18'N	42°25'E
Samuel, i., Can. (săm'ū-ĕl)	116d	48°50'N	123°10'W
Samur, r. (sä-mo͞or')	181	41°40'N	47°20'E
San, Mali (sän)	230	13°18'N	4°54'W
San, r., Eur.	161	50°33'N	22°12'E
Şan'ā', Yemen (sän'ä)	198	15°17'N	44°05'E
Sanaga, r., Cam. (sä-nä'gä)	230	4°30'N	12°00'E
San Ambrosio, Isla, i., Chile (ē's-lä-dē-sän äm-brō'zē-ō)	139	26°40'S	80°00'W
Sanana, Pulau, i., Indon.	213	2°15'S	126°38'E
Sanandaj, Iran	198	36°44'N	46°43'E
San Andreas, Ca., U.S. (săn ăn'drē-ăs)	118	38°10'N	120°42'W
San Andreas, l., Ca., U.S.	116b	37°36'N	122°26'W
San Andrés, Col. (sän-än-drĕ's)	142a	6°57'N	75°41'W
San Andrés, Mex. (sän än-drās')	131a	19°15'N	99°10'W
San Andrés, i., Col.	133	12°32'N	81°34'W
San Andres, Laguna de, l., Mex.	131	22°40'N	97°50'W
San Andres Mountains, mts., N.M., U.S. (săn ăn'drē-ăs)	106	33°00'N	106°40'W
San Andrés Tuxtla, Mex. (sän-än-drā's-to͞os'tlä)	128	18°27'N	95°12'W
San Angelo, Tx., U.S. (săn ăn-jĕ-lō)	104	31°28'N	100°22'W
San Antioco, Isola di, i., Italy (ê'sō-lä-dē-sän-än-tyŏ'kō)	174	39°00'N	8°25'E
San Antonio, Chile (sän-án-tō'nyō)	144	33°34'S	71°36'W
San Antonio, Col.	142a	2°57'N	75°06'W
San Antonio, Col.	142a	3°55'N	75°28'W
San Antonio, Phil.	213a	14°57'N	120°05'E
San Antonio, Tx., U.S. (săn ăn-tō'nē-ô)	104	29°25'N	98°30'W
San Antonio, r., Tx., U.S.	123	29°00'N	97°58'W
San Antonio, Cabo, c., Cuba (kä'bô-sän-än-tō'nyō)	129	21°55'N	84°55'W
San Antonio, Lake, res., Ca., U.S.	118	36°00'N	121°13'W
San Antonio Bay, b., Tx., U.S.	123	28°20'N	97°08'W
San Antonio de Areco, Arg. (dā ä-rā'kō)	141c	34°16'S	59°30'W
San Antonio de las Vegas, Cuba	135a	22°51'N	82°23'W
San Antonio de los Baños, Cuba (dā lōs bän'yōs)	134	22°54'N	82°30'W
San Antonio de los Cobres, Arg. (dā lōs kō'brās)	144	24°15'S	66°29'W
San Antônio de Pádua, Braz. (dē-pá'dwä)	141a	21°32'S	42°09'W
San Antonio de Tamanaco, Ven.	143b	9°42'N	66°03'W
San Antonio Oeste, Arg. (sän-nä-tō'nyō ō-ĕs'tā)	144	40°49'S	64°56'W
San Antonio Peak, mtn., Ca., U.S. (săn ăn-tō'nĭ-ō)	117a	34°17'N	117°39'W
Sanarate, Guat. (sä-nä-rä'tĕ)	132	14°47'N	90°12'W
San Augustine, Tx., U.S. (săn ô'gŭs-tēn)	123	31°33'N	94°08'W
San Bartolo, Mex. (sän bär-tō'lō)	131a	19°36'N	99°43'W
San Bartolo, Mex.	122	24°43'N	103°12'W
San Bartolomeo, Italy (bär-tô-lô-mā'ō)	174	41°25'N	15°04'E
San Benedetto del Tronto, Italy (bā'nā-dĕt'tō dĕl trōn'tō)	174	42°58'N	13°54'E
San Benito, Tx., U.S. (săn bĕ-nē'tō)	123	26°07'N	97°37'W
San Benito, r., Ca., U.S.	118	36°40'N	121°20'W
San Bernardino, Ca., U.S. (bûr-när-dē'nō)	104	34°07'N	117°19'W
San Bernardino Mountains, mts., Ca., U.S.	118	34°05'N	116°23'W
San Bernardo, Chile (sän bĕr-när'dō)	141b	33°35'S	70°42'W
San Blas, Mex. (sän bläs')	128	21°33'N	105°19'W
San Blas, Cape, c., Fl., U.S.	107	29°38'N	85°38'W
San Blas, Cordillera de, mts., Pan.	133	9°17'N	78°20'W
San Blas, Golfo de, b., Pan.	133	9°33'N	78°42'W
San Blas, Punta, c., Pan.	133	9°35'N	78°55'W
San Bruno, Ca., U.S. (săn brū-nô)	116b	37°38'N	122°25'W
San Buenaventura, Mex. (bwā'ná-vĕn-to͞o'rá)	122	27°07'N	101°30'W
San Carlos, Chile (sän-ká'r-lōs)	144	36°23'S	71°58'W
San Carlos, Col.	142a	6°11'N	74°58'W
San Carlos, Eq. Gui.	236	3°27'N	8°33'E
San Carlos, Mex. (săn kär'lōs)	131	17°49'N	92°33'W
San Carlos, Mex.	122	24°36'N	98°52'W
San Carlos, Nic. (sän-kä'r-lôs)	133	11°08'N	84°48'W
San Carlos, Phil.	213a	15°56'N	120°20'E
San Carlos, Ca., U.S. (săn kär'lōs)	116b	37°30'N	122°15'W
San Carlos, Ven.	142	9°36'N	68°35'W
San Carlos, r., C.R.	133	10°36'N	84°18'W
San Carlos de Bariloche, Arg.	144	41°15'S	71°26'W
San Carlos Indian Reservation, I.R., Az., U.S. (săn kär'lōs)	119	33°27'N	110°15'W
San Carlos Lake, res., Az., U.S.	119	33°05'N	110°29'W
San Casimiro, Ven. (kä-sē-mē'rō)	143b	10°01'N	67°02'W
San Cataldo, Italy (kä-täl'dō)	174	37°30'N	13°59'E
Sánchez, Dom. Rep. (sän'chĕz)	129	19°15'N	69°40'W
Sanchez, Río de los, r., Mex. (rē'ō-dĕ-lôs)	130	20°31'N	102°29'W
Sánchez Román, Mex. (rô-má'n)	130	21°48'N	103°20'W
San Clemente, Spain (sän klå-mĕn'tā)	172	39°25'N	2°24'W
San Clemente Island, i., Ca., U.S.	106	32°54'N	118°29'W
San Cristóbal, Dom. Rep. (krēs-tō'bäl)	135	18°25'N	70°05'W
San Cristóbal, Guat.	132	15°22'N	90°26'W
San Cristóbal, Ven.	142	7°43'N	72°15'W
San Cristobal, i., Sol. Is.	221	10°47'S	162°17'E
San Cristóbal de las Casas, Mex.	128	16°44'N	92°39'W
Sancti Spíritus, Cuba (säŋk'tē spē'rē-to͞os)	129	21°55'N	79°25'W
Sancti Spíritus, prov., Cuba	134	22°05'N	79°20'W
Sancy, Puy de, mtn., Fr. (pwē-dĕ-säN-sē')	161	45°30'N	2°53'E
Sand, i., Or., U.S. (sănd)	116c	46°16'N	124°01'W
Sand, i., Wi., U.S.	113	46°03'N	91°09'W
Sand, r., S. Afr.	233c	28°30'S	29°30'E
Sand, r., S. Afr.	238c	28°09'S	26°46'E
Sanda, Japan (sän'dä)	211	34°53'N	135°14'E
Sandakan, Malay. (sán-dä'kán)	212	5°51'N	118°03'E
Sanday, i., Scot., U.K. (sănd'ā)	164a	59°17'N	2°25'W
Sandbach, Eng., U.K. (sănd'băch)	158a	53°08'N	2°22'W
Sandefjord, Nor. (sän'dĕ-fyôr')	166	59°09'N	10°14'E
San de Fuca, Wa., U.S. (de-fo͞o-cä)	116a	48°14'N	122°44'W
Sanders, Az., U.S.	119	35°13'N	109°20'W
Sanderson, Tx., U.S. (săn'dēr-sŭn)	122	30°09'N	102°24'W
Sandersville, Ga., U.S. (săn'dērz-vĭl)	125	32°57'N	82°50'W
Sandhammaren, c., Swe. (sänt'häm-mår)	160	55°24'N	14°37'E
Sand Hills, reg., Ne., U.S. (sănd)	112	41°57'N	101°29'W
Sand Hook, N.J., U.S. (sănd hŏk)	110a	40°29'N	74°05'W
Sandhurst, Eng., U.K. (sănd'hûrst)	158b	51°20'N	0°48'W
Sandia Indian Reservation, I.R., N.M., U.S.	119	35°15'N	106°30'W
San Diego, Ca., U.S. (săn dē-ā'gō)	104	32°43'N	117°10'W
San Diego, Tx., U.S.	120	27°47'N	98°13'W
San Diego, r., Ca., U.S.	118	32°53'N	116°57'W
San Diego de la Unión, Mex. (sän dē-å-gō dā lä o͞o-nyōn')	130	21°27'N	100°52'W
Sandies Creek, r., Tx., U.S. (sănd'ēz)	123	29°13'N	97°34'W
San Dimas, Mex. (dē-mäs')	130	24°08'N	105°57'W
San Dimas, Ca., U.S. (săn dē-más)	117a	34°07'N	117°49'W
Sandnes, Nor. (sänd'nĕs)	166	58°52'N	5°44'E
Sandoa, D.R.C. (sän-dō'á)	232	9°39'S	23°00'E
Sandomierz, Pol. (sán-dô'myĕzh)	169	50°39'N	21°45'E
San Doná di Piave, Italy (sän dô ná' dē pyä'vē)	174	45°38'N	12°34'E
Sandoway, Mya. (sän-dô-wī')	199	18°24'N	94°28'E
Sandpoint, Id., U.S. (sănd point)	114	48°17'N	116°34'W
Sandringham, Austl. (săn'drĭng-ăm)	217a	37°57'S	145°01'E
Sandrio, Italy (sä'n-dryô)	174	46°11'N	9°53'E
Sand Springs, Ok., U.S. (sănd sprĭnz)	121	36°08'N	96°06'W
Sandstone, Austl. (sănd'stōn)	218	28°00'S	119°25'E
Sandstone, Mn., U.S.	113	46°08'N	92°53'W
Sanduo, China (sän-dwô)	206	32°49'N	119°39'E
Sandusky, Al., U.S. (săn-dŭs'kē)	110h	33°32'N	86°50'W
Sandusky, Mi., U.S.	108	43°25'N	82°50'W
Sandusky, Oh., U.S.	105	41°25'N	82°45'W
Sandusky, r., Oh., U.S.	108	41°10'N	83°20'W
Sandwich, Il., U.S. (sănd'wĭch)	108	42°35'N	88°53'W
Sandy, Or., U.S. (sănd'ē)	116c	45°24'N	122°16'W
Sandy, Ut., U.S.	117b	40°36'N	111°53'W
Sandy, r., Or., U.S.	116c	45°28'N	122°17'W
Sandy Cape, c., Austl.	221	24°25'S	153°10'E
Sandy Hook, Ct., U.S. (hŏk)	110a	41°25'N	73°17'W
Sandy Lake, l., Can.	102g	53°46'N	113°58'W
Sandy Lake, l., Can.	101	49°16'N	57°00'W
Sandy Lake, l., Can.	97	53°00'N	93°07'W
Sandy Point, Tx., U.S.	123a	29°22'N	95°27'W
Sandy Point, c., Wa., U.S.	116d	48°48'N	122°42'W
Sandy Springs, Ga., U.S. (springz)	110c	33°55'N	84°23'W
San Estanislao, Para. (ĕs-tä-nēs-lá'ô)	144	24°38'S	56°20'W
San Esteban, Hond. (ĕs-tĕ'bän)	132	15°13'N	85°53'W
San Fabian, Phil. (fä-byä'n)	213a	16°14'N	120°28'E
San Felipe, Chile (fĕ-lē'på)	144	32°45'S	70°43'W
San Felipe, Mex. (fĕ-lē'pĕ)	130	21°29'N	101°13'W
San Felipe, Mex.	130	22°21'N	105°26'W
San Felipe, Ven. (fĕ-lē'pĕ)	142	10°13'N	68°45'W
San Felipe, Cayos de, is., Cuba (kä'yōs-dĕ-sän-fĕ-lē'pĕ)	134	22°00'N	83°30'W

346 San Felipe Creek – San Sebastian PRONOUNCING INDEX

PLACE (Pronunciation)	PAGE	LAT.	LONG.
San Felipe Creek, r., Ca., U.S. (săn fē-lēp′å)	118	33°10′N	116°03′W
San Felipe Indian Reservation, I.R., N.M., U.S.	119	35°26′N	106°26′W
San Félix, Isla, i., Chile (ē′s-lä-dĕ-sän fā-lēks′)	139	26°20′S	80°10′W
San Fernanda, Spain (fĕr-nä′n-dä)	172	36°28′N	6°13′W
San Fernando, Arg. (fĕr-ná′n-dô)	144a	34°26′S	58°34′W
San Fernando, Chile	141b	35°36′S	70°58′W
San Fernando, Mex. (fĕr-nän′dô)	122	24°52′N	98°10′W
San Fernando, Phil. (sän fĕr-nä′n-dô)	212	16°38′N	120°19′E
San Fernando, Ca., U.S. (fĕr-nän′dô)	117a	34°17′N	118°27′W
San Fernando, r., Mex. (sän fĕr-nän′dô)	122	25°07′N	98°25′W
San Fernando de Apure, Ven. (sän-fĕr-nä′n-dō-dĕ-ä-pōō′rā)	142	7°46′N	67°29′W
San Fernando de Atabapo, Ven. (dĕ-ä-tä-bä′pô)	142	3°58′N	67°41′W
San Fernando de Henares, Spain (dĕ-ā-nä′rās)	173a	40°23′N	3°31′W
Sånfjället, mtn., Swe.	160	62°19′N	13°30′E
Sanford, Can. (săn′fērd)	102f	49°41′N	97°27′W
Sanford, Fl., U.S. (săn′fōrd)	105	28°46′N	81°18′W
Sanford, Me., U.S. (săn′fērd)	100	43°26′N	70°47′W
Sanford, N.C., U.S.	125	35°26′N	79°10′W
San Francisco, Arg. (săn frăn′sĭs′kô)	144	31°23′S	62°09′W
San Francisco, El Sal.	132	13°48′N	88°11′W
San Francisco, Ca., U.S.	104	37°45′N	122°26′W
San Francisco, r., N.M., U.S.	119	33°35′N	108°55′W
San Francisco Bay, b., Ca., U.S. (săn frăn′sĭs′kô)	118	37°45′N	122°21′W
San Francisco del Oro, Mex. (dĕl ō′rō)	128	27°00′N	106°37′W
San Francisco del Rincón, Mex. (dĕl rēn-kōn′)	130	21°01′N	101°51′W
San Francisco de Macaira, Ven. (dĕ-mä-kī′rä)	143b	9°58′N	66°17′W
San Francisco de Macoris, Dom. Rep. (dā-mä-kō′rēs)	135	19°20′N	70°15′W
San Francisco de Paula, Cuba (dā pou′lä)	135a	23°04′N	82°18′W
San Gabriel, Ca., U.S. (săn gä-brē-ĕl′) (gā′brē-ĕl)	117a	34°06′N	118°06′W
San Gabriel, r., Ca., U.S.	117a	33°47′N	118°06′W
San Gabriel Chilac, Mex. (sän-gä-brē-ĕl-chē-läk′)	131	18°19′N	97°22′W
San Gabriel Mts, Ca., U.S.	117a	34°17′N	118°03′W
San Gabriel Reservoir, res., Ca., U.S.	117a	34°14′N	117°48′W
Sangamon, r., Il., U.S. (săn′gȧ-msion)	121	40°08′N	90°08′W
Sanger, Ca., U.S. (săng′ēr)	118	36°42′N	119°33′W
Sangerhausen, Ger. (säng′ĕr-hou-zĕn)	168	51°28′N	11°17′E
Sangha, r., Afr.	231	2°40′N	16°10′E
Sangihe, Pulau, i., Indon.	213	3°30′N	125°30′E
San Gil, Col. (sän-κē′l)	142	6°32′N	73°13′W
San Giovanni in Fiore, Italy (sän jô-vän′nē ēn fyō′rā)	174	39°15′N	16°40′E
San Giuseppe Vesuviano, Italy	173c	40°36′N	14°31′E
Sangju, Kor., S. (säng′jōō′)	210	36°20′N	128°07′E
Sāngli, India	199	16°56′N	74°38′E
Sangmélima, Cam.	235	2°56′N	11°59′E
San Gorgonio Mountain, mtn., Ca., U.S. (săn gôr-gō′nĭ-ō)	117a	34°06′N	116°50′W
Sangre de Cristo Mountains, mts., U.S.	106	37°45′N	105°50′W
San Gregoria, Ca., U.S. (săn grĕ-gôr′ā)	116b	37°20′N	122°23′W
Sangro, r., Italy (säŋ′grô)	174	41°38′N	13°56′E
Sangüesa, Spain (sän-gwĕ′sä)	172	42°36′N	1°15′W
Sanhe, China (sän-hŭ)	206	39°59′N	117°06′E
Sanibel Island, i., Fl., U.S. (săn′ĭ-bĕl)	125a	26°26′N	82°15′W
San Ignacio, Belize	132a	17°11′N	89°04′W
San Ildefonso, Cape, c., Phil. (sän-ēl-dĕ-fōn-sō)	213a	16°03′N	122°10′E
San Ildefonso o la Granja, Spain (ō lä grän′khä)	172	40°54′N	4°02′W
San Isidro, Arg. (ē-sē′drō)	141c	34°28′S	58°31′W
San Isidro, C.R.	133	9°24′N	83°43′W
San Jacinto, Phil. (sän hä-sēn′tô)	213a	12°33′N	123°43′E
San Jacinto, Ca., U.S. (săn jȧ-sĭn′tô)	117a	33°47′N	116°57′W
San Jacinto, r., Ca., U.S. (săn jȧ-sĭn′tô)	117a	33°44′N	117°14′W
San Jacinto, r., Tx., U.S.	123	30°25′N	95°05′W
San Jacinto, West Fork, r., Tx., U.S.	123	30°35′N	95°37′W
San Javier, Chile (sän-hà-vē′ĕr)	141b	35°35′S	71°43′W
San Jerónimo, Mex.	131a	19°31′N	98°46′W
San Jerónimo de Juárez, Mex. (hā-rō′nē-mô dā hwä′rāz)	130	17°08′N	100°30′W
San Joaquin, Ven.	143b	10°16′N	67°47′W
San Joaquin, r., Ca., U.S. (săn hwä-kēn′)	118	37°10′N	120°51′W
San Joaquin Valley, Ca., U.S.	118	36°45′N	120°30′W
San Jorge, Golfo, b., Arg. (gôl-fô-sän-κô′r-κĕ)	144	46°15′S	66°45′W
San José, C.R. (săn hō-sā′)	129	9°57′N	84°05′W
San Jose, Phil.	213a	12°22′N	121°04′E
San Jose, Phil.	213a	15°49′N	120°57′E
San Jose, Ca., U.S. (săn hō-zā′)	104	37°20′N	121°54′W
San José, i., Mex. (κô-sĕ′)	128	25°00′N	110°35′W
San José, Isla de, i., Pan. (ē′s-lä-dĕ-sän hō-sā′)	133	8°17′N	79°20′W

PLACE (Pronunciation)	PAGE	LAT.	LONG.
San Jose, Rio, r., N.M., U.S. (săn hō-zā′)	119	35°15′N	108°10′W
San José de Feliciano, Arg. (dā lä ĕs-kē′ná)	144	30°26′S	58°44′W
San José de Gauribe, Ven. (sän-hô-sĕ′dĕ-gàōō-rē′bĕ)	143b	9°51′N	65°49′W
San José de las Lajas, Cuba (sän-κô-sĕ′dĕ-läs-lä′käs)	135a	22°58′N	82°10′W
San José Iturbide, Mex. (ē-tōōr-bē′dĕ)	130	21°00′N	100°24′W
San Juan, Arg. (hwän′)	144	31°36′S	68°29′W
San Juan, Col. (hòá′n)	142a	3°23′N	73°48′W
San Juan, Dom. Rep. (sän hwän′)	135	18°50′N	71°15′W
San Juan, Phil.	213a	16°41′N	120°20′E
San Juan, P.R. (sän hwän′)	129	18°30′N	66°10′W
San Juan, prov., Arg.	144	31°00′S	69°30′W
San Juan, r., Mex. (sän-hōō-än′)	131	18°10′N	95°23′W
San Juan, r., N.A.	129	10°58′N	84°18′W
San Juan, r., U.S.	106	36°30′N	109°00′W
San Juan, Cabezas de, c., P.R.	129b	18°29′N	65°30′W
San Juan, Cabo, c., Eq. Gui.	236	1°08′N	9°23′E
San Juan, Pico, mtn., Cuba (pē′kô-sän-κòá′n)	134	21°55′N	80°00′W
San Juan, Río, r., Mex. (rē′ō-sän-hwän)	122	25°35′N	99°15′W
San Juan Bautista, Para. (sän hwän′ bou-tēs′tä)	144	26°48′S	57°09′W
San Juan Capistrano, Mex. (sän-hōō-än′ kä-pēs-trä′nō)	130	22°41′N	104°07′W
San Juan Creek, r., Ca., U.S. (săn hwän′)	118	35°24′N	120°12′W
San Juan de Guadalupe, Mex. (sän hwan dā gwä-dhä-lōō′pā)	122	24°37′N	102°43′W
San Juan del Norte, Nic.	133	10°55′N	83°44′W
San Juan del Norte, Bahía de, b., Nic.	133	11°12′N	83°40′W
San Juan de los Lagos, Mex. (sän-hōō-än′dā los lä′gôs)	130	21°15′N	102°18′W
San Juan de los Lagos, r., Mex. (dā lōs lä′gôs)	130	21°13′N	102°12′W
San Juan de los Morros, Ven. (dĕ-lôs-mô′r-rôs)	143b	9°54′N	67°22′W
San Juan del Río, Mex.	130	20°21′N	99°59′W
San Juan del Río, Mex. (sän hwän del rē′ō)	122	24°47′N	104°29′W
San Juan del Sur, Nic. (dĕl sōōr)	128	11°15′N	85°53′W
San Juan Evangelista, Mex. (sän-hōō-ä′n-å-väŋ-kå-lĕs′tä′)	131	17°57′N	95°08′W
San Juan Island, i., Wa., U.S.	116a	48°28′N	123°08′W
San Juan Islands, is., Can. (săn hwän)	94	48°49′N	123°14′W
San Juan Islands, is., Wa., U.S.	186a	48°36′N	122°50′W
San Juan Ixtenco, Mex. (ēx-tĕ′n-kô)	131	19°14′N	97°52′W
San Juan Martínez, Cuba	134	22°15′N	83°50′W
San Juan Mountains, mts., Co., U.S. (san hwän′)	106	37°50′N	107°30′W
San Julián, Arg. (sän hōō-lyá′n)	144	49°17′S	68°02′W
San Justo, Arg. (hōōs′tô)	144a	34°40′S	58°33′W
Sankanbiriwa, mtn., S.L.	234	8°56′N	10°48′W
Sankarani, r., Afr. (sän′kä-rä′nē)	230	11°10′N	8°35′W
Sankt Gallen, Switz.	161	47°25′N	9°22′E
Sankt Moritz, Switz. (sånt mō′rĭts) (zäŋkt mō′rēts)	168	46°31′N	9°50′E
Sankt Pölten, Aus. (zäŋkt-pûl′tĕn)	168	48°12′N	15°38′E
Sankt Veit, Aus. (zäŋkt vīt′)	168	46°46′N	14°20′E
Sankuru, r., D.R.C. (säŋ-kōō′rōō)	232	4°00′S	22°35′E
San Lázaro, Cabo, c., Mex. (sän-lá′zä-rō)	128	24°58′N	113°30′W
San Leandro, Ca., U.S. (săn lē-ăn′drô)	116b	37°43′N	122°10′W
Şanlıurfa, Tur.	198	37°20′N	38°45′E
San Lorenzo, Arg. (sän lô-rĕn′zô)	144	32°46′S	60°44′W
San Lorenzo, Hond. (sän lô-rĕn′zô)	132	13°24′N	87°24′W
San Lorenzo, Ca., U.S. (săn lô-rĕn′zô)	116b	37°41′N	122°08′W
San Lorenzo de El Escorial, Spain	172	40°36′N	4°09′W
Sanlúcar de Barrameda, Spain (sän-lōō′kär)	162	36°46′N	6°21′W
San Lucas, Bol. (lōō′kás)	142	20°12′S	65°06′W
San Lucas, Cabo, c., Mex.	128	22°45′N	109°45′W
San Luis, Arg. (lô-ēs′)	144	33°16′S	66°15′W
San Luis, Col. (lôē′s)	142a	6°03′N	74°57′W
San Luis, Cuba	135	20°15′N	75°50′W
San Luis, Guat.	132	14°38′N	89°42′W
San Luis, prov., Arg.	144	32°45′S	66°00′W
San Luis de la Paz, Mex. (dā lä päz′)	130	21°17′N	100°32′W
San Luis del Cordero, Mex. (dĕl kôr-dä′rô)	122	25°25′N	104°20′W
San Luis Obispo, Ca., U.S. (ô-bĭs′pō)	104	35°18′N	120°40′W
San Luis Obispo Bay, b., Ca., U.S.	118	35°07′N	121°05′W
San Luis Potosí, Mex.	128	22°08′N	100°58′W
San Luis Potosí, state, Mex.	128	22°45′N	101°45′W
San Luis Rey, r., Ca., U.S. (rā′ē)	118	33°22′N	117°06′W
San Manuel, Az., U.S. (săn măn′ū-ĕl)	119	32°30′N	110°45′W
San Marcial, N.M., U.S. (săn mȧr-shäl′)	119	33°40′N	107°00′W
San Marco, Italy (sän mär′kô)	174	41°53′N	15°50′E
San Marcos, Guat. (mär′kôs)	132	14°57′N	91°49′W
San Marcos, Mex.	130	16°46′N	99°23′W
San Marcos, Tx., U.S. (săn mär′kôs)	123	29°53′N	97°56′W
San Marcos, r., Tx., U.S.	122	30°08′N	98°15′W
San Marcos de Colón, Hond. (sän-má′r-kōs-dĕ-kô-lô′n)	132	13°17′N	86°50′W
San Maria di Léuca, Cape, c., Italy (dē-lĕ′ōō-kä)	163	39°47′N	18°20′E
San Marino, S. Mar. (sän mä-rē′nô)	174	44°55′N	12°26′E
San Marino, Ca., U.S. (săn mĕr-ē′nô)	117a	34°07′N	118°06′W

PLACE (Pronunciation)	PAGE	LAT.	LONG.
San Marino, nation, Eur.	154	43°40′N	13°00′E
San Martín, Col. (sän mär-tē′n)	142a	3°42′N	73°44′W
San Martín, vol., Mex. (mär-tē′n)	131	18°36′N	95°11′W
San Martín, l., S.A.	144	48°15′S	72°30′W
San Martín Chalchicuautla, Mex.	130	21°22′N	98°39′W
San Martin de la Vega, Spain (sän mär ten′ dā lä vā′gä)	173a	40°12′N	3°34′W
San Martín Hidalgo, Mex. (sän mär-tē′n-ē-däl′gô)	130	20°27′N	103°55′W
San Mateo, Mex.	131	16°59′N	97°04′W
San Mateo, Ca., U.S. (săn mä-tā′ô)	116b	37°34′N	122°20′W
San Mateo, Ven. (sän má-tĕ′ô)	143b	9°45′N	64°34′W
San Matías, Golfo, b., Arg. (sän mä-tē′äs)	144	41°30′S	63°45′W
Sanmen Wan, b., China	209	29°00′N	122°15′E
San Miguel, El Sal. (sän mē-gāl′)	128	13°28′N	88°11′W
San Miguel, Mex. (sän mē-gāl′)	131	18°18′N	97°09′W
San Miguel, Pan.	133	8°26′N	78°55′W
San Miguel, Phil. (sän mē-gĕ′l)	213a	15°09′N	120°56′E
San Miguel, Ven. (sän mē-gĕ′l)	143b	9°56′N	64°58′W
San Miguel, vol., El Sal.	132	13°27′N	88°17′W
San Miguel, i., Ca., U.S.	118	34°03′N	120°23′W
San Miguel, r., Bol. (sän-mē-gĕl′)	142	13°34′S	63°58′W
San Miguel, r., N.A. (sän mē-gāl′)	131	15°27′N	92°00′W
San Miguel, r., Co., U.S. (săn mē-gĕl′)	119	38°15′N	108°40′W
San Miguel, Bahía, b., Pan. (bä-ē′ä-sän mē-gāl′)	133	8°17′N	78°26′W
San Miguel Bay, b., Phil.	213a	13°55′N	123°12′E
San Miguel de Allende, Mex. (dā ä-lyĕn′dā)	130	20°54′N	100°44′W
San Miguel el Alto, Mex. (ĕl äl′tô)	130	21°03′N	102°26′W
Sannār, Sudan	231	14°25′N	33°30′E
San Narciso, Phil. (sän när-sē′sô)	213a	15°01′N	120°05′E
San Narciso, Phil.	213a	13°34′N	122°33′E
San Nicolás, Arg. (sän nē-kô-lá′s)	144	33°20′S	60°14′W
San Nicolas, Phil. (nē-kô-läs′)	213a	16°05′N	120°45′E
San Nicolas, i., Ca., U.S. (săn nĭ′kô-là)	118	33°14′N	119°10′W
San Nicolás, r., Mex.	130	19°40′N	105°08′W
Sanniquellie, Lib.	234	7°22′N	8°43′W
Sannūr, Wādī, Egypt	238b	28°48′N	31°12′E
Sanok, Pol. (sä′nôk)	169	49°31′N	22°13′E
San Pablo, Phil. (sän-pä-blô)	213a	14°05′N	121°20′E
San Pablo, Ca., U.S. (săn păb′lô)	116b	37°58′N	122°21′W
San Pablo, Ven. (sän-pá′blô)	143b	9°46′N	65°04′W
San Pablo, r., Pan. (sän päb′lô)	133	8°12′N	81°12′W
San Pablo Bay, b., Ca., U.S. (săn păb′lô)	116b	38°04′N	122°25′W
San Pablo Res, Ca., U.S.	116b	37°55′N	122°12′W
San Pascual, Phil. (päs-kwäl′)	213a	13°08′N	122°59′E
San Pedro, Arg. (sän pā′drô)	144	24°15′S	64°15′W
San Pedro, Arg.	141c	33°41′S	59°42′W
San Pedro, Chile (sän pĕ′drô)	141b	33°54′S	71°27′W
San Pedro, El Sal. (sän pā′drô)	132	13°49′N	88°58′W
San Pedro, Mex. (sän pā′drô)	131	18°38′N	92°25′W
San Pedro, Para. (sän-pĕ′drô)	144	24°13′S	57°00′W
San Pedro, Ca., U.S. (săn pē′drô)	117a	33°44′N	118°17′W
San Pedro, r., Cuba (sän-pĕ′drô)	134	21°05′N	78°15′W
San Pedro, r., Mex. (sän pā′drô)	130	22°08′N	104°59′W
San Pedro, r., Mex.	122	27°56′N	105°50′W
San Pedro, r., Az., U.S.	119	32°48′N	110°37′W
San Pedro, Río de, r., Mex.	130	21°51′N	102°24′W
San Pedro, Río de, r., N.A.	131	18°23′N	92°13′W
San Pedro Bay, b., Ca., U.S. (săn pē′drō)	117a	33°42′N	118°12′W
San Pedro de las Colonias, Mex. (dĕ-läs-kô-lô′nyäs)	122	25°47′N	102°58′W
San Pedro de Macorís, Dom. Rep. (sän-pĕ′drō-dā mä-kô-rēs′)	135	18°30′N	69°30′W
San Pedro Lagunillas, Mex. (sän pā′drô lä-gōō-nēl′yäs)	130	21°12′N	104°47′W
San Pedro Sula, Hond. (sän pā′drô sōō′lä)	132	15°29′N	88°01′W
San Pietro, Isola di, i., Italy (ē′sō-lä-dē-sän pyā′trô)	174	39°09′N	8°15′E
San Quentin, Ca., U.S. (săn kwĕn-tēn′)	116b	37°57′N	122°29′W
San Quintin, Phil. (sän kēn-tēn′)	213a	15°59′N	120°47′E
San Rafael, Arg. (sän-rä-fä-ĕl′)	144	34°30′S	68°13′W
San Rafael, Col. (sän-rä-fä-ĕ′l)	142a	6°18′N	75°02′W
San Rafael, Ca., U.S. (săn rá-fĕl)	116b	37°58′N	122°31′W
San Rafael, r., Ut., U.S. (săn rá-fĕl′)	119	39°05′N	110°50′W
San Rafael, Cabo, c., Dom. Rep. (ká′bô)	135	19°00′N	68°50′W
San Ramón, C.R.	133	10°07′N	84°30′W
San Ramon, Ca., U.S. (săn rä-mōn′)	116b	37°47′N	122°59′W
San Remo, Italy (sän rā′mô)	174	43°48′N	7°46′E
San Roque, Col. (sän-rô′kĕ)	142a	6°29′N	75°00′W
San Roque, Spain	172	36°13′N	5°23′W
San Saba, Tx., U.S. (săn să′bà)	122	31°12′N	98°43′W
San Saba, r., Tx., U.S.	122	30°58′N	99°12′W
San Salvador, El Sal. (sän säl-vä-dôr)	128	13°45′N	89°11′W
San Salvador (Watling), i., Bah. (săn săl′và-dôr)	135	24°05′N	74°30′W
San Salvador, i., Ec.	142	0°14′S	90°50′W
San Salvador, r., Ur. (sän-säl-vä-dô′r)	141c	33°42′S	58°04′W
Sansanné-Mango, Togo (sän-sà-nā′ män′gô)	230	10°21′N	0°28′E
San Sebastian, Spain (sän sȧ-bås-tyän′)	230	28°09′N	17°11′W

ăt; finȧl; rāte; senåte; ärm; åsk; sofȧ; fâre; ch-choose; dh-as th in other; bē; ēvent; bĕt; recĕnt; cratẽr; g-gō; gh-guttural g; bĭt; ĭ-short neutral; rīde; κ-guttural k as ch in German ich;

PRONOUNCING INDEX San Sebastián – Sapitwa 347

PLACE (Pronunciation)	PAGE	LAT.	LONG.
San Sebastián *see* Donostia-San Sebastián, Spain	154	43°19'N	1°59'W
San Sebastián, Ven. (sän-sĕ-bäs-tyá'n)	143b	9°58'N	67°11'W
San Sebastiàn de los Reyes, Spain	173a	40°33'N	3°38'W
San Severo, Italy (sän sĕ-vâ'rō)	163	41°43'N	15°24'E
Sanshui, China (sän-shwā)	205	23°14'N	112°51'E
San Simon Creek, r., Az., U.S. (sán sī-mōn')	119	32°45'N	109°30'W
Santa Ana, El Sal.	128	14°02'N	89°35'W
Santa Ana, Mex. (sän'tä ä'nä)	130	19°18'N	98°10'W
Santa Ana, Ca., U.S. (săn'tá ăn'á)	104	33°45'N	117°52'W
Santa Ana, r., Ca., U.S.	117a	33°41'N	117°57'W
Santa Ana Mountains, mts., Ca., U.S.	117a	33°44'N	117°36'W
Santa Anna, Tx., U.S.	122	31°44'N	99°18'W
Santa Antão, i., C.V. (sä-tä-á'n-zhĕ-lô)	230b	17°20'N	26°05'W
Santa Bárbara, Braz. (sän-tä-bá'r-bä-rä)	143	19°57'S	43°25'W
Santa Bárbara, Hond.	132	14°52'N	88°20'W
Santa Barbara, Mex.	122	26°48'N	105°50'W
Santa Barbara, Ca., U.S.	104	34°26'N	119°43'W
Santa Barbara, i., Ca., U.S.	118	33°30'N	118°44'W
Santa Barbara Channel, strt., Ca., U.S.	118	34°15'N	120°00'W
Santa Branca, Braz. (sän-tä-brä'N-kä)	141a	23°25'S	45°52'W
Santa Catalina, i., Ca., U.S.	106	33°29'N	118°37'W
Santa Catalina, Cerro de, mtn., Pan.	133	8°39'N	81°36'W
Santa Catalina, Gulf of, b., Ca., U.S. (săn'tá kă-tá-lē'ná)	118	33°00'N	117°58'W
Santa Catarina, Mex. (sän'tä kä-tä-rē'nä)	122	25°41'N	100°27'W
Santa Catarina, state, Braz. (sän-tä-kä-tä-rē'nà)	144	27°15'S	50°30'W
Santa Catarina, r., Mex.	130	16°31'N	98°39'W
Santa Clara, Cuba (sän't klä'rá)	129	22°25'N	80°00'W
Santa Clara, Mex.	122	24°29'N	103°22'W
Santa Clara, Ur.	144	32°46'S	54°51'W
Santa Clara, Ca., U.S. (săn'tá klârá)	114	37°21'N	121°56'W
Santa Clara, vol., Nic.	132	12°44'N	87°00'W
Santa Clara, r., Ca., U.S. (săn'tá klă'rá)	118	34°22'N	118°53'W
Santa Clara, Bahía de, b., Cuba (bä-ē'ä-dĕ-sän-tä-klä-rä)	134	23°05'N	80°50'W
Santa Clara, Sierra, mts., Mex. (sē-ĕ'r-rä-sän'tà klä'rà)	128	27°30'N	113°50'W
Santa Clara Indian Reservation, I.R., N.M., U.S.	119	35°59'N	106°10'W
Santa Cruz, Bol. (sän'tà krōōz')	142	17°45'S	63°03'W
Santa Cruz, Braz. (sän-tä-krōō's)	144	29°43'S	52°15'W
Santa Cruz, Braz.	144b	22°55'S	43°41'W
Santa Cruz, Chile	141b	34°38'S	71°21'W
Santa Cruz, C.R.	132	10°16'N	85°37'W
Santa Cruz, Mex.	122	25°50'N	105°25'W
Santa Cruz, Phil.	213a	13°28'N	122°02'E
Santa Cruz, Phil.	213a	15°46'N	119°53'E
Santa Cruz, Phil.	213a	14°17'N	121°25'E
Santa Cruz, Ca., U.S.	104	36°59'N	122°02'W
Santa Cruz, prov., Arg.	144	48°00'S	70°00'W
Santa Cruz, i., Ec. (sän-tä-krōō'z)	142	0°38'S	90°20'W
Santa Cruz, r., Arg. (sän'tà krōōz')	144	50°05'S	71°00'W
Santa Cruz, r., Az., U.S. (săn'tá krōōz')	119	32°30'N	111°30'W
Santa Cruz Barillas, Guat. (sän-tä-krōō'z-bä-rē'l-yäs)	132	15°47'N	91°22'W
Santa Cruz del Sur, Cuba (sän-tä-krōō's-dĕl-sōō'r)	134	20°45'N	78°00'W
Santa Cruz de Tenerife, Spain (sän'tä krōōz dā tā-nå-rē'fā)	228	28°07'N	15°27'W
Santa Cruz Islands, is., Sol. Is.	221	10°58'S	166°47'E
Santa Cruz Mountains, mts., Ca., U.S. (săn'tà krōōz')	116b	37°30'N	122°19'W
Santa Domingo, Cay, i., Bah.	135	21°50'N	75°45'W
Santa Fe, Arg. (sän'tä fā')	144	31°33'S	60°45'W
Santa Fé, Cuba (sän-tä-fĕ')	134	21°45'N	82°40'W
Santa Fe, Spain (sän'tä-fā')	172	37°12'N	3°43'W
Santa Fe, N.M., U.S. (săn'tá fā')	104	35°40'N	106°00'W
Santa Fe, prov., Arg. (sän'tä fā')	144	32°00'S	61°15'W
Santa Fe de Bogotá *see* Bogotá, Col.	142	4°36'N	74°05'W
Santa Filomena, Braz. (sän-tä-fē-lô-mĕ'nä)	143	9°09'S	44°45'W
Santa Genoveva, mtn., Mex. (sän-tä-hĕ-nō-vĕ'vä)	128	23°30'N	110°00'W
Santai, China (san-tī)	204	31°02'N	105°02'E
Santa Inés, Ven. (sän'tä ē-nĕ's)	143b	9°54'N	64°21'W
Santa Inés, i., Chile (sän'tä ê-näs')	144	53°45'S	74°15'W
Santa Isabel, i., Sol. Is.	221	7°57'S	159°28'E
Santa Isabel, Pico de, mtn., Eq. Gui.	235	3°35'N	8°46'E
Santa Lucia, Cuba (sän'tä lōō-sē'ä)	134	21°15'N	77°30'W
Santa Lucia, Ur. (sän-tä-lōō-sē'ä)	144	34°27'S	56°23'W
Santa Lucia, Ven.	143b	10°18'N	66°40'W
Santa Lucia, r., Ur.	141c	34°19'S	56°13'W
Santa Lucia Bay, b., Cuba (sän'tä lōō-sē'ä)	134	22°55'N	84°20'W
Santa Margarita, i., Mex. (sän'tä mär-gä-rē'tä)	128	24°15'N	112°00'W
Santa Maria, Braz. (sän'tä mä-rē'ä)	144	29°40'S	54°00'W
Santa Maria, Italy (sän-tä mä-rē'ä)	174	41°05'N	14°15'E
Santa Maria, Phil. (sän-tä-mä-rē'ä)	213a	14°48'N	120°57'E
Santa Maria, Ca., U.S. (săn-tá má-rē'á)	118	34°57'N	120°28'W
Santa María, vol., Guat.	132	14°45'N	91°33'W
Santa Maria, r., Mex. (sän'tä mä-rē'ä)	130	21°33'N	100°17'W
Santa Maria, Cabo de, c., Port. (ká'bō-dĕ-sän-tä-mä-rē'ä)	172	36°58'N	7°54'W
Santa Maria, Cape, c., Bah.	135	23°45'N	75°30'W
Santa Maria, Cayo, i., Cuba	134	22°40'N	79°00'W
Santa María del Oro, Mex. (sän'tä-mä-rē'ä-dĕl-ô-rô)	130	21°21'N	104°35'W
Santa Maria de los Angeles, Mex. (dĕ-lôs-á'n-hĕ-lĕs)	130	22°10'N	103°34'W
Santa María del Río, Mex.	130	21°46'N	100°43'W
Santa María de Ocotán, Mex.	130	22°56'N	104°30'W
Santa Maria Island, i., Port. (sän-tä-mä-rē'ä)	230a	37°09'N	26°02'W
Santa Maria Madalena, Braz.	141a	22°00'S	42°00'W
Santa Marta, Col. (sän'tà mär'tà)	142	11°15'N	74°13'W
Santa Marta, Cabo de, c., Ang.	236	13°52'S	12°25'E
Santa Monica, Ca., U.S. (săn'tá mŏn'ĭ-ká)	104	34°01'N	118°29'W
Santa Monica Mountains, mts., Ca., U.S.	117a	34°08'N	118°38'W
Santana, r., Braz. (sän-tä'nä)	144b	22°33'S	43°37'W
Santander, Col. (sän-tän-dĕr')	142a	3°00'N	76°25'W
Santander, Spain (sän-tän-dâr')	154	43°27'N	3°50'W
Sant Antoni de Portmany, Spain	173	38°59'N	1°17'E
Santa Paula, Ca., U.S. (săn'tá pô'lá)	118	34°24'N	119°05'W
Santarém, Braz. (sän-tä-rĕN')	143	2°28'S	54°37'W
Santarém, Port.	172	39°18'N	8°48'W
Santaren Channel, strt., Bah. (săn-tá-rĕn')	134	24°15'N	79°30'W
Santa Rita do Sapucai, Braz. (sä-pô-ká'ē)	141a	22°15'S	45°41'W
Santa Rosa, Arg. (sän-tä-rô-sä)	144	36°45'S	64°10'W
Santa Rosa, Col. (sän-tä-rô-sä)	142a	6°38'N	75°26'W
Santa Rosa, Ec.	142	3°29'S	79°55'W
Santa Rosa, Guat. (sän'tä rō'sá)	132	14°21'N	90°16'W
Santa Rosa, Hond.	132	14°45'N	88°51'W
Santa Rosa, Ca., U.S. (săn'tá rō'zá)	104	38°27'N	122°42'W
Santa Rosa, N.M., U.S. (săn'tá rō'sá)	120	34°55'N	104°41'W
Santa Rosa, Ven. (sän-tä-rô-sä)	143b	9°37'N	64°10'W
Santa Rosa de Cabal, Col. (sän-tä-rô-sä-dĕ-kä-bä'l)	142a	4°53'N	75°38'W
Santa Rosa de Viterbo, Braz. (sän-tä-rô-sá-dĕ-vē-tĕr'-bô)	141a	21°30'S	47°21'W
Santa Rosa Indian Reservation, I.R., Ca., U.S. (săn'tá rō'zá')	118	33°28'N	116°50'W
Santa Rosalía, Mex. (sän'tä rô-zä'lê-á)	128	27°13'N	112°15'W
Santa Rosa Range, mts., Nv., U.S. (săn'tá rō'zá)	114	41°33'N	117°50'W
Santa Susana, Ca., U.S. (săn'tá sōō-zä'ná)	117a	34°16'N	118°42'W
Santa Teresa, Arg. (sän-tä-tĕ-rĕ'sä)	141c	33°27'S	60°47'W
Santa Teresa, Ven.	143b	10°14'N	66°40'W
Santa Uxia, Spain	172	42°34'N	8°55'W
Santa Vitória do Palmar, Braz. (sän-tä-vē-tō'ryä-dô-päl-már)	144	33°30'S	53°16'W
Santa Ynez, r., Ca., U.S. (săn'tá ē-nĕz')	118	34°40'N	120°20'W
Santa Ysabel Indian Reservation, I.R., Ca., U.S. (săn'tá ĭ-zá-bĕl')	118	33°05'N	116°46'W
Santee, Ca., U.S. (săn tē')	118a	32°50'N	116°58'W
Santee, r., S.C., U.S.	107	33°00'N	79°45'W
Sant' Eufemia, Golfo di, b., Italy (gôl-fô-dē-sän-tĕ'ŏ-fĕ'myä)	174	38°53'N	15°53'E
Sant Feliu de Guixols, Spain	173	41°45'N	3°01'E
Santiago, Braz. (sän-tyá'gô)	144	29°05'S	54°46'W
Santiago, Chile (sän-tē-ä'gô)	144	33°26'S	70°40'W
Santiago, Pan.	129	8°07'N	80°58'W
Santiago, Phil. (sän-tyä'gô)	213a	16°42'N	121°33'E
Santiago, prov., Chile (sän-tyá'gō)	141b	33°28'S	70°55'W
Santiago, i., Phil.	213a	16°29'N	120°03'E
Santiago de Compostela, Spain	162	42°52'N	8°32'W
Santiago de Cuba, Cuba (sän-tyá'gô-dā kōō'bá)	129	20°00'N	75°50'W
Santiago de Cuba, prov., Cuba	134	20°20'N	76°05'W
Santiago de las Vegas, Cuba (sän-tyá'gô-dĕ-läs-vĕ'gäs)	135a	22°58'N	82°23'W
Santiago del Estero, Arg.	144	27°50'S	64°14'W
Santiago del Estero, prov., Arg. (sän-tē-á'gō-dĕl ĕs-tä-rô)	144	27°15'S	63°30'W
Santiago de los Cabelleros, Dom. Rep.	129	19°30'N	70°45'W
Santiago Mountains, mts., Tx., U.S. (săn-tē-ä'gô)	106	30°00'N	103°30'W
Santiago Reservoir, res., Ca., U.S.	117a	33°47'N	117°42'W
Santiago Rodriguez, Dom. Rep. (sän-tyá'gô-rô-drē'gĕz)	135	19°30'N	71°25'W
Santiago Tuxtla, Mex. (sän-tyá'gô-tōō'x-tlä)	131	18°28'N	95°18'W
Santiaguillo, Laguna de, l., Mex. (lä-oō'nä-dĕ-sän-tē-a-gēl'yô)	122	24°51'N	104°43'W
Santisteban del Puerto, Spain (sän'tē stâ-bän'dĕl pwĕr'tô)	172	38°15'N	3°12'W
Sant Mateu, Spain	173	40°26'N	0°09'E
Santo Amaro, Braz. (sän'tô ä-mä'rô)	143	12°32'S	38°33'W
Santo Amaro de Campos, Braz.	141a	22°01'S	41°05'W
Santo André, Braz.	141a	23°40'S	46°31'W
Santo Angelo, Braz. (sän-tô-á'n-zhĕ-lô)	144	28°16'S	53°59'W
Santo Antônio do Monte, Braz. (sän-tô-än-tô'nyô-dô-môn'tĕ)	141a	20°06'S	45°18'W
Santo Domingo, Cuba (sän'tô-dōmĭŋ'gô)	134	22°35'N	80°20'W
Santo Domingo, Dom. Rep. (sän'tô-mĭn'gô)	129	18°30'N	69°55'W
Santo Domingo, Nic. (sän-tô-dô-mē'n-gō)	133	12°15'N	84°56'W
Santo Domingo de la Caizada, Spain (dā lä käl-thä'dä)	172	42°27'N	2°55'W
Santoña, Spain (sän-tō'nyä)	172	43°25'N	3°27'W
Santos, Braz. (sän'tozh)	143	23°58'S	46°20'W
Santos Dumont, Braz. (sän'tôs-dō-mô'nt)	143	21°28'S	43°33'W
Sanuki, Japan (sä'nōō-kê)	211a	35°16'N	139°53'E
San Urbano, Arg. (sän-ōr-bä'nô)	141c	33°39'S	61°28'W
San Valentin, Monte, mtn., Chile (sän-vä-lĕn-tē'n)	144	46°41'S	73°30'W
San Vicente, Arg. (sän-vē-sĕn'tĕ)	141c	35°00'S	58°26'W
San Vicente, Chile	141b	34°25'S	71°06'W
San Vicente, El Sal. (sän vê-sĕn'tå)	132	13°41'N	88°43'W
San Vicente de Alcántara, Spain	172	39°24'N	7°08'W
San Vito al Tagliamento, Italy (san vē'tô)	174	45°53'N	12°52'E
San Xavier Indian Reservation, I.R., Az., U.S. (x-ä'vīĕr)	119	32°07'N	111°12'W
San Ysidro, Ca., U.S. (săn ysĭ-drō')	118a	32°33'N	117°02'W
Sanyuanli, China (sän-yûän-lē)	207a	23°11'N	113°16'E
São Bernardo do Campo, Braz. (souN-bĕr-nár'dô-dô-kä'm-pô)	141a	23°44'S	46°33'W
São Borja, Braz. (souN-bôr-zhä)	144	28°44'S	55°59'W
São Carlos, Braz. (souN kär'lōzh)	143	22°02'S	47°54'W
São Cristovão, Braz. (souN-krēs-tō-vouN)	143	11°04'S	37°11'W
São Fidélis, Braz. (souN-fē-dĕ'lĕs)	141a	21°41'S	41°45'W
São Francisco, Braz. (souN frän-sēsh'kō)	143	15°59'S	44°42'W
São Francisco, r., Braz. (sän-frän-sĕ's-kō)	143	8°56'S	40°20'W
São Francisco do Sul, Braz. (souN frän-sēsh'kô-dô-sōō'l)	144	26°15'S	48°42'W
São Gabriel, Braz. (souN'gä-brē-ĕl')	144	30°28'S	54°11'W
São Geraldo, Braz. (souN-zhĕ-rä'l-dô)	141a	21°01'S	42°49'W
São Gonçalo, Braz. (souN'gōŋ-sä'lō)	141a	22°55'S	43°04'W
Sao Hill, Tan.	237	8°20'S	35°12'E
São João, Gui.-B.	234	11°32'N	15°26'W
São João da Barra, Braz. (souN-zhôun-dä-bà'rä)	141a	21°40'S	41°03'W
São João da Boa Vista, Braz. (souN-zhôun-dä-bôä-vē's-tä)	141a	21°58'S	46°45'W
São João del Reî, Braz. (souN zhô-ouN'dĕl-rā)	144	21°08'S	44°14'W
São João de Meriti, Braz. (souN-zhôun-dĕ-mĕ-rē-tē)	144b	22°47'S	43°22'W
São João do Araguaia, Braz. (souN zhô-ouN'dô-ä-rä-gwä'yä)	143	5°29'S	48°44'W
São João dos Lampas, Port. (souN' zhô-ouN' dōzh län-päzh')	173b	38°52'N	9°24'W
São João Nepomuceno, Braz. (souN-zhôun-nĕ-pô-mōō-sĕ-nō)	141a	21°33'S	43°00'W
São Jorge Island, i., Port. (souN zhôr'zhĕ)	230a	38°28'N	27°34'W
São José do Rio Pardo, Braz. (souN-zhô-sĕ'dô-rē'ō-pá'r-dō)	141a	21°36'S	46°50'W
São José do Rio Prêto, Braz. (souN zhô-zĕ'dô-re'ō-prĕ-tō)	143	20°57'S	49°12'W
São José dos Campos, Braz. (souN zhô-zā'dōzh käN pōzh')	141a	23°12'S	45°53'W
São Leopoldo, Braz. (souN-lĕ-ô-pôl'dô)	144	29°46'S	51°09'W
São Luis, Braz.	143	2°31'S	43°14'W
São Luis do Paraitinga, Braz. (souN-lōōē's-dô-pä-rä-ē-tē'n-gä)	141a	23°15'S	45°18'W
São Manuel, r., Braz.	143	8°28'S	57°07'E
São Mateus, Braz. (souN mä-tā'ōzh)	143	18°44'S	39°45'W
São Mateus, Braz.	144b	22°49'S	43°23'W
São Miguel Arcanjo, Braz. (souN-mē-gĕ'l-ár-kän-zhō)	141a	23°54'S	47°59'W
São Miguel Island, i., Port.	230a	37°59'N	26°38'W
Saona, i., Dom. Rep. (sä-ō'nä)	135	18°10'N	68°55'W
Saône, r., Fr. (sōn)	156	47°00'N	5°30'E
São Nicolau, i., C.V. (souN' nĕ-kô-louN')	230b	16°19'N	25°19'W
São Paulo, Braz. (souN' pou'lō)	143	23°34'S	46°38'W
São Paulo, state, Braz. (souN pou'lò)	143	21°45'S	50°47'W
São Paulo de Olivença, Braz. (souN'pou'lōdá ō-lê-vĕn'sá)	142	3°32'S	68°46'W
São Pedro, Braz. (souN-pĕ'drô)	141a	22°34'S	47°54'W
São Pedro de Aldeia, Braz. (souN-pĕ'drô-dĕ-äl-dĕ'yä)	141a	22°50'S	42°04'W
São Pedro e São Paulo, Rocedos, rocks, Braz.	139	1°50'N	30°00'W
São Raimundo Nonato, Braz. (souN' rī-mō'n-do nō-nä'tō)	143	9°09'S	42°32'W
São Roque, Braz. (souN' rō'kĕ)	141a	23°32'S	47°08'W
São Roque, Cabo de, c., Braz. (kä'bo-dĕ-souN' rō'kĕ)	143	5°06'S	35°11'W
São Sebastião, Braz. (souN sâ-bäs-tê-ouN')	141a	23°48'S	45°25'W
São Sebastião, Ilha de, i., Braz.	141a	23°52'S	45°22'W
São Sebastião do Paraíso, Braz.	141a	20°54'S	46°58'W
São Simão, Braz. (souN-sē-mouN)	141a	21°30'S	47°33'W
São Tiago, i., C.V. (souN tê-ä'gô)	230b	15°09'N	24°45'W
São Tomé, S. Tom./P.	230	0°20'N	6°44'E
Sao Tome and Principe, nation, Afr. (prēn'sē-pĕ)	230	1°00'N	6°00'E
Saoura, Oued, r., Alg.	230	29°39'N	1°42'W
São Vicente, Braz. (souN ve-se'n-tĕ)	143	23°57'S	46°25'W
São Vicente, i., C.V. (souN vê-sĕn'tå)	230b	16°51'N	24°35'W
São Vicente, Cabo de, c., Port. (ká'bō-dĕ-sän-vē-sĕ'n-tĕ)	156	37°03'N	9°31'W
Sapele, Nig. (sä-pā'lā)	230	5°54'N	5°41'E
Sapitwa, mtn., Mwi.	237	15°58'S	35°38'E

348 Sa Pobla – Segura PRONOUNCING INDEX

PLACE (Pronunciation)	PAGE	LAT.	LONG.
Sa Pobla, Spain	173	39°46'N	3°02'E
Sapozhok, Russia (sä-pô-zhôk')	176	53°58'N	40°44'E
Sapporo, Japan (säp-pô'rô)	205	43°02'N	141°29'E
Sapronovo, Russia (sȧp-rô'nô-vô)	186b	55°13'N	38°25'E
Sapucaí, r., Braz. (sä-pōō-kȧ-ē')	141a	22°20'S	45°53'W
Sapucaia, Braz. (sä-pōō-kä'yȧ)	141a	22°01'S	42°54'W
Sapucaí Mirim, r., Braz. (sä-pōō-kȧ-ē'mē-rēɴ)	141a	21°06'S	47°03'W
Sapulpa, Ok., U.S. (sȧ-pŭl'pȧ)	121	36°01'N	96°05'W
Saqqez, Iran	201	36°14'N	46°16'E
Saquarema, Braz. (sä-kwä-rĕ-mä)	141a	22°56'S	42°32'W
Sara, Wa., U.S. (sä'rä)	116c	45°45'N	122°42'W
Sara, Bahr, r., Chad (bär)	231	8°19'N	17°44'E
Sarajevo, Bos. (sä-rä-yĕv'ô) (sȧ-rä'ya-vô)	154	43°50'N	18°26'E
Sarakhs, Iran	201	36°32'N	61°11'E
Sarana, Russia (sá-rä'ná)	186a	56°31'N	57°44'E
Saranac Lake, N.Y., U.S.	109	44°20'N	74°05'W
Saranac Lake, I., N.Y., U.S. (săr'ȧ-năk)	109	44°15'N	74°20'W
Sarandi, Arg. (sä-rän'dê)	144a	34°41'S	58°21'W
Sarandi Grande, Ur. (sä-rän'dē-grän'dē)	141c	33°42'S	56°21'W
Saranley, Som.	238a	2°28'N	42°15'E
Saransk, Russia (sȧ-ränsk')	178	54°10'N	45°10'E
Sarany, Russia (sá-rá'nĭ)	186a	58°33'N	58°48'E
Sara Peak, mtn., Nig.	235	9°37'N	9°25'E
Sarapul, Russia (sä-räpôl')	180	56°28'N	53°50'E
Sarasota, Fl., U.S. (săr-ȧ-sōtȧ)	125a	27°27'N	82°30'W
Saratoga, Tx., U.S. (săr-ȧ-tō'gȧ)	123	30°17'N	94°31'W
Saratoga, Wa., U.S.	116a	48°04'N	122°29'W
Saratoga Pass, Wa., U.S.	116a	48°09'N	122°33'W
Saratoga Springs, N.Y., U.S. (sprĭngz)	109	43°05'N	74°50'W
Saratov, Russia (sȧ rä'tôf)	178	51°30'N	45°30'E
Saravane, Laos	209	15°48'N	106°40'E
Sarawak, hist. reg., Malay. (sȧ-rä'wäk)	212	2°30'N	112°45'E
Sárbogárd, Hung. (shär'bô-gärd)	169	46°53'N	18°38'E
Sarcee Indian Reserve, I.R., Can. (sär'sē)	102e	50°58'N	114°23'W
Sarcelles, Fr.	171b	49°00'N	2°23'E
Sardalas, Libya	230	25°59'N	10°33'E
Sardinia, i., Italy (sär-dĭn'ĭȧ)	156	40°08'N	9°05'E
Sardis, Ms., U.S. (sär'dĭs)	124	34°26'N	89°55'W
Sardis Lake, res., Ms., U.S.	124	34°27'N	89°43'W
Sargent, Ne., U.S. (sär'jĕnt)	112	41°40'N	99°38'W
Sarh, Chad (är-chaɴ-bô')	231	9°09'N	18°23'E
Sarikamis, Tur.	181	40°30'N	42°40'E
Sariñena, Spain (sä-rēn-yĕ'nä)	173	41°46'N	0°11'W
Sark, i., Guern. (särk)	170	49°28'N	2°22'W
Şarköy, Tur. (shär'kû-ē)	175	40°39'N	27°07'E
Sarmiento, Monte, mtn., Chile (mô'n-tĕ-sär-myĕn'tō)	144	54°28'S	70°40'W
Sarnia, Can. (sär'nē-ȧ)	91	43°00'N	82°25'W
Sarno, Italy (sä'r-nô)	173c	40°35'N	14°38'E
Sarny, Ukr. (sär'nê)	181	51°17'N	26°39'E
Saronikós Kólpos, b., Grc.	175	37°51'N	23°30'E
Saros Körfezi, b., Tur. (sä'rôs)	175	40°30'N	26°20'E
Sárospatak, Hung. (shä'rôsh-pô'tôk)	169	48°19'N	21°35'E
Šar Planina, mts., Serb. (shär plä'nê-na)	175	42°07'N	21°54'E
Sarpsborg, Nor. (särps'bôrg)	166	59°17'N	11°07'E
Sarrebourg, Fr. (sär-bōōr')	171	48°44'N	7°02'E
Sarreguemines, Fr. (sär-gē-mēn')	161	49°06'N	7°05'E
Sarria, Spain (sär'ê-ä)	162	42°14'N	7°17'W
Sarstun, r., N.A. (särs-tōō'n)	132	15°50'N	89°26'W
Sartène, Fr. (sär-tĕn')	174	41°36'N	8°59'E
Sarthe, r., Fr. (särt)	161	47°44'N	0°32'W
Şarur, Azer.	182	39°33'N	44°58'E
Sárvár, Hung. (shär'vär)	168	47°14'N	16°55'E
Sarych, Mys, c., Ukr. (mĭs sä-rēch')	181	44°25'N	33°00'E
Saryesik-Atyraū, des., Kaz.	183	45°30'N	76°00'E
Sary-Ishikotrau, Peski, des., Kyrg. (sä'rē ē' shĕk-ō'trou)	183	46°12'N	75°30'E
Sarysū, r., Kaz. (sä'rē-sōō)	183	47°47'N	69°14'E
Sasarām, India (sŭs-ŭ-räm')	199	25°00'N	84°00'E
Sasayama, Japan (sä'sä-yä'mä)	211	35°05'N	135°14'E
Sasebo, Japan (sä'sȧ-bô)	205	33°12'N	129°43'E
Saskatchewan, prov., Can.	90	54°46'N	107°40'W
Saskatchewan, r., Can. (săs-kăch'ê-wän)	92	53°45'N	103°20'W
Saskatoon, Can. (săs-kȧ-tōōn')	90	52°07'N	106°38'W
Sasolburg, S. Afr.	238c	26°52'S	27°47'E
Sasovo, Russia (sȧs'ô-vô)	180	54°20'N	42°00'E
Saspamco, Tx., U.S. (săs-păm'cō)	117d	29°13'N	98°18'W
Sassandra, C. Iv.	234	4°58'N	6°05'W
Sassandra, r., C. Iv. (sȧs-sän'drȧ)	230	5°35'N	6°25'W
Sassari, Italy (säs'sä-rê)	162	40°44'N	8°33'E
Sassnitz, Ger. (säs'nēts)	168	54°31'N	13°37'E
Satadougou, Mali (sä-tȧ-dōō-gōō')	234	12°21'N	12°07'W
Säter, Swe. (sĕ'tĕr)	166	60°21'N	15°50'E
Satilla, r., Ga., U.S. (sȧ-tĭl'ȧ)	125	31°15'N	82°13'W
Satka, Russia (sät'kȧ)	180	55°03'N	59°02'E
Sátoraljaujhely, Hung. (shä'tô-rô-lyô-ōō'yĕl')	169	48°24'N	21°40'E
Satu Mare, Rom. (sá'tōō-má'rĕ)	163	47°50'N	22°53'E
Saturna, Can. (sȧ-tûr'nȧ)	116d	48°48'N	123°12'W
Saturna, i., Can.	116d	48°47'N	123°03'W
Sauda, Nor.	160	59°40'N	6°21'E
Saudárkrókur, Ice.	154	65°41'N	19°38'W
Saudi Arabia, nation, Asia (sȧ-ŏ'dĭ ȧ-rä'bĭ-ȧ)	198	22°40'N	46°00'E
Sauerlach, Ger. (zou'ĕr-läκ)	159d	47°58'N	11°39'E
Saugatuck, Mi., U.S. (sô'gȧ-tŭk)	108	42°40'N	86°10'W
Saugeen, r., Can.	98	44°20'N	81°20'W
Saugerties, N.Y., U.S. (sô'gēr-tēz)	109	42°05'N	73°55'W
Saugus, Ma., U.S. (sô'gŭs)	101a	42°28'N	71°01'W
Sauk, r., Mn., U.S. (sôk)	113	45°30'N	94°45'W
Sauk Centre, Mn., U.S.	113	45°43'N	94°58'W
Sauk City, Wi., U.S.	113	43°16'N	89°45'W
Sauk Rapids, Mn., U.S. (răp'ĭd)	113	45°35'N	94°08'W
Sault Sainte Marie, Can.	91	46°31'N	84°20'W
Sault Sainte Marie, Mi., U.S. (sōō sānt mȧ-rē')	105	46°29'N	84°21'W
Saumatre, Étang, I., Haiti	135	18°40'N	72°10'W
Saunders Lake, I., Can. (sän'dĕrs)	102g	53°18'N	113°25'W
Saurimo, Ang.	232	9°39'S	20°24'E
Sausalito, Ca., U.S. (sô-sȧ-lē'tô)	116b	37°51'N	122°29'W
Sausset-les-Pins, Fr. (sō-sĕ'lā-pàɴ')	170a	43°20'N	5°08'E
Saútar, Ang.	236	11°06'S	18°27'E
Sauvie Island, i., Or., U.S. (sô'vē)	116c	45°43'N	123°49'W
Sava, r., Serb. (sä'vä)	156	44°50'N	18°30'E
Savage, Md., U.S. (săv'ĕj)	110e	39°07'N	76°49'W
Savage, Mn., U.S.	117g	44°47'N	93°20'W
Savai'i, i., Samoa	214a	13°35'S	172°25'W
Savalen, I., Nor.	166	62°19'N	10°15'E
Savalou, Benin	230	7°56'N	1°58'E
Savanna, Il., U.S. (sȧ-văn'ȧ)	113	42°05'N	90°09'W
Savannah, Ga., U.S. (sȧ-văn'ȧ)	105	32°04'N	81°07'W
Savannah, Mo., U.S.	121	39°58'N	94°49'W
Savannah, Tn., U.S.	124	35°13'N	88°14'W
Savannah, r., U.S.	107	33°11'N	81°51'W
Savannakhét, Laos	212	16°33'N	104°45'E
Savanna la Mar, Jam. (sȧ-vän'ȧ lȧ mär')	134	18°10'N	78°10'W
Save, r., Fr.	170	43°32'N	0°50'E
Save, Rio (Sabi), r., Afr. (rē'ō-sä'vĕ)	232	21°28'S	34°14'E
Sāveh, Iran	201	35°01'N	50°20'E
Saverne, Fr. (sȧ-vĕrn')	171	48°40'N	7°22'E
Savigliano, Italy (sä-vēl-yä'nô)	174	44°38'N	7°42'E
Savigny-sur-Orge, Fr.	171b	48°41'N	2°22'E
Savona, Italy (sä-nō'nä)	162	44°19'N	8°28'E
Savonlinna, Fin. (sá'vôn-lēn'nȧ)	167	61°53'N	28°49'E
Savran', Ukr. (säv-rän')	177	48°07'N	30°09'E
Sawahlunto, Indon.	212	0°37'S	100°50'E
Sawākin, Sudan	231	19°02'N	37°19'E
Sawda, Jabal as, mts., Libya	231	28°14'N	13°46'E
Sawhāj, Egypt	231	26°34'N	31°40'E
Sawknah, Libya	231	29°04'N	15°53'E
Sawu, Laut (Savu Sea), sea, Asia	212	9°15'S	122°15'E
Sawyer, I., Wa., U.S. (sô'yēr)	116a	47°20'N	122°02'W
Saxony *see* Sachsen, hist. reg., Ger.	168	50°45'N	12°17'E
Say, Niger (sä'ê)	230	13°09'N	2°16'E
Sayan Khrebet, mts., Russia (sŭ-yän')	179	51°30'N	90°00'E
Sayhūt, Yemen	198	15°23'N	51°28'E
Sayre, Ok., U.S. (sā'ēr)	120	35°19'N	99°40'W
Sayre, Pa., U.S.	109	41°55'N	76°30'W
Sayreton, Al., U.S. (sā'ēr-tŭn)	110h	33°34'N	86°51'W
Sayreville, N.J., U.S. (sâr'vĭl)	110a	40°28'N	74°21'W
Sayr Usa, Mong.	204	44°15'N	107°00'E
Sayula, Mex. (sä-yōō'lä)	131	17°51'N	94°56'W
Sayula, Mex.	130	19°50'N	103°33'W
Sayula, Luguna de, I., Mex. (lä-gô'nä-dē)	130	20°00'N	103°33'W
Say'un, Yemen	198	16°00'N	48°59'E
Sayville, N.Y., U.S. (sā'vĭl)	109	40°45'N	73°10'W
Sazanit, i., Alb.	163	40°30'N	19°17'E
Sázava, r., Czech Rep.	168	49°36'N	15°24'E
Sazhino, Russia (sȧz-hē'nô)	186a	56°20'N	58°15'E
Scandinavian Peninsula, pen., Eur.	196	62°00'N	14°00'E
Scanlon, Mn., U.S. (skăn'lôn)	117h	46°27'N	92°26'W
Scappoose, Or., U.S. (skă-pōōs')	116c	45°46'N	122°53'W
Scappoose, r., Or., U.S.	116c	45°47'N	122°57'W
Scarborough, Eng., U.K. (skär'bŭr-ô)	164	54°16'N	0°19'W
Scarsdale, N.Y., U.S. (skärz'dāl)	110a	41°01'N	73°47'W
Scatari I, Can. (skăt'ȧ-rē)	101	46°00'N	59°44'W
Schaerbeek, Bel. (skär'bāk)	159a	50°50'N	4°23'E
Schaffhausen, Switz. (shäf'hou-zĕn)	161	47°42'N	8°38'E
Schefferville, Can.	91	54°52'N	67°01'W
Schelde,, r., Eur.	165	51°04'N	3°55'E
Schenectady, N.Y., U.S. (skĕ-nĕk'tȧ-dê)	105	42°50'N	73°55'W
Scheveningen, Neth.	159a	52°06'N	4°15'E
Schiedam, Neth.	159a	51°55'N	4°23'E
Schiltigheim, Fr. (shēl'tegh-hīm)	171	48°48'N	7°47'E
Schio, Italy (skē'ô)	174	45°43'N	11°23'E
Schleswig, Ger. (shĕls'vēgh)	160	54°32'N	9°32'E
Schleswig , hist. reg., Ger. (shĕls'vēgh)	168	54°40'N	9°10'E
Schleswig-Holstein, state, Ger. (shlĕs'vēgh-hōl'shtīn)	159c	53°40'N	9°45'E
Schmalkalden, Ger. (shmäl'käl-dĕn)	168	50°41'N	10°25'E
Schneider, In., U.S. (schnīd'ēr)	111a	41°12'N	87°26'W
Schofield, Wi., U.S. (skō'fēld)	113	44°52'N	89°37'W
Schönebeck, Ger. (shû'nĕ-bergh)	168	52°01'N	11°44'E
Schoonhoven, Neth.	159a	51°56'N	4°51'E
Schramberg, Ger. (shräm'bĕrgh)	168	48°14'N	8°24'E
Schreiber, Can.	98	48°50'N	87°10'W
Schroon, I., N.Y., U.S. (skrōōn)	109	43°50'N	73°50'W
Schultzendorf, Ger. (shōōl'tzĕn-dōrf)	159b	52°21'N	13°55'E
Schumacher, Can.	98	48°30'N	81°30'W
Schuyler, Ne., U.S. (slī'ler)	112	41°28'N	97°05'W
Schuylkill, r., Pa., U.S. (skōōl'kĭl)	110f	40°10'N	75°31'W
Schuylkill-Haven, Pa., U.S. (skōōl'kĭl hā-vĕn)	109	40°35'N	76°10'W
Schwabach, Ger. (shvä'bäk)	168	49°19'N	11°02'E
Schwäbische Alb, mts., Ger. (shvă'bē-shĕ älb)	168	48°11'N	9°09'E
Schwäbisch Gmünd, Ger. (shvă'bēsh gmünd)	168	48°47'N	9°49'E
Schwäbisch Hall, Ger. (häl)	168	49°08'N	9°44'E
Schwandorf, Ger. (shvän'dôrf)	168	49°19'N	12°08'E
Schwaner, Pegunungan, mts., Indon. (sκvän'ēr)	212	1°05'S	112°30'E
Schwarzwald, for., Ger. (shvärts'väld)	168	47°54'N	7°57'E
Schwaz, Aus.	168	47°20'N	11°45'E
Schwechat, Aus. (shvĕk'ät)	168	48°09'N	16°29'E
Schwedt, Ger. (shvĕt)	168	53°04'N	14°17'E
Schweinfurt, Ger. (shvīn'fōrt)	168	50°03'N	10°14'E
Schwelm, Ger. (shvĕlm)	171c	51°17'N	7°18'E
Schwerin, Ger. (shvĕ-rēn')	168	53°36'N	11°25'E
Schweriner See, I., Ger. (shvĕ'rē-nĕr zā)	168	53°40'N	11°06'E
Schwerte, Ger. (shvĕr'tĕ)	171c	51°26'N	7°34'E
Schwielowsee, I., Ger. (shvē'lōv zā)	159b	52°20'N	12°52'E
Schwyz, Switz. (schēts)	168	47°01'N	8°38'E
Sciacca, Italy (shê-äk'kä)	174	37°30'N	13°09'E
Scilly, Isles of, is., Eng., U.K. (sĭl'ê)	156	49°56'N	6°50'W
Scioto, r., Oh., U.S. (sī-ō'tō)	107	39°10'N	82°55'W
Scituate, Ma., U.S. (sĭt'ŭ-āt)	101a	42°12'N	70°45'W
Scobey, Mt., U.S. (skō'bê)	115	48°48'N	105°29'W
Scoggin, Or., U.S. (skŏ'gĭn)	116c	45°28'N	123°14'W
Scotch, r., Can. (skŏch)	102c	45°21'N	74°56'W
Scotia, Ca., U.S. (skō'shȧ)	114	40°29'N	124°06'W
Scotland, S.D., U.S.	112	43°08'N	97°43'W
Scotland, state, U.K. (skŏt'lȧnd)	154	57°05'N	5°10'W
Scotland Neck, N.C., U.S. (nĕk)	125	36°06'N	77°25'W
Scotstown, Can. (skŏts'toun)	109	45°35'N	71°15'W
Scott, r., Ca., U.S.	114	41°20'N	122°55'W
Scott, Cape, c., Can. (skŏt)	92	50°47'N	128°26'W
Scott, Mount, mtn., Or., U.S.	116c	45°27'N	122°33'W
Scott, Mount, mtn., Or., U.S.	114	42°55'N	122°00'W
Scott Air Force Base, Il., U.S.	117e	38°33'N	89°52'W
Scottburgh, S. Afr. (skŏt'bŭr-ô)	232	30°18'S	30°42'E
Scott City, Ks., U.S.	120	38°28'N	100°54'W
Scottdale, Ga., U.S. (skŏt'dāl)	110c	33°47'N	84°16'W
Scott Islands, is., Ant.	224	67°00'S	178°00'E
Scottsbluff, Ne., U.S. (skŏts'blŭf)	112	41°52'N	103°40'W
Scottsboro, Al., U.S. (skŏts'bŭro)	124	34°40'N	86°03'W
Scottsburg, In., U.S. (skŏts'bûrg)	108	38°40'N	85°50'W
Scottsdale, Austl. (skŏts'dāl)	222	41°12'S	147°37'E
Scottsville, Ky., U.S. (skŏts'vĭl)	124	36°45'N	86°10'W
Scottville, Mi., U.S.	108	44°00'N	86°20'W
Scranton, Pa., U.S. (skrăn'tŭn)	105	41°15'N	75°45'W
Scugog, I., Can. (skū'gôg)	99	44°05'N	78°55'W
Scunthorpe, Eng., U.K. (skŭn'thôrp)	158a	53°36'N	0°38'W
Scutari *see* Shkodër, Alb.	154	42°04'N	19°30'E
Scutari, Lake, I., Eur. (skōō'tä-rē)	163	42°14'N	19°33'E
Seabeck, Wa., U.S. (sē'bĕck)	116a	47°38'N	122°50'W
Sea Bright, N.J., U.S. (sē brīt)	110a	40°22'N	73°58'W
Seabrook, Tx., U.S. (sē'brŏk)	123	29°34'N	95°01'W
Seaford, De., U.S. (sē'fērd)	109	38°35'N	75°40'W
Seagraves, Tx., U.S. (sē'grāvs)	120	32°51'N	102°38'W
Sea Islands, is., Ga., U.S. (sē)	125	31°21'N	81°05'W
Seal, r., Can.	92	59°08'N	96°37'W
Seal Beach, Ca., U.S.	117a	33°44'N	118°06'W
Seal Cays, is., Bah.	135	22°40'N	75°55'W
Seal Cays, is., T./C. Is.	135	21°10'N	71°45'W
Seal Island, i., S. Afr. (sēl)	232a	34°07'S	18°36'E
Sealy, Tx., U.S. (sē'lê)	123	29°46'N	96°10'W
Searcy, Ar., U.S. (sûr'sê)	121	35°13'N	91°43'W
Searles, I., Ca., U.S. (sûrl's)	118	35°44'N	117°22'W
Searsport, Me., U.S. (sērz'pōrt)	100	44°28'N	68°55'W
Seaside, Or., U.S. (sē'sīd)	114	45°59'N	123°55'W
Seattle, Wa., U.S. (sē-ăt''l)	104	47°36'N	122°20'W
Sebaco, Nic. (sĕ-bä'kô)	132	12°50'N	86°03'W
Sebago, Me., U.S. (sē-bā'gō)	100	43°52'N	70°20'W
Sebastián Vizcaíno, Bahía, b., Mex.	128	28°45'N	115°15'W
Sebastopol, Ca., U.S. (sê-bȧs'tô-pôl)	118	38°27'N	122°50'W
Sebderat, Erit.	231	15°30'N	36°45'E
Sebewaing, Mi., U.S. (se'bê-wăng)	108	43°45'N	83°25'W
Sebezh, Russia (syĕ'bĕzh)	176	56°16'N	28°29'E
Sebinkarahisar, Tur.	163	40°15'N	38°10'E
Sebnitz, Ger. (zĕb'nēts)	168	51°01'N	14°16'E
Sebou, Oued, r., Mor.	230	34°23'N	5°18'W
Sebree, Ky., U.S. (sē-brē')	108	37°35'N	87°30'W
Sebring, Fl., U.S. (sē'brĭng)	125a	27°30'N	81°26'W
Sebring, Oh., U.S.	108	40°55'N	81°05'W
Secchia, r., Italy (sĕ'kyä)	174	44°25'N	10°25'E
Seco, r., Mex. (sĕ'kô)	131	18°11'N	93°18'W
Sedalia, Mo., U.S.	105	38°42'N	93°12'W
Sedan, Fr. (sē-däɴ)	161	49°49'N	4°55'E
Sedan, Ks., U.S. (sê-dăn')	121	37°07'N	96°08'W
Sedom, Isr.	197a	31°04'N	35°24'E
Sedro Woolley, Wa., U.S. (sē'drô-wŏŏl'ê)	116a	48°30'N	122°14'W
Šeduva, Lith. (shĕ'dŏ-vȧ)	167	55°46'N	23°45'E
Seestall, Ger. (zā'shtäl)	159d	47°58'N	10°52'E
Sefrou, Mor. (sē-frōō')	162	33°49'N	4°46'W
Seg, I., Russia (syĕgh)	180	63°20'N	33°30'E
Segamat, Malay. (sā'gȧ-mȧt)	197b	2°30'N	102°49'E
Segang, China (sŭ-găŋ)	206	31°59'N	114°13'E
Segbana, Benin	235	10°56'N	3°42'E
Segorbe, Spain (sĕ-gôr-bĕ)	173	39°50'N	0°30'W
Ségou, Mali (sā-gōō)	230	13°27'N	6°16'W
Segovia, Col. (sĕ-gô'vēä)	142a	7°08'N	74°42'W
Segovia, Spain (sā-gō'vē-ä)	162	40°58'N	4°05'W
Segre, r., Spain (sā'grä)	173	41°54'N	1°10'E
Seguam, i., Ak., U.S. (sē'gwäm)	103a	52°16'N	172°10'W
Seguam Passage, strt., Ak., U.S.	103a	52°20'N	173°00'W
Séguédine, Niger	235	20°12'N	12°59'E
Séguéla, C. Iv. (sā-gā-lä')	230	7°57'N	6°40'W
Seguin, Tx., U.S. (sĕ-gēn')	123	29°35'N	97°58'W
Segula, i., Ak., U.S. (sē-gū'lä)	103a	52°08'N	178°35'E
Segura, r., Spain	162	38°24'N	2°12'W

ăt; finȧl; rāte; senȧte; ärm; ȧsk; sofȧ; fâre; ch-choose; dh-as th in other; bē; ėvent; bĕt; recĕnt; cratēr; g-gō; gh-guttural g; bĭt; ĭ-short neutral; rīde; κ-guttural k as ch in German ich;

ng-sing; ŋ-baŋk; ɴ-nasalized n; nŏd; cŏmmit; ōld; ōbey; ôrder; oi-boil; fōōd; ò-as oo in foot; ou-out; s-soft; sh-dish; th-thin; pūre; ûnite; ûrn; stŭd; circŭs; ü-as in French tu; ´-indeterminate vowel.

350 Shelagskiy – Silverdale PRONOUNCING INDEX

PLACE (Pronunciation)	PAGE	LAT.	LONG.
Shelagskiy, Mys, c., Russia (shĭ-läg'skē)	179	70°08'N	170°52'E
Shelbina, Ar., U.S. (shěl-bī'nȧ)	121	39°41'N	92°03'W
Shelburn, In., U.S. (shěl'bŭrn)	108	39°10'N	87°30'W
Shelburne, Can.	91	43°46'N	65°19'W
Shelburne, Can.	99	44°04'N	80°12'W
Shelby, In., U.S. (shěl'bė)	111a	41°12'N	87°21'W
Shelby, Mi., U.S.	108	43°35'N	86°20'W
Shelby, Ms., U.S.	124	33°56'N	90°44'W
Shelby, Mt., U.S.	115	48°35'N	111°55'W
Shelby, N.C., U.S.	125	35°16'N	81°35'W
Shelby, Oh., U.S.	108	40°50'N	82°40'W
Shelbyville, Il., U.S. (shěl'bė-vĭl)	108	39°20'N	88°45'W
Shelbyville, In., U.S.	108	39°30'N	85°45'W
Shelbyville, Ky., U.S.	108	38°10'N	85°15'W
Shelbyville, Tn., U.S.	124	35°30'N	86°28'W
Shelbyville Reservoir, res., Il., U.S.	108	39°30'N	88°45'W
Sheldon, Ia., U.S. (shěl'dŭn)	112	43°10'N	95°50'W
Sheldon, Tx., U.S.	123a	29°52'N	95°07'W
Shelekhova, Zaliv, b., Russia	179	60°00'N	156°00'E
Shelikof Strait, strt., Ak., U.S. (shě'lē-kôf)	103	57°56'N	154°20'W
Shellbrook, Can.	96	53°15'N	106°22'W
Shelley, Id., U.S. (shěl'lė)	115	43°24'N	112°06'W
Shellrock, r., Ia., U.S. (shěl'rŏk)	113	43°25'N	93°19'W
Shelon', r., Russia (shå'lôn)	176	57°50'N	29°40'E
Shelton, Ct., U.S. (shěl'tŭn)	109	41°15'N	73°05'W
Shelton, Ne., U.S.	120	40°46'N	98°41'W
Shelton, Wa., U.S.	114	47°14'N	123°05'W
Shemakha, Russia (shě-mȧ-kä')	186a	56°16'N	59°19'E
Shenandoah, Ia., U.S. (shěn-ăn-dō'ȧ)	121	40°46'N	95°23'W
Shenandoah, Va., U.S.	109	38°30'N	78°30'W
Shenandoah, r., Va., U.S.	109	38°55'N	78°05'W
Shenandoah National Park, rec., Va., U.S.	107	38°35'N	78°25'W
Shendam, Nig.	235	8°53'N	9°32'E
Shengfang, China (shengfäng)	206	39°05'N	116°40'E
Shenkursk, Russia (shěn-kōōrsk')	178	62°10'N	43°08'E
Shenmu, China	208	38°55'N	110°35'E
Shenqiu, China	208	33°11'N	115°06'E
Shenxian, China (shŭn shyän)	208	38°02'N	115°33'E
Shenxian, China (shŭn shyĕn)	206	36°14'N	115°38'E
Shenyang, China (shŭn-yäŋ)	205	41°45'N	123°22'E
Shenze, China (shŭn-dzŭ)	206	38°12'N	115°12'E
Shenzhen, China	209	22°32'N	114°08'E
Sheopur, India	199	25°37'N	77°10'E
Shepard, Can. (shě'pärd)	102e	50°57'N	113°55'W
Shepetivka, Ukr.	181	50°10'N	27°01'E
Shepparton, Austl. (shěp'ár-tŭn)	222	36°15'S	145°25'E
Sherborn, Ma., U.S. (shûr'bŭrn)	101a	42°15'N	71°22'W
Sherbrooke, Can.	91	45°24'N	71°54'W
Sherburn, Eng., U.K. (shûr'bŭrn)	158a	53°47'N	1°15'W
Shereshevo, Bela. (shě-rě-shě-vô)	169	52°31'N	24°08'E
Sheridan, Ar., U.S. (shěr'ĭ-dăn)	121	34°19'N	92°21'W
Sheridan, Or., U.S.	114	45°06'N	123°22'W
Sheridan, Wy., U.S.	104	44°48'N	106°56'W
Sherman, Tx., U.S. (shěr'măn)	104	33°39'N	96°37'W
Sherna, r., Russia (shěr'nȧ)	186b	56°08'N	38°45'E
Sherridon, Can.	97	55°10'N	101°10'W
's Hertogenbosch, Neth. (sěr-tō'ghěn-bôs)	165	51°41'N	5°19'E
Sherwood, Or., U.S.	116c	45°21'N	122°50'W
Sherwood Forest, for., Eng., U.K.	158a	53°11'N	1°07'W
Sherwood Park, Can.	95	53°31'N	113°19'W
Shetland Islands, is., Scot., U.K. (shět'lănd)	156	60°35'N	2°10'W
Shewa Gimira, Eth.	231	7°13'N	35°49'E
Shexian, China (shŭ shyĕn)	206	36°34'N	113°42'E
Sheyang, r., China (she-yäŋ)	206	33°42'N	119°40'E
Sheyenne, r., N.D., U.S. (shī-ĕn')	112	46°42'N	97°52'W
Shi, r., China (shr)	206	31°58'N	115°50'E
Shi, r., China	206	32°09'N	114°11'E
Shiawassee, r., Mi., U.S. (shī-ȧ-wôs'ē)	108	43°15'N	84°05'W
Shibām, Yemen (shē'bäm)	198	16°02'N	48°40'E
Shibīn al Kawn, Egypt (shē-bēn'ĕl kōm')	238b	30°31'N	31°01'E
Shibīn al Qanāṭir, Egypt (kȧ-nä'tēr)	238b	30°18'N	31°21'E
Shicun, China (shr-tsôn)	206	33°47'N	117°18'E
Shields, r., Mt., U.S. (shēldz)	115	45°54'N	110°40'W
Shifnal, Eng., U.K. (shĭf'năl)	158a	52°40'N	2°22'W
Shijian, China (shr-jyĕn)	206	31°27'N	117°51'E
Shijiazhuang, China (shr-jyä-jůäŋ)	205	38°04'N	114°31'E
Shijiu Hu, l., China (shr-jyō hōō)	206	31°29'N	119°07'E
Shikārpur, Pak.	199	27°51'N	68°52'E
Shiki, Japan (shē'kė)	211a	35°50'N	139°35'E
Shikoku, i., Japan (shē'kō'kōō)	205	33°43'N	133°33'E
Shilka, r., Russia (shĭl'kȧ)	185	53°00'N	118°45'E
Shilla, mtn., India	202	32°18'N	78°17'E
Shillong, India (shėl-lông')	199	25°39'N	91°58'E
Shiloh, Il., U.S. (shī'lō)	117e	38°34'N	89°54'W
Shilong, China (shr-lôŋ)	209	23°05'N	113°58'E
Shilou, China	207a	22°58'N	113°29'E
Shimabara, Japan (shē'mä-bä'rä)	211	32°46'N	130°22'E
Shimada, Japan (shē'mä-dä)	211	34°49'N	138°13'E
Shimbiris, mtn., Som.	238a	10°40'N	47°23'E
Shimizu, Japan (shē'mē-zōō)	210	35°00'N	138°29'E
Shimminato, Japan (shĕm'mē'nä-tō)	211	36°47'N	137°05'E
Shimoda, Japan (shē'mô-dȧ)	211	34°41'N	138°58'E
Shimoga, India	203	13°59'N	75°38'E
Shimoni, Kenya	237	4°39'S	39°23'E
Shimonoseki, Japan	205	33°58'N	130°55'E
Shimo-Saga, Japan (shē'mō sä'gä)	211b	35°01'N	135°41'E
Shin, Loch, l., Scot., U.K. (lŏĸ shĭn)	164	58°08'N	4°02'W

PLACE (Pronunciation)	PAGE	LAT.	LONG.
Shinagawa-Wan, b., Japan (shē'nä-gä'wä wän)	211a	35°37'N	139°49'E
Shinano-Gawa, r., Japan (shė-nä'nô gä'wä)	211	36°43'N	138°22'E
Shīndand, Afg.	201	33°18'N	62°08'E
Shinji, l., Japan (shĭn'jė)	211	35°23'N	133°05'E
Shinkolobwe, D.R.C.	237	11°02'S	26°35'E
Shinyanga, Tan. (shĭn-yäŋ'gä)	232	3°40'S	33°26'E
Shiono Misaki, c., Japan (shė-ō'nō mē'sä-kė)	210	33°20'N	136°10'E
Shipai, China (shr-pī)	207a	23°07'N	113°23'E
Ship Channel Cay, i., Bah. (shĭp chă-nĕl kē)	134	24°50'N	76°50'W
Shipley, Eng., U.K. (shĭp'lė)	158a	53°50'N	1°47'W
Shippegan, Can. (shĭ'pē-găn)	100	47°45'N	64°42'W
Shippegan Island, i., Can.	100	47°50'N	64°38'W
Shippenburg, Pa., U.S. (shĭp'ĕn bûrg)	109	40°00'N	77°30'W
Shipshaw, r., Can. (shĭp'shô)	99	48°50'N	71°03'W
Shiqma, r., Isr.	197a	31°31'N	34°40'E
Shirane-san, mtn., Japan (shē'rä'nȧ-sän')	211	35°44'N	138°14'E
Shirati, Tan. (shė-rä'tē)	232	1°15'S	34°02'E
Shīrāz, Iran (shē-räz')	198	29°32'N	52°27'E
Shire, r., Afr. (shē'rȧ)	232	15°00'S	35°00'E
Shiriya Saki, c., Japan (shē'rä sä'kė)	210	41°25'N	142°10'E
Shirley, Ma., U.S. (shûr'lė)	101a	42°33'N	71°39'W
Shishaldin Volcano, vol., Ak., U.S. (shī-shăl'dĭn)	103a	54°48'N	164°00'W
Shively, Ky., U.S. (shīv'lė)	111h	38°11'N	85°47'W
Shivpuri, India	199	25°31'N	77°46'E
Shivta, Horvot, hist., Isr.	197a	30°54'N	34°36'E
Shivwits Plateau, plat., Az., U.S.	119	36°13'N	113°42'W
Shiwan, China (shr-wän)	207a	23°01'N	113°04'E
Shiwan Dashan, mts., China (shr-wän dä-shän)	209	22°10'N	107°30'E
Shizuki, Japan (shĭ'zōō-kė)	211	34°29'N	134°51'E
Shizuoka, Japan (shē'zōō'ōkȧ)	210	34°58'N	138°24'E
Shklow, Bela.	176	54°11'N	30°23'E
Shkodër, Alb. (shkô'dûr) (skōō'tárē)	154	42°04'N	19°30'E
Shkotovo, Russia (shkô'tô-vô)	210	43°15'N	132°21'E
Shoal Creek, r., Il., U.S. (shōl)	121	38°37'N	89°25'W
Shoal Lake, l., Can.	97	49°32'N	95°00'W
Shoals, In., U.S. (shōlz)	108	38°40'N	86°45'W
Shōdo, i., Japan (shō'dō)	211	34°27'N	134°27'E
Sholāpur, India (shō'lä-pōōr)	199	17°42'N	75°51'E
Shorewood, Wi., U.S. (shōr'wŏŏd)	111a	43°05'N	87°54'W
Shoshone, Id., U.S. (shȯ-shōn'tė)	115	42°56'N	114°24'W
Shoshone, r., Wy., U.S.	115	44°35'N	108°50'W
Shoshone Lake, l., Wy., U.S.	115	44°17'N	110°50'W
Shoshoni, Wy., U.S.	115	43°14'N	108°05'W
Shostka, Ukr. (shôst'kȧ)	177	51°51'N	33°31'E
Shouguang, China (shō-gůän)	206	36°53'N	118°45'E
Shouxian, China (shō shyĕn)	206	32°36'N	116°45'E
Shpola, Ukr. (shpô'lȧ)	181	49°01'N	31°36'E
Shreveport, La., U.S. (shrēv'pôrt)	105	32°30'N	93°46'W
Shrewsbury, Eng., U.K. (shrōōz'bēr-ĭ)	164	52°43'N	2°44'W
Shrewsbury, Ma., U.S.	101a	42°18'N	71°43'W
Shropshire, co., Eng., U.K.	158a	52°36'N	2°45'W
Shroud Cay, i., Bah.	134	24°20'N	76°40'W
Shuangcheng, China (shůäŋ-chŭŋ)	208	45°18'N	126°18'E
Shuanghe, China (shůäŋ-hŭ)	206	31°33'N	116°48'E
Shuangliao, China	205	43°37'N	123°30'E
Shuangyang, China	208	43°28'N	125°45'E
Shuhedun, China (shōō-hŭ-dòn)	206	31°33'N	117°01'E
Shuiye, China (shwā-yŭ)	206	36°08'N	114°07'E
Shule, r., China (shōō-lŭ)	204	40°53'N	94°55'E
Shullsburg, Wi., U.S. (shŭlz'bûrg)	113	42°35'N	90°16'W
Shumagin, is., Ak., U.S. (shōō'mȧ-gĕn)	103	55°22'N	159°20'W
Shumen, Blg.	163	43°15'N	26°54'E
Shunde, China (shòn-dŭ)	207a	22°50'N	113°15'E
Shungnak, Ak., U.S. (shŭng'nák)	103	66°55'N	157°20'W
Shunut, Gora, mtn., Russia (gȧ-rä shōō'nôt)	186a	56°33'N	59°45'E
Shunyi, China (shòn-yē)	206	40°09'N	116°38'E
Shuqrah, Yemen	198	13°32'N	46°02'E
Shūrāb, r., Iran (shōō räb)	198	31°08'N	55°30'E
Shuri, Japan (shōō'rė)	210	26°10'N	127°48'E
Shurugwi, Zimb.	232	19°34'S	30°03'E
Shūshtar, Iran (shōōsh'tŭr)	198	31°50'N	48°46'E
Shuswap Lake, l., Can. (shōōs'wŏp)	95	50°57'N	119°15'W
Shuya, Russia (shōō'yȧ)	178	56°52'N	41°23'E
Shuyang, China (shōō yäng)	206	34°09'N	118°47'E
Shweba, Mya.	199	22°23'N	96°13'E
Shymkent, Kaz.	183	42°17'N	69°42'E
Shyroke, Ukr.	177	47°40'N	33°18'E
Siak Kecil, r., Indon.	197b	1°01'N	101°45'E
Siaksriinderapura, Indon. (sė-äks'rĭ ĕn'drȧ-pōō'rä)	197b	0°48'N	102°05'E
Siālkot, Pak. (sė-äl'kōt)	199	32°39'N	74°30'E
Siátista, Grc. (syä'tĭs-ta)	175	40°15'N	21°32'E
Siau, Pulau, i., Indon.	213	2°40'N	126°00'E
Šiauliai, Lith. (shė-ou'lė-ī)	180	55°57'N	23°19'E
Šibay, Russia (sē'báy)	186a	52°41'N	58°40'E
Šibenik, Cro. (shė-bā'nĕk)	163	43°44'N	15°55'E
Siberia, reg., Russia	196	57°00'N	97°00'E
Siberut, Pulau, i., Indon. (sē'bȧ-rōōt)	212	1°22'S	99°45'E
Sibiti, Congo (sė-bė-tē')	232	3°41'S	13°21'E
Sibiu, Rom. (sė-bĭ-ōō')	163	45°47'N	24°09'E
Sibley, Ia., U.S. (sĭb'lė)	112	43°24'N	95°33'W
Sibolga, Indon. (sė-bō'gȧ)	212	1°45'N	98°45'E
Sibsāgar, India (sēb-sŭ'gŭr)	199	26°47'N	94°45'E
Sibutu Island, i., Phil.	212	4°40'N	119°30'E
Sibuyan, i., Phil. (sē-bōō-yän')	213a	12°19'N	122°25'E
Sibuyan Sea, sea, Phil.	212	12°43'N	122°38'E

PLACE (Pronunciation)	PAGE	LAT.	LONG.
Sichuan, prov., China (sz-chůän)	204	31°20'N	103°00'E
Sicily, i., Italy (sĭs'ĭ-lė)	156	37°38'N	13°30'E
Sico, r., Hond. (sė-kō)	132	15°32'N	85°42'W
Sidamo, hist. reg., Eth. (sē-dä'mô)	231	5°08'N	37°45'E
Siderno Marina, Italy (sė-dĕr'nô mä-rē'nä)	174	38°18'N	16°19'E
Sídheros, Ákra, c., Grc.	174a	35°19'N	26°20'E
Sidi Aïssa, Alg.	173	35°53'N	3°44'E
Sidi bel Abbès, Alg. (sē'dē-bĕl ȧ-bĕs')	230	35°15'N	0°43'W
Sidi Ifni, Mor. (ēf'nė)	230	29°22'N	10°15'W
Sidirókastro, Grc.	175	41°13'N	23°27'E
Sidley, Mount, mtn., Ant. (sĭd'lė)	224	77°25'S	129°00'W
Sidney, Can.	94	48°39'N	123°24'W
Sidney, Mt., U.S. (sĭd'nė)	115	47°43'N	104°07'W
Sidney, Ne., U.S.	112	41°10'N	103°00'W
Sidney, Oh., U.S.	108	40°20'N	84°10'W
Sidney Lanier, Lake, res., Ga., U.S. (lăn'yĕr)	107	34°27'N	83°56'W
Sido, Mali	234	11°40'N	7°36'W
Sidon *see* Saydā, Leb.	198	33°34'N	35°23'E
Sidr, Wādī, r., Egypt	197a	29°43'N	32°58'E
Sidra, Gulf of *see* Surt, Khalīj, b., Libya	231	31°30'N	18°28'E
Siedlce, Pol. (syĕd''l-tsĕ)	169	52°09'N	22°20'E
Siegburg, Ger. (zēg'bōōrgh)	168	50°48'N	7°13'E
Siegen, Ger. (zē'ghĕn)	168	50°52'N	8°01'E
Sieghartskirchen, Aus.	159e	48°16'N	16°00'E
Siemiatycze, Pol. (syĕm'yä'tė-chĕ)	169	52°26'N	22°52'E
Siemionówka, Pol. (sĕĕ-mĕō'nōf-kä)	169	52°53'N	23°50'E
Siem Reap, Camb. (syĕm'rä'áp)	212	13°32'N	103°54'E
Siena, Italy (sė-ĕn'ä)	162	43°19'N	11°21'E
Sieradz, Pol. (syĕ'rädz)	169	51°35'N	18°45'E
Sierpc, Pol. (syĕrpts)	169	52°51'N	19°42'E
Sierra Blanca, Tx., U.S. (sē-ĕ'rȧ blaŋ-kä)	122	31°10'N	105°20'W
Sierra Blanca Peak, mtn., N.M., U.S. (blăn'kȧ)	106	33°25'N	105°50'W
Sierra Leone, nation, Afr. (sė-ĕr'rä lå-ō'nå)	230	8°48'N	12°30'W
Sierra Madre, Ca., U.S. (mă'drē)	117a	34°10'N	118°03'W
Sierra Mojada, Mex. (sē-ĕ'r-rä-mô-ĸä'dä)	122	27°22'N	103°42'W
Sífnos, i., Grc.	175	36°58'N	24°30'E
Sigean, Fr. (sē-zhŏn')	170	43°02'N	2°56'E
Sigeurney, Ia., U.S. (sē-gûr-nĭ)	113	41°16'N	92°10'W
Sighetu Marmaţiei, Rom.	169	47°57'N	23°55'E
Sighişoara, Rom. (sē-gė-shwä'rȧ)	169	46°11'N	24°48'E
Siglufjördur, Ice.	160	66°06'N	18°45'W
Signakhi, Geor.	181	41°45'N	45°50'E
Signal Hill, Ca., U.S. (sĭg'năl hĭl)	117a	33°48'N	118°11'W
Sigsig, Ec. (sėg-sēg')	142	3°04'S	78°44'W
Sigtuna, Swe. (sēgh-tōō'nȧ)	166	59°40'N	17°39'E
Siguanea, Ensenada de la, b., Cuba	134	21°45'N	83°15'W
Siguatepeque, Hond. (sē-gwá'tĕ-pĕ-kĕ)	132	14°33'N	87°51'W
Sigüenza, Spain (sē-gwĕ'n-zä)	162	41°03'N	2°38'W
Siguiri, Gui. (sė-gė-rē')	230	11°25'N	9°10'W
Sihong, China (sz-hôŋ)	206	33°25'N	118°13'E
Siirt, Tur. (sĭ-ērt')	181	38°00'N	42°00'E
Sikalongo, Zam.	237	16°46'S	27°07'E
Sikasso, Mali (sė-käs'sō)	230	11°19'N	5°40'W
Sikeston, Mo., U.S. (sīks'tŭn)	121	36°50'N	89°35'W
Sikhote Alin', Khrebet, mts., Russia (se-ĸô'ta a-lēn')	179	45°00'N	135°45'E
Sikinos, i., Grc. (sĭ'kĭ-nōs)	175	36°45'N	24°55'E
Sikkim, state, India	199	27°42'N	88°25'E
Siklós, Hung. (sĭ'klōsh)	169	45°51'N	18°18'E
Sil, r., Spain (sē'l)	172	42°20'N	7°13'W
Silang, Phil. (sė-läng')	213a	14°14'N	120°58'E
Silao, Mex. (sė-lä'ō)	130	20°56'N	101°25'W
Silchar, India (sĭl-chär')	199	24°52'N	92°50'E
Silent Valley, S. Afr. (sī'lĕnt vă'lē)	238c	24°32'S	26°40'E
Siler City, N.C., U.S. (sī'lĕr)	125	35°45'N	79°29'W
Silesia, hist. reg., Pol. (sĭ-lē'shȧ)	168	50°58'N	16°53'E
Silifke, Tur.	163	36°20'N	34°00'E
Siling Co, l., China	204	32°05'N	89°10'E
Silistra, Blg. (sė-lēs'trȧ)	163	44°01'N	27°13'E
Siljan, l., Swe. (sēl'yän)	160	60°48'N	14°28'E
Silkeborg, Den. (sĭl'kĕ-bôr')	166	56°10'N	9°33'E
Sillery, Can. (sēl'-re')	102b	46°46'N	71°15'W
Siloam Springs, Ar., U.S. (sī-lōm)	121	36°10'N	94°32'W
Siloana Plains, pl., Zam.	236	16°55'S	23°10'E
Silocayoápan, Mex. (sē-lō-kä-yō-ä'pän)	130	17°29'N	98°09'W
Silsbee, Tx., U.S. (sĭlz' bė)	123	30°19'N	94°09'W
Šilutė, Lith.	167	55°21'N	21°29'E
Silva Jardim, Braz. (sė'l-vä-zhär-dēn)	141a	22°40'N	42°24'W
Silvana, Wa., U.S. (sĭ-văn'ȧ)	116a	48°12'N	122°16'W
Silvânia, Braz. (sēl-vá'nyä)	143	16°43'S	48°33'W
Silvassa, India	202	20°10'N	73°00'E
Silver, l., Mo., U.S.	121	39°38'N	93°12'W
Silverado, Ca., U.S. (sĭl-vĕr-ä'dō)	117a	33°45'N	117°40'W
Silver Bank, bk.	135	20°40'N	69°40'W
Silver Bank Passage, strt., N.A.	135	20°40'N	70°20'W
Silver Bay, Mn., U.S.	113	47°24'N	91°07'W
Silver City, Pan.	133	9°20'N	79°54'W
Silver City, N.M., U.S. (sĭl'vĕr sĭ'tĭ)	119	32°45'N	108°20'W
Silver Creek, N.Y., U.S. (crēk)	109	42°35'N	79°10'W
Silver Creek, r., Az., U.S.	119	34°30'N	110°05'W
Silver Creek, r., In., U.S.	111h	38°20'N	85°45'W
Silver Creek, Muddy Fork, r., In., U.S.	111h	38°26'N	85°52'W
Silverdale, Wa., U.S. (sĭl'vĕr-dāl)	116a	49°39'N	122°42'W

ng-sing; ŋ-baŋk; N-nasalized n; nŏd; cŏmmit; ōld; ôbey; ôrder; oi-boil; fōōd; ó-as oo in foot; ou-out; s-soft; sh-dish; th-thin; pūre; ûnite; ûrn; stŭd; circŭs; ü-as in French tu; ′-indeterminate vowel.

352 Sofia – Spas-Klepiki PRONOUNCING INDEX

PLACE (Pronunciation)	PAGE	LAT.	LONG.
Sofia (Sofiya), Blg. (sô′fē-yȧ) (sô′fē-ȧ)	154	42°43′N	23°20′E
Sofiïvka, Ukr.	177	48°03′N	33°53′E
Sofiya see Sofia, Blg.	154	42°43′N	23°20′E
Soga, Japan (sô′gä)	211a	35°35′N	140°08′E
Sogamoso, Col. (sô-gä-mô′sō)	142	5°42′N	72°51′W
Sognafjorden, b., Nor.	156	61°09′N	5°30′E
Sogozha, r., Russia (sô′gô-zhȧ)	176	58°35′N	39°08′E
Sohano, Pap. N. Gui.	214e	5°27′S	154°40′E
Soissons, Fr. (swä-sôɴ′)	170	49°23′N	3°17′E
Sōka, Japan (sō′kä)	211a	35°50′N	139°49′E
Sokal′, Ukr. (sô′käl′)	169	50°28′N	24°20′E
Söke, Tur. (sû′kĕ)	163	37°40′N	27°10′E
Sokółka, Pol. (sô-ko̤ol′kȧ)	169	53°23′N	23°30′E
Sokolo, Mali (sô-kô-lō′)	230	14°51′N	6°09′W
Sokołów Podlaski, Pol. (sô-kô-wôf′ pŭd-lä′skĭ)	169	52°24′N	22°15′E
Sokone, Sen.	234	13°53′N	16°22′W
Sokoto, Nig. (sō′kô-tō)	230	13°04′N	5°16′E
Sola de Vega, Mex.	131	16°31′N	96°58′W
Solander, Cape, c., Austl.	217b	34°03′S	151°16′E
Solano, Phil. (sō-lä′nō)	213a	16°31′N	121°11′E
Soledad, Col. (sō-lĕ-dä′d)	142	10°47′N	75°00′W
Soledad Díez Gutiérrez, Mex.	130	22°19′N	100°54′W
Soleduck, r., Wa., U.S. (sōl′dŭk)	114	47°59′N	124°28′W
Solentiname, Islas de, is., Nic. (ē′s-läs-dĕ-sô-lĕn-tē-nä′mȧ)	132	11°15′N	85°16′W
Solihull, Eng., U.K. (sō′lĭ-hŭl)	158a	52°25′N	1°46′W
Solihull, co., Eng., U.K.	158a	52°25′N	1°42′W
Solikamsk, Russia (sô-lē-kȧmsk′)	180	59°38′N	56°48′E
Sol′-Iletsk, Russia	178	51°10′N	55°05′E
Solimões see Amazon, r., Braz.	142	2°45′S	67°44′W
Solingen, Ger. (zō′lĭng-ĕn)	168	51°10′N	7°05′E
Sóller, Spain (sō′lyĕr)	173	39°45′N	2°40′E
Sologne, reg., Fr. (sō-lōn′yĕ)	170	47°36′N	1°53′E
Solola, Guat. (sô-lō′lä)	132	14°45′N	91°12′W
Solomon, r., Ks., U.S.	120	39°24′N	98°19′W
Solomon, North Fork, r., Ks., U.S.	120	39°34′N	99°52′W
Solomon, South Fork, r., Ks., U.S.	120	39°19′N	99°52′W
Solomon Islands, nation, Oc. (sŏ′lō-mŭn)	3	7°00′S	160°00′E
Solon, China (swo-lo͞on)	205	46°32′N	121°18′E
Solon, Oh., U.S. (sō′lŭn)	111d	41°23′N	81°26′W
Solothurn, Switz. (zō′lō-tho͞orn)	168	47°13′N	7°30′E
Solovetskiye Ostrova, is., Russia	180	65°10′N	35°40′E
Šolta, i., Serb. (shôl′tä)	174	43°20′N	16°15′E
Soltau, Ger. (sōl′tou)	168	53°00′N	9°50′E
Sol′tsy, Russia (sôl′tsē)	176	58°04′N	30°13′E
Solvay, N.Y., U.S. (sŏl′vā)	109	43°05′N	76°10′W
Sölvesborg, Swe. (sûl′vĕs-bôrg)	166	56°04′N	14°35′E
Sol′vychegodsk, Russia (sôl′vê-chĕ-gôtsk′)	180	61°18′N	46°58′E
Solway Firth, b., U.K. (sŏl′wā′fûrth′)	160	54°42′N	3°55′W
Solwezi, Zam.	237	12°11′S	26°25′E
Soly, Bela.	166	54°31′N	26°11′E
Somalia, nation, Afr. (sō-mä′lē-ȧ)	238a	3°28′N	44°47′E
Somanga, Tan.	237	8°24′S	39°17′E
Sombor, Serb. (sôm′bôr)	163	45°45′N	19°10′E
Sombrerete, Mex. (sōm-brå-rā′tå)	130	23°38′N	103°37′W
Sombrero, Cayo, i., Ven. (kä-yô-sôm-brĕ′rô)	143b	10°52′N	68°12′W
Somerset, Ky., U.S. (sŭm′ẽr-sĕt)	124	37°05′N	84°35′W
Somerset, Ma., U.S.	110b	41°46′N	71°05′W
Somerset, Pa., U.S.	109	40°00′N	79°05′W
Somerset, Tx., U.S.	117d	29°13′N	98°39′W
Somerset East, S. Afr.	233c	32°44′S	25°36′E
Somersworth, N.H., U.S. (sŭm′ẽrz-wûrth)	100	43°16′N	70°53′W
Somerton, Az., U.S. (sŭm′ẽr-tŭn)	119	32°36′N	114°43′W
Somerville, Ma., U.S. (sŭm′ẽr-vĭl)	101a	42°23′N	71°06′W
Somerville, N.J., U.S.	110a	40°34′N	74°37′W
Somerville, Tn., U.S.	124	35°14′N	89°21′W
Somerville, Tx., U.S.	123	30°21′N	96°31′W
Someș, r., Eur.	169	47°43′N	23°09′E
Somma Vesuviana, Italy (sôm′mä vā-zo͞o-vē-ä′nä)	173c	40°38′N	14°27′E
Somme, r., Fr. (sŏm)	170	50°02′N	2°04′E
Sommerfeld, Ger. (zō′mĕr-fĕld)	159b	52°48′N	13°02′E
Sommerville, Austl.	217a	38°14′S	145°10′E
Somoto, Nic. (sô-mō′tō)	132	13°28′N	86°37′W
Son, r., India (sōn)	199	24°40′N	82°35′E
Sŏnchŏn, Kor., N. (sŭn′shŭn)	210	39°49′N	124°56′E
Sondags, r., S. Afr.	233c	33°17′S	25°14′E
Sønderborg, Den. (sûn″er-bôrgh)	160	54°55′N	9°47′E
Sondershausen, Ger. (zôn′dĕrz-hou′zĕn)	168	51°17′N	10°45′E
Song Ca, r., Viet.	209	19°15′N	105°00′E
Songea, Tan. (sôn-gā′ȧ)	232	10°41′S	35°39′E
Songjiang, China	205	31°01′N	121°14′E
Sŏngjin, Kor., N. (sŭng′jĭn′)	210	40°38′N	129°10′E
Songkhla, Thai. (sông′klä′)	212	7°09′N	100°34′E
Songwe, D.R.C.	237	12°25′S	29°40′E
Sonneberg, Ger. (sôn′ē-bĕrgh)	168	50°20′N	11°14′E
Sonora, Ca., U.S. (sô-nō′rȧ)	118	37°58′N	120°22′W
Sonora, Tx., U.S.	122	30°33′N	100°38′W
Sonora, state, Mex.	128	29°45′N	111°15′W
Sonora, r., Mex.	128	28°45′N	111°35′W
Sonora Peak, mtn., Ca., U.S.	106	38°22′N	119°39′W
Sonseca, Spain (sôn-sā′kä)	172	39°41′N	3°56′W
Sonsón, Col. (sôn-sôn′)	142	5°42′N	75°28′W
Sonsonate, El Sal. (sōn-sô-nä′tå)	132	13°46′N	89°43′W
Sonsorol Islands, is., Palau (sŏn-sô-rōl′)	213	5°03′N	132°33′E
Sooke Basin, b., Can. (so͝ok)	116a	48°21′N	123°47′W
Soo Locks, trans., Mi., U.S. (so͞o lŏks)	117a	46°30′N	84°30′W
Sopetrán, Col. (sô-pĕ-trä′n)	142a	6°30′N	75°44′W
Sopot, Pol. (sô′pôt)	169	54°26′N	18°25′E
Sopron, Hung. (shŏp′rôn)	163	47°41′N	16°36′E
Sora, Italy (sō′rä)	174	41°43′N	13°37′E
Sorbas, Spain (sôr′bäs)	172	37°05′N	2°07′W
Sordo, r., Mex. (sô′r-dō)	131	16°39′N	97°33′W
Sorel, Can. (sô-rĕl′)	91	46°01′N	73°07′W
Sorell, Cape, c., Austl.	222	42°10′S	144°50′E
Soresina, Italy (sō-rå-zē′nä)	174	45°17′N	9°51′E
Soria, Spain (sō′rē-ä)	162	41°46′N	2°28′W
Soriano, dept., Ur. (sō-rēä′nō)	141c	33°25′S	58°00′W
Soroca, Mol.	181	48°09′N	28°17′E
Sorocaba, Braz. (sô-rô-kä′bȧ)	143	23°29′S	47°27′W
Sorong, Indon. (sō-rông′)	213	1°00′S	131°20′E
Sorot′, r., Russia (sô-rō′tzh)	176	57°08′N	29°23′E
Soroti, Ug. (sō-rō′tē)	231	1°43′N	33°37′E
Sørøya, i., Nor.	160	70°37′N	20°58′E
Sorraia, r., Port. (sôr-rī′ȧ)	172	38°55′N	8°42′W
Sorrento, Italy (sôr-rĕn′tō)	174	40°23′N	14°23′E
Sorsogon, Phil. (sôr-sôgōn′)	213	12°51′N	124°02′E
Sortavala, Russia (sôr′tä-vä-lä)	178	61°43′N	30°40′E
Sosna, r., Russia (sôs′nȧ)	177	50°33′N	38°15′E
Sosnogorsk, Russia	178	63°13′N	54°09′E
Sosnowiec, Pol. (sôs-nô′vyĕts)	169	50°17′N	19°10′E
Sosnytsia, Ukr.	177	51°30′N	32°29′E
Sosunova, Mys, c., Russia (mĭs sô′sô-nôf′ȧ)	210	46°28′N	138°06′E
Sos′va, r., Russia (sôs′vȧ)	186a	59°55′N	60°40′E
Sos′va, r., Russia (sôs′vȧ)	180	63°10′N	63°30′E
Sota, r., Benin	235	11°10′N	3°20′E
Sota la Marina, Mex. (sô-tä-lä-mä-rē′nä)	130	23°45′N	98°11′W
Soteapan, Mex. (sō-tå-ä′pän)	131	18°14′N	94°51′W
Soto la Marina, Río, r., Mex. (rē′ō-so′tō lä mä-rē′nä)	130	23°55′N	98°30′W
Sotuta, Mex. (sô-to͞o′tä)	132a	20°35′N	89°00′W
Soublette, Ven. (sō-o͞o-blĕ′tĕ)	143b	9°55′N	66°06′W
Souflí, Grc.	175	41°12′N	26°17′E
Soufrière, St. Luc. (so͞o-frē-âr′)	133b	13°50′N	61°03′W
Soufrière, mtn., St. Vin.	133b	13°19′N	61°12′W
Soufrière, vol., Guad. (so͞o-frē-âr′)	133b	16°06′N	61°42′W
Sŏul see Seoul, Kor., S.	205	37°35′N	127°03′E
Sounding Creek, r., Can. (soun′dĭng)	96	51°35′N	111°00′W
Souq Ahras, Alg.	161	36°23′N	8°00′E
Sources, Mount aux, mtn., Afr. (môn′tō sôrs′)	232	28°47′S	29°04′E
Soure, Port. (sōr-ĕ)	172	40°04′N	8°37′W
Souris, Can. (so͞o′rē′)	101	46°20′N	62°17′W
Souris, Can.	90	49°38′N	100°15′W
Souris, r., N.A.	92	48°30′N	101°30′W
Sourlake, Tx., U.S. (sour′lāk)	123	30°09′N	94°24′W
Sousse, Tun. (so͞os)	230	36°00′N	10°39′E
South, r., Ga., U.S.	110c	33°40′N	84°15′W
South, r., N.C., U.S.	125	34°49′N	78°33′W
South Africa, nation, Afr.	232	28°00′S	24°50′E
South Amboy, N.J., U.S. (south′ăm′boi)	110a	40°28′N	74°17′W
South America, cont.	139	15°00′S	60°00′W
Southampton, Eng., U.K. (south-ămp′tŭn)	154	50°54′N	1°30′W
Southampton, N.Y., U.S.	109	40°53′N	72°24′W
Southampton Island, i., Can.	93	64°38′N	84°00′W
South Andaman Island, i., India (ăn-dȧ-măn′)	212	11°57′N	93°24′E
South Australia, state, Austl. (ôs-trā′lĭ-ȧ)	218	29°45′S	132°00′E
South Bay, b., Bah.	135	20°55′N	73°35′W
South Bend, In., U.S. (bĕnd)	105	41°40′N	86°20′W
South Bend, Wa., U.S. (bĕnd)	114	46°39′N	123°48′W
South Bight, b., Bah.	134	24°20′N	77°35′W
South Bimini, i., Bah. (bē′mē-nē)	134	25°40′N	79°20′W
Southborough, Ma., U.S. (south′bŭr-ô)	101a	42°18′N	71°33′W
South Boston, Va., U.S. (bôs′tŭn)	125	36°41′N	78°55′W
Southbridge, Ma., U.S. (south′brĭj)	109	42°05′N	72°00′W
South Caicos, i., T./C. Is. (kī′kōs)	135	21°30′N	71°35′W
South Carolina, state, U.S. (kăr-ô-lī′nȧ)	105	34°15′N	81°10′W
South Cave, Eng., U.K. (cāv)	158a	53°45′N	0°35′W
South Charleston, W.V., U.S.	108	38°20′N	81°40′W
South China Sea, sea, Asia (chī′nȧ)	212	15°23′N	114°12′E
South Creek, r., Austl.	217b	33°43′S	150°50′E
South Dakota, state, U.S. (dȧ-kō′tȧ)	104	44°20′N	101°55′W
South Downs, Eng., U.K. (dounz)	164	50°55′N	1°13′W
South Dum-Dum, India	202a	22°36′N	88°25′E
South East Cape, c., Austl.	221	43°47′S	146°03′E
Southend-on-Sea, Eng., U.K. (south-ĕnd′)	165	51°33′N	0°41′E
Southern Alps, mts., N.Z. (sŭ-thûrn ălps)	221a	43°35′S	170°00′E
Southern Cross, Austl.	218	31°13′S	119°30′E
Southern Indian, l., Can. (sŭth′ẽrn ĭn′dĭ-ăn)	92	56°46′N	98°57′W
Southern Pines, N.C., U.S. (sŭth′ẽrn pīnz)	125	35°10′N	79°23′W
Southern Ute Indian Reservation, I.R., Co., U.S. (ūt)	119	37°05′N	108°23′W
South Euclid, Oh., U.S. (ū′klĭd)	111d	41°30′N	81°34′W
South Fox, i., Mi., U.S. (fŏks)	108	45°25′N	85°55′W
South Gate, Ca., U.S. (gāt)	117a	33°57′N	118°13′W
South Georgia, i., S. Geor. (jôr′jȧ)	139	54°00′S	37°00′W
South Haven, Mi., U.S. (hāv′′n)	108	42°25′N	86°15′W
South Hill, Va., U.S.	125	36°44′N	78°08′W
South Holston Lake, res., U.S.	125	36°35′N	82°00′W
South Indian Lake, Can.	97	56°50′N	99°00′W
Southington, Ct., U.S. (sŭdh′ĭng-tŭn)	109	41°35′N	72°55′W
South Island, i., N.Z.	221a	42°40′S	169°00′E
South Loup, r., Ne., U.S. (lo͞op)	112	41°21′N	100°08′W
South Magnetic Pole, pt. of i.	224	65°18′S	139°30′E
South Merrimack, N.H., U.S. (mĕr′ĭ-măk)	101a	42°47′N	71°36′W
South Milwaukee, Wi., U.S. (mĭl-wô′kē)	111a	42°55′N	87°52′W
South Moose Lake, l., Can.	97	53°51′N	100°20′W
South Nation, r., Can.	99	45°00′N	75°25′W
South Negril Point, c., Jam. (nå-grĕl′)	134	18°15′N	78°25′W
South Ogden, Ut., U.S. (ŏg′dĕn)	117b	41°12′N	111°58′W
South Orkney Islands, is., Ant.	139	57°00′S	45°00′W
South Ossetia, hist. reg., Geor.	182	42°20′N	44°00′E
South Paris, Me., U.S. (păr′ĭs)	100	44°13′N	70°32′W
South Park, Ky., U.S. (pärk)	111h	38°06′N	85°43′W
South Pasadena, Ca., U.S. (păs-ȧ-dē′nȧ)	117a	34°06′N	118°08′W
South Pease, r., Tx., U.S. (pēz)	120	33°54′N	100°45′W
South Pender, i., Can. (pĕn′dẽr)	116d	48°45′N	123°09′W
South Pittsburg, Tn., U.S. (pĭs′bûrg)	124	35°00′N	85°42′W
South Platte, r., U.S. (plăt)	106	40°40′N	102°40′W
South Point, c., Barb.	133b	13°00′N	59°43′W
South Point, c., Mi., U.S.	108	44°50′N	83°20′W
South Pole, pt. of i., Ant.	224	90°00′S	0°00′
South Porcupine, Can.	98	48°28′N	81°13′W
Southport, Austl. (south′pōrt)	219	27°57′S	153°27′E
Southport, Eng., U.K. (south′pôrt)	164	53°38′N	3°00′W
Southport, In., U.S.	111g	39°40′N	86°07′W
Southport, N.C., U.S.	125	35°55′N	78°02′W
South Portland, Me., U.S. (pōrt-lănd)	100	43°37′N	70°15′W
South Prairie, Wa., U.S. (prā′rĭ)	116a	47°08′N	122°06′W
South Range, Wi., U.S. (rānj)	117h	46°37′N	91°59′W
South River, N.J., U.S. (rĭv′ẽr)	110a	40°27′N	74°23′W
South Ronaldsay, i., Scot., U.K. (rŏn′ăld-s′ā)	164a	58°48′N	2°55′W
South Saint Paul, Mn., U.S.	117g	44°54′N	93°02′W
South Salt Lake, Ut., U.S. (sôlt lāk)	117b	40°44′N	111°53′W
South Sandwich Islands, is., S. Geor. (sănd′wĭch)	139	58°00′S	27°00′W
South Sandwich Trench, deep	139	55°00′S	27°00′W
South San Francisco, Ca., U.S. (săn frăn-sĭs′kô)	116b	37°39′N	122°24′W
South Saskatchewan, r., Can. (săs-kach′ĕ-wän)	92	50°30′N	110°30′W
South Shetland Islands, is., Ant.	139	62°00′S	70°00′W
South Shields, Eng., U.K. (shēldz)	160	55°00′N	1°22′W
South Sioux City, Ne., U.S. (so͞o sĭt′ē)	112	42°48′N	96°26′W
South Taranaki Bight, b., N.Z. (tä-rä-nä′kē)	221a	39°35′S	173°50′E
South Thompson, r., Can. (tŏmp′sŭn)	95	50°41′N	120°21′W
Southton, Tx., U.S. (south′tŭn)	117d	29°18′N	98°26′W
South Uist, i., Scot., U.K. (û′ĭst)	164	57°15′N	7°24′W
South Umpqua, r., Or., U.S. (ŭmp′kwȧ)	114	43°00′N	122°54′W
Southwell, Eng., U.K. (south′wĕl)	158a	53°04′N	0°56′W
South West Africa see Namibia, nation, Afr.	232	19°30′S	16°13′E
Southwest Miramichi, r., Can. (mĭr ȧ-mė′shē)	100	46°35′N	66°17′W
Southwest Point, c., Bah.	134	25°50′N	77°10′W
Southwest Point, c., Bah.	135	23°55′N	74°30′W
South Yorkshire, hist. reg., Eng., U.K.	158a	53°29′N	1°35′W
Sovetsk, Russia (sô-vyĕtsk′)	180	55°04′N	21°54′E
Sovetskaya Gavan′, Russia (sŭ-vyĕt′skĭ-u gä′vŭn′)	179	48°59′N	140°14′E
Sow, r., Eng., U.K. (sou)	158a	52°45′N	2°12′W
Soya Kaikyō, strt., Asia	210	45°45′N	141°38′E
Sōya Misaki, c., Japan (sō′yȧ mē′sä-kē)	210	45°35′N	141°25′E
Soyo, Ang.	232	6°10′S	12°25′E
Sozh, r., Eur. (sôzh)	181	52°50′N	31°00′E
Sozopol, Blg. (sôz′ô-pôl′)	175	42°18′N	27°50′E
Spa, Bel. (spä)	165	50°30′N	5°50′E
Spain, nation, Eur. (spān)	154	40°15′N	4°30′W
Spalding, Ne., U.S. (spôl′dĭng)	112	41°43′N	98°23′W
Spanaway, Wa., U.S. (spăn′ȧ-wā)	116a	47°06′N	122°26′W
Spangler, Pa., U.S. (spăng′lẽr)	109	40°40′N	78°50′W
Spanish Fork, Ut., U.S. (spăn′ĭsh fôrk)	119	40°10′N	111°40′W
Spanish Town, Jam.	129	18°00′N	76°55′W
Sparks, Nv., U.S. (spärks)	118	39°34′N	119°45′W
Sparrows Point, Md., U.S. (spăr′ōz)	110e	39°13′N	76°29′W
Sparta see Spárti, Grc.	175	37°07′N	22°28′E
Sparta, Ga., U.S. (spär′tȧ)	125	33°16′N	82°59′W
Sparta, Il., U.S.	121	38°07′N	89°42′W
Sparta, Mi., U.S.	108	43°10′N	85°45′W
Sparta, Tn., U.S.	124	35°54′N	85°26′W
Sparta, Wi., U.S.	113	43°56′N	90°50′W
Sparta Mountains, mts., N.J., U.S.	110a	41°00′N	74°38′W
Spartanburg, S.C., U.S. (spär′tăn-bûrg)	105	34°57′N	82°13′W
Spartel, Cap, c., Mor. (spär-tĕl′)	172	35°48′N	5°50′W
Spárti (Sparta), Grc.	175	37°07′N	22°28′E
Spartivento, Cape, c., Italy (spär-tē-vĕn′tô)	174	37°55′N	16°09′E
Spartivento, Cape, c., Italy	156	38°54′N	8°52′E
Spas-Demensk, Russia (spȧs dyĕ-mĕnsk′)	176	54°24′N	34°02′E
Spas-Klepiki, Russia (spȧs klĕp′ĕ-kē)	176	55°09′N	40°11′E

ăt; finăl; rāte; senåte; ärm; åsk; sofȧ; fâre; ch-choose; dh-as th in other; bē; ėvent; bĕt; recĕnt; cratẽr; g-gō; gh-guttural g; bĭt; ĭ-short neutral; rīde; ĸ-guttural k as ch in German ich;

PLACE (Pronunciation)	PAGE	LAT.	LONG.
Spassik-Ryazanskiy, Russia (ryä-zän´skĭ)	176	54°24'N	40°21'E
Spassk-Dal'niy, Russia (spŭsk´däl´nyē)	179	44°30'N	133°00'E
Spátha, Ákra, c., Grc.	174a	35°42'N	23°45'E
Spaulding, Al., U.S. (spôl´dĭng)	110h	33°27'N	86°50'W
Spear, Cape, c., Can. (spēr)	101	47°32'N	52°32'W
Spearfish, S.D., U.S. (spēr´fĭsh)	112	44°28'N	103°52'W
Speed, In., U.S. (spēd)	111h	38°25'N	85°45'W
Speedway, In., U.S. (spēd´wā)	111g	39°47'N	86°14'W
Speichersee, l., Ger.	159d	48°12'N	11°47'E
Spencer, Ia., U.S.	112	43°09'N	95°08'W
Spencer, In., U.S. (spĕn´sẽr)	108	39°15'N	86°45'W
Spencer, N.C., U.S.	125	35°43'N	80°25'W
Spencer, W.V., U.S.	108	38°55'N	81°20'W
Spencer Gulf, b., Austl. (spĕn´sẽr)	220	34°20'S	136°55'E
Sperenberg, Ger. (shpĕ´rĕn-bĕrgh)	159b	52°09'N	13°22'E
Spey, l., Scot., U.K. (spā)	164	57°25'N	3°29'W
Speyer, Ger. (shpī´ĕr)	168	49°18'N	8°26'E
Sphinx, hist., Egypt (sfĭnks)	238b	29°57'N	31°08'E
Spijkenisse, Neth.	159a	51°51'N	4°18'E
Spinazzola, Italy (spē-nät´zô-lä)	174	40°58'N	16°05'E
Spirit Lake, Ia., U.S. (lāk)	112	43°25'N	95°08'W
Spirit Lake, Id., U.S. (spĭr´ĭt)	114	47°58'N	116°51'W
Spišská Nová Ves, Slvk. (spēsh´skä nō´vä vĕs)	161	48°56'N	20°35'E
Spitsbergen *see* Svalbard, dep., Nor.	178	77°00'N	20°00'E
Split, Cro. (splēt)	154	43°30'N	16°28'E
Split Lake, l., Can.	97	56°08'N	96°15'W
Spokane, Wa., U.S. (spōkăn´)	104	47°39'N	117°25'W
Spokane, r., Wa., U.S.	114	47°47'N	118°00'W
Spokane Indian Reservation, I.R., Wa., U.S.	114	47°55'N	118°00'W
Spoleto, Italy (spô-lā´tō)	174	42°44'N	12°44'E
Spoon, r., Il., U.S. (spo͞on)	121	40°36'N	90°22'W
Spooner, Wi., U.S. (spo͞on´ẽr)	113	45°50'N	91°53'W
Spotswood, N.J., U.S. (spŏtz´wo͝od)	110a	40°23'N	74°22'W
Sprague, r., Or., U.S. (sprāg)	114	42°30'N	121°42'W
Spratly, i., Asia (sprăt´lē)	212	8°38'N	111°54'E
Spray, N.C., U.S. (sprā)	125	36°30'N	79°44'W
Spree, r., Ger. (shprā)	168	51°53'N	14°08'E
Spremberg, Ger. (shprĕm´bĕrgh)	168	51°35'N	14°23'E
Spring, r., Ar., U.S.	121	36°25'N	91°35'W
Springbok, S. Afr. (spring´bŏk)	232	29°35'S	17°55'E
Spring Creek, r., Nv., U.S. (spring)	118	40°18'N	117°45'W
Spring Creek, r., Tx., U.S.	123	30°03'N	95°43'W
Spring Creek, r., Tx., U.S.	122	31°08'N	100°50'W
Springdale, Can.	101	49°30'N	56°05'W
Springdale, Ar., U.S. (spring´dāl)	121	36°10'N	94°07'W
Springdale, Pa., U.S.	111e	40°33'N	79°46'W
Springer, N.M., U.S. (spring´ẽr)	120	36°21'N	104°37'W
Springerville, Az., U.S.	119	34°08'N	109°17'W
Springfield, Co., U.S. (spring´fēld)	120	37°24'N	102°04'W
Springfield, Il., U.S.	105	39°46'N	89°37'W
Springfield, Ky., U.S.	108	37°35'N	85°10'W
Springfield, Ma., U.S.	105	42°05'N	72°35'W
Springfield, Mn., U.S.	113	44°14'N	94°59'W
Springfield, Mo., U.S.	105	37°13'N	93°17'W
Springfield, Oh., U.S.	105	39°55'N	83°50'W
Springfield, Or., U.S.	114	44°01'N	123°02'W
Springfield, Tn., U.S.	124	36°30'N	86°53'W
Springfield, Vt., U.S.	109	43°20'N	72°35'W
Springfontein, S. Afr. (spring´fōn-tīn)	232	30°16'S	25°45'E
Springhill, Can. (spring-hĭl´)	91	45°39'N	64°03'W
Spring Mountains, mts., Nv., U.S.	118	36°18'N	115°49'W
Springs, S. Afr. (springs)	238c	26°16'S	28°27'E
Springstein, Can. (spring´stīn)	102f	49°49'N	97°29'W
Springton Reservoir, res., Pa., U.S. (spring-tŭn)	110f	39°57'N	75°26'W
Springvale, Austl.	217a	37°57'N	145°09'E
Spring Valley, Ca., U.S.	118a	32°46'N	117°01'W
Springvalley, Il., U.S. (spring-văl´ĭ)	108	41°20'N	89°15'W
Spring Valley, Mn., U.S.	113	43°41'N	92°26'W
Spring Valley, N.Y., U.S.	110a	41°07'N	74°03'W
Springville, Ut., U.S. (spring-vĭl)	119	40°10'N	111°40'W
Springwood, Austl.	217b	33°42'S	150°34'E
Spruce Grove, Can. (spro͞os grōv)	102g	53°32'N	113°55'W
Spur, Tx., U.S. (spûr)	120	33°29'N	100°51'W
Squam, l., N.H., U.S. (skwôm)	109	43°45'N	71°30'W
Squamish, Can. (skwŏ´mĭsh)	94	49°42'N	123°09'W
Squamish, r., Can.	94	50°10'N	123°30'W
Squillace, Golfo di, b., Italy (go͞o´l-fō-dē skwēl-lä´chå)	174	38°44'N	16°47'E
Srbija (Serbia), hist. reg., Serb. (sr bē-yä) (sĕr´bē-ä)	175	44°05'N	20°35'E
Srbobran, Serb. (s'r´bô-brän´)	175	45°32'N	19°50'E
Sredne-Kolymsk, Russia (s'rĕd´nyĕ kô-lēmsk´)	179	67°49'N	154°55'E
Sredne Rogatka, Russia (s'red´nȧ-ya) (rô gär´tkȧ)	186c	59°49'N	30°20'E
Sredniy Ik, r., Russia (srĕd´nĭ ĭk)	186a	55°46'N	58°50'E
Sredniy Ural, mts., Russia (ó´räl)	186a	57°47'N	59°00'E
Śrem, Pol. (shrĕm)	169	52°06'N	17°01'E
Sremska Karlovci, Serb. (srĕm´skē kär´lov-tsĕ)	175	45°10'N	19°57'E
Sremska Mitrovica, Serb. (srĕm´skä mē´trô-vē-tsä´)	175	44°59'N	19°39'E
Sretensk, Russia (s'rĕ´tĕnsk)	179	52°13'N	117°39'E
Sri Jayewardenepura Kotte, Sri L.	203	6°50'N	80°05'E
Sri Lanka, nation, Asia	203	8°45'N	82°30'E
Srīnagar, India (srē-nŭg´ŭr)	199	34°11'N	74°49'E
Środa, Pol. (shrô´dȧ)	169	52°14'N	17°17'E
Stabroek, Bel.	159a	51°20'N	4°21'E
Stade, Ger. (shtä´dĕ)	168	53°36'N	9°28'E
Städjan, mtn., Swe. (stĕd´yän)	166	61°53'N	12°50'E
Stafford, Eng., U.K. (stăf´fẽrd)	164	52°48'N	2°06'W
Stafford, Ks., U.S.	120	37°58'N	98°37'W
Staffordshire, co., Eng., U.K.	158a	52°45'N	2°00'W
Stahnsdorf, Ger. (shtäns´dôrf)	159b	52°22'N	13°10'E
Staines, Eng., U.K.	158b	51°26'N	0°13'W
Stakhanov, Ukr.	181	48°34'N	38°37'E
Stalingrad *see* Volgograd, Russia	178	48°40'N	42°20'E
Stalybridge, Eng., U.K.	158a	53°29'N	2°03'W
Stambaugh, Mi., U.S. (stăm´bô)	113	46°03'N	88°38'W
Stamford, Eng., U.K.	158a	52°39'N	0°28'W
Stamford, Ct., U.S. (stăm´fẽrd)	110a	41°03'N	73°32'W
Stamford, Tx., U.S.	120	32°57'N	99°48'W
Stammersdorf, Aus. (shtäm´ĕrs-dôrf)	159e	48°19'N	16°25'E
Stamps, Ar., U.S. (stămps)	121	33°22'N	93°31'W
Stanberry, Mo., U.S. (stan´bĕr-ē)	121	40°12'N	94°34'W
Standerton, S. Afr. (stăn´dẽr-tŭn)	232	26°57'S	29°17'E
Standing Rock Indian Reservation, I.R., N.D., U.S. (stănd´ĭng rŏk)	112	47°07'N	101°05'W
Standish, Eng., U.K. (stăn´dĭsh)	158a	53°36'N	2°39'W
Stanford, Ky., U.S. (stăn´fẽrd)	124	37°29'N	84°40'W
Stanger, S. Afr. (stăŋ-ger)	233c	29°22'S	31°18'E
Staniard Creek, Bah.	134	24°50'N	77°55'W
Stanislaus, r., Ca., U.S. (stăn´ĭs-lô)	118	38°10'N	120°16'W
Stanley, Can. (stăn´lē)	100	46°17'N	66°44'W
Stanley, Falk. Is.	144	51°46'S	57°59'W
Stanley, N.D., U.S.	112	48°20'N	102°25'W
Stanley, Wi., U.S.	113	44°56'N	90°56'W
Stanley Pool, l., Afr.	232	4°07'S	15°40'E
Stanley Reservoir, res., India (stăn´lē)	203	12°07'N	77°27'E
Stanleyville *see* Kisangani, D.R.C.	231	0°30'S	25°12'E
Stann Creek, Belize (stăn krēk)	132a	17°01'N	88°14'W
Stanovoy Khrebet, mts., Russia (stŭn-ȧ-voi´)	179	56°12'N	127°12'E
Stanton, Ca., U.S. (stăn´tŭn)	117a	33°48'N	118°00'W
Stanton, Ne., U.S.	112	41°57'N	97°15'W
Stanton, Tx., U.S.	122	32°08'N	101°46'W
Stanwood, Wa., U.S. (stăn´wo͝od)	116a	48°14'N	122°23'W
Staples, Mn., U.S. (stā´p'lz)	113	46°21'N	94°48'W
Stapleton, Al., U.S.	124	30°45'N	87°48'W
Stara Planina, mts., Blg.	156	42°50'N	24°45'E
Staraya Kupavna, Russia (stä´rȧ-yȧ kû-päf´nȧ)	186b	55°48'N	38°10'E
Staraya Russa, Russia (stä´rȧ-yȧ ro͞osȧ)	180	57°58'N	31°21'E
Stara Zagora, Blg. (zä´gô-rȧ)	163	42°26'N	25°37'E
Starbuck, Can. (stär´bŭk)	102f	49°46'N	97°36'W
Stargard Szczeciński, Pol. (shtär´gärt shchĕ-chyn´skē)	160	53°19'N	15°03'E
Staritsa, Russia (stä´rē-tsȧ)	176	56°29'N	34°58'E
Starke, Fl., U.S. (stärk)	125	29°55'N	82°07'W
Starkville, Co., U.S. (stärk´vĭl)	120	37°06'N	104°34'W
Starkville, Ms., U.S.	124	33°27'N	88°47'W
Starnberg, Ger. (shtärn-bĕrgh)	159d	47°59'N	11°20'E
Starnberger See, l., Ger.	168	47°58'N	11°30'E
Starobil's'k, Ukr.	181	49°19'N	38°57'E
Starodub, Russia (stä-rô-dróp´)	176	52°25'N	32°49'E
Starogard Gdański, Pol. (stä´rō-grad gdĕn´skē)	160	53°58'N	18°33'E
Starokostiantyniv, Ukr.	181	49°45'N	27°12'E
Staro-Minskaya, Russia (stä´rô mĭn´skȧ-yȧ)	181	46°19'N	38°51'E
Staro-Shcherbinovskaya, Russia	177	46°38'N	38°38'E
Staro-Subkhangulovo, Russia (stäro-so͞ob-kan-go͞o´lôvô)	186a	53°08'N	57°24'E
Staroutkinsk, Russia (stȧ-rô-o͞ot´kĭnsk)	186a	57°14'N	59°21'E
Starovirivka, Ukr.	177	49°31'N	35°48'E
Start Point, c., Eng., U.K. (stärt)	161	50°14'N	3°34'W
Staryi Ostropil', Ukr.	177	49°48'N	27°32'E
Stary Sącz, Pol. (stä-rē sônch´)	169	49°32'N	20°36'E
Staryy Oskol, Russia (stä´rē ôs-kôl´)	181	51°18'N	37°51'E
Stassfurt, Ger. (shtäs´fo͞ort)	168	51°52'N	11°35'E
Staszów, Pol. (stä´shôf)	169	50°32'N	21°13'E
State College, Pa., U.S. (stāt kŏl´ĕj)	109	40°50'N	77°55'W
State Line, Mn., U.S. (līn)	117h	46°36'N	92°18'W
Staten Island, i., N.Y., U.S. (stăt´ĕn)	110a	40°35'N	74°10'W
Statesboro, Ga., U.S. (stāts´bŭr-ō)	125	32°26'N	81°47'W
Statesville, N.C., U.S. (stās´vĭl)	125	34°45'N	80°54'W
Staunton, Il., U.S. (stôn´tŭn)	117e	39°01'N	89°47'W
Staunton, Va., U.S.	109	38°10'N	79°05'W
Stavanger, Nor. (stä´väng´ẽr)	154	58°59'N	5°44'E
Stave, r., Can. (stāv)	116d	49°12'N	122°24'W
Staveley, Eng., U.K. (stāv´lē)	158a	53°17'N	1°21'W
Stavenisse, Neth.	159a	51°35'N	3°59'E
Stavropol', Russia	178	45°05'N	41°50'E
Steamboat Springs, Co., U.S. (stēm´bōt´)	120	40°30'N	106°48'W
Stebliv, Ukr.	177	49°23'N	31°03'E
Steel, r., Can. (stēl)	98	49°08'N	86°55'W
Steelton, Pa., U.S. (stēl´tŭn)	109	40°15'N	76°45'W
Steenbergen, Neth.	159a	51°35'N	4°18'E
Steens Mountain, mts., Or., U.S. (stēnz)	114	42°15'N	118°52'W
Steep Point, c., Austl. (stēp)	220	26°15'N	112°05'E
Stefanie, Lake *see* Chew Bahir, l., Afr.	231	4°46'N	37°31'E
Steinbach, Can.	90	49°32'N	96°41'W
Steinkjer, Nor. (stēĭn-kyĕr)	160	64°00'N	11°19'E
Stella, Wa., U.S. (stĕl´ȧ)	116c	46°11'N	123°12'W
Stellarton, Can. (stĕl´ȧr-tŭn)	91	45°34'N	62°40'W
Stendal, Ger. (shtĕn´däl)	168	52°37'N	11°51'E
Stepanakert *see* Xankändi, Azer.	180	39°50'N	46°40'E
Stephens, Port, b., Austl. (stē´fĕns)	222	32°43'N	152°55'E
Stephenville, Can. (stē´vĕn-vĭl)	93a	48°33'N	58°35'W
Stepnogorsk, Kaz.	183	52°20'N	72°05'E
Sterkrade, Ger. (shtĕr´krädē)	171c	51°31'N	6°51'E
Sterkstroom, S. Afr.	233c	31°33'S	26°36'E
Sterling, Co., U.S. (stûr´lĭng)	104	40°38'N	103°14'W
Sterling, Il., U.S.	108	41°48'N	89°42'W
Sterling, Ks., U.S.	120	38°11'N	98°11'W
Sterling, Ma., U.S.	101a	42°26'N	71°41'W
Sterling, Tx., U.S.	122	31°53'N	100°58'W
Sterlitamak, Russia (styĕr´lē-ta-mȧk´)	178	53°38'N	55°56'E
Šternberk, Czech Rep. (shtĕrn´bĕrk)	169	49°44'N	17°18'E
Stettin *see* Szczecin, Pol.	154	53°25'N	14°35'E
Stettler, Can.	90	52°19'N	112°43'W
Steubenville, Oh., U.S. (stū´bĕn-vĭl)	108	40°20'N	80°40'W
Stevens, l., Wa., U.S. (stē´vĕnz)	116a	47°59'N	122°06'W
Stevens Point, Wi., U.S.	113	44°30'N	89°35'W
Stevensville, Mt., U.S. (stē´vĕnz-vĭl)	115	46°31'N	114°03'E
Stewart, r., Can. (stū´ẽrt)	92	63°27'N	138°48'W
Stewart Island, i., N.Z.	221a	46°56'S	167°40'E
Stewiacke, Can. (stū´wē-ăk)	100	45°08'N	63°21'W
Steynsrus, S. Afr. (stīns´ro͞os)	238c	27°58'S	27°33'E
Steyr, Aus. (shtīr)	161	48°03'N	14°24'E
Stif, Alg.	230	36°18'N	5°21'E
Stikine, r., Can. (stĭ-kēn´)	92	58°17'N	130°10'W
Stikine Ranges, Can.	90	59°05'N	130°00'W
Stillaguamish, r., Wa., U.S.	116a	48°11'N	122°18'W
Stillaguamish, South Fork, r., Wa., U.S. (stĭl-ȧ-gwä´mĭsh)	116a	48°05'N	121°59'W
Stillwater, Mn., U.S. (stĭl´wô-tẽr)	117g	45°04'N	92°48'W
Stillwater, Mt., U.S.	115	45°23'N	109°45'W
Stillwater, Ok., U.S.	121	36°06'N	97°03'W
Stillwater, r., Mt., U.S.	115	48°47'N	114°40'W
Stillwater Range, mts., Nv., U.S.	118	39°43'N	118°11'W
Štip, Mac. (shtĭp)	175	41°43'N	22°07'E
Stirling, Scot., U.K. (stûr´lĭng)	164	56°05'N	3°59'W
Stittsville, Can. (stĭts´vĭl)	102c	45°15'N	75°54'W
Stizef, Alg. (mĕr-syā´ lä-kônb)	173	35°18'N	0°11'W
Stjördalshalsen, Nor. (styûr-däls-hälsĕn)	166	63°26'N	11°00'E
Stockbridge Munsee Indian Reservation, I.R., Wi., U.S. (stŏk´brĭdj mŭn-sē)	113	44°49'N	89°00'W
Stockerau, Aus. (shtô´kĕ-rou)	168	48°24'N	16°13'E
Stockholm, Swe. (stôk´hôlm)	154	59°23'N	18°00'E
Stockholm, Me., U.S. (stŏk´hōlm)	100	47°05'N	68°08'W
Stockport, Eng., U.K. (stŏk´pôrt)	164	53°24'N	2°09'W
Stockton, Eng., U.K.	164	54°35'N	1°25'W
Stockton, Ca., U.S. (stŏk´tŭn)	104	37°56'N	121°16'W
Stockton, Ks., U.S.	120	39°26'N	99°16'W
Stockton, i., Wi., U.S.	113	46°56'N	90°25'W
Stockton Plateau, plat., Tx., U.S.	106	30°34'N	102°35'W
Stockton Reservoir, res., Mo., U.S.	121	37°40'N	93°45'W
Stöde, Swe. (stû´dĕ)	166	62°26'N	16°35'E
Stoeng Trêng, Camb. (stông´trĕng´)	212	13°36'N	106°00'E
Stoke-on-Trent, Eng., U.K. (stōk-ŏn-trĕnt)	160	53°01'N	2°12'W
Stokhid, r., Ukr.	169	51°24'N	25°20'E
Stolac, Bos. (stō´läts)	175	43°03'N	17°59'E
Stolbovoy, is., Russia (stôl-bô-voi´)	185	74°05'N	136°00'E
Stolin, Bela. (stô´lēn)	169	51°54'N	26°52'E
Stömstad, Swe.	166	58°58'N	11°09'E
Stone, Eng., U.K.	158a	52°54'N	2°09'W
Stoneham, Can. (stōn´ȧm)	102b	46°59'N	71°22'W
Stoneham, Ma., U.S.	101a	42°30'N	71°05'W
Stonehaven, Scot., U.K. (stōn´hā-v'n)	164	56°57'N	2°09'W
Stone Mountain, Ga., U.S. (stōn)	110c	33°49'N	84°10'W
Stonewall, Can. (stōn´wôl)	102f	50°09'N	97°21'W
Stonewall, Ms., U.S.	124	32°08'N	88°44'W
Stoney Creek, Can. (stō´nē)	102d	43°13'N	79°45'W
Stonington, Ct., U.S. (stōn´ĭng-tŭn)	109	41°20'N	71°55'W
Stony Indian Reserve, I.R., Can.	102e	51°10'N	114°45'W
Stony Mountain, Can.	102f	50°05'N	97°13'W
Stony Plain, Can. (stō´nē plān)	102g	53°32'N	114°00'W
Stony Plain Indian Reserve, I.R., Can.	102g	53°29'N	113°48'W
Stony Point, N.Y., U.S.	110a	41°13'N	73°58'W
Stora Sotra, i., Nor.	166	60°24'N	4°35'E
Stord, i., Nor. (stōrd)	166	59°54'N	5°15'E
Store Baelt, strt., Den.	166	55°25'N	10°50'E
Storfjorden, b., Nor.	166	62°17'N	6°19'E
Stormberg, mts., S. Afr. (stôrm´bûrg)	233c	31°28'S	26°35'E
Storm Lake, Ia., U.S.	112	42°39'N	95°12'W
Stormy Point, c., V.I.U.S. (stôr´mē)	129c	18°22'N	65°01'W
Stornoway, Scot., U.K. (stôr´nô-wā)	160	58°13'N	6°21'W
Storozhynets', Ukr.	169	48°10'N	25°44'E
Störsjo, Swe. (stör´shû)	166	62°49'N	13°08'E
Störsjoen, l., Nor. (stôr-syûĕn)	166	61°32'N	11°30'E
Störsjön, l., Swe.	160	63°06'N	14°00'E
Storvik, Swe.	166	60°37'N	16°31'E
Stoughton, Wi., U.S.	113	42°54'N	89°15'W
Stour, r., Eng., U.K. (stour)	165	52°09'N	0°29'E
Stourbridge, Eng., U.K. (stour´brĭj)	158a	52°27'N	2°08'W
Stow, Ma., U.S. (stō)	101a	42°56'N	71°31'W
Stow, Oh., U.S.	111d	41°09'N	81°26'W
Straatsdrif, S. Afr.	238c	25°19'S	26°22'E
Strabane, N. Ire., U.K. (stră-băn´)	164	54°59'N	7°27'W
Straelen, Ger. (shtrā´lĕn)	171c	51°26'N	6°16'E
Strahan, Austl. (strā´ăn)	219	42°08'S	145°28'E
Strakonice, Czech Rep. (strä´kô-nyē-tsĕ)	168	49°18'N	13°52'E
Straldzha, Blg. (sträl´dzhȧ)	175	42°37'N	26°44'E
Stralsund, Ger. (shräl´sônt)	160	54°18'N	13°04'E
Strangford Lough, l., N. Ire., U.K.	164	54°30'N	5°34'W
Strängnäs, Swe. (strĕng´nĕs)	166	59°23'N	16°59'E

ng-sing; ŋ-baŋk; ɴ-nasalized n; nŏd; cŏmmit; ōld; ôbey; ôrder; oi-boil; fo͞od; ŏ-as oo in foot; ou-out; s-soft; sh-dish; th-thin; pūre; ûnite; ûrn; stŭd; circŭs; ü-as in French tu; ´-indeterminate vowel.

354 Stranraer – Svyatoy Nos
PRONOUNCING INDEX

PLACE (Pronunciation)	PAGE	LAT.	LONG.
Stranraer, Scot., U.K. (străn-rär′)	164	54°55′N	5°05′W
Strasbourg, Fr. (stràs-bo͞or′)	154	48°36′N	7°49′E
Stratford, Can. (străt′fērd)	98	43°20′N	81°05′W
Stratford, Ct., U.S.	109	41°10′N	73°05′W
Stratford, Wi., U.S.	113	44°16′N	90°02′W
Stratford-upon-Avon, Eng., U.K.	164	52°13′N	1°41′W
Straubing, Ger. (strou′bĭng)	168	48°52′N	12°36′E
Strausberg, Ger. (strous′bĕrgh)	168	52°35′N	13°50′E
Strawberry, r., Ut., U.S.	119	40°05′N	110°55′W
Strawn, Tx., U.S. (strôn)	122	32°38′N	98°28′W
Streator, Il., U.S. (strē′tēr)	108	41°05′N	88°50′W
Streeter, N.D., U.S.	112	46°40′N	99°22′W
Streetsville, Can. (strētz′vĭl)	102d	43°34′N	79°43′W
Strehaia, Rom. (strĕ-κä′yȧ)	175	44°37′N	23°13′E
Strel′na, Russia (strĕl′nȧ)	186c	59°52′N	30°01′E
Stretford, Eng., U.K. (strĕt′fērd)	158a	53°25′N	2°19′W
Strickland, r., Pap. N. Gui. (strĭk′lănd)	213	6°15′S	142°00′E
Strijen, Neth.	159a	51°44′N	4°32′E
Stromboli, Italy (strŏm′bô-lē)	163	38°46′N	15°16′E
Stromyn, Russia (strô′mĭn)	186b	56°02′N	38°29′E
Strong, r., Ms., U.S. (strông)	124	32°03′N	89°42′W
Strongsville, Oh., U.S. (strôngz′vĭl)	111d	41°19′N	81°50′W
Stronsay, i., Scot., U.K. (strŏn′sā)	164a	59°09′N	2°35′W
Stroudsburg, Pa., U.S. (stroudz′bûrg)	109	41°00′N	75°15′W
Struer, Den.	166	56°29′N	8°34′E
Strugi Krasnyye, Russia (stro͞o′gĭ kră′s-ny′yĕ)	176	58°14′N	29°10′E
Struma, r., Eur. (stro͞o′mȧ)	175	41°55′N	23°05′E
Strumica, Mac. (stro͞o′mĭ-tsȧ)	175	41°26′N	22°38′E
Strunino, Russia	186b	56°23′N	38°34′E
Struthers, Oh., U.S. (strŭdh′ērz)	108	41°00′N	80°35′W
Struvenhütten, Ger. (shtro͞o′vĕn-hü-tĕn)	159c	53°52′N	10°04′E
Strydpoortberge, mts., S. Afr.	238c	24°08′N	29°18′E
Stryi, Ukr.	169	49°16′N	23°51′E
Strzelce Opolskie, Pol. (stzhĕl′tsĕ o-pōl′skyĕ)	169	50°31′N	18°20′E
Strzelin, Pol. (stzhĕ-lĭn)	169	50°48′N	17°06′E
Strzelno, Pol. (stzhål′nô)	169	52°37′N	18°10′E
Stuart, Fl., U.S. (stū′ērt)	125a	27°10′N	80°14′W
Stuart, Ia., U.S.	113	41°31′N	94°20′W
Stuart, i., Ak., U.S.	103	63°25′N	162°45′W
Stuart, i., Wa., U.S.	116d	48°42′N	123°10′W
Stuart Lake, l., Can.	94	54°32′N	124°35′W
Stuart Range, mts., Austl.	220	29°00′S	134°30′E
Sturgeon, r., Can.	102g	53°41′N	113°46′W
Sturgeon, r., Mi., U.S.	113	46°43′N	88°43′W
Sturgeon Bay, Wi., U.S.	113	44°50′N	87°22′W
Sturgeon Bay, b., Can.	97	52°00′N	98°00′W
Sturgeon Falls, Can.	91	46°19′N	79°49′W
Sturgis, Ky., U.S.	108	37°35′N	88°00′W
Sturgis, Mi., U.S.	108	41°45′N	85°25′W
Sturgis, S.D., U.S.	112	44°25′N	103°31′W
Sturt Creek, r., Austl.	220	19°40′S	127°40′E
Sturtevant, Wi., U.S. (stŭr′tĕ-vănt)	111a	42°42′N	87°54′W
Stutterheim, S. Afr. (stŭrt′ēr-hīm)	233c	32°34′S	27°27′E
Stuttgart, Ger. (shto͞ot′gärt)	154	48°48′N	9°15′E
Stuttgart, Ar., U.S. (stŭt′gärt)	121	34°30′N	91°33′W
Stykkishólmur, Ice.	160	65°00′N	21°48′W
Styr′, r., Eur. (stēr)	169	51°44′N	26°07′E
Suao, Tai. (so͞oŏu)	209	24°35′N	121°45′E
Subarnarekha, r., India	202	22°38′N	86°26′E
Subata, Lat. (so͝′bȧ-tȧ)	167	56°02′N	25°54′E
Subic, Phil. (so͞o′bĭk)	213a	14°52′N	120°15′E
Subic Bay, b., Phil.	213a	14°41′N	120°11′E
Subotica, Serb. (so͞o′bô′tē-tsȧ)	154	46°06′N	19°41′E
Subugo, mtn., Kenya	237	1°40′S	35°49′E
Succasunna, N.J., U.S. (sŭk′kȧ-sŭn′nȧ)	110a	40°52′N	74°37′W
Suceava, Rom. (so͞o-chȧ-ä′vȧ)	169	47°39′N	26°17′E
Suceava, r., Rom.	169	47°45′N	26°10′E
Sucha, Pol. (so͞o′κȧ)	169	49°44′N	19°40′E
Suchiapa, Mex. (so͞o-chē-ä′pä)	131	16°38′N	93°08′W
Suchiapa, r., Mex.	131	16°27′N	93°26′W
Suchitoto, El Sal. (so͞o-chē-tō′tō)	132	13°58′N	89°03′W
Sucio, r., Col. (so͞o′syō)	142a	6°55′N	76°15′W
Suck, r., Ire. (sŭk)	164	53°34′N	8°16′W
Sucre, Bol. (so͞o′krā)	142	19°06′S	65°16′W
Sucre, dept., Ven. (so͞o′krĕ)	143b	10°18′N	64°12′W
Sud, Canal du, strt., Haiti	135	18°40′N	73°15′W
Sud, Rivière du, r., Can. (rē-vyâr′dü süd′)	102b	46°56′N	70°35′W
Suda, Russia (so͝′dá)	186a	56°58′N	56°45′E
Suda, r., Russia (so͝′dȧ)	176	59°24′N	36°40′E
Sudair, Sau. Ar. (sŭ-dä′ēr)	198	25°48′N	46°28′E
Sudalsvatnet, l., Nor.	166	59°35′N	6°59′E
Sudan, nation, Afr.	231	14°00′N	28°00′E
Sudan, reg., Afr. (so͞o-dän′)	230	15°00′N	7°00′E
Sudbury, Can. (sŭd′bēr-ē)	91	46°28′N	81°00′W
Sudbury, Ma., U.S.	101a	42°23′N	71°25′W
Sudetes, mts., Eur.	156	50°41′N	15°37′E
Sudogda, Russia (so͝′dôk-dȧ)	176	55°57′N	40°29′E
Sudost′, r., Eur. (so͝-dôst′)	176	52°43′N	33°13′E
Sudzha, Russia (so͝d′zhȧ)	177	51°14′N	35°11′E
Sueca, Spain (swā′kä)	173	39°12′N	0°18′W
Suez, Egypt	231	29°58′N	32°34′E
Suez, Gulf of, b., Egypt (so͞o-ĕz′)	231	29°53′N	32°33′E
Suez Canal, can., Egypt	231	30°53′N	32°21′E
Suffern, N.Y., U.S. (sŭf′fērn)	110a	41°07′N	74°09′W
Suffolk, Va., U.S. (sŭf′ŭk)	110g	36°43′N	76°35′W
Sugar City, Co., U.S.	120	38°12′N	103°42′W
Sugar Creek, Mo., U.S.	117f	39°07′N	94°27′W
Sugar Creek, r., Il., U.S. (sho͝g′ēr)	121	40°14′N	89°28′W
Sugar Creek, r., In., U.S.	108	39°55′N	87°10′W
Sugar Island, i., Mi., U.S.	117k	46°31′N	84°12′W
Sugarloaf Point, c., Austl. (so͝gēr′lōf)	222	32°19′S	153°04′E
Suggi Lake, l., Can.	97	54°22′N	102°47′W
Sühbaatar, Mong.	204	50°18′N	106°31′E
Suhl, Ger. (zo͞ol)	168	50°37′N	10°41′E
Suichuan, mtn., China	209	26°25′N	114°10′E
Suide, China (swā-dŭ)	208	37°32′N	110°12′E
Suifenhe, China (swā-fŭn-hŭ)	205	44°47′N	131°13′E
Suihua, China	205	46°38′N	126°50′E
Suining, China (so͞o′ē-nĭng′)	206	33°54′N	117°57′E
Suipacha, Arg. (swē-pä′chä)	141c	34°45′S	59°43′W
Suiping, China (swā-pĭŋ)	206	33°09′N	113°58′E
Suir, r., Ire. (sūr)	164	52°20′N	7°32′W
Suisun Bay, b., Ca., U.S. (so͞oē-so͞on′)	116b	38°07′N	122°02′W
Suita, Japan (so͝′ē-tä)	211b	34°45′N	135°32′E
Suitland, Md., U.S. (so͝t′lănd)	110e	38°51′N	76°57′W
Suixian, China (swā shyĕn)	209	31°42′N	113°20′E
Suiyüan, hist. reg., China (swā-yüĕn)	204	41°31′N	107°04′E
Suizhong, China (swā-jôŋ)	208	40°22′N	120°20′E
Sukabumi, Indon.	212	6°52′S	106°56′E
Sukadana, Indon.	212	1°15′S	110°30′E
Sukagawa, Japan (so͞o′kä-gä′wä)	211	37°08′N	140°07′E
Sukhinichi, Russia (so͞o′κē′nē-chē)	180	54°07′N	35°18′E
Sukhona, r., Russia (so͝-κô′nȧ)	180	59°30′N	42°20′E
Sukhoy Log, Russia (so͞o′kôy lôg)	186a	56°55′N	62°03′E
Sukhumi, Geor. (so͝-ko͝m′)	181	43°00′N	41°00′E
Sukkur, Pak. (sŭk′ŭr)	199	27°49′N	68°50′E
Sukkwan Island, i., Ak., U.S.	94	55°05′N	132°45′W
Suksun, Russia (so͝k′so͝n)	186a	57°08′N	57°22′E
Sukumo, Japan (so͞o′ko͝-mō)	211	32°58′N	132°45′E
Sukunka, r., Can.	95	55°00′N	121°50′W
Sula, r., Ukr. (so͞o-lȧ′)	177	50°36′N	33°13′E
Sula, Kepulauan, is., Indon.	213	2°20′S	125°20′E
Sulaco, r., Hond. (so͞o-lä′kō)	132	14°55′N	87°31′W
Sulaimān Range, mts., Pak. (so͝-lä-ē-män′)	199	29°47′N	69°10′E
Sulak, r., Russia (so͞o-läk′)	181	43°30′N	47°00′E
Sulfeld, Ger. (zo͞o′fĕld)	159c	53°48′N	10°13′E
Sulina, Rom. (so͞o-lē′nȧ)	163	45°08′N	29°38′E
Sulitelma, mtn., Eur. (so͞o-lē-tyĕl′mȧ)	160	67°03′N	16°35′E
Sullana, Peru (so͞o-lyä′nä)	142	4°57′S	80°47′W
Sulligent, Al., U.S. (sŭl′ĭ-jĕnt)	124	33°52′N	88°06′W
Sullivan, Il., U.S. (sŭl′ĭ-văn)	108	41°35′N	88°35′W
Sullivan, In., U.S.	108	39°05′N	87°20′W
Sullivan, Mo., U.S.	121	38°13′N	91°09′W
Sulmona, Italy (so͞ol-mō′nä)	174	42°02′N	13°58′E
Sulphur, Ok., U.S. (sŭl′fŭr)	121	34°31′N	96°58′W
Sulphur, r., Tx., U.S.	121	33°26′N	95°06′W
Sulphur Springs, Tx., U.S. (sprĭngz)	121	33°09′N	95°36′W
Sultan, Wa., U.S. (sŭl′tăn)	116a	47°52′N	121°49′W
Sultan, r., Wa., U.S.	116a	47°55′N	121°49′W
Sultepec, Mex. (so͞ol-tå-pĕk′)	130	18°50′N	99°51′W
Sulu Archipelago, is., Phil. (so͞o′lo͞o)	212	5°52′N	122°00′E
Suluntah, Libya	163	32°39′N	21°49′E
Sulūq, Libya	231	31°39′N	20°15′E
Sulu Sea, sea, Asia	212	8°25′N	119°00′E
Suma, Japan (so͞o′mä)	211b	34°39′N	135°08′E
Sumas, Wa., U.S. (sū′mȧs)	116d	49°00′N	122°16′W
Sumatera, i., Indon. (so͝-mä-trȧ)	212	2°06′N	99°40′E
Sumatra *see* Sumatera, i., Indon.	212	2°06′N	99°40′E
Sumba, i., Indon. (sŭm′bȧ)	212	9°52′S	119°00′E
Sumba, Île, i., D.R.C.	236	1°44′N	19°32′E
Sumbawa, i., Indon. (so͝m-bä′wä)	212	9°00′S	118°18′E
Sumbawa-Besar, Indon.	212	8°32′S	117°20′E
Sumbawanga, Tan.	237	7°58′S	31°37′E
Sumbe, Ang.	232	11°13′S	13°50′E
Sümeg, Hung. (shü′mĕg)	169	46°59′N	17°19′E
Sumida, r., Japan (so͞o′mē-dä)	211	36°01′N	139°24′E
Sumidouro, Braz. (so͞o-mē-dō′ro͝)	141a	22°04′S	42°41′W
Sumiyoshi, Japan (so͞o′mē-yō′shē)	211b	34°43′N	135°16′E
Summer Lake, l., Or., U.S. (sŭm′ēr)	114	42°50′N	120°35′W
Summerland, Can. (sŭ′mēr-lănd)	95	49°39′N	119°40′W
Summerside, Can. (sŭm′ēr-sīd)	91	46°25′N	63°47′W
Summerton, S.C., U.S. (sŭm′ēr-tŭn)	125	33°37′N	80°22′W
Summerville, S.C., U.S. (sŭm′ēr-vĭl)	125	33°00′N	80°10′W
Summit, Il., U.S. (sŭm′mĭt)	111a	41°47′N	87°48′W
Summit, N.J., U.S.	110a	40°43′N	74°21′W
Summit Lake Indian Reservation, I.R., Nv., U.S.	114	41°35′N	119°30′W
Summit Peak, mtn., Co., U.S.	119	37°20′N	106°40′W
Sumner, Wa., U.S. (sŭm′nĕr)	116a	47°12′N	122°14′W
Šumperk, Czech Rep. (sho͝m′pĕrk)	169	49°57′N	17°02′E
Sumqayıt, Azer.	182	40°36′N	49°38′E
Sumrall, Ms., U.S. (sŭm′rôl)	124	31°25′N	89°34′W
Sumter, S.C., U.S. (sŭm′tēr)	125	33°55′N	80°21′W
Sumy, Ukr. (so͞o′mĭ)	178	50°54′N	34°47′E
Sumy, prov., Ukr.	177	51°02′N	34°05′E
Sun, r., Mt., U.S. (sŭn)	115	47°34′N	111°53′W
Sunburst, Mt., U.S.	115	48°53′N	111°55′W
Sunda, Selat, strt., Indon.	212	5°45′S	106°15′E
Sundance, Wy., U.S. (sŭn′dăns)	115	44°24′N	104°27′W
Sundarbans, sw., Asia (so͝n′dēr-bŭns)	199	21°50′N	89°00′E
Sunday Strait, strt., Austl. (sŭn′dā)	220	15°50′S	122°45′E
Sundbyberg, Swe. (so͝n′bü-bĕrgh)	166	59°24′N	17°56′E
Sunderland, Eng., U.K. (sŭn′dēr-lănd)	160	54°55′N	1°25′W
Sunderland, Md., U.S.	110e	38°41′N	76°36′W
Sundsvall, Swe. (so͝nds′väl)	154	62°24′N	19°19′E
Sungari (Songhua), r., China	205	46°09′N	127°53′E
Sungari Reservoir, res., China	208	42°55′N	127°50′E
Sungurlu, Tur. (so͞on′go͝r-lo͝′)	163	40°08′N	34°20′E
Sun Kosi, r., Nepal	202	27°13′N	85°52′E
Sunland, Ca., U.S. (sŭn-lănd)	117a	34°16′N	118°18′W
Sunne, Swe. (so͞on′ĕ)	166	59°51′N	13°07′E
Sunninghill, Eng., U.K. (sŭnĭng′hĭl)	158b	51°23′N	0°40′W
Sunnymead, Ca., U.S. (sŭn′ĭ-mēd)	117a	33°56′N	117°15′W
Sunnyside, Ut., U.S.	119	39°35′N	110°20′W
Sunnyside, Wa., U.S.	114	46°19′N	120°00′W
Sunnyvale, Ca., U.S. (sŭn-nē-vāl)	116b	37°23′N	122°02′W
Sunol, Ca., U.S. (so͞o′nŭl)	116b	37°36′N	122°53′W
Sunset, Ut., U.S. (sŭn-sĕt)	117b	41°08′N	112°02′W
Sunset Crater National Monument, rec., Az., U.S. (krā′tēr)	119	35°20′N	111°30′W
Sunshine, Austl.	217a	37°47′S	144°50′E
Suntar, Russia (so͝n-tȧr′)	179	62°14′N	117°49′E
Sunyani, Ghana	234	7°20′N	2°20′W
Suoyarvi, Russia (so͞o′ô-yĕr′vē)	180	62°12′N	32°29′E
Superior, Az., U.S. (su-pē′rĭ-ēr)	119	33°15′N	111°10′W
Superior, Ne., U.S.	120	40°04′N	98°05′W
Superior, Wi., U.S.	105	46°44′N	92°06′W
Superior, Wy., U.S.	115	41°45′N	108°57′W
Superior, Laguna, l., Mex. (lä-go͞o′nȧ so͞o-pā-rē-ōr′)	131	16°20′N	94°55′W
Superior, Lake, l., N.A.	107	47°38′N	89°20′W
Superior Village, Wi., U.S.	117h	46°38′N	92°07′W
Sup′ung Reservoir, res., Asia (so͞o′po͞ong)	210	40°35′N	126°00′E
Suqian, China (so͞o-chyĕn)	206	33°57′N	118°17′E
Suquamish, Wa., U.S. (so͞o-gwä′mĭsh)	116a	47°44′N	122°34′W
Suquṭrā (Socotra), i., Yemen (sō-kō′trȧ)	198	13°00′N	52°30′E
Şūr, Leb. (so͞or) (tīr)	197a	33°16′N	35°13′E
Şūr, Oman	198	22°23′N	59°28′E
Surabaya, Indon.	212	7°23′S	112°45′E
Surakarta, Indon.	212	7°35′S	110°45′E
Šurany, Slvk. (sho͞o′rȧ-nû′)	169	48°05′N	18°11′E
Surat, Austl. (sū-răt)	222	27°18′S	149°00′E
Surat, India (so͝′rŭt)	199	21°08′N	73°22′E
Surat Thani, Thai.	212	8°59′N	99°14′E
Surazh, Bela.	176	55°24′N	30°46′E
Surazh, Russia (so͞o-rȧzh′)	176	53°02′N	32°27′E
Surgères, Fr. (sür-zhâr′)	170	46°06′N	0°51′W
Surgut, Russia (so͝r-go͝t′)	178	61°18′N	73°38′E
Suriname, nation, S.A. (so͞o-rē-näm′)	143	4°00′N	56°00′W
Sūrmaq, Iran	201	31°03′N	52°48′E
Surt, Libya	231	31°14′N	16°37′E
Surt, Khalīj, b., Libya	231	31°30′N	18°28′E
Suruga-Wan, b., Japan (so͞o′ro͞o-gä wän)	210	34°52′N	138°36′E
Susa, Japan	211	34°40′N	131°39′E
Sušak, i., Serb.	174	42°45′N	16°30′E
Susak, Otok, i., Serb.	174	44°31′N	14°15′E
Susaki, Japan (so͞o′sä-kē)	211	33°23′N	133°16′E
Sušice, Czech Rep.	168	49°14′N	13°31′E
Susitna, Ak., U.S. (so͞o-sĭt′nȧ)	103	61°28′N	150°28′W
Susitna, r., Ak., U.S.	103	62°00′N	150°28′W
Susong, China (so͞o-sôŋ)	209	30°18′N	116°08′E
Susquehanna, Pa., U.S. (sŭs′kwē-hăn′ȧ)	109	41°55′N	73°55′W
Susquehanna, r., U.S.	109	39°50′N	76°20′W
Sussex, Can. (sŭs′ĕks)	91	45°43′N	65°31′W
Sussex, N.J., U.S.	110a	41°12′N	74°36′W
Sussex, Wi., U.S.	111a	43°08′N	88°12′W
Sutherland, Austl. (sŭdh′ēr-lănd)	217b	34°02′S	151°04′E
Sutherland, S. Afr. (sŭ′thēr-lănd)	232	32°25′S	20°40′E
Sutlej, r., Asia (sŭt′lĕj)	199	30°15′N	73°00′E
Sutton, Eng., U.K. (sut′′n)	158b	51°21′N	0°12′W
Sutton, Ma., U.S.	101a	42°09′N	71°46′W
Sutton Coldfield, Eng., U.K. (kōld′fēld)	158a	52°34′N	1°49′W
Sutton-in-Ashfield, Eng., U.K. (ĭn-ăsh′fēld)	158a	53°07′N	1°15′W
Suurberge, mts., S. Afr.	233c	33°15′S	25°32′E
Suva, Fiji	214g	18°08′S	178°25′E
Suwa, Japan (so͞o′wä)	211	36°03′N	138°08′E
Suwałki, Pol. (so͝-vou′kē)	169	54°05′N	22°58′E
Suwanee Lake, l., Can.	97	56°08′N	100°10′W
Suwannee, r., U.S. (so͝-wô′nē)	107	29°42′N	83°00′W
Suways al Ḩulwah, Tur′ at as, can., Egypt	238d	30°15′N	32°20′E
Suxian, China (so͞o shyĕn)	208	33°29′N	117°51′E
Suzdal′, Russia (so͞oz′dȧl)	176	56°26′N	40°29′E
Suzhou, China (so͞o-jō)	205	31°19′N	120°37′E
Suzu Misaki, c., Japan (so͞o′zo͞o mē′sä-kē)	210	37°30′N	137°35′E
Svalbard (Spitsbergen), dep., Nor. (sväl′bärt) (spĭts′bûr-gĕn)	178	77°00′N	20°00′E
Svaneke, Den. (svä′nĕ-kĕ)	166	55°08′N	15°07′E
Svatove, Ukr.	181	49°23′N	38°10′E
Svedala, Swe. (svĕ′dä-lä)	166	55°29′N	13°11′E
Sveg, Swe.	166	62°03′N	14°22′E
Svelvik, Nor. (svĕl′vēk)	166	59°37′N	10°18′E
Svenčionys, Lith.	167	55°09′N	26°09′E
Svendborg, Den. (svĕn-bôrgh)	166	55°05′N	10°35′E
Svensen, Or., U.S. (svĕn′sĕn)	116c	46°10′N	123°39′W
Sverdlovsk *see* Yekaterinburg, Russia	178	56°51′N	60°36′E
Svetlaya, Russia (svyĕt′lȧ-yȧ)	210	46°09′N	137°53′E
Svicha, r., Ukr.	169	49°09′N	24°10′E
Svilajnac, Serb. (svē′lȧ-ē-nȧts)	175	44°12′N	21°14′E
Svilengrad, Blg. (svĕl′ĕn-grȧt)	175	41°44′N	26°11′E
Svir′, r., Russia	180	60°55′N	33°40′E
Svir Kanal, can., Russia (kȧ-näl′)	167	60°10′N	32°40′E
Svishtov, Blg. (svēsh′tôf)	163	43°36′N	25°21′E
Svisloch′, r., Bela. (svēs′lôκ)	176	53°38′N	28°10′E
Svitavy, Czech Rep.	168	49°46′N	16°28′E
Svobodnyy, Russia (svô-bôd′nĭ)	179	51°28′N	128°28′E
Svolvaer, Nor. (svôl′vĕr)	160	68°15′N	14°29′E
Svyatoy Nos, Mys, c., Russia (svyŭ′toi nôs)	179	72°18′N	139°28′E

ăt; finăl; rāte; senåte; ärm; åsk; sofȧ; fâre; ch-choose; dh-as th in other; bē; ēvent; bĕt; recĕnt; cratēr; g-gō; gh-guttural g; bĭt; ĭ-short neutral; rīde; κ-guttural k as ch in German ich;

PRONOUNCING INDEX
Swadlincote – Tamiahua 355

PLACE (Pronunciation)	PAGE	LAT.	LONG.
Swadlincote, Eng., U.K. (swŏd′lĭn-kōt)	158a	52°46′N	1°33′W
Swain Reefs, rf., Austl. (swān)	221	22°12′S	152°08′E
Swainsboro, Ga., U.S. (swānz′bŭr-ô)	125	32°37′N	82°21′W
Swakopmund, Nmb. (svä′kôp-mònt) (swȧ′kôp-mònd)	232	22°40′S	14°30′E
Swallowfield, Eng., U.K. (swŏl′ô-fēld)	158b	51°21′N	0°58′W
Swampscott, Ma., U.S. (swômp′skŏt)	101a	42°28′N	70°55′W
Swan, r., Austl.	220	31°30′S	116°30′E
Swan, r., Can.	97	51°58′N	101°45′W
Swan, r., Mt., U.S.	115	47°50′N	113°40′W
Swan Hill, Austl.	219	35°20′S	143°30′E
Swan Hills, Can. (hĭlz)	90	54°52′N	115°45′W
Swan Island, i., Austl. (swŏn)	217a	38°15′S	144°41′E
Swan Lake, l., Can.	97	52°30′N	100°45′W
Swanland, reg., Austl. (swŏn′lănd)	220	31°45′S	119°15′E
Swan Range, mts., Mt., U.S.	115	47°50′N	113°40′W
Swan River, Can. (swŏn rĭv′ēr)	90	52°06′N	101°16′W
Swansea, Wales, U.K.	161	51°37′N	3°59′W
Swansea, Il., U.S. (swŏn′sē)	117e	38°32′N	89°59′W
Swansea, Ma., U.S.	110b	41°45′N	71°09′W
Swanson Reservoir, res., Ne., U.S. (swŏn′sŭn)	120	40°13′N	101°30′W
Swartberg, mtn., Afr.	233c	30°08′S	29°34′E
Swartkop, mtn., S. Afr.	232a	34°13′S	18°27′E
Swartruggens, S. Afr.	238c	25°40′S	26°40′E
Swartspruit, S. Afr.	233b	25°44′S	28°01′E
Swatow see Shantou, China	205	23°20′N	116°40′E
Swaziland, nation, Afr. (Swä′zē-lănd)	232	26°45′S	31°30′E
Sweden, nation, Eur. (swē′dĕn)	154	60°10′N	14°10′E
Swedesboro, N.J., U.S. (swēdz′bē-rô)	110f	39°45′N	75°22′W
Sweetwater, Tn., U.S. (swēt′wô-tēr)	124	35°36′N	84°29′W
Sweetwater, Tx., U.S.	104	32°28′N	100°25′W
Sweetwater, l., N.D., U.S.	112	48°15′N	98°35′W
Sweetwater, r., Wy., U.S.	115	42°19′N	108°35′W
Sweetwater Reservoir, res., Ca., U.S.	118a	32°42′N	116°54′W
Świdnica, Pol. (shvĭd-nē′tsȧ)	168	50°50′N	16°30′E
Świdwin, Pol. (shvĭd′vĭn)	168	53°46′N	15°48′E
Świebodzice, Pol.	168	50°51′N	16°17′E
Świebodzin, Pol. (shvyĕn-bo′jĕts)	168	52°16′N	15°36′E
Świecie, Pol. (shvyăn′tsyĕ)	169	53°23′N	18°26′E
Świętokrzyskie, Góry, mts., Pol. (shvyĕn-tō-kzhĭ′skyĕ gōō′rĭ)	169	50°57′N	21°02′E
Swift, r., Eng., U.K.	158a	52°26′N	1°08′W
Swift, r., Me., U.S. (swĭft)	101	44°42′N	70°40′W
Swift Creek Reservoir, res., Wa., U.S.	114	46°03′N	122°10′W
Swift Current, Can. (swĭft kûr′ĕnt)	90	50°17′N	107°50′W
Swindle Island, i., Can.	94	52°32′N	128°35′W
Swindon, Eng., U.K. (swĭn′dŭn)	164	51°35′N	1°55′W
Swinomish Indian Reservation, I.R., Wa., U.S. (swĭ-nō′mĭsh)	116a	48°25′N	122°27′W
Świnoujście, Pol. (shvĭ-nĭ-ô-wĕsh′chyĕ)	168	53°56′N	14°14′E
Swinton, Eng., U.K. (swĭn′tŭn)	158a	53°30′N	1°19′W
Swissvale, Pa., U.S. (swĭs′vāl)	111e	40°25′N	79°53′W
Switzerland, nation, Eur. (swĭt′zēr-lănd)	154	46°30′N	7°43′E
Syanno, Bela. (syĕ′nô)	176	54°48′N	29°43′E
Syas′, r., Russia (syäs)	176	59°28′N	33°24′E
Sycamore, Il., U.S. (sĭk′ȧ-mōr)	113	42°00′N	88°42′W
Sycan, r., Or., U.S.	114	42°45′N	121°00′W
Sychëvka, Russia (sē-chôf′kȧ)	176	55°52′N	34°18′E
Sydney, Austl. (sĭd′nē)	219	33°55′S	151°17′E
Sydney, Can.	91	46°09′N	60°11′W
Sydney Mines, Can.	91	46°14′N	60°14′W
Syktyvkar, Russia (sük-tüf′kär)	178	61°35′N	50°40′E
Sylacauga, Al., U.S. (sĭl-ȧ-kô′gȧ)	124	33°10′N	86°15′W
Sylarna, mtn., Eur.	166	63°00′N	12°10′E
Sylt, i., Ger. (sĭlt)	168	54°55′N	8°30′E
Sylvania, Ga., U.S. (sĭl-vā′nĭ-ȧ)	125	32°44′N	81°40′W
Sylvester, Ga., U.S. (sĭl-vĕs′tēr)	124	31°32′N	83°50′W
Sými, i., Grc.	163	36°27′N	27°41′E
Synel′nykove, Ukr.	181	48°19′N	35°33′E
Syracuse, Ks., U.S. (sĭr′ȧ-kūs)	120	37°59′N	101°44′W
Syracuse, N.Y., U.S.	105	43°05′N	76°10′W
Syracuse, Ut., U.S.	117b	41°06′N	112°04′W
Syr Darya, r., Asia	178	44°15′N	65°45′E
Syria, nation, Asia (sĭr′ĭ-ȧ)	198	35°00′N	37°15′E
Syrian Desert, des., Asia	198	32°00′N	40°00′E
Sýros, i., Grc.	163	37°23′N	24°55′E
Sysert′, Russia (sĕ′sĕrt)	186a	56°30′N	60°48′E
Sysola, r., Russia	180	60°50′N	50°40′E
Syvash, zatoka, b., Ukr.	177	45°55′N	34°42′E
Syzran′, Russia (sĕz-rän′)	178	53°09′N	48°27′E
Szamotuły, Pol. (shȧ-mô-tōō′wē)	168	52°36′N	16°34′E
Szarvas, Hung. (sôr′vôsh)	169	46°51′N	20°36′E
Szczebrzeszyn, Pol. (shchĕ-bzhä′shĕn)	169	50°41′N	22°58′E
Szczecin, Pol. (shchĕ′tsĭn)	154	53°25′N	14°35′E
Szczecinek, Pol. (shchĕ′tsĭ-nĕk)	160	53°41′N	16°42′E
Szczuczyn, Pol. (shchōō′chĕn)	169	53°32′N	22°17′E
Szczytno, Pol. (shchĭt′nô)	169	53°33′N	21°00′E
Szechwan Basin, basin, China	204	30°45′N	104°40′E
Szeged, Hung. (sĕ′gĕd)	154	46°15′N	20°12′E
Székesfehérvár, Hung. (sā′kĕsh-fĕ′hār-vär)	163	47°12′N	18°26′E
Szekszárd, Hung. (sĕk′särd)	163	46°19′N	18°42′E
Szentendre, Hung. (sĕnt′ĕn-drĕ)	169	47°40′N	19°07′E
Szentes, Hung. (sĕn′tĕsh)	169	46°38′N	20°18′E
Szigetvar, Hung. (sē′gĕt-vär)	169	46°05′N	17°50′E
Szolnok, Hung.	169	47°11′N	20°12′E
Szombathely, Hung. (sôm′bôt-hĕl′)	163	47°13′N	16°35′E
Szprotawa, Pol. (shprō-tä′vä)	168	51°34′N	15°29′E
Szydłowiec, Pol. (shid-wô′vyets)	169	51°13′N	20°53′E

T

PLACE (Pronunciation)	PAGE	LAT.	LONG.
Taal, l., Phil. (tä-äl′)	213a	13°58′N	121°06′E
Tabaco, Phil. (tä-bä′kō)	213a	13°27′N	123°40′E
Tabankulu, S. Afr. (tä-bän-kōō′la)	233c	30°56′S	29°19′E
Tabasará, Serranía de, mts., Pan.	133	8°29′N	81°22′W
Tabasco, Mex. (tä-bäs′kô)	130	21°47′N	103°04′W
Tabasco, state, Mex.	128	18°10′N	93°00′W
Taber, Can.	90	49°47′N	112°08′W
Tablas, i., Phil. (tä′bläs)	213a	12°26′N	122°00′E
Tablas Strait, strt., Phil.	213a	12°17′N	121°41′E
Table Bay, b., S. Afr. (tā′b′l)	232a	33°41′S	18°27′E
Table Mountain, mtn., S. Afr.	232a	33°58′S	18°26′E
Table Rock Lake, Mo., U.S.	121	36°37′N	93°29′W
Tabligbo, Togo	234	6°35′N	1°30′E
Taboga, i., Pan. (tä-bō′gä)	128a	8°48′N	79°35′W
Taboguilla, i., Pan. (tä-bô-gē′l-yä)	128a	8°48′N	79°31′W
Tábor, Czech Rep. (tä′bôr)	168	49°25′N	14°40′E
Tabora, Tan. (tä-bō′rä)	232	5°01′S	32°48′E
Tabou, C. Iv. (tȧ-bōō′)	230	4°25′N	7°21′W
Tabrīz, Iran (tȧ-brēz′)	198	38°00′N	46°13′E
Tabuaeran, i., Kir.	2	3°52′N	159°20′W
Tabwémasana, Mont, mtn., Vanuatu	214f	15°20′S	166°44′E
Tacámbaro, r., Mex. (tä-käm′bä-rō)	130	18°55′N	101°25′W
Tacámbaro de Codallos, Mex.	130	19°12′N	101°28′W
Tacarigua, Laguna de la, l., Ven.	143b	10°18′N	65°43′W
Tacheng, China (tä-chŭŋ)	204	46°50′N	83°24′E
Tachie, r., Can.	94	54°30′N	125°00′W
Tacloban, Phil. (tä-klō′bän)	213	11°06′N	124°58′E
Tacna, Peru (täk′nä)	142	18°34′S	70°16′W
Tacoma, Wa., U.S. (tȧ-kō′mȧ)	104	47°14′N	122°27′W
Taconic Range, mts., N.Y., U.S. (tȧ-kŏn′ĭk)	109	41°55′N	73°40′W
Tacotalpa, Mex. (tä-kô-täl′pä)	131	17°37′N	92°51′W
Tacotalpa, r., Mex.	131	17°24′N	92°38′W
Tademaït, Plateau du, plat., Alg. (tä-dē-mä′ēt)	230	28°00′N	2°15′E
Tadio, Lagune, b., C. Iv.	234	5°20′N	5°25′W
Tadjoura, Dji. (tȧd-zhōō′rȧ)	238a	11°48′N	42°54′E
Tadley, Eng., U.K. (tăd′lē)	158b	51°19′N	1°08′W
Tadotsu, Japan (tä′dô-tsò)	211	34°14′N	133°43′E
Tadoussac, Can. (tȧ-dōō-sȧk′)	99	48°09′N	69°43′W
Tadzhikistan see Tajikistan, nation, Asia	178	39°22′N	69°30′E
Taebaek Sanmaek, mts., Asia (tī-bĭk′ sän-mĭk′)	210	37°20′N	128°50′E
Taedong, r., Kor., N. (tī-dŏng)	210	38°38′N	124°32′E
Taegu, Kor., S. (tī′gōō′)	205	35°49′N	128°41′E
Taejŏn, Kor., S.	210	36°20′N	127°26′E
Tafalla, Spain (tä-fäl′yä)	172	42°30′N	1°42′W
Tafna, r., Alg. (täf′nä)	172	35°28′N	1°00′W
Taft, Ca., U.S. (tȧft)	118	35°09′N	119°27′W
Tagama, reg., Niger	235	15°50′N	6°30′E
Taganrog, Russia (tȧ-gȧn-rôk′)	181	47°12′N	38°56′E
Taganrogskiy Zaliv, b., Eur. (tȧ-gȧn-rôk′skĭ zä′lĭf)	181	46°55′N	38°17′E
Tagula, i., Pap. N. Gui. (tä′gōō-lȧ)	221	11°45′S	153°46′E
Tagus (Tajo), r., Eur. (tā′gŭs)	156	39°40′N	5°07′W
Tahan, Gunong, mtn., Malay.	212	4°33′N	101°52′E
Tahat, mtn., Alg. (tä-hät′)	230	23°22′N	5°21′E
Tahiti, i., Fr. Poly. (tä-hē′tē) (tä′ē-tē′)	2	17°30′S	149°30′W
Tahkuna Nina, c., Est. (tȧh-kōō′nȧ nē′nȧ)	167	59°08′N	22°03′E
Tahlequah, Ok., U.S. (tä-lĕ-kwä′)	121	35°54′N	94°58′W
Tahoe, l., U.S. (tä′hō)	106	39°09′N	120°18′W
Tahoua, Niger (tä′ōō-ä)	230	14°54′N	5°16′E
Tahtsa Lake, l., Can.	94	53°33′N	127°47′W
Tahuya, Wa., U.S. (tȧ-hū-yā′)	116a	47°23′N	123°03′W
Tahuya, r., Wa., U.S.	116a	47°28′N	122°55′W
Tai′an, China (tī-än)	208	36°13′N	117°08′E
Taibai Shan, mtn., China (tī-bī shän)	208	33°42′N	107°25′E
Taibus Qi, China (tī-bōō-sz chyē)	208	41°52′N	115°25′E
Taicang, China (tī-tsäŋ)	206	31°26′N	121°06′E
T′aichung, Tai. (tī′chòng)	205	24°10′N	120°42′E
Tai′erzhuang, China (tī-är-jůäŋ)	206	34°34′N	117°44′E
Taigu, China (tī-gōō)	208	37°25′N	112°35′E
Taihang Shan, mts., China (tī-häŋ shän)	208	35°45′N	112°00′E
Taihe, China (tī-hŭ)	206	33°10′N	115°38′E
Tai Hu, l., China (tī hōō)	205	31°13′N	120°00′E
Tailagoin, reg., Mong. (tī′lȧ-gän′ kä′rä)	204	43°39′N	105°54′E
Tailai, China (tī-lī)	208	46°20′N	123°10′E
Tailem Bend, Austl. (tā-lĕm)	222	35°15′S	139°30′E
T′ainan, Tai. (tī′nan′)	205	23°08′N	120°18′E
Taínaro, c., Grc.	162	37°45′N	22°00′E
Taining, China (tī′nĭng′)	209	26°58′N	117°15′E
T′aipei, Tai. (tī′pā′)	205	25°02′N	121°38′E
Taiping, pt. of i., Malay.	212	4°56′N	100°39′E
Taiping Ling, mtn., China	208	47°03′N	120°30′E
Taisha, Japan (tī′shä)	211	35°23′N	132°40′E
Taishan, China (tī-shän)	209	22°15′N	112°50′E
Tai Shan, mts., China (tī shän)	208	36°16′N	117°05′E
Taitao, Península de, pen., Chile	144	46°20′S	77°15′W
T′aitung, Tai. (tī′tōōng′)	209	22°45′N	121°02′E
Taiwan, nation, Asia (tī-wän) (fōr-mō′sȧ)	205	23°30′N	122°20′E
Taiwan Strait, strt., Asia	205	24°30′N	120°00′E
Taixian, China (tī shyĕn)	206	32°31′N	119°54′E
Taixing, China (tī-shyĭŋ)	206	32°12′N	119°58′E
Taiyuan, China (tī-yůän)	205	37°32′N	112°38′E
Taizhou, China (tī-jō)	206	32°23′N	119°41′E
Ta′Izz, Yemen	201	13°38′N	44°04′E

PLACE (Pronunciation)	PAGE	LAT.	LONG.
Tajano de Morais, Braz. (tĕ-zhä′nô-dĕ-mô-rä′ĕs)	141a	22°05′S	42°04′W
Tajikistan, nation, Asia	178	39°22′N	69°30′E
Tajumulco, vol., Guat. (tä-hōō-mōōl′kô)	132	15°03′N	91°53′W
Tajuña, r., Spain (tä-kōō′n-yä)	172	40°23′N	2°36′W
Tājūrā′, Libya	162	32°56′N	13°24′W
Tak, Thai.	212	16°57′N	99°12′E
Taka, i., Japan (tä′kä)	211	30°47′N	130°23′E
Takada, Japan (tä′kȧ-dä)	210	37°08′N	138°30′E
Takahashi, Japan (tä′kä′hä-shĭ)	211	34°47′N	133°35′E
Takaishi, Japan	211b	34°32′N	135°27′E
Takamatsu, Japan (tä′kä′mä-tsōō′)	205	34°20′N	134°02′E
Takamori, Japan (tä′kä′mô-rē′)	211	32°50′N	131°08′E
Takaoka, Japan (tä′kä′ô-kä′)	210	36°45′N	136°59′E
Takapuna, N.Z.	223	36°48′S	174°47′E
Takarazuka, Japan (tä′kä-rä-zōō′kä)	211b	34°48′N	135°22′E
Takasaki, Japan (tä′kät′sōō-kē′)	210	36°20′N	139°00′E
Takatsu, Japan (tä-kät′sōō) (mĕ′zō-nô-kô′chĕ)	211a	35°36′N	139°37′E
Takatsuki, Japan (tä′kät′sōō-kē′)	211b	34°51′N	135°38′E
Takayama, Japan (tä′kä′yä′mä)	211	36°11′N	137°16′E
Takefu, Japan (tä′kĕ-fōō)	210	35°57′N	136°09′E
Take-shima, is., Asia	210	37°15′N	131°51′E
Takla Lake, l., Can.	92	55°25′N	125°53′W
Takla Makan, des., China (mä-kän′)	204	39°22′N	82°34′E
Takoma Park, Md., U.S. (tȧ′kōmȧ pȧrk)	110e	38°59′N	77°00′W
Takum, Nig.	235	7°17′N	9°59′E
Tala, Mex. (tä′lä)	130	20°39′N	103°42′W
Talagante, Chile (tä-lä-gá′n-tĕ)	141b	33°39′S	70°54′W
Talamanca, Cordillera de, mts., C.R.	133	9°37′N	83°55′W
Talanga, Hond. (tä-lä′n-gä)	132	14°21′N	87°09′W
Talara, Peru (tä-lä′rä)	142	4°32′S	81°17′W
Talasea, Pap. N. Gui. (tä-lä-sā′ä)	213	5°20′S	150°00′E
Talata Mafara, Nig.	235	12°35′N	6°04′E
Talaud, Kepulauan, is., Indon. (tä-lout′)	213	4°17′N	127°30′E
Talavera de la Reina, Spain	162	39°58′N	4°51′W
Talca, Chile (täl′kä)	144	35°25′S	71°39′W
Talca, prov., Chile	141b	35°23′S	71°15′W
Talca, Punta, c., Chile (pōō′n-tä-täl′kä)	141b	33°25′S	71°42′W
Talcahuano, Chile (täl-kä-wä′nō)	144	36°41′S	73°05′W
Taldom, Russia (täl-dôm)	176	56°44′N	37°33′E
Taldyqorghan, Kaz.	183	45°03′N	77°18′E
Talea de Castro, Mex. (tä′lā-ä dā käs′trō)	131	17°22′N	96°14′W
Talibu, Pulau, i., Indon.	213	1°30′S	125°00′E
Talim, i., Phil. (tä-lēm′)	213a	14°21′N	121°14′E
Talisay, Phil. (tä-lē′sī)	213a	14°08′N	122°56′E
Talkeetna, Ak., U.S. (tȧl-kēt′nȧ)	103	62°18′N	150°02′W
Talladega, Al., U.S. (tăl-ȧ-dē′gȧ)	124	33°25′N	86°06′W
Tallahassee, Fl., U.S. (tăl-ȧ-hăs′ē)	105	30°25′N	84°17′W
Tallahatchie, r., Ms., U.S. (tal-ȧ hăch′ē)	124	34°21′N	90°03′W
Tallapoosa, Ga., U.S. (tăl-ȧ-pōō′sȧ)	124	33°44′N	85°15′W
Tallapoosa, r., Al., U.S.	124	32°22′N	86°08′W
Tallassee, Al., U.S. (tăl′ȧ-sē)	124	32°30′N	85°54′W
Tallinn, Est. (tȧl′lĕn) (rā′väl)	178	59°26′N	24°44′E
Tallmadge, Oh., U.S. (tăl′mĭj)	111d	41°06′N	81°26′W
Tallulah, La., U.S. (tă-lōō′lȧ)	123	32°25′N	91°13′W
Tal′ne, Ukr.	177	48°52′N	30°43′E
Talo, mtn., Eth.	231	10°45′N	37°55′E
Taloje Budrukh, India	203b	19°05′N	73°05′E
Talpa de Allende, Mex. (täl′pä dā äl-yĕn′dā)	130	20°25′N	104°48′W
Talquin, Lake, res., Fl., U.S.	124	30°26′N	84°33′W
Talsi, Lat. (tal′sĭ)	167	57°16′N	22°35′E
Taltal, Chile (täl-täl′)	144	25°26′S	70°32′W
Taly, Russia (täl′ĭ)	177	49°51′N	40°07′E
Tama, Ia., U.S. (tā′mä)	113	41°57′N	92°36′W
Tama, r., Japan	211a	35°38′N	139°35′E
Tamale, Ghana (tä-mä′lȧ)	230	9°25′N	0°50′W
Taman′, Russia (tȧ-män′′)	177	45°13′N	36°46′E
Tamanaco, r., Ven. (tä-mä-nä′kō)	143b	9°32′N	66°00′W
Tamaqua, Pa., U.S. (tȧ-mô′kwȧ)	109	40°45′N	75°50′W
Tamar, r., Eng., U.K. (tā′mär)	164	50°35′N	4°15′W
Tamarite de Litera, Spain (tä-mä-rē′tā)	173	41°52′N	0°24′E
Tamaulipas, state, Mex. (tä-mä-ōō-lē′päs′)	128	23°45′N	98°30′W
Tamazula de Gordiano, Mex.	130	19°44′N	103°09′W
Tamazulapan del Progreso, Mex.	131	17°41′N	97°34′W
Tamazunchale, Mex. (tä-mä-zòn-chä′lȧ)	130	21°16′N	98°46′W
Tambacounda, Sen. (täm-bä-kōōn′dä)	230	13°47′N	13°40′W
Tambador, Serra do, mts., Braz. (sĕ′r-rä-dô-täm′bä-dōr)	143	10°33′S	41°16′W
Tambelan, Kepulauan, is., Indon. (täm-bȧ-län′)	212	0°38′N	107°38′E
Tambo, Austl. (tăm′bō)	219	24°50′S	146°15′E
Tambov, Russia (tȧm-bôf′)	178	52°45′N	41°10′E
Tambov, prov., Russia	176	52°50′N	40°42′E
Tambre, r., Spain (täm′brā)	172	42°59′N	8°33′W
Tambura, Sudan (täm-bōō′rä)	231	5°34′N	27°30′E
Tame, r., Eng., U.K. (tām)	158a	52°41′N	1°42′W
Tâmega, r., Port. (tȧ-mā′gȧ)	172	41°30′N	7°45′W
Tamenghest, Alg.	230	22°34′N	5°34′E
Tamenghest, Oued, r., Alg.	230	22°15′N	2°51′E
Tamgak, Monts, mtn., Niger (tam-gäk′)	230	18°40′N	8°40′E
Tamgué, Massif du, mtn., Gui.	230	12°15′N	12°35′W
Tamiahua, Mex. (tä-myä-wä)	131	21°17′N	97°26′W

ng-sing; ŋ-baŋk; ɴ-nasalized n; nŏd; cŏmmit; ōld; ôbey; ôrder; oi-boil; fōōd; ŏŏ-as oo in foot; ou-out; s-soft; sh-dish; th-thin; pūre; ûnite; ûrn; stŭd; circŭs; ü-as in French tu; ′-indeterminate vowel.

356 Tamiahua – Temoaya PRONOUNCING INDEX

PLACE (Pronunciation)	PAGE	LAT.	LONG.
Tamiahua, Laguna, l., Mex. (lä-gȯ′nä-tä-myä-wä)	131	21°38′N	97°33′W
Tamiami Canal, can., Fl., U.S. (tă-mī-ăm′ĭ)	125a	25°52′N	80°08′W
Tamil Nadu, state, India	199	11°30′N	78°00′E
Tampa, Fl., U.S. (tăm′pȧ)	105	27°57′N	82°25′W
Tampa Bay, b., Fl., U.S.	107	27°35′N	82°38′W
Tampere, Fin. (tȧm′pě-rě)	160	61°21′N	23°39′E
Tampico, Mex. (täm-pē′kō)	128	22°14′N	97°51′W
Tampico Alto, Mex. (täm-pē′kō äl′tō)	131	22°07′N	97°48′W
Tampin, Malay.	197b	2°28′N	102°15′E
Tam Quan, Viet.	209	14°20′N	109°10′E
Tamuín, Mex. (tä-mōō-ē′n)	130	22°04′N	98°47′W
Tamworth, Austl. (tăm′wûrth)	219	31°01′S	151°00′E
Tamworth, Eng., U.K.	158a	52°38′N	1°41′W
Tana, i., Vanuatu	221	19°32′S	169°27′E
Tana, r., Kenya (tä′nä)	233	0°30′S	39°30′E
Tanabe, Japan (tä-nä′bā)	210	33°45′N	135°21′E
Tanabe, Japan	211b	34°49′N	135°46′E
Tanacross, Ak., U.S. (tă′nȧ-crōs)	103	63°20′N	143°30′W
Tanaga, i., Ak., U.S. (tä-nä′gä)	103a	51°28′N	178°10′W
Tanahbala, Pulau, i., Indon. (tȧ-nä-bä′lä)	212	0°30′S	98°22′E
Tanahmasa, Pulau, i., Indon. (tȧ-nä-mä′sä)	212	0°03′S	97°30′E
Tanakpur, India (tăn′ăk-pȯr)	202	29°10′N	80°07′E
Tana Lake, l., Eth.	231	12°09′N	36°41′E
Tanami, Austl. (tȧ-nā′mē)	218	19°45′S	129°50′E
Tanana, Ak., U.S. (tă′nȧ-nô)	103	65°18′N	152°20′W
Tanana, r., Ak., U.S.	103	64°26′N	148°40′W
Tanaro, r., Italy (tä-nä′rô)	174	44°45′N	8°02′E
Tanashi, Japan	211a	35°44′N	139°34′E
Tanbu, China (tän-bōō)	207a	23°20′N	113°06′E
Tancheng, China (tän-chŭŋ)	208	34°37′N	118°22′E
Tanchŏn, Kor., N. (tän′chŭn)	210	40°29′N	128°50′E
Tancítaro, Mex. (tän-sē′tä-rō)	130	19°16′N	102°24′W
Tancítaro, Cerro de, mtn., Mex. (sĕ′r-rō-dĕ)	130	19°24′N	102°19′W
Tancoco, Mex. (tän-kō′kō)	131	21°16′N	97°45′W
Tandil, Arg. (tän-dēl′)	144	36°18′S	59°01′W
Tandil, Sierra del, mts., Arg.	144	38°40′S	59°40′W
Tanega, i., Japan (tä′nå-gä′)	205	30°36′N	131°11′E
Tanezrouft, reg., Alg. (tä′nĕz-rȯft)	230	24°17′N	0°30′W
Tang, r., China (täŋ)	206	33°38′N	117°29′E
Tang, r., China	206	39°13′N	114°45′E
Tanga, Tan. (tăŋ′gȧ)	233	5°04′S	39°06′E
Tangancícuaro, Mex. (täŋ-gän-sē′kwa-rō)	130	19°52′N	102°13′W
Tanganyika, Lake, l., Afr.	232	5°15′S	29°40′E
Tanger, Mor. (tăn-jēr′)	230	35°52′N	5°55′W
Tangermünde, Ger. (täŋ′ĕr-mün′de)	168	52°33′N	11°58′E
Tanggu, China (täŋ-gōō)	206	39°04′N	117°41′E
Tanggula Shan, mts., China (täŋ-gōō-lä shän)	204	33°15′N	89°07′E
Tanghe, China	208	32°40′N	112°50′E
Tangier *see* Tanger, Mor.	230	35°52′N	5°55′W
Tangipahoa, r., La., U.S. (tăn′jē-pȧ-hō′ȧ)	123	30°48′N	90°28′W
Tangra Yumco, l., China (täŋ-rä yōōm-tswo)	202	30°50′N	85°40′E
T′angshan, China	208	39°38′N	118°11′E
Tangxian, China (täŋ shyĕn)	206	38°49′N	115°00′E
Tangzha, China (täŋ-jä)	206	32°06′N	120°48′E
Tanimbar, Kepulauan, is., Indon.	213	8°00′S	132°00′E
Tanjong Piai, c., Malay.	197b	1°16′N	103°11′E
Tanjong Ramunia, c., Malay.	197b	1°27′N	104°44′E
Tanjungbalai, Indon. (tän′jông-bä′lå)	197b	1°00′N	103°26′E
Tanjungpandan, Indon.	212	2°47′S	107°51′E
Tanjungpinang, Indon. (tän′jŏng-pē′näng)	197b	0°55′N	104°29′E
Tannu-Ola, mts., Asia	179	51°00′N	94°00′E
Tannūrah, Ra′s at, c., Sau. Ar.	198	26°45′N	49°59′E
Tano, r., Afr.	234	5°40′N	2°30′W
Tanquijo, Arrecife, i., Mex. (är-rĕ-sē′fĕ-tän-kē′kô)	131	21°07′N	97°16′W
Ţanţā, Egypt	231	30°47′N	31°00′E
Tantoyuca, Mex. (tän-tō-yōō′kä)	130	21°22′N	98°13′W
Tanyang, Kor., S.	210	36°53′N	128°20′E
Tanzania, nation, Afr.	232	6°48′S	33°58′E
Tao, r., China (tou)	208	35°30′N	103°40′E
Tao′an, China (tou-än)	205	45°15′N	122°45′E
Tao′er, r., China (tou-är)	205	45°40′N	122°00′E
Taormina, Italy (tä-ôr-mē′nä)	174	37°53′N	15°18′E
Taos, N.M., U.S. (tä′ōs)	119	36°25′N	105°35′W
Taoudenni, Mali (tä′ōō-dĕ-nē′)	230	22°57′N	3°37′W
Taoussa, Mali	234	16°55′N	0°35′W
Taoyuan, China (tou-yůän)	209	29°00′N	111°15′E
Tapa, Est. (tȧ′pȧ)	167	59°16′N	25°56′E
Tapachula, Mex.	132	14°55′N	92°20′W
Tapajós, r., Braz. (tä-pä-zhô′s)	143	3°27′S	55°33′W
Tapalque, Arg. (tä-päl-kĕ′)	141c	36°22′S	60°05′W
Tapanatepec, Mex. (tä-pä-nä-tĕ-pĕk)	131	16°22′N	94°19′W
Tāpi, r., India	199	21°00′N	76°30′E
Tappi Saki, c., Japan (täp′pē sä′kē)	210	41°05′N	139°40′E
Tapps, l., Wa., U.S. (tăpz)	116a	47°20′N	122°12′W
Taquara, Serra de, mts., Braz. (sĕ′r-rä-dĕ-tä-kwä′rä)	143	15°28′S	54°33′W
Taquari, r., Braz. (tä-kwä′rĭ)	143	18°35′S	56°50′W
Tar, r., N.C., U.S. (tär)	125	35°58′N	78°06′W
Tara, Russia (tä′rȧ)	178	56°58′N	74°13′E
Tara, i., Phil. (tä′rä)	213a	12°18′N	120°28′E
Tara, r., Russia (tä′rȧ)	184	56°32′N	76°13′E
Ţarābulus, Leb. (tȧ-rä′bȯ-lōōs)	198	34°25′N	35°50′E
Ţarābulus (Tripolitania), hist. reg., Libya	230	31°00′N	12°26′E
Tarakan, Indon.	212	3°17′N	118°04′E
Taranaki, Mount, vol., N.Z.	223	39°18′S	174°04′E
Tarancón, Spain (tä-rän-kōn′)	172	40°01′N	3°00′W
Taranto, Italy (tä′rän-tô)	163	40°30′N	17°15′E
Taranto, Golfo di, b., Italy (gōl-fō-dē tä′rän-tô)	156	40°03′N	17°10′E
Tarapoto, Peru (tä-rä-pō′tō)	142	6°29′S	76°26′W
Tarare, Fr. (tȧ-rär′)	170	45°55′N	4°23′E
Tarascon, Fr. (tȧ-rȧs-kôɴ′)	170	42°53′N	1°35′E
Tarascon, Fr. (tä-räs-kôɴ)	170	43°47′N	4°41′E
Tarashcha, Ukr. (tä′rȧsh-chȧ)	177	49°34′N	30°52′E
Tarata, Bol. (tä-rä′tä)	142	17°43′S	66°00′W
Taravo, r., Fr.	174	41°54′N	8°58′E
Tarazit, Massif de, mts., Niger	235	20°05′N	7°35′E
Tarazona, Spain (tä-rä-thō′nä)	172	41°54′N	1°45′W
Tarazona de la Mancha, Spain (tä-rä-zō′nä-dĕ-lä-mä′n-chä)	172	39°13′N	1°50′W
Tarbes, Fr. (tȧrb)	161	43°04′N	0°05′E
Tarboro, N.C., U.S. (tär′bŭr-ō)	125	35°53′N	77°34′W
Taree, Austl. (tă-rē′)	222	31°52′S	152°21′E
Tarentum, Pa., U.S. (tȧ-rĕn′tŭm)	111e	40°36′N	79°44′W
Tarfa, Wādī at, val., Egypt	238b	28°14′N	31°00′E
Târgoviște, Rom.	163	44°54′N	25°29′E
Târgu Jiu, Rom.	163	45°02′N	23°17′E
Târgu Mureș, Rom.	163	46°33′N	24°33′E
Târgu Neamț, Rom.	169	47°14′N	26°23′E
Târgu Ocna, Rom.	169	46°18′N	26°38′E
Târgu Secuiesc, Rom.	169	46°04′N	26°06′E
Tarhūnah, Libya	200	32°26′N	13°38′E
Tarija, Bol. (tär-rē′hä)	142	21°42′S	64°52′W
Tarīm, Yemen (tȧ-rĭm′)	198	16°13′N	49°08′E
Tarim, r., China (tȧ-rĭm′)	204	40°45′N	85°39′E
Tarim Basin, basin, China (tȧ-rĭm′)	204	39°52′N	82°34′E
Tarka, r., S. Afr. (tä′kȧ)	233c	32°15′S	26°00′E
Tarkastad, S. Afr.	233c	32°01′S	26°18′E
Tarkhankut, Mys, c., Ukr. (mĭs tȧr-ĸän′kȯt)	181	45°21′N	32°30′E
Tarkio, Mo., U.S. (tär′kĭ-ō)	121	40°27′N	95°22′W
Tarkwa, Ghana (tärk′wä)	230	5°19′N	1°59′W
Tarlac, Phil. (tär′läk)	212	15°29′N	120°36′E
Tarlton, S. Afr. (tärl′tŭn)	233b	26°05′S	27°38′E
Tarma, Peru (tär′mä)	142	11°20′S	75°40′W
Tarn, r., Fr. (tärn)	161	43°45′N	2°00′E
Târnăveni, Rom.	169	46°19′N	24°18′E
Tarnów, Pol. (tär′nȯf)	161	50°02′N	21°00′E
Taro, r., Italy (tä′rō)	174	44°41′N	10°03′E
Taroudant, Mor. (tȧ-rōō-dänt′)	230	30°39′N	8°52′W
Tarpon Springs, Fl., U.S. (tär′pŏn)	125a	28°07′N	82°44′W
Tarporley, Eng., U.K. (tär′pēr-lē)	158a	53°09′N	2°40′W
Tarpum Bay, b., Bah. (tär′pŭm)	134	25°05′N	76°20′W
Tarquinia, Italy (tär-kwē′nē-ä)	174	42°16′N	11°46′E
Tarragona, Spain (tär-rä-gō′nä)	154	41°05′N	1°15′E
Tarrant, Al., U.S. (tăr′ănt)	110h	33°35′N	86°46′W
Tárrega, Spain (tä rå-gä)	173	41°40′N	1°09′E
Tarrejón de Ardoz, Spain (tär-rĕ-ĸō′n-dĕ-är-dōz)	173a	40°28′N	3°29′W
Tarrytown, N.Y., U.S. (tär′ĭ-toun)	110a	41°04′N	73°52′W
Tarsus, Tur. (tȧr′sȯs) (tär′sŭs)	198	37°00′N	34°50′E
Tartagal, Arg. (tär-tä-gȧ′l)	144	23°31′S	63°47′W
Tartu, Est. (tär′tōō) (dôr′pät)	178	58°23′N	26°44′E
Ţarţūs, Syria	200	34°54′N	35°59′E
Tarumi, Japan (tä′rōō-mē)	211b	34°38′N	135°04′E
Tarusa, Russia (tä-rōōs′ȧ)	176	54°43′N	37°11′E
Tarzana, Ca., U.S. (tär-ză′ȧ)	117a	34°10′N	118°32′W
Tashkent, Uzb. (tȧsh′kĕnt)	183	41°23′N	69°04′E
Tasman Bay, b., N.Z. (tăz′măn)	221a	40°50′S	173°20′E
Tasmania, state, Austl.	219	41°28′S	142°30′E
Tasman Peninsula, pen., Austl.	222	43°00′S	148°30′E
Tasman Sea, sea, Oc.	241	29°30′S	155°00′E
Tasquillo, Mex. (täs-kē′lyō)	130	20°34′N	99°21′W
Tatarsk, Russia (tȧ-tärsk′)	178	55°13′N	75°58′E
Tatarstan, prov., Russia	180	55°00′N	51°00′E
Tatar Strait, strt., Russia	179	51°00′N	141°45′E
Tater Hill, mtn., Or., U.S. (tāt′ēr hĭl)	116c	45°47′N	123°02′W
Tateyama, Japan (tä′tē-yä′mä)	211	35°04′N	139°52′E
Tatlow, Mount, mtn., Can.	94	51°23′N	123°52′W
Tau, Nor.	166	59°05′N	5°59′E
Tauern Tunnel, trans., Aus.	168	47°12′N	13°17′E
Taung, S. Afr. (tä′ȯng)	232	27°25′S	24°47′E
Taunton, Ma., U.S. (tän′tŭn)	109	41°54′N	71°03′W
Taunton, r., R.I., U.S.	110b	41°50′N	71°02′W
Taupo, Lake, l., N.Z. (tä′ōō-pō)	221a	38°42′S	175°55′E
Taurage, Lith. (tou′rȧ-gā)	167	55°15′N	22°18′E
Taurus Mountains *see* Toros Dağları, mts., Tur.	198	37°00′N	32°40′E
Tauste, Spain (tä-ōōs′tå)	172	41°55′N	1°15′W
Tavda, Russia (tȧv-dȧ′)	178	58°00′N	64°44′E
Tavda, r., Russia	184	58°30′N	64°15′E
Taverny, Fr. (tȧ-vĕr-nē′)	171b	49°02′N	2°13′E
Taviche, Mex. (tä-vē′chĕ)	131	16°43′N	96°35′W
Tavira, Port. (tä-vē′rȧ)	172	37°09′N	7°42′W
Tavşanlı, Tur. (tȧv′shän-lĭ)	181	39°30′N	29°30′E
Tawakoni, l., Tx., U.S.	123	32°51′N	95°59′W
Tawaramoto, Japan (tä′wä-rä-mō-tō)	211b	34°33′N	135°48′E
Tawas City, Mi., U.S.	108	44°15′N	83°30′W
Tawas Point, c., Mi., U.S. (tô′wȧs)	108	44°15′N	83°25′W
Tawitawi Group, is., Phil. (tä′wē-tä′wē)	212	4°52′N	120°35′E
Tawkar, Sudan	231	18°28′N	37°46′E
Taxco de Alarcón, Mex. (täs′kō dĕ ä-lär-kō′n)	130	18°34′N	99°37′W
Tay, r., Scot., U.K.	164	56°35′N	3°37′W
Tay, Loch, l., Scot., U.K.	164	56°25′N	4°07′W
Tayabas Bay, b., Phil. (tä-yä′bäs)	213a	13°44′N	121°40′E
Tayga, Russia (tī′gä)	184	56°12′N	85°47′E
Taygonos, Mys, c., Russia	179	60°37′N	160°17′E
Taylor, Tx., U.S.	123	30°35′N	97°25′W
Taylor, Mount, mtn., N.M., U.S.	106	35°20′N	107°40′W
Taylorville, Il., U.S. (tā′lēr-vĭl)	108	39°30′N	89°20′W
Taymyr, l., Russia (tī-mĭr′)	179	74°13′N	100°45′E
Taymyr, Poluostrov, pen., Russia	179	75°15′N	95°00′E
Tayshet, Russia (tī-shĕt′)	179	56°09′N	97°49′E
Tayug, Phil.	213a	16°01′N	120°45′E
Taz, r., Russia (tȧz)	184	67°15′N	80°45′E
Taza, Mor. (tä′zä)	230	34°08′N	4°00′W
Tazovskoye, Russia	178	66°58′N	78°28′E
Tbessa, Alg.	230	35°27′N	8°13′E
Tbilisi, Geor. (′tbĭl-yē′sē)	181	41°40′N	44°45′E
Tchentlo Lake, l., Can.	94	55°11′N	125°00′W
Tchibanga, Gabon (chē-bäŋ′gä)	232	2°51′S	11°02′E
Tchien, Lib.	234	6°04′N	8°08′W
Tchigai, Plateau du, plat., Afr.	235	21°20′N	14°50′E
Tczew, Pol. (t′chĕf′)	160	54°06′N	18°48′E
Teabo, Mex. (tĕ-ä′bō)	132a	20°25′N	89°14′W
Teague, Tx., U.S.	123	31°39′N	96°16′W
Teapa, Mex. (tā-ä′pä)	131	17°35′N	92°56′W
Tebing Tinggi, i., Indon. (teb′ĭng-tĭng′gä)	197b	0°54′N	102°39′E
Tecalitlán, Mex. (tā-kä-lē-tlän′)	130	19°28′N	103°17′W
Techiman, Ghana	234	7°35′N	1°56′W
Tecoanapa, Mex. (tāk-wä-nä-pä′)	130	16°33′N	98°46′W
Tecoh, Mex. (tĕ-kō)	132a	20°46′N	89°27′W
Tecolotlán, Mex. (tā-kō-lō-tlän′)	130	20°13′N	103°57′W
Tecolutla, Mex. (tā-kō-lōō′tlä)	131	20°33′N	97°00′W
Tecolutla, r., Mex.	131	20°16′N	97°14′W
Tecomán, Mex. (tā-kō-män′)	130	18°53′N	103°53′W
Tecómitl, Mex. (tĕ-kŏ′mētl)	131a	19°13′N	98°59′W
Tecozautla, Mex. (tā′kō-zä-ōō′tlä)	130	20°33′N	99°38′W
Tecpan de Galeana, Mex. (tĕk-pän′ dā gä-lā-ä′nä)	130	17°13′N	100°41′W
Tecpatán, Mex. (tĕk-pä-tȧ′n)	131	17°08′N	93°18′W
Tecuala, Mex. (tĕ-kwä-lä)	130	22°24′N	105°29′W
Tecuci, Rom. (ta-kȯch′)	163	45°51′N	27°30′E
Tecumseh, Can. (tē-kŭm′sĕ)	111b	42°19′N	82°53′W
Tecumseh, Mi., U.S.	108	42°00′N	84°00′W
Tecumseh, Ne., U.S.	121	40°21′N	96°09′W
Tecumseh, Ok., U.S.	121	35°18′N	96°55′W
Tees, r., Eng., U.K. (tēz)	164	54°40′N	2°10′W
Teganuna, l., Japan (tā′gä-nōō′nä)	211a	35°50′N	140°02′E
Tegucigalpa, Hond. (tå-gōō-sē-gäl′pä)	128	14°08′N	87°15′W
Tehachapi Mountains, mts., Ca., U.S. (tĕ-hă-shā′pĭ)	118	34°50′N	118°55′W
Tehrān, Iran (tĕ-hrän′)	198	35°45′N	51°30′E
Tehuacan, Mex. (tā-wä-kän′)	128	18°27′N	97°23′W
Tehuantepec, Mex.	128	16°20′N	95°14′W
Tehuantepec, r., Mex.	131	16°30′N	95°23′W
Tehuantepec, Golfo de, b., Mex. (gōl-fô dĕ)	128	15°45′N	95°00′W
Tehuantepec, Istmo de, isth., Mex. (ē′st-mô dĕ)	131	17°55′N	94°35′W
Tehuehuetla, Arroyo, r., Mex. (tĕ-wĕ-wĕ′tlä ȧr-rō-yō)	130	17°54′N	100°26′W
Tehuitzingo, Mex. (tā-wē-tzĭŋ′gō)	130	18°21′N	98°16′W
Tejeda, Sierra de, mts., Spain (sē-ĕ′r-rä dĕ tĕ-kĕ′dä)	172	36°55′N	4°00′W
Tejúpan, Mex. (tĕ-ĸōō-pä′n) (sän-tyȧ′gô)	131	17°39′N	97°34′W
Tejúpan, Punta, c., Mex.	130	18°19′N	103°30′W
Tejupilco de Hidalgo, Mex. (tå-hōō-pēl′kō dā ē-dhäl′gō)	130	18°52′N	100°07′W
Tekamah, Ne., U.S. (tē-kā′mȧ)	112	41°46′N	96°13′W
Tekax de Alvaro Obregon, Mex.	132a	20°12′N	89°11′W
Tekeze, r., Afr.	231	13°38′N	38°00′E
Tekit, Mex. (tĕ-kē′t)	132a	20°35′N	89°18′W
Tekoa, Wa., U.S. (tē-kō′ȧ)	114	47°15′N	117°03′W
Tela, Hond. (tā′lä)	128	15°45′N	87°25′W
Tela, Bahía de, b., Hond.	132	15°53′N	87°29′W
Telapa Burok, Gunong, mtn., Malay.	197b	2°51′N	102°04′E
Telavi, Geor.	181	42°00′N	45°20′E
Tel Aviv-Yafo, Isr. (tĕl-ä-vēv′jȧ′jȧ′fȧ)	198	32°03′N	34°46′E
Telegraph Creek, Can. (tĕl′ē-grȧf)	90	57°59′N	131°22′W
Teleneşti, Mol.	177	47°31′N	28°22′E
Telescope Peak, mtn., Ca., U.S. (tĕl′ē skōp)	106	36°12′N	117°05′W
Telesung, Indon.	197b	1°07′N	102°53′E
Telica, vol., Nic. (tå-lē′kä)	132	12°38′N	86°52′W
Tell City, In., U.S. (tĕl)	108	38°00′N	86°45′W
Teller, Ak., U.S. (tĕl′ēr)	103	65°17′N	166°28′W
Tello, Col. (tĕ′l-yō)	142a	3°05′N	75°08′W
Telluride, Co., U.S. (tĕl′ū-rīd)	119	37°55′N	107°50′W
Telok Datok, Malay.	197b	2°51′N	101°33′E
Teloloapan, Mex. (tā′lō-lō-ä′pän)	130	18°19′N	99°54′W
Tel′pos-Iz, Gora, mtn., Russia (tyĕl′pōs-ēz′)	178	63°50′N	59°20′E
Telšiai, Lith. (tĕl′sha′ē)	167	55°59′N	22°17′E
Teltow, Ger. (tĕl′tō)	159b	52°24′N	13°12′E
Teluklecak, Indon.	197b	1°53′N	101°45′E
Tema, Ghana	234	5°38′N	0°01′E
Temascalcingo, Mex. (tā′mäs-käl-sĭŋ′gō)	130	19°55′N	100°00′W
Temascaltepec, Mex. (tā′mäs-käl-tå pĕk)	130	19°00′N	100°03′W
Temax, Mex. (tĕ′mäx)	128	21°10′N	88°51′W
Temir, Kaz.	183	49°10′N	57°15′E
Temirtaū, Kaz.	183	50°08′N	73°13′E
Temiscouata, l., Can. (tĕ′mĭs-kō-ä′tä)	100	47°40′N	68°50′W
Témiskaming, Can. (tē-mĭs′kȧ-mĭng)	91	46°41′N	79°01′W
Temoaya, Mex. (tĕ-mô-a-um-yä)	131a	19°28′N	99°36′W

ăt; finăl; rāte; senåte; ärm; ȧsk; sofȧ; fâre; ch-choose; dh-as th in other; bē; ēvent; bĕt; recĕnt; cratẽr; g-gō; gh-guttural g; bĭt; ĭ-short neutral; rīde; ĸ-guttural k as ch in German ich;

ng-sing; ŋ-bank; N-nasalized n; nŏd; cŏmmit; ōld; ôbey; ôrder; oi-boil; fōōd; ȯ-as oo in foot; ou-out; s-soft; sh-dish; th-thin; pūre; ûnite; ûrn; stŭd; circŭs; ü-as in French tu; '-indeterminate vowel.

358 Tidra – Topol'čany PRONOUNCING INDEX

PLACE (Pronunciation)	PAGE	LAT.	LONG.
Tidra, Île, i., Maur.	234	19°50'N	16°45'W
Tieling, China (tĭĕ-lĭŋ)	205	42°18'N	123°50'E
Tielmes, Spain (tyâl-màs')	173a	40°15'N	3°20'W
Tienen, Bel.	159a	50°49'N	4°58'E
Tien Shan, mts., Asia	204	42°00'N	78°46'E
Tientsin *see* Tianjin, China	205	39°08'N	117°14'E
Tierp, Swe. (tyĕrp)	166	60°21'N	17°28'E
Tierpoort, S. Afr.	233b	25°53'S	28°26'E
Tierra Blanca, Mex. (tyĕ'r-rä-blä'n-kä)	131	18°28'N	96°19'W
Tierra del Fuego, i., S.A. (tyĕr'rä dĕl fwā'gō)	144	53°50'S	68°45'W
Tiétar, r., Spain (tê-ā'tär)	172	39°56'N	5°44'W
Tiffin, Oh., U.S. (tĭf'ĭn)	108	41°10'N	83°15'W
Tifton, Ga., U.S. (tĭf'tŭn)	124	31°25'N	83°34'W
Tigard, Or., U.S. (tī'gärd)	116c	45°25'N	122°46'W
Tighina, Mol.	181	46°49'N	29°29'E
Tignish, Can. (tĭg'nĭsh)	100	46°57'N	64°02'W
Tigoda, r., Russia (tē'gô-dà)	186c	59°29'N	31°15'E
Tigre, r., Peru	142	2°20'S	75°41'W
Tigres, Península dos, pen., Ang. (pĕ-nē'ŋ-sōō-lä-dôs-tē'grĕs)	232	16°30'S	11°45'E
Tigris, r., Asia	198	34°45'N	44°10'E
Tīh, Jabal at, mts., Egypt	197a	29°23'N	34°05'E
Tihert, Alg.	230	35°28'N	1°15'E
Tihuatlán, Mex. (tē-wä-tlän')	131	20°43'N	97°34'W
Tijuana, Mex. (tē-hwä'nä)	128	32°32'N	117°02'W
Tijuca, Pico da, mtn., Braz. (pē'kō-dä-tē-zhōō'kà)	144b	22°56'S	43°17'W
Tikal, hist., Guat. (tē-käl')	132a	17°16'N	89°49'W
Tikhoretsk, Russia (tē-kôr-yĕtsk')	181	45°55'N	40°05'E
Tikhvin, Russia (tēk-vēn')	178	59°36'N	33°38'E
Tikrīt, Iraq	198	34°36'N	43°31'E
Tiksi, Russia (tēk-sē')	179	71°42'N	128°32'E
Tilburg, Neth. (tĭl'bûrg)	161	51°33'N	5°05'E
Tilbury, Eng., U.K.	158b	51°28'N	0°23'E
Tilemsi, Vallée du, val., Mali	234	17°50'N	0°25'E
Tilichiki, Russia (tyĭ-le-chĭ-kē)	179	60°49'N	166°14'E
Tilimsen, Alg.	230	34°53'N	1°21'W
Tillabéry, Niger (tē-yá-bā-rē')	230	14°14'N	1°30'E
Tillamook, Or., U.S. (tĭl'á-mŏŏk)	114	45°27'N	123°50'W
Tillamook Bay, b., Or., U.S.	114	45°32'N	124°26'W
Tillberga, Swe. (tēl-bĕr'ghá)	166	59°40'N	16°34'E
Tillsonburg, Can. (tĭl'sŭn-bûrg)	99	42°50'N	80°50'W
Tim, Russia (têm)	177	51°39'N	37°07'E
Timaru, N.Z. (tĭm'á-rōō)	221a	44°26'S	171°17'E
Timashevskaya, Russia (tēmă-shĕfs-kă'yă)	181	45°47'N	38°57'E
Timbalier Bay, b., La., U.S. (tĭm'bá-lēr)	123	28°55'N	90°14'W
Timber, Or., U.S. (tĭm'bēr)	116c	45°43'N	123°17'W
Timbo, Gui. (tĭm'bō)	230	10°41'N	11°51'W
Timbuktu *see* Tombouctou, Mali	230	16°46'N	3°01'W
Timétrine Monts, mts., Mali	234	19°50'N	0°30'W
Timimoun, Alg. (tē-mē-mōōn')	230	29°14'N	0°22'E
Timiris, Cap, c., Maur.	230	19°23'N	16°32'W
Timiş, r., Eur.	175	45°28'N	21°06'E
Timişoara, Rom.	163	45°44'N	21°21'E
Timmins, Can. (tĭm'ĭnz)	91	48°25'N	81°22'W
Timmonsville, S.C., U.S. (tĭm'ŭnz-vĭl)	125	34°09'N	79°55'W
Timok, r., Eur.	175	43°35'N	22°13'E
Timor, i., Asia (tē-mōr')	213	10°08'S	125°00'E
Timor Sea, sea	220	12°40'S	125°00'E
Timpanogos Cave National Monument, rec., Ut., U.S. (tĭ-măn'ō-gŏz)	119	40°25'N	111°45'W
Timpson, Tx., U.S. (tĭmp'sŭn)	123	31°55'N	94°24'W
Timsâh, l., Egypt (tĭm'sä)	238b	30°34'N	32°22'E
Tina, r., S. Afr. (tē'nȧ)	233c	30°50'S	28°44'E
Tina, Monte, mtn., Dom. Rep. (mô'n-tĕ-tē'nà)	135	18°50'N	70°40'W
Tinaguillo, Ven. (tē-nä-gē'l-yō)	143b	9°55'N	68°18'W
Tīnah, Khalīj at, b., Egypt	197a	31°06'N	32°42'E
Tindouf, Alg. (tēn-dōōf')	230	27°43'N	7°44'W
Tinggi, i., Malay.	197b	2°16'N	104°16'E
Tinghert, Plateau du, plat., Alg.	230	27°30'N	7°30'E
Tingi Mountains, mts., S.L.	234	9°00'N	10°50'W
Tinglin, China	207b	30°53'N	121°18'E
Tingo María, Peru (tē'ngô-mä-rē'ä)	142	9°15'S	76°04'W
Tingréla, C. Iv.	234	10°29'N	6°24'W
Tingsryd, Swe. (tĭngs'rüd)	166	56°32'N	14°58'E
Tinguindio, Mex.	130	19°38'N	102°02'W
Tinguiririca, r., Chile (tē'n-gē-rē-rē'kä)	141b	34°48'S	70°45'W
Tinley Park, Il., U.S. (tĭn'lē)	111a	41°34'N	87°47'W
Tinnoset, Nor. (tēn'nôs'sĕt)	166	59°44'N	9°00'E
Tinogasta, Arg. (tē-nô-gäs'tä)	144	28°07'S	67°30'W
Tínos, i., Grc.	163	37°45'N	25°12'E
Tinsukia, India (tin-sōō'kĭ-à)	198	27°18'N	95°29'W
Tintic, Ut., U.S. (tĭn'tĭk)	119	39°55'N	112°15'W
Tio, Pic de, mtn., Gui.	234	8°55'N	8°55'W
Tioman, i., Malay.	197b	2°50'N	104°15'E
Tipitapa, Nic. (tē-pē-tä'pä)	132	12°14'N	86°05'W
Tipitapa, r., Nic.	132	12°13'N	85°57'W
Tippah Creek, r., Ms., U.S. (tĭp'pȧ)	124	34°43'N	88°15'W
Tippecanoe, r., In., U.S. (tĭp-ē-kȧ-nōō')	108	40°55'N	86°45'W
Tipperary, Ire. (tĭ-pē-râ'rē)	161	52°28'N	8°13'W
Tippo Bay, Ms., U.S. (tĭp'ō bīōō')	121	33°35'N	90°06'W
Tipton, Ia., U.S.	113	41°46'N	91°10'W
Tipton, In., U.S.	108	40°15'N	86°00'W
Tiranë, Alb. (tē-rä'nä)	154	41°48'N	19°50'E
Tirano, Italy (tē-rä'nō)	174	46°12'N	10°09'E
Tiraspol, Mol.	181	46°52'N	29°38'E
Tire, Tur. (tē'rĕ)	163	38°05'N	27°48'E
Tiree, i., Scot., U.K. (tī-rē')	160	56°34'N	6°30'W
Tirlyanskiy, Russia (tĭr-lyän'skĭ)	186a	54°13'N	58°37'E
Tiruchchirāppalli, India (tĭr'ŏ-chĭ-rä'pá-lĭ)	199	10°49'N	78°48'E
Tirunelveli, India	203	8°53'N	77°43'E
Tiruppur, India	203	11°11'N	77°08'E
Tisdale, Can. (tĭz'dāl)	90	52°51'N	104°04'W
Tista, r., Asia	202	26°00'N	89°30'E
Tisza, r., Eur. (tĭ'sä)	156	47°30'N	21°00'E
Titāgarh, India	202a	22°44'N	88°23'E
Titicaca, Lago, l., S.A. (lä'gô-tē-tē-kä'kä)	142	16°12'S	70°33'W
Titiribi, Col. (tē-tē-rē-bē')	142a	6°05'N	75°47'W
Titiro, Lagh, r., Kenya	237	2°25'N	39°05'E
Titov Veles, Mac. (tē'tôv vĕ'lĕs)	175	41°42'N	21°50'E
Titterstone Clee Hill, hill, Eng., U.K. (klē)	158a	52°24'N	2°37'W
Titule, D.R.C.	237	3°17'N	25°32'E
Titusville, Fl., U.S. (tī'tŭs-vĭl)	125a	28°37'N	80°44'W
Titusville, Pa., U.S.	109	40°40'N	79°40'W
Titz, Ger. (tētz)	171c	51°00'N	6°26'E
Tiverton, R.I., U.S. (tĭv'ēr-tun)	110b	41°38'N	71°11'W
Tivoli, Italy (tē'vô-lē)	162	41°38'N	12°48'E
Tixkokob, Mex. (tēx-kō-kō'b)	132a	21°01'N	89°23'W
Tixtla de Guerrero, Mex. (tē'x-tlä-dĕ-gĕr-rĕ'rô)	130	17°36'N	99°24'W
Tizard Bank and Reef, rf., Asia (tĭz'ȧrd)	212	10°51'N	113°20'E
Tizimín, Mex. (tē-zē-mē'n)	132a	21°08'N	88°10'W
Tizi-Ouzou, Alg. (tē'zē-ōō-zōō')	230	36°44'N	4°04'E
Tiznados, r., Ven. (tēz-nä'dôs)	143b	9°53'N	67°49'W
Tiznit, Mor. (têz-nēt)	230	29°52'N	9°39'W
Tkvarcheli, Geor.	182	42°15'N	41°41'E
Tlacolula de Matamoros, Mex.	131	16°56'N	96°29'W
Tlacotálpan, Mex. (tlä-kô-täl'pän)	131	18°39'N	95°40'W
Tlacotepec, Mex. (tlä-kô-tå-pĕ'k)	130	17°46'N	99°57'W
Tlacotepec, Mex.	130	19°11'N	99°41'W
Tlacotepec, Mex.	131	18°41'N	97°40'W
Tláhuac, Mex. (tlä-wäk')	131a	19°16'N	99°00'W
Tlajomulco de Zúñiga, Mex. (tlä-hô-mōō'l-ko-dĕ-zōō'n-yē-gä)	130	20°30'N	103°27'W
Tlalchapa, Mex. (tläl-chä'pä)	130	18°26'N	100°29'W
Tlalixcoyan, Mex. (tlä-lēs'kō-yän')	131	18°53'N	96°04'W
Tlalmanalco, Mex. (tläl-mä-nä'l-kô)	131a	19°12'N	98°48'W
Tlalnepantla, Mex.	131a	19°32'N	99°13'W
Tlalnepantla, Mex. (tläl-nå-pån'tlä)	131a	18°59'N	99°01'W
Tlalpan, Mex. (tläl-pä'n)	130	19°17'N	99°10'W
Tlalpujahua, Mex. (tläl-pōō-kä'wä)	130	19°50'N	100°10'W
Tlapa, Mex. (tlä'pä)	130	17°30'N	98°30'W
Tlapacoyan, Mex. (tlä-pä-kô-yä'n)	131	19°57'N	97°11'W
Tlapehuala, Mex. (tlä-på-wä'lä)	130	18°17'N	100°30'W
Tlaquepaque, Mex. (tlä-kĕ-pä'kĕ)	130	20°39'N	103°17'W
Tlaltaya, Mex. (tlä-tlä'yä)	130	18°36'N	100°14'W
Tlaxcala, Mex. (tläs-kä'lä)	128	19°16'N	98°14'W
Tlaxcala, state, Mex.	130	19°30'N	98°15'W
Tlaxco, Mex. (tläs'kō)	130	19°37'N	98°06'W
Tlaxiaco Santa María Asunción, Mex.	131	17°16'N	97°41'W
Tlayacapan, Mex. (tlä-yä-kä-pä'n)	131a	18°57'N	99°00'W
Tlevak Strait, strt., Ak., U.S.	94	53°03'N	132°58'W
Tlumach, Ukr. (t'lû-mäch')	169	48°47'N	25°00'E
Toa, r., Cuba (tō'ä)	135	20°25'N	74°35'W
Toamasina, Madag.	233	18°14'S	49°25'E
Toar, Cuchillas de, mts., Cuba (kōō-chē'l-lyäs-dĕ-tô-ä'r)	135	20°20'N	74°50'W
Tobago, i., Trin. (tô-bā'gō)	129	11°15'N	60°30'W
Toba Inlet, b., Can.	94	50°20'N	124°50'W
Tobarra, Spain (tô-bär'rä)	172	38°37'N	1°42'W
Tobol (Tobyl), r., Asia	184	56°00'N	66°30'E
Tobol'sk, Russia (tô-bôlsk')	184	58°09'N	68°28'E
Tobyl *see* Tobol, r., Asia	184	52°00'N	62°00'E
Tocaima, Col. (tô-kā'y-mä)	142a	4°28'N	74°38'W
Tocantinópolis, Braz. (tō-kän-tē-nō'pō-lēs)	143	6°27'S	47°18'W
Tocantins, state, Braz.	143	10°00'S	48°00'W
Tocantins, r., Braz. (tō-kän-tēns')	143	3°28'S	49°22'W
Toccoa, Ga., U.S. (tŏk'ō-ȧ)	124	34°35'N	83°20'W
Toccoa, r., Ga., U.S.	124	34°53'N	84°24'W
Tochigi, Japan (tō'chē-gĭ)	211	36°25'N	139°45'E
Tocoa, Hond. (tō-kô'ä)	132	15°37'N	86°01'W
Tocopilla, Chile (tō-kō-pēl'yä)	144	22°03'S	70°08'W
Tocuyo de la Costa, Ven. (tô-kōō'yō-dĕ-lä-kôs'tä)	143b	11°03'N	68°24'W
Toda, Japan	211a	35°48'N	139°42'E
Todmorden, Eng., U.K. (tŏd'môr-dĕn)	158a	53°43'N	2°05'W
Tofino, Can. (tō-fē'nō)	94	49°09'N	125°54'W
Töfsingdalens National Park, rec., Swe.	166	62°09'N	13°05'E
Tōgane, Japan (tō'gä-nä)	211	35°29'N	140°16'E
Togian, Kepulauan, is., Indon.	212	0°20'S	122°00'E
Togo, nation, Afr. (tō'gō)	230	8°00'N	0°52'E
Toguzak, r., Russia (tō'gō-zák)	186a	53°40'N	61°42'E
Tohono O'odham Indian Reservation, I.R., Az., U.S.	119	32°33'N	112°12'W
Tohopekaliga, Lake, l., Fl., U.S. (tō'hō-pē'kȧ-lĭ'gȧ)	125a	28°16'N	81°09'W
Tohor, Tanjong, c., Malay.	197b	1°53'N	102°29'E
Toijala, Fin. (toi'yȧ-lä)	167	61°11'N	23°46'E
Toi-Misaki, c., Japan (toi mē'sä-kē)	210	31°20'N	131°20'E
Toiyabe, Nv., U.S. (toi'yä-bē)	118	38°59'N	117°22'W
Tokachi Gawa, r., Japan (tō-kä'chē gä'wä)	210	43°10'N	142°30'E
Tokaj, Hung. (tô'kō-ē)	169	48°06'N	21°24'E
Tokat, Tur. (tō-kät')	198	40°20'N	36°30'E
Tokelau, dep., Oc. (tō-kē-lä'ō)	2	8°00'S	176°00'W
Tokmak, Kyrg. (tôk'mák)	183	42°44'N	75°41'E
Tokmak, Ukr.	177	47°17'N	35°48'E
Tokorozawa, Japan (tô'kô-rô-zä'wä)	211a	35°47'N	139°29'E
Tok-to, atoll, Asia	210	37°15'N	131°51'E
Tokuno, i., Japan (tô-kōō'nō)	205	27°42'N	129°25'E
Tokushima, Japan (tō'kô'shē-mä)	205	34°06'N	134°31'E
Tokuyama, Japan (tō'kō'yä-mä)	211	34°04'N	131°49'E
Tōkyō, Japan	205	35°42'N	139°46'E
Tōkyō-Wan, b., Japan (tō'kyō wän)	211	35°56'N	139°56'E
Tolcayuca, Mex. (tôl-kä-yōō'kä)	130	19°55'N	98°54'W
Toledo, Spain (tô-lĕ'dô)	162	39°53'N	4°02'W
Toledo, Ia., U.S. (tô-lē'dō)	113	41°59'N	92°35'W
Toledo, Oh., U.S.	105	41°40'N	83°35'W
Toledo, Or., U.S.	114	44°37'N	123°58'W
Toledo, Montes de, mts., Spain (mô'n-tĕs-dĕ-tô-lĕ'dô)	172	39°33'N	4°40'W
Toledo Bend Reservoir, res., U.S.	107	31°30'N	93°30'W
Toliara, Madag.	233	23°16'S	43°44'E
Tolima, dept., Col. (tô-lē'mä)	142a	4°07'N	75°20'W
Tolima, Nevado del, mtn., Col. (nĕ-vä-dô-dĕl-tô-lē'mä)	142a	4°40'N	75°20'W
Tolimán, Mex. (tô-lē-män')	130	20°54'N	99°54'W
Tollesbury, Eng., U.K. (tōl'z-bēr'ĭ)	158b	51°46'N	0°49'E
Tolmezzo, Italy (tôl-mĕt'zô)	174	46°25'N	13°03'E
Tolmin, Slvn. (tôl'mēn)	174	46°12'N	13°45'E
Tolna, Hung. (tôl'nô)	169	46°25'N	18°47'E
Tolo, Teluk, b., Indon. (tō'lō)	212	2°00'S	122°06'E
Tolosa, Spain (tô-lō'sä)	162	43°10'N	2°05'W
Tolt, r., Wa., U.S. (tōlt)	116a	47°13'N	121°49'W
Toluca, Mex. (tô-lōō'kä)	128	19°17'N	99°40'W
Toluca, Il., U.S. (tô-lōō'kȧ)	108	41°00'N	89°10'W
Toluca, Nevado de, mtn., Mex. (nĕ-vä-dô-dĕ-tô-lōō'kä)	128	19°09'N	99°42'W
Tolyatti, Russia	180	53°30'N	49°10'E
Tom', r., Russia	184	55°33'N	85°00'E
Tomah, Wi., U.S. (tō'mȧ)	113	43°58'N	90°31'W
Tomahawk, Wi., U.S. (tŏm'ȧ-hôk)	113	45°27'N	89°44'W
Tomakivka, Ukr.	177	47°49'N	34°43'E
Tomanivi, mtn., Fiji	214g	17°37'S	178°01'E
Tomar, Port. (tō-mär')	172	39°36'N	8°26'W
Tomashovka, Bela.	169	51°34'N	23°37'E
Tomaszów Lubelski, Pol. (tô-mä'shôf lōō-bĕl'skĭ)	169	50°20'N	23°27'E
Tomaszów Mazowiecki, Pol. (tô-mä'shôf mä-zô'vyĕt-skĭ)	169	51°33'N	20°00'E
Tomatlán, Mex. (tô-mä-tlä'n)	130	19°54'N	105°14'W
Tombadonkéa, Gui.	234	11°00'N	14°23'W
Tombador, Serra do, mts., Braz. (sĕr'rȧ dô tôm-bä-dôr')	143	11°31'S	57°33'W
Tombigbee, r., U.S. (tŏm-bĭg'bē)	107	33°00'N	88°30'W
Tombos, Braz. (tô'm-bōs)	141a	20°53'S	42°00'W
Tombouctou, Mali	230	16°46'N	3°01'W
Tombstone, Az., U.S. (tōōm'stōn)	119	31°40'N	110°00'W
Tombua, Ang. (à-lĕ-zhän'drĕ)	232	15°49'S	11°53'E
Tomelilla, Swe. (tô'mĕ-lēl-lä)	166	55°34'N	13°55'E
Tomelloso, Spain (tō-mâl-lyō'sō)	172	39°09'N	3°02'W
Tommot, Russia (tŏm-mōt')	179	59°13'N	126°22'E
Tomsk, Russia (tŏmsk)	178	56°29'N	84°57'E
Tonala, Mex.	130	20°38'N	103°14'W
Tonalá, r., Mex.	131	18°05'N	94°08'W
Tonawanda, N.Y., U.S. (tôn-ȧ-wŏn'dȧ)	111c	43°01'N	78°53'W
Tonawanda Creek, r., N.Y., U.S.	111c	43°05'N	78°43'W
Tonbridge, Eng., U.K. (tŭn-brĭj)	158b	51°11'N	0°17'E
Tonda, Japan (tôn'dä)	211b	34°51'N	135°38'E
Tondabayashi, Japan (tôn-dä-bä'yä-shē)	211b	34°29'N	135°36'E
Tondano, Indon. (tôn-dä'nō)	213	1°15'N	124°50'E
Tønder, Den. (tûn'nēr)	166	54°47'N	8°49'E
Tone-Gawa, r., Japan (tō'nĕ gä'wa)	211	36°12'N	139°19'E
Tonga, nation, Oc. (tŏŋ'gȧ)	240	18°50'S	175°20'W
Tong'an, China (tôŋ-än)	209	24°48'N	118°02'E
Tonga Trench, deep	240	23°00'S	172°30'W
Tongbei, China (tôŋ-bā)	205	48°00'N	126°48'E
Tongguan, China (tôŋ-gūän)	205	34°48'N	110°25'E
Tonghe, China (tôŋ-hŭ)	208	45°58'N	128°40'E
Tonghua, China (tôŋ-hwä)	205	41°43'N	125°50'E
Tongjiang, China (tôŋ-jyäŋ)	205	47°38'N	132°54'E
Tongliao, China (tôŋ-lĭou)	208	43°30'N	122°15'E
Tongo, Cam.	235	5°11'N	14°00'E
Tongoy, Chile (tōn-goi')	144	30°16'S	71°29'W
Tongren, China (tôŋ-rŭn)	204	27°45'N	109°12'E
Tongshan, China (tôŋ-shän)	206	34°27'N	116°27'E
Tongtian, r., China (tôŋ-tĭĕn)	204	33°00'N	97°00'E
Tongue, r., Mt., U.S. (tŭng)	115	45°08'N	106°40'W
Tongxian, China (tôŋ shyĕn)	206	39°55'N	116°40'E
Tonj, r., Sudan (tônj)	231	6°18'N	28°33'E
Tonk, India (Tōŋk)	199	26°13'N	75°45'E
Tonkawa, Ok., U.S. (tŏŋ kȧ-wô)	121	36°42'N	97°19'W
Tonkin, Gulf of, b., Asia (tôn-kăn')	212	20°30'N	108°10'E
Tonle Sap, l., Camb. (tôn'lā săp')	212	13°03'N	102°49'E
Tonneins, Fr. (tō-năn')	170	44°24'N	0°18'E
Tönning, Ger. (tû'nēng)	168	54°20'N	8°55'E
Tonopah, Nv., U.S. (tō-nō-pä')	104	38°04'N	117°15'W
Tönsberg, Nor. (tûns'bĕrgh)	160	59°19'N	10°25'E
Tonto, r., Mex. (tōn'tō)	131	18°15'N	96°13'W
Tonto Creek, r., Az., U.S.	119	34°05'N	111°15'W
Tonto National Monument, rec., Az., U.S. (tôn'tô)	119	33°33'N	111°08'W
Tooele, Ut., U.S. (tōō-ĕl ē)	117b	40°33'N	112°17'W
Toowoomba, Austl. (tô wōōm'bȧ)	219	27°32'S	152°10'E
Topanga, Ca., U.S. (tō'păn-gȧ)	117a	34°05'N	118°36'W
Topeka, Ks., U.S. (tô-pē'kȧ)	105	39°02'N	95°41'W
Topilejo, Mex. (tô-pē-lĕ'hô)	131a	19°12'N	99°09'W
Topock, Az., U.S.	119	34°40'N	114°20'W
Topol'čany, Slvk. (tô-pôl'chä-nü)	169	48°38'N	18°10'E

ăt; finăl; rāte; senåte; ärm; ȧsk; sofȧ; fâre; ch-choose; dh-as th in other; bē; ēvent; bĕt; recĕnt; cratēr; g-gō; gh-guttural g; bĭt; ĭ-short neutral; rīde; ĸ-guttural k as ch in German ich;

PRONOUNCING INDEX
Topolobampo – Tsiafajovona 359

PLACE (Pronunciation)	PAGE	LAT.	LONG.
Topolobampo, Mex. (tō-pō-lô-bä′m-pô)	128	25°45′N	109°00′W
Topolovgrad, Blg.	175	42°05′N	26°19′E
Toppenish, Wa., U.S. (tôp′ĕn-ĭsh)	114	46°22′N	120°00′W
Torbat-e Ḩeydarīyeh, Iran	201	35°16′N	59°13′E
Torbat-e Jām, Iran	201	35°14′N	60°36′E
Torbay, Can. (tôr-bā′)	101	47°40′N	52°43′W
Torbay see Torquay, Eng., U.K.	164	50°30′N	3°26′W
Torbreck, Mount, mtn., Austl. (tōr-brĕk)	222	37°05′S	146°55′E
Torch, l., Mi., U.S. (tôrch)	108	45°00′N	85°30′W
Töreboda, Swe. (tû′rĕ-bō′dä)	166	58°44′N	14°04′E
Torhout, Bel.	165	51°01′N	3°04′E
Toribío, Col. (tô-rē-bē′ô)	142a	2°58′N	76°14′W
Toride, Japan (tô′rē-dā)	211a	35°54′N	140°04′E
Torino see Turin, Italy	154	45°05′N	7°44′E
Tormes, r., Spain (tōr′mās)	172	41°12′N	6°15′W
Torneälven, r., Eur.	156	67°00′N	22°30′E
Torneträsk, l., Swe. (tôr′nĕ trĕsk)	160	68°10′N	20°36′E
Torngat Mountains, mts., Can.	93	59°18′N	64°35′W
Tornio, Fin. (tôr′nĭ-ô)	154	65°55′N	24°09′E
Toro, Lac, l., Can.	99	46°53′N	73°46′W
Toronto, Can. (tô-rŏn′tō)	91	43°40′N	79°23′W
Toronto, Oh., U.S.	108	40°30′N	80°35′W
Toronto, res., Mex.	122	27°35′N	105°37′W
Toropets, Russia (tô′rô-pyĕts)	180	56°31′N	31°37′E
Toros Dağları, mts., Tur. (tô′rŭs)	198	37°00′N	32°40′E
Torote, r., Spain (tô-rō′tä)	173a	40°36′N	3°24′W
Torquay, Eng., U.K. (tôr-kē′)	164	50°30′N	3°26′W
Torra, Cerro, mtn., Col. (sĕ′r-rô-tô′r-rä)	142a	4°41′N	76°22′W
Torrance, Ca., U.S. (tŏr′rănc)	117a	33°50′N	118°20′W
Torre Annunziata, Italy (tôr′rā ä-nōōn-tsē-ä′tä)	173c	40°31′N	14°27′E
Torreblanca, Spain	173	40°18′N	0°12′E
Torre del Greco, Italy (tôr′rā dĕl grā′kô)	174	40°32′N	14°23′E
Torrejoncillo, Spain (tôr′rā-hōn-thē′lyō)	172	39°54′N	6°26′W
Torrelavega, Spain (tôr-rā′lä-vā′gä)	172	43°22′N	4°02′W
Torre Maggiore, Italy (tôr′rā mäd-jō′rā)	174	41°41′N	15°18′E
Torrens, Lake, l., Austl. (tōr-ĕns)	220	30°07′S	137°40′E
Torrent, Spain	173	39°25′N	0°28′W
Torreón, Mex. (tôr-rā-ōn′)	128	25°32′N	103°26′W
Torres Islands, is., Vanuatu (tôr′rĕs) (tōr′ĕz)	221	13°18′N	165°59′E
Torres Martinez Indian Reservation, I.R., Ca., U.S. (tôr′ĕz mär-tē′nĕz)	118	33°33′N	116°21′W
Torres Novas, Port. (tôr′rĕzh nō′väzh)	172	39°28′N	8°37′W
Torres Strait, strt., Austl. (tôr′rĕs)	221	10°30′S	141°30′E
Torres Vedras, Port. (tôr′rĕsh vĕ′dräzh)	172	39°08′N	9°18′W
Torrevieja, Spain (tôr-rā-vyā′hä)	173	37°58′N	0°40′W
Torrijos, Phil. (tôr-rē′hōs)	213a	13°19′N	122°06′E
Torrington, Ct., U.S. (tŏr′ĭng-tŭn)	109	41°50′N	73°10′W
Torrington, Wy., U.S.	112	42°04′N	104°11′W
Torro, Spain (tô′r-rō)	172	41°27′N	5°23′W
Torsby, Swe. (tôrs′bü)	166	60°07′N	12°56′E
Torshälla, Swe. (tôrs′hĕl-ä)	166	59°26′N	16°21′E
Tórshavn, Far. Is. (tôrs-houn′)	154	62°00′N	6°55′W
Tortola, i., Br. Vir. Is. (tôr-tō′lä)	129b	18°34′N	64°40′W
Tortona, Italy (tôr-tō′nä)	174	44°52′N	8°52′W
Tortosa, Spain (tôr-tō′sä)	154	40°59′N	0°33′E
Tortosa, Cap de, c., Spain	173	40°42′N	0°55′E
Tortue, Canal de la, strt., Haiti (tôr-tü′)	135	20°05′N	73°20′W
Tortue, Île de la, i., Haiti	135	20°10′N	73°00′W
Tortue, Rivière de la, r., Can. (lä tōr-tü′)	102a	45°12′N	73°32′W
Toruń, Pol.	154	53°02′N	18°35′E
Tõrva, Est. (t′r′vȧ)	167	58°02′N	25°56′E
Torzhok, Russia (tôr′zhôk)	180	57°03′N	34°53′E
Toscana, hist. reg., Italy (tôs-kä′nä)	174	43°23′N	11°08′E
Tosna, r., Russia	186c	59°28′N	30°53′E
Tosno, Russia (tôs′nô)	176	59°32′N	30°52′E
Tostado, Arg. (tôs-tä′dô)	144	29°10′S	61°43′W
Tosya, Tur. (tôz′yȧ)	163	41°00′N	34°00′E
Totana, Spain (tô-tä-nä)	172	37°45′N	1°28′W
Tot′ma, Russia (tôt′mȧ)	180	60°00′N	42°20′E
Totness, Sur.	143	5°51′N	56°17′W
Totonicapán, Guat. (tôtō-nē-kä′pän)	128	14°55′N	91°20′W
Totoras, Arg. (tō-tô′räs)	141c	32°33′S	61°13′W
Totsuka, Japan (tōt′sōō-kä)	211a	35°24′N	139°32′E
Tottenham, Eng., U.K. (tŏt′ĕn-ȧm)	158b	51°35′N	0°06′W
Tottori, Japan (tô′tô-rē)	205	35°30′N	134°15′E
Touba, C. Iv.	234	8°17′N	7°41′W
Touba, Sen.	234	14°51′N	15°53′W
Toubkal, Jebel, mtn., Mor.	230	31°15′N	7°46′W
Tougan, Burkina	234	13°04′N	3°04′W
Touggourt, Alg. (tô-gōōrt′) (tōō-gōōr′)	230	33°09′N	6°07′E
Touil, Oued, r., Alg. (tōō-ēl′)	162	34°42′N	2°16′E
Toul, Fr. (tōōl)	161	48°39′N	5°51′E
Toulon, Fr. (tōō-lôn′)	154	43°09′N	5°54′E
Toulouse, Fr. (tōō-lōōz′)	154	43°37′N	1°27′E
Toungoo, Mya. (tŏ-ŏŋ-gōō′)	212	19°00′N	96°29′E
Tourcoing, Fr. (tòr-kwăn′)	161	50°44′N	3°06′E
Tournan-en-Brie, Fr. (tōōr-nän-ĕn-brē′)	171b	48°45′N	2°47′E
Tours, Fr. (tōōr)	154	47°23′N	0°39′E
Touside, Pic, mtn., Chad (tōō-sē-dā′)	231	21°10′N	16°30′E
Tovdalselva, r., Nor. (tôv-däls-ĕlvȧ)	166	58°23′N	8°16′E
Towanda, Pa., U.S. (tô-wän′dȧ)	109	41°45′N	76°30′W
Town Bluff Lake, l., Tx., U.S.	123	30°52′N	94°30′W
Towner, N.D., U.S. (tou′nẽr)	112	48°21′N	100°24′W
Townsend, Ma., U.S. (toun′zĕnd)	101a	42°41′N	71°42′W
Townsend, Mt., U.S.	115	46°19′N	111°35′W
Townsend, Mount, mtn., Wa., U.S.	116a	47°52′N	123°03′W
Townsville, Austl. (tounz′vĭl)	219	19°18′S	146°50′E
Towson, Md., U.S. (tou′sŭn)	110e	39°24′N	76°36′W
Towuti, Danau, l., Indon. (tō-wōō′tē)	212	3°00′S	121°45′E
Toxkan, r., China	204	40°34′N	77°15′E
Toyah, Tx., U.S. (tô′yȧ)	122	31°19′N	103°46′W
Toyama, Japan (tō′yä-mä)	205	36°42′N	137°14′E
Toyama-Wan, b., Japan	211	36°58′N	137°16′E
Toyohashi, Japan (tō′yô-hä′shē)	210	34°44′N	137°21′E
Toyonaka, Japan (tō′yô-nä′kȧ)	211b	34°47′N	135°28′E
Tozeur, Tun. (tô-zûr′)	162	33°59′N	8°11′E
Trabzon, Tur. (tràb′zôn)	198	41°00′N	39°45′E
Tracy, Can.	99	46°00′N	73°13′W
Tracy, Ca., U.S. (trā′sē)	118	37°45′N	121°27′W
Tracy, Mn., U.S.	112	44°13′N	95°37′W
Tracy City, Tn., U.S.	124	35°15′N	85°44′W
Trafalgar, Cabo, c., Spain (kȧ′bô-trä-fäl-gä′r)	172	36°10′N	6°02′W
Trafonomby, mtn., Madag.	233	24°32′S	46°35′E
Trail, Can. (trāl)	90	49°06′N	117°42′W
Traisen, r., Aus.	159e	48°15′N	15°55′E
Traiskirchen, Aus.	159e	48°01′N	16°18′E
Trakai, Lith. (trȧ-kāy)	167	54°38′N	24°59′E
Trakiszki, Pol. (trȧ-kē′-sh-kē)	169	54°16′N	23°07′E
Tralee, Ire. (trȧ-lē′)	161	52°16′N	9°20′W
Tranås, Swe. (trän′ôs)	166	58°03′N	14°56′E
Trancoso, Port. (träŋ-kō′sò)	172	40°46′N	7°23′W
Trangan, Pulau, i., Indon. (träŋ′gän)	213	6°52′S	133°30′E
Trani, Italy (trä′nē)	174	41°15′N	16°25′E
Transylvania, hist. reg., Rom. (trăn-sĭl-vā′nĭ-ȧ)	169	46°30′N	22°35′E
Trapani, Italy	162	38°01′N	12°31′E
Trappes, Fr. (tràp)	171b	48°47′N	2°01′E
Traralgon, Austl. (tră′răl-gŏn)	222	38°15′S	146°33′E
Trarza, reg., Maur.	234	17°35′N	15°15′W
Trasimeno, Lago, l., Italy (lä′gō trä-sē-mā′nō)	174	43°00′N	12°12′E
Trás-os-Montes, hist. reg., Port. (träzh′ōzh mōn′tāzh)	162	41°33′N	7°13′W
Traun, r., Aus. (troun)	168	48°10′N	14°15′E
Traunstein, Ger. (troun′stīn)	168	47°52′N	12°38′E
Traverse, Lake, l., Mn., U.S. (trăv′ẽrs)	112	45°46′N	96°53′W
Traverse City, Mi., U.S.	108	44°45′N	85°40′W
Travnik, Bos. (träv′nēk)	175	44°13′N	17°43′E
Treasure Island, i., Ca., U.S. (trĕzh′ẽr)	116b	37°49′N	122°22′W
Trebbin, Ger. (trĕ′bēn)	159b	52°13′N	13°13′E
Trebinje, Bos. (trȧ′bēn-yĕ)	175	42°43′N	18°21′E
Trebišov, Slvk. (trĕ′bē-shôf)	169	48°36′N	21°32′E
Tregrosse Islands, is., Austl. (trē-grōs′)	221	18°08′S	150°53′E
Treinta y Tres, Ur. (trà-ēn′tä ē träs′)	144	33°14′S	54°17′W
Trelew, Arg. (trē′lū)	144	43°15′S	65°25′W
Trelleborg, Swe.	166	55°24′N	13°07′E
Tremiti, Isole, is., Italy (ē′sō-lĕ trä-mē′tē)	174	42°07′N	16°33′E
Trenčín, Czech Rep. (trĕn′chēn)	161	48°52′N	18°02′E
Trenque Lauquén, Arg. (trĕn′kĕ-lä′ōo-kĕ′n)	144	35°50′S	62°44′W
Trent, r., Can. (trĕnt)	99	44°15′N	77°55′W
Trent, r., Eng., U.K.	158a	53°25′N	0°45′W
Trent and Mersey Canal, can., Eng., U.K. (trĕnt) (mûr zē)	158a	53°11′N	2°24′W
Trentino-Alto Adige, hist. reg., Italy	174	46°16′N	10°47′E
Trento, Italy (trĕn′tô)	162	46°04′N	11°07′E
Trenton, Can. (trĕn′tŭn)	91	44°05′N	77°35′W
Trenton, Can.	101	45°37′N	62°38′W
Trenton, Mi., U.S.	111b	42°08′N	83°12′W
Trenton, Mo., U.S.	121	40°05′N	93°36′W
Trenton, N.J., U.S.	105	40°13′N	74°46′W
Trenton, Tn., U.S.	124	35°57′N	88°55′W
Trepassey, Can. (trē-păs′ē)	101	46°44′N	53°22′W
Trepassey Bay, b., Can.	101	46°40′N	53°20′W
Tres Arroyos, Arg. (träs′är-rō′yōs)	144	38°18′S	60°16′W
Três Corações, Braz. (trĕ′s kō-rä-zô′ĕs)	141a	21°41′S	45°14′W
Tres Cumbres, Mex. (trĕ′s kōō′m-brĕs)	131a	19°03′N	99°14′W
Três Lagoas, Braz. (trĕ′s lä-gô′ás)	143	20°48′S	51°42′W
Três Marias, Represa, res., Braz.	143	18°15′S	45°30′W
Tres Morros, Alto de, mtn., Col. (á′l-tô dĕ trĕ′s mô′r-rôs)	142a	7°08′N	76°10′W
Três Pontas, Braz. (trĕ′pô′n-täs)	141a	21°22′S	45°30′W
Três Pontas, Cabo das, c., Ang.	236	10°23′S	13°32′E
Três Rios, Braz. (trĕ′s rē′ōs)	141a	22°07′S	43°13′W
Très-Saint Rédempteur, Can. (săn rā-dänp-tûr′)	102a	45°26′N	74°23′W
Treuenbrietzen, Ger. (troi′ĕn-brē-tzĕn)	159b	52°06′N	12°52′E
Treviglio, Italy (trā-vē′lyô)	174	45°30′N	9°34′E
Treviso, Italy (trĕ-vē′sô)	162	45°39′N	12°15′E
Trichardt, S. Afr. (trĭ-kärt′)	238c	26°32′N	29°16′E
Trier, Ger.	161	49°45′N	6°38′E
Trieste, Italy (trē-ĕs′tä)	154	45°39′N	13°48′E
Triglav, mtn., Slvn.	174	46°23′N	13°50′E
Trigueros, Spain (trē-gā′rōs)	172	37°23′N	6°50′W
Tríkala, Grc.	163	39°33′N	21°49′E
Trikora, Puncak, mtn., Indon.	213	4°15′S	138°45′E
Trim Creek, r., Il., U.S. (trĭm)	111a	41°19′N	87°39′W
Trincomalee, Sri L. (trĭŋ-kô-mȧ-lē′)	203	8°39′N	81°12′E
Tring, Eng., U.K. (trĭng)	158b	51°46′N	0°40′W
Trinidad, Bol. (trē-nē-dhädh′)	142	14°48′S	64°43′W
Trinidad, Cuba (trē-nē-dhädh′)	129	21°50′N	80°00′W
Trinidad, Ur.	144	33°29′S	56°55′W
Trinidad, Co., U.S. (trĭn′ĭdăd)	104	37°11′N	104°31′W
Trinidad, i., Trin. (trĭn′ĭ-dăd)	143	10°00′N	61°00′W
Trinidad, r., Pan.	128a	8°55′N	80°01′W
Trinidad, Sierra de, mts., Cuba (sē-ĕ′r-rä dĕ trē-nē-dä′d)	134	21°50′N	79°55′W
Trinidad and Tobago, nation, N.A. (trĭn′ĭ-dăd) (tô-bā′gō)	129	11°00′N	61°00′W
Trinitaria, Mex. (trē-nē-tä′ryä)	131	16°09′N	92°04′W
Trinity, Can. (trĭn′ĭ-tē)	101	48°59′N	53°55′W
Trinity, Tx., U.S.	123	30°52′N	95°27′W
Trinity, is., Ak., U.S.	103	56°25′N	153°15′W
Trinity, r., Ca., U.S.	114	40°50′N	123°20′W
Trinity, r., Tx., U.S.	107	30°50′N	95°09′W
Trinity, East Fork, r., Tx., U.S.	121	33°24′N	96°42′W
Trinity, West Fork, r., Tx., U.S.	120	33°22′N	98°26′W
Trinity Bay, b., Can.	93	48°00′N	53°40′W
Trino, Italy (trē′nô)	174	45°11′N	8°16′E
Trion, Ga., U.S. (trī′ŏn)	124	34°32′N	85°18′W
Trípoli, Grc.	163	37°32′N	22°32′E
Tripoli (Tarābulus), Libya	231	32°50′N	13°13′E
Tripolitania see Tarābulus, hist. reg., Libya	230	31°00′N	12°26′E
Tripura, state, India	199	24°00′N	92°00′E
Tristan da Cunha Islands, is., St. Hel. (três-tän′dä kōōn′yȧ)	2	35°30′S	12°15′W
Triste, Golfo, b., Ven. (gôl-fô trē′s-tĕ)	143b	10°40′N	68°05′W
Triticus Reservoir, res., N.Y., U.S. (trī tĭ-cŭs)	110a	41°20′N	73°36′W
Trnava, Slvk. (t′r′nȧ-vȧ)	169	48°22′N	17°34′E
Trobriand Islands, is., Pap. N. Gui. (trō-brē-änd′)	213	8°25′S	151°45′E
Trogir, Cro. (trô′gēr)	174	43°32′N	16°17′E
Trois Fourches, Cap des, c., Mor.	172	35°28′N	2°58′W
Trois-Rivières, Can. (trwä′rē-vyâ′)	91	46°21′N	72°35′W
Troitsk, Russia (trô′ètsk)	184	54°06′N	61°35′E
Troits′ke, Ukr.	177	47°39′N	30°16′E
Troitsko-Pechorsk, Russia (trô′ĭtsk-ô-pyĕ-chôrsk′)	178	62°18′N	56°07′E
Trollhättan, Swe. (trôl′hĕt-ĕn)	160	58°17′N	12°17′E
Trollheimen, mts., Nor. (trôll-hĕĭm)	166	62°48′N	9°05′E
Trona, Ca., U.S. (trō′nȧ)	118	35°49′N	117°20′W
Tronador, Cerro, mtn., S.A. (sĕ′r-rō trō-nä′dôr)	144	41°17′S	71°56′W
Troncoso, Mex. (trôn-kô′sō)	130	22°43′N	102°22′W
Trondheim, Nor. (trôn′hâm)	154	63°25′N	11°35′E
Trosa, Swe. (trô′sä)	166	58°54′N	17°25′E
Trout, l., Can.	93	51°16′N	92°46′W
Trout, l., Can.	92	61°10′N	121°30′W
Trout Creek, r., Or., U.S.	114	42°18′N	118°31′W
Troutdale, Or., U.S. (trout′dāl)	116c	45°32′N	122°23′W
Trout Lake, Mi., U.S.	113	46°20′N	85°02′W
Trouville, Fr. (trōō-vēl′)	170	49°23′N	0°05′E
Troy, Al., U.S. (troi)	124	31°47′N	85°46′W
Troy, Il., U.S.	117e	38°44′N	89°53′W
Troy, Ks., U.S.	121	39°46′N	95°07′W
Troy, Mo., U.S.	120	38°56′N	99°57′W
Troy, Mt., U.S.	114	48°28′N	115°56′W
Troy, N.C., U.S.	125	35°21′N	79°58′W
Troy, N.Y., U.S.	105	42°45′N	73°45′W
Troy, Oh., U.S.	108	40°00′N	84°10′W
Troy, hist., Tur.	198	39°59′N	26°14′E
Troyes, Fr. (trwä)	161	48°18′N	4°03′E
Trstenik, Serb. (t′r′stĕ-nĕk)	163	43°36′N	21°00′E
Trubchëvsk, Russia (tròp′chĕfsk)	181	52°36′N	33°46′E
Trucial States see United Arab Emirates, nation, Asia	198	24°00′N	54°00′E
Truckee, Ca., U.S. (trŭk′ē)	118	39°20′N	120°12′W
Truckee, r., Ca., U.S.	118	39°25′N	120°07′W
Truganina, Austl.	217a	37°49′N	144°44′E
Trujillo, Col. (trò-κē′l-yō)	142a	4°10′N	76°20′W
Trujillo, Peru	142	8°08′S	79°00′W
Trujillo, Spain (trōō-κē′l-yô)	162	39°27′N	5°50′W
Trujillo, Ven.	142	9°15′N	70°28′W
Trujillo, r., Mex.	130	23°12′N	103°10′W
Trujin, Lago, l., Dom. Rep. (trōō-κēn′)	135	17°45′N	71°25′W
Truk see Chuuk, is., Micron.	214c	7°25′N	151°47′E
Trumann, Ar., U.S. (trōō′măn)	121	35°41′N	90°31′W
Trŭn, Blg. (trŭn)	175	42°49′N	22°39′E
Truro, Can. (trōō′rō)	91	45°22′N	63°16′W
Truro, Eng., U.K.	164	50°17′N	5°05′W
Trussville, Al., U.S. (trŭs′vĭl)	110h	33°37′N	86°37′W
Truth or Consequences, N.M., U.S. (trōōth ŏr kŏn′sē-kwĕn-sĭs)	119	33°10′N	107°20′W
Trutnov, Czech Rep. (tròt′nôf)	168	50°36′N	15°36′E
Trzcianka, Pol. (tchyän′kȧ)	168	53°02′N	16°27′E
Trzebiatów, Pol. (tchĕ-byä′tò-v)	168	54°03′N	15°16′E
Tsaidam Basin, basin, China (tsī-däm)	204	37°19′N	94°08′E
Tsala Apopka Lake, l., Fl., U.S. (tsä′lȧ ă-pŏp′kȧ)	125	28°57′N	82°11′W
Tsast Bogd, mtn., Mong.	204	46°44′N	92°34′E
Tsavo National Park, rec., Kenya	237	2°35′S	38°45′E
Tsawwassen Indian Reserve, I.R., Can.	116d	49°03′N	123°11′W
Tsentral′nyy-Kospashskiy, Russia (tsĕn-träl′nyĭ-kôs-pàsh′skĭ)	186a	59°03′N	57°48′E
Tshela, D.R.C. (tshā′lȧ)	232	4°59′S	12°56′E
Tshikapa, D.R.C. (tshē-kä′pä)	232	6°25′S	20°48′E
Tshofa, D.R.C.	237	5°14′S	25°15′E
Tshuapa, r., D.R.C.	232	0°30′S	22°00′E
Tsiafajovona, mtn., Madag.	233	19°17′S	47°27′E

ng-sing; ŋ-baŋk; n-nasalized n; nŏd; cŏmmit; ōld; ôbey; ôrder; oi-boil; fōōd; ò-as oo in foot; ou-out; s-soft; sh-dish; th-thin; pūre; ûnite; ûrn; stŭd; circŭs; ü-as in French tu; ′-indeterminate vowel.

U

ăt; fināl; rāte; senāte; ärm; àsk; sofá; fãre; ch-choose; dh-as th in other; bē; ĕvent; bĕt; recĕnt; cratẽr; g-gō; gh-guttural g; bǐt; ĭ-short neutral; rīde; ĸ-guttural k as ch in German ich;

PLACE (Pronunciation)	PAGE	LAT.	LONG.
Ugleural'sk, Russia (ŏg-lĕ-ò-rálsk')	186a	58°58′N	57°35′E
Uglich, Russia (ōōg-lêch')	176	57°33′N	38°19′E
Uglitskiy, Russia (ŏg-lĭt'skĭ)	186a	53°50′N	60°18′E
Uglovka, Russia (ōōg-lôf'kå)	176	58°14′N	33°24′E
Ugra, r., Russia (ōōg'rå)	180	54°43′N	34°20′E
Ugŭrchin, Blg.	175	43°06′N	24°23′E
Uhrichsville, Oh., U.S. (ū'rĭks-vĭl)	108	40°25′N	81°20′W
Uíge, Ang.	232	7°37′S	15°03′E
Uiju, Kor., N. (ò'éjōō)	205	40°09′N	124°33′E
Uinkaret Plateau, plat., Az., U.S. (ù-ĭn'kår-ĕt)	119	36°43′N	113°15′W
Uinskoye, Russia (ò-ĭn'skô-yĕ)	186a	56°53′N	56°25′E
Uinta, r., Ut., U.S. (ù-ĭn'tä)	119	40°25′N	109°55′W
Uintah and Ouray Indian Reservation, I.R., U.S.	119	40°20′N	110°20′W
Uinta Mountains, mts., Ut., U.S.	106	40°35′N	111°00′W
Uitenhage, S. Afr.	232	33°46′S	25°26′E
Uithoorn, Neth.	159a	52°13′N	4°49′E
Uji, Japan (ōō'jē)	211b	34°53′N	135°49′E
Ujiji, Tan. (ōō-jē'jē)	232	4°55′S	29°41′E
Ujjain, India (ōō-jŭĕn)	199	23°18′N	75°37′E
Ujungpandang, Indon.	212	5°08′S	119°28′E
Ukerewe Island, i., Tan.	237	2°00′S	32°40′E
Ukhta, Russia (ōōk'tä)	180	65°22′N	31°30′E
Ukhta, Russia	180	63°08′N	53°42′E
Ukiah, Ca., U.S. (ū-kī'å)	118	39°09′N	122°12′W
Ukmerge, Lith. (òk'mĕr-ghå)	180	55°16′N	24°45′E
Ukraine, nation, Eur.	178	49°15′N	30°15′E
Uku, i., Japan (ōōk'ōō)	211	33°18′N	129°02′E
Ulaangom, Mong.	204	50°23′N	92°14′E
Ulan Bator (Ulaanbaatar), Mong.	204	47°56′N	107°00′E
Ulan-Ude, Russia (ōō'län ōō'då)	179	51°59′N	107°41′E
Ulchin, Kor., S. (ōōl'chên')	210	36°57′N	129°26′E
Ulcinj, Serb. (ōōl'tsên')	163	41°56′N	19°15′E
Ulhās, r., India	203b	19°13′N	73°03′E
Ulhāsnagar, India	202	19°10′N	73°07′E
Uliastay, Mong.	204	47°49′N	97°00′E
Ulindi, r., D.R.C. (ōō-lĭn'dê)	232	1°55′S	26°17′E
Ulla, Bela. (òl'á)	176	55°14′N	29°15′E
Ulla, r., Bela.	176	54°58′N	29°03′E
Ulla, r., Spain (ōō'lä)	172	42°45′N	8°33′W
Ullŭng, i., Kor., S. (ōōl'lóng')	210	37°29′N	130°50′E
Ulm, Ger. (òlm)	161	48°24′N	9°59′E
Ulmer, Mount, mtn., Ant. (ùl'mûr')	224	77°30′S	86°00′W
Ulricehamn, Swe. (òl-rē'sĕ-häm)	166	57°49′N	13°23′E
Ulsan, Kor., S. (ōōl'sän')	210	35°35′N	129°22′E
Ulster, hist. reg., Eur. (ùl'stēr)	164	54°41′N	7°10′W
Ulua, r., Hond. (ōō-lōō'ä)	132	15°49′N	87°45′W
Ulubăria, India	202a	22°27′N	88°09′E
Ulukışla, Tur. (ōō-lōō-kêsh'lá)	163	36°40′N	34°30′E
Ulunga, Russia (ò-lōōn'gá)	210	46°16′N	136°29′E
Ulungur, r., China (ōō-lōōn-gŭr)	204	46°31′N	88°00′E
Uluru (Ayers Rock), mtn., Austl.	220	25°23′S	131°05′E
Ulu-Telyak, Russia (ōō ló'tĕlyäk)	186a	54°54′N	57°01′E
Ulverstone, Austl. (ùl'vēr-stŭn)	219	41°20′S	146°22′E
Ul'yanovska, Russia	186c	59°38′N	30°47′E
Ul'yanovsk, Russia (ōō-lyä'nôfsk)	178	54°20′N	48°24′E
Ulysses, Ks., U.S. (ū-lĭs'ēz)	120	37°34′N	101°25′W
Umán, Mex. (ōō-män')	132a	20°52′N	89°44′W
Uman', Ukr. (ò-mán')	181	48°44′N	30°13′E
Umatilla Indian Reservation, I.R., Or., U.S. (ū-má-tĭl'á)	114	45°38′N	118°35′W
Umberpāda, India	203b	19°28′N	73°04′E
Umbria, hist. reg., Italy (ùm'brĭ-á)	174	42°53′N	12°22′E
Umeålven, r., Swe.	156	64°57′N	18°51′E
Umhlatuzi, r., S. Afr. (òm'hlà-tōō'zĭ)	233c	28°47′S	31°17′E
Umiat, Ak., U.S. (ōō'mĭ-ăt)	106a	69°20′N	152°28′W
Umkomaas, S. Afr. (òm-kō'mäs)	233c	30°12′S	30°48′E
Umnak, i., Ak., U.S. (ōōm'năk)	106b	53°10′N	169°08′W
Umnak Pass, Ak., U.S.	103a	53°10′N	168°04′W
Umniati, r., Zimb.	232	17°08′S	29°11′E
Umpqua, r., Or., U.S.	114	43°42′N	123°50′W
Umtata, S. Afr. (òm-tä'tä)	232	31°36′S	28°47′E
Umtentweni, S. Afr.	233c	30°41′S	30°29′E
Umzimkulu, S. Afr. (òm-zêm-kōō'lōō)	233c	30°12′S	29°53′E
Umzinto, S. Afr. (òm-zĭn'tô)	233c	30°19′S	30°41′E
Una, r., Serb. (ōō'nä)	174	44°38′N	16°10′E
Unalakleet, Ak., U.S. (ù-ná-lák'lēt)	103	63°50′N	160°42′W
Unalaska, Ak., U.S. (ū-ná-lás'kä)	103a	53°30′N	166°20′W
Unare, r., Ven.	143b	9°45′N	65°12′W
Unare, Laguna de, l., Ven. (lä-gò'nä-de-ōō-nä'rĕ)	143b	10°07′N	65°23′W
Unayzah, Sau. Ar.	198	25°50′N	44°02′E
Uncas, Can. (ùn'kás)	102g	53°30′N	113°02′W
Uncia, Bol. (ōōn'sĕ-ä)	142	18°28′S	66°32′W
Uncompahgre, r., Co., U.S.	119	38°20′N	107°45′W
Uncompahgre Peak, mtn., Co., U.S. (ùn-kŭm-pä'grĕ)	119	38°00′N	107°30′W
Uncompahgre Plateau, plat., Co., U.S.	119	38°40′N	108°40′W
Underberg, S. Afr. (ùn'dēr-bûrg)	233c	29°51′S	29°32′E
Unecha, Russia (ò-nĕ'chá)	176	52°51′N	32°44′E
Ungava, Péninsule d', pen., Can.	93	59°55′N	74°00′W
Ungava Bay, b., Can.	93	59°46′N	67°18′W
União da Vitória, Braz. (ōō-nĕ-ouN' dä vē-tô'ryä)	144	26°17′S	51°13′W
Unije, i., Serb. (ōō'nē-yĕ)	174	44°39′N	14°10′E
Unimak, i., Ak., U.S. (ōō-nĕ-mák')	103	54°30′N	163°35′W
Unimak Pass, Ak., U.S.	103a	54°22′N	165°22′W
Union, Mo., U.S.	121	38°28′N	90°59′W
Union, Ms., U.S. (ūn'yŭn)	124	32°35′N	89°07′W
Union, N.C., U.S.	125	34°42′N	81°40′W
Union, Or., U.S.	114	45°13′N	117°52′W
Union City, Ca., U.S.	116b	37°36′N	122°01′W
Union City, In., U.S.	108	40°10′N	85°00′W
Union City, Mi., U.S.	108	42°00′N	85°10′W
Union City, Pa., U.S.	109	41°50′N	79°50′W
Union City, Tn., U.S.	124	36°25′N	89°04′W
Unión de Reyes, Cuba	134	22°45′N	81°30′W
Unión de San Antonio, Mex.	130	21°07′N	101°56′W
Unión de Tula, Mex.	130	19°57′N	104°14′W
Union Grove, Wi., U.S. (ūn-yŭn grōv)	111a	42°41′N	88°03′W
Unión Hidalgo, Mex. (ê-dä'lgô)	131	16°29′N	94°51′W
Union Point, Ga., U.S.	124	33°37′N	83°08′W
Union Springs, Al., U.S. (sprĭngz)	124	32°08′N	85°43′W
Uniontown, Al., U.S. (ūn'yŭn-toun)	124	32°26′N	87°30′W
Uniontown, Oh., U.S.	111d	40°58′N	81°25′W
Uniontown, Pa., U.S.	108	39°55′N	79°45′W
Unionville, Mo., U.S. (ūn'yŭn-vĭl)	121	40°28′N	92°58′W
Unisan, Phil. (ōō-nē'sän)	213a	13°50′N	121°59′E
United Arab Emirates, nation, Asia	198	24°00′N	54°00′E
United Kingdom, nation, Eur.	154	56°30′N	1°40′W
United States, nation, N.A.	104	38°00′N	110°00′W
Unity, Can.	96	52°27′N	109°10′W
Universal, In., U.S. (ū-nĭ-vûr'sál)	108	39°35′N	87°30′W
University City, Mo., U.S. (ū'nĭ-vûr'sĭ-tĭ)	117e	38°40′N	90°19′W
University Park, Tx., U.S.	117c	32°51′N	96°48′W
Unna, Ger. (ōō'nä)	171c	51°32′N	7°41′E
Uno, Canal Numero, can., Arg.	141c	36°35′S	58°14′W
Unterhaching, Ger. (ōōn'tĕr-hä-kēng)	159d	48°03′N	11°38′E
Ünye, Tur. (ün'yĕ)	163	41°00′N	37°10′E
Unzha, r., Russia (òn'zhá)	180	57°45′N	44°10′E
Upa, r., Russia (ò'pá)	176	53°54′N	36°48′E
Upata, Ven. (ōō-pä'tä)	142	7°58′N	62°27′W
Upemba, Parc National de l', rec., D.R.C.	237	9°10′S	26°15′E
Upington, S. Afr. (ùp'ĭng-tŭn)	232	28°25′S	21°15′E
Upland, Ca., U.S. (ùp'lănd)	117a	34°06′N	117°38′W
Upolu, i., Samoa	214a	13°55′S	171°45′W
Upolu Point, c., Hi., U.S. (ōō-pô'lōō)	126a	20°15′N	155°48′W
Upper Arrow Lake, l., Can. (ăr'ō)	95	50°30′N	117°55′W
Upper Darby, Pa., U.S. (där'bǐ)	110f	39°58′N	75°16′W
Upper des Lacs, l., N.A. (dĕ läk)	112	48°58′N	101°55′W
Upper Kapuas Mountains, mts., Asia	212	1°45′N	112°06′E
Upper Klamath Lake, l., Or., U.S.	114	42°23′N	122°55′W
Upper Lake, l., Nv., U.S. (ùp'ĕr)	114	41°42′N	119°59′W
Upper Marlboro, Md., U.S. (ùp'ēr märl'bôrô)	110e	38°49′N	76°46′W
Upper Mill, Wa., U.S. (mĭl)	116a	47°11′N	121°55′W
Upper Red Lake, l., Mn., U.S. (rĕd)	113	48°14′N	94°53′W
Upper Sandusky, Oh., U.S. (săn-dŭs'kê)	108	40°50′N	83°20′W
Upper San Leandro Reservoir, res., Ca., U.S. (ùp'ĕr săn lê-ăn'drô)	116b	37°47′N	122°04′W
Upper Volta see Burkina Faso, nation, Afr.	230	13°00′N	2°00′W
Uppingham, Eng., U.K. (ùp'ĭng-ăm)	158a	52°35′N	0°43′W
Uppsala, Swe. (ōōp'sä-lä)	154	59°53′N	17°39′E
Uptown, Ma., U.S. (ùp'toun)	101a	42°10′N	71°36′W
Uraga, Japan (ōō'rä-gá')	211a	35°15′N	139°43′E
Ural, r., (ò-räl') (ù-rôl)	178	48°00′N	51°00′E
Urals, mts., Russia	178	56°28′N	58°13′E
Uran, India (ōō-rän')	203b	18°53′N	72°46′E
Uranium City, Can.	90	59°34′N	108°59′W
Urawa, Japan (ōō'rä-wä')	210	35°52′N	139°39′E
Urayasu, Japan (ōō'rä-yä'sōō)	211a	35°40′N	139°54′W
Urazovo, Russia (ò-rä'zô-vô)	177	50°08′N	38°03′E
Urbana, Il., U.S. (ûr-băn'á)	108	40°10′N	88°15′W
Urbana, Oh., U.S.	108	40°05′N	83°50′W
Urbino, Italy (ōōr-bē'nô)	174	43°43′N	12°37′E
Urdaneta, Phil. (ōōr-dä-nā'tä)	213a	15°59′N	120°34′E
Urdinarrain, Arg. (ōōr-dē-när-räĕ'n)	141c	32°43′S	58°53′W
Uritsk, Russia (ōō'rĭtsk)	186c	59°50′N	30°11′E
Urla, Tur. (òr'lä)	175	38°20′N	26°44′E
Urman, Russia (òr'mán)	186a	54°53′N	56°52′E
Urmi, r., Russia (òr'mê)	210	48°50′N	134°00′E
Uromi, Nig.	235	6°44′N	6°18′E
Urrao, Col. (ōōr-rá'ô)	142	6°19′N	76°11′W
Urshel'skiy, Russia (ōōr-shĕl'skêĕ)	176	55°50′N	40°11′E
Ursus, Pol.	169	52°12′N	20°53′E
Urubamba, r., Peru (ōō-rōō-bäm'bä)	142	11°48′S	72°34′W
Uruguaiana, Braz.	144	29°45′S	57°00′W
Uruguay, nation, S.A. (ōō-rōō-gwä') (ū'rōō-gwä)	144	32°45′S	56°00′W
Uruguay, r., S.A. (ōō-rōō-gwī')	144	27°05′S	55°15′W
Ürümqi, China (ù-rŭm-chyē)	204	43°49′N	87°43′E
Urup, i., Russia (ōō'rŭp)	205	46°00′N	150°00′E
Uryupinsk, Russia (òr'yò-pēn-sk')	181	50°50′N	42°00′E
Urzhar, Kaz.	183	47°28′N	82°00′E
Urziceni, Rom. (ò-zē-chĕn'')	175	44°45′N	26°42′E
Usa, Japan	210	33°31′N	131°22′E
Usa, r., Russia (ò'sá)	180	66°00′N	58°20′E
Uşak, Tur. (ōō'shäk)	163	38°45′N	29°15′E
Usakos, Nmb. (ōō-sä'kôs)	232	22°00′S	15°40′E
Usambara Mountains, mts., Tan.	237	4°40′S	38°25′E
Usangu Flats, sw., Tan.	237	8°10′S	34°00′E
Ushaki, Russia (ōō'shá-kĭ)	186c	59°28′N	31°00′E
Ushakovskoye, Russia (ò-shá-kôv'skô-yĕ)	186a	56°18′N	62°23′E
Ushashi, Tan.	237	2°00′S	33°57′E
Ushiku, Japan (ōō'shē-kōō)	211a	35°24′N	140°09′E
Ushimado, Japan (ōō'shē-mä'dô)	211	34°37′N	134°09′E
Ushuaia, Arg. (ōō-shōō-ī'ä)	144	54°46′S	68°24′W
Usman', Russia (ōōs-mán')	181	52°03′N	39°40′E
Usol'ye, Russia (ò-sô'lyĕ)	186a	59°24′N	56°40′E
Usol'ye-Sibirskoye, Russia (ò-sô'lyĕsĭ' bĕr'skô-yĕ)	184	52°44′N	103°46′E
Uspallata Pass, p., S.A. (ōōs-pä-lyä'tä)	144	32°47′S	70°08′W
Uspanapa, r., Mex. (ōōs-pä-nä'pä)	131	17°43′N	94°14′W
Ussel, Fr. (üs'ĕl)	170	45°33′N	2°17′E
Ussuri, r., Asia (ōō-sōō'rê)	185	47°30′N	134°00′E
Ussuriysk, Russia	179	43°48′N	132°09′E
Ust'-Bol'sheretsk, Russia	179	52°41′N	157°00′E
Ústica, Isola di, i., Italy	174	38°43′N	12°11′E
Ústí nad Labem, Czech Rep.	168	50°40′N	14°02′E
Ust'-Izhora, Russia (òst-ēz'hô-rá)	186c	59°49′N	30°35′E
Ustka, Pol. (ōōst'ká)	168	54°34′N	16°52′E
Ust'-Kamchatsk, Russia	179	56°13′N	162°18′E
Ust'-Katav, Russia (òst ká'táf)	186a	54°55′N	58°12′E
Ust'-Kishert', Russia (òst kē'shĕrt)	186a	57°21′N	57°13′E
Ust'-Kulom, Russia (kó'lŭm)	178	61°38′N	54°00′E
Ust'-Maya, Russia (má'yá)	179	60°33′N	134°43′E
Ust' Olenëk, Russia	179	72°52′N	120°15′E
Ust-Ordynskiy, Russia (òst-ôr-dyĕnsk'ĭ)	184	52°47′N	104°39′E
Ust' Penzhino, Russia	185	63°00′N	165°10′E
Ust' Port, Russia (òst'pôrt')	178	69°20′N	83°41′E
Ust'-Tsil'ma, Russia (tsĭl'má)	178	65°25′N	52°10′E
Ust'-Tyrma, Russia (tur'má)	179	50°27′N	131°17′E
Ust' Uls, Russia	186a	60°35′N	58°32′E
Ust-Urt, Plateau, plat., Asia	178	44°03′N	54°58′E
Ustyuzhna, Russia (yōōzh'ná)	180	58°49′N	36°19′E
Usu, China (ù-sōō)	204	44°28′N	84°07′E
Usuki, Japan (ōō'sōō-kē')	211	33°06′N	131°47′E
Usulutan, El Sal. (ōō-sōō-lä-tän')	132	13°22′N	88°25′W
Usumacinta, r., N.A. (ōō-sōō-mä-sēn'tô)	131	18°24′N	92°30′W
Us'va, Russia (ōōs'vá)	186a	58°41′N	57°38′E
Utah, state, U.S. (ū'tô)	104	39°25′N	112°40′W
Utah Lake, l., Ut., U.S.	119	40°10′N	111°55′W
Utan, India	203b	19°17′N	72°43′E
Ute Mountain Indian Reservation, I.R., N.M., U.S.	119	36°57′N	108°34′W
Utena, Lith. (ōō'tä-nä)	167	55°32′N	25°40′E
Utete, Tan. (ōō-tā'tä)	233	8°05′S	38°47′E
Utica, In., U.S. (ū'tĭ-ká)	111h	38°20′N	85°39′W
Utica, N.Y., U.S.	105	43°05′N	75°10′W
Utiel, Spain (ōō-tyäl')	172	39°34′N	1°13′W
Utika, Mi., U.S. (ū'tĭ-ká)	111b	42°37′N	83°02′W
Utik Lake, l., Can.	97	55°16′N	96°00′W
Utikuma Lake, l., Can.	95	55°50′N	115°25′W
Utila, i., Hond. (ōō-tē'lä)	132	16°07′N	87°05′W
Uto, Japan (ōō'tô')	210	32°43′N	130°39′E
Utrecht, Neth. (ū'trĕkt) (ü'trĕkt)	161	52°05′N	5°06′E
Utrera, Spain (ōō-trā'rä)	162	37°12′N	5°48′W
Utsunomiya, Japan (ōōt'sô-nô-mē-yá')	205	36°35′N	139°52′E
Uttaradit, Thai.	212	17°47′N	100°10′E
Uttaranchal, state, India	199	29°30′N	78°30′E
Uttarpara-Kotrung, India	202a	22°40′N	88°21′E
Uttar Pradesh, state, India (òt-tär-prä-dĕsh')	199	27°00′N	80°00′E
Uttoxeter, Eng., U.K. (ŭt-tôk'sĕ-tēr)	158a	52°54′N	1°52′W
Utuado, P.R. (ōō-tōō-ä'dhô)	129b	18°16′N	66°40′W
Uusikaupunki, Fin.	167	60°48′N	21°24′E
Uvalde, Tx., U.S. (ū-väl'dĕ)	122	29°14′N	99°47′W
Uvel'skiy, Russia (ò-vyĕl'skĭ)	186a	54°27′N	61°22′E
Uvinza, Tan.	237	5°06′S	30°22′E
Uvira, D.R.C. (ōō-vē'rä)	232	3°28′S	29°03′E
Uvod', r., Russia (ò-vôd')	176	56°40′N	41°10′E
Uvongo Beach, S. Afr.	233c	30°49′S	30°23′E
Uvs Nuur, l., Asia	204	50°29′N	93°32′E
Uwajima, Japan	210	33°12′N	132°35′E
Uxbridge, Ma., U.S. (ùks'brĭj)	101a	42°05′N	71°38′W
Uxmal, hist., Mex. (ōō'x-mä'l)	132a	20°22′N	89°44′W
Uy, r., Russia (ōō'ê)	186a	54°05′N	62°11′E
Uyskoye, Russia (ùy'skô-yĕ)	186a	54°22′N	60°01′E
Uyuni, Bol. (ōō-yōō'nê)	142	20°28′S	66°45′W
Uyuni, Salar de, pl., Bol. (sä-lär-dĕ)	142	20°58′S	67°09′W
Uzbekistan, nation, Asia	178	42°42′N	60°00′E
Uzh, r., Ukr. (ōzh)	181	51°07′N	29°05′E
Uzhhorod, Ukr.	169	48°38′N	22°18′E
Užice, Serb. (ōō'zhĕ-tsĕ)	175	43°51′N	19°53′E
Uzunköprü, Tur.	175	41°17′N	26°42′E

V

PLACE (Pronunciation)	PAGE	LAT.	LONG.
Vaal, r., S. Afr. (väl)	232	28°15′S	24°30′E
Vaaldam, res., S. Afr.	238c	26°58′S	28°37′E
Vaalplaas, S. Afr.	238c	25°39′S	28°56′E
Vaalwater, S. Afr.	238c	24°17′S	28°08′E
Vaasa, Fin. (vä'sä)	154	63°06′N	21°39′E
Vác, Hung. (väts)	169	47°46′N	19°10′E
Vache, Île à, i., Haiti	135	18°05′N	73°40′W
Vadstena, Swe. (väd'stĭ'ná)	166	58°27′N	14°53′E
Vaduz, Liech. (vä'dôts)	161	47°10′N	9°32′E
Vaga, r., Russia (vä'gà)	180	61°55′N	42°30′E
Vah, r., Slvk. (väk)	161	48°07′N	17°52′E
Vaigai, r., India	203	10°20′N	78°13′E
Vakh, r., Russia (väk)	184	61°30′N	81°33′E
Valachia, hist. reg., Rom.	175	44°45′N	24°17′E
Valcartier-Village, Can. (väl-kärt-yĕ'vē-läzh')	102b	46°56′N	71°28′W
Valdai Hills, hills, Russia (väl-dī' gô'rĭ)	180	57°50′N	32°35′E
Valday, Russia (väl-dī')	180	57°58′N	33°13′E
Valdecañas, Embalse de, res., Spain	172	39°45′N	5°30′W

362 Valdemārpils – Vernon PRONOUNCING INDEX

PLACE (Pronunciation)	PAGE	LAT.	LONG.
Valdemārpils, Lat.	167	57°22'N	22°34'E
Valdemorillo, Spain (väl-då-mô-rēl'yō)	173a	40°30'N	4°04'W
Valdepeñas, Spain (väl-då-pān'yäs)	162	38°46'N	3°22'W
Valderaduey, r., Spain (väl-dĕ-rä-dwĕ'y)	172	41°39'N	5°35'W
Valdés, Península, pen., Arg. (vål-dĕ's)	144	42°15'S	63°15'W
Valdez, Ak., U.S. (văl'dĕz)	103	61°10'N	146°18'W
Valdilecha, Spain (väl-dē-lā'chä)	173a	40°17'N	3°19'W
Valdivia, Chile (väl-dē'vä)	144	39°47'S	73°13'W
Valdivia, Col. (väl-dē'vēä)	142a	7°10'N	75°26'W
Val-d'Or, Can.	91	48°03'N	77°50'W
Valdosta, Ga., U.S. (văl-dŏs'tȧ)	105	30°50'N	83°18'W
Vale, Or., U.S. (vāl)	114	43°59'N	117°14'W
Valença, Braz. (vä-lĕn'sȧ)	143	13°43'S	38°58'W
Valença, Port.	172	42°03'N	8°36'W
Valence, Fr. (vä-lĕnns)	161	44°56'N	4°54'E
València, Spain	154	39°26'N	0°23'W
Valencia, Ven. (vä-lĕn'syä)	142	10°11'N	68°00'W
València, hist. reg., Spain	173	39°08'N	0°43'W
València, Golf de, b., Spain	173	39°50'N	0°30'E
Valencia, Lago de, l., Ven.	143b	10°11'N	67°45'W
Valencia de Alcántara, Spain	172	39°34'N	7°13'W
Valenciennes, Fr. (vá-län-syĕn')	170	50°24'N	3°36'E
Valentine, Ne., U.S. (vă lăn-tē-nyē')	114	42°52'N	100°34'W
Valera, Ven. (vä-lĕ'rä)	142	9°12'N	70°45'W
Valerianovsk, Russia (vȧ-lĕ-rĭ-ä'nôvsk)	186a	58°47'N	59°34'E
Valga, Est. (väl'gȧ)	180	57°47'N	26°03'E
Valhalla, S. Afr. (vål-hăl-ȧ)	233b	25°49'S	28°09'E
Valier, Mt., U.S. (vä-lēr')	115	48°17'N	112°14'W
Valjevo, Serb. (väl'yȧ-vô)	175	44°17'N	19°57'E
Valky, Ukr.	177	49°49'N	35°40'E
Valladolid, Mex. (väl-yä-dhō-lēdh')	128	20°39'N	88°13'W
Valladolid, Spain (väl-yä-dhō-lēdh')	154	41°41'N	4°41'W
Valle, Arroyo del, Ca., U.S. (ä-rō'yō dĕl väl'yå)	118	37°36'N	121°43'W
Vallecas, Spain (väl-yā'käs)	173a	40°23'N	3°37'W
Valle de Allende, Mex. (väl'yā dā äl-yĕn'då)	122	26°55'N	105°25'W
Valle de Bravo, Mex. (brä'vô)	130	19°12'N	100°07'W
Valle de Guanape, Ven. (vä'l-yĕ-dĕ-gwä-nä'pĕ)	143b	9°54'N	65°41'W
Valle de la Pascua, Ven. (lä-pä's-kōōä)	142	9°12'N	65°08'W
Valle del Cauca, dept., Col. (vä'l-yĕ del kou'kä)	142a	4°03'N	76°13'W
Valle de Santiago, Mex. (sän-tē-ä'gō)	130	20°23'N	101°11'W
Valledupar, Col. (dōō-pär')	142	10°13'N	73°39'W
Valle Grande, Bol. (grän'dā)	142	18°27'S	64°03'W
Vallejo, Ca., U.S. (vä-yä'hō) (vä-lā'hō)	104	38°06'N	122°15'W
Vallejo, Sierra de, mts., Mex. (sē-ĕ'r-rä-dĕ-väl-yĕ'kô)	130	21°00'N	105°10'W
Vallenar, Chile (väl-yå-när')	144	28°39'S	70°52'W
Valles, Mex.	128	21°59'N	99°02'W
Valletta, Malta (väl-lĕt'ä)	162	35°50'N	14°29'E
Valle Vista, Ca., U.S. (văl'yȧ vĭs'tȧ)	117a	33°45'N	116°53'W
Valley City, N.D., U.S.	104	46°55'N	97°59'W
Valley City, Oh., U.S. (văl'ĭ)	111d	41°14'N	81°56'W
Valley Falls, Ks., U.S.	121	39°25'N	95°26'W
Valleyfield, Can. (văl'ē-fēld)	91	45°16'N	74°09'W
Valley Park, Mo., U.S. (văl'ē pärk)	117e	38°33'N	90°30'W
Valley Stream, N.Y., U.S. (văl'ĭ strēm)	110a	40°39'N	73°42'W
Valli di Comácchio, l., Italy (vå'lē-dē-kô-mä'chyō)	174	44°38'N	12°15'E
Vallière, Haiti (väl-yâr')	135	19°30'N	71°55'W
Vallimanca, r., Arg. (väl-yē-mä'n-kä)	141c	36°21'S	60°55'W
Valls, Spain (väls)	162	41°15'N	1°15'E
Valmiera, Lat. (vål'myĕ-rȧ)	180	57°34'N	25°54'E
Valognes, Fr. (vå-lôn'y')	170	49°32'N	1°30'W
Valona see Vlorë, Alb.	163	40°28'N	19°31'E
Valozhyn, Bela.	176	54°04'N	26°38'E
Valparaíso, Chile (väl'pä-rä-ē'sô)	144	33°02'S	71°32'W
Valparaíso, Mex.	130	22°49'N	103°33'W
Valparaiso, In., U.S. (văl-pȧ-rā'zō)	108	41°25'N	87°05'W
Valpariso, prov., Chile	141b	32°58'S	71°23'W
Valréas, Fr. (vál-rȧ-ä')	170	44°25'N	4°56'E
Vals, r., S. Afr.	238c	27°32'S	26°51'E
Vals, Tanjung, c., Indon.	213	8°30'S	137°15'E
Valsbaai, b., S. Afr.	232a	34°14'S	18°35'E
Valuyevo, Russia (vá-lōō'yĕ-vô)	186b	55°34'N	37°21'E
Valuyki, Russia (vá-lò-ē'kē)	181	50°14'N	38°04'E
Valverde del Camino, Spain (väl-vĕr-dĕ-dĕl-kä-mē'nō)	172	37°34'N	6°44'W
Vammala, Fin.	167	61°19'N	22°51'E
Van, Tur. (vån)	198	38°04'N	43°10'E
Van Buren, Ar., U.S. (văn bū'rĕn)	121	35°26'N	94°20'W
Van Buren, Me., U.S.	100	47°09'N	67°58'W
Vanceburg, Ky., U.S. (văns'bûrg)	108	38°35'N	83°20'W
Vancouver, Can. (văn-kōō'vẽr)	90	49°16'N	123°06'W
Vancouver, Wa., U.S.	104	45°37'N	122°40'W
Vancouver Island, i., Can.	92	49°50'N	125°05'W
Vancouver Island Ranges, mts., Can.	94	49°25'N	125°25'W
Vandalia, Il., U.S. (văn-dā'lĭ-ȧ)	108	39°00'N	89°00'W
Vandalia, Mo., U.S.	121	39°19'N	91°30'W
Vanderbijlpark, S. Afr.	238c	26°43'S	27°50'E
Vanderhoof, Can.	90	54°01'N	124°01'W
Van Diemen, Cape, c., Austl. (văndē'mĕn)	220	11°05'S	130°15'E
Van Diemen Gulf, b., Austl.	220	11°50'S	131°30'E
Vanegas, Mex. (vä-nĕ'gäs)	128	23°54'N	100°54'W
Vänern, l., Swe.	156	58°52'N	13°17'E
Vänersborg, Swe. (vĕ'nĕrs-bôr')	160	58°24'N	12°15'E
Vanga, Kenya (väŋ'gä)	233	4°38'S	39°10'E
Vangani, India	203b	19°07'N	73°15'E
Van Gölü, l., Tur.	180	38°33'N	42°46'E
Van Horn, Tx., U.S.	122	31°03'N	104°50'W
Vanier, Can.	102c	45°27'N	75°39'W
Van Lear, Ky., U.S. (văn lēr')	108	37°45'N	82°50'W
Vannes, Fr. (vån)	161	47°42'N	2°46'W
Van Nuys, Ca., U.S. (văn nīz')	117a	34°11'N	118°27'W
Van Rees, Pegunungan, mts., Indon.	213	2°30'S	138°45'E
Vantaan, r., Fin.	167	60°25'N	24°43'E
Vanua Levu, i., Fiji	214g	16°33'S	179°15'E
Vanuatu, nation, Oc.	219	16°02'S	169°15'E
Van Wert, Oh., U.S. (văn wûrt')	108	40°50'N	84°35'W
Vara, Swe. (vä'rä)	166	58°17'N	12°55'E
Varaklāni, Lat.	167	56°38'N	26°46'E
Varallo, Italy (vä-räl'lō)	174	45°44'N	8°14'E
Vārānasi (Benares), India	199	25°25'N	83°00'E
Varangerfjorden, b., Nor.	157	70°05'N	30°20'E
Varano, Lago di, l., Italy (lä'gō-dē-vä-rä'nō)	174	41°52'N	15°55'E
Varaždin, Cro. (vä'räzh'dĭn)	163	46°17'N	16°20'E
Varazze, Italy (vä-rät'sä)	174	44°23'N	8°34'E
Varberg, Swe. (vär'bĕrg)	166	57°06'N	12°16'E
Vardar, r., Serb. (vär'där)	175	41°40'N	21°50'E
Varėna, Lith. (vä-rä'nȧ)	167	54°16'N	24°35'E
Varennes, Can. (vȧ-rĕn')	102a	45°41'N	73°27'W
Vareš, Bos. (vä'rĕsh)	175	44°10'N	18°20'E
Varese, Italy (vä-rā'så)	174	45°45'N	8°49'E
Varginha, Braz. (vär-zhē'n-yä)	143	21°33'S	45°25'W
Varkaus, Fin. (vär'kous)	167	62°19'N	27°51'E
Varlamovo, Russia (vár-lá'mô-vô)	186a	54°37'N	60°41'E
Varna, Blg. (vär'nȧ)	154	43°14'N	27°58'E
Varna, Russia	186a	53°22'N	60°59'E
Värnamo, Swe. (vĕr'ná-mô)	166	57°11'N	13°45'E
Varnsdorf, Czech Rep. (värns'dôrf)	168	50°54'N	14°36'E
Varnville, S.C., U.S. (värn'vĭl)	125	32°49'N	81°05'W
Vasa, India	203b	19°20'N	72°47'E
Vascongadas see Basque Provinces, hist. reg., Spain	172	43°00'N	2°40'W
Vashka, r., Russia	180	64°00'N	48°00'E
Vashon, Wa., U.S. (văsh'ŭn)	116a	47°27'N	122°28'W
Vashon Heights, Wa., U.S. (hītz)	116a	47°30'N	122°28'W
Vashon Island, i., Wa., U.S.	116a	47°27'N	122°27'W
Vaslui, Rom. (vås-lōō'ē)	169	46°39'N	27°49'E
Vassar, Mi., U.S. (văs'ẽr)	108	43°25'N	83°35'W
Vassouras, Braz. (väs-sō'räzh)	141a	22°25'S	43°40'W
Västerås, Swe. (vĕs'tĕr-ôs)	160	59°39'N	16°30'E
Västerdalälven, r., Swe.	160	61°06'N	13°10'E
Västervik, Swe. (vĕs'tĕr-vēk)	160	57°45'N	16°35'E
Vasto, Italy (väs'tô)	162	42°06'N	12°42'E
Vasyl'kiv, Ukr.	181	50°10'N	30°22'E
Vasyugan, r., Russia (vås-yōō-gån')	184	58°52'N	77°30'E
Vatican City, nation, Eur.	174	41°54'N	12°22'E
Vaticano, Cape, c., Italy (vä-tē-kä'nô)	174	38°38'N	15°52'E
Vatnajökull, ice, Ice. (våt'ná-yû-kòl)	160	64°34'N	16°41'W
Vatomandry, Madag.	233	18°53'S	48°13'E
Vatra Dornei, Rom. (våt'rȧ dôr'nā')	169	47°22'N	25°20'E
Vättern, l., Swe.	156	58°15'N	14°24'E
Vattholma, Swe.	166	60°01'N	17°40'E
Vaudreuil, Can. (vô-drû'y')	102a	45°24'N	74°02'W
Vaugh, Wa., U.S. (vôn)	116a	47°21'N	122°47'W
Vaughan, Can.	102d	43°47'N	79°36'W
Vaughn, N.M., U.S.	120	34°37'N	105°13'W
Vaupés, r., S.A. (vá'ōō-pĕ's)	142	1°18'N	71°14'W
Vawkavysk, Bela. (vôl-kô-vēsk')	169	53°11'N	24°29'E
Vaxholm, Swe. (väks'hôlm)	166	59°26'N	18°19'E
Växjo, Swe. (vĕks'shû)	160	56°53'N	14°46'E
Vaygach, i., Russia (vī-gåch')	178	70°00'N	59°00'E
Veadeiros, Chapadas dos, hills, Braz. (shä-pä'däs-dôs-vĕ-å-dā'rōs)	143	14°00'S	47°00'W
Vedea, r., Rom. (vå'dyå)	175	44°25'N	24°45'E
Vedia, Arg. (vĕ'dyä)	141c	34°29'S	61°30'W
Veedersburg, In., U.S. (vē'dẽrz-bûrg)	108	40°05'N	87°15'W
Vega, i., Nor.	160	65°38'N	10°51'E
Vega de Alatorre, Mex. (vā'gä dā ä-lä-tōr'rå)	131	20°02'N	96°39'W
Vega Real, reg., Dom. Rep. (vĕ'gä-rĕ-ä'l)	135	19°30'N	71°05'W
Vegreville, Can.	90	53°30'N	112°03'W
Vehār Lake, l., India	203b	19°11'N	72°52'E
Veinticinco de Mayo, Arg.	141c	35°26'S	60°09'W
Vejer de la Frontera, Spain	172	36°15'N	5°58'W
Vejle, Den. (vī'lĕ)	160	55°41'N	9°29'E
Velbert, Ger. (fĕl'bĕrt)	171c	51°20'N	7°03'E
Velebit, mts., Serb. (vā'lĕ-bēt)	163	44°25'N	15°23'E
Velen, Ger. (fĕ'lĕn)	171c	51°54'N	7°00'E
Vélez-Málaga, Spain (vā'lāth-mä'lä-gä)	172	36°48'N	4°05'W
Vélez-Rubio, Spain (rōō'bē-ô)	172	37°38'N	2°05'W
Velika Kapela, mts., Serb. (vĕ'lē-kä kä-pĕ'lä)	163	45°03'N	15°20'E
Velika Morava, r., Serb. (mô'rä-vä)	163	44°00'N	21°30'E
Velikaya, r., Russia (vå-lē'kȧ-yȧ)	176	57°25'N	28°07'E
Velikiye Luki, Russia (vyē-lē'-kyē lōō'ke)	178	56°19'N	30°32'E
Velikiy Ustyug, Russia (vå-lē'kĭ ōōs-tyòg')	178	60°45'N	46°38'E
Veliko Tŭrnovo, Blg.	163	43°06'N	25°38'E
Velikoye, Russia (vå-lē'kô-yĕ)	176	57°21'N	39°45'E
Velikoye, l., Russia	176	57°00'N	36°53'E
Veli Lošinj, Cro. (lō'shēn')	174	44°30'N	14°29'E
Velizh, Russia (vå'lēzh)	180	55°37'N	31°11'E
Vella Lavella, i., Sol. Is.	221	8°00'S	156°42'E
Velletri, Italy (vĕl-lā'trē)	174	41°42'N	12°48'E
Vellore, India (vĕl-lōr')	199	12°57'N	79°09'E
Vels, Russia (vĕls)	186a	60°35'N	58°47'E
Vel'sk, Russia (vĕlsk)	178	61°00'N	42°18'E
Velten, Ger. (fel'tĕn)	159b	52°41'N	13°11'E
Velya, r., Russia (vĕl'yȧ)	186b	56°23'N	37°54'E
Velyka Lepetykha, Ukr.	177	47°11'N	33°58'E
Velykyi Bychkiv, Ukr.	169	47°59'N	24°01'E
Venadillo, Col. (vĕ-nä-dē'l-yō)	142a	4°43'N	74°55'W
Venado, Mex. (vå-mä'dō)	130	22°54'N	101°07'W
Venado Tuerto, Arg. (vĕ-nä'dô-tōōĕ'r-tô)	144	33°28'S	61°47'W
Vendôme, Fr. (väɴ-dōm')	170	47°46'N	1°05'E
Veneto, hist. reg., Italy (vĕ-nĕ'tô)	174	45°58'N	11°24'E
Venëv, Russia (vĕn-ĕf')	180	54°19'N	38°14'E
Venezia see Venice, Italy	154	45°25'N	12°18'E
Venezuela, nation, S.A. (vĕn-ĕ-zwē'lȧ)	142	8°00'N	65°00'W
Venezuela, Golfo de, b., S.A. (gôl-fô-dĕ)	142	11°34'N	71°02'W
Veniaminof, Mount, mtn., Ak., U.S.	103	56°12'N	159°20'W
Venice, Italy	154	45°25'N	12°18'E
Venice, Ca., U.S. (vĕn'ĭs)	117a	33°59'N	118°28'W
Venice, Il., U.S.	117e	38°40'N	90°10'W
Venice, Gulf of, b., Italy	162	45°23'N	13°00'E
Venlo, Neth.	171c	51°22'N	6°11'E
Venta, r., Eur. (vĕn'tȧ)	167	57°05'N	21°45'E
Ventana, Sierra de la, mts., Arg. (sē-ĕ'-rá-dĕ-lä-vĕn-tä'nä)	144	38°00'S	63°00'W
Ventersburg, S. Afr. (vĕn-tẽrs'bûrg)	238c	28°06'S	27°10'E
Ventersdorp, S. Afr. (vĕn-tẽrs'dôrp)	238c	26°20'S	26°48'E
Ventimiglia, Italy (vĕn-tē-mēl'yä)	174	43°46'N	7°37'E
Ventnor, N.J., U.S. (vĕnt'nẽr)	109	39°20'N	74°25'W
Ventspils, Lat. (vĕnt'spĕls)	180	57°24'N	21°41'E
Ventuari, r., Ven. (vĕn-tōōä'rē)	142	4°47'N	65°56'W
Ventura, Ca., U.S. (vĕn-tōō'rȧ)	118	34°18'N	119°18'W
Venukovsky, Russia (vĕ-nōō'kôv-skĭ)	186b	55°10'N	37°26'E
Venustiano Carranza, Mex. (vĕ-nōōs-tyä'nō-kär-rä'n-zä)	130	19°44'N	103°48'W
Venustiano Carranzo, Mex. (kär-rä'n-zô)	131	16°21'N	92°36'W
Vera, Arg. (vĕ-rä)	144	29°22'S	60°09'W
Vera, Spain (vā'rä)	172	37°18'N	1°53'W
Veracruz, Mex.	128	19°13'N	96°07'W
Vera Cruz, state, Mex. (vā-rä-krōōz')	128	20°30'N	97°15'W
Verāval, India (vĕr'vŭ-väl)	199	20°59'N	70°49'E
Vercelli, Italy (vĕr-chĕl'lē)	174	45°18'N	8°27'E
Verchères, Can. (vĕr-shâr')	102a	45°46'N	73°21'W
Verde, i., Phil. (vĕr'då)	213a	13°34'N	121°11'E
Verde, r., Mex.	130	21°48'N	99°50'W
Verde, r., Mex.	130	20°50'N	103°00'W
Verde, r., Mex.	131	16°05'N	97°44'W
Verde, r., Az., U.S. (vûrd)	119	34°04'N	111°40'W
Verde, Cap, c., Bah.	135	22°50'N	75°00'W
Verde, Cay, i., Bah.	135	22°00'N	75°05'W
Verde Island Passage, strt., Phil. (vĕr'dē)	213a	13°36'N	120°39'E
Verdemont, Ca., U.S. (vûr'dē-mŏnt)	117a	34°12'N	117°22'W
Verden, Ger. (fĕr'dĕn)	168	52°55'N	9°15'E
Verdigris, r., Ok., U.S. (vûr'dē-grēs)	121	36°50'N	95°29'W
Verdun, Can. (vĕr'dŭn')	99	45°27'N	73°34'W
Verdun, Fr. (vâr-dûn')	161	49°09'N	5°21'E
Verdun, Fr.	171	43°48'N	1°10'E
Vereeniging, S. Afr. (vĕ-rā'nĭ-gĭng)	238c	26°40'S	27°56'E
Verena, S. Afr. (vĕr-ĕn ȧ)	238c	25°30'S	29°02'E
Vereya, Russia (vĕ-rĕ'yȧ)	176	55°21'N	36°08'E
Verín, Spain (vå-rēn')	172	41°56'N	7°26'W
Verkhne-Kamchatsk, Russia (vyĕrk'nyĕ kám-chatsk')	179	54°42'N	158°41'E
Verkhne Neyvinskiy, Russia (nā-vĭn'skĭ)	186a	57°17'N	60°10'E
Verkhne Ural'sk, Russia (ò-ralsk')	178	53°53'N	59°13'E
Verkhniy Avzyan, Russia (vyĕrk'nyĕ áv-zyán')	186a	53°32'N	57°30'E
Verkhniye Kigi, Russia (vyĕrk'nĭ-yĕ kĭ'gĭ)	186a	55°23'N	58°37'E
Verkhniy Ufaley, Russia (ò-fá'lā)	186a	56°04'N	60°15'E
Verkhnyaya Pyshma, Russia (vyĕrk'nyä-yä pōōsh'má)	186a	56°57'N	60°37'E
Verkhnyaya Salda, Russia (säl'dä)	186a	58°03'N	60°33'E
Verkhnyaya Tunguska (Angara), r., Russia (tòn-gōs'kä)	184	58°13'N	97°00'E
Verkhnyaya Tura, Russia (tò'rä)	186a	58°22'N	59°51'E
Verkhnyaya Yayva, Russia (yäy'vá)	186a	59°28'N	57°38'E
Verkhotur'ye, Russia (vyĕr-kô-tōōr'yĕ)	186a	58°52'N	60°47'E
Verkhoyansk, Russia (vyĕr-kô-yänsk')	179	67°43'N	133°33'E
Verkhoyanskiy Khrebet, mts., Russia (vyĕr-kô-yänskĭ)	179	67°45'N	128°00'E
Vermilion, Can. (vẽr-mĭl'yŭn)	90	53°22'N	110°51'W
Vermilion, l., Mn., U.S.	113	47°49'N	92°35'W
Vermilion, r., Can.	99	47°30'N	73°15'W
Vermilion, r., Can.	96	53°30'N	111°00'W
Vermilion, r., Il., U.S.	108	41°05'N	89°00'W
Vermilion, r., Mn., U.S.	113	48°09'N	92°31'W
Vermilion Hills, hills, Can.	96	50°43'N	106°50'W
Vermilion Range, mts., Mn., U.S.	113	47°55'N	91°59'W
Vermillion, S.D., U.S.	112	42°46'N	96°56'W
Vermillion, r., S.D., U.S.	112	43°54'N	97°14'W
Vermillion Bay, b., La., U.S.	123	29°47'N	92°00'W
Vermont, state, U.S. (vẽr-mŏnt')	105	43°50'N	72°50'W
Vernal, Ut., U.S. (vûr'nȧl)	115	40°29'N	109°40'W
Verneuk Pan, pl., S. Afr. (vĕr-nŭk')	232	30°10'S	21°46'E
Vernon, Can. (vĕr-nōn')	90	50°18'N	119°15'W
Vernon, Can.	102c	45°10'N	75°27'W
Vernon, Ca., U.S. (vûr'nŭn)	117a	34°01'N	118°12'W

ăt; finȧl; rāte; senåte; ärm; ȧsk; sofȧ; fâre; ch-choose; dh-as th in other; bē; ēvent; bĕt; recĕnt; cratẽr; g-gō; gh-guttural g; bĭt; ĭ-short neutral; rīde; ᴋ-guttural k as ch in German ich;

PLACE (Pronunciation)	PAGE	LAT.	LONG.
Vernon, In., U.S. (vûr'nŭn)	108	39°00′N	85°40′W
Vernon, N.J., U.S.	110a	39°00′N	85°40′W
Vernon, Tx., U.S.	120	34°09′N	99°16′W
Vernonia, Or., U.S. (vûr-nō'nya)	116c	45°52′N	123°12′W
Vero Beach, Fl., U.S. (vē'rō)	125a	27°36′N	80°25′W
Véroia, Grc.	175	40°30′N	22°13′E
Verona, Italy (vā-rō'nä)	162	45°28′N	11°02′E
Versailles, Fr. (věr-sī'y')	161	48°48′N	2°07′E
Versailles, Ky., U.S. (vēr-sālz')	108	38°05′N	84°45′W
Versailles, Mo., U.S.	121	38°27′N	92°52′W
Vert, Cap, c., Sen.	230	14°43′N	17°30′W
Verulam, S. Afr. (vě-ro͞o-lăm)	233c	29°39′S	31°08′E
Verviers, Bel. (věr-vyā')	165	50°35′N	5°57′E
Vesele, Ukr.	177	46°59′N	34°56′E
Vesijärvi, l., Fin.	167	61°09′N	25°10′E
Vesoul, Fr. (vē-so͞ol')	171	47°38′N	6°11′E
Vestavia Hills, Al., U.S.	110h	33°26′N	86°46′W
Vesterålen, is., Nor. (věs'tēr ô'lĕn)	160	68°54′N	14°03′E
Vestfjord, b., Nor.	156	67°33′N	12°59′E
Vestmannaeyjar, Ice. (věst'män-ä-ā'yär)	160	63°12′N	20°17′W
Vesuvio, vol., Italy (vě-so͞o'vyä)	156	40°35′N	14°26′E
Ves'yegonsk, Russia (vě-syě-gônsk')	176	58°42′N	37°09′E
Veszprem, Hung. (věs'prăm)	169	47°05′N	17°53′E
Vészto, Hung. (věs'tû)	169	46°55′N	21°18′E
Vet, r., S. Afr. (vět)	238c	28°25′S	26°37′E
Vetlanda, Swe. (vět-län'dä)	166	57°26′N	15°05′E
Vetluga, Russia (vyět-lo͞o'gȧ)	180	57°50′N	45°42′E
Vetluga, r., Russia	180	56°50′N	45°50′E
Vetovo, Blg. (vā'tô-vô)	175	43°42′N	26°18′E
Vetren, Blg. (vět'rěn')	175	42°16′N	24°04′E
Vevay, In., U.S. (vē'vā)	108	38°45′N	85°05′W
Veynes, Fr. (vān'')	171	44°31′N	5°47′E
Vézère, r., Fr. (vā-zer')	170	45°01′N	1°00′E
Viacha, Bol. (vēȧ'chȧ)	142	16°43′S	68°16′W
Viadana, Italy (vē-ä-dä'nä)	174	44°55′N	10°30′E
Vian, Ok., U.S. (vī'ăn)	121	35°30′N	95°00′W
Viana, Braz. (vē-ä'nä)	143	3°09′S	44°44′W
Viana do Alentejo, Port. (vē-ä'nȧ dò ä-lěn-tā'hò)	172	38°20′N	8°02′W
Viana do Bolo, Spain	172	42°10′N	7°07′W
Viana do Castelo, Port. (dò käs-tā'lò)	162	41°41′N	8°45′W
Viangchan, Laos	212	18°07′N	102°33′E
Viar, r., Spain (vē-ä'rä)	172	38°15′N	6°08′W
Viareggio, Italy (vē-ä-rěd'jô)	174	43°52′N	10°14′E
Viborg, Den. (vē'bôr)	166	56°27′N	9°22′E
Vibo Valentia, Italy (vē'bô-vä-lě'n-tyä)	174	38°47′N	16°06′E
Vic, Spain	173	41°55′N	2°14′E
Vicálvaro, Spain	173a	40°25′N	3°37′W
Vicente López, Arg. (vē-sě'n-tě-lô'pěz)	144a	34°31′S	58°29′W
Vicenza, Italy (vē-chěnt'sä)	162	45°33′N	11°33′E
Vichuga, Russia (vē-cho͞o'gȧ)	180	57°13′N	41°58′E
Vichy, Fr. (vē-shē')	161	46°06′N	3°28′E
Vickersund, Nor.	166	60°00′N	9°59′E
Vicksburg, Mi., U.S. (vĭks'bûrg)	108	42°10′N	85°30′W
Vicksburg, Ms., U.S.	105	32°20′N	90°50′W
Viçosa, Braz. (vē-sô'sä)	141a	20°46′S	42°51′W
Victoria, Arg. (vēk-tô'rēä)	144	32°36′S	60°09′W
Victoria, Can. (vĭk-tō'rĭ-ȧ)	90	48°26′N	123°23′W
Victoria, Chile (vēk-tô-rēä)	144	38°15′S	72°16′W
Victoria, Col. (vēk-tô'rēä)	142a	5°19′N	74°54′W
Victoria, Phil. (vēk-tô-ryä)	213a	15°34′N	120°41′E
Victoria, Tx., U.S. (vĭk-tō'rĭ-ȧ)	123	28°48′N	97°00′W
Victoria, Va., U.S.	125	36°57′N	78°13′W
Victoria, state, Austl.	219	36°46′S	143°15′E
Victoria, l., Afr.	232	0°50′S	32°50′E
Victoria, r., Austl.	220	17°25′S	130°50′E
Victoria, Mount, mtn., Mya.	199	21°26′N	93°59′E
Victoria, Mount, mtn., Pap. N. Gui.	213	9°35′S	147°45′E
Victoria de las Tunas, Cuba (vēk-tō'rē-ä dā läs to͞o'näs)	134	20°55′N	77°05′W
Victoria Falls, wtfl., Afr.	232	17°55′S	25°51′E
Victoria Island, i., Can.	89	70°13′N	107°45′W
Victoria Lake, l., Can.	101	48°20′N	57°40′W
Victoria Land, reg., Ant.	224	75°00′S	160°00′E
Victoria Nile, r., Ug.	237	2°20′N	31°35′E
Victoria Peak, mtn., Belize (vēk-tōrĭ'ȧ)	132a	16°47′N	88°40′W
Victoria Peak, mtn., Can.	94	50°03′N	126°06′W
Victoria River Downs, Austl. (vĭc-tôr'ĭȧ)	218	16°30′S	131°10′E
Victoria Strait, strt., Can. (vĭk-tō'rĭ-ȧ)	92	69°10′N	100°58′W
Victoriaville, Can. (vĭk-tō'rĭ-ȧ-vĭl)	91	46°04′N	71°59′W
Victoria West, S. Afr. (wěst)	232	31°25′S	23°10′E
Vidalia, Ga., U.S. (vĭ-dā'lĭ-ȧ)	125	32°10′N	82°26′W
Vidalia, La., U.S.	123	31°33′N	91°28′W
Vidin, Blg. (vĭ'dēn)	163	44°00′N	22°53′E
Vidnoye, Russia	186b	55°33′N	37°41′E
Vidzy, Bela. (vē'dzĭ)	176	55°23′N	26°46′E
Viedma, Arg. (vyād'mä)	144	40°55′S	63°03′W
Viedma, l., Arg.	144	49°40′S	72°35′W
Viejo, r., Nic. (vyā'hō)	132	12°45′N	86°19′W
Vienna (Wien), Aus.	154	48°13′N	16°22′E
Vienna, Ga., U.S. (vē-ěn'ȧ)	124	32°03′N	83°50′W
Vienna, Il., U.S.	121	37°24′N	88°50′W
Vienna, Va., U.S.	110e	38°54′N	77°16′W
Vienne, Fr. (vyěn')	161	45°31′N	4°54′E
Vienne, r., Fr.	170	47°06′N	0°20′E
Vientiane *see* Viangchan, Laos	212	18°07′N	102°33′E
Vieques, P.R. (vyā'kās)	129b	18°09′N	65°27′W
Vieques, i., P.R. (vyā'kās)	129b	18°05′N	65°28′W
Vierfontein, S. Afr. (vēr'fōn-tān)	238c	27°06′S	26°45′E
Viersen, Ger. (fēr'zěn)	171c	51°15′N	6°24′E
Vierwaldstätter See, l., Switz.	168	46°54′N	8°36′E
Vierzon, Fr. (vyâr-zôN')	161	47°14′N	2°04′E
Viesca, Mex. (vē-ās'kä)	122	25°21′N	102°47′W
Viesca, Laguna de, l., Mex. (lä-ò'nä-dě)	122	25°30′N	102°40′W
Vieste, Italy (vyěs'tå)	174	41°52′N	16°10′E
Vietnam, nation, Asia (vyět'näm')	212	18°00′N	107°00′E
Vigan, Phil. (vēgän)	212	17°36′N	120°22′E
Vigevano, Italy (vē-jå-vä'nô)	174	45°18′N	8°52′E
Vigny, Fr. (vēn-y'ē')	171b	49°05′N	1°54′E
Vigo, Spain (vē'gō)	154	42°18′N	8°42′W
Vihti, Fin. (vē'tĭ)	167	60°27′N	24°18′E
Vijayawāda, India	199	16°31′N	80°37′E
Viksøyri, Nor.	166	61°06′N	6°35′E
Vila Caldas Xavier, Moz.	237	15°59′S	34°12′E
Vila de Manica, Moz. (vē'lä dā mä-nē'kȧ)	232	18°48′S	32°49′E
Vila de Rei, Port. (vē'lȧ dā rā'ĭ)	172	39°42′N	8°03′W
Vila do Conde, Port. (vē'lȧ dò kôn'dě)	172	41°21′N	8°44′W
Vilafranca del Penedès, Spain	173	41°20′N	1°40′E
Vilafranca de Xira, Port. (frăn'kȧ dā shē'rȧ)	172	38°58′N	8°59′W
Vilaine, r., Fr. (vē-lån')	170	47°34′N	2°15′W
Vilalba, Spain	172	43°18′N	7°43′W
Vilanculos, Moz. (vē-län-ko͞o'lòs)	232	22°03′S	35°13′E
Vilāni, Lat. (vē'lå-nĭ)	167	56°31′N	27°00′E
Vila Nova de Foz Côa, Port. (nō'vȧ dā fôz-kō'ȧ)	172	41°08′N	7°11′W
Vila Nova de Gaia, Port. (vē'lȧ nō'vȧ dā gä'yä)	172	41°08′N	8°40′W
Vila Nova de Milfontes, Port. (nō'vȧ dā mēl-fôn'tāzh)	172	37°44′N	8°48′W
Vila Real, Port. (rā-äl')	162	41°18′N	7°48′W
Vila-real, Spain	173	39°55′N	0°07′W
Vila Real de Santo Antonio, Port.	172	37°14′N	7°25′W
Vila Viçosa, Port. (vē-sō'zȧ)	172	38°47′N	7°24′W
Vileyka, Bela. (vē-lā'ē-kȧ)	176	54°19′N	26°58′E
Vilhelmina, Swe.	160	64°37′N	16°30′E
Viljandi, Est. (vēl'yän-dē)	180	58°24′N	25°34′E
Viljoenskroon, S. Afr.	238c	27°13′S	26°58′E
Vilkaviškis, Lith. (vēl-kȧ-vēsh'kēs)	167	54°40′N	23°08′E
Vil'kitskogo, i., Russia (vyl-kēts-kōgō)	184	73°25′N	76°00′E
Villa Acuña, Mex. (vēl'yä-ko͞o'n-yä)	122	29°20′N	100°56′W
Villa Ahumada, Mex. (ä-o͞o-mä'dä)	122	30°43′N	106°30′W
Villa Alta, Mex. (äl'tä)(sän ēl-dȧ-fōn'sō)	131	17°20′N	96°08′W
Villa Angela, Arg. (vē'l-yä á'n-kě-lä)	144	27°31′S	60°42′W
Villa Ballester, Arg. (vē'l-yä-bål-yěs-těr)	144a	34°33′S	58°33′W
Villa Bella, Bol. (bě'l-yä)	142	10°25′S	65°22′W
Villablino, Spain (vēl-yä-blē'nō)	172	42°58′N	6°18′W
Villacañas, Spain (vēl-yä-kän'yäs)	172	39°39′N	3°20′W
Villacarrillo, Spain (vēl-yä-kä-rēl'yō)	172	38°09′N	3°07′W
Villach, Aus. (fē'läk)	161	46°38′N	13°50′E
Villacidro, Italy (vē-lä-chē'drō)	174	39°28′N	8°41′E
Villa Clara, prov., Cuba	134	22°40′N	80°10′W
Villa Constitución, Arg. (kōn-stē-to͞o-syōn')	141c	33°15′S	60°19′W
Villa Coronado, Mex. (kō-rō-nä'dhō)	122	26°45′N	105°10′W
Villa Cuauhtémoc, Mex. (vēl'yä-ko͞o-äò-tě'mòk)	131	22°11′N	97°50′W
Villa de Allende, Mex. (vēl'yä'dā äl-yěn'då)	122	25°18′N	100°01′W
Villa de Alvarez, Mex. (vēl'yä-dě-ä'l-vä-rěz)	130	19°17′N	103°44′W
Villa de Cura, Ven. (dě-ko͞o'rä)	143b	10°03′N	67°29′W
Villa de Guadalupe, Mex. (dě-gwä-dhä-lo͞o'på)	130	23°22′N	100°44′W
Villa de Mayo, Arg.	144a	34°31′S	58°41′W
Villa Dolores, Arg. (vēl'yä dō-lō'räs)	144	31°50′S	65°05′W
Villa Escalante, Mex. (vē'l-yä-ěs-kä-lån'tě)	130	19°24′N	101°36′W
Villa Flores, Mex. (vēl'yä-flō'räs)	131	16°13′N	93°17′W
Villafranca, Italy (vēl-lä-frän'kä)	174	45°22′N	10°53′E
Villafranca del Bierzo, Spain	172	42°37′N	6°49′W
Villafranca de los Barros, Spain	172	38°34′N	6°22′W
Villafranche-de-Rouergue, Fr. (dē-ro͞o-ěrg')	170	44°21′N	2°02′E
Villa García, Mex. (gär-sē'ä)	130	22°07′N	101°55′W
Villagarcía, Spain	172	42°38′N	8°43′W
Villagrán, Mex.	122	24°28′N	99°30′W
Villa Grove, Il., U.S. (vĭl'ȧ grōv')	108	39°55′N	88°15′W
Villaguay, Arg. (vē'l-yä-gwī)	144	31°47′S	58°53′W
Villa Hayes, Para. (vēl'yä äyås)(hāz)	144	25°07′S	57°31′W
Villahermosa, Mex. (vēl'yä-ěr-mō'sä)	128	17°59′N	92°56′W
Villa Hidalgo, Mex. (vēl'yäē-däl'gō)	130	21°39′N	102°41′W
Villaldama, Mex. (vēl-yäl-dä'mä)	128	26°30′N	100°26′W
Villa Lopez, Mex. (vēl'yä lō'pěz)	122	27°00′N	105°02′W
Villalpando, Spain (vēl-yäl-pän'dō)	172	41°54′N	5°24′W
Villa María, Arg. (vē'l-yä-mä-rē'ä)	144	32°17′S	63°08′W
Villamatín, Spain (vēl-yä-mä-tēn')	172	36°50′N	5°38′W
Villa Mercedes, Arg. (měr-sā'dås)	144	33°38′S	65°16′W
Villa Montes, Bol. (vē'l-yä-mô'n-těs)	142	21°13′S	63°26′W
Villa Morelos, Mex. (mô-rě'lomcs)	130	20°01′N	101°24′W
Villanueva, Col. (vē'l-yä-nòě'vä)	142	10°44′N	73°08′W
Villanueva, Hond. (vēl'yä-nwā'vä)	132	15°19′N	88°02′W
Villanueva, Mex. (vēl'yä-nòě'vä)	130	22°25′N	102°53′W
Villanueva de Córdoba, Spain (vēl-yä-nwě'vä-dā kôr'dō-bä)	172	38°18′N	4°38′W
Villanueva de la Serena, Spain (lä sā-rā'nä)	172	38°59′N	5°56′W
Villa Obregón, Mex. (vē'l-yä-ô-brě-gô'n)	131a	19°21′N	99°11′W
Villa Ocampo, Mex. (ô-käm'pō)	122	26°26′N	105°30′W
Villa Pedro Montoya, Mex. (vēl'yä-pě'drô-môn-tô'yȧ)	130	21°38′N	99°51′W
Villard-Bonnot, Fr. (vēl-yär'bôn-nô')	171	45°15′N	5°53′E
Villarrica, Para. (vēl-yä-rē'kä)	144	25°55′S	56°23′W
Villarrobledo, Spain (vēl-yär-rō-blā'dhō)	162	39°15′N	2°37′W
Villa Unión, Mex. (vēl'yä-o͞o-nyōn')	130	23°10′N	106°14′W
Villavicencio, Col. (vē'l-yä-vē-sě'n-syō)	142	4°09′N	73°38′W
Villaviciosa de Odón, Spain	173a	40°22′N	3°38′W
Villavieja, Col. (vē'l-yä-vē-ě'kȧ)	142a	3°13′N	75°13′W
Villazón, Bol. (vē'l-yä-zô'n)	142	22°02′S	65°42′W
Villefranche, Fr.	161	45°59′N	4°43′E
Villejuif, Fr. (vēl'zhüst')	171b	48°48′N	2°22′E
Ville-Marie, Can.	91	47°18′N	79°22′W
Villena, Spain (vē-lyā'nȧ)	162	38°37′N	0°52′W
Villeneuve, Can. (vēl'nûv')	102g	53°40′N	113°49′W
Villeneuve-Saint Georges, Fr. (săN-zhôrzh')	171b	48°43′N	2°27′E
Villeneuve-sur-Lot, Fr. (sür-lō')	170	44°25′N	0°41′E
Ville Platte, La., U.S. (vēl plåt')	123	30°41′N	92°17′W
Villers Cotterêts, Fr. (vē-ār'kô-trā')	171b	49°15′N	3°05′E
Villerupt, Fr. (vēl'rüp')	171	49°28′N	6°16′E
Ville-Saint Georges, Can. (vĭl-sěN-zhôrzh')	99	46°07′N	70°40′W
Villeta, Col. (vē'l-yě'tȧ)	142a	5°02′N	74°29′W
Villeurbanne, Fr. (vēl-ûr-bän')	161	45°43′N	4°55′E
Villiers, S. Afr. (vĭl'ĭ-ěrs)	238c	27°03′S	28°38′E
Villingen-Schwenningen, Ger.	168	48°04′N	8°33′E
Villisca, Ia., U.S. (vĭ-lĭs'kȧ)	113	40°56′N	94°56′W
Villupuram, India	203	11°59′N	79°33′E
Vilnius, Lith. (vĭl'nē-ós)	178	54°40′N	25°26′E
Vilppula, Fin. (vĭl'pŭ-lå)	167	62°01′N	24°24′E
Vil'shanka, Ukr.	177	48°14′N	30°52′E
Vil'shany, Ukr.	177	50°02′N	35°54′E
Vilvoorde, Bel.	159a	50°56′N	4°25′E
Vilyuy, r., Russia (vēl'yĭ)	179	63°00′N	121°00′E
Vilyuysk, Russia (vē-lyo͞o'ĭsk')	179	63°41′N	121°47′E
Vimmerby, Swe. (vĭm'ěr-bü)	166	57°41′N	15°51′E
Vimperk, Czech Rep. (vĭm-pěrk')	168	49°04′N	13°41′E
Viña del Mar, Chile (vē'nyä děl mär')	144	33°00′S	71°33′W
Vinalhaven, Me., U.S. (vī-năl-hā'věn)	100	44°03′N	68°49′W
Vinaròs, Spain	173	40°29′N	0°27′E
Vincennes, Fr. (văN-sěn')	171b	48°51′N	2°27′E
Vincennes, In., U.S. (vĭn-zěnz')	105	38°40′N	87°30′W
Vincent, Al., U.S. (vĭn'sěnt)	124	33°21′N	86°25′W
Vindelälven, r., Swe.	160	65°02′N	18°30′E
Vindeln, Swe. (vĭn'děln)	160	64°10′N	19°52′E
Vindhya Range, mts., India (vĭnd'yä)	199	22°30′N	75°50′E
Vineland, N.J., U.S. (vīn'lănd)	109	39°30′N	75°00′W
Vinh, Viet. (vēn'y')	212	18°38′N	105°42′E
Vinhais, Port. (vēn-yä'ēzh)	172	41°51′N	7°00′W
Vinings, Ga., U.S. (vī'nĭngz)	110c	33°52′N	84°28′W
Vinita, Ok., U.S. (vĭ-nē'tȧ)	121	36°38′N	95°09′W
Vinkovci, Cro. (vēn'kôv-tsē)	175	45°17′N	18°47′E
Vinnytsia, Ukr.	178	49°13′N	28°31′E
Vinnytsya, prov., Ukr.	177	48°45′N	28°01′E
Vinogradovo, Russia (vĭ-nô-grä'do-vô)	186b	55°25′N	38°33′E
Vinson Massif, mtn., Ant.	224	77°40′S	87°00′W
Vinton, Ia., U.S. (vĭn'tŭn)	113	42°08′N	92°01′W
Vinton, La., U.S.	123	30°12′N	93°35′W
Violet, La., U.S. (vī'ō-lět)	110d	29°54′N	89°54′W
Virac, Phil. (vē-räk')	209	13°38′N	124°20′E
Virbalis, Lith. (vĭr'bȧ-lēs)	167	54°38′N	22°55′E
Virden, Can. (vûr'děn)	90	49°51′N	101°55′W
Virden, Il., U.S.	121	39°28′N	89°46′W
Virgin, r., U.S.	119	36°51′N	113°50′W
Virginia, S. Afr.	238c	28°07′S	26°54′E
Virginia, Mn., U.S. (věr-jĭn'yȧ)	105	47°32′N	92°36′W
Virginia, state, U.S.	105	37°00′N	80°45′W
Virginia Beach, Va., U.S.	109	36°50′N	75°58′W
Virginia City, Nv., U.S.	118	39°18′N	119°40′W
Virgin Islands, is., N.A. (vûr'jĭn)	129	18°15′N	64°00′W
Viroqua, Wi., U.S. (vĭ-rō'kwȧ)	113	43°33′N	90°54′W
Virovitica, Cro. (vē-rô-vē'tē-tsȧ)	175	45°50′N	17°24′E
Virpazar, Serb. (vēr'pä-zär')	175	42°16′N	19°06′E
Virrat, Fin. (vĭr'ät)	167	62°15′N	23°45′E
Virserum, Swe. (vĭr'sě-róm)	166	57°22′N	15°35′E
Vis, Cro. (vēs)	174	43°03′N	16°11′E
Vis, i., Serb.	163	43°00′N	16°10′E
Visalia, Ca., U.S. (vĭ-sā'lĭ-ȧ)	118	36°20′N	119°18′W
Visby, Swe. (vĭs'bü)	154	57°39′N	18°19′E
Viscount Melville Sound, strt., Can.	89	74°00′N	110°00′W
Višegrad, Bos. (vē'shě-gräd)	175	43°48′N	19°17′E
Vishākhapatnam, India	199	17°48′N	83°21′E
Vishera, r., Russia (vĭ'shě-rȧ)	186a	60°40′N	58°46′E
Vishnyakovo, Russia	186b	55°44′N	38°10′E
Vishoek, S. Afr.	232a	34°13′S	18°26′E
Visim, Russia (vē'sĭm)	186a	57°38′N	59°32′E
Viskan, r., Swe.	166	57°20′N	12°25′E
Viški, Lat. (vēs'kĭ)	167	56°02′N	26°47′E
Visoko, Bos. (vē'sô-kô)	175	43°59′N	18°10′E
Vistula *see* Wisła, r., Pol.	156	52°30′N	20°00′E
Vitebsk, prov., Bela.	176	55°05′N	29°18′E
Viterbo, Italy (vē-těr'bō)	162	42°24′N	12°08′E
Viti Levu, i., Fiji	214g	18°00′S	178°00′E
Vitim, Russia (vē'tēm)	179	59°22′N	112°43′E
Vitim, r., Russia (vē'tēm)	179	54°00′N	115°00′E
Vitino, Russia (vē'tĭ-nô)	186c	59°40′N	29°51′E
Vitória, Braz. (vē-tō'rē-ä)	143	20°09′S	40°17′W
Vitoria, Spain (vē-tô-ryä)	162	42°43′N	2°43′W

364 Vitória de Conquista – Wanzhi PRONOUNCING INDEX

PLACE (Pronunciation)	PAGE	LAT.	LONG.
Vitória de Conquista, Braz. (vē-tō′rē-ä-dä-kōn-kwē′s-tä)	143	14°51′S	40°44′W
Vitry-le-François, Fr. (vē-trē′lē-fräN-swä′)	170	48°44′N	4°34′E
Vitsyebsk, Bela. (vē′tyĕpsk)	180	55°12′N	30°16′E
Vittorio, Italy (vē-tô′rē-ô)	174	45°59′N	12°17′E
Viveiro, Spain	172	43°39′N	7°37′W
Vivian, La., U.S. (vĭv′ĭ-ăn)	123	32°51′N	93°59′W
Vizianagaram, India	199	18°10′N	83°29′E
Vlaardingen, Neth. (vlär′dĭng-ĕn)	165	51°54′N	4°20′E
Vladikavkaz, Russia	181	43°05′N	44°35′E
Vladimir, Russia (vlá-dyē′mēr)	178	56°08′N	40°24′E
Vladimir, prov., Russia (vlä-dyē′mēr)	176	56°08′N	39°53′E
Vladimiro-Aleksandrovskoye, Russia	210	42°50′N	133°00′E
Vladivostok, Russia (vlá-dē-vôs-tŏk′)	179	43°06′N	131°47′E
Vlasenica, Bos. (vlä′sĕ-nēt′sá)	175	44°11′N	18°58′E
Vlasotince, Serb. (vlä′sô-tēn-tsĕ)	175	42°58′N	22°08′E
Vlieland, i., Neth. (vlē′länt)	165	53°19′N	4°55′E
Vlissingen, Neth. (vlĭs′sĭng-ĕn)	165	51°30′N	3°34′E
Vlorë, Alb.	163	40°27′N	19°30′E
Vltava, r., Czech Rep.	168	49°24′N	14°18′E
Vodl, l., Russia (vôd′'l)	180	62°20′N	37°20′E
Voerde, Ger.	171c	51°35′N	6°41′E
Voghera, Italy (vô-gā′rä)	174	44°58′N	9°02′E
Voight, r., Wa., U.S.	116a	47°03′N	122°08′W
Voinjama, Lib.	234	8°25′N	9°45′W
Voiron, Fr. (vwá-rôN′)	171	45°23′N	5°48′E
Voisin, Lac, l., Can. (vwŏ′-zĭn)	96	54°13′N	107°15′W
Volchansk, Ukr. (vôl-chänsk′)	181	50°18′N	36°56′E
Volga, r., Russia (vôl′gä)	178	47°30′N	46°20′E
Volga, Mouths of the, mth.	181	46°00′N	49°10′E
Volgograd, Russia (vŏl-gō-grā′t)	178	48°40′N	42°20′E
Volgogradskoye, res., Russia (vôl-gō-grad′skô-yĕ)	178	51°10′N	45°10′E
Volkhov, Russia (vôl′kôf)	167	59°54′N	32°21′E
Volkhov, r., Russia	180	58°45′N	31°40′E
Volodarskiy, Russia (vô-lô-där′skĭ)	186c	59°49′N	30°06′E
Volodymyr-Volyns′kyi, Ukr.	169	50°50′N	24°20′E
Vologda, Russia (vô′lôg-dá)	178	59°12′N	39°52′E
Vologda, prov., Russia	176	59°00′N	37°26′E
Volokolamsk, Russia (vô-lô-kôlámsk)	176	56°02′N	35°58′E
Volokonovka, Russia (vô-lô-kô′nôf-ká)	177	50°28′N	37°52′E
Vol′sk, Russia (vôl′sk)	181	52°02′N	47°23′E
Volta, r., Ghana	234	6°05′N	0°30′E
Volta, Lake, res., Ghana (vôl′tá)	230	7°10′N	0°30′W
Volta Blanche (White Volta), r., Afr.	234	11°30′N	0°40′W
Volta Noire *see* Black Volta, r., Afr.	230	11°30′N	4°00′W
Volta Redonda, Braz. (vôl′tä-rā-dôn′dä)	143	22°32′S	44°05′W
Volterra, Italy (vōl-tĕr′rä)	174	43°22′N	10°51′E
Voltri, Italy (vōl′trē)	174	44°25′N	8°45′E
Volturno, r., Italy (vôl-tōōr′nô)	174	41°12′N	14°20′E
Vólvi, Límni, l., Grc.	175	40°41′N	23°23′E
Volzhskoye, l., Russia (vôl′sh-skô-yĕ)	176	56°43′N	36°18′E
Von Ormy, Tx., U.S. (vŏn ôr′mē)	117d	29°18′N	98°36′W
Võõpsu, Est. (vōōp′sò)	167	58°06′N	27°30′E
Voorburg, Neth.	159a	52°04′N	4°21′E
Voortrekkerhoogte, S. Afr.	233b	25°48′S	28°10′E
Vop′, r., Russia (vôp)	176	55°20′N	32°55′E
Vopnafjördur, Ice.	160	65°43′N	14°58′W
Vordingborg, Den. (vôr′dĭng-bôr)	166	55°10′N	11°55′E
Vóreioi Sporades, is., Grc.	175	38°55′N	24°05′E
Vóreios Evvoïkós Kólpos, b., Grc.	175	38°48′N	23°02′E
Vorkuta, Russia (vôr-kōō′tá)	178	67°28′N	63°40′E
Vormsi, i., Est. (vôrm′sĭ)	167	59°06′N	23°05′E
Vorona, r., Russia (vô-rô′na)	181	51°50′N	42°00′E
Voronava, Bela.	169	54°07′N	25°16′E
Voronezh, Russia (vô-rô′nyĕzh)	178	51°39′N	39°11′E
Voronezh, prov., Russia	177	51°10′N	39°13′E
Voronezh, r., Russia	181	52°17′N	39°32′E
Vorontsovka, Russia (vô-rônt′sôv-ká)	186a	59°40′N	60°14′E
Voron′ya, r., Russia (vô-rônyá)	180	68°20′N	35°20′E
Võrts-Järv, l., Est. (vôrts yärv)	167	58°15′N	26°12′E
Võru, Est. (vô′rû)	180	57°50′N	26°58′E
Vorya, r., Russia (vôr′yá)	186b	55°55′N	38°15′E
Vosges, mts., Fr. (vōzh)	161	48°09′N	6°57′E
Voskresensk, Russia (vôs-krĕ-sĕnsk′)	186b	55°20′N	38°42′E
Voss, Nor. (vôs)	160	60°40′N	6°24′E
Vostryakovo, Russia	186b	55°23′N	37°49′E
Votkinsk, Russia (vôt-kēnsk′)	180	57°00′N	54°00′E
Votkinskoye Vodokhranilishche, res., Russia	180	57°30′N	55°00′E
Vouga, r., Port. (vō′gä)	172	40°43′N	7°51′W
Vouziers, Fr. (vōō-zyā′)	170	49°25′N	4°40′E
Voxnan, r., Swe.	166	61°30′N	15°24′E
Voyageurs National Park, rec., Mn., U.S.	113	48°30′N	92°40′W
Vozhe, l., Russia (vôzh′yĕ)	180	60°40′N	39°00′E
Voznesens′k, Ukr.	181	47°34′N	31°22′E
Vradiïvka, Ukr.	177	47°51′N	30°38′E
Vrangelya (Wrangel), i., Russia	178	71°25′N	178°30′W
Vranje, Serb. (vrän′yĕ)	175	42°33′N	21°55′E
Vratsa, Blg. (vrät′tsá)	163	43°12′N	23°31′E
Vrbas, Serb. (v′r′bäs)	175	45°34′N	19°43′E
Vrbas, r., Serb.	175	44°25′N	17°17′E
Vrchlabi, Czech Rep. (v′r′chlä-bē)	168	50°32′N	15°51′E
Vrede, S. Afr. (vrĭ′dĕ)(vrēd)	238c	27°25′S	29°11′E
Vredefort, S. Afr. (vrĭ′dĕ-fōrt)(vrēd′fōrt)	238c	27°00′S	27°21′E
Vreeswijk, Neth.	159a	52°00′N	5°06′E
Vršac, Serb. (v′r′shäts)	163	45°08′N	21°18′E
Vrutky, Slvk. (vrōōt′kē)	169	49°09′N	18°55′E
Vryburg, S. Afr. (vrī′bûrg)	232	26°55′S	24°45′E
Vryheid, S. Afr. (vrī′hīt)	232	27°43′S	30°58′E
Vsetín, Czech Rep. (fsĕt′yēn)	169	49°21′N	18°01′E
Vsevolozhskiy, Russia (vsyĕ′vôlô′zh-skēē)	186c	60°01′N	30°41′E
Vuelta Abajo, reg., Cuba (vwĕl′tä ä-bä′hō)	134	22°20′N	83°45′W
Vught, Neth.	159a	51°38′N	5°18′E
Vukovar, Cro. (vō′kô-vär)	175	45°20′N	19°00′E
Vulcan, Mi., U.S. (vŭl′kăn)	108	45°45′N	87°50′W
Vulcano, i., Italy (vōōl-kä′nô)	174	38°23′N	15°00′E
Vŭlchedrŭma, Blg.	175	43°43′N	23°29′E
Vuntut National Park, rec., Can.	92	68°27′N	139°58′W
Vyartsilya, Russia (vyár-tsē′lyá)	167	62°10′N	30°40′E
Vyatka, r., Russia (vyát′ká)	180	59°20′N	51°25′E
Vyazemskiy, Russia (vyá-zĕm′skĭ)	210	47°29′N	134°39′E
Vyaz′ma, Russia (vyáz′má)	180	55°12′N	34°17′E
Vyazniki, Russia (vyáz′nē-kē)	180	56°10′N	42°10′E
Vyborg, Russia (vwē′bôrk)	178	60°43′N	28°46′E
Vychegda, r., Russia (vē′chĕg-dá)	180	61°40′N	48°00′E
Vyerkhnyadzvinsk, Bela.	176	55°48′N	27°59′E
Vyetka, Bela. (vyĕt′ká)	176	52°36′N	31°05′E
Vylkove, Ukr.	181	45°24′N	29°36′E
Vym, r., Russia (vwēm)	180	63°15′N	51°20′E
Vyritsa, Russia (vē′rĭ-tsá)	186c	59°24′N	30°20′E
Vyshnevolotskoye, l., Russia (vŭy′sh-nĕ-vōlôt′s-kô′yĕ)	176	57°30′N	34°27′E
Vyshniy Volochëk, Russia (vēsh′nyĭ vôl-ô-chĕk′)	178	57°34′N	34°35′E
Vyškov, Czech Rep. (vēsh′kôf)	168	49°17′N	16°58′E
Vysoké Mýto, Czech Rep. (vû′sô-kā mû′tô)	168	49°58′N	16°07′E
Vysokovsk, Russia (vĭ-sô′kôfsk)	176	56°16′N	36°32′E
Vytegra, Russia (vû′tĕg-rá)	178	61°00′N	36°20′E
Vyzhnytsia, Ukr.	169	48°16′N	25°12′E

W

PLACE (Pronunciation)	PAGE	LAT.	LONG.
W, Parcs Nationaux du, rec., Niger	235	12°20′N	2°40′E
Waal, r., Neth. (väl)	165	51°46′N	5°00′E
Waalwijk, Neth.	159a	51°41′N	5°05′E
Wabamun, Grc.	163	39°23′N	22°56′E
Wabamuno, Can. (wŏ′bă-mŭn)	95	53°33′N	114°28′W
Wabasca, Can. (wŏ-băs′kă)	95	56°00′N	113°53′W
Wabash, In., U.S. (wô′băsh)	108	40°45′N	85°50′W
Wabash, r., U.S.	107	38°00′N	88°00′W
Wabasha, Mn., U.S. (wä′bá-shô)	113	44°24′N	92°04′W
Wabe Gestro, r., Eth.	231	6°25′N	41°21′E
Wabowden, Can. (wă-bō′d'n)	97	54°55′N	98°38′W
Wąbrzeźno, Pol. (vôŋ-bzĕzh′nô)	169	53°17′N	18°59′E
Wabu Hu, l., China (wä-bōō hōō)	206	32°25′N	116°35′E
W. A. C. Bennett Dam, dam, Can.	95	56°01′N	122°10′W
Waccamaw, r., S.C., U.S. (wăk′ă-mô)	125	33°47′N	78°55′W
Waccasassa Bay, b., Fl., U.S. (wă-ká-să′sá)	124	29°02′N	83°10′W
Wachow, Ger. (vä′kōv)	159b	53°32′N	12°46′E
Waco, Tx., U.S. (wā′kō)	104	31°35′N	97°06′W
Waconda Lake, res., Ks., U.S.	120	39°45′N	98°15′W
Wadayama, Japan (wä′dä′yä-mä)	211	35°19′N	134°49′E
Waddenzee, sea, Neth.	165	53°00′N	4°50′E
Waddington, Mount, mtn., Can. (wŏd′dĭng-tŭn)	92	51°23′N	125°15′W
Wadena, Can.	96	51°57′N	103°50′W
Wadena, Mn., U.S. (wŏ-dē′ná)	112	46°26′N	95°09′W
Wadesboro, N.C., U.S. (wādz′bŭr-ô)	125	34°57′N	80°05′W
Wadley, Ga., U.S. (wŭd′lē)	125	32°54′N	82°25′W
Wad Madani, Sudan (wäd mĕ-dä′nē)	231	14°27′N	33°31′E
Wadowice, Pol. (vá-dô′vēt-sĕ)	169	49°53′N	19°31′E
Wadsworth, Oh., U.S. (wŏdz′wûrth)	111d	41°01′N	81°44′W
Wager Bay, b., Can. (wā′jēr)	93	65°48′N	88°19′W
Wagga Wagga, Austl. (wôg′á wôg′á)	219	35°10′S	147°30′E
Wagoner, Ok., U.S. (wăg′ŭn-ēr)	121	35°58′N	95°22′W
Wagon Mound, N.M., U.S. (wăg′ŭn mound)	120	35°59′N	104°45′W
Wągrowiec, Pol. (vôŋ-grô′vyĕts)	169	52°47′N	17°14′E
Waha, Libya	200	28°16′N	19°54′E
Wahiawā, Hi., U.S.	106d	21°30′N	158°03′W
Wahoo, Ne., U.S. (wä-hōō′)	112	41°14′N	96°39′W
Wahpeton, N.D., U.S. (wô′pē-tŭn)	112	46°17′N	96°38′W
Waialua, Hi., U.S. (wä′ē-ä-lōō′ä)	126a	21°33′N	158°08′W
Wai′anae, Hi., U.S. (wä′ē-á-nä′ä)	126a	21°25′N	158°11′W
Waidhofen, Aus. (vīd′hôf-ĕn)	168	47°58′N	14°46′E
Waigeo, Pulau, i., Indon. (wä-ē-gā′ô)	213	0°07′N	131°00′E
Waikato, r., N.Z. (wä′ē-kä′to)	221a	38°10′S	175°35′E
Waikerie, Austl. (wā′kēr-ē)	222	34°15′S	140°00′E
Wailuku, Hi., U.S. (wä′ē-lōō′kōō)	106c	20°55′N	156°30′W
Waimānalo, Hi., U.S. (wä-ē-mä′nä-lo)	126a	21°19′N	157°43′W
Waimea, Hi., U.S. (wä-ē-mā′ä)	126a	21°56′N	159°38′W
Wainganga, r., India (wä-ēn-gŭŋ′gä)	199	20°30′N	80°15′E
Waingapu, Indon.	212	9°32′S	120°00′E
Wainwright, Can.	90	52°49′N	110°52′W
Wainwright, Ak., U.S. (wān-rīt)	103	74°40′N	159°00′W
Waipahu, Hi., U.S. (wä′ē-pä′hōō)	106d	21°20′N	158°02′W
Waiska, r., Mi., U.S. (wà-ĭz-ká)	117k	46°20′N	84°38′W
Waitsburg, Wa., U.S. (wāts′bûrg)	114	46°17′N	118°08′W
Wajima, Japan (wä′jē-mä)	211	37°23′N	136°56′E
Wajir, Kenya	237	1°45′N	40°04′E
Wakami, r., Can.	98	47°43′N	82°22′W
Wakasa-Wan, b., Japan (wä′kä-sä wän)	210	35°43′N	135°39′E
Wakatipu, l., N.Z. (wä-kä-tē′pōō)	221a	45°04′S	168°30′E
Wakayama, Japan (wä-kä′yä-mä)	205	34°14′N	135°11′E
Wake, i., Oc. (wāk)	3	19°25′N	167°00′E
Wa Keeney, Ks., U.S. (wô-kē′nē)	120	39°01′N	99°53′W
Wakefield, Can. (wāk-fēld)	102c	45°39′N	75°55′W
Wakefield, Eng., U.K.	164	53°41′N	1°25′W
Wakefield, Ma., U.S.	101a	42°31′N	71°05′W
Wakefield, Mi., U.S.	113	46°28′N	89°55′W
Wakefield, Ne., U.S.	112	42°15′N	96°52′W
Wakefield, R.I., U.S.	110b	41°26′N	71°30′W
Wakefield, co., Eng., U.K.	158a	53°12′N	1°25′W
Wake Forest, N.C., U.S. (wāk fŏr′ĕst)	125	35°58′N	78°31′W
Waki, Japan (wä′kē)	211	34°05′N	134°10′E
Wakkanai, Japan (wä′kä-nä′ē)	205	45°19′N	141°43′E
Wakkerstroom, S. Afr. (vák′ēr-strōm)(wăk′ēr-strōōm)	232	27°19′S	30°04′E
Wakonassin, r., Can.	98	46°35′N	82°10′W
Waku Kundo, Ang.	232	11°25′S	15°07′E
Wałbrzych, Pol. (väl′bzhûk)	168	50°46′N	16°16′E
Walcott, Lake, res., Id., U.S.	115	42°40′N	113°23′W
Wałcz, Pol. (välch)	168	53°11′N	16°30′E
Waldoboro, Me., U.S. (wôl′dô-bŭr-ô)	100	44°06′N	69°22′W
Waldo Lake, l., Or., U.S. (wôl′dō)	114	43°46′N	122°10′W
Waldorf, Md., U.S. (wăl′dôrf)	110e	38°37′N	76°57′W
Waldron, Mo., U.S.	117f	39°14′N	94°47′W
Waldron, i., Wa., U.S.	116d	48°42′N	123°02′W
Wales, Ak., U.S. (wālz)	103	65°35′N	168°14′W
Wales, state, U.K.	154	52°12′N	3°40′W
Walewale, Ghana	234	10°21′N	0°48′W
Walgett, Austl. (wôl′gĕt)	219	30°00′S	148°10′E
Walhalla, S.C., U.S. (wŭl-hăl′á)	124	34°45′N	83°04′W
Walikale, D.R.C.	237	1°25′S	28°03′E
Walkden, Eng., U.K.	158a	53°32′N	2°24′W
Walker, Mn., U.S. (wôk′ēr)	113	47°06′N	94°37′W
Walker, r., Nv., U.S.	118	39°07′N	119°10′W
Walker, Mount, mtn., Wa., U.S.	116a	47°47′N	122°54′W
Walker Lake, l., Can.	97	54°42′N	96°57′W
Walker Lake, l., Nv., U.S.	118	38°46′N	118°30′W
Walker River Indian Reservation, I.R., Nv., U.S.	118	39°06′N	118°20′W
Walkerville, Mt., U.S. (wôk′ēr-vĭl)	115	46°20′N	112°32′W
Wallace, Id., U.S. (wŏl′ås)	114	47°27′N	115°55′W
Wallaceburg, Can.	98	42°39′N	82°25′W
Wallacia, Austl.	217b	33°52′S	150°40′E
Wallaroo, Austl. (wŏl-á-rōō)	218	33°52′S	137°45′E
Wallasey, Eng., U.K. (wŏl′á-sē)	158a	53°25′N	3°03′W
Walla Walla, Wa., U.S. (wŏl′á wŏl′á)	104	46°03′N	118°20′W
Walled Lake, Mi., U.S. (wôl′d lāk)	111b	42°32′N	83°29′W
Wallel, Tulu, mtn., Eth.	231	9°00′N	34°52′E
Wallingford, Eng., U.K. (wŏl′ĭng-fērd)	158b	51°34′N	1°08′W
Wallingford, Vt., U.S.	109	43°30′N	72°55′W
Wallis and Futuna Islands, dep., Oc.	241	13°00′S	176°10′E
Wallisville, Tx., U.S. (wôl′ĭs-vĭl)	123a	29°50′N	94°44′W
Wallowa, Or., U.S. (wôl′ô-wá)	114	45°34′N	117°32′W
Wallowa, r., Or., U.S.	114	45°28′N	117°28′W
Wallowa Mountains, mts., Or., U.S.	114	45°10′N	117°22′W
Wallula, Wa., U.S.	114	46°08′N	118°55′W
Walnut, Ca., U.S. (wôl′nŭt)	117a	34°00′N	117°51′W
Walnut, r., Ks., U.S.	121	37°28′N	97°06′W
Walnut Canyon National Mon, rec., Az., U.S.	119	35°10′N	111°30′W
Walnut Creek, Ca., U.S.	116b	37°54′N	122°04′W
Walnut Creek, r., Tx., U.S.	117c	32°37′N	97°03′W
Walnut Ridge, Ar., U.S. (rĭj)	121	36°04′N	90°56′W
Walpole, Ma., U.S. (wôl′pōl)	101a	42°09′N	71°15′W
Walpole, N.H., U.S.	109	43°05′N	72°25′W
Walsall, Eng., U.K. (wôl-sôl)	164	52°35′N	1°58′W
Walsenburg, Co., U.S. (wôl′sĕn-bûrg)	120	37°38′N	104°46′W
Walsum, Ger.	171c	51°32′N	6°41′E
Walter F. George Reservoir, res., U.S.	124	32°00′N	85°00′W
Walters, Ok., U.S. (wôl′tērz)	120	34°21′N	98°19′W
Waltham, Ma., U.S. (wôl′thăm)	101a	42°22′N	71°14′W
Walthamstow, Eng., U.K. (wôl′tăm-stō)	158b	51°34′N	0°01′W
Walton, N.Y., U.S.	109	42°10′N	75°05′W
Walton-le-Dale, Eng., U.K. (lē-dāl′)	158a	53°44′N	2°40′W
Walvis Bay, Nmb. (wôl′vĭs)	232	22°50′S	14°30′E
Walworth, Wi., U.S. (wôl′wûrth)	113	42°33′N	88°39′W
Wama, Ang.	236	12°14′S	15°33′E
Wamba, r., D.R.C.	232	7°00′S	18°00′E
Wamego, Ks., U.S. (wŏ-mē′gō)	121	39°13′N	96°17′W
Wami, r., Tan. (wä′mē)	233	6°31′S	37°17′E
Wanapitei Lake, l., Can.	99	46°45′N	80°45′W
Wanaque, N.J., U.S. (wŏn′á-kū)	110a	41°03′N	74°16′W
Wanaque Reservoir, res., N.J., U.S.	110a	41°06′N	74°20′W
Wanda Shan, mts., China (wän-dä shän)	205	45°54′N	131°45′E
Wandoan, Austl.	222	26°09′S	149°51′E
Wandsbek, Ger. (vänds′bĕk)	159c	53°34′N	10°07′E
Wandsworth, Eng., U.K. (wôndz′wûrth)	158b	51°26′N	0°12′W
Wanganui, N.Z. (wôŋ′gá-nōō′ē)	221a	39°53′S	175°01′E
Wangaratta, Austl. (wŏŋ′gá-răt′á)	222	36°23′S	146°18′E
Wangeroog, i., Ger. (vän′gĕ-rōg)	168	53°49′N	7°57′E
Wangqingtuo, China (wäŋ-chyĭŋ-twô)	206	39°14′N	116°56′E
Wangsi, China (wäŋ-sē)	206	37°59′N	116°57′E
Wantage, Eng., U.K. (wŏn′tăj)	158b	51°33′N	1°26′W
Wantagh, N.Y., U.S.	110a	40°41′N	73°30′W
Wanxian, China (wän shyĕn)	206	38°51′N	115°10′E
Wanxian, China (wän-shyĕn)	204	30°48′N	108°22′E
Wanzai, China (wän-dzī)	209	28°05′N	114°25′E
Wanzhi, China (wän-jr)	206	31°11′N	118°31′E

ăt; finăl; rāte; senåte; ärm; åsk; sofá; fåre; ch-choose; dh-as th in other; bē; ēvent; bĕt; recĕnt; cratēr; g-gō; gh-guttural g; bĭt; ĭ-short neutral; rīde; K-guttural k as ch in German ich;

PRONOUNCING INDEX

Wapakoneta – Wessel Islands 365

PLACE (Pronunciation)	PAGE	LAT.	LONG.
Wapakoneta, Oh., U.S. (wä'pȧ-kō-nĕt'ȧ)	108	40°35'N	84°10'W
Wapawekka Hills, hills, Can. (wŏ'pȧ-wē'kă-hĭlz)	96	54°45'N	104°20'W
Wapawekka Lake, l., Can.	96	54°55'N	104°40'W
Wapello, Ia., U.S. (wŏ-pĕl'ō)	113	41°10'N	91°11'W
Wappapello Reservoir, res., Mo., U.S. (wă'pȧ-pĕl-lō)	107	37°07'N	90°10'W
Wappingers Falls, N.Y., U.S. (wŏp'ĭn-jẽrz)	109	41°35'N	73°55'W
Wapsipinicon, r., Ia., U.S. (wŏp'sĭ-pĭn'ĭ-kŏn)	113	42°16'N	91°35'W
Wapusk National Park, rec., Can.	92	58°00'N	94°15'W
Warabi, Japan (wä'rä-bē)	211a	35°50'N	139°41'E
Warangal, India (wŭ'raŋ-gal)	199	18°03'N	79°45'E
Warburton, The, r., Austl. (wŏr'bûr-tŭn)	220	27°30'S	138°45'E
Wardān, Wādī, r., Egypt	197a	29°22'N	33°00'E
Ward Cove, Ak., U.S.	94	55°24'N	131°43'W
Warden, S. Afr. (wôr'dĕn)	238c	27°52'N	28°59'E
Wardha, India (wŭr'dä)	199	20°46'N	78°42'E
War Eagle, W.V., U.S. (wôr ē'g'l)	108	37°30'N	81°50'W
Waren, Ger. (vä'rĕn)	168	53°32'N	12°43'E
Warendorf, Ger. (vä'rĕn-dōrf)	171c	51°57'N	7°59'E
Wargla, Alg.	230	32°00'N	5°18'E
Warialda, Austl.	222	29°32'S	150°34'E
Warmbad, Nmb. (värm'bäd) (wôrm'băd)	232	28°25'S	18°45'E
Warmbad, S. Afr.	238c	24°52'S	28°18'E
Warm Beach, Wa., U.S. (wôrm)	116a	48°10'N	122°22'W
Warm Springs Indian Reservation, I.R., Or., U.S. (wôrm sprĭnz)	114	44°55'N	121°30'W
Warm Springs Reservoir, res., Or., U.S.	114	43°42'N	118°40'W
Warner Mountains, mts., Ca., U.S.	106	41°30'N	120°17'W
Warner Robins, Ga., U.S.	124	32°37'N	83°36'W
Warnow, r., Ger. (vär'nō)	168	53°51'N	11°55'E
Warracknabeal, Austl.	222	36°20'S	142°28'E
Warragamba Reservoir, res., Austl.	222	33°40'S	150°00'E
Warrego, r., Austl. (wôr'ē-gō)	221	27°13'S	145°58'E
Warren, Can.	102f	50°08'N	97°32'W
Warren, Ar., U.S. (wŏr'ĕn)	121	33°37'N	92°03'W
Warren, In., U.S.	108	40°40'N	85°25'W
Warren, Mi., U.S.	111b	42°33'N	83°03'W
Warren, Mn., U.S.	112	48°11'N	96°44'W
Warren, Oh., U.S.	108	41°15'N	80°50'W
Warren, Or., U.S.	116c	45°49'N	122°51'W
Warren, Pa., U.S.	109	41°50'N	79°10'W
Warren, R.I., U.S.	110b	41°44'N	71°14'W
Warrendale, Pa., U.S. (wŏr'ĕn-dāl)	111e	40°39'N	80°04'W
Warrensburg, Mo., U.S. (wŏr'ĕnz-bûrg)	121	38°45'N	93°42'W
Warrenton, Ga., U.S. (wŏr'ĕn-tŭn)	125	33°26'N	82°37'W
Warrenton, Or., U.S.	116c	46°10'N	123°56'W
Warrenton, Va., U.S.	109	38°45'N	77°50'W
Warri, Nig. (wär'ē)	230	5°33'N	5°43'E
Warrington, Eng., U.K.	158a	53°22'N	2°30'W
Warrington, Fl., U.S. (wŏ'ĭng-tŭn)	124	30°21'N	87°15'W
Warrnambool, Austl. (wôr'năm-bōōl)	219	38°20'S	142°28'E
Warroad, Mn., U.S. (wôr'rōd)	112	48°55'N	95°20'W
Warrumbungle Range, mts., Austl. (wôr'ŭm-bŭŋ-g'l)	221	31°18'S	150°00'E
Warsaw, Pol.	154	52°15'N	21°05'E
Warsaw, Il., U.S. (wôr'sô)	121	40°21'N	91°26'W
Warsaw, In., U.S.	108	41°15'N	85°50'W
Warsaw, N.Y., U.S.	109	42°45'N	78°10'W
Warsaw, NC, N.C., U.S.	125	35°00'N	78°07'W
Warsop, Eng., U.K. (wôr'sŭp)	158a	53°13'N	1°05'W
Warszawa *see* Warsaw, Pol.	154	52°15'N	21°05'E
Warta, r., Pol. (vär'tȧ)	161	52°30'N	16°00'E
Wartburg, S. Afr.	233c	29°26'S	30°39'E
Warwick, Austl. (wŏr'ĭk)	219	28°05'S	152°10'E
Warwick, Can.	99	45°58'N	71°57'W
Warwick, Eng., U.K.	164	52°19'N	1°46'W
Warwick, N.Y., U.S.	110a	41°15'N	74°22'W
Warwick, R.I., U.S.	109	41°42'N	71°27'W
Warwickshire, co., Eng., U.K.	158a	52°30'N	1°35'W
Wasatch Mountains, mts., Ut., U.S. (wô'săch)	117b	40°45'N	111°46'W
Wasatch Plateau, plat., Ut., U.S.	119	38°55'N	111°40'W
Wasatch Range, mts., U.S.	106	39°10'N	111°30'W
Wasbank, S. Afr.	233c	28°27'S	30°09'E
Wasco, Or., U.S. (wäs'kō)	114	45°36'N	120°42'W
Waseca, Mn., U.S. (wô-sē'kȧ)	113	44°04'N	93°31'W
Wash, The, Eng., U.K. (wŏsh)	160	53°00'N	0°20'E
Washburn, Me., U.S. (wŏsh'bŭrn)	100	46°46'N	68°10'W
Washburn, Wi., U.S.	113	46°41'N	90°55'W
Washburn, Mount, mtn., Wy., U.S.	115	44°55'N	110°10'W
Washington, D.C., U.S. (wŏsh'ĭng-tŭn)	105	38°50'N	77°00'W
Washington, Ga., U.S.	125	33°43'N	82°46'W
Washington, Ia., U.S.	113	41°17'N	91°42'W
Washington, In., U.S.	108	38°40'N	87°10'W
Washington, Ks., U.S.	121	39°48'N	97°04'W
Washington, Mo., U.S.	121	38°33'N	91°00'W
Washington, N.C., U.S.	125	35°32'N	77°01'W
Washington, Pa., U.S.	108	40°10'N	80°14'W
Washington, state, U.S.	104	47°30'N	121°10'W
Washington, i., Wi., U.S.	113	45°18'N	86°42'W
Washington, Lake, l., Wa., U.S.	116a	47°34'N	122°12'W
Washington, Mount, mtn., N.H., U.S.	107	44°15'N	71°15'W
Washington Court House, Oh., U.S.	108	39°30'N	83°25'W
Washington Park, Il., U.S.	117e	38°38'N	90°06'W
Washita, r., Ok., U.S. (wŏsh'ĭ-tô)	120	35°33'N	99°16'W
Washougal, Wa., U.S. (wŏ-shōō'gȧl)	116c	45°35'N	122°21'W
Washougal, r., Wa., U.S.	116c	45°38'N	122°17'W
Wasilków, Pol. (vȧ-sēl'kôf)	169	53°12'N	23°13'E
Waskaiowaka Lake, l., Can. (wŏ'skă-yō'wŏ-kă)	97	56°30'N	96°20'W
Wassenberg, Ger. (vä'sĕn-bĕrgh)	171c	51°06'N	6°07'E
Wassuk Range, mts., Nv., U.S. (wȧs'sŭk)	118	38°58'N	119°00'W
Waswanipi, Lac, l., Can.	99	49°35'N	76°15'W
Water, i., V.I.U.S. (wô'tẽr)	129c	18°20'N	64°57'W
Waterberge, mts., S. Afr. (wôrtẽr'bûrg)	238c	24°25'S	27°53'E
Waterboro, S.C., U.S. (wô'tẽr-bûr-ō)	125	32°50'N	80°40'W
Waterbury, Ct., U.S. (wô'tẽr-bĕr-ē)	109	41°30'N	73°00'W
Water Cay, i., Bah.	135	22°55'N	75°50'W
Waterdown, Can. (wô'tẽr-doun)	102d	43°20'N	79°54'W
Wateree Lake, res., S.C., U.S. (wô'tẽr-ē)	125	34°40'N	80°48'W
Waterford, Ire. (wô'tẽr-fẽrd)	161	52°20'N	7°03'W
Waterford, Wi., U.S.	111a	42°46'N	88°13'W
Waterloo, Bel.	159a	50°44'N	4°24'E
Waterloo, Can. (wô-tẽr-lōō')	99	43°30'N	80°40'W
Waterloo, Can.	99	45°25'N	72°30'W
Waterloo, Ia., U.S.	105	42°30'N	92°22'W
Waterloo, Il., U.S.	121	38°19'N	90°08'W
Waterloo, Md., U.S.	110e	39°11'N	76°50'W
Waterloo, N.Y., U.S.	109	42°55'N	76°50'W
Waterton-Glacier International Peace Park, rec., N.A. (wô'ter-tŭn-glā'shûr)	106	48°55'N	114°10'W
Waterton Lakes National Park, rec., Can.	95	49°05'N	113°50'W
Watertown, Ma., U.S. (wô'tẽr-toun)	101a	42°22'N	71°11'W
Watertown, N.Y., U.S.	105	44°00'N	75°55'W
Watertown, S.D., U.S.	104	44°53'N	97°07'W
Watertown, Wi., U.S.	113	43°13'N	88°40'W
Water Valley, Ms., U.S. (văl'ē)	124	34°08'N	89°38'W
Waterville, Me., U.S.	100	44°34'N	69°37'W
Waterville, Mn., U.S.	113	44°10'N	93°35'W
Waterville, Wa., U.S.	114	47°38'N	120°04'W
Watervliet, N.Y., U.S. (wô'tẽr-vlēt')	109	42°45'N	73°54'W
Watford, Eng., U.K. (wŏt'fŏrd)	164	51°38'N	0°24'W
Wathaman Lake, l., Can.	96	56°55'N	103°43'W
Watlington, Eng., U.K.	158b	51°37'N	1°01'W
Watonga, Ok., U.S. (wŏ-tôŋ'gȧ)	121	35°50'N	98°26'E
Watsa, D.R.C. (wät'sä)	231	3°03'N	29°32'E
Watseka, Il., U.S. (wŏt-sē'kȧ)	108	40°45'N	87°45'W
Watson, In., U.S. (wŏt'sŭn)	111h	38°21'N	85°42'W
Watson Lake, Can.	90	60°18'N	128°50'W
Watsonville, Ca., U.S. (wŏt'sŭn-vĭl)	118	36°55'N	121°46'W
Wattenscheid, Ger. (vä'tĕn-shīd)	171c	51°30'N	7°07'E
Watts, Ca., U.S. (wŏts)	117a	33°56'N	118°15'W
Watts Bar Lake, res., Tn., U.S. (bär)	124	35°45'N	84°49'W
Waubay, S.D., U.S. (wô'bā)	112	45°19'N	97°18'W
Wauchula, Fl., U.S. (wô-chōō'lȧ)	125a	27°32'N	81°48'W
Wauconda, Il., U.S. (wô-kŏn'dȧ)	111a	42°15'N	88°08'W
Waukegan, Il., U.S. (wô-kē'găn)	105	42°22'N	87°51'W
Waukesha, Wi., U.S. (wô'kē-shô)	111a	43°01'N	88°13'W
Waukon, Ia., U.S. (wô kŏn)	113	43°15'N	91°30'W
Waupaca, Wi., U.S. (wô-păk'ȧ)	113	44°22'N	89°06'W
Waupun, Wi., U.S. (wô-pŭn')	113	43°37'N	88°45'W
Waurika, Ok., U.S. (wô-rē'kȧ)	121	34°09'N	97°59'W
Wausau, Wi., U.S. (wô'sô)	105	44°58'N	89°40'W
Wausaukee, Wi., U.S. (wô-sô'kē)	113	45°22'N	87°58'W
Wauseon, Oh., U.S. (wô'sē-ŏn)	108	41°30'N	84°10'W
Wautoma, Wi., U.S. (wô-tō'mȧ)	113	44°04'N	89°11'W
Wauwatosa, Wi., U.S. (wô-wȧ-t'ō'sȧ)	111a	43°03'N	88°00'W
Waveney, r., Eng., U.K. (wāv'nē)	165	52°27'N	1°17'E
Waverly, S. Afr.	233c	31°54'S	26°29'E
Waverly, Ia., U.S. (wā'vẽr-lē)	113	42°43'N	92°29'W
Waverly, Tn., U.S.	124	36°04'N	87°46'W
Wāw, Sudan	231	7°41'N	28°00'E
Wawa, Can.	98	47°59'N	84°47'W
Wāw al-Kabir, Libya	231	25°23'N	16°52'E
Wawanesa, Can. (wŏ'wŏ-nē'sȧ)	97	49°36'N	99°41'W.
Wawasee, l., In., U.S. (wô-wô-sē')	108	41°25'N	85°45'W
Waxahachie, Tx., U.S. (wăk-sȧ-hăch'ē)	123	32°23'N	96°50'W
Wayland, Ky., U.S. (wā'lănd)	125	37°25'N	82°47'W
Wayland, Ma., U.S.	101a	42°23'N	71°22'W
Wayne, Mi., U.S.	111b	42°17'N	83°23'W
Wayne, Ne., U.S.	112	42°13'N	97°03'W
Wayne, N.J., U.S.	110a	40°56'N	74°16'W
Wayne, Pa., U.S.	110f	40°03'N	75°22'W
Waynesboro, Ga., U.S. (wānz'bŭr-ō)	125	33°05'N	82°02'W
Waynesboro, Pa., U.S.	109	39°45'N	77°35'W
Waynesboro, Va., U.S.	109	38°05'N	78°50'W
Waynesburg, Pa., U.S. (wānz'bûrg)	108	39°55'N	80°10'W
Waynesville, N.C., U.S. (wānz'vĭl)	125	35°28'N	82°58'W
Waynoka, Ok., U.S. (wā-nō'kȧ)	120	36°34'N	98°52'W
Wayzata, Mn., U.S. (wā-zä-tȧ)	117g	44°58'N	93°31'W
Wazīrbad, Pak.	202	32°39'N	74°11'E
Weagamow Lake, l., Can. (wē'ăg-ă-mou)	97	52°53'N	91°22'W
Weald, The, reg., Eng., U.K. (wēld)	164	50°58'N	0°15'W
Weatherford, Ok., U.S. (wĕ-dhẽr-fẽrd)	120	85°32'N	98°41'W
Weatherford, Tx., U.S.	123	32°45'N	97°46'W
Weaver, r., Eng., U.K. (wē'vẽr)	158a	53°09'N	2°31'W
Weaverville, Ca., U.S. (wē'vẽr-vĭl)	114	40°44'N	122°55'W
Webb City, Mo., U.S.	121	37°10'N	94°26'W
Weber, r., Ut., U.S.	117b	41°13'N	112°07'W
Webster, Ma., U.S.	101a	42°04'N	71°52'W
Webster, S.D., U.S.	112	45°19'N	97°30'W
Webster City, Ia., U.S.	113	42°28'N	93°49'W
Webster Groves, Mo., U.S. (grōvz)	117e	38°36'N	90°22'W
Webster Springs, W.V., U.S. (sprĭngz)	108	38°30'N	80°20'W
Weddell Sea, sea, Ant. (wĕd'ĕl)	224	73°00'S	45°00'W
Wedel, Ger. (vā'dĕl)	159c	53°35'N	9°42'E
Wedge Mountain, mtn., Can. (wĕj)	95	50°10'N	122°50'W
Wedgeport, Can. (wĕj'pōrt)	100	43°44'N	65°59'W
Wednesfield, Eng., U.K. (wĕd''nz-fēld)	158a	52°36'N	2°04'W
Weed, Ca., U.S. (wēd)	114	41°35'N	122°21'W
Weenen, S. Afr. (vā'nĕn)	233c	28°52'S	30°05'E
Weert, Neth.	165	51°16'N	5°39'E
Weesp, Neth.	159a	52°18'N	5°01'E
Węgorzewo, Pol. (vôŋ-gô'zhĕ-vô)	169	54°14'N	21°46'E
Węgrow, Pol. (vôŋ'grôf)	169	52°23'N	22°02'E
Wei, r., China (wā)	206	35°47'N	114°27'E
Wei, r., China (wā)	204	34°00'N	108°10'E
Weichang, China (wā-chäŋ)	205	41°50'N	118°00'E
Weiden, Ger.	168	49°41'N	12°09'E
Weifang, China	205	36°43'N	119°08'E
Weihai, China (wa'hăī')	205	37°30'N	122°05'E
Weilheim, Ger. (vīl'hīm')	168	47°50'N	11°06'E
Weimar, Ger. (vī'mär)	161	50°59'N	11°20'E
Weinan, China	208	34°32'N	109°40'E
Weipa, Austl.	219	12°25'S	141°54'E
Weir, r., Can. (wẽr-rĭv-ẽr)	97	56°49'N	94°04'W
Weirton, W.V., U.S.	108	40°25'N	80°35'W
Weiser, Id., U.S. (wē'zẽr)	114	44°15'N	116°58'W
Weiser, r., Id., U.S.	114	44°26'N	116°40'W
Weishi, China (wā-shr)	208	34°23'N	114°12'E
Weissenburg, Ger.	168	49°04'N	11°20'E
Weissenfels, Ger. (vī'sĕn-fĕlz)	168	51°13'N	11°58'E
Weiss Lake, res., Al., U.S.	124	34°15'N	85°35'W
Weixi, China (wā-shyĕ)	204	27°27'N	99°30'E
Weixian, China (wā shyĕn)	206	36°59'N	115°17'E
Wejherowo, Pol. (vā-hĕ-rô'vô)	169	54°36'N	18°15'E
Welch, W.V., U.S. (wĕlch)	125	37°24'N	81°28'W
Weldon, N.C., U.S. (wĕl'dŭn)	125	36°24'N	77°36'W
Weldon, r., Mo., U.S.	121	40°22'N	93°39'W
Weleetka, Ok., U.S. (wē-lēt'kȧ)	121	35°19'N	96°08'W
Welford, Austl. (wĕl'fẽrd)	222	25°08'S	144°43'E
Welkom, S. Afr. (wĕl'kŏm)	232	27°57'S	26°45'E
Welland, Can. (wĕl'ănd)	99	42°59'N	79°13'W
Wellesley, Ma., U.S. (wĕlz'lē)	101a	42°18'N	71°17'W
Wellesley Islands, is., Austl.	220	16°15'S	139°25'E
Wellington, Austl. (wĕl'lĭng-tŭn)	222	32°40'S	148°50'E
Wellington, N.Z.	221a	41°15'S	174°45'E
Wellington, Eng., U.K.	158a	52°42'N	2°30'W
Wellington, Ks., U.S.	121	37°16'N	97°24'W
Wellington, Oh., U.S.	108	41°10'N	82°10'W
Wellington, Tx., U.S.	120	34°51'N	100°12'W
Wellington, i., Chile (ŏĕ'lēng-tŏn)	144	49°30'S	76°30'W
Wells, Can.	90	53°06'N	121°34'W
Wells, Mi., U.S.	108	45°50'N	87°00'W
Wells, Mn., U.S.	113	43°44'N	93°43'W
Wells, Nv., U.S.	114	41°07'N	115°04'W
Wells, l., Austl. (wĕlz)	220	26°35'S	123°40'E
Wellsboro, Pa., U.S. (wĕlz'bŭ-rō)	109	41°45'N	77°15'W
Wellsburg, W.V., U.S. (wĕlz'bûrg)	108	40°10'N	80°40'W
Wells Dam, dam, Wa., U.S.	114	48°00'N	119°39'W
Wellston, Oh., U.S. (wĕlz'tŭn)	108	39°05'N	82°30'W
Wellsville, Mo., U.S. (wĕlz'vĭl)	121	39°04'N	91°33'W
Wellsville, N.Y., U.S.	109	42°10'N	78°00'W
Wellsville, Oh., U.S.	108	40°35'N	80°40'W
Wellsville, Ut., U.S.	115	41°38'N	111°57'W
Wels, Aus. (vĕls)	161	48°10'N	14°01'E
Welshpool, Wales, U.K. (wĕlsh'pōōl)	164	52°44'N	3°10'W
Welverdiend, S. Afr. (vĕl-vẽr-dēnd')	238c	26°23'S	27°16'E
Welwyn Garden City, Eng., U.K. (wĕlĭn)	158b	51°46'N	0°17'W
Wem, Eng., U.K. (wĕm)	158a	52°51'N	2°44'W
Wembere, r., Tan.	237	4°35'S	33°55'E
Wen, r., China (wŭn)	206	36°24'N	119°00'E
Wenan Wa, sw., China (wĕn'än' wä)	206	38°56'N	116°29'E
Wenatchee, Wa., U.S. (wē-năch'ē)	114	47°24'N	120°18'W
Wenatchee Mountains, mts., Wa., U.S.	114	47°28'N	121°10'W
Wenchang, China (wŭn-chäŋ)	209	19°32'N	110°42'E
Wenchi, Ghana	234	7°42'N	2°07'W
Wendeng, China (wŭn-dŭŋ)	206	37°14'N	122°03'E
Wendo, Eth.	231	6°37'N	38°29'E
Wendorer, Ut., U.S.	115	40°47'N	114°01'W
Wendover, Can. (wĕn-dōv'ẽr)	102c	45°34'N	75°07'W
Wendover, Eng., U.K.	158b	51°44'N	0°45'W
Wenham, Ma., U.S. (wĕn'ăm)	101a	42°36'N	70°53'W
Wenquan, China (wŭn-chyůän)	205	47°10'N	120°00'E
Wenshan, China	204	23°20'N	104°15'E
Wenshang, China (wĕn'shäng)	206	35°43'N	116°31'E
Wensu, China (wĕn-sò)	204	41°45'N	80°30'E
Wentworth, Austl. (wĕnt'wûrth)	219	34°03'S	141°53'E
Wenzhou, China (wŭn-jō)	205	28°00'N	120°40'E
Wepener, S. Afr. (wē'pĕn-ẽr) (vā'pĕn-ẽr)	232	29°43'S	27°04'E
Werder, Ger. (vĕr'dĕr)	159b	52°23'N	12°56'E
Were Ilu, Eth.	231	10°39'N	39°21'E
Werl, Ger. (vĕrl)	171c	51°33'N	7°55'E
Wermelskirchen, Ger.	171c	51°08'N	7°13'E
Werneuchen, Ger. (vĕr'hoi-kĕn)	159b	52°38'N	13°44'E
Werra, r., Ger. (vĕr'ä)	168	51°16'N	9°54'E
Werribee, Austl.	217a	37°54'S	144°40'E
Werribee, r., Austl.	217a	37°40'S	144°37'E
Wertach, r., Ger. (vĕr'täk)	168	48°12'N	10°40'E
Weseke, Ger. (vĕ'zĕ-kĕ)	171c	51°54'N	6°51'E
Wesel, Ger. (vā'zĕl)	171c	51°39'N	6°37'E
Weser, r., Ger. (vā'zẽr)	156	51°00'N	10°30'E
Weslaco, Tx., U.S. (wĕs-lā'kō)	123	26°10'N	97°59'W
Weslemkoon, l., Can.	99	45°02'N	77°25'W
Wesleyville, Can. (wĕs'lē-vĭl)	101	49°09'N	53°34'W
Wessel Islands, is., Austl. (wĕs'ĕl)	220	11°45'S	136°25'E

ng-sing; ŋ-baŋk; N-nasalized n; nŏd; cŏmmit; ōld; ôbey; ôrder; oi-boil; fōōd; ò-as oo in foot; ou-out; s-soft; sh-dish; th-thin; pūre; ûnite; ûrn; stŭd; circŭs; ü-as in French tu; '-indeterminate vowel.

366 Wesselsbron – William Creek PRONOUNCING INDEX

PLACE (Pronunciation)	PAGE	LAT.	LONG.
Wesselsbron, S. Afr. (wĕs′ĕl-brŏn)	238c	27°51′S	26°22′E
Wessington Springs, S.D., U.S. (wĕs′ĭng-tŭn)	112	44°06′N	98°35′W
West, Mount, mtn., Pan.	128a	9°10′N	79°52′W
West Allis, Wi., U.S. (wĕst-ăl′ĭs)	111a	43°01′N	88°01′W
West Alton, Mo., U.S. (ôl′tŭn)	117e	38°52′N	90°13′W
West Bay, b., Fl., U.S.	124	30°20′N	85°45′W
West Bay, b., Tx., U.S.	123a	29°11′N	95°03′W
West Bend, Wi., U.S. (wĕst bĕnd)	113	43°25′N	88°13′W
West Bengal, state, India (bĕn-gôl′)	199	23°30′N	87°30′E
West Blocton, Al., U.S. (blŏk′tŭn)	124	33°05′N	87°05′W
Westborough, Ma., U.S. (wĕst′bŭr-ô)	101a	42°17′N	71°37′W
West Boylston, Ma., U.S. (boil′stŭn)	101a	42°22′N	71°46′W
West Branch, Mi., U.S. (wĕst brănch)	108	44°15′N	84°10′W
West Bridgford, Eng., U.K. (brĭj′fērd)	158a	52°55′N	1°08′W
West Bromwich, Eng., U.K. (wĕst brŭm′ĭj)	158a	52°32′N	1°59′W
Westbrook, Me., U.S. (wĕst′brŏŏk)	100	43°41′N	70°23′W
Westby, Wi., U.S. (wĕst′bē)	113	43°40′N	90°52′W
West Caicos, i., T./C. Is. (käē′kō) (kī′kōs)	135	21°40′N	72°30′W
West Cape Howe, c., Austl.	220	35°15′S	117°30′E
West Chester, Oh., U.S. (chĕs′tēr)	111f	39°20′N	84°24′W
West Chester, Pa., U.S.	110f	39°57′N	75°36′W
West Chicago, Il., U.S. (chĭ-kă′gō)	111a	41°53′N	88°12′W
West Columbia, S.C., U.S. (cŏl′ŭm-bē-ȧ)	125	33°58′N	81°05′W
West Columbia, Tx., U.S.	123	29°08′N	95°39′W
West Cote Blanche Bay, b., La., U.S.	123	29°30′N	92°17′W
West Covina, Ca., U.S. (wĕst kō-vē′nȧ)	117a	34°04′N	117°55′W
West Des Moines, Ia., U.S. (dē moin′)	113	41°35′N	93°42′W
West Des Moines, r., Ia., U.S.	113	42°52′N	94°32′W
West End, Bah.	134	26°40′N	78°55′W
Westerham, Eng., U.K. (wĕ′stēr′ŭm)	158b	51°15′N	0°05′E
Westerhörn, Ger. (vĕs′tĕr-hōrn)	159c	53°52′N	9°41′E
Westerlo, Bel.	159a	51°05′N	4°57′E
Westerly, R.I., U.S. (wĕs′tēr-lē)	109	41°25′N	71°50′W
Western Australia, state, Austl. (ôs-trā′lĭ-ȧ)	218	24°15′S	121°30′E
Western Dvina, r., Eur.	167	55°30′N	28°27′E
Western Ghāts, mts., India	199	17°35′N	74°00′E
Western Port, Md., U.S. (wĕs′tērn pōrt)	109	39°30′N	79°00′W
Western Sahara, dep., Afr. (sȧ-hä′rȧ)	230	23°05′N	15°33′W
Western Samoa *see* Samoa, nation, Oc.	2	14°30′S	172°00′W
Western Siberian Lowland, depr., Russia	178	63°37′N	72°45′E
Westerville, Oh., U.S. (wĕs′tēr-vĭl)	108	40°10′N	83°00′W
Westerwald, for., Ger. (vĕs′tĕr-väld)	168	50°35′N	7°45′E
Westfalen, hist. reg., Ger. (vĕst-fä-lĕn)	168	51°20′N	8°30′E
Westfield, Ma., U.S. (wĕst′fēld)	109	42°05′N	72°45′W
Westfield, N.J., U.S.	110a	40°39′N	74°21′W
Westfield, N.Y., U.S. (wĕst′fēld)	110a	42°20′N	79°40′W
Westford, Ma., U.S. (wĕst′fērd)	101a	42°35′N	71°26′W
West Frankfort, Il., U.S. (frănk′fŭrt)	108	37°55′N	88°55′W
West Ham, Eng., U.K.	158b	51°30′N	0°00′W
West Hartford, Ct., U.S. (härt′fērd)	109	41°45′N	72°45′W
West Helena, Ar., U.S. (hĕl′ĕn-ȧ)	121	34°32′N	90°39′W
West Indies, is. (ĭn′dēz)	129	19°00′N	78°30′W
West Jordon, Ut., U.S. (jôr′dăn)	117b	40°37′N	111°56′W
West Kirby, Eng., U.K. (kûr′bē)	158a	53°22′N	3°11′W
West Lafayette, In., U.S. (lä-fā-yĕt′)	108	40°25′N	86°55′W
Westlake, Oh., U.S.	111d	41°27′N	81°55′W
Westleigh, S. Afr. (wĕst-lē)	238c	27°39′S	27°18′E
West Liberty, Ia., U.S. (wĕst lĭb′ēr-tĭ)	113	41°34′N	91°15′W
West Linn, Or., U.S. (lĭn)	116c	45°22′N	122°37′W
Westlock, Can. (wĕst′lŏk)	95	54°09′N	113°52′W
West Memphis, Ar., U.S.	121	35°08′N	90°11′W
West Midlands, hist. reg., Eng., U.K.	158a	52°26′N	1°50′W
Westminster, Ca., U.S. (wĕst′min-stēr)	117a	33°45′N	117°59′W
Westminster, Md., U.S.	109	39°40′N	76°55′W
Westminster, S.C., U.S.	124	34°38′N	83°10′W
Westmount, Can. (wĕst′mount)	102a	45°29′N	73°36′W
West Newbury, Ma., U.S. (nū′bēr-ē)	101a	42°47′N	70°57′W
West Newton, Pa., U.S. (nū′tŭn)	111e	40°12′N	79°45′W
West New York, N.J., U.S. (nū yŏrk)	110a	40°47′N	74°01′W
West Nishnabotna, r., Ia., U.S. (nĭsh-nȧ-bŏt′nȧ)	112	40°56′N	95°37′W
Weston, Ma., U.S. (wĕs′tŭn)	101a	42°22′N	71°18′W
Weston, W.V., U.S.	108	39°00′N	80°30′W
Westonaria, S. Afr.	238c	26°19′S	27°38′E
Weston-super-Mare, Eng., U.K. (wĕs′tŭn sū′pēr-mā′rē)	164	51°23′N	3°00′W
West Orange, N.J., U.S. (wĕst ŏr′ĕnj)	110a	40°46′N	74°14′W
West Palm Beach, Fl., U.S. (päm bēch)	105	26°44′N	80°04′W
West Pensacola, Fl., U.S. (pĕn-sȧ-kō′lȧ)	124	30°24′N	87°18′W
West Pittsburg, Ca., U.S. (pĭts′bûrg)	116b	38°02′N	121°56′W
Westplains, Mo., U.S. (wĕst-plānz′)	121	36°42′N	91°51′W
West Point, Ga., U.S.	124	32°52′N	85°10′W
West Point, Ms., U.S.	124	33°36′N	88°39′W
Westpoint, Ne., U.S.	112	41°50′N	96°00′W
West Point, N.Y., U.S.	110a	41°23′N	73°58′W
West Point, Ut., U.S.	117b	41°07′N	112°05′W
West Point, Va., U.S.	109	37°25′N	76°50′W
West Point Lake, res., U.S.	124	33°00′N	85°10′W
Westport, Ire.	164	53°44′N	9°36′W
Westport, Ct., U.S. (wĕst′pōrt)	110a	41°07′N	73°22′W
Westport, Or., U.S. (wĕst′pōrt)	116c	46°08′N	123°22′W
Westray, i., Scot., U.K. (wĕs′trā)	164a	59°19′N	3°05′W

PLACE (Pronunciation)	PAGE	LAT.	LONG.
West Road, r., Can. (rōd)	94	53°00′N	124°00′W
West Saint Paul, Mn., U.S. (sānt pôl′)	117g	44°55′N	93°05′W
West Sand Spit, i., T./C. Is.	135	21°25′N	72°10′W
West Slope, Or., U.S.	116c	45°30′N	122°46′W
West Tavaputs Plateau, plat., Ut., U.S. (wĕst tăv′ȧ-pŏts)	119	39°45′N	110°35′W
West Terre Haute, In., U.S. (tĕr-ē hōt′)	108	39°30′N	87°30′W
West Union, Ia., U.S. (ūn′yŭn)	113	42°58′N	91°48′W
West University Place, Tx., U.S.	123a	29°43′N	95°26′W
Westview, Oh., U.S. (wĕst′vū)	111d	41°21′N	81°54′W
West View, Pa., U.S.	111e	40°31′N	80°02′W
Westville, Can. (wĕst′vĭl)	101	45°35′N	62°43′W
Westville, Il., U.S.	108	40°00′N	87°40′W
West Virginia, state, U.S. (wĕst vẽr-jĭn′ĭ-ȧ)	105	39°00′N	80°50′W
West Walker, r., Ca., U.S. (wôk′ẽr)	118	38°25′N	119°25′W
West Warwick, R.I., U.S. (wŏr′ĭk)	110b	41°42′N	71°31′W
Westwego, La., U.S. (wĕst-wē′gō)	110d	29°55′N	90°09′W
Westwood, Ca., U.S. (wĕst′wŏŏd)	118	40°18′N	121°00′W
Westwood, Ks., U.S.	117f	39°03′N	94°37′W
Westwood, Ma., U.S.	101a	42°13′N	71°14′W
Westwood, N.J., U.S.	110a	40°59′N	74°02′W
West Wyalong, Austl. (wīălông)	219	34°00′S	147°20′E
West Yorkshire, hist. reg., Eng., U.K.	158a	53°37′N	1°48′W
Wetar, Pulau, i., Indon. (wĕt′ȧr)	213	7°34′S	126°00′E
Wetaskiwin, Can. (wĕ-tăs′kē-wŏn)	90	52°58′N	113°22′W
Wetmore, Tx., U.S. (wĕt′mōr)	117d	29°34′N	98°25′W
Wetter, Ger.	171c	51°23′N	7°23′E
Wetumpka, Al., U.S. (wē-tŭmp′kȧ)	124	32°33′N	86°12′W
Wetzlar, Ger. (vĕts′lär)	168	50°35′N	8°30′E
Wewak, Pap. N. Gui. (wā-wäk′)	213	3°19′S	143°30′E
Wewoka, Ok., U.S. (wē-wō′kȧ)	121	35°09′N	96°30′W
Wexford, Ire. (wĕks′fẽrd)	161	52°20′N	6°30′W
Weybridge, Eng., U.K. (wā′brĭj)	158b	51°20′N	0°26′W
Weyburn, Can. (wā′bûrn)	90	49°41′N	103°52′W
Weymouth, Eng., U.K. (wā′mŭth)	164	50°37′N	2°34′W
Weymouth, Ma., U.S.	101a	42°44′N	70°57′W
Weymouth, Oh., U.S.	111d	41°11′N	81°48′W
Whale Cay, i., Bah.	134	25°20′N	77°45′W
Whale Cay Channels, strt., Bah.	134	26°45′N	77°10′W
Wharton, N.J., U.S. (hwôr′tŭn)	110a	40°54′N	74°35′W
Wharton, Tx., U.S.	123	29°19′N	96°06′W
What Cheer, Ia., U.S. (hwŏt chēr)	113	41°23′N	92°24′W
Whatcom, Lake, l., Wa., U.S. (hwät′kŭm)	116c	48°44′N	123°34′W
Whatshan Lake, l., Can. (wŏt′shăn)	95	50°00′N	118°03′W
Wheatland, Wy., U.S. (hwēt′lănd)	115	42°04′N	104°52′W
Wheatland Reservoir Number 2, res., Wy., U.S.	115	41°52′N	105°36′W
Wheaton, Il., U.S. (hwē′tŭn)	111a	41°52′N	88°06′W
Wheaton, Md., U.S.	110e	39°05′N	77°05′W
Wheaton, Mn., U.S.	112	45°48′N	96°29′W
Wheeler Peak, mtn., N.M., U.S.	120	36°34′N	105°25′W
Wheeler Peak, mtn., Nv., U.S.	106	38°58′N	114°15′W
Wheeling, Il., U.S. (hwēl′ĭng)	111a	42°08′N	87°54′W
Wheeling, W.V., U.S.	108	40°05′N	80°45′W
Wheelwright, Arg. (ŏē′l-rē′gt)	141c	33°46′S	61°14′W
Whidbey Island, i., Wa., U.S. (hwĭd′bē)	116a	48°13′N	122°50′W
Whippany, N.J., U.S. (hwĭp′ȧ-nē)	110a	40°49′N	74°25′W
Whitby, Can. (hwĭt′bē)	91	43°50′N	79°00′W
Whitchurch, Eng., U.K. (hwĭt′chûrch)	158a	52°58′N	2°49′W
White, l., Can.	98	48°47′N	85°50′W
White, l., Can.	99	45°15′N	76°35′W
White, r., Can.	98	48°34′N	85°46′W
White, r., In., U.S.	108	39°15′N	86°45′W
White, r., S.D., U.S.	112	43°13′N	101°04′W
White, r., Tx., U.S.	120	36°25′N	102°20′W
White, r., Vt., U.S.	109	43°45′N	72°35′W
White, r., Wa., U.S.	114	47°07′N	121°48′W
White, r., U.S.	107	35°30′N	92°00′W
White, r., U.S.	112	43°41′N	99°48′W
White, r., U.S.	119	40°10′N	108°55′W
White, East Fork, r., In., U.S.	108	38°45′N	86°20′W
White Bay, b., Can.	93a	50°00′N	56°30′W
White Bear Indian Reserve, I.R., Can.	97	49°50′N	102°15′W
White Bear Lake, l., Mn., U.S.	117g	45°04′N	92°58′W
White Castle, La., U.S.	123	30°10′N	91°09′W
White Center, Wa., U.S.	116a	47°31′N	122°21′W
White Cloud, Mi., U.S.	108	43°35′N	85°45′W
Whitecourt, Can. (wīt′côrt)	90	54°09′N	115°41′W
White Earth, r., N.D., U.S.	112	48°30′N	102°44′W
White Earth Indian Reservation, I.R., Mn., U.S.	112	47°18′N	95°42′W
Whiteface, r., Mn., U.S. (whīt′fās)	113	47°12′N	92°13′W
Whitefield, N.H., U.S. (hwīt′fēld)	109	44°20′N	71°35′W
Whitefish Bay, Wi., U.S.	111a	43°07′N	77°54′W
Whitefish Bay, b., Can.	97	49°26′N	94°14′W
Whitefish Bay, b., N.A.	113	46°36′N	84°50′W
White Hall, Il., U.S.	121	39°26′N	90°23′W
Whitehall, Mi., U.S. (hwīt′hôl)	108	43°20′N	86°20′W
Whitehall, N.Y., U.S.	109	43°30′N	73°25′W
Whitehaven, Eng., U.K. (hwīt′hā-vĕn)	164	54°35′N	3°30′W
Whitehorn, Point, c., Wa., U.S. (hwīt′hôrn)	116d	48°54′N	122°48′W
Whitehorse, Can. (whīt′hôrs)	90	60°39′N	135°01′W
White Lake, l., La., U.S.	123	29°40′N	92°35′W
White Mountain Peak, mtn., Ca., U.S.	118	37°38′N	118°13′W
White Mountains, mts., Me., U.S.	100	44°22′N	71°15′W
White Mountains, mts., N.H., U.S.	109	42°20′N	71°05′W
Whitemouth, l., Can.	97	49°14′N	95°40′W
White Nile (Al Bahr al Abyad), r., Sudan	231	12°30′N	32°30′E
White Otter, l., Can.	98	49°15′N	91°48′W

PLACE (Pronunciation)	PAGE	LAT.	LONG.
White Pass, p., N.A.	103	59°35′N	135°03′W
White Plains, N.Y., U.S.	110a	41°02′N	73°47′W
White River, Can.	98	48°38′N	85°23′W
White Rock, Can.	95	49°01′N	122°49′W
Whiterock Reservoir, res., Tx., U.S. (hwīt′rŏk)	117c	32°51′N	96°40′W
White Russia *see* Belarus, nation, Eur.	178	53°30′N	25°33′E
Whitesail Lake, l., Can. (whīt′sāl)	94	53°30′N	127°00′W
White Sands National Monument, rec., N.M., U.S.	119	32°50′N	106°20′W
White Sea, sea, Russia	178	66°00′N	40°00′E
White Settlement, Tx., U.S.	117c	32°45′N	97°28′W
White Sulphur Springs, Mt., U.S.	115	46°32′N	110°49′W
White Umfolzi, r., S. Afr. (ŭm-fô-lō′zē)	233c	28°12′S	30°55′E
Whiteville, N.C., U.S. (hwīt′vĭl)	125	34°18′N	78°45′W
White Volta (Volta Blanche), r., Afr.	234	9°40′N	1°10′W
Whitewater, Wi., U.S. (whīt-wŏt′ẽr)	113	42°49′N	88°40′W
Whitewater, l., Can.	97	49°14′N	100°39′W
Whitewater, r., In., U.S.	111f	39°19′N	84°55′W
Whitewater Bay, b., Fl., U.S.	125a	25°16′N	80°21′W
Whitewater Creek, r., Mt., U.S.	115	48°50′N	107°50′W
Whitewell, Tn., U.S. (hwīt′wĕl)	124	35°11′N	85°31′W
Whitewright, Tx., U.S. (hwīt′rīt)	121	33°33′N	96°25′W
Whitham, r., Eng., U.K. (wĭth′ŭm)	158a	53°08′N	0°15′W
Whiting, In., U.S. (hwīt′ĭng)	111a	41°41′N	87°30′W
Whitinsville, Ma., U.S. (hwīt′ĕns-vĭl)	101a	42°06′N	71°40′W
Whitman, Ma., U.S. (hwĭt′măn)	101a	42°05′N	70°57′W
Whitmire, S.C., U.S. (hwĭt′mīr)	125	34°30′N	81°40′W
Whitney, Mount, mtn., Ca., U.S.	106	36°34′N	118°18′W
Whitney Lake, l., Tx., U.S. (hwĭt′nē)	123	32°02′N	97°36′W
Whitstable, Eng., U.K. (wĭt′stăb′l)	158b	51°22′N	1°03′E
Whitsunday, i., Austl. (hwĭt′s′n-dā)	221	20°16′S	149°00′E
Whittier, Ca., U.S. (hwĭt′ĭ-ẽr)	117a	33°58′N	118°02′W
Whittlesea, S. Afr. (wĭt′l′sē)	233c	32°11′S	26°51′E
Whitworth, Eng., U.K. (hwĭt′wŭrth)	158a	53°40′N	2°10′W
Whyalla, Austl. (hwī-ăl′ȧ)	218	33°00′S	137°32′E
Whymper, Mount, mtn., Can. (wĭm′pẽr)	94	48°57′N	124°10′W
Wiarton, Can. (wī′ȧr-tŭn)	91	44°45′N	80°45′W
Wichita, Ks., U.S. (wĭch′ĭ-tô)	104	37°42′N	97°21′W
Wichita, r., Tx., U.S.	120	33°50′N	99°38′W
Wichita Falls, Tx., U.S. (fôls)	104	33°54′N	98°29′W
Wichita Mountains, mts., Ok., U.S.	106	34°48′N	98°43′W
Wick, Scot., U.K. (wĭk)	160	58°25′N	3°05′W
Wickatunk, N.J., U.S. (wĭk′ȧ-tŭnk)	110a	40°21′N	74°15′W
Wickenburg, Az., U.S.	119	33°58′N	112°44′W
Wickiup Reservoir, res., Or., U.S.	114	43°40′N	121°43′W
Wickliffe, Oh., U.S. (wĭk′klĭf)	111d	41°37′N	81°29′W
Wicklow, Ire.	164	52°59′N	6°06′W
Wicklow Mountains, mts., Ire. (wĭk′lō)	164	52°49′N	6°20′W
Wickup Mountain, mtn., Or., U.S. (wĭk′ŭp)	116c	46°06′N	123°35′W
Wiconisco, Pa., U.S. (wĭ-kŏn′ĭs-kō)	109	43°35′N	76°45′W
Widen, W.V., U.S. (wī′dĕn)	108	38°25′N	80°55′W
Widnes, Eng., U.K. (wĭd′nĕs)	158a	53°21′N	2°44′W
Wieliczka, Pol. (vyĕ-lēch′kȧ)	169	49°58′N	20°06′E
Wien *see* Vienna, Aus.	154	48°13′N	16°22′E
Wien, state, Aus.	159e	48°11′N	16°23′E
Wiener Neustadt, Aus. (vē′nĕr noi′shtät)	161	47°48′N	16°15′E
Wiener Wald, for., Aus.	159e	48°09′N	16°05′E
Wieprz, r., Pol. (vyĕpzh)	169	51°25′N	22°45′E
Wiergate, Tx., U.S. (wẽr′gāt)	123	31°00′N	93°42′W
Wiesbaden, Ger. (vēs′bä-dĕn)	161	50°05′N	8°15′E
Wigan, Eng., U.K. (wĭg′ăn)	164	53°33′N	2°37′W
Wiggins, Ms., U.S. (wĭg′ĭnz)	124	30°51′N	89°05′W
Wight, Isle of, i., Eng., U.K. (wīt)	164	50°44′N	1°17′W
Wilber, Ne., U.S. (wĭl′bẽr)	121	40°29′N	96°57′W
Wilburton, Ok., U.S. (wĭl′bẽr-tŭn)	121	34°54′N	95°18′W
Wilcannia, Austl. (wĭl-căn-ĭȧ)	219	31°30′S	143°30′E
Wildau, Ger. (vĕl′dou)	159b	52°20′N	13°39′E
Wildberg, Ger. (vĕl′bĕrgh)	159b	52°52′N	12°39′E
Wildcat Hill, hill, Can. (wīld′kăt)	97	53°17′N	102°30′W
Wildhay, r., Can. (wīld′hā)	95	53°15′N	117°20′W
Wildomar, Ca., U.S. (wĭl′dô-mär)	117a	33°35′N	117°17′W
Wild Rice, r., Mn., U.S.	112	47°10′N	96°40′W
Wild Rice, r., N.D., U.S.	112	46°10′N	97°12′W
Wild Rice Lake, l., Mn., U.S.	117h	46°54′N	92°10′W
Wildspitze, mtn., Aus.	168	46°55′N	10°50′E
Wildwood, N.J., U.S.	109	39°00′N	74°50′W
Wiley, Co., U.S. (wī′lē)	120	38°08′N	102°41′W
Wilge, r., S. Afr. (wĭl′jē)	238c	25°38′S	29°09′E
Wilge, r., S. Afr.	238c	27°27′S	28°46′E
Wilhelm, Mount, mtn., Pap. N. Gui.	213	5°58′S	144°58′E
Wilhelmina Gebergte, mts., Sur.	143	4°30′N	57°00′W
Wilhelmina Kanaal, can., Neth.	159a	51°37′N	4°55′E
Wilhelmshaven, Ger. (vēl-hĕlms-hä′fĕn)	160	53°30′N	8°10′E
Wilkes-Barre, Pa., U.S. (wĭlks′băr-ē)	105	41°15′N	75°50′W
Wilkes Land, reg., Ant.	224	71°00′S	126°00′E
Wilkeson, Wa., U.S. (wĭl-kē′sŭn)	116a	47°06′N	122°03′W
Wilkie, Can. (wĭlk′ē)	90	52°25′N	108°43′W
Wilkinsburg, Pa., U.S. (wĭl′kĭnz-bûrg)	111e	40°26′N	79°53′W
Willamette, r., Or., U.S.	106	45°00′N	123°00′W
Willapa Bay, b., Wa., U.S.	114	46°37′N	124°00′W
Willard, Oh., U.S. (wĭl′ȧrd)	108	41°00′N	82°50′W
Willard, Ut., U.S.	117b	41°24′N	112°02′W
Willcox, Az., U.S. (wĭl′kŏks)	119	32°15′N	109°50′W
Willcox Playa, l., Az., U.S.	119	32°08′N	109°51′W
Willemstad, Neth. Ant.	142	12°12′N	68°58′W
Willesden, Eng., U.K. (wĭlz′dĕn)	158b	51°31′N	0°17′W
William "Bill" Dannelly Reservoir, res., Al., U.S.	124	32°10′N	87°15′W
William Creek, Austl. (wĭl′yăm)	218	28°45′S	136°20′E

ăt; finăl; rāte; senâte; ärm; åsk; sofȧ; fâre; ch-choose; dh-as th in other; bē; ēvent; bĕt; recĕnt; cratẽr; g-gō; gh-guttural g; bĭt; ĭ-short neutral; rīde; κ-guttural k as ch in German ich;

PLACE (Pronunciation)	PAGE	LAT.	LONG.
Williams, Az., U.S. (wĭl′yămz)	119	35°15′N	112°15′W
Williams, i., Bah.	134	24°30′N	78°30′W
Williamsburg, Ky., U.S. (wĭl′yămz-bûrg)	124	36°42′N	84°09′W
Williamsburg, Oh., U.S.	111f	39°04′N	84°02′W
Williamsburg, Va., U.S.	125	37°15′N	76°41′W
Williams Lake, Can.	95	52°08′N	122°09′W
Williamson, W.V., U.S. (wĭl′yăm-sŭn)	108	37°40′N	82°15′W
Williamsport, Md., U.S.	109	39°35′N	77°45′W
Williamsport, Pa., U.S.	109	41°15′N	77°05′W
Williamston, N.C., U.S. (wĭl′yămz-tŭn)	125	35°50′N	77°04′W
Williamston, S.C., U.S.	125	34°36′N	82°30′W
Williamstown, Austl.	217a	37°52′S	144°54′E
Williamstown, W.V., U.S. (wĭl′yămz-toun)	108	39°20′N	81°30′W
Williamsville, N.Y., U.S. (wĭl′yăm-vĭl)	111c	42°58′N	78°46′W
Willimantic, Ct., U.S. (wĭl-ĭ-măn′tĭk)	109	41°40′N	72°10′W
Willis, Tx., U.S. (wĭl′ĭs)	123	30°24′N	95°29′W
Willis Islands, is., Austl.	221	16°15′S	150°30′E
Williston, N.D., U.S. (wĭl′ĭs-tŭn)	104	48°08′N	103°38′W
Williston, Lake, l., Can.	92	55°40′N	123°40′W
Willmar, Mn., U.S. (wĭl′mär)	112	45°07′N	95°05′W
Willoughby, Oh., U.S. (wĭl′ô-bē)	111d	41°39′N	81°25′W
Willow, Ak., U.S.	103	61°50′N	150°00′W
Willow Creek, r., Or., U.S.	114	44°21′N	117°34′W
Willow Grove, Pa., U.S.	110f	40°07′N	75°07′W
Willowick, Oh., U.S. (wĭl′ô-wĭk)	111d	41°39′N	81°28′W
Willowmore, S. Afr. (wĭl′ô-môr)	232	33°15′S	23°37′E
Willow Run, Mi., U.S. (wĭl′ô rŭn)	111b	42°16′N	83°34′W
Willows, Ca., U.S. (wĭl′ōz)	118	39°32′N	122°11′W
Willow Springs, Mo., U.S. (sprĭngz)	121	36°59′N	91°56′W
Willowvale, S. Afr. (wĭ-lô′văl)	233c	32°17′S	28°32′E
Wills Point, Tx., U.S. (wĭlz point)	123	32°42′N	96°02′W
Wilmer, Tx., U.S. (wĭl′mēr)	117c	32°35′N	96°40′W
Wilmette, Il., U.S. (wĭl-mĕt′)	111a	42°04′N	87°42′W
Wilmington, Austl.	222	32°39′S	138°07′E
Wilmington, Ca., U.S. (wĭl′mĭng-tŭn)	117a	33°46′N	118°16′W
Wilmington, De., U.S.	105	39°45′N	75°33′W
Wilmington, Il., U.S.	111a	41°19′N	88°09′W
Wilmington, Ma., U.S.	101a	42°34′N	71°10′W
Wilmington, N.C., U.S.	105	34°12′N	77°56′W
Wilmington, Oh., U.S.	108	39°20′N	83°50′W
Wilmore, Ky., U.S. (wĭl′mōr)	108	37°50′N	84°35′W
Wilmslow, Eng., U.K. (wĭlmz′lō)	158a	53°19′N	2°14′W
Wilno *see* Vilnius, Lith.	178	54°40′N	25°26′E
Wilpoort, S. Afr.	238c	26°57′S	26°17′E
Wilson, Ar., U.S. (wĭl′sŭn)	121	35°35′N	90°02′W
Wilson, N.C., U.S.	125	35°42′N	77°55′W
Wilson, Ok., U.S.	121	34°09′N	97°27′W
Wilson, r., Al., U.S.	124	34°53′N	87°28′W
Wilson, Mount, mtn., Ca., U.S.	117a	34°15′N	118°06′W
Wilson, Point, c., Austl.	217a	38°05′S	144°31′E
Wilson Lake, res., Al., U.S.	107	34°45′N	87°30′W
Wilson's Promontory, pen., Austl. (wĭl′sŭnz)	221	39°05′S	146°50′E
Wilsonville, Il., U.S. (wĭl′sŭn-vĭl)	117e	39°04′N	89°52′W
Wilstedt, Ger. (vēl′shtĕt)	159c	53°45′N	10°04′E
Wilster, Ger. (vēl′stĕr)	159c	53°55′N	9°23′E
Wilton, Ct., U.S. (wĭl′tŭn)	110a	41°11′N	73°25′W
Wilton, N.D., U.S.	112	47°09′N	100°47′W
Wiluna, Austl. (wĭ-lōō′nȧ)	218	26°35′S	120°25′E
Winamac, In., U.S. (wĭn′ȧ măk)	108	41°05′N	86°40′W
Winburg, S. Afr. (wĭm-bûrg)	238c	28°31′S	27°02′E
Winchester, Eng., U.K.	164	51°04′N	1°20′W
Winchester, Ca., U.S. (wĭn′chĕs-tēr)	117a	33°41′N	117°06′W
Winchester, Id., U.S.	114	46°14′N	116°39′W
Winchester, In., U.S.	108	40°10′N	84°50′W
Winchester, Ky., U.S.	108	38°00′N	84°15′W
Winchester, Ma., U.S.	101a	42°28′N	71°09′W
Winchester, N.H., U.S.	109	42°45′N	72°25′W
Winchester, Tn., U.S.	124	35°11′N	86°06′W
Winchester, Va., U.S.	109	39°10′N	78°10′W
Wind, r., Wy., U.S.	115	43°17′N	109°02′W
Windber, Pa., U.S. (wĭnd′bēr)	109	40°15′N	78°45′W
Wind Cave National Park, rec., S.D., U.S.	112	43°36′N	103°53′W
Winder, Ga., U.S. (wĭn′dēr)	124	33°58′N	83°43′W
Windermere, Eng., U.K. (wĭn′dēr-mēr)	164	54°25′N	2°59′W
Windham, Ct., U.S. (wĭnd′ăm)	109	41°45′N	72°05′W
Windham, N.H., U.S.	101a	42°49′N	71°21′W
Windhoek, Nmb. (vĭnt′hŏk)	232	22°05′S	17°10′E
Wind Lake, l., Wi., U.S.	111a	42°49′N	88°06′W
Wind Mountain, mtn., N.M., U.S.	122	32°02′N	105°30′W
Windom, Mn., U.S. (wĭn′dŭm)	112	43°50′N	95°04′W
Windora, Austl. (wĭn-dō′rȧ)	219	25°15′S	142°50′E
Wind River Indian Reservation, I.R., Wy., U.S.	115	43°26′N	109°00′W
Wind River Range, mts., Wy., U.S.	106	43°19′N	109°47′W
Windsor, Austl. (wĭn′zēr)	217b	33°37′S	150°49′E
Windsor, Can.	91	42°19′N	83°00′W
Windsor, Can.	93a	48°57′N	55°40′W
Windsor, Can.	91	44°59′N	64°08′W
Windsor, Eng., U.K.	164	51°27′N	0°37′W
Windsor, Co., U.S.	120	40°27′N	104°51′W
Windsor, Mo., U.S.	121	38°32′N	93°31′W
Windsor, N.C., U.S.	125	35°58′N	76°57′W
Windsor, Vt., U.S.	109	43°30′N	72°25′W
Windward Islands, is., N.A. (wĭnd′wērd)	129	12°45′N	61°40′W
Windward Passage, strt., N.A.	129	19°30′N	74°20′W
Winefred Lake, l., Can.	96	55°30′N	110°35′W
Winfield, Ks., U.S.	121	37°14′N	97°00′W
Winifred, Mt., U.S. (wĭn ĭ frĕd)	115	47°35′N	109°20′W
Winisk, r., Can.	93	54°30′N	86°30′W
Wink, Tx., U.S. (wĭŋk)	122	31°48′N	103°06′W
Winkler, Can. (wĭnk′lēr)	97	49°11′N	97°56′W
Winneba, Ghana (wĭn′ē-bȧ)	234	5°25′N	0°36′W
Winnebago, Mn., U.S. (wĭn′ē-bā′gō)	113	43°45′N	94°08′W
Winnebago, Lake, l., Wi., U.S.	113	44°09′N	88°10′W
Winnebago Indian Reservation, I.R., Ne., U.S.	112	42°15′N	96°06′W
Winnemucca, Nv., U.S. (wĭn-ē-mŭk′ȧ)	104	40°59′N	117°43′W
Winnemucca, l., Nv., U.S.	118	40°06′N	119°07′W
Winner, S.D., U.S. (wĭn′ēr)	112	43°22′N	99°50′W
Winnetka, Il., U.S. (wĭ-nĕt′kȧ)	111a	42°07′N	87°44′W
Winnett, Mt., U.S. (wĭn′ĕt)	115	47°01′N	108°20′W
Winnfield, La., U.S. (wĭn′fēld)	123	31°56′N	92°39′W
Winnibigoshish, l., Mn., U.S. (wĭn′ĭ-bĭ-gō′shĭsh)	113	47°30′N	93°45′W
Winnipeg, Can. (wĭn′ĭ-pĕg)	90	49°53′N	97°09′W
Winnipeg, r., Can.	92	50°30′N	95°00′W
Winnipeg, Lake, l., Can.	92	52°00′N	97°00′W
Winnipegosis, Can. (wĭn′ĭ-pē-gō′sĭs)	90	51°39′N	99°56′W
Winnipegosis, l., Can.	92	52°30′N	100°00′W
Winnipesaukee, l., N.H., U.S. (wĭn′ē-pē-sô′kē)	109	43°40′N	71°20′W
Winnsboro, La., U.S. (wĭnz′bŭr′ô)	123	32°09′N	91°42′W
Winnsboro, S.C., U.S.	125	34°29′N	81°05′W
Winnsboro, Tx., U.S.	121	32°56′N	95°15′W
Winona, Can. (wĭ-nō′nȧ)	102d	43°13′N	79°39′W
Winona, Mn., U.S.	105	44°03′N	91°40′W
Winona, Ms., U.S.	124	33°29′N	89°43′W
Winooski, Vt., U.S. (wĭ-nōōs′kē)	109	44°30′N	73°10′W
Winsen, Ger. (vēn′zĕn)	159c	53°22′N	10°13′E
Winsford, Eng., U.K. (wĭnz′fērd)	158a	53°11′N	2°30′W
Winslow, Az., U.S. (wĭnz′lō)	119	35°00′N	110°45′W
Winslow, Wa., U.S.	116a	47°38′N	122°31′W
Winsted, Ct., U.S. (wĭn′stĕd)	109	41°55′N	73°05′W
Winster, Eng., U.K. (wĭn′stēr)	158a	53°08′N	1°38′W
Winston-Salem, N.C., U.S. (wĭn stŭn-sā′lĕm)	105	36°05′N	80°15′W
Winterberge, mts., Afr.	233c	32°18′S	26°25′E
Winter Garden, Fl., U.S. (wĭn′tēr gär′d′n)	125a	28°32′N	81°35′W
Winter Haven, Fl., U.S. (hā′vĕn)	125a	28°01′N	81°38′W
Winter Park, Fl., U.S. (pärk)	125a	28°35′N	81°21′W
Winters, Tx., U.S. (wĭn′tērz)	122	31°59′N	99°58′W
Winterset, Ia., U.S. (wĭn′tēr-sĕt)	113	41°19′N	94°03′W
Winterswijk, Neth.	171c	51°58′N	6°44′E
Winterthur, Switz. (vĭn′tĕr-tōōr)	168	47°30′N	8°32′E
Winterton, S. Afr.	233c	28°51′S	29°33′E
Winthrop, Ma., U.S.	101a	42°23′N	70°59′W
Winthrop, Me., U.S. (wĭn′thrŭp)	100	44°19′N	70°00′W
Winthrop, Mn., U.S.	113	44°31′N	94°20′W
Winton, Austl. (wĭn-tŭn)	219	22°17′S	143°08′E
Wipperfürth, Ger. (vĕ′pĕr-fürt)	171c	51°07′N	7°23′E
Wirksworth, Eng., U.K. (wûrks′wûrth)	158a	53°05′N	1°35′W
Wisconsin, state, U.S. (wĭs-kŏn′sĭn)	105	44°30′N	91°00′W
Wisconsin, r., Wi., U.S.	107	43°14′N	90°34′W
Wisconsin Dells, Wi., U.S.	113	43°38′N	89°46′W
Wisconsin Rapids, Wi., U.S.	113	44°24′N	89°50′W
Wishek, N.D., U.S. (wĭsh′ĕk)	112	46°15′N	99°34′W
Wisła, r., Pol. (vēs′wȧ)	156	52°30′N	20°00′E
Wisłoka, r., Pol. (vēs-wô′kȧ)	169	49°55′N	21°26′E
Wismar, Ger. (vĭs′mär)	160	53°53′N	11°28′E
Wismar, Guy. (wĭs′mȧr)	143	5°58′N	58°15′W
Wisner, Ne., U.S. (wĭz′nēr)	112	42°00′N	96°55′W
Wissembourg, Fr. (vē-sän-bōōr′)	171	49°03′N	7°58′E
Wister, Lake, l., Ok., U.S. (vĭs′tēr)	121	35°02′N	94°52′W
Witbank, S. Afr. (wĭt-băŋk)	238c	25°53′S	29°14′E
Witberg, mtn., Afr.	233c	30°32′S	27°18′E
Witham, Eng., U.K. (wĭdh′ăm)	158b	51°48′N	0°37′E
Witham, r., Eng., U.K.	158a	53°11′N	0°20′W
Withamsville, Oh., U.S. (wĭdh′ămz-vĭl)	111f	39°04′N	84°16′W
Withlacoochee, r., Fl., U.S. (wĭth-lȧ-kōō′chē)	125a	28°58′N	82°30′W
Withlacoochee, r., Ga., U.S.	124	31°15′N	83°30′W
Withrow, Mn., U.S. (wĭdh′rō)	117g	45°08′N	92°54′W
Witney, Eng., U.K. (wĭt′nē)	158b	51°45′N	1°30′W
Witt, Il., U.S. (vĭt)	108	39°10′N	89°15′W
Witten, Ger. (vē′tĕn)	171c	51°26′N	7°19′E
Wittenberg, Ger. (vē′tĕn-bĕrgh)	168	51°53′N	12°40′E
Wittenberge, Ger. (vĭt-ĕn-bĕr′gē)	168	52°59′N	11°45′E
Wittlich, Ger. (vĭt′lĭk)	168	49°58′N	6°54′E
Witu, Kenya (wē′tōō)	233	2°18′S	40°28′E
Witu Islands, is., Pap. N. Gui.	213	4°45′S	149°50′E
Witwatersberg, mts., S. Afr. (wĭt-wôr-tērz-bûrg)	233b	25°58′S	27°53′E
Witwatersrand, mtn., S. Afr. (wĭt-wôr′tērs-rănd)	238c	25°55′S	26°27′E
Wkra, r., Pol. (f′krȧ)	169	52°40′N	20°35′E
Włocławek, Pol. (vwô-tswä′vĕk)	169	52°38′N	19°08′E
Włodawa, Pol. (vwô-dä′vä)	169	51°33′N	23°33′E
Włoszczowa, Pol. (vwôsh-chô′vä)	169	50°51′N	19°58′E
Woburn, Ma., U.S. (wō′bŭrn) (wō′bŭrn)	101a	42°29′N	71°10′W
Woerden, Neth.	159a	52°05′N	4°52′E
Woking, Eng., U.K.	158b	51°18′N	0°33′W
Wokingham, Eng., U.K. (wō′kĭng-hăm)	158b	51°23′N	0°50′W
Wolcott, Ks., U.S. (wōl′kŏt)	117f	39°12′N	94°47′W
Wolf, i., Can. (wōlf)	99	44°10′N	76°25′W
Wolf, r., Ms., U.S.	124	30°45′N	89°36′W
Wolf, r., Wi., U.S.	113	45°14′N	88°45′W
Wolfenbüttel, Ger. (vôl′fĕn-büt-ĕl)	168	52°10′N	10°32′E
Wolf Lake, l., Il., U.S.	111a	41°39′N	87°33′W
Wolf Point, Mt., U.S. (wŏlf point)	115	48°07′N	105°40′W
Wolfratshausen, Ger. (vôlf′räts-hou-zĕn)	159d	47°55′N	11°25′E
Wolfsburg, Ger. (vôlfs′bōōrgh)	168	52°30′N	10°37′E
Wolfville, Can. (wŏlf′vĭl)	100	45°05′N	64°22′W
Wolgast, Ger. (vôl′găst)	168	54°04′N	13°46′E
Wolhuterskop, S. Afr.	233b	25°41′S	27°40′E
Wolkersdorf, Aus.	159e	48°24′N	16°31′E
Wollaston, l., Can. (wŏl′ȧs-tŭn)	92	58°15′N	103°20′W
Wollaston Peninsula, pen., Can.	92	70°00′N	115°00′W
Wollongong, Austl. (wŏol′ŭn-gŏng)	219	34°26′S	151°05′E
Wołomin, Pol. (vô-wō′mēn)	169	52°19′N	21°17′E
Wolseley, Can.	96	50°25′N	103°15′W
Woltersdorf, Ger. (vōl′tĕs-dŏrf)	159b	52°07′N	13°13′E
Wolverhampton, Eng., U.K. (wŏol′vēr-hămp-tŭn)	161	52°35′N	2°07′W
Wolwehoek, S. Afr.	238c	26°55′S	27°50′E
Wŏnsan, Kor., N. (wŭn′sän′)	205	39°08′N	127°24′E
Wonthaggi, Austl. (wŏnt-hăg′ē)	219	38°45′S	145°42′E
Wood, S.D., U.S. (wŏod)	112	43°26′N	100°25′W
Woodbine, Ia., U.S. (wŏod′bīn)	112	41°44′N	95°42′W
Woodbridge, N.J., U.S. (wŏod′brĭj′)	110a	40°33′N	74°18′W
Wood Buffalo National Park, rec., Can.	92	59°50′N	118°53′W
Woodburn, Il., U.S. (wŏod′bûrn)	117e	39°03′N	90°01′W
Woodburn, Or., U.S.	114	45°10′N	122°51′W
Woodbury, N.J., U.S. (wŏod′bĕr-ē)	110f	39°50′N	75°14′W
Woodcrest, Ca., U.S. (wŏod′krĕst)	117a	33°53′N	117°18′W
Woodinville, Wa., U.S. (wŏod′ĭn-vĭl)	116a	47°46′N	122°09′W
Woodland, Ca., U.S. (wŏod′lănd)	118	38°41′N	121°47′W
Woodland, Wa., U.S.	116c	45°54′N	122°45′W
Woodland Hills, Ca., U.S.	117a	34°10′N	118°36′W
Woodlark Island, i., Pap. N. Gui. (wŏod′lärk)	213	9°07′S	152°00′E
Woodlawn Beach, N.Y., U.S. (wŏod′lôn bēch)	111c	42°48′N	78°51′W
Wood Mountain, mtn., Can.	96	49°14′N	106°20′W
Wood River, Il., U.S.	117e	38°52′N	90°06′W
Woodroffe, Mount, mtn., Austl. (wŏod′rŭf)	220	26°05′S	132°00′E
Woodruff, S.C., U.S. (wŏod′rŭf)	125	34°43′N	82°03′W
Woods, l., Austl. (wŏodz)	220	18°00′S	133°18′E
Woods, Lake of the, l., N.A.	93	49°25′N	93°25′W
Woods Cross, Ut., U.S. (krôs)	117b	40°53′N	111°54′W
Woodsfield, Oh., U.S. (wŏodz-fēld)	108	39°45′N	81°10′W
Woodson, Or., U.S. (wŏod sŭn)	116c	46°07′N	123°20′W
Woodstock, Can. (wŏod′stŏk)	99	43°10′N	80°50′W
Woodstock, Can.	91	46°09′N	67°34′W
Woodstock, Eng., U.K.	158b	51°48′N	1°22′W
Woodstock, Il., U.S.	113	42°20′N	88°29′W
Woodstock, Va., U.S.	109	38°55′N	78°25′W
Woodsville, N.H., U.S. (wŏodz′vĭl)	109	44°10′N	72°00′W
Woodville, Ms., U.S. (wŏod′vĭl)	124	31°06′N	91°11′W
Woodville, Tx., U.S.	123	30°48′N	94°25′W
Woodward, Ok., U.S. (wŏod′wôrd)	120	36°25′N	99°24′W
Woolwich, Eng., U.K. (wŏol′ĭj)	158b	51°28′N	0°05′E
Woomera, Austl. (wōōm′ĕrȧ)	218	31°15′S	136°43′E
Woonsocket, R.I., U.S. (wōōn-sŏk′ĕt)	110b	42°00′N	71°30′W
Woonsocket, S.D., U.S.	112	44°03′N	98°17′W
Wooster, Oh., U.S. (wŏos′tēr)	108	40°50′N	81°55′W
Worcester, S. Afr. (wōōs′tēr)	232	33°35′S	19°31′E
Worcester, Eng., U.K. (wŏo′stēr)	161	52°09′N	2°14′W
Worcester, Ma., U.S. (wŏos′tēr)	105	42°16′N	71°49′W
Worcestershire, co., Eng., U.K.	158a	52°25′N	2°10′W
Worden, Il., U.S. (wôr′dĕn)	117e	38°56′N	89°50′W
Workington, Eng., U.K. (wûr′kĭng-tŭn)	164	54°40′N	3°30′W
Worksop, Eng., U.K. (wûrk′sŏp) (wûr′sŭp)	158a	53°18′N	1°07′W
Worland, Wy., U.S. (wûr′lănd)	115	44°02′N	107°56′W
Worms, Ger. (vōrms)	161	49°37′N	8°22′E
Worona Reservoir, res., Austl.	217b	34°12′S	150°55′E
Worth, Il., U.S. (wûrth)	111a	41°42′N	87°47′W
Wortham, Tx., U.S. (wûr′dhăm)	123	31°46′N	96°22′W
Worthing, Eng., U.K. (wûr′dhĭng)	164	50°48′N	0°29′W
Worthington, In., U.S. (wûr′dhĭng-tŭn)	108	39°05′N	87°00′W
Worthington, Mn., U.S.	112	43°38′N	95°36′W
Worth Lake, l., Tx., U.S.	117c	32°48′N	97°32′W
Wowoni, Pulau, i., Indon. (wō-wō′nē)	213	4°05′S	123°45′E
Wragby, Eng., U.K. (răg′bē)	158a	53°17′N	0°19′W
Wrangell, Ak., U.S. (răn′gĕl)	106a	56°28′N	132°25′W
Wrangell, Cape, c., Ak., U.S.	103a	52°55′N	172°30′E
Wrangell, Mount, mtn., Ak., U.S.	103	61°58′N	143°50′W
Wrangell Mountains, mts., Ak., U.S.	103	62°28′N	142°40′W
Wrangell-Saint Elias National Park, rec., Ak., U.S.	103	61°00′N	142°00′W
Wrath, Cape, c., Scot., U.K. (răth)	164	58°34′N	5°01′W
Wray, Co., U.S. (rā)	120	40°06′N	102°14′W
Wreak, r., Eng., U.K. (rēk)	158a	52°45′N	0°59′W
Wreck Reefs, rf., Austl. (rĕk)	221	22°00′S	155°52′E
Wrekin, The, mtn., Eng., U.K. (rĕk′ĭn)	158a	52°40′N	2°33′W
Wrens, Ga., U.S. (rĕnz)	125	33°15′N	82°25′W
Wrentham, Ma., U.S.	101a	42°04′N	71°20′W
Wrexham, Wales, U.K. (rĕk′săm)	164	53°03′N	3°00′W
Wrexham, co., Wales, U.K.	158a	53°00′N	2°57′W
Wrights Corners, N.Y., U.S. (rĭtz kôr′nērz)	111c	43°14′N	78°42′W
Wrightsville, Ga., U.S. (rīts′vĭl)	125	32°44′N	82°44′W
Wrocław, Pol. (vrôtsläv) (brĕs′lou)	169	51°07′N	17°10′E
Wrotham, Eng., U.K. (rōōt′ŭm)	158b	51°18′N	0°19′E
Września, Pol. (vzhăsh′nyȧ)	169	52°19′N	17°33′E
Wu, r., China (wōō′)	204	27°30′N	107°00′E
Wuchang, China	208	44°59′N	127°00′E
Wuchang, China (wōō-chäŋ)	205	30°32′N	114°25′E
Wucheng, China (wōō-chŭŋ)	206	37°14′N	116°03′E
Wuhan, China	205	30°30′N	114°15′E

ng-sing; ŋ-baŋk; N-nasalized n; nŏd; cŏmmit; ōld; ôbey; ôrder; oi-boil; fōōd; ŏo-as oo in foot; ou-out; s-soft; sh-dish; th-thin; pūre; ûnite; ûrn; stŭd; circŭs; ü-as in French tu; ′-indeterminate vowel.

ăt; finăl; rāte; senåte; ärm; åsk; sofá; fåre; ch-choose; dh-as th in other; bē; ĕvent; bĕt; recĕnt; cratĕr; g-gō; gh-guttural g; bĭt; ĭ-short neutral; rīde; ᴋ-guttural k as ch in German ich;

PRONOUNCING INDEX Yellowstone National Park – Zeya 369

PLACE (Pronunciation)	PAGE	LAT.	LONG.
Yellowstone National Park, rec., U.S. (yĕl′o̊-stōn)	106	44°45′N	110°35′W
Yel′nya, Russia (yĕl′nyȧ)	176	54°34′N	33°12′E
Yemanzhelinsk, Russia (yĕ-mȧn-zhâ′lĭnsk)	186a	54°47′N	61°24′E
Yemen, nation, Asia (yĕm′ĕn)	198	15°00′N	47°00′E
Yemetsk, Russia	180	63°28′N	41°28′E
Yenangyaung, Mya. (yā′nän-d oung)	199	20°27′N	94°59′E
Yencheng, China	204	37°30′N	79°26′E
Yendi, Ghana (yĕn′de̊)	230	9°26′N	0°01′W
Yengisar, China (yŭn-gē-sär)	204	39°01′N	75°29′E
Yenice, r., Tur.	181	41°10′N	33°00′E
Yenisey, r., Russia (yĕ-ne̊-sĕ′e̊)	178	71°00′N	82°00′E
Yeniseysk, Russia (yĕ-nĭĕsā′ĭsk)	179	58°27′N	90°28′E
Yeo, l., Austl. (yō)	220	28°15′S	124°00′E
Yerevan, Arm. (yĕ-rĕ-vän′)	181	40°10′N	44°30′E
Yerington, Nv., U.S. (ye̊′rĭng-tŭn)	118	38°59′N	119°10′W
Yermak, i., Russia	180	66°45′N	71°30′E
Yeste, Spain (yĕs′tå)	172	38°23′N	2°19′W
Yeu, Île d′, i., Fr. (ēl dyû)	161	46°43′N	2°45′W
Yevlax, Azer.	182	40°36′N	47°09′E
Yexian, China (yŭ-shyĕn)	206	37°09′N	119°57′E
Yeya, r., Russia (yă′yȧ)	177	46°25′N	39°17′E
Yeysk, Russia (yĕysk)	181	46°41′N	38°13′E
Yi, r., China	206	34°38′N	118°07′E
Yibin, China (yē-bĭn)	204	28°50′N	104°40′E
Yichang, China (yē-chäŋ)	205	30°38′N	111°22′E
Yidu, China (yē-do͞o)	208	36°42′N	118°30′E
Yilan, China (yē-län)	205	46°10′N	129°40′E
Yinchuan, China (yĭn-chůän)	204	38°22′N	106°22′E
Yingkou, China (yĭŋ-kō)	205	40°35′N	122°10′E
Yining, China (yē-nĭŋ)	204	43°58′N	80°40′E
Yin Shan, mts., China (yĭng′shän′)	208	40°50′N	110°30′E
Yishan, China (yē-shän)	204	24°32′N	108°42′E
Yishui, China (yē-shwā)	206	35°49′N	118°40′E
Yitong, China (yē-to̊ŋ)	205	43°15′N	125°10′E
Yixian, China (yē shyĕn)	208	41°30′N	121°15′E
Yixing, China	206	31°26′N	119°57′E
Yiyang, China (yē-yäŋ)	209	28°52′N	112°12′E
Yoakum, Tx., U.S. (yō′kŭm)	123	29°18′N	97°09′W
Yockanookany, r., Ms., U.S. (yŏk′ȧ-no͞o-kă-nī)	124	32°47′N	89°38′W
Yodo-Gawa, strt., Japan (yō′dō′gä-wä)	211b	34°46′N	135°35′E
Yog Point, c., Phil. (yōg)	209	14°00′N	124°30′E
Yogyakarta, Indon. (yŏg-yȧ-kär′tȧ)	212	7°50′S	110°20′E
Yoho National Park, rec., Can. (yō′hō)	90	51°26′N	116°30′W
Yojoa, Lago de, l., Hond. (lä′gô dĕ yo̊-hō′ä)	132	14°49′N	87°53′W
Yokkaichi, Japan (yo̊′kä′e̊-che̊)	210	34°58′N	136°35′E
Yokohama, Japan (yō′ko̊-hä′mą)	205	35°37′N	139°40′E
Yokosuka, Japan (yo̊-kō′sȯ-kä)	210	35°17′N	139°40′E
Yokota, Japan (yō-kō′tä)	211a	35°23′N	140°02′E
Yola, Nig. (yō′lä)	230	9°13′N	12°27′E
Yolaina, Cordillera de, mts., Nic.	133	11°34′N	84°34′W
Yomou, Gui.	234	7°34′N	9°16′W
Yonago, Japan (yō′nä-gō)	210	35°27′N	133°19′E
Yonezawa, Japan (yō′nĕ′zȧ-wä)	210	37°50′N	140°07′E
Yong′an, China (yo̊ŋ-än)	209	26°00′N	117°22′E
Yongding, r., China (yo̊ŋ-dĭŋ)	208	40°25′N	115°00′E
Yŏngdŏk, Kor., S. (yŭng′dŭk′)	210	36°28′N	129°25′E
Yŏnghŭng, Kor., N. (yŭng′hȯng′)	210	39°31′N	127°11′E
Yonghŭng Man, b., Kor., N.	210	39°10′N	128°00′E
Yongnian, China (yo̊ŋ-nĭĕn)	208	36°47′N	114°32′E
Yongqing, China (yo̊ŋ-chyĭŋ)	208a	39°18′N	116°27′E
Yongshun, China (yo̊ŋ-shȯn)	204	29°05′N	109°58′E
Yonkers, N.Y., U.S. (yŏŋ′kẽrz)	110a	40°57′N	73°54′W
Yonne, r., Fr. (yo̊n)	170	48°18′N	3°15′E
Yono, Japan (yō′nō)	211a	35°53′N	139°36′E
Yorba Linda, Ca., U.S. (yôr′bă lĭn′dȧ)	117a	33°55′N	117°51′W
York, Austl.	218	32°00′S	117°00′E
York, Eng., U.K.	160	53°58′N	1°10′W
York, Al., U.S. (yôrk)	124	32°33′N	88°16′W
York, Ne., U.S.	121	40°52′N	97°36′W
York, Pa., U.S.	105	40°00′N	76°40′W
York, S.C., U.S.	125	34°59′N	81°14′W
York, Cape, c., Austl.	221	10°45′S	142°35′E
York, Kap, c., Grnld.	89	75°30′N	73°00′W
Yorke Peninsula, pen., Austl.	222	34°24′S	137°20′E
Yorketown, Austl.	222	35°00′S	137°28′E
York Factory, Can.	97	57°05′N	92°18′W
Yorkshire Wolds, Eng., U.K. (yôrk′shĭr)	164	54°00′N	0°35′W
Yorkton, Can. (yôrk′tŭn)	90	51°13′N	102°28′W
Yorktown, Tx., U.S. (yôrk′toun)	123	28°57′N	97°30′W
Yorktown, Va., U.S.	125	37°12′N	76°31′W
Yoro, Hond. (yō′ro̊)	132	15°09′N	87°05′W
Yoron, i., Japan	210	26°48′N	128°40′E
Yosemite National Park, rec., Ca., U.S. (yo̊-sĕm′ĭ-te̊)	106	38°03′N	119°36′W
Yoshida, Japan (yō′she̊-dȧ)	211	34°39′N	132°41′E
Yoshikawa, Japan (yō-she̊′kä′wä′)	211a	35°53′N	139°51′E
Yoshino, r., Japan (yō′shē-nō)	211	34°04′N	133°57′E
Yoshkar-Ola, Russia (yôsh-kär′o̊-lä′)	180	56°35′N	48°05′E
Yos Sudarsa, Pulau, i., Indon.	213	7°20′S	138°30′E
Yŏsu, Kor., S. (yŭ′so͞o′)	210	34°42′N	127°42′W
You, r., China (yō)	209	23°55′N	106°50′E
Youghal, Ire. (yo͞o′ôl) (yôl)	165	51°58′N	7°57′E
Youghal Bay, b., Ire.	164	51°52′N	7°46′W
Young, Austl. (yŭng)	222	34°15′S	148°18′E
Young, Ur. (yô-o͞o′ng)	141c	32°42′S	57°38′W
Youngs, l., Wa., U.S. (yŭngz)	116a	47°25′N	122°08′W
Youngstown, N.Y., U.S.	111c	43°15′N	79°02′W
Youngstown, Oh., U.S.	108	41°05′N	80°40′W
Yozgat, Tur. (yo̊z′gȧd)	198	39°50′N	34°50′E
Ypsilanti, Mi., U.S. (ĭp-sĭ-lăn′tĭ)	111b	42°15′N	83°37′W
Yreka, Ca., U.S. (wī-rē′kȧ)	114	41°43′N	122°36′W
Yrghyz, Kaz.	183	48°30′N	61°17′E
Yrghyz, r., Kaz.	156	49°30′N	60°32′E
Ysleta, Tx., U.S. (e̊z-lĕ′tȧ)	122	31°42′N	106°18′W
Yssingeaux, Fr. (ē-săɴ-zhō)	170	45°09′N	4°08′E
Ystad, Swe.	160	55°25′N	13°49′E
Ystādeh-ye Moqor, Āb-e, l., Afg.	202	32°35′N	68°00′E
Yu′alliq, Jabal, mts., Egypt	197a	30°12′N	33°42′E
Yuan, r., China (yůän)	205	28°50′N	110°50′E
Yuan′an, China (yůän-än)	209	31°08′N	111°28′E
Yuanling, China (yůän-lĭŋ)	209	28°30′N	110°18′E
Yuanshi, China (yůän-shr)	208	37°45′N	114°32′E
Yuasa, Japan	211	34°02′N	135°10′E
Yuba City, Ca., U.S. (yo͞o′bȧ)	118	39°08′N	121°38′W
Yucaipa, Ca., Ca., U.S. (yŭ-kȧ-ē′pȧ)	117a	34°02′N	117°02′W
Yucatán, state, Mex. (yo͞o-kä-tän′)	128	20°45′N	89°00′W
Yucatan Channel, strt., N.A.	128	22°30′N	87°00′W
Yucatan Peninsula, pen., N.A.	132	19°30′N	89°00′W
Yucheng, China (yo͞o-chŭŋ)	206	34°31′N	115°54′E
Yucheng, China	208	36°55′N	116°39′E
Yuci, China (yo͞o-tsz)	208	37°32′N	112°40′E
Yudoma, r., Russia (yo͞o-dō′mȧ)	185	59°13′N	137°00′E
Yueqing, China (yůĕ-chyĭn)	209	28°02′N	120°40′E
Yueyang, China (yůĕ-yäŋ)	205	29°25′N	113°05′E
Yuezhuang, China (yůĕ-jůäŋ)	206	36°13′N	118°17′E
Yug, r., Russia (yȯg)	180	59°50′N	45°55′E
Yugoslavia, *see* Serbia and Montenegro, nation, Eur. (yo͞o-go̊-slä-vĭ-ȧ)	154	44°00′N	21°00′E
Yukhnov, Russia (yȯk′nof)	176	54°44′N	35°15′E
Yukon, ter., Can. (yo͞o′kŏn)	90	63°16′N	135°30′W
Yukon, r., N.A.	106a	64°00′N	159°30′W
Yukutat Bay, b., Ak., U.S. (yo͞o-kū tăt′)	103	59°34′N	140°50′W
Yuldybayevo, Russia (yȯld′bä′yĕ-vô)	186a	52°20′N	57°52′E
Yulin, China (yo͞o-lĭn)	209	22°38′N	110°10′E
Yulin, China	204	38°18′N	109°45′E
Yuma, Az., U.S. (yo͞o′mä)	104	32°40′N	114°40′W
Yuma, Co., U.S.	120	40°08′N	102°50′W
Yuma, r., Dom. Rep.	135	19°05′N	70°05′W
Yumbi, D.R.C.	237	1°14′S	26°14′E
Yumen, China (yo͞o-mŭn)	204	40°14′N	96°56′E
Yuncheng, China (yȯn-chŭŋ)	208	35°00′N	110°40′E
Yunnan, prov., China (yun′nän′)	204	24°23′N	101°03′E
Yunnan Plat, plat., China (yȯ-nän)	204	26°03′N	101°26′E
Yunxian, China (yȯn shyĕn)	205	32°50′N	110°55′E
Yunxiao, China (yȯn-shyou)	209	24°00′N	117°20′E
Yura, Japan (yo͞o′rä)	211	34°18′N	134°54′E
Yurécuaro, Mex. (yo͞o-rā′kwä-ro̊)	130	20°21′N	102°16′W
Yurimaguas, Peru (yo͞o-re̊-mä′gwäs)	142	5°59′S	76°12′W
Yuriria, Mex. (yo͞o′re̊-rē′ä)	130	20°11′N	101°08′W
Yurovo, Russia	186b	55°30′N	38°24′E
Yur′yevets, Russia	180	57°15′N	43°08′E
Yuscarán, Hond. (yo͞os-kä-rän′)	132	13°57′N	86°48′W
Yushan, China (yo͞o-shän)	209	28°42′N	118°20′E
Yü Shan, mtn., Tai.	205	23°38′N	121°05′E
Yushu, China (yo͞o-sho͞o)	208	44°58′N	126°32′E
Yutian, China (yo͞o-tĭĕn)	208	39°54′N	117°45′E
Yutian, China (yo͞o-tĭĕn) (kŭ-r-yä)	204	36°55′N	81°39′E
Yuty, Para. (yo͞o-tē′)	144	26°45′S	56°13′W
Yuwangcheng, China (yü′wäng′chĕng)	206	31°32′N	114°26′E
Yuxian, China (yo͞o shyĕn)	208	39°40′N	114°38′E
Yuzha, Russia (yo͞o′zhȧ)	180	56°38′N	42°20′E
Yuzhno-Sakhalinsk, Russia (yo͞ozh′nô-sä-кä-lĭnsk′)	179	47°11′N	143°04′E
Yuzhnoural′skiy, Russia (yo͞ozh-nô-ȯ-rál′skĭ)	186a	54°26′N	61°17′E
Yuzhnyy Ural, mts., Russia (yo͞o′zhnĭ ȯ-räl′)	186a	52°51′N	57°48′E
Yverdon, Switz. (e̊-vĕr-dôn)	168	46°46′N	6°35′E
Yvetot, Fr. (ēv-tō′)	170	49°39′N	0°45′E

Z

PLACE (Pronunciation)	PAGE	LAT.	LONG.
Za, r., Mor.	162	34°19′N	2°23′W
Zaachila, Mex. (sä-ä-chē′lȧ)	131	16°56′N	96°45′W
Zaandam, Neth. (zän′dȧm)	165	52°25′N	4°49′E
Ząbkowice Śląskie, Pol.	168	50°35′N	16°48′E
Zabrze, Pol. (zäb′zhĕ)	161	50°18′N	18°48′E
Zacapa, Guat. (sä-kä′pä)	132	14°56′N	89°30′W
Zacapoaxtla, Mex. (sä-kä-pō-äs′tlä)	131	19°51′N	97°34′W
Zacatecas, Mex. (sä-kä-tā′käs)	128	22°44′N	102°32′W
Zacatecas, state, Mex.	128	24°00′N	102°45′W
Zacatecoluca, El Sal. (sä-kä-tå-ko̊-lo͞o′kä)	132	13°31′N	88°50′W
Zacatelco, Mex.	130	19°12′N	98°12′W
Zacatepec, Mex. (sä-kä-tå-pĕk′) (sän-te̊-ä′go̊)	131	17°10′N	95°53′W
Zacatlán, Mex. (sä-kä-tlän′)	131	19°55′N	97°57′W
Zacoalco de Torres, Mex. (sä-ko̊-äl′ko̊ dā tōr′rĕs)	130	20°12′N	103°33′W
Zacualpan, Mex. (sä-kȯ-äl-pän′)	130	18°43′N	99°46′W
Zacualtipan, Mex. (sȧ-kȯ-äl-tē-pän′)	130	20°38′N	98°39′W
Zadar, Cro. (zä′där)	154	44°08′N	15°16′E
Zadonsk, Russia (zä-dônsk′)	176	52°22′N	38°55′E
Žagare, Lat. (zhȧgȧrĕ)	167	56°21′N	23°14′E
Zagarolo, Italy (tzä-gä-rô′lo̊)	173d	41°51′N	12°53′E
Zaghouan, Tun. (zȧ-gwäɴ′)	230	36°30′N	10°04′E
Zagreb, Cro. (zä′grĕb)	154	45°50′N	15°58′E
Zagros Mountains, mts., Iran	198	33°30′N	46°30′E
Zāhedān, Iran (zä′hå-dān)	198	29°37′N	60°31′E
Zahlah, Leb. (zä′lā′)	197a	33°50′N	35°54′E
Zaire *see* Congo, Democratic Republic of the , nation, Afr.	232	1°00′S	22°15′E
Zaječar, Serb. (zä′yĕ-chär′)	175	43°54′N	22°16′E
Zakhidnyi Buh (Bug), r., Eur.	168	52°29′N	21°20′E
Zakopane, Pol. (zȧ-kô-pä′nĕ)	169	49°18′N	19°57′E
Zakouma, Parc National de, rec., Chad	235	10°50′N	19°20′E
Zákynthos, Grc.	175	37°48′N	20°55′E
Zákynthos, i., Grc.	163	37°45′N	20°32′E
Zalaegerszeg, Hung. (zŏ′lô-ĕ′gĕr-sĕg)	168	46°50′N	16°50′E
Zalău, Rom. (zȧ-lŭ′ȯ)	169	47°11′N	23°06′E
Zalţan, Libya	231	28°20′N	19°40′E
Zaltbommel, Neth.	159a	51°48′N	5°15′E
Zambezi, r., Afr. (zȧm-bā′ze̊)	232	16°00′S	29°45′E
Zambia, nation, Afr. (zăm′be̊-ȧ)	232	14°23′S	24°15′E
Zamboanga, Phil. (säm-bo̊-aŋ′gä)	212	6°58′N	122°02′E
Zambrów, Pol. (zäm′brȯf)	169	52°29′N	22°17′E
Zamora, Mex. (sä-mō′rä)	128	19°59′N	102°16′W
Zamora, Spain (thä-mō′rä)	162	41°32′N	5°43′W
Zanatepec, Mex.	131	16°30′N	94°22′W
Zandvoort, Neth.	159a	52°22′N	4°30′E
Zanesville, Oh., U.S. (zānz′vĭl)	108	39°55′N	82°00′W
Zangasso, Mali	234	12°09′N	5°37′W
Zanjān, Iran	198	36°26′N	48°24′E
Zanzibar, Tan. (zăn′zĭ-bär)	233	6°10′S	39°11′E
Zanzibar, i., Tan.	233	6°20′S	39°37′E
Zanzibar Channel, strt., Tan.	237	6°05′S	39°00′E
Zaozhuang, China (dzou-jůäŋ)	206	34°51′N	117°34′E
Zapadnaya Dvina *see* Western Dvina, r., Eur.	167	55°30′N	28°27′E
Zapala, Arg. (zä-pä′lä)	144	38°53′S	70°02′W
Zapata, Tx., U.S. (sä-pä′tä)	122	26°52′N	99°18′W
Zapata, Ciénaga de, sw., Cuba (syĕ′nä-gä-dĕ-zä-pȧ′tä)	134	22°30′N	81°20′W
Zapata, Península de, pen., Cuba (pĕ-ne̊′n-so͞o-lä-dĕ-zä-pȧ′tä)	134	22°20′N	81°30′W
Zapatera, Isla, i., Nic. (e̊′s-lä-sä-pä-tā′rō)	132	11°45′N	85°45′W
Zapopan, Mex. (sä-pō′pän)	130	20°42′N	103°23′W
Zaporizhzhia, Ukr.	178	47°50′N	35°10′E
Zaporizhzhia, prov., Ukr.	177	47°20′N	35°05′E
Zaporoshskoye, Russia (zȧ-po̊-rôsh′sko̊-yĕ)	167	60°36′N	30°31′E
Zapotiltic, Mex. (sä-po̊-te̊l-tēk′)	130	19°37′N	103°25′W
Zapotitlán, Mex. (sä-po̊-te̊-tlän′)	130	17°13′N	98°58′W
Zapotitlán, Punta, c., Mex.	131	18°34′N	94°48′W
Zapotlanejo, Mex. (sä-po̊-tlä-nā′ho̊)	130	20°38′N	103°05′W
Zaragoza, Mex. (sä-rä-gō′sä)	130	23°59′N	99°45′W
Zaragoza, Mex.	130	22°02′N	100°45′W
Zaragoza, Spain (thä-rä-gō′thä)	154	41°39′N	0°53′W
Zarand, Munţii, mts., Rom.	169	46°07′N	22°21′E
Zaranda Hill, mtn., Nig.	235	10°15′N	9°35′E
Zaranj, Afg.	201	31°06′N	61°53′E
Zarasai, Lith. (zä-rä-sī′)	167	55°45′N	26°18′E
Zárate, Arg. (zä-rä′tā)	144	34°05′S	59°05′W
Zaraysk, Russia (zä-rä′e̊sk)	180	54°46′N	38°53′E
Zaria, Nig. (zä′re̊-ä)	230	11°07′N	7°44′E
Zarqā′, r., Jord.	197a	32°13′N	35°43′E
Zarzal, Col. (zär-zȧ′l)	142a	4°23′N	76°04′W
Zashiversk, Russia (zȧ′shĭ-vĕrsk′)	179	67°08′N	144°02′E
Zastavna, Ukr. (zȧs-täf′nȧ)	169	48°32′N	25°50′E
Zastron, S. Afr. (zȧs′trŭn)	233c	30°19′S	27°07′E
Žatec, Czech Rep. (zhä′tĕts)	168	50°19′N	13°32′E
Zavitinsk, Russia	185	50°12′N	129°44′E
Zawiercie, Pol. (zȧ-vyĕr′tsyĕ)	169	50°28′N	19°25′E
Zāwiyat al-Baydā′, Libya	231	32°49′N	21°46′E
Zāyandeh, r., Iran	198	32°15′N	51°00′E
Zaysan, Kaz. (zī′sȧn)	183	47°43′N	84°44′E
Zaza, r., Cuba (zȧ′zȧ)	134	21°40′N	79°25′W
Zbarazh, Ukr. (zbä-räzh′)	169	49°39′N	25°48′E
Zbruch, r., Ukr. (zbrȯch)	169	48°56′N	26°18′E
Zdolbuniv, Ukr.	169	50°31′N	26°17′E
Zduńska Wola, Pol. (zdo͞on′′skä vō′lä)	169	51°36′N	18°27′E
Zebediela, S. Afr.	238c	24°19′S	29°21′E
Zeeland, Mi., U.S. (zē′lănd)	108	42°50′N	86°00′W
Zefat, Isr.	197a	32°58′N	35°30′E
Zehdenick, Ger. (tsā′dĕ-ne̊k)	168	52°59′N	13°20′E
Zehlendorf, Ger. (tsā′lĕn-dôrf)	159b	52°47′N	13°23′E
Zeist, Neth.	159a	52°05′N	5°14′E
Zelenogorsk, Russia (zĕ-lă′no̊-go̊rsk)	167	60°13′N	29°39′E
Zella-Mehlis, Ger. (tsâl′ȧ-mā′le̊s)	168	50°40′N	10°38′E
Zémio, C.A.R. (za-myō′)	231	5°03′N	25°11′E
Zemlya Frantsa-Iosifa (Franz Josef Land), is., Russia	178	81°32′N	40°00′E
Zempoala, Punta, c., Mex. (po͞o′n-tä-sĕm-po̊-ä′lä)	131	19°30′N	96°18′W
Zempoatlépetl, mtn., Mex. (sĕm-po̊-ä-tlā′pĕt′l)	131	17°13′N	95°59′W
Zemun, Serb. (zĕ′mo͞on) (sĕm′lĭn)	163	44°50′N	20°25′E
Zengcheng, China (dzŭŋ-chŭŋ)	207a	23°18′N	113°49′E
Zenica, Bos. (zĕ′ne̊t-sä)	175	44°10′N	17°54′E
Zeni-Su, is., Japan (zĕ′nē so͞o)	211	33°55′N	138°55′E
Žepče, Bos. (zhĕp′chĕ)	177	44°26′N	18°01′E
Zepernick, Ger. (tsĕ′pĕr-nēk)	159b	52°39′N	13°32′E
Zerbst, Ger. (tsĕrbst)	168	51°58′N	12°03′E
Zerpenschleuse, Ger. (tsĕr′pĕn-shloi-zĕ)	159b	52°51′N	13°30′E
Zeuthen, Ger. (tsoi′tĕn)	159b	52°21′N	13°38′E
Zevenaar, Neth.	171c	51°56′N	6°06′E
Zevenbergen, Neth.	159a	51°38′N	4°36′E
Zeya, Russia (zå′yȧ)	179	53°43′N	127°29′E

ng-sing; ŋ-baŋk; ɴ-nasalized n; nŏd; cŏmmit; ōld; o̊bey; ôrder; oi-boil; fo͞od; ȯ-as oo in foot; ou-out; s-soft; sh-dish; th-thin; pūre; ůnite; ûrn; stŭd; circŭs; ü-as in French tu; ′-indeterminate vowel.

PLACE (Pronunciation)	PAGE	LAT.	LONG.
Zeya, r., Russia	185	52°31'N	128°30'E
Zeytun, Tur. (zā-tōōn')	181	38°00'N	36°40'E
Zezere, r., Port. (zě'zå-rě)	172	39°54'N	8°12'W
Zgierz, Pol. (zgyězh)	169	51°51'N	19°26'E
Zhambyl, Kaz.	183	42°51'N	71°29'E
Zhangaqazaly, Kaz.	183	45°47'N	62°00'E
Zhangbei, China (jän-bā)	205	41°12'N	114°50'E
Zhanggezhuang, China (jän-gŭ-jůän)	206	40°09'N	116°56'E
Zhangguangcai Ling, mts., China (jän-gůän-tsī lǐŋ)	208	43°50'N	127°55'E
Zhangjiakou, China	205	40°45'N	114°58'E
Zhangqiu, China (jän-chyǒ)	206	36°50'N	117°29'E
Zhangye, China (jän-yu)	204	38°46'N	101°00'E
Zhangzhou, China (jän-jō)	205	24°35'N	117°45'E
Zhangzi Dao, i., China (jän-dz dou)	206	39°02'N	122°44'E
Zhanhua, China (jän-hwä)	206	37°42'N	117°49'E
Zhanjiang, China (jän-jyäŋ)	205	21°20'N	110°28'E
Zhanyu, China (jän-yōō)	208	44°30'N	122°30'E
Zhao'an, China (jou-än)	209	23°48'N	117°10'E
Zhaodong, China (jou-dôŋ)	208	45°58'N	126°00'E
Zhaotong, China (jou-tôŋ)	204	27°18'N	103°50'E
Zhaoxian, China (jou shyěn)	206	37°46'N	114°48'E
Zhaoyuan, China (jou-yuän)	206	37°22'N	120°23'E
Zharkent, Kaz.	183	44°12'N	79°58'E
Zhaysang köli, l., Kaz.	183	48°16'N	84°05'E
Zhecheng, China (jǔ-chǔŋ)	208	34°05'N	115°19'E
Zhegao, China (jǔ-gou)	206	31°47'N	117°44'E
Zhejiang, prov., China (jǔ-jyäŋ)	205	29°30'N	120°00'E
Zhelaniya, Mys, c., Russia (zhě'lä-nǐ-yà)	178	75°43'N	69°10'E
Zhem, r., Kaz.	181	46°50'N	54°10'E
Zhengding, China (jüŋ-dǐŋ)	208	38°10'N	114°35'E
Zhengyang, China (jüŋ-yäŋ)	206	32°34'N	114°22'E
Zhengzhou, China (jüŋ-jō)	205	34°46'N	113°42'E
Zhenjiang, China (jüŋ-jyäŋ)	205	32°13'N	119°24'E
Zhenyuan, China (jün-yůän)	209	27°08'N	108°30'E
Zhetiqara, Kaz.	183	52°12'N	61°18'E
Zhigalovo, Russia (zhě-gä'lô-vô)	179	54°52'N	105°05'E
Zhigansk, Russia (zhě-gänsk')	170	66°45'N	123°20'E
Zhijiang, China (jr-jyäŋ)	209	27°25'N	109°45'E
Zhizdra, Russia (zhěz'drá)	176	53°47'N	34°41'E
Zhizhitskoye, l., Russia (zhě-zhět'skô-yě)	176	56°08'N	31°34'E
Zhmerynka, Ukr.	181	49°02'N	28°09'E
Zhongwei, China (jôŋ-wā)	204	37°32'N	105°10'E
Zhongxian, China (jôŋ shyěn)	204	30°20'N	108°00'E
Zhongxin, China (jôŋ-shyǐn)	207a	23°16'N	113°38'E
Zhoucun, China (jō-tsōōn)	208	36°49'N	117°52'E
Zhoukouzhen, China (jō-kō-jǔn)	206	33°39'N	114°40'E
Zhoupu, China (jō-pōō)	206	31°07'N	121°33'E
Zhoushan Qundao, is., China (jō-shän-chyôn-dou)	205	30°00'N	123°00'E
Zhouxian, China (jō shyěn)	208	39°30'N	115°59'E
Zhovkva, Ukr.	169	50°03'N	23°58'E
Zhu, r., China (jōō)	207a	22°48'N	113°36'E
Zhuanghe, China (jůäŋ-hŭ)	208	39°40'N	123°00'E
Zhuanqiao, China (jůäŋ-chyou)	207b	31°02'N	121°24'E
Zhucheng, China (jōō-chǔŋ)	208	36°01'N	119°24'E
Zhuji, China (jōō-jyě)	209	29°58'N	120°10'E
Zhujiang Kou, b., Asia (jōō-jyäŋ kō)	209	22°00'N	114°00'E
Zhukovskiy, Russia (zhô-kôf'skǐ)	186b	55°33'N	38°09'E
Zhurivka, Ukr.	177	50°31'N	31°43'E
Zhytomyr, Ukr.	178	50°15'N	28°40'E
Zhytomyr, prov., Ukr.	177	50°40'N	28°07'E
Zi, r., China (dzě)	209	26°50'N	111°00'E
Zia Indian Reservation, I.R., N.M., U.S.	119	35°30'N	106°43'W
Zibo, China (dzě-bwo)	206	36°48'N	118°04'E
Ziel, Mount, mtn., Austl. (zēl)	220	23°15'S	132°45'E
Zielona Góra, Pol. (zhyě-lô'nä gōō'rä)	168	51°56'N	15°30'E
Zigazinskiy, Russia (zī-gazinskēē)	186a	53°50'N	57°18'E
Ziguinchor, Sen.	230	12°35'N	16°16'W
Zile, Tur. (zē-lě')	163	40°20'N	35°50'E
Žilina, Slvk. (zhě'lǐ-nä)	161	49°14'N	18°45'E
Zillah, Libya	231	28°26'N	17°52'E
Zima, Russia (zē'má)	184	53°58'N	102°08'E
Zimapan, Mex. (sē-mä'pän)	130	20°43'N	99°23'W
Zimatlán de Alvarez, Mex.	131	16°52'N	96°47'W
Zimba, Zam.	237	17°19'S	26°13'E
Zimbabwe, nation, Afr. (rô-dē'zhǐ-á)	232	17°50'S	29°30'E
Zimnicea, Rom. (zěm-nē'chá)	175	43°39'N	25°22'E
Zin, r., Isr.	197a	30°50'N	35°12'E
Zinacatepec, Mex. (zē-nä-kä-tě'pěk)	131	18°19'N	97°15'W
Zinapécuaro, Mex. (sē-nä-pā'kwä-rô)	130	19°50'N	100°49'W
Zinder, Niger (zǐn'děr)	230	13°48'N	8°59'E
Zin'kiv, Ukr.	177	50°13'N	34°23'E
Zion, Il., U.S. (zī'ŭn)	111a	42°27'N	87°50'W
Zion National Park, rec., Ut., U.S.	106	37°20'N	113°00'W
Zionsville, In., U.S. (zīŭnz-vǐl)	111g	39°57'N	86°15'W
Zirandaro, Mex. (sē-rän-dä'rô)	130	18°28'N	101°02'W
Zitacuaro, Mex. (sē-tá-kwä'rô)	130	19°25'N	100°22'W
Zitlala, Mex. (sē-tlä'lä)	130	17°38'N	99°09'W
Zittau, Ger. (tsē'tou)	168	50°55'N	14°48'E
Ziway, l., Eth.	231	8°08'N	39°11'E
Ziya, r., China (dzē-yä)	206	38°38'N	116°31'E
Zlatograd, Blg.	175	41°24'N	25°05'E
Zlatoust, Russia (zlá-tô-óst')	178	55°13'N	59°39'E
Zlītan, Libya	231	32°27'N	14°33'E
Złoczew, Pol. (zwô'chěf)	169	51°23'N	18°34'E
Zlynka, Russia (zlěn'ká)	176	52°28'N	31°39'E
Znamensk, Russia (znä'měnsk)	167	54°37'N	21°13'E
Znamianka, Ukr.	177	48°43'N	32°35'E
Znojmo, Czech Rep. (znoi'mô)	161	48°52'N	16°03'E
Zoetermeer, Neth.	159a	52°08'N	4°29'E
Zoeterwoude, Neth.	159a	52°08'N	4°29'E
Zolochiv, Ukr.	169	49°48'N	24°55'E
Zolotonosha, Ukr. (zô'lô-tô-nô'shá)	181	49°41'N	32°03'E
Zolotoy, Mys, c., Russia (mǐs zô-lô-tôy')	210	47°24'N	139°10'E
Zomba, Mwi. (zôm'bá)	232	15°23'S	35°18'E
Zongo, D.R.C. (zôŋ'gô)	231	4°19'N	18°36'E
Zonguldak, Tur. (zôn'gōōl'dák)	198	41°25'N	31°50'E
Zonhoven, Bel.	159a	50°59'N	5°24'E
Zoquitlán, Mex. (sô-kět-län')	131	18°09'N	97°02'W
Zorita, Spain (thō-rē'tä)	172	39°18'N	5°41'W
Zossen, Ger. (tsō'sěn)	159b	52°13'N	13°27'E
Zouar, Chad	235	20°27'N	16°32'E
Zouxian, China (dzō shyěn)	208	35°24'N	116°54'E
Zubtsov, Russia (zôp-tsôf')	176	56°13'N	34°34'E
Zuera, Spain (thwä'rä)	173	41°40'N	0°48'W
Zugdidi, Geor.	182	42°30'N	41°53'E
Zuger See, l., Switz. (tsōōg)	168	47°10'N	8°40'E
Zugspitze, mtn., Eur.	168	47°25'N	11°00'E
Zuidelijk Flevoland, reg., Neth.	159a	52°22'N	5°20'E
Zújar, r., Spain (zō'kär)	172	38°55'N	5°05'W
Zújar, Embalse del, res., Spain	172	38°50'N	5°20'W
Zulueta, Cuba (zōō-lô-č'tä)	134	22°20'N	79°35'W
Zumbo, Moz. (zōōm'bò)	232	15°36'S	30°25'E
Zumbro, r., Mn., U.S. (zŭm'brô)	113	44°18'N	92°14'W
Zumbrota, Mn., U.S. (zŭm-brô'tá)	113	44°16'N	92°39'W
Zumpango, Mex. (sôm-päŋ-gô)	131	19°48'N	99°06'W
Zundert, Neth.	159a	51°28'N	4°39'E
Zungeru, Nig. (zôŋ-gā'rōō)	230	9°48'N	6°09'E
Zunhua, China (dzòn-hwä)	208	40°12'N	117°55'E
Zuni, r., Az., U.S.	119	34°40'N	109°30'W
Zuni Indian Reservation, I.R., N.M., U.S. (zōō'nē)	119	35°10'N	108°40'W
Zuni Mountains, mts., N.M., U.S.	119	35°10'N	108°10'W
Zunyi, China	204	27°58'N	106°40'E
Zürich, Switz. (tsü'rǐk)	154	47°22'N	8°32'E
Zürichsee, l., Switz.	168	47°18'N	8°47'E
Zushi, Japan (zōō'shē)	211a	35°17'N	139°35'E
Zuwārah, Libya	230	32°58'N	12°07'E
Zuwayzā, Jord.	197a	31°42'N	35°55'E
Zvenigorod, Russia (zvä-nē'gô-rót)	176	55°46'N	36°54'E
Zvenyhorodka, Ukr.	181	49°07'N	30°59'E
Zvishavane, Zimb.	232	20°15'S	30°28'E
Zvolen, Slvk. (zvô'lěn)	169	48°35'N	19°10'E
Zvornik, Bos. (zvôr'něk)	175	44°24'N	19°08'E
Zweibrücken, Ger. (tsvī-brük'ěn)	168	49°16'N	7°20'E
Zwickau, Ger. (tsvī'kôu)	161	50°43'N	12°30'E
Zwolle, Neth. (zvôl'ě)	161	52°33'N	6°05'E
Żyrardów, Pol. (zhě-rär'dôf)	169	52°04'N	20°28'E
Zyryanka, Russia (zě-ryän'ká)	179	65°45'N	151°15'E
Zyryanovsk, Kaz.	183	49°43'N	84°20'E

ăt; finǎl; rāte; senåte; ärm; åsk; sofà; fåre; ch-choose; dh-as th in other; bē; ĕvent; bĕt; recĕnt; cratĕr; g-gō; gh-guttural g; bĭt; ĭ-short neutral; rīde; κ-guttural k as ch in German ich;

SUBJECT INDEX

sted below are major topics covered by the thematic maps, graphs and/or statistics.
age citations are for world, continent and country maps and for world tables.

SOURCES

The sources listed below have been consulted during the process of creating and updating the thematic maps and statistics for the 20th Edition.

AAMA Motor Vehicle Facts and Figures, American Automobile Manufacturers Association

Agricultural Atlas of the United States, U.S. Dept. of Commerce, Bureau of the Census

Agricultural Statistics, U.S. Dept. of Agriculture

Anuario Estatistico do Brasil, Fundacao Instituto Brasileiro de Geografia e Estatistica

Atlas of African Agriculture, United Nations, Food and Agriculture Organization

Atlas of India, TT Maps and Publications, Government of India

Atlas of the Middle East, U.S. Dept. of State, Central Intelligence Agency

Canada Year Book, Statistics Canada, Minister of Industry, Science and Technology

Census of Agriculture, U.S. Dept. of Commerce, Bureau of the Census

Census of Canada, Statistics Canada, Minister of Supplies and Services

Census of Population Characteristics: United States, U.S. Dept. of Commerce, Economics and Statistics Administration

Census of Population, U.S. Dept. of Commerce, Bureau of the Census

China Statistical Yearbook, State Statistical Bureau of the People's Republic of China

City and County Data Book, U.S. Dept. of Commerce, Bureau of the Census

Coal Production, U.S. Dept. of Energy, Energy Information Administration

Compendium of Social Statistics and Indicators, United Nations, Department of International Economic and Social Affairs

Contemporary Conflicts, Canadian Forces College Information Resource Centre, Dept. of National Defence

The Defense Monitor, Center for Defense Information

Demographic Yearbook, United Nations, Department of International Economic and Social Affairs

Earthquakes and Volcanoes, U.S. Dept. of the Interior, U.S. Geological Survey

Ecoregions of the Continents, U.S. Dept. of the Agriculture, Forest Service

Energy Information Administration Country Analysis Briefs, U.S. Dept. of Energy, Energy Information Administration

Energy Map of Central Asia, The Petroleum Economist, Ltd.

Energy Map of the World, The Petroleum Economist, Ltd.

Energy Statistics Yearbook (UN), United Nations, Department of International Economic and Social Affairs

Estimated Use of Water in the United States, U.S. Dept of the Interior, U.S. Geological Survey

FAA Statistical Handbook of Aviation, U.S. Dept. of Transportation, Federal Aviation Administration

FAO Atlas of the Living Resources of the Seas, United Nations, Food and Agriculture Organization

FAO Production Yearbook, United Nations, Food and Agriculture Organization

FAO Trade Yearbook, United Nations, Food and Agriculture Organization

FAOSTAT, United Nations, Food and Agriculture Organization

FAS Online, U.S. Dept. of Agriculture, Foreign Agriculture Service

Fiber Organon World Man-made Fiber Survey, Fiber Economics Bureau, Inc.

Geothermal Energy Worldwide, Geothermal Education Office

Global Volcanism Program, Smithsonian Institution, National Museum of Natural History

A Guide to Your National Forests, U.S. Dept. of Agriculture, Forest Service

Handbook of International Economic Statistics, U.S. Dept. of State, Central Intelligence Agency

Handbook of International Trade and Development Statistics, United Nations, Conference on Trade and Development

ILO Yearbook of Labour Statistics, International Labour Organisation

International Data Base, U.S. Dept. of Commerce, Bureau of the Census

International Energy Annual, U.S. Dept. of Energy, Energy Information Administration

International Petroleum Encyclopedia, PennWell Publishing Co.

International Trade Statistics Yearbook, United Nations, Dept. of Economic and Social Development

International Water Power and Dam Construction Handbook, Reed Business Publishing Ltd.

IUCN Red List of Threatened Animals, World Conservation Union / World Conservation Monitoring Centre

Maritime Transport, Organization for Economic and Social Co-operation and Development

Merchant Fleets of the World, United States Maritime Administration, Office of Trade Analysis and Insurance

Mineral Industries of Africa and Middle East, U.S. Dept of the Interior, U.S. Geological Survey

Mineral Industries of Latin America and Canada, U.S. Dept of the Interior, U.S. Geological Survey

Mineral Industries of the Asia and the Pacific, U.S. Dept of the Interior, U.S. Geological Survey

Mineral Industry Surveys, U.S. Dept of the Interior, U.S. Geological Survey

Minerals Yearbook, U.S. Dept of the Interior, U.S. Geological Survey

Monthly Bulletin of Statistics, United Nations, Dept. of Economic and Social Development

National Atlas - Canada, Dept. of Energy, Mines, and Resources

National Atlas - Chile, Instituto Geografico Militar

National Atlas - China, Cartographic Publishing House

National Atlas - Japan, Geographical Survey Institute

National Atlas - United States, U.S. Dept of the Interior, U.S. Geological Survey

National Priorities List, U.S. Environmental Protection Agency

Natural Gas Annual, U.S. Dept. of Energy, Energy Information Administration

Nuclear Power Reactors in the World, International Atomic Energy Agency

Oxford Economic Atlas of the World, Oxford University Press

Petroleum Supply Annual, U.S. Dept. of Energy, Energy Information Administration

Population and Dwelling Counts: A National Overview, Minister of Industry, Science and Technology, Statistics Canada

Population and Vital Statistics Reports, United Nations, Dept. for Economic and Social Information and Policy Analysis

Populations of Concern to UNHCR, United Nations, United Nations High Commissioner for Refugees (UNHCR)

Post-Soviet Geography, V.H. Winston and Son, Inc.

Public Land Surveys, U.S. Dept of the Interior, U.S. Geological Survey

Rail in Canada, Statistics Canada, Transport Division, Surface and Marine Transport Section

Rand McNally Road Atlas, Rand McNally

Rubber Statistical Bulletin, International Rubber Study Group

Significant Earthquake Database, National Oceanic and Atmospheric Administration, National Geophysical Data Center

Statistical Abstract of India, Central Statistical Organisation

Statistical Abstract of the United States, U.S. Dept. of Commerce, Bureau of the Census

Statistical Pocket-Book of Yugoslavia, Federal Statistical Office

Statistical Yearbook, United Nations, Department of International Economic and Social Affairs

Statistical Yearbook, United Nations, Educational, Scientific and Cultural Organization (UNESCO)

Status of Armed Conflicts, International Institute for Strategic Studies

Sugar Yearbook, International Sugar Organization

Survey of Energy Resources, World Energy Council

United Nations List of Protected Areas, World Conservation Monitoring Centre

Uranium Resources, Production and Demand, United Nations, Organization for Economic Co-operation and Development

This Dynamic Planet: World Map of Volcanoes, Earthquakes and Plate Tectonics, Smithsonian Institution / U.S. Geological Survey

Volcanoes of the World, Geoscience Press

WHO Estimates of Health Personnel, United Nations, World Health Organization

World Atlas of Agriculture, Instituto Geografico De Agostini

World Atlas of Geology and Mineral Deposits, Mining Journal Books, Ltd.

The World's Busiest Airport, Airports Council International

World Coal Resources and Major Trade Routes, Miller Freeman Publications, Inc.

World Conflict List, National Defense Council Foundation

World Development Report, World Bank

World Directory of Manufactured Fiber Producers, Fiber Economics Bureau, Inc.

World Factbook, U.S. Dept. of State, Central Intelligence Agency

World Gas Map, The Petroleum Economist, Ltd.

World Mineral Statistics, British Geological Survey

World Oil International Outlook, Gulf Publishing Company

World Population Profile, U.S. Dept. of Commerce, Bureau of the Census

World Population Prospects, United Nations, Department of International Economic and Social Affairs

World Transport Statistics, International Road Transport Union, Dept. of Economic Affairs

World Urbanization Prospects, United Nations, Department of International Economic and Social Affairs

Year Book Australia, Australian Bureau of Statistics